D1574997

30
YEARS
OF
NME
NEW MUSICAL EXPRESS
ALBUM
CHARTS

BOXTREE

The Complete NME Album Charts is designed and produced by:

Osborne Books, 70 High Street, Snainton, North Yorkshire YO13 9AJ

The commentaries on the charts for the years 1962 to 1979, were written by Michael Gray, copyright and all rights reserved.
The commentaries on the charts for the years 1980 to 1993, were written by Barry Lazell, copyright and all rights reserved.
Remaining text, Copyright Roger Osborne, all rights reserved.

The compilers and authors would like to thank the following people who have helped in various and invaluable ways: Eileen Buss, Michael Randolfi, Alan Lewis, Fiona Foulgar, Steve Sutherland, Dick Whincup, Sarah Beattie, Nigel Hinton, Phil Hardy, Andy Lineham, J Blackmore Reed, Arthur Berman, Bryan Hodgson.

Cover design by Design 23, London
Photo research by Cate Jago

This edition published 1995 by
BOXTREE Ltd

First published in the UK 1993 by:
BOXTREE Ltd
Broadwall House
21 Broadwall
London SE1 9PL

10 9 8 7 6 5 4 3 2 1

NME Album Charts June 1962 to May 1988, Copyright IPC Magazines Ltd.
NME Album Charts June 1988 to December 1994, Copyright MRIB Ltd.

Linotronic output by AdverSet, Scarborough
Printed and bound in Great Britain by
Cox & Wyman Ltd, Reading, Berkshire

ISBN: 0 7522 0824 1

A CIP catalogue entry for this book is available from the British Library

The Complete NME Album Charts

This updated edition of *The Complete NME Album Charts* includes all the charts up to the end of 1994. As in previous editions, the charts differ in some important respects from those printed weekly in the NME. As in the sister volume to this book, *The Complete NME Singles Charts,* the date at the head of each chart is the Saturday at the end of the week in which the chart was published. Under intense pressure of producing the best music weekly in Britain, mistakes were sometimes made in compiling the chart.

These have been corrected wherever possible.
Along with most other papers and magazines the NME usually misses one or two issues over the Christmas and New Year period. We have not duplicated the previous week's chart for these missing weeks, but gone on to the next published chart.
The Title Index and Artist Index at the end of the book are both a guide to locating records in the charts, and a complete guide to the chart career of every artist that has appeared in the NME Album Chart.

9 June 1962
(last week / this week)

last	this	Title — Artist (Label)
-	1	BLUE HAWAII — Elvis Presley (RCA)
-	2	WEST SIDE STORY — Soundtrack (Philips)
-	3	IT'S TRAD DAD — Soundtrack (Columbia)
-	4	SOUTH PACIFIC — Soundtrack (RCA)
-	5	THE YOUNG ONES — Cliff Richard & the Shadows (Columbia)
-	6	I REMEMBER TOMMY — Frank Sinatra (Reprise)
-	7	SINATRA AND STRINGS — Frank Sinatra (Reprise)
-	8	THE BLACK AND WHITE MINSTREL SHOW — George Mitchell Minstrels (HMV)
-	9	THE SOUND OF MUSIC — London Cast (HMV)
-	10	HONEY HIT PARADE — Various Artists (Golden Guinea)

16 June 1962

last	this	Title — Artist (Label)
1	1	BLUE HAWAII — Elvis Presley (RCA)
2	2	WEST SIDE STORY — Soundtrack (Philips)
3	3	IT'S TRAD DAD — Soundtrack (Columbia)
5	4	THE YOUNG ONES — Cliff Richard & the Shadows (Columbia)
4	5	SOUTH PACIFIC — Soundtrack (RCA)
8	6	THE BLACK AND WHITE MINSTREL SHOW — George Mitchell Minstrels (HMV)
7	7	SINATRA AND STRINGS — Frank Sinatra (Reprise)
	8	THE ROARING TWENTIES - SONGS FROM THE TV SERIES — Dorothy Provine (Warner Bros.)
6	9	I REMEMBER TOMMY — Frank Sinatra (Reprise)
	10	THE SHADOWS — Shadows (Columbia)

23 June 1962

last	this	Title — Artist (Label)
2	1	WEST SIDE STORY — Soundtrack (Philips)
1	2	BLUE HAWAII — Elvis Presley (RCA)
7	3	SINATRA AND STRINGS — Frank Sinatra (Reprise)
6	4	THE BLACK AND WHITE MINSTREL SHOW — George Mitchell Minstrels (HMV)
4	5	THE YOUNG ONES — Cliff Richard & the Shadows (Columbia)
5	6	SOUTH PACIFIC — Soundtrack (RCA)
3	7	IT'S TRAD DAD — Soundtrack (Columbia)
10	8	THE SHADOWS — Shadows (Columbia)
6	9	I REMEMBER TOMMY — Frank Sinatra (Reprise)
8	10	THE ROARING TWENTIES - SONGS FROM THE TV SERIES — Dorothy Provine (Warner Bros.)

30 June 1962

last	this	Title — Artist (Label)
1	1	WEST SIDE STORY — Soundtrack (Philips)
2	2	BLUE HAWAII — Elvis Presley (RCA)
6	3	SOUTH PACIFIC — Soundtrack (RCA)
4	4	THE BLACK AND WHITE MINSTREL SHOW — George Mitchell Minstrels (HMV)
6	5	IT'S TRAD DAD — Soundtrack (Columbia)
3	6	SINATRA AND STRINGS — Frank Sinatra (Reprise)
5	7	THE YOUNG ONES — Cliff Richard & the Shadows (Columbia)
10	8	THE ROARING TWENTIES - SONGS FROM THE TV SERIES — Dorothy Provine (Warner Bros.)
-	9	ANOTHER BLACK AND WHITE MINSTREL SHOW — George Mitchell Minstrels (HMV)
-	10	WIMOWEH — Karl Denver (Ace of Clubs)
9	10	I REMEMBER TOMMY — Frank Sinatra (Reprise)

7 July 1962

last	this	Title — Artist (Label)
-	1	POT LUCK — Elvis Presley (RCA)
1	2	WEST SIDE STORY — Soundtrack (Philips)
2	3	BLUE HAWAII — Elvis Presley (RCA)
4	4	THE BLACK AND WHITE MINSTREL SHOW — George Mitchell Minstrels (HMV)
6	5	SINATRA AND STRINGS — Frank Sinatra (Reprise)
5	6	IT'S TRAD DAD — Soundtrack (Columbia)
8	7	THE ROARING TWENTIES - SONGS FROM THE TV SERIES — Dorothy Provine (Warner Bros.)
3	8	SOUTH PACIFIC — Soundtrack (RCA)
9	9	ANOTHER BLACK AND WHITE MINSTREL SHOW — George Mitchell Minstrels (HMV)
-	10	STRANGER ON THE SHORE — Mr. Acker Bilk (Columbia)

14 July 1962

last	this	Title — Artist (Label)
1	1	POT LUCK — Elvis Presley (RCA)
2	2	WEST SIDE STORY — Soundtrack (Philips)
3	3	BLUE HAWAII — Elvis Presley (RCA)
8	4	SOUTH PACIFIC — Soundtrack (RCA)
4	5	THE BLACK AND WHITE MINSTREL SHOW — George Mitchell Minstrels (HMV)
6	6	IT'S TRAD DAD — Soundtrack (Columbia)
5	7	SINATRA AND STRINGS — Frank Sinatra (Reprise)
-	8	BLITZ! — Original Cast (HMV)
7	9	THE ROARING TWENTIES - SONGS FROM THE TV SERIES — Dorothy Provine (Warner Bros.)
-	10	THE YOUNG ONES — Cliff Richard & the Shadows (Columbia)
-	10	TWISTIN' 'N' TWANGIN' — Duane Eddy (London)

21 July 1962

last	this	Title — Artist (Label)
1	1	POT LUCK — Elvis Presley (RCA)
2	2	WEST SIDE STORY — Soundtrack (Philips)
3	3	BLUE HAWAII — Elvis Presley (RCA)
5	4	THE BLACK AND WHITE MINSTREL SHOW — George Mitchell Minstrels (HMV)
4	5	SOUTH PACIFIC — Soundtrack (RCA)
6	6	IT'S TRAD DAD — Soundtrack (Columbia)
8	7	BLITZ! — Original Cast (HMV)
7	7	SINATRA AND STRINGS — Frank Sinatra (Reprise)
10	9	THE YOUNG ONES — Cliff Richard & the Shadows (Columbia)
9	10	THE ROARING TWENTIES - SONGS FROM THE TV SERIES — Dorothy Provine (Warner Bros.)

28 July 1962

last	this	Title — Artist (Label)
1	1	POT LUCK — Elvis Presley (RCA)
2	2	WEST SIDE STORY — Soundtrack (Philips)
4	3	THE BLACK AND WHITE MINSTREL SHOW — George Mitchell Minstrels (HMV)
5	4	SOUTH PACIFIC — Soundtrack (RCA)
3	5	BLUE HAWAII — Elvis Presley (RCA)
7	6	BLITZ! — Original Cast (HMV)
6	7	IT'S TRAD DAD — Soundtrack (Columbia)
-	8	MODERN SOUNDS IN COUNTRY AND WESTERN MUSIC — Ray Charles (HMV)
7	8	SINATRA AND STRINGS — Frank Sinatra (Reprise)
-	10	THE SOUND OF MUSIC — London Cast (HMV)

The album chart was born - but the single still ruled. Most LPs were greatest hits compilations, film soundtracks or spin-offs from TV. Aside from "sophisticated artistes" (Frank Sinatra) only the very biggest-sellers in pop made LPs of new material at all, and even these offered potential singles plus filler tracks. Exceptions were Ray Charles' *Modern Sounds In Country And Western* (a prototype Concept Album: a radical fusion of country and soul) and *Honey Hit Parade*, a spin-off from a Radio Luxembourg show.

August – September 1962

4 August 1962

last	this	
2	1	WEST SIDE STORY Soundtrack (Philips)
1	2	POT LUCK Elvis Presley (RCA)
5	3	BLUE HAWAII Elvis Presley (RCA)
3	4	THE BLACK AND WHITE MINSTREL SHOW George Mitchell Minstrels (HMV)
4	5	SOUTH PACIFIC Soundtrack (RCA)
8	6	MODERN SOUNDS IN COUNTRY AND WESTERN MUSIC Ray Charles (HMV)
-	7	THE SHADOWS Shadows (Columbia)
8	8	SINATRA AND STRINGS Frank Sinatra (Reprise)
-	9	THE BUDDY HOLLY STORY VOL. 1 Buddy Holly (Coral)
7	10	IT'S TRAD DAD Soundtrack (Columbia)

11 August 1962

2	1	POT LUCK Elvis Presley (RCA)
1	2	WEST SIDE STORY Soundtrack (Philips)
5	3	SOUTH PACIFIC Soundtrack (RCA)
4	4	THE BLACK AND WHITE MINSTREL SHOW George Mitchell Minstrels (HMV)
-	5	BLITZ! Original Cast (HMV)
3	6	BLUE HAWAII Elvis Presley (RCA)
6	7	MODERN SOUNDS IN COUNTRY AND WESTERN MUSIC Ray Charles (HMV)
-	8	TWISTIN' 'N' TWANGIN' Duane Eddy (London)
-	9	THE YOUNG ONES Cliff Richard & the Shadows (Columbia)
8	10	SINATRA AND STRINGS Frank Sinatra (Reprise)

18 August 1962

1	1	POT LUCK Elvis Presley (RCA)
2	2	WEST SIDE STORY Soundtrack (Philips)
4	3	THE BLACK AND WHITE MINSTREL SHOW George Mitchell Minstrels (HMV)
5	4	BLITZ! Original Cast (HMV)
3	4	SOUTH PACIFIC Soundtrack (RCA)
6	6	BLUE HAWAII Elvis Presley (RCA)
8	7	TWISTIN' 'N' TWANGIN' Duane Eddy (London)
7	8	MODERN SOUNDS IN COUNTRY AND WESTERN MUSIC Ray Charles (HMV)
-	9	LONDON BY NIGHT Frank Sinatra (Reprise)
10	10	SINATRA AND STRINGS Frank Sinatra (Reprise)

25 August 1962

2	1	WEST SIDE STORY Soundtrack (Philips)
1	2	POT LUCK Elvis Presley (RCA)
3	3	THE BLACK AND WHITE MINSTREL SHOW George Mitchell Minstrels (HMV)
6	4	BLUE HAWAII Elvis Presley (RCA)
4	5	SOUTH PACIFIC Soundtrack (RCA)
4	6	BLITZ! Original Cast (HMV)
8	7	MODERN SOUNDS IN COUNTRY AND WESTERN MUSIC Ray Charles (HMV)
7	8	TWISTIN' 'N' TWANGIN' Duane Eddy (London)
-	9	THE SHADOWS Shadows (Columbia)
-	10	A PICTURE OF YOU Joe Brown (Golden Guinea)
-	10	STRANGER ON THE SHORE Mr. Acker Bilk (Columbia)

1 September 1962

1	1	WEST SIDE STORY Soundtrack (Philips)
2	2	POT LUCK Elvis Presley (RCA)
-	3	THE BEST OF BALL, BARBER AND BILK Kenny Ball, Chris Barber & Acker Bilk (Golden Guinea)
-	4	A GOLDEN AGE OF DONEGAN Lonnie Donegan (Golden Guinea)
3	5	THE BLACK AND WHITE MINSTREL SHOW George Mitchell Minstrels (HMV)
5	5	SOUTH PACIFIC Soundtrack (RCA)
4	7	BLUE HAWAII Elvis Presley (RCA)
10	7	A PICTURE OF YOU Joe Brown (Golden Guinea)
6	9	BLITZ! Original Cast (HMV)
7	10	MODERN SOUNDS IN COUNTRY AND WESTERN MUSIC Ray Charles (HMV)

8 September 1962

1	1	WEST SIDE STORY Soundtrack (Philips)
4	2	A GOLDEN AGE OF DONEGAN Lonnie Donegan (Golden Guinea)
2	3	POT LUCK Elvis Presley (RCA)
3	4	THE BEST OF BALL, BARBER AND BILK Kenny Ball, Chris Barber & Acker Bilk (Golden Guinea)
5	5	THE BLACK AND WHITE MINSTREL SHOW George Mitchell Minstrels (HMV)
5	6	SOUTH PACIFIC Soundtrack (RCA)
7	7	A PICTURE OF YOU Joe Brown (Golden Guinea)
7	8	BLUE HAWAII Elvis Presley (RCA)
9	9	BLITZ! Original Cast (HMV)
-	10	THE MUSIC MAN Soundtrack (Warner Bros.)

15 September 1962

1	1	WEST SIDE STORY Soundtrack (Philips)
2	2	A GOLDEN AGE OF DONEGAN Lonnie Donegan (Golden Guinea)
4	3	THE BEST OF BALL, BARBER AND BILK Kenny Ball, Chris Barber & Acker Bilk (Golden Guinea)
3	4	POT LUCK Elvis Presley (RCA)
7	5	A PICTURE OF YOU Joe Brown (Golden Guinea)
6	6	THE BLACK AND WHITE MINSTREL SHOW George Mitchell Minstrels (HMV)
6	7	SOUTH PACIFIC Soundtrack (RCA)
8	8	BLUE HAWAII Elvis Presley (RCA)
-	9	MODERN SOUNDS IN COUNTRY AND WESTERN MUSIC Ray Charles (HMV)
-	10	THE SOUND OF MUSIC London Cast (HMV)
-	10	'S WONDERFUL 'S MARVELLOUS Ray Conniff (CBS)

22 September 1962

1	1	WEST SIDE STORY Soundtrack (Philips)
2	2	A GOLDEN AGE OF DONEGAN Lonnie Donegan (Golden Guinea)
3	3	THE BEST OF BALL, BARBER AND BILK Kenny Ball, Chris Barber & Acker Bilk (Golden Guinea)
4	4	POT LUCK Elvis Presley (RCA)
6	5	THE BLACK AND WHITE MINSTREL SHOW George Mitchell Minstrels (HMV)
5	6	A PICTURE OF YOU Joe Brown (Golden Guinea)
7	7	SOUTH PACIFIC Soundtrack (RCA)
8	8	BLUE HAWAII Elvis Presley (RCA)
9	9	MODERN SOUNDS IN COUNTRY AND WESTERN MUSIC Ray Charles (HMV)
-	10	32 MINUTES AND 17 SECONDS Cliff Richard (Columbia)

Radio Luxembourg was the only respite from the BBC Light Programme: it actually played lots of records, because it sold airtime to record companies. The big ones (EMI and Decca, embracing exciting American-music labels: London, Coral, RCA) had half-hour shows, like Jimmy Savile's Teen And 20 Disc Club (Elvis was member no. 11321). Smaller companies (Pye, Philips) had quarter-hours they struggled to fill with Britishers – note the hits on Pye's cheap label Golden Guinea.

6

September – November 1962

29 September 1962 (last week / this week)

1 1 WEST SIDE STORY Soundtrack (Philips)
2 2 A GOLDEN AGE OF DONEGAN Lonnie Donegan (Golden Guinea)
3 3 THE BEST OF BALL, BARBER AND BILK Kenny Ball, Chris Barber & Acker Bilk (Golden Guinea)
6 4 A PICTURE OF YOU Joe Brown (Golden Guinea)
4 5 POT LUCK Elvis Presley (RCA)
10 6 32 MINUTES AND 17 SECONDS Cliff Richard (Columbia)
5 7 THE BLACK AND WHITE MINSTREL SHOW George Mitchell Minstrels (HMV)
8 8 BLUE HAWAII Elvis Presley (RCA)
7 9 SOUTH PACIFIC Soundtrack (RCA)
9 10 MODERN SOUNDS IN COUNTRY AND WESTERN MUSIC Ray Charles (HMV)

6 October 1962

1 1 WEST SIDE STORY Soundtrack (Philips)
3 2 THE BEST OF BALL, BARBER AND BILK Kenny Ball, Chris Barber & Acker Bilk (Golden Guinea)
2 3 A GOLDEN AGE OF DONEGAN Lonnie Donegan (Golden Guinea)
4 4 A PICTURE OF YOU
7 5 THE BLACK AND WHITE MINSTREL SHOW George Mitchell Minstrels (HMV)
5 6 POT LUCK Elvis Presley (RCA)
6 7 32 MINUTES AND 17 SECONDS Cliff Richard (Columbia)
10 8 MODERN SOUNDS IN COUNTRY AND WESTERN MUSIC Ray Charles (HMV)
- 9 'S WONDERFUL 'S MARVELLOUS Ray Conniff (CBS)
- 9 RAY CONNIFF HI-FI COMPANION Ray Conniff (Philips)
- 9 A PICTURE OF JOE BROWN Joe Brown (Ace of Clubs)

13 October 1962

1 1 WEST SIDE STORY Soundtrack (Philips)
3 2 A GOLDEN AGE OF DONEGAN Lonnie Donegan (Golden Guinea)
2 3 THE BEST OF BALL, BARBER AND BILK Kenny Ball, Chris Barber & Acker Bilk (Golden Guinea)
- 4 OUT OF THE SHADOWS Shadows (Columbia)
5 5 THE BLACK AND WHITE MINSTREL SHOW George Mitchell Minstrels (HMV)
4 6 A PICTURE OF YOU Joe Brown (Golden Guinea)
7 7 32 MINUTES AND 17 SECONDS Cliff Richard (Columbia)
8 8 SOUTH PACIFIC Soundtrack (RCA)
9 9 THE SOUND OF MUSIC London Cast (HMV)
- 10 BLITZ! Original Cast (HMV)

20 October 1962

1 1 WEST SIDE STORY Soundtrack (Philips)
4 2 OUT OF THE SHADOWS Shadows (Columbia)
3 3 THE BEST OF BALL, BARBER AND BILK Kenny Ball, Chris Barber & Acker Bilk (Golden Guinea)
2 4 A GOLDEN AGE OF DONEGAN Lonnie Donegan (Golden Guinea)
6 5 A PICTURE OF YOU Joe Brown (Golden Guinea)
5 6 THE BLACK AND WHITE MINSTREL SHOW George Mitchell Minstrels (HMV)
7 7 32 MINUTES AND 17 SECONDS Cliff Richard (Columbia)
- 8 POT LUCK Elvis Presley (RCA)
- 9 MODERN SOUNDS IN COUNTRY AND WESTERN MUSIC Ray Charles (HMV)
- 9 PORGY AND BESS Soundtrack (Philips)

27 October 1962

2 1 OUT OF THE SHADOWS Shadows (Columbia)
1 2 WEST SIDE STORY Soundtrack (CBS)
3 3 THE BEST OF BALL, BARBER AND BILK Kenny Ball, Chris Barber & Acker Bilk (Golden Guinea)
4 4 A GOLDEN AGE OF DONEGAN Lonnie Donegan (Golden Guinea)
- 5 ON STAGE WITH THE GEORGE MITCHELL MINSTRELS George Mitchell Minstrels (HMV)
7 6 32 MINUTES & 17 SECONDS Cliff Richard (Columbia)
5 7 A PICTURE OF YOU Joe Brown (Golden Guinea)
- 8 SOUTH PACIFIC Soundtrack (RCA)
8 9 POT LUCK Elvis Presley (RCA)
6 10 THE BLACK AND WHITE MINSTREL SHOW George Mitchell Minstrels (HMV)
- 10 NAT 'KING' COLE SINGS, THE GEORGE SHEARING QUINTET PLAYS Nat 'King' Cole & George Shearing (Capitol)

3 November 1962

2 1 WEST SIDE STORY Soundtrack (CBS)
1 2 OUT OF THE SHADOWS Shadows (Columbia)
5 3 ON STAGE WITH THE GEORGE MITCHELL MINSTRELS George Mitchell Minstrels (HMV)
3 4 THE BEST OF BALL, BARBER AND BILK Kenny Ball, Chris Barber & Acker Bilk (Golden Guinea)
4 5 A GOLDEN AGE OF DONEGAN Lonnie Donegan (Golden Guinea)
8 6 SOUTH PACIFIC Soundtrack (RCA)
9 6 POT LUCK Elvis Presley (RCA)
10 8 THE BLACK AND WHITE MINSTREL SHOW George Mitchell Minstrels (HMV)
- 9 MODERN SOUNDS IN COUNTRY AND WESTERN MUSIC Ray Charles (HMV)
7 10 A PICTURE OF YOU Joe Brown (Golden Guinea)

10 November 1962

1 1 WEST SIDE STORY Soundtrack (CBS)
2 2 OUT OF THE SHADOWS Shadows (Columbia)
3 3 ON STAGE WITH THE GEORGE MITCHELL MINSTRELS George Mitchell Minstrels (HMV)
4 4 THE BEST OF BALL, BARBER AND BILK Kenny Ball, Chris Barber & Acker Bilk (Golden Guinea)
5 5 A GOLDEN AGE OF DONEGAN Lonnie Donegan (Golden Guinea)
6 6 SOUTH PACIFIC Soundtrack (RCA)
- 7 NAT 'KING' COLE SINGS, THE GEORGE SHEARING QUINTET PLAYS Nat 'King' Cole & George Shearing (Capitol)
8 8 THE BLACK AND WHITE MINSTREL SHOW George Mitchell Minstrels (HMV)
10 8 A PICTURE OF YOU Joe Brown (Golden Guinea)
6 10 POT LUCK Elvis Presley (RCA)

17 November 1962

1 1 WEST SIDE STORY Soundtrack (CBS)
3 2 ON STAGE WITH THE GEORGE MITCHELL MINSTRELS George Mitchell Minstrels (HMV)
2 3 OUT OF THE SHADOWS Shadows (Columbia)
8 4 THE BLACK AND WHITE MINSTREL SHOW George Mitchell Minstrels (HMV)
5 5 A GOLDEN AGE OF DONEGAN Lonnie Donegan (Golden Guinea)
4 6 THE BEST OF BALL, BARBER AND BILK Kenny Ball, Chris Barber & Acker Bilk (Golden Guinea)
6 7 SOUTH PACIFIC Soundtrack (RCA)
8 8 A PICTURE OF YOU Joe Brown (Golden Guinea)
- 9 BOBBY VEE MEETS THE CRICKETS Bobby Vee & the Crickets (Liberty)
7 10 NAT 'KING' COLE SINGS, THE GEORGE SHEARING QUINTET PLAYS Nat 'King' Cole & George Shearing (Capitol)

BBC DJ Brian Matthew wrote in his book *Trad Mad* that "the sixties may well come to be labelled the ten years of Trad..." Mercifully he was mistaken. Trad was to prove a short-lived craze, though this autumn was its zenith. Not content with pastiches of pre-war jazz for people alarmed by anything more modern, adults also bought huge numbers of Black And White Minstrel records, stimulated by TV series in which white Britons parodied Dixieland. In the real Deep South segregation remained.

7

November – December 1962

24 November 1962

2	1	ON STAGE WITH THE GEORGE MITCHELL MINSTRELS George Mitchell Minstrels (HMV)
1	2	WEST SIDE STORY Soundtrack (CBS)
3	3	OUT OF THE SHADOWS Shadows (Columbia)
6	4	THE BEST OF BALL, BARBER AND BILK Kenny Ball, Chris Barber & Acker Bilk (Golden Guinea)
4	5	THE BLACK AND WHITE MINSTREL SHOW George Mitchell Minstrels (HMV)
5	5	A GOLDEN AGE OF DONEGAN Lonnie Donegan (Golden Guinea)
-	7	POT LUCK Elvis Presley (RCA)
8	8	A PICTURE OF YOU Joe Brown (Golden Guinea)
7	9	SOUTH PACIFIC Soundtrack (RCA)
9	9	BOBBY VEE MEETS THE CRICKETS Bobby Vee & the Crickets (Liberty)

1 December 1962

1	1	ON STAGE WITH THE GEORGE MITCHELL MINSTRELS George Mitchell Minstrels (HMV)
2	2	WEST SIDE STORY Soundtrack (CBS)
4	3	THE BEST OF BALL, BARBER AND BILK Kenny Ball, Chris Barber & Acker Bilk (Golden Guinea)
3	4	OUT OF THE SHADOWS Shadows (Columbia)
5	5	THE BLACK AND WHITE MINSTREL SHOW George Mitchell Minstrels (HMV)
5	6	A GOLDEN AGE OF DONEGAN Lonnie Donegan (Golden Guinea)
9	7	BOBBY VEE MEETS THE CRICKETS Bobby Vee & the Crickets (Liberty)
8	8	A PICTURE OF YOU Joe Brown (Golden Guinea)
9	9	SOUTH PACIFIC Soundtrack (RCA)
7	10	POT LUCK Elvis Presley (RCA)

8 December 1962

1	1	ON STAGE WITH THE GEORGE MITCHELL MINSTRELS George Mitchell Minstrels (HMV)
2	2	WEST SIDE STORY Soundtrack (CBS)
5	3	THE BLACK AND WHITE MINSTREL SHOW George Mitchell Minstrels (HMV)
4	4	OUT OF THE SHADOWS Shadows (Columbia)
3	5	THE BEST OF BALL, BARBER AND BILK Kenny Ball, Chris Barber & Acker Bilk (Golden Guinea)
6	6	A GOLDEN AGE OF DONEGAN Lonnie Donegan (Golden Guinea)
7	7	BOBBY VEE MEETS THE CRICKETS Bobby Vee & the Crickets (Liberty)
-	8	ROCK 'N' ROLL NO. 2 Elvis Presley (RCA)
9	9	SOUTH PACIFIC Soundtrack (RCA)
10	10	POT LUCK Elvis Presley (RCA)

15 December 1962

1	1	ON STAGE WITH THE GEORGE MITCHELL MINSTRELS George Mitchell Minstrels (HMV)
2	2	WEST SIDE STORY Soundtrack (CBS)
8	3	ROCK 'N' ROLL NO. 2 Elvis Presley (RCA)
3	4	THE BLACK AND WHITE MINSTREL SHOW George Mitchell Minstrels (HMV)
7	5	BOBBY VEE MEETS THE CRICKETS Bobby Vee & the Crickets (Liberty)
4	6	OUT OF THE SHADOWS Shadows (Columbia)
9	7	SOUTH PACIFIC Soundtrack (RCA)
-	8	ANOTHER BLACK AND WHITE MINSTREL SHOW George Mitchell Minstrels (HMV)
-	9	32 MINUTES AND 17 SECONDS Cliff Richard (Columbia)
5	10	THE BEST OF BALL, BARBER AND BILK Kenny Ball, Chris Barber & Acker Bilk (Golden Guinea)

22 December 1962

1	1	ON STAGE WITH THE GEORGE MITCHELL MINSTRELS George Mitchell Minstrels (HMV)
4	2	THE BLACK AND WHITE MINSTREL SHOW George Mitchell Minstrels (HMV)
2	3	WEST SIDE STORY Soundtrack (CBS)
3	4	ROCK 'N' ROLL NO. 2 Elvis Presley (RCA)
8	5	ANOTHER BLACK AND WHITE MINSTREL SHOW George Mitchell Minstrels (HMV)
5	6	BOBBY VEE MEETS THE CRICKETS Bobby Vee & the Crickets (Liberty)
6	6	OUT OF THE SHADOWS Shadows (Columbia)
7	8	SOUTH PACIFIC Soundtrack (RCA)
10	9	THE BEST OF BALL, BARBER AND BILK Kenny Ball, Chris Barber & Acker Bilk (Golden Guinea)
-	10	SINATRA AND SWINGING BRASS Frank Sinatra (Reprise)

29 December 1962

1	1	ON STAGE WITH THE GEORGE MITCHELL MINSTRELS George Mitchell Minstrels (HMV)
2	2	THE BLACK AND WHITE MINSTREL SHOW George Mitchell Minstrels (HMV)
4	3	ROCK 'N' ROLL NO. 2 Elvis Presley (RCA)
3	4	WEST SIDE STORY Soundtrack (CBS)
6	5	OUT OF THE SHADOWS Shadows (Columbia)
5	6	ANOTHER BLACK AND WHITE MINSTREL SHOW George Mitchell Minstrels (HMV)
9	7	THE BEST OF BALL, BARBER AND BILK Kenny Ball, Chris Barber & Acker Bilk (Golden Guinea)
10	8	SINATRA AND SWINGING BRASS Frank Sinatra (Reprise)
6	8	BOBBY VEE MEETS THE CRICKETS Bobby Vee & the Crickets (Liberty)
8	10	SOUTH PACIFIC Soundtrack (RCA)

The grown-ups dreamed of a white Christmas with the Black And White Minstrels at Nos 1,2 and 5. While parents also bought each other soundtracks of musicals, trad, Sinatra and swinging brass, there was room in the charts for just three pop acts: Bobby Vee meeting the Crickets, the Shadows and Elvis. Vee personified tne legendary clean-cut Bobbies of post-rock'n'roll; the Shadows were big because they had headed another craze of the day: for guitar-based instrumental hit singles.

5 January 1963

last week	this week	
1	1	ON STAGE WITH THE GEORGE MITCHELL MINSTRELS George Mitchell Minstrels (HMV)
4	2	WEST SIDE STORY Soundtrack (CBS)
2	3	THE BLACK AND WHITE MINSTREL SHOW George Mitchell Minstrels (HMV)
5	4	OUT OF THE SHADOWS Shadows (Columbia)
3	5	ROCK 'N' ROLL NO. 2 Elvis Presley (RCA)
8	6	BOBBY VEE MEETS THE CRICKETS Bobby Vee & the Crickets (Liberty)
6	7	ANOTHER BLACK AND WHITE MINSTREL SHOW George Mitchell Minstrels (HMV)
10	7	SOUTH PACIFIC Soundtrack (RCA)
7	9	THE BEST OF BALL, BARBER AND BILK Kenny Ball, Chris Barber & Acker Bilk (Golden Guinea)
8	9	SINATRA AND SWINGING BRASS Frank Sinatra (Reprise)

12 January 1963

2	1	WEST SIDE STORY Soundtrack (CBS)
1	2	ON STAGE WITH THE GEORGE MITCHELL MINSTRELS George Mitchell Minstrels (HMV)
4	3	OUT OF THE SHADOWS Shadows (Columbia)
6	4	BOBBY VEE MEETS THE CRICKETS Bobby Vee & the Crickets (Liberty)
5	5	ROCK 'N' ROLL NO. 2 Elvis Presley (RCA)
3	6	THE BLACK AND WHITE MINSTREL SHOW George Mitchell Minstrels (HMV)
7	7	SOUTH PACIFIC Soundtrack (RCA)
-	8	A PICTURE OF YOU Joe Brown (Golden Guinea)
7	9	ANOTHER BLACK AND WHITE MINSTREL SHOW George Mitchell Minstrels (HMV)
9	9	SINATRA AND SWINGING BRASS Frank Sinatra (Reprise)

19 January 1963

1	1	WEST SIDE STORY Soundtrack (CBS)
4	2	BOBBY VEE MEETS THE CRICKETS Bobby Vee & the Crickets (Liberty)
3	3	OUT OF THE SHADOWS Shadows (Columbia)
5	4	ROCK 'N' ROLL NO. 2 Elvis Presley (RCA)
2	5	ON STAGE WITH THE GEORGE MITCHELL MINSTRELS George Mitchell Minstrels (HMV)
6	6	THE BLACK AND WHITE MINSTREL SHOW George Mitchell Minstrels (HMV)
7	7	SOUTH PACIFIC Soundtrack (RCA)
-	8	32 MINUTES AND 17 SECONDS Cliff Richard (Columbia)
9	9	SINATRA AND SWINGING BRASS Frank Sinatra (Reprise)
-	10	A BOBBY VEE RECORDING SESSION Bobby Vee (Liberty)

26 January 1963

1	1	WEST SIDE STORY Soundtrack (CBS)
-	2	SUMMER HOLIDAY Cliff Richard & the Shadows (Columbia)
-	3	GIRLS! GIRLS! GIRLS! Elvis Presley (RCA)
3	4	OUT OF THE SHADOWS Shadows (Columbia)
5	5	ON STAGE WITH THE GEORGE MITCHELL MINSTRELS George Mitchell Minstrels (HMV)
2	6	BOBBY VEE MEETS THE CRICKETS Bobby Vee & the Crickets (Liberty)
4	7	ROCK 'N' ROLL NO. 2 Elvis Presley (RCA)
6	8	THE BLACK AND WHITE MINSTREL SHOW George Mitchell Minstrels (HMV)
7	9	SOUTH PACIFIC Soundtrack (RCA)
-	10	THE BEST OF BALL, BARBER AND BILK Kenny Ball, Chris Barber & Acker Bilk (Golden Guinea)

2 February 1963

2	1	SUMMER HOLIDAY Cliff Richard & the Shadows (Columbia)
3	2	GIRLS! GIRLS! GIRLS! Elvis Presley (RCA)
1	3	WEST SIDE STORY Soundtrack (CBS)
4	4	OUT OF THE SHADOWS Shadows (Columbia)
9	5	SOUTH PACIFIC Soundtrack (RCA)
6	6	BOBBY VEE MEETS THE CRICKETS Bobby Vee & the Crickets (Liberty)
7	6	ROCK 'N' ROLL NO. 2 Elvis Presley (RCA)
5	8	ON STAGE WITH THE GEORGE MITCHELL MINSTRELS George Mitchell Minstrels (HMV)
8	9	THE BLACK AND WHITE MINSTREL SHOW George Mitchell Minstrels (HMV)
-	10	A GOLDEN AGE OF DONEGAN VOL 2 Lonnie Donegan (Golden Guinea)

9 February 1963

1	1	SUMMER HOLIDAY Cliff Richard & the Shadows (Columbia)
2	2	GIRLS! GIRLS! GIRLS! Elvis Presley (RCA)
3	3	WEST SIDE STORY Soundtrack (CBS)
4	4	OUT OF THE SHADOWS Shadows (Columbia)
5	5	SOUTH PACIFIC Soundtrack (RCA)
9	6	THE BLACK AND WHITE MINSTREL SHOW George Mitchell Minstrels (HMV)
10	7	A GOLDEN AGE OF DONEGAN VOL 2 Lonnie Donegan (Golden Guinea)
8	8	ON STAGE WITH THE GEORGE MITCHELL MINSTRELS George Mitchell Minstrels (HMV)
9	9	BOBBY VEE MEETS THE CRICKETS Bobby Vee & the Crickets (Liberty)
-	10	A BOBBY VEE RECORDING SESSION Bobby Vee (Liberty)
-	10	GYPSY Soundtrack (Warner Bros.)

16 February 1963

1	1	SUMMER HOLIDAY Cliff Richard & the Shadows (Columbia)
2	2	GIRLS! GIRLS! GIRLS! Elvis Presley (RCA)
3	3	WEST SIDE STORY Soundtrack (CBS)
-	4	I'LL REMEMBER YOU Frank Ifield (Columbia)
4	5	OUT OF THE SHADOWS Shadows (Columbia)
5	6	SOUTH PACIFIC Soundtrack (RCA)
6	7	THE BLACK AND WHITE MINSTREL SHOW George Mitchell Minstrels (HMV)
9	8	BOBBY VEE MEETS THE CRICKETS Bobby Vee & the Crickets (Liberty)
-	9	MODERN SOUNDS IN COUNTRY AND WESTERN MUSIC, VOL. 2 Ray Charles (HMV)
-	10	THE BUDDY HOLLY STORY VOL 1 Buddy Holly (Coral)

23 February 1963

1	1	SUMMER HOLIDAY Cliff Richard & the Shadows (Columbia)
2	2	GIRLS! GIRLS! GIRLS! Elvis Presley (RCA)
4	3	I'LL REMEMBER YOU Frank Ifield (Columbia)
3	4	WEST SIDE STORY Soundtrack (CBS)
-	5	SINATRA/BASIE Frank Sinatra & Count Basie (Reprise)
7	6	THE BLACK AND WHITE MINSTREL SHOW George Mitchell Minstrels (HMV)
5	7	OUT OF THE SHADOWS Shadows (Columbia)
6	7	SOUTH PACIFIC Soundtrack (RCA)
8	9	BOBBY VEE MEETS THE CRICKETS Bobby Vee & the Crickets (Liberty)
-	10	ON STAGE WITH THE GEORGE MITCHELL MINSTRELS George Mitchell Minstrels (HMV)

Shads boss Cliff Richard leapt straight in at No.2 with the LP of his film about taking a London double-decker for a *Summer Holiday* in Europe. This cheer reached the top slot in freezing February (it was the coldest winter in living memory; Sylvia Plath killed herself in London that month). Cliff held the latest Presley movie-soundtrack at bay and was to remain at No.1 right through till May, when The Beatles would introduce themselves to the LP top spot and hold on to it for five months straight.

March – April 1963

2 March 1963

(last week / this week)

1	1	SUMMER HOLIDAY — Cliff Richard & the Shadows (Columbia)
3	2	I'LL REMEMBER YOU — Frank Ifield (Columbia)
2	3	GIRLS! GIRLS! GIRLS! — Elvis Presley (RCA)
5	4	SINATRA/BASIE — Frank Sinatra & Count Basie (Reprise)
4	5	WEST SIDE STORY — Soundtrack (CBS)
7	6	OUT OF THE SHADOWS — Shadows (Columbia)
10	7	ON STAGE WITH THE GEORGE MITCHELL MINSTRELS — George Mitchell Minstrels (HMV)
7	8	SOUTH PACIFIC — Soundtrack (RCA)
6	9	THE BLACK AND WHITE MINSTREL SHOW — George Mitchell Minstrels (HMV)
9	10	BOBBY VEE MEETS THE CRICKETS — Bobby Vee & the Crickets (Liberty)

9 March 1963

1	1	SUMMER HOLIDAY — Cliff Richard & the Shadows (Columbia)
4	2	SINATRA/BASIE — Frank Sinatra & Count Basie (Reprise)
3	3	GIRLS! GIRLS! GIRLS! — Elvis Presley (RCA)
2	4	I'LL REMEMBER YOU — Frank Ifield (Columbia)
5	5	WEST SIDE STORY — Soundtrack (CBS)
-	6	ALL STAR FESTIVAL — Various Artists (United Nations)
6	7	OUT OF THE SHADOWS — Shadows (Columbia)
-	7	STEPTOE AND SON — TV Cast (Pye)
8	9	SOUTH PACIFIC — Soundtrack (RCA)
7	10	ON STAGE WITH THE GEORGE MITCHELL MINSTRELS — George Mitchell Minstrels (HMV)
9	10	THE BLACK AND WHITE MINSTREL SHOW — George Mitchell Minstrels (HMV)

16 March 1963

1	1	SUMMER HOLIDAY — Cliff Richard & the Shadows (Columbia)
2	2	SINATRA/BASIE — Frank Sinatra & Count Basie (Reprise)
4	3	I'LL REMEMBER YOU — Frank Ifield (Columbia)
3	4	GIRLS! GIRLS! GIRLS! — Elvis Presley (RCA)
6	5	ALL STAR FESTIVAL — Various Artists (United Nations)
5	6	WEST SIDE STORY — Soundtrack (CBS)
9	7	SOUTH PACIFIC — Soundtrack (RCA)
7	8	STEPTOE AND SON — TV Cast (Pye)
7	9	OUT OF THE SHADOWS — Shadows (Columbia)
10	10	THE BLACK AND WHITE MINSTREL SHOW — George Mitchell Minstrels (HMV)

23 March 1963

1	1	SUMMER HOLIDAY — Cliff Richard & the Shadows (Columbia)
2	2	SINATRA/BASIE — Frank Sinatra & Count Basie (Reprise)
3	3	I'LL REMEMBER YOU — Frank Ifield (Columbia)
4	4	GIRLS! GIRLS! GIRLS! — Elvis Presley (RCA)
5	5	ALL STAR FESTIVAL — Various Artists (United Nations)
6	6	WEST SIDE STORY — Soundtrack (CBS)
7	7	SOUTH PACIFIC — Soundtrack (RCA)
9	8	OUT OF THE SHADOWS — Shadows (Columbia)
8	9	STEPTOE AND SON — TV Cast (Pye)
-	10	RICHARD CHAMBERLAIN SINGS — Richard Chamberlain (MGM)

30 March 1963

1	1	SUMMER HOLIDAY — Cliff Richard & the Shadows (Columbia)
2	2	SINATRA/BASIE — Frank Sinatra & Count Basie (Reprise)
3	3	I'LL REMEMBER YOU — Frank Ifield (Columbia)
5	4	ALL STAR FESTIVAL — Various Artists (United Nations)
4	5	GIRLS! GIRLS! GIRLS! — Elvis Presley (RCA)
-	6	REMINISCING — Buddy Holly (Coral)
6	7	WEST SIDE STORY — Soundtrack (CBS)
7	8	SOUTH PACIFIC — Soundtrack (RCA)
-	9	PLEASE PLEASE ME — Beatles (Parlophone)
7	10	OUT OF THE SHADOWS — Shadows (Columbia)

6 April 1963

1	1	SUMMER HOLIDAY — Cliff Richard & the Shadows (Columbia)
6	2	REMINISCING — Buddy Holly (Coral)
2	3	SINATRA/BASIE — Frank Sinatra & Count Basie (Reprise)
3	3	I'LL REMEMBER YOU — Frank Ifield (Columbia)
5	5	GIRLS! GIRLS! GIRLS! — Elvis Presley (RCA)
9	6	PLEASE PLEASE ME — Beatles (Parlophone)
4	7	ALL STAR FESTIVAL — Various Artists (United Nations)
7	8	WEST SIDE STORY — Soundtrack (CBS)
10	9	OUT OF THE SHADOWS — Shadows (Columbia)
8	10	SOUTH PACIFIC — Soundtrack (RCA)

13 April 1963

1	1	SUMMER HOLIDAY — Cliff Richard & the Shadows (Columbia)
2	2	REMINISCING — Buddy Holly (Coral)
7	3	ALL STAR FESTIVAL — Various Artists (United Nations)
3	4	SINATRA/BASIE — Frank Sinatra & Count Basie (Reprise)
6	5	PLEASE PLEASE ME — Beatles (Parlophone)
3	6	I'LL REMEMBER YOU — Frank Ifield (Columbia)
5	7	GIRLS! GIRLS! GIRLS! — Elvis Presley (RCA)
8	8	WEST SIDE STORY — Soundtrack (CBS)
9	9	OUT OF THE SHADOWS — Shadows (Columbia)
-	10	THE EDDIE COCHRAN MEMORIAL ALBUM — Eddie Cochran (Liberty)

20 April 1963

1	1	SUMMER HOLIDAY — Cliff Richard & the Shadows (Columbia)
2	2	REMINISCING — Buddy Holly (Coral)
5	3	PLEASE PLEASE ME — Beatles (Parlophone)
3	4	ALL STAR FESTIVAL — Various Artists (United Nations)
6	5	I'LL REMEMBER YOU — Frank Ifield (Columbia)
8	6	WEST SIDE STORY — Soundtrack (CBS)
4	7	SINATRA/BASIE — Frank Sinatra & Count Basie (Reprise)
9	8	OUT OF THE SHADOWS — Shadows (Columbia)
-	9	SOUTH PACIFIC — Soundtrack (RCA)
6	9	ON STAGE WITH THE GEORGE MITCHELL MINSTRELS — George Mitchell Minstrels (HMV)
-	9	BOBBY VEE'S GOLDEN GREATS — Bobby Vee (Liberty)

The Beatles' LP chart arrival came at No.9 that March, three places below a curious posthumous album by Buddy Holly. *Reminiscing* offered some previously-unissued Holly overdubbed by The Fireballs at the behest of producer Norman Petty, whose studio in Clovis New Mexico was almost as famous as Sam Phillips' Sun studio in Memphis. At this time record-buyers knew nothing of such matters as outtakes; each time "new" Holly material emerged, they were surprised there was any left.

April – June 1963

last week	this week	27 April 1963
1	1	SUMMER HOLIDAY Cliff Richard & the Shadows (Columbia)
3	2	PLEASE PLEASE ME Beatles (Parlophone)
2	3	REMINISCING Buddy Holly (Coral)
6	4	WEST SIDE STORY Soundtrack (CBS)
4	5	ALL STAR FESTIVAL Various Artists (United Nations)
5	6	I'LL REMEMBER YOU Frank Ifield (Columbia)
-	7	GIRLS! GIRLS! GIRLS! Elvis Presley (RCA)
7	8	SINATRA/BASIE Frank Sinatra & Count Basie (Reprise)
9	9	SOUTH PACIFIC Soundtrack (RCA)
-	10	HATS OFF TO DEL SHANNON Del Shannon (London)

4 May 1963

1	1	SUMMER HOLIDAY Cliff Richard & the Shadows (Columbia)
2	2	PLEASE PLEASE ME Beatles (Parlophone)
3	3	REMINISCING Buddy Holly (Coral)
4	4	WEST SIDE STORY Soundtrack (CBS)
6	5	I'LL REMEMBER YOU Frank Ifield (Columbia)
7	6	GIRLS! GIRLS! GIRLS! Elvis Presley (RCA)
5	7	ALL STAR FESTIVAL Various Artists (United Nations)
8	7	SINATRA/BASIE Frank Sinatra & Count Basie (Reprise)
-	9	ALL ALONE AM I Brenda Lee (Brunswick)
-	9	STEPTOE AND SON TV Cast (Pye)

11 May 1963

2	1	PLEASE PLEASE ME Beatles (Parlophone)
1	2	SUMMER HOLIDAY Cliff Richard & the Shadows (Columbia)
3	3	REMINISCING Buddy Holly (Coral)
-	4	IT HAPPENED AT THE WORLD'S FAIR Elvis Presley (RCA)
5	5	I'LL REMEMBER YOU Frank Ifield (Columbia)
4	6	WEST SIDE STORY Soundtrack (CBS)
-	7	JUST FOR FUN Soundtrack (Decca)
6	8	GIRLS! GIRLS! GIRLS! Elvis Presley (RCA)
7	8	ALL STAR FESTIVAL Various Artists (United Nations)
7	10	SINATRA/BASIE Frank Sinatra & Count Basie (Reprise)

18 May 1963

1	1	PLEASE PLEASE ME Beatles (Parlophone)
2	2	SUMMER HOLIDAY Cliff Richard & the Shadows (Columbia)
4	3	IT HAPPENED AT THE WORLD'S FAIR Elvis Presley (RCA)
3	4	REMINISCING Buddy Holly (Coral)
6	5	WEST SIDE STORY Soundtrack (CBS)
5	6	I'LL REMEMBER YOU Frank Ifield (Columbia)
7	7	JUST FOR FUN Soundtrack (Decca)
8	7	GIRLS! GIRLS! GIRLS! Elvis Presley (RCA)
10	7	SINATRA/BASIE Frank Sinatra & Count Basie (Reprise)
-	10	ALL ALONE AM I Brenda Lee (Brunswick)

25 May 1963

1	1	PLEASE PLEASE ME Beatles (Parlophone)
3	2	IT HAPPENED AT THE WORLD'S FAIR Elvis Presley (RCA)
2	3	SUMMER HOLIDAY Cliff Richard & the Shadows (Columbia)
4	4	REMINISCING Buddy Holly (Coral)
5	5	WEST SIDE STORY Soundtrack (CBS)
-	6	BILLY Billy Fury (Decca)
-	7	ALL STAR FESTIVAL Various Artists (United Nations)
6	8	I'LL REMEMBER YOU Frank Ifield (Columbia)
-	9	SAMMY DAVIS JR. AT THE COCONUT GROVE Sammy Davis Jnr. (Reprise)
7	10	SINATRA/BASIE Frank Sinatra & Count Basie (Reprise)

1 June 1963

1	1	PLEASE PLEASE ME Beatles (Parlophone)
3	2	SUMMER HOLIDAY Cliff Richard & the Shadows (Columbia)
2	3	IT HAPPENED AT THE WORLD'S FAIR Elvis Presley (RCA)
5	4	WEST SIDE STORY Soundtrack (CBS)
4	5	REMINISCING Buddy Holly (Coral)
6	6	BILLY Billy Fury (Decca)
10	7	SINATRA/BASIE Frank Sinatra & Count Basie (Reprise)
7	8	ALL STAR FESTIVAL Various Artists (United Nations)
8	9	I'LL REMEMBER YOU Frank Ifield (Columbia)
-	10	HATS OFF TO DEL SHANNON Del Shannon (London)

8 June 1963

1	1	PLEASE PLEASE ME Beatles (Parlophone)
2	2	SUMMER HOLIDAY Cliff Richard & the Shadows (Columbia)
3	3	IT HAPPENED AT THE WORLD'S FAIR Elvis Presley (RCA)
4	4	WEST SIDE STORY Soundtrack (CBS)
6	5	BILLY Billy Fury (Decca)
5	5	REMINISCING Buddy Holly (Coral)
9	7	I'LL REMEMBER YOU Frank Ifield (Columbia)
-	8	SOUTH PACIFIC Soundtrack (RCA)
-	9	ALL ALONE AM I Brenda Lee (Brunswick)
-	9	RAY CHARLES' GREATEST HITS Ray Charles (HMV)

15 June 1963

1	1	PLEASE PLEASE ME Beatles (Parlophone)
2	2	SUMMER HOLIDAY Cliff Richard & the Shadows (Columbia)
3	3	IT HAPPENED AT THE WORLD'S FAIR Elvis Presley (RCA)
5	4	REMINISCING Buddy Holly (Coral)
-	5	THE SHADOWS' GREATEST HITS Shadows (Columbia)
6	5	BILLY Billy Fury (Decca)
4	7	WEST SIDE STORY Soundtrack (CBS)
7	8	I'LL REMEMBER YOU Frank Ifield (Columbia)
	9	THE EDDIE COCHRAN MEMORIAL ALBUM Eddie Cochran (Liberty)
	10	HATS OFF TO DEL SHANNON Del Shannon (London)

Eddie Cochran had died in 1960, Holly in 1959. Here they were charting three and four years on. This gave the lie to the prevalent notion that pop was ephemeral rubbish by nine-day wonders without the staying-power of "real entertainers". Yet to look back on this first year's LP chart is to ask whatever happened to the George Mitchell Minstrels, the Ray Conniff Singers, Dorothy Provine? What Sammy Davis Jnr record remains even an "easy listening" favourite? 30 years on, Holly, Presley and Cliff are the survivors.

June – August 1963

22 June 1963

last	this	
1	1	PLEASE PLEASE ME — Beatles (Parlophone)
2	2	SUMMER HOLIDAY — Cliff Richard & the Shadows (Columbia)
5	3	THE SHADOWS' GREATEST HITS — Shadows (Columbia)
3	4	IT HAPPENED AT THE WORLD'S FAIR — Elvis Presley (RCA)
7	5	WEST SIDE STORY — Soundtrack (CBS)
4	6	REMINISCING — Buddy Holly (Coral)
6	7	BILLY — Billy Fury (Decca)
8	8	I'LL REMEMBER YOU — Frank Ifield (Columbia)
-	9	SOUTH PACIFIC — Soundtrack (RCA)
-	10	BOBBY VEE'S GOLDEN GREATS — Bobby Vee (Liberty)

29 June 1963

last	this	
1	1	PLEASE PLEASE ME — Beatles (Parlophone)
3	2	THE SHADOWS' GREATEST HITS — Shadows (Columbia)
2	3	SUMMER HOLIDAY — Cliff Richard & the Shadows (Columbia)
5	4	WEST SIDE STORY — Soundtrack (CBS)
4	5	IT HAPPENED AT THE WORLD'S FAIR — Elvis Presley (RCA)
8	6	I'LL REMEMBER YOU — Frank Ifield (Columbia)
6	7	REMINISCING — Buddy Holly (Coral)
7	8	BILLY — Billy Fury (Decca)
9	9	SOUTH PACIFIC — Soundtrack (RCA)
-	10	GIRLS! GIRLS! GIRLS! — Elvis Presley (RCA)

6 July 1963

last	this	
1	1	PLEASE PLEASE ME — Beatles (Parlophone)
2	2	THE SHADOWS' GREATEST HITS — Shadows (Columbia)
5	3	IT HAPPENED AT THE WORLD'S FAIR — Elvis Presley (RCA)
4	4	WEST SIDE STORY — Soundtrack (CBS)
3	5	SUMMER HOLIDAY — Cliff Richard & the Shadows (Columbia)
7	6	REMINISCING — Buddy Holly (Coral)
8	7	BILLY — Billy Fury (Decca)
9	8	SOUTH PACIFIC — Soundtrack (RCA)
6	9	I'LL REMEMBER YOU — Frank Ifield (Columbia)
-	9	SINATRA/BASIE — Frank Sinatra & Count Basie (Reprise)

13 July 1963

last	this	
1	1	PLEASE PLEASE ME — Beatles (Parlophone)
2	2	THE SHADOWS' GREATEST HITS — Shadows (Columbia)
5	3	SUMMER HOLIDAY — Cliff Richard & the Shadows (Columbia)
4	4	WEST SIDE STORY — Soundtrack (CBS)
3	5	IT HAPPENED AT THE WORLD'S FAIR — Elvis Presley (RCA)
9	6	I'LL REMEMBER YOU — Frank Ifield (Columbia)
-	7	CLIFF'S HIT ALBUM — Cliff Richard (Columbia)
6	8	REMINISCING — Buddy Holly (Coral)
-	9	BASSEY SPECTACULAR — Shirley Bassey (Philips)
7	10	BILLY — Billy Fury (Decca)

20 July 1963

last	this	
1	1	PLEASE PLEASE ME — Beatles (Parlophone)
2	2	THE SHADOWS' GREATEST HITS — Shadows (Columbia)
7	3	CLIFF'S HIT ALBUM — Cliff Richard (Columbia)
5	4	IT HAPPENED AT THE WORLD'S FAIR — Elvis Presley (RCA)
4	5	WEST SIDE STORY — Soundtrack (CBS)
3	6	SUMMER HOLIDAY — Cliff Richard & the Shadows (Columbia)
9	7	BASSEY SPECTACULAR — Shirley Bassey (Philips)
6	8	I'LL REMEMBER YOU — Frank Ifield (Columbia)
8	9	REMINISCING — Buddy Holly (Coral)
-	10	SOUTH PACIFIC — Soundtrack (RCA)

27 July 1963

last	this	
1	1	PLEASE PLEASE ME — Beatles (Parlophone)
2	2	THE SHADOWS' GREATEST HITS — Shadows (Columbia)
3	3	CLIFF'S HIT ALBUM — Cliff Richard (Columbia)
4	4	IT HAPPENED AT THE WORLD'S FAIR — Elvis Presley (RCA)
5	5	WEST SIDE STORY — Soundtrack (CBS)
6	6	SUMMER HOLIDAY — Cliff Richard & the Shadows (Columbia)
9	7	REMINISCING — Buddy Holly (Coral)
8	8	I'LL REMEMBER YOU — Frank Ifield (Columbia)
-	9	THE CONCERT SINATRA — Frank Sinatra (Reprise)
7	10	BASSEY SPECTACULAR — Shirley Bassey (Philips)

3 August 1963

last	this	
1	1	PLEASE PLEASE ME — Beatles (Parlophone)
2	2	THE SHADOWS' GREATEST HITS — Shadows (Columbia)
3	3	CLIFF'S HIT ALBUM — Cliff Richard (Columbia)
5	4	WEST SIDE STORY — Soundtrack (CBS)
4	5	IT HAPPENED AT THE WORLD'S FAIR — Elvis Presley (RCA)
6	6	SUMMER HOLIDAY — Cliff Richard & the Shadows (Columbia)
8	7	I'LL REMEMBER YOU — Frank Ifield (Columbia)
7	8	REMINISCING — Buddy Holly (Coral)
8	9	THE CONCERT SINATRA — Frank Sinatra (Reprise)
10	10	BASSEY SPECTACULAR — Shirley Bassey (Philips)
-	10	BILLY — Billy Fury (Decca)

10 August 1963

last	this	
1	1	PLEASE PLEASE ME — Beatles (Parlophone)
2	2	THE SHADOWS' GREATEST HITS — Shadows (Columbia)
3	3	CLIFF'S HIT ALBUM — Cliff Richard (Columbia)
4	4	WEST SIDE STORY — Soundtrack (CBS)
5	5	IT HAPPENED AT THE WORLD'S FAIR — Elvis Presley (RCA)
7	6	I'LL REMEMBER YOU — Frank Ifield (Columbia)
8	7	REMINISCING — Buddy Holly (Coral)
-	8	MEET THE SEARCHERS — Searchers (Pye)
9	9	THE CONCERT SINATRA — Frank Sinatra (Reprise)
6	10	SUMMER HOLIDAY — Cliff Richard & the Shadows (Columbia)

Many other enduring pop artists were around, but most were in the singles charts. Hit 45ers of 1962-1963 included the Everlys, Shirelles, Crystals, Drifters, Rick Nelson, Jerry Lee Lewis, Sam Cooke and Roy Orbison. Now, however, with the Beatles topping the LP chart, it was the Mersey Sound that threatened them. Merseybeat was the punk of its day: grassroots music anyone could play, it was (to begin with) rough stuff. It was now big enough for another Liverpool group, the Searchers, to chart with an LP.

August – October 1963

17 August 1963

last week	this week		
1	1	PLEASE PLEASE ME	Beatles (Parlophone)
2	2	THE SHADOWS' GREATEST HITS	Shadows (Columbia)
3	3	CLIFF'S HIT ALBUM	Cliff Richard (Columbia)
8	4	MEET THE SEARCHERS	Searchers (Pye)
4	5	WEST SIDE STORY	Soundtrack (CBS)
5	6	IT HAPPENED AT THE WORLD'S FAIR	Elvis Presley (RCA)
9	7	THE CONCERT SINATRA	Frank Sinatra (Reprise)
-	8	BILLY	Billy Fury (Decca)
-	9	SOUTH PACIFIC	Soundtrack (RCA)
-	10	THE BUDDY HOLLY STORY VOL 1	Buddy Holly (Coral)

24 August 1963

1	1	PLEASE PLEASE ME	Beatles (Parlophone)
4	2	MEET THE SEARCHERS	Searchers (Pye)
2	3	THE SHADOWS' GREATEST HITS	Shadows (Columbia)
3	3	CLIFF'S HIT ALBUM	Cliff Richard (Columbia)
5	5	WEST SIDE STORY	Soundtrack (CBS)
6	6	IT HAPPENED AT THE WORLD'S FAIR	Elvis Presley (RCA)
7	7	THE CONCERT SINATRA	Frank Sinatra (Reprise)
-	8	SUMMER HOLIDAY	Cliff Richard & the Shadows (Columbia)
-	9	I'LL REMEMBER YOU	Frank Ifield (Columbia)
10	10	THE BUDDY HOLLY STORY VOL 1	Buddy Holly (Coral)
-	10	STEPTOE AND SON	TV Cast (Pye)
-	10	PICKWICK	London Cast (Philips)

31 August 1963

1	1	PLEASE PLEASE ME	Beatles (Parlophone)
3	2	THE SHADOWS' GREATEST HITS	Shadows (Columbia)
3	3	CLIFF'S HIT ALBUM	Cliff Richard (Columbia)
2	4	MEET THE SEARCHERS	Searchers (Pye)
5	5	WEST SIDE STORY	Soundtrack (CBS)
-	6	KENNY BALL'S GOLDEN HITS	Kenny Ball (Golden Guinea)
10	7	STEPTOE AND SON	TV Cast (Pye)
6	8	IT HAPPENED AT THE WORLD'S FAIR	Elvis Presley (RCA)
7	8	THE CONCERT SINATRA	Frank Sinatra (Reprise)
-	10	SOUTH PACIFIC	Soundtrack (RCA)

7 September 1963

1	1	PLEASE PLEASE ME	Beatles (Parlophone)
2	2	THE SHADOWS' GREATEST HITS	Shadows (Columbia)
3	3	CLIFF'S HIT ALBUM	Cliff Richard (Columbia)
4	4	MEET THE SEARCHERS	Searchers (Pye)
6	5	KENNY BALL'S GOLDEN HITS	Kenny Ball (Golden Guinea)
5	6	WEST SIDE STORY	Soundtrack (CBS)
7	7	STEPTOE AND SON	TV Cast (Pye)
8	8	THE CONCERT SINATRA	Frank Sinatra (Reprise)
-	9	RAY CHARLES' GREATEST HITS	Ray Charles (HMV)
-	10	I'LL REMEMBER YOU	Frank Ifield (Columbia)

14 September 1963

1	1	PLEASE PLEASE ME	Beatles (Parlophone)
2	2	THE SHADOWS' GREATEST HITS	Shadows (Columbia)
4	3	MEET THE SEARCHERS	Searchers (Pye)
3	4	CLIFF'S HIT ALBUM	Cliff Richard (Columbia)
5	5	KENNY BALL'S GOLDEN HITS	Kenny Ball (Golden Guinea)
7	6	STEPTOE AND SON	TV Cast (Pye)
6	7	WEST SIDE STORY	Soundtrack (CBS)
10	8	I'LL REMEMBER YOU	Frank Ifield (Columbia)
-	9	REMINISCING	Buddy Holly (Coral)
8	10	THE CONCERT SINATRA	Frank Sinatra (Reprise)

21 September 1963

1	1	PLEASE PLEASE ME	Beatles (Parlophone)
2	2	THE SHADOWS' GREATEST HITS	Shadows (Columbia)
3	3	MEET THE SEARCHERS	Searchers (Pye)
4	4	CLIFF'S HIT ALBUM	Cliff Richard (Columbia)
5	5	KENNY BALL'S GOLDEN HITS	Kenny Ball (Golden Guinea)
7	6	WEST SIDE STORY	Soundtrack (CBS)
-	7	BORN FREE	Frank Ifield (Columbia)
6	8	STEPTOE AND SON	TV Cast (Pye)
10	9	THE CONCERT SINATRA	Frank Sinatra (Reprise)
8	10	I'LL REMEMBER YOU	Frank Ifield (Columbia)

28 September 1963

1	1	PLEASE PLEASE ME	Beatles (Parlophone)
3	2	MEET THE SEARCHERS	Searchers (Pye)
7	3	BORN FREE	Frank Ifield (Columbia)
2	4	THE SHADOWS' GREATEST HITS	Shadows (Columbia)
5	5	KENNY BALL'S GOLDEN HITS	Kenny Ball (Golden Guinea)
4	6	CLIFF'S HIT ALBUM	Cliff Richard (Columbia)
6	7	WEST SIDE STORY	Soundtrack (CBS)
-	8	WHEN IN SPAIN	Cliff Richard (Columbia)
8	9	STEPTOE AND SON	TV Cast (Pye)
-	10	HITSVILLE	Various Artists (Golden Guinea)

5 October 1963

1	1	PLEASE PLEASE ME	Beatles (Parlophone)
2	2	MEET THE SEARCHERS	Searchers (Pye)
3	3	BORN FREE	Frank Ifield (Columbia)
4	4	THE SHADOWS' GREATEST HITS	Shadows (Columbia)
8	5	WHEN IN SPAIN	Cliff Richard (Columbia)
5	6	KENNY BALL'S GOLDEN HITS	Kenny Ball (Golden Guinea)
-	7	SINATRA'S SINATRA	Frank Sinatra (Reprise)
-	8	CHUCK BERRY ON STAGE	Chuck Berry (Pye International)
7	9	WEST SIDE STORY	Soundtrack (CBS)
6	10	CLIFF'S HIT ALBUM	Cliff Richard (Columbia)

The LP chart said less about the new beat groups' success than about the medium. Cheap and ideal for the short guitar-bass-drum number, the single and Merseybeat seemed made for each other, even while the music really thrived live in small venues for the young working-class. So the LP chart showed only the tip of the tip of this sweaty iceberg; the real tip remained the singles chart, topped August-October by the Searchers, Billy J. Kramer (his second No.1), the Beatles and counterfeit-Merseysiders the Tremeloes.

October – November 1963

12 October 1963

last week	this week	
1	1	PLEASE PLEASE ME — Beatles (Parlophone)
2	2	MEET THE SEARCHERS — Searchers (Pye)
3	3	BORN FREE — Frank Ifield (Columbia)
6	4	KENNY BALL'S GOLDEN HITS — Kenny Ball (Golden Guinea)
5	5	WHEN IN SPAIN — Cliff Richard (Columbia)
4	6	THE SHADOWS' GREATEST HITS — Shadows (Columbia)
7	7	SINATRA'S SINATRA — Frank Sinatra (Reprise)
8	8	CHUCK BERRY ON STAGE — Chuck Berry (Pye International)
9	9	WEST SIDE STORY — Soundtrack (CBS)
-	9	STEPTOE AND SON — TV Cast (Pye)

19 October 1963

last week	this week	
1	1	PLEASE PLEASE ME — Beatles (Parlophone)
2	2	MEET THE SEARCHERS — Searchers (Pye)
3	3	BORN FREE — Frank Ifield (Columbia)
4	4	KENNY BALL'S GOLDEN HITS — Kenny Ball (Golden Guinea)
6	5	THE SHADOWS' GREATEST HITS — Shadows (Columbia)
5	6	WHEN IN SPAIN — Cliff Richard (Columbia)
8	7	CHUCK BERRY ON STAGE — Chuck Berry (Pye International)
9	8	WEST SIDE STORY — Soundtrack (CBS)
-	9	HOW DO YOU LIKE IT — Gerry & the Pacemakers (Columbia)
7	10	SINATRA'S SINATRA — Frank Sinatra (Reprise)
-	10	FOOL BRITANNIA — Original Cast (Ember)

26 October 1963

last week	this week	
1	1	PLEASE PLEASE ME — Beatles (Parlophone)
3	2	BORN FREE — Frank Ifield (Columbia)
2	3	MEET THE SEARCHERS — Searchers (Pye)
9	4	HOW DO YOU LIKE IT — Gerry & the Pacemakers (Columbia)
4	5	KENNY BALL'S GOLDEN HITS — Kenny Ball (Golden Guinea)
5	6	THE SHADOWS' GREATEST HITS — Shadows (Columbia)
6	7	WHEN IN SPAIN — Cliff Richard (Columbia)
10	8	SINATRA'S SINATRA — Frank Sinatra (Reprise)
8	9	WEST SIDE STORY — Soundtrack (CBS)
-	10	TRINI LOPEZ AT P.J.'S — Trini Lopez (Reprise)

2 November 1963

last week	this week	
1	1	PLEASE PLEASE ME — Beatles (Parlophone)
3	2	MEET THE SEARCHERS — Searchers (Pye)
2	3	BORN FREE — Frank Ifield (Columbia)
4	4	HOW DO YOU LIKE IT — Gerry & the Pacemakers (Columbia)
6	5	THE SHADOWS' GREATEST HITS — Shadows (Columbia)
8	6	SINATRA'S SINATRA — Frank Sinatra (Reprise)
10	7	TRINI LOPEZ AT P.J.'S — Trini Lopez (Reprise)
9	8	WEST SIDE STORY — Soundtrack (CBS)
-	9	CHUCK BERRY ON STAGE — Chuck Berry (Pye International)
5	10	KENNY BALL'S GOLDEN HITS — Kenny Ball (Golden Guinea)

9 November 1963

last week	this week	
1	1	PLEASE PLEASE ME — Beatles (Parlophone)
4	2	HOW DO YOU LIKE IT — Gerry & the Pacemakers (Columbia)
2	3	MEET THE SEARCHERS — Searchers (Pye)
5	4	THE SHADOWS' GREATEST HITS — Shadows (Columbia)
7	5	TRINI LOPEZ AT P.J.'S — Trini Lopez (Reprise)
3	6	BORN FREE — Frank Ifield (Columbia)
6	7	SINATRA'S SINATRA — Frank Sinatra (Reprise)
8	8	WEST SIDE STORY — Soundtrack (CBS)
-	9	FREDDIE AND THE DREAMERS — Freddie & the Dreamers (Columbia)
10	10	KENNY BALL'S GOLDEN HITS — Kenny Ball (Golden Guinea)

16 November 1963

last week	this week	
1	1	PLEASE PLEASE ME — Beatles (Parlophone)
2	2	HOW DO YOU LIKE IT — Gerry & the Pacemakers (Columbia)
3	3	MEET THE SEARCHERS — Searchers (Pye)
10	4	KENNY BALL'S GOLDEN HITS — Kenny Ball (Golden Guinea)
-	5	SUGAR AND SPICE — Searchers (Pye)
9	6	FREDDIE AND THE DREAMERS — Freddie & the Dreamers (Columbia)
6	7	BORN FREE — Frank Ifield (Columbia)
4	8	THE SHADOWS' GREATEST HITS — Shadows (Columbia)
8	9	WEST SIDE STORY — Soundtrack (CBS)
-	10	ON TOUR WITH THE GEORGE MITCHELL MINSTRELS — George Mitchell Minstrels (HMV)

23 November 1963

last week	this week	
1	1	PLEASE PLEASE ME — Beatles (Parlophone)
2	2	HOW DO YOU LIKE IT — Gerry & the Pacemakers (Columbia)
3	3	MEET THE SEARCHERS — Searchers (Pye)
6	4	FREDDIE AND THE DREAMERS — Freddie & the Dreamers (Columbia)
9	5	WEST SIDE STORY — Soundtrack (CBS)
-	6	TRINI LOPEZ AT P.J.'S — Trini Lopez (Reprise)
10	7	ON TOUR WITH THE GEORGE MITCHELL MINSTRELS — George Mitchell Minstrels (HMV)
8	8	THE SHADOWS' GREATEST HITS — Shadows (Columbia)
5	9	SUGAR AND SPICE — Searchers (Pye)
7	10	BORN FREE — Frank Ifield (Columbia)

30 November 1963

last week	this week	
-	1	WITH THE BEATLES — Beatles (Parlophone)
1	2	PLEASE PLEASE ME — Beatles (Parlophone)
2	3	HOW DO YOU LIKE IT — Gerry & the Pacemakers (Columbia)
9	4	SUGAR AND SPICE — Searchers (Pye)
5	5	WEST SIDE STORY — Soundtrack (CBS)
3	6	MEET THE SEARCHERS — Searchers (Pye)
7	7	ON TOUR WITH THE GEORGE MITCHELL MINSTRELS — George Mitchell Minstrels (HMV)
6	8	TRINI LOPEZ AT P.J.'S — Trini Lopez (Reprise)
-	9	SINATRA'S SINATRA — Frank Sinatra (Reprise)
4	10	FREDDIE AND THE DREAMERS — Freddie & the Dreamers (Columbia)

As Billy J. Kramer and Brian Poole made clear, the raw excitement of the new beat groups was to remain largely uncaptured on record, while vinyl success met those who made the music chirpy, clean and sweet. So the LP chart opened up also to Merseyside's Gerry & the Pacemakers, whose hit singles were written by Tin Pan Alley's Mitch Murray, and Manchester's gruesome Freddie & the Dreamers, more novelty act than beat group, whose first hit had been a limp cover of an inspired, weird R&B classic by James Ray.

14

December 1963

It was a tradition for DJs to play US originals once and their "home-grown" covers interminably. This obtained both before Merseybeat (Marty Wilde vastly outsold Richie Valens with *Donna*, despite Valens dying in the Holly plane-crash as his disc was released) and after it. In 1965 the TV show *Thank Your Lucky Stars* claimed that the Righteous Brothers' *You've Lost That Loving Feeling* was too dull to hit and that Cilla Black's was superior. For beat groups, though, it was different: they covered obscure R&B because they loved it. This Christmas, beat groups occupied four of the top five LP slots.

15

From the sublime to the ridiculous.
Roy Orbison (left) has charted in every decade, as have the Shadows (below

The heyday of the Black and White Minstrels has thankfully passed, but they are still playing at a theatre somewhere...

January – February 1964

last / this week

4 January 1964

last	this		
1	1	WITH THE BEATLES	Beatles (Parlophone)
2	2	PLEASE PLEASE ME	Beatles (Parlophone)
6	3	HOW DO YOU LIKE IT	Gerry & the Pacemakers (Columbia)
4	4	ON TOUR WITH THE GEORGE MITCHELL MINSTRELS	George Mitchell Minstrels (HMV)
7	4	FREDDIE AND THE DREAMERS	Freddie & the Dreamers (Columbia)
3	6	WEST SIDE STORY	Soundtrack (CBS)
5	7	KATHY KIRBY SINGS 16 HITS FROM STARS AND GARTERS	Kathy Kirby (Decca)
10	8	KENNY BALL'S GOLDEN HITS	Kenny Ball (Golden Guinea)
7	9	MRS. MILLS' PARTY	Mrs. Mills (Parlophone)
7	10	SINATRA'S SINATRA	Frank Sinatra (Reprise)
-	10	MEET THE SEARCHERS	Searchers (Pye)

11 January 1964

1	1	WITH THE BEATLES	Beatles (Parlophone)
2	2	PLEASE PLEASE ME	Beatles (Parlophone)
3	3	HOW DO YOU LIKE IT	Gerry & the Pacemakers (Columbia)
-	4	FUN IN ACAPULCO	Elvis Presley (RCA)
6	5	WEST SIDE STORY	Soundtrack (CBS)
4	6	FREDDIE AND THE DREAMERS	Freddie & the Dreamers (Columbia)
7	7	KATHY KIRBY SINGS 16 HITS FROM STARS AND GARTERS	Kathy Kirby (Decca)
4	8	ON TOUR WITH THE GEORGE MITCHELL MINSTRELS	George Mitchell Minstrels (HMV)
8	9	KENNY BALL'S GOLDEN HITS	Kenny Ball (Golden Guinea)
-	10	TRINI LOPEZ AT P.J.'S	Trini Lopez (Reprise)

18 January 1964

1	1	WITH THE BEATLES	Beatles (Parlophone)
2	2	PLEASE PLEASE ME	Beatles (Parlophone)
4	3	FUN IN ACAPULCO	Elvis Presley (RCA)
3	4	HOW DO YOU LIKE IT	Gerry & the Pacemakers (Columbia)
5	5	WEST SIDE STORY	Soundtrack (CBS)
7	6	KATHY KIRBY SINGS 16 HITS FROM STARS AND GARTERS	Kathy Kirby (Decca)
-	7	BORN FREE	Frank Ifield (Columbia)
8	8	ON TOUR WITH THE GEORGE MITCHELL MINSTRELS	George Mitchell Minstrels (HMV)
6	9	FREDDIE AND THE DREAMERS	Freddie & the Dreamers (Columbia)
10	9	TRINI LOPEZ AT P.J.'S	Trini Lopez (Reprise)

25 January 1964

1	1	WITH THE BEATLES	Beatles (Parlophone)
2	2	PLEASE PLEASE ME	Beatles (Parlophone)
4	3	HOW DO YOU LIKE IT	Gerry & the Pacemakers (Columbia)
5	4	WEST SIDE STORY	Soundtrack (CBS)
3	5	FUN IN ACAPULCO	Elvis Presley (RCA)
6	6	KATHY KIRBY SINGS 16 HITS FROM STARS AND GARTERS	Kathy Kirby (Decca)
7	7	BORN FREE	Frank Ifield (Columbia)
9	7	FREDDIE AND THE DREAMERS	Freddie & the Dreamers (Columbia)
8	9	ON TOUR WITH THE GEORGE MITCHELL MINSTRELS	George Mitchell Minstrels (HMV)
-	10	PICKWICK	London Cast (Philips)

1 February 1964

1	1	WITH THE BEATLES	Beatles (Parlophone)
2	2	PLEASE PLEASE ME	Beatles (Parlophone)
4	3	WEST SIDE STORY	Soundtrack (CBS)
3	4	HOW DO YOU LIKE IT	Gerry & the Pacemakers (Columbia)
-	5	MEET THE SEARCHERS	Searchers (Pye)
6	6	KATHY KIRBY SINGS 16 HITS FROM STARS AND GARTERS	Kathy Kirby (Decca)
9	7	ON TOUR WITH THE GEORGE MITCHELL MINSTRELS	George Mitchell Minstrels (HMV)
7	8	BORN FREE	Frank Ifield (Columbia)
7	9	FREDDIE AND THE DREAMERS	Freddie & the Dreamers (Columbia)
-	9	SUGAR AND SPICE	Searchers (Pye)
-	9	I LEFT MY HEART IN SAN FRANCISCO	Tony Bennett (CBS)

8 February 1964

1	1	WITH THE BEATLES	Beatles (Parlophone)
2	2	PLEASE PLEASE ME	Beatles (Parlophone)
3	3	WEST SIDE STORY	Soundtrack (CBS)
4	4	HOW DO YOU LIKE IT	Gerry & the Pacemakers (Columbia)
9	5	SUGAR AND SPICE	Searchers (Pye)
6	6	KATHY KIRBY SINGS 16 HITS FROM STARS AND GARTERS	Kathy Kirby (Decca)
8	6	BORN FREE	Frank Ifield (Columbia)
5	8	MEET THE SEARCHERS	Searchers (Pye)
-	8	READY STEADY GO!	Various Artists (Decca)
9	10	I LEFT MY HEART IN SAN FRANCISCO	Tony Bennett (CBS)

15 February 1964

1	1	WITH THE BEATLES	Beatles (Parlophone)
2	2	PLEASE PLEASE ME	Beatles (Parlophone)
3	3	WEST SIDE STORY	Soundtrack (CBS)
4	4	HOW DO YOU LIKE IT	Gerry & the Pacemakers (Columbia)
8	5	MEET THE SEARCHERS	Searchers (Pye)
8	5	READY STEADY GO!	Various Artists (Decca)
-	7	STAY WITH THE HOLLIES	Hollies (Parlophone)
5	8	SUGAR AND SPICE	Searchers (Pye)
6	8	BORN FREE	Frank Ifield (Columbia)
-	10	KENNY BALL'S GOLDEN HITS	Kenny Ball (Golden Guinea)

22 February 1964

1	1	WITH THE BEATLES	Beatles (Parlophone)
2	2	PLEASE PLEASE ME	Beatles (Parlophone)
3	3	WEST SIDE STORY	Soundtrack (CBS)
4	4	HOW DO YOU LIKE IT	Gerry & the Pacemakers (Columbia)
7	5	STAY WITH THE HOLLIES	Hollies (Parlophone)
-	6	KATHY KIRBY SINGS 16 HITS FROM STARS AND GARTERS	Kathy Kirby (Decca)
5	7	MEET THE SEARCHERS	Searchers (Pye)
-	8	ON TOUR WITH THE GEORGE MITCHELL MINSTRELS	George Mitchell Minstrels (HMV)
-	9	JAZZ SEBASTIAN BACH	Les Swingle Singers (Philips)
8	10	SUGAR AND SPICE	Searchers (Pye)
8	10	BORN FREE	Frank Ifield (Columbia)

By now the real 1960s had begun, but the old guard fought on. The cash for LP-buying still belonged to adults whose ideas of "good music" pre-dated rock'n'roll. Despite the civil rights struggle in the USA (summer 1963 had seen Martin Luther King's "I have a dream" speech) the Minstrels were back. So was Kathy Kirby, a young dance-band-era revivalist with glossy red lipstick and black-seamed nylons. Mrs Mills' image was more cleaning-lady than star; she tinkled singalongable medleys on her joanna.

February – April 1964

last week	this week	29 February 1964
1	1	WITH THE BEATLES Beatles (Parlophone)
2	2	PLEASE PLEASE ME Beatles (Parlophone)
3	3	WEST SIDE STORY Soundtrack (CBS)
4	4	HOW DO YOU LIKE IT Gerry & the Pacemakers (Columbia)
5	5	STAY WITH THE HOLLIES Hollies (Parlophone)
7	6	MEET THE SEARCHERS Searchers (Pye)
-	7	READY STEADY GO! Various Artists (Decca)
8	8	ON TOUR WITH THE GEORGE MITCHELL MINSTRELS George Mitchell Minstrels (HMV)
-	8	IN DREAMS Roy Orbison (London)
10	10	BORN FREE Frank Ifield (Columbia)

		7 March 1964
1	1	WITH THE BEATLES Beatles (Parlophone)
2	2	PLEASE PLEASE ME Beatles (Parlophone)
3	3	WEST SIDE STORY Soundtrack (CBS)
5	4	STAY WITH THE HOLLIES Hollies (Parlophone)
4	5	HOW DO YOU LIKE IT Gerry & the Pacemakers (Columbia)
7	6	READY STEADY GO! Various Artists (Decca)
-	7	FUN IN ACAPULCO Elvis Presley (RCA)
8	8	IN DREAMS Roy Orbison (London)
10	9	BORN FREE Frank Ifield (Columbia)
-	10	SUGAR AND SPICE Searchers (Pye)
-	10	TEEN SCENE Chet Atkins (RCA)

		14 March 1964
1	1	WITH THE BEATLES Beatles (Parlophone)
2	2	PLEASE PLEASE ME Beatles (Parlophone)
3	3	WEST SIDE STORY Soundtrack (CBS)
4	4	STAY WITH THE HOLLIES Hollies (Parlophone)
9	5	BORN FREE Frank Ifield (Columbia)
5	6	HOW DO YOU LIKE IT Gerry & the Pacemakers (Columbia)
-	7	KATHY KIRBY SINGS 16 HITS FROM STARS AND GARTERS Kathy Kirby (Decca)
-	7	RHYTHM AND BLUES AT THE FLAMINGO Georgie Fame (Columbia)
9	9	TRINI LOPEZ AT P.J.'S Trini Lopez (Reprise)
-	10	SOUTH PACIFIC Soundtrack (RCA)

		21 March 1964
1	1	WITH THE BEATLES Beatles (Parlophone)
4	2	STAY WITH THE HOLLIES Hollies (Parlophone)
3	3	WEST SIDE STORY Soundtrack (CBS)
2	4	PLEASE PLEASE ME Beatles (Parlophone)
6	5	HOW DO YOU LIKE IT Gerry & the Pacemakers (Columbia)
10	6	SOUTH PACIFIC Soundtrack (RCA)
-	7	ON TOUR WITH THE GEORGE MITCHELL MINSTRELS George Mitchell Minstrels (HMV)
-	7	MORE TRINI LOPEZ AT P.J.'S Trini Lopez (Reprise)
-	9	BLUE SKIES Frank Ifield (Columbia)
-	9	FREDDIE AND THE DREAMERS Freddie & the Dreamers (Columbia)

		28 March 1964
1	1	WITH THE BEATLES Beatles (Parlophone)
4	2	PLEASE PLEASE ME Beatles (Parlophone)
3	3	WEST SIDE STORY Soundtrack (CBS)
2	4	STAY WITH THE HOLLIES Hollies (Parlophone)
5	5	HOW DO YOU LIKE IT Gerry & the Pacemakers (Columbia)
-	6	THE SHADOWS' GREATEST HITS Shadows (Columbia)
-	7	KATHY KIRBY SINGS 16 HITS FROM STARS AND GARTERS Kathy Kirby (Decca)
6	8	SOUTH PACIFIC Soundtrack (RCA)
7	8	MORE TRINI LOPEZ AT P.J.'S Trini Lopez (Reprise)
-	10	SUGAR AND SPICE Searchers (Pye)

		4 April 1964
1	1	WITH THE BEATLES Beatles (Parlophone)
2	2	PLEASE PLEASE ME Beatles (Parlophone)
3	3	WEST SIDE STORY Soundtrack (CBS)
4	4	STAY WITH THE HOLLIES Hollies (Parlophone)
-	5	ELVIS' GOLDEN RECORDS VOL 3 Elvis Presley (RCA)
8	6	SOUTH PACIFIC Soundtrack (RCA)
6	7	THE SHADOWS' GREATEST HITS Shadows (Columbia)
-	7	GOOD 'N' COUNTRY Jim Reeves (RCA)
5	9	HOW DO YOU LIKE IT Gerry & the Pacemakers (Columbia)
7	9	KATHY KIRBY SINGS 16 HITS FROM STARS AND GARTERS Kathy Kirby (Decca)

		11 April 1964
1	1	WITH THE BEATLES Beatles (Parlophone)
2	2	PLEASE PLEASE ME Beatles (Parlophone)
4	3	STAY WITH THE HOLLIES Hollies (Parlophone)
3	4	WEST SIDE STORY Soundtrack (CBS)
5	5	ELVIS' GOLDEN RECORDS VOL 3 Elvis Presley (RCA)
9	6	HOW DO YOU LIKE IT Gerry & the Pacemakers (Columbia)
7	7	GOOD 'N' COUNTRY Jim Reeves (RCA)
-	8	AT THE DROP OF ANOTHER HAT Michael Flanders & Donald Swann (Parlophone)
-	9	BLUE SKIES Frank Ifield (Columbia)
-	10	FREDDIE AND THE DREAMERS Freddie & the Dreamers (Columbia)

		18 April 1964
1	1	WITH THE BEATLES Beatles (Parlophone)
4	2	WEST SIDE STORY Soundtrack (CBS)
2	3	PLEASE PLEASE ME Beatles (Parlophone)
3	4	STAY WITH THE HOLLIES Hollies (Parlophone)
-	5	A GIRL CALLED DUSTY Dusty Springfield (Philips)
-	6	A SESSION WITH THE DAVE CLARK FIVE Dave Clark Five (Columbia)
5	7	ELVIS' GOLDEN RECORDS VOL 3 Elvis Presley (RCA)
8	8	AT THE DROP OF ANOTHER HAT Michael Flanders & Donald Swann (Parlophone)
-	9	JAZZ SEBASTIAN BACH Les Swingle Singers (Philips)
-	9	IN THE WIND Peter, Paul & Mary (Warner Bros.)

Beatlemania was such that the sleevenotes of the Fab Four's LP *Please Please Me* already sounded quaint: "Possibly," these had dared boast, "the most exciting British group since the Shadows." The LP sold in such huge numbers that it had reached No.11 in the singles chart the previous December, while on 28 March 1964 the American Top 5 was all Beatles. Australian Frank Ifield, meanwhile, was nearing the end as a big star in Britain, with four No.1 singles behind him, plus many smaller hits, 4 in 1964 alone.

25 April 1964

last week	this week	
-	1	THE ROLLING STONES — Rolling Stones (Decca)
1	2	WITH THE BEATLES — Beatles (Parlophone)
2	3	WEST SIDE STORY — Soundtrack (CBS)
6	4	A SESSION WITH THE DAVE CLARK FIVE — Dave Clark Five (Columbia)
3	5	PLEASE PLEASE ME — Beatles (Parlophone)
4	6	STAY WITH THE HOLLIES — Hollies (Parlophone)
5	7	A GIRL CALLED DUSTY — Dusty Springfield (Philips)
9	8	IN THE WIND — Peter, Paul & Mary (Warner Bros.)
-	8	SOUTH PACIFIC — Soundtrack (RCA)
7	10	ELVIS' GOLDEN RECORDS VOL 3 — Elvis Presley (RCA)

2 May 1964

1	1	THE ROLLING STONES — Rolling Stones (Decca)
2	2	WITH THE BEATLES — Beatles (Parlophone)
3	3	WEST SIDE STORY — Soundtrack (CBS)
4	4	A SESSION WITH THE DAVE CLARK FIVE — Dave Clark Five (Columbia)
6	5	STAY WITH THE HOLLIES — Hollies (Parlophone)
5	6	PLEASE PLEASE ME — Beatles (Parlophone)
7	7	A GIRL CALLED DUSTY — Dusty Springfield (Philips)
10	8	ELVIS' GOLDEN RECORDS VOL 3 — Elvis Presley (RCA)
8	9	IN THE WIND — Peter, Paul & Mary (Warner Bros.)
-	10	BLUE SKIES — Frank Ifield (Columbia)
-	10	TRIBUTE TO EDDIE — Heinz (Decca)

9 May 1964

1	1	THE ROLLING STONES — Rolling Stones (Decca)
2	2	WITH THE BEATLES — Beatles (Parlophone)
3	3	WEST SIDE STORY — Soundtrack (CBS)
4	4	A SESSION WITH THE DAVE CLARK FIVE — Dave Clark Five (Columbia)
7	5	A GIRL CALLED DUSTY — Dusty Springfield (Philips)
-	6	DANCE WITH THE SHADOWS — Shadows (Columbia)
5	7	STAY WITH THE HOLLIES — Hollies (Parlophone)
6	8	PLEASE PLEASE ME — Beatles (Parlophone)
-	9	SOUTH PACIFIC — Soundtrack (RCA)
-	10	ON TOUR WITH THE GEORGE MITCHELL MINSTRELS — George Mitchell Minstrels (HMV)

16 May 1964

1	1	THE ROLLING STONES — Rolling Stones (Decca)
2	2	WITH THE BEATLES — Beatles (Parlophone)
4	3	A SESSION WITH THE DAVE CLARK FIVE — Dave Clark Five (Columbia)
6	4	DANCE WITH THE SHADOWS — Shadows (Columbia)
3	5	WEST SIDE STORY — Soundtrack (CBS)
5	6	A GIRL CALLED DUSTY — Dusty Springfield (Philips)
7	7	STAY WITH THE HOLLIES — Hollies (Parlophone)
-	8	JAZZ SEBASTIAN BACH — Les Swingle Singers (Philips)
8	9	PLEASE PLEASE ME — Beatles (Parlophone)
10	10	ON TOUR WITH THE GEORGE MITCHELL MINSTRELS — George Mitchell Minstrels (HMV)

23 May 1964

1	1	THE ROLLING STONES — Rolling Stones (Decca)
2	2	WITH THE BEATLES — Beatles (Parlophone)
4	3	DANCE WITH THE SHADOWS — Shadows (Columbia)
5	4	WEST SIDE STORY — Soundtrack (CBS)
3	5	A SESSION WITH THE DAVE CLARK FIVE — Dave Clark Five (Columbia)
6	6	A GIRL CALLED DUSTY — Dusty Springfield (Philips)
-	7	SOUTH PACIFIC — Soundtrack (RCA)
-	8	IN DREAMS — Roy Orbison (London)
-	8	THE LATEST AND THE GREATEST — Chuck Berry (Pye International)
8	10	JAZZ SEBASTIAN BACH — Les Swingle Singers (Philips)
9	10	PLEASE PLEASE ME — Beatles (Parlophone)

30 May 1964

1	1	THE ROLLING STONES — Rolling Stones (Decca)
2	2	WITH THE BEATLES — Beatles (Parlophone)
3	3	DANCE WITH THE SHADOWS — Shadows (Columbia)
5	4	A SESSION WITH THE DAVE CLARK FIVE — Dave Clark Five (Columbia)
-	5	IT'S THE SEARCHERS — Searchers (Pye)
4	6	WEST SIDE STORY — Soundtrack (CBS)
8	7	THE LATEST AND THE GREATEST — Chuck Berry (Pye International)
-	8	STAY WITH THE HOLLIES — Hollies (Parlophone)
-	9	ELVIS' GOLDEN RECORDS VOL 3 — Elvis Presley (RCA)
8	10	IN DREAMS — Roy Orbison (London)

6 June 1964

1	1	THE ROLLING STONES — Rolling Stones (Decca)
2	2	WITH THE BEATLES — Beatles (Parlophone)
5	3	IT'S THE SEARCHERS — Searchers (Pye)
3	4	DANCE WITH THE SHADOWS — Shadows (Columbia)
7	4	THE LATEST AND THE GREATEST — Chuck Berry (Pye International)
6	6	A SESSION WITH THE DAVE CLARK FIVE — Dave Clark Five (Columbia)
6	7	WEST SIDE STORY — Soundtrack (CBS)
9	8	ELVIS' GOLDEN RECORDS VOL 3 — Elvis Presley (RCA)
-	8	MORE CHUCK BERRY — Chuck Berry (Pye International)
8	10	STAY WITH THE HOLLIES — Hollies (Parlophone)

13 June 1964

1	1	THE ROLLING STONES — Rolling Stones (Decca)
4	2	DANCE WITH THE SHADOWS — Shadows (Columbia)
3	3	IT'S THE SEARCHERS — Searchers (Pye)
2	4	WITH THE BEATLES — Beatles (Parlophone)
4	5	THE LATEST AND THE GREATEST — Chuck Berry (Pye International)
6	5	A SESSION WITH THE DAVE CLARK FIVE — Dave Clark Five (Columbia)
7	5	WEST SIDE STORY — Soundtrack (CBS)
-	8	SHOWCASE — Buddy Holly (Coral)
-	8	PRESENTING DIONNE WARWICK — Dionne Warwick (Pye International)
10	10	STAY WITH THE HOLLIES — Hollies (Parlophone)

The Rolling Stones' debut LP also sold strongly enough to enter the singles chart, jumping straight to No.1 in the LPs. They managed this despite ignoring co-manager Eric Easton's advice to Andrew Loog Oldham in 1963: "The singer," said Easton, "will have to go. The BBC won't like him." The Folk Revival, a major US trend since 1961, brushed the LP chart via Peter, Paul & Mary. Bob Dylan's LP chart debut was as their sleevenote-writer, and composer of *Blowin' In The Wind,*

June – August 1964

last week	this week	20 June 1964
1	1	THE ROLLING STONES Rolling Stones (Decca)
3	2	IT'S THE SEARCHERS Searchers (Pye)
4	3	WITH THE BEATLES Beatles (Parlophone)
8	4	SHOWCASE Buddy Holly (Coral)
2	5	DANCE WITH THE SHADOWS Shadows (Columbia)
5	6	WEST SIDE STORY Soundtrack (CBS)
5	7	A SESSION WITH THE DAVE CLARK FIVE Dave Clark Five (Columbia)
10	8	STAY WITH THE HOLLIES Hollies (Parlophone)
-	8	IN DREAMS Roy Orbison (London)
5	10	THE LATEST AND THE GREATEST Chuck Berry (Pye International)

		27 June 1964
1	1	THE ROLLING STONES Rolling Stones (Decca)
4	2	SHOWCASE Buddy Holly (Coral)
3	3	WITH THE BEATLES Beatles (Parlophone)
5	4	DANCE WITH THE SHADOWS Shadows (Columbia)
2	5	IT'S THE SEARCHERS Searchers (Pye)
-	6	KISSIN' COUSINS Elvis Presley (RCA)
6	7	WEST SIDE STORY Soundtrack (CBS)
-	7	THE BACHELORS PLUS 16 GREAT SONGS Bachelors (Decca)
-	7	THE MERSEYBEATS Merseybeats (Fontana)
8	10	IN DREAMS Roy Orbison (London)

		4 July 1964
1	1	THE ROLLING STONES Rolling Stones (Decca)
7	2	THE BACHELORS PLUS 16 GREAT SONGS Bachelors (Decca)
2	3	SHOWCASE Buddy Holly (Coral)
3	4	WITH THE BEATLES Beatles (Parlophone)
6	5	KISSIN' COUSINS Elvis Presley (RCA)
10	6	IN DREAMS Roy Orbison (London)
4	7	DANCE WITH THE SHADOWS Shadows (Columbia)
5	8	IT'S THE SEARCHERS Searchers (Pye)
7	9	WEST SIDE STORY Soundtrack (CBS)
7	10	THE MERSEYBEATS Merseybeats (Fontana)

		11 July 1964
1	1	THE ROLLING STONES Rolling Stones (Decca)
5	2	KISSIN' COUSINS Elvis Presley (RCA)
-	3	WONDERFUL LIFE Cliff Richard & the Shadows (Columbia)
2	4	THE BACHELORS PLUS 16 GREAT SONGS Bachelors (Decca)
8	5	IT'S THE SEARCHERS Searchers (Pye)
3	6	SHOWCASE Buddy Holly (Coral)
7	7	DANCE WITH THE SHADOWS Shadows (Columbia)
4	8	WITH THE BEATLES Beatles (Parlophone)
9	9	WEST SIDE STORY Soundtrack (CBS)
-	10	THE LATEST AND THE GREATEST Chuck Berry (Pye International)

		18 July 1964
-	1	A HARD DAY'S NIGHT Beatles (Parlophone)
1	2	THE ROLLING STONES Rolling Stones (Decca)
3	3	WONDERFUL LIFE Cliff Richard & the Shadows (Columbia)
4	4	THE BACHELORS PLUS 16 GREAT SONGS Bachelors (Decca)
2	5	KISSIN' COUSINS Elvis Presley (RCA)
9	6	WEST SIDE STORY Soundtrack (CBS)
5	7	IT'S THE SEARCHERS Searchers (Pye)
7	8	DANCE WITH THE SHADOWS Shadows (Columbia)
8	9	WITH THE BEATLES Beatles (Parlophone)
6	10	SHOWCASE Buddy Holly (Coral)

		25 July 1964
1	1	A HARD DAY'S NIGHT Beatles (Parlophone)
2	2	THE ROLLING STONES Rolling Stones (Decca)
3	3	WONDERFUL LIFE Cliff Richard & the Shadows (Columbia)
5	4	KISSIN' COUSINS Elvis Presley (RCA)
9	5	WITH THE BEATLES Beatles (Parlophone)
6	6	WEST SIDE STORY Soundtrack (CBS)
4	7	THE BACHELORS PLUS 16 GREAT SONGS Bachelors (Decca)
7	8	IT'S THE SEARCHERS Searchers (Pye)
8	9	DANCE WITH THE SHADOWS Shadows (Columbia)
10	10	SHOWCASE Buddy Holly (Coral)

		1 August 1964
1	1	A HARD DAY'S NIGHT Beatles (Parlophone)
2	2	THE ROLLING STONES Rolling Stones (Decca)
3	3	WONDERFUL LIFE Cliff Richard & the Shadows (Columbia)
7	4	THE BACHELORS PLUS 16 GREAT SONGS Bachelors (Decca)
4	5	KISSIN' COUSINS Elvis Presley (RCA)
6	6	WEST SIDE STORY Soundtrack (CBS)
5	7	WITH THE BEATLES Beatles (Parlophone)
-	8	A GIRL CALLED DUSTY Dusty Springfield (Philips)
8	9	IT'S THE SEARCHERS Searchers (Pye)
9	10	DANCE WITH THE SHADOWS Shadows (Columbia)

		8 August 1964
1	1	A HARD DAY'S NIGHT Beatles (Parlophone)
2	2	THE ROLLING STONES Rolling Stones (Decca)
3	3	WONDERFUL LIFE Cliff Richard & the Shadows (Columbia)
4	4	THE BACHELORS PLUS 16 GREAT SONGS Bachelors (Decca)
8	5	A GIRL CALLED DUSTY Dusty Springfield (Philips)
5	6	KISSIN' COUSINS Elvis Presley (RCA)
6	7	WEST SIDE STORY Soundtrack (CBS)
9	8	IT'S THE SEARCHERS Searchers (Pye)
-	9	PRESENTING DIONNE WARWICK Dionne Warwick (Pye International)
7	10	WITH THE BEATLES Beatles (Parlophone)

The title *Stay With The Hollies* referred to their revival of an 88-second masterpiece by Maurice Williams & the Zodiacs, *Stay* (to re-chart in 1978 by Jackson Browne), which they followed up with Doris Troy's *Just One Look*. Chuck Berry was surprised to be charting (he was also riding high with the 45 *No Particular Place To Go*), for despite his legendary status he had gone from 1958 till 1963 with no UK hit. (His only No.1 was to be 1972's *My Ding-A-Ling*, a ponderous novelty-item.)

August – October 1964

15 August 1964

last	this	Title	Artist (Label)
1	1	A HARD DAY'S NIGHT	Beatles (Parlophone)
2	2	THE ROLLING STONES	Rolling Stones (Decca)
3	3	WONDERFUL LIFE	Cliff Richard & the Shadows (Columbia)
4	4	THE BACHELORS PLUS 16 GREAT SONGS	Bachelors (Decca)
6	5	KISSIN' COUSINS	Elvis Presley (RCA)
-	6	A TOUCH OF VELVET	Jim Reeves (RCA)
10	7	WITH THE BEATLES	Beatles (Parlophone)
-	8	GENTLEMAN JIM	Jim Reeves (RCA)
7	9	WEST SIDE STORY	Soundtrack (CBS)
-	9	HELLO DOLLY	Louis Armstrong (London)

22 August 1964

last	this	Title	Artist (Label)
1	1	A HARD DAY'S NIGHT	Beatles (Parlophone)
2	2	THE ROLLING STONES	Rolling Stones (Decca)
3	3	WONDERFUL LIFE	Cliff Richard & the Shadows (Columbia)
4	4	THE BACHELORS PLUS 16 GREAT SONGS	Bachelors (Decca)
8	5	GENTLEMAN JIM	Jim Reeves (RCA)
6	6	A TOUCH OF VELVET	Jim Reeves (RCA)
9	7	WEST SIDE STORY	Soundtrack (CBS)
5	8	KISSIN' COUSINS	Elvis Presley (RCA)
7	9	WITH THE BEATLES	Beatles (Parlophone)
-	10	IT'S THE SEARCHERS	Searchers (Pye)

29 August 1964

last	this	Title	Artist (Label)
1	1	A HARD DAY'S NIGHT	Beatles (Parlophone)
2	2	THE ROLLING STONES	Rolling Stones (Decca)
3	3	WONDERFUL LIFE	Cliff Richard & the Shadows (Columbia)
4	4	THE BACHELORS PLUS 16 GREAT SONGS	Bachelors (Decca)
5	5	GENTLEMAN JIM	Jim Reeves (RCA)
7	6	WEST SIDE STORY	Soundtrack (CBS)
8	7	KISSIN' COUSINS	Elvis Presley (RCA)
-	8	GOOD 'N' COUNTRY	Jim Reeves (RCA)
6	9	A TOUCH OF VELVET	Jim Reeves (RCA)
-	10	HE'LL HAVE TO GO	Jim Reeves (RCA)

5 September 1964

last	this	Title	Artist (Label)
1	1	A HARD DAY'S NIGHT	Beatles (Parlophone)
2	2	THE ROLLING STONES	Rolling Stones (Decca)
-	3	MOONLIGHT AND ROSES	Jim Reeves (RCA)
3	4	WONDERFUL LIFE	Cliff Richard & the Shadows (Columbia)
4	5	THE BACHELORS PLUS 16 GREAT SONGS	Bachelors (Decca)
5	6	GENTLEMAN JIM	Jim Reeves (RCA)
6	7	WEST SIDE STORY	Soundtrack (CBS)
9	8	A TOUCH OF VELVET	Jim Reeves (RCA)
8	9	GOOD 'N' COUNTRY	Jim Reeves (RCA)
7	10	KISSIN' COUSINS	Elvis Presley (RCA)

12 September 1964

last	this	Title	Artist (Label)
1	1	A HARD DAY'S NIGHT	Beatles (Parlophone)
3	2	MOONLIGHT AND ROSES	Jim Reeves (RCA)
2	3	THE ROLLING STONES	Rolling Stones (Decca)
-	4	FIVE FACES OF MANFRED MANN	Manfred Mann (HMV)
5	5	GENTLEMAN JIM	Jim Reeves (RCA)
4	6	WONDERFUL LIFE	Cliff Richard & the Shadows (Columbia)
5	7	THE BACHELORS PLUS 16 GREAT SONGS	Bachelors (Decca)
8	7	A TOUCH OF VELVET	Jim Reeves (RCA)
-	9	A GIRL CALLED DUSTY	Dusty Springfield (Philips)
7	10	WEST SIDE STORY	Soundtrack (CBS)

19 September 1964

last	this	Title	Artist (Label)
1	1	A HARD DAY'S NIGHT	Beatles (Parlophone)
3	2	THE ROLLING STONES	Rolling Stones (Decca)
2	3	MOONLIGHT AND ROSES	Jim Reeves (RCA)
4	4	FIVE FACES OF MANFRED MANN	Manfred Mann (HMV)
6	5	WONDERFUL LIFE	Cliff Richard & the Shadows (Columbia)
7	6	THE BACHELORS PLUS 16 GREAT SONGS	Bachelors (Decca)
5	7	GENTLEMAN JIM	Jim Reeves (RCA)
10	8	WEST SIDE STORY	Soundtrack (CBS)
-	9	GOD BE WITH YOU	Jim Reeves (RCA)
7	10	A TOUCH OF VELVET	Jim Reeves (RCA)

26 September 1964

last	this	Title	Artist (Label)
1	1	A HARD DAY'S NIGHT	Beatles (Parlophone)
2	2	MOONLIGHT AND ROSES	Jim Reeves (RCA)
3	3	THE ROLLING STONES	Rolling Stones (Decca)
4	4	FIVE FACES OF MANFRED MANN	Manfred Mann (HMV)
7	5	GENTLEMAN JIM	Jim Reeves (RCA)
6	6	THE BACHELORS PLUS 16 GREAT SONGS	Bachelors (Decca)
5	7	WONDERFUL LIFE	Cliff Richard & the Shadows (Columbia)
9	8	GOD BE WITH YOU	Jim Reeves (RCA)
8	9	WEST SIDE STORY	Soundtrack (CBS)
10	9	A TOUCH OF VELVET	Jim Reeves (RCA)
-	9	GOOD 'N' COUNTRY	Jim Reeves (RCA)

3 October 1964

last	this	Title	Artist (Label)
1	1	A HARD DAY'S NIGHT	Beatles (Parlophone)
3	2	THE ROLLING STONES	Rolling Stones (Decca)
3	3	FIVE FACES OF MANFRED MANN	Manfred Mann (HMV)
2	4	MOONLIGHT AND ROSES	Jim Reeves (RCA)
6	5	THE BACHELORS PLUS 16 GREAT SONGS	Bachelors (Decca)
7	6	WONDERFUL LIFE	Cliff Richard & the Shadows (Columbia)
5	7	GENTLEMAN JIM	Jim Reeves (RCA)
9	8	A TOUCH OF VELVET	Jim Reeves (RCA)
9	9	WEST SIDE STORY	Soundtrack (CBS)
-	10	IT MIGHT AS WELL BE SWING	Frank Sinatra/Count Basie (Reprise)

If Chuck Berry was a relative chart stranger, rock and blues classics remained in the public ear. Berry's *Johnny B. Goode*, Little Richard songs and Muddy Waters' *Got My Mojo Working* were core repertoire for every beat group, and now they were on vinyl. The Swinging Blue Jeans had hit with *Good Golly Miss Molly*, the Beatles with their *Long Tall Sally* EP, and in November the Stones would be No.1 with *Little Red Rooster*, learnt from Howlin' Wolf. Oldest originator with a hit was Louis Armstrong.

October – November 1964

10 October 1964

last	this		
1	1	A HARD DAY'S NIGHT	Beatles (Parlophone)
2	2	THE ROLLING STONES	Rolling Stones (Decca)
3	3	FIVE FACES OF MANFRED MANN	Manfred Mann (HMV)
4	4	MOONLIGHT AND ROSES	Jim Reeves (RCA)
5	5	THE BACHELORS PLUS 16 GREAT SONGS	Bachelors (Decca)
6	6	WONDERFUL LIFE	Cliff Richard & the Shadows (Columbia)
-	6	THE KINKS	Kinks (Pye)
7	8	GENTLEMAN JIM	Jim Reeves (RCA)
9	9	WEST SIDE STORY	Soundtrack (CBS)
-	10	FAME AT LAST	Georgie Fame (Columbia)

17 October 1964

1	1	A HARD DAY'S NIGHT	Beatles (Parlophone)
2	2	THE ROLLING STONES	Rolling Stones (Decca)
3	3	FIVE FACES OF MANFRED MANN	Manfred Mann (HMV)
4	4	MOONLIGHT AND ROSES	Jim Reeves (RCA)
6	5	THE KINKS	Kinks (Pye)
6	6	WONDERFUL LIFE	Cliff Richard & the Shadows (Columbia)
5	6	THE BACHELORS PLUS 16 GREAT SONGS	Bachelors (Decca)
9	8	WEST SIDE STORY	Soundtrack (CBS)
8	9	GENTLEMAN JIM	Jim Reeves (RCA)
-	10	IN DREAMS	Roy Orbison (London)

24 October 1964

1	1	A HARD DAY'S NIGHT	Beatles (Parlophone)
3	2	FIVE FACES OF MANFRED MANN	Manfred Mann (HMV)
2	3	THE ROLLING STONES	Rolling Stones (Decca)
5	4	THE KINKS	Kinks (Pye)
4	5	MOONLIGHT AND ROSES	Jim Reeves (RCA)
6	6	THE BACHELORS PLUS 16 GREAT SONGS	Bachelors (Decca)
-	7	IN THE HOLLIES STYLE	Hollies (Parlophone)
8	8	WEST SIDE STORY	Soundtrack (CBS)
-	9	GOLDFINGER	Soundtrack (United Artists)
9	10	GENTLEMAN JIM	Jim Reeves (RCA)
6	10	WONDERFUL LIFE	Cliff Richard & the Shadows (Columbia)

31 October 1964

1	1	A HARD DAY'S NIGHT	Beatles (Parlophone)
3	2	THE ROLLING STONES	Rolling Stones (Decca)
4	3	THE KINKS	Kinks (Pye)
2	4	FIVE FACES OF MANFRED MANN	Manfred Mann (HMV)
5	5	MOONLIGHT AND ROSES	Jim Reeves (RCA)
6	6	THE BACHELORS PLUS 16 GREAT SONGS	Bachelors (Decca)
-	7	IN DREAMS	Roy Orbison (London)
10	8	GENTLEMAN JIM	Jim Reeves (RCA)
7	9	IN THE HOLLIES STYLE	Hollies (Parlophone)
10	10	WONDERFUL LIFE	Cliff Richard & the Shadows (Columbia)

7 November 1964

1	1	A HARD DAY'S NIGHT	Beatles (Parlophone)
2	2	THE ROLLING STONES	Rolling Stones (Decca)
4	3	FIVE FACES OF MANFRED MANN	Manfred Mann (HMV)
3	4	THE KINKS	Kinks (Pye)
5	5	MOONLIGHT AND ROSES	Jim Reeves (RCA)
7	6	IN DREAMS	Roy Orbison (London)
6	7	THE BACHELORS PLUS 16 GREAT SONGS	Bachelors (Decca)
10	8	WONDERFUL LIFE	Cliff Richard & the Shadows (Columbia)
9	9	IN THE HOLLIES STYLE	Hollies (Parlophone)
-	10	FRANK IFIELD'S GREATEST HITS	Frank Ifield (Columbia)
8	10	GENTLEMAN JIM	Jim Reeves (RCA)

14 November 1964

1	1	A HARD DAY'S NIGHT	Beatles (Parlophone)
4	2	THE KINKS	Kinks (Pye)
2	3	THE ROLLING STONES	Rolling Stones (Decca)
-	4	THE ANIMALS	Animals (Columbia)
3	5	FIVE FACES OF MANFRED MANN	Manfred Mann (HMV)
-	6	THE FREEWHEELIN' BOB DYLAN	Bob Dylan (CBS)
5	7	MOONLIGHT AND ROSES	Jim Reeves (RCA)
6	8	IN DREAMS	Roy Orbison (London)
8	9	WONDERFUL LIFE	Cliff Richard & the Shadows (Columbia)
9	10	IN THE HOLLIES STYLE	Hollies (Parlophone)

21 November 1964

1	1	A HARD DAY'S NIGHT	Beatles (Parlophone)
4	2	THE ANIMALS	Animals (Columbia)
3	3	THE ROLLING STONES	Rolling Stones (Decca)
2	4	THE KINKS	Kinks (Pye)
5	5	FIVE FACES OF MANFRED MANN	Manfred Mann (HMV)
10	6	IN THE HOLLIES STYLE	Hollies (Parlophone)
6	7	THE FREEWHEELIN' BOB DYLAN	Bob Dylan (CBS)
7	8	MOONLIGHT AND ROSES	Jim Reeves (RCA)
-	9	THE BACHELORS PLUS 16 GREAT SONGS	Bachelors (Decca)
9	10	WONDERFUL LIFE	Cliff Richard & the Shadows (Columbia)

28 November 1964

1	1	A HARD DAY'S NIGHT	Beatles (Parlophone)
3	2	THE ROLLING STONES	Rolling Stones (Decca)
2	3	THE ANIMALS	Animals (Columbia)
4	4	THE KINKS	Kinks (Pye)
8	5	MOONLIGHT AND ROSES	Jim Reeves (RCA)
5	6	FIVE FACES OF MANFRED MANN	Manfred Mann (HMV)
9	7	THE BACHELORS PLUS 16 GREAT SONGS	Bachelors (Decca)
-	8	MEET THE SUPREMES	Supremes (Stateside)
-	9	ANOTHER SIDE OF BOB DYLAN	Bob Dylan (CBS)
-	10	IN DREAMS	Roy Orbison (London)

Plane-crash victim Jim Reeves enjoyed phenomenal success in 1964. By October he had only two LPs in the Top 10, but there had been six of them since mid-August. In the last week of September, five of the Top 10 were Jim Reeves LPs. Another would arrive for Christmas. By year's end, he was the artist with the most chart weeks to his credit, Beatles notwithstanding. Meanwhile November saw Bob Dylan's first entry to the chart in his own right, with (oddly) both his second LP and his fourth.

December 1964

last week / this week

5 December 1964

last	this	Title / Artist
1	1	A HARD DAY'S NIGHT — Beatles (Parlophone)
2	2	THE ROLLING STONES — Rolling Stones (Decca)
3	3	THE ANIMALS — Animals (Columbia)
5	4	MOONLIGHT AND ROSES — Jim Reeves (RCA)
4	5	THE KINKS — Kinks (Pye)
7	6	THE BACHELORS PLUS 16 GREAT SONGS — Bachelors (Decca)
-	7	12 SONGS OF CHRISTMAS — Jim Reeves (RCA)
-	8	OH, PRETTY WOMAN — Roy Orbison (London)
6	9	FIVE FACES OF MANFRED MANN — Manfred Mann (HMV)
-	10	ALADDIN AND HIS WONDERFUL LAMP — Cliff Richard & the Shadows (Columbia)
8	10	MEET THE SUPREMES — Supremes (Stateside)

12 December 1964

last	this	Title / Artist
-	1	BEATLES FOR SALE — Beatles (Parlophone)
1	2	A HARD DAY'S NIGHT — Beatles (Parlophone)
2	3	THE ROLLING STONES — Rolling Stones (Decca)
7	4	12 SONGS OF CHRISTMAS — Jim Reeves (RCA)
5	5	THE KINKS — Kinks (Pye)
8	6	OH, PRETTY WOMAN — Roy Orbison (London)
4	7	MOONLIGHT AND ROSES — Jim Reeves (RCA)
3	8	THE ANIMALS — Animals (Columbia)
9	9	FIVE FACES OF MANFRED MANN — Manfred Mann (HMV)
6	9	THE BACHELORS PLUS 16 GREAT SONGS — Bachelors (Decca)
10	9	ALADDIN AND HIS WONDERFUL LAMP — Cliff Richard & the Shadows (Columbia)

19 December 1964

last	this	Title / Artist
1	1	BEATLES FOR SALE — Beatles (Parlophone)
4	2	12 SONGS OF CHRISTMAS — Jim Reeves (RCA)
2	3	A HARD DAY'S NIGHT — Beatles (Parlophone)
9	4	THE BACHELORS PLUS 16 GREAT SONGS — Bachelors (Decca)
6	5	OH, PRETTY WOMAN — Roy Orbison (London)
3	6	THE ROLLING STONES — Rolling Stones (Decca)
7	7	MOONLIGHT AND ROSES — Jim Reeves (RCA)
5	8	THE KINKS — Kinks (Pye)
9	9	ALADDIN AND HIS WONDERFUL LAMP — Cliff Richard & the Shadows (Columbia)
-	10	LUCKY 13 SHADES OF VAL DOONICAN — Val Doonican (Decca)

26 December 1964

last	this	Title / Artist
1	1	BEATLES FOR SALE — Beatles (Parlophone)
4	2	THE BACHELORS PLUS 16 GREAT SONGS — Bachelors (Decca)
10	3	LUCKY 13 SHADES OF VAL DOONICAN — Val Doonican (Decca)
2	4	12 SONGS OF CHRISTMAS — Jim Reeves (RCA)
3	5	A HARD DAY'S NIGHT — Beatles (Parlophone)
6	6	THE ROLLING STONES — Rolling Stones (Decca)
5	6	OH, PRETTY WOMAN — Roy Orbison (London)
7	8	MOONLIGHT AND ROSES — Jim Reeves (RCA)
9	9	ALADDIN AND HIS WONDERFUL LAMP — Cliff Richard & the Shadows (Columbia)
-	10	THE ANIMALS — Animals (Columbia)

Both Dylan LPs dropped out of the Top 10 after only a week but the wonder is that they had made it at all, with no chart single to stimulate sales. Every other act in the LP Top 10 at the time had big hit singles behind them. The Beatles, the Animals, the Kinks and Manfred Mann had all had recent No.1s; the Bachelors had scored a No.1 and three other Top 5 singles this year; the Supremes had had a No.2 in September and a No.1 earlier in November; Cliff Richard was about to get his fourth Top 10 of the year; the Hollies had already had four Top 10s in the last twelve months; Roy Orbison had just enjoyed his second No.1 of the year; and the Stones were at No.1 now. In contrast, Bob Dylan was not to enter the Top 10 singles chart until the following year. His success with two unsupported LPs, therefore, was something special - and hinted at the changes he was almost singlehandedly to bring about in the near future. Even as Beatlemania raged on both sides of the Atlantic, Dylan was to be the catalyst for the imminent split between "pop" and "rock", revolutionising what songs could say, calling radio's bluff in demanding the 3-minute single, deposing the 45 from its pre-eminent position, and empowering the LP as a medium in its own right. Thus the LP became the album. Dylan was to change the language of the industry as well as of the song. He would even change the Beatles.

January – February 1965

2 January 1965

1	1	BEATLES FOR SALE	Beatles (Parlophone)
4	2	12 SONGS OF CHRISTMAS	Jim Reeves (RCA)
2	3	THE BACHELORS PLUS 16 GREAT SONGS	Bachelors (Decca)
5	4	A HARD DAY'S NIGHT	Beatles (Parlophone)
3	5	LUCKY 13 SHADES OF VAL DOONICAN	Val Doonican (Decca)
8	6	MOONLIGHT AND ROSES	Jim Reeves (RCA)
6	7	OH, PRETTY WOMAN	Roy Orbison (London)
9	8	ALADDIN AND HIS WONDERFUL LAMP	Cliff Richard & the Shadows (Columbia)
-	9	SPOTLIGHT ON THE MINSTRELS	George Mitchell Minstrels (HMV)
6	10	THE ROLLING STONES	Rolling Stones (Decca)

9 January 1965

1	1	BEATLES FOR SALE	Beatles (Parlophone)
5	2	LUCKY 13 SHADES OF VAL DOONICAN	Val Doonican (Decca)
3	3	THE BACHELORS PLUS 16 GREAT SONGS	Bachelors (Decca)
4	4	A HARD DAY'S NIGHT	Beatles (Parlophone)
10	5	THE ROLLING STONES	Rolling Stones (Decca)
7	6	OH, PRETTY WOMAN	Roy Orbison (London)
8	7	ALADDIN AND HIS WONDERFUL LAMP	Cliff Richard & the Shadows (Columbia)
6	8	MOONLIGHT AND ROSES	Jim Reeves (RCA)
-	9	THE ANIMALS	Animals (Columbia)
-	10	FAME AT LAST	Georgie Fame (Columbia)

16 January 1965

1	1	BEATLES FOR SALE	Beatles (Parlophone)
3	2	THE BACHELORS PLUS 16 GREAT SONGS	Bachelors (Decca)
2	3	LUCKY 13 SHADES OF VAL DOONICAN	Val Doonican (Decca)
4	4	A HARD DAY'S NIGHT	Beatles (Parlophone)
6	5	OH, PRETTY WOMAN	Roy Orbison (London)
5	6	THE ROLLING STONES	Rolling Stones (Decca)
7	7	ALADDIN AND HIS WONDERFUL LAMP	Cliff Richard & the Shadows (Columbia)
-	8	THE KINKS	Kinks (Pye)
9	9	THE ANIMALS	Animals (Columbia)
10	10	FAME AT LAST	Georgie Fame (Columbia)

23 January 1965

-	1	THE ROLLING STONES NO 2	Rolling Stones (Decca)
1	2	BEATLES FOR SALE	Beatles (Parlophone)
3	3	LUCKY 13 SHADES OF VAL DOONICAN	Val Doonican (Decca)
2	4	THE BACHELORS PLUS 16 GREAT SONGS	Bachelors (Decca)
4	5	A HARD DAY'S NIGHT	Beatles (Parlophone)
8	6	THE KINKS	Kinks (Pye)
5	7	OH, PRETTY WOMAN	Roy Orbison (London)
7	8	ALADDIN AND HIS WONDERFUL LAMP	Cliff Richard & the Shadows (Columbia)
6	9	THE ROLLING STONES	Rolling Stones (Decca)
-	10	GENE PITNEY'S BIG SIXTEEN	Gene Pitney (Stateside)

30 January 1965

1	1	THE ROLLING STONES NO 2	Rolling Stones (Decca)
2	2	BEATLES FOR SALE	Beatles (Parlophone)
3	3	LUCKY 13 SHADES OF VAL DOONICAN	Val Doonican (Decca)
-	4	THE BEST OF JIM REEVES	Jim Reeves (RCA)
4	5	THE BACHELORS PLUS 16 GREAT SONGS	Bachelors (Decca)
6	6	THE KINKS	Kinks (Pye)
5	7	A HARD DAY'S NIGHT	Beatles (Parlophone)
-	8	THE LENNON-McCARTNEY SONGBOOK	Keely Smith (Reprise)
10	9	GENE PITNEY'S BIG SIXTEEN	Gene Pitney (Stateside)
8	10	ALADDIN AND HIS WONDERFUL LAMP	Cliff Richard & the Shadows (Columbia)

6 February 1965

1	1	THE ROLLING STONES NO 2	Rolling Stones (Decca)
2	2	BEATLES FOR SALE	Beatles (Parlophone)
3	3	THE BEST OF JIM REEVES	Jim Reeves (RCA)
4	4	LUCKY 13 SHADES OF VAL DOONICAN	Val Doonican (Decca)
5	5	THE KINKS	Kinks (Pye)
5	6	THE BACHELORS PLUS 16 GREAT SONGS	Bachelors (Decca)
8	7	THE LENNON-McCARTNEY SONGBOOK	Keely Smith (Reprise)
7	8	A HARD DAY'S NIGHT	Beatles (Parlophone)
-	9	THE VOICE OF WINSTON CHURCHILL	Winston Churchill (Decca)
-	10	ANOTHER SIDE OF BOB DYLAN	Bob Dylan (CBS)

13 February 1965

1	1	THE ROLLING STONES NO 2	Rolling Stones (Decca)
2	2	BEATLES FOR SALE	Beatles (Parlophone)
3	3	THE BEST OF JIM REEVES	Jim Reeves (RCA)
4	4	LUCKY 13 SHADES OF VAL DOONICAN	Val Doonican (Decca)
-	5	CILLA	Cilla Black (Parlophone)
9	6	THE VOICE OF WINSTON CHURCHILL	Winston Churchill (Decca)
5	7	THE KINKS	Kinks (Pye)
6	8	THE BACHELORS PLUS 16 GREAT SONGS	Bachelors (Decca)
10	9	ANOTHER SIDE OF BOB DYLAN	Bob Dylan (CBS)
-	10	THE ANIMALS	Animals (Columbia)

20 February 1965

1	1	THE ROLLING STONES NO 2	Rolling Stones (Decca)
2	2	BEATLES FOR SALE	Beatles (Parlophone)
3	3	THE BEST OF JIM REEVES	Jim Reeves (RCA)
5	4	CILLA	Cilla Black (Parlophone)
4	5	LUCKY 13 SHADES OF VAL DOONICAN	Val Doonican (Decca)
6	6	THE VOICE OF WINSTON CHURCHILL	Winston Churchill (Decca)
-	7	I'M GONNA BE STRONG	Gene Pitney (Stateside)
9	8	ANOTHER SIDE OF BOB DYLAN	Bob Dylan (CBS)
7	9	THE KINKS	Kinks (Pye)
10	10	THE ANIMALS	Animals (Columbia)

Winston Churchill, born 1874, took the Jim Reeves chart-route. Like Dylan, he had no supporting 45. The LP emphasised wartime speech extracts. More curious was The Keely Smith *Lennon-McCartney Songbook*. (This US female vocalist didn't really co-write the Beatles' songs). One of chart history's least-remembered entries, its success was due partly to the magic label "Lennon-McCartney", and partly to Frank Sinatra's label Reprise – it had already achieved chart placings for eleven albums.

February – April 1965

27 February 1965

last week	this week		
1	1	THE ROLLING STONES NO 2	Rolling Stones (Decca)
2	2	BEATLES FOR SALE	Beatles (Parlophone)
3	3	THE BEST OF JIM REEVES	Jim Reeves (RCA)
4	4	CILLA Cilla Black (Parlophone)	
6	5	THE VOICE OF WINSTON CHURCHILL	Winston Churchill (Decca)
5	6	LUCKY 13 SHADES OF VAL DOONICAN	Val Doonican (Decca)
8	7	ANOTHER SIDE OF BOB DYLAN	Bob Dylan (CBS)
9	8	THE KINKS	Kinks (Pye)
7	9	I'M GONNA BE STRONG	Gene Pitney (Stateside)
-	10	SANDIE	Sandie Shaw (Pye)

6 March 1965

1	1	THE ROLLING STONES NO 2	Rolling Stones (Decca)
2	2	BEATLES FOR SALE	Beatles (Parlophone)
10	3	SANDIE Sandie Shaw (Pye)	
3	4	THE BEST OF JIM REEVES	Jim Reeves (RCA)
5	5	THE VOICE OF WINSTON CHURCHILL	Winston Churchill (Decca)
6	6	LUCKY 13 SHADES OF VAL DOONICAN	Val Doonican (Decca)
8	7	THE KINKS Kinks (Pye)	
9	8	I'M GONNA BE STRONG	Gene Pitney (Stateside)
4	9	CILLA Cilla Black (Parlophone)	
-	10	THE BACHELORS PLUS 16 GREAT SONGS	Bachelors (Decca)

13 March 1965

1	1	THE ROLLING STONES NO 2	Rolling Stones (Decca)
2	2	BEATLES FOR SALE	Beatles (Parlophone)
4	3	THE BEST OF JIM REEVES	Jim Reeves (RCA)
3	4	SANDIE Sandie Shaw (Pye)	
-	5	KINDA KINKS Kinks (Pye)	
6	6	LUCKY 13 SHADES OF VAL DOONICAN	Val Doonican (Decca)
9	7	CILLA Cilla Black (Parlophone)	
5	8	THE VOICE OF WINSTON CHURCHILL	Winston Churchill (Decca)
-	9	THE FREEWHEELIN' BOB DYLAN	Bob Dylan (CBS)
-	10	MARY POPPINS	Soundtrack (HMV)

20 March 1965

1	1	THE ROLLING STONES NO 2	Rolling Stones (Decca)
5	2	KINDA KINKS Kinks (Pye)	
2	3	BEATLES FOR SALE	Beatles (Parlophone)
4	4	SANDIE Sandie Shaw (Pye)	
-	5	THE PRETTY THINGS	Pretty Things (Fontana)
7	6	CILLA Cilla Black (Parlophone)	
9	7	THE FREEWHEELIN' BOB DYLAN	Bob Dylan (CBS)
-	8	ANOTHER SIDE OF BOB DYLAN	Bob Dylan (CBS)
-	9	THE UNFORGETTABLE NAT 'KING' COLE	Nat 'King' Cole (Capitol)
6	10	LUCKY 13 SHADES OF VAL DOONICAN	Val Doonican (Decca)

27 March 1965

1	1	THE ROLLING STONES NO 2	Rolling Stones (Decca)
2	2	KINDA KINKS Kinks (Pye)	
3	3	BEATLES FOR SALE	Beatles (Parlophone)
4	4	SANDIE Sandie Shaw (Pye)	
7	5	THE FREEWHEELIN' BOB DYLAN	Bob Dylan (CBS)
5	6	THE PRETTY THINGS	Pretty Things (Fontana)
-	7	THE BEST OF JIM REEVES	Jim Reeves (RCA)
-	8	THE TIMES THEY ARE A-CHANGIN' Bob Dylan (CBS)	
8	9	ANOTHER SIDE OF BOB DYLAN	Bob Dylan (CBS)
6	10	CILLA Cilla Black (Parlophone)	

3 April 1965

1	1	THE ROLLING STONES NO 2	Rolling Stones (Decca)
3	2	BEATLES FOR SALE	Beatles (Parlophone)
5	3	THE FREEWHEELIN' BOB DYLAN	Bob Dylan (CBS)
2	4	KINDA KINKS Kinks (Pye)	
8	5	THE TIMES THEY ARE A-CHANGIN' Bob Dylan (CBS)	
6	6	THE PRETTY THINGS	Pretty Things (Fontana)
4	6	SANDIE Sandie Shaw (Pye)	
7	8	THE BEST OF JIM REEVES	Jim Reeves (RCA)
-	9	LUCKY 13 SHADES OF VAL DOONICAN	Val Doonican (Decca)
-	10	A COLLECTION OF 16 TAMLA MOTOWN HITS Various Artists	(Tamla Motown)

10 April 1965

1	1	THE ROLLING STONES NO 2	Rolling Stones (Decca)
3	2	THE FREEWHEELIN' BOB DYLAN Bob Dylan (CBS)	
2	3	BEATLES FOR SALE	Beatles (Parlophone)
4	4	KINDA KINKS Kinks (Pye)	
5	5	THE TIMES THEY ARE A-CHANGIN' Bob Dylan (CBS)	
6	6	THE PRETTY THINGS	Pretty Things (Fontana)
-	6	CLIFF RICHARD	Cliff Richard (Columbia)
-	8	SOUNDS LIKE THE SEARCHERS Searchers (Pye)	
-	9	HAVE I TOLD YOU LATELY THAT I LOVE YOU	Jim Reeves (RCA)
-	10	THE UNFORGETTABLE NAT 'KING' COLE	Nat 'King' Cole (Capitol)

17 April 1965

1	1	THE ROLLING STONES NO 2	Rolling Stones (Decca)
3	2	BEATLES FOR SALE	Beatles (Parlophone)
2	3	THE FREEWHEELIN' BOB DYLAN Bob Dylan (CBS)	
5	4	THE TIMES THEY ARE A-CHANGIN' Bob Dylan (CBS)	
9	5	HAVE I TOLD YOU LATELY THAT I LOVE YOU	Jim Reeves (RCA)
6	6	THE PRETTY THINGS	Pretty Things (Fontana)
3	7	KINDA KINKS Kinks (Pye)	
6	8	CLIFF RICHARD	Cliff Richard (Columbia)
-	9	MARY POPPINS	Soundtrack (HMV)
-	10	THE SOUND OF MUSIC	Soundtrack (RCA)

February saw *Another Side Of Bob Dylan*, his fourth LP, back in the Top 10, and by the end of March he was in the lists with a vengeance, with his second album, *Freewheelin'*, re-entering alongside his newly-arrived third LP, while its title-track, aptly named *The Times They Are A-Changin'*, finally took him into the singles chart. In April this went Top 10, as he came to Britain for what would prove his last solo-acoustic tour, captured on D.A. Pennebaker's pioneering rock-doc *Don't Look Back*.

25

April – June 1965

24 April 1965

LW	TW	Title
2	1	BEATLES FOR SALE — Beatles (Parlophone)
1	2	THE ROLLING STONES NO 2 — Rolling Stones (Decca)
3	3	THE FREEWHEELIN' BOB DYLAN — Bob Dylan (CBS)
9	4	MARY POPPINS — Soundtrack (HMV)
10	5	THE SOUND OF MUSIC — Soundtrack (RCA)
4	6	THE TIMES THEY ARE A-CHANGIN' — Bob Dylan (CBS)
-	7	ANOTHER SIDE OF BOB DYLAN — Bob Dylan (CBS)
7	8	KINDA KINKS — Kinks (Pye)
6	9	THE PRETTY THINGS — Pretty Things (Fontana)
8	10	CLIFF RICHARD — Cliff Richard (Columbia)

1 May 1965

LW	TW	Title
1	1	BEATLES FOR SALE — Beatles (Parlophone)
2	2	THE ROLLING STONES NO 2 — Rolling Stones (Decca)
3	3	THE FREEWHEELIN' BOB DYLAN — Bob Dylan (CBS)
4	4	MARY POPPINS — Soundtrack (HMV)
10	5	CLIFF RICHARD — Cliff Richard (Columbia)
-	6	GIRL HAPPY — Elvis Presley (RCA)
5	7	THE SOUND OF MUSIC — Soundtrack (RCA)
5	8	THE TIMES THEY ARE A-CHANGIN' — Bob Dylan (CBS)
9	9	THE PRETTY THINGS — Pretty Things (Fontana)
8	10	KINDA KINKS — Kinks (Pye)

8 May 1965

LW	TW	Title
1	1	BEATLES FOR SALE — Beatles (Parlophone)
3	2	THE FREEWHEELIN' BOB DYLAN — Bob Dylan (CBS)
2	3	THE ROLLING STONES NO 2 — Rolling Stones (Decca)
6	4	GIRL HAPPY — Elvis Presley (RCA)
4	5	MARY POPPINS — Soundtrack (HMV)
7	6	THE SOUND OF MUSIC — Soundtrack (RCA)
8	7	THE TIMES THEY ARE A-CHANGIN' — Bob Dylan (CBS)
-	8	ANOTHER SIDE OF BOB DYLAN — Bob Dylan (CBS)
-	9	THE JIM REEVES WAY — Jim Reeves (RCA)
9	10	THE PRETTY THINGS — Pretty Things (Fontana)
-	10	MARIANNE FAITHFULL — Marianne Faithfull (Decca)

15 May 1965

LW	TW	Title
2	1	THE FREEWHEELIN' BOB DYLAN — Bob Dylan (CBS)
1	2	BEATLES FOR SALE — Beatles (Parlophone)
4	3	GIRL HAPPY — Elvis Presley (RCA)
5	3	MARY POPPINS — Soundtrack (HMV)
7	5	THE TIMES THEY ARE A-CHANGIN' — Bob Dylan (CBS)
6	6	THE SOUND OF MUSIC — Soundtrack (RCA)
-	7	ANIMAL TRACKS — Animals (Columbia)
3	8	THE ROLLING STONES NO 2 — Rolling Stones (Decca)
9	9	THE JIM REEVES WAY — Jim Reeves (RCA)
-	10	BRINGING IT ALL BACK HOME — Bob Dylan (CBS)
-	10	CLIFF RICHARD — Cliff Richard (Columbia)

22 May 1965

LW	TW	Title
10	1	BRINGING IT ALL BACK HOME — Bob Dylan (CBS)
7	2	ANIMAL TRACKS — Animals (Columbia)
-	3	HIT MAKER — Burt Bacharach (London)
2	4	BEATLES FOR SALE — Beatles (Parlophone)
1	5	THE FREEWHEELIN' BOB DYLAN — Bob Dylan (CBS)
3	6	MARY POPPINS — Soundtrack (HMV)
5	7	THE TIMES THEY ARE A-CHANGIN' — Bob Dylan (CBS)
9	7	THE JIM REEVES WAY — Jim Reeves (RCA)
6	9	THE SOUND OF MUSIC — Soundtrack (RCA)
-	10	WHAT'S BIN DID AND WHAT'S BIN HID — Donovan (Pye)

29 May 1965

LW	TW	Title
1	1	BRINGING IT ALL BACK HOME — Bob Dylan (CBS)
3	2	HIT MAKER — Burt Bacharach (London)
5	3	THE FREEWHEELIN' BOB DYLAN — Bob Dylan (CBS)
9	4	THE SOUND OF MUSIC — Soundtrack (RCA)
4	5	BEATLES FOR SALE — Beatles (Parlophone)
10	6	WHAT'S BIN DID AND WHAT'S BIN HID — Donovan (Pye)
6	7	MARY POPPINS — Soundtrack (HMV)
7	8	THE JIM REEVES WAY — Jim Reeves (RCA)
2	9	ANIMAL TRACKS — Animals (Columbia)
-	10	THE ROLLING STONES NO 2 — Rolling Stones (Decca)

5 June 1965

LW	TW	Title
1	1	BRINGING IT ALL BACK HOME — Bob Dylan (CBS)
4	2	THE SOUND OF MUSIC — Soundtrack (RCA)
2	3	HIT MAKER — Burt Bacharach (London)
7	4	MARY POPPINS — Soundtrack (HMV)
5	5	BEATLES FOR SALE — Beatles (Parlophone)
6	6	WHAT'S BIN DID AND WHAT'S BIN HID — Donovan (Pye)
9	6	ANIMAL TRACKS — Animals (Columbia)
3	8	THE FREEWHEELIN' BOB DYLAN — Bob Dylan (CBS)
10	9	THE ROLLING STONES NO 2 — Rolling Stones (Decca)
8	10	THE JIM REEVES WAY — Jim Reeves (RCA)

12 June 1965

LW	TW	Title
1	1	BRINGING IT ALL BACK HOME — Bob Dylan (CBS)
2	2	THE SOUND OF MUSIC — Soundtrack (RCA)
3	3	HIT MAKER — Burt Bacharach (London)
8	4	THE FREEWHEELIN' BOB DYLAN — Bob Dylan (CBS)
6	5	ANIMAL TRACKS — Animals (Columbia)
6	6	WHAT'S BIN DID AND WHAT'S BIN HID — Donovan (Pye)
4	7	MARY POPPINS — Soundtrack (HMV)
5	7	BEATLES FOR SALE — Beatles (Parlophone)
	9	THE SEEKERS — Seekers (Decca)
-	10	'14' — Various Artists (Decca)

In mid-tour, Dylan was told by the Sheriff of Nottingham's wife: "everybody loves you... I think the songs are very wonderful. And you write them yourself, too, don't you, sometimes?" By May Day, Dylan's "electric" single, *Subterranean Homesick Blues,* was in the Top 20 alongside his two-year-old "protest" song; soon after, his new album, with one acoustic and one electric side, topped the LP chart. The Sheriff's wife surely preferred the LPs just below it in early June: *The Sound of Music* and *Hit Maker.*

June – August 1965

last week	this week	19 June 1965
1	1	BRINGING IT ALL BACK HOME Bob Dylan (CBS)
2	2	THE SOUND OF MUSIC Soundtrack (RCA)
3	3	HIT MAKER Burt Bacharach (London)
6	4	WHAT'S BIN DID AND WHAT'S BIN HID Donovan (Pye)
7	5	MARY POPPINS Soundtrack (HMV)
7	6	BEATLES FOR SALE Beatles (Parlophone)
4	7	THE FREEWHEELIN' BOB DYLAN Bob Dylan (CBS)
9	8	THE SEEKERS Seekers (Decca)
-	9	ALONG CAME JONES Tom Jones (Decca)
-	10	JOAN BAEZ/5 Joan Baez (Fontana)

		26 June 1965
2	1	THE SOUND OF MUSIC Soundtrack (RCA)
1	2	BRINGING IT ALL BACK HOME Bob Dylan (CBS)
4	3	WHAT'S BIN DID AND WHAT'S BIN HID Donovan (Pye)
3	4	HIT MAKER Burt Bacharach (London)
5	5	MARY POPPINS Soundtrack (HMV)
10	6	JOAN BAEZ/5 Joan Baez (Fontana)
7	7	THE FREEWHEELIN' BOB DYLAN Bob Dylan (CBS)
6	8	BEATLES FOR SALE Beatles (Parlophone)
-	9	HOLLY IN THE HILLS Buddy Holly (Coral)
8	10	THE SEEKERS Seekers (Decca)

		3 July 1965
2	1	BRINGING IT ALL BACK HOME Bob Dylan (CBS)
1	2	THE SOUND OF MUSIC Soundtrack (RCA)
6	3	JOAN BAEZ/5 Joan Baez (Fontana)
3	4	WHAT'S BIN DID AND WHAT'S BIN HID Donovan (Pye)
5	5	MARY POPPINS Soundtrack (HMV)
4	6	HIT MAKER Burt Bacharach (London)
-	7	A WORLD OF OUR OWN Seekers (Columbia)
9	8	HOLLY IN THE HILLS Buddy Holly (Coral)
8	9	BEATLES FOR SALE Beatles (Parlophone)
-	9	THE ROLLING STONES NO 2 Rolling Stones (Decca)

		10 July 1965
1	1	BRINGING IT ALL BACK HOME Bob Dylan (CBS)
2	2	THE SOUND OF MUSIC Soundtrack (RCA)
3	3	JOAN BAEZ/5 Joan Baez (Fontana)
7	4	A WORLD OF OUR OWN Seekers (Columbia)
4	5	WHAT'S BIN DID AND WHAT'S BIN HID Donovan (Pye)
5	6	MARY POPPINS Soundtrack (HMV)
6	7	HIT MAKER Burt Bacharach (London)
-	8	THE FREEWHEELIN' BOB DYLAN Bob Dylan (CBS)
-	9	JOAN BAEZ Joan Baez (Fontana)
8	10	HOLLY IN THE HILLS Buddy Holly (Coral)

		17 July 1965
1	1	BRINGING IT ALL BACK HOME Bob Dylan (CBS)
2	2	THE SOUND OF MUSIC Soundtrack (RCA)
3	3	JOAN BAEZ/5 Joan Baez (Fontana)
4	4	A WORLD OF OUR OWN Seekers (Columbia)
6	5	MARY POPPINS Soundtrack (HMV)
-	6	THE SOUND OF THE SHADOWS Shadows (Columbia)
7	7	HIT MAKER Burt Bacharach (London)
5	8	WHAT'S BIN DID AND WHAT'S BIN HID Donovan (Pye)
8	9	THE FREEWHEELIN' BOB DYLAN Bob Dylan (CBS)
10	9	HOLLY IN THE HILLS Buddy Holly (Coral)

		24 July 1965
2	1	THE SOUND OF MUSIC Soundtrack (RCA)
1	2	BRINGING IT ALL BACK HOME Bob Dylan (CBS)
3	3	JOAN BAEZ/5 Joan Baez (Fontana)
6	4	THE SOUND OF THE SHADOWS Shadows (Columbia)
5	5	MARY POPPINS Soundtrack (HMV)
7	6	HIT MAKER Burt Bacharach (London)
9	7	HOLLY IN THE HILLS Buddy Holly (Coral)
9	8	THE FREEWHEELIN' BOB DYLAN Bob Dylan (CBS)
8	9	WHAT'S BIN DID AND WHAT'S BIN HID Donovan (Pye)
-	10	JOAN BAEZ IN CONCERT, VOL. 2 Joan Baez (Fontana)
-	10	ALMOST THERE Andy Williams (CBS)

		31 July 1965
1	1	THE SOUND OF MUSIC Soundtrack (RCA)
2	2	BRINGING IT ALL BACK HOME Bob Dylan (CBS)
3	3	JOAN BAEZ/5 Joan Baez (Fontana)
5	4	MARY POPPINS Soundtrack (HMV)
4	5	THE SOUND OF THE SHADOWS Shadows (Columbia)
10	6	ALMOST THERE Andy Williams (CBS)
10	7	JOAN BAEZ IN CONCERT, VOL. 2 Joan Baez (Fontana)
9	8	WHAT'S BIN DID AND WHAT'S BIN HID Donovan (Pye)
-	9	A WORLD OF OUR OWN Seekers (Columbia)
8	10	THE FREEWHEELIN' BOB DYLAN Bob Dylan (CBS)

		7 August 1965
1	1	THE SOUND OF MUSIC Soundtrack (RCA)
4	2	MARY POPPINS Soundtrack (HMV)
2	3	BRINGING IT ALL BACK HOME Bob Dylan (CBS)
3	4	JOAN BAEZ/5 Joan Baez (Fontana)
-	5	THE MAGNIFICENT MOODIES Moody Blues (Decca)
6	5	ALMOST THERE Andy Williams (CBS)
5	7	THE SOUND OF THE SHADOWS Shadows (Columbia)
7	8	JOAN BAEZ IN CONCERT, VOL. 2 Joan Baez (Fontana)
9	9	A WORLD OF OUR OWN Seekers (Columbia)
-	10	BEATLES FOR SALE Beatles (Parlophone)

Burt Bacharach and Hal David were a "sophisticat" Goffin-King: a series of their songs became unfailing hits for whoever recorded them, while being instantly recognisable as Bacharach-Davids. There was *Walk On By* and *You'll Never Get To Heaven* by Dionne Warwick - the former would chart again for the Stranglers in 1978 - *Anyone Who Had A Heart* by Dionne Warwick and by Cilla Black. *Trains And Boats And Planes* was a 1965 hit by Billy J. Kramer and by Bacharach himself.

August – October 1965

14 August 1965

LW	TW	Title / Artist
-	1	HELP! Beatles (Parlophone)
1	2	THE SOUND OF MUSIC Soundtrack (RCA)
2	3	MARY POPPINS Soundtrack (HMV)
4	4	JOAN BAEZ/5 Joan Baez (Fontana)
3	5	BRINGING IT ALL BACK HOME Bob Dylan (CBS)
5	6	THE MAGNIFICENT MOODIES Moody Blues (Decca)
5	7	ALMOST THERE Andy Williams (CBS)
7	8	THE SOUND OF THE SHADOWS Shadows (Columbia)
8	9	JOAN BAEZ IN CONCERT, VOL. 2 Joan Baez (Fontana)
9	10	A WORLD OF OUR OWN Seekers (Columbia)

21 August 1965

LW	TW	Title / Artist
1	1	HELP! Beatles (Parlophone)
2	2	THE SOUND OF MUSIC Soundtrack (RCA)
3	3	MARY POPPINS Soundtrack (HMV)
4	4	JOAN BAEZ/5 Joan Baez (Fontana)
6	5	THE MAGNIFICENT MOODIES Moody Blues (Decca)
5	5	BRINGING IT ALL BACK HOME Bob Dylan (CBS)
7	7	ALMOST THERE Andy Williams (CBS)
8	8	THE SOUND OF THE SHADOWS Shadows (Columbia)
-	9	MR. TAMBOURINE MAN Byrds (CBS)
9	10	JOAN BAEZ IN CONCERT. VOL. 2 Joan Baez (Fontana)

28 August 1965

LW	TW	Title / Artist
1	1	HELP! Beatles (Parlophone)
2	2	THE SOUND OF MUSIC Soundtrack (RCA)
3	3	MARY POPPINS Soundtrack (HMV)
4	4	JOAN BAEZ/5 Joan Baez (Fontana)
9	5	MR. TAMBOURINE MAN Byrds (CBS)
7	6	ALMOST THERE Andy Williams (CBS)
5	7	BRINGING IT ALL BACK HOME Bob Dylan (CBS)
8	8	THE SOUND OF THE SHADOWS Shadows (Columbia)
-	8	CATCH US IF YOU CAN Dave Clark Five (Columbia)
-	10	THE TIMES THEY ARE A-CHANGIN' Bob Dylan (CBS)

4 September 1965

LW	TW	Title / Artist
1	1	HELP! Beatles (Parlophone)
2	2	THE SOUND OF MUSIC Soundtrack (RCA)
3	3	MARY POPPINS Soundtrack (HMV)
4	4	JOAN BAEZ/5 Joan Baez (Fontana)
7	5	BRINGING IT ALL BACK HOME Bob Dylan (CBS)
6	6	ALMOST THERE Andy Williams (CBS)
5	7	MR. TAMBOURINE MAN Byrds (CBS)
8	8	THE SOUND OF THE SHADOWS Shadows (Columbia)
-	9	THE FREEWHEELIN' BOB DYLAN Bob Dylan (CBS)
-	10	FLAMING STAR AND SUMMER KISSES Elvis Presley (RCA)

11 September 1965

LW	TW	Title / Artist
1	1	HELP! Beatles (Parlophone)
2	2	THE SOUND OF MUSIC Soundtrack (RCA)
3	3	MARY POPPINS Soundtrack (HMV)
5	4	BRINGING IT ALL BACK HOME Bob Dylan (CBS)
6	5	ALMOST THERE Andy Williams (CBS)
4	6	JOAN BAEZ/5 Joan Baez (Fontana)
10	7	FLAMING STAR AND SUMMER KISSES Elvis Presley (RCA)
-	8	JOAN BAEZ IN CONCERT, VOL. 2 Joan Baez (Fontana)
-	9	CATCH US IF YOU CAN Dave Clark Five (Columbia)
-	10	THE ROLLING STONES NO 2 Rolling Stones (Decca)

18 September 1965

LW	TW	Title / Artist
1	1	HELP! Beatles (Parlophone)
2	2	THE SOUND OF MUSIC Soundtrack (RCA)
3	3	MARY POPPINS Soundtrack (HMV)
5	4	ALMOST THERE Andy Williams (CBS)
6	5	JOAN BAEZ/5 Joan Baez (Fontana)
4	6	BRINGING IT ALL BACK HOME Bob Dylan (CBS)
7	7	FLAMING STAR AND SUMMER KISSES Elvis Presley (RCA)
-	8	MORE GREAT SONG HITS Bachelors (Decca)
-	9	THERE IS ONLY ONE ROY ORBISON Roy Orbison (London)
8	10	JOAN BAEZ IN CONCERT, VOL. 2 Joan Baez (Fontana)
-	10	MY FAIR LADY Soundtrack (CBS)

25 September 1965

LW	TW	Title / Artist
1	1	HELP! Beatles (Parlophone)
2	2	THE SOUND OF MUSIC Soundtrack (RCA)
3	3	MARY POPPINS Soundtrack (HMV)
4	4	ALMOST THERE Andy Williams (CBS)
6	5	BRINGING IT ALL BACK HOME Bob Dylan (CBS)
5	6	JOAN BAEZ/5 Joan Baez (Fontana)
9	7	THERE IS ONLY ONE ROY ORBISON Roy Orbison (London)
7	8	FLAMING STAR AND SUMMER KISSES Elvis Presley (RCA)
-	9	ALL I REALLY WANT TO DO Cher (Liberty)
10	10	JOAN BAEZ IN CONCERT, VOL. 2 Joan Baez (Fontana)

2 October 1965

LW	TW	Title / Artist
1	1	HELP! Beatles (Parlophone)
2	2	THE SOUND OF MUSIC Soundtrack (RCA)
-	3	OUT OF OUR HEADS Rolling Stones (Decca)
3	4	MARY POPPINS Soundtrack (HMV)
4	5	ALMOST THERE Andy Williams (CBS)
9	6	ALL I REALLY WANT TO DO Cher (Liberty)
5	7	BRINGING IT ALL BACK HOME Bob Dylan (CBS)
6	8	JOAN BAEZ/5 Joan Baez (Fontana)
-	9	HOLLIES Hollies (Parlophone)
8	10	FLAMING STAR AND SUMMER KISSES Elvis Presley (RCA)

And then came Joan Baez. Since mid-June she'd been quietly storming the chart (in parallel with the single *There But For Fortune*), with her exciting LP titles *Joan Baez In Concert No.5*, *Joan Baez*, and *Joan Baez In Concert No.2* (in that order). The first and last of these were to stay in and around the Top 10 all through August and September, by which time she had another hit single with Dylan's *It's All Over Now Baby Blue*, while he rode the charts with the 6-minute long single *Like A Rolling Stone*.

October – November 1965

9 October 1965

1	1 HELP!	Beatles (Parlophone)
3	2 OUT OF OUR HEADS	Rolling Stones (Decca)
2	3 THE SOUND OF MUSIC	Soundtrack (RCA)
4	4 MARY POPPINS	Soundtrack (HMV)
5	5 ALMOST THERE	Andy Williams (CBS)
-	6 HIGHWAY 61 REVISITED	Bob Dylan (CBS)
-	7 LOOK AT US	Sonny & Cher (Atlantic)
9	8 HOLLIES	Hollies (Parlophone)
6	9 ALL I REALLY WANT TO DO	Cher (Liberty)
7	9 BRINGING IT ALL BACK HOME	Bob Dylan (CBS)

16 October 1965

1	1 HELP!	Beatles (Parlophone)
3	2 THE SOUND OF MUSIC	Soundtrack (RCA)
2	3 OUT OF OUR HEADS	Rolling Stones (Decca)
4	4 MARY POPPINS	Soundtrack (HMV)
6	5 HIGHWAY 61 REVISITED	Bob Dylan (CBS)
5	6 ALMOST THERE	Andy Williams (CBS)
7	7 LOOK AT US	Sonny & Cher (Atlantic)
-	8 EVERYTHING'S COMING UP DUSTY	Dusty Springfield (Philips)
8	9 HOLLIES	Hollies (Parlophone)
-	10 FLAMING STAR AND SUMMER KISSES	Elvis Presley (RCA)

23 October 1965

1	1 HELP!	Beatles (Parlophone)
2	2 THE SOUND OF MUSIC	Soundtrack (RCA)
3	3 OUT OF OUR HEADS	Rolling Stones (Decca)
4	3 MARY POPPINS	Soundtrack (HMV)
5	5 HIGHWAY 61 REVISITED	Bob Dylan (CBS)
6	6 ALMOST THERE	Andy Williams (CBS)
8	7 EVERYTHING'S COMING UP DUSTY	Dusty Springfield (Philips)
7	8 LOOK AT US	Sonny & Cher (Atlantic)
-	9 MANN MADE	Manfred Mann (HMV)
-	10 MORE GREAT SONG HITS	Bachelors (Decca)

30 October 1965

2	1 THE SOUND OF MUSIC	Soundtrack (RCA)
1	2 HELP!	Beatles (Parlophone)
3	3 OUT OF OUR HEADS	Rolling Stones (Decca)
3	4 MARY POPPINS	Soundtrack (HMV)
6	5 ALMOST THERE	Andy Williams (CBS)
5	6 HIGHWAY 61 REVISITED	Bob Dylan (CBS)
7	7 EVERYTHING'S COMING UP DUSTY	Dusty Springfield (Philips)
8	8 LOOK AT US	Sonny & Cher (Atlantic)
9	9 MANN MADE	Manfred Mann (HMV)
-	10 ALL I REALLY WANT TO DO	Cher (Liberty)

6 November 1965

1	1 THE SOUND OF MUSIC	Soundtrack (RCA)
3	2 OUT OF OUR HEADS	Rolling Stones (Decca)
2	3 HELP!	Beatles (Parlophone)
4	4 MARY POPPINS	Soundtrack (HMV)
5	5 ALMOST THERE	Andy Williams (CBS)
6	6 HIGHWAY 61 REVISITED	Bob Dylan (CBS)
7	7 EVERYTHING'S COMING UP DUSTY	Dusty Springfield (Philips)
8	8 LOOK AT US	Sonny & Cher (Atlantic)
9	9 MANN MADE	Manfred Mann (HMV)
-	10 FAIRYTALE	Donovan (Pye)

13 November 1965

1	1 THE SOUND OF MUSIC	Soundtrack (RCA)
3	2 HELP!	Beatles (Parlophone)
4	3 MARY POPPINS	Soundtrack (HMV)
2	4 OUT OF OUR HEADS	Rolling Stones (Decca)
7	5 EVERYTHING'S COMING UP DUSTY	Dusty Springfield (Philips)
5	6 ALMOST THERE	Andy Williams (CBS)
6	7 HIGHWAY 61 REVISITED	Bob Dylan (CBS)
8	8 LOOK AT US	Sonny & Cher (Atlantic)
9	9 MANN MADE	Manfred Mann (HMV)
10	10 FAIRYTALE	Donovan (Pye)
-	10 FAREWELL ANGELINA	Joan Baez (Fontana)

20 November 1965

1	1 THE SOUND OF MUSIC	Soundtrack (RCA)
2	2 HELP!	Beatles (Parlophone)
4	3 OUT OF OUR HEADS	Rolling Stones (Decca)
3	4 MARY POPPINS	Soundtrack (HMV)
6	5 ALMOST THERE	Andy Williams (CBS)
7	6 HIGHWAY 61 REVISITED	Bob Dylan (CBS)
5	7 EVERYTHING'S COMING UP DUSTY	Dusty Springfield (Philips)
10	8 FAREWELL ANGELINA	Joan Baez (Fontana)
8	9 LOOK AT US	Sonny & Cher (Atlantic)
9	10 MANN MADE	Manfred Mann (HMV)

27 November 1965

1	1 THE SOUND OF MUSIC	Soundtrack (RCA)
2	2 HELP!	Beatles (Parlophone)
4	3 MARY POPPINS	Soundtrack (HMV)
3	4 OUT OF OUR HEADS	Rolling Stones (Decca)
5	5 ALMOST THERE	Andy Williams (CBS)
6	6 HIGHWAY 61 REVISITED	Bob Dylan (CBS)
10	7 MANN MADE	Manfred Mann (HMV)
8	8 FAREWELL ANGELINA	Joan Baez (Fontana)
-	9 MY FAIR LADY	Soundtrack (CBS)
9	10 LOOK AT US	Sonny & Cher (Atlantic)

Baez wasn't the only Dylan-associated artist straddling both charts. The Byrds' *Mr Tambourine Man* had been a No.1 single and a No.5 album; now Dylan's *All I Really Want To Do* went Top 10 for them and Cher, giving her a hit album too. Manfred Mann, after a hit EP featuring *God On Our Side*, went Top 3 with the Dylan song, *If You Gotta Go Go Now*, and LP-charted in October. Donovan, "Britain's Dylan", now had a hit album too, while Baez had yet another in *Farewell Angelina* - again a Dylan title.

December 1965

last this week

	4 December 1965		11 December 1965		18 December 1965		25 December 1965
1	1 THE SOUND OF MUSIC Soundtrack (RCA)	-	1 RUBBER SOUL Beatles (Parlophone)	1	1 RUBBER SOUL Beatles (Parlophone)	1	1 RUBBER SOUL Beatles (Parlophone)
3	2 MARY POPPINS Soundtrack (HMV)	1	2 THE SOUND OF MUSIC Soundtrack (RCA)	2	2 THE SOUND OF MUSIC Soundtrack (RCA)	2	2 THE SOUND OF MUSIC Soundtrack (RCA)
2	3 HELP! Beatles (Parlophone)	2	3 MARY POPPINS Soundtrack (HMV)	3	3 MARY POPPINS Soundtrack (HMV)	3	3 MARY POPPINS Soundtrack (HMV)
4	4 OUT OF OUR HEADS Rolling Stones (Decca)	3	4 HELP! Beatles (Parlophone)	4	4 HELP! Beatles (Parlophone)	5	4 TAKE IT EASY WITH THE WALKER BROTHERS Walker Brothers (Philips)
-	5 ELVIS FOR EVERYONE Elvis Presley (RCA)	5	5 ELVIS FOR EVERYONE Elvis Presley (RCA)	-	5 TAKE IT EASY WITH THE WALKER BROTHERS Walker Brothers (Philips)	8	4 FAREWELL ANGELINA Joan Baez (Fontana)
5	6 ALMOST THERE Andy Williams (CBS)	4	6 OUT OF OUR HEADS Rolling Stones (Decca)	-	6 MY GENERATION Who (Brunswick)	6	6 MY GENERATION Who (Brunswick)
8	7 FAREWELL ANGELINA Joan Baez (Fontana)	6	7 ALMOST THERE Andy Williams (CBS)	6	7 OUT OF OUR HEADS Rolling Stones (Decca)	4	7 HELP! Beatles (Parlophone)
6	8 HIGHWAY 61 REVISITED Bob Dylan (CBS)	7	8 FAREWELL ANGELINA Joan Baez (Fontana)	5	8 ELVIS FOR EVERYONE Elvis Presley (RCA)	-	7 MY FAIR LADY Soundtrack (CBS)
-	9 I LEFT MY HEART IN SAN FRANCISCO Tony Bennett (CBS)	9	9 I LEFT MY HEART IN SAN FRANCISCO Tony Bennett (CBS)	8	8 FAREWELL ANGELINA Joan Baez (Fontana)	9	9 I LEFT MY HEART IN SAN FRANCISCO Tony Bennett (CBS)
-	10 THE OTHER SIDE OF DUDLEY MOORE Dudley Moore (Decca)	-	10 KINKS KONTROVERSY Kinks (Pye)	7	10 ALMOST THERE Andy Williams (CBS)	7	10 OUT OF OUR HEADS Rolling Stones (Decca)

On the other hand *The Sound Of Music*, *Mary Poppins*, Andy Williams, Tony Bennett, Dudley Moore and *My Fair Lady* told a different Christmas story. That Elvis' album couldn't sustain its place in the Top 10 on the big day reflected two trends: first, it was a ragbag collection of tracks, typifying his label's disrespect for his catalogue; second, it mirrored his falling status, both because of all the awful formula-movies he'd been making and because, since the birth of the Beatles, he was yesterday's man. The Beatles still ruled – they had a new No.1 LP and the No.1 single (*Day Tripper/We Can Work It Out*). If Mary and Tony and Andy (and even Elvis) suggested Christmas past, and the Beatles the Christmas present, one future was surely hinted at by the puns lurking unsubtlely in both the Beatles' single title *Day Tripper* and the title of the Stones' latest LP *Out Of Our Heads*.

1 January 1966

last / this week

1	1	RUBBER SOUL Beatles (Parlophone)
2	2	THE SOUND OF MUSIC Soundtrack (RCA)
3	3	MARY POPPINS Soundtrack (HMV)
6	4	MY GENERATION Who (Brunswick)
7	5	MY FAIR LADY Soundtrack (CBS)
4	6	TAKE IT EASY WITH THE WALKER BROTHERS Walker Brothers (Philips)
-	7	ALMOST THERE Andy Williams (CBS)
-	7	TEARS OF HAPPINESS Ken Dodd (Columbia)
7	9	HELP! Beatles (Parlophone)
4	9	FAREWELL ANGELINA Joan Baez (Fontana)

8 January 1966

1	1	RUBBER SOUL Beatles (Parlophone)
2	2	THE SOUND OF MUSIC Soundtrack (RCA)
3	3	MARY POPPINS Soundtrack (HMV)
9	4	HELP! Beatles (Parlophone)
4	5	MY GENERATION Who (Brunswick)
7	6	TEARS OF HAPPINESS Ken Dodd (Columbia)
6	7	TAKE IT EASY WITH THE WALKER BROTHERS Walker Brothers (Philips)
-	8	OUT OF OUR HEADS Rolling Stones (Decca)
-	9	I LEFT MY HEART IN SAN FRANCISCO Tony Bennett (CBS)
-	10	HAREM HOLIDAY Elvis Presley (RCA)

15 January 1966

1	1	RUBBER SOUL Beatles (Parlophone)
2	2	THE SOUND OF MUSIC Soundtrack (RCA)
3	3	MARY POPPINS Soundtrack (HMV)
4	4	HELP! Beatles (Parlophone)
5	4	MY GENERATION Who (Brunswick)
6	6	TEARS OF HAPPINESS Ken Dodd (Columbia)
7	7	TAKE IT EASY WITH THE WALKER BROTHERS Walker Brothers (Philips)
8	7	OUT OF OUR HEADS Rolling Stones (Decca)
-	9	GOING PLACES Herb Alpert & the Tijuana Brass (Pye International)
-	10	MY FAIR LADY Soundtrack (CBS)
-	10	THE OTHER SIDE OF DUDLEY MOORE Dudley Moore (Decca)

22 January 1966

1	1	RUBBER SOUL Beatles (Parlophone)
2	2	THE SOUND OF MUSIC Soundtrack (RCA)
3	3	MARY POPPINS Soundtrack (HMV)
-	4	SECOND ALBUM Spencer Davis Group (Fontana)
4	5	MY GENERATION Who (Brunswick)
7	6	TAKE IT EASY WITH THE WALKER BROTHERS Walker Brothers (Philips)
6	7	TEARS OF HAPPINESS Ken Dodd (Columbia)
4	8	HELP! Beatles (Parlophone)
-	9	MY NAME IS BARBRA, TWO Barbra Streisand (CBS)
-	10	THEIR FIRST LP Spencer Davis Group (Fontana)

29 January 1966

1	1	RUBBER SOUL Beatles (Parlophone)
2	2	THE SOUND OF MUSIC Soundtrack (RCA)
4	3	SECOND ALBUM Spencer Davis Group (Fontana)
3	4	MARY POPPINS Soundtrack (HMV)
-	5	A MAN AND HIS MUSIC Frank Sinatra (Reprise)
6	6	TAKE IT EASY WITH THE WALKER BROTHERS Walker Brothers (Philips)
5	7	MY GENERATION Who (Brunswick)
10	8	THEIR FIRST LP Spencer Davis Group (Fontana)
7	9	TEARS OF HAPPINESS Ken Dodd (Columbia)
-	10	GOING PLACES Herb Alpert & the Tijuana Brass (Pye International)
-	10	A WORLD OF OUR OWN Seekers (Columbia)

5 February 1966

1	1	RUBBER SOUL Beatles (Parlophone)
3	2	SECOND ALBUM Spencer Davis Group (Fontana)
2	3	THE SOUND OF MUSIC Soundtrack (RCA)
5	4	A MAN AND HIS MUSIC Frank Sinatra (Reprise)
4	5	MARY POPPINS Soundtrack (HMV)
6	6	TAKE IT EASY WITH THE WALKER BROTHERS Walker Brothers (Philips)
-	7	OTIS BLUE Otis Redding (Atlantic)
-	8	MY NAME IS BARBRA, TWO Barbra Streisand (CBS)
-	9	OUT OF OUR HEADS Rolling Stones (Decca)
-	10	HAREM HOLIDAY Elvis Presley (RCA)

12 February 1966

1	1	RUBBER SOUL Beatles (Parlophone)
3	2	THE SOUND OF MUSIC Soundtrack (RCA)
2	3	SECOND ALBUM Spencer Davis Group (Fontana)
4	4	A MAN AND HIS MUSIC Frank Sinatra (Reprise)
6	5	TAKE IT EASY WITH THE WALKER BROTHERS Walker Brothers (Philips)
5	6	MARY POPPINS Soundtrack (HMV)
8	7	MY NAME IS BARBRA, TWO Barbra Streisand (CBS)
7	8	OTIS BLUE Otis Redding (Atlantic)
9	8	OUT OF OUR HEADS Rolling Stones (Decca)
-	10	HELP! Beatles (Parlophone)

19 February 1966

1	1	RUBBER SOUL Beatles (Parlophone)
2	2	THE SOUND OF MUSIC Soundtrack (RCA)
3	3	SECOND ALBUM Spencer Davis Group (Fontana)
4	4	A MAN AND HIS MUSIC Frank Sinatra (Reprise)
5	5	TAKE IT EASY WITH THE WALKER BROTHERS Walker Brothers (Philips)
6	5	MARY POPPINS Soundtrack (HMV)
-	7	BEACH BOYS' PARTY! Beach Boys (Capitol)
8	8	OTIS BLUE Otis Redding (Atlantic)
10	9	HELP! Beatles (Parlophone)
7	10	MY NAME IS BARBRA, TWO Barbra Streisand (CBS)

Crispian St. Peters, with three 1966 hit 45s (*You Were On My Mind, Pied Piper and Changes*), claimed in the music press: "My songs are better than the Beatles' songs. You just wait. People will be singing my songs when they've forgotten who the Beatles were." He never reached the LP chart. In contrast, *The Sound Of Music*, in there since the chart began, would still be selling enough to stay in the Top 10 as the 1970s dawned, and still in the chart when the Beatles broke up.

February – April 1966

26 February 1966

- 1 1 RUBBER SOUL — Beatles (Parlophone)
- 2 2 THE SOUND OF MUSIC — Soundtrack (RCA)
- 3 3 SECOND ALBUM — Spencer Davis Group (Fontana)
- 7 4 BEACH BOYS' PARTY! — Beach Boys (Capitol)
- 8 4 OTIS BLUE — Otis Redding (Atlantic)
- 5 6 MARY POPPINS — Soundtrack (HMV)
- - 6 GOING PLACES — Herb Alpert & the Tijuana Brass (Pye International)
- - 8 BYE BYE BLUES — Bert Kaempfert (Polydor)
- - 9 OUT OF OUR HEADS — Rolling Stones (Decca)
- 4 10 A MAN AND HIS MUSIC — Frank Sinatra (Reprise)
- - 10 IN TOWN — P.J. Proby (Liberty)

5 March 1966

- 2 1 THE SOUND OF MUSIC — Soundtrack (RCA)
- 1 2 RUBBER SOUL — Beatles (Parlophone)
- 8 3 BYE BYE BLUES — Bert Kaempfert (Polydor)
- 4 4 BEACH BOYS' PARTY! — Beach Boys (Capitol)
- 6 5 MARY POPPINS — Soundtrack (HMV)
- 3 6 SECOND ALBUM — Spencer Davis Group (Fontana)
- 4 7 OTIS BLUE — Otis Redding (Atlantic)
- 10 8 IN TOWN — P.J. Proby (Liberty)
- 6 9 GOING PLACES — Herb Alpert & the Tijuana Brass (Pye International)
- - 10 TAKE IT EASY WITH THE WALKER BROTHERS — Walker Brothers (Philips)

12 March 1966

- 1 1 THE SOUND OF MUSIC — Soundtrack (RCA)
- 2 2 RUBBER SOUL — Beatles (Parlophone)
- 4 3 BEACH BOYS' PARTY! — Beach Boys (Capitol)
- 10 4 TAKE IT EASY WITH THE WALKER BROTHERS — Walker Brothers (Philips)
- 6 5 SECOND ALBUM — Spencer Davis Group (Fontana)
- 5 6 MARY POPPINS — Soundtrack (HMV)
- 7 7 OTIS BLUE — Otis Redding (Atlantic)
- 9 7 GOING PLACES — Herb Alpert & the Tijuana Brass (Pye International)
- - 9 A-TOM-IC JONES — Tom Jones (Decca)
- - 10 A STRING OF TONY'S HITS — Tony Bennett (CBS)
- 3 10 BYE BYE BLUES — Bert Kaempfert (Polydor)
- 8 10 IN TOWN — P.J. Proby (Liberty)

19 March 1966

- 1 1 THE SOUND OF MUSIC — Soundtrack (RCA)
- 2 2 RUBBER SOUL — Beatles (Parlophone)
- 3 3 BEACH BOYS' PARTY! — Beach Boys (Capitol)
- 10 4 BYE BYE BLUES — Bert Kaempfert (Polydor)
- 4 5 TAKE IT EASY WITH THE WALKER BROTHERS — Walker Brothers (Philips)
- 6 5 MARY POPPINS — Soundtrack (HMV)
- - 7 A MAN AND HIS MUSIC — Frank Sinatra (Reprise)
- 7 8 OTIS BLUE — Otis Redding (Atlantic)
- - 9 MAY EACH DAY — Andy Williams (CBS)
- 5 10 SECOND ALBUM — Spencer Davis Group (Fontana)
- 7 10 GOING PLACES — Herb Alpert & the Tijuana Brass (Pye International)

26 March 1966

- 1 1 THE SOUND OF MUSIC — Soundtrack (RCA)
- 2 2 RUBBER SOUL — Beatles (Parlophone)
- 3 3 BEACH BOYS' PARTY! — Beach Boys (Capitol)
- 5 4 TAKE IT EASY WITH THE WALKER BROTHERS — Walker Brothers (Philips)
- 4 5 BYE BYE BLUES — Bert Kaempfert (Polydor)
- 10 5 GOING PLACES — Herb Alpert & the Tijuana Brass (Pye International)
- 10 7 SECOND ALBUM — Spencer Davis Group (Fontana)
- 5 8 MARY POPPINS — Soundtrack (HMV)
- 8 9 OTIS BLUE — Otis Redding (Atlantic)
- 9 10 MAY EACH DAY — Andy Williams (CBS)

2 April 1966

- 1 1 THE SOUND OF MUSIC — Soundtrack (RCA)
- 2 2 RUBBER SOUL — Beatles (Parlophone)
- 4 3 TAKE IT EASY WITH THE WALKER BROTHERS — Walker Brothers (Philips)
- 5 4 GOING PLACES — Herb Alpert & the Tijuana Brass (Pye International)
- 8 5 MARY POPPINS — Soundtrack (HMV)
- 5 6 BYE BYE BLUES — Bert Kaempfert (Polydor)
- 3 7 BEACH BOYS' PARTY! — Beach Boys (Capitol)
- 10 8 MAY EACH DAY — Andy Williams (CBS)
- 9 9 OTIS BLUE — Otis Redding (Atlantic)
- - 10 MY NAME IS BARBRA, TWO — Barbra Streisand (CBS)

9 April 1966

- 1 1 THE SOUND OF MUSIC — Soundtrack (RCA)
- 2 2 RUBBER SOUL — Beatles (Parlophone)
- 3 3 TAKE IT EASY WITH THE WALKER BROTHERS — Walker Brothers (Philips)
- 4 4 GOING PLACES — Herb Alpert & the Tijuana Brass (Pye International)
- 5 5 MARY POPPINS — Soundtrack (HMV)
- 6 6 BYE BYE BLUES — Bert Kaempfert (Polydor)
- - 7 SECOND ALBUM — Spencer Davis Group (Fontana)
- 9 8 OTIS BLUE — Otis Redding (Atlantic)
- 10 8 MY NAME IS BARBRA, TWO — Barbra Streisand (CBS)
- - 10 SOLID GOLD SOUL — Various Artists (Atlantic)

16 April 1966

- 1 1 THE SOUND OF MUSIC — Soundtrack (RCA)
- 2 2 RUBBER SOUL — Beatles (Parlophone)
- 3 3 TAKE IT EASY WITH THE WALKER BROTHERS — Walker Brothers (Philips)
- 7 4 SECOND ALBUM — Spencer Davis Group (Fontana)
- 4 5 GOING PLACES — Herb Alpert & the Tijuana Brass (Pye International)
- 5 6 MARY POPPINS — Soundtrack (HMV)
- 6 7 BYE BYE BLUES — Bert Kaempfert (Polydor)
- 8 8 MY NAME IS BARBRA, TWO — Barbra Streisand (CBS)
- 8 9 OTIS BLUE — Otis Redding (Atlantic)
- 10 10 SOLID GOLD SOUL — Various Artists (Atlantic)

P.J.Proby was another whose chart profile shortchanges his talent. Blessed with an immense vocal range, his Top 10 hits on Decca in 1964, *Hold Me* and *Together*, upbeat white R&B using a high, near-demented voice flailing in the mix, were instantly followed by ballads on Liberty with a deep, rich, voice, starting with an inspired *Somewhere*, from *West Side Story*, and, later, the same show's *Maria*, on which a post-climactic falsetto swooped down to operatic full-throated declamation. Great.

April – June 1966

23 April 1966

last week	this week	Title / Artist
1	1	THE SOUND OF MUSIC — Soundtrack (RCA)
-	2	AFTERMATH — Rolling Stones (Decca)
2	3	RUBBER SOUL — Beatles (Parlophone)
3	4	TAKE IT EASY WITH THE WALKER BROTHERS — Walker Brothers (Philips)
6	5	MARY POPPINS — Soundtrack (HMV)
7	6	BYE BYE BLUES — Bert Kaempfert (Polydor)
4	7	SECOND ALBUM — Spencer Davis Group (Fontana)
5	8	GOING PLACES — Herb Alpert & the Tijuana Brass (Pye International)
10	9	SOLID GOLD SOUL — Various Artists (Atlantic)
-	10	BEACH BOYS' PARTY! — Beach Boys (Capitol)
-	10	MANTOVANI MAGIC — Mantovani (Decca)

30 April 1966

last week	this week	Title / Artist
2	1	AFTERMATH — Rolling Stones (Decca)
1	2	THE SOUND OF MUSIC — Soundtrack (RCA)
3	3	RUBBER SOUL — Beatles (Parlophone)
4	4	TAKE IT EASY WITH THE WALKER BROTHERS — Walker Brothers (Philips)
10	5	MANTOVANI MAGIC — Mantovani (Decca)
5	6	MARY POPPINS — Soundtrack (HMV)
8	7	GOING PLACES — Herb Alpert & the Tijuana Brass (Pye International)
-	8	FRANKIE AND JOHNNY — Elvis Presley (RCA)
6	9	BYE BYE BLUES — Bert Kaempfert (Polydor)
9	10	SOLID GOLD SOUL — Various Artists (Atlantic)

7 May 1966

last week	this week	Title / Artist
1	1	AFTERMATH — Rolling Stones (Decca)
2	2	THE SOUND OF MUSIC — Soundtrack (RCA)
3	3	RUBBER SOUL — Beatles (Parlophone)
4	4	TAKE IT EASY WITH THE WALKER BROTHERS — Walker Brothers (Philips)
5	5	MANTOVANI MAGIC — Mantovani (Decca)
8	6	FRANKIE AND JOHNNY — Elvis Presley (RCA)
-	7	THE MOST OF THE ANIMALS — Animals (Columbia)
7	8	GOING PLACES — Herb Alpert & the Tijuana Brass (Pye International)
-	9	SECOND ALBUM — Spencer Davis Group (Fontana)
10	10	SOLID GOLD SOUL — Various Artists (Atlantic)

14 May 1966

last week	this week	Title / Artist
1	1	AFTERMATH — Rolling Stones (Decca)
2	2	SOUND OF MUSIC — Soundtrack (RCA)
3	3	RUBBER SOUL — Beatles (Parlophone)
5	4	MANTOVANI MAGIC — Mantovani (Decca)
7	5	THE MOST OF THE ANIMALS — Animals (Columbia)
4	6	TAKE IT EASY WITH THE WALKER BROTHERS — Walker Brothers (Philips)
6	7	FRANKIE AND JOHNNY — Elvis Presley (RCA)
-	8	CILLA SINGS A RAINBOW — Cilla Black (Parlophone)
8	9	GOING PLACES — Herb Alpert & the Tijuana Brass (Pye International)
-	10	SHADOW MUSIC — Shadows (Columbia)

21 May 1966

last week	this week	Title / Artist
1	1	AFTERMATH — Rolling Stones (Decca)
2	2	THE SOUND OF MUSIC — Soundtrack (RCA)
-	3	SMALL FACES — Small Faces (Decca)
3	4	RUBBER SOUL — Beatles (Parlophone)
8	5	CILLA SINGS A RAINBOW — Cilla Black (Parlophone)
-	5	SWEET THINGS — Georgie Fame (Columbia)
5	7	THE MOST OF THE ANIMALS — Animals (Columbia)
10	8	SHADOW MUSIC — Shadows (Columbia)
4	9	MANTOVANI MAGIC — Mantovani (Decca)
-	10	DAYDREAM — Lovin' Spoonful (Pye)
6	10	TAKE IT EASY WITH THE WALKER BROTHERS — Walker Brothers (Philips)

28 May 1966

last week	this week	Title / Artist
1	1	AFTERMATH — Rolling Stones (Decca)
2	2	THE SOUND OF MUSIC — Soundtrack (RCA)
3	3	SMALL FACES — Small Faces (Decca)
4	4	RUBBER SOUL — Beatles (Parlophone)
7	5	THE MOST OF THE ANIMALS — Animals (Columbia)
8	6	SHADOW MUSIC — Shadows (Columbia)
5	7	SWEET THINGS — Georgie Fame (Columbia)
10	8	TAKE IT EASY WITH THE WALKER BROTHERS — Walker Brothers (Philips)
-	9	ANIMALISMS — Animals (Columbia)
9	10	MANTOVANI MAGIC — Mantovani (Decca)
-	10	THE SONNY SIDE OF CHER — Cher (Liberty)

4 June 1966

last week	this week	Title / Artist
1	1	AFTERMATH — Rolling Stones (Decca)
2	2	THE SOUND OF MUSIC — Soundtrack (RCA)
3	3	SMALL FACES — Small Faces (Decca)
7	4	SWEET THINGS — Georgie Fame (Columbia)
9	5	ANIMALISMS — Animals (Columbia)
4	6	RUBBER SOUL — Beatles (Parlophone)
-	7	CILLA SINGS A RAINBOW — Cilla Black (Parlophone)
5	8	THE MOST OF THE ANIMALS — Animals (Columbia)
8	9	TAKE IT EASY WITH THE WALKER BROTHERS — Walker Brothers (Philips)
10	10	MANTOVANI MAGIC — Mantovani (Decca)

11 June 1966

last week	this week	Title / Artist
1	1	AFTERMATH — Rolling Stones (Decca)
2	2	THE SOUND OF MUSIC — Soundtrack (RCA)
3	3	SMALL FACES — Small Faces (Decca)
5	4	ANIMALISMS — Animals (Columbia)
4	5	SWEET THINGS — Georgie Fame (Columbia)
7	6	CILLA SINGS A RAINBOW — Cilla Black (Parlophone)
6	7	RUBBER SOUL — Beatles (Parlophone)
8	8	THE MOST OF THE ANIMALS — Animals (Columbia)
-	8	SHADOW MUSIC — Shadows (Columbia)
9	10	TAKE IT EASY WITH THE WALKER BROTHERS — Walker Brothers (Philips)

Without ruffling the LP chart, Dusty Springfield, Manfred Mann and Frank Sinatra all scored No.1 singles in this period. *You Don't Have To Say You Love Me* was Dusty's first, *Pretty Flamingo* Manfred Mann's second. Meanwhile Bob Dylan toured Britain again, now backed by rocker Ronnie Hawkins' ex-musos The Hawks (later The Band). Led by guitarist Robbie Robertson, they and Bob got booed nightly. The famous audience cry of "Judas!", long attributed to London, actually happened in Manchester.

June – August 1966

18 June 1966

last	this	
1	1	AFTERMATH — Rolling Stones (Decca)
2	2	THE SOUND OF MUSIC — Soundtrack (RCA)
3	3	SMALL FACES — Small Faces (Decca)
4	4	ANIMALISMS — Animals (Columbia)
7	5	RUBBER SOUL — Beatles (Parlophone)
5	6	SWEET THINGS — Georgie Fame (Columbia)
6	7	CILLA SINGS A RAINBOW — Cilla Black (Parlophone)
8	8	SHADOW MUSIC — Shadows (Columbia)
10	9	TAKE IT EASY WITH THE WALKER BROTHERS — Walker Brothers (Philips)
8	10	THE MOST OF THE ANIMALS — Animals (Columbia)

25 June 1966

last	this	
1	1	AFTERMATH — Rolling Stones (Decca)
2	2	THE SOUND OF MUSIC — Soundtrack (RCA)
3	3	SMALL FACES — Small Faces (Decca)
6	4	SWEET THINGS — Georgie Fame (Columbia)
7	5	CILLA SINGS A RAINBOW — Cilla Black (Parlophone)
4	6	ANIMALISMS — Animals (Columbia)
-	7	THE MAMAS & THE PAPAS — Mamas & Papas (RCA)
5	8	RUBBER SOUL — Beatles (Parlophone)
10	9	THE MOST OF THE ANIMALS — Animals (Columbia)
8	10	SHADOW MUSIC — Shadows (Columbia)

2 July 1966

last	this	
2	1	THE SOUND OF MUSIC — Soundtrack (RCA)
1	2	AFTERMATH — Rolling Stones (Decca)
3	3	SMALL FACES — Small Faces (Decca)
7	4	THE MAMAS & THE PAPAS — Mamas & Papas (RCA)
4	5	SWEET THINGS — Georgie Fame (Columbia)
5	6	CILLA SINGS A RAINBOW — Cilla Black (Parlophone)
-	7	TAKE IT EASY WITH THE WALKER BROTHERS — Walker Brothers (Philips)
6	8	ANIMALISMS — Animals (Columbia)
-	9	STRANGERS IN THE NIGHT — Frank Sinatra (Reprise)
9	10	THE MOST OF THE ANIMALS — Animals (Columbia)

9 July 1966

last	this	
1	1	THE SOUND OF MUSIC — Soundtrack (RCA)
2	2	AFTERMATH — Rolling Stones (Decca)
4	3	THE MAMAS & THE PAPAS — Mamas & Papas (RCA)
9	4	STRANGERS IN THE NIGHT — Frank Sinatra (Reprise)
5	5	SWEET THINGS — Georgie Fame (Columbia)
-	6	PET SOUNDS — Beach Boys (Capitol)
3	7	SMALL FACES — Small Faces (Decca)
6	8	CILLA SINGS A RAINBOW — Cilla Black (Parlophone)
7	9	TAKE IT EASY WITH THE WALKER BROTHERS — Walker Brothers (Philips)
-	9	DAVE DEE, DOZY, BEAKY, MICK & TICH — Dave Dee, Dozy, Beaky, Mick & Tich (Fontana)

16 July 1966

last	this	
1	1	THE SOUND OF MUSIC — Soundtrack (RCA)
2	2	AFTERMATH — Rolling Stones (Decca)
6	3	PET SOUNDS — Beach Boys (Capitol)
5	4	SWEET THINGS — Georgie Fame (Columbia)
4	5	STRANGERS IN THE NIGHT — Frank Sinatra (Reprise)
3	6	THE MAMAS & THE PAPAS — Mamas & Papas (RCA)
9	7	DAVE DEE, DOZY, BEAKY, MICK & TICH — Dave Dee, Dozy, Beaky, Mick & Tich (Fontana)
-	8	SUMMER DAYS (AND SUMMER NIGHTS!!) — Beach Boys (Capitol)
7	9	SMALL FACES — Small Faces (Decca)
-	9	WOULD YOU BELIEVE — Hollies (Parlophone)

23 July 1966

last	this	
1	1	THE SOUND OF MUSIC — Soundtrack (RCA)
2	2	AFTERMATH — Rolling Stones (Decca)
3	3	PET SOUNDS — Beach Boys (Capitol)
6	4	THE MAMAS & THE PAPAS — Mamas & Papas (RCA)
8	5	SUMMER DAYS (AND SUMMER NIGHTS!!) — Beach Boys (Capitol)
5	6	STRANGERS IN THE NIGHT — Frank Sinatra (Reprise)
4	7	SWEET THINGS — Georgie Fame (Columbia)
9	8	WOULD YOU BELIEVE — Hollies (Parlophone)
9	9	SMALL FACES — Small Faces (Decca)
7	10	DAVE DEE, DOZY, BEAKY, MICK & TICH — Dave Dee, Dozy, Beaky, Mick & Tich (Fontana)
-	10	YARDBIRDS — Yardbirds (Columbia)

30 July 1966

last	this	
1	1	THE SOUND OF MUSIC — Soundtrack (RCA)
3	2	PET SOUNDS — Beach Boys (Capitol)
2	3	AFTERMATH — Rolling Stones (Decca)
5	4	SUMMER DAYS (AND SUMMER NIGHTS!!) — Beach Boys (Capitol)
6	5	STRANGERS IN THE NIGHT — Frank Sinatra (Reprise)
7	5	SWEET THINGS — Georgie Fame (Columbia)
10	7	YARDBIRDS — Yardbirds (Columbia)
4	8	THE MAMAS & THE PAPAS — Mamas & Papas (RCA)
-	9	BLUES BREAKERS — John Mayall with Eric Clapton (Decca)
8	10	WOULD YOU BELIEVE — Hollies (Parlophone)

6 August 1966

last	this	
1	1	THE SOUND OF MUSIC — Soundtrack (RCA)
2	2	PET SOUNDS — Beach Boys (Capitol)
3	3	AFTERMATH — Rolling Stones (Decca)
4	4	SUMMER DAYS (AND SUMMER NIGHTS!!) — Beach Boys (Capitol)
5	5	STRANGERS IN THE NIGHT — Frank Sinatra (Reprise)
5	6	SWEET THINGS — Georgie Fame (Columbia)
-	7	PARADISE HAWAIIAN STYLE — Elvis Presley (RCA)
8	8	THE MAMAS & THE PAPAS — Mamas & Papas (RCA)
7	9	YARDBIRDS — Yardbirds (Columbia)
10	9	WOULD YOU BELIEVE — Hollies (Parlophone)

While the Stones suffered the ignominy of being knocked off the top slot by *The Sound Of Music* instead of by the Beatles, the Beach Boys turned from muscle-bound WASPs (recent charting album *Beach Boys' Party!*) into serious artists of radical musical complexity with their new LP entry, the limpid *Pet Sounds*, and its single, *Good Vibrations*, which alone had taken the same gestation period as a human baby. It was the peak of writer/producer Brian Wilson's career, and hung the term "genius" around his neck.

August – October 1966

last this week

13 August 1966
- - 1 REVOLVER — Beatles (Parlophone)
- 1 2 THE SOUND OF MUSIC — Soundtrack (RCA)
- 2 3 PET SOUNDS — Beach Boys (Capitol)
- 3 4 AFTERMATH — Rolling Stones (Decca)
- 4 5 SUMMER DAYS (AND SUMMER NIGHTS!!) — Beach Boys (Capitol)
- - 6 BLUES BREAKERS — John Mayall with Eric Clapton (Decca)
- 6 7 FROM NOWHERE ... THE TROGGS — Troggs (Fontana)
- 7 8 PARADISE HAWAIIAN STYLE — Elvis Presley (RCA)
- - 9 STRANGERS IN THE NIGHT — Bert Kaempfert (Polydor)
- - 10 I COULDN'T LIVE WITHOUT YOUR LOVE — Petula Clark (Pye)

20 August 1966
- 1 1 REVOLVER — Beatles (Parlophone)
- 2 2 THE SOUND OF MUSIC — Soundtrack (RCA)
- 3 3 PET SOUNDS — Beach Boys (Capitol)
- 4 4 AFTERMATH — Rolling Stones (Decca)
- - 5 BLONDE ON BLONDE — Bob Dylan (CBS)
- 5 6 SUMMER DAYS (AND SUMMER NIGHTS!!) — Beach Boys (Capitol)
- 6 7 BLUES BREAKERS — John Mayall with Eric Clapton (Decca)
- 6 8 FROM NOWHERE ... THE TROGGS — Troggs (Fontana)
- 8 9 PARADISE HAWAIIAN STYLE — Elvis Presley (RCA)
- 9 10 STRANGERS IN THE NIGHT — Bert Kaempfert (Polydor)

27 August 1966
- 1 1 REVOLVER — Beatles (Parlophone)
- 2 2 THE SOUND OF MUSIC — Soundtrack (RCA)
- 3 3 PET SOUNDS — Beach Boys (Capitol)
- 5 4 BLONDE ON BLONDE — Bob Dylan (CBS)
- 8 5 FROM NOWHERE ... THE TROGGS — Troggs (Fontana)
- 6 6 SUMMER DAYS (AND SUMMER NIGHTS!!) — Beach Boys (Capitol)
- 4 7 AFTERMATH — Rolling Stones (Decca)
- 7 8 BLUES BREAKERS — John Mayall with Eric Clapton (Decca)
- 9 9 PARADISE HAWAIIAN STYLE — Elvis Presley (RCA)
- - 10 SMALL FACES — Small Faces (Decca)

3 September 1966
- 1 1 REVOLVER — Beatles (Parlophone)
- 2 2 THE SOUND OF MUSIC — Soundtrack (RCA)
- 3 3 PET SOUNDS — Beach Boys (Capitol)
- 4 4 BLONDE ON BLONDE — Bob Dylan (CBS)
- 6 5 SUMMER DAYS (AND SUMMER NIGHTS!!) — Beach Boys (Capitol)
- 8 5 BLUES BREAKERS — John Mayall with Eric Clapton (Decca)
- - 7 GOING PLACES — Herb Alpert & the Tijuana Brass (Pye International)
- 5 8 FROM NOWHERE ... THE TROGGS — Troggs (Fontana)
- 7 8 AFTERMATH — Rolling Stones (Decca)
- 10 10 SMALL FACES — Small Faces (Decca)

10 September 1966
- 1 1 REVOLVER — Beatles (Parlophone)
- 2 2 THE SOUND OF MUSIC — Soundtrack (RCA)
- 3 3 PET SOUNDS — Beach Boys (Capitol)
- - 4 PORTRAIT — Walker Brothers (Philips)
- 4 5 BLONDE ON BLONDE — Bob Dylan (CBS)
- 5 6 BLUES BREAKERS — John Mayall with Eric Clapton (Decca)
- 5 7 SUMMER DAYS (AND SUMMER NIGHTS!!) — Beach Boys (Capitol)
- 10 8 SMALL FACES — Small Faces (Decca)
- 8 9 FROM NOWHERE ... THE TROGGS — Troggs (Fontana)
- 8 10 AFTERMATH — Rolling Stones (Decca)

17 September 1966
- 1 1 REVOLVER — Beatles (Parlophone)
- 2 2 THE SOUND OF MUSIC — Soundtrack (RCA)
- 4 3 PORTRAIT — Walker Brothers (Philips)
- 3 4 PET SOUNDS — Beach Boys (Capitol)
- - 5 WELL RESPECTED KINKS — Kinks (Marble Arch)
- 5 6 BLONDE ON BLONDE — Bob Dylan (CBS)
- 6 7 BLUES BREAKERS — John Mayall with Eric Clapton (Decca)
- - 8 AUTUMN '66 — Spencer Davis Group (Fontana)
- - 9 STARS CHARITY FANTASIA — Various Artists (Philips)
- 9 10 FROM NOWHERE ... THE TROGGS — Troggs (Fontana)

24 September 1966
- 1 1 REVOLVER — Beatles (Parlophone)
- 2 2 THE SOUND OF MUSIC — Soundtrack (RCA)
- 3 3 PORTRAIT — Walker Brothers (Philips)
- 4 4 PET SOUNDS — Beach Boys (Capitol)
- 8 5 AUTUMN '66 — Spencer Davis Group (Fontana)
- 6 6 BLONDE ON BLONDE — Bob Dylan (CBS)
- 7 7 BLUES BREAKERS — John Mayall with Eric Clapton (Decca)
- 5 8 WELL RESPECTED KINKS — Kinks (Marble Arch)
- - 9 THE CLASSIC ROY ORBISON — Roy Orbison (London)
- 9 10 STARS CHARITY FANTASIA — Various Artists (Philips)

1 October 1966
- 2 1 THE SOUND OF MUSIC — Soundtrack (RCA)
- 1 2 REVOLVER — Beatles (Parlophone)
- 3 3 PORTRAIT — Walker Brothers (Philips)
- 4 4 PET SOUNDS — Beach Boys (Capitol)
- 8 5 WELL RESPECTED KINKS — Kinks (Marble Arch)
- 6 6 BLONDE ON BLONDE — Bob Dylan (CBS)
- 5 7 AUTUMN '66 — Spencer Davis Group (Fontana)
- 10 8 STARS CHARITY FANTASIA — Various Artists (Philips)
- - 9 GOING PLACES — Herb Alpert & the Tijuana Brass (Pye International)
- 7 10 BLUES BREAKERS — John Mayall with Eric Clapton (Decca)

In the Beach Boys' *Pet Sounds* and the newly-arrived *Blonde On Blonde*, a double-album, the LP chart had two classics. They heralded the age of Progressive Rock. From now until about 1973, when the real 1970s began, this movement would prove a force for good, producing some of the most creative, richly diverse, musically fresh and longest-lasting work in popular music history. Only later would its decay into self-indulgent elitism and murky torpor make the very term Progressive Rock one of abuse.

October – November 1966

8 October 1966

1	1	THE SOUND OF MUSIC Soundtrack (RCA)
2	2	REVOLVER Beatles (Parlophone)
-3	3	PORTRAIT Walker Brothers (Philips)
4	4	PET SOUNDS Beach Boys (Capitol)
7	5	AUTUMN '66 Spencer Davis Group (Fontana)
5	6	WELL RESPECTED KINKS Kinks (Marble Arch)
8	7	STARS CHARITY FANTASIA Various Artists (Philips)
9	8	GOING PLACES Herb Alpert & the Tijuana Brass (Pye International)
6	9	BLONDE ON BLONDE Bob Dylan (CBS)
-	9	SINATRA AT THE SANDS Frank Sinatra (Reprise)

15 October 1966

1	1	THE SOUND OF MUSIC Soundtrack (RCA)
2	2	REVOLVER Beatles (Parlophone)
3	3	PORTRAIT Walker Brothers (Philips)
4	4	PET SOUNDS Beach Boys (Capitol)
9	5	BLONDE ON BLONDE Bob Dylan (CBS)
6	6	WELL RESPECTED KINKS Kinks (Marble Arch)
5	7	AUTUMN '66 Spencer Davis Group (Fontana)
8	8	GOING PLACES Herb Alpert & the Tijuana Brass (Pye International)
9	9	SINATRA AT THE SANDS Frank Sinatra (Reprise)
-	10	BLUES BREAKERS John Mayall with Eric Clapton (Decca)

22 October 1966

1	1	THE SOUND OF MUSIC Soundtrack (RCA)
2	2	REVOLVER Beatles (Parlophone)
3	3	PORTRAIT Walker Brothers (Philips)
6	4	WELL RESPECTED KINKS Kinks (Marble Arch)
4	5	PET SOUNDS Beach Boys (Capitol)
-	6	SOUND VENTURE Georgie Fame (Columbia)
5	7	BLONDE ON BLONDE Bob Dylan (CBS)
-	8	STARS CHARITY FANTASIA Various Artists (Philips)
9	9	GOING PLACES Herb Alpert & the Tijuana Brass (Pye International)
7	10	AUTUMN '66 Spencer Davis Group (Fontana)

29 October 1966

1	1	THE SOUND OF MUSIC Soundtrack (RCA)
2	2	REVOLVER Beatles (Parlophone)
-	3	GOLDEN HITS Dusty Springfield (Philips)
3	4	PORTRAIT Walker Brothers (Philips)
5	5	PET SOUNDS Beach Boys (Capitol)
4	6	WELL RESPECTED KINKS Kinks (Marble Arch)
6	7	SOUND VENTURE Georgie Fame (Columbia)
9	8	GOING PLACES Herb Alpert & the Tijuana Brass (Pye International)
10	9	AUTUMN '66 Spencer Davis Group (Fontana)
8	10	STARS CHARITY FANTASIA Various Artists (Philips)

5 November 1966

1	1	THE SOUND OF MUSIC Soundtrack (RCA)
2	2	REVOLVER Beatles (Parlophone)
3	3	GOLDEN HITS Dusty Springfield (Philips)
-	4	DISTANT DRUMS Jim Reeves (RCA)
5	5	PET SOUNDS Beach Boys (Capitol)
4	6	PORTRAIT Walker Brothers (Philips)
7	7	SOUND VENTURE Georgie Fame (Columbia)
8	8	GOING PLACES Herb Alpert & the Tijuana Brass (Pye International)
6	9	WELL RESPECTED KINKS Kinks (Marble Arch)
-	10	DRIVIN' YOU WILD Cliff Bennett (Music for Pleasure)

12 November 1966

1	1	THE SOUND OF MUSIC Soundtrack (RCA)
2	2	REVOLVER Beatles (Parlophone)
4	3	DISTANT DRUMS Jim Reeves (RCA)
3	4	GOLDEN HITS Dusty Springfield (Philips)
-	5	BEST OF THE BEACH BOYS Beach Boys (Capitol)
-	6	BIG HITS (HIGH TIDE AND GREEN GRASS) Rolling Stones (Decca)
5	7	PET SOUNDS Beach Boys (Capitol)
6	8	PORTRAIT Walker Brothers (Philips)
8	9	GOING PLACES Herb Alpert & the Tijuana Brass (Pye International)
9	9	WELL RESPECTED KINKS Kinks (Marble Arch)

19 November 1966

1	1	THE SOUND OF MUSIC Soundtrack (RCA)
5	2	BEST OF THE BEACH BOYS Beach Boys (Capitol)
3	3	DISTANT DRUMS Jim Reeves (RCA)
6	4	BIG HITS (HIGH TIDE AND GREEN GRASS) Rolling Stones (Decca)
2	5	REVOLVER Beatles (Parlophone)
4	6	GOLDEN HITS Dusty Springfield (Philips)
7	7	PET SOUNDS Beach Boys (Capitol)
-	8	COME THE DAY Seekers (Columbia)
9	9	GOING PLACES Herb Alpert & the Tijuana Brass (Pye International)
-	10	SOUND VENTURE Georgie Fame (Columbia)

26 November 1966

1	1	THE SOUND OF MUSIC Soundtrack (RCA)
2	2	BEST OF THE BEACH BOYS Beach Boys (Capitol)
3	3	DISTANT DRUMS Jim Reeves (RCA)
4	4	BIG HITS (HIGH TIDE AND GREEN GRASS) Rolling Stones (Decca)
6	5	GOLDEN HITS Dusty Springfield (Philips)
8	6	COME THE DAY Seekers (Columbia)
-	7	CALIFORNIA HOLIDAY Elvis Presley (RCA)
5	8	REVOLVER Beatles (Parlophone)
7	9	PET SOUNDS Beach Boys (Capitol)
-	10	FOUR TOPS ON TOP Four Tops (Tamla Motown)

Matching those *Well Respected Kinks*, which was on Pye's cheap-LP label Marble Arch (successor to Golden Guinea), Cliff Bennett & The Rebel Rousers' November chart-entry marked the debut of EMI's cheap label Music for Pleasure. While the group's name commemorated a venerable (1958) Duane Eddy hit, they played, extremely well for British copyists, Drifters-style mid-60s soul. Their third and final hit single, *Got To Get You Into My Life* (revisited in 1978 by Earth Wind & Fire), had peaked in September.

36

last week	this week	3 December 1966
1	1	THE SOUND OF MUSIC Soundtrack (RCA)
2	2	BEST OF THE BEACH BOYS Beach Boys (Capitol)
3	3	DISTANT DRUMS Jim Reeves (RCA)
6	4	COME THE DAY Seekers (Columbia)
4	5	BIG HITS (HIGH TIDE AND GREEN GRASS) Rolling Stones (Decca)
5	6	GOLDEN HITS Dusty Springfield (Philips)
8	7	REVOLVER Beatles (Parlophone)
10	7	FOUR TOPS ON TOP Four Tops (Tamla Motown)
9	9	PET SOUNDS Beach Boys (Capitol)
7	10	CALIFORNIA HOLIDAY Elvis Presley (RCA)

10 December 1966

1	1	THE SOUND OF MUSIC Soundtrack (RCA)
2	2	BEST OF THE BEACH BOYS Beach Boys (Capitol)
3	3	DISTANT DRUMS Jim Reeves (RCA)
4	4	COME THE DAY Seekers (Columbia)
5	5	BIG HITS (HIGH TIDE AND GREEN GRASS) Rolling Stones (Decca)
6	6	GOLDEN HITS Dusty Springfield (Philips)
-	7	GOING PLACES Herb Alpert & the Tijuana Brass (Pye International)
-	8	GENTLE SHADES OF VAL DOONICAN Val Doonican (Decca)
9	9	PET SOUNDS Beach Boys (Capitol)
-	10	HERE COME THE MINSTRELS George Mitchell Minstrels (HMV)

17 December 1966

1	1	THE SOUND OF MUSIC Soundtrack (RCA)
2	2	BEST OF THE BEACH BOYS Beach Boys (Capitol)
4	3	COME THE DAY Seekers (Columbia)
3	4	DISTANT DRUMS Jim Reeves (RCA)
8	5	GENTLE SHADES OF VAL DOONICAN Val Doonican (Decca)
6	6	GOLDEN HITS Dusty Springfield (Philips)
-	7	A COLLECTION OF BEATLES OLDIES (BUT GOLDIES) Beatles (Parlophone)
-	8	REVOLVER Beatles (Parlophone)
-	8	HAND CLAPPIN' - FOOT STOMPIN' - FUNKY BUTT - LIVE! Geno Washington (Pye)
-	10	COME TO MY PARTY Mrs. Mills (Parlophone)
7	11	GOING PLACES Herb Alpert & the Tijuana Brass (Pye International)
-	12	SUPREMES A-GO-GO Supremes (Tamla Motown)
-	13	THE BEST OF JIM REEVES Jim Reeves (RCA)
5	14	BIG HITS (HIGH TIDE AND GREEN GRASS) Rolling Stones (Decca)
-	14	12 SONGS OF CHRISTMAS Jim Reeves (RCA)

24 December 1966

1	1	THE SOUND OF MUSIC Soundtrack (RCA)
2	2	BEST OF THE BEACH BOYS Beach Boys (Capitol)
4	3	DISTANT DRUMS Jim Reeves (RCA)
3	4	COME THE DAY Seekers (Columbia)
5	5	GENTLE SHADES OF VAL DOONICAN Val Doonican (Decca)
8	6	HAND CLAPPIN' - FOOT STOMPIN' - FUNKY BUTT - LIVE! Geno Washington (Pye)
7	7	A COLLECTION OF BEATLES OLDIES (BUT GOLDIES) Beatles (Parlophone)
-	8	A QUICK ONE Who (Reaction)
14	9	12 SONGS OF CHRISTMAS Jim Reeves (RCA)
-	10	FRESH CREAM Cream (Reaction)
14	11	BIG HITS (HIGH TIDE AND GREEN GRASS) Rolling Stones (Decca)
-	12	STARS CHARITY FANTASIA Various Artists (Philips)
11	13	GOING PLACES Herb Alpert & the Tijuana Brass (Pye International)
-	14	HERE COME THE MINSTRELS George Mitchell Minstrels (HMV)
-	15	BACHELORS' GIRLS Bachelors (Decca)

31 December 1966

1	1	THE SOUND OF MUSIC Soundtrack (RCA)
2	2	BEST OF THE BEACH BOYS Beach Boys (Capitol)
5	3	GENTLE SHADES OF VAL DOONICAN Val Doonican (Decca)
3	4	DISTANT DRUMS Jim Reeves (RCA)
-	5	FINDERS KEEPERS Cliff Richard & the Shadows (Columbia)
4	6	COME THE DAY Seekers (Columbia)
7	6	A COLLECTION OF BEATLES OLDIES (BUT GOLDIES) Beatles (Parlophone)
6	8	HAND CLAPPIN' - FOOT STOMPIN' - FUNKY BUTT - LIVE! Geno Washington (Pye)
8	8	A QUICK ONE Who (Reaction)
11	10	BIG HITS (HIGH TIDE AND GREEN GRASS) Rolling Stones (Decca)
9	11	12 SONGS OF CHRISTMAS Jim Reeves (RCA)
10	12	FRESH CREAM Cream (Reaction)
12	13	STARS CHARITY FANTASIA Various Artists (Philips)
13	14	GOING PLACES Herb Alpert & the Tijuana Brass (Pye International)
14	15	HERE COME THE MINSTRELS George Mitchell Minstrels (HMV)

The NME now began to publish the Top 15 albums rather than the Top 10. While this acknowledged the growing importance of the album as a medium for artists and listeners, and thus of LP sales to the industry, no surprises or delights were immediately revealed by the records making it into the extra published places. If this is Christmas it has to be time for more of Mrs Mills, Jim Reeves, the Bachelors, Herb Alpert & the Tijuana Brass, and oh dear, here come the Black & White Minstrels.

Sgt Pepper was to be the album to have in 1967. By the end of the year Otis Redding was dead and Dylan had gone to the country.
Andy Williams kept on smiling.

January – February 1967

7 January 1967

last	this	Album — Artist (Label)
1	1	THE SOUND OF MUSIC Soundtrack (RCA)
2	2	BEST OF THE BEACH BOYS Beach Boys (Capitol)
6	3	COME THE DAY Seekers (Columbia)
3	4	GENTLE SHADES OF VAL DOONICAN Val Doonican (Decca)
8	5	A QUICK ONE Who (Reaction)
4	6	DISTANT DRUMS Jim Reeves (RCA)
8	7	HAND CLAPPIN'-FOOT STOMPIN'-FUNKY BUTT–LIVE Geno Washington (Piccadilly)
12	8	FRESH CREAM Cream (Reaction)
5	9	FINDERS KEEPERS Cliff Richard & the Shadows (Columbia)
6	10	A COLLECTION OF BEATLES OLDIES (BUT GOLDIES) Beatles (Parlophone)
10	11	BIG HITS (HIGH TIDE & GREEN GRASS) Rolling Stones (Decca)
15	12	HERE COME THE MINSTRELS George Mitchell Minstrels (HMV)
-	13	REVOLVER Beatles (Parlophone)
-	14	GOLDEN HITS Dusty Springfield (Philips)
-	15	THE BEST OF JIM REEVES Jim Reeves (RCA)

14 January 1967

last	this	Album — Artist (Label)
1	1	THE SOUND OF MUSIC Soundtrack (RCA)
2	2	BEST OF THE BEACH BOYS Beach Boys (Capitol)
3	3	COME THE DAY Seekers (Columbia)
5	4	A QUICK ONE Who (Reaction)
6	5	DISTANT DRUMS Jim Reeves (RCA)
4	6	GENTLE SHADES OF VAL DOONICAN Val Doonican (Decca)
8	7	FRESH CREAM Cream (Reaction)
14	8	GOLDEN HITS Dusty Springfield (Philips)
10	9	A COLLECTION OF BEATLES OLDIES (BUT GOLDIES) Beatles (Parlophone)
7	10	HAND CLAPPIN'-FOOT STOMPIN'-FUNKY BUTT–LIVE Geno Washington (Piccadilly)
-	11	GOING PLACES Herb Alpert & the Tijuana Brass (Pye International)
9	12	FINDERS KEEPERS Cliff Richard & the Shadows (Columbia)
-	13	PET SOUNDS Beach Boys (Capitol)
11	14	BIG HITS (HIGH TIDE & GREEN GRASS) Rolling Stones (Decca)
13	15	REVOLVER Beatles (Parlophone)

21 January 1967

last	this	Album — Artist (Label)
1	1	THE SOUND OF MUSIC Soundtrack (RCA)
2	2	BEST OF THE BEACH BOYS Beach Boys (Capitol)
3	3	COME THE DAY Seekers (Columbia)
4	4	A QUICK ONE Who (Reaction)
5	5	DISTANT DRUMS Jim Reeves (RCA)
12	6	FINDERS KEEPERS Cliff Richard & the Shadows (Columbia)
7	7	FRESH CREAM Cream (Reaction)
10	8	GOING PLACES Herb Alpert & the Tijuana Brass (Pye International)
6	9	GENTLE SHADES OF VAL DOONICAN Val Doonican (Decca)
9	10	A COLLECTION OF BEATLES OLDIES (BUT GOLDIES) Beatles (Parlophone)
10	11	HAND CLAPPIN'-FOOT STOMPIN'-FUNKY BUTT–LIVE Geno Washington (Piccadilly)
-	12	BOB DYLAN'S GREATEST HITS Bob Dylan (CBS)
8	13	GOLDEN HITS Dusty Springfield (Philips)
14	14	BIG HITS (HIGH TIDE & GREEN GRASS) Rolling Stones (Decca)
13	15	PET SOUNDS Beach Boys (Capitol)

28 January 1967

last	this	Album — Artist (Label)
1	1	THE SOUND OF MUSIC Soundtrack (RCA)
-	2	THE MONKEES Monkees (RCA)
2	3	BEST OF THE BEACH BOYS Beach Boys (Capitol)
-	4	BETWEEN THE BUTTONS Rolling Stones (Decca)
7	5	FRESH CREAM Cream (Reaction)
3	6	COME THE DAY Seekers (Columbia)
4	7	A QUICK ONE Who (Reaction)
6	8	FINDERS KEEPERS Cliff Richard & the Shadows (Columbia)
5	9	DISTANT DRUMS Jim Reeves (RCA)
11	10	HAND CLAPPIN'-FOOT STOMPIN'-FUNKY BUTT–LIVE Geno Washington (Piccadilly)
9	11	GENTLE SHADES OF VAL DOONICAN Val Doonican (Decca)
10	12	A COLLECTION OF BEATLES OLDIES (BUT GOLDIES) Beatles (Parlophone)
14	13	BIG HITS (HIGH TIDE & GREEN GRASS) Rolling Stones (Decca)
8	14	GOING PLACES Herb Alpert & the Tijuana Brass (Pye International)
-	15	REVOLVER Beatles (Parlophone)

4 February 1967

last	this	Album — Artist (Label)
2	1	THE MONKEES Monkees (RCA)
1	2	THE SOUND OF MUSIC Soundtrack (RCA)
4	3	BETWEEN THE BUTTONS Rolling Stones (Decca)
3	4	BEST OF THE BEACH BOYS Beach Boys (Capitol)
6	5	COME THE DAY Seekers (Columbia)
5	6	FRESH CREAM Cream (Reaction)
7	7	A QUICK ONE Who (Reaction)
8	8	FINDERS KEEPERS Cliff Richard & the Shadows (Columbia)
11	9	GENTLE SHADES OF VAL DOONICAN Val Doonican (Decca)
10	10	HAND CLAPPIN'-FOOT STOMPIN'-FUNKY BUTT–LIVE Geno Washington (Piccadilly)
8	11	DISTANT DRUMS Jim Reeves (RCA)
12	12	A COLLECTION OF BEATLES OLDIES (BUT GOLDIES) Beatles (Parlophone)
13	13	GOING PLACES Herb Alpert & the Tijuana Brass (Pye International)
-	14	FOUR TOPS ON TOP Four Tops (Tamla Motown)
-	15	FROM THE HEART Tom Jones (Decca)

11 February 1967

last	this	Album — Artist (Label)
1	1	THE MONKEES Monkees (RCA)
2	2	THE SOUND OF MUSIC Soundtrack (RCA)
3	3	BETWEEN THE BUTTONS Rolling Stones (Decca)
4	4	BEST OF THE BEACH BOYS Beach Boys (Capitol)
7	5	A QUICK ONE Who (Reaction)
5	6	COME THE DAY Seekers (Columbia)
11	7	DISTANT DRUMS Jim Reeves (RCA)
8	8	FINDERS KEEPERS Cliff Richard & the Shadows (Columbia)
6	9	FRESH CREAM Cream (Reaction)
10	10	HAND CLAPPIN'-FOOT STOMPIN' –FUNKY BUTT–LIVE Geno Washington (Piccadilly)
-	11	FOUR TOPS LIVE Four Tops (Tamla Motown)
13	12	GOING PLACES Herb Alpert & the Tijuana Brass (Pye International)
9	13	GENTLE SHADES OF VAL DOONICAN Val Doonican (Decca)
12	14	A COLLECTION OF BEATLES OLDIES (BUT GOLDIES) Beatles (Parlophone)
-	15	SRO Herb Alpert & the Tijuana Brass (Pye International)

18 February 1967

last	this	Album — Artist (Label)
1	1	THE MONKEES Monkees (RCA)
2	2	THE SOUND OF MUSIC Soundtrack (RCA)
3	3	BETWEEN THE BUTTONS Rolling Stones (Decca)
4	4	BEST OF THE BEACH BOYS Beach Boys (Capitol)
6	5	COME THE DAY Seekers (Columbia)
11	6	FOUR TOPS LIVE Four Tops (Tamla Motown)
7	7	DISTANT DRUMS Jim Reeves (RCA)
8	8	FINDERS KEEPERS Cliff Richard & the Shadows (Columbia)
12	9	GOING PLACES Herb Alpert & the Tijuana Brass (Pye International)
9	10	FRESH CREAM Cream (Reaction)
10	12	HAND CLAPPIN'-FOOT STOMPIN' –FUNKY BUTT–LIVE Geno Washington (Piccadilly)
15	13	SRO Herb Alpert & the Tijuana Brass (Pye International)
14	14	A COLLECTION OF BEATLES OLDIES (BUT GOLDIES) Beatles (Parlophone)
13	15	GENTLE SHADES OF VAL DOONICAN Val Doonican (Decca)

25 February 1967

last	this	Album — Artist (Label)
1	1	THE MONKEES Monkees (RCA)
2	2	THE SOUND OF MUSIC Soundtrack (RCA)
3	3	BETWEEN THE BUTTONS Rolling Stones (Decca)
4	4	BEST OF THE BEACH BOYS Beach Boys (Capitol)
5	5	COME THE DAY Seekers (Columbia)
6	6	FOUR TOPS LIVE Four Tops (Tamla Motown)
13	7	SRO Herb Alpert & the Tijuana Brass (Pye International)
12	8	HAND CLAPPIN'-FOOT STOMPIN'–FUNKY BUTT–LIVE Geno Washington (Piccadilly)
9	9	GOING PLACES Herb Alpert & the Tijuana Brass (Pye International)
-	10	TROGGLODYNAMITE Troggs (Page One)
7	11	DISTANT DRUMS Jim Reeves (RCA)
8	12	FINDERS KEEPERS Cliff Richard & the Shadows (Columbia)
-	13	BOB DYLAN'S GREATEST HITS Bob Dylan (CBS)
15	14	GENTLE SHADES OF VAL DOONICAN Val Doonican (Decca)
10	15	FRESH CREAM Cream (Reaction)

Geno Washington & the Ram Jam Band were surely thrilled to find themselves high in the chart, and for so long, with *Hand Clappin'-Footstompin'-Funky Butt Live*. As this ponderously wacky title hints, Geno was felt to be great live but unreproduceable on disc. On February 18, his album at No.12, he achieved his highest-ever singles placing: the forgettable *Michael (The Lover)* made No.30 for one week. Yet he was an institution for many years, seemingly second on the bill at every student ball ever held.

March – April 1967

4 March 1967

last	this	Title / Artist (Label)
1	1	THE MONKEES Monkees (RCA)
2	2	THE SOUND OF MUSIC Soundtrack (RCA)
3	3	BETWEEN THE BUTTONS Rolling Stones (Decca)
4	4	BEST OF THE BEACH BOYS Beach Boys (Capitol)
8	5	HAND CLAPPIN'-FOOT STOMPIN' -FUNKY BUTT-LIVE Geno Washington (Piccadilly)
5	6	COME THE DAY Seekers (Columbia)
6	7	FOUR TOPS LIVE Four Tops (Tamla Motown)
9	8	GOING PLACES Herb Alpert & the Tijuana Brass (Pye International)
7	9	SRO Herb Alpert & the Tijuana Brass (Pye International)
-	10	MANTOVANI'S GOLDEN HITS Mantovani (Decca)
10	11	TROGGLODYNAMITE Troggs (Page One)
13	12	BOB DYLAN'S GREATEST HITS Bob Dylan (CBS)
15	13	FRESH CREAM Cream (Reaction)
11	14	DISTANT DRUMS Jim Reeves (RCA)
12	15	FINDERS KEEPERS Cliff Richard & the Shadows (Columbia)

11 March 1967

last	this	Title / Artist (Label)
1	1	THE MONKEES Monkees (RCA)
2	2	THE SOUND OF MUSIC Soundtrack (RCA)
4	3	BEST OF THE BEACH BOYS Beach Boys (Capitol)
3	4	BETWEEN THE BUTTONS Rolling Stones (Decca)
6	5	COME THE DAY Seekers (Columbia)
5	6	HAND CLAPPIN'-FOOT STOMPIN' -FUNKY BUTT-LIVE Geno Washington (Piccadilly)
11	7	TROGGLODYNAMITE Troggs (Page One)
6	8	FOUR TOPS LIVE Four Tops (Tamla Motown)
8	9	GOING PLACES Herb Alpert & the Tijuana Brass (Pye International)
9	10	SRO Herb Alpert & the Tijuana Brass (Pye International)
14	11	DISTANT DRUMS Jim Reeves (RCA)
-	12	COLOUR MY WORLD Petula Clark (Pye)
10	13	MANTOVANI'S GOLDEN HITS Mantovani (Decca)
15	14	FINDERS KEEPERS Cliff Richard & the Shadows (Columbia)
12	15	BOB DYLAN'S GREATEST HITS Bob Dylan (CBS)

18 March 1967

last	this	Title / Artist (Label)
1	1	THE MONKEES Monkees (RCA)
2	2	THE SOUND OF MUSIC Soundtrack (RCA)
4	3	BETWEEN THE BUTTONS Rolling Stones (Decca)
3	4	BEST OF THE BEACH BOYS Beach Boys (Capitol)
8	5	FOUR TOPS LIVE Four Tops (Tamla Motown)
10	6	SRO Herb Alpert & the Tijuana Brass (Pye International)
9	7	GOING PLACES Herb Alpert & the Tijuana Brass (Pye International)
5	8	HAND CLAPPIN'-FOOT STOMPIN' -FUNKY BUTT-LIVE Geno Washington (Piccadilly)
7	9	TROGGLODYNAMITE Troggs (Page One)
5	10	COME THE DAY Seekers (Columbia)
11	11	DISTANT DRUMS Jim Reeves (RCA)
13	12	MANTOVANI'S GOLDEN HITS Mantovani (Decca)
-	13	THE TEMPTATIONS' GREATEST HITS Temptations (Tamla Motown)
-	14	HALL OF FAME Georgie Fame (Columbia)
-	15	A HARD ROAD John Mayall's Bluesbreakers (Decca)

25 March 1967

last	this	Title / Artist (Label)
2	1	THE SOUND OF MUSIC Soundtrack (RCA)
1	2	THE MONKEES Monkees (RCA)
3	3	BETWEEN THE BUTTONS Rolling Stones (Decca)
4	4	BEST OF THE BEACH BOYS Beach Boys (Capitol)
-	5	IMAGES Walker Brothers (Philips)
8	6	HAND CLAPPIN'-FOOT STOMPIN' -FUNKY BUTT-LIVE Geno Washington (Piccadilly)
5	7	FOUR TOPS LIVE Four Tops (Tamla Motown)
9	8	TROGGLODYNAMITE Troggs (Page One)
10	9	COME THE DAY Seekers (Columbia)
7	10	GOING PLACES Herb Alpert & the Tijuana Brass (Pye International)
6	11	SRO Herb Alpert & the Tijuana Brass (Pye International)
12	12	MANTOVANI'S GOLDEN HITS Mantovani (Decca)
14	13	HALL OF FAME Georgie Fame (Columbia)
15	14	A HARD ROAD John Mayall's Bluesbreakers (Decca)
11	15	DISTANT DRUMS Jim Reeves (RCA)

1 April 1967

last	this	Title / Artist (Label)
2	1	THE MONKEES Monkees (RCA)
1	2	THE SOUND OF MUSIC Soundtrack (RCA)
4	3	BEST OF THE BEACH BOYS Beach Boys (Capitol)
9	4	COME THE DAY Seekers (Columbia)
5	5	IMAGES Walker Brothers (Philips)
7	6	FOUR TOPS LIVE Four Tops (Tamla Motown)
3	7	BETWEEN THE BUTTONS Rolling Stones (Decca)
11	8	SRO Herb Alpert & the Tijuana Brass (Pye International)
13	9	HALL OF FAME Georgie Fame (Columbia)
10	10	GOING PLACES Herb Alpert & the Tijuana Brass (Pye International)
-	11	SURFER GIRL Beach Boys (Capitol)
14	12	A HARD ROAD John Mayall's Bluesbreakers (Decca)
6	13	HAND CLAPPIN'-FOOT STOMPIN'-FUNKY BUTT-LIVE Geno Washington (Piccadilly)
11	14	MANTOVANI'S GOLDEN HITS Mantovani (Decca)
8	15	TROGGLODYNAMITE Troggs (Page One)

8 April 1967

last	this	Title / Artist (Label)
2	1	THE SOUND OF MUSIC Soundtrack (RCA)
1	2	THE MONKEES Monkees (RCA)
3	3	BEST OF THE BEACH BOYS Beach Boys (Capitol)
5	4	IMAGES Walker Brothers (Philips)
4	5	COME THE DAY Seekers (Columbia)
-	6	GREEN GREEN GRASS OF HOME Tom Jones (Decca)
7	7	BETWEEN THE BUTTONS Rolling Stones (Decca)
8	8	FOUR TOPS LIVE Four Tops (Tamla Motown)
13	9	HAND CLAPPIN'-FOOTSTOMPIN' -FUNKY BUTT-LIVE Geno Washington (Piccadilly)
9	10	HALL OF FAME Georgie Fame (Columbia)
12	11	A HARD ROAD John Mayall's Bluesbreakers (Decca)
10	12	GOING PLACES Herb Alpert & the Tijuana Brass (Pye International)
11	13	SURFER GIRL Beach Boys (Capitol)
14	14	MANTOVANI'S GOLDEN HITS Mantovani (Decca)
-	15	TRINI LOPEZ IN LONDON Trini Lopez (Reprise)

15 April 1967

last	this	Title / Artist (Label)
1	1	THE SOUND OF MUSIC Soundtrack (RCA)
-	2	MORE OF THE MONKEES Monkees (RCA)
2	3	THE MONKEES Monkees (RCA)
3	4	BEST OF THE BEACH BOYS Beach Boys (Capitol)
6	5	GREEN GREEN GRASS OF HOME Tom Jones (Decca)
4	6	IMAGES Walker Brothers (Philips)
5	7	COME THE DAY Seekers (Columbia)
8	8	FOUR TOPS LIVE Four Tops (Tamla Motown)
10	9	HALL OF FAME Georgie Fame (Columbia)
15	10	TRINI LOPEZ IN LONDON Trini Lopez (Reprise)
9	11	HAND CLAPPIN'-FOOT STOMPIN'-FUNKY BUTT-LIVE Geno Washington (Piccadilly)
-	12	MATTHEW AND SON Cat Stevens (Deram)
12	13	GOING PLACES Herb Alpert & the Tijuana Brass (Pye International)
-	13	DR. ZHIVAGO Soundtrack (MGM)
-	15	FIDDLER ON THE ROOF London Cast (CBS)

22 April 1967

last	this	Title / Artist (Label)
2	1	MORE OF THE MONKEES Monkees (RCA)
1	2	THE SOUND OF MUSIC Soundtrack (RCA)
3	3	THE MONKEES Monkees (RCA)
5	4	GREEN GREEN GRASS OF HOME Tom Jones (Decca)
4	5	BEST OF THE BEACH BOYS Beach Boys (Capitol)
6	6	IMAGES Walker Brothers (Philips)
8	7	FOUR TOPS LIVE Four Tops (Tamla Motown)
7	8	COME THE DAY Seekers (Columbia)
15	9	FIDDLER ON THE ROOF London Cast (CBS)
13	10	DR. ZHIVAGO Soundtrack (MGM)
11	11	MATTHEW AND SON Cat Stevens (Deram)
10	12	TRINI LOPEZ IN LONDON Trini Lopez (Reprise)
9	13	HALL OF FAME Georgie Fame (Columbia)
-	14	THIS IS JAMES LAST James Last (Polydor)
11	15	HAND CLAPPIN'-FOOT STOMPIN'-FUNKY BUTT-LIVE Geno Washington (Piccadilly)

An extra-good couple of months for Easy Listening music. Why is it called this? Do you know anyone who finds it easy to listen to? Imagine, after two Herb Alpert albums and *Distant Drums*, rushing to listen easily to these new entries: *Mantovani's Golden Hits*, the soundtracks of *Dr Zhivago* and *Fiddler On The Roof* and, Last but not least, *This Is James L.* Not the sounds we generally think of as vintage Early 1967. *Fresh Cream* did manage to get in there too – now that was more like it.

April – June 1967

29 April 1967

last week	this week	
2	1	THE SOUND OF MUSIC — Soundtrack (RCA)
1	2	MORE OF THE MONKEES — Monkees (RCA)
3	3	THE MONKEES — Monkees (RCA)
4	4	GREEN GREEN GRASS OF HOME — Tom Jones (Decca)
5	5	BEST OF THE BEACH BOYS — Beach Boys (Capitol)
9	6	FIDDLER ON THE ROOF — London Cast (CBS)
6	7	IMAGES — Walker Brothers (Philips)
14	8	THIS IS JAMES LAST — James Last (Polydor)
7	9	FOUR TOPS LIVE — Four Tops (Tamla Motown)
11	10	MATTHEW AND SON — Cat Stevens (Deram)
8	11	COME THE DAY — Seekers (Columbia)
10	11	DR. ZHIVAGO Soundtrack (MGM)
12	13	TRINI LOPEZ IN LONDON — Trini Lopez (Reprise)
15	14	HAND CLAPPIN'–FOOT STOMPIN' –FUNKY BUTT–LIVE — Geno Washington (Piccadilly)
–	15	SECOMBE'S PERSONAL CHOICE — Harry Secombe (Philips)

6 May 1967

last week	this week	
1	1	THE SOUND OF MUSIC — Soundtrack (RCA)
2	2	MORE OF THE MONKEES — Monkees (RCA)
3	3	THE MONKEES — Monkees (RCA)
4	4	GREEN GREEN GRASS OF HOME — Tom Jones (Decca)
5	5	BEST OF THE BEACH BOYS — Beach Boys (Capitol)
6	6	FIDDLER ON THE ROOF — London Cast (CBS)
8	7	THIS IS JAMES LAST — James Last (Polydor)
10	8	MATTHEW AND SON — Cat Stevens (Deram)
11	9	COME THE DAY — Seekers (Columbia)
7	10	IMAGES — Walker Brothers (Philips)
–	11	HALL OF FAME — Georgie Fame (Columbia)
14	12	HAND CLAPPIN'–FOOT STOMPIN' –FUNKY BUTT–LIVE — Geno Washington (Piccadilly)
9	13	FOUR TOPS LIVE — Four Tops (Tamla Motown)
–	14	HIT THE ROAD STAX — Various Artists (Stax)
11	15	DR. ZHIVAGO Soundtrack (MGM)

13 May 1967

last week	this week	
1	1	THE SOUND OF MUSIC — Soundtrack (RCA)
2	2	MORE OF THE MONKEES — Monkees (RCA)
3	3	THE MONKEES — Monkees (RCA)
4	4	GREEN GREEN GRASS OF HOME — Tom Jones (Decca)
5	5	BEST OF THE BEACH BOYS — Beach Boys (Capitol)
6	6	FIDDLER ON THE ROOF — London Cast (CBS)
7	7	THIS IS JAMES LAST — James Last (Polydor)
10	8	IMAGES — Walker Brothers (Philips)
9	9	COME THE DAY — Seekers (Columbia)
13	10	FOUR TOPS LIVE — Four Tops (Tamla Motown)
8	11	MATTHEW AND SON — Cat Stevens (Deram)
11	12	HALL OF FAME — Georgie Fame (Columbia)
–	13	SECOMBE'S PERSONAL CHOICE — Harry Secombe (Philips)
14	14	DR. ZHIVAGO Soundtrack (MGM)
12	15	HAND CLAPPIN'–FOOT STOMPIN' –FUNKY BUTT–LIVE — Geno Washington (Piccadilly)

20 May 1967

last week	this week	
1	1	THE SOUND OF MUSIC — Soundtrack (RCA)
2	2	MORE OF THE MONKEES — Monkees (RCA)
4	3	GREEN GREEN GRASS OF HOME — Tom Jones (Decca)
3	4	THE MONKEES — Monkees (RCA)
5	5	BEST OF THE BEACH BOYS — Beach Boys (Capitol)
6	6	FIDDLER ON THE ROOF — London Cast (CBS)
7	7	THIS IS JAMES LAST — James Last (Polydor)
–	8	A DROP OF THE HARD STUFF — Dubliners (Major Minor)
13	9	SECOMBE'S PERSONAL CHOICE — Harry Secombe (Philips)
11	10	MATTHEW AND SON — Cat Stevens (Deram)
8	11	IMAGES — Walker Brothers (Philips)
–	12	GOING PLACES — Herb Alpert & the Tijuana Brass (Pye International)
9	13	COME THE DAY — Seekers (Columbia)
15	14	HAND CLAPPIN'–FOOT STOMPIN' –FUNKY BUTT–LIVE — Geno Washington (Piccadilly)
14	15	DR. ZHIVAGO Soundtrack (MGM)

27 May 1967

last week	this week	
1	1	THE SOUND OF MUSIC — Soundtrack (RCA)
2	2	MORE OF THE MONKEES — Monkees (RCA)
–	3	ARE YOU EXPERIENCED — Jimi Hendrix Experience (Track)
3	4	GREEN GREEN GRASS OF HOME — Tom Jones (Decca)
8	5	A DROP OF THE HARD STUFF — Dubliners (Major Minor)
4	6	THE MONKEES — Monkees (RCA)
6	7	FIDDLER ON THE ROOF — London Cast (CBS)
5	8	BEST OF THE BEACH BOYS — Beach Boys (Capitol)
7	9	THIS IS JAMES LAST — James Last (Polydor)
9	10	SECOMBE'S PERSONAL CHOICE — Harry Secombe (Philips)
12	11	GOING PLACES — Herb Alpert & the Tijuana Brass (Pye International)
14	12	HAND CLAPPIN'–FOOT STOMPIN' –FUNKY BUTT–LIVE — Geno Washington (Piccadilly)
–	13	RELEASE ME — Engelbert Humperdinck (Decca)
15	14	DR. ZHIVAGO Soundtrack (MGM)
10	15	MATTHEW AND SON — Cat Stevens (Deram)
13	15	COME THE DAY — Seekers (Columbia)

3 June 1967

last week	this week	
–	1	SGT. PEPPER'S LONELY HEARTS CLUB BAND — Beatles (Parlophone)
1	2	THE SOUND OF MUSIC — Soundtrack (RCA)
3	3	ARE YOU EXPERIENCED — Jimi Hendrix Experience (Track)
2	4	MORE OF THE MONKEES — Monkees (RCA)
5	5	A DROP OF THE HARD STUFF — Dubliners (Major Minor)
4	6	GREEN GREEN GRASS OF HOME — Tom Jones (Decca)
7	7	FIDDLER ON THE ROOF — London Cast (CBS)
8	8	BEST OF THE BEACH BOYS — Beach Boys (Capitol)
9	9	THIS IS JAMES LAST — James Last (Polydor)
6	10	THE MONKEES — Monkees (RCA)
13	11	RELEASE ME — Engelbert Humperdinck (Decca)
–	12	GOING PLACES — Herb Alpert & the Tijuana Brass (Pye International)
14	13	DR. ZHIVAGO Soundtrack (MGM)
15	14	MATTHEW AND SON — Cat Stevens (Deram)
10	15	SECOMBE'S PERSONAL CHOICE — Harry Secombe (Philips)

10 June 1967

last week	this week	
1	1	SGT. PEPPER'S LONELY HEARTS CLUB BAND — Beatles (Parlophone)
2	2	THE SOUND OF MUSIC — Soundtrack (RCA)
3	3	ARE YOU EXPERIENCED — Jimi Hendrix Experience (Track)
4	4	MORE OF THE MONKEES — Monkees (RCA)
5	5	A DROP OF THE HARD STUFF — Dubliners (Major Minor)
8	6	BEST OF THE BEACH BOYS — Beach Boys (Capitol)
6	7	GREEN GREEN GRASS OF HOME — Tom Jones (Decca)
7	8	FIDDLER ON THE ROOF — London Cast (CBS)
11	9	RELEASE ME — Engelbert Humperdinck (Decca)
9	10	THIS IS JAMES LAST — James Last (Polydor)
10	11	THE MONKEES — Monkees (RCA)
12	12	GOING PLACES — Herb Alpert & the Tijuana Brass (Pye International)
13	13	DR. ZHIVAGO Soundtrack (MGM)
–	14	HERE COME THE TREMELOES — Tremeloes (CBS)
15	15	SECOMBE'S PERSONAL CHOICE — Harry Secombe (Philips)

17 June 1967

last week	this week	
1	1	SGT. PEPPER'S LONELY HEARTS CLUB BAND — Beatles (Parlophone)
2	2	THE SOUND OF MUSIC — Soundtrack (RCA)
3	3	ARE YOU EXPERIENCED — Jimi Hendrix Experience (Track)
4	4	MORE OF THE MONKEES — Monkees (RCA)
8	5	FIDDLER ON THE ROOF — London Cast (CBS)
7	6	GREEN GREEN GRASS OF HOME — Tom Jones (Decca)
9	7	RELEASE ME — Engelbert Humperdinck (Decca)
6	8	BEST OF THE BEACH BOYS — Beach Boys (Capitol)
5	9	A DROP OF THE HARD STUFF — Dubliners (Major Minor)
10	10	THIS IS JAMES LAST — James Last (Polydor)
12	11	GOING PLACES — Herb Alpert & the Tijuana Brass (Pye International)
11	12	THE MONKEES — Monkees (RCA)
13	13	DR. ZHIVAGO Soundtrack (MGM)
14	14	HERE COME THE TREMELOES — Tremeloes (CBS)

It was the age of Motown (Detroit) and Stax (Memphis). The Four Tops had just been No.1 with their fourth hit since '65; other Motowners included the Supremes (five Top 10s since 1964), Temptations (five hits already) and Martha & the Vandellas (four). Stax couldn't quite compete but had Otis Redding, Sam & Dave, Carla Thomas, Rufus Thomas, Booker T. and more. Between them they created not just hits but instant classics. *Hit The Road Stax* captured perhaps the most exciting, soul tour package ever.

41

June – August 1967

24 June 1967

last	this	Album (Artist / Label)
1	1	SGT. PEPPER'S LONELY HEARTS CLUB BAND Beatles (Parlophone)
2	2	THE SOUND OF MUSIC Soundtrack (RCA)
3	3	ARE YOU EXPERIENCED Jimi Hendrix Experience (Track)
4	4	MORE OF THE MONKEES Monkees (RCA)
5	5	FIDDLER ON THE ROOF London Cast (CBS)
7	6	RELEASE ME Engelbert Humperdinck (Decca)
6	7	GREEN GREEN GRASS OF HOME Tom Jones (Decca)
8	8	BEST OF THE BEACH BOYS Beach Boys (Capitol)
9	9	A DROP OF THE HARD STUFF Dubliners (Major Minor)
11	10	GOING PLACES Herb Alpert & the Tijuana Brass (Pye International)
10	11	THIS IS JAMES LAST James Last (Polydor)
13	12	EVOLUTION Hollies (Parlophone)
12	13	THE MONKEES Monkees (RCA)
15	14	HERE COME THE TREMELOES Tremeloes (CBS)
14	15	DR. ZHIVAGO Soundtrack (MGM)

1 July 1967

last	this	Album (Artist / Label)
1	1	SGT. PEPPER'S LONELY HEARTS CLUB BAND Beatles (Parlophone)
2	2	THE SOUND OF MUSIC Soundtrack (RCA)
3	3	ARE YOU EXPERIENCED Jimi Hendrix Experience (Track)
4	4	MORE OF THE MONKEES Monkees (RCA)
5	5	FIDDLER ON THE ROOF London Cast (CBS)
9	6	A DROP OF THE HARD STUFF Dubliners (Major Minor)
7	7	GREEN GREEN GRASS OF HOME Tom Jones (Decca)
8	8	BEST OF THE BEACH BOYS Beach Boys (Capitol)
6	9	RELEASE ME Engelbert Humperdinck (Decca)
13	10	THE MONKEES Monkees (RCA)
12	11	EVOLUTION Hollies (Parlophone)
11	12	THIS IS JAMES LAST James Last (Polydor)
10	13	GOING PLACES Herb Alpert & the Tijuana Brass (Pye International)
-	14	TOM JONES LIVE AT THE TALK OF THE TOWN Tom Jones (Decca)
-	15	THE MAMAS AND PAPAS DELIVER Mamas & Papas (RCA)

8 July 1967

last	this	Album (Artist / Label)
1	1	SGT. PEPPER'S LONELY HEARTS CLUB BAND Beatles (Parlophone)
2	2	THE SOUND OF MUSIC Soundtrack (RCA)
-	3	HEADQUARTERS Monkees (RCA)
3	4	ARE YOU EXPERIENCED Jimi Hendrix Experience (Track)
4	5	MORE OF THE MONKEES Monkees (RCA)
5	6	FIDDLER ON THE ROOF London Cast (CBS)
6	7	A DROP OF THE HARD STUFF Dubliners (Major Minor)
9	8	RELEASE ME Engelbert Humperdinck (Decca)
11	9	EVOLUTION Hollies (Parlophone)
8	10	BEST OF THE BEACH BOYS Beach Boys (Capitol)
7	11	GREEN GREEN GRASS OF HOME Tom Jones (Decca)
14	12	TOM JONES LIVE AT THE TALK OF THE TOWN Tom Jones (Decca)
13	13	GOING PLACES Herb Alpert & the Tijuana Brass (Pye International)
12	14	THIS IS JAMES LAST James Last (Polydor)
15	15	THE MAMAS AND PAPAS DELIVER Mamas & Papas (RCA)

15 July 1967

last	this	Album (Artist / Label)
1	1	SGT. PEPPER'S LONELY HEARTS CLUB BAND Beatles (Parlophone)
3	2	HEADQUARTERS Monkees (RCA)
2	3	THE SOUND OF MUSIC Soundtrack (RCA)
4	4	ARE YOU EXPERIENCED Jimi Hendrix Experience (Track)
6	5	FIDDLER ON THE ROOF London Cast (CBS)
5	6	MORE OF THE MONKEES Monkees (RCA)
8	7	RELEASE ME Engelbert Humperdinck (Decca)
10	8	BEST OF THE BEACH BOYS Beach Boys (Capitol)
12	9	TOM JONES LIVE AT THE TALK OF THE TOWN Tom Jones (Decca)
9	10	EVOLUTION Hollies (Parlophone)
15	11	THE MAMAS AND PAPAS DELIVER Mamas & Papas (RCA)
11	12	DR. ZHIVAGO Soundtrack (MGM)
-	13	SMALL FACES Small Faces (Immediate)
13	14	GOING PLACES Herb Alpert & the Tijuana Brass (Pye International)
7	15	A DROP OF THE HARD STUFF Dubliners (Major Minor)

22 July 1967

last	this	Album (Artist / Label)
1	1	SGT. PEPPER'S LONELY HEARTS CLUB BAND Beatles (Parlophone)
2	2	HEADQUARTERS Monkees (RCA)
3	3	THE SOUND OF MUSIC Soundtrack (RCA)
4	4	ARE YOU EXPERIENCED Jimi Hendrix Experience (Track)
5	5	FIDDLER ON THE ROOF London Cast (CBS)
8	6	BEST OF THE BEACH BOYS Beach Boys (Capitol)
6	7	MORE OF THE MONKEES Monkees (RCA)
10	8	EVOLUTION Hollies (Parlophone)
11	9	THE MAMAS AND PAPAS DELIVER Mamas & Papas (RCA)
7	10	RELEASE ME Engelbert Humperdinck (Decca)
-	11	SOUNDS LIKE Herb Alpert & the Tijuana Brass (A&M)
12	12	DR. ZHIVAGO Soundtrack (MGM)
15	13	A DROP OF THE HARD STUFF Dubliners (Major Minor)
13	14	SMALL FACES Small Faces (Immediate)
9	15	TOM JONES LIVE AT THE TALK OF THE TOWN Tom Jones (Decca)

29 July 1967

last	this	Album (Artist / Label)
1	1	SGT. PEPPER'S LONELY HEARTS CLUB BAND Beatles (Parlophone)
2	2	HEADQUARTERS Monkees (RCA)
3	3	THE SOUND OF MUSIC Soundtrack (RCA)
4	4	ARE YOU EXPERIENCED Jimi Hendrix Experience (Track)
5	5	FIDDLER ON THE ROOF London Cast (CBS)
6	6	BEST OF THE BEACH BOYS Beach Boys (Capitol)
8	7	THE MAMAS AND PAPAS DELIVER Mamas & Papas (RCA)
7	8	MORE OF THE MONKEES Monkees (RCA)
15	9	TOM JONES LIVE AT THE TALK OF THE TOWN Tom Jones (Decca)
12	10	DR. ZHIVAGO Soundtrack (MGM)
-	11	THIS IS JAMES LAST James Last (Polydor)
11	12	SOUNDS LIKE Herb Alpert & the Tijuana Brass (A&M)
13	13	JIGSAW Shadows (Columbia)
10	14	RELEASE ME Engelbert Humperdinck (Decca)
-	15	GOING PLACES Herb Alpert & the Tijuana Brass (Pye International)

5 August 1967

last	this	Album (Artist / Label)
1	1	SGT. PEPPER'S LONELY HEARTS CLUB BAND Beatles (Parlophone)
2	2	HEADQUARTERS Monkees (RCA)
3	3	THE SOUND OF MUSIC Soundtrack (RCA)
4	4	ARE YOU EXPERIENCED Jimi Hendrix Experience (Track)
9	5	TOM JONES LIVE AT THE TALK OF THE TOWN Tom Jones (Decca)
5	6	FIDDLER ON THE ROOF London Cast (CBS)
6	7	BEST OF THE BEACH BOYS Beach Boys (Capitol)
13	8	JIGSAW Shadows (Columbia)
7	9	THE MAMAS AND PAPAS DELIVER Mamas & Papas (RCA)
8	10	MORE OF THE MONKEES Monkees (RCA)
10	11	DR. ZHIVAGO Soundtrack (MGM)
14	12	RELEASE ME Engelbert Humperdinck (Decca)
12	13	SOUNDS LIKE Herb Alpert & the Tijuana Brass (A&M)
11	14	THIS IS JAMES LAST James Last (Polydor)
-	15	SMALL FACES Small Faces (Immediate)

12 August 1967

last	this	Album (Artist / Label)
1	1	SGT. PEPPER'S LONELY HEARTS CLUB BAND Beatles (Parlophone)
2	2	HEADQUARTERS Monkees (RCA)
3	3	THE SOUND OF MUSIC Soundtrack (RCA)
4	4	ARE YOU EXPERIENCED Jimi Hendrix Experience (Track)
-	5	THE PIPER AT THE GATES OF DAWN Pink Floyd (Columbia)
7	6	BEST OF THE BEACH BOYS Beach Boys (Capitol)
5	7	TOM JONES LIVE AT THE TALK OF THE TOWN Tom Jones (Decca)
6	8	FIDDLER ON THE ROOF London Cast (CBS)
8	9	JIGSAW Shadows (Columbia)
10	10	DR. ZHIVAGO Soundtrack (MGM)
9	11	THE MAMAS AND PAPAS DELIVER Mamas & Papas (RCA)
14	12	THIS IS JAMES LAST James Last (Polydor)
12	13	RELEASE ME Engelbert Humperdinck (Decca)
10	14	MORE OF THE MONKEES Monkees (RCA)
15	15	SMALL FACES Small Faces (Immediate)

By now the chart was enriched by Jimi Hendrix's *Are You Experienced?*, which had crashed straight into May's Top 3. Seattle's James Marshall Hendrix, brought to Britain by the Animals' Chas Chandler, had been feted by the guitar-gods of Swinging London, the Who's Pete Townshend and ex-Yardbird Cream-member Eric Clapton. The Jimi Henrix Experience had charted with *Hey Joe* in January, *Purple Haze* in April and *The Wind Cries Mary* in May. *Burning of the Midnight Lamp* followed.

last week	this week	19 August 1967
1	1	SGT. PEPPER'S LONELY HEARTS CLUB BAND Beatles (Parlophone)
3	2	THE SOUND OF MUSIC Soundtrack (RCA)
2	3	HEADQUARTERS Monkees (RCA)
5	4	THE PIPER AT THE GATES OF DAWN Pink Floyd (Columbia)
4	5	ARE YOU EXPERIENCED Jimi Hendrix Experience (Track)
6	6	BEST OF THE BEACH BOYS Beach Boys (Capitol)
9	7	JIGSAW Shadows (Columbia)
7	8	TOM JONES LIVE AT THE TALK OF THE TOWN Tom Jones (Decca)
8	9	FIDDLER ON THE ROOF London Cast (CBS)
11	10	THE MAMAS AND PAPAS DELIVER Mamas & Papas (RCA)
9	11	DR. ZHIVAGO Soundtrack (MGM)
12	12	THIS IS JAMES LAST James Last (Polydor)
15	13	SMALL FACES Small Faces (Immediate)
14	14	MORE OF THE MONKEES Monkees (RCA)
-	15	GOING PLACES Herb Alpert & the Tijuana Brass (Pye International)

		26 August 1967
1	1	SGT. PEPPER'S LONELY HEARTS CLUB BAND Beatles (Parlophone)
2	2	THE SOUND OF MUSIC Soundtrack (RCA)
3	3	HEADQUARTERS Monkees (RCA)
4	4	THE PIPER AT THE GATES OF DAWN Pink Floyd (Columbia)
6	5	BEST OF THE BEACH BOYS Beach Boys (Capitol)
8	6	TOM JONES LIVE AT THE TALK OF THE TOWN Tom Jones (Decca)
5	7	ARE YOU EXPERIENCED Jimi Hendrix Experience (Track)
11	8	DR. ZHIVAGO Soundtrack (MGM)
7	9	JIGSAW Shadows (Columbia)
10	9	FIDDLER ON THE ROOF London Cast (CBS)
13	11	SMALL FACES Small Faces (Immediate)
12	12	THIS IS JAMES LAST James Last (Polydor)
15	13	GOING PLACES Herb Alpert & the Tijuana Brass (Pye International)
10	14	THE MAMAS AND PAPAS DELIVER Mamas & Papas (RCA)
-	15	A DROP OF THE HARD STUFF Dubliners (Major Minor)

		2 September 1967
1	1	SGT. PEPPER'S LONELY HEARTS CLUB BAND Beatles (Parlophone)
2	2	THE SOUND OF MUSIC Soundtrack (RCA)
3	3	HEADQUARTERS Monkees (RCA)
4	4	THE PIPER AT THE GATES OF DAWN Pink Floyd (Columbia)
5	5	BEST OF THE BEACH BOYS Beach Boys (Capitol)
8	6	DR. ZHIVAGO Soundtrack (MGM)
6	7	TOM JONES LIVE AT THE TALK OF THE TOWN Tom Jones (Decca)
7	8	ARE YOU EXPERIENCED Jimi Hendrix Experience (Track)
14	9	THE MAMAS AND PAPAS DELIVER Mamas & Papas (RCA)
9	10	JIGSAW Shadows (Columbia)
12	11	THIS IS JAMES LAST James Last (Polydor)
15	11	A DROP OF THE HARD STUFF Dubliners (Major Minor)
10	13	FIDDLER ON THE ROOF London Cast (CBS)
13	14	GOING PLACES Herb Alpert & the Tijuana Brass (Pye International)
11	15	SMALL FACES Small Faces (Immediate)

		9 September 1967
1	1	SGT. PEPPER'S LONELY HEARTS CLUB BAND Beatles (Parlophone)
2	2	THE SOUND OF MUSIC Soundtrack (RCA)
4	3	PIPER AT THE GATES OF DAWN Pink Floyd (Columbia)
3	4	HEADQUARTERS Monkees (RCA)
5	5	BEST OF THE BEACH BOYS Beach Boys (Capitol)
-	6	SCOTT Scott Walker (Philips)
8	7	ARE YOU EXPERIENCED Jimi Hendrix Experience (Track)
6	8	DR ZHIVAGO Soundtrack (MGM)
9	9	THE MAMAS AND PAPAS DELIVER Mamas & Papas (RCA)
13	10	FIDDLER ON THE ROOF London Cast (CBS)
10	11	JIGSAW Shadows (Columbia)
7	12	TOM JONES LIVE AT THE TALK OF THE TOWN Tom Jones (Decca)
14	13	GOING PLACES Herb Alpert & the Tijuana Brass (Pye International)
-	13	RELEASE ME Engelbert Humperdinck (Decca)
15	15	SMALL FACES Small Faces (Immediate)

		16 September 1967
1	1	SGT. PEPPER'S LONELY HEARTS CLUB BAND Beatles (Parlophone)
2	2	THE SOUND OF MUSIC Soundtrack (RCA)
5	3	BEST OF THE BEACH BOYS Beach Boys (Capitol)
4	4	HEADQUARTERS Monkees (RCA)
6	5	SCOTT Scott Walker (Philips)
3	6	THE PIPER AT THE GATES OF DAWN Pink Floyd (Columbia)
8	7	DR. ZHIVAGO Soundtrack (MGM)
12	8	TOM JONES LIVE AT THE TALK OF THE TOWN Tom Jones (Decca)
13	9	RELEASE ME Engelbert Humperdinck (Decca)
7	10	ARE YOU EXPERIENCED Jimi Hendrix Experience (Track)
10	11	FIDDLER ON THE ROOF London Cast (CBS)
11	12	JIGSAW Shadows (Columbia)
15	13	SMALL FACES Small Faces (Immediate)
9	14	THE MAMAS AND PAPAS DELIVER Mamas & Papas (RCA)
13	15	GOING PLACES Herb Alpert & the Tijuana Brass (Pye International)

		23 September 1967
1	1	SGT. PEPPER'S LONELY HEARTS CLUB BAND Beatles (Parlophone)
2	2	THE SOUND OF MUSIC Soundtrack (RCA)
5	3	SCOTT Scott Walker (Philips)
3	4	BEST OF THE BEACH BOYS Beach Boys (Capitol)
4	4	HEADQUARTERS Monkees (RCA)
7	6	DR. ZHIVAGO Soundtrack (MGM)
6	7	THE PIPER AT THE GATES OF DAWN Pink Floyd (Columbia)
8	8	TOM JONES LIVE AT THE TALK OF THE TOWN Tom Jones (Decca)
10	9	ARE YOU EXPERIENCED Jimi Hendrix Experience (Track)
9	10	RELEASE ME Engelbert Humperdinck (Decca)
-	11	THE WALKER BROTHERS STORY Walker Brothers (Philips)
12	12	CRUSADE John Mayall (Decca)
11	13	FIDDLER ON THE ROOF London Cast (CBS)
14	14	THE MAMAS AND PAPAS DELIVER Mamas & Papas (RCA)
-	15	BUDDY HOLLY'S GREATEST HITS Buddy Holly (Ace of Hearts)

		30 September 1967
1	1	SGT. PEPPER'S LONELY HEARTS CLUB BAND Beatles (Parlophone)
2	2	THE SOUND OF MUSIC Soundtrack (RCA)
3	3	SCOTT Scott Walker (Philips)
4	4	BEST OF THE BEACH BOYS Beach Boys (Capitol)
6	5	DR. ZHIVAGO Soundtrack (MGM)
5	6	HEADQUARTERS Monkees (RCA)
7	7	THE PIPER AT THE GATES OF DAWN Pink Floyd (Columbia)
8	8	TOM JONES LIVE AT THE TALK OF THE TOWN Tom Jones (Decca)
-	9	HIPSTERS, FLIPSTERS, FINGER-POPPIN' DADDIES Geno Washington (Piccadilly)
-	10	RAYMOND LEFEVRE Raymond Lefevre (Major Minor)
11	11	THE WALKER BROTHERS STORY Walker Brothers (Philips)
12	11	CRUSADE John Mayall (Decca)
10	13	RELEASE ME Engelbert Humperdinck (Decca)
9	14	ARE YOU EXPERIENCED Jimi Hendrix Experience (Track)
13	15	FIDDLER ON THE ROOF London Cast (CBS)

		7 October 1967
1	1	SGT. PEPPER'S LONELY HEARTS CLUB BAND Beatles (Parlophone)
2	2	THE SOUND OF MUSIC Soundtrack (RCA)
3	3	SCOTT Scott Walker (Philips)
4	4	BEST OF THE BEACH BOYS Beach Boys (Capitol)
5	5	DR. ZHIVAGO Soundtrack (MGM)
13	6	RELEASE ME Engelbert Humperdinck (Decca)
9	7	HIPSTERS, FLIPSTERS, FINGER-POPPIN' DADDIES Geno Washington (Piccadilly)
6	8	HEADQUARTERS Monkees (RCA)
11	9	CRUSADE John Mayall (Decca)
11	10	THE WALKER BROTHERS STORY Walker Brothers (Philips)
7	11	THE PIPER AT THE GATES OF DAWN Pink Floyd (Columbia)
10	12	RAYMOND LEFEVRE Raymond Lefevre (Major Minor)
8	13	TOM JONES LIVE AT THE TALK OF THE TOWN Tom Jones (Decca)
15	14	FIDDLER ON THE ROOF Topol & London Cast (CBS)
-	15	MORE OF THE HARD STUFF Dubliners (Major Minor)

Watch out, Geno's back. *Hipsters, Flipsters, Fingerpoppin' Daddies* indeed. But loopy titles, becoming de rigeur, seemed more drugster than funkster. It wasn't fingers these people were poppin'. With the singles topped by Scott McKenzie's *San Francisco*, bottomed by Procol Harum's ex-No.1 *Whiter Shade of Pale* and embracing Pink Floyd, Flowerpot Men, *All You Need Is Love* and even the Stones claiming *We Love You*, the LP chart had *Sgt Pepper* and *Piper At The Gates of Dawn*.

October – December 1967

last week / this week

14 October 1967

last	this		
1	1	SGT. PEPPER'S LONELY HEARTS CLUB BAND	Beatles (Parlophone)
2	2	THE SOUND OF MUSIC	Soundtrack (RCA)
3	3	SCOTT	Scott Walker (Philips)
5	4	DR. ZHIVAGO Soundtrack (MGM)	
4	5	BEST OF THE BEACH BOYS	Beach Boys (Capitol)
7	6	HIPSTERS, FLIPSTERS, FINGER-POPPIN' DADDIES	Geno Washington (Piccadilly)
12	7	RAYMOND LEFEVRE	Raymond Lefevre (Major Minor)
15	8	MORE OF THE HARD STUFF	Dubliners (Major Minor)
6	9	RELEASE ME	Engelbert Humperdinck (Decca)
10	10	THE WALKER BROTHERS STORY	Walker Brothers (Philips)
-	11	BEST OF THE BEACH BOYS VOL 2	Beach Boys (Capitol)
9	12	CRUSADE	John Mayall (Decca)
8	13	HEADQUARTERS	Monkees (RCA)
11	14	THE PIPER AT THE GATES OF DAWN	Pink Floyd (Columbia)
13	15	TOM JONES LIVE AT THE TALK OF THE TOWN	Tom Jones (Decca)

21 October 1967

last	this		
2	1	THE SOUND OF MUSIC	Soundtrack (RCA)
1	2	SGT. PEPPER'S LONELY HEARTS CLUB BAND	Beatles (Parlophone)
3	3	SCOTT	Scott Walker (Philips)
4	4	DR. ZHIVAGO Soundtrack (MGM)	
-	5	BREAKTHROUGH	Various Artists (Studio 2)
11	6	BEST OF THE BEACH BOYS VOL 2	Beach Boys (Capitol)
5	7	BEST OF THE BEACH BOYS	Beach Boys (Capitol)
8	8	MORE OF THE HARD STUFF	Dubliners (Major Minor)
7	9	RAYMOND LEFEVRE	Raymond Lefevre (Major Minor)
6	10	HIPSTERS, FLIPSTERS, FINGER-POPPIN' DADDIES	Geno Washington (Piccadilly)
9	11	RELEASE ME	Engelbert Humperdinck (Decca)
12	12	CRUSADE	John Mayall (Decca)
-	13	VANILLA FUDGE	Donovan (Marble Arch)
-	14	BRITISH MOTOWN CHARTBUSTERS	Various Artists (Tamla Motown)
14	15	THE PIPER AT THE GATES OF DAWN	Pink Floyd (Columbia)

28 October 1967

last	this		
1	1	THE SOUND OF MUSIC	Soundtrack (RCA)
2	2	SGT. PEPPER'S LONELY HEARTS CLUB BAND	Beatles (Parlophone)
5	3	BREAKTHROUGH	Various Artists (Studio 2)
6	4	BEST OF THE BEACH BOYS VOL 2	Beach Boys (Capitol)
4	5	DR. ZHIVAGO Soundtrack (MGM)	
14	6	BRITISH MOTOWN CHARTBUSTERS	Various Artists (Tamla Motown)
13	7	UNIVERSAL SOLDIER	Donovan (Marble Arch)
3	8	SCOTT	Scott Walker (Philips)
9	9	RAYMOND LEFEVRE	Raymond Lefevre (Major Minor)
8	10	MORE OF THE HARD STUFF	Dubliners (Major Minor)
7	11	BEST OF THE BEACH BOYS	Beach Boys (Capitol)
11	12	RELEASE ME	Engelbert Humperdinck (Decca)
-	13	VANILLA FUDGE	Vanilla Fudge (Atlantic)
9	14	HIPSTERS, FLIPSTERS, FINGER-POPPIN' DADDIES	Geno Washington (Piccadilly)
-	15	THOROUGHLY MODERN MILLIE	Soundtrack (Brunswick)

4 November 1967

last	this		
1	1	THE SOUND OF MUSIC	Soundtrack (RCA)
2	2	SGT. PEPPER'S LONELY HEARTS CLUB BAND	Beatles (Parlophone)
3	3	BREAKTHROUGH	Various Artists (Studio 2)
4	4	BEST OF THE BEACH BOYS VOL 2	Beach Boys (Capitol)
6	5	BRITISH MOTOWN CHARTBUSTERS	Various Artists (Tamla Motown)
5	6	DR. ZHIVAGO Soundtrack (MGM)	Donovan (Marble Arch)
8	8	SCOTT	Scott Walker (Philips)
11	9	BEST OF THE BEACH BOYS	Beach Boys (Capitol)
12	10	RELEASE ME	Engelbert Humperdinck (Decca)
10	11	MORE OF THE HARD STUFF	Dubliners (Major Minor)
9	12	RAYMOND LEFEVRE	Raymond Lefevre (Major Minor)
-	13	THE BEE GEES' FIRST	Bee Gees (Polydor)
15	14	THOROUGHLY MODERN MILLIE	Soundtrack (Brunswick)
14	15	HIPSTERS, FLIPSTERS, FINGER-POPPIN' DADDIES	Geno Washington (Piccadilly)

11 November 1967

last	this		
1	1	THE SOUND OF MUSIC	Soundtrack (RCA)
2	2	SGT. PEPPER'S LONELY HEARTS CLUB BAND	Beatles (Parlophone)
3	3	BREAKTHROUGH	Various Artists (Studio 2)
5	4	BRITISH MOTOWN CHARTBUSTERS	Various Artists (Tamla Motown)
4	5	BEST OF THE BEACH BOYS VOL 2	Beach Boys (Capitol)
-	6	SMILEY SMILE	Beach Boys (Capitol)
7	7	UNIVERSAL SOLDIER	Donovan (Marble Arch)
6	8	DR. ZHIVAGO Soundtrack (MGM)	
8	9	SCOTT	Scott Walker (Philips)
-	10	DISRAELI GEARS	Cream (Reaction)
11	11	MORE OF THE HARD STUFF	Dubliners (Major Minor)
9	12	BEST OF THE BEACH BOYS	Beach Boys (Capitol)
10	13	RELEASE ME	Engelbert Humperdinck (Decca)
12	14	RAYMOND LEFEVRE	Raymond Lefevre (Major Minor)
13	15	THE BEE GEES' FIRST	Bee Gees (Polydor)

18 November 1967

last	this		
1	1	THE SOUND OF MUSIC	Soundtrack (RCA)
2	2	SGT. PEPPER'S LONELY HEARTS CLUB BAND	Beatles (Parlophone)
4	3	BRITISH MOTOWN CHARTBUSTERS	Various Artists (Tamla Motown)
3	4	BREAKTHROUGH	Various Artists (Studio 2)
10	5	DISRAELI GEARS	Cream (Reaction)
5	6	BEST OF THE BEACH BOYS VOL 2	Beach Boys (Capitol)
7	7	UNIVERSAL SOLDIER	Donovan (Marble Arch)
6	8	SMILEY SMILE	Beach Boys (Capitol)
8	9	DR. ZHIVAGO Soundtrack (MGM)	
-	10	THE LAST WALTZ	Engelbert Humperdinck (Decca)
-	11	THOROUGHLY MODERN MILLIE	Soundtrack (Brunswick)
11	12	MORE OF THE HARD STUFF	Dubliners (Major Minor)
12	13	BEST OF THE BEACH BOYS	Beach Boys (Capitol)
15	14	THE BEE GEES' FIRST	Bee Gees (Polydor)
13	15	RELEASE ME	Engelbert Humperdinck (Decca)

25 November 1967

last	this		
1	1	THE SOUND OF MUSIC	Soundtrack (RCA)
2	2	SGT. PEPPER'S LONELY HEARTS CLUB BAND	Beatles (Parlophone)
4	3	BREAKTHROUGH	Various Artists (Studio 2)
5	4	DISRAELI GEARS	Cream (Reaction)
3	5	BRITISH MOTOWN CHARTBUSTERS	Various Artists (Tamla Motown)
10	6	THE LAST WALTZ	Engelbert Humperdinck (Decca)
6	7	BEST OF THE BEACH BOYS VOL 2	Beach Boys (Capitol)
7	8	UNIVERSAL SOLDIER	Donovan (Marble Arch)
8	9	SMILEY SMILE	Beach Boys (Capitol)
-	10	UNEQUALLED EQUALS (President)	
15	11	RELEASE ME	Engelbert Humperdinck (Decca)
-	12	REACH OUT	Four Tops (Tamla Motown)
13	13	BEST OF THE BEACH BOYS	Beach Boys (Capitol)
9	14	DR. ZHIVAGO Soundtrack (MGM)	
11	15	THOROUGHLY MODERN MILLIE	Soundtrack (Brunswick)

2 December 1967

last	this		
1	1	THE SOUND OF MUSIC	Soundtrack (RCA)
4	2	DISRAELI GEARS	Cream (Reaction)
2	3	SGT. PEPPER'S LONELY HEARTS CLUB BAND	Beatles (Parlophone)
5	4	BRITISH MOTOWN CHARTBUSTERS	Various Artists (Tamla Motown)
6	5	THE LAST WALTZ	Engelbert Humperdinck (Decca)
3	6	BREAKTHROUGH	Various Artists (Studio 2)
7	7	BEST OF THE BEACH BOYS VOL 2	Beach Boys (Capitol)
10	8	UNEQUALLED EQUALS (President)	
8	9	UNIVERSAL SOLDIER	Donovan (Marble Arch)
9	10	SMILEY SMILE	Beach Boys (Capitol)
14	11	DR. ZHIVAGO Soundtrack (MGM)	
-	12	TOM JONES LIVE AT THE TALK OF THE TOWN	Tom Jones (Decca)
12	13	REACH OUT	Four Tops (Tamla Motown)
-	14	SUNNY AFTERNOON	Kinks (Marble Arch)
13	15	BEST OF THE BEACH BOYS	Beach Boys (Capitol)

Bringing in *Disraeli Gears* and *Smiley Smile*, this was the Indian summer of love. Donovan, with a hit LP named after a Buffy St. Marie protest song, had said on TV: "When you are aware, there are no such things as hate and envy: there is only love... My job is writing beautiful things about beauty. You see, my life is beautiful." Paul McCartney had declared that "God is in everything. People who are hungry, who are sick and dying, should try to show love." Too much.

44

9 December 1967

last week	this week		
1	1	THE SOUND OF MUSIC	Soundtrack (RCA)
3	2	SGT. PEPPER'S LONELY HEARTS CLUB BAND	Beatles (Parlophone)
6	3	BREAKTHROUGH	Various Artists (Studio 2)
4	4	BRITISH MOTOWN CHARTBUSTERS	Various Artists (Tamla Motown)
2	5	DISRAELI GEARS	Cream (Reaction)
5	6	THE LAST WALTZ	Engelbert Humperdinck (Decca)
-	7	VAL DOONICAN ROCKS, BUT GENTLY	Val Doonican (Pye)
7	8	BEST OF THE BEACH BOYS VOL 2	Beach Boys (Capitol)
11	9	DR. ZHIVAGO	Soundtrack (MGM)
14	10	SUNNY AFTERNOON	Kinks (Marble Arch)
12	11	TOM JONES LIVE AT THE TALK OF THE TOWN	Tom Jones (Decca)
9	12	UNIVERSAL SOLDIER	Donovan (Marble Arch)
10	13	SMILEY SMILE	Beach Boys (Capitol)
13	14	REACH OUT	Four Tops (Tamla Motown)
15	15	BEST OF THE BEACH BOYS	Beach Boys (Capitol)
8	15	UNEQUALLED	Equals (President)

16 December 1967

1	1	THE SOUND OF MUSIC	Soundtrack (RCA)
2	2	SGT. PEPPER'S LONELY HEARTS CLUB BAND	Beatles (Parlophone)
7	3	VAL DOONICAN ROCKS, BUT GENTLY	Val Doonican (Pye)
4	4	BRITISH MOTOWN CHARTBUSTERS	Various Artists (Tamla Motown)
3	5	BREAKTHROUGH	Various Artists (Studio 2)
6	6	THE LAST WALTZ	Engelbert Humperdinck (Decca)
5	7	DISRAELI GEARS	Cream (Reaction)
-	8	AXIS: BOLD AS LOVE	Jimi Hendrix Experience (Track)
9	9	DR. ZHIVAGO	Soundtrack (MGM)
8	10	BEST OF THE BEACH BOYS VOL 2	Beach Boys (Capitol)
14	11	REACH OUT	Four Tops (Tamla Motown)
-	12	GREAT WALTZES	Roberto Mann (Deram)
11	13	TOM JONES LIVE AT THE TALK OF THE TOWN	Tom Jones (Decca)
15	14	BEST OF THE BEACH BOYS	Beach Boys (Capitol)
15	15	UNEQUALLED	Equals (President)

23 December 1967

1	1	THE SOUND OF MUSIC	Soundtrack (RCA)
2	2	SGT. PEPPER'S LONELY HEARTS CLUB BAND	Beatles (Parlophone)
3	3	VAL DOONICAN ROCKS, BUT GENTLY	Val Doonican (Pye)
6	3	THE LAST WALTZ	Engelbert Humperdinck (Decca)
4	5	BRITISH MOTOWN CHARTBUSTERS	Various Artists (Tamla Motown)
7	6	DISRAELI GEARS	Cream (Reaction)
13	7	TOM JONES LIVE AT THE TALK OF THE TOWN	Tom Jones (Decca)
5	8	BREAKTHROUGH	Various Artists (Studio 2)
8	9	AXIS: BOLD AS LOVE	Jimi Hendrix Experience (Track)
-	10	THEIR SATANIC MAJESTIES REQUEST	Rolling Stones (Decca)
11	11	REACH OUT	Four Tops (Tamla Motown)
9	12	DR. ZHIVAGO	Soundtrack (MGM)
10	13	BEST OF THE BEACH BOYS VOL 2	Beach Boys (Capitol)
14	14	BEST OF THE BEACH BOYS	Beach Boys (Capitol)
12	15	GREAT WALTZES	Roberto Mann (Deram)

30 December 1967

1	1	THE SOUND OF MUSIC	Soundtrack (RCA)
2	2	SGT. PEPPER'S LONELY HEARTS CLUB BAND	Beatles (Parlophone)
3	3	VAL DOONICAN ROCKS, BUT GENTLY	Val Doonican (Pye)
3	4	THE LAST WALTZ	Engelbert Humperdinck (Decca)
5	5	BRITISH MOTOWN CHARTBUSTERS	Various Artists (Tamla Motown)
6	6	DISRAELI GEARS	Cream (Reaction)
10	7	THEIR SATANIC MAJESTIES REQUEST	Rolling Stones (Decca)
7	8	TOM JONES LIVE AT THE TALK OF THE TOWN	Tom Jones (Decca)
8	9	BREAKTHROUGH	Various Artists (Studio 2)
11	10	REACH OUT	Four Tops (Tamla Motown)
9	11	AXIS: BOLD AS LOVE	Jimi Hendrix Experience (Track)
12	12	DR. ZHIVAGO	Soundtrack (MGM)
13	13	BEST OF THE BEACH BOYS VOL 2	Beach Boys (Capitol)
15	14	GREAT WALTZES	Roberto Mann (Deram)
14	15	BEST OF THE BEACH BOYS	Beach Boys (Capitol)

The late David Widgery, one radical journalist not beguiled by the heady smell of flower power, offered this rejoinder in OZ magazine: "We believe a lot of lies... The world's turned on... it's the psychedelic storming of the Winter Palace... Which is a pity. Because at the moment the hippies in England represent about as powerful a challenge to the power of the state as the people who put foreign coins in their gas meters." But, armed with *Sgt. Pepper's Lonely Hearts Club Band, Their Satanic Majesties Request* and *Axis: Bold As Love*, at least they had deposed the Minstrels.

January – February 1968

6 January 1968
(last week / this week)

Last	This	Title	Artist (Label)
2	1	SGT. PEPPER'S LONELY HEARTS CLUB BAND	Beatles (Parlophone)
3	2	VAL DOONICAN ROCKS, BUT GENTLY	Val Doonican (Pye)
1	3	THE SOUND OF MUSIC	Soundtrack (RCA)
7	4	THEIR SATANIC MAJESTIES REQUEST	Rolling Stones (Decca)
4	5	THE LAST WALTZ	Engelbert Humperdinck (Decca)
5	6	BRITISH MOTOWN CHARTBUSTERS	Various Artists (Tamla Motown)
10	7	REACH OUT	Four Tops (Tamla Motown)
11	8	AXIS: BOLD AS LOVE	Jimi Hendrix Experience (Track)
-	9	13 SMASH HITS	Tom Jones (Decca)
6	10	DISRAELI GEARS	Cream (Reaction)
9	10	BREAKTHROUGH	Various Artists (Studio 2)
8	12	TOM JONES LIVE AT THE TALK OF THE TOWN	Tom Jones (Decca)
-	13	PISCES, AQUARIUS, CAPRICORN & JONES LTD	Monkees (RCA Victor)
15	14	BEST OF THE BEACH BOYS	Beach Boys (Capitol)
-	15	MR. FANTASY	Traffic (Island)

13 January 1968

Last	This	Title	Artist (Label)
1	1	SGT. PEPPER'S LONELY HEARTS CLUB BAND	Beatles (Parlophone)
3	2	THE SOUND OF MUSIC	Soundtrack (RCA)
2	3	VAL DOONICAN ROCKS, BUT GENTLY	Val Doonican (Pye)
7	4	REACH OUT	Four Tops (Tamla Motown)
6	5	BRITISH MOTOWN CHARTBUSTERS	Various Artists (Tamla Motown)
4	6	THEIR SATANIC MAJESTIES REQUEST	Rolling Stones (Decca)
5	7	THE LAST WALTZ	Engelbert Humperdinck (Decca)
9	8	13 SMASH HITS	Tom Jones (Decca)
8	9	AXIS: BOLD AS LOVE	Jimi Hendrix Experience (Track)
13	10	PISCES, AQUARIUS, CAPRICORN & JONES LTD	Monkees (RCA Victor)
10	11	DISRAELI GEARS	Cream (Reaction)
15	12	MR. FANTASY	Traffic (Island)
10	13	BREAKTHROUGH	Various Artists (Studio 2)
12	14	TOM JONES LIVE AT THE TALK OF THE TOWN	Tom Jones (Decca)
-	15	DR. ZHIVAGO	Soundtrack (MGM)

20 January 1968

Last	This	Title	Artist (Label)
3	1	VAL DOONICAN ROCKS, BUT GENTLY	Val Doonican (Pye)
1	2	SGT. PEPPER'S LONELY HEARTS CLUB BAND	Beatles (Parlophone)
2	3	THE SOUND OF MUSIC	Soundtrack (RCA)
6	4	THEIR SATANIC MAJESTIES REQUEST	Rolling Stones (Decca)
4	5	REACH OUT	Four Tops (Tamla Motown)
5	6	BRITISH MOTOWN CHARTBUSTERS	Various Artists (Tamla Motown)
7	7	THE LAST WALTZ	Engelbert Humperdinck (Decca)
-	8	SUPREMES' GREATEST HITS	Supremes (Tamla Motown)
8	9	13 SMASH HITS	Tom Jones (Decca)
10	10	PISCES, AQUARIUS, CAPRICORN & JONES LTD	Monkees (RCA Victor)
-	11	FOUR TOPS' GREATEST HITS	Four Tops (Tamla Motown)
9	12	AXIS: BOLD AS LOVE	Jimi Hendrix Experience (Track)
-	13	THE WHO SELL OUT	Who (Reaction)
12	14	MR. FANTASY	Traffic (Island)
11	15	DISRAELI GEARS	Cream (Reaction)

27 January 1968

Last	This	Title	Artist (Label)
3	1	THE SOUND OF MUSIC	Soundtrack (RCA)
5	2	REACH OUT	Four Tops (Tamla Motown)
1	3	VAL DOONICAN ROCKS, BUT GENTLY	Val Doonican (Pye)
8	4	SUPREMES' GREATEST HITS	Supremes (Tamla Motown)
2	5	SGT. PEPPER'S LONELY HEARTS CLUB BAND	Beatles (Parlophone)
11	6	FOUR TOPS' GREATEST HITS	Four Tops (Tamla Motown)
4	7	THEIR SATANIC MAJESTIES REQUEST	Rolling Stones (Decca)
6	8	BRITISH MOTOWN CHARTBUSTERS	Various Artists (Tamla Motown)
9	9	13 SMASH HITS	Tom Jones (Decca)
12	10	AXIS: BOLD AS LOVE	Jimi Hendrix Experience (Track)
10	11	PISCES, AQUARIUS, CAPRICORN & JONES LTD	Monkees (RCA Victor)
7	12	THE LAST WALTZ	Engelbert Humperdinck (Decca)
13	13	THE WHO SELL OUT	Who (Reaction)
15	14	DISRAELI GEARS	Cream (Reaction)
14	15	MR. FANTASY	Traffic (Island)

3 February 1968

Last	This	Title	Artist (Label)
4	1	SUPREMES' GREATEST HITS	Supremes (Tamla Motown)
1	2	THE SOUND OF MUSIC	Soundtrack (RCA)
6	3	FOUR TOPS' GREATEST HITS	Four Tops (Tamla Motown)
2	4	REACH OUT	Four Tops (Tamla Motown)
3	4	VAL DOONICAN ROCKS, BUT GENTLY	Val Doonican (Pye)
5	6	SGT. PEPPER'S LONELY HEARTS CLUB BAND	Beatles (Parlophone)
8	7	BRITISH MOTOWN CHARTBUSTERS	Various Artists (Tamla Motown)
9	8	13 SMASH HITS	Tom Jones (Decca)
11	9	PISCES, AQUARIUS, CAPRICORN & JONES LTD	Monkees (RCA Victor)
12	10	THE LAST WALTZ	Engelbert Humperdinck (Decca)
7	11	THEIR SATANIC MAJESTIES REQUEST	Rolling Stones (Decca)
-	12	BREAKTHROUGH	Various Artists (Studio 2)
10	13	AXIS: BOLD AS LOVE	Jimi Hendrix Experience (Track)
13	14	THE WHO SELL OUT	Who (Reaction)
15	15	MR. FANTASY	Traffic (Island)

10 February 1968

Last	This	Title	Artist (Label)
1	1	SUPREMES' GREATEST HITS	Supremes (Tamla Motown)
2	2	THE SOUND OF MUSIC	Soundtrack (RCA)
3	3	FOUR TOPS' GREATEST HITS	Four Tops (Tamla Motown)
6	4	SGT. PEPPER'S LONELY HEARTS CLUB BAND	Beatles (Parlophone)
4	5	VAL DOONICAN ROCKS, BUT GENTLY	Val Doonican (Pye)
4	6	REACH OUT	Four Tops (Tamla Motown)
8	7	13 SMASH HITS	Tom Jones (Decca)
7	8	BRITISH MOTOWN CHARTBUSTERS	Various Artists (Tamla Motown)
10	9	THE LAST WALTZ	Engelbert Humperdinck (Decca)
11	10	THEIR SATANIC MAJESTIES REQUEST	Rolling Stones (Decca)
-	11	OTIS BLUE	Otis Redding (Atlantic)
14	12	THE WHO SELL OUT	Who (Reaction)
9	13	PISCES, AQUARIUS, CAPRICORN & JONES LTD	Monkees (RCA Victor)
12	14	BREAKTHROUGH	Various Artists (Studio 2)
-	15	PARADISE LOST	Herd (Fontana)

17 February 1968

Last	This	Title	Artist (Label)
1	1	SUPREMES' GREATEST HITS	Supremes (Tamla Motown)
2	2	THE SOUND OF MUSIC	Soundtrack (RCA)
3	3	FOUR TOPS' GREATEST HITS	Four Tops (Tamla Motown)
7	4	13 SMASH HITS	Tom Jones (Decca)
4	5	SGT. PEPPER'S LONELY HEARTS CLUB BAND	Beatles (Parlophone)
5	6	VAL DOONICAN ROCKS, BUT GENTLY	Val Doonican (Pye)
8	7	BRITISH MOTOWN CHARTBUSTERS	Various Artists (Tamla Motown)
14	8	BREAKTHROUGH	Various Artists (Studio 2)
6	9	REACH OUT	Four Tops (Tamla Motown)
9	10	THE LAST WALTZ	Engelbert Humperdinck (Decca)
13	11	PISCES, AQUARIUS, CAPRICORN & JONES LTD	Monkees (RCA Victor)
-	12	THIS IS CHAQUITO AND QUEDO BRASS	Chaquito & Quedo Brass (Fontana)
11	13	OTIS BLUE	Otis Redding (Atlantic)
12	14	THE WHO SELL OUT	Who (Reaction)
10	15	THEIR SATANIC MAJESTIES REQUEST	Rolling Stones (Decca)

24 February 1968

Last	This	Title	Artist (Label)
1	1	SUPREMES' GREATEST HITS	Supremes (Tamla Motown)
3	2	FOUR TOPS' GREATEST HITS	Four Tops (Tamla Motown)
2	3	THE SOUND OF MUSIC	Soundtrack (RCA)
4	4	13 SMASH HITS	Tom Jones (Decca)
5	5	SGT. PEPPER'S LONELY HEARTS CLUB BAND	Beatles (Parlophone)
8	6	BREAKTHROUGH	Various Artists (Studio 2)
6	7	VAL DOONICAN ROCKS, BUT GENTLY	Val Doonican (Pye)
7	8	BRITISH MOTOWN CHARTBUSTERS	Various Artists (Tamla Motown)
11	9	PISCES, AQUARIUS, CAPRICORN & JONES LTD	Monkees (RCA Victor)
10	10	THE LAST WALTZ	Engelbert Humperdinck (Decca)
13	11	OTIS BLUE	Otis Redding (Atlantic)
9	12	REACH OUT	Four Tops (Tamla Motown)
12	13	THIS IS CHAQUITO AND QUEDO BRASS	Chaquito & Quedo Brass (Fontana)
-	14	HORIZONTAL	Bee Gees (Polydor)
14	15	THE WHO SELL OUT	Who (Reaction)

Statistics say the Beatles' new year began well. Pepper was top again; in the singles chart they were No.1 with *Hello Goodbye* and No.2 with the *Magical Mystery Tour* double-EP (an album in the USA). Yet the TV-film behind this lead-ballooned. It was the first thumb's down for the Fab Four. Famously thumbs-up Paul commented: "If everything Beethoven had written had been great it would have been one grey sludge, but... There were good bits and bad bits, and that's the way we are."

March – April 1968

2 March 1968

last	this		
1	1	SUPREMES' GREATEST HITS	Supremes (Tamla Motown)
-	2	JOHN WESLEY HARDING	Bob Dylan (CBS)
2	3	FOUR TOPS' GREATEST HITS	Four Tops (Tamla Motown)
3	4	THE SOUND OF MUSIC	Soundtrack (RCA)
4	5	13 SMASH HITS	Tom Jones (Decca)
6	6	BREAKTHROUGH	Various Artists (Studio 2)
5	7	SGT. PEPPER'S LONELY HEARTS CLUB BAND	Beatles (Parlophone)
8	8	BRITISH MOTOWN CHARTBUSTERS	Various Artists (Tamla Motown)
-	9	THIS IS BERT KAEMPFERT	Bert Kaempfert (Polydor)
-	10	HISTORY OF OTIS REDDING	Otis Redding (Volt)
11	11	OTIS BLUE	Otis Redding (Volt)
13	12	THIS IS CHAQUITO AND QUEDO BRASS	Chaquito & Quedo Brass (Fontana)
9	13	PISCES, AQUARIUS, CAPRICORN & JONES LTD	Monkees (RCA Victor)
14	14	HORIZONTAL	Bee Gees (Polydor)
10	15	THE LAST WALTZ	Engelbert Humperdinck (Decca)

9 March 1968

last	this		
1	1	SUPREMES' GREATEST HITS	Supremes (Tamla Motown)
2	2	JOHN WESLEY HARDING	Bob Dylan (CBS)
3	3	FOUR TOPS' GREATEST HITS	Four Tops (Tamla Motown)
4	4	THE SOUND OF MUSIC	Soundtrack (RCA)
10	5	HISTORY OF OTIS REDDING	Otis Redding (Volt)
5	6	13 SMASH HITS	Tom Jones (Decca)
8	7	BRITISH MOTOWN CHARTBUSTERS	Various Artists (Tamla Motown)
9	8	THIS IS BERT KAEMPFERT	Bert Kaempfert (Polydor)
14	9	HORIZONTAL	Bee Gees (Polydor)
6	10	BREAKTHROUGH	Various Artists (Studio 2)
-	11	WILD HONEY	Beach Boys (Capitol)
-	12	2 IN 3	Esther & Abi Ofarim (Philips)
7	13	SGT. PEPPER'S LONELY HEARTS CLUB BAND	Beatles (Parlophone)
-	14	PETER GREEN'S FLEETWOOD MAC	Fleetwood Mac (Blue Horizon)
-	15	VAL DOONICAN ROCKS, BUT GENTLY	Val Doonican (Pye)

16 March 1968

last	this		
2	1	JOHN WESLEY HARDING	Bob Dylan (CBS)
1	2	SUPREMES' GREATEST HITS	Supremes (Tamla Motown)
4	3	THE SOUND OF MUSIC	Soundtrack (RCA)
5	4	HISTORY OF OTIS REDDING	Otis Redding (Volt)
3	5	FOUR TOPS' GREATEST HITS	Four Tops (Tamla Motown)
12	6	2 IN 3	Esther & Abi Ofarim (Philips)
8	7	THIS IS BERT KAEMPFERT	Bert Kaempfert (Polydor)
6	8	13 SMASH HITS	Tom Jones (Decca)
11	9	WILD HONEY	Beach Boys (Capitol)
14	10	PETER GREEN'S FLEETWOOD MAC	Fleetwood Mac (Blue Horizon)
9	11	HORIZONTAL	Bee Gees (Polydor)
7	12	BRITISH MOTOWN CHARTBUSTERS	Various Artists (Tamla Motown)
13	13	SGT. PEPPER'S LONELY HEARTS CLUB BAND	Beatles (Parlophone)
15	14	VAL DOONICAN ROCKS, BUT GENTLY	Val Doonican (Pye)
-	15	OTIS BLUE	Otis Redding (Atlantic)

23 March 1968

last	this		
1	1	JOHN WESLEY HARDING	Bob Dylan (CBS)
2	2	SUPREMES' GREATEST HITS	Supremes (Tamla Motown)
4	3	HISTORY OF OTIS REDDING	Otis Redding (Volt)
3	4	THE SOUND OF MUSIC	Soundtrack (RCA)
-	5	THIS IS SOUL	Various Artists (Atlantic)
5	6	FOUR TOPS' GREATEST HITS	Four Tops (Tamla Motown)
6	7	2 IN 3	Esther & Abi Ofarim (Philips)
9	8	WILD HONEY	Beach Boys (Capitol)
8	9	13 SMASH HITS	Tom Jones (Decca)
10	10	PETER GREEN'S FLEETWOOD MAC	Fleetwood Mac (Blue Horizon)
13	11	SGT. PEPPER'S LONELY HEARTS CLUB BAND	Beatles (Parlophone)
12	12	BRITISH MOTOWN CHARTBUSTERS	Various Artists (Tamla Motown)
7	13	THIS IS BERT KAEMPFERT	Bert Kaempfert (Polydor)
11	14	HORIZONTAL	Bee Gees (Polydor)
14	15	VAL DOONICAN ROCKS, BUT GENTLY	Val Doonican (Pye)

30 March 1968

last	this		
1	1	JOHN WESLEY HARDING	Bob Dylan (CBS)
5	2	THIS IS SOUL	Various Artists (Atlantic)
3	3	HISTORY OF OTIS REDDING	Otis Redding (Volt)
2	4	SUPREMES' GREATEST HITS	Supremes (Tamla Motown)
4	5	THE SOUND OF MUSIC	Soundtrack (RCA)
6	6	FOUR TOPS' GREATEST HITS	Four Tops (Tamla Motown)
8	7	WILD HONEY	Beach Boys (Capitol)
10	8	PETER GREEN'S FLEETWOOD MAC	Fleetwood Mac (Blue Horizon)
7	9	2 IN 3	Esther & Abi Ofarim (Philips)
9	10	13 SMASH HITS	Tom Jones (Decca)
12	11	BRITISH MOTOWN CHARTBUSTERS	Various Artists (Tamla Motown)
-	12	LIVE AT THE TALK OF THE TOWN	Diana Ross & the Supremes (Tamla Motown)
-	13	OTIS BLUE	Otis Redding (Atlantic)
11	14	SGT. PEPPER'S LONELY HEARTS CLUB BAND	Beatles (Parlophone)
13	15	THIS IS BERT KAEMPFERT	Bert Kaempfert (Polydor)

6 April 1968

last	this		
1	1	JOHN WESLEY HARDING	Bob Dylan (CBS)
2	2	THIS IS SOUL	Various Artists (Atlantic)
3	3	HISTORY OF OTIS REDDING	Otis Redding (Volt)
5	4	THE SOUND OF MUSIC	Soundtrack (RCA)
4	5	SUPREMES' GREATEST HITS	Supremes (Tamla Motown)
6	6	FOUR TOPS' GREATEST HITS	Four Tops (Tamla Motown)
7	7	WILD HONEY	Beach Boys (Capitol)
8	8	PETER GREEN'S FLEETWOOD MAC	Fleetwood Mac (Blue Horizon)
9	9	2 IN 3	Esther & Abi Ofarim (Philips)
12	10	LIVE AT THE TALK OF THE TOWN	Diana Ross & the Supremes (Tamla Motown)
10	11	13 SMASH HITS	Tom Jones (Decca)
14	12	SGT. PEPPER'S LONELY HEARTS CLUB BAND	Beatles (Parlophone)
-	13	THE HANGMAN'S BEAUTIFUL DAUGHTER	Incredible String Band (Elektra)
-	14	OTIS REDDING IN EUROPE	Otis Redding (Stax)
-	15	MOVE	Move (Regal Zonophone)

13 April 1968

last	this		
1	1	JOHN WESLEY HARDING	Bob Dylan (CBS)
2	2	THIS IS SOUL	Various Artists (Atlantic)
3	3	HISTORY OF OTIS REDDING	Otis Redding (Volt)
4	4	THE SOUND OF MUSIC	Soundtrack (RCA)
8	5	PETER GREEN'S FLEETWOOD MAC	Fleetwood Mac (Blue Horizon)
5	6	SUPREMES' GREATEST HITS	Supremes (Tamla Motown)
6	7	FOUR TOPS' GREATEST HITS	Four Tops (Tamla Motown)
13	8	THE HANGMAN'S BEAUTIFUL DAUGHTER	Incredible String Band (Elektra)
7	9	WILD HONEY	Beach Boys (Capitol)
9	10	2 IN 3	Esther & Abi Ofarim (Philips)
10	11	LIVE AT THE TALK OF THE TOWN	Diana Ross & the Supremes (Tamla Motown)
-	12	SCOTT 2	Scott Walker (Philips)
15	13	MOVE	Move (Regal Zonophone)
-	14	ROUND AMEN CORNER	Amen Corner (Deram)
14	15	OTIS REDDING IN EUROPE	Otis Redding (Stax)

20 April 1968

last	this		
1	1	JOHN WESLEY HARDING	Bob Dylan (CBS)
2	2	THIS IS SOUL	Various Artists (Atlantic)
4	3	THE SOUND OF MUSIC	Soundtrack (RCA)
6	4	SUPREMES' GREATEST HITS	Supremes (Tamla Motown)
3	5	HISTORY OF OTIS REDDING	Otis Redding (Volt)
7	6	FOUR TOPS' GREATEST HITS	Four Tops (Tamla Motown)
5	7	PETER GREEN'S FLEETWOOD MAC	Fleetwood Mac (Blue Horizon)
8	8	THE HANGMAN'S BEAUTIFUL DAUGHTER	Incredible String Band (Elektra)
9	9	WILD HONEY	Beach Boys (Capitol)
10	10	2 IN 3	Esther & Abi Ofarim (Philips)
12	11	SCOTT 2	Scott Walker (Philips)
11	12	LIVE AT THE TALK OF THE TOWN	Diana Ross & the Supremes (Tamla Motown)
15	13	OTIS REDDING IN EUROPE	Otis Redding (Stax)
-	14	13 SMASH HITS	Tom Jones (Decca)
13	15	MOVE	Move (Regal Zonophone)

Back came Bob Dylan, after motorcycle-crashing from the public eye in 1966, on the eve of *Blonde On Blonde*'s release. CBS concocted a *Bob Dylan's Greatest Hits* - which seemed, at the time, a vulgar title - but there had been no new release in eighteen months. In a period when pop acts averaged two albums a year, it felt like aeons. John Wesley Harding proved spare, demanding, countrified: and as fierce a stance as possible against psychedelic overkill. The public sent it to No.1 for seven weeks.

April – June 1968

27 April 1968

LW	TW	Album	Artist (Label)
1	1	JOHN WESLEY HARDING	Bob Dylan (CBS)
2	2	THIS IS SOUL	Various Artists (Atlantic)
5	3	HISTORY OF OTIS REDDING	Otis Redding (Volt)
3	4	THE SOUND OF MUSIC	Soundtrack (RCA)
6	5	FOUR TOPS' GREATEST HITS	Four Tops (Tamla Motown)
11	6	SCOTT 2	Scott Walker (Philips)
4	7	SUPREMES' GREATEST HITS	Supremes (Tamla Motown)
7	8	PETER GREEN'S FLEETWOOD MAC	Fleetwood Mac (Blue Horizon)
8	8	THE HANGMAN'S BEAUTIFUL DAUGHTER	Incredible String Band (Elektra)
10	10	2 IN 3	Esther & Abi Ofarim (Philips)
13	11	OTIS REDDING IN EUROPE	Otis Redding (Stax)
12	12	LIVE AT THE TALK OF THE TOWN	Supremes (Tamla Motown)
15	13	MOVE	Move (Regal Zonophone)
9	14	WILD HONEY	Beach Boys (Capitol)
-	15	SHER-OO!	Cilla Black (Parlophone)

4 May 1968

LW	TW	Album	Artist (Label)
2	1	THIS IS SOUL	Various Artists (Atlantic)
1	2	JOHN WESLEY HARDING	Bob Dylan (CBS)
3	3	HISTORY OF OTIS REDDING	Otis Redding (Volt)
4	4	THE SOUND OF MUSIC	Soundtrack (RCA)
7	5	SUPREMES' GREATEST HITS	Supremes (Tamla Motown)
6	6	SCOTT 2	Scott Walker (Philips)
8	7	PETER GREEN'S FLEETWOOD MAC	Fleetwood Mac (Blue Horizon)
8	8	THE HANGMAN'S BEAUTIFUL DAUGHTER	Incredible String Band (Elektra)
-	9	SMASH HITS	Jimi Hendrix Experience (Track)
5	10	FOUR TOPS' GREATEST HITS	Four Tops (Tamla Motown)
15	11	SHER-OO!	Cilla Black (Parlophone)
-	12	THE JUNGLE BOOK	Soundtrack (Disneyland)
13	13	MOVE	Move (Regal Zonophone)
-	14	A GIFT FROM A FLOWER TO A GARDEN	Donovan (Pye)
14	15	WILD HONEY	Beach Boys (Capitol)

11 May 1968

LW	TW	Album	Artist (Label)
1	1	THIS IS SOUL	Various Artists (Atlantic)
2	2	JOHN WESLEY HARDING	Bob Dylan (CBS)
6	3	SCOTT 2	Scott Walker (Philips)
3	4	HISTORY OF OTIS REDDING	Otis Redding (Volt)
4	5	THE SOUND OF MUSIC	Soundtrack (RCA)
9	6	SMASH HITS	Jimi Hendrix Experience (Track)
5	7	SUPREMES' GREATEST HITS	Supremes (Tamla Motown)
7	8	PETER GREEN'S FLEETWOOD MAC	Fleetwood Mac (Blue Horizon)
-	9	LIVE AT THE TALK OF THE TOWN	Diana Ross & the Supremes (Tamla Motown)
8	10	THE HANGMAN'S BEAUTIFUL DAUGHTER	Incredible String Band (Elektra)
10	11	FOUR TOPS' GREATEST HITS	Four Tops (Tamla Motown)
14	12	A GIFT FROM A FLOWER TO A GARDEN	Donovan (Pye)
12	13	THE JUNGLE BOOK	Soundtrack (Disneyland)
11	14	SHER-OO!	Cilla Black (Parlophone)
-	15	2 IN 3	Esther & Abi Ofarim (Philips)

18 May 1968

LW	TW	Album	Artist (Label)
1	1	THIS IS SOUL	Various Artists (Atlantic)
2	2	JOHN WESLEY HARDING	Bob Dylan (CBS)
3	3	SCOTT 2	Scott Walker (Philips)
4	4	HISTORY OF OTIS REDDING	Otis Redding (Volt)
5	5	THE SOUND OF MUSIC	Soundtrack (RCA)
6	6	SMASH HITS	Jimi Hendrix Experience (Track)
7	7	SUPREMES' GREATEST HITS	Supremes (Tamla Motown)
10	8	THE HANGMAN'S BEAUTIFUL DAUGHTER	Incredible String Band (Elektra)
13	9	THE JUNGLE BOOK	Soundtrack (Disneyland)
8	10	PETER GREEN'S FLEETWOOD MAC	Fleetwood Mac (Blue Horizon)
11	11	FOUR TOPS' GREATEST HITS	Four Tops (Tamla Motown)
12	12	A GIFT FROM A FLOWER TO A GARDEN	Donovan (Pye)
9	13	LIVE AT THE TALK OF THE TOWN	Diana Ross & the Supremes (Tamla Motown)
14	14	SHER-OO!	Cilla Black (Parlophone)
-	15	13 SMASH HITS	Tom Jones (Decca)

25 May 1968

LW	TW	Album	Artist (Label)
1	1	THIS IS SOUL	Various Artists (Atlantic)
2	2	JOHN WESLEY HARDING	Bob Dylan (CBS)
3	3	SCOTT 2	Scott Walker (Philips)
4	4	HISTORY OF OTIS REDDING	Otis Redding (Volt)
6	5	SMASH HITS	Jimi Hendrix Experience (Track)
5	6	THE SOUND OF MUSIC	Soundtrack (RCA)
7	7	SUPREMES' GREATEST HITS	Supremes (Tamla Motown)
10	8	PETER GREEN'S FLEETWOOD MAC	Fleetwood Mac (Blue Horizon)
-	9	THE DOCK OF THE BAY	Otis Redding (Stax)
9	10	THE JUNGLE BOOK	Soundtrack (Disneyland)
8	11	THE HANGMAN'S BEAUTIFUL DAUGHTER	Incredible String Band (Elektra)
12	12	A GIFT FROM A FLOWER TO A GARDEN	Donovan (Pye)
11	13	FOUR TOPS' GREATEST HITS	Four Tops (Tamla Motown)
-	14	LOVE ANDY	Andy Williams (CBS)
-	15	BUDDY HOLLY'S GREATEST HITS	Buddy Holly (Ace of Hearts)

1 June 1968

LW	TW	Album	Artist (Label)
1	1	THIS IS SOUL	Various Artists (Atlantic)
3	2	SCOTT 2	Scott Walker (Philips)
2	3	JOHN WESLEY HARDING	Bob Dylan (CBS)
6	4	THE SOUND OF MUSIC	Soundtrack (RCA)
4	5	HISTORY OF OTIS REDDING	Otis Redding (Volt)
5	6	SMASH HITS	Jimi Hendrix Experience (Track)
9	7	THE DOCK OF THE BAY	Otis Redding (Stax)
8	8	PETER GREEN'S FLEETWOOD MAC	Fleetwood Mac (Blue Horizon)
13	9	LOVE ANDY	Andy Williams (CBS)
10	10	THE JUNGLE BOOK	Soundtrack (Disneyland)
11	11	THE HANGMAN'S BEAUTIFUL DAUGHTER	Incredible String Band (Elektra)
7	12	SUPREMES' GREATEST HITS	Supremes (Tamla Motown)
13	13	FOUR TOPS' GREATEST HITS	Four Tops (Tamla Motown)
-	14	VALLEY OF THE DOLLS	Dionne Warwick (Pye)
12	15	A GIFT FROM A FLOWER TO A GARDEN	Donovan (Pye)

8 June 1968

LW	TW	Album	Artist (Label)
1	1	THIS IS SOUL	Various Artists (Atlantic)
2	2	SCOTT 2	Scott Walker (Philips)
3	3	JOHN WESLEY HARDING	Bob Dylan (CBS)
7	4	THE DOCK OF THE BAY	(CBS)
9	5	LOVE ANDY	Andy Williams (CBS)
4	6	THE SOUND OF MUSIC	Soundtrack (RCA)
5	7	HISTORY OF OTIS REDDING	Otis Redding (Volt)
6	8	SMASH HITS	Jimi Hendrix Experience (Track)
8	8	PETER GREEN'S FLEETWOOD MAC	Fleetwood Mac (Blue Horizon)
-	10	TOM JONES LIVE AT THE TALK OF THE TOWN	Tom Jones (Decca)
11	11	THE HANGMAN'S BEAUTIFUL DAUGHTER	Incredible String Band (Elektra)
10	12	THE JUNGLE BOOK	Soundtrack (Disneyland)
12	13	SUPREMES' GREATEST HITS	Supremes (Tamla Motown)
14	14	VALLEY OF THE DOLLS	Dionne Warwick (Pye)
15	15	A GIFT FROM A FLOWER TO A GARDEN	Donovan (Pye)

15 June 1968

LW	TW	Album	Artist (Label)
1	1	THIS IS SOUL	Various Artists (Atlantic)
3	2	JOHN WESLEY HARDING	Bob Dylan (CBS)
2	3	SCOTT 2	Scott Walker (Philips)
5	4	LOVE ANDY	Andy Williams (CBS)
6	5	THE SOUND OF MUSIC	Soundtrack (RCA)
8	6	SMASH HITS	Jimi Hendrix Experience (Track)
7	7	HISTORY OF OTIS REDDING	Otis Redding (Volt)
4	8	THE DOCK OF THE BAY	Otis Redding (Stax)
-	9	OGDENS NUT GONE FLAKE	Small Faces (Immediate)
13	10	SUPREMES' GREATEST HITS	Supremes (Tamla Motown)
11	11	PETER GREEN'S FLEETWOOD MAC	Fleetwood Mac (Blue Horizon)
12	12	THE JUNGLE BOOK	Soundtrack (Disneyland)
14	13	VALLEY OF THE DOLLS	Dionne Warwick (Pye)
11	14	THE HANGMAN'S BEAUTIFUL DAUGHTER	Incredible String Band (Elektra)
10	15	TOM JONES LIVE AT THE TALK OF THE TOWN	Tom Jones (Decca)

Otis Redding died in December 1967, his plane crashing into a lake. He'd had a British mod following since 1965, with hit singles and an album; for whites his 1967 Monterey Pop Festival performance (besuited, while all around him wore kaftans and bells) had clinched his status as Mr Soul. Now *Otis Blue* had re-entered the charts in February, followed by *History Of Otis Redding*, *Otis Redding In Europe*, and *Dock of the Bay* in May. The posthumous single of that title proved his biggest hit.

June – August 1968

22 June 1968

last week	this week	Title / Artist (label)
1	1	THIS IS SOUL — Various Artists (Atlantic)
9	2	OGDENS NUT GONE FLAKE — Small Faces (Immediate)
4	3	LOVE ANDY — Andy Williams (CBS)
5	4	THE SOUND OF MUSIC — Soundtrack (RCA)
2	5	JOHN WESLEY HARDING — Bob Dylan (CBS)
11	6	PETER GREEN'S FLEETWOOD MAC — Fleetwood Mac (Blue Horizon)
6	7	SMASH HITS — Jimi Hendrix Experience (Track)
3	8	SCOTT 2 — Scott Walker (Philips)
8	9	THE DOCK OF THE BAY — Otis Redding (Stax)
13	10	VALLEY OF THE DOLLS — Dionne Warwick (Pye)
–	11	OPEN — Julie Driscoll & the Brian Auger Trinity (Marmalade)
7	12	HISTORY OF OTIS REDDING — Otis Redding (Volt)
10	13	SUPREMES' GREATEST HITS — Supremes (Tamla Motown)
12	14	THE JUNGLE BOOK — Soundtrack (Disneyland)
14	15	THE HANGMAN'S BEAUTIFUL DAUGHTER — Incredible String Band (Elektra)

29 June 1968

last week	this week	Title / Artist (label)
1	1	THIS IS SOUL — Various Artists (Atlantic)
2	2	OGDENS NUT GONE FLAKE — Small Faces (Immediate)
3	3	LOVE ANDY — Andy Williams (CBS)
5	4	JOHN WESLEY HARDING — Bob Dylan (CBS)
8	5	SCOTT 2 — Scott Walker (Philips)
7	6	SMASH HITS — Jimi Hendrix Experience (Track)
12	7	HISTORY OF OTIS REDDING — Otis Redding (Volt)
4	8	THE SOUND OF MUSIC — Soundtrack (RCA)
11	9	OPEN — Julie Driscoll & the Brian Auger Trinity (Marmalade)
6	10	PETER GREEN'S FLEETWOOD MAC — Fleetwood Mac (Blue Horizon)
9	11	THE DOCK OF THE BAY — Otis Redding (Stax)
10	12	VALLEY OF THE DOLLS — Dionne Warwick (Pye)
–	13	40 BLUE FINGERS FRESHLY PACKED AND READY TO SERVE — Chicken Shack (Blue Horizon)
14	14	THE JUNGLE BOOK — Soundtrack (Disneyland)
–	15	CRAZY WORLD OF ARTHUR BROWN — Crazy World Of Arthur Brown (Track)

6 July 1968

last week	this week	Title / Artist (label)
2	1	OGDENS NUT GONE FLAKE — Small Faces (Immediate)
1	2	THIS IS SOUL — Various Artists (Atlantic)
3	3	LOVE ANDY — Andy Williams (CBS)
8	4	THE SOUND OF MUSIC — Soundtrack (RCA)
10	5	THE DOCK OF THE BAY — Otis Redding (Stax)
5	6	SCOTT 2 — Scott Walker (Philips)
7	7	HONEY — Andy Williams (CBS)
4	8	JOHN WESLEY HARDING — Bob Dylan (CBS)
6	9	SMASH HITS — Jimi Hendrix Experience (Track)
14	10	THE JUNGLE BOOK — Soundtrack (Disneyland)
9	11	OPEN — Julie Driscoll & the Brian Auger Trinity (Marmalade)
15	12	CRAZY WORLD OF ARTHUR — Crazy World Of Arthur Brown (Track)
13	13	40 BLUE FINGERS FRESHLY PACKED AND READY TO SERVE — Chicken Shack (Blue Horizon)
7	14	HISTORY OF OTIS REDDING — Otis Redding (Volt)
10	15	PETER GREEN'S FLEETWOOD MAC — Fleetwood Mac (Blue Horizon)

13 July 1968

last week	this week	Title / Artist (label)
1	1	OGDENS NUT GONE FLAKE — Small Faces (Immediate)
2	2	THIS IS SOUL — Various Artists (Atlantic)
4	3	THE SOUND OF MUSIC — Soundtrack (RCA)
7	4	HONEY — Andy Williams (CBS)
5	5	THE DOCK OF THE BAY — Otis Redding (Stax)
3	6	LOVE ANDY — Andy Williams (CBS)
12	7	CRAZY WORLD OF ARTHUR BROWN — Crazy World Of Arthur Brown (Track)
8	8	JOHN WESLEY HARDING — Bob Dylan (CBS)
11	9	OPEN — Julie Driscoll & the Brian Auger Trinity (Marmalade)
10	10	THE JUNGLE BOOK — Soundtrack (Disneyland)
–	11	BARE WIRES — John Mayall (Decca)
15	12	PETER GREEN'S FLEETWOOD MAC — Fleetwood Mac (Blue Horizon)
–	13	THE BIRDS, THE BEES AND THE MONKEES — Monkees (RCA)
9	14	SMASH HITS — Jimi Hendrix Experience (Track)
6	15	SCOTT 2 — Scott Walker (Philips)

20 July 1968

last week	this week	Title / Artist (label)
1	1	OGDENS NUT GONE FLAKE — Small Faces (Immediate)
3	2	THE SOUND OF MUSIC — Soundtrack (RCA)
2	3	THIS IS SOUL — Various Artists (Atlantic)
4	4	HONEY — Andy Williams (CBS)
7	5	CRAZY WORLD OF ARTHUR BROWN — Crazy World Of Arthur Brown (Track)
10	6	THE JUNGLE BOOK — Soundtrack (Disneyland)
13	7	THE BIRDS, THE BEES AND THE MONKEES — Monkees (RCA)
14	8	SMASH HITS — Jimi Hendrix Experience (Track)
9	9	OPEN — Julie Driscoll & the Brian Auger Trinity (Marmalade)
6	10	LOVE ANDY — Andy Williams (CBS)
12	11	PETER GREEN'S FLEETWOOD MAC — Fleetwood Mac (Blue Horizon)
–	12	40 BLUE FINGERS FRESHLY PACKED AND READY TO SERVE — Chicken Shack (Blue Horizon)
5	13	THE DOCK OF THE BAY — Otis Redding (Stax)
–	14	A SAUCERFUL OF SECRETS — Pink Floyd (Columbia)
8	15	JOHN WESLEY HARDING — Bob Dylan (CBS)

27 July 1968

last week	this week	Title / Artist (label)
1	1	OGDENS NUT GONE FLAKE — Small Faces (Immediate)
3	2	THIS IS SOUL — Various Artists (Atlantic)
5	3	CRAZY WORLD OF ARTHUR BROWN — Crazy World Of Arthur Brown (Track)
–	4	DELILAH — Tom Jones (Decca)
–	5	BOOKENDS — Simon & Garfunkel (CBS)
2	6	THE SOUND OF MUSIC — Soundtrack (RCA)
–	7	A MAN WITHOUT LOVE — Engelbert Humperdinck (Decca)
4	8	HONEY — Andy Williams (CBS)
7	9	THE BIRDS, THE BEES AND THE MONKEES — Monkees (RCA)
14	10	A SAUCERFUL OF SECRETS — Pink Floyd (Columbia)
6	11	THE JUNGLE BOOK — Soundtrack (Disneyland)
11	12	PETER GREEN'S FLEETWOOD MAC — Fleetwood Mac (Blue Horizon)
10	13	LOVE ANDY — Andy Williams (CBS)
8	14	SMASH HITS — Jimi Hendrix Experience (Track)
–	15	TYRANNOSAURUS REX — Tyrannosaurus Rex (Regal Zonophone)

3 August 1968

last week	this week	Title / Artist (label)
5	1	BOOKENDS — Simon & Garfunkel (CBS)
4	2	DELILAH — Tom Jones (Decca)
1	3	OGDENS NUT GONE FLAKE — Small Faces (Immediate)
3	4	CRAZY WORLD OF ARTHUR BROWN — Crazy World Of Arthur Brown (Track)
7	5	A MAN WITHOUT LOVE — Engelbert Humperdinck (Decca)
10	6	BARE WIRES — John Mayall (Decca)
2	7	THIS IS SOUL — Various Artists (Atlantic)
6	8	THE SOUND OF MUSIC — Soundtrack (RCA)
8	9	HONEY — Andy Williams (CBS)
11	10	A SAUCERFUL OF SECRETS — Pink Floyd (Columbia)
15	11	SMASH HITS — Jimi Hendrix Experience (Track)
–	12	THE ROCK MACHINE TURNS YOU ON — Various Artists (CBS)
12	13	THE JUNGLE BOOK — Soundtrack (Disneyland)
–	14	IN SEARCH OF THE LOST CHORD — Moody Blues (Deram)
12	15	PETER GREEN'S FLEETWOOD MAC — Fleetwood Mac (Blue Horizon)

10 August 1968

last week	this week	Title / Artist (label)
2	1	DELILAH — Tom Jones (Decca)
1	2	BOOKENDS — Simon & Garfunkel (CBS)
5	3	A MAN WITHOUT LOVE — Engelbert Humperdinck (Decca)
4	4	CRAZY WORLD OF ARTHUR BROWN — Crazy World Of Arthur Brown (Track)
3	5	OGDENS NUT GONE FLAKE — Small Faces (Immediate)
7	6	THIS IS SOUL — Various Artists (Atlantic)
8	7	THE SOUND OF MUSIC — Soundtrack (RCA)
6	8	BARE WIRES — John Mayall (Decca)
12	9	THE ROCK MACHINE TURNS YOU ON — Various Artists (CBS)
13	10	THE JUNGLE BOOK — Soundtrack (Disneyland)
10	11	A SAUCERFUL OF SECRETS — Pink Floyd (Columbia)
11	12	SMASH HITS — Jimi Hendrix Experience (Track)
14	13	IN SEARCH OF THE LOST CHORD — Moody Blues (Deram)
15	14	PETER GREEN'S FLEETWOOD MAC — Fleetwood Mac (Blue Horizon)
9	15	HONEY — Andy Williams (CBS)

The Incredible String Band, whose third (and classic) album was ending its chart run, were THE British hippy band; led by Celtic folkie Robin Williamson and ex-R&B guitarist Mike Heron, they patented the alternative life: love, peace and rural communality. Their wonderfully wiffly songs, on exotic instruments, wriggled between the charming, the mystical and the twee. It's taken 25 years to restore them from unpersondom to history - and to learn that Mike and Robin loathed each other all along.

August – October 1968

17 August 1968

last week	this week	Title	Artist (Label)
2	1	BOOKENDS	Simon & Garfunkel (CBS)
1	2	DELILAH	Tom Jones (Decca)
3	3	A MAN WITHOUT LOVE	Engelbert Humperdinck (Decca)
7	4	THE SOUND OF MUSIC	Soundtrack (RCA)
4	5	CRAZY WORLD OF ARTHUR BROWN	Crazy World Of Arthur Brown (Track)
8	6	BARE WIRES	John Mayall (Decca)
5	7	OGDENS NUT GONE FLAKE	Small Faces (Immediate)
-	8	HOLLIES' GREATEST HITS	Hollies (Parlophone)
6	9	THIS IS SOUL	Various Artists (Atlantic)
13	9	IN SEARCH OF THE LOST CHORD	Moody Blues (Deram)
11	11	A SAUCERFUL OF SECRETS	Pink Floyd (Columbia)
10	12	THE JUNGLE BOOK	Soundtrack (Disneyland)
-	12	BOOGIE WITH CANNED HEAT	Canned Heat (Liberty)
-	14	WHEELS OF FIRE	Cream (Polydor)
9	15	THE ROCK MACHINE TURNS YOU ON	Various Artists (CBS)

24 August 1968

last week	this week	Title	Artist (Label)
1	1	BOOKENDS	Simon & Garfunkel (CBS)
2	2	DELILAH	Tom Jones (Decca)
8	3	HOLLIES' GREATEST HITS	Hollies (Parlophone)
3	4	A MAN WITHOUT LOVE	Engelbert Humperdinck (Decca)
5	5	CRAZY WORLD OF ARTHUR BROWN	Crazy World Of Arthur Brown (Track)
6	6	BARE WIRES	John Mayall (Decca)
14	7	WHEELS OF FIRE	Cream (Polydor)
9	8	IN SEARCH OF THE LOST CHORD	Moody Blues (Deram)
9	9	THIS IS SOUL	Various Artists (Atlantic)
7	10	OGDENS NUT GONE FLAKE	Small Faces (Immediate)
12	11	THE JUNGLE BOOK	Soundtrack (Disneyland)
12	12	BOOGIE WITH CANNED HEAT	Canned Heat (Liberty)
4	13	THE SOUND OF MUSIC	Soundtrack (RCA)
11	14	A SAUCERFUL OF SECRETS	Pink Floyd (Columbia)
-	15	WHEELS OF FIRE IN THE STUDIO	Cream (Polydor)

31 August 1968

last week	this week	Title	Artist (Label)
1	1	BOOKENDS	Simon & Garfunkel (CBS)
2	2	DELILAH	Tom Jones (Decca)
3	3	HOLLIES' GREATEST HITS	Hollies (Parlophone)
7	4	WHEELS OF FIRE	Cream (Polydor)
8	5	IN SEARCH OF THE LOST CHORD	Moody Blues (Deram)
4	6	A MAN WITHOUT LOVE	Engelbert Humperdinck (Decca)
6	6	BARE WIRES	John Mayall (Decca)
4	8	CRAZY WORLD OF ARTHUR BROWN	Crazy World Of Arthur Brown (Track)
13	9	THE SOUND OF MUSIC	Soundtrack (RCA)
12	10	BOOGIE WITH CANNED HEAT	Canned Heat (Liberty)
11	11	THE JUNGLE BOOK	Soundtrack (Disneyland)
15	11	WHEELS OF FIRE IN THE STUDIO	Cream (Polydor)
9	13	THIS IS SOUL	Various Artists (Atlantic)
10	14	OGDENS NUT GONE FLAKE	Small Faces (Immediate)
-	15	MR. WONDERFUL	Fleetwood Mac (Blue Horizon)

7 September 1968

last week	this week	Title	Artist (Label)
1	1	BOOKENDS	Simon & Garfunkel (CBS)
3	2	HOLLIES' GREATEST HITS	Hollies (Parlophone)
2	3	DELILAH	Tom Jones (Decca)
4	4	WHEELS OF FIRE	Cream (Polydor)
5	5	IN SEARCH OF THE LOST CHORD	Moody Blues (Deram)
6	6	A MAN WITHOUT LOVE	Engelbert Humperdinck (Decca)
9	7	THE SOUND OF MUSIC	Soundtrack (RCA)
8	8	CRAZY WORLD OF ARTHUR BROWN	Crazy World Of Arthur Brown (Track)
6	9	BARE WIRES	John Mayall (Decca)
10	10	BOOGIE WITH CANNED HEAT	Canned Heat (Liberty)
15	10	MR WONDERFUL	Fleetwood Mac (Blue Horizon)
13	12	THIS IS SOUL	Various Artists (Atlantic)
11	13	WHEELS OF FIRE IN THE STUDIO	Cream (Polydor)
11	14	THE JUNGLE BOOK	Soundtrack (Disneyland)
14	15	OGDENS NUT GONE FLAKE	Small Faces (Immediate)

14 September 1968

last week	this week	Title	Artist (Label)
1	1	BOOKENDS	Simon & Garfunkel (CBS)
2	2	HOLLIES' GREATEST HITS	Hollies (Parlophone)
3	3	DELILAH	Tom Jones (Decca)
4	4	WHEELS OF FIRE	Cream (Polydor)
10	5	MR. WONDERFUL	Fleetwood Mac (Blue Horizon)
5	6	IN SEARCH OF THE LOST CHORD	Moody Blues (Deram)
7	7	THE SOUND OF MUSIC	Soundtrack (RCA)
10	8	BOOGIE WITH CANNED HEAT	Canned Heat (Liberty)
6	9	A MAN WITHOUT LOVE	Engelbert Humperdinck (Decca)
12	10	THIS IS SOUL	Various Artists (Atlantic)
-	11	THE SEEKERS AT THE TALK OF THE TOWN	Seekers (Columbia)
14	12	THE JUNGLE BOOK	Soundtrack (Disneyland)
8	13	CRAZY WORLD OF ARTHUR BROWN	Crazy World Of Arthur Brown (Track)
9	14	BARE WIRES	John Mayall (Decca)
-	15	JOHNNY CASH AT FOLSOM PRISON	Johnny Cash (CBS)

21 September 1968

last week	this week	Title	Artist (Label)
2	1	HOLLIES' GREATEST HITS	Hollies (Parlophone)
1	2	BOOKENDS	Simon & Garfunkel (CBS)
3	3	DELILAH	Tom Jones (Decca)
5	4	MR. WONDERFUL	Fleetwood Mac (Blue Horizon)
4	5	WHEELS OF FIRE	Cream (Polydor)
11	5	THE SEEKERS AT THE TALK OF THE TOWN	Seekers (Columbia)
8	7	BOOGIE WITH CANNED HEAT	Canned Heat (Liberty)
6	8	IN SEARCH OF THE LOST CHORD	Moody Blues (Deram)
9	9	A MAN WITHOUT LOVE	Engelbert Humperdinck (Decca)
-	10	WAITING FOR THE SUN	Doors (Elektra)
7	11	THE SOUND OF MUSIC	Soundtrack (RCA)
10	12	THIS IS SOUL	Various Artists (Atlantic)
-	13	ARETHA NOW	Aretha Franklin (Atlantic)
12	14	THE JUNGLE BOOK	Soundtrack (Disneyland)
14	15	BARE WIRES	John Mayall (Decca)

28 September 1968

last week	this week	Title	Artist (Label)
1	1	HOLLIES' GREATEST HITS	Hollies (Parlophone)
3	2	DELILAH	Tom Jones (Decca)
2	3	BOOKENDS	Simon & Garfunkel (CBS)
5	4	THE SEEKERS AT THE TALK OF THE TOWN	Seekers (Columbia)
5	5	WHEELS OF FIRE	Cream (Polydor)
9	6	A MAN WITHOUT LOVE	Engelbert Humperdinck (Decca)
7	7	BOOGIE WITH CANNED HEAT	Canned Heat (Liberty)
11	7	THE SOUND OF MUSIC	Soundtrack (RCA)
4	9	MR. WONDERFUL	Fleetwood Mac (Blue Horizon)
10	10	WAITING FOR THE SUN	Doors (Elektra)
8	11	IN SEARCH OF THE LOST CHORD	Moody Blues (Deram)
13	12	ARETHA NOW	Aretha Franklin (Atlantic)
14	13	THE JUNGLE BOOK	Soundtrack (Disneyland)
-	14	IDEA	Bee Gees (Polydor)
-	15	JOHNNY CASH AT FOLSOM PRISON	Johnny Cash (CBS)

5 October 1968

last week	this week	Title	Artist (Label)
1	1	HOLLIES' GREATEST HITS	Hollies (Parlophone)
4	2	THE SEEKERS AT THE TALK OF THE TOWN	Seekers (Columbia)
3	3	BOOKENDS	Simon & Garfunkel (CBS)
2	4	DELILAH	Tom Jones (Decca)
7	5	BOOGIE WITH CANNED HEAT	Canned Heat (Liberty)
5	6	WHEELS OF FIRE	Cream (Polydor)
7	7	THE SOUND OF MUSIC	Soundtrack (RCA)
11	8	IN SEARCH OF THE LOST CHORD	Moody Blues (Deram)
10	9	WAITING FOR THE SUN	Doors (Elektra)
6	10	A MAN WITHOUT LOVE	Engelbert Humperdinck (Decca)
14	11	IDEA	Bee Gees (Polydor)
9	12	MR. WONDERFUL	Fleetwood Mac (Blue Horizon)
12	13	ARETHA NOW	Aretha Franklin (Atlantic)
13	13	THE JUNGLE BOOK	Soundtrack (Disneyland)
15	15	JOHNNY CASH AT FOLSOM PRISON	Johnny Cash (CBS)

Most unusual was the charting of both a single-LP and a double of Cream's *Wheels Of Fire* - the double far more successfully. September saw the launch of the Beatles' Apple label. CBS' prog-rock compilation *Rock Machine Turns You On* was an interesting title.

The previous year the BBC had banned the Beatles' Day In The Life because it included "I'd love to turn you on." Now it was already a hip marketing phrase. Later the BBC would adapt it for their jingle "Radio 1 really turns you on".

12 October 1968

last week	this week	
1	1	HOLLIES' GREATEST HITS Hollies (Parlophone)
2	2	THE SEEKERS AT THE TALK OF THE TOWN Seekers (Columbia)
3	3	BOOKENDS Simon & Garfunkel (CBS)
11	4	IDEA Bee Gees (Polydor)
7	5	THE SOUND OF MUSIC Soundtrack (RCA)
5	6	BOOGIE WITH CANNED HEAT Canned Heat (Liberty)
4	7	DELILAH Tom Jones (Decca)
9	8	WAITING FOR THE SUN Doors (Elektra)
8	9	IN SEARCH OF THE LOST CHORD Moody Blues (Deram)
6	10	WHEELS OF FIRE Cream (Polydor)
10	11	A MAN WITHOUT LOVE Engelbert Humperdinck (Decca)
15	12	JOHNNY CASH AT FOLSOM PRISON Johnny Cash (CBS)
12	13	MR. WONDERFUL Fleetwood Mac (Blue Horizon)
13	14	ARETHA NOW Aretha Franklin (Atlantic)
13	15	THE JUNGLE BOOK Soundtrack (Disneyland)

19 October 1968

last week	this week	
1	1	HOLLIES' GREATEST HITS Hollies (Parlophone)
2	2	THE SEEKERS AT THE TALK OF THE TOWN Seekers (Columbia)
3	3	BOOKENDS Simon & Garfunkel (CBS)
5	4	THE SOUND OF MUSIC Soundtrack (RCA)
4	5	IDEA Bee Gees (Polydor)
7	6	DELILAH Tom Jones (Decca)
10	7	WHEELS OF FIRE Cream (Polydor)
11	8	A MAN WITHOUT LOVE Engelbert Humperdinck (Decca)
6	9	BOOGIE WITH CANNED HEAT Canned Heat (Liberty)
8	10	WAITING FOR THE SUN Doors (Elektra)
9	11	IN SEARCH OF THE LOST CHORD Moody Blues (Deram)
14	12	ARETHA NOW Aretha Franklin (Atlantic)
12	13	JOHNNY CASH AT FOLSOM PRISON Johnny Cash (CBS)
-	14	THE WORLD OF MANTOVANI Mantovani (Decca)
-	15	TRAFFIC Traffic (Island)

26 October 1968

last week	this week	
1	1	HOLLIES' GREATEST HITS Hollies (Parlophone)
2	2	THE SEEKERS AT THE TALK OF THE TOWN Seekers (Columbia)
5	3	IDEA Bee Gees (Polydor)
3	4	BOOKENDS Simon & Garfunkel (CBS)
4	5	THE SOUND OF MUSIC Soundtrack (RCA)
6	6	DELILAH Tom Jones (Decca)
15	7	TRAFFIC Traffic (Island)
-	8	THIS WAS Jethro Tull (Island)
14	9	THE WORLD OF MANTOVANI Mantovani (Decca)
7	10	WHEELS OF FIRE Cream (Polydor)
8	11	A MAN WITHOUT LOVE Engelbert Humperdinck (Decca)
11	12	IN SEARCH OF THE LOST CHORD Moody Blues (Deram)
9	13	BOOGIE WITH CANNED HEAT Canned Heat (Liberty)
10	14	WAITING FOR THE SUN Doors (Elektra)
13	15	JOHNNY CASH AT FOLSOM PRISON Johnny Cash (CBS)

2 November 1968

last week	this week	
1	1	HOLLIES' GREATEST HITS Hollies (Parlophone)
2	2	THE SEEKERS AT THE TALK OF THE TOWN Seekers (Columbia)
3	3	IDEA Bee Gees (Polydor)
5	4	THE SOUND OF MUSIC Soundtrack (RCA)
8	5	THIS WAS Jethro Tull (Island)
4	6	BOOKENDS Simon & Garfunkel (CBS)
7	7	TRAFFIC Traffic (Island)
6	8	DELILAH Tom Jones (Decca)
-	9	THE GOOD, THE BAD & THE UGLY Soundtrack (United Artists)
-	10	ELECTRIC LADYLAND Jimi Hendrix Experience (Track)
11	11	A MAN WITHOUT LOVE Engelbert Humperdinck (Decca)
14	12	WAITING FOR THE SUN Doors (Elektra)
10	13	WHEELS OF FIRE Cream (Polydor)
-	14	THE JUNGLE BOOK Soundtrack (Disneyland)
13	15	BOOGIE WITH CANNED HEAT Canned Heat (Liberty)

9 November 1968

last week	this week	
1	1	HOLLIES' GREATEST HITS Hollies (Parlophone)
2	2	THE SEEKERS AT THE TALK OF THE TOWN Seekers (Columbia)
3	3	IDEA Bee Gees (Polydor)
4	4	THE SOUND OF MUSIC Soundtrack (RCA)
10	5	ELECTRIC LADYLAND Jimi Hendrix Experience (Track)
6	6	BOOKENDS Simon & Garfunkel (CBS)
5	7	THIS WAS Jethro Tull (Island)
9	8	THE GOOD, THE BAD & THE UGLY Soundtrack (United Artists)
8	9	DELILAH Tom Jones (Decca)
7	10	TRAFFIC Traffic (Island)
11	11	A MAN WITHOUT LOVE Engelbert Humperdinck (Decca)
-	12	FELICIANO Jose Feliciano (RCA)
-	13	JOHNNY CASH AT FOLSOM PRISON Johnny Cash (CBS)
13	14	WHEELS OF FIRE Cream (Polydor)
-	15	THE WORLD OF MANTOVANI Mantovani (Decca)

16 November 1968

last week	this week	
1	1	HOLLIES' GREATEST HITS Hollies (Parlophone)
2	2	THE SEEKERS AT THE TALK OF THE TOWN Seekers (Columbia)
8	3	THE GOOD, THE BAD & THE UGLY Soundtrack (United Artists)
5	4	ELECTRIC LADYLAND Jimi Hendrix Experience (Track)
4	5	THE SOUND OF MUSIC Soundtrack (RCA)
7	6	THIS WAS Jethro Tull (Island)
3	7	IDEA Bee Gees (Polydor)
6	8	BOOKENDS Simon & Garfunkel (CBS)
-	9	THE GRADUATE Soundtrack (CBS)
12	10	FELICIANO Jose Feliciano (RCA)
15	11	THE WORLD OF MANTOVANI Mantovani (Decca)
-	12	BEST OF THE SEEKERS Seekers (Columbia)
13	13	THE JUNGLE BOOK Soundtrack (Disneyland)
9	14	DELILAH Tom Jones (Decca)
11	15	A MAN WITHOUT LOVE Engelbert Humperdinck (Decca)

23 November 1968

last week	this week	
1	1	HOLLIES' GREATEST HITS Hollies (Parlophone)
4	2	ELECTRIC LADYLAND Jimi Hendrix Experience (Track)
2	3	THE SEEKERS AT THE TALK OF THE TOWN Seekers (Columbia)
3	4	THE GOOD, THE BAD & THE UGLY Soundtrack (United Artists)
9	5	THE GRADUATE Soundtrack (CBS)
12	6	BEST OF THE SEEKERS Seekers (Columbia)
5	7	THE SOUND OF MUSIC Soundtrack (RCA)
10	8	FELICIANO Jose Feliciano (RCA)
6	9	THIS WAS Jethro Tull (Island)
11	10	THE WORLD OF MANTOVANI Mantovani (Decca)
-	11	BEST OF THE BEACH BOYS VOL 3 Beach Boys (Capitol)
14	12	DELILAH Tom Jones (Decca)
7	13	IDEA Bee Gees (Polydor)
8	13	BOOKENDS Simon & Garfunkel (CBS)
	15	A MAN WITHOUT LOVE Engelbert Humperdinck (Decca)

30 November 1968

last week	this week	
-	1	THE BEATLES Beatles (Apple)
6	2	BEST OF THE SEEKERS Seekers (Columbia)
2	3	ELECTRIC LADYLAND Jimi Hendrix Experience (Track)
1	4	HOLLIES' GREATEST HITS Hollies (Parlophone)
7	5	THE SOUND OF MUSIC Soundtrack (RCA)
4	6	THE GOOD, THE BAD & THE UGLY Soundtrack (United Artists)
5	7	THE GRADUATE Soundtrack (CBS)
3	8	THE SEEKERS AT THE TALK OF THE TOWN Seekers (Columbia)
10	9	THE WORLD OF MANTOVANI Mantovani (Decca)
8	10	FELICIANO Jose Feliciano (RCA)
11	11	BEST OF THE BEACH BOYS VOL 3 Beach Boys (Capitol)
9	12	THIS WAS Jethro Tull (Island)
13	13	IDEA Bee Gees (Polydor)
-	14	VAL Val Doonican (Pye)
12	15	DELILAH Tom Jones (Decca)

This period starts with an Apple single topping the chart, Mary Hopkins' *Those Were The Days*; it ends with an Apple album topping it, the Beatles' White Album. This displaced *Hollies' Greatest Hits*, top for ten weeks. By now the Hollies had racked up eighteen hit singles, starting with minor 1963 hit *Just Like Me*, running through thirteen Top 10s to *Listen To Me*, peaking at 7 this October/November. And you never met anyone who admitted to liking them: not even their own Graham Nash.

December 1968

last this
week

		7 December 1968			**14 December 1968**			**21 December 1968**
1	1	THE BEATLES Beatles (Apple)	1	1	THE BEATLES Beatles (Apple)	1	1	THE BEATLES Beatles (Apple)
2	2	BEST OF THE SEEKERS	2	2	BEST OF THE SEEKERS	2	2	BEST OF THE SEEKERS
		Seekers (Columbia)			Seekers (Columbia)			Seekers (Columbia)
4	3	HOLLIES' GREATEST HITS	-	3	BEGGARS BANQUET	3	3	BEGGARS BANQUET
		Hollies (Parlophone)			Rolling Stones (Decca)			Rolling Stones (Decca)
3	4	ELECTRIC LADYLAND	10	4	THE WORLD OF VAL DOONICAN	4	4	THE WORLD OF VAL DOONICAN
		Jimi Hendrix Experience (Track)			Val Doonican (Decca)			Val Doonican (Decca)
6	5	THE GOOD, THE BAD & THE	3	5	HOLLIES' GREATEST HITS	7	5	THE SOUND OF MUSIC
		UGLY			Hollies (Parlophone)			Soundtrack (RCA)
		Soundtrack (United Artists)	5	6	THE GOOD, THE BAD & THE	9	6	THE GRADUATE
7	5	THE GRADUATE			UGLY			Soundtrack (CBS)
		Soundtrack (CBS)			Soundtrack (United Artists)	15	7	HELP YOURSELF
5	7	THE SOUND OF MUSIC	7	7	THE SOUND OF MUSIC			Tom Jones (Decca)
		Soundtrack (RCA)			Soundtrack (RCA)	11	8	THE WORLD OF MANTOVANI
9	8	THE WORLD OF MANTOVANI	4	8	ELECTRIC LADYLAND			Mantovani (Decca)
		Mantovani (Decca)			Jimi Hendrix Experience (Track)	8	9	ELECTRIC LADYLAND
8	9	THE SEEKERS AT THE TALK OF	5	9	THE GRADUATE			Jimi Hendrix Experience (Track)
		THE TOWN Seekers (Columbia)			Soundtrack (CBS)	5	10	HOLLIES' GREATEST HITS
-	10	THE WORLD OF VAL DOONICAN	11	10	BEST OF THE BEACH BOYS			Hollies (Parlophone)
		Val Doonican (Decca)			VOL 3 Beach Boys (Capitol)	12	11	VAL Val Doonican Pye)
11	11	BEST OF THE BEACH BOYS	8	11	THE WORLD OF MANTOVANI	6	12	THE GOOD, THE BAD & THE
		VOL 3 Beach Boys (Capitol)			Mantovani (Decca)			UGLY
12	11	THIS WAS Jethro Tull (Island)	14	12	VAL Val Doonican (Pye)			Soundtrack (United Artists)
10	13	FELICIANO Jose Feliciano (RCA)	13	13	FELICIANO Jose Feliciano (RCA)	-	13	I PRETEND
14	14	VAL Val Doonican (Pye)	-	14	THE WORLD OF THE			Des O'Connor (Columbia)
15	15	DELILAH Tom Jones (Decca)			BACHELORS Bachelors (Decca)	14	14	THE WORLD OF THE
			-	15	HELP YOURSELF			BACHELORS Bachelors (Decca)
					Tom Jones (Decca)	13	15	FELICIANO Jose Feliciano (RCA)

December is the gruellest month. The spirit of the Black & White Minstrels conjured up a chart embracing not just Mantovani (and of course *The Sound Of Music*) but TWO Val Doonicans and TWO Seekers albums. Perhaps after all those psychedelic epic records called *Piper At The Gates of Dawn* and *In Search of the Lost Chord* (Pink Floyd and Moody Blues), some people's aunties bought them *The Seekers At The Talk Of The Town* by mistake. NME staff certainly made a mistake. No doubt too busy seeking that lost chord at the gates of dawn, they couldn't quite get it together to sort out the year-end's chart, man. Those were the days, my friend.

January – February 1969

4 January 1969

last week	this week	Title	Artist (Label)
1	1	THE BEATLES	Beatles (Apple)
2	2	BEST OF THE SEEKERS	Seekers (Columbia)
3	3	BEGGARS BANQUET	Rolling Stones (Decca)
4	4	THE WORLD OF VAL DOONICAN	Val Doonican (Decca)
5	5	THE SOUND OF MUSIC	Soundtrack (RCA)
6	6	THE GRADUATE	Soundtrack (CBS)
7	7	HELP YOURSELF	Tom Jones (Decca)
12	8	THE GOOD, THE BAD & THE UGLY	Soundtrack (United Artists)
10	9	HOLLIES' GREATEST HITS	Hollies (Parlophone)
14	10	THE WORLD OF THE BACHELORS	Bachelors (Decca)
11	11	VAL	Val Doonican (Pye)
8	12	THE WORLD OF MANTOVANI	Mantovani (Decca)
13	12	I PRETEND	Des O'Connor (Columbia)
9	14	ELECTRIC LADYLAND	Jimi Hendrix (Track)
-	15	A TOUCH OF SADNESS	Jim Reeves (RCA)

11 January 1969

last week	this week	Title	Artist (Label)
1	1	THE BEATLES	Beatles (Apple)
2	2	BEST OF THE SEEKERS	Seekers (Columbia)
3	3	BEGGARS BANQUET	Rolling Stones (Decca)
4	4	THE WORLD OF VAL DOONICAN	Val Doonican (Decca)
5	5	THE SOUND OF MUSIC	Soundtrack (RCA)
6	6	THE GRADUATE	Soundtrack (CBS)
9	7	HOLLIES' GREATEST HITS	Hollies (Parlophone)
7	8	HELP YOURSELF	Tom Jones (Decca)
12	9	THE WORLD OF MANTOVANI	Mantovani (Decca)
-	10	FELICIANO	Jose Feliciano (RCA)
14	11	ELECTRIC LADYLAND	Jimi Hendrix (Track)
11	12	VAL	Val Doonican (Pye)
-	13	BOOKENDS	Simon & Garfunkel (CBS)
14	THIS WAS	Jethro Tull (Island)
8	15	THE GOOD, THE BAD & THE UGLY	Soundtrack (United Artists)

18 January 1969

last week	this week	Title	Artist (Label)
1	1	THE BEATLES	Beatles (Apple)
2	2	BEST OF THE SEEKERS	Seekers (Columbia)
5	3	THE SOUND OF MUSIC	Soundtrack (RCA)
3	4	BEGGARS BANQUET	Rolling Stones (Decca)
4	4	THE WORLD OF VAL DOONICAN	Val Doonican (Decca)
8	6	HELP YOURSELF	Tom Jones (Decca)
9	7	THE WORLD OF MANTOVANI	Mantovani (Decca)
6	8	THE GRADUATE	Soundtrack (CBS)
7	9	HOLLIES' GREATEST HITS	Hollies (Parlophone)
-	10	DIANA ROSS & THE SUPREMES' GREATEST HITS	Diana Ross & the Supremes (Tamla Motown)
11	BEST OF NAT 'KING' COLE	Nat 'King' Cole (Capitol)
11	BEST OF THE BEACH BOYS VOL 3	Beach Boys (Capitol)
12	13	VAL	Val Doonican (Pye)
10	14	FELICIANO	Jose Feliciano (RCA)
-	15	FOUR TOPS' GREATEST HITS	Four Tops (Tamla Motown)

25 January 1969

last week	this week	Title	Artist (Label)
1	1	THE BEATLES	Beatles (Apple)
2	2	BEST OF THE SEEKERS	Seekers (Columbia)
8	3	THE GRADUATE	Soundtrack (CBS)
4	4	BEGGARS BANQUET	Rolling Stones (Decca)
4	5	THE WORLD OF VAL DOONICAN	Val Doonican (Decca)
3	6	THE SOUND OF MUSIC	Soundtrack (RCA)
6	7	HELP YOURSELF	Tom Jones (Decca)
-	8	DIANA ROSS AND THE SUPREMES JOIN THE TEMPTATIONS	Diana Ross & the Supremes with the Temptations (Tamla Motown)
-	9	YELLOW SUBMARINE	Beatles (Apple)
11	10	BEST OF THE BEACH BOYS VOL 3	Beach Boys (Capitol)
9	11	HOLLIES' GREATEST HITS	Hollies (Parlophone)
-	12	HAIR	London Cast (Polydor)
13	13	VAL	Val Doonican (Pye)
7	13	THE WORLD OF MANTOVANI	Mantovani (Decca)
10	15	DIANA ROSS & THE SUPREMES' GREATEST HITS	Diana Ross & the Supremes (Tamla Motown)

1 February 1969

last week	this week	Title	Artist (Label)
2	1	BEST OF THE SEEKERS	Seekers (Columbia)
1	2	THE BEATLES	Beatles (Apple)
9	3	YELLOW SUBMARINE	Beatles (Apple)
8	4	DIANA ROSS AND THE SUPREMES JOIN THE TEMPTATIONS	Diana Ross & the Supremes with the Temptations (Tamla Motown)
3	5	THE GRADUATE	Soundtrack (CBS)
6	6	THE SOUND OF MUSIC	Soundtrack (RCA)
4	7	BEGGARS BANQUET	Rolling Stones (Decca)
5	8	THE WORLD OF VAL DOONICAN	Val Doonican (Decca)
7	9	HELP YOURSELF	Tom Jones (Decca)
12	10	HAIR	London Cast (Polydor)
-	11	FELICIANO	Jose Feliciano (RCA)
-	12	SOUNDS OF SILENCE	Simon & Garfunkel (CBS)
-	12	LOVE CHILD	Diana Ross & the Supremes (Tamla Motown)
13	14	WORLD OF MANTOVANI	Mantovani (Decca)
10	14	BEST OF THE BEACH BOYS VOL 3	Beach Boys (Capitol)

8 February 1969

last week	this week	Title	Artist (Label)
4	1	DIANA ROSS AND THE SUPREMES JOIN THE TEMPTATIONS	Diana Ross & the Supremes with the Temptations (Tamla Motown)
2	2	THE BEATLES	Beatles (Apple)
1	3	BEST OF THE SEEKERS	Seekers (Columbia)
5	4	THE GRADUATE	Soundtrack (CBS)
3	5	YELLOW SUBMARINE	Beatles (Apple)
6	6	THE SOUND OF MUSIC	Soundtrack (RCA)
8	7	THE WORLD OF VAL DOONICAN	Val Doonican (Decca)
7	8	BEGGARS BANQUET	Rolling Stones (Decca)
10	9	HAIR	London Cast (Polydor)
11	10	FELICIANO	Jose Feliciano (RCA)
12	11	LOVE CHILD	Diana Ross & the Supremes (Tamla Motown)
-	12	HOLLIES' GREATEST HITS	Hollies (Parlophone)
9	13	HELP YOURSELF	Tom Jones (Decca)
-	13	BEST OF NAT 'KING' COLE	Nat 'King' Cole (Capitol)
-	15	BRITISH MOTOWN CHARTBUSTERS VOL 2	Various Artists (Tamla Motown)

Week 1's only real new entrant was Jim Reeves. In May, a rather different country would top the charts, Dylan's *Nashville Skyline*, with his 1962 song *Girl Of The North Country* as a duet with Johnny Cash, whose own *Johnny Cash At Folsom Prison* had hit in 1968. But the new country rock owed more to a highly influential LP that hadn't made the charts at all, *Sweetheart Of The Rodeo* by the Byrds.

February – April 1969

15 February 1969

1	1	DIANA ROSS AND THE SUPREMES JOIN THE TEMPTATIONS Diana Ross & the Supremes with the Temptations (Tamla Motown)
3	2	BEST OF THE SEEKERS Seekers (Columbia)
5	3	YELLOW SUBMARINE Beatles (Apple)
2	4	THE BEATLES Beatles (Apple)
4	5	THE GRADUATE Soundtrack (CBS)
6	6	THE SOUND OF MUSIC Soundtrack (RCA)
9	7	HAIR London Cast (Polydor)
8	8	BEGGARS BANQUET Rolling Stones (Decca)
11	8	LOVE CHILD Diana Ross & the Supremes (Tamla Motown)
7	10	THE WORLD OF VAL DOONICAN Val Doonican (Decca)
10	11	FELICIANO Jose Feliciano (RCA)
-	12	THE GOOD, THE BAD & THE UGLY Soundtrack (United Artists)
13	13	HELP YOURSELF Tom Jones (Decca)
12	13	HOLLIES' GREATEST HITS Hollies (Parlophone)
15	15	BRITISH MOTOWN CHARTBUSTERS VOL 2 Various Artists (Tamla Motown)

22 February 1969

1	1	DIANA ROSS AND THE SUPREMES JOIN THE TEMPTATIONS Diana Ross & the Supremes with the Temptations (Tamla Motown)
2	2	BEST OF THE SEEKERS Seekers (Columbia)
4	3	THE BEATLES Beatles (Apple)
3	4	YELLOW SUBMARINE Beatles (Apple)
6	5	THE SOUND OF MUSIC Soundtrack (RCA)
5	6	THE GRADUATE Soundtrack (CBS)
7	7	HAIR London Cast (Polydor)
10	8	THE WORLD OF VAL DOONICAN Val Doonican (Decca)
8	9	BEGGARS BANQUET Rolling Stones (Decca)
13	9	HELP YOURSELF Tom Jones (Decca)
11	11	FELICIANO Jose Feliciano (RCA)
-	12	THE WORLD OF MANTOVANI Mantovani (Decca)
8	13	LOVE CHILD Diana Ross & the Supremes (Tamla Motown)
-	14	EARLY ALPERT Herb Alpert (Marble Arch)
-	15	'NUFF SAID Nina Simone (RCA)

1 March 1969

1	1	DIANA ROSS AND THE SUPREMES JOIN THE TEMPTATIONS Diana Ross & the Supremes with the Temptations (Tamla Motown)
2	2	BEST OF THE SEEKERS Seekers (Columbia)
3	3	THE BEATLES Beatles (Apple)
4	4	YELLOW SUBMARINE Beatles (Apple)
7	4	HAIR London Cast (Polydor)
6	6	THE GRADUATE Soundtrack (CBS)
5	7	THE SOUND OF MUSIC Soundtrack (RCA)
8	8	THE WORLD OF VAL DOONICAN Val Doonican (Decca)
-	9	ENGELBERT Engelbert Humperdinck (Decca)
-	10	DISRAELI GEARS Cream (Reaction)
9	11	BEGGARS BANQUET Rolling Stones (Decca)
-	12	STONEDHENGE Ten Years After (Deram)
12	13	THE WORLD OF MANTOVANI Mantovani (Decca)
9	14	HELP YOURSELF Tom Jones (Decca)
11	15	FELICIANO Jose Feliciano (RCA)

8 March 1969

1	1	DIANA ROSS AND THE SUPREMES JOIN THE TEMPTATIONS Diana Ross & the Supremes with the Temptations (Tamla Motown)
2	2	BEST OF THE SEEKERS Seekers (Columbia)
-	3	GOODBYE Cream (Polydor)
9	4	ENGELBERT Engelbert Humperdinck (Decca)
-	5	POSTCARD Mary Hopkin (Apple)
3	6	THE BEATLES Beatles (Apple)
7	7	THE SOUND OF MUSIC Soundtrack (RCA)
6	8	THE GRADUATE Soundtrack (CBS)
12	9	STONEDHENGE Ten Years After (Deram)
4	10	HAIR London Cast (Polydor)
4	11	YELLOW SUBMARINE Beatles (Apple)
8	12	THE WORLD OF VAL DOONICAN Val Doonican (Decca)
-	13	BEST OF CILLA BLACK Cilla Black (Parlophone)
13	14	THE WORLD OF MANTOVANI Mantovani (Decca)
11	15	BEGGARS BANQUET Rolling Stones (Decca)

15 March 1969

1	1	DIANA ROSS AND THE SUPREMES JOIN THE TEMPTATIONS Diana Ross & the Supremes with the Temptations (Tamla Motown)
3	2	GOODBYE Cream (Polydor)
2	3	BEST OF THE SEEKERS Seekers (Columbia)
4	4	ENGELBERT Engelbert Humperdinck (Decca)
12	5	THE WORLD OF VAL DOONICAN Val Doonican (Decca)
5	6	POSTCARD Mary Hopkin (Apple)
6	7	THE BEATLES Beatles (Apple)
7	8	THE SOUND OF MUSIC Soundtrack (RCA)
-	9	ROCK MACHINE I LOVE YOU Various Artists (CBS)
9	10	STONEDHENGE Ten Years After (Deram)
10	11	HAIR London Cast (Polydor)
-	12	YOU CAN ALL JOIN IN Various Artists (Island)
14	13	THE WORLD OF MANTOVANI Mantovani (Decca)
11	14	YELLOW SUBMARINE Beatles (Apple)
-	15	20/20 Beach Boys (Capitol)

22 March 1969

2	1	GOODBYE Cream (Polydor)
3	2	BEST OF THE SEEKERS Seekers (Columbia)
1	3	DIANA ROSS AND THE SUPREMES JOIN THE TEMPTATIONS Diana Ross & the Supremes with the Temptations (Tamla Motown)
4	4	ENGELBERT Engelbert Humperdinck (Decca)
6	5	POSTCARD Mary Hopkin (Apple)
8	6	THE SOUND OF MUSIC Soundtrack (RCA)
11	7	HAIR London Cast (Polydor)
9	8	ROCK MACHINE I LOVE YOU Various Artists (CBS)
-	9	PETER SARSTEDT Peter Sarstedt (United Artists)
7	10	THE BEATLES Beatles (Apple)
10	11	STONEDHENGE Ten Years After (Deram)
13	12	THE WORLD OF MANTOVANI Mantovani (Decca)
5	13	THE WORLD OF VAL DOONICAN Val Doonican (Decca)
-	14	THE FOUR AND ONLY SEEKERS Seekers (Music for Pleasure)
-	15	GENTLE ON MY MIND Dean Martin (Reprise)

29 March 1969

1	1	GOODBYE Cream (Polydor)
2	2	BEST OF THE SEEKERS Seekers (Columbia)
3	3	DIANA ROSS AND THE SUPREMES JOIN THE TEMPTATIONS Diana Ross & the Supremes with the Temptations (Tamla Motown)
4	4	ENGELBERT Engelbert Humperdinck (Decca)
6	5	THE SOUND OF MUSIC Soundtrack (RCA)
8	6	ROCK MACHINE I LOVE YOU Various Artists (CBS)
5	7	POSTCARD Mary Hopkin (Apple)
-	8	ODESSA Bee Gees (Polydor)
11	9	STONEDHENGE Ten Years After (Deram)
10	10	THE BEATLES Beatles (Apple)
9	11	PETER SARSTEDT Peter Sarstedt (United Artists)
13	12	THE WORLD OF VAL DOONICAN Val Doonican (Decca)
7	13	HAIR London Cast (Polydor)
14	14	THE FOUR AND ONLY SEEKERS Seekers (Music for Pleasure)
-	15	YOU CAN ALL JOIN IN Various Artists (Island)

5 April 1969

1	1	GOODBYE Cream (Polydor)
2	2	BEST OF THE SEEKERS Seekers (Columbia)
3	3	DIANA ROSS AND THE SUPREMES JOIN THE TEMPTATIONS Diana Ross & the Supremes with the Temptations (Tamla Motown)
6	4	ROCK MACHINE I LOVE YOU Various Artists (CBS)
4	5	ENGELBERT Engelbert Humperdinck (Decca)
11	6	PETER SARSTEDT Peter Sarstedt (United Artists)
5	7	THE SOUND OF MUSIC Soundtrack (RCA)
15	8	YOU CAN ALL JOIN IN Various Artists (Island)
-	8	20/20 Beach Boys (Capitol)
10	10	THE BEATLES Beatles (Apple)
12	11	THE WORLD OF VAL DOONICAN Val Doonican (Decca)
-	12	GENTLE ON MY MIND Dean Martin (Reprise)
8	13	ODESSA Bee Gees (Polydor)
-	14	SCOTT 3 Scott Walker (Philips)
-	15	FAMILY ENTERTAINMENT Family (Reprise)

Cream returned, straight in at No.3 with the apt *Goodbye*. Cream was disbanding, becoming so-called supergroup Blind Faith, which was so ego-unwieldy it would manage only two gigs and one LP. Another sign of the times was the entry of Nina Simone, long a favourite of those who said Ray Charles was too pop. An accomplished pianist, Simone responded to the new Black Power politics, her rich voice articulating this anger on a 1968 single still in the charts in February, *Ain't Got No - I Got Life*.

12 April 1969

last week	this week	Title / Artist (Label)
1	1	GOODBYE Cream (Polydor)
2	2	BEST OF THE SEEKERS Seekers (Columbia)
5	3	ENGELBERT Engelbert Humperdinck (Decca)
7	4	THE SOUND OF MUSIC Soundtrack (RCA)
14	5	SCOTT 3 Scott Walker (Philips)
3	6	DIANA ROSS AND THE SUPREMES JOIN THE TEMPTATIONS Diana Ross & the Supremes with the Temptations (Tamla Motown)
12	7	GENTLE ON MY MIND Dean Martin (Reprise)
8	8	20/20 Beach Boys (Capitol)
-	9	POSTCARD Mary Hopkin (Apple)
-	10	WORLD STAR FESTIVAL Various Artists (Philips)
11	11	THE WORLD OF VAL DOONICAN Val Doonican (Decca)
13	12	ODESSA Bee Gees (Polydor)
4	13	ROCK MACHINE I LOVE YOU Various Artists (CBS)
10	14	THE BEATLES Beatles (Apple)
15	15	FAMILY ENTERTAINMENT Family (Reprise)

19 April 1969

this week	Title / Artist (Label)
2 1	BEST OF THE SEEKERS Seekers (Columbia)
1 2	GOODBYE Cream (Polydor)
5 3	SCOTT 3 Scott Walker (Philips)
4 4	THE SOUND OF MUSIC Soundtrack (RCA)
6 5	DIANA ROSS AND THE SUPREMES JOIN THE TEMPTATIONS Diana Ross & the Supremes with the Temptations (Tamla Motown)
9 6	POSTCARD Mary Hopkin (Apple)
- 7	OLIVER! Soundtrack (RCA)
- 8	LED ZEPPELIN Led Zeppelin (Atlantic)
- 9	HAIR London Cast (Polydor)
3 10	ENGELBERT Engelbert Humperdinck (Decca)
8 11	20/20 Beach Boys (Capitol)
7 12	GENTLE ON MY MIND Dean Martin (Reprise)
13 13	ROCK MACHINE I LOVE YOU Various Artists (CBS)
14 14	THE BEATLES Beatles (Apple)
11 15	THE WORLD OF VAL DOONICAN Val Doonican (Decca)

26 April 1969

this week	Title / Artist (Label)
1 1	GOODBYE Cream (Polydor)
1 2	BEST OF THE SEEKERS Seekers (Columbia)
3 3	SCOTT 3 Scott Walker (Philips)
7 4	OLIVER! Soundtrack (RCA)
4 5	THE SOUND OF MUSIC Soundtrack (RCA)
- 6	ELVIS: NBC TV SPECIAL Elvis Presley (RCA)
9 7	HAIR London Cast (Polydor)
6 8	POSTCARD Mary Hopkin (Apple)
8 9	LED ZEPPELIN Led Zeppelin (Atlantic)
- 10	ON THE THRESHOLD OF A DREAM Moody Blues (Deram)
12 11	GENTLE ON MY MIND Dean Martin (Reprise)
11 12	20/20 Beach Boys (Capitol)
5 13	DIANA ROSS AND THE SUPREMES JOIN THE TEMPTATIONS Diana Ross & the Supremes with the Temptations (Tamla Motown)
- 14	THE WORLD OF BLUES POWER Various Artists (Decca)
15 15	THE WORLD OF VAL DOONICAN Val Doonican (Decca)

3 May 1969

this week	Title / Artist (Label)
1 1	GOODBYE Cream (Polydor)
2 2	BEST OF THE SEEKERS Seekers (Columbia)
9 3	ON THE THRESHOLD OF A DREAM Moody Blues (Deram)
7 4	HAIR London Cast (Polydor)
9 5	LED ZEPPELIN Led Zeppelin (Atlantic)
11 6	GENTLE ON MY MIND Dean Martin (Reprise)
4 7	OLIVER! Soundtrack (RCA)
5 8	THE SOUND OF MUSIC Soundtrack (RCA)
3 9	SCOTT 3 Scott Walker (Philips)
8 10	POSTCARD Mary Hopkin (Apple)
6 11	ELVIS: NBC TV SPECIAL Elvis Presley (RCA)
12 12	20/20 Beach Boys (Capitol)
- 13	SONGS FROM A ROOM Leonard Cohen (CBS)
13 14	DIANA ROSS AND THE SUPREMES JOIN THE TEMPTATIONS Diana Ross & the Supremes with the Temptations (Tamla Motown)
14 15	THE WORLD OF BLUES POWER Various Artists (Decca)

10 May 1969

this week	Title / Artist (Label)
3 1	ON THE THRESHOLD OF A DREAM Moody Blues (Deram)
2 2	BEST OF THE SEEKERS Seekers (Columbia)
1 3	GOODBYE Cream (Polydor)
11 4	ELVIS: NBC TV SPECIAL Elvis Presley (RCA)
13 5	SONGS FROM A ROOM Leonard Cohen (CBS)
7 6	OLIVER! Soundtrack (RCA)
6 7	GENTLE ON MY MIND Dean Martin (Reprise)
5 8	LED ZEPPELIN Led Zeppelin (Atlantic)
4 9	HAIR London Cast (Polydor)
8 10	THE SOUND OF MUSIC Soundtrack (RCA)
10 11	POSTCARD Mary Hopkin (Apple)
9 12	SCOTT 3 Scott Walker (Philips)
- 13	NASHVILLE SKYLINE Bob Dylan (CBS)
- 14	HOLLIES SING DYLAN Hollies (Parlophone)
- 15	DUSTY IN MEMPHIS Dusty Springfield (Philips)

17 May 1969

this week	Title / Artist (Label)
1 1	ON THE THRESHOLD OF A DREAM Moody Blues (Deram)
13 2	NASHVILLE SKYLINE Bob Dylan (CBS)
2 3	BEST OF THE SEEKERS Seekers (Columbia)
4 4	ELVIS: NBC TV SPECIAL Elvis Presley (RCA)
3 5	GOODBYE Cream (Polydor)
5 6	SONGS FROM A ROOM Leonard Cohen (CBS)
6 7	OLIVER! Soundtrack (RCA)
14 8	HOLLIES SING DYLAN Hollies (Parlophone)
9 9	HAIR London Cast (Polydor)
8 10	LED ZEPPELIN Led Zeppelin (Atlantic)
7 11	GENTLE ON MY MIND Dean Martin (Reprise)
10 12	THE SOUND OF MUSIC Soundtrack (RCA)
- 13	20/20 Beach Boys (Capitol)
11 14	POSTCARD Mary Hopkin (Apple)
15 15	DUSTY IN MEMPHIS Dusty Springfield (Philips)

24 May 1969

this week	Title / Artist (Label)
2 1	NASHVILLE SKYLINE Bob Dylan (CBS)
1 2	ON THE THRESHOLD OF A DREAM Moody Blues (Deram)
3 3	BEST OF THE SEEKERS Seekers (Columbia)
8 4	HOLLIES SING DYLAN Hollies (Parlophone)
5 5	GOODBYE Cream (Polydor)
4 6	ELVIS: NBC TV SPECIAL Elvis Presley (RCA)
6 7	SONGS FROM A ROOM Leonard Cohen (CBS)
7 8	OLIVER! Soundtrack (RCA)
9 9	HAIR London Cast (Polydor)
10 10	LED ZEPPELIN Led Zeppelin (Atlantic)
12 11	THE SOUND OF MUSIC Soundtrack (RCA)
11 12	GENTLE ON MY MIND Dean Martin (Reprise)
- 13	THE BEATLES Beatles (Apple)
- 14	THE WORLD OF MANTOVANI Mantovani (Decca)
- 15	THE FOUR AND ONLY SEEKERS Seekers (Music for Pleasure)

31 May 1969

this week	Title / Artist (Label)
1 1	NASHVILLE SKYLINE Bob Dylan (CBS)
2 2	ON THE THRESHOLD OF A DREAM Moody Blues (Deram)
4 3	HOLLIES SING DYLAN Hollies (Parlophone)
3 4	BEST OF THE SEEKERS Seekers (Columbia)
6 5	ELVIS: NBC TV SPECIAL Elvis Presley (RCA)
9 6	HAIR London Cast (Polydor)
5 7	GOODBYE Cream (Polydor)
7 8	SONGS FROM A ROOM Leonard Cohen (CBS)
- 9	TOMMY Who (Track)
10 10	LED ZEPPELIN Led Zeppelin (Atlantic)
8 11	OLIVER! Soundtrack (RCA)
11 12	THE SOUND OF MUSIC Soundtrack (RCA)
14 13	THE WORLD OF MANTOVANI Mantovani (Decca)
- 14	SURROUND YOURSELF WITH CILLA Cilla Black (Parlophone)
12 15	GENTLE ON MY MIND Dean Martin (Reprise)

Pop journalist, and later film-maker Tony Palmer, at this time the Observer's pop critic, paid this tribute to the disbanding group Cream (Eric Clapton, Jack Bruce and Ginger Baker): "Cream have almost single-handedly given pop a musical authority which only the deaf cannot acknowledge and only the ignorant cannot hear." Which was odd because he also said that the Beatles had given us "a deluge of joyful music-making which only the ignorant will not hear and only the deaf will not acknowledge."

June – July 1969

7 June 1969

last week	this week	entry
1	1	NASHVILLE SKYLINE — Bob Dylan (CBS)
2	2	ON THE THRESHOLD OF A DREAM — Moody Blues (Deram)
3	3	HOLLIES SING DYLAN — Hollies (Parlophone)
7	4	GOODBYE — Cream (Polydor)
4	5	BEST OF THE SEEKERS — Seekers (Columbia)
6	6	HAIR — London Cast (Polydor)
8	7	SONGS FROM A ROOM — Leonard Cohen (CBS)
11	8	OLIVER! — Soundtrack (RCA)
5	9	ELVIS: NBC TV SPECIAL — Elvis Presley (RCA)
9	10	TOMMY — Who (Track)
-	11	MY WAY — Frank Sinatra (Reprise)
12	12	THE SOUND OF MUSIC — Soundtrack (RCA)
10	13	LED ZEPPELIN — Led Zeppelin (Atlantic)
-	13	2001: A SPACE ODYSSEY — Soundtrack (MGM)
13	15	THE WORLD OF MANTOVANI — Mantovani (Decca)
14	16	SURROUND YOURSELF WITH CILLA — Cilla Black (Parlophone)
15	17	GENTLE ON MY MIND — Dean Martin (Reprise)
-	18	OVER AND OVER — Nana Mouskouri (Fontana)
-	19	THE WORLD OF VAL DOONICAN — Val Doonican (Decca)
-	19	SOUNDS OF SILENCE — Simon & Garfunkel (CBS)

14 June 1969

last week	this week	entry
1	1	NASHVILLE SKYLINE — Bob Dylan (CBS)
2	2	ON THE THRESHOLD OF A DREAM — Moody Blues (Deram)
6	3	HAIR — London Cast (Polydor)
11	4	MY WAY — Frank Sinatra (Reprise)
5	5	BEST OF THE SEEKERS — Seekers (Columbia)
8	6	OLIVER! — Soundtrack (RCA)
10	7	TOMMY — Who (Track)
3	8	HOLLIES SING DYLAN — Hollies (Parlophone)
4	9	GOODBYE — Cream (Polydor)
13	10	2001: A SPACE ODYSSEY — Soundtrack (MGM)
7	11	SONGS FROM A ROOM — Leonard Cohen (CBS)
9	12	ELVIS: NBC TV SPECIAL — Elvis Presley (RCA)
12	13	THE SOUND OF MUSIC — Soundtrack (RCA)
17	14	GENTLE ON MY MIND — Dean Martin (Reprise)
-	15	20/20 — Beach Boys (Capitol)
15	16	THE WORLD OF MANTOVANI — Mantovani (Decca)
13	17	LED ZEPPELIN — Led Zeppelin (Atlantic)
-	18	THE BEATLES — Beatles (Apple)
19	19	THE WORLD OF VAL DOONICAN — Val Doonican (Decca)
-	19	UNICORN — Tyrannosaurus Rex (Regal Zonophone)

21 June 1969

last week	this week	entry
4	1	MY WAY — Frank Sinatra (Reprise)
1	2	NASHVILLE SKYLINE — Bob Dylan (CBS)
2	3	ON THE THRESHOLD OF A DREAM — Moody Blues (Deram)
10	4	2001: A SPACE ODYSSEY — Soundtrack (MGM)
6	5	OLIVER! — Soundtrack (RCA)
3	6	HAIR — London Cast (Polydor)
5	7	BEST OF THE SEEKERS — Seekers (Columbia)
9	8	GOODBYE — Cream (Polydor)
7	9	TOMMY — Who (Track)
8	10	HOLLIES SING DYLAN — Hollies (Parlophone)
-	11	THIS IS TOM JONES — Tom Jones (Decca)
19	12	THE WORLD OF VAL DOONICAN — Val Doonican (Decca)
14	13	GENTLE ON MY MIND — Dean Martin (Reprise)
12	14	ELVIS: NBC TV SPECIAL — Elvis Presley (RCA)
17	15	LED ZEPPELIN — Led Zeppelin (Atlantic)
13	16	THE SOUND OF MUSIC — Soundtrack (RCA)
11	16	SONGS FROM A ROOM — Leonard Cohen (CBS)
16	18	THE WORLD OF MANTOVANI — Mantovani (Decca)
-	19	RAY CONNIFF, HIS ORCHESTRA, HIS CHORUS, HIS SINGERS, HIS SOUND — Ray Conniff (CBS)
19	20	UNICORN — Tyrannosaurus Rex (Regal Zonophone)

28 June 1969

last week	this week	entry
1	1	MY WAY — Frank Sinatra (Reprise)
11	2	THIS IS TOM JONES — Tom Jones (Decca)
2	3	NASHVILLE SKYLINE — Bob Dylan (CBS)
9	4	TOMMY — Who (Track)
6	5	HAIR — London Cast (Polydor)
4	6	2001: A SPACE ODYSSEY — Soundtrack (MGM)
3	7	ON THE THRESHOLD OF A DREAM — Moody Blues (Deram)
5	8	OLIVER! — Soundtrack (RCA)
19	9	RAY CONNIFF, HIS ORCHESTRA, HIS CHORUS, HIS SINGERS, HIS SOUND — Ray Conniff (CBS)
-	10	OVER AND OVER — Nana Mouskouri (Fontana)
7	11	BEST OF THE SEEKERS — Seekers (Columbia)
-	12	FLAMING STAR — Elvis Presley (RCA International)
-	13	ACCORDING TO MY HEART — Jim Reeves (RCA International)
18	14	THE WORLD OF MANTOVANI — Mantovani (Decca)
13	15	GENTLE ON MY MIND — Dean Martin (Reprise)
10	16	HOLLIES SING DYLAN — Hollies (Parlophone)
14	17	ELVIS: NBC TV SPECIAL — Elvis Presley (RCA)
12	18	THE WORLD OF VAL DOONICAN — Val Doonican (Decca)
15	19	LED ZEPPELIN — Led Zeppelin (Atlantic)
-	19	THE WORLD OF CHARLIE KUNZ — Charlie Kunz (Decca)

5 July 1969

last week	this week	entry
2	1	THIS IS TOM JONES — Tom Jones (Decca)
1	2	MY WAY — Frank Sinatra (Reprise)
3	3	NASHVILLE SKYLINE — Bob Dylan (CBS)
7	4	ON THE THRESHOLD OF A DREAM — Moody Blues (Deram)
12	5	FLAMING STAR — Elvis Presley (RCA International)
13	6	ACCORDING TO MY HEART — Jim Reeves (RCA International)
5	7	HAIR — London Cast (Polydor)
9	8	RAY CONNIFF, HIS ORCHESTRA, HIS CHORUS, HIS SINGERS, HIS SOUND — Ray Conniff (CBS)
6	9	2001: A SPACE ODYSSEY — Soundtrack (MGM)
4	10	TOMMY — Who (Track)
8	11	OLIVER! — Soundtrack (RCA)
11	12	BEST OF THE SEEKERS — Seekers (Columbia)
17	13	ELVIS: NBC TV SPECIAL — Elvis Presley (RCA)
-	14	SOUNDTRACK FROM THE FILM 'MORE' — Pink Floyd (Columbia)
15	15	HOLLIES SING DYLAN — Hollies (Parlophone)
-	16	TCB — Diana Ross & the Supremes & the Temptations (Tamla Motown)
-	16	SCOTT WALKER SINGS SONGS FROM HIS TV SERIES — Scott Walker (Philips)
18	18	THE WORLD OF VAL DOONICAN — Val Doonican (Decca)
-	19	THE SOUND OF MUSIC — Soundtrack (RCA)
15	20	GENTLE ON MY MIND — Dean Martin (Reprise)

12 July 1969

last week	this week	entry
1	1	THIS IS TOM JONES — Tom Jones (Decca)
5	2	FLAMING STAR — Elvis Presley (RCA International)
6	3	ACCORDING TO MY HEART — Jim Reeves (RCA International)
2	4	MY WAY — Frank Sinatra (Reprise)
3	5	NASHVILLE SKYLINE — Bob Dylan (CBS)
4	6	ON THE THRESHOLD OF A DREAM — Moody Blues (Deram)
16	7	SCOTT WALKER SINGS SONGS FROM HIS TV SERIES — Scott Walker (Philips)
8	8	RAY CONNIFF, HIS ORCHESTRA, HIS CHORUS, HIS SINGERS, HIS SOUND — Ray Conniff (CBS)
7	9	HAIR — London Cast (Polydor)
11	10	OLIVER! — Soundtrack (RCA)
9	11	2001: A SPACE ODYSSEY — Soundtrack (MGM)
10	12	TOMMY — Who (Track)
16	13	TCB — Diana Ross & the Supremes & the Temptations (Tamla Motown)
-	14	LED ZEPPELIN — Led Zeppelin (Atlantic)
13	15	ELVIS: NBC TV SPECIAL — Elvis Presley (RCA)
12	16	BEST OF THE SEEKERS — Seekers (Columbia)
14	16	SOUNDTRACK FROM THE FILM 'MORE' — Pink Floyd (Columbia)
-	18	THE BEST OF CLIFF — Cliff Richard (Columbia)
15	19	HOLLIES SING DYLAN — Hollies (Parlophone)
18	20	THE WORLD OF VAL DOONICAN — Val Doonican (Decca)

The Top 15 became the Top 20; mad titles abounded. The Moody Blues, a competent beat group with an excellent debut single, Go Now, copied from Bessie Banks, had metamorphosed rapidly into mystical-twaddle concept-album makers, their latest being On *The Threshold Of A Dream*, temporarily on the threshold of the top. Listening to the Moody Blues, a reviewer was later to suggest, was "like mainlining yoghurt". Preferable, surely, to the practice urged by June 7's No.16: *Surround Yourself With Cilla*.

July – August 1969

19 July 1969

last week	this week	Title	Artist (label)
1	1	THIS IS TOM JONES	Tom Jones (Decca)
3	2	ACCORDING TO MY HEART	Jim Reeves (RCA International)
2	3	FLAMING STAR	Elvis Presley (RCA International)
4	4	MY WAY	Frank Sinatra (Reprise)
6	5	ON THE THRESHOLD OF A DREAM	Moody Blues (Deram)
5	6	NASHVILLE SKYLINE	Bob Dylan (CBS)
7	7	SCOTT WALKER SINGS SONGS FROM HIS TV SERIES	Scott Walker (Philips)
11	8	2001: A SPACE ODYSSEY	Soundtrack (MGM)
10	9	OLIVER!	Soundtrack (RCA)
16	10	SOUNDTRACK FROM THE FILM 'MORE'	Pink Floyd (Columbia)
9	11	HAIR	London Cast (Polydor)
8	12	RAY CONNIFF, HIS ORCHESTRA, HIS CHORUS, HIS SINGERS, HIS SOUND	Ray Conniff (CBS)
13	13	TCB	Diana Ross & the Supremes & the Temptations (Tamla Motown)
18	14	THE BEST OF CLIFF	Cliff Richard (Columbia)
20	15	THE WORLD OF VAL DOONICAN	Val Doonican (Decca)
-	16	THE BEATLES	Beatles (Apple)
14	17	LED ZEPPELIN	Led Zeppelin (Atlantic)
16	18	BEST OF THE SEEKERS	Seekers (Columbia)
15	19	ELVIS: NBC TV SPECIAL	Elvis Presley (RCA)
12	20	TOMMY	Who (Track)

26 July 1969

last week	this week	Title	Artist (label)
1	1	THIS IS TOM JONES	Tom Jones (Decca)
3	2	FLAMING STAR	Elvis Presley (RCA International)
2	3	ACCORDING TO MY HEART	Jim Reeves (RCA International)
4	4	MY WAY	Frank Sinatra (Reprise)
8	5	2001: A SPACE ODYSSEY	Soundtrack (MGM)
14	6	THE BEST OF CLIFF	Cliff Richard (Columbia)
13	7	TCB	Diana Ross & the Supremes & the Temptations (Tamla Motown)
6	8	NASHVILLE SKYLINE	Bob Dylan (CBS)
11	9	HAIR	London Cast (Polydor)
9	10	OLIVER!	Soundtrack (RCA)
17	11	LED ZEPPELIN	Led Zeppelin (Atlantic)
5	12	ON THE THRESHOLD OF A DREAM	Moody Blues (Deram)
7	13	SCOTT WALKER SINGS SONGS FROM HIS TV SERIES	Scott Walker (Philips)
10	14	SOUNDTRACK FROM THE FILM 'MORE'	Pink Floyd (Columbia)
-	15	THE WORLD OF MANTOVANI	Mantovani (Decca)
12	16	RAY CONNIFF, HIS ORCHESTRA, HIS CHORUS, HIS SINGERS, HIS SOUND	Ray Conniff (CBS)
15	17	THE WORLD OF VAL DOONICAN	Val Doonican (Decca)
-	18	THE SOUND OF MUSIC	Soundtrack (RCA)
-	19	GOODBYE	Cream (Polydor)
-	20	THE WORLD OF THE BACHELORS	Bachelors (Decca)

2 August 1969

last week	this week	Title	Artist (label)
2	1	FLAMING STAR	Elvis Presley (RCA International)
3	2	ACCORDING TO MY HEART	Jim Reeves (RCA International)
5	3	2001: A SPACE ODYSSEY	Soundtrack (MGM)
1	4	THIS IS TOM JONES	Tom Jones (Decca)
6	5	THE BEST OF CLIFF	Cliff Richard (Columbia)
10	6	OLIVER!	Soundtrack (RCA)
9	7	HAIR	London Cast (Polydor)
8	8	NASHVILLE SKYLINE	Bob Dylan (CBS)
-	8	STAND UP	Jethro Tull (Island)
4	10	MY WAY	Frank Sinatra (Reprise)
17	11	THE WORLD OF VAL DOONICAN	Val Doonican (Decca)
-	12	UNHALFBRICKING	Fairport Convention (Island)
-	13	BEST OF THE SEEKERS	Seekers (Columbia)
11	14	LED ZEPPELIN	Led Zeppelin (Atlantic)
20	15	THE WORLD OF THE BACHELORS	Bachelors (Decca)
16	16	RAY CONNIFF, HIS ORCHESTRA, HIS CHORUS, HIS SINGERS, HIS SOUND	Ray Conniff (CBS)
7	17	TCB	Diana Ross & the Supremes & the Temptations (Tamla Motown)
18	18	THE SOUND OF MUSIC	Soundtrack (RCA)
12	18	ON THE THRESHOLD OF A DREAM	Moody Blues (Deram)
-	20	WARM	Herb Alpert & the Tijuana Brass (A&M)

9 August 1969

last week	this week	Title	Artist (label)
8	1	STAND UP	Jethro Tull (Island)
1	2	FLAMING STAR	Elvis Presley (RCA International)
2	3	ACCORDING TO MY HEART	Jim Reeves (RCA International)
3	4	2001: A SPACE ODYSSEY	Soundtrack (MGM)
4	5	THIS IS TOM JONES	Tom Jones (Decca)
7	6	HAIR	London Cast (Polydor)
10	7	MY WAY	Frank Sinatra (Reprise)
8	8	NASHVILLE SKYLINE	Bob Dylan (CBS)
12	9	UNHALFBRICKING	Fairport Convention (Island)
5	10	THE BEST OF CLIFF	Cliff Richard (Columbia)
16	11	RAY CONNIFF, HIS ORCHESTRA, HIS CHORUS, HIS SINGERS, HIS SOUND	Ray Conniff (CBS)
14	12	LED ZEPPELIN	Led Zeppelin (Atlantic)
11	13	THE WORLD OF VAL DOONICAN	Val Doonican (Decca)
17	14	TCB	Diana Ross & the Supremes & the Temptations (Tamla Motown)
-	15	AHEAD RINGS OUT	Blodwyn Pig (Island)
18	16	ON THE THRESHOLD OF A DREAM	Moody Blues (Deram)
13	17	BEST OF THE SEEKERS	Seekers (Columbia)
6	18	OLIVER!	Soundtrack (RCA)
-	19	THE BEST OF GLENN MILLER	Glenn Miller (RCA International)
20	20	WARM	Herb Alpert & the Tijuana Brass (A&M)

16 August 1969

last week	this week	Title	Artist (label)
1	1	STAND UP	Jethro Tull (Island)
4	2	2001: A SPACE ODYSSEY	Soundtrack (MGM)
3	3	ACCORDING TO MY HEART	Jim Reeves (RCA International)
2	4	FLAMING STAR	Elvis Presley (RCA International)
6	5	HAIR	London Cast (Polydor)
5	6	THIS IS TOM JONES	Tom Jones (Decca)
18	7	OLIVER!	Soundtrack (RCA)
-	8	FROM ELVIS IN MEMPHIS	Elvis Presley (RCA)
8	9	UNHALFBRICKING	Fairport Convention (Island)
10	10	THE BEST OF CLIFF	Cliff Richard (Columbia)
16	11	ON THE THRESHOLD OF A DREAM	Moody Blues (Deram)
17	12	BEST OF THE SEEKERS	Seekers (Columbia)
15	12	AHEAD RINGS OUT	Blodwyn Pig (Island)
12	14	LED ZEPPELIN	Led Zeppelin (Atlantic)
7	15	MY WAY	Frank Sinatra (Reprise)
-	15	JOHNNY CASH AT SAN QUENTIN	Johnny Cash (CBS)
19	17	THE BEST OF GLENN MILLER	Glenn Miller (RCA International)
11	18	RAY CONNIFF, HIS ORCHESTRA, HIS CHORUS, HIS SINGERS, HIS SOUND	Ray Conniff (CBS)
8	19	NASHVILLE SKYLINE	Bob Dylan (CBS)
13	20	THE WORLD OF VAL DOONICAN	Val Doonican (Decca)

23 August 1969

last week	this week	Title	Artist (label)
1	1	STAND UP	Jethro Tull (Island)
2	2	2001: A SPACE ODYSSEY	Soundtrack (MGM)
3	3	ACCORDING TO MY HEART	Jim Reeves (RCA International)
8	4	FROM ELVIS IN MEMPHIS	Elvis Presley (RCA)
4	5	FLAMING STAR	Elvis Presley (RCA International)
7	6	OLIVER!	Soundtrack (RCA)
9	7	UNHALFBRICKING	Fairport Convention (Island)
5	8	HAIR	London Cast (Polydor)
6	9	THIS IS TOM JONES	Tom Jones (Decca)
12	10	AHEAD RINGS OUT	Blodwyn Pig (Island)
15	11	JOHNNY CASH AT SAN QUENTIN	Johnny Cash (CBS)
10	12	THE BEST OF CLIFF	Cliff Richard (Columbia)
14	13	LED ZEPPELIN	Led Zeppelin (Atlantic)
20	14	THE WORLD OF VAL DOONICAN	Val Doonican (Decca)
-	15	AS SAFE AS YESTERDAY IS	Humble Pie (Immediate)
11	16	ON THE THRESHOLD OF A DREAM	Moody Blues (Deram)
18	16	RAY CONNIFF, HIS ORCHESTRA, HIS CHORUS, HIS SINGERS, HIS SOUND	Ray Conniff (CBS)
15	18	MY WAY	Frank Sinatra (Reprise)
-	19	THE PIOUS BIRD OF GOOD OMEN	Fleetwood Mac (Blue Horizon)
17	20	THE BEST OF GLENN MILLER	Glenn Miller (RCA International)

In 1968, signalling the end of his run of abysmal movies, Elvis made his momentous TV "comeback": but this didn't get shown on TV in Britain till 1969, so a renewal of interest in Presley was only now reflected in healthy chart returns. Even now, one of the charting albums was *Flaming Star*, a typically careless compilation and named after an old film, 1960's *Flaming Star*. Meanwhile on July 3, aged 25, the most genuinely sinister of the Rolling Stones, Brian Jones, died in his swimming pool.

August – October 1969

last this week

30 August 1969

LW	TW	Title	Artist (Label)
1	1	STAND UP	Jethro Tull (Island)
4	2	FROM ELVIS IN MEMPHIS	Elvis Presley (RCA)
2	3	2001: A SPACE ODYSSEY	Soundtrack (MGM)
3	4	ACCORDING TO MY HEART	Jim Reeves (RCA International)
11	5	JOHNNY CASH AT SAN QUENTIN	Johnny Cash (CBS)
7	6	UNHALFBRICKING	Fairport Convention (Island)
8	7	HAIR	London Cast (Polydor)
5	8	FLAMING STAR	Elvis Presley (RCA International)
6	9	OLIVER!	Soundtrack (RCA)
13	10	LED ZEPPELIN	Led Zeppelin (Atlantic)
10	11	AHEAD RINGS OUT	Blodwyn Pig (Island)
-	12	LOOKING BACK	John Mayall (Decca)
9	13	THIS IS TOM JONES	Tom Jones (Decca)
16	14	RAY CONNIFF, HIS ORCHESTRA, HIS CHORUS, HIS SINGERS, HIS SOUND	Ray Conniff (CBS)
12	15	THE BEST OF CLIFF	Cliff Richard (Columbia)
15	16	AS SAFE AS YESTERDAY IS	Humble Pie (Immediate)
-	17	THE SOUND OF MUSIC	Soundtrack (RCA)
14	18	THE WORLD OF VAL DOONICAN	Val Doonican (Decca)
-	19	CROSBY, STILLS & NASH	Crosby, Stills & Nash (Atlantic)
-	20	JIM REEVES AND SOME FRIENDS	Jim Reeves (RCA)

6 September 1969

LW	TW	Title	Artist (Label)
1	1	STAND UP	Jethro Tull (Island)
2	2	FROM ELVIS IN MEMPHIS	Elvis Presley (RCA)
5	3	JOHNNY CASH AT SAN QUENTIN	Johnny Cash (CBS)
7	4	HAIR	London Cast (Polydor)
3	5	2001: A SPACE ODYSSEY	Soundtrack (MGM)
9	6	OLIVER!	Soundtrack (RCA)
4	7	ACCORDING TO MY HEART	Jim Reeves (RCA)
6	8	UNHALFBRICKING	Fairport Convention (Island)
11	9	AHEAD RINGS OUT	Blodwyn Pig (Island)
12	10	LOOKING BACK	John Mayall (Decca)
8	11	FLAMING STAR	Elvis Presley (RCA International)
-	12	THE PIOUS BIRD OF GOOD OMEN	Fleetwood Mac (Blue Horizon)
17	13	THE SOUND OF MUSIC	Soundtrack (RCA)
-	13	NICE	Nice (Immediate)
-	15	ON THE THRESHOLD OF A DREAM	Moody Blues (Deram)
16	16	THE WORLD OF MANTOVANI	Mantovani (Decca)
10	17	LED ZEPPELIN	Led Zeppelin (Atlantic)
16	17	AS SAFE AS YESTERDAY IS	Humble Pie (Immediate)
13	19	THIS IS TOM JONES	Tom Jones (Decca)
14	20	RAY CONNIFF, HIS ORCHESTRA, HIS CHORUS, HIS SINGERS, HIS SOUND	Ray Conniff (CBS)

13 September 1969

LW	TW	Title	Artist (Label)
1	1	STAND UP	Jethro Tull (Island)
-	2	BLIND FAITH	Blind Faith (Polydor)
3	3	JOHNNY CASH AT SAN QUENTIN	Johnny Cash (CBS)
2	4	FROM ELVIS IN MEMPHIS	Elvis Presley (RCA)
6	5	OLIVER!	Soundtrack (RCA)
13	6	NICE	Nice (Immediate)
4	7	HAIR	London Cast (Polydor)
7	8	ACCORDING TO MY HEART	Jim Reeves (RCA)
5	9	2001: A SPACE ODYSSEY	Soundtrack (MGM)
9	10	AHEAD RINGS OUT	Blodwyn Pig (Island)
8	11	UNHALFBRICKING	Fairport Convention (Island)
10	12	LOOKING BACK	John Mayall (Decca)
11	13	FLAMING STAR	Elvis Presley (RCA International)
-	14	THE BEST OF CLIFF	Cliff Richard (Columbia)
17	15	LED ZEPPELIN	Led Zeppelin (Atlantic)
17	16	AS SAFE AS YESTERDAY IS	Humble Pie (Immediate)
-	17	NASHVILLE SKYLINE	Bob Dylan (CBS)
-	18	BEST OF THE SEEKERS	Seekers (Columbia)
20	19	RAY CONNIFF, HIS ORCHESTRA, HIS CHORUS, HIS SINGERS, HIS SOUND	Ray Conniff (CBS)
-	20	CROSBY, STILLS & NASH	Crosby, Stills & Nash (Atlantic)

20 September 1969

LW	TW	Title	Artist (Label)
3	1	JOHNNY CASH AT SAN QUENTIN	Johnny Cash (CBS)
2	2	BLIND FAITH	Blind Faith (Polydor)
1	3	STAND UP	Jethro Tull (Island)
6	4	NICE	Nice (Immediate)
4	5	FROM ELVIS IN MEMPHIS	Elvis Presley (RCA)
7	6	HAIR	London Cast (Polydor)
8	7	ACCORDING TO MY HEART	Jim Reeves (RCA International)
5	8	OLIVER!	Soundtrack (RCA)
11	9	UNHALFBRICKING	Fairport Convention (Island)
17	10	NASHVILLE SKYLINE	Bob Dylan (CBS)
9	11	2001: A SPACE ODYSSEY	Soundtrack (MGM)
-	12	THE SOUND OF MUSIC	Soundtrack (RCA)
12	13	LOOKING BACK	John Mayall (Decca)
-	14	THROUGH THE PAST DARKLY (BIG HITS VOL 2)	Rolling Stones (Decca)
15	15	LED ZEPPELIN	Led Zeppelin (Atlantic)
-	16	THE WORLD OF VAL DOONICAN	Val Doonican (Decca)
10	17	AHEAD RINGS OUT	Blodwyn Pig (Island)
13	18	FLAMING STAR	Elvis Presley (RCA International)
20	19	CROSBY, STILLS & NASH	Crosby, Stills & Nash (Atlantic)
16	20	AS SAFE AS YESTERDAY IS	Humble Pie (Immediate)

27 September 1969

LW	TW	Title	Artist (Label)
1	1	JOHNNY CASH AT SAN QUENTIN	Johnny Cash (CBS)
2	2	BLIND FAITH	Blind Faith (Polydor)
3	3	STAND UP	Jethro Tull (Island)
14	4	THROUGH THE PAST DARKLY (BIG HITS VOL 2)	Rolling Stones (Decca)
10	5	NASHVILLE SKYLINE	Bob Dylan (CBS)
4	6	NICE	Nice (Immediate)
6	7	HAIR	London Cast (Polydor)
11	7	2001: A SPACE ODYSSEY	Soundtrack (MGM)
-	10	BEST OF GENE PITNEY	Gene Pitney (Stateside)
8	11	OLIVER!	Soundtrack (RCA)
7	11	ACCORDING TO MY HEART	Jim Reeves (RCA International)
13	13	LOOKING BACK	John Mayall (Decca)
-	14	CLOUD NINE	Temptations (Tamla Motown)
-	15	SONGS FOR A TAILOR	Jack Bruce (Polydor)
16	16	THIS IS TOM JONES	Tom Jones (Decca)
-	17	FUNNY GIRL	Soundtrack (CBS)
-	18	BEST OF THE SEEKERS	Seekers (Columbia)
16	18	THE WORLD OF VAL DOONICAN	Val Doonican (Decca)
-	18	THE BEST OF CLIFF	Cliff Richard (Columbia)

4 October 1969

LW	TW	Title	Artist (Label)
-	1	ABBEY ROAD	Beatles (Apple)
1	2	JOHNNY CASH AT SAN QUENTIN	Johnny Cash (CBS)
4	3	THROUGH THE PAST DARKLY (BIG HITS VOL 2)	Rolling Stones (Decca)
2	4	BLIND FAITH	Blind Faith (Polydor)
3	5	STAND UP	Jethro Tull (Island)
7	6	HAIR	London Cast (Polydor)
11	7	ACCORDING TO MY HEART	Jim Reeves (RCA International)
6	8	NICE	Nice (Immediate)
9	9	FROM ELVIS IN MEMPHIS	Elvis Presley (RCA)
-	9	THE WORLD OF MANTOVANI	Mantovani (Decca)
5	11	NASHVILLE SKYLINE	Bob Dylan (CBS)
12	12	OLIVER!	Soundtrack (RCA)
18	13	THE WORLD OF VAL DOONICAN	Val Doonican (Decca)
15	14	SONGS FOR A TAILOR	Jack Bruce (Polydor)
-	15	SSSSH	Ten Years After (Deram)
7	16	2001: A SPACE ODYSSEY	Soundtrack (MGM)
-	17	RAY CONNIFF, HIS ORCHESTRA, HIS CHORUS, HIS SINGERS, HIS SOUND	Ray Conniff (CBS)
-	18	THE SOUND OF MUSIC	Soundtrack (RCA)
-	19	AHEAD RINGS OUT	Blodwyn Pig (Island)
-	20	LED ZEPPELIN	Led Zeppelin (Atlantic)

More classics in the chart: Fairport Convention's *Unhalfbricking*, a highpoint of English folk-rock, and *Led Zeppelin*, the epoch-making debut album by the biggest white group on Atlantic Records, a group famous for refusing to issue singles. Meanwhile supergroup Blind Faith had played their debut gig in Hyde Park in June, the USA had gone to Woodstock and now 250,000 here went to the 2nd Isle of Wight Festival, at the end of August, for The Who, Marsha Hunt, Richie Havens and Bob Dylan and The Band.

October – November 1969

11 October 1969

last week	this week		
1	1	ABBEY ROAD	Beatles (Apple)
2	2	JOHNNY CASH AT SAN QUENTIN	Johnny Cash (CBS)
3	3	THROUGH THE PAST DARKLY (BIG HITS VOL 2)	Rolling Stones (Decca)
4	4	BLIND FAITH	Blind Faith (Polydor)
15	5	SSSSH	Ten Years After (Deram)
6	6	HAIR	London Cast (Polydor)
11	7	NASHVILLE SKYLINE	Bob Dylan (CBS)
9	8	THE WORLD OF MANTOVANI VOL 2	Mantovani (Decca)
5	9	STAND UP	Jethro Tull (Island)
-	10	THEN PLAY ON	Fleetwood Mac (Reprise)
14	11	SONGS FOR A TAILOR	Jack Bruce (Polydor)
8	12	NICE	Nice (Immediate)
-	13	BEST OF GENE PITNEY	Gene Pitney (Stateside)
12	14	OLIVER!	Soundtrack (RCA)
7	15	ACCORDING TO MY HEART	Jim Reeves (RCA International)
9	16	FROM ELVIS IN MEMPHIS	Elvis Presley (RCA)
13	17	THE WORLD OF VAL DOONICAN	Val Doonican (Decca)
20	18	LED ZEPPELIN	Led Zeppelin (Atlantic)
-	19	THE WORLD OF VAL DOONICAN VOL 2	Val Doonican (Decca)
16	20	2001: A SPACE ODYSSEY	Soundtrack (MGM)

18 October 1969

last week	this week		
1	1	ABBEY ROAD	Beatles (Apple)
2	2	JOHNNY CASH AT SAN QUENTIN	Johnny Cash (CBS)
3	3	THROUGH THE PAST DARKLY (BIG HITS VOL 2)	Rolling Stones (Decca)
5	4	SSSSH	Ten Years After (Deram)
10	5	THEN PLAY ON	Fleetwood Mac (Reprise)
4	6	BLIND FAITH	Blind Faith (Polydor)
6	7	HAIR	London Cast (Polydor)
7	8	NASHVILLE SKYLINE	Bob Dylan (CBS)
11	8	SONGS FOR A TAILOR	Jack Bruce (Polydor)
8	10	THE WORLD OF MANTOVANI VOL 2	Mantovani (Decca)
14	11	OLIVER!	Soundtrack (RCA)
9	12	STAND UP	Jethro Tull (Island)
12	13	NICE	Nice (Immediate)
13	14	BEST OF GENE PITNEY	Gene Pitney (Stateside)
-	15	THE COUNTRY SIDE OF JIM REEVES	Jim Reeves (RCA Camden)
-	16	BEST OF THE SEEKERS	Seekers (Columbia)
18	17	LED ZEPPELIN	Led Zeppelin (Atlantic)
19	18	THE WORLD OF VAL DOONICAN VOL 2	Val Doonican (Decca)
16	19	FROM ELVIS IN MEMPHIS	Elvis Presley (RCA)
-	20	A MAN ALONE	Frank Sinatra (Reprise)

25 October 1969

last week	this week		
1	1	ABBEY ROAD	Beatles (Apple)
2	2	JOHNNY CASH AT SAN QUENTIN	Johnny Cash (CBS)
3	3	THROUGH THE PAST DARKLY (BIG HITS VOL 2)	Rolling Stones (Decca)
-	4	MOTOWN CHARTBUSTERS VOL 3	Various Artists (Tamla Motown)
4	5	SSSSH	Ten Years After (Deram)
5	6	THEN PLAY ON	Fleetwood Mac (Reprise)
8	7	NASHVILLE SKYLINE	Bob Dylan (CBS)
8	8	SONGS FOR A TAILOR	Jack Bruce (Polydor)
6	9	BLIND FAITH	Blind Faith (Polydor)
10	10	THE WORLD OF MANTOVANI VOL 2	Mantovani (Decca)
7	11	HAIR	London Cast (Polydor)
11	12	OLIVER!	Soundtrack (RCA)
-	13	IN THE COURT OF THE CRIMSON KING	King Crimson (Island)
14	14	THE SOUND OF MUSIC	Soundtrack (RCA)
15	15	THE COUNTRY SIDE OF JIM REEVES	Jim Reeves (RCA Camden)
12	16	STAND UP	Jethro Tull (Island)
17	17	2001: A SPACE ODYSSEY	Soundtrack (MGM)
16	18	BEST OF THE SEEKERS	Seekers (Columbia)
13	19	NICE	Nice (Immediate)
14	20	BEST OF GENE PITNEY	Gene Pitney (Stateside)

1 November 1969

last week	this week		
1	1	ABBEY ROAD	Beatles (Apple)
2	2	JOHNNY CASH AT SAN QUENTIN	Johnny Cash (CBS)
4	3	MOTOWN CHARTBUSTERS VOL 3	Various Artists (Tamla Motown)
3	4	THROUGH THE PAST DARKLY (BIG HITS VOL 2)	Rolling Stones (Decca)
13	5	IN THE COURT OF THE CRIMSON KING	King Crimson (Island)
6	6	THEN PLAY ON	Fleetwood Mac (Reprise)
5	7	SSSSH	Ten Years After (Deram)
7	8	NASHVILLE SKYLINE	Bob Dylan (CBS)
11	9	HAIR	London Cast (Polydor)
8	10	SONGS FOR A TAILOR	Jack Bruce (Polydor)
-	11	BEST OF CREAM	Cream (Polydor)
15	12	THE COUNTRY SIDE OF JIM REEVES	Jim Reeves (RCA Camden)
20	13	BEST OF GENE PITNEY	Gene Pitney (Stateside)
10	13	THE WORLD OF MANTOVANI VOL 2	Mantovani (Decca)
14	15	THE SOUND OF MUSIC	Soundtrack (RCA)
-	16	A MAN ALONE	Frank Sinatra (Reprise)
9	17	BLIND FAITH	Blind Faith (Polydor)
12	18	OLIVER!	Soundtrack (RCA)
-	19	BEST OF THE BEE GEES	Bee Gees (Polydor)
16	20	STAND UP	Jethro Tull (Island)

8 November 1969

last week	this week		
1	1	ABBEY ROAD	Beatles (Apple)
2	2	JOHNNY CASH AT SAN QUENTIN	Johnny Cash (CBS)
3	3	MOTOWN CHARTBUSTERS VOL 3	Various Artists (Tamla Motown)
5	4	IN THE COURT OF THE CRIMSON KING	King Crimson (Island)
4	5	THROUGH THE PAST DARKLY (BIG HITS VOL 2)	Rolling Stones (Decca)
6	6	THEN PLAY ON	Fleetwood Mac (Reprise)
-	7	LED ZEPPELIN II	Led Zeppelin (Atlantic)
19	8	BEST OF THE BEE GEES	Bee Gees (Polydor)
11	9	BEST OF CREAM	Cream (Polydor)
7	10	SSSSH	Ten Years After (Deram)
-	11	TOM JONES LIVE IN LAS VEGAS	Tom Jones (Decca)
15	12	THE SOUND OF MUSIC	Soundtrack (RCA)
9	13	HAIR	London Cast (Polydor)
8	14	NASHVILLE SKYLINE	Bob Dylan (CBS)
-	15	UMMAGUMMA	Pink Floyd (Harvest)
-	15	NICE ENOUGH TO EAT	Various Artists (Island)
13	17	BEST OF GENE PITNEY	Gene Pitney (Stateside)
16	18	A MAN ALONE	Frank Sinatra (Reprise)
13	19	THE WORLD OF MANTOVANI VOL 2	Mantovani (Decca)
-	20	NICE	Nice (Immediate)
17	20	BLIND FAITH	Blind Faith (Polydor)

15 November 1969

last week	this week		
1	1	ABBEY ROAD	Beatles (Apple)
3	2	MOTOWN CHARTBUSTERS VOL 3	Various Artists (Tamla Motown)
2	3	JOHNNY CASH AT SAN QUENTIN	Johnny Cash (CBS)
7	4	LED ZEPPELIN II	Led Zeppelin (Atlantic)
4	5	IN THE COURT OF THE CRIMSON KING	King Crimson (Island)
8	6	BEST OF THE BEE GEES	Bee Gees (Polydor)
11	7	TOM JONES LIVE IN LAS VEGAS	Tom Jones (Decca)
9	8	BEST OF CREAM	Cream (Polydor)
5	9	THROUGH THE PAST DARKLY (BIG HITS VOL 2)	Rolling Stones (Decca)
6	10	THEN PLAY ON	Fleetwood Mac (Reprise)
15	11	UMMAGUMMA	Pink Floyd (Harvest)
10	12	SSSSH	Ten Years After (Deram)
13	13	HAIR	London Cast (Polydor)
-	14	OLIVER!	Soundtrack (RCA)
14	14	NASHVILLE SKYLINE	Bob Dylan (CBS)
-	16	BEST OF THE SEEKERS	Seekers (Columbia)
15	17	NICE ENOUGH TO EAT	Various Artists (Island)
-	18	THE COUNTRY SIDE OF JIM REEVES	Jim Reeves (RCA Camden)
-	19	STAND UP	Jethro Tull (Island)
19	20	THE WORLD OF MANTOVANI VOL 2	Mantovani (Decca)
18	20	A MAN ALONE	Frank Sinatra (Reprise)

Yet more classics: *Abbey Road*, the avant-garde *In The Court Of The Crimson King* and *Ummagumma*. Geoffrey Cannon was still remembering summer: "Like love, or a child's face, some events keep an unanalysable beautify and vivacity... and what they are depends upon the thoughts directed to and contained in them... so with the Blind Faith concert... I'd no need to telephone friends; everyone I knew would be in the park... thinking the same thoughts as me." This man became editor of *Radio Times*.

59

November – December 1969

22 November 1969

last week	this week	Title	Artist (label)
1	1	ABBEY ROAD	Beatles (Apple)
2	2	MOTOWN CHARTBUSTERS VOL 3	Various Artists (Tamla Motown)
3	3	JOHNNY CASH AT SAN QUENTIN	Johnny Cash (CBS)
4	4	LED ZEPPELIN II	Led Zeppelin (Atlantic)
7	5	TOM JONES LIVE IN LAS VEGAS	Tom Jones (Decca)
11	6	UMMAGUMMA	Pink Floyd (Harvest)
5	7	IN THE COURT OF THE CRIMSON KING	King Crimson (Island)
6	8	BEST OF THE BEE GEES	Bee Gees (Polydor)
8	9	BEST OF CREAM	Cream (Polydor)
10	10	THEN PLAY ON	Fleetwood Mac (Reprise)
9	11	THROUGH THE PAST DARKLY (BIG HITS VOL 2)	Rolling Stones (Decca)
-	12	THE SOUND OF MUSIC	Soundtrack (RCA)
14	13	NASHVILLE SKYLINE	Bob Dylan (CBS)
12	14	SSSSH	Ten Years After (Deram)
17	15	NICE ENOUGH TO EAT	Various Artists (Island)
16	16	OLIVER!	Soundtrack (RCA)
18	17	THE COUNTRY SIDE OF JIM REEVES	Jim Reeves (RCA Camden)
19	18	STAND UP	Jethro Tull (Island)
20	19	THE WORLD OF MANTOVANI VOL 2	Mantovani (Decca)
13	20	HAIR	London Cast (Polydor)

29 November 1969

last week	this week	Title	Artist (label)
1	1	ABBEY ROAD	Beatles (Apple)
3	2	JOHNNY CASH AT SAN QUENTIN	Johnny Cash (CBS)
2	3	MOTOWN CHARTBUSTERS VOL 3	Various Artists (Tamla Motown)
4	4	LED ZEPPELIN II	Led Zeppelin (Atlantic)
5	5	TOM JONES LIVE IN LAS VEGAS	Tom Jones (Decca)
8	6	BEST OF THE BEE GEES	Bee Gees (Polydor)
-	7	TO OUR CHILDREN'S CHILDREN'S CHILDREN	Moody Blues (Threshold)
9	8	BEST OF CREAM	Cream (Polydor)
6	9	UMMAGUMMA	Pink Floyd (Harvest)
7	10	IN THE COURT OF THE CRIMSON KING	King Crimson (Island)
11	11	THROUGH THE PAST DARKLY (BIG HITS VOL 2)	Rolling Stones (Decca)
19	12	THE WORLD OF MANTOVANI VOL 2	Mantovani (Decca)
-	13	ENGELBERT HUMPERDINCK	Engelbert Humperdinck (Decca)
16	14	OLIVER!	Soundtrack (RCA)
-	15	BEST OF THE SEEKERS	Seekers (Columbia)
10	16	THEN PLAY ON	Fleetwood Mac (Reprise)
12	17	THE SOUND OF MUSIC	Soundtrack (RCA)
17	18	THE COUNTRY SIDE OF JIM REEVES	Jim Reeves (RCA/Camden)
-	19	TURNING POINT	John Mayall (Polydor)
15	20	NICE ENOUGH TO EAT	Various Artists (Island)

6 December 1969

last week	this week	Title	Artist (label)
1	1	ABBEY ROAD	Beatles (Apple)
3	2	MOTOWN CHARTBUSTERS VOL 3	Various Artists (Tamla Motown)
2	3	JOHNNY CASH AT SAN QUENTIN	Johnny Cash (CBS)
5	4	TOM JONES LIVE IN LAS VEGAS	Tom Jones (Decca)
4	5	LED ZEPPELIN II	Led Zeppelin (Atlantic)
7	6	TO OUR CHILDREN'S CHILDREN'S CHILDREN	Moody Blues (Threshold)
8	7	BEST OF CREAM	Cream (Polydor)
6	8	BEST OF THE BEE GEES	Bee Gees (Polydor)
9	9	UMMAGUMMA	Pink Floyd (Harvest)
13	10	ENGELBERT HUMPERDINCK	Engelbert Humperdinck (Decca)
17	11	THE SOUND OF MUSIC	Soundtrack (RCA)
10	12	IN THE COURT OF THE CRIMSON KING	King Crimson (Island)
15	13	BEST OF THE SEEKERS	Seekers (Columbia)
11	14	THROUGH THE PAST DARKLY (BIG HITS VOL 2)	Rolling Stones (Decca)
14	15	OLIVER!	Soundtrack (RCA)
12	16	THE WORLD OF MANTOVANI VOL 2	Mantovani (Decca)
16	17	THEN PLAY ON	Fleetwood Mac (Reprise)
-	18	STAND UP	Jethro Tull (Island)
20	19	NICE ENOUGH TO EAT	Various Artists (Island)
18	20	THE COUNTRY SIDE OF JIM REEVES	Jim Reeves (RCA Camden)

13 December 1969

last week	this week	Title	Artist (label)
1	1	ABBEY ROAD	Beatles (Apple)
2	2	MOTOWN CHARTBUSTERS VOL 3	Various Artists (Tamla Motown)
4	3	TOM JONES LIVE IN LAS VEGAS	Tom Jones (Decca)
-	4	LET IT BLEED	Rolling Stones (Decca)
6	5	TO OUR CHILDREN'S CHILDREN'S CHILDREN	Moody Blues (Threshold)
3	6	JOHNNY CASH AT SAN QUENTIN	Johnny Cash (CBS)
5	7	LED ZEPPELIN II	Led Zeppelin (Atlantic)
10	8	ENGELBERT HUMPERDINCK	Engelbert Humperdinck (Decca)
19	9	NICE ENOUGH TO EAT	Various Artists (Island)
11	10	THE SOUND OF MUSIC	Soundtrack (RCA)
8	11	BEST OF THE BEE GEES	Bee Gees (Polydor)
7	12	BEST OF CREAM	Cream (Polydor)
15	13	OLIVER!	Soundtrack (RCA)
9	14	UMMAGUMMA	Pink Floyd (Harvest)
15	15	THE WORLD OF MANTOVANI VOL 2	Mantovani (Decca)
14	16	THROUGH THE PAST DARKLY (BIG HITS VOL 2)	Rolling Stones (Decca)
18	17	STAND UP	Jethro Tull (Island)
12	17	IN THE COURT OF THE CRIMSON KING	Crimson King (Island)
-	19	AMERICA	Herb Alpert & the Tijuana Brass (A&M)
-	20	HAIR	London Cast (Polydor)

20 December 1969

last week	this week	Title	Artist (label)
1	1	ABBEY ROAD	Beatles (Apple)
2	2	MOTOWN CHARTBUSTERS VOL 3	Various Artists (Tamla Motown)
3	3	TOM JONES LIVE IN LAS VEGAS	Tom Jones (Decca)
4	4	LET IT BLEED	Rolling Stones (Decca)
6	5	JOHNNY CASH AT SAN QUENTIN	Johnny Cash (CBS)
5	6	TO OUR CHILDREN'S CHILDREN'S CHILDREN	Moody Blues (Threshold)
8	7	ENGELBERT HUMPERDINCK	Engelbert Humperdinck (Decca)
10	8	THE SOUND OF MUSIC	Soundtrack (RCA)
7	9	LED ZEPPELIN II	Led Zeppelin (Atlantic)
15	10	THE WORLD OF MANTOVANI VOL 2	Mantovani (Decca)
-	11	BEST OF THE SEEKERS	Seekers (Columbia)
13	12	OLIVER!	Soundtrack (RCA)
-	13	TIGHTEN UP VOL. 2	Various Artists (Trojan)
12	14	BEST OF CREAM	Cream (Polydor)
-	15	MY CHERIE AMOUR	Stevie Wonder (Tamla Motown)
17	16	STAND UP	Jethro Tull (Island)
11	16	BEST OF THE BEE GEES	Bee Gees (Polydor)
20	17	HAIR	London Cast (Polydor)
-	17	GET TOGETHER WITH ANDY WILLIAMS	Andy Williams (CBS)
14	19	UMMAGUMMA	Pink Floyd (Harvest)
17	20	IN THE COURT OF THE CRIMSON KING	King Crimson (Island)

27 December 1969

last week	this week	Title	Artist (label)
1	1	ABBEY ROAD	Beatles (Apple)
3	2	TOM JONES LIVE IN LAS VEGAS	Tom Jones (Decca)
4	3	LET IT BLEED	Rolling Stones (Decca)
2	4	MOTOWN CHARTBUSTERS VOL 3	Various Artists (Tamla Motown)
5	5	JOHNNY CASH AT SAN QUENTIN	Johnny Cash (CBS)
6	6	TO OUR CHILDREN'S CHILDREN'S CHILDREN	Moody Blues (Threshold)
7	7	ENGELBERT HUMPERDINCK	Engelbert Humperdinck (Decca)
9	8	LED ZEPPELIN II	Led Zeppelin (Atlantic)
12	9	OLIVER!	Soundtrack (RCA)
8	10	THE SOUND OF MUSIC	Soundtrack (RCA)
13	11	TIGHTEN UP VOL. 2	Various Artists (Trojan)
11	12	BEST OF THE SEEKERS	Seekers (Columbia)
14	13	BEST OF CREAM	Cream (Polydor)
-	14	EASY RIDER	Soundtrack (Stateside)
16	15	BEST OF THE BEE GEES	Bee Gees (Polydor)
10	17	THE WORLD OF MANTOVANI VOL 2	Mantovani (Decca)
17	18	GET TOGETHER WITH ANDY WILLIAMS	Andy Williams (CBS)
-	20	SYD LAWRENCE PLAYS GLENN MILLER	Syd Lawrence (Fontana)

The years that technically ended the 1960s had been spectacularly eventful. 1968 had seen the zenith of student radicalism, a period in which it had been possible not only to bring down President Johnson but to believe that, via socialism, anarchy and/or dropping out, tuning in and turning on, the revolution was coming. In 1969 Woodstock was talked of in America as Woodstock Nation, a coming-together of tribes. In Britain, people were torn between International Socialism and International Times. The old folks at home were shamelessly tuning in and dropping out to *Sid Lawrence Plays Glen Miller*.

*Decadence and facial hair at
the end of the 60s.
From the top: Jethro Tull,
Jimi Hendrix, the Faces,
Pink Floyd*

January – February 1970

last week	this week	3 January 1970
1	1	ABBEY ROAD — Beatles (Apple)
3	2	LET IT BLEED — Rolling Stones (Decca)
2	3	TOM JONES LIVE IN LAS VEGAS — Tom Jones (Decca)
4	4	MOTOWN CHARTBUSTERS VOL 3 — Various Artists (Tamla Motown)
5	5	JOHNNY CASH AT SAN QUENTIN — Johnny Cash (CBS)
6	6	TO OUR CHILDREN'S CHILDREN'S CHILDREN — Moody Blues (Threshold)
7	7	ENGELBERT HUMPERDINCK — Engelbert Humperdinck (Decca)
8	8	LED ZEPPELIN II — Led Zeppelin (Atlantic)
-	9	AMERICA — Herb Alpert & the Tijuana Brass (A&M)
10	10	THE SOUND OF MUSIC — Soundtrack (RCA)
9	11	OLIVER! — Soundtrack (RCA)
11	12	TIGHTEN UP VOL 2 — Various Artists (Trojan)
12	13	BEST OF THE SEEKERS — Seekers (Columbia)
14	14	EASY RIDER — Soundtrack (Stateside)
13	15	BEST OF CREAM — Cream (Polydor)
17	16	THE WORLD OF MANTOVANI VOL 2 — Mantovani (Decca)
15	17	BEST OF THE BEE GEES — Bee Gees (Polydor)
18	18	GET TOGETHER WITH ANDY WILLIAMS — Andy Williams (CBS)
20	19	SYD LAWRENCE PLAYS GLENN MILLER — Syd Lawrence (Fontana)
-	20	HAIR — London Cast (Polydor)

last	this	10 January 1970
1	1	ABBEY ROAD — Beatles (Apple)
4	2	MOTOWN CHARTBUSTERS VOL 3 — Various Artists (Tamla Motown)
2	3	LET IT BLEED — Rolling Stones (Decca)
3	4	TOM JONES LIVE IN LAS VEGAS — Tom Jones (Decca)
8	5	LED ZEPPELIN II — Led Zeppelin (Atlantic)
6	6	TO OUR CHILDREN'S CHILDREN'S CHILDREN — Moody Blues (Threshold)
5	7	JOHNNY CASH AT SAN QUENTIN — Johnny Cash (CBS)
7	8	ENGELBERT HUMPERDINCK — Engelbert Humperdinck (Decca)
9	9	AMERICA — Herb Alpert & the Tijuana Brass (A&M)
12	10	TIGHTEN UP VOL 2 — Various Artists (Trojan)
11	11	OLIVER! — Soundtrack (RCA)
15	12	BEST OF CREAM — Cream (Polydor)
10	13	THE SOUND OF MUSIC — Soundtrack (RCA)
20	14	HAIR — London Cast (Polydor)
16	15	THE WORLD OF MANTOVANI VOL 2 — Mantovani (Decca)
-	16	MY CHERIE AMOUR — Stevie Wonder (Tamla Motown)
14	17	EASY RIDER — Soundtrack (Stateside)
18	18	GET TOGETHER WITH ANDY WILLIAMS — Andy Williams (CBS)
-	19	IN THE COURT OF THE CRIMSON KING — King Crimson (Island)
-	20	NICE ENOUGH TO EAT — Various Artists (Island)

last	this	17 January 1970
1	1	ABBEY ROAD — Beatles (Apple)
2	2	MOTOWN CHARTBUSTERS VOL 3 — Various Artists (Tamla Motown)
5	3	LED ZEPPELIN II — Led Zeppelin (Atlantic)
3	4	LET IT BLEED — Rolling Stones (Decca)
4	5	TOM JONES LIVE IN LAS VEGAS — Tom Jones (Decca)
6	6	TO OUR CHILDREN'S CHILDREN — Moody Blues (Threshold)
7	7	JOHNNY CASH AT SAN QUENTIN — Johnny Cash (CBS)
10	8	TIGHTEN UP VOL 2 — Various Artists (Trojan)
17	9	EASY RIDER — Soundtrack (Stateside)
8	10	ENGELBERT HUMPERDINCK — Engelbert Humperdinck (Decca)
9	11	AMERICA — Herb Alpert & the Tijuana Brass (A&M)
-	12	BASKET OF LIGHT — Pentangle (Transatlantic)
13	13	THE SOUND OF MUSIC — Soundtrack (RCA)
12	14	BEST OF CREAM — Cream (Polydor)
11	15	OLIVER! — Soundtrack (RCA)
20	16	NICE ENOUGH TO EAT — Various Artists (Island)
19	17	IN THE COURT OF THE CRIMSON KING — King Crimson (Island)
-	18	BEST OF THE SEEKERS — Seekers (Columbia)
16	19	MY CHERIE AMOUR — Stevie Wonder (Tamla Motown)
-	20	THE GLENN MILLER STORY — Glenn Miller (RCA)

last	this	24 January 1970
1	1	ABBEY ROAD — Beatles (Apple)
2	2	MOTOWN CHARTBUSTERS VOL 3 — Various Artists (Tamla Motown)
3	3	LED ZEPPELIN II — Led Zeppelin (Atlantic)
4	4	LET IT BLEED — Rolling Stones (Decca)
6	5	TO OUR CHILDREN'S CHILDREN'S CHILDREN — Moody Blues (Threshold)
5	6	TOM JONES LIVE IN LAS VEGAS — Tom Jones (Decca)
7	7	JOHNNY CASH AT SAN QUENTIN — Johnny Cash (CBS)
8	8	TIGHTEN UP VOL 2 — Various Artists (Trojan)
9	9	EASY RIDER — Soundtrack (Stateside)
11	10	AMERICA — Herb Alpert & the Tijuana Brass (A&M)
13	11	THE SOUND OF MUSIC — Soundtrack (RCA)
14	12	BEST OF CREAM — Cream (Polydor)
12	13	BASKET OF LIGHT — Pentangle (Transatlantic)
17	14	IN THE COURT OF THE CRIMSON KING — King Crimson (Island)
-	15	LIEGE AND LIEF — Fairport Convention (Island)
-	16	THE WORLD OF JOHN MAYALL — John Mayall (Decca)
18	17	BEST OF THE SEEKERS — Seekers (Columbia)
-	18	THE WORLD OF MANTOVANI VOL 2 — Mantovani (Decca)
15	19	OLIVER! — Soundtrack (RCA)
10	20	ENGELBERT HUMPERDINCK — Engelbert Humperdinck (Decca)

last	this	31 January 1970
1	1	ABBEY ROAD — Beatles (Apple)
2	1	MOTOWN CHARTBUSTERS VOL 3 — Various Artists (Tamla Motown)
3	3	LED ZEPPELIN II — Led Zeppelin (Atlantic)
4	4	LET IT BLEED — Rolling Stones (Decca)
6	5	TOM JONES LIVE IN LAS VEGAS — Tom Jones (Decca)
9	6	EASY RIDER — Soundtrack (Stateside)
5	7	TO OUR CHILDREN'S CHILDREN — Moody Blues (Threshold)
7	8	JOHNNY CASH AT SAN QUENTIN — Johnny Cash (CBS)
8	9	TIGHTEN UP VOL 2 — Various Artists (Trojan)
10	10	BASKET OF LIGHT — Pentangle (Transatlantic)
11	11	AMERICA — Herb Alpert & the Tijuana Brass (A&M)
12	12	BEST OF CREAM — Cream (Polydor)
16	13	THE WORLD OF JOHN MAYALL — John Mayall (Decca)
14	14	IN THE COURT OF THE CRIMSON KING — King Crimson (Island)
20	15	ENGELBERT HUMPERDINCK — Engelbert Humperdinck (Decca)
-	16	CHICAGO TRANSIT AUTHORITY — Chicago (CBS)
11	17	THE SOUND OF MUSIC — Soundtrack (RCA)
17	18	BEST OF THE SEEKERS — Seekers (Columbia)
15	19	LIEGE AND LIEF — Fairport Convention (Island)
19	20	OLIVER! — Soundtrack (RCA)

last	this	7 February 1970
3	1	LED ZEPPELIN II — Led Zeppelin (Atlantic)
2	2	MOTOWN CHARTBUSTERS VOL 3 — Various Artists (Tamla Motown)
1	3	ABBEY ROAD — Beatles (Apple)
4	4	LET IT BLEED — Rolling Stones (Decca)
5	5	EASY RIDER — Soundtrack (Stateside)
6	6	TOM JONES LIVE IN LAS VEGAS — Tom Jones (Decca)
10	7	BASKET OF LIGHT — Pentangle (Transatlantic)
8	8	JOHNNY CASH AT SAN QUENTIN — Johnny Cash (CBS)
9	9	TIGHTEN UP VOL 2 — Various Artists (Trojan)
11	10	AMERICA — Herb Alpert & the Tijuana Brass (A&M)
19	11	LIEGE AND LIEF — Fairport Convention (Island)
7	12	TO OUR CHILDREN'S CHILDREN'S CHILDREN — Moody Blues (Threshold)
-	13	FUNNY GIRL — Soundtrack (CBS)
-	14	A SONG FOR ME — Family (Reprise)
16	15	CHICAGO TRANSIT AUTHORITY — Chicago (CBS)
13	16	THE WORLD OF JOHN MAYALL — John Mayall (Decca)
17	17	THE SOUND OF MUSIC — Soundtrack (RCA)
12	18	BEST OF CREAM — Cream (Polydor)
-	19	PAINT YOUR WAGON — Soundtrack (Paramount)
18	20	BEST OF THE SEEKERS — Seekers (Columbia)

1970: but first, let it be remembered that some who contributed crucially to the music of the late 1960s never showed up in the chart at all, despite making seminal albums of the period. Van Morrison was one of these. He had disbanded his Northern Ireland beat group, Them, recorded some tentative material in New York, and then, out of nowhere, in 1968, made *Astral Weeks*: way ahead of its time, visionary and bright, celebratory, youthful, timeless. It would be hard to name a more important 1960s album.

February – March 1970

Another whose influential, innovative albums had never charted was Frank Zappa. His Mothers of Invention had made their recording debut with a double-album (at first a single LP in Britain). 1966's *Freak Out!* had been followed by *Absolutely Free* and, its cover splendidly parodying Sgt Pepper's, *We're Only In It For The Money*, a title that mocked hippies as much as their parents. Zappa finally charted with 1969's *Hot Rats*, showcasing his fierce proficiency as guitarist, composer and producer.

March – May 1970

28 March 1970

last	this		
1	1	BRIDGE OVER TROUBLED WATER	Simon & Garfunkel (CBS)
2	2	PAINT YOUR WAGON	Soundtrack (Paramount)
3	3	LED ZEPPELIN II	Led Zeppelin (Atlantic)
4	4	EASY RIDER	Soundtrack (Stateside)
5	5	MOTOWN CHARTBUSTERS VOL 3	Various Artists (Tamla Motown)
10	5	FILL YOUR HEAD WITH ROCK	Various Artists (CBS)
7	7	HELLO I'M JOHNNY CASH	Johnny Cash (CBS)
6	8	FROM MEMPHIS TO VEGAS - FROM VEGAS TO MEMPHIS	Elvis Presley (RCA)
-	9	JIM REEVES' GOLDEN RECORDS	Jim Reeves (RCA International)
8	10	ABBEY ROAD	Beatles (Apple)
11	11	FUNNY GIRL	Soundtrack (CBS)
9	12	CANNED HEAT COOKBOOK	Canned Heat (Liberty)
-	13	DIANA ROSS PRESENTS THE JACKSON FIVE	Jackson Five (Tamla Motown)
-	14	BUDDY HOLLY'S GREATEST HITS	Buddy Holly (Coral)
12	15	BASKET OF LIGHT	Pentangle (Transatlantic)
16	16	WILLY AND THE POOR BOYS	Creedence Clearwater Revival (Liberty)
-	17	CHICAGO TRANSIT AUTHORITY	Chicago (CBS)
-	18	BEST OF THE SEEKERS	Seekers (Columbia)
13	19	TIGHTEN UP VOL 2	Various Artists (Trojan)
20	20	THE SOUND OF MUSIC	Soundtrack (RCA)

4 April 1970

1	1	BRIDGE OVER TROUBLED WATER	Simon & Garfunkel (CBS)
4	2	EASY RIDER	Soundtrack (Stateside)
2	3	PAINT YOUR WAGON	Soundtrack (Paramount)
3	4	LED ZEPPELIN II	Led Zeppelin (Atlantic)
5	5	FILL YOUR HEAD WITH ROCK	Various Artists (CBS)
5	6	MOTOWN CHARTBUSTERS VOL 3	Various Artists (Tamla Motown)
7	7	HELLO I'M JOHNNY CASH	Johnny Cash (CBS)
8	8	FROM MEMPHIS TO VEGAS - FROM VEGAS TO MEMPHIS	Elvis Presley (RCA)
10	9	ABBEY ROAD	Beatles (Apple)
16	10	WILLY AND THE POOR BOYS	Creedence Clearwater Revival (Liberty)
17	11	CHICAGO TRANSIT AUTHORITY	Chicago (CBS)
9	12	JIM REEVES' GOLDEN RECORDS	Jim Reeves (RCA International)
-	13	ANDY WILLIAMS' GREATEST HITS	Andy Williams (CBS)
-	14	BLACK SABBATH	Black Sabbath (Vertigo)
-	15	JOHNNY CASH AT SAN QUENTIN	Johnny Cash (CBS)
12	16	CANNED HEAT COOKBOOK	Canned Heat (Liberty)
15	17	BASKET OF LIGHT	Pentangle (Transatlantic)
-	18	LIVE AT THE TALK OF THE TOWN	Temptations (Tamla Motown)
-	19	HOT RATS	Frank Zappa (Reprise)
14	20	BUDDY HOLLY'S GREATEST HITS	Buddy Holly (Coral)

11 April 1970

1	1	BRIDGE OVER TROUBLED WATER	Simon & Garfunkel (CBS)
2	2	EASY RIDER	Soundtrack (Stateside)
3	3	PAINT YOUR WAGON	Soundtrack (Paramount)
5	4	FILL YOUR HEAD WITH ROCK	Various Artists (CBS)
4	5	LED ZEPPELIN II	Led Zeppelin (Atlantic)
13	6	ANDY WILLIAMS' GREATEST HITS	Andy Williams (CBS)
6	7	MOTOWN CHARTBUSTERS VOL 3	Various Artists (Tamla Motown)
-	8	CHICAGO	Chicago (CBS)
8	9	FROM MEMPHIS TO VEGAS - FROM VEGAS TO MEMPHIS	Elvis Presley (RCA)
12	10	JIM REEVES' GOLDEN RECORDS	Jim Reeves (RCA International)
9	11	ABBEY ROAD	Beatles (Apple)
-	12	THE EXQUISITE NANA MOUSKOURI	Nana Mouskouri (Fontana)
10	13	WILLY AND THE POOR BOYS	Creedence Clearwater Revival (Liberty)
7	14	HELLO I'M JOHNNY CASH	Johnny Cash (CBS)
19	15	HOT RATS	Frank Zappa (Reprise)
11	16	CHICAGO TRANSIT AUTHORITY	Chicago (CBS)
-	17	HAIR	London Cast (Polydor)
-	18	FUNNY GIRL	Soundtrack (CBS)
-	19	TIGHTEN UP VOL 2	Various Artists (Trojan)
16	20	CANNED HEAT COOKBOOK	Canned Heat (Liberty)

18 April 1970

1	1	BRIDGE OVER TROUBLED WATER	Simon & Garfunkel (CBS)
6	2	ANDY WILLIAMS' GREATEST HITS	Andy Williams (CBS)
2	3	EASY RIDER	Soundtrack (Stateside)
3	4	PAINT YOUR WAGON	Soundtrack (Paramount)
5	5	LED ZEPPELIN II	Led Zeppelin (Atlantic)
4	6	FILL YOUR HEAD WITH ROCK	Various Artists (CBS)
8	7	CHICAGO	Chicago (CBS)
7	8	MOTOWN CHARTBUSTERS VOL 3	Various Artists (Tamla Motown)
-	9	BLACK SABBATH	Black Sabbath (Vertigo)
-	10	TOM	Tom Jones (Decca)
11	11	ABBEY ROAD	Beatles (Apple)
12	12	THE EXQUISITE NANA MOUSKOURI	Nana Mouskouri (Fontana)
10	13	JIM REEVES' GOLDEN RECORDS	Jim Reeves (RCA International)
9	14	FROM MEMPHIS TO VEGAS - FROM VEGAS TO MEMPHIS	Elvis Presley (RCA)
15	14	HOT RATS	Frank Zappa (Reprise)
-	16	EMPTY ROOMS	John Mayall (Polydor)
14	17	HELLO I'M JOHNNY CASH	Johnny Cash (CBS)
-	18	BASKET OF LIGHT	Pentangle (Transatlantic)
18	19	FUNNY GIRL	Soundtrack (CBS)
19	20	TIGHTEN UP VOL 2	Various Artists (Trojan)

25 April 1970

1	1	BRIDGE OVER TROUBLED WATER	Simon & Garfunkel (CBS)
2	2	ANDY WILLIAMS' GREATEST HITS	Andy Williams (CBS)
5	3	LED ZEPPELIN II	Led Zeppelin (Atlantic)
3	4	EASY RIDER	Soundtrack (Stateside)
6	5	FILL YOUR HEAD WITH ROCK	Various Artists (CBS)
-	6	McCARTNEY	Paul McCartney (Apple)
4	7	PAINT YOUR WAGON	Soundtrack (Paramount)
9	8	BLACK SABBATH	Black Sabbath (Vertigo)
7	9	CHICAGO	Chicago (CBS)
14	10	HOT RATS	Frank Zappa (Reprise)
11	11	ABBEY ROAD	Beatles (Apple)
8	12	MOTOWN CHARTBUSTERS VOL 3	Various Artists (Tamla Motown)
10	13	TOM	Tom Jones (Decca)
18	14	BASKET OF LIGHT	Pentangle (Transatlantic)
13	15	JIM REEVES' GOLDEN RECORDS	Jim Reeves (RCA International)
-	16	SENTIMENTAL JOURNEY	Ringo Starr (Apple)
-	17	WILLY AND THE POOR BOYS	Creedence Clearwater Revival (Liberty)
14	18	FROM MEMPHIS TO VEGAS - FROM VEGAS TO MEMPHIS	Elvis Presley (RCA)
12	19	THE EXQUISITE NANA MOUSKOURI	Nana Mouskouri (Fontana)
20	19	TIGHTEN UP VOL 2	Various Artists (Trojan)

2 May 1970

1	1	BRIDGE OVER TROUBLED WATER	Simon & Garfunkel (CBS)
6	2	McCARTNEY	Paul McCartney (Apple)
2	3	ANDY WILLIAMS' GREATEST HITS	Andy Williams (CBS)
3	4	LED ZEPPELIN II	Led Zeppelin (Atlantic)
4	5	EASY RIDER	Soundtrack (Stateside)
7	6	PAINT YOUR WAGON	Soundtrack (Paramount)
5	7	FILL YOUR HEAD WITH ROCK	Various Artists (CBS)
13	8	TOM	Tom Jones (Decca)
9	9	CHICAGO	Chicago (CBS)
8	10	BLACK SABBATH	Black Sabbath (Vertigo)
-	11	GETTING TO THIS	Blodwyn Pig (Island)
11	12	ABBEY ROAD	Beatles (Apple)
12	13	MOTOWN CHARTBUSTERS VOL 3	Various Artists (Tamla Motown)
17	14	WILLY AND THE POOR BOYS	Creedence Clearwater Revival (Liberty)
16	15	SENTIMENTAL JOURNEY	Ringo Starr (Apple)
-	16	REGGAE CHARTBUSTERS	Various Artists (Trojan)
-	17	CRICKLEWOOD GREEN	Ten Years After (Deram)
15	18	JIM REEVES' GOLDEN RECORDS	Jim Reeves (RCA International)
-	19	A MEMORIAL 1944-1969	Glenn Miller (RCA)
-	20	LET'S BE FRIENDS	Elvis Presley (RCA Camden)

Unlike Morrison and Zappa, Simon & Garfunkel never had problems charting. *Bridge Over Troubled Water* leapt to No.1 and would remain there till June, when the Beatles would temporarily dislodge it. By mid-August *Bridge* would be top again, and remain so, but for a brief disruption from the Moodies, till October. Never leaving the Top 5, it would return to No.1 in March 1971, and again that July-August. It would still be in the Top 10 in September 1972, more than 2 AND A HARRRRRRF years after entering it.

9 May 1970

last week	this week	title
1	1	BRIDGE OVER TROUBLED WATER Simon & Garfunkel (CBS)
2	2	McCARTNEY Paul McCartney (Apple)
3	3	ANDY WILLIAMS' GREATEST HITS Andy Williams (CBS)
4	4	LED ZEPPELIN II Led Zeppelin (Atlantic)
5	5	EASY RIDER Soundtrack (Stateside)
8	6	TOM Tom Jones (Decca)
6	7	PAINT YOUR WAGON Soundtrack (Paramount)
10	8	BLACK SABBATH Black Sabbath (Vertigo)
-	8	BENEFIT Jethro Tull (Chrysalis)
11	10	GETTING TO THIS Blodwyn Pig (Island)
12	11	ABBEY ROAD Beatles (Apple)
17	12	CRICKLEWOOD GREEN Ten Years After (Deram)
7	13	FILL YOUR HEAD WITH ROCK Various Artists (CBS)
13	14	MOTOWN CHARTBUSTERS VOL 3 Various Artists (Tamla Motown)
-	15	BEST OF THE SEEKERS Seekers (Columbia)
9	16	CHICAGO Chicago (CBS)
14	17	WILLY AND THE POOR BOYS Creedence Clearwater Revival (Liberty)
-	18	SACHA Sacha Distel (Warner Bros.)
15	19	SENTIMENTAL JOURNEY Ringo Starr (Apple)
-	20	MORRISON HOTEL Doors (Elektra)

16 May 1970

last week	this week	title
1	1	BRIDGE OVER TROUBLED WATER Simon & Garfunkel (CBS)
2	2	McCARTNEY Paul McCartney (Apple)
-	3	LET IT BE Beatles (Apple)
3	4	ANDY WILLIAMS' GREATEST HITS Andy Williams (CBS)
8	5	BENEFIT Jethro Tull (Chrysalis)
5	6	EASY RIDER Soundtrack (Stateside)
4	7	LED ZEPPELIN II Led Zeppelin (Atlantic)
6	8	TOM Tom Jones (Decca)
17	9	CRICKLEWOOD GREEN Ten Years After (Deram)
17	10	WILLY AND THE POOR BOYS Creedence Clearwater Revival (Liberty)
13	10	FILL YOUR HEAD WITH ROCK Various Artists (CBS)
7	12	PAINT YOUR WAGON Soundtrack (Paramount)
-	13	THE WORLD BEATERS SING THE WORLD BEATERS England Football World Cup Squad (Pye)
8	14	BLACK SABBATH Black Sabbath (Vertigo)
14	15	MOTOWN CHARTBUSTERS VOL 3 Various Artists (Tamla Motown)
-	16	REGGAE CHARTBUSTERS Various Artists (Trojan)
10	18	GETTING TO THIS Blodwyn Pig (Island)
19	19	SENTIMENTAL JOURNEY Ringo Starr (Apple)
11	20	ABBEY ROAD Beatles (Apple)

23 May 1970

last week	this week	title
1	1	BRIDGE OVER TROUBLED WATER Simon & Garfunkel (CBS)
3	2	LET IT BE Beatles (Apple)
2	3	McCARTNEY Paul McCartney (Apple)
4	4	ANDY WILLIAMS' GREATEST HITS Andy Williams (CBS)
5	5	BENEFIT Jethro Tull (Chrysalis)
6	6	EASY RIDER Soundtrack (Stateside)
12	6	PAINT YOUR WAGON Soundtrack (Paramount)
9	8	CRICKLEWOOD GREEN Ten Years After (Deram)
13	9	THE WORLD BEATERS SING THE WORLD BEATERS England Football World Cup Squad (Pye)
8	10	TOM Tom Jones (Decca)
14	11	BLACK SABBATH Black Sabbath (Vertigo)
17	12	LET'S BE FRIENDS Elvis Presley (RCA Camden)
7	13	LED ZEPPELIN II Led Zeppelin (Atlantic)
-	14	IN THE WAKE OF POSEIDON King Crimson (Island)
20	15	ABBEY ROAD Beatles (Apple)
10	16	WILLY AND THE POOR BOYS Creedence Clearwater Revival (Liberty)
10	16	FILL YOUR HEAD WITH ROCK Various Artists (CBS)
15	18	MOTOWN CHARTBUSTERS VOL 3 Various Artists (Tamla Motown)
-	19	DIANA ROSS AND THE SUPREMES' GREATEST HITS VOL 2 Diana Ross & the Supremes (Tamla Motown)
-	19	BEST OF THE SEEKERS Seekers (Columbia)

30 May 1970

last week	this week	title
1	1	BRIDGE OVER TROUBLED WATER Simon & Garfunkel (CBS)
2	2	LET IT BE Beatles (Apple)
3	3	McCARTNEY Paul McCartney (Apple)
4	4	ANDY WILLIAMS' GREATEST HITS Andy Williams (CBS)
5	4	BENEFIT Jethro Tull (Chrysalis)
6	6	TOM Tom Jones (Decca)
13	7	LED ZEPPELIN II Led Zeppelin (Atlantic)
9	8	THE WORLD BEATERS SING THE WORLD BEATERS England Football World Cup Squad (Pye)
6	9	EASY RIDER Soundtrack (Stateside)
11	10	BLACK SABBATH Black Sabbath (Vertigo)
6	11	PAINT YOUR WAGON Soundtrack (Paramount)
16	12	FILL YOUR HEAD WITH ROCK Various Artists (CBS)
8	13	CRICKLEWOOD GREEN Ten Years After (Deram)
-	14	WATERTOWN Frank Sinatra (Reprise)
-	15	DEJA VU Crosby, Stills, Nash & Young (Atlantic)
16	16	WILLY AND THE POOR BOYS Creedence Clearwater Revival (Liberty)
12	17	LET'S BE FRIENDS Elvis Presley (RCA Camden)
15	18	ABBEY ROAD Beatles (Apple)
14	19	IN THE WAKE OF POSEIDON King Crimson (Island)
18	20	MOTOWN CHARTBUSTERS VOL 3 Various Artists (Tamla Motown)

6 June 1970

last week	this week	title
2	1	LET IT BE Beatles (Apple)
1	2	BRIDGE OVER TROUBLED WATER Simon & Garfunkel (CBS)
3	3	McCARTNEY Paul McCartney (Apple)
4	4	ANDY WILLIAMS' GREATEST HITS Andy Williams (CBS)
9	5	EASY RIDER Soundtrack (Stateside)
4	6	BENEFIT Jethro Tull (Chrysalis)
15	7	DEJA VU Crosby, Stills, Nash & Young (Atlantic)
7	8	LED ZEPPELIN II Led Zeppelin (Atlantic)
-	9	LIVE AT LEEDS Who (Track)
11	10	PAINT YOUR WAGON Soundtrack (Paramount)
8	11	THE WORLD BEATERS SING THE WORLD BEATERS England Football World Cup Squad (Pye)
19	12	IN THE WAKE OF POSEIDON King Crimson (Island)
10	13	BLACK SABBATH Black Sabbath (Vertigo)
6	14	TOM Tom Jones (Decca)
13	15	CRICKLEWOOD GREEN Ten Years After (Deram)
12	16	FILL YOUR HEAD WITH ROCK Various Artists (CBS)
17	17	LET'S BE FRIENDS Elvis Presley (RCA Camden)
16	18	WILLY AND THE POOR BOYS Creedence Clearwater Revival (Liberty)
20	19	MOTOWN CHARTBUSTERS VOL 3 Various Artists (Tamla Motown)
18	20	ABBEY ROAD Beatles (Apple)

13 June 1970

last week	this week	title
1	1	LET IT BE Beatles (Apple)
2	2	BRIDGE OVER TROUBLED WATER Simon & Garfunkel (CBS)
3	3	McCARTNEY Paul McCartney (Apple)
9	4	LIVE AT LEEDS Who (Track)
5	5	EASY RIDER Soundtrack (Stateside)
4	6	ANDY WILLIAMS' GREATEST HITS Andy Williams (CBS)
7	7	DEJA VU Crosby, Stills, Nash & Young (Atlantic)
11	8	THE WORLD BEATERS SING THE WORLD BEATERS England Football World Cup Squad (Pye)
10	9	PAINT YOUR WAGON Soundtrack (Paramount)
8	10	LED ZEPPELIN II Led Zeppelin (Atlantic)
14	11	TOM Tom Jones (Decca)
6	12	BENEFIT Jethro Tull (Chrysalis)
15	13	CRICKLEWOOD GREEN Ten Years After (Deram)
12	14	IN THE WAKE OF POSEIDON King Crimson (Island)
18	15	WILLY AND THE POOR BOYS Creedence Clearwater Revival (Liberty)
-	16	DIANA ROSS AND THE SUPREMES' GREATEST HITS VOL 2 Diana Ross & the Supremes (Tamla Motown)
-	17	HOT RATS Frank Zappa (Reprise)
-	18	REGGAE CHARTBUSTERS Various Artists (Trojan)
13	19	BLACK SABBATH Black Sabbath (Vertigo)
17	20	LET'S BE FRIENDS Elvis Presley (RCA Camden)

The Beatles were disintegrating, but they were spilling all over the charts in the process. May 16 shows McCartney at No.2 with *Let It Be* at No.3, and, echoing that pattern lower down, Ringo Starr's album at No.19, immediately above *Abbey Road*. Allen Klein plus John George and Ringo had tried to delay McCartney's album so as to not to detract from sales of *Let It Be*. Ringo was sent to Paul's house to tell him. Paul flew into such a fearful bate that they all backed down.

June – July 1970

20 June 1970

last	this		
1	1	LET IT BE	Beatles (Apple)
2	2	BRIDGE OVER TROUBLED WATER	
			Simon & Garfunkel (CBS)
3	3	McCARTNEY	Paul McCartney (Apple)
4	4	LIVE AT LEEDS	Who (Track)
5	5	EASY RIDER	Soundtrack (Stateside)
7	6	DEJA VU Crosby, Stills, Nash & Young (Atlantic)
6	7	ANDY WILLIAMS' GREATEST HITS	
			Andy Williams (CBS)
10	8	LED ZEPPELIN II	Led Zeppelin (Atlantic)
8	9	THE WORLD BEATERS SING THE WORLD
		BEATERS	
		England Football World Cup Squad (Pye)
14	10	IN THE WAKE OF POSEIDON	
			King Crimson (Island)
9	11	PAINT YOUR WAGON	Soundtrack (Paramount)
12	12	BENEFIT	Jethro Tull (Chrysalis)
-	13	LADIES OF THE CANYON Joni Mitchell (Reprise)
19	14	BLACK SABBATH	Black Sabbath (Vertigo)
11	15	TOM	Tom Jones (Decca)
-	16	BUMPERS	Various Artists (Island)
-	17	FILL YOUR HEAD WITH ROCK	
			Various Artists (CBS)
17	18	HOT RATS	Frank Zappa (Reprise)
18	19	REGGAE CHARTBUSTERS	
			Various Artists (Trojan)
15	20	WILLY AND THE POOR BOYS	
		Creedence Clearwater Revival (Liberty)

27 June 1970

last	this		
2	1	BRIDGE OVER TROUBLED WATER	
			Simon & Garfunkel (CBS)
1	2	LET IT BE	Beatles (Apple)
4	3	LIVE AT LEEDS	Who (Track)
3	4	McCARTNEY	Paul McCartney (Apple)
5	5	EASY RIDER	Soundtrack (Stateside)
7	6	ANDY WILLIAMS' GREATEST HITS	
			Andy Williams (CBS)
6	7	DEJA VU Crosby, Stills, Nash & Young (Atlantic)
8	8	LED ZEPPELIN II	Led Zeppelin (Atlantic)
-	9	CAN'T HELP FALLING IN LOVE	
			Andy Williams (CBS)
9	10	THE WORLD BEATERS SING THE WORLD
		BEATERS	
		England Football World Cup Squad (Pye)
16	11	BUMPERS	Various Artists (Island)
-	12	LIVE CREAM	Cream (Polydor)
-	13	DEEP PURPLE IN ROCK	Deep Purple (Harvest)
12	14	BENEFIT	Jethro Tull (Chrysalis)
5	15	FIVE BRIDGES	Nice (Charisma)
-	16	HERB ALPERT'S GREATEST HITS	
		Herb Alpert & the Tijuana Brass (A&M)
10	17	IN THE WAKE OF POSEIDON	
			King Crimson (Island)
11	18	PAINT YOUR WAGON	Soundtrack (Paramount)
13	19	LADIES OF THE CANYON	
			Joni Mitchell (Reprise)
-	20	THE SOUND OF MUSIC	Soundtrack (RCA)

4 July 1970

last	this		
1	1	BRIDGE OVER TROUBLED WATER	
			Simon & Garfunkel (CBS)
2	2	LET IT BE	Beatles (Apple)
5	3	EASY RIDER	Soundtrack (Stateside)
3	4	LIVE AT LEEDS	Who (Track)
13	5	DEEP PURPLE IN ROCK	Deep Purple (Harvest)
4	6	McCARTNEY	Paul McCartney (Apple)
11	7	BUMPERS	Various Artists (Island)
-	8	SELF PORTRAIT	Bob Dylan (CBS)
12	9	LIVE CREAM	Cream (Polydor)
7	10	DEJA VU Crosby, Stills, Nash & Young (Atlantic)
9	11	CAN'T HELP FALLING IN LOVE	
			Andy Williams (CBS)
8	12	LED ZEPPELIN II	Led Zeppelin (Atlantic)
15	13	FIVE BRIDGES	Nice (Charisma)
6	14	ANDY WILLIAMS' GREATEST HITS	
			Andy Williams (CBS)
18	15	PAINT YOUR WAGON	Soundtrack (Paramount)
-	16	BAND OF GYPSIES	Jimi Hendrix (Track)
17	17	IN THE WAKE OF POSEIDON	
			King Crimson (Island)
19	18	LADIES OF THE CANYON	
			Joni Mitchell (Reprise)
14	19	BENEFIT	Jethro Tull (Chrysalis)
-	20	PICNIC - A BREATH OF FRESH AIR	
			Various Artists (Harvest)

11 July 1970

last	this		
1	1	BRIDGE OVER TROUBLED WATER	
			Simon & Garfunkel (CBS)
2	2	LET IT BE	Beatles (Apple)
4	3	LIVE AT LEEDS	Who (Track)
8	4	SELF PORTRAIT	Bob Dylan (CBS)
7	5	BUMPERS	Various Artists (Island)
3	6	EASY RIDER	Soundtrack (Stateside)
5	7	DEEP PURPLE IN ROCK	Deep Purple (Harvest)
13	8	FIVE BRIDGES	Nice (Charisma)
6	9	McCARTNEY	Paul McCartney (Apple)
-	10	FIRE AND WATER	Free (Island)
9	11	LIVE CREAM	Cream (Polydor)
12	12	LED ZEPPELIN II	Led Zeppelin (Atlantic)
16	13	BAND OF GYPSIES	Jimi Hendrix (Track)
10	14	DEJA VU Crosby, Stills, Nash & Young (Atlantic)
11	15	CAN'T HELP FALLING IN LOVE	
			Andy Williams (CBS)
15	16	PAINT YOUR WAGON	Soundtrack (Paramount)
14	17	ANDY WILLIAMS' GREATEST HITS	
			Andy Williams (CBS)
20	18	PICNIC - A BREATH OF FRESH AIR	
			Various Artists (Harvest)
-	19	THIRD	Soft Machine (CBS)
-	20	WE MADE IT HAPPEN	
			Engelbert Humperdinck (Decca)

18 July 1970

last	this		
2	1	LET IT BE	Beatles (Apple)
1	2	BRIDGE OVER TROUBLED WATER	
			Simon & Garfunkel (CBS)
4	3	SELF PORTRAIT	Bob Dylan (CBS)
10	4	FIRE AND WATER	Free (Island)
5	5	BUMPERS	Various Artists (Island)
9	6	McCARTNEY	Paul McCartney (Apple)
11	7	LIVE CREAM	Cream (Polydor)
6	8	EASY RIDER	Soundtrack (Stateside)
14	9	DEJA VU Crosby, Stills, Nash & Young (Atlantic)
7	10	DEEP PURPLE IN ROCK	Deep Purple (Harvest)
8	11	FIVE BRIDGES	Nice (Charisma)
13	12	BAND OF GYPSIES	Jimi Hendrix (Track)
12	13	LED ZEPPELIN II	Led Zeppelin (Atlantic)
3	14	LIVE AT LEEDS	Who (Track)
16	15	PAINT YOUR WAGON	Soundtrack (Paramount)
15	16	CAN'T HELP FALLING IN LOVE	
			Andy Williams (CBS)
17	17	ANDY WILLIAMS' GREATEST HITS	
			Andy Williams (CBS)
18	18	PICNIC - A BREATH OF FRESH AIR	
			Various Artists (Harvest)
20	19	WE MADE IT HAPPEN	
			Engelbert Humperdinck (Decca)
-	20	FILL YOUR HEAD WITH ROCK	
			Various Artists (CBS)

25 July 1970

last	this		
2	1	BRIDGE OVER TROUBLED WATER	
			Simon & Garfunkel (CBS)
4	2	FIRE AND WATER	Free (Island)
1	3	LET IT BE	Beatles (Apple)
3	4	SELF PORTRAIT	Bob Dylan (CBS)
5	5	BUMPERS	Various Artists (Island)
10	6	DEEP PURPLE IN ROCK	Deep Purple (Harvest)
11	7	FIVE BRIDGES	Nice (Charisma)
7	8	LIVE CREAM	Cream (Polydor)
6	9	McCARTNEY	Paul McCartney (Apple)
8	10	EASY RIDER	Soundtrack (Stateside)
15	11	PAINT YOUR WAGON	Soundtrack (Paramount)
-	12	ON STAGE: FEBRUARY 1970	
			Elvis Presley (RCA)
14	13	LIVE AT LEEDS	Who (Track)
9	14	DEJA VU Crosby, Stills, Nash & Young (Atlantic)
13	15	LED ZEPPELIN II	Led Zeppelin (Atlantic)
12	16	BAND OF GYPSIES	Jimi Hendrix (Track)
-	17	FULL HOUSE	Fairport Convention (Island)
18	18	PICNIC - A BREATH OF FRESH AIR	
			Various Artists (Harvest)
17	19	ANDY WILLIAMS' GREATEST HITS	
			Andy Williams (CBS)
-	20	STEPPENWOLF LIVE	Steppenwolf (Dunhill)

The Who's vivid *Live At Leeds* (their first album since *Tommy*) had charted earlier in June. Now it rose to 3 before suddenly plunging, from 3 to 14 in one week. Pete Townshend, interviewed this spring, had said of his work: "If you look at any form of art, you can find something in the best of pop which completely eliminates the old form... If you think Mahler's 9th Symphony is overwhelming, I can play you a tape I made in my studio at home which is MORE overwhelming."

August – September 1970

1 August 1970

last	this	title	artist
3	1	LET IT BE	Beatles (Apple)
4	2	SELF PORTRAIT	Bob Dylan (CBS)
1	3	BRIDGE OVER TROUBLED WATER	Simon & Garfunkel (CBS)
2	4	FIRE AND WATER	Free (Island)
9	5	McCARTNEY	Paul McCartney (Apple)
6	6	DEEP PURPLE IN ROCK	Deep Purple (Harvest)
15	7	LED ZEPPELIN II	Led Zeppelin (Atlantic)
10	8	EASY RIDER	Soundtrack (Stateside)
7	9	FIVE BRIDGES	Nice (Charisma)
11	10	PAINT YOUR WAGON	Soundtrack (Paramount)
8	11	LIVE CREAM	Cream (Polydor)
12	12	ON STAGE: FEBRUARY 1970	Elvis Presley (RCA)
19	13	ANDY WILLIAMS' GREATEST HITS	Andy Williams (CBS)
5	14	BUMPERS	Various Artists (Island)
13	15	LIVE AT LEEDS	Who (Track)
14	16	DEJA VU	Crosby, Stills, Nash & Young (Atlantic)
-	17	MOTOWN CHARTBUSTERS VOL 3	Various Artists (Tamla Motown)
16	18	BAND OF GYPSIES	Jimi Hendrix (Track)
-	19	WOODSTOCK	Soundtrack (Atlantic)
-	20	CRICKLEWOOD GREEN	Ten Years After (Deram)

8 August 1970

last	this	title	artist
1	1	LET IT BE	Beatles (Apple)
3	2	BRIDGE OVER TROUBLED WATER	Simon & Garfunkel (CBS)
4	3	FIRE AND WATER	Free (Island)
12	4	ON STAGE: FEBRUARY 1970	Elvis Presley (RCA)
2	5	SELF PORTRAIT	Bob Dylan (CBS)
6	6	DEEP PURPLE IN ROCK	Deep Purple (Harvest)
5	7	McCARTNEY	Paul McCartney (Apple)
10	8	PAINT YOUR WAGON	Soundtrack (Paramount)
7	9	LED ZEPPELIN II	Led Zeppelin (Atlantic)
14	10	BUMPERS	Various Artists (Island)
9	11	FIVE BRIDGES	Nice (Charisma)
8	12	EASY RIDER	Soundtrack (Stateside)
13	13	ANDY WILLIAMS' GREATEST HITS	Andy Williams (CBS)
16	14	DEJA VU	Crosby, Stills, Nash & Young (Atlantic)
11	15	LIVE CREAM	Cream (Polydor)
15	16	LIVE AT LEEDS	Who (Track)
-	17	A QUESTION OF BALANCE	Moody Blues (Threshold)
19	18	WOODSTOCK	Soundtrack (Atlantic)
-	19	FULL HOUSE	Fairport Convention (Island)
-	20	JOHN BARLEYCORN MUST DIE	Traffic (Island)

15 August 1970

last	this	title	artist
2	1	BRIDGE OVER TROUBLED WATER	Simon & Garfunkel (CBS)
1	2	LET IT BE	Beatles (Apple)
3	3	FIRE AND WATER	Free (Island)
4	4	ON STAGE: FEBRUARY 1970	Elvis Presley (RCA)
17	5	A QUESTION OF BALANCE	Moody Blues (Threshold)
5	6	SELF PORTRAIT	Bob Dylan (CBS)
6	7	DEEP PURPLE IN ROCK	Deep Purple (Harvest)
9	8	LED ZEPPELIN II	Led Zeppelin (Atlantic)
8	9	PAINT YOUR WAGON	Soundtrack (Paramount)
11	10	EASY RIDER	Soundtrack (Stateside)
7	11	McCARTNEY	Paul McCartney (Apple)
10	12	BUMPERS	Various Artists (Island)
13	13	ANDY WILLIAMS' GREATEST HITS	Andy Williams (CBS)
16	14	LIVE AT LEEDS	Who (Track)
-	15	THE WORLD OF JOHNNY CASH	Johnny Cash (CBS)
-	16	STEPPENWOLF LIVE	Steppenwolf (Dunhill)
20	17	JOHN BARLEYCORN MUST DIE	Traffic (Island)
14	18	DEJA VU	Crosby, Stills, Nash & Young (Atlantic)
12	19	FIVE BRIDGES	Nice (Charisma)
15	20	LIVE CREAM	Cream (Polydor)

22 August 1970

last	this	title	artist
1	1	BRIDGE OVER TROUBLED WATER	Simon & Garfunkel (CBS)
5	2	A QUESTION OF BALANCE	Moody Blues (Threshold)
4	3	ON STAGE: FEBRUARY 1970	Elvis Presley (RCA)
2	4	LET IT BE	Beatles (Apple)
3	5	FIRE AND WATER	Free (Island)
6	6	SELF PORTRAIT	Bob Dylan (CBS)
9	7	PAINT YOUR WAGON	Soundtrack (Paramount)
7	8	DEEP PURPLE IN ROCK	Deep Purple (Harvest)
8	9	LED ZEPPELIN II	Led Zeppelin (Atlantic)
10	10	EASY RIDER	Soundtrack (Stateside)
13	11	ANDY WILLIAMS' GREATEST HITS	Andy Williams (CBS)
11	12	McCARTNEY	Paul McCartney (Apple)
-	13	BLOOD SWEAT AND TEARS	Blood Sweat & Tears (CBS)
15	14	THE WORLD OF JOHNNY CASH	Johnny Cash (CBS)
17	15	JOHN BARLEYCORN MUST DIE	Traffic (Island)
12	16	BUMPERS	Various Artists (Island)
-	17	MUNGO JERRY	Mungo Jerry (Dawn)
20	18	LIVE CREAM	Cream (Polydor)
19	19	FIVE BRIDGES	Nice (Charisma)
18	20	DEJA VU	Crosby, Stills, Nash & Young (Atlantic)

29 August 1970

last	this	title	artist
1	1	BRIDGE OVER TROUBLED WATER	Simon & Garfunkel (CBS)
2	2	A QUESTION OF BALANCE	Moody Blues (Threshold)
4	3	LET IT BE	Beatles (Apple)
3	4	ON STAGE: FEBRUARY 1970	Elvis Presley (RCA)
5	5	FIRE AND WATER	Free (Island)
8	6	DEEP PURPLE IN ROCK	Deep Purple (Harvest)
9	7	LED ZEPPELIN II	Led Zeppelin (Atlantic)
7	8	PAINT YOUR WAGON	Soundtrack (Paramount)
6	9	SELF PORTRAIT	Bob Dylan (CBS)
10	10	BUMPERS	Various Artists (Island)
10	11	EASY RIDER	Soundtrack (Stateside)
14	12	THE WORLD OF JOHNNY CASH	Johnny Cash (CBS)
12	13	McCARTNEY	Paul McCartney (Apple)
13	14	BLOOD SWEAT AND TEARS	Blood Sweat & Tears (CBS)
11	15	ANDY WILLIAMS' GREATEST HITS	Andy Williams (CBS)
15	16	JOHN BARLEYCORN MUST DIE	Traffic (Island)
-	17	LIVE AT LEEDS	Who (Track)
18	18	WOODSTOCK	Soundtrack (Atlantic)
18	19	LIVE CREAM	Cream (Polydor)
20	20	DEJA VU	Crosby, Stills, Nash & Young (Atlantic)

5 September 1970

last	this	title	artist
2	1	A QUESTION OF BALANCE	Moody Blues (Threshold)
1	2	BRIDGE OVER TROUBLED WATER	Simon & Garfunkel (CBS)
3	3	LET IT BE	Beatles (Apple)
4	4	ON STAGE: FEBRUARY 1970	Elvis Presley (RCA)
5	5	FIRE AND WATER	Free (Island)
7	6	LED ZEPPELIN II	Led Zeppelin (Atlantic)
-	7	SOMETHING	Shirley Bassey (United Artists)
6	8	DEEP PURPLE IN ROCK	Deep Purple (Harvest)
11	9	EASY RIDER	Soundtrack (Stateside)
-	10	COSMO'S FACTORY	Creedence Clearwater Revival (Liberty)
8	11	PAINT YOUR WAGON	Soundtrack (Paramount)
15	12	ANDY WILLIAMS' GREATEST HITS	Andy Williams (CBS)
13	13	McCARTNEY	Paul McCartney (Apple)
9	14	SELF PORTRAIT	Bob Dylan (CBS)
10	15	BUMPERS	Various Artists (Island)
12	16	THE WORLD OF JOHNNY CASH	Johnny Cash (CBS)
18	17	WOODSTOCK	Soundtrack (Atlantic)
14	18	BLOOD SWEAT AND TEARS	Blood Sweat & Tears (CBS)
19	19	LIVE CREAM	Cream (Polydor)
16	20	JOHN BARLEYCORN MUST DIE	Traffic (Island)

Dylan had issued *Self Portrait*, a double album of other people's songs and far too many musicians, and although it was in the charts, suddenly Bob Dylan wasn't hip any more. Still very hip were the stars of this August's Isle Of Wight Music Festival, Jimi Hendrix and the Doors. Yet while 1970's Doors' album, *Morrison Hotel*, was up to standard, Jim Morrison himself was by this point giving bleary performances verging on self-parody. Hendrix gave a great performance. It was, in the event, his last.

September – October 1970

last week	this week	12 September 1970
1	1	A QUESTION OF BALANCE — Moody Blues (Threshold)
2	2	BRIDGE OVER TROUBLED WATER — Simon & Garfunkel (CBS)
4	3	ON STAGE: FEBRUARY 1970 — Elvis Presley (RCA)
3	4	LET IT BE — Beatles (Apple)
-	5	'GET YOUR YA-YA'S OUT!' — Rolling Stones (Decca)
5	6	FIRE AND WATER — Free (Island)
11	7	PAINT YOUR WAGON — Soundtrack (Paramount)
10	8	COSMO'S FACTORY — Creedence Clearwater Revival (Liberty)
9	9	EASY RIDER — Soundtrack (Stateside)
16	10	THE WORLD OF JOHNNY CASH — Johnny Cash (CBS)
7	11	SOMETHING — Shirley Bassey (United Artists)
8	12	DEEP PURPLE IN ROCK — Deep Purple (Harvest)
6	13	LED ZEPPELIN II — Led Zeppelin (Atlantic)
13	14	McCARTNEY — Paul McCartney (Apple)
15	15	BUMPERS — Various Artists (Island)
14	16	SELF PORTRAIT — Bob Dylan (CBS)
12	17	ANDY WILLIAMS' GREATEST HITS — Andy Williams (CBS)
18	18	BLOOD SWEAT AND TEARS — Blood Sweat & Tears (CBS)
20	19	JOHN BARLEYCORN MUST DIE — Traffic (Island)
-	20	CAN'T HELP FALLING IN LOVE — Andy Williams (CBS)

last week	this week	19 September 1970
1	1	A QUESTION OF BALANCE — Moody Blues (Threshold)
2	2	BRIDGE OVER TROUBLED WATER — Simon & Garfunkel (CBS)
8	3	COSMO'S FACTORY — Creedence Clearwater Revival (Liberty)
3	4	ON STAGE: FEBRUARY 1970 — Elvis Presley (RCA)
5	5	'GET YOUR YA-YA'S OUT!' — Rolling Stones (Decca)
4	6	LET IT BE — Beatles (Apple)
11	7	SOMETHING — Shirley Bassey (United Artists)
7	8	PAINT YOUR WAGON — Soundtrack (Paramount)
12	9	DEEP PURPLE IN ROCK — Deep Purple (Harvest)
13	10	LED ZEPPELIN II — Led Zeppelin (Atlantic)
10	11	THE WORLD OF JOHNNY CASH — Johnny Cash (CBS)
6	12	FIRE AND WATER — Free (Island)
9	13	EASY RIDER — Soundtrack (Stateside)
20	14	CAN'T HELP FALLING IN LOVE — Andy Williams (CBS)
-	15	ERIC CLAPTON — Eric Clapton (Polydor)
14	16	McCARTNEY — Paul McCartney (Apple)
17	17	SELF PORTRAIT — Bob Dylan (CBS)
-	18	MAD DOGS AND ENGLISHMEN — Joe Cocker (A&M)
17	19	ANDY WILLIAMS' GREATEST HITS — Andy Williams (CBS)
-	19	THE SPINNERS ARE IN TOWN — Spinners (Fontana)

last week	this week	26 September 1970
2	1	BRIDGE OVER TROUBLED WATER — Simon & Garfunkel (CBS)
3	2	COSMO'S FACTORY — Creedence Clearwater Revival (Liberty)
5	3	'GET YOUR YA-YA'S OUT!' — Rolling Stones (Decca)
1	4	A QUESTION OF BALANCE — Moody Blues (Threshold)
4	5	ON STAGE: FEBRUARY 1970 — Elvis Presley (RCA)
10	6	LED ZEPPELIN II — Led Zeppelin (Atlantic)
8	7	PAINT YOUR WAGON — Soundtrack (Paramount)
7	8	SOMETHING — Shirley Bassey (United Artists)
6	9	LET IT BE — Beatles (Apple)
9	10	DEEP PURPLE IN ROCK — Deep Purple (Harvest)
-	11	MOTOWN CHARTBUSTERS VOL 3 — Various Artists (Tamla Motown)
-	12	THE BEACH BOYS' GREATEST HITS — Beach Boys (Capitol)
14	13	CAN'T HELP FALLING IN LOVE — Andy Williams (CBS)
12	14	FIRE AND WATER — Free (Island)
19	15	ANDY WILLIAMS' GREATEST HITS — Andy Williams (CBS)
-	15	THE EVERLY BROTHERS' ORIGINAL GREATEST HITS — Various Artists (CBS)
17	17	PARANOID — Black Sabbath (Vertigo)
18	18	MAD DOGS AND ENGLISHMEN — Joe Cocker (A&M)
-	19	OVER AND OVER — Nana Mouskouri (Fontana)
13	20	EASY RIDER — Soundtrack (Stateside)

last week	this week	3 October 1970
1	1	BRIDGE OVER TROUBLED WATER — Simon & Garfunkel (CBS)
3	2	'GET YOUR YA-YA'S OUT!' — Rolling Stones (Decca)
2	3	COSMO'S FACTORY — Creedence Clearwater Revival (Liberty)
4	4	A QUESTION OF BALANCE — Moody Blues (Threshold)
10	5	DEEP PURPLE IN ROCK — Deep Purple (Harvest)
17	6	PARANOID — Black Sabbath (Vertigo)
5	7	ON STAGE: FEBRUARY 1970 — Elvis Presley (RCA)
6	8	LED ZEPPELIN II — Led Zeppelin (Atlantic)
7	9	PAINT YOUR WAGON — Soundtrack (Paramount)
12	10	THE BEACH BOYS' GREATEST HITS — Beach Boys (Capitol)
8	11	SOMETHING — Shirley Bassey (United Artists)
13	12	CAN'T HELP FALLING IN LOVE — Andy Williams (CBS)
9	13	LET IT BE — Beatles (Apple)
15	14	THE EVERLY BROTHERS' ORIGINAL GREATEST HITS — Everly Brothers (CBS)
11	15	MOTOWN CHARTBUSTERS VOL 3 — Various Artists (Tamla Motown)
18	16	MAD DOGS AND ENGLISHMEN — Joe Cocker (A&M)
20	17	EASY RIDER — Soundtrack (Stateside)
15	18	ANDY WILLIAMS' GREATEST HITS — Andy Williams (CBS)
-	19	THE WORLD OF JOHNNY CASH — Johnny Cash (CBS)
-	20	CANDLES IN THE RAIN — Melanie (Buddah)

last week	this week	10 October 1970
1	1	BRIDGE OVER TROUBLED WATER — Simon & Garfunkel (CBS)
2	2	'GET YOUR YA-YA'S OUT!' — Rolling Stones (Decca)
4	3	A QUESTION OF BALANCE — Moody Blues (Threshold)
6	4	PARANOID — Black Sabbath (Vertigo)
8	5	LED ZEPPELIN II — Led Zeppelin (Atlantic)
3	6	COSMO'S FACTORY — Creedence Clearwater Revival (Liberty)
5	7	DEEP PURPLE IN ROCK — Deep Purple (Harvest)
11	8	SOMETHING — Shirley Bassey (United Artists)
20	9	CANDLES IN THE RAIN — Melanie (Buddah)
14	10	THE EVERLY BROTHERS' ORIGINAL GREATEST HITS — Everly Brothers (CBS)
13	11	LET IT BE — Beatles (Apple)
9	12	PAINT YOUR WAGON — Soundtrack (Paramount)
17	13	EASY RIDER — Soundtrack (Stateside)
10	14	THE BEACH BOYS' GREATEST HITS — Beach Boys (Capitol)
7	15	ON STAGE: FEBRUARY 1970 — Elvis Presley (RCA)
12	16	CAN'T HELP FALLING IN LOVE — Andy Williams (CBS)
19	17	WORLD OF JOHNNY CASH — Johnny Cash (CBS)
15	18	MOTOWN CHARTBUSTERS VOL 3 — Various Artists (Tamla Motown)
-	19	BAND OF GYPSIES — Jimi Hendrix (Track)
18	20	ANDY WILLIAMS' GREATEST HITS — Andy Williams (CBS)

last week	this week	17 October 1970
4	1	PARANOID — Black Sabbath (Vertigo)
1	2	BRIDGE OVER TROUBLED WATER — Simon & Garfunkel (CBS)
2	3	'GET YOUR YA-YA'S OUT!' — Rolling Stones (Decca)
3	4	A QUESTION OF BALANCE — Moody Blues (Threshold)
9	5	CANDLES IN THE RAIN — Melanie (Buddah)
5	6	LED ZEPPELIN II — Led Zeppelin (Atlantic)
6	7	COSMO'S FACTORY — Creedence Clearwater Revival (Liberty)
7	8	DEEP PURPLE IN ROCK — Deep Purple (Harvest)
-	9	ROCK BUSTER — Various Artists (CBS)
12	10	PAINT YOUR WAGON — Soundtrack (Paramount)
-	11	ATOM HEART MOTHER — Pink Floyd (Harvest)
-	12	MOTOWN CHARTBUSTERS VOL 4 — Various Artists (Tamla Motown)
8	13	SOMETHING — Shirley Bassey (United Artists)
11	14	LET IT BE — Beatles (Apple)
10	15	THE BEACH BOYS' GREATEST HITS — Beach Boys (Capitol)
15	16	ON STAGE: FEBRUARY 1970 — Elvis Presley (RCA)
10	17	THE EVERLY BROTHERS' ORIGINAL GREATEST HITS — Everly Brothers (CBS)
-	18	FUTURE BLUES — Canned Heat (Liberty)
-	19	STAGE FRIGHT — Band (Capitol)
-	20	BAND OF GYPSIES — Jimi Hendrix (Track)

James Marshall Hendrix died on September 18. Sixteen days later, on October 4, Janis Joplin died of a heroin overdose. Hendrix had once said: "It's funny the way most people love the dead. Once you are dead you are made for life." Yet Hendrix's *Band Of Gypsies*, entering the chart on October 10, dropped out again only two weeks later. The posthumous release of Hendrix albums - many times more than ever issued in his lifetime - was slow to happen. Nor did death deliver Janis Joplin to the charts.

October – November 1970

24 October 1970

last	this		
1	1	PARANOID	Black Sabbath (Vertigo)
2	2	BRIDGE OVER TROUBLED WATER	Simon & Garfunkel (CBS)
3	3	'GET YOUR YA-YA'S OUT!'	Rolling Stones (Decca)
12	4	MOTOWN CHARTBUSTERS VOL 4	Various Artists (Tamla Motown)
8	5	DEEP PURPLE IN ROCK	Deep Purple (Harvest)
4	6	A QUESTION OF BALANCE	Moody Blues (Threshold)
6	7	LED ZEPPELIN II	Led Zeppelin (Atlantic)
7	8	COSMO'S FACTORY	Creedence Clearwater Revival (Liberty)
11	9	ATOM HEART MOTHER	Pink Floyd (Harvest)
5	10	CANDLES IN THE RAIN	Melanie (Buddah)
9	11	ROCK BUSTER	Various Artists (CBS)
19	12	STAGE FRIGHT	Band (Capitol)
13	13	SOMETHING	Shirley Bassey (United Artists)
15	14	THE BEACH BOYS' GREATEST HITS	Beach Boys (Capitol)
-	15	TIGHTEN UP VOL 3	Various Artists (Trojan)
10	16	PAINT YOUR WAGON	Soundtrack (Paramount)
16	17	ON STAGE	Elvis Presley (RCA)
-	18	THIS GUY'S IN LOVE WITH YOU	Herb Alpert & the Tijuana Brass (A&M)
17	19	THE EVERLY BROTHERS' ORIGINAL GREATEST HITS	Everly Brothers (CBS)
14	20	LET IT BE	Beatles (Apple)

31 October 1970

last	this		
-	1	LED ZEPPELIN III	Led Zeppelin (Atlantic)
4	2	MOTOWN CHARTBUSTERS VOL 4	Various Artists (Tamla Motown)
1	3	PARANOID	Black Sabbath (Vertigo)
9	4	ATOM HEART MOTHER	Pink Floyd (Harvest)
2	5	BRIDGE OVER TROUBLED WATER	Simon & Garfunkel (CBS)
5	6	DEEP PURPLE IN ROCK	Deep Purple (Harvest)
3	7	'GET YOUR YA-YA'S OUT!'	Rolling Stones (Decca)
8	8	CANDLES IN THE RAIN	Melanie (Buddah)
7	9	COSMO'S FACTORY	Creedence Clearwater Revival (Liberty)
11	10	ROCK BUSTER	Various Artists (CBS)
7	11	LED ZEPPELIN II	Led Zeppelin (Atlantic)
6	12	A QUESTION OF BALANCE	Moody Blues (Threshold)
16	13	PAINT YOUR WAGON	Soundtrack (Paramount)
-	14	EASY LISTENING	Various Artists (Polydor)
14	15	THE BEACH BOYS' GREATEST HITS	Beach Boys (Capitol)
15	16	TIGHTEN UP VOL 3	Various Artists (Trojan)
19	17	THE EVERLY BROTHERS' ORIGINAL GREATEST HITS	Everly Brothers (CBS)
18	18	THIS GUY'S IN LOVE WITH YOU	Herb Alpert & the Tijuana Brass (A&M)
-	19	DEJA VU	Crosby, Stills, Nash & Young (Atlantic)
-	20	TOTAL SOUND	Various Artists (Studio Two)

7 November 1970

last	this		
2	1	MOTOWN CHARTBUSTERS VOL 4	Various Artists (Tamla Motown)
1	2	LED ZEPPELIN III	Led Zeppelin (Atlantic)
8	3	CANDLES IN THE RAIN	Melanie (Buddah)
5	4	BRIDGE OVER TROUBLED WATER	Simon & Garfunkel (CBS)
3	5	PARANOID	Black Sabbath (Vertigo)
4	6	ATOM HEART MOTHER	Pink Floyd (Harvest)
6	7	DEEP PURPLE IN ROCK	Deep Purple (Harvest)
11	8	LED ZEPPELIN II	Led Zeppelin (Atlantic)
7	9	'GET YOUR YA-YA'S OUT!'	Rolling Stones (Decca)
9	10	COSMO'S FACTORY	Creedence Clearwater Revival (Liberty)
10	11	ROCK BUSTER	Various Artists (CBS)
13	12	PAINT YOUR WAGON	Soundtrack (Paramount)
14	13	EASY LISTENING	Various Artists (Polydor)
-	14	AFTER THE GOLD RUSH	Neil Young (Reprise)
16	15	TIGHTEN UP VOL 3	Various Artists (Trojan)
17	16	THE EVERLY BROTHERS' ORIGINAL GREATEST HITS	Everly Brothers (CBS)
15	17	THE BEACH BOYS' GREATEST HITS	Beach Boys (Capitol)
20	18	TOTAL SOUND	Various Artists (Studio Two)
-	19	OVER AND OVER	Nana Mouskouri (Fontana)
12	20	A QUESTION OF BALANCE	Moody Blues (Threshold)

14 November 1970

last	this		
2	1	LED ZEPPELIN III	Led Zeppelin (Atlantic)
1	2	MOTOWN CHARTBUSTERS VOL 4	Various Artists (Tamla Motown)
4	3	BRIDGE OVER TROUBLED WATER	Simon & Garfunkel (CBS)
5	4	PARANOID	Black Sabbath (Vertigo)
3	5	CANDLES IN THE RAIN	Melanie (Buddah)
6	6	ATOM HEART MOTHER	Pink Floyd (Harvest)
7	7	DEEP PURPLE IN ROCK	Deep Purple (Harvest)
14	8	AFTER THE GOLD RUSH	Neil Young (Reprise)
13	9	EASY LISTENING	Various Artists (Polydor)
9	10	'GET YOUR YA-YA'S OUT!'	Rolling Stones (Decca)
12	11	PAINT YOUR WAGON	Soundtrack (Paramount)
8	12	LED ZEPPELIN II	Led Zeppelin (Atlantic)
10	13	COSMO'S FACTORY	Creedence Clearwater Revival (Liberty)
11	14	ROCK BUSTER	Various Artists (CBS)
18	15	TOTAL SOUND	Various Artists (Studio Two)
-	16	I WHO HAVE NOTHING	Tom Jones (Decca)
16	17	THE EVERLY BROTHERS' ORIGINAL GREATEST HITS	Everly Brothers (CBS)
15	18	TIGHTEN UP VOL 3	Various Artists (Trojan)
-	19	FULL CREAM	Cream (Polydor)
17	20	THE BEACH BOYS' GREATEST HITS	Beach Boys (Capitol)

21 November 1970

last	this		
1	1	LED ZEPPELIN III	Led Zeppelin (Atlantic)
2	2	MOTOWN CHARTBUSTERS VOL 4	Various Artists (Tamla Motown)
4	3	PARANOID	Black Sabbath (Vertigo)
3	4	BRIDGE OVER TROUBLED WATER	Simon & Garfunkel (CBS)
7	5	DEEP PURPLE IN ROCK	Deep Purple (Harvest)
6	6	ATOM HEART MOTHER	Pink Floyd (Harvest)
5	7	CANDLES IN THE RAIN	Melanie (Buddah)
-	8	NEW MORNING	Bob Dylan (CBS)
9	9	EASY LISTENING	Various Artists (Polydor)
8	10	AFTER THE GOLD RUSH	Neil Young (Reprise)
16	11	I WHO HAVE NOTHING	Tom Jones (Decca)
12	12	LED ZEPPELIN II	Led Zeppelin (Atlantic)
11	13	PAINT YOUR WAGON	Soundtrack (Paramount)
14	14	ROCK BUSTER	Various Artists (CBS)
10	15	'GET YOUR YA-YA'S OUT!'	Rolling Stones (Decca)
13	16	COSMO'S FACTORY	Creedence Clearwater Revival (Liberty)
15	17	TOTAL SOUND	Various Artists (Studio Two)
-	18	JOHNNY CASH AT SAN QUENTIN	Johnny Cash (CBS)
20	19	THE BEACH BOYS' GREATEST HITS	Beach Boys (Capitol)
-	20	ANYWAY	Family (Reprise)

28 November 1970

last	this		
1	1	LED ZEPPELIN III	Led Zeppelin (Atlantic)
2	2	MOTOWN CHARTBUSTERS VOL 4	Various Artists (Tamla Motown)
4	3	BRIDGE OVER TROUBLED WATER	Simon & Garfunkel (CBS)
7	4	CANDLES IN THE RAIN	Melanie (Buddah)
5	5	DEEP PURPLE IN ROCK	Deep Purple (Harvest)
3	6	PARANOID	Black Sabbath (Vertigo)
10	7	AFTER THE GOLD RUSH	Neil Young (Reprise)
9	8	EASY LISTENING	Various Artists (Polydor)
8	9	NEW MORNING	Bob Dylan (CBS)
6	10	ATOM HEART MOTHER	Pink Floyd (Harvest)
-	11	EMERSON LAKE AND PALMER	Emerson Lake & Palmer (Island)
-	12	ANDY WILLIAMS' GREATEST HITS	Andy Williams (CBS)
12	13	LED ZEPPELIN II	Led Zeppelin (Atlantic)
11	14	I WHO HAVE NOTHING	Tom Jones (Decca)
18	15	JOHNNY CASH AT SAN QUENTIN	Johnny Cash (CBS)
-	16	SWEET BABY JAMES	James Taylor (Warner Bros.)
20	17	ANYWAY	Family (Reprise)
13	18	PAINT YOUR WAGON	Soundtrack (Paramount)
19	19	THE BEACH BOYS' GREATEST HITS	Beach Boys (Capitol)
15	20	'GET YOUR YA-YA'S OUT!'	Rolling Stones (Decca)
17	21	TOTAL SOUND	Various Artists (Studio Two)
-	22	ABRAXAS	Santana (CBS)
-	23	EASY RIDER	Soundtrack (Stateside)
16	24	COSMO'S FACTORY	Creedence Clearwater Revival (Liberty)
-	25	CAN'T HELP FALLING IN LOVE	Andy Williams (CBS)
-	26	ELVIS' CHRISTMAS ALBUM	Elvis Presley (RCA)
14	27	ROCK BUSTER	Various Artists (CBS)
-	28	SOMETHING	Shirley Bassey (United Artists)
-	29	THE SOUND OF MUSIC	Soundtrack (RCA)
-	30	THIS GUY'S IN LOVE WITH YOU	Herb Alpert & the Tijuana Brass (A&M)

The genre later called Heavy Metal was spreading fast. Led Zeppelin II was joined by Led Zeppelin III, making a dramatic entrance straight in at No.1, and in the process knocking one of the Zeppelin wannabe groups off the top spot, Black Sabbath and Paranoid, while a few rungs down lurked *Deep Purple In Rock*. (The term wannabe hadn't arrived yet either.) Meanwhile, as from November 28, the NME chart expanded again, this time to offer the Top 30.

December 1970

It's that Jim Reeves time of year again, and a great encouragement to the public, apparently, to buy Andy Williams records. Andy, a replacement Perry Como, was born wearing a cardigan. This yuletide saw him with three Top 20 albums. Shirley Bassey reached the charts with *Something*, titled after the song that had given her a Top 5 single earlier in the year and that, along with *Here Comes The Sun*, had been proving to an embattled Lennon and McCartney that George Harrison really could write songs. The year ended with the entry of George's own (triple) solo album *All Things Must Pass*, destined for immense success.

2 January 1971

last week	this week	Title / Artist
2	1	ANDY WILLIAMS' GREATEST HITS Andy Williams (CBS)
1	2	LED ZEPPELIN III Led Zeppelin (Atlantic)
3	3	BRIDGE OVER TROUBLED WATER Simon & Garfunkel (CBS)
5	4	MOTOWN CHARTBUSTERS VOL 4 Various Artist (Tamla Motown)
7	5	FRANK SINATRA'S GREATEST HITS VOL 2 Frank Sinatra (Reprise)
11	6	ALL THINGS MUST PASS George Harrison (Apple)
6	7	EMERSON LAKE & PALMER Emerson, Lake & Palmer (Island)
15	8	PAINT YOUR WAGON Soundtrack (Paramount)
12	9	JOHNNY CASH AT SAN QUENTIN Johnny Cash (CBS)
16	10	CAN'T HELP FALLING IN LOVE Andy Williams (CBS)
9	11	DEEP PURPLE IN ROCK Deep Purple (Harvest)
17	12	THE SOUND OF MUSIC Soundtrack (RCA)
8	13	SWEET BABY JAMES James Taylor (Warner Bros.)
24	14	12 SONGS OF CHRISTMAS Jim Reeves (RCA International)
4	15	NEW MORNING Bob Dylan (CBS)
18	16	THE GLEN CAMPBELL ALBUM Glen Campbell (Capitol)
10	17	EASY LISTENING Various Artists (Polydor)
25	18	AIR CONDITIONING Curved Air (Warner Bros.)
20	19	ABRAXAS Santana (CBS)
26	20	LET IT BE Beatles (Apple)
13	21	ANDY WILLIAMS SHOW Andy Williams (CBS)
27	22	JOHNNY CASH SHOW Johnny Cash (CBS)
21	23	CANDLES IN THE RAIN Melanie (Buddah)
-	24	THE BEACH BOYS' GREATEST HITS Beach Boys (Capitol)
19	25	AFTER THE GOLD RUSH Neil Young (Reprise)
23	26	OVER AND OVER Nana Mouskouri (Fontana)
22	27	ANYWAY Family (Reprise)
28	28	PARANOID Black Sabbath (Vertigo)
30	29	ELVIS' CHRISTMAS ALBUM Elvis Presley (RCA)
-	30	ATOM HEART MOTHER Pink Floyd (Harvest)

9 January 1971

last week	this week	Title / Artist
1	1	ANDY WILLIAMS' GREATEST HITS Andy Williams (CBS)
4	2	MOTOWN CHARTBUSTERS VOL 4 Various Artists (Tamla Motown)
3	3	BRIDGE OVER TROUBLED WATER Simon & Garfunkel (CBS)
2	4	LED ZEPPELIN III Led Zeppelin (Atlantic)
6	5	ALL THINGS MUST PASS George Harrison (Apple)
11	6	DEEP PURPLE IN ROCK Deep Purple (Harvest)
9	7	JOHNNY CASH AT SAN QUENTIN Johnny Cash (CBS)
7	8	EMERSON LAKE & PALMER Emerson, Lake & Palmer (Island)
8	9	PAINT YOUR WAGON Soundtrack (Paramount)
5	10	FRANK SINATRA'S GREATEST HITS VOL 2 Frank Sinatra (Reprise)
10	11	CAN'T HELP FALLING IN LOVE Andy Williams (CBS)
18	12	AIR CONDITIONING Curved Air (Warner Bros.)
23	13	CANDLES IN THE RAIN Melanie (Buddah)
26	14	OVER AND OVER Nana Mouskouri (Fontana)
12	15	THE SOUND OF MUSIC Soundtrack (RCA)
16	16	THE GLEN CAMPBELL ALBUM Glen Campbell (Capitol)
20	17	LET IT BE Beatles (Apple)
13	18	SWEET BABY JAMES James Taylor (Warner Bros.)
15	19	NEW MORNING Bob Dylan (CBS)
17	20	EASY LISTENING Various Artists (Polydor)
21	21	ANDY WILLIAMS SHOW Andy Williams (CBS)
22	22	THE BEACH BOYS' GREATEST HITS Beach Boys (Capitol)
-	23	TOTAL SOUND Various Artists (Studio Two)
24	24	STEPHEN STILLS Stephen Stills (Atlantic)
30	25	ATOM HEART MOTHER Pink Floyd (Harvest)
-	26	LED ZEPPELIN II Led Zeppelin (Atlantic)
27	27	ANYWAY Family (Reprise)
22	28	JOHNNY CASH SHOW Johnny Cash (CBS)
19	29	ABRAXAS Santana (CBS)
28	30	PARANOID Black Sabbath (Vertigo)

16 January 1971

last week	this week	Title / Artist
3	1	BRIDGE OVER TROUBLED WATER Simon & Garfunkel (CBS)
1	2	ANDY WILLIAMS' GREATEST HITS Andy Williams (CBS)
2	3	MOTOWN CHARTBUSTERS VOL 4 Various Artists (Tamla Motown)
4	4	LED ZEPPELIN III Led Zeppelin (Atlantic)
5	5	ALL THINGS MUST PASS George Harrison (Apple)
8	6	EMERSON LAKE & PALMER Emerson, Lake & Palmer (Island)
18	7	SWEET BABY JAMES James Taylor (Warner Bros.)
6	8	DEEP PURPLE IN ROCK Deep Purple (Harvest)
13	9	CANDLES IN THE RAIN Melanie (Buddah)
9	10	PAINT YOUR WAGON Soundtrack (Paramount)
10	11	FRANK SINATRA'S GREATEST HITS VOL 2 Frank Sinatra (Reprise)
7	12	JOHNNY CASH AT SAN QUENTIN Johnny Cash (CBS)
25	13	ATOM HEART MOTHER Pink Floyd (Harvest)
19	14	NEW MORNING Bob Dylan (CBS)
11	15	CAN'T HELP FALLING IN LOVE Andy Williams (CBS)
20	16	EASY LISTENING Various Artists (Polydor)
-	17	JOHN LENNON/PLASTIC ONO BAND John Lennon & the Plastic Ono Band (Apple)
-	18	AFTER THE GOLD RUSH Neil Young (Reprise)
16	19	THE GLEN CAMPBELL ALBUM Glen Campbell (Capitol)
22	20	THE BEACH BOYS' GREATEST HITS Beach Boys (Capitol)
-	21	T. REX T. Rex (Fly)
26	22	LED ZEPPELIN II Led Zeppelin (Atlantic)
14	23	OVER AND OVER Nana Mouskouri (Fontana)
15	24	THE SOUND OF MUSIC Soundtrack (RCA)
29	25	ABRAXAS Santana (CBS)
12	26	AIR CONDITIONING Curved Air (Warner Bros.)
-	27	WATT Ten Years After (Deram)
17	28	LET IT BE Beatles (Apple)
-	29	SOMETHING Shirley Bassey (United Artists)
-	30	LEFTOVER WINE Melanie (Buddah)

23 January 1971

last week	this week	Title / Artist
2	1	ANDY WILLIAMS' GREATEST HITS Andy Williams (CBS)
1	2	BRIDGE OVER TROUBLED WATER Simon & Garfunkel (CBS)
4	3	LED ZEPPELIN III Led Zeppelin (Atlantic)
3	4	MOTOWN CHARTBUSTERS VOL 4 Various Artists (Tamla Motown)
5	5	ALL THINGS MUST PASS George Harrison (Apple)
6	6	EMERSON LAKE & PALMER Emerson, Lake & Palmer (Island)
7	7	SWEET BABY JAMES James Taylor (Warner Bros.)
8	8	DEEP PURPLE IN ROCK Deep Purple (Harvest)
11	9	FRANK SINATRA'S GREATEST HITS VOL 2 Frank Sinatra (Reprise)
18	10	AFTER THE GOLD RUSH Neil Young (Reprise)
-	11	TUMBLEWEED CONNECTION Elton John (DJM)
21	12	T. REX T. Rex (Fly)
27	13	WATT Ten Years After (Deram)
13	14	ATOM HEART MOTHER Pink Floyd (Harvest)
10	15	PAINT YOUR WAGON Soundtrack (Paramount)
25	16	ABRAXAS Santana (CBS)
16	17	EASY LISTENING Various Artists (Polydor)
12	18	JOHNNY CASH AT SAN QUENTIN Johnny Cash (CBS)
26	19	AIR CONDITIONING Curved Air (Warner Bros.)
28	20	LET IT BE Beatles (Apple)
15	21	CAN'T HELP FALLING IN LOVE Andy Williams (CBS)
9	22	CANDLES IN THE RAIN Melanie (Buddah)
17	23	JOHN LENNON/PLASTIC ONO BAND John Lennon & the Plastic One Band (Apple)
24	24	THE SOUND OF MUSIC Soundtrack (RCA)
22	25	LED ZEPPELIN II Led Zeppelin (Atlantic)
19	26	THE GLEN CAMPBELL ALBUM Glen Campbell (Capitol)
14	27	NEW MORNING Bob Dylan (CBS)
-	28	STEPHEN STILLS Stephen Stills (Atlantic)
30	29	LEFTOVER WINE Melanie (Buddah)
23	30	OVER AND OVER Nana Mouskouri (Fontana)

No wonder people were grateful when George Harrison jumped up the January singles chart from No.14 to No.1 with *My Sweet Lord*: it displaced *Grandad* by Clive Dunn, which T. Rex's *Ride A White Swan* had failed to do. Others currently with hit singles were the Jackson Five, Neil Diamond, Glen Campbell, Gilbert O'Sullivan, Ken Dodd, White Plains, Ann Murray, Chairmen of the Board, Dorothy Squires (a querulous *My Way*) and Roger Whittaker. All things must pass.

January – February 1971

last this
week

30 January 1971

last	this		
5	1	ALL THINGS MUST PASS	George Harrison (Apple)
2	2	BRIDGE OVER TROUBLED WATER	Simon & Garfunkel (CBS)
1	3	ANDY WILLIAMS' GREATEST HITS	Andy Williams (CBS)
4	4	MOTOWN CHARTBUSTERS VOL 4	Various Artists (Tamla Motown)
3	5	LED ZEPPELIN III	Led Zeppelin (Atlantic)
7	6	SWEET BABY JAMES	James Taylor (Warner Bros.)
6	7	EMERSON LAKE & PALMER	Emerson, Lake & Palmer (Island)
9	8	FRANK SINATRA'S GREATEST HITS VOL 2	Frank Sinatra (Reprise)
13	9	WATT	Ten Years After (Deram)
10	10	AFTER THE GOLD RUSH	Neil Young (Reprise)
11	11	TUMBLEWEED CONNECTION	Elton John (DJM)
12	12	T. REX	T. Rex (Fly)
15	13	PAINT YOUR WAGON	Soundtrack (Paramount)
17	14	EASY LISTENING	Various Artists (Polydor)
19	15	AIR CONDITIONING	Curved Air (Warner Bros.)
8	16	DEEP PURPLE IN ROCK	Deep Purple (Harvest)
23	17	JOHN LENNON/PLASTIC ONO BAND	John Lennon & the Plastic Ono Band (Apple)
25	18	LED ZEPPELIN II	Led Zeppelin (Atlantic)
22	19	CANDLES IN THE RAIN	Melanie (Buddah)
16	20	ABRAXAS	Santana (CBS)
18	21	JOHNNY CASH AT SAN QUENTIN	Johnny Cash (CBS)
-	22	ELVIS: THAT'S THE WAY IT IS	Elvis Presley (RCA)
28	23	STEPHEN STILLS	Stephen Stills (Atlantic)
-	24	PENDULUM	Creedence Clearwater Revival (Liberty)
29	25	LEFTOVER WINE	Melanie (Buddah)
-	26	ELTON JOHN	Elton John (DJM)
14	27	ATOM HEART MOTHER	Pink Floyd (Harvest)
26	28	THE GLEN CAMPBELL ALBUM	Glen Campbell (Capitol)
-	29	GOLD	Neil Diamond (UNI)
20	30	LET IT BE	Beatles (Apple)

6 February 1971

1	1	ALL THINGS MUST PASS	George Harrison (Apple)
2	2	BRIDGE OVER TROUBLED WATER	Simon & Garfunkel (CBS)
3	3	ANDY WILLIAMS' GREATEST HITS	Andy Williams (CBS)
4	4	MOTOWN CHARTBUSTERS VOL 4	Various Artists (Tamla Motown)
5	5	LED ZEPPELIN III	Led Zeppelin (Atlantic)
11	6	TUMBLEWEED CONNECTION	Elton John (DJM)
6	7	SWEET BABY JAMES	James Taylor (Warner Bros.)
7	8	EMERSON LAKE & PALMER	Emerson, Lake & Palmer (Island)
8	9	FRANK SINATRA'S GREATEST HITS VOL 2	Frank Sinatra (Reprise)
16	10	DEEP PURPLE IN ROCK	Deep Purple (Harvest)
30	11	LET IT BE	Beatles (Apple)
9	12	WATT	Ten Years After (Deram)
17	13	JOHN LENNON/PLASTIC ONO BAND	John Lennon & the Plastic Ono Band (Apple)
18	14	LED ZEPPELIN II	Led Zeppelin (Atlantic)
-	15	CAN'T HELP FALLING IN LOVE	Andy Williams (CBS)
19	16	CANDLES IN THE RAIN	Melanie (Buddah)
15	17	AIR CONDITIONING	Curved Air (Warner Bros.)
22	18	ELVIS: THAT'S THE WAY IT IS	Elvis Presley (RCA)
12	19	T. REX	T. Rex (Fly)
24	20	PENDULUM	Creedence Clearwater Revival (Liberty)
21	21	JOHNNY CASH AT SAN QUENTIN	Johnny Cash (CBS)
23	22	STEPHEN STILLS	Stephen Stills (Atlantic)
10	23	AFTER THE GOLD RUSH	Neil Young (Reprise)
14	24	EASY LISTENING	Various Artists (Polydor)
13	25	PAINT YOUR WAGON	Soundtrack (Paramount)
-	26	OVER AND OVER	Nana Mouskouri (Fontana)
-	27	McGUINNESS FLINT	McGuinness Flint (Capitol)
26	28	ELTON JOHN	Elton John (DJM)
25	29	LEFTOVER WINE	Melanie (Buddah)
20	30	ABRAXAS	Santana (CBS)

13 February 1971

1	1	ALL THINGS MUST PASS	George Harrison (Apple)
2	2	BRIDGE OVER TROUBLED WATER	Simon & Garfunkel (CBS)
6	3	TUMBLEWEED CONNECTION	Elton John (DJM)
3	4	ANDY WILLIAMS' GREATEST HITS	Andy Williams (CBS)
4	5	MOTOWN CHARTBUSTERS VOL 4	Various Artists (Tamla Motown)
7	6	SWEET BABY JAMES	James Taylor (Warner Bros.)
5	7	LED ZEPPELIN III	Led Zeppelin (Atlantic)
17	8	AIR CONDITIONING	Curved Air (Warner Bros.)
8	9	EMERSON LAKE & PALMER	Emerson, Lake & Palmer (Island)
10	10	DEEP PURPLE IN ROCK	Deep Purple (Harvest)
9	11	FRANK SINATRA'S GREATEST HITS VOL 2	Frank Sinatra (Reprise)
23	12	AFTER THE GOLD RUSH	Neil Young (Reprise)
13	13	JOHN LENNON/PLASTIC ONO BAND	John Lennon & the Plastic Ono Band (Apple)
24	14	EASY LISTENING	Various Artists (Polydor)
18	15	ELVIS: THAT'S THE WAY IT IS	Elvis Presley (RCA)
20	16	PENDULUM	Creedence Clearwater Revival (Liberty)
19	17	T. REX	T. Rex (Fly)
27	18	McGUINNESS FLINT	McGuinness Flint (Capitol)
-	19	DEJA VU	Crosby Stills Nash & Young (Atlantic)
15	20	CAN'T HELP FALLING IN LOVE	Andy Williams (CBS)
12	21	WATT	Ten Years After (Deram)
22	22	STEPHEN STILLS	Stephen Stills (Atlantic)
21	23	JOHNNY CASH AT SAN QUENTIN	Johnny Cash (CBS)
16	24	CANDLES IN THE RAIN	Melanie (Buddah)
14	25	LED ZEPPELIN II	Led Zeppelin (Atlantic)
26	26	OVER AND OVER	Nana Mouskouri (Fontana)
25	27	PAINT YOUR WAGON	Soundtrack (Paramount)
29	28	LEFTOVER WINE	Melanie (Buddah)
-	29	WISHBONE ASH	Wishbone Ash (MCA)
28	30	ELTON JOHN	Elton John (DJM)

20 February 1971

1	1	ALL THINGS MUST PASS	George Harrison (Apple)
2	2	BRIDGE OVER TROUBLED WATER	Simon & Garfunkel (CBS)
3	3	TUMBLEWEED CONNECTION	Elton John (DJM)
4	4	ANDY WILLIAMS' GREATEST HITS	Andy Williams (CBS)
5	5	MOTOWN CHARTBUSTERS VOL 4	Various Artists (Tamla Motown)
7	6	LED ZEPPELIN III	Led Zeppelin (Atlantic)
8	7	AIR CONDITIONING	Curved Air (Warner Bros.)
11	8	FRANK SINATRA'S GREATEST HITS VOL 2	Frank Sinatra (Reprise)
6	9	SWEET BABY JAMES	James Taylor (Warner Bros.)
10	10	DEEP PURPLE IN ROCK	Deep Purple (Harvest)
9	11	EMERSON LAKE & PALMER	Emerson, Lake & Palmer (Island)
14	12	EASY LISTENING	Various Artists (Polydor)
13	13	JOHN LENNON/PLASTIC ONO BAND	John Lennon & the Plastic Ono Band (Apple)
21	14	WATT	Ten Years After (Deram)
30	15	ELTON JOHN	Elton John (DJM)
12	16	AFTER THE GOLD RUSH	Neil Young (Reprise)
16	17	PENDULUM	Creedence Clearwater Revival (Liberty)
15	18	ELVIS: THAT'S THE WAY IT IS	Elvis Presley (RCA)
17	19	T. REX	T. Rex (Fly)
20	20	CAN'T HELP FALLING IN LOVE	Andy Williams (CBS)
25	21	LED ZEPPELIN II	Led Zeppelin (Atlantic)
24	22	CANDLES IN THE RAIN	Melanie (Buddah)
19	23	DEJA VU	Crosby Stills Nash & Young (Atlantic)
29	24	WISHBONE ASH	Wishbone Ash (MCA)
28	25	LEFTOVER WINE	Melanie (Buddah)
23	26	JOHNNY CASH AT SAN QUENTIN	Johnny Cash (CBS)
18	27	McGUINNESS FLINT	McGuinness Flint (Capitol)
-	28	CLOSE TO YOU	Carpenters (A&M)
-	29	MY WAY	Frank Sinatra (Reprise)
-	30	LET IT BE	Beatles (Apple)

John Lennon & The Plastic Ono Band was not an album that much pleased the public. However, a new superstar did: Elton John, at first perceived as an "authentic-sounding" Brit R&B singer good at southern fried ballads with soulful piano. An English Leon Russell, almost. Signed to little DJM - it stood for Dick James Music, and had once had the Beatles' song-publishing - suddenly in February Elton had two Top 20 albums at once, (his 2nd and 3rd LPs) helped by just one hit single, *Your Song*.

February – March 1971

27 February 1971

last week	this week	Title	Artist
1	1	ALL THINGS MUST PASS	George Harrison (Apple)
2	2	BRIDGE OVER TROUBLED WATER	Simon & Garfunkel (CBS)
3	3	TUMBLEWEED CONNECTION	Elton John (DJM)
9	4	SWEET BABY JAMES	James Taylor (Warner Bros.)
4	5	ANDY WILLIAMS' GREATEST HITS	Andy Williams (CBS)
5	6	MOTOWN CHARTBUSTERS VOL 4	Various Artists (Tamla Motown)
6	7	LED ZEPPELIN III	Led Zeppelin (Atlantic)
8	8	FRANK SINATRA'S GREATEST HITS VOL 2	Frank Sinatra (Reprise)
7	9	AIR CONDITIONING	Curved Air (Warner Bros.)
11	10	EMERSON LAKE & PALMER	Emerson, Lake & Palmer (Island)
10	11	DEEP PURPLE IN ROCK	Deep Purple (Harvest)
18	12	ELVIS: THAT'S THE WAY IT IS	Elvis Presley (RCA)
17	13	PENDULUM	Creedence Clearwater Revival (Liberty)
-	14	CHICAGO 3	Chicago (CBS)
19	15	T. REX	T. Rex (Fly)
16	16	AFTER THE GOLD RUSH	Neil Young (Reprise)
12	17	EASY LISTENING	Various Artists (Polydor)
-	18	STEPHEN STILLS	Stephen Stills (Atlantic)
14	19	WATT	Ten Years After (Deram)
-	20	THE SOUND OF MUSIC	Soundtrack (RCA)
15	21	ELTON JOHN	Elton John (DJM)
-	22	PAINT YOUR WAGON	Soundtrack (Paramount)
13	23	JOHN LENNON/PLASTIC ONO BAND	John Lennon & the Plastic Ono Band (Apple)
22	24	CANDLES IN THE RAIN	Melanie (Buddah)
-	25	GOLD	Neil Diamond (UNI)
20	26	CAN'T HELP FALLING IN LOVE	Andy Williams (CBS)
25	27	LEFTOVER WINE	Melanie (Buddah)
29	28	MY WAY	Frank Sinatra (Reprise)
23	29	DEJA VU	Crosby Stills Nash & Young (Atlantic)
24	30	WISHBONE ASH	Wishbone Ash (MCA)

6 March 1971

last week	this week	Title	Artist
1	1	ALL THINGS MUST PASS	George Harrison (Apple)
2	2	BRIDGE OVER TROUBLED WATER	Simon & Garfunkel (CBS)
3	3	TUMBLEWEED CONNECTION	Elton John (DJM)
5	4	ANDY WILLIAMS' GREATEST HITS	Andy Williams (CBS)
4	5	SWEET BABY JAMES	James Taylor (Warner Bros.)
6	6	MOTOWN CHARTBUSTERS VOL 4	Various Artists (Tamla Motown)
7	7	LED ZEPPELIN III	Led Zeppelin (Atlantic)
9	8	AIR CONDITIONING	Curved Air (Warner Bros.)
13	9	PENDULUM	Creedence Clearwater Revival (Liberty)
11	10	DEEP PURPLE IN ROCK	Deep Purple (Harvest)
8	11	FRANK SINATRA'S GREATEST HITS VOL 2	Frank Sinatra (Reprise)
19	12	WATT	Ten Years After (Deram)
23	13	JOHN LENNON/PLASTIC ONO BAND	John Lennon & the Plastic Ono Band (Apple)
21	14	ELTON JOHN	Elton John (DJM)
15	15	CHICAGO 3	Chicago (CBS)
16	16	AFTER THE GOLD RUSH	Neil Young (Reprise)
10	17	EMERSON LAKE & PALMER	Emerson, Lake & Palmer (Island)
12	18	ELVIS: THAT'S THE WAY IT IS	Elvis Presley (RCA)
18	19	STEPHEN STILLS	Stephen Stills (Atlantic)
17	20	EASY LISTENING	Various Artists (Polydor)
-	21	LED ZEPPELIN II	Led Zeppelin (Atlantic)
24	22	CANDLES IN THE RAIN	Melanie (Buddah)
25	23	GOLD	Neil Diamond (UNI)
-	24	ABRAXAS	Santana (CBS)
15	25	T. REX	T. Rex (Fly)
-	26	TAP ROOT MANUSCRIPT	Neil Diamond (UNI)
20	27	THE SOUND OF MUSIC	Soundtrack (RCA)
-	28	THE YES ALBUM	Yes (Atlantic)
-	29	LET IT BE	Beatles (Apple)
27	30	LEFTOVER WINE	Melanie (Buddah)

13 March 1971

last week	this week	Title	Artist
1	1	ALL THINGS MUST PASS	George Harrison (Apple)
2	2	BRIDGE OVER TROUBLED WATER	Simon & Garfunkel (CBS)
3	3	TUMBLEWEED CONNECTION	Elton John (DJM)
4	4	ANDY WILLIAMS' GREATEST HITS	Andy Williams (CBS)
5	5	SWEET BABY JAMES	James Taylor (Warner Bros.)
7	6	LED ZEPPELIN III	Led Zeppelin (Atlantic)
14	7	ELTON JOHN	Elton John (DJM)
9	8	PENDULUM	Creedence Clearwater Revival (Liberty)
11	9	FRANK SINATRA'S GREATEST HITS VOL 2	Frank Sinatra (Reprise)
28	10	THE YES ALBUM	Yes (Atlantic)
8	11	AIR CONDITIONING	Curved Air (Warner Bros.)
10	12	DEEP PURPLE IN ROCK	Deep Purple (Harvest)
17	13	EMERSON LAKE & PALMER	Emerson, Lake & Palmer (Island)
6	14	MOTOWN CHARTBUSTERS VOL 4	Various Artists (Tamla Motown)
-	15	THE BEST OF T. REX	T. Rex (Fly)
19	16	STEPHEN STILLS	Stephen Stills (Atlantic)
26	17	TAP ROOT MANUSCRIPT	Neil Diamond (UNI)
-	18	WHALES AND NIGHTINGALES	Judy Collins (Elektra)
23	19	GOLD	Neil Diamond (UNI)
16	20	AFTER THE GOLD RUSH	Neil Young (Reprise)
15	21	CHICAGO 3	Chicago (CBS)
-	22	STONE AGE	Rolling Stones (Decca)
-	23	HOME LOVIN' MAN	Andy Williams (CBS)
21	24	LED ZEPPELIN II	Led Zeppelin (Atlantic)
18	25	ELVIS: THAT'S THE WAY IT IS	Elvis Presley (RCA)
20	26	EASY LISTENING	Various Artists (Polydor)
13	27	JOHN LENNON/ PLASTIC ONO BAND	John Lennon & the Plastic Ono Band (Apple)
-	28	LIVE TASTE	Taste (Polydor)
12	29	WATT	Ten Years After (Deram)
29	30	LET IT BE	Beatles (Apple)

20 March 1971

last week	this week	Title	Artist
2	1	BRIDGE OVER TROUBLED WATER	Simon & Garfunkel (CBS)
1	2	ALL THINGS MUST PASS	George Harrison (Apple)
3	3	TUMBLEWEED CONNECTION	Elton John (DJM)
23	4	HOME LOVIN' MAN	Andy Williams (CBS)
4	5	ANDY WILLIAMS' GREATEST HITS	Andy Williams (CBS)
15	6	THE BEST OF T. REX	T. Rex (Fly)
6	7	LED ZEPPELIN III	Led Zeppelin (Atlantic)
9	8	FRANK SINATRA'S GREATEST HITS VOL 2	Frank Sinatra (Reprise)
12	9	DEEP PURPLE IN ROCK	Deep Purple (Harvest)
10	10	THE YES ALBUM	Yes (Atlantic)
22	11	STONE AGE	Rolling Stones (Decca)
26	12	EASY LISTENING	Various Artists (Polydor)
5	13	SWEET BABY JAMES	James Taylor (Warner Bros.)
7	14	ELTON JOHN	Elton John (DJM)
14	15	MOTOWN CHARTBUSTERS VOL 4	Various Artists (Tamla Motown)
13	16	EMERSON LAKE & PALMER	Emerson, Lake & Palmer (Island)
8	17	PENDULUM	Creedence Clearwater Revival (Liberty)
11	18	AIR CONDITIONING	Curved Air (Warner Bros.)
19	19	GOLD	Neil Diamond (UNI)
21	20	CHICAGO 3	Chicago (CBS)
27	21	JOHN LENNON/PLASTIC ONO BAND	John Lennon & the Plastic Ono Band (Apple)
24	22	LED ZEPPELIN II	Led Zeppelin (Atlantic)
-	23	THE WORLD OF YOUR 100 BEST TUNES	Various Artists (Decca)
-	24	THE SOUND OF MUSIC	Soundtrack (RCA)
-	25	PORTRAIT IN MUSIC	Burt Bacharach (A&M)
17	26	TAP ROOT MANUSCRIPT	Neil Diamond (UNI)
18	27	WHALES AND NIGHTINGALES	Judy Collins (Elektra)
16	28	STEPHEN STILLS	Stephen Stills (Atlantic)
28	29	LIVE TASTE	Taste (Polydor)
20	30	AFTER THE GOLD RUSH	Neil Young (Reprise)

Symptomatic of the age was a chart that included *Deja Vu* by supplemented supergroup Crosby Stills Nash & Young (Young was the supplement), plus Wishbone Ash, Yes, Judy Collins' *Whales And Nightingales*, two Melanie albums and Ten Years After. Ten Years After, fronted by Alvin Lee, a faster-than-thou guitarist, had been one of the unexpected popular successes at Woodstock. While their one hit single, *Love Like A Man*, had reached No.7 the previous August, *Watt* was not their first hit album.

March – April 1971

27 March 1971

last week	this week	Album	Artist (Label)
1	1	BRIDGE OVER TROUBLED WATER	Simon & Garfunkel (CBS)
4	2	HOME LOVIN' MAN	Andy Williams (CBS)
2	3	ALL THINGS MUST PASS	George Harrison (Apple)
5	4	ANDY WILLIAMS' GREATEST HITS	Andy Williams (CBS)
-	5	CRY OF LOVE	Jimi Hendrix (Track)
3	6	TUMBLEWEED CONNECTION	Elton John (DJM)
10	7	THE YES ALBUM	Yes (Atlantic)
7	8	LED ZEPPELIN III	Led Zeppelin (Atlantic)
8	9	FRANK SINATRA'S GREATEST HITS VOL 2	Frank Sinatra (Reprise)
9	10	DEEP PURPLE IN ROCK	Deep Purple (Harvest)
11	11	STONE AGE	Rolling Stones (Decca)
20	12	CHICAGO 3	Chicago (CBS)
15	13	MOTOWN CHARTBUSTERS VOL 4	Various Artists (Tamla Motown)
12	14	EASY LISTENING	Various Artists (Polydor)
16	15	EMERSON LAKE & PALMER	Emerson, Lake & Palmer (Island)
6	16	THE BEST OF T. REX	T. Rex (Fly)
19	17	GOLD	Neil Diamond (UNI)
-	18	AQUALUNG	Jethro Tull (Chrysalis)
-	19	T. REX	T. Rex (Fly)
13	20	SWEET BABY JAMES	James Taylor (Warner Bros.)
14	21	ELTON JOHN	Elton John (DJM)
17	22	PENDULUM	Creedence Clearwater Revival (Liberty)
18	23	AIR CONDITIONING	Curved Air (Warner Bros.)
-	24	ABRAXAS	Santana (CBS)
-	25	WATT	Ten Years After (Deram)
26	26	TAP ROOT MANUSCRIPT	Neil Diamond (UNI)
-	27	PAINT YOUR WAGON	Soundtrack (Paramount)
24	28	THE SOUND OF MUSIC	Soundtrack (RCA)
28	29	STEPHEN STILLS	Stephen Stills (Atlantic)
29	30	LIVE TASTE	Taste (Polydor)

3 April 1971

last week	this week	Album	Artist (Label)
1	1	BRIDGE OVER TROUBLED WATER	Simon & Garfunkel (CBS)
2	2	HOME LOVIN' MAN	Andy Williams (CBS)
3	3	ALL THINGS MUST PASS	George Harrison (Apple)
5	4	CRY OF LOVE	Jimi Hendrix (Track)
4	5	ANDY WILLIAMS' GREATEST HITS	Andy Williams (CBS)
6	6	TUMBLEWEED CONNECTION	Elton John (DJM)
8	7	LED ZEPPELIN III	Led Zeppelin (Atlantic)
16	8	THE BEST OF T. REX	T. Rex (Fly)
13	9	MOTOWN CHARTBUSTERS VOL 4	Various Artists (Tamla Motown)
9	10	FRANK SINATRA'S GREATEST HITS VOL 2	Frank Sinatra (Reprise)
7	11	THE YES ALBUM	Yes (Atlantic)
14	12	EASY LISTENING	Various Artists (Polydor)
11	13	STONE AGE	Rolling Stones (Decca)
22	14	PENDULUM	Creedence Clearwater Revival (Liberty)
10	15	DEEP PURPLE IN ROCK	Deep Purple (Harvest)
24	16	ABRAXAS	Santana (CBS)
15	17	EMERSON LAKE & PALMER	Emerson, Lake & Palmer (Island)
18	18	AQUALUNG	Jethro Tull (Chrysalis)
17	19	GOLD	Neil Diamond (UNI)
21	20	ELTON JOHN	Elton John (DJM)
23	21	AIR CONDITIONING	Curved Air (Warner Bros.)
12	22	CHICAGO 3	Chicago (CBS)
20	23	SWEET BABY JAMES	James Taylor (Warner Bros.)
28	24	THE SOUND OF MUSIC	Soundtrack (RCA)
29	25	STEPHEN STILLS	Stephen Stills (Atlantic)
-	26	LED ZEPPELIN II	Led Zeppelin (Atlantic)
26	27	TAP ROOT MANUSCRIPT	Neil Diamond (UNI)
-	28	ELVIS COUNTRY	Elvis Presley (RCA)
25	29	WATT	Ten Years After (Deram)
30	30	LIVE TASTE	Taste (Polydor)

10 April 1971

last week	this week	Album	Artist (Label)
2	1	HOME LOVIN' MAN	Andy Williams (CBS)
1	2	BRIDGE OVER TROUBLED WATER	Simon & Garfunkel (CBS)
3	3	ALL THINGS MUST PASS	George Harrison (Apple)
4	4	CRY OF LOVE	Jimi Hendrix (Track)
13	5	STONE AGE	Rolling Stones (Decca)
6	6	TUMBLEWEED CONNECTION	Elton John (DJM)
5	7	ANDY WILLIAMS' GREATEST HITS	Andy Williams (CBS)
-	8	MOTOWN CHARTBUSTERS VOL 5	Various Artists (Tamla Motown)
10	9	FRANK SINATRA'S GREATEST HITS VOL 2	Frank Sinatra (Reprise)
12	10	EASY LISTENING	Various Artists (Polydor)
9	11	MOTOWN CHARTBUSTERS VOL 4	Various Artists (Tamla Motown)
28	12	ELVIS COUNTRY	Elvis Presley (RCA)
7	13	LED ZEPPELIN III	Led Zeppelin (Atlantic)
8	14	THE BEST OF T. REX	T. Rex (Fly)
11	15	THE YES ALBUM	Yes (Atlantic)
18	16	AQUALUNG	Jethro Tull (Chrysalis)
-	17	PORTRAIT IN MUSIC	Burt Bacharach (A&M)
14	18	PENDULUM	Creedence Clearwater Revival (Liberty)
17	19	EMERSON LAKE & PALMER	Emerson, Lake & Palmer (Island)
15	20	DEEP PURPLE IN ROCK	Deep Purple (Harvest)
20	21	ELTON JOHN	Elton John (DJM)
19	22	GOLD	Neil Diamond (UNI)
16	23	ABRAXAS	Santana (CBS)
23	24	SWEET BABY JAMES	James Taylor (Warner Bros.)
21	25	AIR CONDITIONING	Curved Air (Warner Bros.)
27	26	TAP ROOT MANUSCRIPT	Neil Diamond (UNI)
22	27	CHICAGO 3	Chicago (CBS)
30	28	LIVE TASTE	Taste (Polydor)
24	29	THE SOUND OF MUSIC	Soundtrack (RCA)
26	30	LED ZEPPELIN II	Led Zeppelin (Atlantic)

17 April 1971

last week	this week	Album	Artist (Label)
2	1	BRIDGE OVER TROUBLED WATER	Simon & Garfunkel (CBS)
1	2	HOME LOVIN' MAN	Andy Williams (CBS)
4	3	CRY OF LOVE	Jimi Hendrix (Track)
6	4	TUMBLEWEED CONNECTION	Elton John (DJM)
8	5	MOTOWN CHARTBUSTERS VOL 5	Various Artists (Tamla Motown)
3	6	ALL THINGS MUST PASS	George Harrison (Apple)
16	7	AQUALUNG	Jethro Tull (Chrysalis)
9	8	FRANK SINATRA'S GREATEST HITS VOL 2	Frank Sinatra (Reprise)
14	9	THE BEST OF T. REX	T. Rex (Fly)
12	10	ELVIS COUNTRY	Elvis Presley (RCA)
7	11	ANDY WILLIAMS' GREATEST HITS	Andy Williams (CBS)
15	12	THE YES ALBUM	Yes (Atlantic)
19	13	EMERSON LAKE & PALMER	Emerson, Lake & Palmer (Island)
10	14	EASY LISTENING	Various Artists (Polydor)
5	15	STONE AGE	Rolling Stones (Decca)
11	16	MOTOWN CHARTBUSTERS VOL 4	Various Artists (Tamla Motown)
13	17	LED ZEPPELIN III	Led Zeppelin (Atlantic)
27	18	CHICAGO 3	Chicago (CBS)
25	19	AIR CONDITIONING	Curved Air (Warner Bros.)
18	20	PENDULUM	Creedence Clearwater Revival (Liberty)
20	21	DEEP PURPLE IN ROCK	Deep Purple (Harvest)
23	22	ABRAXAS	Santana (CBS)
21	23	ELTON JOHN	Elton John (DJM)
24	24	SWEET BABY JAMES	James Taylor (Warner Bros.)
30	25	LED ZEPPELIN II	Led Zeppelin (Atlantic)
26	26	LIVE TASTE	Taste (Polydor)
22	27	GOLD	Neil Diamond (UNI)
28	28	TAP ROOT MANUSCRIPT	Neil Diamond (UNI)
29	29	THE SOUND OF MUSIC	Soundtrack (RCA)
17	30	PORTRAIT IN MUSIC	Burt Bacharach (A&M)

Jimi Hendrix's first posthumous hit LP arrived, but unlike Andy Williams' *Home Lovin' Man*, it couldn't displace *Bridge Over Troubled Water* from the top slot. While Andy was leering down over the LP charts, his prototype, Perry Como himself, was enjoying a revival. He was drifting down from the No.2 slot in the singles chart (his first time in this Top 20 since 1960) with *It's Impossible*; the album of the same name would chart in June. His last Top 20 album had been *Como's Golden Records*, in 1958-59.

24 April 1971

last week	this week	Album	Artist
2	1	HOME LOVIN' MAN	Andy Williams (CBS)
5	2	MOTOWN CHARTBUSTERS VOL 5	Various Artists (Tamla Motown)
1	3	BRIDGE OVER TROUBLED WATER	Simon & Garfunkel (CBS)
7	4	AQUALUNG	Jethro Tull (Chrysalis)
3	5	CRY OF LOVE	Jimi Hendrix (Track)
12	6	THE YES ALBUM	Yes (Atlantic)
-	7	ELEGY	Nice (Chrisma)
11	8	ANDY WILLIAMS' GREATEST HITS	Andy Williams (CBS)
30	9	PORTRAIT IN MUSIC	Burt Bacharach (A&M)
15	10	STONE AGE	Rolling Stones (Decca)
-	11	SONGS OF LOVE & HATE	Leonard Cohen (CBS)
4	12	TUMBLEWEED CONNECTION	Elton John (DJM)
8	13	FRANK SINATRA'S GREATEST HITS VOL 2	Frank Sinatra (Reprise)
6	14	ALL THINGS MUST PASS	George Harrison (Apple)
-	15	IF I COULD ONLY REMEMBER MY NAME	David Crosby (Atlantic)
14	16	EASY LISTENING	Various Artists (Polydor)
-	17	SPLIT	Groundhogs (Liberty)
-	18	DEATH WALKS BEHIND YOU	Atomic Rooster (Charisma)
21	19	DEEP PURPLE IN ROCK	Deep Purple (Harvest)
9	20	THE BEST OF T. REX	T. Rex (Fly)
-	21	2001: A SPACE ODYSSEY	Soundtrack (MGM)
10	22	ELVIS COUNTRY	Elvis Presley (RCA)
23	23	ELTON JOHN	Elton John (DJM)
25	24	LED ZEPPELIN II	Led Zeppelin (Atlantic)
-	25	T. REX	T. Rex (Fly)
17	26	LED ZEPPELIN III	Led Zeppelin (Atlantic)
19	27	AIR CONDITIONING	Curved Air (Warner Bros.)
13	28	EMERSON, LAKE & PALMER	Emerson, Lake & Palmer (Island)
22	29	ABRAXAS	Santana (CBS)
24	30	SWEET BABY JAMES	James Taylor (Warner Bros.)

1 May 1971

last week	this week	Album	Artist
2	1	MOTOWN CHARTBUSTERS VOL 5	Various Artists (Tamla Motown)
1	2	HOME LOVIN' MAN	Andy Williams (CBS)
-	3	STICKY FINGERS	Rolling Stones (Rolling Stones)
3	4	BRIDGE OVER TROUBLED WATER	Simon & Garfunkel (CBS)
11	5	SONGS OF LOVE & HATE	Leonard Cohen (CBS)
4	6	AQUALUNG	Jethro Tull (Chrysalis)
6	7	THE YES ALBUM	Yes (Atlantic)
5	8	CRY OF LOVE	Jimi Hendrix (Track)
7	9	ELEGY	Nice (Chrisma)
23	10	ELTON JOHN	Elton John (DJM)
17	11	SPLIT	Groundhogs (Liberty)
15	12	IF I COULD ONLY REMEMBER MY NAME	David Crosby (Atlantic)
13	13	FRANK SINATRA'S GREATEST HITS VOL 2	Frank Sinatra (Reprise)
22	14	ELVIS COUNTRY	Elvis Presley (RCA)
8	15	ANDY WILLIAMS' GREATEST HITS	Andy Williams (CBS)
-	16	IT'S IMPOSSIBLE	Perry Como (RCA)
12	17	TUMBLEWEED CONNECTION	Elton John (DJM)
14	18	ALL THINGS MUST PASS	George Harrison (Apple)
9	19	PORTRAIT IN MUSIC	Burt Bacharach (A&M)
16	20	EASY LISTENING	Various Artists (Polydor)
19	21	DEEP PURPLE IN ROCK	Deep Purple (Harvest)
24	22	LED ZEPPELIN II	Led Zeppelin (Atlantic)
-	23	PAINT YOUR WAGON	Soundtrack (Paramount)
25	24	T. REX	T. Rex (Fly)
26	25	LED ZEPPELIN III	Led Zeppelin (Atlantic)
-	26	ELECTRONICALLY TESTED	Mungo Jerry (Dawn)
21	27	2001: A SPACE ODYSSEY	Soundtrack (MGM)
28	28	EMERSON LAKE & PALMER	Emerson, Lake & Palmer (Island)
-	29	THE COMPLEAT TOM PAXTON	Tom Paxton (Elektra)
27	30	AIR CONDITIONING	Curved Air (Warner Bros.)

8 May 1971

last week	this week	Album	Artist
3	1	STICKY FINGERS	Rolling Stones (Rolling Stones)
1	2	MOTOWN CHARTBUSTERS VOL 5	Various Artists (Tamla Motown)
2	3	HOME LOVIN' MAN	Andy Williams (CBS)
4	4	BRIDGE OVER TROUBLED WATER	Simon & Garfunkel (CBS)
5	5	SONGS OF LOVE & HATE	Leonard Cohen (CBS)
7	6	THE YES ALBUM	Yes (Atlantic)
9	7	ELEGY	Nice (Chrisma)
12	8	IF I COULD ONLY REMEMBER MY NAME	David Crosby (Atlantic)
8	9	CRY OF LOVE	Jimi Hendrix (Track)
15	10	ANDY WILLIAMS' GREATEST HITS	Andy Williams (CBS)
11	11	SPLIT	Groundhogs (Liberty)
6	12	AQUALUNG	Jethro Tull (Chrysalis)
20	13	EASY LISTENING	Various Artists (Polydor)
14	14	ELVIS COUNTRY	Elvis Presley (RCA)
10	15	ELTON JOHN	Elton John (DJM)
-	16	SYMPHONIES FOR THE 70s	Waldo de los Rios (A&M)
18	17	ALL THINGS MUST PASS	George Harrison (Apple)
22	18	LED ZEPPELIN II	Led Zeppelin (Atlantic)
19	19	PORTRAIT IN MUSIC	Burt Bacharach (A&M)
-	20	17.11.70	Elton John (DJM)
-	21	FRIENDS	Soundtrack (Paramount)
-	22	SOMETHING ELSE	Shirley Bassey (United Artists)
13	23	FRANK SINATRA'S GREATEST HITS VOL 2	Frank Sinatra (Reprise)
23	24	PAINT YOUR WAGON	Soundtrack (Paramount)
26	25	ELECTRONICALLY TESTED	Mungo Jerry (Dawn)
21	26	DEEP PURPLE IN ROCK	Deep Purple (Harvest)
-	27	AFTER THE GOLD RUSH	Neil Young (Reprise)
16	28	IT'S IMPOSSIBLE	Perry Como (RCA)
17	29	TUMBLEWEED CONNECTION	Elton John (DJM)
-	30	DEATH WALKS BEHIND YOU	Atomic Rooster (Charisma)

15 May 1971

last week	this week	Album	Artist
1	1	STICKY FINGERS	Rolling Stones (Rolling Stones)
2	2	MOTOWN CHARTBUSTERS VOL 5	Various Artists (Tamla Motown)
3	3	HOME LOVIN' MAN	Andy Williams (CBS)
5	4	SONGS OF LOVE & HATE	Leonard Cohen (CBS)
4	5	BRIDGE OVER TROUBLED WATER	Simon & Garfunkel (CBS)
9	6	CRY OF LOVE	Jimi Hendrix (Track)
-	7	FOUR WAY STREET	Crosby Stills Nash & Young (Atlantic)
6	8	THE YES ALBUM	Yes (Atlantic)
14	9	ELVIS COUNTRY	Elvis Presley (RCA)
23	10	FRANK SINATRA'S GREATEST HITS VOL 2	Frank Sinatra (Reprise)
10	11	ANDY WILLIAMS' GREATEST HITS	Andy Williams (CBS)
12	12	AQUALUNG	Jethro Tull (Chrysalis)
11	13	SPLIT	Groundhogs (Liberty)
7	14	ELEGY	Nice (Chrisma)
16	15	SYMPHONIES FOR THE 70s	Waldo de los Rios (A&M)
13	16	EASY LISTENING	Various Artists (Polydor)
17	17	LED ZEPPELIN II	Led Zeppelin (Atlantic)
26	18	DEEP PURPLE IN ROCK	Deep Purple (Harvest)
22	19	SOMETHING ELSE	Shirley Bassey (United Artists)
8	20	IF I COULD ONLY REMEMBER MY NAME	David Crosby (Atlantic)
24	21	PAINT YOUR WAGON	Soundtrack (Paramount)
15	22	ELTON JOHN	Elton John (DJM)
19	23	PORTRAIT IN MUSIC	Burt Bacharach (A&M)
17	24	ALL THINGS MUST PASS	George Harrison (Apple)
20	25	17.11.70	Elton John (DJM)
25	26	ELECTRONICALLY TESTED	Mungo Jerry (Dawn)
-	27	SWEET BABY JAMES	James Taylor (Warner Bros.)
-	28	OVER AND OVER	Nana Mouskouri (Fontana)
-	29	CLUB REGGAE	Various Artists (Trojan)
-	30	ABRAXAS	Santana (CBS)

A curious error arose in these charts (now corrected). April 24 showed *Elvis Country* plummet to No.26, and *I'm 10,000 Years Old* arrive at 22. This then disappeared and *Elvis Country* regained the Top 20. In fact *I'm 10,000 Years Old* was *Elvis Country*'s sub-title, not another album. It's the name of a song used on the LP only in short extracts, in place of the gaps between the proper tracks. This daft attempt to make Elvis "modern" marred an LP rightly popular as his best in ages.

May – June 1971

22 May 1971

last	this	Title / Artist (Label)
1	1	STICKY FINGERS Rolling Stones (Rolling Stones)
3	2	HOME LOVIN' MAN Andy Williams (CBS)
2	3	MOTOWN CHARTBUSTERS VOL 5 Various Artists (Tamla Motown)
4	4	SONGS OF LOVE & HATE Leonard Cohen (CBS)
5	5	BRIDGE OVER TROUBLED WATER Simon & Garfunkel (CBS)
7	6	FOUR WAY STREET Crosby Stills Nash & Young (Atlantic)
15	7	SYMPHONIES FOR THE 70s Waldo de los Rios (A&M)
6	8	CRY OF LOVE Jimi Hendrix (Track)
8	9	THE YES ALBUM Yes (Atlantic)
13	10	SPLIT Groundhogs (Liberty)
10	11	FRANK SINATRA'S GREATEST HITS VOL 2 Frank Sinatra (Reprise)
14	12	ELEGY Nice (Chrisma)
12	13	AQUALUNG Jethro Tull (Chrysalis)
11	14	ANDY WILLIAMS' GREATEST HITS Andy Williams (CBS)
-	15	MUD SLIDE SLIM AND THE BLUE HORIZON James Taylor (Warner Bros.)
9	16	ELVIS COUNTRY Elvis Presley (RCA)
19	17	SOMETHING ELSE Shirley Bassey (United Artists)
20	18	IF I COULD ONLY REMEMBER MY NAME David Crosby (Atlantic)
16	19	EASY LISTENING Various Artists (Polydor)
18	20	DEEP PURPLE IN ROCK Deep Purple (Harvest)
30	21	ABRAXAS Santana (CBS)
28	22	OVER AND OVER Nana Mouskouri (Fontana)
17	23	LED ZEPPELIN II Led Zeppelin (Atlantic)
21	24	PAINT YOUR WAGON Soundtrack (Paramount)
-	25	IT'S IMPOSSIBLE Perry Como (RCA)
-	26	THE BEST OF T. REX T. Rex (Fly)
22	27	ELTON JOHN Elton John (DJM)
25	28	17.11.70 Elton John (DJM)
27	29	SWEET BABY JAMES James Taylor (Warner Bros.)
23	30	PORTRAIT IN MUSIC Burt Bacharach (A&M)

29 May 1971

last	this	Title / Artist (Label)
1	1	STICKY FINGERS Rolling Stones (Rolling Stones)
2	2	HOME LOVIN' MAN Andy Williams (CBS)
3	3	MOTOWN CHARTBUSTERS VOL 5 Various Artists (Tamla Motown)
5	4	BRIDGE OVER TROUBLED WATER Simon & Garfunkel (CBS)
4	5	SONGS OF LOVE & HATE Leonard Cohen (CBS)
7	6	SYMPHONIES FOR THE 70s Waldo de los Rios (A&M)
10	7	SPLIT Groundhogs (Liberty)
6	8	FOUR WAY STREET Crosby Stills Nash & Young (Atlantic)
25	9	IT'S IMPOSSIBLE Perry Como (RCA)
-	10	RAM Paul McCartney (Apple)
13	11	AQUALUNG Jethro Tull (Chrysalis)
14	12	ANDY WILLIAMS' GREATEST HITS Andy Williams (CBS)
15	13	MUD SLIDE SLIM AND THE BLUE HORIZON James Taylor (Warner Bros.)
11	14	FRANK SINATRA'S GREATEST HITS VOL 2 Frank Sinatra (Reprise)
8	15	CRY OF LOVE Jimi Hendrix (Track)
9	16	THE YES ALBUM Yes (Atlantic)
30	17	PORTRAIT IN MUSIC Burt Bacharach (A&M)
23	18	LED ZEPPELIN II Led Zeppelin (Atlantic)
-	19	ALL THINGS MUST PASS George Harrison (Apple)
12	20	ELEGY Nice (Chrisma)
21	21	DEEP PURPLE IN ROCK Deep Purple (Harvest)
17	22	SOMETHING ELSE Shirley Bassey (United Artists)
19	23	EASY LISTENING Various Artists (Polydor)
24	24	SWEET BABY JAMES James Taylor (Warner Bros.)
-	25	THE GOOD BOOK Melanie (Buddah)
-	26	AFTER THE GOLD RUSH Neil Young (Reprise)
27	27	ABRAXAS Santana (CBS)
-	28	SHE'S A LADY Tom Jones (Decca)
22	29	OVER AND OVER Nana Mouskouri (Fontana)
24	30	PAINT YOUR WAGON Soundtrack (Paramount)

5 June 1971

last	this	Title / Artist (Label)
1	1	STICKY FINGERS Rolling Stones (Rolling Stones)
3	2	MOTOWN CHARTBUSTERS VOL 5 Various Artists (Tamla Motown)
2	3	HOME LOVIN' MAN Andy Williams (CBS)
4	4	BRIDGE OVER TROUBLED WATER Simon & Garfunkel (CBS)
10	5	RAM Paul McCartney (Apple)
5	6	SONGS OF LOVE & HATE Leonard Cohen (CBS)
6	7	SYMPHONIES FOR THE 70s Waldo de los Rios (A&M)
7	8	SPLIT Groundhogs (Liberty)
13	9	MUD SLIDE SLIM AND THE BLUE HORIZON James Taylor (Warner Bros.)
8	10	FOUR WAY STREET Crosby Stills Nash & Young (Atlantic)
12	11	ANDY WILLIAMS' GREATEST HITS Andy Williams (CBS)
25	12	THE GOOD BOOK Melanie (Buddah)
15	13	CRY OF LOVE Jimi Hendrix (Track)
9	14	IT'S IMPOSSIBLE Perry Como (RCA)
27	15	ABRAXAS Santana (CBS)
29	16	OVER AND OVER Nana Mouskouri (Fontana)
28	17	SHE'S A LADY Tom Jones (Decca)
16	18	THE YES ALBUM Yes (Atlantic)
24	19	SWEET BABY JAMES James Taylor (Warner Bros.)
-	20	RELICS Pink Floyd (Starline)
14	21	FRANK SINATRA'S GREATEST HITS VOL 2 Frank Sinatra (Reprise)
-	22	OSIBISA Osibisa (Decca)
11	23	AQUALUNG Jethro Tull (Chrysalis)
20	24	ELEGY Nice (Chrisma)
19	25	ALL THINGS MUST PASS George Harrison (Apple)
21	26	DEEP PURPLE IN ROCK Deep Purple (Harvest)
17	27	PORTRAIT IN MUSIC Burt Bacharach (A&M)
22	28	SOMETHING ELSE Shirley Bassey (United Artists)
18	29	LED ZEPPELIN II Led Zeppelin (Atlantic)
26	30	AFTER THE GOLD RUSH Neil Young (Reprise)

12 June 1971

last	this	Title / Artist (Label)
1	1	STICKY FINGERS Rolling Stones (Rolling Stones)
2	2	MOTOWN CHARTBUSTERS VOL 5 Various Artists (Tamla Motown)
4	3	BRIDGE OVER TROUBLED WATER Simon & Garfunkel (CBS)
5	4	RAM Paul McCartney (Apple)
8	5	SPLIT Groundhogs (Liberty)
7	6	SYMPHONIES FOR THE 70s Waldo de los Rios (A&M)
3	7	HOME LOVIN' MAN Andy Williams (CBS)
9	8	MUD SLIDE SLIM AND THE BLUE HORIZON James Taylor (Warner Bros.)
10	9	FOUR WAY STREET Crosby Stills Nash & Young (Atlantic)
6	10	SONGS OF LOVE & HATE Leonard Cohen (CBS)
11	11	ANDY WILLIAMS' GREATEST HITS Andy Williams (CBS)
17	12	SHE'S A LADY Tom Jones (Decca)
28	13	SOMETHING ELSE Shirley Bassey (United Artists)
18	14	THE YES ALBUM Yes (Atlantic)
21	15	FRANK SINATRA'S GREATEST HITS VOL 2 Frank Sinatra (Reprise)
-	16	SINATRA & COMPANY Frank Sinatra (Reprise)
12	17	THE GOOD BOOK Melanie (Buddah)
26	18	DEEP PURPLE IN ROCK Deep Purple (Harvest)
29	19	LED ZEPPELIN II Led Zeppelin (Atlantic)
16	20	OVER AND OVER Nana Mouskouri (Fontana)
-	21	TARKUS Emerson Lake & Palmer (Island)
-	22	DEJA VU Crosby Stills Nash & Young (Atlantic)
13	23	CRY OF LOVE Jimi Hendrix (Track)
-	24	ELVIS: THAT'S THE WAY IT IS Elvis Presley (RCA)
30	25	AFTER THE GOLD RUSH Neil Young (Reprise)
19	26	SWEET BABY JAMES James Taylor (Warner Bros.)
14	27	IT'S IMPOSSIBLE Perry Como (RCA)
15	28	ABRAXAS Santana (CBS)
27	29	PORTRAIT IN MUSIC Burt Bacharach (A&M)
20	30	RELICS Pink Floyd (Starline)

Sticky Fingers, the Stones' 13th album (counting hits packages), was the first on their own label, and free of Decca. It introduced the famous lolling-tongue-and-lips design. Rock groups had long been keen on these corporate logos; oddly, the Stones chose one that used the personality cult of Mick Jagger, well-known owner of said lips, to symbolise the world's greatest rock band. *Sticky Fingers* was their fourth No.1 album (some charts said their sixth), and perhaps their best. Ultimate highlight: *Moonlight Mile*.

19 June 1971

last week	this week	
1	1	STICKY FINGERS Rolling Stones (Rolling Stones)
4	2	RAM Paul McCartney (Apple)
3	3	BRIDGE OVER TROUBLED WATER Simon & Garfunkel (CBS)
2	4	MOTOWN CHARTBUSTERS VOL 5 Various Artists (Tamla Motown)
8	5	MUD SLIDE SLIM AND THE BLUE HORIZON James Taylor (Warner Bros.)
5	6	SPLIT Groundhogs (Liberty)
7	7	HOME LOVIN' MAN Andy Williams (CBS)
21	8	TARKUS Emerson Lake & Palmer (Island)
6	9	SYMPHONIES FOR THE 70s Waldo de los Rios (A&M)
9	10	FOUR WAY STREET Crosby Stills Nash & Young (Atlantic)
10	11	SONGS OF LOVE & HATE Leonard Cohen (CBS)
17	12	THE GOOD BOOK Melanie (Buddah)
11	13	ANDY WILLIAMS' GREATEST HITS Andy Williams (CBS)
14	14	THE YES ALBUM Yes (Atlantic)
20	15	OVER AND OVER Nana Mouskouri (Fontana)
30	16	RELICS Pink Floyd (Starline)
13	17	SOMETHING ELSE Shirley Bassey (United Artists)
16	18	SINATRA & COMPANY Frank Sinatra (Reprise)
15	19	FRANK SINATRA'S GREATEST HITS VOL 2 Frank Sinatra (Reprise)
26	20	SWEET BABY JAMES James Taylor (Warner Bros.)
19	21	LED ZEPPELIN II Led Zeppelin (Atlantic)
12	22	SHE'S A LADY Tom Jones (Decca)
27	23	IT'S IMPOSSIBLE Perry Como (RCA)
18	24	DEEP PURPLE IN ROCK Deep Purple (Harvest)
-	25	THE MAGNIFICENT SEVEN Supremes & Four Tops (Tamla Motown)
22	26	DEJA VU Crosby Stills Nash & Young (Atlantic)
25	27	AFTER THE GOLD RUSH Neil Young (Reprise)
29	28	PORTRAIT IN MUSIC Burt Bacharach (A&M)
-	29	THIS IS MANUEL Manuel & His Music of the Mountains (Studio Two)
-	30	AQUALUNG Jethro Tull (Chrysalis)

26 June 1971

1	1	STICKY FINGERS Rolling Stones (Rolling Stones)
2	2	RAM Paul McCartney (Apple)
8	3	TARKUS Emerson Lake & Palmer (Island)
3	4	BRIDGE OVER TROUBLED WATER Simon & Garfunkel (CBS)
4	5	MOTOWN CHARTBUSTERS VOL 5 Various Artists (Tamla Motown)
6	6	SPLIT Groundhogs (Liberty)
5	7	MUD SLIDE SLIM AND THE BLUE HORIZON James Taylor (Warner Bros.)
7	8	HOME LOVIN' MAN Andy Williams (CBS)
10	9	FOUR WAY STREET Crosby Stills Nash & Young (Atlantic)
9	10	SYMPHONIES FOR THE 70s Waldo de los Rios (A&M)
11	11	SONGS OF LOVE & HATE Leonard Cohen (CBS)
18	12	SINATRA & COMPANY Frank Sinatra (Reprise)
13	13	ANDY WILLIAMS' GREATEST HITS Andy Williams (CBS)
-	14	FREE LIVE Free (Island)
-	15	SONGS FOR BEGINNERS Graham Nash (Atlantic)
16	16	RELICS Pink Floyd (Starline)
12	17	THE GOOD BOOK Melanie (Buddah)
-	18	ABRAXAS Santana (CBS)
19	19	FRANK SINATRA'S GREATEST HITS VOL 2 Frank Sinatra (Reprise)
-	20	COLOSSEUM LIVE Colosseum (Bronze)
27	21	AFTER THE GOLD RUSH Neil Young (Reprise)
22	22	SHE'S A LADY Tom Jones (Decca)
15	23	OVER AND OVER Nana Mouskouri (Fontana)
30	24	AQUALUNG Jethro Tull (Chrysalis)
14	25	THE YES ALBUM Yes (Atlantic)
-	26	TAP ROOT MANUSCRIPT Neil Diamond (UNI)
25	27	THE MAGNIFICENT SEVEN Supremes & Four Tops (Tamla Motown)
20	28	SWEET BABY JAMES James Taylor (Warner Bros.)
23	29	IT'S IMPOSSIBLE Perry Como (RCA)
28	30	PORTRAIT IN MUSIC Burt Bacharach (A&M)

3 July 1971

4	1	BRIDGE OVER TROUBLED WATER Simon & Garfunkel (CBS)
2	2	RAM Paul McCartney (Apple)
1	3	STICKY FINGERS Rolling Stones (Rolling Stones)
3	4	TARKUS Emerson Lake & Palmer (Island)
5	5	MOTOWN CHARTBUSTERS VOL 5 Various Artists (Tamla Motown)
14	6	FREE LIVE Free (Island)
8	7	HOME LOVIN' MAN Andy Williams (CBS)
6	8	SPLIT Groundhogs (Liberty)
7	9	MUD SLIDE SLIM AND THE BLUE HORIZON James Taylor (Warner Bros.)
10	10	SYMPHONIES FOR THE 70s Waldo de los Rios (A&M)
12	11	SINATRA & COMPANY Frank Sinatra (Reprise)
15	12	SONGS FOR BEGINNERS Graham Nash (Atlantic)
-	13	THIS IS MANUEL Manuel & His Music of the Mountains (Studio Two)
-	14	THE SOUND OF MUSIC Soundtrack (RCA)
13	15	ANDY WILLIAMS' GREATEST HITS Andy Williams (CBS)
9	16	FOUR WAY STREET Crosby Stills Nash & Young (Atlantic)
16	17	RELICS Pink Floyd (Starline)
11	18	SONGS OF LOVE & HATE Leonard Cohen (CBS)
-	19	LED ZEPPELIN II Led Zeppelin (Atlantic)
-	20	DEJA VU Crosby Stills Nash & Young (Atlantic)
19	21	FRANK SINATRA'S GREATEST HITS VOL 2 Frank Sinatra (Reprise)
-	22	BACK TO THE ROOTS John Mayall (Polydor)
20	23	COLOSSEUM LIVE Colosseum (Bronze)
-	24	OSIBISA Osibisa (Decca)
25	25	THE YES ALBUM Yes (Atlantic)
-	26	TURN ON THE SUN Nana Mouskouri (Fontana)
23	27	OVER AND OVER Nana Mouskouri (Fontana)
21	28	AFTER THE GOLD RUSH Neil Young (Reprise)
30	29	PORTRAIT IN MUSIC Burt Bacharach (A&M)
18	30	ABRAXAS Santana (CBS)
27	30	THE MAGNIFICENT SEVEN Supremes & Four Tops (Tamla Motown)

10 July 1971

2	1	RAM Paul McCartney (Apple)
1	2	BRIDGE OVER TROUBLED WATER Simon & Garfunkel (CBS)
4	3	TARKUS Emerson Lake & Palmer (Island)
5	4	MOTOWN CHARTBUSTERS VOL 5 Various Artists (Tamla Motown)
6	5	FREE LIVE Free (Island)
3	6	STICKY FINGERS Rolling Stones (Rolling Stones)
10	7	SYMPHONIES FOR THE 70s Waldo de los Rios (A&M)
9	8	MUD SLIDE SLIM AND THE BLUE HORIZON James Taylor (Warner Bros.)
7	9	HOME LOVIN' MAN Andy Williams (CBS)
8	10	SPLIT Groundhogs (Liberty)
-	11	ANGEL DELIGHT Fairport Convention (Island)
11	12	SINATRA & COMPANY Frank Sinatra (Reprise)
15	13	ANDY WILLIAMS' GREATEST HITS Andy Williams (CBS)
13	14	THIS IS MANUEL Manuel & His Music of the Mountains (Studio Two)
21	15	FRANK SINATRA'S GREATEST HITS VOL 2 Frank Sinatra (Reprise)
19	16	LED ZEPPELIN II Led Zeppelin (Atlantic)
-	17	THE GOOD BOOK Melanie (Buddah)
16	18	FOUR WAY STREET Crosby Stills Nash & Young (Atlantic)
25	19	THE YES ALBUM Yes (Atlantic)
17	20	RELICS Pink Floyd (Starline)
14	21	THE SOUND OF MUSIC Soundtrack (RCA)
18	22	SONGS OF LOVE & HATE Leonard Cohen (CBS)
27	23	OVER AND OVER Nana Mouskouri (Fontana)
-	24	THE WORLD OF YOUR 100 BEST TUNES Various Artists (Decca)
12	25	SONGS FOR BEGINNERS Graham Nash (Atlantic)
30	26	THE MAGNIFICENT SEVEN Supremes & Four Tops (Tamla Motown)
28	27	AFTER THE GOLD RUSH Neil Young (Reprise)
30	28	ABRAXAS Santana (CBS)
22	29	BACK TO THE ROOTS John Mayall (Polydor)
26	30	TURN ON THE SUN Nana Mouskouri (Fontana)

This Is Manuel was an album that would yo-yo in and out of the charts over the coming weeks (in at 29, out again, in at 13, then 14, then out, back in at 18, back out again). It was not a comedy album by the Spanish waiter character from Fawlty Towers, but an "easy listening" LP by Manuel & His Music Of The Mountains. In turn, these happy peasants from the foothills of the Andes were not forerunners of World Music; they were British bandleader Geoff Love and His Orchestra.

July – August 1971

Geoff Love was having a busy year. Under his own name he would soon make the chart with the LP *Big War Movie Themes*, and then the parts too low for NME to reach, with *Big Western Movie Themes* and *Big Love Movie Themes*. In July, Jim Morrison died in his bath in Paris, and in August, sax maestro King Curtis was murdered back in the USA. August also saw George Harrison organise and star in the Concert For Bangla Desh in New York City – a Live Aid before its time.

14 August 1971

last week	this week	Title	Artist (Label)
4	1	EVERY GOOD BOY DESERVES FAVOUR	Moody Blues (Threshold)
1	2	BRIDGE OVER TROUBLED WATER	Simon & Garfunkel (CBS)
7	3	BLUE	Joni Mitchell (Reprise)
2	4	RAM	Paul McCartney (Apple)
3	5	MOTOWN CHARTBUSTERS VOL 5	Various Artists (Tamla Motown)
5	6	STICKY FINGERS	Rolling Stones (Rolling Stones)
8	7	TARKUS	Emerson Lake & Palmer (Island)
9	8	MUD SLIDE SLIM AND THE BLUE HORIZON	James Taylor (Warner Bros.)
11	9	EVERY PICTURE TELLS A STORY	Rod Stewart (Mercury)
10	10	LOVE STORY	Andy Williams (CBS)
-	11	TAPESTRY	Carole King (A&M)
-	12	HOT HITS SIX	Various Artists (Music for Pleasure)
-	13	STEPHEN STILLS 2	Stephen Stills (Atlantic)
-	14	MASTER OF REALITY	Black Sabbath (Vertigo)
20	15	AFTER THE GOLD RUSH	Neil Young (Reprise)
19	16	JIM REEVES' GOLDEN RECORDS	Jim Reeves (RCA)
24	17	THE YES ALBUM	Yes (Atlantic)
13	18	SWEET BABY JAMES	James Taylor (Warner Bros.)
29	19	LED ZEPPELIN II	Led Zeppelin (Atlantic)
-	20	HOME LOVIN' MAN	Andy Williams (CBS)
12	21	LOVE LETTERS FROM ELVIS	Elvis Presley (RCA)
23	22	L.A. WOMAN	Doors (Elektra)
-	23	BS&T 4	Blood Sweat & Tears (CBS)
26	24	RELICS	Pink Floyd (Starline)
16	25	SPLIT	Groundhogs (Liberty)
15	26	THE MAGNIFICENT SEVEN	Supremes & Four Tops (Tamla Motown)
17	27	ANDY WILLIAMS' GREATEST HITS	Andy Williams (CBS)
21	28	C'MON EVERYBODY	Elvis Presley (RCA International)
22	29	PAINT YOUR WAGON	Soundtrack (Paramount)
28	30	SONGS OF LOVE & HATE	Leonard Cohen (CBS)

21 August 1971

last week	this week	Title	Artist (Label)
1	1	EVERY GOOD BOY DESERVES FAVOUR	Moody Blues (Threshold)
2	2	BRIDGE OVER TROUBLED WATER	Simon & Garfunkel (CBS)
4	3	RAM	Paul McCartney (Apple)
5	4	MOTOWN CHARTBUSTERS VOL 5	Various Artists (Tamla Motown)
8	5	MUD SLIDE SLIM AND THE BLUE HORIZON	James Taylor (Warner Bros.)
3	6	BLUE	Joni Mitchell (Reprise)
6	7	STICKY FINGERS	Rolling Stones (Rolling Stones)
11	8	TAPESTRY	Carole King (A&M)
7	9	TARKUS	Emerson Lake & Palmer (Island)
10	10	LOVE STORY	Andy Williams (CBS)
28	11	C'MON EVERYBODY	Elvis Presley (RCA International)
18	12	SWEET BABY JAMES	James Taylor (Warner Bros.)
14	13	MASTER OF REALITY	Black Sabbath (Vertigo)
-	14	TOP OF THE POPS 18	Various Artists (Hallmark)
27	15	ANDY WILLIAMS' GREATEST HITS	Andy Williams (CBS)
15	16	AFTER THE GOLD RUSH	Neil Young (Reprise)
9	17	EVERY PICTURE TELLS A STORY	Rod Stewart (Mercury)
12	18	HOT HITS SIX	Various Artists (Music for Pleasure)
13	19	STEPHEN STILLS 2	Stephen Stills (Atlantic)
25	20	SPLIT	Groundhogs (Liberty)
-	21	FREE LIVE	Free (Island)
29	22	PAINT YOUR WAGON	Soundtrack (Paramount)
26	23	THE MAGNIFICENT SEVEN	Supremes & Four Tops (Tamla Motown)
24	24	RELICS	Pink Floyd (Starline)
19	25	LED ZEPPELIN II	Led Zeppelin (Atlantic)
17	26	THE YES ALBUM	Yes (Atlantic)
-	27	DEEP PURPLE IN ROCK	Deep Purple (Harvest)
20	28	HOME LOVIN' MAN	Andy Williams (CBS)
-	29	SYMPHONIES FOR THE 70s	Waldo de los Rios (A&M)
30	30	SONGS OF LOVE & HATE	Leonard Cohen (CBS)

28 August 1971

last week	this week	Title	Artist (Label)
1	1	EVERY GOOD BOY DESERVES FAVOUR	Moody Blues (Threshold)
2	2	BRIDGE OVER TROUBLED WATER	Simon & Garfunkel (CBS)
6	3	BLUE	Joni Mitchell (Reprise)
3	4	RAM	Paul McCartney (Apple)
5	5	MUD SLIDE SLIM AND THE BLUE HORIZON	James Taylor (Warner Bros.)
9	6	TARKUS	Emerson Lake & Palmer (Island)
17	7	EVERY PICTURE TELLS A STORY	Rod Stewart (Mercury)
8	8	TAPESTRY	Carole King (A&M)
4	9	MOTOWN CHARTBUSTERS VOL 5	Various Artists (Tamla Motown)
7	10	STICKY FINGERS	Rolling Stones (Rolling Stones)
13	11	MASTER OF REALITY	Black Sabbath (Vertigo)
14	12	TOP OF THE POPS 18	Various Artists (Hallmark)
10	13	LOVE STORY	Andy Williams (CBS)
11	14	C'MON EVERYBODY	Elvis Presley (RCA International)
18	15	HOT HITS SIX	Various Artists (Music for Pleasure)
15	16	ANDY WILLIAMS' GREATEST HITS	Andy Williams (CBS)
12	17	SWEET BABY JAMES	James Taylor (Warner Bros.)
-	18	EXPERIENCE	Jimi Hendrix Experience (Ember)
19	19	THE INTIMATE JIM REEVES	Jim Reeves (RCA International)
16	20	AFTER THE GOLD RUSH	Neil Young (Reprise)
22	21	PAINT YOUR WAGON	Soundtrack (Paramount)
21	22	FREE LIVE	Free (Island)
-	23	LIVE PERFORMANCE	Spinners (Fontana)
24	24	RELICS	Pink Floyd (Starline)
20	25	SPLIT	Groundhogs (Liberty)
26	26	STEPHEN STILLS 2	Stephen Stills (Atlantic)
-	27	LOVE STORY	Soundtrack (Paramount)
25	28	LED ZEPPELIN II	Led Zeppelin (Atlantic)
27	29	DEEP PURPLE IN ROCK	Deep Purple (Harvest)
30	30	HOME LOVIN' MAN	Andy Williams (CBS)

4 September 1971

last week	this week	Title	Artist (Label)
1	1	EVERY GOOD BOY DESERVES FAVOUR	Moody Blues (Threshold)
2	2	BRIDGE OVER TROUBLED WATER	Simon & Garfunkel (CBS)
5	3	MUD SLIDE SLIM AND THE BLUE HORIZON	James Taylor (Warner Bros.)
8	4	TAPESTRY	Carole King (A&M)
4	5	RAM	Paul McCartney (Apple)
3	6	BLUE	Joni Mitchell (Reprise)
11	7	MASTER OF REALITY	Black Sabbath (Vertigo)
9	8	MOTOWN CHARTBUSTERS VOL 5	Various Artists (Tamla Motown)
10	9	STICKY FINGERS	Rolling Stones (Rolling Stones)
12	10	TOP OF THE POPS 18	Various Artists (Hallmark)
14	11	C'MON EVERYBODY	Elvis Presley (RCA International)
7	12	EVERY PICTURE TELLS A STORY	Rod Stewart (Mercury)
13	13	LOVE STORY	Andy Williams (CBS)
17	14	SWEET BABY JAMES	James Taylor (Warner Bros.)
6	15	TARKUS	Emerson Lake & Palmer (Island)
15	16	HOT HITS SIX	Various Artists (Music for Pleasure)
-	17	WHO'S NEXT	Who (Polydor)
-	18	EVERYTHING IS EVERYTHING	Diana Ross (Tamla Motown)
21	19	PAINT YOUR WAGON	Soundtrack (Paramount)
25	20	SPLIT	Groundhogs (Liberty)
18	21	EXPERIENCE	Jimi Hendrix Experience (Ember)
22	22	FREE LIVE	Free (Island)
20	23	AFTER THE GOLD RUSH	Neil Young (Reprise)
23	24	LIVE PERFORMANCE	Spinners (Fontana)
30	25	HOME LOVIN' MAN	Andy Williams (CBS)
24	26	RELICS	Pink Floyd (Starline)
16	27	ANDY WILLIAMS' GREATEST HITS	Andy Williams (CBS)
19	28	THE INTIMATE JIM REEVES	Jim Reeves (RCA International)
-	29	IN HEARING OF	Atomic Rooster (Pegasus)
28	30	LED ZEPPELIN II	Led Zeppelin (Atlantic)

Every Picture Tells A Story was not Rod Stewart's first album since leaving the Faces. *Gasoline Alley* had come first; but *Every Picture Tells A Story* was to prove the huge turning-point in Rod the Mod's career: the first of six consecutive No.1 albums, issued at the rate of one a year from now till 1976's *Night On The Town*, by which time Rod was the tabloids' Richard Burton of rock, street cred blown, while back in gasoline alley the punks were baying at the garage door.

September – October 1971

Carole King's *Tapestry* typified a movement whereby those who had made ultra-successful pop hits now apologised for this sordid and vulgar attainment, and sought to prove themselves serious artists with albums of deliberately uncommercial songs of great length and wiffliness. As producer and writer, Carole King and her ex-partner Jerry Goffin had been pop hit factories, even making their babysitter, Little Eva, a star. Shocking. *Tapestry* was King's penance; it would enjoy some 90 weeks in the chart.

9 October 1971

last week	this week	Title	Artist (label)
1	1	EVERY PICTURE TELLS A STORY	Rod Stewart (Mercury)
2	2	TAPESTRY	Carole King (A&M)
6	3	BRIDGE OVER TROUBLED WATER	Simon & Garfunkel (CBS)
5	4	MUD SLIDE SLIM AND THE BLUE HORIZON	James Taylor (Warner Bros.)
4	5	FIREBALL	Deep Purple (Harvest)
7	6	EVERY GOOD BOY DESERVES FAVOUR	Moody Blues (Threshold)
15	7	TEASER & THE FIRECAT	Cat Stevens (Island)
3	8	WHO'S NEXT	Who (Polydor)
9	9	BLUE	Joni Mitchell (Reprise)
10	10	SWEET BABY JAMES	James Taylor (Warner Bros.)
8	11	RAM	Paul McCartney (Apple)
12	12	ELECTRIC WARRIOR	T. Rex (Fly)
11	13	MOTOWN CHARTBUSTERS VOL 5	Various Artists (Tamla Motown)
13	14	MASTER OF REALITY	Black Sabbath (Vertigo)
17	15	I'M STILL WAITING	Diana Ross (Tamla Motown)
16	16	ANDY WILLIAMS' GREATEST HITS	Andy Williams (CBS)
-	17	TOP OF THE POPS 19	Various Artists (Halimark)
23	18	MAN IN BLACK	Johnny Cash (CBS)
19	19	LOVE STORY	Andy Williams (CBS)
14	20	DIANA!	Diana Ross (Tamla Motown)
24	21	CURVED AIR	Curved Air (Warner Bros.)
25	22	TARKUS	Emerson Lake & Palmer (Island)
26	23	C'MON EVERYBODY	Elvis Presley (RCA International)
27	24	SYMPHONIES FOR THE 70s	Waldo de los Rios (A&M)
-	25	PAINT YOUR WAGON	Soundtrack (Paramount)
-	26	EXPERIENCE	Jimi Hendrix Experience (Ember)
-	27	LOVE STORY	Soundtrack (Paramount)
-	28	CARPENTERS	Carpenters (A&M)
-	29	LOVELACE WATKINS LIVE AT THE TALK OF THE TOWN	Lovelace Watkins (York)
29	30	THIS IS MANUEL	Manuel & His Music of the Mountains (Studio Two)

16 October 1971

last week	this week	Title	Artist (label)
1	1	EVERY PICTURE TELLS A STORY	Rod Stewart (Mercury)
2	2	TAPESTRY	Carole King (A&M)
12	3	ELECTRIC WARRIOR	T. Rex (Fly)
5	4	FIREBALL	Deep Purple (Harvest)
3	5	BRIDGE OVER TROUBLED WATER	Simon & Garfunkel (CBS)
4	6	MUD SLIDE SLIM AND THE BLUE HORIZON	James Taylor (Warner Bros.)
8	7	WHO'S NEXT	Who (Polydor)
6	8	EVERY GOOD BOY DESERVES FAVOUR	Moody Blues (Threshold)
10	9	SWEET BABY JAMES	James Taylor (Warner Bros.)
7	10	TEASER & THE FIRECAT	Cat Stevens (Island)
15	11	I'M STILL WAITING	Diana Ross (Tamla Motown)
9	12	BLUE	Joni Mitchell (Reprise)
17	13	TOP OF THE POPS 19	Various Artists (Hallmark)
-	14	MOTOWN CHARTBUSTERS VOL 6	Various Artists (Tamla Motown)
-	15	PILGRIMAGE	Wishbone Ash (MCA)
21	16	CURVED AIR	Curved Air (Warner Bros.)
18	17	MAN IN BLACK	Johnny Cash (CBS)
14	18	MASTER OF REALITY	Black Sabbath (Vertigo)
23	19	C'MON EVERYBODY	Elvis Presley (RCA International)
20	20	DIANA!	Diana Ross (Tamla Motown)
11	21	RAM	Paul McCartney (Apple)
19	22	LOVE STORY	Andy Williams (CBS)
16	23	ANDY WILLIAMS' GREATEST HITS	Andy Williams (CBS)
13	24	MOTOWN CHARTBUSTERS VOL 5	Various Artists (Tamla Motown)
24	25	SYMPHONIES FOR THE 70s	Waldo de los Rios (A&M)
25	26	PAINT YOUR WAGON	Soundtrack (Paramount)
27	27	LOVE STORY	Soundtrack (Paramount)
28	28	THE CARPENTERS	Carpenters (A&M)
22	29	TARKUS	Emerson Lake & Palmer (Island)
-	30	THE WORLD OF YOUR 100 BEST TUNES VOL 2	Various Artists (Decca)

23 October 1971

last week	this week	Title	Artist (label)
1	1	EVERY PICTURE TELLS A STORY	Rod Stewart (Mercury)
2	2	TAPESTRY	Carole King (A&M)
4	3	FIREBALL	Deep Purple (Harvest)
3	4	ELECTRIC WARRIOR	T. Rex (Fly)
5	5	BRIDGE OVER TROUBLED WATER	Simon & Garfunkel (CBS)
6	6	MUD SLIDE SLIM AND THE BLUE HORIZON	James Taylor (Warner Bros.)
10	7	TEASER & THE FIRECAT	Cat Stevens (Island)
7	8	WHO'S NEXT	Who (Polydor)
8	9	EVERY GOOD BOY DESERVES FAVOUR	Moody Blues (Threshold)
14	10	MOTOWN CHARTBUSTERS VOL 6	Various Artists (Tamla Motown)
-	11	IMAGINE	John Lennon (Apple)
15	12	PILGRIMAGE	Wishbone Ash (MCA)
11	13	I'M STILL WAITING	Diana Ross (Tamla Motown)
16	14	CURVED AIR	Curved Air (Warner Bros.)
9	15	SWEET BABY JAMES	James Taylor (Warner Bros.)
21	16	RAM	Paul McCartney (Apple)
30	17	THE WORLD OF YOUR 100 BEST TUNES VOL. 2	Various Artists (Decca)
12	18	BLUE	Joni Mitchell (Reprise)
13	19	TOP OF THE POPS 19	Various Artists (Hallmark)
28	20	THE CARPENTERS	Carpenters (A&M)
18	21	MASTER OF REALITY	Black Sabbath (Vertigo)
-	22	BIG WAR MOVIE THEMES	Geoff Love & His Orchestra (Music for Pleasure)
24	23	MOTOWN CHARTBUSTERS VOL 5	Various Artists (Tamla Motown)
27	24	LOVE STORY	Soundtrack (Paramount)
26	25	PAINT YOUR WAGON	Soundtrack (Paramount)
29	26	TARKUS	Emerson Lake & Palmer (Island)
19	27	C'MON EVERYBODY	Elvis Presley (RCA International)
22	28	LOVE STORY	Andy Williams (CBS)
17	29	MAN IN BLACK	Johnny Cash (CBS)
-	30	THE INTIMATE JIM REEVES	Jim Reeves (RCA International)

30 October 1971

last week	this week	Title	Artist (label)
1	1	EVERY PICTURE TELLS A STORY	Rod Stewart (Mercury)
10	2	MOTOWN CHARTBUSTERS VOL 6	Various Artists (Tamla Motown)
4	3	ELECTRIC WARRIOR	T. Rex (Fly)
2	4	TAPESTRY	Carole King (A&M)
5	5	BRIDGE OVER TROUBLED WATER	Simon & Garfunkel (CBS)
11	6	IMAGINE	John Lennon (Apple)
6	7	MUD SLIDE SLIM AND THE BLUE HORIZON	James Taylor (Warner Bros.)
7	8	TEASER & THE FIRECAT	Cat Stevens (Island)
8	9	WHO'S NEXT	Who (Polydor)
3	10	FIREBALL	Deep Purple (Harvest)
13	11	I'M STILL WAITING	Diana Ross (Tamla Motown)
-	12	HOT HITS SEVEN	Various Artists (Music for Pleasure)
12	13	PILGRIMAGE	Wishbone Ash (MCA)
9	14	EVERY GOOD BOY DESERVES FAVOUR	Moody Blues (Threshold)
15	15	SWEET BABY JAMES	James Taylor (Warner Bros.)
14	16	CURVED AIR	Curved Air (Warner Bros.)
-	17	THE WORLD OF YOUR 100 BEST TUNES	Various Artists (Decca)
17	18	THE WORLD OF YOUR 100 BEST TUNES VOL. 2	Various Artists (Decca)
24	19	LOVE STORY	Soundtrack (Paramount)
20	20	THE CARPENTERS	Carpenters (A&M)
16	21	RAM	Paul McCartney (Apple)
18	22	BLUE	Joni Mitchell (Reprise)
19	23	TOP OF THE POPS 19	Various Artists (Hallmark)
23	24	MOTOWN CHARTBUSTERS VOL 5	Various Artists (Hallmark)
-	25	ANDY WILLIAMS' GREATEST HITS	Andy Williams (CBS)
29	26	MAN IN BLACK	Johnny Cash (CBS)
21	27	MASTER OF REALITY	Black Sabbath (Vertigo)
-	28	LED ZEPPELIN II	Led Zeppelin (Atlantic)
22	29	BIG WAR MOVIE THEMES	Geoff Love & His Orchestra (Music for Pleasure)
25	30	PAINT YOUR WAGON	Soundtrack (Paramount)

On October 29, gifted lead guitarist Duane Allman died in a motorcycle crash in Macon, Georgia: his hometown and that of his record-company, Capricorn. Duane would soon ride the charts on Clapton's Derek & The Dominoes LP *Layla* (duelling with Eric/Derek on the title track). The Allmans had never made the British charts in Duane's lifetime, and wouldn't do so till 1973. Nor would Van Morrison, though his first albums were his most influential. Jerry Lee Lewis has never been in the NME chart.

November 1971

6 November 1971

last	this	
1	1	EVERY PICTURE TELLS A STORY Rod Stewart (Mercury)
2	2	MOTOWN CHARTBUSTERS VOL 6 Various Artists (Tamla Motown)
6	3	IMAGINE John Lennon (Apple)
3	4	ELECTRIC WARRIOR T. Rex (Fly)
4	5	TAPESTRY Carole King (A&M)
5	6	BRIDGE OVER TROUBLED WATER Simon & Garfunkel (CBS)
8	7	TEASER & THE FIRECAT Cat Stevens (Island)
7	8	MUD SLIDE SLIM AND THE BLUE HORIZON James Taylor (Warner Bros.)
9	9	WHO'S NEXT Who (Polydor)
11	10	I'M STILL WAITING Diana Ross (Tamla Motown)
10	11	FIREBALL Deep Purple (Harvest)
16	12	CURVED AIR Curved Air (Warner Bros.)
12	13	HOT HITS SEVEN Various Artists (Music for Pleasure)
13	14	PILGRIMAGE Wishbone Ash (MCA)
-	15	SANTANA 3 Santana (CBS)
20	16	THE CARPENTERS Carpenters (A&M)
22	17	BLUE Joni Mitchell (Reprise)
-	18	FOG ON THE TYNE Lindisfarne (Charisma)
18	19	THE WORLD OF YOUR 100 BEST TUNES VOL. 2 Various Artists (Decca)
15	20	SWEET BABY JAMES James Taylor (Warner Bros.)
14	21	EVERY GOOD BOY DESERVES FAVOUR Moody Blues (Threshold)
24	22	MOTOWN CHARTBUSTERS VOL 5 Various Artists (Tamla Motown)
-	23	SPACE IN TIME Ten Years After (Chrysalis)
-	24	AFTER THE GOLD RUSH Neil Young (Reprise)
25	25	ANDY WILLIAMS' GREATEST HITS Andy Williams (CBS)
26	26	MAN IN BLACK Johnny Cash (CBS)
29	27	BIG WAR MOVIE THEMES Geoff Love & His Orchestra (Music for Pleasure)
27	28	MASTER OF REALITY Black Sabbath (Vertigo)
-	29	NANCY & LEE Nancy Sinatra & Lee Hazlewood (Reprise)
30	30	PAINT YOUR WAGON Soundtrack (Paramount)

13 November 1971

last	this	
1	1	EVERY PICTURE TELLS A STORY Rod Stewart (Mercury)
3	2	IMAGINE John Lennon (Apple)
5	3	TAPESTRY Carole King (A&M)
2	4	MOTOWN CHARTBUSTERS VOL 6 Various Artists (Tamla Motown)
4	5	ELECTRIC WARRIOR T. Rex (Fly)
7	6	TEASER & THE FIRECAT Cat Stevens (Island)
6	7	BRIDGE OVER TROUBLED WATER Simon & Garfunkel (CBS)
8	8	MUD SLIDE SLIM AND THE BLUE HORIZON James Taylor (Warner Bros.)
9	9	WHO'S NEXT Who (Polydor)
15	10	SANTANA 3 Santana (CBS)
16	11	THE CARPENTERS Carpenters (A&M)
18	12	FOG ON THE TYNE Lindisfarne (Charisma)
10	13	I'M STILL WAITING Diana Ross (Tamla Motown)
11	14	FIREBALL Deep Purple (Harvest)
14	15	PILGRIMAGE Wishbone Ash (MCA)
13	16	HOT HITS SEVEN Various Artists (Music for Pleasure)
17	17	MEDDLE Pink Floyd (Harvest)
20	18	SWEET BABY JAMES James Taylor (Warner Bros.)
19	19	FEARLESS Family (Reprise)
-	20	TOP OF THE POPS 20 Various Artists (Hallmark)
21	21	JIMI HENDRIX AT THE ISLE OF WIGHT, 1970 Jimi Hendrix (Polydor)
12	22	CURVED AIR Curved Air (Warner Bros.)
17	23	BLUE Joni Mitchell (Reprise)
25	24	ANDY WILLIAMS' GREATEST HITS Andy Williams (CBS)
21	25	EVERY GOOD BOY DESERVES FAVOUR Moody Blues (Threshold)
-	26	IN SEARCH OF SPACE Hawkwind (United Artists)
24	27	AFTER THE GOLD RUSH Neil Young (Reprise)
-	28	RAM Paul McCartney (Apple)
19	29	THE WORLD OF YOUR 100 BEST TUNES VOL. 2 Various Artists (Decca)
-	30	ANOTHER MONTY PYTHON RECORD Monty Python's Flying Circus (Charisma)

20 November 1971

last	this	
1	1	EVERY PICTURE TELLS A STORY Rod Stewart (Mercury)
2	2	IMAGINE John Lennon (Apple)
4	3	MOTOWN CHARTBUSTERS VOL 6 Various Artists (Tamla Motown)
3	4	TAPESTRY Carole King (A&M)
5	5	ELECTRIC WARRIOR T. Rex (Fly)
6	6	TEASER & THE FIRECAT Cat Stevens (Island)
7	7	BRIDGE OVER TROUBLED WATER Simon & Garfunkel (CBS)
10	8	SANTANA 3 Santana (CBS)
8	9	MUD SLIDE SLIM AND THE BLUE HORIZON James Taylor (Warner Bros.)
9	10	WHO'S NEXT Who (Polydor)
12	11	FOG ON THE TYNE Lindisfarne (Charisma)
17	12	MEDDLE Pink Floyd (Harvest)
11	13	THE CARPENTERS Carpenters (A&M)
-	14	LED ZEPPELIN IV Led Zeppelin (Atlantic)
14	15	FIREBALL Deep Purple (Harvest)
29	16	THE WORLD OF YOUR 100 BEST TUNES VOL. 2 Various Artists (Decca)
15	17	PILGRIMAGE Wishbone Ash (MCA)
16	18	HOT HITS SEVEN Various Artists (Music for Pleasure)
-	19	FRAGILE Yes (Atlantic)
21	20	JIMI HENDRIX AT THE ISLE OF WIGHT, 1970 Jimi Hendrix (Polydor)
25	21	EVERY GOOD BOY DESERVES FAVOUR Moody Blues (Threshold)
20	22	TOP OF THE POPS 20 Various Artists (Hallmark)
26	23	IN SEARCH OF SPACE Hawkwind (United Artists)
-	24	TOM JONES AT CAESAR'S PALACE LAS VEGAS Tom Jones (Decca)
-	25	SPACE IN TIME Ten Years After (Chrysalis)
19	26	FEARLESS Family (Reprise)
-	27	THE WORLD OF YOUR 100 BEST TUNES Various Artists (Decca)
18	28	SWEET BABY JAMES James Taylor (Warner Bros.)
13	29	I'M STILL WAITING Diana Ross (Tamla Motown)
22	30	CURVED AIR Curved Air (Warner Bros.)

27 November 1971

last	this	
2	1	IMAGINE John Lennon (Apple)
1	2	EVERY PICTURE TELLS A STORY Rod Stewart (Mercury)
5	3	ELECTRIC WARRIOR T. Rex (Fly)
4	4	TAPESTRY Carole King (A&M)
12	5	MEDDLE Pink Floyd (Harvest)
8	6	SANTANA 3 Santana (CBS)
14	7	LED ZEPPELIN IV Led Zeppelin (Atlantic)
3	8	MOTOWN CHARTBUSTERS VOL 6 Various Artists (Tamla Motown)
7	9	BRIDGE OVER TROUBLED WATER Simon & Garfunkel (CBS)
6	10	TEASER & THE FIRECAT Cat Stevens (Island)
20	11	JIMI HENDRIX AT THE ISLE OF WIGHT, 1970 Jimi Hendrix (Polydor)
22	12	TOP OF THE POPS 20 Various Artists (Hallmark)
-	13	PICTURES AT AN EXHIBITION Emerson, Lake & Palmer (Island)
26	14	FEARLESS Family (Reprise)
19	15	FRAGILE Yes (Atlantic)
11	16	FOG ON THE TYNE Lindisfarne (Charisma)
10	17	WHO'S NEXT Who (Polydor)
15	18	FIREBALL Deep Purple (Harvest)
9	19	MUD SLIDE SLIM AND THE BLUE HORIZON James Taylor (Warner Bros.)
13	20	THE CARPENTERS Carpenters (A&M)
-	21	THIS IS POURCEL Franck Pourcel (Studio Two)
-	22	SURF'S UP Beach Boys (Stateside)
16	23	THE WORLD OF YOUR 100 BEST TUNES VOL. 2 Various Artists (Decca)
29	24	I'M STILL WAITING Diana Ross (Tamla Motown)
24	25	TOM JONES AT CAESAR'S PALACE LAS VEGAS Tom Jones (Decca)
23	26	IN SEARCH OF SPACE Hawkwind (United Artists)
18	27	HOT HITS SEVEN Various Artists (Music for Pleasure)
27	28	THE WORLD OF YOUR 100 BEST TUNES Various Artists (Decca)
17	29	PILGRIMAGE Wishbone Ash (MCA)
30	30	CURVED AIR Curved Air (Warner Bros.)

Imagine had entered the charts on October 23, and took its time to reach the top. McCartney's album *Ram*, released hard on its heels, jumped in at No.28 on November 13 and then dropped out again. *Imagine* there's no gloating. It was to be Lennon's longest-lingering chart album, not least because its title-track was so sumptuous. Only much later was it issued as a single: it first entered in November 1975 (without especial success), and was a hit again when reissued after Lennon's death in 1980.

December 1971

last week	this week	4 December 1971
1	1	IMAGINE John Lennon (Apple)
2	2	EVERY PICTURE TELLS A STORY Rod Stewart (Mercury)
3	3	ELECTRIC WARRIOR T. Rex (Fly)
7	4	LED ZEPPELIN IV Led Zeppelin (Atlantic)
8	5	MOTOWN CHARTBUSTERS VOL 6 Various Artists (Tamla Motown)
4	6	TAPESTRY Carole King (A&M)
13	7	PICTURES AT AN EXHIBITION Emerson, Lake & Palmer (Island)
6	8	SANTANA 3 Santana (CBS)
9	9	BRIDGE OVER TROUBLED WATER Simon & Garfunkel (CBS)
10	10	TEASER & THE FIRECAT Cat Stevens (Island)
5	11	MEDDLE Pink Floyd (Harvest)
15	12	FRAGILE Yes (Atlantic)
20	13	THE CARPENTERS Carpenters (A&M)
19	14	MUD SLIDE SLIM AND THE BLUE HORIZON James Taylor (Warner Bros.)
16	15	FOG ON THE TYNE Lindisfarne (Charisma)
-	16	FOUR TOPS GREATEST HITS VOL. 2 Four Tops (Tamla Motown)
22	17	SURF'S UP Beach Boys (Stateside)
11	18	JIMI HENDRIX AT THE ISLE OF WIGHT, 1970 Jimi Hendrix (Polydor)
17	19	WHO'S NEXT Who (Polydor)
21	20	THIS IS POURCEL Franck Pourcel (Studio Two)
25	21	TOM JONES AT CAESAR'S PALACE LAS VEGAS Tom Jones (Decca)
-	22	PERFORMANCE-ROCKIN' AT THE FILLMORE Humble Pie (A&M)
-	23	SHAFT Isaac Hayes (Stax)
12	24	TOP OF THE POPS 20 Various Artists (Hallmark)
23	25	THE WORLD OF YOUR 100 BEST TUNES VOL. 2 Various Artists (Decca)
14	26	FEARLESS Family (Reprise)
24	27	I'M STILL WAITING Diana Ross (Tamla Motown)
26	28	IN SEARCH OF SPACE Hawkwind (United Artists)
28	29	THE WORLD OF YOUR 100 BEST TUNES Various Artists (Decca)
27	30	HOT HITS SEVEN Various Artists (Music for Pleasure)

last week	this week	11 December 1971
1	1	IMAGINE John Lennon (Apple)
4	2	LED ZEPPELIN IV Led Zeppelin (Atlantic)
3	3	ELECTRIC WARRIOR T. Rex (Fly)
2	4	EVERY PICTURE TELLS A STORY Rod Stewart (Mercury)
7	5	PICTURES AT AN EXHIBITION Emerson, Lake & Palmer (Island)
6	6	TAPESTRY Carole King (A&M)
5	7	MOTOWN CHARTBUSTERS VOL 6 Various Artists (Tamla Motown)
12	8	FRAGILE Yes (Atlantic)
11	9	MEDDLE Pink Floyd (Harvest)
13	10	THE CARPENTERS Carpenters (A&M)
10	11	TEASER & THE FIRECAT Cat Stevens (Island)
8	12	SANTANA 3 Santana (CBS)
9	13	BRIDGE OVER TROUBLED WATER Simon & Garfunkel (CBS)
23	14	SHAFT Isaac Hayes (Stax)
14	15	MUD SLIDE SLIM AND THE BLUE HORIZON James Taylor (Warner Bros.)
17	16	SURF'S UP Beach Boys (Stateside)
24	17	TOP OF THE POPS 20 Various Artists (Hallmark)
-	18	MEATY BEATY BIG AND BOUNCY Who (Track)
-	19	RAINBOW BRIDGE Jimi Hendrix (Reprise)
-	20	12 SONGS OF CHRISTMAS Jim Reeves (RCA International)
19	21	WHO'S NEXT Who (Polydor)
21	22	TOM JONES AT CAESAR'S PALACE LAS VEGAS Tom Jones (Decca)
-	23	GLEN CAMPBELL'S GREATEST HITS Glen Campbell (Capitol)
15	24	FOG ON THE TYNE Lindisfarne (Charisma)
22	25	PERFORMANCE-ROCKIN' AT THE FILLMORE Humble Pie (A&M)
20	26	THIS IS POURCEL Franck Pourcel (Studio Two)
-	27	CLOSE TO YOU Carpenters (A&M)
-	28	HOT HITS EIGHT Various Artists (Music for Pleasure)
26	29	FEARLESS Family (Reprise)
18	30	JIMI HENDRIX AT THE ISLE OF WIGHT, 1970 Jimi Hendrix (Polydor)

last week	this week	18 December 1971
2	1	LED ZEPPELIN IV Led Zeppelin (Atlantic)
1	2	IMAGINE John Lennon (Apple)
3	3	ELECTRIC WARRIOR T. Rex (Fly)
4	4	EVERY PICTURE TELLS A STORY Rod Stewart (Mercury)
7	5	MOTOWN CHARTBUSTERS VOL 6 Various Artists (Tamla Motown)
5	6	PICTURES AT AN EXHIBITION Emerson, Lake & Palmer (Island)
13	7	BRIDGE OVER TROUBLED WATER Simon & Garfunkel (CBS)
6	8	TAPESTRY Carole King (A&M)
8	9	FRAGILE Yes (Atlantic)
11	10	TEASER & THE FIRECAT Cat Stevens (Island)
10	11	THE CARPENTERS Carpenters (A&M)
9	12	MEDDLE Pink Floyd (Harvest)
-	13	WILD LIFE Wings (Parlophone)
20	14	12 SONGS OF CHRISTMAS Jim Reeves (RCA International)
14	15	SHAFT Isaac Hayes (Stax)
17	16	TOP OF THE POPS 20 Various Artists (Hallmark)
18	17	MEATY BEATY BIG AND BOUNCY Who (Track)
28	18	HOT HITS EIGHT Various Artists (Music for Pleasure)
-	19	A NOD'S AS GOOD AS A WINK ... TO A BLIND HORSE Faces (Warner Bros.)
26	20	THIS IS POURCEL Franck Pourcel (Studio Two)
19	21	RAINBOW BRIDGE Jimi Hendrix (Reprise)
15	22	MUD SLIDE SLIM AND THE BLUE HORIZON James Taylor (Warner Bros.)
23	23	GLEN CAMPBELL'S GREATEST HITS Glen Campbell (Capitol)
-	24	THE SOUND OF MUSIC Soundtrack (RCA)
16	25	SURF'S UP Beach Boys (Stateside)
21	26	WHO'S NEXT Who (Polydor)
-	27	WORDS AND MUSIC Benny Hill (Columbia)
12	28	SANTANA 3 Santana (CBS)
-	29	THE WORLD OF YOUR 100 BEST TUNES VOL. 2 Various Artists (Decca)
-	30	ELVIS' CHRISTMAS ALBUM Elvis Presley (RCA International)

last week	this week	25 December 1971
1	1	LED ZEPPELIN IV Led Zeppelin (Atlantic)
3	2	ELECTRIC WARRIOR T. Rex (Fly)
2	3	IMAGINE John Lennon (Apple)
4	4	EVERY PICTURE TELLS A STORY Rod Stewart (Mercury)
19	5	A NOD'S AS GOOD AS A WINK ... TO A BLIND HORSE Faces (Warner Bros.)
5	6	MOTOWN CHARTBUSTERS VOL 6 Various Artists (Tamla Motown)
10	7	TEASER & THE FIRECAT Cat Stevens (Island)
7	8	BRIDGE OVER TROUBLED WATER Simon & Garfunkel (CBS)
6	9	PICTURES AT AN EXHIBITION Emerson, Lake & Palmer (Island)
15	10	SHAFT Isaac Hayes (Stax)
13	11	WILD LIFE Wings (Parlophone)
17	12	MEATY BEATY BIG AND BOUNCY Who (Track)
8	13	TAPESTRY Carole King (A&M)
14	14	12 SONGS OF CHRISTMAS Jim Reeves (RCA International)
11	15	THE CARPENTERS Carpenters (A&M)
28	16	SANTANA 3 Santana (CBS)
30	17	ELVIS' CHRISTMAS ALBUM Elvis Presley (RCA International)
22	18	MUD SLIDE SLIM AND THE BLUE HORIZON James Taylor (Warner Bros.)
9	19	FRAGILE Yes (Atlantic)
12	20	MEDDLE Pink Floyd (Harvest)
-	21	FIREBALL Deep Purple (Harvest)
-	22	TOP OF THE POPS 21 Various Artists (Hallmark)
-	23	A SONG FOR YOU Andy Williams (CBS)
21	24	RAINBOW BRIDGE Jimi Hendrix (Reprise)
16	25	TOP OF THE POPS 20 Various Artists (Hallmark)
26	26	WHO'S NEXT Who (Polydor)
20	27	THIS IS POURCEL Franck Pourcel (Studio Two)
27	28	WORDS AND MUSIC Benny Hill (Columbia)
18	29	HOT HITS EIGHT Various Artists (Music for Pleasure)
25	30	SURF'S UP Beach Boys (Stateside)

Emerson Lake & Palmer were overblowing Modest Petrovich Mussorgsky in the Top 10. John Peel on their London debut gig: "a tragic waste of talent and electricity." Other 1971 quotes by album chart entrants: When John and Yoko wanted a New York apartment, and Yoko found one on the Bowery, John said: "Oh no, luv, no there. I don't want to walk out me door and see people dying in the gutter - really I don't." And from the rehearsals for the Concert For Bangla Desh at Madison Square Garden: George Harrison asked Bob Dylan if he planned to sing his early hit Blowin' In The Wind; Dylan replied, "Well George, are you gonna sing I Want To Hold Your Hand?"

January 1972

The double-album called (here) *More Bob Dylan Greatest Hits*, released some months after its American issue, was in its way oddly titled, since Dylan fans rushed to buy it because it offered a number of tracks never previously released, including a 1963 concert recording of *Tomorrow Is A Long Time*, one of the two Dylan songs that Elvis Presley recorded. This, and *Don't Think Twice It's Alright*, were "bonus tracks" used to pad out one of Elvis' mid-60s film soundtrack albums.

January – February 1972

29 January 1972

last week	this week	Title	Artist
1	1	TEASER AND THE FIRECAT	Cat Stevens (Island)
2	2	A NOD'S AS GOOD AS A WINK ... TO A BLIND HORSE	Faces (Warner Bros.)
3	3	ELECTRIC WARRIOR	T. Rex (Fly)
6	4	THE CONCERT FOR BANGLA DESH	Various Artists (Apple)
4	5	IMAGINE	John Lennon (Apple)
7	6	BRIDGE OVER TROUBLED WATER	Simon & Garfunkel (CBS)
8	7	HIMSELF	Gilbert O'Sullivan (MAM)
5	8	LED ZEPPELIN IV	Led Zeppelin (Atlantic)
14	9	JESUS CHRIST SUPERSTAR	Various Artists (MCA)
10	10	TAPESTRY	Carole King (A&M)
11	11	EVERY PICTURE TELLS A STORY	Rod Stewart (Philips)
20	12	GATHER ME	Melanie (Buddah)
12	13	FIREBALL	Deep Purple (Harvest)
21	14	PICTURES AT AN EXHIBITION	Emerson Lake & Palmer (Island)
15	15	MUSIC	Carole King (A&M)
9	16	MOTOWN CHARTBUSTERS VOL 6	Various Artists (Tamla Motown)
25	17	MORE BOB DYLAN GREATEST HITS	Bob Dylan (CBS)
26	18	HOT HITS NINE	Various Artists (Music for Pleasure)
24	19	FRAGILE	Yes (Atlantic)
13	20	MEATY BEATY BIG AND BOUNCY	Who (Track)
27	21	AMERICA	America (Warner Bros.)
29	22	STONES	Neil Diamond (Uni)
16	23	THE CARPENTERS	Carpenters (A&M)
17	24	MUD SLIDE SLIM AND THE BLUE HORIZON	James Taylor (Warner Bros.)
28	25	SHAFT	Isaac Hayes (Stax)
-	26	HENDRIX IN THE WEST	Jimi Hendrix (Polydor)
18	27	MEDDLE	Pink Floyd (Harvest)
22	28	FOG ON THE TYNE	Lindisfarne (Charisma)
19	30	ANDY WILLIAMS' GREATEST HITS	Andy Williams (CBS)

5 February 1972

last week	this week	Title	Artist
1	1	TEASER AND THE FIRECAT	Cat Stevens (Island)
2	2	A NOD'S AS GOOD AS A WINK ... TO A BLIND HORSE	Faces (Warner Bros.)
3	3	ELECTRIC WARRIOR	T. Rex (Fly)
4	4	THE CONCERT FOR BANGLA DESH	Various Artists (Apple)
5	5	IMAGINE	John Lennon (Apple)
6	6	BRIDGE OVER TROUBLED WATER	Simon & Garfunkel (CBS)
8	7	LED ZEPPELIN IV	Led Zeppelin (Atlantic)
9	8	JESUS CHRIST SUPERSTAR	Various Artists (MCA)
11	9	EVERY PICTURE TELLS A STORY	Rod Stewart (Philips)
26	10	HENDRIX IN THE WEST	Jimi Hendrix (Polydor)
12	11	GATHER ME	Melanie (Buddah)
7	12	HIMSELF	Gilbert O'Sullivan (MAM)
17	13	MORE BOB DYLAN GREATEST HITS	Bob Dylan (CBS)
-	14	NEIL REID	Neil Reid (Decca)
23	15	THE CARPENTERS	Carpenters (A&M)
21	16	AMERICA	America (Warner Bros.)
14	17	PICTURES AT AN EXHIBITION	Emerson Lake & Palmer (Island)
19	18	FRAGILE	Yes (Atlantic)
25	19	SHAFT	Isaac Hayes (Stax)
15	20	MUSIC	Carole King (A&M)
13	21	FIREBALL	Deep Purple (Harvest)
16	22	MOTOWN CHARTBUSTERS VOL 6	Various Artists (Tamla Motown)
10	23	TAPESTRY	Carole King (A&M)
24	24	MUD SLIDE SLIM AND THE BLUE HORIZON	James Taylor (Warner Bros.)
30	25	ANDY WILLIAMS' GREATEST HITS	Andy Williams (CBS)
20	26	MEATY BEATY BIG AND BOUNCY	Who (Track)
18	27	HOT HITS NINE	Various Artists (Music for Pleasure)
22	28	STONES	Neil Diamond (Uni)
-	29	TEA FOR THE TILLERMAN	Cat Stevens (Island)
-	30	RAINBOW BRIDGE	Jimi Hendrix (Reprise)

12 February 1972

last week	this week	Title	Artist
1	1	TEASER AND THE FIRECAT	Cat Stevens (Island)
3	2	ELECTRIC WARRIOR	T. Rex (Fly)
2	3	A NOD'S AS GOOD AS A WINK ... TO A BLIND HORSE	Faces (Warner Bros.)
6	4	BRIDGE OVER TROUBLED WATER	Simon & Garfunkel (CBS)
7	5	LED ZEPPELIN IV	Led Zeppelin (Atlantic)
5	6	IMAGINE	John Lennon (Apple)
4	7	THE CONCERT FOR BANGLA DESH	Various Artists (Apple)
14	8	NEIL REID	Neil Reid (Decca)
12	9	HIMSELF	Gilbert O'Sullivan (MAM)
9	10	EVERY PICTURE TELLS A STORY	Rod Stewart (Philips)
10	11	HENDRIX IN THE WEST	Jimi Hendrix (Polydor)
16	12	AMERICA	America (Warner Bros.)
11	13	GATHER ME	Melanie (Buddah)
20	14	MUSIC	Carole King (A&M)
13	15	MORE BOB DYLAN GREATEST HITS	Bob Dylan (CBS)
22	16	MOTOWN CHARTBUSTERS VOL 6	Various Artists (Tamla Motown)
19	17	SHAFT	Isaac Hayes (Stax)
23	18	TAPESTRY	Carole King (A&M)
17	19	PICTURES AT AN EXHIBITION	Emerson Lake & Palmer (Island)
-	20	MEDDLE	Pink Floyd (Harvest)
26	21	MEATY BEATY BIG AND BOUNCY	Who (Track)
-	22	GLEN CAMPBELL'S GREATEST HITS	Glen Campbell (Capitol)
-	23	THERE'S A RIOT GOIN' ON	Sly & the Family Stone (Epic)
28	24	STONES	Neil Diamond (Uni)
18	25	FRAGILE	Yes (Atlantic)
-	26	FOG ON THE TYNE	Lindisfarne (Charisma)
-	27	WILD LIFE	Wings (Parlophone)
27	28	HOT HITS NINE	Various Artists (Music for Pleasure)
21	29	FIREBALL	Deep Purple (Harvest)
-	30	NILSSON SCHMILSSON	Nilsson (RCA)

19 February 1972

last week	this week	Title	Artist
1	1	TEASER AND THE FIRECAT	Cat Stevens (Island)
2	2	ELECTRIC WARRIOR	T. Rex (Fly)
3	3	A NOD'S AS GOOD AS A WINK ... TO A BLIND HORSE	Faces (Warner Bros.)
8	4	NEIL REID	Neil Reid (Decca)
7	5	THE CONCERT FOR BANGLA DESH	Various Artists (Apple)
11	6	HENDRIX IN THE WEST	Jimi Hendrix (Polydor)
4	7	BRIDGE OVER TROUBLED WATER	Simon & Garfunkel (CBS)
6	8	IMAGINE	John Lennon (Apple)
-	9	PAUL SIMON	Paul Simon (CBS)
5	10	LED ZEPPELIN IV	Led Zeppelin (Atlantic)
13	11	GATHER ME	Melanie (Buddah)
-	12	JESUS CHRIST SUPERSTAR	Various Artists (MCA)
14	13	MUSIC	Carole King (A&M)
18	15	TAPESTRY	Carole King (A&M)
9	16	HIMSELF	Gilbert O'Sullivan (MAM)
12	17	AMERICA	America (Warner Bros.)
-	18	WOYAMA	Osibisa (MCA)
19	19	PICTURES AT AN EXHIBITION	Emerson Lake & Palmer (Island)
15	20	MORE BOB DYLAN GREATEST HITS	Bob Dylan (CBS)
16	21	MOTOWN CHARTBUSTERS VOL 6	Various Artists (Tamla Motown)
10	22	EVERY PICTURE TELLS A STORY	Rod Stewart (Philips)
-	23	TEA FOR THE TILLERMAN	Cat Stevens (Island)
22	24	GLEN CAMPBELL'S GREATEST HITS	Glen Campbell (Capitol)
21	25	MEATY BEATY BIG AND BOUNCY	Who (Track)
30	26	NILSSON SCHMILSSON	Nilsson (RCA)
26	27	FOG ON THE TYNE	Lindisfarne (Charisma)
24	28	STONES	Neil Diamond (UNI)
27	29	WILD LIFE	Wings (Parlophone)
20	30	MEDDLE	Pink Floyd (Harvest)

Teaser And The Firecat was not only Cat Stevens' No.1 album (his fourth LP, his third for Chris Blackwell's Island label and to prove his longest-lasting chart contender). *Teaser And The Firecat* was also the title of Stevens' children's book. The story is told in Chinese, English, French, German, Italian, Greek, Hebrew, Japanese, Russian, Spanish and Welsh. Stevens' previous album, *Tea For The Tillerman*, was sufficiently boosted by the great success of *Firecat* to re-enter the chart in February.

February – March 1972

	26 February 1972		4 March 1972		11 March 1972		18 March 1972
4	1 NEIL REID Neil Reid (Decca)	4	1 PAUL SIMON Paul Simon (CBS)	1	1 PAUL SIMON Paul Simon (CBS)	1	1 PAUL SIMON Paul Simon (CBS)
2	2 ELECTRIC WARRIOR	3	2 TEASER AND THE FIRECAT	7	2 HARVEST Neil Young (Reprise)	2	2 HARVEST Neil Young (Reprise)
	T. Rex (Fly)		Cat Stevens (Island)	2	3 TEASER AND THE FIRECAT	3	3 TEASER AND THE FIRECAT
1	3 TEASER AND THE FIRECAT	1	3 NEIL REID Neil Reid (Decca)		Cat Stevens (Island)		Cat Stevens (Island)
	Cat Stevens (Island)	2	4 ELECTRIC WARRIOR	3	4 NEIL REID Neil Reid (Decca)	9	4 NILSSON SCHMILSSON
9	4 PAUL SIMON Paul Simon (CBS)		T. Rex (Fly)	4	5 ELECTRIC WARRIOR		Nilsson (RCA)
3	5 A NOD'S AS GOOD AS A WINK ...	5	5 A NOD'S AS GOOD AS A WINK ...		T. Rex (Fly)	6	5 BRIDGE OVER TROUBLED
	TO A BLIND HORSE		TO A BLIND HORSE	6	6 BRIDGE OVER TROUBLED		WATER
	Faces (Warner Bros.)		Faces (Warner Bros.)		WATER		Simon & Garfunkel (CBS)
7	6 BRIDGE OVER TROUBLED	6	6 BRIDGE OVER TROUBLED		Simon & Garfunkel (CBS)	4	6 NEIL REID Neil Reid (Decca)
	WATER		WATER	5	7 A NOD'S AS GOOD AS A WINK ...	8	7 HIMSELF
	Simon & Garfunkel (CBS)		Simon & Garfunkel (CBS)		TO A BLIND HORSE		Gilbert O'Sullivan (MAM)
8	7 IMAGINE John Lennon (Apple)	10	7 HARVEST Neil Young (Reprise)		Faces (Warner Bros.)	10	8 FOG ON THE TYNE
5	8 THE CONCERT FOR BANGLA	13	8 HIMSELF	8	8 HIMSELF		Lindisfarne (Charisma)
	DESH Various Artists (Apple)		Gilbert O'Sullivan (MAM)		Gilbert O'Sullivan (MAM)	16	9 AMERICAN PIE
10	9 LED ZEPPELIN IV	12	9 NILSSON SCHMILSSON	9	9 NILSSON SCHMILSSON		Don McLean (United Artists)
	Led Zeppelin (Atlantic)		Nilsson (RCA)		Nilsson (RCA)	5	10 ELECTRIC WARRIOR
-	10 HARVEST Neil Young (Reprise)	7	10 IMAGINE John Lennon (Apple)	11	10 FOG ON THE TYNE		T. Rex (Fly)
17	11 AMERICA	21	11 FOG ON THE TYNE	20	11 GRAVE NEW WORLD	23	11 THICK AS A BRICK
	America (Warner Bros.)		Lindisfarne (Charisma)		Strawbs (A&M)		Jethro Tull (Chrysalis)
26	12 NILSSON SCHMILSSON	19	12 MOTOWN CHARTBUSTERS	13	12 HENDRIX IN THE WEST	7	12 A NOD'S AS GOOD AS A WINK ...
	Nilsson (RCA)		VOL 6		Jimi Hendrix (Polydor)		TO A BLIND HORSE
16	13 HIMSELF		Various Artists (Tamla Motown)	10	13 IMAGINE John Lennon (Apple)		Faces (Warner Bros.)
	Gilbert O'Sullivan (MAM)	15	13 HENDRIX IN THE WEST	17	14 LED ZEPPELIN IV	11	13 GRAVE NEW WORLD
12	14 JESUS CHRIST SUPERSTAR		Jimi Hendrix (Polydor)		Led Zeppelin (Atlantic)		Strawbs (A&M)
	Various Artists (MCA)	8	14 THE CONCERT FOR BANGLA	14	15 THE CONCERT FOR BANGLA	13	14 IMAGINE John Lennon (Apple)
6	15 HENDRIX IN THE WEST		DESH Various Artists (Apple)		DESH	12	15 HENDRIX IN THE WEST
	Jimi Hendrix (Polydor)	22	15 TOP OF THE POPS 22		Various Artists (Apple)		Jimi Hendrix (Polydor)
15	16 TAPESTRY Carole King (A&M)		Various Artists (Hallmark)	-	16 AMERICAN PIE	14	16 LED ZEPPELIN IV
18	17 WOYAYA Osibisa (MCA)	11	16 AMERICA		Don McLean (United Artists)		Led Zeppelin (Atlantic)
22	18 EVERY PICTURE TELLS A		America (Warner Bros.)	15	17 TOP OF THE POPS 22	-	17 BABY I'M A WANT-YOU
	STORY Rod Stewart (Philips)	9	17 LED ZEPPELIN IV		Various Artists (Hallmark)		Bread (Elektra)
21	19 MOTOWN CHARTBUSTERS VOL 6		Led Zeppelin (Atlantic)	12	18 MOTOWN CHARTBUSTERS VOL 6	22	18 THE CARPENTERS
	Various Artists (Tamla Motown)	18	18 EVERY PICTURE TELLS A		Various Artists (Tamla Motown)		Carpenters (A&M)
-	20 THE PERSUADERS		STORY Rod Stewart (Philips)	22	19 JESUS CHRIST SUPERSTAR	-	19 WHO WILL SAVE THE WORLD?
	John Barry Orchestra (CBS)	25	19 GATHER ME Melanie (Buddah)		Various Artists (MCA)		Groundhogs (United Artists)
27	21 FOG ON THE TYNE	-	20 GRAVE NEW WORLD	24	20 FRAGILE Yes (Atlantic)	21	20 TEA FOR THE TILLERMAN
	Lindisfarne (Charisma)		Strawbs (A&M)	-	21 TEA FOR THE TILLERMAN		Cat Stevens (Island)
-	22 TOP OF THE POPS 22	16	21 TAPESTRY Carole King (A&M)		Cat Stevens (Island)	24	21 TAPESTRY Carole King (A&M)
	Various Artists (Hallmark)	14	22 JESUS CHRIST SUPERSTAR	-	22 THE CARPENTERS	15	22 THE CONCERT FOR BANGLA
14	23 FRAGILE Yes (Atlantic)		Various Artists (MCA)		Carpenters (A&M)		DESH Various Artists (Apple)
30	24 MEDDLE Pink Floyd (Harvest)	-	23 I CAPRICORN	-	23 THICK AS A BRICK	27	23 MEDDLE Pink Floyd (Harvest)
11	25 GATHER ME Melanie (Buddah)		Shirley Bassey (United Artists)		Jethro Tull (Chrysalis)	17	25 TOP OF THE POPS 22
25	26 MEATY BEATY BIG AND	23	24 FRAGILE Yes (Atlantic)	21	24 TAPESTRY Carole King (A&M)		Various Artists (Hallmark)
	BOUNCY Who (Track)	27	25 MUSIC Carole King (A&M)	29	25 ANDY WILLIAMS' GREATEST	19	26 JESUS CHRIST SUPERSTAR
13	27 MUSIC Carole King (A&M)	24	26 MEDDLE Pink Floyd (Harvest)		HITS Andy Williams (CBS)		Various Artists (MCA)
20	28 MORE BOB DYLAN GREATEST	-	27 ELVIS: THAT'S THE WAY IT IS	-	26 PICTURES AT AN EXHIBITION	30	27 GATHER ME Melanie (Buddah)
	HITS Bob Dylan (CBS)		Elvis Presley (RCA)		Emerson Lake & Palmer (Island)	18	28 MOTOWN CHARTBUSTERS VOL 6
23	29 TEA FOR THE TILLERMAN	20	28 THE PERSUADERS	26	27 MEDDLE Pink Floyd (Harvest)		Various Artists (Tamla Motown)
	Cat Stevens (Island)		John Barry Orchestra (CBS)	-	28 MILESTONES	-	29 TOP TV THEMES
24	30 GLEN CAMPBELL'S GREATEST	-	29 ANDY WILLIAMS' GREATEST		Rolling Stones (Decca)		Johnny Keating (Studio Two)
	HITS Glen Campbell (Capitol)		HITS Andy Williams (CBS)	18	29 EVERY PICTURE TELLS A	29	30 EVERY PICTURE TELLS A
		-	30 FLEETWOOD MAC'S GREATEST		STORY Rod Stewart (Philips)		STORY Rod Stewart (Philips)
			HITS Fleetwood Mac (CBS)	19	30 GATHER ME Melanie (Buddah)		

The "modern" musical had shifted from *West Side Story* to *Hair* to *Jesus Christ Superstar*. The cast of the latter included Yvonne Elliman and Murray Head, and a one-week hit maxi-single taken from the show featured *I Don't Know How To Love Him* by Elliman and *Superstar* by Head. Elliman would sing with Eric Clapton on his *461 Ocean Boulevard* (1974) and have Top 10 singles in 1976-7 (*Love Me*) and 1978 (*If I Can't Have You*); Murray Head would have a 1984 hit with *One Night In Bangkok*.

March – April 1972

last week	this week	25 March 1972
1	1	PAUL SIMON Paul Simon (CBS)
2	2	HARVEST Neil Young (Reprise)
4	3	NILSSON SCHMILSSON Nilsson (RCA)
7	4	HIMSELF Gilbert O'Sullivan (MAM)
6	5	NEIL REID Neil Reid (Decca)
3	6	TEASER AND THE FIRECAT Cat Stevens (Island)
5	7	BRIDGE OVER TROUBLED WATER Simon & Garfunkel (CBS)
11	8	THICK AS A BRICK Jethro Tull (Chrysalis)
8	9	FOG ON THE TYNE Lindisfarne (Charisma)
10	10	ELECTRIC WARRIOR T. Rex (Fly)
9	11	AMERICAN PIE Don McLean (United Artists)
13	12	GRAVE NEW WORLD Strawbs (A&M)
12	13	A NOD'S AS GOOD AS A WINK ... TO A BLIND HORSE Faces (Warner Bros.)
19	14	WHO WILL SAVE THE WORLD? Groundhogs (United Artists)
14	15	IMAGINE John Lennon (Apple)
15	16	HENDRIX IN THE WEST Jimi Hendrix (Polydor)
-	17	MILESTONES Rolling Stones (Decca)
25	18	TOP OF THE POPS 22 Various Artists (Hallmark)
18	19	THE CARPENTERS Carpenters (A&M)
21	20	TAPESTRY Carole King (A&M)
26	21	JESUS CHRIST SUPERSTAR Various Artists (MCA)
29	22	TOP TV THEMES Johnny Keating (Studio Two)
-	23	WE'D LIKE TO TEACH THE WORLD TO SING New Seekers (Polydor)
20	24	TEA FOR THE TILLERMAN Cat Stevens (Island)
22	25	THE CONCERT FOR BANGLA DESH Various Artists (Apple)
16	26	LED ZEPPELIN IV Led Zeppelin (Atlantic)
28	27	MOTOWN CHARTBUSTERS VOL 6 Various Artists (Tamla Motown)
30	28	EVERY PICTURE TELLS A STORY Rod Stewart (Philips)
17	29	BABY I'M A WANT-YOU Bread (Elektra)
23	30	MEDDLE Pink Floyd (Harvest)

last week	this week	1 April 1972
1	1	PAUL SIMON Paul Simon (CBS)
3	2	NILSSON SCHMILSSON Nilsson (RCA)
2	3	HARVEST Neil Young (Reprise)
4	4	HIMSELF Gilbert O'Sullivan (MAM)
9	5	FOG ON THE TYNE Lindisfarne (Charisma)
11	6	AMERICAN PIE Don McLean (United Artists)
6	7	TEASER AND THE FIRECAT Cat Stevens (Island)
8	8	THICK AS A BRICK Jethro Tull (Chrysalis)
5	9	NEIL REID Neil Reid (Decca)
7	10	BRIDGE OVER TROUBLED WATER Simon & Garfunkel (CBS)
10	11	ELECTRIC WARRIOR T. Rex (Fly)
23	12	WE'D LIKE TO TEACH THE WORLD TO SING New Seekers (Polydor)
14	13	WHO WILL SAVE THE WORLD? Groundhogs (United Artists)
12	14	GRAVE NEW WORLD Strawbs (A&M)
15	15	IMAGINE John Lennon (Apple)
26	16	LED ZEPPELIN IV Led Zeppelin (Atlantic)
16	17	HENDRIX IN THE WEST Jimi Hendrix (Polydor)
-	18	FAREWELL TO THE GREYS Band of the Royal Scots Guards (RCA)
13	19	A NOD'S AS GOOD AS A WINK ... TO A BLIND HORSE Faces (Warner Bros.)
29	20	BABY I'M A WANT-YOU Bread (Elektra)
19	21	THE CARPENTERS Carpenters (A&M)
-	22	SLADE ALIVE Slade (Polydor)
17	23	MILESTONES Rolling Stones (Decca)
22	24	TOP TV THEMES Johnny Keating (Studio Two)
-	25	NEW AGE OF ATLANTIC Various Artists (Atlantic)
-	26	HOT HITS TEN Various Artists (Music for Pleasure)
-	27	WOYAYA Osibisa (MCA)
28	28	EVERY PICTURE TELLS A STORY Rod Stewart (Philips)
20	29	TAPESTRY Carole King (A&M)
21	30	JESUS CHRIST SUPERSTAR Various Artists (MCA)

last week	this week	8 April 1972
5	1	FOG ON THE TYNE Lindisfarne (Charisma)
3	2	HARVEST Neil Young (Reprise)
2	3	NILSSON SCHMILSSON Nilsson (RCA)
4	4	HIMSELF Gilbert O'Sullivan (MAM)
10	5	BRIDGE OVER TROUBLED WATER Simon & Garfunkel (CBS)
1	6	PAUL SIMON Paul Simon (CBS)
7	7	TEASER AND THE FIRECAT Cat Stevens (Island)
12	8	WE'D LIKE TO TEACH THE WORLD TO SING New Seekers (Polydor)
6	9	AMERICAN PIE Don McLean (United Artists)
8	10	THICK AS A BRICK Jethro Tull (Chrysalis)
9	11	NEIL REID Neil Reid (Decca)
11	12	ELECTRIC WARRIOR T. Rex (Fly)
-	13	MACHINE HEAD Deep Purple (Purple)
-	14	GARDEN IN THE CITY Melanie (Buddah)
15	15	IMAGINE John Lennon (Apple)
19	16	A NOD'S AS GOOD AS A WINK ... TO A BLIND HORSE Faces (Warner Bros.)
26	17	HOT HITS TEN Various Artists (Music for Pleasure)
30	18	JESUS CHRIST SUPERSTAR Various Artists (MCA)
23	19	MILESTONES Rolling Stones (Decca)
14	20	GRAVE NEW WORLD Strawbs (A&M)
13	21	WHO WILL SAVE THE WORLD? Groundhogs (United Artists)
29	22	TAPESTRY Carole King (A&M)
20	23	BABY I'M A WANT-YOU Bread (Elektra)
22	24	SLADE ALIVE Slade (Polydor)
-	24	MOTOWN CHARTBUSTERS VOL 6 Various Artists (Tamla Motown)
-	26	GLEN CAMPBELL'S GREATEST HITS Glen Campbell (Capitol)
18	27	FAREWELL TO THE GREYS Band of the Royal Scots Guards (RCA)
24	28	FRAGILE Yes (Atlantic)
17	29	HENDRIX IN THE WEST Jimi Hendrix (Polydor)
16	30	LED ZEPPELIN IV Led Zeppelin (Atlantic)

last week	this week	15 April 1972
2	1	HARVEST Neil Young (Reprise)
1	2	FOG ON THE TYNE Lindisfarne (Charisma)
4	3	HIMSELF Gilbert O'Sullivan (MAM)
3	4	NILSSON SCHMILSSON Nilsson (RCA)
6	5	PAUL SIMON Paul Simon (CBS)
8	6	WE'D LIKE TO TEACH THE WORLD TO SING New Seekers (Polydor)
10	7	THICK AS A BRICK Jethro Tull (Chrysalis)
5	8	BRIDGE OVER TROUBLED WATER Simon & Garfunkel (CBS)
9	9	AMERICAN PIE Don McLean (United Artists)
7	10	TEASER AND THE FIRECAT Cat Stevens (Island)
24	11	SLADE ALIVE Slade (Polydor)
13	12	MACHINE HEAD Deep Purple (Purple)
20	13	GRAVE NEW WORLD Strawbs (A&M)
12	14	ELECTRIC WARRIOR T. Rex (Fly)
16	15	IMAGINE John Lennon (Apple)
16	16	A NOD'S AS GOOD AS A WINK ... TO A BLIND HORSE Faces (Warner Bros.)
27	17	FAREWELL TO THE GREYS Band of the Royal Scots Guards (RCA)
17	18	HOT HITS TEN Various Artists (Music for Pleasure)
11	19	NEIL REID Neil Reid (Decca) C.C.S. (RAK)
14	21	GARDEN IN THE CITY Melanie (Buddah)
22	22	TAPESTRY Carole King (A&M)
28	23	FRAGILE Yes (Atlantic)
21	24	WHO WILL SAVE THE WORLD? Groundhogs (United Artists)
23	25	BABY I'M A WANT-YOU Bread (Elektra)
-	26	NEW AGE OF ATLANTIC Various Artists (Atlantic)
29	27	HENDRIX IN THE WEST Jimi Hendrix (Polydor)
30	28	LED ZEPPELIN IV Led Zeppelin (Atlantic)
18	29	JESUS CHRIST SUPERSTAR Various Artists (MCA)
24	30	MOTOWN CHARTBUSTERS VOL 6 Various Artists (Tamla Motown)

Neil Reid's excitingly-titled ex-No.1 album *Neil Reid*, now slipping down the Top 10, must be one of the least-remembered No.1 albums of the post-war years, by one of the least-remembered artists. Reid, a television talent-show find, had entered the singles chart on Christmas Day 1971 with *Mother Of Mine*, which peaked at No.4 in February. His follow-up single would barely scrape the bottom of the Top 50; his second album, *Smile*, would do no better, later in the year.

April – May 1972

22 April 1972

last week	this week		
1	1	HARVEST	Neil Young (Reprise)
2	2	FOG ON THE TYNE	Lindisfarne (Charisma)
12	3	MACHINE HEAD	Deep Purple (Purple)
5	4	PAUL SIMON	Paul Simon (CBS)
6	5	WE'D LIKE TO TEACH THE WORLD TO SING	New Seekers (Polydor)
4	6	NILSSON SCHMILSSON	Nilsson (RCA)
3	7	HIMSELF	Gilbert O'Sullivan (MAM)
8	8	BRIDGE OVER TROUBLED WATER	Simon & Garfunkel (CBS)
17	9	FAREWELL TO THE GREYS	Band of the Royal Scots Guards (RCA)
7	10	THICK AS A BRICK	Jethro Tull (Chrysalis)
11	11	SLADE ALIVE	Slade (Polydor)
10	12	TEASER AND THE FIRECAT	Cat Stevens (Island)
14	13	ELECTRIC WARRIOR	T. Rex (Fly)
-	14	PROPHETS, SEERS AND SAGES THE ANGELS OF THE AGES/MY PEOPLE WERE FAIR AND HAD SKY IN THEIR HAIR, BUT NOW THEY'RE CONTENT TO WEAR STARS ON THEIR BROWS	Tyrannosaurus Rex (Fly)
9	15	AMERICAN PIE	Don McLean (United Artists)
25	16	BABY I'M A WANT-YOU	Bread (Elektra)
13	17	GRAVE NEW WORLD	Strawbs (A&M)
15	18	IMAGINE	John Lennon (Apple)
21	19	GARDEN IN THE CITY	Melanie (Buddah)
18	20	HOT HITS TEN	Various Artists (Music for Pleasure)
16	21	A NOD'S AS GOOD AS A WINK ... TO A BLIND HORSE	Faces (Warner Bros.)
22	22	TAPESTRY	Carole King (A&M)
-	23	TOP OF THE POPS 23	Various Artists (Hallmark)
-	24	SMOKIN'	Humble Pie (A&M)
30	25	MOTOWN CHARTBUSTERS VOL 6	Various Artists (Tamla Motown)
27	26	HENDRIX IN THE WEST	Jimi Hendrix (Polydor)
-	27	THE CARPENTERS	Carpenters (A&M)
24	28	WHO WILL SAVE THE WORLD?	Groundhogs (United Artists)
23	29	FRAGILE	Yes (Atlantic)
20	30	C.C.S.	C.C.S. (RAK)

29 April 1972

last week	this week		
1	1	HARVEST	Neil Young (Reprise)
3	2	MACHINE HEAD	Deep Purple (Purple)
2	3	FOG ON THE TYNE	Lindisfarne (Charisma)
6	4	NILSSON SCHMILSSON	Nilsson (RCA)
7	5	HIMSELF	Gilbert O'Sullivan (MAM)
5	6	WE'D LIKE TO TEACH THE WORLD TO SING	New Seekers (Polydor)
8	7	BRIDGE OVER TROUBLED WATER	Simon & Garfunkel (CBS)
4	8	PAUL SIMON	Paul Simon (CBS)
10	9	THICK AS A BRICK	Jethro Tull (Chrysalis)
9	10	FAREWELL TO THE GREYS	Band of the Royal Scots Guards (RCA)
14	11	PROPHETS, SEERS AND SAGES THE ANGELS OF THE AGES/MY PEOPLE WERE FAIR AND HAD SKY IN THEIR HAIR, BUT NOW THEY'RE CONTENT TO WEAR STARS ON THEIR BROWS	Tyrannosaurus Rex (Fly)
13	12	ELECTRIC WARRIOR	T. Rex (Fly)
11	13	SLADE ALIVE	Slade (Polydor)
12	14	TEASER AND THE FIRECAT	Cat Stevens (Island)
15	15	AMERICAN PIE	Don McLean (United Artists)
16	16	BABY I'M A WANT-YOU	Bread (Elektra)
17	17	GRAVE NEW WORLD	Strawbs (A&M)
-	18	GODSPELL	London Cast (Bell)
19	19	GARDEN IN THE CITY	Melanie (Buddah)
23	20	TOP OF THE POPS 23	Various Artists (Hallmark)
18	21	IMAGINE	John Lennon (Apple)
21	22	A NOD'S AS GOOD AS A WINK ... TO A BLIND HORSE	Faces (Warner Bros.)
28	23	WHO WILL SAVE THE WORLD?	Groundhogs (United Artists)
24	24	NEIL REID	Neil Reid (Decca)
25	25	MOTOWN CHARTBUSTERS VOL 6	Various Artists (Tamla Motown)
-	26	THE PARTRIDGE FAMILY ... SOUND MAGAZINE	Partridge Family (Bell)
24	27	SMOKIN'	Humble Pie (A&M)
-	28	ALL TOGETHER NOW	Argent (Epic)
22	29	TAPESTRY	Carole King (A&M)
-	30	LED ZEPPELIN IV	Led Zeppelin (Atlantic)

6 May 1972

last week	this week		
2	1	MACHINE HEAD	Deep Purple (Purple)
1	2	HARVEST	Neil Young (Reprise)
11	3	PROPHETS, SEERS AND SAGES THE ANGELS OF THE AGES/MY PEOPLE WERE FAIR AND HAD SKY IN THEIR HAIR, BUT NOW THEY'RE CONTENT TO WEAR STARS ON THEIR BROWS	Tyrannosaurus Rex (Fly)
3	4	FOG ON THE TYNE	Lindisfarne (Charisma)
8	5	PAUL SIMON	Paul Simon (CBS)
7	6	BRIDGE OVER TROUBLED WATER	Simon & Garfunkel (CBS)
5	7	HIMSELF	Gilbert O'Sullivan (MAM)
13	8	SLADE ALIVE	Slade (Polydor)
4	9	NILSSON SCHMILSSON	Nilsson (RCA)
9	10	THICK AS A BRICK	Jethro Tull (Chrysalis)
10	11	FAREWELL TO THE GREYS	Band of the Royal Scots Guards (RCA)
6	12	WE'D LIKE TO TEACH THE WORLD TO SING	New Seekers (Polydor)
12	13	ELECTRIC WARRIOR	T. Rex (Fly)
21	14	IMAGINE	John Lennon (Apple)
14	15	TEASER AND THE FIRECAT	Cat Stevens (Island)
16	16	BABY I'M A WANT-YOU	Bread (Elektra)
15	17	AMERICAN PIE	Don McLean (United Artists)
18	18	GODSPELL	London Cast (Bell)
29	19	TAPESTRY	Carole King (A&M)
26	20	THE PARTRIDGE FAMILY ... SOUND MAGAZINE	Partridge Family (Bell)
-	21	GLEN CAMPBELL'S GREATEST HITS	Glen Campbell (Capitol)
-	22	JESUS CHRIST SUPERSTAR	Various Artists (MCA)
28	23	ALL TOGETHER NOW	Argent (Epic)
20	24	TOP OF THE POPS 23	Various Artists (Hallmark)
22	25	A NOD'S AS GOOD AS A WINK ... TO A BLIND HORSE	Faces (Warner Bros.)
19	26	GARDEN IN THE CITY	Melanie (Buddah)
-	27	TICKET TO RIDE	Carpenters (A&M)
17	28	GRAVE NEW WORLD	Strawbs (A&M)
24	29	NEIL REID	Neil Reid (Decca)
-	30	TEA FOR THE TILLERMAN	Cat Stevens (Island)

13 May 1972

last week	this week		
1	1	MACHINE HEAD	Deep Purple (Purple)
2	2	HARVEST	Neil Young (Reprise)
4	3	FOG ON THE TYNE	Lindisfarne (Charisma)
3	4	PROPHETS, SEERS AND SAGES THE ANGELS OF THE AGES/MY PEOPLE WERE FAIR AND HAD SKY IN THEIR HAIR, BUT NOW THEY'RE CONTENT TO WEAR STARS ON THEIR BROWS	Tyrannosaurus Rex (Fly)
11	5	FAREWELL TO THE GREYS	Band of the Royal Scots Guards (RCA)
6	6	BRIDGE OVER TROUBLED WATER	Simon & Garfunkel (CBS)
12	7	WE'D LIKE TO TEACH THE WORLD TO SING	New Seekers (Polydor)
5	8	PAUL SIMON	Paul Simon (CBS)
-	9	BOLAN BOOGIE	T. Rex (Fly)
7	10	HIMSELF	Gilbert O'Sullivan (MAM)
9	11	NILSSON SCHMILSSON	Nilsson (RCA)
15	12	TEASER AND THE FIRECAT	Cat Stevens (Island)
13	13	ELECTRIC WARRIOR	T. Rex (Fly)
8	14	SLADE ALIVE	Slade (Polydor)
16	15	BABY I'M A WANT-YOU	Bread (Elektra)
17	16	AMERICAN PIE	Don McLean (United Artists)
23	17	ALL TOGETHER NOW	Argent (Epic)
28	18	GRAVE NEW WORLD	Strawbs (A&M)
24	19	TOP OF THE POPS 23	Various Artists (Hallmark)
19	20	TAPESTRY	Carole King (A&M)
-	21	HOT HITS ELEVEN	Various Artists (Music for Pleasure)
26	22	GARDEN IN THE CITY	Melanie (Buddah)
-	23	DAVID CROSBY AND GRAHAM NASH	David Crosby & Graham Nash (Atlantic)
-	24	MANASSAS	Stephen Stills' Manassas (Atlantic)
10	25	THICK AS A BRICK	Jethro Tull (Chrysalis)
21	26	GLEN CAMPBELL'S GREATEST HITS	Glen Campbell (Capitol)
18	27	GODSPELL	London Cast (Bell)
-	28	CHERISH	David Cassidy (Bell)
-	29	NICELY OUT OF TIME	Lindisfarne (Charisma)
-	30	A THING CALLED LOVE	Johnny Cash (CBS)

Neil Young was top with his great album *Harvest*, and the other members of CSN&Y charted too, David Crosby & Graham Nash with an LP so-titled, and Stephen Stills with his band and LP *Manassas* (a re-entry). NB.: it was beyond the pale for anyone at this time to use the term "LP"; this was as prohibited by hipness and cool as saying "group". Part of punk's war on the old hip would be the defiant use of these long-scorned labels, not only by punters but by the younger, shorter-haired people in the music industry.

May – June 1972

20 May 1972

- 3 1 FOG ON THE TYNE — Lindisfarne (Charisma)
- 1 2 MACHINE HEAD — Deep Purple (Purple)
- 2 3 HARVEST — Neil Young (Reprise)
- 9 4 BOLAN BOOGIE — T. Rex (Fly)
- 5 5 FAREWELL TO THE GREYS — Band of the Royal Scots Guards (RCA)
- 6 6 BRIDGE OVER TROUBLED WATER — Simon & Garfunkel (CBS)
- 8 7 PAUL SIMON — Paul Simon (CBS)
- 4 8 PROPHETS, SEERS AND SAGES THE ANGELS OF THE AGES/MY PEOPLE WERE FAIR AND HAD SKY IN THEIR HAIR, BUT NOW THEY'RE CONTENT TO WEAR STARS ON THEIR BROWS — Tyrannosaurus Rex (Fly)
- 10 9 HIMSELF — Gilbert O'Sullivan (MAM)
- 14 10 SLADE ALIVE — Slade (Polydor)
- 7 11 WE'D LIKE TO TEACH THE WORLD TO SING — New Seekers (Polydor)
- 13 12 ELECTRIC WARRIOR — T. Rex (Fly)
- 12 13 TEASER AND THE FIRECAT — Cat Stevens (Island)
- 15 13 BABY I'M A WANT-YOU — Bread (Elektra)
- 25 15 THICK AS A BRICK — Jethro Tull (Chrysalis)
- 28 16 CHERISH — David Cassidy (Bell)
- 11 17 NILSSON SCHMILSSON — Nilsson (RCA)
- 30 18 A THING CALLED LOVE — Johnny Cash (CBS)
- 21 19 HOT HITS ELEVEN — Various Artists (Music for Pleasure)
- 16 20 AMERICAN PIE — Don McLean (United Artists)
- 24 21 MANASSAS — Stephen Stills' Manassas (Atlantic)
- 20 22 TAPESTRY — Carole King (A&M)
- 26 23 GLEN CAMPBELL'S GREATEST HITS — Glen Campbell (Capitol)
- - 24 ARGUS — Wishbone Ash (MCA)
- - 25 A SONG FOR YOU — Jack Jones (RCA)
- - 26 IMAGINE — John Lennon (Apple)
- 23 27 DAVID CROSBY AND GRAHAM NASH — David Crosby & Graham Nash (Atlantic)
- 27 28 GODSPELL — London Cast (Bell)
- 18 29 GRAVE NEW WORLD — Strawbs (A&M)
- - 30 THE PARTRIDGE FAMILY ... SOUND MAGAZINE — Partridge Family (Bell)

27 May 1972

- 4 1 BOLAN BOOGIE — T. Rex (Fly)
- 1 2 FOG ON THE TYNE — Lindisfarne (Charisma)
- 3 3 HARVEST — Neil Young (Reprise)
- 7 4 PAUL SIMON — Paul Simon (CBS)
- 2 5 MACHINE HEAD — Deep Purple (Purple)
- 16 6 CHERISH — David Cassidy (Bell)
- 6 7 BRIDGE OVER TROUBLED WATER — Simon & Garfunkel (CBS)
- 5 8 FAREWELL TO THE GREYS — Band of the Royal Scots Guards (RCA)
- 24 9 ARGUS — Wishbone Ash (MCA)
- 20 10 AMERICAN PIE — Don McLean (United Artists)
- 12 11 ELECTRIC WARRIOR — T. Rex (Fly)
- 9 12 HIMSELF — Gilbert O'Sullivan (MAM)
- 18 13 A THING CALLED LOVE — Johnny Cash (CBS)
- - 14 HONKY CHATEAU — Elton John (DJM)
- 26 15 IMAGINE — John Lennon (Apple)
- 17 16 NILSSON SCHMILSSON — Nilsson (RCA)
- 11 17 WE'D LIKE TO TEACH THE WORLD TO SING — New Seekers (Polydor)
- 13 18 BABY I'M A WANT-YOU — Bread (Elektra)
- 8 19 PROPHETS, SEERS AND SAGES THE ANGELS OF THE AGES/MY PEOPLE WERE FAIR AND HAD SKY IN THEIR HAIR, BUT NOW THEY'RE CONTENT TO WEAR STARS ON THEIR BROWS — Tyrannosaurus Rex (Fly)
- 10 20 SLADE ALIVE — Slade (Polydor)
- 13 21 TEASER AND THE FIRECAT — Cat Stevens (Island)
- - 22 LIVE IN EUROPE — Rory Gallagher (Polydor)
- - 23 THE MUSIC PEOPLE — Various Artists (CBS)
- 27 24 DAVID CROSBY AND GRAHAM NASH — David Crosby & Graham Nash (Atlantic)
- 19 25 HOT HITS ELEVEN — Various Artists (Music for Pleasure)
- - 26 BREADWINNERS — Jack Jones (RCA)
- 22 27 TAPESTRY — Carole King (A&M)
- 21 28 MANASSAS — Stephen Stills' Manassas (Atlantic)
- - 29 NICELY OUT OF TIME — Lindisfarne (Charisma)
- 25 30 A SONG FOR YOU — Jack Jones (RCA)

3 June 1972

- 1 1 BOLAN BOOGIE — T. Rex (Fly)
- - 2 EXILE ON MAIN STREET — Rolling Stones (Rolling Stones)
- 14 3 HONKY CHATEAU — Elton John (DJM)
- 6 4 CHERISH — David Cassidy (Bell)
- - 5 20 DYNAMIC HITS — Various Artists (K-Tel)
- 7 6 BRIDGE OVER TROUBLED WATER — Simon & Garfunkel (CBS)
- 2 7 FOG ON THE TYNE — Lindisfarne (Charisma)
- 5 8 MACHINE HEAD — Deep Purple (Purple)
- 22 9 LIVE IN EUROPE — Rory Gallagher (Polydor)
- 9 10 ARGUS — Wishbone Ash (MCA)
- 26 11 BREADWINNERS — Jack Jones (RCA)
- 3 12 HARVEST — Neil Young (Reprise)
- 8 13 FAREWELL TO THE GREYS — Band of the Royal Scots Guards (RCA)
- 19 14 PROPHETS, SEERS AND SAGES THE ANGELS OF THE AGES/MY PEOPLE WERE FAIR AND HAD SKY IN THEIR HAIR, BUT NOW THEY'RE CONTENT TO WEAR STARS ON THEIR BROWS — Tyrannosaurus Rex (Fly)
- 10 15 AMERICAN PIE — Don McLean (United Artists)
- 4 16 PAUL SIMON — Paul Simon (CBS)
- 18 17 BABY I'M A WANT-YOU — Bread (Elektra)
- 23 18 THE MUSIC PEOPLE — Various Artists (CBS)
- 25 19 HOT HITS ELEVEN — Various Artists (for Pleasure)
- 11 20 ELECTRIC WARRIOR — T. Rex (Fly)
- 21 21 TEASER AND THE FIRECAT — Cat Stevens (Island)
- - 22 ELVIS NOW — Elvis Presley (RCA)
- - 23 MOONLIGHT AND ROSES — Jim Reeves (RCA International)
- 12 24 HIMSELF — Gilbert O'Sullivan (MAM)
- 15 25 IMAGINE — John Lennon (Apple)
- 16 26 NILSSON SCHMILSSON — Nilsson (RCA)
- 27 27 TAPESTRY — Carole King (A&M)
- 28 28 MANASSAS — Stephen Stills' Manassas (Atlantic)
- 13 29 A THING CALLED LOVE — Johnny Cash (CBS)
- 20 30 SLADE ALIVE — Slade (Polydor)

10 June 1972

- 1 1 BOLAN BOOGIE — T. Rex (Fly)
- 3 2 HONKY CHATEAU — Elton John (DJM)
- 2 3 EXILE ON MAIN STREET — Rolling Stones (Rolling Stones)
- 4 4 CHERISH — David Cassidy (Bell)
- 15 5 AMERICAN PIE — Don McLean (United Artists)
- 6 6 BRIDGE OVER TROUBLED WATER — Simon & Garfunkel (CBS)
- 8 7 MACHINE HEAD — Deep Purple (Purple)
- 7 8 FOG ON THE TYNE — Lindisfarne (Charisma)
- 11 9 BREADWINNERS — Jack Jones (RCA)
- 5 10 20 DYNAMIC HITS — Various Artists (K-Tel)
- 12 11 HARVEST — Neil Young (Reprise)
- 10 12 ARGUS — Wishbone Ash (MCA)
- 16 13 PAUL SIMON — Paul Simon (CBS)
- 9 14 LIVE IN EUROPE — Rory Gallagher (Polydor)
- 13 15 FAREWELL TO THE GREYS — Band of the Royal Scots Guards (RCA)
- 29 16 A THING CALLED LOVE — Johnny Cash (CBS)
- 21 17 TEASER AND THE FIRECAT — Cat Stevens (Island)
- 24 18 HIMSELF — Gilbert O'Sullivan (MAM)
- 30 19 SLADE ALIVE — Slade (Polydor)
- 17 20 BABY I'M A WANT-YOU — Bread (Elektra)
- 18 21 THE MUSIC PEOPLE — Various Artists (CBS)
- - 22 NICELY OUT OF TIME — Lindisfarne (Charisma)
- 22 23 ELVIS NOW — Elvis Presley (RCA)
- 27 24 TAPESTRY — Carole King (A&M)
- 14 25 PROPHETS, SEERS AND SAGES THE ANGELS OF THE AGES/MY PEOPLE WERE FAIR AND HAD SKY IN THEIR HAIR, BUT NOW THEY'RE CONTENT TO WEAR STARS ON THEIR BROWS — Tyrannosaurus Rex (Fly)
- - 26 THE WORLD OF 100 BEST TUNES VOL 3 — Various Artists (Decca)
- 20 27 ELECTRIC WARRIOR — T. Rex (Fly)
- 28 28 MANASSAS — Stephen Stills' Manassas (Atlantic)
- - 29 GODSPELL — London Cast (Bell)
- - 30 FREE AT LAST — Free (Island)

Tynesiders Lindisfarne made No.1 again. The title track was not the band's big hit: *Meet Me On The Corner* and *Lady Eleanor* reached No.5 and No.7. Others in the singles chart the same week included *Vincent* (Don MacLean), *Sister Jane* (New World), *Rockin' Robin* (Michael Jackson) *Mary Had A Little Lamb* (Wings) and *Me And Julio Down By The School Yard* (Paul Simon) Meanwhile album entrant *Godspell* was by the London cast, among whom were David Essex and Jeremy Irons.

June – July 1972

last this week

17 June 1972	24 June 1972	1 July 1972	8 July 1972
3 1 EXILE ON MAIN STREET Rolling Stones (Rolling Stones)	1 1 EXILE ON MAIN STREET Rolling Stones (Rolling Stones)	3 1 AMERICAN PIE Don McLean (United Artists)	1 1 AMERICAN PIE Don McLean (United Artists)
1 2 BOLAN BOOGIE T. Rex (Fly)	2 2 BOLAN BOOGIE T. Rex (Fly)	1 2 EXILE ON MAIN STREET Rolling Stones (Rolling Stones)	4 2 20 DYNAMIC HITS Various Artists (K-Tel)
5 3 AMERICAN PIE Don McLean (United Artists)	3 3 AMERICAN PIE Don McLean (United Artists)	4 3 HONKY CHATEAU Elton John (DJM)	5 3 BOLAN BOOGIE T. Rex (Fly)
2 4 HONKY CHATEAU Elton John (DJM)	4 4 HONKY CHATEAU Elton John (DJM)	6 4 20 DYNAMIC HITS Various Artists (K-Tel)	2 4 EXILE ON MAIN STREET Rolling Stones (Rolling Stones)
8 5 FOG ON THE TYNE Lindisfarne (Charisma)	5 5 FOG ON THE TYNE Lindisfarne (Charisma)	2 5 BOLAN BOOGIE T. Rex (Fly)	3 5 HONKY CHATEAU Elton John (DJM)
9 6 BREADWINNERS Jack Jones (RCA)	9 6 20 DYNAMIC HITS Various Artists (K-Tel)	13 6 BRIDGE OVER TROUBLED WATER Simon & Garfunkel (CBS)	6 6 BRIDGE OVER TROUBLED WATER Simon & Garfunkel (CBS)
4 7 CHERISH David Cassidy (Bell)	7 7 CHERISH David Cassidy (Bell)	9 7 OBSCURED BY CLOUDS Pink Floyd (Harvest)	7 7 OBSCURED BY CLOUDS Pink Floyd (Harvest)
6 8 BRIDGE OVER TROUBLED WATER Simon & Garfunkel (CBS)	10 8 ARGUS Wishbone Ash (MCA)	10 8 SLADE ALIVE Slade (Polydor)	8 7 SLADE ALIVE Slade (Polydor)
10 9 20 DYNAMIC HITS Various Artists (K-Tel)	17 9 OBSCURED BY CLOUDS Pink Floyd (Harvest)	5 9 FOG ON THE TYNE Lindisfarne (Charisma)	- 9 TRILOGY Emerson Lake & Palmer (Island)
12 10 ARGUS Wishbone Ash (MCA)	13 10 SLADE ALIVE Slade (Polydor)	7 10 CHERISH David Cassidy (Bell)	12 10 BREADWINNERS Jack Jones (RCA)
7 11 MACHINE HEAD Deep Purple (Purple)	6 11 BREADWINNERS Jack Jones (RCA)	14 11 FREE AT LAST Free (Island)	19 11 THE RISE AND FALL OF ZIGGY STARDUST AND THE SPIDERS FROM MARS David Bowie (RCA)
11 12 HARVEST Neil Young (Reprise)	11 12 MACHINE HEAD Deep Purple (Purple)	11 12 BREADWINNERS Jack Jones (RCA)	9 12 FOG ON THE TYNE Lindisfarne (Charisma)
19 13 SLADE ALIVE Slade (Polydor)	8 13 BRIDGE OVER TROUBLED WATER Simon & Garfunkel (CBS)	27 13 THE DRIFTERS' GREATEST HITS Drifters (Atlantic)	10 13 CHERISH David Cassidy (Bell)
13 14 PAUL SIMON Paul Simon (CBS)	- 14 FREE AT LAST Free (Island)	- 14 TAPESTRY Don McLean (United Artists)	24 14 HARVEST Neil Young (Reprise)
15 15 FAREWELL TO THE GREYS Band of the Royal Scots Guards (RCA)	12 15 HARVEST Neil Young (Reprise)	8 15 ARGUS Wishbone Ash (MCA)	21 15 LIVE IN EUROPE Rory Gallagher (Polydor)
20 16 BABY I'M A WANT-YOU Bread (Elektra)	21 16 ELECTRIC WARRIOR T. Rex (Fly)	- 16 CLOSE UP Tom Jones (Decca)	23 16 LIVING IN THE PAST Jethro Tull (Chrysalis)
- 17 OBSCURED BY CLOUDS Pink Floyd (Harvest)	30 16 DEMONS AND WIZARDS Uriah Heep (Bronze)	12 17 MACHINE HEAD Deep Purple (Purple)	11 17 FREE AT LAST Free (Island)
18 18 HIMSELF Gilbert O'Sullivan (MAM)	24 18 LIVE IN EUROPE Rory Gallagher (Polydor)	16 17 ELECTRIC WARRIOR T. Rex (Fly)	15 18 ARGUS Wishbone Ash (MCA)
17 19 TEASER AND THE FIRECAT Cat Stevens (Island)	14 19 PAUL SIMON Paul Simon (CBS)	22 19 THE RISE AND FALL OF ZIGGY STARDUST AND THE SPIDERS FROM MARS David Bowie (RCA)	28 19 HIMSELF Gilbert O'Sullivan (MAM)
24 20 TAPESTRY Carole King (A&M)	16 20 BABY I'M A WANT-YOU Bread (Elektra)	21 20 NICELY OUT OF TIME Lindisfarne (Charisma)	30 19 PAUL SIMON Paul Simon (CBS)
27 21 ELECTRIC WARRIOR T. Rex (Fly)	27 21 NICELY OUT OF TIME Lindisfarne (Charisma)	18 21 LIVE IN EUROPE Rory Gallagher (Polydor)	- 21 DEMONS AND WIZARDS Uriah Heep (Bronze)
- 22 GLEN CAMPBELL'S GREATEST HITS Glen Campbell (Capitol)	- 22 THE RISE AND FALL OF ZIGGY STARDUST AND THE SPIDERS FROM MARS David Bowie (RCA)	- 22 GOLD Neil Diamond (Uni)	29 22 TEASER AND THE FIRECAT Cat Stevens (Island)
25 23 PROPHETS, SEERS AND SAGES THE ANGELS OF THE AGES/MY PEOPLE WERE FAIR AND HAD SKY IN THEIR HAIR, BUT NOW THEY'RE CONTENT TO WEAR STARS ON THEIR BROWS Tyrannosaurus Rex (Fly)	15 23 FAREWELL TO THE GREYS Band of the Royal Scots Guards (RCA)	- 23 LIVING IN THE PAST Jethro Tull (Chrysalis)	17 23 MACHINE HEAD Deep Purple (Purple)
14 24 LIVE IN EUROPE Rory Gallagher (Polydor)	20 24 TAPESTRY Carole King (A&M)	15 24 HARVEST Neil Young (Reprise)	16 24 CLOSE UP Tom Jones (Decca)
21 25 THE MUSIC PEOPLE Various Artists (CBS)	26 25 A THING CALLED LOVE Johnny Cash (CBS)	20 25 BABY I'M A WANT-YOU Bread (Elektra)	26 25 A THING CALLED LOVE Johnny Cash (CBS)
16 26 A THING CALLED LOVE Johnny Cash (CBS)	29 26 ELVIS NOW Elvis Presley (RCA)	25 26 A THING CALLED LOVE Johnny Cash (CBS)	22 26 GOLD Neil Diamond (Uni)
22 27 NICELY OUT OF TIME Lindisfarne (Charisma)	- 27 THE DRIFTERS' GREATEST HITS Drifters (Atlantic)	- 27 IMAGINE John Lennon (Apple)	17 27 ELECTRIC WARRIOR T. Rex (Fly)
28 28 MANASSAS Stephen Stills' Manassas (Atlantic)	19 28 TEASER AND THE FIRECAT Cat Stevens (Island)	- 28 HIMSELF Gilbert O'Sullivan (MAM)	14 28 TAPESTRY Don McLean (United Artists)
23 29 ELVIS NOW Elvis Presley (RCA)	- 29 NILSSON SCHMILSSON Nilsson (RCA)	28 29 TEASER AND THE FIRECAT Cat Stevens (Island)	20 29 NICELY OUT OF TIME Lindisfarne (Charisma)
- 30 DEMONS AND WIZARDS Uriah Heep (Bronze)	22 30 GLEN CAMPBELL'S GREATEST HITS Glen Campbell (Capitol)	19 30 PAUL SIMON Paul Simon (CBS)	- 30 ELVIS NOW Elvis Presley (RCA)

The rise of *The Rise And Fall Of Ziggy Stardust And The Spiders From Mars* marked the album chart arrival of David Bowie, that ex-One Hit Wonder c/o 1969's *Space Oddity*. Bowie's first record was *Liza Jane*, by Davie Jones With The King Bees, 1964. Others included two 1966 Pye singles produced by Tony Hatch. His debut LP was 1967's *David Bowie*, his next 1969's, um, *David Bowie. The Man Who Sold The World* and *Hunky Dory*, both 1971, would chart AFTER Ziggy Stardust.

July – August 1972

15 July 1972

last	this	title	artist
2	1	20 DYNAMIC HITS	Various Artists (K-Tel)
1	2	AMERICAN PIE	Don McLean (United Artists)
7	3	SLADE ALIVE	Slade (Polydor)
3	4	BOLAN BOOGIE	T. Rex (Fly)
4	5	EXILE ON MAIN STREET	Rolling Stones (Rolling Stones)
5	6	HONKY CHATEAU	Elton John (DJM)
11	7	THE RISE AND FALL OF ZIGGY STARDUST AND THE SPIDERS FROM MARS	David Bowie (RCA)
6	8	BRIDGE OVER TROUBLED WATER	Simon & Garfunkel (CBS)
9	9	TRILOGY	Emerson Lake & Palmer (Island)
12	10	FOG ON THE TYNE	Lindisfarne (Charisma)
7	11	OBSCURED BY CLOUDS	Pink Floyd (Harvest)
10	12	BREADWINNERS	Jack Jones (RCA)
19	13	HIMSELF	Gilbert O'Sullivan (MAM)
-	14	SIMON AND GARFUNKEL'S GREATEST HITS	Simon & Garfunkel (CBS)
-	15	ELVIS AS RECORDED LIVE AT MADISON SQUARE GARDEN	Elvis Presley (RCA)
17	16	FREE AT LAST	Free (Island)
16	17	LIVING IN THE PAST	Jethro Tull (Chrysalis)
13	18	CHERISH	David Cassidy (Bell)
-	19	LIVE CREAM VOL 2	Cream (Polydor)
14	20	HARVEST	Neil Young (Reprise)
28	21	TAPESTRY	Don McLean (United Artists)
18	22	ARGUS	Wishbone Ash (MCA)
15	23	LIVE IN EUROPE	Rory Gallagher (Polydor)
23	24	MACHINE HEAD	Deep Purple (Purple)
21	25	DEMONS AND WIZARDS	Uriah Heep (Bronze)
19	26	PAUL SIMON	Paul Simon (CBS)
29	27	NICELY OUT OF TIME	Lindisfarne (Charisma)
-	28	STONES	Neil Diamond (Uni)
24	29	CLOSE UP	Tom Jones (Decca)
26	30	GOLD	Neil Diamond (Uni)

22 July 1972

last	this	title	artist
2	1	AMERICAN PIE	Don McLean (United Artists)
14	2	SIMON AND GARFUNKEL'S GREATEST HITS	Simon & Garfunkel (CBS)
1	3	20 DYNAMIC HITS	Various Artists (K-Tel)
7	4	THE RISE AND FALL OF ZIGGY STARDUST AND THE SPIDERS FROM MARS	David Bowie (RCA)
3	5	SLADE ALIVE	Slade (Polydor)
8	6	BRIDGE OVER TROUBLED WATER	Simon & Garfunkel (CBS)
9	7	TRILOGY	Emerson Lake & Palmer (Island)
4	8	BOLAN BOOGIE	T. Rex (Fly)
15	9	ELVIS AS RECORDED LIVE AT MADISON SQUARE GARDEN	Elvis Presley (RCA)
17	10	LIVING IN THE PAST	Jethro Tull (Chrysalis)
6	11	HONKY CHATEAU	Elton John (DJM)
5	12	EXILE ON MAIN STREET	Rolling Stones (Rolling Stones)
11	13	OBSCURED BY CLOUDS	Pink Floyd (Harvest)
-	14	SCHOOL'S OUT	Alice Cooper (Warner Bros.)
12	15	BREADWINNERS	Jack Jones (RCA)
18	16	CHERISH	David Cassidy (Bell)
10	17	FOG ON THE TYNE	Lindisfarne (Charisma)
20	18	HARVEST	Neil Young (Reprise)
13	19	HIMSELF	Gilbert O'Sullivan (MAM)
16	20	FREE AT LAST	Free (Island)
28	21	STONES	Neil Diamond (Uni)
25	22	DEMONS AND WIZARDS	Uriah Heep (Bronze)
22	23	ARGUS	Wishbone Ash (MCA)
23	24	LIVE IN EUROPE	Rory Gallagher (Polydor)
29	25	CLOSE UP	Tom Jones (Decca)
-	26	ELECTRIC WARRIOR	T. Rex (Fly)
-	27	THE WORLD OF YOUR 100 BEST TUNES VOL 3	Various Artists (Decca)
-	28	THE DRIFTERS' GREATEST HITS	Drifters (Atlantic)
26	29	PAUL SIMON	Paul Simon (CBS)
-	30	TWENTY FANTASTIC HITS	Various Artists (Arcade)

29 July 1972

last	this	title	artist
2	1	SIMON AND GARFUNKEL'S GREATEST HITS	Simon & Garfunkel (CBS)
1	2	AMERICAN PIE	Don McLean (United Artists)
3	3	20 DYNAMIC HITS	Various Artists (K-Tel)
14	4	SCHOOL'S OUT	Alice Cooper (Warner Bros.)
4	5	THE RISE AND FALL OF ZIGGY STARDUST AND THE SPIDERS FROM MARS	David Bowie (RCA)
5	6	SLADE ALIVE	Slade (Polydor)
6	7	BRIDGE OVER TROUBLED WATER	Simon & Garfunkel (CBS)
9	8	ELVIS AS RECORDED LIVE AT MADISON SQUARE GARDEN	Elvis Presley (RCA)
-	9	THE SLIDER	T. Rex (T. Rex Wax Co)
-	10	NEVER A DULL MOMENT	Rod Stewart (Mercury)
19	11	HIMSELF	Gilbert O'Sullivan (MAM)
7	12	TRILOGY	Emerson Lake & Palmer (Island)
12	13	EXILE ON MAIN STREET	Rolling Stones (Rolling Stones)
11	14	HONKY CHATEAU	Elton John (DJM)
30	15	TWENTY FANTASTIC HITS	Various Artists (Arcade)
8	16	BOLAN BOOGIE	T. Rex (Fly)
10	17	LIVING IN THE PAST	Jethro Tull (Chrysalis)
-	18	MOODS	Neil Diamond (Uni)
15	19	BREADWINNERS	Jack Jones (RCA)
16	20	CHERISH	David Cassidy (Bell)
17	21	FOG ON THE TYNE	Lindisfarne (Charisma)
18	22	HARVEST	Neil Young (Reprise)
23	23	ARGUS	Wishbone Ash (MCA)
13	24	OBSCURED BY CLOUDS	Pink Floyd (Harvest)
-	25	RIDE A WHITE SWAN	T. Rex (Music for Pleasure)
20	26	FREE AT LAST	Free (Island)
-	27	LIVE CREAM VOL 2	Cream (Polydor)
28	28	LOVE THEME FROM THE GODFATHER	Andy Williams (CBS)
22	29	DEMONS AND WIZARDS	Uriah Heep (Bronze)
21	30	STONES	Neil Diamond (Uni)

5 August 1972

last	this	title	artist
1	1	SIMON AND GARFUNKEL'S GREATEST HITS	Simon & Garfunkel (CBS)
9	2	THE SLIDER	T. Rex (T. Rex Wax Co)
4	3	SCHOOL'S OUT	Alice Cooper (Warner Bros.)
10	4	NEVER A DULL MOMENT	Rod Stewart (Mercury)
3	5	20 DYNAMIC HITS	Various Artists (K-Tel)
2	6	AMERICAN PIE	Don McLean (United Artists)
5	7	THE RISE AND FALL OF ZIGGY STARDUST AND THE SPIDERS FROM MARS	David Bowie (RCA)
6	8	SLADE ALIVE	Slade (Polydor)
12	9	TRILOGY	Emerson Lake & Palmer (Island)
15	10	TWENTY FANTASTIC HITS	Various Artists (Arcade)
8	11	ELVIS AS RECORDED LIVE AT MADISON SQUARE GARDEN	Elvis Presley (RCA)
7	12	BRIDGE OVER TROUBLED WATER	Simon & Garfunkel (CBS)
18	13	MOODS	Neil Diamond (Uni)
20	14	CHERISH	David Cassidy (Bell)
14	15	HONKY CHATEAU	Elton John (DJM)
17	16	LIVING IN THE PAST	Jethro Tull (Chrysalis)
-	17	ROXY MUSIC	Roxy Music (Island)
28	18	LOVE THEME FROM THE GODFATHER	Andy Williams (CBS)
13	19	EXILE ON MAIN STREET	Rolling Stones (Rolling Stones)
16	20	BOLAN BOOGIE	T. Rex (Fly)
11	21	HIMSELF	Gilbert O'Sullivan (MAM)
-	22	KILLER	Alice Cooper (Warner Bros.)
19	23	HARVEST	Neil Young (Reprise)
22	24	BREADWINNERS	Jack Jones (RCA)
21	25	FOG ON THE TYNE	Lindisfarne (Charisma)
24	26	OBSCURED BY CLOUDS	Pink Floyd (Harvest)
-	27	TAPESTRY	Don McLean (United Artists)
25	28	RIDE A WHITE SWAN	T. Rex (Music for Pleasure)
-	29	SON OF SCHMILSSON	Nilsson (RCA)
26	30	FREE AT LAST	Free (Island)

It had surely been an odd decision by Don MacLean and his record company to call his post-*American Pie* album *Tapestry*, when Carole King's LP of the same name had been one of the most prominent records of the previous couple of years. There were now signs that the 1970s were beginning properly to emerge: a new emphasis on glam, and on a knowing, detached manipulation of style, was beginning to be evident in a chart that now included not only Bowie but Roxy Music and Alice Cooper.

August – September 1972

12 August 1972

last week	this week	
1	1	SIMON AND GARFUNKEL'S GREATEST HITS — Simon & Garfunkel (CBS)
4	2	NEVER A DULL MOMENT — Rod Stewart (Mercury)
2	3	THE SLIDER — T. Rex (T. Rex Wax Co)
3	4	SCHOOL'S OUT — Alice Cooper (Warner Bros.)
5	5	20 DYNAMIC HITS — Various Artists (K-Tel)
7	6	SLADE ALIVE — Slade (Polydor)
7	7	THE RISE AND FALL OF ZIGGY STARDUST AND THE SPIDERS FROM MARS — David Bowie (RCA)
6	8	AMERICAN PIE — Don McLean (United Artists)
13	9	MOODS — Neil Diamond (Uni)
12	10	BRIDGE OVER TROUBLED WATER — Simon & Garfunkel (CBS)
11	11	ELVIS AS RECORDED LIVE AT MADISON SQUARE GARDEN — Elvis Presley (RCA)
9	12	TRILOGY — Emerson Lake & Palmer (Island)
21	13	HIMSELF — Gilbert O'Sullivan (MAM)
10	14	TWENTY FANTASTIC HITS — Various Artists (Arcade)
18	15	LOVE THEME FROM THE GODFATHER — Andy Williams (CBS)
16	16	LIVING IN THE PAST — Jethro Tull (Chrysalis)
14	17	CHERISH — David Cassidy (Bell)
19	18	EXILE ON MAIN STREET — Rolling Stones (Rolling Stones)
27	19	TAPESTRY — Don McLean (United Artists)
15	20	HONKY CHATEAU — Elton John (DJM)
25	21	FOG ON THE TYNE — Lindisfarne (Charisma)
-	22	JANIS JOPLIN IN CONCERT — Janis Joplin (CBS)
20	23	BOLAN BOOGIE — T. Rex (Fly)
-	24	ARGUS — Wishbone Ash (MCA)
-	25	MACHINE HEAD — Deep Purple (Purple)
24	26	BREADWINNERS — Jack Jones (RCA)
17	27	ROXY MUSIC — Roxy Music (Island)
26	28	OBSCURED BY CLOUDS — Pink Floyd (Harvest)
29	29	SON OF SCHMILSSON — Nilsson (RCA)
28	30	RIDE A WHITE SWAN — T. Rex (Music for Pleasure)

19 August 1972

last	this	
2	1	NEVER A DULL MOMENT — Rod Stewart (Mercury)
1	2	SIMON AND GARFUNKEL'S GREATEST HITS — Simon & Garfunkel (CBS)
3	3	THE SLIDER — T. Rex (T. Rex Wax Co)
4	4	SCHOOL'S OUT — Alice Cooper (Warner Bros.)
9	5	MOODS — Neil Diamond (Uni)
14	6	TWENTY FANTASTIC HITS — Various Artists (Arcade)
7	7	THE RISE AND FALL OF ZIGGY STARDUST AND THE SPIDERS FROM MARS — David Bowie (RCA)
5	8	20 DYNAMIC HITS — Various Artists (K-Tel)
6	9	SLADE ALIVE — Slade (Polydor)
8	10	AMERICAN PIE — Don McLean (United Artists)
11	11	ELVIS AS RECORDED LIVE AT MADISON SQUARE GARDEN — Elvis Presley (RCA)
12	12	TRILOGY — Emerson Lake & Palmer (Island)
-	13	SIMPLY — Jack Jones (Coral)
10	14	BRIDGE OVER TROUBLED WATER — Simon & Garfunkel (CBS)
13	15	HIMSELF — Gilbert O'Sullivan (MAM)
20	16	HONKY CHATEAU — Elton John (DJM)
15	17	LOVE THEME FROM THE GODFATHER — Andy Williams (CBS)
27	18	ROXY MUSIC — Roxy Music (Island)
-	19	IN SEARCH OF SPACE — Hawkwind (United Artists)
26	20	BREADWINNERS — Jack Jones (RCA)
17	21	CHERISH — David Cassidy (Bell)
19	22	TAPESTRY — Don McLean (United Artists)
24	23	ARGUS — Wishbone Ash (MCA)
28	24	OBSCURED BY CLOUDS — Pink Floyd (Harvest)
16	25	LIVING IN THE PAST — Jethro Tull (Chrysalis)
18	26	EXILE ON MAIN STREET — Rolling Stones (Rolling Stones)
-	27	HARVEST — Neil Young (Reprise)
21	28	FOG ON THE TYNE — Lindisfarne (Charisma)
22	29	JANIS JOPLIN IN CONCERT — Janis Joplin (CBS)
25	30	MACHINE HEAD — Deep Purple (Purple)

26 August 1972

last	this	
1	1	NEVER A DULL MOMENT — Rod Stewart (Mercury)
2	2	SIMON AND GARFUNKEL'S GREATEST HITS — Simon & Garfunkel (CBS)
4	3	SCHOOL'S OUT — Alice Cooper (Warner Bros.)
3	4	THE SLIDER — T. Rex (T. Rex Wax Co)
5	5	MOODS — Neil Diamond (Uni)
6	6	TWENTY FANTASTIC HITS — Various Artists (Arcade)
9	7	SLADE ALIVE — Slade (Polydor)
10	8	AMERICAN PIE — Don McLean (United Artists)
8	9	20 DYNAMIC HITS — Various Artists (K-Tel)
7	10	THE RISE AND FALL OF ZIGGY STARDUST AND THE SPIDERS FROM MARS — David Bowie (RCA)
14	11	BRIDGE OVER TROUBLED WATER — Simon & Garfunkel (CBS)
12	12	TRILOGY — Emerson Lake & Palmer (Island)
15	13	HIMSELF — Gilbert O'Sullivan (MAM)
11	14	ELVIS AS RECORDED LIVE AT MADISON SQUARE GARDEN — Elvis Presley (RCA)
19	15	IN SEARCH OF SPACE — Hawkwind (United Artists)
18	16	ROXY MUSIC — Roxy Music (Island)
-	17	THE EDWARD WOODWARD ALBUM — Edward Woodward (Jam)
17	18	LOVE THEME FROM THE GODFATHER — Andy Williams (CBS)
13	19	SIMPLY — Jack Jones (Coral)
20	20	BREADWINNERS — Jack Jones (RCA)
27	21	HARVEST — Neil Young (Reprise)
16	22	HONKY CHATEAU — Elton John (DJM)
21	23	CHERISH — David Cassidy (Bell)
26	24	EXILE ON MAIN STREET — Rolling Stones (Rolling Stones)
22	25	TAPESTRY — Don McLean (United Artists)
28	26	FOG ON THE TYNE — Lindisfarne (Charisma)
24	27	OBSCURED BY CLOUDS — Pink Floyd (Harvest)
25	28	LIVING IN THE PAST — Jethro Tull (Chrysalis)
-	29	CARLOS SANTANA AND BUDDY MILES LIVE! — Carlos Santana & Buddy Miles (CBS)
-	30	BOLAN BOOGIE — T. Rex (Fly)

2 September 1972

last	this	
1	1	NEVER A DULL MOMENT — Rod Stewart (Mercury)
2	2	SIMON AND GARFUNKEL'S GREATEST HITS — Simon & Garfunkel (CBS)
3	3	SCHOOL'S OUT — Alice Cooper (Warner Bros.)
6	4	TWENTY FANTASTIC HITS — Various Artists (Arcade)
5	5	MOODS — Neil Diamond (Uni)
7	6	SLADE ALIVE — Slade (Polydor)
4	7	THE SLIDER — T. Rex (T. Rex Wax Co)
8	8	AMERICAN PIE — Don McLean (United Artists)
10	9	THE RISE AND FALL OF ZIGGY STARDUST AND THE SPIDERS FROM MARS — David Bowie (RCA)
11	10	BRIDGE OVER TROUBLED WATER — Simon & Garfunkel (CBS)
12	11	TRILOGY — Emerson Lake & Palmer (Island)
13	12	HIMSELF — Gilbert O'Sullivan (MAM)
9	13	20 DYNAMIC HITS — Various Artists (K-Tel)
18	14	LOVE THEME FROM THE GODFATHER — Andy Williams (CBS)
20	15	BREADWINNERS — Jack Jones (RCA)
23	16	CHERISH — David Cassidy (Bell)
28	17	LIVING IN THE PAST — Jethro Tull (Chrysalis)
14	18	ELVIS AS RECORDED LIVE AT MADISON SQUARE GARDEN — Elvis Presley (RCA)
16	19	ROXY MUSIC — Roxy Music (Island)
26	20	FOG ON THE TYNE — Lindisfarne (Charisma)
17	21	THE EDWARD WOODWARD ALBUM — Edward Woodward (Jam)
21	22	HARVEST — Neil Young (Reprise)
15	23	IN SEARCH OF SPACE — Hawkwind (United Artists)
-	24	JACKSON FIVE'S GREATEST HITS — Jackson Five (Tamla Motown)
22	25	HONKY CHATEAU — Elton John (DJM)
27	26	OBSCURED BY CLOUDS — Pink Floyd (Harvest)
29	27	CARLOS SANTANA AND BUDDY MILES LIVE! — Santana & Buddy Miles (CBS)
19	28	SIMPLY — Jack Jones (Coral)
25	29	TAPESTRY — Don McLean (United Artists)
24	30	EXILE ON MAIN STREET — Rolling Stones (Rolling Stones)

It was a year since British singer-songwriter-pianist Gilbert O'Sullivan's *Himself* had first charted; a quiet success, it was re-climbing the Top 20. In November, its follow-up, *Back To Front*, would jump in at No.9 and top the chart two weeks later. O'Sullivan had first appeared dressed as a Dickensian urchin to plug his successful single *Nothing Rhymed* (No.7 in December 1990); a year and several minor hits later came *No Matter How I Try* (a No.5) and then this year his "classic", *Alone Again (Naturally)*.

last week / this week

9 September 1972

- 1 / 1 NEVER A DULL MOMENT — Rod Stewart (Mercury)
- 2 / 2 SIMON AND GARFUNKEL'S GREATEST HITS — Simon & Garfunkel (CBS)
- 3 / 3 SCHOOL'S OUT — Alice Cooper (Warner Bros.)
- 6 / 4 SLADE ALIVE — Slade (Polydor)
- 7 / 5 THE SLIDER — T. Rex (T. Rex Wax Co)
- 4 / 6 TWENTY FANTASTIC HITS — Various Artists (Arcade)
- 5 / 7 MOODS — Neil Diamond (Uni)
- 8 / 8 AMERICAN PIE — Don McLean (United Artists)
- 9 / 9 THE RISE AND FALL OF ZIGGY STARDUST AND THE SPIDERS FROM MARS — David Bowie (RCA)
- 10 / 10 BRIDGE OVER TROUBLED WATER — Simon & Garfunkel (CBS)
- 19 / 11 ROXY MUSIC — Roxy Music (Island)
- 11 / 12 TRILOGY — Emerson Lake & Palmer (Island)
- 13 / 13 20 DYNAMIC HITS — Various Artists (K-Tel)
- 23 / 14 IN SEARCH OF SPACE — Hawkwind (United Artists)
- 15 /
- 14 / 16 LOVE THEME FROM THE GODFATHER — Andy Williams (CBS)
- 15 / 17 BREADWINNERS — Jack Jones (RCA)
- 26 / 18 OBSCURED BY CLOUDS — Pink Floyd (Harvest)
- 17 / 19 LIVING IN THE PAST — Jethro Tull (Chrysalis)
- 27 / 20 CARLOS SANTANA AND BUDDY MILES LIVE! — Carlos Santana & Buddy Miles (CBS)
- – / 21 MACHINE HEAD — Deep Purple (Purple)
- – / 22 EVERY PICTURE TELLS A STORY — Rod Stewart (Philips)
- 23 /
- 25 / 24 HONKY CHATEAU — Elton John (DJM)
- 20 / 25 FOG ON THE TYNE — Lindisfarne (Charisma)
- 16 / 26 CHERISH — David Cassidy (Bell)
- – / 27 HISTORY OF ERIC CLAPTON — Eric Clapton (Polydor)
- 28 /
- 29 /
- – / 30 KILLER — Alice Cooper (Warner Bros.)

16 September 1972

- 1 / 1 NEVER A DULL MOMENT — Rod Stewart (Mercury)
- 2 / 2 SIMON AND GARFUNKEL'S GREATEST HITS — Simon & Garfunkel (CBS)
- 6 / 3 TWENTY FANTASTIC HITS — Various Artists (Arcade)
- 3 / 4 SCHOOL'S OUT — Alice Cooper (Warner Bros.)
- 5 / 5 THE SLIDER — T. Rex (T. Rex Wax Co)
- 4 / 6 SLADE ALIVE — Slade (Polydor)
- 11 / 7 ROXY MUSIC — Roxy Music (Island)
- 9 / 8 THE RISE AND FALL OF ZIGGY STARDUST AND THE SPIDERS FROM MARS — David Bowie (RCA)
- 10 / 9 BRIDGE OVER TROUBLED WATER — Simon & Garfunkel (CBS)
- 26 / 10 CHERISH — David Cassidy (Bell)
- 7 / 11 MOODS — Neil Diamond (Uni)
- 16 / 12 LOVE THEME FROM THE GODFATHER — Andy Williams (CBS)
- 13 / 13 20 DYNAMIC HITS — Various Artists (K-Tel)
- 8 / 14 AMERICAN PIE — Don McLean (United Artists)
- 17 / 15 BREADWINNERS — Jack Jones (RCA)
- 24 / 16 HONKY CHATEAU — Elton John (DJM)
- 12 / 17 TRILOGY — Emerson Lake & Palmer (Island)
- 14 / 18 IN SEARCH OF SPACE — Hawkwind (United Artists)
- 30 / 19 KILLER — Alice Cooper (Warner Bros.)
- 25 / 20 FOG ON THE TYNE — Lindisfarne (Charisma)
- – / 21 LOVE IT TO DEATH — Alice Cooper (Warner Bros.)
- – / 22 CLOSE TO THE EDGE — Yes (Atlantic)
- – / 23 TEASER AND THE FIRECAT — Cat Stevens (Island)
- 27 / 24 HISTORY OF ERIC CLAPTON — Eric Clapton (Polydor)
- – / 25 THE EDWARD WOODWARD ALBUM — Edward Woodward (Jam)
- 20 / 26 CARLOS SANTANA AND BUDDY MILES LIVE! — Carlos Santana & Buddy Miles (CBS)
- 22 / 27 EVERY PICTURE TELLS A STORY — Rod Stewart (Philips)
- 18 / 28 OBSCURED BY CLOUDS — Pink Floyd (Harvest)
- 19 / 29 LIVING IN THE PAST — Jethro Tull (Chrysalis)
- 21 / 30 MACHINE HEAD — Deep Purple (Purple)

23 September 1972

- 2 / 1 SIMON AND GARFUNKEL'S GREATEST HITS — Simon & Garfunkel (CBS)
- 1 / 2 NEVER A DULL MOMENT — Rod Stewart (Mercury)
- 5 / 3 THE SLIDER — T. Rex (T. Rex Wax Co)
- 6 / 4 SLADE ALIVE — Slade (Polydor)
- 3 / 5 TWENTY FANTASTIC HITS — Various Artists (Arcade)
- 7 / 6 ROXY MUSIC — Roxy Music (Island)
- 4 / 7 SCHOOL'S OUT — Alice Cooper (Warner Bros.)
- 11 / 8 MOODS — Neil Diamond (Uni)
- 9 / 9 BRIDGE OVER TROUBLED WATER — Simon & Garfunkel (CBS)
- 10 / 10 CHERISH — David Cassidy (Bell)
- 14 / 11 AMERICAN PIE — Don McLean (United Artists)
- 8 / 12 THE RISE AND FALL OF ZIGGY STARDUST AND THE SPIDERS FROM MARS — David Bowie (RCA)
- 17 / 13 TRILOGY — Emerson Lake & Palmer (Island)
- 22 / 14 CLOSE TO THE EDGE — Yes (Atlantic)
- – / 15 20 ALL TIME GREATS OF THE 50s — Various Artists (K-Tel)
- 16 / 16 HONKY CHATEAU — Elton John (DJM)
- 18 / 17 IN SEARCH OF SPACE — Hawkwind (United Artists)
- 12 / 18 LOVE THEME FROM THE GODFATHER — Andy Williams (CBS)
- 25 / 19 THE EDWARD WOODWARD ALBUM — Edward Woodward (Jam)
- 23 / 20 TEASER AND THE FIRECAT — Cat Stevens (Island)
- – / 21 HIMSELF — Gilbert O'Sullivan (MAM)
- 27 / 22 EVERY PICTURE TELLS A STORY — Rod Stewart (Philips)
- 21 / 23 LOVE IT TO DEATH — Alice Cooper (Warner Bros.)
- 13 / 24 20 DYNAMIC HITS — Various Artists (K-Tel)
- 20 / 25 FOG ON THE TYNE — Lindisfarne (Charisma)
- 24 / 26 HISTORY OF ERIC CLAPTON — Eric Clapton (Polydor)
- 15 / 27 BREADWINNERS — Jack Jones (RCA)
- – / 28 BLACK SABBATH VOL 4 — Black Sabbath (Vertigo)
- – / 29 HARVEST — Neil Young (Reprise)
- – / 30 NICELY OUT OF TIME — Lindisfarne (Charisma)

30 September 1972

- 2 / 1 NEVER A DULL MOMENT — Rod Stewart (Mercury)
- 1 / 2 SIMON AND GARFUNKEL'S GREATEST HITS — Simon & Garfunkel (CBS)
- 14 / 3 CLOSE TO THE EDGE — Yes (Atlantic)
- 4 / 4 SLADE ALIVE — Slade (Polydor)
- – / 5 CATCH BULL AT FOUR — Cat Stevens (Island)
- 15 / 6 20 ALL TIME GREATS OF THE 50s — Various Artists (K-Tel)
- 6 / 7 ROXY MUSIC — Roxy Music (Island)
- 3 / 8 THE SLIDER — T. Rex (T. Rex Wax Co)
- 8 / 9 MOODS — Neil Diamond (Uni)
- 28 / 10 BLACK SABBATH VOL 4 — Black Sabbath (Vertigo)
- – / 11 DINGLY DELL — Lindisfarne (Charisma)
- 7 / 12 SCHOOL'S OUT — Alice Cooper (Warner Bros.)
- 5 / 13 TWENTY FANTASTIC HITS — Various Artists (Arcade)
- 9 / 14 BRIDGE OVER TROUBLED WATER — Simon & Garfunkel (CBS)
- 11 / 15 AMERICAN PIE — Don McLean (United Artists)
- 10 / 16 CHERISH — David Cassidy (Bell)
- 19 / 17 THE EDWARD WOODWARD ALBUM — Edward Woodward (Jam)
- 16 / 18 HONKY CHATEAU — Elton John (DJM)
- – / 19 SING ALONG WITH MAX — Max Bygraves (Pye)
- 12 / 20 THE RISE AND FALL OF ZIGGY STARDUST AND THE SPIDERS FROM MARS — David Bowie (RCA)
- 13 / 21 TRILOGY — Emerson Lake & Palmer (Island)
- – / 22 CHICAGO V — Chicago (CBS)
- 22 / 23 EVERY PICTURE TELLS A STORY — Rod Stewart (Philips)
- 29 / 24 HARVEST — Neil Young (Reprise)
- – / 25 KILLER — Alice Cooper (Warner Bros.)
- 18 / 26 LOVE THEME FROM THE GODFATHER — Andy Williams (CBS)
- 25 / 27 FOG ON THE TYNE — Lindisfarne (Charisma)
- 21 / 28 HIMSELF — Gilbert O'Sullivan (MAM)
- 24 / 29 20 DYNAMIC HITS — Various Artists (K-Tel)
- – / 30 ALL THE YOUNG DUDES — Mott the Hoople (CBS)

Yes, 21 years ago people were already buying retrospective Clapton albums: *History of Eric Clapton* was in fact only the second LP under Eric's own name. Three Alice Cooper chart LPs reflected the popularity of *School's Out*, a No.1 single. Similarly Rod Stewart's second No.1 album, *Never A Dull Moment*, coincided with his topping the singles chart with *You Wear It Well*, soon displaced by Slade's *Mama Weer All Crazee Now*. This singalonga-noddyholda group also boasted a Top 5 album.

October 1972

last this
week

7 October 1972

last week	this week	
1	1	NEVER A DULL MOMENT Rod Stewart (Mercury)
2	2	SIMON AND GARFUNKEL'S GREATEST HITS Simon & Garfunkel (CBS)
3	3	CLOSE TO THE EDGE Yes (Atlantic)
4	4	SLADE ALIVE Slade (Polydor)
5	5	CATCH BULL AT FOUR Cat Stevens (Island)
11	6	DINGLY DELL Lindisfarne (Charisma)
7	7	ROXY MUSIC Roxy Music (Island)
10	8	BLACK SABBATH VOL 4 Black Sabbath (Vertigo)
9	9	MOODS Neil Diamond (Uni)
20	10	THE RISE AND FALL OF ZIGGY STARDUST AND THE SPIDERS FROM MARS David Bowie (RCA)
6	11	20 ALL TIME GREATS OF THE 50s Various Artists (K-Tel)
8	12	THE SLIDER T. Rex (T. Rex Wax Co)
13	13	TWENTY FANTASTIC HITS Various Artists (Arcade)
14	14	BRIDGE OVER TROUBLED WATER Simon & Garfunkel (CBS)
19	15	SING ALONG WITH MAX Max Bygraves (Pye)
21	16	TRILOGY Emerson Lake & Palmer (Island)
23	16	EVERY PICTURE TELLS A STORY Rod Stewart (Philips)
22	18	CHICAGO V Chicago (CBS)
30	19	ALL THE YOUNG DUDES Mott the Hoople (CBS)
16	20	CHERISH David Cassidy (Bell)
12	21	SCHOOL'S OUT Alice Cooper (Warner Bros.)
-	22	BANDSTAND Family (Reprise)
25	23	KILLER Alice Cooper (Warner Bros.)
-	24	TEASER AND THE FIRECAT Cat Stevens (Island)
-	25	LAYLA AND OTHER ASSORTED LOVE SONGS Derek & the Dominoes (Polydor)
-	26	PORTRAIT OF DONNY Donny Osmond (MGM)
-	27	LOVE IT TO DEATH Alice Cooper (Warner Bros.)
17	28	THE EDWARD WOODWARD ALBUM Edward Woodward (Jam)
-	29	IN SEARCH OF SPACE Hawkwind (United Artists)
28	30	HIMSELF Gilbert O'Sullivan (MAM)

14 October 1972

last week	this week	
1	1	NEVER A DULL MOMENT Rod Stewart (Mercury)
5	2	CATCH BULL AT FOUR Cat Stevens (Island)
2	3	SIMON AND GARFUNKEL'S GREATEST HITS Simon & Garfunkel (CBS)
3	4	CLOSE TO THE EDGE Yes (Atlantic)
4	5	SLADE ALIVE Slade (Polydor)
8	6	BLACK SABBATH VOL 4 Black Sabbath (Vertigo)
7	7	ROXY MUSIC Roxy Music (Island)
6	8	DINGLY DELL Lindisfarne (Charisma)
10	9	THE RISE AND FALL OF ZIGGY STARDUST AND THE SPIDERS FROM MARS David Bowie (RCA)
11	10	20 ALL TIME GREATS OF THE 50s Various Artists (K-Tel)
20	11	CHERISH David Cassidy (Bell)
13	12	TWENTY FANTASTIC HITS Various Artists (Arcade)
9	13	MOODS Neil Diamond (Uni)
21	14	SCHOOL'S OUT Alice Cooper (Warner Bros.)
15	15	SING ALONG WITH MAX Max Bygraves (Pye)
18	16	CHICAGO V Chicago (CBS)
14	17	BRIDGE OVER TROUBLED WATER Simon & Garfunkel (CBS)
-	18	AMERICAN PIE Don McLean (United Artists)
16	19	TRILOGY Emerson Lake & Palmer (Island)
29	20	IN SEARCH OF SPACE Hawkwind (United Artists)
22	21	BANDSTAND Family (Reprise)
-	22	SOMETIME IN NEW YORK CITY John & Yoko Lennon (Apple)
12	23	THE SLIDER T. Rex (T. Rex Wax Co)
-	24	THE FOUR SIDES OF MELANIE Melanie (Buddah)
24	25	TEASER AND THE FIRECAT Cat Stevens (Island)
-	26	HONKY CHATEAU Elton John (DJM)
-	27	ELVIS AS RECORDED LIVE AT MADISON SQUARE GARDEN Elvis Presley (RCA)
23	28	KILLER Alice Cooper (Warner Bros.)
26	29	PORTRAIT OF DONNY Donny Osmond (MGM)
16	30	EVERY PICTURE TELLS A STORY Rod Stewart (Philips)

21 October 1972

last week	this week	
3	1	SIMON AND GARFUNKEL'S GREATEST HITS Simon & Garfunkel (CBS)
1	2	NEVER A DULL MOMENT Rod Stewart (Mercury)
2	3	CATCH BULL AT FOUR Cat Stevens (Island)
6	4	BLACK SABBATH VOL 4 Black Sabbath (Vertigo)
4	5	CLOSE TO THE EDGE Yes (Atlantic)
5	6	SLADE ALIVE Slade (Polydor)
10	7	20 ALL TIME GREATS OF THE 50s Various Artists (K-Tel)
8	8	DINGLY DELL Lindisfarne (Charisma)
15	9	SING ALONG WITH MAX Max Bygraves (Pye)
11	10	CHERISH David Cassidy (Bell)
13	11	MOODS Neil Diamond (Uni)
9	12	THE RISE AND FALL OF ZIGGY STARDUST AND THE SPIDERS FROM MARS David Bowie (RCA)
-	13	20 STAR TRACKS Various Artists (Ronco)
7	14	ROXY MUSIC Roxy Music (Island)
21	15	BANDSTAND Family (Reprise)
17	16	BRIDGE OVER TROUBLED WATER Simon & Garfunkel (CBS)
19	17	TRILOGY Emerson Lake & Palmer (Island)
14	18	SCHOOL'S OUT Alice Cooper (Warner Bros.)
12	19	TWENTY FANTASTIC HITS Various Artists (Arcade)
-	20	STAR PORTRAIT Johnny Cash (CBS)
28	21	KILLER Alice Cooper (Warner Bros.)
24	22	THE FOUR SIDES OF MELANIE Melanie (Buddah)
29	23	PORTRAIT OF DONNY Donny Osmond (MGM)
20	24	IN SEARCH OF SPACE Hawkwind (United Artists)
22	25	SOMETIME IN NEW YORK CITY John & Yoko Lennon (Apple)
-	26	CIRCLES New Seekers (Polydor)
-	27	NICE 'N' EASY Various Artists (Philips)
-	28	WHO CAME FIRST Pete Townshend (Track)
30	29	EVERY PICTURE TELLS A STORY Rod Stewart (Philips)
18	30	AMERICAN PIE Don McLean (United Artists)

28 October 1972

last week	this week	
1	1	SIMON AND GARFUNKEL'S GREATEST HITS Simon & Garfunkel (CBS)
3	2	CATCH BULL AT FOUR Cat Stevens (Island)
2	3	NEVER A DULL MOMENT Rod Stewart (Mercury)
7	4	20 ALL TIME GREATS OF THE 50s Various Artists (K-Tel)
5	5	CLOSE TO THE EDGE Yes (Atlantic)
9	6	SING ALONG WITH MAX Max Bygraves (Pye)
4	7	BLACK SABBATH VOL 4 Black Sabbath (Vertigo)
8	8	DINGLY DELL Lindisfarne (Charisma)
6	9	SLADE ALIVE Slade (Polydor)
10	10	CHERISH David Cassidy (Bell)
13	11	20 STAR TRACKS Various Artists (Ronco)
12	12	THE RISE AND FALL OF ZIGGY STARDUST AND THE SPIDERS FROM MARS David Bowie (RCA)
17	13	TRILOGY Emerson Lake & Palmer (Island)
19	14	TWENTY FANTASTIC HITS Various Artists (Arcade)
29	15	EVERY PICTURE TELLS A STORY Rod Stewart (Phillips)
16	16	BRIDGE OVER TROUBLED WATER Simon & Garfunkel (CBS)
-	17	A SONG FOR YOU Carpenters (A&M)
11	18	MOODS Neil Diamond (Uni)
18	19	SCHOOL'S OUT Alice Cooper (Warner Bros.)
20	20	STAR PORTRAIT Johnny Cash (CBS)
25	21	SOMETIME IN NEW YORK CITY John & Yoko Lennon (Apple)
23	22	PORTRAIT OF DONNY Donny Osmond (MGM)
-	23	GLITTER Gary Glitter (Bell)
30	24	AMERICAN PIE Don McLean (United Artists)
15	25	BANDSTAND Family (Reprise)
26	26	CIRCLES New Seekers (Polydor)
28	27	WHO CAME FIRST Pete Townshend (Track)
-	28	HIMSELF Gilbert O'Sullivan (MAM)
14	29	ROXY MUSIC Roxy Music (Island)
-	30	THE SLIDER T. Rex (T. Rex Wax Co)

From now until year's end, the No.1 singles would be David Cassidy's *How Can I Be Sure*, Lieutenant Pidgeon's *Mouldy Old Dough*, Gilbert O'Sullivan's *Clair*, Chuck Berry's *My Ding-A-Ling*, Slade's *Gudbuy T'Jane* and Little Jimmy Osmond's *Long-Haired Lover From Liverpool*. In this climate, an albums chart that embraced *Sing Along With Max* and *Portrait Of Donny* (Osmond), might be said to make sense. John & Yoko Lennon, now so billed, seemed under-appreciated with *Sometime In New York City*.

4 November 1972

last week	this week	entry
1	1	SIMON AND GARFUNKEL'S GREATEST HITS — Simon & Garfunkel (CBS)
2	2	CATCH BULL AT FOUR — Cat Stevens (Island)
3	3	NEVER A DULL MOMENT — Rod Stewart (Mercury)
4	4	20 ALL TIME GREATS OF THE 50s — Various Artists (K-Tel)
23	5	GLITTER — Gary Glitter (Bell)
9	6	SLADE ALIVE — Slade (Polydor)
6	7	SING ALONG WITH MAX — Max Bygraves (Pye)
5	8	CLOSE TO THE EDGE — Yes (Atlantic)
7	9	BLACK SABBATH VOL 4 — Black Sabbath (Vertigo)
11	10	20 STAR TRACKS — Various Artists (Ronco)
12	11	THE RISE AND FALL OF ZIGGY STARDUST AND THE SPIDERS FROM MARS — David Bowie (RCA)
8	12	DINGLY DELL — Lindisfarne (Charisma)
-	13	BEST OF BREAD — Bread (Elektra)
16	14	BRIDGE OVER TROUBLED WATER — Simon & Garfunkel (CBS)
10	15	CHERISH — David Cassidy (Bell)
14	16	TWENTY FANTASTIC HITS — Various Artists (Arcade)
25	17	BANDSTAND — Family (Reprise)
18	18	MOODS — Neil Diamond (Uni)
29	19	ROXY MUSIC — Roxy Music (Island)
21	20	SOMETIME IN NEW YORK CITY — John & Yoko Lennon (Apple)
-	21	HOT HITS 14 — Various Artists (Music for Pleasure)
28	22	HIMSELF — Gilbert O'Sullivan (MAM)
13	23	TRILOGY — Emerson Lake & Palmer (Island)
24	24	AMERICAN PIE — Don McLean (United Artists)
19	25	SCHOOL'S OUT — Alice Cooper (Warner Bros.)
17	26	A SONG FOR YOU — Carpenters (A&M)
15	27	EVERY PICTURE TELLS A STORY — Rod Stewart (Philips)
-	28	BREADWINNERS — Jack Jones (RCA)
20	29	STAR PORTRAIT — Johnny Cash (CBS)
22	30	PORTRAIT OF DONNY — Donny Osmond (MGM)

11 November 1972

last week	this week	entry
1	1	SIMON AND GARFUNKEL'S GREATEST HITS — Simon & Garfunkel (CBS)
2	2	CATCH BULL AT FOUR — Cat Stevens (Island)
3	3	NEVER A DULL MOMENT — Rod Stewart (Mercury)
4	4	20 ALL TIME GREATS OF THE 50s — Various Artists (K-Tel)
9	5	BLACK SABBATH VOL 4 — Black Sabbath (Vertigo)
6	6	GLITTER — Gary Glitter (Bell)
10	7	20 STAR TRACKS — Various Artists (Ronco)
7	8	SING ALONG WITH MAX — Max Bygraves (Pye)
-	9	BACK TO FRONT — Gilbert O'Sullivan (MAM)
15	10	CHERISH — David Cassidy (Bell)
6	11	SLADE ALIVE — Slade (Polydor)
13	12	BEST OF BREAD — Bread (Elektra)
8	13	CLOSE TO THE EDGE — Yes (Atlantic)
17	14	BANDSTAND — Family (Reprise)
11	15	THE RISE AND FALL OF ZIGGY STARDUST AND THE SPIDERS FROM MARS — David Bowie (RCA)
30	16	PORTRAIT OF DONNY — Donny Osmond (MGM)
14	17	BRIDGE OVER TROUBLED WATER — Simon & Garfunkel (CBS)
18	18	MOODS — Neil Diamond (Uni)
20	19	SOMETIME IN NEW YORK CITY — John & Yoko Lennon (Apple)
12	20	DINGLY DELL — Lindisfarne (Charisma)
26	21	A SONG FOR YOU — Carpenters (A&M)
27	22	EVERY PICTURE TELLS A STORY — Rod Stewart (Philips)
22	23	HIMSELF — Gilbert O'Sullivan (MAM)
16	24	TWENTY FANTASTIC HITS — Various Artists (Arcade)
-	25	FOXTROT — Genesis (Charisma)
-	26	KILLER — Alice Cooper (Warner Bros.)
29	27	STAR PORTRAIT — Johnny Cash (CBS)
25	28	SCHOOL'S OUT — Alice Cooper (Warner Bros.)
-	29	DIANA ROSS' GREATEST HITS — Diana Ross (Tamla Motown)
24	30	AMERICAN PIE — Don McLean (United Artists)

18 November 1972

last week	this week	entry
1	1	SIMON AND GARFUNKEL'S GREATEST HITS — Simon & Garfunkel (CBS)
4	2	20 ALL TIME GREATS OF THE 50s — Various Artists (K-Tel)
2	3	CATCH BULL AT FOUR — Cat Stevens (Island)
9	4	BACK TO FRONT — Gilbert O'Sullivan (MAM)
3	5	NEVER A DULL MOMENT — Rod Stewart (Mercury)
12	6	BEST OF BREAD — Bread (Elektra)
8	7	SING ALONG WITH MAX — Max Bygraves (Pye)
7	8	20 STAR TRACKS — Various Artists (Ronco)
6	9	GLITTER — Gary Glitter (Bell)
10	10	CHERISH — David Cassidy (Bell)
5	11	BLACK SABBATH VOL 4 — Black Sabbath (Vertigo)
11	12	SLADE ALIVE — Slade (Polydor)
-	13	22 DYNAMIC HITS — Various Artists (K-Tel)
13	14	CLOSE TO THE EDGE — Yes (Atlantic)
16	15	PORTRAIT OF DONNY — Donny Osmond (MGM)
17	16	BRIDGE OVER TROUBLED WATER — Simon & Garfunkel (CBS)
21	17	A SONG FOR YOU — Carpenters (A&M)
-	18	WAR HEROES — Jimi Hendrix (Polydor)
15	19	THE RISE AND FALL OF ZIGGY STARDUST AND THE SPIDERS FROM MARS — David Bowie (RCA)
-	20	20 FANTASTIC HITS VOL 2 — Various Artists (Arcade)
20	21	DINGLY DELL — Lindisfarne (Charisma)
-	22	CARAVANSERAI — Santana (CBS)
29	23	DIANA ROSS' GREATEST HITS — Diana Ross (Tamla Motown)
-	24	TRILOGY — Emerson Lake & Palmer (Island)
14	25	BANDSTAND — Family (Reprise)
28	26	SCHOOL'S OUT — Alice Cooper (Warner Bros.)
-	27	THE LAST GOON SHOW OF ALL — Goons (BBC)
22	28	EVERY PICTURE TELLS A STORY — Rod Stewart (Philips)
-	29	JACKSON FIVE'S GREATEST HITS — Jackson Five (Tamla Motown)
-	30	I CAN SEE CLEARLY NOW — Johnny Nash (CBS)

25 November 1972

last week	this week	entry
4	1	BACK TO FRONT — Gilbert O'Sullivan (MAM)
1	2	SIMON AND GARFUNKEL'S GREATEST HITS — Simon & Garfunkel (CBS)
3	3	CATCH BULL AT FOUR — Cat Stevens (Island)
5	4	NEVER A DULL MOMENT — Rod Stewart (Mercury)
2	5	20 ALL TIME GREATS OF THE 50s — Various Artists (K-Tel)
13	6	22 DYNAMIC HITS — Various Artists (K-Tel)
7	7	SING ALONG WITH MAX — Max Bygraves (Pye)
12	8	SLADE ALIVE — Slade (Polydor)
-	9	SEVENTH SOJOURN — Moody Blues (Threshold)
6	10	BEST OF BREAD — Bread (Elektra)
8	11	20 STAR TRACKS — Various Artists (Ronco)
9	12	GLITTER — Gary Glitter (Bell)
11	13	BLACK SABBATH VOL 4 — Black Sabbath (Vertigo)
14	14	20 FANTASTIC HITS VOL 2 — Various Artists (Arcade)
22	15	CARAVANSERAI — Santana (CBS)
15	16	PORTRAIT OF DONNY — Donny Osmond (MGM)
27	17	THE LAST GOON SHOW OF ALL — Goons (BBC)
14	18	CLOSE TO THE EDGE — Yes (Atlantic)
17	19	A SONG FOR YOU — Carpenters (A&M)
21	20	DINGLY DELL — Lindisfarne (Charisma)
26	21	SCHOOL'S OUT — Alice Cooper (Warner Bros.)
28	22	EVERY PICTURE TELLS A STORY — Rod Stewart (Philips)
10	23	CHERISH — David Cassidy (Bell)
16	24	BRIDGE OVER TROUBLED WATER — Simon & Garfunkel (CBS)
19	25	THE RISE AND FALL OF ZIGGY STARDUST AND THE SPIDERS FROM MARS — David Bowie (RCA)
24	26	TRILOGY — Emerson Lake & Palmer (Island)
18	27	WAR HEROES — Jimi Hendrix (Polydor)
-	28	MOODS — Neil Diamond (Uni)
29	29	JACKSON FIVE'S GREATEST HITS — Jackson Five (Tamla Motown)
25	30	BANDSTAND — Family (Reprise)

Much of the chart was now hits compilations, both of the *Jackson Five's Greatest Hits* sort and the *20 All Time Greats Of The 50s* by Various Artists sort: the latter thrown together by specialist companies, like K-Tel, Arcade and Ronco, which signed no acts themselves but repackaged others' back-catalogues. So dominant were these becoming that the industry discussed changing the rules of chart-entry to exclude them. Current hit singles included the Shangri-Las' *Leader Of The Pack* and Neil Sedaka's *Oh Carol*.

December 1972

2 December 1972

9 December 1972

16 December 1972

23 December 1972

With everything from the Goons onwards in the charts, David Widgery wrote in this month's Socialist Worker that "on the principle that almost anything would be better than the 1970s, the pioneering pop singles of the late 1950s and 1960s are being remorselessly re-released to swamp any originality which might be struggling to the surface. This has reached such a point that half the record-buying public appears to be awash with nostalgia over experiences they never had in the first place."

last week	this week		
		30 December 1972	
2	1	SLAYED	Slade (Polydor)
7	2	20 ALL TIME GREATS OF THE 50s	Various Artists (K-Tel)
1	3	BACK TO FRONT	Gilbert O'Sullivan (MAM)
3	4	25 ROCKIN' AND ROLLIN' GREATS	Various Artists (K-Tel)
5	5	PORTRAIT OF DONNY	Donny Osmond (MGM)
4	6	SIMON AND GARFUNKEL'S GREATEST HITS	Simon & Garfunkel (CBS)
6	7	22 DYNAMIC HITS	Various Artists (K-Tel)
11	8	TOO YOUNG	Donny Osmond (MGM)
16	9	CATCH BULL AT FOUR	Cat Stevens (Island)
9	10	NEVER A DULL MOMENT	Rod Stewart (Mercury)
8	11	SEVENTH SOJOURN	Moody Blues (Threshold)
13	12	20 FANTASTIC HITS VOL 2	Various Artists (Arcade)
10	13	SING ALONG WITH MAX	Max Bygraves (Pye)
15	14	CRAZY HORSES	Osmonds (MGM)
12	15	CHERISH	David Cassidy (Bell)
20	16	MADE IN JAPAN	Deep Purple (Purple)
-	17	PHIL SPECTOR'S CHRISTMAS ALBUM	Various Artists (Apple)
30	18	BRIDGE OVER TROUBLED WATER	Simon & Garfunkel (CBS)
29	19	IMAGINE	John Lennon (Apple)
27	20	20 STAR TRACKS	Various Artists (Ronco)
14	21	MOTOWN CHARTBUSTERS VOL 7	Various Artists (Tamla Motown)
21	22	LOOKIN' THROUGH THE WINDOWS	Jackson Five (Tamla Motown)
19	23	CARAVANSERAI	Santana (CBS)
17	24	DOREMI FASOL LATIDO	Hawkwind (United Artists)
26	25	BEST OF BREAD	Bread (Elektra)
23	26	BOBBY CRUSH	Bobby Crush (Philips)
28	27	ANDY WILLIAMS' GREATEST HITS VOL 2	Andy Williams (CBS)
18	28	SING ALONG WITH MAX VOL 2	Max Bygraves (Pye)
-	29	SLADE ALIVE	Slade (Polydor)
24	30	A SONG FOR YOU	Carpenters (A&M)

The new and the old:
Slade (top) and
The Who

January 1973

6 January 1973

Last week	This week	Title	Artist
1	1	SLAYED	Slade (Polydor)
3	2	BACK TO FRONT	Gilbert O'Sullivan (MAM)
6	3	SIMON & GARFUNKEL'S GREATEST HITS	Simon & Garfunkel (CBS)
5	4	PORTRAIT OF DONNY	Donny Osmond (MGM)
2	5	20 ALL TIME GREATS OF THE 50s	Various Artists (K-Tel)
4	6	25 ROCKIN' & ROLLIN' GREATS	Various Artists (K-Tel)
9	7	CATCH BULL AT FOUR	Cat Stevens (Island)
7	8	22 DYNAMIC HITS	Various Artists (K-Tel)
10	9	NEVER A DULL MOMENT	Rod Stewart (Mercury)
14	10	CRAZY HORSES	Osmonds (MGM)
12	11	20 FANTASTIC HITS VOL 2	Various Artists (Arcade)
15	12	CHERISH	David Cassidy (Bell)
8	13	TOO YOUNG	Donny Osmond (MGM)
11	14	SEVENTH SOJOURN	Moody Blues (Threshold)
13	15	SING ALONG WITH MAX	Max Bygraves (Pye)
16	16	MADE IN JAPAN	Deep Purple (Purple)
-	17	THE STRAUSS FAMILY	Cyril Ornadel & the London Symphony Orchestra (Polydor)
21	18	MOTOWN CHARTBUSTERS VOL 7	Various Artists (Tamla Motown)
29	19	SLADE ALIVE	Slade (Polydor)
20	20	20 STAR TRACKS	Various Artists (Ronco)
24	21	DOREMI FASOL LATIDO	Hawkwind (United Artists)
23	22	CARAVANSERAI	Santana (CBS)
-	23	BEN	Michael Jackson (Tamla Motown)
-	24	HIMSELF	Gilbert O'Sullivan (MAM)
28	25	SING ALONG WITH MAX VOL 2	Max Bygraves (Pye)
18	26	BRIDGE OVER TROUBLED WATER	Simon & Garfunkel (CBS)
22	27	LOOKIN' THROUGH THE WINDOWS	Jackson Five (Tamla Motown)
19	28	IMAGINE	John Lennon (Apple)
25	29	BEST OF BREAD	Bread (Elektra)
30	30	A SONG FOR YOU	Carpenters (A&M)

13 January 1973

Last week	This week	Title	Artist
1	1	SLAYED	Slade (Polydor)
2	2	BACK TO FRONT	Gilbert O'Sullivan (MAM)
4	3	PORTRAIT OF DONNY	Donny Osmond (MGM)
3	4	SIMON & GARFUNKEL'S GREATEST HITS	Simon & Garfunkel (CBS)
5	5	NEVER A DULL MOMENT	Rod Stewart (Mercury)
7	6	CATCH BULL AT FOUR	Cat Stevens (Island)
10	7	CRAZY HORSES	Osmonds (MGM)
14	8	SEVENTH SOJOURN	Moody Blues (Threshold)
16	9	MADE IN JAPAN	Deep Purple (Purple)
5	10	20 ALL TIME GREATS OF THE 50s	Various Artists (K-Tel)
13	11	TOO YOUNG	Donny Osmond (MGM)
-	12	NO SECRETS	Carly Simon (Elektra)
18	13	MOTOWN CHARTBUSTERS VOL 7	Various Artists (Tamla Motown)
17	14	THE STRAUSS FAMILY	Cyril Ornadel & the London Symphony Orchestra (Polydor)
21	15	DOREMI FASOL LATIDO	Hawkwind (United Artists)
6	16	25 ROCKIN' & ROLLIN' GREATS	Various Artists (K-Tel)
23	17	BEN	Michael Jackson (Tamla Motown)
11	18	20 FANTASTIC HITS VOL 2	Various Artists (Arcade)
12	19	CHERISH	David Cassidy (Bell)
8	20	22 DYNAMIC HITS	Various Artists (K-Tel)
15	21	SING ALONG WITH MAX	Max Bygraves (Pye)
19	22	SLADE ALIVE	Slade (Polydor)
-	23	TOMMY	London Symphony Orchestra & Chamber Choir with Guest Soloists (A&M)
26	24	BRIDGE OVER TROUBLED WATER	Simon & Garfunkel (CBS)
29	25	BEST OF BREAD	Bread (Elektra)
-	26	OSMONDS LIVE	Osmonds (MGM)
24	27	HIMSELF	Gilbert O'Sullivan (MAM)
-	28	MOVING WAVES	Focus (Polydor)
-	29	ALL DIRECTIONS	Temptations (Tamla Motown)
22	30	CARAVANSERAI	Santana (CBS)

20 January 1973

Last week	This week	Title	Artist
1	1	SLAYED	Slade (Polydor)
2	2	BACK TO FRONT	Gilbert O'Sullivan (MAM)
4	3	SIMON & GARFUNKEL'S GREATEST HITS	Simon & Garfunkel (CBS)
6	4	CATCH BULL AT FOUR	Cat Stevens (Island)
7	5	CRAZY HORSES	Osmonds (MGM)
5	6	NEVER A DULL MOMENT	Rod Stewart (Mercury)
3	7	PORTRAIT OF DONNY	Donny Osmond (MGM)
9	8	MADE IN JAPAN	Deep Purple (Purple)
-	9	THE RISE AND FALL OF ZIGGY STARDUST AND THE SPIDERS FROM MARS	David Bowie (RCA)
12	10	NO SECRETS	Carly Simon (Elektra)
8	11	SEVENTH SOJOURN	Moody Blues (Threshold)
30	12	CARAVANSERAI	Santana (CBS)
17	13	BEN	Michael Jackson (Tamla Motown)
13	14	MOTOWN CHARTBUSTERS VOL 7	Various Artists (Tamla Motown)
14	15	THE STRAUSS FAMILY	Cyril Ornadel & the London Symphony Orchestra (Polydor)
11	16	TOO YOUNG	Donny Osmond (MGM)
16	17	25 ROCKIN' & ROLLIN' GREATS	Various Artists (K-Tel)
20	18	22 DYNAMIC HITS	Various Artists (K-Tel)
18	19	20 FANTASTIC HITS VOL 2	Various Artists (Arcade)
24	20	BRIDGE OVER TROUBLED WATER	Simon & Garfunkel (CBS)
22	21	SLADE ALIVE	Slade (Polydor)
26	22	OSMONDS LIVE	Osmonds (MGM)
21	23	SING ALONG WITH MAX	Max Bygraves (Pye)
23	24	TOMMY	London Symphony Orchestra & Chamber Choir with Guest Soloists (A&M)
10	25	20 ALL TIME GREATS OF THE 50s	Various Artists (K-Tel)
15	26	DOREMI FASOL LATIDO	Hawkwind (United Artists)
19	27	CHERISH	David Cassidy (Bell)
-	28	BREADWINNERS	Jack Jones (RCA)
-	29	FOR THE ROSES	Joni Mitchell (Asylum)
28	30	MOVING WAVES	Focus (Polydor)

27 January 1973

Last week	This week	Title	Artist
1	1	SLAYED	Slade (Polydor)
2	2	BACK TO FRONT	Gilbert O'Sullivan (MAM)
10	3	NO SECRETS	Carly Simon (Elektra)
3	4	SIMON & GARFUNKEL'S GREATEST HITS	Simon & Garfunkel (CBS)
7	5	PORTRAIT OF DONNY	Donny Osmond (MGM)
4	6	CATCH BULL AT FOUR	Cat Stevens (Island)
6	7	NEVER A DULL MOMENT	Rod Stewart (Mercury)
9	8	THE RISE AND FALL OF ZIGGY STARDUST AND THE SPIDERS FROM MARS	David Bowie (RCA)
16	9	TOO YOUNG	Donny Osmond (MGM)
8	10	MADE IN JAPAN	Deep Purple (Purple)
11	11	SEVENTH SOJOURN	Moody Blues (Threshold)
15	12	THE STRAUSS FAMILY	Cyril Ornadel & the London Symphony Orchestra (Polydor)
30	13	MOVING WAVES	Focus (Polydor)
5	14	CRAZY HORSES	Osmonds (MGM)
-	15	PILEDRIVER	Status Quo (Vertigo)
17	16	25 ROCKIN' & ROLLIN' GREATS	Various Artists (K-Tel)
13	17	BEN	Michael Jackson (Tamla Motown)
19	18	20 FANTASTIC HITS VOL 2	Various Artists (Arcade)
-	19	ALL DIRECTIONS	Temptations (Tamla Motown)
20	20	BRIDGE OVER TROUBLED WATER	Simon & Garfunkel (CBS)
27	21	CHERISH	David Cassidy (Bell)
14	22	MOTOWN CHARTBUSTERS VOL 7	Various Artists (Tamla Motown)
-	23	TRILOGY	Emerson Lake & Palmer (Island)
-	24	BEST OF BREAD	Bread (Elektra)
29	25	FOR THE ROSES	Joni Mitchell (Asylum)
12	26	CARAVANSERAI	Santana (CBS)
24	27	TOMMY	London Symphony Orchestra & Chamber Choir with Guest Soloists (A&M)
-	28	IMAGINE	John Lennon (Apple)
21	29	SLADE ALIVE	Slade (Polydor)
23	30	SING ALONG WITH MAX	Max Bygraves (Pye)

Carly Simon, of America's wealthy elite, one of the Simons of the Simon & Schuster publishing empire, was doing very nicely with her album *No Secrets* and the hit single *You're So Vain*. Its punch-line "You're so vain you prob'ly think this song is about you, don't you?" made the song a self-reflexive text, though since this post-structuralist term was not yet available, people had to content themselves with surmising that Carly had aimed it at Warren Beatty, the well-known film-star and womaniser.

February 1973

3 February 1973

LW	TW	Title	Artist (Label)
1	1	SLAYED	Slade (Polydor)
2	2	BACK TO FRONT	Gilbert O'Sullivan (MAM)
4	3	SIMON & GARFUNKEL'S GREATEST HITS	Simon & Garfunkel (CBS)
3	4	NO SECRETS	Carly Simon (Elektra)
6	5	CATCH BULL AT FOUR	Cat Stevens (Island)
-	6	DON'T SHOOT ME I'M ONLY THE PIANO PLAYER	Elton John (DJM)
12	7	THE STRAUSS FAMILY	Cyril Ornadel & the London Symphony Orchestra (Polydor)
8	8	THE RISE AND FALL OF ZIGGY STARDUST AND THE SPIDERS FROM MARS	David Bowie (RCA)
11	9	SEVENTH SOJOURN	Moody Blues (Threshold)
5	10	PORTRAIT OF DONNY	Donny Osmond (MGM)
7	11	NEVER A DULL MOMENT	Rod Stewart (Mercury)
15	12	PILEDRIVER	Status Quo (Vertigo)
13	13	MOVING WAVES	Focus (Polydor)
14	14	CRAZY HORSES	Osmonds (MGM)
10	15	MADE IN JAPAN	Deep Purple (Purple)
19	16	ALL DIRECTIONS	Temptations (Tamla Motown)
9	17	TOO YOUNG	Donny Osmond (MGM)
-	18	FOCUS 3	Focus (Polydor)
20	19	BRIDGE OVER TROUBLED WATER	Simon & Garfunkel (CBS)
-	20	TALKING BOOK	Stevie Wonder (Tamla Motown)
18	21	20 FANTASTIC HITS VOL 2	Various Artists (Arcade)
-	22	BREADWINNERS	Jack Jones (RCA)
17	23	BEN	Michael Jackson (Tamla Motown)
-	24	HEARTBREAKER	Free (Island)
22	25	MOTOWN CHARTBUSTERS VOL 7	Various Artists (Tamla Motown)
16	26	25 ROCKIN' & ROLLIN' GREATS	Various Artists (K-Tel)
-	27	HIMSELF	Gilbert O'Sullivan (MAM)
29	28	SLADE ALIVE	Slade (Polydor)
23	29	TRILOGY	Emerson Lake & Palmer (Island)
28	30	IMAGINE	John Lennon (Apple)

10 February 1973

LW	TW	Title	Artist (Label)
6	1	DON'T SHOOT ME I'M ONLY THE PIANO PLAYER	Elton John (DJM)
4	2	NO SECRETS	Carly Simon (Elektra)
2	3	BACK TO FRONT	Gilbert O'Sullivan (MAM)
1	4	SLAYED	Slade (Polydor)
5	5	CATCH BULL AT FOUR	Cat Stevens (Island)
3	6	SIMON & GARFUNKEL'S GREATEST HITS	Simon & Garfunkel (CBS)
13	7	MOVING WAVES	Focus (Polydor)
12	8	PILEDRIVER	Status Quo (Vertigo)
7	9	THE STRAUSS FAMILY	Cyril Ornadel & the London Symphony Orchestra (Polydor)
8	10	THE RISE AND FALL OF ZIGGY STARDUST AND THE SPIDERS FROM MARS	David Bowie (RCA)
24	11	HEARTBREAKER	Free (Island)
18	12	FOCUS 3	Focus (Polydor)
11	13	NEVER A DULL MOMENT	Rod Stewart (Mercury)
14	14	MADE IN JAPAN	Deep Purple (Purple)
15	15	CRAZY HORSES	Osmonds (MGM)
-	16	WHO DO YOU THINK WE ARE	Deep Purple (Purple)
10	17	PORTRAIT OF DONNY	Donny Osmond (MGM)
17	18	TOO YOUNG	Donny Osmond (MGM)
9	19	SEVENTH SOJOURN	Moody Blues (Threshold)
20	20	TALKING BOOK	Stevie Wonder (Tamla Motown)
19	21	BRIDGE OVER TROUBLED WATER	Simon & Garfunkel (CBS)
26	22	25 ROCKIN' & ROLLIN' GREATS	Various Artists (K-Tel)
-	23	BEST OF BREAD	Bread (Elektra)
16	24	ALL DIRECTIONS	Temptations (Tamla Motown)
23	25	BEN	Michael Jackson (Tamla Motown)
22	26	BREADWINNERS	Jack Jones (RCA)
29	27	TRILOGY	Emerson Lake & Palmer (Island)
-	28	KILLER JOE	Little Jimmy Osmond (MGM)
-	29	A SONG FOR YOU	Carpenters (A&M)
-	30	OSMONDS LIVE	Osmonds (MGM)

17 February 1973

LW	TW	Title	Artist (Label)
1	1	DON'T SHOOT ME I'M ONLY THE PIANO PLAYER	Elton John (DJM)
2	2	NO SECRETS	Carly Simon (Elektra)
4	3	SLAYED	Slade (Polydor)
3	4	BACK TO FRONT	Gilbert O'Sullivan (MAM)
6	5	SIMON & GARFUNKEL'S GREATEST HITS	Simon & Garfunkel (CBS)
11	6	HEARTBREAKER	Free (Island)
12	7	FOCUS 3	Focus (Polydor)
9	8	THE STRAUSS FAMILY	Cyril Ornadel & the London Symphony Orchestra (Polydor)
7	9	MOVING WAVES	Focus (Polydor)
8	10	PILEDRIVER	Status Quo (Vertigo)
5	11	CATCH BULL AT FOUR	Cat Stevens (Island)
10	12	THE RISE AND FALL OF ZIGGY STARDUST AND THE SPIDERS FROM MARS	David Bowie (RCA)
19	13	SEVENTH SOJOURN	Moody Blues (Threshold)
17	14	PORTRAIT OF DONNY	Donny Osmond (MGM)
16	15	WHO DO YOU THINK WE ARE	Deep Purple (Purple)
13	16	NEVER A DULL MOMENT	Rod Stewart (Mercury)
26	17	BREADWINNERS	Jack Jones (RCA)
15	18	CRAZY HORSES	Osmonds (MGM)
-	19	THE SIX WIVES OF HENRY VIII	Rick Wakeman (A&M)
14	20	MADE IN JAPAN	Deep Purple (Purple)
18	21	TOO YOUNG	Donny Osmond (MGM)
21	22	BRIDGE OVER TROUBLED WATER	Simon & Garfunkel (CBS)
23	23	BEST OF BREAD	Bread (Elektra)
20	24	TALKING BOOK	Stevie Wonder (Tamla Motown)
-	25	SING ALONG WITH MAX	Max Bygraves (Pye)
-	26	HOT AUGUST NIGHT	Neil Diamond (Uni)
27	27	GLITTER	Gary Glitter (Bell)
28	28	KILLER JOE	Little Jimmy Osmond (MGM)
-	29	MOTOWN CHARTBUSTERS VOL 7	Various Artists (Tamla Motown)
-	30	SLADE ALIVE	Slade (Polydor)

24 February 1973

LW	TW	Title	Artist (Label)
1	1	DON'T SHOOT ME I'M ONLY THE PIANO PLAYER	Elton John (DJM)
2	2	NO SECRETS	Carly Simon (Elektra)
3	3	SLAYED	Slade (Polydor)
9	4	MOVING WAVES	Focus (Polydor)
4	5	BACK TO FRONT	Gilbert O'Sullivan (MAM)
10	6	PILEDRIVER	Status Quo (Vertigo)
15	7	WHO DO YOU THINK WE ARE	Deep Purple (Purple)
7	8	FOCUS 3	Focus (Polydor)
8	9	THE STRAUSS FAMILY	Cyril Ornadel & the London Symphony Orchestra (Polydor)
11	10	CATCH BULL AT FOUR	Cat Stevens (Island)
5	11	SIMON & GARFUNKEL'S GREATEST HITS	Simon & Garfunkel (CBS)
19	12	THE SIX WIVES OF HENRY VIII	Rick Wakeman (A&M)
6	13	HEARTBREAKER	Free (Island)
13	14	SEVENTH SOJOURN	Moody Blues (Threshold)
24	15	TALKING BOOK	Stevie Wonder (Tamla Motown)
12	16	THE RISE AND FALL OF ZIGGY STARDUST AND THE SPIDERS FROM MARS	David Bowie (RCA)
-	17	ROCK ME BABY	David Cassidy (Bell)
20	18	MADE IN JAPAN	Deep Purple (Purple)
-	19	BURSTING AT THE SEAMS	Strawbs (A&M)
16	20	NEVER A DULL MOMENT	Rod Stewart (Mercury)
28	21	KILLER JOE	Little Jimmy Osmond (MGM)
26	22	HOT AUGUST NIGHT	Neil Diamond (Uni)
-	23	HOLLAND	Beach Boys (Reprise)
14	24	PORTRAIT OF DONNY	Donny Osmond (MGM)
23	25	BEST OF BREAD	Bread (Elektra)
22	26	BRIDGE OVER TROUBLED WATER	Simon & Garfunkel (CBS)
25	27	SING ALONG WITH MAX	Max Bygraves (Pye)
21	28	TOO YOUNG	Donny Osmond (MGM)
18	29	CRAZY HORSES	Osmonds (MGM)
-	30	TRILOGY	Emerson Lake & Palmer (Island)

Canadian Joni Mitchell's minor hit album *For The Roses* had just left the Top 30 after peaking at 25. Mitchell, singer-songwriter of several anthemic 1960s songs, was slowly acquiring gravitas, through the dexterity of her very personal writing and performance (on piano as well as guitar). About to move among the rock superstar elite, she would soon make more heavily promoted albums and go off at many jazzy tangents, but *For The Roses* was a true classic; its warm, intelligent appeal is undiminished today.

March 1973

3 March 1973

last	this		
1	1	DON'T SHOOT ME I'M ONLY THE PIANO PLAYER	Elton John (DJM)
2	2	NO SECRETS	Carly Simon (Elektra)
5	3	BACK TO FRONT	Gilbert O'Sullivan (MAM)
3	4	SLAYED	Slade (Polydor)
7	5	WHO DO YOU THINK WE ARE	Deep Purple (Purple)
4	6	MOVING WAVES	Focus (Polydor)
8	7	FOCUS 3	Focus (Polydor)
11	8	SIMON & GARFUNKEL'S GREATEST HITS	Simon & Garfunkel (CBS)
9	9	THE STRAUSS FAMILY	Cyril Ornadel & the London Symphony Orchestra (Polydor)
6	10	PILEDRIVER	Status Quo (Vertigo)
10	11	CATCH BULL AT FOUR	Cat Stevens (Island)
17	12	ROCK ME BABY	David Cassidy (Bell)
12	13	THE SIX WIVES OF HENRY VIII	Rick Wakeman (A&M)
19	14	BURSTING AT THE SEAMS	Strawbs (A&M)
13	15	HEARTBREAKER	Free (Island)
-	16	ALOHA FROM HAWAII VIA SATELLITE	Elvis Presley (RCA)
-	17	BLUEPRINT	Rory Gallagher (Polydor)
26	18	BRIDGE OVER TROUBLED WATER	Simon & Garfunkel (CBS)
16	19	THE RISE AND FALL OF ZIGGY STARDUST AND THE SPIDERS FROM MARS	David Bowie (RCA)
-	20	A CLOCKWORK ORANGE	Soundtrack (Warner Bros.)
14	21	SEVENTH SOJOURN	Moody Blues (Threshold)
-	22	JAMES LAST IN RUSSIA	James Last (Polydor)
23	23	HOLLAND	Beach Boys (Reprise)
20	24	NEVER A DULL MOMENT	Rod Stewart (Mercury)
15	25	TALKING BOOK	Stevie Wonder (Tamla Motown)
22	26	HOT AUGUST NIGHT	Neil Diamond (Uni)
-	27	MOTOWN CHARTBUSTERS VOL 7	Various Artists (Tamla Motown)
24	28	PORTRAIT OF DONNY	Donny Osmond (MGM)
-	29	GLITTER	Gary Glitter (Bell)
28	30	TOO YOUNG	Donny Osmond (MGM)

10 March 1973

last	this		
1	1	DON'T SHOOT ME I'M ONLY THE PIANO PLAYER	Elton John (DJM)
6	2	MOVING WAVES	Focus (Polydor)
14	3	BURSTING AT THE SEAMS	Strawbs (A&M)
2	4	NO SECRETS	Carly Simon (Elektra)
4	5	SLAYED	Slade (Polydor)
12	6	ROCK ME BABY	David Cassidy (Bell)
3	7	BACK TO FRONT	Gilbert O'Sullivan (MAM)
13	8	THE SIX WIVES OF HENRY VIII	Rick Wakeman (A&M)
5	9	WHO DO YOU THINK WE ARE	Deep Purple (Purple)
8	10	SIMON & GARFUNKEL'S GREATEST HITS	Simon & Garfunkel (CBS)
10	11	PILEDRIVER	Status Quo (Vertigo)
7	12	FOCUS 3	Focus (Polydor)
9	13	THE STRAUSS FAMILY	Cyril Ornadel & the London Symphony Orchestra (Polydor)
17	14	BLUEPRINT	Rory Gallagher (Polydor)
20	15	A CLOCKWORK ORANGE	Soundtrack (Warner Bros.)
25	16	TALKING BOOK	Stevie Wonder (Tamla Motown)
11	17	CATCH BULL AT FOUR	Cat Stevens (Island)
26	18	HOT AUGUST NIGHT	Neil Diamond (Uni)
19	19	THE RISE AND FALL OF ZIGGY STARDUST AND THE SPIDERS FROM MARS	David Bowie (RCA)
30	20	TOO YOUNG	Donny Osmond (MGM)
23	21	HOLLAND	Beach Boys (Reprise)
16	22	ALOHA FROM HAWAII VIA SATELLITE	Elvis Presley (RCA)
15	23	HEARTBREAKER	Free (Island)
22	24	JAMES LAST IN RUSSIA	James Last (Polydor)
18	25	BRIDGE OVER TROUBLED WATER	Simon & Garfunkel (CBS)
28	26	PORTRAIT OF DONNY	Donny Osmond (MGM)
24	27	NEVER A DULL MOMENT	Rod Stewart (Mercury)
-	28	KILLER JOE	Little Jimmy Osmond (MGM)
29	29	GLITTER	Gary Glitter (Bell)
21	30	SEVENTH SOJOURN	Moody Blues (Threshold)

17 March 1973

last	this		
1	1	DON'T SHOOT ME I'M ONLY THE PIANO PLAYER	Elton John (DJM)
2	2	MOVING WAVES	Focus (Polydor)
-	3	BILLION DOLLAR BABIES	Alice Cooper (Warner Bros.)
4	4	NO SECRETS	Carly Simon (Elektra)
3	5	BURSTING AT THE SEAMS	Strawbs (A&M)
8	6	THE SIX WIVES OF HENRY VIII	Rick Wakeman (A&M)
5	7	SLAYED	Slade (Polydor)
6	8	ROCK ME BABY	David Cassidy (Bell)
12	9	FOCUS 3	Focus (Polydor)
7	10	BACK TO FRONT	Gilbert O'Sullivan (MAM)
15	11	A CLOCKWORK ORANGE	Soundtrack (Warner Bros.)
9	12	WHO DO YOU THINK WE ARE	Deep Purple (Purple)
11	13	PILEDRIVER	Status Quo (Vertigo)
14	14	BLUEPRINT	Rory Gallagher (Polydor)
10	15	SIMON & GARFUNKEL'S GREATEST HITS	Simon & Garfunkel (CBS)
22	16	ALOHA FROM HAWAII VIA SATELLITE	Elvis Presley (RCA)
26	17	PORTRAIT OF DONNY	Donny Osmond (MGM)
16	18	TALKING BOOK	Stevie Wonder (Tamla Motown)
19	19	THE RISE AND FALL OF ZIGGY STARDUST AND THE SPIDERS FROM MARS	David Bowie (RCA)
13	20	THE STRAUSS FAMILY	Cyril Ornadel & the London Symphony Orchestra (Polydor)
18	21	HOT AUGUST NIGHT	Neil Diamond (Uni)
17	22	CATCH BULL AT FOUR	Cat Stevens (Island)
21	23	HOLLAND	Beach Boys (Reprise)
-	24	20 FLASHBACK GREATS OF THE 60s	Various Artists (K-Tel)
27	25	NEVER A DULL MOMENT	Rod Stewart (Mercury)
25	26	BRIDGE OVER TROUBLED WATER	Simon & Garfunkel (CBS)
-	27	COSMIC WHEELS	Donovan (Epic)
-	28	CRAZY HORSES	Osmonds (MGM)
24	29	JAMES LAST IN RUSSIA	James Last (Polydor)
23	30	HEARTBREAKER	Free (Island)

24 March 1973

last	this		
1	1	DON'T SHOOT ME I'M ONLY THE PIANO PLAYER	Elton John (DJM)
2	2	MOVING WAVES	Focus (Polydor)
3	3	BILLION DOLLAR BABIES	Alice Cooper (Warner Bros.)
-	4	THE DARK SIDE OF THE MOON	Pink Floyd (Harvest)
7	5	SLAYED	Slade (Polydor)
5	6	BURSTING AT THE SEAMS	Strawbs (A&M)
-	7	TANX	T. Rex (T. Rex)
15	8	SIMON & GARFUNKEL'S GREATEST HITS	Simon & Garfunkel (CBS)
10	9	BACK TO FRONT	Gilbert O'Sullivan (MAM)
8	10	ROCK ME BABY	David Cassidy (Bell)
12	11	WHO DO YOU THINK WE ARE	Deep Purple (Purple)
24	12	20 FLASHBACK GREATS OF THE 60s	Various Artists (K-Tel)
11	13	A CLOCKWORK ORANGE	Soundtrack (Warner Bros.)
9	14	FOCUS 3	Focus (Polydor)
6	15	THE SIX WIVES OF HENRY VIII	Rick Wakeman (A&M)
4	16	NO SECRETS	Carly Simon (Elektra)
13	17	PILEDRIVER	Status Quo (Vertigo)
20	18	THE STRAUSS FAMILY	Cyril Ornadel & the London Symphony Orchestra (Polydor)
14	19	BLUEPRINT	Rory Gallagher (Polydor)
17	20	PORTRAIT OF DONNY	Donny Osmond (MGM)
16	21	ALOHA FROM HAWAII VIA SATELLITE	Elvis Presley (RCA)
-	22	TOO YOUNG	Donny Osmond (MGM)
26	23	BRIDGE OVER TROUBLED WATER	Simon & Garfunkel (CBS)
25	24	NEVER A DULL MOMENT	Rod Stewart (Mercury)
21	25	HOT AUGUST NIGHT	Neil Diamond (Uni)
22	26	CATCH BULL AT FOUR	Cat Stevens (Island)
23	27	HOLLAND	Beach Boys (Reprise)
-	28	SEVENTH SOJOURN	Moody Blues (Threshold)
29	29	JAMES LAST IN RUSSIA	James Last (Polydor)
30	30	HEARTBREAKER	Free (Island)

Elvis' *Aloha From Hawaii* was in the 9-day wonder of quadrophonic sound. Elton John's No.1 was his eighth LP, and his last before the bloating effects of superstardom disfigured his work. Though it offered the fatuous *Crocodile Rock*, there was also *Daniel* and *High Flying Bird*. Next would come double-LP *Goodbye Yellowbrick Road*, *Caribou* and the desperately-titled, lavish *Captain Fantastic And The Brown Dirt Cowboy*. By 1976 John's sales would account for 2% of all record sales worldwide.

last week	this week	31 March 1973
3	1	BILLION DOLLAR BABIES — Alice Cooper (Warner Bros.)
1	2	DON'T SHOOT ME I'M ONLY THE PIANO PLAYER — Elton John (DJM)
4	3	THE DARK SIDE OF THE MOON — Pink Floyd (Harvest)
7	4	TANX — T. Rex (T. Rex)
10	5	ROCK ME BABY — David Cassidy (Bell)
12	6	20 FLASHBACK GREATS OF THE 60s — Various Artists (K-Tel)
2	7	MOVING WAVES — Focus (Polydor)
6	8	BURSTING AT THE SEAMS — Strawbs (A&M)
5	9	SLAYED — Slade (Polydor)
8	10	SIMON & GARFUNKEL'S GREATEST HITS — Simon & Garfunkel (CBS)
9	11	BACK TO FRONT — Gilbert O'Sullivan (MAM)
13	12	A CLOCKWORK ORANGE — Soundtrack (Warner Bros.)
-	13	40 FANTASTIC HITS OF THE 50s AND 60s — Various Artists (Arcade)
11	14	WHO DO YOU THINK WE ARE — Deep Purple (Purple)
15	15	THE SIX WIVES OF HENRY VIII — Rick Wakeman (A&M)
-	15	FOR YOUR PLEASURE — Roxy Music (Island)
19	17	BLUEPRINT — Rory Gallagher (Polydor)
16	18	NO SECRETS — Carly Simon (Elektra)
14	19	FOCUS 3 — Focus (Polydor)
-	20	COSMIC WHEELS — Donovan (Epic)
17	21	PILEDRIVER — Status Quo (Vertigo)
27	22	HOLLAND — Beach Boys (Reprise)
20	23	PORTRAIT OF DONNY — Donny Osmond (MGM)
24	24	NEVER A DULL MOMENT — Rod Stewart (Mercury)
25	25	HOT AUGUST NIGHT — Neil Diamond (Uni)
-	26	THE RISE AND FALL OF ZIGGY STARDUST AND THE SPIDERS FROM MARS — David Bowie (RCA)
-	27	ELO 2 — Electric Light Orchestra (Harvest)
29	28	JAMES LAST IN RUSSIA — James Last (Polydor)
23	29	BRIDGE OVER TROUBLED WATER — Simon & Garfunkel (CBS)
26	29	CATCH BULL AT FOUR — Cat Stevens (Island)

last week	this week	7 April 1973
3	1	THE DARK SIDE OF THE MOON — Pink Floyd (Harvest)
4	2	TANX — T. Rex (T. Rex)
2	3	DON'T SHOOT ME I'M ONLY THE PIANO PLAYER — Elton John (DJM)
1	4	BILLION DOLLAR BABIES — Alice Cooper (Warner Bros.)
-	5	HOUSES OF THE HOLY — Led Zeppelin (Atlantic)
6	6	20 FLASHBACK GREATS OF THE 60s — Various Artists (K-Tel)
15	7	FOR YOUR PLEASURE — Roxy Music (Island)
18	8	NO SECRETS — Carly Simon (Elektra)
11	9	BACK TO FRONT — Gilbert O'Sullivan (MAM)
13	10	40 FANTASTIC HITS OF THE 50s AND 60s — Various Artists (Arcade)
9	11	SLAYED — Slade (Polydor)
12	12	A CLOCKWORK ORANGE — Soundtrack (Warner Bros.)
10	13	SIMON & GARFUNKEL'S GREATEST HITS — Simon & Garfunkel (CBS)
7	14	MOVING WAVES — Focus (Polydor)
8	15	BURSTING AT THE SEAMS — Strawbs (A&M)
5	16	ROCK ME BABY — David Cassidy (Bell)
17	17	BLUEPRINT — Rory Gallagher (Polydor)
14	18	WHO DO YOU THINK WE ARE — Deep Purple (Purple)
23	19	PORTRAIT OF DONNY — Donny Osmond (MGM)
24	20	NEVER A DULL MOMENT — Rod Stewart (Mercury)
29	21	BRIDGE OVER TROUBLED WATER — Simon & Garfunkel (CBS)
26	22	THE RISE AND FALL OF ZIGGY STARDUST AND THE SPIDERS FROM MARS — David Bowie (RCA)
15	23	THE SIX WIVES OF HENRY VIII — Rick Wakeman (A&M)
20	23	COSMIC WHEELS — Donovan (Epic)
25	25	HOT AUGUST NIGHT — Neil Diamond (Uni)
-	26	EAT IT — Humble Pie (A&M)
-	27	HARVEST — Neil Young (Reprise)
-	28	HOT HITS SEVENTEEN — Various Artists (Music for Pleasure)
-	29	ALOHA FROM HAWAII VIA SATELLITE — Elvis Presley (RCA)
21	30	PILEDRIVER — Status Quo (Vertigo)

last week	this week	14 April 1973
3	1	DON'T SHOOT ME I'M ONLY THE PIANO PLAYER — Elton John (DJM)
4	2	BILLION DOLLAR BABIES — Alice Cooper (Warner Bros.)
7	3	FOR YOUR PLEASURE — Roxy Music (Island)
1	4	THE DARK SIDE OF THE MOON — Pink Floyd (Harvest)
5	5	HOUSES OF THE HOLY — Led Zeppelin (Atlantic)
2	6	TANX — T. Rex (T. Rex)
6	7	20 FLASHBACK GREATS OF THE 60s — Various Artists (K-Tel)
9	8	BACK TO FRONT — Gilbert O'Sullivan (MAM)
-	9	OOH LA LA — Faces (Warner Bros.)
12	10	A CLOCKWORK ORANGE — Soundtrack (Warner Bros.)
10	11	40 FANTASTIC HITS OF THE 50s AND 60s — Various Artists (Arcade)
16	12	ROCK ME BABY — David Cassidy (Bell)
11	13	SLAYED — Slade (Polydor)
13	14	SIMON & GARFUNKEL'S GREATEST HITS — Simon & Garfunkel (CBS)
14	14	MOVING WAVES — Focus (Polydor)
8	16	NO SECRETS — Carly Simon (Elektra)
-	17	TOGETHER — Jack Jones (RCA)
15	18	BURSTING AT THE SEAMS — Strawbs (A&M)
30	19	PILEDRIVER — Status Quo (Vertigo)
19	20	PORTRAIT OF DONNY — Donny Osmond (MGM)
-	21	LIZA WITH A Z — Liza Minnelli (CBS)
23	22	THE SIX WIVES OF HENRY VIII — Rick Wakeman (A&M)
-	23	FOCUS 3 — Focus (Polydor)
18	24	WHO DO YOU THINK WE ARE — Deep Purple (Purple)
23	25	COSMIC WHEELS — Donovan (Epic)
-	26	BIRDS OF FIRE — Mahavishnu Orchestra (CBS)
-	27	TOO YOUNG — Donny Osmond (MGM)
17	28	BLUEPRINT — Rory Gallagher (Polydor)
25	29	HOT AUGUST NIGHT — Neil Diamond (Uni)
-	30	TALKING BOOK — Stevie Wonder (Tamla Motown)

last week	this week	21 April 1973
5	1	HOUSES OF THE HOLY — Led Zeppelin (Atlantic)
3	2	FOR YOUR PLEASURE — Roxy Music (Island)
2	3	BILLION DOLLAR BABIES — Alice Cooper (Warner Bros.)
1	4	DON'T SHOOT ME I'M ONLY THE PIANO PLAYER — Elton John (DJM)
9	5	OOH LA LA — Faces (Warner Bros.)
4	6	THE DARK SIDE OF THE MOON — Pink Floyd (Harvest)
10	7	A CLOCKWORK ORANGE — Soundtrack (Warner Bros.)
6	8	TANX — T. Rex (T. Rex)
8	9	BACK TO FRONT — Gilbert O'Sullivan (MAM)
11	10	40 FANTASTIC HITS OF THE 50s AND 60s — Various Artists (Arcade)
7	11	20 FLASHBACK GREATS OF THE 60s — Various Artists (K-Tel)
13	12	SLAYED — Slade (Polydor)
-	13	BELIEVE IN MUSIC — Various Artists (K-Tel)
12	14	ROCK ME BABY — David Cassidy (Bell)
14	15	SIMON & GARFUNKEL'S GREATEST HITS — Simon & Garfunkel (CBS)
16	16	NO SECRETS — Carly Simon (Elektra)
21	17	LIZA WITH A Z — Liza Minnelli (CBS)
14	18	MOVING WAVES — Focus (Polydor)
17	19	TOGETHER — Jack Jones (RCA)
18	20	BURSTING AT THE SEAMS — Strawbs (A&M)
29	21	HOT AUGUST NIGHT — Neil Diamond (Uni)
22	22	THE SIX WIVES OF HENRY VIII — Rick Wakeman (A&M)
-	23	LARKS' TONGUES IN ASPIC — King Crimson (Island)
25	24	COSMIC WHEELS — Donovan (Epic)
19	25	PILEDRIVER — Status Quo (Vertigo)
-	26	HIMSELF — Gilbert O'Sullivan (MAM)
30	27	TALKING BOOK — Stevie Wonder (Tamla Motown)
23	28	FOCUS 3 — Focus (Polydor)
-	28	BECK, BOGERT & APPICE — Jeff Beck, Tim Bogert & Carmine Appice (Epic)
27	30	TOO YOUNG — Donny Osmond (MGM)

Atlantic Records held a 25th Anniversary weekend in Paris – a lavish get-together of 500 salesmen and their wives from across the USA ("rack-jobbers from Kansas", as the music-writers sniffily said) plus execs, PR and press. Everyone was given a pink sampler-cassette of Atlantic's forthcoming "product". The music-press muttered darkly about how white the label had become. As the UK chart of the time shows, Atlantic acts included Led Zeppelin, whose *Houses Of The Holy* reached No.1 the next weekend.

April – May 1973

28 April 1973

Last	This	Title	Artist (Label)
5	1	OOH LA LA	Faces (Warner Bros.)
1	2	HOUSES OF THE HOLY	Led Zeppelin (Atlantic)
3	3	BILLION DOLLAR BABIES	Alice Cooper (Warner Bros.)
2	4	FOR YOUR PLEASURE	Roxy Music (Island)
6	5	THE DARK SIDE OF THE MOON	Pink Floyd (Harvest)
-	6	ALADDIN SANE	David Bowie (RCA)
9	7	BACK TO FRONT	Gilbert O'Sullivan (MAM)
4	8	DON'T SHOOT ME I'M ONLY THE PIANO PLAYER	Elton John (DJM)
7	9	A CLOCKWORK ORANGE	Soundtrack (Warner Bros.)
8	10	TANX	T. Rex (T. Rex)
11	11	20 FLASHBACK GREATS OF THE 60s	Various Artists (K-Tel)
10	12	40 FANTASTIC HITS OF THE 50s AND 60s	Various Artists (Arcade)
13	13	BELIEVE IN MUSIC	Various Artists (K-Tel)
14	14	ROCK ME BABY	David Cassidy (Bell)
15	15	SIMON & GARFUNKEL'S GREATEST HITS	Simon & Garfunkel (CBS)
16	16	NO SECRETS	Carly Simon (Elektra)
-	17	THE BEATLES 1962-1966	Beatles (Apple)
24	18	COSMIC WHEELS	Donovan (Epic)
22	19	THE SIX WIVES OF HENRY VIII	Rick Wakeman (A&M)
12	20	SLAYED	Slade (Polydor)
17	21	LIZA WITH A Z	Liza Minnelli (CBS)
-	21	20 FANTASTIC HITS VOL 3	Various Artists (Arcade)
26	23	HIMSELF	Gilbert O'Sullivan (MAM)
21	24	HOT AUGUST NIGHT	Neil Diamond (Uni)
18	25	MOVING WAVES	Focus (Polydor)
27	26	TALKING BOOK	Stevie Wonder (Tamla Motown)
-	27	THE BEATLES 1967-1970	Beatles (Apple)
28	28	FOCUS 3	Focus (Polydor)
-	29	BLUEPRINT	Rory Gallagher (Polydor)
-	30	BRIDGE OVER TROUBLED WATER	Simon & Garfunkel (CBS)

5 May 1973

Last	This	Title	Artist (Label)
6	1	ALADDIN SANE	David Bowie (RCA)
1	2	OOH LA LA	Faces (Warner Bros.)
3	3	BILLION DOLLAR BABIES	Alice Cooper (Warner Bros.)
2	4	HOUSES OF THE HOLY	Led Zeppelin (Atlantic)
5	5	THE DARK SIDE OF THE MOON	Pink Floyd (Harvest)
7	6	BACK TO FRONT	Gilbert O'Sullivan (MAM)
12	7	40 FANTASTIC HITS OF THE 50s AND 60s	Various Artists (Arcade)
4	8	FOR YOUR PLEASURE	Roxy Music (Island)
8	9	DON'T SHOOT ME I'M ONLY THE PIANO PLAYER	Elton John (DJM)
21	10	20 FANTASTIC HITS VOL 3	Various Artists (Arcade)
10	11	TANX	T. Rex (T. Rex)
11	12	20 FLASHBACK GREATS OF THE 60s	Various Artists (K-Tel)
13	13	BELIEVE IN MUSIC	Various Artists (K-Tel)
14	14	ROCK ME BABY	David Cassidy (Bell)
17	15	THE BEATLES 1962-1966	Beatles (Apple)
27	16	THE BEATLES 1967-1970	Beatles (Apple)
20	17	SLAYED	Slade (Polydor)
-	18	TOGETHER	Jack Jones (RCA)
9	19	A CLOCKWORK ORANGE	Soundtrack (Warner Bros.)
-	20	PORTRAIT OF DONNY	Donny Osmond (MGM)
-	21	PILEDRIVER	Status Quo (Vertigo)
15	22	SIMON & GARFUNKEL'S GREATEST HITS	Simon & Garfunkel (CBS)
18	23	COSMIC WHEELS	Donovan (Epic)
25	24	MOVING WAVES	Focus (Polydor)
26	25	TALKING BOOK	Stevie Wonder (Tamla Motown)
16	26	NO SECRETS	Carly Simon (Elektra)
28	27	FOCUS 3	Focus (Polydor)
23	28	HIMSELF	Gilbert O'Sullivan (MAM)
30	29	BRIDGE OVER TROUBLED WATER	Simon & Garfunkel (CBS)
21	30	LIZA WITH A Z	Liza Minnelli (CBS)

12 May 1973

Last	This	Title	Artist (Label)
1	1	ALADDIN SANE	David Bowie (RCA)
16	2	THE BEATLES 1967-1970	Beatles (Apple)
15	3	THE BEATLES 1962-1966	Beatles (Apple)
2	4	OOH LA LA	Faces (Warner Bros.)
3	5	BILLION DOLLAR BABIES	Alice Cooper (Warner Bros.)
4	6	HOUSES OF THE HOLY	Led Zeppelin (Atlantic)
5	7	THE DARK SIDE OF THE MOON	Pink Floyd (Harvest)
6	8	BACK TO FRONT	Gilbert O'Sullivan (MAM)
8	9	FOR YOUR PLEASURE	Roxy Music (Island)
9	10	DON'T SHOOT ME I'M ONLY THE PIANO PLAYER	Elton John (DJM)
13	11	BELIEVE IN MUSIC	Various Artists (K-Tel)
26	12	NO SECRETS	Carly Simon (Elektra)
7	13	40 FANTASTIC HITS OF THE 50s AND 60s	Various Artists (Arcade)
-	14	SINGALONGAMAX	Max Bygraves (Pye)
10	15	20 FANTASTIC HITS VOL 3	Various Artists (Arcade)
-	16	CABARET	Soundtrack (Probe)
-	17	RED ROSE SPEEDWAY	Paul McCartney & Wings (Apple)
22	18	SIMON & GARFUNKEL'S GREATEST HITS	Simon & Garfunkel (CBS)
12	19	20 FLASHBACK GREATS OF THE 60s	Various Artists (K-Tel)
11	20	TANX	T. Rex (T. Rex)
19	21	A CLOCKWORK ORANGE	Soundtrack (Warner Bros.)
14	22	ROCK ME BABY	David Cassidy (Bell)
20	23	PORTRAIT OF DONNY	Donny Osmond (MGM)
30	24	LIZA WITH A Z	Liza Minnelli (CBS)
17	25	SLAYED	Slade (Polydor)
29	26	BRIDGE OVER TROUBLED WATER	Simon & Garfunkel (CBS)
-	27	CATCH BULL AT FOUR	Cat Stevens (Island)
21	28	PILEDRIVER	Status Quo (Vertigo)
-	29	TRANSFORMER	Lou Reed (RCA)
-	30	THE SIX WIVES OF HENRY VIII	Rick Wakeman (A&M)

19 May 1973

Last	This	Title	Artist (Label)
2	1	THE BEATLES 1967-1970	Beatles (Apple)
1	2	ALADDIN SANE	David Bowie (RCA)
3	3	THE BEATLES 1962-1966	Beatles (Apple)
6	4	HOUSES OF THE HOLY	Led Zeppelin (Atlantic)
4	5	OOH LA LA	Faces (Warner Bros.)
5	6	BILLION DOLLAR BABIES	Alice Cooper (Warner Bros.)
7	7	THE DARK SIDE OF THE MOON	Pink Floyd (Harvest)
9	8	FOR YOUR PLEASURE	Roxy Music (Island)
17	9	RED ROSE SPEEDWAY	Paul McCartney & Wings (Apple)
8	10	BACK TO FRONT	Gilbert O'Sullivan (MAM)
-	11	YESSONGS	Yes (Atlantic)
24	12	LIZA WITH A Z	Liza Minnelli (CBS)
14	13	SINGALONGAMAX	Max Bygraves (Pye)
16	14	CABARET	Soundtrack (Probe)
-	15	DALTREY	Roger Daltrey (Track)
12	16	NO SECRETS	Carly Simon (Elektra)
11	17	BELIEVE IN MUSIC	Various Artists (K-Tel)
18	18	SIMON & GARFUNKEL'S GREATEST HITS	Simon & Garfunkel (CBS)
15	19	20 FANTASTIC HITS VOL 3	Various Artists (Arcade)
10	20	DON'T SHOOT ME I'M ONLY THE PIANO PLAYER	Elton John (DJM)
-	21	ALONE TOGETHER	Donny Osmond (MGM)
13	22	40 FANTASTIC HITS OF THE 50s AND 60s	Various Artists (Arcade)
21	23	A CLOCKWORK ORANGE	Soundtrack (Warner Bros.)
20	24	TANX	T. Rex (T. Rex)
29	25	TRANSFORMER	Lou Reed (RCA)
22	26	ROCK ME BABY	David Cassidy (Bell)
-	27	FOCUS 3	Focus (Polydor)
-	28	URIAH HEEP LIVE	Uriah Heep (Bronze)
28	29	PILEDRIVER	Status Quo (Vertigo)
-	30	COSMIC WHEELS	Donovan (Epic)

Bowie's *Aladdin Sane* would twice be knocked off the No.1 slot in the coming weeks, and would twice regain it. The records that displaced him were *The Beatles 1967-1970* and *The Beatles 1962-1966*. These simultaneous releases leapt up the chart in parallel (27 and 17, 16 and 15, 2 and 3, 1 and 3, 2 and 3, 2 and 3, 2 and 1) and each topped the chart during May and June. Containing singles and other selected tracks, they would each remain in the Top 50 for more than two years.

last week	this week	26 May 1973
2	1	ALADDIN SANE David Bowie (RCA)
1	2	THE BEATLES 1967-1970 Beatles (Apple)
3	3	THE BEATLES 1962-1966 Beatles (Apple)
9	4	RED ROSE SPEEDWAY Paul McCartney & Wings (Apple)
7	5	THE DARK SIDE OF THE MOON Pink Floyd (Harvest)
5	6	OOH LA LA Faces (Warner Bros.)
11	7	YESSONGS Yes (Atlantic)
8	8	FOR YOUR PLEASURE Roxy Music (Island)
4	9	HOUSES OF THE HOLY Led Zeppelin (Atlantic)
6	10	BILLION DOLLAR BABIES Alice Cooper (Warner Bros.)
10	11	BACK TO FRONT Gilbert O'Sullivan (MAM)
14	12	CABARET Soundtrack (Probe)
13	13	SINGALONGAMAX Max Bygraves (Pye)
12	14	LIZA WITH A Z Liza Minnelli (CBS)
15	15	DALTREY Roger Daltrey (Track)
25	16	TRANSFORMER Lou Reed (RCA)
17	17	BELIEVE IN MUSIC Various Artists (K-Tel)
16	18	NO SECRETS Carly Simon (Elektra)
23	19	A CLOCKWORK ORANGE Soundtrack (Warner Bros.)
18	20	SIMON & GARFUNKEL'S GREATEST HITS Simon & Garfunkel (CBS)
22	21	40 FANTASTIC HITS OF THE 50s AND 60s Various Artists (Arcade)
-	22	THERE GOES RHYMIN' SIMON Paul Simon (CBS)
20	23	DON'T SHOOT ME I'M ONLY THE PIANO PLAYER Elton John (DJM)
21	24	ALONE TOGETHER Donny Osmond (MGM)
28	25	URIAH HEEP LIVE Uriah Heep (Bronze)
-	26	NEVER NEVER NEVER Shirley Bassey (United Artists)
26	27	ROCK ME BABY David Cassidy (Bell)
-	28	SLAYED Slade (Polydor)
30	29	COSMIC WHEELS Donovan (Epic)
-	30	SONGS FROM HER TV SERIES Nana Mouskouri (Philips)

last week	this week	2 June 1973
1	1	ALADDIN SANE David Bowie (RCA)
2	2	THE BEATLES 1967-1970 Beatles (Apple)
3	3	THE BEATLES 1962-1966 Beatles (Apple)
5	4	THE DARK SIDE OF THE MOON Pink Floyd (Harvest)
4	5	RED ROSE SPEEDWAY Paul McCartney & Wings (Apple)
-	6	20 FANTASTIC HITS VOL 3 Various Artists (Arcade)
7	7	YESSONGS Yes (Atlantic)
-	8	PURE GOLD Various Artists (EMI)
14	9	LIZA WITH A Z Liza Minnelli (CBS)
10	10	BILLION DOLLAR BABIES Alice Cooper (Warner Bros.)
15	11	DALTREY Roger Daltrey (Track)
12	12	CABARET Soundtrack (Probe)
11	13	BACK TO FRONT Gilbert O'Sullivan (MAM)
-	14	20 ORIGINAL CHART HITS Various Artists (Philips)
-	15	WISHBONE 4 Wishbone Ash (MCA)
19	16	A CLOCKWORK ORANGE Soundtrack (Warner Bros.)
-	17	THAT'LL BE THE DAY - SOUNDTRACK Various Artists (Ronco)
9	18	HOUSES OF THE HOLY Led Zeppelin (Atlantic)
16	19	TRANSFORMER Lou Reed (RCA)
17	20	BELIEVE IN MUSIC Various Artists (K-Tel)
18	21	NO SECRETS Carly Simon (Elektra)
8	22	FOR YOUR PLEASURE Roxy Music (Island)
6	23	OOH LA LA Faces (Warner Bros.)
21	24	40 FANTASTIC HITS OF THE 50s AND 60s Various Artists (Arcade)
24	25	ALONE TOGETHER Donny Osmond (MGM)
-	26	ROCKY MOUNTAIN HIGH John Denver (RCA)
22	27	THERE GOES RHYMIN' SIMON Paul Simon (CBS)
13	28	SINGALONGAMAX Max Bygraves (Pye)
29	29	COSMIC WHEELS Donovan (Epic)
25	30	URIAH HEEP LIVE Uriah Heep (Bronze)

last week	this week	9 June 1973
3	1	THE BEATLES 1962-1966 Beatles (Apple)
2	2	THE BEATLES 1967-1970 Beatles (Apple)
1	3	ALADDIN SANE David Bowie (RCA)
5	4	RED ROSE SPEEDWAY Paul McCartney & Wings (Apple)
8	5	PURE GOLD Various Artists (EMI)
4	6	THE DARK SIDE OF THE MOON Pink Floyd (Harvest)
-	7	TOUCH ME Gary Glitter (Bell)
15	8	WISHBONE 4 Wishbone Ash (MCA)
7	9	YESSONGS Yes (Atlantic)
27	10	THERE GOES RHYMIN' SIMON Paul Simon (CBS)
6	11	20 FANTASTIC HITS VOL 3 Various Artists (Arcade)
9	12	LIZA WITH A Z Liza Minnelli (CBS)
11	13	DALTREY Roger Daltrey (Track)
16	14	A CLOCKWORK ORANGE Soundtrack (Warner Bros.)
13	15	BACK TO FRONT Gilbert O'Sullivan (MAM)
17	16	THAT'LL BE THE DAY - SOUNDTRACK Various Artists (Ronco)
10	17	BILLION DOLLAR BABIES Alice Cooper (Warner Bros.)
25	18	ALONE TOGETHER Donny Osmond (MGM)
-	19	SIMON & GARFUNKEL'S GREATEST HITS Simon & Garfunkel (CBS)
23	20	OOH LA LA Faces (Warner Bros.)
19	21	TRANSFORMER Lou Reed (RCA)
-	22	NEVER NEVER NEVER Shirley Bassey (United Artists)
18	23	HOUSES OF THE HOLY Led Zeppelin (Atlantic)
26	24	ROCKY MOUNTAIN HIGH John Denver (RCA)
30	25	URIAH HEEP LIVE Uriah Heep (Bronze)
-	26	SPACE RITUAL ALIVE Hawkwind (United Artists)
21	27	NO SECRETS Carly Simon (Elektra)
12	28	CABARET Soundtrack (Probe)
22	29	FOR YOUR PLEASURE Roxy Music (Island)
-	30	FAUST TAPES Faust (Virgin)

last week	this week	16 June 1973
3	1	ALADDIN SANE David Bowie (RCA)
5	2	PURE GOLD Various Artists (EMI)
2	3	THE BEATLES 1967-1970 Beatles (Apple)
1	4	THE BEATLES 1962-1966 Beatles (Apple)
4	5	RED ROSE SPEEDWAY Paul McCartney & Wings (Apple)
6	6	THE DARK SIDE OF THE MOON Pink Floyd (Harvest)
10	7	THERE GOES RHYMIN' SIMON Paul Simon (CBS)
9	8	YESSONGS Yes (Atlantic)
7	9	TOUCH ME Gary Glitter (Bell)
16	10	THAT'LL BE THE DAY - SOUNDTRACK Various Artists (Ronco)
8	11	WISHBONE 4 Wishbone Ash (MCA)
18	12	ALONE TOGETHER Donny Osmond (MGM)
21	13	TRANSFORMER Lou Reed (RCA)
11	14	20 FANTASTIC HITS VOL 3 Various Artists (Arcade)
12	15	LIZA WITH A Z Liza Minnelli (CBS)
13	16	DALTREY Roger Daltrey (Track)
26	17	SPACE RITUAL ALIVE Hawkwind (United Artists)
14	18	A CLOCKWORK ORANGE Soundtrack (Warner Bros.)
-	19	20 ORIGINAL CHART HITS Various Artists (Philips)
24	20	ROCKY MOUNTAIN HIGH John Denver (RCA)
22	21	NEVER NEVER NEVER Shirley Bassey (United Artists)
15	22	BACK TO FRONT Gilbert O'Sullivan (MAM)
28	23	CABARET Soundtrack (Probe)
30	24	FAUST TAPES Faust (Virgin)
19	25	SIMON & GARFUNKEL'S GREATEST HITS Simon & Garfunkel (CBS)
29	26	FOR YOUR PLEASURE Roxy Music (Island)
17	27	BILLION DOLLAR BABIES Alice Cooper (Warner Bros.)
25	28	URIAH HEEP LIVE Uriah Heep (Bronze)
23	29	HOUSES OF THE HOLY Led Zeppelin (Atlantic)
-	30	TALKING BOOK Stevie Wonder (Tamla Motown)

The top rungs of the chart had The Beatles at No.2 and No.3, with Paul McCartney at No.4. In the concurrent singles charts, Paul & Wings were dropping down the Top 20 with *My Love* while George was jumping in with *Give Me Love (Give Me Peace On Earth)*. He would soon rejoin the album chart too, with *Living In The Material World*. Other typically 1973ish acts in the chart included Faust, Uriah Heep, Hawkwind, Lou Reed and John Denver. Donny Osmond and David Cassidy were still there.

June – July 1973

last week	this week	23 June 1973
2	1	PURE GOLD — Various Artists (EMI)
1	2	ALADDIN SANE — David Bowie (RCA)
4	3	THE BEATLES 1962-1966 — Beatles (Apple)
3	4	THE BEATLES 1967-1970 — Beatles (Apple)
7	5	THERE GOES RHYMIN' SIMON — Paul Simon (CBS)
5	6	RED ROSE SPEEDWAY — Paul McCartney & Wings (Apple)
10	7	THAT'LL BE THE DAY - SOUNDTRACK — Various Artists (Ronco)
6	8	THE DARK SIDE OF THE MOON — Pink Floyd (Harvest)
9	9	TOUCH ME — Gary Glitter (Bell)
21	10	NEVER NEVER NEVER — Shirley Bassey (United Artists)
12	11	ALONE TOGETHER — Donny Osmond (MGM)
13	12	TRANSFORMER — Lou Reed (RCA)
16	13	DALTREY — Roger Daltrey (Track)
14	14	20 FANTASTIC HITS VOL 3 — Various Artists (Arcade)
27	15	BILLION DOLLAR BABIES — Alice Cooper (Warner Bros.)
18	16	A CLOCKWORK ORANGE — Soundtrack (Warner Bros.)
8	17	YESSONGS — Yes (Atlantic)
20	18	ROCKY MOUNTAIN HIGH — John Denver (RCA)
11	19	WISHBONE 4 — Wishbone Ash (MCA)
-	20	RAZAMANAZ — Nazareth (Mooncrest)
15	21	LIZA WITH A Z — Liza Minnelli (CBS)
17	22	SPACE RITUAL ALIVE — Hawkwind (United Artists)
25	23	SIMON & GARFUNKEL'S GREATEST HITS — Simon & Garfunkel (CBS)
23	24	CABARET — Soundtrack (Probe)
22	25	BACK TO FRONT — Gilbert O'Sullivan (MAM)
30	26	TALKING BOOK — Stevie Wonder (Tamla Motown)
19	27	20 ORIGINAL CHART HITS — Various Artists (Philips)
-	28	OOH LA LA — Faces (Warner Bros.)
28	29	URIAH HEEP LIVE — Uriah Heep (Bronze)
-	30	40 FANTASTIC HITS OF THE 50s AND 60s — Various Artists (Arcade)

last week	this week	30 June 1973
2	1	ALADDIN SANE — David Bowie (RCA)
4	2	THE BEATLES 1967-1970 — Beatles (Apple)
7	3	THAT'LL BE THE DAY - SOUNDTRACK — Various Artists (Ronco)
3	4	THE BEATLES 1962-1966 — Beatles (Apple)
5	5	THERE GOES RHYMIN' SIMON — Paul Simon (CBS)
1	6	PURE GOLD — Various Artists (EMI)
8	7	THE DARK SIDE OF THE MOON — Pink Floyd (Harvest)
-	8	LIVING IN THE MATERIAL WORLD — George Harrison (Apple)
9	9	TOUCH ME — Gary Glitter (Bell)
6	10	RED ROSE SPEEDWAY — Paul McCartney & Wings (Apple)
16	11	A CLOCKWORK ORANGE — Soundtrack (Warner Bros.)
18	12	ROCKY MOUNTAIN HIGH — John Denver (RCA)
17	13	YESSONGS — Yes (Atlantic)
-	14	MASTERPIECE — Temptations (Tamla Motown)
11	15	ALONE TOGETHER — Donny Osmond (MGM)
27	16	20 ORIGINAL CHART HITS — Various Artists (Philips)
-	17	AND I LOVE YOU SO — Perry Como (RCA)
19	18	WISHBONE 4 — Wishbone Ash (MCA)
15	19	BILLION DOLLAR BABIES — Alice Cooper (Warner Bros.)
22	20	SPACE RITUAL ALIVE — Hawkwind (United Artists)
26	21	TALKING BOOK — Stevie Wonder (Tamla Motown)
14	22	20 FANTASTIC HITS VOL 3 — Various Artists (Arcade)
10	23	NEVER NEVER NEVER — Shirley Bassey (United Artists)
-	24	FOR YOUR PLEASURE — Roxy Music (Island)
24	25	CABARET — Soundtrack (Probe)
12	26	TRANSFORMER — Lou Reed (RCA)
25	27	BACK TO FRONT — Gilbert O'Sullivan (MAM)
23	28	SIMON & GARFUNKEL'S GREATEST HITS — Simon & Garfunkel (CBS)
-	29	FAUST TAPES — Faust (Virgin)
20	30	RAZAMANAZ — Nazareth (Mooncrest)

last week	this week	7 July 1973
1	1	ALADDIN SANE — David Bowie (RCA)
3	2	THAT'LL BE THE DAY - SOUNDTRACK — Various Artists (Ronco)
2	3	THE BEATLES 1967-1970 — Beatles (Apple)
5	4	THERE GOES RHYMIN' SIMON — Paul Simon (CBS)
4	5	THE BEATLES 1962-1966 — Beatles (Apple)
8	6	LIVING IN THE MATERIAL WORLD — George Harrison (Apple)
10	7	RED ROSE SPEEDWAY — Paul McCartney & Wings (Apple)
7	8	THE DARK SIDE OF THE MOON — Pink Floyd (Harvest)
11	9	A CLOCKWORK ORANGE — Soundtrack (Warner Bros.)
9	10	TOUCH ME — Gary Glitter (Bell)
17	11	AND I LOVE YOU SO — Perry Como (RCA)
6	12	PURE GOLD — Various Artists (EMI)
-	13	WE CAN MAKE IT — Peters & Lee (Philips)
28	14	SIMON & GARFUNKEL'S GREATEST HITS — Simon & Garfunkel (CBS)
18	15	WISHBONE 4 — Wishbone Ash (MCA)
27	16	BACK TO FRONT — Gilbert O'Sullivan (MAM)
14	17	MASTERPIECE — Temptations (Tamla Motown)
12	18	ROCKY MOUNTAIN HIGH — John Denver (RCA)
15	19	ALONE TOGETHER — Donny Osmond (MGM)
-	20	NOW AND THEN — Carpenters (A&M)
13	21	YESSONGS — Yes (Atlantic)
26	22	TRANSFORMER — Lou Reed (RCA)
30	23	RAZAMANAZ — Nazareth (Mooncrest)
23	24	NEVER NEVER NEVER — Shirley Bassey (United Artists)
20	25	SPACE RITUAL ALIVE — Hawkwind (United Artists)
29	26	FAUST TAPES — Faust (Virgin)
-	27	HUNKY DORY — David Bowie (RCA)
19	28	BILLION DOLLAR BABIES — Alice Cooper (Warner Bros.)
25	29	CABARET — Soundtrack (Probe)
21	30	TALKING BOOK — Stevie Wonder (Tamla Motown)

last week	this week	14 July 1973
1	1	ALADDIN SANE — David Bowie (RCA)
2	2	THAT'LL BE THE DAY - SOUNDTRACK — Various Artists (Ronco)
11	3	AND I LOVE YOU SO — Perry Como (RCA)
3	4	THE BEATLES 1967-1970 — Beatles (Apple)
4	5	THERE GOES RHYMIN' SIMON — Paul Simon (CBS)
13	6	WE CAN MAKE IT — Peters & Lee (Philips)
5	7	THE BEATLES 1962-1966 — Beatles (Apple)
6	8	LIVING IN THE MATERIAL WORLD — George Harrison (Apple)
8	9	THE DARK SIDE OF THE MOON — Pink Floyd (Harvest)
10	10	TOUCH ME — Gary Glitter (Bell)
20	11	NOW AND THEN — Carpenters (A&M)
27	12	HUNKY DORY — David Bowie (RCA)
9	13	A CLOCKWORK ORANGE — Soundtrack (Warner Bros.)
18	14	ROCKY MOUNTAIN HIGH — John Denver (RCA)
14	15	SIMON & GARFUNKEL'S GREATEST HITS — Simon & Garfunkel (CBS)
7	16	RED ROSE SPEEDWAY — Paul McCartney & Wings (Apple)
19	17	ALONE TOGETHER — Donny Osmond (MGM)
26	18	FAUST TAPES — Faust (Virgin)
-	19	FOREIGNER — Cat Stevens (Island)
21	20	YESSONGS — Yes (Atlantic)
24	21	NEVER NEVER NEVER — Shirley Bassey (United Artists)
12	22	PURE GOLD — Various Artists (EMI)
16	23	BACK TO FRONT — Gilbert O'Sullivan (MAM)
15	24	WISHBONE 4 — Wishbone Ash (MCA)
-	25	BRIDGE OVER TROUBLED WATER — Simon & Garfunkel (CBS)
25	26	SPACE RITUAL ALIVE — Hawkwind (United Artists)
-	27	LIZA WITH A Z — Liza Minnelli (CBS)
23	28	RAZAMANAZ — Nazareth (Mooncrest)
30	29	TALKING BOOK — Stevie Wonder (Tamla Motown)
22	30	TRANSFORMER — Lou Reed (RCA)

With *Aladdin Sane* back on top, Bowie's earlier album *Hunky Dory* began a climb up the chart. Mid-August would find both in the Top 5. *That'll Be The Day* was the soundtrack album from a surprisingly successful film starring ex-Godspell actor David Essex as a fairground lad, and featuring Rosemary Leach and Ringo Starr. A follow-up, *Stardust*, more lavish but less convincing, starred David Essex again. His debut in the singles chart would be in August, with *Rock On*, a No.1 for a week in September.

July – August 1973

21 July 1973

last	this	Title / Artist
6	1	WE CAN MAKE IT — Peters & Lee (Philips)
1	2	ALADDIN SANE — David Bowie (RCA)
2	3	THAT'LL BE THE DAY - SOUNDTRACK — Various Artists (Ronco)
5	4	THERE GOES RHYMIN' SIMON — Paul Simon (CBS)
8	5	LIVING IN THE MATERIAL WORLD — George Harrison (Apple)
4	6	THE BEATLES 1967-1970 — Beatles (Apple)
3	7	AND I LOVE YOU SO — Perry Como (RCA)
7	8	THE BEATLES 1962-1966 — Beatles (Apple)
9	9	THE DARK SIDE OF THE MOON — Pink Floyd (Harvest)
12	10	HUNKY DORY — David Bowie (RCA)
19	11	FOREIGNER — Cat Stevens (Island)
10	12	TOUCH ME — Gary Glitter (Bell)
11	13	NOW AND THEN — Carpenters (A&M)
16	14	RED ROSE SPEEDWAY — Paul McCartney & Wings (Apple)
13	15	A CLOCKWORK ORANGE — Soundtrack (Warner Bros.)
15	16	SIMON & GARFUNKEL'S GREATEST HITS — Simon & Garfunkel (CBS)
18	17	FAUST TAPES — Faust (Virgin)
-	18	THE RISE AND FALL OF ZIGGY STARDUST AND THE SPIDERS FROM MARS — David Bowie (RCA)
17	19	ALONE TOGETHER — Donny Osmond (MGM)
20	20	YESSONGS — Yes (Atlantic)
-	21	TUBULAR BELLS — Mike Oldfield (Virgin)
22	22	PURE GOLD — Various Artists (EMI)
21	23	NEVER NEVER NEVER — Shirley Bassey (United Artists)
23	24	BACK TO FRONT — Gilbert O'Sullivan (MAM)
-	25	LOVE DEVOTION SURRENDER — Carlos Santana & Mahavishnu John McLaughlin (CBS)
25	26	BRIDGE OVER TROUBLED WATER — Simon & Garfunkel (CBS)
14	27	ROCKY MOUNTAIN HIGH — John Denver (RCA)
30	28	TRANSFORMER — Lou Reed (RCA)
-	29	A PASSION PLAY — Jethro Tull (Chrysalis)
-	30	20 ORIGINAL CHART HITS — Various Artists (Philips)

28 July 1973

last	this	Title / Artist
2	1	ALADDIN SANE — David Bowie (RCA)
1	2	WE CAN MAKE IT — Peters & Lee (Philips)
5	3	LIVING IN THE MATERIAL WORLD — George Harrison (Apple)
3	4	THAT'LL BE THE DAY - SOUNDTRACK — Various Artists (Ronco)
6	5	THE BEATLES 1967-1970 — Beatles (Apple)
11	6	FOREIGNER — Cat Stevens (Island)
4	7	THERE GOES RHYMIN' SIMON — Paul Simon (CBS)
7	8	AND I LOVE YOU SO — Perry Como (RCA)
8	9	THE BEATLES 1962-1966 — Beatles (Apple)
13	10	NOW AND THEN — Carpenters (A&M)
9	11	THE DARK SIDE OF THE MOON — Pink Floyd (Harvest)
10	12	HUNKY DORY — David Bowie (RCA)
12	13	TOUCH ME — Gary Glitter (Bell)
15	14	A CLOCKWORK ORANGE — Soundtrack (Warner Bros.)
19	15	ALONE TOGETHER — Donny Osmond (MGM)
14	16	RED ROSE SPEEDWAY — Paul McCartney & Wings (Apple)
29	17	A PASSION PLAY — Jethro Tull (Chrysalis)
25	18	LOVE DEVOTION SURRENDER — Carlos Santana & Mahavishnu John McLaughlin (CBS)
21	19	TUBULAR BELLS — Mike Oldfield (Virgin)
30	20	20 ORIGINAL CHART HITS — Various Artists (Philips)
18	21	THE RISE AND FALL OF ZIGGY STARDUST AND THE SPIDERS FROM MARS — David Bowie (RCA)
24	22	BACK TO FRONT — Gilbert O'Sullivan (MAM)
16	23	SIMON & GARFUNKEL'S GREATEST HITS — Simon & Garfunkel (CBS)
-	24	MY MERRY GO ROUND — Johnny Nash (CBS)
-	25	SCHOOL DAYS — Alice Cooper (Warner Bros.)
20	26	YESSONGS — Yes (Atlantic)
17	27	FAUST TAPES — Faust (Virgin)
22	28	PURE GOLD — Various Artists (EMI)
-	29	FANTASY — Carole King (Ode)
23	30	NEVER NEVER NEVER — Shirley Bassey (United Artists)

4 August 1973

last	this	Title / Artist
2	1	WE CAN MAKE IT — Peters & Lee (Philips)
1	2	ALADDIN SANE — David Bowie (RCA)
4	3	THAT'LL BE THE DAY - SOUNDTRACK — Various Artists (Ronco)
6	4	FOREIGNER — Cat Stevens (Island)
5	5	THE BEATLES 1967-1970 — Beatles (Apple)
10	6	NOW AND THEN — Carpenters (A&M)
3	7	LIVING IN THE MATERIAL WORLD — George Harrison (Apple)
7	8	THERE GOES RHYMIN' SIMON — Paul Simon (CBS)
12	9	HUNKY DORY — David Bowie (RCA)
9	10	THE BEATLES 1962-1966 — Beatles (Apple)
11	11	THE DARK SIDE OF THE MOON — Pink Floyd (Harvest)
8	12	AND I LOVE YOU SO — Perry Como (RCA)
18	13	LOVE DEVOTION SURRENDER — Carlos Santana & Mahavishnu John McLaughlin (CBS)
14	14	A CLOCKWORK ORANGE — Soundtrack (Warner Bros.)
13	15	TOUCH ME — Gary Glitter (Bell)
23	16	SIMON & GARFUNKEL'S GREATEST HITS — Simon & Garfunkel (CBS)
16	17	RED ROSE SPEEDWAY — Paul McCartney & Wings (Apple)
17	18	A PASSION PLAY — Jethro Tull (Chrysalis)
19	19	TUBULAR BELLS — Mike Oldfield (Virgin)
-	20	MOTT — Mott the Hoople (CBS)
-	21	FOR YOUR PLEASURE — Roxy Music (Island)
25	22	SCHOOL DAYS — Alice Cooper (Warner Bros.)
-	23	HARD NOSE THE HIGHWAY — Van Morrison (Warner Bros.)
-	24	A LITTLE TOUCH OF SCHMILSSON IN THE NIGHT — Nilsson (RCA)
21	25	THE RISE AND FALL OF ZIGGY STARDUST AND THE SPIDERS FROM MARS — David Bowie (RCA)
22	26	BACK TO FRONT — Gilbert O'Sullivan (MAM)
-	27	PIPEDREAM — Alan Hull (Charisma)
-	28	GOLDEN GREATS OF THE 60s — Various Artists (K-Tel)
-	29	RECORDED LIVE — Ten Years After (Chrysalis)
-	30	GENESIS LIVE — Genesis (Charisma)

11 August 1973

last	this	Title / Artist
1	1	WE CAN MAKE IT — Peters & Lee (Philips)
3	2	THAT'LL BE THE DAY - SOUNDTRACK — Various Artists (Ronco)
2	3	ALADDIN SANE — David Bowie (RCA)
6	4	NOW AND THEN — Carpenters (A&M)
9	5	HUNKY DORY — David Bowie (RCA)
4	6	FOREIGNER — Cat Stevens (Island)
5	7	THE BEATLES 1967-1970 — Beatles (Apple)
12	8	AND I LOVE YOU SO — Perry Como (RCA)
11	9	THE DARK SIDE OF THE MOON — Pink Floyd (Harvest)
15	10	TOUCH ME — Gary Glitter (Bell)
10	11	THE BEATLES 1962-1966 — Beatles (Apple)
8	12	THERE GOES RHYMIN' SIMON — Paul Simon (CBS)
13	13	LOVE DEVOTION SURRENDER — Carlos Santana & Mahavishnu John McLaughlin (CBS)
16	14	SIMON & GARFUNKEL'S GREATEST HITS — Simon & Garfunkel (CBS)
19	15	TUBULAR BELLS — Mike Oldfield (Virgin)
14	16	A CLOCKWORK ORANGE — Soundtrack (Warner Bros.)
18	17	A PASSION PLAY — Jethro Tull (Chrysalis)
7	18	LIVING IN THE MATERIAL WORLD — George Harrison (Apple)
-	19	RAZAMANAZ — Nazareth (Mooncrest)
22	20	SCHOOL DAYS — Alice Cooper (Warner Bros.)
17	21	RED ROSE SPEEDWAY — Paul McCartney & Wings (Apple)
26	22	BACK TO FRONT — Gilbert O'Sullivan (MAM)
24	23	A LITTLE TOUCH OF SCHMILSSON IN THE NIGHT — Nilsson (RCA)
25	24	THE RISE AND FALL OF ZIGGY STARDUST AND THE SPIDERS FROM MARS — David Bowie (RCA)
-	25	CLOSE TO YOU — Carpenters (A&M)
23	26	HARD NOSE THE HIGHWAY — Van Morrison (Warner Bros.)
-	27	PURE GOLD — Various Artists (EMI)
28	28	FOR YOUR PLEASURE — Roxy Music (Island)
30	29	GENESIS LIVE — Genesis (Charisma)
-	30	SLAYED — Slade (Polydor)

Mike Oldfield's *Tubular Bells* arrived in the chart. It had been a long journey for Oldfield to get it there. Turned down by every record label in Britain, it became the bedrock big seller of Richard Branson's young Virgin label. Another historic entry was the debut, at last, by Van Morrison, whose *Hard Nose The Highway* now succeeded where such albums as *Moondance* (1970) and the great *St.Dominic's Preview* (1972) had failed. Even now, No.23 was as high as Van the Man could manage.

August – September 1973

17 August 1973

last	this		
1	1	WE CAN MAKE IT	Peters & Lee (Philips)
3	2	ALADDIN SANE	David Bowie (RCA)
4	3	NOW AND THEN	Carpenters (A&M)
5	4	HUNKY DORY	David Bowie (RCA)
2	5	THAT'LL BE THE DAY - SOUNDTRACK	Various Artists (Ronco)
6	6	FOREIGNER	Cat Stevens (Island)
7	7	THE BEATLES 1967-1970	Beatles (Apple)
9	8	THE DARK SIDE OF THE MOON	Pink Floyd (Harvest)
11	9	THE BEATLES 1962-1966	Beatles (Apple)
-	10	SING IT AGAIN ROD	Rod Stewart (Mercury)
8	11	AND I LOVE YOU SO	Perry Como (RCA)
13	12	LOVE DEVOTION SURRENDER	Carlos Santana & Mahavishnu John McLaughlin (CBS)
10	13	TOUCH ME	Gary Glitter (Bell)
12	14	THERE GOES RHYMIN' SIMON	Paul Simon (CBS)
-	15	MOTT	Mott The Hoople (CBS)
18	16	LIVING IN THE MATERIAL WORLD	George Harrison (Apple)
20	17	SCHOOL DAYS	Alice Cooper (Warner Bros.)
24	18	THE RISE AND FALL OF ZIGGY STARDUST AND THE SPIDERS FROM MARS	David Bowie (RCA)
15	19	TUBULAR BELLS	Mike Oldfield (Virgin)
17	20	A PASSION PLAY	Jethro Tull (Chrysalis)
14	21	SIMON & GARFUNKEL'S GREATEST HITS	Simon & Garfunkel (CBS)
16	22	A CLOCKWORK ORANGE	Soundtrack (Warner Bros.)
26	23	HARD NOSE THE HIGHWAY	Van Morrison (Warner Bros.)
23	24	A LITTLE TOUCH OF SCHMILSSON IN THE NIGHT	Nilsson (RCA)
19	25	RAZAMANAZ	Nazareth (Mooncrest)
-	26	THE PLAN	Osmonds (MGM)
29	27	GENESIS LIVE	Genesis (Charisma)
-	28	SPACE ODDITY	David Bowie (RCA)
22	29	BACK TO FRONT	Gilbert O'Sullivan (MAM)
-	30	CABARET	Soundtrack (Probe)

25 August 1973

last	this		
3	1	NOW AND THEN	Carpenters (A&M)
1	2	WE CAN MAKE IT	Peters & Lee (Philips)
2	3	ALADDIN SANE	David Bowie (RCA)
4	4	HUNKY DORY	David Bowie (RCA)
6	5	FOREIGNER	Cat Stevens (Island)
10	6	SING IT AGAIN ROD	Rod Stewart (Mercury)
11	7	AND I LOVE YOU SO	Perry Como (RCA)
13	8	TOUCH ME	Gary Glitter (Bell)
5	9	THAT'LL BE THE DAY - SOUNDTRACK	Various Artists (Ronco)
7	10	THE BEATLES 1967-1970	Beatles (Apple)
12	11	LOVE DEVOTION SURRENDER	Carlos Santana & Mahavishnu John McLaughlin (CBS)
15	12	MOTT	Mott The Hoople (CBS)
8	13	THE DARK SIDE OF THE MOON	Pink Floyd (Harvest)
19	14	TUBULAR BELLS	Mike Oldfield (Virgin)
26	15	THE PLAN	Osmonds (MGM)
18	16	THE RISE AND FALL OF ZIGGY STARDUST AND THE SPIDERS FROM MARS	David Bowie (RCA)
21	17	SIMON & GARFUNKEL'S GREATEST HITS	Simon & Garfunkel (CBS)
-	18	BOULDERS	Roy Wood (Harvest)
27	19	GENESIS LIVE	Genesis (Charisma)
25	20	RAZAMANAZ	Nazareth (Mooncrest)
9	21	THE BEATLES 1962-1966	Beatles (Apple)
-	22	INNERVISIONS	Stevie Wonder (Tamla Motown)
17	23	SCHOOL DAYS	Alice Cooper (Warner Bros.)
20	24	A PASSION PLAY	Jethro Tull (Chrysalis)
29	25	BACK TO FRONT	Gilbert O'Sullivan (MAM)
28	26	SPACE ODDITY	David Bowie (RCA)
22	27	A CLOCKWORK ORANGE	Soundtrack (Warner Bros.)
-	28	20 EXPLOSIVE HITS	Various Artists (K-Tel)
24	29	A LITTLE TOUCH OF SCHMILSSON IN THE NIGHT	Nilsson (RCA)
-	30	LINDISFARNE LIVE	Lindisfarne (Charisma)

1 September 1973

last	this		
1	1	NOW AND THEN	Carpenters (A&M)
3	2	ALADDIN SANE	David Bowie (RCA)
6	3	SING IT AGAIN ROD	Rod Stewart (Mercury)
2	4	WE CAN MAKE IT	Peters & Lee (Philips)
4	5	HUNKY DORY	David Bowie (RCA)
15	6	THE PLAN	Osmonds (MGM)
9	7	THAT'LL BE THE DAY - SOUNDTRACK	Various Artists (Ronco)
7	8	AND I LOVE YOU SO	Perry Como (RCA)
16	9	THE RISE AND FALL OF ZIGGY STARDUST AND THE SPIDERS FROM MARS	David Bowie (RCA)
10	10	THE BEATLES 1967-1970	Beatles (Apple)
8	11	TOUCH ME	Gary Glitter (Bell)
17	12	SIMON & GARFUNKEL'S GREATEST HITS	Simon & Garfunkel (CBS)
13	13	THE DARK SIDE OF THE MOON	Pink Floyd (Harvest)
19	14	GENESIS LIVE	Genesis (Charisma)
12	15	MOTT	Mott the Hoople (CBS)
5	16	FOREIGNER	Cat Stevens (Island)
21	17	THE BEATLES 1962-1966	Beatles (Apple)
27	18	A CLOCKWORK ORANGE	Soundtrack (Warner Bros.)
20	19	RAZAMANAZ	Nazareth (Mooncrest)
14	20	TUBULAR BELLS	Mike Oldfield (Virgin)
18	21	BOULDERS	Roy Wood (Harvest)
-	22	TOUCH ME IN THE MORNING	Diana Ross (Tamla Motown)
22	23	INNERVISIONS	Stevie Wonder (Tamla Motown)
24	24	PASSION PLAY	Jethro Tull (Chrysalis)
-	25	24 GOLDEN GREATS OF THE 60s	Various Artists (K-Tel)
28	26	20 EXPLOSIVE HITS	Various Artists (K-Tel)
29	27	A LITTLE TOUCH OF SCHMILSSON IN THE NIGHT	Nilsson (RCA)
-	28	THERE GOES RHYMIN' SIMON	Paul Simon (CBS)
-	29	BRIDGE OVER TROUBLED WATER	Simon & Garfunkel (CBS)
11	30	LOVE DEVOTION SURRENDER	Carlos Santana & Mahavishnu John McLaughlin (CBS)

8 September 1973

last	this		
3	1	SING IT AGAIN ROD	Rod Stewart (Mercury)
1	2	NOW AND THEN	Carpenters (A&M)
4	3	WE CAN MAKE IT	Peters & Lee (Philips)
5	4	HUNKY DORY	David Bowie (RCA)
2	5	ALADDIN SANE	David Bowie (RCA)
6	6	THE PLAN	Osmonds (MGM)
7	7	THAT'LL BE THE DAY	Various Artists (Ronco)
16	8	FOREIGNER	Cat Stevens (Island)
13	9	DARK SIDE OF THE MOON	Pink Floyd (Harvest)
22	10	TOUCH ME IN THE MORNING	Diana Ross (Tamla Motown)
15	11	MOTT	Mott the Hoople (CBS)
21	12	BOULDERS	Roy Wood (Harvest)
20	13	TUBULAR BELLS	Mike Oldfield (Virgin)
8	14	AND I LOVE YOU SO	Perry Como (RCA)
10	15	THE BEATLES 1967-1970	Beatles (Apple)
11	16	TOUCH ME	Gary Glitter (Bell)
12	17	SIMON & GARFUNKEL'S GREATEST HITS	Simon & Garfunkel (CBS)
23	18	INNERVISIONS	Stevie Wonder (Tamla Motown)
9	19	THE RISE AND FALL OF ZIGGY STARDUST AND THE SPIDERS FROM MARS	David Bowie (RCA)
25	20	24 GOLDEN GREATS OF THE 60s	Various Artists (K-Tel)
14	21	GENESIS LIVE	Genesis (Charisma)
17	22	THE BEATLES 1962-1966	Beatles (Apple)
26	23	20 EXPLOSIVE HITS	Various Artists (K-Tel)
24	24	PASSION PLAY	Jethro Tull (Chrysalis)
30	25	LOVE DEVOTION SURRENDER	Carlos Santana & Mahavishnu John McLaughlin (CBS)
-	26	SCHOOL DAYS	Alice Cooper (Warner Bros.)
19	27	RAZAMANAZ	Nazareth (Mooncrest)
27	28	A LITTLE TOUCH OF SCHMILSSON IN THE NIGHT	Nilsson (RCA)
-	29	LINDISFARNE LIVE	Lindisfarne (Charisma)
28	30	THERE GOES RHYMIN' SIMON	Paul Simon (CBS)

Glam-rock's ugliest star, Gary Glitter, loitered around the Top 10 with his uninvitingly-titled album *Touch Me*, and scored a No.1 single with *I'm The Leader Of The Gang*, though this soon gave way to Donny Osmond's *Young Love* and Wizzard's *Angel Fingers*.

Talking of which, Mr Glitter had declared in May: "There's a scene in Last Tango In Paris where Brando says 'I don't need to talk but we can still communicate.' And he grunts and groans. That's pretty similar to what I achieve."

September – October 1973

15 September 1973

last	this		
1	1	SING IT AGAIN ROD	Rod Stewart (Mercury)
2	2	NOW AND THEN	Carpenters (A&M)
5	3	ALADDIN SANE	David Bowie (RCA)
3	4	WE CAN MAKE IT	Peters & Lee (Philips)
4	5	HUNKY DORY	David Bowie (RCA)
6	6	THE PLAN	Osmonds (MGM)
-	7	GOAT'S HEAD SOUP	Rolling Stones (Rolling Stones)
10	8	TOUCH ME IN THE MORNING	Diana Ross (Tamla Motown)
18	9	INNERVISIONS	Stevie Wonder (Tamla Motown)
14	10	AND I LOVE YOU SO	Perry Como (RCA)
7	11	THAT'LL BE THE DAY - SOUNDTRACK	Various Artists (Ronco)
17	12	SIMON & GARFUNKEL'S GREATEST HITS	Simon & Garfunkel (CBS)
15	13	THE BEATLES 1967-1970	Beatles (Apple)
11	14	MOTT	Mott The Hoople (CBS)
20	15	24 GOLDEN GREATS OF THE 60s	Various Artists (K-Tel)
23	16	20 EXPLOSIVE HITS	Various Artists (K-Tel)
16	17	TOUCH ME	Gary Glitter (Bell)
12	18	BOULDERS	Roy Wood (Harvest)
19	19	THE RISE AND FALL OF ZIGGY STARDUST AND THE SPIDERS FROM MARS	David Bowie (RCA)
13	20	TUBULAR BELLS	Mike Oldfield (Virgin)
9	21	THE DARK SIDE OF THE MOON	Pink Floyd (Harvest)
21	22	GENESIS LIVE	Genesis (Charisma)
25	23	LOVE DEVOTION SURRENDER	Carlos Santana & Mahavishnu John McLaughlin (CBS)
-	24	TRANSFORMER	Lou Reed (RCA)
8	25	FOREIGNER	Cat Stevens (Island)
30	26	THERE GOES RHYMIN' SIMON	Paul Simon (CBS)
22	27	THE BEATLES 1962-1966	Beatles (Apple)
-	28	SINGALONGAMAX	Max Bygraves (Pye)
27	29	RAZAMANAZ	Nazareth (Mooncrest)
-	30	THE TRA-LA DAYS ARE OVER	Neil Sedaka (MGM)

22 September 1973

1	1	SING IT AGAIN ROD	Rod Stewart (Mercury)
7	2	GOAT'S HEAD SOUP	Rolling Stones (Rolling Stones)
3	3	ALADDIN SANE	David Bowie (RCA)
2	4	NOW AND THEN	Carpenters (A&M)
4	5	WE CAN MAKE IT	Peters & Lee (Philips)
5	6	HUNKY DORY	David Bowie (RCA)
13	7	THE BEATLES 1967-1970	Beatles (Apple)
9	8	INNERVISIONS	Stevie Wonder (Tamla Motown)
8	9	TOUCH ME IN THE MORNING	Diana Ross (Tamla Motown)
6	10	THE PLAN	Osmonds (MGM)
14	11	MOTT	Mott The Hoople (CBS)
10	12	AND I LOVE YOU SO	Perry Como (RCA)
12	13	SIMON & GARFUNKEL'S GREATEST HITS	Simon & Garfunkel (CBS)
15	14	24 GOLDEN GREATS OF THE 60s	Various Artists (K-Tel)
23	15	LOVE DEVOTION SURRENDER	Carlos Santana & Mahavishnu John McLaughlin (CBS)
18	16	BOULDERS	Roy Wood (Harvest)
11	17	THAT'LL BE THE DAY - SOUNDTRACK	Various Artists (Ronco)
27	18	THE BEATLES 1962-1966	Beatles (Apple)
20	19	TUBULAR BELLS	Mike Oldfield (Virgin)
19	20	THE RISE AND FALL OF ZIGGY STARDUST AND THE SPIDERS FROM MARS	David Bowie (RCA)
16	21	20 EXPLOSIVE HITS	Various Artists (K-Tel)
17	22	TOUCH ME	Gary Glitter (Bell)
22	23	THE DARK SIDE OF THE MOON	Pink Floyd (Harvest)
22	24	GENESIS LIVE	Genesis (Charisma)
26	25	THERE GOES RHYMIN' SIMON	Paul Simon (CBS)
29	26	RAZAMANAZ	Nazareth (Mooncrest)
25	27	FOREIGNER	Cat Stevens (Island)
24	28	TRANSFORMER	Lou Reed (RCA)
-	29	ELVIS	Elvis Presley (RCA)
-	30	BRIDGE OVER TROUBLED WATER	Simon & Garfunkel (CBS)

29 September 1973

2	1	GOAT'S HEAD SOUP	Rolling Stones (Rolling Stones)
1	2	SING IT AGAIN ROD	Rod Stewart (Mercury)
4	3	NOW AND THEN	Carpenters (A&M)
3	4	ALADDIN SANE	David Bowie (RCA)
5	5	WE CAN MAKE IT	Peters & Lee (Philips)
6	6	HUNKY DORY	David Bowie (RCA)
7	7	THE BEATLES 1967-1970	Beatles (Apple)
13	8	SIMON & GARFUNKEL'S GREATEST HITS	Simon & Garfunkel (CBS)
12	9	AND I LOVE YOU SO	Perry Como (RCA)
-	10	SINGALONGAMAX VOL 4	Max Bygraves (Pye)
-	11	SLADEST	Slade (Polydor)
19	12	TUBULAR BELLS	Mike Oldfield (Virgin)
8	13	INNERVISIONS	Stevie Wonder (Tamla Motown)
10	14	THE PLAN	Osmonds (MGM)
21	15	20 EXPLOSIVE HITS	Various Artists (K-Tel)
11	16	MOTT	Mott The Hoople (CBS)
16	17	BOULDERS	Roy Wood (Harvest)
20	18	THE RISE AND FALL OF ZIGGY STARDUST AND THE SPIDERS FROM MARS	David Bowie (RCA)
-	19	A LITTLE TOUCH OF SCHMILSSON IN THE NIGHT	Nilsson (RCA)
-	20	HELLO	Status Quo (Vertigo)
-	21	GOOD VIBRATIONS	Various Artists (Ronco)
24	22	GENESIS LIVE	Genesis (Charisma)
23	23	THE DARK SIDE OF THE MOON	Pink Floyd (Harvest)
-	24	I'M A WRITER NOT A FIGHTER	Gilbert O'Sullivan (MAM)
18	25	THE BEATLES 1962-1966	Beatles (Apple)
9	26	TOUCH ME IN THE MORNING	Diana Ross (Tamla Motown)
25	27	THERE GOES RHYMIN' SIMON	Paul Simon (CBS)
29	28	ELVIS	Elvis Presley (RCA)
17	29	THAT'LL BE THE DAY - SOUNDTRACK	Various Artists (Ronco)
28	30	TRANSFORMER	Lou Reed (RCA)'

6 October 1973

1	1	GOAT'S HEAD SOUP	Rolling Stones (Rolling Stones)
2	2	SING IT AGAIN ROD	Rod Stewart (Mercury)
11	3	SLADEST	Slade (Polydor)
3	4	NOW AND THEN	Carpenters (A&M)
4	5	ALADDIN SANE	David Bowie (RCA)
24	6	I'M A WRITER NOT A FIGHTER	Gilbert O'Sullivan (MAM)
9	7	AND I LOVE YOU SO	Perry Como (RCA)
6	8	HUNKY DORY	David Bowie (RCA)
10	9	SINGALONGAMAX VOL 4	Max Bygraves (Pye)
5	10	WE CAN MAKE IT	Peters & Lee (Philips)
16	11	MOTT	Mott The Hoople (CBS)
15	12	20 EXPLOSIVE HITS	Various Artists (K-Tel)
20	13	HELLO	Status Quo (Vertigo)
21	14	GOOD VIBRATIONS	Various Artists (Ronco)
7	15	THE BEATLES 1967-1970	Beatles (Apple)
-	16	CLASSICS 100	Various Orchestras (K-Tel)
8	17	SIMON & GARFUNKEL'S GREATEST HITS	Simon & Garfunkel (CBS)
14	18	THE PLAN	Osmonds (MGM)
13	19	INNERVISIONS	Stevie Wonder (Tamla Motown)
12	20	TUBULAR BELLS	Mike Oldfield (Virgin)
26	21	TOUCH ME IN THE MORNING	Diana Ross (Tamla Motown)
22	22	GENESIS LIVE	Genesis (Charisma)
-	23	ALL TIME CLASSICS	London Symphony Orchestra (Arcade)
-	24	SWEET FREEDOM	Uriah Heep (Island)
17	25	BOULDERS	Roy Wood (Harvest)
25	26	THE BEATLES 1962-1966	Beatles (Apple)
18	27	THE RISE AND FALL OF ZIGGY STARDUST AND THE SPIDERS FROM MARS	David Bowie (RCA)
23	28	THE DARK SIDE OF THE MOON	Pink Floyd (Harvest)
-	29	A CLOCKWORK ORANGE	Soundtrack (Warner Bros.)
19	30	A LITTLE TOUCH OF SCHMILSSON IN THE NIGHT	Nilsson (RCA)

On September 19, Gram Parsons died of an overdose. As suggested already, Parsons had shitkick-started country rock with the Byrds on their 1968 *Sweetheart Of The Rodeo* album. Then he formed the *Flying Burrito Brothers* but quit this excellent non-charting band in 1970. Later Parsons made two solo albums, in the course of which he helped his old friend Emmylou Harris head for stardom. He was also a friend of Keith Richards, whose new Stones album now topped the chart.

October – November 1973

13 October 1973

last week	this week		
3	1	SLADEST	Slade (Polydor)
1	2	GOAT'S HEAD SOUP	Rolling Stones (Rolling Stones)
13	3	HELLO	Status Quo (Vertigo)
2	4	SING IT AGAIN ROD	Rod Stewart (Mercury)
4	5	NOW AND THEN	Carpenters (A&M)
6	6	I'M A WRITER NOT A FIGHTER	Gilbert O'Sullivan (MAM)
7	7	AND I LOVE YOU SO	Perry Como (RCA)
9	8	SINGALONGAMAX VOL 4	Max Bygraves (Pye)
5	9	ALADDIN SANE	David Bowie (RCA)
8	10	HUNKY DORY	David Bowie (RCA)
21	11	TOUCH ME IN THE MORNING	Diana Ross (Tamla Motown)
17	12	SIMON & GARFUNKEL'S GREATEST HITS	Simon & Garfunkel (CBS)
11	13	MOTT	Mott The Hoople (CBS)
10	14	WE CAN MAKE IT	Peters & Lee (Philips)
19	15	INNERVISIONS	Stevie Wonder (Tamla Motown)
23	16	ALL TIME CLASSICS	London Symphony Orchestra (Arcade)
24	17	SWEET FREEDOM	Uriah Heep (Island)
20	18	TUBULAR BELLS	Mike Oldfield (Virgin)
15	19	THE BEATLES 1967-1970	Beatles (Apple)
-	20	SING ALONG WITH MAX VOL 2	Max Bygraves (Pye)
16	21	CLASSICS 100	Various Orchestras (K-Tel)
-	22	THE TRA-LA DAYS ARE OVER	Neil Sedaka (MGM)
12	23	20 EXPLOSIVE HITS	Various Artists (K-Tel)
-	24	SELLING ENGLAND BY THE POUND	Genesis (Charisma)
14	25	GOOD VIBRATIONS	Various Artists (Ronco)
-	26	THESE FOOLISH THINGS	Bryan Ferry (Island)
22	27	GENESIS LIVE	Genesis (Charisma)
18	28	THE PLAN	Osmonds (MGM)
26	29	THE BEATLES 1962-1966	Beatles (Apple)
-	30	BRIDGE OVER TROUBLED WATER	Simon & Garfunkel (CBS)

20 October 1973

1	1	SLADEST	Slade (Polydor)
4	2	SING IT AGAIN ROD	Rod Stewart (Mercury)
3	3	HELLO	Status Quo (Vertigo)
2	4	GOAT'S HEAD SOUP	Rolling Stones (Rolling Stones)
6	5	I'M A WRITER NOT A FIGHTER	Gilbert O'Sullivan (MAM)
5	6	NOW AND THEN	Carpenters (A&M)
8	7	SINGALONGAMAX VOL 4	Max Bygraves (Pye)
9	8	ALADDIN SANE	David Bowie (RCA)
10	9	HUNKY DORY	David Bowie (RCA)
7	10	AND I LOVE YOU SO	Perry Como (RCA)
16	11	ALL TIME CLASSICS	London Symphony Orchestra (Arcade)
24	12	SELLING ENGLAND BY THE POUND	Genesis (Charisma)
15	13	INNERVISIONS	Stevie Wonder (Tamla Motown)
12	14	SIMON & GARFUNKEL'S GREATEST HITS	Simon & Garfunkel (CBS)
26	15	THESE FOOLISH THINGS	Bryan Ferry (Island)
21	16	CLASSICS 100	Various Orchestras (K-Tel)
-	17	THE DARK SIDE OF THE MOON	Pink Floyd (Harvest)
25	18	GOOD VIBRATIONS	Various Artists (Ronco)
-	19	GOODBYE YELLOW BRICK ROAD	Elton John (DJM)
19	20	THE BEATLES 1967-1970	Beatles (Apple)
13	21	MOTT	Mott The Hoople (CBS)
29	22	THE BEATLES 1962-1966	Beatles (Apple)
18	23	TUBULAR BELLS	Mike Oldfield (Virgin)
11	24	TOUCH ME IN THE MORNING	Diana Ross (Tamla Motown)
-	25	THE RISE AND FALL OF ZIGGY STARDUST AND THE SPIDERS FROM MARS	David Bowie (RCA)
-	26	ANGEL CLARE	Art Garfunkel (CBS)
14	27	WE CAN MAKE IT	Peters & Lee (Philips)
20	28	SING ALONG WITH MAX VOL 2	Max Bygraves (Pye)
17	29	SWEET FREEDOM	Uriah Heep (Island)
23	30	20 EXPLOSIVE HITS	Various Artists (K-Tel)

27 October 1973

3	1	HELLO	Status Quo (Vertigo)
5	2	I'M A WRITER NOT A FIGHTER	Gilbert O'Sullivan (MAM)
1	3	SLADEST	Slade (Polydor)
2	4	SING IT AGAIN ROD	Rod Stewart (Mercury)
-	5	BOWIE PIN-UPS	David Bowie (RCA)
4	6	GOAT'S HEAD SOUP	Rolling Stones (Rolling Stones)
19	7	GOODBYE YELLOW BRICK ROAD	Elton John (DJM)
12	8	SELLING ENGLAND BY THE POUND	Genesis (Charisma)
6	9	NOW AND THEN	Carpenters (A&M)
8	10	ALADDIN SANE	David Bowie (RCA)
17	11	THE DARK SIDE OF THE MOON	Pink Floyd (Harvest)
10	12	AND I LOVE YOU SO	Perry Como (RCA)
9	13	HUNKY DORY	David Bowie (RCA)
7	14	SINGALONGAMAX VOL 4	Max Bygraves (Pye)
24	15	TOUCH ME IN THE MORNING	Diana Ross (Tamla Motown)
16	16	CLASSICS 100	Various Orchestras (K-Tel)
15	17	THESE FOOLISH THINGS	Bryan Ferry (Island)
26	18	ANGEL CLARE	Art Garfunkel (CBS)
13	19	INNERVISIONS	Stevie Wonder (Tamla Motown)
18	20	GOOD VIBRATIONS	Various Artists (Ronco)
21	21	MOTT	Mott The Hoople (CBS)
11	22	ALL TIME CLASSICS	London Symphony Orchestra (Arcade)
30	23	20 EXPLOSIVE HITS	Various Artists (K-Tel)
27	24	WE CAN MAKE IT	Peters & Lee (Philips)
22	25	THE BEATLES 1962-1966	Beatles (Apple)
20	26	THE BEATLES 1967-1970	Beatles (Apple)
23	27	TUBULAR BELLS	Mike Oldfield (Virgin)
-	28	THE PLAN	Osmonds (MGM)
-	29	BERLIN	Lou Reed (RCA)
-	30	SUZI QUATRO	Suzi Quatro (RAK)

3 November 1973

5	1	BOWIE PIN-UPS	David Bowie (RCA)
1	2	HELLO	Status Quo (Vertigo)
9	3	NOW AND THEN	Carpenters (A&M)
3	4	SLADEST	Slade (Polydor)
2	5	I'M A WRITER NOT A FIGHTER	Gilbert O'Sullivan (MAM)
8	6	SELLING ENGLAND BY THE POUND	Genesis (Charisma)
12	7	AND I LOVE YOU SO	Perry Como (RCA)
6	8	GOAT'S HEAD SOUP	Rolling Stones (Rolling Stones)
14	9	SINGALONGAMAX VOL 4	Max Bygraves (Pye)
11	10	THE DARK SIDE OF THE MOON	Pink Floyd (Harvest)
4	11	SING IT AGAIN ROD	Rod Stewart (Mercury)
7	12	GOODBYE YELLOW BRICK ROAD	Elton John (DJM)
17	13	THESE FOOLISH THINGS	Bryan Ferry (Island)
10	14	ALADDIN SANE	David Bowie (RCA)
16	15	CLASSICS 100	Various Orchestras (K-Tel)
22	16	ALL TIME CLASSICS	London Symphony Orchestra (Arcade)
29	17	BERLIN	Lou Reed (RCA)
15	18	TOUCH ME IN THE MORNING	Diana Ross (Tamla Motown)
-	19	TIME FADES AWAY	Neil Young (Warner Bros.)
26	20	THE BEATLES 1967-1970	Beatles (Apple)
20	21	GOOD VIBRATIONS	Various Artists (Ronco)
-	22	SIMON & GARFUNKEL'S GREATEST HITS	Simon & Garfunkel (CBS)
28	23	THE PLAN	Osmonds (MGM)
27	24	TUBULAR BELLS	Mike Oldfield (Virgin)
13	25	HUNKY DORY	David Bowie (RCA)
25	26	THE BEATLES 1962-1966	Beatles (Apple)
19	27	INNERVISIONS	Stevie Wonder (Tamla Motown)
-	28	FOCUS AT THE RAINBOW	Focus (Polydor)
18	29	ANGEL CLARE	Art Garfunkel (CBS)
23	30	20 EXPLOSIVE HITS	Various Artists (K-Tel)

Revisiting other people's old songs was a trend of the day. The Band's 1973 album *Moondog Matinee* was entirely covers of oldies, such as Clarence Frogman Henry's *Ain't Got No Home*, Junior Parker's *Mystery Train* and Chuck Berry's *Promised Land*. The album didn't chart, but two similar projects did: Bryan Ferry's LP *These Foolish Things* (in at No.26) was similarly, if less affectionately, retro – and so was Bowie's *Pin Ups*, a collection of his British 1960s favourites, including the Merseybeats' song *Sorrow*.

November – December 1973

last week	this week	10 November 1973
1	1	BOWIE PIN-UPS — David Bowie (RCA)
2	2	HELLO — Status Quo (Vertigo)
12	3	GOODBYE YELLOW BRICK ROAD — Elton John (DJM)
7	4	AND I LOVE YOU SO — Perry Como (RCA)
4	5	SLADEST — Slade (Polydor)
3	6	NOW AND THEN — Carpenters (A&M)
13	7	THESE FOOLISH THINGS — Bryan Ferry (Island)
5	8	I'M A WRITER NOT A FIGHTER — Gilbert O'Sullivan (MAM)
6	9	SELLING ENGLAND BY THE POUND — Genesis (Charisma)
14	10	ALADDIN SANE — David Bowie (RCA)
8	11	GOAT'S HEAD SOUP — Rolling Stones (Rolling Stones)
10	12	THE DARK SIDE OF THE MOON — Pink Floyd (Harvest)
11	13	SING IT AGAIN ROD — Rod Stewart (Mercury)
-	14	20 POWER HITS — Various Artists (K-Tel)
9	15	SINGALONGAMAX VOL 4 — Max Bygraves (Pye)
-	16	MOTOWN CHARTBUSTERS VOL 8 — Various Artists (Tamla Motown)
25	17	HUNKY DORY — David Bowie (RCA)
15	18	CLASSICS 100 — Various Orchestras (K-Tel)
18	19	TOUCH ME IN THE MORNING — Diana Ross (Tamla Motown)
29	20	ANGEL CLARE — Art Garfunkel (CBS)
23	21	THE PLAN — Osmonds (MGM)
16	22	ALL TIME CLASSICS — London Symphony Orchestra (Arcade)
21	23	GOOD VIBRATIONS — Various Artists (Ronco)
22	24	SIMON & GARFUNKEL'S GREATEST HITS — Simon & Garfunkel (CBS)
-	25	THE RISE AND FALL OF ZIGGY STARDUST AND THE SPIDERS FROM MARS — David Bowie (RCA)
-	26	SING ALONG WITH MAX VOL 2 — Max Bygraves (Pye)
-	27	ERIC CLAPTON'S RAINBOW CONCERT — Eric Clapton (RSO)
20	28	THE BEATLES 1967-1970 — Beatles (Apple)
26	29	THE BEATLES 1962-1966 — Beatles (Apple)
28	30	FOCUS AT THE RAINBOW — Focus (Polydor)

last week	this week	17 November 1973
1	1	BOWIE PIN-UPS — David Bowie (RCA)
3	2	GOODBYE YELLOW BRICK ROAD — Elton John (DJM)
2	3	HELLO — Status Quo (Vertigo)
4	4	AND I LOVE YOU SO — Perry Como (RCA)
5	5	SLADEST — Slade (Polydor)
7	6	THESE FOOLISH THINGS — Bryan Ferry (Island)
8	7	I'M A WRITER NOT A FIGHTER — Gilbert O'Sullivan (MAM)
6	8	NOW AND THEN — Carpenters (A&M)
12	9	THE DARK SIDE OF THE MOON — Pink Floyd (Harvest)
-	10	QUADROPHENIA — Who (Track)
13	11	SING IT AGAIN ROD — Rod Stewart (Mercury)
15	12	SINGALONGAMAX VOL 4 — Max Bygraves (Pye)
9	13	SELLING ENGLAND BY THE POUND — Genesis (Charisma)
14	14	20 POWER HITS — Various Artists (K-Tel)
17	15	HUNKY DORY — David Bowie (RCA)
16	16	MOTOWN CHARTBUSTERS VOL 8 — Various Artists (Tamla Motown)
11	17	GOAT'S HEAD SOUP — Rolling Stones (Rolling Stones)
21	18	THE PLAN — Osmonds (MGM)
10	19	ALADDIN SANE — David Bowie (RCA)
27	20	ERIC CLAPTON'S RAINBOW CONCERT — Eric Clapton (RSO)
-	21	SINGALONGAMAX — Max Bygraves (Pye)
30	22	FOCUS AT THE RAINBOW — Focus (Polydor)
28	23	THE BEATLES 1967-1970 — Beatles (Apple)
18	24	CLASSICS 100 — Various Orchestras (K-Tel)
24	25	SIMON & GARFUNKEL'S GREATEST HITS — Simon & Garfunkel (CBS)
25	26	THE RISE AND FALL OF ZIGGY STARDUST AND THE SPIDERS FROM MARS — David Bowie (RCA)
23	27	GOOD VIBRATIONS — Various Artists (Ronco)
-	28	TUBULAR BELLS — Mike Oldfield (Virgin)
-	29	INNERVISIONS — Stevie Wonder (Tamla Motown)
-	30	WE CAN MAKE IT — Peters & Lee (Philips)

last week	this week	24 November 1973
1	1	BOWIE PIN-UPS — David Bowie (RCA)
2	2	GOODBYE YELLOW BRICK ROAD — Elton John (DJM)
10	3	QUADROPHENIA — Who (Track)
3	4	HELLO — Status Quo (Vertigo)
8	5	NOW AND THEN — Carpenters (A&M)
7	6	I'M A WRITER NOT A FIGHTER — Gilbert O'Sullivan (MAM)
4	7	AND I LOVE YOU SO — Perry Como (RCA)
6	8	THESE FOOLISH THINGS — Bryan Ferry (Island)
5	9	SLADEST — Slade (Polydor)
9	10	THE DARK SIDE OF THE MOON — Pink Floyd (Harvest)
14	11	20 POWER HITS — Various Artists (K-Tel)
11	12	SING IT AGAIN ROD — Rod Stewart (Mercury)
13	13	SELLING ENGLAND BY THE POUND — Genesis (Charisma)
19	14	ALADDIN SANE — David Bowie (RCA)
18	15	THE PLAN — Osmonds (MGM)
17	16	GOAT'S HEAD SOUP — Rolling Stones (Rolling Stones)
16	17	MOTOWN CHARTBUSTERS VOL 8 — Various Artists (Tamla Motown)
12	18	SINGALONGAMAX VOL 4 — Max Bygraves (Pye)
15	19	HUNKY DORY — David Bowie (RCA)
-	20	DREAMS ARE NOTHIN' MORE THAN WISHES — David Cassidy (Bell)
-	21	ROCK ON — David Essex (CBS)
23	22	THE BEATLES 1967-1970 — Beatles (Apple)
27	23	GOOD VIBRATIONS — Various Artists (Ronco)
25	24	SIMON & GARFUNKEL'S GREATEST HITS — Simon & Garfunkel (CBS)
-	25	THE BEATLES 1962-1966 — Beatles (Apple)
-	26	STRANDED — Roxy Music (Island)
24	27	CLASSICS 100 — Various Orchestras (K-Tel)
28	28	TUBULAR BELLS — Mike Oldfield (Virgin)
-	29	JESUS CHRIST SUPERSTAR — Soundtrack (MCA)
20	30	ERIC CLAPTON'S RAINBOW CONCERT — Eric Clapton (RSO)

last week	this week	1 December 1973
1	1	BOWIE PIN-UPS — David Bowie (RCA)
2	2	GOODBYE YELLOW BRICK ROAD — Elton John (DJM)
3	3	QUADROPHENIA — Who (Track)
6	4	I'M A WRITER NOT A FIGHTER — Gilbert O'Sullivan (MAM)
7	5	AND I LOVE YOU SO — Perry Como (RCA)
5	6	NOW AND THEN — Carpenters (A&M)
11	7	20 POWER HITS — Various Artists (K-Tel)
8	8	THESE FOOLISH THINGS — Bryan Ferry (Island)
4	9	HELLO — Status Quo (Vertigo)
9	10	SLADEST — Slade (Polydor)
26	11	STRANDED — Roxy Music (Island)
15	12	THE PLAN — Osmonds (MGM)
10	13	THE DARK SIDE OF THE MOON — Pink Floyd (Harvest)
21	14	ROCK ON — David Essex (CBS)
-	15	LOUD 'N' PROUD — Nazareth (Mooncrest)
20	16	DREAMS ARE NOTHIN' MORE THAN WISHES — David Cassidy (Bell)
14	17	ALADDIN SANE — David Bowie (RCA)
13	18	SELLING ENGLAND BY THE POUND — Genesis (Charisma)
18	19	SINGALONGAMAX VOL 4 — Max Bygraves (Pye)
12	20	SING IT AGAIN ROD — Rod Stewart (Mercury)
-	21	RINGO — Ringo Starr (Apple)
16	22	GOAT'S HEAD SOUP — Rolling Stones (Rolling Stones)
17	23	MOTOWN CHARTBUSTERS VOL 8 — Various Artists (Tamla Motown)
23	24	GOOD VIBRATIONS — Various Artists (Ronco)
-	25	A SONG FOR YOU — Carpenters (A&M)
22	26	THE BEATLES 1967-1970 — Beatles (Apple)
19	27	HUNKY DORY — David Bowie (RCA)
-	28	TATTOO — Rory Gallagher (Polydor)
24	29	SIMON & GARFUNKEL'S GREATEST HITS — Simon & Garfunkel (CBS)
-	30	SINGALONGAMAX — Max Bygraves (Pye)

Frank Zappa hadn't charted since 1970's *Weasels Ripped My Flesh*, but his *Grand Wazoo* sleevenotes summed up the current chart: "The enemy... has 5000 dynamic male vocalists in tuxedos who stand in the middle of the road, loosen their bowties and arch one eyebrow... 5000 dynamic (but carefully understated) male vocalists in old Levi clothes who cry, sulk, whimper and play harmonica, plus 5000 more... of indeterminate sex who can't sing at all but dance good and do hot moves with the mike wire."

December 1973

8 December 1973

last week	this week	Title	Artist
1	1	BOWIE PIN-UPS	David Bowie (RCA)
3	2	QUADROPHENIA	Who (Track)
11	3	STRANDED	Roxy Music (Island)
4	4	I'M A WRITER NOT A FIGHTER	Gilbert O'Sullivan (MAM)
5	5	AND I LOVE YOU SO	Perry Como (RCA)
2	6	GOODBYE YELLOW BRICK ROAD	Elton John (DJM)
16	7	DREAMS ARE NOTHIN' MORE THAN WISHES	David Cassidy (Bell)
7	8	20 POWER HITS	Various Artists (K-Tel)
9	9	HELLO	Status Quo (Vertigo)
6	10	NOW AND THEN	Carpenters (A&M)
8	11	THESE FOOLISH THINGS	Bryan Ferry (Island)
10	12	SLADEST	Slade (Polydor)
13	13	THE DARK SIDE OF THE MOON	Pink Floyd (Harvest)
26	14	THE BEATLES 1967-1970	Beatles (Apple)
12	15	THE PLAN	Osmonds (MGM)
15	16	LOUD 'N' PROUD	Nazareth (Mooncrest)
-	17	WELCOME	Santana (CBS)
21	18	RINGO	Ringo Starr (Apple)
-	19	CLASSICS 100	Various Orchestras (K-Tel)
29	20	SIMON & GARFUNKEL'S GREATEST HITS	Simon & Garfunkel (CBS)
-	21	MIND GAMES	John Lennon (Apple)
14	22	ROCK ON	David Essex (CBS)
23	23	MOTOWN CHARTBUSTERS VOL 8	Various Artists (Tamla Motown)
17	24	ALADDIN SANE	David Bowie (RCA)
18	25	SELLING ENGLAND BY THE POUND	Genesis (Charisma)
20	26	SING IT AGAIN ROD	Rod Stewart (Mercury)
-	27	THE BEATLES 1962-1966	Beatles (Apple)
-	28	SABBATH BLOODY SABBATH	Black Sabbath (WWA)
27	29	HUNKY DORY	David Bowie (RCA)
24	30	GOOD VIBRATIONS	Various Artists (Ronco)

15 December 1973

last week	this week	Title	Artist
1	1	BOWIE PIN-UPS	David Bowie (RCA)
6	2	GOODBYE YELLOW BRICK ROAD	Elton John (DJM)
3	3	STRANDED	Roxy Music (Island)
2	4	QUADROPHENIA	Who (Track)
4	5	I'M A WRITER NOT A FIGHTER	Gilbert O'Sullivan (MAM)
10	6	NOW AND THEN	Carpenters (A&M)
18	7	RINGO	Ringo Starr (Apple)
5	8	AND I LOVE YOU SO	Perry Como (RCA)
7	9	DREAMS ARE NOTHIN' MORE THAN WISHES	David Cassidy (Bell)
21	10	MIND GAMES	John Lennon (Apple)
-	11	BRAIN SALAD SURGERY	Emerson, Lake & Palmer (Manticore)
28	12	SABBATH BLOODY SABBATH	Black Sabbath (WWA)
13	13	THE DARK SIDE OF THE MOON	Pink Floyd (Harvest)
-	14	TALES FROM TOPOGRAPHIC OCEANS	Yes (Atlantic)
12	15	SLADEST	Slade (Polydor)
9	16	HELLO	Status Quo (Vertigo)
22	17	ROCK ON	David Essex (CBS)
8	18	20 POWER HITS	Various Artists (K-Tel)
-	19	OL' BLUE EYES IS BACK	Frank Sinatra (Reprise)
20	20	SIMON & GARFUNKEL'S GREATEST HITS	Simon & Garfunkel (CBS)
17	21	WELCOME	Santana (CBS)
14	22	THE BEATLES 1967-1970	Beatles (Apple)
-	23	BAND ON THE RUN	Paul McCartney & Wings (Parlophone)
16	24	LOUD 'N' PROUD	Nazareth (Mooncrest)
24	25	ALADDIN SANE	David Bowie (RCA)
15	26	THE PLAN	Osmonds (MGM)
11	27	THESE FOOLISH THINGS	Bryan Ferry (Island)
25	28	SELLING ENGLAND BY THE POUND	Genesis (Charisma)
-	29	SINGALONGAPARTY SONG	Max Bygraves (Pye)
-	30	COMMAND PERFORMANCE	Various Artists (Ronco)

22 December 1973

last week	this week	Title	Artist
3	1	STRANDED	Roxy Music (Island)
1	2	BOWIE PIN-UPS	David Bowie (RCA)
9	3	DREAMS ARE NOTHIN' MORE THAN WISHES	David Cassidy (Bell)
2	4	GOODBYE YELLOW BRICK ROAD	Elton John (DJM)
5	5	I'M A WRITER NOT A FIGHTER	Gilbert O'Sullivan (MAM)
4	6	QUADROPHENIA	Who (Track)
7	7	RINGO	Ringo Starr (Apple)
6	8	NOW AND THEN	Carpenters (A&M)
8	9	AND I LOVE YOU SO	Perry Como (RCA)
14	10	TALES FROM TOPOGRAPHIC OCEANS	Yes (Atlantic)
10	11	MIND GAMES	John Lennon (Apple)
29	12	SINGALONGAPARTY SONG	Max Bygraves (Pye)
-	13	20 EVERLASTING MEMORIES OF THE 50s	Various Artists (K-Tel)
18	14	20 POWER HITS	Various Artists (K-Tel)
11	15	BRAIN SALAD SURGERY	Emerson, Lake & Palmer (Manticore)
16	16	HELLO	Status Quo (Vertigo)
12	17	SABBATH BLOODY SABBATH	Black Sabbath (WWA)
13	18	THE DARK SIDE OF THE MOON	Pink Floyd (Harvest)
17	19	ROCK ON	David Essex (CBS)
30	20	COMMAND PERFORMANCE	Various Artists (Ronco)
21	21	WELCOME	Santana (CBS)
23	22	BAND ON THE RUN	Paul McCartney & Wings (Parlophone)
15	23	SLADEST	Slade (Polydor)
19	24	OL' BLUE EYES IS BACK	Frank Sinatra (Reprise)
-	25	CLASSICS 100	Various Orchestras (K-Tel)
26	26	A TIME FOR US	Donny Osmond (MGM)
-	27	TUBULAR BELLS	Mike Oldfield (Virgin)
-	28	TOUCH ME	Gary Glitter (Bell)
24	29	LOUD 'N' PROUD	Nazareth (Mooncrest)
-	30	MOTOWN CHARTBUSTERS VOL 8	Various Artists (Tamla Motown)

This month's chart included John, Paul and Ringo as well as two Beatles LPs. In fact Ringo's album was notable for featuring all four ex-Beatles on it, though never all at once. He was also enjoying a hit single with *Photograph*, which had peaked at No.4, while Paul's *Helen Wheels* only reached No.12 and John's single of *Mind Games* couldn't better No.19. Deep Purple ended the year officially acclaimed as the world's Loudest Performing Rock Band (117 decibels) in the Guinness Book of Records.

5 January 1974

last week	this week	Title	Artist
4	1	GOODBYE YELLOW BRICK ROAD	Elton John (DJM)
2	2	BOWIE PIN-UPS	David Bowie (RCA)
23	3	SLADEST	Slade (Polydor)
1	4	STRANDED	Roxy Music (Island)
5	5	I'M A WRITER NOT A FIGHTER	Gilbert O'Sullivan (MGM)
7	6	RINGO	Ringo Starr (Apple)
15	7	BRAIN SALAD SURGERY	Emerson, Lake & Palmer (Manticore)
3	8	DREAMS ARE NOTHIN' MORE THAN WISHES	David Cassidy (Bell)
11	9	MIND GAMES	John Lennon (Apple)
10	10	TALES FROM TOPOGRAPHIC OCEANS	Yes (Atlantic)
22	11	BAND ON THE RUN	Paul McCartney & Wings (Parlophone)
-	12	SING IT AGAIN ROD	Rod Stewart (Mercury)
9	13	AND I LOVE YOU SO	Perry Como (RCA)
8	14	NOW AND THEN	Carpenters (A&M)
20	15	COMMAND PERFORMANCE	Various Artists (Ronco)
18	16	THE DARK SIDE OF THE MOON	Pink Floyd (Harvest)
17	17	SABBATH BLOODY SABBATH	Black Sabbath (WWA)
26	18	A TIME FOR US	Donny Osmond (MGM)
19	19	ROCK ON	David Essex (CBS)
-	20	THE PLAN	Osmonds (MGM)
28	21	TOUCH ME	Gary Glitter (Bell)
-	22	SILVERBIRD	Leo Sayer (Chrysalis)
-	23	SIMON AND GARFUNKEL'S GREATEST HITS	Simon & Garfunkel (CBS)
-	24	THE BEATLES 1967-1970	Beatles (Apple)
16	25	HELLO	Status Quo (Vertigo)
-	26	THE BEATLES 1962-1966	Beatles (Apple)
6	27	QUADROPHENIA	Who (Track)
-	28	TWENTY NO. 1s	Various Artists (Arcade)
14	29	20 POWER HITS	Various Artists (K-Tel)
27	30	TUBULAR BELLS	Mike Oldfield (Virgin)

12 January 1974

last week	this week	Title	Artist
1	1	GOODBYE YELLOW BRICK ROAD	Elton John (DJM)
2	2	BOWIE PIN-UPS	David Bowie (RCA)
5	3	I'M A WRITER NOT A FIGHTER	Gilbert O'Sullivan (MGM)
7	4	BRAIN SALAD SURGERY	Emerson, Lake & Palmer (Manticore)
10	5	TALES FROM TOPOGRAPHIC OCEANS	Yes (Atlantic)
3	6	SLADEST	Slade (Polydor)
11	7	BAND ON THE RUN	Paul McCartney & Wings (Parlophone)
18	8	A TIME FOR US	Donny Osmond (MGM)
22	9	SILVERBIRD	Leo Sayer (Chrysalis)
8	10	DREAMS ARE NOTHIN' MORE THAN WISHES	David Cassidy (Bell)
13	11	AND I LOVE YOU SO	Perry Como (RCA)
21	12	TOUCH ME	Gary Glitter (Bell)
4	13	STRANDED	Roxy Music (Island)
14	14	NOW AND THEN	Carpenters (A&M)
6	15	RINGO	Ringo Starr (Apple)
9	16	MIND GAMES	John Lennon (Apple)
27	17	QUADROPHENIA	Who (Track)
24	18	THE BEATLES 1967-1970	Beatles (Apple)
-	19	BACK TO FRONT	Gilbert O'Sullivan (MGM)
19	20	ROCK ON	David Essex (CBS)
-	21	OL' BLUE EYES IS BACK	Frank Sinatra (Reprise)
23	22	SIMON AND GARFUNKEL'S GREATEST HITS	Simon & Garfunkel (CBS)
20	23	THE PLAN	Osmonds (MGM)
16	24	THE DARK SIDE OF THE MOON	Pink Floyd (Harvest)
26	25	THE BEATLES 1962-1966	Beatles (Apple)
-	26	20 EVERLASTING MEMORIES OF THE 50s	Various Artists (K-Tel)
-	27	THE RISE AND FALL OF ZIGGY STARDUST AND THE SPIDERS FROM MARS	David Bowie (RCA)
25	28	HELLO	Status Quo (Vertigo)
-	29	DIANA AND MARVIN	Diana Ross & Marvin Gaye (Tamla Motown)
-	30	WELCOME	Santana (CBS)

19 January 1974

last week	this week	Title	Artist
4	1	BRAIN SALAD SURGERY	Emerson, Lake & Palmer (Manticore)
1	2	GOODBYE YELLOW BRICK ROAD	Elton John (DJM)
2	3	BOWIE PIN-UPS	David Bowie (RCA)
5	4	TALES FROM TOPOGRAPHIC OCEANS	Yes (Atlantic)
3	5	I'M A WRITER NOT A FIGHTER	Gilbert O'Sullivan (MGM)
10	6	DREAMS ARE NOTHIN' MORE THAN WISHES	David Cassidy (Bell)
13	7	STRANDED	Roxy Music (Island)
11	8	AND I LOVE YOU SO	Perry Como (RCA)
6	9	SLADEST	Slade (Polydor)
-	10	OVERTURE AND BEGINNERS	Rod Stewart & the Faces (Mercury)
12	11	TOUCH ME	Gary Glitter (Bell)
24	12	THE DARK SIDE OF THE MOON	Pink Floyd (Harvest)
21	13	OL' BLUE EYES IS BACK	Frank Sinatra (Reprise)
8	14	A TIME FOR US	Donny Osmond (MGM)
-	15	THE SINGLES 1969-1973	Carpenters (A&M)
9	16	SILVERBIRD	Leo Sayer (Chrysalis)
15	17	RINGO	Ringo Starr (Apple)
17	18	QUADROPHENIA	Who (Track)
14	19	NOW AND THEN	Carpenters (A&M)
7	20	BAND ON THE RUN	Paul McCartney & Wings (Parlophone)
-	21	TUBULAR BELLS	Mike Oldfield (Virgin)
20	22	ROCK ON	David Essex (CBS)
18	23	THE BEATLES 1967-1970	Beatles (Apple)
-	24	SABBATH BLOODY SABBATH	Black Sabbath (WWA)
28	25	HELLO	Status Quo (Vertigo)
-	26	BRIDGE OVER TROUBLED WATER	Simon & Garfunkel (CBS)
23	27	THE PLAN	Osmonds (MGM)
16	28	MIND GAMES	John Lennon (Apple)
-	29	MUSCLE OF LOVE	Alice Cooper (Warner Bros.)
22	30	SIMON AND GARFUNKEL'S GREATEST HITS	Simon & Garfunkel (CBS)

26 January 1974

last week	this week	Title	Artist
1	1	BRAIN SALAD SURGERY	Emerson, Lake & Palmer (Manticore)
3	2	BOWIE PIN-UPS	David Bowie (RCA)
2	3	GOODBYE YELLOW BRICK ROAD	Elton John (DJM)
4	4	TALES FROM TOPOGRAPHIC OCEANS	Yes (Atlantic)
9	5	SLADEST	Slade (Polydor)
20	6	BAND ON THE RUN	Paul McCartney & Wings (Parlophone)
5	7	I'M A WRITER NOT A FIGHTER	Gilbert O'Sullivan (MGM)
15	8	THE SINGLES 1969-1973	Carpenters (A&M)
7	9	STRANDED	Roxy Music (Island)
12	10	THE DARK SIDE OF THE MOON	Pink Floyd (Harvest)
16	11	SILVERBIRD	Leo Sayer (Chrysalis)
8	12	AND I LOVE YOU SO	Perry Como (RCA)
22	13	ROCK ON	David Essex (CBS)
14	14	A TIME FOR US	Donny Osmond (MGM)
10	15	OVERTURE AND BEGINNERS	Rod Stewart & the Faces (Mercury)
6	16	DREAMS ARE NOTHIN' MORE THAN WISHES	David Cassidy (Bell)
21	17	TUBULAR BELLS	Mike Oldfield (Virgin)
-	18	GLITTER	Gary Glitter (Bell)
18	19	QUADROPHENIA	Who (Track)
29	20	MUSCLE OF LOVE	Alice Cooper (Warner Bros.)
19	21	NOW AND THEN	Carpenters (A&M)
11	22	TOUCH ME	Gary Glitter (Bell)
30	23	SIMON AND GARFUNKEL'S GREATEST HITS	Simon & Garfunkel (CBS)
13	24	OL' BLUE EYES IS BACK	Frank Sinatra (Reprise)
-	25	THESE FOOLISH THINGS	Bryan Ferry (Island)
-	26	ALADDIN SANE	David Bowie (RCA)
25	27	HELLO	Status Quo (Vertigo)
-	28	DIANA AND MARVIN	Diana Ross & Marvin Gaye (Tamla Motown)
28	29	MIND GAMES	John Lennon (Apple)
17	30	RINGO	Ringo Starr (Apple)

Silverbird (No.22) marked the debut of Adam Faith protege Leo Sayer, whose debut single *The Show Must Go On* would top the charts this month. Leo Sayer looked and sounded like a Gilbert O'Sullivan without the image problem. John Lennon seemed to have an image problem too. He turned up this month at the LA Troubadour club with a Kotex [sanitary towel] on his head. Glared at by a waitress, he asked "D'you know who I am?" "Yes, you're some asshole with a Kotex on your head."

February 1974

2 February 1974

last week	this week	title / artist (label)
8	1	THE SINGLES 1969-1973 — Carpenters (A&M)
11	2	SILVERBIRD — Leo Sayer (Chrysalis)
12	3	AND I LOVE YOU SO — Perry Como (RCA)
1	4	BRAIN SALAD SURGERY — Emerson, Lake & Palmer (Manticore)
6	5	BAND ON THE RUN — Paul McCartney & Wings (Parlophone)
15	6	OVERTURE AND BEGINNERS — Rod Stewart & the Faces (Mercury)
2	7	BOWIE PIN-UPS — David Bowie (RCA)
10	8	THE DARK SIDE OF THE MOON — Pink Floyd (Harvest)
4	9	TALES FROM TOPOGRAPHIC OCEANS — Yes (Atlantic)
9	10	STRANDED — Roxy Music (Island)
7	11	I'M A WRITER NOT A FIGHTER — Gilbert O'Sullivan (MGM)
5	12	SLADEST — Slade (Polydor)
3	13	GOODBYE YELLOW BRICK ROAD — Elton John (DJM)
13	14	ROCK ON — David Essex (CBS)
17	15	TUBULAR BELLS — Mike Oldfield (Virgin)
-	16	SOLITAIRE — Andy Williams (CBS)
28	17	DIANA AND MARVIN — Diana Ross & Marvin Gaye (Tamla Motown)
23	18	SIMON AND GARFUNKEL'S GREATEST HITS — Simon & Garfunkel (CBS)
18	19	GLITTER — Gary Glitter (Bell)
24	20	OL' BLUE EYES IS BACK — Frank Sinatra (Reprise)
19	21	QUADROPHENIA — Who (Track)
-	22	HUNKY DORY — David Bowie (RCA)
-	23	THE BEATLES 1967-1970 — Beatles (Apple)
27	24	HELLO — Status Quo (Vertigo)
30	25	RINGO — Ringo Starr (Apple)
21	26	NOW AND THEN — Carpenters (A&M)
20	27	MUSCLE OF LOVE — Alice Cooper (Warner Bros.)
22	28	TOUCH ME — Gary Glitter (Bell)
-	29	THE BEATLES 1962-1966 — Beatles (Apple)
-	30	BRIDGE OVER TROUBLED WATER — Simon & Garfunkel (CBS)

9 February 1974

last week	this week	title / artist (label)
1	1	THE SINGLES 1969-1973 — Carpenters (A&M)
2	2	SILVERBIRD — Leo Sayer (Chrysalis)
3	3	AND I LOVE YOU SO — Perry Como (RCA)
5	4	BAND ON THE RUN — Paul McCartney & Wings (Parlophone)
6	5	OVERTURE AND BEGINNERS — Rod Stewart & the Faces (Mercury)
7	6	BOWIE PIN-UPS — David Bowie (RCA)
4	7	BRAIN SALAD SURGERY — Emerson, Lake & Palmer (Manticore)
8	8	THE DARK SIDE OF THE MOON — Pink Floyd (Harvest)
9	9	TALES FROM TOPOGRAPHIC OCEANS — Yes (Atlantic)
11	10	I'M A WRITER NOT A FIGHTER — Gilbert O'Sullivan (MGM)
12	11	SLADEST — Slade (Polydor)
15	12	TUBULAR BELLS — Mike Oldfield (Virgin)
13	13	GOODBYE YELLOW BRICK ROAD — Elton John (DJM)
10	14	STRANDED — Roxy Music (Island)
16	15	SOLITAIRE — Andy Williams (CBS)
-	16	TOUCH ME IN THE MORNING — Diana Ross (Tamla Motown)
18	17	SIMON AND GARFUNKEL'S GREATEST HITS — Simon & Garfunkel (CBS)
-	18	TOM JONES' GREATEST HITS — Tom Jones (Decca)
14	19	ROCK ON — David Essex (CBS)
23	20	THE BEATLES 1967-1970 — Beatles (Apple)
-	21	TWENTY NO. 1s — Various Artists (Arcade)
26	22	NOW AND THEN — Carpenters (A&M)
17	23	DIANA AND MARVIN — Diana Ross & Marvin Gaye (Tamla Motown)
20	24	OL' BLUE EYES IS BACK — Frank Sinatra (Reprise)
-	25	MOONTAN — Golden Earring (Track)
-	26	ALADDIN SANE — David Bowie (RCA)
25	27	RINGO — Ringo Starr (Apple)
30	28	BRIDGE OVER TROUBLED WATER — Simon & Garfunkel (CBS)
29	29	THE BEATLES 1962-1966 — Beatles (Apple)
22	30	HUNKY DORY — David Bowie (RCA)

16 February 1974

last week	this week	title / artist (label)
1	1	THE SINGLES 1969-1973 — Carpenters (A&M)
2	2	SILVERBIRD — Leo Sayer (Chrysalis)
3	3	AND I LOVE YOU SO — Perry Como (RCA)
-	4	OLD NEW BORROWED AND BLUE — Slade (Polydor)
4	5	BAND ON THE RUN — Paul McCartney & Wings (Parlophone)
15	6	SOLITAIRE — Andy Williams (CBS)
8	7	THE DARK SIDE OF THE MOON — Pink Floyd (Harvest)
5	8	OVERTURE AND BEGINNERS — Rod Stewart & the Faces (Mercury)
12	9	TUBULAR BELLS — Mike Oldfield (Virgin)
7	10	BRAIN SALAD SURGERY — Emerson, Lake & Palmer (Manticore)
21	11	TWENTY NO. 1s — Various Artists (Arcade)
10	12	I'M A WRITER NOT A FIGHTER — Gilbert O'Sullivan (MGM)
14	13	STRANDED — Roxy Music (Island)
9	14	TALES FROM TOPOGRAPHIC OCEANS — Yes (Atlantic)
-	15	PLANET WAVES — Bob Dylan (Island)
6	16	BOWIE PIN-UPS — David Bowie (RCA)
17	17	SIMON AND GARFUNKEL'S GREATEST HITS — Simon & Garfunkel (CBS)
-	18	HARBOUR — Jack Jones (RCA)
13	19	GOODBYE YELLOW BRICK ROAD — Elton John (DJM)
23	20	DIANA AND MARVIN — Diana Ross & Marvin Gaye (Tamla Motown)
22	21	NOW AND THEN — Carpenters (A&M)
18	22	TOM JONES' GREATEST HITS — Tom Jones (Decca)
16	23	TOUCH ME IN THE MORNING — Diana Ross (Tamla Motown)
25	24	MOONTAN — Golden Earring (Track)
26	25	ALADDIN SANE — David Bowie (RCA)
19	26	ROCK ON — David Essex (CBS)
-	27	INNERVISIONS — Stevie Wonder (Tamla Motown)
-	28	LET'S GET IT ON — Marvin Gaye (Tamla Motown)
29	29	THE BEATLES 1962-1966 — Beatles (Apple)
27	30	RINGO — Ringo Starr (Apple)

23 February 1974

last week	this week	title / artist (label)
1	1	THE SINGLES 1969-1973 — Carpenters (A&M)
4	2	OLD NEW BORROWED AND BLUE — Slade (Polydor)
2	3	SILVERBIRD — Leo Sayer (Chrysalis)
3	4	AND I LOVE YOU SO — Perry Como (RCA)
5	5	BAND ON THE RUN — Paul McCartney & Wings (Parlophone)
6	6	SOLITAIRE — Andy Williams (CBS)
8	7	OVERTURE AND BEGINNERS — Rod Stewart & the Faces (Mercury)
12	8	I'M A WRITER NOT A FIGHTER — Gilbert O'Sullivan (MGM)
11	9	TWENTY NO. 1s — Various Artists (Arcade)
15	10	PLANET WAVES — Bob Dylan (Island)
7	11	THE DARK SIDE OF THE MOON — Pink Floyd (Harvest)
9	12	TUBULAR BELLS — Mike Oldfield (Virgin)
19	13	GOODBYE YELLOW BRICK ROAD — Elton John (DJM)
10	14	BRAIN SALAD SURGERY — Emerson, Lake & Palmer (Manticore)
17	15	SIMON AND GARFUNKEL'S GREATEST HITS — Simon & Garfunkel (CBS)
16	16	BOWIE PIN-UPS — David Bowie (RCA)
14	17	TALES FROM TOPOGRAPHIC OCEANS — Yes (Atlantic)
23	18	TOUCH ME IN THE MORNING — Diana Ross (Tamla Motown)
20	19	DIANA AND MARVIN — Diana Ross & Marvin Gaye (Tamla Motown)
21	20	NOW AND THEN — Carpenters (A&M)
-	21	THE BEATLES 1967-1970 — Beatles (Apple)
30	22	RINGO — Ringo Starr (Apple)
13	23	STRANDED — Roxy Music (Island)
-	24	OL' BLUE EYES IS BACK — Frank Sinatra (Reprise)
18	25	HARBOUR — Jack Jones (RCA)
22	26	TOM JONES' GREATEST HITS — Tom Jones (Decca)
-	27	A NICE PAIR — Pink Floyd (Harvest)
29	28	THE BEATLES 1962-1966 — Beatles (Apple)
-	29	BURN — Deep Purple (Purple)
24	30	MOONTAN — Golden Earring (Track)

Emerson Lake & Palmer's *Brain Salad Surgery* would be their last No.1 album; it had now been displaced by the Carpenters' *The Singles 1969-1973*, which was to manage more weeks at No.1 than anything since Simon & Garfunkel's *Bridge Over Troubled Water*. It would sit there for 19 weeks... which was odd, because they'd only had four Top 10 hits. *Tom Jones' Greatest Hits*, which jumped into the Top 20 on February 9, were selected from his nineteen Top 20 singles and five minor hits.

March 1974

2 March 1974

last week	this week	Title	Artist (Label)
1	1	THE SINGLES 1969-1973	Carpenters (A&M)
2	2	OLD NEW BORROWED AND BLUE	Slade (Polydor)
3	3	SILVERBIRD	Leo Sayer (Chrysalis)
5	4	BAND ON THE RUN	Paul McCartney & Wings (Parlophone)
6	5	SOLITAIRE	Andy Williams (CBS)
4	6	AND I LOVE YOU SO	Perry Como (RCA)
10	7	PLANET WAVES	Bob Dylan (Island)
11	8	THE DARK SIDE OF THE MOON	Pink Floyd (Harvest)
15	9	SIMON & GARFUNKEL'S GREATEST HITS	Simon & Garfunkel (CBS)
12	10	TUBULAR BELLS	Mike Oldfield (Virgin)
13	11	GOODBYE YELLOW BRICK ROAD	Elton John (DJM)
17	12	TALES FROM TOPOGRAPHIC OCEANS	Yes (Atlantic)
27	13	A NICE PAIR	Pink Floyd (Harvest)
14	14	BRAIN SALAD SURGERY	Emerson, Lake & Palmer (Manticore)
25	15	HARBOUR	Jack Jones (RCA)
22	16	RINGO	Ringo Starr (Apple)
29	17	BURN	Deep Purple (Purple)
9	18	TWENTY NO. 1s	Various Artists (Arcade)
16	19	BOWIE PIN-UPS	David Bowie (RCA)
-	20	DYNAMITE	Various Artists (K-Tel)
7	21	OVERTURE AND BEGINNERS	Rod Stewart & the Faces (Mercury)
18	22	TOUCH ME IN THE MORNING	Diana Ross (Tamla Motown)
8	23	I'M A WRITER NOT A FIGHTER	Gilbert O'Sullivan (MGM)
20	24	NOW AND THEN	Carpenters (A&M)
-	25	THE RISE AND FALL OF ZIGGY STARDUST AND THE SPIDERS FROM MARS	David Bowie (RCA)
21	26	THE BEATLES 1967-1970	Beatles (Apple)
24	27	OL' BLUE EYES IS BACK	Frank Sinatra (Reprise)
19	28	DIANA AND MARVIN	Diana Ross & Marvin Gaye (Tamla Motown)
28	29	THE BEATLES 1962-1966	Beatles (Apple)
23	30	STRANDED	Roxy Music (Island)

9 March 1974

last week	this week	Title	Artist (Label)
1	1	THE SINGLES 1969-1973	Carpenters (A&M)
2	2	OLD NEW BORROWED AND BLUE	Slade (Polydor)
4	3	BAND ON THE RUN	Paul McCartney & Wings (Parlophone)
7	4	PLANET WAVES	Bob Dylan (Island)
3	5	SILVERBIRD	Leo Sayer (Chrysalis)
6	6	AND I LOVE YOU SO	Perry Como (RCA)
17	7	BURN	Deep Purple (Purple)
11	8	GOODBYE YELLOW BRICK ROAD	Elton John (DJM)
5	9	SOLITAIRE	Andy Williams (CBS)
8	10	THE DARK SIDE OF THE MOON	Pink Floyd (Harvest)
15	11	HARBOUR	Jack Jones (RCA)
10	12	TUBULAR BELLS	Mike Oldfield (Virgin)
16	13	RINGO	Ringo Starr (Apple)
20	14	DYNAMITE	Various Artists (K-Tel)
23	15	I'M A WRITER NOT A FIGHTER	Gilbert O'Sullivan (MGM)
24	16	NOW AND THEN	Carpenters (A&M)
14	17	BRAIN SALAD SURGERY	Emerson, Lake & Palmer (Manticore)
9	18	SIMON AND GARFUNKEL'S GREATEST HITS	Simon & Garfunkel (CBS)
21	19	OVERTURE AND BEGINNERS	Rod Stewart & the Faces (Mercury)
26	20	THE BEATLES 1967-1970	Beatles (Apple)
-	21	A LEGENDARY PERFORMER VOL 1	Elvis Presley (RCA)
22	22	TOUCH ME IN THE MORNING	Diana Ross (Tamla Motown)
12	23	TALES FROM TOPOGRAPHIC OCEANS	Yes (Atlantic)
-	24	THE UNTOUCHABLE	Alvin Stardust (Magnet)
13	25	A NICE PAIR	Pink Floyd (Harvest)
-	26	BRIDGE OVER TROUBLED WATER	Simon & Garfunkel (CBS)
29	27	THE BEATLES 1962-1966	Beatles (Apple)
19	28	BOWIE PIN-UPS	David Bowie (RCA)
30	29	STRANDED	Roxy Music (Island)
-	30	ALADDIN SANE	David Bowie (RCA)

16 March 1974

last week	this week	Title	Artist (Label)
1	1	THE SINGLES 1969-1973	Carpenters (A&M)
2	2	OLD NEW BORROWED AND BLUE	Slade (Polydor)
3	3	BAND ON THE RUN	Paul McCartney & Wings (Parlophone)
7	4	BURN	Deep Purple (Purple)
8	5	GOODBYE YELLOW BRICK ROAD	Elton John (DJM)
6	6	AND I LOVE YOU SO	Perry Como (RCA)
9	7	SOLITAIRE	Andy Williams (CBS)
12	8	TUBULAR BELLS	Mike Oldfield (Virgin)
4	9	PLANET WAVES	Bob Dylan (Island)
10	10	THE DARK SIDE OF THE MOON	Pink Floyd (Harvest)
5	11	SILVERBIRD	Leo Sayer (Chrysalis)
14	12	DYNAMITE	Various Artists (K-Tel)
16	13	NOW AND THEN	Carpenters (A&M)
18	14	SIMON AND GARFUNKEL'S GREATEST HITS	Simon & Garfunkel (CBS)
24	15	THE UNTOUCHABLE	Alvin Stardust (Magnet)
17	16	BRAIN SALAD SURGERY	Emerson, Lake & Palmer (Manticore)
11	17	HARBOUR	Jack Jones (RCA)
13	18	RINGO	Ringo Starr (Apple)
23	19	TALES FROM TOPOGRAPHIC OCEANS	Yes (Atlantic)
-	20	ALAN FREEMAN'S HISTORY OF POP	Various Artists (Arcade)
20	21	THE BEATLES 1967-1970	Beatles (Apple)
27	22	THE BEATLES 1962-1966	Beatles (Apple)
21	23	A LEGENDARY PERFORMER VOL 1	Elvis Presley (RCA)
25	24	A NICE PAIR	Pink Floyd (Harvest)
-	25	THE FREE STORY	Free (Island)
-	26	STONE GON'	Barry White (Pye)
28	27	BOWIE PIN-UPS	David Bowie (RCA)
-	28	MA, HE'S MAKING EYES AT ME	Lena Zavaroni (Philips)
-	29	ZINC ALLOY AND THE HIDDEN RIDERS OF TOMORROW	Marc Bolan & T. Rex (EMI)
-	30	COURT AND SPARK	Joni Mitchell (Asylum)

23 March 1974

last week	this week	Title	Artist (Label)
1	1	THE SINGLES 1969-1973	Carpenters (A&M)
5	2	GOODBYE YELLOW BRICK ROAD	Elton John (DJM)
4	3	BURN	Deep Purple (Purple)
2	4	OLD NEW BORROWED AND BLUE	Slade (Polydor)
3	5	BAND ON THE RUN	Paul McCartney & Wings (Parlophone)
8	6	TUBULAR BELLS	Mike Oldfield (Virgin)
6	7	AND I LOVE YOU SO	Perry Como (RCA)
10	8	THE DARK SIDE OF THE MOON	Pink Floyd (Harvest)
7	9	SOLITAIRE	Andy Williams (CBS)
15	10	THE UNTOUCHABLE	Alvin Stardust (Magnet)
20	11	ALAN FREEMAN'S HISTORY OF POP	Various Artists (Arcade)
25	12	THE FREE STORY	Free (Island)
9	13	PLANET WAVES	Bob Dylan (Island)
12	14	DYNAMITE	Various Artists (K-Tel)
13	15	NOW AND THEN	Carpenters (A&M)
14	16	SIMON AND GARFUNKEL'S GREATEST HITS	Simon & Garfunkel (CBS)
11	17	SILVERBIRD	Leo Sayer (Chrysalis)
-	18	HOT CAKES	Carly Simon (Elektra)
30	19	COURT AND SPARK	Joni Mitchell (Asylum)
16	20	BRAIN SALAD SURGERY	Emerson, Lake & Palmer (Manticore)
-	21	DIANA AND MARVIN	Diana Ross & Marvin Gaye (Tamla Motown)
18	22	RINGO	Ringo Starr (Apple)
17	23	HARBOUR	Jack Jones (RCA)
29	24	ZINC ALLOY AND THE HIDDEN RIDERS OF TOMORROW	Marc Bolan & T. Rex (EMI)
-	25	SLAUGHTER ON TENTH AVENUE	Mick Ronson (RCA)
-	26	MILLICAN AND NESBIT	Millican & Nesbit (Pye)
-	27	THE STORY OF POP	Various Artists (K-Tel)
24	28	A NICE PAIR	Pink Floyd (Harvest)
26	29	STONE GON'	Barry White (Pye)
21	30	THE BEATLES 1967-1970	Beatles (Apple)

It was odd to see Dylan on Island instead of CBS. His Columbia contract had expired in 1972; for *Planet Waves*, cut with The Band in five days in November 1973, Dylan did a one-off US deal with David Geffen's Elektra/Asylum company (part of WEA, Columbia's chief rival); here, Chris Blackwell's Island label was used. The forthcoming live album from Dylan's mega-successful 1974 "come-back" tour would also go to Asylum and Island. CBS, forced to renegotiate with Dylan, would then re-sign him.

March – April 1974

30 March 1974

last week	this week	Album
1	1	THE SINGLES 1969-1973 — Carpenters (A&M)
5	2	BAND ON THE RUN — Paul McCartney & Wings (Parlophone)
2	3	GOODBYE YELLOW BRICK ROAD — Elton John (DJM)
4	4	OLD NEW BORROWED AND BLUE — Slade (Polydor)
3	5	BURN — Deep Purple (Purple)
7	6	AND I LOVE YOU SO — Perry Como (RCA)
8	7	THE DARK SIDE OF THE MOON — Pink Floyd (Harvest)
6	8	TUBULAR BELLS — Mike Oldfield (Virgin)
26	9	MILLICAN AND NESBIT — Millican & Nesbit (Pye)
10	10	THE UNTOUCHABLE — Alvin Stardust (Magnet)
11	11	ALAN FREEMAN'S HISTORY OF POP — Various Artists (Arcade)
15	12	NOW AND THEN — Carpenters (A&M)
12	13	THE FREE STORY — Free (Island)
9	14	SOLITAIRE — Andy Williams (CBS)
14	15	DYNAMITE — Various Artists (K-Tel)
18	16	HOT CAKES — Carly Simon (Elektra)
19	17	COURT AND SPARK — Joni Mitchell (Asylum)
-	18	BEHIND CLOSED DOORS — Charlie Rich (Epic)
25	19	SLAUGHTER ON TENTH AVENUE — Mick Ronson (RCA)
-	20	NOW WE ARE SIX — Steeleye Span (Chrysalis)
16	21	SIMON AND GARFUNKEL'S GREATEST HITS — Simon & Garfunkel (CBS)
-	22	QUEEN II — Queen (EMI)
21	23	DIANA AND MARVIN — Diana Ross & Marvin Gaye (Tamla Motown)
-	24	TOGETHER — New Seekers (Polydor)
24	25	ZINC ALLOY AND THE HIDDEN RIDERS OF TOMORROW — Marc Bolan & T. Rex (EMI)
13	26	PLANET WAVES — Bob Dylan (Island)
-	27	BUDDAH AND THE CHOCOLATE BOX — Cat Stevens (Island)
22	28	RINGO — Ringo Starr (Apple)
17	29	SILVERBIRD — Leo Sayer (Chrysalis)
29	30	STONE GON' — Barry White (Pye)

6 April 1974

last week	this week	Album
1	1	THE SINGLES 1969-1973 — Carpenters (A&M)
9	2	MILLICAN AND NESBIT — Millican & Nesbit (Pye)
2	3	BAND ON THE RUN — Paul McCartney & Wings (Parlophone)
3	4	GOODBYE YELLOW BRICK ROAD — Elton John (DJM)
4	5	OLD NEW BORROWED AND BLUE — Slade (Polydor)
22	6	QUEEN II — Queen (EMI)
5	7	BURN — Deep Purple (Purple)
8	8	TUBULAR BELLS — Mike Oldfield (Virgin)
23	9	DIANA AND MARVIN — Diana Ross & Marvin Gaye (Tamla Motown)
6	10	AND I LOVE YOU SO — Perry Como (RCA)
11	11	ALAN FREEMAN'S HISTORY OF POP — Various Artists (Arcade)
15	12	DYNAMITE — Various Artists (K-Tel)
7	13	THE DARK SIDE OF THE MOON — Pink Floyd (Harvest)
12	14	NOW AND THEN — Carpenters (A&M)
24	15	TOGETHER — New Seekers (Polydor)
20	16	NOW WE ARE SIX — Steeleye Span (Chrysalis)
17	17	COURT AND SPARK — Joni Mitchell (Asylum)
27	18	BUDDAH AND THE CHOCOLATE BOX — Cat Stevens (Island)
21	19	SIMON AND GARFUNKEL'S GREATEST HITS — Simon & Garfunkel (CBS)
10	20	THE UNTOUCHABLE — Alvin Stardust (Magnet)
-	21	MA, HE'S MAKING EYES AT ME — Lena Zavaroni (Philips)
13	22	THE FREE STORY — Free (Island)
-	23	THE STING — Soundtrack (MCA)
-	24	THE HOOPLE — Mott The Hoople (CBS)
19	25	SLAUGHTER ON TENTH AVENUE — Mick Ronson (RCA)
26	26	PLANET WAVES — Bob Dylan (Island)
18	27	BEHIND CLOSED DOORS — Charlie Rich (Epic)
-	28	THE STORY OF POP — Various Artists (K-Tel)
28	29	RINGO — Ringo Starr (Apple)
-	30	HARBOUR — Jack Jones (RCA)

13 April 1974

last week	this week	Album
1	1	THE SINGLES 1969-1973 — Carpenters (A&M)
4	2	GOODBYE YELLOW BRICK ROAD — Elton John (DJM)
3	3	BAND ON THE RUN — Paul McCartney & Wings (Parlophone)
18	4	BUDDAH AND THE CHOCOLATE BOX — Cat Stevens (Island)
6	5	QUEEN II — Queen (EMI)
8	6	TUBULAR BELLS — Mike Oldfield (Virgin)
11	7	ALAN FREEMAN'S HISTORY OF POP — Various Artists (Arcade)
2	8	MILLICAN AND NESBIT — Millican & Nesbit (Pye)
5	9	OLD NEW BORROWED AND BLUE — Slade (Polydor)
9	10	DIANA AND MARVIN — Diana Ross & Marvin Gaye (Tamla Motown)
7	11	BURN — Deep Purple (Purple)
12	12	DYNAMITE — Various Artists (K-Tel)
14	13	NOW AND THEN — Carpenters (A&M)
10	14	AND I LOVE YOU SO — Perry Como (RCA)
24	15	THE HOOPLE — Mott The Hoople (CBS)
28	16	THE STORY OF POP — Various Artists (K-Tel)
22	17	THE FREE STORY — Free (Island)
13	18	THE DARK SIDE OF THE MOON — Pink Floyd (Harvest)
-	19	GLEN CAMPBELL'S GREATEST HITS — Glen Campbell (Capitol)
17	20	COURT AND SPARK — Joni Mitchell (Asylum)
15	21	TOGETHER — New Seekers (Polydor)
20	22	THE UNTOUCHABLE — Alvin Stardust (Magnet)
16	23	NOW WE ARE SIX — Steeleye Span (Chrysalis)
23	24	THE STING — Soundtrack (MCA)
19	25	SIMON AND GARFUNKEL'S GREATEST HITS — Simon & Garfunkel (CBS)
27	26	BEHIND CLOSED DOORS — Charlie Rich (Epic)
-	27	HOT CAKES — Carly Simon (Elektra)
-	28	SOLITAIRE — Andy Williams (CBS)
21	29	MA, HE'S MAKING EYES AT ME — Lena Zavaroni (Philips)
-	30	PHAEDRA — Tangerine Dream (Virgin)

20 April 1974

last week	this week	Album
1	1	THE SINGLES 1969-1973 — Carpenters (A&M)
3	2	BAND ON THE RUN — Paul McCartney & Wings (Parlophone)
2	3	GOODBYE YELLOW BRICK ROAD — Elton John (DJM)
5	4	QUEEN II — Queen (EMI)
4	5	BUDDAH AND THE CHOCOLATE BOX — Cat Stevens (Island)
10	6	DIANA AND MARVIN — Diana Ross & Marvin Gaye (Tamla Motown)
9	7	OLD NEW BORROWED AND BLUE — Slade (Polydor)
6	8	TUBULAR BELLS — Mike Oldfield (Virgin)
8	9	MILLICAN AND NESBIT — Millican & Nesbit (Pye)
19	10	GLEN CAMPBELL'S GREATEST HITS — Glen Campbell (Capitol)
7	11	ALAN FREEMAN'S HISTORY OF POP — Various Artists (Arcade)
24	12	THE STING — Soundtrack (MCA)
13	13	NOW AND THEN — Carpenters (A&M)
15	14	THE HOOPLE — Mott The Hoople (CBS)
11	15	BURN — Deep Purple (Purple)
14	16	AND I LOVE YOU SO — Perry Como (RCA)
12	17	DYNAMITE — Various Artists (K-Tel)
18	18	THE DARK SIDE OF THE MOON — Pink Floyd (Harvest)
26	19	BEHIND CLOSED DOORS — Charlie Rich (Epic)
28	20	SOLITAIRE — Andy Williams (CBS)
23	21	NOW WE ARE SIX — Steeleye Span (Chrysalis)
21	22	TOGETHER — New Seekers (Polydor)
22	23	THE UNTOUCHABLE — Alvin Stardust (Magnet)
25	24	SIMON AND GARFUNKEL'S GREATEST HITS — Simon & Garfunkel (CBS)
30	25	PHAEDRA — Tangerine Dream (Virgin)
27	26	HOT CAKES — Carly Simon (Elektra)
20	27	COURT AND SPARK — Joni Mitchell (Asylum)
-	28	INNERVISIONS — Stevie Wonder (Tamla Motown)
-	29	BY YOUR SIDE — Peters & Lee (Philips)
17	30	THE FREE STORY — Free (Island)

Charlie Rich's *Behind Closed Doors* album made a shaky start, entering but then dropping from the Top 20 for two weeks before re-climbing, eventually to No.5. The album arrived as Rich's *The Most Beautiful Girl In The World* was peaking at No.2 in the singles chart. The follow-up single would be the album's title track, which would prove his second huge crossover country hit. Rich, a fine singer and excellent pianist, had been one of the early stars of Sun Records subsidiary Phillips International in Memphis.

April – May 1974

27 April 1974

last	this	Title	Artist (Label)
1	1	THE SINGLES 1969-1973	Carpenters (A&M)
3	2	GOODBYE YELLOW BRICK ROAD	Elton John (DJM)
2	3	BAND ON THE RUN	Paul McCartney & Wings (Parlophone)
5	4	BUDDAH AND THE CHOCOLATE BOX	Cat Stevens (Island)
8	5	TUBULAR BELLS	Mike Oldfield (Virgin)
6	6	DIANA AND MARVIN	Diana Ross & Marvin Gaye (Tamla Motown)
4	7	QUEEN II	Queen (EMI)
12	8	THE STING	Soundtrack (MCA)
14	9	THE HOOPLE	Mott The Hoople (CBS)
19	10	BEHIND CLOSED DOORS	Charlie Rich (Epic)
18	11	THE DARK SIDE OF THE MOON	Pink Floyd (Harvest)
13	12	NOW AND THEN	Carpenters (A&M)
9	13	MILLICAN AND NESBIT	Millican & Nesbit (Pye)
15	14	BURN	Deep Purple (Purple)
7	15	OLD NEW BORROWED AND BLUE	Slade (Polydor)
11	16	ALAN FREEMAN'S HISTORY OF POP	Various Artists (Arcade)
25	17	PHAEDRA	Tangerine Dream (Virgin)
28	18	INNERVISIONS	Stevie Wonder (Tamla Motown)
10	19	GLEN CAMPBELL'S GREATEST HITS	Glen Campbell (Capitol)
-	20	THE STORY OF POP	Various Artists (K-Tel)
21	21	NOW WE ARE SIX	Steeleye Span (Chrysalis)
23	22	THE UNTOUCHABLE	Alvin Stardust (Magnet)
16	23	AND I LOVE YOU SO	Perry Como (RCA)
-	24	THE BEATLES 1967-1970	Beatles (Apple)
22	25	TOGETHER	New Seekers (Polydor)
20	26	SOLITAIRE	Andy Williams (CBS)
29	27	BY YOUR SIDE	Peters & Lee (Philips)
-	28	SELLING ENGLAND BY THE POUND	Genesis (Charisma)
-	29	JOURNEY THROUGH THE '60S	Various Artists (Ronco)
26	30	HOT CAKES	Carly Simon (Elektra)

4 May 1974

last	this	Title	Artist (Label)
1	1	THE SINGLES 1969-1973	Carpenters (A&M)
2	2	GOODBYE YELLOW BRICK ROAD	Elton John (DJM)
3	3	BAND ON THE RUN	Paul McCartney & Wings (Parlophone)
4	4	BUDDAH AND THE CHOCOLATE BOX	Cat Stevens (Island)
6	5	DIANA AND MARVIN	Diana Ross & Marvin Gaye (Tamla Motown)
5	6	TUBULAR BELLS	Mike Oldfield (Virgin)
7	7	QUEEN II	Queen (EMI)
15	8	OLD NEW BORROWED AND BLUE	Slade (Polydor)
9	9	THE STING	Soundtrack (MCA)
10	10	BEHIND CLOSED DOORS	Charlie Rich (Epic)
18	11	INNERVISIONS	Stevie Wonder (Tamla Motown)
13	12	MILLICAN AND NESBIT	Millican & Nesbit (Pye)
11	13	THE DARK SIDE OF THE MOON	Pink Floyd (Harvest)
12	14	NOW AND THEN	Carpenters (A&M)
17	15	PHAEDRA	Tangerine Dream (Virgin)
19	16	GLEN CAMPBELL'S GREATEST HITS	Glen Campbell (Capitol)
9	17	THE HOOPLE	Mott The Hoople (CBS)
14	18	BURN	Deep Purple (Purple)
22	19	THE UNTOUCHABLE	Alvin Stardust (Magnet)
16	20	ALAN FREEMAN'S HISTORY OF POP	Various Artists (Arcade)
23	21	AND I LOVE YOU SO	Perry Como (RCA)
24	22	THE BEATLES 1967-1970	Beatles (Apple)
27	23	BY YOUR SIDE	Peters & Lee (Philips)
-	24	SIMON AND GARFUNKEL'S GREATEST HITS	Simon & Garfunkel (CBS)
21	25	NOW WE ARE SIX	Steeleye Span (Chrysalis)
25	26	TOGETHER	New Seekers (Polydor)
29	27	JOURNEY THROUGH THE '60S	Various Artists (Ronco)
-	28	COURT AND SPARK	Joni Mitchell (Asylum)
28	29	SELLING ENGLAND BY THE POUND	Genesis (Charisma)
-	30	AMERICAN GRAFFITI	Soundtrack (MCA)

11 May 1974

last	this	Title	Artist (Label)
1	1	THE SINGLES 1969-1973	Carpenters (A&M)
2	2	GOODBYE YELLOW BRICK ROAD	Elton John (DJM)
3	3	BAND ON THE RUN	Paul McCartney & Wings (Parlophone)
4	4	BUDDAH AND THE CHOCOLATE BOX	Cat Stevens (Island)
10	5	BEHIND CLOSED DOORS	Charlie Rich (Epic)
6	6	TUBULAR BELLS	Mike Oldfield (Virgin)
5	7	DIANA AND MARVIN	Diana Ross & Marvin Gaye (Tamla Motown)
8	8	QUEEN II	Queen (EMI)
11	9	INNERVISIONS	Stevie Wonder (Tamla Motown)
8	10	OLD NEW BORROWED AND BLUE	Slade (Polydor)
17	11	THE HOOPLE	Mott The Hoople (CBS)
12	12	MILLICAN AND NESBIT	Millican & Nesbit (Pye)
14	13	NOW AND THEN	Carpenters (A&M)
13	14	THE DARK SIDE OF THE MOON	Pink Floyd (Harvest)
9	15	THE STING	Soundtrack (MCA)
21	16	AND I LOVE YOU SO	Perry Como (RCA)
-	17	SUPER BAD	Various Artists (K-Tel)
15	18	PHAEDRA	Tangerine Dream (Virgin)
-	19	QUO	Status Quo (Vertigo)
25	20	NOW WE ARE SIX	Steeleye Span (Chrysalis)
18	21	BURN	Deep Purple (Purple)
22	22	THE BEATLES 1967-1970	Beatles (Apple)
29	23	SELLING ENGLAND BY THE POUND	Genesis (Charisma)
-	24	JOURNEY TO THE CENTRE OF THE EARTH	Rick Wakeman (A&M)
24	25	SIMON AND GARFUNKEL'S GREATEST HITS	Simon & Garfunkel (CBS)
28	26	COURT AND SPARK	Joni Mitchell (Asylum)
-	27	SWEET FANNY ADAMS	Sweet (RCA)
16	28	GLEN CAMPBELL'S GREATEST HITS	Glen Campbell (Capitol)
27	29	JOURNEY THROUGH THE '60S	Various Artists (Ronco)
19	30	THE UNTOUCHABLE	Alvin Stardust (Magnet)

18 May 1974

last	this	Title	Artist (Label)
1	1	THE SINGLES 1969-1973	Carpenters (A&M)
2	2	GOODBYE YELLOW BRICK ROAD	Elton John (DJM)
4	3	BUDDAH AND THE CHOCOLATE BOX	Cat Stevens (Island)
3	4	BAND ON THE RUN	Paul McCartney & Wings (Parlophone)
6	5	TUBULAR BELLS	Mike Oldfield (Virgin)
7	6	DIANA AND MARVIN	Diana Ross & Marvin Gaye (Tamla Motown)
5	7	BEHIND CLOSED DOORS	Charlie Rich (Epic)
15	8	THE STING	Soundtrack (MCA)
19	9	QUO	Status Quo (Vertigo)
8	10	QUEEN II	Queen (EMI)
17	11	SUPER BAD	Various Artists (K-Tel)
12	12	MILLICAN AND NESBIT	Millican & Nesbit (Pye)
14	13	THE DARK SIDE OF THE MOON	Pink Floyd (Harvest)
24	14	JOURNEY TO THE CENTRE OF THE EARTH	Rick Wakeman (A&M)
9	15	INNERVISIONS	Stevie Wonder (Tamla Motown)
10	16	OLD NEW BORROWED AND BLUE	Slade (Polydor)
11	17	THE HOOPLE	Mott The Hoople (CBS)
13	18	NOW AND THEN	Carpenters (A&M)
18	19	PHAEDRA	Tangerine Dream (Virgin)
21	20	BURN	Deep Purple (Purple)
29	21	JOURNEY THROUGH THE '60S	Various Artists (Ronco)
16	22	AND I LOVE YOU SO	Perry Como (RCA)
22	23	THE BEATLES 1967-1970	Beatles (Apple)
25	24	SIMON AND GARFUNKEL'S GREATEST HITS	Simon & Garfunkel (CBS)
-	25	RAMPANT	Nazareth (Mooncrest)
26	26	GLEN CAMPBELL'S GREATEST HITS	Glen Campbell (Capitol)
-	27	WOMBLING SONGS	Wombles (CBS)
-	28	SGT PEPPER'S LONELY HEARTS CLUB BAND	Beatles (Parlophone)
-	29	THE BEATLES 1962-1966	Beatles (Apple)
23	30	SELLING ENGLAND BY THE POUND	Genesis (Charisma)

Who were Millican And Nesbit? Their next album would be called *Everybody Knows Millican And Nesbit*, but this was a large claim then, let alone now. Although this UK male vocal duo had reached No.2 with the LP now hovering around the No.12 slot, their only previous celebrity had been via the very minor hit single *Vaya Con Dios*, which had reached No.21 and promptly vanished again. That follow-up album would make the lower reaches of the chart, for three weeks only, in 1975. Who were they? Coalminers.

May – June 1974

25 May 1974

1	1	THE SINGLES 1969-1973 Carpenters (A&M)
2	2	GOODBYE YELLOW BRICK ROAD Elton John (DJM)
9	3	QUO Status Quo (Vertigo)
14	4	JOURNEY TO THE CENTRE OF THE EARTH Rick Wakeman (A&M)
5	5	TUBULAR BELLS Mike Oldfield (Virgin)
4	6	BAND ON THE RUN Paul McCartney & Wings (Parlophone)
7	7	BEHIND CLOSED DOORS Charlie Rich (Epic)
8	8	THE STING Soundtrack (MCA)
6	9	DIANA AND MARVIN Diana Ross & Marvin Gaye (Tamla Motown)
3	10	BUDDAH AND THE CHOCOLATE BOX Cat Stevens (Island)
18	11	NOW AND THEN Carpenters (A&M)
12	12	MILLICAN AND NESBIT Millican & Nesbit (Pye)
15	13	INNERVISIONS Stevie Wonder (Tamla Motown)
13	14	THE DARK SIDE OF THE MOON Pink Floyd (Harvest)
11	15	SUPER BAD Various Artists (K-Tel)
22	16	AND I LOVE YOU SO Perry Como (RCA)
25	17	RAMPANT Nazareth (Mooncrest)
-	18	SWEET FANNY ADAMS Sweet (RCA)
20	19	BURN Deep Purple (Purple)
10	20	QUEEN II Queen (EMI)
19	21	PHAEDRA Tangerine Dream (Virgin)
27	22	WOMBLING SONGS Wombles (CBS)
-	23	BY YOUR SIDE Peters & Lee (Philips)
24	24	SIMON AND GARFUNKEL'S GREATEST HITS Simon & Garfunkel (CBS)
30	25	SELLING ENGLAND BY THE POUND Genesis (Charisma)
17	26	THE HOOPLE Mott The Hoople (CBS)
26	27	GLEN CAMPBELL'S GREATEST HITS Glen Campbell (Capitol)
16	28	OLD NEW BORROWED AND BLUE Slade (Polydor)
-	29	SOLITAIRE Andy Williams (CBS)
-	30	BEST OF BREAD Bread (Elektra)

1 June 1974

1	1	THE SINGLES 1969-1973 Carpenters (A&M)
4	2	JOURNEY TO THE CENTRE OF THE EARTH Rick Wakeman (A&M)
-	3	DIAMOND DOGS David Bowie (RCA)
6	4	BAND ON THE RUN Paul McCartney & Wings (Parlophone)
3	5	QUO Status Quo (Vertigo)
5	6	TUBULAR BELLS Mike Oldfield (Virgin)
2	7	GOODBYE YELLOW BRICK ROAD Elton John (DJM)
8	8	THE STING Soundtrack (MCA)
7	9	BEHIND CLOSED DOORS Charlie Rich (Epic)
10	10	BUDDAH AND THE CHOCOLATE BOX Cat Stevens (Island)
9	11	DIANA AND MARVIN Diana Ross & Marvin Gaye (Tamla Motown)
11	12	NOW AND THEN Carpenters (A&M)
21	13	PHAEDRA Tangerine Dream (Virgin)
14	14	THE DARK SIDE OF THE MOON Pink Floyd (Harvest)
15	15	SUPER BAD Various Artists (K-Tel)
24	16	SIMON AND GARFUNKEL'S GREATEST HITS Simon & Garfunkel (CBS)
25	17	SELLING ENGLAND BY THE POUND Genesis (Charisma)
16	18	AND I LOVE YOU SO Perry Como (RCA)
-	19	KIMONO MY HOUSE Sparks (Island)
13	20	INNERVISIONS Stevie Wonder (Tamla Motown)
27	21	GLEN CAMPBELL'S GREATEST HITS Glen Campbell (Capitol)
18	22	SWEET FANNY ADAMS Sweet (RCA)
-	23	RHINOS WINOS AND LUNATICS Man (United Artists)
-	24	EASY EASY Scotland World Cup Squad (Polydor)
23	25	BY YOUR SIDE Peters & Lee (Philips)
22	26	WOMBLING SONGS Wombles (CBS)
-	27	THE BEATLES 1967-1970 Beatles (Apple)
12	28	MILLICAN AND NESBIT Millican & Nesbit (Pye)
19	29	BURN Deep Purple (Purple)
-	30	SCOTT JOPLIN/PIANO RAGS Joshua Rifkin (Nonesuch)

8 June 1974

1	1	THE SINGLES 1969-1973 Carpenters (A&M)
2	2	JOURNEY TO THE CENTRE OF THE EARTH Rick Wakeman (A&M)
3	3	DIAMOND DOGS David Bowie (RCA)
6	4	TUBULAR BELLS Mike Oldfield (Virgin)
5	5	QUO Status Quo (Vertigo)
4	6	BAND ON THE RUN Paul McCartney & Wings (Parlophone)
7	7	GOODBYE YELLOW BRICK ROAD Elton John (DJM)
9	8	BEHIND CLOSED DOORS Charlie Rich (Epic)
8	9	THE STING Soundtrack (MCA)
15	10	SUPER BAD Various Artists (K-Tel)
19	11	KIMONO MY HOUSE Sparks (Island)
25	12	BY YOUR SIDE Peters & Lee (Philips)
14	13	THE DARK SIDE OF THE MOON Pink Floyd (Harvest)
11	14	DIANA AND MARVIN Diana Ross & Marvin Gaye (Tamla Motown)
18	15	AND I LOVE YOU SO Perry Como (RCA)
20	16	INNERVISIONS Stevie Wonder (Tamla Motown)
21	17	GLEN CAMPBELL'S GREATEST HITS Glen Campbell (Capitol)
10	18	BUDDAH AND THE CHOCOLATE BOX Cat Stevens (Island)
-	19	HAMBURGER CONCERTO Focus (Polydor)
12	20	NOW AND THEN Carpenters (A&M)
16	21	SIMON AND GARFUNKEL'S GREATEST HITS Simon & Garfunkel (CBS)
23	22	RHINOS WINOS AND LUNATICS Man (United Artists)
13	23	PHAEDRA Tangerine Dream (Virgin)
24	24	EASY EASY Scotland World Cup Squad (Polydor)
28	25	MILLICAN AND NESBIT Millican & Nesbit (Pye)
-	26	BAD COMPANY Bad Company (Island)
26	27	WOMBLING SONGS Wombles (CBS)
-	28	WE CAN MAKE IT Peters & Lee (Philips)
22	29	SWEET FANNY ADAMS Sweet (RCA)
-	30	SOLITAIRE Andy Williams (CBS)

15 June 1974

3	1	DIAMOND DOGS David Bowie (RCA)
1	2	THE SINGLES 1969-1973 Carpenters (A&M)
5	3	QUO Status Quo (Vertigo)
2	4	JOURNEY TO THE CENTRE OF THE EARTH Rick Wakeman (A&M)
4	5	TUBULAR BELLS Mike Oldfield (Virgin)
11	6	KIMONO MY HOUSE Sparks (Island)
7	7	GOODBYE YELLOW BRICK ROAD Elton John (DJM)
6	8	BAND ON THE RUN Paul McCartney & Wings (Parlophone)
10	9	SUPER BAD Various Artists (K-Tel)
13	10	THE DARK SIDE OF THE MOON Pink Floyd (Harvest)
9	11	THE STING Soundtrack (MCA)
8	12	BEHIND CLOSED DOORS Charlie Rich (Epic)
14	13	DIANA AND MARVIN Diana Ross & Marvin Gaye (Tamla Motown)
12	14	BY YOUR SIDE Peters & Lee (Philips)
26	15	BAD COMPANY Bad Company (Island)
15	16	AND I LOVE YOU SO Perry Como (RCA)
23	17	PHAEDRA Tangerine Dream (Virgin)
17	18	GLEN CAMPBELL'S GREATEST HITS Glen Campbell (Capitol)
16	19	INNERVISIONS Stevie Wonder (Tamla Motown)
24	20	EASY EASY Scotland World Cup Squad (Polydor)
18	21	BUDDAH AND THE CHOCOLATE BOX Cat Stevens (Island)
21	22	SIMON AND GARFUNKEL'S GREATEST HITS Simon & Garfunkel (CBS)
-	23	BETWEEN TODAY AND YESTERDAY Alan Price (Warner Bros.)
-	24	RAMPANT Nazareth (Mooncrest)
20	25	NOW AND THEN Carpenters (A&M)
19	26	HAMBURGER CONCERTO Focus (Polydor)
-	27	MONKEY GRIP Bill Wyman (Rolling Stones)
-	28	IN FOR THE KILL Budgie (MCA)
-	29	THESE FOOLISH THINGS Bryan Ferry (Island)
27	30	WOMBLING SONGS Wombles (CBS)

Rhinos Winos And Lunatics was Welsh band Man's second minor hit album; *Back Into The Future* had made some charts, though not NME's. Fronted by Deke Leonard, who had a cult following, Man was a self-deprecating guitar band. A later, cut-priced LP would have the splendid title *Man Live At The Paget Rooms, Penarth*. Also Welsh were Budgie, a self-deprecating name in itself. *In For The Kill*, their first and biggest LP, entered the chart at No.28. It was downhill all the way after that.

22 June 1974

last week / this week

1. 1 — DIAMOND DOGS — David Bowie (RCA)
2. 2 — THE SINGLES 1969-1973 — Carpenters (A&M)
3. 4 → 3 — JOURNEY TO THE CENTRE OF THE EARTH — Rick Wakeman (A&M)
4. 3 → 4 — QUO — Status Quo (Vertigo)
5. 6 → 5 — KIMONO MY HOUSE — Sparks (Island)
6. 15 → 6 — BAD COMPANY — Bad Company (Island)
7. 8 → 7 — BAND ON THE RUN — Paul McCartney & Wings (Parlophone)
8. 5 → 8 — TUBULAR BELLS — Mike Oldfield (Virgin)
9. 7 → 9 — GOODBYE YELLOW BRICK ROAD — Elton John (DJM)
10. 12 → 10 — BEHIND CLOSED DOORS — Charlie Rich (Epic)
11. 14 → 11 — BY YOUR SIDE — Peters & Lee (Philips)
12. 9 → 12 — SUPER BAD — Various Artists (K-Tel)
13. 16 → 13 — AND I LOVE YOU SO — Perry Como (RCA)
14. - → 14 — SHEET MUSIC — 10 C.C. (UK)
15. 13 → 15 — DIANA AND MARVIN — Diana Ross & Marvin Gaye (Tamla Motown)
16. 11 → 16 — THE STING — Soundtrack (MCA)
17. 18 → 17 — GLEN CAMPBELL'S GREATEST HITS — Glen Campbell (Capitol)
18. 20 → 18 — EASY EASY — Scotland World Cup Squad (Polydor)
19. - → 19 — REMEMBER ME THIS WAY — Gary Glitter (Bell)
20. - → 20 — THE WAY WE WERE — Andy Williams (CBS)
21. 10 → 21 — THE DARK SIDE OF THE MOON — Pink Floyd (Harvest)
22. 22 — SIMON AND GARFUNKEL'S GREATEST HITS — Simon & Garfunkel (CBS)
23. 25 → 23 — NOW AND THEN — Carpenters (A&M)
24. - → 24 — DIANA ROSS LIVE — Diana Ross (Tamla Motown)
25. 21 → 25 — BUDDAH AND THE CHOCOLATE BOX — Cat Stevens (Island)
26. 19 → 26 — INNERVISIONS — Stevie Wonder (Tamla Motown)
27. - → 27 — QUEEN II — Queen (EMI)
28. - → 28 — SCOTT JOPLIN/PIANO RAGS — Joshua Rifkin (Nonesuch)
29. - → 29 — CAMEMBERT ELECTRIQUE — Gong (Virgin)
30. 28 → 30 — IN FOR THE KILL — Budgie (MCA)

29 June 1974

1. 1 — DIAMOND DOGS — David Bowie (RCA)
2. 2 — THE SINGLES 1969-1973 — Carpenters (A&M)
3. 6 → 3 — BAD COMPANY — Bad Company (Island)
4. 5 → 4 — KIMONO MY HOUSE — Sparks (Island)
5. 3 → 5 — JOURNEY TO THE CENTRE OF THE EARTH — Rick Wakeman (A&M)
6. 8 → 6 — TUBULAR BELLS — Mike Oldfield (Virgin)
7. 7 — BAND ON THE RUN — Paul McCartney & Wings (Parlophone)
8. 9 → 8 — GOODBYE YELLOW BRICK ROAD — Elton John (DJM)
9. 4 → 9 — QUO — Status Quo (Vertigo)
10. 14 → 10 — SHEET MUSIC — 10 C.C. (UK)
11. 10 → 11 — BEHIND CLOSED DOORS — Charlie Rich (Epic)
12. 19 → 12 — REMEMBER ME THIS WAY — Gary Glitter (Bell)
13. 16 → 13 — THE STING — Soundtrack (MCA)
14. 12 → 14 — SUPER BAD — Various Artists (K-Tel)
15. 21 → 15 — THE DARK SIDE OF THE MOON — Pink Floyd (Harvest)
16. 13 → 16 — AND I LOVE YOU SO — Perry Como (RCA)
17. 17 — GLEN CAMPBELL'S GREATEST HITS — Glen Campbell (Capitol)
18. 20 → 18 — THE WAY WE WERE — Andy Williams (CBS)
19. 15 → 19 — DIANA AND MARVIN — Diana Ross & Marvin Gaye (Tamla Motown)
20. 18 → 20 — EASY EASY — Scotland World Cup Squad (Polydor)
21. 11 → 21 — BY YOUR SIDE — Peters & Lee (Philips)
22. - → 22 — ATLANTIC BLACK GOLD — Various Artists (Atlantic)
23. - → 23 — PHAEDRA — Tangerine Dream (Virgin)
24. 23 → 24 — NOW AND THEN — Carpenters (A&M)
25. - → 25 — THE PSYCHOMODO — Cockney Rebel (EMI)
26. 26 — INNERVISIONS — Stevie Wonder (Tamla Motown)
27. - → 27 — HAMBURGER CONCERTO — Focus (Polydor)
28. - → 28 — WOMBLING SONGS — Wombles (CBS)
29. - → 29 — BETWEEN TODAY AND YESTERDAY — Alan Price (Warner Bros.)
30. - → 30 — BEST OF BREAD — Bread (Elektra)

6 July 1974

1. 1 — DIAMOND DOGS — David Bowie (RCA)
2. 2 — THE SINGLES 1969-1973 — Carpenters (A&M)
3. 6 → 3 — TUBULAR BELLS — Mike Oldfield (Virgin)
4. 7 → 4 — BAND ON THE RUN — Paul McCartney & Wings (Parlophone)
5. - → 5 — CARIBOU — Elton John (DJM)
6. 12 → 6 — REMEMBER ME THIS WAY — Gary Glitter (Bell)
7. 4 → 7 — KIMONO MY HOUSE — Sparks (Island)
8. 3 → 8 — BAD COMPANY — Bad Company (Island)
9. 5 → 9 — JOURNEY TO THE CENTRE OF THE EARTH — Rick Wakeman (A&M)
10. 9 → 10 — QUO — Status Quo (Vertigo)
11. 8 → 11 — GOODBYE YELLOW BRICK ROAD — Elton John (DJM)
12. - → 12 — AZNAVOUR SINGS AZNAVOUR VOL 3 — Charles Aznavour (Barclay)
13. 10 → 13 — SHEET MUSIC — 10 C.C. (UK)
14. - → 14 — 22 ELECTRIFYING HITS — Various Artists (K-Tel)
15. 15 — THE DARK SIDE OF THE MOON — Pink Floyd (Harvest)
16. 25 → 16 — THE PSYCHOMODO — Cockney Rebel (EMI)
17. 11 → 17 — BEHIND CLOSED DOORS — Charlie Rich (Epic)
18. 19 → 18 — DIANA AND MARVIN — Diana Ross & Marvin Gaye (Tamla Motown)
19. 16 → 19 — AND I LOVE YOU SO — Perry Como (RCA)
20. 18 → 20 — THE WAY WE WERE — Andy Williams (CBS)
21. 14 → 21 — SUPER BAD — Various Artists (K-Tel)
22. 24 → 22 — NOW AND THEN — Carpenters (A&M)
23. 20 → 23 — EASY EASY — Scotland World Cup Squad (Polydor)
24. - → 24 — HIS 12 GREATEST HITS — Neil Diamond (MCA)
25. 13 → 25 — THE STING — Soundtrack (MCA)
26. - → 26 — LAUGHTER IN THE RAIN — Neil Sedaka (Polydor)
27. 27 — DIANA ROSS LIVE — Diana Ross (Tamla Motown)
28. 21 → 28 — BY YOUR SIDE — Peters & Lee (Philips)
29. 28 → 29 — WOMBLING SONGS — Wombles (CBS)
30. 23 → 30 — PHAEDRA — Tangerine Dream (Virgin)

13 July 1974

1. 4 → 1 — BAND ON THE RUN — Paul McCartney & Wings (Parlophone)
2. 2 — THE SINGLES 1969-1973 — Carpenters (A&M)
3. 5 → 3 — CARIBOU — Elton John (DJM)
4. 3 → 4 — TUBULAR BELLS — Mike Oldfield (Virgin)
5. 1 → 5 — DIAMOND DOGS — David Bowie (RCA)
6. 6 — REMEMBER ME THIS WAY — Gary Glitter (Bell)
7. 9 → 7 — JOURNEY TO THE CENTRE OF THE EARTH — Rick Wakeman (A&M)
8. 8 — BAD COMPANY — Bad Company (Island)
9. 7 → 9 — KIMONO MY HOUSE — Sparks (Island)
10. 11 → 10 — GOODBYE YELLOW BRICK ROAD — Elton John (DJM)
11. 13 → 11 — SHEET MUSIC — 10 C.C. (UK)
12. 15 → 12 — THE DARK SIDE OF THE MOON — Pink Floyd (Harvest)
13. 20 → 13 — THE WAY WE WERE — Andy Williams (CBS)
14. 17 → 14 — BEHIND CLOSED DOORS — Charlie Rich (Epic)
15. 25 → 15 — THE STING — Soundtrack (MCA)
16. 12 → 16 — AZNAVOUR SINGS AZNAVOUR VOL 3 — Charles Aznavour (Barclay)
17. 19 → 17 — AND I LOVE YOU SO — Perry Como (RCA)
18. - → 18 — BETWEEN TODAY AND YESTERDAY — Alan Price (Warner Bros.)
19. - → 19 — ANOTHER TIME, ANOTHER PLACE — Bryan Ferry (Island)
20. 16 → 20 — THE PSYCHOMODO — Cockney Rebel (EMI)
21. 14 → 21 — 22 ELECTRIFYING HITS — Various Artists (K-Tel)
22. 24 → 22 — HIS 12 GREATEST HITS — Neil Diamond (MCA)
23. 18 → 23 — DIANA AND MARVIN — Diana Ross & Marvin Gaye (Tamla Motown)
24. 21 → 24 — SUPER BAD — Various Artists (K-Tel)
25. - → 25 — CAMEMBERT ELECTRIQUE — Gong (Virgin)
26. 30 → 26 — PHAEDRA — Tangerine Dream (Virgin)
27. - → 27 — ATLANTIC BLACK GOLD — Various Artists (Atlantic)
28. - → 28 — GLEN CAMPBELL'S GREATEST HITS — Glen Campbell (Capitol)
29. 10 → 29 — QUO — Status Quo (Vertigo)
30. - → 30 — SIMON AND GARFUNKEL'S GREATEST HITS — Simon & Garfunkel (CBS)

This period ends with a Top 5 of real mega-sellers. McCartney's *Band On The Run* had been a slow riser (first charting the previous December) but would end up the second best-selling LP of the year, in Britain and the USA. The Carpenters' *The Singles 1969-1973* would beat it in the UK, with Mike Oldfield's *Tubular Bells* third (17th in the USA). Elton John's *Caribou* would be 1974's 15th best-seller here and its 12th in the USA. Bowie's *Diamond Dogs* would be Britain's 14th best-seller.

July – August 1974

Bob Dylan and the Band's live double-album *Before The Flood* charted. Dylan's first live album, it set a precedent in failing to capture anything remotely close to the highlights of the tour it tried to represent. Later, the triple-LP *Bob Dylan At Budokan* would offer no hint at all of the rigorous splendours of the 1978 tours; nor would *Real Live*, 1984, illuminate that year's march through Europe.

In a London hotel-room on July 29, 1974, Mama Cass Elliott died, aged 31.

August – September 1974

17 August 1974

1	1	BAND ON THE RUN	Paul McCartney & Wings (Parlophone)
2	2	TUBULAR BELLS	Mike Oldfield (Virgin)
5	3	THE SINGLES 1969-1973	Carpenters (A&M)
3	4	CARIBOU	Elton John (DJM)
4	5	ANOTHER TIME, ANOTHER PLACE	Bryan Ferry (Island)
6	6	KIMONO MY HOUSE	Sparks (Island)
8	7	THE DARK SIDE OF THE MOON	Pink Floyd (Harvest)
7	8	JOURNEY TO THE CENTRE OF THE EARTH	Rick Wakeman (A&M)
9	9	AND I LOVE YOU SO	Perry Como (RCA)
11	10	DIAMOND DOGS	David Bowie (RCA)
12	11	SHEET MUSIC	10 C.C. (UK)
21	12	DAVID CASSIDY LIVE	David Cassidy (Bell)
14	13	FULFILLINGNESS' FIRST FINALE	Stevie Wonder (Tamla Motown)
15	14	HIS 12 GREATEST HITS	Neil Diamond (MCA)
-	15	WELCOME BACK MY FRIENDS TO THE SHOW THAT NEVER ENDS	Emerson, Lake & Palmer (Manticore)
10	16	GOODBYE YELLOW BRICK ROAD	Elton John (DJM.)
13	17	REMEMBER ME THIS WAY	Gary Glitter (Bell)
-	18	ROCK YOUR BABY	George McCrae (Jay Boy)
19	19	BEFORE THE FLOOD	Bob Dylan (Island)
27	20	DIANA AND MARVIN	Diana Ross & Marvin Gaye (Tamla Motown)
-	21	461 OCEAN BOULEVARD	Eric Clapton (RSO)
23	22	SOLO CONCERT	Billy Connolly (Transatlantic)
22	23	20 SMASH HITS	Various Artists (Arcade)
17	24	SIMON AND GARFUNKEL'S GREATEST HITS	Simon & Garfunkel (CBS)
18	25	LAUGHTER IN THE RAIN	Neil Sedaka (Polydor)
16	26	BAD COMPANY	Bad Company (Island)
-	27	GLEN CAMPBELL'S GREATEST HITS	Glen Campbell (Capitol)
-	28	PERRY	Perry Como (RCA)
29	29	INNERVISIONS	Stevie Wonder (Tamla Motown)
-	30	THE THREE DEGREES	Three Degrees (Philadelphia International)

24 August 1974

1	1	BAND ON THE RUN	Paul McCartney & Wings (Parlophone)
2	2	TUBULAR BELLS	Mike Oldfield (Virgin)
6	3	KIMONO MY HOUSE	Sparks (Island)
5	4	ANOTHER TIME, ANOTHER PLACE	Bryan Ferry (Island)
3	5	THE SINGLES 1969-1973	Carpenters (A&M)
4	6	CARIBOU	Elton John (DJM)
7	7	THE DARK SIDE OF THE MOON	Pink Floyd (Harvest)
8	8	JOURNEY TO THE CENTRE OF THE EARTH	Rick Wakeman (A&M)
13	9	FULFILLINGNESS' FIRST FINALE	Stevie Wonder (Tamla Motown)
18	10	ROCK YOUR BABY	George McCrae (Jay Boy)
14	11	HIS 12 GREATEST HITS	Neil Diamond (MCA)
9	12	AND I LOVE YOU SO	Perry Como (RCA)
21	13	461 OCEAN BOULEVARD	Eric Clapton (RSO)
17	14	REMEMBER ME THIS WAY	Gary Glitter (Bell)
16	15	GOODBYE YELLOW BRICK ROAD	Elton John (DJM)
11	16	SHEET MUSIC	10 C.C. (UK)
20	17	DIANA AND MARVIN	Diana Ross & Marvin Gaye (Tamla Motown)
15	18	WELCOME BACK MY FRIENDS TO THE SHOW THAT NEVER ENDS	Emerson, Lake & Palmer (Manticore)
-	19	THE PSYCHOMODO	Cockney Rebel (EMI)
10	20	DIAMOND DOGS	David Bowie (RCA)
28	21	PERRY	Perry Como (RCA)
26	22	BAD COMPANY	Bad Company (Island)
22	23	SOLO CONCERT	Billy Connolly (Transatlantic)
19	24	BEFORE THE FLOOD	Bob Dylan (Island)
30	25	THE THREE DEGREES	Three Degrees (Philadelphia International)
29	26	INNERVISIONS	Stevie Wonder (Tamla Motown)
24	27	SIMON AND GARFUNKEL'S GREATEST HITS	Simon & Garfunkel (CBS)
-	28	LIVE AT DRURY LANE	Monty Python's Flying Circus (Charisma)
-	29	OUR BEST TO YOU	Osmonds (MGM)
-	30	EDDY AND THE FALCONS	Wizzard (Warner Bros.)

31 August 1974

1	1	BAND ON THE RUN	Paul McCartney & Wings (Parlophone)
2	2	TUBULAR BELLS	Mike Oldfield (Virgin)
5	3	THE SINGLES 1969-1973	Carpenters (A&M)
4	4	ANOTHER TIME, ANOTHER PLACE	Bryan Ferry (Island)
18	5	WELCOME BACK MY FRIENDS TO THE SHOW THAT NEVER ENDS	Emerson, Lake & Palmer (Manticore)
3	6	KIMONO MY HOUSE	Sparks (Island)
7	7	THE DARK SIDE OF THE MOON	Pink Floyd (Harvest)
6	8	CARIBOU	Elton John (DJM)
13	9	461 OCEAN BOULEVARD	Eric Clapton (RSO)
9	10	FULFILLINGNESS' FIRST FINALE	Stevie Wonder (Tamla Motown)
19	11	THE PSYCHOMODO	Cockney Rebel (EMI)
11	12	HIS 12 GREATEST HITS	Neil Diamond (MCA)
8	13	JOURNEY TO THE CENTRE OF THE EARTH	Rick Wakeman (A&M)
25	14	THE THREE DEGREES	Three Degrees (Philadelphia International)
16	15	SHEET MUSIC	10 C.C. (UK)
27	16	SIMON AND GARFUNKEL'S GREATEST HITS	Simon & Garfunkel (CBS)
21	17	PERRY	Perry Como (RCA)
14	18	REMEMBER ME THIS WAY	Gary Glitter (Bell)
23	19	SOLO CONCERT	Billy Connolly (Transatlantic)
12	20	AND I LOVE YOU SO	Perry Como (RCA)
29	21	OUR BEST TO YOU	Osmonds (MGM)
-	22	DAVID CASSIDY LIVE	David Cassidy (Bell)
10	23	ROCK YOUR BABY	George McCrae (Jay Boy)
28	24	LIVE AT DRURY LANE	Monty Python's Flying Circus (Charisma)
17	25	DIANA AND MARVIN	Diana Ross & Marvin Gaye (Tamla Motown)
22	26	BAD COMPANY	Bad Company (Island)
24	27	BEFORE THE FLOOD	Bob Dylan (Island)
15	28	GOODBYE YELLOW BRICK ROAD	Elton John (DJM)
26	29	INNERVISIONS	Stevie Wonder (Tamla Motown)
30	30	BLACK EXPLOSION	Various Artists (Ronco)

7 September 1974

1	1	BAND ON THE RUN	Paul McCartney & Wings (Parlophone)
2	2	TUBULAR BELLS	Mike Oldfield (Virgin)
3	3	THE SINGLES 1969-1973	Carpenters (A&M)
9	4	461 OCEAN BOULEVARD	Eric Clapton (RSO)
4	5	ANOTHER TIME, ANOTHER PLACE	Bryan Ferry (Island)
6	6	KIMONO MY HOUSE	Sparks (Island)
-	7	HERGEST RIDGE	Mike Oldfield (Virgin)
21	8	OUR BEST TO YOU	Osmonds (MGM)
10	9	FULFILLINGNESS' FIRST FINALE	Stevie Wonder (Tamla Motown)
5	10	WELCOME BACK MY FRIENDS TO THE SHOW THAT NEVER ENDS	Emerson, Lake & Palmer (Manticore)
8	11	CARIBOU	Elton John (DJM)
7	12	THE DARK SIDE OF THE MOON	Pink Floyd (Harvest)
13	13	JOURNEY TO THE CENTRE OF THE EARTH	Rick Wakeman (A&M)
11	14	THE PSYCHOMODO	Cockney Rebel (EMI)
23	15	ROCK YOUR BABY	George McCrae (Jay Boy)
20	16	AND I LOVE YOU SO	Perry Como (RCA)
14	17	THE THREE DEGREES	Three Degrees (Philadelphia International)
15	18	SHEET MUSIC	10 C.C. (UK)
28	19	GOODBYE YELLOW BRICK ROAD	Elton John (DJM)
12	20	HIS 12 GREATEST HITS	Neil Diamond (MCA)
24	21	LIVE AT DRURY LANE	Monty Python's Flying Circus (Charisma)
-	22	BACK HOME AGAIN	John Denver (RCA)
16	23	SIMON AND GARFUNKEL'S GREATEST HITS	Simon & Garfunkel (CBS)
22	24	DAVID CASSIDY LIVE	David Cassidy (Bell)
30	25	BLACK EXPLOSION	Various Artists (Ronco)
19	26	SOLO CONCERT	Billy Connolly (Transatlantic)
-	27	REMEMBER YOU'RE A WOMBLE	Wombles (CBS)
17	28	PERRY	Perry Como (RCA)
-	29	GLEN CAMPBELL'S GREATEST HITS	Glen Campbell (Capitol)
-	30	EDDY AND THE FALCONS	Wizzard (Warner Bros.)

Billy Connolly's *Solo Concert* was the first of several hit albums by Scotland's great comic. The title *Solo Concert* referred to the fact that he'd been half of the Humblebums, along with singer-songwriter Gerry Rafferty, who had made a well-regarded but non-charting LP of his own, *Can I Have My Money Back?* (also on the British indie label Transatlantic), before forming Stealer's Wheel, which had had a big 1973 hit with *Stuck In The Middle With You* and the more modest *Star* earlier in 1974.

September – October 1974

14 September 1974

1	1	BAND ON THE RUN — Paul McCartney & Wings (Parlophone)
2	2	TUBULAR BELLS — Mike Oldfield (Virgin)
3	3	THE SINGLES 1969-1973 — Carpenters (A&M)
4	4	461 OCEAN BOULEVARD — Eric Clapton (RSO)
8	5	OUR BEST TO YOU — Osmonds (MGM)
7	6	HERGEST RIDGE — Mike Oldfield (Virgin)
5	7	ANOTHER TIME, ANOTHER PLACE — Bryan Ferry (Island)
14	8	THE PSYCHOMODO — Cockney Rebel (EMI)
22	9	BACK HOME AGAIN — John Denver (RCA)
12	10	THE DARK SIDE OF THE MOON — Pink Floyd (Harvest)
11	11	CARIBOU — Elton John (DJM)
9	12	FULFILLINGNESS' FIRST FINALE — Stevie Wonder (Tamla Motown)
13	13	JOURNEY TO THE CENTRE OF THE EARTH — Rick Wakeman (A&M)
16	14	AND I LOVE YOU SO — Perry Como (RCA)
17	15	THE THREE DEGREES — Three Degrees (Philadelphia International)
10	16	WELCOME BACK MY FRIENDS TO THE SHOW THAT NEVER ENDS — Emerson, Lake & Palmer (Manticore)
6	17	KIMONO MY HOUSE — Sparks (Island)
-	18	TAPESTRY OF DREAMS — Charles Aznavour (Barclay)
26	19	SOLO CONCERT — Billy Connolly (Transatlantic)
19	20	GOODBYE YELLOW BRICK ROAD — Elton John (DJM)
15	21	ROCK YOUR BABY — George McCrae (Jay Boy)
28	22	PERRY — Perry Como (RCA)
23	23	SIMON AND GARFUNKEL'S GREATEST HITS — Simon & Garfunkel (CBS)
-	24	THE STING — Soundtrack (MCA)
-	25	THE BEATLES 1967-1970 — Beatles (Apple)
20	26	HIS 12 GREATEST HITS — Neil Diamond (MCA)
27	27	REMEMBER YOU'RE A WOMBLE — Wombles (CBS)
18	28	SHEET MUSIC — 10 C.C. (UK)
-	29	DIAMOND DOGS — David Bowie (RCA)
-	30	BEST OF BREAD — Bread (Elektra)

21 September 1974

6	1	HERGEST RIDGE — Mike Oldfield (Virgin)
2	2	TUBULAR BELLS — Mike Oldfield (Virgin)
1	3	BAND ON THE RUN — Paul McCartney & Wings (Parlophone)
7	4	ANOTHER TIME, ANOTHER PLACE — Bryan Ferry (Island)
9	5	BACK HOME AGAIN — John Denver (RCA)
3	6	THE SINGLES 1969-1973 — Carpenters (A&M)
4	7	461 OCEAN BOULEVARD — Eric Clapton (RSO)
10	8	THE DARK SIDE OF THE MOON — Pink Floyd (Harvest)
12	9	FULFILLINGNESS' FIRST FINALE — Stevie Wonder (Tamla Motown)
8	10	THE PSYCHOMODO — Cockney Rebel (EMI)
5	11	OUR BEST TO YOU — Osmonds (MGM)
-	12	HEY! — Glitter Band (Bell)
17	13	KIMONO MY HOUSE — Sparks (Island)
-	14	BLACK EXPLOSION — Various Artists (Ronco)
11	15	CARIBOU — Elton John (DJM)
-	16	RAINBOW — Peters & Lee (Philips)
23	17	SIMON AND GARFUNKEL'S GREATEST HITS — Simon & Garfunkel (CBS)
16	18	WELCOME BACK MY FRIENDS TO THE SHOW THAT NEVER ENDS — Emerson, Lake & Palmer (Manticore)
26	19	HIS 12 GREATEST HITS — Neil Diamond (MCA)
13	20	JOURNEY TO THE CENTRE OF THE EARTH — Rick Wakeman (A&M)
15	21	THE THREE DEGREES — Three Degrees (Philadelphia International)
14	22	AND I LOVE YOU SO — Perry Como (RCA)
28	23	SHEET MUSIC — 10 C.C. (UK)
-	24	IN THE HALL OF THE MOUNTAIN GRILL — Hawkwind (United Artists)
-	25	DIANA AND MARVIN — Diana Ross & Marvin Gaye (Tamla Motown)
-	26	BY YOUR SIDE — Peters & Lee (Philips)
-	27	THE BEST OF JOHN DENVER — John Denver (RCA)
-	28	SANTANA'S GREATEST HITS — Santana (CBS)
29	29	DIAMOND DOGS — David Bowie (RCA)
22	30	PERRY — Perry Como (RCA)

28 September 1974

1	1	HERGEST RIDGE — Mike Oldfield (Virgin)
2	2	TUBULAR BELLS — Mike Oldfield (Virgin)
3	3	BAND ON THE RUN — Paul McCartney & Wings (Parlophone)
5	4	BACK HOME AGAIN — John Denver (RCA)
4	5	ANOTHER TIME, ANOTHER PLACE — Bryan Ferry (Island)
6	6	THE SINGLES 1969-1973 — Carpenters (A&M)
11	7	OUR BEST TO YOU — Osmonds (MGM)
15	8	CARIBOU — Elton John (DJM)
7	9	461 OCEAN BOULEVARD — Eric Clapton (RSO)
9	10	FULFILLINGNESS' FIRST FINALE — Stevie Wonder (Tamla Motown)
10	11	THE PSYCHOMODO — Cockney Rebel (EMI)
16	12	RAINBOW — Peters & Lee (Philips)
8	13	THE DARK SIDE OF THE MOON — Pink Floyd (Harvest)
28	14	SANTANA'S GREATEST HITS — Santana (CBS)
21	15	THE THREE DEGREES — Three Degrees (Philadelphia International)
12	16	HEY! — Glitter Band (Bell)
23	17	SHEET MUSIC — 10 C.C. (UK)
14	18	BLACK EXPLOSION — Various Artists (Ronco)
13	19	KIMONO MY HOUSE — Sparks (Island)
17	20	SIMON AND GARFUNKEL'S GREATEST HITS — Simon & Garfunkel (CBS)
20	21	JOURNEY TO THE CENTRE OF THE EARTH — Rick Wakeman (A&M)
24	22	IN THE HALL OF THE MOUNTAIN GRILL — Hawkwind (United Artists)
-	23	MUD ROCK — Mud (RAK)
-	24	TAPESTRY OF DREAMS — Charles Aznavour (Barclay)
27	25	THE BEST OF JOHN DENVER — John Denver (RCA)
19	26	HIS 12 GREATEST HITS — Neil Diamond (MCA)
-	27	ROCK YOUR BABY — George McCrae (Jay Boy)
-	28	INNERVISIONS — Stevie Wonder (Tamla Motown)
25	29	DIANA AND MARVIN — Diana Ross & Marvin Gaye (Tamla Motown)
18	30	WELCOME BACK MY FRIENDS TO THE SHOW THAT NEVER ENDS — Emerson, Lake & Palmer (Manticore)

5 October 1974

2	1	TUBULAR BELLS — Mike Oldfield (Virgin)
1	2	HERGEST RIDGE — Mike Oldfield (Virgin)
4	3	BACK HOME AGAIN — John Denver (RCA)
3	4	BAND ON THE RUN — Paul McCartney & Wings (Parlophone)
5	5	ANOTHER TIME, ANOTHER PLACE — Bryan Ferry (Island)
6	6	THE SINGLES 1969-1973 — Carpenters (A&M)
12	7	RAINBOW — Peters & Lee (Philips)
13	8	THE DARK SIDE OF THE MOON — Pink Floyd (Harvest)
8	9	CARIBOU — Elton John (DJM)
-	10	ROLLIN' — Bay City Rollers (Bell)
9	11	461 OCEAN BOULEVARD — Eric Clapton (RSO)
7	12	OUR BEST TO YOU — Osmonds (MGM)
10	13	FULFILLINGNESS' FIRST FINALE — Stevie Wonder (Tamla Motown)
14	14	SANTANA'S GREATEST HITS — Santana (CBS)
23	15	MUD ROCK — Mud (RAK)
17	16	SHEET MUSIC — 10 C.C. (UK)
11	17	THE PSYCHOMODO — Cockney Rebel (EMI)
24	18	TAPESTRY OF DREAMS — Charles Aznavour (Barclay)
18	19	BLACK EXPLOSION — Various Artists (Ronco)
15	20	THE THREE DEGREES — Three Degrees (Philadelphia International)
21	21	JOURNEY TO THE CENTRE OF THE EARTH — Rick Wakeman (A&M)
16	22	HEY! — Glitter Band (Bell)
22	23	IN THE HALL OF THE MOUNTAIN GRILL — Hawkwind (United Artists)
19	24	KIMONO MY HOUSE — Sparks (Island)
25	25	GOODBYE YELLOW BRICK ROAD — Elton John (DJM)
25	26	THE BEST OF JOHN DENVER — John Denver (RCA)
26	27	HIS 12 GREATEST HITS — Neil Diamond (MCA)
27	28	ROCK YOUR BABY — George McCrae (Jay Boy)
28	29	INNERVISIONS — Stevie Wonder (Tamla Motown)
-	30	SOLO CONCERT — Billy Connolly (Transatlantic)

Mike Oldfield's second album, *Hergest Ridge*, was named after a real place on the Welsh border. Another second album, *Remember You're A Womble*, referred to a set of children's TV characters. The Wombles picked up litter on Wimbledon Common. The creator of their jolly, whimsical, and insufferably twee music, Mike Batt, picked up a fortune. The year would end not with a bang but a Womble: the No.3 single for the last week of 1974 was to be *A Wombling Merry Christmas*, their fifth Top 20 hit.

October – November 1974

12 October 1974

last week	this week	Album
1	1	TUBULAR BELLS — Mike Oldfield (Virgin)
2	2	HERGEST RIDGE — Mike Oldfield (Virgin)
3	3	BACK HOME AGAIN — John Denver (RCA)
-	4	SMILER Rod Stewart (Mercury)
4	5	BAND ON THE RUN — Paul McCartney & Wings (Parlophone)
5	6	ANOTHER TIME, ANOTHER PLACE Bryan Ferry (Island)
11	7	461 OCEAN BOULEVARD Eric Clapton (RSO)
16	8	SHEET MUSIC 10 C.C. (UK)
10	9	ROLLIN' Bay City Rollers (Bell)
6	10	THE SINGLES 1969-1973 Carpenters (A&M)
15	11	MUD ROCK Mud (RAK)
9	12	CARIBOU Elton John (DJM)
14	13	SANTANA'S GREATEST HITS Santana (CBS)
8	14	THE DARK SIDE OF THE MOON Pink Floyd (Harvest)
7	15	RAINBOW Peters & Lee (Philips)
19	16	BLACK EXPLOSION Various Artists (Ronco)
-	17	HANG ON IN THERE BABY Johnny Bristol (MGM)
20	18	THE THREE DEGREES Three Degrees (Philadelphia International)
12	19	OUR BEST TO YOU Osmonds (MGM)
22	20	HEY! Glitter Band (Bell)
18	21	TAPESTRY OF DREAMS Charles Aznavour (Barclay)
13	22	FULLFILLINGNESS' FIRST FINALE Stevie Wonder (Tamla Motown)
-	23	WALLS AND BRIDGES John Lennon (Apple)
26	24	THE BEST OF JOHN DENVER John Denver (RCA)
21	25	JOURNEY TO THE CENTRE OF THE EARTH Rick Wakeman (A&M)
23	26	IN THE HALL OF THE MOUNTAIN GRILL Hawkwind (United Artists)
-	27	SIMON AND GARFUNKEL'S GREATEST HITS Simon & Garfunkel (CBS)
17	28	THE PSYCHOMODO Cockney Rebel (EMI)
-	29	THESE FOOLISH THINGS Bryan Ferry (Island)
-	30	DAVID ESSEX David Essex (CBS)
-	30	NEW SKIN FOR THE OLD CEREMONY Leonard Cohen (CBS)

19 October 1974

last week	this week	Album
3	1	BACK HOME AGAIN John Denver (RCA)
9	2	ROLLIN' Bay City Rollers (Bell)
5	3	BAND ON THE RUN Paul McCartney & Wings (Parlophone)
1	4	TUBULAR BELLS Mike Oldfield (Virgin)
4	5	SMILER Rod Stewart (Mercury)
2	6	HERGEST RIDGE Mike Oldfield (Virgin)
6	7	ANOTHER TIME, ANOTHER PLACE Bryan Ferry (Island)
8	8	SHEET MUSIC 10 C.C. (UK)
13	9	SANTANA'S GREATEST HITS Santana (CBS)
23	10	WALLS AND BRIDGES John Lennon (Apple)
10	11	THE SINGLES 1969-1973 Carpenters (A&M)
11	12	MUD ROCK Mud (RAK)
17	13	HANG ON IN THERE BABY Johnny Bristol (MGM)
15	14	RAINBOW Peters & Lee (Philips)
24	15	THE BEST OF JOHN DENVER John Denver (RCA)
22	16	FULFILLINGNESS' FIRST FINALE Stevie Wonder (Tamla Motown)
16	17	BLACK EXPLOSION Various Artists (Ronco)
20	18	HEY! Glitter Band (Bell)
-	19	JUST A BOY Leo Sayer (Chrysalis)
18	20	THE THREE DEGREES Three Degrees (Philadelphia International)
7	21	461 OCEAN BOULEVARD Eric Clapton (RSO)
12	22	CARIBOU Elton John (DJM)
-	23	MOTOWN CHARTBUSTERS VOL 9 Various Artists (Tamla Motown)
14	24	THE DARK SIDE OF THE MOON Pink Floyd (Harvest)
-	25	ODDS 'N' SODS Who (Track)
-	26	A STRANGER IN MY OWN BACK YARD Gilbert O'Sullivan (MAM)
-	27	SO FAR Crosby Stills Nash & Young (Atlantic)
19	28	OUR BEST TO YOU Osmonds (MGM)
-	29	ROCK YOUR BABY George McCrae (Jay Boy)
30	30	DAVID ESSEX David Essex (CBS)

26 October 1974

last week	this week	Album
5	1	SMILER Rod Stewart (Mercury)
4	2	TUBULAR BELLS Mike Oldfield (Virgin)
2	3	ROLLIN' Bay City Rollers (Bell)
1	4	BACK HOME AGAIN John Denver (RCA)
6	5	HERGEST RIDGE Mike Oldfield (Virgin)
3	6	BAND ON THE RUN Paul McCartney & Wings (Parlophone)
10	7	WALLS AND BRIDGES John Lennon (Apple)
9	8	SANTANA'S GREATEST HITS Santana (CBS)
11	9	THE SINGLES 1969-1973 Carpenters (A&M)
7	10	ANOTHER TIME, ANOTHER PLACE Bryan Ferry (Island)
19	11	JUST A BOY Leo Sayer (Chrysalis)
30	12	DAVID ESSEX David Essex (CBS)
8	13	SHEET MUSIC 10 C.C. (UK)
-	14	IT'S ONLY ROCK 'N' ROLL Rolling Stones (Rolling Stones)
26	15	A STRANGER IN MY OWN BACK YARD Gilbert O'Sullivan (MAM)
12	16	MUD ROCK Mud (RAK)
24	17	THE DARK SIDE OF THE MOON Pink Floyd (Harvest)
14	18	RAINBOW Peters & Lee (Philips)
13	19	HANG ON IN THERE BABY Johnny Bristol (MGM)
22	20	CARIBOU Elton John (DJM)
25	20	ODDS 'N' SODS Who (Track)
15	22	THE BEST OF JOHN DENVER John Denver (RCA)
17	23	BLACK EXPLOSION Various Artists (Ronco)
29	24	ROCK YOUR BABY George McCrae (Jay Boy)
-	25	TAPESTRY OF DREAMS Charles Aznavour (Barclay)
18	26	HEY! Glitter Band (Bell)
28	27	OUR BEST TO YOU Osmonds (MGM)
21	28	461 OCEAN BOULEVARD Eric Clapton (RSO)
23	29	MOTOWN CHARTBUSTERS VOL 9 Various Artists (Tamla Motown)
16	30	FULFILLINGNESS' FIRST FINALE Stevie Wonder (Tamla Motown)

2 November 1974

last week	this week	Album
1	1	SMILER Rod Stewart (Mercury)
3	2	ROLLIN' Bay City Rollers (Bell)
2	3	TUBULAR BELLS Mike Oldfield (Virgin)
14	4	IT'S ONLY ROCK 'N' ROLL Rolling Stones (Rolling Stones)
7	5	WALLS AND BRIDGES John Lennon (Apple)
6	6	BAND ON THE RUN Paul McCartney & Wings (Parlophone)
5	7	HERGEST RIDGE Mike Oldfield (Virgin)
11	8	JUST A BOY Leo Sayer (Chrysalis)
4	9	BACK HOME AGAIN John Denver (RCA)
12	10	DAVID ESSEX David Essex (CBS)
10	11	ANOTHER TIME, ANOTHER PLACE Bryan Ferry (Island)
20	12	ODDS 'N' SODS Who (Track)
9	13	THE SINGLES 1969-1973 Carpenters (A&M)
8	14	SANTANA'S GREATEST HITS Santana (CBS)
15	15	A STRANGER IN MY OWN BACK YARD Gilbert O'Sullivan (MAM)
17	16	THE DARK SIDE OF THE MOON Pink Floyd (Harvest)
29	17	MOTOWN CHARTBUSTERS VOL 9 Various Artists (Tamla Motown)
16	18	MUD ROCK Mud (RAK)
13	19	SHEET MUSIC 10 C.C. (UK)
-	20	THE IMPOSSIBLE DREAM Sensational Alex Harvey Band (Vertigo)
-	21	CAN'T GET ENOUGH OF YOUR LOVE BABE Barry White (20th Century)
24	22	ROCK YOUR BABY George McCrae (Jay Boy)
19	23	HANG ON IN THERE BABY Johnny Bristol (MGM)
23	24	BLACK EXPLOSION Various Artists (Ronco)
-	25	STARDUST - SOUNDTRACK Various Artists (Ronco)
22	26	THE BEST OF JOHN DENVER John Denver (RCA)
26	27	HEY! Glitter Band (Bell)
-	28	STONE GON' Barry White (Pye)
27	29	OUR BEST TO YOU Osmonds (MGM)
18	30	RAINBOW Peters & Lee (Philips)

October 12 was the last of four remarkable weeks in which Mike Oldfield had held both the No.1 and the No.2 positions in the album chart. He had no concurrent hit single. The top singles in this four-week period were Carl Douglas' *Kung Fu Fighting*, Peter Shelley's *Gee Baby* (not the Buzzcocks' future lead singer) and Ken Boothe's *Everything I Own*, a cover of an old Bread song done again later by Boy George. None of these 1974 No.1 single-makers would ever have a hit album.

November 1974

9 November 1974

last week	this week	Title	Artist
2	1	ROLLIN'	Bay City Rollers (Bell)
1	2	SMILER	Rod Stewart (Mercury)
8	3	JUST A BOY	Leo Sayer (Chrysalis)
4	4	IT'S ONLY ROCK 'N' ROLL	Rolling Stones (Rolling Stones)
3	5	TUBULAR BELLS	Mike Oldfield (Virgin)
6	6	BAND ON THE RUN	Paul McCartney & Wings (Parlophone)
5	7	WALLS AND BRIDGES	John Lennon (Apple)
10	8	DAVID ESSEX	David Essex (CBS)
13	9	THE SINGLES 1969-1973	Carpenters (A&M)
7	10	HERGEST RIDGE	Mike Oldfield (Virgin)
-	11	DAVID LIVE	David Bowie (RCA)
15	12	A STRANGER IN MY OWN BACK YARD	Gilbert O'Sullivan (MAM)
9	13	BACK HOME AGAIN	John Denver (RCA)
21	14	CAN'T GET ENOUGH OF YOUR LOVE BABE	Barry White (20th Century)
16	15	THE DARK SIDE OF THE MOON	Pink Floyd (Harvest)
25	16	STARDUST - SOUNDTRACK	Various (Ronco)
11	17	ANOTHER TIME, ANOTHER PLACE	Bryan Ferry (Island)
12	18	ODDS 'N' SODS	Who (Track)
14	18	SANTANA'S GREATEST HITS	Santana (CBS)
18	20	MUD ROCK	Mud (RAK)
-	21	WAR CHILD	Jethro Tull (Chrysalis)
-	22	I'M LEAVING IT ALL UP TO YOU	Donny & Marie Osmond (MGM)
22	23	ROCK YOUR BABY	George McCrae (Jay Boy)
30	24	RAINBOW	Peters & Lee (Philips)
17	25	MOTOWN CHARTBUSTERS VOL 9	Various Artists (Tamla Motown)
20	26	THE IMPOSSIBLE DREAM	Sensational Alex Harvey Band (Vertigo)
28	27	STONE GON'	Barry White (Pye)
26	28	THE BEST OF JOHN DENVER	John Denver (RCA)
19	29	SHEET MUSIC	10 C.C. (UK)
23	30	HANG ON IN THERE BABY	Johnny Bristol (MGM)

16 November 1974

last week	this week	Title	Artist
1	1	ROLLIN'	Bay City Rollers (Bell)
2	2	SMILER	Rod Stewart (Mercury)
5	3	TUBULAR BELLS	Mike Oldfield (Virgin)
3	4	JUST A BOY	Leo Sayer (Chrysalis)
4	5	IT'S ONLY ROCK 'N' ROLL	Rolling Stones (Rolling Stones)
8	6	DAVID ESSEX	David Essex (CBS)
6	7	BAND ON THE RUN	Paul McCartney & Wings (Parlophone)
14	8	CAN'T GET ENOUGH OF YOUR LOVE BABE	Barry White (20th Century)
13	9	BACK HOME AGAIN	John Denver (RCA)
11	10	DAVID LIVE	David Bowie (RCA)
15	11	THE DARK SIDE OF THE MOON	Pink Floyd (Harvest)
-	12	ELVIS PRESLEY'S 40 GREATEST HITS	Elvis Presley (Arcade)
7	13	WALLS AND BRIDGES	John Lennon (Apple)
9	14	THE SINGLES 1969-1973	Carpenters (A&M)
-	15	ELTON JOHN'S GREATEST HITS	Elton John (DJM)
12	16	A STRANGER IN MY OWN BACK YARD	Gilbert O'Sullivan (MAM)
10	17	HERGEST RIDGE	Mike Oldfield (Virgin)
-	18	SHEER HEART ATTACK	Queen (EMI)
18	19	ODDS 'N' SODS	Who (Track)
16	20	STARDUST - SOUNDTRACK	Various (Ronco)
-	21	PROPAGANDA	Sparks (Island)
21	22	WAR CHILD	Jethro Tull (Chrysalis)
18	23	SANTANA'S GREATEST HITS	Santana (CBS)
17	24	ANOTHER TIME, ANOTHER PLACE	Bryan Ferry (Island)
-	25	BLACK EXPLOSION	Various Artists (Ronco)
22	26	I'M LEAVING IT ALL UP TO YOU	Donny & Marie Osmond (MGM)
-	27	MEDDLE	Pink Floyd (Harvest)
-	28	STORMBRINGER	Deep Purple (Purple)
29	29	SHEET MUSIC	10 C.C. (UK)
-	30	HEY!	Glitter Band (Bell)

23 November 1974

last week	this week	Title	Artist
6	1	DAVID ESSEX	David Essex (CBS)
1	2	ROLLIN'	Bay City Rollers (Bell)
2	3	SMILER	Rod Stewart (Mercury)
12	4	ELVIS PRESLEY'S 40 GREATEST HITS	Elvis Presley (Arcade)
15	5	ELTON JOHN'S GREATEST HITS	Elton John (DJM)
3	6	TUBULAR BELLS	Mike Oldfield (Virgin)
10	7	DAVID LIVE	David Bowie (RCA)
8	8	CAN'T GET ENOUGH OF YOUR LOVE BABE	Barry White (20th Century)
4	9	JUST A BOY	Leo Sayer (Chrysalis)
7	10	BAND ON THE RUN	Paul McCartney & Wings (Parlophone)
5	11	IT'S ONLY ROCK 'N' ROLL	Rolling Stones (Rolling Stones)
21	12	PROPAGANDA	Sparks (Island)
-	13	THIS IS THE MOODY BLUES	Moody Blues (Threshold)
18	14	SHEER HEART ATTACK	Queen (EMI)
14	15	THE SINGLES 1969-1973	Carpenters (A&M)
-	16	COUNTRY LIFE	Roxy Music (Island)
11	17	THE DARK SIDE OF THE MOON	Pink Floyd (Harvest)
-	18	SERENADE	Neil Diamond (CBS)
13	19	WALLS AND BRIDGES	John Lennon (Apple)
16	20	A STRANGER IN MY OWN BACK YARD	Gilbert O'Sullivan (MAM)
20	21	STARDUST - SOUNDTRACK	Various (Ronco)
9	22	BACK HOME AGAIN	John Denver (RCA)
28	23	STORMBRINGER	Deep Purple (Purple)
-	24	MOTOWN CHARTBUSTERS VOL 9	Various Artists (Tamla Motown)
-	25	MUSIC EXPLOSION	Various Artists (K-Tel)
17	26	HERGEST RIDGE	Mike Oldfield (Virgin)
-	27	MUD ROCK	Mud (RAK)
22	28	WAR CHILD	Jethro Tull (Chrysalis)
-	29	THE BEST OF JOHN DENVER	John Denver (RCA)
24	30	ANOTHER TIME, ANOTHER PLACE	Bryan Ferry (Island)

30 November 1974

last week	this week	Title	Artist
5	1	ELTON JOHN'S GREATEST HITS	Elton John (DJM)
2	2	ROLLIN'	Bay City Rollers (Bell)
8	3	CAN'T GET ENOUGH OF YOUR LOVE BABE	Barry White (20th Century)
4	4	ELVIS PRESLEY'S 40 GREATEST HITS	Elvis Presley (Arcade)
1	5	DAVID ESSEX	David Essex (CBS)
14	6	SHEER HEART ATTACK	Queen (EMI)
6	7	TUBULAR BELLS	Mike Oldfield (Virgin)
7	8	DAVID LIVE	David Bowie (RCA)
3	9	SMILER	Rod Stewart (Mercury)
23	10	STORMBRINGER	Deep Purple (Purple)
12	11	PROPAGANDA	Sparks (Island)
10	12	BAND ON THE RUN	Paul McCartney & Wings (Parlophone)
13	13	THIS IS THE MOODY BLUES	Moody Blues (Threshold)
15	14	THE SINGLES 1969-1973	Carpenters (A&M)
16	15	COUNTRY LIFE	Roxy Music (Island)
21	16	STARDUST - SOUNDTRACK	Various (Ronco)
17	17	THE DARK SIDE OF THE MOON	Pink Floyd (Harvest)
11	18	IT'S ONLY ROCK 'N' ROLL	Rolling Stones (Rolling Stones)
9	19	JUST A BOY	Leo Sayer (Chrysalis)
24	20	MOTOWN CHARTBUSTERS VOL 9	Various Artists (Tamla Motown)
25	21	MUSIC EXPLOSION	Various Artists (K-Tel)
19	22	WALLS AND BRIDGES	John Lennon (Apple)
27	23	MUD ROCK	Mud (RAK)
18	24	SERENADE	Neil Diamond (CBS)
22	25	BACK HOME AGAIN	John Denver (RCA)
-	26	30 SMASH HITS OF THE WAR YEARS	Concert Band & Chorus of the RAF (Crest)
28	27	WAR CHILD	Jethro Tull (Chrysalis)
-	28	I'M LEAVING IT ALL UP TO YOU	Donny & Marie Osmond (MGM)
-	29	40 ALL TIME HONKY TONK HITS	Warren Carr (Robin)
20	30	A STRANGER IN MY OWN BACK YARD	Gilbert O'Sullivan (MAM)

Topping both charts was David Essex (single: *Gonna Make You A Star*) above the Rollers (No.5 in the singles). Despite these successes, the LP chart little indicated the prevalence of teenybop acts. Arty albums by people like Yes and Rick Wakeman wearied the grown-ups, let alone teenagers. Grown-ups could opt for pub-rock; the pubescent only had *Top Of The Pops* and puppy-faced idols: Essex, the Rollers, Rubettes, Pilot, Donny, Shawaddywaddy and at a push on the airbrush, Glitter and Suzi Quatro.

December 1974

7 December 1974

last	this		
1	1	ELTON JOHN'S GREATEST HITS	Elton John (DJM)
4	2	ELVIS PRESLEY'S 40 GREATEST HITS	Elvis Presley (Arcade)
2	3	ROLLIN'	Bay City Rollers (Bell)
6	4	SHEER HEART ATTACK	Queen (EMI)
15	5	COUNTRY LIFE	Roxy Music (Island)
5	6	DAVID ESSEX	David Essex (CBS)
3	7	CAN'T GET ENOUGH OF YOUR LOVE BABE	Barry White (20th Century)
7	8	TUBULAR BELLS	Mike Oldfield (Virgin)
10	9	STORMBRINGER	Deep Purple (Purple)
11	10	PROPAGANDA	Sparks (Island)
9	11	SMILER	Rod Stewart (Mercury)
14	12	THE SINGLES 1969-1973	Carpenters (A&M)
13	13	THIS IS THE MOODY BLUES	Moody Blues (Threshold)
8	14	DAVID LIVE	David Bowie (RCA)
-	15	THERE'S THE RUB	Wishbone Ash (EMI)
16	16	STARDUST - SOUNDTRACK	Various (Ronco)
17	17	THE DARK SIDE OF THE MOON	Pink Floyd (Harvest)
19	18	JUST A BOY	Leo Sayer (Chrysalis)
12	19	BAND ON THE RUN	Paul McCartney & Wings (Parlophone)
23	20	MUD ROCK	Mud (RAK)
24	21	SERENADE	Neil Diamond (CBS)
21	22	MUSIC EXPLOSION	Various Artists (K-Tel)
-	23	SLADE IN FLAME	Slade (Polydor)
25	24	BACK HOME AGAIN	John Denver (RCA)
18	25	IT'S ONLY ROCK 'N' ROLL	Rolling Stones (Rolling Stones)
-	26	BARBOLETTA	Santana (CBS)
26	27	30 SMASH HITS OF THE WAR YEARS	Concert Band & Chorus of the RAF (Crest)
-	28	CRIME OF THE CENTURY	Supertramp (A&M)
-	29	AND I LOVE YOU SO	Perry Como (RCA)
20	30	MOTOWN CHARTBUSTERS VOL 9	Various Artists (Tamla Motown)

14 December 1974

last	this		
1	1	ELTON JOHN'S GREATEST HITS	Elton John (DJM)
2	2	ELVIS PRESLEY'S 40 GREATEST HITS	Elvis Presley (Arcade)
6	3	DAVID ESSEX	David Essex (CBS)
7	4	CAN'T GET ENOUGH OF YOUR LOVE BABE	Barry White (20th Century)
3	5	ROLLIN'	Bay City Rollers (Bell)
4	6	SHEER HEART ATTACK	Queen (EMI)
5	7	COUNTRY LIFE	Roxy Music (Island)
9	8	STORMBRINGER	Deep Purple (Purple)
11	9	SMILER	Rod Stewart (Mercury)
8	10	TUBULAR BELLS	Mike Oldfield (Virgin)
17	11	THE DARK SIDE OF THE MOON	Pink Floyd (Harvest)
10	12	PROPAGANDA	Sparks (Island)
-	13	SHOWADDYWADDY	Showaddywaddy (Bell)
13	14	THIS IS THE MOODY BLUES	Moody Blues (Threshold)
19	15	BAND ON THE RUN	Paul McCartney & Wings (Parlophone)
-	16	THE LAMB LIES DOWN ON BROADWAY	Genesis (Charisma)
12	17	THE SINGLES 1969-1973	Carpenters (A&M)
20	18	MUD ROCK	Mud (RAK)
-	19	RELAYER	Yes (Atlantic)
22	20	MUSIC EXPLOSION	Various Artists (K-Tel)
14	21	DAVID LIVE	David Bowie (RCA)
24	22	BACK HOME AGAIN	John Denver (RCA)
15	23	THERE'S THE RUB	Wishbone Ash (EMI)
-	24	GOODNIGHT VIENNA	Ringo Starr (Apple)
16	25	STARDUST - SOUNDTRACK	Various (Ronco)
23	26	SLADE IN FLAME	Slade (Polydor)
-	27	SANTANA'S GREATEST HITS	Santana (CBS)
-	28	A STRANGER IN MY OWN BACK YARD	Gilbert O'Sullivan (MAM)
29	29	AND I LOVE YOU SO	Perry Como (RCA)
30	30	MOTOWN CHARTBUSTERS VOL 9	Various Artists (Tamla Motown)

21 December 1974

last	this		
1	1	ELTON JOHN'S GREATEST HITS	Elton John (DJM)
3	2	DAVID ESSEX	David Essex (CBS)
4	3	CAN'T GET ENOUGH OF YOUR LOVE BABE	Barry White (20th Century)
2	4	ELVIS PRESLEY'S 40 GREATEST HITS	Elvis Presley (Arcade)
5	5	ROLLIN'	Bay City Rollers (Bell)
6	6	SHEER HEART ATTACK	Queen (EMI)
10	7	TUBULAR BELLS	Mike Oldfield (Virgin)
9	8	SMILER	Rod Stewart (Mercury)
17	9	THE SINGLES 1969-1973	Carpenters (A&M)
15	10	BAND ON THE RUN	Paul McCartney & Wings (Parlophone)
26	11	SLADE IN FLAME	Slade (Polydor)
11	12	THE DARK SIDE OF THE MOON	Pink Floyd (Harvest)
7	13	COUNTRY LIFE	Roxy Music (Island)
13	14	SHOWADDYWADDY	Showaddywaddy (Bell)
20	15	MUSIC EXPLOSION	Various Artists (K-Tel)
8	16	STORMBRINGER	Deep Purple (Purple)
18	17	MUD ROCK	Mud (RAK)
29	18	AND I LOVE YOU SO	Perry Como (RCA)
21	19	DAVID LIVE	David Bowie (RCA)
19	20	RELAYER	Yes (Atlantic)
14	21	THIS IS THE MOODY BLUES	Moody Blues (Threshold)
22	22	BACK HOME AGAIN	John Denver (RCA)
25	23	STARDUST - SOUNDTRACK	Soundtrack (Ronco)
-	24	LOVE ME FOR A REASON	Osmonds (MGM)
12	25	PROPAGANDA	Sparks (Island)
-	26	JUST A BOY	Leo Sayer (Chrysalis)
-	27	ENGELBERT HUMPERDINCK'S GREATEST HITS	Engelbert Humperdinck (Decca)
27	28	SANTANA'S GREATEST HITS	Santana (CBS)
-	29	COP YER WHACK OF THIS	Billy Connolly (Transatlantic)
-	30	GOODBYE YELLOW BRICK ROAD	Elton John (DJM)

28 December 1974

last	this		
1	1	ELTON JOHN'S GREATEST HITS	Elton John (DJM)
2	2	DAVID ESSEX	David Essex (CBS)
5	3	ROLLIN'	Bay City Rollers (Bell)
3	4	CAN'T GET ENOUGH OF YOUR LOVE BABE	Barry White (20th Century)
4	5	ELVIS PRESLEY'S 40 GREATEST HITS	Elvis Presley (Arcade)
7	6	TUBULAR BELLS	Mike Oldfield (Virgin)
12	7	THE DARK SIDE OF THE MOON	Pink Floyd (Harvest)
14	8	SHOWADDYWADDY	Showaddywaddy (Bell)
6	9	SHEER HEART ATTACK	Queen (EMI)
11	10	SLADE IN FLAME	Slade (Polydor)
13	11	COUNTRY LIFE	Roxy Music (Island)
8	12	SMILER	Rod Stewart (Mercury)
20	13	RELAYER	Yes (Atlantic)
27	14	ENGELBERT HUMPERDINCK'S GREATEST HITS	Engelbert Humperdinck (Decca)
9	15	THE SINGLES 1969-1973	Carpenters (A&M)
16	16	STORMBRINGER	Deep Purple (Purple)
24	17	LOVE ME FOR A REASON	Osmonds (MGM)
17	18	MUD ROCK	Mud (RAK)
10	19	BAND ON THE RUN	Paul McCartney & Wings (Parlophone)
18	20	AND I LOVE YOU SO	Perry Como (RCA)
15	21	MUSIC EXPLOSION	Various Artists (K-Tel)
29	22	COP YER WHACK OF THIS	Billy Connolly (Transatlantic)
21	23	THIS IS THE MOODY BLUES	Moody Blues (Threshold)
19	24	DAVID LIVE	David Bowie (RCA)
-	25	OUR BEST TO YOU	Osmonds (MGM)
23	26	STARDUST - SOUNDTRACK	Various (Ronco)
-	27	SINGALONGAMAXMAS	Max Bygraves (Pye)
-	28	SERENADE	Neil Diamond (CBS)
25	29	PROPAGANDA	Sparks (Island)
-	30	40 ALL TIME HONKY TONK HITS	Warren Carr (Robin)

Typically, Elvis Presley's record-company had leased out the tracks for his 40 Greatest Hits collection to cheapo specialist Arcade. This didn't happen to the other artists with charting hits collections: not Elton John, holding Elvis off the top of the chart, not the Carpenters, Santana nor Engelbert Humperdinck, whose *Greatest Hits* jumped to No.14 over the Christmas period. Engelbert's hits had begun in 1967, with Release Me; his 12th and last Top 30 single had been 1972's *Too Beautiful To Last*.

*All sorts charting in the mid
70s:
Tom Jones (top)
Left to right at bottom:
Slim Whitman
Mike Oldfield
Marc Bolan*

January 1975

last week	this week	4 January 1975
1	1	ELTON JOHN'S GREATEST HITS Elton John (DJM)
2	2	DAVID ESSEX David Essex (CBS)
4	3	CAN'T GET ENOUGH OF YOUR LOVE Barry White (20th Century)
3	4	ROLLIN' Bay City Rollers (Bell)
6	5	TUBULAR BELLS Mike Oldfield (Virgin)
5	6	ELVIS PRESLEY'S 40 GREATEST HITS Elvis Presley (Arcade)
13	7	RELAYER Yes (Atlantic)
9	8	SHEER HEART ATTACK Queen (EMI)
10	9	SLADE IN FLAME Slade (Polydor)
18	10	MUD ROCK Mud (RAK)
7	11	THE DARK SIDE OF THE MOON Pink Floyd (Harvest)
8	12	SHOWADDYWADDY Showaddywaddy (Bell)
11	13	COUNTRY LIFE Roxy Music (Island)
12	14	SMILER Rod Stewart (Mercury)
14	15	ENGELBERT HUMPERDINCK'S GREATEST HITS Engelbert Humperdinck (Decca)
15	16	THE SINGLES 1969-1973 Carpenters (A&M)
16	17	STORMBRINGER Deep Purple (Purple)
26	18	STARDUST - SOUNDTRACK Various (Ronco)
24	19	DAVID LIVE David Bowie (RCA)
20	20	AND I LOVE YOU SO Perry Como (RCA)
19	21	BAND ON THE RUN Paul McCartney & Wings (Parlophone)
17	22	LOVE ME FOR A REASON Osmonds (MGM)
30	23	40 ALL TIME HONKY TONK HITS Various Artists (Robin)
23	24	THIS IS THE MOODY BLUES Moody Blues (Threshold)
-	25	KEEP ON WOMBLING Wombles (CBS)
21	26	MUSIC EXPLOSION Various Artists (K-Tel)
-	27	HERGEST RIDGE Mike Oldfield (Virgin)
-	28	JUST A BOY Leo Sayer (Chrysalis)
-	29	RAINBOW Peters & Lee (Philips)
-	30	SIMON & GARFUNKEL'S GREATEST HITS Simon & Garfunkel (CBS)

last week	this week	11 January 1975
1	1	ELTON JOHN'S GREATEST HITS Elton John (DJM)
2	2	DAVID ESSEX David Essex (CBS)
3	3	CAN'T GET ENOUGH OF YOUR LOVE Barry White (20th Century)
5	4	TUBULAR BELLS Mike Oldfield (Virgin)
4	5	ROLLIN' Bay City Rollers (Bell)
11	6	THE DARK SIDE OF THE MOON Pink Floyd (Harvest)
8	7	SHEER HEART ATTACK Queen (EMI)
10	8	MUD ROCK Mud (RAK)
7	9	RELAYER Yes (Atlantic)
6	10	ELVIS PRESLEY'S 40 GREATEST HITS Elvis Presley (Arcade)
15	11	ENGELBERT HUMPERDINCK'S GREATEST HITS Engelbert Humperdinck (Decca)
14	12	SMILER Rod Stewart (Mercury)
12	13	SHOWADDYWADDY Showaddywaddy (Bell)
9	14	SLADE IN FLAME Slade (Polydor)
21	15	BAND ON THE RUN Paul McCartney & Wings (Parlophone)
16	16	THE SINGLES 1969-1973 Carpenters (A&M)
22	17	LOVE ME FOR A REASON Osmonds (MGM)
13	18	COUNTRY LIFE Roxy Music (Island)
20	19	AND I LOVE YOU SO Perry Como (RCA)
30	20	SIMON & GARFUNKEL'S GREATEST HITS Simon & Garfunkel (CBS)
19	21	DAVID LIVE David Bowie (RCA)
18	22	STARDUST - SOUNDTRACK Various (Ronco)
24	23	THIS IS THE MOODY BLUES Moody Blues (Threshold)
17	24	STORMBRINGER Deep Purple (Purple)
-	25	MEDDLE Pink Floyd (Harvest)
-	26	MOTOWN CHARTBUSTERS VOL 9 Various Artists (Tamla Motown)
-	27	NOT FRAGILE Bachman Turner Overdrive (Mercury)
-	28	REMEMBER YOU'RE A WOMBLE Wombles (CBS)
26	29	MUSIC EXPLOSION Various Artists (K-Tel)
-	30	COP YER WHACK OF THIS Billy Connolly (Polydor)

last week	this week	18 January 1975
1	1	ELTON JOHN'S GREATEST HITS Elton John (DJM)
2	2	DAVID ESSEX David Essex (CBS)
3	3	CAN'T GET ENOUGH OF YOUR LOVE Barry White (20th Century)
5	4	ROLLIN' Bay City Rollers (Bell)
4	5	TUBULAR BELLS Mike Oldfield (Virgin)
11	6	ENGELBERT HUMPERDINCK'S GREATEST HITS Engelbert Humperdinck (Decca)
6	7	THE DARK SIDE OF THE MOON Pink Floyd (Harvest)
7	8	SHEER HEART ATTACK Queen (EMI)
9	9	RELAYER Yes (Atlantic)
8	10	MUD ROCK Mud (RAK)
19	11	AND I LOVE YOU SO Perry Como (RCA)
16	12	THE SINGLES 1969-1973 Carpenters (A&M)
10	13	ELVIS PRESLEY'S 40 GREATEST HITS Elvis Presley (Arcade)
12	14	SMILER Rod Stewart (Mercury)
15	15	BAND ON THE RUN Paul McCartney & Wings (Parlophone)
17	16	LOVE ME FOR A REASON Osmonds (MGM)
14	17	SLADE IN FLAME Slade (Polydor)
13	18	SHOWADDYWADDY Showaddywaddy (Bell)
18	19	COUNTRY LIFE Roxy Music (Island)
27	20	NOT FRAGILE Bachman Turner Overdrive (Mercury)
20	21	SIMON & GARFUNKEL'S GREATEST HITS Simon & Garfunkel (CBS)
-	22	CRIME OF THE CENTURY Supertramp (A&M)
-	23	ROCK YOUR BABY George McCrae (Jayboy)
24	24	STORMBRINGER Deep Purple (Purple)
29	25	MUSIC EXPLOSION Various Artists (K-Tel)
23	26	THIS IS THE MOODY BLUES Moody Blues (Threshold)
21	27	DAVID LIVE David Bowie (RCA)
-	28	KEEP ON WOMBLING Wombles (CBS)
-	29	PROPAGANDA Sparks (Island)
22	30	STARDUST - SOUNDTRACK Various (Ronco)

last week	this week	25 January 1975
1	1	ELTON JOHN'S GREATEST HITS Elton John (DJM)
5	2	TUBULAR BELLS Mike Oldfield (Virgin)
2	3	DAVID ESSEX David Essex (CBS)
8	4	SHEER HEART ATTACK Queen (EMI)
6	5	ENGELBERT HUMPERDINCK'S GREATEST HITS Engelbert Humperdinck (Decca)
4	6	ROLLIN' Bay City Rollers (Bell)
3	7	CAN'T GET ENOUGH OF YOUR LOVE Barry White (20th Century)
7	8	THE DARK SIDE OF THE MOON Pink Floyd (Harvest)
10	9	MUD ROCK Mud (RAK)
15	10	BAND ON THE RUN Paul McCartney & Wings (Parlophone)
12	11	THE SINGLES 1969-1973 Carpenters (A&M)
11	12	AND I LOVE YOU SO Perry Como (RCA)
13	13	ELVIS PRESLEY'S 40 GREATEST HITS Elvis Presley (Arcade)
21	14	SIMON & GARFUNKEL GREATEST HITS Simon & Garfunkel (CBS)
9	15	RELAYER Yes (Atlantic)
22	16	CRIME OF THE CENTURY Supertramp (A&M)
14	17	SMILER Rod Stewart (Mercury)
20	18	NOT FRAGILE Bachman Turner Overdrive (Mercury)
30	19	STARDUST - SOUNDTRACK Various (Ronco)
19	20	COUNTRY LIFE Roxy Music (Island)
-	21	SERENADE Neil Diamond (CBS)
-	22	GOODBYE YELLOW BRICK ROAD Elton John (DJM)
17	23	SLADE IN FLAME Slade (Polydor)
16	24	LOVE ME FOR A REASON Osmonds (MGM)
-	25	MEDDLE Pink Floyd (Harvest)
-	26	HIS 12 GREATEST HITS Neil Diamond (MCA)
-	27	COP YER WHACK OF THIS Billy Connolly (Polydor)
18	28	SHOWADDYWADDY Showaddywaddy (Bell)
-	29	MOTOWN CHARTBUSTERS VOL 9 Various Artists (Tamla Motown)
-	30	THE THREE DEGREES Three Degrees (Philadelphia International)

The year began with *Mud Rock* at No.10, while Mud were top of the singles chart with *Lonely This Christmas*, their seventh hit and their third No.1. (The first had been the immortal dance-hall favourite *Tiger Feet*, and the second the less memorable *The Cat Crept In*, top for one week, both in 1974.) Mud, fronted by the decidedly post-adolescent Les Gray, was one of the most successful of the retro-pop bands. *Mud Rock* was the first and most successful of their three Top 30 albums.

February 1975

Chart tables for February 1975 follow.

1 February 1975

last week	this week	Title — Artist (Label)
1	1	ELTON JOHN'S GREATEST HITS — Elton John (DJM)
5	2	ENGELBERT HUMPERDINCK'S GREATEST HITS — Engelbert Humperdinck (Decca)
3	3	DAVID ESSEX — David Essex (CBS)
2	4	TUBULAR BELLS — Mike Oldfield (Virgin)
4	5	SHEER HEART ATTACK — Queen (EMI)
11	6	THE SINGLES 1969-1973 — Carpenters (A&M)
6	7	ROLLIN' — Bay City Rollers (Bell)
10	8	BAND ON THE RUN — Paul McCartney & Wings (Parlophone)
7	9	CAN'T GET ENOUGH OF YOUR LOVE — Barry White (20th Century)
8	10	THE DARK SIDE OF THE MOON — Pink Floyd (Harvest)
9	11	MUD ROCK — Mud (RAK)
16	12	CRIME OF THE CENTURY — Supertramp (A&M)
13	13	ELVIS PRESLEY'S 40 GREATEST HITS — Elvis Presley (Arcade)
14	14	SIMON & GARFUNKEL'S GREATEST HITS — Simon & Garfunkel (CBS)
18	15	NOT FRAGILE — Bachman Turner Overdrive (Mercury)
15	16	RELAYER — Yes (Atlantic)
17	17	SMILER — Rod Stewart (Mercury)
20	18	COUNTRY LIFE — Roxy Music (Island)
12	19	AND I LOVE YOU SO — Perry Como (RCA)
27	20	COP YER WHACK OF THIS — Billy Connolly (Polydor)
19	21	STARDUST - SOUNDTRACK — Various (Ronco)
26	22	HIS 12 GREATEST HITS — Neil Diamond (MCA)
-	23	STORMBRINGER — Deep Purple (Purple)
-	24	PROPAGANDA — Sparks (Island)
-	25	GET DANCING — Various Artists (K-Tel)
-	26	BRIDGE OVER TROUBLED WATER — Simon & Garfunkel (CBS)
28	27	SHOWADDYWADDY — Showaddywaddy (Bell)
21	28	SERENADE — Neil Diamond (CBS)
-	29	BACK HOME AGAIN — John Denver (RCA)
-	30	ROCK YOUR BABY — George McCrae (Jayboy)

8 February 1975

last week	this week	Title — Artist (Label)
1	1	ELTON JOHN'S GREATEST HITS — Elton John (DJM)
2	2	ENGELBERT HUMPERDINCK'S GREATEST HITS — Engelbert Humperdinck (Decca)
4	3	TUBULAR BELLS — Mike Oldfield (Virgin)
5	4	SHEER HEART ATTACK — Queen (EMI)
9	5	CAN'T GET ENOUGH OF YOUR LOVE — Barry White (20th Century)
3	6	DAVID ESSEX — David Essex (CBS)
7	7	ROLLIN' — Bay City Rollers (Bell)
10	8	THE DARK SIDE OF THE MOON — Pink Floyd (Harvest)
12	9	CRIME OF THE CENTURY — Supertramp (A&M)
6	10	THE SINGLES 1969-1973 — Carpenters (A&M)
8	11	BAND ON THE RUN — Paul McCartney & Wings (Parlophone)
11	12	MUD ROCK — Mud (RAK)
13	13	ELVIS PRESLEY'S 40 GREATEST HITS — Elvis Presley (Arcade)
15	14	NOT FRAGILE — Bachman Turner Overdrive (Mercury)
14	15	SIMON & GARFUNKEL GREATEST HITS — Simon & Garfunkel (CBS)
21	16	STARDUST - SOUNDTRACK — Various (Ronco)
27	17	SHOWADDYWADDY — Showaddywaddy (Bell)
25	18	GET DANCING — Various Artists (K-Tel)
16	19	RELAYER — Yes (Atlantic)
22	20	HIS 12 GREATEST HITS — Neil Diamond (MCA)
19	21	AND I LOVE YOU SO — Perry Como (RCA)
17	22	SMILER — Rod Stewart (Mercury)
24	23	PROPAGANDA — Sparks (Island)
30	24	ROCK YOUR BABY — George McCrae (Jayboy)
-	25	BLOOD ON THE TRACKS — Bob Dylan (CBS)
-	26	THE BEST OF JOHN DENVER — John Denver (RCA)
-	27	DAVID LIVE — David Bowie (RCA)
-	28	FREE AND EASY — Helen Reddy (Capitol)
28	29	SERENADE — Neil Diamond (CBS)
20	30	COP YER WHACK OF THIS — Billy Connolly (Polydor)

15 February 1975

last week	this week	Title — Artist (Label)
2	1	ENGELBERT HUMPERDINCK'S GREATEST HITS — Engelbert Humperdinck (Decca)
1	2	ELTON JOHN'S GREATEST HITS — Elton John (DJM)
3	3	TUBULAR BELLS — Mike Oldfield (Virgin)
4	4	SHEER HEART ATTACK — Queen (EMI)
10	5	THE SINGLES 1969-1973 — Carpenters (A&M)
18	6	GET DANCING — Various Artists (K-Tel)
5	7	CAN'T GET ENOUGH OF YOUR LOVE — Barry White (20th Century)
6	8	DAVID ESSEX — David Essex (CBS)
8	9	THE DARK SIDE OF THE MOON — Pink Floyd (Harvest)
7	10	ROLLIN' — Bay City Rollers (Bell)
12	11	MUD ROCK — Mud (RAK)
11	12	BAND ON THE RUN — Paul McCartney & Wings (Parlophone)
9	13	CRIME OF THE CENTURY — Supertramp (A&M)
15	14	SIMON & GARFUNKEL'S GREATEST HITS — Simon & Garfunkel (CBS)
13	15	ELVIS PRESLEY'S 40 GREATEST HITS — Elvis Presley (Arcade)
16	16	STARDUST - SOUNDTRACK — Various (Ronco)
28	17	FREE AND EASY — Helen Reddy (Capitol)
17	18	SHOWADDYWADDY — Showaddywaddy (Bell)
-	19	THE ORCHESTRAL TUBULAR BELLS — Royal Philharmonic Orchestra & Mike Oldfield (Virgin)
-	20	DONNY — Donny Osmond (MGM)
20	21	HIS 12 GREATEST HITS — Neil Diamond (MCA)
21	22	AND I LOVE YOU SO — Perry Como (RCA)
25	23	BLOOD ON THE TRACKS — Bob Dylan (CBS)
14	24	NOT FRAGILE — Bachman Turner Overdrive (Mercury)
30	25	COP YER WHACK OF THIS — Billy Connolly (Polydor)
19	26	RELAYER — Yes (Atlantic)
-	27	SLADE IN FLAME — Slade (Polydor)
-	28	COUNTRY LIFE — Roxy Music (Island)
-	29	BRIDGE OVER TROUBLED WATER — Simon & Garfunkel (CBS)
23	30	PROPAGANDA — Sparks (Island)

22 February 1975

last week	this week	Title — Artist (Label)
1	1	ENGELBERT HUMPERDINCK'S GREATEST HITS — Engelbert Humperdinck (Decca)
2	2	ELTON JOHN'S GREATEST HITS — Elton John (DJM)
4	3	SHEER HEART ATTACK — Queen (EMI)
3	4	TUBULAR BELLS — Mike Oldfield (Virgin)
23	5	BLOOD ON THE TRACKS — Bob Dylan (CBS)
9	6	THE DARK SIDE OF THE MOON — Pink Floyd (Harvest)
7	7	CAN'T GET ENOUGH OF YOUR LOVE — Barry White (20th Century)
5	8	THE SINGLES 1969-1973 — Carpenters (A&M)
8	9	DAVID ESSEX — David Essex (CBS)
10	10	ROLLIN' — Bay City Rollers (Bell)
13	11	CRIME OF THE CENTURY — Supertramp (A&M)
6	12	GET DANCING — Various Artists (K-Tel)
-	13	ON THE LEVEL — Status Quo (Vertigo)
14	14	SIMON & GARFUNKEL'S GREATEST HITS — Simon & Garfunkel (CBS)
12	15	BAND ON THE RUN — Paul McCartney & Wings (Parlophone)
11	16	MUD ROCK — Mud (RAK)
22	17	AND I LOVE YOU SO — Perry Como (RCA)
-	18	STREETS — Ralph McTell (Warner Bros.)
15	19	ELVIS PRESLEY'S 40 GREATEST HITS — Elvis Presley (Arcade)
16	20	STARDUST - SOUNDTRACK — Various (Ronco)
20	21	DONNY — Donny Osmond (MGM)
24	22	NOT FRAGILE — Bachman Turner Overdrive (Mercury)
18	23	SHOWADDYWADDY — Showaddywaddy (Bell)
25	24	COP YER WHACK OF THIS — Billy Connolly (Polydor)
21	25	HIS 12 GREATEST HITS — Neil Diamond (MCA)
19	26	THE ORCHESTRAL TUBULAR BELLS — Royal Philharmonic Orchestra & Mike Oldfield (Virgin)
-	27	RAINBOW — Peters & Lee (Philips)
-	28	THE MAIN EVENT — Frank Sinatra (Reprise)
-	29	COMMONER'S CROWN — Steeleye Span (Chrysalis)
-	30	MEDDLE — Pink Floyd (Harvest)

Bob Dylan, unhip for years, now charted with *Blood On The Tracks*, which would never go beyond a briefly-held No.5, yet would prove arguably the decade's best "rock" album; even NME made it Album of the Year. Charting the same week was a singer much bigger in America than in Britain, Helen Reddy. *Angie Baby*, her one significant UK single, was about to peak at No.5. Her records claimed a feminist alignment; but British writer Nigel Fountain commented: "I know an Auntie Tom when I see one."

March 1975

1 March 1975

last	this	Album
2	1	ELTON JOHN'S GREATEST HITS Elton John (DJM)
3	2	SHEER HEART ATTACK Queen (EMI)
4	3	TUBULAR BELLS Mike Oldfield (Virgin)
1	4	ENGELBERT HUMPERDINCK'S GREATEST HITS Engelbert Humperdinck (Decca)
13	5	ON THE LEVEL Status Quo (Vertigo)
5	6	BLOOD ON THE TRACKS Bob Dylan (CBS)
11	7	CRIME OF THE CENTURY Supertramp (A&M)
8	8	THE SINGLES 1969-1973 Carpenters (A&M)
20	9	STARDUST - SOUNDTRACK Various (Ronco)
6	10	THE DARK SIDE OF THE MOON Pink Floyd (Harvest)
12	11	GET DANCING Various Artists (K-Tel)
10	12	ROLLIN' Bay City Rollers (Bell)
14	13	SIMON & GARFUNKEL'S GREATEST HITS Simon & Garfunkel (CBS)
9	14	DAVID ESSEX David Essex (CBS)
7	15	CAN'T GET ENOUGH OF YOUR LOVE Barry White (20th Century)
22	16	NOT FRAGILE Bachman Turner Overdrive (Mercury)
15	17	BAND ON THE RUN Paul McCartney & Wings (Parlophone)
19	18	ELVIS PRESLEY'S 40 GREATEST HITS Elvis Presley (Arcade)
25	19	HIS 12 GREATEST HITS Neil Diamond (MCA)
17	20	AND I LOVE YOU SO Perry Como (RCA)
18	21	STREETS Ralph McTell (Warner Bros.)
23	22	SHOWADDYWADDY Showaddywaddy (Bell)
26	23	THE ORCHESTRAL TUBULAR BELLS Royal Philharmonic Orchestra & Mike Oldfield (Virgin)
24	24	COP YER WHACK OF THIS Billy Connolly (Polydor)
-	25	PROMISED LAND Elvis Presley (RCA)
-	26	THE BEST OF JOHN DENVER John Denver (RCA)
-	27	BRIDGE OVER TROUBLED WATER Simon & Garfunkel (CBS)
-	28	AVERAGE WHITE BAND Average White Band (Atlantic)
-	29	BEST OF BREAD Bread (Elektra)
-	30	MUSIC EXPLOSION Various Artists (K-Tel)

8 March 1975

last	this	Album
5	1	ON THE LEVEL Status Quo (Vertigo)
1	2	ELTON JOHN'S GREATEST HITS Elton John (DJM)
3	3	TUBULAR BELLS Mike Oldfield (Virgin)
7	4	CRIME OF THE CENTURY Supertramp (A&M)
2	5	SHEER HEART ATTACK Queen (EMI)
4	6	ENGELBERT HUMPERDINCK'S GREATEST HITS Engelbert Humperdinck (Decca)
6	7	BLOOD ON THE TRACKS Bob Dylan (CBS)
-	8	PHYSICAL GRAFFITI Led Zeppelin (Swansong)
8	9	THE SINGLES 1969-1973 Carpenters (A&M)
15	10	CAN'T GET ENOUGH OF YOUR LOVE Barry White (20th Century)
10	11	THE DARK SIDE OF THE MOON Pink Floyd (Harvest)
13	12	SIMON & GARFUNKEL'S GREATEST HITS Simon & Garfunkel (CBS)
11	13	GET DANCING Various Artists (K-Tel)
12	14	ROLLIN' Bay City Rollers (Bell)
19	15	HIS 12 GREATEST HITS Neil Diamond (MCA)
21	16	STREETS Ralph McTell (Warner Bros.)
18	17	ELVIS PRESLEY'S 40 GREATEST HITS Elvis Presley (Arcade)
14	18	DAVID ESSEX David Essex (CBS)
16	19	NOT FRAGILE Bachman Turner Overdrive (Mercury)
17	20	BAND ON THE RUN Paul McCartney & Wings (Parlophone)
-	21	THE 10TH ANNIVERSARY ALBUM/20 GREATEST HITS Tom Jones (Decca)
9	22	STARDUST - SOUNDTRACK Various (Ronco)
-	23	ROCK 'N' ROLL John Lennon (Apple)
-	24	FOR EARTH BELOW Robin Trower (Chrysalis)
-	25	MUD ROCK Mud (RAK)
20	26	AND I LOVE YOU SO Perry Como (RCA)
-	27	SLADE IN FLAME Slade (Polydor)
-	28	FREE AND EASY Helen Reddy (Capitol)
28	29	AVERAGE WHITE BAND Average White Band (Atlantic)
24	30	COP YER WHACK OF THIS Billy Connolly (Polydor)

15 March 1975

last	this	Album
1	1	ON THE LEVEL Status Quo (Vertigo)
2	2	ELTON JOHN'S GREATEST HITS Elton John (DJM)
8	3	PHYSICAL GRAFFITI Led Zeppelin (Swansong)
3	4	TUBULAR BELLS Mike Oldfield (Virgin)
7	5	BLOOD ON THE TRACKS Bob Dylan (CBS)
4	6	CRIME OF THE CENTURY Supertramp (A&M)
21	7	THE 10TH ANNIVERSARY ALBUM/20 GREATEST HITS Tom Jones (Decca)
5	8	SHEER HEART ATTACK Queen (EMI)
6	9	ENGELBERT HUMPERDINCK'S GREATEST HITS Engelbert Humperdinck (Decca)
9	10	THE SINGLES 1969-1973 Carpenters (A&M)
29	11	AVERAGE WHITE BAND Average White Band (Atlantic)
13	12	GET DANCING Various Artists (K-Tel)
23	13	ROCK 'N' ROLL John Lennon (Apple)
11	14	THE DARK SIDE OF THE MOON Pink Floyd (Harvest)
12	15	SIMON & GARFUNKEL'S GREATEST HITS Simon & Garfunkel (CBS)
10	16	CAN'T GET ENOUGH OF YOUR LOVE Barry White (20th Century)
14	17	ROLLIN' Bay City Rollers (Bell)
-	18	THE BEST YEARS OF OUR LIVES Steve Harley & Cockney Rebel (EMI)
-	19	SOULED OUT Various Artists (K-Tel)
16	20	STREETS Ralph McTell (Warner Bros.)
20	21	BAND ON THE RUN Paul McCartney & Wings (Parlophone)
-	22	THE SHIRLEY BASSEY SINGLES ALBUM Shirley Bassey (United Artists)
28	23	FREE AND EASY Helen Reddy (Capitol)
30	24	COP YER WHACK OF THIS Billy Connolly (Polydor)
19	25	NOT FRAGILE Bachman Turner Overdrive (Mercury)
15	26	HIS 12 GREATEST HITS Neil Diamond (MCA)
25	27	MUD ROCK Mud (RAK)
17	28	ELVIS PRESLEY'S 40 GREATEST HITS Elvis Presley (Arcade)
-	29	THE ORCHESTRAL TUBULAR BELLS Royal Philharmonic Orchestra & Mike Oldfield (Virgin)
22	30	STARDUST - SOUNDTRACK Various (Ronco)

22 March 1975

last	this	Album
1	1	ON THE LEVEL Status Quo (Vertigo)
3	2	PHYSICAL GRAFFITI Led Zeppelin (Swansong)
6	3	CRIME OF THE CENTURY Supertramp (A&M)
7	4	THE 10TH ANNIVERSARY ALBUM/20 GREATEST HITS Tom Jones (Decca)
2	5	ELTON JOHN'S GREATEST HITS Elton John (DJM)
4	6	TUBULAR BELLS Mike Oldfield (Virgin)
11	7	AVERAGE WHITE BAND Average White Band (Atlantic)
9	8	ENGELBERT HUMPERDINCK'S GREATEST HITS Engelbert Humperdinck (Decca)
22	9	THE SHIRLEY BASSEY SINGLES ALBUM Shirley Bassey (United Artists)
13	10	ROCK 'N' ROLL John Lennon (Apple)
18	11	THE BEST YEARS OF OUR LIVES Steve Harley & Cockney Rebel (EMI)
10	12	THE SINGLES 1969-1973 Carpenters (A&M)
5	13	BLOOD ON THE TRACKS Bob Dylan (CBS)
16	14	CAN'T GET ENOUGH OF YOUR LOVE Barry White (20th Century)
15	15	SIMON & GARFUNKEL'S GREATEST HITS Simon & Garfunkel (CBS)
8	16	SHEER HEART ATTACK Queen (EMI)
19	17	SOULED OUT Various Artists (K-Tel)
14	18	THE DARK SIDE OF THE MOON Pink Floyd (Harvest)
26	19	HIS 12 GREATEST HITS Neil Diamond (MCA)
-	20	WELCOME TO MY NIGHTMARE Alice Cooper (Anchor)
17	21	ROLLIN' Bay City Rollers (Bell)
21	22	BAND ON THE RUN Wings (Parlophone)
12	23	GET DANCING Various Artists (K-Tel)
-	24	BLACK MUSIC Various Artists (Arcade)
-	25	BRIDGE OVER TROUBLED WATER Simon & Garfunkel (CBS)
-	26	YESTERDAYS Yes (Atlantic)
-	27	BLUE JAYS Justin Hayward & John Lodge (Threshold)
20	28	STREETS Ralph McTell (Warner Bros.)
-	29	SLADE IN FLAME Slade (Polydor)
-	30	BEST OF BREAD Bread (Elektra)

Folkie Ralph McTell had charted in late February with *Streets*, and now spent March on the lower rungs before slipping off again. This must have disappointed Warners, who, in the tradition of the day, had tried to take a modest artist and, by pouring money into a heavily-marketed album, transform the scale of his career. The title *Streets* referred to McTell's song *Streets Of London*, which, in his repertoire for years, had topped January's singles chart for a fortnight. It would be his only Top 30 hit

March – April 1975

29 March 1975

last week	this week	
2	1	PHYSICAL GRAFFITI — Led Zeppelin (Swansong)
1	2	ON THE LEVEL — Status Quo (Vertigo)
3	3	CRIME OF THE CENTURY — Supertramp (A&M)
4	4	THE 10TH ANNIVERSARY ALBUM/20 GREATEST HITS — Tom Jones (Decca)
5	5	ELTON JOHN'S GREATEST HITS — Elton John (DJM)
11	6	THE BEST YEARS OF OUR LIVES — Steve Harley & Cockney Rebel (EMI)
6	7	TUBULAR BELLS — Mike Oldfield (Virgin)
9	8	THE SHIRLEY BASSEY SINGLES ALBUM — Shirley Bassey (United Artists)
7	9	AVERAGE WHITE BAND — Average White Band (Atlantic)
-	10	THE ORIGINAL SOUNDTRACK — 10 C.C. (Mercury)
13	11	BLOOD ON THE TRACKS — Bob Dylan (CBS)
12	12	THE SINGLES 1969-1973 — Carpenters (A&M)
14	13	CAN'T GET ENOUGH OF YOUR LOVE — Barry White (20th Century)
27	14	BLUE JAYS — Justin Hayward & John Lodge (Threshold)
8	15	ENGELBERT HUMPERDINCK'S GREATEST HITS — Engelbert Humperdinck (Decca)
15	16	SIMON & GARFUNKEL'S GREATEST HITS — Simon & Garfunkel (CBS)
10	17	ROCK 'N' ROLL — John Lennon (Apple)
-	18	TOMMY Soundtrack (Polydor)
-	19	I'M COMING HOME — Johnny Mathis (CBS)
18	20	THE DARK SIDE OF THE MOON — Pink Floyd (Harvest)
16	21	SHEER HEART ATTACK — Queen (EMI)
23	22	GET DANCING — Various Artists (K-Tel)
-	23	YOUNG AMERICANS — David Bowie (RCA)
21	24	ROLLIN' Bay City Rollers (Bell)
-	25	COP YER WHACK OF THIS — Billy Connolly (Polydor)
20	26	WELCOME TO MY NIGHTMARE — Alice Cooper (Anchor)
-	27	TELLY Telly Savalas (MCA)
22	28	BAND ON THE RUN — Paul McCartney & Wings (Parlophone)
17	29	SOULED OUT — Various Artists (K-Tel)
-	30	AN EVENING WITH JOHN DENVER — John Denver (RCA)

5 April 1975

last week	this week	
1	1	PHYSICAL GRAFFITI — Led Zeppelin (Swansong)
4	2	THE 10TH ANNIVERSARY ALBUM/20 GREATEST HITS — Tom Jones (Decca)
2	3	ON THE LEVEL — Status Quo (Vertigo)
3	4	CRIME OF THE CENTURY — Supertramp (A&M)
6	5	THE BEST YEARS OF OUR LIVES — Steve Harley & Cockney Rebel (EMI)
5	6	ELTON JOHN'S GREATEST HITS — Elton John (DJM)
9	7	AVERAGE WHITE BAND — Average White Band (Atlantic)
16	8	SIMON & GARFUNKEL'S GREATEST HITS — Simon & Garfunkel (CBS)
10	9	THE ORIGINAL SOUNDTRACK — 10 C.C. (Mercury)
8	10	THE SHIRLEY BASSEY SINGLES ALBUM — Shirley Bassey (United Artists)
17	11	ROCK 'N' ROLL — John Lennon (Apple)
7	12	TUBULAR BELLS — Mike Oldfield (Virgin)
23	13	YOUNG AMERICANS — David Bowie (RCA)
14	14	BLUE JAYS — Justin Hayward & John Lodge (Threshold)
-	15	STRAIGHT SHOOTER — Bad Company (Island)
-	16	YESTERDAYS Yes (Atlantic)
-	17	THERE'S ONE IN EVERY CROWD — Eric Clapton (RSO)
21	18	SHEER HEART ATTACK — Queen (EMI)
-	19	THE MYTHS AND LEGENDS OF KING ARTHUR AND THE KNIGHTS OF THE ROUND TABLE — Rick Wakeman & the English Rock Ensemble (A&M)
15	20	ENGELBERT HUMPERDINCK'S GREATEST HITS — Engelbert Humperdinck (Decca)
12	21	THE SINGLES 1969-1973 — Carpenters (A&M)
20	22	THE DARK SIDE OF THE MOON — Pink Floyd (Harvest)
27	23	TELLY Telly Savalas (MCA)
24	24	ROLLIN' Bay City Rollers (Bell)
11	25	BLOOD ON THE TRACKS — Bob Dylan (CBS)
29	26	SOULED OUT — Various Artists (K-Tel)
-	27	BEST OF BREAD — Bread (Elektra)
13	28	CAN'T GET ENOUGH OF YOUR LOVE — Barry White (20th Century)
-	29	BLACK MUSIC — Various Artists (Arcade)
28	30	BAND ON THE RUN — Paul McCartney & Wings (Parlophone)

12 April 1975

last week	this week	
1	1	PHYSICAL GRAFFITI — Led Zeppelin (Swansong)
13	2	YOUNG AMERICANS — David Bowie (RCA)
10	3	THE SHIRLEY BASSEY SINGLES ALBUM — Shirley Bassey (United Artists)
14	4	BLUE JAYS — Justin Hayward & John Lodge (Threshold)
2	5	THE 10TH ANNIVERSARY ALBUM/20 GREATEST HITS — Tom Jones (Decca)
9	6	THE ORIGINAL SOUNDTRACK — 10 C.C. (Mercury)
4	7	CRIME OF THE CENTURY — Supertramp (A&M)
5	8	THE BEST YEARS OF OUR LIVES — Steve Harley & Cockney Rebel (EMI)
3	9	ON THE LEVEL — Status Quo (Vertigo)
19	10	THE MYTHS AND LEGENDS OF KING ARTHUR AND THE KNIGHTS OF THE ROUND TABLE — Rick Wakeman & the English Rock Ensemble (A&M)
15	11	STRAIGHT SHOOTER — Bad Company (Island)
6	12	ELTON JOHN'S GREATEST HITS — Elton John (DJM)
-	13	THE BEST OF THE STYLISTICS — Stylistics (Avco)
26	14	SOULED OUT — Various Artists (K-Tel)
12	15	TUBULAR BELLS — Mike Oldfield (Virgin)
7	16	AVERAGE WHITE BAND — Average White Band (Atlantic)
24	17	ROLLIN' Bay City Rollers (Bell)
25	18	BLOOD ON THE TRACKS — Bob Dylan (CBS)
23	19	TELLY Telly Savalas (MCA)
11	20	ROCK 'N' ROLL — John Lennon (Apple)
28	21	CAN'T GET ENOUGH OF YOUR LOVE — Barry White (20th Century)
17	22	THERE'S ONE IN EVERY CROWD — Eric Clapton (RSO)
16	23	YESTERDAYS Yes (Atlantic)
18	24	TOMMY Soundtrack (Polydor)
18	25	SHEER HEART ATTACK — Queen (EMI)
21	26	THE SINGLES 1969-1973 — Carpenters (A&M)
22	27	THE DARK SIDE OF THE MOON — Pink Floyd (Harvest)
30	28	BLACK MUSIC — Various Artists (Arcade)
8	29	SIMON & GARFUNKEL'S GREATEST HITS — Simon & Garfunkel (CBS)
30	30	BAND ON THE RUN — Paul McCartney & Wings (Parlophone)

19 April 1975

last week	this week	
2	1	YOUNG AMERICANS — David Bowie (RCA)
10	2	THE MYTHS AND LEGENDS OF KING ARTHUR AND THE KNIGHTS OF THE ROUND TABLE — Rick Wakeman & the English Rock Ensemble (A&M)
3	3	THE SHIRLEY BASSEY SINGLES ALBUM — Shirley Bassey (United Artists)
6	4	THE ORIGINAL SOUNDTRACK — 10 C.C. (Mercury)
1	5	PHYSICAL GRAFFITI — Led Zeppelin (Swansong)
13	6	THE BEST OF THE STYLISTICS — Stylistics (Avco)
4	7	BLUE JAYS — Justin Hayward & John Lodge (Threshold)
11	8	STRAIGHT SHOOTER — Bad Company (Island)
5	9	THE 10TH ANNIVERSARY ALBUM/20 GREATEST HITS — Tom Jones (Decca)
12	10	ELTON JOHN'S GREATEST HITS — Elton John (DJM)
15	11	TUBULAR BELLS — Mike Oldfield (Virgin)
8	12	THE BEST YEARS OF OUR LIVES — Steve Harley & Cockney Rebel (EMI)
9	13	ON THE LEVEL — Status Quo (Vertigo)
24	14	TOMMY Soundtrack (Polydor)
7	15	CRIME OF THE CENTURY — Supertramp (A&M)
17	16	ROLLIN' Bay City Rollers (Bell)
22	17	THERE'S ONE IN EVERY CROWD — Eric Clapton (RSO)
14	18	SOULED OUT — Various Artists (K-Tel)
16	19	AVERAGE WHITE BAND — Average White Band (Atlantic)
26	20	THE SINGLES 1969-1973 — Carpenters (A&M)
19	21	TELLY Telly Savalas (MCA)
18	22	BLOOD ON THE TRACKS — Bob Dylan (CBS)
29	23	SIMON & GARFUNKEL'S GREATEST HITS — Simon & Garfunkel (CBS)
23	24	YESTERDAYS Yes (Atlantic)
-	25	JUST ANOTHER WAY TO SAY I LOVE YOU — Barry White (20th Century)
-	26	RUBYCON — Tangerine Dream (Virgin)
-	27	ENGELBERT HUMPERDINCK'S GREATEST HITS — Engelbert Humperdinck (Decca)
28	28	IAN HUNTER Ian Hunter (CBS)
20	29	ROCK 'N' ROLL — John Lennon (Apple)
-	30	COP YER WHACK OF THIS — Billy Connolly (Polydor)

The Average White Band had entered the chart on March 1, and was now peaking at No.7. They were a modest British group, very 1975: they played quiet funk - as if for themselves, rather than an audience - that somehow managed to sound wholly unrelated in spirit to the black music it was based upon. Their first and biggest hit single, *Pick Up The Pieces*, had peaked at No.6 in March. Founding member Robbie McIntosh had died of a drugs overdose the previous September.

last this week

26 April 1975

LW	TW	Album (Artist/Label)
-	1	ONCE UPON A STAR Bay City Rollers (Bell)
2	2	THE MYTHS AND LEGENDS OF KING ARTHUR AND THE KNIGHTS OF THE ROUND TABLE Rick Wakeman & the English Rock Ensemble (A&M)
6	3	THE BEST OF THE STYLISTICS Stylistics (Avco)
4	4	THE ORIGINAL SOUNDTRACK 10 C.C. (Mercury)
3	5	THE SHIRLEY BASSEY SINGLES ALBUM Shirley Bassey (United Artists)
7	6	BLUE JAYS Justin Hayward & John Lodge (Threshold)
8	7	STRAIGHT SHOOTER Bad Company (Island)
5	8	PHYSICAL GRAFFITI Led Zeppelin (Swansong)
1	9	YOUNG AMERICANS David Bowie (RCA)
14	10	TOMMY Soundtrack (Polydor)
9	11	THE 10TH ANNIVERSARY ALBUM/20 GREATEST HITS Tom Jones (Decca)
16	12	ROLLIN' Bay City Rollers (Bell)
10	13	ELTON JOHN'S GREATEST HITS Elton John (DJM)
12	14	THE BEST YEARS OF OUR LIVES Steve Harley & Cockney Rebel (EMI)
15	15	CRIME OF THE CENTURY Supertramp (A&M)
11	16	TUBULAR BELLS Mike Oldfield (Virgin)
17	17	THERE'S ONE IN EVERY CROWD Eric Clapton (RSO)
13	18	ON THE LEVEL Status Quo (Vertigo)
26	19	RUBYCON Tangerine Dream (Virgin)
18	20	SOULED OUT Various (K-Tel)
19	21	AVERAGE WHITE BAND Average White Band (Atlantic)
-	22	ROCK 'N' ROLL DUDES Glitter Band (Bell)
-	23	MEMORIES ARE MADE OF HITS Perry Como (RCA)
20	24	THE SINGLES 1969-1973 Carpenters (A&M)
21	25	TELLY Telly Savalas (MCA)
27	26	ENGELBERT HUMPERDINCK'S GREATEST HITS Engelbert Humperdinck (Decca)
25	27	JUST ANOTHER WAY TO SAY I LOVE YOU Barry White (20th Century)
-	28	THE DARK SIDE OF THE MOON Pink Floyd (Harvest)
22	29	BLOOD ON THE TRACKS Bob Dylan (CBS)
23	30	SIMON & GARFUNKEL GREATEST HITS Simon & Garfunkel (CBS)

3 May 1975

LW	TW	Album (Artist/Label)
1	1	ONCE UPON A STAR Bay City Rollers (Bell)
3	2	THE BEST OF THE STYLISTICS Stylistics (Avco)
2	3	THE MYTHS AND LEGENDS OF KING ARTHUR AND THE KNIGHTS OF THE ROUND TABLE Rick Wakeman & the English Rock Ensemble (A&M)
6	4	BLUE JAYS Justin Hayward & John Lodge (Threshold)
5	5	THE SHIRLEY BASSEY SINGLES ALBUM Shirley Bassey (United Artists)
4	6	THE ORIGINAL SOUNDTRACK 10 C.C. (Mercury)
7	7	STRAIGHT SHOOTER Bad Company (Island)
16	8	TUBULAR BELLS Mike Oldfield (Virgin)
8	9	PHYSICAL GRAFFITI Led Zeppelin (Swansong)
11	10	THE 10TH ANNIVERSARY ALBUM/20 GREATEST HITS Tom Jones (Decca)
12	11	ROLLIN' Bay City Rollers (Bell)
9	12	YOUNG AMERICANS David Bowie (RCA)
13	13	ELTON JOHN'S GREATEST HITS Elton John (DJM)
27	14	JUST ANOTHER WAY TO SAY I LOVE YOU Barry White (20th Century)
10	15	TOMMY Soundtrack (Polydor)
17	16	THERE'S ONE IN EVERY CROWD Eric Clapton (RSO)
18	17	ON THE LEVEL Status Quo (Vertigo)
14	18	THE BEST YEARS OF OUR LIVES Steve Harley & Cockney Rebel (EMI)
23	19	MEMORIES ARE MADE OF HITS Perry Como (RCA)
24	20	THE SINGLES 1969-1973 Carpenters (A&M)
19	21	RUBYCON Tangerine Dream (Virgin)
21	22	AVERAGE WHITE BAND Average White Band (Atlantic)
20	23	SOULED OUT Various Artists (K-Tel)
15	24	CRIME OF THE CENTURY Supertramp (A&M)
29	25	BLOOD ON THE TRACKS Bob Dylan (CBS)
22	26	ROCK 'N' ROLL DUDES Glitter Band (Bell)
30	27	SIMON & GARFUNKEL GREATEST HITS Simon & Garfunkel (CBS)
28	28	THE DARK SIDE OF THE MOON Pink Floyd (Harvest)
25	29	TELLY Telly Savalas (MCA)
-	30	YESTERDAYS Yes (Atlantic)

10 May 1975

LW	TW	Album (Artist/Label)
1	1	ONCE UPON A STAR Bay City Rollers (Bell)
2	2	THE BEST OF THE STYLISTICS Stylistics (Avco)
3	3	THE MYTHS AND LEGENDS OF KING ARTHUR AND THE KNIGHTS OF THE ROUND TABLE Rick Wakeman & the English Rock Ensemble (A&M)
4	4	BLUE JAYS Justin Hayward & John Lodge (Threshold)
7	5	STRAIGHT SHOOTER Bad Company (Island)
5	6	THE SHIRLEY BASSEY SINGLES ALBUM Shirley Bassey (United Artists)
6	7	THE ORIGINAL SOUNDTRACK 10 C.C. (Mercury)
8	8	TUBULAR BELLS Mike Oldfield (Virgin)
13	9	ELTON JOHN'S GREATEST HITS Elton John (DJM)
26	10	ROCK 'N' ROLL DUDES Glitter Band (Bell)
10	11	THE 10TH ANNIVERSARY ALBUM/20 GREATEST HITS Tom Jones (Decca)
21	12	RUBYCON Tangerine Dream (Virgin)
11	13	ROLLIN' Bay City Rollers (Bell)
14	14	JUST ANOTHER WAY TO SAY I LOVE YOU Barry White (20th Century)
9	15	PHYSICAL GRAFFITI Led Zeppelin (Swansong)
28	16	THE DARK SIDE OF THE MOON Pink Floyd (Harvest)
-	17	KATY LIED Steely Dan (ABC)
19	18	MEMORIES ARE MADE OF HITS Perry Como (RCA)
17	19	ON THE LEVEL Status Quo (Vertigo)
25	20	BLOOD ON THE TRACKS Bob Dylan (CBS)
20	21	THE SINGLES 1969-1973 Carpenters (A&M)
12	22	YOUNG AMERICANS David Bowie (RCA)
23	23	TOMMY Soundtrack (Polydor)
16	24	THERE'S ONE IN EVERY CROWD Eric Clapton (RSO)
23	25	SOULED OUT Various Artists (K-Tel)
27	26	SIMON & GARFUNKEL GREATEST HITS Simon & Garfunkel (CBS)
-	27	ROCK 'N' ROLL John Lennon (Apple)
22	28	AVERAGE WHITE BAND Average White Band (Atlantic)
-	29	AL GREEN'S GREATEST HITS Al Green (London)
18	30	THE BEST YEARS OF OUR LIVES Steve Harley & Cockney Rebel (EMI)

17 May 1975

LW	TW	Album (Artist/Label)
1	1	ONCE UPON A STAR Bay City Rollers (Bell)
2	2	THE BEST OF THE STYLISTICS Stylistics (Avco)
6	3	THE SHIRLEY BASSEY SINGLES ALBUM Shirley Bassey (United Artists)
13	4	ROLLIN' Bay City Rollers (Bell)
3	5	THE MYTHS AND LEGENDS OF KING ARTHUR AND THE KNIGHTS OF THE ROUND TABLE Rick Wakeman & the English RocK Ensemble (A&M)
5	6	STRAIGHT SHOOTER Bad Company (Island)
7	7	THE ORIGINAL SOUNDTRACK 10 C.C. (Mercury)
8	8	TUBULAR BELLS Mike Oldfield (Virgin)
4	9	BLUE JAYS Justin Hayward & John Lodge (Threshold)
21	10	THE SINGLES 1969-1973 Carpenters (A&M)
14	11	JUST ANOTHER WAY TO SAY I LOVE YOU Barry White (20th Century)
9	12	ELTON JOHN'S GREATEST HITS Elton John (DJM)
11	13	THE 10TH ANNIVERSARY ALBUM/20 GREATEST HITS Tom Jones (Decca)
27	14	ROCK 'N' ROLL John Lennon (Apple)
10	15	ROCK 'N' ROLL DUDES Glitter Band (Bell)
12	16	RUBYCON Tangerine Dream (Virgin)
15	17	PHYSICAL GRAFFITI Led Zeppelin (Swansong)
26	18	SIMON & GARFUNKEL GREATEST HITS Simon & Garfunkel (CBS)
18	19	MEMORIES ARE MADE OF HITS Perry Como (RCA)
16	20	THE DARK SIDE OF THE MOON Pink Floyd (Harvest)
-	21	IAN HUNTER Ian Hunter (CBS)
24	22	THERE'S ONE IN EVERY CROWD Eric Clapton (RSO)
-	23	THE BEST OF TAMMY WYNETTE Tammy Wynette (Epic)
-	24	GLEN CAMPBELL'S GREATEST HITS Glen Campbell (Capitol)
25	25	SOULED OUT Various Artists (K-Tel)
29	26	AL GREEN'S GREATEST HITS Al Green (London)
-	27	TOMORROW BELONGS TO ME Sensational Alex Harvey Band (Phonogram)
23	28	TOMMY Soundtrack (Polydor)
-	29	STAMPEDE Doobie Brothers (Warner Bros.)
-	30	CRIME OF THE CENTURY Supertramp (A&M)

Once Upon A Star leapt in at No.1, above the Stylistics, a group no-one seemed to notice was always charting. Their hit 45s had started in 1972, with *Betcha By Golly Wow* and *I'm Stone In Love With You*; they regained the Top 10 with 1974's *Rockin' Roll Baby, You Make Me Feel Brand New* and *Let's Put It All Together*. *Star On A TV Show* had made No.13; *Sing Baby Sing* would soon reach No.3; in August *I Can't Give You Anything (But My Love)* would be No.1.

May – June 1975

	24 May 1975		31 May 1975		7 June 1975		14 June 1975
1 1	ONCE UPON A STAR Bay City Rollers (Bell)	1 1	ONCE UPON A STAR Bay City Rollers (Bell)	1 1	ONCE UPON A STAR Bay City Rollers (Bell)	3 1	CAPTAIN FANTASTIC AND THE BROWN DIRT COWBOY Elton John (DJM)
2 2	THE BEST OF THE STYLISTICS Stylistics (Avco)	2 2	THE BEST OF THE STYLISTICS Stylistics (Avco)	2 2	THE BEST OF THE STYLISTICS Stylistics (Avco)	2 2	THE BEST OF THE STYLISTICS Stylistics (Avco)
5 3	THE MYTHS AND LEGENDS OF KING ARTHUR AND THE KNIGHTS OF THE ROUND TABLE Rick Wakeman & The English Rock Ensemble (A&M)	17 3	THE BEST OF TAMMY WYNETTE Tammy Wynette (Epic)	4 3	CAPTAIN FANTASTIC AND THE BROWN DIRT COWBOY Elton John (DJM)	1 3	ONCE UPON A STAR Bay City Rollers (Bell)
7 4	THE ORIGINAL SOUNDTRACK 10 C.C. (Mercury)	- 4	CAPTAIN FANTASTIC AND THE BROWN DIRT COWBOY Elton John (DJM)	3 4	THE BEST OF TAMMY WYNETTE Tammy Wynette (Epic)	5 4	THE ORIGINAL SOUNDTRACK 10 C.C. (Mercury)
9 5	BLUE JAYS Justin Hayward & John Lodge (Threshold)	12 5	AUTOBAHN Kraftwerk (Vertigo)	6 5	THE ORIGINAL SOUNDTRACK 10 C.C. (Mercury)	4 5	THE BEST OF TAMMY WYNETTE Tammy Wynette (Epic)
3 6	THE SHIRLEY BASSEY SINGLES ALBUM Shirley Bassey (United Artists)	4 6	THE ORIGINAL SOUNDTRACK 10 C.C. (Mercury)	5 6	AUTOBAHN Kraftwerk (Vertigo)	6 6	AUTOBAHN Kraftwerk (Vertigo)
13 7	THE 10TH ANNIVERSARY ALBUM/20 GREATEST HITS Tom Jones (Decca)	18 7	FOX Fox (GTO)	7 7	FOX Fox (GTO)	12 7	JUDITH Judy Collins (Elektra)
11 8	JUST ANOTHER WAY TO SAY I LOVE YOU Barry White (20th Century)	14 8	TUBULAR BELLS Mike Oldfield (Virgin)	9 8	THE SINGLES 1969-1973 Carpenters (A&M)	- 8	VENUS AND MARS Wings (Apple)
4 9	ROLLIN' Bay City Rollers (Bell)	13 9	THE SINGLES 1969-1973 Carpenters (A&M)	15 9	JUST ANOTHER WAY TO SAY I LOVE YOU Barry White (20th Century)	7 9	FOX Fox (GTO)
12 10	ELTON JOHN'S GREATEST HITS Elton John (DJM)	6 10	THE SHIRLEY BASSEY SINGLES ALBUM Shirley Bassey (United Artists)	8 10	TUBULAR BELLS Mike Oldfield (Virgin)	10 10	TUBULAR BELLS Mike Oldfield (Virgin)
- 11	TAKE CARE OF YOURSELF Three Degrees (Philadelphia International)	10 11	ELTON JOHN'S GREATEST HITS Elton John (DJM)	12 11	ROLLIN' Bay City Rollers (Bell)	14 11	TAKE GOOD CARE OF YOURSELF Three Degrees (Philadelphia International)
- 12	AUTOBAHN Kraftwerk (Vertigo)	9 12	ROLLIN' Bay City Rollers (Bell)	28 12	JUDITH Judy Collins (Elektra)	20 12	PHYSICAL GRAFFITI Led Zeppelin (Swansong)
10 13	THE SINGLES 1969-1973 Carpenters (A&M)	11 13	TAKE GOOD CARE OF YOURSELF Three Degrees (Philadelphia International)	10 13	THE SHIRLEY BASSEY SINGLES ALBUM Shirley Bassey (United Artists)	8 13	THE SINGLES 1969-1973 Carpenters (A&M)
8 14	TUBULAR BELLS Mike Oldfield (Virgin)	7 14	THE 10TH ANNIVERSARY ALBUM/20 GREATEST HITS Tom Jones (Decca)	13 14	TAKE GOOD CARE OF YOURSELF Three Degrees (Philadelphia International)	9 14	JUST ANOTHER WAY TO SAY I LOVE YOU Barry White (20th Century)
6 15	STRAIGHT SHOOTER Bad Company (Island)	8 15	JUST ANOTHER WAY TO SAY I LOVE YOU Barry White (20th Century)	17 15	BLUE JAYS Justin Hayward & John Lodge (Threshold)	15 15	ELTON JOHN'S GREATEST HITS Elton John (DJM)
16 16	RUBYCON Tangerine Dream (Virgin)	26 16	24 CARAT PURPLE Deep Purple (Purple)	11 16	ELTON JOHN'S GREATEST HITS Elton John (DJM)	11 16	ROLLIN' Bay City Rollers (Bell)
23 17	THE BEST OF TAMMY WYNETTE Tammy Wynette (Epic)	5 17	BLUE JAYS Justin Hayward & John Lodge (Threshold)	14 17	THE 10TH ANNIVERSARY ALBUM/20 GREATEST HITS Tom Jones (Decca)	23 17	24 CARAT PURPLE Deep Purple (Purple)
- 18	FOX Fox (GTO)	- 18	STAMPEDE Doobie Brothers (Warner Bros.)	19 18	STRAIGHT SHOOTER Bad Company (Island)	19 18	THE MYTHS AND LEGENDS OF KING ARTHUR AND THE KNIGHTS OF THE ROUND TABLE Rick Wakeman & the English Rock Ensemble (A&M)
14 19	ROCK 'N' ROLL John Lennon (Apple)	15 19	STRAIGHT SHOOTER Bad Company (Island)	22 19	THE MYTHS AND LEGENDS OF KING ARTHUR AND THE KNIGHTS OF THE ROUND TABLE Rick Wakeman & the English Rock Ensemble (A&M)	- 19	I FEEL A SONG Gladys Knight & the Pips (Buddah)
27 20	TOMORROW BELONGS TO ME Sensational Alex Harvey Band (Phonogram)	23 20	PHYSICAL GRAFFITI Led Zeppelin (Swansong)	20 20	PHYSICAL GRAFFITI Led Zeppelin (Swansong)	17 20	THE 10TH ANNIVERSARY ALBUM/20 GREATEST HITS Tom Jones (Decca)
20 21	THE DARK SIDE OF THE MOON Pink Floyd (Harvest)	16 21	RUBYCON Tangerine Dream (Virgin)	21 21	RUBYCON Tangerine Dream (Virgin)	15 21	BLUE JAYS Justin Hayward & John Lodge (Threshold)
- 22	CAN'T GET ENOUGH OF YOUR LOVE Barry White (20th Century)	3 22	THE MYTHS AND LEGENDS OF KING ARTHUR AND THE KNIGHTS OF THE ROUND TABLE Rick Wakeman & the English Rock Ensemble (A&M)	29 22	SIMON & GARFUNKEL GREATEST HITS Simon & Garfunkel (CBS)	18 22	STRAIGHT SHOOTER Bad Company (Island)
17 23	PHYSICAL GRAFFITI Led Zeppelin (Swansong)	19 23	ROCK 'N' ROLL John Lennon (Apple)	16 23	24 CARAT PURPLE Deep Purple (Purple)	22 23	SIMON & GARFUNKEL GREATEST HITS Simon & Garfunkel (CBS)
25 24	SOULED OUT Various (K-Tel)	25 24	AL GREEN'S GREATEST HITS Al Green (London)	27 24	THE DARK SIDE OF THE MOON Pink Floyd (Harvest)	26 24	STAMPEDE Doobie Brothers (Warner Bros.)
26 25	AL GREEN'S GREATEST HITS Al Green (London)	- 25	ROCKET Various Artists (Arcade)	24 25	AL GREEN'S GREATEST HITS Al Green (London)	- 25	WARRIOR ON THE EDGE OF TIME Hawkwind (United Artists)
- 26	24 CARAT PURPLE Deep Purple (Purple)	- 26	IAN HUNTER Ian Hunter (CBS)	18 26	STAMPEDE Doobie Brothers (Warner Bros.)	- 26	GREATEST HITS OF 10 C.C. 10 C.C. (UK)
18 27	SIMON & GARFUNKEL'S GREATEST HITS Simon & Garfunkel (CBS)	21 27	THE DARK SIDE OF THE MOON Pink Floyd (Harvest)	25 27	ROCKET Various Artists (Arcade)	28 27	MUSIC POWER Various Artists (K-Tel)
- 28	ON THE LEVEL Status Quo (Vertigo)	- 28	JUDITH Judy Collins (Elektra)	- 28	MUSIC POWER Various Artists (K-Tel)	21 28	RUBYCON Tangerine Dream (Virgin)
- 29	ENGELBERT HUMPERDINCK'S GREATEST HITS Engelbert Humperdinck (Decca)	27 29	SIMON & GARFUNKEL GREATEST HITS Simon & Garfunkel (CBS)	23 29	ROCK 'N' ROLL John Lennon (Apple)	24 29	THE DARK SIDE OF THE MOON Pink Floyd (Harvest)
24 30	GLEN CAMPBELL'S GREATEST HITS Glen Campbell (Capitol)	20 30	TOMORROW BELONGS TO ME Sensational Alex Harvey Band (Phonogram)	- 30	KATY LIED Steely Dan (ABC)	13 30	THE SHIRLEY BASSEY SINGLES ALBUM Shirley Bassey (United Artists)

John Lennon's retro-album *Rock'N'Roll*, produced by Phil Spector, was not reviving his chart fortunes. Entering at No.27 in mid-May, it had jumped to No.14 only to fall back to No.19, then 23, 29, out. The week it left, Paul McCartney's Wings jumped straight into the Top 10 at No.8 with *Venus And Mars*. Barry White, a large man with a curiously tuneless voice and a certain sexual *je ne sais quoi* for Medallion Woman, was enjoying, briefly, two hit albums.

21 June 1975

last week	this week	Title
1	1	CAPTAIN FANTASTIC AND THE BROWN DIRT COWBOY Elton John (DJM)
2	2	THE BEST OF THE STYLISTICS Stylistics (Avco)
3	3	ONCE UPON A STAR Bay City Rollers (Bell)
4	4	THE ORIGINAL SOUNDTRACK 10 C.C. (Mercury)
5	5	THE BEST OF TAMMY WYNETTE Tammy Wynette (Epic)
8	6	VENUS AND MARS Wings (Apple)
6	7	AUTOBAHN Kraftwerk (Vertigo)
11	8	TAKE GOOD CARE OF YOURSELF Three Degrees (Philadelphia International)
10	9	TUBULAR BELLS Mike Oldfield (Virgin)
9	10	FOX Fox (GTO)
7	11	JUDITH Judy Collins (Elektra)
26	12	GREATEST HITS OF 10 C.C. 10 C.C. (UK)
29	13	THE DARK SIDE OF THE MOON Pink Floyd (Harvest)
15	14	ELTON JOHN'S GREATEST HITS Elton John (DJM)
-	15	HORIZON Carpenters (A&M)
16	16	ROLLIN' Bay City Rollers (Bell)
-	17	I'M STILL GONNA NEED YOU Osmonds (MGM)
13	18	THE SINGLES 1969-1973 Carpenters (A&M)
19	19	I FEEL A SONG Gladys Knight & the Pips (Buddah)
18	20	THE MYTHS AND LEGENDS OF KING ARTHUR AND THE KNIGHTS OF THE ROUND TABLE Rick Wakeman & the English Rock Ensemble (A&M)
24	21	STAMPEDE Doobie Brothers (Warner Bros.)
23	22	SIMON & GARFUNKEL'S GREATEST HITS Simon & Garfunkel (CBS)
17	23	24 CARAT PURPLE Deep Purple (Purple)
14	24	JUST ANOTHER WAY TO SAY I LOVE YOU Barry White (20th Century)
12	25	PHYSICAL GRAFFITI Led Zeppelin (Swansong)
20	26	THE 10TH ANNIVERSARY ALBUM/20 GREATEST HITS Tom Jones (Decca)
30	27	THE SHIRLEY BASSEY SINGLES ALBUM Shirley Bassey (United Artists)
-	28	GLEN CAMPBELL'S GREATEST HITS Glen Campbell (Capitol)
-	29	ROCK 'N' ROLL John Lennon (Apple)
22	30	STRAIGHT SHOOTER Bad Company (Island)

28 June 1975

last week	this week	Title
1	1	CAPTAIN FANTASTIC AND THE BROWN DIRT COWBOY Elton John (DJM)
6	2	VENUS AND MARS Wings (Apple)
4	3	THE ORIGINAL SOUNDTRACK 10 C.C. (Mercury)
2	4	THE BEST OF THE STYLISTICS Stylistics (Avco)
3	5	ONCE UPON A STAR Bay City Rollers (Bell)
15	6	HORIZON Carpenters (A&M)
7	7	AUTOBAHN Kraftwerk (Vertigo)
8	8	TAKE GOOD CARE OF YOURSELF Three Degrees (Philadelphia International)
5	9	THE BEST OF TAMMY WYNETTE Tammy Wynette (Epic)
14	10	ELTON JOHN'S GREATEST HITS Elton John (DJM)
9	11	TUBULAR BELLS Mike Oldfield (Virgin)
12	12	GREATEST HITS OF 10 C.C. 10 C.C. (UK)
11	13	JUDITH Judy Collins (Elektra)
10	14	FOX Fox (GTO)
18	15	THE SINGLES 1969-1973 Carpenters (A&M)
16	16	ROLLIN' Bay City Rollers (Bell)
19	17	I FEEL A SONG Gladys Knight & the Pips (Buddah)
17	18	I'M STILL GONNA NEED YOU Osmonds (MGM)
13	19	THE DARK SIDE OF THE MOON Pink Floyd (Harvest)
-	20	STAND BY YOUR MAN Tammy Wynette (Epic)
25	21	PHYSICAL GRAFFITI Led Zeppelin (Swansong)
20	22	THE MYTHS AND LEGENDS OF KING ARTHUR AND THE KNIGHTS OF THE ROUND TABLE Rick Wakeman & the English Rock Ensemble (A&M)
22	23	SIMON & GARFUNKEL'S GREATEST HITS Simon & Garfunkel (CBS)
-	24	BEST OF BREAD Bread (Elektra)
30	25	STRAIGHT SHOOTER Bad Company (Island)
21	26	STAMPEDE Doobie Brothers (Warner Bros.)
23	27	24 CARAT PURPLE Deep Purple (Purple)
-	28	ON THE LEVEL Status Quo (Vertigo)
24	29	JUST ANOTHER WAY TO SAY I LOVE YOU Barry White (20th Century)
27	30	THE SHIRLEY BASSEY SINGLES ALBUM Shirley Bassey (United Artists)

5 July 1975

last week	this week	Title
2	1	VENUS AND MARS Wings (Apple)
1	2	CAPTAIN FANTASTIC AND THE BROWN DIRT COWBOY Elton John (DJM)
6	3	HORIZON Carpenters (A&M)
3	4	THE ORIGINAL SOUNDTRACK 10 C.C. (Mercury)
4	5	THE BEST OF THE STYLISTICS Stylistics (Avco)
5	6	ONCE UPON A STAR Bay City Rollers (Bell)
12	7	GREATEST HITS OF 10 C.C. 10 C.C. (UK)
7	8	AUTOBAHN Kraftwerk (Vertigo)
8	9	TAKE GOOD CARE OF YOURSELF Three Degrees (Philadelphia International)
16	10	ROLLIN' Bay City Rollers (Bell)
13	11	JUDITH Judy Collins (Elektra)
11	12	TUBULAR BELLS Mike Oldfield (Virgin)
9	13	THE BEST OF TAMMY WYNETTE Tammy Wynette (Epic)
15	14	THE SINGLES 1969-1973 Carpenters (A&M)
19	15	THE DARK SIDE OF THE MOON Pink Floyd (Harvest)
14	16	FOX Fox (GTO)
-	17	MADE IN THE SHADE Rolling Stones (Atlantic)
24	18	BEST OF BREAD Bread (Elektra)
10	19	ELTON JOHN'S GREATEST HITS Elton John (DJM)
20	20	STAND BY YOUR MAN Tammy Wynette (Epic)
-	21	ONE OF THESE NIGHTS Eagles (Asylum)
17	22	I FEEL A SONG Gladys Knight & the Pips (Buddah)
27	23	24 CARAT PURPLE Deep Purple (Purple)
22	24	THE MYTHS AND LEGENDS OF KING ARTHUR AND THE KNIGHTS OF THE ROUND TABLE Rick Wakeman & the English Rock Ensemble (A&M)
-	25	SNOWFLAKES ARE DANCING Tomita (Red Seal)
18	26	I'M STILL GONNA NEED YOU Osmonds (MGM)
-	27	RUBYCON Tangerine Dream (Virgin)
-	28	BAND ON THE RUN Paul McCartney & Wings (Parlophone)
23	29	SIMON & GARFUNKEL'S GREATEST HITS Simon & Garfunkel (CBS)
-	30	CUT THE CAKE Average White Band (Atlantic)

12 July 1975

last week	this week	Title
1	1	VENUS AND MARS Wings (Apple)
3	2	HORIZON Carpenters (A&M)
2	3	CAPTAIN FANTASTIC AND THE BROWN DIRT COWBOY Elton John (DJM)
4	4	THE ORIGINAL SOUNDTRACK 10 C.C. (Mercury)
6	5	ONCE UPON A STAR Bay City Rollers (Bell)
5	6	THE BEST OF THE STYLISTICS Stylistics (Avco)
13	7	THE BEST OF TAMMY WYNETTE Tammy Wynette (Epic)
7	8	GREATEST HITS OF 10 C.C. 10 C.C. (UK)
12	9	TUBULAR BELLS Mike Oldfield (Virgin)
14	10	THE SINGLES 1969-1973 Carpenters (A&M)
8	11	AUTOBAHN Kraftwerk (Vertigo)
9	12	TAKE GOOD CARE OF YOURSELF Three Degrees (Philadelphia International)
23	13	24 CARAT PURPLE Deep Purple (Purple)
19	14	ELTON JOHN'S GREATEST HITS Elton John (DJM)
17	15	MADE IN THE SHADE Rolling Stones (Atlantic)
10	16	ROLLIN' Bay City Rollers (Bell)
11	17	JUDITH Judy Collins (Elektra)
-	18	PHYSICAL GRAFFITI Led Zeppelin (Swansong)
25	19	SNOWFLAKES ARE DANCING Tomita (Red Seal)
-	20	RETURN TO FANTASY Uriah Heep (Bronze)
20	21	STAND BY YOUR MAN Tammy Wynette (Epic)
22	22	I FEEL A SONG Gladys Knight & the Pips (Buddah)
-	23	THANK YOU BABY Stylistics (Avco)
15	24	THE DARK SIDE OF THE MOON Pink Floyd (Harvest)
-	25	STEP TWO Showaddywaddy (Bell)
29	26	SIMON & GARFUNKEL GREATEST HITS Simon & Garfunkel (CBS)
28	27	BAND ON THE RUN Paul McCartney & Wings (Parlophone)
16	28	FOX Fox (GTO)
21	29	ONE OF THESE NIGHTS Eagles (Asylum)
18	30	BEST OF BREAD Bread (Elektra)

Lennon's *Rock'N'Roll* resurfaced briefly at No.29 and then left again. Two weeks later, McCartney had the satisfaction of seeing Wings replace the mega-selling *Captain Fantastic And The Brown Dirt Cowboy* at No.1, where *Venus And Mars* would stay for six weeks. Rick Wakeman was recovering from the shock of the May 31 chart, which had seen the humiliating plummet from No.3 to No.22 of his *Myths And Legends Of King Arthur And The Knights Of The Round Table* (to give it its full if uninteresting title).

July – August 1975

19 July 1975

last	this	album
1	1	VENUS AND MARS — Wings (Apple)
2	2	HORIZON — Carpenters (A&M)
4	3	THE ORIGINAL SOUNDTRACK — 10 C.C. (Mercury)
3	4	CAPTAIN FANTASTIC AND THE BROWN DIRT COWBOY — Elton John (DJM)
5	5	ONCE UPON A STAR — Bay City Rollers (Bell)
6	6	THE BEST OF THE STYLISTICS — Stylistics (Avco)
29	7	ONE OF THESE NIGHTS — Eagles (Asylum)
7	8	THE BEST OF TAMMY WYNETTE — Tammy Wynette (Epic)
9	9	TUBULAR BELLS — Mike Oldfield (Virgin)
8	10	GREATEST HITS OF 10 C.C. — 10 C.C. (UK)
25	11	STEP TWO — Showaddywaddy (Bell)
10	12	THE SINGLES 1969-1973 — Carpenters (A&M)
16	13	ROLLIN' — Bay City Rollers (Bell)
12	14	TAKE GOOD CARE OF YOURSELF — Three Degrees (Philadelphia International)
15	15	MADE IN THE SHADE — Rolling Stones (Atlantic)
13	16	24 CARAT PURPLE — Deep Purple (Purple)
20	17	RETURN TO FANTASY — Uriah Heep (Bronze)
11	18	AUTOBAHN — Kraftwerk (Vertigo)
14	19	ELTON JOHN'S GREATEST HITS — Elton John (DJM)
17	20	JUDITH — Judy Collins (Elektra)
23	21	THANK YOU BABY — Stylistics (Avco)
24	22	THE DARK SIDE OF THE MOON — Pink Floyd (Harvest)
26	23	SIMON & GARFUNKEL GREATEST HITS — Simon & Garfunkel (CBS)
-	24	MUD ROCK II — Mud (RAK)
18	25	PHYSICAL GRAFFITI — Led Zeppelin (Swansong)
-	26	THE SNOW GOOSE — Camel (Decca)
-	27	THE BASEMENT TAPES — Bob Dylan (CBS)
-	28	CUT THE CAKE — Average White Band (Atlantic)
21	29	STAND BY YOUR MAN — Tammy Wynette (Epic)
22	30	I FEEL A SONG — Gladys Knight & the Pips (Buddah)

26 July 1975

last	this	album
1	1	VENUS AND MARS — Wings (Apple)
5	2	ONCE UPON A STAR — Bay City Rollers (Bell)
4	3	CAPTAIN FANTASTIC AND THE BROWN DIRT COWBOY — Elton John (DJM)
2	4	HORIZON — Carpenters (A&M)
3	5	THE ORIGINAL SOUNDTRACK — 10 C.C. (Mercury)
6	6	THE BEST OF THE STYLISTICS — Stylistics (Avco)
8	7	THE BEST OF TAMMY WYNETTE — Tammy Wynette (Epic)
7	8	ONE OF THESE NIGHTS — Eagles (Asylum)
-	9	CAT STEVENS' GREATEST HITS — Cat Stevens (Island)
10	10	GREATEST HITS OF 10 C.C. — 10 C.C. (UK)
11	11	STEP TWO — Showaddywaddy (Bell)
9	12	TUBULAR BELLS — Mike Oldfield (Virgin)
12	13	THE SINGLES 1969-1973 — Carpenters (A&M)
16	14	24 CARAT PURPLE — Deep Purple (Purple)
21	15	THANK YOU BABY — Stylistics (Avco)
22	16	THE DARK SIDE OF THE MOON — Pink Floyd (Harvest)
19	17	ELTON JOHN'S GREATEST HITS — Elton John (DJM)
15	18	MADE IN THE SHADE — Rolling Stones (Atlantic)
13	19	ROLLIN' — Bay City Rollers (Bell)
-	20	SNOWFLAKES ARE DANCING — Tomita (Red Seal)
14	21	TAKE GOOD CARE OF YOURSELF — Three Degrees (Philadelphia International)
20	22	JUDITH — Judy Collins (Elektra)
24	23	MUD ROCK II — Mud (RAK)
-	24	DISCO BABY — Van McCoy (Avco)
27	25	THE BASEMENT TAPES — Bob Dylan (CBS)
25	26	PHYSICAL GRAFFITI — Led Zeppelin (Swansong)
26	27	THE SNOW GOOSE — Camel (Decca)
17	28	RETURN TO FANTASY — Uriah Heep (Bronze)
18	29	AUTOBAHN — Kraftwerk (Vertigo)
-	30	BAND ON THE RUN — Paul McCartney & Wings (Parlophone)

2 August 1975

last	this	album
1	1	VENUS AND MARS — Wings (Apple)
4	2	HORIZON — Carpenters (A&M)
3	3	CAPTAIN FANTASTIC AND THE BROWN DIRT COWBOY — Elton John (DJM)
2	4	ONCE UPON A STAR — Bay City Rollers (Bell)
5	5	THE ORIGINAL SOUNDTRACK — 10 C.C. (Mercury)
6	6	THE BEST OF THE STYLISTICS — Stylistics (Avco)
23	7	MUD ROCK II — Mud (RAK)
8	8	ONE OF THESE NIGHTS — Eagles (Asylum)
11	9	STEP TWO — Showaddywaddy (Bell)
25	10	THE BASEMENT TAPES — Bob Dylan (CBS)
12	11	TUBULAR BELLS — Mike Oldfield (Virgin)
17	12	ELTON JOHN'S GREATEST HITS — Elton John (DJM)
9	13	CAT STEVENS' GREATEST HITS — Cat Stevens (Island)
19	14	ROLLIN' — Bay City Rollers (Bell)
16	15	THE DARK SIDE OF THE MOON — Pink Floyd (Harvest)
13	16	THE SINGLES 1969-1973 — Carpenters (A&M)
7	17	THE BEST OF TAMMY WYNETTE — Tammy Wynette (Epic)
15	18	THANK YOU BABY — Stylistics (Avco)
18	19	MADE IN THE SHADE — Rolling Stones (Atlantic)
-	20	WHEN WILL I SEE YOU AGAIN — Johnny Mathis (CBS)
27	21	THE SNOW GOOSE — Camel (Decca)
10	22	GREATEST HITS OF 10 C.C. — 10 C.C. (UK)
14	23	24 CARAT PURPLE — Deep Purple (Purple)
-	24	SIMON & GARFUNKEL'S GREATEST HITS — Simon & Garfunkel (CBS)
22	25	JUDITH — Judy Collins (Elektra)
20	26	SNOWFLAKES ARE DANCING — Tomita (Red Seal)
-	27	TEN YEARS NON STOP JUBILEE — James Last (Polydor)
26	28	PHYSICAL GRAFFITI — Led Zeppelin (Swansong)
-	29	RIDE A ROCK HORSE — Roger Daltrey (Polydor)
24	30	DISCO BABY — Van McCoy (Avco)

9 August 1975

last	this	album
1	1	VENUS AND MARS — Wings (Apple)
2	2	HORIZON — Carpenters (A&M)
3	3	CAPTAIN FANTASTIC AND THE BROWN DIRT COWBOY — Elton John (DJM)
4	4	ONCE UPON A STAR — Bay City Rollers (Bell)
7	5	MUD ROCK II — Mud (RAK)
5	6	THE ORIGINAL SOUNDTRACK — 10 C.C. (Mercury)
8	7	ONE OF THESE NIGHTS — Eagles (Asylum)
10	8	THE BASEMENT TAPES — Bob Dylan (CBS)
6	9	THE BEST OF THE STYLISTICS — Stylistics (Avco)
9	10	STEP TWO — Showaddywaddy (Bell)
13	11	CAT STEVENS' GREATEST HITS — Cat Stevens (Island)
11	12	TUBULAR BELLS — Mike Oldfield (Virgin)
18	13	THANK YOU BABY — Stylistics (Avco)
21	14	THE SNOW GOOSE — Camel (Decca)
16	15	THE SINGLES 1969-1973 — Carpenters (A&M)
17	16	THE BEST OF TAMMY WYNETTE — Tammy Wynette (Epic)
15	17	THE DARK SIDE OF THE MOON — Pink Floyd (Harvest)
26	18	SNOWFLAKES ARE DANCING — Tomita (Red Seal)
12	19	ELTON JOHN'S GREATEST HITS — Elton John (DJM)
14	20	ROLLIN' — Bay City Rollers (Bell)
27	21	TEN YEARS NON STOP JUBILEE — James Last (Polydor)
22	22	GREATEST HITS OF 10 C.C. — 10 C.C. (UK)
23	23	24 CARAT PURPLE — Deep Purple (Purple)
24	24	SIMON & GARFUNKEL'S GREATEST HITS — Simon & Garfunkel (CBS)
29	25	RIDE A ROCK HORSE — Roger Daltrey (Polydor)
28	26	PHYSICAL GRAFFITI — Led Zeppelin (Swansong)
19	27	MADE IN THE SHADE — Rolling Stones (Atlantic)
-	28	MAKE THE WORLD GO AWAY — Donny & Marie Osmond (MGM)
20	29	WHEN WILL I SEE YOU AGAIN — Johnny Mathis (CBS)
-	30	PICTURES AT AN EXHIBITION — Tomita (Red Seal)

The singles chart was, even by 1970s standards, now oldie-mad. To the old songs revisited were added old records reissued: The Chi-Lites were No.5 with *Have You Seen Her* (their 1972 hit); Brian Hyland was about to peak at No.6 with *Sealed With A Kiss* (one of his 1962 hits); Desmond Dekker was just leaving with *The Israelites* (his 1969 hit). The LP chart oldies collections were joined by Dylan's double-album *The Basement Tapes*, recorded on a home tape machine with the Band in 1967.

16 August 1975

last week	this week	Title	Artist (Label)
9	1	THE BEST OF THE STYLISTICS	Stylistics (Avco)
1	2	VENUS AND MARS	Wings (Apple)
2	3	HORIZON	Carpenters (A&M)
4	4	ONCE UPON A STAR	Bay City Rollers (Bell)
3	5	CAPTAIN FANTASTIC AND THE BROWN DIRT COWBOY	Elton John (DJM)
13	6	THANK YOU BABY	Stylistics (Avco)
5	7	MUD ROCK II	Mud (RAK)
7	8	ONE OF THESE NIGHTS	Eagles (Asylum)
11	9	CAT STEVENS' GREATEST HITS	Cat Stevens (Island)
8	10	THE BASEMENT TAPES	Bob Dylan (CBS)
6	11	THE ORIGINAL SOUNDTRACK	10 C.C. (Mercury)
21	12	TEN YEARS NON STOP JUBILEE	James Last (Polydor)
15	13	THE SINGLES 1969-1973	Carpenters (A&M)
20	14	ROLLIN'	Bay City Rollers (Bell)
10	15	STEP TWO	Showaddywaddy (Bell)
29	16	WHEN WILL I SEE YOU AGAIN	Johnny Mathis (CBS)
12	17	TUBULAR BELLS	Mike Oldfield (Virgin)
17	18	THE DARK SIDE OF THE MOON	Pink Floyd (Harvest)
18	19	SNOWFLAKES ARE DANCING	Tomita (Red Seal)
16	20	THE BEST OF TAMMY WYNETTE	Tammy Wynette (Epic)
19	21	ELTON JOHN'S GREATEST HITS	Elton John (DJM)
25	22	RIDE A ROCK HORSE	Roger Daltrey (Polydor)
23	23	24 CARAT PURPLE	Deep Purple (Purple)
24	24	SIMON & GARFUNKEL'S GREATEST HITS	Simon & Garfunkel (CBS)
-	25	FROM MIGHTY OAKS	Ray Thomas (Threshold)
-	26	THE HIGHER THEY CLIMB	David Cassidy (RCA)
22	27	GREATEST HITS OF 10 C.C.	10 C.C. (UK)
-	28	BAND ON THE RUN	Paul McCartney & Wings (Parlophone)
14	29	THE SNOW GOOSE	Camel (Decca)
-	30	TAKE TWO	Diane Solomon (Philips)

23 August 1975

last	this	Title	Artist (Label)
1	1	THE BEST OF THE STYLISTICS	Stylistics (Avco)
2	2	VENUS AND MARS	Wings (Apple)
3	3	HORIZON	Carpenters (A&M)
6	4	THANK YOU BABY	Stylistics (Avco)
4	5	ONCE UPON A STAR	Bay City Rollers (Bell)
8	6	ONE OF THESE NIGHTS	Eagles (Asylum)
5	7	CAPTAIN FANTASTIC AND THE BROWN DIRT COWBOY	Elton John (DJM)
9	8	CAT STEVENS' GREATEST HITS	Cat Stevens (Island)
11	9	THE ORIGINAL SOUNDTRACK	10 C.C. (Mercury)
7	10	MUD ROCK II	Mud (RAK)
20	11	THE BEST OF TAMMY WYNETTE	Tammy Wynette (Epic)
12	12	TEN YEARS NON STOP JUBILEE	James Last (Polydor)
16	13	WHEN WILL I SEE YOU AGAIN	Johnny Mathis (CBS)
-	14	ATLANTIC CROSSING	Rod Stewart (Warner Bros.)
10	15	THE BASEMENT TAPES	Bob Dylan (CBS)
18	16	THE DARK SIDE OF THE MOON	Pink Floyd (Harvest)
13	17	THE SINGLES 1969-1973	Carpenters (A&M)
24	18	SIMON & GARFUNKEL'S GREATEST HITS	Simon & Garfunkel (CBS)
17	19	TUBULAR BELLS	Mike Oldfield (Virgin)
22	20	RIDE A ROCK HORSE	Roger Daltrey (Polydor)
15	21	STEP TWO	Showaddywaddy (Bell)
14	22	ROLLIN'	Bay City Rollers (Bell)
21	23	ELTON JOHN'S GREATEST HITS	Elton John (DJM)
23	24	24 CARAT PURPLE	Deep Purple (Purple)
19	25	SNOWFLAKES ARE DANCING	Tomita (Red Seal)
29	26	THE SNOW GOOSE	Camel (Decca)
26	27	THE HIGHER THEY CLIMB	David Cassidy (RCA)
27	28	GREATEST HITS OF 10 C.C.	10 C.C. (UK)
-	29	DISCO BABY	Van McCoy (Avco)
-	30	MADE IN THE SHADE	Rolling Stones (Atlantic)

30 August 1975

last	this	Title	Artist (Label)
1	1	THE BEST OF THE STYLISTICS	Stylistics (Avco)
3	2	HORIZON	Carpenters (A&M)
5	3	ONCE UPON A STAR	Bay City Rollers (Bell)
2	4	VENUS AND MARS	Wings (Apple)
14	5	ATLANTIC CROSSING	Rod Stewart (Warner Bros.)
4	6	THANK YOU BABY	Stylistics (Avco)
6	7	ONE OF THESE NIGHTS	Eagles (Asylum)
7	8	CAPTAIN FANTASTIC AND THE BROWN DIRT COWBOY	Elton John (DJM)
8	9	CAT STEVENS' GREATEST HITS	Cat Stevens (Island)
10	10	MUD ROCK II	Mud (RAK)
19	11	TUBULAR BELLS	Mike Oldfield (Virgin)
12	12	TEN YEARS NON STOP JUBILEE	James Last (Polydor)
20	13	RIDE A ROCK HORSE	Roger Daltrey (Polydor)
9	14	THE ORIGINAL SOUNDTRACK	10 C.C. (Mercury)
16	15	THE DARK SIDE OF THE MOON	Pink Floyd (Harvest)
17	16	THE SINGLES 1969-1973	Carpenters (A&M)
15	17	THE BASEMENT TAPES	Bob Dylan (CBS)
13	18	WHEN WILL I SEE YOU AGAIN	Johnny Mathis (CBS)
22	19	ROLLIN'	Bay City Rollers (Bell)
25	20	SNOWFLAKES ARE DANCING	Tomita (Red Seal)
28	21	GREATEST HITS OF 10 C.C.	10 C.C. (UK)
27	22	THE HIGHER THEY CLIMB	David Cassidy (RCA)
24	23	24 CARAT PURPLE	Deep Purple (Purple)
30	24	MADE IN THE SHADE	Rolling Stones (Atlantic)
18	25	SIMON & GARFUNKEL'S GREATEST HITS	Simon & Garfunkel (CBS)
26	26	THE SNOW GOOSE	Camel (Decca)
-	27	NEXT	Sensational Alex Harvey Band (Vertigo)
11	28	THE BEST OF TAMMY WYNETTE	Tammy Wynette (Epic)
21	29	STEP TWO	Showaddywaddy (Bell)
-	30	PICTURES AT AN EXHIBITION	Tomita (Red Seal)

6 September 1975

last	this	Title	Artist (Label)
5	1	ATLANTIC CROSSING	Rod Stewart (Warner Bros.)
1	2	THE BEST OF THE STYLISTICS	Stylistics (Avco)
6	3	THANK YOU BABY	Stylistics (Avco)
2	4	HORIZON	Carpenters (A&M)
4	5	VENUS AND MARS	Wings (Apple)
7	6	ONE OF THESE NIGHTS	Eagles (Asylum)
3	7	ONCE UPON A STAR	Bay City Rollers (Bell)
9	8	CAT STEVENS' GREATEST HITS	Cat Stevens (Island)
10	9	MUD ROCK II	Mud (RAK)
11	10	TUBULAR BELLS	Mike Oldfield (Virgin)
8	11	CAPTAIN FANTASTIC AND THE BROWN DIRT COWBOY	Elton John (DJM)
14	12	THE ORIGINAL SOUNDTRACK	10 C.C. (Mercury)
15	13	THE DARK SIDE OF THE MOON	Pink Floyd (Harvest)
12	14	TEN YEARS NON STOP JUBILEE	James Last (Polydor)
13	15	RIDE A ROCK HORSE	Roger Daltrey (Polydor)
16	16	THE SINGLES 1969-1973	Carpenters (A&M)
23	17	24 CARAT PURPLE	Deep Purple (Purple)
19	18	ROLLIN'	Bay City Rollers (Bell)
29	19	STEP TWO	Showaddywaddy (Bell)
-	20	E.C. WAS HERE	Eric Clapton (Polydor)
-	21	THE VERY BEST OF ROGER WHITTAKER	Roger Whittaker (EMI)
-	22	RAINBOW	Ritchie Blackmore (Oyster)
17	23	THE BASEMENT TAPES	Bob Dylan (CBS)
20	24	SNOWFLAKES ARE DANCING	Tomita (Red Seal)
26	25	THE SNOW GOOSE	Camel (Decca)
28	26	THE BEST OF TAMMY WYNETTE	Tammy Wynette (Epic)
18	27	WHEN WILL I SEE YOU AGAIN	Johnny Mathis (CBS)
-	28	TOMMY	Soundtrack (Polydor)
27	29	NEXT	Sensational Alex Harvey Band (Vertigo)
-	30	ELTON JOHN'S GREATEST HITS	Elton John (DJM)

Stylistics time again, with their long-serving *Best Of* album now jumping right back up, this time to No.1, while *Thank You Baby* rose so high that the week the group lost the top spot, September 6, they found themselves at Nos.2 and 3 instead. Their single *I Can't Give You Anything (But My Love)* was knocked off the No.1 slot by Rod Stewart's *Sailing* the week before his album *Atlantic Crossing* knocked *Best Of The Stylistics* from the No.1 LP slot. It was Stewart's fifth consecutive No.1 LP.

September – October 1975

13 September 1975

last week	this week	Album	Artist (label)
1	1	ATLANTIC CROSSING	Rod Stewart (Warner Bros.)
2	2	THE BEST OF THE STYLISTICS	Stylistics (Avco)
4	3	HORIZON	Carpenters (A&M)
6	4	ONE OF THESE NIGHTS	Eagles (Asylum)
3	5	THANK YOU BABY	Stylistics (Avco)
5	6	VENUS AND MARS	Wings (Apple)
8	7	CAT STEVENS' GREATEST HITS	Cat Stevens (Island)
21	8	THE VERY BEST OF ROG ER WHITTAKER	Roger Whittaker (EMI)
7	9	ONCE UPON A STAR	Bay City Rollers (Bell)
11	10	CAPTAIN FANTASTIC AND THE BROWN DIRT COWBOY	Elton John (DJM)
10	11	TUBULAR BELLS	Mike Oldfield (Virgin)
13	12	THE DARK SIDE OF THE MOON	Pink Floyd (Harvest)
12	13	THE ORIGINAL SOUNDTRACK	10 C.C. (Mercury)
9	14	MUD ROCK II	Mud (RAK)
16	15	THE SINGLES 1969-1973	Carpenters (A&M)
20	16	E.C. WAS HERE	Eric Clapton (Polydor)
17	17	24 CARAT PURPLE	Deep Purple (Purple)
-	18	STRAIGHT SHOOTER	Bad Company (Island)
-	19	ANOTHER YEAR	Leo Sayer (Chrysalis)
22	20	RAINBOW	Ritchie Blackmore (Oyster)
15	21	RIDE A ROCK HORSE	Roger Daltrey (Polydor)
19	22	STEP TWO	Showaddywaddy (Bell)
26	23	THE BEST OF TAMMY WYNETTE	Tammy Wynette (Epic)
-	24	THE SUN COLLECTION	Elvis Presley (RCA)
24	25	SNOWFLAKES ARE DANCING	Tomita (Red Seal)
14	26	TEN YEARS NON STOP JUBILEE	James Last (Polydor)
28	27	TOMMY	Soundtrack (Polydor)
18	28	ROLLIN'	Bay City Rollers (Bell)
-	29	SIMON & GARFUNKEL'S GREATEST HITS	Simon & Garfunkel (CBS)
-	30	MRS. 'ARDIN'S KID	Mike Harding (Transatlantic)

20 September 1975

last week	this week	Album	Artist (label)
1	1	ATLANTIC CROSSING	Rod Stewart (Warner Bros.)
2	2	THE BEST OF THE STYLISTICS	Stylistics (Avco)
3	3	HORIZON	Carpenters (A&M)
8	4	THE VERY BEST OF ROG ER WHITTAKER	Roger Whittaker (EMI)
7	5	CAT STEVENS' GREATEST HITS	Cat Stevens (Island)
4	6	ONE OF THESE NIGHTS	Eagles (Asylum)
5	7	THANK YOU BABY	Stylistics (Avco)
6	8	VENUS AND MARS	Wings (Apple)
9	9	ONCE UPON A STAR	Bay City Rollers (Bell)
20	10	RAINBOW	Ritchie Blackmore (Oyster)
19	11	ANOTHER YEAR	Leo Sayer (Chrysalis)
11	12	TUBULAR BELLS	Mike Oldfield (Virgin)
12	13	THE DARK SIDE OF THE MOON	Pink Floyd (Harvest)
10	14	CAPTAIN FANTASTIC AND THE BROWN DIRT COWBOY	Elton John (DJM)
16	15	E.C. WAS HERE	Eric Clapton (Polydor)
-	16	WISH YOU WERE HERE	Pink Floyd (Harvest)
13	17	THE ORIGINAL SOUNDTRACK	10 C.C. (Mercury)
15	18	THE SINGLES 1969-1973	Carpenters (A&M)
26	19	TEN YEARS NON STOP JUBILEE	James Last (Polydor)
18	20	STRAIGHT SHOOTER	Bad Company (Island)
-	21	SABOTAGE	Black Sabbath (Vertigo)
21	22	RIDE A ROCK HORSE	Roger Daltrey (Polydor)
-	23	ALL THE FUN OF THE FAIR	David Essex (CBS)
17	24	24 CARAT PURPLE	Deep Purple (Purple)
29	25	SIMON & GARFUNKEL'S GREATEST HITS	Simon & Garfunkel (CBS)
14	26	MUD ROCK II	Mud (RAK)
24	27	THE SUN COLLECTION	Elvis Presley (RCA)
-	28	LIVE	Sensational Alex Harvey Band (Vertigo)
22	29	STEP TWO	Showaddywaddy (Bell)
-	30	ELTON JOHN'S GREATEST HITS	Elton John (DJM)

27 September 1975

last week	this week	Album	Artist (label)
1	1	ATLANTIC CROSSING	Rod Stewart (Warner Bros.)
2	2	THE BEST OF THE STYLISTICS	Stylistics (Avco)
16	3	WISH YOU WERE HERE	Pink Floyd (Harvest)
5	4	CAT STEVENS' GREATEST HITS	Cat Stevens (Island)
4	5	THE VERY BEST OF ROG ER WHITTAKER	Roger Whittaker (EMI)
3	6	HORIZON	Carpenters (A&M)
8	7	VENUS AND MARS	Wings (Apple)
6	8	ONE OF THESE NIGHTS	Eagles (Asylum)
7	9	THANK YOU BABY	Stylistics (Avco)
9	10	ONCE UPON A STAR	Bay City Rollers (Bell)
12	11	TUBULAR BELLS	Mike Oldfield (Virgin)
11	12	ANOTHER YEAR	Leo Sayer (Chrysalis)
23	13	ALL THE FUN OF THE FAIR	David Essex (CBS)
10	14	RAINBOW	Ritchie Blackmore (Oyster)
15	15	E.C. WAS HERE	Eric Clapton (Polydor)
14	16	CAPTAIN FANTASTIC AND THE BROWN DIRT COWBOY	Elton John (DJM)
25	17	SIMON & GARFUNKEL'S GREATEST HITS	Simon & Garfunkel (CBS)
13	18	THE DARK SIDE OF THE MOON	Pink Floyd (Harvest)
18	19	THE SINGLES 1969-1973	Carpenters (A&M)
21	20	SABOTAGE	Black Sabbath (Vertigo)
28	21	LIVE	Sensational Alex Harvey Band (Vertigo)
20	22	STRAIGHT SHOOTER	Bad Company (Island)
17	23	THE ORIGINAL SOUNDTRACK	10 C.C. (Mercury)
27	24	THE SUN COLLECTION	Elvis Presley (RCA)
19	25	TEN YEARS NON STOP JUBILEE	James Last (Polydor)
-	26	THE MYTHS AND LEGENDS OF KING ARTHUR AND THE KNIGHTS OF THE ROUND TABLE	Rick Wakeman & the English Rock Ensemble (A&M)
27	27	TOMMY	Soundtrack (Polydor)
-	28	MRS. 'ARDIN'S KID	Mike Harding (Transatlantic)
-	29	ROLLIN'	Bay City Rollers (Bell)
-	30	40 SINGALONG PUB SONGS	Various Artists (K-Tel)

4 October 1975

last week	this week	Album	Artist (label)
1	1	ATLANTIC CROSSING	Rod Stewart (Warner Bros.)
3	2	WISH YOU WERE HERE	Pink Floyd (Harvest)
2	3	THE BEST OF THE STYLISTICS	Stylistics (Avco)
5	4	THE VERY BEST OF ROG ER WHITTAKER	Roger Whittaker (EMI)
4	5	CAT STEVENS' GREATEST HITS	Cat Stevens (Island)
6	6	HORIZON	Carpenters (A&M)
13	7	ALL THE FUN OF THE FAIR	David Essex (CBS)
20	8	SABOTAGE	Black Sabbath (Vertigo)
7	9	VENUS AND MARS	Wings (Apple)
12	10	ANOTHER YEAR	Leo Sayer (Chrysalis)
21	11	LIVE	Sensational Alex Harvey Band (Vertigo)
9	12	THANK YOU BABY	Stylistics (Avco)
11	13	TUBULAR BELLS	Mike Oldfield (Virgin)
8	14	ONE OF THESE NIGHTS	Eagles (Asylum)
10	15	ONCE UPON A STAR	Bay City Rollers (Bell)
19	16	THE SINGLES 1969-1973	Carpenters (A&M)
17	17	SIMON & GARFUNKEL'S GREATEST HITS	Simon & Garfunkel (CBS)
16	18	CAPTAIN FANTASTIC AND THE BROWN DIRT COWBOY	Elton John (DJM)
15	19	E.C. WAS HERE	Eric Clapton (Polydor)
-	20	ELTON JOHN'S GREATEST HITS	Elton John (DJM)
25	21	TEN YEARS NON STOP JUBILEE	James Last (Polydor)
18	22	THE DARK SIDE OF THE MOON	Pink Floyd (Harvest)
-	23	MISTY	Ray Stevens (Janus)
23	24	THE ORIGINAL SOUNDTRACK	10 C.C. (Mercury)
14	25	RAINBOW	Ritchie Blackmore (Oyster)
-	26	JIM REEVES' 40 GOLDEN GREATS	Jim Reeves (Arcade)
26	27	THE MYTHS AND LEGENDS OF KING ARTHUR AND THE KNIGHTS OF THE ROUND TABLE	Rick Wakeman & the English Rock Ensemble (A&M)
-	28	MINSTREL IN THE GALLERY	Jethro Tull (Chrysalis)
24	29	THE SUN COLLECTION	Elvis Presley (RCA)
-	30	FAVOURITES	Peters & Lee (Philips)

Several of those now charting had done so in a previous life. The crucial part of Wings had emerged from the Beatles; Bad Company, now with its second chart album beginning an erratic climb, had been formed around Paul Rodgers and Simon Kirke of Free; Ritchie Blackmore, ex-Deep Purple, was in the chart with Rainbow, which would become the name of his new band; Rick Wakeman was ex-Yes; and Roger Daltrey, though he hadn't quit the Who, was making his solo album debut.

October – November 1975

11 October 1975

last week	this week	
1	1	ATLANTIC CROSSING Rod Stewart (Warner Bros.)
2	2	WISH YOU WERE HERE Pink Floyd (Harvest)
7	3	ALL THE FUN OF THE FAIR David Essex (CBS)
5	4	CAT STEVENS' GREATEST HITS Cat Stevens (Island)
3	5	THE BEST OF THE STYLISTICS Stylistics (Avco)
4	6	THE VERY BEST OF ROGER WHITTAKER Roger Whittaker (EMI)
10	7	ANOTHER YEAR Leo Sayer (Chrysalis)
6	8	HORIZON Carpenters (A&M)
8	9	SABOTAGE Black Sabbath (Vertigo)
9	10	VENUS AND MARS Wings (Apple)
14	11	ONE OF THESE NIGHTS Eagles (Asylum)
30	12	FAVOURITES Peters & Lee (Philips)
11	13	LIVE Sensational Alex Harvey Band (Vertigo)
13	14	TUBULAR BELLS Mike Oldfield (Virgin)
-	15	STRAIGHT SHOOTER Bad Company (Island)
12	16	THANK YOU BABY Stylistics (Avco)
26	17	JIM REEVES' 40 GOLDEN GREATS Jim Reeves (Arcade)
15	18	ONCE UPON A STAR Bay City Rollers (Bell)
16	19	THE SINGLES 1969-1973 Carpenters (A&M)
22	20	THE DARK SIDE OF THE MOON Pink Floyd (Harvest)
19	21	E.C. WAS HERE Eric Clapton (Polydor)
28	22	MINSTREL IN THE GALLERY Jethro Tull (Chrysalis)
17	23	SIMON & GARFUNKEL'S GREATEST HITS Simon & Garfunkel (CBS)
18	24	CAPTAIN FANTASTIC AND THE BROWN DIRT COWBOY Elton John (DJM)
25	25	RAINBOW Ritchie Blackmore (Oyster)
-	26	40 SINGALONG PUB SONGS Various Artists (K-Tel)
24	27	THE ORIGINAL SOUNDTRACK 10 C.C. (Mercury)
29	28	THE SUN COLLECTION Elvis Presley (RCA)
20	29	ELTON JOHN'S GREATEST HITS Elton John (DJM)
21	30	TEN YEARS NON STOP JUBILEE James Last (Polydor)

18 October 1975

last week	this week	
1	1	ATLANTIC CROSSING Rod Stewart (Warner Bros.)
2	2	WISH YOU WERE HERE Pink Floyd (Harvest)
3	3	ALL THE FUN OF THE FAIR David Essex (CBS)
6	4	THE VERY BEST OF ROG ER WHITTAKER (EMI)
5	5	THE BEST OF THE STYLISTICS Stylistics (Avco)
12	6	FAVOURITES Peters & Lee (Philips)
4	7	CAT STEVENS' GREATEST HITS Cat Stevens (Island)
10	8	VENUS AND MARS Wings (Apple)
8	9	HORIZON Carpenters (A&M)
9	10	SABOTAGE Black Sabbath (Vertigo)
7	11	ANOTHER YEAR Leo Sayer (Chrysalis)
17	12	JIM REEVES' 40 GOLDEN GREATS Jim Reeves (Arcade)
11	13	ONE OF THESE NIGHTS Eagles (Asylum)
18	14	ONCE UPON A STAR Bay City Rollers (Bell)
13	15	LIVE Sensational Alex Harvey Band (Vertigo)
24	16	CAPTAIN FANTASTIC AND THE BROWN DIRT COWBOY Elton John (DJM)
16	17	THANK YOU BABY Stylistics (Avco)
19	18	THE SINGLES 1969-1973 Carpenters (A&M)
15	19	STRAIGHT SHOOTER Bad Company (Island)
14	20	TUBULAR BELLS Mike Oldfield (Virgin)
20	21	THE DARK SIDE OF THE MOON Pink Floyd (Harvest)
23	22	SIMON & GARFUNKEL'S GREATEST HITS Simon & Garfunkel (CBS)
29	23	ELTON JOHN'S GREATEST HITS Elton John (DJM)
28	24	THE SUN COLLECTION Elvis Presley (RCA)
-	25	EXTRA TEXTURE George Harrison (Apple)
22	26	MINSTREL IN THE GALLERY Jethro Tull (Chrysalis)
-	27	WINDSONG John Denver (RCA)
-	28	MAXIMUM DARKNESS Man (United Artists)
-	29	INDISCREET Sparks (Island)
-	30	STEP TWO Showaddywaddy (Bell)

25 October 1975

last week	this week	
2	1	WISH YOU WERE HERE Pink Floyd (Harvest)
1	2	ATLANTIC CROSSING Rod Stewart (Warner Bros.)
3	3	ALL THE FUN OF THE FAIR David Essex (CBS)
6	4	FAVOURITES Peters & Lee (Philips)
12	5	JIM REEVES' 40 GOLDEN GREATS Jim Reeves (Arcade)
4	6	THE VERY BEST OF ROG ER WHITTAKER (EMI)
-	7	THE WHO BY NUMBERS Who (Polydor)
7	8	CAT STEVENS' GREATEST HITS Cat Stevens (Island)
5	9	THE BEST OF THE STYLISTICS Stylistics (Avco)
11	10	ANOTHER YEAR Leo Sayer (Chrysalis)
8	11	VENUS AND MARS Wings (Apple)
10	12	SABOTAGE Black Sabbath (Vertigo)
9	13	HORIZON Carpenters (A&M)
13	14	ONE OF THESE NIGHTS Eagles (Asylum)
-	15	BREAKAWAY Art Garfunkel (CBS)
19	16	STRAIGHT SHOOTER Bad Company (Island)
22	17	SIMON & GARFUNKEL'S GREATEST HITS Simon & Garfunkel (CBS)
29	18	INDISCREET Sparks (Island)
-	19	STILL CRAZY AFTER ALL THESE YEARS Paul Simon (CBS)
20	20	TUBULAR BELLS Mike Oldfield (Virgin)
-	21	GOOD BAD BUT BEAUTIFUL Shirley Bassey (United Artists)
15	22	LIVE Sensational Alex Harvey Band (Vertigo)
27	23	WINDSONG John Denver (RCA)
18	24	THE SINGLES 1969-1973 Carpenters (A&M)
-	25	PERRY COMO'S 40 GREATEST HITS Perry Como (K-Tel)
-	26	40 SINGALONG PUB SONGS Various Artists (K-Tel)
21	27	THE DARK SIDE OF THE MOON Pink Floyd (Harvest)
26	28	MINSTREL IN THE GALLERY Jethro Tull (Chrysalis)
-	29	MALPRACTICE Dr. Feelgood (United Artists)
-	30	TIME HONOURED GHOSTS Barclay James Harvest (Polydor)

1 November 1975

last week	this week	
2	1	ATLANTIC CROSSING Rod Stewart (Warner Bros.)
5	2	JIM REEVES' 40 GOLDEN GREATS Jim Reeves (Arcade)
1	3	WISH YOU WERE HERE Pink Floyd (Harvest)
4	4	FAVOURITES Peters & Lee (Philips)
3	5	ALL THE FUN OF THE FAIR David Essex (CBS)
6	6	THE VERY BEST OF ROG ER WHITTAKER Roger Whittaker (EMI)
9	7	THE BEST OF THE STYLISTICS Stylistics (Avco)
7	8	THE WHO BY NUMBERS Who (Polydor)
15	9	BREAKAWAY Art Garfunkel (CBS)
8	10	CAT STEVENS' GREATEST HITS Cat Stevens (Island)
-	11	SIREN Roxy Music (Island)
-	12	ROCK OF THE WESTIES Elton John (DJM)
11	13	VENUS AND MARS Wings (Apple)
18	14	INDISCREET Sparks (Island)
10	15	ANOTHER YEAR Leo Sayer (Chrysalis)
13	16	HORIZON Carpenters (A&M)
25	17	PERRY COMO'S 40 GREATEST HITS Perry Como (K-Tel)
21	18	GOOD BAD BUT BEAUTIFUL Shirley Bassey (United Artists)
14	19	ONE OF THESE NIGHTS Eagles (Asylum)
23	20	WINDSONG John Denver (RCA)
19	21	STILL CRAZY AFTER ALL THESE YEARS Paul Simon (CBS)
-	22	EXTRA TEXTURE George Harrison (Apple)
12	23	SABOTAGE Black Sabbath (Vertigo)
17	24	SIMON & GARFUNKEL'S GREATEST HITS Simon & Garfunkel (CBS)
29	25	MALPRACTICE Dr. Feelgood (United Artists)
20	26	TUBULAR BELLS Mike Oldfield (Virgin)
-	27	RABBITS ON AND ON Jasper Carrott (DJM)
16	28	STRAIGHT SHOOTER Bad Company (Island)
-	29	TOMMY Soundtrack (Polydor)
-	30	WORDS AND MUSIC Billy Connolly (Transatlantic)

The god of MOR was ready for Christmas: hence we found chart homage offered to James Last; the re-entry of Perry Como's *40 Greatest Hits* (he'd never had 40 hits); Peters & Lee; the newly-devised *40 Singalong Pub Songs* torture; the Carpenters twice over; the predictable ascent of Jim Reeves again (his 22nd posthumous Top 30 album); the arrival of the *Good Bad But Beautiful* (not necessarily in that order) Shirley Bassey; and, Top 10, the circumspectly-titled *Very Best Of Roger Whittaker*.

November 1975

8 November 1975

Last	This	Title — Artist (Label)
2	1	JIM REEVES' 40 GOLDEN GREATS Jim Reeves (Arcade)
3	2	WISH YOU WERE HERE Pink Floyd (Harvest)
4	3	FAVOURITES Peters & Lee (Philips)
1	4	ATLANTIC CROSSING Rod Stewart (Warner Bros.)
5	5	ALL THE FUN OF THE FAIR David Essex (CBS)
9	6	BREAKAWAY Art Garfunkel (CBS)
17	7	PERRY COMO'S 40 GREATEST HITS Perry Como (K-Tel)
6	8	THE VERY BEST OF ROG ER WHITTAKER Roger Whittaker (EMI)
12	9	ROCK OF THE WESTIES Elton John (DJM)
11	10	SIREN Roxy Music (Island)
7	11	THE BEST OF THE STYLISTICS Stylistics (Avco)
8	12	THE WHO BY NUMBERS Who (Polydor)
18	13	GOOD BAD BUT BEAUTIFUL Shirley Bassey (United Artists)
21	14	STILL CRAZY AFTER ALL THESE YEARS Paul Simon (CBS)
-	15	ALL AROUND MY HAT Steeleye Span (Chrysalis)
19	16	ONE OF THESE NIGHTS Eagles (Asylum)
10	17	CAT STEVENS' GREATEST HITS Cat Stevens (Island)
20	18	WINDSONG John Denver (RCA)
-	19	MUD'S GREATEST HITS Mud (RAK)
-	20	WE ALL HAD DOCTOR'S PAPERS Max Boyce (EMI)
-	21	OMMADAWN Mike Oldfield (Virgin)
24	22	SIMON & GARFUNKEL'S GREATEST HITS Simon & Garfunkel (CBS)
13	23	VENUS AND MARS Wings (Apple)
15	24	ANOTHER YEAR Leo Sayer (Chrysalis)
16	25	HORIZON Carpenters (A&M)
25	26	MALPRACTICE Dr. Feelgood (United Artists)
26	27	TUBULAR BELLS Mike Oldfield (Virgin)
-	28	CHANGING ALL THE TIME Smokie (RAK)
14	29	INDISCREET Sparks (Island)
27	30	RABBITS ON AND ON Jasper Carrott (DJM)

15 November 1975

Last	This	Title — Artist (Label)
1	1	JIM REEVES' 40 GOLDEN GREATS Jim Reeves (Arcade)
10	2	SIREN Roxy Music (Island)
7	3	PERRY COMO'S 40 GREATEST HITS Perry Como (K-Tel)
9	4	ROCK OF THE WESTIES Elton John (DJM)
3	5	FAVOURITES Peters & Lee (Philips)
6	6	BREAKAWAY Art Garfunkel (CBS)
4	7	ATLANTIC CROSSING Rod Stewart (Warner Bros.)
2	8	WISH YOU WERE HERE Pink Floyd (Harvest)
5	9	ALL THE FUN OF THE FAIR David Essex (CBS)
21	10	OMMADAWN Mike Oldfield (Virgin)
8	11	THE VERY BEST OF ROG ER WHITTAKER Roger Whittaker (EMI)
11	12	THE BEST OF THE STYLISTICS Stylistics (Avco)
20	13	WE ALL HAD DOCTOR'S PAPERS Max Boyce (EMI)
14	14	STILL CRAZY AFTER ALL THESE YEARS Paul Simon (CBS)
15	15	ALL AROUND MY HAT Steeleye Span (Chrysalis)
12	16	THE WHO BY NUMBERS Who (Polydor)
16	17	ONE OF THESE NIGHTS Eagles (Asylum)
13	18	GOOD BAD BUT BEAUTIFUL Shirley Bassey (United Artists)
-	19	SHAVED FISH John Lennon (Apple)
18	20	WINDSONG John Denver (RCA)
28	21	CHANGING ALL THE TIME Smokie (RAK)
-	22	BLAZING BULLETS Various Artists (Ronco)
19	23	MUD'S GREATEST HITS Mud (RAK)
17	24	CAT STEVENS' GREATEST HITS Cat Stevens (Island)
-	25	SABOTAGE Black Sabbath (Vertigo)
-	26	RHINESTONE COWBOY Glen Campbell (Capitol)
-	27	DOWN THE DUST PIPE Status Quo (Golden Hour)
30	28	RABBITS ON AND ON Jasper Carrott (DJM)
22	29	SIMON & GARFUNKEL'S GREATEST HITS Simon & Garfunkel (CBS)
24	30	ANOTHER YEAR Leo Sayer (Chrysalis)

22 November 1975

Last	This	Title — Artist (Label)
1	1	JIM REEVES' 40 GOLDEN GREATS Jim Reeves (Arcade)
3	2	PERRY COMO'S 40 GREATEST HITS Perry Como (K-Tel)
4	3	ROCK OF THE WESTIES Elton John (DJM)
2	4	SIREN Roxy Music (Island)
5	5	FAVOURITES Peters & Lee (Philips)
7	6	ATLANTIC CROSSING Rod Stewart (Warner Bros.)
10	7	OMMADAWN Mike Oldfield (Virgin)
8	8	WISH YOU WERE HERE Pink Floyd (Harvest)
6	9	BREAKAWAY Art Garfunkel (CBS)
19	10	SHAVED FISH John Lennon (Apple)
15	11	ALL AROUND MY HAT Steeleye Span (Chrysalis)
9	12	ALL THE FUN OF THE FAIR David Essex (CBS)
13	13	WE ALL HAD DOCTOR'S PAPERS Max Boyce (EMI)
11	14	THE VERY BEST OF ROG ER WHITTAKER Roger Whittaker (EMI)
17	15	ONE OF THESE NIGHTS Eagles (Asylum)
12	16	THE BEST OF THE STYLISTICS Stylistics (Avco)
18	17	GOOD BAD BUT BEAUTIFUL Shirley Bassey (United Artists)
-	18	MOTOWN GOLD Various Artists (Tamla Motown)
-	19	BEGINNINGS Steve Howe (Atlantic)
-	20	GOOFY GREATS Various Artists (K-Tel)
14	21	STILL CRAZY AFTER ALL THESE YEARS Paul Simon (CBS)
20	22	WINDSONG John Denver (RCA)
-	23	COME TASTE THE BAND Deep Purple (Purple)
16	24	THE WHO BY NUMBERS Who (Polydor)
24	25	CAT STEVENS' GREATEST HITS Cat Stevens (Island)
23	26	MUD'S GREATEST HITS Mud (RAK)
29	27	SIMON & GARFUNKEL GREATEST HITS Simon & Garfunkel (CBS)
-	28	TUBULAR BELLS Mike Oldfield (Virgin)
-	29	MAKE THE PARTY LAST James Last (Polydor)
-	30	DISCO HITS '75 Various Artists (Arcade)

29 November 1975

Last	This	Title — Artist (Label)
2	1	PERRY COMO'S 40 GREATEST HITS Perry Como (K-Tel)
1	2	JIM REEVES' 40 GOLDEN GREATS Jim Reeves (Arcade)
5	3	FAVOURITES Peters & Lee (Philips)
7	4	OMMADAWN Mike Oldfield (Virgin)
6	5	ATLANTIC CROSSING Rod Stewart (Warner Bros.)
11	6	ALL AROUND MY HAT Steeleye Span (Chrysalis)
10	7	SHAVED FISH John Lennon (Apple)
4	8	SIREN Roxy Music (Island)
3	9	ROCK OF THE WESTIES Elton John (DJM)
15	10	ONE OF THESE NIGHTS Eagles (Asylum)
8	11	WISH YOU WERE HERE Pink Floyd (Harvest)
12	12	ALL THE FUN OF THE FAIR David Essex (CBS)
9	13	BREAKAWAY Art Garfunkel (CBS)
14	14	THE VERY BEST OF ROG ER WHITTAKER Roger Whittaker (EMI)
16	15	THE BEST OF THE STYLISTICS Stylistics (Avco)
29	16	MAKE THE PARTY LAST James Last (Polydor)
13	17	WE ALL HAD DOCTOR'S PAPERS Max Boyce (EMI)
18	18	MOTOWN GOLD Various Artists (Tamla Motown)
17	19	GOOD BAD BUT BEAUTIFUL Shirley Bassey (United Artists)
-	20	BARRY WHITE'S GREATEST HITS Barry White (20th Century)
19	21	BEGINNINGS Steve Howe (Atlantic)
23	22	COME TASTE THE BAND Deep Purple (Purple)
27	23	SIMON & GARFUNKEL GREATEST HITS Simon & Garfunkel (CBS)
-	24	BORN TO RUN Bruce Springsteen (CBS)
24	25	THE WHO BY NUMBERS Who (Polydor)
-	26	HOT CHOCOLATE Hot Chocolate (RAK)
20	27	GOOFY GREATS Various Artists (K-Tel)
-	28	RHINESTONE COWBOY Glen Campbell (Capitol)
-	29	GET RIGHT INTAE HIM Billy Connolly (Polydor)
30	30	DISCO HITS '75 Various Artists (Arcade)

What year was it? Jim Reeves battled with Perry Como for top place (two more RCA artists leased to the cheapo labels). Meanwhile Art Garfunkel battled with Paul Simon and with Simon & Garfunkel, Max Boyce and Jasper Carrott battled with Billy Connolly (*Get Right Intae Him* was his third Top 30 album) and Mike Oldfield with Mike Oldfield. John Lennon's *Shaved Fish*, surprisingly, didn't have to battle it out with Paul McCartney's anything. A one-week-only chart debut by Bruce Springsteen proved it was 1975.

6 December 1975

last week	this week	Title / Artist (Label)
1	1	PERRY COMO'S 40 GREATEST HITS Perry Como (K-Tel)
2	2	JIM REEVES' 40 GOLDEN GREATS Jim Reeves (Arcade)
3	3	FAVOURITES Peters & Lee (Philips)
-	4	A NIGHT AT THE OPERA Queen (EMI)
4	5	OMMADAWN Mike Oldfield (Virgin)
5	6	ATLANTIC CROSSING Rod Stewart (Warner Bros.)
6	7	ALL AROUND MY HAT Steeleye Span (Chrysalis)
8	8	SIREN Roxy Music (Island)
7	9	SHAVED FISH John Lennon (Apple)
9	10	ROCK OF THE WESTIES Elton John (DJM)
16	11	MAKE THE PARTY LAST James Last (Polydor)
10	12	ONE OF THESE NIGHTS Eagles (Asylum)
11	13	WISH YOU WERE HERE Pink Floyd (Harvest)
12	14	ALL THE FUN OF THE FAIR David Essex (CBS)
-	15	CRISIS? WHAT CRISIS? Supertramp (A&M)
-	16	WOULDN'T YOU LIKE IT? Bay City Rollers (Bell)
15	17	THE BEST OF THE STYLISTICS Stylistics (Avco)
30	18	DISCO HITS '75 Various Artists (Arcade)
-	19	ROLLED GOLD Rolling Stones (Decca)
13	20	BREAKAWAY Art Garfunkel (CBS)
29	21	GET RIGHT INTAE HIM Billy Connolly (Polydor)
14	22	THE VERY BEST OF ROG ER WHITTAKER Roger Whittaker (EMI)
20	23	BARRY WHITE'S GREATEST HITS Barry White (20th Century)
17	24	WE ALL HAD DOCTOR'S PAPERS Max Boyce (EMI)
22	25	COME TASTE THE BAND Deep Purple (Purple)
-	26	THE DARK SIDE OF THE MOON Pink Floyd (Harvest)
-	27	SONGS OF JOY Nigel Brooks Singers (K-Tel)
18	28	MOTOWN GOLD Various Artists (Tamla Motown)
28	29	RHINESTONE COWBOY Glen Campbell (Capitol)
25	30	THE WHO BY NUMBERS Who (Polydor)

13 December 1975

last week	this week	Title / Artist (Label)
1	1	PERRY COMO'S 40 GREATEST HITS Perry Como (K-Tel)
4	2	A NIGHT AT THE OPERA Queen (EMI)
3	3	FAVOURITES Peters & Lee (Philips)
2	4	JIM REEVES' 40 GOLDEN GREATS Jim Reeves (Arcade)
11	5	MAKE THE PARTY LAST James Last (Polydor)
9	6	SHAVED FISH John Lennon (Apple)
19	7	ROLLED GOLD Rolling Stones (Decca)
7	8	ALL AROUND MY HAT Steeleye Span (Chrysalis)
6	9	ATLANTIC CROSSING Rod Stewart (Warner Bros.)
15	10	CRISIS? WHAT CRISIS? Supertramp (A&M)
21	11	GET RIGHT INTAE HIM Billy Connolly (Polydor)
5	12	OMMADAWN Mike Oldfield (Virgin)
16	13	WOULDN'T YOU LIKE IT? Bay City Rollers (Bell)
8	14	SIREN Roxy Music (Island)
18	15	DISCO HITS '75 Various Artists (Arcade)
14	16	ALL THE FUN OF THE FAIR David Essex (CBS)
12	17	ONE OF THESE NIGHTS Eagles (Asylum)
13	18	WISH YOU WERE HERE Pink Floyd (Harvest)
10	19	ROCK OF THE WESTIES Elton John (DJM)
-	20	24 ORIGINAL HITS Drifters (Atlantic)
17	21	THE BEST OF THE STYLISTICS Stylistics (Avco)
27	22	SONGS OF JOY Nigel Brooks Singers (K-Tel)
24	23	WE ALL HAD DOCTOR'S PAPERS Max Boyce (EMI)
28	24	MOTOWN GOLD Various Artists (Tamla Motown)
-	25	YOU ARE BEAUTIFUL Stylistics (Avco)
23	26	BARRY WHITE'S GREATEST HITS Barry White (20th Century)
-	27	ELVIS PRESLEY'S 40 GREATEST HITS Elvis Presley (Arcade)
22	28	THE VERY BEST OF ROG ER WHITTAKER Roger Whittaker (EMI)
-	29	LIVE! Bob Marley & the Wailers (Island)
-	30	BLAZING BULLETS Various Artists (Ronco)

20 December 1975

last week	this week	Title / Artist (Label)
1	1	PERRY COMO'S 40 GREATEST HITS Perry Como (K-Tel)
2	2	A NIGHT AT THE OPERA Queen (EMI)
4	3	JIM REEVES' 40 GOLDEN GREATS Jim Reeves (Arcade)
5	4	MAKE THE PARTY LAST James Last (Polydor)
13	5	WOULDN'T YOU LIKE IT? Bay City Rollers (Bell)
8	6	ALL AROUND MY HAT Steeleye Span (Chrysalis)
6	7	SHAVED FISH John Lennon (Apple)
12	8	OMMADAWN Mike Oldfield (Virgin)
9	9	ATLANTIC CROSSING Rod Stewart (Warner Bros.)
7	10	ROLLED GOLD Rolling Stones (Decca)
22	11	SONGS OF JOY Nigel Brooks Singers (K-Tel)
3	12	FAVOURITES Peters & Lee (Philips)
11	13	GET RIGHT INTAE HIM Billy Connolly (Polydor)
21	14	THE BEST OF THE STYLISTICS Stylistics (Avco)
10	15	CRISIS? WHAT CRISIS? Supertramp (A&M)
18	16	WISH YOU WERE HERE Pink Floyd (Harvest)
20	17	24 ORIGINAL HITS Drifters (Atlantic)
16	18	ALL THE FUN OF THE FAIR David Essex (CBS)
14	19	SIREN Roxy Music (Island)
15	20	DISCO HITS '75 Various Artists (Arcade)
17	21	ONE OF THESE NIGHTS Eagles (Asylum)
26	22	BARRY WHITE'S GREATEST HITS Barry White (20th Century)
24	23	MOTOWN GOLD Various Artists (Tamla Motown)
27	24	ELVIS PRESLEY'S 40 GREATEST HITS Elvis Presley (Arcade)
25	25	YOU ARE BEAUTIFUL Stylistics (Avco)
23	26	WE ALL HAD DOCTOR'S PAPERS Max Boyce (EMI)
28	27	THE VERY BEST OF ROG ER WHITTAKER Roger Whittaker (EMI)
19	28	ROCK OF THE WESTIES Elton John (DJM)
-	29	THE GREATEST HITS OF WALT DISNEY Various Artists (Ronco)
-	30	40 SUPER GREATS Various Artists (K-Tel)

27 December 1975

last week	this week	Title / Artist (Label)
2	1	A NIGHT AT THE OPERA Queen (EMI)
1	2	PERRY COMO'S 40 GREATEST HITS Perry Como (K-Tel)
3	3	JIM REEVES' 40 GOLDEN GREATS Jim Reeves (Arcade)
5	4	WOULDN'T YOU LIKE IT? Bay City Rollers (Bell)
4	5	MAKE THE PARTY LAST James Last (Polydor)
17	6	24 ORIGINAL HITS Drifters (Atlantic)
12	7	FAVOURITES Peters & Lee (Philips)
8	8	OMMADAWN Mike Oldfield (Virgin)
9	9	ATLANTIC CROSSING Rod Stewart (Warner Bros.)
7	10	SHAVED FISH John Lennon (Apple)
11	11	SONGS OF JOY Nigel Brooks Singers (K-Tel)
10	12	ROLLED GOLD Rolling Stones (Decca)
6	13	ALL AROUND MY HAT Steeleye Span (Chrysalis)
18	14	ALL THE FUN OF THE FAIR David Essex (CBS)
24	15	ELVIS PRESLEY'S 40 GREATEST HITS Elvis Presley (Arcade)
13	16	GET RIGHT INTAE HIM Billy Connolly (Polydor)
15	17	CRISIS? WHAT CRISIS? Supertramp (A&M)
16	18	WISH YOU WERE HERE Pink Floyd (Harvest)
29	19	THE GREATEST HITS OF WALT DISNEY Various Artists (Ronco)
20	20	DISCO HITS '75 Various Artists (Arcade)
22	21	BARRY WHITE'S GREATEST HITS Barry White (20th Century)
30	22	40 SUPER GREATS Various Artists (K-Tel)
21	23	ONE OF THESE NIGHTS Eagles (Asylum)
14	24	THE BEST OF THE STYLISTICS Stylistics (Avco)
23	25	MOTOWN GOLD Various Artists (Tamla Motown)
27	26	THE VERY BEST OF ROG ER WHITTAKER Roger Whittaker (EMI)
28	27	ROCK OF THE WESTIES Elton John (DJM)
-	28	SIMON & GARFUNKEL'S GREATEST HITS Simon & Garfunkel (CBS)
26	29	WE ALL HAD DOCTOR'S PAPERS Max Boyce (EMI)
-	30	THE NEW GOODIES LP Goodies (Bradley's)

Queen's *A Night At The Opera* would be followed by *A Day At The Races*, both Marx Brothers film titles. Their first No.1 LP ran parallel with their first No.1 single, *Bohemian Rhapsody*, top throughout December. Supertramp, now largely forgotten, was hugely successful, very '70s, and lingered on in the charts as late as 1986. Our most commercial folk-rock group, Steeleye Span, built around Tim Hart and Maddy Prior, were having their biggest hit LP, while *All Around My Hat* was also a Top 10 single.

January 1976

3 January 1976

last week	this week	Title	Artist (Label)
1	1	A NIGHT AT THE OPERA	Queen (EMI)
2	2	PERRY COMO'S 40 GREATEST HITS	Perry Como (K-Tel)
5	3	MAKE THE PARTY LAST	James Last (Polydor)
3	4	JIM REEVES' 40 GOLDEN GREATS	Jim Reeves (Arcade)
4	5	WOULDN'T YOU LIKE IT?	Bay City Rollers (Bell)
6	6	24 ORIGINAL HITS	Drifters (Atlantic)
8	7	OMMADAWN	Mike Oldfield (Virgin)
7	8	FAVOURITES	Peters & Lee (Philips)
9	9	ATLANTIC CROSSING	Rod Stewart (Warner Bros.)
14	10	ALL THE FUN OF THE FAIR	David Essex (CBS)
22	11	40 SUPER GREATS	Various Artists (K-Tel)
16	12	GET RIGHT INTAE HIM	Billy Connolly (Polydor)
11	13	SONGS OF JOY	Nigel Brooks Singers (K-Tel)
13	14	ALL AROUND MY HAT	Steeleye Span (Chrysalis)
15	15	ELVIS PRESLEY'S 40 GREATEST HITS	Elvis Presley (Arcade)
20	16	DISCO HITS '75	Various Artists (Arcade)
12	17	ROLLED GOLD	Rolling Stones (Decca)
10	18	SHAVED FISH	John Lennon (Apple)
24	19	BEST OF THE STYLISTICS	Stylistics (Avco)
19	20	THE GREATEST HITS OF WALT DISNEY	Various Artists (Ronco)
18	21	WISH YOU WERE HERE	Pink Floyd (Harvest)
17	22	CRISIS? WHAT CRISIS?	Supertramp (A&M)
23	23	ONE OF THESE NIGHTS	Eagles (Asylum)
-	24	SUPERSONIC	Various Artists (Stallion)
-	25	GOOFY GREATS	Various Artists (K-Tel)
-	26	BREAKAWAY	Art Garfunkel (CBS)
21	27	BARRY WHITE'S GREATEST HITS	Barry White (20th Century)
26	28	THE VERY BEST OF ROGER WHITTAKER	Roger Whittaker (EMI)
-	29	FISH OUT OF WATER	Chris Squire (Atlantic)
28	30	SIMON & GARFUNKEL'S GREATEST HITS	Simon & Garfunkel (CBS)

10 January 1976

last week	this week	Title	Artist (Label)
1	1	A NIGHT AT THE OPERA	Queen (EMI)
2	2	PERRY COMO'S 40 GREATEST HITS	Perry Como (K-Tel)
7	3	OMMADAWN	Mike Oldfield (Virgin)
3	4	MAKE THE PARTY LAST	James Last (Polydor)
6	5	24 ORIGINAL HITS	Drifters (Atlantic)
9	6	ATLANTIC CROSSING	Rod Stewart (Warner Bros.)
5	7	WOULDN'T YOU LIKE IT?	Bay City Rollers (Bell)
14	8	ALL AROUND MY HAT	Steeleye Span (Chrysalis)
4	9	JIM REEVES' 40 GOLDEN GREATS	Jim Reeves (Arcade)
8	10	FAVOURITES	Peters & Lee (Philips)
10	11	ALL THE FUN OF THE FAIR	David Essex (CBS)
18	12	SHAVED FISH	John Lennon (Apple)
22	13	CRISIS? WHAT CRISIS?	Supertramp (A&M)
17	14	ROLLED GOLD	Rolling Stones (Decca)
12	15	GET RIGHT INTAE HIM	Billy Connolly (Polydor)
19	16	BEST OF THE STYLISTICS	Stylistics (Avco)
23	17	ONE OF THESE NIGHTS	Eagles (Asylum)
21	18	WISH YOU WERE HERE	Pink Floyd (Harvest)
29	19	FISH OUT OF WATER	Chris Squire (Atlantic)
11	20	40 SUPER GREATS	Various Artists (K-Tel)
26	21	BREAKAWAY	Art Garfunkel (CBS)
15	22	ELVIS PRESLEY'S 40 GREATEST HITS	Elvis Presley (Arcade)
28	23	THE VERY BEST OF ROGER WHITTAKER	Roger Whittaker (EMI)
13	24	SONGS OF JOY	Nigel Brooks Singers (K-Tel)
16	25	DISCO HITS '75	Various Artists (Arcade)
20	26	THE GREATEST HITS OF WALT DISNEY	Various Artists (Ronco)
-	27	THE TOP 25 FROM YOUR 100 BEST TUNES	Various Artists (Decca)
-	28	THE HISSING OF SUMMER LAWNS	Joni Mitchell (Asylum)
27	29	BARRY WHITE'S GREATEST HITS	Barry White (20th Century)
-	30	TUBULAR BELLS	Mike Oldfield (Virgin)

17 January 1976

last week	this week	Title	Artist (Label)
1	1	A NIGHT AT THE OPERA	Queen (EMI)
2	2	PERRY COMO'S 40 GREATEST HITS	Perry Como (K-Tel)
3	3	OMMADAWN	Mike Oldfield (Virgin)
5	4	24 ORIGINAL HITS	Drifters (Atlantic)
7	5	WOULDN'T YOU LIKE IT?	Bay City Rollers (Bell)
4	6	MAKE THE PARTY LAST	James Last (Polydor)
6	7	ATLANTIC CROSSING	Rod Stewart (Warner Bros.)
9	8	JIM REEVES' 40 GOLDEN GREATS	Jim Reeves (Arcade)
8	9	ALL AROUND MY HAT	Steeleye Span (Chrysalis)
16	10	BEST OF THE STYLISTICS	Stylistics (Avco)
15	11	GET RIGHT INTAE HIM	Billy Connolly (Polydor)
14	12	ROLLED GOLD	Rolling Stones (Decca)
10	13	FAVOURITES	Peters & Lee (Philips)
11	14	ALL THE FUN OF THE FAIR	David Essex (CBS)
12	15	SHAVED FISH	John Lennon (Apple)
18	16	WISH YOU WERE HERE	Pink Floyd (Harvest)
17	17	ONE OF THESE NIGHTS	Eagles (Asylum)
13	18	CRISIS? WHAT CRISIS?	Supertramp (A&M)
29	19	BARRY WHITE'S GREATEST HITS	Barry White (20th Century)
-	20	THE BEST OF ROY ORBISON	Roy Orbison (Arcade)
19	21	FISH OUT OF WATER	Chris Squire (Atlantic)
-	22	STILL CRAZY AFTER ALL THESE YEARS	Paul Simon (CBS)
24	23	SONGS OF JOY	Nigel Brooks Singers (K-Tel)
22	24	ELVIS PRESLEY'S 40 GREATEST HITS	Elvis Presley (Arcade)
28	25	THE HISSING OF SUMMER LAWNS	Joni Mitchell (Asylum)
-	26	MOTOWN GOLD	Various Artists (Tamla Motown)
21	27	BREAKAWAY	Art Garfunkel (CBS)
25	28	DISCO HITS '75	Various Artists (Arcade)
30	29	TUBULAR BELLS	Mike Oldfield (Virgin)
-	30	SIMON & GARFUNKEL'S GREATEST HITS	Simon & Garfunkel (CBS)

24 January 1976

last week	this week	Title	Artist (Label)
1	1	A NIGHT AT THE OPERA	Queen (EMI)
3	2	OMMADAWN	Mike Oldfield (Virgin)
4	3	24 ORIGINAL HITS	Drifters (Atlantic)
2	4	PERRY COMO'S 40 GREATEST HITS	Perry Como (K-Tel)
20	5	THE BEST OF ROY ORBISON	Roy Orbison (Arcade)
7	6	ATLANTIC CROSSING	Rod Stewart (Warner Bros.)
5	7	WOULDN'T YOU LIKE IT?	Bay City Rollers (Bell)
-	8	HOW DARE YOU	10 C.C. (Mercury)
22	9	STILL CRAZY AFTER ALL THESE YEARS	Paul Simon (CBS)
6	10	MAKE THE PARTY LAST	James Last (Polydor)
12	11	ROLLED GOLD	Rolling Stones (Decca)
10	12	BEST OF THE STYLISTICS	Stylistics (Avco)
16	13	WISH YOU WERE HERE	Pink Floyd (Harvest)
8	14	JIM REEVES' 40 GOLDEN GREATS	Jim Reeves (Arcade)
9	15	ALL AROUND MY HAT	Steeleye Span (Chrysalis)
14	16	ALL THE FUN OF THE FAIR	David Essex (CBS)
-	17	DESIRE	Bob Dylan (CBS)
11	18	GET RIGHT INTAE HIM	Billy Connolly (Polydor)
13	19	FAVOURITES	Peters & Lee (Philips)
17	20	ONE OF THESE NIGHTS	Eagles (Asylum)
25	21	THE HISSING OF SUMMER LAWNS	Joni Mitchell (Asylum)
18	22	CRISIS? WHAT CRISIS?	Supertramp (A&M)
15	23	SHAVED FISH	John Lennon (Apple)
-	24	MUSIC EXPRESS	Various Artists (K-Tel)
23	25	SONGS OF JOY	Nigel Brooks Singers (K-Tel)
29	26	TUBULAR BELLS	Mike Oldfield (Virgin)
27	27	BREAKAWAY	Art Garfunkel (CBS)
-	28	40 SUPER GREATS	Various Artists (K-Tel)
19	29	BARRY WHITE'S GREATEST HITS	Barry White (20th Century)
-	30	SHEER HEART ATTACK	Queen (EMI)

This was the first year since album charts began that Frank Sinatra didn't enter the Top 30 at least once. Britain's first LP chart, Melody Maker's, began in 1958; from then till the NME chart arrived, Sinatra had 16 Top 20 hit LPs. Then, from *I Remember Tommy* and *Sinatra And Strings*, both in the first NME chart (Top 10 only) back in June 1962, through to *Main Event* in February 1975, this remarkable singer (and convincing screen actor) had racked up some 26 further Top 30 album successes.

January – February 1976

31 January 1976

last week	this week	Album
1	1	A NIGHT AT THE OPERA — Queen (EMI)
3	2	24 ORIGINAL HITS — Drifters (Atlantic)
5	3	THE BEST OF ROY ORBISON — Roy Orbison (Arcade)
2	4	OMMADAWN — Mike Oldfield (Virgin)
9	5	STILL CRAZY AFTER ALL THESE YEARS — Paul Simon (CBS)
4	6	PERRY COMO'S 40 GREATEST HITS — Perry Como (K-Tel)
8	7	HOW DARE YOU — 10 C.C. (Mercury)
6	8	ATLANTIC CROSSING — Rod Stewart (Warner Bros.)
17	9	DESIRE — Bob Dylan (CBS)
13	10	WISH YOU WERE HERE — Pink Floyd (Harvest)
10	11	MAKE THE PARTY LAST — James Last (Polydor)
24	12	MUSIC EXPRESS — Various Artists (K-Tel)
7	13	WOULDN'T YOU LIKE IT? — Bay City Rollers (Bell)
22	14	CRISIS? WHAT CRISIS? — Supertramp (A&M)
11	15	ROLLED GOLD — Rolling Stones (Decca)
12	16	BEST OF THE STYLISTICS — Stylistics (Avco)
21	17	THE HISSING OF SUMMER LAWNS — Joni Mitchell (Asylum)
16	18	ALL THE FUN OF THE FAIR — David Essex (CBS)
20	19	ONE OF THESE NIGHTS — Eagles (Asylum)
-	20	THE VERY BEST OF SLIM WHITMAN — Slim Whitman (United Artists)
14	21	JIM REEVES' 40 GOLDEN GREATS — Jim Reeves (Arcade)
-	22	MOTOWN GOLD — Various Artists (Tamla Motown)
30	23	SHEER HEART ATTACK — Queen (EMI)
15	24	ALL AROUND MY HAT — Steeleye Span (Chrysalis)
25	25	SONGS OF JOY — Nigel Brooks Singers (K-Tel)
-	26	THE VERY BEST OF ROGER WHITTAKER — Roger Whittaker (EMI)
18	27	GET RIGHT INTAE HIM — Billy Connolly (Polydor)
26	28	TUBULAR BELLS — Mike Oldfield (Virgin)
23	29	SHAVED FISH — John Lennon (Apple)
-	30	STATION TO STATION — David Bowie (RCA)

7 February 1976

last week	this week	Album
7	1	HOW DARE YOU — 10 C.C. (Mercury)
9	2	DESIRE — Bob Dylan (CBS)
1	3	A NIGHT AT THE OPERA — Queen (EMI)
3	4	THE BEST OF ROY ORBISON — Roy Orbison (Arcade)
2	5	24 ORIGINAL HITS — Drifters (Atlantic)
4	6	OMMADAWN — Mike Oldfield (Virgin)
5	7	STILL CRAZY AFTER ALL THESE YEARS — Paul Simon (CBS)
12	8	MUSIC EXPRESS — Various Artists (K-Tel)
6	9	PERRY COMO'S 40 GREATEST HITS — Perry Como (K-Tel)
8	10	ATLANTIC CROSSING — Rod Stewart (Warner Bros.)
20	11	THE VERY BEST OF SLIM WHITMAN — Slim Whitman (United Artists)
30	12	STATION TO STATION — David Bowie (RCA)
-	13	SING LOFTY — Don Estelle & Windsor Davies (EMI)
17	14	THE HISSING OF SUMMER LAWNS — Joni Mitchell (Asylum)
23	15	SHEER HEART ATTACK — Queen (EMI)
15	16	ROLLED GOLD — Rolling Stones (Decca)
-	17	STAR TRACKING '76 — Various Artists (Ronco)
13	18	WOULDN'T YOU LIKE IT? — Bay City Rollers (Bell)
-	19	ABBA — Abba (Epic)
-	20	SUNBURST FINISH — Be-Bop Deluxe (Harvest)
14	21	CRISIS? WHAT CRISIS? — Supertramp (A&M)
10	22	WISH YOU WERE HERE — Pink Floyd (Harvest)
19	23	ONE OF THESE NIGHTS — Eagles (Asylum)
22	24	MOTOWN GOLD — Various Artists (Tamla Motown)
16	25	BEST OF THE STYLISTICS — Stylistics (Avco)
-	26	BARRY WHITE'S GREATEST HITS — Barry White (20th Century)
21	27	JIM REEVES' 40 GOLDEN GREATS — Jim Reeves (Arcade)
11	28	MAKE THE PARTY LAST — James Last (Polydor)
28	29	TUBULAR BELLS — Mike Oldfield (Virgin)
-	30	SIMON & GARFUNKEL'S GREATEST HITS — Simon & Garfunkel (CBS)

14 February 1976

last week	this week	Album
2	1	DESIRE — Bob Dylan (CBS)
1	2	HOW DARE YOU — 10 C.C. (Mercury)
3	3	A NIGHT AT THE OPERA — Queen (EMI)
4	4	THE BEST OF ROY ORBISON — Roy Orbison (Arcade)
11	5	THE VERY BEST OF SLIM WHITMAN — Slim Whitman (United Artists)
6	6	OMMADAWN — Mike Oldfield (Virgin)
5	7	24 ORIGINAL HITS — Drifters (Atlantic)
12	8	STATION TO STATION — David Bowie (RCA)
8	9	MUSIC EXPRESS — Various Artists (K-Tel)
24	10	MOTOWN GOLD — Various Artists (Tamla Motown)
7	11	STILL CRAZY AFTER ALL THESE YEARS — Paul Simon (CBS)
9	12	PERRY COMO'S 40 GREATEST HITS — Perry Como (K-Tel)
14	13	THE HISSING OF SUMMER LAWNS — Joni Mitchell (Asylum)
19	14	ABBA — Abba (Epic)
10	15	ATLANTIC CROSSING — Rod Stewart (Warner Bros.)
15	16	SHEER HEART ATTACK — Queen (EMI)
29	17	TUBULAR BELLS — Mike Oldfield (Virgin)
-	18	BREAKAWAY — Art Garfunkel (CBS)
13	19	SING LOFTY — Don Estelle & Windsor Davies (EMI)
-	20	RUN WITH THE PACK — Bad Company (Island)
21	21	CRISIS? WHAT CRISIS? — Supertramp (A&M)
20	22	SUNBURST FINISH — Be-Bop Deluxe (Harvest)
-	23	CARNIVAL — Manuel & His Music of the Mountains (Studio Two)
23	24	ONE OF THESE NIGHTS — Eagles (Asylum)
16	25	ROLLED GOLD — Rolling Stones (Decca)
-	26	LOVE TO LOVE YOU BABY — Donna Summer (GTO)
-	27	QUEEN II — Queen (EMI)
27	28	JIM REEVES' 40 GOLDEN GREATS — Jim Reeves (Arcade)
22	29	WISH YOU WERE HERE — Pink Floyd (Harvest)
25	30	BEST OF THE STYLISTICS — Stylistics (Avco)

21 February 1976

last week	this week	Album
1	1	DESIRE — Bob Dylan (CBS)
5	2	THE VERY BEST OF SLIM WHITMAN — Slim Whitman (United Artists)
2	3	HOW DARE YOU — 10 C.C. (Mercury)
4	4	THE BEST OF ROY ORBISON — Roy Orbison (Arcade)
8	5	STATION TO STATION — David Bowie (RCA)
3	6	A NIGHT AT THE OPERA — Queen (EMI)
9	7	MUSIC EXPRESS — Various Artists (K-Tel)
7	8	24 ORIGINAL HITS — Drifters (Atlantic)
6	9	OMMADAWN — Mike Oldfield (Virgin)
11	10	STILL CRAZY AFTER ALL THESE YEARS — Paul Simon (CBS)
12	11	PERRY COMO'S 40 GREATEST HITS — Perry Como (K-Tel)
-	12	THE BEST OF HELEN REDDY — Helen Reddy (Capitol)
20	13	RUN WITH THE PACK — Bad Company (Island)
14	14	ABBA — Abba (Epic)
10	15	MOTOWN GOLD — Various Artists (Tamla Motown)
23	16	CARNIVAL — Manuel & His Music of the Mountains (Studio Two)
22	17	SUNBURST FINISH — Be-Bop Deluxe (Harvest)
18	18	BREAKAWAY — Art Garfunkel (CBS)
15	19	ATLANTIC CROSSING — Rod Stewart (Warner Bros.)
13	20	THE HISSING OF SUMMER LAWNS — Joni Mitchell (Asylum)
-	21	TIMELESS FLIGHT — Steve Harley & Cockney Rebel (EMI)
26	22	LOVE TO LOVE YOU BABY — Donna Summer (GTO)
17	23	TUBULAR BELLS — Mike Oldfield (Virgin)
25	24	ROLLED GOLD — Rolling Stones (Decca)
29	25	WISH YOU WERE HERE — Pink Floyd (Harvest)
19	26	SING LOFTY — Don Estelle & Windsor Davies (EMI)
21	27	CRISIS? WHAT CRISIS? — Supertramp (A&M)
24	28	ONE OF THESE NIGHTS — Eagles (Asylum)
16	29	SHEER HEART ATTACK — Queen (EMI)
-	30	SONGS OF JOY — Nigel Brooks Singers (K-Tel)

Roy Orbison hadn't been in the singles chart since 1969, and hadn't had a real hit since 1966; when *Roy Orbison's Greatest Hits* had been issued in 1967, and his *All-Time Greatest Hits* in 1973, they had barely sold. Now the power of TV-advertising proved itself for the cheapo Arcade label and *The Best Of Roy Orbison* reached the Top 3. Orbison himself spent the mid-70s playing cabaret circuits, unloved by most of those who would proclaim their eternal devotion to him when he died.

February – March 1976

last week	this week	28 February 1976
1	1	DESIRE — Bob Dylan (CBS)
2	2	THE VERY BEST OF SLIM WHITMAN — Slim Whitman (United Artists)
4	3	THE BEST OF ROY ORBISON — Roy Orbison (Arcade)
13	3	RUN WITH THE PACK — Bad Company (Island)
6	5	A NIGHT AT THE OPERA — Queen (EMI)
5	6	STATION TO STATION — David Bowie (RCA)
16	7	CARNIVAL — Manuel & His Music of the Mountains (Studio Two)
8	8	24 ORIGINAL HITS — Drifters (Atlantic)
15	9	MOTOWN GOLD — Various Artists (Tamla Motown)
9	10	OMMADAWN — Mike Oldfield (Virgin)
3	11	HOW DARE YOU — 10 C.C. (Mercury)
12	12	THE BEST OF HELEN REDDY — Helen Reddy (Capitol)
7	13	MUSIC EXPRESS — Various Artists (K-Tel)
17	14	SUNBURST FINISH — Be-Bop Deluxe (Harvest)
11	15	PERRY COMO'S 40 GREATEST HITS — Perry Como (K-Tel)
21	16	TIMELESS FLIGHT — Steve Harley & Cockney Rebel (EMI)
14	17	ABBA — Abba (Epic)
22	18	LOVE TO LOVE YOU BABY — Donna Summer (GTO)
-	19	A TRICK OF THE TAIL — Genesis (Charisma)
10	20	STILL CRAZY AFTER ALL THESE YEARS — Paul Simon (CBS)
24	21	ROLLED GOLD — Rolling Stones (Decca)
29	22	SHEER HEART ATTACK — Queen (EMI)
27	23	CRISIS? WHAT CRISIS? — Supertramp (A&M)
18	24	BREAKAWAY — Art Garfunkel (CBS)
-	25	NO REGRETS — Walker Brothers (GTO)
23	26	TUBULAR BELLS — Mike Oldfield (Virgin)
25	27	WISH YOU WERE HERE — Pink Floyd (Harvest)
20	28	THE HISSING OF SUMMER LAWNS — Joni Mitchell (Asylum)
-	29	THE BEST OF THE STYLISTICS — Stylistics (Avco)
30	30	SONGS OF JOY — Nigel Brooks Singers (K-Tel)

this week	6 March 1976
1	THE VERY BEST OF SLIM WHITMAN — Slim Whitman (United Artists)
2	CARNIVAL — Manuel & His Music of the Mountains (Studio Two)
3	THE BEST OF ROY ORBISON — Roy Orbison (Arcade)
4	RUN WITH THE PACK — Bad Company (Island)
5	A TRICK OF THE TAIL — Genesis (Charisma)
6	A NIGHT AT THE OPERA — Queen (EMI)
7	DESIRE — Bob Dylan (CBS)
8	HOW DARE YOU — 10 C.C. (Mercury)
9	OMMADAWN — Mike Oldfield (Virgin)
10	THE BEST OF HELEN REDDY — Helen Reddy (Capitol)
11	STATION TO STATION — David Bowie (RCA)
12	ABBA — Abba (Epic)
13	24 ORIGINAL HITS — Drifters (Atlantic)
14	MUSIC EXPRESS — Various Artists (K-Tel)
15	MOTOWN GOLD — Various Artists (Tamla Motown)
16	PERRY COMO'S 40 GREATEST HITS — Perry Como (K-Tel)
17	TIMELESS FLIGHT — Steve Harley & Cockney Rebel (EMI)
18	SUNBURST FINISH — Be-Bop Deluxe (Harvest)
19	STILL CRAZY AFTER ALL THESE YEARS — Paul Simon (CBS)
20	THE BEST OF GLADYS KNIGHT & THE PIPS — Gladys Knight & the Pips (Buddah)
21	SHEER HEART ATTACK — Queen (EMI)
22	ONE OF THESE NIGHTS — Eagles (Asylum)
23	SONGS OF JOY — Nigel Brooks Singers (K-Tel)
24	BREAKAWAY — Art Garfunkel (CBS)
25	BREAKAWAY — Gallagher & Lyle (A&M)
26	ELITE HOTEL — Emmylou Harris (Reprise)
27	ROLLED GOLD — Rolling Stones (Decca)
28	QUEEN II — Queen (EMI)
29	LET THE MUSIC PLAY — Barry White (20th Century)
30	WISH YOU WERE HERE — Pink Floyd (Harvest)

this week	13 March 1976
1	THE VERY BEST OF SLIM WHITMAN — Slim Whitman (United Artists)
2	CARNIVAL — Manuel & His Music of the Mountains (Studio Two)
3	THE BEST OF ROY ORBISON — Roy Orbison (Arcade)
4	RUN WITH THE PACK — Bad Company (Island)
5	A TRICK OF THE TAIL — Genesis (Charisma)
6	A NIGHT AT THE OPERA — Queen (EMI)
7	DESIRE — Bob Dylan (CBS)
8	HOW DARE YOU — 10 C.C. (Mercury)
9	OMMADAWN — Mike Oldfield (Virgin)
10	THE BEST OF HELEN REDDY — Helen Reddy (Capitol)
11	STATION TO STATION — David Bowie (RCA)
12	ABBA — Abba (Epic)
13	24 ORIGINAL HITS — Drifters (Atlantic)
14	MUSIC EXPRESS — Various Artists (K-Tel)
15	MOTOWN GOLD — Various Artists (Tamla Motown)
16	PERRY COMO'S 40 GREATEST HITS — Perry Como (K-Tel)
17	TIMELESS FLIGHT — Steve Harley & Cockney Rebel (EMI)
18	SUNBURST FINISH — Be-Bop Deluxe (Harvest)
19	STILL CRAZY AFTER ALL THESE YEARS — Paul Simon (CBS)
20	THE BEST OF GLADYS KNIGHT & THE PIPS — Gladys Knight & the Pips (Buddah)
21	SHEER HEART ATTACK — Queen (EMI)
22	ONE OF THESE NIGHTS — Eagles (Asylum)
23	SONGS OF JOY — Nigel Brooks Singers (K-Tel)
24	BREAKAWAY — Art Garfunkel (CBS)
25	BREAKAWAY — Gallagher & Lyle (A&M)
26	ELITE HOTEL — Emmylou Harris (Reprise)
27	ROLLED GOLD — Rolling Stones (Decca)
28	QUEEN II — Queen (EMI)
29	LET THE MUSIC PLAY — Barry White (20th Century)
30	WISH YOU WERE HERE — Pink Floyd (Harvest)

last week	this week	20 March 1976
7	1	DESIRE — Bob Dylan (CBS)
2	2	CARNIVAL — Manuel & His Music of the Mountains (Studio Two)
5	3	A TRICK OF THE TAIL — Genesis (Charisma)
1	4	THE VERY BEST OF SLIM WHITMAN — Slim Whitman (United Artists)
-	5	THEIR GREATEST HITS 1971–1975 — Eagles (Asylum)
8	6	HOW DARE YOU — 10 C.C. (Mercury)
4	7	RUN WITH THE PACK — Bad Company (Island)
10	8	THE BEST OF HELEN REDDY — Helen Reddy (Capitol)
3	9	THE BEST OF ROY ORBISON — Roy Orbison (Arcade)
-	10	BLUE FOR YOU — Status Quo (Vertigo)
6	11	A NIGHT AT THE OPERA — Queen (EMI)
25	12	BREAKAWAY — Gallagher & Lyle (A&M)
20	13	THE BEST OF GLADYS KNIGHT & THE PIPS — Gladys Knight & the Pips (Buddah)
13	14	24 ORIGINAL HITS — Drifters (Atlantic)
-	15	THE FOUR SEASONS STORY — Four Seasons (Private Stock)
11	16	STATION TO STATION — David Bowie (RCA)
15	17	MOTOWN GOLD — Various Artists (Tamla Motown)
9	18	OMMADAWN — Mike Oldfield (Virgin)
26	19	ELITE HOTEL — Emmylou Harris (Reprise)
18	20	SUNBURST FINISH — Be-Bop Deluxe (Harvest)
-	21	GLENN MILLER - A MEMORIAL 1944-1968 — Glenn Miller (RCA)
12	22	ABBA — Abba (Epic)
29	23	LET THE MUSIC PLAY — Barry White (20th Century)
14	24	MUSIC EXPRESS — Various Artists (K-Tel)
-	25	THE BEST OF JOHN DENVER — John Denver (RCA)
27	26	ROLLED GOLD — Rolling Stones (Decca)
-	27	THE HISSING OF SUMMER LAWNS — Joni Mitchell (Asylum)
-	28	LIVE — Robin Trower (Chrysalis)
-	29	WHO LOVES YOU — Four Seasons (Warner Bros.)
-	30	CRISIS? WHAT CRISIS? — Supertramp (A&M)

In February, destitute ex-Supreme Florence Ballard died of a heart attack. On March 19, on a transatlantic flight, so did Paul Kossoff of Free; his second heart attack, both had been drug-induced. So was the death of Uriah Heep's Gary Thain, also in March. In April, US folk-singer Phil Ochs would commit suicide. Meanwhile February-March saw Ochs' old Greenwich Village rival Bob Dylan topping the LP charts (for four weeks), for the first time in years. He hasn't done it again since.

March – April 1976

27 March 1976

last	this	Album
10	1	BLUE FOR YOU — Status Quo (Vertigo)
5	2	THEIR GREATEST HITS 1971–1975 — Eagles (Asylum)
2	3	CARNIVAL — Manuel & the Music of the Mountains (Studio Two)
3	4	A TRICK OF THE TAIL — Genesis (Charisma)
1	5	DESIRE — Bob Dylan (CBS)
7	6	RUN WITH THE PACK — Bad Company (Island)
6	7	HOW DARE YOU — 10 C.C. (Mercury)
4	8	THE VERY BEST OF SLIM WHITMAN — Slim Whitman (United Artists)
8	9	THE BEST OF HELEN REDDY — Helen Reddy (Capitol)
12	10	BREAKAWAY — Gallagher & Lyle (A&M)
9	11	THE BEST OF ROY ORBISON — Roy Orbison (Arcade)
11	12	A NIGHT AT THE OPERA — Queen (EMI)
14	13	24 ORIGINAL HITS — Drifters (Atlantic)
13	14	THE BEST OF GLADYS KNIGHT & THE PIPS — Gladys Knight & the Pips (Buddah)
17	15	MOTOWN GOLD — Various Artists (Tamla Motown)
19	16	ELITE HOTEL — Emmylou Harris (Reprise)
15	17	THE FOUR SEASONS STORY — Four Seasons (Private Stock)
23	18	LET THE MUSIC PLAY — Barry White (20th Century)
18	19	OMMADAWN — Mike Oldfield (Virgin)
21	20	GLENN MILLER - A MEMORIAL 1944-1968 — Glenn Miller (RCA)
25	21	THE BEST OF JOHN DENVER — John Denver (RCA)
-	22	BRASS CONSTRUCTION — Brass Construction (United Artists)
-	23	WALK RIGHT BACK WITH THE EVERLYS — Everly Brothers (Warner Bros.)
20	24	SUNBURST FINISH — Be-Bop Deluxe (Harvest)
-	25	DIANA ROSS — Diana Ross (Tamla Motown)
-	26	RAISIN' HELL — Fatback Band (Polydor)
24	27	MUSIC EXPRESS — Various Artists (K-Tel)
-	28	RODRIGO: CONCIERTO DE ARANJUEZ — John Williams with the English Chamber Orchestra (CBS)
22	29	ABBA — Abba (Epic)
29	30	WHO LOVES YOU — Four Seasons (Warner Bros.)

3 April 1976

last	this	Album
1	1	BLUE FOR YOU — Status Quo (Vertigo)
2	2	THEIR GREATEST HITS 1971–1975 — Eagles (Asylum)
4	3	A TRICK OF THE TAIL — Genesis (Charisma)
10	4	BREAKAWAY — Gallagher & Lyle (A&M)
3	5	CARNIVAL — Manuel & His Music of the Mountains (Studio Two)
8	6	THE VERY BEST OF SLIM WHITMAN — Slim Whitman (United Artists)
7	7	HOW DARE YOU — 10 C.C. (Mercury)
5	8	DESIRE — Bob Dylan (CBS)
25	9	DIANA ROSS — Diana Ross (Tamla Motown)
6	10	RUN WITH THE PACK — Bad Company (Island)
21	11	THE BEST OF JOHN DENVER — John Denver (RCA)
9	12	THE BEST OF HELEN REDDY — Helen Reddy (Capitol)
-	13	REBEL — John Miles (Decca)
17	14	THE FOUR SEASONS STORY — Four Seasons (Private Stock)
11	15	THE BEST OF ROY ORBISON — Roy Orbison (Arcade)
16	16	ELITE HOTEL — Emmylou Harris (Reprise)
-	17	NOBODY'S FOOL — Slade (Polydor)
12	18	A NIGHT AT THE OPERA — Queen (EMI)
14	19	THE BEST OF GLADYS KNIGHT & THE PIPS — Gladys Knight & the Pips (Buddah)
-	20	JUKE BOX JIVE — Various Artists (K-Tel)
-	21	LIVE — Robin Trower (Chrysalis)
22	22	BRASS CONSTRUCTION — Brass Construction (United Artists)
13	23	24 ORIGINAL HITS — Drifters (Atlantic)
-	24	GREATEST HITS — Abba (Epic)
24	25	SUNBURST FINISH — Be-Bop Deluxe (Harvest)
-	26	ROCK FOLLIES — Soundtrack (Island)
18	27	LET THE MUSIC PLAY — Barry White (20th Century)
19	28	OMMADAWN — Mike Oldfield (Virgin)
15	29	MOTOWN GOLD — Various Artists (Tamla Motown)
-	30	BY INVITATION ONLY — Various Artists (Atlantic)

10 April 1976

last	this	Album
2	1	THEIR GREATEST HITS 1971–1975 — Eagles (Asylum)
1	2	BLUE FOR YOU — Status Quo (Vertigo)
26	3	ROCK FOLLIES — Soundtrack (Island)
13	4	REBEL — John Miles (Decca)
3	5	BREAKAWAY — Gallagher & Lyle (A&M)
9	6	DIANA ROSS — Diana Ross (Tamla Motown)
8	7	DESIRE — Bob Dylan (CBS)
3	8	A TRICK OF THE TAIL — Genesis (Charisma)
-	9	WINGS AT THE SPEED OF SOUND — Wings (EMI)
5	10	CARNIVAL — Manuel & the Music of the Mountains (Studio Two)
7	11	HOW DARE YOU — 10 C.C. (Mercury)
11	12	THE BEST OF JOHN DENVER — John Denver (RCA)
12	13	THE BEST OF HELEN REDDY — Helen Reddy (Capitol)
19	14	THE BEST OF GLADYS KNIGHT & THE PIPS — Gladys Knight & the Pips (Buddah)
24	15	GREATEST HITS — Abba (Epic)
20	16	JUKE BOX JIVE — Various Artists (K-Tel)
6	17	THE VERY BEST OF SLIM WHITMAN — Slim Whitman (United Artists)
-	18	WALK RIGHT BACK WITH THE EVERLYS — Everly Brothers (Warner Bros.)
10	19	RUN WITH THE PACK — Bad Company (Island)
27	20	LET THE MUSIC PLAY — Barry White (20th Century)
18	21	A NIGHT AT THE OPERA — Queen (EMI)
16	22	ELITE HOTEL — Emmylou Harris (Reprise)
-	23	PENTHOUSE TAPES — Sensational Alex Harvey Band (Vertigo)
15	24	THE BEST OF ROY ORBISON — Roy Orbison (Arcade)
22	25	BRASS CONSTRUCTION — Brass Construction (United Artists)
30	26	BY INVITATION ONLY — Various Artists (Atlantic)
28	27	OMMADAWN — Mike Oldfield (Virgin)
14	28	THE FOUR SEASONS STORY — Four Seasons (Private Stock)
23	29	24 ORIGINAL HITS — Drifters (Atlantic)
-	30	GARY GLITTER'S GREATEST HITS — Gary Glitter (Bell)

17 April 1976

last	this	Album
3	1	ROCK FOLLIES — Soundtrack (Island)
1	2	THEIR GREATEST HITS 1971–1975 — Eagles (Asylum)
5	3	DIANA ROSS — Diana Ross (Tamla Motown)
4	4	REBEL — John Miles (Decca)
16	5	JUKE BOX JIVE — Various Artists (K-Tel)
7	6	DESIRE — Bob Dylan (CBS)
11	7	HOW DARE YOU — 10 C.C. (Mercury)
2	8	BLUE FOR YOU — Status Quo (Vertigo)
5	9	BREAKAWAY — Gallagher & Lyle (A&M)
8	10	WINGS AT THE SPEED OF SOUND — Wings (EMI)
23	11	PENTHOUSE TAPES — Sensational Alex Harvey Band (Vertigo)
10	12	CARNIVAL — Manuel & His Music of the Mountains (Studio Two)
15	13	GREATEST HITS — Abba (Epic)
12	14	THE BEST OF JOHN DENVER — John Denver (RCA)
-	15	PRESENCE — Led Zeppelin (Swansong)
17	16	THE VERY BEST OF SLIM WHITMAN — Slim Whitman (United Artists)
8	17	A TRICK OF THE TAIL — Genesis (Charisma)
24	18	THE BEST OF ROY ORBISON — Roy Orbison (Arcade)
-	19	AMIGOS — Santana (CBS)
13	20	THE BEST OF HELEN REDDY — Helen Reddy (Capitol)
21	21	A NIGHT AT THE OPERA — Queen (EMI)
25	22	BRASS CONSTRUCTION — Brass Construction (United Artists)
-	23	LIVE — Joe Walsh (ABC)
26	24	BY INVITATION ONLY — Various Artists (Atlantic)
19	25	RUN WITH THE PACK — Bad Company (Island)
-	26	JAILBREAK — Thin Lizzy (Vertigo)
20	27	LET THE MUSIC PLAY — Barry White (20th Century)
-	28	CRY TOUGH — Nils Lofgren (A&M)
14	29	THE BEST OF GLADYS KNIGHT & THE PIPS — Gladys Knight & the Pips (Buddah)
-	30	SUNBURST FINISH — Be-Bop Deluxe (Harvest)

Blue For You was the fifth mega-album by Britain's lowest common denominators of rock, Status Quo. The Eagles' *Greatest Hits*, their fourth LP, was their biggest: which was odd, because they were the classic 1970s American albums band and had only had three hit singles, *One Of These Nights, Lyin' Eyes* and, now, *Take It To The Limit*. Their least chart-successful LP had been their finest, *Desperado*. Soon would come *Hotel California*, an artifact held in special contempt by the newly-emerging punks.

April – May 1976

24 April 1976

last	this		
1	1	ROCK FOLLIES	Soundtrack (Island)
10	2	WINGS AT THE SPEED OF SOUND	Wings (EMI)
5	3	JUKE BOX JIVE	Various Artists (K-Tel)
13	4	GREATEST HITS	Abba (Epic)
3	5	DIANA ROSS	Diana Ross (Tamla Motown)
8	6	BLUE FOR YOU	Status Quo (Vertigo)
15	7	PRESENCE	Led Zeppelin (Swansong)
2	8	THEIR GREATEST HITS 1971–1975	Eagles (Asylum)
4	9	REBEL	John Miles (Decca)
6	10	DESIRE	Bob Dylan (CBS)
17	11	A TRICK OF THE TAIL	Genesis (Charisma)
28	12	CRY TOUGH	Nils Lofgren (A&M)
7	13	HOW DARE YOU	10 C.C. (Mercury)
-	14	MOONMADNESS	Camel (Decca)
22	15	BRASS CONSTRUCTION	Brass Construction (United Artists)
11	16	PENTHOUSE TAPES	Sensational Alex Harvey Band (Vertigo)
9	17	BREAKAWAY	Gallagher & Lyle (A&M)
-	18	NO EARTHLY CONNECTION	Rick Wakeman (A&M)
29	19	THE BEST OF GLADYS KNIGHT & THE PIPS	Gladys Knight & the Pips (Buddah)
19	20	AMIGOS	Santana (CBS)
14	21	THE BEST OF JOHN DENVER	John Denver (RCA)
27	22	LET THE MUSIC PLAY	Barry White (20th Century)
20	23	THE BEST OF HELEN REDDY	Helen Reddy (Capitol)
25	24	RUN WITH THE PACK	Bad Company (Island)
-	25	INSTRUMENTAL GOLD	Various Artists (Warwick)
-	26	PATRICK MORAZ	Patrick Moraz (Charisma)
-	27	TUBULAR BELLS	Mike Oldfield (Virgin)
-	28	THE FOUR SEASONS STORY	Four Seasons (Private Stock)
16	29	THE VERY BEST OF SLIM WHITMAN	Slim Whitman (United Artists)
18	30	THE BEST OF ROY ORBISON	Roy Orbison (Arcade)

1 May 1976

last	this		
1	1	ROCK FOLLIES	Soundtrack (Island)
7	2	PRESENCE	Led Zeppelin (Swansong)
2	3	WINGS AT THE SPEED OF SOUND	Wings (EMI)
4	4	GREATEST HITS	Abba (Epic)
3	5	JUKE BOX JIVE	Various Artists (K-Tel)
6	6	BLUE FOR YOU	Status Quo (Vertigo)
5	7	DIANA ROSS	Diana Ross (Tamla Motown)
8	8	THEIR GREATEST HITS 1971–1975	Eagles (Asylum)
9	9	REBEL	John Miles (Decca)
18	10	NO EARTHLY CONNECTION	Rick Wakeman (A&M)
13	11	HOW DARE YOU	10 C.C. (Mercury)
10	12	DESIRE	Bob Dylan (CBS)
14	13	MOONMADNESS	Camel (Decca)
11	14	A TRICK OF THE TAIL	Genesis (Charisma)
21	15	THE BEST OF JOHN DENVER	John Denver (RCA)
-	16	BLACK AND BLUE	Rolling Stones (Rolling Stones)
19	17	THE BEST OF GLADYS KNIGHT & THE PIPS	Gladys Knight & the Pips (Buddah)
12	18	CRY TOUGH	Nils Lofgren (A&M)
16	19	PENTHOUSE TAPES	Sensational Alex Harvey Band (Vertigo)
15	20	BRASS CONSTRUCTION	Brass Construction (United Artists)
20	21	AMIGOS	Santana (CBS)
25	22	INSTRUMENTAL GOLD	Various Artists (Warwick)
-	23	CARNIVAL	Manuel & His Music of the Mountains (Studio Two)
-	24	PAT BOONE ORIGINALS	Pat Boone (ABC)
-	25	LOVE AND KISSES FROM	Brotherhood of Man (Pye)
22	26	LET THE MUSIC PLAY	Barry White (20th Century)
-	27	HAPPY TO BE	Demis Roussos (Philips)
26	28	PATRICK MORAZ	Patrick Moraz (Charisma)
17	29	BREAKAWAY	Gallagher & Lyle (A&M)
29	30	THE VERY BEST OF SLIM WHITMAN	Slim Whitman (United Artists)

8 May 1976

last	this		
1	1	ROCK FOLLIES	Soundtrack (Island)
4	2	GREATEST HITS	Abba (Epic)
2	3	PRESENCE	Led Zeppelin (Swansong)
3	4	WINGS AT THE SPEED OF SOUND	Wings (EMI)
10	5	NO EARTHLY CONNECTION	Rick Wakeman (A&M)
8	6	THEIR GREATEST HITS 1971–1975	Eagles (Asylum)
11	7	HOW DARE YOU	10 C.C. (Mercury)
7	8	DIANA ROSS	Diana Ross (Tamla Motown)
5	9	JUKE BOX JIVE	Various Artists (K-Tel)
6	10	BLUE FOR YOU	Status Quo (Vertigo)
9	11	REBEL	John Miles (Decca)
12	12	DESIRE	Bob Dylan (CBS)
16	13	BLACK AND BLUE	Rolling Stones (Rolling Stones)
-	14	WHO LOVES YOU	Four Seasons (Warner Bros.)
25	15	LOVE AND KISSES FROM	Brotherhood of Man (Pye)
-	16	LIVE IN LONDON	John Denver (RCA)
15	17	THE BEST OF JOHN DENVER	John Denver (RCA)
22	18	INSTRUMENTAL GOLD	Various Artists (Warwick)
21	19	AMIGOS	Santana (CBS)
14	20	A TRICK OF THE TAIL	Genesis (Charisma)
24	21	PAT BOONE ORIGINALS	Pat Boone (ABC)
13	22	MOONMADNESS	Camel (Decca)
-	23	HERE AND THERE	Elton John (DJM)
-	24	DOUBLY DEVINE	Sydney Devine (Philips)
-	25	HIT MACHINE	Various Artists (K-Tel)
17	26	THE BEST OF GLADYS KNIGHT & THE PIPS	Gladys Knight & the Pips (Buddah)
30	27	THE VERY BEST OF SLIM WHITMAN	Slim Whitman (United Artists)
18	28	CRY TOUGH	Nils Lofgren (A&M)
-	29	24 ORIGINAL HITS	Drifters (Atlantic)
19	30	PENTHOUSE TAPES	Sensational Alex Harvey Band (Vertigo)

15 May 1976

last	this		
2	1	GREATEST HITS	Abba (Epic)
13	2	BLACK AND BLUE	Rolling Stones (Rolling Stones)
4	3	WINGS AT THE SPEED OF SOUND	Wings (EMI)
3	4	PRESENCE	Led Zeppelin (Swansong)
8	5	DIANA ROSS	Diana Ross (Tamla Motown)
1	6	ROCK FOLLIES	Soundtrack (Island)
7	7	HOW DARE YOU	10 C.C. (Mercury)
9	8	JUKE BOX JIVE	Various Artists (K-Tel)
6	9	THEIR GREATEST HITS 1971–1975	Eagles (Asylum)
18	10	INSTRUMENTAL GOLD	Various Artists (Warwick)
5	11	NO EARTHLY CONNECTION	Rick Wakeman (A&M)
10	12	BLUE FOR YOU	Status Quo (Vertigo)
11	13	REBEL	John Miles (Decca)
20	14	A TRICK OF THE TAIL	Genesis (Charisma)
12	15	DESIRE	Bob Dylan (CBS)
26	16	THE BEST OF GLADYS KNIGHT & THE PIPS	Gladys Knight & the Pips (Buddah)
14	17	WHO LOVES YOU	Four Seasons (Warner Bros.)
15	18	LOVE AND KISSES FROM	Brotherhood of Man (Pye)
16	19	LIVE IN LONDON	John Denver (RCA)
25	20	HIT MACHINE	Various Artists (K-Tel)
17	21	THE BEST OF JOHN DENVER	John Denver (RCA)
24	22	DOUBLY DEVINE	Sydney Devine (Philips)
19	23	AMIGOS	Santana (CBS)
-	24	THE BEATLES 1962-1966	Beatles (Apple)
21	25	PAT BOONE ORIGINALS	Pat Boone (ABC)
30	26	PENTHOUSE TAPES	Sensational Alex Harvey Band (Vertigo)
23	27	HERE AND THERE	Elton John (DJM)
29	28	24 ORIGINAL HITS	Drifters (Atlantic)
-	29	BREAKAWAY	Gallagher & Lyle (A&M)
27	30	THE VERY BEST OF SLIM WHITMAN	Slim Whitman (United Artists)

Rock Follies came from TV series about a group of three female singers, one of whom was played by Rula Lenska, later an item with Dennis Waterman, another actor who imagined he could sing. Hello again to Manuel, Pat Boone (his first chart LP since 1960), and Demis Roussos (see description for Barry White, May-June 1975). But goodbye to ex-Yardbird Keith Relf: he was electrocuted in May. His only solo chart appearance had been at No.50 in the singles for one week in 1966 with *Mr Zero*.

22 May 1976

last week	this week		
1	1	GREATEST HITS	Abba (Epic)
3	2	WINGS AT THE SPEED OF SOUND	Wings (EMI)
2	3	BLACK AND BLUE	Rolling Stones (Rolling Stones)
4	4	PRESENCE	Led Zeppelin (Swansong)
19	5	LIVE IN LONDON	John Denver (RCA)
6	6	ROCK FOLLIES	Soundtrack (Island)
5	7	DIANA ROSS	Diana Ross (Tamla Motown)
7	8	HOW DARE YOU	10 C.C. (Mercury)
27	9	HERE AND THERE	Elton John (DJM)
20	10	HIT MACHINE	Various Artists (K-Tel)
9	11	THEIR GREATEST HITS 1971–1975	Eagles (Asylum)
11	12	NO EARTHLY CONNECTION	Rick Wakeman (A&M)
10	13	INSTRUMENTAL GOLD	Various Artists (Warwick)
16	14	THE BEST OF GLADYS KNIGHT & THE PIPS	Gladys Knight & the Pips (Buddah)
15	15	DESIRE	Bob Dylan (CBS)
18	16	LOVE AND KISSES FROM	Brotherhood of Man (Pye)
12	17	BLUE FOR YOU	Status Quo (Vertigo)
29	18	BREAKAWAY	Gallagher & Lyle (A&M)
13	19	REBEL	John Miles (Decca)
8	20	JUKE BOX JIVE	Various Artists (K-Tel)
-	21	SOME OF ME POEMS AND SONGS	Pam Ayres (Galaxy)
17	22	WHO LOVES YOU	Four Seasons (Warner Bros.)
14	23	A TRICK OF THE TAIL	Genesis (Charisma)
-	24	I'M NEARLY FAMOUS	Cliff Richard (EMI)
-	25	THE ROYAL SCAM	Steely Dan (ABC)
-	26	PATRICK MORAZ	Patrick Moraz (Charisma)
-	27	RASTAMAN VIBRATION	Bob Marley & the Wailers (Island)
23	28	AMIGOS	Santana (CBS)
-	29	I WANT YOU	Marvin Gaye (Tamla Motown)
25	30	PAT BOONE ORIGINALS	Pat Boone (ABC)

29 May 1976

last week	this week		
1	1	GREATEST HITS	Abba (Epic)
3	2	BLACK AND BLUE	Rolling Stones (Rolling Stones)
2	3	WINGS AT THE SPEED OF SOUND	Wings (EMI)
5	4	LIVE IN LONDON	John Denver (RCA)
4	5	PRESENCE	Led Zeppelin (Swansong)
7	6	DIANA ROSS	Diana Ross (Tamla Motown)
13	7	INSTRUMENTAL GOLD	Various Artists (Warwick)
14	8	THE BEST OF GLADYS KNIGHT & THE PIPS	Gladys Knight & the Pips (Buddah)
10	9	HIT MACHINE	Various Artists (K-Tel)
6	10	ROCK FOLLIES	Soundtrack (Island)
11	11	THEIR GREATEST HITS 1971–1975	Eagles (Asylum)
9	12	HERE AND THERE	Elton John (DJM)
22	13	WHO LOVES YOU	Four Seasons (Warner Bros.)
12	14	NO EARTHLY CONNECTION	Rick Wakeman (A&M)
24	15	I'M NEARLY FAMOUS	Cliff Richard (EMI)
20	16	JUKE BOX JIVE	Various Artists (K-Tel)
8	17	HOW DARE YOU	10 C.C. (Mercury)
-	18	A TOUCH OF COUNTRY	Various Artists (Topaz)
15	19	DESIRE	Bob Dylan (CBS)
21	20	SOME OF ME POEMS AND SONGS	Pam Ayres (Galaxy)
18	21	BREAKAWAY	Gallagher & Lyle (A&M)
23	22	A TRICK OF THE TAIL	Genesis (Charisma)
-	23	ON TOUR	David Essex (CBS)
28	24	AMIGOS	Santana (CBS)
-	25	WINDSONG	John Denver (RCA)
19	26	REBEL	John Miles (Decca)
16	27	LOVE AND KISSES FROM	Brotherhood of Man (Pye)
-	28	LOVE, LIFE AND FEELINGS	Shirley Bassey (United Artists)
-	29	TOO OLD TO ROCK 'N' ROLL, TOO YOUNG TO DIE	Jethro Tull (Chrysalis)
25	30	THE ROYAL SCAM	Steely Dan (ABC)

5 June 1976

last week	this week		
1	1	GREATEST HITS	Abba (Epic)
4	2	LIVE IN LONDON	John Denver (RCA)
3	3	WINGS AT THE SPEED OF SOUND	Wings (EMI)
2	4	BLACK AND BLUE	Rolling Stones (Rolling Stones)
6	5	DIANA ROSS	Diana Ross (Tamla Motown)
5	6	PRESENCE	Led Zeppelin (Swansong)
15	7	I'M NEARLY FAMOUS	Cliff Richard (EMI)
8	8	THE BEST OF GLADYS KNIGHT & THE PIPS	Gladys Knight & the Pips (Buddah)
9	9	HIT MACHINE	Various Artists (K-Tel)
-	10	FRAMPTON COMES ALIVE	Peter Frampton (A&M)
10	11	ROCK FOLLIES	Soundtrack (Island)
13	12	WHO LOVES YOU	Four Seasons (Warner Bros.)
30	13	THE ROYAL SCAM	Steely Dan (ABC)
11	14	THEIR GREATEST HITS 1971–1975	Eagles (Asylum)
7	15	INSTRUMENTAL GOLD	Various Artists (Warwick)
21	16	BREAKAWAY	Gallagher & Lyle (A&M)
18	17	A TOUCH OF COUNTRY	Various Artists (Topaz)
16	18	JUKE BOX JIVE	Various Artists (K-Tel)
12	19	HERE AND THERE	Elton John (DJM)
17	20	HOW DARE YOU	10 C.C. (Mercury)
14	21	NO EARTHLY CONNECTION	Rick Wakeman (A&M)
22	22	A TRICK OF THE TAIL	Genesis (Charisma)
-	23	STATION TO STATION	David Bowie (RCA)
19	24	DESIRE	Bob Dylan (CBS)
-	25	SIMON & GARFUNKEL'S GREATEST HITS	Simon & Garfunkel (CBS)
-	26	REACH FOR THE SKY	Sutherland Brothers & Quiver (CBS)
27	27	LOVE AND KISSES FROM	Brotherhood of Man (Pye)
-	28	CRY TOUGH	Nils Lofgren (A&M)
-	29	BLUE FOR YOU	Status Quo (Vertigo)
-	30	ROLLED GOLD	Rolling Stones (Decca)

12 June 1976

last week	this week		
1	1	GREATEST HITS	Abba (Epic)
2	2	LIVE IN LONDON	John Denver (RCA)
3	3	WINGS AT THE SPEED OF SOUND	Wings (EMI)
4	4	BLACK AND BLUE	Rolling Stones (Rolling Stones)
7	5	I'M NEARLY FAMOUS	Cliff Richard (EMI)
8	6	THE BEST OF GLADYS KNIGHT & THE PIPS	Gladys Knight & the Pips (Buddah)
15	7	INSTRUMENTAL GOLD	Various Artists (Warwick)
10	8	FRAMPTON COMES ALIVE	Peter Frampton (A&M)
5	9	DIANA ROSS	Diana Ross (Tamla Motown)
6	10	PRESENCE	Led Zeppelin (Swansong)
-	11	CHANGESONEBOWIE	David Bowie (WEA)
9	12	HIT MACHINE	Various Artists (K-Tel)
12	13	WHO LOVES YOU	Four Seasons (Warner Bros.)
16	14	BREAKAWAY	Gallagher & Lyle (A&M)
19	15	HERE AND THERE	Elton John (DJM)
13	16	THE ROYAL SCAM	Steely Dan (ABC)
17	17	A TOUCH OF COUNTRY	Various Artists (Topaz)
20	18	HOW DARE YOU	10 C.C. (Mercury)
14	19	THEIR GREATEST HITS 1971–1975	Eagles (Asylum)
11	20	ROCK FOLLIES	Soundtrack (Island)
26	21	REACH FOR THE SKY	Sutherland Brothers & Quiver (CBS)
-	22	DESTROYER	Kiss (Casablanca)
18	23	JUKE BOX JIVE	Various Artists (K-Tel)
-	24	THE BEST OF JOHN DENVER	John Denver (RCA)
-	25	JAILBREAK	Thin Lizzy (Vertigo)
22	26	A TRICK OF THE TAIL	Genesis (Charisma)
25	27	SIMON & GARFUNKEL'S GREATEST HITS	Simon & Garfunkel (CBS)
21	28	NO EARTHLY CONNECTION	Rick Wakeman (A&M)
-	29	LOVE, LIFE AND FEELINGS	Shirley Bassey (United Artists)
28	30	CRY TOUGH	Nils Lofgren (A&M)

Howlin' Wolf (Chester Burnett) had died in Chicago in January, so Keith Relf had just outlived one of the grandest old heroes of the beat-groups. Relf was the third British musician electrocuted in modern times, after Les Harvey of Stone the Crows (May 1972) and John Rostill of the Shadows (November 1973). Shads boss Cliff Richard now returned to the album chart with the gruesomely coy title *I'm Nearly Famous*; John Denvermania now returned the risible title *Windsong* to the chart, to join two other Denver LPs.

June – July 1976

19 June 1976

last week	this week	Title	Artist (Label)
1	1	GREATEST HITS	Abba (Epic)
2	2	LIVE IN LONDON	John Denver (RCA)
3	3	WINGS AT THE SPEED OF SOUND	Wings (EMI)
4	4	BLACK AND BLUE	Rolling Stones (Rolling Stones)
11	5	CHANGESONEBOWIE	David Bowie (WEA)
5	6	I'M NEARLY FAMOUS	Cliff Richard (EMI)
8	7	FRAMPTON COMES ALIVE	Peter Frampton (A&M)
6	8	THE BEST OF GLADYS KNIGHT & THE PIPS	Gladys Knight & the Pips (Buddah)
7	9	INSTRUMENTAL GOLD	Various Artists (Warwick)
14	10	BREAKAWAY	Gallagher & Lyle (A&M)
9	11	DIANA ROSS	Diana Ross (Tamla Motown)
10	12	PRESENCE	Led Zeppelin (Swansong)
12	13	HIT MACHINE	Various Artists (K-Tel)
15	14	HERE AND THERE	Elton John (DJM)
19	15	THEIR GREATEST HITS 1971–1975	Eagles (Asylum)
-	16	RAINBOW RISING	Ritchie Blackmore (Polydor)
16	17	THE ROYAL SCAM	Steely Dan (ABC)
-	18	RED CARD	Streetwalkers (Vertigo)
-	19	ROCK 'N' ROLL MUSIC	Beatles (Apple)
13	20	WHO LOVES YOU	Four Seasons (Warner Bros.)
24	21	THE BEST OF JOHN DENVER	John Denver (RCA)
20	22	ROCK FOLLIES	Soundtrack (Island)
-	23	FABULOUS	Stylistics (Avco)
22	24	DESTROYER	Kiss (Casablanca)
25	25	JAILBREAK	Thin Lizzy (Vertigo)
23	26	JUKE BOX JIVE	Various Artists (K-Tel)
17	27	A TOUCH OF COUNTRY	Various Artists (Topaz)
-	28	FLY LIKE AN EAGLE	Steve Miller Band (Mercury)
18	29	HOW DARE YOU	10 C.C. (Mercury)
21	30	REACH FOR THE SKY	Sutherland Brothers & Quiver (CBS)

26 June 1976

last week	this week	Title	Artist (Label)
1	1	GREATEST HITS	Abba (Epic)
3	2	WINGS AT THE SPEED OF SOUND	Wings (EMI)
2	3	LIVE IN LONDON	John Denver (RCA)
5	4	CHANGESONEBOWIE	David Bowie (WEA)
6	5	I'M NEARLY FAMOUS	Cliff Richard (EMI)
7	6	FRAMPTON COMES ALIVE	Peter Frampton (A&M)
4	7	BLACK AND BLUE	Rolling Stones (Rolling Stones)
10	8	BREAKAWAY	Gallagher & Lyle (A&M)
-	9	A NIGHT ON THE TOWN	Rod Stewart (Riva)
8	10	THE BEST OF GLADYS KNIGHT & THE PIPS	Gladys Knight & the Pips (Buddah)
9	11	INSTRUMENTAL GOLD	Various Artists (Warwick)
11	12	DIANA ROSS	Diana Ross (Tamla Motown)
15	13	THEIR GREATEST HITS 1971–1975	Eagles (Asylum)
17	14	THE ROYAL SCAM	Steely Dan (ABC)
16	15	RAINBOW RISING	Ritchie Blackmore (Polydor)
21	16	THE BEST OF JOHN DENVER	John Denver (RCA)
28	17	FLY LIKE AN EAGLE	Steve Miller Band (Mercury)
-	18	BELLAMY BROTHERS	Bellamy Brothers (Warner Bros.)
25	19	JAILBREAK	Thin Lizzy (Vertigo)
19	20	ROCK 'N' ROLL MUSIC	Beatles (Apple)
14	21	HERE AND THERE	Elton John (DJM)
20	22	WHO LOVES YOU	Four Seasons (Warner Bros.)
18	23	RED CARD	Streetwalkers (Vertigo)
23	24	FABULOUS	Stylistics (Avco)
-	25	SOME OF ME POEMS AND SONGS	Pam Ayres (Galaxy)
13	26	HIT MACHINE	Various Artists (K-Tel)
27	27	A TOUCH OF COUNTRY	Various Artists (Topaz)
12	28	PRESENCE	Led Zeppelin (Swansong)
30	29	REACH FOR THE SKY	Sutherland Brothers & Quiver (CBS)
24	30	DESTROYER	Kiss (Casablanca)

3 July 1976

last week	this week	Title	Artist (Label)
1	1	GREATEST HITS	Abba (Epic)
2	2	WINGS AT THE SPEED OF SOUND	Wings (EMI)
3	3	LIVE IN LONDON	John Denver (RCA)
4	4	CHANGESONEBOWIE	David Bowie (WEA)
-	5	HAPPY TO BE	Demis Roussos (Philips)
6	6	FRAMPTON COMES ALIVE	Peter Frampton (A&M)
9	7	A NIGHT ON THE TOWN	Rod Stewart (Riva)
10	8	THE BEST OF GLADYS KNIGHT & THE PIPS	Gladys Knight & the Pips (Buddah)
7	9	BLACK AND BLUE	Rolling Stones (Rolling Stones)
20	10	ROCK 'N' ROLL MUSIC	Beatles (Apple)
5	11	I'M NEARLY FAMOUS	Cliff Richard (EMI)
19	12	JAILBREAK	Thin Lizzy (Vertigo)
8	13	BREAKAWAY	Gallagher & Lyle (A&M)
13	14	THEIR GREATEST HITS 1971–1975	Eagles (Asylum)
11	15	INSTRUMENTAL GOLD	Various Artists (Warwick)
15	16	RAINBOW RISING	Ritchie Blackmore (Polydor)
-	17	20 GOLDEN GREATS	Beach Boys (Capitol)
-	18	A KIND OF HUSH	Carpenters (A&M)
-	19	FOREVER AND EVER	Demis Roussos (Philips)
12	20	DIANA ROSS	Diana Ross (Tamla Motown)
-	21	MUSIC OF AMERICA	Various Artists (Ronco)
23	22	RED CARD	Streetwalkers (Vertigo)
28	23	PRESENCE	Led Zeppelin (Swansong)
17	24	FLY LIKE AN EAGLE	Steve Miller Band (Mercury)
14	25	THE ROYAL SCAM	Steely Dan (ABC)
26	26	HIT MACHINE	Various Artists (K-Tel)
22	27	WHO LOVES YOU	Four Seasons (Warner Bros.)
-	28	LAUGHTER AND TEARS - THE BEST OF NEIL SEDAKA TODAY	Neil Sedaka (Polydor)
-	29	A LITTLE BIT MORE	Dr. Hook (Capitol)
21	30	HERE AND THERE	Elton John (DJM)

10 July 1976

last week	this week	Title	Artist (Label)
7	1	A NIGHT ON THE TOWN	Rod Stewart (Riva)
1	2	GREATEST HITS	Abba (Epic)
3	3	LIVE IN LONDON	John Denver (RCA)
2	4	WINGS AT THE SPEED OF SOUND	Wings (EMI)
5	5	HAPPY TO BE	Demis Roussos (Philips)
18	6	A KIND OF HUSH	Carpenters (A&M)
17	7	20 GOLDEN GREATS	Beach Boys (Capitol)
4	8	CHANGESONEBOWIE	David Bowie (WEA)
19	9	FOREVER AND EVER	Demis Roussos (Philips)
6	10	FRAMPTON COMES ALIVE	Peter Frampton (A&M)
8	11	THE BEST OF GLADYS KNIGHT & THE PIPS	Gladys Knight & the Pips (Buddah)
10	12	ROCK 'N' ROLL MUSIC	Beatles (Apple)
12	13	JAILBREAK	Thin Lizzy (Vertigo)
9	14	BLACK AND BLUE	Rolling Stones (Rolling Stones)
14	15	THEIR GREATEST HITS 1971–1975	Eagles (Asylum)
16	16	RAINBOW RISING	Ritchie Blackmore (Polydor)
25	17	THE ROYAL SCAM	Steely Dan (ABC)
15	18	INSTRUMENTAL GOLD	Various Artists (Warwick)
29	19	A LITTLE BIT MORE	Dr. Hook (Capitol)
21	20	MUSIC OF AMERICA	Various Artists (Ronco)
11	21	I'M NEARLY FAMOUS	Cliff Richard (EMI)
24	22	FLY LIKE AN EAGLE	Steve Miller Band (Mercury)
13	23	BREAKAWAY	Gallagher & Lyle (A&M)
-	24	I ONLY HAVE EYES FOR YOU	Johnny Mathis (CBS)
-	25	KING COTTON	Fivepenny Piece (EMI)
-	26	SOUVENIRS	Demis Roussos (Philips)
22	27	RED CARD	Streetwalkers (Vertigo)
26	28	HIT MACHINE	Various Artists (K-Tel)
-	29	PASSPORT	Nana Mouskouri (Philips)
-	30	ROCK FOLLIES	Soundtrack (Island)

Odd figures here. Bob Marley had entered the album chart at No.27 in May with *Rastaman Vibration*, but had promptly disappeared again. Yet in other charts, this album rose as high as No.15, consolidating Marley's position as reggae's international star, after 1975's *Natty Dread* and his celebrated London Lyceum concert that summer. Nonetheless, Marley's biggest LP hits were still to come, with *Exodus* (1977), *Kaya* (1978), *Uprising* (1980) and more albums after Marley's death from cancer in 1981.

17 July 1976

last week	this week	Album / Artist (Label)
1	1	A NIGHT ON THE TOWN — Rod Stewart (Riva)
2	2	GREATEST HITS — Abba (Epic)
5	3	HAPPY TO BE — Demis Roussos (Philips)
7	4	20 GOLDEN GREATS — Beach Boys (Capitol)
4	5	WINGS AT THE SPEED OF SOUND — Wings (EMI)
3	6	LIVE IN LONDON — John Denver (RCA)
8	7	CHANGESONEBOWIE — David Bowie (WEA)
6	8	A KIND OF HUSH — Carpenters (A&M)
9	9	FOREVER AND EVER — Demis Roussos (Philips)
10	10	FRAMPTON COMES ALIVE — Peter Frampton (A&M)
29	11	PASSPORT — Nana Mouskouri (Philips)
19	12	A LITTLE BIT MORE — Dr. Hook (Capitol)
-	13	LAUGHTER AND TEARS - THE BEST OF NEIL SEDAKA TODAY — Neil Sedaka (Polydor)
15	14	THEIR GREATEST HITS 1971–1975 — Eagles (Asylum)
12	15	ROCK 'N' ROLL MUSIC — Beatles (Apple)
13	16	JAILBREAK — Thin Lizzy (Vertigo)
11	17	THE BEST OF GLADYS KNIGHT & THE PIPS — Gladys Knight & the Pips (Buddah)
16	18	RAINBOW RISING — Ritchie Blackmore (Polydor)
23	19	BREAKAWAY — Gallagher & Lyle (A&M)
21	20	I'M NEARLY FAMOUS — Cliff Richard (EMI)
-	21	DIANA ROSS — Diana Ross (Tamla Motown)
17	22	THE ROYAL SCAM — Steely Dan (ABC)
24	23	I ONLY HAVE EYES FOR YOU — Johnny Mathis (CBS)
-	24	BEAUTIFUL NOISE — Neil Diamond (CBS)
18	25	INSTRUMENTAL GOLD — Various Artists (Warwick)
22	26	FLY LIKE AN EAGLE — Steve Miller Band (Mercury)
25	27	KING COTTON — Fivepenny Piece (EMI)
28	28	HIT MACHINE — Various Artists (K-Tel)
27	29	RED CARD — Streetwalkers (Vertigo)
-	30	BELLAMY BROTHERS — Bellamy Brothers (Warner Bros.)

24 July 1976

lw	tw	Album / Artist (Label)
4	1	20 GOLDEN GREATS — Beach Boys (Capitol)
1	2	A NIGHT ON THE TOWN — Rod Stewart (Riva)
9	3	FOREVER AND EVER — Demis Roussos (Philips)
3	4	HAPPY TO BE — Demis Roussos (Philips)
2	5	GREATEST HITS — Abba (Epic)
13	6	LAUGHTER AND TEARS - THE BEST OF NEIL SEDAKA TODAY — Neil Sedaka (Polydor)
8	7	A KIND OF HUSH — Carpenters (A&M)
7	8	CHANGESONEBOWIE — David Bowie (WEA)
12	9	A LITTLE BIT MORE — Dr. Hook (Capitol)
11	10	PASSPORT — Nana Mouskouri (Philips)
6	11	LIVE IN LONDON — John Denver (RCA)
24	12	BEAUTIFUL NOISE — Neil Diamond (CBS)
5	13	WINGS AT THE SPEED OF SOUND — Wings (EMI)
14	14	THEIR GREATEST HITS 1971–1975 — Eagles (Asylum)
10	15	FRAMPTON COMES ALIVE — Peter Frampton (A&M)
16	16	JAILBREAK — Thin Lizzy (Vertigo)
15	17	ROCK 'N' ROLL MUSIC — Beatles (Apple)
17	18	THE BEST OF GLADYS KNIGHT & THE PIPS — Gladys Knight & the Pips (Buddah)
21	19	DIANA ROSS — Diana Ross (Tamla Motown)
-	20	VIVA! — Roxy Music (Island)
26	21	FLY LIKE AN EAGLE — Steve Miller Band (Mercury)
-	22	OLIAS OF SUNHILLOW — Jon Anderson (Atlantic)
-	23	BLACK AND BLUE — Rolling Stones (Rolling Stones)
19	24	BREAKAWAY — Gallagher & Lyle (A&M)
20	25	I'M NEARLY FAMOUS — Cliff Richard (EMI)
23	26	I ONLY HAVE EYES FOR YOU — Johnny Mathis (CBS)
-	27	ONE MAN SHOW — Mike Harding (Philips)
25	28	INSTRUMENTAL GOLD — Various Artists (Warwick)
-	29	COMBINE HARVESTER — Wurzels (One Up)
-	30	15 BIG ONES — Beach Boys (Reprise)

31 July 1976

lw	tw	Album / Artist (Label)
1	1	20 GOLDEN GREATS — Beach Boys (Capitol)
3	2	FOREVER AND EVER — Demis Roussos (Philips)
2	3	A NIGHT ON THE TOWN — Rod Stewart (Riva)
6	4	LAUGHTER AND TEARS - THE BEST OF NEIL SEDAKA TODAY — Neil Sedaka (Polydor)
7	5	A KIND OF HUSH — Carpenters (A&M)
10	6	PASSPORT — Nana Mouskouri (Philips)
5	7	GREATEST HITS — Abba (Epic)
4	8	HAPPY TO BE — Demis Roussos (Philips)
9	9	A LITTLE BIT MORE — Dr. Hook (Capitol)
8	10	CHANGESONEBOWIE — David Bowie (WEA)
12	11	BEAUTIFUL NOISE — Neil Diamond (CBS)
15	12	FRAMPTON COMES ALIVE — Peter Frampton (A&M)
13	13	WINGS AT THE SPEED OF SOUND — Wings (EMI)
11	14	LIVE IN LONDON — John Denver (RCA)
22	15	OLIAS OF SUNHILLOW — Jon Anderson (Atlantic)
17	16	ROCK 'N' ROLL MUSIC — Beatles (Apple)
16	17	JAILBREAK — Thin Lizzy (Vertigo)
20	18	VIVA! — Roxy Music (Island)
19	19	DIANA ROSS — Diana Ross (Tamla Motown)
14	20	THEIR GREATEST HITS 1971–1975 — Eagles (Asylum)
18	21	THE BEST OF GLADYS KNIGHT & THE PIPS — Gladys Knight & the Pips (Buddah)
27	22	ONE MAN SHOW — Mike Harding (Philips)
24	23	BREAKAWAY — Gallagher & Lyle (A&M)
-	24	ALICE COOPER GOES TO HELL — Alice Cooper (Warner Bros.)
-	25	HOW DARE YOU — 10 C.C. (Mercury)
30	26	15 BIG ONES — Beach Boys (Reprise)
25	27	I'M NEARLY FAMOUS — Cliff Richard (EMI)
23	28	BLACK AND BLUE — Rolling Stones (Rolling Stones)
-	29	SOUVENIRS — Demis Roussos (Philips)
-	30	WIRED — Jeff Beck (CBS)

7 August 1976

lw	tw	Album / Artist (Label)
1	1	20 GOLDEN GREATS — Beach Boys (Capitol)
2	2	FOREVER AND EVER — Demis Roussos (Philips)
6	3	PASSPORT — Nana Mouskouri (Philips)
4	4	LAUGHTER AND TEARS - THE BEST OF NEIL SEDAKA TODAY — Neil Sedaka (Polydor)
3	5	A NIGHT ON THE TOWN — Rod Stewart (Riva)
9	6	A LITTLE BIT MORE — Dr. Hook (Capitol)
7	7	GREATEST HITS — Abba (Epic)
8	8	HAPPY TO BE — Demis Roussos (Philips)
10	9	CHANGESONEBOWIE — David Bowie (WEA)
5	10	A KIND OF HUSH — Carpenters (A&M)
11	11	BEAUTIFUL NOISE — Neil Diamond (CBS)
14	12	LIVE IN LONDON — John Denver (RCA)
15	13	OLIAS OF SUNHILLOW — Jon Anderson (Atlantic)
13	14	WINGS AT THE SPEED OF SOUND — Wings (EMI)
18	15	VIVA! — Roxy Music (Island)
20	16	THEIR GREATEST HITS 1971–1975 — Eagles (Asylum)
12	17	FRAMPTON COMES ALIVE — Peter Frampton (A&M)
-	18	SAHB STORIES — Sensational Alex Harvey Band (Mountain)
17	19	JAILBREAK — Thin Lizzy (Vertigo)
16	20	ROCK 'N' ROLL MUSIC — Beatles (Apple)
24	21	ALICE COOPER GOES TO HELL — Alice Cooper (Warner Bros.)
22	22	ONE MAN SHOW — Mike Harding (Philips)
21	23	THE BEST OF GLADYS KNIGHT & THE PIPS — Gladys Knight & the Pips (Buddah)
-	24	DON WILLIAMS' GREATEST HITS VOL 1 — Don Williams (ABC)
19	25	DIANA ROSS — Diana Ross (Tamla Motown)
-	26	YOUNG HEARTS RUN FREE — Candi Staton (Warner Bros.)
-	27	SIMON & GARFUNKEL'S GREATEST HITS — Simon & Garfunkel (CBS)
26	28	15 BIG ONES — Beach Boys (Reprise)
23	29	BREAKAWAY — Gallagher & Lyle (A&M)
30	30	WIRED — Jeff Beck (CBS)

Rod Stewart's *Night On The Town* was the first on his own label, Riva. *Atlantic Crossing* should have been on Rod's own label but at the last moment had to appear on Warners. Rod's first name-choice had been Rampant Records but, after spending extravagantly on artwork, his management found that Rampant Records was a registered business name, owned by, well, me. Stewart, notoriously mean (he once got a Rembrandt for Christmas from Elton John, and gave an ice-bucket in return), declined to buy the name.

145

August – September 1976

14 August 1976

last	this	
1	1	20 GOLDEN GREATS Beach Boys (Capitol)
2	2	FOREVER AND EVER Demis Roussos (Philips)
4	3	LAUGHTER AND TEARS - THE BEST OF NEIL SEDAKA TODAY Neil Sedaka (Polydor)
6	4	A LITTLE BIT MORE Dr. Hook (Capitol)
3	5	PASSPORT Nana Mouskouri (Philips)
5	6	A NIGHT ON THE TOWN Rod Stewart (Riva)
7	7	GREATEST HITS Abba (Epic)
8	8	HAPPY TO BE Demis Roussos (Philips)
10	9	A KIND OF HUSH Carpenters (A&M)
9	10	CHANGESONEBOWIE David Bowie (WEA)
15	11	VIVA! Roxy Music (Island)
14	12	WINGS AT THE SPEED OF SOUND Wings (EMI)
18	13	SAHB STORIES Sensational Alex Harvey Band (Mountain)
13	14	OLIAS OF SUNHILLOW Jon Anderson (Atlantic)
12	15	LIVE IN LONDON John Denver (RCA)
11	16	BEAUTIFUL NOISE Neil Diamond (CBS)
19	17	JAILBREAK Thin Lizzy (Vertigo)
17	18	FRAMPTON COMES ALIVE Peter Frampton (A&M)
16	19	THEIR GREATEST HITS 1971-1975 Eagles (Asylum)
23	20	THE BEST OF GLADYS KNIGHT & THE PIPS Gladys Knight & the Pips (Buddah)
20	21	ROCK 'N' ROLL MUSIC Beatles (Apple)
21	22	ALICE COOPER GOES TO HELL Alice Cooper (Warner Bros.)
-	23	COMBINE HARVESTER Wurzels (One Up)
27	24	SIMON & GARFUNKEL'S GREATEST HITS Simon & Garfunkel (CBS)
28	25	15 BIG ONES Beach Boys (Reprise)
24	26	DON WILLIAMS' GREATEST HITS VOL 1 Don Williams (ABC)
22	27	ONE MAN SHOW Mike Harding (Philips)
-	28	DIANA ROSS' GREATEST HITS II Diana Ross (Tamla Motown)
-	29	THE DARK SIDE OF THE MOON Pink Floyd (Harvest)
25	30	DIANA ROSS Diana Ross (Tamla Motown)

21 August 1976

last	this	
1	1	20 GOLDEN GREATS Beach Boys (Capitol)
3	2	LAUGHTER AND TEARS - THE BEST OF NEIL SEDAKA TODAY Neil Sedaka (Polydor)
6	3	A NIGHT ON THE TOWN Rod Stewart (Riva)
4	4	A LITTLE BIT MORE Dr. Hook (Capitol)
5	5	PASSPORT Nana Mouskouri (Philips)
2	6	FOREVER AND EVER Demis Roussos (Philips)
12	7	WINGS AT THE SPEED OF SOUND Wings (EMI)
7	8	GREATEST HITS Abba (Epic)
11	9	VIVA! Roxy Music (Island)
10	10	CHANGESONEBOWIE David Bowie (WEA)
28	11	DIANA ROSS' GREATEST HITS II Diana Ross (Tamla Motown)
9	12	A KIND OF HUSH Carpenters (A&M)
16	13	BEAUTIFUL NOISE Neil Diamond (CBS)
8	14	HAPPY TO BE Demis Roussos (Philips)
17	15	JAILBREAK Thin Lizzy (Vertigo)
15	16	LIVE IN LONDON John Denver (RCA)
13	17	SAHB STORIES Sensational Alex Harvey Band (Mountain)
14	18	OLIAS OF SUNHILLOW Jon Anderson (Atlantic)
18	19	FRAMPTON COMES ALIVE Peter Frampton (A&M)
19	20	THEIR GREATEST HITS 1971-1975 Eagles (Asylum)
20	21	THE BEST OF GLADYS KNIGHT & THE PIPS Gladys Knight & the Pips (Buddah)
21	22	ROCK 'N' ROLL MUSIC Beatles (Apple)
24	23	SIMON & GARFUNKEL'S GREATEST HITS Simon & Garfunkel (CBS)
29	24	THE DARK SIDE OF THE MOON Pink Floyd (Harvest)
30	25	DIANA ROSS Diana Ross (Tamla Motown)
23	26	COMBINE HARVESTER Wurzels (One Up)
26	27	DON WILLIAMS' GREATEST HITS VOL 1 Don Williams (ABC)
-	28	BLUE FOR YOU Status Quo (Vertigo)
27	29	ONE MAN SHOW Mike Harding (Philips)
22	30	ALICE COOPER GOES TO HELL Alice Cooper (Warner Bros.)

28 August 1976

last	this	
2	1	LAUGHTER AND TEARS - THE BEST OF NEIL SEDAKA TODAY Neil Sedaka (Polydor)
1	2	20 GOLDEN GREATS Beach Boys (Capitol)
3	3	A NIGHT ON THE TOWN Rod Stewart (Riva)
4	4	A LITTLE BIT MORE Dr. Hook (Capitol)
6	5	FOREVER AND EVER Demis Roussos (Philips)
5	6	PASSPORT Nana Mouskouri (Philips)
11	7	DIANA ROSS' GREATEST HITS II Diana Ross (Tamla Motown)
7	8	WINGS AT THE SPEED OF SOUND Wings (EMI)
13	9	BEAUTIFUL NOISE Neil Diamond (CBS)
10	10	VIVA! Roxy Music (Island)
8	11	GREATEST HITS Abba (Epic)
12	12	CHANGESONEBOWIE David Bowie (WEA)
15	13	JAILBREAK Thin Lizzy (Vertigo)
14	14	A KIND OF HUSH Carpenters (A&M)
16	15	LIVE IN LONDON John Denver (RCA)
17	16	SAHB STORIES Sensational Alex Harvey Band (Mountain)
19	17	FRAMPTON COMES ALIVE Peter Frampton (A&M)
28	18	BLUE FOR YOU Status Quo (Vertigo)
14	19	HAPPY TO BE Demis Roussos (Philips)
18	20	OLIAS OF SUNHILLOW Jon Anderson (Atlantic)
20	21	THEIR GREATEST HITS 1971-1975 Eagles (Asylum)
22	22	ROCK 'N' ROLL MUSIC Beatles (Apple)
21	23	THE BEST OF GLADYS KNIGHT & THE PIPS Gladys Knight & the Pips (Buddah)
30	24	ALICE COOPER GOES TO HELL Alice Cooper (Warner Bros.)
24	25	THE DARK SIDE OF THE MOON Pink Floyd (Harvest)
23	26	SIMON & GARFUNKEL'S GREATEST HITS Simon & Garfunkel (CBS)
26	27	COMBINE HARVESTER Wurzels (One Up)
-	28	WHAT I'VE GOT IN MIND Billie Joe Spears (United Artists)
-	29	15 BIG ONES Beach Boys (Reprise)
-	30	TWIGGY Twiggy (Mercury)

4 September 1976

last	this	
2	1	20 GOLDEN GREATS Beach Boys (Capitol)
7	2	DIANA ROSS' GREATEST HITS II Diana Ross (Tamla Motown)
1	3	LAUGHTER AND TEARS - THE BEST OF NEIL SEDAKA TODAY Neil Sedaka (Polydor)
3	4	A NIGHT ON THE TOWN Rod Stewart (Riva)
5	5	FOREVER AND EVER Demis Roussos (Philips)
11	6	GREATEST HITS Abba (Epic)
10	7	VIVA! Roxy Music (Island)
4	8	A LITTLE BIT MORE Dr. Hook (Capitol)
8	9	WINGS AT THE SPEED OF SOUND Wings (EMI)
6	10	PASSPORT Nana Mouskouri (Philips)
13	11	JAILBREAK Thin Lizzy (Vertigo)
9	12	BEAUTIFUL NOISE Neil Diamond (CBS)
12	13	CHANGESONEBOWIE David Bowie (WEA)
14	14	A KIND OF HUSH Carpenters (A&M)
15	15	LIVE IN LONDON John Denver (RCA)
17	16	FRAMPTON COMES ALIVE Peter Frampton (A&M)
19	17	HAPPY TO BE Demis Roussos (Philips)
21	18	THEIR GREATEST HITS 1971-1975 Eagles (Asylum)
16	19	SAHB STORIES Sensational Alex Harvey Band (Mountain)
25	20	THE DARK SIDE OF THE MOON Pink Floyd (Harvest)
-	21	SPIRIT John Denver (RCA)
-	22	ATLANTIC CROSSING Rod Stewart (Warner Bros.)
27	23	COMBINE HARVESTER Wurzels (One Up)
20	24	OLIAS OF SUNHILLOW Jon Anderson (Atlantic)
18	25	BLUE FOR YOU Status Quo (Vertigo)
30	26	TWIGGY Twiggy (Mercury)
-	27	I'M NEARLY FAMOUS Cliff Richard (EMI)
29	28	15 BIG ONES Beach Boys (Reprise)
-	29	SPITFIRE Jefferson Starship (Grunt)
-	30	SKY HIGH Tavares (Capitol)

Roussosmania, as Demis reposed twice over in the Top 10, with *Forever And Ever* titled after a single that had got nowhere when first released but was now also the selling-point of the extraordinary EP *The Roussos Phenomenon*, which had topped the singles chart in July. This was also a time of comedy hits: the Wurzels re-entry *Combine Harvester* had, weeks earlier, charted alongside Mike Harding and just after Pam Ayres. Of course, some said Demis Roussos was the biggest comic of them all.

September – October 1976

11 September 1976

last week	this week	Album
1	1	20 GOLDEN GREATS — Beach Boys (Capitol)
3	2	LAUGHTER AND TEARS - THE BEST OF NEIL SEDAKA TODAY — Neil Sedaka (Polydor)
4	3	A NIGHT ON THE TOWN — Rod Stewart (Riva)
5	4	FOREVER AND EVER — Demis Roussos (Philips)
6	5	GREATEST HITS — Abba (Epic)
9	6	WINGS AT THE SPEED OF SOUND — Wings (EMI)
2	7	DIANA ROSS' GREATEST HITS — Diana Ross (Tamla Motown)
8	8	A LITTLE BIT MORE — Dr. Hook (Capitol)
10	9	PASSPORT — Nana Mouskouri (Philips)
12	10	BEAUTIFUL NOISE — Neil Diamond (CBS)
7	11	VIVA! — Roxy Music (Island)
11	12	JAILBREAK — Thin Lizzy (Vertigo)
15	13	LIVE IN LONDON — John Denver (RCA)
25	14	BLUE FOR YOU — Status Quo (Vertigo)
17	15	HAPPY TO BE — Demis Roussos (Philips)
18	16	THEIR GREATEST HITS 1971–1975 — Eagles (Asylum)
14	17	A KIND OF HUSH — Carpenters (A&M)
16	18	FRAMPTON COMES ALIVE — Peter Frampton (A&M)
13	19	CHANGESONEBOWIE — David Bowie (WEA)
26	20	TWIGGY — Twiggy (Mercury)
24	21	OLIAS OF SUNHILLOW — Jon Anderson (Atlantic)
-	22	THE BEST OF GLADYS KNIGHT & THE PIPS — Gladys Knight & the Pips (Buddah)
19	23	SAHB STORIES — Sensational Alex Harvey Band (Mountain)
22	24	ATLANTIC CROSSING — Rod Stewart (Warner Bros.)
21	25	SPIRIT — John Denver (RCA)
-	26	BREAKAWAY — Gallagher & Lyle (A&M)
20	27	THE DARK SIDE OF THE MOON — Pink Floyd (Harvest)
-	28	HASTEN DOWN THE WIND — Linda Ronstadt (Asylum)
-	29	ROCK 'N' ROLL MUSIC — Beatles (Apple)
27	30	I'M NEARLY FAMOUS — Cliff Richard (EMI)

18 September 1976

last	this	Album
1	1	20 GOLDEN GREATS — Beach Boys (Capitol)
2	2	LAUGHTER AND TEARS - THE BEST OF NEIL SEDAKA TODAY — Neil Sedaka (Polydor)
5	3	GREATEST HITS — Abba (Epic)
3	4	A NIGHT ON THE TOWN — Rod Stewart (Riva)
6	5	WINGS AT THE SPEED OF SOUND — Wings (EMI)
7	6	DIANA ROSS' GREATEST HITS II — Diana Ross (Tamla Motown)
8	7	A LITTLE BIT MORE — Dr. Hook (Capitol)
4	8	FOREVER AND EVER — Demis Roussos (Philips)
9	9	PASSPORT — Nana Mouskouri (Philips)
25	10	SPIRIT — John Denver (RCA)
26	11	BREAKAWAY — Gallagher & Lyle (A&M)
18	12	FRAMPTON COMES ALIVE — Peter Frampton (A&M)
11	13	VIVA! — Roxy Music (Island)
10	14	BEAUTIFUL NOISE — Neil Diamond (CBS)
12	15	JAILBREAK — Thin Lizzy (Vertigo)
-	16	NO REASON TO CRY — Eric Clapton (RSO)
16	17	THEIR GREATEST HITS 1971–1975 — Eagles (Asylum)
24	18	ATLANTIC CROSSING — Rod Stewart (Warner Bros.)
20	19	TWIGGY — Twiggy (Mercury)
19	20	CHANGESONEBOWIE — David Bowie (WEA)
14	21	BLUE FOR YOU — Status Quo (Vertigo)
23	22	SAHB STORIES — Sensational Alex Harvey Band (Mountain)
-	23	THE BEST OF THE STYLISTICS VOL.2 — Stylistics (Avco)
27	24	THE DARK SIDE OF THE MOON — Pink Floyd (Harvest)
28	25	HASTEN DOWN THE WIND — Linda Ronstadt (Asylum)
13	26	LIVE IN LONDON — John Denver (RCA)
22	27	THE BEST OF GLADYS KNIGHT & THE PIPS — Gladys Knight & the Pips (Buddah)
30	28	I'M NEARLY FAMOUS — Cliff Richard (EMI)
21	29	OLIAS OF SUNHILLOW — Jon Anderson (Atlantic)
-	30	THE ROARING SILENCE — Manfred Mann Earthband (Bronze)

25 September 1976

last	this	Album
4	1	A NIGHT ON THE TOWN — Rod Stewart (Riva)
3	2	GREATEST HITS — Abba (Epic)
10	3	SPIRIT — John Denver (RCA)
2	4	LAUGHTER AND TEARS - THE BEST OF NEIL SEDAKA TODAY — Neil Sedaka (Polydor)
6	5	DIANA ROSS' GREATEST HITS II — Diana Ross (Tamla Motown)
1	6	20 GOLDEN GREATS — Beach Boys (Capitol)
5	7	WINGS AT THE SPEED OF SOUND — Wings (EMI)
8	8	FOREVER AND EVER — Demis Roussos (Philips)
7	9	A LITTLE BIT MORE — Dr. Hook (Capitol)
16	10	NO REASON TO CRY — Eric Clapton (RSO)
15	11	JAILBREAK — Thin Lizzy (Vertigo)
11	12	BREAKAWAY — Gallagher & Lyle (A&M)
12	13	FRAMPTON COMES ALIVE — Peter Frampton (A&M)
14	14	BEAUTIFUL NOISE — Neil Diamond (CBS)
9	15	PASSPORT — Nana Mouskouri (Philips)
18	16	ATLANTIC CROSSING — Rod Stewart (Warner Bros.)
13	17	VIVA! — Roxy Music (Island)
23	18	THE BEST OF THE STYLISTICS VOL.2 — Stylistics (Avco)
20	19	CHANGESONEBOWIE — David Bowie (WEA)
30	20	THE ROARING SILENCE — Manfred Mann Earthband (Bronze)
17	21	THEIR GREATEST HITS 1971–1975 — Eagles (Asylum)
27	22	THE BEST OF GLADYS KNIGHT & THE PIPS — Gladys Knight & the Pips (Buddah)
29	23	OLIAS OF SUNHILLOW — Jon Anderson (Atlantic)
19	24	TWIGGY — Twiggy (Mercury)
-	25	JOAN ARMATRADING — Joan Armatrading (A&M)
-	26	BIGGER THAN BOTH OF US — Darryl Hall & John Oates (RCA)
-	27	MODERN MUSIC — Be-Bop Deluxe (Harvest)
21	28	BLUE FOR YOU — Status Quo (Vertigo)
-	29	HAPPY TO BE — Demis Roussos (Philips)
26	30	LIVE IN LONDON — John Denver (RCA)

2 October 1976

last	this	Album
2	1	GREATEST HITS — Abba (Epic)
6	2	20 GOLDEN GREATS — Beach Boys (Capitol)
1	3	A NIGHT ON THE TOWN — Rod Stewart (Riva)
5	4	DIANA ROSS' GREATEST HITS II — Diana Ross (Tamla Motown)
4	5	LAUGHTER AND TEARS - THE BEST OF NEIL SEDAKA TODAY — Neil Sedaka (Polydor)
3	6	SPIRIT — John Denver (RCA)
8	7	FOREVER AND EVER — Demis Roussos (Philips)
7	8	WINGS AT THE SPEED OF SOUND — Wings (EMI)
18	9	THE BEST OF THE STYLISTICS VOL.2 — Stylistics (Avco)
9	10	A LITTLE BIT MORE — Dr. Hook (Capitol)
12	11	BREAKAWAY — Gallagher & Lyle (A&M)
13	12	FRAMPTON COMES ALIVE — Peter Frampton (A&M)
14	13	BEAUTIFUL NOISE — Neil Diamond (CBS)
16	14	ATLANTIC CROSSING — Rod Stewart (Warner Bros.)
10	15	NO REASON TO CRY — Eric Clapton (RSO)
22	16	THE BEST OF GLADYS KNIGHT & THE PIPS — Gladys Knight & the Pips (Buddah)
11	17	JAILBREAK — Thin Lizzy (Vertigo)
15	18	PASSPORT — Nana Mouskouri (Philips)
-	19	DEDICATION — Bay City Rollers (Bell)
30	20	LIVE IN LONDON — John Denver (RCA)
20	21	THE ROARING SILENCE — Manfred Mann Earthband (Bronze)
21	22	THEIR GREATEST HITS 1971–1975 — Eagles (Asylum)
17	23	VIVA! — Roxy Music (Island)
-	24	DEREK AND CLIVE LIVE — Peter Cook & Dudley Moore (Island)
25	25	HARD RAIN — Bob Dylan (CBS)
25	26	JOAN ARMATRADING — Joan Armatrading (A&M)
27	27	MODERN MUSIC — Be-Bop Deluxe (Harvest)
-	28	LET'S STICK TOGETHER — Bryan Ferry (Atlantic)
19	29	CHANGESONEBOWIE — David Bowie (WEA)
26	30	BIGGER THAN BOTH OF US — Darryl Hall & John Oates (RCA)

Joan Armatrading, born in St.Kitts but raised in Birmingham, can be said to be not only the UK's first black woman singer-songwriter but our most credible singer-songwriter full stop. *Joan Armatrading* was not her first album: that had been on Fly/Cube, a London music-publisher's small subsidiary label. However, now signed to A&M, she was starting to build a sustained career on her own quiet terms. She would be THE favourite of the British women's movement, yet remain a highly individual artist.

October 1976

9 October 1976

last week	this week	Title	Artist
1	1	GREATEST HITS	Abba (Epic)
3	2	A NIGHT ON THE TOWN	Rod Stewart (Riva)
9	3	THE BEST OF THE STYLISTICS VOL.2	Stylistics (Avco)
2	4	20 GOLDEN GREATS	Beach Boys (Capitol)
8	5	WINGS AT THE SPEED OF SOUND	Wings (EMI)
7	6	FOREVER AND EVER	Demis Roussos (Philips)
4	7	DIANA ROSS' GREATEST HITS II	Diana Ross (Tamla Motown)
5	8	LAUGHTER AND TEARS - THE BEST OF NEIL SEDAKA TODAY	Neil Sedaka (Polydor)
-	9	STUPIDITY	Dr. Feelgood (United Artists)
19	10	DEDICATION	Bay City Rollers (Bell)
6	11	SPIRIT	John Denver (RCA)
14	12	ATLANTIC CROSSING	Rod Stewart (Warner Bros.)
24	13	DEREK AND CLIVE LIVE	Peter Cook & Dudley Moore (Island)
26	14	JOAN ARMATRADING	Joan Armatrading (A&M)
21	15	THE ROARING SILENCE	Manfred Mann Earthband (Bronze)
12	16	FRAMPTON COMES ALIVE	Peter Frampton (A&M)
10	17	A LITTLE BIT MORE	Dr. Hook (Capitol)
22	18	THEIR GREATEST HITS 1971–1975	Eagles (Asylum)
13	19	BEAUTIFUL NOISE	Neil Diamond (CBS)
-	20	20 ITALIAN LOVE SONGS	Various Artists (K-Tel)
16	21	THE BEST OF GLADYS KNIGHT & THE PIPS	Gladys Knight & the Pips (Buddah)
25	22	HARD RAIN	Bob Dylan (CBS)
11	23	BREAKAWAY	Gallagher & Lyle (A&M)
28	24	LET'S STICK TOGETHER	Bryan Ferry (Atlantic)
27	25	MODERN MUSIC	Be-Bop Deluxe (Harvest)
30	26	BIGGER THAN BOTH OF US	Darryl Hall & John Oates (RCA)
15	27	NO REASON TO CRY	Eric Clapton (RSO)
23	28	VIVA!	Roxy Music (Island)
-	29	THE WHO STORY	Who (Polydor)
18	30	PASSPORT	Nana Mouskouri (Philips)

16 October 1976

last week	this week	Title	Artist
2	1	A NIGHT ON THE TOWN	Rod Stewart (Riva)
1	2	GREATEST HITS	Abba (Epic)
3	3	THE BEST OF THE STYLISTICS VOL.2	Stylistics (Avco)
4	4	20 GOLDEN GREATS	Beach Boys (Capitol)
9	5	STUPIDITY	Dr. Feelgood (United Artists)
8	6	LAUGHTER AND TEARS - THE BEST OF NEIL SEDAKA TODAY	Neil Sedaka (Polydor)
12	7	ATLANTIC CROSSING	Rod Stewart (Warner Bros.)
22	8	HARD RAIN	Bob Dylan (CBS)
6	9	FOREVER AND EVER	Demis Roussos (Philips)
7	10	DIANA ROSS' GREATEST HITS II	Diana Ross (Tamla Motown)
10	11	DEDICATION	Bay City Rollers (Bell)
29	12	THE WHO STORY	Who (Polydor)
16	13	FRAMPTON COMES ALIVE	Peter Frampton (A&M)
5	14	WINGS AT THE SPEED OF SOUND	Wings (EMI)
-	15	SONGS IN THE KEY OF LIFE	Stevie Wonder (Tamla Motown)
11	16	SPIRIT	John Denver (RCA)
20	17	20 ITALIAN LOVE SONGS	Various Artists (K-Tel)
15	18	THE ROARING SILENCE	Manfred Mann Earthband (Bronze)
-	19	SOUL MOTION	Various Artists (K-Tel)
14	20	JOAN ARMATRADING	Joan Armatrading (A&M)
19	21	BEAUTIFUL NOISE	Neil Diamond (CBS)
21	22	THE BEST OF GLADYS KNIGHT & THE PIPS	Gladys Knight & the Pips (Buddah)
13	23	DEREK AND CLIVE LIVE	Peter Cook & Dudley Moore (Island)
17	24	A LITTLE BIT MORE	Dr. Hook (Capitol)
18	25	THEIR GREATEST HITS 1971–1975	Eagles (Asylum)
25	26	MODERN MUSIC	Be-Bop Deluxe (Harvest)
24	27	LET'S STICK TOGETHER	Bryan Ferry (Atlantic)
27	28	NO REASON TO CRY	Eric Clapton (RSO)
-	29	GENE PITNEY'S GREATEST HITS	Gene Pitney (Arcade)
23	30	BREAKAWAY	Gallagher & Lyle (A&M)

23 October 1976

last week	this week	Title	Artist
2	1	GREATEST HITS	Abba (Epic)
12	2	THE WHO STORY	Who (Polydor)
1	3	A NIGHT ON THE TOWN	Rod Stewart (Riva)
8	4	HARD RAIN	Bob Dylan (CBS)
3	5	THE BEST OF THE STYLISTICS VOL.2	Stylistics (Avco)
15	6	SONGS IN THE KEY OF LIFE	Stevie Wonder (Tamla Motown)
5	7	STUPIDITY	Dr. Feelgood (United Artists)
6	8	LAUGHTER AND TEARS - THE BEST OF NEIL SEDAKA TODAY	Neil Sedaka (Polydor)
11	9	DEDICATION	Bay City Rollers (Bell)
4	10	20 GOLDEN GREATS	Beach Boys (Capitol)
10	11	DIANA ROSS' GREATEST HITS II	Diana Ross (Tamla Motown)
19	12	SOUL MOTION	Various Artists (K-Tel)
7	13	ATLANTIC CROSSING	Rod Stewart (Warner Bros.)
9	14	FOREVER AND EVER	Demis Roussos (Philips)
20	15	JOAN ARMATRADING	Joan Armatrading (A&M)
14	16	WINGS AT THE SPEED OF SOUND	Wings (EMI)
-	17	COUNTRY COMFORT	Various Artists (K-Tel)
23	18	DEREK AND CLIVE LIVE	Peter Cook & Dudley Moore (Island)
13	19	FRAMPTON COMES ALIVE	Peter Frampton (A&M)
16	20	SPIRIT	John Denver (RCA)
17	21	20 ITALIAN LOVE SONGS	Various Artists (K-Tel)
29	22	GENE PITNEY'S GREATEST HITS	Gene Pitney (Arcade)
-	23	LONG MAY YOU RUN	Stills-Young Band (Reprise)
-	24	ALBEDO 0.39	Vangelis (RCA)
21	25	BEAUTIFUL NOISE	Neil Diamond (CBS)
18	26	THE ROARING SILENCE	Manfred Mann Earthband (Bronze)
-	27	JAILBREAK	Thin Lizzy (Vertigo)
-	28	"L"	Steve Hillage (Virgin)
25	29	THEIR GREATEST HITS 1971–1975	Eagles (Asylum)
22	30	THE BEST OF GLADYS KNIGHT & THE PIPS	Gladys Knight & the Pips (Buddah)

30 October 1976

last week	this week	Title	Artist
2	1	THE WHO STORY	Who (Polydor)
1	2	GREATEST HITS	Abba (Epic)
6	3	SONGS IN THE KEY OF LIFE	Stevie Wonder (Tamla Motown)
3	4	A NIGHT ON THE TOWN	Rod Stewart (Riva)
5	5	THE BEST OF THE STYLISTICS VOL.2	Stylistics (Avco)
12	6	SOUL MOTION	Various Artists (K-Tel)
13	7	ATLANTIC CROSSING	Rod Stewart (Warner Bros.)
7	8	STUPIDITY	Dr. Feelgood (United Artists)
19	9	FRAMPTON COMES ALIVE	Peter Frampton (A&M)
14	10	FOREVER AND EVER	Demis Roussos (Philips)
10	11	20 GOLDEN GREATS	Beach Boys (Capitol)
4	12	HARD RAIN	Bob Dylan (CBS)
15	13	JOAN ARMATRADING	Joan Armatrading (A&M)
8	14	LAUGHTER AND TEARS - THE BEST OF NEIL SEDAKA TODAY	Neil Sedaka (Polydor)
-	15	THE SONG REMAINS THE SAME	Led Zeppelin (Swansong)
11	16	DIANA ROSS' GREATEST HITS II	Diana Ross (Tamla Motown)
22	17	GENE PITNEY'S GREATEST HITS	Gene Pitney (Arcade)
17	18	COUNTRY COMFORT	Various Artists (K-Tel)
9	19	DEDICATION	Bay City Rollers (Bell)
16	20	WINGS AT THE SPEED OF SOUND	Wings (EMI)
26	21	THE ROARING SILENCE	Manfred Mann Earthband (Bronze)
20	22	SPIRIT	John Denver (RCA)
29	23	THEIR GREATEST HITS 1971–1975	Eagles (Asylum)
25	24	BEAUTIFUL NOISE	Neil Diamond (CBS)
-	25	BLUE MOVES	Elton John (Rocket)
21	26	20 ITALIAN LOVE SONGS	Various Artists (K-Tel)
18	27	DEREK AND CLIVE LIVE	Peter Cook & Dudley Moore (Island)
-	28	OUT ON THE STREET	David Essex (CBS)
30	29	THE BEST OF GLADYS KNIGHT & THE PIPS	Gladys Knight & the Pips (Buddah)
28	30	"L"	Steve Hillage (Virgin)

Enter the rude *Derek And Clive Live* by comedian and *Private Eye* owner Peter Cook and jazz-pianist turned comic Dudley Moore. It was the second of three LPs taken into the charts by Cook and Moore, each on a different label. *Once Moore With Cook* had been a minor hit in 1966; *Derek and Clive Come Again* would climax at No.22 in January 1978. "Cuddly" Dudley Moore would metamorphose into a 1980s Hollywood superstar, while Cook would make a US TV series that flopped.

November 1976

6 November 1976

last week	this week	
3	1	SONGS IN THE KEY OF LIFE — Stevie Wonder (Tamla Motown)
1	2	THE WHO STORY — Who (Polydor)
2	3	GREATEST HITS Abba (Epic)
4	4	A NIGHT ON THE TOWN — Rod Stewart (Riva)
6	5	SOUL MOTION — Various Artists (K-Tel)
7	6	ATLANTIC CROSSING — Rod Stewart (Warner Bros.)
8	7	STUPIDITY — Dr. Feelgood (United Artists)
9	8	FRAMPTON COMES ALIVE — Peter Frampton (A&M)
10	9	FOREVER AND EVER — Demis Roussos (Philips)
25	10	BLUE MOVES — Elton John (Rocket)
5	11	THE BEST OF THE STYLISTICS VOL.2 Stylistics (Avco)
13	12	JOAN ARMATRADING — Joan Armatrading (A&M)
24	13	BEAUTIFUL NOISE — Neil Diamond (CBS)
15	14	THE SONG REMAINS THE SAME — Led Zeppelin (Swansong)
-	15	100 GOLDEN GREATS — Max Bygraves (Ronco)
11	16	20 GOLDEN GREATS — Beach Boys (Capitol)
18	17	COUNTRY COMFORT — Various Artists (K-Tel)
12	18	HARD RAIN Bob Dylan (CBS)
30	19	"L" Steve Hillage (Virgin)
17	20	GENE PITNEY'S GREATEST HITS Gene Pitney (Arcade)
-	21	BERT WEEDON'S 22 GOLDEN GUITAR GREATS — Bert Weedon (Warwick)
14	22	LAUGHTER AND TEARS - THE BEST OF NEIL SEDAKA TODAY — Neil Sedaka (Polydor)
-	23	JOHNNY THE FOX — Thin Lizzy (Vertigo)
28	24	OUT ON THE STREET — David Essex (CBS)
-	25	OCTOBERON — Barclay James Harvest (Polydor)
22	26	SPIRIT John Denver (RCA)
27	27	DEREK AND CLIVE LIVE — Peter Cook & Dudley Moore (Island)
-	28	ALBEDO 0.39 Vangelis (RCA)
16	29	DIANA ROSS' GREATEST HITS II — Diana Ross (Tamla Motown)
21	30	THE ROARING SILENCE — Manfred Mann Earthband (Bronze)

13 November 1976

last week	this week	
1	1	SONGS IN THE KEY OF LIFE — Stevie Wonder (Tamla Motown)
5	2	SOUL MOTION — Various Artists (K-Tel)
3	3	GREATEST HITS Abba (Epic)
2	4	THE WHO STORY — Who (Polydor)
14	5	THE SONG REMAINS THE SAME — Led Zeppelin (Swansong)
10	6	BLUE MOVES — Elton John (Rocket)
8	7	FRAMPTON COMES ALIVE — Peter Frampton (A&M)
9	8	FOREVER AND EVER — Demis Roussos (Philips)
11	9	THE BEST OF THE STYLISTICS VOL.2 Stylistics (Avco)
23	10	JOHNNY THE FOX — Thin Lizzy (Vertigo)
12	11	JOAN ARMATRADING — Joan Armatrading (A&M)
4	12	A NIGHT ON THE TOWN — Rod Stewart (Riva)
20	13	GENE PITNEY'S GREATEST HITS Gene Pitney (Arcade)
13	14	BEAUTIFUL NOISE — Neil Diamond (CBS)
6	15	ATLANTIC CROSSING — Rod Stewart (Warner Bros.)
-	16	20 GOLDEN GREATS — Glen Campbell (Capitol)
17	17	COUNTRY COMFORT — Various Artists (K-Tel)
-	18	A LITTLE BIT MORE — Dr. Hook (Capitol)
7	19	STUPIDITY — Dr. Feelgood (United Artists)
21	20	BERT WEEDON'S 22 GOLDEN GUITAR GREATS — Bert Weedon (Warwick)
29	21	DIANA ROSS' GREATEST HITS II — Diana Ross (Tamla Motown)
19	22	"L" Steve Hillage (Virgin)
-	23	TECHNICAL ECSTASY — Black Sabbath (Vertigo)
15	24	100 GOLDEN GREATS — Max Bygraves (Ronco)
-	25	ONE MORE FROM THE ROAD — Lynyrd Skynyrd (MCA)
-	26	FRANKIE VALLI & THE FOUR SEASONS' GREATEST HITS — Frankie Valli & the Four Seasons (K-Tel)
18	27	HARD RAIN Bob Dylan (CBS)
24	28	OUT ON THE STREET — David Essex (CBS)
22	29	LAUGHTER AND TEARS - THE BEST OF NEIL SEDAKA TODAY — Neil Sedaka (Polydor)
-	30	CHICAGO X Chicago (CBS)

20 November 1976

last week	this week	
1	1	SONGS IN THE KEY OF LIFE — Stevie Wonder (Tamla Motown)
2	2	SOUL MOTION — Various Artists (K-Tel)
4	3	THE WHO STORY Who (Polydor)
6	4	BLUE MOVES — Elton John (Rocket)
3	5	GREATEST HITS Abba (Epic)
5	6	THE SONG REMAINS THE SAME — Led Zeppelin (Swansong)
8	7	FOREVER AND EVER — Demis Roussos (Philips)
24	8	100 GOLDEN GREATS — Max Bygraves (Ronco)
10	9	JOHNNY THE FOX — Thin Lizzy (Vertigo)
20	10	BERT WEEDON'S 22 GOLDEN GUITAR GREATS — Bert Weedon (Warwick)
11	11	JOAN ARMATRADING — Joan Armatrading (A&M)
7	12	FRAMPTON COMES ALIVE — Peter Frampton (A&M)
9	13	THE BEST OF THE STYLISTICS VOL.2 Stylistics (Avco)
15	14	ATLANTIC CROSSING — Rod Stewart (Warner Bros.)
-	15	ARRIVAL Abba (Epic)
12	16	A NIGHT ON THE TOWN — Rod Stewart (Riva)
16	17	20 GOLDEN GREATS — Glen Campbell (Capitol)
18	18	A LITTLE BIT MORE — Dr. Hook (Capitol)
-	19	HOT CHOCOLATE'S GREATEST HITS — Hot Chocolate (RAK)
30	20	CHICAGO X Chicago (CBS)
13	21	GENE PITNEY'S GREATEST HITS Gene Pitney (Arcade)
14	22	BEAUTIFUL NOISE — Neil Diamond (CBS)
23	23	TECHNICAL ECSTASY — Black Sabbath (Vertigo)
26	24	FRANKIE VALLI & THE FOUR SEASONS' GREATEST HITS — Frankie Valli & the Four Seasons (K-Tel)
-	25	DEREK AND CLIVE LIVE — Peter Cook & Dudley Moore (Island)
22	26	"L" Steve Hillage (Virgin)
-	27	FLEETWOOD MAC — Fleetwood Mac (Reprise)
-	28	20 ORIGINAL DEAN MARTIN HITS — Dean Martin (Reprise)
28	29	OUT ON THE STREET — David Essex (CBS)
21	30	DIANA ROSS' GREATEST HITS II — Diana Ross (Tamla Motown)

27 November 1976

last week	this week	
17	1	20 GOLDEN GREATS — Glen Campbell (Capitol)
1	2	SONGS IN THE KEY OF LIFE — Stevie Wonder (Tamla Motown)
10	3	BERT WEEDON'S 22 GOLDEN GUITAR GREATS — Bert Weedon (Warwick)
8	4	100 GOLDEN GREATS — Max Bygraves (Ronco)
6	5	THE SONG REMAINS THE SAME — Led Zeppelin (Swansong)
4	6	BLUE MOVES — Elton John (Rocket)
2	7	SOUL MOTION — Various Artists (K-Tel)
3	8	THE WHO STORY — Who (Polydor)
15	9	ARRIVAL Abba (Epic)
5	10	GREATEST HITS Abba (Epic)
7	11	FOREVER AND EVER — Demis Roussos (Philips)
28	12	20 ORIGINAL DEAN MARTIN HITS — Dean Martin (Reprise)
12	13	FRAMPTON COMES ALIVE — Peter Frampton (A&M)
19	14	HOT CHOCOLATE'S GREATEST HITS — Hot Chocolate (RAK)
16	15	A NIGHT ON THE TOWN — Rod Stewart (Riva)
24	16	FRANKIE VALLI & THE FOUR SEASONS' GREATEST HITS — Frankie Valli & the Four Seasons (K-Tel)
12	17	THE BEST OF THE STYLISTICS VOL.2 Stylistics (Avco)
18	18	A LITTLE BIT MORE — Dr. Hook (Capitol)
9	19	JOHNNY THE FOX — Thin Lizzy (Vertigo)
11	20	JOAN ARMATRADING — Joan Armatrading (A&M)
20	21	CHICAGO X Chicago (CBS)
22	22	BEAUTIFUL NOISE — Neil Diamond (CBS)
25	23	DEREK AND CLIVE LIVE — Peter Cook & Dudley Moore (Island)
27	24	FLEETWOOD MAC — Fleetwood Mac (Reprise)
14	25	ATLANTIC CROSSING — Rod Stewart (Warner Bros.)
-	26	20 GOLDEN GREATS — Beach Boys (Capitol)
-	27	ALL THIS AND WORLD WAR II — Various Artists (Riva)
-	28	BOXED Mike Oldfield (Virgin)
-	29	THE INCREDIBLE PLAN — Max Boyce (EMI)
-	30	HENRY MANCINI — Henry Mancini (Arcade)

TV-advertised albums had brought many unlikely, even unwelcome, artists back into the charts, decades after their heyday: none so unexpectedly as Bert Weedon, Britain's first rock'n'roll guitar star. His very name had always made people guffaw (more so even than Conway Twitty's), and even as he was enjoying his hits - which were only in the period 1959-1961 - they were felt to be hopelessly feeble and, well, British. His real achievement, indeed, had been to make the Shadows sound exciting.

December 1976

4 December 1976

last	this	Album	Artist (Label)
1	1	20 GOLDEN GREATS	Glen Campbell (Capitol)
9	2	ARRIVAL	Abba (Epic)
2	3	SONGS IN THE KEY OF LIFE	Stevie Wonder (Tamla Motown)
3	4	BERT WEEDON'S 22 GOLDEN GUITAR GREATS	Bert Weedon (Warwick)
4	5	100 GOLDEN GREATS	Max Bygraves (Ronco)
5	6	THE SONG REMAINS THE SAME	Led Zeppelin (Swansong)
7	7	SOUL MOTION	Various Artists (K-Tel)
10	8	GREATEST HITS	Abba (Epic)
6	9	BLUE MOVES	Elton John (Rocket)
14	10	HOT CHOCOLATE'S GREATEST HITS	Hot Chocolate (RAK)
12	11	20 ORIGINAL DEAN MARTIN HITS	Dean Martin (Reprise)
16	12	FRANKIE VALLI & THE FOUR SEASONS' GREATEST HITS	Frankie Valli & the Four Seasons (K-Tel)
8	13	THE WHO STORY	Who (Polydor)
17	14	THE BEST OF THE STYLISTICS VOL.2	Stylistics (Avco)
13	15	FRAMPTON COMES ALIVE	Peter Frampton (A&M)
-	16	LIVE IN EUROPE	Deep Purple (Purple)
11	17	FOREVER AND EVER	Demis Roussos (Philips)
21	18	CHICAGO X	Chicago (CBS)
-	19	SOUNDS OF GLORY	Various Artists (Arcade)
-	20	DISCO ROCKET	Various Artists (K-Tel)
27	21	ALL THIS AND WORLD WAR II	Various Artists (Riva)
18	22	A LITTLE BIT MORE	Dr. Hook (Capitol)
24	23	FLEETWOOD MAC	Fleetwood Mac (Reprise)
15	24	A NIGHT ON THE TOWN	Rod Stewart (Riva)
25	25	ATLANTIC CROSSING	Rod Stewart (Warner Bros.)
-	26	A NEW WORLD RECORD	Electric Light Orchestra (Jet)
-	27	GENE PITNEY'S GREATEST HITS	Gene Pitney (Arcade)
20	28	JOAN ARMATRADING	Joan Armatrading (A&M)
-	29	DAVID SOUL	David Soul (Private Stock)
29	30	THE INCREDIBLE PLAN	Max Boyce (EMI)

11 December 1976

last	this	Album	Artist (Label)
1	1	20 GOLDEN GREATS	Glen Campbell (Capitol)
2	2	ARRIVAL	Abba (Epic)
3	3	SONGS IN THE KEY OF LIFE	Stevie Wonder (Tamla Motown)
5	4	100 GOLDEN GREATS	Max Bygraves (Ronco)
4	5	BERT WEEDON'S 22 GOLDEN GUITAR GREATS	Bert Weedon (Warwick)
8	6	GREATEST HITS	Abba (Epic)
12	7	FRANKIE VALLI & THE FOUR SEASONS' GREATEST HITS	Frankie Valli & the Four Seasons (K-Tel)
10	8	HOT CHOCOLATE'S GREATEST HITS	Hot Chocolate (RAK)
9	9	BLUE MOVES	Elton John (Rocket)
11	10	20 ORIGINAL DEAN MARTIN HITS	Dean Martin (Reprise)
6	11	THE SONG REMAINS THE SAME	Led Zeppelin (Swansong)
20	12	DISCO ROCKET	Various Artists (K-Tel)
16	13	LIVE IN EUROPE	Deep Purple (Purple)
13	14	THE WHO STORY	Who (Polydor)
7	15	SOUL MOTION	Various Artists (K-Tel)
18	16	CHICAGO X	Chicago (CBS)
17	17	FOREVER AND EVER	Demis Roussos (Philips)
14	18	THE BEST OF THE STYLISTICS VOL.2	Stylistics (Avco)
15	19	FRAMPTON COMES ALIVE	Peter Frampton (A&M)
29	20	DAVID SOUL	David Soul (Private Stock)
22	21	A LITTLE BIT MORE	Dr. Hook (Capitol)
-	22	THOUGHTS OF LOVE	Shirley Bassey (United Artists)
-	23	ENDLESS FLIGHT	Leo Sayer (Chrysalis)
19	24	SOUNDS OF GLORY	Various Artists (Arcade)
-	25	JOHNNY THE FOX	Thin Lizzy (Vertigo)
26	26	A NEW WORLD RECORD	Electric Light Orchestra (Jet)
24	27	A NIGHT ON THE TOWN	Rod Stewart (Riva)
21	28	ALL THIS AND WORLD WAR II	Various Artists (Riva)
25	29	ATLANTIC CROSSING	Rod Stewart (Warner Bros.)
23	30	FLEETWOOD MAC	Fleetwood Mac (Reprise)

18 December 1976

last	this	Album	Artist (Label)
1	1	20 GOLDEN GREATS	Glen Campbell (Capitol)
2	2	ARRIVAL	Abba (Epic)
5	3	BERT WEEDON'S 22 GOLDEN GUITAR GREATS	Bert Weedon (Warwick)
7	4	FRANKIE VALLI & THE FOUR SEASONS' GREATEST HITS	Frankie Valli & the Four Seasons (K-Tel)
4	5	100 GOLDEN GREATS	Max Bygraves (Ronco)
3	6	SONGS IN THE KEY OF LIFE	Stevie Wonder (Tamla Motown)
6	7	GREATEST HITS	Abba (Epic)
12	8	DISCO ROCKET	Various Artists (K-Tel)
26	9	A NEW WORLD RECORD	Electric Light Orchestra (Jet)
8	10	HOT CHOCOLATE'S GREATEST HITS	Hot Chocolate (RAK)
20	11	DAVID SOUL	David Soul (Private Stock)
-	12	A DAY AT THE RACES	Queen (EMI)
9	13	BLUE MOVES	Elton John (Rocket)
14	14	THE WHO STORY	Who (Polydor)
17	15	FOREVER AND EVER	Demis Roussos (Philips)
10	16	20 ORIGINAL DEAN MARTIN HITS	Dean Martin (Reprise)
22	17	THOUGHTS OF LOVE	Shirley Bassey (United Artists)
11	18	THE SONG REMAINS THE SAME	Led Zeppelin (Swansong)
18	19	THE BEST OF THE STYLISTICS VOL.2	Stylistics (Avco)
15	20	SOUL MOTION	Various Artists (K-Tel)
21	21	A LITTLE BIT MORE	Dr. Hook (Capitol)
19	22	FRAMPTON COMES ALIVE	Peter Frampton (A&M)
-	23	DEREK AND CLIVE LIVE	Peter Cook & Dudley Moore (Island)
-	24	SHOWADDYWADDY'S GREATEST HITS	Showaddywaddy (Arista)
-	25	THE INCREDIBLE PLAN	Max Boyce (EMI)
16	26	CHICAGO X	Chicago (CBS)
28	27	ALL THIS AND WORLD WAR II	Various Artists (Riva)
24	28	SOUNDS OF GLORY	Various Artists (Arcade)
23	29	ENDLESS FLIGHT	Leo Sayer (Chrysalis)
27	30	A NIGHT ON THE TOWN	Rod Stewart (Riva)

25 December 1976

last	this	Album	Artist (Label)
2	1	ARRIVAL	Abba (Epic)
1	2	20 GOLDEN GREATS	Glen Campbell (Capitol)
6	3	SONGS IN THE KEY OF LIFE	Stevie Wonder (Tamla Motown)
5	4	100 GOLDEN GREATS	Max Bygraves (Ronco)
4	5	FRANKIE VALLI & THE FOUR SEASONS' GREATEST HITS	Frankie Valli & the Four Seasons (K-Tel)
12	6	A DAY AT THE RACES	Queen (EMI)
7	7	GREATEST HITS	Abba (Epic)
3	8	22 GOLDEN GUITAR GREATS	Bert Weedon (Warwick)
9	9	A NEW WORLD RECORD	Electric Light Orchestra (Jet)
11	10	DAVID SOUL	David Soul (Private Stock)
8	11	DISCO ROCKET	Various Artists (K-Tel)
10	12	HOT CHOCOLATE'S GREATEST HITS	Hot Chocolate (RAK)
13	13	BLUE MOVES	Elton John (Rocket)
24	14	SHOWADDYWADDY'S GREATEST HITS	Showaddywaddy (Arista)
14	15	THE WHO STORY	Who (Polydor)
16	16	20 ORIGINAL DEAN MARTIN HITS	Dean Martin (Reprise)
17	17	THOUGHTS OF LOVE	Shirley Bassey (United Artists)
15	18	FOREVER AND EVER	Demis Roussos (Philips)
-	19	HOTEL CALIFORNIA	Eagles (Asylum)
19	20	THE BEST OF THE STYLISTICS VOL.2	Stylistics (Avco)
-	21	GILBERT O'SULLIVAN'S GREATEST HITS	Gilbert O'Sullivan (MAM)
18	22	THE SONG REMAINS THE SAME	Led Zeppelin (Swansong)
22	23	FRAMPTON COMES ALIVE	Peter Frampton (A&M)
-	24	SOME MORE OF ME POEMS AND SONGS	Pam Ayres (Galaxy)
21	25	A LITTLE BIT MORE	Dr. Hook (Capitol)
-	26	44 SUPERSTARS	Various Artists (K-Tel)
20	27	SOUL MOTION	Various Artists (K-Tel)
30	28	A NIGHT ON THE TOWN	Rod Stewart (Riva)
-	29	ATLANTIC BRIDGE	Billy Connolly (Polydor)
23	30	DEREK AND CLIVE LIVE	Peter Cook & Dudley Moore (Island)

Signs were abroad that rock's rococo period was doomed. Elton John's two latest albums, the live *Here And There* and the studio-cut *Blue Moves*, had done hopelessly badly by his sales standards, while a live album of crude pub-rock, *Stupidity* by Dr Feelgood (fronted by guitar-ace Wilko Johnson and vocalist Lee Brilleaux) had reached No.1 in every chart but the NME's. September had seen a two-day "punk" festival at London's 100 Club, with debuts by the Clash, Buzzcocks, Siouxsie & the Banshees (including Sid Vicious), the Damned, Vibrators and... the Sex Pistols. In December, TV's Bill Grundy made the Pistols national heroes of unwholesomeness, and they made their single *Anarchy In The UK*.

8 January 1977

last week	this week	Title / Artist (Label)
1	1	ARRIVAL — Abba (Epic)
3	2	SONGS IN THE KEY OF LIFE — Stevie Wonder (Tamla Motown)
2	3	20 GOLDEN GREATS — Glen Campbell (Capitol)
14	4	SHOWADDYWADDY'S GREATEST HITS — Showaddywaddy (Arista)
6	5	A DAY AT THE RACES — Queen (EMI)
4	6	100 GOLDEN GREATS — Max Bygraves (Ronco)
11	7	DISCO ROCKET — Various Artists (K-Tel)
7	8	GREATEST HITS — Abba (Epic)
5	9	FRANKIE VALLI & THE FOUR SEASONS' GREATEST HITS — Frankie Valli & the Four Seasons (K-Tel)
9	10	A NEW WORLD RECORD — Electric Light Orchestra (Jet)
10	11	DAVID SOUL — David Soul (Private Stock)
19	12	HOTEL CALIFORNIA — Eagles (Asylum)
8	13	BERT WEEDON'S 22 GOLDEN GUITAR GREATS — Bert Weedon (Warwick)
13	14	BLUE MOVES — Elton John (Rocket)
12	15	HOT CHOCOLATE'S GREATEST HITS — Hot Chocolate (RAK)
17	16	THOUGHTS OF LOVE — Shirley Bassey (United Artists)
15	17	THE WHO STORY — Who (Polydor)
21	18	GILBERT O'SULLIVAN'S GREATEST HITS — Gilbert O'Sullivan (MAM)
24	19	SOME MORE OF ME POEMS AND SONGS — Pam Ayres (Galaxy)
16	20	20 ORIGINAL DEAN MARTIN HITS — Dean Martin (Reprise)
-	21	WINGS OVER AMERICA — Wings (EMI)
22	22	THE SONG REMAINS THE SAME — Led Zeppelin (Swan Song)
18	23	FOREVER AND EVER — Demis Roussos (Philips)
20	24	BEST OF THE STYLISTICS VOL 2 — Stylistics (Avco)
-	25	THIRTY THREE AND A THIRD — George Harrison (Dark Horse)
-	26	ATLANTIC CROSSING — Rod Stewart (Warner Bros.)
-	27	SOUNDS OF GLORY — Various Artists (Arcade)
26	28	44 SUPERSTARS — Various Artists (K-Tel)
29	29	ATLANTIC BRIDGE — Billy Connolly (Polydor)
-	30	BOXED — Mike Oldfield (Virgin)

15 January 1977

this week	Title / Artist (Label)
1	ARRIVAL — Abba (Epic)
2	A DAY AT THE RACES — Queen (EMI)
3	DAVID SOUL — David Soul (Private Stock)
4	GREATEST HITS — Abba (Epic)
5	SONGS IN THE KEY OF LIFE — Stevie Wonder (Tamla Motown)
6	HOTEL CALIFORNIA — Eagles (Asylum)
7	SHOWADDYWADDY'S GREATEST HITS — Showaddywaddy (Arista)
8	A NEW WORLD RECORD — Electric Light Orchestra (Jet)
9	20 GOLDEN GREATS — Glen Campbell (Capitol)
10	RED RIVER VALLEY — Slim Whitman (United Artists)
11	MAX BYGRAVES' 100 GOLDEN GREATS — Max Bygraves (Ronco)
12	FRANKIE VALLI & THE FOUR SEASONS' GREATEST HITS — Frankie Valli & the Four Seasons (K-Tel)
13	WINGS OVER AMERICA — Wings (EMI)
14	DISCO ROCKET — Various Artists (K-Tel)
15	THOUGHTS OF LOVE — Shirley Bassey (United Artists)
16	HOT CHOCOLATE'S GREATEST HITS — Hot Chocolate (RAK)
17	GILBERT O'SULLIVAN'S GREATEST HITS — Gilbert O'Sullivan (MAM)
18	BLUE MOVES — Elton John (Rocket)
19	BOXED — Mike Oldfield (Virgin)
20	I ONLY HAVE EYES FOR YOU — Johnny Mathis (CBS)
21	BERT WEEDON'S 22 GOLDEN GUITAR GREATS — Bert Weedon (Warwick)
22	BEST OF THE STYLISTICS VOL 2 — Stylistics (Avco)
23	THE WHO STORY — Who (Polydor)
24	WIND AND WUTHERING — Genesis (Charisma)
25	SOME MORE OF ME POEMS AND SONGS — Pam Ayres (Galaxy)
26	FOREVER AND EVER — Demis Roussos (Philips)
27	EVITA — Various Artists (MCA)
28	44 SUPERSTARS — Various Artists (K-Tel)
29	GREATEST HITS — Linda Ronstadt (Asylum)
30	THE SONG REMAINS THE SAME — Led Zeppelin (Swan Song)

22 January 1977

this week	Title / Artist (Label)
1	RED RIVER VALLEY — Slim Whitman (United Artists)
2	ARRIVAL — Abba (Epic)
3	A DAY AT THE RACES — Queen (EMI)
4	HOTEL CALIFORNIA — Eagles (Asylum)
5	DAVID SOUL — David Soul (Private Stock)
6	SONGS IN THE KEY OF LIFE — Stevie Wonder (Tamla Motown)
7	GREATEST HITS — Abba (Epic)
8	SHOWADDYWADDY'S GREATEST HITS — Showaddywaddy (Arista)
9	WINGS OVER AMERICA — Wings (EMI)
10	WIND AND WUTHERING — Genesis (Charisma)
11	FRANKIE VALLI & THE FOUR SEASONS' GREATEST HITS — Frankie Valli & the Four Seasons (K-Tel)
12	A NEW WORLD RECORD — Electric Light Orchestra (Jet)
13	DISCO ROCKET — Various Artists (K-Tel)
14	100 GOLDEN GREATS — Max Bygraves (Ronco)
15	20 GOLDEN GREATS — Glen Campbell (Capitol)
16	HOT CHOCOLATE'S GREATEST HITS — Hot Chocolate (RAK)
17	EVITA — Various Artists (MCA)
18	GILBERT O'SULLIVAN'S GREATEST HITS — Gilbert O'Sullivan (MAM)
19	BLUE MOVES — Elton John (Rocket)
20	44 SUPERSTARS — Various Artists (K-Tel)
21	FOREVER AND EVER — Demis Roussos (Philips)
22	THEIR GREATEST HITS 1971-1975 — Eagles (Asylum)
23	BOXED — Mike Oldfield (Virgin)
24	LOW — David Bowie (RCA)
25	THE WHO STORY — Who (Polydor)
26	DIANA ROSS GREATEST HITS 2 — Diana Ross (Tamla Motown)
27	SOUL MOTION — Various Artists (K-Tel)
28	BEST OF THE STYLISTICS VOL 2 — Stylistics (Avco)
29	ATLANTIC CROSSING — Rod Stewart (Warner Bros.)
30	BERT WEEDON'S 22 GOLDEN GUITAR GREATS — Bert Weedon (Warwick)

29 January 1977

this week	Title / Artist (Label)
1	RED RIVER VALLEY — Slim Whitman (United Artists)
2	DAVID SOUL — David Soul (Private Stock)
3	ARRIVAL — Abba (Epic)
4	HOTEL CALIFORNIA — Eagles (Asylum)
5	A DAY AT THE RACES — Queen (EMI)
6	GREATEST HITS — Abba (Epic)
7	SONGS IN THE KEY OF LIFE — Stevie Wonder (Tamla Motown)
8	WIND AND WUTHERING — Genesis (Charisma)
9	WINGS OVER AMERICA — Wings (EMI)
10	SHOWADDYWADDY'S GREATEST HITS — Showaddywaddy (Arista)
11	EVITA — Various Artists (MCA)
12	A NEW WORLD RECORD — Electric Light Orchestra (Jet)
13	20 GOLDEN GREATS — Glen Campbell (Capitol)
14	DISCO ROCKET — Various Artists (K-Tel)
15	LOW — David Bowie (RCA)
16	FRANKIE VALLI & THE FOUR SEASONS' GREATEST HITS — Frankie Valli & the Four Seasons (K-Tel)
17	HOT CHOCOLATE'S GREATEST HITS — Hot Chocolate (RAK)
18	ENDLESS FLIGHT — Leo Sayer (Chrysalis)
19	A NIGHT ON THE TOWN — Rod Stewart (Riva)
20	100 GOLDEN GREATS — Max Bygraves (Ronco)
21	GILBERT O'SULLIVAN'S GREATEST HITS — Gilbert O'Sullivan (MAM)
22	THE SONG REMAINS THE SAME — Led Zeppelin (Swan Song)
23	BLUE MOVES — Elton John (Rocket)
24	I ONLY HAVE EYES FOR YOU — Johnny Mathis (CBS)
25	ATLANTIC CROSSING — Rod Stewart (Warner Bros.)
26	THE WHO STORY — Who (Polydor)
27	THOUGHTS OF LOVE — Shirley Bassey (United Artists)
28	FOREVER AND EVER — Demis Roussos (Philips)
29	LOST WITHOUT YOUR LOVE — Bread (Elektra)
30	SOUL MOTION — Various Artists (K-Tel)

Bert Weedon had reached No.3! In 1976! So for everyone who remembered the guitar world of Britain 1959-1961, where was Max Harris' Greatest Hits? Where was The Best Of Wout Steenhuis? Rhet Stoller's 22 Golden Greats? The punters of 1977 could have charted them alongside Max Bygraves' *100 Golden Greats* - his last real hit (an aberrational 1973 *Deck Of Cards* aside) had been in 1960 - and Slim Whitman's *Red River Valley*; HIS last real hit (1974's *Happy Anniversary* aside) had been in 1957.

February 1977

last week	this week	5 February 1977
1	1	RED RIVER VALLEY — Slim Whitman (United Artists)
2	2	DAVID SOUL — David Soul (Private Stock)
7	3	SONGS IN THE KEY OF LIFE — Stevie Wonder (Tamla Motown)
3	4	ARRIVAL — Abba (Epic)
4	5	HOTEL CALIFORNIA — Eagles (Asylum)
11	6	EVITA — Various Artists (MCA)
6	7	GREATEST HITS — Abba (Epic)
9	8	WINGS OVER AMERICA — Wings (EMI)
8	9	WIND AND WUTHERING — Genesis (Charisma)
10	10	SHOWADDYWADDY'S GREATEST HITS — Showaddywaddy (Arista)
5	11	A DAY AT THE RACES — Queen (EMI)
12	12	A NEW WORLD RECORD — Electric Light Orchestra (Jet)
15	13	LOW — David Bowie (RCA)
14	14	DISCO ROCKET — Various Artists (K-Tel)
18	15	ENDLESS FLIGHT — Leo Sayer (Chrysalis)
16	16	FRANKIE VALLI & THE FOUR SEASONS' GREATEST HITS — Frankie Valli & the Four Seasons (K-Tel)
-	17	THEIR GREATEST HITS 1971–1975 — Eagles (Asylum)
17	18	HOT CHOCOLATE'S GREATEST HITS — Hot Chocolate (RAK)
-	19	JOHNNY THE FOX — Thin Lizzy (Vertigo)
13	20	20 GOLDEN GREATS — Glen Campbell (Capitol)
20	21	100 GOLDEN GREATS — Max Bygraves (Ronco)
-	22	LOVE ON THE AIRWAVES — Gallagher & Lyle (A&M)
29	23	LOST WITHOUT YOUR LOVE — Bread (Elektra)
-	24	MOTORVATIN' — Chuck Berry (Chess)
21	25	GILBERT O'SULLIVAN'S GREATEST HITS — Gilbert O'Sullivan (MAM)
-	26	WHITE ROCK — Rick Wakeman (A&M)
-	27	BOXED — Mike Oldfield (Virgin)
-	28	20 GOLDEN GREATS — Shadows (EMI)
25	29	ATLANTIC CROSSING — Rod Stewart (Warner Bros.)
27	30	THOUGHTS OF LOVE — Shirley Bassey (United Artists)

last	this	12 February 1977
1	1	RED RIVER VALLEY — Slim Whitman (United Artists)
6	2	EVITA — Various Artists (MCA)
2	3	DAVID SOUL — David Soul (Private Stock)
4	4	ARRIVAL — Abba (Epic)
3	5	SONGS IN THE KEY OF LIFE — Stevie Wonder (Tamla Motown)
5	6	HOTEL CALIFORNIA — Eagles (Asylum)
15	7	ENDLESS FLIGHT — Leo Sayer (Chrysalis)
8	8	WINGS OVER AMERICA — Wings (EMI)
13	9	LOW — David Bowie (RCA)
28	10	20 GOLDEN GREATS — Shadows (EMI)
7	11	GREATEST HITS — Abba (Epic)
11	12	A DAY AT THE RACES — Queen (EMI)
-	13	ANIMALS — Pink Floyd (Harvest)
10	14	SHOWADDYWADDY'S GREATEST HITS — Showaddywaddy (Arista)
12	15	A NEW WORLD RECORD — Electric Light Orchestra (Jet)
9	16	WIND AND WUTHERING — Genesis (Charisma)
-	17	20 GREAT HEARTBREAKERS — Various Artists (K-Tel)
14	18	DISCO ROCKET — Various Artists (K-Tel)
19	19	JOHNNY THE FOX — Thin Lizzy (Vertigo)
17	20	THEIR GREATEST HITS 1971–1975 — Eagles (Asylum)
24	21	MOTORVATIN' — Chuck Berry (Chess)
16	22	FRANKIE VALLI & THE FOUR SEASONS' GREATEST HITS — Frankie Valli & the Four Seasons (K-Tel)
23	23	LOST WITHOUT YOUR LOVE — Bread (Elektra)
-	24	LUXURY LINER — Emmylou Harris (Warner Bros.)
26	25	WHITE ROCK — Rick Wakeman (A&M)
22	26	LOVE ON THE AIRWAVES — Gallagher & Lyle (A&M)
-	27	DANCE TO THE MUSIC — Various Artists (K-Tel)
-	28	BOSTON — Boston (Epic)
21	29	100 GOLDEN GREATS — Max Bygraves (Ronco)
-	30	YEAR OF THE CAT — Al Stewart (RCA)

last	this	19 February 1977
2	1	EVITA — Various Artists (MCA)
3	2	DAVID SOUL — David Soul (Private Stock)
10	3	20 GOLDEN GREATS — Shadows (EMI)
1	4	RED RIVER VALLEY — Slim Whitman (United Artists)
7	5	ENDLESS FLIGHT — Leo Sayer (Chrysalis)
4	6	ARRIVAL — Abba (Epic)
5	7	SONGS IN THE KEY OF LIFE — Stevie Wonder (Tamla Motown)
9	8	LOW — David Bowie (RCA)
6	9	HOTEL CALIFORNIA — Eagles (Asylum)
13	10	ANIMALS — Pink Floyd (Harvest)
8	11	WINGS OVER AMERICA — Wings (EMI)
11	12	GREATEST HITS — Abba (Epic)
25	13	WHITE ROCK — Rick Wakeman (A&M)
17	14	20 GREAT HEARTBREAKERS — Various Artists (K-Tel)
21	15	MOTORVATIN' — Chuck Berry (Chess)
14	16	SHOWADDYWADDY'S GREATEST HITS — Showaddywaddy (Arista)
16	17	WIND AND WUTHERING — Genesis (Charisma)
12	18	A DAY AT THE RACES — Queen (EMI)
15	19	A NEW WORLD RECORD — Electric Light Orchestra (Jet)
28	20	BOSTON — Boston (Epic)
23	21	LOST WITHOUT YOUR LOVE — Bread (Elektra)
27	22	DANCE TO THE MUSIC — Various Artists (K-Tel)
24	23	LUXURY LINER — Emmylou Harris (Warner Bros.)
26	24	LOVE ON THE AIRWAVES — Gallagher & Lyle (A&M)
19	25	JOHNNY THE FOX — Thin Lizzy (Vertigo)
22	26	FRANKIE VALLI & THE FOUR SEASONS' GREATEST HITS — Frankie Valli & the Four Seasons (K-Tel)
-	27	FESTIVAL — Santana (CBS)
20	28	THEIR GREATEST HITS 1971–1975 — Eagles (Asylum)
-	29	20 GOLDEN GREATS — Glen Campbell (Capitol)
-	30	GILBERT O'SULLIVAN'S GREATEST HITS — Gilbert O'Sullivan (MAM)

last	this	26 February 1977
3	1	20 GOLDEN GREATS — Shadows (EMI)
10	2	ANIMALS — Pink Floyd (Harvest)
1	3	EVITA — Various Artists (MCA)
5	4	ENDLESS FLIGHT — Leo Sayer (Chrysalis)
2	5	DAVID SOUL — David Soul (Private Stock)
14	6	20 GREAT HEARTBREAKERS — Various Artists (K-Tel)
7	7	SONGS IN THE KEY OF LIFE — Stevie Wonder (Tamla Motown)
9	8	HOTEL CALIFORNIA — Eagles (Asylum)
4	9	RED RIVER VALLEY — Slim Whitman (United Artists)
8	10	LOW — David Bowie (RCA)
6	11	ARRIVAL — Abba (Epic)
15	12	MOTORVATIN' — Chuck Berry (Chess)
12	13	GREATEST HITS — Abba (Epic)
11	14	WINGS OVER AMERICA — Wings (EMI)
19	15	A NEW WORLD RECORD — Electric Light Orchestra (Jet)
20	16	BOSTON — Boston (Epic)
22	17	DANCE TO THE MUSIC — Various Artists (K-Tel)
-	18	SONGS FROM THE WOOD — Jethro Tull (Chrysalis)
17	19	WIND AND WUTHERING — Genesis (Charisma)
13	20	WHITE ROCK — Rick Wakeman (A&M)
25	21	JOHNNY THE FOX — Thin Lizzy (Vertigo)
18	22	A DAY AT THE RACES — Queen (EMI)
-	23	DOWNTOWN TONIGHT — Racing Cars (Chrysalis)
-	24	BERT WEEDON'S 22 GOLDEN GUITAR GREATS — Bert Weedon (Warwick)
16	25	SHOWADDYWADDY'S GREATEST HITS — Showaddywaddy (Arista)
24	26	LOVE ON THE AIRWAVES — Gallagher & Lyle (A&M)
21	27	LOST WITHOUT YOUR LOVE — Bread (Elektra)
-	28	IN YOUR MIND — Bryan Ferry (Polydor)
23	29	LUXURY LINER — Emmylou Harris (Warner Bros.)
-	30	RUMOURS — Fleetwood Mac (Warner Bros.)

David Soul, of TV cop series *Starsky & Hutch*, topped the singles chart with UK million-seller *Don't Give Up On Us*. Hence his Top 3 album. No surprise either to see the 7th Genesis album, *Wind And Wuthering*, in the Top 10, though it had charted only in January and was already falling. Their first hit LPs had been 1972's *Foxtrot* and 1973's *Genesis Live* and *Selling England By The Pound*. 1974's *Nursery Cryme* had flopped. Their biggest LPs were to be from 1978 onwards.

March 1977

Chuck Berry *Motorvatin'* up into the Top 10 WAS a surprise: the album was on a real label, the legendary Chicago blues label Chess, no hit single fuelled Chuck's ride up the album chart, and he'd had no hit album since 1964's non-Top 10er *You Never Can Tell*. His endless fund of classic rock and roll songs, however, had never ceased to give others chart material, including on the Beatles' hit compilation album of 1976, *Rock'N'Roll Music*, itself a Chuck Berry song-title.

April 1977

2 April 1977

LW	TW	Title	Artist (Label)
1	1	20 GOLDEN GREATS	Shadows (EMI)
3	2	PORTRAIT OF SINATRA	Frank Sinatra (Reprise)
2	3	ARRIVAL	Abba (Epic)
4	4	ANIMALS	Pink Floyd (Harvest)
5	5	ENDLESS FLIGHT	Leo Sayer (Chrysalis)
12	6	COMING OUT	Manhattan Transfer (Atlantic)
17	7	HOLLIES LIVE HITS	Hollies (Polydor)
7	8	STATUS QUO LIVE	Status Quo (Vertigo)
8	9	IN YOUR MIND	Bryan Ferry (Polydor)
6	10	20 GREAT HEARTBREAKERS	Various Artists (K-Tel)
9	11	EVITA	Various Artists (MCA)
13	12	GREATEST HITS	Abba (Epic)
11	13	RUMOURS	Fleetwood Mac (Warner Bros.)
10	14	LOW	David Bowie (RCA)
15	15	A NEW WORLD RECORD	Electric Light Orchestra (Jet)
14	16	PETER GABRIEL	Peter Gabriel (Charisma)
20	17	DAVID SOUL	David Soul (Private Stock)
23	18	EVERY FACE TELLS A STORY	Cliff Richard (EMI)
19	19	HOTEL CALIFORNIA	Eagles (Asylum)
27	20	BURNIN' SKY	Bad Company (Island)
26	21	THE BEST OF LENA MARTELL	Lena Martell (Pye)
16	22	SONGS IN THE KEY OF LIFE	Stevie Wonder (Tamla Motown)
30	23	RED RIVER VALLEY	Slim Whitman (United Artists)
24	24	THE BEST OF JOHN DENVER VOL.2	John Denver (RCA)
25	25	SONGS FROM THE WOOD	Jethro Tull (Chrysalis)
29	26	BOSTON	Boston (Epic)
18	27	VISIONS	Don Williams (ABC)
-	28	WORKS	Emerson Lake & Palmer (Manticore)
-	29	KIKI DEE	Kiki Dee (Rocket)
-	30	MARQUEE MOON	Television (Elektra)

9 April 1977

LW	TW	Title	Artist (Label)
2	1	PORTRAIT OF SINATRA	Frank Sinatra (Reprise)
3	2	ARRIVAL	Abba (Epic)
1	3	20 GOLDEN GREATS	Shadows (EMI)
5	4	ENDLESS FLIGHT	Leo Sayer (Chrysalis)
8	5	STATUS QUO LIVE	Status Quo (Vertigo)
4	6	ANIMALS	Pink Floyd (Harvest)
7	7	HOLLIES LIVE HITS	Hollies (Polydor)
12	8	GREATEST HITS	Abba (Epic)
6	9	COMING OUT	Manhattan Transfer (Atlantic)
13	10	RUMOURS	Fleetwood Mac (Warner Bros.)
11	11	EVITA	Various Artists (MCA)
18	12	EVERY FACE TELLS A STORY	Cliff Richard (EMI)
10	13	20 GREAT HEARTBREAKERS	Various Artists (K-Tel)
15	14	A NEW WORLD RECORD	Electric Light Orchestra (Jet)
16	15	PETER GABRIEL	Peter Gabriel (Charisma)
9	16	IN YOUR MIND	Bryan Ferry (Polydor)
14	17	LOW	David Bowie (RCA)
24	18	THE BEST OF JOHN DENVER VOL.2	John Denver (RCA)
19	19	HOTEL CALIFORNIA	Eagles (Asylum)
21	20	THE BEST OF LENA MARTELL	Lena Martell (Pye)
28	21	WORKS	Emerson Lake & Palmer (Manticore)
17	22	DAVID SOUL	David Soul (Private Stock)
22	23	SONGS IN THE KEY OF LIFE	Stevie Wonder (Tamla Motown)
20	24	BURNIN' SKY	Bad Company (Island)
-	25	THE UNFORGETTABLE GLENN MILLER	Glenn Miller (RCA)
30	26	MARQUEE MOON	Television (Elektra)
25	27	SONGS FROM THE WOOD	Jethro Tull (Chrysalis)
-	28	DAMNED DAMNED DAMNED	Damned (Stiff)
23	29	RED RIVER VALLEY	Slim Whitman (United Artists)
26	30	BOSTON	Boston (Epic)

16 April 1977

LW	TW	Title	Artist (Label)
2	1	ARRIVAL	Abba (Epic)
4	2	ENDLESS FLIGHT	Leo Sayer (Chrysalis)
1	3	PORTRAIT OF SINATRA	Frank Sinatra (Reprise)
3	4	20 GOLDEN GREATS	Shadows (EMI)
7	5	HOLLIES LIVE HITS	Hollies (Polydor)
6	6	ANIMALS	Pink Floyd (Harvest)
9	7	COMING OUT	Manhattan Transfer (Atlantic)
10	8	RUMOURS	Fleetwood Mac (Warner Bros.)
8	9	GREATEST HITS	Abba (Epic)
5	10	STATUS QUO LIVE	Status Quo (Vertigo)
12	11	EVERY FACE TELLS A STORY	Cliff Richard (EMI)
11	12	EVITA	Various Artists (MCA)
18	13	THE BEST OF JOHN DENVER VOL.2	John Denver (RCA)
21	14	WORKS	Emerson Lake & Palmer (Manticore)
16	15	IN YOUR MIND	Bryan Ferry (Polydor)
15	16	PETER GABRIEL	Peter Gabriel (Charisma)
13	17	20 GREAT HEARTBREAKERS	Various Artists (K-Tel)
14	18	A NEW WORLD RECORD	Electric Light Orchestra (Jet)
22	19	DAVID SOUL	David Soul (Private Stock)
17	20	LOW	David Bowie (RCA)
25	21	THE UNFORGETTABLE GLENN MILLER	Glenn Miller (RCA)
-	22	A STAR IS BORN	Soundtrack (CBS)
19	23	HOTEL CALIFORNIA	Eagles (Asylum)
-	24	BARRY WHITE'S GREATEST HITS VOL 2	Barry White (20th Century)
23	25	SONGS IN THE KEY OF LIFE	Stevie Wonder (Tamla Motown)
24	26	BURNIN' SKY	Bad Company (Island)
-	27	LIVING LEGENDS	Everly Brothers (Warwick)
30	28	BOSTON	Boston (Epic)
-	29	DANDY IN THE UNDERWORLD	T. Rex (EMI)
28	30	DAMNED DAMNED DAMNED	Damned (Stiff)

23 April 1977

LW	TW	Title	Artist (Label)
1	1	ARRIVAL	Abba (Epic)
2	2	ENDLESS FLIGHT	Leo Sayer (Chrysalis)
3	3	PORTRAIT OF SINATRA	Frank Sinatra (Reprise)
4	4	20 GOLDEN GREATS	Shadows (EMI)
5	5	HOLLIES LIVE HITS	Hollies (Polydor)
6	6	ANIMALS	Pink Floyd (Harvest)
14	7	WORKS	Emerson Lake & Palmer (Manticore)
9	8	GREATEST HITS	Abba (Epic)
8	9	RUMOURS	Fleetwood Mac (Warner Bros.)
10	10	STATUS QUO LIVE	Status Quo (Vertigo)
16	11	PETER GABRIEL	Peter Gabriel (Charisma)
23	12	HOTEL CALIFORNIA	Eagles (Asylum)
7	13	COMING OUT	Manhattan Transfer (Atlantic)
21	14	THE UNFORGETTABLE GLENN MILLER	Glenn Miller (RCA)
18	15	A NEW WORLD RECORD	Electric Light Orchestra (Jet)
11	16	EVERY FACE TELLS A STORY	Cliff Richard (EMI)
11	17	EVITA	Various Artists (MCA)
22	18	A STAR IS BORN	Soundtrack (CBS)
20	19	LOW	David Bowie (RCA)
13	20	THE BEST OF JOHN DENVER VOL.2	John Denver (RCA)
25	21	SONGS IN THE KEY OF LIFE	Stevie Wonder (Tamla Motown)
24	22	BARRY WHITE'S GREATEST HITS VOL 2	Barry White (20th Century)
15	23	IN YOUR MIND	Bryan Ferry (Polydor)
19	24	DAVID SOUL	David Soul (Private Stock)
-	25	THE CLASH	Clash (CBS)
26	26	BURNIN' SKY	Bad Company (Island)
-	27	SMOKIE'S GREATEST HITS	Smokie (RAK)
27	28	LIVING LEGENDS	Everly Brothers (Warwick)
17	29	20 GREAT HEARTBREAKERS	Various Artists (K-Tel)
-	30	THE MAGIC OF DEMIS ROUSSOS	Demis Roussos (Philips)

Fleetwood Mac's *Rumours* was making an unobtrusive start to its long career: eventually 440-odd weeks in the Top 100, thus beating even *Dark Side Of The Moon* by Pink Floyd; their *Animals*, still in the Top 10 after peaking at No.2 in March, was their 11th hit LP. Floyd hadn't bothered with hit singles since *See Emily Play*, ten years earlier. Another huge UK band, Jethro Tull, were struggling with THEIR 11th Top 30 album, *Songs From The Wood*, but had recently had an EP in the singles chart.

30 April 1977

last week	this week	Album / Artist (Label)
1	1	ARRIVAL — Abba (Epic)
2	2	ENDLESS FLIGHT — Leo Sayer (Chrysalis)
3	3	PORTRAIT OF SINATRA — Frank Sinatra (Reprise)
4	4	20 GOLDEN GREATS — Shadows (EMI)
8	5	GREATEST HITS — Abba (Epic)
12	6	HOTEL CALIFORNIA — Eagles (Asylum)
6	7	ANIMALS — Pink Floyd (Harvest)
14	8	THE UNFORGETTABLE GLENN MILLER — Glenn Miller (RCA)
5	9	HOLLIES LIVE HITS — Hollies (Polydor)
7	10	WORKS — Emerson Lake & Palmer (Manticore)
18	11	A STAR IS BORN — Soundtrack (CBS)
9	12	RUMOURS — Fleetwood Mac (Warner Bros.)
11	13	PETER GABRIEL — Peter Gabriel (Charisma)
10	14	STATUS QUO LIVE — Status Quo (Vertigo)
21	15	SONGS IN THE KEY OF LIFE — Stevie Wonder (Tamla Motown)
17	16	EVITA — Various Artists (MCA)
15	17	A NEW WORLD RECORD — Electric Light Orchestra (Jet)
16	18	EVERY FACE TELLS A STORY — Cliff Richard (EMI)
30	19	THE MAGIC OF DEMIS ROUSSOS — Demis Roussos (Philips)
27	20	SMOKIE'S GREATEST HITS — Smokie (RAK)
28	21	LIVING LEGENDS — Everly Brothers (Warwick)
22	22	BARRY WHITE'S GREATEST HITS VOL 2 — Barry White (20th Century)
20	23	THE BEST OF JOHN DENVER VOL.2 — John Denver (RCA)
19	24	LOW — David Bowie (RCA)
-	25	EVEN IN THE QUIETEST MOMENTS — Supertramp (A&M)
13	26	COMING OUT — Manhattan Transfer (Atlantic)
-	27	SHOWADDYWADDY'S GREATEST HITS — Showaddywaddy (Arista)
25	28	THE CLASH — Clash (CBS)
24	29	DAVID SOUL — David Soul (Private Stock)
23	30	IN YOUR MIND — Bryan Ferry (Polydor)

7 May 1977

last week	this week	Album / Artist (Label)
1	1	ARRIVAL — Abba (Epic)
6	2	HOTEL CALIFORNIA — Eagles (Asylum)
3	3	PORTRAIT OF SINATRA — Frank Sinatra (Reprise)
2	4	ENDLESS FLIGHT — Leo Sayer (Chrysalis)
5	5	GREATEST HITS — Abba (Epic)
12	6	RUMOURS — Fleetwood Mac (Warner Bros.)
4	7	20 GOLDEN GREATS — Shadows (EMI)
9	8	HOLLIES LIVE HITS — Hollies (Polydor)
20	9	SMOKIE'S GREATEST HITS — Smokie (RAK)
7	10	ANIMALS — Pink Floyd (Harvest)
11	11	A STAR IS BORN — Soundtrack (CBS)
8	12	THE UNFORGETTABLE GLENN MILLER — Glenn Miller (RCA)
10	13	WORKS — Emerson Lake & Palmer (Manticore)
25	14	EVEN IN THE QUIETEST MOMENTS — Supertramp (A&M)
21	15	LIVING LEGENDS — Everly Brothers (Warwick)
15	16	SONGS IN THE KEY OF LIFE — Stevie Wonder (Tamla Motown)
13	17	PETER GABRIEL — Peter Gabriel (Charisma)
14	18	STATUS QUO LIVE — Status Quo (Vertigo)
17	19	A NEW WORLD RECORD — Electric Light Orchestra (Jet)
28	20	THE CLASH — Clash (CBS)
-	21	STRANGLERS IV (RATTUS NORVEGICUS) — Stranglers (United Artists)
18	22	EVERY FACE TELLS A STORY — Cliff Richard (EMI)
-	23	DECEPTIVE BENDS — 10 C.C. (Philips)
22	24	BARRY WHITE'S GREATEST HITS VOL 2 — Barry White (20th Century)
19	25	THE MAGIC OF DEMIS ROUSSOS — Demis Roussos (Philips)
23	26	THE BEST OF JOHN DENVER VOL.2 — John Denver (RCA)
27	27	THEIR GREATEST HITS 1971–1975 — Eagles (Asylum)
16	28	EVITA — Various Artists (MCA)
29	29	DAVID SOUL — David Soul (Private Stock)
26	30	COMING OUT — Manhattan Transfer (Atlantic)

14 May 1977

last week	this week	Album / Artist (Label)
1	1	ARRIVAL — Abba (Epic)
2	2	HOTEL CALIFORNIA — Eagles (Asylum)
4	3	ENDLESS FLIGHT — Leo Sayer (Chrysalis)
11	4	A STAR IS BORN — Soundtrack (CBS)
7	5	20 GOLDEN GREATS — Shadows (EMI)
6	6	RUMOURS — Fleetwood Mac (Warner Bros.)
5	7	GREATEST HITS — Abba (Epic)
3	8	PORTRAIT OF SINATRA — Frank Sinatra (Reprise)
9	9	SMOKIE'S GREATEST HITS — Smokie (RAK)
10	10	ANIMALS — Pink Floyd (Harvest)
17	11	PETER GABRIEL — Peter Gabriel (Charisma)
21	12	STRANGLERS IV (RATTUS NORVEGICUS) — Stranglers (United Artists)
8	13	HOLLIES LIVE HITS — Hollies (Polydor)
16	14	SONGS IN THE KEY OF LIFE — Stevie Wonder (Tamla Motown)
14	15	EVEN IN THE QUIETEST MOMENTS — Supertramp (A&M)
-	16	THE BEATLES AT THE HOLLYWOOD BOWL — Beatles (Parlophone)
27	17	THEIR GREATEST HITS 1971–1975 — Eagles (Asylum)
15	18	LIVING LEGENDS — Everly Brothers (Warwick)
13	19	WORKS — Emerson Lake & Palmer (Manticore)
18	20	STATUS QUO LIVE — Status Quo (Vertigo)
19	21	A NEW WORLD RECORD — Electric Light Orchestra (Jet)
12	22	THE UNFORGETTABLE GLENN MILLER — Glenn Miller (RCA)
23	23	DECEPTIVE BENDS — 10 C.C. (Philips)
20	24	THE CLASH — Clash (CBS)
-	25	HIT ACTION — Various Artists (K-Tel)
-	26	A PERIOD OF TRANSITION — Van Morrison (Warner Bros.)
28	27	EVITA — Various Artists (MCA)
25	28	THE MAGIC OF DEMIS ROUSSOS — Demis Roussos (Philips)
22	29	EVERY FACE TELLS A STORY — Cliff Richard (EMI)
-	30	ALL TO YOURSELF — Jack Jones (RCA)

21 May 1977

last week	this week	Album / Artist (Label)
1	1	ARRIVAL — Abba (Epic)
2	2	HOTEL CALIFORNIA — Eagles (Asylum)
4	3	A STAR IS BORN — Soundtrack (CBS)
23	4	DECEPTIVE BENDS — 10 C.C. (Philips)
7	5	GREATEST HITS — Abba (Epic)
12	6	STRANGLERS IV (RATTUS NORVEGICUS) — Stranglers (United Artists)
3	7	ENDLESS FLIGHT — Leo Sayer (Chrysalis)
5	8	20 GOLDEN GREATS — Shadows (EMI)
6	9	RUMOURS — Fleetwood Mac (Warner Bros.)
16	10	THE BEATLES AT THE HOLLYWOOD BOWL — Beatles (Parlophone)
7	11	PORTRAIT OF SINATRA — Frank Sinatra (Reprise)
10	12	ANIMALS — Pink Floyd (Harvest)
9	13	SMOKIE'S GREATEST HITS — Smokie (RAK)
11	14	PETER GABRIEL — Peter Gabriel (Charisma)
14	15	SONGS IN THE KEY OF LIFE — Stevie Wonder (Tamla Motown)
17	16	THEIR GREATEST HITS 1971–1975 — Eagles (Asylum)
15	17	EVEN IN THE QUIETEST MOMENTS — Supertramp (A&M)
19	18	WORKS — Emerson Lake & Palmer (Manticore)
13	19	HOLLIES LIVE HITS — Hollies (Polydor)
21	20	A NEW WORLD RECORD — Electric Light Orchestra (Jet)
20	21	STATUS QUO LIVE — Status Quo (Vertigo)
22	22	THE UNFORGETTABLE GLENN MILLER — Glenn Miller (RCA)
18	23	LIVING LEGENDS — Everly Brothers (Warwick)
24	24	THE CLASH — Clash (CBS)
30	25	ALL TO YOURSELF — Jack Jones (RCA)
-	26	IZITSO — Cat Stevens (Island)
-	27	ATLANTIC CROSSING — Rod Stewart (Warner Bros.)
-	28	DETROIT SPINNERS' SMASH HITS — Detroit Spinners (Atlantic)
-	29	THE BEST OF THE FACES — Faces (Riva)
-	30	TIME LOVES A HERO — Little Feat (Warner Bros.)

Damned Damned Damned was the first punk album to chart, on April 9, followed by *The Clash* and now *Stranglers IV (Rattus Norvegicus)*. The Stranglers were a band risen from the streets, and with the possible exception of boyish-looking Jean-Jacques Burnel (the Paul McCartney of the group) they were rather elderly to be fronting a youth movement. However, their 2nd hit single was imminent and they were cleverly marketed by United Artists, which had also signed Buzzcocks.

May – June 1977

28 May 1977

last week	this week	
2	1	HOTEL CALIFORNIA Eagles (Asylum)
1	2	ARRIVAL Abba (Epic)
4	3	DECEPTIVE BENDS 10 C.C. (Philips)
3	4	A STAR IS BORN Soundtrack (CBS)
10	5	THE BEATLES AT THE HOLLYWOOD BOWL Beatles (Parlophone)
13	6	SMOKIE'S GREATEST HITS Smokie (RAK)
5	7	GREATEST HITS Abba (Epic)
8	8	20 GOLDEN GREATS Shadows (EMI)
6	9	STRANGLERS IV (RATTUS NORVEGICUS) Stranglers (United Artists)
7	10	ENDLESS FLIGHT Leo Sayer (Chrysalis)
9	11	RUMOURS Fleetwood Mac (Warner Bros.)
11	12	PORTRAIT OF SINATRA Frank Sinatra (Reprise)
14	13	PETER GABRIEL Peter Gabriel (Charisma)
12	14	ANIMALS Pink Floyd (Harvest)
15	15	SONGS IN THE KEY OF LIFE Stevie Wonder (Tamla Motown)
16	16	THEIR GREATEST HITS 1971–1975 Eagles (Asylum)
23	17	LIVING LEGENDS Everly Brothers (Warwick)
24	18	THE CLASH Clash (CBS)
25	19	ALL TO YOURSELF Jack Jones (RCA)
20	20	A NEW WORLD RECORD Electric Light Orchestra (Jet)
26	21	IZITSO Cat Stevens (Island)
19	22	HOLLIES LIVE HITS Hollies (Polydor)
17	23	EVEN IN THE QUIETEST MOMENTS Supertramp (A&M)
-	24	HIT ACTION Various Artists (K-Tel)
-	25	SIN AFTER SIN Judas Priest (CBS)
-	26	IN THE CITY Jam (Polydor)
27	27	ATLANTIC CROSSING Rod Stewart (Warner Bros.)
-	28	MOROCCAN ROLL Brand X (Charisma)
21	29	STATUS QUO LIVE Status Quo (Vertigo)
30	30	TIME LOVES A HERO Little Feat (Warner Bros.)

4 June 1977

1	1	HOTEL CALIFORNIA Eagles (Asylum)
2	2	ARRIVAL Abba (Epic)
3	3	DECEPTIVE BENDS 10 C.C. (Philips)
4	4	A STAR IS BORN Soundtrack (CBS)
5	5	THE BEATLES AT THE HOLLYWOOD BOWL Beatles (Parlophone)
10	6	ENDLESS FLIGHT Leo Sayer (Chrysalis)
9	7	STRANGLERS IV (RATTUS NORVEGICUS) Stranglers (United Artists)
11	8	RUMOURS Fleetwood Mac (Warner Bros.)
7	9	GREATEST HITS Abba (Epic)
16	10	THEIR GREATEST HITS 1971–1975 Eagles (Asylum)
8	11	20 GOLDEN GREATS Shadows (EMI)
19	12	ALL TO YOURSELF Jack Jones (RCA)
13	13	PETER GABRIEL Peter Gabriel (Charisma)
14	14	ANIMALS Pink Floyd (Harvest)
6	15	SMOKIE'S GREATEST HITS Smokie (RAK)
12	16	PORTRAIT OF SINATRA Frank Sinatra (Reprise)
20	17	A NEW WORLD RECORD Electric Light Orchestra (Jet)
21	18	IZITSO Cat Stevens (Island)
-	19	THE MUPPET SHOW Muppets (Pye)
30	20	TIME LOVES A HERO Little Feat (Warner Bros.)
-	21	A NIGHT ON THE TOWN Rod Stewart (Riva)
24	22	HIT ACTION Various Artists (K-Tel)
15	23	SONGS IN THE KEY OF LIFE Stevie Wonder (Tamla Motown)
27	24	ATLANTIC CROSSING Rod Stewart (Warner Bros.)
23	25	EVEN IN THE QUIETEST MOMENTS Supertramp (A&M)
18	26	THE CLASH Clash (CBS)
29	27	STATUS QUO LIVE Status Quo (Vertigo)
-	28	BOOK OF DREAMS Steve Miller Band (Mercury)
-	29	THE BEATLES LIVE AT THE STAR CLUB IN HAMBURG, GERMANY 1962 Beatles (Lingasong)
22	30	HOLLIES LIVE HITS Hollies (Polydor)

11 June 1977

2	1	ARRIVAL Abba (Epic)
3	2	DECEPTIVE BENDS 10 C.C. (Philips)
1	3	HOTEL CALIFORNIA Eagles (Asylum)
4	4	A STAR IS BORN Soundtrack (CBS)
5	5	THE BEATLES AT THE HOLLYWOOD BOWL Beatles (Parlophone)
6	6	ENDLESS FLIGHT Leo Sayer (Chrysalis)
10	7	THEIR GREATEST HITS 1971–1975 Eagles (Asylum)
8	8	RUMOURS Fleetwood Mac (Warner Bros.)
12	9	ALL TO YOURSELF Jack Jones (RCA)
7	10	STRANGLERS IV (RATTUS NORVEGICUS) Stranglers (United Artists)
15	11	SMOKIE'S GREATEST HITS Smokie (RAK)
28	12	BOOK OF DREAMS Steve Miller Band (Mercury)
9	13	GREATEST HITS Abba (Epic)
21	14	A NIGHT ON THE TOWN Rod Stewart (Riva)
17	15	A NEW WORLD RECORD Electric Light Orchestra (Jet)
19	16	THE MUPPET SHOW Muppets (Pye)
24	17	ATLANTIC CROSSING Rod Stewart (Warner Bros.)
25	18	EVEN IN THE QUIETEST MOMENTS Supertramp (A&M)
14	19	ANIMALS Pink Floyd (Harvest)
-	20	THE BEST OF THE FACES Faces (Riva)
-	21	SNEAKIN' SUSPICION Dr. Feelgood (United Artists)
23	22	SONGS IN THE KEY OF LIFE Stevie Wonder (Tamla Motown)
13	23	PETER GABRIEL Peter Gabriel (Charisma)
18	24	IZITSO Cat Stevens (Island)
20	25	TIME LOVES A HERO Little Feat (Warner Bros.)
16	26	PORTRAIT OF SINATRA Frank Sinatra (Reprise)
29	27	THE BEATLES LIVE AT THE STAR CLUB IN HAMBURG, GERMANY 1962 Beatles (Lingasong)
-	28	THIS IS NIECY Deniece Williams (CBS)
30	29	HOLLIES LIVE HITS Hollies (Polydor)
11	30	20 GOLDEN GREATS Shadows (EMI)

18 June 1977

1	1	ARRIVAL Abba (Epic)
4	2	A STAR IS BORN Soundtrack (CBS)
3	3	HOTEL CALIFORNIA Eagles (Asylum)
5	4	THE BEATLES AT THE HOLLYWOOD BOWL Beatles (Parlophone)
2	5	DECEPTIVE BENDS 10 C.C. (Philips)
16	6	THE MUPPET SHOW Muppets (Pye)
10	7	STRANGLERS IV (RATTUS NORVEGICUS) Stranglers (United Artists)
15	8	A NEW WORLD RECORD Electric Light Orchestra (Jet)
8	9	RUMOURS Fleetwood Mac (Warner Bros.)
13	10	GREATEST HITS Abba (Epic)
7	11	THEIR GREATEST HITS 1971–1975 Eagles (Asylum)
6	12	ENDLESS FLIGHT Leo Sayer (Chrysalis)
30	13	20 GOLDEN GREATS Shadows (EMI)
-	14	EXODUS Bob Marley & the Wailers (Island)
11	15	SMOKIE'S GREATEST HITS Smokie (RAK)
19	16	ANIMALS Pink Floyd (Harvest)
17	17	ATLANTIC CROSSING Rod Stewart (Warner Bros.)
24	18	IZITSO Cat Stevens (Island)
12	19	BOOK OF DREAMS Steve Miller Band (Mercury)
-	20	IN FLIGHT George Benson (Warner Bros.)
9	21	ALL TO YOURSELF Jack Jones (RCA)
-	22	SHEER MAGIC Acker Bilk (Warwick)
-	23	TOM PETTY & THE HEARTBREAKERS Tom Petty & the Heartbreakers (Shelter)
-	24	THE CLASH Clash (CBS)
-	25	WORKS Emerson Lake & Palmer (Manticore)
21	26	SNEAKIN' SUSPICION Dr. Feelgood (United Artists)
14	27	A NIGHT ON THE TOWN Rod Stewart (Riva)
-	28	I'M IN YOU Peter Frampton (A&M)
18	29	EVEN IN THE QUIETEST MOMENTS Supertramp (A&M)
23	30	PETER GABRIEL Peter Gabriel (Charisma)

The Jam joined the album chart, as the Stranglers held onto the Top 10 and the Clash faltered way below. The ideal medium for punk was of course live performance, and next best was the single. As with Merseybeat 15 years before, album charts couldn't reflect the scale of punk's penetration, but only hint at events in the singles market. The Clash had no big single; the Stranglers did. How appropriate to the spirit of the times that *The Beatles Live At The Star Club Hamburg* should now chart.

25 June 1977

last week	this week	Title	Artist (Label)
4	1	THE BEATLES AT THE HOLLYWOOD BOWL	Beatles (Parlophone)
1	2	ARRIVAL	Abba (Epic)
6	3	THE MUPPET SHOW	Muppets (Pye)
3	4	HOTEL CALIFORNIA	Eagles (Asylum)
2	5	A STAR IS BORN	Soundtrack (CBS)
5	6	DECEPTIVE BENDS	10 C.C. (Philips)
7	7	STRANGLERS IV (RATTUS NORVEGICUS)	Stranglers (United Artists)
8	8	A NEW WORLD RECORD	Electric Light Orchestra (Jet)
22	9	SHEER MAGIC	Acker Bilk (Warwick)
12	10	ENDLESS FLIGHT	Leo Sayer (Chrysalis)
9	11	RUMOURS	Fleetwood Mac (Warner Bros.)
-	12	ROCK FOLLIES 77	Various Artists (Polydor)
-	13	THE JOHNNY MATHIS COLLECTION	Johnny Mathis (CBS)
14	14	EXODUS	Bob Marley & the Wailers (Island)
10	15	GREATEST HITS	Abba (Epic)
11	16	THEIR GREATEST HITS 1971–1975	Eagles (Asylum)
17	17	ATLANTIC CROSSING	Rod Stewart (Warner Bros.)
27	18	A NIGHT ON THE TOWN	Rod Stewart (Riva)
16	19	ANIMALS	Pink Floyd (Harvest)
13	20	20 GOLDEN GREATS	Shadows (EMI)
20	21	IN FLIGHT	George Benson (Warner Bros.)
21	22	ALL TO YOURSELF	Jack Jones (RCA)
28	23	I'M IN YOU Peter Frampton (A&M)	
19	24	BOOK OF DREAMS	Steve Miller Band (Mercury)
-	25	SILK DEGREES	Boz Scaggs (CBS)
23	26	TOM PETTY & THE HEARTBREAKERS	Tom Petty & the Heartbreakers (Shelter)
30	27	PETER GABRIEL	Peter Gabriel (Charisma)
-	28	KENNY ROGERS	Kenny Rogers (United Artists)
15	29	SMOKIE'S GREATEST HITS	Smokie (RAK)
26	30	SNEAKIN' SUSPICION	Dr. Feelgood (United Artists)

2 July 1977

last week	this week	Title	Artist (Label)
3	1	THE MUPPET SHOW	Muppets (Pye)
5	2	A STAR IS BORN	Soundtrack (CBS)
4	3	HOTEL CALIFORNIA	Eagles (Asylum)
2	4	ARRIVAL	Abba (Epic)
1	5	THE BEATLES AT THE HOLLYWOOD BOWL	Beatles (Parlophone)
7	6	STRANGLERS IV (RATTUS NORVEGICUS)	Stranglers (United Artists)
11	7	RUMOURS	Fleetwood Mac (Warner Bros.)
6	8	DECEPTIVE BENDS	10 C.C. (Philips)
8	9	A NEW WORLD RECORD	Electric Light Orchestra (Jet)
13	10	THE JOHNNY MATHIS COLLECTION	Johnny Mathis (CBS)
25	11	SILK DEGREES	Boz Scaggs (CBS)
14	12	EXODUS	Bob Marley & the Wailers (Island)
21	13	IN FLIGHT	George Benson (Warner Bros.)
15	14	GREATEST HITS	Abba (Epic)
9	15	SHEER MAGIC	Acker Bilk (Warwick)
16	16	THEIR GREATEST HITS 1971–1975	Eagles (Asylum)
12	17	ROCK FOLLIES 77	Various Artists (Polydor)
23	18	I'M IN YOU Peter Frampton (A&M)	
17	19	ATLANTIC CROSSING	Rod Stewart (Warner Bros.)
10	20	ENDLESS FLIGHT	Leo Sayer (Chrysalis)
-	21	I REMEMBER YESTERDAY	Donna Summer (GTO)
26	22	TOM PETTY & THE HEARTBREAKERS	Tom Petty & the Heartbreakers (Shelter)
-	23	LOVE AT THE GREEK	Neil Diamond (CBS)
28	24	KENNY ROGERS	Kenny Rogers (United Artists)
18	25	A NIGHT ON THE TOWN	Rod Stewart (Riva)
-	26	EVEN IN THE QUIETEST MOMENTS	Supertramp (A&M)
29	27	SMOKIE'S GREATEST HITS	Smokie (RAK)
-	28	WORKS	Emerson Lake & Palmer (Manticore)
-	29	CAT SCRATCH FEVER	Ted Nugent (Epic)
24	30	BOOK OF DREAMS	Steve Miller Band (Mercury)

9 July 1977

last week	this week	Title	Artist (Label)
2	1	A STAR IS BORN	Soundtrack (CBS)
1	2	THE MUPPET SHOW	Muppets (Pye)
3	3	HOTEL CALIFORNIA	Eagles (Asylum)
4	4	ARRIVAL	Abba (Epic)
9	5	A NEW WORLD RECORD	Electric Light Orchestra (Jet)
10	6	THE JOHNNY MATHIS COLLECTION	Johnny Mathis (CBS)
8	7	DECEPTIVE BENDS	10 C.C. (Philips)
6	8	STRANGLERS IV (RATTUS NORVEGICUS)	Stranglers (United Artists)
5	9	THE BEATLES AT THE HOLLYWOOD BOWL	Beatles (Parlophone)
23	10	LOVE AT THE GREEK	Neil Diamond (CBS)
12	11	EXODUS	Bob Marley & the Wailers (Island)
7	12	RUMOURS	Fleetwood Mac (Warner Bros.)
28	13	WORKS	Emerson Lake & Palmer (Manticore)
14	14	GREATEST HITS	Abba (Epic)
18	15	I'M IN YOU Peter Frampton (A&M)	
20	16	ENDLESS FLIGHT	Leo Sayer (Chrysalis)
-	17	THE ROXY, LONDON WC2	Various Artists (Harvest)
21	18	I REMEMBER YESTERDAY	Donna Summer (GTO)
13	19	IN FLIGHT	George Benson (Warner Bros.)
24	20	KENNY ROGERS	Kenny Rogers (United Artists)
-	21	COMING OUT	Manhattan Transfer (Atlantic)
26	22	EVEN IN THE QUIETEST MOMENTS	Supertramp (A&M)
-	23	STEVE WINWOOD	Steve Winwood (Island)
15	24	SHEER MAGIC	Acker Bilk (Warwick)
-	25	AMERICAN STARS 'N' BARS	Neil Young (Reprise)
22	26	TOM PETTY & THE HEARTBREAKERS	Tom Petty & the Heartbreakers (Shelter)
29	27	CAT SCRATCH FEVER	Ted Nugent (Epic)
11	28	SILK DEGREES	Boz Scaggs (CBS)
16	29	ROCK FOLLIES 77	Various Artists (Polydor)
-	30	PURE MANIA	Vibrators (Epic)

16 July 1977

last week	this week	Title	Artist (Label)
1	1	A STAR IS BORN	Soundtrack (CBS)
6	2	THE JOHNNY MATHIS COLLECTION	Johnny Mathis (CBS)
4	3	ARRIVAL	Abba (Epic)
2	4	THE MUPPET SHOW	Muppets (Pye)
3	5	HOTEL CALIFORNIA	Eagles (Asylum)
8	6	STRANGLERS IV (RATTUS NORVEGICUS)	Stranglers (United Artists)
18	7	I REMEMBER YESTERDAY	Donna Summer (GTO)
7	8	DECEPTIVE BENDS	10 C.C. (Philips)
11	9	EXODUS	Bob Marley & the Wailers (Island)
9	10	THE BEATLES AT THE HOLLYWOOD BOWL	Beatles (Parlophone)
10	11	LOVE AT THE GREEK	Neil Diamond (CBS)
12	12	RUMOURS	Fleetwood Mac (Warner Bros.)
5	13	A NEW WORLD RECORD	Electric Light Orchestra (Jet)
13	14	WORKS	Emerson Lake & Palmer (Manticore)
19	15	IN FLIGHT	George Benson (Warner Bros.)
-	16	THE BEST OF THE MAMAS AND THE PAPAS	Mamas & Papas (Arcade)
-	17	20 ALL TIME GREATS	Connie Francis (Polydor)
25	18	AMERICAN STARS 'N' BARS	Neil Young (Reprise)
15	19	I'M IN YOU Peter Frampton (A&M)	
16	20	ENDLESS FLIGHT	Leo Sayer (Chrysalis)
23	21	STEVE WINWOOD	Steve Winwood (Island)
26	22	TOM PETTY & THE HEARTBREAKERS	Tom Petty & the Heartbreakers (Shelter)
-	23	CSN	Crosby Stills & Nash (Atlantic)
20	24	KENNY ROGERS	Kenny Rogers (United Artists)
27	25	CAT SCRATCH FEVER	Ted Nugent (Epic)
17	26	THE ROXY, LONDON WC2	Various Artists (Harvest)
24	27	SHEER MAGIC	Acker Bilk (Warwick)
30	28	PURE MANIA	Vibrators (Epic)
22	29	EVEN IN THE QUIETEST MOMENTS	Supertramp (A&M)
28	30	SILK DEGREES	Boz Scaggs (CBS)

More punk charted: *The Roxy, London WC2* (a prinicipal venue for the music, pogo-ing and gobbing) and the Vibrators. Ranged against it was music from every previous era: 50s crooners Jack Jones and Johnny Mathis, the latter enjoying a career revival; 1961 Trad craze artist Acker Bilk; re-born '60s British blues-boom group Fleetwood Mac; hippies Crosby Stills & Nash and, at the top, *The Beatles At The Hollywood Bowl* and the soundtrack of a remake of an old Judy Garland film.

July – August 1977

23 July 1977

last	this	
2	1	THE JOHNNY MATHIS COLLECTION — Johnny Mathis (CBS)
1	2	A STAR IS BORN — Soundtrack (CBS)
7	3	I REMEMBER YESTERDAY — Donna Summer (GTO)
4	4	THE MUPPET SHOW — Muppets (Pye)
3	5	ARRIVAL — Abba (Epic)
12	6	RUMOURS — Fleetwood Mac (Warner Bros.)
6	7	STRANGLERS IV (RATTUS NORVEGICUS) — Stranglers (United Artists)
5	8	HOTEL CALIFORNIA — Eagles (Asylum)
14	9	WORKS — Emerson Lake & Palmer (Manticore)
9	10	EXODUS — Bob Marley & the Wailers (Island)
11	11	LOVE AT THE GREEK — Neil Diamond (CBS)
10	12	THE BEATLES AT THE HOLLYWOOD BOWL — Beatles (Parlophone)
13	13	A NEW WORLD RECORD — Electric Light Orchestra (Jet)
8	14	DECEPTIVE BENDS — 10 C.C. (Philips)
16	15	THE BEST OF THE MAMAS AND THE PAPAS — Mamas & Papas (Arcade)
-	16	GOING FOR THE ONE — Yes (Atlantic)
21	17	STEVE WINWOOD — Steve Winwood (Island)
19	18	I'M IN YOU — Peter Frampton (A&M)
17	19	20 ALL TIME GREATS — Connie Francis (Polydor)
26	20	THE ROXY, LONDON WC2 — Various Artists (Harvest)
30	21	SILK DEGREES — Boz Scaggs (CBS)
18	22	AMERICAN STARS 'N' BARS — Neil Young (Reprise)
29	23	EVEN IN THE QUIETEST MOMENTS — Supertramp (A&M)
-	24	THE BEST OF ROD STEWART — Rod Stewart (Mercury)
25	25	CAT SCRATCH FEVER — Ted Nugent (Epic)
-	26	GREATEST HITS — Abba (Epic)
15	27	IN FLIGHT — George Benson (Warner Bros.)
-	28	SMOKIE'S GREATEST HITS — Smokie (RAK)
20	29	ENDLESS FLIGHT — Leo Sayer (Chrysalis)
23	30	CSN — Crosby Stills & Nash (Atlantic)

30 July 1977

this		
1		THE JOHNNY MATHIS COLLECTION — Johnny Mathis (CBS)
2		A STAR IS BORN — Soundtrack (CBS)
3		I REMEMBER YESTERDAY — Donna Summer (GTO)
7	4	STRANGLERS IV (RATTUS NORVEGICUS) — Stranglers (United Artists)
11	5	LOVE AT THE GREEK — Neil Diamond (CBS)
6	6	RUMOURS — Fleetwood Mac (Warner Bros.)
16	7	GOING FOR THE ONE — Yes (Atlantic)
8	8	HOTEL CALIFORNIA — Eagles (Asylum)
5	9	ARRIVAL — Abba (Epic)
4	10	THE MUPPET SHOW — Muppets (Pye)
17	11	STEVE WINWOOD — Steve Winwood (Island)
13	12	A NEW WORLD RECORD — Electric Light Orchestra (Jet)
9	13	WORKS — Emerson Lake & Palmer (Manticore)
15	14	THE BEST OF THE MAMAS AND THE PAPAS — Mamas & Papas (Arcade)
19	15	20 ALL TIME GREATS — Connie Francis (Polydor)
10	16	EXODUS — Bob Marley & the Wailers (Island)
14	17	DECEPTIVE BENDS — 10 C.C. (Philips)
12	18	THE BEATLES AT THE HOLLYWOOD BOWL — Beatles (Parlophone)
-	19	ON STAGE — Rainbow (Polydor)
18	20	I'M IN YOU — Peter Frampton (A&M)
-	21	SORCERER — Tangerine Dream (MCA)
-	22	LIVE! IN THE AIR AGE — Be Bop Deluxe (Harvest)
30	22	CSN — Crosby Stills & Nash (Atlantic)
25	24	CAT SCRATCH FEVER — Ted Nugent (Epic)
-	25	LITTLE QUEEN — Heart (Portrait)
22	26	AMERICAN STARS 'N' BARS — Neil Young (Reprise)
27	27	ANIMALS — Pink Floyd (Harvest)
27	28	IN FLIGHT — George Benson (Warner Bros.)
21	29	SILK DEGREES — Boz Scaggs (CBS)
24	30	THE BEST OF ROD STEWART — Rod Stewart (Mercury)

6 August 1977

this		
1		THE JOHNNY MATHIS COLLECTION — Johnny Mathis (CBS)
2		A STAR IS BORN — Soundtrack (CBS)
7	3	GOING FOR THE ONE — Yes (Atlantic)
5	4	LOVE AT THE GREEK — Neil Diamond (CBS)
3	5	I REMEMBER YESTERDAY — Donna Summer (GTO)
6	6	RUMOURS — Fleetwood Mac (Warner Bros.)
13	7	WORKS — Emerson Lake & Palmer (Manticore)
15	8	20 ALL TIME GREATS — Connie Francis (Polydor)
4	9	STRANGLERS IV (RATTUS NORVEGICUS) — Stranglers (United Artists)
8	10	HOTEL CALIFORNIA — Eagles (Asylum)
9	10	ARRIVAL — Abba (Epic)
10	12	THE MUPPET SHOW — Muppets (Pye)
12	13	A NEW WORLD RECORD — Electric Light Orchestra (Jet)
19	14	ON STAGE — Rainbow (Polydor)
11	15	STEVE WINWOOD — Steve Winwood (Island)
14	16	THE BEST OF THE MAMAS AND THE PAPAS — Mamas & Papas (Arcade)
17	17	DECEPTIVE BENDS — 10 C.C. (Philips)
16	18	EXODUS — Bob Marley & the Wailers (Island)
21	19	SORCERER — Tangerine Dream (MCA)
27	20	ANIMALS — Pink Floyd (Harvest)
30	21	THE BEST OF ROD STEWART — Rod Stewart (Mercury)
-	22	EVEN IN THE QUIETEST MOMENTS — Supertramp (A&M)
-	23	STREISAND SUPERMAN — Barbra Streisand (CBS)
-	24	LOVE FOR SALE — Boney M (Atlantic)
22	25	CSN — Crosby Stills & Nash (Atlantic)
22	26	LIVE! IN THE AIR AGE — Be Bop Deluxe (Harvest)
20	27	I'M IN YOU — Peter Frampton (A&M)
-	28	FACE TO FACE – A LIVE RECORDING — Steve Harley & Cockney Rebel (EMI)
28	29	IN FLIGHT — George Benson (Warner Bros.)
-	30	SMOKIE'S GREATEST HITS — Smokie (RAK)

13 August 1977

this		
1		THE JOHNNY MATHIS COLLECTION — Johnny Mathis (CBS)
3	2	GOING FOR THE ONE — Yes (Atlantic)
5	3	I REMEMBER YESTERDAY — Donna Summer (GTO)
2	4	A STAR IS BORN — Soundtrack (CBS)
8	5	20 ALL TIME GREATS — Connie Francis (Polydor)
4	6	LOVE AT THE GREEK — Neil Diamond (CBS)
10	7	HOTEL CALIFORNIA — Eagles (Asylum)
6	8	RUMOURS — Fleetwood Mac (Warner Bros.)
10	9	ARRIVAL — Abba (Epic)
12	10	THE MUPPET SHOW — Muppets (Pye)
9	11	STRANGLERS IV (RATTUS NORVEGICUS) — Stranglers (United Artists)
18	12	EXODUS — Bob Marley & the Wailers (Island)
17	13	DECEPTIVE BENDS — 10 C.C. (Philips)
7	14	WORKS — Emerson Lake & Palmer (Manticore)
13	15	A NEW WORLD RECORD — Electric Light Orchestra (Jet)
14	16	ON STAGE — Rainbow (Polydor)
26	17	LIVE! IN THE AIR AGE — Be Bop Deluxe (Harvest)
21	18	THE BEST OF ROD STEWART — Rod Stewart (Mercury)
16	19	THE BEST OF THE MAMAS AND THE PAPAS — Mamas & Papas (Arcade)
29	20	IN FLIGHT — George Benson (Warner Bros.)
30	21	SMOKIE'S GREATEST HITS — Smokie (RAK)
24	22	LOVE FOR SALE — Boney M (Atlantic)
27	23	I'M IN YOU — Peter Frampton (A&M)
20	24	ANIMALS — Pink Floyd (Harvest)
-	25	GREATEST HITS — Abba (Epic)
-	26	COMING OUT — Manhattan Transfer (Atlantic)
23	27	STREISAND SUPERMAN — Barbra Streisand-(CBS)
15	28	STEVE WINWOOD — Steve Winwood (Island)
19	29	SORCERER — Tangerine Dream (MCA)
-	30	ENDLESS FLIGHT — Leo Sayer (Chrysalis)

Exodus gave Bob Marley a deserved substantial hit. No such hit for US punks Television (though punk was different there: more James Dean-Brando-early Elvis-to-Velvet Underground in look, more precise yet garage-band in sound). Television, led by guitarist Tom Verlaine, had recently had a minor hit, *Marquee Moon*, title song from their perfect debut album, and now reached the Top 20 with another single from it (*Prove It*): but the album had barely scraped the Top 30 for a fortnight in April.

last week	this week	20 August 1977
2	1	GOING FOR THE ONE — Yes (Atlantic)
3	2	I REMEMBER YESTERDAY — Donna Summer (GTO)
4	3	A STAR IS BORN — Soundtrack (CBS)
5	4	20 ALL TIME GREATS — Connie Francis (Polydor)
8	5	RUMOURS — Fleetwood Mac (Warner Bros.)
1	5	THE JOHNNY MATHIS COLLECTION — Johnny Mathis (CBS)
11	7	STRANGLERS IV (RATTUS NORVEGICUS) — Stranglers (United Artists)
7	8	HOTEL CALIFORNIA — Eagles (Asylum)
10	9	THE MUPPET SHOW — Muppets (Pye)
6	10	LOVE AT THE GREEK — Neil Diamond (CBS)
22	11	LOVE FOR SALE — Boney M (Atlantic)
9	12	ARRIVAL — Abba (Epic)
14	13	WORKS — Emerson Lake & Palmer (Manticore)
16	14	ON STAGE — Rainbow (Polydor)
18	15	THE BEST OF ROD STEWART — Rod Stewart (Mercury)
15	16	A NEW WORLD RECORD — Electric Light Orchestra (Jet)
-	17	NEW WAVE — Various Artists (Vertigo)
12	18	EXODUS — Bob Marley & the Wailers (Island)
21	19	SMOKIE'S GREATEST HITS — Smokie (RAK)
13	20	DECEPTIVE BENDS — 10 C.C. (Philips)
-	21	OXYGENE — Jean-Michel Jarre (Polydor)
17	22	LIVE! IN THE AIR AGE — Be Bop Deluxe (Harvest)
27	23	STREISAND SUPERMAN — Barbra Streisand (CBS)
-	24	MY AIM IS TRUE — Elvis Costello (Stiff)
26	25	COMING OUT — Manhattan Transfer (Atlantic)
-	26	IN THE CITY — Jam (Polydor)
30	27	ENDLESS FLIGHT — Leo Sayer (Chrysalis)
24	28	ANIMALS — Pink Floyd (Harvest)
19	29	THE BEST OF THE MAMAS AND THE PAPAS — Mamas & Papas (Arcade)
-	30	FLOATERS — Floaters (ABC)

		27 August 1977
1	1	GOING FOR THE ONE — Yes (Atlantic)
3	2	A STAR IS BORN — Soundtrack (CBS)
4	2	20 ALL TIME GREATS — Connie Francis (Polydor)
2	4	I REMEMBER YESTERDAY — Donna Summer (GTO)
5	5	RUMOURS — Fleetwood Mac (Warner Bros.)
5	6	THE JOHNNY MATHIS COLLECTION — Johnny Mathis (CBS)
21	7	OXYGENE — Jean-Michel Jarre (Polydor)
8	8	HOTEL CALIFORNIA — Eagles (Asylum)
12	9	ARRIVAL — Abba (Epic)
7	10	STRANGLERS IV (RATTUS NORVEGICUS) — Stranglers (United Artists)
-	11	MOODY BLUE — Elvis Presley (RCA)
11	12	LOVE FOR SALE — Boney M (Atlantic)
10	13	LOVE AT THE GREEK — Neil Diamond (CBS)
15	14	THE BEST OF ROD STEWART — Rod Stewart (Mercury)
13	15	WORKS — Emerson Lake & Palmer (Manticore)
-	16	40 GREATEST — Elvis Presley (RCA)
9	17	THE MUPPET SHOW — Muppets (Pye)
17	18	NEW WAVE — Various Artists (Vertigo)
14	19	ON STAGE — Rainbow (Polydor)
22	20	LIVE! IN THE AIR AGE — Be Bop Deluxe (Harvest)
-	21	WELCOME TO MY WORLD — Elvis Presley (RCA)
30	22	FLOATERS — Floaters (ABC)
18	23	EXODUS — Bob Marley & the Wailers (Island)
20	24	DECEPTIVE BENDS — 10 C.C. (Philips)
25	25	IN THE CITY — Jam (Polydor)
16	26	A NEW WORLD RECORD — Electric Light Orchestra (Jet)
19	27	SMOKIE'S GREATEST HITS — Smokie (RAK)
24	28	MY AIM IS TRUE — Elvis Costello (Stiff)
23	29	STREISAND SUPERMAN — Barbra Streisand (CBS)
29	30	THE BEST OF THE MAMAS AND THE PAPAS — Mamas & Papas (Arcade)

		3 September 1977
11	1	MOODY BLUE — Elvis Presley (RCA)
2	2	A STAR IS BORN — Soundtrack (CBS)
7	3	OXYGENE — Jean-Michel Jarre (Polydor)
2	4	20 ALL TIME GREATS — Connie Francis (Polydor)
4	5	I REMEMBER YESTERDAY — Donna Summer (GTO)
1	6	GOING FOR THE ONE — Yes (Atlantic)
5	7	RUMOURS — Fleetwood Mac (Warner Bros.)
6	8	THE JOHNNY MATHIS COLLECTION — Johnny Mathis (CBS)
10	9	STRANGLERS IV (RATTUS NORVEGICUS) — Stranglers (United Artists)
9	10	ARRIVAL — Abba (Epic)
8	11	HOTEL CALIFORNIA — Eagles (Asylum)
12	12	LOVE FOR SALE — Boney M (Atlantic)
23	13	EXODUS — Bob Marley & the Wailers (Island)
16	14	40 GREATEST — Elvis Presley (RCA)
18	15	NEW WAVE — Various Artists (Vertigo)
21	16	WELCOME TO MY WORLD — Elvis Presley (RCA)
17	17	THE MUPPET SHOW — Muppets (Pye)
22	18	FLOATERS — Floaters (ABC)
28	19	MY AIM IS TRUE — Elvis Costello (Stiff)
14	20	THE BEST OF ROD STEWART — Rod Stewart (Mercury)
13	21	LOVE AT THE GREEK — Neil Diamond (CBS)
24	21	DECEPTIVE BENDS — 10 C.C. (Philips)
27	23	SMOKIE'S GREATEST HITS — Smokie (RAK)
-	24	I, ROBOT — Alan Parsons Project (Arista)
-	25	STEVE WINWOOD — Steve Winwood (Island)
15	26	WORKS — Emerson Lake & Palmer (Manticore)
20	27	LIVE! IN THE AIR AGE — Be Bop Deluxe (Harvest)
-	28	THIS IS NIECY — Deniece Williams (CBS)
26	29	A NEW WORLD RECORD — Electric Light Orchestra (Jet)
19	30	ON STAGE — Rainbow (Polydor)

		10 September 1977
3	1	OXYGENE — Jean-Michel Jarre (Polydor)
1	2	MOODY BLUE — Elvis Presley (RCA)
7	3	RUMOURS — Fleetwood Mac (Warner Bros.)
2	4	A STAR IS BORN — Soundtrack (CBS)
4	5	20 ALL TIME GREATS — Connie Francis (Polydor)
16	6	WELCOME TO MY WORLD — Elvis Presley (RCA)
6	7	GOING FOR THE ONE — Yes (Atlantic)
5	8	I REMEMBER YESTERDAY — Donna Summer (GTO)
14	9	40 GREATEST — Elvis Presley (RCA)
9	10	STRANGLERS IV (RATTUS NORVEGICUS) — Stranglers (United Artists)
11	11	HOTEL CALIFORNIA — Eagles (Asylum)
15	12	NEW WAVE — Various Artists (Vertigo)
10	13	ARRIVAL — Abba (Epic)
8	14	THE JOHNNY MATHIS COLLECTION — Johnny Mathis (CBS)
12	15	LOVE FOR SALE — Boney M (Atlantic)
19	16	MY AIM IS TRUE — Elvis Costello (Stiff)
-	17	20 GOLDEN GREATS — Diana Ross & the Supremes (Motown)
20	18	THE BEST OF ROD STEWART — Rod Stewart (Mercury)
13	19	EXODUS — Bob Marley & the Wailers (Island)
-	20	G.I. BLUES — Elvis Presley (RCA)
29	21	A NEW WORLD RECORD — Electric Light Orchestra (Jet)
-	22	ELVIS IN DEMAND — Elvis Presley (RCA)
26	23	WORKS — Emerson Lake & Palmer (Manticore)
21	24	LOVE AT THE GREEK — Neil Diamond (CBS)
-	25	MAGIC FLY — Space (Pye)
-	26	BLUE HAWAII — Elvis Presley (RCA)
17	27	THE MUPPET SHOW — Muppets (Pye)
-	28	ROCK 'N' ROLL WITH THE MODERN LOVERS — Jonathan Richman & the Modern Lovers (Beserkeley)
-	29	CABRETTA — Mink De Ville (Capitol)
30	30	ON STAGE — Rainbow (Polydor)

Elvis Presley died on August 16. The dramatic impact on sales of his rich, randomly available catalogue began to show in the August 27 chart. *Moody Blue*, his most recent album, recorded live and at his Graceland home-studio, was not a wholly unworthy last testament. Its chilling 1977 live performance of *Unchained Melody* seemed to express Presley's lonely despair and yet to show that, whatever shape he was in, his bravery of voice, especially in hitting the high notes, was undiminished.

September – October 1977

17 September 1977

last week	this week		
1	1	OXYGENE	Jean-Michel Jarre (Polydor)
2	2	MOODY BLUE	Elvis Presley (RCA)
3	3	RUMOURS	Fleetwood Mac (Warner Bros.)
4	4	20 ALL TIME GREATS	Connie Francis (Polydor)
4	5	A STAR IS BORN	Soundtrack (CBS)
17	6	20 GOLDEN GREATS	Diana Ross & the Supremes (Motown)
7	7	GOING FOR THE ONE	Yes (Atlantic)
6	8	WELCOME TO MY WORLD	Elvis Presley (RCA)
8	9	I REMEMBER YESTERDAY	Donna Summer (GTO)
10	10	STRANGLERS IV (RATTUS NORVEGICUS)	Stranglers (United Artists)
11	11	HOTEL CALIFORNIA	Eagles (Asylum)
22	12	ELVIS IN DEMAND	Elvis Presley (RCA)
9	13	40 GREATEST	Elvis Presley (RCA)
14	14	THE JOHNNY MATHIS COLLECTION	Johnny Mathis (CBS)
19	15	EXODUS	Bob Marley & the Wailers (Island)
20	16	G.I. BLUES	Elvis Presley (RCA)
25	17	MAGIC FLY	Space (Pye)
13	18	ARRIVAL	Abba (Epic)
12	19	NEW WAVE	Various Artists (Vertigo)
18	20	THE BEST OF ROD STEWART	Rod Stewart (Mercury)
-	21	FLOATERS	Floaters (ABC)
-	22	ELVIS' GOLDEN RECORDS	Elvis Presley (RCA)
15	23	LOVE FOR SALE	Boney M (Atlantic)
-	24	ELVIS' GOLDEN RECORDS VOL.2	Elvis Presley (RCA)
24	25	LOVE AT THE GREEK	Neil Diamond (CBS)
-	26	THE SUN COLLECTION	Elvis Presley (RCA)
23	27	WORKS	Emerson Lake & Palmer (Manticore)
16	28	MY AIM IS TRUE	Elvis Costello (Stiff)
21	29	A NEW WORLD RECORD	Electric Light Orchestra (Jet)
30	30	ON STAGE	Rainbow (Polydor)

24 September 1977

6	1	20 GOLDEN GREATS	Diana Ross & the Supremes (Motown)
1	2	OXYGENE	Jean-Michel Jarre (Polydor)
2	3	MOODY BLUE	Elvis Presley (RCA)
5	4	A STAR IS BORN	Soundtrack (CBS)
17	5	MAGIC FLY	Space (Pye)
3	6	RUMOURS	Fleetwood Mac (Warner Bros.)
8	7	WELCOME TO MY WORLD	Elvis Presley (RCA)
9	8	I REMEMBER YESTERDAY	Donna Summer (GTO)
4	9	20 ALL TIME GREATS	Connie Francis (Polydor)
13	10	40 GREATEST	Elvis Presley (RCA)
10	11	STRANGLERS IV (RATTUS NORVEGICUS)	Stranglers (United Artists)
7	12	GOING FOR THE ONE	Yes (Atlantic)
11	13	HOTEL CALIFORNIA	Eagles (Asylum)
15	14	EXODUS	Bob Marley & the Wailers (Island)
18	15	ARRIVAL	Abba (Epic)
-	16	PLAYING TO AN AUDIENCE OF ONE	David Soul (Private Stock)
19	17	NEW WAVE	Various Artists (Vertigo)
12	18	ELVIS IN DEMAND	Elvis Presley (RCA)
14	19	THE JOHNNY MATHIS COLLECTION	Johnny Mathis (CBS)
21	20	FLOATERS	Floaters (ABC)
26	21	THE SUN COLLECTION	Elvis Presley (RCA)
20	22	THE BEST OF ROD STEWART	Rod Stewart (Mercury)
-	23	BAD REPUTATION	Thin Lizzy (Vertigo)
16	24	G.I. BLUES	Elvis Presley (RCA)
-	25	THIS IS NIECY	Deniece Williams (CBS)
-	26	SHOW SOME EMOTION	Joan Armatrading (A&M)
28	27	MY AIM IS TRUE	Elvis Costello (Stiff)
25	28	LOVE AT THE GREEK	Neil Diamond (CBS)
-	29	IN FULL BLOOM	Rose Royce (Whitfield)
-	30	RAIN DANCES	Camel (Decca)

1 October 1977

1	1	20 GOLDEN GREATS	Diana Ross & the Supremes (Motown)
2	2	OXYGENE	Jean-Michel Jarre (Polydor)
3	3	MOODY BLUE	Elvis Presley (RCA)
4	4	A STAR IS BORN	Soundtrack (CBS)
6	5	RUMOURS	Fleetwood Mac (Warner Bros.)
9	6	20 ALL TIME GREATS	Connie Francis (Polydor)
5	7	MAGIC FLY	Space (Pye)
12	8	GOING FOR THE ONE	Yes (Atlantic)
16	9	PLAYING TO AN AUDIENCE OF ONE	David Soul (Private Stock)
8	10	I REMEMBER YESTERDAY	Donna Summer (GTO)
7	11	WELCOME TO MY WORLD	Elvis Presley (RCA)
-	12	NO MORE HEROES	Stranglers (United Artists)
14	13	EXODUS	Bob Marley & the Wailers (Island)
11	14	STRANGLERS IV (RATTUS NORVEGICUS)	Stranglers (United Artists)
10	15	40 GREATEST	Elvis Presley (RCA)
23	16	BAD REPUTATION	Thin Lizzy (Vertigo)
13	17	HOTEL CALIFORNIA	Eagles (Asylum)
-	18	LOVE YOU LIVE	Rolling Stones (Rolling Stones)
22	19	THE BEST OF ROD STEWART	Rod Stewart (Mercury)
18	20	THE JOHNNY MATHIS COLLECTION	Johnny Mathis (CBS)
26	21	SHOW SOME EMOTION	Joan Armatrading (A&M)
15	22	ARRIVAL	Abba (Epic)
20	23	FLOATERS	Floaters (ABC)
24	24	G.I. BLUES	Elvis Presley (RCA)
-	25	THE VERY BEST OF FRANKIE LAINE	Frankie Laine (Warwick)
-	26	BOOMTOWN RATS	Boomtown Rats (Ensign)
17	27	NEW WAVE	Various Artists (Vertigo)
21	28	THE SUN COLLECTION	Elvis Presley (RCA)
-	29	AJA	Steely Dan (ABC)
30	30	RAIN DANCES	Camel (Decca)

8 October 1977

1	1	20 GOLDEN GREATS	Diana Ross & the Supremes (Motown)
2	2	OXYGENE	Jean-Michel Jarre (Polydor)
3	3	MOODY BLUE	Elvis Presley (RCA)
4	4	A STAR IS BORN	Soundtrack (CBS)
7	5	MAGIC FLY	Space (Pye)
6	6	20 ALL TIME GREATS	Connie Francis (Polydor)
5	7	RUMOURS	Fleetwood Mac (Warner Bros.)
12	8	NO MORE HEROES	Stranglers (United Artists)
8	9	GOING FOR THE ONE	Yes (Atlantic)
9	10	PLAYING TO AN AUDIENCE OF ONE	David Soul (Private Stock)
16	11	BAD REPUTATION	Thin Lizzy (Vertigo)
21	12	SHOW SOME EMOTION	Joan Armatrading (A&M)
13	13	EXODUS	Bob Marley & the Wailers (Island)
11	14	WELCOME TO MY WORLD	Elvis Presley (RCA)
10	15	I REMEMBER YESTERDAY	Donna Summer (GTO)
18	16	LOVE YOU LIVE	Rolling Stones (Rolling Stones)
17	17	HOTEL CALIFORNIA	Eagles (Asylum)
25	18	THE VERY BEST OF FRANKIE LAINE	Frankie Laine (Warwick)
-	19	HOME ON THE RANGE	Slim Whitman (United Artists)
15	20	40 GREATEST	Elvis Presley (RCA)
27	21	NEW WAVE	Various Artists (Vertigo)
26	22	BOOMTOWN RATS	Boomtown Rats (Ensign)
22	23	ARRIVAL	Abba (Epic)
19	24	THE BEST OF ROD STEWART	Rod Stewart (Mercury)
-	25	SIMPLE DREAMS	Linda Ronstadt (Asylum)
-	26	TWO DAYS AWAY	Elkie Brooks (A&M)
24	27	G.I. BLUES	Elvis Presley (RCA)
20	28	THE JOHNNY MATHIS COLLECTION	Johnny Mathis (CBS)
29	29	PASSAGE	Carpenters (A&M)
29	30	AJA	Steely Dan (ABC)

By September 10, three Presley albums were Top 10 and another two were joining the 30. Now three more entered. Stocks ran out all over the world. People bought whatever was available: *GI Blues*, for example, the soundtrack album from his lacklustre first post-Army movie, made in 1960 but wholly lacking the genius evident on that year's *Elvis Is Back* LP. *Elvis In Demand* was a compilation supposedly requested by UK fanclub members. Marc Bolan died on September 16, to no immediate chart effect.

October – November 1977

15 October 1977

last	this	title / artist
1	1	20 GOLDEN GREATS — Diana Ross & the Supremes (Motown)
2	2	OXYGENE — Jean-Michel Jarre (Polydor)
8	3	NO MORE HEROES — Stranglers (United Artists)
7	4	RUMOURS — Fleetwood Mac (Warner Bros.)
3	5	MOODY BLUE — Elvis Presley (RCA)
16	6	LOVE YOU LIVE — Rolling Stones (Rolling Stones)
11	7	BAD REPUTATION — Thin Lizzy (Vertigo)
4	8	A STAR IS BORN — Soundtrack (CBS)
5	9	MAGIC FLY — Space (Pye)
9	10	GOING FOR THE ONE — Yes (Atlantic)
30	11	AJA — Steely Dan (ABC)
10	12	PLAYING TO AN AUDIENCE OF ONE — David Soul (Private Stock)
12	13	SHOW SOME EMOTION — Joan Armatrading (A&M)
15	14	I REMEMBER YESTERDAY — Donna Summer (GTO)
6	15	20 ALL TIME GREATS — Connie Francis (Polydor)
-	16	40 GOLDEN GREATS — Cliff Richard (EMI)
22	17	BOOMTOWN RATS — Boomtown Rats (Ensign)
19	18	HOME ON THE RANGE — Slim Whitman (United Artists)
29	19	PASSAGE — Carpenters (A&M)
17	20	HOTEL CALIFORNIA — Eagles (Asylum)
26	21	TWO DAYS AWAY — Elkie Brooks (A&M)
-	22	THUNDER IN MY HEART — Leo Sayer (Chrysalis)
18	23	THE VERY BEST OF FRANKIE LAINE — Frankie Laine (Warwick)
-	24	RAIN DANCES — Camel (Decca)
13	25	EXODUS — Bob Marley & the Wailers (Island)
14	26	WELCOME TO MY WORLD — Elvis Presley (RCA)
24	27	THE BEST OF ROD STEWART — Rod Stewart (Mercury)
23	28	ARRIVAL — Abba (Epic)
-	29	FAREWELL TO KINGS — Rush (Mercury)
-	30	GOLD AND IVORY — David Essex (CBS)

22 October 1977

last	this	title / artist
1	1	20 GOLDEN GREATS — Diana Ross & the Supremes (Motown)
3	2	NO MORE HEROES — Stranglers (United Artists)
2	3	OXYGENE — Jean-Michel Jarre (Polydor)
4	4	RUMOURS — Fleetwood Mac (Warner Bros.)
5	5	MOODY BLUE — Elvis Presley (RCA)
10	6	GOING FOR THE ONE — Yes (Atlantic)
19	7	PASSAGE — Carpenters (A&M)
18	8	HOME ON THE RANGE — Slim Whitman (United Artists)
7	9	BAD REPUTATION — Thin Lizzy (Vertigo)
8	10	A STAR IS BORN — Soundtrack (CBS)
6	11	LOVE YOU LIVE — Rolling Stones (Rolling Stones)
12	12	PLAYING TO AN AUDIENCE OF ONE — David Soul (Private Stock)
11	13	AJA — Steely Dan (ABC)
16	14	40 GOLDEN GREATS — Cliff Richard (EMI)
9	15	MAGIC FLY — Space (Pye)
13	16	SHOW SOME EMOTION — Joan Armatrading (A&M)
14	17	I REMEMBER YESTERDAY — Donna Summer (GTO)
21	18	TWO DAYS AWAY — Elkie Brooks (A&M)
22	19	THUNDER IN MY HEART — Leo Sayer (Chrysalis)
-	20	STRANGLERS IV (RATTUS NORVEGICUS) — Stranglers (United Artists)
20	21	HOTEL CALIFORNIA — Eagles (Asylum)
-	22	ELTON JOHN'S GREATEST HITS VOL 2 — Elton John (DJM)
-	23	GREATEST HITS — Abba (Epic)
-	24	SECONDS OUT — Genesis (Charisma)
15	25	20 ALL TIME GREATS — Connie Francis (Polydor)
17	26	BOOMTOWN RATS — Boomtown Rats (Ensign)
27	27	THE BEST OF ROD STEWART — Rod Stewart (Mercury)
24	28	RAIN DANCES — Camel (Decca)
25	29	EXODUS — Bob Marley & the Wailers (Island)
-	30	GONE TO EARTH — Barclay James Harvest (Polydor)

29 October 1977

last	this	title / artist
1	1	20 GOLDEN GREATS — Diana Ross & the Supremes (Motown)
2	2	NO MORE HEROES — Stranglers (United Artists)
14	3	40 GOLDEN GREATS — Cliff Richard (EMI)
8	4	HOME ON THE RANGE — Slim Whitman (United Artists)
4	5	RUMOURS — Fleetwood Mac (Warner Bros.)
11	6	LOVE YOU LIVE — Rolling Stones (Rolling Stones)
3	7	OXYGENE — Jean-Michel Jarre (Polydor)
5	8	MOODY BLUE — Elvis Presley (RCA)
10	9	A STAR IS BORN — Soundtrack (CBS)
6	10	GOING FOR THE ONE — Yes (Atlantic)
6	11	PASSAGE — Carpenters (A&M)
8	12	BAD REPUTATION — Thin Lizzy (Vertigo)
-	13	HEROES — David Bowie (RCA)
12	14	PLAYING TO AN AUDIENCE OF ONE — David Soul (Private Stock)
17	15	I REMEMBER YESTERDAY — Donna Summer (GTO)
19	16	THUNDER IN MY HEART — Leo Sayer (Chrysalis)
18	17	TWO DAYS AWAY — Elkie Brooks (A&M)
22	18	ELTON JOHN'S GREATEST HITS VOL 2 — Elton John (DJM)
15	19	SHOW SOME EMOTION — Joan Armatrading (A&M)
-	20	SOUL CITY — Various Artists (K-Tel)
15	21	MAGIC FLY — Space (Pye)
24	22	SECONDS OUT — Genesis (Charisma)
13	23	AJA — Steely Dan (ABC)
-	24	COUNTRY BOY — Don Williams (ABC)
24	25	20 ALL TIME GREATS — Connie Francis (Polydor)
-	26	THE JOHNNY MATHIS COLLECTION — Johnny Mathis (CBS)
21	27	HOTEL CALIFORNIA — Eagles (Asylum)
23	28	GREATEST HITS — Abba (Epic)
20	29	STRANGLERS IV (RATTUS NORVEGICUS) — Stranglers (United Artists)
27	30	THE BEST OF ROD STEWART — Rod Stewart (Mercury)

5 November 1977

last	this	title / artist
1	1	20 GOLDEN GREATS — Diana Ross & the Supremes (Motown)
3	2	40 GOLDEN GREATS — Cliff Richard (EMI)
2	3	NO MORE HEROES — Stranglers (United Artists)
5	4	RUMOURS — Fleetwood Mac (Warner Bros.)
13	5	HEROES — David Bowie (RCA)
4	6	HOME ON THE RANGE — Slim Whitman (United Artists)
7	7	OXYGENE — Jean-Michel Jarre (Polydor)
22	8	SECONDS OUT — Genesis (Charisma)
16	9	THUNDER IN MY HEART — Leo Sayer (Chrysalis)
9	10	A STAR IS BORN — Soundtrack (CBS)
10	11	GOING FOR THE ONE — Yes (Atlantic)
6	12	LOVE YOU LIVE — Rolling Stones (Rolling Stones)
7	13	MOODY BLUE — Elvis Presley (RCA)
18	14	ELTON JOHN'S GREATEST HITS VOL 2 — Elton John (DJM)
-	15	THE SOUND OF BREAD — Bread (Elektra)
11	16	PASSAGE — Carpenters (A&M)
28	17	GREATEST HITS — Abba (Epic)
14	18	PLAYING TO AN AUDIENCE OF ONE — David Soul (Private Stock)
23	19	AJA — Steely Dan (ABC)
20	20	SOUL CITY — Various Artists (K-Tel)
-	21	NEVER MIND THE BOLLOCKS HERE'S THE SEX PISTOLS — Sex Pistols (Virgin)
12	22	BAD REPUTATION — Thin Lizzy (Vertigo)
14	23	I REMEMBER YESTERDAY — Donna Summer (GTO)
-	24	NEWS OF THE WORLD — Queen (EMI)
21	25	MAGIC FLY — Space (Pye)
30	26	THE BEST OF ROD STEWART — Rod Stewart (Mercury)
-	27	FRONT PAGE NEWS — Wishbone Ash (MCA)
-	28	THEIR GREATEST HITS 1971–1975 — Eagles (Asylum)
-	29	ELVIS IN CONCERT — Elvis Presley (RCA)
-	30	OUT OF THE BLUE — Electric Light Orchestra (Jet)

Electric Light Orchestra were fronted by Jeff Lynne, once Roy Wood's lesser half in the Move. Roy later had some slight success with Wizzard but Lynne's ELO was far bigger. The overblown double-album *Out Of The Blue* would be their longest-charting. Jet Records belonged to notorious former Small Faces manager Don Arden, who'd said in 1972: "In an industry riddled with drug addicts, homosexuals and hangers-on, I am one of the few real men left." But *Never Mind The Bollocks Here's The Sex Pistols*.

November 1977

12 November 1977

last	this	Title / Artist (Label)
15	1	THE SOUND OF BREAD — Bread (Elektra)
2	2	40 GOLDEN GREATS — Cliff Richard (EMI)
1	3	20 GOLDEN GREATS — Diana Ross & the Supremes (Motown)
21	4	NEVER MIND THE BOLLOCKS HERE'S THE SEX PISTOLS — Sex Pistols (Virgin)
3	5	NO MORE HEROES — Stranglers (United Artists)
4	6	RUMOURS — Fleetwood Mac (Warner Bros.)
-	7	FOOTLOOSE & FANCY FREE — Rod Stewart (Riva)
9	8	THUNDER IN MY HEART — Leo Sayer (Chrysalis)
8	9	SECONDS OUT — Genesis (Charisma)
5	10	HEROES — David Bowie (RCA)
11	11	GOING FOR THE ONE — Yes (Atlantic)
7	12	OXYGENE — Jean-Michel Jarre (Polydor)
10	13	A STAR IS BORN — Soundtrack (CBS)
16	13	PASSAGE — Carpenters (A&M)
6	15	HOME ON THE RANGE — Slim Whitman (United Artists)
-	16	MOONFLOWER — Santana (CBS)
14	16	ELTON JOHN'S GREATEST HITS VOL 2 — Elton John (DJM)
23	18	NEWS OF THE WORLD — Queen (EMI)
30	19	OUT OF THE BLUE — Electric Light Orchestra (Jet)
20	20	SOUL CITY — Various Artists (K-Tel)
-	21	FEELINGS — Various Artists (K-Tel)
29	22	ELVIS IN CONCERT — Elvis Presley (RCA)
18	23	PLAYING TO AN AUDIENCE OF ONE — David Soul (Private Stock)
-	24	ONCE UPON A TIME — Donna Summer (GTO)
23	25	I REMEMBER YESTERDAY — Donna Summer (GTO)
12	26	LOVE YOU LIVE — Rolling Stones (Rolling Stones)
17	27	GREATEST HITS — Abba (Epic)
-	28	30 GREATEST — Gladys Knight & the Pips (K-Tel)
13	29	MOODY BLUE — Elvis Presley (RCA)
22	30	BAD REPUTATION — Thin Lizzy (Vertigo)

19 November 1977

last	this	Title / Artist (Label)
1	1	THE SOUND OF BREAD — Bread (Elektra)
4	2	NEVER MIND THE BOLLOCKS HERE'S THE SEX PISTOLS — Sex Pistols (Virgin)
3	3	20 GOLDEN GREATS — Diana Ross & the Supremes (Motown)
5	4	NO MORE HEROES — Stranglers (United Artists)
21	5	FEELINGS — Various Artists (K-Tel)
2	6	40 GOLDEN GREATS — Cliff Richard (EMI)
18	7	NEWS OF THE WORLD — Queen (EMI)
7	8	FOOTLOOSE & FANCY FREE — Rod Stewart (Riva)
16	9	MOONFLOWER — Santana (CBS)
6	10	RUMOURS — Fleetwood Mac (Warner Bros.)
16	11	ELTON JOHN'S GREATEST HITS VOL 2 — Elton John (DJM)
9	11	SECONDS OUT — Genesis (Charisma)
10	13	HEROES — David Bowie (RCA)
19	14	OUT OF THE BLUE — Electric Light Orchestra (Jet)
8	15	THUNDER IN MY HEART — Leo Sayer (Chrysalis)
-	15	ROCKIN' ALL OVER THE WORLD — Status Quo (Vertigo)
12	17	OXYGENE — Jean-Michel Jarre (Polydor)
13	18	PASSAGE — Carpenters (A&M)
11	19	GOING FOR THE ONE — Yes (Atlantic)
22	20	ELVIS IN CONCERT — Elvis Presley (RCA)
28	20	30 GREATEST — Gladys Knight & the Pips (K-Tel)
20	22	SOUL CITY — Various Artists (K-Tel)
27	23	GREATEST HITS — Abba (Epic)
15	24	HOME ON THE RANGE — Slim Whitman (United Artists)
-	25	ECHOES OF THE 60s — Various Artists (Phil Spector International)
-	26	STREET SURVIVORS — Lynyrd Skynyrd (MCA)
-	27	30 GOLDEN GREATS — George Mitchell Minstrels (EMI)
13	28	A STAR IS BORN — Soundtrack (CBS)
-	29	GET STONED — Rolling Stones (Arcade)
29	30	MOODY BLUE — Elvis Presley (RCA)

26 November 1977

last	this	Title / Artist (Label)
1	1	THE SOUND OF BREAD — Bread (Elektra)
2	2	NEVER MIND THE BOLLOCKS HERE'S THE SEX PISTOLS — Sex Pistols (Virgin)
8	3	FOOTLOOSE & FANCY FREE — Rod Stewart (Riva)
7	4	NEWS OF THE WORLD — Queen (EMI)
14	5	OUT OF THE BLUE — Electric Light Orchestra (Jet)
9	6	MOONFLOWER — Santana (CBS)
10	7	RUMOURS — Fleetwood Mac (Warner Bros.)
5	8	FEELINGS — Various Artists (K-Tel)
6	9	40 GOLDEN GREATS — Cliff Richard (EMI)
11	10	SECONDS OUT — Genesis (Charisma)
3	11	20 GOLDEN GREATS — Diana Ross & the Supremes (Motown)
4	12	NO MORE HEROES — Stranglers (United Artists)
-	13	DISCO FEVER — Various Artists (K-Tel)
20	14	30 GREATEST — Gladys Knight & the Pips (K-Tel)
15	15	ROCKIN' ALL OVER THE WORLD — Status Quo (Vertigo)
29	16	GET STONED — Rolling Stones (Arcade)
20	17	ELVIS IN CONCERT — Elvis Presley (RCA)
13	18	HEROES — David Bowie (RCA)
23	19	GREATEST HITS — Abba (Epic)
11	20	ELTON JOHN'S GREATEST HITS VOL 2 — Elton John (DJM)
15	20	THUNDER IN MY HEART — Leo Sayer (Chrysalis)
-	22	ROXY MUSIC'S GREATEST HITS — Roxy Music (Polydor)
18	23	PASSAGE — Carpenters (A&M)
27	24	30 GOLDEN GREATS — George Mitchell Minstrels (EMI)
-	25	STICK TO ME — Graham Parker & the Rumour (Vertigo)
19	26	GOING FOR THE ONE — Yes (Atlantic)
26	27	STREET SURVIVORS — Lynyrd Skynyrd (MCA)
-	28	LET THERE BE ROCK — AC/DC (Atlantic)
-	29	RED STAR — Showaddywaddy (Arista)
-	30	BLACK JOY — Soundtrack (Ronco)

3 December 1977

last	this	Title / Artist (Label)
1	1	THE SOUND OF BREAD — Bread (Elektra)
3	2	FOOTLOOSE & FANCY FREE — Rod Stewart (Riva)
2	3	NEVER MIND THE BOLLOCKS HERE'S THE SEX PISTOLS — Sex Pistols (Virgin)
15	4	ROCKIN' ALL OVER THE WORLD — Status Quo (Vertigo)
4	5	NEWS OF THE WORLD — Queen (EMI)
13	6	DISCO FEVER — Various Artists (K-Tel)
5	7	OUT OF THE BLUE — Electric Light Orchestra (Jet)
6	8	MOONFLOWER — Santana (CBS)
8	9	FEELINGS — Various Artists (K-Tel)
9	10	40 GOLDEN GREATS — Cliff Richard (EMI)
14	11	30 GREATEST — Gladys Knight & the Pips (K-Tel)
11	12	20 GOLDEN GREATS — Diana Ross & the Supremes (Motown)
7	13	RUMOURS — Fleetwood Mac (Warner Bros.)
16	13	GET STONED — Rolling Stones (Arcade)
24	15	30 GOLDEN GREATS — George Mitchell Minstrels (EMI)
12	16	NO MORE HEROES — Stranglers (United Artists)
17	17	ELVIS IN CONCERT — Elvis Presley (RCA)
20	18	ELTON JOHN'S GREATEST HITS VOL 2 — Elton John (DJM)
10	19	SECONDS OUT — Genesis (Charisma)
19	20	GREATEST HITS — Abba (Epic)
18	21	HEROES — David Bowie (RCA)
-	22	ECHOES OF THE 60s — Various Artists (Phil Spector International)
-	23	WORKS VOL 2 — Emerson Lake & Palmer (Manticore)
26	24	GOING FOR THE ONE — Yes (Atlantic)
-	25	HOME ON THE RANGE — Slim Whitman (United Artists)
-	26	SOUL CITY — Various Artists (K-Tel)
23	27	PASSAGE — Carpenters (A&M)
20	28	THUNDER IN MY HEART — Leo Sayer (Chrysalis)
22	29	ROXY MUSIC'S GREATEST HITS — Roxy Music (Polydor)
28	30	LET THERE BE ROCK — AC/DC (Atlantic)

Up from No.21 to No.4 for the Pistols, who then reached No.1 in most charts, though not the NME's, the music paper that had championed them first. It was almost a year after the first of their unarguable singles, *Anarchy In The UK* had charted on Christmas Day, 1976. *God Save The Queen*, a timely poke at British attitudes in Jubilee Year, had made No.1 in June, despite an airplay and W.H.Smith ban. *Pretty Vacant*, issued with *Queen* still Top 5, had peaked at 5 in July-August.

December 1977

10 December 1977

last week	this week	Title
1	1	THE SOUND OF BREAD — Bread (Elektra)
6	2	DISCO FEVER — Various Artists (K-Tel)
11	3	30 GREATEST — Gladys Knight & the Pips (K-Tel)
9	4	FEELINGS — Various Artists (K-Tel)
2	5	FOOTLOOSE & FANCY FREE — Rod Stewart (Riva)
4	6	ROCKIN' ALL OVER THE WORLD — Status Quo (Vertigo)
5	7	NEWS OF THE WORLD — Queen (EMI)
3	8	NEVER MIND THE BOLLOCKS HERE'S THE SEX PISTOLS — Sex Pistols (Virgin)
7	9	OUT OF THE BLUE — Electric Light Orchestra (Jet)
13	10	RUMOURS — Fleetwood Mac (Warner Bros.)
13	11	GET STONED — Rolling Stones (Arcade)
8	12	MOONFLOWER — Santana (CBS)
10	13	40 GOLDEN GREATS — Cliff Richard (EMI)
15	14	30 GOLDEN GREATS — George Mitchell Minstrels (EMI)
-	15	ONCE UPON A TIME — Donna Summer (GTO)
17	16	ELVIS IN CONCERT — Elvis Presley (RCA)
18	17	ELTON JOHN'S GREATEST HITS VOL 2 — Elton John (DJM)
20	18	GREATEST HITS — Abba (Epic)
16	19	NO MORE HEROES — Stranglers (United Artists)
-	20	ARRIVAL — Abba (Epic)
29	21	ROXY MUSIC'S GREATEST HITS — Roxy Music (Polydor)
24	22	GOING FOR THE ONE — Yes (Atlantic)
-	22	SLOWHAND — Eric Clapton (RSO)
21	24	HEROES — David Bowie (RCA)
12	25	20 GOLDEN GREATS — Diana Ross & the Supremes (Motown)
28	26	THUNDER IN MY HEART — Leo Sayer (Chrysalis)
-	27	GREATEST HITS, ETC. — Paul Simon (CBS)
-	28	CRIMINAL RECORD — Rick Wakeman (A&M)
-	29	A STAR IS BORN — Soundtrack (CBS)
-	30	RED STAR — Showaddywaddy (Arista)

17 December 1977

last week	this week	Title
2	1	DISCO FEVER — Various Artists (K-Tel)
1	2	THE SOUND OF BREAD — Bread (Elektra)
4	3	FEELINGS — Various Artists (K-Tel)
8	4	NEVER MIND THE BOLLOCKS HERE'S THE SEX PISTOLS — Sex Pistols (Virgin)
3	5	30 GREATEST — Gladys Knight & the Pips (K-Tel)
5	6	FOOTLOOSE & FANCY FREE — Rod Stewart (Riva)
10	7	RUMOURS — Fleetwood Mac (Warner Bros.)
6	8	ROCKIN' ALL OVER THE WORLD — Status Quo (Vertigo)
7	8	NEWS OF THE WORLD — Queen (EMI)
11	10	GET STONED — Rolling Stones (Arcade)
12	11	MOONFLOWER — Santana (CBS)
27	12	GREATEST HITS, ETC. — Paul Simon (CBS)
-	13	DEREK AND CLIVE COME AGAIN — Peter Cook & Dudley Moore (Virgin)
13	14	40 GOLDEN GREATS — Cliff Richard (EMI)
9	15	OUT OF THE BLUE — Electric Light Orchestra (Jet)
19	16	NO MORE HEROES — Stranglers (United Artists)
16	17	ELVIS IN CONCERT — Elvis Presley (RCA)
30	17	RED STAR — Showaddywaddy (Arista)
18	19	GREATEST HITS — Abba (Epic)
14	20	30 GOLDEN GREATS — George Mitchell Minstrels (EMI)
-	21	I'M GLAD YOU'RE HERE WITH ME TONIGHT — Neil Diamond (CBS)
-	22	WORKS VOL 2 — Emerson Lake & Palmer (Manticore)
17	23	ELTON JOHN'S GREATEST HITS VOL 2 — Elton John (DJM)
25	24	20 GOLDEN GREATS — Diana Ross & the Supremes (Motown)
15	25	ONCE UPON A TIME — Donna Summer (GTO)
28	26	CRIMINAL RECORD — Rick Wakeman (A&M)
22	27	SLOWHAND — Eric Clapton (RSO)
21	28	ROXY MUSIC'S GREATEST HITS — Roxy Music (Polydor)
-	29	SECONDS OUT — Genesis (Charisma)
20	30	ARRIVAL — Abba (Epic)

24 December 1977

last week	this week	Title
1	1	DISCO FEVER — Various Artists (K-Tel)
2	2	THE SOUND OF BREAD — Bread (Elektra)
4	3	NEVER MIND THE BOLLOCKS HERE'S THE SEX PISTOLS — Sex Pistols (Virgin)
5	4	30 GREATEST — Gladys Knight & the Pips (K-Tel)
6	5	FOOTLOOSE & FANCY FREE — Rod Stewart (Riva)
7	6	RUMOURS — Fleetwood Mac (Warner Bros.)
8	6	NEWS OF THE WORLD — Queen (EMI)
12	6	GREATEST HITS, ETC. — Paul Simon (CBS)
3	9	FEELINGS — Various Artists (K-Tel)
24	10	20 GOLDEN GREATS — Diana Ross & the Supremes (Motown)
11	11	MOONFLOWER — Santana (CBS)
10	12	GET STONED — Rolling Stones (Arcade)
8	13	ROCKIN' ALL OVER THE WORLD — Status Quo (Vertigo)
15	14	OUT OF THE BLUE — Electric Light Orchestra (Jet)
-	15	20 COUNTRY CLASSICS — Tammy Wynette (CBS)
14	16	40 GOLDEN GREATS — Cliff Richard (EMI)
19	17	GREATEST HITS — Abba (Epic)
21	18	I'M GLAD YOU'RE HERE WITH ME TONIGHT — Neil Diamond (CBS)
20	19	30 GOLDEN GREATS — George Mitchell Minstrels (EMI)
13	20	DEREK AND CLIVE COME AGAIN — Peter Cook & Dudley Moore (Virgin)
16	21	NO MORE HEROES — Stranglers (United Artists)
30	22	ARRIVAL — Abba (Epic)
23	23	ELTON JOHN'S GREATEST HITS VOL 2 — Elton John (DJM)
-	24	THE MUPPET SHOW — Muppets (Pye)
25	25	ONCE UPON A TIME — Donna Summer (GTO)
27	26	SLOWHAND — Eric Clapton (RSO)
-	27	THE BEST OF BING — Bing Crosby (MCA)
-	28	LIVE AND LET LIVE — 10 C.C. (Mercury)
17	29	RED STAR — Showaddywaddy (Arista)
-	30	SEASONS — Bing Crosby (Polydor)

After this year's *Izitso* no Cat Stevens album (aside from a 1990 *Very Best Of*) would chart again. Farewell too to November plane-crash fatalities Ronnie Van Zandt, lead singer, and other members of Lynyrd Skynyrd, a rootsier Allman Brothers whose LPs and chart placings never matched their live grandeur and popularity. Their 1974 UK tour as support to Dutch group Golden Earring, was their first time out of the American south. Their anthemic *Free Bird* would become a hit single in 1982.

*Punk offered no
worries to
Frank Sinatra
(top);
below:
Johnny Rotten
and the original
Bat Out Of Hell
– Meatloaf*

January 1978

7 January 1978

last week	this week	title	artist (label)
1	1	DISCO FEVER	Various Artists (K-Tel)
2	2	THE SOUND OF BREAD	Bread (WEA)
9	3	FEELINGS	Various Artists (K-Tel)
3	4	NEVER MIND THE BOLLOCKS HERE'S THE SEX PISTOLS	Sex Pistols (Virgin)
4	5	30 GREATEST	Gladys Knight & the Pips (K-Tel)
5	6	FOOTLOOSE & FANCY FREE	Rod Stewart (Riva)
6	7	RUMOURS	Fleetwood Mac (Warner Bros.)
8	8	NEWS OF THE WORLD	Queen (EMI)
15	9	20 COUNTRY CLASSICS	Tammy Wynette (CBS)
13	10	ROCKIN' ALL OVER THE WORLD	Status Quo (Vertigo)
12	11	GET STONED	Rolling Stones (Arcade)
11	12	MOONFLOWER	Santana (CBS)
14	13	OUT OF THE BLUE	Electric Light Orchestra (Jet)
18	14	I'M GLAD YOU'RE HERE WITH ME TONIGHT	Neil Diamond (CBS)
10	15	20 GREATEST	Diana Ross & the Supremes (Tamla Motown)
-	16	ELVIS IN CONCERT	Elvis Presley (RCA)
6	17	GREATEST HITS, ETC.	Paul Simon (CBS)
16	18	40 GOLDEN GREATS	Cliff Richard (EMI)
30	19	SEASONS	Bing Crosby (Polydor)
27	20	THE BEST OF BING	Bing Crosby (MCA)
17	21	GREATEST HITS	Abba (Epic)
19	22	30 GOLDEN GREATS	George Mitchell Minstrels (EMI)
-	23	THUNDER IN MY HEART	Leo Sayer (Chrysalis)
-	24	ECHOES OF THE 60s	Various Artists (Phil Spector International)
-	25	THE JOHNNY NASH COLLECTION	Johnny Nash (Epic)
22	26	ARRIVAL	Abba (Epic)
29	27	RED STAR	Showaddywaddy (Arista)
21	28	NO MORE HEROES	Stranglers (United Artists)
24	29	THE MUPPET SHOW	Muppets (Pye)
23	30	ELTON JOHN'S GREATEST HITS VOL 2	Elton John (DJM)

14 January 1978

	title	artist (label)
1 DISCO FEVER	Various Artists (K-Tel)	
2 THE SOUND OF BREAD	Bread (WEA)	
3 RUMOURS	Fleetwood Mac (Warner Bros.)	
4 FOOTLOOSE & FANCY FREE	Rod Stewart (Riva)	
5 20 COUNTRY CLASSICS	Tammy Wynette (CBS)	
6 30 GREATEST	Gladys Knight & the Pips (K-Tel)	
7 DONNA SUMMER'S GREATEST HITS	Donna Summer (GTO)	
8 NEWS OF THE WORLD	Queen (EMI)	
9 OUT OF THE BLUE	Electric Light Orchestra (Jet)	
10 GREATEST HITS, ETC.	Paul Simon (CBS)	
11 FEELINGS	Various Artists (K-Tel)	
12 ROCKIN' ALL OVER THE WORLD	Status Quo (Vertigo)	
13 ELTON JOHN'S GREATEST HITS VOL 2	Elton John (DJM)	
14 NEVER MIND THE BOLLOCKS HERE'S THE SEX PISTOLS	Sex Pistols (Virgin)	
15 20 GOLDEN GREATS	Diana Ross & the Supremes (Tamla Motown)	
16 GREATEST HITS	Abba (Epic)	
17 GET STONED	Rolling Stones (Arcade)	
18 I'M GLAD YOU'RE HERE WITH ME TONIGHT	Neil Diamond (CBS)	
19 MOONFLOWER	Santana (CBS)	
20 RED STAR	Showaddywaddy (Arista)	
21 LIVE AND LET LIVE	10 c.c. (Mercury)	
22 ARRIVAL	Abba (Epic)	
23 EXODUS	Bob Marley & the Wailers (Island)	
24 DEREK AND CLIVE COME AGAIN	Peter Cook & Dudley Moore (Virgin)	
25 ELVIS IN CONCERT	Elvis Presley (RCA)	
26 THE JOHNNY NASH COLLECTION	Johnny Nash (Epic)	
27 GOING FOR THE ONE	Yes (Atlantic)	
28 BY REQUEST	Salvation Army (Warwick)	
29 NEW BOOTS & PANTIES!!	Ian Dury and the Blockheads (Stiff)	
30 THE MUPPET SHOW	Muppets (Pye)	

21 January 1978

last	this	title	artist (label)
3	1	RUMOURS	Fleetwood Mac (Warner Bros.)
2	2	THE SOUND OF BREAD	Bread (WEA)
1	3	DISCO FEVER	Various Artists (K-Tel)
7	4	DONNA SUMMER'S GREATEST HITS	Donna Summer (GTO)
13	5	NEVER MIND THE BOLLOCKS HERE'S THE SEX PISTOLS	Sex Pistols (Virgin)
5	6	20 COUNTRY CLASSICS	Tammy Wynette (CBS)
11	7	FEELINGS	Various Artists (K-Tel)
13	8	ELTON JOHN'S GREATEST HITS VOL 2	Elton John (DJM)
4	9	FOOTLOOSE & FANCY FREE	Rod Stewart (Riva)
9	10	OUT OF THE BLUE	Electric Light Orchestra (Jet)
15	11	20 GOLDEN GREATS	Diana Ross & the Supremes (Tamla Motown)
10	12	GREATEST HITS, ETC.	Paul Simon (CBS)
6	13	30 GREATEST	Gladys Knight & the Pips (K-Tel)
8	14	NEWS OF THE WORLD	Queen (EMI)
15	15	GREATEST HITS	Abba (Epic)
19	16	MOONFLOWER	Santana (CBS)
23	17	EXODUS	Bob Marley & the Wailers (Island)
22	18	ARRIVAL	Abba (Epic)
20	19	RED STAR	Showaddywaddy (Arista)
17	20	GET STONED	Rolling Stones (Arcade)
12	21	ROCKIN' ALL OVER THE WORLD	Status Quo (Vertigo)
24	22	DEREK AND CLIVE COME AGAIN	Peter Cook & Dudley Moore (Virgin)
29	23	NEW BOOTS & PANTIES!!	Ian Dury and the Blockheads (Stiff)
-	24	ALL 'N' ALL	Earth Wind & Fire (CBS)
28	25	BY REQUEST	Salvation Army (Warwick)
-	26	LOVE SONGS	Beatles (Parlophone)
25	27	ELVIS IN CONCERT	Elvis Presley (RCA)
-	28	40 GOLDEN GREATS	Cliff Richard (EMI)
-	29	SECONDS OUT	Genesis (Charisma)
-	30	DARTS	Darts (Magnet)

28 January 1978

last	this	title	artist (label)
1	1	RUMOURS	Fleetwood Mac (Warner Bros.)
2	2	THE SOUND OF BREAD	Bread (WEA)
3	3	DISCO FEVER	Various Artists (K-Tel)
4	4	DONNA SUMMER'S GREATEST HITS	Donna Summer (GTO)
4	5	NEVER MIND THE BOLLOCKS HERE'S THE SEX PISTOLS	Sex Pistols (Virgin)
6	6	20 COUNTRY CLASSICS	Tammy Wynette (CBS)
7	7	THE ALBUM	Abba (Epic)
9	8	FOOTLOOSE & FANCY FREE	Rod Stewart (Riva)
10	9	OUT OF THE BLUE	Electric Light Orchestra (Jet)
8	9	ELTON JOHN'S GREATEST HITS VOL 2	Elton John (DJM)
13	11	30 GREATEST	
15	12	MOONFLOWER	Santana (CBS)
26	13	LOVE SONGS	Beatles (Parlophone)
7	14	FEELINGS	Various Artists (K-Tel)
13	15	NEWS OF THE WORLD	Queen (EMI)
18	16	ARRIVAL	Abba (Epic)
17	17	EXODUS	Bob Marley & the Wailers (Island)
21	18	ROCKIN' ALL OVER THE WORLD	Status Quo (Vertigo)
12	19	GREATEST HITS, ETC.	Paul Simon (CBS)
11	20	20 GOLDEN GREATS	Diana Ross & the Supremes (Tamla Motown)
15	21	GREATEST HITS	Abba (Epic)
22	22	DEREK AND CLIVE COME AGAIN	Peter Cook & Dudley Moore (Virgin)
20	23	GET STONED	Rolling Stones (Arcade)
-	24	I'M GLAD YOU'RE HERE WITH ME TONIGHT	Neil Diamond (CBS)
-	25	OLIVIA NEWTON-JOHN'S GREATEST HITS	Olivia Newton-John (EMI)
24	26	ALL 'N' ALL	Earth Wind & Fire (CBS)
-	27	THE JOHNNY NASH COLLECTION	Johnny Nash (Epic)
28	28	40 GOLDEN GREATS	Cliff Richard (EMI)
-	29	DON JUAN'S RECKLESS DAUGHTER	Joni Mitchell (Asylum)
-	30	RUNNING ON EMPTY	Jackson Browne (Asylum)

Current disco was like Donna Summer music: it owed more to 1970s Bee Gees than to the late '60s disco funk of people like Isaac Hayes. By the end of January the ex-No.1 album *Disco Fever* and Donna were together in the Top 3. Ms Summer's current hit single, *Love's Unkind*, was also in the Top 3. She'd had other high-flyers like *Love To Love You Baby* (her 1976 chart debut) and August 1977's chart-topper *I Feel Love*, and many minor hits. More would follow.

February 1978

4 February 1978

last	this	Title	Artist (Label)
1	1	RUMOURS	Fleetwood Mac (Warner Bros.)
7	2	THE ALBUM	Abba (Epic)
2	3	THE SOUND OF BREAD	Bread (WEA)
4	4	DONNA SUMMER'S GREATEST HITS	Donna Summer (GTO)
8	5	FOOTLOOSE & FANCY FREE	Rod Stewart (Riva)
9	6	ELTON JOHN'S GREATEST HITS VOL 2	Elton John (DJM)
6	7	20 COUNTRY CLASSICS	Tammy Wynette (CBS)
3	8	DISCO FEVER	Various Artists (K-Tel)
5	9	NEVER MIND THE BOLLOCKS HERE'S THE SEX PISTOLS	Sex Pistols (Virgin)
9	10	OUT OF THE BLUE	Electric Light Orchestra (Jet)
-	11	REFLECTIONS	Andy Williams (CBS)
13	12	LOVE SONGS	Beatles (Parlophone)
21	13	GREATEST HITS	Abba (Epic)
15	14	NEWS OF THE WORLD	Queen (EMI)
24	15	I'M GLAD YOU'RE HERE WITH ME TONIGHT	Neil Diamond (CBS)
12	16	MOONFLOWER	Santana (CBS)
-	17	FLORAL DANCE	Brighouse & Rastrick Brass Band (Logo)
17	18	EXODUS	Bob Marley & the Wailers (Island)
19	19	GREATEST HITS, ETC.	Paul Simon (CBS)
26	20	ALL 'N' ALL	Earth Wind & Fire (CBS)
20	21	20 GOLDEN GREATS	Diana Ross & the Supremes (Tamla Motown)
14	22	FEELINGS	Various Artists (K-Tel)
25	23	OLIVIA NEWTON-JOHN'S GREATEST HITS	Olivia Newton-John (EMI)
11	24	30 GREATEST	Gladys Knight & the Pips (K-Tel)
-	25	NEW BOOTS & PANTIES!!	Ian Dury & the Blockheads (Stiff)
18	26	ROCKIN' ALL OVER THE WORLD	Status Quo (Vertigo)
16	27	ARRIVAL	Abba (Epic)
-	28	VARIATONS	Andrew Lloyd Webber (MCA)
-	29	WE MUST BELIEVE IN MAGIC	Crystal Gayle (United Artists)
29	29	DON JUAN'S RECKLESS DAUGHTER	Joni Mitchell (Asylum)

11 February 1978

last	this	Title	Artist (Label)
2	1	THE ALBUM	Abba (Epic)
1	2	RUMOURS	Fleetwood Mac (Warner Bros.)
4	3	DONNA SUMMER'S GREATEST HITS	Donna Summer (GTO)
5	4	FOOTLOOSE & FANCY FREE	Rod Stewart (Riva)
3	5	THE SOUND OF BREAD	Bread (WEA)
18	6	EXODUS	Bob Marley & the Wailers (Island)
9	7	NEVER MIND THE BOLLOCKS HERE'S THE SEX PISTOLS	Sex Pistols (Virgin)
8	8	DISCO FEVER	Various Artists (K-Tel)
10	9	OUT OF THE BLUE	Electric Light Orchestra (Jet)
7	10	20 COUNTRY CLASSICS	Tammy Wynette (CBS)
25	11	NEW BOOTS & PANTIES!!	Ian Dury & the Blockheads (Stiff)
12	12	LOVE SONGS	Beatles (Parlophone)
11	13	REFLECTIONS	Andy Williams (CBS)
6	14	ELTON JOHN'S GREATEST HITS VOL 2	Elton John (DJM)
17	15	FLORAL DANCE	Brighouse & Rastrick Brass Band (Logo)
20	16	ALL 'N' ALL	Earth Wind & Fire (CBS)
22	16	FEELINGS	Various Artists (K-Tel)
28	18	VARIATONS	Andrew Lloyd Webber (MCA)
16	19	MOONFLOWER	Santana (CBS)
24	20	30 GREATEST	Gladys Knight & the Pips (K-Tel)
14	21	NEWS OF THE WORLD	Queen (EMI)
13	22	GREATEST HITS	Abba (Epic)
23	23	OLIVIA NEWTON-JOHN'S GREATEST HITS	Olivia Newton-John (EMI)
21	24	20 GOLDEN GREATS	Diana Ross & the Supremes (Tamla Motown)
15	25	I'M GLAD YOU'RE HERE WITH ME TONIGHT	Neil Diamond (CBS)
27	26	ARRIVAL	Abba (Epic)
29	27	DON JUAN'S RECKLESS DAUGHTER	Joni Mitchell (Asylum)
-	28	BEST FRIENDS	Cleo Laine & John Williams (RCA)
-	29	STAR WARS	Soundtrack (20th Century)
19	30	GREATEST HITS, ETC.	Paul Simon (CBS)

18 February 1978

last	this	Title	Artist (Label)
1	1	THE ALBUM	Abba (Epic)
2	2	RUMOURS	Fleetwood Mac (Warner Bros.)
9	3	OUT OF THE BLUE	Electric Light Orchestra (Jet)
3	4	DONNA SUMMER'S GREATEST HITS	Donna Summer (GTO)
6	5	EXODUS	Bob Marley & the Wailers (Island)
4	6	FOOTLOOSE & FANCY FREE	Rod Stewart (Riva)
5	7	THE SOUND OF BREAD	Bread (WEA)
18	8	VARIATONS	Andrew Lloyd Webber (MCA)
11	9	NEW BOOTS & PANTIES!!	Ian Dury & the Blockheads (Stiff)
13	10	REFLECTIONS	Andy Williams (CBS)
8	11	DISCO FEVER	Various Artists (K-Tel)
12	12	LOVE SONGS	Beatles (Parlophone)
14	13	ELTON JOHN'S GREATEST HITS VOL 2	Elton John (DJM)
19	14	MOONFLOWER	Santana (CBS)
7	15	NEVER MIND THE BOLLOCKS HERE'S THE SEX PISTOLS	Sex Pistols (Virgin)
15	16	FLORAL DANCE	Brighouse & Rastrick Brass Band (Logo)
16	17	ALL 'N' ALL	Earth Wind & Fire (CBS)
10	18	20 COUNTRY CLASSICS	Tammy Wynette (CBS)
16	19	FEELINGS	Various Artists (K-Tel)
22	20	GREATEST HITS	Abba (Epic)
25	21	I'M GLAD YOU'RE HERE WITH ME TONIGHT	Neil Diamond (CBS)
-	22	WHITE MUSIC	XTC (Virgin)
-	23	RUNNING ON EMPTY	Jackson Browne (Asylum)
-	24	PLASTIC LETTERS	Blondie (Chrysalis)
29	25	STAR WARS	Soundtrack (20th Century)
-	26	DARTS	Darts (Magnet)
-	27	THE MUPPET SHOW VOL. 2	Muppets (Pye)
-	28	DISCO STARS	Various Artists (K-Tel)
20	29	30 GREATEST	Gladys Knight & the Pips (K-Tel)
27	30	DON JUAN'S RECKLESS DAUGHTER	Joni Mitchell (Asylum)

25 February 1978

last	this	Title	Artist (Label)
1	1	THE ALBUM	Abba (Epic)
2	2	RUMOURS	Fleetwood Mac (Warner Bros.)
8	3	VARIATONS	Andrew Lloyd Webber (MCA)
6	4	FOOTLOOSE & FANCY FREE	Rod Stewart (Riva)
3	5	OUT OF THE BLUE	Electric Light Orchestra (Jet)
4	6	DONNA SUMMER'S GREATEST HITS	Donna Summer (GTO)
9	7	NEW BOOTS & PANTIES!!	Ian Dury & the Blockheads (Stiff)
11	8	DISCO FEVER	Various Artists (K-Tel)
5	9	EXODUS	Bob Marley & the Wailers (Island)
15	9	NEVER MIND THE BOLLOCKS HERE'S THE SEX PISTOLS	Sex Pistols (Virgin)
10	11	REFLECTIONS	Andy Williams (CBS)
7	12	THE SOUND OF BREAD	Bread (WEA)
13	12	ELTON JOHN'S GREATEST HITS VOL 2	Elton John (DJM)
16	14	FLORAL DANCE	Brighouse & Rastrick Brass Band (Logo)
17	15	ALL 'N' ALL	Earth Wind & Fire (CBS)
12	16	LOVE SONGS	Beatles (Parlophone)
22	17	WHITE MUSIC	XTC (Virgin)
-	18	I WANT TO LIVE	John Denver (RCA)
-	19	ARRIVAL	Abba (Epic)
19	20	FEELINGS	Various Artists (K-Tel)
21	21	I'M GLAD YOU'RE HERE WITH ME TONIGHT	Neil Diamond (CBS)
-	22	ROCKIN' ALL OVER THE WORLD	Status Quo (Vertigo)
27	23	THE MUPPET SHOW VOL. 2	Muppets (Pye)
20	24	GREATEST HITS	Abba (Epic)
-	25	BEST FRIENDS	Cleo Laine & John Williams (RCA)
-	26	COUNTRY GIRL MEETS COUNTRY BOY	Various Artists (CBS/Warwick)
-	27	WE MUST BELIEVE IN MAGIC	Crystal Gayle (United Artists)
28	28	DISCO STARS	Various Artists (K-Tel)
25	29	STAR WARS	Soundtrack (20th Century)
-	30	OLIVIA NEWTON-JOHN'S GREATEST HITS	Olivia Newton-John (EMI)

Another Donna arose. Celebrations took place all over Britain, specially in Scotland, as an act destined never to make the album chart knocked Wings' *Mull Of Kintyre* off the top of the singles chart, where it had solidified for nine weeks. The further achievement of Althia and Donna's delightfully loopy *Uptown Top Ranking* was of course to give another meaning to the brand-name Rank other than as in the long-popular expression "having a J.Arthur". In the LP chart, solemn Swedish glam ruled.

March 1978

4 March 1978

last week	this week	title / artist
1	1	THE ALBUM — Abba (Epic)
2	2	RUMOURS — Fleetwood Mac (Warner Bros.)
3	3	VARIATONS — Andrew Lloyd Webber (MCA)
6	4	DONNA SUMMER'S GREATEST HITS — Donna Summer (GTO)
5	5	OUT OF THE BLUE — Electric Light Orchestra (Jet)
11	6	REFLECTIONS — Andy Williams (CBS)
4	7	FOOTLOOSE & FANCY FREE — Rod Stewart (Riva)
7	8	NEW BOOTS & PANTIES!! — Ian Dury & the Blockheads (Stiff)
12	9	THE SOUND OF BREAD — Bread (WEA)
-	10	20 GOLDEN GREATS — Buddy Holly & the Crickets (MCA)
28	11	DISCO STARS — Various Artists (K-Tel)
24	12	GREATEST HITS — Abba (Epic)
-	13	DARTS — Darts (Magnet)
15	14	ALL 'N' ALL — Earth Wind & Fire (CBS)
9	15	EXODUS — Bob Marley & the Wailers (Island)
9	16	NEVER MIND THE BOLLOCKS HERE'S THE SEX PISTOLS — Sex Pistols (Virgin)
-	17	THE KICK INSIDE — Kate Bush (EMI)
-	18	DRASTIC PLASTIC — Be-Bop Deluxe (Harvest)
20	19	FEELINGS — Various Artists (K-Tel)
-	20	PASTICHE — Manhattan Transfer (Atlantic)
-	21	30 GREATEST — Gladys Knight & the Pips (K-Tel)
8	22	DISCO FEVER — Various Artists (K-Tel)
16	23	LOVE SONGS — Beatles (Parlophone)
-	24	IN FULL BLOOM — Rose Royce (Warner Bros.)
12	25	ELTON JOHN'S GREATEST HITS VOL 2 — Elton John (DJM)
29	26	STAR WARS — Soundtrack (20th Century)
17	27	WHITE MUSIC — XTC (Virgin)
-	28	CITY TO CITY — Gerry Rafferty (United Artists)
23	29	THE MUPPET SHOW VOL. 2 — Muppets (Pye)
25	30	BEST FRIENDS — Cleo Laine & John Williams (RCA)

11 March 1978

this week	title / artist
1	THE ALBUM — Abba (Epic)
2	RUMOURS — Fleetwood Mac (Warner Bros.)
3	VARIATONS — Andrew Lloyd Webber (MCA)
4	OUT OF THE BLUE — Electric Light Orchestra (Jet)
5	REFLECTIONS — Andy Williams (CBS)
6	20 GOLDEN GREATS — Buddy Holly & the Crickets (MCA)
7	FOOTLOOSE & FANCY FREE — Rod Stewart (Riva)
8	NEW BOOTS & PANTIES!! — Ian Dury & the Blockheads (Stiff)
9	DARTS — Darts (Magnet)
10	DISCO STARS — Various Artists (K-Tel)
11	THE KICK INSIDE — Kate Bush (EMI)
12	DONNA SUMMER'S GREATEST HITS — Donna Summer (GTO)
13	25 THUMPING GREAT HITS — Dave Clark Five (Polydor)
14	CITY TO CITY — Gerry Rafferty (United Artists)
15	THE SOUND OF BREAD — Bread (WEA)
16	BOOGIE NIGHTS — Bob Marley & the Wailers (Island)
17	ARRIVAL — Abba (Epic)
18	EXODUS — Bob Marley & the Wailers (Island)
19	ALL 'N' ALL — Earth Wind & Fire (CBS)
20	GREATEST HITS — Abba (Epic)
21	THE MUPPET SHOW VOL. 2 — Muppets (Pye)
22	IN FULL BLOOM — Rose Royce (Warner Bros.)
23	LOVE SONGS — Beatles (Parlophone)
24	PLASTIC LETTERS — Blondie (Chrysalis)
25	WAITING FOR COLUMBUS — Little Feat (Warner Bros.)
26	STAR WARS — Soundtrack (20th Century)
27	JESUS OF COOL — Nick Lowe (Radar)
28	BEST FRIENDS — Cleo Laine & John Williams (RCA)
29	DRASTIC PLASTIC — Be-Bop Deluxe (Harvest)
30	PASTICHE — Manhattan Transfer (Atlantic)

18 March 1978

last week	this week	title / artist
1	1	THE ALBUM — Abba (Epic)
6	2	20 GOLDEN GREATS — Buddy Holly & the Crickets (MCA)
5	3	REFLECTIONS — Andy Williams (CBS)
11	4	THE KICK INSIDE — Kate Bush (EMI)
2	5	RUMOURS — Fleetwood Mac (Warner Bros.)
3	6	VARIATONS — Andrew Lloyd Webber (MCA)
4	7	OUT OF THE BLUE — Electric Light Orchestra (Jet)
9	8	DARTS — Darts (Magnet)
13	9	25 THUMPING GREAT HITS — Dave Clark Five (Polydor)
7	10	FOOTLOOSE & FANCY FREE — Rod Stewart (Riva)
15	11	THE SOUND OF BREAD — Bread (WEA)
19	12	ALL 'N' ALL — Earth Wind & Fire (CBS)
14	13	CITY TO CITY — Gerry Rafferty (United Artists)
8	14	NEW BOOTS & PANTIES!! — Ian Dury & the Blockheads (Stiff)
-	15	FONZIE'S FAVOURITES — Various Artists (Warwick)
12	16	DONNA SUMMER'S GREATEST HITS — Donna Summer (GTO)
24	17	PLASTIC LETTERS — Blondie (Chrysalis)
10	18	DISCO STARS — Various Artists (K-Tel)
17	19	ARRIVAL — Abba (Epic)
22	20	IN FULL BLOOM — Rose Royce (Warner Bros.)
20	21	GREATEST HITS — Abba (Epic)
30	22	PASTICHE — Manhattan Transfer (Atlantic)
-	23	SATURDAY NIGHT FEVER — Soundtrack (RSO)
16	24	BOOGIE NIGHTS — Various Artists (Ronco)
27	25	JESUS OF COOL — Nick Lowe (Radar)
18	26	EXODUS — Bob Marley & the Wailers (Island)
-	27	NEVER MIND THE BOLLOCKS HERE'S THE SEX PISTOLS — Sex Pistols (Virgin)
21	28	THE MUPPET SHOW VOL. 2 — Muppets (Pye)
23	29	LOVE SONGS — Beatles (Parlophone)
28	30	BEST FRIENDS — Cleo Laine & John Williams (RCA)

25 March 1978

last week	this week	title / artist
1	1	THE ALBUM — Abba (Epic)
2	2	20 GOLDEN GREATS — Buddy Holly & the Crickets (MCA)
4	3	THE KICK INSIDE — Kate Bush (EMI)
3	4	REFLECTIONS — Andy Williams (CBS)
7	5	OUT OF THE BLUE — Electric Light Orchestra (Jet)
5	6	RUMOURS — Fleetwood Mac (Warner Bros.)
6	7	VARIATONS — Andrew Lloyd Webber (MCA)
13	8	CITY TO CITY — Gerry Rafferty (United Artists)
17	9	PLASTIC LETTERS — Blondie (Chrysalis)
24	10	BOOGIE NIGHTS — Various Artists (Ronco)
18	11	DISCO STARS — Various Artists (K-Tel)
8	12	DARTS — Darts (Magnet)
14	13	NEW BOOTS & PANTIES!! — Ian Dury & the Blockheads (Stiff)
15	14	FONZIE'S FAVOURITES — Various Artists (Warwick)
21	15	PASTICHE — Manhattan Transfer (Atlantic)
26	16	EXODUS — Bob Marley & the Wailers (Island)
10	17	FOOTLOOSE & FANCY FREE — Rod Stewart (Riva)
9	18	25 THUMPING GREAT HITS — Dave Clark Five (Polydor)
-	19	KAYA — Bob Marley & the Wailers (Island)
11	20	THE SOUND OF BREAD — Bread (WEA)
-	21	THIS YEAR'S MODEL — Elvis Costello (Radar)
25	22	JESUS OF COOL — Nick Lowe (Radar)
21	23	GREATEST HITS — Abba (Epic)
16	24	DONNA SUMMER'S GREATEST HITS — Donna Summer (GTO)
12	25	ALL 'N' ALL — Earth Wind & Fire (CBS)
19	26	ARRIVAL — Abba (Epic)
-	27	THEIR GREATEST HITS 1971-1975 — Eagles (Asylum)
-	28	ANOTHER MUSIC IN A DIFFERENT KITCHEN — Buzzcocks (United Artists)
-	29	BAT OUT OF HELL — Meatloaf (Epic)
23	30	SATURDAY NIGHT FEVER — Soundtrack (RSO)

"New" arrivals included old pub-rocker Ian Dury, on the punk indie label Stiff; New Boots & Panties, a sleeper that had first pottered into the chart basement the previous October, first made the 30 for a fortnight in January and then re-entered with more conviction in February. Kate Bush debuted with *The Kick Inside*, which kicked up high, as did Gerry Rafferty's first post-Stealers Wheel solo album *City To City*. Bush's *Wuthering Heights* single was No.1; Rafferty's *Baker Street* would peak at No.2 in early April.

April 1978

1 April 1978

last	this	album	artist (label)
3	1	THE KICK INSIDE	Kate Bush (EMI)
1	2	THE ALBUM	Abba (Epic)
2	3	20 GOLDEN GREATS	Buddy Holly & the Crickets (MCA)
6	4	RUMOURS	Fleetwood Mac (Warner Bros.)
4	5	REFLECTIONS	Andy Williams (CBS)
5	6	OUT OF THE BLUE	Electric Light Orchestra (Jet)
9	7	PLASTIC LETTERS	Blondie (Chrysalis)
7	8	CITY TO CITY	Gerry Rafferty (United Artists)
7	9	VARIATONS	Andrew Lloyd Webber (MCA)
13	10	FONZIE'S FAVOURITES	Various Artists (Warwick)
10	11	BOOGIE NIGHTS	Various Artists (Ronco)
18	12	25 THUMPING GREAT HITS	Dave Clark Five (Polydor)
12	13	DARTS	Darts (Magnet)
15	14	PASTICHE	Manhattan Transfer (Atlantic)
19	15	KAYA	Bob Marley & the Wailers (Island)
30	16	SATURDAY NIGHT FEVER	Soundtrack (RSO)
25	17	ALL 'N' ALL	Earth Wind & Fire (CBS)
21	18	THIS YEAR'S MODEL	Elvis Costello (Radar)
26	19	ARRIVAL	Abba (Epic)
-	20	IN FULL BLOOM	Rose Royce (Warner Bros.)
5	21	20 GOLDEN GREATS	Nat 'King' Cole (Capitol)
13	22	NEW BOOTS & PANTIES!!	Ian Dury & the Blockheads (Stiff)
16	23	EXODUS	Bob Marley & the Wailers (Island)
23	24	GREATEST HITS	Abba (Epic)
-	25	WATERMARK	Art Garfunkel (CBS)
17	26	FOOTLOOSE & FANCY FREE	Rod Stewart (Riva)
11	27	DISCO STARS	Various Artists (K-Tel)
22	28	JESUS OF COOL	Nick Lowe (Radar)
24	29	DONNA SUMMER'S GREATEST HITS	Donna Summer (GTO)
29	30	BAT OUT OF HELL	Meatloaf (Epic)

8 April 1978

last	this	album	artist (label)
1	1	THE KICK INSIDE	Kate Bush (EMI)
3	2	20 GOLDEN GREATS	Buddy Holly & the Crickets (MCA)
8	3	THE ALBUM	Abba (Epic)
4	4	CITY TO CITY	Gerry Rafferty (United Artists)
21	5	20 GOLDEN GREATS	Nat 'King' Cole (Capitol)
16	6	SATURDAY NIGHT FEVER	Soundtrack (RSO)
5	7	REFLECTIONS	Andy Williams (CBS)
6	8	OUT OF THE BLUE	Electric Light Orchestra (Jet)
4	9	RUMOURS	Fleetwood Mac (Warner Bros.)
15	10	KAYA	Bob Marley & the Wailers (Island)
7	11	PLASTIC LETTERS	Blondie (Chrysalis)
10	12	FONZIE'S FAVOURITES	Various Artists (Warwick)
-	13	LONDON TOWN	Wings (EMI)
18	14	THIS YEAR'S MODEL	Elvis Costello (Radar)
14	15	PASTICHE	Manhattan Transfer (Atlantic)
-	16	AND THEN THERE WERE THREE	Genesis (Charisma)
11	17	BOOGIE NIGHTS	Various Artists (Ronco)
12	18	25 THUMPING GREAT HITS	Dave Clark Five (Polydor)
27	19	DISCO STARS	Various Artists (K-Tel)
9	20	VARIATONS	Andrew Lloyd Webber (MCA)
-	21	THE SOUND OF BREAD	Bread (WEA)
13	22	DARTS	Darts (Magnet)
24	23	GREATEST HITS	Abba (Epic)
17	24	ALL 'N' ALL	Earth Wind & Fire (CBS)
-	25	ANOTHER MUSIC IN A DIFFERENT KITCHEN	Buzzcocks (United Artists)
-	26	THE STRANGER	Billy Joel (CBS)
30	27	BAT OUT OF HELL	Meatloaf (Epic)
22	28	NEW BOOTS & PANTIES!!	Ian Dury & the Blockheads (Stiff)
20	29	IN FULL BLOOM	Rose Royce (Warner Bros.)
25	30	WATERMARK	Art Garfunkel (CBS)

15 April 1978

last	this	album	artist (label)
5	1	20 GOLDEN GREATS	Nat 'King' Cole (Capitol)
3	2	THE ALBUM	Abba (Epic)
6	3	SATURDAY NIGHT FEVER	Soundtrack (RSO)
2	4	20 GOLDEN GREATS	Buddy Holly & the Crickets (MCA)
1	5	THE KICK INSIDE	Kate Bush (EMI)
10	6	KAYA	Bob Marley & the Wailers (Island)
4	7	CITY TO CITY	Gerry Rafferty (United Artists)
14	8	THIS YEAR'S MODEL	Elvis Costello (Radar)
13	9	LONDON TOWN	Wings (EMI)
11	10	PLASTIC LETTERS	Blondie (Chrysalis)
16	11	AND THEN THERE WERE THREE	Genesis (Charisma)
7	12	REFLECTIONS	Andy Williams (CBS)
8	13	OUT OF THE BLUE	Electric Light Orchestra (Jet)
15	14	PASTICHE	Manhattan Transfer (Atlantic)
8	15	RUMOURS	Fleetwood Mac (Warner Bros.)
25	16	ANOTHER MUSIC IN A DIFFERENT KITCHEN	Buzzcocks (United Artists)
12	17	FONZIE'S FAVOURITES	Various Artists (Warwick)
-	18	ARRIVAL	Abba (Epic)
17	19	BOOGIE NIGHTS	Various Artists (Ronco)
20	20	VARIATONS	Andrew Lloyd Webber (MCA)
-	21	EXODUS	Bob Marley & the Wailers (Island)
27	22	BAT OUT OF HELL	Meatloaf (Epic)
22	23	DARTS	Darts (Magnet)
18	24	25 THUMPING GREAT HITS	Dave Clark Five (Polydor)
21	25	THE SOUND OF BREAD	Bread (WEA)
28	26	NEW BOOTS & PANTIES!!	Ian Dury & the Blockheads (Stiff)
-	27	BEST FRIENDS	Cleo Laine & John Williams (RCA)
24	28	ALL 'N' ALL	Earth Wind & Fire (CBS)
-	29	TELL US THE TRUTH	Sham 69 (Phonogram)
-	30	THE RUTLES	Rutles (Warner Bros.)

22 April 1978

last	this	album	artist (label)
1	1	20 GOLDEN GREATS	Nat 'King' Cole (Capitol)
3	2	SATURDAY NIGHT FEVER	Soundtrack (RSO)
11	3	AND THEN THERE WERE THREE	Genesis (Charisma)
9	4	LONDON TOWN	Wings (EMI)
2	5	THE ALBUM	Abba (Epic)
6	6	KAYA	Bob Marley & the Wailers (Island)
4	7	20 GOLDEN GREATS	Buddy Holly & the Crickets (MCA)
7	8	CITY TO CITY	Gerry Rafferty (United Artists)
5	9	THE KICK INSIDE	Kate Bush (EMI)
8	10	THIS YEAR'S MODEL	Elvis Costello (Radar)
-	11	THE STUD - SOUNDTRACK	Various Artists (Ronco)
10	12	PLASTIC LETTERS	Blondie (Chrysalis)
15	13	RUMOURS	Fleetwood Mac (Warner Bros.)
13	14	OUT OF THE BLUE	Electric Light Orchestra (Jet)
30	15	THE RUTLES	Rutles (Warner Bros.)
14	16	PASTICHE	Manhattan Transfer (Atlantic)
26	17	NEW BOOTS & PANTIES!!	Ian Dury & the Blockheads (Stiff)
17	18	FONZIE'S FAVOURITES	Various Artists (Warwick)
12	19	REFLECTIONS	Andy Williams (CBS)
22	20	BAT OUT OF HELL	Meatloaf (Epic)
-	21	ANYTIME, ANYWHERE	Rita Coolidge (A&M)
-	22	PENNIES FROM HEAVEN	Various Artists (World Records)
-	23	YOU LIGHT UP MY LIFE	Johnny Mathis (CBS)
16	24	ANOTHER MUSIC IN A DIFFERENT KITCHEN	Buzzcocks (United Artists)
20	25	VARIATONS	Andrew Lloyd Webber (MCA)
-	26	DISCO STARS	Various Artists (K-Tel)
28	27	ALL 'N' ALL	Earth Wind & Fire (CBS)
27	28	BEST FRIENDS	Cleo Laine & John Williams (RCA)
24	29	25 THUMPING GREAT HITS	Dave Clark Five (Polydor)
-	30	20 CLASSIC HITS	Platters (Mercury)

Elvis Costello's second album, *This Year's Model*, followed 1977's model, *My Aim Is True*. New Wave rather than punk, Costello was an old folkie really, but his remarkable lyrics had indeed contributed to the abrasion of the moment. Buzzcocks charted with debut LP *Another Music In A Different Kitchen*, a title typical of their ex-artschool management's style. Meat Loaf's *Bat Out Of Hell* was starting a chart run of 400+ weeks: longer than every other LP between 1958 and 1992 except Fleetwood Mac's *Rumours*.

29 April 1978

last week	this week	Title	Artist (Label)
2	1	SATURDAY NIGHT FEVER	Soundtrack (RSO)
3	2	AND THEN THERE WERE THREE	Genesis (Charisma)
1	3	20 GOLDEN GREATS	Nat 'King' Cole (Capitol)
4	4	LONDON TOWN	Wings (EMI)
5	5	THE ALBUM	Abba (Epic)
6	6	KAYA	Bob Marley & the Wailers (Island)
8	7	CITY TO CITY	Gerry Rafferty (United Artists)
10	8	THIS YEAR'S MODEL	Elvis Costello (Radar)
7	9	20 GOLDEN GREATS	Buddy Holly & the Crickets (MCA)
9	10	THE KICK INSIDE	Kate Bush (EMI)
11	11	THE STUD - SOUNDTRACK	Various Artists (Ronco)
12	12	PLASTIC LETTERS	Blondie (Chrysalis)
16	13	PASTICHE	Manhattan Transfer (Atlantic)
15	14	THE RUTLES	Rutles (Warner Bros.)
13	15	RUMOURS	Fleetwood Mac (Warner Bros.)
-	16	LONG LIVE ROCK & ROLL	Rainbow (Polydor)
14	17	OUT OF THE BLUE	Electric Light Orchestra (Jet)
22	18	PENNIES FROM HEAVEN	Various Artists (World Records)
18	19	FONZIE'S FAVOURITES	Various Artists (Warwick)
17	20	NEW BOOTS & PANTIES!!	Ian Dury & the Blockheads (Stiff)
20	21	BAT OUT OF HELL	Meatloaf (Epic)
-	22	ADVENTURE	Television (Elektra)
23	23	YOU LIGHT UP MY LIFE	Johnny Mathis (CBS)
-	24	EASTER	Patti Smith (Arista)
30	25	20 CLASSIC HITS	Platters (Mercury)
-	26	GREEN	Steve Hillage (Virgin Records)
19	27	REFLECTIONS	Andy Williams (CBS)
-	28	THE STRANGER	Billy Joel (CBS)
-	29	GREATEST HITS	Abba (Epic)
21	30	ANYTIME, ANYWHERE	Rita Coolidge (A&M)

6 May 1978

last week	this week	Title	Artist (Label)
1	1	SATURDAY NIGHT FEVER	Soundtrack (RSO)
2	2	AND THEN THERE WERE THREE	Genesis (Charisma)
3	3	20 GOLDEN GREATS	Nat 'King' Cole (Capitol)
4	4	LONDON TOWN	Wings (EMI)
5	5	THE ALBUM	Abba (Epic)
7	6	CITY TO CITY	Gerry Rafferty (United Artists)
11	7	THE STUD - SOUNDTRACK	Various Artists (Ronco)
6	8	KAYA	Bob Marley & the Wailers (Island)
9	9	20 GOLDEN GREATS	Buddy Holly & the Crickets (MCA)
14	10	THE RUTLES	Rutles (Warner Bros.)
10	11	THE KICK INSIDE	Kate Bush (EMI)
15	12	RUMOURS	Fleetwood Mac (Warner Bros.)
8	13	THIS YEAR'S MODEL	Elvis Costello (Radar)
23	14	YOU LIGHT UP MY LIFE	Johnny Mathis (CBS)
22	15	ADVENTURE	Television (Elektra)
12	16	PLASTIC LETTERS	Blondie (Chrysalis)
16	16	LONG LIVE ROCK & ROLL	Rainbow (Polydor)
13	18	PASTICHE	Manhattan Transfer (Atlantic)
21	19	BAT OUT OF HELL	Meatloaf (Epic)
19	20	FONZIE'S FAVOURITES	Various Artists (Warwick)
17	21	OUT OF THE BLUE	Electric Light Orchestra (Jet)
25	22	20 CLASSIC HITS	Platters (Mercury)
18	23	PENNIES FROM HEAVEN	Various Artists (World Records)
24	24	EASTER	Patti Smith (Arista)
20	25	NEW BOOTS & PANTIES!!	Ian Dury & the Blockheads (Stiff)
30	26	ANYTIME, ANYWHERE	Rita Coolidge (A&M)
-	27	ANOTHER MUSIC IN A DIFFERENT KITCHEN	Buzzcocks (United Artists)
-	28	HEAVY HORSES	Jethro Tull (Chrysalis)
26	29	GREEN	Steve Hillage (Virgin Records)
-	30	HERMIT OF MINK HOLLOW	Todd Rundgren (Bearsville)

13 May 1978

last week	this week	Title	Artist (Label)
1	1	SATURDAY NIGHT FEVER	Soundtrack (RSO)
2	2	AND THEN THERE WERE THREE	Genesis (Charisma)
3	3	20 GOLDEN GREATS	Nat 'King' Cole (Capitol)
7	4	THE STUD - SOUNDTRACK	Various Artists (Ronco)
4	5	LONDON TOWN	Wings (EMI)
6	6	CITY TO CITY	Gerry Rafferty (United Artists)
5	7	THE ALBUM	Abba (Epic)
13	8	YOU LIGHT UP MY LIFE	Johnny Mathis (CBS)
12	9	RUMOURS	Fleetwood Mac (Warner Bros.)
16	10	LONG LIVE ROCK & ROLL	Rainbow (Polydor)
8	11	KAYA	Bob Marley & the Wailers (Island)
23	12	PENNIES FROM HEAVEN	Various Artists (World Records)
19	13	BAT OUT OF HELL	Meatloaf (Epic)
9	14	20 GOLDEN GREATS	Buddy Holly & the Crickets (MCA)
16	15	PLASTIC LETTERS	Blondie (Chrysalis)
-	16	20 GOLDEN GREATS	Frank Sinatra (EMI)
13	17	THIS YEAR'S MODEL	Elvis Costello (Radar)
24	18	EASTER	Patti Smith (Arista)
10	19	THE RUTLES	Rutles (Warner Bros.)
26	20	ANYTIME, ANYWHERE	Rita Coolidge (A&M)
25	21	NEW BOOTS & PANTIES!!	Ian Dury & the Blockheads (Stiff)
18	22	PASTICHE	Manhattan Transfer (Atlantic)
28	23	HEAVY HORSES	Jethro Tull (Chrysalis)
-	24	A LITTLE BIT MORE	Dr. Hook (Capitol)
11	25	THE KICK INSIDE	Kate Bush (EMI)
22	26	20 CLASSIC HITS	Platters (Mercury)
-	27	SHOOTING STAR	Elkie Brooks (A&M)
21	28	OUT OF THE BLUE	Electric Light Orchestra (Jet)
20	29	FONZIE'S FAVOURITES	Various Artists (Warwick)
29	30	GREEN	Steve Hillage (Virgin Records)

20 May 1978

last week	this week	Title	Artist (Label)
1	1	SATURDAY NIGHT FEVER	Soundtrack (RSO)
2	2	AND THEN THERE WERE THREE	Genesis (Charisma)
4	3	THE STUD - SOUNDTRACK	Various Artists (Ronco)
3	4	20 GOLDEN GREATS	Nat 'King' Cole (Capitol)
8	5	YOU LIGHT UP MY LIFE	Johnny Mathis (CBS)
7	6	THE ALBUM	Abba (Epic)
16	7	20 GOLDEN GREATS	Frank Sinatra (EMI)
10	8	LONG LIVE ROCK & ROLL	Rainbow (Polydor)
5	9	LONDON TOWN	Wings (EMI)
9	10	RUMOURS	Fleetwood Mac (Warner Bros.)
6	10	CITY TO CITY	Gerry Rafferty (United Artists)
18	12	EASTER	Patti Smith (Arista)
20	13	ANYTIME, ANYWHERE	Rita Coolidge (A&M)
11	14	KAYA	Bob Marley & the Wailers (Island)
13	15	BAT OUT OF HELL	Meatloaf (Epic)
21	16	NEW BOOTS & PANTIES!!	Ian Dury & the Blockheads (Stiff)
23	17	HEAVY HORSES	Jethro Tull (Chrysalis)
22	18	PASTICHE	Manhattan Transfer (Atlantic)
12	19	PENNIES FROM HEAVEN	Various Artists (World Records)
18	20	THE RUTLES	Rutles (Warner Bros.)
26	21	20 CLASSIC HITS	Platters (Mercury)
15	22	PLASTIC LETTERS	Blondie (Chrysalis)
17	23	THIS YEAR'S MODEL	Elvis Costello (Radar)
25	24	THE KICK INSIDE	Kate Bush (EMI)
14	25	20 GOLDEN GREATS	Buddy Holly & the Crickets (MCA)
30	26	GREEN	Steve Hillage (Virgin Records)
-	27	ANOTHER MUSIC IN A DIFFERENT KITCHEN	Buzzcocks (United Artists)
24	28	A LITTLE BIT MORE	Dr. Hook (Capitol)
27	29	SHOOTING STAR	Elkie Brooks (A&M)
-	30	THE LAST WALTZ	Soundtrack (Warner Bros.)

Easter was New York City punk poet Patti Smith's first, and only sizeable, hit LP. Credited to the Patti Smith Group, it featured her thumping great classic single *Because The Night*, written by Bruce Springsteen, which charted on May 6 and peaked at No.3 two weeks later. The Platters, 1950s giants still on every pub jukebox in Britain to this day with *Great Pretender/Only You*, had never had a hit LP and hadn't had a hit single since *Harbour Lights* dropped out of the Top 20 in April 1960.

May – June 1978

27 May 1978

last week	this week	Title / Artist (Label)
1	1	SATURDAY NIGHT FEVER — Soundtrack (RSO)
3	2	THE STUD - SOUNDTRACK — Various Artists (Ronco)
6	3	THE ALBUM — Abba (Epic)
5	4	YOU LIGHT UP MY LIFE — Johnny Mathis (CBS)
2	5	AND THEN THERE WERE THREE — Genesis (Charisma)
7	6	20 GOLDEN GREATS — Frank Sinatra (EMI)
4	7	20 GOLDEN GREATS — Nat 'King' Cole (Capitol)
8	8	LONG LIVE ROCK & ROLL — Rainbow (Polydor)
9	9	LONDON TOWN — Wings (EMI)
19	10	PENNIES FROM HEAVEN — Various Artists (World Records)
-	11	BLACK AND WHITE — Stranglers (United Artists)
10	12	RUMOURS — Fleetwood Mac (Warner Bros.)
18	13	PASTICHE — Manhattan Transfer (Atlantic)
12	14	EASTER — Patti Smith (Arista)
15	15	BAT OUT OF HELL — Meatloaf (Epic)
21	16	20 CLASSIC HITS — Platters (Mercury)
-	16	THANK GOD IT'S FRIDAY — Soundtrack (Casablanca)
16	18	NEW BOOTS & PANTIES!! — Ian Dury & the Blockheads (Stiff)
13	19	ANYTIME, ANYWHERE — Rita Coolidge (A&M)
-	20	POWER IN THE DARK — Tom Robinson Band (EMI)
-	21	EVERYONE PLAYS DARTS — Darts (Magnet)
25	22	20 GOLDEN GREATS — Buddy Holly & the Crickets (MCA)
10	23	CITY TO CITY — Gerry Rafferty (United Artists)
14	24	KAYA — Bob Marley & the Wailers (Island)
23	25	THIS YEAR'S MODEL — Elvis Costello (Radar)
-	26	OUT OF THE BLUE — Electric Light Orchestra (Jet)
24	27	THE KICK INSIDE — Kate Bush (EMI)
29	28	SHOOTING STAR — Elkie Brooks (A&M)
22	29	PLASTIC LETTERS — Blondie (Chrysalis)
-	30	POWERAGE — AC/DC (Atlantic)

3 June 1978

last week	this week	Title / Artist (Label)
1	1	SATURDAY NIGHT FEVER — Soundtrack (RSO)
3	2	THE ALBUM — Abba (Epic)
5	3	AND THEN THERE WERE THREE — Genesis (Charisma)
2	4	THE STUD - SOUNDTRACK — Various Artists (Ronco)
11	5	BLACK AND WHITE — Stranglers (United Artists)
14	6	EASTER — Patti Smith (Arista)
7	7	20 GOLDEN GREATS — Nat 'King' Cole (Capitol)
18	8	NEW BOOTS & PANTIES!! — Ian Dury & the Blockheads (Stiff)
6	9	20 GOLDEN GREATS — Frank Sinatra (EMI)
19	10	ANYTIME, ANYWHERE — Rita Coolidge (A&M)
15	11	BAT OUT OF HELL — Meatloaf (Epic)
12	12	RUMOURS — Fleetwood Mac (Warner Bros.)
4	13	YOU LIGHT UP MY LIFE — Johnny Mathis (CBS)
-	14	THE PARKERILLA — Graham Parker & the Rumour (Vertigo)
9	14	LONDON TOWN — Wings (EMI)
23	16	CITY TO CITY — Gerry Rafferty (United Artists)
13	17	PASTICHE — Manhattan Transfer (Atlantic)
8	18	LONG LIVE ROCK & ROLL — Rainbow (Polydor)
24	19	KAYA — Bob Marley & the Wailers (Island)
29	20	PLASTIC LETTERS — Blondie (Chrysalis)
20	21	POWER IN THE DARK — Tom Robinson Band (EMI)
16	22	20 CLASSIC HITS — Platters (Mercury)
21	23	EVERYONE PLAYS DARTS — Darts (Magnet)
22	24	20 GOLDEN GREATS — Buddy Holly & the Crickets (MCA)
10	25	PENNIES FROM HEAVEN — Various Artists (World Records)
-	26	I KNOW 'COS I WAS THERE — Max Boyce (EMI)
27	27	THE KICK INSIDE — Kate Bush (EMI)
30	28	POWERAGE — AC/DC (Atlantic)
-	29	BUT SERIOUSLY FOLKS — Joe Walsh (Asylum)
-	30	APPROVED BY THE MOTORS — Motors (Virgin)

10 June 1978

last week	this week	Title / Artist (Label)
1	1	SATURDAY NIGHT FEVER — Soundtrack (RSO)
5	2	BLACK AND WHITE — Stranglers (United Artists)
2	3	THE ALBUM — Abba (Epic)
4	4	THE STUD - SOUNDTRACK — Various Artists (Ronco)
3	5	AND THEN THERE WERE THREE — Genesis (Charisma)
10	6	ANYTIME, ANYWHERE — Rita Coolidge (A&M)
17	7	PASTICHE — Manhattan Transfer (Atlantic)
9	8	20 GOLDEN GREATS — Frank Sinatra (EMI)
7	9	20 GOLDEN GREATS — Nat 'King' Cole (Capitol)
23	10	EVERYONE PLAYS DARTS — Darts (Magnet)
8	11	NEW BOOTS & PANTIES!! — Ian Dury & the Blockheads (Stiff)
21	12	POWER IN THE DARK — Tom Robinson Band (EMI)
6	13	EASTER — Patti Smith (Arista)
11	14	BAT OUT OF HELL — Meatloaf (Epic)
13	15	YOU LIGHT UP MY LIFE — Johnny Mathis (CBS)
26	16	I KNOW 'COS I WAS THERE — Max Boyce (EMI)
14	17	THE PARKERILLA — Graham Parker & the Rumour (Vertigo)
18	18	LONDON TOWN — Wings (EMI)
12	19	RUMOURS — Fleetwood Mac (Warner Bros.)
19	20	KAYA — Bob Marley & the Wailers (Island)
-	21	THE LENA MARTELL COLLECTION — Lena Martell (Ronco)
20	22	PLASTIC LETTERS — Blondie (Chrysalis)
18	23	LONG LIVE ROCK & ROLL — Rainbow (Polydor)
-	24	SHOOTING STAR — Elkie Brooks (A&M)
28	25	POWERAGE — AC/DC (Atlantic)
25	26	PENNIES FROM HEAVEN — Various Artists (World Records)
-	27	THIS YEAR'S MODEL — Elvis Costello (Radar)
-	28	THE STRANGER — Billy Joel (CBS)
29	29	LIVE AND DANGEROUS — Thin Lizzy (Vertigo)
30	30	APPROVED BY THE MOTORS — Motors (Virgin)

17 June 1978

last week	this week	Title / Artist (Label)
2	1	BLACK AND WHITE — Stranglers (United Artists)
1	2	SATURDAY NIGHT FEVER — Soundtrack (RSO)
3	3	THE ALBUM — Abba (Epic)
4	4	THE STUD - SOUNDTRACK — Various Artists (Ronco)
10	5	EVERYONE PLAYS DARTS — Darts (Magnet)
5	6	AND THEN THERE WERE THREE — Genesis (Charisma)
6	7	ANYTIME, ANYWHERE — Rita Coolidge (A&M)
7	8	PASTICHE — Manhattan Transfer (Atlantic)
-	9	DISCO DOUBLE — Various Artists (K-Tel)
15	10	YOU LIGHT UP MY LIFE — Johnny Mathis (CBS)
-	11	SOME GIRLS — Rolling Stones (EMI)
11	12	NEW BOOTS & PANTIES!! — Ian Dury & the Blockheads (Stiff)
12	13	POWER IN THE DARK — Tom Robinson Band (EMI)
9	14	20 GOLDEN GREATS — Nat 'King' Cole (Capitol)
16	15	I KNOW 'COS I WAS THERE — Max Boyce (EMI)
29	16	LIVE AND DANGEROUS — Thin Lizzy (Vertigo)
13	17	EASTER — Patti Smith (Arista)
14	18	BAT OUT OF HELL — Meatloaf (Epic)
19	19	RUMOURS — Fleetwood Mac (Warner Bros.)
-	20	THE KICK INSIDE — Kate Bush (EMI)
-	21	NATURAL HIGH — Commodores (Motown)
-	22	DAVID GILMOUR — David Gilmour (Harvest)
24	23	SHOOTING STAR — Elkie Brooks (A&M)
8	24	20 GOLDEN GREATS — Frank Sinatra (EMI)
-	25	OUT OF THE BLUE — Electric Light Orchestra (Jet)
23	26	LONG LIVE ROCK & ROLL — Rainbow (Polydor)
-	27	OCTAVE — Moody Blues (Threshold)
28	28	THE STRANGER — Billy Joel (CBS)
27	29	THIS YEAR'S MODEL — Elvis Costello (Radar)
20	30	KAYA — Bob Marley & the Wailers (Island)

While the custard of the singles chart bubbled under the unyieldingly thick skin of John Travolta & Olivia Newton-John's *You're The One That I Want*, from the film (but not the stage-show) of *Grease*, the album chart shivered with *Saturday Night Fever*. These long occupancies of the top slots confirmed that both singles and albums were, after some doldrum years, enjoying huge sales again. Punk had re-activated the power of music in people's lives, as Beatlemania had done in days of yore.

June – July 1978

24 June 1978

last week	this week	Album	Artist (Label)
2	1	SATURDAY NIGHT FEVER	Soundtrack (RSO)
16	2	LIVE AND DANGEROUS	Thin Lizzy (Vertigo)
1	3	BLACK AND WHITE	Stranglers (United Artists)
3	4	THE ALBUM	Abba (Epic)
12	5	NEW BOOTS & PANTIES!!	Ian Dury & the Blockheads (Stiff)
13	6	POWER IN THE DARK	Tom Robinson Band (EMI)
4	7	THE STUD - SOUNDTRACK	Various Artists (Ronco)
18	8	BAT OUT OF HELL	Meatloaf (Epic)
10	9	YOU LIGHT UP MY LIFE	Johnny Mathis (CBS)
11	10	SOME GIRLS	Rolling Stones (EMI)
5	11	EVERYONE PLAYS DARTS	Darts (Magnet)
14	12	20 GOLDEN GREATS	Nat 'King' Cole (Capitol)
-	13	PETER GABRIEL	Peter Gabriel (Charisma)
-	14	DARKNESS ON THE EDGE OF TOWN	Bruce Springsteen (CBS)
7	15	ANYTIME, ANYWHERE	Rita Coolidge (A&M)
15	16	I KNOW 'COS I WAS THERE	Max Boyce (EMI)
9	17	DISCO DOUBLE	Various Artists (K-Tel)
8	18	PASTICHE	Manhattan Transfer (Atlantic)
22	19	DAVID GILMOUR	David Gilmour (Harvest)
20	20	THE KICK INSIDE	Kate Bush (EMI)
-	21	STREET LEGAL	Bob Dylan (CBS)
6	22	AND THEN THERE WERE THREE	Genesis (Charisma)
19	23	RUMOURS	Fleetwood Mac (Warner Bros.)
24	24	20 GOLDEN GREATS	Frank Sinatra (EMI)
27	25	OCTAVE	Moody Blues (Threshold)
17	26	EASTER	Patti Smith (Arista)
-	27	PENNIES FROM HEAVEN	Various Artists (World Records)
28	28	THE STRANGER	Billy Joel (CBS)
30	29	KAYA	Bob Marley & the Wailers (Island)
21	30	NATURAL HIGH	Commodores (Motown)

1 July 1978

last week	this week	Album	Artist (Label)
1	1	SATURDAY NIGHT FEVER	Soundtrack (RSO)
2	2	LIVE AND DANGEROUS	Thin Lizzy (Vertigo)
10	3	SOME GIRLS	Rolling Stones (EMI)
4	4	THE ALBUM	Abba (Epic)
3	5	BLACK AND WHITE	Stranglers (United Artists)
8	6	BAT OUT OF HELL	Meatloaf (Epic)
5	7	NEW BOOTS & PANTIES!!	Ian Dury & the Blockheads (Stiff)
9	8	YOU LIGHT UP MY LIFE	Johnny Mathis (CBS)
20	9	THE KICK INSIDE	Kate Bush (EMI)
7	10	THE STUD - SOUNDTRACK	Various Artists (Ronco)
25	11	OCTAVE	Moody Blues (Threshold)
11	12	EVERYONE PLAYS DARTS	Darts (Magnet)
21	13	STREET LEGAL	Bob Dylan (CBS)
16	14	I KNOW 'COS I WAS THERE	Max Boyce (EMI)
6	15	POWER IN THE DARK	Tom Robinson Band (EMI)
18	16	PASTICHE	Manhattan Transfer (Atlantic)
22	17	AND THEN THERE WERE THREE	Genesis (Charisma)
17	18	DISCO DOUBLE	Various Artists (K-Tel)
13	19	PETER GABRIEL	Peter Gabriel (Charisma)
14	20	DARKNESS ON THE EDGE OF TOWN	Bruce Springsteen (CBS)
23	21	RUMOURS	Fleetwood Mac (Warner Bros.)
24	22	20 GOLDEN GREATS	Frank Sinatra (EMI)
19	23	DAVID GILMOUR	David Gilmour (Harvest)
15	24	ANYTIME, ANYWHERE	Rita Coolidge (A&M)
-	25	OUT OF THE BLUE	Electric Light Orchestra (Jet)
12	26	20 GOLDEN GREATS	Nat 'King' Cole (Capitol)
-	27	REAL LIFE	Magazine (Virgin)
29	28	KAYA	Bob Marley & the Wailers (Island)
27	29	PENNIES FROM HEAVEN	Various Artists (World Records)
-	30	THE LENA MARTELL COLLECTION	Lena Martell (Ronco)

8 July 1978

last week	this week	Album	Artist (Label)
1	1	SATURDAY NIGHT FEVER	Soundtrack (RSO)
2	2	LIVE AND DANGEROUS	Thin Lizzy (Vertigo)
3	3	SOME GIRLS	Rolling Stones (EMI)
11	4	OCTAVE	Moody Blues (Threshold)
13	5	STREET LEGAL	Bob Dylan (CBS)
4	6	THE ALBUM	Abba (Epic)
9	7	THE KICK INSIDE	Kate Bush (EMI)
7	8	NEW BOOTS & PANTIES!!	Ian Dury & the Blockheads (Stiff)
7	9	YOU LIGHT UP MY LIFE	Johnny Mathis (CBS)
6	10	BAT OUT OF HELL	Meatloaf (Epic)
5	11	BLACK AND WHITE	Stranglers (United Artists)
17	12	AND THEN THERE WERE THREE	Genesis (Charisma)
15	13	POWER IN THE DARK	Tom Robinson Band (EMI)
10	14	THE STUD - SOUNDTRACK	Various Artists (Ronco)
-	15	A TONIC FOR THE TROOPS	Boomtown Rats (Ensign)
14	16	I KNOW 'COS I WAS THERE	Max Boyce (EMI)
16	17	PASTICHE	Manhattan Transfer (Atlantic)
21	18	RUMOURS	Fleetwood Mac (Warner Bros.)
20	19	DARKNESS ON THE EDGE OF TOWN	Bruce Springsteen (CBS)
23	19	DAVID GILMOUR	David Gilmour (Harvest)
19	21	PETER GABRIEL	Peter Gabriel (Charisma)
22	22	20 GOLDEN GREATS	Frank Sinatra (EMI)
27	23	REAL LIFE	Magazine (Virgin)
18	24	DISCO DOUBLE	Various Artists (K-Tel)
25	25	OUT OF THE BLUE	Electric Light Orchestra (Jet)
-	26	WAR OF THE WORLDS	Jeff Wayne (CBS)
12	27	EVERYONE PLAYS DARTS	Darts (Magnet)
29	28	PENNIES FROM HEAVEN	Various Artists (World Records)
24	29	ANYTIME, ANYWHERE	Rita Coolidge (A&M)
-	30	CITY TO CITY	Gerry Rafferty (United Artists)

15 July 1978

last week	this week	Album	Artist (Label)
1	1	SATURDAY NIGHT FEVER	Soundtrack (RSO)
5	2	STREET LEGAL	Bob Dylan (CBS)
3	3	SOME GIRLS	Rolling Stones (EMI)
2	4	LIVE AND DANGEROUS	Thin Lizzy (Vertigo)
4	5	OCTAVE	Moody Blues (Threshold)
7	6	THE KICK INSIDE	Kate Bush (EMI)
6	7	THE ALBUM	Abba (Epic)
15	8	A TONIC FOR THE TROOPS	Boomtown Rats (Ensign)
-	9	20 GOLDEN GREATS	Hollies (EMI)
8	10	NEW BOOTS & PANTIES!!	Ian Dury & the Blockheads (Stiff)
26	11	WAR OF THE WORLDS	Jeff Wayne (CBS)
12	12	AND THEN THERE WERE THREE	Genesis (Charisma)
10	13	BAT OUT OF HELL	Meatloaf (Epic)
-	14	GREASE	Soundtrack (RSO)
9	15	YOU LIGHT UP MY LIFE	Johnny Mathis (CBS)
17	16	PASTICHE	Manhattan Transfer (Atlantic)
14	17	THE STUD - SOUNDTRACK	Various Artists (Ronco)
21	18	PETER GABRIEL	Peter Gabriel (Charisma)
11	19	BLACK AND WHITE	Stranglers (United Artists)
-	20	ROCK RULES	Various Artists (K-Tel)
16	21	I KNOW 'COS I WAS THERE	Max Boyce (EMI)
23	22	REAL LIFE	Magazine (Virgin)
-	23	GOODBYE GIRL	David Gates (Elektra)
-	24	BACK & FOURTH	Lindisfarne (Mercury)
19	25	DARKNESS ON THE EDGE OF TOWN	Bruce Springsteen (CBS)
-	26	YOU'RE GONNA GET IT	Tom Petty & the Heartbreakers (Shelter)
-	27	THE LENA MARTELL COLLECTION	Lena Martell (Ronco)
-	28	20 GOLDEN GREATS	Nat 'King' Cole (Capitol)
13	29	POWER IN THE DARK	Tom Robinson Band (EMI)
19	30	DAVID GILMOUR	David Gilmour (Harvest)

Bob Dylan's six June nights at Earls Court, followed by July 15's Picnic at Blackbushe (his first UK tour for 12 years) gained him extraordinarily good press (especially considering that for many New Wavers, in and outside the industry, he was a useful symbol of the hated old order), and pulled in massive crowds. It wasn't quite enough to put his new studio album *Street Legal* to the No.1 slot. Nor could the Rolling Stones quite manage this with their best LP in years, *Some Girls*.

July – August 1978

last week	this week	22 July 1978
1	1	SATURDAY NIGHT FEVER — Soundtrack (RSO)
2	2	STREET LEGAL — Bob Dylan (CBS)
3	3	SOME GIRLS — Rolling Stones (EMI)
4	4	LIVE AND DANGEROUS — Thin Lizzy (Vertigo)
5	5	OCTAVE — Moody Blues (Threshold)
6	6	THE KICK INSIDE — Kate Bush (EMI)
9	7	20 GOLDEN GREATS — Hollies (EMI)
11	8	WAR OF THE WORLDS — Jeff Wayne (CBS)
8	9	A TONIC FOR THE TROOPS — Boomtown Rats (Ensign)
12	10	AND THEN THERE WERE THREE — Genesis (Charisma)
14	11	GREASE — Soundtrack (RSO)
16	12	PASTICHE — Manhattan Transfer (Atlantic)
-	13	RUMOURS — Fleetwood Mac (Warner Bros.)
7	14	THE ALBUM — Abba (Epic)
15	15	YOU LIGHT UP MY LIFE — Johnny Mathis (CBS)
20	16	ROCK RULES — Various Artists (K-Tel)
10	17	NEW BOOTS & PANTIES!! — Ian Dury & the Blockheads (Stiff)
-	18	KAYA — Bob Marley & the Wailers (Island)
-	19	EVERYONE PLAYS DARTS — Darts (Magnet)
19	20	BLACK AND WHITE — Stranglers (United Artists)
-	21	NIGHT FLIGHT TO VENUS — Boney M (Atlantic/Hansa)
29	22	POWER IN THE DARK — Tom Robinson Band (EMI)
-	23	BUT SERIOUSLY FOLKS — Joe Walsh (Asylum)
-	24	OUT OF THE BLUE — Electric Light Orchestra (Jet)
24	25	BACK & FOURTH — Lindisfarne (Mercury)
-	26	OBSESSION — UFO (Chrysalis)
13	27	BAT OUT OF HELL — Meatloaf (Epic)
17	28	THE STUD - SOUNDTRACK — Various Artists(Ronco)
21	29	I KNOW 'COS I WAS THERE — Max Boyce (EMI)
22	30	REAL LIFE — Magazine (Virgin)

		29 July 1978
1	1	SATURDAY NIGHT FEVER — Soundtrack (RSO)
4	2	LIVE AND DANGEROUS — Thin Lizzy (Vertigo)
3	3	SOME GIRLS — Rolling Stones (EMI)
2	4	STREET LEGAL — Bob Dylan (CBS)
7	5	20 GOLDEN GREATS — Hollies (EMI)
5	6	OCTAVE — Moody Blues (Threshold)
8	7	WAR OF THE WORLDS — Jeff Wayne (CBS)
6	8	THE KICK INSIDE — Kate Bush (EMI)
9	9	A TONIC FOR THE TROOPS — Boomtown Rats (Ensign)
11	10	GREASE — Soundtrack (RSO)
14	11	THE ALBUM — Abba (Epic)
17	12	NEW BOOTS & PANTIES!! — Ian Dury & the Blockheads (Stiff)
27	13	BAT OUT OF HELL — Meatloaf (Epic)
10	14	AND THEN THERE WERE THREE — Genesis (Charisma)
12	15	PASTICHE — Manhattan Transfer (Atlantic)
24	16	OUT OF THE BLUE — Electric Light Orchestra (Jet)
21	17	NIGHT FLIGHT TO VENUS — Boney M (Atlantic/Hansa)
20	18	BLACK AND WHITE — Stranglers (United Artists)
13	19	RUMOURS — Fleetwood Mac (Warner Bros.)
28	20	THE STUD - SOUNDTRACK — Various Artists (Ronco)
15	21	YOU LIGHT UP MY LIFE — Johnny Mathis (CBS)
16	22	ROCK RULES — Various Artists (K-Tel)
-	23	THE LENA MARTELL COLLECTION — Lena Martell (Ronco)
-	24	20 GIANT HITS — Nolan Sisters (Target)
25	25	BACK & FOURTH — Lindisfarne (Mercury)
18	26	KAYA — Bob Marley & the Wailers (Island)
23	27	BUT SERIOUSLY FOLKS — Joe Walsh (Asylum)
-	28	NATURAL HIGH — Commodores (Motown)
-	29	THANK GOD ITS FRIDAY — Soundtrack (Casablanca)
26	30	OBSESSION — UFO (Chrysalis)

		5 August 1978
1	1	SATURDAY NIGHT FEVER — Soundtrack (RSO)
4	2	STREET LEGAL — Bob Dylan (CBS)
5	3	20 GOLDEN GREATS — Hollies (EMI)
2	4	LIVE AND DANGEROUS — Thin Lizzy (Vertigo)
10	5	GREASE — Soundtrack (RSO)
8	6	THE KICK INSIDE — Kate Bush (EMI)
9	7	A TONIC FOR THE TROOPS — Boomtown Rats (Ensign)
3	8	SOME GIRLS — Rolling Stones (EMI)
6	9	OCTAVE — Moody Blues (Threshold)
17	10	NIGHT FLIGHT TO VENUS — Boney M (Atlantic/Hansa)
14	11	AND THEN THERE WERE THREE — Genesis (Charisma)
27	12	BUT SERIOUSLY FOLKS — Joe Walsh (Asylum)
16	13	OUT OF THE BLUE — Electric Light Orchestra (Jet)
24	14	20 GIANT HITS — Nolan Sisters (Target)
7	15	WAR OF THE WORLDS — Jeff Wayne (CBS)
28	16	NATURAL HIGH — Commodores (Motown)
19	17	RUMOURS — Fleetwood Mac (Warner Bros.)
25	18	BACK & FOURTH — Lindisfarne (Mercury)
15	19	PASTICHE — Manhattan Transfer (Atlantic)
12	20	NEW BOOTS & PANTIES!! — Ian Dury & the Blockheads (Stiff)
11	21	THE ALBUM — Abba (Epic)
-	22	MORE SONGS ABOUT BUILDINGS AND FOOD — Talking Heads (Sire)
13	23	BAT OUT OF HELL — Meatloaf (Epic)
22	24	ROCK RULES — Various Artists (K-Tel)
29	25	THANK GOD ITS FRIDAY — Soundtrack (Casablanca)
-	26	HANDSWORTH REVOLUTION — Steel Pulse (Island)
-	27	IMAGES — Don Williams (K-Tel)
-	28	EVERYONE PLAYS DARTS — Darts (Magnet)
-	29	SUNLIGHT — Herbie Hancock (CBS)
20	30	THE STUD - SOUNDTRACK — Various Artists (Ronco)

		12 August 1978
1	1	SATURDAY NIGHT FEVER — Soundtrack (RSO)
3	2	20 GOLDEN GREATS — Hollies (EMI)
2	3	STREET LEGAL — Bob Dylan (CBS)
10	4	NIGHT FLIGHT TO VENUS — Boney M (Atlantic/Hansa)
5	5	GREASE — Soundtrack (RSO)
4	6	LIVE AND DANGEROUS — Thin Lizzy (Vertigo)
8	7	SOME GIRLS — Rolling Stones (EMI)
14	8	20 GIANT HITS — Nolan Sisters (Target)
13	9	OUT OF THE BLUE — Electric Light Orchestra (Jet)
6	10	THE KICK INSIDE — Kate Bush (EMI)
15	11	WAR OF THE WORLDS — Jeff Wayne (CBS)
9	12	OCTAVE — Moody Blues (Threshold)
16	13	NATURAL HIGH — Commodores (Motown)
7	14	A TONIC FOR THE TROOPS — Boomtown Rats (Ensign)
12	15	BUT SERIOUSLY FOLKS — Joe Walsh (Asylum)
20	16	NEW BOOTS & PANTIES!! — Ian Dury & the Blockheads (Stiff)
25	17	THANK GOD ITS FRIDAY — Soundtrack (Casablanca)
26	17	HANDSWORTH REVOLUTION — Steel Pulse (Island)
-	19	CAN'T STAND THE REZILLOS — Rezillos (Sire)
24	20	ROCK RULES — Various Artists (K-Tel)
22	21	MORE SONGS ABOUT BUILDINGS AND FOOD — Talking Heads (Sire)
17	22	RUMOURS — Fleetwood Mac (Warner Bros.)
21	23	THE ALBUM — Abba (Epic)
27	24	IMAGES — Don Williams (K-Tel)
-	25	SHOOTING STAR — Elkie Brooks (A&M)
23	26	BAT OUT OF HELL — Meatloaf (Epic)
-	27	BLACK AND WHITE — Stranglers (United Artists)
11	28	AND THEN THERE WERE THREE — Genesis (Charisma)
-	29	CLASSIC ROCK — London Symphony Orchestra (K-Tel)
18	30	PASTICHE — Manhattan Transfer (Atlantic)

Boney M's *Night Flight To Venus* was launched up the chart by their single *Rivers Of Babylon* / *Brown Girl In The Ring*, a June No.1 and a 2-million-seller in the UK alone. (Wonder how these West Indian girls and boys regarded the Stones' LP, with its title song's "Black girls just wanna get fucked all night".) Thin Lizzy's *Live And Dangerous* was their fourth hit album, and followed a concert at the Rainbow in March which had been televised in many countries (though not Britain).

19 August 1978

(last week / this week)

1	1	SATURDAY NIGHT FEVER — Soundtrack (RSO)
8	2	20 GIANT HITS — Nolan Sisters (Target)
2	3	20 GOLDEN GREATS — Hollies (EMI)
3	4	STREET LEGAL — Bob Dylan (CBS)
4	5	NIGHT FLIGHT TO VENUS — Boney M (Atlantic/Hansa)
5	6	GREASE — Soundtrack (RSO)
11	7	WAR OF THE WORLDS — Jeff Wayne (CBS)
6	8	LIVE AND DANGEROUS — Thin Lizzy (Vertigo)
14	9	A TONIC FOR THE TROOPS — Boomtown Rats (Ensign)
9	10	OUT OF THE BLUE — Electric Light Orchestra (Jet)
10	11	THE KICK INSIDE — Kate Bush (EMI)
-	11	STAR PARTY — Various Artists (K-Tel)
17	13	HANDSWORTH REVOLUTION — Steel Pulse (Island)
12	14	OCTAVE — Moody Blues (Threshold)
7	14	SOME GIRLS — Rolling Stones (EMI)
13	16	NATURAL HIGH — Commodores (Motown)
15	17	BUT SERIOUSLY FOLKS — Joe Walsh (Asylum)
26	18	BAT OUT OF HELL — Meatloaf (Epic)
22	19	RUMOURS — Fleetwood Mac (Warner Bros.)
23	20	THE ALBUM — Abba (Epic)
24	21	IMAGES — Don Williams (K-Tel)
16	22	NEW BOOTS & PANTIES!! — Ian Dury & the Blockheads (Stiff)
29	23	CLASSIC ROCK — London Symphony Orchestra (K-Tel)
28	24	AND THEN THERE WERE THREE — Genesis (Charisma)
19	25	CAN'T STAND THE REZILLOS — Rezillos (Sire)
-	26	BLAM!! — Brothers Johnson (A&M)
27	27	BLACK AND WHITE — Stranglers (United Artists)
-	28	LOVE ME AGAIN — Rita Coolidge (A&M)
20	29	ROCK RULES — Various Artists (K-Tel)
17	30	THANK GOD ITS FRIDAY — Soundtrack (Casablanca)

26 August 1978

1	1	SATURDAY NIGHT FEVER — Soundtrack (RSO)
5	2	NIGHT FLIGHT TO VENUS — Boney M (Atlantic/Hansa)
4	3	STREET LEGAL — Bob Dylan (CBS)
7	4	WAR OF THE WORLDS — Jeff Wayne (CBS)
6	5	GREASE — Soundtrack (RSO)
2	6	20 GIANT HITS — Nolan Sisters (Target)
16	7	NATURAL HIGH — Commodores (Motown)
8	8	LIVE AND DANGEROUS — Thin Lizzy (Vertigo)
3	9	20 GOLDEN GREATS — Hollies (EMI)
14	10	SOME GIRLS — Rolling Stones (EMI)
23	11	CLASSIC ROCK — London Symphony Orchestra (K-Tel)
11	12	STAR PARTY — Various Artists (K-Tel)
14	13	OCTAVE — Moody Blues (Threshold)
10	14	OUT OF THE BLUE — Electric Light Orchestra (Jet)
11	15	THE KICK INSIDE — Kate Bush (EMI)
18	15	BAT OUT OF HELL — Meatloaf (Epic)
25	17	CAN'T STAND THE REZILLOS — Rezillos (Sire)
17	18	BUT SERIOUSLY FOLKS — Joe Walsh (Asylum)
22	19	NEW BOOTS & PANTIES!! — Ian Dury & the Blockheads (Stiff)
21	20	IMAGES — Don Williams (K-Tel)
20	21	THE ALBUM — Abba (Epic)
29	22	ROCK RULES — Various Artists (K-Tel)
13	23	HANDSWORTH REVOLUTION — Steel Pulse (Island)
9	24	A TONIC FOR THE TROOPS — Boomtown Rats (Ensign)
-	25	PASTICHE — Manhattan Transfer (Atlantic)
26	26	BLAM!! — Brothers Johnson (A&M)
24	27	AND THEN THERE WERE THREE — Genesis (Charisma)
-	28	SHADOW DANCING — Andy Gibb (RSO)
-	29	EVERYONE PLAYS DARTS — Darts (Magnet)
19	30	RUMOURS — Fleetwood Mac (Warner Bros.)

2 September 1978

1	1	SATURDAY NIGHT FEVER — Soundtrack (RSO)
3	2	STREET LEGAL — Bob Dylan (CBS)
2	3	NIGHT FLIGHT TO VENUS — Boney M (Atlantic/Hansa)
4	4	WAR OF THE WORLDS — Jeff Wayne (CBS)
5	5	GREASE — Soundtrack (RSO)
6	6	20 GIANT HITS — Nolan Sisters (Target)
7	7	LIVE AND DANGEROUS — Thin Lizzy (Vertigo)
10	8	SOME GIRLS — Rolling Stones (EMI)
9	9	20 GOLDEN GREATS — Hollies (EMI)
7	10	NATURAL HIGH — Commodores (Motown)
13	11	OCTAVE — Moody Blues (Threshold)
11	12	CLASSIC ROCK — London Symphony Orchestra (K-Tel)
12	13	STAR PARTY — Various Artists (K-Tel)
14	14	OUT OF THE BLUE — Electric Light Orchestra (Jet)
-	15	WHO ARE YOU — Who (Polydor)
15	16	THE KICK INSIDE — Kate Bush (EMI)
17	17	CAN'T STAND THE REZILLOS — Rezillos (Sire)
20	18	IMAGES — Don Williams (K-Tel)
24	19	A TONIC FOR THE TROOPS — Boomtown Rats (Ensign)
18	20	BUT SERIOUSLY FOLKS — Joe Walsh (Asylum)
19	21	NEW BOOTS & PANTIES!! — Ian Dury & the Blockheads (Stiff)
15	22	BAT OUT OF HELL — Meatloaf (Epic)
-	23	DOUBLE VISION — Foreigner (Atlantic)
23	24	HANDSWORTH REVOLUTION — Steel Pulse (Island)
27	25	AND THEN THERE WERE THREE — Genesis (Charisma)
21	26	THE ALBUM — Abba (Epic)
-	27	JAMES GALWAY PLAYS SONGS FOR ANNIE — James Galway (RCA Red Seal)
22	28	ROCK RULES — Various Artists (K-Tel)
26	29	BLAM!! — Brothers Johnson (A&M)
29	30	EVERYONE PLAYS DARTS — Darts (Magnet)

9 September 1978

3	1	NIGHT FLIGHT TO VENUS — Boney M (Atlantic/Hansa)
5	2	GREASE — Soundtrack (RSO)
4	3	WAR OF THE WORLDS — Jeff Wayne (CBS)
1	4	SATURDAY NIGHT FEVER — Soundtrack (RSO)
12	5	CLASSIC ROCK — London Symphony Orchestra (K-Tel)
6	5	20 GIANT HITS — Nolan Sisters (Target)
10	7	NATURAL HIGH — Commodores (Motown)
18	8	IMAGES — Don Williams (K-Tel)
2	9	STREET LEGAL — Bob Dylan (CBS)
13	10	STAR PARTY — Various Artists (K-Tel)
8	11	SOME GIRLS — Rolling Stones (EMI)
7	12	LIVE AND DANGEROUS — Thin Lizzy (Vertigo)
14	13	OUT OF THE BLUE — Electric Light Orchestra (Jet)
22	14	BAT OUT OF HELL — Meatloaf (Epic)
15	15	WHO ARE YOU — Who (Polydor)
11	16	OCTAVE — Moody Blues (Threshold)
9	17	20 GOLDEN GREATS — Hollies (EMI)
19	18	A TONIC FOR THE TROOPS — Boomtown Rats (Ensign)
17	19	CAN'T STAND THE REZILLOS — Rezillos (Sire)
26	20	THE ALBUM — Abba (Epic)
16	21	THE KICK INSIDE — Kate Bush (EMI)
-	22	THE LENA MARTELL COLLECTION — Lena Martell (Ronco)
21	23	NEW BOOTS & PANTIES!! — Ian Dury & the Blockheads (Stiff)
-	24	WHO PAYS THE FERRYMAN — Yannis Markopoulos (BBC)
25	25	AND THEN THERE WERE THREE — Genesis (Charisma)
-	26	RUMOURS — Fleetwood Mac (Warner Bros.)
29	27	BLAM!! — Brothers Johnson (A&M)
23	28	DOUBLE VISION — Foreigner (Atlantic)
24	29	HANDSWORTH REVOLUTION — Steel Pulse (Island)
-	30	REAL LIFE — Magazine (Virgin)

The Who's 13th Top 30 album, *Who Are You*, joined the chart at No.15 on September 2. Five days later, Keith Moon died of an overdose of sedatives used as a "treatment" for alcoholism. He had been the group's drummer since its inception in 1962, and had long been a well-loved British institution (for acting as if he should have been in one). Pete Townshend said of his death: "It's something we have been expecting for twenty years." He was eventually replaced by Kenny Jones, formerly of the Faces.

September – October 1978

16 September 1978

last week	this week		
1	1	NIGHT FLIGHT TO VENUS	Boney M (Atlantic/Hansa)
3	2	WAR OF THE WORLDS	Jeff Wayne (CBS)
5	3	CLASSIC ROCK	London Symphony Orchestra (K-Tel)
2	4	GREASE	Soundtrack (RSO)
15	5	WHO ARE YOU	Who (Polydor)
8	6	IMAGES	Don Williams (K-Tel)
9	7	STREET LEGAL	Bob Dylan (CBS)
4	8	SATURDAY NIGHT FEVER	Soundtrack (RSO)
7	9	NATURAL HIGH	Commodores (Motown)
10	10	STAR PARTY	Various Artists (K-Tel)
-	11	JAMES GALWAY PLAYS SONGS FOR ANNIE	James Galway (RCA Red Seal)
-	12	DON'T LOOK BACK	Boston (Epic)
17	12	20 GOLDEN GREATS	Hollies (EMI)
5	14	20 GIANT HITS	Nolan Sisters (Target)
19	15	CAN'T STAND THE REZILLOS	Rezillos (Sire)
13	16	OUT OF THE BLUE	Electric Light Orchestra (Jet)
16	17	OCTAVE	Moody Blues (Threshold)
20	18	THE ALBUM	Abba (Epic)
14	19	BAT OUT OF HELL	Meatloaf (Epic)
12	20	LIVE AND DANGEROUS	Thin Lizzy (Vertigo)
23	21	NEW BOOTS & PANTIES!!	Ian Dury & the Blockheads (Stiff)
25	22	AND THEN THERE WERE THREE	Genesis (Charisma)
-	23	SHADOW DANCING	Andy Gibb (RSO)
29	24	HANDSWORTH REVOLUTION	Steel Pulse (Island)
-	25	SUNLIGHT	Herbie Hancock (CBS)
-	26	EVERYONE PLAYS DARTS	Darts (Magnet)
11	27	SOME GIRLS	Rolling Stones (EMI)
26	28	RUMOURS	Fleetwood Mac (Warner Bros.)
-	29	Q: ARE WE NOT MEN? A: WE ARE DEVO!	Devo (Virgin)
-	30	LEO SAYER	Leo Sayer (Chrysalis)

23 September 1978

last week	this week		
1	1	NIGHT FLIGHT TO VENUS	Boney M (Atlantic/Hansa)
6	2	IMAGES	Don Williams (K-Tel)
4	3	GREASE	Soundtrack (RSO)
2	4	WAR OF THE WORLDS	Jeff Wayne (CBS)
3	5	CLASSIC ROCK	London Symphony Orchestra (K-Tel)
8	6	SATURDAY NIGHT FEVER	Soundtrack (RSO)
5	7	WHO ARE YOU	Who (Polydor)
11	8	JAMES GALWAY PLAYS SONGS FOR ANNIE	James Galway (RCA Red Seal)
9	9	NATURAL HIGH	Commodores (Motown)
12	10	DON'T LOOK BACK	Boston (Epic)
7	11	STREET LEGAL	Bob Dylan (CBS)
-	12	BLOODY TOURISTS	10 c.c. (Mercury)
10	13	STAR PARTY	Various Artists (K-Tel)
16	14	OUT OF THE BLUE	Electric Light Orchestra (Jet)
14	15	20 GIANT HITS	Nolan Sisters (Target)
12	16	20 GOLDEN GREATS	Hollies (EMI)
15	17	CAN'T STAND THE REZILLOS	Rezillos (Sire)
22	18	AND THEN THERE WERE THREE	Genesis (Charisma)
29	19	Q: ARE WE NOT MEN? A: WE ARE DEVO!	Devo (Virgin)
27	20	SOME GIRLS	Rolling Stones (EMI)
28	21	RUMOURS	Fleetwood Mac (Warner Bros.)
19	22	BAT OUT OF HELL	Meatloaf (Epic)
20	23	LIVE AND DANGEROUS	Thin Lizzy (Vertigo)
23	24	SHADOW DANCING	Andy Gibb (RSO)
-	25	PARALLEL LINES	Blondie (Chrysalis)
18	26	THE ALBUM	Abba (Epic)
-	27	DOUBLE VISION	Foreigner (Atlantic)
-	28	THE BRIDE STRIPPED BARE	Bryan Ferry (Polydor)
-	29	THE LENA MARTELL COLLECTION	Lena Martell (Ronco)
30	30	LEO SAYER	Leo Sayer (Chrysalis)

30 September 1978

last week	this week		
3	1	GREASE	Soundtrack (RSO)
1	2	NIGHT FLIGHT TO VENUS	Boney M (Atlantic/Hansa)
2	3	IMAGES	Don Williams (K-Tel)
4	4	WAR OF THE WORLDS	Jeff Wayne (CBS)
6	5	SATURDAY NIGHT FEVER	Soundtrack (RSO)
5	6	CLASSIC ROCK	London Symphony Orchestra (K-Tel)
25	7	PARALLEL LINES	Blondie (Chrysalis)
7	8	WHO ARE YOU	Who (Polydor)
12	9	BLOODY TOURISTS	10 c.c. (Mercury)
10	10	DON'T LOOK BACK	Boston (Epic)
9	11	NATURAL HIGH	Commodores (Motown)
11	12	STREET LEGAL	Bob Dylan (CBS)
8	13	JAMES GALWAY PLAYS SONGS FOR ANNIE	James Galway (RCA Red Seal)
14	14	OUT OF THE BLUE	Electric Light Orchestra (Jet)
23	15	LIVE AND DANGEROUS	Thin Lizzy (Vertigo)
19	16	Q: ARE WE NOT MEN? A: WE ARE DEVO!	Devo (Virgin)
-	17	BIG WHEELS OF MOTOWN	Various Artists (Motown)
-	18	NEW BOOTS & PANTIES!!	Ian Dury & the Blockheads (Stiff)
30	19	LEO SAYER	Leo Sayer (Chrysalis)
13	20	STAR PARTY	Various Artists (K-Tel)
21	21	RUMOURS	Fleetwood Mac (Warner Bros.)
-	22	OCTAVE	Moody Blues (Threshold)
-	23	SUNLIGHT	Herbie Hancock (CBS)
24	24	TORMATO	Yes (Atlantic)
22	25	BAT OUT OF HELL	Meatloaf (Epic)
28	26	THE BRIDE STRIPPED BARE	Bryan Ferry (Polydor)
27	27	DOUBLE VISION	Foreigner (Atlantic)
-	28	THE KICK INSIDE	Kate Bush (EMI)
17	29	CAN'T STAND THE REZILLOS	Rezillos (Sire)
26	30	THE ALBUM	Abba (Epic)

7 October 1978

last week	this week		
1	1	GREASE	Soundtrack (RSO)
2	2	NIGHT FLIGHT TO VENUS	Boney M (Atlantic/Hansa)
9	3	BLOODY TOURISTS	10 c.c. (Mercury)
3	4	IMAGES	Don Williams (K-Tel)
4	5	WAR OF THE WORLDS	Jeff Wayne (CBS)
5	5	SATURDAY NIGHT FEVER	Soundtrack (RSO)
7	7	PARALLEL LINES	Blondie (Chrysalis)
6	8	CLASSIC ROCK	London Symphony Orchestra (K-Tel)
10	9	DON'T LOOK BACK	Boston (Epic)
8	10	WHO ARE YOU	Who (Polydor)
-	11	ROSE ROYCE STRIKES AGAIN	Rose Royce (Whitfield)
17	12	BIG WHEELS OF MOTOWN	Various Artists (Motown)
12	13	STREET LEGAL	Bob Dylan (CBS)
19	14	LEO SAYER	Leo Sayer (Chrysalis)
24	15	TORMATO	Yes (Atlantic)
16	16	Q: ARE WE NOT MEN? A: WE ARE DEVO!	Devo (Virgin)
13	17	JAMES GALWAY PLAYS SONGS FOR ANNIE	James Galway (RCA Red Seal)
11	18	NATURAL HIGH	Commodores (Motown)
26	19	THE BRIDE STRIPPED BARE	Bryan Ferry (Polydor)
20	20	STAR PARTY	Various Artists (K-Tel)
14	21	OUT OF THE BLUE	Electric Light Orchestra (Jet)
-	22	ROAD TO RUIN	Ramones (Sire)
25	23	BAT OUT OF HELL	Meatloaf (Epic)
-	24	STAGE	David Bowie (RCA)
-	25	BREATHLESS	Camel (Decca)
15	26	LIVE AND DANGEROUS	Thin Lizzy (Vertigo)
21	27	RUMOURS	Fleetwood Mac (Warner Bros.)
-	28	LIVING IN THE USA	Linda Ronstadt (Asylum)
-	29	GHOSTS OF PRINCES IN TOWERS	Rich Kids (EMI)
22	30	OCTAVE	Moody Blues (Threshold)

The Ramones were an important iconic American punky group on Sire Records; the Rezillos were an unimportant British punky group on Sire, whose only hit single, the mistitled *Top Of The Pops*, had just peaked at No.13. For 1980 *Motorbike Beat*, they tried to improve their luck with a radical name-change... to the Revillos. *James Galway Plays Songs For Annie* referred to this flute-toting professional Irishman's recent revival (No.4 in June) of John Denver's mawkish *Annie's Song* (No.2 for Denver in 1974).

174

October – November 1978

14 October 1978

last week	this week	Album	Artist (Label)
1	1	GREASE	Soundtrack (RSO)
4	2	IMAGES	Don Williams (K-Tel)
2	3	NIGHT FLIGHT TO VENUS	Boney M (Atlantic/Hansa)
3	4	BLOODY TOURISTS	10 c.c. (Mercury)
5	5	WAR OF THE WORLDS	Jeff Wayne (CBS)
12	6	BIG WHEELS OF MOTOWN	Various Artists (Motown)
5	7	SATURDAY NIGHT FEVER	Soundtrack (RSO)
7	8	PARALLEL LINES	Blondie (Chrysalis)
8	9	CLASSIC ROCK	London Symphony Orchestra (K-Tel)
15	10	TORMATO	Yes (Atlantic)
10	11	WHO ARE YOU	Who (Polydor)
19	12	THE BRIDE STRIPPED BARE	Bryan Ferry (Polydor)
11	13	ROSE ROYCE STRIKES AGAIN	Rose Royce (Whitfield)
9	14	DON'T LOOK BACK	Boston (Epic)
24	15	STAGE	David Bowie (RCA)
21	15	OUT OF THE BLUE	Electric Light Orchestra (Jet)
23	17	BAT OUT OF HELL	Meatloaf (Epic)
-	18	BROTHERHOOD OF MAN	Brotherhood of Man (K-Tel)
22	19	ROAD TO RUIN	Ramones (Sire)
13	20	STREET LEGAL	Bob Dylan (CBS)
18	21	NATURAL HIGH	Commodores (Motown)
26	22	LIVE AND DANGEROUS	Thin Lizzy (Vertigo)
27	23	RUMOURS	Fleetwood Mac (Warner Bros.)
16	24	Q: ARE WE NOT MEN? A: WE ARE DEVO!	Devo (Virgin)
17	25	JAMES GALWAY PLAYS SONGS FOR ANNIE	James Galway (RCA Red Seal)
14	26	LEO SAYER	Leo Sayer (Chrysalis)
-	27	LOVE BITES	Buzzcocks (United Artists)
-	28	NEVER SAY DIE	Black Sabbath (Vertigo)
-	29	THAT'S WHAT FRIENDS ARE FOR	Johnny Mathis & Deniece Williams (CBS)
-	30	20 GOLDEN GREATS	Kinks (Ronco)

21 October 1978

last week	this week	Album	Artist (Label)
1	1	GREASE	Soundtrack (RSO)
6	2	BIG WHEELS OF MOTOWN	Various Artists (Motown)
3	3	NIGHT FLIGHT TO VENUS	Boney M (Atlantic/Hansa)
4	4	BLOODY TOURISTS	10 c.c. (Mercury)
5	5	WAR OF THE WORLDS	Jeff Wayne (CBS)
9	6	CLASSIC ROCK	London Symphony Orchestra (K-Tel)
2	7	IMAGES	Don Williams (K-Tel)
15	8	STAGE	David Bowie (RCA)
10	9	TORMATO	Yes (Atlantic)
13	10	ROSE ROYCE STRIKES AGAIN	Rose Royce (Whitfield)
8	11	PARALLEL LINES	Blondie (Chrysalis)
7	12	SATURDAY NIGHT FEVER	Soundtrack (RSO)
27	13	LOVE BITES	Buzzcocks (United Artists)
15	14	OUT OF THE BLUE	Electric Light Orchestra (Jet)
14	15	DON'T LOOK BACK	Boston (Epic)
18	16	BROTHERHOOD OF MAN	Brotherhood of Man (K-Tel)
28	17	NEVER SAY DIE	Black Sabbath (Vertigo)
21	18	NATURAL HIGH	Commodores (Motown)
-	19	LIVE & MORE	Donna Summer (Casablanca)
11	20	WHO ARE YOU	Who (Polydor)
26	21	LEO SAYER	Leo Sayer (Chrysalis)
-	22	LIVE BURSTING OUT	Jethro Tull (Chrysalis)
-	23	TO THE LIMIT	Joan Armatrading (A&M)
24	24	Q: ARE WE NOT MEN? A: WE ARE DEVO!	Devo (Virgin)
19	25	ROAD TO RUIN	Ramones (Sire)
30	26	20 GOLDEN GREATS	Kinks (Ronco)
12	27	THE BRIDE STRIPPED BARE	Bryan Ferry (Polydor)
-	28	BREATHLESS	Camel (Decca)
-	29	GREEN LIGHT	Cliff Richard (EMI)
-	30	JOURNEY TO ADDIS	Third World (Island)

28 October 1978

last week	this week	Album	Artist (Label)
1	1	GREASE	Soundtrack (RSO)
5	2	WAR OF THE WORLDS	Jeff Wayne (CBS)
3	3	NIGHT FLIGHT TO VENUS	Boney M (Atlantic/Hansa)
2	3	BIG WHEELS OF MOTOWN	Various Artists (Motown)
7	5	IMAGES	Don Williams (K-Tel)
6	6	CLASSIC ROCK	London Symphony Orchestra (K-Tel)
4	7	BLOODY TOURISTS	10 c.c. (Mercury)
10	8	ROSE ROYCE STRIKES AGAIN	Rose Royce (Whitfield)
12	9	SATURDAY NIGHT FEVER	Soundtrack (RSO)
17	10	NEVER SAY DIE	Black Sabbath (Vertigo)
19	11	LIVE & MORE	Donna Summer (Casablanca)
13	12	LOVE BITES	Buzzcocks (United Artists)
8	13	STAGE	David Bowie (RCA)
16	14	BROTHERHOOD OF MAN	Brotherhood of Man (K-Tel)
14	15	OUT OF THE BLUE	Electric Light Orchestra (Jet)
-	16	SATIN CITY	Various Artists (CBS)
11	17	PARALLEL LINES	Blondie (Chrysalis)
22	18	LIVE BURSTING OUT	Jethro Tull (Chrysalis)
30	19	JOURNEY TO ADDIS	Third World (Island)
9	20	TORMATO	Yes (Atlantic)
-	21	WELL, WELL, SAID THE ROCKING CHAIR	Dean Friedman (Lifesong)
26	22	20 GOLDEN GREATS	Kinks (Ronco)
-	23	JAMES GALWAY PLAYS SONGS FOR ANNIE	James Galway (RCA Red Seal)
23	24	TO THE LIMIT	Joan Armatrading (A&M)
21	25	LEO SAYER	Leo Sayer (Chrysalis)
-	26	STREET LEGAL	Bob Dylan (CBS)
29	27	GREEN LIGHT	Cliff Richard (EMI)
-	28	ECSTASY	Various Artists (Lotus)
15	29	DON'T LOOK BACK	Boston (Epic)
-	30	A TONIC FOR THE TROOPS	Boomtown Rats (Ensign)

4 November 1978

last week	this week	Album	Artist (Label)
1	1	GREASE	Soundtrack (RSO)
3	2	NIGHT FLIGHT TO VENUS	Boney M (Atlantic/Hansa)
3	3	BIG WHEELS OF MOTOWN	Various Artists (Motown)
2	4	WAR OF THE WORLDS	Jeff Wayne (CBS)
14	5	BROTHERHOOD OF MAN	Brotherhood of Man (K-Tel)
9	6	SATURDAY NIGHT FEVER	Soundtrack (RSO)
5	7	IMAGES	Don Williams (K-Tel)
17	8	PARALLEL LINES	Blondie (Chrysalis)
13	9	STAGE	David Bowie (RCA)
-	10	EMOTIONS	Various Artists (K-Tel)
8	11	ROSE ROYCE STRIKES AGAIN	Rose Royce (Whitfield)
15	12	OUT OF THE BLUE	Electric Light Orchestra (Jet)
6	13	CLASSIC ROCK	London Symphony Orchestra (K-Tel)
30	14	A TONIC FOR THE TROOPS	Boomtown Rats (Ensign)
25	15	LEO SAYER	Leo Sayer (Chrysalis)
7	16	BLOODY TOURISTS	10 c.c. (Mercury)
20	17	TORMATO	Yes (Atlantic)
18	18	LIVE BURSTING OUT	Jethro Tull (Chrysalis)
-	19	SOME ENCHANTED EVENING	Blue Oyster Cult (CBS)
12	20	LOVE BITES	Buzzcocks (United Artists)
24	21	TO THE LIMIT	Joan Armatrading (A&M)
-	22	GO 2	XTC (Virgin)
11	23	LIVE & MORE	Donna Summer (Casablanca)
-	24	25TH ANNIVERSARY ALBUM	Shirley Bassey (United Artists)
-	25	MANHATTAN TRANSFER LIVE	Manhattan Transfer (Atlantic)
-	26	MOVING TARGETS	Penetration (Virgin)
10	27	NEVER SAY DIE	Black Sabbath (Vertigo)
-	28	A SINGLE MAN	Elton John (Rocket)
-	29	EVEN NOW	Barry Manilow (Arista)
-	30	IF YOU CAN'T STAND THE HEAT	Status Quo (Vertigo)

The Buzzcocks' second LP, *Love Bites*, charted mid-October, peaked at 12 and would quit by mid-November. This also typified what happened with the classic singles of Manchester's finest. *What Do I Get* had peaked at 28; *I Don't Mind* never made the 30; *Love You More* had peaked at 22; *Ever Fallen In Love (With Someone You Shouldn't've)* was peaking at No.13 now. They never topped that. *Ever Fallen* would be a bigger hit for Fine Young Cannibals in 1987; Buzzcocks would re-form in the 1990s.

November – December 1978

Some disingenuous titles entered the charts. *All Mod Cons*, by the Jam, punned on the fact that this nifty and resourceful punk band had been founded on re-inventing the spirit of the early Who, Mod heroes supreme. *Ecstasy*, by Various Artists, did not refer with uncanny foresight to the designer-drug of the 1980s, and Queen's 6th hit album *Jazz* did not refer to its musical contents, which no more resembled jazz than *Classic Rock* resembled either rock or the classics (let alone classic rock).

December 1978

last this week 9 December 1978

2 1 20 GOLDEN GREATS
Neil Diamond (MCA)
1 2 GREASE Soundtrack (RSO)
25 3 THE SINGLES 1974-1978
Carpenters (A&M)
4 4 NIGHT FLIGHT TO VENUS
Boney M (Atlantic/Hansa)
7 5 MIDNIGHT HUSTLE
Various Artists (K-Tel)
6 6 JAZZ Queen (EMI)
16 7 BLONDES HAVE MORE FUN
Rod Stewart (Riva)
20 8 THE AMAZING DARTS
Darts (K-Tel/Magnet)
11 9 A TONIC FOR THE TROOPS
Boomtown Rats (Ensign)
5 10 EMOTIONS
Various Artists (K-Tel)
3 11 GIVE 'EM ENOUGH ROPE
Clash (CBS)
21 12 LIONHEART Kate Bush (EMI)
9 13 A SINGLE MAN
Elton John (Rocket)
11 14 IMAGES Don Williams (K-Tel)
28 15 THAT'S LIFE
Sham 69 (Polydor)
19 16 EVERGREEN
Acker Bilk (Warwick)
10 17 WAR OF THE WORLDS
Jeff Wayne (CBS)
22 18 OUT OF THE BLUE
Electric Light Orchestra (Jet)
8 19 IF YOU CAN'T STAND THE HEAT
Status Quo (Vertigo)
- 20 THE SCREAM
Siouxsie & the Banshees
(Polydor)
15 21 25TH ANNIVERSARY ALBUM
Shirley Bassey (United Artists)
- 22 COMMODORES' GREATEST HITS
Commodores (Motown)
- 23 GREATEST HITS 1976-1978
Showaddywaddy (Arista)
17 24 BOOGIE FEVER
Various Artists (Ronco)
- 25 FATHER ABRAHAM IN
SMURFLAND
Father Abraham & the Smurfs
(Decca)
13 26 ALL MOD CONS Jam (Polydor)
- 27 DON'T WALK BOOGIE
Various Artists (EMI)
23 28 SATURDAY NIGHT FEVER
Soundtrack (RSO)
14 29 MANHATTAN TRANSFER LIVE
Manhattan Transfer (Atlantic)
18 30 LIVE & MORE
Donna Summer (Casablanca)

16 December 1978

1 1 20 GOLDEN GREATS
Neil Diamond (MCA)
7 2 BLONDES HAVE MORE FUN
Rod Stewart (Riva)
2 3 GREASE Soundtrack (RSO)
3 4 THE SINGLES 1974-1978
Carpenters (A&M)
13 5 A SINGLE MAN
Elton John (Rocket)
5 6 MIDNIGHT HUSTLE
Various Artists (K-Tel)
4 7 NIGHT FLIGHT TO VENUS
Boney M (Atlantic/Hansa)
10 7 EMOTIONS
Various Artists (K-Tel)
6 9 JAZZ Queen (EMI)
8 10 THE AMAZING DARTS
Darts (K-Tel/Magnet)
23 11 GREATEST HITS 1976-1978
Showaddywaddy (Arista)
16 12 EVERGREEN
Acker Bilk (Warwick)
12 13 LIONHEART Kate Bush (EMI)
11 14 GIVE 'EM ENOUGH ROPE
Clash (CBS)
17 15 WAR OF THE WORLDS
Jeff Wayne (CBS)
29 16 MANHATTAN TRANSFER LIVE
Manhattan Transfer (Atlantic)
25 17 FATHER ABRAHAM IN
SMURFLAND
Father Abraham & the Smurfs
(Decca)
- 18 NIGHT GALLERY
Barron Knights (Epic)
15 19 THAT'S LIFE Sham 69 (Polydor)
14 20 IMAGES Don Williams (K-Tel)
22 21 COMMODORES' GREATEST HITS
Commodores (Motown)
9 22 A TONIC FOR THE TROOPS
Boomtown Rats (Ensign)
20 23 THE SCREAM
Siouxsie & the Banshees
(Polydor)
27 24 DON'T WALK BOOGIE
Various Artists (EMI)
- 25 BACKLESS Eric Clapton (RSO)
18 26 OUT OF THE BLUE
Electric Light Orchestra (Jet)
26 27 ALL MOD CONS Jam (Polydor)
- 28 GERM FREE ADOLESCENTS
X Ray Spex (EMI International)
- 29 BOTH SIDES
Dolly Parton (Lotus)
19 30 IF YOU CAN'T STAND THE HEAT
Status Quo (Vertigo)

23 December 1978

3 1 GREASE Soundtrack (RSO)
4 2 THE SINGLES 1974-1978
Carpenters (A&M)
1 3 20 GOLDEN GREATS
Neil Diamond (MCA)
7 4 NIGHT FLIGHT TO VENUS
Boney M (Atlantic/Hansa)
2 5 BLONDES HAVE MORE FUN
Rod Stewart (Riva)
6 6 MIDNIGHT HUSTLE
Various Artists (K-Tel)
10 7 THE AMAZING DARTS
Darts (K-Tel/Magnet)
11 8 GREATEST HITS 1976-1978
Showaddywaddy (Arista)
5 9 A SINGLE MAN
Elton John (Rocket)
22 10 A TONIC FOR THE TROOPS
Boomtown Rats (Ensign)
7 11 EMOTIONS
Various Artists (K-Tel)
25 12 BACKLESS Eric Clapton (RSO)
9 13 JAZZ Queen (EMI)
14 14 GIVE 'EM ENOUGH ROPE
Clash (CBS)
15 15 WAR OF THE WORLDS
Jeff Wayne (CBS)
20 16 IMAGES Don Williams (K-Tel)
- 17 EQUINOXE
Jean-Michel Jarre (Polydor)
- 18 INCANTATIONS
Mike Oldfield (Virgin)
18 19 NIGHT GALLERY
Barron Knights (Epic)
- 20 SATURDAY NIGHT FEVER
Soundtrack (RSO)
- 21 CLASSICAL GOLD VOL 2
Various Artists (K-Tel)
- 22 20 SONGS OF JOY
Harry Secombe (Warwick)
- 23 WINGS' GREATEST
Wings (Parlophone)
- 24 20 GOLDEN GREATS
Nat 'King' Cole (Capitol)
13 25 LIONHEART Kate Bush (EMI)
12 26 EVERGREEN
Acker Bilk (Warwick)
26 27 OUT OF THE BLUE
Electric Light Orchestra (Jet)
- 28 25TH ANNIVERSARY ALBUM
Shirley Bassey (United Artists)
- 29 PARALLEL LINES
Blondie (Chrysalis)
29 30 BOTH SIDES
Dolly Parton (Lotus)

The second LP of Carpenters 45s leapt into the Top 3. Their 1974-78 hit singles had included revisits to perfectly harmless old songs like Hank Williams' *Jambalaya* and the Marvelettes' *Please Mr Postman*, plus songs that more readily deserved the Carpenter treatment – *Solitaire* and *There's A Kind Of Hush All Over The World* – plus something called *Calling Occupants Of Interplanetary Craft (The Recognized Anthem Of World Contact Day)* from 1977. Meanwhile enter Siouxsie & the Banshees and X Ray Spex.

January 1979

6 January 1979

last week	this week	Title / Artist (Label)
8	1	GREATEST HITS 1976-1978 — Showaddywaddy (Arista)
2	2	THE SINGLES 1974-1978 — Carpenters (A&M)
6	3	MIDNIGHT HUSTLE — Various Artists (K-Tel)
3	4	20 GOLDEN GREATS — Neil Diamond (MCA)
1	5	GREASE Soundtrack (RSO)
4	6	NIGHT FLIGHT TO VENUS — Boney M (Atlantic/Hansa)
5	7	BLONDES HAVE MORE FUN — Rod Stewart (Riva)
11	8	EMOTIONS — Various Artists (K-Tel)
7	9	THE AMAZING DARTS — Darts (K-Tel/Magnet)
19	10	NIGHT GALLERY — Barron Knights (Epic)
22	11	20 SONGS OF JOY — Harry Secombe (Warwick)
9	12	A SINGLE MAN — Elton John (Rocket)
10	13	A TONIC FOR THE TROOPS — Boomtown Rats (Ensign)
18	14	INCANTATIONS — Mike Oldfield (Virgin)
-	15	PUBLIC IMAGE — Public Image Ltd. (Virgin)
12	16	JAZZ — Queen (EMI)
17	17	EQUINOXE — Jean-Michel Jarre (Polydor)
16	18	IMAGES Don Williams (K-Tel)
15	19	WAR OF THE WORLDS — Jeff Wayne (CBS)
14	20	GIVE 'EM ENOUGH ROPE — Clash (CBS)
12	21	BACKLESS Eric Clapton (RSO)
23	22	WINGS' GREATEST — Wings (Parlophone)
21	23	CLASSICAL GOLD VOL 2 — Various Artists (K-Tel)
24	24	20 GOLDEN GREATS — Nat 'King' Cole (Capitol)
-	25	SANDY John Travolta (Polydor)
-	26	COMMODORES' GREATEST HITS — Commodores (Motown)
25	27	LIONHEART Kate Bush (EMI)
28	28	25TH ANNIVERSARY ALBUM — Shirley Bassey (United Artists)
-	29	FATHER ABRAHAM IN SMURFLAND — Father Abraham & the Smurfs (Decca)
-	30	DON'T WALK, BOOGIE — Various Artists (EMI)

13 January 1979

last week	this week	Title / Artist (Label)
1	1	GREATEST HITS 1976-1978 — Showaddywaddy (Arista)
2	2	THE SINGLES 1974-1978 — Carpenters (A&M)
5	3	GREASE Soundtrack (RSO)
4	4	20 GOLDEN GREATS
7	5	BLONDES HAVE MORE FUN — Rod Stewart (Riva)
6	6	NIGHT FLIGHT TO VENUS — Boney M (Atlantic/Hansa)
3	7	MIDNIGHT HUSTLE — Various Artists (K-Tel)
19	8	WAR OF THE WORLDS — Jeff Wayne (CBS)
30	9	DON'T WALK, BOOGIE — Various Artists (EMI)
12	10	A SINGLE MAN — Elton John (Rocket)
8	11	EMOTIONS — Various Artists (K-Tel)
13	12	A TONIC FOR THE TROOPS — Boomtown Rats (Ensign)
11	13	20 SONGS OF JOY — Harry Secombe (Warwick)
-	14	YOU DON'T BRING ME FLOWERS — Neil Diamond (CBS)
9	15	THE AMAZING DARTS — Darts (K-Tel/Magnet)
22	16	WINGS' GREATEST — Wings (Parlophone)
17	17	EQUINOXE — Jean-Michel Jarre (Polydor)
-	18	PARALLEL LINES — Blondie (Chrysalis)
15	19	PUBLIC IMAGE — Public Image Ltd. (Virgin)
10	20	NIGHT GALLERY — Barron Knights (Epic)
16	21	JAZZ — Queen (EMI)
14	22	INCANTATIONS — Mike Oldfield (Virgin)
-	23	THAT'S LIFE Sham 69 (Polydor)
21	24	BACKLESS Eric Clapton (RSO)
-	25	OUT OF THE BLUE — Electric Light Orchestra (Jet)
-	26	52ND STREET Billy Joel (CBS)
20	27	GIVE 'EM ENOUGH ROPE — Clash (CBS)
-	28	THE BEST OF EARTH WIND & FIRE, VOL. 1 — Earth Wind & Fire (CBS)
-	29	TOTALLY HOT — Olivia Newton-John (EMI)
27	30	LIONHEART Kate Bush (EMI)

20 January 1979

last week	this week	Title / Artist (Label)
1	1	GREATEST HITS 1976-1978 — Showaddywaddy (Arista)
9	2	DON'T WALK, BOOGIE — Various Artists (EMI)
2	3	THE SINGLES 1974-1978 — Carpenters (A&M)
5	4	BLONDES HAVE MORE FUN — Rod Stewart (Riva)
7	5	MIDNIGHT HUSTLE — Various Artists (K-Tel)
4	6	20 GOLDEN GREATS — Neil Diamond (MCA)
6	7	NIGHT FLIGHT TO VENUS — Boney M (Atlantic/Hansa)
8	8	WAR OF THE WORLDS — Jeff Wayne (CBS)
16	9	WINGS' GREATEST — Wings (Parlophone)
15	10	THE AMAZING DARTS — Darts (K-Tel/Magnet)
10	11	A SINGLE MAN — Elton John (Rocket)
3	12	GREASE Soundtrack (RSO)
11	13	EMOTIONS — Various Artists (K-Tel)
12	14	A TONIC FOR THE TROOPS — Boomtown Rats (Ensign)
13	15	20 SONGS OF JOY — Harry Secombe (Warwick)
18	16	PARALLEL LINES — Blondie (Chrysalis)
28	17	THE BEST OF EARTH WIND & FIRE, VOL. 1 — Earth Wind & Fire (CBS)
-	18	ACTION REPLAY — Various Artists (K-Tel)
22	19	INCANTATIONS — Mike Oldfield (Virgin)
17	20	EQUINOXE — Jean-Michel Jarre (Polydor)
-	21	COMMODORES' GREATEST HITS — Commodores (Motown)
22	22	20 GOLDEN GREATS — Doris Day (Warwick)
27	23	GIVE 'EM ENOUGH ROPE — Clash (CBS)
20	24	NIGHT GALLERY — Barron Knights (Epic)
30	25	LIONHEART Kate Bush (EMI)
-	26	ARMED FORCES — Elvis Costello (Radar)
-	27	NEW BOOTS AND PANTIES!! — Ian Dury & the Blockheads (Stiff)
21	28	JAZZ — Queen (EMI)
14	29	YOU DON'T BRING ME FLOWERS — Neil Diamond (CBS)
-	30	DREAM MUSIC — Various Artists (Lotus)

27 January 1979

last week	this week	Title / Artist (Label)
2	1	DON'T WALK, BOOGIE — Various Artists (EMI)
3	2	THE SINGLES 1974-1978 — Carpenters (A&M)
9	3	WINGS' GREATEST — Wings (Parlophone)
1	4	GREATEST HITS 1976-1978 — Showaddywaddy (Arista)
16	5	PARALLEL LINES — Blondie (Chrysalis)
18	6	ACTION REPLAY — Various Artists (K-Tel)
26	7	ARMED FORCES — Elvis Costello (Radar)
10	8	A SINGLE MAN — Elton John (Rocket)
4	9	BLONDES HAVE MORE FUN — Rod Stewart (Riva)
12	10	GREASE Soundtrack (RSO)
17	11	THE BEST OF EARTH WIND & FIRE, VOL. 1 — Earth Wind & Fire (CBS)
7	12	NIGHT FLIGHT TO VENUS — Boney M (Atlantic/Hansa)
5	13	MIDNIGHT HUSTLE — Various Artists (K-Tel)
20	14	EQUINOXE — Jean-Michel Jarre (Polydor)
6	15	20 GOLDEN GREATS — Neil Diamond (MCA)
8	16	WAR OF THE WORLDS — Jeff Wayne (CBS)
14	17	A TONIC FOR THE TROOPS — Boomtown Rats (Ensign)
-	18	OUT OF THE BLUE — Electric Light Orchestra (Jet)
27	19	NEW BOOTS AND PANTIES!! — Ian Dury & the Blockheads (Stiff)
22	20	20 GOLDEN GREATS — Doris Day (Warwick)
23	21	GIVE 'EM ENOUGH ROPE — Clash (CBS)
24	22	NIGHT GALLERY — Barron Knights (Epic)
29	23	YOU DON'T BRING ME FLOWERS — Neil Diamond (CBS)
13	24	EMOTIONS — Various Artists (K-Tel)
-	25	EVEN NOW — Barry Manilow (Arista)
19	26	INCANTATIONS — Mike Oldfield (Virgin)
25	27	LIONHEART Kate Bush (EMI)
28	28	JAZZ — Queen (EMI)
21	29	COMMODORES' GREATEST HITS — Commodores (Motown)
30	30	DREAM MUSIC — Various Artists (Lotus)

MOR ruled, most "new" entries were re-entries and the biggest new arrival, John Lydon's Public Image Ltd, was much less interesting than the Sex Pistols. The singles chart was almost as moribund: Village People's *Y.M.C.A.* was displaced at No.1 by Ian Dury's *Hit Me With Your Rhythm Stick* and other entrants included Buzzcocks' *Promises* (another re-entry) and *Hello This Is Joanie* by Paul Evans, his first appearance since *Seven Little Girls (Sitting In The Back Seat)*, No.25 for one week in 1959.

February 1979

3 February 1979

last week	this week	Title	Artist
1	1	DON'T WALK, BOOGIE	Various Artists (EMI)
5	2	PARALLEL LINES	Blondie (Chrysalis)
4	3	GREATEST HITS 1976-1978	Showaddywaddy (Arista)
7	4	ARMED FORCES	Elvis Costello (Radar)
2	5	THE SINGLES 1974-1978	Carpenters (A&M)
6	6	ACTION REPLAY	Various Artists (K-Tel)
14	7	EQUINOXE	Jean-Michel Jarre (Polydor)
10	8	GREASE	Soundtrack (RSO)
19	9	NEW BOOTS AND PANTIES!!	Ian Dury & the Blockheads (Stiff)
8	10	A SINGLE MAN	Elton John (Rocket)
17	11	A TONIC FOR THE TROOPS	Boomtown Rats (Ensign)
12	12	NIGHT FLIGHT TO VENUS	Boney M (Atlantic/Hansa)
3	12	WINGS' GREATEST	Wings (Parlophone)
11	14	THE BEST OF EARTH WIND & FIRE, VOL. 1	Earth Wind & Fire (CBS)
25	15	EVEN NOW	Barry Manilow (Arista)
8	16	BLONDES HAVE MORE FUN	Rod Stewart (Riva)
26	17	INCANTATIONS	Mike Oldfield (Virgin)
20	18	20 GOLDEN GREATS	Doris Day (Warwick)
16	19	WAR OF THE WORLDS	Jeff Wayne (CBS)
-	20	CRUISIN'	Village People (Mercury)
23	21	YOU DON'T BRING ME FLOWERS	Neil Diamond (CBS)
24	22	EMOTIONS	Various Artists (K-Tel)
15	23	20 GOLDEN GREATS	Neil Diamond (MCA)
-	24	52ND STREET	Billy Joel (CBS)
-	25	BAT OUT OF HELL	Meatloaf (Epic)
-	26	THE AMAZING DARTS	Darts (K-Tel/Magnet)
18	27	OUT OF THE BLUE	Electric Light Orchestra (Jet)
21	28	GIVE 'EM ENOUGH ROPE	Clash (CBS)
-	29	TOTALLY HOT	Olivia Newton-John (EMI)
13	30	MIDNIGHT HUSTLE	Various Artists (K-Tel)

10 February 1979

last week	this week	Title	Artist
2	1	PARALLEL LINES	Blondie (Chrysalis)
6	2	ACTION REPLAY	Various Artists (K-Tel)
1	3	DON'T WALK, BOOGIE	Various Artists (EMI)
4	4	ARMED FORCES	Elvis Costello (Radar)
14	5	THE BEST OF EARTH WIND & FIRE, VOL. 1	Earth Wind & Fire (CBS)
15	6	EVEN NOW	Barry Manilow (Arista)
9	7	NEW BOOTS AND PANTIES!!	Ian Dury & the Blockheads (Stiff)
3	8	GREATEST HITS 1976-1978	Showaddywaddy (Arista)
10	9	A SINGLE MAN	Elton John (Rocket)
5	10	THE SINGLES 1974-1978	Carpenters (A&M)
7	11	EQUINOXE	Jean-Michel Jarre (Polydor)
8	11	GREASE	Soundtrack (RSO)
12	13	WINGS' GREATEST	Wings (Parlophone)
16	14	BLONDES HAVE MORE FUN	Rod Stewart (Riva)
27	15	OUT OF THE BLUE	Electric Light Orchestra (Jet)
12	16	NIGHT FLIGHT TO VENUS	Boney M (Atlantic/Hansa)
11	17	A TONIC FOR THE TROOPS	Boomtown Rats (Ensign)
-	18	C'EST CHIC	Chic (Atlantic)
21	19	YOU DON'T BRING ME FLOWERS	Neil Diamond (CBS)
20	20	CRUISIN'	Village People (Mercury)
-	21	SPIRITS HAVING FLOWN	Bee Gees (RSO)
25	22	BAT OUT OF HELL	Meatloaf (Epic)
24	23	52ND STREET	Billy Joel (CBS)
23	24	20 GOLDEN GREATS	Neil Diamond (MCA)
17	25	INCANTATIONS	Mike Oldfield (Virgin)
-	26	COMMODORES' GREATEST HITS	Commodores (Motown)
-	27	THREE LIGHT YEARS	Electric Light Orchestra (Jet)
22	28	JAZZ	Queen (EMI)
19	29	WAR OF THE WORLDS	Jeff Wayne (CBS)
22	30	EMOTIONS	Various Artists (K-Tel)

17 February 1979

last week	this week	Title	Artist
1	1	PARALLEL LINES	Blondie (Chrysalis)
2	2	ACTION REPLAY	Various Artists (K-Tel)
4	3	ARMED FORCES	Elvis Costello (Radar)
3	4	DON'T WALK, BOOGIE	Various Artists (EMI)
5	5	THE BEST OF EARTH WIND & FIRE, VOL. 1	Earth Wind & Fire (CBS)
11	6	EQUINOXE	Jean-Michel Jarre (Polydor)
6	7	EVEN NOW	Barry Manilow (Arista)
13	8	WINGS' GREATEST	Wings (Parlophone)
7	9	NEW BOOTS AND PANTIES!!	Ian Dury & the Blockheads (Stiff)
21	10	GREASE	Soundtrack (RSO)
21	11	SPIRITS HAVING FLOWN	Bee Gees (RSO)
-	12	THE MARTY ROBBINS COLLECTION	Marty Robbins (Lotus)
14	12	BLONDES HAVE MORE FUN	Rod Stewart (Riva)
9	14	A SINGLE MAN	Elton John (Rocket)
-	15	STRANGERS IN THE NIGHT	UFO (Chrysalis)
18	16	C'EST CHIC	Chic (Atlantic)
25	17	INCANTATIONS	Mike Oldfield (Virgin)
23	18	52ND STREET	Billy Joel (CBS)
24	19	20 GOLDEN GREATS	Neil Diamond (MCA)
8	20	GREATEST HITS 1976-1978	Showaddywaddy (Arista)
17	21	A TONIC FOR THE TROOPS	Boomtown Rats (Ensign)
28	22	JAZZ	Queen (EMI)
29	23	WAR OF THE WORLDS	Jeff Wayne (CBS)
10	24	THE SINGLES 1974-1978	Carpenters (A&M)
15	25	OUT OF THE BLUE	Electric Light Orchestra (Jet)
-	26	TOTALLY HOT	Olivia Newton-John (EMI)
19	27	YOU DON'T BRING ME FLOWERS	Neil Diamond (CBS)
-	28	LIVE AND DANGEROUS	Thin Lizzy (Vertigo)
22	29	BAT OUT OF HELL	Meatloaf (Epic)
-	30	PLASTIC LETTERS	Blondie (Chrysalis)

24 February 1979

last week	this week	Title	Artist
1	1	PARALLEL LINES	Blondie (Chrysalis)
11	2	SPIRITS HAVING FLOWN	Bee Gees (RSO)
2	3	ACTION REPLAY	Various Artists (K-Tel)
3	4	ARMED FORCES	Elvis Costello (Radar)
5	5	THE BEST OF EARTH WIND & FIRE, VOL. 1	Earth Wind & Fire (CBS)
4	6	DON'T WALK, BOOGIE	Various Artists (EMI)
9	7	NEW BOOTS AND PANTIES!!	Ian Dury & the Blockheads (Stiff)
15	8	STRANGERS IN THE NIGHT	UFO (Chrysalis)
12	9	THE MARTY ROBBINS COLLECTION	Marty Robbins (Lotus)
6	10	EQUINOXE	Jean-Michel Jarre (Polydor)
8	11	WINGS' GREATEST	Wings (Parlophone)
-	12	THANK YOU VERY MUCH – REUNION CONCERT AT THE LONDON PALLADIUM	Cliff Richard & the Shadows (EMI)
16	13	C'EST CHIC	Chic (Atlantic)
12	14	BLONDES HAVE MORE FUN	Rod Stewart (Riva)
23	15	WAR OF THE WORLDS	Jeff Wayne (CBS)
7	16	EVEN NOW	Barry Manilow (Arista)
25	17	OUT OF THE BLUE	Electric Light Orchestra (Jet)
14	18	A SINGLE MAN	Elton John (Rocket)
19	19	20 GOLDEN GREATS	Neil Diamond (MCA)
-	20	NIGHT FLIGHT TO VENUS	Boney M (Atlantic/Hansa)
-	21	CRUISIN'	Village People (Mercury)
-	22	FORCE MAJEURE	Tangerine Dream (Virgin)
-	23	REFLECTIONS	George Hamilton IV (Lotus)
27	24	YOU DON'T BRING ME FLOWERS	Neil Diamond (CBS)
-	25	THE INCREDIBLE SHRINKING DICKIES	Dickies (A&M)
29	26	BAT OUT OF HELL	Meatloaf (Epic)
10	27	GREASE	Soundtrack (RSO)
18	28	52ND STREET	Billy Joel (CBS)
17	29	INCANTATIONS	Mike Oldfield (Virgin)
-	30	VALLEY OF THE DOLLS	Generation X (Chrysalis)

This month saw the death of Sid Vicious, whose solid contribution to music was his extraordinary filmed performance of *My Way*. He OD'd while on trial for the murder of girlfriend Nancy Spungen in New York's legendary Chelsea Hotel, where, among many other things, Bob Dylan said he'd written *Blonde On Blonde*'s *Sad-Eyed Lady Of The Lowlands*. Meanwhile Blondie, essentially Debbie Harry and guitarist Chris Stein, hit No.1. *Parallel Lines*, the group's third LP, would eventually sell 20 million worldwide.

March 1979

	3 March 1979		10 March 1979		17 March 1979		24 March 1979
1 1	PARALLEL LINES Blondie (Chrysalis)	1 1	PARALLEL LINES Blondie (Chrysalis)	1 1	PARALLEL LINES Blondie (Chrysalis)	2 1	SPIRITS HAVING FLOWN Bee Gees (RSO)
4 2	ARMED FORCES Elvis Costello (Radar)	3 2	SPIRITS HAVING FLOWN Bee Gees (RSO)	2 2	SPIRITS HAVING FLOWN Bee Gees (RSO)	1 2	PARALLEL LINES Blondie (Chrysalis)
2 3	SPIRITS HAVING FLOWN Bee Gees (RSO)	2 3	ARMED FORCES Elvis Costello (Radar)	10 3	MANILOW MAGIC Barry Manilow (Arista)	4 3	ARMED FORCES Elvis Costello (Radar)
3 4	ACTION REPLAY Various Artists (K-Tel)	4 4	ACTION REPLAY Various Artists (K-Tel)	3 4	ARMED FORCES Elvis Costello (Radar)	5 4	C'EST CHIC Chic (Atlantic)
14 5	BLONDES HAVE MORE FUN Rod Stewart (Riva)	7 5	THANK YOU VERY MUCH – REUNION CONCERT AT THE LONDON PALLADIUM Cliff Richard & the Shadows (EMI)	16 5	C'EST CHIC Chic (Atlantic)	3 5	MANILOW MAGIC Barry Manilow (Arista)
9 6	THE MARTY ROBBINS COLLECTION Marty Robbins (Lotus)	6 5	THE MARTY ROBBINS COLLECTION Marty Robbins (Lotus)	5 6	THANK YOU VERY MUCH – REUNION CONCERT AT THE LONDON PALLADIUM Cliff Richard & the Shadows (EMI)	10 6	THE GREAT ROCK'N'ROLL SWINDLE Sex Pistols (Virgin)
12 7	THANK YOU VERY MUCH – REUNION CONCERT AT THE LONDON PALLADIUM Cliff Richard & the Shadows (EMI)	5 7	BLONDES HAVE MORE FUN Rod Stewart (Riva)	5 7	THE MARTY ROBBINS COLLECTION Marty Robbins (Lotus)	7 7	THE MARTY ROBBINS COLLECTION Marty Robbins (Lotus)
6 8	DON'T WALK, BOOGIE Various Artists (EMI)	15 8	NEW BOOTS AND PANTIES!! Ian Dury & the Blockheads (Stiff)	12 8	THE BEST OF EARTH WIND & FIRE, VOL. 1 Earth Wind & Fire (CBS)	18 8	DIRE STRAITS Dire Straits (Vertigo)
8 9	STRANGERS IN THE NIGHT UFO (Chrysalis)	9 9	STRANGERS IN THE NIGHT UFO (Chrysalis)	7 9	BLONDES HAVE MORE FUN Rod Stewart (Riva)	22 9	A COLLECTION OF THEIR 20 GREATEST HITS Three Degrees (Epic)
19 10	20 GOLDEN GREATS Neil Diamond (MCA)	- 10	MANILOW MAGIC Barry Manilow (Arista)	21 10	THE GREAT ROCK'N'ROLL SWINDLE Sex Pistols (Virgin)	- 10	BARBRA STREISAND'S GREATEST HITS VOL 2 Barbra Streisand (CBS)
20 11	NIGHT FLIGHT TO VENUS Boney M (Atlantic/Hansa)	17 11	BAT OUT OF HELL Meatloaf (Epic)	15 11	52ND STREET Billy Joel (CBS)	12 11	LIVE (X CERT) Stranglers (United Artists)
5 12	THE BEST OF EARTH WIND & FIRE, VOL. 1 Earth Wind & Fire (CBS)	12 12	THE BEST OF EARTH WIND & FIRE, VOL. 1 Earth Wind & Fire (CBS)	- 12	LIVE (X CERT) Stranglers (United Artists)	6 12	THANK YOU VERY MUCH – REUNION CONCERT AT THE LONDON PALLADIUM Cliff Richard & the Shadows (EMI)
10 13	EQUINOXE Jean-Michel Jarre (Polydor)	17 13	WINGS' GREATEST HITS Wings (Parlophone)	4 13	ACTION REPLAY Various Artists (K-Tel)	8 13	THE BEST OF EARTH WIND & FIRE, VOL. 1 Earth Wind & Fire (CBS)
18 14	A SINGLE MAN Elton John (Rocket)	13 14	EQUINOXE Jean-Michel Jarre (Polydor)	9 14	STRANGERS IN THE NIGHT UFO (Chrysalis)	15 13	NEW BOOTS AND PANTIES!! Ian Dury & the Blockheads (Stiff)
7 15	NEW BOOTS AND PANTIES!! Ian Dury & the Blockheads (Stiff)	30 15	52ND STREET Billy Joel (CBS)	8 15	NEW BOOTS AND PANTIES!! Ian Dury & the Blockheads (Stiff)	17 15	EQUINOXE Jean-Michel Jarre (Polydor)
17 16	OUT OF THE BLUE Electric Light Orchestra (Jet)	19 16	C'EST CHIC Chic (Atlantic)	11 16	BAT OUT OF HELL Meatloaf (Epic)	11 16	52ND STREET Billy Joel (CBS)
26 17	BAT OUT OF HELL Meatloaf (Epic)	17 17	DIRE STRAITS Dire Straits (Vertigo)	14 17	EQUINOXE Jean-Michel Jarre (Polydor)	- 17	DESOLATION ANGELS Bad Company (Swan Song)
11 17	WINGS' GREATEST Wings (Parlophone)	10 17	20 GOLDEN GREATS Neil Diamond (MCA)	17 18	DIRE STRAITS Dire Straits (Vertigo)	27 18	TURN THE MUSIC UP Players Association (Vanguard)
13 19	C'EST CHIC Chic (Atlantic)	26 19	THE INCREDIBLE SHRINKING DICKIES Dickies (A&M)	22 19	GREASE Soundtrack (RSO)	- 19	SCARED TO DANCE Skids (Virgin)
27 20	GREASE Soundtrack (RSO)	16 20	OUT OF THE BLUE Electric Light Orchestra (Jet)	20 20	OUT OF THE BLUE Electric Light Orchestra (Jet)	24 20	THE INCREDIBLE SHRINKING DICKIES Dickies (A&M)
16 21	EVEN NOW Barry Manilow (Arista)	- 21	THE GREAT ROCK'N'ROLL SWINDLE Sex Pistols (Virgin)	13 21	WINGS' GREATEST Wings (Parlophone)	- 21	STATELESS Lene Lovich (Stiff)
21 22	CRUISIN' Village People (Mercury)	20 22	GREASE Soundtrack (RSO)	30 22	A COLLECTION OF THEIR 20 GREATEST HITS Three Degrees (Epic)	20 22	OUT OF THE BLUE Electric Light Orchestra (Jet)
22 23	FORCE MAJEURE Tangerine Dream (Virgin)	- 23	YOU DON'T BRING ME FLOWERS Neil Diamond (CBS)	- 23	CHEAP TRICK AT BUDOKAN Cheap Trick (Epic)	16 23	BAT OUT OF HELL Meatloaf (Epic)
15 24	WAR OF THE WORLDS Jeff Wayne (CBS)	8 24	DON'T WALK, BOOGIE Various Artists (EMI)	19 24	THE INCREDIBLE SHRINKING DICKIES Dickies (A&M)	9 24	BLONDES HAVE MORE FUN Rod Stewart (Riva)
- 25	A COLLECTION OF THEIR 20 GREATEST HITS Three Degrees (Epic)	- 25	TURN THE MUSIC UP Players Association (Vanguard)	28 25	WAR OF THE WORLDS Jeff Wayne (CBS)	- 25	SHEIK YERBOUTI Frank Zappa (CBS)
25 26	THE INCREDIBLE SHRINKING DICKIES Dickies (A&M)	21 26	EVEN NOW Barry Manilow (Arista)	29 26	INFLAMMABLE MATERIAL Stiff Little Fingers (Rough Trade)	23 26	CHEAP TRICK AT BUDOKAN Cheap Trick (Epic)
- 27	THE CARS Cars (Elektra)	- 27	CLASSIC ROCK - THE SECOND MOVEMENT London Symphony Orchestra (K-Tel)	25 27	TURN THE MUSIC UP Players Association (Vanguard)	- 27	FEEL NO FRET Average White Band (RCA)
- 28	LIVE HERALD Steve Hillage (Virgin)	24 28	WAR OF THE WORLDS Jeff Wayne (CBS)	28 28	NEW DIMENSIONS Three Degrees (Ariola)	- 28	TRB 2 Tom Robinson Band (EMI)
- 29	IMAGES Don Williams (K-Tel)	- 29	INFLAMMABLE MATERIAL Stiff Little Fingers (Rough Trade)	- 29	FEETS DON'T FAIL ME NOW Herbie Hancock (CBS)	9 29	NIGHT FLIGHT TO VENUS Boney M (Atlantic/Hansa)
28 30	52ND STREET Billy Joel (CBS)	25 30	A COLLECTION OF THEIR 20 GREATEST HITS Three Degrees (Epic)	17 30	20 GOLDEN GREATS Neil Diamond (MCA)	26 30	INFLAMMABLE MATERIAL Stiff Little Fingers (Rough Trade)

March 10 saw the first arrival of a band so cosily 1970s-progressive-rock that it was surprising they'd secured a record deal at all in the prevailing climate: Dire Straits. *The Great Rock & Roll Swindle*, released after the Sex Pistols were no longer functioning, would peak at No.5. A Derek Jarman-style film of the same name was more interesting in prospect than reality. A single, coupling *Swindle* with *Rock Around The Clock*, would manage just three weeks in the Top 30 in October-November.

March – April 1979

31 March 1979

last week	this week	Title / Artist
4	1	C'EST CHIC — Chic (Atlantic)
5	2	MANILOW MAGIC — Barry Manilow (Arista)
1	3	SPIRITS HAVING FLOWN — Bee Gees (RSO)
2	4	PARALLEL LINES — Blondie (Chrysalis)
6	5	THE GREAT ROCK'N'ROLL SWINDLE — Sex Pistols (Virgin)
10	6	BARBRA STREISAND'S GREATEST HITS VOL 2 — Barbra Streisand (CBS)
3	7	ARMED FORCES — Elvis Costello (Radar)
8	8	DIRE STRAITS — Dire Straits (Vertigo)
9	9	A COLLECTION OF THEIR 20 GREATEST HITS — Three Degrees (Epic)
16	10	52ND STREET — Billy Joel (CBS)
23	11	BAT OUT OF HELL — Meatloaf (Epic)
7	12	THE MARTY ROBBINS COLLECTION — Marty Robbins (Lotus)
12	13	THANK YOU VERY MUCH – REUNION CONCERT AT THE LONDON PALLADIUM — Cliff Richard & the Shadows (EMI)
11	14	LIVE (X CERT) — Stranglers (United Artists)
15	15	EQUINOXE — Jean-Michel Jarre (Polydor)
17	16	DESOLATION ANGELS — Bad Company (Swan Song)
-	17	MANIFESTO — Roxy Music (Polydor)
13	18	THE BEST OF EARTH WIND & FIRE, VOL. 1 — Earth Wind & Fire (CBS)
27	19	FEEL NO FRET — Average White Band (RCA)
28	20	TRB 2 — Tom Robinson Band (EMI)
24	21	BLONDES HAVE MORE FUN — Rod Stewart (Riva)
-	22	ACTION REPLAY — Various Artists (K-Tel)
22	23	OUT OF THE BLUE — Electric Light Orchestra (Jet)
-	24	20 GOLDEN GREATS — Neil Diamond (MCA)
-	25	REFLECTIONS — George Hamilton IV (Lotus)
19	26	SCARED TO DANCE — Skids (Virgin)
25	27	SHEIK YERBOUTI — Frank Zappa (CBS)
13	28	NEW BOOTS AND PANTIES!! — Ian Dury & the Blockheads (Stiff)
29	29	NIGHT FLIGHT TO VENUS — Boney M (Atlantic/Hansa)
-	30	BREAKFAST IN AMERICA — Supertramp (A&M)

7 April 1979

last week	this week	Title / Artist
6	1	BARBRA STREISAND'S GREATEST HITS VOL 2 — Barbra Streisand (CBS)
2	2	MANILOW MAGIC — Barry Manilow (Arista)
4	3	PARALLEL LINES — Blondie (Chrysalis)
3	4	SPIRITS HAVING FLOWN — Bee Gees (RSO)
1	5	C'EST CHIC — Chic (Atlantic)
5	6	THE GREAT ROCK'N'ROLL SWINDLE — Sex Pistols (Virgin)
8	7	DIRE STRAITS — Dire Straits (Vertigo)
7	8	ARMED FORCES — Elvis Costello (Radar)
-	8	THE VERY BEST OF LEO SAYER — Leo Sayer (Chrysalis)
9	10	A COLLECTION OF THEIR 20 GREATEST HITS — Three Degrees (Epic)
30	11	BREAKFAST IN AMERICA — Supertramp (A&M)
16	12	DESOLATION ANGELS — Bad Company (Swan Song)
11	13	BAT OUT OF HELL — Meatloaf (Epic)
12	14	THE MARTY ROBBINS COLLECTION — Marty Robbins (Lotus)
18	15	THE BEST OF EARTH WIND & FIRE, VOL. 1 — Earth Wind & Fire (CBS)
10	16	52ND STREET — Billy Joel (CBS)
13	17	THANK YOU VERY MUCH – REUNION CONCERT AT THE LONDON PALLADIUM — Cliff Richard & the Shadows (EMI)
19	18	FEEL NO FRET — Average White Band (RCA)
-	19	TURN THE MUSIC UP — Players Association (Vanguard)
28	20	NEW BOOTS AND PANTIES!! — Ian Dury & the Blockheads (Stiff)
17	21	LIONHEART — Kate Bush (EMI)
17	22	MANIFESTO — Roxy Music (Polydor)
14	23	LIVE (X CERT) — Stranglers (United Artists)
20	24	TRB 2 — Tom Robinson Band (EMI)
15	25	EQUINOXE — Jean-Michel Jarre (Polydor)
-	26	OVERKILL — Motorhead (Bronze)
26	27	SCARED TO DANCE — Skids (Virgin)
-	28	LOVE LIFE — Gloria Gaynor (Polydor)
-	29	THE INCREDIBLE SHRINKING DICKIES — Dickies (A&M)
-	30	STATELESS — Lene Lovich (Stiff)

14 April 1979

last week	this week	Title / Artist
1	1	BARBRA STREISAND'S GREATEST HITS VOL 2 — Barbra Streisand (CBS)
11	2	BREAKFAST IN AMERICA — Supertramp (A&M)
5	3	C'EST CHIC — Chic (Atlantic)
2	4	MANILOW MAGIC — Barry Manilow (Arista)
7	5	DIRE STRAITS — Dire Straits (Vertigo)
8	6	THE VERY BEST OF LEO SAYER — Leo Sayer (Chrysalis)
3	7	PARALLEL LINES — Blondie (Chrysalis)
4	8	SPIRITS HAVING FLOWN — Bee Gees (RSO)
6	9	THE GREAT ROCK'N'ROLL SWINDLE — Sex Pistols (Virgin)
8	10	ARMED FORCES — Elvis Costello (Radar)
12	11	DESOLATION ANGELS — Bad Company (Swan Song)
16	12	52ND STREET — Billy Joel (CBS)
-	13	COUNTRY PORTRAITS — Various Artists (Warwick)
22	14	MANIFESTO — Roxy Music (Polydor)
21	15	LIONHEART — Kate Bush (EMI)
10	16	A COLLECTION OF THEIR 20 GREATEST HITS — Three Degrees (Epic)
14	17	THE MARTY ROBBINS COLLECTION — Marty Robbins (Lotus)
18	18	FEEL NO FRET — Average White Band (RCA)
13	19	BAT OUT OF HELL — Meatloaf (Epic)
24	20	TRB 2 — Tom Robinson Band (EMI)
27	21	SCARED TO DANCE — Skids (Virgin)
-	22	YOU DON'T BRING ME FLOWERS — Neil Diamond (CBS)
-	23	SQUEEZING OUT SPARKS — Graham Parker & the Rumour (Vertigo)
25	24	EQUINOXE — Jean-Michel Jarre (Polydor)
-	25	COUNTRY LIFE — Various Artists (EMI)
15	26	THE BEST OF EARTH WIND & FIRE, VOL. 1 — Earth Wind & Fire (CBS)
-	27	VAN HALEN II — Van Halen (Warner Bros.)
19	28	TURN THE MUSIC UP — Players Association (Vanguard)
-	29	IMPERIAL WIZARD — David Essex (Mercury)
-	30	DISCO INFERNO — Various Artists (K-Tel)

21 April 1979

last week	this week	Title / Artist
1	1	BARBRA STREISAND'S GREATEST HITS VOL 2 — Barbra Streisand (CBS)
6	2	THE VERY BEST OF LEO SAYER — Leo Sayer (Chrysalis)
3	3	C'EST CHIC — Chic (Atlantic)
5	4	DIRE STRAITS — Dire Straits (Vertigo)
4	5	MANILOW MAGIC — Barry Manilow (Arista)
8	6	SPIRITS HAVING FLOWN — Bee Gees (RSO)
7	7	PARALLEL LINES — Blondie (Chrysalis)
9	8	THE GREAT ROCK'N'ROLL SWINDLE — Sex Pistols (Virgin)
2	9	BREAKFAST IN AMERICA — Supertramp (A&M)
15	10	LIONHEART — Kate Bush (EMI)
13	11	COUNTRY PORTRAITS — Various Artists (Warwick)
10	12	ARMED FORCES — Elvis Costello (Radar)
30	13	DISCO INFERNO — Various Artists (K-Tel)
17	14	THE MARTY ROBBINS COLLECTION — Marty Robbins (Lotus)
14	15	MANIFESTO — Roxy Music (Polydor)
18	16	FEEL NO FRET — Average White Band (RCA)
26	17	THE BEST OF EARTH WIND & FIRE, VOL. 1 — Earth Wind & Fire (CBS)
19	18	BAT OUT OF HELL — Meatloaf (Epic)
16	19	A COLLECTION OF THEIR 20 GREATEST HITS — Three Degrees (Epic)
29	20	IMPERIAL WIZARD — David Essex (Mercury)
25	21	COUNTRY LIFE — Various Artists (EMI)
28	22	TURN THE MUSIC UP — Players Association (Vanguard)
-	23	SECOND HAND DAYLIGHT — Magazine (Virgin)
11	24	DESOLATION ANGELS — Bad Company (Swan Song)
27	25	VAN HALEN II — Van Halen (Warner Bros.)
23	26	SQUEEZING OUT SPARKS — Graham Parker & the Rumour (Vertigo)
-	27	THE CARS — Cars (Elektra)
-	28	THE INCREDIBLE SHRINKING DICKIES — Dickies (A&M)
12	29	52ND STREET — Billy Joel (CBS)
20	30	TRB 2 — Tom Robinson Band (EMI)

Frank Zappa had signed to Columbia, and *Sheik Yerbouti* (in at No.25 in March), the first LP of the partnership, thus got a special push, giving Zappa his biggest UK hit since 1969's *Hot Rats*. Motorhead's *Overkill* was their 2nd LP but their first Top 30 hit. Likewise with Van Halen's *Van Halen II*. Neither had yet had a single. Original Buzzcock Howard Devoto's band Magazine had already a (minor) hit single with the beautfully picture-sleeved *Shot By Both Sides*. *Secondhand Daylight* was their 2nd album.

April – May 1979

last week	this week	28 April 1979
2	1	THE VERY BEST OF LEO SAYER — Leo Sayer (Chrysalis)
1	2	BARBRA STREISAND'S GREATEST HITS VOL 2 — Barbra Streisand (CBS)
3	3	C'EST CHIC — Chic (Atlantic)
4	4	DIRE STRAITS — Dire Straits (Vertigo)
9	5	BREAKFAST IN AMERICA — Supertramp (A&M)
7	6	PARALLEL LINES — Blondie (Chrysalis)
6	7	SPIRITS HAVING FLOWN — Bee Gees (RSO)
8	8	THE GREAT ROCK'N'ROLL SWINDLE — Sex Pistols (Virgin)
19	9	A COLLECTION OF THEIR 20 GREATEST HITS — Three Degrees (Epic)
21	10	COUNTRY LIFE — Various Artists (EMI)
13	11	DISCO INFERNO — Various Artists (K-Tel)
25	12	VAN HALEN II — Van Halen (Warner Bros.)
10	13	LIONHEART — Kate Bush (EMI)
16	14	FEEL NO FRET — Average White Band (RCA)
11	15	COUNTRY PORTRAITS — Various Artists (Warwick)
5	16	MANILOW MAGIC — Barry Manilow (Arista)
-	17	FATE FOR BREAKFAST — Art Garfunkel (CBS)
18	18	BAT OUT OF HELL — Meatloaf (Epic)
-	19	LAST THE WHOLE NIGHT THROUGH — James Last (Polydor)
12	20	ARMED FORCES — Elvis Costello (Radar)
20	21	IMPERIAL WIZARD — David Essex (Mercury)
15	22	MANIFESTO — Roxy Music (Polydor)
-	23	LA (LIGHT ALBUM) — Beach Boys (Caribou)
-	24	THE MARK II PURPLE SINGLES — Deep Purple (Purple)
24	25	DESOLATION ANGELS — Bad Company (Swan Song)
29	26	52ND STREET — Billy Joel (CBS)
-	27	YOU DON'T BRING ME FLOWERS — Neil Diamond (CBS)
-	28	STRANGERS IN THE NIGHT — UFO (Chrysalis)
27	29	THE CARS — Cars (Elektra)
14	30	THE MARTY ROBBINS COLLECTION — Marty Robbins (Lotus)

last week	this week	5 May 1979
1	1	THE VERY BEST OF LEO SAYER — Leo Sayer (Chrysalis)
2	2	BARBRA STREISAND'S GREATEST HITS VOL 2 — Barbra Streisand (CBS)
5	3	BREAKFAST IN AMERICA — Supertramp (A&M)
3	4	C'EST CHIC — Chic (Atlantic)
10	5	COUNTRY LIFE — Various Artists (EMI)
4	6	DIRE STRAITS — Dire Straits (Vertigo)
6	7	PARALLEL LINES — Blondie (Chrysalis)
11	8	DISCO INFERNO — Various Artists (K-Tel)
17	9	FATE FOR BREAKFAST — Art Garfunkel (CBS)
7	10	SPIRITS HAVING FLOWN — Bee Gees (RSO)
13	11	LIONHEART — Kate Bush (EMI)
16	12	MANILOW MAGIC — Barry Manilow (Arista)
8	13	THE GREAT ROCK'N'ROLL SWINDLE — Sex Pistols (Virgin)
22	14	MANIFESTO — Roxy Music (Polydor)
15	15	COUNTRY PORTRAITS — Various Artists (Warwick)
20	16	ARMED FORCES — Elvis Costello (Radar)
14	17	FEEL NO FRET — Average White Band (RCA)
19	18	LAST THE WHOLE NIGHT THROUGH — James Last (Polydor)
21	19	IMPERIAL WIZARD — David Essex (Mercury)
9	20	A COLLECTION OF THEIR 20 GREATEST HITS — Three Degrees (Epic)
-	21	LIVIN' INSIDE YOUR LOVE — George Benson (Warner Bros.)
-	22	BLACK ROSE — Thin Lizzy (Phonogram)
23	23	LA (LIGHT ALBUM) — Beach Boys (Caribou)
-	24	WINGS' GREATEST — Wings (Parlophone)
12	25	VAN HALEN II — Van Halen (Warner Bros.)
17	26	BAT OUT OF HELL — Meatloaf (Epic)
24	27	THE MARK II PURPLE SINGLES — Deep Purple (Purple)
30	28	THE MARTY ROBBINS COLLECTION — Marty Robbins (Lotus)
-	29	WAR OF THE WORLDS — Jeff Wayne (CBS)
-	30	OVERKILL — Motorhead (Bronze)

last week	this week	12 May 1979
1	1	THE VERY BEST OF LEO SAYER — Leo Sayer (Chrysalis)
3	2	BREAKFAST IN AMERICA — Supertramp (A&M)
9	3	FATE FOR BREAKFAST — Art Garfunkel (CBS)
4	4	C'EST CHIC — Chic (Atlantic)
10	5	SPIRITS HAVING FLOWN — Bee Gees (RSO)
6	6	COUNTRY LIFE — Various Artists (EMI)
7	7	DIRE STRAITS — Dire Straits (Vertigo)
7	8	PARALLEL LINES — Blondie (Chrysalis)
2	9	BARBRA STREISAND'S GREATEST HITS VOL 2 — Barbra Streisand (CBS)
22	10	BLACK ROSE — Thin Lizzy (Phonogram)
18	11	LAST THE WHOLE NIGHT THROUGH — James Last (Polydor)
12	12	MANILOW MAGIC — Barry Manilow (Arista)
-	13	OUT OF THE BLUE — Electric Light Orchestra (Jet)
11	14	LIONHEART — Kate Bush (EMI)
20	15	A COLLECTION OF THEIR 20 GREATEST HITS — Three Degrees (Epic)
8	16	DISCO INFERNO — Various Artists (K-Tel)
13	17	THE GREAT ROCK'N'ROLL SWINDLE — Sex Pistols (Virgin)
-	18	VOULEZ VOUS — Abba (Epic)
14	19	MANIFESTO — Roxy Music (Polydor)
-	20	HI ENERGY — Various Artists (K-Tel)
-	21	OUTLANDOS D'AMOUR — Police (A&M)
26	22	BAT OUT OF HELL — Meatloaf (Epic)
27	23	THE MARK II PURPLE SINGLES — Deep Purple (Purple)
17	24	FEEL NO FRET — Average White Band (RCA)
16	25	ARMED FORCES — Elvis Costello (Radar)
21	26	LIVIN' INSIDE YOUR LOVE — George Benson (Warner Bros.)
19	27	IMPERIAL WIZARD — David Essex (Mercury)
29	28	WAR OF THE WORLDS — Jeff Wayne (CBS)
15	29	COUNTRY PORTRAITS — Various Artists (Warwick)
-	30	COOL FOR CATS — Squeeze (A&M)

last week	this week	19 May 1979
1	1	THE VERY BEST OF LEO SAYER — Leo Sayer (Chrysalis)
10	2	BLACK ROSE — Thin Lizzy (Phonogram)
3	3	FATE FOR BREAKFAST — Art Garfunkel (CBS)
2	4	BREAKFAST IN AMERICA — Supertramp (A&M)
7	5	DIRE STRAITS — Dire Straits (Vertigo)
6	6	COUNTRY LIFE — Various Artists (EMI)
8	7	PARALLEL LINES — Blondie (Chrysalis)
4	8	C'EST CHIC — Chic (Atlantic)
21	9	OUTLANDOS D'AMOUR — Police (A&M)
5	10	SPIRITS HAVING FLOWN — Bee Gees (RSO)
9	11	BARBRA STREISAND'S GREATEST HITS VOL 2 — Barbra Streisand (CBS)
18	12	VOULEZ VOUS — Abba (Epic)
11	13	LAST THE WHOLE NIGHT THROUGH — James Last (Polydor)
15	14	A COLLECTION OF THEIR 20 GREATEST HITS — Three Degrees (Epic)
19	15	MANIFESTO — Roxy Music (Polydor)
20	16	HI ENERGY — Various Artists (K-Tel)
14	17	LIONHEART — Kate Bush (EMI)
-	18	WE ARE FAMILY — Sister Sledge (Atlantic)
12	19	MANILOW MAGIC — Barry Manilow (Arista)
17	20	THE GREAT ROCK'N'ROLL SWINDLE — Sex Pistols (Virgin)
26	21	LIVIN' INSIDE YOUR LOVE — George Benson (Warner Bros.)
24	22	FEEL NO FRET — Average White Band (RCA)
27	23	IMPERIAL WIZARD — David Essex (Mercury)
16	24	DISCO INFERNO — Various Artists (K-Tel)
-	25	THE INCREDIBLE SHRINKING DICKIES — Dickies (A&M)
13	26	OUT OF THE BLUE — Electric Light Orchestra (Jet)
22	27	BAT OUT OF HELL — Meatloaf (Epic)
28	28	WAR OF THE WORLDS — Jeff Wayne (CBS)
23	29	THE MARK II PURPLE SINGLES — Deep Purple (Purple)
-	30	GO WEST — Village People (Mercury)

The chart of May 12 saw Police's Top 30 entry with debut album *Outlandos D'Amour*, a week after the single *Roxanne* (possibly their best) joined the other Top 30. *Roxanne* was not their first 45: *Can't Stand Losing You* had been issued in 1978 but would be released after the success of *Roxanne* and the band's album, and would peak at No.2 in August; October would see *Message In A Bottle* give them their first No.1 single and, with *Regatta de Blanc*, a No.1 album to go with it.

182

26 May 1979

last week	this week	
12	1	VOULEZ VOUS — Abba (Epic)
1	2	THE VERY BEST OF LEO SAYER — Leo Sayer (Chrysalis)
3	3	FATE FOR BREAKFAST — Art Garfunkel (CBS)
4	4	BREAKFAST IN AMERICA — Supertramp (A&M)
2	5	BLACK ROSE — Thin Lizzy (Phonogram)
7	6	PARALLEL LINES — Blondie (Chrysalis)
10	7	SPIRITS HAVING FLOWN — Bee Gees (RSO)
8	8	C'EST CHIC — Chic (Atlantic)
5	9	DIRE STRAITS — Dire Straits (Vertigo)
13	10	LAST THE WHOLE NIGHT THROUGH — James Last (Polydor)
15	11	MANIFESTO — Roxy Music (Polydor)
5	12	COUNTRY LIFE — Various Artists (EMI)
11	13	BARBRA STREISAND'S GREATEST HITS VOL 2 — Barbra Streisand (CBS)
26	14	OUT OF THE BLUE — Electric Light Orchestra (Jet)
9	15	OUTLANDOS D'AMOUR — Police (A&M)
17	16	LIONHEART — Kate Bush (EMI)
19	17	MANILOW MAGIC — Barry Manilow (Arista)
16	18	HI ENERGY — Various Artists (K-Tel)
-	19	THE BILLIE JO SPEARS SINGLES ALBUM — Billie Jo Spears (United Artists)
14	20	A COLLECTION OF THEIR 20 GREATEST HITS — Three Degrees (Epic)
-	21	ARMED FORCES — Elvis Costello (Radar)
30	22	GO WEST — Village People (Mercury)
-	23	BOB DYLAN AT BUDOKAN — Bob Dylan (CBS)
21	24	LIVIN' INSIDE YOUR LOVE — George Benson (Warner Bros.)
-	25	THE UNDERTONES — Undertones (Sire)
-	26	BOOGIE BUS — Various Artists (Polystar)
18	27	WE ARE FAMILY — Sister Sledge (Atlantic)
20	28	THE GREAT ROCK'N'ROLL SWINDLE — Sex Pistols (Virgin)
28	29	WAR OF THE WORLDS — Jeff Wayne (CBS)
-	30	DO IT YOURSELF — Ian Dury & the Blockheads (Stiff)

2 June 1979

1	VOULEZ VOUS — Abba (Epic)
2	THE VERY BEST OF LEO SAYER — Leo Sayer (Chrysalis)
3	FATE FOR BREAKFAST — Art Garfunkel (CBS)
4	BREAKFAST IN AMERICA — Supertramp (A&M)
5	PARALLEL LINES — Blondie (Chrysalis)
6	MANIFESTO — Roxy Music (Polydor)
7	BLACK ROSE — Thin Lizzy (Phonogram)
8	DIRE STRAITS — Dire Straits (Vertigo)
9	DO IT YOURSELF — Ian Dury & the Blockheads (Stiff)
10	THE BILLIE JO SPEARS SINGLES ALBUM — Billie Jo Spears (United Artists)
11	BOB DYLAN AT BUDOKAN — Bob Dylan (CBS)
12	SPIRITS HAVING FLOWN — Bee Gees (RSO)
13	LAST THE WHOLE NIGHT THROUGH — James Last (Polydor)
14	OUT OF THE BLUE — Electric Light Orchestra (Jet)
15	BARBRA STREISAND'S GREATEST HITS VOL 2 — Barbra Streisand (CBS)
16	C'EST CHIC — Chic (Atlantic)
17	OUTLANDOS D'AMOUR — Police (A&M)
18	A MONUMENT TO BRITISH ROCK — Various Artists (Harvest)
19	THE UNDERTONES — Undertones (Sire)
20	COUNTRY LIFE — Various Artists (EMI)
21	MANILOW MAGIC — Barry Manilow (Arista)
22	LIONHEART — Kate Bush (EMI)
23	WE ARE FAMILY — Sister Sledge (Atlantic)
24	BAT OUT OF HELL — Meatloaf (Epic)
25	GO WEST — Village People (Mercury)
26	LIVIN' INSIDE YOUR LOVE — George Benson (Warner Bros.)
27	HI ENERGY — Various Artists (K-Tel)
28	THE GREAT ROCK'N'ROLL SWINDLE — Sex Pistols (Virgin)
29	SPECTRAL MORNINGS — Steve Hackett (Charisma)
30	ROCK LEGENDS — Various Artists (Ronco)

9 June 1979

1	VOULEZ VOUS — Abba (Epic)
2	DO IT YOURSELF — Ian Dury & the Blockheads (Stiff)
3	PARALLEL LINES — Blondie (Chrysalis)
4	FATE FOR BREAKFAST — Art Garfunkel (CBS)
5	MANIFESTO — Roxy Music (Polydor)
6	THE VERY BEST OF LEO SAYER — Leo Sayer (Chrysalis)
7	BREAKFAST IN AMERICA — Supertramp (A&M)
8	CHEAP TRICK AT BUDOKAN — Bob Dylan (CBS)
9	BLACK ROSE — Thin Lizzy (Phonogram)
10	DISCOVERY — Electric Light Orchestra (Jet)
11	THE BILLIE JO SPEARS SINGLES ALBUM — Billie Jo Spears (United Artists)
12	DIRE STRAITS — Dire Straits (Vertigo)
13	OUTLANDOS D'AMOUR — Police (A&M)
14	LAST THE WHOLE NIGHT THROUGH — James Last (Polydor)
15	THE UNDERTONES — Undertones (Sire)
16	C'EST CHIC — Chic (Atlantic)
17	A MONUMENT TO BRITISH ROCK — Various Artists (Harvest)
18	SPIRITS HAVING FLOWN — Bee Gees (RSO)
19	COUNTRY LIFE — Various Artists (EMI)
20	WE ARE FAMILY — Sister Sledge (Atlantic)
21	GO WEST — Village People (Mercury)
22	OUT OF THE BLUE — Electric Light Orchestra (Jet)
23	BARBRA STREISAND'S GREATEST HITS VOL 2 — Barbra Streisand (CBS)
24	LOVEDRIVE — Scorpions (Harvest)
25	SPECTRAL MORNINGS — Steve Hackett (Charisma)
26	KNUCKLE SANDWICH — Various Artists (EMI Int)
27	BOOGIE BUS — Various Artists (Polystar)
28	THIS IS IT — Various Artists (CBS)
29	LIVIN' INSIDE YOUR LOVE — George Benson (Warner Bros.)
30	MANILOW MAGIC — Barry Manilow (Arista)

16 June 1979

1	VOULEZ VOUS — Abba (Epic)
2	DO IT YOURSELF — Ian Dury & the Blockheads (Stiff)
3	PARALLEL LINES — Blondie (Chrysalis)
4	DISCOVERY — Electric Light Orchestra (Jet)
5	MANIFESTO — Roxy Music (Polydor)
6	BREAKFAST IN AMERICA — Supertramp (A&M)
7	LODGER — David Bowie (RCA)
8	FATE FOR BREAKFAST — Art Garfunkel (CBS)
9	THIS IS IT — Various Artists (CBS)
10	LAST THE WHOLE NIGHT THROUGH
11	THE VERY BEST OF LEO SAYER — Leo Sayer (Chrysalis)
12	BOB DYLAN AT BUDOKAN — Bob Dylan (CBS)
13	BLACK ROSE — Thin Lizzy (Phonogram)
14	THE BILLIE JO SPEARS SINGLES ALBUM — Billie Jo Spears (United Artists)
15	NIGHT OWL — Gerry Rafferty (United Artists)
16	OUTLANDOS D'AMOUR — Police (A&M)
17	A MONUMENT TO BRITISH ROCK — Various Artists (Harvest)
18	DIRE STRAITS — Dire Straits (Vertigo)
19	KNUCKLE SANDWICH — Various Artists (EMI Int)
20	SKY — Sky (Ariola)
21	BAD GIRLS — Donna Summer (Casablanca)
22	BOOGIE BUS — Various Artists (Polystar)
23	COMMUNIQUE — Dire Straits (Phonogram)
24	THE UNDERTONES — Undertones (Sire)
25	SPIRITS HAVING FLOWN — Bee Gees (RSO)
26	I AM — Earth Wind & Fire (CBS)
27	ARMED FORCES — Elvis Costello (Radar)
28	C'EST CHIC — Chic (Atlantic)
29	CHEAP TRICK AT BUDOKAN — Cheap Trick (Epic)
30	RHAPSODIES — Rick Wakeman (A&M)

At the other No.10, the woman with the handbag entered. It would have seemed laughable if predicted in 1968 when posters declared "London Paris Rome Berlin, We Shall Fight And We Shall Win", the police attack on the Vietnam demo outside London's US Embassy politicised many hippies, and revolution was in the air. Now Margaret Thatcher was voted in, not least by thrusting young record-execs. Within months, huge musicbiz cutbacks meant that many found they'd voted themselves out of work.

June – July 1979

Tubeway Army's *Replicas* entered at No.16, and leapt on its way to the top of the album chart. Tubeway Army, not longhand for the Tubes, was actually Gary Numan, a small British wannabowie who would famously fly aeroplanes as a hobby. Tubeway Army had come from nowhere to top the singles chart of July 7 with *Are Friends Electric*. In their vapourtrails, debut album *Tubeway Army* would chart in August, and, credited to Numan, follow-up single *Cars* would be a second No.1 single in September.

July – August 1979

21 July 1979

last	this	Album / Artist (Label)
2	1	REPLICAS — Tubeway Army (Beggars Banquet)
4	2	I AM — Earth Wind & Fire (CBS)
3	3	DISCOVERY — Electric Light Orchestra (Jet)
11	4	BRIDGES — John Williams (Lotus)
7	5	VOULEZ VOUS — Abba (Epic)
17	6	LIVE KILLERS — Queen (EMI)
1	7	PARALLEL LINES — Blondie (Chrysalis)
9	8	BREAKFAST IN AMERICA — Supertramp (A&M)
5	9	LAST THE WHOLE NIGHT THROUGH — James Last (Polydor)
8	10	BACK TO THE EGG — Wings (Parlophone)
6	11	COMMUNIQUE — Dire Straits (Phonogram)
10	12	NIGHT OWL — Gerry Rafferty (United Artists)
29	13	THE BEST DISCO ALBUM IN THE WORLD — Various Artists (Warner Bros.)
15	14	RICKIE LEE JONES — Rickie Lee Jones (Warner Bros.)
12	15	SKY — Sky (Ariola)
14	16	LODGER — David Bowie (RCA)
13	17	MANIFESTO — Roxy Music (Polydor)
19	18	DO IT YOURSELF — Ian Dury and the Blockheads (Stiff)
16	19	MANILOW MAGIC — Barry Manilow (Arista)
-	20	THE WORLD IS FULL OF MARRIED MEN - SOUNDTRACK — Various Artists (Ronco)
-	21	RUST NEVER SLEEPS — Neil Young (Reprise)
20	22	BAD GIRLS — Donna Summer (Casablanca)
-	23	THE BEST OF THE DOOLEYS — Dooleys (GTO)
-	24	CANDY-O — Cars (Elektra)
25	25	THIS IS IT — Various Artists (CBS)
27	26	OUTLANDOS D'AMOUR — Police (A&M)
-	27	THE WARRIORS — Soundtrack (A&M)
-	28	MORNING DANCE — Spyro Gyra (Infinity)
-	29	REPEAT WHEN NECESSARY — Dave Edmunds (Swan Song)
23	30	BLACK ROSE — Thin Lizzy (Phonogram)

28 July 1979

last	this	Album / Artist (Label)
1	1	REPLICAS — Tubeway Army (Beggars Banquet)
3	2	DISCOVERY — Electric Light Orchestra (Jet)
13	3	THE BEST DISCO ALBUM IN THE WORLD — Various Artists (Warner Bros.)
8	4	BREAKFAST IN AMERICA — Supertramp (A&M)
7	5	PARALLEL LINES — Blondie (Chrysalis)
4	6	BRIDGES — John Williams (Lotus)
11	7	COMMUNIQUE — Dire Straits (Phonogram)
2	8	I AM — Earth Wind & Fire (CBS)
5	9	VOULEZ VOUS — Abba (Epic)
6	10	LIVE KILLERS — Queen (EMI)
12	11	NIGHT OWL — Gerry Rafferty (United Artists)
9	12	LAST THE WHOLE NIGHT THROUGH — James Last (Polydor)
10	13	BACK TO THE EGG — Wings (Parlophone)
21	14	RUST NEVER SLEEPS — Neil Young (Reprise)
19	15	MANILOW MAGIC — Barry Manilow (Arista)
18	16	DO IT YOURSELF — Ian Dury and the Blockheads (Stiff)
26	17	OUTLANDOS D'AMOUR — Police (A&M)
16	18	LODGER — David Bowie (RCA)
14	19	RICKIE LEE JONES — Rickie Lee Jones (Warner Bros.)
22	20	BAD GIRLS — Donna Summer (Casablanca)
23	21	THE BEST OF THE DOOLEYS — Dooleys (GTO)
-	22	FATE FOR BREAKFAST — Art Garfunkel (CBS)
15	23	SKY — Sky (Ariola)
17	24	MANIFESTO — Roxy Music (Polydor)
-	25	THE VERY BEST OF LEO SAYER — Leo Sayer (Chrysalis)
24	26	CANDY-O — Cars (Elektra)
28	27	MORNING DANCE — Spyro Gyra (Infinity)
-	28	STREET LIFE — Crusaders (MCA)
-	29	DIRE STRAITS — Dire Straits (Vertigo)
-	30	THE GREAT ROCK'N'ROLL SWINDLE — Sex Pistols (Virgin)

4 August 1979

last	this	Album / Artist (Label)
3	1	THE BEST DISCO ALBUM IN THE WORLD — Various Artists (Warner Bros.)
1	2	REPLICAS — Tubeway Army (Beggars Banquet)
2	3	DISCOVERY — Electric Light Orchestra (Jet)
9	4	VOULEZ VOUS — Abba (Epic)
7	5	COMMUNIQUE — Dire Straits (Phonogram)
5	6	PARALLEL LINES — Blondie (Chrysalis)
8	7	I AM — Earth Wind & Fire (CBS)
4	8	BREAKFAST IN AMERICA — Supertramp (A&M)
6	9	BRIDGES — John Williams (Lotus)
17	10	OUTLANDOS D'AMOUR — Police (A&M)
11	11	NIGHT OWL — Gerry Rafferty (United Artists)
9	12	LIVE KILLERS — Queen (EMI)
19	13	RICKIE LEE JONES — Rickie Lee Jones (Warner Bros.)
18	14	LODGER — David Bowie (RCA)
12	15	LAST THE WHOLE NIGHT THROUGH — James Last (Polydor)
15	16	MANILOW MAGIC — Barry Manilow (Arista)
13	17	BACK TO THE EGG — Wings (Parlophone)
14	18	RUST NEVER SLEEPS — Neil Young (Reprise)
15	19	DO IT YOURSELF — Ian Dury and the Blockheads (Stiff)
21	20	THE BEST OF THE DOOLEYS — Dooleys (GTO)
22	21	FATE FOR BREAKFAST — Art Garfunkel (CBS)
20	22	BAD GIRLS — Donna Summer (Casablanca)
25	23	THE VERY BEST OF LEO SAYER — Leo Sayer (Chrysalis)
24	24	MANIFESTO — Roxy Music (Polydor)
30	25	THE GREAT ROCK'N'ROLL SWINDLE — Sex Pistols (Virgin)
27	26	MORNING DANCE — Spyro Gyra (Infinity)
26	27	CANDY-O — Cars (Elektra)
28	28	STREET LIFE — Crusaders (MCA)
-	29	GOLDEN GREATS — Beach Boys (Capitol)
-	30	SOME PRODUCT - CARRI ON SEX PISTOLS — Sex Pistols (Virgin)

11 August 1979

last	this	Album / Artist (Label)
1	1	THE BEST DISCO ALBUM IN THE WORLD — Various Artists (Warner Bros.)
2	2	REPLICAS — Tubeway Army (Beggars Banquet)
3	3	DISCOVERY — Electric Light Orchestra (Jet)
7	4	I AM — Earth Wind & Fire (CBS)
8	5	BREAKFAST IN AMERICA — Supertramp (A&M)
4	6	VOULEZ VOUS — Abba (Epic)
9	7	BRIDGES — John Williams (Lotus)
6	8	PARALLEL LINES — Blondie (Chrysalis)
5	9	COMMUNIQUE — Dire Straits (Phonogram)
20	10	THE BEST OF THE DOOLEYS — Dooleys (GTO)
10	11	OUTLANDOS D'AMOUR — Police (A&M)
14	12	LODGER — David Bowie (RCA)
19	13	DO IT YOURSELF — Ian Dury and the Blockheads (Stiff)
11	14	LIVE KILLERS — Queen (EMI)
17	15	BACK TO THE EGG — Wings (Parlophone)
28	16	STREET LIFE — Crusaders (MCA)
11	17	NIGHT OWL — Gerry Rafferty (United Artists)
26	18	MORNING DANCE — Spyro Gyra (Infinity)
18	19	RUST NEVER SLEEPS — Neil Young (Reprise)
30	20	SOME PRODUCT - CARRI ON SEX PISTOLS — Sex Pistols (Virgin)
22	21	BAD GIRLS — Donna Summer (Casablanca)
29	22	GOLDEN GREATS — Beach Boys (Capitol)
23	23	THE VERY BEST OF LEO SAYER — Leo Sayer (Chrysalis)
-	24	THE KIDS ARE ALRIGHT — Who (Polydor)
27	25	CANDY-O — Cars (Elektra)
-	26	GO WEST — Village People (Mercury)
16	27	MANILOW MAGIC — Barry Manilow (Arista)
13	28	RICKIE LEE JONES — Rickie Lee Jones (Warner Bros.)
-	29	THE BOSS — Diana Ross (Motown)
24	30	MANIFESTO — Roxy Music (Polydor)

Jazz-funk outfit the Crusaders were jumping up the singles chart with the title track of their *Street Life* LP. The single, which featured Randy Crawford as uncredited vocalist, would peak at No.4, the album at 5, both on September 22. They would enjoy an extremely minor 1981 hit single, *I'm So Glad I'm Standing Here Today*, with "featured vocalist Joe Cocker". Veteran Neil Young shared the credits with his sometime band Crazy Horse on *Rust Never Sleeps*, his most successful album since 1972's *Harvest*.

August – September 1979

18 August 1979

last week / this week

last	this	Album	Artist (Label)
1	1	THE BEST DISCO ALBUM IN THE WORLD	Various Artists (Warner Bros.)
3	2	DISCOVERY	Electric Light Orchestra (Jet)
2	3	REPLICAS	Tubeway Army (Beggars Banquet)
4	4	I AM	Earth Wind & Fire (CBS)
5	5	BREAKFAST IN AMERICA	Supertramp (A&M)
6	6	VOULEZ VOUS	Abba (Epic)
11	7	OUTLANDOS D'AMOUR	Police (A&M)
20	8	SOME PRODUCT - CARRI ON SEX PISTOLS	Sex Pistols (Virgin)
10	9	THE BEST OF THE DOOLEYS	Dooleys (GTO)
8	10	PARALLEL LINES	Blondie (Chrysalis)
9	11	COMMUNIQUE	Dire Straits (Phonogram)
7	12	BRIDGES	John Williams (Lotus)
16	13	STREET LIFE	Crusaders (MCA)
17	14	NIGHT OWL	Gerry Rafferty (United Artists)
13	15	DO IT YOURSELF	Ian Dury & the Blockheads (Stiff)
18	16	MORNING DANCE	Spyro Gyra (Infinity)
19	17	RUST NEVER SLEEPS	Neil Young (Reprise)
14	18	LIVE KILLERS	Queen (EMI)
-	19	EXPOSED	Mike Oldfield (Virgin)
27	20	MANILOW MAGIC	Barry Manilow (Arista)
12	21	LODGER	David Bowie (RCA)
26	22	GO WEST	Village People (Mercury)
22	23	20 GOLDEN GREATS	Beach Boys (Capitol)
30	24	MANIFESTO	Roxy Music (Polydor)
-	25	OUT OF THE BLUE	Electric Light Orchestra (Jet)
23	26	THE VERY BEST OF LEO SAYER	Leo Sayer (Chrysalis)
-	27	WELCOME TO THE CRUISE	Judie Tzuke (Rocket)
-	28	DIRE STRAITS	Dire Straits (Vertigo)
-	29	B-52s	B-52s (Island)
15	30	BACK TO THE EGG	Wings (Parlophone)

25 August 1979

last	this	Album	Artist (Label)
2	1	DISCOVERY	Electric Light Orchestra (Jet)
1	2	THE BEST DISCO ALBUM IN THE WORLD	Various Artists (Warner Bros.)
3	3	REPLICAS	Tubeway Army (Beggars Banquet)
5	4	BREAKFAST IN AMERICA	Supertramp (A&M)
4	5	I AM	Earth Wind & Fire (CBS)
6	6	VOULEZ VOUS	Abba (Epic)
8	7	SOME PRODUCT - CARRI ON SEX PISTOLS	Sex Pistols (Virgin)
9	8	THE BEST OF THE DOOLEYS	Dooleys (GTO)
16	9	MORNING DANCE	Spyro Gyra (Infinity)
13	10	STREET LIFE	Crusaders (MCA)
7	11	OUTLANDOS D'AMOUR	Police (A&M)
19	12	EXPOSED	Mike Oldfield (Virgin)
10	13	PARALLEL LINES	Blondie (Chrysalis)
18	14	LIVE KILLERS	Queen (EMI)
-	15	HIGHWAY TO HELL	AC/DC (Atlantic)
12	16	BRIDGES	John Williams (Lotus)
14	17	NIGHT OWL	Gerry Rafferty (United Artists)
20	18	MANILOW MAGIC	Barry Manilow (Arista)
-	19	DOWN TO EARTH	Rainbow (Polydor)
23	20	20 GOLDEN GREATS	Beach Boys (Capitol)
11	21	COMMUNIQUE	Dire Straits (Phonogram)
26	22	THE VERY BEST OF LEO SAYER	Leo Sayer (Chrysalis)
15	23	DO IT YOURSELF	Ian Dury & the Blockheads (Stiff)
-	24	MIDNIGHT MAGIC	Commodores (Motown)
-	25	TEENAGE WARNING	Angelic Upstarts (Warner Bros.)
-	26	BAD GIRLS	Donna Summer (Casablanca)
-	27	RISQUE	Chic (Atlantic)
27	28	WELCOME TO THE CRUISE	Judie Tzuke (Rocket)
17	29	RUST NEVER SLEEPS	Neil Young (Reprise)
-	30	THE WARRIORS	Soundtrack (A&M)

1 September 1979

last	this	Album	Artist (Label)
2	1	THE BEST DISCO ALBUM IN THE WORLD	Various Artists (Warner Bros.)
1	2	DISCOVERY	Electric Light Orchestra (Jet)
3	3	REPLICAS	Tubeway Army (Beggars Banquet)
5	4	I AM	Earth Wind & Fire (CBS)
4	5	BREAKFAST IN AMERICA	Supertramp (A&M)
10	6	STREET LIFE	Crusaders (MCA)
19	7	DOWN TO EARTH	Rainbow (Polydor)
7	8	SOME PRODUCT - CARRI ON SEX PISTOLS	Sex Pistols (Virgin)
9	9	MORNING DANCE	Spyro Gyra (Infinity)
15	10	HIGHWAY TO HELL	AC/DC (Atlantic)
6	11	VOULEZ VOUS	Abba (Epic)
-	12	IN THROUGH THE OUT DOOR	Led Zeppelin (Swan Song)
13	13	PARALLEL LINES	Blondie (Chrysalis)
11	14	OUTLANDOS D'AMOUR	Police (A&M)
16	15	BRIDGES	John Williams (Lotus)
8	16	THE BEST OF THE DOOLEYS	Dooleys (GTO)
-	17	SLOW TRAIN COMING	Bob Dylan (CBS)
12	18	EXPOSED	Mike Oldfield (Virgin)
14	19	LIVE KILLERS	Queen (EMI)
21	20	COMMUNIQUE	Dire Straits (Phonogram)
17	21	NIGHT OWL	Gerry Rafferty (United Artists)
-	22	MANIFESTO	Roxy Music (Polydor)
-	23	TUBEWAY ARMY	Tubeway Army (Beggars Banquet)
23	24	DO IT YOURSELF	Ian Dury & the Blockheads (Stiff)
27	25	RISQUE	Chic (Atlantic)
28	26	WELCOME TO THE CRUISE	Judie Tzuke (Rocket)
18	27	MANILOW MAGIC	Barry Manilow (Arista)
29	28	RUST NEVER SLEEPS	Neil Young (Reprise)
25	29	TEENAGE WARNING	Angelic Upstarts (Warner Bros.)
26	30	BAD GIRLS	Donna Summer (Casablanca)

8 September 1979

last	this	Album	Artist (Label)
2	1	DISCOVERY	Electric Light Orchestra (Jet)
4	2	I AM	Earth Wind & Fire (CBS)
5	3	BREAKFAST IN AMERICA	Supertramp (A&M)
1	4	THE BEST DISCO ALBUM IN THE WORLD	Various Artists (Warner Bros.)
6	5	STREET LIFE	Crusaders (MCA)
13	6	PARALLEL LINES	Blondie (Chrysalis)
9	7	MORNING DANCE	Spyro Gyra (Infinity)
11	8	VOULEZ VOUS	Abba (Epic)
8	9	SOME PRODUCT - CARRI ON SEX PISTOLS	Sex Pistols (Virgin)
10	10	HIGHWAY TO HELL	AC/DC (Atlantic)
19	11	LIVE KILLERS	Queen (EMI)
14	12	OUTLANDOS D'AMOUR	Police (A&M)
3	13	REPLICAS	Tubeway Army (Beggars Banquet)
7	14	DOWN TO EARTH	Rainbow (Polydor)
12	15	IN THROUGH THE OUT DOOR	Led Zeppelin (Swan Song)
21	16	NIGHT OWL	Gerry Rafferty (United Artists)
25	17	RISQUE	Chic (Atlantic)
15	18	BRIDGES	John Williams (Lotus)
26	19	WELCOME TO THE CRUISE	Judie Tzuke (Rocket)
16	20	THE BEST OF THE DOOLEYS	Dooleys (GTO)
-	21	MIDNIGHT MAGIC	Commodores (Motown)
23	22	TUBEWAY ARMY	Tubeway Army (Beggars Banquet)
18	23	EXPOSED	Mike Oldfield (Virgin)
20	24	COMMUNIQUE	Dire Straits (Phonogram)
24	25	DO IT YOURSELF	Ian Dury & the Blockheads (Stiff)
17	26	SLOW TRAIN COMING	Bob Dylan (CBS)
28	27	RUST NEVER SLEEPS	Neil Young (Reprise)
-	28	RUMOURS	Fleetwood Mac (Warner Bros.)
29	29	TEENAGE WARNING	Angelic Upstarts (Warner Bros.)
22	30	MANIFESTO	Roxy Music (Polydor)

Bob Dylan's controversial *Slow Train Coming*, an evangelising Christian harangue that had the old New Leftie tagged as Born Again, came in at No.17, plummeted to No.26 and would leap straight up to No.2 the following week. This suggested supply or distribution problems on release, rather than a very wayward public response. The album, musically and lyrically rich, had been produced at Muscle Shoals studios in Sheffield Alabama using Atlantic Records veteran producer and atheist Jerry Wexler.

15 September 1979

LW	TW	Title	Artist (Label)
1	1	DISCOVERY	Electric Light Orchestra (Jet)
26	2	SLOW TRAIN COMING	Bob Dylan (CBS)
2	3	I AM	Earth Wind & Fire (CBS)
15	4	IN THROUGH THE OUT DOOR	Led Zeppelin (Swan Song)
8	5	VOULEZ VOUS	Abba (Epic)
12	6	REPLICAS	Tubeway Army (Beggars Banquet)
3	7	BREAKFAST IN AMERICA	Supertramp (A&M)
4	8	THE BEST DISCO ALBUM IN THE WORLD	Various Artists (Warner Bros.)
5	9	STREET LIFE	Crusaders (MCA)
14	10	DOWN TO EARTH	Rainbow (Polydor)
6	11	PARALLEL LINES	Blondie (Chrysalis)
30	12	MANIFESTO	Roxy Music (Polydor)
12	13	OUTLANDOS D'AMOUR	Police (A&M)
9	14	SOME PRODUCT - CARRI ON SEX PISTOLS	Sex Pistols (Virgin)
20	15	THE BEST OF THE DOOLEYS	Dooleys (GTO)
7	16	MORNING DANCE	Spyro Gyra (Infinity)
-	17	ROCK 'N' ROLL JUVENILE	Cliff Richard (EMI)
21	18	MIDNIGHT MAGIC	Commodores (Motown)
-	19	THE PLEASURE PRINCIPLE	Gary Numan (Beggars Banquet)
16	20	NIGHT OWL	Gerry Rafferty (United Artists)
10	21	HIGHWAY TO HELL	AC/DC (Atlantic)
22	22	TUBEWAY ARMY	Tubeway Army (Beggars Banquet)
19	23	WELCOME TO THE CRUISE	Judie Tzuke (Rocket)
-	24	STRING OF HITS	Shadows (EMI)
18	25	BRIDGES	John Williams (Lotus)
25	26	DO IT YOURSELF	Ian Dury and the Blockheads (Stiff)
11	27	LIVE KILLERS	Queen (EMI)
-	28	LOOK SHARP	Joe Jackson (A&M)
-	29	INTO THE MUSIC	Van Morrison (Vertigo)
-	30	DRUMS AND WIRES	XTC (Virgin)

22 September 1979

LW	TW	Title	Artist (Label)
1	1	DISCOVERY	Electric Light Orchestra (Jet)
4	2	IN THROUGH THE OUT DOOR	Led Zeppelin (Swan Song)
2	3	SLOW TRAIN COMING	Bob Dylan (CBS)
17	4	ROCK 'N' ROLL JUVENILE	Cliff Richard (EMI)
9	5	STREET LIFE	Crusaders (MCA)
3	6	I AM	Earth Wind & Fire (CBS)
8	7	THE BEST DISCO ALBUM IN THE WORLD	Various Artists (Warner Bros.)
7	8	BREAKFAST IN AMERICA	Supertramp (A&M)
19	9	THE PLEASURE PRINCIPLE	Gary Numan (Beggars Banquet)
24	10	STRING OF HITS	Shadows (EMI)
5	11	VOULEZ VOUS	Abba (Epic)
11	12	PARALLEL LINES	Blondie (Chrysalis)
18	13	MIDNIGHT MAGIC	Commodores (Motown)
13	14	OUTLANDOS D'AMOUR	Police (A&M)
20	15	NIGHT OWL	Gerry Rafferty (United Artists)
6	16	REPLICAS	Tubeway Army (Beggars Banquet)
-	17	MANILOW MAGIC	Barry Manilow (Arista)
-	18	OCEANS OF FANTASY	Boney M (Atlantic/Hansa)
16	19	MORNING DANCE	Spyro Gyra (Infinity)
10	20	DOWN TO EARTH	Rainbow (Polydor)
25	21	BRIDGES	John Williams (Lotus)
14	22	SOME PRODUCT - CARRI ON SEX PISTOLS	Sex Pistols (Virgin)
29	23	INTO THE MUSIC	Van Morrison (Vertigo)
21	24	HIGHWAY TO HELL	AC/DC (Atlantic)
-	25	THE SINGLES ALBUM	Eddie Cochran (United Artists)
15	26	THE BEST OF THE DOOLEYS	Dooleys (GTO)
-	27	WAR OF THE WORLDS	Jeff Wayne (CBS)
23	28	WELCOME TO THE CRUISE	Judie Tzuke (Rocket)
27	29	LIVE KILLERS	Queen (EMI)
12	30	MANIFESTO	Roxy Music (Polydor)

29 September 1979

LW	TW	Title	Artist (Label)
4	1	ROCK 'N' ROLL JUVENILE	Cliff Richard (EMI)
9	2	THE PLEASURE PRINCIPLE	Gary Numan (Beggars Banquet)
2	3	IN THROUGH THE OUT DOOR	Led Zeppelin (Swan Song)
1	4	DISCOVERY	Electric Light Orchestra (Jet)
3	5	SLOW TRAIN COMING	Bob Dylan (CBS)
10	6	STRING OF HITS	Shadows (EMI)
6	7	I AM	Earth Wind & Fire (CBS)
5	8	STREET LIFE	Crusaders (MCA)
16	9	REPLICAS	Tubeway Army (Beggars Banquet)
11	10	VOULEZ VOUS	Abba (Epic)
13	11	MIDNIGHT MAGIC	Commodores (Motown)
14	12	OUTLANDOS D'AMOUR	Police (A&M)
12	13	PARALLEL LINES	Blondie (Chrysalis)
8	14	BREAKFAST IN AMERICA	Supertramp (A&M)
20	15	DOWN TO EARTH	Rainbow (Polydor)
-	16	JOIN HANDS	Siouxsie & the Banshees (Polydor)
7	17	THE BEST DISCO ALBUM IN THE WORLD	Various Artists (Warner Bros.)
24	18	HIGHWAY TO HELL	AC/DC (Atlantic)
30	19	MANIFESTO	Roxy Music (Polydor)
15	20	NIGHT OWL	Gerry Rafferty (United Artists)
18	21	OCEANS OF FANTASY	Boney M (Atlantic/Hansa)
-	22	OFF THE WALL	Michael Jackson (Epic)
19	23	MORNING DANCE	Spyro Gyra (Infinity)
21	24	BRIDGES	John Williams (Lotus)
17	25	MANILOW MAGIC	Barry Manilow (Arista)
23	26	INTO THE MUSIC	Van Morrison (Vertigo)
27	27	HERE	Leo Sayer (Chrysalis)
28	28	WELCOME TO THE CRUISE	Judie Tzuke (Rocket)
-	29	CUT	Slits (Island)
25	30	THE SINGLES ALBUM	Eddie Cochran (United Artists)

6 October 1979

LW	TW	Title	Artist (Label)
2	1	THE PLEASURE PRINCIPLE	Gary Numan (Beggars Banquet)
21	2	OCEANS OF FANTASY	Boney M (Atlantic/Hansa)
1	3	ROCK 'N' ROLL JUVENILE	Cliff Richard (EMI)
6	4	STRING OF HITS	Shadows (EMI)
4	5	DISCOVERY	Electric Light Orchestra (Jet)
3	6	IN THROUGH THE OUT DOOR	Led Zeppelin (Swan Song)
5	7	SLOW TRAIN COMING	Bob Dylan (CBS)
-	8	THE ADVENTURES OF THE HERSHAM BOYS	Sham 69 (Polydor)
7	9	I AM	Earth Wind & Fire (CBS)
12	10	OUTLANDOS D'AMOUR	Police (A&M)
8	11	STREET LIFE	Crusaders (MCA)
14	12	BREAKFAST IN AMERICA	Supertramp (A&M)
11	13	MIDNIGHT MAGIC	Commodores (Motown)
10	14	VOULEZ VOUS	Abba (Epic)
22	15	OFF THE WALL	Michael Jackson (Epic)
-	16	EAT TO THE BEAT	Blondie (Chrysalis)
9	17	REPLICAS	Tubeway Army (Beggars Banquet)
13	18	PARALLEL LINES	Blondie (Chrysalis)
19	19	MANIFESTO	Roxy Music (Polydor)
16	20	JOIN HANDS	Siouxsie & the Banshees (Polydor)
17	21	THE BEST DISCO ALBUM IN THE WORLD	Various Artists (Warner Bros.)
15	22	DOWN TO EARTH	Rainbow (Polydor)
-	23	THE LONG RUN	Eagles (Asylum)
-	24	HOT TRACKS	Various Artists (K-Tel)
-	25	WAR OF THE WORLDS	Jeff Wayne (CBS)
20	26	NIGHT OWL	Gerry Rafferty (United Artists)
23	27	MORNING DANCE	Spyro Gyra (Infinity)
28	28	WELCOME TO THE CRUISE	Judie Tzuke (Rocket)
-	29	LIVE KILLERS	Queen (EMI)
29	30	CUT	Slits (Island)

Off The Wall was Michael Jackson's first solo album since quitting Motown and signing with Columbia subsidiary Epic. It would peak at No.3 and last in the chart for 170-odd weeks, slightly LONGER than 1982's *Thriller*. Sham 69's *Adventures Of The Hersham Boys* peaked as it entered. Its title plugged hit single *Hersham Boys*, a No.5 in August. Neither success would be repeated. The Eagles' *The Long Run* would be their last Top 5er too, though not such a long runner as 1985's *Best Of The Eagles*.

October – November 1979

13 October 1979

last	this	title
1	1	THE PLEASURE PRINCIPLE — Gary Numan (Beggars Banquet)
3	2	ROCK 'N' ROLL JUVENILE — Cliff Richard (EMI)
2	3	OCEANS OF FANTASY — Boney M (Atlantic/Hansa)
4	4	STRING OF HITS — Shadows (EMI)
5	5	DISCOVERY — Electric Light Orchestra (Jet)
16	6	EAT TO THE BEAT — Blondie (Chrysalis)
-	7	THE RAVEN — Stranglers (United Artists)
14	8	OFF THE WALL — Michael Jackson (Epic)
-	9	REGGATTA DE BLANC — Police (A&M)
7	10	SLOW TRAIN COMING — Bob Dylan (CBS)
10	11	OUTLANDOS D'AMOUR — Police (A&M)
8	12	THE ADVENTURES OF THE HERSHAM BOYS — Sham 69 (Polydor)
9	13	I AM — Earth Wind & Fire (CBS)
13	14	MIDNIGHT MAGIC — Commodores (Motown)
-	15	10 C.C.'s GREATEST HITS — 10 C.C. (Mercury)
11	16	STREET LIFE — Crusaders (MCA)
6	17	IN THROUGH THE OUT DOOR — Led Zeppelin (Swan Song)
-	18	UNLEASHED IN THE EAST — Judas Priest (CBS)
26	19	NIGHT OWL — Gerry Rafferty (United Artists)
12	20	BREAKFAST IN AMERICA — Supertramp (A&M)
22	21	DOWN TO EARTH — Rainbow (Polydor)
17	22	REPLICAS — Tubeway Army (Beggars Banquet)
14	23	VOULEZ VOUS — Abba (Epic)
18	24	PARALLEL LINES — Blondie (Chrysalis)
23	25	THE LONG RUN — Eagles (Asylum)
21	26	THE BEST DISCO ALBUM IN THE WORLD — Various Artists (Warner Bros.)
20	27	JOIN HANDS — Siouxsie & the Banshees (Polydor)
25	28	WAR OF THE WORLDS — Jeff Wayne (CBS)
-	29	SURVIVAL — Bob Marley & the Wailers (Island)
-	30	A DIFFERENT KIND OF TENSION — Buzzcocks (United Artists)

20 October 1979

last	this	title
9	1	REGGATTA DE BLANC — Police (A&M)
7	2	THE RAVEN — Stranglers (United Artists)
6	3	EAT TO THE BEAT — Blondie (Chrysalis)
25	4	THE LONG RUN — Eagles (Asylum)
1	5	THE PLEASURE PRINCIPLE — Gary Numan (Beggars Banquet)
5	6	DISCOVERY — Electric Light Orchestra (Jet)
8	7	OFF THE WALL — Michael Jackson (Epic)
3	8	OCEANS OF FANTASY — Boney M (Atlantic/Hansa)
11	9	OUTLANDOS D'AMOUR — Police (A&M)
4	10	STRING OF HITS — Shadows (EMI)
2	11	ROCK 'N' ROLL JUVENILE — Cliff Richard (EMI)
17	12	IN THROUGH THE OUT DOOR — Led Zeppelin (Swan Song)
18	13	UNLEASHED IN THE EAST — Judas Priest (CBS)
13	14	I AM — Earth Wind & Fire (CBS)
20	15	BREAKFAST IN AMERICA — Supertramp (A&M)
10	16	SLOW TRAIN COMING — Bob Dylan (CBS)
21	17	DOWN TO EARTH — Rainbow (Polydor)
14	18	MIDNIGHT MAGIC — Commodores (Motown)
15	19	10 C.C.'s GREATEST HITS — 10 C.C. (Mercury)
23	20	VOULEZ VOUS — Abba (Epic)
24	21	PARALLEL LINES — Blondie (Chrysalis)
12	22	THE ADVENTURES OF THE HERSHAM BOYS — Sham 69 (Polydor)
16	23	STREET LIFE — Crusaders (MCA)
-	24	I'M THE MAN — Joe Jackson (A&M)
22	25	REPLICAS — Tubeway Army (Beggars Banquet)
-	26	QUADROPHENIA — Soundtrack (Polydor)
19	27	NIGHT OWL — Gerry Rafferty (United Artists)
-	28	LOVE HUNTER — Whitesnake (United Artists)
-	29	LENA'S MUSIC ALBUM — Lena Martell (Pye)
29	30	SURVIVAL — Bob Marley & the Wailers (Island)

27 October 1979

last	this	title
1	1	REGGATTA DE BLANC — Police (A&M)
3	2	EAT TO THE BEAT — Blondie (Chrysalis)
7	3	OFF THE WALL — Michael Jackson (Epic)
4	4	THE LONG RUN — Eagles (Asylum)
-	5	WHATEVER YOU WANT — Status Quo (Vertigo)
10	6	STRING OF HITS — Shadows (EMI)
5	7	THE PLEASURE PRINCIPLE — Gary Numan (Beggars Banquet)
6	8	DISCOVERY — Electric Light Orchestra (Jet)
2	9	THE RAVEN — Stranglers (United Artists)
8	10	OCEANS OF FANTASY — Boney M (Atlantic/Hansa)
-	11	TUSK — Fleetwood Mac (Warner Bros.)
29	12	LENA'S MUSIC ALBUM — Lena Martell (Pye)
17	13	DOWN TO EARTH — Rainbow (Polydor)
12	14	IN THROUGH THE OUT DOOR — Led Zeppelin (Swan Song)
11	15	ROCK 'N' ROLL JUVENILE — Cliff Richard (EMI)
14	16	I AM — Earth Wind & Fire (CBS)
19	17	10 C.C.'s GREATEST HITS — 10 C.C. (Mercury)
9	18	OUTLANDOS D'AMOUR — Police (A&M)
15	19	BREAKFAST IN AMERICA — Supertramp (A&M)
18	20	MIDNIGHT MAGIC — Commodores (Motown)
-	21	ONE VOICE — Barry Manilow (Arista)
25	22	REPLICAS — Tubeway Army (Beggars Banquet)
-	23	THE CRACK — Ruts (Virgin)
30	24	SURVIVAL — Bob Marley & the Wailers (Island)
13	25	UNLEASHED IN THE EAST — Judas Priest (CBS)
22	26	THE ADVENTURES OF THE HERSHAM BOYS — Sham 69 (Polydor)
28	27	LOVE HUNTER — Whitesnake (United Artists)
-	28	THE UNRECORDED JASPER CARROTT — Jasper Carrott (DJM)
16	29	SLOW TRAIN COMING — Bob Dylan (CBS)
24	30	I'M THE MAN — Joe Jackson (A&M)

3 November 1979

last	this	title
1	1	REGGATTA DE BLANC — Police (A&M)
4	2	THE LONG RUN — Eagles (Asylum)
2	3	EAT TO THE BEAT — Blondie (Chrysalis)
11	4	TUSK — Fleetwood Mac (Warner Bros.)
3	5	OFF THE WALL — Michael Jackson (Epic)
12	6	LENA'S MUSIC ALBUM — Lena Martell (Pye)
5	7	WHATEVER YOU WANT — Status Quo (Vertigo)
7	8	THE PLEASURE PRINCIPLE — Gary Numan (Beggars Banquet)
16	9	I AM — Earth Wind & Fire (CBS)
21	10	ONE VOICE — Barry Manilow (Arista)
8	11	DISCOVERY — Electric Light Orchestra (Jet)
-	12	BOMBER — Motorhead (Bronze)
13	13	MR. UNIVERSE — Gillan (Acrobat)
13	14	DOWN TO EARTH — Rainbow (Polydor)
6	15	STRING OF HITS — Shadows (EMI)
10	16	OCEANS OF FANTASY — Boney M (Atlantic/Hansa)
28	17	THE UNRECORDED JASPER CARROTT — Jasper Carrott (DJM)
18	18	OUTLANDOS D'AMOUR — Police (A&M)
9	19	THE RAVEN — Stranglers (United Artists)
17	20	10 C.C.'s GREATEST HITS — 10 C.C. (Mercury)
29	21	SLOW TRAIN COMING — Bob Dylan (CBS)
24	22	SURVIVAL — Bob Marley & the Wailers (Island)
-	23	SPECIALS — Specials (2-Tone)
15	24	ROCK 'N' ROLL JUVENILE — Cliff Richard (EMI)
-	25	WAR OF THE WORLDS — Jeff Wayne (CBS)
-	26	MARATHON — Santana (CBS)
14	27	IN THROUGH THE OUT DOOR — Led Zeppelin (Swan Song)
19	28	BREAKFAST IN AMERICA — Supertramp (A&M)
22	29	REPLICAS — Tubeway Army (Beggars Banquet)
23	30	THE CRACK — Ruts (Virgin)

Charting by 2 Tone Records' the Specials proved the presence of the punk-influenced Ska Revival. Heavy Metal had never gone away but was enjoying what seemed a revival. Ozzy Osbourne had quit Black Sabbath, but here were not only Led Zeppelin, Rainbow and Motorhead (led by ex-Hawkwind roadie Lemmie) but also Judas Priest's first Top 20 LP, the live *Unleashed In The East*, Whitesnake's first Top 30 LP, and ex-Deep Purple member Ian Gillan's band Gillan (previously the Ian Gillan Band).

November – December 1979

10 November 1979

last week	this week	Title / Artist (Label)
1	1	REGGATTA DE BLANC — Police (A&M)
4	2	TUSK — Fleetwood Mac (Warner Bros.)
3	3	EAT TO THE BEAT — Blondie (Chrysalis)
6	4	LENA'S MUSIC ALBUM — Lena Martell (Pye)
2	5	THE LONG RUN — Eagles (Asylum)
7	6	WHATEVER YOU WANT — Status Quo (Vertigo)
5	7	OFF THE WALL — Michael Jackson (Epic)
-	8	ROCK 'N' ROLLER DISCO — Various Artists (Ronco)
23	9	SPECIALS — Specials (2-Tone)
20	10	10 C.C.'s GREATEST HITS — 10 C.C. (Mercury)
15	11	STRING OF HITS — Shadows (EMI)
12	12	BOMBER — Motorhead (Bronze)
11	13	DISCOVERY — Electric Light Orchestra (Jet)
19	14	THE RAVEN — Stranglers (United Artists)
16	15	OCEANS OF FANTASY — Boney M (Atlantic/Hansa)
13	16	MR UNIVERSE — Gillan (Acrobat)
9	17	I AM — Earth Wind & Fire (CBS)
-	18	GREATEST HITS VOL 2 — Abba (Epic)
-	19	THE FINE ART OF SURFACING — Boomtown Rats (Ensign)
-	20	PARALLEL LINES — Blondie (Chrysalis)
-	21	JOURNEY THROUGH THE SECRET LIFE OF PLANTS — Stevie Wonder (Motown)
14	22	DOWN TO EARTH — Rainbow (Polydor)
-	23	MIDNIGHT MAGIC — Commodores (Motown)
22	24	SURVIVAL — Bob Marley & the Wailers (Island)
-	25	HOT TRACKS — Various Artists (K-Tel)
8	26	THE PLEASURE PRINCIPLE — Gary Numan (Beggars Banquet)
10	27	ONE VOICE — Barry Manilow (Arista)
-	28	ONE STEP BEYOND — Madness (Stiff)
24	29	ROCK 'N' ROLL JUVENILE — Cliff Richard (EMI)
-	30	A CURIOUS FEELING — Tony Banks (Charisma)

17 November 1979

last week	this week	Title / Artist (Label)
1	1	REGGATTA DE BLANC — Police (A&M)
2	2	TUSK — Fleetwood Mac (Warner Bros.)
18	3	GREATEST HITS VOL 2 — Abba (Epic)
8	4	ROCK 'N' ROLLER DISCO — Various Artists (Ronco)
10	5	10 C.C.'s GREATEST HITS — 10 C.C. (Mercury)
4	6	LENA'S MUSIC ALBUM — Lena Martell (Pye)
19	7	THE FINE ART OF SURFACING — Boomtown Rats (Ensign)
-	8	ROD STEWART VOL. 1 GREATEST HITS — Rod Stewart (Riva)
9	9	SPECIALS — Specials (2-Tone)
5	10	THE LONG RUN — Eagles (Asylum)
21	11	JOURNEY THROUGH THE SECRET LIFE OF PLANTS — Stevie Wonder (Motown)
7	12	OFF THE WALL — Michael Jackson (Epic)
3	13	EAT TO THE BEAT — Blondie (Chrysalis)
6	14	WHATEVER YOU WANT — Status Quo (Vertigo)
23	15	MIDNIGHT MAGIC — Commodores (Motown)
-	16	MANTOVANI'S 20 GOLDEN GREATS — Mantovani (Warwick)
11	17	STRING OF HITS — Shadows (EMI)
28	18	ONE STEP BEYOND — Madness (Stiff)
-	19	OUT OF THIS WORLD — Moody Blues (K-Tel)
-	20	BREAKFAST IN AMERICA — Supertramp (A&M)
-	21	QUADROPHENIA — Soundtrack (Polydor)
-	22	ON THE RADIO – GREATEST HITS VOLS 1 & 2 — Donna Summer (Casablanca)
-	23	PLEASURE AND PAIN — Dr Hook (Capitol)
20	24	PARALLEL LINES — Blondie (Chrysalis)
-	25	BAT OUT OF HELL — Meatloaf (Epic)
17	26	I AM — Earth Wind & Fire (CBS)
12	27	BOMBER — Motorhead (Bronze)
22	28	DOWN TO EARTH — Rainbow (Polydor)
-	29	BEE GEES' GREATEST HITS — Bee Gees (RSO)
14	30	THE RAVEN — Stranglers (United Artists)

24 November 1979

last week	this week	Title / Artist (Label)
8	1	ROD STEWART VOL. 1 GREATEST HITS — Rod Stewart (Riva)
3	2	GREATEST HITS VOL 2 — Abba (Epic)
1	3	REGGATTA DE BLANC — Police (A&M)
2	4	TUSK — Fleetwood Mac (Warner Bros.)
12	5	OFF THE WALL — Michael Jackson (Epic)
6	6	LENA'S MUSIC ALBUM — Lena Martell (Pye)
-	7	20 GOLDEN GREATS — Diana Ross (Motown)
5	8	10 C.C.'s GREATEST HITS — 10 C.C. (Mercury)
9	9	SPECIALS — Specials (2-Tone)
4	10	ROCK 'N' ROLLER DISCO — Various Artists (Ronco)
11	11	JOURNEY THROUGH THE SECRET LIFE OF PLANTS — Stevie Wonder (Motown)
19	12	OUT OF THIS WORLD — Moody Blues (K-Tel)
10	13	THE LONG RUN — Eagles (Asylum)
7	14	THE FINE ART OF SURFACING — Boomtown Rats (Ensign)
16	15	MANTOVANI'S 20 GOLDEN GREATS — Mantovani (Warwick)
29	16	BEE GEES' GREATEST HITS — Bee Gees (RSO)
26	17	I AM — Earth Wind & Fire (CBS)
18	18	ONE STEP BEYOND — Madness (Stiff)
15	19	MIDNIGHT MAGIC — Commodores (Motown)
22	20	ON THE RADIO – GREATEST HITS VOLS 1 & 2 — Donna Summer (Casablanca)
17	21	STRING OF HITS — Shadows (EMI)
-	22	OUTLANDOS D'AMOUR — Police (A&M)
13	23	EAT TO THE BEAT — Blondie (Chrysalis)
-	24	DISCOVERY — Electric Light Orchestra (Jet)
25	25	SOMETIMES YOU WIN — Dr Hook (Capitol)
-	26	RISE — Herb Alpert (A&M)
23	27	PLEASURE AND PAIN — Dr Hook (Capitol)
-	28	CREPES AND DRAPES — Showaddywaddy (Arista)
-	29	WET — Barbra Streisand (CBS)
-	30	SETTING SONS — Jam (Polydor)

1 December 1979

last week	this week	Title / Artist (Label)
2	1	GREATEST HITS VOL 2 — Abba (Epic)
7	2	20 GOLDEN GREATS — Diana Ross (Motown)
1	3	ROD STEWART VOL. 1 GREATEST HITS — Rod Stewart (Riva)
3	4	REGGATTA DE BLANC — Police (A&M)
10	5	ROCK 'N' ROLLER DISCO — Various Artists (Ronco)
15	6	MANTOVANI'S 20 GOLDEN GREATS — Mantovani (Warwick)
4	7	TUSK — Fleetwood Mac (Warner Bros.)
5	8	OFF THE WALL — Michael Jackson (Epic)
30	9	SETTING SONS — Jam (Polydor)
6	10	LENA'S MUSIC ALBUM — Lena Martell (Pye)
12	11	OUT OF THIS WORLD — Moody Blues (K-Tel)
-	12	LOVE SONGS — Elvis Presley (K-Tel)
8	13	SPECIALS — Specials (2-Tone)
8	14	10 C.C.'s GREATEST HITS — 10 C.C. (Mercury)
24	15	DISCOVERY — Electric Light Orchestra (Jet)
18	16	ONE STEP BEYOND — Madness (Stiff)
23	17	EAT TO THE BEAT — Blondie (Chrysalis)
11	18	JOURNEY THROUGH THE SECRET LIFE OF PLANTS — Stevie Wonder (Motown)
25	19	SOMETIMES YOU WIN — Dr Hook (Capitol)
29	20	WET — Barbra Streisand (CBS)
17	21	I AM — Earth Wind & Fire (CBS)
16	22	BEE GEES' GREATEST HITS — Bee Gees (RSO)
13	23	THE LONG RUN — Eagles (Asylum)
21	24	STRING OF HITS — Shadows (EMI)
-	25	NIGHT MOVES — Various Artists (K-Tel)
14	26	THE FINE ART OF SURFACING — Boomtown Rats (Ensign)
20	27	ON THE RADIO – GREATEST HITS VOLS 1 & 2 — Donna Summer (Casablanca)
26	28	RISE — Herb Alpert (A&M)
22	29	OUTLANDOS D'AMOUR — Police (A&M)
19	30	MIDNIGHT MAGIC — Commodores (Motown)

A double dose of Dr Hook reflected the success of *When You're In Love With A Beautiful Woman*, infinitely less memorable than their first big hit, 1972's *Sylvia's Mother*. Likewise the Stevie Wonder of *The Secret Life Of Plants* seemed far less engaging than the 12-year-old harmonica star of *Fingertips Part 2*, his live debut single from 1963, the only US No.1 ever made on which you hear a musician shout "What key?! What key?!" By December 1, the Top 3 was congealing for Christmas.

December 1979

Over a third of the chart comprised records called Greatest Hits or Golden Greats; others were similarly retrospective. Across three Top 10s, there were only four genuinely current albums: Police's *Regatta de Blanc*, the Jam's *Setting Sons*, Pink Floyd's *The Wall*

and Blondie's *Eat To The Beat*. Meanwhile the singles chart revived old Dusty Springfield and Miracles songs, and included the Moody Blues' 1967/1972 hit *Nights In White Satin*. The decade was ending as it had begun, awash in recycled nostalgia.

January – February 1980

Despite (or perhaps because of) the near-million-selling success of Pink Floyd's *Another Brick In The Wall* single, the band's double album *The Wall*, from which it was extracted, failed to top the chart, or even break the still-continuing Abba/Rod Stewart/Police stranglehold on the Top 3. More fortunate, though, were the Pretenders, whose eponymous debut album hit the top immediately on the heels of their *Brass In Pocket* single, while Madness finally made No.2 after an almost 3-month climb through the lower reaches.

February – March 1980

9 February 1980

Last	This	Title / Artist (Label)
1	1	PRETENDERS — Pretenders (Real)
2	2	ONE STEP BEYOND — Madness (Stiff)
3	3	REGATTA DE BLANC — Police (A&M)
4	4	VIDEO STARS — Various Artists (K-Tel)
25	5	SHORT STORIES — Jon & Vangelis (Polydor)
12	6	BEE GEES' GREATEST HITS — Bee Gees (RSO)
11	7	THE SPECIALS — Specials (2-Tone)
18	8	PERMANENT WAVES — Rush (Mercury)
5	9	ABBA'S GREATEST HITS VOL 2 — Abba (Epic)
8	10	OFF THE WALL — Michael Jackson (Epic)
9	11	EAT TO THE BEAT — Blondie (Chrysalis)
-	12	THE KENNY ROGERS SINGLES ALBUM — Kenny Rogers (United Artists)
-	13	I'M THE MAN — Joe Jackson (A&M)
26	14	ASTAIRE — Peter Skellern (Mercury)
13	15	NO PLACE TO RUN — UFO (Chrysalis)
19	16	SEPTEMBER MORN — Neil Diamond (CBS)
16	17	PARALLEL LINES — Blondie (Chrysalis)
10	18	ROD STEWART'S GREATEST HITS — Rod Stewart (Riva)
23	19	THE SUMMIT — Various Artists (K-Tel)
17	20	TUSK — Fleetwood Mac (Warner Bros.)
14	21	20 GOLDEN GREATS — Diana Ross (Motown)
22	22	SEMI DETACHED SUBURBAN — Manfred Mann (EMI)
27	23	OUTLANDOS D'AMOUR — Police (A&M)
-	24	SID SINGS — Sid Vicious (Virgin)
20	25	FAWLTY TOWERS — TV Soundtrack (BBC)
7	26	20 HOTTEST HITS — Hot Chocolate (RAK)
30	27	SETTING SONS — Jam (Polydor)
24	28	SOMETIMES YOU WIN — Dr Hook (Capitol)
-	29	THE LAST DANCE — Various Artists (EMI)
-	30	GOLDEN COLLECTION — Charley Pride (K-Tel)

16 February 1980

Last	This	Title / Artist (Label)
1	1	PRETENDERS — Pretenders (Real)
29	2	THE LAST DANCE — Various Artists (EMI)
2	3	ONE STEP BEYOND — Madness (Stiff)
3	4	REGATTA DE BLANC — Police (A&M)
10	5	OFF THE WALL — Michael Jackson (Epic)
5	6	SHORT STORIES — Jon & Vangelis (Polydor)
7	7	THE SPECIALS — Specials (2-Tone)
8	8	PERMANENT WAVES — Rush (Mercury)
6	9	BEE GEES' GREATEST HITS — Bee Gees (RSO)
13	10	I'M THE MAN — Joe Jackson (A&M)
-	11	KENNY — Kenny Rogers (United Artists)
28	12	SOMETIMES YOU WIN — Dr Hook (Capitol)
16	12	SEPTEMBER MORN — Neil Diamond (CBS)
9	14	ABBA'S GREATEST HITS VOL 2 — Abba (Epic)
-	15	METAMATIC — John Foxx (Metalbeat)
18	16	ROD STEWART'S GREATEST HITS — Rod Stewart (Riva)
4	17	VIDEO STARS — Various Artists (K-Tel)
-	18	THE WALL — Pink Floyd (Harvest)
17	19	PARALLEL LINES — Blondie (Chrysalis)
23	20	OUTLANDOS D'AMOUR — Police (A&M)
26	21	20 HOTTEST HITS — Hot Chocolate (RAK)
-	22	FLEX — Lene Lovich (Stiff)
-	23	STRING OF HITS — Shadows (EMI)
11	24	EAT TO THE BEAT — Blondie (Chrysalis)
19	25	THE SUMMIT — Various Artists (K-Tel)
20	26	TUSK — Fleetwood Mac (Warner Bros.)
15	27	NO PLACE TO RUN — UFO (Chrysalis)
-	28	END OF THE CENTURY — Ramones (Sire)
-	29	SUNBURN - ORIGINAL SOUNDTRACK — Various Artists (Warwick)
21	30	20 GOLDEN GREATS — Diana Ross (Motown)

23 February 1980

Last	This	Title / Artist (Label)
2	1	THE LAST DANCE — Various Artists (EMI)
3	2	ONE STEP BEYOND — Madness (Stiff)
1	3	PRETENDERS — Pretenders (Real)
4	4	REGATTA DE BLANC — Police (A&M)
5	5	SHORT STORIES — Jon & Vangelis (Polydor)
11	6	KENNY — Kenny Rogers (United Artists)
7	7	THE SPECIALS — Specials (2-Tone)
15	8	METAMATIC — John Foxx (Metalbeat)
10	9	I'M THE MAN — Joe Jackson (A&M)
5	10	OFF THE WALL — Michael Jackson (Epic)
28	11	END OF THE CENTURY — Ramones (Sire)
-	12	THE NOLAN SISTERS — Nolans (Epic)
8	13	PERMANENT WAVES — Rush (Mercury)
-	14	JUST FOR YOU — Des O'Connor (Warwick)
-	15	GET HAPPY! — Elvis Costello (F Beat)
9	16	BEE GEES' GREATEST HITS — Bee Gees (RSO)
12	16	SEPTEMBER MORN — Neil Diamond (CBS)
14	18	ABBA'S GREATEST HITS VOL 2 — Abba (Epic)
20	19	OUTLANDOS D'AMOUR — Police (A&M)
19	20	PARALLEL LINES — Blondie (Chrysalis)
-	21	LONDON CALLING — Clash (CBS)
-	22	GOLDEN COLLECTION — Charley Pride (K-Tel)
29	23	SUNBURN - ORIGINAL SOUNDTRACK — Various Artists (Warwick)
22	24	FLEX — Lene Lovich (Stiff)
24	25	EAT TO THE BEAT — Blondie (Chrysalis)
-	26	CAPTAIN BEAKY AND HIS BAND — Keith Michell (Polydor)
-	27	THE FINE ART OF SURFACING — Boomtown Rats (Ensign)
18	28	THE WALL — Pink Floyd (Harvest)
-	29	THE KENNY ROGERS SINGLES ALBUM — Kenny Rogers (United Artists)
17	30	VIDEO STARS — Various Artists (K-Tel)

1 March 1980

Last	This	Title / Artist (Label)
1	1	THE LAST DANCE — Various Artists (EMI)
15	2	GET HAPPY! — Elvis Costello (F Beat)
-	3	TOO MUCH PRESSURE — Selecter (2-Tone)
2	4	ONE STEP BEYOND — Madness (Stiff)
3	5	PRETENDERS — Pretenders (Real)
4	6	REGATTA DE BLANC — Police (A&M)
10	7	OFF THE WALL — Michael Jackson (Epic)
5	8	SHORT STORIES — Jon & Vangelis (Polydor)
6	9	KENNY — Kenny Rogers (United Artists)
7	10	THE SPECIALS — Specials (2-Tone)
-	11	TELL ME ON A SUNDAY — Marti Webb (Polydor)
-	12	STRING OF HITS — Shadows (EMI)
9	13	I'M THE MAN — Joe Jackson (A&M)
28	14	THE WALL — Pink Floyd (Harvest)
-	15	LIGHT UP THE NIGHT — Brothers Johnson (A&M)
14	16	JUST FOR YOU — Des O'Connor (Warwick)
16	16	SEPTEMBER MORN — Neil Diamond (CBS)
25	18	EAT TO THE BEAT — Blondie (Chrysalis)
12	19	THE NOLAN SISTERS — Nolans (Epic)
-	20	FLOGGING A DEAD HORSE — Sex Pistols (Virgin)
23	21	SUNBURN - ORIGINAL SOUNDTRACK — Various Artists (Warwick)
-	22	SOMETIMES YOU WIN — Dr Hook (Capitol)
16	23	BEE GEES' GREATEST HITS — Bee Gees (RSO)
26	24	CAPTAIN BEAKY AND HIS BAND — Keith Michell (Polydor)
13	25	PERMANENT WAVES — Rush (Mercury)
11	26	END OF THE CENTURY — Ramones (Sire)
-	27	CATCHING THE SUN — Spyro Gyra (MCA)
-	28	ROCK AND ROLL JUVENILE — Cliff Richard (EMI)
18	29	ABBA'S GREATEST HITS VOL 2 — Abba (Epic)
22	30	GOLDEN COLLECTION — Charley Pride (K-Tel)

The big-selling *Last Dance* compilation was, though its title disguised the fact, part of EMI's "EMTV" series (the 20th such, in fact), usually devoted to an artist's 20 Golden Greats. This one was a collection of classic ballads from the Motown back-catalogue, and had a successful TV ad campaign, becoming the first chart-topping Various Artists compilation of the '80s. Former Ultravox vocalist John Foxx scored an unexpected top-tenner with *Metamatic*, though the album's sales (and chart) span was extremely limited.

8 March 1980

last week	this week	Title / Artist (Label)
1	1	THE LAST DANCE — Various Artists (EMI)
6	2	REGATTA DE BLANC — Police (A&M)
5	3	PRETENDERS — Pretenders (Real)
9	4	KENNY — Kenny Rogers (United Artists)
2	5	GET HAPPY! — Elvis Costello (F Beat)
7	6	OFF THE WALL — Michael Jackson (Epic)
11	7	TELL ME ON A SUNDAY — Marti Webb (Polydor)
12	8	STRING OF HITS — Shadows (EMI)
8	9	SHORT STORIES — Jon & Vangelis (Polydor)
4	10	ONE STEP BEYOND — Madness (Stiff)
3	11	TOO MUCH PRESSURE — Selecter (2-Tone)
10	12	THE SPECIALS — Specials (2-Tone)
-	13	OUTLANDOS D'AMOUR — Police (A&M)
30	14	GOLDEN COLLECTION — Chareye Pride (K-Tel)
18	15	EAT TO THE BEAT — Blondie (Chrysalis)
15	16	LIGHT UP THE NIGHT — Brothers Johnson (A&M)
-	17	THE AGE OF PLASTIC — Buggles (Island)
-	18	THE KENNY ROGERS SINGLES ALBUM — Kenny Rogers (United Artists)
16	18	SEPTEMBER MORN — Neil Diamond (CBS)
20	20	FLOGGING A DEAD HORSE — Sex Pistols (Virgin)
16	21	JUST FOR YOU — Des O'Connor (Warwick)
13	22	I'M THE MAN — Joe Jackson (A&M)
14	23	THE WALL — Pink Floyd (Harvest)
29	24	ABBA'S GREATEST HITS VOL 2 — Abba (Epic)
-	25	METAL FOR MUTHAS — Various Artists (EMI)
25	26	PERMANENT WAVES — Rush (Mercury)
19	27	THE NOLAN SISTERS — Nolans (Epic)
28	28	ROCK AND ROLL JUVENILE — Cliff Richard (EMI)
-	29	PARALLEL LINES — Blondie (Chrysalis)
22	30	SOMETIMES YOU WIN — Dr Hook (Capitol)

15 March 1980

last week	this week	Title / Artist (Label)
8	1	STRING OF HITS — Shadows (EMI)
2	2	REGATTA DE BLANC — Police (A&M)
1	3	THE LAST DANCE — Various Artists (EMI)
3	4	PRETENDERS — Pretenders (Real)
15	5	EAT TO THE BEAT — Blondie (Chrysalis)
4	6	KENNY — Kenny Rogers (United Artists)
7	7	TELL ME ON A SUNDAY — Marti Webb (Polydor)
5	8	GET HAPPY! — Elvis Costello (F Beat)
-	9	ROSE ROYCE'S GREATEST HITS — Rose Royce (Whitfield)
14	10	GOLDEN COLLECTION — Charlie Pride (K-Tel)
11	11	TOO MUCH PRESSURE — Selecter (2-Tone)
10	12	ONE STEP BEYOND — Madness (Stiff)
13	13	OUTLANDOS D'AMOUR — Police (A&M)
9	13	SHORT STORIES — Jon & Vangelis (Polydor)
12	15	THE SPECIALS — Specials (2-Tone)
-	16	REALITY EFFECT — Tourists (Logo)
16	17	LIGHT UP THE NIGHT — Brothers Johnson (A&M)
25	18	METAL FOR MUTHAS — Various Artists (EMI)
6	19	OFF THE WALL — Michael Jackson (Epic)
27	20	THE NOLAN SISTERS — Nolans (Epic)
28	21	ROCK AND ROLL JUVENILE — Cliff Richard (EMI)
-	22	DOWN TO EARTH — Rainbow (Polydor)
-	23	K C & THE SUNSHINE BAND'S GREATEST HITS — K C & the Sunshine Band (TK)
23	24	THE WALL — Pink Floyd (Harvest)
26	25	PERMANENT WAVES — Rush (Mercury)
-	26	SMALLCREEP'S DAY — Mike Rutherford (Charisma)
20	27	FLOGGING A DEAD HORSE — Sex Pistols (Virgin)
-	28	ON THE RADIO: GREATEST HITS VOLS. 1 & 2 — Donna Summer (Casablanca)
29	29	TEARS AND LAUGHTER — Johnny Mathis (CBS)
24	30	ABBA'S GREATEST HITS VOL 2 — Abba (Epic)

22 March 1980

last week	this week	Title / Artist (Label)
29	1	TEARS AND LAUGHTER — Johnny Mathis (CBS)
1	2	STRING OF HITS — Shadows (EMI)
7	3	TELL ME ON A SUNDAY — Marti Webb (Polydor)
3	4	THE LAST DANCE — Various Artists (EMI)
9	5	ROSE ROYCE'S GREATEST HITS — Rose Royce (Whitfield)
2	6	REGATTA DE BLANC — Police (A&M)
8	7	GET HAPPY! — Elvis Costello (F Beat)
5	8	EAT TO THE BEAT — Blondie (Chrysalis)
-	9	NOBODY'S HERO — Stiff Little Fingers (Chrysalis)
10	10	GOLDEN COLLECTION — Charlie Pride (K-Tel)
22	11	DOWN TO EARTH — Rainbow (Polydor)
-	12	HEARTBREAKERS — Matt Monro (EMI)
19	13	OFF THE WALL — Michael Jackson (Epic)
4	14	PRETENDERS — Pretenders (Real)
-	15	THE CRYSTAL GAYLE SINGLES ALBUM — Crystal Gayle (United Artists)
12	16	ONE STEP BEYOND — Madness (Stiff)
11	17	TOO MUCH PRESSURE — Selecter (2-Tone)
17	18	LIGHT UP THE NIGHT — Brothers Johnson (A&M)
15	19	THE SPECIALS — Specials (2-Tone)
6	20	KENNY — Kenny Rogers (United Artists)
13	21	OUTLANDOS D'AMOUR — Police (A&M)
-	22	THE WHISPERS — Whispers (Solar)
23	23	K C & THE SUNSHINE BAND'S GREATEST HITS — K C & the Sunshine Band (TK)
-	24	AGAINST THE WIND — Bob Seger (Capitol)
-	25	OFFICIAL BOOTLEG ALBUM — Blues Band (Arista)
16	26	REALITY EFFECT — Tourists (Logo)
25	27	PERMANENT WAVES — Rush (Mercury)
21	28	ROCK AND ROLL JUVENILE — Cliff Richard (EMI)
-	29	FREEDOM AT POINT ZERO — Jefferson Starship (Grunt)
-	30	METRO MUSIC — Martha & the Muffins (Dindisc)

29 March 1980

last week	this week	Title / Artist (Label)
1	1	TEARS AND LAUGHTER — Johnny Mathis (CBS)
3	2	TELL ME ON A SUNDAY — Marti Webb (Polydor)
6	3	REGATTA DE BLANC — Police (A&M)
5	4	ROSE ROYCE'S GREATEST HITS — Rose Royce (Whitfield)
2	5	STRING OF HITS — Shadows (EMI)
-	6	GLASS HOUSES — Billy Joel (CBS)
7	7	GET HAPPY! — Elvis Costello (F Beat)
12	8	HEARTBREAKERS — Matt Monro (EMI)
21	9	OUTLANDOS D'AMOUR — Police (A&M)
9	10	NOBODY'S HERO — Stiff Little Fingers (Chrysalis)
4	11	THE LAST DANCE — Various Artists (EMI)
15	12	THE CRYSTAL GAYLE SINGLES ALBUM — Crystal Gayle (United Artists)
10	13	GOLDEN COLLECTION — Charlie Pride (K-Tel)
11	14	DOWN TO EARTH — Rainbow (Polydor)
19	15	THE SPECIALS — Specials (2-Tone)
-	16	12 GOLD BARS — Status Quo (Vertigo)
13	17	OFF THE WALL — Michael Jackson (Epic)
8	18	EAT TO THE BEAT — Blondie (Chrysalis)
18	19	LIGHT UP THE NIGHT — Brothers Johnson (A&M)
20	20	KENNY — Kenny Rogers (United Artists)
14	21	PRETENDERS — Pretenders (Real)
-	22	LOUD AND CLEAR — Sammy Hagar (Capitol)
16	23	ONE STEP BEYOND — Madness (Stiff)
17	24	TOO MUCH PRESSURE — Selecter (2-Tone)
24	25	AGAINST THE WIND — Bob Seger (Capitol)
-	26	MAKE YOUR MOVE — Captain & Tennille (Casablanca)
27	27	PERMANENT WAVES — Rush (Mercury)
-	28	PSYCHEDELIC FURS — Psychedelic Furs (CBS)
-	29	COCKNEY REJECTS' GREATEST HITS VOL 1 — Cockney Rejects (Zonophone)
23	30	K C & THE SUNSHINE BAND'S GREATEST HITS — K C & the Sunshine Band (TK)

String Of Hits - a collection of interpretations of other people's hits, rather than their own successes - was to be one of the Shadows' biggest-selling albums of all-time, second only to their *20 Golden Greats* package. Its sudden resurrection to the top of the chart after months on the market was down to clever marketing - EMI ran a new TV ad campaign for it. Also heavily TV-featured was Johnny Mathis' *Tears And Laughter*, a 20-track compilation which included his recent hit singles.

April 1980

5 April 1980

last week	this week	title / artist (label)
4	1	ROSE ROYCE'S GREATEST HITS - / Rose Royce (Whitfield)
2	2	TELL ME ON A SUNDAY / Marti Webb (Polydor)
1	3	TEARS AND LAUGHTER / Johnny Mathis (CBS)
-	4	STAR TRACKS / Various Artists (K-Tel)
12	5	THE CRYSTAL GAYLE SINGLES ALBUM / Crystal Gayle (United Artists)
16	6	12 GOLD BARS / Status Quo (Vertigo)
8	7	HEARTBREAKERS / Matt Monro (EMI)
3	8	REGATTA DE BLANC / Police (A&M)
5	9	STRING OF HITS / Shadows (EMI)
6	10	GLASS HOUSES / Billy Joel (CBS)
14	11	DOWN TO EARTH / Rainbow (Polydor)
10	12	NOBODY'S HERO / Stiff Little Fingers (Chrysalis)
11	13	LAST DANCE / Various Artists (EMI)
15	14	THE SPECIALS / Specials (2-Tone)
9	15	OUTLANDOS D'AMOUR / Police (A&M)
7	16	GET HAPPY! / Elvis Costello (F Beat)
19	17	LIGHT UP THE NIGHT / Brothers Johnson (A&M)
22	18	LOUD AND CLEAR / Sammy Hagar (Capitol)
18	19	EAT TO THE BEAT / Blondie (Chrysalis)
21	20	PRETENDERS / Pretenders (Real)
-	21	DUKE / Genesis (Charisma)
17	22	OFF THE WALL / Michael Jackson (Epic)
26	23	MAKE YOUR MOVE / Captain & Tennille (Casablanca)
24	24	TOO MUCH PRESSURE / Selecter (2-Tone)
20	25	KENNY / Kenny Rogers (United Artists)
-	26	ON THROUGH THE NIGHT / Def Leppard (Vertigo)
27	27	PERMANENT WAVES / Rush (Mercury)
23	28	ONE STEP BEYOND / Madness (Stiff)
-	29	FACADES / Sad Cafe (RCA)
29	30	GREATEST HITS VOL 1 / Cockney Rejects (Zonophone)

12 April 1980

this week		title / artist (label)
21	1	DUKE / Genesis (Charisma)
1	2	ROSE ROYCE'S GREATEST HITS / Rose Royce (Whitfield)
3	3	TEARS AND LAUGHTER / Johnny Mathis (CBS)
4	4	STAR TRACKS / Various Artists (K-Tel)
7	5	HEARTBREAKERS / Matt Monro (EMI)
6	6	12 GOLD BARS / Status Quo (Vertigo)
9	7	STRING OF HITS / Shadows (EMI)
8	8	REGATTA DE BLANC / Police (A&M)
14	9	THE SPECIALS / Specials (2-Tone)
10	10	GLASS HOUSES / Billy Joel (CBS)
4	11	THE CRYSTAL GAYLE SINGLES ALBUM / Crystal Gayle (United Artists)
2	12	TELL ME ON A SUNDAY / Marti Webb (Polydor)
20	13	PRETENDERS / Pretenders (Real)
11	14	DOWN TO EARTH / Rainbow (Polydor)
15	15	OUTLANDOS D'AMOUR / Police (A&M)
28	16	ONE STEP BEYOND / Madness (Stiff)
29	17	FACADES / Sad Cafe (RCA)
-	18	THE WALL / Pink Floyd (Harvest)
-	19	WOMEN AND CHILDREN FIRST / Van Halen (Warner Bros.)
16	20	GET HAPPY! / Elvis Costello (F Beat)
19	21	EAT TO THE BEAT / Blondie (Chrysalis)
22	22	OFF THE WALL / Michael Jackson (Epic)
24	23	TOO MUCH PRESSURE / Selecter (2-Tone)
18	24	LOUD AND CLEAR / Sammy Hagar (Capitol)
17	25	LIGHT UP THE NIGHT / Brothers Johnson (A&M)
-	26	HER BEST SONGS / Emmylou Harris (K-Tel)
26	27	ON THROUGH THE NIGHT / Def Leppard (Vertigo)
27	28	PERMANENT WAVES / Rush (Mercury)
12	29	NOBODY'S HERO / Stiff Little Fingers (Chrysalis)
23	30	MAKE YOUR MOVE / Captain & Tennille (Casablanca)

19 April 1980

this week		title / artist (label)
2	1	ROSE ROYCE'S GREATEST HITS / Rose Royce (Whitfield)
1	2	DUKE / Genesis (Charisma)
6	3	12 GOLD BARS / Status Quo (Vertigo)
3	4	TEARS AND LAUGHTER / Johnny Mathis (CBS)
8	5	REGATTA DE BLANC / Police (A&M)
4	6	STAR TRACKS / Various Artists (K-Tel)
5	7	HEARTBREAKERS / Matt Monro (EMI)
11	8	THE CRYSTAL GAYLE SINGLES ALBUM / Crystal Gayle (United Artists)
-	9	THE MAGIC OF BONEY M / Boney M (Atlantic/Hansa)
12	10	TELL ME ON A SUNDAY / Marti Webb (Polydor)
10	11	GLASS HOUSES / Billy Joel (CBS)
25	12	LIGHT UP THE NIGHT / Brothers Johnson (A&M)
7	13	STRING OF HITS / Shadows (EMI)
16	14	ONE STEP BEYOND / Madness (Stiff)
-	15	THE BARBARA DICKSON ALBUM / Barbara Dickson (Epic)
-	16	WHEELS OF STEEL / Saxon (Carrere)
19	17	WOMEN AND CHILDREN FIRST / Van Halen (Warner Bros.)
24	18	LOUD AND CLEAR / Sammy Hagar (Capitol)
22	19	OFF THE WALL / Michael Jackson (Epic)
27	20	ON THROUGH THE NIGHT / Def Leppard (Vertigo)
29	21	NOBODY'S HERO / Stiff Little Fingers (Chrysalis)
13	22	PRETENDERS / Pretenders (Real)
23	23	TOO MUCH PRESSURE / Selecter (2-Tone)
-	24	SOMETIMES YOU WIN / Dr Hook (Capitol)
9	25	THE SPECIALS / Specials (2-Tone)
17	26	FACADES / Sad Cafe (RCA)
-	27	OFFICIAL BOOTLEG ALBUM / Blues Band (Arista)
-	28	COUNTRY NUMBER ONE / Don Gibson (Warwick)
-	29	LOOK HEAR / 10 c.c. (Mercury)
14	30	DOWN TO EARTH / Rainbow (Polydor)

26 April 1980

this week		title / artist (label)
1	1	ROSE ROYCE'S GREATEST HITS / Rose Royce (Whitfield)
3	2	12 GOLD BARS / Status Quo (Vertigo)
2	3	DUKE / Genesis (Charisma)
-	4	BRITISH STEEL / Judas Priest (CBS)
9	5	THE MAGIC OF BONEY M / Boney M (Atlantic/Hansa)
5	6	REGATTA DE BLANC / Police (A&M)
15	7	THE BARBARA DICKSON ALBUM / Barbara Dickson (Epic)
16	8	WHEELS OF STEEL / Saxon (Carrere)
4	9	TEARS AND LAUGHTER / Johnny Mathis (CBS)
6	10	STAR TRACKS / Various Artists (K-Tel)
-	11	THE BOBBY VEE SINGLES ALBUM / Bobby Vee (United Artists)
11	12	GLASS HOUSES / Billy Joel (CBS)
14	13	ONE STEP BEYOND / Madness (Stiff)
28	14	COUNTRY NUMBER ONE / Don Gibson (Warwick)
10	15	TELL ME ON A SUNDAY / Marti Webb (Polydor)
26	16	FACADES / Sad Cafe (RCA)
-	17	OUTLANDOS D'AMOUR / Police (A&M)
-	18	SKY 2 / Sky (Ariola)
7	19	HEARTBREAKERS / Matt Monro (EMI)
17	20	WOMEN AND CHILDREN FIRST / Van Halen (Warner Bros.)
22	21	PRETENDERS / Pretenders (Real)
-	22	GOING STEADY / Various Artists (Warwick)
-	23	EAT TO THE BEAT / Blondie (Chrysalis)
25	24	THE SPECIALS / Specials (2-Tone)
8	25	THE CRYSTAL GAYLE SINGLES ALBUM / Crystal Gayle (United Artists)
12	26	LIGHT UP THE NIGHT / Brothers Johnson (A&M)
13	27	STRING OF HITS / Shadows (EMI)
-	28	BRAND NEW AGE / U K Subs (Gem)
-	29	BY REQUEST / Lena Martell (Ronco)
18	30	LOUD AND CLEAR / Sammy Hagar (Capitol)

It was a widely-accepted truism in the British record business of the late-1970s and early 1980s, when disco held sway in the singles charts, that disco or dance-based acts just couldn't sell albums in large quantities. Nobody had told Rose Royce about this, however, with the result that their hits compilation was the biggest LP seller of April 1980, outdoing not only the new Genesis album *Duke*, but also the more predictably big-selling hits package *12 Gold Bars* by Status Quo.

May 1980

3 May 1980

last	this	title / artist (label)
1	1	ROSE ROYCE'S GREATEST HITS — Rose Royce (Whitfield)
2	2	12 GOLD BARS — Status Quo (Vertigo)
18	3	SKY 2 — Sky (Ariola)
5	4	THE MAGIC OF BONEY M — Boney M (Atlantic/Hansa)
-	5	IRON MAIDEN — Iron Maiden (EMI)
11	6	THE BOBBY VEE SINGLES ALBUM — Bobby Vee (United Artists)
3	7	DUKE — Genesis (Charisma)
-	8	SUZI QUATRO'S GREATEST HITS — Suzi Quatro (RAK)
29	9	BY REQUEST — Lena Martell (Ronco)
-	10	HYPNOTISED — Undertones (Sire)
-	11	SNAKES AND LADDERS — Gerry Rafferty (United Artists)
7	12	THE BARBARA DICKSON ALBUM — Barbara Dickson (Epic)
-	13	HEAVEN AND HELL — Black Sabbath (Vertigo)
4	14	BRITISH STEEL — Judas Priest (CBS)
14	15	COUNTRY NUMBER ONE — Don Gibson (Warwick)
6	16	REGATTA DE BLANC — Police (A&M)
-	17	SOMETIMES YOU WIN — Dr Hook (Capitol)
15	18	TELL ME ON A SUNDAY — Marti Webb (Polydor)
16	19	FACADES — Sad Cafe (RCA)
21	20	PRETENDERS — Pretenders (Real)
8	21	WHEELS OF STEEL — Saxon (Carrere)
-	22	SNAP, CRACKLE AND BOP — John Cooper-Clark (Epic)
23	23	EAT TO THE BEAT — Blondie (Chrysalis)
9	24	TEARS AND LAUGHTER — Johnny Mathis (CBS)
19	25	HEARTBREAKERS — Matt Monro (EMI)
24	26	THE SPECIALS — Specials (2-Tone)
-	27	SKA 'N' B — Bad Manners (Magnet)
28	28	BRAND NEW AGE — U K Subs (Gem)
-	29	OFF THE WALL — Michael Jackson (Epic)
13	30	ONE STEP BEYOND — Madness (Stiff)

10 May 1980

last	this	title / artist (label)
4	1	THE MAGIC OF BONEY M — Boney M (Atlantic/Hansa)
1	2	ROSE ROYCE'S GREATEST HITS — Rose Royce (Whitfield)
3	3	SKY 2 — Sky (Ariola)
8	4	SUZI QUATRO'S GREATEST HITS — Suzi Quatro (RAK)
7	5	DUKE — Genesis (Charisma)
2	6	12 GOLD BARS — Status Quo (Vertigo)
-	7	EMPTY GLASS — Pete Townshend (Atco)
10	8	HYPNOTISED — Undertones (Sire)
6	9	THE BOBBY VEE SINGLES ALBUM — Bobby Vee (United Artists)
9	10	BY REQUEST — Lena Martell (Ronco)
11	11	SNAKES AND LADDERS — Gerry Rafferty (United Artists)
12	12	THE BARBARA DICKSON ALBUM — Barbara Dickson (Epic)
5	13	IRON MAIDEN — Iron Maiden (EMI)
16	14	REGATTA DE BLANC — Police (A&M)
29	15	OFF THE WALL — Michael Jackson (Epic)
14	16	BRITISH STEEL — Judas Priest (CBS)
13	17	HEAVEN AND HELL — Black Sabbath (Vertigo)
21	18	WHEELS OF STEEL — Saxon (Carrere)
20	19	PRETENDERS — Pretenders (Real)
17	20	SOMETIMES YOU WIN — Dr Hook (Capitol)
-	21	WILD HORSES — Wild Horses (EMI)
19	22	FACADES — Sad Cafe (RCA)
30	23	ONE STEP BEYOND — Madness (Stiff)
27	24	SKA 'N' B — Bad Manners (Magnet)
24	25	TEARS AND LAUGHTER — Johnny Mathis (CBS)
-	26	17 SECONDS — Cure (Fiction)
-	27	GLASS HOUSES — Billy Joel (CBS)
15	28	COUNTRY NUMBER ONE — Don Gibson (Warwick)
23	29	EAT TO THE BEAT — Blondie (Chrysalis)
-	30	BRAND NEW AGE — UK Subs (Gem)

17 May 1980

last	this	title / artist (label)
1	1	THE MAGIC OF BONEY M — Boney M (Atlantic/Hansa)
3	2	SKY 2 — Sky (Ariola)
2	3	ROSE ROYCE'S GREATEST HITS — Rose Royce (Whitfield)
4	4	SUZI QUATRO'S GREATEST HITS — Suzi Quatro (RAK)
9	5	THE BOBBY VEE SINGLES ALBUM — Bobby Vee (United Artists)
5	6	DUKE — Genesis (Charisma)
20	7	SOMETIMES YOU WIN — Dr Hook (Capitol)
8	8	HYPNOTISED — Undertones (Sire)
6	9	12 GOLD BARS — Status Quo (Vertigo)
10	10	BY REQUEST — Lena Martell (Ronco)
17	11	HEAVEN AND HELL — Black Sabbath (Vertigo)
15	12	OFF THE WALL — Michael Jackson (Epic)
7	13	EMPTY GLASS — Pete Townshend (Atco)
12	14	THE BARBARA DICKSON ALBUM — Barbara Dickson (Epic)
13	15	IRON MAIDEN — Iron Maiden (EMI)
11	16	SNAKES AND LADDERS — Gerry Rafferty (United Artists)
-	17	JUST ONE NIGHT — Eric Clapton (RSO)
14	18	REGATTA DE BLANC — Police (A&M)
-	19	SPORTS CAR — Judie Tzuke (Rocket)
18	20	WHEELS OF STEEL — Saxon (Carrere)
23	21	ONE STEP BEYOND — Madness (Stiff)
27	22	GLASS HOUSES — Billy Joel (CBS)
24	23	SKA 'N' B — Bad Manners (Magnet)
25	24	TEARS AND LAUGHTER — Johnny Mathis (CBS)
26	25	17 SECONDS — Cure (Fiction)
30	26	BRAND NEW AGE — UK Subs (Gem)
22	27	FACADES — Sad Cafe (RCA)
21	28	WILD HORSES — Wild Horses (EMI)
-	29	THE CORRECT USE OF SOAP — Magazine (Virgin)
-	30	ANIMAL MAGNETISM — Scorpions (Harvest)

24 May 1980

last	this	title / artist (label)
1	1	THE MAGIC OF BONEY M — Boney M (Atlantic/Hansa)
2	2	SKY 2 — Sky (Ariola)
3	3	ROSE ROYCE'S GREATEST HITS — Rose Royce (Whitfield)
4	4	SUZI QUATRO'S GREATEST HITS — Suzi Quatro (RAK)
19	5	SPORTS CAR — Judie Tzuke (Rocket)
9	6	12 GOLD BARS — Status Quo (Vertigo)
17	7	JUST ONE NIGHT — Eric Clapton (RSO)
6	8	DUKE — Genesis (Charisma)
7	9	SOMETIMES YOU WIN — Dr Hook (Capitol)
5	10	THE BOBBY VEE SINGLES ALBUM — Bobby Vee (United Artists)
14	11	THE BARBARA DICKSON ALBUM — Barbara Dickson (Epic)
10	12	BY REQUEST — Lena Martell (Ronco)
12	13	OFF THE WALL — Michael Jackson (Epic)
12	14	EMPTY GLASS — Pete Townshend (Atco)
11	15	HEAVEN AND HELL — Black Sabbath (Vertigo)
8	16	HYPNOTISED — Undertones (Sire)
18	17	REGATTA DE BLANC — Police (A&M)
16	18	SNAKES AND LADDERS — Gerry Rafferty (United Artists)
15	19	IRON MAIDEN — Iron Maiden (EMI)
-	20	GOOD MORNING AMERICA — Various Artists (K-Tel)
-	21	EAT TO THE BEAT — Blondie (Chrysalis)
24	22	TEARS AND LAUGHTER — Johnny Mathis (CBS)
-	23	WAR OF THE WORLDS — Jeff Wayne (CBS)
-	24	HAPPY DAYS — Various Artists (K-Tel)
21	25	ONE STEP BEYOND — Madness (Stiff)
26	26	BRAND NEW AGE — UK Subs (Gem)
22	27	GLASS HOUSES — Billy Joel (CBS)
29	28	THE CORRECT USE OF SOAP — Magazine (Virgin)
20	29	WHEELS OF STEEL — Saxon (Carrere)
-	30	SOLO IN SOHO — Philip Lynott (Vertigo)

Boney M's *The Magic Of* compilation took the best part of a month to get into high gear, but once at the chart top it fended off *Sky 2*, the pop/classical instrumental group's biggest-selling album. The chart was heavy with greatest hits sets (on May 17, the whole Top Five except *Sky 2* were hits compilations), and particularly remarkable among them was *The Bobby Vee Singles album*, which was the former teen idol's first UK top twenty entry of any kind for 17 years.

May – June 1980

last week	this week	**31 May 1980**
1	1	THE MAGIC OF BONEY M — Boney M (Atlantic/Hansa)
2	2	SKY 2 — Sky (Ariola)
3	3	ROSE ROYCE'S GREATEST HITS — Rose Royce (Whitfield)
13	4	OFF THE WALL — Michael Jackson (Epic)
7	5	JUST ONE NIGHT — Eric Clapton (RSO)
8	6	DUKE — Genesis (Charisma)
5	7	SPORTS CAR — Judie Tzuke (Rocket)
15	8	HEAVEN AND HELL — Black Sabbath (Vertigo)
6	9	12 GOLD BARS — Status Quo (Vertigo)
-	10	ME MYSELF I — Joan Armatrading (A&M)
25	11	ONE STEP BEYOND — Madness (Stiff)
16	12	HYPNOTISED — Undertones (Sire)
18	13	SNAKES AND LADDERS — Gerry Rafferty (United Artists)
-	14	PRETENDERS — Pretenders (Real)
4	15	SUZI QUATRO'S GREATEST HITS — Suzi Quatro (RAK)
-	16	McCARTNEY 2 — Paul McCartney (Parlophone)
10	17	THE BOBBY VEE SINGLES ALBUM — Bobby Vee (United Artists)
17	18	REGATTA DE BLANC — Police (A&M)
-	19	I JUST CAN'T STOP IT — Beat (Go Feet)
-	20	MAGIC REGGAE — Various Artists (K-Tel)
9	21	SOMETIMES YOU WIN — Dr Hook (Capitol)
-	22	LITTLE DREAMER — Peter Green (PVK)
20	23	GOOD MORNING AMERICA — Various Artists (K-Tel)
29	24	WHEELS OF STEEL — Saxon (Carrere)
-	25	SO FAR AWAY — Chords (Polydor)
11	26	THE BARBARA DICKSON ALBUM — Barbara Dickson (Epic)
14	27	EMPTY GLASS — Pete Townshend (Atco)
-	28	17 SECONDS — Cure (Fiction)
19	29	IRON MAIDEN — Iron Maiden (EMI)
23	30	WAR OF THE WORLDS — Jeff Wayne (CBS)

7 June 1980

16	1	McCARTNEY 2 — Paul McCartney (Parlophone)
2	2	SKY 2 — Sky (Ariola)
19	3	I JUST CAN'T STOP IT — Beat (Go Feet)
1	4	THE MAGIC OF BONEY M — Boney M (Atlantic/Hansa)
-	5	FLESH AND BLOOD — Roxy Music (Polydor)
10	6	ME MYSELF I — Joan Armatrading (A&M)
3	7	ROSE ROYCE'S GREATEST HITS — Rose Royce (Whitfield)
-	8	CHAMPAGNE AND ROSES — Various Artists (Polydor)
5	9	JUST ONE NIGHT — Eric Clapton (RSO)
4	10	OFF THE WALL — Michael Jackson (Epic)
6	11	DUKE — Genesis (Charisma)
7	12	SPORTS CAR — Judie Tzuke (Rocket)
13	13	SNAKES AND LADDERS — Gerry Rafferty (United Artists)
-	14	TRAVELOGUE — Human League (Virgin)
8	15	HEAVEN AND HELL — Black Sabbath (Vertigo)
21	16	SOMETIMES YOU WIN — Dr Hook (Capitol)
9	17	12 GOLD BARS — Status Quo (Vertigo)
15	18	SUZI QUATRO'S GREATEST HITS — Suzi Quatro (RAK)
26	19	THE BARBARA DICKSON ALBUM — Barbara Dickson (Epic)
18	20	REGATTA DE BLANC — Police (A&M)
11	21	ONE STEP BEYOND — Madness (Stiff)
-	22	21 AT 33 — Elton John (Rocket)
-	23	SHINE — Average White Band (RCA)
28	24	17 SECONDS — Cure (Fiction)
-	25	PETER GABRIEL — Peter Gabriel (Charisma)
-	26	FROM A TO B — New Musik (GTO)
-	27	LET'S GET SERIOUS — Jermaine Jackson (Motown)
29	28	IRON MAIDEN — Iron Maiden (EMI)
20	29	MAGIC REGGAE — Various Artists (K-Tel)
22	30	LITTLE DREAMER — Peter Green (PVK)

14 June 1980

1	1	McCARTNEY 2 — Paul McCartney (Parlophone)
5	2	FLESH AND BLOOD — Roxy Music (Polydor)
25	3	PETER GABRIEL — Peter Gabriel (Charisma)
6	4	ME MYSELF I — Joan Armatrading (A&M)
3	5	I JUST CAN'T STOP IT — Beat (Go Feet)
4	6	THE MAGIC OF BONEY M — Boney M (Atlantic/Hansa)
8	7	CHAMPAGNE AND ROSES — Various Artists (Polydor)
2	8	SKY 2 — Sky (Ariola)
10	9	OFF THE WALL — Michael Jackson (Epic)
22	10	21 AT 33 — Elton John (Rocket)
7	11	ROSE ROYCE'S GREATEST HITS — Rose Royce (Whitfield)
-	12	READY AND WILLING — Whitesnake (United Artists)
17	13	12 GOLD BARS — Status Quo (Vertigo)
9	14	JUST ONE NIGHT — Eric Clapton (RSO)
11	15	DUKE — Genesis (Charisma)
-	16	GOOD MORNING AMERICA — Various Artists (K-Tel)
-	17	THE UP ESCALATOR — Graham Parker & the Rumour (Stiff)
16	18	SOMETIMES YOU WIN — Dr Hook (Capitol)
20	19	REGATTA DE BLANC — Police (A&M)
27	20	LET'S GET SERIOUS — Jermaine Jackson (Motown)
28	21	IRON MAIDEN — Iron Maiden (EMI)
29	22	MAGIC REGGAE — Various Artists (K-Tel)
15	23	HEAVEN AND HELL — Black Sabbath (Vertigo)
14	24	TRAVELOGUE — Human League (Virgin)
18	25	SUZI QUATRO'S GREATEST HITS — Suzi Quatro (RAK)
13	26	SNAKES AND LADDERS — Gerry Rafferty (United Artists)
-	27	THEMES FOR DREAMS — Various Artists (K-Tel)
-	28	SOMETIMES WHEN WE TOUCH — Cleo Laine/James Galway (RCA)
23	29	SHINE — Average White Band (RCA)
21	30	ONE STEP BEYOND — Madness (Stiff)

21 June 1980

2	1	FLESH AND BLOOD — Roxy Music (Polydor)
1	2	McCARTNEY 2 — Paul McCartney (Parlophone)
3	3	PETER GABRIEL — Peter Gabriel (Charisma)
7	4	CHAMPAGNE AND ROSES — Various Artists (Polydor)
12	5	READY AND WILLING — Whitesnake (United Artists)
9	6	OFF THE WALL — Michael Jackson (Epic)
6	7	THE MAGIC OF BONEY M — Boney M (Atlantic/Hansa)
5	8	I JUST CAN'T STOP IT — Beat (Go Feet)
22	9	MAGIC REGGAE — Various Artists (K-Tel)
8	10	SKY 2 — Sky (Ariola)
4	11	ME MYSELF I — Joan Armatrading (A&M)
10	12	21 AT 33 — Elton John (Rocket)
15	13	DUKE — Genesis (Charisma)
11	14	ROSE ROYCE'S GREATEST HITS — Rose Royce (Whitfield)
-	15	HOT WAX — Various Artists (K-Tel)
19	16	REGATTA DE BLANC — Police (A&M)
14	17	JUST ONE NIGHT — Eric Clapton (RSO)
20	18	LET'S GET SERIOUS — Jermaine Jackson (Motown)
-	19	ORCHESTRAL MANOEUVRES IN THE DARK — Orchestral Manoeuvres in the Dark (Dindisc)
28	20	SOMETIMES WHEN WE TOUCH — Cleo Laine/James Galway (RCA)
-	21	THE GREAT ROCK AND ROLL SWINDLE — Soundtrack (Virgin)
13	22	12 GOLD BARS — Status Quo (Vertigo)
18	23	SOMETIMES YOU WIN — Dr Hook (Capitol)
16	24	GOOD MORNING AMERICA — Various Artists (K-Tel)
-	25	LADY T — Teena Marie (Motown)
-	26	TANGRAM — Tangerine Dream (Virgin)
29	27	SHINE — Average White Band (RCA)
17	28	THE UP ESCALATOR — Graham Parker & the Rumour (Stiff)
24	29	TRAVELOGUE — Human League (Virgin)
27	30	THEMES FOR DREAMS — Various Artists (K-Tel)

After a decade of billing himself and his ever-changing group as Wings, Paul McCartney finally issued an album credited to himself as a soloist once again - and emphasised the point by linking it, title-wise, to his first solo effort *McCartney* 10 years earlier in May 1970. Peter Gabriel, meanwhile, was taking the my-work-bears-my-name game to extraordinary lengths - *Peter Gabriel* was his third album to carry that title in just over three years, and would not be the last!

28 June 1980

last week	this week	Album	Artist (Label)
3	1	PETER GABRIEL	Peter Gabriel (Charisma)
15	2	HOT WAX	Various Artists (K-Tel)
1	3	FLESH AND BLOOD	Roxy Music (Polydor)
2	4	McCARTNEY 2	Paul McCartney (Parlophone)
11	5	ME MYSELF I	Joan Armatrading (A&M)
7	6	I JUST CAN'T STOP IT	Beat (Go Feet)
9	7	MAGIC REGGAE	Various Artists (K-Tel)
10	8	SKY 2	Sky (Ariola)
4	9	CHAMPAGNE AND ROSES	Various Artists (Polydor)
5	10	READY AND WILLING	Whitesnake (United Artists)
6	11	OFF THE WALL	Michael Jackson (Epic)
7	12	THE MAGIC OF BONEY M	Boney M (Atlantic/Hansa)
27	13	SHINE	Average White Band (RCA)
14	14	ROSE ROYCE'S GREATEST HITS	Rose Royce (Whitfield)
21	15	THE GREAT ROCK AND ROLL SWINDLE	Soundtrack (Virgin)
-	16	DIANA	Diana Ross (Motown)
-	17	CHAIN LIGHTNING	Don McLean (EMI America)
13	18	DUKE	Genesis (Charisma)
16	19	REGATTA DE BLANC	Police (A&M)
-	20	THE PHOTOS	Photos (CBS)
-	21	DREAMS	Grace Slick (RCA)
22	22	AT 33	Elton John (Rocket)
-	23	ROBERTA FLACK AND DONNY HATHAWAY	Roberta Flack & Donny Hathaway (Atlantic)
20	24	SOMETIMES WHEN WE TOUCH	Cleo Laine/James Galway (RCA)
-	25	DEFECTOR	Steve Hackett (Charisma)
28	26	THE UP ESCALATOR	Graham Parker & the Rumour (Stiff)
23	27	SOMETIMES YOU WIN	Dr Hook (Capitol)
19	28	ORCHESTRAL MANOEUVRES IN THE DARK	Orchestral Manoeuvres in the Dark (Dindisc)
17	29	JUST ONE NIGHT	Eric Clapton (RSO)
-	30	THE WANDERERS - ORIGINAL SOUNDTRACK	Various Artists (GEM)

5 July 1980

last week	this week	Album	Artist (Label)
3	1	FLESH AND BLOOD	Roxy Music (Polydor)
2	2	HOT WAX	Various Artists (K-Tel)
4	3	McCARTNEY 2	Paul McCartney (Parlophone)
7	4	MAGIC REGGAE	Various Artists (K-Tel)
1	5	PETER GABRIEL	Peter Gabriel (Charisma)
-	6	UPRISING	Bob Marley & the Wailers (Island)
8	7	SKY 2	Sky (Ariola)
-	8	SAVED	Bob Dylan (CBS)
20	9	THE PHOTOS	Photos (CBS)
5	10	ME MYSELF I	Joan Armatrading (A&M)
9	11	CHAMPAGNE AND ROSES	Various Artists (Polydor)
6	12	I JUST CAN'T STOP IT	Beat (Go Feet)
19	13	REGATTA DE BLANC	Police (A&M)
16	14	DIANA	Diana Ross (Motown)
18	15	DUKE	Genesis (Charisma)
22	16	21 AT 33	Elton John (Rocket)
10	17	READY AND WILLING	Whitesnake (United Artists)
-	18	EMOTIONAL RESCUE	Rolling Stones (Rolling Stones)
23	19	ROBERTA FLACK AND DONNY HATHAWAY	Roberta Flack & Donny Hathaway (Atlantic)
13	20	SHINE	Average White Band (RCA)
11	21	OFF THE WALL	Michael Jackson (Epic)
17	22	CHAIN LIGHTNING	Don McLean (EMI America)
12	23	THE MAGIC OF BONEY M	Boney M (Atlantic/Hansa)
14	24	ROSE ROYCE'S GREATEST HITS	Rose Royce (Whitfield)
15	25	THE GREAT ROCK AND ROLL SWINDLE	Soundtrack (Virgin)
25	26	DEFECTOR	Steve Hackett (Charisma)
26	27	THE UP ESCALATOR	Graham Parker & the Rumour (Stiff)
30	28	THE WANDERERS - ORIGINAL SOUNDTRACK	Various Artists (GEM)
28	29	ORCHESTRAL MANOEUVRES IN THE DARK	Orchestral Manoeuvres in the Dark (Dindisc)
29	30	JUST ONE NIGHT	Eric Clapton (RSO)

12 July 1980

last week	this week	Album	Artist (Label)
1	1	FLESH AND BLOOD	Roxy Music (Polydor)
18	2	EMOTIONAL RESCUE	Rolling Stones (Rolling Stones)
3	3	McCARTNEY 2	Paul McCartney (Parlophone)
2	4	HOT WAX	Various Artists (K-Tel)
10	5	ME MYSELF I	Joan Armatrading (A&M)
7	6	SKY 2	Sky (Ariola)
6	7	UPRISING	Bob Marley & the Wailers (Island)
21	8	OFF THE WALL	Michael Jackson (Epic)
5	9	PETER GABRIEL	Peter Gabriel (Charisma)
8	10	SAVED	Bob Dylan (CBS)
15	11	DUKE	Genesis (Charisma)
12	12	I JUST CAN'T STOP IT	Beat (Go Feet)
11	13	CHAMPAGNE AND ROSES	Various Artists (Polydor)
23	14	THE MAGIC OF BONEY M	Boney M (Atlantic/Hansa)
13	15	REGATTA DE BLANC	Police (A&M)
22	16	CHAIN LIGHTNING	Don McLean (EMI America)
17	17	READY AND WILLING	Whitesnake (United Artists)
20	18	SHINE	Average White Band (RCA)
14	19	DIANA	Diana Ross (Motown)
9	20	THE PHOTOS	Photos (CBS)
26	21	DEFECTOR	Steve Hackett (Charisma)
-	22	BLACK SABBATH LIVE AT LAST	Black Sabbath (NEMS)
27	23	THE UP ESCALATOR	Graham Parker & the Rumour (Stiff)
4	24	MAGIC REGGAE	Various Artists (K-Tel)
-	25	KING OF THE ROAD	Boxcar Willie (Warwick)
-	26	SOUNDS SENSATIONAL	Bert Kaempfert (Polydor)
-	27	KILLER WATTS	Various Artists (Epic)
16	28	21 AT 33	Elton John (Rocket)
24	29	ROSE ROYCE'S GREATEST HITS	Rose Royce (Whitfield)
28	30	THE WANDERERS	Soundtrack (GEM)

19 July 1980

last week	this week	Album	Artist (Label)
2	1	EMOTIONAL RESCUE	Rolling Stones (Rolling Stones)
1	2	FLESH AND BLOOD	Roxy Music (Polydor)
-	3	THE GAME	Queen (EMI)
5	4	ME MYSELF I	Joan Armatrading (A&M)
3	5	McCARTNEY 2	Paul McCartney (Parlophone)
6	6	SKY 2	Sky (Ariola)
22	7	BLACK SABBATH LIVE AT LAST	Black Sabbath (NEMS)
7	8	UPRISING	Bob Marley & the Wailers (Island)
9	9	PETER GABRIEL	Peter Gabriel (Charisma)
12	10	I JUST CAN'T STOP IT	Beat (Go Feet)
8	11	OFF THE WALL	Michael Jackson (Epic)
11	12	DUKE	Genesis (Charisma)
17	13	READY AND WILLING	Whitesnake (United Artists)
16	14	CHAIN LIGHTNING	Don McLean (EMI America)
10	15	SAVED	Bob Dylan (CBS)
4	16	HOT WAX	Various Artists (K-Tel)
18	17	SHINE	Average White Band (RCA)
26	18	SOUNDS SENSATIONAL	Bert Kaempfert (Polydor)
25	19	KING OF THE ROAD	Boxcar Willie (Warwick)
19	20	DIANA	Diana Ross (Motown)
20	21	THE PHOTOS	Photos (CBS)
29	22	ROSE ROYCE'S GREATEST HITS	Rose Royce (Whitfield)
15	23	REGATTA DE BLANC	Police (A&M)
24	24	MAGIC REGGAE	Various Artists (K-Tel)
14	25	THE MAGIC OF BONEY M	Boney M (Atlantic/Hansa)
13	26	CHAMPAGNE AND ROSES	Various Artists (Polydor)
-	27	WHEELS OF STEEL	Saxon (Carrere)
-	28	XANADU	Soundtrack (Jet)
-	29	BEAT BOYS IN THE JET AGE	Lambrettas (Rocket)
21	30	DEFECTOR	Steve Hackett (Charisma)

The Photos, a UK group led by striking girl vocalist Wendy Wu, surprised many with the Top 10 success of their eponymous album, particularly since they never managed to have single success, at this or any other time (it must have been down to all that heavy music paper coverage focusing on the extremely photogenic Wendy). The Rolling Stones and Joan Armatrading, meanwhile, both charted albums of which they simultaneously issued the title song as a single - in both cases, the LP sold better.

July – August 1980

last this week

26 July 1980

last	this	
3	1	THE GAME — Queen (EMI)
1	2	EMOTIONAL RESCUE — Rolling Stones (Rolling Stones)
28	3	XANADU — Soundtrack (Jet)
8	4	UPRISING — Bob Marley & the Wailers (Island)
2	5	FLESH AND BLOOD — Roxy Music (Polydor)
11	6	OFF THE WALL — Michael Jackson (Epic)
5	7	McCARTNEY 2 — Paul McCartney (Parlophone)
19	8	KING OF THE ROAD — Boxcar Willie (Warwick)
6	9	SKY 2 — Sky (Ariola)
4	10	ME MYSELF I — Joan Armatrading (A&M)
-	11	DEEPEST PURPLE — Deep Purple (Harvest)
20	12	DIANA — Diana Ross (Motown)
16	13	HOT WAX — Various Artists (K-Tel)
23	14	REGATTA DE BLANC — Police (A&M)
9	15	PETER GABRIEL — Peter Gabriel (Charisma)
-	16	GIVE ME THE NIGHT — George Benson (Warner Bros.)
12	17	DUKE — Genesis (Charisma)
17	18	SHINE — Average White Band (RCA)
7	19	BLACK SABBATH LIVE AT LAST — Black Sabbath (NEMS)
13	20	READY AND WILLING — Whitesnake (United Artists)
-	21	VIENNA — Ultravox (Chrysalis)
25	22	THE MAGIC OF BONEY M — Boney M (Atlantic/Hansa)
14	23	CHAIN LIGHTNING — Don McLean (EMI America)
15	24	SAVED — Bob Dylan (CBS)
-	25	CULTOSAURUS ERECTUS — Blue Oyster Cult (CBS)
-	26	THEMES FOR DREAMS — Pierre Belmonde (K-Tel)
10	27	I JUST CAN'T STOP IT — Beat (Go Feet)
-	28	DEMOLITION — Girlschool (Bronze)
-	29	HOT LOVE — David Essex (Phonogram)
-	30	BAT OUT OF HELL — Meatloaf (Epic)

2 August 1980

last	this	
3	1	XANADU — Soundtrack (Jet)
2	2	EMOTIONAL RESCUE — Rolling Stones (Rolling Stones)
5	3	FLESH AND BLOOD — Roxy Music (Polydor)
4	4	UPRISING — Bob Marley & the Wailers (Island)
16	5	GIVE ME THE NIGHT — George Benson (Warner Bros.)
1	6	THE GAME — Queen (EMI)
11	7	DEEPEST PURPLE — Deep Purple (Harvest)
6	8	OFF THE WALL — Michael Jackson (Epic)
7	9	McCARTNEY 2 — Paul McCartney (Parlophone)
10	10	ME MYSELF I — Joan Armatrading (A&M)
9	11	SKY 2 — Sky (Ariola)
8	12	KING OF THE ROAD — Boxcar Willie (Warwick)
27	13	I JUST CAN'T STOP IT — Beat (Go Feet)
19	14	BLACK SABBATH LIVE AT LAST — Black Sabbath (NEMS)
-	15	SEARCHING FOR THE YOUNG SOUL REBELS — Dexy's Midnight Runners (Parlophone)
12	16	DIANA — Diana Ross (Motown)
24	17	SAVED — Bob Dylan (CBS)
-	18	ALL FOR YOU — Johnny Mathis (CBS)
-	19	MAGIC REGGAE — Various Artists (K-Tel)
15	20	PETER GABRIEL — Peter Gabriel (Charisma)
20	21	READY AND WILLING — Whitesnake (United Artists)
21	22	VIENNA — Ultravox (Chrysalis)
13	23	HOT WAX — Various Artists (K-Tel)
17	24	DUKE — Genesis (Charisma)
-	25	CLOSER — Joy Division (Factory)
-	26	SMALL FACES BIG HITS — Small Faces (Immediate/Virgin)
14	27	REGATTA DE BLANC — Police (A&M)
18	28	SHINE — Average White Band (RCA)
25	29	CULTOSAURUS ERECTUS — Blue Oyster Cult (CBS)
-	30	MANILOW MAGIC — Barry Manilow (Arista)

9 August 1980

last	this	
1	1	XANADU — Soundtrack (Jet)
7	2	DEEPEST PURPLE — Deep Purple (Harvest)
6	3	THE GAME — Queen (EMI)
3	4	FLESH AND BLOOD — Roxy Music (Polydor)
5	5	GIVE ME THE NIGHT — George Benson (Warner Bros.)
2	6	EMOTIONAL RESCUE — Rolling Stones (Rolling Stones)
4	7	UPRISING — Bob Marley & the Wailers (Island)
8	8	OFF THE WALL — Michael Jackson (Epic)
15	9	SEARCHING FOR THE YOUNG SOUL REBELS — Dexy's Midnight Runners (Parlophone)
-	10	ANOTHER STRING OF HOT HITS — Shadows (EMI)
10	11	ME MYSELF I — Joan Armatrading (A&M)
9	12	McCARTNEY 2 — Paul McCartney (Parlophone)
11	13	SKY 2 — Sky (Ariola)
13	14	I JUST CAN'T STOP IT — Beat (Go Feet)
25	15	CLOSER — Joy Division (Factory)
16	16	DIANA — Diana Ross (Motown)
22	17	VIENNA — Ultravox (Chrysalis)
30	18	MANILOW MAGIC — Barry Manilow (Arista)
19	19	MAGIC REGGAE — Various Artists (K-Tel)
12	20	KING OF THE ROAD — Boxcar Willie (Warwick)
-	21	RHAPSODY AND BLUES — Crusaders (MCA)
27	22	REGATTA DE BLANC — Police (A&M)
14	23	BLACK SABBATH LIVE AT LAST — Black Sabbath (NEMS)
20	24	PETER GABRIEL — Peter Gabriel (Charisma)
18	25	ALL FOR YOU — Johnny Mathis (CBS)
-	26	WHEELS OF STEEL — Saxon (Carrere)
17	27	SAVED — Bob Dylan (CBS)
-	28	BRAZILIAN LOVE AFFAIR — George Duke (Epic)
-	29	ROMANTIC GUITAR — Paul Brett (K-Tel)
-	30	CROCODILES — Echo & the Bunnymen (Korova)

16 August 1980

last	this	
4	1	FLESH AND BLOOD — Roxy Music (Polydor)
1	2	XANADU — Soundtrack (Jet)
-	3	BACK IN BLACK — AC/DC (Atlantic)
2	4	DEEPEST PURPLE — Deep Purple (Harvest)
7	5	UPRISING — Bob Marley & the Wailers (Island)
5	6	GIVE ME THE NIGHT — George Benson (Warner Bros.)
16	7	DIANA — Diana Ross (Motown)
6	8	EMOTIONAL RESCUE — Rolling Stones (Rolling Stones)
15	9	CLOSER — Joy Division (Factory)
8	10	OFF THE WALL — Michael Jackson (Epic)
9	11	SEARCHING FOR THE YOUNG SOUL REBELS — Dexy's Midnight Runners (Parlophone)
24	12	PETER GABRIEL — Peter Gabriel (Charisma)
14	13	I JUST CAN'T STOP IT — Beat (Go Feet)
3	14	THE GAME — Queen (EMI)
13	15	SKY 2 — Sky (Ariola)
10	16	ANOTHER STRING OF HOT HITS — Shadows (EMI)
17	17	VIENNA — Ultravox (Chrysalis)
22	18	REGATTA DE BLANC — Police (A&M)
20	19	KING OF THE ROAD — Boxcar Willie (Warwick)
18	20	MANILOW MAGIC — Barry Manilow (Arista)
19	21	MAGIC REGGAE — Various Artists (K-Tel)
-	22	BEAT BOYS IN THE JET AGE — Lambrettas (Rocket)
-	22	LIVE 1979 — Hawkwind (Bronze)
-	24	XOO MULTIPLIES — Yellow Magic Orchestra (A&M)
-	25	DO A RUNNER — Athletico Spizz '80 (A&M)
21	26	RHAPSODY AND BLUES — Crusaders (MCA)
12	27	McCARTNEY 2 — Paul McCartney (Parlophone)
11	28	ME MYSELF I — Joan Armatrading (A&M)
-	29	BREAKING GLASS — Hazel O'Connor (A&M)
-	30	SMALL FACES BIG HITS — Small Faces (Immediate/Virgin)

Xanadu, an extraordinarily inane film musical which Olivia Newton-John and Gene Kelly should have known better than to approach with a bargepole, nonetheless proved a big commercial success in terms of its spin-off recordings. In addition to the soundtrack album topping the chart, the title song by Olivia and ELO was a No.1 single, and there were *three* more hit singles from the movie - Olivia's *Magic*, ELO's *I'm Alive*, and the Newton-John/Cliff Richard duet *Suddenly*.

August – September 1980

last week	this week	23 August 1980
1	1	FLESH AND BLOOD — Roxy Music (Polydor)
6	2	GIVE ME THE NIGHT — George Benson (Warner Bros.)
2	3	XANADU — Soundtrack (Jet)
4	4	DEEPEST PURPLE — Deep Purple (Harvest)
3	5	BACK IN BLACK — AC/DC (Atlantic)
7	6	DIANA — Diana Ross (Motown)
8	7	EMOTIONAL RESCUE — Rolling Stones (Rolling Stones)
5	8	UPRISING — Bob Marley & the Wailers (Island)
15	9	SKY 2 — Sky (Ariola)
9	10	CLOSER — Joy Division (Factory)
10	11	OFF THE WALL — Michael Jackson (Epic)
-	12	GLORY ROAD — Gillan (Virgin)
11	13	SEARCHING FOR THE YOUNG SOUL REBELS — Dexy's Midnight Runners (Parlophone)
20	14	MANILOW MAGIC — Barry Manilow (Arista)
14	15	THE GAME — Queen (EMI)
13	16	I JUST CAN'T STOP IT — Beat (Go Feet)
19	17	KING OF THE ROAD — Boxcar Willie (Warwick)
22	18	LIVE 1979 — Hawkwind (Bronze)
17	19	VIENNA — Ultravox (Chrysalis)
18	20	REGATTA DE BLANC — Police (A&M)
-	21	KALEIDOSCOPE — Siouxsie & the Banshees (Polydor)
29	22	BREAKING GLASS — Hazel O'Connor (A&M)
-	23	BAT OUT OF HELL — Meatloaf (Epic)
-	24	THE WALL — Pink Floyd (Harvest)
-	25	WAR OF THE WORLDS — Jeff Wayne (CBS)
27	26	McCARTNEY 2 — Paul McCartney (Parlophone)
-	27	CAN'T STOP THE MUSIC — Soundtrack (Mercury)
-	28	DUKE — Genesis (Charisma)
28	28	DUMB WAITERS — Korgis (Rialto)
-	30	SKA 'N' B — Bad Manners (Magnet)

last week	this week	30 August 1980
2	1	GIVE ME THE NIGHT — George Benson (Warner Bros.)
1	2	FLESH AND BLOOD — Roxy Music (Polydor)
3	3	XANADU — Soundtrack (Jet)
5	4	BACK IN BLACK — AC/DC (Atlantic)
4	5	DEEPEST PURPLE — Deep Purple (Harvest)
6	6	DIANA — Diana Ross (Motown)
19	7	VIENNA — Ultravox (Chrysalis)
9	8	SKY 2 — Sky (Ariola)
26	9	McCARTNEY 2 — Paul McCartney (Parlophone)
11	10	OFF THE WALL — Michael Jackson (Epic)
16	11	I JUST CAN'T STOP IT — Beat (Go Feet)
13	12	SEARCHING FOR THE YOUNG SOUL REBELS — Dexy's Midnight Runners (Parlophone)
-	13	LIVING IN A FANTASY — Leo Sayer (Chrysalis)
7	14	EMOTIONAL RESCUE — Rolling Stones (Rolling Stones)
-	15	ELVIS ARON PRESLEY — Elvis Presley (RCA)
21	16	KALEIDOSCOPE — Siouxsie & the Banshees (Polydor)
14	17	MANILOW MAGIC — Barry Manilow (Arista)
20	18	REGATTA DE BLANC — Police (A&M)
17	19	KING OF THE ROAD — Boxcar Willie (Warwick)
30	20	SKA 'N' B — Bad Manners (Magnet)
25	21	WAR OF THE WORLDS — Jeff Wayne (CBS)
12	22	GLORY ROAD — Gillan (Virgin)
8	23	UPRISING — Bob Marley & the Wailers (Island)
23	24	BAT OUT OF HELL — Meatloaf (Epic)
15	25	THE GAME — Queen (EMI)
10	26	CLOSER — Joy Division (Factory)
27	27	CAN'T STOP THE MUSIC — Soundtrack (Mercury)
-	28	ME MYSELF I — Joan Armatrading (A&M)
18	29	LIVE 1979 — Hawkwind (Bronze)
28	30	DUMB WAITERS — Korgis (Rialto)

last week	this week	6 September 1980
1	1	GIVE ME THE NIGHT — George Benson (Warner Bros.)
2	2	FLESH AND BLOOD — Roxy Music (Polydor)
10	3	OFF THE WALL — Michael Jackson (Epic)
6	3	DIANA — Diana Ross (Motown)
4	5	BACK IN BLACK — AC/DC (Atlantic)
-	5	BREAKING GLASS — Hazel O'Connor (A&M)
8	7	SKY 2 — Sky (Ariola)
3	8	XANADU — Soundtrack (Jet)
-	9	DRAMA — Yes (Atlantic)
23	10	UPRISING — Bob Marley & the Wailers (Island)
16	11	KALEIDOSCOPE — Siouxsie & the Banshees (Polydor)
17	12	MANILOW MAGIC — Barry Manilow (Arista)
5	13	DEEPEST PURPLE — Deep Purple (Harvest)
22	14	GLORY ROAD — Gillan (Virgin)
28	15	ME MYSELF I — Joan Armatrading (A&M)
7	16	VIENNA — Ultravox (Chrysalis)
13	17	LIVING IN A FANTASY — Leo Sayer (Chrysalis)
11	18	I JUST CAN'T STOP IT — Beat (Go Feet)
15	19	ELVIS ARON PRESLEY — Elvis Presley (RCA)
9	20	McCARTNEY 2 — Paul McCartney (Parlophone)
26	21	CLOSER — Joy Division (Factory)
27	22	CAN'T STOP THE MUSIC — Soundtrack (Mercury)
14	23	EMOTIONAL RESCUE — Rolling Stones (Rolling Stones)
12	24	SEARCHING FOR THE YOUNG SOUL REBELS — Dexy's Midnight Runners (Parlophone)
25	25	THE GAME — Queen (EMI)
20	26	SKA 'N' B — Bad Manners (Magnet)
24	27	BAT OUT OF HELL — Meatloaf (Epic)
18	28	REGATTA DE BLANC — Police (A&M)
-	29	PETER GABRIEL — Peter Gabriel (Charisma)
30	30	DUMB WAITERS — Korgis (Rialto)

last week	this week	13 September 1980
2	1	FLESH AND BLOOD — Roxy Music (Polydor)
1	2	GIVE ME THE NIGHT — George Benson (Warner Bros.)
8	3	XANADU — Soundtrack (Jet)
5	4	BREAKING GLASS — Hazel O'Connor (A&M)
5	5	BACK IN BLACK — AC/DC (Atlantic)
-	6	SIGNING OFF — UB40 (Graduate)
3	7	OFF THE WALL — Michael Jackson (Epic)
14	8	GLORY ROAD — Gillan (Virgin)
22	9	CAN'T STOP THE MUSIC — Soundtrack (Mercury)
9	10	DRAMA — Yes (Atlantic)
18	11	I JUST CAN'T STOP IT — Beat (Go Feet)
10	12	UPRISING — Bob Marley & the Wailers (Island)
7	13	SKY 2 — Sky (Ariola)
3	14	DIANA — Diana Ross (Motown)
15	15	ME MYSELF I — Joan Armatrading (A&M)
11	16	KALEIDOSCOPE — Siouxsie & the Banshees (Polydor)
16	17	VIENNA — Ultravox (Chrysalis)
12	18	MANILOW MAGIC — Barry Manilow (Arista)
-	19	I'M NO HERO — Cliff Richard (EMI)
13	20	DEEPEST PURPLE — Deep Purple (Harvest)
-	21	TELEKON — Gary Numan (Beggars Banquet)
24	22	SEARCHING FOR THE YOUNG SOUL REBELS — Dexy's Midnight Runners (Parlophone)
17	23	LIVING IN A FANTASY — Leo Sayer (Chrysalis)
-	24	ONE TRICK PONY — Paul Simon (Warner Bros.)
19	25	ELVIS ARON PRESLEY — Elvis Presley (RCA)
21	26	CLOSER — Joy Division (Factory)
-	27	WARM LEATHERETTE — Grace Jones (Island)
-	28	CLUES — Robert Palmer (Island)
-	29	ON THE RIVIERA — Gibson Brothers (Island)
-	30	WILD CAT — Tygers Of Pan Tang (MCA)

Elvis Aron Presley was an 8-LP boxed set, issued to commemorate the third anniversary of Presley's death, and containing mostly rare or previously unreleased material by him. Retailing at over £30, it became both the most expensive and largest album package yet to reach the UK Top 20. Hazel O'Connor's *Breaking Glass* album, which gave her a Top 5 debut, contained the songs from the British film of the same name, in which the singer had a starring role as a manipulated punk vocalist.

September – October 1980

20 September 1980

last week	this week	Title	Artist (Label)
6	1	SIGNING OFF	UB40 (Graduate)
21	2	TELEKON	Gary Numan (Beggars Banquet)
1	3	FLESH AND BLOOD	Roxy Music (Polydor)
2	4	GIVE ME THE NIGHT	George Benson (Warner Bros.)
4	5	BREAKING GLASS	Hazel O'Connor (A&M)
5	6	BACK IN BLACK	AC/DC (Atlantic)
19	7	I'M NO HERO	Cliff Richard (EMI)
10	8	DRAMA	Yes (Atlantic)
18	9	MANILOW MAGIC	Barry Manilow (Arista)
14	10	DIANA	Diana Ross (Motown)
-	11	FAME	Soundtrack (Jet)
3	12	XANADU	Soundtrack (Jet)
7	13	OFF THE WALL	Michael Jackson (Epic)
11	14	I JUST CAN'T STOP IT	Beat (Go Feet)
13	15	SKY 2	Sky (Ariola)
-	16	NEVER FOR EVER	Kate Bush (EMI)
24	17	ONE TRICK PONY	Paul Simon (Warner Bros.)
9	18	CAN'T STOP THE MUSIC	Soundtrack (Mercury)
-	19	WILD PLANET	B52s (Island)
8	20	GLORY ROAD	Gillan (Virgin)
-	21	NOW WE MAY BEGIN	Randy Crawford (Warner Bros.)
-	22	GLASS HOUSES	Billy Joel (CBS)
-	23	FRESH FRUIT FOR ROTTING VEGETABLES	Dead Kennedys (Cherry Red)
15	24	ME MYSELF I	Joan Armatrading (A&M)
-	25	CHANGE OF ADDRESS	Shadows (Polydor)
12	26	UPRISING	Bob Marley & the Wailers (Island)
16	27	KALEIDOSCOPE	Siouxsie & the Banshees (Polydor)
20	28	DEEPEST PURPLE	Deep Purple (Harvest)
23	29	LIVING IN A FANTASY	Leo Sayer (Chrysalis)
29	30	ON THE RIVIERA	Gibson Brothers (Island)

27 September 1980

last week	this week	Title	Artist (Label)
2	1	TELEKON	Gary Numan (Beggars Banquet)
1	2	SIGNING OFF	UB40 (Graduate)
16	3	NEVER FOR EVER	Kate Bush (EMI)
7	4	I'M NO HERO	Cliff Richard (EMI)
9	5	MANILOW MAGIC	Barry Manilow (Arista)
21	6	NOW WE MAY BEGIN	Randy Crawford (Warner Bros.)
4	7	GIVE ME THE NIGHT	George Benson (Warner Bros.)
3	8	FLESH AND BLOOD	Roxy Music (Polydor)
-	9	OZZY OSBOURNE'S BLIZZARD OF OZ	Ozzy Osbourne (Jet)
25	10	CHANGE OF ADDRESS	Shadows (Polydor)
6	11	BACK IN BLACK	AC/DC (Atlantic)
5	12	BREAKING GLASS	Hazel O'Connor (A&M)
-	13	SCARY MONSTERS AND SUPER CREEPS	David Bowie (RCA)
10	14	DIANA	Diana Ross (Motown)
15	15	SKY 2	Sky (Ariola)
8	16	DRAMA	Yes (Atlantic)
17	17	ONE TRICK PONY	Paul Simon (Warner Bros.)
12	18	XANADU	Soundtrack (Jet)
-	19	HANX	Stiff Little Fingers (Chrysalis)
-	20	BLACK SEA	XTC (Virgin)
11	21	FAME	Soundtrack (Jet)
-	22	THE GAME	Queen (EMI)
18	23	CAN'T STOP THE MUSIC	Soundtrack (Mercury)
-	24	REGATTA DE BLANC	Police (A&M)
26	25	UPRISING	Bob Marley & the Wailers (Island)
29	26	LIVING IN A FANTASY	Leo Sayer (Chrysalis)
20	27	GLORY ROAD	Gillan (Virgin)
-	28	McVICAR	Roger Daltrey (Polydor)
22	29	GLASS HOUSES	Billy Joel (CBS)
13	30	OFF THE WALL	Michael Jackson (Epic)

4 October 1980

last week	this week	Title	Artist (Label)
3	1	NEVER FOR EVER	Kate Bush (EMI)
13	2	SCARY MONSTERS AND SUPER CREEPS	David Bowie (RCA)
2	3	SIGNING OFF	UB40 (Graduate)
-	4	MOUNTING EXCITEMENT	Various Artists (K-Tel)
6	5	NOW WE MAY BEGIN	Randy Crawford (Warner Bros.)
1	6	TELEKON	Gary Numan (Beggars Banquet)
8	7	FLESH AND BLOOD	Roxy Music (Polydor)
-	8	THE ABSOLUTE GAME	Skids (Virgin)
4	9	I'M NO HERO	Cliff Richard (EMI)
-	10	THE VERY BEST OF DON McLEAN	Don McLean (United Artists)
5	11	MANILOW MAGIC	Barry Manilow (Arista)
7	12	GIVE ME THE NIGHT	George Benson (Warner Bros.)
19	13	HANX	Stiff Little Fingers (Chrysalis)
-	14	LIVE CRASH COURSE	UK Subs (Gem)
12	15	BREAKING GLASS	Hazel O'Connor (A&M)
22	16	THE GAME	Queen (EMI)
9	17	OZZY OSBOURNE'S BLIZZARD OF OZ	Ozzy Osbourne (Jet)
20	18	BLACK SEA	XTC (Virgin)
14	19	DIANA	Diana Ross (Motown)
-	20	GOLD	Three Degrees (Ariola)
-	21	I JUST CAN'T STOP IT	Beat (Go Feet)
15	22	SKY 2	Sky (Ariola)
30	23	OFF THE WALL	Michael Jackson (Epic)
-	24	I AM WOMAN	Various Artists (Polydor)
10	25	CHANGE OF ADDRESS	Shadows (Polydor)
18	26	XANADU	Soundtrack (Jet)
-	27	THE LOVE ALBUM	Various Artists (K-Tel)
-	28	FRESH FRUIT FOR ROTTING VEGETABLES	Dead Kennedys (Cherry Red)
29	29	GLASS HOUSES	Billy Joel (CBS)
-	30	ABSOLUTELY	Madness (Stiff)

11 October 1980

last week	this week	Title	Artist (Label)
2	1	SCARY MONSTERS AND SUPER CREEPS	David Bowie (RCA)
1	2	NEVER FOR EVER	Kate Bush (EMI)
4	3	MOUNTING EXCITEMENT	Various Artists (K-Tel)
-	4	ZENYATTA MONDATTA	Police (A&M)
9	5	THE VERY BEST OF DON McLEAN	Don McLean (United Artists)
4	6	NOW WE MAY BEGIN	Randy Crawford (Warner Bros.)
9	7	I'M NO HERO	Cliff Richard (EMI)
30	8	ABSOLUTELY	Madness (Stiff)
3	9	SIGNING OFF	UB40 (Graduate)
-	10	MORE SPECIALS	Specials (2-Tone)
15	11	BREAKING GLASS	Hazel O'Connor (A&M)
11	12	MANILOW MAGIC	Barry Manilow (Arista)
12	13	GIVE ME THE NIGHT	George Benson (Warner Bros.)
-	14	PARIS	Supertramp (A&M)
7	15	FLESH AND BLOOD	Roxy Music (Polydor)
6	16	TELEKON	Gary Numan (Beggars Banquet)
7	17	THE ABSOLUTE GAME	Skids (Virgin)
20	18	GOLD	Three Degrees (Ariola)
13	19	HANX	Stiff Little Fingers (Chrysalis)
14	20	LIVE CRASH COURSE	UK Subs (Gem)
22	21	SKY 2	Sky (Ariola)
28	22	FRESH FRUIT FOR ROTTING VEGETABLES	Dead Kennedys (Cherry Red)
17	23	OZZY OSBOURNE'S BLIZZARD OF OZ	Ozzy Osbourne (Jet)
-	24	A TOUCH OF LOVE	Gladys Knight & the Pips (K-Tel)
23	25	OFF THE WALL	Michael Jackson (Epic)
-	26	MIDNITE DYNAMOS	Matchbox (Magnet)
-	27	BACK IN BLACK	AC/DC (Atlantic)
27	28	THE LOVE ALBUM	Various Artists (K-Tel)
16	29	THE GAME	Queen (EMI)
24	30	I AM WOMAN	Various Artists (Polydor)

With *Signing Off* (the title being a wry allusion to their own band name), UB40 joined the elite to have scored a chart-topper with their first album release, and also gave a rare Number 1 album to a small indie label - in this case, the West Midland-based Graduate Records. Kate Bush, meanwhile, made it two Number 1's from her first three releases, and Gary Numan three chart-toppers in a row. The Shadows' title appeared to note their label move from EMI to Polydor.

October – November 1980

18 October 1980

last week	this week	Album	Artist (Label)
4	1	ZENYATTA MONDATTA	Police (A&M)
8	2	ABSOLUTELY	Madness (Stiff)
1	3	SCARY MONSTERS AND SUPER CREEPS	David Bowie (RCA)
2	4	NEVER FOR EVER	Kate Bush (EMI)
-	5	GUILTY	Barbra Streisand (CBS)
3	6	MOUNTING EXCITEMENT	Various Artists (K-Tel)
5	7	THE VERY BEST OF DON McLEAN	Don McLean (United Artists)
12	8	MANILOW MAGIC	Barry Manilow (Arista)
10	9	MORE SPECIALS	Specials (2-Tone)
11	10	BREAKING GLASS	Hazel O'Connor (A&M)
14	11	PARIS	Supertramp (A&M)
8	12	SIGNING OFF	UB40 (Graduate)
-	13	TRIUMPH	Jacksons (Epic)
26	14	MIDNITE DYNAMOS	Matchbox (Magnet)
6	15	NOW WE MAY BEGIN	Randy Crawford (Warner Bros.)
13	16	GIVE ME THE NIGHT	George Benson (Warner Bros.)
16	17	TELEKON	Gary Numan (Beggars Banquet)
15	18	FLESH AND BLOOD	Roxy Music (Polydor)
7	19	I'M NO HERO	Cliff Richard (EMI)
-	20	DIANA	Diana Ross (Motown)
30	21	I AM WOMAN	Various Artists (Polydor)
18	22	GOLD	Three Degrees (Ariola)
24	23	A TOUCH OF LOVE	Gladys Knight & the Pips (K-Tel)
-	24	PAULINE MURRAY & THE INVISIBLE GIRLS	Pauline Murray & the Invisible Girls (Elusive)
21	25	SKY 2	Sky (Ariola)
27	26	BACK IN BLACK	AC/DC (Atlantic)
17	27	THE ABSOLUTE GAME	Skids (Virgin)
28	28	THE LOVE ALBUM	Various Artists (K-Tel)
29	29	THE GAME	Queen (EMI)
-	30	BLACK SEA	XTC (Virgin)

25 October 1980

last week	this week	Album	Artist (Label)
1	1	ZENYATTA MONDATTA	Police (A&M)
5	2	GUILTY	Barbra Streisand (CBS)
2	3	ABSOLUTELY	Madness (Stiff)
6	4	MOUNTING EXCITEMENT	Various Artists (K-Tel)
4	5	NEVER FOR EVER	Kate Bush (EMI)
3	6	SCARY MONSTERS AND SUPER CREEPS	David Bowie (RCA)
11	7	PARIS	Supertramp (A&M)
9	8	MORE SPECIALS	Specials (2-Tone)
8	9	MANILOW MAGIC	Barry Manilow (Arista)
-	10	CHINATOWN	Thin Lizzy (Vertigo)
7	11	THE VERY BEST OF DON McLEAN	Don McLean (United Artists)
10	12	BREAKING GLASS	Hazel O'Connor (A&M)
13	13	TRIUMPH	Jacksons (Epic)
12	14	SIGNING OFF	UB40 (Graduate)
23	15	A TOUCH OF LOVE	Gladys Knight & the Pips (K-Tel)
18	16	FLESH AND BLOOD	Roxy Music (Polydor)
28	17	THE LOVE ALBUM	Various Artists (K-Tel)
16	18	GIVE ME THE NIGHT	George Benson (Warner Bros.)
22	19	GOLD	Three Degrees (Ariola)
21	20	I AM WOMAN	Various Artists (Polydor)
15	21	NOW WE MAY BEGIN	Randy Crawford (Warner Bros.)
14	22	MIDNITE DYNAMOS	Matchbox (Magnet)
-	23	REGATTA DE BLANC	Police (A&M)
19	24	I'M NO HERO	Cliff Richard (EMI)
17	25	TELEKON	Gary Numan (Beggars Banquet)
-	26	MONSTERS OF ROCK	Various Artists (Polydor)
24	27	PAULINE MURRAY & THE INVISIBLE GIRLS	Pauline Murray & the Invisible Girls (Elusive)
-	28	BEAT CRAZY	Joe Jackson (A&M)
-	29	CONTRACTUAL OBLIGATION ALBUM	Monty Python's Flying Circus (Charisma)
27	30	THE ABSOLUTE GAME	Skids (Virgin)

1 November 1980

last week	this week	Album	Artist (Label)
1	1	ZENYATTA MONDATTA	Police (A&M)
2	2	GUILTY	Barbra Streisand (CBS)
-	3	JUST SUPPOSIN'	Status Quo (Vertigo)
-	4	THE RIVER	Bruce Springsteen (CBS)
5	5	SCARY MONSTERS AND SUPER CREEPS	David Bowie (RCA)
3	6	ABSOLUTELY	Madness (Stiff)
29	7	CONTRACTUAL OBLIGATION ALBUM	Monty Python's Flying Circus (Charisma)
17	8	THE LOVE ALBUM	Various Artists (K-Tel)
7	9	PARIS	Supertramp (A&M)
4	10	MOUNTING EXCITEMENT	Various Artists (K-Tel)
5	11	NEVER FOR EVER	Kate Bush (EMI)
20	12	I AM WOMAN	Various Artists (Polydor)
13	13	TRIUMPH	Jacksons (Epic)
11	14	THE VERY BEST OF DON McLEAN	Don McLean (United Artists)
10	15	CHINATOWN	Thin Lizzy (Vertigo)
18	16	GIVE ME THE NIGHT	George Benson (Warner Bros.)
9	17	MANILOW MAGIC	Barry Manilow (Arista)
12	18	BREAKING GLASS	Hazel O'Connor (A&M)
-	19	MAKIN' MOVIES	Dire Straits (Vertigo)
24	20	I'M NO HERO	Cliff Richard (EMI)
19	21	GOLD	Three Degrees (Ariola)
-	22	MY GENERATION	Who (Virgin)
14	23	SIGNING OFF	UB40 (Graduate)
-	24	KILLING JOKE	Killing Joke (Polydor)
23	25	REGATTA DE BLANC	Police (A&M)
16	26	FLESH AND BLOOD	Roxy Music (Polydor)
-	27	FULL HOUSE	Dooleys (GTO)
22	28	MIDNITE DYNAMOS	Matchbox (Magnet)
21	29	NOW WE MAY BEGIN	Randy Crawford (Warner Bros.)
-	30	FACES	Earth, Wind & Fire (CBS)

8 November 1980

last week	this week	Album	Artist (Label)
1	1	ZENYATTA MONDATTA	Police (A&M)
2	2	GUILTY	Barbra Streisand (CBS)
-	3	ORGANISATION	Orchestral Manoeuvres in the Dark (Dindisc)
3	4	JUST SUPPOSIN'	Status Quo (Vertigo)
8	5	THE LOVE ALBUM	Various Artists (K-Tel)
4	6	THE RIVER	Bruce Springsteen (CBS)
21	7	GOLD	Three Degrees (Ariola)
30	8	FACES	Earth, Wind & Fire (CBS)
17	9	MANILOW MAGIC	Barry Manilow (Arista)
-	10	HOTTER THAN JULY	Stevie Wonder (Motown)
11	11	NEVER FOR EVER	Kate Bush (EMI)
13	12	TRIUMPH	Jacksons (Epic)
7	13	CONTRACTUAL OBLIGATION ALBUM	Monty Python's Flying Circus (Charisma)
6	14	ABSOLUTELY	Madness (Stiff)
5	15	SCARY MONSTERS AND SUPER CREEPS	David Bowie (RCA)
-	16	REMAIN IN LIGHT	Talking Heads (Sire)
12	17	I AM WOMAN	Various Artists (Polydor)
19	18	MAKIN' MOVIES	Dire Straits (Vertigo)
17	19	BREAKING GLASS	Hazel O'Connor (A&M)
-	20	THE VERY BEST OF ELTON JOHN	Elton John (K-Tel)
16	21	GIVE ME THE NIGHT	George Benson (Warner Bros.)
-	22	A TOUCH OF LOVE	Gladys Knight & the Pips (K-Tel)
15	23	CHINATOWN	Thin Lizzy (Vertigo)
25	24	REGATTA DE BLANC	Police (A&M)
-	25	LITTLE MISS DYNAMITE	Brenda Lee (Warwick)
9	26	PARIS	Supertramp (A&M)
-	27	INHERIT THE WIND	Wilton Felder (MCA)
14	28	THE VERY BEST OF DON McLEAN	Don McLean (United Artists)
22	29	MY GENERATION	Who (Virgin)
10	30	MOUNTING EXCITEMENT	Various Artists (K-Tel)

The Police dominated album sales for a full month with their third release (and second chart-topper) *Zenyatta Mondatta*, buoyed by the simultaneous Number 1 success of the extracted single *Don't Stand So Close To Me*. This consistent run denied chart-topping success both to Madness' second album *Absolutely*, and to Barbra Streisand with her Bee Gees-produced set *Guilty*, though the latter was to make the runner-up slot virtually its own for more than two months, up until the end of the year.

November – December 1980

15 November 1980

last	this		
10	1	HOTTER THAN JULY	Stevie Wonder (Motown)
2	2	GUILTY	Barbra Streisand (CBS)
1	3	ZENYATTA MONDATTA	Police (A&M)
7	4	GOLD Three Degrees (Ariola)	
-	5	ACE OF SPADES	Motorhead (Bronze)
3	6	ORGANISATION	Orchestral Manoeuvres in the Dark (Dindisc)
8	7	FACES	Earth, Wind & Fire (CBS)
6	8	THE RIVER	Bruce Springsteen (CBS)
-	9	LIVE IN THE HEART OF THE CITY	Whitesnake (United Artists)
-	10	LEVITATION	Hawkwind (Bronze)
9	11	MANILOW MAGIC	Barry Manilow (Arista)
4	12	JUST SUPPOSIN'	Status Quo (Vertigo)
15	13	SCARY MONSTERS AND SUPER CREEPS	David Bowie (RCA)
18	14	MAKIN' MOVIES	Dire Straits (Vertigo)
11	15	NEVER FOR EVER	Kate Bush (EMI)
12	16	TRIUMPH	Jacksons (Epic)
5	17	THE LOVE ALBUM	Various Artists (K-Tel)
-	18	NOT THE 9 O'CLOCK NEWS	TV Cast (BBC)
14	19	ABSOLUTELY	Madness (Stiff)
16	20	REMAIN IN LIGHT	Talking Heads (Sire)
21	21	GIVE ME THE NIGHT	George Benson (Warner Bros.)
-	22	MAKING WAVES	Nolans (Epic)
-	22	SIGNING OFF	UB40 (Graduate)
-	24	MIDNITE DYNAMOS	Matchbox (Magnet)
20	25	THE VERY BEST OF ELTON JOHN	Elton John (K-Tel)
13	26	CONTRACTUAL OBLIGATION ALBUM	Monty Python's Flying Circus (Charisma)
26	27	PARIS	Supertramp (A&M)
19	28	BREAKING GLASS	Hazel O'Connor (A&M)
-	29	MORE SPECIALS	Specials (2-Tone)
30	29	MOUNTING EXCITEMENT	Various Artists (K-Tel)

22 November 1980

1	1	HOTTER THAN JULY	Stevie Wonder (Motown)
2	2	GUILTY	Barbra Streisand (CBS)
3	3	ZENYATTA MONDATTA	Police (A&M)
18	4	NOT THE 9 O'CLOCK NEWS	TV Cast (BBC)
4	5	GOLD Three Degrees (Ariola)	
5	6	ACE OF SPADES	Motorhead (Bronze)
-	7	KINGS OF THE WILD FRONTIER	Adam & the Ants (CBS)
6	8	ORGANISATION	Orchestral Manoeuvres in the Dark (Dindisc)
11	9	MANILOW MAGIC	Barry Manilow (Arista)
9	10	LIVE IN THE HEART OF THE CITY	Whitesnake (United Artists)
12	11	JUST SUPPOSIN'	Status Quo (Vertigo)
-	12	SUPER TROUPER	Abba (Epic)
22	13	MAKING WAVES	Nolans (Epic)
13	14	SCARY MONSTERS AND SUPER CREEPS	David Bowie (RCA)
-	15	LITTLE MISS DYNAMITE	Brenda Lee (Warwick)
8	16	THE RIVER	Bruce Springsteen (CBS)
15	17	NEVER FOR EVER	Kate Bush (EMI)
7	18	FACES	Earth, Wind & Fire (CBS)
-	19	COUNTRY LEGENDS	Various Artists (Ronco)
-	20	QE2	Mike Oldfield (Virgin)
17	21	THE LOVE ALBUM	Various Artists (K-Tel)
25	22	THE VERY BEST OF ELTON JOHN	Elton John (K-Tel)
10	23	LEVITATION	Hawkwind (Bronze)
16	24	TRIUMPH	Jacksons (Epic)
-	25	THE TURN OF A FRIENDLY CARD	Alan Parsons Project (Arista)
19	26	ABSOLUTELY	Madness (Stiff)
-	27	STRONG ARM OF THE LAW	Saxon (Carrere)
-	28	RADIOACTIVE	Various Artists (Ronco)
14	29	MAKIN' MOVIES	Dire Straits (Vertigo)
28	30	BREAKING GLASS	Hazel O'Connor (A&M)

29 November 1980

12	1	SUPER TROUPER	Abba (Epic)
2	2	GUILTY	Barbra Streisand (CBS)
-	3	FOOLISH BEHAVIOUR	Rod Stewart (Riva)
3	4	ZENYATTA MONDATTA	Police (A&M)
1	5	HOTTER THAN JULY	Stevie Wonder (Motown)
15	6	LITTLE MISS DYNAMITE	Brenda Lee (Warwick)
4	7	NOT THE 9 O'CLOCK NEWS	TV Cast (BBC)
-	8	THE JAZZ SINGER	Neil Diamond (Capitol)
-	9	DOUBLE FANTASY	John Lennon & Yoko Ono (Warner Bros./Geffen)
8	10	ORGANISATION	Orchestral Manoeuvres in the Dark (Dindisc)
-	11	AUTOAMERICAN	Blondie (Chrysalis)
13	12	MAKING WAVES	Nolans (Epic)
28	13	RADIOACTIVE	Various Artists (Ronco)
7	14	KINGS OF THE WILD FRONTIER	Adam & the Ants (CBS)
26	15	ABSOLUTELY	Madness (Stiff)
-	16	EAGLES LIVE	Eagles (Asylum)
9	17	MANILOW MAGIC	Barry Manilow (Arista)
19	18	COUNTRY LEGENDS	Various Artists (Ronco)
16	19	THE RIVER	Bruce Springsteen (CBS)
5	20	GOLD Three Degrees (Ariola)	
27	21	STRONG ARM OF THE LAW	Saxon (Carrere)
21	22	THE LOVE ALBUM	Various Artists (K-Tel)
6	23	ACE OF SPADES	Motorhead (Bronze)
14	24	SCARY MONSTERS AND SUPER CREEPS	David Bowie (RCA)
10	25	LIVE IN THE HEART OF THE CITY	Whitesnake (United Artists)
22	26	THE VERY BEST OF ELTON JOHN	Elton John (K-Tel)
20	27	QE2	Mike Oldfield (Virgin)
-	28	MASTERWORKS	Various Artists (K-Tel)
11	29	JUST SUPPOSIN'	Status Quo (Vertigo)
-	30	INSPIRATIONS	Elvis Presley (K-Tel)

6 December 1980

1	1	SUPER TROUPER	Abba (Epic)
11	2	AUTOAMERICAN	Blondie (Chrysalis)
2	3	GUILTY	Barbra Streisand (CBS)
3	4	FOOLISH BEHAVIOUR	Rod Stewart (Riva)
-	5	BARRY	Barry Manilow (Arista)
4	6	ZENYATTA MONDATTA	Police (A&M)
-	7	CHART EXPLOSION	Various Artists (K-Tel)
9	8	DOUBLE FANTASY	John Lennon & Yoko Ono (Warner Bros./Geffen)
30	9	INSPIRATIONS	Elvis Presley (K-Tel)
7	10	NOT THE 9 O'CLOCK NEWS	Cast (BBC)
14	11	KINGS OF THE WILD FRONTIER	Adam & the Ants (CBS)
8	12	THE JAZZ SINGER	Neil Diamond (Capitol)
19	13	THE RIVER	Bruce Springsteen (CBS)
18	14	COUNTRY LEGENDS	Various Artists (Ronco)
6	15	LITTLE MISS DYNAMITE	Brenda Lee (Warwick)
-	16	LOONIE TUNES	Bad Manners (Magnet)
24	17	SCARY MONSTERS AND SUPER CREEPS	David Bowie (RCA)
22	18	THE LOVE ALBUM	Various Artists (K-Tel)
23	19	ACE OF SPADES	Motorhead (Bronze)
-	20	FLESH AND BLOOD	Roxy Music (Polydor)
10	20	ORGANISATION	Orchestral Manoeuvres in the Dark (Dindisc)
13	22	RADIOACTIVE	Various Artists (Ronco)
5	23	HOTTER THAN JULY	Stevie Wonder (Motown)
16	24	EAGLES LIVE	Eagles (Asylum)
12	25	MAKING WAVES	Nolans (Epic)
-	25	THE BLACK ALBUM	Damned (Chiswick)
15	27	ABSOLUTELY	Madness (Stiff)
20	28	GOLD Three Degrees (Ariola)	
-	29	STEPHANIE MILLS	Stephanie Mills (RCA)
-	30	AXE ATTACK	Various Artists (K-Tel)

In a familiar pattern, many of the big name acts started releasing albums as the lucrative year-end sales period drew near, and inevitably there was not room for all of them at the top of the chart, though Stevie Wonder leapt in early to give Motown a now not-too-frequent chart-topper with his long-awaited *Hotter Than July*. The return of Brenda Lee to the album chart after more 17 years was, inevitably, down to Warwick TV-marketing a compilation of her old hit singles.

December 1980

Abba once again hugely outsold the competition at Christmas, as in 1979 – this time with a set of new material, *Super Trouper,* rather than a hits collection. Almost inevitably, the title song was simultaneously a Number 1 single.

January 1981

3 January 1981

last week	this week	Title / Artist (Label)
1	1	SUPER TROUPER — Abba (Epic)
5	2	DOUBLE FANTASY — John Lennon & Yoko Ono (Geffen)
7	3	DR HOOK'S GREATEST HITS — Dr Hook (Capitol)
13	4	BARRY — Barry Manilow (Arista)
2	5	GUILTY — Barbra Streisand (CBS)
9	6	CHART EXPLOSION — Various Artists (K-Tel)
-	6	FLASH GORDON — Queen (EMI)
6	8	INSPIRATIONS — Elvis Presley (K-Tel)
10	8	NOT THE NINE O'CLOCK NEWS — TV Cast (BBC)
8	10	ZENYATTA MONDATTA — Police (A&M)
3	11	AUTOAMERICAN — Blondie (Chrysalis)
27	12	20 GOLDEN GREATS OF KEN DODD — Ken Dodd (Warwick)
12	13	THE JAZZ SINGER — Neil Diamond (Capitol)
14	14	MANILOW MAGIC — Barry Manilow (Arista)
20	15	SING 20 NUMBER ONE HITS — Brotherhood Of Man (Warwick)
21	16	ABSOLUTELY — Madness (Stiff)
3	17	SOUND AFFECTS — Jam (Polydor)
11	18	CLASSICS FOR DREAMING — James Last (Polydor)
17	19	FOOLISH BEHAVIOUR — Rod Stewart (Riva)
26	20	ACE OF SPADES — Motorhead (Bronze)
-	21	BEATLES BALLADS — Beatles (Parlophone)
16	22	KINGS OF THE WILD FRONTIER — Adam & the Ants (CBS)
24	23	HOTTER THAN JULY — Stevie Wonder (Motown)
-	24	AXE ATTACK — Various Artists (K-Tel)
-	25	BRIGHT LIGHTS — Showaddywaddy (Arista)
22	26	SIGNING OFF — UB40 (Graduate)
25	27	SANDINISTA — Clash (CBS)
-	28	SCARY MONSTERS AND SUPER CREEPS — David Bowie (RCA)
-	29	SLADE SMASHES — Slade (Polydor)
15	30	BEST OF BARRY MANILOW — Barry Manilow (Arista)

10 January 1981

last week	this week	Title / Artist (Label)
2	1	DOUBLE FANTASY — John Lennon & Yoko Ono (Geffen)
1	2	SUPER TROUPER — Abba (Epic)
8	3	NOT THE NINE O'CLOCK NEWS — TV Cast (BBC)
3	4	DR HOOK'S GREATEST HITS — Dr Hook (Capitol)
11	5	AUTOAMERICAN — Blondie (Chrysalis)
22	6	KINGS OF THE WILD FRONTIER — Adam & the Ants (CBS)
10	7	ZENYATTA MONDATTA — Police (A&M)
4	8	BARRY — Barry Manilow (Arista)
5	9	GUILTY — Barbra Streisand (CBS)
16	10	ABSOLUTELY — Madness (Stiff)
6	11	FLASH GORDON — Queen (EMI)
14	12	MANILOW MAGIC — Barry Manilow (Arista)
13	13	THE JAZZ SINGER — Neil Diamond (Capitol)
12	14	20 GOLDEN GREATS OF KEN DODD — Ken Dodd (Warwick)
18	15	CLASSICS FOR DREAMING — James Last (Polydor)
19	16	FOOLISH BEHAVIOUR — Rod Stewart (Riva)
6	17	CHART EXPLOSION — Various Artists (K-Tel)
8	18	INSPIRATIONS — Elvis Presley (K-Tel)
28	19	SCARY MONSTERS AND SUPER CREEPS — David Bowie (RCA)
27	20	SANDINISTA — Clash (CBS)
26	21	SIGNING OFF — UB40 (Graduate)
29	22	SLADE SMASHES — Slade (Polydor)
23	23	HOTTER THAN JULY — Stevie Wonder (Motown)
24	24	AXE ATTACK — Various Artists (K-Tel)
30	25	BEST OF BARRY MANILOW — Barry Manilow (Arista)
-	26	YESSHOWS — Yes (Atlantic)
-	27	GAUCHO — Steely Dan (MCA)
-	28	NIGHT LIFE — Various Artists (K-Tel)
17	29	SOUND AFFECTS — Jam (Polydor)
25	30	BRIGHT LIGHTS — Showaddywaddy (Arista)

17 January 1981

last week	this week	Title / Artist (Label)
1	1	SUPER TROUPER — Abba (Epic)
4	2	DR HOOK'S GREATEST HITS — Dr Hook (Capitol)
1	3	DOUBLE FANTASY — John Lennon & Yoko Ono (Geffen)
-	4	IMAGINE — John Lennon (Apple)
12	5	MANILOW MAGIC — Barry Manilow (Arista)
7	6	ZENYATTA MONDATTA — Police (A&M)
11	7	FLASH GORDON — Queen (EMI)
8	8	KINGS OF THE WILD FRONTIER — Adam & the Ants (CBS)
3	9	NOT THE NINE O'CLOCK NEWS — TV Cast (BBC)
8	10	BARRY — Barry Manilow (Arista)
9	11	GUILTY — Barbra Streisand (CBS)
14	12	20 GOLDEN GREATS OF KEN DODD — Ken Dodd (Warwick)
10	13	ABSOLUTELY — Madness (Stiff)
23	14	HOTTER THAN JULY — Stevie Wonder (Motown)
-	15	THE VERY BEST OF DAVID BOWIE — David Bowie (K-Tel)
5	16	AUTOAMERICAN — Blondie (Chrysalis)
16	17	FOOLISH BEHAVIOUR — Rod Stewart (Riva)
15	18	CLASSICS FOR DREAMING — James Last (Polydor)
18	19	INSPIRATIONS — Elvis Presley (K-Tel)
17	20	CHART EXPLOSION — Various Artists (K-Tel)
29	21	SOUND AFFECTS — Jam (Polydor)
13	22	THE JAZZ SINGER — Neil Diamond (Capitol)
26	23	YESSHOWS — Yes (Atlantic)
19	24	SCARY MONSTERS AND SUPER CREEPS — David Bowie (RCA)
-	25	SHAVED FISH — John Lennon (Apple)
21	26	SIGNING OFF — UB40 (Graduate)
25	27	BEST OF BARRY MANILOW — Barry Manilow (Arista)
22	28	SLADE SMASHES — Slade (Polydor)
-	29	MAKIN' MOVIES — Dire Straits (Vertigo)
20	30	SANDINISTA — Clash (CBS)

24 January 1981

last week	this week	Title / Artist (Label)
3	1	DOUBLE FANTASY — John Lennon & Yoko Ono (Geffen)
15	2	THE VERY BEST OF DAVID BOWIE — David Bowie (K-Tel)
1	3	SUPER TROUPER — Abba (Epic)
2	4	DR HOOK'S GREATEST HITS — Dr Hook (Capitol)
8	5	KINGS OF THE WILD FRONTIER — Adam & the Ants (CBS)
6	6	ZENYATTA MONDATTA — Police (A&M)
11	7	GUILTY — Barbra Streisand (CBS)
9	8	NOT THE NINE O'CLOCK NEWS — TV Cast (BBC)
7	9	FLASH GORDON — Queen (EMI)
5	9	MANILOW MAGIC — Barry Manilow (Arista)
4	11	IMAGINE — John Lennon (Apple)
13	12	ABSOLUTELY — Madness (Stiff)
16	13	AUTOAMERICAN — Blondie (Chrysalis)
10	14	BARRY — Barry Manilow (Arista)
14	15	HOTTER THAN JULY — Stevie Wonder (Motown)
22	16	THE JAZZ SINGER — Neil Diamond (Capitol)
26	17	SIGNING OFF — UB40 (Graduate)
12	18	20 GOLDEN GREATS OF KEN DODD — Ken Dodd (Warwick)
-	19	SKY 2 — Sky (Ariola)
-	20	ARC OF A DIVER — Steve Winwood (Island)
29	21	MAKIN' MOVIES — Dire Straits (Vertigo)
25	22	SHAVED FISH — John Lennon (Apple)
17	23	FOOLISH BEHAVIOUR — Rod Stewart (Riva)
23	24	YESSHOWS — Yes (Atlantic)
-	25	NIGHT LIFE — Various Artists (K-Tel)
-	26	MAKING WAVES — Nolans (Epic)
18	27	CLASSICS FOR DREAMING — James Last (Polydor)
19	28	INSPIRATIONS — Elvis Presley (K-Tel)
30	29	SANDINISTA — Clash (CBS)
-	30	DIRK WEARS WHITE SOX — Adam & the Ants (Do It)

The shocking assassination of John Lennon pushed his and Yoko's "comeback" *Double Fantasy* album, which had not exhibited chart-topping potential during its first weeks on sale, to No.1 in the New Year, while the Lennon tragedy was also responsible for returning his *Imagine* album (again, alongside a chart-topping single - the title track) and the *Shaved Fish* compilation of his earlier hits, to the chart. *Not The Nine O'Clock News* achieved the extraordinary feat for a comedy album of a Top 3 place.

January – February 1981

31 January 1981

last week	this week	
5	1	KINGS OF THE WILD FRONTIER — Adam & the Ants (CBS)
4	2	DR HOOK'S GREATEST HITS — Dr Hook (Capitol)
2	3	THE VERY BEST OF DAVID BOWIE — David Bowie (K-Tel)
1	4	DOUBLE FANTASY — John Lennon & Yoko Ono (Geffen)
3	5	SUPER TROUPER — Abba (Epic)
11	6	IMAGINE — John Lennon (Apple)
7	7	GUILTY — Barbra Streisand (CBS)
9	8	MANILOW MAGIC — Barry Manilow (Arista)
9	9	FLASH GORDON — Queen (EMI)
14	10	BARRY — Barry Manilow (Arista)
-	11	MONDO BONGO — Boomtown Rats (Mercury)
21	12	MAKIN' MOVIES — Dire Straits (Vertigo)
22	13	SHAVED FISH — John Lennon (Apple)
6	14	ZENYATTA MONDATTA — Police (A&M)
15	15	HOTTER THAN JULY — Stevie Wonder (Motown)
20	16	ARC OF A DIVER — Steve Winwood (Island)
8	17	NOT THE NINE O'CLOCK NEWS — TV Cast (BBC)
-	18	PARADISE THEATER — Styx (A&M)
12	19	ABSOLUTELY — Madness (Stiff)
-	20	THE WILD, THE WILLING & THE INNOCENT — UFO (Chrysalis)
17	21	SIGNING OFF — UB40 (Graduate)
13	22	AUTOAMERICAN — Blondie (Chrysalis)
29	23	SANDINISTA — Clash (CBS)
24	24	YESSHOWS — Yes (Atlantic)
19	25	SKY 2 — Sky (Ariola)
-	26	THE RIVER — Bruce Springsteen (CBS)
-	27	SCARY MONSTERS AND SUPER CREEPS — David Bowie (RCA)
26	28	MAKING WAVES — Nolans (Epic)
27	29	CLASSICS FOR DREAMING — James Last (Polydor)
16	30	THE JAZZ SINGER — Neil Diamond (Capitol)

7 February 1981

this week	
1	KINGS OF THE WILD FRONTIER — Adam & the Ants (CBS)
2	THE VERY BEST OF DAVID BOWIE — David Bowie (K-Tel)
3	MANILOW MAGIC — Barry Manilow (Arista)
4	DOUBLE FANTASY — John Lennon & Yoko Ono (Geffen)
5	IMAGINE — John Lennon (Apple)
6	BARRY — Barry Manilow (Arista)
7	DR HOOK'S GREATEST HITS — Dr Hook (Capitol)
8	GUILTY — Barbra Streisand (CBS)
9	MONDO BONGO — Boomtown Rats (Mercury)
10	MAKIN' MOVIES — Dire Straits (Vertigo)
11	PARADISE THEATER — Styx (A&M)
12	SIGNING OFF — UB40 (Graduate)
13	HOTTER THAN JULY — Stevie Wonder (Motown)
13	TRUST — Elvis Costello & the Attractions (F-Beat)
15	TAKE MY TIME — Sheena Easton (EMI)
16	VIENNA — Ultravox (Chrysalis)
17	ABSOLUTELY — Madness (Stiff)
18	THE JAZZ SINGER — Neil Diamond (Capitol)
19	SHAVED FISH — John Lennon (Apple)
19	SUPER TROUPER — Abba (Epic)
21	ARC OF A DIVER — Steve Winwood (Island)
22	FLASH GORDON — Queen (EMI)
23	NOT THE NINE O'CLOCK NEWS — TV Cast (BBC)
23	VISAGE — Visage (Polydor)
25	AUTOAMERICAN — Blondie (Chrysalis)
26	LADY — Kenny Rogers (Liberty)
27	SCARY MONSTERS AND SUPER CREEPS — David Bowie (RCA)
28	GAP BAND 3 — Gap Band (Mercury)
29	BACK IN BLACK — AC/DC (Atlantic)
29	LOONEE TUNES — Bad Manners (Magnet)

14 February 1981

this week	
1	DOUBLE FANTASY — John Lennon & Yoko Ono (Geffen)
2	KINGS OF THE WILD FRONTIER — Adam & the Ants (CBS)
3	THE VERY BEST OF DAVID BOWIE — David Bowie (K-Tel)
4	MANILOW MAGIC — Barry Manilow (Arista)
5	IMAGINE — John Lennon (Apple)
6	THE JAZZ SINGER — Neil Diamond (Capitol)
7	MAKIN' MOVIES — Dire Straits (Vertigo)
8	VIENNA — Ultravox (Chrysalis)
9	MONDO BONGO — Boomtown Rats (Mercury)
10	DR HOOK'S GREATEST HITS — Dr Hook (Capitol)
11	HOTTER THAN JULY — Stevie Wonder (Motown)
12	BARRY — Barry Manilow (Arista)
13	GUILTY — Barbra Streisand (CBS)
13	SHAVED FISH — John Lennon (Apple)
15	VISAGE — Visage (Polydor)
16	ARC OF A DIVER — Steve Winwood (Island)
17	TAKE MY TIME — Sheena Easton (EMI)
18	PARADISE THEATER — Styx (A&M)
19	SUPER TROUPER — Abba (Epic)
20	SIGNING OFF — UB40 (Graduate)
21	FLASH GORDON — Queen (EMI)
22	SOUTHERN FREEEZ — Freeez (Beggars Banquet)
23	AUTOAMERICAN — Blondie (Chrysalis)
24	ABSOLUTELY — Madness (Stiff)
25	TRUST — Elvis Costello & the Attractions (F-Beat)
26	DIRK WEARS WHITE SOX — Adam & the Ants (Do It)
27	SOUND AFFECTS — Jam (Polydor)
28	THE RIVER — Bruce Springsteen (CBS)
29	NIGHT LIFE — Various Artists (K-Tel)
30	SCARY MONSTERS AND SUPER CREEPS — David Bowie (RCA)

21 February 1981

last week	this week	
2	1	KINGS OF THE WILD FRONTIER — Adam & the Ants (CBS)
8	2	VIENNA — Ultravox (Chrysalis)
1	3	DOUBLE FANTASY — John Lennon & Yoko Ono (Geffen)
3	4	THE VERY BEST OF DAVID BOWIE — David Bowie (K-Tel)
7	5	MAKIN' MOVIES — Dire Straits (Vertigo)
5	6	IMAGINE — John Lennon (Apple)
13	7	SHAVED FISH — John Lennon (Apple)
-	8	DANCE CRAZE — Soundtrack (2-Tone)
6	9	THE JAZZ SINGER — Neil Diamond (Capitol)
4	10	MANILOW MAGIC — Barry Manilow (Arista)
-	11	FACE VALUE — Phil Collins (Virgin)
15	12	VISAGE — Visage (Polydor)
13	13	GUILTY — Barbra Streisand (CBS)
12	14	BARRY — Barry Manilow (Arista)
9	15	MONDO BONGO — Boomtown Rats (Mercury)
17	16	TAKE MY TIME — Sheena Easton (EMI)
10	17	DR HOOK'S GREATEST HITS — Dr Hook (Capitol)
24	18	ABSOLUTELY — Madness (Stiff)
16	19	ARC OF A DIVER — Steve Winwood (Island)
11	20	HOTTER THAN JULY — Stevie Wonder (Motown)
26	21	DIRK WEARS WHITE SOX — Adam & the Ants (Do It)
-	22	MOVING PICTURES — Rush (Mercury)
23	23	AUTOAMERICAN — Blondie (Chrysalis)
18	24	PARADISE THEATER — Styx (A&M)
20	25	SIGNING OFF — UB40 (Graduate)
18	26	SUPER TROUPER — Abba (Epic)
22	27	SOUTHERN FREEEZ — Freeez (Beggars Banquet)
-	28	REMAIN IN LIGHT — Talking Heads (Sire)
-	29	CANDLES — Heatwave (GTO)
25	30	TRUST — Elvis Costello & the Attractions (F-Beat)

Adam & The Ants' *King Of The Wild Frontier* had been hanging around the upper part of the chart for over two months when it was vaulted to the top by an explosion of what the press inevitably dubbd "Antmania", as the group suddenly emerged as the newest teen fad and put two singles, *Antmusic* and *Young Parisians*, simultaneously into the Top 10. The normally MOR/pop-orientated K-Tel, meanwhile, broke successful new ground by licensing a package of familiar David Bowie material from RCA.

February – March 1981

28 February 1981

last	this		
3	1	DOUBLE FANTASY	John Lennon & Yoko Ono (Geffen)
11	2	FACE VALUE	Phil Collins (Virgin)
1	3	KINGS OF THE WILD FRONTIER	Adam & the Ants (CBS)
2	4	VIENNA	Ultravox (Chrysalis)
-	5	DIFFICULT TO CURE	Rainbow (Polydor)
9	6	THE JAZZ SINGER	Neil Diamond (Capitol)
22	7	MOVING PICTURES	Rush (Mercury)
4	8	THE VERY BEST OF DAVID BOWIE	David Bowie (K-Tel)
8	9	DANCE CRAZE	Soundtrack (2-Tone)
10	10	MANILOW MAGIC	Barry Manilow (Arista)
5	11	MAKIN' MOVIES	Dire Straits (Vertigo)
17	12	DR HOOK'S GREATEST HITS	Dr Hook (Capitol)
-	13	THEMENINBLACK	Stranglers (Liberty)
14	14	BARRY	Barry Manilow (Arista)
7	15	SHAVED FISH	John Lennon (Apple)
27	16	SOUTHERN FREEEZ	Freeez (Beggars Banquet)
26	17	SUPER TROUPER	Abba (Epic)
6	18	IMAGINE	John Lennon (Apple)
12	18	VISAGE	Visage (Polydor)
19	20	ARC OF A DIVER	Steve Winwood (Island)
15	21	MONDO BONGO	Boomtown Rats (Mercury)
20	22	HOTTER THAN JULY	Stevie Wonder (Motown)
18	23	ABSOLUTELY	Madness (Stiff)
23	24	AUTOAMERICAN	Blondie (Chrysalis)
-	25	FAWLTY TOWERS VOLUME 2	TV Cast (BBC)
25	26	SIGNING OFF	UB40 (Graduate)
13	27	GUILTY	Barbra Streisand (CBS)
29	28	CANDLES	Heatwave (GTO)
28	29	REMAIN IN LIGHT	Talking Heads (Sire)
30	30	TRUST	Elvis Costello & the Attractions (F-Beat)

7 March 1981

2	1	FACE VALUE	Phil Collins (Virgin)
3	2	KINGS OF THE WILD FRONTIER	Adam & the Ants (CBS)
4	3	VIENNA	Ultravox (Chrysalis)
5	4	DIFFICULT TO CURE	Rainbow (Polydor)
-	5	STRAY CATS	Stray Cats (Arista)
1	6	DOUBLE FANTASY	John Lennon & Yoko Ono (Geffen)
6	7	THE JAZZ SINGER	Neil Diamond (Capitol)
9	8	DANCE CRAZE	Soundtrack (2-Tone)
11	9	MAKIN' MOVIES	Dire Straits (Vertigo)
18	10	VISAGE	Visage (Polydor)
27	11	GUILTY	Barbra Streisand (CBS)
8	12	THE VERY BEST OF DAVID BOWIE	David Bowie (K-Tel)
7	13	MOVING PICTURES	Rush (Mercury)
10	14	MANILOW MAGIC	Barry Manilow (Arista)
-	15	KILLERS	Iron Maiden (EMI)
16	16	SOUTHERN FREEEZ	Freeez (Beggars Banquet)
13	17	THEMENINBLACK	Stranglers (Liberty)
-	18	DIRK WEARS WHITE SOX	Adam & the Ants (Do It)
25	19	FAWLTY TOWERS VOLUME 2	TV Cast (BBC)
18	20	IMAGINE	John Lennon (Apple)
23	21	ABSOLUTELY	Madness (Stiff)
20	22	ARC OF A DIVER	Steve Winwood (Island)
-	23	IN OUR LIFETIME	Marvin Gaye (Motown)
-	24	HIT MACHINE	Various Artists (K-Tel)
14	25	BARRY	Barry Manilow (Arista)
12	26	DR HOOK'S GREATEST HITS	Dr Hook (Capitol)
15	27	SHAVED FISH	John Lennon (Apple)
-	28	BEATLES BALLADS	Beatles (Parlophone)
22	28	HOTTER THAN JULY	Stevie Wonder (Motown)
-	30	FLESH AND BLOOD	Roxy Music (Polydor)

14 March 1981

2	1	KINGS OF THE WILD FRONTIER	Adam & the Ants (CBS)
1	2	FACE VALUE	Phil Collins (Virgin)
3	3	VIENNA	Ultravox (Chrysalis)
5	4	STRAY CATS	Stray Cats (Arista)
7	5	THE JAZZ SINGER	Neil Diamond (Capitol)
8	6	DANCE CRAZE	Soundtrack (2-Tone)
6	7	DOUBLE FANTASY	John Lennon & Yoko Ono (Geffen)
13	8	MOVING PICTURES	Rush (Mercury)
4	9	DIFFICULT TO CURE	Rainbow (Polydor)
9	10	MAKIN' MOVIES	Dire Straits (Vertigo)
-	11	POINT OF ENTRY	Judas Priest (CBS)
14	12	MANILOW MAGIC	Barry Manilow (Arista)
10	13	VISAGE	Visage (Polydor)
16	14	SOUTHERN FREEEZ	Freeez (Beggars Banquet)
15	15	KILLERS	Iron Maiden (EMI)
25	16	BARRY	Barry Manilow (Arista)
21	17	ABSOLUTELY	Madness (Stiff)
11	18	GUILTY	Barbra Streisand (CBS)
-	19	REMAIN IN LIGHT	Talking Heads (Sire)
12	20	THE VERY BEST OF DAVID BOWIE	David Bowie (K-Tel)
-	21	ANOTHER TICKET	Eric Clapton (RSO)
-	22	JOURNEYS TO GLORY	Spandau Ballet (Reformation)
22	23	ARC OF A DIVER	Steve Winwood (Island)
28	24	HOTTER THAN JULY	Stevie Wonder (Motown)
20	25	IMAGINE	John Lennon (Apple)
-	25	McCARTNEY INTERVIEW	Paul McCartney (EMI)
-	27	CLOSER	Joy Division (Factory)
18	28	DIRK WEARS WHITE SOX	Adam & the Ants (Do It)
-	29	CHRISTOPHER CROSS	Christopher Cross (Warner Bros.)
19	30	FAWLTY TOWERS VOLUME 2	TV Cast (BBC)

21 March 1981

1	1	KINGS OF THE WILD FRONTIER	Adam & the Ants (CBS)
2	2	FACE VALUE	Phil Collins (Virgin)
3	3	VIENNA	Ultravox (Chrysalis)
4	4	STRAY CATS	Stray Cats (Arista)
22	5	JOURNEYS TO GLORY	Spandau Ballet (Reformation)
5	6	THE JAZZ SINGER	Neil Diamond (Capitol)
6	7	DANCE CRAZE	Soundtrack (2-Tone)
7	8	DOUBLE FANTASY	John Lennon & Yoko Ono (Geffen)
9	9	DIFFICULT TO CURE	Rainbow (Polydor)
10	10	MAKIN' MOVIES	Dire Straits (Vertigo)
12	11	MANILOW MAGIC	Barry Manilow (Arista)
14	12	SOUTHERN FREEEZ	Freeez (Beggars Banquet)
11	13	POINT OF ENTRY	Judas Priest (CBS)
8	14	MOVING PICTURES	Rush (Mercury)
19	15	REMAIN IN LIGHT	Talking Heads (Sire)
-	16	VERY BEST OF RITA COOLIDGE	Rita Coolidge (A&M)
13	17	VISAGE	Visage (Polydor)
17	18	ABSOLUTELY	Madness (Stiff)
21	19	ANOTHER TICKET	Eric Clapton (RSO)
-	20	MY LIFE IN THE BUSH OF GHOSTS	Brian Eno & David Byrne (Polydor)
15	21	KILLERS	Iron Maiden (EMI)
28	22	DIRK WEARS WHITE SOX	Adam & the Ants (Do It)
16	23	BARRY	Barry Manilow (Arista)
18	23	GUILTY	Barbra Streisand (CBS)
29	25	CHRISTOPHER CROSS	Christopher Cross (Warner Bros.)
-	26	TOYAH TOYAH TOYAH	Toyah (Safari)
23	27	ARC OF A DIVER	Steve Winwood (Island)
-	28	FLESH AND BLOOD	Roxy Music (Polydor)
27	29	CLOSER	Joy Division (Factory)
-	30	THE RIVER	Bruce Springsteen (CBS)

Phil Collins' first solo album *Face Value* emulated his group Genesis' *Duke* the previous year by giving him a week at Number 1, shortly after his *In The Air Tonight* had dropped from that position on the singles chart. The Number 1 slot was something of which

Phil Collins was to see a great deal, particularly as a soloist, over the decade to come. Ultravox' *Vienna*, like its title track as a single, was the first big album success for the band, now led by Midge Ure.
A second Adam & the Ants album hit the charts.

March – April 1981

28 March 1981

last week	this week		
1	1	KINGS OF THE WILD FRONTIER	Adam & the Ants (CBS)
2	2	FACE VALUE	Phil Collins (Virgin)
5	3	JOURNEYS TO GLORY	Spandau Ballet (Reformation)
6	4	THE JAZZ SINGER	Neil Diamond (Capitol)
3	5	VIENNA	Ultravox (Chrysalis)
10	6	MAKIN' MOVIES	Dire Straits (Vertigo)
7	7	DANCE CRAZE	Soundtrack (2-Tone)
9	7	DIFFICULT TO CURE	Rainbow (Polydor)
4	9	STRAY CATS	Stray Cats (Arista)
12	10	SOUTHERN FREEEZ	Freeez (Beggars Banquet)
11	11	MANILOW MAGIC	Barry Manilow (Arista)
17	12	VISAGE	Visage (Polydor)
-	13	FACE DANCES	Who (Polydor)
8	14	DOUBLE FANTASY	John Lennon & Yoko Ono (Geffen)
15	15	REMAIN IN LIGHT	Talking Heads (Sire)
16	16	VERY BEST OF RITA COOLIDGE	Rita Coolidge (A&M)
22	17	DIRK WEARS WHITE SOX	Adam & the Ants (Do It)
-	18	HOTTER THAN JULY	Stevie Wonder (Motown)
-	19	NEVER TOO LATE	Status Quo (Vertigo)
19	20	ANOTHER TICKET	Eric Clapton (RSO)
-	21	20 GOLDEN GREATS OF AL JOLSON	Al Jolson (MCA)
-	22	FROM THE TEAROOMS OF MARS TO THE HELLHOLES OF URANUS	Landscape (RCA)
-	23	SOUND AFFECTS	Jam (Polydor)
14	24	MOVING PICTURES	Rush (Mercury)
23	25	GUILTY	Barbra Streisand (CBS)
-	25	IMAGINATION	Whispers (Solar)
-	25	SOLID GOLD	Gang of Four (EMI)
21	28	KILLERS	Iron Maiden (EMI)
23	29	BARRY	Barry Manilow (Arista)
-	30	HE WHO DARES WINS	Theatre of Hate (SSSSS)

4 April 1981

last week	this week		
1	1	KINGS OF THE WILD FRONTIER	Adam & the Ants (CBS)
2	2	FACE VALUE	Phil Collins (Virgin)
19	3	NEVER TOO LATE	Status Quo (Vertigo)
4	4	THE JAZZ SINGER	Neil Diamond (Capitol)
-	5	SKY 3	Sky (Ariola)
13	6	FACE DANCES	Who (Polydor)
3	7	JOURNEYS TO GLORY	Spandau Ballet (Reformation)
18	8	HOTTER THAN JULY	Stevie Wonder (Motown)
9	9	STRAY CATS	Stray Cats (Arista)
11	10	MANILOW MAGIC	Barry Manilow (Arista)
14	11	DOUBLE FANTASY	John Lennon & Yoko Ono (Geffen)
12	12	VISAGE	Visage (Polydor)
10	13	SOUTHERN FREEEZ	Freeez (Beggars Banquet)
5	14	VIENNA	Ultravox (Chrysalis)
30	15	HE WHO DARES WINS	Theatre of Hate (SSSSS)
25	16	SOLID GOLD	Gang of Four (EMI)
16	17	VERY BEST OF RITA COOLIDGE	Rita Coolidge (A&M)
21	18	20 GOLDEN GREATS OF AL JOLSON	Al Jolson (MCA)
6	19	MAKIN' MOVIES	Dire Straits (Vertigo)
7	20	DANCE CRAZE	Soundtrack (2-Tone)
24	21	MOVING PICTURES	Rush (Mercury)
17	22	DIRK WEARS WHITE SOX	Adam & the Ants (Do It)
15	23	REMAIN IN LIGHT	Talking Heads (Sire)
25	24	GUILTY	Barbra Streisand (CBS)
-	25	FLESH AND BLOOD	Roxy Music (Polydor)
-	25	MY LIFE IN THE BUSH OF GHOSTS	Brian Eno & David Byrne (Polydor)
20	27	ANOTHER TICKET	Eric Clapton (RSO)
-	28	TOYAH TOYAH TOYAH	Toyah (Safari)
-	29	LEAGUE OF GENTLEMEN	Robert Fripp (EG)
-	30	KILIMANJARO	Teardrop Explodes (Mercury)

11 April 1981

last week	this week		
1	1	KINGS OF THE WILD FRONTIER	Adam & the Ants (CBS)
14	2	VIENNA	Ultravox (Chrysalis)
5	3	SKY 3	Sky (Ariola)
2	4	FACE VALUE	Phil Collins (Virgin)
6	5	FACE DANCES	Who (Polydor)
8	6	HOTTER THAN JULY	Stevie Wonder (Motown)
4	7	THE JAZZ SINGER	Neil Diamond (Capitol)
10	8	MANILOW MAGIC	Barry Manilow (Arista)
3	9	NEVER TOO LATE	Status Quo (Vertigo)
12	10	VISAGE	Visage (Polydor)
11	11	DOUBLE FANTASY	John Lennon & Yoko Ono (Geffen)
-	12	INTUITION	Linx (Chrysalis)
7	13	JOURNEYS TO GLORY	Spandau Ballet (Reformation)
-	14	BARRY	Barry Manilow (Arista)
15	15	MAKIN' MOVIES	Dire Straits (Vertigo)
-	16	THIS OLE HOUSE	Shakin' Stevens (Epic)
17	17	VERY BEST OF RITA COOLIDGE	Rita Coolidge (A&M)
9	18	STRAY CATS	Stray Cats (Arista)
24	19	GUILTY	Barbra Streisand (CBS)
25	20	FLESH AND BLOOD	Roxy Music (Polydor)
-	21	DIFFICULT TO CURE	Rainbow (Polydor)
-	22	TO LOVE AGAIN	Diana Ross (Motown)
-	23	THE RIVER	Bruce Springsteen (CBS)
22	24	DIRK WEARS WHITE SOX	Adam & the Ants (Do It)
28	24	TOYAH TOYAH TOYAH	Toyah (Safari)
-	26	THE ROGER WHITTAKER ALBUM	Roger Whittaker (K-Tel)
20	27	DANCE CRAZE	Soundtrack (2-Tone)
-	28	FROM THE TEAROOMS OF MARS TO THE HELLHOLES OF URANUS	Landscape (RCA)
30	29	KILIMANJARO	Teardrop Explodes (Mercury)
13	29	SOUTHERN FREEEZ	Freeez (Beggars Banquet)

18 April 1981

last week	this week		
1	1	KINGS OF THE WILD FRONTIER	Adam & the Ants (CBS)
6	2	HOTTER THAN JULY	Stevie Wonder (Motown)
15	3	MAKIN' MOVIES	Dire Straits (Vertigo)
3	3	SKY 3	Sky (Ariola)
9	5	NEVER TOO LATE	Status Quo (Vertigo)
4	6	FACE VALUE	Phil Collins (Virgin)
5	7	FACE DANCES	Who (Polydor)
7	8	THE JAZZ SINGER	Neil Diamond (Capitol)
16	9	THIS OLE HOUSE	Shakin' Stevens (Epic)
2	10	VIENNA	Ultravox (Chrysalis)
10	11	VISAGE	Visage (Polydor)
13	12	JOURNEYS TO GLORY	Spandau Ballet (Reformation)
8	13	MANILOW MAGIC	Barry Manilow (Arista)
12	14	INTUITION	Linx (Chrysalis)
-	15	FLOWERS OF ROMANCE	Public Image Limited (Virgin)
-	16	CHRISTOPHER CROSS	Christopher Cross (Warner Bros.)
24	17	DIRK WEARS WHITE SOX	Adam & the Ants (Do It)
17	18	VERY BEST OF RITA COOLIDGE	Rita Coolidge (A&M)
29	19	KILIMANJARO	Teardrop Explodes (Mercury)
-	20	390 DEGREES OF SIMULATED STEREO	Pere Ubu (Rough Trade)
-	21	COME AN' GET IT	Whitesnake (Liberty)
11	22	DOUBLE FANTASY	John Lennon & Yoko Ono (Geffen)
28	23	FROM THE TEAROOMS OF MARS TO THE HELLHOLES OF URANUS	Landscape (RCA)
-	24	REMIXTURE	Various Artists (Champagne)
20	25	FLESH AND BLOOD	Roxy Music (Polydor)
18	26	STRAY CATS	Stray Cats (Arista)
-	27	THE ADVENTURES OF THIN LIZZY	Thin Lizzy (Vertigo)
-	28	HE WHO DARES WINS	Theatre of Hate (SSSSS)
-	29	AUTHOR! AUTHOR!	Scars (Pre)
-	30	FUN IN SPACE	Roger Taylor (EMI)

Adam & The Ants' *Kings Of The Wild Frontier* finally put down the opposition and settled down into an unchallenged period of 12 weeks - or virtually a quarter of the year - as the country's best-selling album, continually being given new impetus by successive hit singles like its title track and the Number 1 seller *Stand And Deliver*. Spandau Ballet made the Top 3 with their debut set, and the tiny independent SSSS label sold (albeit briefly) remarkably well with new-wavers Theatre Of Hate.

April – May 1981

25 April 1981

last	this	Title / Artist (Label)
1	1	KINGS OF THE WILD FRONTIER — Adam & the Ants (CBS)
2	2	HOTTER THAN JULY — Stevie Wonder (Motown)
15	3	FLOWERS OF ROMANCE — Public Image Limited (Virgin)
21	4	COME AN' GET IT — Whitesnake (Liberty)
9	5	THIS OLE HOUSE — Shakin' Stevens (Epic)
8	6	THE JAZZ SINGER — Neil Diamond (Capitol)
3	7	SKY 3 — Sky (Ariola)
3	8	MAKIN' MOVIES — Dire Straits (Vertigo)
6	9	FACE VALUE — Phil Collins (Virgin)
14	10	INTUITION — Linx (Chrysalis)
30	11	FUN IN SPACE — Roger Taylor (EMI)
10	12	VIENNA — Ultravox (Chrysalis)
12	13	JOURNEYS TO GLORY — Spandau Ballet (Reformation)
5	14	NEVER TOO LATE — Status Quo (Vertigo)
13	15	MANILOW MAGIC — Barry Manilow (Arista)
-	16	FAITH — Cure (Fiction)
7	17	FACE DANCES — Who (Polydor)
11	18	VISAGE — Visage (Polydor)
-	19	HIT AND RUN — Girlschool (Bronze)
29	20	AUTHOR! AUTHOR! — Scars (Pre)
27	21	THE ADVENTURES OF THIN LIZZY — Thin Lizzy (Vertigo)
22	22	DOUBLE FANTASY — John Lennon & Yoko Ono (Geffen)
23	23	FROM THE TEAROOMS OF MARS TO THE HELLHOLES OF URANUS — Landscape (RCA)
-	24	FUTURE SHOCK — Gillan (Virgin)
16	25	CHRISTOPHER CROSS — Christopher Cross (Warner Bros.)
-	26	SPELLBOUND — Tygers of Pan Tang (MCA)
28	27	HE WHO DARES WINS — Theatre of Hate (SSSSS)
-	28	TO LOVE AGAIN — Diana Ross (Motown)
-	29	JAZZ FUNK — Incognito (Ensign)
20	30	390 DEGREES OF SIMULATED STEREO — Pere Ubu (Rough Trade)

2 May 1981

last	this	Title / Artist (Label)
1	1	KINGS OF THE WILD FRONTIER — Adam & the Ants (CBS)
2	2	HOTTER THAN JULY — Stevie Wonder (Motown)
24	3	FUTURE SHOCK — Gillan (Virgin)
4	4	COME AN' GET IT — Whitesnake (Liberty)
3	4	FLOWERS OF ROMANCE — Public Image Limited (Virgin)
8	6	MAKIN' MOVIES — Dire Straits (Vertigo)
7	6	SKY 3 — Sky (Ariola)
16	8	FAITH — Cure (Fiction)
5	9	THIS OLE HOUSE — Shakin' Stevens (Epic)
6	10	THE JAZZ SINGER — Neil Diamond (Capitol)
13	11	JOURNEYS TO GLORY — Spandau Ballet (Reformation)
19	12	HIT AND RUN — Girlschool (Bronze)
9	13	FACE VALUE — Phil Collins (Virgin)
-	14	GO FOR IT — Stiff Little Fingers (Chrysalis)
10	15	INTUITION — Linx (Chrysalis)
-	16	LIVING ORNAMENTS 1979-1980 — Gary Numan (Beggars Banquet)
15	17	MANILOW MAGIC — Barry Manilow (Arista)
23	18	FROM THE TEAROOMS OF MARS TO THE HELLHOLES OF URANUS — Landscape (RCA)
17	19	FACE DANCES — Who (Polydor)
12	20	VIENNA — Ultravox (Chrysalis)
-	21	TO EACH — A Certain Ratio (Factory)
14	22	NEVER TOO LATE — Status Quo (Vertigo)
-	23	PSYCHEDELIC JUNGLE — Cramps (IRS)
11	24	FUN IN SPACE — Roger Taylor (EMI)
-	25	BARRY — Barry Manilow (Arista)
-	26	THE ROGER WHITTAKER ALBUM — Roger Whittaker (K-Tel)
20	27	AUTHOR! AUTHOR! — Scars (Pre)
18	28	VISAGE — Visage (Polydor)
21	29	THE ADVENTURES OF THIN LIZZY — Thin Lizzy (Vertigo)
-	30	CHART BUSTERS '81 — Various Artists (K-Tel)

9 May 1981

last	this	Title / Artist (Label)
1	1	KINGS OF THE WILD FRONTIER — Adam & the Ants (CBS)
2	2	HOTTER THAN JULY — Stevie Wonder (Motown)
16	3	LIVING ORNAMENTS 1979-1980 — Gary Numan (Beggars Banquet)
10	4	THE JAZZ SINGER — Neil Diamond (Capitol)
3	5	FUTURE SHOCK — Gillan (Virgin)
30	6	CHART BUSTERS '81 — Various Artists (K-Tel)
8	7	FAITH — Cure (Fiction)
4	8	COME AN' GET IT — Whitesnake (Liberty)
4	9	FLOWERS OF ROMANCE — Public Image Limited (Virgin)
12	10	HIT AND RUN — Girlschool (Bronze)
6	11	MAKIN' MOVIES — Dire Straits (Vertigo)
13	12	FACE VALUE — Phil Collins (Virgin)
11	13	JOURNEYS TO GLORY — Spandau Ballet (Reformation)
14	14	GO FOR IT — Stiff Little Fingers (Chrysalis)
20	15	VIENNA — Ultravox (Chrysalis)
6	16	SKY 3 — Sky (Ariola)
21	17	TO EACH — A Certain Ratio (Factory)
-	18	DOUBLE FANTASY — John Lennon & Yoko Ono (Geffen)
-	19	CHARIOTS OF FIRE — Vangelis (Polydor)
17	20	MANILOW MAGIC — Barry Manilow (Arista)
15	21	INTUITION — Linx (Chrysalis)
-	22	CHRISTOPHER CROSS — Christopher Cross (Warner Bros.)
-	23	THE DUDE — Quincy Jones (A&M)
-	24	HI INFIDELITY — REO Speedwagon (Epic)
-	24	VERY BEST OF RITA COOLIDGE — Rita Coolidge (A&M)
19	26	FACE DANCES — Who (Polydor)
27	27	AUTHOR! AUTHOR! — Scars (Pre)
-	27	MAKING WAVES — Nolans (Epic)
18	29	FROM THE TEAROOMS OF MARS TO THE HELLHOLES OF URANUS — Landscape (RCA)
23	30	PSYCHEDELIC JUNGLE — Cramps (A&M)

16 May 1981

last	this	Title / Artist (Label)
1	1	KINGS OF THE WILD FRONTIER — Adam & the Ants (CBS)
3	2	LIVING ORNAMENTS 1979-1980 — Gary Numan (Beggars Banquet)
2	3	HOTTER THAN JULY — Stevie Wonder (Motown)
13	4	JOURNEYS TO GLORY — Spandau Ballet (Reformation)
-	5	THIS OLE HOUSE — Shakin' Stevens (Epic)
4	6	THE JAZZ SINGER — Neil Diamond (Capitol)
6	7	CHART BUSTERS '81 — Various Artists (K-Tel)
5	8	FUTURE SHOCK — Gillan (Virgin)
14	9	GO FOR IT — Stiff Little Fingers (Chrysalis)
11	10	MAKIN' MOVIES — Dire Straits (Vertigo)
-	11	ROLL ON — Various Artists (Polystar)
20	12	MANILOW MAGIC — Barry Manilow (Arista)
8	13	COME AN' GET IT — Whitesnake (Liberty)
16	14	SKY 3 — Sky (Ariola)
12	15	FACE VALUE — Phil Collins (Virgin)
19	16	CHARIOTS OF FIRE — Vangelis (Polydor)
7	17	FAITH — Cure (Fiction)
10	18	HIT AND RUN — Girlschool (Bronze)
17	19	TO EACH — A Certain Ratio (Factory)
23	20	THE DUDE — Quincy Jones (A&M)
9	21	FLOWERS OF ROMANCE — Public Image Limited (Virgin)
-	22	WHA'PPEN? — Beat (Go Feet)
27	23	MAKING WAVES — Nolans (Epic)
-	24	PUNKS NOT DEAD — Exploited (Secret)
24	25	HI INFIDELITY — REO Speedwagon (Epic)
15	26	VIENNA — Ultravox (Chrysalis)
30	27	PSYCHEDELIC JUNGLE — Cramps (IRS)
18	28	DOUBLE FANTASY — John Lennon & Yoko Ono (Geffen)
-	29	POSITIVE TOUCH — Undertones (Ardeck)
-	30	BARRY — Barry Manilow (Arista)
-	30	THIS IS ENNIO MORICONE — Ennio Morricone (EMI)

The resurgence to Number 2 by Stevie Wonder's *Hotter Than July* had much to do with the huge succes of the latest single extracted from it, the ballad *Lately*. Meanwhile, there was a sudden bigger-than-usual presence by heavy rock bands in the Top 10, via albums by Gillan and Whitesnake (both led by former Deep Purple vocalists), and the all-girl metal quartet Girlschool, who had far bigger success with their *Hit And Run* set than they ever managed with any of their singles.

May – June 1981

last week	this week	23 May 1981
1	1	KINGS OF THE WILD FRONTIER — Adam & the Ants (CBS)
22	2	WHA'PPEN? — Beat (Go Feet)
5	3	THIS OLE HOUSE — Shakin' Stevens (Epic)
-	4	STARS ON 45 — Starsound (CBS)
3	5	HOTTER THAN JULY — Stevie Wonder (Motown)
29	6	POSITIVE TOUCH — Undertones (Ardeck)
16	7	CHARIOTS OF FIRE — Vangelis (Polydor)
11	8	ROLL ON — Various Artists (Polystar)
2	9	LIVING ORNAMENTS 1979-1980 — Gary Numan (Beggars Banquet)
24	10	PUNKS NOT DEAD — Exploited (Secret)
25	11	HI INFIDELITY — REO Speedwagon (Epic)
4	12	JOURNEYS TO GLORY — Spandau Ballet (Reformation)
7	13	CHART BUSTERS '81 — Various Artists (K-Tel)
9	14	GO FOR IT — Stiff Little Fingers (Chrysalis)
6	15	THE JAZZ SINGER — Neil Diamond (Capitol)
8	16	FUTURE SHOCK — Gillan (Virgin)
13	17	COME AN' GET IT — Whitesnake (Liberty)
10	18	MAKIN' MOVIES — Dire Straits (Vertigo)
-	19	STRAY CATS — Stray Cats (Arista)
17	20	FAITH — Cure (Fiction)
19	21	TO EACH — A Certain Ratio (Factory)
30	22	BARRY — Barry Manilow (Arista)
14	23	SKY 3 — Sky (Ariola)
15	24	FACE VALUE — Phil Collins (Virgin)
-	25	COMPUTER WORLD — Kraftwerk (EMI)
-	26	NIGHTCLUBBING — Grace Jones (Island)
-	27	I AM THE PHOENIX — Judy Tzuke (Rocket)
18	28	HIT AND RUN — Girlschool (Bronze)
-	29	BAD FOR GOOD — Jim Steinman (Epic)
27	30	PSYCHEDELIC JUNGLE — Cramps (IRS)

last week	this week	30 May 1981
1	1	KINGS OF THE WILD FRONTIER — Adam & the Ants (CBS)
4	2	STARS ON 45 — Starsound (CBS)
2	3	WHA'PPEN? — Beat (Go Feet)
3	4	THIS OLE HOUSE — Shakin' Stevens (Epic)
-	5	QUIT DREAMING AND GET ON THE BEAM — Bill Nelson (Mercury)
5	6	HOTTER THAN JULY — Stevie Wonder (Motown)
25	7	COMPUTER WORLD — Kraftwerk (EMI)
-	8	TALK TALK TALK — Psychedelic Furs (CBS)
11	9	HI INFIDELITY — REO Speedwagon (Epic)
-	10	LONG DISTANCE VOYAGER — Moody Blues (Threshold)
7	11	CHARIOTS OF FIRE — Vangelis (Polydor)
29	12	BAD FOR GOOD — Jim Steinman (Epic)
10	13	PUNKS NOT DEAD — Exploited (Secret)
-	14	THE ADVENTURES OF THIN LIZZY — Thin Lizzy (Vertigo)
6	15	POSITIVE TOUCH — Undertones (Ardeck)
19	16	STRAY CATS — Stray Cats (Arista)
27	17	I AM THE PHOENIX — Judy Tzuke (Rocket)
-	18	PLAYING WITH A DIFFERENT SEX — Au Pairs (Human)
-	19	THE DUDE — Quincy Jones (A&M)
20	20	FAITH — Cure (Fiction)
8	21	ROLL ON — Various Artists (Polystar)
14	22	GO FOR IT — Stiff Little Fingers (Chrysalis)
-	23	EAST SIDE STORY — Squeeze (A&M)
-	24	DISCO DAZE AND DISCO NITES — Various Artists (Ronco)
18	25	MAKIN' MOVIES — Dire Straits (Vertigo)
12	26	JOURNEYS TO GLORY — Spandau Ballet (Reformation)
9	27	LIVING ORNAMENTS 1979-1980 — Gary Numan (Beggars Banquet)
13	28	CHART BUSTERS '81 — Various Artists (K-Tel)
22	29	BARRY — Barry Manilow (Arista)
-	30	FAIR WARNING — Van Halen (Warner Bros.)

last week	this week	6 June 1981
2	1	STARS ON 45 — Starsound (CBS)
1	2	KINGS OF THE WILD FRONTIER — Adam & the Ants (CBS)
-	3	ANTHEM — Toyah (Safari)
3	4	WHA'PPEN? — Beat (Go Feet)
4	5	THIS OLE HOUSE — Shakin' Stevens (Epic)
24	6	DISCO DAZE AND DISCO NITES — Various Artists (Ronco)
6	7	HOTTER THAN JULY — Stevie Wonder (Motown)
10	8	LONG DISTANCE VOYAGER — Moody Blues (Threshold)
9	9	THE JAZZ SINGER — Neil Diamond (Capitol)
14	10	THE ADVENTURES OF THIN LIZZY — Thin Lizzy (Vertigo)
-	11	SECRET COMBINATION — Randy Crawford (Warner Bros.)
5	12	QUIT DREAMING AND GET ON THE BEAM — Bill Nelson (Mercury)
9	13	HI INFIDELITY — REO Speedwagon (Epic)
15	14	POSITIVE TOUCH — Undertones (Ardeck)
11	15	CHARIOTS OF FIRE — Vangelis (Polydor)
16	16	STRAY CATS — Stray Cats (Arista)
12	17	BAD FOR GOOD — Jim Steinman (Epic)
23	18	EAST SIDE STORY — Squeeze (A&M)
18	19	PLAYING WITH A DIFFERENT SEX — Au Pairs (Human)
19	20	THE DUDE — Quincy Jones (A&M)
7	21	COMPUTER WORLD — Kraftwerk (EMI)
-	22	THEMES — Various Artists (K-Tel)
17	23	I AM THE PHOENIX — Judy Tzuke (Rocket)
13	24	PUNKS NOT DEAD — Exploited (Secret)
25	25	MAKIN' MOVIES — Dire Straits (Vertigo)
-	26	TO EACH — A Certain Ratio (Factory)
-	27	CAN'T GET ENOUGH — Eddy Grant (Ice)
20	27	FAITH — Cure (Fiction)
-	27	FUTURE SHOCK — Gillan (Virgin)
26	30	JOURNEYS TO GLORY — Spandau Ballet (Reformation)

last week	this week	13 June 1981
3	1	ANTHEM — Toyah (Safari)
1	2	STARS ON 45 — Starsound (CBS)
-	3	PRESENT ARMS — UB40 (DEP Int)
-	4	HEAVEN UP THERE — Echo & the Bunnymen (Korova)
2	5	KINGS OF THE WILD FRONTIER — Adam & the Ants (CBS)
5	6	THIS OLE HOUSE — Shakin' Stevens (Epic)
4	7	WHA'PPEN? — Beat (Go Feet)
15	8	CHARIOTS OF FIRE — Vangelis (Polydor)
17	9	BAD FOR GOOD — Jim Steinman (Epic)
19	10	PLAYING WITH A DIFFERENT SEX — Au Pairs (Human)
-	10	THE FOX — Elton John (Rocket)
22	10	THEMES — Various Artists (K-Tel)
6	13	DISCO DAZE AND DISCO NITES — Various Artists (Ronco)
7	14	HOTTER THAN JULY — Stevie Wonder (Motown)
21	15	COMPUTER WORLD — Kraftwerk (EMI)
8	16	LONG DISTANCE VOYAGER — Moody Blues (Threshold)
13	17	HI INFIDELITY — REO Speedwagon (Epic)
12	18	QUIT DREAMING AND GET ON THE BEAM — Bill Nelson (Mercury)
24	19	PUNKS NOT DEAD — Exploited (Secret)
17	20	EAST SIDE STORY — Squeeze (A&M)
11	21	SECRET COMBINATION — Randy Crawford (Warner Bros.)
25	22	MAKIN' MOVIES — Dire Straits (Vertigo)
-	23	MAGNETIC FIELDS — Jean Michael Jarre (Polydor)
-	24	NIGHT PEOPLE — Classix Nouveaux (Liberty)
14	25	POSITIVE TOUCH — Undertones (Ardeck)
-	26	NIGHTCLUBBING — Grace Jones (Island)
-	27	KILIMANJARO — Teardrop Explodes (Mercury)
-	28	SOMEWHERE IN ENGLAND — George Harrison (Dark Horse)
-	29	GO FOR IT — Stiff Little Fingers (Chrysalis)
-	30	THE RIVER — Bruce Springsteen (CBS)

The first album to break Adam & The Ants' stranglehold at Number 1 was the album-length version of the Continentally-recorded *Stars On 45* soundalike medley, credited to Starsound and actually the brainchild of Dutch producer Jaap Eggermont. The concept sparked a whole fad for such re-creations, and umpteen hit singles by assorted copyists, though only the Dutch original troubled the upper reaches of the album chart. Another surprise in the Top 10 were hardcore punk band the Exploited.

June – July 1981

20 June 1981

last week	this week	Title / Artist (Label)
3	1	PRESENT ARMS — UB40 (DEP Int)
2	2	STARS ON 45 — Starsound (CBS)
1	3	ANTHEM — Toyah (Safari)
13	4	DISCO DAZE AND DISCO NITES — Various Artists (Ronco)
5	5	KINGS OF THE WILD FRONTIER — Adam & the Ants (CBS)
7	6	WHA'PPEN? — Beat (Go Feet)
18	7	QUIT DREAMING AND GET ON THE BEAM — Bill Nelson (Mercury)
8	8	CHARIOTS OF FIRE — Vangelis (Polydor)
4	9	HEAVEN UP THERE — Echo & the Bunnymen (Korova)
10	10	THEMES — Various Artists (K-Tel)
23	11	MAGNETIC FIELDS — Jean Michael Jarre (Polydor)
6	12	THIS OLE HOUSE — Shakin' Stevens (Epic)
28	13	SOMEWHERE IN ENGLAND — George Harrison (Dark Horse)
16	14	LONG DISTANCE VOYAGER — Moody Blues (Threshold)
-	15	FACE VALUE — Phil Collins (Virgin)
10	16	PLAYING WITH A DIFFERENT SEX — Au Pairs (Human)
17	17	HI INFIDELITY — REO Speedwagon (Epic)
-	18	VIENNA — Ultravox (Chrysalis)
15	19	COMPUTER WORLD — Kraftwerk (EMI)
19	20	PUNKS NOT DEAD — Exploited (Secret)
21	21	SECRET COMBINATION — Randy Crawford (Warner Bros.)
30	22	THE RIVER — Bruce Springsteen (CBS)
10	23	THE FOX — Elton John (Rocket)
26	24	NIGHTCLUBBING — Grace Jones (Island)
27	25	KILIMANJARO — Teardrop Explodes (Mercury)
20	26	EAST SIDE STORY — Squeeze (A&M)
-	27	WHAT'S THIS FOR — Killing Joke (Malicious Damage)
-	28	I AM THE PHOENIX — Judy Tzuke (Rocket)
9	29	BAD FOR GOOD — Jim Steinman (Epic)
-	30	THE DUDE — Quincy Jones (A&M)

27 June 1981

last week	this week	Title / Artist (Label)
2	1	STARS ON 45 — Starsound (CBS)
3	2	ANTHEM — Toyah (Safari)
4	3	DISCO DAZE AND DISCO NITES — Various Artists (Ronco)
5	4	KINGS OF THE WILD FRONTIER — Adam & the Ants (CBS)
1	5	PRESENT ARMS — UB40 (DEP Int)
8	6	CHARIOTS OF FIRE — Vangelis (Polydor)
12	7	THIS OLE HOUSE — Shakin' Stevens (Epic)
11	8	MAGNETIC FIELDS — Jean Michael Jarre (Polydor)
18	9	VIENNA — Ultravox (Chrysalis)
6	10	WHA'PPEN? — Beat (Go Feet)
15	11	FACE VALUE — Phil Collins (Virgin)
9	12	HEAVEN UP THERE — Echo & the Bunnymen (Korova)
-	13	NO SLEEP 'TIL HAMMERSMITH — Motorhead (Bronze)
14	14	LONG DISTANCE VOYAGER — Moody Blues (Threshold)
17	15	HI INFIDELITY — REO Speedwagon (Epic)
22	16	THE RIVER — Bruce Springsteen (CBS)
10	17	THEMES — Various Artists (K-Tel)
16	18	PLAYING WITH A DIFFERENT SEX — Au Pairs (Human)
-	19	JUJU — Siouxsie and the Banshees (Polydor)
20	20	PUNKS NOT DEAD — Exploited (Secret)
27	21	WHAT'S THIS FOR — Killing Joke (Malicious Damage)
21	22	SECRET COMBINATION — Randy Crawford (Warner Bros.)
-	23	BEING WITH YOU — Smokey Robinson (Motown)
-	24	MISTAKEN IDENTITY — Kim Carnes (EMI America)
13	25	SOMEWHERE IN ENGLAND — George Harrison (Dark Horse)
-	26	MAKIN' MOVIES — Dire Straits (Vertigo)
25	27	KILIMANJARO — Teardrop Explodes (Mercury)
-	28	HOTTER THAN JULY — Stevie Wonder (Motown)
-	29	TALK TALK TALK — Psychedelic Furs (CBS)
-	30	RED — Black Uhuru (Island)

4 July 1981

last week	this week	Title / Artist (Label)
5	1	PRESENT ARMS — UB40 (DEP Int)
13	2	NO SLEEP 'TIL HAMMERSMITH — Motorhead (Bronze)
1	3	STARS ON 45 — Starsound (CBS)
3	4	DISCO DAZE AND DISCO NITES — Various Artists (Ronco)
2	5	ANTHEM — Toyah (Safari)
19	6	JUJU — Siouxsie & the Banshees (Polydor)
-	7	DURAN DURAN — Duran Duran (EMI)
11	8	FACE VALUE — Phil Collins (Virgin)
6	9	CHARIOTS OF FIRE — Vangelis (Polydor)
15	10	HI INFIDELITY — REO Speedwagon (Epic)
4	11	KINGS OF THE WILD FRONTIER — Adam & the Ants (CBS)
8	12	MAGNETIC FIELDS — Jean Michael Jarre (Polydor)
22	13	SECRET COMBINATION — Randy Crawford (Warner Bros.)
23	14	BEING WITH YOU — Smokey Robinson (Motown)
-	15	BAD FOR GOOD — Jim Steinman (Epic)
16	16	THEMES — Various Artists (K-Tel)
9	17	VIENNA — Ultravox (Chrysalis)
14	18	LONG DISTANCE VOYAGER — Moody Blues (Threshold)
7	19	THIS OLE HOUSE — Shakin' Stevens (Epic)
26	20	MAKIN' MOVIES — Dire Straits (Vertigo)
-	21	2,000,000 VOICES — Angelic Upstarts (Zonophone)
27	22	KILIMANJARO — Teardrop Explodes (Mercury)
29	23	TALK TALK TALK — Psychedelic Furs (CBS)
-	24	EAST SIDE STORY — Squeeze (A&M)
21	25	WHAT'S THIS FOR — Killing Joke (Malicious Damage)
10	26	WHA'PPEN? — Beat (Go Feet)
-	27	MADE IN AMERICA — Carpenters (A&M)
16	28	THE RIVER — Bruce Springsteen (CBS)
-	29	POLECATS ARE GO — Polecats (Mercury)
18	30	PLAYING WITH A DIFFERENT SEX — Au Pairs (Human)

11 July 1981

last week	this week	Title / Artist (Label)
2	1	NO SLEEP 'TIL HAMMERSMITH — Motorhead (Bronze)
1	2	PRESENT ARMS — UB40 (DEP Int)
3	3	STARS ON 45 — Starsound (CBS)
4	4	DISCO DAZE AND DISCO NITES — Various Artists (Ronco)
5	5	ANTHEM — Toyah (Safari)
-	6	LOVE SONGS — Cliff Richard (EMI)
7	7	DURAN DURAN — Duran Duran (EMI)
11	8	KINGS OF THE WILD FRONTIER — Adam & the Ants (CBS)
9	9	CHARIOTS OF FIRE — Vangelis (Polydor)
6	10	JUJU — Siouxsie & the Banshees (Polydor)
12	11	MAGNETIC FIELDS — Jean Michael Jarre (Polydor)
13	12	SECRET COMBINATION — Randy Crawford (Warner Bros.)
8	13	FACE VALUE — Phil Collins (Virgin)
29	14	POLECATS ARE GO — Polecats (Mercury)
28	15	THE RIVER — Bruce Springsteen (CBS)
16	16	THEMES — Various Artists (K-Tel)
27	17	MADE IN AMERICA — Carpenters (A&M)
15	18	BAD FOR GOOD — Jim Steinman (Epic)
-	19	KIM WILDE — Kim Wilde (RAK)
19	20	THIS OLE HOUSE — Shakin' Stevens (Epic)
22	21	KILIMANJARO — Teardrop Explodes (Mercury)
-	22	JUMPIN' JIVE — Joe Jackson (A&M)
-	23	THE JAZZ SINGER — Neil Diamond (Capitol)
17	24	VIENNA — Ultravox (Chrysalis)
-	25	HOTTER THAN JULY — Stevie Wonder (Motown)
-	26	BAT OUT OF HELL — Meatloaf (Epic/Cleveland Int)
-	27	THE DUDE — Quincy Jones (A&M)
10	28	HI INFIDELITY — REO Speedwagon (Epic)
14	29	BEING WITH YOU — Smokey Robinson (Motown)
21	30	2,000,000 VOICES — Angelic Upstarts (Zonophone)

The successful *Disco Daze And Disco Nites* package was actually two separate dance compilation albums - *Disco Daze* and *Disco Nites*, the thrust of whose TV campaign was that you bought one and received the other free. Neither was available separately, but the set's Top 3 success suggests that the gimmick was a successful one. Toyah became one of the few female soloists to have a Number 1 album, while Vangelis' *Chariots Of Fire* contained his Oscar-winning music from the film of the same title.

July – August 1981

18 July 1981

last week	this week	Title	Artist (Label)
1	1	NO SLEEP 'TIL HAMMERSMITH	Motorhead (Bronze)
4	2	DISCO DAZE AND DISCO NITES	Various Artists (Ronco)
6	3	LOVE SONGS	Cliff Richard (EMI)
2	4	PRESENT ARMS	UB40 (DEP Int)
19	5	KIM WILDE	Kim Wilde (RAK)
7	6	DURAN DURAN	Duran Duran (EMI)
3	7	STARS ON 45	Starsound (CBS)
12	8	SECRET COMBINATION	Randy Crawford (Warner Bros.)
5	9	ANTHEM	Toyah (Safari)
8	10	KINGS OF THE WILD FRONTIER	Adam & the Ants (CBS)
10	11	JUJU	Siouxsie & the Banshees (Polydor)
9	12	CHARIOTS OF FIRE	Vangelis (Polydor)
-	13	PENIS ENVY	Crass (Crass)
25	14	HOTTER THAN JULY	Stevie Wonder (Motown)
11	15	MAGNETIC FIELDS	Jean Michael Jarre (Polydor)
-	16	NAH POO THE ART OF BLUFF	Wah! (Eternal)
17	17	MADE IN AMERICA	Carpenters (A&M)
18	18	BAD FOR GOOD	Jim Steinman (Epic)
28	19	HI INFIDELITY	REO Speedwagon (Epic)
22	20	JUMPIN' JIVE	Joe Jackson (A&M)
19	21	THIS OLE HOUSE	Shakin' Stevens (Epic)
23	22	VIENNA	Ultravox (Chrysalis)
-	23	BEST OF MICHAEL JACKSON	Michael Jackson (Motown)
-	24	THE PARTY MIX ALBUM	B52's (Island)
-	25	HEAVEN UP THERE	Echo & the Bunnymen (Korova)
-	26	MAGIC, MURDER & THE WEATHER	Magazine (Virgin)
-	27	WHAT'S THIS FOR	Killing Joke (Malicious Damage)
26	28	BAT OUT OF HELL	Meatloaf (Epic)
16	29	THEMES	Various Artists (K-Tel)
15	30	THE RIVER	Bruce Springsteen (CBS)

25 July 1981

this week	Title	Artist (Label)
3 1	LOVE SONGS	Cliff Richard (EMI)
1 2	NO SLEEP 'TIL HAMMERSMITH	Motorhead (Bronze)
5 3	KIM WILDE	Kim Wilde (RAK)
7 4	STARS ON 45	Starsound (CBS)
6 5	DURAN DURAN	Duran Duran (EMI)
9 6	ANTHEM	Toyah (Safari)
2 7	DISCO DAZE AND DISCO NITES	Various Artists (Ronco)
10 8	KINGS OF THE WILD FRONTIER	Adam & the Ants (CBS)
18 9	BAD FOR GOOD	Jim Steinman (Epic)
11 10	JUJU	Siouxsie & the Banshees (Polydor)
8 11	SECRET COMBINATION	Randy Crawford (Warner Bros.)
16 12	NAH POO THE ART OF BLUFF	Wah! (Eternal)
4 13	PRESENT ARMS	UB40 (DEP Int)
23 14	BEST OF MICHAEL JACKSON	Michael Jackson (Motown)
13 15	PENIS ENVY	Crass (Crass)
15 16	MAGNETIC FIELDS	Jean Michael Jarre (Polydor)
12 17	CHARIOTS OF FIRE	Vangelis (Polydor)
20 18	JUMPIN' JIVE	Joe Jackson (A&M)
19 19	HI INFIDELITY	REO Speedwagon (Epic)
14 20	HOTTER THAN JULY	Stevie Wonder (Motown)
- 21	I'VE GOT THE MELODY	Odyssey (RCA)
21 22	THIS OLE HOUSE	Shakin' Stevens (Epic)
17 23	MADE IN AMERICA	Carpenters (A&M)
- 24	TALK TALK TALK	Psychedelic Furs (CBS)
25 25	HEAVEN UP THERE	Echo & the Bunnymen (Korova)
- 26	EAST SIDE STORY	Squeeze (A&M)
28 27	BAT OUT OF HELL	Meatloaf (Epic)
- 28	PUNKS NOT DEAD	Exploited (Secret)
- 29	THE ONLY FUN IN TOWN	Josef K (Postcard)
30 30	THE RIVER	Bruce Springsteen (CBS)

1 August 1981

this week	Title	Artist (Label)
1 1	LOVE SONGS	Cliff Richard (EMI)
3 2	KIM WILDE	Kim Wilde (RAK)
4 3	STARS ON 45	Starsound (CBS)
2 4	NO SLEEP 'TIL HAMMERSMITH	Motorhead (Bronze)
11 5	SECRET COMBINATION	Randy Crawford (Warner Bros.)
5 6	DURAN DURAN	Duran Duran (EMI)
8 7	KINGS OF THE WILD FRONTIER	Adam & the Ants (CBS)
9 8	BAD FOR GOOD	Jim Steinman (Epic)
20 9	HOTTER THAN JULY	Stevie Wonder (Motown)
13 10	PRESENT ARMS	UB40 (DEP Int)
7 11	DISCO DAZE AND DISCO NITES	Various Artists (Ronco)
6 12	ANTHEM	Toyah (Safari)
14 13	BEST OF MICHAEL JACKSON	Michael Jackson (Motown)
18 14	JUMPIN' JIVE	Joe Jackson (A&M)
19 15	HI INFIDELITY	REO Speedwagon (Epic)
10 16	JUJU	Siouxsie & the Banshees (Polydor)
16 17	MAGNETIC FIELDS	Jean Michael Jarre (Polydor)
12 18	NAH POO THE ART OF BLUFF	Wah! (Eternal)
- 19	PRECIOUS TIME	Pat Benatar (Chrysalis)
30 20	THE RIVER	Bruce Springsteen (CBS)
17 21	CHARIOTS OF FIRE	Vangelis (Polydor)
15 22	PENIS ENVY	Crass (Crass)
25 23	HEAVEN UP THERE	Echo & the Bunnymen (Korova)
- 24	FIRE OF UNKNOWN ORIGIN	Blue Oyster Cult (CBS)
27 25	BAT OUT OF HELL	Meatloaf (Epic)
- 26	HIGH & DRY	Def Leppard (Vertigo)
23 27	MADE IN AMERICA	Carpenters (A&M)
- 28	JOURNEYS TO GLORY	Spandau Ballet (Reformation)
22 29	THIS OLE HOUSE	Shakin' Stevens (Epic)
- 30	FACE VALUE	Phil Collins (Virgin)

8 August 1981

this week	Title	Artist (Label)
1 1	LOVE SONGS	Cliff Richard (EMI)
2 2	KIM WILDE	Kim Wilde (RAK)
4 3	NO SLEEP 'TIL HAMMERSMITH	Motorhead (Bronze)
7 4	KINGS OF THE WILD FRONTIER	Adam & the Ants (CBS)
3 5	STARS ON 45	Starsound (CBS)
13 6	BEST OF MICHAEL JACKSON	Michael Jackson (Motown)
5 7	SECRET COMBINATION	Randy Crawford (Warner Bros.)
9 8	HOTTER THAN JULY	Stevie Wonder (Motown)
6 9	DURAN DURAN	Duran Duran (EMI)
15 10	HI INFIDELITY	REO Speedwagon (Epic)
10 11	PRESENT ARMS	UB40 (DEP Int)
8 12	BAD FOR GOOD	Jim Steinman (Epic)
16 13	JUJU	Siouxsie & the Banshees (Polydor)
12 14	ANTHEM	Toyah (Safari)
20 15	THE RIVER	Bruce Springsteen (CBS)
- 16	CATS	Various Artists (Polydor)
- 17	ROCK CLASSICS	London Symphony Orchestra & Royal Chorale Society (K-Tel)
30 18	FACE VALUE	Phil Collins (Virgin)
21 19	CHARIOTS OF FIRE	Vangelis (Polydor)
- 20	BELLA DONNA	Stevie Nicks (WEA)
29 21	THIS OLE HOUSE	Shakin' Stevens (Epic)
11 22	DISCO DAZE AND DISCO NITES	Various Artists (Ronco)
14 23	JUMPIN' JIVE	Joe Jackson (A&M)
- 24	4	Foreigner (Atlantic)
18 25	NAH POO THE ART OF BLUFF	Wah! (Eternal)
26 26	BAT OUT OF HELL	Meatloaf (Epic)
26 27	HIGH & DRY	Def Leppard (Vertigo)
23 28	HEAVEN UP THERE	Echo & the Bunnymen (Korova)
- 29	PUNKS NOT DEAD	Exploited (Secret)
- 30	ARC OF A DIVER	Steve Winwood (Island)
- 30	I'VE GOT THE MELODY	Odyssey (RCA)

Love Songs, which was to be one of Cliff Richard's all-time best-selling albums, was not a new set, but a collection of his most popular ballads, stretching from contemporary recordings right back to the early 1960s. Its success prevented the first album by Marty Wilde's daughter Kim from topping the chart (though it went a place higher than her debut single *Kids In America*). The Number 1 Cliff deposed was heavy metal trio Motorhead's biggest-ever seller, capturing their storming stage act.

August – September 1981

15 August 1981

last week	this week		
1	1	LOVE SONGS	Cliff Richard (EMI)
-	2	TIME	Electric Light Orchestra (Jet)
9	3	DURAN DURAN	Duran Duran (EMI)
5	4	STARS ON 45	Starsound (CBS)
7	5	SECRET COMBINATION	Randy Crawford (Warner Bros.)
2	6	KIM WILDE	Kim Wilde (RAK)
-	7	KOO KOO	Debbie Harry (Chrysalis)
8	8	HOTTER THAN JULY	Stevie Wonder (Motown)
17	9	ROCK CLASSICS	London Symphony Orchestra & Royal Chorale Society (K-Tel)
3	10	NO SLEEP 'TIL HAMMERSMITH	Motorhead (Bronze)
20	11	BELLA DONNA	Stevie Nicks (WEA)
10	12	HI INFIDELITY	REO Speedwagon (Epic)
4	13	KINGS OF THE WILD FRONTIER	Adam & the Ants (CBS)
11	14	PRESENT ARMS	UB40 (DEP Int)
-	15	THE OFFICIAL BBC ALBUM OF THE ROYAL WEDDING	BBC Recording (BBC)
16	16	CATS	Various Artists (Polydor)
21	17	THIS OLE HOUSE	Shakin' Stevens (Epic)
23	18	JUMPIN' JIVE	Joe Jackson (A&M)
14	19	ANTHEM	Toyah (Safari)
12	20	BAD FOR GOOD	Jim Steinman (Epic)
26	21	BAT OUT OF HELL	Meatloaf (Epic)
-	22	PRETENDERS II	Pretenders (Real)
15	23	THE RIVER	Bruce Springsteen (CBS)
-	24	STARTRAX CLUB DISCO	Various Artists (Picksy)
6	25	BEST OF MICHAEL JACKSON	Michael Jackson (Motown)
22	26	DISCO DAZE AND DISCO NITES	Various Artists (Ronco)
25	27	NAH POO THE ART OF BLUFF	Wah! (Eternal)
-	28	PIRATES	Rickie Lee Jones (Warner Bros.)
13	29	JUJU	Siouxsie and the Banshees (Polydor)
28	30	HEAVEN UP THERE	Echo & the Bunnymen (Korova)

22 August 1981

last week	this week		
2	1	TIME	Electric Light Orchestra (Jet)
1	2	LOVE SONGS	Cliff Richard (EMI)
3	3	DURAN DURAN	Duran Duran (EMI)
12	4	HI INFIDELITY	REO Speedwagon (Epic)
7	5	KOO KOO	Debbie Harry (Chrysalis)
5	6	SECRET COMBINATION	Randy Crawford (Warner Bros.)
8	7	HOTTER THAN JULY	Stevie Wonder (Motown)
22	8	PRETENDERS II	Pretenders (Real)
6	9	KIM WILDE	Kim Wilde (RAK)
21	10	BAT OUT OF HELL	Meatloaf (Epic)
13	11	KINGS OF THE WILD FRONTIER	Adam & the Ants (CBS)
4	12	STARS ON 45	Starsound (CBS)
15	13	THE OFFICIAL BBC ALBUM OF THE ROYAL WEDDING	BBC Recording (BBC)
16	14	CATS	Various Artists (Polydor)
10	15	NO SLEEP 'TIL HAMMERSMITH	Motorhead (Bronze)
11	16	BELLA DONNA	Stevie Nicks (WEA)
17	17	THIS OLE HOUSE	Shakin' Stevens (Epic)
20	18	BAD FOR GOOD	Jim Steinman (Epic)
14	19	PRESENT ARMS	UB40 (DEP Int)
-	20	BUCKS FIZZ	Bucks Fizz (RCA)
9	21	ROCK CLASSICS	London Symphony Orchestra & Royal Chorale Society (K-Tel)
25	22	BEST OF MICHAEL JACKSON	Michael Jackson (Motown)
18	23	JUMPIN' JIVE	Joe Jackson (A&M)
26	24	DISCO DAZE AND DISCO NITES	Various Artists (Ronco)
19	25	ANTHEM	Toyah (Safari)
-	26	JOURNEYS TO GLORY	Spandau Ballet (Reformation)
27	27	THE PARTY MIX ALBUM	B52's (Island)
-	28	THE JAZZ SINGER	Neil Diamond (Capitol)
23	29	THE RIVER	Bruce Springsteen (CBS)
-	30	FACE VALUE	Phil Collins (Virgin)

29 August 1981

last week	this week		
1	1	TIME	Electric Light Orchestra (Jet)
3	2	DURAN DURAN	Duran Duran (EMI)
2	3	LOVE SONGS	Cliff Richard (EMI)
13	4	THE OFFICIAL BBC ALBUM OF THE ROYAL WEDDING	BBC Recording (BBC)
6	5	SECRET COMBINATION	Randy Crawford (Warner Bros.)
8	6	PRETENDERS II	Pretenders (Real)
9	7	KIM WILDE	Kim Wilde (RAK)
7	8	HOTTER THAN JULY	Stevie Wonder (Motown)
5	9	KOO KOO	Debbie Harry (Chrysalis)
10	10	BAT OUT OF HELL	Meatloaf (Epic)
12	11	STARS ON 45	Starsound (CBS)
16	12	BELLA DONNA	Stevie Nicks (WEA)
11	13	KINGS OF THE WILD FRONTIER	Adam & the Ants (CBS)
17	14	THIS OLE HOUSE	Shakin' Stevens (Epic)
19	15	PRESENT ARMS	UB40 (DEP Int)
15	16	NO SLEEP 'TIL HAMMERSMITH	Motorhead (Bronze)
4	17	HI INFIDELITY	REO Speedwagon (Epic)
20	18	BUCKS FIZZ	Bucks Fizz (RCA)
21	19	ROCK CLASSICS	London Symphony Orchestra & Royal Chorale Society (K-Tel)
18	20	BAD FOR GOOD	Jim Steinman (Epic)
22	21	BEST OF MICHAEL JACKSON	Michael Jackson (Motown)
-	22	CURED	Steve Hackett (Charisma)
29	23	THE RIVER	Bruce Springsteen (CBS)
-	24	JUJU	Siouxsie & the Banshees (Polydor)
25	25	ANTHEM	Toyah (Safari)
14	26	CATS	Various Artists (Polydor)
-	27	THE LAST CALL	Anti-Pasti (Rondelet)
30	28	FACE VALUE	Phil Collins (Virgin)
-	29	MADE IN AMERICA	Carpenters (A&M)
-	30	20 GOLDEN GREATS	Beach Boys (Capitol)

5 September 1981

last week	this week		
1	1	TIME	Electric Light Orchestra (Jet)
3	2	LOVE SONGS	Cliff Richard (EMI)
5	3	SECRET COMBINATION	Randy Crawford (Warner Bros.)
15	4	PRESENT ARMS	UB40 (DEP Int)
2	5	DURAN DURAN	Duran Duran (EMI)
-	6	SHOT OF LOVE	Bob Dylan (CBS)
14	7	THIS OLE HOUSE	Shakin' Stevens (Epic)
4	8	THE OFFICIAL BBC ALBUM OF THE ROYAL WEDDING	BBC Recording (BBC)
10	9	BAT OUT OF HELL	Meatloaf (Epic)
7	10	KIM WILDE	Kim Wilde (RAK)
6	11	PRETENDERS II	Pretenders (Real)
12	12	BELLA DONNA	Stevie Nicks (WEA)
22	13	CURED	Steve Hackett (Charisma)
8	14	HOTTER THAN JULY	Stevie Wonder (Motown)
-	15	TRAVELOGUE	Human League (Virgin)
17	16	HI INFIDELITY	REO Speedwagon (Epic)
13	17	KINGS OF THE WILD FRONTIER	Adam & the Ants (CBS)
21	18	BEST OF MICHAEL JACKSON	Michael Jackson (Motown)
25	19	ANTHEM	Toyah (Safari)
28	20	FACE VALUE	Phil Collins (Virgin)
20	21	BAD FOR GOOD	Jim Steinman (Epic)
18	22	BUCKS FIZZ	Bucks Fizz (RCA)
-	23	BOY	U2 (Island)
9	24	KOO KOO	Debbie Harry (Chrysalis)
-	25	LEVEL 42	Level 42 (Polydor)
26	26	CATS	Various Artists (Polydor)
-	27	4	Foreigner (Atlantic)
11	28	STARS ON 45	Starsound (CBS)
19	29	ROCK CLASSICS	London Symphony Orchestra & Royal Chorale Society (K-Tel)
-	30	VIENNA	Ultravox (Chrysalis)

Time was ELO's first new album for over two years, but its almost immediate ascent to, and four-week stay at, the chart top underlined the Jeff Lynne-led group's continuing huge popularity - they were up to their 21st hit single at this time, with *Hold On Tight*, taken from *Time*. Meanwhile, BBC Records' souvenir album of the highlights of Charles and Diana's wedding became one of the very few documentary LPs ever to reach the Top 10. How many of those buyers still play it?

12 September 1981

last week	this week	Title / Artist (Label)
1	1	TIME — Electric Light Orchestra (Jet)
2	2	LOVE SONGS — Cliff Richard (EMI)
5	3	DURAN DURAN — Duran Duran (EMI)
3	4	SECRET COMBINATION — Randy Crawford (Warner Bros.)
16	5	HI INFIDELITY — REO Speedwagon (Epic)
4	6	PRESENT ARMS — UB40 (DEP Int)
-	7	DEAD RINGER — Meatloaf (Epic)
10	8	KIM WILDE — Kim Wilde (RAK)
6	9	SHOT OF LOVE — Bob Dylan (CBS)
11	10	PRETENDERS II — Pretenders (Real)
22	11	BUCKS FIZZ — Bucks Fizz (RCA)
8	12	THE OFFICIAL BBC ALBUM OF THE ROYAL WEDDING — BBC Recording (BBC)
7	13	THIS OLE HOUSE — Shakin' Stevens (Epic)
-	14	TATTOO YOU — Rolling Stones (Rolling Stones)
9	15	BAT OUT OF HELL — Meatloaf (Epic)
17	16	KINGS OF THE WILD FRONTIER — Adam & the Ants (CBS)
14	17	HOTTER THAN JULY — Stevie Wonder (Motown)
15	18	TRAVELOGUE — Human League (Virgin)
12	19	BELLA DONNA — Stevie Nicks (WEA)
19	20	ANTHEM — Toyah (Safari)
24	21	KOO KOO — Debbie Harry (Chrysalis)
-	22	NO SLEEP 'TIL HAMMERSMITH — Motorhead (Bronze)
25	23	LEVEL 42 — Level 42 (Polydor)
23	24	BOY — U2 (Island)
13	25	CURED — Steve Hackett (Charisma)
27	26	4 — Foreigner (Atlantic)
21	27	BAD FOR GOOD — Jim Steinman (Epic)
-	28	JUJU — Siouxsie & the Banshees (Polydor)
28	29	STARS ON 45 — Starsound (CBS)
-	30	CHRISTOPHER CROSS — Christopher Cross (Warner Bros.)

19 September 1981

last week	this week	Title / Artist (Label)
7	1	DEAD RINGER — Meatloaf (Epic)
14	2	TATTOO YOU — Rolling Stones (Rolling Stones)
-	3	DANCE — Gary Numan (Beggars Banquet)
2	4	LOVE SONGS — Cliff Richard (EMI)
4	5	SECRET COMBINATION — Randy Crawford (Warner Bros.)
-	6	SONS & FASCINATION/SISTERS FEELINGS CALL — Simple Minds (Virgin)
1	7	TIME — Electric Light Orchestra (Jet)
3	8	DURAN DURAN — Duran Duran (EMI)
5	9	HI INFIDELITY — REO Speedwagon (Epic)
-	10	WALK UNDER LADDERS — Joan Armatrading (A&M)
15	11	BAT OUT OF HELL — Meatloaf (Epic)
6	12	PRESENT ARMS — UB40 (DEP Int)
-	13	RAGE IN EDEN — Ultravox (Chrysalis)
10	14	PRETENDERS II — Pretenders (Real)
20	15	ANTHEM — Toyah (Safari)
9	16	SHOT OF LOVE — Bob Dylan (CBS)
13	17	THIS OLE HOUSE — Shakin' Stevens (Epic)
8	18	KIM WILDE — Kim Wilde (RAK)
-	19	COVER PLUS — Hazel O'Connor (Albion)
11	20	BUCKS FIZZ — Bucks Fizz (RCA)
24	21	BOY — U2 (Island)
17	22	HOTTER THAN JULY — Stevie Wonder (Motown)
23	23	KINGS OF THE WILD FRONTIER — Adam & the Ants (CBS)
18	24	TRAVELOGUE — Human League (Virgin)
19	25	BELLA DONNA — Stevie Nicks (WEA)
23	26	LEVEL 42 — Level 42 (Polydor)
28	27	JUJU — Siouxsie & the Banshees (Polydor)
-	28	20 GOLDEN GREATS — Beach Boys (Capitol)
-	29	ROCK CLASSICS — London Symphony Orchestra & Royal Chorale Society (K-Tel)
22	30	NO SLEEP 'TIL HAMMERSMITH — Motorhead (Bronze)

26 September 1981

last week	this week	Title / Artist (Label)
1	1	DEAD RINGER — Meatloaf (Epic)
2	2	TATTOO YOU — Rolling Stones (Rolling Stones)
13	3	RAGE IN EDEN — Ultravox (Chrysalis)
3	4	DANCE — Gary Numan (Beggars Banquet)
7	5	TIME — Electric Light Orchestra (Jet)
-	6	SHAKY — Shakin' Stevens (Epic)
4	7	LOVE SONGS — Cliff Richard (EMI)
-	8	STARS ON 45 VOL 2 — Starsound (CBS)
-	9	WIRED FOR SOUND — Cliff Richard (EMI)
8	10	DURAN DURAN — Duran Duran (EMI)
5	11	SECRET COMBINATION — Randy Crawford (Warner Bros.)
12	12	PRESENT ARMS — UB40 (DEP Int)
11	13	BAT OUT OF HELL — Meatloaf (Epic)
-	14	CELEBRATION — Johnny Mathis (CBS)
10	15	WALK UNDER LADDERS — Joan Armatrading (A&M)
6	16	SONS & FASCINATION/SISTERS FEELINGS CALL — Simple Minds (Virgin)
-	17	ABACAB — Genesis (Charisma)
-	18	HITS RIGHT UP YOUR STREET — Shadows (Polydor)
-	19	HAPPY BIRTHDAY — Altered Images (Epic)
-	20	DANCE DANCE DANCE — Various Artists (K-Tel)
23	21	KINGS OF THE WILD FRONTIER — Adam & the Ants (CBS)
-	22	SUPER HITS 1 & 2 — Various Artists (Ronco)
-	23	MICHAEL SCHENKER GROUP — Michael Schenker Group (Chrysalis)
-	24	PENTHOUSE AND PAVEMENT — Heaven 17 (BEF/Virgin)
17	25	THIS OLE HOUSE — Shakin' Stevens (Epic)
-	26	BLACK & WHITE — Pointer Sisters (Planet)
24	27	TRAVELOGUE — Human League (Virgin)
9	28	HI INFIDELITY — REO Speedwagon (Epic)
16	29	SHOT OF LOVE — Bob Dylan (CBS)
-	30	SLEEP NO MORE — Comsat Angels (Polydor)

3 October 1981

last week	this week	Title / Artist (Label)
17	1	ABACAB — Genesis (Charisma)
1	2	DEAD RINGER — Meatloaf (Epic)
2	3	TATTOO YOU — Rolling Stones (Rolling Stones)
3	4	RAGE IN EDEN — Ultravox (Chrysalis)
6	5	SHAKY — Shakin' Stevens (Epic)
5	6	TIME — Electric Light Orchestra (Jet)
9	7	WIRED FOR SOUND — Cliff Richard (EMI)
22	8	SUPER HITS 1 & 2 — Various Artists (Ronco)
-	9	HOOKED ON CLASSICS — Louis Clark & the Royal Philharmonic Orchestra (K-Tel)
14	10	CELEBRATION — Johnny Mathis (CBS)
15	11	WALK UNDER LADDERS — Joan Armatrading (A&M)
24	12	PENTHOUSE AND PAVEMENT — Heaven 17 (BEF/Virgin)
11	13	SECRET COMBINATION — Randy Crawford (Warner Bros.)
13	14	BAT OUT OF HELL — Meatloaf (Epic)
12	15	PRESENT ARMS — UB40 (DEP Int)
4	16	DANCE — Gary Numan (Beggars Banquet)
21	17	KINGS OF THE WILD FRONTIER — Adam & the Ants (CBS)
10	18	DURAN DURAN — Duran Duran (EMI)
7	19	LOVE SONGS — Cliff Richard (EMI)
-	20	ANGELIC UPSTARTS — Angelic Upstarts (Zonophone)
19	21	HAPPY BIRTHDAY — Altered Images (Epic)
8	22	STARS ON 45 VOL 2 — Starsound (CBS)
-	23	LEVEL 42 — Level 42 (Polydor)
18	24	HITS RIGHT UP YOUR STREET — Shadows (Polydor)
23	25	MICHAEL SCHENKER GROUP — Michael Schenker Group (Chrysalis)
-	26	BUCKS FIZZ — Bucks Fizz (RCA)
26	27	BLACK & WHITE — Pointer Sisters (Planet)
20	28	DANCE DANCE DANCE — Various Artists (K-Tel)
-	29	DENIM AND LEATHER — Saxon (Carrere)
-	30	THE GARDEN — John Foxx (Virgin)

Meatloaf's *Dead Ringer* was the belated follow-up to his huge 1978 seller *Bat Out Of Hell*, and though it proved to have nothing like the chart staying power of its predecessor, it initially sold much more quickly, securing a Number 1 position which held the Rolling Stones' *Tattoo You* to runner-up status. With the release of *Wired For Sound* and continuing success of *Love Songs*, Cliff Richard had two albums in the Top Ten simultaneously for the first time since the heady days of 1963.

October 1981

10 October 1981

Last	This	Title / Artist (Label)
2	1	DEAD RINGER — Meatloaf (Epic)
1	2	ABACAB — Genesis (Charisma)
9	3	HOOKED ON CLASSICS — Louis Clark & the Royal Philharmonic Orchestra (K-Tel)
8	4	SUPER HITS 1 & 2 — Various Artists (Ronco)
-	5	IF I SHOULD LOVE AGAIN — Barry Manilow (Arista)
7	6	WIRED FOR SOUND — Cliff Richard (EMI)
5	7	SHAKY — Shakin' Stevens (Epic)
4	8	RAGE IN EDEN — Ultravox (Chrysalis)
-	9	GHOST IN THE MACHINE — Police (A&M)
3	10	TATTOO YOU — Rolling Stones (Rolling Stones)
10	11	CELEBRATION — Johnny Mathis (CBS)
15	12	PRESENT ARMS — UB40 (DEP Int)
6	13	TIME — Electric Light Orchestra (Jet)
12	14	PENTHOUSE AND PAVEMENT — Heaven 17 (BEF/Virgin)
13	15	SECRET COMBINATION — Randy Crawford (Warner Bros.)
29	16	DENIM AND LEATHER — Saxon (Carrere)
19	17	LOVE SONGS — Cliff Richard (EMI)
-	18	BEAT THE CARROTT — Jasper Carrott (DJM)
18	19	DURAN DURAN — Duran Duran (EMI)
-	20	SONS & FASCINATION/SISTERS FEELINGS CALL — Simple Minds (Virgin)
24	21	HITS RIGHT UP YOUR STREET — Shadows (Polydor)
-	22	YOU COULD HAVE BEEN WITH ME — Sheena Easton (EMI)
30	23	THE GARDEN — John Foxx (Virgin)
11	24	WALK UNDER LADDERS — Joan Armatrading (A&M)
-	25	ANTHEM — Toyah (Safari)
28	26	DANCE DANCE DANCE — Various Artists (K-Tel)
-	27	ASSEMBLAGE — Japan (Hansa)
16	28	DANCE — Gary Numan (Beggars Banquet)
-	29	DISCIPLINE — King Crimson (Polydor)
-	30	THE VERY BEST OF ANNE MURRAY — Anne Murray (Capitol)

17 October 1981

Last	This	Title / Artist (Label)
9	1	GHOST IN THE MACHINE — Police (A&M)
-	2	7 — Madness (Stiff)
4	3	SUPER HITS 1 & 2 — Various Artists (Ronco)
2	4	ABACAB — Genesis (Charisma)
7	5	SHAKY — Shakin' Stevens (Epic)
5	6	IF I SHOULD LOVE AGAIN — Barry Manilow (Arista)
1	7	DEAD RINGER — Meatloaf (Epic)
10	8	TATTOO YOU — Rolling Stones (Rolling Stones)
6	9	WIRED FOR SOUND — Cliff Richard (EMI)
3	10	HOOKED ON CLASSICS — Louis Clark & the Royal Philharmonic Orchestra (K-Tel)
8	11	RAGE IN EDEN — Ultravox (Chrysalis)
11	12	CELEBRATION — Johnny Mathis (CBS)
15	13	SECRET COMBINATION — Randy Crawford (Warner Bros.)
16	14	DENIM AND LEATHER — Saxon (Carrere)
27	15	ASSEMBLAGE — Japan (Hansa)
14	16	PENTHOUSE AND PAVEMENT — Heaven 17 (BEF/Virgin)
17	17	LOVE SONGS — Cliff Richard (EMI)
20	18	SONS & FASCINATION/SISTERS FEELINGS CALL — Simple Minds (Virgin)
12	19	PRESENT ARMS — UB40 (DEP Int)
18	20	BEAT THE CARROTT — Jasper Carrott (DJM)
30	21	THE VERY BEST OF ANNE MURRAY — Anne Murray (Capitol)
13	22	TIME — Electric Light Orchestra (Jet)
22	23	YOU COULD HAVE BEEN WITH ME — Sheena Easton (EMI)
-	24	HAPPY BIRTHDAY — Altered Images (Epic)
-	25	NINE TONIGHT — Bob Seger & the Silver Bullet Band (Capitol)
23	26	THE GARDEN — John Foxx (Virgin)
-	27	20 GOLDEN GREATS — Diana Ross (Motown)
-	28	FRESH QUOTA — Status Quo (Phonogram)
-	29	BAT OUT OF HELL — Meatloaf (Epic)
-	30	BLACK & WHITE — Pointer Sisters (Planet)

24 October 1981

Last	This	Title / Artist (Label)
1	1	GHOST IN THE MACHINE — Police (A&M)
5	2	SHAKY — Shakin' Stevens (Epic)
2	3	7 — Madness (Stiff)
6	4	IF I SHOULD LOVE AGAIN — Barry Manilow (Arista)
7	5	DEAD RINGER — Meatloaf (Epic)
3	6	SUPER HITS 1 & 2 — Various Artists (Ronco)
8	7	TATTOO YOU — Rolling Stones (Rolling Stones)
4	8	ABACAB — Genesis (Charisma)
10	9	HOOKED ON CLASSICS — Louis Clark & the Royal Philharmonic Orchestra (K-Tel)
-	10	STILL — Joy Division (Factory)
9	11	WIRED FOR SOUND — Cliff Richard (EMI)
11	12	RAGE IN EDEN — Ultravox (Chrysalis)
12	13	CELEBRATION — Johnny Mathis (CBS)
14	14	DENIM AND LEATHER — Saxon (Carrere)
19	15	PRESENT ARMS — UB40 (DEP Int)
-	16	DARE — Human League (Virgin)
16	17	PENTHOUSE AND PAVEMENT — Heaven 17 (BEF/Virgin)
24	18	HAPPY BIRTHDAY — Altered Images (Epic)
-	19	HITS RIGHT UP YOUR STREET — Shadows (Polydor)
13	20	SECRET COMBINATION — Randy Crawford (Warner Bros.)
-	21	OCTOBER — U2 (Island)
-	22	ROCK CLASSICS — London Symphony Orchestra & Royal Chorale Society (K-Tel)
26	23	THE GARDEN — John Foxx (Virgin)
-	24	ISMISM — Godley & Creme (Polydor)
21	25	THE VERY BEST OF ANNE MURRAY — Anne Murray (Capitol)
22	26	TIME — Electric Light Orchestra (Jet)
-	27	KINGS OF THE WILD FRONTIER — Adam & the Ants (CBS)
15	28	ASSEMBLAGE — Japan (Hansa)
-	29	DURAN DURAN — Duran Duran (EMI)
-	30	WALK UNDER LADDERS — Joan Armatrading (A&M)

31 October 1981

Last	This	Title / Artist (Label)
1	1	GHOST IN THE MACHINE — Police (A&M)
16	2	DARE — Human League (Virgin)
4	3	IF I SHOULD LOVE AGAIN — Barry Manilow (Arista)
2	4	SHAKY — Shakin' Stevens (Epic)
3	5	7 — Madness (Stiff)
9	6	HOOKED ON CLASSICS — Philharmonic Orchestra (K-Tel)
6	7	SUPER HITS 1 & 2 — Various Artists (Ronco)
8	8	ABACAB — Genesis (Charisma)
5	9	DEAD RINGER — Meatloaf (Epic)
-	10	HEDGEHOG SANDWICH — Not the Nine O'clock News (BBC)
20	11	OCTOBER — U2 (Island)
10	12	STILL — Joy Division (Factory)
-	13	BODY TALK — Imagination (R&B)
-	14	GOSH IT'S BAD MANNERS — Bad Manners (Magnet)
11	15	WIRED FOR SOUND — Cliff Richard (EMI)
7	16	TATTOO YOU — Rolling Stones (Rolling Stones)
13	17	CELEBRATION — Johnny Mathis (CBS)
12	18	RAGE IN EDEN — Ultravox (Chrysalis)
26	19	TIME — Electric Light Orchestra (Jet)
16	20	PENTHOUSE AND PAVEMENT — Heaven 17 (BEF/Virgin)
14	21	DENIM AND LEATHER — Saxon (Carrere)
22	22	ROCK CLASSICS — London Symphony Orchestra & Royal Chorale Society (K-Tel)
24	23	ISMISM — Godley & Creme (Polydor)
-	24	SONIC ATTACK — Hawkwind (RCA)
-	25	MASK — Bauhaus (Beggars Banquet)
20	26	SECRET COMBINATION — Randy Crawford (Warner Bros.)
25	27	THE VERY BEST OF ANNE MURRAY — Anne Murray (Capitol)
18	28	HAPPY BIRTHDAY — Altered Images (Epic)
-	29	TOM TOM CLUB — Tom Tom Club (Island)
28	30	ASSEMBLAGE — Japan (Hansa)

The Police proved their consistency by completing a hat-trick of Number 1 albums with *Ghost In The Machine*. Its three weeks atop the chart prevented likely contenders like Madness, Shakin' Stevens and Barry Manilow from making Number 1 - although the trio's current single *Invisible Sun* stalled at Number 2. *Hedgehog Sandwich* gave Not The Nine O'Clock News a second Top-Tenner, a unique achievement for a comedy team, while *Hooked On Classics* was a classical variation on the Stars On 45 formula.

7 November 1981

last week	this week		
2	1	DARE	Human League (Virgin)
4	2	SHAKY	Shakin' Stevens (Epic)
1	3	GHOST IN THE MACHINE	Police (A&M)
3	4	IF I SHOULD LOVE AGAIN	Barry Manilow (Arista)
5	5	7	Madness (Stiff)
6	6	HOOKED ON CLASSICS	Louis Clark & the Royal Philharmonic Orchestra (K-Tel)
7	7	SUPER HITS 1 & 2	Various Artists (Ronco)
-	8	ALMOST BLUE	Elvis Costello (F-Beat)
-	9	LOVE IS	Various Artists (K-Tel)
-	10	BEST OF BLONDIE	Blondie (Chrysalis)
11	11	OCTOBER	U2 (Island)
28	12	HAPPY BIRTHDAY	Altered Images (Epic)
12	13	STILL	Joy Division (Factory)
10	14	HEDGEHOG SANDWICH	Not the Nine O'clock News (BBC)
14	15	GOSH IT'S BAD MANNERS	Bad Manners (Magnet)
8	16	ABACAB	Genesis (Charisma)
17	17	CELEBRATION	Johnny Mathis (CBS)
21	18	DENIM AND LEATHER	Saxon (Carrere)
12	19	BODY TALK	Imagination (R&B)
16	20	TATTOO YOU	Rolling Stones (Rolling Stones)
26	21	SECRET COMBINATION	Randy Crawford (Warner Bros.)
24	22	SONIC ATTACK	Hawkwind (RCA)
-	23	CARRY ON OI!	Various Artists (Secret)
-	24	SEE JUNGLE! SEE JUNGLE! GO JOIN YOUR GANG YEAH CITY ALL OVER! GO APE CRAZY	Bow Wow Wow (RCA)
9	25	DEAD RINGER	Meatloaf (Epic)
18	25	RAGE IN EDEN	Ultravox (Chrysalis)
-	27	PHYSICAL	Olivia Newton-John (EMI)
25	28	MASK	Bauhaus (Beggars Banquet)
-	29	EXIT STAGE LEFT	Rush (Mercury)
-	29	NO CAUSE FOR CONCERN	Vice Squad (Zonophone)

14 November 1981

last	this		
1	1	DARE	Human League (Virgin)
-	2	QUEEN'S GREATEST HITS	Queen (EMI)
2	3	SHAKY	Shakin' Stevens (Epic)
10	4	BEST OF BLONDIE	Blondie (Chrysalis)
3	5	GHOST IN THE MACHINE	Police (A&M)
8	6	ALMOST BLUE	Elvis Costello (F-Beat)
29	7	EXIT STAGE LEFT	Rush (Mercury)
4	8	IF I SHOULD LOVE AGAIN	Barry Manilow (Arista)
-	9	PRINCE CHARMING	Adam & the Ants (CBS)
5	10	7	Madness (Stiff)
-	11	DOUBLE TROUBLE	Gillan (Virgin)
13	12	STILL	Joy Division (Factory)
9	13	LOVE IS	Various Artists (K-Tel)
-	14	ARCHITECTURE AND MORALITY	Orchestral Manoeuvres in the Dark (Dindisc)
16	15	ABACAB	Genesis (Charisma)
-	16	DIARY OF A MADMAN	Ozzy Osbourne (Jet)
14	17	HEDGEHOG SANDWICH	Not the Nine O'clock News (BBC)
6	18	HOOKED ON CLASSICS	Louis Clark & the Royal Philharmonic Orchestra (K-Tel)
-	19	WIRED FOR SOUND	Cliff Richard (EMI)
7	20	SUPER HITS 1 & 2	Various Artists (Ronco)
11	21	OCTOBER	U2 (Island)
12	22	HAPPY BIRTHDAY	Altered Images (Epic)
19	23	BODY TALK	Imagination (R&B)
-	24	MONSTER TRACKS	Various Artists (Polydor)
-	25	SPEAK AND SPELL	Depeche Mode (Mute)
-	26	WHY DO FOOLS FALL IN LOVE	Diana Ross (Capitol)
29	27	NO CAUSE FOR CONCERN	Vice Squad (Zonophone)
-	28	PLEASURE	Girls At Our Best (Happy Birthday)
27	29	PHYSICAL	Olivia Newton-John (EMI)
15	30	GOSH IT'S BAD MANNERS	Bad Manners (Magnet)

21 November 1981

last	this		
9	1	PRINCE CHARMING	Adam & the Ants (CBS)
1	2	DARE	Human League (Virgin)
14	3	ARCHITECTURE AND MORALITY	Orchestral Manoeuvres in the Dark (Dindisc)
2	4	QUEEN'S GREATEST HITS	Queen (EMI)
5	5	GHOST IN THE MACHINE	Police (A&M)
25	6	SPEAK AND SPELL	Depeche Mode (Mute)
3	7	SHAKY	Shakin' Stevens (Epic)
-	8	TONIGHT I'M YOURS	Rod Stewart (Riva)
4	9	BEST OF BLONDIE	Blondie (Chrysalis)
-	10	MOB RULES	Black Sabbath (Vertigo)
7	11	EXIT STAGE LEFT	Rush (Mercury)
6	12	ALMOST BLUE	Elvis Costello (F-Beat)
16	13	DIARY OF A MADMAN	Ozzy Osbourne (Jet)
13	14	LOVE IS	Various Artists (K-Tel)
-	15	RAISE!	Earth Wind & Fire (CBS)
17	16	HEDGEHOG SANDWICH	Not the Nine O'clock News (BBC)
12	17	STILL	Joy Division (Factory)
-	18	PUNKS NOT DEAD	Exploited (Secret)
-	19	PEARLS	Elkie Brooks (A&M)
10	20	7	Madness (Stiff)
20	21	SUPER HITS 1 & 2	Various Artists (Ronco)
11	22	DOUBLE TROUBLE	Gillan (Virgin)
8	23	IF I SHOULD LOVE AGAIN	Barry Manilow (Arista)
-	24	THE GEORGE BENSON COLLECTION	George Benson (Warner Bros.)
-	25	SECRET COMBINATION	Randy Crawford (Warner Bros.)
18	26	HOOKED ON CLASSICS	Louis Clark & the Royal Philharmonic Orchestra (K-Tel)
-	27	BEST OF RAINBOW	Rainbow (Polydor)
15	28	ABACAB	Genesis (Charisma)
-	28	SEE JUNGLE! SEE JUNGLE! GO JOIN YOUR GANG YEAH CITY ALL OVER! GO APE CRAZY	Bow Wow Wow (RCA)
21	30	OCTOBER	U2 (Island)

28 November 1981

last	this		
1	1	PRINCE CHARMING	Adam & the Ants (CBS)
4	2	QUEEN'S GREATEST HITS	Queen (EMI)
3	3	ARCHITECTURE AND MORALITY	Orchestral Manoeuvres in the Dark (Dindisc)
5	4	GHOST IN THE MACHINE	Police (A&M)
2	5	DARE	Human League (Virgin)
9	6	BEST OF BLONDIE	Blondie (Chrysalis)
7	7	SHAKY	Shakin' Stevens (Epic)
8	8	TONIGHT I'M YOURS	Rod Stewart (Riva)
12	9	ALMOST BLUE	Elvis Costello (F-Beat)
19	10	PEARLS	Elkie Brooks (A&M)
15	11	RAISE!	Earth Wind & Fire (CBS)
6	12	SPEAK AND SPELL	Depeche Mode (Mute)
-	13	CHART HITS '81	Various Artists (K-Tel)
26	14	HOOKED ON CLASSICS	Louis Clark & the Royal Philharmonic Orchestra (K-Tel)
10	15	MOB RULES	Black Sabbath (Vertigo)
11	16	EXIT STAGE LEFT	Rush (Mercury)
-	17	TIN DRUM	Japan (Virgin)
28	18	ABACAB	Genesis (Charisma)
-	19	WIRED FOR SOUND	Cliff Richard (EMI)
14	20	LOVE IS	Various Artists (K-Tel)
23	21	IF I SHOULD LOVE AGAIN	Barry Manilow (Arista)
-	22	ALL THE GREAT HITS	Diana Ross (Motown)
-	23	DE NINA A MUJER	Julio Iglesias (CBS)
24	24	THE GEORGE BENSON COLLECTION	George Benson (Warner Bros.)
17	25	STILL	Joy Division (Factory)
21	26	SUPER HITS 1 & 2	Various Artists (Ronco)
27	27	BEST OF RAINBOW	Rainbow (Polydor)
20	28	7	Madness (Stiff)
16	29	HEDGEHOG SANDWICH	Not the Nine O'clock News (BBC)
-	30	BODY TALK	Imagination (R&B)

As always, the hot chart names came out to play for the pre-Christmas market. Human League's *Dare* initially gave way quite quickly at the top to Adam & The Ants' *Prince Charming*, though would get a second boost when the million-selling single *Don't You Want Me* was extracted from it. *Queen's Greatest Hits*, rounding up most of the quartet's major hit singles to date, would eventually become the best-selling compilation album of all time in the UK, remaining a steady seller throughout the decade.

December 1981

5 December 1981

last week	this week		
2	1	QUEEN'S GREATEST HITS	Queen (EMI)
13	2	CHART HITS '81	Various Artists (K-Tel)
5	3	DARE	Human League (Virgin)
6	4	BEST OF BLONDIE	Blondie (Chrysalis)
1	5	PRINCE CHARMING	Adam & the Ants (CBS)
3	6	ARCHITECTURE AND MORALITY	Orchestral Manoeuvres in the Dark (Dindisc)
23	7	DE NINA A MUJER	Julio Iglesias (CBS)
7	8	SHAKY	Shakin' Stevens (Epic)
17	9	TIN DRUM	Japan (Virgin)
10	10	PEARLS	Elkie Brooks (A&M)
4	11	GHOST IN THE MACHINE	Police (A&M)
8	12	TONIGHT I'M YOURS	Rod Stewart (Riva)
12	13	SPEAK AND SPELL	Depeche Mode (Mute)
-	14	THE SIMON & GARFUNKEL COLLECTION	Simon & Garfunkel (CBS)
11	15	RAISE!	Earth Wind & Fire (CBS)
16	16	EXIT STAGE LEFT	Rush (Mercury)
-	17	MOVEMENT	New Order (Factory)
9	18	ALMOST BLUE	Elvis Costello (F-Beat)
-	19	HANSIMANIA	James Last (Polydor)
22	20	ALL THE GREAT HITS	Diana Ross (Motown)
28	21	7	Madness (Stiff)
27	22	BEST OF RAINBOW	Rainbow (Polydor)
20	23	LOVE IS	Various Artists (K-Tel)
-	24	NON-STOP EROTIC CABARET	Soft Cell (Some Bizzare)
-	25	WHY DO FOOLS FALL IN LOVE	Diana Ross (Capitol)
14	26	HOOKED ON CLASSICS	Louis Clark & the Royal Philharmonic Orchestra (K-Tel)
21	27	IF I SHOULD LOVE AGAIN	Barry Manilow (Arista)
-	28	THE VERY BEST OF SHOWADDYWADDY	Showaddywaddy (Arista)
-	29	LA FOLIE	Stranglers (Liberty)
19	30	WIRED FOR SOUND	Cliff Richard (EMI)

12 December 1981

2	1	CHART HITS '81	Various Artists (K-Tel)
1	2	QUEEN'S GREATEST HITS	Queen (EMI)
-	3	FOR THOSE ABOUT TO ROCK	AC/DC (Atlantic)
5	4	PRINCE CHARMING	Adam & the Ants (CBS)
10	5	PEARLS	Elkie Brooks (A&M)
3	6	DARE	Human League (Virgin)
4	7	BEST OF BLONDIE	Blondie (Chrysalis)
14	8	THE SIMON & GARFUNKEL COLLECTION	Simon & Garfunkel (CBS)
24	9	NON-STOP EROTIC CABARET	Soft Cell (Some Bizzare)
12	10	TONIGHT I'M YOURS	Rod Stewart (Riva)
6	11	ARCHITECTURE AND MORALITY	Orchestral Manoeuvres in Dark (Dindisc)
7	12	DE NINA A MUJER	Julio Iglesias (CBS)
8	13	SHAKY	Shakin' Stevens (Epic)
9	14	TIN DRUM	Japan (Virgin)
15	15	RAISE!	Earth Wind & Fire (CBS)
20	16	ALL THE GREAT HITS	Diana Ross (Motown)
30	17	WIRED FOR SOUND	Cliff Richard (EMI)
22	18	BEST OF RAINBOW	Rainbow (Polydor)
26	19	HOOKED ON CLASSICS	Louis Clark & Philharmonic Orchestra (K-Tel)
11	20	GHOST IN THE MACHINE	Police (A&M)
28	21	THE VERY BEST OF SHOWADDYWADDY	Showaddywaddy (Arista)
19	22	HANSIMANIA	James Last (Polydor)
18	23	ALMOST BLUE	Elvis Costello (F-Beat)
-	24	WILDER	Teardrop Explodes (Mercury)
-	25	BEGIN THE BEGUINE	Julio Iglesias (CBS)
13	26	SPEAK AND SPELL	Depeche Mode (Mute)
-	27	RENEGADE	Thin Lizzy (Vertigo)
-	28	PERHAPS LOVE	Placido Domingo & John Denver (CBS)
-	29	COUNTRY GIRL	Billy Jo Spears (Warwick)
-	30	THE PICK OF BILLY CONNOLLY	Billy Connolly (Polydor)

19 December 1981

6	1	DARE	Human League (Virgin)
4	2	PRINCE CHARMING	Adam & the Ants (CBS)
1	3	CHART HITS '81	Various Artists (K-Tel)
2	4	QUEEN'S GREATEST HITS	Queen (EMI)
5	5	PEARLS	Elkie Brooks (A&M)
25	6	BEGIN THE BEGUINE	Julio Iglesias (CBS)
7	7	BEST OF BLONDIE	Blondie (Chrysalis)
8	8	THE SIMON & GARFUNKEL COLLECTION	Simon & Garfunkel (CBS)
3	9	FOR THOSE ABOUT TO ROCK	AC/DC (Atlantic)
20	10	GHOST IN THE MACHINE	Police (A&M)
13	11	SHAKY	Shakin' Stevens (Epic)
10	12	TONIGHT I'M YOURS	Rod Stewart (Riva)
9	13	NON-STOP EROTIC CABARET	Soft Cell (Some Bizzare)
11	14	ARCHITECTURE AND MORALITY	Orchestral Manoeuvres in the Dark (Dindisc)
-	15	THE VISITORS	Abba (Epic)
19	16	HOOKED ON CLASSICS	Louis Clark & Philharmonic Orchestra (K-Tel)
29	17	COUNTRY GIRL	Billy Jo Spears (Warwick)
15	18	RAISE!	Earth Wind & Fire (CBS)
14	19	TIN DRUM	Japan (Virgin)
16	20	ALL THE GREAT HITS	Diana Ross (Motown)
-	21	ONCE UPON A TIME	Siouxsie & the Banshees (Polydor)
22	22	HANSIMANIA	James Last (Polydor)
17	23	WIRED FOR SOUND	Cliff Richard (EMI)
12	24	DE NINA A MUJER	Julio Iglesias (CBS)
28	25	PERHAPS LOVE	Placido Domingo & John Denver (CBS)
-	26	MOVEMENT	New Order (Factory)
24	27	WILDER	Teardrop Explodes (Mercury)
23	28	ALMOST BLUE	Elvis Costello (F-Beat)
18	29	BEST OF RAINBOW	Rainbow (Polydor)
30	30	THE PICK OF BILLY CONNOLLY	Billy Connolly (Polydor)

Topping the pre-Christmas singles chart with *Begin The Beguine*, Latin hearthrob vocalist Julio Iglesias suddenly found the kind of success in the UK that he enjoyed elsewhere in the world, manifested in two albums in the Top 30 simultaneously. Elkie Brooks scored the biggest-selling album of her career with *Pearls*, a collection of classic song covers, while Blondie, Diana Ross, Rainbow, Showaddywaddy and the long-split Simon & Garfunkel all had big-selling hit singles collections for Christmas.

Clockwise from top left: Debbie (later Deborah) Harry, Bob Marley (without the Wailers), Madness and Adam (without the Ants)

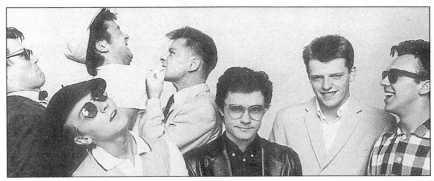

217

January 1982

2 January 1982

last week	this week	Album	Artist
15	1	THE VISITORS	Abba (Epic)
1	2	DARE	Human League (Virgin)
3	3	CHART HITS '81	Various Artists (K-Tel)
4	4	QUEEN'S GREATEST HITS	Queen (EMI)
2	5	PRINCE CHARMING	Adam & the Ants (CBS)
7	6	BEST OF BLONDIE	Blondie (Chrysalis)
8	7	THE SIMON & GARFUNKEL COLLECTION	Simon & Garfunkel (CBS)
5	8	PEARLS	Elkie Brooks (A&M)
6	9	BEGIN THE BEGUINE	Julio Iglesias (CBS)
23	10	WIRED FOR SOUND	Cliff Richard (EMI)
12	11	TONIGHT I'M YOURS	Rod Stewart (Riva)
10	12	GHOST IN THE MACHINE	Police (A&M)
11	13	SHAKY	Shakin' Stevens (Epic)
9	14	FOR THOSE ABOUT TO ROCK	AC/DC (Atlantic)
20	15	ALL THE GREAT HITS	Diana Ross (Motown)
14	16	ARCHITECTURE AND MORALITY	Orchestral Manoeuvres In The Dark (DinDisc)
25	17	PERHAPS LOVE	Placido Domingo & John Denver (CBS)
-	18	IF I SHOULD LOVE AGAIN	Barry Manilow (Arista)
-	19	CHANGESTWOBOWIE	David Bowie (RCA)
22	20	HANSIMANIA	James Last (Polydor)
-	21	CHAS AND DAVE'S CHRISTMAS JAMBOREE BAG	Chas & Dave (Warwick)
18	22	RAISE!	Earth Wind & Fire (CBS)
-	23	DURAN DURAN	Duran Duran (EMI)
-	24	LOVE SONGS	Cliff Richard (EMI)
-	25	REJOICE	St. Paul's Boys Choir (K-Tel)
-	26	HAWAIIAN PARADISE/CHRISTMAS	Woot Steenhuis (Warwick)
-	27	HEDGEHOG SANDWICH	Not The Nine O'Clock News (BBC)
-	28	ISMISM	Godley & Creme (Polydor)
-	29	THE OFFICIAL BBC ALBUM OF THE ROYAL WEDDING	BBC Recording (BBC)
-	30	WE ARE MOST AMUSED – THE VERY BEST OF BRITISH COMEDY	Various Artists (Ronco)

9 January 1982

last week	this week	Album	Artist
2	1	DARE	Human League (Virgin)
4	2	QUEEN'S GREATEST HITS	Queen (EMI)
1	3	THE VISITORS	Abba (Epic)
10	4	WIRED FOR SOUND	Cliff Richard (EMI)
3	5	CHART HITS '81	Various Artists (K-Tel)
6	6	BEST OF BLONDIE	Blondie (Chrysalis)
8	7	PEARLS	Elkie Brooks (A&M)
5	8	PRINCE CHARMING	Adam & the Ants (CBS)
12	9	GHOST IN THE MACHINE	Police (A&M)
13	10	SHAKY	Shakin' Stevens (Epic)
16	11	ARCHITECTURE AND MORALITY	Orchestral Manoeuvres In The Dark (DinDisc)
11	12	TONIGHT I'M YOURS	Rod Stewart (Riva)
7	13	THE SIMON & GARFUNKEL COLLECTION	Simon & Garfunkel (CBS)
-	14	HITS HITS HITS	Various Artists (Ronco)
21	15	CHAS AND DAVE'S CHRISTMAS JAMBOREE BAG	Chas & Dave (Warwick)
23	16	DURAN DURAN	Duran Duran (EMI)
9	17	BEGIN THE BEGUINE	Julio Iglesias (CBS)
-	18	HOOKED ON CLASSICS	Louis Clark & the Royal Philharmonic Orchestra (K-Tel)
15	19	ALL THE GREAT HITS	Diana Ross (Motown)
24	20	LOVE SONGS	Cliff Richard (EMI)
19	21	CHANGESTWOBOWIE	David Bowie (RCA)
20	22	HANSIMANIA	James Last (Polydor)
14	23	FOR THOSE ABOUT TO ROCK	AC/DC (Atlantic)
-	24	NON-STOP EROTIC CABARET	Soft Cell (Some Bizzare)
18	25	IF I SHOULD LOVE AGAIN	Barry Manilow (Arista)
-	26	MADNESS 7	Madness (Stiff)
26	27	HAWAIIAN PARADISE/CHRISTMAS	Woot Steenhuis (Warwick)
22	28	RAISE!	Earth Wind & Fire (CBS)
28	29	ISMISM	Godley & Creme (Polydor)
27	30	HEDGEHOG SANDWICH	Not The Nine O'Clock News (BBC)

16 January 1982

last week	this week	Album	Artist
1	1	DARE	Human League (Virgin)
2	2	QUEEN'S GREATEST HITS	Queen (EMI)
3	3	THE VISITORS	Abba (Epic)
8	4	PRINCE CHARMING	Adam & the Ants (CBS)
5	5	CHART HITS '81	Various Artists (K-Tel)
14	6	HITS HITS HITS	Various Artists (Ronco)
4	7	WIRED FOR SOUND	Cliff Richard (EMI)
7	8	PEARLS	Elkie Brooks (A&M)
9	9	GHOST IN THE MACHINE	Police (A&M)
11	10	ARCHITECTURE AND MORALITY	Orchestral Manoeuvres In The Dark (DinDisc)
13	11	THE SIMON & GARFUNKEL COLLECTION	Simon & Garfunkel (CBS)
24	12	NON-STOP EROTIC CABARET	Soft Cell (Some Bizzare)
10	13	SHAKY	Shakin' Stevens (Epic)
6	14	BEST OF BLONDIE	Blondie (Chrysalis)
-	15	TIN DRUM	Japan (Virgin)
-	16	ONCE UPON A TIME	Siouxsie & the Banshees (Polydor)
17	17	BEGIN THE BEGUINE	Julio Iglesias (CBS)
28	18	RAISE!	Earth Wind & Fire (CBS)
23	19	FOR THOSE ABOUT TO ROCK	AC/DC (Atlantic)
26	20	MADNESS 7	Madness (Stiff)
12	21	TONIGHT I'M YOURS	Rod Stewart (Riva)
20	22	LOVE SONGS	Cliff Richard (EMI)
-	23	CHRISTOPHER CROSS	Christopher Cross (Warner Bros.)
21	24	CHANGESTWOBOWIE	David Bowie (RCA)
25	25	IF I SHOULD LOVE AGAIN	Barry Manilow (Arista)
-	26	HAPPY BIRTHDAY	Altered Images (Epic)
-	27	THE GEORGE BENSON COLLECTION	George Benson (Warner Bros.)
-	28	BEST OF RAINBOW	Rainbow (Polydor)
19	29	ALL THE GREAT HITS	Diana Ross (Motown)
-	30	4	Foreigner (Atlantic)

23 January 1982

last week	this week	Album	Artist
1	1	DARE	Human League (Virgin)
2	2	QUEEN'S GREATEST HITS	Queen (EMI)
3	3	THE VISITORS	Abba (Epic)
6	4	HITS HITS HITS	Various Artists (Ronco)
4	5	PRINCE CHARMING	Adam & the Ants (CBS)
7	6	WIRED FOR SOUND	Cliff Richard (EMI)
8	7	PEARLS	Elkie Brooks (A&M)
9	8	GHOST IN THE MACHINE	Police (A&M)
-	9	LOVE SONGS	Barbra Streisand (CBS)
5	10	CHART HITS '81	Various Artists (K-Tel)
14	11	BEST OF BLONDIE	Blondie (Chrysalis)
10	12	ARCHITECTURE AND MORALITY	Orchestral Manoeuvres In The Dark (DinDisc)
22	13	LOVE SONGS	Cliff Richard (EMI)
13	14	SHAKY	Shakin' Stevens (Epic)
12	15	NON-STOP EROTIC CABARET	Soft Cell (Some Bizzare)
-	16	MODERN DANCE	Various Artists (K-Tel)
30	17	4	Foreigner (Atlantic)
-	18	DURAN DURAN	Duran Duran (EMI)
20	19	MADNESS 7	Madness (Stiff)
11	20	THE SIMON & GARFUNKEL COLLECTION	Simon & Garfunkel (CBS)
15	21	TIN DRUM	Japan (Virgin)
21	22	TONIGHT I'M YOURS	Rod Stewart (Riva)
23	23	CHRISTOPHER CROSS	Christopher Cross (Warner Bros.)
16	24	ONCE UPON A TIME	Siouxsie & the Ba (Polydor)
19	25	FOR THOSE ABOUT TO ROCK	AC/DC (Atlantic)
-	26	ANTHEM	Toyah (Safari)
-	27	SOMETHING SPECIAL	Kool & the Gang (De-Lite)
-	28	TRAVELOGUE	Human League (Virgin)
17	29	BEGIN THE BEGUINE	Julio Iglesias (CBS)
-	30	DEAD RINGER	Meatloaf (Epic)

Abba, as was becoming their habit, celebrated a change of year with a chart-topping album, *The Visitors*. It was the Swedish quartet's seventh Number 1 LP, but with a break-up looming, this would be the last set of original material from them. Human League's *Dare* was to be their biggest-selling album, and the UK's best seller for most of the first two months of 1982. And who could possibly have been buying Chas And Dave's Christmas set during the week after New Year?

218

January – February 1982

30 January 1982

last	this	Title / Artist (Label)
1	1	DARE — Human League (Virgin)
3	2	THE VISITORS — Abba (Epic)
4	3	HITS HITS HITS — Various Artists (Ronco)
2	4	QUEEN'S GREATEST HITS — Queen (EMI)
9	5	LOVE SONGS — Barbra Streisand (CBS)
16	6	MODERN DANCE — Various Artists (K-Tel)
12	7	ARCHITECTURE AND MORALITY — Orchestral Manoeuvres In The Dark (DinDisc)
8	8	GHOST IN THE MACHINE — Police (A&M)
5	9	PRINCE CHARMING — Adam & the Ants (CBS)
7	10	PEARLS — Elkie Brooks (A&M)
27	11	SOMETHING SPECIAL — Kool & the Gang (De-Lite)
10	12	CHART HITS '81 — Various Artists (K-Tel)
13	13	LOVE SONGS — Cliff Richard (EMI)
30	14	DEAD RINGER — Meatloaf (Epic)
6	15	WIRED FOR SOUND — Cliff Richard (EMI)
28	16	TRAVELOGUE — Human League (Virgin)
14	17	SHAKY — Shakin' Stevens (Epic)
18	18	DURAN DURAN — Duran Duran (EMI)
22	19	TONIGHT I'M YOURS — Rod Stewart (Riva)
11	20	BEST OF BLONDIE — Blondie (Chrysalis)
19	21	MADNESS 7 — Madness (Stiff)
17	22	4 — Foreigner (Atlantic)
23	23	CHRISTOPHER CROSS — Christopher Cross (Warner Bros.)
20	24	THE SIMON & GARFUNKEL COLLECTION — Simon & Garfunkel (CBS)
29	25	BEGIN THE BEGUINE — Julio Iglesias (CBS)
15	26	NON-STOP EROTIC CABARET — Soft Cell (Some Bizzare)
-	27	CHANGESTWOBOWIE — David Bowie (RCA)
-	28	SECRET COMBINATION — Randy Crawford (Warner Bros.)
25	29	FOR THOSE ABOUT TO ROCK — AC/DC (Atlantic)
21	30	TIN DRUM — Japan (Virgin)

6 February 1982

last	this	Title / Artist (Label)
5	1	LOVE SONGS — Barbra Streisand (CBS)
1	2	DARE — Human League (Virgin)
3	3	HITS HITS HITS — Various Artists (Ronco)
2	4	THE VISITORS — Abba (Epic)
10	5	PEARLS — Elkie Brooks (A&M)
6	6	MODERN DANCE — Various Artists (K-Tel)
7	7	ARCHITECTURE AND MORALITY — Orchestral Manoeuvres In The Dark (DinDisc)
11	8	SOMETHING SPECIAL — Kool & the Gang (De-Lite)
22	9	4 — Foreigner (Atlantic)
4	10	QUEEN'S GREATEST HITS — Queen (EMI)
-	11	THE FRIENDS OF MR CAIRO — Jon & Vangelis (Polydor)
14	12	DEAD RINGER — Meatloaf (Epic)
8	13	GHOST IN THE MACHINE — Police (A&M)
9	14	PRINCE CHARMING — Adam & the Ants (CBS)
23	15	CHRISTOPHER CROSS — Christopher Cross (Warner Bros.)
16	16	IF I SHOULD LOVE AGAIN — Barry Manilow (Arista)
26	17	NON-STOP EROTIC CABARET — Soft Cell (Some Bizzare)
-	18	LA FOLIE — Stranglers (Liberty)
13	19	LOVE SONGS — Cliff Richard (EMI)
30	20	TIN DRUM — Japan (Virgin)
24	21	THE SIMON & GARFUNKEL COLLECTION — Simon & Garfunkel (CBS)
19	22	TONIGHT I'M YOURS — Rod Stewart (Riva)
17	23	SHAKY — Shakin' Stevens (Epic)
-	24	THE MAN MACHINE — Kraftwerk (Capitol)
16	25	TRAVELOGUE — Human League (Virgin)
12	26	CHART HITS '81 — Various Artists (K-Tel)
-	27	PERHAPS LOVE — Placido Domingo & John Denver (CBS)
20	28	BEST OF BLONDIE — Blondie (Chrysalis)
-	29	SEXTET — A Certain Ratio (Factory)
15	30	WIRED FOR SOUND — Cliff Richard (EMI)

13 February 1982

last	this	Title / Artist (Label)
2	1	DARE — Human League (Virgin)
1	2	LOVE SONGS — Barbra Streisand (CBS)
7	3	ARCHITECTURE AND MORALITY — Orchestral Manoeuvres In The Dark (DinDisc)
5	4	PEARLS — Elkie Brooks (A&M)
12	5	DEAD RINGER — Meatloaf (Epic)
9	6	4 — Foreigner (Atlantic)
8	7	SOMETHING SPECIAL — Kool & the Gang (De-Lite)
15	8	CHRISTOPHER CROSS — Christopher Cross (Warner Bros.)
10	9	QUEEN'S GREATEST HITS — Queen (EMI)
17	10	NON-STOP EROTIC CABARET — Soft Cell (Some Bizzare)
11	11	THE FRIENDS OF MR CAIRO — Jon & Vangelis (Polydor)
6	12	MODERN DANCE — Various Artists (K-Tel)
24	13	THE MAN MACHINE — Kraftwerk (Capitol)
4	14	THE VISITORS — Abba (Epic)
3	15	HITS HITS HITS — Various Artists (Ronco)
-	16	THE GEORGE BENSON COLLECTION — George Benson (Warner Bros.)
-	17	BAT OUT OF HELL — Meatloaf (Epic)
-	18	ALL FOR A SONG — Barbara Dickson (Epic)
18	19	LA FOLIE — Stranglers (Liberty)
16	20	IF I SHOULD LOVE AGAIN — Barry Manilow (Arista)
20	21	TIN DRUM — Japan (Virgin)
-	22	TRANS-EUROPE EXPRESS — Kraftwerk (Capitol)
19	23	LOVE SONGS — Cliff Richard (EMI)
27	24	PERHAPS LOVE — Placido Domingo & John Denver (CBS)
-	25	PRIVATE EYES — Daryl Hall & John Oates (RCA)
14	26	PRINCE CHARMING — Adam & the Ants (CBS)
23	27	SHAKY — Shakin' Stevens (Epic)
21	28	THE SIMON & GARFUNKEL COLLECTION — Simon & Garfunkel (CBS)
-	29	PENTHOUSE AND PAVEMENT — Heaven 17 (Virgin)
-	30	SPEAK AND SPELL — Depeche Mode (Mute)

20 February 1982

last	this	Title / Artist (Label)
1	1	DARE — Human League (Virgin)
2	2	LOVE SONGS — Barbra Streisand (CBS)
3	3	ARCHITECTURE AND MORALITY — Orchestral Manoeuvres In The Dark (DinDisc)
4	4	PEARLS — Elkie Brooks (A&M)
10	5	NON-STOP EROTIC CABARET — Soft Cell (Some Bizzare)
13	6	THE MAN MACHINE — Kraftwerk (Capitol)
11	7	THE FRIENDS OF MR CAIRO — Jon & Vangelis (Polydor)
6	8	4 — Foreigner (Atlantic)
5	9	DEAD RINGER — Meatloaf (Epic)
25	10	PRIVATE EYES — Daryl Hall & John Oates (RCA)
14	11	THE VISITORS — Abba (Epic)
12	12	MODERN DANCE — Various Artists (K-Tel)
20	13	IF I SHOULD LOVE AGAIN — Barry Manilow (Arista)
19	14	LA FOLIE — Stranglers (Liberty)
17	15	BAT OUT OF HELL — Meatloaf (Epic)
9	16	QUEEN'S GREATEST HITS — Queen (EMI)
8	17	CHRISTOPHER CROSS — Christopher Cross (Warner Bros.)
18	18	ALL FOR A SONG — Barbara Dickson (Epic)
21	19	TIN DRUM — Japan (Virgin)
27	20	SHAKY — Shakin' Stevens (Epic)
-	21	THE SOUND OF YOUR CRY — Elvis Presley (RCA)
-	22	GHOST IN THE MACHINE — Police (A&M)
-	23	ENGLISH SETTLEMENT — XTC (Virgin)
7	24	SOMETHING SPECIAL — Kool & the Gang (De-Lite)
29	25	PENTHOUSE AND PAVEMENT — Heaven 17 (Virgin)
24	26	PERHAPS LOVE — Placido Domingo & John Denver (CBS)
-	27	PRESENT ARMS — UB40 (DEP International)
15	28	HITS HITS HITS — Various Artists (Ronco)
16	29	THE GEORGE BENSON COLLECTION — George Benson (Warner Bros.)
22	30	TRANS-EUROPE EXPRESS — Kraftwerk (Capitol)

Although probably unaware of the coincidence, Barbra Streisand emulated Cliff Richard with a compilation of favourite ballads titled *Love Songs*, and sold even more prodigiously with it - this was to be one of 1982's top albums, and a chart fixture for many months. Foreigner, the Anglo-American band led by ex-Spooky Tooth guitarist Mick Jones, had found only minor UK success with their first three albums, but *4* was helped to Top 10 status by their hit single *Waiting For A Girl Like You.*

February – March 1982

27 February 1982

last	this		
2	1	LOVE SONGS	Barbra Streisand (CBS)
3	2	ARCHITECTURE AND MORALITY	Orchestral Manoeuvres In The Dark (DinDisc)
1	3	DARE	Human League (Virgin)
4	4	PEARLS	Elkie Brooks (A&M)
6	5	THE MAN MACHINE	Kraftwerk (Capitol)
10	6	PRIVATE EYES	Daryl Hall & John Oates (RCA)
5	7	NON-STOP EROTIC CABARET	Soft Cell (Some Bizzare)
23	8	ENGLISH SETTLEMENT	XTC (Virgin)
7	9	THE FRIENDS OF MR CAIRO	Jon & Vangelis (Polydor)
14	10	LA FOLIE	Stranglers (Liberty)
8	11	4	Foreigner (Atlantic)
15	12	BAT OUT OF HELL	Meatloaf (Epic)
-	13	DREAMING	Various Artists (K-Tel)
9	14	DEAD RINGER	Meatloaf (Epic)
-	15	MECHANIX	UFO (Chrysalis)
17	16	CHRISTOPHER CROSS	Christopher Cross (Warner Bros.)
-	17	PHYSICAL	Olivia Newton-John (EMI)
-	18	TRAVELOGUE	Human League (Virgin)
-	19	COMPUTER WORLD	Kraftwerk (EMI)
12	20	MODERN DANCE	Various Artists (K-Tel)
18	21	ALL FOR A SONG	Barbara Dickson (Epic)
13	22	IF I SHOULD LOVE AGAIN	Barry Manilow (Arista)
29	23	THE GEORGE BENSON COLLECTION	George Benson (Warner Bros.)
10	24	THE VISITORS	Abba (Epic)
25	25	PENTHOUSE AND PAVEMENT	Heaven 17 (Virgin)
19	26	TIN DRUM	Japan (Virgin)
-	27	ACTION TRAX	Various Artists (K-Tel)
24	28	SOMETHING SPECIAL	Kool & the Gang (De-Lite)
16	29	QUEEN'S GREATEST HITS	Queen (EMI)
26	30	PERHAPS LOVE	Placido Domingo & John Denver (CBS)

6 March 1982

1	1	LOVE SONGS	Barbra Streisand (CBS)
3	2	DARE	Human League (Virgin)
4	3	PEARLS	Elkie Brooks (A&M)
13	4	DREAMING	Various Artists (K-Tel)
2	5	ARCHITECTURE AND MORALITY	Orchestral Manoeuvres In The Dark (DinDisc)
8	6	ENGLISH SETTLEMENT	XTC (Virgin)
7	7	NON-STOP EROTIC CABARET	Soft Cell (Some Bizzare)
6	8	PRIVATE EYES	Daryl Hall & John Oates (RCA)
9	9	THE FRIENDS OF MR CAIRO	Jon & Vangelis (Polydor)
21	10	ALL FOR A SONG	Barbara Dickson (Epic)
12	11	BAT OUT OF HELL	Meatloaf (Epic)
14	12	DEAD RINGER	Meatloaf (Epic)
5	13	THE MAN MACHINE	Kraftwerk (Capitol)
29	14	QUEEN'S GREATEST HITS	Queen (EMI)
17	15	PHYSICAL	Olivia Newton-John (EMI)
-	16	MESOPOTAMIA	B52s (Island)
18	17	TRAVELOGUE	Human League (Virgin)
-	18	PELICAN WEST	Haircut 100 (Arista)
11	19	4	Foreigner (Atlantic)
10	20	LA FOLIE	Stranglers (Liberty)
24	21	THE VISITORS	Abba (Epic)
16	22	CHRISTOPHER CROSS	Christopher Cross (Warner Bros.)
30	23	PERHAPS LOVE	Placido Domingo & John Denver (CBS)
-	24	FREEZE FRAME	J Geils Band (EMI America)
23	25	THE GEORGE BENSON COLLECTION	George Benson (Warner Bros.)
-	26	TONIGHT	Four Tops (Casablanca)
25	27	PENTHOUSE AND PAVEMENT	Heaven 17 (Virgin)
-	28	FOR THOSE ABOUT TO ROCK	AC/DC (Atlantic)
-	29	WORD OF MOUTH	Toni Basil (Radialchoice)
28	30	SOMETHING SPECIAL	Kool & the Gang (De-Lite)

13 March 1982

1	1	LOVE SONGS	Barbra Streisand (CBS)
4	2	DREAMING	Various Artists (K-Tel)
18	3	PELICAN WEST	Haircut 100 (Arista)
-	4	ACTION TRAX	Various Artists (K-Tel)
7	5	NON-STOP EROTIC CABARET	Soft Cell (Some Bizzare)
3	6	PEARLS	Elkie Brooks (A&M)
5	7	ARCHITECTURE AND MORALITY	Orchestral Manoeuvres In The Dark (DinDisc)
10	8	ALL FOR A SONG	Barbara Dickson (Epic)
2	9	DARE	Human League (Virgin)
6	10	ENGLISH SETTLEMENT	XTC (Virgin)
8	11	PRIVATE EYES	Daryl Hall & John Oates (RCA)
29	12	WORD OF MOUTH	Toni Basil (Radialchoice)
9	13	THE FRIENDS OF MR CAIRO	Jon & Vangelis (Polydor)
-	14	CHASE THE DRAGON	Magnum (Jet)
-	15	TWENTY WITH A BULLET	Various Artists (EMI)
12	16	DEAD RINGER	Meatloaf (Epic)
16	17	MESOPOTAMIA	B52s (Island)
11	18	BAT OUT OF HELL	Meatloaf (Epic)
20	19	LA FOLIE	Stranglers (Liberty)
24	20	FREEZE FRAME	J Geils Band (EMI America)
-	21	YOU CAN'T HIDE YOUR LOVE FOREVER	Orange Juice (Polydor)
13	22	THE MAN MACHINE	Kraftwerk (Capitol)
21	23	THE VISITORS	Abba (Epic)
19	24	4	Foreigner (Atlantic)
-	25	SEE JUNGLE! SEE JUNGLE! GO JOIN YOUR GANG YEAH CITY ALL OVER! GO APE CRAZY	Bow Wow Wow (RCA)
-	26	WESTWORLD	Theatre Of Hate (Burning Rome)
-	27	ANTHEM	Toyah (Safari)
25	28	THE GEORGE BENSON COLLECTION	George Benson (Warner Bros.)
-	29	SPEAK AND SPELL	Depeche Mode (Mute)
15	30	PHYSICAL	Olivia Newton-John (EMI)

20 March 1982

3	1	PELICAN WEST	Haircut 100 (Arista)
1	2	LOVE SONGS	Barbra Streisand (CBS)
4	3	ACTION TRAX	Various Artists (K-Tel)
9	4	DARE	Human League (Virgin)
5	5	NON-STOP EROTIC CABARET	Soft Cell (Some Bizzare)
8	6	ALL FOR A SONG	Barbara Dickson (Epic)
7	7	PEARLS	Elkie Brooks (A&M)
-	8	THE GIFT	Jam (Polydor)
7	9	ARCHITECTURE AND MORALITY	Orchestral Manoeuvres In The Dark (DinDisc)
2	10	DREAMING	Various Artists (K-Tel)
11	11	PRIVATE EYES	Daryl Hall & John Oates (RCA)
10	12	ENGLISH SETTLEMENT	XTC (Virgin)
20	13	FREEZE FRAME	J Geils Band (EMI America)
-	14	ONE NIGHT AT BUDOKAN	Michael Schenker Group (Chrysalis)
26	15	WESTWORLD	Theatre Of Hate (Burning Rome)
18	16	BAT OUT OF HELL	Meatloaf (Epic)
-	17	DIAMOND	Spandau Ballet (Reformation)
16	18	DEAD RINGER	Meatloaf (Epic)
24	19	4	Foreigner (Atlantic)
12	20	WORD OF MOUTH	Toni Basil (Radialchoice)
15	21	TWENTY WITH A BULLET	Various Artists (EMI)
14	22	CHASE THE DRAGON	Magnum (Jet)
19	23	LA FOLIE	Stranglers (Liberty)
13	24	THE FRIENDS OF MR CAIRO	Jon & Vangelis (Polydor)
28	25	THE GEORGE BENSON COLLECTION	George Benson (Warner Bros.)
23	26	THE VISITORS	Abba (Epic)
25	27	SEE JUNGLE! SEE JUNGLE! GO JOIN YOUR GANG YEAH CITY ALL OVER! GO APE CRAZY	Bow Wow Wow (RCA)
-	28	BEGIN THE BEGUINE	Julio Iglesias (CBS)
-	29	DR HECKLE AND MR JIVE	Pigbag (Y)
17	30	MESOPOTAMIA	B52s (Island)

Haircut 100 topped the chart with their debut album *Pelican West* just as their second (and biggest) hit single *Love Plus One* was peaking at Number 3, while another Top 10 album boosted by a current single was Hall & Oates' *Private Eyes* - none of their previous LPs had made the UK Top 20, but this one had the Top-Tenner *I Can't Go For That* batting for it. Malcolm McLaren protegees Bow Wow Wow, meanwhile, had probably the most stupidly-titled chart album ever.

March – April 1982

27 March 1982

last week	this week	Title	Artist (Label)
8	1	THE GIFT	Jam (Polydor)
1	2	PELICAN WEST	Haircut 100 (Arista)
2	3	LOVE SONGS	Barbra Streisand (CBS)
3	4	ACTION TRAX	Various Artists (K-Tel)
9	5	ARCHITECTURE AND MORALITY	Orchestral Manoeuvres In T Dark (DinDisc)
-	6	FUN BOY THREE	Fun Boy Three (Chrysalis)
7	7	PEARLS	Elkie Brooks (A&M)
5	8	NON-STOP EROTIC CABARET	Soft Cell (Some Bizzare)
4	9	DARE	Human League (Virgin)
6	10	ALL FOR A SONG	Barbra Dickson (Epic)
14	11	ONE NIGHT AT BUDOKAN	Michael Schenker Group (Chrysalis)
17	12	DIAMOND	Spandau Ballet (Reformation)
21	13	TWENTY WITH A BULLET	Various Artists (EMI)
10	14	DREAMING	Various Artists (K-Tel)
28	15	BEGIN THE BEGUINE	Julio Iglesias (CBS)
-	16	SPEAK AND SPELL	Depeche Mode (Mute)
16	17	BAT OUT OF HELL	Meatloaf (Epic)
15	18	WESTWORLD	Theatre Of Hate (Burning Rome)
13	19	FREEZE FRAME	J Geils Band (EMI America)
12	20	ENGLISH SETTLEMENT	XTC (Virgin)
11	21	PRIVATE EYES	Daryl Hall & John Oates (RCA)
20	22	WORD OF MOUTH	Toni Basil (Radialchoice)
29	23	DR HECKLE AND MR JIVE	Pigbag (Y)
-	24	PHYSICAL	Olivia Newton-John (EMI)
27	25	SEE JUNGLE! SEE JUNGLE! GO JOIN YOUR GANG YEAH CITY ALL OVER! GO APE CRAZY	Bow Wow Wow (RCA)
-	26	QUEEN'S GREATEST HITS	Queen (EMI)
26	27	THE VISITORS	Abba (Epic)
30	28	MESOPOTAMIA	B52s (Island)
-	29	FILTH HOUNDS OF HADES	Tank (Kamaflage)
23	30	LA FOLIE	Stranglers (Liberty)

3 April 1982

last week	this week	Title	Artist (Label)
1	1	THE GIFT	Jam (Polydor)
3	2	LOVE SONGS	Barbra Streisand (CBS)
2	3	PELICAN WEST	Haircut 100 (Arista)
15	4	BEGIN THE BEGUINE	Julio Iglesias (CBS)
10	5	ALL FOR A SONG	Barbara Dickson (Epic)
7	6	PEARLS	Elkie Brooks (A&M)
4	7	ACTION TRAX	Various Artists (K-Tel)
9	8	DARE	Human League (Virgin)
6	9	FUN BOY THREE	Fun Boy Three (Chrysalis)
-	10	FIVE MILES OUT	Mike Oldfield (Virgin)
14	11	DREAMING	Various Artists (K-Tel)
-	12	TIN DRUM	Japan (Virgin)
-	13	THE BEST OF THE FOUR TOPS	Four Tops (K-Tel)
11	14	ONE NIGHT AT BUDOKAN	Michael Schenker Group (Chrysalis)
-	15	KEEP FIT AND DANCE	Peter Powell (K-Tel)
8	16	NON-STOP EROTIC CABARET	Soft Cell (Some Bizzare)
-	17	THE CONCERT IN CENTRAL PARK	Simon & Garfunkel (CBS)
13	18	TWENTY WITH A BULLET	Various Artists (EMI)
12	19	DIAMOND	Spandau Ballet (Reformation)
5	20	ARCHITECTURE AND MORALITY	Orchestral Manoeuvres In The Dark (DinDisc)
17	21	BAT OUT OF HELL	Meatloaf (Epic)
-	22	PORTRAIT	Nolans (Epic)
22	23	WORD OF MOUTH	Toni Basil (Radialchoice)
20	24	ENGLISH SETTLEMENT	XTC (Virgin)
19	25	FREEZE FRAME	J Geils Band (EMI America)
-	26	JAMES BOND'S GREATEST HITS	Various Artists (Liberty)
-	27	THE SECRET POLICEMAN'S OTHER BALL	Various Artists (Springtime)
23	28	DR HECKLE AND MR JIVE	Pigbag (Y)
30	29	LA FOLIE	Stranglers (Liberty)
18	30	WESTWORLD	Theatre Of Hate (Burning Rome)

10 April 1982

last week	this week	Title	Artist (Label)
3	1	PELICAN WEST	Haircut 100 (Arista)
2	2	LOVE SONGS	Barbra Streisand (CBS)
1	3	THE GIFT	Jam (Polydor)
-	4	THE ANVIL	Visage (Polydor)
4	5	BEGIN THE BEGUINE	Julio Iglesias (CBS)
12	6	TIN DRUM	Japan (Virgin)
6	7	PEARLS	Elkie Brooks (A&M)
5	8	ALL FOR A SONG	Barbara Dickson (Epic)
7	9	ACTION TRAX	Various Artists (K-Tel)
19	10	DIAMOND	Spandau Ballet (Reformation)
26	11	JAMES BOND'S GREATEST HITS	Various Artists (Liberty)
22	12	PORTRAIT	Nolans (Epic)
9	13	FUN BOY THREE	Fun Boy Three (Chrysalis)
10	14	FIVE MILES OUT	Mike Oldfield (Virgin)
21	15	BAT OUT OF HELL	Meatloaf (Epic)
8	16	DARE	Human League (Virgin)
-	17	SKY 4 - FORTHCOMING	Sky (Ariola)
14	18	ONE NIGHT AT BUDOKAN	Michael Schenker Group (Chrysalis)
-	19	BODY TALK	Imagination (R&B)
20	20	ARCHITECTURE AND MORALITY	Orchestral Manoeuvres In The Dark (DinDisc)
28	21	DR HECKLE AND MR JIVE	Pigbag (Y)
23	22	WORD OF MOUTH	Toni Basil (Radialchoice)
11	23	DREAMING	Various Artists (K-Tel)
-	24	MAYBE IT'S LIVE	Robert Palmer (Island)
15	25	KEEP FIT AND DANCE	Peter Powell (K-Tel)
-	26	CHARIOTS OF FIRE	Vangelis (Polydor)
-	27	CHRISTOPHER CROSS	Christopher Cross (Warner Bros.)
17	28	THE CONCERT IN CENTRAL PARK	Simon & Garfunkel (CBS)
13	29	THE BEST OF THE FOUR TOPS	Four Tops (K-Tel)
27	30	THE SECRET POLICEMAN'S OTHER BALL	Various Artists (Springtime)

17 April 1982

last week	this week	Title	Artist (Label)
-	1	THE NUMBER OF THE BEAST	Iron Maiden (EMI)
2	2	LOVE SONGS	Barbra Streisand (CBS)
8	3	ALL FOR A SONG	Barbara Dickson (Epic)
1	4	PELICAN WEST	Haircut 100 (Arista)
6	5	TIN DRUM	Japan (Virgin)
5	6	BEGIN THE BEGUINE	Julio Iglesias (CBS)
4	7	THE ANVIL	Visage (Polydor)
3	8	THE GIFT	Jam (Polydor)
17	9	SKY 4 - FORTHCOMING	Sky (Ariola)
-	10	BLACKOUT	Scorpions (Harvest)
-	11	THE NAME OF THIS BAND IS TALKING HEADS	Talking Heads (Sire)
7	12	PEARLS	Elkie Brooks (A&M)
19	13	BODY TALK	Imagination (R&B)
14	14	FIVE MILES OUT	Mike Oldfield (Virgin)
9	15	ACTION TRAX	Various Artists (K-Tel)
-	16	FREEZE FRAME	J Geils Band (EMI America)
-	17	IRON FIST	Motorhead (Bronze)
11	18	JAMES BOND'S GREATEST HITS	Various Artists (Liberty)
26	19	CHARIOTS OF FIRE	Vangelis (Polydor)
10	20	ASIA	Asia (Geffen)
10	21	DIAMOND	Spandau Ballet (Reformation)
16	22	DARE	Human League (Virgin)
-	23	100PERCENT COTTON	Jets (EMI)
25	24	KEEP FIT AND DANCE	Peter Powell (K-Tel)
12	25	PORTRAIT	Nolans (Epic)
18	26	ONE NIGHT AT BUDOKAN	Michael Schenker Group (Chrysalis)
28	27	THE CONCERT IN CENTRAL PARK	Simon & Garfunkel (CBS)
-	28	PENTHOUSE AND PAVEMENT	Heaven 17 (Virgin)
15	29	BAT OUT OF HELL	Meatloaf (Epic)
-	30	20 WITH A BULLET	Various Artists (EMI)

Though albums by the Jam, Haircut 100 and Iron Maiden came and went at Number 1 around it, Barbra Streisand's *Love Songs* was overall, the best-selling album through March and April - a demonstration of its continued selling power two months after release. Iron Maiden's *Number Of The Beast* was the band's third album but first chart-topper, and it led a new heavy metal assault onto the chart, which also included German band the Scorpions at No.10, and the UK's Motorhead at 17.

April – May 1982

24 April 1982

last week	this week	Title / Artist (Label)
2	1	LOVE SONGS — Barbra Streisand (CBS)
4	2	PELICAN WEST — Haircut 100 (Arista)
17	3	IRON FIST — Motorhead (Bronze)
1	4	THE NUMBER OF THE BEAST — Iron Maiden (EMI)
3	5	ALL FOR A SONG — Barbara Dickson (Epic)
18	6	JAMES BOND'S GREATEST HITS — Various Artists (Liberty)
8	7	THE GIFT — Jam (Polydor)
25	8	PORTRAIT — Nolans (Epic)
6	9	BEGIN THE BEGUINE — Julio Iglesias (CBS)
5	10	TIN DRUM — Japan (Virgin)
9	11	SKY 4 – FORTHCOMING — Sky (Ariola)
14	12	FIVE MILES OUT — Mike Oldfield (Virgin)
7	13	THE ANVIL — Visage (Polydor)
12	14	PEARLS — Elkie Brooks (A&M)
19	15	CHARIOTS OF FIRE — Vangelis (Polydor)
-	16	1982 — Status Quo (Vertigo)
29	17	BAT OUT OF HELL — Meatloaf (Epic)
-	18	SEVEN TEARS — Goombay Dance Band (Epic)
15	19	ACTION TRAX — Various Artists (K-Tel)
20	20	ASIA — Asia (Geffen)
13	21	BODY TALK — Imagination (R&B)
22	22	DARE — Human League (Virgin)
-	23	BRITISH ELECRIC FOUNDATION PRESENTS MUSIC OF QUALITY AND DISTINCTION, VOL.1 — British Electric Foundation (Virgin)
-	24	JUMP UP — Elton John (Rocket)
10	25	BLACKOUT — Scorpions (Harvest)
-	26	FUN BOY THREE — Fun Boy Three (Chrysalis)
11	27	THE NAME OF THIS BAND IS TALKING HEADS — Talking Heads (Sire)
-	28	HEDGEHOG SANDWICH — Not The Nine O'Clock News (BBC)
24	29	KEEP FIT AND DANCE — Peter Powell (K-Tel)
-	30	DR HECKLE AND MR JIVE — Pigbag (Y)

1 May 1982

last week	this week	Title / Artist (Label)
2	1	PELICAN WEST — Haircut 100 (Arista)
4	2	THE NUMBER OF THE BEAST — Iron Maiden (EMI)
16	3	1982 — Status Quo (Vertigo)
1	4	LOVE SONGS — Barbra Streisand (CBS)
-	5	STRAIGHT BETWEEN THE EYES — Rainbow (Polydor)
15	6	CHARIOTS OF FIRE — Vangelis (Polydor)
5	7	ALL FOR A SONG — Barbara Dickson (Epic)
8	8	PORTRAIT — Nolans (Epic)
11	9	SKY 4 – FORTHCOMING — Sky (Ariola)
3	10	IRON FIST — Motorhead (Bronze)
6	11	JAMES BOND'S GREATEST HITS — Various Artists (Liberty)
24	12	JUMP UP — Elton John (Rocket)
20	13	ASIA — Asia (Geffen)
7	14	THE GIFT — Jam (Polydor)
10	15	TIN DRUM — Japan (Virgin)
-	16	BARRY LIVE IN BRITAIN — Barry Manilow (Arista)
17	17	BAT OUT OF HELL — Meatloaf (Epic)
-	18	THE SLIDE AREA — Ry Cooder (Warner Bros.)
23	19	BRITISH ELECRIC FOUNDATION PRESENTS MUSIC OF QUALITY AND DISTINCTION, VOL.1 — British Electric Foundation (Virgin)
-	20	SHOOT THE MOON — Judy Tzuke (Chrysalis)
13	21	THE ANVIL — Visage (Polydor)
-	22	COMPLETE MADNESS — Madness (Stiff)
14	23	PEARLS — Elkie Brooks (A&M)
18	24	SEVEN TEARS — Goombay Dance Band (Epic)
-	25	NON-STOP EROTIC CABARET — Soft Cell (Some Bizzare)
21	26	BODY TALK — Imagination (R&B)
26	27	FUN BOY THREE — Fun Boy Three (Chrysalis)
9	28	BEGIN THE BEGUINE — Julio Iglesias (CBS)
12	29	FIVE MILES OUT — Mike Oldfield (Virgin)
30	30	DR HECKLE AND MR JIVE — Pigbag (Y)

8 May 1982

last week	this week	Title / Artist (Label)
16	1	BARRY LIVE IN BRITAIN — Barry Manilow (Arista)
22	2	COMPLETE MADNESS — Madness (Stiff)
3	3	1982 — Status Quo (Vertigo)
1	4	PELICAN WEST — Haircut 100 (Arista)
2	5	THE NUMBER OF THE BEAST — Iron Maiden (EMI)
4	6	LOVE SONGS — Barbra Streisand (CBS)
-	7	DISCO UK AND DISCO USA — Various Artists (Ronco)
6	8	CHARIOTS OF FIRE — Vangelis (Polydor)
12	9	JUMP UP — Elton John (Rocket)
5	10	STRAIGHT BETWEEN THE EYES — Rainbow (Polydor)
-	11	TUG OF WAR — Paul McCartney (Parlophone)
9	12	SKY 4 – FORTHCOMING — Sky (Ariola)
13	13	ASIA — Asia (Geffen)
14	14	TIN DRUM — Japan (Virgin)
8	15	PORTRAIT — Nolans (Epic)
-	16	MUSTN'T GRUMBLE — Chas & Dave (Rockney)
23	17	PEARLS — Elkie Brooks (A&M)
17	18	BAT OUT OF HELL — Meatloaf (Epic)
-	19	SHAPE UP AND DANCE VOL 2 — Angela Rippon (Lifestyle)
11	20	JAMES BOND'S GREATEST HITS — Various Artists (Liberty)
7	21	ALL FOR A SONG — Barbara Dickson (Epic)
21	22	THE ANVIL — Visage (Polydor)
-	23	DIVER DOWN — Van Halen (Warner Bros.)
30	24	DR HECKLE AND MR JIVE — Pigbag (Y)
10	25	IRON FIST — Motorhead (Bronze)
-	26	TIME PIECES – THE BEST OF ERIC CLAPTON — Eric Clapton (RSO)
29	27	FIVE MILES OUT — Mike Oldfield (Virgin)
19	28	BRITISH ELECRIC FOUNDATION PRESENTS MUSIC OF QUALITY, VOL.1 — British Electric Foundation (Virgin)
-	29	THE BROADSWORD AND THE BEAST — Jethro Tull (Chrysalis)
·14	30	THE GIFT — Jam (Polydor)

15 May 1982

last week	this week	Title / Artist (Label)
11	1	TUG OF WAR — Paul McCartney (Parlophone)
1	2	BARRY LIVE IN BRITAIN — Barry Manilow (Arista)
2	3	COMPLETE MADNESS — Madness (Stiff)
3	4	1982 — Status Quo (Vertigo)
4	5	PELICAN WEST — Haircut 100 (Arista)
7	6	DISCO UK AND DISCO USA — Various Artists (Ronco)
8	7	CHARIOTS OF FIRE — Vangelis (Polydor)
6	8	LOVE SONGS — Barbra Streisand (CBS)
-	9	ARE YOU READY? — Bucks Fizz (RCA)
5	10	THE NUMBER OF THE BEAST — Iron Maiden (EMI)
-	11	DIAMOND — Spandau Ballet (Reformation)
19	12	SHAPE UP AND DANCE VOL 2 — Angela Rippon (Lifestyle)
18	13	BAT OUT OF HELL — Meatloaf (Epic)
9	14	JUMP UP — Elton John (Rocket)
10	15	STRAIGHT BETWEEN THE EYES — Rainbow (Polydor)
-	16	REVELATIONS — Killing Joke (Malicious Damage)
12	17	SKY 4 – FORTHCOMING — Sky (Ariola)
21	18	ALL FOR A SONG — Barbara Dickson (Epic)
14	19	TIN DRUM — Japan (Virgin)
17	20	PEARLS — Elkie Brooks (A&M)
-	21	FUN BOY THREE — Fun Boy Three (Chrysalis)
32	22	THE GIFT — Jam (Polydor)
13	23	ASIA — Asia (Geffen)
27	24	FIVE MILES OUT — Mike Oldfield (Virgin)
20	25	JAMES BOND'S GREATEST HITS — Various Artists (Liberty)
24	26	DR HECKLE AND MR JIVE — Pigbag (Y)
25	27	IRON FIST — Motorhead (Bronze)
15	28	PORTRAIT — Nolans (Epic)
16	29	MUSTN'T GRUMBLE — Chas & Dave (Rockney)
26	30	TIME PIECES – THE BEST OF ERIC CLAPTON — Eric Clapton (RSO)

James Bond's Greatest Hits was not a gimmicky attempt to present Roger Moore or Sean Connery singing, but was a TV-advertised compilation which gathered up the themes and some of the incidental musical pieces from all the Bond films (except *Casino Royale*) to date, most of them co-written, played or accompanied by John Barry. Barry Manilow's *Live In Britain* was custom-released for the UK market, and despite topping the chart here, it was not released in his native USA at all.

May – June 1982

22 May 1982

last week	this week	title / artist (label)
3	1	COMPLETE MADNESS — Madness (Stiff)
1	2	TUG OF WAR — Paul McCartney (Parlophone)
2	3	BARRY LIVE IN BRITAIN — Barry Manilow (Arista)
5	4	PELICAN WEST — Haircut 100 (Arista)
-	5	HOT SPACE — Queen (EMI)
-	6	NIGHT BIRDS — Shakatak (Polydor)
-	7	CHARTBUSTERS '82 — Various Artists (Ronco)
-	8	THE CONCERTS IN CHINA — Jean-Michel Jarre (Polydor)
9	9	ARE YOU READY? — Bucks Fizz (RCA)
7	10	CHARIOTS OF FIRE — Vangelis (Polydor)
6	11	DISCO UK AND DISCO USA — Various Artists (Ronco)
-	12	PINKY BLUE — Altered Images (Epic)
-	13	PORNOGRAPHY — Cure (Fiction)
-	14	SWEETS FROM A STRANGER — Squeeze (A&M)
10	15	THE NUMBER OF THE BEAST — Iron Maiden (EMI)
8	16	LOVE SONGS — Barbra Streisand (CBS)
4	17	1982 — Status Quo (Vertigo)
11	18	DIAMOND — Spandau Ballet (Reformation)
13	19	BAT OUT OF HELL — Meatloaf (Epic)
-	20	I LOVE ROCK 'N' ROLL — Joan Jett & the Blackhearts (Epic)
12	21	SHAPE UP AND DANCE VOL 2 — Angela Rippon (Lifestyle)
15	22	STRAIGHT BETWEEN THE EYES — Rainbow (Polydor)
-	23	COMBAT ROCK — Clash (CBS)
20	24	PEARLS — Elkie Brooks (A&M)
18	25	ALL FOR A SONG — Barbara Dickson (Epic)
-	26	STRAIGHT FROM THE HEART — Patrice Rushen (Elektra)
19	27	TIN DRUM — Japan (Virgin)
14	28	JUMP UP — Elton John (Rocket)
21	29	FUN BOY THREE — Fun Boy Three (Chrysalis)
29	30	MUSTN'T GRUMBLE — Chas & Dave (Rockney)

29 May 1982

last	this	title / artist (label)
1	1	COMPLETE MADNESS — Madness (Stiff)
2	2	TUG OF WAR — Paul McCartney (Parlophone)
7	3	CHARTBUSTERS '82 — Various Artists (Ronco)
3	4	BARRY LIVE IN BRITAIN — Barry Manilow (Arista)
-	5	RIO — Duran Duran (EMI)
23	6	COMBAT ROCK — Clash (CBS)
5	7	HOT SPACE — Queen (EMI)
4	8	PELICAN WEST — Haircut 100 (Arista)
6	9	NIGHT BIRDS — Shakatak (Polydor)
-	10	THE EAGLE HAS LANDED — Saxon (Carrere)
8	11	THE CONCERTS IN CHINA — Jean-Michel Jarre (Polydor)
16	12	LOVE SONGS — Barbra Streisand (CBS)
17	13	1982 — Status Quo (Vertigo)
15	14	THE NUMBER OF THE BEAST — Iron Maiden (EMI)
12	15	PINKY BLUE — Altered Images (Epic)
19	16	BAT OUT OF HELL — Meatloaf (Epic)
-	17	CHURCH OF HAWKWIND — Hawkwind (RCA)
11	18	DISCO UK AND DISCO USA — Various Artists (Ronco)
9	19	ARE YOU READY? — Bucks Fizz (RCA)
18	20	DIAMOND — Spandau Ballet (Reformation)
-	21	SULK — Associates (Associates)
24	22	PEARLS — Elkie Brooks (A&M)
10	23	CHARIOTS OF FIRE — Vangelis (Polydor)
-	24	STEVIE WONDER'S ORIGINAL MUSIQUARIUM 1 — Stevie Wonder (Motown)
26	25	STRAIGHT FROM THE HEART — Patrice Rushen (Elektra)
-	26	WE ARE ...THE LEAGUE — Anti-Nowhere League (WXYZ)
27	27	TIN DRUM — Japan (Virgin)
-	28	DARE — Human League (Virgin)
13	29	PORNOGRAPHY — Cure (Fiction)
28	30	JUMP UP — Elton John (Rocket)

5 June 1982

last	this	title / artist (label)
1	1	COMPLETE MADNESS — Madness (Stiff)
5	2	RIO — Duran Duran (EMI)
3	3	CHARTBUSTERS '82 — Various Artists (Ronco)
2	4	TUG OF WAR — Paul McCartney (Parlophone)
4	5	BARRY LIVE IN BRITAIN — Barry Manilow (Arista)
24	6	STEVIE WONDER'S ORIGINAL MUSIQUARIUM 1 — Stevie Wonder (Motown)
7	7	HOT SPACE — Queen (EMI)
10	8	THE EAGLE HAS LANDED — Saxon (Carrere)
14	9	THE NUMBER OF THE BEAST — Iron Maiden (EMI)
6	10	COMBAT ROCK — Clash (CBS)
9	11	NIGHT BIRDS — Shakatak (Polydor)
8	12	PELICAN WEST — Haircut 100 (Arista)
23	13	CHARIOTS OF FIRE — Vangelis (Polydor)
21	14	SULK — Associates (Associates)
-	15	SELECT — Kim Wilde (RAK)
19	16	ARE YOU READY? — Bucks Fizz (RCA)
13	17	1982 — Status Quo (Vertigo)
11	18	THE CONCERTS IN CHINA — Jean-Michel Jarre (Polydor)
25	19	STRAIGHT FROM THE HEART — Patrice Rushen (Elektra)
22	20	PEARLS — Elkie Brooks (A&M)
-	21	TROPICAL GANGSTERS — Kid Creole & the Coconuts (Ze)
-	22	THE HUNTER — Blondie (Chrysalis)
-	23	AVALON — Roxy Music (EG)
12	24	LOVE SONGS — Barbra Streisand (CBS)
15	25	PINKY BLUE — Altered Images (Epic)
16	26	BAT OUT OF HELL — Meatloaf (Epic)
20	27	DIAMOND — Spandau Ballet (Reformation)
18	28	DISCO UK AND DISCO USA — Various Artists (Ronco)
28	29	DARE — Human League (Virgin)
26	30	WE ARE ...THE LEAGUE — Anti-Nowhere League (WXYZ)

12 June 1982

last	this	title / artist (label)
1	1	COMPLETE MADNESS — Madness (Stiff)
7	2	HOT SPACE — Queen (EMI)
2	3	RIO — Duran Duran (EMI)
23	4	AVALON — Roxy Music (EG)
4	5	TUG OF WAR — Paul McCartney (Parlophone)
5	6	BARRY LIVE IN BRITAIN — Barry Manilow (Arista)
3	7	CHARTBUSTERS '82 — Various Artists (Ronco)
11	8	NIGHT BIRDS — Shakatak (Polydor)
6	9	STEVIE WONDER'S ORIGINAL MUSIQUARIUM 1 — Stevie Wonder (Motown)
9	10	THE NUMBER OF THE BEAST — Iron Maiden (EMI)
22	11	THE HUNTER — Blondie (Chrysalis)
8	12	THE EAGLE HAS LANDED — Saxon (Carrere)
12	13	PELICAN WEST — Haircut 100 (Arista)
19	13	STRAIGHT FROM THE HEART — Patrice Rushen (Elektra)
21	15	TROPICAL GANGSTERS — Kid Creole & the Coconuts (Ze)
25	16	PINKY BLUE — Altered Images (Epic)
13	17	CHARIOTS OF FIRE — Vangelis (Polydor)
18	18	THE CONCERTS IN CHINA — Jean-Michel Jarre (Polydor)
14	19	SULK — Associates (Associates)
26	20	BAT OUT OF HELL — Meatloaf (Epic)
10	21	COMBAT ROCK — Clash (CBS)
24	22	LOVE SONGS — Barbra Streisand (CBS)
-	23	THE GIFT — Jam (Polydor)
-	24	STILL LIFE (AMERICAN CONCERTS 1981) — Rolling Stones (Rolling Stones)
-	25	PhD — PhD (WEA)
30	26	WE ARE ...THE LEAGUE — Anti-Nowhere League (WXYZ)
-	26	NON-STOP EROTIC CABARET — Soft Cell (Some Bizzare)
-	28	ANIMATION — Jon Anderson (Polydor)
15	29	SELECT — Kim Wilde (RAK)
20	30	PEARLS — Elkie Brooks (A&M)

May 22 had an album chart particularly notable for its turnover rate - exactly a third of the Top 30 were new entries, four of them debuting in the Top 10. Oddly, though, the sales of virtually every one of those newcomers dropped away in their second week, the notable exception being the Clash's *Combat Rock*, which started chart life quite modestly before snatching two weeks of Top 10 action. Madness' four-week chart-topper *Complete Madness* was a compilation of their hit singles to date.

June – July 1982

last this week

19 June 1982

Last	This	Album	Artist (Label)
4	1	AVALON	Roxy Music (EG)
24	2	STILL LIFE (AMERICAN CONCERTS 1981)	Rolling Stones (Rolling Stones)
1	3	COMPLETE MADNESS	Madness (Stiff)
-	4	THREE SIDES LIVE	Genesis (Charisma)
3	5	RIO	Duran Duran (EMI)
9	6	STEVIE WONDER'S ORIGINAL MUSIQUARIUM 1	Stevie Wonder (Motown)
8	7	NIGHT BIRDS	Shakatak (Polydor)
11	8	THE HUNTER	Blondie (Chrysalis)
-	9	WINDSONG	Randy Crawford (Warner Bros.)
13	10	PELICAN WEST	Haircut 100 (Arista)
5	11	BARRY LIVE IN BRITAIN	Barry Manilow (Arista)
-	12	ARE YOU READY?	Bucks Fizz (RCA)
17	13	CHARIOTS OF FIRE	Vangelis (Polydor)
19	14	SULK	Associates (Associates)
2	15	HOT SPACE	Queen (EMI)
15	16	TROPICAL GANGSTERS	Kid Creole & the Coconuts (Ze)
5	17	TUG OF WAR	Paul McCartney (Parlophone)
12	18	THE EAGLE HAS LANDED	Saxon (Carrere)
10	19	THE NUMBER OF THE BEAST	Iron Maiden (EMI)
-	20	JI	Junior (Mercury)
20	21	BAT OUT OF HELL	Meatloaf (Epic)
7	22	CHARTBUSTERS '82	Various Artists (Ronco)
29	23	SELECT	Kim Wilde (RAK)
16	24	PINKY BLUE	Altered Images (Epic)
18	25	THE CONCERTS IN CHINA	Jean-Michel Jarre (Polydor)
-	26	SCREAMING BLUE MURDER	Girlschool (Bronze)
21	27	COMBAT ROCK	Clash (CBS)
26	28	NON-STOP EROTIC CABARET	Soft Cell (Some Bizzare)
13	29	STRAIGHT FROM THE HEART	Patrice Rushen (Elektra)
25	30	PhD	PhD (WEA)

26 June 1982

Last	This	Album	Artist (Label)
1	1	AVALON	Roxy Music (EG)
3	2	COMPLETE MADNESS	Madness (Stiff)
4	3	THREE SIDES LIVE	Genesis (Charisma)
2	4	STILL LIFE (AMERICAN CONCERTS 1981)	Rolling Stones (Rolling Stones)
5	5	RIO	Duran Duran (EMI)
6	6	THE CHANGELING	Toyah (Safari)
16	7	TROPICAL GANGSTERS	Kid Creole & the Coconuts (Ze)
10	8	PELICAN WEST	Haircut 100 (Arista)
19	9	THE NUMBER OF THE BEAST	Iron Maiden (EMI)
15	10	HOT SPACE	Queen (EMI)
9	11	WINDSONG	Randy Crawford (Warner Bros.)
11	12	BARRY LIVE IN BRITAIN	Barry Manilow (Arista)
6	13	STEVIE WONDER'S ORIGINAL MUSIQUARIUM 1	Stevie Wonder (Motown)
20	14	JI	Junior (Mercury)
28	15	NON-STOP EROTIC CABARET	Soft Cell (Some Bizzare)
14	16	SULK	Associates (Associates)
7	17	NIGHT BIRDS	Shakatak (Polydor)
13	18	CHARIOTS OF FIRE	Vangelis (Polydor)
8	19	THE HUNTER	Blondie (Chrysalis)
12	20	ARE YOU READY?	Bucks Fizz (RCA)
17	21	TUG OF WAR	Paul McCartney (Parlophone)
-	22	ASIA	Asia (Geffen)
-	23	ABRACADABRA	Steve Miller Band (Mercury)
27	24	COMBAT ROCK	Clash (CBS)
24	25	PINKY BLUE	Altered Images (Epic)
21	26	BAT OUT OF HELL	Meatloaf (Epic)
-	27	CHILL OUT	Black Uhuru (Island)
-	28	TIN DRUM	Japan (Virgin)
-	29	FUN BOY THREE	Fun Boy Three (Chrysalis)
-	30	TURBO TRAX	Various Artists (K-Tel)

3 July 1982

Last	This	Album	Artist (Label)
1	1	AVALON	Roxy Music (EG)
4	2	STILL LIFE (AMERICAN CONCERTS 1981)	Rolling Stones (Rolling Stones)
2	3	COMPLETE MADNESS	Madness (Stiff)
-	4	NON-STOP ECSTATIC DANCING	Soft Cell (Some Bizzare)
5	5	RIO	Duran Duran (EMI)
7	6	TROPICAL GANGSTERS	Kid Creole & the Coconuts (Ze)
3	7	THREE SIDES LIVE	Genesis (Charisma)
10	8	HOT SPACE	Queen (EMI)
11	9	WINDSONG	Randy Crawford (Warner Bros.)
21	10	TUG OF WAR	Paul McCartney (Parlophone)
6	11	THE CHANGELING	Toyah (Safari)
17	12	NIGHT BIRDS	Shakatak (Polydor)
9	13	THE NUMBER OF THE BEAST	Iron Maiden (EMI)
13	14	STEVIE WONDER'S ORIGINAL MUSIQUARIUM 1	Stevie Wonder (Motown)
18	15	CHARIOTS OF FIRE	Vangelis (Polydor)
12	16	BARRY LIVE IN BRITAIN	Barry Manilow (Arista)
22	17	ASIA	Asia (Geffen)
-	18	THE LEXICON OF LOVE	ABC (Neutron)
20	19	ARE YOU READY?	Bucks Fizz (RCA)
-	20	KILLERS	Kiss (Casablanca)
18	21	THE HUNTER	Blondie (Chrysalis)
-	22	LOVE SONGS	Barbra Streisand (CBS)
-	23	1982	Status Quo (Vertigo)
23	24	ABRACADABRA	Steve Miller Band (Mercury)
26	25	BAT OUT OF HELL	Meatloaf (Epic)
-	26	PEARLS	Elkie Brooks (A&M)
-	27	WE ARE ...THE LEAGUE	Anti-Nowhere League (WXYZ)
-	28	DARE	Human League (Virgin)
30	29	TURBO TRAX	Various Artists (K-Tel)
14	30	JI	Junior (Mercury)

10 July 1982

Last	This	Album	Artist (Label)
1	1	AVALON	Roxy Music (EG)
18	2	THE LEXICON OF LOVE	ABC (Neutron)
3	3	COMPLETE MADNESS	Madness (Stiff)
2	4	STILL LIFE (AMERICAN CONCERTS 1981)	Rolling Stones (Rolling Stones)
6	5	TROPICAL GANGSTERS	Kid Creole & the Coconuts (Ze)
4	6	NON-STOP ECSTATIC DANCING	Soft Cell (Some Bizzare)
5	7	RIO	Duran Duran (EMI)
12	8	NIGHT BIRDS	Shakatak (Polydor)
7	9	THREE SIDES LIVE	Genesis (Charisma)
8	10	HOT SPACE	Queen (EMI)
11	11	THE CHANGELING	Toyah (Safari)
-	12	FABRIQUE	Fashion (Arista)
10	13	TUG OF WAR	Paul McCartney (Parlophone)
24	14	ABRACADABRA	Steve Miller Band (Mercury)
29	15	TURBO TRAX	Various Artists (K-Tel)
14	16	STEVIE WONDER'S ORIGINAL MUSIQUARIUM 1	Stevie Wonder (Motown)
-	17	THE LOVE THAT WHIRLS (DIARY OF A THINKING HEART)	Bill Nelson (Mercury)
9	18	WINDSONG	Randy Crawford (Warner Bros.)
-	19	ALL THE BEST COWBOYS HAVE CHINESE EYES	Pete Townshend (Atco)
20	20	PELICAN WEST	Haircut 100 (Arista)
17	21	ASIA	Asia (Geffen)
-	22	OVERLOAD	Various Artists (Ronco)
15	23	CHARIOTS OF FIRE	Vangelis (Polydor)
-	24	ALL THE GREAT HITS	Diana Ross (Motown)
-	25	THE CONCERT IN CENTRAL PARK	Simon & Garfunkel (CBS)
21	26	THE HUNTER	Blondie (Chrysalis)
-	27	THE EAGLE HAS LANDED	Saxon (Carrere)
28	28	COMBAT ROCK	Clash (CBS)
-	29	BODY TALK	Imagination (R&B)
24	30	BAT OUT OF HELL	Meatloaf (Epic)

Appearing a full two years after their previous album *Flesh And Blood*, Roxy Music's *Avalon* indicated no loss of commercial appeal for Bryan Ferry and Co, emulating its predecessor's Number 1 status, and holding the top slot for four straight weeks - consigning the Rolling Stones, in the process, to yet another Number 2 album with their live set *Still Life*. The Genesis set *Three Sides Live* was exactly that - a double set consisting of one double-sided LP and one single-sided disc!

July – August 1982

last week / this week	17 July 1982		24 July 1982		31 July 1982		7 August 1982
2	1 THE LEXICON OF LOVE ABC (Neutron)	1	1 THE LEXICON OF LOVE ABC (Neutron)	1	1 THE LEXICON OF LOVE ABC (Neutron)	14	1 THE KIDS FROM FAME Kids From Fame (BBC)
1	2 AVALON Roxy Music (EG)	3	2 FAME Soundtrack (RSO)	2	2 FAME Soundtrack (RSO)	2	2 FAME Soundtrack (RSO)
-	3 FAME Soundtrack (RSO)	2	3 AVALON Roxy Music (EG)	4	3 LOVE AND DANCE League Unlimited Orchestra (Virgin)	1	3 THE LEXICON OF LOVE ABC (Neutron)
14	4 ABRACADABRA Steve Miller Band (Mercury)	15	4 LOVE AND DANCE League Unlimited Orchestra (Virgin)	3	4 AVALON Roxy Music (EG)	6	4 COMPLETE MADNESS Madness (Stiff)
5	5 TROPICAL GANGSTERS Kid Creole & the Coconuts (Ze)	10	5 PICTURES AT ELEVEN Robert Plant (Swansong)	8	5 ABRACADABRA Steve Miller Band (Mercury)	4	5 AVALON Roxy Music (EG)
3	6 COMPLETE MADNESS Madness (Stiff)	6	6 STILL LIFE (AMERICAN CONCERTS 1981) Rolling Stones (Rolling Stones)	9	6 COMPLETE MADNESS Madness (Stiff)	7	6 TROPICAL GANGSTERS Kid Creole & the Coconuts (Ze)
4	6 STILL LIFE (AMERICAN CONCERTS 1981) Rolling Stones (Rolling Stones)	-	7 SCREAMING FOR VENGEANCE Judas Priest (CBS)	11	7 TROPICAL GANGSTERS Kid Creole & the Coconuts (Ze)	9	7 PICTURES AT ELEVEN Robert Plant (Swansong)
7	8 RIO Duran Duran (EMI)	4	8 ABRACADABRA Steve Miller Band (Mercury)	15	8 THE CONCERT IN CENTRAL PARK Simon & Garfunkel (CBS)	3	8 LOVE AND DANCE League Unlimited Orchestra (Virgin)
15	9 TURBO TRAX Various Artists (K-Tel)	6	9 COMPLETE MADNESS Madness (Stiff)	6	9 STILL LIFE (AMERICAN CONCERTS 1981) Rolling Stones (Rolling Stones)	5	9 ABRACADABRA Steve Miller Band (Mercury)
-	10 PICTURES AT ELEVEN Robert Plant (Swansong)	13	10 IMPERIAL BEDROOM Elvis Costello & the Attractions (F-Beat)	5	9 PICTURES AT ELEVEN Robert Plant (Swansong)	8	10 THE CONCERT IN CENTRAL PARK Simon & Garfunkel (CBS)
6	11 NON-STOP ECSTATIC DANCING Soft Cell (Some Bizzare)	5	11 TROPICAL GANGSTERS Kid Creole & the Coconuts (Ze)	14	11 MIRAGE Fleetwood Mac (Warner Bros.)	17	11 FRIENDS Shalamar (Solar)
-	12 MIRAGE Fleetwood Mac (Warner Bros.)	-	12 GOOD TROUBLE REO Speedwagon (Epic)	16	12 ASIA Asia (Geffen)	28	12 TUG OF WAR Paul McCartney (Parlophone)
-	13 IMPERIAL BEDROOM Elvis Costello & the Attraction (F-Beat)	19	13 OVERLOAD Various Artists (Ronco)	17	13 RIO Duran Duran (EMI)	9	13 STILL LIFE (AMERICAN CONCERTS 1981) Rolling Stones (Rolling Stones)
11	14 THE CHANGELING Toyah (Safari)	12	14 MIRAGE Fleetwood Mac (Warner Bros.)	-	14 THE KIDS FROM FAME Kids From Fame (BBC)	23	14 SCREAMING FOR VENGEANCE Judas Priest (CBS)
-	15 LOVE AND DANCE League Unlimited Orchestra (Virgin)	-	15 THE CONCERT IN CENTRAL PARK Simon & Garfunkel (CBS)	13	15 OVERLOAD Various Artists (Ronco)	-	15 DONNA SUMMER Donna Summer (Warner Bros.)
9	16 THREE SIDES LIVE Genesis (Charisma)	18	16 ASIA Asia (Geffen)	18	16 HAPPY TOGETHER Odyssey (RCA)	11	16 MIRAGE Fleetwood Mac (Warner Bros.)
13	17 TUG OF WAR Paul McCartney (Parlophone)	8	17 RIO Duran Duran (EMI)	22	17 FRIENDS Shalamar (Solar)	12	17 ASIA Asia (Geffen)
21	18 ASIA Asia (Geffen)	-	18 HAPPY TOGETHER Odyssey (RCA)	24	18 THREE SIDES LIVE Genesis (Charisma)	-	18 CAN'T STOP THE CLASSICS – HOOKED ON CLASSICS 2 Louis Clark & the Royal Philharmonic Orchestra (K-Tel)
22	19 OVERLOAD Various Artists (Ronco)	22	19 NIGHT BIRDS Shakatak (Polydor)	19	19 NIGHT BIRDS Shakatak (Polydor)	15	19 OVERLOAD Various Artists (Ronco)
10	20 HOT SPACE Queen (EMI)	11	20 NON-STOP ECSTATIC DANCING Soft Cell (Some Bizzare)	12	19 GOOD TROUBLE REO Speedwagon (Epic)	16	20 HAPPY TOGETHER Odyssey (RCA)
23	21 CHARIOTS OF FIRE Vangelis (Polydor)	17	21 TUG OF WAR Paul McCartney (Parlophone)	20	21 NON-STOP ECSTATIC DANCING Soft Cell (Some Bizzare)	21	21 IMPERIAL BEDROOM Elvis Costello & the Attractions (F-Beat)
8	22 NIGHT BIRDS Shakatak (Polydor)	25	22 FRIENDS Shalamar (Solar)	10	21 IMPERIAL BEDROOM Elvis Costello & the Attractions (F-Beat)	13	22 RIO Duran Duran (EMI)
12	23 FABRIQUE Fashion (Arista)	20	23 HOT SPACE Queen (EMI)	7	23 SCREAMING FOR VENGEANCE Judas Priest (CBS)	-	23 WINDSONG Randy Crawford (Warner Bros.)
20	24 PELICAN WEST Haircut 100 (Arista)	16	24 THREE SIDES LIVE Genesis (Charisma)	23	24 HOT SPACE Queen (EMI)	-	24 TOO-RYE-AY Dexy's Midnight Runners (Mercury)
-	25 FRIENDS Shalamar (Solar)	9	24 TURBO TRAX Various Artists (K-Tel)	29	25 THE CHANGELING Toyah (Safari)	21	25 NON-STOP ECSTATIC DANCING Soft Cell (Some Bizzare)
-	26 ARE YOU READY? Bucks Fizz (RCA)	24	26 PELICAN WEST Haircut 100 (Arista)	-	26 COMBAT ROCK Clash (CBS)	19	26 NIGHT BIRDS Shakatak (Polydor)
18	27 WINDSONG Randy Crawford (Warner Bros.)	21	27 CHARIOTS OF FIRE Vangelis (Polydor)	-	27 A CONCERT FOR THE PEOPLE (BERLIN) Barclay James Harvest (Polydor)	-	27 PELICAN WEST Haircut 100 (Arista)
-	28 CHILL OUT Black Uhuru (Island)	-	28 LOVE SONGS Barbra Streisand (CBS)	21	28 TUG OF WAR Paul McCartney (Parlophone)	-	28 ARE YOU READY? Bucks Fizz (RCA)
-	29 BARRY LIVE IN BRITAIN Barry Manilow (Arista)	14	29 THE CHANGELING Toyah (Safari)	27	29 CHARIOTS OF FIRE Vangelis (Polydor)	-	29 I WANT CANDY Bow Wow Wow (EMI)
-	30 1982 Status Quo (Vertigo)	23	30 FABRIQUE Fashion (Arista)	-	30 MUSTN'T GRUMBLE Chas & Dave (Rockney)	18	30 THREE SIDES LIVE Genesis (Charisma)

ABC's debut album, following after two Top 10 singles, was the clear best-seller in July, though closely followed by the two-year-old soundtrack from the film *Fame*. This, together with its title track single performed by Irene Cara (which hit Number 1 on July 24) were sudden if belated British successes due to the success of the spin-off *Fame* TV series. The new BBC album *The Kids From Fame*, containing music from the television series, was an almost instant chart-topper.

last week	this week	14 August 1982		
1	1	THE KIDS FROM FAME	Kids From Fame (BBC)	
24	2	TOO-RYE-AY	Dexy's Midnight Runners (Mercury)	
2	3	FAME	Soundtrack (RSO)	
3	4	THE LEXICON OF LOVE	ABC (Neutron)	
8	5	LOVE AND DANCE	League Unlimited Orchestra (Virgin)	
4	6	COMPLETE MADNESS	Madness (Stiff)	
5	7	AVALON	Roxy Music (EG)	
6	8	TROPICAL GANGSTERS	Kid Creole & the Coconuts (Ze)	
10	9	THE CONCERT IN CENTRAL PARK	Simon & Garfunkel (CBS)	
9	10	ABRACADABRA	Steve Miller Band (Mercury)	
13	11	STILL LIFE (AMERICAN CONCERTS 1981)	Rolling Stones (Rolling Stones)	
16	12	MIRAGE	Fleetwood Mac (Warner Bros.)	
11	13	FRIENDS	Shalamar (Solar)	
7	14	PICTURES AT ELEVEN	Robert Plant (Swansong)	
29	15	I WANT CANDY	Bow Wow Wow (EMI)	
12	16	TUG OF WAR	Paul McCartney (Parlophone)	
15	17	DONNA SUMMER	Donna Summer (Warner Bros.)	
17	18	ASIA	Asia (Geffen)	
22	19	RIO	Duran Duran (EMI)	
18	20	CAN'T STOP THE CLASSICS – HOOKED ON CLASSICS 2	Louis Clark & the Royal Philharmonic Orchestra (K-Tel)	
-	21	A CONCERT FOR THE PEOPLE (BERLIN)	Barclay James Harvest (Polydor)	
-	22	DARE	Human League (Virgin)	
-	23	ASSEMBLAGE	Japan (Hansa)	
26	24	NIGHT BIRDS	Shakatak (Polydor)	
30	25	THREE SIDES LIVE	Genesis (Charisma)	
-	26	BAT OUT OF HELL	Meatloaf (Epic)	
23	27	WINDSONG	Randy Crawford (Warner Bros.)	
25	28	NON-STOP ECSTATIC DANCING	Soft Cell (Some Bizzare)	
21	29	IMPERIAL BEDROOM	Elvis Costello & the Attractions (F-Beat)	
20	30	HAPPY TOGETHER	Odyssey (RCA)	

		21 August 1982	
2	1	TOO-RYE-AY	Dexy's Midnight Runners (Mercury)
1	2	THE KIDS FROM FAME	Kids From Fame (BBC)
3	3	FAME	Soundtrack (RSO)
8	4	TROPICAL GANGSTERS	Kid Creole & the Coconuts (Ze)
6	5	COMPLETE MADNESS	Madness (Stiff)
4	6	THE LEXICON OF LOVE	ABC (Neutron)
5	7	LOVE AND DANCE	League Unlimited Orchestra (Virgin)
9	8	THE CONCERT IN CENTRAL PARK	Simon & Garfunkel (CBS)
7	9	AVALON	Roxy Music (EG)
17	10	DONNA SUMMER	Donna Summer (Warner Bros.)
-	11	LOVE SONGS	Commodores (K-Tel)
13	12	FRIENDS	Shalamar (Solar)
-	13	TALKING BACK TO THE NIGHT	Steve Winwood (Island)
12	14	MIRAGE	Fleetwood Mac (Warner Bros.)
19	15	RIO	Duran Duran (EMI)
11	16	STILL LIFE (AMERICAN CONCERTS 1981)	Rolling Stones (Rolling Stones)
10	17	ABRACADABRA	Steve Miller Band (Mercury)
20	18	CAN'T STOP THE CLASSICS – HOOKED ON CLASSICS 2	Louis Clark & the Royal Philharmonic Orchestra (K-Tel)
16	19	TUG OF WAR	Paul McCartney (Parlophone)
-	20	THE JIMI HENDRIX CONCERTS	Jimi Hendrix (CBS)
-	21	SHANGO	Santana (CBS)
14	22	PICTURES AT ELEVEN	Robert Plant (Swansong)
15	23	I WANT CANDY	Bow Wow Wow (EMI)
24	24	NIGHT BIRDS	Shakatak (Polydor)
21	25	A CONCERT FOR THE PEOPLE (BERLIN)	Barclay James Harvest (Polydor)
26	26	BAT OUT OF HELL	Meatloaf (Epic)
-	27	THE NUMBER OF THE BEAST	Iron Maiden (EMI)
28	28	NON-STOP ECSTATIC DANCING	Soft Cell (Some Bizzare)
25	29	THREE SIDES LIVE	Genesis (Charisma)
18	30	ASIA	Asia (Geffen)

		28 August 1982	
1	1	TOO-RYE-AY	Dexy's Midnight Runners (Mercury)
2	2	THE KIDS FROM FAME	Kids From Fame (BBC)
7	3	LOVE AND DANCE	League Unlimited Orchestra (Virgin)
6	4	THE LEXICON OF LOVE	ABC (Neutron)
4	5	TROPICAL GANGSTERS	Kid Creole & the Coconuts (Ze)
3	6	FAME	Soundtrack (RSO)
8	7	THE CONCERT IN CENTRAL PARK	Simon & Garfunkel (CBS)
5	8	COMPLETE MADNESS	Madness (Stiff)
9	9	AVALON	Roxy Music (EG)
15	10	RIO	Duran Duran (EMI)
13	11	TALKING BACK TO THE NIGHT	Steve Winwood (Island)
14	12	MIRAGE	Fleetwood Mac (Warner Bros.)
19	13	TUG OF WAR	Paul McCartney (Parlophone)
17	14	ABRACADABRA	Steve Miller Band (Mercury)
11	15	LOVE SONGS	Commodores (K-Tel)
10	16	DONNA SUMMER	Donna Summer (Warner Bros.)
20	17	THE JIMI HENDRIX CONCERTS	Jimi Hendrix (CBS)
28	18	NON-STOP ECSTATIC DANCING	Soft Cell (Some Bizzare)
-	19	DARE	Human League (Virgin)
30	20	ASIA	Asia (Geffen)
24	21	NIGHT BIRDS	Shakatak (Polydor)
16	22	STILL LIFE (AMERICAN CONCERTS 1981)	Rolling Stones (Rolling Stones)
22	23	PICTURES AT ELEVEN	Robert Plant (Swansong)
-	24	ASSEMBLAGE	Japan (Hansa)
12	25	FRIENDS	Shalamar (Solar)
26	26	BAT OUT OF HELL	Meatloaf (Epic)
-	27	EYE OF THE TIGER	Survivor (Scotti Bros.)
21	28	SHANGO	Santana (CBS)
18	29	CAN'T STOP THE CLASSICS – HOOKED ON CLASSICS 2	Louis Clark & the Royal Philharmonic Orchestra (K-Tel)
23	30	I WANT CANDY	Bow Wow Wow (EMI)

		4 September 1982	
2	1	THE KIDS FROM FAME	Kids From Fame (BBC)
1	2	TOO-RYE-AY	Dexy's Midnight Runners (Mercury)
3	3	LOVE AND DANCE	League Unlimited Orchestra (Virgin)
4	4	THE LEXICON OF LOVE	ABC (Neutron)
5	5	TROPICAL GANGSTERS	Kid Creole & the Coconuts (Ze)
10	6	RIO	Duran Duran (EMI)
8	7	COMPLETE MADNESS	Madness (Stiff)
27	8	EYE OF THE TIGER	Survivor (Scotti Bros.)
9	9	AVALON	Roxy Music (EG)
6	10	FAME	Soundtrack (RSO)
16	11	DONNA SUMMER	Donna Summer (Warner Bros.)
11	12	TALKING BACK TO THE NIGHT	Steve Winwood (Island)
29	13	CAN'T STOP THE CLASSICS – HOOKED ON CLASSICS 2	Louis Clark & the Royal Philharmonic Orchestra (K-Tel)
-	14	THE CAGE	Tygers Of Pan Tang (MCA)
15	15	LOVE SONGS	Commodores (K-Tel)
-	16	THE SINGLES ALBUM	UB40 (Graduate)
14	17	ABRACADABRA	Steve Miller Band (Mercury)
12	18	MIRAGE	Fleetwood Mac (Warner Bros.)
7	19	THE CONCERT IN CENTRAL PARK	Simon & Garfunkel (CBS)
-	20	CHRIST THE ALBUM	Crass (Crass)
17	21	THE JIMI HENDRIX CONCERTS	Jimi Hendrix (CBS)
18	22	NON-STOP ECSTATIC DANCING	Soft Cell (Some Bizzare)
-	23	ROUGH DIAMONDS	Bad Company (Swansong)
-	24	NOW YOU SEE ME, NOW YOU DON'T	Cliff Richard (EMI)
13	25	TUG OF WAR	Paul McCartney (Parlophone)
24	26	ASSEMBLAGE	Japan (Hansa)
21	27	NIGHT BIRDS	Shakatak (Polydor)
26	28	BAT OUT OF HELL	Meatloaf (Epic)
22	29	STILL LIFE (AMERICAN CONCERTS 1981)	Rolling Stones (Rolling Stones)
23	30	PICTURES AT ELEVEN	Robert Plant (Swansong)

Dexy's Midnight Runners' million-selling single *Come On Eileen* was instrumental in making its parent album *Too-Rye-Ay* (this title being a key phrase from the single's lyric) the group's most successful yet, snatching a two-week stay at Number 1 from *The Kids From Fame*. The Commodores became the third major act with a few months to release a ballads compilation titled *Love Songs* and score a hit with it, though this package was not destined to follow Cliff and Streisand to Number 1.

11 September 1982

(last week / this week)

- / 1 UPSTAIRS AT ERIC'S — Yazoo (Mute)
1 / 2 THE KIDS FROM FAME — Kids From Fame (BBC)
2 / 3 TOO-RYE-AY — Dexy's Midnight Runners (Mercury)
6 / 4 RIO — Duran Duran (EMI)
4 / 5 THE LEXICON OF LOVE — ABC (Neutron)
5 / 6 TROPICAL GANGSTERS — Kid Creole & the Coconuts (Ze)
24 / 7 NOW YOU SEE ME, NOW YOU DON'T — Cliff Richard (EMI)
15 / 8 LOVE SONGS — Commodores (K-Tel)
3 / 9 LOVE AND DANCE — League Unlimited Orch (Virgin)
7 / 10 COMPLETE MADNESS — Madness (Stiff)
10 / 11 FAME — Soundtrack (RSO)
12 / 12 TALKING BACK TO THE NIGHT — Steve Winwood (Island)
9 / 13 AVALON — Roxy Music (EG)
8 / 14 EYE OF THE TIGER — Survivor (Scotti Bros.)
16 / 15 THE SINGLES ALBUM — UB40 (Graduate)
18 / 16 MIRAGE — Fleetwood Mac (Warner Bros.)
21 / 17 THE JIMI HENDRIX CONCERTS — Jimi Hendrix (CBS)
23 / 18 ROUGH DIAMONDS — Bad Company (Swansong)
- / 19 DEEP PURPLE LIVE IN LONDON — Deep Purple (Harvest)
- / 20 ROCKY III — Soundtrack (Liberty)
22 / 21 NON-STOP ECSTATIC DANCING — Soft Cell (Some Bizzare)
13 / 22 CAN'T STOP THE CLASSICS – HOOKED ON CLASSICS 2 — Louis Clark & the Royal Philharmonic Orchestra (K-Tel)
14 / 23 THE CAGE — Tygers Of Pan Tang (MCA)
- / 24 WELL KEPT SECRET — John Martyn (WEA)
25 / 25 ASIA — Asia (Geffen)
- / 26 THE PARTY'S OVER — Talk Talk (EMI)
19 / 27 THE CONCERT IN CENTRAL PARK — Simon & Garfunkel (CBS)
27 / 28 NIGHT BIRDS — Shakatak (Polydor)
11 / 29 DONNA SUMMER — Donna Summer (Warner Bros.)
20 / 30 CHRIST THE ALBUM — Crass (Crass)

18 September 1982

2 / 1 THE KIDS FROM FAME — Kids From Fame (BBC)
3 / 2 TOO-RYE-AY — Dexy's Midnight Runners (Mercury)
1 / 3 UPSTAIRS AT ERIC'S — Yazoo (Mute)
4 / 4 RIO — Duran Duran (EMI)
7 / 5 NOW YOU SEE ME, NOW YOU DON'T — Cliff Richard (EMI)
9 / 6 LOVE AND DANCE — League Unlimited Orch (Virgin)
5 / 7 THE LEXICON OF LOVE — ABC (Neutron)
- / 8 IN THE HEAT OF THE NIGHT — Imagination (R&B)
- / 9 BREAKOUT — Various Artists (Ronco)
10 / 10 COMPLETE MADNESS — Madness (Stiff)
- / 11 IT'S HARD — Who (Polydor)
14 / 12 EYE OF THE TIGER — Survivor (Scotti Bros.)
8 / 13 LOVE SONGS — Commodores (K-Tel)
11 / 14 FAME — Soundtrack (RSO)
6 / 15 TROPICAL GANGSTERS — Kid Creole & the Coconuts (Ze)
16 / 16 MIRAGE — Fleetwood Mac (Warner Bros.)
12 / 17 TALKING BACK TO THE NIGHT — Steve Winwood (Island)
- / 18 HIGHWAY SONG – BLACKFOOT LIVE — Blackfoot (Atco)
15 / 19 THE SINGLES ALBUM — UB40 (Graduate)
13 / 20 AVALON — Roxy Music (EG)
17 / 21 THE JIMI HENDRIX CONCERTS — Jimi Hendrix (CBS)
- / 22 SIGNALS — Rush (Mercury)
- / 23 I, ASSASSIN — Gary Numan (Beggars Banquet)
21 / 24 NON-STOP ECSTATIC DANCING — Soft Cell (Some Bizzare)
27 / 25 THE CONCERT IN CENTRAL PARK — Simon & Garfunkel (CBS)
- / 26 PETER GABRIEL — Peter Gabriel (Charisma)
20 / 27 ROCKY III — Soundtrack (Liberty)
- / 28 SONGS TO REMEMBER — Scritti Politti (Rough Trade)
26 / 29 THE PARTY'S OVER — Talk Talk (EMI)
- / 30 MAKIN' MOVIES — Dire Straits (Vertigo)

25 September 1982

1 / 1 THE KIDS FROM FAME — Kids From Fame (BBC)
3 / 2 UPSTAIRS AT ERIC'S — Yazoo (Mute)
7 / 3 THE LEXICON OF LOVE — ABC (Neutron)
26 / 4 PETER GABRIEL — Peter Gabriel (Charisma)
4 / 5 RIO — Duran Duran (EMI)
8 / 6 IN THE HEAT OF THE NIGHT — Imagination (R&B)
23 / 7 I, ASSASSIN — Gary Numan (Beggars Banquet)
9 / 8 BREAKOUT — Various Artists (Ronco)
22 / 9 SIGNALS — Rush (Mercury)
5 / 10 NOW YOU SEE ME, NOW YOU DON'T — Cliff Richard (EMI)
2 / 11 TOO-RYE-AY — Dexy's Midnight Runners (Mercury)
10 / 12 COMPLETE MADNESS — Madness (Stiff)
- / 13 CHART BEAT, CHART HEAT — Various Artists (K-Tel)
11 / 14 IT'S HARD — Who (Polydor)
6 / 15 LOVE AND DANCE — League Unlimited Orch (Virgin)
13 / 16 LOVE SONGS — Commodores (K-Tel)
- / 17 THE DREAMING — Kate Bush (EMI)
18 / 18 NEW GOLD DREAM (81,82,83,84) — Simple Minds (Virgin)
19 / 19 HIGHWAY SONG – BLACKFOOT LIVE — Blackfoot (Atco)
15 / 20 TROPICAL GANGSTERS — Kid Creole & the Coconuts (Ze)
20 / 21 AVALON — Roxy Music (EG)
14 / 22 FAME — Soundtrack (RSO)
- / 23 ASIA — Asia (Geffen)
- / 24 FICTION — Comsat Angels (Polydor)
28 / 25 SONGS TO REMEMBER — Scritti Politti (Rough Trade)
12 / 26 EYE OF THE TIGER — Survivor (Scotti Bros.)
- / 27 ACTING VERY STRANGE — Mike Rutherford (WEA)
27 / 28 ROCKY III — Soundtrack (Liberty)
- / 29 MYSTERY — Hot Chocolate (RAK)
- / 30 THE COLLECTION 1977-1982 — Stranglers (Liberty)

2 October 1982

1 / 1 THE KIDS FROM FAME — Kids From Fame (BBC)
3 / 2 THE LEXICON OF LOVE — ABC (Neutron)
2 / 3 UPSTAIRS AT ERIC'S — Yazoo (Mute)
13 / 4 CHART BEAT, CHART HEAT — Various Artists (K-Tel)
- / 5 LOVE OVER GOLD — Dire Straits (Vertigo)
6 / 6 IN THE HEAT OF THE NIGHT — Imagination (R&B)
17 / 7 THE DREAMING — Kate Bush (EMI)
5 / 8 RIO — Duran Duran (EMI)
18 / 9 NEW GOLD DREAM (81,82,83,84) — Simple Minds (Virgin)
11 / 10 TOO-RYE-AY — Dexy's Midnight Runners (Mercury)
30 / 11 THE COLLECTION 1977-1982 — Stranglers (Liberty)
8 / 12 BREAKOUT — Various Artists (Ronco)
7 / 13 I, ASSASSIN — Gary Numan (Beggars Banquet)
4 / 14 PETER GABRIEL — Peter Gabriel (Charisma)
9 / 15 SIGNALS — Rush (Mercury)
16 / 16 LOVE SONGS — Commodores (K-Tel)
29 / 17 MYSTERY — Hot Chocolate (RAK)
15 / 18 LOVE AND DANCE — League Unlimited Orch (Virgin)
10 / 19 NOW YOU SEE ME, NOW YOU DON'T — Cliff Richard (EMI)
- / 20 FRIENDS — Shalamar (Solar)
- / 21 LIFE IN THE JUNGLE/ LIVE AT ABBEY ROAD — Shadows (Polydor)
- / 22 NEBRASKA — Bruce Springsteen (CBS)
20 / 23 TROPICAL GANGSTERS — Kid Creole & the Coconuts (Ze)
- / 24 SOMETHING'S GOING ON — Frida (Epic)
21 / 25 AVALON — Roxy Music (EG)
- / 26 MIRAGE — Fleetwood Mac (Warner Bros.)
27 / 27 ACTING VERY STRANGE — Mike Rutherford (WEA)
24 / 28 FICTION — Comsat Angels (Polydor)
26 / 29 EYE OF THE TIGER — Survivor (Scotti Bros.)
12 / 30 COMPLETE MADNESS — Madness (Stiff)

Yazoo, the duo formed by ex-Depeche Mode keyboards player Vince Clark and vocalist Alison Moyet became one of only a handful of acts in history to debut in the Number 1 slot with their first album, *Upstairs At Eric's* (the title being a refence to the studio where the LP was recorded). Peter Gabriel charted with his fourth album (and the last, fortunately) to be called just *Peter Gabriel*, while the Shadows' album was a studio set with a free live LP attached.

October 1982

last week	this	9 October 1982
5	1	LOVE OVER GOLD Dire Straits (Vertigo)
1	2	THE KIDS FROM FAME Kids From Fame (BBC)
4	3	CHART BEAT, CHART HEAT Various Artists (K-Tel)
9	4	NEW GOLD DREAM (81,82,83,84) Simple Minds (Virgin)
3	5	UPSTAIRS AT ERIC'S Yazoo (Mute)
6	6	IN THE HEAT OF THE NIGHT Imagination (R&B)
22	7	NEBRASKA Bruce Springsteen (CBS)
7	8	THE DREAMING Kate Bush (EMI)
20	9	FRIENDS Shalamar (Solar)
2	10	THE LEXICON OF LOVE ABC (Neutron)
10	11	TOO-RYE-AY Dexy's Midnight Runners (Mercury)
8	12	RIO Duran Duran (EMI)
16	13	LOVE SONGS Commodores (K-Tel)
11	14	THE COLLECTION 1977-1982 Stranglers (Liberty)
-	15	FOREVER NOW Psychedelic Furs (CBS)
18	16	LOVE AND DANCE League Unlimited Orchestra (Virgin)
12	17	BREAKOUT Various Artists (Ronco)
14	18	PETER GABRIEL Peter Gabriel (Charisma)
-	19	UB44 UB40 (DEP International)
-	20	MAGIC Gillan (Virgin)
17	21	MYSTERY Hot Chocolate (RAK)
19	22	NOW YOU SEE ME, NOW YOU DON'T Cliff Richard (EMI)
15	23	SIGNALS Rush (Mercury)
-	24	A BROKEN FRAME Depeche Mode (Mute)
-	25	NOW THEN Stiff Little Fingers (Chrysalis)
-	26	SHALAMAR'S GREATEST HITS Shalamar (Solar)
29	27	EYE OF THE TIGER Survivor (Scotti Bros.)
21	28	LIFE IN THE JUNGLE – LIVE AT ABBEY ROAD Shadows (Polydor)
-	29	AS ONE Kool & the Gang (De-Lite)
24	30	SOMETHING'S GOING ON Frida (Epic)

16 October 1982

1	1	LOVE OVER GOLD Dire Straits (Vertigo)
19	2	UB44 UB40 (DEP International)
7	3	NEBRASKA Bruce Springsteen (CBS)
2	4	THE KIDS FROM FAME Kids From Fame (BBC)
5	5	UPSTAIRS AT ERIC'S Yazoo (Mute)
4	6	NEW GOLD DREAM (81,82,83,84) Simple Minds (Virgin)
24	7	A BROKEN FRAME Depeche Mode (Mute)
10	8	THE LEXICON OF LOVE ABC (Neutron)
-	9	GIVE ME YOUR HEART TONIGHT Shakin' Stevens (Epic)
11	10	TOO-RYE-AY Dexy's Midnight Runners (Mercury)
3	11	CHART BEAT, CHART HEAT Various Artists (K-Tel)
13	12	LOVE SONGS Commodores (K-Tel)
-	13	AVALON Roxy Music (EG)
6	14	IN THE HEAT OF THE NIGHT Imagination (R&B)
9	15	FRIENDS Shalamar (Solar)
20	16	MAGIC Gillan (Virgin)
8	17	THE DREAMING Kate Bush (EMI)
-	18	SPECIAL BEAT SERVICE Beat (Go-Feet)
12	19	RIO Duran Duran (EMI)
18	20	PETER GABRIEL Peter Gabriel (Charisma)
15	21	FOREVER NOW Psychedelic Furs (CBS)
-	22	MIRAGE Fleetwood Mac (Warner Bros.)
-	23	TROPICAL GANGSTERS Kid Creole & the Coconuts (Ze)
26	24	SHALAMAR'S GREATEST HITS Shalamar (Solar)
14	25	THE COLLECTION 1977-1982 Stranglers (Liberty)
23	26	SIGNALS Rush (Mercury)
-	27	SOUL DAZE, SOUL NITES Various Artists ((Ronco)
-	28	GET LOOSE Evelyn King (RCA)
17	29	BREAKOUT Various Artists (Ronco)
21	30	MYSTERY Hot Chocolate (RAK)

23 October 1982

1	1	LOVE OVER GOLD Dire Straits (Vertigo)
-	2	THE KIDS FROM FAME AGAIN Kids From Fame (RCA)
9	3	GIVE ME YOUR HEART TONIGHT Shakin' Stevens (Epic)
2	4	UB44 UB40 (DEP International)
-	5	CHART ATTACK Various Artists (Telstar)
6	6	NEW GOLD DREAM (81,82,83,84) Simple Minds (Virgin)
-	7	KISSING TO BE CLEVER Culture Club (Virgin)
14	8	IN THE HEAT OF THE NIGHT Imagination (R&B)
5	9	UPSTAIRS AT ERIC'S Yazoo (Mute)
7	10	A BROKEN FRAME Depeche Mode (Mute)
10	11	TOO-RYE-AY Dexy's Midnight Runners (Mercury)
8	12	THE LEXICON OF LOVE ABC (Neutron)
3	13	NEBRASKA Bruce Springsteen (CBS)
-	14	FRIEND OR FOE Adam Ant (CBS)
12	15	LOVE SONGS Commodores (K-Tel)
23	16	TROPICAL GANGSTERS Kid Creole & the Coconuts (Ze)
-	17	REFLECTIONS Various Artists (CBS)
-	18	AMOR Julio Iglesias (CBS)
11	19	CHART BEAT, CHART HEAT Various Artists (K-Tel)
15	20	FRIENDS Shalamar (Solar)
4	21	THE KIDS FROM FAME Kids From Fame (BBC)
24	22	SHALAMAR'S GREATEST HITS Shalamar (Solar)
13	23	AVALON Roxy Music (EG)
30	24	MYSTERY Hot Chocolate (RAK)
20	25	PETER GABRIEL Peter Gabriel (Charisma)
18	26	SPECIAL BEAT SERVICE Beat (Go-Feet)
17	27	THE DREAMING Kate Bush (EMI)
-	28	HAPPY FAMILIES Blancmange (London)
19	29	RIO Duran Duran (EMI)
26	30	SIGNALS Rush (Mercury)

30 October 1982

2	1	THE KIDS FROM FAME AGAIN Kids From Fame (RCA)
1	2	LOVE OVER GOLD Dire Straits (Vertigo)
21	3	THE KIDS FROM FAME Kids From Fame (BBC)
14	4	FRIEND OR FOE Adam Ant (CBS)
7	5	KISSING TO BE CLEVER Culture Club (Virgin)
-	6	QUARTET Ultravox (Chrysalis)
17	7	REFLECTIONS Various Artists (CBS)
3	8	GIVE ME YOUR HEART TONIGHT Shakin' Stevens (Epic)
4	9	UB44 UB40 (DEP International)
5	10	CHART ATTACK Various Artists (Telstar)
9	11	UPSTAIRS AT ERIC'S Yazoo (Mute)
12	12	THE LEXICON OF LOVE ABC (Neutron)
-	13	THE SKY'S GONE OUT Bauhaus (Beggars Banquet)
8	14	IN THE HEAT OF THE NIGHT Imagination (R&B)
10	15	A BROKEN FRAME Depeche Mode (Mute)
-	16	STRAWBERRIES Damned (Bronze)
20	17	FRIENDS Shalamar (Solar)
11	18	TOO-RYE-AY Dexy's Midnight Runners (Mercury)
15	19	LOVE SONGS Commodores (K-Tel)
18	20	AMOR Julio Iglesias (CBS)
13	21	NEBRASKA Bruce Springsteen (CBS)
6	22	NEW GOLD DREAM (81,82,83,84) Simple Minds (Virgin)
16	23	TROPICAL GANGSTERS Kid Creole & the Coconuts (Ze)
-	24	20 GREATEST HITS Beatles (Parlophone)
-	25	BORROWED TIME Diamond Head (MCA)
-	26	CHOOSE YOUR MASQUES Hawkwind (RCA)
29	27	RIO Duran Duran (EMI)
-	28	SILK ELECTRIC Diana Ross (Capitol)
-	29	ENDLESS LOVE Various Artists (TV)
-	30	OLIVIA NEWTON-JOHN'S GREATEST HITS Olivia Newton-John (EMI)

Love Over Gold was only the fourth album from the not hugely prolific Dire Straits in five years, and became their first to top the chart, hitting Number 1 two weeks after the extracted *Private Investigations* gave them their debut Number 1 single. *The Kids From Fame Again*, the next LP chart-topper, was released by RCA, which did not repeat its (in retrospect) dumb move of declining the first *Kids* album and allowing BBC Records to licence - and sell vast quantities of - it.

6 November 1982

last week	this week	
2	1	LOVE OVER GOLD — Dire Straits (Vertigo)
1	2	THE KIDS FROM FAME AGAIN — Kids From Fame (RCA)
3	3	THE KIDS FROM FAME — Kids From Fame (BBC)
5	4	KISSING TO BE CLEVER — Culture Club (Virgin)
13	5	THE SKY'S GONE OUT — Bauhaus (Beggars Banquet)
23	6	TROPICAL GANGSTERS — Kid Creole & the Coconuts (Ze)
6	7	QUARTET — Ultravox (Chrysalis)
7	8	REFLECTIONS — Various Artists (CBS)
24	9	20 GREATEST HITS — Beatles (Parlophone)
8	10	GIVE ME YOUR HEART TONIGHT — Shakin' Stevens (Epic)
30	11	OLIVIA NEWTON-JOHN'S GREATEST HITS — Olivia Newton-John (EMI)
4	12	FRIEND OR FOE — Adam Ant (CBS)
10	13	CHART ATTACK — Various Artists (Telstar)
20	14	AMOR — Julio Iglesias (CBS)
12	15	THE LEXICON OF LOVE — ABC (Neutron)
11	16	UPSTAIRS AT ERIC'S — Yazoo (Mute)
-	17	THE LOVE SONGS ALBUM — Various Artists (K-Tel)
-	18	THE DOLLAR ALBUM — Dollar (WEA)
15	19	A BROKEN FRAME — Depeche Mode (Mute)
-	20	HEARTBREAKER — Dionne Warwick (Arista)
19	21	LOVE SONGS — Commodores (K-Tel)
29	22	ENDLESS LOVE — Various Artists (TV)
17	23	FRIENDS — Shalamar (Solar)
28	24	SILK ELECTRIC — Diana Ross (Capitol)
9	25	UB44 — UB40 (DEP International)
-	26	CHART BEAT, CHART HEAT — Various Artists (K-Tel)
-	27	THE NIGHTFLY — Donald Fagen (Warner Bros.)
22	28	NEW GOLD DREAM (81,82,83,84) — Simple Minds (Virgin)
-	29	ASSAULT ATTACK — Michael Schenker Group (Chrysalis)
16	30	STRAWBERRIES — Damned (Bronze)

13 November 1982

last week	this week	
3	1	THE KIDS FROM FAME — Kids From Fame (BBC)
4	2	KISSING TO BE CLEVER — Culture Club (Virgin)
1	3	LOVE OVER GOLD — Dire Straits (Vertigo)
2	4	THE KIDS FROM FAME AGAIN — Kids From Fame (RCA)
-	5	FAMOUS LAST WORDS — Supertramp (A&M)
-	6	SINGLES – 45s AND UNDER — Squeeze (A&M)
6	7	TROPICAL GANGSTERS — Kid Creole & the Coconuts (Ze)
8	8	REFLECTIONS — Various Artists (CBS)
14	9	AMOR — Julio Iglesias (CBS)
5	10	THE SKY'S GONE OUT — Bauhaus (Beggars Banquet)
20	11	HEARTBREAKER — Dionne Warwick (Arista)
9	12	20 GREATEST HITS — Beatles (Parlophone)
11	13	OLIVIA NEWTON-JOHN'S GREATEST HITS — Olivia Newton-John (EMI)
10	14	GIVE ME YOUR HEART TONIGHT — Shakin' Stevens (Epic)
-	15	H20 — Daryl Hall & John Oates (RCA)
7	16	QUARTET — Ultravox (Chrysalis)
15	17	THE LEXICON OF LOVE — ABC (Neutron)
-	18	HELLO, I MUST BE GOING! — Phil Collins (Virgin)
21	19	LOVE SONGS — Commodores (K-Tel)
16	20	UPSTAIRS AT ERIC'S — Yazoo (Mute)
18	21	THE DOLLAR ALBUM — Dollar (WEA)
-	22	IN THE HEAT OF THE NIGHT — Imagination (R&B)
17	23	THE LOVE SONGS ALBUM — Various Artists (K-Tel)
-	24	CREATURES OF THE NIGHT — Kiss (Casablanca)
-	25	FLASH TRACKS — Various Artists (TV)
-	26	HITS OF THE SCREAMING SIXTIES — Various Artists (Warwick)
24	27	SILK ELECTRIC — Diana Ross (Capitol)
-	28	VOICE OF A GENERATION — Blitz (No Future)
12	29	FRIEND OR FOE — Adam Ant (CBS)
25	30	UB44 — UB40 (DEP International)

20 November 1982

last week	this week	
1	1	THE KIDS FROM FAME — Kids From Fame (BBC)
6	2	SINGLES – 45s AND UNDER — Squeeze (A&M)
-	3	FROM THE MAKERS OF ... — Status Quo (Vertigo)
11	4	HEARTBREAKER — Dionne Warwick (Arista)
4	5	THE KIDS FROM FAME AGAIN — Kids From Fame (RCA)
18	6	HELLO, I MUST BE GOING! — Phil Collins (Virgin)
8	7	REFLECTIONS — Various Artists (CBS)
3	8	LOVE OVER GOLD — Dire Straits (Vertigo)
2	9	KISSING TO BE CLEVER — Culture Club (Virgin)
5	10	FAMOUS LAST WORDS — Supertramp (A&M)
14	11	GIVE ME YOUR HEART TONIGHT — Shakin' Stevens (Epic)
-	12	MADNESS PRESENTS THE RISE AND FALL — Madness (Stiff)
7	13	TROPICAL GANGSTERS — Kid Creole & the Coconuts (Ze)
-	14	A KISS IN THE DREAMHOUSE — Siouxsie & the Banshees (Polydor)
-	15	WARRIOR ROCK – TOYAH ON TOUR — Toyah (Safari)
19	16	LOVE SONGS — Commodores (K-Tel)
12	17	20 GREATEST HITS — Beatles (Parlophone)
10	18	THE SKY'S GONE OUT — Bauhaus (Beggars Banquet)
25	19	FLASH TRACKS — Various Artists (TV)
-	20	PEARLS II — Elkie Brooks (A&M)
27	21	SILK ELECTRIC — Diana Ross (Capitol)
20	22	UPSTAIRS AT ERIC'S — Yazoo (Mute)
13	23	OLIVIA NEWTON-JOHN'S GREATEST HITS — Olivia Newton-John (EMI)
-	24	WAXWORKS – SOME SINGLES (1977-82) — XTC (Virgin)
26	25	HITS OF THE SCREAMING SIXTIES — Various Artists (Warwick)
21	26	THE DOLLAR ALBUM — Dollar (WEA)
15	27	H20 — Daryl Hall & John Oates (RCA)
-	28	GET NERVOUS — Pat Benatar (Chrysalis)
22	29	IN THE HEAT OF THE NIGHT — Imagination (R&B)
-	30	LOVE SONGS — Elton John (TV)

27 November 1982

last week	this week	
4	1	HEARTBREAKER — Dionne Warwick (Arista)
6	2	HELLO, I MUST BE GOING! — Phil Collins (Virgin)
-	3	THE SINGLES – THE FIRST TEN YEARS — Abba (Epic)
1	3	THE KIDS FROM FAME — Kids From Fame (BBC)
2	5	SINGLES – 45s AND UNDER — Squeeze (A&M)
3	6	FROM THE MAKERS OF ... — Status Quo (Vertigo)
12	7	MADNESS PRESENTS THE RISE AND FALL — Madness (Stiff)
7	8	REFLECTIONS — Various Artists (CBS)
-	9	THE JOHN LENNON COLLECTION — John Lennon (Parlophone)
20	10	PEARLS II — Elkie Brooks (A&M)
-	11	MIDNIGHT LOVE — Marvin Gaye (CBS)
-	12	CHART HITS '82 — Various Artists (K-Tel)
5	13	THE KIDS FROM FAME AGAIN — Kids From Fame (RCA)
10	14	FAMOUS LAST WORDS — Supertramp (A&M)
-	15	LINING MY LIFE — Grace Jones (Island)
9	16	KISSING TO BE CLEVER — Culture Club (Virgin)
11	17	GIVE ME YOUR HEART TONIGHT — Shakin' Stevens (Epic)
8	18	LOVE OVER GOLD — Dire Straits (Vertigo)
-	19	RIO — Duran Duran (EMI)
14	20	A KISS IN THE DREAMHOUSE — Siouxsie & the Banshees (Polydor)
13	21	TROPICAL GANGSTERS — Kid Creole & the Coconuts (Ze)
17	22	20 GREATEST HITS — Beatles (Parlophone)
15	23	WARRIOR ROCK – TOYAH ON TOUR — Toyah (Safari)
-	24	HAPPY FAMILIES — Blancmange (London)
19	25	FLASH TRACKS — Various Artists (TV)
22	26	UPSTAIRS AT ERIC'S — Yazoo (Mute)
-	27	RIP IT UP — Orange Juice (Holden Caulfield Universal)
26	28	THE DOLLAR ALBUM — Dollar (WEA)
-	29	GREATEST LOVE SONGS — Nat 'King' Cole (Capitol)
30	30	LOVE SONGS — Elton John (TV)

Interestingly, the first *Kids From Fame* album resurged to outsell its successor during November, grabbing two further weeks at Number 1 after *Kids From Fame Again* had dropped. The Beatles Top 10 album *20 Greatest Hits* was a new compilation issued to coincide with the 20th anniversary of the release of their first EMI single *Love Me Do* - this track was not only included on the album but also successfully re-promoted on single, reaching Number 3 (24 places higher than the first time around!).

December 1982

4 December 1982

last	this	Title	Artist (Label)
3	1	THE SINGLES – THE FIRST TEN YEARS	Abba (Epic)
1	2	HEARTBREAKER	Dionne Warwick (Arista)
-	3	I WANNA DO IT WITH YOU	Barry Manilow (Arista)
3	4	THE KIDS FROM FAME	Kids From Fame (BBC)
2	5	HELLO, I MUST BE GOING!	Phil Collins (Virgin)
6	6	FROM THE MAKERS OF ...	Status Quo (Vertigo)
9	7	THE JOHN LENNON COLLECTION	John Lennon (Parlophone)
5	8	SINGLES – 45s AND UNDER	Squeeze (A&M)
10	9	PEARLS II	Elkie Brooks (A&M)
29	10	GREATEST LOVE SONGS	Nat 'King' Cole (Capitol)
-	11	SAINTS 'N' SINNERS	Whitesnake (Liberty)
19	12	RIO	Duran Duran (EMI)
11	13	MIDNIGHT LOVE	Marvin Gaye (CBS)
8	14	REFLECTIONS	Various Artists (CBS)
-	15	CHART WARS – MAY THE HITS BE WITH YOU	Various Artists (Ronco)
13	16	THE KIDS FROM FAME AGAIN	Kids From Fame (RCA)
17	17	GIVE ME YOUR HEART TONIGHT	Shakin' Stevens (Epic)
26	18	UPSTAIRS AT ERIC'S	Yazoo (Mute)
-	19	KILLER ON THE RAMPAGE	Eddy Grant (Ice)
7	20	MADNESS PRESENTS THE RISE AND FALL	Madness (Stiff)
14	21	FAMOUS LAST WORDS	Supertramp (A&M)
16	22	KISSING TO BE CLEVER	Culture Club (Virgin)
21	23	TROPICAL GANGSTERS	Kid Creole & the Coconuts (Ze)
-	24	INVITATIONS	Shakatak (Polydor)
-	25	LIONEL RICHIE	Lionel Richie (Motown)
12	26	CHART HITS '82	Various Artists (K-Tel)
18	27	LOVE OVER GOLD	Dire Straits (Vertigo)
22	28	20 GREATEST HITS	Beatles (Parlophone)
24	29	HAPPY FAMILIES	Blancmange (London)
20	30	A KISS IN THE DREAMHOUSE	Siouxsie & the Banshees (Polydor)

11 December 1982

last	this	Title	Artist (Label)
1	1	THE SINGLES – THE FIRST TEN YEARS	Abba (Epic)
7	2	THE JOHN LENNON COLLECTION	John Lennon (Parlophone)
9	3	PEARLS II	Elkie Brooks (A&M)
6	4	FROM THE MAKERS OF ...	Status Quo (Vertigo)
4	5	THE KIDS FROM FAME	Kids From Fame (BBC)
10	6	GREATEST LOVE SONGS	Nat 'King' Cole (Capitol)
-	7	CODA	Led Zeppelin (Swansong)
2	8	HEARTBREAKER	Dionne Warwick (Arista)
12	9	RIO	Duran Duran (EMI)
8	10	SINGLES – 45s AND UNDER	Squeeze (A&M)
3	11	I WANNA DO IT WITH YOU	Barry Manilow (Arista)
5	12	HELLO, I MUST BE GOING!	Phil Collins (Virgin)
14	13	REFLECTIONS	Various Artists (CBS)
13	14	MIDNIGHT LOVE	Marvin Gaye (CBS)
26	15	CHART HITS '82	Various Artists (K-Tel)
-	16	THE YOUTH OF TODAY	Musical Youth (MCA)
25	17	LIONEL RICHIE	Lionel Richie (Motown)
17	18	GIVE ME YOUR HEART TONIGHT	Shakin' Stevens (Epic)
27	19	LOVE OVER GOLD	Dire Straits (Vertigo)
15	20	CHART WARS – MAY THE HITS BE WITH YOU	Various Artists (Ronco)
11	21	SAINTS 'N' SINNERS	Whitesnake (Liberty)
19	22	KILLER ON THE RAMPAGE	Eddy Grant (Ice)
-	23	OLIVIA NEWTON-JOHN'S GREATEST HITS	Olivia Newton-John (EMI)
20	24	MADNESS PRESENTS THE RISE AND FALL	Madness (Stiff)
21	25	FAMOUS LAST WORDS	Supertramp (A&M)
22	26	KISSING TO BE CLEVER	Culture Club (Virgin)
18	27	UPSTAIRS AT ERIC'S	Yazoo (Mute)
16	28	THE KIDS FROM FAME AGAIN	Kids From Fame (RCA)
-	29	WILD THINGS RUN FAST	Joni Mitchell (Geffen)
-	30	LOVE SONGS	Diana Ross (K-Tel)

18 December 1982

last	this	Title	Artist (Label)
1	1	THE SINGLES – THE FIRST TEN YEARS	Abba (Epic)
2	2	THE JOHN LENNON COLLECTION	John Lennon (Parlophone)
9	3	RIO	Duran Duran (EMI)
3	4	PEARLS II	Elkie Brooks (A&M)
7	5	CODA	Led Zeppelin (Swansong)
30	6	LOVE SONGS	Diana Ross (K-Tel)
15	7	CHART HITS '82	Various Artists (K-Tel)
5	8	THE KIDS FROM FAME	Kids From Fame (BBC)
8	9	HEARTBREAKER	Dionne Warwick (Arista)
6	10	GREATEST LOVE SONGS	Nat 'King' Cole (Capitol)
4	11	FROM THE MAKERS OF ...	Status Quo (Vertigo)
28	12	THE KIDS FROM FAME AGAIN	Kids From Fame (RCA)
-	13	QUARTET	Ultravox (Chrysalis)
12	14	HELLO, I MUST BE GOING!	Phil Collins (Virgin)
26	15	KISSING TO BE CLEVER	Culture Club (Virgin)
24	16	MADNESS PRESENTS THE RISE AND FALL	Madness (Stiff)
-	17	THRILLER	Michael Jackson (Epic)
11	18	I WANNA DO IT WITH YOU	Barry Manilow (Arista)
19	19	LOVE OVER GOLD	Dire Straits (Vertigo)
10	20	SINGLES – 45s AND UNDER	Squeeze (A&M)
17	21	LIONEL RICHIE	Lionel Richie (Motown)
14	22	MIDNIGHT LOVE	Marvin Gaye (CBS)
-	23	RICHARD CLAYDERMAN	Richard Clayderman (Delphine)
-	24	THE STORY OF THE STONES	Rolling Stones (K-Tel)
-	25	BEST OF CLASSIC ROCK	London Symphony Orchestra & the Royal Choral Society (K-Tel)
23	26	OLIVIA NEWTON-JOHN'S GREATEST HITS	Olivia Newton-John (EMI)
18	27	GIVE ME YOUR HEART TONIGHT	Shakin' Stevens (Epic)
16	28	THE YOUTH OF TODAY	Musical Youth (MCA)
21	29	SAINTS 'N' SINNERS	Whitesnake (Liberty)
13	30	REFLECTIONS	Various Artists (CBS)

25 December 1982

last	this	Title	Artist (Label)
2	1	THE JOHN LENNON COLLECTION	John Lennon (Parlophone)
1	2	THE SINGLES – THE FIRST TEN YEARS	Abba (Epic)
-	3	DIG THE NEW BREED	Jam (Polydor)
3	4	RIO	Duran Duran (EMI)
9	5	HEARTBREAKER	Dionne Warwick (Arista)
10	6	GREATEST LOVE SONGS	Nat 'King' Cole (Capitol)
4	7	PEARLS II	Elkie Brooks (A&M)
6	8	LOVE SONGS	Diana Ross (K-Tel)
11	9	FROM THE MAKERS OF ...	Status Quo (Vertigo)
8	10	THE KIDS FROM FAME	Kids From Fame (BBC)
23	11	RICHARD CLAYDERMAN	Richard Clayderman (Delphine)
15	12	KISSING TO BE CLEVER	Culture Club (Virgin)
18	13	I WANNA DO IT WITH YOU	Barry Manilow (Arista)
16	14	MADNESS PRESENTS THE RISE AND FALL	Madness (Stiff)
-	15	FRIENDS	Shalamar (Solar)
5	16	CODA	Led Zeppelin (Swansong)
21	17	LIONEL RICHIE	Lionel Richie (Motown)
27	18	GIVE ME YOUR HEART TONIGHT	Shakin' Stevens (Epic)
20	19	SINGLES – 45s AND UNDER	Squeeze (A&M)
7	20	CHART HITS '82	Various Artists (K-Tel)
24	21	THE STORY OF THE STONES	Rolling Stones (K-Tel)
-	22	FLOCK OF SEAGULLS	Flock Of Seagulls (Jive)
12	23	THE KIDS FROM FAME AGAIN	Kids From Fame (RCA)
17	24	THRILLER	Michael Jackson (Epic)
-	25	CACHARPAYA (PANPIPES OF THE ANDES)	Incantation (Beggars Banquet)
19	26	LOVE OVER GOLD	Dire Straits (Vertigo)
30	27	REFLECTIONS	Various Artists (CBS)
-	28	RAIDERS OF THE POP CHARTS	Various Artists (Ronco)
14	29	HELLO, I MUST BE GOING!	Phil Collins (Virgin)
29	30	SAINTS 'N' SINNERS	Whitesnake (Liberty)

True to form, the now all-but-defunct Abba had December's biggest-selling album, this time with their third (and biggest) hit singles compilation. The actual Christmas chart-topper, though, was another singles compilation, the TV-promoted *John Lennon Collection*. Meanwhile, the *Love Songs* saga continued, with Diana Ross being the fourth act in close recent memory to use that title. Nat 'King' Cole at least had *Greatest...* added to his similar album with which Diana shared the Top 10.

8 January 1983

last week	this week	Title	Artist (Label)
1	1	THE JOHN LENNON COLLECTION	John Lennon (Parlophone)
3	2	DIG THE NEW BREED	Jam (Polydor)
2	3	THE SINGLES - THE FIRST TEN YEARS	Abba (Epic)
15	4	FRIENDS	Shalamar (Solar)
14	5	MADNESS PRESENTS THE RISE AND FALL	Madness (Stiff)
7	6	PEARLS II	Elkie Brooks (A&M)
8	7	LOVE SONGS	Diana Ross (K-Tel)
4	8	RIO	Duran Duran (EMI)
5	9	HEARTBREAKER	Dionne Warwick (Arista)
11	10	RICHARD CLAYDERMAN	Richard Clayderman (Decca/Delphine)
17	11	LIONEL RICHIE	Lionel Richie (Motown)
12	12	KISSING TO BE CLEVER	Culture Club (Virgin)
29	13	HELLO, I MUST BE GOING!	Phil Collins (Virgin)
6	14	GREATEST LOVE SONGS	Nat 'King' Cole (Capitol)
13	15	I WANNA DO IT WITH YOU	Barry Manilow (Arista)
10	16	THE KIDS FROM FAME	Various Artists (BBC)
8	17	FROM THE MAKERS OF	Status Quo (Vertigo)
28	18	RAIDERS OF THE POP CHARTS	Various Artists (Ronco)
22	19	FLOCK OF SEAGULLS	Flock of Seagulls (Jive)
18	20	GIVE ME YOUR HEART TONIGHT	Shakin' Stevens (Epic)
21	21	THE STORY OF THE STONES	Rolling Stones (K-Tel)
20	22	CHART HITS '82	Various Artists (K-Tel)
23	23	THE KIDS FROM FAME AGAIN	Various Artists (K-Tel)
19	24	SINGLES - 45s AND UNDER	Squeeze (A&M)
24	25	THRILLER	Michael Jackson (EPIC)
16	26	CODA	Led Zeppelin (Swansong)
-	27	QUARTET	Ultravox (Chrysalis)
-	28	ET - THE EXTRA-TERRESTRIAL	John Williams (MCA)
-	29	UPSTAIRS AT ERIC'S	Yazoo (Mute)
25	30	CACHARPAYA (PANPIPES OF THE ANDES)	Incantation (Beggars Banquet)

15 January 1983

last week	this week	Title	Artist (Label)
1	1	THE JOHN LENNON COLLECTION	John Lennon (Parlophone)
9	2	HEARTBREAKER	Dionne Warwick (Arista)
8	3	RIO	Duran Duran (EMI)
18	4	RAIDERS OF THE POP CHARTS	Various Artists (Ronco)
2	5	DIG THE NEW BREED	Jam (Polydor)
3	6	THE SINGLES - THE FIRST TEN YEARS	Abba (Epic)
4	7	FRIENDS	Shalamar (Solar)
6	8	PEARLS II	Elkie Brooks (A&M)
11	9	LIONEL RICHIE	Lionel Richie (Motown)
13	10	HELLO, I MUST BE GOING!	Phil Collins (Virgin)
12	11	KISSING TO BE CLEVER	Culture Club (Virgin)
7	12	LOVE SONGS	Diana Ross (K-Tel)
5	12	MADNESS PRESENTS THE RISE AND FALL	Madness (Stiff)
10	14	RICHARD CLAYDERMAN	Richard Clayderman (Decca/Delphine)
17	15	FROM THE MAKERS OF	Status Quo (Vertigo)
16	16	THE KIDS FROM FAME	Various Artists (BBC)
-	17	OLIVIA NEWTON-JOHN'S GREATEST HITS	Olivia Newton-John (EMI)
-	18	COMPLETE MADNESS	Madness (Stiff)
-	19	20 GREATEST HITS	Beatles (Parlophone)
23	20	THE KIDS FROM FAME AGAIN	Various Artists (K-Tel)
-	21	BUSINESS AS USUAL	Men at Work (Epic)
25	22	THRILLER	Michael Jackson (Epic)
14	23	GREATEST LOVE SONGS	Nat 'King' Cole (Capitol)
27	24	QUARTET	Ultravox (Chrysalis)
-	25	TOO-RYE-AY	Dexy's Midnight Runners (Mercury)
22	26	CHART HITS '82	Various Artists (K-Tel)
24	27	SINGLES - 45s AND UNDER	Squeeze (A&M)
15	28	I WANNA DO IT WITH YOU	Barry Manilow (Arista)
28	29	ET - THE EXTRA-TERRESTRIAL	John Williams (MCA)
29	30	UPSTAIRS AT ERIC'S	Yazoo (Mute)

22 January 1983

last week	this week	Title	Artist (Label)
1	1	THE JOHN LENNON COLLECTION	John Lennon (Parlophone)
21	2	BUSINESS AS USUAL	Men at Work (Epic)
3	3	RIO	Duran Duran (EMI)
10	4	HELLO, I MUST BE GOING!	Phil Collins (Virgin)
2	5	HEARTBREAKER	Dionne Warwick (Arista)
4	6	RAIDERS OF THE POP CHARTS	Various Artists (Ronco)
11	7	KISSING TO BE CLEVER	Culture Club (Virgin)
6	8	THE SINGLES - THE FIRST TEN YEARS	Abba (Epic)
-	9	CACHARPAYA (PANPIPES OF THE ANDES)	Incantation (Beggars Banquet)
7	10	FRIENDS	Shalamar (Solar)
8	11	PEARLS II	Elkie Brooks (A&M)
14	12	RICHARD CLAYDERMAN	Richard Clayderman (Decca/Delphine)
17	13	OLIVIA NEWTON-JOHN'S GREATEST HITS	Olivia Newton-John (EMI)
24	14	QUARTET	Ultravox (Chrysalis)
5	15	DIG THE NEW BREED	Jam (Polydor)
18	16	COMPLETE MADNESS	Madness (Stiff)
-	17	LOVE OVER GOLD	Dire Straits (Vertigo)
22	18	THRILLER	Michael Jackson (Epic)
15	19	FROM THE MAKERS OF	Status Quo (Vertigo)
16	20	THE KIDS FROM FAME	Various Artists (BBC)
25	21	TOO-RYE-AY	Dexy's Midnight Runners (Mercury)
12	22	MADNESS PRESENTS THE RISE AND FALL	Madness (Stiff)
9	23	LIONEL RICHIE	Lionel Richie (Motown)
30	24	UPSTAIRS AT ERIC'S	Yazoo (Mute)
27	25	SINGLES - 45s AND UNDER	Squeeze (A&M)
-	26	MIDNIGHT LOVE	Marvin Gaye (CBS)
-	27	FELINE	Stranglers (Epic)
-	28	THE ART OF FALLING APART	Soft Cell (Some Bizzare)
19	29	20 GREATEST HITS	Beatles (Parlophone)
-	30	LIVE EVIL	Black Sabbath (Vertigo)

The Jam's *Dig The New Breed* (a phrase appropriated from James Brown) was their last album prior to splitting, while Lionel Richie's eponymous set was his first solo release since leaving the Commodores. It started slowly on the chart and gradually built to huge sales - as, interestingly, did Michael Jackson's *Thriller*.

January – February 1983

29 January 1983

last week	this week		
2	1	BUSINESS AS USUAL	Men at Work (Epic)
4	2	HELLO, I MUST BE GOING!	Phil Collins (Virgin)
1	3	THE JOHN LENNON COLLECTION	John Lennon (Parlophone)
6	4	RAIDERS OF THE POP CHARTS	Various Artists (Ronco)
5	5	HEARTBREAKER	Dionne Warwick (Arista)
27	6	FELINE	Stranglers (Epic)
28	7	THE ART OF FALLING APART	Soft Cell (Some Bizzare)
3	8	RIO	Duran Duran (EMI)
10	9	FRIENDS	Shalamar (Solar)
12	10	RICHARD CLAYDERMAN	Richard Clayderman (Decca/Delphine)
30	11	LIVE EVIL	Black Sabbath (Vertigo)
9	12	CACHARPAYA (PANPIPES OF THE ANDES)	Incantation (Beggars Banquet)
7	13	KISSING TO BE CLEVER	Culture Club (Virgin)
-	14	LOVE SONGS	Diana Ross (K-Tel)
8	15	THE SINGLES - THE FIRST TEN YEARS	Abba (Epic)
13	16	OLIVIA NEWTON-JOHN'S GREATEST HITS	Olivia Newton-John (EMI)
16	17	COMPLETE MADNESS	Madness (Stiff)
26	18	MIDNIGHT LOVE	Marvin Gaye (CBS)
17	19	LOVE OVER GOLD	Dire Straits (Vertigo)
-	20	NIGHT AND DAY	Joe Jackson (A&M)
18	21	THRILLER	Michael Jackson (Epic)
14	22	QUARTET	Ultravox (Chrysalis)
-	23	RARE	David Bowie (RCA)
-	24	KILLER ON THE RAMPAGE	Eddy Grant (Ice)
19	25	FROM THE MAKERS OF	Status Quo (Vertigo)
11	26	PEARLS II	Elkie Brooks (A&M)
27	27	SKY FIVE LIVE	Sky (Ariola)
15	28	DIG THE NEW BREED	Jam (Polydor)
29	29	20 GREATEST HITS	Beatles (Parlophone)
21	30	TOO-RYE-AY	Dexy's Midnight Runners (Mercury)

5 February 1983

last	this		
1	1	BUSINESS AS USUAL	Men at Work (Epic)
2	2	HELLO, I MUST BE GOING!	Phil Collins (Virgin)
3	3	THE JOHN LENNON COLLECTION	John Lennon (Parlophone)
20	4	NIGHT AND DAY	Joe Jackson (A&M)
6	5	FELINE	Stranglers (Epic)
10	6	RICHARD CLAYDERMAN	Richard Clayderman (Decca/Delphine)
5	7	HEARTBREAKER	Dionne Warwick (Arista)
7	8	THE ART OF FALLING APART	Soft Cell (Some Bizzare)
24	9	KILLER ON THE RAMPAGE	Eddy Grant (Ice)
8	10	RIO	Duran Duran (EMI)
12	11	CACHARPAYA (PANPIPES OF THE ANDES)	Incantation (Beggars Banquet)
4	12	RAIDERS OF THE POP CHARTS	Various Artists (Ronco)
13	13	KISSING TO BE CLEVER	Culture Club (Virgin)
26	14	PEARLS II	Elkie Brooks (A&M)
9	15	FRIENDS	Shalamar (Solar)
19	16	LOVE OVER GOLD	Dire Straits (Vertigo)
16	17	OLIVIA NEWTON-JOHN'S GREATEST HITS	Olivia Newton-John (EMI)
11	18	LIVE EVIL	Black Sabbath (Vertigo)
21	19	THRILLER	Michael Jackson (Epic)
-	20	LIONEL RICHIE	Lionel Richie (Motown)
15	21	THE SINGLES - THE FIRST TEN YEARS	Abba (Epic)
25	22	FROM THE MAKERS OF	Status Quo (Vertigo)
-	23	THE VERY BEST OF CILLA BLACK	Cilla Black (Parlophone)
17	24	COMPLETE MADNESS	Madness (Stiff)
27	25	SKY FIVE LIVE	Sky (Ariola)
22	26	QUARTET	Ultravox (Chrysalis)
28	27	DIG THE NEW BREED	Jam (Polydor)
23	28	RARE	David Bowie (RCA)
18	29	MIDNIGHT LOVE	Marvin Gaye (CBS)
-	30	DIFFICULT SHAPES AND PASSIVE RHYTHMS	China Crisis (Virgin)

12 February 1983

last	this		
1	1	BUSINESS AS USUAL	Men at Work (Epic)
2	2	HELLO, I MUST BE GOING!	Phil Collins (Virgin)
3	3	NIGHT AND DAY	Joe Jackson (A&M)
6	4	RICHARD CLAYDERMAN	Richard Clayderman (Decca/delphine)
5	5	FELINE	Stranglers (Epic)
9	6	KILLER ON THE RAMPAGE	Eddy Grant (Ice)
3	7	THE JOHN LENNON COLLECTION	John Lennon (Parlophone)
12	8	RAIDERS OF THE POP CHARTS	Various Artists (Ronco)
19	9	THRILLER	Michael Jackson (Epic)
10	10	TRANS	Neil Young (Geffen)
11	11	CACHARPAYA (PANPIPES OF THE ANDES)	Incantation (Beggars Banquet)
7	12	HEARTBREAKER	Dionne Warwick (Arista)
13	13	THE ART OF FALLING APART	Soft Cell (Some Bizzare)
14	14	PEARLS II	Elkie Brooks (A&M)
23	15	THE VERY BEST OF CILLA BLACK	Cilla Black (Parlophone)
16	16	LIVE EVIL	Black Sabbath (Vertigo)
10	17	RIO	Duran Duran (EMI)
17	18	OLIVIA NEWTON-JOHN'S GREATEST HITS	Olivia Newton-John (EMI)
30	19	DIFFICULT SHAPES AND PASSIVE RHYTHMS	China Crisis (Virgin)
20	20	THE NIGHTFLY	Donald Fagen (Warner Bros.)
-	21	PORCUPINE	Echo & the Bunnymen (Korova)
25	22	SKY FIVE LIVE	Sky (Ariola)
15	23	FRIENDS	Shalamar (Solar)
22	24	FROM THE MAKERS OF	Status Quo (Vertigo)
16	25	LOVE OVER GOLD	Dire Straits (Vertigo)
-	26	THE BELLE STARS	Belle Stars (Stiff)
13	27	KISSING TO BE CLEVER	Culture Club (Virgin)
-	28	VISIONS	Various Artists (K-Tel)
29	29	MIDNIGHT LOVE	Marvin Gaye (CBS)
21	30	THE SINGLES - THE FIRST TEN YEARS	Abba (Epic)

19 February 1983

last	this		
1	1	BUSINESS AS USUAL	Men at Work (Epic)
21	2	PORCUPINE	Echo & the Bunnymen (Korova)
7	3	THE JOHN LENNON COLLECTION	John Lennon (Parlophone)
3	4	NIGHT AND DAY	Joe Jackson (A&M)
9	5	THRILLER	Michael Jackson (Epic)
12	6	HEARTBREAKER	Dionne Warwick (Arista)
2	7	HELLO, I MUST BE GOING!	Phil Collins (Virgin)
6	8	KILLER ON THE RAMPAGE	Eddy Grant (Ice)
5	9	FELINE	Stranglers (Epic)
4	10	RICHARD CLAYDERMAN	Richard Clayderman (Decca/Delphine)
-	11	MAKING CONTACT	UFO (Chrysalis)
8	12	RAIDERS OF THE POP CHARTS	Various Artists (Ronco)
28	13	VISIONS	Various Artists (K-Tel)
-	14	ALL THE BEST	Stiff Little Fingers (Chrysalis)
-	15	GREATEST LOVE SONGS	Nat 'King' Cole (Capitol)
-	16	FRONTIERS	Journey (CBS)
22	17	SKY FIVE LIVE	Sky (Ariola)
14	18	PEARLS II	Elkie Brooks (A&M)
-	19	SWEET DREAMS (ARE MADE OF THIS)	Eurythmics (RCA)
10	20	TRANS	Neil Young (Geffen)
19	21	DIFFICULT SHAPES AND PASSIVE RHYTHMS	China Crisis (Virgin)
26	22	THE BELLE STARS	Belle Stars (Stiff)
11	23	CACHARPAYA (PANPIPES OF THE ANDES)	Incantation (Beggars Banquet)
16	24	LIVE EVIL	Black Sabbath (Vertigo)
17	25	RIO	Duran Duran (EMI)
25	26	LOVE OVER GOLD	Dire Straits (Vertigo)
-	27	OCTOBER	U2 (Island)
13	28	THE ART OF FALLING APART	Soft Cell (Some Bizzare)
-	29	SHAPE UP AND DANCE VOL 1	Felicity Kendall (Lifestyle)
-	30	MONEY & CIGARETTES	Eric Clapton (Duck)

Australia's Men At Work had already found Number 1 US success in 1982, so the UK was catching up in February 1983 when their *Business As Usual* album topped the chart simultaneously with the single *Down Under*. The album actually outlived the 45 at the top, logging five straight Number 1 weeks, and holding Phil Collins' second solo set *Hello I Must Be Going* (also boosted by a Number 1 single) in second place.

26 February 1983

last week	this week	Title / Artist
1	1	BUSINESS AS USUAL — Men at Work (Epic)
5	2	THRILLER — Michael Jackson (Epic)
4	3	NIGHT AND DAY — Joe Jackson (A&M)
2	3	PORCUPINE — Echo & the Bunnymen (Korova)
3	5	THE JOHN LENNON COLLECTION — John Lennon (Parlophone)
7	6	HELLO, I MUST BE GOING! — Phil Collins (Virgin)
-	7	WAITING — Fun Boy Three (Chrysalis)
-	8	ANOTHER PAGE — Christopher Cross (Warner Bros.)
10	9	RICHARD CLAYDERMAN — Richard Clayderman (Decca/Delphine)
16	9	FRONTIERS — Journey (CBS)
6	11	HEARTBREAKER — Dionne Warwick (Arista)
18	12	PEARLS II — Elkie Brooks (A&M)
22	13	THE BELLE STARS — Belle Stars (Stiff)
13	14	VISIONS — Various Artists (K-Tel)
21	15	DIFFICULT SHAPES AND PASSIVE RHYTHMS — China Crisis (Virgin)
14	16	ALL THE BEST — Stiff Little Fingers (Chrysalis)
30	17	MONEY & CIGARETTES — Eric Clapton (Duck)
8	18	KILLER ON THE RAMPAGE — Eddy Grant (Ice)
25	19	RIO — Duran Duran (EMI)
-	20	POWERLIGHT — Earth Wind & Fire (CBS)
12	21	RAIDERS OF THE POP CHARTS — Various Artists (Ronco)
15	22	GREATEST LOVE SONGS — Nat 'King' Cole (Capitol)
9	23	FELINE — Stranglers (Epic)
19	24	SWEET DREAMS (ARE MADE OF THIS) — Eurythmics (RCA)
23	25	CACHARPAYA (PANPIPES OF THE ANDES) — Incantation (Beggars Banquet)
-	26	LIONEL RICHIE — Lionel Richie (Motown)
-	27	COMPLETE MADNESS — Madness (Stiff)
11	28	MAKING CONTACT — UFO (Chrysalis)
20	29	TRANS — Neil Young (Geffen)
26	30	LOVE OVER GOLD — Dire Straits (Vertigo)

5 March 1983

last week	this week	Title / Artist
2	1	THRILLER — Michael Jackson (Epic)
1	1	BUSINESS AS USUAL — Men at Work (Epic)
8	3	ANOTHER PAGE — Christopher Cross (Warner Bros.)
-	4	QUICK STEP AND SIDE KICK — Thompson Twins (Arista)
3	5	NIGHT AND DAY — Joe Jackson (A&M)
11	6	HEARTBREAKER — Dionne Warwick (Arista)
-	7	TOTO IV — Toto (CBS)
3	8	PORCUPINE — Echo & the Bunnymen (Korova)
5	9	THE JOHN LENNON COLLECTION — John Lennon (Parlophone)
14	10	VISIONS — Various Artists (K-Tel)
9	11	RICHARD CLAYDERMAN — Richard Clayderman (Decca/Delphine)
6	12	HELLO, I MUST BE GOING! — Phil Collins (Virgin)
13	13	FRONTIERS — Journey (CBS)
7	14	WAITING — Fun Boy Three (Chrysalis)
17	15	MONEY & CIGARETTES — Eric Clapton (Duck)
-	16	JANE FONDA'S WORKOUT RECORD — Jane Fonda (CBS)
-	17	WRECKIN' CREW — Meteors (Identity)
13	18	THE BELLE STARS — Belle Stars (Stiff)
19	19	RIO — Duran Duran (EMI)
-	20	SHOW PEOPLE — Mari Wilson (Compact)
26	21	LIONEL RICHIE — Lionel Richie (Motown)
-	22	WHAT'S WORDS WORTH — Motorhead (Big Beat)
16	23	ALL THE BEST — Stiff Little Fingers (Chrysalis)
-	24	UB40 LIVE — UB40 (DEP Int)
15	25	DIFFICULT SHAPES AND PASSIVE RHYTHMS — China Crisis (Virgin)
24	26	SWEET DREAMS (ARE MADE OF THIS) — Eurythmics (RCA)
27	27	COMPLETE MADNESS — Madness (Stiff)
18	28	KILLER ON THE RAMPAGE — Eddy Grant (Ice)
12	29	PEARLS II — Elkie Brooks (A&M)
22	30	GREATEST LOVE SONGS — Nat 'King' Cole (Capitol)

12 March 1983

last week	this week	Title / Artist
1	1	THRILLER — Michael Jackson (Epic)
4	2	QUICK STEP AND SIDE KICK — Thompson Twins (Arista)
7	3	TOTO IV — Toto (CBS)
1	4	BUSINESS AS USUAL — Men at Work (Epic)
26	5	SWEET DREAMS (ARE MADE OF THIS) — Eurythmics (RCA)
3	6	ANOTHER PAGE — Christopher Cross (Warner Bros.)
5	7	NIGHT AND DAY — Joe Jackson (A&M)
-	8	WAR — U2 (Island)
11	9	RICHARD CLAYDERMAN — Richard Clayderman (Decca/Delphine)
16	10	JANE FONDA'S WORKOUT RECORD — Jane Fonda (CBS)
18	11	THE BELLE STARS — Belle Stars (Stiff)
6	12	HEARTBREAKER — Dionne Warwick (Arista)
9	13	THE JOHN LENNON COLLECTION — John Lennon (Parlophone)
19	14	RIO — Duran Duran (EMI)
14	15	WAITING — Fun Boy Three (Chrysalis)
-	16	THUNDER AND LIGHTNING — Thin Lizzy (Vertigo)
8	17	PORCUPINE — Echo & the Bunnymen (Korova)
10	18	VISIONS — Various Artists (K-Tel)
12	19	HELLO, I MUST BE GOING! — Phil Collins (Virgin)
21	20	LIONEL RICHIE — Lionel Richie (Motown)
13	21	FRONTIERS — Journey (CBS)
28	22	KILLER ON THE RAMPAGE — Eddy Grant (Ice)
20	23	SHOW PEOPLE — Mari Wilson (Compact)
15	24	MONEY & CIGARETTES — Eric Clapton (Duck)
29	25	PEARLS II — Elkie Brooks (A&M)
-	26	HOTLINE — Various Artists (K-Tel)
-	27	PYROMANIA — Def Leppard (Vertigo)
17	28	WRECKIN' CREW — Meteors (Identity)
-	29	BATTLE HYMNS FOR CHILDREN SINGING — Haysi Fantayzee (Regard)
25	30	DIFFICULT SHAPES AND PASSIVE RHYTHMS — China Crisis (Virgin)

19 March 1983

last week	this week	Title / Artist
1	1	THRILLER — Michael Jackson (Epic)
16	2	THUNDER AND LIGHTNING — Thin Lizzy (Vertigo)
8	3	WAR — U2 (Island)
5	4	SWEET DREAMS (ARE MADE OF THIS) — Eurythmics (RCA)
-	5	TRUE — Spandau Ballet (Reformation)
-	6	DAZZLE SHIPS — Orchestral Manoeuvres in the Dark (Telegraph)
26	7	HOTLINE — Various Artists (K-Tel)
3	8	TOTO IV — Toto (CBS)
-	9	THE KEY — Joan Armatrading (A&M)
4	10	BUSINESS AS USUAL — Men at Work (Epic)
2	11	QUICK STEP AND SIDE KICK — Thompson Twins (Arista)
18	12	VISIONS — Various Artists (K-Tel)
10	13	JANE FONDA'S WORKOUT RECORD — Jane Fonda (CBS)
15	14	WAITING — Fun Boy Three (Chrysalis)
6	15	ANOTHER PAGE — Christopher Cross (Warner Bros.)
27	16	PYROMANIA — Def Leppard (Vertigo)
-	17	THE HURTING — Tears for Fears (Mercury)
9	18	RICHARD CLAYDERMAN — Richard Clayderman (Decca/Delphine)
11	19	THE BELLE STARS — Belle Stars (Stiff)
19	20	HELLO, I MUST BE GOING! — Phil Collins (Virgin)
7	21	NIGHT AND DAY — Joe Jackson (A&M)
12	22	HEARTBREAKER — Dionne Warwick (Arista)
17	23	PORCUPINE — Echo & the Bunnymen (Korova)
13	24	THE JOHN LENNON COLLECTION — John Lennon (Parlophone)
23	25	SHOW PEOPLE — Mari Wilson (Compact)
-	26	COMPLETE MADNESS — Madness (Stiff)
-	27	DEEP SEA SKIVING — Bananarama (London)
21	28	FRONTIERS — Journey (CBS)
24	29	MONEY & CIGARETTES — Eric Clapton (Duck)
14	30	RIO — Duran Duran (EMI)

Given a boost by the extracted single *Billie Jean*, which hit Number 1 on March 5, Michael Jackson's *Thriller* album also finally topped the chart on the same day - the beginning of a very long stay at or near Number 1 which would eventually see the album as one of the UK's all-time Top 5 sellers (it would also be, globally, the best-selling album of all time, moving more than 40 million copies by 1985).

March – April 1983

26 March 1983

last	this	Title / Artist
1	1	THRILLER — Michael Jackson (Epic)
4	2	SWEET DREAMS (ARE MADE OF THIS) — Eurythmics (RCA)
17	3	THE HURTING — Tears for Fears (Mercury)
3	4	WAR — U2 (Island)
18	5	RICHARD CLAYDERMAN — Richard Clayderman (Decca/Delphine)
2	6	THUNDER AND LIGHTNING — Thin Lizzy (Vertigo)
7	7	HOTLINE — Various Artists (K-Tel)
6	8	DAZZLE SHIPS — Orchestral Manoeuvres in the Dark (Telegraph)
27	9	DEEP SEA SKIVING — Bananarama (London)
9	9	THE KEY — Joan Armatrading (A&M)
5	11	TRUE — Spandau Ballet (Reformation)
11	12	QUICK STEP AND SIDE KICK — Thompson Twins (Arista)
13	13	JANE FONDA'S WORKOUT RECORD — Jane Fonda (CBS)
8	14	TOTO IV — Toto (CBS)
-	15	LIONEL RICHIE — Lionel Richie (Motown)
12	16	VISIONS — Various Artists (K-Tel)
30	17	RIO — Duran Duran (EMI)
20	18	HELLO, I MUST BE GOING! — Phil Collins (Virgin)
22	19	HEARTBREAKER — Dionne Warwick (Arista)
-	20	CHARTRUNNERS — Various Artists (Ronco)
-	21	HAND CUT — Bucks Fizz (RCA)
21	22	NIGHT AND DAY — Joe Jackson (A&M)
24	23	THE JOHN LENNON COLLECTION — John Lennon (Parlophone)
-	24	THE SIN OF PRIDE — Undertones (Ardeck)
10	25	BUSINESS AS USUAL — Men at Work (Epic)
-	26	THE HIGH ROAD — Roxy Music (EG)
-	27	THE VERY BEST OF CILLA BLACK — Cilla Black (Parlophone)
15	28	ANOTHER PAGE — Christopher Cross (Warner Bros.)
-	29	DIFFICULT SHAPES AND PASSIVE RHYTHMS — China Crisis (Virgin)
25	30	SHOW PEOPLE — Mari Wilson (Compact)

2 April 1983

last	this	Title / Artist
2	1	SWEET DREAMS (ARE MADE OF THIS) — Eurythmics (RCA)
3	2	THE HURTING — Tears for Fears (Mercury)
1	3	THRILLER — Michael Jackson (Epic)
-	4	SCRIPT FOR A JESTER'S TEAR — Marillion (EMI)
4	5	WAR — U2 (Island)
6	6	THUNDER AND LIGHTNING — Thin Lizzy (Vertigo)
9	7	THE KEY — Joan Armatrading (A&M)
11	8	TRUE — Spandau Ballet (Reformation)
-	9	INARTICULATE SPEECH OF THE HEART — Van Morrison (Mercury)
-	10	POWER AND THE GLORY — Saxon (Carrere)
14	11	TOTO IV — Toto (CBS)
20	12	CHARTRUNNERS — Various Artists (Ronco)
9	13	DEEP SEA SKIVING — Bananarama (London)
7	14	HOTLINE — Various Artists (K-Tel)
-	15	THE FINAL CUT — Pink Floyd (Harvest)
12	16	QUICK STEP AND SIDE KICK — Thompson Twins (Arista)
5	17	RICHARD CLAYDERMAN — Richard Clayderman (Decca/delphine)
21	18	HAND CUT — Bucks Fizz (RCA)
26	19	THE HIGH ROAD — Roxy Music (EG)
17	20	RIO — Duran Duran (EMI)
8	21	DAZZLE SHIPS — Orchestral Manoeuvres in the Dark (Telegraph)
-	22	SURPRISE, SURPRISE — Mezzoforte (Steinar)
16	23	VISIONS — Various Artists (K-Tel)
18	24	HELLO, I MUST BE GOING! — Phil Collins (Virgin)
-	25	WAITING — Fun Boy Three (Chrysalis)
13	26	JANE FONDA'S WORKOUT RECORD — Jane Fonda (CBS)
25	27	BUSINESS AS USUAL — Men at Work (Epic)
15	28	LIONEL RICHIE — Lionel Richie (Motown)
28	29	ANOTHER PAGE — Christopher Cross (Warner Bros.)
-	30	RIP IT UP — Orange Juice (Polydor)

9 April 1983

last	this	Title / Artist
15	1	THE FINAL CUT — Pink Floyd (Harvest)
2	2	THE HURTING — Tears for Fears (Mercury)
3	3	THRILLER — Michael Jackson (Epic)
1	4	SWEET DREAMS (ARE MADE OF THIS) — Eurythmics (RCA)
5	5	WAR — U2 (Island)
13	6	DEEP SEA SKIVING — Bananarama (London)
12	7	CHARTRUNNERS — Various Artists (Ronco)
4	7	SCRIPT FOR A JESTER'S TEAR — Marillion (EMI)
20	9	RIO — Duran Duran (EMI)
7	10	THE KEY — Joan Armatrading (A&M)
11	11	TOTO IV — Toto (CBS)
9	12	INARTICULATE SPEECH OF THE HEART — Van Morrison (Mercury)
18	13	HAND CUT — Bucks Fizz (RCA)
10	14	POWER AND THE GLORY — Saxon (Carrere)
14	15	HOTLINE — Various Artists (K-Tel)
8	16	TRUE — Spandau Ballet (Reformation)
21	17	DAZZLE SHIPS — Orchestral Manoeuvres in the Dark (Telegraph)
16	18	QUICK STEP AND SIDE KICK — Thompson Twins (Arista)
6	19	THUNDER AND LIGHTNING — Thin Lizzy (Vertigo)
24	20	HELLO, I MUST BE GOING! — Phil Collins (Virgin)
29	21	ANOTHER PAGE — Christopher Cross (Warner Bros.)
19	22	THE HIGH ROAD — Roxy Music (EG)
17	23	RICHARD CLAYDERMAN — Richard Clayderman (Decca/delphine)
-	24	HEARTBREAKER — Dionne Warwick (Arista)
-	25	THE JOHN LENNON COLLECTION — John Lennon (Parlophone)
26	26	JANE FONDA'S WORKOUT RECORD — Jane Fonda (CBS)
23	27	VISIONS — Various Artists (K-Tel)
-	28	SHAPE UP AND DANCE VOL 1 — Felicity Kendall (Lifestyle)
22	29	SURPRISE, SURPRISE — Mezzoforte (Steinar)
-	30	THE BILLY FURY HIT PARADE — Billy Fury (Decca)

16 April 1983

last	this	Title / Artist
1	1	THE FINAL CUT — Pink Floyd (Harvest)
2	2	THE HURTING — Tears for Fears (Mercury)
5	3	WAR — U2 (Island)
3	4	THRILLER — Michael Jackson (Epic)
9	5	RIO — Duran Duran (EMI)
4	5	SWEET DREAMS (ARE MADE OF THIS) — Eurythmics (RCA)
11	7	TOTO IV — Toto (CBS)
20	8	HELLO, I MUST BE GOING! — Phil Collins (Virgin)
10	9	THE KEY — Joan Armatrading (A&M)
7	10	CHARTRUNNERS — Various Artists (Ronco)
5	11	SCRIPT FOR A JESTER'S TEAR — Marillion (EMI)
16	12	TRUE — Spandau Ballet (Reformation)
13	13	HAND CUT — Bucks Fizz (RCA)
17	14	DAZZLE SHIPS — Orchestral Manoeuvres in the Dark (Telegraph)
6	15	DEEP SEA SKIVING — Bananarama (London)
18	16	QUICK STEP AND SIDE KICK — Thompson Twins (Arista)
-	17	BUSINESS AS USUAL — Men at Work (Epic)
14	18	POWER AND THE GLORY — Saxon (Carrere)
19	19	THUNDER AND LIGHTNING — Thin Lizzy (Vertigo)
29	20	SURPRISE, SURPRISE — Mezzoforte (Steinar)
12	21	INARTICULATE SPEECH OF THE HEART — Van Morrison (Mercury)
22	22	THE HIGH ROAD — Roxy Music (EG)
23	23	RICHARD CLAYDERMAN — Richard Clayderman (Decca/delphine)
24	24	HEARTBREAKER — Dionne Warwick (Arista)
-	25	MAGICAL RING — Clannad (RCA)
-	26	RARE — David Bowie (RCA)
-	27	NIGHT AND DAY — Joe Jackson (A&M)
-	28	LIONEL RICHIE — Lionel Richie (Motown)
-	29	KISSING TO BE CLEVER — Culture Club (Virgin)
-	30	THE KIDS FROM FAME LIVE — Kids From Fame (BBC)

The Eurythmics and Tears For Fears, both now major names on the singles chart, swung confidently into contention with their first successful albums. The Eurythmics snatched a week at Number 1 from *Thriller* with *Sweet Dreams*, but Tears For Fears' *The Hurting* was held at 2 by *The Final Cut*, the first new release since 1979's *The Wall* by Pink Floyd - who had supposedly already irrevocably broken up.

April 1983

23 April 1983

last	this	Title	Artist
4	1	THRILLER	Michael Jackson (Epic)
1	2	THE FINAL CUT	Pink Floyd (Harvest)
-	3	FASTER THAN THE SPEED OF NIGHT	Bonnie Tyler (CBS)
5	4	SWEET DREAMS (ARE MADE OF THIS)	Eurythmics (RCA)
2	5	THE HURTING	Tears for Fears (Mercury)
3	6	WAR	U2 (Island)
12	7	TRUE	Spandau Ballet (Reformation)
16	8	QUICK STEP AND SIDE KICK	Thompson Twins (Arista)
-	9	LET'S DANCE	David Bowie (EMI America)
5	10	RIO	Duran Duran (EMI)
11	11	SCRIPT FOR A JESTER'S TEAR	Marillion (EMI)
9	12	THE KEY	Joan Armatrading (A&M)
-	13	LOCAL HERO	Mark Knopfler (Vertigo)
7	14	TOTO IV	Toto (CBS)
10	15	CHARTRUNNERS	Various Artists (Ronco)
15	16	DEEP SEA SKIVING	Bananarama (London)
14	17	DAZZLE SHIPS	Orchestral Manoeuvres in the Dark (Telegraph)
21	18	INARTICULATE SPEECH OF THE HEART	Van Morrison (Mercury)
8	19	HELLO, I MUST BE GOING!	Phil Collins (Virgin)
17	20	BUSINESS AS USUAL	Men at Work (Epic)
30	21	THE KIDS FROM FAME LIVE	Kids From Fame (BBC)
27	22	NIGHT AND DAY	Joe Jackson (A&M)
29	23	KISSING TO BE CLEVER	Culture Club (Virgin)
-	24	HIGH LAND, HARD RAIN	Aztec Camera (Rough Trade)
-	25	HEADHUNTER	Krokus (Arista)
22	26	THE HIGH ROAD	Roxy Music (EG)
-	27	PRIDE	Robert Palmer (Island)
13	28	HAND CUT	Bucks Fizz (RCA)
-	29	A CHILD'S ADVENTURE	Marianne Faithful (Island)
26	30	RARE	David Bowie (RCA)
18	31	POWER AND THE GLORY	Saxon (Carrere)
28	32	LIONEL RICHIE	Lionel Richie (Motown)
-	33	WAITING	Fun Boy Three (Chrysalis)
20	34	SURPRISE, SURPRISE	Mezzoforte (Steinar)
-	35	LAZY WAYS	Marine Girls (Cherry Red)
19	36	THUNDER AND LIGHTNING	Thin Lizzy (Vertigo)
-	37	THE SIN OF PRIDE	Undertones (Ardeck)
-	38	ANOTHER PAGE	Christopher Cross (Warner Bros.)
-	39	WORKOUT	Jane Fonda (CBS)
24	40	HEARTBREAKER	Dionne Warwick (Arista)
25	41	MAGICAL RING	Clannad (RCA)
-	42	MONEY & CIGARETTES	Eric Clapton (Duck)
-	43	LIVING MY LIFE	Grace Jones (Island)
-	44	STREET SOUNDS EDITION 3	Various Artists (Street Sounds)
-	45	SHOW PEOPLE	Mari Wilson (Compact)
-	46	ELIMINATOR	ZZ Top (WEA)
-	47	BAT OUT OF HELL	Meatloaf (Epic)
-	48	JARREAU	Al Jarreau (WEA)
-	49	RIP IT UP	Orange Juice (Polydor)
-	50	JOURNEY THROUGH THE CLASSICS	Louis Clark and the Royal Philharmonic Orchestra (K-Tel)

30 April 1983

this	Title	Artist
1	LET'S DANCE	David Bowie (EMI America)
2	THRILLER	Michael Jackson (Epic)
3	FASTER THAN THE SPEED OF NIGHT	Bonnie Tyler (CBS)
4	THE FINAL CUT	Pink Floyd (Harvest)
5	SWEET DREAMS (ARE MADE OF THIS)	Eurythmics (RCA)
6	TRUE	Spandau Ballet (Reformation)
7	WAR	U2 (Island)
8	THE HURTING	Tears for Fears (Mercury)
9	QUICK STEP AND SIDE KICK	Thompson Twins (Arista)
10	LOCAL HERO	Mark Knopfler (Vertigo)
11	TOTO IV	Toto (CBS)
12	HIGH LAND, HARD RAIN	Aztec Camera (Rough Trade)
13	RIO	Duran Duran (EMI)
14	BUSINESS AS USUAL	Men at Work (Epic)
15	PRIDE	Robert Palmer (Island)
16	THE KIDS FROM FAME LIVE	Kids From Fame (BBC)
17	WHITE FEATHERS	Kajagoogoo (EMI)
18	SCRIPT FOR A JESTER'S TEAR	Marillion (EMI)
19	THE KEY	Joan Armatrading (A&M)
20	CARGO	Men At Work (Epic)
21	HELLO, I MUST BE GOING!	Phil Collins (Virgin)
22	KISSING TO BE CLEVER	Culture Club (Virgin)
23	GRAPES OF WRATH	Spear of Destiny (Epic)
24	CHARTRUNNERS	Various Artists (Ronco)
25	DEEP SEA SKIVING	Bananarama (London)
26	STREET SOUNDS EDITION 3	Various Artists (Street Sounds)
27	DAZZLE SHIPS	Orchestral Manoeuvres in the Dark (Telegraph)
28	INARTICULATE SPEECH OF THE HEART	Van Morrison (Mercury)
29	HIGHLY STRUNG	Steve Hackett (Charisma)
30	JARREAU	Al Jarreau (WEA)
31	JOURNEY THROUGH THE CLASSICS	Louis Clark and the Royal Philharmonic Orchestra (K-Tel)
32	NIGHT AND DAY	Joe Jackson (A&M)
33	LIONEL RICHIE	Lionel Richie (Motown)
34	POWER AND THE GLORY	Saxon (Carrere)
35	FASTWAY	Fastway (CBS)
36	ELIMINATOR	ZZ Top (WEA)
37	SUBTERRANEAN JUNGLE	Ramones (Sire)
38	RIP IT UP	Orange Juice (Polydor)
39	MONEY & CIGARETTES	Eric Clapton (Duck)
40	THE PERFECT BEAT	Various Artists (Polydor)
41	WAITING	Fun Boy Three (Chrysalis)
42	THE RISE AND FALL OF ZIGGY STARDUST AND THE SPIDERS FROM MARS	David Bowie (RCA)
43	YELLOW MOON	Don Williams (MCA)
44	PRIMITIVE MAN	Icehouse (Chrysalis)
45	SURPRISE, SURPRISE	Mezzoforte (Steinar)
46	HEADHUNTER	Krokus (Arista)
47	THE HIGH ROAD	Roxy Music (EG)
48	HAND CUT	Bucks Fizz (RCA)
49	TRICK OF THE LIGHT	Modern Romance (WEA)
50	PORCUPINE	Echo & the Bunnymen (Korova)

7 May 1983

this	Title	Artist
1	LET'S DANCE	David Bowie (EMI America)
2	THRILLER	Michael Jackson (Epic)
3	CARGO	Men At Work (Epic)
4	TRUE	Spandau Ballet (Reformation)
5	SWEET DREAMS (ARE MADE OF THIS)	Eurythmics (RCA)
6	FASTER THAN THE SPEED OF NIGHT	Bonnie Tyler (CBS)
7	THE FINAL CUT	Pink Floyd (Harvest)
8	WHITE FEATHERS	Kajagoogoo (EMI)
9	QUICK STEP AND SIDE KICK	Thompson Twins (Arista)
10	THE LUXURY GAP	Heaven 17 (Virgin)
11	MIDNIGHT AT THE LOST AND FOUND	Meatloaf (Epic)
12	TOTO IV	Toto (CBS)
13	WAR	U2 (Island)
14	THE HURTING	Tears for Fears (Mercury)
15	HIGH LAND, HARD RAIN	Aztec Camera (Rough Trade)
16	HIGHLY STRUNG	Steve Hackett (Charisma)
17	RIO	Duran Duran (EMI)
18	LOCAL HERO	Mark Knopfler (Vertigo)
19	THE KEY	Joan Armatrading (A&M)
20	YOU CAN'T STOP ROCK 'N' ROLL	Twisted Sister (Atlantic)
21	PRIDE	Robert Palmer (Island)
22	LISTEN	Flock of Seagulls (Jive)
23	SCRIPT FOR A JESTER'S TEAR	Marillion (EMI)
24	JARREAU	Al Jarreau (WEA)
25	KISSING TO BE CLEVER	Culture Club (Virgin)
26	GRAPES OF WRATH	Spear of Destiny (Epic)
27	THE KIDS FROM FAME LIVE	Kids From Fame (BBC)
28	ELIMINATOR	ZZ Top (WEA)
29	FASTWAY	Fastway (CBS)
30	SUBTERRANEAN JUNGLE	Ramones (Sire)
31	HELLO, I MUST BE GOING!	Phil Collins (Virgin)
32	CHARTRUNNERS	Various Artists (Ronco)
33	STREET SOUNDS EDITION 3	Various Artists (Street Sounds)
34	STONEKILLERS	Prince Charles & the City Band (Virgin)
35	BUSINESS AS USUAL	Men at Work (Epic)
36	POWER AND THE GLORY	Saxon (Carrere)
37	LIVING MY LIFE	Grace Jones (Island)
38	LIONEL RICHIE	Lionel Richie (Motown)
39	DAZZLE SHIPS	Orchestral Manoeuvres in the Dark (Telegraph)
40	TWICE AS KOOL	Kool & the Gang (De-Lite)
41	STEVE MILLER BAND LIVE!	Steve Miller Band (Mercury)
42	JOURNEY THROUGH THE CLASSICS	Louis Clark and the Royal Philharmonic Orchestra (K-Tel)
43	SURPRISE, SURPRISE	Mezzoforte (Steinar)
44	THE RISE AND FALL OF ZIGGY STARDUST AND THE SPIDERS FROM MARS	David Bowie (RCA)
45	JAILHOUSE ROCK	Elvis Presley (RCA)
46	THE PERFECT BEAT	Various Artists (Polydor)
47	PHIL EVERLY	Phil Everly (Capitol)
48	MAMA AFRICA	Peter Tosh (EMI)
49	THE MAN WHO SOLD THE WORLD	David Bowie (RCA)
50	MONEY & CIGARETTES	Eric Clapton (Duck)

After its longest-ever period of stable length, the NME Top 30 album chart finally expanded to a Top 50, in reflection of the growth of album sales against those of singles during the 1980s. Michael Jackson returned to the top of the first expanded chart, but was then immediately dislodged by David Bowie's comeback album under his new deal with EMI. Its title track had already been a Number 1 single.

May 1983

14 May 1983

last week	this week	Title	Artist (Label)
1	1	LET'S DANCE	David Bowie (EMI America)
2	2	THRILLER	Michael Jackson (Epic)
4	3	TRUE	Spandau Ballet (Reformation)
11	4	MIDNIGHT AT THE LOST AND FOUND	Meatloaf (Epic)
10	5	THE LUXURY GAP	Heaven 17 (Virgin)
6	6	FASTER THAN THE SPEED OF NIGHT	Bonnie Tyler (CBS)
3	7	CARGO	Men at Work (Epic)
5	8	SWEET DREAMS (ARE MADE OF THIS)	Eurythmics (RCA)
9	9	QUICK STEP AND SIDE KICK	Thompson Twins (Arista)
7	10	THE FINAL CUT	Pink Floyd (Harvest)
8	11	WHITE FEATHERS	Kajagoogoo (EMI)
14	12	THE HURTING	Tears for Fears (Mercury)
22	13	LISTEN	Flock of Seagulls (Jive)
12	14	TOTO IV	Toto (CBS)
-	15	POWER, CORRUPTION AND LIES	New Order (Factory)
20	16	YOU CAN'T STOP ROCK 'N' ROLL	Twisted Sister (Atlantic)
-	17	SONGS	Kids from Fame (BBC)
17	18	RIO	Duran Duran (EMI)
15	19	HIGH LAND, HARD RAIN	Aztec Camera (Rough Trade)
13	20	WAR	U2 (Island)
19	21	THE KEY	Joan Armatrading (A&M)
21	22	PRIDE	Robert Palmer (Island)
40	23	TWICE AS KOOL	Kool & the Gang (De-Lite)
28	24	ELIMINATOR	ZZ Top (WEA)
18	25	LOCAL HERO	Mark Knopfler (Vertigo)
32	26	CHARTRUNNERS	Various Artists (Ronco)
16	27	HIGHLY STRUNG	Steve Hackett (Charisma)
23	28	SCRIPT FOR A JESTER'S TEAR	Marillion (EMI)
34	29	STONEKILLERS	Prince Charles & the City Band (Virgin)
38	30	LIONEL RICHIE	Lionel Richie (Motown)
-	31	WE ARE ONE	Maze (Capitol)
27	32	THE KIDS FROM FAME LIVE	Kids From Fame (BBC)
31	33	HELLO, I MUST BE GOING!	Phil Collins (Virgin)
25	34	KISSING TO BE CLEVER	Culture Club (Virgin)
-	35	MAGICAL RING	Clannad (RCA)
30	36	SUBTERRANEAN JUNGLE	Ramones (Sire)
33	37	STREET SOUNDS EDITION 3	Various Art (Street Sounds)
-	38	CHIMERA	Bill Nelson (Mercury)
26	39	GRAPES OF WRATH	Spear of Destiny (Epic)
39	40	DAZZLE SHIPS	Orchestral Manoeuvres in Dark (Telegraph)
24	41	JARREAU	Al Jarreau (WEA)
41	42	STEVE MILLER BAND LIVE!	Steve Miller Ban (Mercury)
-	43	NIGHT DUBBING	Imagination (R&B)
-	44	WAITING	Fun Boy Three (Chrysalis)
35	45	BUSINESS AS USUAL	Men at Work (Epic)
50	46	MONEY & CIGARETTES	Eric Clapton (Duck)
-	47	THE HEIGHT OF BAD MANNERS	Bad Manners (Telstar)
29	48	FASTWAY	Fastway (CBS)
36	49	POWER AND THE GLORY	Saxon (Carrere)
37	50	LIVING MY LIFE	Grace Jones (Island)

21 May 1983

last week	this week	Title	Artist (Label)
3	1	TRUE	Spandau Ballet (Reformation)
1	2	LET'S DANCE	David Bowie (EMI America)
5	3	THE LUXURY GAP	Heaven 17 (Virgin)
2	4	THRILLER	Michael Jackson (Epic)
15	5	POWER, CORRUPTION AND LIES	New Order (Factory)
12	6	THE HURTING	Tears for Fears (Mercury)
7	7	CARGO	Men At Work (Epic)
4	8	MIDNIGHT AT THE LOST AND FOUND	Meatloaf (Epic)
8	9	SWEET DREAMS (ARE MADE OF THIS)	Eurythmics (RCA)
6	10	FASTER THAN THE SPEED OF NIGHT	Bonnie Tyler (CBS)
10	11	THE FINAL CUT	Pink Floyd (Harvest)
9	12	QUICK STEP AND SIDE KICK	Thompson Twins (Arista)
38	13	CHIMERA	Bill Nelson (Mercury)
13	14	LISTEN	Flock of Seagulls (Jive)
11	15	WHITE FEATHERS	Kajagoogoo (EMI)
43	16	NIGHT DUBBING	Imagination (R&B)
17	17	SONGS	Kids from Fame (BBC)
23	18	TWICE AS KOOL	Kool & the Gang (De-Lite)
16	19	YOU CAN'T STOP ROCK 'N' ROLL	Twisted Sister (Atlantic)
14	20	TOTO IV	Toto (CBS)
-	21	DRESSED FOR THE OCCASION	Cliff Richard (EMI)
44	22	WAITING	Fun Boy Three (Chrysalis)
18	23	RIO	Duran Duran (EMI)
25	24	LOCAL HERO	Mark Knopfler (Vertigo)
19	25	HIGH LAND, HARD RAIN	Aztec Camera (Rough Trade)
20	26	WAR	U2 (Island)
31	27	WE ARE ONE	Maze (Capitol)
35	28	MAGICAL RING	Clannad (RCA)
-	29	SIAGO	Blackfoot (Atco)
24	30	ELIMINATOR	ZZ Top (WEA)
-	31	HAPPY FAMILIES	Blancmange (London)
47	32	THE HEIGHT OF BAD MANNERS	Bad Manners (Telstar)
-	33	THE LAUGHTER AND TEARS COLLECTION	Various Artists (WEA)
22	34	PRIDE	Robert Palmer (Island)
33	35	HELLO, I MUST BE GOING!	Phil Collins (Virgin)
41	36	JARREAU	Al Jarreau (WEA)
37	37	H2 O	Daryl Hall & John Oates (RCA)
27	38	HIGHLY STRUNG	Steve Hackett (Charisma)
21	39	THE KEY	Joan Armatrading (A&M)
30	40	LIONEL RICHIE	Lionel Richie (Motown)
-	41	THE RISE AND FALL OF ZIGGY STARDUST AND THE SPIDERS FROM MARS	David Bowie (RCA)
28	42	SCRIPT FOR A JESTER'S TEAR	Marillion (EMI)
-	43	TOO-RYE-AY	Dexy's Midnight Runners (Mercury)
42	44	STEVE MILLER BAND LIVE!	
-	45	THE FORMER 12 YEAR-OLD GENIUS	Coati Mundi (Virgin)
45	46	BUSINESS AS USUAL	Men at Work (Epic)
34	47	KISSING TO BE CLEVER	Culture Club (Virgin)
37	48	STREET SOUNDS EDITION 3	Various Artists (Street Sounds)
-	49	WORDS	F R David (Carrere)
29	50	STONEKILLERS	Prince Charles & the City Band (Virgin)

28 May 1983

last week	this week	Title	Artist (Label)
3	1	THE LUXURY GAP	Heaven 17 (Virgin)
1	2	TRUE	Spandau Ballet (Reformation)
4	3	THRILLER	Michael Jackson (Epic)
2	4	LET'S DANCE	David Bowie (EMI America)
5	5	POWER, CORRUPTION AND LIES	New Or (Factory)
6	6	CARGO	Men At Work (Epic)
6	7	THE HURTING	Tears for Fears (Mercury)
8	8	MIDNIGHT AT THE LOST AND FOUND	Meatloaf (Epic)
16	9	NIGHT DUBBING	Imagination (R&B)
21	10	DRESSED FOR THE OCCASION	Cliff Richard (EMI)
10	11	FASTER THAN THE SPEED OF NIGHT	Bonnie Tyler (CBS)
12	12	QUICK STEP AND SIDE KICK	Thompson Twins (Arista)
9	13	SWEET DREAMS (ARE MADE OF THIS)	Eurythmics (RCA)
-	14	PIECE OF MIND	Iron Maiden (EMI)
-	15	FEAST	Creatures (Polydor)
18	16	TWICE AS KOOL	Kool & the Gang (De-Lite)
-	17	CONFRONTATION	Bob Marley & the Wailers (Island)
11	18	THE FINAL CUT	Pink Floyd (Harvest)
-	19	WHAMMY!	B52s (Island)
20	20	TOTO IV	Toto (CBS)
13	21	CHIMERA	Bill Nelson (Mercury)
-	22	CHART ENCOUNTERS OF THE HIT KIND	Various Artists (Ronco)
29	23	SIAGO	Blackfoot (Atco)
17	24	SONGS	Kids from Fame (BBC)
15	25	WHITE FEATHERS	Kajagoogoo (EMI)
22	26	WAITING	Fun Boy Three (Chrysalis)
37	27	H2 O	Daryl Hall & John Oates (RCA)
19	28	YOU CAN'T STOP ROCK 'N' ROLL	Twisted Sister (Atlantic)
27	29	WE ARE ONE	Maze (Capitol)
14	30	LISTEN	Flock of Seagulls (Jive)
-	31	THE ELEVENTH HOUR	Magnum (Jet)
25	32	HIGH LAND, HARD RAIN	Aztec Camera (Rough Trade)
40	33	LIONEL RICHIE	Lionel Richie (Motown)
23	34	RIO	Duran Duran (EMI)
26	35	WAR	U2 (Island)
-	36	THE COLLECTION	Dionne Warwick (Arista)
-	37	RING OF CHANGES	Barclay James Ha (Polydor)
41	38	THE RISE AND FALL OF ZIGGY STARDUST AND THE SPIDERS FROM MARS	David Bowie (RCA)
35	39	HELLO, I MUST BE GOING!	Phil Collins (Virgin)
36	40	JARREAU	Al Jarreau (WEA)
34	41	PRIDE	Robert Palmer (Island)
-	42	A TRICK OF THE LIGHT	Modern Romance (WEA)
30	43	ELIMINATOR	ZZ Top (WEA)
33	44	THE LAUGHTER AND TEARS COLLECTION	Various Artists (WEA)
24	45	LOCAL HERO	Mark Knopfler (Vertigo)
46	46	LIVING MY LIFE	Grace Jones (Island)
32	47	THE HEIGHT OF BAD MANNERS	Bad Manners (Telstar)
42	48	SCRIPT FOR A JESTER'S TEAR	Marillion (EMI)
-	49	REACH THE BEACH	Fixx (MCA)
46	50	BUSINESS AS USUAL	Men at Work (Epic)

Spandau Ballet had the country's best-selling single and album on May 21 with the same title, *True*. Meatloaf this time failed to reach the Top 3, though Heaven 17, boosted by their Number 2 single *Temptation*, also scored a (one-week) chart-topper. Meanwhile, the appeal of the Kids From Fame had noticeably cooled, as their new album *Songs* stuck at its debut peak of Number 17 before sinking away.

June 1983

4 June 1983

last week	this week	Title	Artist
3	1	THRILLER	Michael Jackson (Epic)
2	2	TRUE	Spandau Ballet (Reformation)
17	3	CONFRONTATION	Bob Marley & the Wailers (Island)
1	4	THE LUXURY GAP	Heaven 17 (Virgin)
14	5	PIECE OF MIND	Iron Maiden (EMI)
4	6	LET'S DANCE	David Bowie (EMI America)
5	7	POWER, CORRUPTION AND LIES	New Order (Factory)
15	8	FEAST	Creatures (Polydor)
16	9	TWICE AS KOOL	Kool & the Gang (De-Lite)
10	10	DRESSED FOR THE OCCASION	Cliff Richard (EMI)
7	11	THE HURTING	Tears for Fears (Mercury)
9	12	NIGHT DUBBING	Imagination (R&B)
6	13	CARGO	Men At Work (Epic)
12	14	QUICK STEP AND SIDE KICK	Thompson Twins (Arista)
8	15	MIDNIGHT AT THE LOST AND FOUND	Meatloaf (Epic)
11	16	FASTER THAN THE SPEED OF NIGHT	Bonnie Tyler (CBS)
22	17	CHART ENCOUNTERS OF THE HIT KIND	Various Artists (Ronco)
19	18	WHAMMY!	B52s (Island)
13	19	SWEET DREAMS (ARE MADE OF THIS)	Eurythmics (RCA)
20	20	TOTO IV	Toto (CBS)
-	21	DUCK ROCK	Malcolm McLaren (Charisma)
37	22	RING OF CHANGES	Barclay James Harvest (Polydor)
18	23	THE FINAL CUT	Pink Floyd (Harvest)
24	24	SONGS	Kids from Fame (BBC)
25	25	WHITE FEATHERS	Kajagoogoo (EMI)
-	26	CRISES	Mike Oldfield (Virgin)
36	27	THE COLLECTION	Dionne Warwick (Arista)
-	28	ANOTHER PERFECT DAY	Motorhead (Bronze)
21	29	CHIMERA	Bill Nelson (Mercury)
27	30	H2O	Daryl Hall & John Oates (RCA)
23	31	SIAGO	Blackfoot (Atco)
32	32	HIGH LAND, HARD RAIN	Aztec Camera (Rough Trade)
40	33	JARREAU	Al Jarreau (WEA)
26	34	WAITING	Fun Boy Three (Chrysalis)
30	35	LISTEN	Flock of Seagulls (Jive)
28	36	YOU CAN'T STOP ROCK 'N' ROLL	Twisted Sister (Atlantic)
41	37	PRIDE	Robert Palmer (Island)
44	38	THE LAUGHTER AND TEARS COLLECTION	Various Artists (WEA)
-	39	OUTSIDE INSIDE	Tubes (Capitol)
-	40	NAKED	Kissing the Pink (Magnet)
29	41	WE ARE ONE	Maze (Capitol)
31	42	THE ELEVENTH HOUR	Magnum (Jet)
39	43	HELLO, I MUST BE GOING!	Phil Collins (Virgin)
-	44	HUNKY DORY	David Bowie (RCA)
38	45	THE RISE AND FALL OF ZIGGY STARDUST AND THE SPIDERS FROM MARS	David Bowie (RCA)
34	46	RIO	Duran Duran (EMI)
48	47	SCRIPT FOR A JESTER'S TEAR	Marillion (EMI)
35	48	WAR	U2 (Island)
45	49	LOCAL HERO	Mark Knopfler (Vertigo)
33	50	LIONEL RICHIE	Lionel Richie (Motown)

11 June 1983

last week	this week	Title	Artist
1	1	THRILLER	Michael Jackson (Epic)
6	2	LET'S DANCE	David Bowie (EMI America)
2	3	TRUE	Spandau Ballet (Reformation)
3	4	CONFRONTATION	Bob Marley & the Wailers (Island)
5	5	PIECE OF MIND	Iron Maiden (EMI)
4	6	THE LUXURY GAP	Heaven 17 (Virgin)
7	7	POWER, CORRUPTION AND LIES	New Order (Factory)
8	8	FEAST	Creatures (Polydor)
26	9	CRISES	Mike Oldfield (Virgin)
9	10	TWICE AS KOOL	Kool & the Gang (De-Lite)
21	11	DUCK ROCK	Malcolm McLaren (Charisma)
12	12	NIGHT DUBBING	Imagination (R&B)
13	13	CARGO	Men At Work (Epic)
11	14	THE HURTING	Tears for Fears (Mercury)
10	15	DRESSED FOR THE OCCASION	Cliff Richard (EMI)
28	16	ANOTHER PERFECT DAY	Motorhead (Bronze)
15	17	MIDNIGHT AT THE LOST AND FOUND	Meatloaf (Epic)
14	18	QUICK STEP AND SIDE KICK	Thompson Twins (Arista)
20	19	TOTO IV	Toto (CBS)
17	20	CHART ENCOUNTERS OF THE HIT KIND	Various Artists (Ronco)
-	21	TOO LATE FOR ZERO	Elton John (Rocket)
19	22	SWEET DREAMS (ARE MADE OF THIS)	Eurythmics (RCA)
16	23	FASTER THAN THE SPEED OF NIGHT	Bonnie Tyler (CBS)
-	24	IN YOUR EYES	George Benson (WEA)
-	25	WHAT IS BEAT? (THE BEST OF THE BEAT)	Beat (Go Feet)
22	26	RING OF CHANGES	Barclay James Harvest (Polydor)
18	27	WHAMMY!	B52s (Island)
27	28	THE COLLECTION	Dionne Warwick (Arista)
25	29	WHITE FEATHERS	Kajagoogoo (EMI)
23	30	THE FINAL CUT	Pink Floyd (Harvest)
-	31	HOLY DIVER	Dio (Vertigo)
34	32	WAITING	Fun Boy Three (Chrysalis)
24	33	SONGS	Kids from Fame (BBC)
43	34	HELLO, I MUST BE GOING!	Phil Collins (Virgin)
40	35	NAKED	Kissing the Pink (Magnet)
-	36	TUBULAR BELLS	Mike Oldfield (Virgin)
33	37	JARREAU	Al Jarreau (WEA)
32	38	HIGH LAND, HARD RAIN	Aztec Camera (Rough Trade)
30	39	H2O	Daryl Hall & John Oates (RCA)
39	40	OUTSIDE INSIDE	Tubes (Capitol)
-	41	WRAP YOUR ARMS AROUND ME	Agnetha Faltskog (Epic)
-	42	YES SIR I WILL	Crass (Crass)
44	43	HUNKY DORY	David Bowie (RCA)
37	44	PRIDE	Robert Palmer (Island)
45	45	THE RISE AND FALL OF ZIGGY STARDUST AND THE SPIDERS FROM MARS	David Bowie (RCA)
31	46	SIAGO	Blackfoot (Atco)
29	47	CHIMERA	Bill Nelson (Mercury)
41	48	WE ARE ONE	Maze (Capitol)
38	49	THE LAUGHTER AND TEARS COLLECTION	Various Artists (WEA)
-	50	MARY JANE GIRLS	Mary Jane Girls (Gordy)

18 June 1983

last week	this week	Title	Artist
2	1	LET'S DANCE	David Bowie (EMI America)
1	2	THRILLER	Michael Jackson (Epic)
3	3	TRUE	Spandau Ballet (Reformation)
4	4	CONFRONTATION	Bob Marley & the Wailers (Island)
9	5	CRISES	Mike Oldfield (Virgin)
21	6	TOO LATE FOR ZERO	Elton John (Rocket)
10	7	TWICE AS KOOL	Kool & the Gang (De-Lite)
6	8	THE LUXURY GAP	Heaven 17 (Virgin)
24	9	IN YOUR EYES	George Benson (WEA)
25	10	WHAT IS BEAT? (THE BEST OF THE BEAT)	Beat (Go Feet)
5	11	PIECE OF MIND	Iron Maiden (EMI)
31	12	HOLY DIVER	Dio (Vertigo)
14	13	THE HURTING	Tears for Fears (Mercury)
-	14	PETER GABRIEL PLAYS LIVE	Peter Gabriel (Charisma)
11	15	DUCK ROCK	Malcolm McLaren (Charisma)
16	16	CHART ENCOUNTERS OF THE HIT KIND	Various Artists (Ronco)
28	17	THE COLLECTION	Dionne Warwick (Arista)
13	18	CARGO	Men At Work (Epic)
-	19	SPEAKING IN TONGUES	Talking Heads (Sire)
29	20	WHITE FEATHERS	Kajagoogoo (EMI)
12	21	NIGHT DUBBING	Imagination (R&B)
7	22	POWER, CORRUPTION AND LIES	New Order (Factory)
-	23	BODY WISHES	Rod Stewart (Warner Bros.)
8	24	FEAST	Creatures (Wonderland)
-	25	OIL ON CANVAS	Japan (Virgin)
16	26	ANOTHER PERFECT DAY	Motorhead (Bronze)
41	27	WRAP YOUR ARMS AROUND ME	Agnetha Faltskog (Epic)
17	28	MIDNIGHT AT THE LOST AND FOUND	Meatloaf (Epic)
22	29	SWEET DREAMS (ARE MADE OF THIS)	Eurythmics (RCA)
27	30	WHAMMY!	B52s (Island)
15	31	DRESSED FOR THE OCCASION	Cliff Richard (EMI)
19	32	TOTO IV	Toto (CBS)
18	33	QUICK STEP AND SIDE KICK	Thompson Twins (Arista)
36	34	TUBULAR BELLS	Mike Oldfield (Virgin)
23	35	FASTER THAN THE SPEED OF NIGHT	Bonnie Tyler (CBS)
-	36	SOUTHERN DEATH CULT	Southern Death Cult (Beggars Banquet)
35	37	NAKED	Kissing the Pink (Magnet)
37	38	JARREAU	Al Jarreau (WEA)
30	39	THE FINAL CUT	Pink Floyd (Harvest)
-	40	WATER SIGN	Chris Rea (Magnet)
39	41	H2O	Daryl Hall & John Oates (RCA)
-	42	SAMURAI	Grand Prix (Chrysalis)
42	43	YES SIR I WILL	Crass (Crass)
43	44	HUNKY DORY	David Bowie (RCA)
50	45	MARY JANE GIRLS	Mary Jane Girls (Gordy)
-	46	HEAD FIRST	Uriah Heep (Bronze)
33	47	SONGS	Kids from Fame (BBC)
26	48	RING OF CHANGES	Barclay James Harvest (Polydor)
45	49	THE RISE AND FALL OF ZIGGY STARDUST AND THE SPIDERS FROM MARS	David Bowie (RCA)
32	50	WAITING	Fun Boy Three (Chrysalis)

A posthumous set of previous unheard Bob Marley recordings, *Confrontation*, was the major challenge to the ongoing Jackson/Bowie/Spandau stranglehold at the chart-top. *Duck Rock*, the first album by former Sex Pistols manager Malcolm McLaren, now a maverick music-maker in his own right, raised a few eyebrows when it climbed to Number 11. Mike Oldfield's *Tubular Bells* followed his new album in!

June – July 1983

25 June 1983

last week	this week	Title	Artist (Label)
1	1	LET'S DANCE	David Bowie (EMI America)
2	2	THRILLER	Michael Jackson (Epic)
25	3	OIL ON CANVAS	Japan (Virgin)
6	4	TOO LATE FOR ZERO	Elton John (Rocket)
23	5	BODY WISHES	Rod Stewart (Warner Bros.)
9	6	IN YOUR EYES	George Benson (WEA)
5	7	CRISES	Mike Oldfield (Virgin)
14	8	PETER GABRIEL PLAYS LIVE	Peter Gabriel (Charisma)
4	9	CONFRONTATION	Bob Marley & the Wailers (Island)
7	10	TWICE AS KOOL	Kool & the Gang (De-Lite)
10	11	WHAT IS BEAT? (THE BEST OF THE BEAT)	Beat (Go Feet)
3	12	TRUE	Spandau Ballet (Reformation)
19	13	SPEAKING IN TONGUES	Talking Heads (Sire)
-	14	SYNCHRONICITY	Police (A&M)
8	15	THE LUXURY GAP	Heaven 17 (Virgin)
36	16	SOUTHERN DEATH CULT	Southern Death Cult (Beggars Banquet)
12	17	HOLY DIVER	Dio (Vertigo)
11	18	PIECE OF MIND	Iron Maiden (EMI)
13	19	THE HURTING	Tears for Fears (Mercury)
22	20	POWER, CORRUPTION AND LIES	New Order (Factory)
16	21	CHART ENCOUNTERS OF THE HIT KIND	Various Artists (Ronco)
-	22	CHART STARS	Various Artists (K-Tel)
17	23	THE COLLECTION	Dionne Warwick (Arista)
27	24	WRAP YOUR ARMS AROUND ME	Agnetha Faltskog (Epic)
18	25	CARGO	Men At Work (Epic)
15	26	DUCK ROCK	Malcolm McLaren (Charisma)
20	27	WHITE FEATHERS	Kajagoogoo (EMI)
46	28	HEAD FIRST	Uriah Heep (Bronze)
35	29	FASTER THAN THE SPEED OF NIGHT	Bonnie Tyler (CBS)
29	30	SWEET DREAMS (ARE MADE OF THIS)	Eurythmics (RCA)
33	31	QUICK STEP AND SIDE KICK	Thompson Twins (Arista)
-	32	BITE	Altered Images (Epic)
30	33	WHAMMY!	B52s (Island)
42	34	SAMURAI	Grand Prix (Chrysalis)
21	35	NIGHT DUBBING	Imagination (R&B)
-	36	OFF THE BONE	Cramps (Illegal)
28	37	MIDNIGHT AT THE LOST AND FOUND	Meatloaf (Epic)
34	38	TUBULAR BELLS	Mike Oldfield (Virgin)
26	39	ANOTHER PERFECT DAY	Motorhead (Bronze)
-	40	STREET SOUNDS EDITION 4	Various Artists (Street Sounds)
-	41	THE FUGITIVE	Tony Banks (Charisma)
24	42	FEAST	Creatures (Wonderland)
37	43	NAKED	Kissing the Pink (Magnet)
-	44	SYNCHRO SYSTEM	King Sunny Ade (Island)
31	45	DRESSED FOR THE OCCASION	Cliff Richard (EMI)
-	46	ELIMINATOR	ZZ Top (WEA)
44	47	HUNKY DORY	David Bowie (RCA)
40	48	WATER SIGN	Chris Rea (Magnet)
47	49	SONGS	Kids from Fame (BBC)
32	50	TOTO IV	Toto (CBS)

2 July 1983

last week	this week	Title	Artist (Label)
14	1	SYNCHRONICITY	Police (A&M)
2	2	THRILLER	Michael Jackson (Epic)
1	3	LET'S DANCE	David Bowie (EMI America)
5	4	BODY WISHES	Rod Stewart (Warner Bros.)
6	5	IN YOUR EYES	George Benson (WEA)
4	6	TOO LATE FOR ZERO	Elton John (Rocket)
3	7	OIL ON CANVAS	Japan (Virgin)
7	8	CRISES	Mike Oldfield (Virgin)
10	9	TWICE AS KOOL	Kool & the Gang (De-Lite)
32	10	BITE	Altered Images (Epic)
11	11	TRUE	Spandau Ballet (Reformation)
13	12	SPEAKING IN TONGUES	Talking Heads (Sire)
8	13	PETER GABRIEL PLAYS LIVE	Peter Gabriel (Charisma)
11	14	WHAT IS BEAT? (THE BEST OF THE BEAT)	Beat (Go Feet)
9	15	CONFRONTATION	Bob Marley & Wailers (Island)
15	16	THE LUXURY GAP	Heaven 17 (Virgin)
22	17	CHART STARS	Various Artists (K-Tel)
-	18	SECRET MESSAGES	Electric Light Orchestra (Jet)
18	19	PIECE OF MIND	Iron Maiden (EMI)
40	20	STREET SOUNDS EDITION 4	Various Artists (Street Sounds)
23	21	THE COLLECTION	Dionne Warwick (Arista)
26	22	DUCK ROCK	Malcolm McLaren (Charisma)
36	23	OFF THE BONE	Cramps (Illegal)
17	24	HOLY DIVER	Dio (Vertigo)
16	25	SOUTHERN DEATH CULT	Southern Death Cult (Beggars Banquet)
25	26	CARGO	Men At Work (Epic)
20	27	POWER, CORRUPTION AND LIES	New Order (Factory)
24	28	WRAP YOUR ARMS AROUND ME	Agnetha Faltskog (Epic)
27	29	WHITE FEATHERS	Kajagoogoo (EMI)
19	30	THE HURTING	Tears for Fears (Mercury)
-	31	THE WILD HEART	Stevie Nicks (WEA)
-	32	THE PRIVATE COLLECTION	Jon & Vangelis (Polydor)
-	33	MARY JANE GIRLS	Mary Jane Girls (Gordy)
44	34	SYNCHRO SYSTEM	King Sunny Ade (Island)
29	35	FASTER THAN THE SPEED OF NIGHT	Bonnie Tyler (CBS)
38	36	TUBULAR BELLS	Mike Oldfield (Virgin)
-	37	HAND OF KINDNESS	Richard Thompson (Hannibal)
30	38	SWEET DREAMS (ARE MADE OF THIS)	Eurythmics (RCA)
39	39	ANOTHER PERFECT DAY	Motorhead (Bronze)
-	40	UPSTAIRS AT ERIC'S	Yazoo (Mute)
-	41	JARREAU	Al Jarreau (WEA International)
-	42	XL-1	Pete Shelley (Genetic)
31	43	QUICK STEP AND SIDE KICK	Thompson Twins (Arista)
50	44	TOTO IV	Toto (CBS)
35	45	NIGHT DUBBING	Imagination (R&B)
-	46	GIRL AT HER VOLCANO	Rickie Lee Jones (Warner Bros.)
-	47	H2 O	Daryl Hall & John Oates (RCA)
21	48	CHART ENCOUNTERS OF THE HIT KIND	Various Artists (Ronco)
41	49	THE FUGITIVE	Tony Banks (Charisma)
28	50	HEAD FIRST	Uriah Heep (Bronze)

9 July 1983

last week	this week	Title	Artist (Label)
1	1	SYNCHRONICITY	Police (A&M)
4	2	BODY WISHES	Rod Stewart (Warner Bros.)
2	3	THRILLER	Michael Jackson (Epic)
18	4	SECRET MESSAGES	Electric Light Orchestra (Jet)
3	5	LET'S DANCE	David Bowie (EMI America)
8	6	CRISES	Mike Oldfield (Virgin)
5	7	IN YOUR EYES	George Benson (WEA)
6	8	TOO LATE FOR ZERO	Elton John (Rocket)
7	9	OIL ON CANVAS	Japan (Virgin)
16	10	THE LUXURY GAP	Heaven 17 (Virgin)
11	11	TRUE	Spandau Ballet (Reformation)
9	12	TWICE AS KOOL	Kool & the Gang (De-Lite)
-	13	FANTASTIC	Wham! (Innervision)
14	14	BITE	Altered Images (Epic)
13	15	PETER GABRIEL PLAYS LIVE	Peter Gabriel (Charisma)
32	16	THE PRIVATE COLLECTION	Jon & Vangelis (Polydor)
14	17	WHAT IS BEAT? (THE BEST OF THE BEAT)	Beat (Go Feet)
12	18	SPEAKING IN TONGUES	Talking Heads (Sire)
-	19	FLASHDANCE	Soundtrack (Casablanca)
22	20	DUCK ROCK	Malcolm McLaren (Charisma)
31	21	THE WILD HEART	Stevie Nicks (WEA)
15	22	CONFRONTATION	Bob Marley & the Wailers (Island)
46	23	GIRL AT HER VOLCANO	Rickie Lee Jones (Warner Bros.)
17	24	CHART STARS	Various Artists (K-Tel)
20	25	STREET SOUNDS EDITION 4	Various Artists (Street Sounds)
-	26	JULIO	Julio Iglesias (CBS)
21	27	THE COLLECTION	Dionne Warwick (Arista)
24	28	HOLY DIVER	Dio (Vertigo)
42	29	XL-1	Pete Shelley (Genetic)
41	30	JARREAU	Al Jarreau (WEA International)
23	31	OFF THE BONE	Cramps (Illegal)
19	32	PIECE OF MIND	Iron Maiden (EMI)
34	33	SYNCHRO SYSTEM	King Sunny Ade (Island)
-	34	WAR	U2 (Island)
30	35	THE HURTING	Tears for Fears (Mercury)
27	36	POWER, CORRUPTION AND LIES	New Order (Factory)
28	37	WRAP YOUR ARMS AROUND ME	Agnetha Faltskog (Epic)
-	38	LOVERS ONLY	Various Artists (Ronco)
35	39	FASTER THAN THE SPEED OF NIGHT	Bonnie Tyler (CBS)
36	40	TUBULAR BELLS	Mike Oldfield (Virgin)
40	41	UPSTAIRS AT ERIC'S	Yazoo (Mute)
-	42	DANCE MIX	Various Artists (Epic)
-	43	RIO	Duran Duran (EMI)
38	44	SWEET DREAMS (ARE MADE OF THIS)	Eurythmics (RCA)
29	45	WHITE FEATHERS	Kajagoogoo (EMI)
33	46	MARY JANE GIRLS	Mary Jane Girls (Gordy)
49	47	THE FUGITIVE	Tony Banks (Charisma)
44	48	TOTO IV	Toto (CBS)
-	49	DON'T TAKE MY COCONUTS	Coconuts (EMI-America)
-	50	PAN-ORAMA	Flash and the Pan (Easy Beat)

It took the new Police album *Synchronicity* to convincingly break up the existing chart-top cartel (although Thriller was not finished with the Number 1 slot yet, as later months would reveal). The Police set topped the chart simultaneously with its extracted single, *Every Breath You Take* - though the latter was quite quickly deposed by Rod Stewart's *Baby Jane*, whereas Rod's *Body Wishes* album was held at 2.

16 July 1983

last week	this week	Title	Artist (Label)
13	1	FANTASTIC	Wham! (Innervision)
1	2	SYNCHRONICITY	Police (A&M)
5	3	LET'S DANCE	David Bowie (EMI America)
2	4	BODY WISHES	Rod Stewart (Warner Bros.)
6	5	CRISES	Mike Oldfield (Virgin)
4	6	SECRET MESSAGES	Electric Light Orchestra (Jet)
3	7	THRILLER	Michael Jackson (Epic)
7	8	IN YOUR EYES	George Benson (WEA)
10	9	THE LUXURY GAP	Heaven 17 (Virgin)
8	10	TOO LATE FOR ZERO	Elton John (Rocket)
19	11	FLASHDANCE	Soundtrack (Casablanca)
-	12	YOU AND ME BOTH	Yazoo (Mute)
9	13	OIL ON CANVAS	Japan (Virgin)
26	14	JULIO	Julio Iglesias (CBS)
20	15	DUCK ROCK	Malcolm McLaren (Charisma)
12	16	TWICE AS KOOL	Kool & the Gang (De-Lite)
18	17	SPEAKING IN TONGUES	Talking Heads (Sire)
21	18	THE WILD HEART	Stevie Nicks (WEA)
22	19	CONFRONTATION	Bob Marley & the Wailers (Island)
32	20	PIECE OF MIND	Iron Maiden (EMI)
16	21	THE PRIVATE COLLECTION	Jon & Vangelis (Polydor)
23	22	GIRL AT HER VOLCANO	Rickie Lee Jones (Warner Bros.)
11	23	TRUE	Spandau Ballet (Reformation)
14	24	BITE	Altered Images (Epic)
30	25	JARREAU	Al Jarreau (WEA International)
15	26	PETER GABRIEL PLAYS LIVE	Peter Gabriel (Charisma)
38	27	LOVERS ONLY	Various Artists (Ronco)
17	28	WHAT IS BEAT? (THE BEST OF THE BEAT)	Beat (Go Feet)
28	29	HOLY DIVER	Dio (Vertigo)
25	30	STREET SOUNDS EDITION 4	Various Artists (Street Sounds)
29	31	XL-1	Pete Shelley (Genetic)
34	32	WAR	U2 (Island)
24	33	CHART STARS	Various Artists (K-Tel)
33	34	SYNCHRO SYSTEM	King Sunny Ade (Island)
27	35	THE COLLECTION	Dionne Warwick (Arista)
-	36	MICHAEL JACKSON & THE JACKSONS' 18 GREATEST HITS	Michael Jackson & the Jacksons (Star)
-	37	IN THE GROOVE	Various Artists (Teistar)
43	38	RIO	Duran Duran (EMI)
35	39	THE HURTING	Tears for Fears (Mercury)
31	40	OFF THE BONE	Cramps (Illegal)
-	41	ROSS	Diana Ross (Capitol)
-	42	SHE WORKS HARD FOR THE MONEY	Donna Summer (Mercury)
-	43	CARGO	Men At Work (Epic)
44	44	SWEET DREAMS (ARE MADE OF THIS)	Eurythmics (RCA)
-	45	SCRIPT FOR A JESTER'S TEAR	Marillion (EMI)
-	46	QUICK STEP AND SIDE KICK	Thompson Twins (Arista)
-	47	I-LEVEL	I-Level (Virgin)
40	48	TUBULAR BELLS	Mike Oldfield (Virgin)
-	49	MAGICAL RING	Clannad (RCA)
36	50	POWER, CORRUPTION AND LIES	New Order (Factory)

23 July 1983

last week	this week	Title	Artist (Label)
1	1	FANTASTIC	Wham! (Innervision)
12	2	YOU AND ME BOTH	Yazoo (Mute)
7	3	THRILLER	Michael Jackson (Epic)
2	4	SYNCHRONICITY	Police (A&M)
4	5	BODY WISHES	Rod Stewart (Warner Bros.)
5	6	CRISES	Mike Oldfield (Virgin)
3	7	LET'S DANCE	David Bowie (EMI America)
9	8	THE LUXURY GAP	Heaven 17 (Virgin)
11	9	FLASHDANCE	Soundtrack (Casablanca)
6	10	SECRET MESSAGES	Electric Light Orchestra (Jet)
8	11	IN YOUR EYES	George Benson (WEA)
14	12	JULIO	Julio Iglesias (CBS)
15	13	DUCK ROCK	Malcolm McLaren (Charisma)
20	14	PIECE OF MIND	Iron Maiden (EMI)
10	15	TOO LATE FOR ZERO	Elton John (Rocket)
-	16	BURNING FROM THE INSIDE	Bauhaus (Beggars Banquet)
42	17	SHE WORKS HARD FOR THE MONEY	Donna Summer (Mercury)
13	18	OIL ON CANVAS	Japan (Virgin)
21	19	THE PRIVATE COLLECTION	Jon & Vangelis (Polydor)
23	20	TRUE	Spandau Ballet (Reformation)
16	21	TWICE AS KOOL	Kool & the Gang (De-Lite)
44	22	SWEET DREAMS (ARE MADE OF THIS)	Eurythmics (RCA)
17	23	SPEAKING IN TONGUES	Talking Heads (Sire)
-	24	FIRE DANCES	Killing Joke (EG)
19	25	CONFRONTATION	Bob Marley & Wailers (Island)
41	26	ROSS	Diana Ross (Capitol)
18	27	THE WILD HEART	Stevie Nicks (WEA)
50	28	POWER, CORRUPTION AND LIES	New Order (Factory)
22	29	GIRL AT HER VOLCANO	Rickie Lee Jones (Warner Bros.)
31	30	XL-1	Pete Shelley (Genetic)
24	31	BITE	Altered Images (Epic)
26	32	PETER GABRIEL PLAYS LIVE	Peter Gabriel (Charisma)
27	33	LOVERS ONLY	Various Artists (Ronco)
32	34	WAR	U2 (Island)
34	35	SYNCHRO SYSTEM	King Sunny Ade (Island)
40	36	OFF THE BONE	Cramps (Illegal)
-	37	MARY JANE GIRLS	Mary Jane Girls (Gordy)
39	38	THE HURTING	Tears for Fears (Mercury)
25	39	JARREAU	Al Jarreau (WEA International)
30	40	STREET SOUNDS EDITION 4	Various Artists (Street Sounds)
46	41	QUICK STEP AND SIDE KICK	Thompson Twins (Arista)
-	42	FASTER THAN THE SPEED OF NIGHT	Bonnie Tyler (CBS)
28	43	WHAT IS BEAT? (THE BEST OF THE BEAT)	Beat (Go Feet)
36	44	MICHAEL JACKSON & THE JACKSONS' 18 GREATEST HITS	Michael Jackson & the Jacksons (Star)
-	45	ELIMINATOR	ZZ Top (WEA)
29	46	HOLY DIVER	Dio (Vertigo)
33	47	CHART STARS	Various Artists (K-Tel)
35	48	THE COLLECTION	Dionne Warwick (Arista)
43	49	CARGO	Men At Work (Epic)
-	50	GET IT RIGHT	Aretha Franklin (Arista)

30 July 1983

last week	this week	Title	Artist (Label)
1	1	FANTASTIC	Wham! (Innervision)
2	2	YOU AND ME BOTH	Yazoo (Mute)
4	3	SYNCHRONICITY	Police (A&M)
3	4	THRILLER	Michael Jackson (Epic)
8	5	THE LUXURY GAP	Heaven 17 (Virgin)
6	6	CRISES	Mike Oldfield (Virgin)
16	7	BURNING FROM THE INSIDE	Bauhaus (Beggars Banquet)
-	8	PRINCIPLE OF MOMENTS	Robert Plant (WEA)
11	9	IN YOUR EYES	George Benson (WEA)
7	10	LET'S DANCE	David Bowie (EMI America)
5	11	BODY WISHES	Rod Stewart (Warner Bros.)
12	12	JULIO	Julio Iglesias (CBS)
9	13	FLASHDANCE	Soundtrack (Casablanca)
10	14	SECRET MESSAGES	Electric Light Orchestra (Jet)
15	15	TOO LATE FOR ZERO	Elton John (Rocket)
13	16	DUCK ROCK	Malcolm McLaren (Charisma)
-	17	THE LOOK	Shalamar (Solar)
-	18	NO PARLEZ	Paul Young (CBS)
24	19	FIRE DANCES	Killing Joke (EG)
22	20	SWEET DREAMS (ARE MADE OF THIS)	Eurythmics (RCA)
18	21	OIL ON CANVAS	Japan (Virgin)
23	22	SPEAKING IN TONGUES	Talking Heads (Sire)
34	23	WAR	U2 (Island)
20	24	TRUE	Spandau Ballet (Reformation)
14	25	PIECE OF MIND	Iron Maiden (EMI)
17	26	SHE WORKS HARD FOR THE MONEY	Donna Summer (Mercury)
25	27	CONFRONTATION	Bob Marley & the Wailers (Island)
29	28	GIRL AT HER VOLCANO	Rickie Lee Jones (Warner Bros.)
21	29	TWICE AS KOOL	Kool & the Gang (De-Lite)
27	30	THE WILD HEART	Stevie Nicks (WEA)
-	31	RIO	Duran Duran (EMI)
37	32	MARY JANE GIRLS	Mary Jane Girls (Gordy)
-	33	HITS ON FIRE	Various Artists (Ronco)
19	34	THE PRIVATE COLLECTION	Jon & Vangelis (Polydor)
26	35	ROSS	Diana Ross (Capitol)
49	36	CARGO	Men At Work (Epic)
39	37	THE HURTING	Tears for Fears (Mercury)
44	38	MICHAEL JACKSON & THE JACKSONS' 18 GREATEST HITS	Michael Jackson & the Jacksons (Star)
35	39	SYNCHRO SYSTEM	King Sunny Ade (Island)
33	40	LOVERS ONLY	Various Artists (Ronco)
42	41	FASTER THAN THE SPEED OF NIGHT	Bonnie Tyler (CBS)
30	42	XL-1	Pete Shelley (Genetic)
43	43	WHAT IS BEAT? (THE BEST OF THE BEAT)	Beat (Go Feet)
48	44	THE COLLECTION	Dionne Warwick (Arista)
31	45	BITE	Altered Images (Epic)
32	46	PETER GABRIEL PLAYS LIVE	Peter Gabriel (Charisma)
36	47	OFF THE BONE	Cramps (Illegal)
28	48	POWER, CORRUPTION AND LIES	New Order (Factory)
-	49	MAKIN' MOVIES	Dire Straits (Vertigo)
47	50	CHART STARS	Various Artists (K-Tel)

Highlighted by the inclusion of their first three big hit singles, the reception for Wham!'s first album *Fantastic* was just that, giving it a three-week initial run (it would return later) at the top which would stop Yazoo's second album *You And Me Both* from emulating the chart-topping achievement of their first. A surprise chartmaker was Rickie Lee Jones, whose new album had no hit single and very little radio play.

August 1983

6 August 1983

last week	this week	title	artist (label)
18	1	NO PARLEZ	Paul Young (CBS)
2	2	YOU AND ME BOTH	Yazoo (Mute)
1	3	FANTASTIC	Wham! (Innervision)
3	4	SYNCHRONICITY	Police (A&M)
4	5	THRILLER	Michael Jackson (Epic)
8	6	PRINCIPLE OF MOMENTS	Robert Plant (WEA)
17	7	THE LOOK	Shalamar (Solar)
5	8	THE LUXURY GAP	Heaven 17 (Virgin)
6	9	CRISES	Mike Oldfield (Virgin)
-	10	THE CROSSING	Big Country (Mercury)
11	11	BODY WISHES	Rod Stewart (Warner Bros.)
16	12	DUCK ROCK	Malcolm McLaren (Charisma)
10	13	LET'S DANCE	David Bowie (EMI America)
7	14	BURNING FROM THE INSIDE	Bauhaus (Beggars Banquet)
15	15	TOO LATE FOR ZERO	Elton John (Rocket)
9	16	IN YOUR EYES	George Benson (WEA)
-	17	THE VERY BEST OF THE BEACH BOYS	Beach Boys (Capitol)
13	18	FLASHDANCE	Soundtrack (Casablanca)
38	19	MICHAEL JACKSON & THE JACKSONS' 18 GREATEST HITS	Michael Jackson & the Jacksons (Star)
12	20	JULIO	Julio Iglesias (CBS)
20	21	SWEET DREAMS (ARE MADE OF THIS)	Eurythmics (RCA)
33	22	HITS ON FIRE	Various Artists (Ronco)
14	23	SECRET MESSAGES	Electric Light Orchestra (Jet)
26	24	SHE WORKS HARD FOR THE MONEY	Donna Summer (Mercury)
23	25	WAR	U2 (Island)
24	26	TRUE	Spandau Ballet (Reformation)
36	27	CARGO	Men At Work (Epic)
19	28	FIRE DANCES	Killing Joke (EG)
25	29	PIECE OF MIND	Iron Maiden (EMI)
-	30	JARREAU	Al Jarreau (WEA International)
48	31	POWER, CORRUPTION AND LIES	New Order (Factory)
45	32	BITE	Altered Images (Epic)
29	33	TWICE AS KOOL	Kool & the Gang (De-Lite)
27	34	CONFRONTATION	Bob Marley & the Wailers (Island)
21	35	OIL ON CANVAS	Japan (Virgin)
37	36	THE HURTING	Tears for Fears (Mercury)
32	37	MARY JANE GIRLS	Mary Jane Girls (Gordy)
35	38	ROSS	Diana Ross (Capitol)
44	39	THE COLLECTION	Dionne Warwick (Arista)
-	40	JERKY VERSIONS OF THE DREAM	Howard Devoto (Virgin)
34	41	THE PRIVATE COLLECTION	Jon & Vangelis (Polydor)
30	42	THE WILD HEART	Stevie Nicks (WEA)
22	43	SPEAKING IN TONGUES	Talking Heads (Sire)
39	44	SYNCHRO SYSTEM	King Sunny Ade (Island)
-	45	PORCUPINE	Echo & the Bunnymen (Korova)
28	46	GIRL AT HER VOLCANO	Rickie Lee Jones (Warner Bros.)
41	47	FASTER THAN THE SPEED OF NIGHT	Bonnie Tyler (CBS)
50	48	CHART STARS	Various Artists (K-Tel)
46	49	PETER GABRIEL PLAYS LIVE	Peter Gabriel (Charisma)
-	50	HOLY DIVER	Dio (Vertigo)

13 August 1983

last week	this week	title	artist (label)
1	1	NO PARLEZ	Paul Young (CBS)
10	2	THE CROSSING	Big Country (Mercury)
3	3	FANTASTIC	Wham! (Innervision)
2	4	YOU AND ME BOTH	Yazoo (Mute)
6	5	PRINCIPLE OF MOMENTS	Robert Plant (WEA)
7	6	THE LOOK	Shalamar (Solar)
5	7	THRILLER	Michael Jackson (Epic)
19	8	MICHAEL JACKSON & THE JACKSONS' 18 GREATEST HITS	Michael Jackson & the Jacksons (Star)
4	9	SYNCHRONICITY	Police (A&M)
-	10	PUNCH THE CLOCK	Elvis Costello (F-Beat)
17	11	THE VERY BEST OF THE BEACH BOYS	Beach Boys (Capitol)
13	12	LET'S DANCE	David Bowie (EMI America)
8	13	THE LUXURY GAP	Heaven 17 (Virgin)
9	14	CRISES	Mike Oldfield (Virgin)
16	15	IN YOUR EYES	George Benson (WEA)
15	16	TOO LATE FOR ZERO	Elton John (Rocket)
12	17	DUCK ROCK	Malcolm McLaren (Charisma)
21	18	SWEET DREAMS (ARE MADE OF THIS)	Eurythmics (RCA)
22	19	HITS ON FIRE	Various Artists (Ronco)
40	20	JERKY VERSIONS OF THE DREAM	Howard Devoto (Virgin)
18	21	FLASHDANCE	Soundtrack (Casablanca)
11	22	BODY WISHES	Rod Stewart (Warner Bros.)
14	23	BURNING FROM THE INSIDE	Bauhaus (Beggars Banquet)
20	24	JULIO	Julio Iglesias (CBS)
23	25	SECRET MESSAGES	Electric Light Orchestra (Jet)
26	26	TRUE	Spandau Ballet (Reformation)
-	27	CLOSE TO THE BONE	Tom Tom Club (Island)
25	28	WAR	U2 (Island)
29	29	PIECE OF MIND	Iron Maiden (EMI)
28	30	FIRE DANCES	Killing Joke (EG)
-	31	CRACKDOWN	Cabaret Voltaire (Some Bizzare)
-	32	LAWYERS IN LOVE	Jackson Browne (Elektra)
-	33	THE WATERBOYS	Waterboys (Chicken Jazz)
-	34	APOLLO ATMOSPHERES AND SOUNDTRACKS	Eno (EG)
31	35	POWER, CORRUPTION AND LIES	New Order (Factory)
30	36	JARREAU	Al Jarreau (WEA International)
24	37	SHE WORKS HARD FOR THE MONEY	Donna Summer (Mercury)
35	38	OIL ON CANVAS	Japan (Virgin)
27	39	CARGO	Men At Work (Epic)
-	40	BAT OUT OF HELL	Meatloaf (Epic)
41	41	THE PRIVATE COLLECTION	Jon & Vangelis (Polydor)
-	42	RIO	Duran Duran (EMI)
-	43	QUICK STEP AND SIDE KICK	Thompson Twins (Arista)
-	44	LIVE	Doobie Brothers (Warner Bros.)
38	45	ROSS	Diana Ross (Capitol)
33	46	TWICE AS KOOL	Kool & the Gang (De-Lite)
-	47	XL-1	Pete Shelley (Genetic)
43	48	SPEAKING IN TONGUES	Talking Heads (Sire)
-	49	ALL THE GOOD ONES ARE TAKEN	Ian Hunter (CBS)
-	50	LIVE IN BERLIN	Au Pairs (AKA)

20 August 1983

last week	this week	title	artist (label)
10	1	PUNCH THE CLOCK	Elvis Costello (F-Beat)
2	2	THE CROSSING	Big Country (Mercury)
1	3	NO PARLEZ	Paul Young (CBS)
3	4	FANTASTIC	Wham! (Innervision)
8	5	MICHAEL JACKSON & THE JACKSONS' 18 GREATEST HITS	Michael Jackson & the Jacksons (Star)
5	6	PRINCIPLE OF MOMENTS	Robert Plant (WEA)
11	7	THE VERY BEST OF THE BEACH BOYS	Beach Boys (Capitol)
7	8	THRILLER	Michael Jackson (Epic)
6	9	THE LOOK	Shalamar (Solar)
9	10	SYNCHRONICITY	Police (A&M)
16	11	TOO LATE FOR ZERO	Elton John (Rocket)
4	12	YOU AND ME BOTH	Yazoo (Mute)
13	13	THE LUXURY GAP	Heaven 17 (Virgin)
12	14	LET'S DANCE	David Bowie (EMI America)
32	15	LAWYERS IN LOVE	Jackson Browne (Elektra)
-	16	ALPHA	Asia (Geffen)
14	17	CRISES	Mike Oldfield (Virgin)
31	18	CRACKDOWN	Cabaret Voltaire (Some Bizzare)
-	19	STREET SOUNDS EDITION 5	Various Artists (Street Sounds)
17	20	DUCK ROCK	Malcolm McLaren (Charisma)
15	21	IN YOUR EYES	George Benson (WEA)
26	22	TRUE	Spandau Ballet (Reformation)
21	23	FLASHDANCE	Soundtrack (Casablanca)
22	24	BODY WISHES	Rod Stewart (Warner Bros.)
28	25	WAR	U2 (Island)
19	26	HITS ON FIRE	Various Artists (Ronco)
18	27	SWEET DREAMS (ARE MADE OF THIS)	Eurythmics (RCA)
24	28	JULIO	Julio Iglesias (CBS)
-	29	GOLDEN YEARS	David Bowie (RCA)
23	30	BURNING FROM THE INSIDE	Bauhaus (Beggars Banquet)
27	31	CLOSE TO THE BONE	Tom Tom Club (Island)
44	32	LIVE	Doobie Brothers (Warner Bros.)
45	33	ROSS	Diana Ross (Capitol)
42	34	RIO	Duran Duran (EMI)
25	35	SECRET MESSAGES	Electric Light Orchestra (Jet)
35	36	POWER, CORRUPTION AND LIES	New Order (Factory)
48	37	SPEAKING IN TONGUES	Talking Heads (Sire)
20	38	JERKY VERSIONS OF THE DREAM	Howard Devoto (Virgin)
40	39	BAT OUT OF HELL	Meatloaf (Epic)
43	40	QUICK STEP AND SIDE KICK	Thompson Twins (Arista)
41	41	OIL ON CANVAS	Japan (Virgin)
46	42	TWICE AS KOOL	Kool & the Gang (De-Lite)
30	43	FIRE DANCES	Killing Joke (EG)
-	44	THE WILD HEART	Stevie Nicks (WEA)
29	45	PIECE OF MIND	Iron Maiden (EMI)
-	46	THE PROPHET RIDES AGAIN	Dennis Brown (A&M)
-	47	TORMENT AND TOREROS	Marc and the Mambas (Some Bizzare)
-	48	FEAST	Creatures (Wonderland)
-	49	WRAP YOUR ARMS AROUND ME	Agnetha Faltskog (Epic)
-	50	ALL IN A NIGHT'S WORK	K C and the Sunshine Band (Epic)

After many years of trying as a group vocalist, Paul Young finally made it as a solist with his chart-topping revival of Marvin Gaye's *Wherever I Lay My Hat*, and his follow-up album *No Parlez* would cement this success, eventually becoming one of the year's biggest sellers. The Jacksons' new Top-Tenner was a TV-advertised package of the group's and Michael's early solo hits, licensed from Motown.

August – September 1983

27 August 1983

last	this	Title	Artist (Label)
4	1	FANTASTIC	Wham! (Innervision)
5	2	MICHAEL JACKSON & THE JACKSONS' 18 GREATEST HITS	Michael Jackson & the Jacksons (Star)
3	3	NO PARLEZ	Paul Young (CBS)
1	4	PUNCH THE CLOCK	Elvis Costello (F-Beat)
6	5	PRINCIPLE OF MOMENTS	Robert Plant (WEA)
16	6	ALPHA	Asia (Geffen)
7	7	THE VERY BEST OF THE BEACH BOYS	Beach Boys (Capitol)
11	8	TOO LATE FOR ZERO	Elton John (Rocket)
8	9	THRILLER	Michael Jackson (Epic)
12	10	YOU AND ME BOTH	Yazoo (Mute)
2	11	THE CROSSING	Big Country (Mercury)
22	12	TRUE	Spandau Ballet (Reformation)
9	13	THE LOOK	Shalamar (Solar)
10	14	SYNCHRONICITY	Police (A&M)
19	15	STREET SOUNDS EDITION 5	Various Artists (Street Sounds)
13	16	THE LUXURY GAP	Heaven 17 (Virgin)
21	17	IN YOUR EYES	George Benson (WEA)
14	18	LET'S DANCE	David Bowie (EMI America)
17	19	CRISES	Mike Oldfield (Virgin)
15	20	LAWYERS IN LOVE	Jackson Browne (Elektra)
18	21	CRACKDOWN	Cabaret Voltaire (Some Bizzare)
20	22	DUCK ROCK	Malcolm McLaren (Charisma)
27	23	SWEET DREAMS (ARE MADE OF THIS)	Eurythmics (RCA)
24	24	BODY WISHES	Rod Stewart (Warner Bros.)
47	25	TORMENT AND TOREROS	Marc and the Mambas (Some Bizzare)
29	26	GOLDEN YEARS	David Bowie (RCA)
26	27	HITS ON FIRE	Various Artists (Ronco)
25	28	WAR	U2 (Island)
23	29	FLASHDANCE	Soundtrack (Casablanca)
34	30	RIO	Duran Duran (EMI)
30	31	BURNING FROM THE INSIDE	Bauhaus (Beggars Banquet)
28	32	JULIO	Julio Iglesias (CBS)
39	33	BAT OUT OF HELL	Meatloaf (Epic)
33	34	ROSS	Diana Ross (Capitol)
31	35	CLOSE TO THE BONE	Tom Tom Club (Island)
36	36	POWER, CORRUPTION AND LIES	New Order (Factory)
-	37	THE PRIVATE COLLECTION	Jon & Vangelis (Polydor)
37	38	SPEAKING IN TONGUES	Talking Heads (Sire)
-	39	OFF THE BONE	Cramps (Illegal)
-	40	FUTURE SHOCK	Herbie Hancock (CBS)
32	41	LIVE	Doobie Brothers (Warner Bros.)
46	42	THE PROPHET RIDES AGAIN	Dennis Brown (A&M)
-	43	LIVE AT RONNIE SCOTT'S	Weekend (Rough Trade)
38	44	JERKY VERSIONS OF THE DREAM	Howard Devoto (Virgin)
40	45	QUICK STEP AND SIDE KICK	Thompson Twins (Arista)
41	46	OIL ON CANVAS	Japan (Virgin)
-	47	SING FOR YOU	Kids from Fame (BBC)
-	48	TOTO IV	Toto (CBS)
-	49	I WAS THE ONE	Elvis Presley (RCA)
-	50	HEROES	David Bowie (RCA)

3 September 1983

last	this	Title	Artist (Label)
1	1	FANTASTIC	Wham! (Innervision)
2	2	MICHAEL JACKSON & THE JACKSONS' 18 GREATEST HITS	Michael Jackson & the Jacksons (Star)
7	3	THE VERY BEST OF THE BEACH BOYS	Beach Boys (Capitol)
6	4	ALPHA	Asia (Geffen)
12	5	TRUE	Spandau Ballet (Reformation)
8	6	TOO LATE FOR ZERO	Elton John (Rocket)
5	7	PRINCIPLE OF MOMENTS	Robert Plant (WEA)
9	8	THRILLER	Michael Jackson (Epic)
3	9	NO PARLEZ	Paul Young (CBS)
4	10	PUNCH THE CLOCK	Elvis Costello (F-Beat)
11	11	THE CROSSING	Big Country (Mercury)
-	12	FLICK OF THE SWITCH	AC/DC (Atlantic)
13	13	THE LOOK	Shalamar (Solar)
14	14	SYNCHRONICITY	Police (A&M)
10	15	YOU AND ME BOTH	Yazoo (Mute)
-	16	CONSTRUCTION TIME AGAIN	Depeche Mode (Mute)
-	17	STANDING IN THE LIGHT	Level 42 (Polydor)
40	18	FUTURE SHOCK	Herbie Hancock (CBS)
15	19	STREET SOUNDS EDITION 5	Various Artists (Street Sounds)
24	20	BODY WISHES	Rod Stewart (Warner Bros.)
26	21	GOLDEN YEARS	David Bowie (RCA)
17	22	IN YOUR EYES	George Benson (WEA)
18	23	LET'S DANCE	David Bowie (EMI America)
23	24	SWEET DREAMS (ARE MADE OF THIS)	Eurythmics (RCA)
-	25	EVERYBODY'S ROCKIN'	Neil Young (Geffen)
-	26	ELIMINATOR	ZZ Top (WEA)
19	27	CRISES	Mike Oldfield (Virgin)
16	28	THE LUXURY GAP	Heaven 17 (Virgin)
25	29	TORMENT AND TOREROS	Marc and the Mambas (Some Bizzare)
-	30	HEADSTONE – BEST OF UFO	UFO (Chrysalis)
33	31	BAT OUT OF HELL	Meatloaf (Epic)
36	32	POWER, CORRUPTION AND LIES	New Order (Factory)
28	33	WAR	U2 (Island)
20	34	LAWYERS IN LOVE	Jackson Browne (Elektra)
22	35	DUCK ROCK	Malcolm McLaren (Charisma)
29	36	FLASHDANCE	Soundtrack (Casablanca)
32	37	JULIO	Julio Iglesias (CBS)
21	38	CRACKDOWN	Cabaret Voltaire (Some Bizzare)
-	39	HITS ON FIRE	Various Artists (Ronco)
-	40	ALL IN A NIGHT'S WORK	K C and the Sunshine Band (Epic)
-	41	TWICE AS KOOL	Kool & the Gang (De-Lite)
-	42	SCRIPT OF THE BRIDGE	Chameleons (Statik)
45	43	QUICK STEP AND SIDE KICK	Thompson Twins (Arista)
-	44	HOLY DIVER	Dio (Vertigo)
27	45	HITS ON FIRE	Various Artists (Ronco)
30	46	RIO	Duran Duran (EMI)
39	47	OFF THE BONE	Cramps (Illegal)
31	48	BURNING FROM THE INSIDE	Bauhaus (Beggars Banquet)
-	49	PIECE OF MIND	Iron Maiden (EMI)
44	50	JERKY VERSIONS OF THE DREAM	Howard Devoto (Virgin)

10 September 1983

last	this	Title	Artist (Label)
12	1	FLICK OF THE SWITCH	AC/DC (Atlantic)
1	2	FANTASTIC	Wham! (Innervision)
3	3	THE VERY BEST OF THE BEACH BOYS	Beach Boys (Capitol)
16	4	CONSTRUCTION TIME AGAIN	Depeche Mode (Mute)
2	5	MICHAEL JACKSON & THE JACKSONS' 18 GREATEST HITS	Michael Jackson & the Jacksons (Star)
17	6	STANDING IN THE LIGHT	Level 42 (Polydor)
4	7	ALPHA	Asia (Geffen)
11	8	THE CROSSING	Big Country (Mercury)
5	9	TRUE	Spandau Ballet (Reformation)
6	10	TOO LATE FOR ZERO	Elton John (Rocket)
7	11	PRINCIPLE OF MOMENTS	Robert Plant (WEA)
8	12	THRILLER	Michael Jackson (Epic)
9	13	NO PARLEZ	Paul Young (CBS)
10	14	PUNCH THE CLOCK	Elvis Costello (F-Beat)
13	15	THE LOOK	Shalamar (Solar)
15	16	YOU AND ME BOTH	Yazoo (Mute)
14	17	SYNCHRONICITY	Police (A&M)
20	18	BODY WISHES	Rod Stewart (Warner Bros.)
18	19	FUTURE SHOCK	Herbie Hancock (CBS)
19	20	STREET SOUNDS EDITION 5	Various Artists (Street Sounds)
30	21	HEADSTONE – BEST OF UFO	UFO (Chrysalis)
22	22	IN YOUR EYES	George Benson (WEA)
28	23	THE LUXURY GAP	Heaven 17 (Virgin)
25	24	EVERYBODY'S ROCKIN'	Neil Young (Geffen)
-	25	BUILT TO DESTROY	Michael Schenker Group (Chrysalis)
33	26	WAR	U2 (Island)
32	27	POWER, CORRUPTION AND LIES	New Order (Factory)
34	28	LAWYERS IN LOVE	Jackson Browne (Elektra)
-	29	MEAN STREAK	Y & T (A&M)
21	30	GOLDEN YEARS	David Bowie (RCA)
27	31	CRISES	Mike Oldfield (Virgin)
-	32	SUNNY AFTERNOON	Various Artists (Impression)
24	33	SWEET DREAMS (ARE MADE OF THIS)	Eurythmics (RCA)
36	34	FLASHDANCE	Soundtrack (Casablanca)
46	35	RIO	Duran Duran (EMI)
47	36	OFF THE BONE	Cramps (Illegal)
-	37	MUMMER	XTC (Virgin)
26	38	ELIMINATOR	ZZ Top (WEA)
-	39	MERRY CHRISTMAS MR LAWRENCE	Ryuichi Sakamoto (Virgin)
29	40	TORMENT AND TOREROS	Marc and the Mambas (Some Bizzare)
23	41	LET'S DANCE	David Bowie (EMI America)
40	42	ALL IN A NIGHT'S WORK	K C and the Sunshine Band (Epic)
-	43	COME WITH CLUB – CLUB TRACKS VOL 2	Various Artists (Club)
37	44	JULIO	Julio Iglesias (CBS)
41	45	TWICE AS KOOL	Kool & the Gang (De-Lite)
-	46	ROCK SYMPHONIES	London Symphony Orchestra (K-Tel)
31	47	BAT OUT OF HELL	Meatloaf (Epic)
43	48	QUICK STEP AND SIDE KICK	Thompson Twins (Arista)
-	49	THE PRESENT	Moody Blues (Threshold)
-	50	BOYS DON'T CRY	Cure (Fiction)

The Beach Boys' *Very Best Of* compilation was no less than their fifth Top 10 album to recycle their Capitol hits of the 1960s and early '70s, the first having been *Best Of The Beach Boys* way back at the end of 1966, and the biggest the trend-setting *20 Golden Greats*, which had launched EMI's successful TV-advertised series in 1976. The newcomer (a double album) also benefited from a TV ad campaign.

September – October 1983

Several titles, mostly among the resurgent flurry of Top 10 sellers by heavy metal bands - AC/DC, Rainbow, Black Sabbath - were displaying a sales pattern which would become ever more apparent by the end of the 1980s: making a solid arrival in the upper reaches, having their best sales in their second week, then dropping away ultra-quickly. Eventually, most hard rock would sell strongest in its *first* week.

October 1983

8 October 1983

last week	this week	Title	Artist (Label)
1	1	LABOUR OF LOVE	UB40 (DEP International)
2	2	NO PARLEZ	Paul Young (CBS)
3	3	THE CROSSING	Big Country (Mercury)
18	4	LET'S DANCE	David Bowie (EMI America)
4	5	BORN AGAIN	Black Sabbath (Vertigo)
6	6	THRILLER	Michael Jackson (Epic)
5	7	FANTASTIC	Wham! (Innervision)
14	8	THE HIT SQUAD	Various Artists (Ronco)
12	9	CONSTRUCTION TIME AGAIN	Depeche Mode (Mute)
11	10	STANDING IN THE LIGHT	Level 42 (Polydor)
7	11	TRUE	Spandau Ballet (Reformation)
9	12	MICHAEL JACKSON & THE JACKSONS' 18 GREATEST HITS	Michael Jackson & the Jacksons (Star)
8	13	THE VERY BEST OF THE BEACH BOYS	Beach Boys (Capitol)
10	14	WARRIORS	Gary Numan (Beggars Banquet)
19	15	THE LUXURY GAP	Heaven 17 (Virgin)
-	16	LICK IT UP	Kiss (Vertigo)
23	17	UNFORGETTABLE	Johnny Mathis & Natalie Cole (CBS)
45	18	RITMO	Judie Tzuke (Chrysalis)
17	19	DOPPELGANGER	Kid Creole & the Coconuts (Island)
15	20	FLICK OF THE SWITCH	AC/DC (Atlantic)
16	21	LIKE GANGBUSTERS	Jo Boxers (RCA)
-	22	LIVE IN TOKYO	Public Image Ltd (Virgin)
22	23	TOO LATE FOR ZERO	Elton John (Rocket)
13	24	BENT OUT OF SHAPE	Rainbow (Polydor)
29	25	BORN TO LOVE	Peabo Bryson & Roberta Flack (Capitol)
-	26	KISSING TO BE CLEVER	Culture Club (Virgin)
21	27	CANTERBURY	Diamond Head (MCA)
24	28	THE PRESENT	Moody Blues (Threshold)
31	29	NO. 8	J J Cale (Mercury)
36	30	IN YOUR EYES	George Benson (WEA)
-	31	A TOUCH MORE MAGIC	Barry Manilow (Arista)
26	32	THE LOOK	Shalamar (Solar)
28	33	SUNNY AFTERNOON	Various Artists (Impression)
-	34	THE GOLDEN SECTION	John Foxx (Virgin)
46	35	SWORDFISHTROMBONE	Tom Waits (Island)
41	36	MERRY CHRISTMAS MR LAWRENCE	Ryuichi Sakamoto (Virgin)
30	37	YOU AND ME BOTH	Yazoo (Mute)
42	38	PUNCH THE CLOCK	Elvis Costello (F-Beat)
20	39	HEADLINE HITS	Various Artists (K-Tel)
39	40	BLUE SUNSHINE	Glove (Wonderland)
-	41	DANCE IN THE MIDNIGHT	Marc Bolan (Marc on Wax)
40	42	POWER, CORRUPTION AND LIES	New Order (Factory)
32	43	BUILT TO DESTROY	Michael Schenker Group (Chrysalis)
35	44	SYNCHRONICITY	Police (A&M)
25	45	PRINCIPLE OF MOMENTS	Robert Plant (WEA)
27	46	BODY WISHES	Rod Stewart (Warner Bros.)
38	47	WAR	U2 (Island)
-	48	STAYIN' ALIVE	Soundtrack (RSO)
47	49	AN INNOCENT MAN	Billy Joel (CBS)
37	50	RIO	Duran Duran (EMI)

15 October 1983

last week	this week	Title	Artist (Label)
1	1	LABOUR OF LOVE	UB40 (DEP International)
2	2	NO PARLEZ	Paul Young (CBS)
3	3	THE CROSSING	Big Country (Mercury)
4	4	LET'S DANCE	David Bowie (EMI America)
7	5	FANTASTIC	Wham! (Innervision)
-	6	GENESIS	Genesis (Charisma/Virgin)
6	7	THRILLER	Michael Jackson (Epic)
16	8	LICK IT UP	Kiss (Vertigo)
22	9	LIVE IN TOKYO	Public Image Ltd (Virgin)
9	10	CONSTRUCTION TIME AGAIN	Depeche Mode (Mute)
31	11	A TOUCH MORE MAGIC	Barry Manilow (Arista)
30	12	IN YOUR EYES	George Benson (WEA)
5	13	BORN AGAIN	Black Sabbath (Vertigo)
14	14	THE LUXURY GAP	Heaven 17 (Virgin)
11	15	TRUE	Spandau Ballet (Reformation)
8	16	THE HIT SQUAD	Various Artists (Ronco)
17	17	UNFORGETTABLE	Johnny Mathis & Natalie Cole (CBS)
14	18	WARRIORS	Gary Numan (Beggars Banquet)
12	19	MICHAEL JACKSON & THE JACKSONS' 18 GREATEST HITS	Michael Jackson & the Jacksons (Star)
18	20	RITMO	Judie Tzuke (Chrysalis)
10	21	STANDING IN THE LIGHT	Level 42 (Polydor)
13	22	THE VERY BEST OF THE BEACH BOYS	Beach Boys (Capitol)
25	23	BORN TO LOVE	Peabo Bryson & Roberta Flack (Capitol)
-	24	STREET SOUNDS EDITION 6	Various Artists (Street Sounds)
48	25	STAYIN' ALIVE	Soundtrack (RSO)
34	26	THE GOLDEN SECTION	John Foxx (Virgin)
23	27	TOO LATE FOR ZERO	Elton John (Rocket)
20	28	FLICK OF THE SWITCH	AC/DC (Atlantic)
-	29	SILVER	Cliff Richard (EMI)
-	30	TWO OF US	Various Artists (K-Tel)
-	31	VICES	Waysted (Chrysalis)
19	32	DOPPELGANGER	Kid Creole & the Coconuts (Island)
21	33	LIKE GANGBUSTERS	Jo Boxers (RCA)
47	34	WAR	U2 (Island)
-	35	THE MUSIC OF RICHARD CLAYDERMAN	Richard Clayderman (Decca/Delphine)
-	36	FLIGHTS OF FANCY	Paul Leoni (Nouveau)
-	37	INTRODUCING	Style Council (Polydor Import)
35	38	SWORDFISHTROMBONE	Tom Waits (Island)
24	39	BENT OUT OF SHAPE	Rainbow (Polydor)
26	40	KISSING TO BE CLEVER	Culture Club (Virgin)
37	41	YOU AND ME BOTH	Yazoo (Mute)
42	42	POWER, CORRUPTION AND LIES	New Order (Factory)
-	43	IS NOTHING SACRED?	Lords of the New Church (LNC)
28	44	THE PRESENT	Moody Blues (Threshold)
32	45	THE LOOK	Shalamar (Solar)
27	46	CANTERBURY	Diamond Head (MCA)
-	47	THE WILD HEART	Stevie Nicks (WEA)
40	48	BLUE SUNSHINE	Glove (Wonderland)
38	49	PUNCH THE CLOCK	Elvis Costello (F-Beat)
-	50	LIVE FROM EARTH	Pat Benatar (Chrysalis)

22 October 1983

last week	this week	Title	Artist (Label)
6	1	GENESIS	Genesis (Charisma/Virgin)
2	2	NO PARLEZ	Paul Young (CBS)
1	3	LABOUR OF LOVE	UB40 (DEP International)
-	4	COLOUR BY NUMBERS	Culture Club (Virgin)
-	5	SNAP!	Jam (Polydor)
3	6	THE CROSSING	Big Country (Mercury)
5	7	FANTASTIC	Wham! (Innervision)
4	8	LET'S DANCE	David Bowie (EMI America)
7	9	THRILLER	Michael Jackson (Epic)
12	10	IN YOUR EYES	George Benson (WEA)
29	11	SILVER	Cliff Richard (EMI)
10	12	CONSTRUCTION TIME AGAIN	Depeche Mode (Mute)
8	13	LICK IT UP	Kiss (Vertigo)
9	14	LIVE IN TOKYO	Public Image Ltd (Virgin)
25	15	STAYIN' ALIVE	Soundtrack (RSO)
11	16	A TOUCH MORE MAGIC	Barry Manilow (Arista)
23	17	BORN TO LOVE	Peabo Bryson & Roberta Flack (Capitol)
16	18	THE HIT SQUAD	Various Artists (Ronco)
27	19	TOO LATE FOR ZERO	Elton John (Rocket)
37	20	INTRODUCING	Style Council (Polydor Import)
-	21	VOICE OF THE HEART	Carpenters (A&M)
22	22	RITMO	Judie Tzuke (Chrysalis)
40	23	KISSING TO BE CLEVER	Culture Club (Virgin)
50	24	LIVE FROM EARTH	Pat Benatar (Chrysalis)
14	25	THE LUXURY GAP	Heaven 17 (Virgin)
38	26	SWORD⁒ISHTROMBONE	Tom Waits (Island)
-	27	MONUMENT (LIVE)	Ultravox (Chrysalis)
21	28	STANDING IN THE LIGHT	Level 42 (Polydor)
-	29	CHAS AND DAVE'S KNEES UP - JAMBOREE BAG NO.2	Chas & Dave (Rockney)
26	30	THE GOLDEN SECTION	John Foxx (Virgin)
15	31	TRUE	Spandau Ballet (Reformation)
19	32	MICHAEL JACKSON & THE JACKSONS' 18 GREATEST HITS	Michael Jackson & the Jacksons (Star)
18	33	WARRIORS	Gary Numan (Beggars Banquet)
-	34	BAT OUT OF HELL	Meatloaf (Epic)
31	35	VICES	Waysted (Chrysalis)
-	36	WINDOW IN THE JUNGLE	10 c.c. (Mercury)
17	37	UNFORGETTABLE	Johnny Mathis & Natalie Cole (CBS)
30	38	TWO OF US	Various Artists (K-Tel)
41	39	YOU AND ME BOTH	Yazoo (Mute)
32	40	DOPPELGANGER	Kid Creole & the Coconuts (Island)
-	41	RESPOND PACKAGE	Various Artists (Respond)
24	42	STREET SOUNDS EDITION 6	Various Artists (Street Sounds)
-	43	MUTINY	David Essex (Mercury)
45	44	THE LOOK	Shalamar (Solar)
36	45	FLIGHTS OF FANCY	Paul Leoni (Nouveau)
42	46	POWER, CORRUPTION AND LIES	New Order (Factory)
28	47	FLICK OF THE SWITCH	AC/DC (Atlantic)
43	48	IS NOTHING SACRED?	Lords of the New Church (LNC)
-	49	BUILT TO DESTROY	Michael Schenker Group (Chrysalis)
35	50	THE MUSIC OF RICHARD CLAYDERMAN	Richard Clayderman (Decca/Delphine)

The return to prominence of David Bowie's *Let's Dance* was down to his Number 2 single *Modern Love*, while Genesis also had a Number 2 single, *Mama*, to kick-start their eponymously-titled new chart-topping album. Kiss' *Lick It Up* was, surprisingly, the 1970s veterans' first UK Top 10 album ever. Cliff Richard's *Silver* was, initially a box set containing a bonus *Rock'n'Roll Silver* oldies set.

243

October – November 1983

Culture Club's million-plus-selling *Karma Chameleon* was 1983's biggest single, and hugely boosted the profile of its parent album *Colour By Numbers*, which would dominate the top of the chart for much of the rest of the year. Culture Club's enormous sales meant, that the Jam's retrospective singles collection *Snap!* was held at 2. The Doors' *Alive, She Cried* was a mini-album containing newly-discovered live tracks.

November – December 1983

19 November 1983

last	this	Title	Artist (Label)
2	1	CAN'T SLOW DOWN	Lionel Richie (Motown)
1	2	COLOUR BY NUMBERS	Culture Club (Virgin)
20	3	INFIDELS	Bob Dylan (CBS)
9	4	PIPES OF PEACE	Paul McCartney (Parlophone)
4	5	LABOUR OF LOVE	UB40 (DEP International)
5	6	GENESIS	Genesis (Charisma/Virgin)
3	7	SNAP!	Jam (Polydor)
14	8	AN INNOCENT MAN	Billy Joel (CBS)
-	9	UNDERCOVER	Rolling Stones (Rolling Stones)
8	10	NO PARLEZ	Paul Young (CBS)
12	11	TWO OF US	Various Artists (K-Tel)
13	12	THRILLER	Michael Jackson (Epic)
6	13	VOICE OF THE HEART	Carpenters (A&M)
10	14	ZIGGY STARDUST - THE MOTION PICTURE	David Bowie (RCA)
11	15	FANTASTIC	Wham! (Innervision)
44	16	THE ATLANTIC YEARS 1973-80	Roxy Music (EG)
16	17	TOO LATE FOR ZERO	Elton John (Rocket)
15	18	ROCK 'N' SOUL (PART 1)	Daryl Hall & John Oates (RCA)
30	19	WORKING WITH FIRE AND STEEL	China Crisis (Virgin)
-	20	HEARTS AND BONES	Paul Simon (Warner Bros.)
7	21	NORTH OF A MIRACLE	Nick Heyward (Arista)
-	22	STRIP	Adam Ant (CBS)
19	23	THE CROSSING	Big Country (Mercury)
21	24	ALIVE, SHE CRIED	Doors (Elektra)
-	25	STARFLEET PROJECT	Brian May (EMI)
-	26	SCANDALOUS	Imagination (Red Bus)
17	27	IN YOUR EYES	George Benson (WEA)
23	28	LET'S DANCE	David Bowie (EMI America)
26	29	SILVER	Cliff Richard (EMI)
24	30	IMAGINATIONS	Various Artists (CBS)
-	31	STAGES	Elaine Paige (K-Tel)
27	32	SOUL MINING	The The (Some Bizzare)
18	33	MONUMENT (LIVE)	Ultravox (Chrysalis)
22	34	HEAD OVER HEELS	Cocteau Twins (4AD)
39	35	MICHAEL JACKSON & THE JACKSONS' 18 GREATEST HITS	Michael Jackson & the Jacksons (Star)
-	36	THANK YOU FOR THE MUSIC	Abba (Epic)
42	37	SYNCHRONICITY	Police (A&M)
25	38	LOVE IS THE LAW	Toyah (Safari)
-	39	HAVE YOU EVER BEEN IN LOVE	Leo Sayer (Chrysalis)
-	40	THE ESSENTIAL JEAN MICHEL JARRE	Jean Michel Jarre (Polydor)
-	41	SNAKE CHARMER	Jah Wobble (Island)
43	42	STREET SOUNDS ELECTRO I	Various Artists (Street Sounds)
32	43	BORN TO LOVE	Peabo Bryson & Roberta Flack (Capitol)
35	44	DAVID GRANT	David Grant (Chrysalis)
-	45	DADA	Alice Cooper (Warner Bros.)
-	46	PLAY DIRTY	Girlschool (Bronze)
-	47	CHART HITS '83	Various Artists (K-Tel)
36	48	LOVE STORIES	Don Williams (K-Tel)
-	49	THE WILD HEART	Stevie Nicks (WEA)
28	50	HYPERBOREA	Tangerine Dream (Virgin)

26 November 1983

last	this	Title	Artist (Label)
2	1	COLOUR BY NUMBERS	Culture Club (Virgin)
1	2	CAN'T SLOW DOWN	Lionel Richie (Motown)
9	3	UNDERCOVER	Rolling Stones (Rolling Stones)
8	4	AN INNOCENT MAN	Billy Joel (CBS)
4	5	PIPES OF PEACE	Paul McCartney (Parlophone)
10	6	NO PARLEZ	Paul Young (CBS)
6	7	GENESIS	Genesis (Charisma/Virgin)
12	8	THRILLER	Michael Jackson (Epic)
5	9	LABOUR OF LOVE	UB40 (DEP International)
3	10	INFIDELS	Bob Dylan (CBS)
7	11	SNAP!	Jam (Polydor)
-	12	BEAUTY STAB	ABC (Neutron)
13	13	VOICE OF THE HEART	Carpenters (A&M)
22	14	STRIP	Adam Ant (CBS)
-	15	TOUCH	Eurythmics (RCA)
31	16	STAGES	Elaine Paige (K-Tel)
16	17	THE ATLANTIC YEARS 1973-80	Roxy Music (EG)
47	18	CHART HITS '83	Various Artists (K-Tel)
15	19	FANTASTIC	Wham! (Innervision)
14	20	ZIGGY STARDUST - THE MOTION PICTURE	David Bowie (RCA)
18	21	ROCK 'N' SOUL (PART 1)	Daryl Hall & John Oates (RCA)
11	22	TWO OF US	Various Artists (K-Tel)
27	23	IN YOUR EYES	George Benson (WEA)
17	24	TOO LATE FOR ZERO	Elton John (Rocket)
21	25	NORTH OF A MIRACLE	Nick Heyward (Arista)
39	26	HAVE YOU EVER BEEN IN LOVE	Leo Sayer (Chrysalis)
36	27	THANK YOU FOR THE MUSIC	Abba (Epic)
25	28	STARFLEET PROJECT	Brian May (EMI)
23	29	THE CROSSING	Big Country (Mercury)
-	30	FADE TO GREY	Visage (Polydor)
-	31	90125	Yes (Atco)
-	32	LIZZY LIFE	Thin Lizzy (Vertigo)
-	33	THE BOP WON'T STOP	Shakin' Stevens (Epic)
-	34	TRACK RECORD	Joan Armatrading (A&M)
-	35	ROOTS REGGAE 'N' REGGAE ROCK	Various Artists (Telstar)
37	36	SYNCHRONICITY	Police (A&M)
-	37	MARVIN GAYE'S GREATEST HITS	Marvin Gaye (Telstar)
-	38	HIT SQUAD - HITS OF '83	Various Artists (Ronco)
19	39	WORKING WITH FIRE AND STEEL	China Crisis (Virgin)
20	40	HEARTS AND BONES	Paul Simon (Warner Bros.)
28	41	LET'S DANCE	David Bowie (EMI America)
-	42	SMELL OF FEMALE	Cramps (Big Beat)
29	43	SILVER	Cliff Richard (EMI)
-	44	SUPERCHART '83	Various Artists (Telstar)
-	45	YENTL	Barbra Streisand (CBS)
34	46	HEAD OVER HEELS	Cocteau Twins (4AD)
-	47	CHAS AND DAVE'S KNEES UP - JAMBOREE BAG NO.2	Chas & Dave (Rockney)
30	48	IMAGINATIONS	Various Artists (CBS)
35	49	MICHAEL JACKSON & THE JACKSONS' 18 GREATEST HITS	Michael Jackson & the Jacksons (Star)
-	50	BAY OF KINGS	Steve Hackett (Lamborghini)

3 December 1983

last	this	Title	Artist (Label)
1	1	COLOUR BY NUMBERS	Culture Club (Virgin)
2	2	CAN'T SLOW DOWN	Lionel Richie (Motown)
3	3	UNDERCOVER	Rolling Stones (Rolling Stones)
15	4	TOUCH	Eurythmics (RCA)
4	5	AN INNOCENT MAN	Billy Joel (CBS)
12	6	BEAUTY STAB	ABC (Neutron)
6	7	NO PARLEZ	Paul Young (CBS)
-	8	SEVEN AND THE RAGGED TIGER	Duran Duran (EMI)
-	9	U2 LIVE: UNDER A BLOOD RED SKY	U2 (Island)
18	10	CHART HITS '83	Various Artists (K-Tel)
8	11	THRILLER	Michael Jackson (Epic)
5	12	PIPES OF PEACE	Paul McCartney (Parlophone)
7	13	GENESIS	Genesis (Charisma/Virgin)
31	14	90125	Yes (Atco)
19	15	FANTASTIC	Wham! (Innervision)
9	16	LABOUR OF LOVE	UB40 (DEP International)
33	17	THE BOP WON'T STOP	Shakin' Stevens (Epic)
16	18	STAGES	Elaine Paige (K-Tel)
-	19	BACK TO BACK	Status Quo (Vertigo)
11	20	SNAP!	Jam (Polydor)
13	21	VOICE OF THE HEART	Carpenters (A&M)
32	22	LIZZY LIFE	Thin Lizzy (Vertigo)
14	23	STRIP	Adam Ant (CBS)
23	24	IN YOUR EYES	George Benson (WEA)
10	25	INFIDELS	Bob Dylan (CBS)
38	26	HIT SQUAD - HITS OF '83	Various Artists (Ronco)
37	27	MARVIN GAYE'S GREATEST HITS	Marvin Gaye (Telstar)
-	28	NOCTURNE	Siouxsie and the Banshees (Wonderland)
21	29	ROCK 'N' SOUL (PART 1)	Daryl Hall & John Oates (RCA)
42	30	SMELL OF FEMALE	Cramps (Big Beat)
26	31	HAVE YOU EVER BEEN IN LOVE	Leo Sayer (Chrysalis)
27	32	THANK YOU FOR THE MUSIC	Abba (Epic)
24	33	TOO LATE FOR ZERO	Elton John (Rocket)
44	34	SUPERCHART '83	Various Artists (Telstar)
34	35	TRACK RECORD	Joan Armatrading (A&M)
22	36	TWO OF US	Various Artists (K-Tel)
20	37	ZIGGY STARDUST - THE MOTION PICTURE	David Bowie (RCA)
17	38	THE ATLANTIC YEARS 1973-80	Roxy Music (EG)
46	39	HEAD OVER HEELS	Cocteau Twins (4AD)
48	40	IMAGINATIONS	Various Artists (CBS)
39	41	WORKING WITH FIRE AND STEEL	China Crisis (Virgin)
45	42	YENTL	Barbra Streisand (CBS)
30	43	FADE TO GREY	Visage (Polydor)
28	44	STARFLEET PROJECT	Brian May (EMI)
29	45	THE CROSSING	Big Country (Mercury)
25	46	NORTH OF A MIRACLE	Nick Heyward (Arista)
-	47	WALK INTO LIGHT	Ian Anderson (Chrysalis)
-	48	ELIMINATOR	ZZ Top (WEA)
-	49	THESE ARE 2-TONE	Various Artists (2-Tone)
35	50	ROOTS REGGAE 'N' REGGAE ROCK	Various Artists (Telstar)

Lionel Richie's second solo album *Can't Slow Down* managed a one-week penetration of Culture Club's armour - compensation for Richie's titled-track single just failing to dislodge either Boy George & Co. or Billy Joel's *Uptown Girl* from atop the singles chart. Joel, meanwhile, aided by his new-found singles success, moved into contention with what would be his all-time best-selling UK album, *An Innocent Man*.

December 1983

10 December 1983

9	1	U2 LIVE: UNDER A BLOOD RED SKY	U2 (Island)
8	2	SEVEN AND THE RAGGED TIGER	Duran Duran (EMI)
1	3	COLOUR BY NUMBERS	Culture Club (Virgin)
2	4	CAN'T SLOW DOWN	Lionel Richie (Motown)
4	5	TOUCH	Eurythmics (RCA)
11	6	THRILLER	Michael Jackson (Epic)
19	7	BACK TO BACK	Status Quo (Vertigo)
7	8	NO PARLEZ	Paul Young (CBS)
3	9	UNDERCOVER	Rolling Stones (Rolling Stones)
5	10	AN INNOCENT MAN	Billy Joel (CBS)
18	11	STAGES	Elaine Paige (K-Tel)
13	12	GENESIS	Genesis (Charisma/Virgin)
28	13	NOCTURNE	Siouxsie and the Banshees (Wonderland)
10	14	CHART HITS '83	Various Artists (K-Tel)
15	15	FANTASTIC	Wham! (Innervision)
12	16	PIPES OF PEACE	Paul McCartney (Parlophone)
14	17	91502	Yes (Atco)
6	18	BEAUTY STAB	ABC (Neutron)
16	19	LABOUR OF LOVE	UB40 (DEP International)
-	20	BARK AT THE MOON	Ozzy Osbourne (Epic)
35	21	TRACK RECORD	Joan Armatrading (A&M)
20	22	SNAP!	Jam (Polydor)
29	23	ROCK 'N' SOUL (PART 1)	Daryl Hall & John Oates (RCA)
-	24	YOU BROKE MY HEART IN 17 PLACES	Tracey Ullman (Stiff)
32	25	THANK YOU FOR THE MUSIC	Abba (Epic)
22	26	LIZZY LIFE	Thin Lizzy (Vertigo)
27	27	MARVIN GAYE'S GREATEST HITS	Marvin Gaye (Telstar)
17	28	THE BOP WON'T STOP	Shakin' Stevens (Epic)
31	29	HAVE YOU EVER BEEN IN LOVE	Leo Sayer (Chrysalis)
42	30	YENTL	Barbra Streisand (CBS)
33	31	TOO LATE FOR ZERO	Elton John (Rocket)
-	32	CHAS AND DAVE'S KNEES UP - JAMBOREE BAG NO.2	Chas & Dave (Rockney)
25	33	INFIDELS	Bob Dylan (CBS)
30	34	SMELL OF FEMALE	Cramps (Big Beat)
26	35	HIT SQUAD - HITS OF '83	Various Artists (Ronco)
34	36	SUPERCHART '83	Various Artists (Telstar)
-	37	BUCKS FIZZ - GREATEST HITS	Bucks Fizz (RCA)
21	38	VOICE OF THE HEART	Carpenters (A&M)
39	39	HEAD OVER HEELS	Cocteau Twins (4AD)
36	40	TWO OF US	Various Artists (K-Tel)
44	41	STARFLEET PROJECT	Brian May (EMI)
37	42	ZIGGY STARDUST - THE MOTION PICTURE	David Bowie (RCA)
48	43	ELIMINATOR	ZZ Top (WEA)
41	44	WORKING WITH FIRE AND STEEL	China Crisis (Virgin)
-	45	FIRE AND WATER	Dave Greenfield & Jean-Jaques Burnel (Epic)
24	46	IN YOUR EYES	George Benson (WEA)
-	47	FORMULA 30	Various Artists (Decca)
23	48	STRIP	Adam Ant (CBS)
38	49	THE ATLANTIC YEARS 1973-80	Roxy Music (EG)
43	50	FADE TO GREY	Visage (Polydor)

17 December 1983

6	1	THRILLER	Michael Jackson (Epic)
1	2	U2 LIVE: UNDER A BLOOD RED SKY	U2 (Island)
3	3	COLOUR BY NUMBERS	Culture Club (Virgin)
2	4	SEVEN AND THE RAGGED TIGER	Duran Duran (EMI)
8	5	NO PARLEZ	Paul Young (CBS)
4	6	CAN'T SLOW DOWN	Lionel Richie (Motown)
11	7	STAGES	Elaine Paige (K-Tel)
5	8	TOUCH	Eurythmics (RCA)
-	9	NOW THAT'S WHAT I CALL MUSIC	Various Artists (EMI/Virgin)
10	10	AN INNOCENT MAN	Billy Joel (CBS)
12	11	GENESIS	Genesis (Charisma/Virgin)
15	12	FANTASTIC	Wham! (Innervision)
20	13	BARK AT THE MOON	Ozzy Osbourne (Epic)
7	14	BACK TO BACK	Status Quo (Vertigo)
9	15	UNDERCOVER	Rolling Stones (Rolling Stones)
14	16	CHART HITS '83	Various Artists (K-Tel)
16	17	PIPES OF PEACE	Paul McCartney (Parlophone)
19	18	LABOUR OF LOVE	UB40 (DEP International)
13	19	NOCTURNE	Siouxsie and the Banshees (Wonderland)
21	20	TRACK RECORD	Joan Armatrading (A&M)
23	21	ROCK 'N' SOUL (PART 1)	Daryl Hall & John Oates (RCA)
32	22	CHAS AND DAVE'S KNEES UP - JAMBOREE BAG NO.2	Chas & Dave (Rockney)
-	23	ALL WRAPPED UP	Undertones (Ardeck)
27	24	MARVIN GAYE'S GREATEST HITS	Marvin Gaye (Telstar)
24	25	YOU BROKE MY HEART IN 17 PLACES	Tracey Ullman (Stiff)
25	26	THANK YOU FOR THE MUSIC	Abba (Epic)
28	27	THE BOP WON'T STOP	Shakin' Stevens (Epic)
22	28	SNAP!	Jam (Polydor)
17	29	91502	Yes (Atco)
29	30	HAVE YOU EVER BEEN IN LOVE	Leo Sayer (Chrysalis)
47	31	FORMULA 30	Various Artists (Decca)
38	32	VOICE OF THE HEART	Carpenters (A&M)
43	33	ELIMINATOR	ZZ Top (WEA)
33	34	INFIDELS	Bob Dylan (CBS)
31	35	TOO LATE FOR ZERO	Elton John (Rocket)
-	36	SILVER	Cliff Richard (EMI)
-	37	PHIL SPECTOR'S GREATEST HITS	Various Artists (Impression)
-	38	STREET SOUNDS EDITION 7	Various Artists (Street Sounds)
-	39	LIVE AND DIRECT	Aswad (Island)
-	40	THESE ARE 2-TONE	Various Artists (2-Tone)
18	41	BEAUTY STAB	ABC (Neutron)
-	42	OOH WALLAH WALLAH	King Kurt (Stiff)
49	43	THE ATLANTIC YEARS 1973-80	Roxy Music (EG)
-	44	LIFE'S A RIOT WITH SPY VS SPY	Billy Bragg (Go! Discs)
46	45	IN YOUR EYES	George Benson (WEA)
30	46	YENTL	Barbra Streisand (CBS)
48	47	STRIP	Adam Ant (CBS)
40	48	TWO OF US	Various Artists (K-Tel)
26	49	LIZZY LIFE	Thin Lizzy (Vertigo)
34	50	SMELL OF FEMALE	Cramps (Big Beat)

24 December 1983

1	1	THRILLER	Michael Jackson (Epic)
3	2	COLOUR BY NUMBERS	Culture Club (Virgin)
5	3	NO PARLEZ	Paul Young (CBS)
9	4	NOW THAT'S WHAT I CALL MUSIC	Various Artists (EMI/Virgin)
2	5	U2 LIVE: UNDER A BLOOD RED SKY	U2 (Island)
7	6	STAGES	Elaine Paige (K-Tel)
4	7	SEVEN AND THE RAGGED TIGER	Duran Duran (EMI)
6	8	CAN'T SLOW DOWN	Lionel Richie (Motown)
12	9	FANTASTIC	Wham! (Innervision)
11	10	GENESIS	Genesis (Charisma/Virgin)
10	11	AN INNOCENT MAN	Billy Joel (CBS)
8	12	TOUCH	Eurythmics (RCA)
31	13	FORMULA 30	Various Artists (Decca)
18	14	LABOUR OF LOVE	UB40 (DEP International)
22	15	CHAS AND DAVE'S KNEES UP - JAMBOREE BAG NO.2	Chas & Dave (Rockney)
14	16	BACK TO BACK	Status Quo (Vertigo)
20	17	TRACK RECORD	Joan Armatrading (A&M)
16	18	CHART HITS '83	Various Artists (K-Tel)
24	19	MARVIN GAYE'S GREATEST HITS	Marvin Gaye (Telstar)
25	20	YOU BROKE MY HEART IN 17 PLACES	Tracey Ullman (Stiff)
37	21	PHIL SPECTOR'S GREATEST HITS	Various Artists (Impression)
13	22	BARK AT THE MOON	Ozzy Osbourne (Epic)
17	23	PIPES OF PEACE	Paul McCartney (Parlophone)
15	24	UNDERCOVER	Rolling Stones (Rolling Stones)
32	25	VOICE OF THE HEART	Carpenters (A&M)
-	26	THE ESSENTIAL JEAN MICHEL JARRE	Jean Michel Jarre (Polydor)
21	27	ROCK 'N' SOUL (PART 1)	Daryl Hall & John Oates (RCA)
30	28	HAVE YOU EVER BEEN IN LOVE	Leo Sayer (Chrysalis)
-	29	MICHAEL JACKSON & THE JACKSONS' 18 GREATEST HITS	Michael Jackson & the Jacksons (Star)
29	30	91502	Yes (Atco)
-	31	GREEN VELVET	Various Artists (Ronco)
-	32	JAPANESE WHISPERS	Cure (Fiction)
34	33	INFIDELS	Bob Dylan (CBS)
38	34	STREET SOUNDS EDITION 7	Various Artists (Street Sounds)
28	35	SNAP!	Jam (Polydor)
27	36	THE BOP WON'T STOP	Shakin' Stevens (Epic)
36	37	SILVER	Cliff Richard (EMI)
19	38	NOCTURNE	Siouxsie and the Banshees (Wonderland)
33	39	ELIMINATOR	ZZ Top (WEA)
39	40	LIVE AND DIRECT	Aswad (Island)
41	41	BEAUTY STAB	ABC (Neutron)
26	42	THANK YOU FOR THE MUSIC	Abba (Epic)
-	43	LOVE STORIES	Don Williams (K-Tel)
-	44	IMAGINATIONS	Various Artists (CBS)
35	45	TOO LATE FOR ZERO	Elton John (Rocket)
45	46	IN YOUR EYES	George Benson (WEA)
-	47	LIVE AT THE ALBANY	Flying Pickets (AVM)
23	48	ALL WRAPPED UP	Undertones (Ardeck)
-	49	PERVERTED BY LANGUAGE	Fall (Rough Trade)
-	50	THE VERY BEST OF NEIL DIAMOND	Neil Diamond (K-Tel)

U2's *Under A Blood Red Sky* was the band's first chart-topper, bettering *War*'s peak of Number 3 earlier in the year. It was also their first live album, recorded at 1983 tour gigs in the US and Germany.

The joint EMI/Virgin various artists compilation *Now That's What I Call Music* was the opener in what would be the best-selling UK compilation series of all time, with some volumes topping a million sales.

last week	this week	7 January 1984	
3	1	NO PARLEZ	Paul Young (CBS)
4	2	NOW THAT'S WHAT I CALL MUSIC	Various Artists (EMI/Virgin)
1	3	THRILLER	Michael Jackson (Epic)
2	4	COLOUR BY NUMBERS	Culture Club (Virgin)
6	5	STAGES	Elaine Paige (K-Tel)
8	6	CAN'T SLOW DOWN	Lionel Richie (Motown)
10	7	GENESIS	Genesis (Charisma)
26	8	THE ESSENTIAL JEAN MICHEL JARRE	Jean Michel Jarre (Polydor)
5	9	U2 LIVE: UNDER A BLOOD RED SKY	U2 (Island)
13	10	FORMULA 30	Various Artists (Decca)
7	11	SEVEN AND THE RAGGED TIGER	Duran Duran (EMI)
14	12	LABOUR OF LOVE	UB40 (DEP International)
9	13	FANTASTIC	Wham! (Innervision)
12	14	TOUCH	Eurythmics (RCA)
11	15	AN INNOCENT MAN	Billy Joel (CBS)
20	16	YOU BROKE MY HEART IN 17 PLACES	Tracey Ullman (Stiff)
23	17	PIPES OF PEACE	Paul McCartney (Parlophone)
-	18	PORTRAIT	Diana Ross (Telstar)
19	19	MARVIN GAYE'S GREATEST HITS	Marvin Gaye (Telstar)
31	20	GREEN VELVET	Various Artists (Ronco)
21	21	PHIL SPECTOR'S GREATEST HITS	Various Artists (Impression)
16	22	BACK TO BACK	Status Quo (Vertigo)
18	23	CHART HITS '83	Various Artists (K-Tel)
15	24	CHAS AND DAVE'S KNEES UP - JAMBOREE BAG NO.2	Chas & Dave (Rockney)
17	25	TRACK RECORD	Joan Armatrading (A&M)
29	26	MICHAEL JACKSON & THE JACKSON FIVE'S 18 GREATEST HITS	Michael Jackson & the Jackson Five (Star)
35	27	SNAP!	Jam (Polydor)
27	28	ROCK 'N' SOUL (PART 1)	Daryl Hall & John Oates (RCA)
24	29	UNDERCOVER	Rolling Stones (Rolling Stones)
47	30	LIVE AT THE ALBANY EMPIRE	Flying Pickets (AVM)
50	31	THE VERY BEST OF NEIL DIAMOND	Neil Diamond (K-Tel)
28	32	HAVE YOU EVER BEEN IN LOVE	Leo Sayer (Chrysalis)
33	33	INFIDELS	Bob Dylan (CBS)
37	34	SILVER	Cliff Richard (EMI)
25	35	VOICE OF THE HEART	Carpenters (A&M)
39	36	ELIMINATOR	ZZ Top (WEA)
-	37	ZIGGY STARDUST – THE MOTION PICTURE	David Bowie (RCA)
22	38	BARK AT THE MOON	Ozzy Osbourne (Epic)
32	39	JAPANESE WHISPERS	Cure (Fiction)
40	40	LIVE AND DIRECT	Aswad (Island)
44	41	IMAGINATIONS	Various Artists (CBS)
45	42	TOO LOW FOR ZERO	Elton John (Rocket)
-	43	HIT SQUAD – HITS OF '83	Various (Ronco)
-	44	OUT DEH	Gregory Isaacs (Island)
30	45	90125	Yes (Atco)
46	46	IN YOUR EYES	George Benson (WEA)
-	47	THE MUSIC OF RICHARD CLAYDERMAN	Richard Clayderman (Decca/Delphine)
34	48	STREETSOUNDS EDITION 7	Various Artists (Street Sounds)
36	49	THE BOP WON'T STOP	Shakin' Stevens (Epic)
-	50	CLASSIC TRANQUILITY	Phil Coulter (K-Tel)

last week	this week	14 January 1984	
3	1	THRILLER	Michael Jackson (Epic)
1	2	NO PARLEZ	Paul Young (CBS)
2	3	NOW THAT'S WHAT I CALL MUSIC	Various Artists (EMI/Virgin)
4	4	COLOUR BY NUMBERS	Culture Club (Virgin)
6	5	CAN'T SLOW DOWN	Lionel Richie (Motown)
5	6	STAGES	Elaine Paige (K-Tel)
17	7	PIPES OF PEACE	Paul McCartney (Parlophone)
15	8	AN INNOCENT MAN	Billy Joel (CBS)
8	9	THE ESSENTIAL JEAN MICHEL JARRE	Jean Michel Jarre (Polydor)
10	10	FORMULA 30	Various Artists (Decca/delphine)
12	11	LABOUR OF LOVE	UB40 (DEP International)
9	12	U2 LIVE: UNDER A BLOOD RED SKY	U2 (Island)
7	12	GENESIS	Genesis (Charisma)
13	14	FANTASTIC	Wham! (Innervision)
20	15	GREEN VELVET	Various Artists (Ronco)
18	16	PORTRAIT	Diana Ross (Telstar)
14	17	TOUCH	Eurythmics (RCA)
11	18	SEVEN AND THE RAGGED TIGER	Duran Duran (EMI)
25	19	TRACK RECORD	Joan Armatrading (A&M)
26	20	MICHAEL JACKSON & THE JACKSON FIVE'S 18 GREATEST HITS	Michael Jackson & the Jackson Five (Star)
19	21	MARVIN GAYE'S GREATEST HITS	Marvin Gaye (Telstar)
24	22	CHAS AND DAVE'S KNEES UP - JAMBOREE BAG NO.2	Chas & Dave (Rockney)
22	23	BACK TO BACK	Status Quo (Vertigo)
39	24	JAPANESE WHISPERS	Cure (Fiction)
16	25	YOU BROKE MY HEART IN 17 PLACES	Tracey Ullman (Stiff)
42	26	TOO LOW FOR ZERO	Elton John (Rocket)
-	27	STREET SOUNDS ELECTRO 2	Various Artists (Street Sounds)
36	28	ELIMINATOR	ZZ Top (WEA)
46	29	IN YOUR EYES	George Benson (WEA)
-	30	CHART TREK VOLUME 1 & 2	Various Artists (Ronco)
28	31	ROCK 'N' SOUL (PART 1)	Daryl Hall & John Oates (RCA)
27	32	SNAP!	Jam (Polydor)
-	33	HEAD OVER HEELS	Cocteau Twins (4AD)
-	34	IN THE HEART	Kool & the Gang (De-Lite)
29	35	UNDERCOVER	Rolling Stones (Rolling Stones)
21	36	PHIL SPECTOR'S GREATEST HITS	Various Artists (Impression)
-	37	YENTL	Barbra Streisand (CBS)
34	38	SILVER	Cliff Richard (EMI)
48	39	STREETSOUNDS EDITION 7	Various Artists (Street Sounds)
-	40	NOCTURNE	Siouxsie & the Banshees (Wonderland)
40	41	LIVE AND DIRECT	Aswad (Island)
23	42	CHART HITS '83	Various Artists (K-Tel)
-	43	QUICK STEP AND SIDE KICK	Thompson Twins (Arista)
30	44	LIVE AT ALBANY EMPIRE	Flying Pickets (AVM)
45	45	90125	Yes (Atco)
-	46	BUCKS FIZZ - GREATEST HITS	Bucks Fizz (RCA)
49	47	THE BOP WON'T STOP	Shakin' Stevens (Epic)
-	48	THE LUXURY GAP	Heaven 17 (BEF/Virgin)
-	49	CADMIUM	Sky (Ariola)
33	50	INFIDELS	Bob Dylan (CBS)

last week	this week	21 January 1984	
1	1	THRILLER	Michael Jackson (Epic)
2	2	NO PARLEZ	Paul Young (CBS)
4	3	COLOUR BY NUMBERS	Culture Club (Virgin)
3	4	NOW THAT'S WHAT I CALL MUSIC	Various Artists (EMI/Virgin)
12	5	U2 LIVE: UNDER A BLOOD RED SKY	U2 (Island)
7	6	PIPES OF PEACE	Paul McCartney (Parlophone)
8	7	AN INNOCENT MAN	Billy Joel (CBS)
11	8	LABOUR OF LOVE	UB40 (DEP International)
5	9	CAN'T SLOW DOWN	Lionel Richie (Motown)
17	10	TOUCH	Eurythmics (RCA)
16	11	PORTRAIT	Diana Ross (Telstar)
12	12	GENESIS	Genesis (Charisma)
13	13	LEARNING TO CRAWL	Pretenders (WEA)
24	14	JAPANESE WHISPERS	Cure (Fiction)
9	15	THE ESSENTIAL JEAN MICHEL JARRE	Jean Michel Jarre (Polydor)
23	16	BACK TO BACK	Status Quo (Vertigo)
18	17	SEVEN AND THE RAGGED TIGER	Duran Duran (EMI)
25	18	YOU BROKE MY HEART IN 17 PLACES	Tracey Ullman (Stiff)
6	19	STAGES	Elaine Paige (K-Tel)
14	20	FANTASTIC	Wham! (Innervision)
10	21	FORMULA 30	Various Artists (Decca/delphine)
19	22	TRACK RECORD	Joan Armatrading (A&M)
26	23	TOO LOW FOR ZERO	Elton John (Rocket)
15	24	GREEN VELVET	Various Artists (Ronco)
21	25	MARVIN GAYE'S GREATEST HITS	Marvin Gaye (Telstar)
28	26	ELIMINATOR	ZZ Top (WEA)
41	27	LIVE AND DIRECT	Aswad (Island)
30	28	CHART TREK VOL 1 & 2	Various Artists (Ronco)
-	29	WORKING WITH FIRE AND STEEL	China Crisis (Virgin)
32	30	SNAP!	Jam (Polydor)
27	31	STREET SOUNDS ELECTRO 2	Various Artists (Street Sounds)
-	32	THE CROSSING	Big Country (Mercury)
-	33	SYNCHRONICITY	Police (A&M)
31	34	ROCK 'N' SOUL (PART 1)	Daryl Hall & John Oates (RCA)
33	35	HEAD OVER HEELS	Cocteau Twins (4AD)
-	36	BUSY BODY	Luther Vandross (Epic)
20	37	MICHAEL JACKSON & THE JACKSON FIVE'S 18 GREATEST HITS	Michael Jackson & the Jackson Five (Star)
-	38	LIFE'S A RIOT WITH SPY VS SPY	Billy Bragg (Go! Discs)
43	39	QUICK STEP AND SIDE KICK	Thompson Twins (Arista)
35	40	UNDERCOVER	Rolling Stones (Rolling Stones)
39	41	STREETSOUNDS 7	Various (Street Sounds)
34	42	IN THE HEART	Kool & the Gang (De-Lite)
29	43	IN YOUR EYES	George Benson (WEA)
-	44	LET'S DANCE	David Bowie (EMI)
22	45	CHAS AND DAVE'S KNEES UP - JAMBOREE BAG NO.2	Chas & Dave (Rockney)
-	46	OUT DEH	Gregory Isaacs (Island)
-	47	PERVERTED BY LANGUAGE	Fall (Rough Trade)
-	48	WAR	U2 (Island)
-	49	HIGH LAND HARD RAIN	Aztec Camera (Rough Trade)
-	50	TRUE	Spandau Ballet (Chrysalis)

Paul McCartney's *Pipes Of Peace* album, after a comparatively modest start, established itself as a firm Top 10 seller on the back of its namesake single's elevation to Number 1. The arrival of Diana Ross' *Portrait* compilation on Telstar, meanwhile, provided another addition to the ranks of Motown hits packages licensed by TV-marketing labels. Marvin Gaye and the Jacksons were already similarly charted.

January – February 1984

28 January 1984

last	this	Album	Artist (Label)
1	1	THRILLER	Michael Jackson (Epic)
2	2	NO PARLEZ	Paul Young (CBS)
6	3	PIPES OF PEACE	Paul McCartney (Parlophone)
13	4	LEARNING TO CRAWL	Pretenders (WEA)
5	5	U2 LIVE: UNDER A BLOOD RED SKY	U2 (Island)
9	6	CAN'T SLOW DOWN	Lionel Richie (Motown)
7	7	AN INNOCENT MAN	Billy Joel (CBS)
4	8	NOW THAT'S WHAT I CALL MUSIC	Various Artists (EMI/Virgin)
10	9	TOUCH	Eurythmics (RCA)
3	10	COLOUR BY NUMBERS	Culture Club (Virgin)
8	11	LABOUR OF LOVE	UB40 (DEP International)
11	12	PORTRAIT	Diana Ross (Telstar)
12	13	GENESIS	Genesis (Charisma)
14	14	JAPANESE WHISPERS	Cure (Fiction)
16	15	BACK TO BACK	Status Quo (Vertigo)
38	16	LIFE'S A RIOT WITH SPY VS SPY	Billy Bragg (Go! Discs)
33	17	SYNCHRONICITY	Police (A&M)
19	18	STAGES	Elaine Paige (K-Tel)
18	19	YOU BROKE MY HEART IN 17 PLACES	Tracey Ullman (Stiff)
23	20	TOO LOW FOR ZERO	Elton John (Rocket)
15	21	THE ESSENTIAL JEAN MICHEL JARRE	Jean Michel Jarre (Polydor)
24	22	GREEN VELVET	Various Artists (Ronco)
32	23	THE CROSSING	Big Country (Mercury)
21	24	FORMULA 30	Various Artists (Decca/delphine)
31	25	STREET SOUNDS ELECTRO 2	Various Artists (Street Sounds)
-	26	DEFENDERS OF THE FAITH	Judas Priest (CBS)
29	27	WORKING WITH FIRE AND STEEL	China Crisis (Virgin)
17	28	SEVEN AND THE RAGGED TIGER	Duran Duran (EMI)
26	29	ELIMINATOR	ZZ Top (WEA)
36	30	BUSY BODY	Luther Vandross (Epic)
27	31	LIVE AND DIRECT	Aswad (Island)
35	32	HEAD OVER HEELS	Cocteau Twins (4AD)
-	33	SOMETIMES WHEN WE TOUCH	Various (Ronco)
20	34	FANTASTIC	Wham! (Innervision)
22	35	TRACK RECORD	Joan Armatrading (A&M)
39	36	QUICK STEP AND SIDE KICK	Thompson Twins (Arista)
-	37	1984	Van Halen (WEA)
40	38	UNDERCOVER	Rolling Stones (Rolling Stones)
34	39	ROCK 'N' SOUL (PART 1)	Daryl Hall & John Oates (RCA)
48	40	WAR	U2 (Island)
49	41	HIGH LAND HARD RAIN	Aztec Camera (Rough Trade)
-	42	WHAT'S NEW?	Linda Ronstadt (Asylum)
28	43	CHART TREK VOLUME 1 & 2	Various (Ronco)
46	44	OUT DEH	Gregory Isaacs (Island)
37	45	MICHAEL JACKSON & THE JACKSON FIVE'S 18 GREATEST HITS	Michael Jackson & the Jackson Five (Star)
47	46	PERVERTED BY LANGUAGE	Fall (Rough Trade)
-	47	BALLS TO THE WALL	Accept (Lark)
25	48	MARVIN GAYE'S GREATEST HITS	Marvin Gaye (Telstar)
43	49	IN YOUR EYES	George Benson (WEA)
42	50	IN THE HEART	Kool & the Gang (De-Lite)

4 February 1984

last	this	Album	Artist (Label)
1	1	THRILLER	Michael Jackson (Epic)
3	2	PIPES OF PEACE	Paul McCartney (Parlophone)
4	3	LEARNING TO CRAWL	Pretenders (WEA)
5	4	U2 LIVE: UNDER A BLOOD RED SKY	U2 (Island)
7	5	AN INNOCENT MAN	Billy Joel (CBS)
-	6	MILK AND HONEY	John Lennon & Yoko Ono (Polydor)
6	7	CAN'T SLOW DOWN	Lionel Richie (Motown)
8	8	NO PARLEZ	Paul Young (CBS)
9	9	NOW THAT'S WHAT I CALL MUSIC	Various Artists (EMI/Virgin)
9	10	TOUCH	Eurythmics (RCA)
10	11	COLOUR BY NUMBERS	Culture Club (Virgin)
12	12	PORTRAIT	Diana Ross (Telstar)
23	13	THE CROSSING	Big Country (Mercury)
11	14	LABOUR OF LOVE	UB40 (DEP International)
26	15	DEFENDERS OF THE FAITH	Judas Priest (CBS)
16	16	LIFE'S A RIOT WITH SPY VS SPY	Billy Bragg (Go! Discs)
27	17	WORKING WITH FIRE AND STEEL	China Crisis (Virgin)
15	18	BACK TO BACK	Status Quo (Vertigo)
14	19	JAPANESE WHISPERS	Cure (Fiction)
37	20	1984	Van Halen (WEA)
13	21	GENESIS	Genesis (Charisma)
17	22	SYNCHRONICITY	Police (A&M)
18	23	STAGES	Elaine Paige (K-Tel)
33	24	SOMETIMES WHEN WE TOUCH	Various (Ronco)
42	25	WHAT'S NEW?	Linda Ronstadt (Asylum)
36	26	QUICK STEP AND SIDE KICK	Thompson Twins (Arista)
21	27	THE ESSENTIAL JEAN MICHEL JARRE	Jean Michel Jarre (Polydor)
32	28	HEAD OVER HEELS	Cocteau Twins (4AD)
30	29	BUSY BODY	Luther Vandross (Epic)
28	30	SEVEN AND THE RAGGED TIGER	Duran Duran (EMI)
31	31	LIVE AND DIRECT	Aswad (Island)
19	32	YOU BROKE MY HEART IN 17 PLACES	Tracey Ullman (Stiff)
20	33	TOO LOW FOR ZERO	Elton John (Rocket)
35	34	TRACK RECORD	Joan Armatrading (A&M)
34	35	FANTASTIC	Wham! (Innervision)
39	36	ROCK 'N' SOUL (PART 1)	Daryl Hall & John Oates (RCA)
25	37	STREET SOUNDS ELECTRO 2	Various Artists (Street Sounds)
22	38	GREEN VELVET	Various Artists (Ronco)
40	39	WAR	U2 (Island)
49	40	IN YOUR EYES	George Benson (WEA)
-	41	BEAUTY STAB	ABC (Neutron)
45	42	MICHAEL JACKSON & THE JACKSON FIVE'S 18 GREATEST HITS	Michael Jackson & the Jackson Five (Star)
-	43	NEW GOLD DREAM	Simple Minds (Virgin)
44	44	LET'S DANCE	David Bowie (EMIAmerica)
50	45	IN THE HEART	Kool & the Gang (De-Lite)
-	46	THE MUSIC OF RICHARD CLAYDERMAN	Richard Clayderman (Decca/delphine)
-	47	THE BOP WON'T STOP	Shakin' Stevens (Epic)
44	48	OUT DEH	Gregory Isaacs (Island)
24	49	FORMULA 30	Various Artists (Decca/delphine)
38	50	UNDERCOVER	Rolling Stones (Rolling Stones)

11 February 1984

last	this	Album	Artist (Label)
6	1	MILK AND HONEY	John Lennon & Yoko Ono (Polydor)
10	2	TOUCH	Eurythmics (RCA)
1	3	THRILLER	Michael Jackson (Epic)
8	4	NO PARLEZ	Paul Young (CBS)
5	5	AN INNOCENT MAN	Billy Joel (CBS)
7	6	CAN'T SLOW DOWN	Lionel Richie (Motown)
3	7	LEARNING TO CRAWL	Pretenders (WEA)
4	8	U2 LIVE: UNDER A BLOOD RED SKY	U2 (Island)
2	9	PIPES OF PEACE	Paul McCartney (Parlophone)
20	10	1984	Van Halen (WEA)
13	11	THE CROSSING	Big Country (Mercury)
-	12	SLIDE IT IN	Whitesnake (Liberty)
9	13	NOW THAT'S WHAT I CALL MUSIC	Various Artists (EMI/Virgin)
12	14	PORTRAIT	Diana Ross (Telstar)
11	15	COLOUR BY NUMBERS	Culture Club (Virgin)
16	16	LIFE'S A RIOT WITH SPY VS SPY	Billy Bragg (Go! Discs)
17	17	WORKING WITH FIRE AND STEEL	China Crisis (Virgin)
14	18	LABOUR OF LOVE	UB40 (DEP International)
26	19	QUICK STEP AND SIDE KICK	Thompson Twins (Arista)
15	20	DEFENDERS OF THE FAITH	Judas Priest (CBS)
21	21	GENESIS	Genesis (Charisma)
-	22	HEAVEN IS WAITING	Danse Society (Arista)
35	23	FANTASTIC	Wham! (Innervision)
19	24	JAPANESE WHISPERS	Cure (Fiction)
22	25	SYNCHRONICITY	Police (A&M)
-	26	CRUSADER	Saxon (Carrerre)
29	27	BUSY BODY	Luther Vandross (Epic)
23	28	STAGES	Elaine Paige (K-Tel)
31	29	LIVE AND DIRECT	Aswad (Island)
28	30	HEAD OVER HEELS	Cocteau Twins (4AD)
18	31	BACK TO BACK	Status Quo (Vertigo)
37	32	STREET SOUNDS ELECTRO 2	Various Artists (Street Sounds)
24	33	SOMETIMES WHEN WE TOUCH	Various (Ronco)
27	34	THE ESSENTIAL JEAN MICHEL JARRE	Jean Michel Jarre (Polydor)
-	35	WHITE FLAME	Snowy White (Towerbell)
30	36	SEVEN AND THE RAGGED TIGER	Duran Duran (EMI)
-	37	4,000 WEEKS HOLIDAY	Ian Dury (Polydor)
32	38	YOU BROKE MY HEART IN 17 PLACES	Tracey Ullman (Stiff)
39	39	WAR	U2 (Island)
33	40	TOO LOW FOR ZERO	Elton John (Rocket)
-	41	ELIMINATOR	ZZ Top (WEA)
40	42	IN YOUR EYES	George Benson (WEA)
-	43	AUF WIEDERSEHEN PET - TV SOUNDTRACK	Various Artists (Towerbell)
-	44	THE COLLECTION - 20 GREATEST HITS	Gladys Knight & The Pips (Star Blend)
-	45	MARVIN GAYE'S GREATEST HITS	Marvin Gaye (Telstar)
45	46	IN THE HEART	Kool & the Gang (De-Lite)
25	47	WHAT'S NEW?	Linda Ronstadt (Asylum)
48	48	HIGH LAND HARD RAIN	Aztec Camera (Rough Trade)
48	49	OUT DEH	Gregory Isaacs (Island)
34	50	TRACK RECORD	Joan Armatrading (A&M)

John and Yoko's *Milk And Honey* set, released more than three years after Lennon's death, was a selection from the material the pair had been working on during 1980, the initial pick of which had been used in their *Double Fantasy* album. Lennon also had a simultaneous posthumous Number 2 hit single with *Nobody Told Me*, taken from the album. Van Halen had the most obviously topical LP title of the year yet.

February – March 1984

18 February 1984

last week	this week		
2	1	TOUCH	Eurythmics (RCA)
3	2	THRILLER	Michael Jackson (Epic)
1	3	MILK AND HONEY	John Lennon & Yoko Ono (Polydor)
12	4	SLIDE IT IN	Whitesnake (Liberty)
6	5	CAN'T SLOW DOWN	Lionel Richie (Motown)
8	6	U2 LIVE: UNDER A BLOOD RED SKY	U2 (Island)
4	7	NO PARLEZ	Paul Young (CBS)
5	8	AN INNOCENT MAN	Billy Joel (CBS)
-	9	SPARKLE IN THE RAIN	Simple Minds (Virgin)
11	10	THE CROSSING	Big Country (Mercury)
7	11	LEARNING TO CRAWL	Pretenders (WEA)
10	12	1984	Van Halen (WEA)
15	13	COLOUR BY NUMBERS	Culture Club (Virgin)
9	14	PIPES OF PEACE	Paul McCartney (Parlophone)
18	15	LABOUR OF LOVE	UB40 (DEP International)
14	16	PORTRAIT	Diana Ross (Telstar)
13	17	NOW THAT'S WHAT I CALL MUSIC	Various Artists (EMI/Virgin)
26	18	CRUSADER	Saxon (Carrere)
21	19	GENESIS	Genesis (Charisma)
19	20	QUICK STEP AND SIDE KICK	Thompson Twins (Arista)
-	21	THE FLAT EARTH	Thomas Dolby (Parlophone)
22	22	HEAVEN IS WAITING	Danse Society (Arista)
-	23	VICTIMS OF THE FUTURE	Gary Moore (Virgin)
16	24	LIFE'S A RIOT WITH SPY VS SPY	Billy Bragg (Go! Discs)
36	25	SEVEN AND THE RAGGED TIGER	Duran Duran (EMI)
17	26	WORKING WITH FIRE AND STEEL	China Crisis (Virgin)
33	27	SOMETIMES WHEN WE TOUCH	Various (Ronco)
28	28	STAGES	Elaine Paige (K-Tel)
35	29	WHITE FLAME	Snowy White (Towerbell)
31	30	BACK TO BACK	Status Quo (Vertigo)
24	31	JAPANESE WHISPERS	Cure (Fiction)
25	32	SYNCHRONICITY	Police (A&M)
27	33	BUSY BODY	Luther Vandross (Epic)
-	34	YENTL	Barbra Streisand (CBS)
20	35	DEFENDERS OF THE FAITH	Judas Priest (CBS)
40	36	TOO LOW FOR ZERO	Elton John (Rocket)
-	37	THE VERY BEST OF MOTOWN LOVE SONGS	Various Artists (Telstar)
30	38	HEAD OVER HEELS	Cocteau Twins (4AD)
-	39	CHRISTINE McVIE	Christine McVie (Warner Bros.)
50	40	TRACK RECORD	Joan Armatrading (A&M)
-	41	BEAUTY STAB	ABC (Neutron)
34	42	THE ESSENTIAL JEAN MICHEL JARRE	Jean Michel Jarre (Polydor)
23	43	FANTASTIC	Wham! (Innervision)
-	44	ROCK 'N' SOUL (PART 1)	Daryl Hall & John Oates (RCA)
38	45	YOU BROKE MY HEART IN 17 PLACES	Tracey Ullman (Stiff)
-	46	LIVING IN OZ	Rick Springfield (RCA)
44	47	THE COLLECTION - 20 GREATEST HITS	Gladys Knight & The Pips (Star Blend)
-	48	LET'S DANCE	David Bowie (EMI America)
29	49	LIVE AND DIRECT	Aswad (Island)
32	50	STREET SOUNDS ELECTRO 2	Various Artists (Street Sounds)

25 February 1984

last week	this week		
9	1	SPARKLE IN THE RAIN	Simple Minds (Virgin)
2	2	THRILLER	Michael Jackson (Epic)
1	3	TOUCH	Eurythmics (RCA)
-	4	INTO THE GAP	Thompson Twins (Arista)
8	5	AN INNOCENT MAN	Billy Joel (CBS)
21	6	THE FLAT EARTH	Thomas Dolby (Parlophone)
5	7	CAN'T SLOW DOWN	Lionel Richie (Motown)
10	8	THE CROSSING	Big Country (Mercury)
6	9	U2 LIVE: UNDER A BLOOD RED SKY	U2 (Island)
7	10	NO PARLEZ	Paul Young (CBS)
23	11	VICTIMS OF THE FUTURE	Gary Moore (Virgin)
4	12	SLIDE IT IN	Whitesnake (Liberty)
3	13	MILK AND HONEY	John Lennon & Yoko Ono (Polydor)
12	14	1984	Van Halen (WEA)
18	15	CRUSADER	Saxon (Carrere)
16	16	LEARNING TO CRAWL	Pretenders (WEA)
14	17	PIPES OF PEACE	Paul McCartney (Parlophone)
37	18	THE VERY BEST OF MOTOWN LOVE SONGS	Various Artists (Telstar)
-	19	DECLARATION	Alarm (Mute)
13	20	COLOUR BY NUMBERS	Culture Club (Virgin)
29	21	WHITE FLAME	Snowy White (Towerbell)
15	22	LABOUR OF LOVE	UB40 (DEP International)
17	23	NOW THAT'S WHAT I CALL MUSIC	Various Artists (EMI/Virgin)
20	24	QUICK STEP AND SIDE KICK	Thompson Twins (Arista)
27	25	SOMETIMES WHEN WE TOUCH	Various Artists (Ronco)
22	26	HEAVEN IS WAITING	Danse Society (Arista)
24	27	LIFE'S A RIOT WITH SPY VS SPY	Billy Bragg (Go! Discs)
19	28	GENESIS	Genesis (Charisma)
34	29	YENTL	Barbra Streisand (CBS)
-	30	SHE'S SO UNUSUAL	Cyndi Lauper (Portrait)
25	31	SEVEN AND THE RAGGED TIGER	Duran Duran (EMI)
30	32	BACK TO BACK	Status Quo (Vertigo)
-	33	MADONNA	Madonna (Sire)
43	34	FANTASTIC	Wham! (Innervision)
49	35	LIVE AND DIRECT	Aswad (Island)
28	36	STAGES	Elaine Paige (K-Tel)
26	37	WORKING WITH FIRE AND STEEL	China Crisis (Virgin)
-	38	SENTINEL	Pallas (Harvest)
46	39	LIVING IN OZ	Rick Springfield (RCA)
16	40	PORTRAIT	Diana Ross (Telstar)
38	41	HEAD OVER HEELS	Cocteau Twins (4AD)
-	42	IT'S MY LIFE	Talk Talk (EMI)
33	43	BUSY BODY	Luther Vandross (Epic)
39	44	CHRISTINE McVIE	Christine McVie (Warner Bros.)
32	45	SYNCHRONICITY	Police (A&M)
42	46	THE ESSENTIAL JEAN MICHEL JARRE	Jean Michel Jarre (Polydor)
47	47	THE COLLECTION - 20 GREATEST HITS	Gladys Knight & The Pips (Star Blend)
45	48	YOU BROKE MY HEART IN 17 PLACES	Tracey Ullman (Stiff)
-	49	BODIES AND SOULS	Manhattan Transfer (Atlantic)
36	50	TOO LOW FOR ZERO	Elton John (Rocket)

3 March 1984

last week	this week		
4	1	INTO THE GAP	Thompson Twins (Arista)
1	2	SPARKLE IN THE RAIN	Simple Minds (Virgin)
2	3	THRILLER	Michael Jackson (Epic)
3	4	TOUCH	Eurythmics (RCA)
5	5	AN INNOCENT MAN	Billy Joel (CBS)
8	6	THE CROSSING	Big Country (Mercury)
19	7	DECLARATION	Alarm (Mute)
7	8	CAN'T SLOW DOWN	Lionel Richie (Motown)
6	9	THE FLAT EARTH	Thomas Dolby (Parlophone)
-	10	THE SMITHS	Smiths (Rough Trade)
9	11	U2 LIVE: UNDER A BLOOD RED SKY	U2 (Island)
10	12	NO PARLEZ	Paul Young (CBS)
14	13	1984	Van Halen (WEA)
16	14	LEARNING TO CRAWL	Pretenders (WEA)
12	15	SLIDE IT IN	Whitesnake (Liberty)
11	16	VICTIMS OF THE FUTURE	Gary Moore (Virgin)
18	17	THE VERY BEST OF MOTOWN LOVE SONGS	Various Artists (Telstar)
13	18	MILK AND HONEY	John Lennon & Yoko Ono (Polydor)
22	19	LABOUR OF LOVE	UB40 (DEP International)
28	20	GENESIS	Genesis (Charisma)
25	21	SOMETIMES WHEN WE TOUCH	Various Artists (Ronco)
33	22	MADONNA	Madonna (Sire)
42	23	IT'S MY LIFE	Talk Talk (EMI)
-	24	KEEP MOVING	Madness (Stiff)
20	25	COLOUR BY NUMBERS	Culture Club (Virgin)
23	26	NOW THAT'S WHAT I CALL MUSIC	Various Artists (EMI/Virgin)
15	27	CRUSADER	Saxon (Carrere)
-	28	LIVE IN BELFAST	Van Morrison (Mercury)
-	29	THE TUBE	Various Artists (K-Tel)
17	30	PIPES OF PEACE	Paul McCartney (Parlophone)
-	31	IN THE HEART	Kool & the Gang (De-Lite)
-	32	WORLD SHUT YOUR MOUTH	Julian Cope (Mercury)
31	33	SEVEN AND THE RAGGED TIGER	Duran Duran (EMI)
26	34	HEAVEN IS WAITING	Danse Society (Arista)
38	35	SENTINEL	Pallas (Liberty)
36	36	STAGES	Elaine Paige (K-Tel)
27	37	LIFE'S A RIOT WITH SPY VS SPY	Billy Bragg (Go! Discs)
-	38	HAIL TO ENGLAND	Manowar (Music for Nations)
24	39	QUICK STEP AND SIDE KICK	Thompson Twins (Arista)
40	40	PORTRAIT	Diana Ross (Telstar)
21	41	WHITE FLAME	Snowy White (Towerbell)
29	42	YENTL	Barbra Streisand (CBS)
-	43	AMMONIA AVENUE	Alan Parsons Project (Arista)
-	44	PRIVATE PARTY	Bobby Nunn (Motown)
-	45	NEW GOLD DREAM	Simple Minds (Virgin)
43	46	BUSY BODY	Luther Vandross (Epic)
-	47	E.S.P.	Millie Jackson (Sire)
41	48	HEAD OVER HEELS	Cocteau Twins (4AD)
30	49	SHE'S SO UNUSUAL	Cyndi Lauper (Portrait)
32	50	BACK TO BACK	Status Quo (Vertigo)

Thriller continued to be the most consistently-selling album in the country, while several other acts and titles took turns with a brief glory moment at Number 1 above it. *Into The Gap* was to be the all-time biggest-selling album for the Thompson Twins (who were a group with the name of a duo), while *Touch* was the second chart-topping LP by the Eurythmics (who were actually a duo with the name of a group!)

March 1984

10 March 1984

last	this	Title	Artist (label)
1	1	INTO THE GAP	Thompson Twins (Arista)
10	2	THE SMITHS	Smiths (Rough Trade)
2	3	SPARKLE IN THE RAIN	Simple Minds (Virgin)
4	4	TOUCH	Eurythmics (RCA)
3	5	THRILLER	Michael Jackson (Epic)
24	6	KEEP MOVING	Madness (Stiff)
5	7	AN INNOCENT MAN	Billy Joel (CBS)
8	8	CAN'T SLOW DOWN	Lionel Richie (Motown)
7	9	DECLARATION	Alarm (Mute)
6	10	THE CROSSING	Big Country (Mercury)
12	11	NO PARLEZ	Paul Young (CBS)
-	12	THE WORKS	Queen (EMI)
13	13	1984	Van Halen (WEA)
11	14	U2 LIVE: UNDER A BLOOD RED SKY	U2 (Island)
9	15	THE FLAT EARTH	Thomas Dolby (Parlophone)
17	16	THE VERY BEST OF MOTOWN LOVE SONGS	Various Artists (Telstar)
31	17	IN THE HEART	Kool & the Gang (De-Lite)
32	18	WORLD SHUT YOUR MOUTH	Julian Cope (Mercury)
43	19	AMMONIA AVENUE	Alan Parsons Project (Arista)
25	20	COLOUR BY NUMBERS	Culture Club (Virgin)
21	21	SOMETIMES WHEN WE TOUCH	Various Artists (Ronco)
28	22	LIVE IN BELFAST	Van Morrison (Mercury)
37	23	LIFE'S A RIOT WITH SPY VS SPY	Billy Bragg (Go! Discs)
19	24	LABOUR OF LOVE	UB40 (DEP International)
26	25	NOW THAT'S WHAT I CALL MUSIC	Various Artists (EMI/Virgin)
30	26	PIPES OF PEACE	Paul McCartney (Parlophone)
20	27	GENESIS	Genesis (Charisma)
15	28	SLIDE IT IN	Whitesnake (Liberty)
16	29	VICTIMS OF THE FUTURE	Gary Moore (Virgin)
18	30	MILK AND HONEY	John Lennon & Yoko Ono (Polydor)
-	31	TEXAS FEVER	Orange Juice (Polydor)
-	32	HUMAN RACING	Nik Kershaw (MCA)
33	33	SEVEN AND THE RAGGED TIGER	Duran Duran (EMI)
39	34	QUICK STEP AND SIDE KICK	Thompson Twins (Arista)
14	35	LEARNING TO CRAWL	Pretenders (WEA)
22	36	MADONNA	Madonna (Sire)
34	37	HEAVEN IS WAITING	Danse Society (Society)
27	38	CRUSADER	Saxon (Carrere)
29	39	THE TUBE	Various Artists (K-Tel)
23	40	IT'S MY LIFE	Talk Talk (EMI)
-	41	STREET SOUNDS EDITION 8	Various Artists (Street Sounds)
48	42	HEAD OVER HEELS	Cocteau Twins (4AD)
-	43	SERENADE	Juan Martin (K-Tel)
40	44	PORTRAIT	Diana Ross (Telstar)
42	45	YENTL	Barbra Streisand (CBS)
-	46	LOVE WARS	Womack & Womack (Elektra)
36	47	STAGES	Elaine Paige (K-Tel)
47	48	E.S.P.	Millie Jackson (Sire)
-	49	FANTASTIC	Wham! (Innervision)
35	50	SENTINEL	Pallas (Liberty)

17 March 1984

last	this	Title	Artist (label)
1	1	INTO THE GAP	Thompson Twins (Arista)
12	2	THE WORKS	Queen (EMI)
2	3	THE SMITHS	Smiths (Rough Trade)
5	4	THRILLER	Michael Jackson (Epic)
3	5	SPARKLE IN THE RAIN	Simple Minds (Virgin)
8	6	CAN'T SLOW DOWN	Lionel Richie (Motown)
4	7	TOUCH	Eurythmics (RCA)
13	8	1984	Van Halen (WEA)
6	9	KEEP MOVING	Madness (Stiff)
7	10	AN INNOCENT MAN	Billy Joel (CBS)
32	11	HUMAN RACING	Nik Kershaw (MCA)
-	12	HUMAN'S LIB	Howard Jones (WEA)
10	13	THE CROSSING	Big Country (Mercury)
11	14	NO PARLEZ	Paul Young (CBS)
9	15	DECLARATION	Alarm (Mute)
16	16	THE VERY BEST OF MOTOWN LOVE SONGS	Various Artists (Telstar)
14	17	U2 LIVE: UNDER A BLOOD RED SKY	U2 (Island)
17	18	IN THE HEART	Kool & the Gang (De-Lite)
15	19	THE FLAT EARTH	Thomas Dolby (Parlophone)
20	20	AMMONIA AVENUE	Alan Parsons Project (Arista)
31	21	TEXAS FEVER	Orange Juice (Polydor)
41	22	STREET SOUNDS EDITION 8	Various Artists (Street Sounds)
20	23	COLOUR BY NUMBERS	Culture Club (Virgin)
-	24	ABOUT FACE	Dave Gilmour (Harvest)
-	25	OFF THE WALL	Michael Jackson (Epic)
21	26	SOMETIMES WHEN WE TOUCH	Various (Ronco)
22	27	LIVE IN BELFAST	Van Morrison (Mercury)
25	28	NOW THAT'S WHAT I CALL MUSIC	Various Artists (EMI/Virgin)
-	29	STREET SOUNDS CRUCIAL ELECTRO	Various Artists (Street Sounds)
-	30	SWOON	Prefab Sprout (Kitchenware)
35	31	LEARNING TO CRAWL	Pretenders (WEA)
33	32	SEVEN AND THE RAGGED TIGER	Duran Duran (EMI)
23	33	LIFE'S A RIOT WITH SPY VS SPY	Billy Bragg (Go! Discs)
39	34	THE TUBE	Various Artists (K-Tel)
18	35	WORLD SHUT YOUR MOUTH	Julian Cope (Mercury)
-	36	MR HEARTBREAK	Laurie Anderson (Warner Bros.)
29	37	VICTIMS OF THE FUTURE	Gary Moore (Virgin)
-	38	MICHAEL JACKSON & THE JACKSON FIVE'S 18 GREATEST HITS	Michael Jackson & the Jackson Five (Star)
24	39	LABOUR OF LOVE	UB40 (DEP International)
40	40	HEAD OVER HEELS	Cocteau Twins (4AD)
27	41	GENESIS	Genesis (Charisma)
34	42	QUICK STEP AND SIDE KICK	Thompson Twins (Arista)
-	43	SOMEBODY'S WATCHING ME	Rockwell (Motown)
44	44	PACIFIC STREET	Pale Fountains (Virgin)
28	45	SLIDE IT IN	Whitesnake (Liberty)
-	46	IN YOUR EYES	George Benson (WEA)
-	47	MAKING HISTORY	Linton Kwesi Johnson (Island)
-	48	BODIES AND SOULS	Manhattan Transfer (Atlantic)
36	49	MADONNA	Madonna (Sire)
38	50	CRUSADER	Saxon (Carrere)

24 March 1984

last	this	Title	Artist (label)
12	1	HUMAN'S LIB	Howard Jones (WEA)
1	2	INTO THE GAP	Thompson Twins (Arista)
2	3	THE WORKS	Queen (EMI)
3	4	THE SMITHS	Smiths (Rough Trade)
-	5	CAFE BLEU	Style Council (Polydor)
4	6	THRILLER	Michael Jackson (Epic)
6	7	CAN'T SLOW DOWN	Lionel Richie (Motown)
-	8	FUGAZI	Marillion (EMI)
10	9	AN INNOCENT MAN	Billy Joel (CBS)
5	10	SPARKLE IN THE RAIN	Simple Minds (Virgin)
11	11	HUMAN RACING	Nik Kershaw (MCA)
-	12	ALCHEMY - DIRE STRAITS LIVE	Dire Straits (Vertigo)
7	13	TOUCH	Eurythmics (RCA)
8	14	1984	Van Halen (WEA)
9	15	KEEP MOVING	Madness (Stiff)
13	16	THE CROSSING	Big Country (Mercury)
30	17	SWOON	Prefab Sprout (Kitchenware)
18	18	IN THE HEART	Kool & the Gang (De-Lite)
24	19	ABOUT FACE	Dave Gilmour (Harvest)
16	20	THE VERY BEST OF MOTOWN LOVE SONGS	Various Artists (Telstar)
21	21	TEXAS FEVER	Orange Juice (Polydor)
29	22	STREET SOUNDS CRUCIAL ELECTRO	Various Artists (Street Sounds)
17	23	U2 LIVE: UNDER A BLOOD RED SKY	U2 (Island)
19	24	THE FLAT EARTH	Thomas Dolby (Parlophone)
14	25	NO PARLEZ	Paul Young (CBS)
25	26	OFF THE WALL	Michael Jackson (Epic)
20	27	AMMONIA AVENUE	Alan Parsons Project (Arista)
-	28	LOVE AT FIRST STING	Scorpions (Harvest)
22	29	STREET SOUNDS EDITION 8	Various Artists (Street Sounds)
23	30	COLOUR BY NUMBERS	Culture Club (Virgin)
-	31	THE DRUM IS EVERYTHING	Carmel (London)
15	32	DECLARATION	Alarm (Mute)
42	33	QUICK STEP AND SIDE KICK	Thompson Twins (Arista)
27	34	LIVE IN BELFAST	Van Morrison (Mercury)
26	35	SOMETIMES WHEN WE TOUCH	Various Artists (Ronco)
28	36	NOW THAT'S WHAT I CALL MUSIC	Various Artists (EMI/Virgin)
-	37	THE FISH PEOPLE TAPES	Alexei Sayle (Island)
39	38	LABOUR OF LOVE	UB40 (DEP International)
-	39	LET THE MUSIC PLAY	Shannon (Club)
-	40	E.S.P.	Millie Jackson (Sire)
33	41	LIFE'S A RIOT WITH SPY VS SPY	Billy Bragg (Go! Discs)
34	42	THE TUBE	Various Artists (K-Tel)
41	43	GENESIS	Genesis (Charisma)
-	44	NENA	Nena (Epic)
-	45	YOU BROKE MY HEART IN 17 PLACES	Tracey Ullman (Stiff)
-	46	G FORCE	Kenny G (Liberty)
32	47	SEVEN AND THE RAGGED TIGER	Duran Duran (EMI)
35	48	WORLD SHUT YOUR MOUTH	Julian Cope (Mercury)
37	49	VICTIMS OF THE FUTURE	Gary Moore (Virgin)
40	50	HEAD OVER HEELS	Cocteau Twins (4AD)

The Smiths' debut album, boosted by the Mancunian group's growing popularity in the singles chart, became the independent Rough Trade label's biggest-selling LP to date. Though neither it nor Queen's *The Works* were able to push aside the Thompson Twins at the top, *Human's Lib*, the first album by new UK hitmaking singer-songwriter Howard Jones, did, also outselling similarly-marketed Nik Kershaw's debut.

March – April 1984

31 March 1984

last week	this week	title	artist
1	1	HUMAN'S LIB	Howard Jones (WEA)
5	2	CAFE BLEU	Style Council (Polydor)
12	3	ALCHEMY - DIRE STRAITS LIVE	Dire Straits (Vertigo)
8	4	FUGAZI	Marillion (EMI)
2	5	INTO THE GAP	Thompson Twins (Arista)
7	6	CAN'T SLOW DOWN	Lionel Richie (Motown)
3	7	THE WORKS	Queen (EMI)
6	8	THRILLER	Michael Jackson (Epic)
9	9	AN INNOCENT MAN	Billy Joel (CBS)
4	10	THE SMITHS	Smiths (Rough Trade)
11	11	HUMAN RACING	Nik Kershaw (MCA)
31	12	THE DRUM IS EVERYTHING	Carmel (London)
10	13	SPARKLE IN THE RAIN	Simple Minds (Virgin)
14	14	1984	Van Halen (WEA)
13	15	TOUCH	Eurythmics (RCA)
16	16	THE CROSSING	Big Country (Mercury)
15	17	KEEP MOVING	Madness (Stiff)
28	18	LOVE AT FIRST STING	Scorpions (Harvest)
19	19	IN THE HEART	Kool & the Gang (De-Lite)
-	20	THIS LAST NIGHT	Soft Cell (Some Bizzare)
26	21	OFF THE WALL	Michael Jackson (Epic)
20	22	THE VERY BEST OF MOTOWN LOVE SONGS	Various Artists (Telstar)
19	23	ABOUT FACE	Dave Gilmour (Harvest)
27	24	AMMONIA AVENUE	Alan Parsons Project (Arista)
44	25	NENA	Nena (Epic)
17	26	SWOON	Prefab Sprout (Kitchenware)
23	27	U2 LIVE: UNDER A BLOOD RED SKY	U2 (Island)
46	28	G FORCE	Kenny G (Ronco)
35	29	SOMETIMES WHEN WE TOUCH	Various Artist (Ronco)
38	30	LABOUR OF LOVE	UB40 (DEP International)
25	31	NO PARLEZ	Paul Young (CBS)
-	32	THREE OF A PERFECT PAIR	King Crimson (EG)
21	33	TEXAS FEVER	Orange Juice (Polydor)
30	34	COLOUR BY NUMBERS	Culture Club (Virgin)
24	35	THE FLAT EARTH	Thomas Dolby (Parlophone)
22	36	STREET SOUNDS CRUCIAL ELECTRO	Various Artists (Street Sounds)
-	37	DOMINO THEORY	Weather Report (CBS)
33	38	QUICK STEP AND SIDE KICK	Thompson Twins (Arista)
40	39	E.S.P.	Millie Jackson (Sire)
36	40	NOW THAT'S WHAT I CALL MUSIC	Various Artists (EMI/Virgin)
48	41	WORLD SHUT YOUR MOUTH	Julian Cope (Mercury)
37	42	THE FISH PEOPLE TAPES	Alexei Sayle (Island)
32	43	DECLARATION	Alarm (Mute)
29	44	STREET SOUNDS EDITION 8	Various Artists (Street Sounds)
-	45	THE ICICLE WORKS	Icicle Works (Beggars Banquet)
-	46	SOMEBODY'S WATCHING ME	Rockwell (Motown)
39	47	LET THE MUSIC PLAY	Shannon (Club/Phonogram)
43	48	GENESIS	Genesis (Charisma)
-	49	YENTL	Barbra Streisand (CBS)
34	50	LIVE IN BELFAST	Van Morrison (Mercury)

7 April 1984

last week	this week	title	artist
6	1	CAN'T SLOW DOWN	Lionel Richie (Motown)
1	2	HUMAN'S LIB	Howard Jones (WEA)
2	3	CAFE BLEU	Style Council (Polydor)
3	4	ALCHEMY - DIRE STRAITS LIVE	Dire Straits (Vertigo)
8	5	THRILLER	Michael Jackson (Epic)
5	6	INTO THE GAP	Thompson Twins (Arista)
4	7	FUGAZI	Marillion (EMI)
9	8	AN INNOCENT MAN	Billy Joel (CBS)
10	9	THE SMITHS	Smiths (Rough Trade)
7	10	THE WORKS	Queen (EMI)
20	11	THIS LAST NIGHT	Soft Cell (Some Bizzare)
13	12	SPARKLE IN THE RAIN	Simple Minds (Virgin)
11	13	HUMAN RACING	Nik Kershaw (MCA)
15	14	TOUCH	Eurythmics (RCA)
14	15	1984	Van Halen (WEA)
30	16	LABOUR OF LOVE	UB40 (DEP International)
45	17	THE ICICLE WORKS	Icicle Works (Beggars Banquet)
12	18	THE DRUM IS EVERYTHING	Carmel (London)
21	19	OFF THE WALL	Michael Jackson (Epic)
22	20	THE VERY BEST OF MOTOWN LOVE SONGS	Various Artists (Telstar)
27	21	U2 LIVE: UNDER A BLOOD RED SKY	U2 (Island)
-	22	NOW THAT'S WHAT I CALL MUSIC 2	Various Artists (EMI/Virgin)
18	23	LOVE AT FIRST STING	Scorpions (Harvest)
32	24	THREE OF A PERFECT PAIR	King Crimson (EG)
34	25	COLOUR BY NUMBERS	Culture Club (Virgin)
26	26	SWOON	Prefab Sprout (Kitchenware)
16	27	THE CROSSING	Big Country (Mercury)
25	28	NENA	Nena (Epic)
17	29	KEEP MOVING	Madness (Stiff)
-	30	CLIMATE OF HUNTER	Scott Walker (Virgin)
35	31	THE FLAT EARTH	Thomas Dolby (Parlophone)
28	32	G FORCE	Kenny G (Arista)
23	33	ABOUT FACE	Dave Gilmour (Harvest)
31	34	NO PARLEZ	Paul Young (CBS)
44	35	STREET SOUNDS EDITION 8	Various Artists (Street Sounds)
36	36	STREET SOUNDS CRUCIAL ELECTRO	Various Artists (Street Sounds)
19	37	IN THE HEART	Kool & the Gang (De-Lite)
24	38	AMMONIA AVENUE	Alan Parsons Project (Arista)
-	39	LIONEL RICHIE	Lionel Richie (Motown)
-	40	THE ROSE OF TRALEE	James Last (Polydor)
-	41	BODY AND SOUL	Joe Jackson (A&M)
29	42	E.S.P.	Millie Jackson (Sire)
33	43	TEXAS FEVER	Orange Juice (Polydor)
42	44	THE FISH PEOPLE TAPES	Alexei Sayle (Island)
-	45	STREET SOUNDS ELECTRO 3	Various Artists (Street Sounds)
41	46	WORLD SHUT YOUR MOUTH	Julian Cope (Mercury)
-	47	IT'S YOUR NIGHT	James Ingram (Qwest)
48	48	GENESIS	Genesis (Charisma)
-	49	THE F C'S TREAT US LIKE PRICKS	A Flux of Pink Indians (Mortarhate)
-	50	VENICE IN PERIL	Rondo Veneziano (Ferroway)

14 April 1984

last week	this week	title	artist
1	1	CAN'T SLOW DOWN	Lionel Richie (Motown)
2	2	HUMAN'S LIB	Howard Jones (WEA)
22	3	NOW THAT'S WHAT I CALL MUSIC 2	Various Artists (EMI/Virgin)
4	4	ALCHEMY - DIRE STRAITS LIVE	Dire Straits (Vertigo)
5	5	THRILLER	Michael Jackson (Epic)
6	6	INTO THE GAP	Thompson Twins (Arista)
3	7	CAFE BLEU	Style Council (Polydor)
8	8	AN INNOCENT MAN	Billy Joel (CBS)
7	9	FUGAZI	Marillion (EMI)
9	10	THE SMITHS	Smiths (Rough Trade)
12	11	SPARKLE IN THE RAIN	Simple Minds (Virgin)
41	12	BODY AND SOUL	Joe Jackson (A&M)
13	13	HUMAN RACING	Nik Kershaw (MCA)
25	14	COLOUR BY NUMBERS	Culture Club (Virgin)
10	15	THE WORKS	Queen (EMI)
14	16	TOUCH	Eurythmics (RCA)
21	17	U2 LIVE: UNDER A BLOOD RED SKY	U2 (Island)
-	18	LAMENT	Ultravox (Chrysalis)
16	19	LABOUR OF LOVE	UB40 (DEP International)
45	20	STREET SOUNDS ELECTRO 3	Various Artists (Street Sounds)
20	21	THE VERY BEST OF MOTOWN LOVE SONGS	Various Artists (Telstar)
-	22	GHETTO BLASTER	Crusaders (MCA)
-	23	YENTL	Barbra Streisand (CBS)
18	24	THE DRUM IS EVERYTHING	Carmel (London)
11	25	THIS LAST NIGHT	Soft Cell (Some Bizzare)
24	26	THREE OF A PERFECT PAIR	King Crimson (EG)
15	27	1984	Van Halen (WEA)
17	28	THE ICICLE WORKS	Icicle Works (Beggars Banquet)
27	29	THE CROSSING	Big Country (Mercury)
-	30	VICTIMS OF CIRCUMSTANCE	Barclay James Harvest (Polydor)
31	31	THE FLAT EARTH	Thomas Dolby (Parlophone)
-	32	SILVER	Cliff Richard (EMI)
-	33	STAGES	Elaine Paige (K-Tel)
-	34	I CAN HELP	Elvis Presley (RCA)
35	35	IN THE HEART	Kool & the Gang (De-Lite)
19	36	OFF THE WALL	Michael Jackson (Epic)
23	37	LOVE AT FIRST STIN	Scorpions (Harvest)
35	38	STREET SOUNDS EDITION 8	Various Artists (Street Sounds)
34	39	NO PARLEZ	Paul Young (CBS)
26	40	SWOON	Prefab Sprout (Kitchenware)
47	41	IT'S YOUR NIGHT	James Ingram (Qwest)
32	42	G FORCE	Kenny G (Arista)
33	43	ABOUT FACE	Dave Gilmour (Harvest)
38	44	AMMONIA AVENUE	Alan Parsons Project (Arista)
-	45	INTIMATE CONNECTION	Kleeer (Atlantic)
-	46	ROBERTA FLACK'S GREATEST HITS	Roberta Flack (K-Tel)
28	47	NENA	Nena (Epic)
29	48	KEEP MOVING	Madness (Stiff)
39	49	LIONEL RICHIE	Lionel Richie (Motown)
30	50	CLIMATE OF HUNTER	Scott Walker (Virgin)

Cafe Bleu was the first album by former Jam leader Paul Weller's new (and contrasting) band the Style Council, who had already had a year's success with five Top 20 singles by the time of its release. Lionel Richie's sudden dash to the top after some months of consistent Top 10 service with *Can't Slow Down* was the result of the boost given by the simultaneous 5-week Number 1 run by its extracted single *Hello*.

251

April – May 1984

last week	this week	21 April 1984	
1	1	CAN'T SLOW DOWN	Lionel Richie (Motown)
5	2	THRILLER	Michael Jackson (Epic)
3	3	NOW THAT'S WHAT I CALL MUSIC 2	Various Artists (EMI/Virgin)
2	4	HUMAN'S LIB	Howard Jones (WEA)
6	5	INTO THE GAP	Thompson Twins (Arista)
4	6	ALCHEMY - DIRE STRAITS LIVE	Dire Straits (Vertigo)
18	7	LAMENT	Ultravox (Chrysalis)
7	8	CAFE BLEU	Style Council (Polydor)
8	9	AN INNOCENT MAN	Billy Joel (CBS)
10	10	THE SMITHS	Smiths (Rough Trade)
-	11	MARVIN GAYE'S GREATEST HITS	Marvin Gaye (Telstar)
11	12	SPARKLE IN THE RAIN	Simple Minds (Virgin)
15	13	THE WORKS	Queen (EMI)
12	14	BODY AND SOUL	Joe Jackson (A&M)
14	15	COLOUR BY NUMBERS	Culture Club (Virgin)
13	16	HUMAN RACING	Nik Kershaw (MCA)
9	17	FUGAZI	Marillion (EMI)
17	18	U2 LIVE: UNDER A BLOOD RED SKY	U2 (Island)
16	19	TOUCH	Eurythmics (RCA)
9	20	LABOUR OF LOVE	UB40 (DEP International)
21	21	THE VERY BEST OF MOTOWN LOVE SONGS	Various Artists (Telstar)
28	22	THE ICICLE WORKS	Icicle Works (Beggars Banquet)
30	23	VICTIMS OF CIRCUMSTANCE	Barclay James Harvest (Polydor)
41	24	IT'S YOUR NIGHT	James Ingram (Qwest)
29	25	THE CROSSING	Big Country (Mercury)
25	26	THIS LAST NIGHT	Soft Cell (Some Bizzare)
22	27	GHETTO BLASTER	Crusaders (MCA)
20	28	STREET SOUNDS ELECTRO 3	Various Artists (Street Sounds)
39	29	NO PARLEZ	Paul Young (CBS)
-	30	THE BOP WON'T STOP	Shakin' Stevens (Epic)
-	31	AND I LOVE YOU SO	Howard Keel (Warwick)
31	32	THE FLAT EARTH	Thomas Dolby (Parlophone)
35	33	IN THE HEART	Kool & the Gang (De-Lite)
-	34	POINTS ON A CURVE	Wang Chung (Geffin)
-	35	THE ROSE OF TRALEE	James Last (Polydor)
-	36	WIRED TO THE MOON	Chris Rea (Magnet)
34	37	I CAN HELP	Elvis Presley (RCA)
38	38	OFF THE WALL	Michael Jackson (Epic)
24	39	THE DRUM IS EVERYTHING	Carmel (London)
-	40	MADONNA	Madonna (Sire)
27	41	1984	Van Halen (WEA)
40	42	SWOON	Prefab Sprout (Kitchenware)
-	43	SEANCE	Church (Carrere)
26	44	THREE OF A PERFECT PAIR	King Crimson (EG)
-	45	IN YOUR EYES	George Benson (WEA)
47	46	NENA	Nena (Epic)
23	47	YENTL	Barbra Streisand (CBS)
38	48	STREET SOUNDS EDITION 8	Various Artists (Street Sounds)
43	49	ABOUT FACE	Dave Gilmour (Harvest)
-	50	THE POET II	Bobby Womack (Motown)

last week	this week	28 April 1984	
3	1	NOW THAT'S WHAT I CALL MUSIC 2	Various Artists (EMI/Virgin)
1	2	CAN'T SLOW DOWN	Lionel Richie (Motown)
5	3	INTO THE GAP	Thompson Twins (Arista)
2	4	THRILLER	Michael Jackson (Epic)
4	5	HUMAN'S LIB	Howard Jones (WEA)
6	6	ALCHEMY - DIRE STRAITS LIVE	Dire Straits (Vertigo)
7	7	LAMENT	Ultravox (Chrysalis)
9	8	AN INNOCENT MAN	Billy Joel (CBS)
13	9	THE WORKS	Queen (EMI)
10	10	THE SMITHS	Smiths (Rough Trade)
8	11	CAFE BLEU	Style Council (Polydor)
14	12	BODY AND SOUL	Joe Jackson (A&M)
16	13	HUMAN RACING	Nik Kershaw (MCA)
15	14	COLOUR BY NUMBERS	Culture Club (Virgin)
-	15	GRACE UNDER PRESSURE	Rush (Vertigo)
12	16	SPARKLE IN THE RAIN	Simple Minds (Virgin)
11	17	MARVIN GAYE'S GREATEST HITS	Marvin Gaye (Telstar)
20	18	LABOUR OF LOVE	UB40 (DEP International)
-	19	SOPHISTICATED BOOM BOOM	Dead or Alive (Epic)
19	20	TOUCH	Eurythmics (RCA)
31	21	OFF THE WALL	Michael Jackson (Epic)
-	22	AND I LOVE YOU SO	Howard Keel (Warwick)
23	23	VICTIMS OF CIRCUMSTANCE	Barclay James Harvest (Polydor)
18	24	U2 LIVE: UNDER A BLOOD RED SKY	U2 (Island)
21	25	THE VERY BEST OF MOTOWN LOVE SONGS	Various Artists (Telstar)
-	26	ONE EYED JACKS	Spear of Destiny (Epic)
17	27	FUGAZI	Marillion (EMI)
34	28	POINTS ON A CURVE	Wang Chung (Geffin)
-	29	STOMPIN' AT THE SAVOY	Rufus with Chaka Khan (Warner Bros.)
24	30	IT'S YOUR NIGHT	James Ingram (Qwest)
-	31	BANANARAMA	Bananarama (London)
36	32	WIRED TO THE MOON	Chris Rea (Magnet)
25	33	THE CROSSING	Big Country (Mercury)
41	34	1984	Van Halen (WEA)
30	35	THE BOP WON'T STOP	Shakin' Stevens (Epic)
-	36	AT WAR WITH SATAN	Venom (Neat)
-	37	A LITTLE SPICE	Loose Ends (Virgin)
-	38	NOW THAT'S WHAT I CALL MUSIC	Various Artists (EMI/Virgin)
39	39	AGAINST ALL ODDS	Soundtrack (Virgin)
29	40	NO PARLEZ	Paul Young (CBS)
40	41	MADONNA	Madonna (Sire)
50	42	THE POET II	Bobby Womack (Motown)
43	43	FOOTLOOSE	Soundtrack (CBS)
22	44	THE ICICLE WORKS	Icicle Works (Beggars Banquet)
47	45	YENTL	Barbra Streisand (CBS)
27	46	RECKONING	REM (IRS)
27	47	GHETTO BLASTER	Crusaders (MCA)
48	48	G FORCE	Kenny G (Arista)
-	49	FAME AND FASHION (ALL TIME GREATEST HITS)	David Bowie (RCA)
-	50	LOVE WARS	Womack & Womack (Elektra)

last week	this week	5 May 1984	
1	1	NOW THAT'S WHAT I CALL MUSIC 2	Various Artists (EMI/Virgin)
2	2	CAN'T SLOW DOWN	Lionel Richie (Motown)
9	3	THE WORKS	Queen (EMI)
4	4	THRILLER	Michael Jackson (Epic)
3	5	INTO THE GAP	Thompson Twins (Arista)
6	6	ALCHEMY - DIRE STRAITS LIVE	Dire Straits (Vertigo)
5	7	HUMAN'S LIB	Howard Jones (WEA)
15	8	GRACE UNDER PRESSURE	Rush (Vertigo)
8	9	AN INNOCENT MAN	Billy Joel (CBS)
7	10	LAMENT	Ultravox (Chrysalis)
13	11	HUMAN RACING	Nik Kershaw (MCA)
22	12	AND I LOVE YOU SO	Howard Keel (Warwick)
17	13	MARVIN GAYE'S GREATEST HITS	Marvin Gaye (Telstar)
12	14	BODY AND SOUL	Joe Jackson (A&M)
19	15	SOPHISTICATED BOOM BOOM	Dead or Alive (Epic)
42	16	THE POET II	Bobby Womack (Motown)
31	17	BANANARAMA	Bananarama (London)
10	18	THE SMITHS	Smiths (Rough Trade)
14	19	COLOUR BY NUMBERS	Culture Club (Virgin)
11	20	CAFE BLEU	Style Council (Polydor)
43	21	FOOTLOOSE	Soundtrack (CBS)
21	22	OFF THE WALL	Michael Jackson (Epic)
18	23	LABOUR OF LOVE	UB40 (DEP International)
16	24	SPARKLE IN THE RAIN	Simple Minds (Virgin)
20	25	TOUCH	Eurythmics (RCA)
49	26	FAME AND FASHION (ALL TIME GREATEST HITS)	David Bowie (RCA)
23	27	VICTIMS OF CIRCUMSTANCE	Barclay James Harvest (Polydor)
29	28	STOMPIN' AT THE SAVOY	Rufus with Chaka Khan (Warner Bros.)
24	29	U2 LIVE: UNDER A BLOOD RED SKY	U2 (Island)
33	30	THE CROSSING	Big Country (Mercury)
32	31	WIRED TO THE MOON	Chris Rea (Magnet)
30	32	IT'S YOUR NIGHT	James Ingram (Qwest)
46	33	RECKONING	REM (IRS)
-	34	IN THE HEART	Kool & the Gang (De-Lite)
35	35	THE FLAT EARTH	Thomas Dolby (Parlophone)
-	36	OASIS	Oasis (WEA)
25	37	THE VERY BEST OF MOTOWN LOVE SONGS	Various Artists (Telstar)
-	38	STREET SOUNDS ELECTRO 3	Various Artists (Street Sounds)
50	39	LOVE WARS	Womack & Womack (Elektra)
48	40	G FORCE	Kenny G (Arista)
-	41	CAUGHT IN THE ACT	Styx (A&M)
-	42	SEVEN AND THE RAGGED TIGER	Duran Duran (EMI)
-	43	BON JOVI	Bon Jovi (Vertigo)
35	44	THE BOP WON'T STOP	Shakin' Stevens (Epic)
38	45	NOW THAT'S WHAT I CALL MUSIC	Various Artists (EMI/Virgin)
27	46	FUGAZI	Marillion (EMI)
45	47	YENTL	Barbra Streisand (CBS)
40	48	NO PARLEZ	Paul Young (CBS)
47	49	GHETTO BLASTER	Crusaders (MCA)
41	50	MADONNA	Madonna (Sire)

The collaborative EMI/Virgin compilation *Now That's What I Call Music 2* proved an even faster seller than its predecessor. The *Now* line, offering an anthology of recent (and often current) big single hits by major names, was to become established through the 1980s as the biggest-selling compilation series ever in the UK. Several would reach triple-platinum status, indicating sales around a million each.

May 1984

12 May 1984

last	this		
1	1	NOW THAT'S WHAT I CALL MUSIC 2	Various Artists (EMI/Virgin)
2	2	CAN'T SLOW DOWN	Lionel Richie (Motown)
3	3	THE WORKS	Queen (EMI)
4	4	THRILLER	Michael Jackson (Epic)
5	5	INTO THE GAP	Thompson Twins (Arista)
6	6	ALCHEMY - DIRE STRAITS LIVE	Dire Straits (Vertigo)
8	7	GRACE UNDER PRESSURE	Rush (Vertigo)
7	8	HUMAN'S LIB	Howard Jones (WEA)
21	9	FOOTLOOSE	Soundtrack (CBS)
12	10	AND I LOVE YOU SO	Howard Keel (Warwick)
-	11	OCEAN RAIN	Echo & the Bunnymen (Korova)
9	12	AN INNOCENT MAN	Billy Joel (CBS)
11	13	HUMAN RACING	Nik Kershaw (MCA)
10	14	LAMENT	Ultravox (Chrysalis)
-	15	JUNK CULTURE	Orchestral Manoeuvres In The Dark (Virgin)
14	16	BODY AND SOUL	Joe Jackson (A&M)
18	17	THE SMITHS	Smiths (Rough Trade)
13	18	MARVIN GAYE'S GREATEST HITS	Marvin Gaye (Telstar)
17	19	BANANARAMA	Bananarama (London)
-	20	ONE EYED JACKS	Spear of Destiny (Epic)
-	21	THE TOP	Cure (Fiction)
16	22	THE POET II	Bobby Womack (Motown)
20	23	CAFE BLEU	Style Council (Polydor)
-	24	THE PROS AND CONS OF HITCH HIKING	Roger Waters (Harvest)
19	25	COLOUR BY NUMBERS	Culture Club (Virgin)
15	26	SOPHISTICATED BOOM BOOM	Dead or Alive (Epic)
22	27	OFF THE WALL	Michael Jackson (Epic)
34	28	IN THE HEART	Kool & the Gang (De-Lite)
37	29	THE VERY BEST OF MOTOWN LOVE SONGS	Various Artists (Telstar)
32	30	IT'S YOUR NIGHT	James Ingram (Qwest)
25	31	TOUCH	Eurythmics (RCA)
28	32	STOMPIN' AT THE SAVOY	Rufus with Chaka Khan (Warner Bros.)
24	33	SPARKLE IN THE RAIN	Simple Minds (Virgin)
29	34	U2 LIVE: UNDER A BLOOD RED SKY	U2 (Island)
39	35	LOVE WARS	Womack & Womack (Elektra)
23	36	LABOUR OF LOVE	UB40 (DEP International)
31	37	WIRED TO THE MOON	Chris Rea (Magnet)
42	38	SEVEN AND THE RAGGED TIGER	Duran Duran (EMI)
-	39	LEGEND (MUSIC FROM ROBIN OF SHERWOOD)	Clannad (RCA)
46	40	FUGAZI	Marillion (EMI)
41	41	CAUGHT IN THE ACT	Styx (A&M)
42	42	LIONEL RICHIE	Lionel Richie (Motown)
-	43	AGAINST ALL ODDS	Soundtrack (Virgin)
-	44	HEAD OVER HEELS	Cocteau Twins (4AD)
33	45	RECKONING	REM (IRS)
-	46	QUICK STEP AND SIDE KICK	Thompson Twins (Arista)
-	47	QUEEN'S GREATEST HITS	Queen (EMI)
30	48	THE CROSSING	Big Country (Mercury)
27	49	VICTIMS OF CIRCUMSTANCE	Barclay James Harvest (Polydor)
26	50	FAME AND FASHION (ALL TIME GREATEST HITS)	David Bowie (RCA)

19 May 1984

last	this		
1	1	NOW THAT'S WHAT I CALL MUSIC 2	Various Artists (EMI/Virgin)
11	2	OCEAN RAIN	Echo & the Bunnymen (Korova)
2	3	CAN'T SLOW DOWN	Lionel Richie (Motown)
4	4	THRILLER	Michael Jackson (Epic)
3	5	THE WORKS	Queen (EMI)
9	6	FOOTLOOSE	Soundtrack (CBS)
21	7	THE TOP	Cure (Fiction)
15	8	JUNK CULTURE	Orchestral Manoeuvres In The Dark (Virgin)
5	9	INTO THE GAP	Thompson Twins (Arista)
6	10	ALCHEMY - DIRE STRAITS LIVE	Dire Straits (Vertigo)
-	11	HYSTERIA	Human League (Virgin)
7	12	GRACE UNDER PRESSURE	Rush (Vertigo)
24	13	THE PROS AND CONS OF HITCH HIKING	Roger Waters (Harvest)
12	14	AN INNOCENT MAN	Billy Joel (CBS)
-	15	LEGEND	Bob Marley & the Wailers (Island)
16	16	MIRROR MOVES	Psychedlic Furs (CBS)
10	17	AND I LOVE YOU SO	Howard Keel (Warwick)
8	18	HUMAN'S LIB	Howard Jones (WEA)
13	19	HUMAN RACING	Nik Kershaw (MCA)
-	20	STREET SOUNDS EDITION 5	Various Artists (Street Sounds)
18	21	MARVIN GAYE'S GREATEST HITS	Marvin Gaye (Telstar)
38	22	SEVEN AND THE RAGGED TIGER	Duran Duran (EMI)
14	23	LAMENT	Ultravox (Chrysalis)
22	24	THE POET II	Bobby Womack (Motown)
17	25	THE SMITHS	Smiths (Rough Trade)
39	26	LEGEND (MUSIC FROM ROBIN OF SHERWOOD)	Clannad (RCA)
19	27	BANANARAMA	Bananarama (London)
20	28	ONE EYED JACKS	Spear of Destiny (Epic)
34	29	U2 LIVE: UNDER A BLOOD RED SKY	U2 (Island)
-	30	MAN ON THE LINE	Chris DeBurgh (A&M)
25	31	COLOUR BY NUMBERS	Culture Club (Virgin)
28	32	IN THE HEART	Kool & the Gang (De-Lite)
27	33	OFF THE WALL	Michael Jackson (Epic)
31	34	TOUCH	Eurythmics (RCA)
16	35	BODY AND SOUL	Joe Jackson (A&M)
23	36	CAFE BLEU	Style Council (Polydor)
26	37	SOPHISTICATED BOOM BOOM	Dead Or Alive (Epic)
40	38	FUGAZI	Marillion (EMI)
-	39	BREAK OUT	Pointer Sisters (Planet)
43	40	AGAINST ALL ODDS	Soundtrack (Virgin)
36	40	LABOUR OF LOVE	UB40 (DEP International)
29	42	THE VERY BEST OF MOTOWN LOVE SONGS	Various Artists (Telstar)
30	43	IT'S YOUR NIGHT	James Ingram (Qwest)
-	44	OASIS	Oasis (WEA)
33	45	SPARKLE IN THE RAIN	Simple Minds (Virgin)
35	46	LOVE WARS	Womack & Womack (Elektra)
37	47	WIRED TO THE MOON	Chris Rea (Magnet)
32	48	STOMPIN' AT THE SAVOY	Rufus with Chaka Khan (Warner Bros.)
41	49	CAUGHT IN THE ACT	Styx (A&M)
42	50	LIONEL RICHIE	Lionel Richie (Motwn)

26 May 1984

last	this		
15	1	LEGEND	Bob Marley & the Wailers (Island)
11	2	HYSTERIA	Human League (Virgin)
2	3	OCEAN RAIN	Echo & the Bunnymen (Korova)
3	4	CAN'T SLOW DOWN	Lionel Richie (Motown)
1	5	NOW THAT'S WHAT I CALL MUSIC 2	Various Artists (EMI/Virgin)
6	6	FOOTLOOSE	Soundtrack (CBS)
5	7	THE WORKS	Queen (EMI)
8	8	JUNK CULTURE	Orchestral Manoeuvres In The Dark (Virgin)
4	9	THRILLER	Michael Jackson (Epic)
7	10	THE TOP	Cure (Fiction)
10	11	ALCHEMY - DIRE STRAITS LIVE	Dire Straits (Vertigo)
30	12	MAN ON THE LINE	Chris DeBurgh (A&M)
16	13	MIRROR MOVES	Psychedlic Furs (CBS)
9	14	INTO THE GAP	Thompson Twins (Arista)
13	15	THE PROS AND CONS OF HITCH HIKING	Roger Waters (Harvest)
17	16	AND I LOVE YOU SO	Howard Keel (Warwick)
14	17	AN INNOCENT MAN	Billy Joel (CBS)
22	18	SEVEN AND THE RAGGED TIGER	Duran Duran (EMI)
18	19	HUMAN'S LIB	Howard Jones (WEA)
-	20	MANGE TOUT	Blancmange (London)
12	21	GRACE UNDER PRESSURE	Rush (Vertigo)
26	22	LEGEND (MUSIC FROM ROBIN OF SHERWOOD)	Clannad (RCA)
19	23	HUMAN RACING	Nik Kershaw (MCA)
21	24	MARVIN GAYE'S GREATEST HITS	Marvin Gaye (Telstar)
20	25	STREET SOUNDS EDITION 5	Various Artists (Street Sounds)
36	26	CAFE BLEU	Style Council (Polydor)
39	27	BREAK OUT	Pointer Sisters (Planet)
24	28	THE POET II	Bobby Womack (Motown)
25	29	THE SMITHS	Smiths (Rough Trade)
44	30	OASIS	Oasis (WEA)
-	31	MASTERPIECES - THE VERY BEST OF SKY	Sky (Telstar)
28	32	ONE EYED JACKS	Spear of Destiny (Epic)
46	33	LOVE WARS	Womack & Womack (Elektra)
31	34	COLOUR BY NUMBERS	Culture Club (Virgin)
35	35	BODY AND SOUL	Joe Jackson (A&M)
23	36	LAMENT	Ultravox (Chrysalis)
33	37	OFF THE WALL	Michael Jackson (Epic)
32	38	IN THE HEART	Kool & the Gang (De-Lite)
40	39	AGAINST ALL ODDS	Soundtrack (Virgin)
40	40	LABOUR OF LOVE	UB40 (DEP International)
27	41	BANANARAMA	Bananarama (London)
-	42	TOUCH SENSITIVE	Bruce Foxton (Arista)
-	43	DYNAMITE	Jermaine Jackson (Arista)
48	44	STOMPIN' AT THE SAVOY	Rufus with Chaka Khan (Warner Bros.)
34	45	TOUCH	Eurythmics (RCA)
38	46	FUGAZI	Marillion (EMI)
29	47	U2 LIVE: UNDER A BLOOD RED SKY	U2 (Island)
-	48	VENGEANCE	New Model Army (Abstract)
-	49	THROUGH THE FIRE	Hagar, Schon, aaronson, Shrlieve (Geffin)
-	50	LOVE YOU TILL TUESDAY	David Bowie (London)

Veteran soul singer Bobby Womack's Top 20 success with *The Poet II* (his first-ever UK chart album) is worthy of note because it was due entirely to word-of-mouth, good reviews and strong club play - there was no accompanying hit single to boost it by getting radio airplay. The album was the sequel to an earlier highly-rated set, *The Poet* (hence this one's title), which had only been available here as an US import.

June 1984

2 June 1984

last	this		
1	1	LEGEND	Bob Marley & the Wailers (Island)
2	2	HYSTERIA	Human League (Virgin)
20	3	MANGE TOUT	Blancmange (London)
7	4	THE WORKS	Queen (EMI)
9	5	THRILLER	Michael Jackson (Epic)
5	6	NOW THAT'S WHAT I CALL MUSIC 2	Various Artists (EMI/Virgin)
4	7	CAN'T SLOW DOWN	Lionel Richie (Motown)
6	8	FOOTLOOSE	Soundtrack (CBS)
3	9	OCEAN RAIN	Echo & the Bunnymen (Korova)
12	10	MAN ON THE LINE	Chris DeBurgh (A&M)
11	11	ALCHEMY - DIRE STRAITS LIVE	Dire Straits (Vertigo)
8	12	JUNK CULTURE	Orchestral Manoeuvres In The Dark (Virgin)
14	13	INTO THE GAP	Thompson Twins (Arista)
13	14	MIRROR MOVES	Psychedlic Furs (CBS)
17	15	AN INNOCENT MAN	Billy Joel (CBS)
10	16	THE TOP	Cure (Fiction)
-	17	HUNGRY FOR HITS	Various Artists (K-Tel)
27	18	BREAK OUT	Pointer Sisters (Planet)
19	19	HUMAN'S LIB	Howard Jones (WEA)
22	20	LEGEND (MUSIC FROM ROBIN OF SHERWOOD)	Clannad (RCA)
36	21	LAMENT	Ultravox (Chrysalis)
-	22	DON'T STOP DANCIN'	Various Artists (Telstar)
24	23	MARVIN GAYE'S GREATEST HITS	Marvin Gaye (Telstar)
16	24	AND I LOVE YOU SO	Howard Keel (Warwick)
18	25	SEVEN AND THE RAGGED TIGER	Duran Duran (EMI)
15	26	THE PROS AND CONS OF HITCH HIKING	Roger Waters (Harvest)
31	27	MASTERPIECES - THE VERY BEST OF SKY	Sky (Telstar)
21	28	GRACE UNDER PRESSURE	Rush (Vertigo)
33	29	LOVE WARS	Womack & Womack (Elektra)
-	30	THEN CAME ROCK 'N' ROLL	Various Artists (EMI)
26	31	CAFE BLEU	Style Council (Polydor)
-	32	CHANGE OF HEART	Change (WEA)
23	33	HUMAN RACING	Nik Kershaw (MCA)
25	34	STREET SOUNDS EDITION 9	Various Artists (Street Sounds)
29	35	THE SMITHS	Smiths (Rough Trade)
-	36	FROM HER TO ETERNITY	Nick Cave & the bad seeds (Mute)
46	37	FUGAZI	Marillion (EMI)
-	38	WOULD YA LIKE MORE SCRATCHIN'	Malcolm McLaren (Virgin/Charisma)
39	39	AGAINST ALL ODDS	Soundtrack (Virgin)
-	40	DANCIN' ON THE EDGE	Lita Ford (Vertigo)
28	41	THE POET II	Bobby Womack (Motown)
30	42	OASIS	Oasis (WEA)
32	43	ONE EYED JACKS	Spear of Destiny (Epic)
-	44	LIFE'S A RIOT WITH SPY VS SPY	Billy Bragg (Go! Discs)
-	45	FROM THE PROMISED LAND	Playdead (Clay)
35	46	BODY AND SOUL	Joe Jackson (A&M)
37	47	OFF THE WALL	Michael Jackson (Epic)
-	48	ISLANDS	Kajagoogoo (EMI)
34	49	COLOUR BY NUMBERS	Culture Club (Virgin)
38	50	IN THE HEART	Kool & the Gang (De-Lite)

9 June 1984

last	this		
1	1	LEGEND	Bob Marley & the Wailers (Island)
4	2	THE WORKS	Queen (EMI)
2	3	HYSTERIA	Human League (Virgin)
6	4	NOW THAT'S WHAT I CALL MUSIC 2	Various Artists (EMI/Virgin)
3	5	MANGE TOUT	Blancmange (London)
7	6	CAN'T SLOW DOWN	Lionel Richie (Motown)
5	7	THRILLER	Michael Jackson (Epic)
8	8	FOOTLOOSE	Soundtrack (CBS)
17	9	HUNGRY FOR HITS	Various Artists (K-Tel)
10	10	MAN ON THE LINE	Chris DeBurgh (A&M)
9	11	OCEAN RAIN	Echo & the Bunnymen (Korova)
19	12	HUMAN'S LIB	Howard Jones (WEA)
13	13	INTO THE GAP	Thompson Twins (Arista)
15	14	AN INNOCENT MAN	Billy Joel (CBS)
30	15	THEN CAME ROCK 'N' ROLL	Various Artists (EMI)
20	16	LEGEND (MUSIC FROM ROBIN OF SHERWOOD)	Clannad (RCA)
31	17	CAFE BLEU	Style Council (Polydor)
11	18	ALCHEMY - DIRE STRAITS LIVE	Dire Straits (Vertigo)
21	19	LAMENT	Ultravox (Chrysalis)
22	20	DON'T STOP DANCIN'	Various Artists (Telstar)
35	21	THE SMITHS	Smiths (Rough Trade)
14	22	MIRROR MOVES	Psychedlic Furs (CBS)
16	23	THE TOP	Cure (Fiction)
18	24	BREAK OUT	Pointer Sisters (Planet)
12	25	JUNK CULTURE	Orchestral Manoeuvres In The Dark (Virgin)
25	26	SEVEN AND THE RAGGED TIGER	Duran Duran (EMI)
36	27	FROM HER TO ETERNITY	Nick Cave & the bad seeds (Mute)
33	28	HUMAN RACING	Nik Kershaw (MCA)
24	29	AND I LOVE YOU SO	Howard Keel (Warwick)
48	30	ISLANDS	Kajagoogoo (EMI)
29	31	LOVE WARS	Womack & Womack (Elektra)
32	32	CHANGE OF HEART	Change (WEA)
41	33	THE POET II	Bobby Womack (Motown)
27	34	MASTERPIECES - THE VERY BEST OF SKY	Sky (Telstar)
23	35	MARVIN GAYE'S GREATEST HITS	Marvin Gaye (Telstar)
26	36	THE PROS AND CONS OF HITCH HIKING	Roger Waters (Harvest)
-	37	STREET SOUNDS ELECTRO 4	Various Artists (Street Sounds)
-	38	TOUCH DANCE	Eurythmics (RCA)
43	39	ONE EYED JACKS	Spear of Destiny (Epic)
28	40	GRACE UNDER PRESSURE	Rush (Vertigo)
-	41	LABOUR OF LOVE	UB40 (DEP International)
-	42	VENGEANCE	New Model Army (Abstract)
43	43	LOST BOYS	Flying Pickets (10 Records)
34	44	STREET SOUNDS EDITION 9	Various Artists (Street Sounds)
42	45	OASIS	Oasis (WEA)
49	47	COLOUR BY NUMBERS	Culture Club (Virgin)
-	48	1984	Van Halen (Warner Bros.)
38	49	WOULD YA LIKE MORE SCRATCHIN'	Malcolm McLaren (Virgin/Charisma)
39	50	AGAINST ALL ODDS	Soundtrack (Virgin)

16 June 1984

last	this		
1	1	LEGEND	Bob Marley & the Wailers (Island)
2	2	THE WORKS	Queen (EMI)
4	3	NOW THAT'S WHAT I CALL MUSIC 2	Various Artists (EMI/Virgin)
14	4	AN INNOCENT MAN	Billy Joel (CBS)
7	5	THRILLER	Michael Jackson (Epic)
6	6	CAN'T SLOW DOWN	Lionel Richie (Motown)
12	7	HUMAN'S LIB	Howard Jones (WEA)
17	8	CAFE BLEU	Style Council (Polydor)
9	9	HUNGRY FOR HITS	Various Artists (K-Tel)
-	10	BORN IN THE USA	Bruce Springsteen (CBS)
8	11	FOOTLOOSE	Soundtrack (CBS)
5	12	MANGE TOUT	Blancmange (London)
15	13	THEN CAME ROCK 'N' ROLL	Various Artists (EMI)
-	14	BREAK MACHINE	Break Machine (Record Shack)
16	15	LEGEND (MUSIC FROM ROBIN OF SHERWOOD)	Clannad (RCA)
3	16	HYSTERIA	Human League (Virgin)
-	17	HYENA	Siouxsie & the Banshees (Wonderland)
21	18	THE SMITHS	Smiths (Rough Trade)
26	19	SEVEN AND THE RAGGED TIGER	Duran Duran (EMI)
43	20	LOST BOYS	Flying Pickets (10 Records)
37	21	STREET SOUNDS ELECTRO 4	Various Artists (Street Sounds)
-	22	FAREWELL MY SUMMER LOVE	Michael Jackson (Motown)
34	23	MASTERPIECES - THE VERY BEST OF SKY	Sky (Telstar)
10	24	MAN ON THE LINE	Chris DeBurgh (A&M)
13	25	INTO THE GAP	Thompson Twins (Arista)
-	26	EDEN	Everything but the Girl (Blanco Y Negro)
19	27	LAMENT	Ultravox (Chrysalis)
20	28	DON'T STOP DANCIN'	Various Artists (Telstar)
18	29	ALCHEMY - DIRE STRAITS LIVE	Dire Straits (Vertigo)
32	30	CHANGE OF HEART	Change (WEA)
38	31	TOUCH DANCE	Eurythmics (RCA)
24	32	BREAK OUT	Pointer Sisters (Planet)
28	33	HUMAN RACING	Nik Kershaw (MCA)
-	34	20 FAMILY FAVOURITES	Vera Lynn (EMI)
11	35	OCEAN RAIN	Echo & the Bunnymen (Korova)
33	36	THE POET II	Bobby Womack (Motown)
29	37	AND I LOVE YOU SO	Howard Keel (Warwick)
25	38	JUNK CULTURE	Orchestral Manoeuvres In The Dark (Virgin)
36	39	THE PROS AND CONS OF HITCH HIKING	Roger Waters (Harvest)
22	40	MIRROR MOVES	Psychedlic Furs (CBS)
27	41	FROM HER TO ETERNITY	Nick Cave & the Bad Seeds (Mute)
41	42	LABOUR OF LOVE	UB40 (DEP International)
23	43	THE TOP	Cure (Fiction)
40	44	GRACE UNDER PRESSURE	Rush (Vertigo)
-	45	BREAKDANCE	Soundtrack (Polydor)
30	46	ISLANDS	Kajagoogoo (EMI)
31	47	LOVE WARS	Womack & Womack (Elektra)
-	48	NEW SENSATION	Lou Reed (RCA)
50	49	AGAINST ALL ODDS	Soundtrack (Virgin)
44	50	STREET SOUNDS EDITION 9	Various Artists (Street Sounds)

Legend, a compilation of the hits and the best of the late Bob Marley, was to be not only Marley's biggest seller, but also the biggest-selling reggae album of all time, and a still very hardy perennial in Island's catalogue by the 1990s. Its nine straight weeks at Number 1 were the longest continuous chart-topping run since Adam & The Ants' three-month stay with *Kings Of The Wild Frontier* in 1981.

254

June – July 1984

last week	this week	23 June 1984	
1	1	LEGEND	Bob Marley & the Wailers (Island)
10	2	BORN IN THE USA	Bruce Springsteen (CBS)
2	3	THE WORKS	Queen (EMI)
4	4	AN INNOCENT MAN	Billy Joel (CBS)
5	5	THRILLER	Michael Jackson (Epic)
6	6	CAN'T SLOW DOWN	Lionel Richie (Motown)
7	7	HUMAN'S LIB	Howard Jones (WEA)
26	8	EDEN Everything but the Girl (Blanco Y Negro)	
17	9	HYENA Siouxsie & the Banshees (Wonderland)	
3	10	NOW THAT'S WHAT I CALL MUSIC 2	
			Various Artists (EMI/Virgin)
9	11	HUNGRY FOR HITS	Various Artists (K-Tel)
20	12	LOST BOYS	Flying Pickets (10 Records)
8	13	CAFE BLEU	Style Council (Polydor)
-	14	CAMOUFLAGE	Rod Stewart (Warner Bros.)
11	15	FOOTLOOSE	Soundtrack (CBS)
13	16	THEN CAME ROCK 'N' ROLL	
			Various Artists (EMI)
28	17	DON'T STOP DANCIN'	Various Artists (Telstar)
18	18	THE SMITHS	Smiths (Rough Trade)
22	19	FAREWELL MY SUMMER LOVE	
			Michael Jackson (Motown)
-	20	AMERICAN HEARTBEAT	Various Artists (Epic)
45	21	BREAKDANCE	Soundtrack (Polydor)
12	22	MANGE TOUT	Blancmange (London)
24	23	MAN ON THE LINE	Chris DeBurgh (A&M)
16	24	HYSTERIA	Human League (Virgin)
21	25	STREET SOUNDS ELECTRO 4	
			Various Artists (Street Sounds)
-	26	IN THE STUDIO	Special AKA (2-Tone)
-	27	STAY HUNGRY	Twisted Sister (Atlantic)
27	28	LAMENT	Ultravox (Chrysalis)
14	29	BREAK MACHINE	
			Break Machine (Record Shack)
23	30	MASTERPIECES - THE VERY BEST OF SKY	
			Sky (Telstar)
-	31	ROCK WILL NEVER DIE	
			Michael Schenker (Chrysalis)
31	32	TOUCH DANCE	Eurythmics (RCA)
25	33	INTO THE GAP	Thompson Twins (Arista)
33	34	HUMAN RACING	Nik Kershaw (MCA)
41	35	FROM HER TO ETERNITY	
			Nick Cave & the Bad Seeds (Mute)
47	36	LOVE WARS	Womack & Womack (Elektra)
32	37	BREAK OUT	Pointer Sisters (Planet)
35	38	OCEAN RAIN	Echo & the Bunnymen (Korova)
30	39	CHANGE OF HEART	Change (WEA)
29	40	ALCHEMY - DIRE STRAITS LIVE	
			Dire Straits (Vertigo)
-	41	VOICE OF AMERICA	
			Little Steven (EMI America)
36	42	THE POET II	Bobby Womack (Motown)
15	43	LEGEND (MUSIC FROM ROBIN OF SHERWOOD)	
			Clannad (RCA)
38	44	JUNK CULTURE	
			Orchestral Manoeuvres In The Dark (Virgin)
19	45	SEVEN AND THE RAGGED TIGER	
			Duran Duran (EMI)
-	46	BACKTRACKIN'	Eric Clapton (Starblend)
39	47	THE PROS AND CONS OF HITCH HIKING	
			Roger Waters (Harvest)
-	48	NOW	Patrice Rushen (Elektra)
-	49	FANTASTIC	Wham! (Innervision)
-	50	CREW CUTS	Various Artists (Island)

last week	this week	30 June 1984	
1	1	LEGEND	Bob Marley & the Wailers (Island)
2	2	BORN IN THE USA	Bruce Springsteen (CBS)
-	3	BREAKING HEARTS	Elton John (Rocket)
4	4	AN INNOCENT MAN	Billy Joel (CBS)
14	5	CAMOUFLAGE	Rod Stewart (Warner Bros.)
6	6	CAN'T SLOW DOWN	Lionel Richie (Motown)
3	7	THE WORKS	Queen (EMI)
20	8	AMERICAN HEARTBEAT Various Artists (Epic)	
8	9	EDEN Everything but the Girl (Blanco Y Negro)	
21	10	BREAKDANCE	Soundtrack (Polydor)
16	11	THEN CAME ROCK 'N' ROLL	
			Various Artists (EMI)
5	12	THRILLER	Michael Jackson (Epic)
7	13	HUMAN'S LIB	Howard Jones (WEA)
31	14	ROCK WILL NEVER DIE	
			Michael Schenker (Chrysalis)
19	15	FAREWELL MY SUMMER LOVE	
			Michael Jackson (Motown)
29	16	BREAK MACHINE Break Machine (Record Shack)	
13	17	CAFE BLEU	Style Council (Polydor)
26	18	IN THE STUDIO	Special AKA (2-Tone)
9	19	HYENA Siouxsie & the Banshees (Wonderland)	
10	20	NOW THAT'S WHAT I CALL MUSIC 2	
			Various Artists (EMI/Virgin)
15	21	FOOTLOOSE	Soundtrack (CBS)
24	22	HYSTERIA	Human League (Virgin)
12	23	LOST BOYS	Flying Pickets (10 Records)
-	24	PRIVATE DANCER	Tina Turner (Capitol)
37	25	BREAK OUT	Pointer Sisters (Planet)
34	26	HUMAN RACING	Nik Kershaw (MCA)
18	27	THE SMITHS	Smiths (Rough Trade)
-	28	HEARTBEATS	Barbara Dickson (Epic)
22	29	MANGE TOUT	Blancmange (London)
23	30	MAN ON THE LINE	Chris DeBurgh (A&M)
25	31	STREET SOUNDS ELECTRO 4	
			Various Artists (Street Sounds)
39	32	CHANGE OF HEART	Change (WEA)
30	33	MASTERPIECES - THE VERY BEST OF SKY	
			Sky (Telstar)
47	34	THE PROS AND CONS OF HITCH HIKING	
			Roger Waters (Harvest)
11	35	HUNGRY FOR HITS	Various Artists (K-Tel)
17	36	DON'T STOP DANCIN'	Various Artists (Telstar)
40	37	ALCHEMY - DIRE STRAITS LIVE	
			Dire Straits (Vertigo)
45	38	SEVEN AND THE RAGGED TIGER	
			Duran Duran (EMI)
44	39	JUNK CULTURE	
			Orchestral Manoeuvres In The Dark (Virgin)
32	40	TOUCH DANCE	Eurythmics (RCA)
35	41	FROM HER TO ETERNITY	
			Nick Cave and the Bad Seeds (Mute)
43	42	LEGEND (MUSIC FROM ROBIN OF SHERWOOD)	
			Clannad (RCA)
-	43	BROKEN DREAMS	Various Artists (Starblend)
-	44	MIRROR MOVES	Psychedelic Furs (CBS)
-	45	STREET SOUNDS NUMBER ONES	
			Various Artists (Street Sounds)
-	46	NYLON CURTAIN	Billy Joel (CBS)
-	47	MADONNA	Madonna (Sire)
-	48	THE THEMES ALBUM	Various Artists (K-Tel)
38	49	OCEAN RAIN	
			Echo & the Bunnymen (Korova)
48	50	NOW	Patrice Rushen (Elektra)

last week	this week	7 July 1984	
1	1	LEGEND	Bob Marley & the Wailers (Island)
3	2	BREAKING HEARTS	Elton John (Rocket)
2	3	BORN IN THE USA	Bruce Springsteen (CBS)
4	4	AN INNOCENT MAN	Billy Joel (CBS)
8	5	AMERICAN HEARTBEAT	
			Various Artists (Epic)
10	6	BREAKDANCE	Soundtrack (Polydor)
-	7	PARADE	Spandau Ballet (Chrysalis)
6	8	CAN'T SLOW DOWN	Lionel Richie (Motown)
5	9	CAMOUFLAGE	Rod Stewart (Warner Bros.)
-	10	BRILLIANT TREES	David Sylvian (Virgin)
24	11	PRIVATE DANCER	Tina Turner (Capitol)
15	12	FAREWELL MY SUMMER LOVE	
			Michael Jackson (Motown)
-	13	GOODBYE CRUEL WORLD	
			Elvis Costello (F Beat)
7	14	THE WORKS	Queen (EMI)
13	15	HUMAN'S LIB	Howard Jones (WEA)
12	16	THRILLER	Michael Jackson (Epic)
26	17	HUMAN RACING	Nik Kershaw (MCA)
25	18	BREAK OUT	Pointer Sisters (Planet)
17	19	CAFE BLEU	Style Council (Polydor)
9	20	EDEN Everything but the Girl (Blanco Y Negro)	
-	21	DISCOVERY	Mike Oldfield (Virgin)
11	22	THEN CAME ROCK 'N' ROLL	
			Various Artists (EMI)
21	23	FOOTLOOSE	Soundtrack (CBS)
19	24	HYENA Siouxsie & the Banshees (Wonderland)	
20	25	NOW THAT'S WHAT I CALL MUSIC 2	
			Various Artists (EMI/Virgin)
22	26	HYSTERIA	Human League (Virgin)
-	27	REWIND 1971-1984 (THE BEST OF THE	
			ROLLING STONES)
			Rolling Stones (Rolling Stones)
28	28	STRANGE FRONTIER	Roger Taylor (EMI)
46	29	NYLON CURTAIN	Billy Joel (CBS)
14	30	ROCK WILL NEVER DIE	
			Michael Schenker (Chrysalis)
40	31	TOUCH DANCE	Eurythmics (RCA)
32	32	CHANGE OF HEART	Change (WEA)
39	33	JUNK CULTURE	
			Orchestral Manoeuvres In The Dark (Virgin)
16	34	BREAK MACHINE	
			Break Machine (Record Shack)
18	35	IN THE STUDIO	Special AKA (2-Tone)
28	36	HEARTBEATS	Barbara Dickson (Epic)
50	37	NOW	Patrice Rushen (Elektra)
-	38	SHE'S SO UNUSUAL	Cyndi Lauper (Portrait)
-	39	MARCUS MILLER	
			Marcus Miller (Warner Bros.)
-	40	LOVE LANGUAGE	
			Teddy Pendergrass (Asylum)
-	41	TOCSIN	X-Mal Deutschland (4AD)
27	42	THE SMITHS	Smiths (Rough Trade)
31	43	MAN ON THE LINE	Chris DeBurgh (A&M)
-	44	STREET SOUNDS ELECTRO 4	
			Various Artists (Street Sounds)
29	45	MANGE TOUT	Blancmange (London)
23	46	LOST BOYS	Flying Pickets (10 Records)
-	47	LAMENT	Ultravox (Chrysalis)
-	48	STREET SOUNDS UK ELECTRO	
			Various Artists (Street Sounds)
35	49	HUNGRY FOR HITS	Various Artists (K-Tel)
-	50	INTO THE GAP	Thompson Twins (Arista)

Bruce Springsteen emerged with what was to be his all-time best-selling (and hit single offloading) album, *Born In The USA*. However, despite US chart-topping success, he was never able to muster enough concentrated sales here initially to dethrone the Bob Marley compilation, and in fact *Born In The USA* would not reach Number 1 in the UK until much later in its prodigious chart run, during February 1985.

July 1984

14 July 1984

last week	this week	Title	Artist (Label)
1	1	LEGEND	Bob Marley & the Wailers (Island)
2	2	BREAKING HEARTS	Elton John (Rocket)
7	3	PARADE	Spandau Ballet (Chrysalis)
10	4	BRILLIANT TREES	David Sylvian (Virgin)
13	5	GOODBYE CRUEL WORLD	Elvis Costello (F Beat)
4	6	AN INNOCENT MAN	Billy Joel (CBS)
5	7	AMERICAN HEARTBEAT	Various Artists (Epic)
8	8	CAN'T SLOW DOWN	Lionel Richie (Motown)
6	9	BREAKDANCE	Soundtrack (Polydor)
17	10	HUMAN RACING	Nik Kershaw (MCA)
21	11	DISCOVERY	Mike Oldfield (Virgin)
11	12	PRIVATE DANCER	Tina Turner (Capitol)
3	13	BORN IN THE USA	Bruce Springsteen (CBS)
27	14	REWIND 1971-1984 (THE BEST OF THE ROLLING STONES)	Rolling Stones (Rolling Stones)
14	15	THE WORKS	Queen (EMI)
12	16	FAREWELL MY SUMMER LOVE	Michael Jackson (Motown)
9	17	CAMOUFLAGE	Rod Stewart (Warner Bros.)
18	18	BREAK OUT	Pointer Sisters (Planet)
33	19	JUNK CULTURE	Orchestral Manoeuvres In The Dark (Virgin)
16	20	THRILLER	Michael Jackson (Epic)
28	21	STRANGE FRONTIER	Roger Taylor (EMI)
15	22	HUMAN'S LIB	Howard Jones (WEA)
-	23	BEAT STREET	Soundtrack (Atlantic)
25	24	NOW THAT'S WHAT I CALL MUSIC 2	Various Artists (EMI)
38	25	SHE'S SO UNUSUAL	Cyndi Lauper (Portrait)
50	26	INTO THE GAP	Thompson Twins (Arista)
26	27	HYSTERIA	Human League (Virgin)
20	28	EDEN Everything but the Girl (Blanco Y Negro)	
22	29	THEN CAME ROCK 'N' ROLL	Various Artists (EMI)
30	30	ROCK WILL NEVER DIE	Michael Schenker (Chrysalis)
24	31	HYENA	Siouxsie & the Banshees (Wonderland)
35	32	IN THE STUDIO	Special AKA (2-Tone)
32	33	CHANGE OF HEART	Change (WEA)
41	34	TOCSIN	X-Mal Deutschland (4AD)
47	35	LAMENT	Ultravox (Chrysalis)
46	36	LOST BOYS	Flying Pickets (10 Records)
37	37	HUNGRY FOR HITS	Various Artists (K-Tel)
42	38	THE SMITHS	Smiths (Rough Trade)
39	39	FOOTLOOSE	Soundtrack (CBS)
19	40	CAFE BLEU	Style Council (Polydor)
-	41	MASTERPIECES - THE VERY BEST OF SKY	Sky (Telstar)
45	42	MANGE TOUT	Blancmange (London)
-	43	ROCK 'N' SOUL (PART 1)	Daryl Hall & John Oates (RCA)
-	44	ALCHEMY - DIRE STRAITS LIVE	Dire Straits (Vertigo)
29	45	NYLON CURTAIN	Billy Joel (CBS)
34	46	BREAK MACHINE	Break Machine (Record Shack)
36	47	HEARTBEATS	Barbara Dickson (Epic)
44	48	STREET SOUNDS ELECTRO 4	Various Artists (Street Sounds)
48	49	STREET SOUNDS UK ELECTRO	Various Artists (Street Sounds)
-	50	COLOUR BY NUMBERS	Culture Club (Virgin)

21 July 1984

last week	this week	Title	Artist (Label)
1	1	LEGEND	Bob Marley & the Wailers (Island)
3	2	PARADE	Spandau Ballet (Chrysalis)
-	3	VICTORY	Jacksons (Epic)
2	4	BREAKING HEARTS	Elton John (Rocket)
8	5	CAN'T SLOW DOWN	Lionel Richie (Motown)
6	6	AN INNOCENT MAN	Billy Joel (CBS)
-	7	THE LAST IN LINE	Dio (Vertigo)
18	8	BREAK OUT	Pointer Sisters (Planet)
9	9	BREAKDANCE	Soundtrack (Polydor)
10	10	HUMAN RACING	Nik Kershaw (MCA)
12	11	PRIVATE DANCER	Tina Turner (Capitol)
5	12	GOODBYE CRUEL WORLD	Elvis Costello (F Beat)
7	13	AMERICAN HEARTBEAT	Various Artists (Epic)
4	14	BRILLIANT TREES	David Sylvian (Virgin)
20	15	THRILLER	Michael Jackson (Epic)
11	16	DISCOVERY	Mike Oldfield (Virgin)
13	17	BORN IN THE USA	Bruce Springsteen (CBS)
15	18	THE WORKS	Queen (EMI)
14	19	REWIND 1971-1984 (THE BEST OF THE ROLLING STONES)	Rolling Stones (Rolling Stones)
22	20	HUMAN'S LIB	Howard Jones (WEA)
25	21	SHE'S SO UNUSUAL	Cyndi Lauper (Portrait)
24	22	NOW THAT'S WHAT I CALL MUSIC 2	Various Artists (EMI/Virgin)
17	23	CAMOUFLAGE	Rod Stewart (Warner Bros.)
16	24	FAREWELL MY SUMMER LOVE	Michael Jackson (Motown)
-	25	PURPLE RAIN	Prince & the Revolution (Warner Bros.)
26	26	INTO THE GAP	Thompson Twins (Arista)
23	27	BEAT STREET	Soundtrack (Atlantic)
28	28	OCEAN RAIN	Echo & the Bunnymen (Korova)
35	29	LAMENT	Ultravox (Chrysalis)
27	30	HYSTERIA	Human League (Virgin)
19	31	JUNK CULTURE	Orchestral Manoeuvres In The Dark (Virgin)
-	32	NOW	Patrice Rushen (Elektra)
39	33	FOOTLOOSE	Soundtrack (CBS)
-	34	20 ORIGINAL GREATS	Cliff Richard & the Shadows (EMI)
-	35	STREET TALK	Steve Perry (CBS)
36	36	THIS IS WHAT YOU WANT	Public Image Ltd (Virgin)
32	37	IN THE STUDIO	Special AKA (2-Tone)
33	38	CHANGE OF HEART	Change (WEA)
34	39	TOCSIN	X-Mal Deutschland (4AD)
28	40	EDEN Everything but the Girl (Blanco Y Negro)	
-	41	MINUTES	Elkie Brooks (A&M)
-	42	CIVILIZED MAN	Joe Cocker (Capitol)
38	43	THE SMITHS	Smiths (Rough Trade)
48	44	STREET SOUNDS ELECTRO 4	Various Artists (Street Sounds)
49	45	STREET SOUNDS UK ELECTRO	Various Artists (Street Sounds)
21	46	STRANGE FRONTIER	Roger Taylor (EMI)
-	47	DIFFORD AND TILBROOK	Difford & Tilbrook (A&M)
-	48	AFTER MIDNIGHT	Eric Clapton (RSO)
-	49	RED OCTOPUS	Jefferson Starship (RCA)
-	50	HALLOWED GROUND	Violent Femmes (London)

28 July 1984

last week	this week	Title	Artist (Label)
3	1	VICTORY	Jacksons (Epic)
1	2	LEGEND	Bob Marley & the Wailers (Island)
7	3	THE LAST IN LINE	Dio (Vertigo)
2	4	PARADE	Spandau Ballet (Chrysalis)
11	5	PRIVATE DANCER	Tina Turner (Capitol)
10	6	HUMAN RACING	Nik Kershaw (MCA)
4	7	BREAKING HEARTS	Elton John (Rocket)
8	8	BREAK OUT	Pointer Sisters (Planet)
6	9	AN INNOCENT MAN	Billy Joel (CBS)
25	10	PURPLE RAIN	Prince & the Revolution (Warner Bros.)
-	11	DIAMOND LIFE	Sade (CBS)
5	12	CAN'T SLOW DOWN	Lionel Richie (Motown)
9	13	BREAKDANCE	Soundtrack (Polydor)
14	14	BRILLIANT TREES	David Sylvian (Virgin)
13	15	AMERICAN HEARTBEAT	Various Artists (Epic)
12	16	GOODBYE CRUEL WORLD	Elvis Costello (F Beat)
15	17	THRILLER	Michael Jackson (Epic)
16	18	DISCOVERY	Mike Oldfield (Virgin)
21	19	SHE'S SO UNUSUAL	Cyndi Lauper (Portrait)
18	20	THE WORKS	Queen (EMI)
-	21	PRIMITIVE	Neil Diamond (CBS)
17	22	BORN IN THE USA	Bruce Springsteen (CBS)
27	23	BEAT STREET	Soundtrack (Atlantic)
20	24	HUMAN'S LIB	Howard Jones (WEA)
19	25	REWIND 1971-1984 (THE BEST OF THE ROLLING STONES)	Rolling Stones (Rolling Stones)
28	26	OCEAN RAIN	Echo & the Bunnymen (Korova)
36	27	THIS IS WHAT YOU WANT	Public Image Ltd (Virgin)
26	28	INTO THE GAP	Thompson Twins (Arista)
22	29	NOW THAT'S WHAT I CALL MUSIC 2	Various Artists (EMI/Virgin)
30	30	CAMOUFLAGE	Rod Stewart (Warner Bros.)
31	31	JUNK CULTURE	Orchestral Manoeuvres In The Dark (Virgin)
41	32	MINUTES	Elkie Brooks (A&M)
29	33	LAMENT	Ultravox (Chrysalis)
24	34	FAREWELL MY SUMMER LOVE	Michael Jackson (Motown)
40	35	EDEN Everything but the Girl (Blanco Y Negro)	
36	36	CHANGE OF HEART	Change (WEA)
37	37	IN THE STUDIO	Special AKA (2-Tone)
35	38	STREET TALK	Steve Perry (CBS)
47	39	DIFFORD AND TILBROOK	Difford & Tilbrook (A&M)
30	40	HYSTERIA	Human League (Virgin)
32	41	NOW	Patrice Rushen (Elektra)
33	42	FOOTLOOSE	Soundtrack (CBS)
39	43	TOCSIN	X-Mal Deutschland (4AD)
-	44	SEND ME YOUR LOVE	Kashif (Arista)
-	45	STREET SOUNDS NUMBER ONES	Various Artists (Street Sounds)
-	46	WIPEOUT	Various Artists (Impression)
-	47	INCREASE THE PRESSURE	Conflict (Mortarhate)
-	48	CAFE BLEU	Style Council (Polydor)
43	49	THE SMITHS	Smiths (Rough Trade)
46	50	STRANGE FRONTIER	Roger Taylor (EMI)

The Jacksons' *Victory* album was their first-ever chart-topping LP as a group, and clearly benefitted from the spin-off effect of the continuing enormous sales of Michael Jackson's *Thriller* and its associated singles. An extra boost also came from *Victory*'s own spin-off 45, *State Of Shock*, which owed little to the traditional Jacksons sound, and instead highlighted a vocal duet between Michael and guest Mick Jagger.

August 1984

4 August 1984

last week	this week		
2	1	LEGEND	Bob Marley & the Wailers (Island)
5	2	PRIVATE DANCER	Tina Turner (Capitol)
11	3	DIAMOND LIFE	Sade (CBS)
4	4	PARADE	Spandau Ballet (Chrysalis)
1	5	VICTORY	Jacksons (Epic)
3	6	THE LAST IN LINE	Dio (Vertigo)
12	7	CAN'T SLOW DOWN	Lionel Richie (Motown)
21	8	PRIMITIVE	Neil Diamond (CBS)
7	9	BREAKING HEARTS	Elton John (Rocket)
10	10	PURPLE RAIN	Prince & the Revolution (Warner Bros.)
9	11	AN INNOCENT MAN	Billy Joel (CBS)
20	12	THE WORKS	Queen (EMI)
6	13	HUMAN RACING	Nik Kershaw (MCA)
13	14	BREAKDANCE	Soundtrack (Polydor)
17	15	THRILLER	Michael Jackson (Epic)
8	16	BREAK OUT	Pointer Sisters (Planet)
19	17	SHE'S SO UNUSUAL	Cyndi Lauper (Portrait)
25	18	REWIND 1971-1984 (THE BEST OF THE ROLLING STONES)	Rolling Stones (Rolling Stones)
16	19	GOODBYE CRUEL WORLD	Elvis Costello (F Beat)
22	20	BORN IN THE USA	Bruce Springsteen (CBS)
15	21	AMERICAN HEARTBEAT	Various Artists (Epic)
26	22	OCEAN RAIN	Echo & the Bunnymen (Korova)
28	23	INTO THE GAP	Thompson Twins (Arista)
24	24	HUMAN'S LIB	Howard Jones (WEA)
18	25	DISCOVERY	Mike Oldfield (Virgin)
14	26	BRILLIANT TREES	David Sylvian (Virgin)
23	27	BEAT STREET	Soundtrack (Atlantic)
40	28	HYSTERIA	Human League (Virgin)
33	29	LAMENT	Ultravox (Chrysalis)
-	30	A WORD TO THE WISE GUY	Mighty Wah (Beggars Banquet)
31	31	JUNK CULTURE	Orchestral Manoeuvres In The Dark (Virgin)
30	32	CAMOUFLAGE	Rod Stewart (Warner Bros.)
35	33	EDEN	Everything but the Girl (Blanco Y Negro)
42	34	FOOTLOOSE	Soundtrack (CBS)
45	35	STREET SOUNDS NUMBER ONES	Various Artists (Street Sounds)
-	36	BREAKDANCE - YOU CAN DO IT	Various Artists (K-Tel)
32	37	MINUTES	Elkie Brooks (A&M)
34	38	FAREWELL MY SUMMER LOVE	Michael Jackson (Motown)
27	39	THIS IS WHAT YOU WANT	Public Image Ltd (Virgin)
29	40	NOW THAT'S WHAT I CALL MUSIC 2	Various Artists (EMI/Virgin)
36	41	CHANGE OF HEART	Change (WEA)
38	42	STREET TALK	Steve Perry (CBS)
39	43	DIFFORD AND TILBROOK	Difford & Tilbrook (A&M)
48	44	CAFE BLEU	Style Council (Polydor)
-	45	GREATEST MESSAGES	Grandmaster Flash (Sugarhill)
-	46	ANTHEM	Black Uhuru (Island)
-	47	CLUB TRACKS	Various Artists (Club)
-	48	BACKTRACKIN'	Eric Clapton (Starblend)
41	49	NOW	Patrice Rushen (Elektra)
50	50	STRANGE FRONTIER	Roger Taylor (EMI)

11 August 1984

last week	this week		
3	1	DIAMOND LIFE	Sade (CBS)
2	2	PRIVATE DANCER	Tina Turner (Capitol)
1	3	LEGEND	Bob Marley & the Wailers (Island)
7	4	CAN'T SLOW DOWN	Lionel Richie (Motown)
4	5	PARADE	Spandau Ballet (Chrysalis)
12	6	THE WORKS	Queen (EMI)
15	7	THRILLER	Michael Jackson (Epic)
10	8	PURPLE RAIN	Prince & the Revolution (Warner Bros.)
11	9	AN INNOCENT MAN	Billy Joel (CBS)
16	10	BREAK OUT	Pointer Sisters (Planet)
8	11	PRIMITIVE	Neil Diamond (CBS)
5	12	VICTORY	Jacksons (Epic)
9	13	BREAKING HEARTS	Elton John (Rocket)
14	14	BREAKDANCE	Soundtrack (Polydor)
6	15	THE LAST IN LINE	Dio (Vertigo)
13	16	HUMAN RACING	Nik Kershaw (MCA)
17	17	SHE'S SO UNUSUAL	Cyndi Lauper (Portrait)
-	18	NOW THAT'S WHAT I CALL MUSIC 3	Various Artists (EMI/Virgin)
24	19	HUMAN'S LIB	Howard Jones (WEA)
-	20	STARLIGHT EXPRESS	Various (Starlight/Polydor)
23	21	INTO THE GAP	Thompson Twins (Arista)
25	22	DISCOVERY	Mike Oldfield (Virgin)
30	23	A WORD TO THE WISE GUY	Mighty Wah (Beggars Banquet)
22	24	OCEAN RAIN	Echo & the Bunnymen (Korova)
20	25	BORN IN THE USA	Bruce Springsteen (CBS)
27	26	BEAT STREET	Soundtrack (Atlantic)
21	27	AMERICAN HEARTBEAT	Various Artists (Epic)
26	28	BRILLIANT TREES	David Sylvian (Virgin)
32	29	CAMOUFLAGE	Rod Stewart (Warner Bros.)
38	30	FAREWELL MY SUMMER LOVE	Michael Jackson (Motown)
-	31	STREET SOUNDS CRUCIAL ELECTRO 2	Various Artists (Street Sounds)
-	32	CONDITION CRITICAL	Quiet Riot (Epic)
18	33	REWIND 1971-1984 (THE BEST OF THE ROLLING STONES)	Rolling Stones (Rolling Stones)
19	34	GOODBYE CRUEL WORLD	Elvis Costello (F Beat)
-	35	SISTERS	Bluebells (London)
36	36	BREAKDANCE - YOU CAN DO IT	Various Artists (K-Tel)
-	37	REVOLUTION	Theatre of Hate (Burning Rome)
-	38	ALCHEMY - DIRE STRAITS LIVE	Dire Straits (Vertigo)
34	39	FOOTLOOSE	Soundtrack (CBS)
-	40	MANGE TOUT	Blancmange (London)
-	41	SEVEN AND THE RAGGED TIGER	Duran Duran (EMI)
40	42	NOW THAT'S WHAT I CALL MUSIC 2	Various Artists (EMI/Virgin)
29	43	LAMENT	Ultravox (Chrysalis)
31	44	JUNK CULTURE	Orchestral Manoeuvres In The Dark (Virgin)
-	45	MAN ON THE LINE	Chris DeBurgh (A&M)
-	46	INTOLERANCE	Tik & Tok (Survival)
41	47	CHANGE OF HEART	Change (WEA)
33	48	EDEN	Everything but the Girl (Blanco Y Negro)
37	49	MINUTES	Elkie Brooks (A&M)
35	50	STREET SOUNDS NUMBER ONES	Various Artists (Street Sounds)

18 August 1984

last week	this week		
18	1	NOW THAT'S WHAT I CALL MUSIC 3	Various Artists (EMI/Virgin)
1	2	DIAMOND LIFE	Sade (CBS)
2	3	PRIVATE DANCER	Tina Turner (Capitol)
3	4	LEGEND	Bob Marley & the Wailers (Island)
6	5	THE WORKS	Queen (EMI)
10	6	BREAK OUT	Pointer Sisters (Planet)
4	7	CAN'T SLOW DOWN	Lionel Richie (Motown)
9	8	AN INNOCENT MAN	Billy Joel (CBS)
8	9	PURPLE RAIN	Prince & the Revolution (Warner Bros.)
7	10	THRILLER	Michael Jackson (Epic)
5	11	PARADE	Spandau Ballet (Chrysalis)
13	12	BREAKING HEARTS	Elton John (Rocket)
14	13	BREAKDANCE	Soundtrack (Polydor)
35	14	SISTERS	Bluebells (London)
11	15	PRIMITIVE	Neil Diamond (CBS)
16	16	HUMAN RACING	Nik Kershaw (MCA)
19	17	HUMAN'S LIB	Howard Jones (WEA)
12	18	VICTORY	Jacksons (Epic)
15	19	THE LAST IN LINE	Dio (Vertigo)
17	20	SHE'S SO UNUSUAL	Cyndi Lauper (Portrait)
24	21	OCEAN RAIN	Echo & the Bunnymen (Korova)
20	22	STARLIGHT EXPRESS	Various (Starlight/Polydor)
21	23	INTO THE GAP	Thompson Twins (Arista)
23	24	A WORD TO THE WISE GUY	Mighty Wah (Beggars Banquet)
25	25	BORN IN THE USA	Bruce Springsteen (CBS)
-	26	THE BEST OF JON AND VANGELIS	Jon & Vangelis (Polydor)
22	27	DISCOVERY	Mike Oldfield (Virgin)
27	28	AMERICAN HEARTBEAT	Various Artists (Epic)
31	29	STREET SOUNDS CRUCIAL ELECTRO 2	Various Artists (Street Sounds)
29	30	CAMOUFLAGE	Rod Stewart (Warner Bros.)
34	31	GOODBYE CRUEL WORLD	Elvis Costello (F Beat)
26	32	BEAT STREET	Soundtrack (Atlantic)
28	33	BRILLIANT TREES	David Sylvian (Virgin)
43	34	LAMENT	Ultravox (Chrysalis)
42	35	NOW THAT'S WHAT I CALL MUSIC 2	Various Artists (EMI/Virgin)
-	36	WELL PLEASED	Chas & Dave (Rockney)
-	37	IN ROCK WE TRUST	Y & T (A&M)
33	38	REWIND 1971-1984 (THE BEST OF THE ROLLING STONES)	Rolling Stones (Rolling Stones)
38	39	ALCHEMY - DIRE STRAITS LIVE	Dire Straits (Vertigo)
47	40	CHANGE OF HEART	Change (WEA)
48	41	EDEN	Everything but the Girl (Blanco Y Negro)
-	42	STREET SOUNDS EDITION 10	Various Artists (Street Sounds)
-	43	CHUNKS OF FUNK	Various Artists (MCA)
37	44	REVOLUTION	Theatre of Hate (Burning Rome)
41	45	SEVEN AND THE RAGGED TIGER	Duran Duran (EMI)
40	46	MANGE TOUT	Blancmange (London)
36	47	BREAKDANCE - YOU CAN DO IT	Various Artists (K-Tel)
-	48	GREATEST MESSAGES	Grandmaster Flash (Sugarhill)
-	49	BACKTRACKIN'	Eric Clapton (Starblend)
39	50	FOOTLOOSE	Soundtrack (CBS)

The Number 1 success of Sade's *Diamond Life* made her only the second female solo singer (after Kate Bush in 1978) to top the UK chart with her debut album - even if its reign at the top was restricted to one week before giving way to the third and best-selling yet of the blockbuster *Now That's What I Call Music* compilations. Tina Turner only just failed to achieve this feat with *Private Dancer*, peaking at 2.

August – September 1984

Prince's *Purple Rain* album, the soundtrack from his film of the same title, was a chart-topper for over 6 months in the US, but did not conquer quite so convincingly in the UK - where it was actually his first album to figure in the chart at all. Its Number 5 placing in August was the highest it would reach, despite a lengthy Top 10 residency and the boosting effect of the Top 3 *When Doves Cry* single.

September 1984

15 September 1984

last week	this week	Title	Artist (Label)
1	1	NOW THAT'S WHAT I CALL MUSIC 3	Various Artists (EMI/Virgin)
3	2	DIAMOND LIFE	Sade (CBS)
2	3	PRIVATE DANCER	Tina Turner (Capitol)
4	4	THE WORKS	Queen (EMI)
5	5	LEGEND	Bob Marley & the Wailers (Island)
6	6	CAN'T SLOW DOWN	Lionel Richie (Motown)
8	7	PARADE	Spandau Ballet (Chrysalis)
7	8	PURPLE RAIN	Prince & the Revolution (Warner Bros.)
11	9	HUMAN'S LIB	Howard Jones (WEA)
31	10	ELIMINATOR	ZZ Top (WEA)
-	11	POWERSLAVE	Iron Maiden (EMI)
12	12	BREAKING HEARTS	Elton John (Rocket)
9	13	PHIL FEARON AND GALAXY	Phil Fearon & Galaxy (Ensign)
37	14	DREAMLINE	Cult (Beggars Banquet)
10	15	BREAK OUT	Pointer Sisters (Planet)
13	16	THRILLER	Michael Jackson (Epic)
23	17	1100 BEL AIR PLACE	Julio Iglesias (CBS)
22	18	SELF CONTROL	Laura Branigan (Atlantic)
-	19	NO REMORSE	Motorhead (Bronze)
15	20	BORN IN THE USA	Bruce Springsteen (CBS)
-	21	UNDER WRAPS	Jethro Tull (Chrysalis)
17	22	AN INNOCENT MAN	Billy Joel (CBS)
18	23	HUMAN RACING	Nik Kershaw (MCA)
14	24	DOWN ON THE STREET	Shakatak (Polydor)
19	25	VICTORY	Jacksons (Epic)
16	26	JUST THE WAY YOU LIKE IT	SOS Band (Tabu/Epic)
-	27	WHOSE SIDE ARE YOU ON	Matt Bianco (WEA)
28	28	SHE'S SO UNUSUAL	Cyndi Lauper (Portrait)
33	29	THE STORY OF A YOUNG HEART	Flock of Seagulls (Jive)
21	30	INTO THE GAP	Thompson Twins (Arista)
26	31	NOW THAT'S WHAT I CALL MUSIC 2	Various Artists (EMI/Virgin)
20	32	BREAKDANCE	Soundtrack (Polydor)
-	33	REFLECTIONS	Rick James (Motown)
46	34	A WORD TO THE WISE GUY	Mighty Wah (Beggars Banquet)
-	35	1999	Prince (Warner Bros.)
43	36	QUEEN'S GREATEST HITS	Queen (EMI)
40	37	THE CROSSING	Big Country (Mercury)
-	38	CHANGE OF HEART	Change (WEA)
25	39	SISTERS	Bluebells (London)
42	40	THE LAST IN LINE	Dio (Vertigo)
50	41	BEAT STREET	Soundtrack (Atlantic)
39	42	L.A. IS MY LADY	Frank Sinatra (Qwest)
34	43	BRILLIANT TREES	David Sylvian (Virgin)
-	44	BURNING OIL	Skeletal Family (Red Rhino)
24	45	STREET SOUNDS EDITION 10	Various Artists (Street Sounds)
27	46	CAMOUFLAGE	Rod Stewart (Warner Bros.)
35	47	BREAKDANCE - YOU CAN DO IT	Various Artists (K-Tel)
-	48	RIDE THE LIGHTNING	Metallica (Music For Nations)
-	49	W.A.S.P.	W.A.S.P. (Capitol)
-	50	THE LAS VEGAS STORY	Gun Club (Animal/Chrysalis)

22 September 1984

last week	this week	Title	Artist (Label)
1	1	NOW THAT'S WHAT I CALL MUSIC 3	Various Artists (EMI/Virgin)
11	2	POWERSLAVE	Iron Maiden (EMI)
3	3	PRIVATE DANCER	Tina Turner (Capitol)
2	4	DIAMOND LIFE	Sade (CBS)
8	5	PURPLE RAIN	Prince & the Revolution (Warner Bros.)
10	6	ELIMINATOR	ZZ Top (WEA)
4	7	THE WORKS	Queen (EMI)
19	8	NO REMORSE	Motorhead (Bronze)
5	9	LEGEND	Bob Marley & the Wailers (Island)
7	10	PARADE	Spandau Ballet (Chrysalis)
6	11	CAN'T SLOW DOWN	Lionel Richie (Motown)
9	12	HUMAN'S LIB	Howard Jones (WEA)
-	13	THE WOMAN IN RED - ORIGINAL SOUNDTRACK	Stevie Wonder (Motown)
18	14	SELF CONTROL	Laura Branigan (Atlantic)
15	15	BREAK OUT	Pointer Sisters (Planet)
12	16	BREAKING HEARTS	Elton John (Rocket)
21	17	UNDER WRAPS	Jethro Tull (Chrysalis)
16	18	THRILLER	Michael Jackson (Epic)
17	19	1100 BEL AIR PLACE	Julio Iglesias (CBS)
14	20	DREAMLINE	Cult (Beggars Banquet)
20	21	BORN IN THE USA	Bruce Springsteen (CBS)
13	22	PHIL FEARON AND GALAXY	Phil Fearon & Galaxy (Ensign)
26	23	JUST THE WAY YOU LIKE IT	SOS Band (Tabu/Epic)
22	24	AN INNOCENT MAN	Billy Joel (CBS)
25	25	VICTORY	Jacksons (Epic)
-	26	CRE-OLE	Kid Creole & the Coconuts (Island)
24	27	DOWN ON THE STREET	Shakatak (Polydor)
32	28	BREAKDANCE	Soundtrack (Polydor)
30	29	INTO THE GAP	Thompson Twins (Arista)
28	30	SHE'S SO UNUSUAL	Cyndi Lauper (Portrait)
-	31	A SPECIAL PART OF ME	Johnny Mathis (CBS)
-	32	SWEET SIXTEEN	Sweet (Anagram)
31	33	NOW THAT'S WHAT I CALL MUSIC 2	Various Artists (EMI/Virgin)
36	34	QUEEN'S GREATEST HITS	Queen (EMI)
23	35	HUMAN RACING	Nik Kershaw (MCA)
46	36	CAMOUFLAGE	Rod Stewart (Warner Bros.)
42	37	L.A. IS MY LADY	Frank Sinatra (Qwest)
33	38	REFLECTIONS	Rick James (Motown)
35	39	1999	Prince (Warner Bros.)
29	40	THE STORY OF A YOUNG HEART	Flock of Seagulls (Jive)
-	41	CATS WITHOUT CLAWS	Donna Summer (Warner Bros.)
45	42	STREET SOUNDS EDITION 10	Various Artists (Street Sounds)
-	43	NIGHT MOVES	Various Artists (K-Tel)
-	44	YOU, ME AND HE	M'Tume (Epic)
27	45	WHOSE SIDE ARE YOU ON	Matt Bianco (WEA)
-	46	ALCHEMY - DIRE STRAITS LIVE	Dire Straits (Vertigo)
-	47	ANTHEM	Black Uhuru (Island)
-	48	IF I KISSED HER	400 Blows (Illuminated)
43	49	BRILLIANT TREES	David Sylvian (Virgin)
-	50	WAR	U2 (Island)

29 September 1984

last week	this week	Title	Artist (Label)
13	1	THE WOMAN IN RED - ORIGINAL SOUNDTRACK	Stevie Wonder (Motown)
4	2	DIAMOND LIFE	Sade (CBS)
3	3	PRIVATE DANCER	Tina Turner (Capitol)
6	4	ELIMINATOR	ZZ Top (WEA)
2	5	POWERSLAVE	Iron Maiden (EMI)
1	6	NOW THAT'S WHAT I CALL MUSIC 3	Various Artists (EMI/Virgin)
5	7	PURPLE RAIN	Prince & the Revolution (Warner Bros.)
8	8	NO REMORSE	Motorhead (Bronze)
7	9	THE WORKS	Queen (EMI)
9	10	LEGEND	Bob Marley & the Wailers (Island)
10	11	PARADE	Spandau Ballet (Chrysalis)
12	12	HUMAN'S LIB	Howard Jones (WEA)
11	13	CAN'T SLOW DOWN	Lionel Richie (Motown)
14	14	SELF CONTROL	Laura Branigan (Atlantic)
16	15	BREAKING HEARTS	Elton John (Rocket)
18	16	THRILLER	Michael Jackson (Epic)
17	17	UNDER WRAPS	Jethro Tull (Chrysalis)
-	18	KNIFE	Aztec Camera (WEA)
19	19	1100 BEL AIR PLACE	Julio Iglesias (CBS)
15	20	BREAK OUT	Pointer Sisters (Planet)
22	21	PHIL FEARON AND GALAXY	Phil Fearon & Galaxy (Ensign)
20	22	DREAMLINE	Cult (Beggars Banquet)
34	23	QUEEN'S GREATEST HITS	Queen (EMI)
23	24	JUST THE WAY YOU LIKE IT	SOS Band (Tabu/Epic)
21	25	BORN IN THE USA	Bruce Springsteen (CBS)
26	26	CRE-OLE	Kid Creole & the Coconuts (Island)
24	27	AN INNOCENT MAN	Billy Joel (CBS)
27	28	DOWN ON THE STREET	Shakatak (Polydor)
-	29	HOPE AND GLORY	Tom Robinson (Castaway)
30	30	GHOSTBUSTERS	Soundtrack (Arista)
35	31	HUMAN RACING	Nik Kershaw (MCA)
-	32	THE SMITHS	Smiths (Rough Trade)
-	33	WE ARE FAMILY	Sister Sledge (Cotillion)
33	34	NOW THAT'S WHAT I CALL MUSIC 2	Various Artists (EMI/Virgin)
37	35	L.A. IS MY LADY	Frank Sinatra (Qwest)
-	36	THE LAST IN LINE	Dio (Vertigo)
-	37	SISTERS	Bluebells (London)
-	38	AMERICAN HEARTBEAT	Various Artists (Epic)
25	39	VICTORY	Jacksons (Epic)
30	40	SHE'S SO UNUSUAL	Cyndi Lauper (Portrait)
28	41	BREAKDANCE	Soundtrack (Polydor)
41	42	CATS WITHOUT CLAWS	Donna Summer (Warner Bros.)
46	43	ALCHEMY - DIRE STRAITS LIVE	Dire Straits (Vertigo)
-	44	BREAKDANCE - YOU CAN DO IT	Various Artists (K-Tel)
-	45	TILL WE HAVE FACES	Steve Hackett (Lamborghini)
-	46	BURNING OIL	Skeletal Family (Red Rhino)
-	47	SOIL FESTIVITIES	Vangelis (Polydor)
29	48	INTO THE GAP	Thompson Twins (Arista)
36	49	CAMOUFLAGE	Rod Stewart (Warner Bros.)
39	50	1999	Prince (Warner Bros.)

The Woman In Red was Stevie Wonder's soundtrack for the Gene Wilder-starring movie of the same title, and proved a better commercial prospect than Stevie's previous soundtrack experimentation with *The Secret Life Of Plants*. The album contained both vocal and instrumental tracks, plus guest vocals by Dionne Warwick, but the obvious highlight was the million-selling single *I Just Called To Say I Love You..*

October 1984

6 October 1984

last	this		
1	1	THE WOMAN IN RED - ORIGINAL SOUNDTRACK	Stevie Wonder (Motown)
4	2	ELIMINATOR	ZZ Top (WEA)
2	3	DIAMOND LIFE	Sade (CBS)
6	4	NOW THAT'S WHAT I CALL MUSIC 3	Various Artists (EMI/Virgin)
3	5	PRIVATE DANCER	Tina Turner (Capitol)
7	6	PURPLE RAIN	Prince & the Revolution (Warner Bros.)
5	7	POWERSLAVE	Iron Maiden (EMI)
18	8	KNIFE	Aztec Camera (WEA)
-	9	TONIGHT	David Bowie (EMI America)
9	10	THE WORKS	Queen (EMI)
13	11	CAN'T SLOW DOWN	Lionel Richie (Motown)
10	12	LEGEND	Bob Marley & the Wailers (Island)
11	13	PARADE	Spandau Ballet (Chrysalis)
33	14	WE ARE FAMILY	Sister Sledge (Cotillion)
29	15	HOPE AND GLORY	Tom Robinson (Castaway)
16	16	THRILLER	Michael Jackson (Epic)
12	17	HUMAN'S LIB	Howard Jones (WEA)
-	18	SOME GREAT REWARD	Depeche Mode (Mute)
-	19	ANIMALIZE	Kiss (Vertigo)
-	20	HOW MEN ARE	Heaven 17 (Virgin)
25	21	BORN IN THE USA	Bruce Springsteen (CBS)
-	22	U2 LIVE: UNDER A BLOOD RED SKY	U2 (Island)
14	23	SELF CONTROL	Laura Branigan (Atlantic)
15	24	BREAKING HEARTS	Elton John (Rocket)
30	25	GHOSTBUSTERS	Soundtrack (Arista)
20	26	BREAK OUT	Pointer Sisters (Planet)
31	27	HUMAN RACING	Nik Kershaw (MCA)
28	28	VERTICAL SMILES	Blackfoot (Atco)
17	29	UNDER WRAPS	Jethro Tull (Chrysalis)
27	30	AN INNOCENT MAN	Billy Joel (CBS)
22	31	DREAMLINE	Cult (Beggars Banquet)
8	32	NO REMORSE	Motorhead (Bronze)
19	33	1100 BEL AIR PLACE	Julio Iglesias (CBS)
26	34	CRE-OLE	Kid Creole & the Coconuts (Island)
21	35	PHIL FEARON AND GALAXY	Phil Fearon & Galaxy (Ensign)
23	36	QUEEN'S GREATEST HITS	Queen (EMI)
-	37	STREET SOUNDS ELECTRO 5	Various Artists (Street Sounds)
-	38	EDEN	Everything but the Girl (Blanco Y Negro)
39	39	VICTORY	Jacksons (Epic)
40	40	SHE'S SO UNUSUAL	Cyndi Lauper (Portrait)
-	41	ALL BY MYSELF	Various Artists (K-Tel)
-	42	THE STORY OF A YOUNG HEART	A Flock of Seagulls (Jive)
-	43	WAR	U2 (Island)
48	44	INTO THE GAP	Thompson Twins (Arista)
24	45	JUST THE WAY YOU LIKE IT	SOS Band (Tabu/Epic)
28	46	DOWN ON THE STREET	Shakatak (Polydor)
34	47	NOW THAT'S WHAT I CALL MUSIC 2	Various Artists (EMI/Virgin)
35	48	L.A. IS MY LADY	Frank Sinatra (Qwest)
32	49	THE SMITHS	Smiths (Rough Trade)
50	50	1999	Prince (Warner Bros.)

13 October 1984

last	this		
9	1	TONIGHT	David Bowie (EMI America)
3	2	DIAMOND LIFE	Sade (CBS)
2	3	ELIMINATOR	ZZ Top (WEA)
1	4	THE WOMAN IN RED - ORIGINAL SOUNDTRACK	Stevie Wonder (Motown)
6	5	PURPLE RAIN	Prince & the Revolution (Warner Bros.)
18	6	SOME GREAT REWARD	Depeche Mode (Mute)
4	7	NOW THAT'S WHAT I CALL MUSIC 3	Various Artists (EMI/Virgin)
20	8	HOW MEN ARE	Heaven 17 (Virgin)
5	9	PRIVATE DANCER	Tina Turner (Capitol)
-	10	WE ARE FAMILY	Sister Sledge (Cotillion)
-	11	THE UNFORGETTABLE FIRE	U2 (Island)
10	12	THE WORKS	Queen (EMI)
8	13	KNIFE	Aztec Camera (WEA)
11	14	CAN'T SLOW DOWN	Lionel Richie (Motown)
13	15	PARADE	Spandau Ballet (Chrysalis)
12	16	LEGEND	Bob Marley & the Wailers (Island)
16	17	THRILLER	Michael Jackson (Epic)
23	18	SELF CONTROL	Laura Branigan (Atlantic)
17	19	HUMAN'S LIB	Howard Jones (WEA)
15	20	HOPE AND GLORY	Tom Robinson (Castaway)
7	21	POWERSLAVE	Iron Maiden (EMI)
19	22	ANIMALIZE	Kiss (Vertigo)
37	23	STREET SOUNDS ELECTRO 5	Various Artists (Street Sounds)
26	24	BREAK OUT	Pointer Sisters (Planet)
30	25	AN INNOCENT MAN	Billy Joel (CBS)
22	26	U2 LIVE: UNDER A BLOOD RED SKY	U2 (Island)
-	27	TRUE COLOURS	Level 42 (Polydor)
24	28	BREAKING HEARTS	Elton John (Rocket)
27	29	HUMAN RACING	Nik Kershaw (MCA)
41	30	ALL BY MYSELF	Various Artists (K-Tel)
31	31	DREAMLINE	Cult (Beggars Banquet)
-	32	SWEPT AWAY	Diana Ross (Capitol)
-	33	THE PLAN	Gary Numan (Beggars Banquet)
21	34	BORN IN THE USA	Bruce Springsteen (CBS)
-	35	THE MAGAZINE	Rickie Lee Jones (Warner Bros.)
25	36	GHOSTBUSTERS	Soundtrack (Arista)
29	37	UNDER WRAPS	Jethro Tull (Chrysalis)
-	38	WE WANT MOORE!	Gary Moore (10/Virgin)
34	39	CRE-OLE	Kid Creole & the Coconuts (Island)
35	40	PHIL FEARON AND GALAXY	Phil Fearon & Galaxy (Ensign)
36	41	QUEEN'S GREATEST HITS	Queen (EMI)
-	42	NIGHT MOVES	Various Artists (K-Tel)
33	43	1100 BEL AIR PLACE	Julio Iglesias (CBS)
32	44	NO REMORSE	Motorhead (Bronze)
40	45	SHE'S SO UNUSUAL	Cyndi Lauper (Portrait)
-	46	YOU, ME AND HE	M'Tume (Epic)
-	47	SIGN OF THE HAMMER	Manowar (10/Virgin)
38	48	EDEN	Everything but the Girl (Blanco Y Negro)
45	49	JUST THE WAY YOU LIKE IT	SOS Band (Tabu/Epic)
-	50	HEARTBEAT CITY	Cars (Elektra)

20 October 1984

last	this		
11	1	THE UNFORGETTABLE FIRE	U2 (Island)
2	2	DIAMOND LIFE	Sade (CBS)
1	3	TONIGHT	David Bowie (EMI America)
4	4	THE WOMAN IN RED - ORIGINAL SOUNDTRACK	Stevie Wonder (Motown)
3	5	ELIMINATOR	ZZ Top (WEA)
5	6	PURPLE RAIN	Prince & the Revolution (Warner Bros.)
6	7	SOME GREAT REWARD	Depeche Mode (Mute)
10	8	WE ARE FAMILY	Sister Sledge (Cotillion)
9	9	PRIVATE DANCER	Tina Turner (Capitol)
7	10	NOW THAT'S WHAT I CALL MUSIC 3	Various Artists (EMI/Virgin)
27	11	TRUE COLOURS	Level 42 (Polydor)
-	12	GEFFREY MORGAN	UB40 (DEP International)
12	13	THE WORKS	Queen (EMI)
8	14	HOW MEN ARE	Heaven 17 (Virgin)
14	15	CAN'T SLOW DOWN	Lionel Richie (Motown)
-	16	RATTLESNAKES	Lloyd Cole & the Commotions (Polydor)
15	17	PARADE	Spandau Ballet (Chrysalis)
13	18	KNIFE	Aztec Camera (WEA)
-	19	THE AGE OF CONSENT	Bronski Beat (London)
23	20	STREET SOUNDS ELECTRO 5	Various Artists (Street Sounds)
35	21	THE MAGAZINE	Rickie Lee Jones (Warner Bros.)
20	22	HOPE AND GLORY	Tom Robinson (Castaway)
16	23	LEGEND	Bob Marley & the Wailers (Island)
22	24	ANIMALIZE	Kiss (Vertigo)
18	25	SELF CONTROL	Laura Branigan (Atlantic)
-	26	HITS, HITS, HITS	Various Artists (Telstar)
30	27	ALL BY MYSELF	Various Artists (K-Tel)
17	28	THRILLER	Michael Jackson (Epic)
38	29	WE WANT MOORE!	Gary Moore (10/Virgin)
-	30	RANDY CRAWFORD'S GREATEST HITS	Randy Crawford (K-Tel)
-	31	BREWING UP WITH BILLY BRAGG	Billy Bragg (Go! Discs)
21	32	POWERSLAVE	Iron Maiden (EMI)
26	33	U2 LIVE: UNDER A BLOOD RED SKY	U2 (Island)
-	34	MUSIC MAGIC	Rose Royce (Streetwave)
19	35	HUMAN'S LIB	Howard Jones (WEA)
42	36	NIGHT MOVES	Various Artists (K-Tel)
34	37	BORN IN THE USA	Bruce Springsteen (CBS)
29	38	HUMAN RACING	Nik Kershaw (MCA)
28	39	BREAKING HEARTS	Elton John (Rocket)
50	40	HEARTBEAT CITY	Cars (Elektra)
-	41	TWO STEPS FROM THE MOVE	Hanoi Rocks (CBS)
-	42	DON'T STOP	Jeffrey Osborne (A&M)
24	43	BREAK OUT	Pointer Sisters (Planet)
25	44	AN INNOCENT MAN	Billy Joel (CBS)
49	45	JUST THE WAY YOU LIKE IT	SOS Band (Tabu/Epic)
-	46	JUST LIKE DREAMING	Terri Wells (London)
47	47	THE PLAN	Gary Numan (Beggars Banquet)
32	48	SWEPT AWAY	Diana Ross (Capitol)
41	49	QUEEN'S GREATEST HITS	Queen (EMI)
31	50	DREAMLINE	Cult (Beggars Banquet)

David Bowie scored a second straight chart-topper with his second EMI America album *Tonight*, but the set did not have the longevity either at Number 1 (just one week) or in the Top 50 chart as a whole that its predecessor *Let's Dance* had displayed. *Eliminator* marked Texan hard boogie band ZZ Top's first UK album chart appearace, and thereby guaranteed them final place in the artist index of this book!

260

27 October 1984

last week	this week	Title	Artist (Label)
1	1	THE UNFORGETTABLE FIRE	U2 (Island)
2	2	DIAMOND LIFE	Sade (CBS)
12	3	GEFFREY MORGAN	UB40 (DEP International)
19	4	THE AGE OF CONSENT	Bronski Beat (London)
3	5	TONIGHT	David Bowie (EMI America)
5	6	ELIMINATOR	ZZ Top (WEA)
4	7	THE WOMAN IN RED - ORIGINAL SOUNDTRACK	Stevie Wonder (Motown)
16	8	RATTLESNAKES	Lloyd Cole & the Commotions (Polydor)
6	9	PURPLE RAIN	Prince & the Revolution (Warner Bros.)
31	10	BREWING UP WITH BILLY BRAGG	Billy Bragg (Go! Discs)
-	11	STEELTOWN	Big Country (Mercury)
8	12	WE ARE FAMILY	Sister Sledge (Cotillion)
11	13	TRUE COLOURS	Level 42 (Polydor)
10	14	NOW THAT'S WHAT I CALL MUSIC 3	Various Artists (EMI/Virgin)
26	15	HITS, HITS, HITS	Various Artists (Telstar)
30	16	RANDY CRAWFORD'S GREATEST HITS	Randy Crawford (K-Tel)
7	17	SOME GREAT REWARD	Depeche Mode (Mute)
27	18	ALL BY MYSELF	Various Artists (K-Tel)
9	19	PRIVATE DANCER	Tina Turner (Capitol)
-	20	IT'LL END IN TEARS	This Mortal Coil (4AD)
15	21	CAN'T SLOW DOWN	Lionel Richie (Motown)
14	22	HOW MEN ARE	Heaven 17 (Virgin)
41	23	TWO STEPS FROM THE MOVE	Hanoi Rocks (CBS)
17	24	PARADE	Spandau Ballet (Chrysalis)
37	25	BORN IN THE USA	Bruce Springsteen (CBS)
13	26	THE WORKS	Queen (EMI)
18	27	KNIFE	Aztec Camera (WEA)
21	28	THE MAGAZINE	Rickie Lee Jones (Warner Bros.)
39	29	BREAKING HEARTS	Elton John (Rocket)
23	30	LEGEND	Bob Marley & the Wailers (Island)
36	31	NIGHT MOVES	Various Artists (K-Tel)
-	32	I FEEL FOR YOU	Chaka Khan (WEA)
20	33	STREET SOUNDS ELECTRO 5	Various Artists (Street Sounds)
-	34	EMOTION	Barbra Streisand (CBS)
-	35	SEA OF TRANQUILITY	Phil Coulter (K-Tel)
-	36	THE WONDERFUL AND FRIGHTENING WORLD OF	Fall (Beggars Banquet)
42	37	DON'T STOP	Jeffrey Osborne (A&M)
-	38	MUSIC FROM THE FILM CAL	Mark Knopfler (Vertigo)
22	39	HOPE AND GLORY	Tom Robinson (Castaway)
29	40	WE WANT MOORE!	Gary Moore (10/Virgin)
28	41	THRILLER	Michael Jackson (Epic)
43	42	BREAK OUT	Pointer Sisters (Planet)
38	43	HUMAN RACING	Nik Kershaw (MCA)
40	44	HEARTBEAT CITY	Cars (Elektra)
24	45	ANIMALIZE	Kiss (Vertigo)
33	46	U2 LIVE: UNDER A BLOOD RED SKY	U2 (Island)
-	47	ELECTRIC DREAMS	Soundtrack (Virgin)
45	48	JUST THE WAY YOU LIKE IT	SOS Band (Tabu/Epic)
47	49	THE PLAN	Gary Numan (Beggars Banquet)
34	50	MUSIC MAGIC	Rose Royce (Streetwave)

3 November 1984

last week	this week	Title	Artist (Label)
11	1	STEELTOWN	Big Country (Mercury)
2	2	DIAMOND LIFE	Sade (CBS)
1	3	THE UNFORGETTABLE FIRE	U2 (Island)
4	4	THE AGE OF CONSENT	Bronski Beat (London)
6	5	ELIMINATOR	ZZ Top (WEA)
3	6	GEFFREY MORGAN	UB40 (DEP International)
-	7	WAKING UP WITH THE HOUSE ON FIRE	Culture Club (Virgin)
7	8	THE WOMAN IN RED - ORIGINAL SOUNDTRACK	Stevie Wonder (Motown)
-	9	GIVE MY REGARDS TO BROAD STREET	Paul McCartney (EMI)
5	10	TONIGHT	David Bowie (EMI America)
10	11	BREWING UP WITH BILLY BRAGG	Billy Bragg (Go! Discs)
8	12	RATTLESNAKES	Lloyd Cole & the Commotions (Polydor)
34	13	EMOTION	Barbra Streisand (CBS)
15	14	HITS, HITS, HITS	Various Artists (Telstar)
14	15	NOW THAT'S WHAT I CALL MUSIC 3	Various Artists (EMI/Virgin)
9	16	PURPLE RAIN	Prince & the Revolution (Warner Bros.)
18	17	ALL BY MYSELF	Various Artists (K-Tel)
12	18	WE ARE FAMILY	Sister Sledge (Cotillion)
16	19	RANDY CRAWFORD'S GREATEST HITS	Randy Crawford (K-Tel)
32	20	I FEEL FOR YOU	Chaka Khan (WEA)
-	21	BIM BAM BOOM	Hall & Oates (RCA)
21	22	CAN'T SLOW DOWN	Lionel Richie (Motown)
13	23	TRUE COLOURS	Level 42 (Polydor)
26	24	THE WORKS	Queen (EMI)
19	25	PRIVATE DANCER	Tina Turner (Capitol)
-	26	YESTERDAY ONCE MORE	Carpenters (EMI/A&M)
24	27	PARADE	Spandau Ballet (Chrysalis)
-	28	VALOTTE	Julian Lennon (Charisma/Virgin)
41	29	THRILLER	Michael Jackson (Epic)
30	30	LEGEND	Bob Marley & the Wailers (Island)
-	31	CINEMA	Elaine Paige (K-Tel)
29	32	BREAKING HEARTS	Elton John (Rocket)
-	33	GREATEST LOVE CLASSICS	Andy Williams (EMI)
-	34	THEM OR US	Frank Zappa (EMI)
17	35	SOME GREAT REWARD	Depeche Mode (Mute)
-	36	STOP MAKING SENSE	Talking Heads (EMI)
28	37	THE MAGAZINE	Rickie Lee Jones (Warner Bros.)
-	38	THE BIG EXPRESS	XTC (Virgin)
-	39	DES O'CONNOR NOW	Des O'Connor (Telstar)
20	40	IT'LL END IN TEARS	This Mortal Coil (4AD)
25	41	BORN IN THE USA	Bruce Springsteen (CBS)
35	42	SEA OF TRANQUILITY	Phil Coulter (K-Tel)
22	43	HOW MEN ARE	Heaven 17 (Virgin)
44	44	HEARTBEAT CITY	Cars (Elektra)
-	45	CREW CUTS - LESSON 2	Various Artists (Island)
36	46	THE WONDERFUL AND FRIGHTENING WORLD OF	Fall (Beggars Banquet)
-	47	CONCERT - THE CURE LIVE	Cure (Fiction)
46	48	U2 LIVE: UNDER A BLOOD RED SKY	U2 (Island)
47	49	ELECTRIC DREAMS	Soundtrack (Virgin)
37	50	DON'T STOP	Jeffrey Osborne (A&M)

10 November 1984

last week	this week	Title	Artist (Label)
-	1	WELCOME TO THE PLEASUREDOME	Frankie Goes To Hollywood (ZTT)
1	2	STEELTOWN	Big Country (Mercury)
9	3	GIVE MY REGARDS TO BROAD STREET	Paul McCartney (EMI)
2	4	DIAMOND LIFE	Sade (CBS)
7	5	WAKING UP WITH THE HOUSE ON FIRE	Culture Club (Virgin)
5	6	ELIMINATOR	ZZ Top (WEA)
3	7	THE UNFORGETTABLE FIRE	U2 (Island)
4	8	THE AGE OF CONSENT	Bronski Beat (London)
6	9	GEFFREY MORGAN	UB40 (DEP International)
19	10	RANDY CRAWFORD'S GREATEST HITS	Randy Crawford (K-Tel)
28	11	VALOTTE	Julian Lennon (Charisma/Virgin)
-	12	PERFECT STRANGERS	Deep Purple (Polydor)
8	13	THE WOMAN IN RED - ORIGINAL SOUNDTRACK	Stevie Wonder (Motown)
20	14	I FEEL FOR YOU	Chaka Khan (WEA)
10	15	TONIGHT	David Bowie (EMI America)
14	16	HITS, HITS, HITS	Various Artists (Telstar)
-	17	THE COLLECTION	Ultravox (Chrysalis)
22	18	CAN'T SLOW DOWN	Lionel Richie (Motown)
15	19	NOW THAT'S WHAT I CALL MUSIC 3	Various Artists (EMI/Virgin)
47	20	CONCERT - THE CURE LIVE	Cure (Fiction)
12	21	RATTLESNAKES	Lloyd Cole & the Commotions (Polydor)
26	22	YESTERDAY ONCE MORE	Carpenters (EMI/A&M)
-	23	BAD ATTITUDE	Meatloaf (Arista)
13	24	EMOTION	Barbra Streisand (CBS)
31	25	CINEMA	Elaine Paige (K-Tel)
25	26	PRIVATE DANCER	Tina Turner (Capitol)
27	27	PARADE	Spandau Ballet (Chrysalis)
11	28	BREWING UP WITH BILLY BRAGG	Billy Bragg (Go! Discs)
36	29	STOP MAKING SENSE	Talking Heads (EMI)
17	30	ALL BY MYSELF	Various Artists (K-Tel)
38	31	THE BIG EXPRESS	XTC (Virgin)
-	32	REBEL SOULS	Aswad (Island)
16	33	PURPLE RAIN	Prince & the Revolution (Warner Bros.)
18	34	WE ARE FAMILY	Sister Sledge (Cotillion)
29	35	THRILLER	Michael Jackson (Epic)
-	36	THE EVERLY BROTHERS	Everly Brothers (Mercury)
21	37	BIM BAM BOOM	Hall & Oates (RCA)
33	38	GREATEST LOVE CLASSICS	Andy Williams (EMI)
41	39	BORN IN THE USA	Bruce Springsteen (CBS)
44	40	HEARTBEAT CITY	Cars (Elektra)
23	41	TRUE COLOURS	Level 42 (Polydor)
24	42	THE WORKS	Queen (EMI)
43	43	HOW MEN ARE	Heaven 17 (Virgin)
-	44	THE FUGITIVE KIND	Swans Way (Balgier)
30	45	LEGEND	Bob Marley & the Wailers (Island)
-	46	VERMIN IN ERMINE	Marc Almond & the Willing Sinners (Some Bizzare)
35	47	SOME GREAT REWARD	Depeche Mode (Mute)
42	48	SEA OF TRANQUILITY	Phil Coulter (K-Tel)
40	49	IT'LL END IN TEARS	This Mortal Coil (4AD)

Paul McCartney's *Give My Regards To Broad Street* was yet another of 1984's big albums based around the artist's soundtrack to a movie - in this case, McCartney's own less-than-blockbuster vehicle of the same title, in which the music, including unexpected revivals of several Beatles oldies, was most definitely the biggest plus factor. (Broad Street, a London rail terminus, has sincebeen obliterated by development!)

November - December 1984

17 November 1984

last week	this week	Title	Artist (Label)
1	1	WELCOME TO THE PLEASUREDOME	Frankie Goes To Hollywood (ZTT)
4	2	DIAMOND LIFE	Sade (CBS)
6	3	ELIMINATOR	ZZ Top (WEA)
17	4	THE COLLECTION	Ultravox (Chrysalis)
3	5	GIVE MY REGARDS TO BROAD STREET	Paul McCartney (EMI)
12	6	PERFECT STRANGERS	Deep Purple (Polydor)
-	7	MAKE IT BIG	Wham! (CBS)
5	8	WAKING UP WITH THE HOUSE ON FIRE	Culture Club (Virgin)
23	9	BAD ATTITUDE	Meatloaf (Arista)
2	10	STEELTOWN	Big Country (Mercury)
7	11	THE UNFORGETTABLE FIRE	U2 (Island)
-	12	ALF	Alison Moyet (CBS)
14	13	I FEEL FOR YOU	Chaka Khan (WEA)
8	14	THE AGE OF CONSENT	Bronski Beat (London)
-	15	AURAL SCULPTURE	Stranglers (Epic)
11	16	VALOTTE	Julian Lennon (Charisma/Virgin)
13	17	THE WOMAN IN RED - ORIGINAL SOUNDTRACK	Stevie Wonder (Motown)
10	18	RANDY CRAWFORD'S GREATEST HITS	Randy Crawford (K-Tel)
24	19	EMOTION	Barbra Streisand (CBS)
22	20	YESTERDAY ONCE MORE	Carpenters (EMI/A&M)
9	21	GEFFREY MORGAN	UB40 (DEP International)
-	22	REAL TO REEL	Marillion (EMI)
18	23	CAN'T SLOW DOWN	Lionel Richie (Motown)
26	24	PRIVATE DANCER	Tina Turner (Capitol)
15	25	TONIGHT	David Bowie (EMI America)
33	26	PURPLE RAIN	Prince & the Revolution (Warner Bros.)
19	27	NOW THAT'S WHAT I CALL MUSIC 3	Various Artists (EMI/Virgin)
16	28	HITS, HITS, HITS	Various Artists (Telstar)
29	29	STOP MAKING SENSE	Talking Heads (EMI)
25	30	CINEMA	Elaine Paige (K-Tel)
21	31	RATTLESNAKES	Lloyd Cole & the Commotions (Polydor)
27	32	PARADE	Spandau Ballet (Chrysalis)
20	33	CONCERT - THE CURE LIVE	Cure (Fiction)
32	34	REBEL SOULS	Aswad (Island)
28	35	BREWING UP WITH BILLY BRAGG	Billy Bragg (Go! Discs)
47	36	VERMIN IN ERMINE	Marc Almond & the Willing Sinners (Some Bizzare)
39	37	BORN IN THE USA	Bruce Springsteen (CBS)
38	38	GREATEST LOVE CLASSICS	Andy Williams (EMI)
30	39	ALL BY MYSELF	Various Artists (K-Tel)
37	40	BIM BAM BOOM	Hall & Oates (RCA)
35	41	THRILLER	Michael Jackson (Epic)
46	42	LEGEND	Bob Marley & the Wailers (Island)
49	43	SEA OF TRANQUILITY	Phil Coulter (K-Tel)
34	44	WE ARE FAMILY	Sister Sledge (Cotillion)
42	45	THE WORKS	Queen (EMI)
41	46	TRUE COLOURS	Level 42 (Polydor)
43	47	HOW MEN ARE	Heaven 17 (Virgin)
40	48	HEARTBEAT CITY	Cars (Elektra)
-	49	NO BRAKES	John Waite (EMI)
31	50	THE BIG EXPRESS	XTC (Virgin)

24 November 1984

last week	this week	Title	Artist (Label)
7	1	MAKE IT BIG	Wham! (CBS)
1	2	WELCOME TO THE PLEASUREDOME	Frankie Goes To Hollywood (ZTT)
12	3	ALF	Alison Moyet (CBS)
4	4	THE COLLECTION	Ultravox (Chrysalis)
2	5	DIAMOND LIFE	Sade (CBS)
3	6	ELIMINATOR	ZZ Top (WEA)
6	7	PERFECT STRANGERS	Deep Purple (Polydor)
22	8	REAL TO REEL	Marillion (EMI)
5	9	GIVE MY REGARDS TO BROAD STREET	Paul McCartney (EMI)
13	10	I FEEL FOR YOU	Chaka Khan (WEA)
15	11	AURAL SCULPTURE	Stranglers (Epic)
11	12	THE UNFORGETTABLE FIRE	U2 (Island)
9	13	BAD ATTITUDE	Meatloaf (Arista)
-	14	ARENA	Duran Duran (EMI)
-	15	HATFUL OF HOLLOW	Smiths (Rough Trade)
8	16	WAKING UP WITH THE HOUSE ON FIRE	Culture Club (Virgin)
10	17	STEELTOWN	Big Country (Mercury)
14	18	THE AGE OF CONSENT	Bronski Beat (London)
18	19	RANDY CRAWFORD'S GREATEST HITS	Randy Crawford (K-Tel)
-	20	WHO'S LAST	Who (MCA)
-	21	SHAKIN' STEVENS GREATEST HITS	Shakin' Stevens (Epic)
-	22	THE ART GARFUNKEL ALBUM	Art Garfunkel (CBS)
20	23	YESTERDAY ONCE MORE	Carpenters (EMI/A&M)
23	24	CAN'T SLOW DOWN	Lionel Richie (Motown)
17	25	THE WOMAN IN RED - ORIGINAL SOUNDTRACK	Stevie Wonder (Motown)
30	26	CINEMA	Elaine Paige (K-Tel)
-	27	GOLDEN DAYS	Fureys with Davey Arthur (K-Tel)
-	28	TREASURE	Cocteau Twins (4AD)
24	29	PRIVATE DANCER	Tina Turner (Capitol)
16	30	VALOTTE	Julian Lennon (Charisma/Virgin)
27	31	NOW THAT'S WHAT I CALL MUSIC 3	Various Artists (EMI/Virgin)
19	32	EMOTION	Barbra Streisand (CBS)
21	33	GEFFREY MORGAN	UB40 (DEP International)
37	34	BORN IN THE USA	Bruce Springsteen (CBS)
-	35	THE VERY BEST OF FOSTER AND ALLEN	Foster & Allen (Ritz)
-	36	ALL BY MYSELF	Various Artists (K-Tel)
41	37	THRILLER	Michael Jackson (Epic)
40	38	BIM BAM BOOM	Hall & Oates (RCA)
-	39	SAPPHIRE	John Martyn (Island)
33	40	SEA OF TRANQUILITY	Phil Coulter (K-Tel)
31	41	RATTLESNAKES	Lloyd Cole & the Commotions (Polydor)
45	42	THE WORKS	Queen (EMI)
-	43	HIGH CRIME	Al Jarreau (WEA)
-	44	ALL THE HITS	Eddy Grant (K-Tel)
-	45	1984 (FOR THE LOVE OF BIG BROTHER)	Eurythmics (Virgin)
28	46	HITS, HITS, HITS	Various Artists (Telstar)
29	47	STOP MAKING SENSE	Talking Heads (EMI)
25	48	TONIGHT	David Bowie (EMI America)
-	49	ORANGE JUICE	Orange Juice (Polydor)
26	50	PURPLE RAIN	Prince & the Revolution (Warner Bros.)

1 December 1984

last week	this week	Title	Artist (Label)
1	1	MAKE IT BIG	Wham! (CBS)
3	2	ALF	Alison Moyet (CBS)
2	3	WELCOME TO THE PLEASUREDOME	Frankie Goes To Hollywood (ZTT)
4	4	THE COLLECTION	Ultravox (Chrysalis)
5	5	ELIMINATOR	ZZ Top (WEA)
14	6	ARENA	Duran Duran (EMI)
5	7	DIAMOND LIFE	Sade (CBS)
15	8	HATFUL OF HOLLOW	Smiths (Rough Trade)
9	9	GIVE MY REGARDS TO BROAD STREET	Paul McCartney (EMI)
8	10	REAL TO REEL	Marillion (EMI)
10	11	I FEEL FOR YOU	Chaka Khan (WEA)
21	12	SHAKIN' STEVENS GREATEST HITS	Shakin' Stevens (Epic)
12	13	THE UNFORGETTABLE FIRE	U2 (Island)
-	14	THE HITS ALBUM	Various Artists (WEA/CBS)
22	15	THE ART GARFUNKEL ALBUM	Art Garfunkel (CBS)
13	16	BAD ATTITUDE	Meatloaf (Arista)
26	17	CINEMA	Elaine Paige (K-Tel)
45	18	1984 (FOR THE LOVE OF BIG BROTHER)	Eurythmics (Virgin)
44	19	ALL THE HITS	Eddy Grant (K-Tel)
-	20	THE RIDDLE	Nik Kershaw (MCA)
23	21	YESTERDAY ONCE MORE	Carpenters (EMI/A&M)
24	22	CAN'T SLOW DOWN	Lionel Richie (Motown)
18	23	THE AGE OF CONSENT	Bronski Beat (London)
7	24	PERFECT STRANGERS	Deep Purple (Polydor)
29	25	PRIVATE DANCER	Tina Turner (Capitol)
11	26	AURAL SCULPTURE	Stranglers (Epic)
17	27	STEELTOWN	Big Country (Mercury)
35	28	THE VERY BEST OF FOSTER AND ALLEN	Foster & Allen (Ritz)
19	29	RANDY CRAWFORD'S GREATEST HITS	Randy Crawford (K-Tel)
27	30	GOLDEN DAYS	Fureys with Davey Arthur (K-Tel)
-	31	ZOOLOOK	Jean Michel Jarre (Polydor)
34	32	BORN IN THE USA	Bruce Springsteen (CBS)
28	33	TREASURE	Cocteau Twins (4AD)
16	34	WAKING UP WITH THE HOUSE ON FIRE	Culture Club (Virgin)
-	35	TWELVE GOLD BARS VOLUMES 1 & 2	Status Quo (Vertigo)
25	36	THE WOMAN IN RED - ORIGINAL SOUNDTRACK	Stevie Wonder (Motown)
-	37	LIKE A VIRGIN	Madonna (Sire)
38	38	GEFFREY MORGAN	UB40 (DEP International)
-	39	BESERKER	Gary Numan (Numa)
40	40	VALOTTE	Julian Lennon (Charisma/Virgin)
31	41	NOW THAT'S WHAT I CALL MUSIC 3	Various Artists (EMI/Virgin)
46	42	HITS, HITS, HITS	Various Artists (Telstar)
-	43	THE LOVE SONGS - 16 CLASSIC HITS	Stevie Wonder (Telstar)
20	44	WHO'S LAST	Who (MCA)
-	45	2 AM PARADISE CAFE	Barry Manilow (Arista)
49	46	ORANGE JUICE	Orange Juice (Polydor)
-	47	THE MUSIC OF LOVE	Richard Clayderman (Decca/Delphine)
-	48	SUDDENLY	Billy Ocean (Jive)
-	49	FRIED	Julian Cope (Mercury)
48	50	TONIGHT	David Bowie (EMI America)

Frankie Goes To Hollywood's *Welcome To The Pleasuredome* album was one of the most eagerly awaited sets of the year, after the group had had two million-selling singles with *Relax* and *Two Tribes*. Despite huge advance orders and big sales for its first couple of weeks, however, it didn't hog the chart top for the extended period many expected, and quickly surrendered to Wham!'s hit-heavy *Make It Big*.

December 1984

8 December 1984

last week	this week	Title	Artist (Label)
1	1	MAKE IT BIG	Wham! (CBS)
2	2	ALF	Alison Moyet (CBS)
14	3	THE HITS ALBUM	Various Artists (WEA/CBS)
4	4	THE COLLECTION	Ultravox (Chrysalis)
7	5	DIAMOND LIFE	Sade (CBS)
3	6	WELCOME TO THE PLEASUREDOME	Frankie Goes To Hollywood (ZTT)
5	7	ELIMINATOR	ZZ Top (WEA)
6	8	ARENA	Duran Duran (EMI)
-	9	NOW THAT'S WHAT I CALL MUSIC 4	Various Artists (EMI/Virgin)
35	10	TWELVE GOLD BARS VOLUMES 1 & 2	Status Quo (Vertigo)
20	11	THE RIDDLE	Nik Kershaw (MCA)
8	12	HATFUL OF HOLLOW	Smiths (Rough Trade)
9	13	GIVE MY REGARDS TO BROAD STREET	Paul McCartney (EMI)
17	14	CINEMA	Elaine Paige (K-Tel)
16	15	BAD ATTITUDE	Meatloaf (Arista)
12	16	SHAKIN' STEVENS GREATEST HITS	Shakin' Stevens (Epic)
21	17	YESTERDAY ONCE MORE	Carpenters (EMI/A&M)
18	18	1984 (FOR THE LOVE OF BIG BROTHER)	Eurythmics (Virgin)
22	19	CAN'T SLOW DOWN	Lionel Richie (Motown)
43	20	THE LOVE SONGS - 16 CLASSIC HITS	Stevie Wonder (Telstar)
11	21	I FEEL FOR YOU	Chaka Khan (WEA)
-	22	CHAS & DAVE'S GREATEST HITS	Chas & Dave (Rockney)
15	23	THE ART GARFUNKEL ALBUM	Art Garfunkel (CBS)
30	24	GOLDEN DAYS	Fureys & Davey Arthur (K-Tel)
28	25	THE VERY BEST OF FOSTER AND ALLEN	Foster & Allen (Ritz)
33	26	TREASURE	Cocteau Twins (4AD)
45	27	2 AM PARADISE CAFE	Barry Manilow (Arista)
29	28	GREATEST HITS	Randy Crawford (K-Tel)
-	29	THE HONEYDRIPPERS VOLUME 1	Honeydrippers (Es Paranza)
-	30	THE 12 INCH ALBUM	Howard Jones (WEA)
25	31	PRIVATE DANCER	Tina Turner (Capitol)
13	32	THE UNFORGETTABLE FIRE	U2 (Island)
23	33	THE AGE OF CONSENT	Bronski Beat (London)
-	34	TRULY FOR YOU	Temptations (Motown)
-	35	EUGENE WILDE	Eugene Wilde (Fourth & Broadway)
38	36	GEFFREY MORGAN	UB40 (DEP International)
27	37	STEELTOWN	Big Country (Mercury)
34	38	WAKING UP WITH THE HOUSE ON FIRE	Culture Club (Virgin)
36	39	THE WOMAN IN RED	Stevie Wonder (Motown)
24	40	PERFECT STRANGERS	Deep Purple (Polydor)
-	41	SEA OF TRANQUILITY	Phil Coulter (K-Tel)
-	42	EXORCISING GHOSTS	Japan (Virgin)
-	43	THE ROCK CONNECTION	Cliff Richard (EMI)
-	44	THE WAKING HOUR	Dali's Car (Paradox)
-	45	THE COLLECTION	John Denver (Telstar)
26	46	AURAL SCULPTURE	Stranglers (Epic)
32	47	BORN IN THE USA	Bruce Springsteen (CBS)
41	48	NOW THAT'S WHAT I CALL MUSIC 3	Various Artists (EMI/Virgin)
49	49	FRIED	Julian Cope (Mercury)
50	50	TONIGHT	David Bowie (EMI America)

15 December 1984

last week	this week	Title	Artist (Label)
3	1	THE HITS ALBUM	Various Artists (WEA/CBS)
9	2	NOW THAT'S WHAT I CALL MUSIC 4	Various Artists (EMI/Virgin)
2	3	ALF	Alison Moyet (CBS)
4	4	THE COLLECTION	Ultravox (Chrysalis)
1	5	MAKE IT BIG	Wham! (CBS)
6	6	WELCOME TO THE PLEASUREDOME	Frankie Goes To Hollywood (ZTT)
5	7	DIAMOND LIFE	Sade (CBS)
7	8	ELIMINATOR	ZZ Top (WEA)
11	9	THE RIDDLE	Nik Kershaw (MCA)
8	10	ARENA	Duran Duran (EMI)
13	11	GIVE MY REGARDS TO BROAD STREET	Paul McCartney (EMI)
10	12	TWELVE GOLD BARS VOLUMES 1 & 2	Status Quo (Vertigo)
16	13	SHAKIN' STEVENS GREATEST HITS	Shakin' Stevens (Epic)
12	14	HATFUL OF HOLLOW	Smiths (Rough Trade)
15	15	YESTERDAY ONCE MORE	Carpenters (EMI/A&M)
30	16	THE 12 INCH ALBUM	Howard Jones (WEA)
14	17	CINEMA	Elaine Paige (K-Tel)
23	18	THE ART GARFUNKEL ALBUM	Art Garfunkel (CBS)
18	19	1984 (FOR THE LOVE OF BRIG BROTHER)	Eurythmics (Virgin)
31	20	PRIVATE DANCER	Tina Turner (Capitol)
42	21	EXORCISING GHOSTS	Japan (Virgin)
-	22	PARTY, PARTY	Black Lace (Flair)
22	23	CHAS & DAVE'S GREATEST HITS	Chas & Dave (Rockney)
15	24	BAD ATTITUDE	Meatloaf (Arista)
24	25	GOLDEN DAYS	Fureys & Davey Arthur (K-Tel)
25	26	THE VERY BEST OF FOSTER AND ALLEN	Foster & Allen (Ritz)
27	27	2 AM PARADISE CAFE	Barry Manilow (Arista)
34	28	TRULY FOR YOU	Temptations (Motown)
20	29	THE LOVE SONGS - 16 CLASSIC HITS	Stevie Wonder (Telstar)
21	30	I FEEL FOR YOU	Chaka Khan (WEA)
29	31	THE HONEYDRIPPERS VOLUME 1	Honeydrippers (Es Paranza)
19	32	CAN'T SLOW DOWN	Lionel Richie (Motown)
32	33	THE UNFORGETTABLE FIRE	U2 (Island)
-	34	ALL THE HITS	Eddy Grant (K-Tel)
-	35	HOOKED ON NUMBER ONES	Various (K-Tel)
41	36	SEA OF TRANQUILITY	Phil Coulter (K-Tel)
26	37	TREASURE	Cocteau Twins (4AD)
-	38	REAL LIVE	Bob Dylan (CBS)
-	39	RATTLESNAKES	Lloyd Cole & the Commotions (Polydor)
35	40	EUGENE WILDE	Eugene Wilde (IFourth & Broadway)
-	41	IN THE DARK	Roy Ayers (CBS)
47	42	BORN IN THE USA	Bruce Springsteen (CBS)
28	43	GREATEST HITS	Randy Crawford (K-Tel)
38	44	WAKING UP WITH THE HOUSE ON FIRE	Culture Club (Virgin)
-	45	BREAK OUT	Pointer Sisters (Planet)
-	46	LEGEND	Bob Marley & the Wailers (Island)
33	47	THE AGE OF CONSENT	Bronski Beat (London)
37	48	STEELTOWN	Big Country (Mercury)
-	49	HIGH CRIME	Al Jarreau (WEA)
46	50	AURAL SCULPTURE	Stranglers (Epic)

22 December 1984

last week	this week	Title	Artist (Label)
1	1	THE HITS ALBUM	Various Artists (WEA/CBS)
2	2	NOW THAT'S WHAT I CALL MUSIC 4	Various Artists (EMI/Virgin)
3	3	ALF	Alison Moyet (CBS)
5	4	MAKE IT BIG	Wham! (CBS)
4	5	THE COLLECTION	Ultravox (Chrysalis)
6	6	WELCOME TO THE PLEASUREDOME	Frankie Goes To Hollywood (ZTT)
8	7	ELIMINATOR	ZZ Top (WEA)
7	8	DIAMOND LIFE	Sade (CBS)
9	9	THE RIDDLE	Nik Kershaw (MCA)
11	10	GIVE MY REGARDS TO BROAD STREET	Paul McCartney (EMI)
10	11	ARENA	Duran Duran (EMI)
12	12	TWELVE GOLD BARS VOLUMES 1 & 2	Status Quo (Vertigo)
22	13	PARTY, PARTY	Black Lace (Flair)
13	14	SHAKIN' STEVENS GREATEST HITS	Shakin' Stevens (Epic)
15	15	YESTERDAY ONCE MORE	Carpenters (EMI/A&M)
23	16	CHAS & DAVE'S GREATEST HITS	Chas & Dave (Rockney)
18	17	THE ART GARFUNKEL ALBUM	Art Garfunkel (CBS)
26	18	THE VERY BEST OF FOSTER AND ALLEN	Foster & Allen (Ritz)
29	19	THE LOVE SONGS - 16 CLASSIC HITS	Stevie Wonder (Telstar)
16	20	THE 12 INCH ALBUM	Howard Jones (WEA)
20	21	PRIVATE DANCER	Tina Turner (Capitol)
17	22	CINEMA	Elaine Paige (K-Tel)
25	23	GOLDEN DAYS	Fureys & Davey Arthur (K-Tel)
19	24	1984 (FOR THE LOVE OF BIG BROTHER)	Eurythmics (Virgin)
38	25	REAL LIVE	Bob Dylan (CBS)
30	26	I FEEL FOR YOU	Chaka Khan (WEA)
-	27	PARADE	Spandau Ballet (Virgin)
48	28	HATFUL OF HOLLOW	Smiths (Rough Trade)
21	29	EXORCISING GHOSTS	Japan (Virgin)
31	30	THE HONEYDRIPPERS VOLUME 1	Honeydrippers (Es Paranza)
-	31	EMERGENCY	Kool & the Gang (De-Lite)
-	32	LIKE A VIRGIN	Madonna (Sire)
42	33	BORN IN THE USA	Bruce Springsteen (CBS)
35	34	HOOKED ON NUMBER ONES	VariousArtists (K-Tel)
-	35	DES O'CONNOR NOW	Des O'Connor (Telstar)
32	36	CAN'T SLOW DOWN	Lionel Richie (Motown)
48	37	STEELTOWN	Big Country (Mercury)
24	38	BAD ATTITUDE	Meatloaf (Arista)
37	39	SEA OF TRANQUILITY	Phil Coulter (K-Tel)
37	40	TREASURE	Cocteau Twins (4AD)
34	41	ALL THE HITS	Eddy Grant (K-Tel)
33	42	THE UNFORGETTABLE FIRE	U2 (Island)
44	43	WAKING UP WITH THE HOUSE ON FIRE	Culture Club (Virgin)
39	44	PERFECT STRANGERS	Deep Purple (Polydor)
39	45	RATTLESNAKES	Lloyd Cole & the Commotions (Polydor)
45	46	BREAK OUT	Pointer Sisters (Planet)
-	47	THRILLER	Michael Jackson (Epic)
-	48	LOVE SONGS	Various Artists (Telstar)
-	49	GREEN VELVET	Various Artists (Telstar)
-	50	I AM WHAT I AM	Shirley Bassey (Towerbell)

Having seen the EMI/Virgin partnership clean up in the compilation field during 1984 with the *Now* series, major record labels CBS and WEA teamed up to fight back with a similar series of their own, adventurously titled *Hits*. The initial *Hits Album* proved sufficiently strong in recent hit content to outsell the latest volume from the opposition (No.4), and capture the coveted Christmas Number 1 slot.

*Faces making the album
charts in the 80s:
Kate Bush (left)
Boy George (bottom left)
ABC (below)*

5 January 1985

last week	this week	Title	Artist (label)
1	1	THE HITS ALBUM	Various Artists (WEA/CBS)
2	2	NOW THAT'S WHAT I CALL MUSIC 4	Various Artists (EMI/Virgin)
4	3	MAKE IT BIG	Wham! (CBS)
3	4	ALF	Alison Moyet (CBS)
5	5	THE COLLECTION	Ultravox (Chrysalis)
6	6	WELCOME TO THE PLEASUREDOME	Frankie Goes to Hollywood (ZTT)
13	7	PARTY, PARTY	Black Lace (Flair)
8	8	DIAMOND LIFE	Sade (CBS)
7	9	ELIMINATOR	ZZ Top (Warner Brothers)
11	10	ARENA	Duran Duran (EMI)
10	11	GIVE MY REGARDS TO BROAD STREET	Paul McCartney (EMI)
17	12	THE ART GARFUNKEL ALBUM	Art Garfunkel (CBS)
12	13	12 GOLD BARS VOLUMES 1 & 2	Status Quo (Vertigo)
16	14	CHAS & DAVE'S GREATEST HITS	Chas & Dave (Rockney)
14	15	SHAKIN' STEVENS GREATEST HITS	Shakin' Stevens (Epic)
9	16	THE RIDDLE	Nik Kershaw (MCA)
23	17	GOLDEN DAYS	Fureys with Davey Arthur (K-Tel)
15	18	YESTERDAY ONCE MORE	Carpenters (EMI/A&M)
18	19	THE VERY BEST OF FOSTER & ALLEN	Foster & Allen (Ritz)
22	20	CINEMA	Elaine Paige (K-Tel)
24	21	1984 (FOR THE LOVE OF BIG BROTHER)	Eurythmics (Virgin)
-	22	AGENT PROVOCATEUR	Foreigner (Atlantic)
21	23	PRIVATE DANCER	Tina Turner (Capitol)
42	24	THE UNFORGETTABLE FIRE	U2 (Island)
41	25	ALL THE HITS	Eddy Grant (K-Tel)
-	26	THE COLLECTION	John Denver (Telstar)
25	27	REAL LIVE	Bob Dylan (CBS)
31	28	EMERGENCY	Kool and the Gang (De-Lite)
32	29	LIKE A VIRGIN	Madonna (Sire)
30	30	DES O'CONNOR NOW	Des O'Connor (Telstar)
19	31	THE LOVE SONGS - 16 CLASSIC HITS	Stevie Wonder (Telstar)
50	32	I AM WHAT I AM	Shirley Bassey (Towerbell)
27	33	PARADE	Spandau Ballet (Chrysalis)
49	34	GREEN VELVET	Various Artists (Telstar)
20	35	THE 12-INCH ALBUM	Howard Jones (WEA)
38	36	BAD ATTITUDE	Meatloaf (Arista)
29	37	HATFUL OF HOLLOW	Smiths (Rough Trade)
-	38	THE MUSIC OF LOVE	Richard Clayderman (Decca/Delphine)
-	39	FANS	Malcolm McLaren (Charisma)
34	40	HOOKED ON NUMBER ONES	Various Artists (K-Tel)
-	41	RANDY CRAWFORD'S GREATEST HITS	Randy Crawford (K-Tel)
36	42	CAN'T SLOW DOWN	Lionel Richie (Motown)
37	43	STEELTOWN	Big Country (Mercury)
26	44	I FEEL FOR YOU	Chaka Khan (WEA)
33	45	BORN IN THE USA	Bruce Springsteen (CBS)
29	46	EXORCISING GHOSTS	Japan (Virgin)
39	47	SEA OF TRANQUILITY	Phil Coulter (K-Tel)
47	48	THRILLER	Michael Jackson (Epic)
48	49	LOVE SONGS	Various Artists (Telstar)
43	50	WAKING UP WITH THE HOUSE ON FIRE	Culture Club (Virgin)

12 January 1985

last week	this week	Title	Artist (label)
1	1	THE HITS ALBUM	Various Artists (WEA/CBS)
2	2	NOW THAT'S WHAT I CALL MUSIC 4	Various Artists (EMI/Virgin)
4	3	ALF	Alison Moyet (CBS)
3	4	MAKE IT BIG	Wham! (CBS)
5	5	THE COLLECTION	Ultravox (Chrysalis)
6	6	WELCOME TO THE PLEASUREDOME	Frankie Goes to Hollywood (ZTT)
8	7	DIAMOND LIFE	Sade (CBS)
7	8	PARTY, PARTY	Black Lace (Flair)
10	9	ARENA	Duran Duran (EMI)
15	10	SHAKIN' STEVENS GREATEST HITS	Shakin' Stevens (Epic)
11	11	GIVE MY REGARDS TO BROAD STREET	Paul McCartney (EMI)
9	12	ELIMINATOR	ZZ Top (Warner Brothers)
23	13	PRIVATE DANCER	Tina Turner (Capitol)
12	14	THE ART GARFUNKEL ALBUM	Art Garfunkel (CBS)
16	15	THE RIDDLE	Nik Kershaw (MCA)
13	16	12 GOLD BARS VOLUMES 1 & 2	Status Quo (Vertigo)
18	17	YESTERDAY ONCE MORE	Carpenters (EMI/A&M)
22	18	AGENT PROVOCATEUR	Foreigner (Atlantic)
39	19	FANS	Malcolm McLaren (Charisma)
-	20	VERY BEST OF CHRIS DE BURGH	Chris De Burgh (Telstar)
-	21	THE AGE OF CONSENT	Bronski Beat (Forbidden Fruit)
47	22	SEA OF TRANQUILITY	Phil Coulter (K-Tel)
-	23	TRULY FOR YOU	Temptations (Motown)
35	24	THE 12-INCH ALBUM	Howard Jones (WEA)
33	25	PARADE	Spandau Ballet (Chrysalis)
28	26	EMERGENCY	Kool and the Gang (De-Lite)
17	27	GOLDEN DAYS Fureys with Davey Arthur (K-Tel)	
21	28	1984 (FOR THE LOVE OF BIG BROTHER)	Eurythmics (Virgin)
20	29	CINEMA	Elaine Paige (K-Tel)
14	30	CHAS & DAVE'S GREATEST HITS	Chas & Dave (Rockney)
31	31	THE LOVE SONGS - 16 CLASSIC HITS	Stevie Wonder (Telstar)
34	32	GREEN VELVET	Various Artists (Telstar)
44	33	I FEEL FOR YOU	Chaka Khan (WEA)
24	34	THE UNFORGETTABLE FIRE	U2 (Island)
19	35	THE VERY BEST OF FOSTER & ALLEN	Foster & Allen (Ritz)
32	36	I AM WHAT I AM	Shirley Bassey (Towerbell)
26	37	THE COLLECTION	John Denver (Telstar)
29	38	LIKE A VIRGIN	Madonna (Sire)
42	39	CAN'T SLOW DOWN	Lionel Richie (Motown)
37	40	HATFUL OF HOLLOW	Smiths (Rough Trade)
45	41	BORN IN THE USA	Bruce Springsteen (CBS)
-	42	EUGENE WILDE	Eugene Wilde (Fourth & Broadway)
-	43	BREAK OUT	Pointer Sisters (Planet)
-	44	RATTLESNAKES	Lloyd Cole & the Commotions (Polydor)
49	45	LOVE SONGS	Various Artists (Telstar)
27	46	REAL LIVE	Bob Dylan (CBS)
48	47	THRILLER	Michael Jackson (Epic)
30	48	NOW	Des O'Connor (Telstar)
46	49	EXORCISING GHOSTS	Japan (Virgin)
25	50	ALL THE HITS	Eddy Grant (K-Tel)

19 January 1985

last week	this week	Title	Artist (label)
1	1	THE HITS ALBUM	Various Artists (WEA/CBS)
3	2	ALF	Alison Moyet (CBS)
2	3	NOW THAT'S WHAT I CALL MUSIC 4	Various Artists (EMI/Virgin)
4	4	MAKE IT BIG	Wham! (CBS)
7	5	DIAMOND LIFE	Sade (CBS)
6	6	WELCOME TO THE PLEASUREDOME	Frankie Goes to Hollywood (ZTT)
5	7	THE COLLECTION	Ultravox (Chrysalis)
12	8	ELIMINATOR	ZZ Top (Warner Brothers)
18	9	AGENT PROVOCATEUR	Foreigner (Atlantic)
9	10	ARENA	Duran Duran (EMI)
21	11	THE AGE OF CONSENT	Bronski Beat (Forbidden Fruit)
38	12	LIKE A VIRGIN	Madonna (Sire)
25	13	PARADE	Spandau Ballet (Chrysalis)
14	14	PRIVATE DANCER	Tina Turner (Capitol)
8	15	PARTY, PARTY	Black Lace (Flair)
15	16	THE RIDDLE	Nik Kershaw (MCA)
24	17	THE 12-INCH ALBUM	Howard Jones (WEA)
34	18	THE UNFORGETTABLE FIRE	U2 (Island)
19	19	FANS	Malcolm McLaren (Charisma)
40	20	HATFUL OF HOLLOW	Smiths (Rough Trade)
10	21	SHAKIN' STEVENS GREATEST HITS	Shakin' Stevens (Epic)
-	22	STEELTOWN	Big Country (Mercury)
28	23	1984 (FOR THE LOVE OF BIG BROTHER)	Eurythmics (Virgin)
44	24	RATTLESNAKES	Lloyd Cole & the Commotions (Polydor)
11	25	GIVE MY REGARDS TO BROAD STREET	Paul McCartney (EMI)
16	26	12 GOLD BARS VOLUMES 1 & 2	Status Quo (Vertigo)
39	27	CAN'T SLOW DOWN	Lionel Richie (Motown)
20	28	VERY BEST OF CHRIS DE BURGH	Chris De Burgh (Telstar)
26	29	EMERGENCY	Kool and the Gang (De-Lite)
35	30	THE VERY BEST OF FOSTER & ALLEN	Foster & Allen (Ritz)
33	31	I FEEL FOR YOU	Chaka Khan (WEA)
-	32	VALOTTE	Julian Lennon (Chrisma)
17	33	YESTERDAY ONCE MORE	Carpenters (EMI/A&M)
-	34	GEFFERY MORGAN	UB40 (Dep International)
-	35	GHOSTBUSTERS	Soundtrack (Arista)
31	36	THE LOVE SONGS - 16 CLASSIC HITS	Stevie Wonder (Telstar)
-	37	THE ESSENTIAL JEAN MICHEL JARRE	Jean Michel Jarre (Polystar)
23	38	TRULY FOR YOU	Temptations (Motown)
14	39	THE ART GARFUNKEL ALBUM	Art Garfunkel (CBS)
-	40	TREASURE	Cocteau Twins (4AD)
45	41	LOVE SONGS	Various Artists (Telstar)
-	42	BIG BAM BOOM	Daryl Hall & John Oates (RCA)
-	43	WAKING UP WITH THE HOUSE ON FIRE	Culture Club (Virgin)
46	44	REAL LIVE	Bob Dylan (CBS)
43	45	BREAK OUT	Pointer Sisters (Planet)
29	46	CINEMA	Elaine Paige (K-Tel)
22	47	SEA OF TRANQUILITY	Phil Coulter (K-Tel)
47	48	THRILLER	Michael Jackson (Epic)
49	49	EXORCISING GHOSTS	Japan (Virgin)
-	50	PERFECT STRANGERS	Deep Purple (Polydor)

Cabaret group Black Lace, the scourge of the mid-80s singles charts with their irritatingly infectious singalongs like *Agadoo*, made a rare appearance among the big album sellers with their *Party, Party* set - intended, and no doubt bought, for Christmas and New Year party play. Many probably acquired *Chas & Dave's Greatest Hits*, which peaked at 14 in the first week of the year, for the same reason.

January – February 1985

		26 January 1985	
2	1	ALF	Alison Moyet (CBS)
9	2	AGENT PROVOCATEUR	Foreigner (Atlantic)
3	3	MAKE IT BIG	Wham! (CBS)
8	4	ELIMINATOR	ZZ Top (Warner Brothers)
1	5	THE HITS ALBUM	Various Artists (WEA/CBS)
5	6	DIAMOND LIFE	Sade (CBS)
6	7	WELCOME TO THE PLEASUREDOME	
			Frankie Goes to Hollywood (ZTT)
7	8	THE COLLECTION	Ultravox (Chrysalis)
-	9	BORN IN THE USA	Bruce Springsteen (CBS)
3	10	NOW THAT'S WHAT I CALL MUSIC 4	
			Various Artists (EMI/Virgin)
12	11	LIKE A VIRGIN	Madonna (Sire)
11	12	THE AGE OF CONSENT	
			Bronski Beat (Forbidden Fruit)
14	13	PRIVATE DANCER	Tina Turner (Capitol)
10	14	ARENA	Duran Duran (EMI)
18	15	THE UNFORGETTABLE FIRE	U2 (Island)
-	16	20/20	George Benson (Warner Bros.)
-	17	THE BARBARA DICKSON SONGBOOK	
			Barbara Dickson (K-Tel)
13	18	PARADE	Spandau Ballet (Chrysalis)
28	19	VERY BEST OF CHRIS DE BURGH	
			Chris De Burgh (Telstar)
16	20	THE RIDDLE	Nik Kershaw (MCA)
23	21	1984 (FOR THE LOVE OF BIG BROTHER)	
			Eurythmics (Virgin)
17	22	THE 12-INCH ALBUM	Howard Jones (WEA)
21	23	SHAKIN' STEVENS GREATEST HITS	
			Shakin' Stevens (Epic)
15	24	PARTY, PARTY	Black Lace (Flair)
19	25	FANS	Malcolm McLaren (Charisma)
-	26	BREAKDANCE II	Various Artists (Polydor)
20	27	HATFUL OF HOLLOW	Smiths (Rough Trade)
24	28	RATTLESNAKES	
			Lloyd Cole & the Commotions (Polydor)
38	29	TRULY FOR YOU	Temptations (Motown)
31	30	I FEEL FOR YOU	Chaka Khan (WEA)
35	31	GHOSTBUSTERS	Soundtrack (Arista)
22	32	STEELTOWN	Big Country (Mercury)
25	33	GIVE MY REGARDS TO BROAD STREET	
			Paul McCartney (EMI)
26	34	12 GOLD BARS VOLUMES 1 & 2	
			Status Quo (Vertigo)
29	35	EMERGENCY	Kool and the Gang (De-Lite)
-	36	CHESS	Original Cast (RCA)
-	37	BAD ATTITUDE	Meatloaf (Arista)
40	38	TREASURE	Cocteau Twins (4AD)
-	39	LOVE HURTS	Everly Brothers (K-Tel)
-	40	1999	Prince (Warner Bros.)
27	41	CAN'T SLOW DOWN	Lionel Richie (Motown)
30	42	THE VERY BEST OF FOSTER & ALLEN	
			Foster & Allen (Ritz)
32	43	VALOTTE	Julian Lennon (Chrisma)
-	44	THE HONEYDRIPPERS VOLUME 1	
			Honeydrippers (Es Paranza)
43	45	WAKING UP WITH THE HOUSE ON FIRE	
			Culture Club (Virgin)
44	46	REAL LIVE	Bob Dylan (CBS)
33	47	YESTERDAY ONCE MORE	Carpenters (EMI/A&M)
41	48	LOVE SONGS	Various Artists (Telstar)
-	49	THE COLLECTION	John Denver (Telstar)
-	50	(WHO'S AFRAID OF) THE ART OF NOISE	
			Art of Noise (ZTT)

		2 February 1985	
2	1	AGENT PROVOCATEUR	Foreigner (Atlantic)
1	2	ALF	Alison Moyet (CBS)
4	3	ELIMINATOR	ZZ Top (Warner Bros.)
9	4	BORN IN THE USA	Bruce Springsteen (CBS)
12	5	THE AGE OF CONSENT	
			Bronski Beat (Forbidden Fruit)
-	6	HITS OUT OF HELL	Meatloaf (Epic)
3	7	MAKE IT BIG	Wham! (CBS)
8	8	THE COLLECTION	Ultravox (Chrysalis)
16	9	20/20	George Benson (Warner Bros.)
5	10	THE HITS ALBUM	Various Artists (WEA/CBS)
11	11	LIKE A VIRGIN	Madonna (Sire)
6	12	DIAMOND LIFE	Sade (CBS)
15	13	THE UNFORGETTABLE FIRE	U2 (Island)
7	14	WELCOME TO THE PLEASUREDOME	
			Frankie Goes to Hollywood (ZTT)
19	15	VERY BEST OF CHRIS DE BURGH	
			Chris De Burgh (Telstar)
10	16	NOW THAT'S WHAT I CALL MUSIC 4	
			Various Artists (EMI/Virgin)
17	17	THE BARBARA DICKSON SONGBOOK	
			Barbara Dickson (K-Tel)
13	18	PRIVATE DANCER	Tina Turner (Capitol)
14	19	ARENA	Duran Duran (EMI)
30	20	I FEEL FOR YOU	Chaka Khan (WEA)
18	21	PARADE	Spandau Ballet (Chrysalis)
21	22	1984 (FOR THE LOVE OF BIG BROTHER)	
			Eurythmics (Virgin)
40	23	1999	Prince (Warner Bros.)
-	24	TOO TOUGH TO DIE	
			Ramones (Beggars Banquet)
32	25	STEELTOWN	Big Country (Mercury)
22	26	THE 12-INCH ALBUM	Howard Jones (WEA)
41	27	CAN'T SLOW DOWN	Lionel Richie (Motown)
27	28	HATFUL OF HOLLOW	
			Smiths (Rough Trade)
25	29	FANS	Malcolm McLaren (Charisma)
28	30	RATTLESNAKES	
			Lloyd Cole & the Commotions (Polydor)
26	31	BREAKDANCE II	Various Artists (Polydor)
24	32	PARTY, PARTY	Black Lace (Flair)
20	33	THE RIDDLE	Nik Kershaw (MCA)
31	34	GHOSTBUSTERS	Soundtrack (Arista)
-	35	CINEMA	Elaine Paige (K-Tel)
36	36	TROPICO	Pat Benatar (Chrysalis)
39	37	LOVE HURTS	Everly Brothers (K-Tel)
50	38	(WHO'S AFRAID OF) THE ART OF NOISE	
			Art of Noise (ZTT)
36	39	CHESS	Original Cast (RCA)
-	40	PURPLE RAIN	
			Prince& The Revolution (Warner Bros.)
35	41	EMERGENCY	Kool and the Gang (De-Lite)
-	42	SCREEN GEMS	Elkie Brooks (EMI)
23	43	SHAKIN' STEVENS GREATEST HITS	
			Shakin' Stevens (Epic)
33	44	GIVE MY REGARDS TO BROAD STREET	
			Paul McCartney (EMI)
29	45	TRULY FOR YOU	Temptations (Motown)
44	46	THE HONEYDRIPPERS VOLUME 1	
			Honeydrippers (Es Paranza)
-	47	THE DEED IS DONE	Molly Hatchet (Epic)
-	48	NO PARLEZ	Paul Young (CBS)
-	49	BREAK OUT	Pointer Sisters (Planet)
38	50	TREASURE	Cocteau Twins (4AD)

		9 February 1985	
1	1	AGENT PROVOCATEUR	Foreigner (Atlantic)
3	2	ELIMINATOR	ZZ Top (Warner Brothers)
4	3	BORN IN THE USA	Bruce Springsteen (CBS)
2	4	ALF	Alison Moyet (CBS)
9	5	20/20	George Benson (Warner Bros.)
6	6	HITS OUT OF HELL	Meatloaf (Epic)
5	7	THE AGE OF CONSENT	
			Bronski Beat (Forbidden Fruit)
7	8	MAKE IT BIG	Wham! (CBS)
15	9	VERY BEST OF CHRIS DE BURGH	
			Chris De Burgh (Telstar)
8	10	THE COLLECTION	Ultravox (Chrysalis)
11	11	LIKE A VIRGIN	Madonna (Sire)
12	12	DIAMOND LIFE	Sade (CBS)
14	13	WELCOME TO THE PLEASUREDOME	
			Frankie Goes to Hollywood (ZTT)
17	14	THE BARBARA DICKSON SONGBOOK	
			Barbara Dickson (K-Tel)
13	15	THE UNFORGETTABLE FIRE	U2 (Island)
23	16	1999	Prince (Warner Bros.)
28	17	HATFUL OF HOLLOW	Smiths (Rough Trade)
10	18	THE HITS ALBUM	Various Artists (WEA/CBS)
39	19	CHESS	Original Cast (RCA)
20	20	I FEEL FOR YOU	Chaka Khan (WEA)
35	21	CINEMA	Elaine Paige (K-Tel)
-	22	STEPS IN TIME	King (CBS)
19	23	ARENA	Duran Duran (EMI)
18	24	PRIVATE DANCER	Tina Turner (Capitol)
-	25	A SENSE OF WONDER	
			Van Morrison (Mercury)
27	26	CAN'T SLOW DOWN	Lionel Richie (Motown)
21	27	PARADE	Spandau Ballet (Chrysalis)
26	28	THE 12-INCH ALBUM	Howard Jones (WEA)
25	29	STEELTOWN	Big Country (Mercury)
16	30	NOW THAT'S WHAT I CALL MUSIC 4	
			Various Artists (EMI/Virgin)
22	31	1984 (FOR THE LOVE OF BIG BROTHER)	
			Eurythmics (Virgin)
24	32	TOO TOUGH TO DIE	
			Ramones (Beggars Banquet)
38	33	(WHO'S AFRAID OF) THE ART OF NOISE	
			Art of Noise (ZTT)
31	34	BREAKDANCE II	Various Artists (Polydor)
-	35	PLANETARY INVASION	Midnight Star (Solar)
36	36	TROPICO	Pat Benatar (Chrysalis)
-	37	CHICAGO 17	Chicago (Full Moon)
-	38	BREWING UP WITH BILLY BRAGG	
			Billy Bragg (Go! Discs)
30	39	RATTLESNAKES	
			Lloyd Cole & the Commotions (Polydor)
-	40	IT'S YOUR NIGHT	James Ingram (Qwest)
-	41	EUGENE WILDE	
			Eugene Wilde (Fourth & Broadway)
50	42	TREASURE	Cocteau Twins (4AD)
-	43	HEARTBEAT CITY	Cars (Elektra)
34	44	GHOSTBUSTERS	Soundtrack (Arista)
44	45	GIVE MY REGARDS TO BROAD STREET	
			Paul McCartney (EMI)
49	46	BREAK OUT	Pointer Sisters (Planet)
32	47	PARTY, PARTY	Black Lace (Flair)
-	48	THRILLER	Michael Jackson (Epic)
40	49	PURPLE RAIN	
			Prince& The Revolution (Warner Bros.)
-	50	SO GOOD	Whispers (Solar)

Alison Moyet's debut solo album *Alf* (the title referred to her nickname) finally topped the chart after nine weeks in the Top 10, only to be eclipsed after a sole week of glory by Foreigner's first UK chart-topping album *Agent Provocateur*. The latter was boosted hugely by the simultaneous Number 1 success of the group's hymnal single *I Want To Know What Love Is*, which the album included.

February – March 1985

16 February 1985

1	1	AGENT PROVOCATEUR	Foreigner (Atlantic)
3	2	BORN IN THE USA	Bruce Springsteen (CBS)
6	3	HITS OUT OF HELL	Meatloaf (Epic)
2	4	ELIMINATOR	ZZ Top (Warner Brothers)
4	5	ALF	Alison Moyet (CBS)
7	6	THE AGE OF CONSENT	Bronski Beat (Forbidden Fruit)
22	7	STEPS IN TIME	King (CBS)
5	8	20/20	George Benson (Warner Bros.)
9	9	VERY BEST OF CHRIS DE BURGH	Chris De Burgh (Telstar)
12	10	DIAMOND LIFE	Sade (CBS)
8	11	MAKE IT BIG	Wham! (CBS)
14	12	THE BARBARA DICKSON SONGBOOK	Barbara Dickson (K-Tel)
10	13	THE COLLECTION	Ultravox (Chrysalis)
25	14	A SENSE OF WONDER	Van Morrison (Mercury)
28	15	THE 12-INCH ALBUM	Howard Jones (WEA)
11	16	LIKE A VIRGIN	Madonna (Sire)
13	17	WELCOME TO THE PLEASUREDOME	Frankie Goes to Hollywood (ZTT)
19	18	CHESS	Original Cast (RCA)
33	19	(WHO'S AFRAID OF) THE ART OF NOISE	Art of Noise (ZTT)
16	20	1999	Prince (Warner Bros.)
21	21	CINEMA	Elaine Paige (K-Tel)
20	22	I FEEL FOR YOU	Chaka Khan (Warner Bros.)
24	23	PRIVATE DANCER	Tina Turner (Capitol)
29	24	STEELTOWN	Big Country (Mercury)
23	25	ARENA	Duran Duran (EMI)
38	26	BREWING UP WITH BILLY BRAGG	Billy Bragg (Go! Discs)
30	27	NOW THAT'S WHAT I CALL MUSIC 4	Various Artists (EMI/Virgin)
-	28	LIFE'S A RIOT WITH SPY VS SPY	Billy Bragg (Go! Discs)
26	29	CAN'T SLOW DOWN	Lionel Richie (Motown)
18	30	THE HITS ALBUM	Various Artists (WEA/CBS)
17	31	HATFUL OF HOLLOW	Smiths (Rough Trade)
-	32	SECRET SECRETS	Joan Armatrading (A&M)
-	33	NO PARLEZ	Paul Young (CBS)
36	34	TROPICO	Pat Benatar (Chrysalis)
15	35	THE UNFORGETTABLE FIRE	U2 (Island)
27	36	PARADE	Spandau Ballet (Chrysalis)
31	37	1984 (FOR THE LOVE OF BIG BROTHER)	Eurythmics (Virgin)
32	38	TOO TOUGH TO DIE	Ramones (Beggars Banquet)
40	39	IT'S YOUR NIGHT	James Ingram (Qwest)
39	40	RATTLESNAKES	Lloyd Cole & the Commotions (Polydor)
-	41	LEGEND	Bob Marley & the Wailers (Island)
-	42	U2 LIVE: UNDER A BLOOD RED SKY	U2 (Island)
-	43	CENTERFIELD	John Fogerty (Warner Bros.)
34	44	BREAKDANCE II	Various Artists (Polydor)
35	45	PLANETARY INVASION	Midnight Star (Solar)
50	46	SO GOOD	Whispers (Solar)
42	47	TREASURE	Cocteau Twins (4AD)
-	48	VARIOUS POSITIONS	Leonard Cohen (CBS)
-	49	PERHAPS	Associates (WEA)
-	50	THE RIDDLE	Nik Kershaw (MCA)

23 February 1985

2	1	BORN IN THE USA	Bruce Springsteen (CBS)
5	2	ALF	Alison Moyet (CBS)
1	3	AGENT PROVOCATEUR	Foreigner (Atlantic)
4	4	ELIMINATOR	ZZ Top (Warner Brothers)
7	5	STEPS IN TIME	King (CBS)
3	6	HITS OUT OF HELL	Meatloaf (Epic)
10	7	DIAMOND LIFE	Sade (CBS)
8	8	20/20	George Benson (Warner Bros.)
32	9	SECRET SECRETS	Joan Armatrading (A&M)
-	10	MEAT IS MURDER	Smiths (Rough Trade)
18	11	CHESS	Original Cast (RCA)
9	12	VERY BEST OF CHRIS DE BURGH	Chris De Burgh (Telstar)
11	13	MAKE IT BIG	Wham! (CBS)
12	14	THE BARBARA DICKSON SONGBOOK	Barbara Dickson (K-Tel)
13	15	THE COLLECTION	Ultravox (Chrysalis)
6	16	THE AGE OF CONSENT	Bronski Beat (Forbidden Fruit)
49	17	PERHAPS	Associates (WEA)
19	18	(WHO'S AFRAID OF) THE ART OF NOISE	Art of Noise (ZTT)
14	19	A SENSE OF WONDER	Van Morrison (Mercury)
20	20	1999	Prince (Warner Bros.)
16	21	CHICAGO 17	Chicago (Full Moon)
22	22	LIKE A VIRGIN	Madonna (Sire)
-	23	THE BAD AND LOWDOWN WORLD OF THE KANE GANG	Kane Gang (Kitchenware)
17	24	WELCOME TO THE PLEASUREDOME	Frankie Goes to Hollywood (ZTT)
15	25	THE 12-INCH ALBUM	Howard Jones (WEA)
23	26	PRIVATE DANCER	Tina Turner (Capitol)
43	27	CENTERFIELD	John Fogerty (Warner Bros.)
22	28	I FEEL FOR YOU	Chaka Khan (WEA)
21	29	CINEMA	Elaine Paige (K-Tel)
24	30	STEELTOWN	Big Country (Mercury)
31	31	HATFUL OF HOLLOW	Smiths (Rough Trade)
-	32	BEYOND THE ASTRAL SKIES	Uli Jon Roth (EMI)
30	33	THE HITS ALBUM	Various Artists (WEA/CBS)
33	34	NO PARLEZ	Paul Young (CBS)
-	35	FROM ACROSS THE KITCHEN TABLE	Pale Fountains (Virgin)
27	36	NOW THAT'S WHAT I CALL MUSIC 4	Various Artists (EMI/Virgin)
28	37	LIFE'S A RIOT WITH SPY VS SPY	Billy Bragg (Go! Discs)
29	38	CAN'T SLOW DOWN	Lionel Richie (Motown)
-	39	FACE VALUE	Phil Collins (Virgin)
25	40	ARENA	Duran Duran (EMI)
26	41	BREWING UP WITH BILLY BRAGG	Billy Bragg (Go! Discs)
35	42	THE UNFORGETTABLE FIRE	U2 (Island)
48	43	VARIOUS POSITIONS	Leonard Cohen (CBS)
-	44	BEVERLY HILLS COP	Soundtrack (MCA)
45	45	V.U.	Velvet Underground (Polydor)
45	46	PLANETARY INVASION	Midnight Star (Solar)
-	47	SOLID	Ashford & Simpson (Capitol)
34	48	TROPICO	Pat Benatar (Chrysalis)
37	49	1984 (FOR THE LOVE OF BIG BROTHER)	Eurythmics (Virgin)
40	50	RATTLESNAKES	Lloyd Cole & the Commotions (Polydor)

2 March 1985

10	1	MEAT IS MURDER	Smiths (Rough Trade)
1	2	BORN IN THE USA	Bruce Springsteen (CBS)
2	3	ALF	Alison Moyet (CBS)
-	4	NO JACKET REQUIRED	Phil Collins (Virgin)
5	5	STEPS IN TIME	King (CBS)
3	6	AGENT PROVOCATEUR	Foreigner (Atlantic)
7	7	DIAMOND LIFE	Sade (CBS)
23	8	THE BAD AND LOWDOWN WORLD OF THE KANE GANG	Kane Gang (Kitchenware)
16	9	THE AGE OF CONSENT	Bronski Beat (Forbidden Fruit)
4	10	ELIMINATOR	ZZ Top (Warner Brothers)
6	11	HITS OUT OF HELL	Meatloaf (Epic)
9	12	SECRET SECRETS	Joan Armatrading (A&M)
8	13	20/20	George Benson (Warner Bros.)
11	14	CHESS	Original Cast (RCA)
13	15	MAKE IT BIG	Wham! (CBS)
14	16	THE BARBARA DICKSON SONGBOOK	Barbara Dickson (K-Tel)
12	17	VERY BEST OF CHRIS DE BURGH	Chris De Burgh (Telstar)
24	18	WELCOME TO THE PLEASUREDOME	Frankie Goes to Hollywood (ZTT)
-	19	NIGHTSHIFT	Commodores (Tamla Motown)
15	20	THE COLLECTION	Ultravox (Chrysalis)
-	21	THE FIRM	Atlantic (Atlantic)
18	22	(WHO'S AFRAID OF) THE ART OF NOISE	Art of Noise (ZTT)
47	23	SOLID	Ashford & Simpson (Capitol)
-	24	RECKLESS	Bryan Adams (A&M)
25	25	THE 12-INCH ALBUM	Howard Jones (WEA)
17	26	PERHAPS	Associates (WEA)
21	27	CHICAGO 17	Chicago (Full Moon)
19	28	A SENSE OF WONDER	Van Morrison (Mercury)
45	29	V.U.	Velvet Underground (Polydor)
20	30	1999	Prince (Warner Bros.)
26	31	PRIVATE DANCER	Tina Turner (Capitol)
32	32	HATFUL OF HOLLOW	Smiths (Rough Trade)
34	33	NO PARLEZ	Paul Young (CBS)
37	34	LIFE'S A RIOT WITH SPY VS SPY	Billy Bragg (Go! Discs)
32	35	BEYOND THE ASTRAL SKIES	Uli Jon Roth (EMI)
-	36	VULTURE CULTURE	Alan Parsons Project (Arista)
27	37	CENTERFIELD	John Fogerty (Warner Bros.)
22	38	LIKE A VIRGIN	Madonna (Sire)
29	39	CINEMA	Elaine Paige (K-Tel)
38	40	CAN'T SLOW DOWN	Lionel Richie (Motown)
-	41	SHAKATAK LIVE!	Shakatak (Polydor)
-	42	SECRETS	Wilton Felder (MCA)
35	43	FROM ACROSS THE KITCHEN TABLE	Pale Fountains (Virgin)
42	44	THE UNFORGETTABLE FIRE	U2 (Island)
-	45	LOST AND FOUND	Jason & the Scorchers (EMI)
-	46	PARIS, TEXAS - SOUNDTRACK	Ry Cooder (Warner Bros.)
33	47	THE HITS ALBUM	Various Artists (WEA/CBS)
40	48	ARENA	Duran Duran (EMI)
28	49	I FEEL FOR YOU	Chaka Khan (WEA)
-	50	STOP MAKING SENSE	Talking Heads (EMI)

Bruce Springsteen's *Born In The USA* had been riding the UK chart for just over eight months when it finally got the extra push to No. 1 on February 23, much of the impetus clearly coming from the success of the extracted single *Dancing In The Dark*, which was now in the Top 5 on its second release, having under-performed in 1984 first time around. Bruce was soon uprooted, though, by the Smiths' first Number 1.

March 1985

9 March 1985

last week	this week		
4	1	NO JACKET REQUIRED	Phil Collins (Virgin)
2	2	BORN IN THE USA	Bruce Springsteen (CBS)
1	3	MEAT IS MURDER	Smiths (Rough Trade)
3	4	ALF	Alison Moyet (CBS)
24	5	RECKLESS	Bryan Adams (A&M)
5	6	STEPS IN TIME	King (CBS)
10	7	ELIMINATOR	ZZ Top (Warner Brothers)
21	8	THE FIRM	Firm (Atlantic)
7	9	DIAMOND LIFE	Sade (CBS)
9	10	THE AGE OF CONSENT	Bronski Beat (Forbidden Fruit)
6	11	AGENT PROVOCATEUR	Foreigner (Atlantic)
11	12	HITS OUT OF HELL	Meatloaf (Epic)
8	13	THE BAD AND LOWDOWN WORLD OF THE KANE GANG	Kane Gang (Kitchenware)
14	14	CHESS	Original Cast (RCA)
16	15	THE BARBARA DICKSON SONGBOOK	Barbara Dickson (K-Tel)
17	16	VERY BEST OF CHRIS DE BURGH	Chris De Burgh (Telstar)
13	17	20/20	George Benson (Warner Bros.)
19	18	NIGHTSHIFT	Commodores (Tamla Motown)
12	19	SECRET SECRETS	Joan Armatrading (A&M)
15	20	MAKE IT BIG	Wham! (CBS)
30	21	1999	Prince (Warner Bros.)
-	22	NIGHT TIME	Killing Joke (EG)
-	23	BUILDING THE PERFECT BEAST	Don Henley (Geffen)
18	24	WELCOME TO THE PLEASUREDOME	Frankie Goes to Hollywood (ZTT)
37	25	CENTERFIELD	John Fogerty (Warner Bros.)
-	26	PURPLE RAIN	Prince & the Revolution (Warner Bros.)
-	27	MODERN LOVE	Various Artists (K-Tel)
23	28	SOLID	Ashford & Simpson (Capitol)
-	29	STREET SOUNDS ELECTRO 6	Various Artists (Street Sounds)
38	30	LIKE A VIRGIN	Madonna (Sire)
27	31	CHICAGO 17	Chicago (Full Moon)
32	32	THE 12-INCH ALBUM	Howard Jones (WEA)
-	33	CRAZY FROM THE HEAT	David Lee Roth (Warner Bros.)
31	34	PRIVATE DANCER	Tina Turner (Capitol)
32	35	HATFUL OF HOLLOW	Smiths (Rough Trade)
-	36	DANGEROUS MUSIC	Robin George (Bronze)
29	37	V.U.	Velvet Underground (Polydor)
-	38	BEVERLY HILLS COP	Soundtrack (MCA)
26	39	PERHAPS	Associates (WEA)
20	40	THE COLLECTION	Ultravox (Chrysalis)
47	41	THE HITS ALBUM	Various Artists (WEA/CBS)
-	42	CASHMERE	Cashmere (Fourth & Broadway)
50	43	STOP MAKING SENSE	Talking Heads (EMI)
22	44	(WHO'S AFRAID OF) THE ART OF NOISE	Art of Noise (ZTT)
28	45	A SENSE OF WONDER	Van Morrison (Mercury)
34	46	LIFE'S A RIOT WITH SPY VS SPY	Billy Bragg (Go! Discs)
35	47	BEYOND THE ASTRAL SKIES	Uli Jon Roth (EMI)
48	48	CAN'T SLOW DOWN	Lionel Richie (Motown)
42	49	SECRETS	Wilton Felder (MCA)
45	50	LOST AND FOUND	Jason & the Scorchers (EMI)

16 March 1985

last week	this week		
1	1	NO JACKET REQUIRED	Phil Collins (Virgin)
2	2	BORN IN THE USA	Bruce Springsteen (CBS)
-	3	SONGS FROM THE BIG CHAIR	Tears For Fears (Mercury)
3	4	MEAT IS MURDER	Smiths (Rough Trade)
5	5	RECKLESS	Bryan Adams (A&M)
4	6	ALF	Alison Moyet (CBS)
23	7	BUILDING THE PERFECT BEAST	Don Henley (Geffen)
7	8	ELIMINATOR	ZZ Top (Warner Brothers)
22	9	NIGHT TIME	Killing Joke (EG)
12	10	HITS OUT OF HELL	Meatloaf (Epic)
9	11	DIAMOND LIFE	Sade (CBS)
-	12	SHE'S THE BOSS	Mick Jagger (CBS)
21	13	1999	Prince (Warner Bros.)
8	14	THE FIRM	Firm (Atlantic)
10	15	THE AGE OF CONSENT	Bronski Beat (Forbidden Fruit)
14	16	CHESS	Original Cast (RCA)
34	17	PRIVATE DANCER	Tina Turner (Capitol)
20	18	MAKE IT BIG	Wham! (CBS)
11	19	AGENT PROVOCATEUR	Foreigner (Atlantic)
18	20	NIGHTSHIFT	Commodores (Tamla Motown)
6	21	STEPS IN TIME	King (CBS)
30	22	LIKE A VIRGIN	Madonna (Sire)
26	23	PURPLE RAIN	Prince & the Revolution (Warner Bros.)
29	24	STREET SOUNDS ELECTRO 6	Various Artists (Street Sounds)
31	25	CHICAGO 17	Chicago (Full Moon)
13	26	THE BAD AND LOWDOWN WORLD OF THE KANE GANG	Kane Gang (Kitchenware)
15	27	THE BARBARA DICKSON SONGBOOK	Barbara Dickson (K-Tel)
17	28	20/20	George Benson (Warner Bros.)
27	29	HATFUL OF HOLLOW	Smiths (Rough Trade)
27	30	MODERN LOVE	Various Artists (K-Tel)
32	31	THE 12-INCH ALBUM	Howard Jones (WEA)
19	32	SECRET SECRETS	Joan Armatrading (A&M)
-	33	CAN'T STOP THE LOVE	Maze (Capitol)
16	34	VERY BEST OF CHRIS DE BURGH	Chris De Burgh (Telstar)
37	35	V.U.	Velvet Underground (Polydor)
28	36	SOLID	Ashford & Simpson (Capitol)
38	37	BEVERLY HILLS COP	Soundtrack (MCA)
24	38	WELCOME TO THE PLEASUREDOME	Frankie Goes to Hollywood (ZTT)
46	39	LIFE'S A RIOT WITH SPY VS SPY	Billy Bragg (Go! Discs)
40	40	THE COLLECTION	Ultravox (Chrysalis)
25	41	CENTERFIELD	John Fogerty (Warner Bros.)
42	42	CASHMERE	Cashmere (Fourth & Broadway)
44	43	(WHO'S AFRAID OF) THE ART OF NOISE	Art of Noise (ZTT)
45	44	A SENSE OF WONDER	Van Morrison (Mercury)
48	45	CAN'T SLOW DOWN	Lionel Richie (Motown)
50	46	LOST AND FOUND	Jason & the Scorchers (EMI)
-	47	BREWING UP WITH BILLY BRAGG	Billy Bragg (Go! Discs)
-	48	FACE VALUE	Phil Collins (Virgin)
39	49	PERHAPS	Associates (WEA)
41	50	THE HITS ALBUM	Various Artists (WEA/CBS)

23 March 1985

last week	this week		
1	1	NO JACKET REQUIRED	Phil Collins (Virgin)
3	2	SONGS FROM THE BIG CHAIR	Tears For Fears (Mercury)
2	3	BORN IN THE USA	Bruce Springsteen (CBS)
12	4	SHE'S THE BOSS	Mick Jagger (CBS)
6	5	ALF	Alison Moyet (CBS)
5	6	RECKLESS	Bryan Adams (A&M)
11	7	DIAMOND LIFE	Sade (CBS)
7	8	BUILDING THE PERFECT BEAST	Don Henley (Geffen)
8	9	ELIMINATOR	ZZ Top (Warner Brothers)
10	10	HITS OUT OF HELL	Meatloaf (Epic)
-	11	DREAM INTO ACTION	Howard Jones (WEA)
9	12	NIGHT TIME	Killing Joke (EG)
22	13	LIKE A VIRGIN	Madonna (Sire)
20	14	NIGHTSHIFT	Commodores (Tamla Motown)
4	15	MEAT IS MURDER	Smiths (Rough Trade)
17	16	PRIVATE DANCER	Tina Turner (Capitol)
23	17	PURPLE RAIN	Prince & the Revolution (Warner Bros.)
-	18	BEHIND THE SUN	Eric Clapton (Duck)
15	19	THE AGE OF CONSENT	Bronski Beat (Forbidden Fruit)
-	20	FIRST AND LAST AND ALWAYS	Sisters of Mercy (Merciful Release)
13	21	1999	Prince (Warner Bros.)
14	22	THE FIRM	Firm (Atlantic)
-	23	WHATEVER HAPPENED TO JUGULA?	Roy Harper & Jimmy Page (Beggars Banquet)
16	24	CHESS	Original Cast (RCA)
18	25	MAKE IT BIG	Wham! (CBS)
24	26	STREET SOUNDS ELECTRO 6	Various Artists (Street Sounds)
39	27	LIFE'S A RIOT WITH SPY VS SPY	Billy Bragg (Go! Discs)
26	28	THE BAD AND LOWDOWN WORLD OF THE KANE GANG	Kane Gang (Kitchenware)
37	29	BEVERLY HILLS COP	Soundtrack (MCA)
21	30	STEPS IN TIME	King (CBS)
33	31	CAN'T STOP THE LOVE	Maze (Capitol)
32	32	SECRET SECRETS	Joan Armatrading (A&M)
-	33	NO PARLEZ	Paul Young (CBS)
31	34	THE 12-INCH ALBUM	Howard Jones (WEA)
36	35	SOLID	Ashford & Simpson (Capitol)
41	36	CENTERFIELD	John Fogerty (Warner Bros.)
38	37	WELCOME TO THE PLEASUREDOME	Frankie Goes to Hollywood (ZTT)
35	38	STOP MAKING SENSE	Talking Heads (EMI)
34	39	VERY BEST OF CHRIS DE BURGH	Chris De Burgh (Telstar)
30	40	MODERN LOVE	Various Artists (K-Tel)
-	41	ALL OVER THE PLACE	Bangles (CBS)
19	42	AGENT PROVOCATEUR	Foreigner (Atlantic)
25	43	CHICAGO 17	Chicago (Full Moon)
29	44	HATFUL OF HOLLOW	Smiths (Rough Trade)
27	45	THE BARBARA DICKSON SONGBOOK	Barbara Dickson (K-Tel)
48	46	FACE VALUE	Phil Collins (Virgin)
28	47	20/20	George Benson (Warner Bros.)
44	48	A SENSE OF WONDER	Van Morrison (Mercury)
50	49	THE HITS ALBUM	Various Artists (WEA/CBS)
40	50	THE COLLECTION	Ultravox (Chrysalis)

Phil Collins' third solo album *No Jacket Required* was to be his biggest seller yet - in fact, it was also to be one of Virgin Records' best sellers yet, and would eventually be the eighth top-selling album of the 1980s. After five consecutive weeks at Number 1, it would remain close to the top of the chart through until the middle of 1985, denying an immediate top place to Tears For Fears' *Songs From The Big Chair*.

March – April 1985

Thanks to Phil Collins' extended run at the chart top, Howard Jones second album (excluding the 12" compilation issued at Christmas) *Dream Into Action* just failed to emulate the Number 1 success of his debut, peaking at 2. Paul Young, whose second solo effort *The Secret Of Association* was (strategically?) released two weeks later, had no such problems, and his was the album to finally end the Collins run.

April – May 1985

20 April 1985

last week	this week	title	artist (label)
1	1	THE SECRET OF ASSOCIATION	Paul Young (CBS)
2	2	NO JACKET REQUIRED	Phil Collins (Virgin)
3	3	SONGS FROM THE BIG CHAIR	Tears For Fears (Mercury)
20	4	HITS 2	Various Artists (CBS/WEA)
5	5	DREAM INTO ACTION	Howard Jones (WEA)
4	6	BORN IN THE USA	Bruce Springsteen (CBS)
6	7	ALF	Alison Moyet (CBS)
7	8	REQUIEM	Andrew Lloyd Webber & Various (HMV)
13	9	WELCOME TO THE PLEASUREDOME	Frankie Goes to Hollywood (ZTT)
8	10	THE POWER STATION	Power Station (Parlophone)
9	11	PRIVATE DANCER	Tina Turner (Capitol)
42	12	GO WEST/BANGS AND CRASHES	Go West (Chrysalis)
10	13	RECKLESS	Bryan Adams (A&M)
12	14	LIKE A VIRGIN	Madonna (Sire)
21	15	WORKING NIGHTS	Working Week (Virgin)
14	16	ELIMINATOR	ZZ Top (Warner Brothers)
18	17	THE NIGHT I FELL IN LOVE	Luther Vandross (Epic)
11	18	BEHIND THE SUN	Eric Clapton (Duck)
15	19	HITS OUT OF HELL	Meatloaf (Epic)
23	20	VERY BEST OF BRENDA LEE	Brenda Lee (MCA)
16	21	CHINESE WALL	Philip Bailey (CBS)
-	22	STRAWBERRY SWITCHBLADE	Strawberry Switchblade (Korova)
28	23	THE AGE OF CONSENT	Bronski Beat (Forbidden Fruit)
19	24	DIAMOND LIFE	Sade (CBS)
-	25	SO WHERE ARE YOU?	Loose Ends (Virgin)
25	26	MAKE IT BIG	Wham! (CBS)
17	27	PURPLE RAIN	Prince & the Revolution (Warner Bros.)
22	28	BUILDING THE PERFECT BEAST	Don Henley (Geffen)
-	29	THE BEST OF ELVIS COSTELLO - THE MAN	Elvis Costello (Telstar)
-	30	TOMMY BOY'S GREATEST BEATS	Various Artists (Tommy Boy)
41	31	HOW WILL THE WOLF SURVIVE?	Los Lobos (Slash)
26	32	NO PARLEZ	Paul Young (CBS)
-	33	THE UPS AND DOWNS	Stephen TinTin Duffy (10)
24	34	SHE'S THE BOSS	Mick Jagger (CBS)
-	35	SOUTHERN ACCENTS	Tom Petty & the Heartbreakers (MCA)
27	36	STEPS IN TIME	King (CBS)
29	37	MEAT IS MURDER	Smiths (Rough Trade)
-	38	WHITE NOISE - LIVE	Gary Numan (Numa)
40	39	DANCIN' IN THE KEY OF LIFE	Steve Arrington (Atlantic)
44	40	MYSTERY	Rah Band (RCA)
49	41	LEGEND	Clannad (RCA)
45	42	STREET SOUNDS ELECTRO 6	Various Artists (Street Sounds)
35	43	LIFE'S A RIOT WITH SPY VS SPY	Billy Bragg (Go! Discs)
30	44	FIRST AND LAST AND ALWAYS	Sisters of Mercy (Merciful Release)
32	45	POWER AND PASSION	Mama's Boys (Jive)
33	46	AGENT PROVOCATEUR	Foreigner (Atlantic)
34	47	REGGAE HITS VOL 1	Various Artists (Jetstar)
38	48	20/20	George Benson (Warner Bros.)
39	49	BIRDY – MUSIC FROM THE FILM	Peter Gabriel (Charisma)
48	50	NIGHT TIME	Killing Joke (EG)

27 April 1985

last week	this week	title	artist (label)
4	1	HITS 2	Various Artists (CBS/WEA)
1	2	THE SECRET OF ASSOCIATION	Paul Young (CBS)
2	3	NO JACKET REQUIRED	Phil Collins (Virgin)
3	4	SONGS FROM THE BIG CHAIR	Tears For Fears (Mercury)
6	5	BORN IN THE USA	Bruce Springsteen (CBS)
12	6	GO WEST/BANGS AND CRASHES	Go West (Chrysalis)
8	7	REQUIEM	Andrew Lloyd Webber/ Various (HMV)
5	8	DREAM INTO ACTION	Howard Jones (WEA)
7	9	ALF	Alison Moyet (CBS)
10	10	THE POWER STATION	Power Station (Parlophone)
9	11	WELCOME TO THE PLEASUREDOME	Frankie Goes to Hollywood (ZTT)
35	12	SOUTHERN ACCENTS	Tom Petty & the Heartbreakers (MCA)
13	13	RECKLESS	Bryan Adams (A&M)
25	14	SO WHERE ARE YOU?	Loose Ends (Virgin)
11	15	PRIVATE DANCER	Tina Turner (Capitol)
14	16	LIKE A VIRGIN	Madonna (Sire)
26	17	MAKE IT BIG	Wham! (CBS)
-	18	LOVE NOT MONEY	Everything But The Girl (Blanco y Negro)
19	19	BEHIND THE SUN	Eric Clapton (Duck)
23	20	THE AGE OF CONSENT	Bronski Beat (Forbidden Fruit)
17	21	THE NIGHT I FELL IN LOVE	Luther Vandross (Epic)
16	22	ELIMINATOR	ZZ Top (Warner Brothers)
24	23	DIAMOND LIFE	Sade (CBS)
15	24	WORKING NIGHTS	Working Week (Virgin)
21	25	CHINESE WALL	Philip Bailey (CBS)
27	26	PURPLE RAIN	Prince & the Revolution (Warner Bros.)
38	27	WHITE NOISE - LIVE	Gary Numan (Numa)
36	28	STEPS IN TIME	King (CBS)
41	29	LEGEND	Clannad (RCA)
29	30	THE BEST OF ELVIS COSTELLO - THE MAN	Elvis Costello (Telstar)
34	31	SHE'S THE BOSS	Mick Jagger (CBS)
22	32	STRAWBERRY SWITCHBLADE	Strawberry Switchblade (Korova)
31	33	HOW WILL THE WOLF SURVIVE?	Los Lobos (Slash)
20	34	VERY BEST OF BRENDA LEE	Brenda Lee(MCA)
39	35	DANCIN' IN THE KEY OF LIFE	Steve Arrington (Atlantic)
19	36	HITS OUT OF HELL	Meatloaf (Epic)
-	37	CAN'T STOP THE LOVE	Maze (Capitol)
43	38	LIFE'S A RIOT WITH SPY VS SPY	Billy Bragg (Go! Discs)
32	39	NO PARLEZ	Paul Young (CBS)
30	40	TOMMY BOY'S GREATEST BEATS	Various Artists (Tommy Boy)
46	41	AGENT PROVOCATEUR	Foreigner (Atlantic)
-	42	TURN ON THE RADIO	Change (Cooltempo)
28	43	BUILDING THE PERFECT BEAST	Don Henley (Geffen)
-	44	TROPICO	Pat Benatar (CBS)
44	45	FIRST AND LAST AND ALWAYS	Sisters of Mercy (Merciful Release)
40	46	MYSTERY	Rah Band (RCA)
47	47	REGGAE HITS VOL 1	Various Artists (Jetstar)
-	48	NIGHTSHIFT	Commodores (Tamla Motown)
-	49	FACE VALUE	Phil Collins (Virgin)
-	50	HELLO, I MUST BE GOING	Phil Collins (Virgin)

4 May 1985

last week	this week	title	artist (label)
1	1	HITS 2	Various Artists (CBS/WEA)
3	2	NO JACKET REQUIRED	Phil Collins (Virgin)
4	3	SONGS FROM THE BIG CHAIR	Tears For Fears (Mercury)
2	4	THE SECRET OF ASSOCIATION	Paul Young (CBS)
8	5	BORN IN THE USA	Bruce Springsteen (CBS)
8	6	DREAM INTO ACTION	Howard Jones (WEA)
6	7	GO WEST/BANGS AND CRASHES	Go West (Chrysalis)
-	8	AROUND THE WORLD IN A DAY	Prince & the Revolution (Warner Bros.)
7	9	REQUIEM	Andrew Lloyd Webber & Various (HMV)
11	10	WELCOME TO THE PLEASUREDOME	Frankie Goes to Hollywood (ZTT)
13	11	RECKLESS	Bryan Adams (A&M)
18	12	LOVE NOT MONEY	Everything But The Girl (Blanco y Negro)
9	13	ALF	Alison Moyet (CBS)
14	14	SO WHERE ARE YOU?	Loose Ends (Virgin)
12	15	SOUTHERN ACCENTS	Tom Petty & the Heartbreakers (MCA)
15	16	PRIVATE DANCER	Tina Turner (Capitol)
16	17	LIKE A VIRGIN	Madonna (Sire)
20	18	THE AGE OF CONSENT	Bronski Beat (Forbidden Fruit)
17	19	MAKE IT BIG	Wham! (CBS)
22	20	ELIMINATOR	ZZ Top (Warner Brothers)
10	21	THE POWER STATION	Power Station (Parlophone)
29	22	LEGEND	Clannad (RCA)
23	23	DIAMOND LIFE	Sade (CBS)
30	24	THE BEST OF ELVIS COSTELLO - THE MAN	Elvis Costello (Telstar)
26	25	PURPLE RAIN	Prince & the Revolution (Warner Bros.)
28	26	STEPS IN TIME	King (CBS)
25	27	CHINESE WALL	Philip Bailey (CBS)
-	28	VIRGINS AND PHILISTINES	Colour Field (Chrysalis)
41	29	AGENT PROVOCATEUR	Foreigner (Atlantic)
42	30	TURN ON THE RADIO	Change (Cooltempo)
21	31	THE NIGHT I FELL IN LOVE	Luther Vandross (Epic)
24	32	WORKING NIGHTS	Working Week (Virgin)
35	33	DANCIN' IN THE KEY OF LIFE	Steve Arrington (Atlantic)
-	34	MOVE CLOSER	Phyllis Nelson (Carrere)
49	35	FACE VALUE	Phil Collins (Virgin)
34	36	VERY BEST OF BRENDA LEE	Brenda Lee (MCA)
27	37	WHITE NOISE - LIVE	Gary Numan (Numa)
38	38	BEHIND THE SUN	Eric Clapton (Duck)
47	39	REGGAE HITS VOL 1	Various Artists (Jetstar)
-	40	VOICES FROM THE HOLY LAND	BBC Welsh Chorus (BBC)
-	41	WILDWEED	Jeffrey Lee Pierce (Statik)
-	42	THE UPS AND DOWNS	Stephen 'Tin Tin' Duffy (10)
-	43	ROSE MARIE SINGS JUST FOR YOU	Rose Marie (A1)
-	44	THE HITS ALBUM	Various Artists (CBS/WEA)
31	45	SHE'S THE BOSS	Mick Jagger (CBS)
32	46	STRAWBERRY SWITCHBLADE	Strawberry Switchblade (Korova)
50	47	HELLO, I MUST BE GOING	Phil Collins (Virgin)
46	48	MYSTERY	Rah Band (RCA)
37	49	CAN'T STOP THE LOVE	Maze (Capitol)
-	50	BAD INFLUENCE	Robert Cray Band (Demon)

The Power Station, finding Top 10 success with their eponymous album, were basically a spin-off from Duran Duran, whose Andy and John Taylor teamed on a studio-only basis with vocalist Robert Palmer and former Chic members Bernard Edwards and Tony Thompson. The studio they used was The Power Station in New York, hence the name of the group. *Hits 2*, meanwhile, equalled the success of *Hits*.

May 1985

11 May 1985

Last	This	Album	Artist (Label)
1	1	HITS 2	Various Artists (CBS/WEA)
2	2	NO JACKET REQUIRED	Phil Collins (Virgin)
3	3	SONGS FROM THE BIG CHAIR	Tears For Fears (Mercury)
4	4	THE SECRET OF ASSOCIATION	Paul Young (CBS)
8	5	AROUND THE WORLD IN A DAY	Prince & the Revolution (Warner Bros.)
5	6	BORN IN THE USA	Bruce Springsteen (CBS)
7	7	GO WEST/BANGS AND CRASHES	Go West (Chrysalis)
6	8	DREAM INTO ACTION	Howard Jones (WEA)
12	9	LOVE NOT MONEY	Everything But The Girl (Blanco y Negro)
13	10	ALF	Alison Moyet (CBS)
-	11	BE YOURSELF TONIGHT	Eurythmics (RCA)
28	12	VIRGINS AND PHILISTINES	Colour Field (Chrysalis)
14	13	SO WHERE ARE YOU?	Loose Ends (Virgin)
18	14	THE AGE OF CONSENT	Bronski Beat (Forbidden Fruit)
9	15	REQUIEM	Andrew Lloyd Webber & Various Artists (HMV)
16	16	PRIVATE DANCER	Tina Turner (Capitol)
11	17	RECKLESS	Bryan Adams (A&M)
24	18	THE BEST OF ELVIS COSTELLO - THE MAN	Elvis Costello (Telstar)
21	19	THE POWER STATION	Power Station (Parlophone)
-	20	MR BAD GUY	Freddie Mercury (CBS)
17	21	LIKE A VIRGIN	Madonna (Sire)
10	22	WELCOME TO THE PLEASUREDOME	Frankie Goes to Hollywood (ZTT)
-	23	FLAUNT THE IMPERFECTION	China Crisis (Virgin)
15	24	SOUTHERN ACCENTS	Tom Petty & the Heartbreakers (MCA)
34	25	MOVE CLOSER	Phyllis Nelson (Carrere)
40	26	VOICES FROM THE HOLY LAND	BBC Welsh Chorus (BBC)
27	27	CHINESE WALL	Philip Bailey (CBS)
-	28	THE UNFORGETTABLE FIRE	U2 (Island)
22	29	LEGEND	Clannad (RCA)
23	30	DIAMOND LIFE	Sade (CBS)
19	31	MAKE IT BIG	Wham! (CBS)
20	32	ELIMINATOR	ZZ Top (Warner Brothers)
33	33	DANCIN' IN THE KEY OF LIFE	Steve Arrington (Atlantic)
30	34	TURN ON THE RADIO	Change (Cooltempo)
26	35	STEPS IN TIME	King (CBS)
31	36	THE NIGHT I FELL IN LOVE	Luther Vandross (Epic)
-	37	SO DELICIOUS	Fatback Band (Cotillion)
-	38	7800 DEGREES FAHRENHEIT	Bon Jovi (Vertigo)
35	39	FACE VALUE	Phil Collins (Virgin)
44	40	THE HITS ALBUM	Various Artists (CBS/WEA)
29	41	AGENT PROVOCATEUR	Foreigner (Atlantic)
25	42	PURPLE RAIN	Prince & the Revolution (Warner Bros.)
42	43	THE UPS AND DOWNS	Stephen 'Tin Tin' Duffy (10)
39	44	REGGAE HITS VOL 1	Various Artists (Jetstar)
-	45	LIVE AND UNCENSORED	Millie Jackson (Important)
-	46	TROPICO	Pat Benatar (Chrysalis)
48	47	MYSTERY	Rah Band (RCA)
41	48	WILDWEED	Jeffrey Lee Pierce (Statik)
32	49	WORKING NIGHTS	Working Week (Virgin)
45	50	SHE'S THE BOSS	Mick Jagger (CBS)

18 May 1985

Last	This	Album	Artist (Label)
1	1	HITS 2	Various Artists (CBS/WEA)
3	2	SONGS FROM THE BIG CHAIR	Tears For Fears (Mercury)
2	3	NO JACKET REQUIRED	Phil Collins (Virgin)
4	4	THE SECRET OF ASSOCIATION	Paul Young (CBS)
5	5	AROUND THE WORLD IN A DAY	Prince & the Revolution (Warner Bros.)
11	6	BE YOURSELF TONIGHT	Eurythmics (RCA)
6	7	BORN IN THE USA	Bruce Springsteen (CBS)
20	8	MR BAD GUY	Freddie Mercury (CBS)
7	9	GO WEST/BANGS AND CRASHES	Go West (Chrysalis)
23	10	FLAUNT THE IMPERFECTION	China Crisis (Virgin)
8	11	DREAM INTO ACTION	Howard Jones (WEA)
10	12	ALF	Alison Moyet (CBS)
18	13	THE BEST OF ELVIS COSTELLO - THE MAN	Elvis Costello (Telstar)
12	14	VIRGINS AND PHILISTINES	Colour Field (Chrysalis)
9	15	LOVE NOT MONEY	Everything But The Girl (Blanco y Negro)
14	16	THE AGE OF CONSENT	Bronski Beat (Forbidden Fruit)
13	17	SO WHERE ARE YOU?	Loose Ends (Virgin)
22	18	WELCOME TO THE PLEASUREDOME	Frankie Goes to Hollywood (ZTT)
19	19	PRIVATE DANCER	Tina Turner (Capitol)
19	20	THE POWER STATION	Power Station (Parlophone)
21	21	RECKLESS	Bryan Adams (A&M)
38	22	7800 DEGREES FAHRENHEIT	Bon Jovi (Vertigo)
26	23	VOICES FROM THE HOLY LAND	BBC Welsh Chorus (BBC)
31	24	MAKE IT BIG	Wham! (CBS)
33	25	DANCIN' IN THE KEY OF LIFE	Steve Arrington (Atlantic)
30	26	DIAMOND LIFE	Sade (CBS)
36	27	THE NIGHT I FELL IN LOVE	Luther Vandross (Epic)
15	28	REQUIEM	Andrew Lloyd Webber & Various Artists (HMV)
21	29	LIKE A VIRGIN	Madonna (Sire)
24	30	SOUTHERN ACCENTS	Tom Petty & the Heartbreakers (MCA)
25	31	MOVE CLOSER	Phyllis Nelson (Carrere)
32	32	ELIMINATOR	ZZ Top (Warner Brothers)
34	33	TURN ON THE RADIO	Change (Cooltempo)
28	34	THE UNFORGETTABLE FIRE	U2 (Island)
-	35	BEST OF THE EAGLES	Eagles (Asylum)
-	36	YOUTHQUAKE	Dead Or Alive (Epic)
42	37	PURPLE RAIN	Prince & the Revolution (Warner Bros.)
35	38	STEPS IN TIME	King (CBS)
-	39	HEARTS OF FORTUNE	Immaculate Fools (A&M)
47	40	MYSTERY	Rah Band (RCA)
46	41	TROPICO	Pat Benatar (Chrysalis)
-	42	CAN'T STOP THE LOVE	Maze (Capitol)
-	43	STREET SOUNDS ELECTRO 7	Various Artists (Street Sounds)
-	44	HITS OUT OF HELL	Meatloaf (Epic)
39	45	FACE VALUE	Phil Collins (Virgin)
27	46	CHINESE WALL	Philip Bailey (CBS)
29	47	LEGEND	Clannad (RCA)
-	48	STREET SOUNDS EDITION 12	Various Artists (Street Sounds)
37	49	SO DELICIOUS	Fatback Band (Cotillion)
-	50	BEST OF THE 20TH CENTURY BOY	Marc Bolan (K-Tel)

25 May 1985

Last	This	Album	Artist (Label)
2	1	SONGS FROM THE BIG CHAIR	Tears For Fears (Mercury)
3	2	NO JACKET REQUIRED	Phil Collins (Virgin)
6	3	BE YOURSELF TONIGHT	Eurythmics (RCA)
1	4	HITS 2	Various Artists (CBS/WEA)
-	5	BROTHERS IN ARMS	Dire Straits (Vertigo)
8	6	MR BAD GUY	Freddie Mercury (CBS)
4	7	THE SECRET OF ASSOCIATION	Paul Young (CBS)
10	8	FLAUNT THE IMPERFECTION	China Crisis (Virgin)
5	9	AROUND THE WORLD IN A DAY	Prince & the Revolution (Warner Bros.)
7	10	BORN IN THE USA	Bruce Springsteen (CBS)
13	11	THE BEST OF ELVIS COSTELLO - THE MAN	Elvis Costello (Telstar)
9	12	GO WEST/BANGS AND CRASHES	Go West (Chrysalis)
16	13	THE AGE OF CONSENT	Bronski Beat (Forbidden Fruit)
36	14	YOUTHQUAKE	Dead Or Alive (Epic)
50	15	BEST OF THE 20TH CENTURY BOY	Marc Bolan (K-Tel)
43	16	STREET SOUNDS ELECTRO 7	Various Artists (Street Sounds)
12	17	ALF	Alison Moyet (CBS)
35	18	BEST OF THE EAGLES	Eagles (Asylum)
15	19	LOVE NOT MONEY	Everything But The Girl (Blanco y Negro)
11	20	DREAM INTO ACTION	Howard Jones (WEA)
-	21	OUT NOW!	Various Artists (Chrysalis/MCA)
20	22	THE POWER STATION	Power Station (Parlophone)
19	23	PRIVATE DANCER	Tina Turner (Capitol)
21	24	RECKLESS	Bryan Adams (A&M)
-	25	SHAMROCK DIARIES	Chris Rea (Magnet)
17	26	SO WHERE ARE YOU?	Loose Ends (Virgin)
-	27	LOW-LIFE	New Order (Factory)
22	28	7800 DEGREES FAHRENHEIT	Bon Jovi (Vertigo)
18	29	WELCOME TO THE PLEASUREDOME	Frankie Goes to Hollywood (ZTT)
31	30	MOVE CLOSER	Phyllis Nelson (Carrere)
23	31	VOICES FROM THE HOLY LAND	BBC Welsh Chorus (BBC)
24	32	MAKE IT BIG	Wham! (CBS)
-	33	ROCK ME TONIGHT	Freddie Jackson (Capitol)
-	34	WEST SIDE STORY	Leonard Bernstein & Studio Cast (Deutsche Grammophon)
14	35	VIRGINS AND PHILISTINES	Colour Field (Chrysalis)
25	36	DANCIN' IN THE KEY OF LIFE	Steve Arrington (Atlantic)
37	37	STREET SOUNDS EDITION 12	Various Artists (Street Sounds)
48	38	TROPICO	Pat Benatar (Chrysalis)
32	39	ELIMINATOR	ZZ Top (Warner Brothers)
26	40	DIAMOND LIFE	Sade (CBS)
46	41	CHINESE WALL	Philip Bailey (CBS)
28	42	REQUIEM	Andrew Lloyd Webber & Various Artists (HMV)
42	43	CAN'T STOP THE LOVE	Maze (Capitol)
33	44	TURN ON THE RADIO	Change (Cooltempo)
-	45	NO REST FOR THE WICKED	New Model Army (EMI)
-	46	BROTHER WHERE YOU BOUND	Supertramp (A&M)
47	47	WE ARE THE WORLD	USA For Africa (CBS)
29	48	LIKE A VIRGIN	Madonna (Sire)
27	49	THE NIGHT I FELL IN LOVE	Luther Vandross (Epic)
34	50	THE UNFORGETTABLE FIRE	U2 (Island)

Queen vocalist Freddie Mercury, who had signed a separate solo recording deal with CBS, unveiled its first fruits on the solo album *Mr Bad Guy*, and was rewarded with Queen-sized sales as the set bounded into the Top 10. Meanwhile, Tears For Fears' *Songs From The Big Chair* finally snatched a week at Number 1 after 10 weeks of almost making it behind Phil Collins, Paul Young and the *Hits 2* compilation.

June 1985

Brothers In Arms was only Dire Straits' sixth album in eight years, but it turned out to be just the release the new upwardly-mobile CD buyers of the 80s were looking for, and quickly outsold everything the band had done previously. After its initial run at the chart top in June, it would keep returning to Number 1 throughout the year (and in 1986), and would prove to be the biggest-selling album (and CD) of the 1980s.

June – July 1985

22 June 1985

last week	this week		
11	1	BOYS AND GIRLS	Bryan Ferry (EG)
4	2	BORN IN THE USA	Bruce Springsteen (CBS)
1	3	BROTHERS IN ARMS	Dire Straits (Vertigo)
2	4	OUR FAVOURITE SHOP	Style Council (Polydor)
3	5	OUT NOW!	Various Artists (Chrysalis/MCA)
8	6	NO JACKET REQUIRED	Phil Collins (Virgin)
5	7	NOW DANCE	Various Artists (EMI/Virgin)
9	8	BEST OF THE 20TH CENTURY BOY	
			Marc Bolan (K-Tel)
6	9	LOW-LIFE	New Order (Factory)
7	10	SONGS FROM THE BIG CHAIR	
			Tears For Fears (Mercury)
12	11	GO WEST/BANGS AND CRASHES	
			Go West (Chrysalis)
15	12	BE YOURSELF TONIGHT	Eurythmics (RCA)
13	13	BEST OF THE EAGLES	Eagles (Asylum)
14	14	SHAMROCK DIARIES	Chris Rea (Magnet)
10	15	HITS 2	Various Artists (CBS/WEA)
-	16	CUPID AND PSYCHE '85	Scritti Politti (Virgin)
19	17	THE SECRET OF ASSOCIATION Paul Young (CBS)	
17	18	FLAUNT THE IMPERFECTION China Crisis (Virgin)	
23	19	KATRINA AND THE WAVES	
			Katrina & the Waves (Capitol)
-	20	STEVE McQUEEN Prefab Sprout (Kitchenware)	
20	21	RECKLESS	Bryan Adams (A&M)
35	22	ROMANCE	David Cassidy (Arista)
26	23	THE POWER STATION	
			Power Station (Parlophone)
-	24	EMPIRE BURLESQUE	Bob Dylan (CBS)
37	25	THE RIVER	Bruce Springsteen (CBS)
24	26	THE AGE OF CONSENT	
			Bronski Beat (Forbidden Fruit)
18	27	YOUTHQUAKE	Dead Or Alive (Epic)
16	28	SHAKEN 'N' STIRRED Robert Plant (Es Paranza)	
-	29	BORN TO RUN	Bruce Springsteen (CBS)
-	30	WATCHING YOU WATCHING ME	
			Bill Withers (CBS)
25	31	WEST SIDE STORY	Leonard Bernstein
			& Studio Cast (Deutsche Grammophon)
34	32	SUDDENLY	Billy Ocean (Jive)
21	33	THE BEST OF ELVIS COSTELLO - THE MAN	
			Elvis Costello (Telstar)
28	34	AROUND THE WORLD IN A DAY	
			Prince & the Revolution (Warner Bros.)
43	35	CHINESE WALL	Philip Bailey (CBS)
22	36	MR BAD GUY	Freddie Mercury (CBS)
27	37	VOICES FROM THE HOLY LAND	
			BBC Welsh Chorus (BBC)
33	38	ALF	Alison Moyet (CBS)
-	39	AS THE BAND TURNS	Atlantic Starr (A&M)
-	40	THE CAT IS OUT	Judy Tzuke (Legacy)
-	41	LIKE A VIRGIN	Madonna (Sire)
-	42	YOU'RE UNDER ARREST	Miles Davis (CBS)
31	43	7800 DEGREES FAHRENHEIT Bon Jovi (Vertigo)	
32	44	BROTHER WHERE YOU BOUND	
			Supertramp (A&M)
36	45	ROCK ME TONIGHT Freddie Jackson (Capitol)	
-	46	DARKNESS ON THE EDGE OF TOWN	
			Bruce Springsteen (CBS)
42	47	THE UNFORGETTABLE FIRE	U2 (Island)
45	48	SO WHERE ARE YOU?	Loose Ends (Virgin)
30	49	DREAM INTO ACTION	Howard Jones (WEA)
-	50	RADIO M.U.S.I.C. MAN	
			Womack & Womack (Elektra)

29 June 1985

last week	this week		
2	1	BORN IN THE USA	Bruce Springsteen (CBS)
3	2	BROTHERS IN ARMS	Dire Straits (Vertigo)
1	3	BOYS AND GIRLS	Bryan Ferry (EG)
4	4	OUR FAVOURITE SHOP Style Council (Polydor)	
16	5	CUPID AND PSYCHE '85	Scritti Politti (Virgin)
-	6	MISPLACED CHILDHOOD	Marillion (EMI)
24	7	EMPIRE BURLESQUE	Bob Dylan (CBS)
5	8	OUT NOW!	Various Artists (Chrysalis/MCA)
10	9	SONGS FROM THE BIG CHAIR	
			Tears For Fears (Mercury)
8	10	BEST OF THE 20TH CENTURY BOY	
			Marc Bolan (K-Tel)
6	11	NO JACKET REQUIRED	Phil Collins (Virgin)
7	12	NOW DANCE	Various Artists (EMI/Virgin)
-	13	LITTLE CREATURES	Talking Heads (EMI)
20	14	STEVE McQUEEN Prefab Sprout (Kitchenware)	
-	15	THE DREAM OF THE BLUE TURTLES	
			Sting (A&M)
32	16	SUDDENLY	Billy Ocean (Jive)
18	17	FLAUNT THE IMPERFECTION China Crisis (Virgin)	
13	18	BEST OF THE EAGLES	Eagles (Asylum)
11	19	GO WEST/BANGS AND CRASHES	
			Go West (Chrysalis)
-	20	WHEN THE BOYS MEET THE GIRLS	
			Sister Sledge (Atlantic)
17	21	THE SECRET OF ASSOCIATION Paul Young (CBS)	
-	22	CRUSH	
			Orchestral Manoeuvres in the Dark (Virgin)
15	23	HITS 2	Various Artists (CBS/WEA)
14	24	SHAMROCK DIARIES	Chris Rea (Magnet)
12	25	BE YOURSELF TONIGHT	Eurythmics (RCA)
19	26	KATRINA AND THE WAVES	
			Katrina & the Waves (Capitol)
25	27	THE RIVER	Bruce Springsteen (CBS)
50	28	RADIO M.U.S.I.C. MAN	
			Womack & Womack (Elektra)
34	29	AROUND THE WORLD IN A DAY	
			Prince & the Revolution (Warner Bros.)
9	30	LOW-LIFE	New Order (Factory)
-	31	FABLES OF THE RECONSTRUCTION REM (IRS)	
-	32	WORLD WIDE LIVE	Scorpions (Harvest)
29	33	BORN TO RUN	Bruce Springsteen (CBS)
26	34	THE AGE OF CONSENT	
			Bronski Beat (Forbidden Fruit)
46	35	DARKNESS ON THE EDGE OF TOWN	
			Bruce Springsteen (CBS)
-	36	DREAM OF A LIFETIME	Marvin Gaye (CBS)
-	37	MAKE IT BIG	Wham! (CBS)
37	38	VOICES FROM THE HOLY LAND	
			BBC Welsh Chorus (BBC)
41	39	LIKE A VIRGIN	Madonna (Sire)
21	40	RECKLESS	Bryan Adams (A&M)
31	41	WEST SIDE STORY	Leonard Bernstein
			& Studio Cast (Deutsche Grammophon)
36	42	MR BAD GUY	Freddie Mercury (CBS)
35	43	CHINESE WALL	Philip Bailey (CBS)
33	44	THE BEST OF ELVIS COSTELLO - THE MAN	
			Elvis Costello (Telstar)
39	45	AS THE BAND TURNS	Atlantic Starr (A&M)
38	46	ALF	Alison Moyet (CBS)
48	47	SO WHERE ARE YOU?	Loose Ends (Virgin)
-	48	THE BEACH BOYS	Beach Boys (Caribou)
22	49	ROMANCE	David Cassidy (Arista)
23	50	THE POWER STATION Power Station (Parlophone)	

6 July 1985

last week	this week		
6	1	MISPLACED CHILDHOOD	Marillion (EMI)
1	2	BORN IN THE USA	Bruce Springsteen (CBS)
3	3	BOYS AND GIRLS	Bryan Ferry (EG)
4	4	OUR FAVOURITE SHOP Style Council (Polydor)	
5	5	CUPID AND PSYCHE '85	Scritti Politti (Virgin)
15	6	THE DREAM OF THE BLUE TURTLES	
			Sting (A&M)
9	7	SONGS FROM THE BIG CHAIR	
			Tears For Fears (Mercury)
13	8	LITTLE CREATURES	Talking Heads (EMI)
4	9	OUR FAVOURITE SHOP Style Council (Polydor)	
22	10	CRUSH	
			Orchestral Manoeuvres in the Dark (Virgin)
32	11	WORLD WIDE LIVE	Scorpions (Harvest)
7	12	EMPIRE BURLESQUE	Bob Dylan (CBS)
10	13	BEST OF THE 20TH CENTURY BOY	
			Marc Bolan (K-Tel)
8	14	OUT NOW!	Various Artists (Chrysalis/MCA)
11	15	NO JACKET REQUIRED	Phil Collins (Virgin)
16	16	SUDDENLY	Billy Ocean (Jive)
12	17	NOW DANCE	Various Artists (EMI/Virgin)
31	18	FABLES OF THE RECONSTRUCTION REM (IRS)	
27	19	THE RIVER	Bruce Springsteen (CBS)
21	20	THE SECRET OF ASSOCIATION	
			Paul Young (CBS)
25	21	BE YOURSELF TONIGHT	Eurythmics (RCA)
20	22	WHEN THE BOYS MEET THE GIRLS	
			Sister Sledge (Atlantic)
-	23	ALL THROUGH THE NIGHT	Aled Jones (BBC)
14	24	STEVE McQUEEN Prefab Sprout (Kitchenware)	
33	25	BORN TO RUN	Bruce Springsteen (CBS)
35	26	BEST OF THE EAGLES	Eagles (Asylum)
35	27	DARKNESS ON THE EDGE OF TOWN	
			Bruce Springsteen (CBS)
26	28	KATRINA AND THE WAVES	
			Katrina & the Waves (Capitol)
19	29	GO WEST/BANGS AND CRASHES	
			Go West (Chrysalis)
38	30	VOICES FROM THE HOLY LAND	
			BBC Welsh Chorus (BBC)
39	31	LIKE A VIRGIN	Madonna (Sire)
23	32	HITS 2	Various Artists (CBS/WEA)
33	33	THE ANTHOLOGY	Deep Purple (Harvest)
45	34	AS THE BAND TURNS	Atlantic Starr (A&M)
-	35	LONE JUSTICE	Lone Justice (Geffen)
36	36	DREAM OF A LIFETIME	Marvin Gaye (CBS)
-	37	FLIP	Nils Lofgren (Towerbell)
24	38	SHAMROCK DIARIES	Chris Rea (Magnet)
-	39	HISTORY	Mai Tai (Virgin)
30	40	LOW-LIFE	New Order (Factory)
29	41	AROUND THE WORLD IN A DAY	
			Prince & the Revolution (Warner Bros.)
34	42	THE AGE OF CONSENT	
			Bronski Beat (Forbidden Fruit)
-	43	BEYOND THE SUNSET	Rain Parade (Island)
-	44	BEVERLY HILLS COP	Soundtrack (MCA)
28	45	RADIO M.U.S.I.C. MAN	
			Womack & Womack (Elektra)
40	46	RECKLESS	Bryan Adams (A&M)
47	47	SO WHERE ARE YOU?	Loose Ends (Virgin)
50	48	THE POWER STATION	
			Power Station (Parlophone)
-	49	DREAM INTO ACTION	Howard Jones (WEA)
43	50	CHINESE WALL	Philip Bailey (CBS)

The arrival of Bruce Springsteen's spectacular Born In The USA tour in Britain created a wave of interest which not only propelled the album of the same title back to Number 1, but also boosted sales on Springsteen's earlier albums *Born To Run*, *The River* and *Darkness On The Edge Of Town* sufficiently to pull all of them into the chart again too. Bryan Ferry and Marillion also snatched a Number 1 week apiece.

273

July 1985

13 July 1985

last	this		
2	1	BORN IN THE USA	Bruce Springsteen (CBS)
1	2	MISPLACED CHILDHOOD	Marillion (EMI)
6	3	THE DREAM OF THE BLUE TURTLES	
			Sting (A&M)
5	4	CUPID AND PSYCHE '85	Scritti Politti (Virgin)
4	5	BROTHERS IN ARMS	Dire Straits (Vertigo)
3	6	BOYS AND GIRLS	Bryan Ferry (EG)
7	7	SONGS FROM THE BIG CHAIR	
			Tears For Fears (Mercury)
8	8	LITTLE CREATURES	Talking Heads (EMI)
10	9	CRUSH	
			Orchestral Manoeuvres in the Dark (Virgin)
11	10	WORLD WIDE LIVE	Scorpions (Harvest)
16	11	SUDDENLY	Billy Ocean (Jive)
13	12	BEST OF THE 20TH CENTURY BOY	
			Marc Bolan (K-Tel)
19	13	THE RIVER	Bruce Springsteen (CBS)
23	14	ALL THROUGH THE NIGHT	Aled Jones (BBC)
20	15	THE SECRET OF ASSOCIATION	
			Paul Young (CBS)
22	16	WHEN THE BOYS MEET THE GIRLS	
			Sister Sledge (Atlantic)
15	17	NO JACKET REQUIRED	Phil Collins (Virgin)
14	18	OUT NOW!	Various Artists (Chrysalis/MCA)
-	19	FLY ON THE WALL	AC/DC (Atlantic)
29	20	GO WEST/BANGS AND CRASHES	
			Go West (Chrysalis)
-	21	A PHYSICAL PRESENCE	Level 42 (Polydor)
18	22	FABLES OF THE RECONSTRUCTION	
			REM (IRS)
9	23	OUR FAVOURITE SHOP	Style Council (Polydor)
17	24	NOW DANCE	Various Artists (EMI/Virgin)
21	25	BE YOURSELF TONIGHT	Eurythmics (RCA)
-	26	THEATRE OF PAIN	Motley Crue (Elektra)
-	27	THE ALLNIGHTER	Glen Frey (MCA)
25	28	BORN TO RUN	Bruce Springsteen (CBS)
-	29	FLAUNT THE IMPERFECTION	
			China Crisis (Virgin)
38	30	SHAMROCK DIARIES	Chris Rea (Magnet)
-	31	A SECRET WISH	Propaganda (ZTT)
-	32	INVASION OF YOUR PRIVACY	Ratt (Atlantic)
12	33	EMPIRE BURLESQUE	Bob Dylan (CBS)
36	34	DREAM OF A LIFETIME	Marvin Gaye (CBS)
37	35	FLIP	Nils Lofgren (Towerbell)
34	36	AS THE BAND TURNS	Atlantic Starr (A&M)
30	37	VOICES FROM THE HOLY LAND	
			BBC Welsh Chorus (BBC)
35	38	LONE JUSTICE	Lone Justice (Geffen)
32	39	HITS 2	Various Artists (CBS/WEA)
24	40	STEVE McQUEEN	Prefab Sprout (Kitchenware)
31	41	LIKE A VIRGIN	Madonna (Sire)
26	42	BEST OF THE EAGLES	Eagles (Asylum)
33	43	THE ANTHOLOGY	Deep Purple (Harvest)
28	44	KATRINA AND THE WAVES	
			Katrina & the Waves (Capitol)
27	45	DARKNESS ON THE EDGE OF TOWN	
			Bruce Springsteen (CBS)
-	46	PHENOMENA	Phenomena (Bronze)
-	47	U2 LIVE: UNDER A BLOOD RED SKY	U2 (Island)
-	48	THE BEST OF ELVIS COSTELLO - THE MAN	
			Elvis Costello (Telstar)
-	49	YOUTHQUAKE	Dead Or Alive (Epic)
-	50	WEST SIDE STORY	Leonard Bernstein
			& Studio Cast (Deutsche Grammophon)

20 July 1985

last	this		
1	1	BORN IN THE USA	Bruce Springsteen (CBS)
2	2	MISPLACED CHILDHOOD	Marillion (EMI)
5	3	BROTHERS IN ARMS	Dire Straits (Vertigo)
19	4	FLY ON THE WALL	AC/DC (Atlantic)
4	5	CUPID AND PSYCHE '85	Scritti Politti (Virgin)
7	6	SONGS FROM THE BIG CHAIR	
			Tears For Fears (Mercury)
6	7	BOYS AND GIRLS	Bryan Ferry (EG)
3	8	THE DREAM OF THE BLUE TURTLES	
			Sting (A&M)
31	9	A SECRET WISH	Propaganda (ZTT)
8	10	LITTLE CREATURES	Talking Heads (EMI)
25	11	BE YOURSELF TONIGHT	Eurythmics (RCA)
13	12	THE RIVER	Bruce Springsteen (CBS)
16	13	WHEN THE BOYS MEET THE GIRLS	
			Sister Sledge (Atlantic)
14	14	ALL THROUGH THE NIGHT	Aled Jones (BBC)
15	15	THE SECRET OF ASSOCIATION	
			Paul Young (CBS)
11	16	SUDDENLY	Billy Ocean (Jive)
26	17	THEATRE OF PAIN	Motley Crue (Elektra)
17	18	NO JACKET REQUIRED	Phil Collins (Virgin)
23	19	OUR FAVOURITE SHOP	Style Council (Polydor)
24	20	NOW DANCE	Various Artists (EMI/Virgin)
18	21	OUT NOW!	Various Artists (Chrysalis/MCA)
10	22	WORLD WIDE LIVE	Scorpions (Harvest)
37	23	VOICES FROM THE HOLY LAND	
			BBC Welsh Chorus (BBC)
41	24	LIKE A VIRGIN	Madonna (Sire)
-	25	STREET SOUNDS ELECTRO 8	
			Various Artists (Street Sounds)
28	26	BORN TO RUN	Bruce Springsteen (CBS)
9	27	CRUSH	
			Orchestral Manoeuvres in the Dark (Virgin)
20	28	GO WEST/BANGS AND CRASHES	
			Go West (Chrysalis)
32	29	INVASION OF YOUR PRIVACY	Ratt (Atlantic)
22	30	FABLES OF THE RECONSTRUCTION	REM (IRS)
27	31	THE ALLNIGHTER	Glen Frey (MCA)
12	32	BEST OF THE 20TH CENTURY BOY	
			Marc Bolan (K-Tel)
-	33	WILD CHILD	Untouchables (Stiff)
21	34	A PHYSICAL PRESENCE	Level 42 (Polydor)
-	35	BILLY JOEL'S GREATEST HITS VOL 1 & VOL 2	
			Billy Joel (CBS)
39	36	HITS 2	Various Artists (CBS/WEA)
29	37	FLAUNT THE IMPERFECTION	
			China Crisis (Virgin)
38	38	LONE JUSTICE	Lone Justice (Geffen)
45	39	DARKNESS ON THE EDGE OF TOWN	
			Bruce Springsteen (CBS)
42	40	BEST OF THE EAGLES	Eagles (Asylum)
-	41	ROCK AIN'T DEAD	Heavy Pettin' (Polydor)
-	42	HISTORY	Mai Tai (Virgin)
-	42	THE ARTISTS VOLUME 2	
			Various Artists (Street Sounds)
34	43	DREAM OF A LIFETIME	Marvin Gaye (CBS)
35	44	FLIP	Nils Lofgren (Towerbell)
46	45	PHENOMENA	Phenomena (Bronze)
49	46	YOUTHQUAKE	Dead Or Alive (Epic)
44	47	KATRINA AND THE WAVES	
			Katrina & the Waves (Capitol)
30	49	SHAMROCK DIARIES	Chris Rea (Magnet)
36	50	AS THE BAND TURNS	Atlantic Starr (A&M)

27 July 1985

last	this		
1	1	BORN IN THE USA	Bruce Springsteen (CBS)
3	2	BROTHERS IN ARMS	Dire Straits (Vertigo)
11	3	BE YOURSELF TONIGHT	Eurythmics (RCA)
2	4	MISPLACED CHILDHOOD	Marillion (EMI)
4	5	FLY ON THE WALL	AC/DC (Atlantic)
6	6	SONGS FROM THE BIG CHAIR	
			Tears For Fears (Mercury)
8	7	THE DREAM OF THE BLUE TURTLES	
			Sting (A&M)
14	8	ALL THROUGH THE NIGHT	Aled Jones (BBC)
35	9	BILLY JOEL'S GREATEST HITS VOL 1 & VOL 2	
			Billy Joel (CBS)
7	10	BOYS AND GIRLS	Bryan Ferry (EG)
18	11	NO JACKET REQUIRED	Phil Collins (Virgin)
5	12	CUPID AND PSYCHE '85	Scritti Politti (Virgin)
12	13	THE RIVER	Bruce Springsteen (CBS)
16	14	SUDDENLY	Billy Ocean (Jive)
13	15	WHEN THE BOYS MEET THE GIRLS	
			Sister Sledge (Atlantic)
24	16	LIKE A VIRGIN	Madonna (Sire)
9	17	A SECRET WISH	Propaganda (ZTT)
15	18	THE SECRET OF ASSOCIATION	
			Paul Young (CBS)
10	19	LITTLE CREATURES	Talking Heads (EMI)
19	20	OUR FAVOURITE SHOP	Style Council (Polydor)
26	21	BORN TO RUN	Bruce Springsteen (CBS)
-	22	PHANTASMAGORIA	Damned (MCA)
-	23	CONTACT	Pointer Sisters (Planet)
23	24	VOICES FROM THE HOLY LAND	
			BBC Welsh Chorus (BBC)
31	25	THE ALLNIGHTER	Glen Frey (MCA)
17	26	THEATRE OF PAIN	Motley Crue (Elektra)
22	27	WORLD WIDE LIVE	Scorpions (Harvest)
-	28	PRIVATE DANCER	Tina Turner (Capitol)
27	29	CRUSH	
			Orchestral Manoeuvres in the Dark (Virgin)
28	30	GO WEST/BANGS AND CRASHES	
			Go West (Chrysalis)
-	31	NIGHT OF A THOUSAND CANDLES	
			Men They Couldn't Hang (Imp)
46	32	YOUTHQUAKE	Dead Or Alive (Epic)
39	33	DARKNESS ON THE EDGE OF TOWN	
			Bruce Springsteen (CBS)
25	34	STREET SOUNDS ELECTRO 8	
			Various Artists (Street Sounds)
32	35	BEST OF THE 20TH CENTURY BOY	
			Marc Bolan (K-Tel)
-	36	ALF	Alison Moyet (CBS)
21	37	OUT NOW!	Various Artists (Chrysalis/MCA)
-	38	DIAMOND LIFE	Sade (CBS)
36	39	HITS 2	Various Artists (CBS/WEA)
-	40	MAKE IT BIG	Wham! (CBS)
41	41	BEVERLY HILLS COP	Soundtrack (MCA)
37	42	FLAUNT THE IMPERFECTION	
			China Crisis (Virgin)
40	43	BEST OF THE EAGLES	Eagles (Asylum)
42	44	THE ARTISTS VOLUME 2	
			Various Artists (Street Sounds)
20	45	NOW DANCE	Various Artists (EMI/Virgin)
29	46	INVASION OF YOUR PRIVACY	Ratt (Atlantic)
34	47	A PHYSICAL PRESENCE	Level 42 (Polydor)
30	48	FABLES OF THE RECONSTRUCTION	REM (IRS)
33	49	WILD CHILD	Untouchables (Stiff)
45	50	PHENOMENA	Phenomena (Bronze)

The Dream Of The Blue Turtles was former Police vocalist Sting's first solo album, and like Freddie Mercury's a few months previously, it found success almost on the same level as the group's releases. *Fly On The Wall*, meanwhile, was Aussie hard rockers AC/DC's first album for two years, but its almost immediate Top 5 placing suggested no drop-off in the hard-touring band's record popularity.

August 1985

3 August 1985

last	this	Title	Artist
1	1	BORN IN THE USA	Bruce Springsteen (CBS)
3	2	BE YOURSELF TONIGHT	Eurythmics (RCA)
2	3	BROTHERS IN ARMS	Dire Straits (Vertigo)
6	4	SONGS FROM THE BIG CHAIR	Tears For Fears (Mercury)
11	5	NO JACKET REQUIRED	Phil Collins (Virgin)
9	6	BILLY JOEL'S GREATEST HITS VOL 1 & VOL 2	Billy Joel (CBS)
16	7	LIKE A VIRGIN	Madonna (Sire)
22	8	PHANTASMAGORIA	Damned (MCA)
4	9	MISPLACED CHILDHOOD	Marillion (EMI)
-	10	THE UNFORGETTABLE FIRE	U2 (Island)
10	11	BOYS AND GIRLS	Bryan Ferry (EG)
7	12	THE DREAM OF THE BLUE TURTLES	Sting (A&M)
18	13	THE SECRET OF ASSOCIATION	Paul Young (CBS)
13	14	THE RIVER	Bruce Springsteen (CBS)
5	15	FLY ON THE WALL	AC/DC (Atlantic)
-	16	U2 LIVE: UNDER A BLOOD RED SKY	U2 (Island)
8	17	ALL THROUGH THE NIGHT	Aled Jones (BBC)
12	18	CUPID AND PSYCHE '85	Scritti Politti (Virgin)
26	19	THEATRE OF PAIN	Motley Crue (Elektra)
-	20	THE KENNY ROGERS STORY	Kenny Rogers (Liberty)
38	21	DIAMOND LIFE	Sade (CBS)
23	22	CONTACT	Pointer Sisters (Planet)
14	23	SUDDENLY	Billy Ocean (Jive)
15	24	WHEN THE BOYS MEET THE GIRLS	Sister Sledge (Atlantic)
19	25	LITTLE CREATURES	Talking Heads (EMI)
24	26	VOICES FROM THE HOLY LAND	BBC Welsh Chorus (BBC)
37	27	OUT NOW!	Various Artists (Chrysalis/MCA)
-	28	QUEEN'S GREATEST HITS	Queen (EMI)
40	29	MAKE IT BIG	Wham! (CBS)
31	30	NIGHT OF A THOUSAND CANDLES	Men They Couldn't Hang (Imp)
-	31	MR BAD GUY	Freddie Mercury (CBS)
20	32	OUR FAVOURITE SHOP	Style Council (Polydor)
21	33	BORN TO RUN	Bruce Springsteen (CBS)
17	34	A SECRET WISH	Propaganda (ZTT)
28	35	PRIVATE DANCER	Tina Turner (Capitol)
-	36	WAR	U2 (Island)
30	37	GO WEST/BANGS AND CRASHES	Go West (Chrysalis)
36	38	ALF	Alison Moyet (CBS)
34	39	STREET SOUNDS ELECTRO 8	Various Artists (Street Sounds)
-	40	BOY	U2 (Island)
-	41	BIG BAM BOOM	Daryll Hall & John Oates (RCA)
-	42	VITAL IDOL	Billy Idol (Chrysalis)
27	43	WORLD WIDE LIVE	Scorpions (Harvest)
-	44	FLIP	Nils Lofgren (Towerbell)
41	45	BEVERLY HILLS COP	Soundtrack (MCA)
44	46	THE ARTISTS VOL II	Various Artists (Street Sounds)
-	47	OPEN FIRE	Y & T (A&M)
-	48	THE WORKS	Queen (EMI)
39	49	HITS 2	Various Artists (CBS/WEA)
33	50	DARKNESS ON THE EDGE OF TOWN	Bruce Springsteen (CBS)

10 August 1985

last	this	Title	Artist
3	1	BROTHERS IN ARMS	Dire Straits (Vertigo)
1	2	BORN IN THE USA	Bruce Springsteen (CBS)
2	3	BE YOURSELF TONIGHT	Eurythmics (RCA)
4	4	SONGS FROM THE BIG CHAIR	Tears For Fears (Mercury)
7	5	LIKE A VIRGIN	Madonna (Sire)
5	6	NO JACKET REQUIRED	Phil Collins (Virgin)
6	7	BILLY JOEL'S GREATEST HITS VOL 1 & VOL 2	Billy Joel (CBS)
10	8	THE UNFORGETTABLE FIRE	U2 (Island)
20	9	THE KENNY ROGERS STORY	Kenny Rogers (Liberty)
13	10	THE SECRET OF ASSOCIATION	Paul Young (CBS)
8	11	PHANTASMAGORIA	Damned (MCA)
9	12	MISPLACED CHILDHOOD	Marillion (EMI)
12	13	THE DREAM OF THE BLUE TURTLES	Sting (A&M)
16	14	U2 LIVE: UNDER A BLOOD RED SKY	U2 (Island)
11	15	BOYS AND GIRLS	Bryan Ferry (EG)
35	16	PRIVATE DANCER	Tina Turner (Capitol)
-	17	MINX	Toyah (Portrait)
17	18	ALL THROUGH THE NIGHT	Aled Jones (BBC)
-	19	LUXURY OF LIFE	Five Star (Tent)
28	20	QUEEN'S GREATEST HITS	Queen (EMI)
18	21	CUPID AND PSYCHE '85	Scritti Politti (Virgin)
14	22	THE RIVER	Bruce Springsteen (CBS)
-	23	MADONNA	Madonna (Sire)
26	24	VOICES FROM THE HOLY LAND	BBC Welsh Chorus (BBC)
22	25	CONTACT	Pointer Sisters (Planet)
25	26	LITTLE CREATURES	Talking Heads (EMI)
34	27	A SECRET WISH	Propaganda (ZTT)
-	28	DRINKING GASOLINE	Cabaret Voltaire (Some Bizzare)
-	29	THE MAGIC OF TORVILL AND DEAN	Various Artists (Stylus)
37	30	GO WEST/BANGS AND CRASHES	Go West (Chrysalis)
30	31	NIGHT OF A THOUSAND CANDLES	Men They Couldn't Hang (Imp)
24	32	WHEN THE BOYS MEET THE GIRLS	Sister Sledge (Atlantic)
33	33	BORN TO RUN	Bruce Springsteen (CBS)
38	34	ALF	Alison Moyet (CBS)
15	35	FLY ON THE WALL	AC/DC (Atlantic)
-	36	PHILIP OAKEY AND GIORGIO MORODER	Philip Oakey & Giorgio Moroder (Virgin)
32	37	OUR FAVOURITE SHOP	Style Council (Polydor)
42	38	VITAL IDOL	Billy Idol (Chrysalis)
-	39	INVASION OF YOUR PRIVACY	Ratt (Island)
-	40	LONE JUSTICE	Lone Justice (Geffen)
36	41	WAR	U2 (Island)
-	42	THE ALLNIGHTER	Glen Frey (MCA)
27	43	OUT NOW!	Various Artists (Chrysalis/MCA)
-	44	CRUSH	Orchestral Manoeuvres in the Dark (Virgin)
-	45	WIDE AWAKE IN AMERICA	U2 (Island)
21	46	DIAMOND LIFE	Sade (CBS)
23	47	SUDDENLY	Billy Ocean (Jive)
19	48	THEATRE OF PAIN	Motley Crue (Elektra)
31	49	MR BAD GUY	Freddie Mercury (CBS)
43	50	WORLD WIDE LIVE	Scorpions (Harvest)

17 August 1985

last	this	Title	Artist
1	1	BROTHERS IN ARMS	Dire Straits (Vertigo)
2	2	BORN IN THE USA	Bruce Springsteen (CBS)
5	3	LIKE A VIRGIN	Madonna (Sire)
3	4	BE YOURSELF TONIGHT	Eurythmics (RCA)
4	5	SONGS FROM THE BIG CHAIR	
6	6	NO JACKET REQUIRED	Phil Collins (Virgin)
-	7	NOW THAT'S WHAT I CALL MUSIC 5	Various Artists (EMI/Virgin)
8	8	THE UNFORGETTABLE FIRE	U2 (Island)
7	9	BILLY JOEL'S GREATEST HITS VOL 1 & VOL 2	Billy Joel (CBS)
9	10	THE KENNY ROGERS STORY	Kenny Rogers (Liberty)
13	11	THE DREAM OF THE BLUE TURTLES	Sting (A&M)
10	12	THE SECRET OF ASSOCIATION	Paul Young (CBS)
23	13	RUM, SODOMY AND THE LASH	Pogues (Stiff)
15	14	MADONNA	Madonna (Sire)
12	15	MISPLACED CHILDHOOD	Marillion (EMI)
10	16	BOYS AND GIRLS	Bryan Ferry (EG)
20	17	QUEEN'S GREATEST HITS	Queen (EMI)
19	18	LUXURY OF LIFE	Five Star (Tent)
16	19	PRIVATE DANCER	Tina Turner (Capitol)
11	20	PHANTASMAGORIA	Damned (MCA)
14	21	U2 LIVE: UNDER A BLOOD RED SKY	U2 (Island)
21	22	CUPID AND PSYCHE '85	Scritti Politti (Virgin)
37	23	OUR FAVOURITE SHOP	Style Council (Polydor)
18	24	ALL THROUGH THE NIGHT	Aled Jones (BBC)
38	25	VITAL IDOL	Billy Idol (Chrysalis)
45	26	WIDE AWAKE IN AMERICA	U2 (Island)
-	27	FLASH	Jeff Beck (Epic)
31	28	NIGHT OF A THOUSAND CANDLES	Men They Couldn't Hang (Imp)
30	29	GO WEST/BANGS AND CRASHES	Go West (Chrysalis)
36	30	PHILIP OAKEY AND GIORGIO MORODER	Philip Oakey & Giorgio Moroder (Virgin)
-	31	RECKLESS	Bryan Adams (A&M)
39	32	INVASION OF YOUR PRIVACY	Ratt (Island)
28	33	DRINKING GASOLINE	Cabaret Voltaire (Some Bizzare)
43	34	OUT NOW!	Various Artists (Chrysalis/MCA)
17	35	MINX	Toyah (Portrait)
46	36	DIAMOND LIFE	Sade (CBS)
-	37	HEARTBEAT CITY	Cars (Elektra)
41	38	WAR	U2 (Island)
25	39	CONTACT	Pointer Sisters (Planet)
27	40	A SECRET WISH	Propaganda (ZTT)
33	41	BORN TO RUN	Bruce Springsteen (CBS)
29	42	THE MAGIC OF TORVILL AND DEAN	Various Artists (Stylus)
32	43	WHEN THE BOYS MEET THE GIRLS	Sister Sledge (Atlantic)
47	44	SUDDENLY	Billy Ocean (Jive)
24	45	VOICES FROM THE HOLY LAND	BBC Welsh Chorus (BBC)
-	46	STREET SOUNDS EDITION 13	Various Artists (Street Sounds)
22	47	THE RIVER	Bruce Springsteen (CBS)
35	48	FLY ON THE WALL	AC/DC (Atlantic)
42	49	THE ALLNIGHTER	Glen Frey (MCA)
-	50	AROUND THE WORLD IN A DAY	Prince & the Revolution (Warner Bros.)

As Springsteen fever died somewhat and his back-catalogue began to slip out of the chart, that for Dire Straits reasserted itself, and *Brothers In Arms* returned to Number 1 in place of *Born In The USA*. The new Straits sales spurt was at least party generated by the simultaneous Top 5 success of the wry *Money For Nothing*, the most successful of the several singles to be extracted from *Brothers In Arms*.

August – September 1985

24 August 1985

last week	this week	Title	Artist (Label)
7	1	NOW THAT'S WHAT I CALL MUSIC 5	Various Artists (EMI/Virgin)
1	2	BROTHERS IN ARMS	Dire Straits (Vertigo)
3	3	LIKE A VIRGIN	Madonna (Sire)
2	4	BORN IN THE USA	Bruce Springsteen (CBS)
14	5	MADONNA	Madonna (Sire)
4	6	BE YOURSELF TONIGHT	Eurythmics (RCA)
6	7	NO JACKET REQUIRED	Phil Collins (Virgin)
5	8	SONGS FROM THE BIG CHAIR	Tears For Fears (Mercury)
8	9	THE UNFORGETTABLE FIRE	U2 (Island)
13	10	RUM, SODOMY AND THE LASH	Pogues (Stiff)
21	11	U2 LIVE: UNDER A BLOOD RED SKY	U2 (Island)
9	12	BILLY JOEL'S GREATEST HITS VOL 1 & VOL 2	Billy Joel (CBS)
10	13	THE KENNY ROGERS STORY	Kenny Rogers (Liberty)
19	14	PRIVATE DANCER	Tina Turner (Capitol)
29	15	GO WEST/BANGS AND CRASHES	Go West (Chrysalis)
11	16	THE DREAM OF THE BLUE TURTLES	Sting (A&M)
16	17	BOYS AND GIRLS	Bryan Ferry (EG)
25	18	VITAL IDOL	Billy Idol (Chrysalis)
17	19	QUEEN'S GREATEST HITS	Queen (EMI)
18	20	LUXURY OF LIFE	Five Star (Tent)
46	21	STREET SOUNDS EDITION 13	Various Artists (Street Sounds)
15	22	MISPLACED CHILDHOOD	Marillion (EMI)
12	23	THE SECRET OF ASSOCIATION	Paul Young (CBS)
-	24	NIGHT BEAT	Various Artists (Styles)
31	25	RECKLESS	Bryan Adams (A&M)
26	26	WIDE AWAKE IN AMERICA	U2 (Island)
-	27	ELIMINATOR	ZZ Top (Warner Bros.)
37	28	HEARTBEAT CITY	Cars (Elektra)
44	29	SUDDENLY	Billy Ocean (Jive)
36	30	DIAMOND LIFE	Sade (CBS)
27	31	FLASH	Jeff Beck (Epic)
20	32	PHANTASMAGORIA	Damned (MCA)
22	33	CUPID AND PSYCHE '85	Scritti Politti (Virgin)
47	34	THE RIVER	Bruce Springsteen (CBS)
48	35	FLY ON THE WALL	AC/DC (Atlantic)
24	36	ALL THROUGH THE NIGHT	Aled Jones (BBC)
40	37	A SECRET WISH	Propaganda (ZTT)
-	38	COLOURBOX	Colourbox (4AD)
-	39	LEGEND	Bob Marley & the Wailers (Island)
-	40	THE WORKS	Queen (EMI)
50	41	AROUND THE WORLD IN A DAY	Prince & the Revolution (Warner Bros.)
30	42	PHILIP OAKEY AND GIORGIO MORODER	Philip Oakey & Giorgio Moroder (Virgin)
39	43	CONTACT	Pointer Sisters (Planet)
38	44	WAR	U2 (Island)
-	45	LITTLE CREATURES	Talking Heads (EMI)
-	46	BEST OF THE EAGLES	Eagles (Asylum)
-	47	SINGLE LIFE	Cameo (Club)
-	48	FLIP	Nils Lofgren (Towerbell)
42	49	THE MAGIC OF TORVILL AND DEAN	Various Artists (Stylus)
28	50	NIGHT OF A THOUSAND CANDLES	Men They Couldn't Hang (Imp)

31 August 1985

last week	this week	Title	Artist (Label)
1	1	NOW THAT'S WHAT I CALL MUSIC 5	Various Artists (EMI/Virgin)
3	2	LIKE A VIRGIN	Madonna (Sire)
2	3	BROTHERS IN ARMS	Dire Straits (Vertigo)
7	4	NO JACKET REQUIRED	Phil Collins (Virgin)
4	5	BORN IN THE USA	Bruce Springsteen (CBS)
8	6	SONGS FROM THE BIG CHAIR	Tears For Fears (Mercury)
5	7	MADONNA	Madonna (Sire)
10	8	RUM, SODOMY AND THE LASH	Pogues (Stiff)
6	9	BE YOURSELF TONIGHT	Eurythmics (RCA)
9	10	THE UNFORGETTABLE FIRE	U2 (Island)
14	11	PRIVATE DANCER	Tina Turner (Capitol)
15	12	GO WEST/BANGS AND CRASHES	Go West (Chrysalis)
18	13	VITAL IDOL	Billy Idol (Chrysalis)
11	14	U2 LIVE: UNDER A BLOOD RED SKY	U2 (Island)
26	15	WIDE AWAKE IN AMERICA	U2 (Island)
16	16	THE DREAM OF THE BLUE TURTLES	Sting (A&M)
21	17	STREET SOUNDS EDITION 13	Various Artists (Street Sounds)
13	18	THE KENNY ROGERS STORY	Kenny Rogers (Liberty)
12	19	BILLY JOEL'S GREATEST HITS VOL 1 & VOL 2	Billy Joel (CBS)
28	20	HEARTBEAT CITY	Cars (Elektra)
19	21	QUEEN'S GREATEST HITS	Queen (EMI)
27	22	ELIMINATOR	ZZ Top (Warner Bros.)
23	23	THE SECRET OF ASSOCIATION	Paul Young (CBS)
22	24	MISPLACED CHILDHOOD	Marillion (EMI)
-	25	SHANGRI-LA	Animal Nightlife (Island)
17	26	BOYS AND GIRLS	Bryan Ferry (EG)
38	27	COLOURBOX	Colourbox (4AD)
24	28	NIGHT BEAT	Various Artists (Styles)
36	29	ALL THROUGH THE NIGHT	Aled Jones (BBC)
30	30	LUXURY OF LIFE	Five Star (Tent)
31	31	DIAMOND LIFE	Sade (CBS)
-	32	HOLD ME	Laura Branigan (Atlantic)
50	33	NIGHT OF A THOUSAND CANDLES	Men They Couldn't Hang (Imp)
-	34	OUR FAVOURITE SHOP	Style Council (Polydor)
-	35	AMERICAN DREAMS	Various Artists (Starblend)
-	36	THE RIDDLE	Nik Kershaw (MCA)
-	37	HELD DOWN AT LAST	Guana Batz (ID)
29	38	SUDDENLY	Billy Ocean (Jive)
47	39	SINGLE LIFE	Cameo (Club)
25	40	RECKLESS	Bryan Adams (A&M)
-	41	STEVE McQUEEN	Prefab Sprout (Kitchenware)
33	42	CUPID AND PSYCHE '85	Scritti Politti (Virgin)
-	43	FORWARD AT BATTLE	English Dogs (Rot)
31	44	FLASH	Jeff Beck (Epic)
32	45	PHANTASMAGORIA	Damned (MCA)
42	46	PHILIP OAKEY AND GIORGIO MORODER	Philip Oakey & Giorgio Moroder (Virgin)
-	48	SPANISH TRAIN AND OTHER STORIES	Chris De Burgh (A&M)
-	49	FACE VALUE	Phil Collins (Virgin)
-	50	BEST OF BLONDIE	Blondie (Chrysalis)

7 September 1985

last week	this week	Title	Artist (Label)
1	1	NOW THAT'S WHAT I CALL MUSIC 5	Various Artists (EMI/Virgin)
3	2	BROTHERS IN ARMS	Dire Straits (Vertigo)
2	3	LIKE A VIRGIN	Madonna (Sire)
5	4	BORN IN THE USA	Bruce Springsteen (CBS)
4	5	NO JACKET REQUIRED	Phil Collins (Virgin)
7	6	MADONNA	Madonna (Sire)
9	7	BE YOURSELF TONIGHT	Eurythmics (RCA)
6	8	SONGS FROM THE BIG CHAIR	Tears For Fears (Mercury)
10	9	THE UNFORGETTABLE FIRE	U2 (Island)
8	10	RUM, SODOMY AND THE LASH	Pogues (Stiff)
11	11	PRIVATE DANCER	Tina Turner (Capitol)
-	12	SACRED HEART	Dio (Vertigo)
15	13	WIDE AWAKE IN AMERICA	U2 (Island)
13	14	VITAL IDOL	Billy Idol (Chrysalis)
12	15	GO WEST/BANGS AND CRASHES	Go West (Chrysalis)
16	16	THE DREAM OF THE BLUE TURTLES	Sting (A&M)
18	17	THE KENNY ROGERS STORY	Kenny Rogers (Liberty)
28	18	NIGHT BEAT	Various Artists (Styles)
14	19	U2 LIVE: UNDER A BLOOD RED SKY	U2 (Island)
26	20	BOYS AND GIRLS	Bryan Ferry (EG)
-	21	THE HEAD ON THE DOOR	Cure (Fiction)
-	22	WORLD SERVICE	Spear Of Destiny (Epic)
21	23	QUEEN'S GREATEST HITS	Queen (EMI)
-	24	COSI FAN TUTTI FRUTTI	Squeeze (A&M)
25	25	SHANGRI-LA	Animal Nightlife (Island)
20	26	HEARTBEAT CITY	Cars (Elektra)
30	27	LUXURY OF LIFE	Five Star (Tent)
17	28	STREET SOUNDS EDITION 13	Various Artists (Street Sounds)
24	29	MISPLACED CHILDHOOD	Marillion (EMI)
19	30	BILLY JOEL'S GREATEST HITS VOL 1 & VOL 2	Billy Joel (CBS)
23	31	THE SECRET OF ASSOCIATION	Paul Young (CBS)
-	32	DISCO BEACH PARTY	Various Artists (Stylus)
49	33	FACE VALUE	Phil Collins (Virgin)
27	34	COLOURBOX	Colourbox (4AD)
39	35	SINGLE LIFE	Cameo (Club)
42	36	CUPID AND PSYCHE '85	Scritti Politti (Virgin)
48	37	SPANISH TRAIN AND OTHER STORIES	Chris De Burgh (A&M)
38	38	SUDDENLY	Billy Ocean (Jive)
31	39	DIAMOND LIFE	Sade (CBS)
29	40	ALL THROUGH THE NIGHT	Aled Jones (BBC)
45	41	PHANTASMAGORIA	Damned (MCA)
-	42	MAKE IT BIG	Wham! (CBS)
-	43	ARISE	Amoebics (Alternative Tentacles)
-	44	FLAUNT THE IMPERFECTION	China Crisis (Virgin)
-	45	ROCK ME TONIGHT	Freddy Jackson (Capitol)
-	46	CONTACT	Pointer Sisters (Planet)
-	47	STREET CALLED DESIRE	Renee & Angela (Club)
-	48	20 HOLIDAY HITS	Various Artists (Creole)
22	49	ELIMINATOR	ZZ Top (Warner Bros.)
40	50	RECKLESS	Bryan Adams (A&M)

Eight months after *Now That's What I Call Music 4* had just failed to top the chart because CBS/WEA's first *Hits* volume pipped it at the post, *Now 5* soared to Number 1 with no such opposition from another mega-hit compilation. Apart from Dire Straits, its biggest challenger was Madonna, whose nine-month-old *Like A Virgin* album was now selling like crazy following her chart-topping *Into The Groove* single.

September 1985

14 September 1985

LW	TW	Title	Artist (Label)
2	1	BROTHERS IN ARMS	Dire Straits (Vertigo)
3	2	LIKE A VIRGIN	Madonna (Sire)
1	3	NOW THAT'S WHAT I CALL MUSIC 5	Various Artists (EMI/Virgin)
22	4	WORLD SERVICE	Spear Of Destiny (Epic)
12	5	SACRED HEART	Dio (Vertigo)
4	6	BORN IN THE USA	Bruce Springsteen (CBS)
21	7	THE HEAD ON THE DOOR	Cure (Fiction)
5	8	NO JACKET REQUIRED	Phil Collins (Virgin)
8	9	SONGS FROM THE BIG CHAIR	Tears For Fears (Mercury)
6	10	MADONNA	Madonna (Sire)
9	11	THE UNFORGETTABLE FIRE	U2 (Island)
11	12	PRIVATE DANCER	Tina Turner (Capitol)
7	13	BE YOURSELF TONIGHT	Eurythmics (RCA)
13	14	WIDE AWAKE IN AMERICA	U2 (Island)
20	15	BOYS AND GIRLS	Bryan Ferry (EG)
17	16	THE KENNY ROGERS STORY	Kenny Rogers (Liberty)
14	17	VITAL IDOL	Billy Idol (Chrysalis)
24	18	COSI FAN TUTTI FRUTTI	Squeeze (A&M)
10	19	RUM, SODOMY AND THE LASH	Pogues (Stiff)
-	20	BAGGARADDIM	UB40 (Dep International)
-	21	RUN FOR COVER	Gary Moore (10/Virgin)
50	22	RECKLESS	Bryan Adams (A&M)
16	23	THE DREAM OF THE BLUE TURTLES	Sting (A&M)
23	24	QUEEN'S GREATEST HITS	Queen (EMI)
19	25	U2 LIVE: UNDER A BLOOD RED SKY	U2 (Island)
15	26	GO WEST/BANGS AND CRASHES	Go (Chrysalis)
26	27	HEARTBEAT CITY	Cars (Elektra)
29	28	MISPLACED CHILDHOOD	Marillion (EMI)
18	29	NIGHT BEAT	Various Artists (Styles)
-	30	VIVE LE ROCK	Adam Ant (CBS)
-	31	OLD WAYS	Neil Young (Geffen)
25	32	SHANGRI-LA	Animal Nightlife (Island)
49	33	ELIMINATOR	ZZ Top (Warner Bros.)
30	34	BILLY JOEL'S GREATEST HITS VOL 1 & VOL 2	Billy Joel (CBS)
27	35	LUXURY OF LIFE	Five Star (Tent)
31	36	THE SECRET OF ASSOCIATION	Paul Young (CBS)
35	37	SINGLE LIFE	Cameo (Club)
33	38	FACE VALUE	Phil Collins (Virgin)
32	39	DISCO BEACH PARTY	Various Artists (Stylus)
40	40	ALL THROUGH THE NIGHT	Aled Jones (BBC)
-	41	LOVE OVER GOLD	Dire Straits (Vertigo)
42	42	MAKE IT BIG	Wham! (CBS)
47	43	SREET CALLED DESIRE	Renee & Angela (Club)
36	44	CUPID AND PSYCHE '85	Scritti Politti (Virgin)
38	45	SUDDENLY	Billy Ocean (Jive)
-	46	INNOCENCE IS NO EXCUSE	Saxon (Parlophone)
-	47	ALCHEMY - DIRE STRAITS LIVE	Dire Straits (Vertigo)
46	48	CONTACT	Pointer Sisters (Planet)
44	49	FLAUNT THE IMPERFECTION	China Crisis (Virgin)
-	50	ALF	Alison Moyet (CBS)

21 September 1985

LW	TW	Title	Artist (Label)
3	1	NOW THAT'S WHAT I CALL MUSIC 5	Various Artists (EMI/Virgin)
2	2	LIKE A VIRGIN	Madonna (Sire)
7	3	THE HEAD ON THE DOOR	Cure (Fiction)
1	4	BROTHERS IN ARMS	Dire Straits (Vertigo)
5	5	SACRED HEART	Dio (Vertigo)
21	6	RUN FOR COVER	Gary Moore (10/Virgin)
9	7	SONGS FROM THE BIG CHAIR	Tears For Fears (Mercury)
8	8	NO JACKET REQUIRED	Phil Collins (Virgin)
6	9	BORN IN THE USA	Bruce Springsteen (CBS)
16	10	THE KENNY ROGERS STORY	Kenny Rogers (Liberty)
20	11	BAGGARADDIM	UB40 (Dep International)
15	12	BOYS AND GIRLS	Bryan Ferry (EG)
4	13	WORLD SERVICE	Spear Of Destiny (Epic)
28	14	MISPLACED CHILDHOOD	Marillion (EMI)
10	15	MADONNA	Madonna (Sire)
46	16	INNOCENCE IS NO EXCUSE	Saxon (Parlophone)
12	17	PRIVATE DANCER	Tina Turner (Capitol)
31	18	OLD WAYS	Neil Young (Geffen)
27	19	HEARTBEAT CITY	Cars (Elektra)
17	20	VITAL IDOL	Billy Idol (Chrysalis)
11	21	THE UNFORGETTABLE FIRE	U2 (Island)
13	22	BE YOURSELF TONIGHT	Eurythmics (RCA)
25	23	U2 LIVE: UNDER A BLOOD RED SKY	U2 (Island)
-	24	DON'T STAND DOWN	Dexys Midnight Runners (Mercury)
19	25	RUM, SODOMY AND THE LASH	Pogues (Stiff)
18	26	COSI FAN TUTTI FRUTTI	Squeeze (A&M)
30	27	VIVE LE ROCK	Adam Ant (CBS)
-	28	OPEN TOP CARS AND GIRLS IN T-SHIRTS	Various Artists (Telstar)
14	29	WIDE AWAKE IN AMERICA	U2 (Island)
23	30	THE DREAM OF THE BLUE TURTLES	Sting (A&M)
26	31	GO WEST/BANGS AND CRASHES	Go West (Chrysalis)
24	32	QUEEN'S GREATEST HITS	Queen (EMI)
22	33	RECKLESS	Bryan Adams (A&M)
-	34	STREET SOUNDS EDITION 13	Various Artists (Street Sounds)
-	35	SPORTS	Huey Lewis & the News (Chrysalis)
-	36	HUNDREDS AND THOUSANDS	Bronski Beat (Forbidden Fruit)
29	37	NIGHT BEAT	Various Artists (Styles)
-	38	HEAVEN KNOWS	Jaki Graham (EMI)
34	39	BILLY JOEL'S GREATEST HITS VOL 1 & VOL 2	Billy Joel (CBS)
-	40	ALEXANDER O'NEAL	Alexander O'Neal (Tabu/Epic)
35	41	LUXURY OF LIFE	Five Star (Tent)
39	43	DISCO BEACH PARTY	Various Artists (Stylus)
-	44	THE RIVER	Bruce Springsteen (CBS)
-	45	HOLD ME	Laura Branigan (Atlantic)
43	46	SREET CALLED DESIRE	Renee & Angela (Club)
32	47	SHANGRI-LA	Animal Nightlife (Island)
36	48	THE SECRET OF ASSOCIATION	Paul Young (CBS)
48	49	CONTACT	Pointer Sisters (Planet)
50	50	ALF	Alison Moyet (CBS)

28 September 1985

LW	TW	Title	Artist (Label)
2	1	LIKE A VIRGIN	Madonna (Sire)
4	2	BROTHERS IN ARMS	Dire Straits (Vertigo)
1	3	NOW THAT'S WHAT I CALL MUSIC 5	Various Artists (EMI/Virgin)
-	4	HOUNDS OF LOVE	Kate Bush (EMI)
10	5	THE KENNY ROGERS STORY	Kenny Rogers (Liberty)
-	6	IN SQUARE CIRCLE	Stevie Wonder (Tamla Motown)
8	7	NO JACKET REQUIRED	Phil Collins (Virgin)
3	8	THE HEAD ON THE DOOR	Cure (Fiction)
14	9	MISPLACED CHILDHOOD	Marillion (EMI)
24	10	DON'T STAND DOWN	Dexys Midnight Runners (Mercury)
6	11	RUN FOR COVER	Gary Moore (10/Virgin)
11	12	BAGGARADDIM	UB40 (Dep International)
15	13	MADONNA	Madonna (Sire)
7	14	SONGS FROM THE BIG CHAIR	Tears For Fears (Mercury)
12	15	BOYS AND GIRLS	Bryan Ferry (EG)
9	16	BORN IN THE USA	Bruce Springsteen (CBS)
-	17	HERE'S TO FUTURE DAYS	Thompson Twins (Arista)
23	18	U2 LIVE: UNDER A BLOOD RED SKY	U2 (Island)
30	19	THE DREAM OF THE BLUE TURTLES	Sting (A&M)
20	20	VITAL IDOL	Billy Idol (Chrysalis)
36	21	HUNDREDS AND THOUSANDS	Bronski Beat (Forbidden Fruit)
5	22	SACRED HEART	Dio (Vertigo)
21	23	THE UNFORGETTABLE FIRE	U2 (Island)
25	24	RUM, SODOMY AND THE LASH	Progues (Stiff)
35	25	SPORTS	Huey Lewis & the News (Chrysalis)
28	26	OPEN TOP CARS AND GIRLS IN T-SHIRTS	Various Artists (Telstar)
26	27	COSI FAN TUTTI FRUTTI	Squeeze (A&M)
-	28	THIS IS THE SEA	Waterboys (Ensign)
13	29	WORLD SERVICE	Spear Of Destiny (Epic)
22	30	BE YOURSELF TONIGHT	Eurythmics (RCA)
18	31	OLD WAYS	Neil Young (Geffen)
-	32	LIVE AT THE APOLLO	Daryll Hall & John Oates (RCA)
33	33	RECKLESS	Bryan Adams (A&M)
32	34	QUEEN'S GREATEST HITS	Queen (EMI)
37	35	NIGHT BEAT	Various Artists (Styles)
19	36	HEARTBEAT CITY	Cars (Elektra)
16	37	INNOCENCE IS NO EXCUSE	Saxon (Parlophone)
38	38	HEAVEN KNOWS	Jaki Graham (EMI)
39	39	BILLY JOEL'S GREATEST HITS VOL 1 & VOL 2	Billy Joel (CBS)
29	40	WIDE AWAKE IN AMERICA	U2 (Island)
48	41	THE SECRET OF ASSOCIATION	Paul Young (CBS)
40	42	ALEXANDER O'NEAL	Alexander O'Neal (Tabu/Epic)
-	43	SO MANY RIVERS	Bobby Womack (MCA)
-	44	SUDDENLY	Billy Ocean (Jive)
-	45	FOUR STAR COUNTRY	Various Artists (K-Tel)
-	46	THE VERSATILE BOBBY DARIN	Bobby Darin (Capitol)
42	47	SINGLE LIFE	Cameo (Club)
-	48	WAITING FOR THE FLOODS	Armoury Show (Parlophone)
-	49	LEAVE THE BEST TO LAST	James Last (Polydor)
17	50	PRIVATE DANCER	Tina Turner (Capitol)

Like A Virgin eventually topped the UK chart for Madonna the best part of a year after its release, as the peroxide singer's star rating grew by leaps and bounds - at the end of August, she had been the first female singer (and only one of a handful of acts altogether) to have held Numbers 1 and 2 on the singles chart simultaneously, with *Into The Groove* and *Holiday*. Her first LP was also still in the Top 10.

October 1985

Despite being her first release since *The Dreaming*, three years earlier, Kate Bush's *Hounds Of Love* easily swept aside the competition to give her another Number 1 album - which it remained for four consecutive weeks. Meanwhile, Ultravox lead vocalist Midge Ure emulated Sting's and Freddie Mercury's recent successes by charting a solo album, *The Gift*, alongside his chart-topping single *If I Was*.

278

October – November 1985

26 October 1985

last week	this week	title	artist (label)
1	1	HOUNDS OF LOVE	Kate Bush (EMI)
2	2	BROTHERS IN ARMS	Dire Straits (Vertigo)
3	3	LIKE A VIRGIN	Madonna (Sire)
12	4	THE GIFT	Midge Ure (Chrysalis)
-	5	LIVE AFTER DEATH	Iron Maiden (EMI)
5	6	MISPLACED CHILDHOOD	Marillion (EMI)
-	7	LOVE	Cult (Beggars Banquet)
6	8	IN SQUARE CIRCLE	Stevie Wonder (Tamla Motown)
8	9	THE HEAD ON THE DOOR	Cure (Fiction)
39	10	THE LOVE SONGS	George Benson (K-Tel)
-	11	OUT NOW! 2	Various Artists (Chrysalis)
9	12	MAD NOT MAD	Madness (Zarjazz)
23	13	RAIN DOGS	Tom Waits (Island)
7	14	NOW THAT'S WHAT I CALL MUSIC 5	Various Artists (EMI/Virgin)
13	15	HERE'S TO FUTURE DAYS	Thompson Twins (Arista)
18	16	EXPRESSIONS	Various Artists (K-Tel)
15	17	BOYS AND GIRLS	Bryan Ferry (EG)
16	18	NO JACKET REQUIRED	Phil Collins (Virgin)
19	19	U2 LIVE: UNDER A BLOOD RED SKY	U2 (Island)
14	20	THE KENNY ROGERS STORY	Kenny Rogers (Liberty)
26	21	SONGS FROM THE BIG CHAIR	Tears For Fears (Mercury)
-	22	WORLD MACHINE	Level 42 (Polydor)
32	23	THE DREAM OF THE BLUE TURTLES	Sting (A&M)
11	24	MADONNA	Madonna (Sire)
4	25	VITAL IDOL	Billy Idol (Chrysalis)
31	26	DIAMOND LIFE	Sade (CBS)
10	27	SPORTS	Huey Lewis & the News (Chrysalis)
27	28	BAGGARADDIM	UB40 (Dep International)
22	29	BORN IN THE USA	Bruce Springsteen (CBS)
24	30	STREET SOUNDS ELECTRO 9	Various Artists (Street Sounds)
-	31	THE SINGLES '81-'85	Depeche Mode (Mute)
-	32	STRENGTH	Alarm (IRS)
-	33	PICTURE BOOK	Simply Red (Elektra)
-	34	BELIEVE YOU	Blancmange (London)
-	35	BILLY JOEL'S GREATEST HITS VOL 1 & VOL 2	Billy Joel (CBS)
17	37	PRIVATE DANCER	Tina Turner (Capitol)
-	38	PEACE AND TRANQUILITY	Phil Coulter (Harmac)
-	39	REELIN' IN THE YEARS	Steely Dan (MCA)
25	40	SO MANY RIVERS	Bobby Womack (MCA)
-	41	FLIP YOUR WIG	Husker Du (SST)
-	42	MACALLA	Clannad (RCA)
45	43	REGGAE HITS VOL 2	Various Artists (Jetstar)
48	44	RUM, SODOMY AND THE LASH	Pogues (Stiff)
28	45	LUXURY OF LIFE	Five Star (Tent)
44	46	SINGLE LIFE	Cameo (Club)
-	47	HOW TO BE A ZILLIONAIRE	ABC (Neutron)
21	48	STORIES OF JOHNNY	Marc Almond (Some Bizzare)
50	49	RECKLESS	Bryan Adams (A&M)
20	50	ASYLUM	Kiss (Vertigo)

2 November 1985

last week	this week	title	artist (label)
5	1	LIVE AFTER DEATH	Iron Maiden (EMI)
1	2	HOUNDS OF LOVE	Kate Bush (EMI)
7	3	LOVE	Cult (Beggars Banquet)
10	4	THE LOVE SONGS	George Benson (K-Tel)
11	5	OUT NOW! 2	Various Artists (Chrysalis)
4	6	THE GIFT	Midge Ure (Chrysalis)
3	7	LIKE A VIRGIN	Madonna (Sire)
31	8	THE SINGLES '81-'85	Depeche Mode (Mute)
-	9	ONCE UPON A TIME	Simple Minds (Virgin)
25	10	VITAL IDOL	Billy Idol (Chrysalis)
2	11	BROTHERS IN ARMS	Dire Straits (Vertigo)
22	12	WORLD MACHINE	Level 42 (Polydor)
13	13	RAIN DOGS	Tom Waits (Island)
-	14	MUSIC FROM MIAMI VICE	Various Artists (BBC)
-	15	WEST SIDE STORY	Leonard Bernstein & Studio Cast (Deutsche Grammophon)
32	16	STRENGTH	Alarm (IRS)
6	17	MISPLACED CHILDHOOD	Marillion (EMI)
8	18	IN SQUARE CIRCLE	Stevie Wonder (Tamla Motown)
14	19	NOW THAT'S WHAT I CALL MUSIC 5	Various Artists (EMI/Virgin)
45	20	LUXURY OF LIFE	Five Star (Tent)
16	21	EXPRESSIONS	Various Artists (K-Tel)
9	22	THE HEAD ON THE DOOR	Cure (Fiction)
33	23	PICTURE BOOK	Simply Red (Elektra)
35	24	BILLY JOEL'S GREATEST HITS VOL 1 & VOL 2	Billy Joel (CBS)
47	25	HOW TO BE A ZILLIONAIRE	ABC (Neutron)
17	26	BOYS AND GIRLS	Bryan Ferry (EG)
20	27	THE KENNY ROGERS STORY	Kenny Rogers (Liberty)
12	28	MAD NOT MAD	Madness (Zarjazz)
23	29	THE DREAM OF THE BLUE TURTLES	Sting (A&M)
15	30	HERE'S TO FUTURE DAYS	Thompson Twins (Arista)
24	31	MADONNA	Madonna (Sire)
39	32	REELIN' IN THE YEARS	Steely Dan (MCA)
-	33	STREET SOUNDS EDITION 13	Various Artists (Street Sounds)
-	34	HEART	Heart (Capitol)
18	35	NO JACKET REQUIRED	Phil Collins (Virgin)
19	36	U2 LIVE: UNDER A BLOOD RED SKY	U2 (Island)
40	37	SO MANY RIVERS	Bobby Womack (MCA)
30	38	STREET SOUNDS ELECTRO 9	Various Artists (Street Sounds)
21	39	SONGS FROM THE BIG CHAIR	Tears For Fears (Mercury)
46	40	SINGLE LIFE	Cameo (Club)
38	41	PEACE AND TRANQUILITY	Phil Coulter (Harmac)
29	42	BORN IN THE USA	Bruce Springsteen (CBS)
42	43	MACALLA	Clannad (RCA)
41	44	FLIP YOUR WIG	Husker Du (SST)
-	45	THIS IS THE SEA	Waterboys (Ensign)
-	46	LITTLE CREATURES	Talking Heads (EMI)
-	47	BLUE SKIES	Kiri Te Kanawa (London)
-	48	THE COVENANT, THE SWORD AND THE LAW OF THE LAW	Cabaret Voltaire (Some Bizzare)
-	49	YOU MIGHT BE SURPRISED	Roy Ayers (CBS)
-	50	LIBRA	Julio Iglesias (CBS)

9 November 1985

last week	this week	title	artist (label)
9	1	ONCE UPON A TIME	Simple Minds (Virgin)
4	2	THE LOVE SONGS	George Benson (K-Tel)
5	3	OUT NOW! 2	Various Artists (Chrysalis)
2	4	HOUNDS OF LOVE	Kate Bush (EMI)
1	5	LIVE AFTER DEATH	Iron Maiden (EMI)
-	6	AFTERBURNER	ZZ Top (Warner Bros.)
7	7	LIKE A VIRGIN	Madonna (Sire)
3	8	LOVE	Cult (Beggars Banquet)
8	9	THE SINGLES '81-'85	Depeche Mode (Mute)
11	10	BROTHERS IN ARMS	Dire Straits (Vertigo)
12	11	WORLD MACHINE	Level 42 (Polydor)
-	12	POWER WINDOWS	Rush (Vertigo)
6	13	THE GIFT	Midge Ure (Chrysalis)
14	14	MUSIC FROM MIAMI VICE	Various Artists (BBC)
10	15	VITAL IDOL	Billy Idol (Chrysalis)
15	16	WEST SIDE STORY	Leonard Bernstein & Studio Cast (Deutsche Grammophon)
-	17	THE CARS' GREATEST HITS	Cars (Elektra)
13	18	RAIN DOGS	Tom Waits (Island)
24	19	BILLY JOEL'S GREATEST HITS VOL 1 & VOL 2	Billy Joel (CBS)
17	20	MISPLACED CHILDHOOD	Marillion (EMI)
21	21	EXPRESSIONS	Various Artists (K-Tel)
39	22	SONGS FROM THE BIG CHAIR	Tears For Fears (Mercury)
-	23	THE LAST COMMAND	W.A.S.P. (Capitol)
20	24	LUXURY OF LIFE	Five Star (Tent)
-	25	DIAMOND LIFE	Sade (CBS)
36	26	U2 LIVE: UNDER A BLOOD RED SKY	U2 (Island)
-	27	SLAVE TO THE RHYTHM	Grace Jones (ZTT)
16	28	STRENGTH	Alarm (IRS)
31	29	MADONNA	Madonna (Sire)
18	30	IN SQUARE CIRCLE	Stevie Wonder (Tamla Motown)
34	31	HEART	Heart (Capitol)
35	32	NO JACKET REQUIRED	Phil Collins (Virgin)
-	33	THE UNFORGETTABLE FIRE	U2 (Island)
19	34	NOW THAT'S WHAT I CALL MUSIC 5	Various Artists (EMI/Virgin)
29	35	THE DREAM OF THE BLUE TURTLES	Sting (A&M)
-	36	PRIVATE DANCER	Tina Turner (Capitol)
37	37	SO MANY RIVERS	Bobby Womack (MCA)
-	38	HAVE A GOOD FOREVER	Cool Notes (Abstract Dance)
-	39	LEAVE THE BEST TO LAST	James Last (Polydor)
-	40	SUZANNE VEGA	Suzanne Vega (A&M)
-	41	THE COMPLETE MIKE OLDFIELD	Mike Oldfield (Virgin)
-	42	JOHN PARR	John Parr (London)
23	43	PICTURE BOOK	Simply Red (Elektra)
30	44	HERE'S TO FUTURE DAYS	Thompson Twins (Arista)
41	45	PEACE AND TRANQUILITY	Phil Coulter (Harmac)
43	46	MACALLA	Clannad (RCA)
45	47	THIS IS THE SEA	Waterboys (Ensign)
46	48	LITTLE CREATURES	Talking Heads (EMI)
40	49	SINGLE LIFE	Cameo (Club)
32	50	REELIN' IN THE YEARS	Steely Dan (MCA)

George Benson's *The Love Songs*, a TV-marketed compilation of former singles and LP tracks, proved even stronger commercially than many of his "official" releases, giving the smooth singer/guitarist his highest-ever UK chart placing. Leonard Bernstein's new studio re-creation of his famed *West Side Story* musical score was an all-star affair with Jose Carreras and Kiri Te Kanawa in the lead roles.

November 1985

16 November 1985

last week	this week	Title	Artist (Label)
1	1	ONCE UPON A TIME	Simple Minds (Virgin)
2	2	THE LOVE SONGS	George Benson (K-Tel)
6	3	AFTERBURNER	ZZ Top (Warner Bros.)
3	4	OUT NOW! 2	Various Artists (Chrysalis)
4	5	HOUNDS OF LOVE	Kate Bush (EMI)
12	6	POWER WINDOWS	Rush (Vertigo)
9	7	THE SINGLES '81-'85	Depeche Mode (Mute)
10	8	BROTHERS IN ARMS	Dire Straits (Vertigo)
-	9	PROMISE	Sade (Epic)
8	10	LOVE	Cult (Beggars Banquet)
11	11	WORLD MACHINE	Level 42 (Polydor)
27	12	SLAVE TO THE RHYTHM	Grace Jones (ZTT)
-	13	JENNIFER RUSH	Jennifer Rush (CBS)
5	14	LIVE AFTER DEATH	Iron Maiden (EMI)
7	15	LIKE A VIRGIN	Madonna (Sire)
-	16	THE SINGLES COLLECTION	Spandau Ballet (Chrysalis)
-	17	ICE ON FIRE	Elton John (Rocket)
-	18	CUT THE CRAP	Clash (CBS)
13	19	THE GIFT	Midge Ure (Chrysalis)
14	20	MUSIC FROM MIAMI VICE	Various Artists (BBC)
17	21	THE CARS' GREATEST HITS	Cars (Elektra)
-	22	HUNTING HIGH AND LOW	A Ha (Warner Bros.)
16	23	WEST SIDE STORY	Leonard Bernstein & Studio Cast (Deutsche Grammophon)
18	24	RAIN DOGS	Tom Waits (Island)
20	25	MISPLACED CHILDHOOD	Marillion (EMI)
15	26	VITAL IDOL	Billy Idol (Chrysalis)
-	27	ROCK ANTHEMS	Various Artists (K-Tel)
32	28	NO JACKET REQUIRED	Phil Collins (Virgin)
19	29	BILLY JOEL'S GREATEST HITS VOL 1 & VOL 2	Billy Joel (CBS)
24	30	LUXURY OF LIFE	Five Star (Tent)
-	31	THE 10-5-60 LP	Long Ryders (PVC)
-	32	UNDER A RAGING SUN	Roger Daltrey (10/Virgin)
-	33	BOYS AND GIRLS	Bryan Ferry (EG)
-	34	EAST ENDERS	Various Artists (BBC)
-	35	LIPSTICK, POWDER AND PAINT	Shakin' Stevens (Epic)
-	36	LOVE HURTS	Elaine Paige (WEA)
-	37	THE HEAD ON THE DOOR	Cure (Fiction)
-	38	THIS IS BIG AUDIO DYNAMITE	Big Audio Dynamite (CBS)
21	39	EXPRESSIONS	Various Artists (K-Tel)
34	40	NOW THAT'S WHAT I CALL MUSIC 5	Various Artists (EMI/Virgin)
-	41	THE POWER OF CLASSIC ROCK	London Symphony Orchestra (Portrait)
28	42	STRENGTH	Alarm (IRS)
35	43	THE DREAM OF THE BLUE TURTLES	Sting (A&M)
41	44	THE COMPLETE MIKE OLDFIELD	Mike Oldfield (Virgin)
43	45	PICTURE BOOK	Simply Red (Elektra)
48	46	LITTLE CREATURES	Talking Heads (EMI)
37	47	SO MANY RIVERS	Bobby Womack (MCA)
25	48	DIAMOND LIFE	Sade (CBS)
26	49	U2 LIVE: UNDER A BLOOD RED SKY	U2 (Island)
23	50	THE LAST COMMAND	W.A.S.P. (Capitol)

23 November 1985

last week	this week	Title	Artist (Label)
9	1	PROMISE	Sade (Epic)
3	2	AFTERBURNER	ZZ Top (Warner Bros.)
2	3	THE LOVE SONGS	George Benson (K-Tel)
1	4	ONCE UPON A TIME	Simple Minds (Virgin)
13	5	JENNIFER RUSH	Jennifer Rush (CBS)
17	6	ICE ON FIRE	Elton John (Rocket)
16	7	THE SINGLES COLLECTION	Spandau Ballet (Chrysalis)
8	8	BROTHERS IN ARMS	Dire Straits (Vertigo)
11	9	WORLD MACHINE	Level 42 (Polydor)
7	10	THE SINGLES '81-'85	Depeche Mode (Mute)
5	11	HOUNDS OF LOVE	Kate Bush (EMI)
18	12	CUT THE CRAP	Clash (CBS)
4	13	OUT NOW! 2	Various Artists (Chrysalis)
12	14	SLAVE TO THE RHYTHM	Grace Jones (ZTT)
15	15	LIKE A VIRGIN	Madonna (Sire)
-	16	SONGS TO LEARN AND SING	Echo & the Bunnymen (Korova)
-	17	BITTER SWEET	King (CBS)
35	18	LIPSTICK, POWDER AND PAINT	Shakin' Stevens (Epic)
27	19	ROCK ANTHEMS	Various Artists (K-Tel)
6	20	POWER WINDOWS	Rush (Vertigo)
-	21	FEARGAL SHARKEY	Feargal Sharkey (Virgin)
41	22	THE POWER OF CLASSIC ROCK	London Symphony Orchestra (Portrait)
14	23	LIVE AFTER DEATH	Iron Maiden (EMI)
-	24	SONGS FROM THE BIG CHAIR	Tears For Fears (Mercury)
36	25	LOVE HURTS	Elaine Paige (WEA)
21	26	THE CARS' GREATEST HITS	Cars (Elektra)
19	27	THE GIFT	Midge Ure (Chrysalis)
-	28	BAGGARADDIM	UB40 (Dep International)
20	29	MUSIC FROM MIAMI VICE	Various Artists (BBC)
22	30	HUNTING HIGH AND LOW	A Ha (Warner Bros.)
29	31	BILLY JOEL'S GREATEST HITS VOL 1 & VOL 2	Billy Joel (CBS)
45	32	PICTURE BOOK	Simply Red (Elektra)
-	33	MANILOW	Barry Manilow (RCA)
-	34	SUZANNE VEGA	Suzanne Vega (A&M)
-	35	STREET SOUNDS EDITION 14	Various Artists (Street Sounds)
26	36	VITAL IDOL	Billy Idol (Chrysalis)
23	37	WEST SIDE STORY	Leonard Bernstein & Studio Cast (Deutsche Grammophon)
24	38	RAIN DOGS	Tom Waits (Island)
31	39	THE 10-5-60 LP	Long Ryders (PVC)
38	40	THIS IS BIG AUDIO DYNAMITE	Big Audio Dynamite (CBS)
34	41	EAST ENDERS	Various Artists (BBC)
46	42	LITTLE CREATURES	Talking Heads (EMI)
43	43	BE YOURSELF TONIGHT	Eurythmics (RCA)
-	44	CHRONICLE OF THE BLACK SWORD	Hawkwind (Flicknife)
-	45	BALLADS	Elvis Presley (Telstar)
-	46	GREATEST HITS OF '85	Various Artists (Telstar)
-	47	JAMBOREE BAG NUMBER THREE	Chas & Dave (Rockney)
42	48	STRENGTH	Alarm (IRS)
47	49	SO MANY RIVERS	Bobby Womack (MCA)
-	50	RIPTIDE	Robert Palmer (Island)

30 November 1985

last week	this week	Title	Artist (Label)
1	1	PROMISE	Sade (Epic)
3	2	THE LOVE SONGS	George Benson (K-Tel)
21	3	FEARGAL SHARKEY	Feargal Sharkey (Virgin)
4	4	ICE ON FIRE	Elton John (Rocket)
16	5	SONGS TO LEARN AND SING	Echo & the Bunnymen (Korova)
4	6	ONCE UPON A TIME	Simple Minds (Virgin)
5	7	JENNIFER RUSH	Jennifer Rush (CBS)
7	8	THE SINGLES COLLECTION	Spandau Ballet (Chrysalis)
8	9	BROTHERS IN ARMS	Dire Straits (Vertigo)
2	10	AFTERBURNER	ZZ Top (Warner Bros.)
17	11	BITTER SWEET	King (CBS)
9	12	WORLD MACHINE	Level 42 (Polydor)
46	13	GREATEST HITS OF '85	Various Artists (Telstar)
-	14	EASY PIECES	Lloyd Cole & the Commotions (Polydor)
15	15	LIKE A VIRGIN	Madonna (Sire)
22	16	THE POWER OF CLASSIC ROCK	London Symphony Orchestra (Portrait)
25	17	LOVE HURTS	Elaine Paige (WEA)
10	18	THE SINGLES '81-'85	Depeche Mode (Mute)
19	19	ROCK ANTHEMS	Various Artists (K-Tel)
11	20	HOUNDS OF LOVE	Kate Bush (EMI)
-	21	PSYCHOCANDY	Jesus & Mary Chain (Blanco y Negro)
-	22	THE LOVE ALBUM	Various Artists (Telstar)
-	23	1979-1983	Bauhaus (Beggars Banquet)
-	24	LOVE	Cult (Beggars Banquet)
-	25	GOLD	Barbara Dickson (K-Tel)
-	26	I LOVE A PARTY	Russ Abbott (K-Tel)
-	27	TELLY HITS - 16 TOP TV THEMES	Various Artists (Stylus)
12	28	CUT THE CRAP	Clash (CBS)
35	29	STREET SOUNDS EDITION 14	Various Artists (Street Sounds)
20	30	POWER WINDOWS	Rush (Vertigo)
13	31	OUT NOW! 2	Various Artists (Chrysalis)
-	32	ALED JONES WITH THE BBC WELSH CHORUS	Aled Jones (10/BBC)
14	33	SLAVE TO THE RHYTHM	Grace Jones (ZTT)
28	34	BAGGARADDIM	UB40 (Dep International)
23	35	LIVE AFTER DEATH	Iron Maiden (EMI)
-	36	PAUL HARDCASTLE	Paul Hardcastle (Chrysalis)
26	37	THE CARS' GREATEST HITS	Cars (Elektra)
32	38	PICTURE BOOK	Simply Red (Elektra)
24	39	SONGS FROM THE BIG CHAIR	Tears For Fears (Mercury)
30	40	HUNTING HIGH AND LOW	A Ha (Warner Bros.)
-	41	WHITE CITY	Pete Townshend (Atco)
-	42	SCARECROW	John Cougar Mellencamp (RCA)
27	43	THE GIFT	Midge Ure (Chrysalis)
-	44	DOG EAT DOG	Joni Mitchell (Geffen)
-	45	NOW - THE CHRISTMAS ALBUM	Various Artists (EMI/Virgin)
-	46	KNEE DEEP IN THE HOOPLA	Starship (Grunt)
-	47	REMINISCING - THE HOWARD KEEL COLLECTION	Howard Keel (Telstar)
50	48	RIPTIDE	Robert Palmer (Island)
41	49	EAST ENDERS	Various Artists (BBC)
47	50	JAMBOREE BAG NUMBER THREE	Chas & Dave (Rockney)

As Simple Minds celebrated their second Number 1 album with *Once Upon A Time*, Sade scored an even more notable double with *Promise*, which gave her two chart-topping albums from two releases. Jennifer Rush's eponymous album found top 10 success on the back of her hit single *The Power Of Love* (the year's biggest-selling single and only million-seller), while ex-Undertone Feargal Sharkey made his solo mark.

December 1985

7 December 1985

9	1	BROTHERS IN ARMS	Dire Straits (Vertigo)
2	2	THE LOVE SONGS	George Benson (K-Tel)
1	3	PROMISE	Sade (Epic)
14	4	EASY PIECES	
			Lloyd Cole & the Commotions (Polydor)
-	5	NOW THAT'S WHAT I CALL MUSIC 6	
			Various Artists (EMI/Virgin)
13	6	GREATEST HITS OF '85 Various Artists (Telstar)
4	7	ICE ON FIRE	Elton John (Rocket)
-	8	HITS 3	Various Artists (CBS/WEA)
8	9	THE SINGLES COLLECTION	
			Spandau Ballet (Chrysalis)
3	10	FEARGAL SHARKEY	Feargal Sharkey (Virgin)
22	11	THE LOVE ALBUM	Various Artists (Telstar)
45	12	NOW - THE CHRISTMAS ALBUM	
			Various Artists (EMI/Virgin)
7	13	JENNIFER RUSH	Jennifer Rush (CBS)
5	14	SONGS TO LEARN AND SING	
			Echo & the Bunnymen (Korova)
17	15	LOVE HURTS	Elaine Paige (WEA)
12	16	WORLD MACHINE	Level 42 (Polydor)
16	17	THE POWER OF CLASSIC ROCK	
			London Symphony Orchestra (Portrait)
19	18	ROCK ANTHEMS	Various Artists (K-Tel)
6	19	ONCE UPON A TIME	Simple Minds (Virgin)
21	20	PSYCHOCANDY	
			Jesus & Mary Chain (Blanco y Negro)
15	21	LIKE A VIRGIN	Madonna (Sire)
11	21	BITTER SWEET	King (CBS)
23	23	1979-1983	Bauhaus (Beggars Banquet)
10	24	AFTERBURNER	ZZ Top (Warner Bros.)
44	25	DOG EAT DOG	Joni Mitchell (Geffen)
-	26	GREATEST HITS VOL 1 & VOL 2	Billy Joel (CBS)
25	27	GOLD	Barbara Dickson (K-Tel)
31	28	OUT NOW! 2	Various Artists (Chrysalis)
47	29	REMINISCING - THE HOWARD KEEL	
		COLLECTION	Howard Keel (Telstar)
-	30	SO RED THE ROSE	Arcadia (EMI)
36	31	PAUL HARDCASTLE	Paul Hardcastle (Chrysalis)
20	32	HOUNDS OF LOVE	Kate Bush (EMI)
26	33	I LOVE A PARTY	Russ Abbott (K-Tel)
-	34	THE VERY BEST OF THE COMMODORES	
			Commodores (Telstar)
29	35	STREET SOUNDS EDITION 14	
			Various Artists (Street Sounds)
34	36	BAGGARADDIM	UB40 (Dep International)
50	37	JAMBOREE BAG NUMBER THREE	
			Chas & Dave (Rockney)
27	38	TELLY HITS - 16 TOP TV THEMES	
			Various Artists (Stylus)
-	39	LEAVE THE BEST TO LAST James Last (Polydor)
37	40	THE CARS' GREATEST HITS	Cars (Elektra)
49	41	EAST ENDERS	Various Artists (BBC)
24	42	LOVE	Cult (Beggars Banquet)
-	43	SEVEN THE HARD WAY	Pat Benatar (Chrysalis)
-	44	WEST SIDE STORY	Leonard Bernstein
			& Studio Cast (Deutsche Grammophon)
-	45	JUST A MILLION DREAMS	Alan Vega (Elektra)
-	46	NO JACKET REQUIRED	Phil Collins (Virgin)
39	47	SONGS FROM THE BIG CHAIR	
			Tears For Fears (Mercury)
43	48	THE GIFT	Midge Ure (Chrysalis)
-	49	NAIL Scraping Foetus off the Wheel (Some Bizzare)
35	50	LIVE AFTER DEATH	Iron Maiden (EMI)

14 December 1985

5	1	NOW THAT'S WHAT I CALL MUSIC 6	
			Various Artists (EMI/Virgin)
8	2	HITS 3	Various Artists (CBS/WEA)
1	3	BROTHERS IN ARMS	Dire Straits (Vertigo)
2	4	THE LOVE SONGS	George Benson (K-Tel)
12	5	NOW - THE CHRISTMAS ALBUM	
			Various Artists (EMI/Virgin)
4	6	EASY PIECES	
			Lloyd Cole & the Commotions (Polydor)
3	7	PROMISE	Sade (Epic)
6	8	GREATEST HITS OF '85 Various Artists (Telstar)
9	9	THE SINGLES COLLECTION	
			Spandau Ballet (Chrysalis)
7	10	ICE ON FIRE	Elton John (Rocket)
11	11	THE LOVE ALBUM	Various Artists (Telstar)
16	12	WORLD MACHINE	Level 42 (Polydor)
15	13	LOVE HURTS	Elaine Paige (WEA)
30	14	SO RED THE ROSE	Arcadia (EMI)
13	15	JENNIFER RUSH	Jennifer Rush (CBS)
27	16	GOLD	Barbara Dickson (K-Tel)
19	17	ONCE UPON A TIME	Simple Minds (Virgin)
21	18	LIKE A VIRGIN	Madonna (Sire)
18	19	ROCK ANTHEMS	Various Artists (K-Tel)
10	20	FEARGAL SHARKEY	Feargal Sharkey (Virgin)
14	21	SONGS TO LEARN AND SING	
			Echo & the Bunnymen (Korova)
26	22	GREATEST HITS VOL 1 & VOL 2	Billy Joel (CBS)
39	23	LEAVE THE BEST TO LAST James Last (Polydor)
24	24	AFTERBURNER	ZZ Top (Warner Bros.)
17	25	THE POWER OF CLASSIC ROCK	
			London Symphony Orchestra (Portrait)
32	26	HOUNDS OF LOVE	Kate Bush (EMI)
-	27	ISLAND LIFE	Grace Jones (Island)
43	28	SEVEN THE HARD WAY Pat Benatar (Chrysalis)
20	29	PSYCHOCANDY	
			Jesus & Mary Chain (Blanco y Negro)
33	30	I LOVE A PARTY	Russ Abbott (K-Tel)
-	31	LITTLE CREATURES	Talking Heads (EMI)
34	32	THE VERY BEST OF THE COMMODORES	
			Commodores (Telstar)
21	33	BITTER SWEET	King (CBS)
-	34	ASTRA	Asia (Geffen)
47	35	SONGS FROM THE BIG CHAIR	
			Tears For Fears (Mercury)
-	36	PARTY PARTY 2	Black Lace (Telstar)
-	37	WHITNEY HOUSTON	Whitney Houston (Arista)
-	38	COME OUT AND PLAY Twisted Sister (Atlantic)
25	39	DOG EAT DOG	Joni Mitchell (Geffen)
-	40	ALED JONES WITH THE BBC WELSH CHORUS	
			Aled Jones (10/BBC)
29	41	REMINISCING - THE HOWARD KEEL	
		COLLECTION	Howard Keel (Telstar)
44	42	WEST SIDE STORY	Leonard Bernstein
			& Studio Cast (Deutsche Grammophon)
36	43	BAGGARADDIM	UB40 (Dep International)
-	44	RECKLESS	Bryan Adams (A&M)
-	45	DONE WITH MIRRORS	Aerosmith (Geffen)
-	46	BORN IN THE USA Bruce Springsteen (CBS)
23	47	1979-1983	Bauhaus (Beggars Banquet)
-	48	PACK UP THE PLANTATION	
			Tom Petty & the Heartbreakers (MCA)
-	49	FRANKENCHRIST	
			Dead Kennedys (Alternative Tentacles)
-	50	VITAL IDOL	Billy Idol (Chrysalis)

21 December 1985

1	1	NOW THAT'S WHAT I CALL MUSIC 6	
			Various Artists (EMI/Virgin)
2	2	HITS 3	Various Artists (CBS/WEA)
5	3	NOW - THE CHRISTMAS ALBUM	
			Various Artists (EMI/Virgin)
4	4	THE LOVE SONGS	George Benson (K-Tel)
9	5	THE SINGLES COLLECTION	
			Spandau Ballet (Chrysalis)
3	6	BROTHERS IN ARMS	Dire Straits (Vertigo)
7	7	PROMISE	Sade (Epic)
11	8	THE LOVE ALBUM	Various Artists (Telstar)
8	9	GREATEST HITS OF '85 Various Artists (Telstar)
10	10	ICE ON FIRE	Elton John (Rocket)
6	11	EASY PIECES	
			Lloyd Cole & the Commotions (Polydor)
18	12	LIKE A VIRGIN	Madonna (Sire)
13	13	LOVE HURTS	Elaine Paige (WEA)
16	14	GOLD	Barbara Dickson (K-Tel)
12	15	WORLD MACHINE	Level 42 (Polydor)
23	16	LEAVE THE BEST TO LAST James Last (Polydor)
30	17	I LOVE A PARTY	Russ Abbott (K-Tel)
37	18	WHITNEY HOUSTON	Whitney Houston (Arista)
27	19	ISLAND LIFE	Grace Jones (Island)
-	20	JAMBOREE BAG NO.3	Chas & Dave (Rockney)
14	21	SO RED THE ROSE	Arcadia (EMI)
15	22	JENNIFER RUSH	Jennifer Rush (CBS)
41	23	REMINISCING - THE HOWARD KEEL	
		COLLECTION	Howard Keel (Telstar)
36	24	PARTY PARTY 2	Black Lace (Telstar)
22	25	GREATEST HITS VOL 1 & VOL 2 Billy Joel (CBS)
19	26	ROCK ANTHEMS	Various Artists (K-Tel)
24	27	AFTERBURNER	ZZ Top (Warner Bros.)
26	28	HOUNDS OF LOVE	Kate Bush (EMI)
20	29	FEARGAL SHARKEY	Feargal Sharkey (Virgin)
-	30	ROCK A LITTLE	Stevie Nicks (Modern)
-	31	FINE YOUNG CANNIBALS	
			Fine Young Cannibals (London)
34	32	ASTRA	Asia (Geffen)
40	33	ALED JONES WITH THE BBC WELSH CHORUS	
			Aled Jones (10/BBC)
35	34	SONGS FROM THE BIG CHAIR	
			Tears For Fears (Mercury)
25	35	THE CLASSIC TOUCH Richard Clayderman (Decca)
2	36	THE POWER OF CLASSIC ROCK LSO (Portrait)
33	37	BITTER SWEET	King (CBS)
48	38	PACK UP THE PLANTATION	
			Tom Petty & the Heartbreakers (MCA)
38	39	COME OUT AND PLAY Twisted Sister (Atlantic)
29	40	PSYCHOCANDY	
			Jesus & Mary Chain (Blanco y Negro)
-	41	THE LEGEND OF BILLIE HOLIDAYBillie Holiday (MCA)
42	42	WEST SIDE STORY	Leonard Bernstein
			& Studio Cast (Deutsche Grammophon)
32	43	THE VERY BEST OF THE COMMODORES	
			Commodores (Telstar)
17	44	ONCE UPON A TIME	Simple Minds (Virgin)
-	45	CLUB NINJA	Blue Oyster Cult (CBS)
49	46	FRANKENCHRIST	
			Dead Kennedys (Alternative Tentacles)
21	47	SONGS TO LEARN AND SING	
			Echo & the Bunnymen (Korova)
-	48	THE SINGLES '81-'85	Depeche Mode (Mute)
39	49	DOG EAT DOG	Joni Mitchell (Geffen)
45	50	DONE WITH MIRRORS	Aerosmith (Geffen)

Following yet another *Brothers In Arms* sales spurt at the beginning of December, the major Christmas sales battle was clearly going to be, as in 1984, between the major labels' mega-hits compilations. This time, the honours went the other way, with EMI/Virgin's *Now 6* holding CBS/WEA's *Hits 3* into second place. Moreover, *The Christmas Album* boosted the *Now* partnership's share, locking in behind at Number 3.

January 1986

4 January 1986

last week	this	Title	Artist (Label)
1	1	NOW THAT'S WHAT I CALL MUSIC 6	Various Artists (EMI/Virgin)
3	2	NOW - THE CHRISTMAS ALBUM	Various Artists (EMI/Virgin)
2	3	HITS 3	Various Artists (CBS/WEA)
6	4	BROTHERS IN ARMS	Dire Straits (Vertigo)
4	5	THE LOVE SONGS	George Benson (K-Tel)
7	6	PROMISE	Sade (Epic)
5	7	THE SINGLES COLLECTION	Spandau Ballet (Chrysalis)
12	8	LIKE A VIRGIN	Madonna (Sire)
8	9	THE LOVE ALBUM	Various Artists (Telstar)
10	10	ICE ON FIRE	Elton John (Rocket)
14	11	GOLD	Barbara Dickson (K-Tel)
22	12	JENNIFER RUSH	Jennifer Rush (CBS)
18	13	WHITNEY HOUSTON	Whitney Houston (Arista)
9	14	GREATEST HITS OF '85	Various Artists (Telstar)
15	15	WORLD MACHINE	Level 42 (Polydor)
16	16	LEAVE THE BEST TO LAST	James Last (Polydor)
13	17	LOVE HURTS	Elaine Paige (WEA)
17	18	I LOVE A PARTY	Russ Abbot (K-Tel)
11	19	EASY PIECES	Lloyd Cole & the Commotions (Polydor)
31	20	FINE YOUNG CANNIBALS	Fine Young Cannibals (London)
20	21	JAMBOREE BAG NO.3	Chas & Dave (Rockney)
19	22	ISLAND LIFE	Grace Jones (Island)
-	23	STREET SOUNDS EDITION 15	Various Artists (Street Sounds)
36	24	THE POWER OF CLASSIC ROCK	London Symphony Orchestra (Portrait)
23	25	REMINISCING – THE HOWARD KEEL COLLECTION	Howard Keel (Telstar)
-	26	CRACKERS – THE SLADE CHRISTMAS PARTY ALBUM	Slade (Telstar)
25	27	GREATEST HITS VOL 1 & VOL 2	Billy Joel (CBS)
43	28	THE VERY BEST OF THE COMMODORES	Commodores (Telstar)
-	29	NO JACKET REQUIRED	Phil Collins (Virgin)
29	30	FEARGAL SHARKEY	Feargal Sharkey (Virgin)
33	31	ALED JONES WITH THE BBC WELSH CHORUS	Aled Jones (10/BBC)
24	32	PARTY PARTY 2	Black Lace (Telstar)
28	33	HOUNDS OF LOVE	Kate Bush (EMI)
44	34	ONCE UPON A TIME	Simple Minds (Virgin)
34	35	SONGS FROM THE BIG CHAIR	Tears for Fears (Mercury)
-	36	GO WEST/BANGS AND CRASHES	Go West (Chrysalis)
47	37	SONGS TO LEARN AND SING	Echo & the Bunnymen (Korova)
49	38	DOG EAT DOG	Joni Mitchell (Geffen)
45	39	CLUB NINJA	Blue Oyster Cult (CBS)
-	40	BALLADS	Elvis Presley (Telstar)
-	41	STREETSOUNDS ELECTRO 10	Various Artists (Street Sounds)
35	42	THE CLASSIC TOUCH	Richard Clayderman (Decca/Delphine)
30	43	ROCK A LITTLE	Stevie Nicks (Modern)
40	44	PSYCHOCANDY	Jesus & Mary Chain (Blanco Y Negro)
21	45	SO RED THE ROSE	Arcadia (EMI)
-	46	VELVET WATERS	Various Artists (Stylus)
-	47	THE HEART OF THE MATTER	Kenny Rogers (RCA)
-	48	HEART AND SOUL	Barry White (K-Tel)
-	49	BEST OF THE DOORS	Doors (Elektra)
-	50	AMAZING GRACE	Judy Collins (Telstar)

11 January 1986

last	this	Title	Artist (Label)
4	1	BROTHERS IN ARMS	Dire Straits (Vertigo)
1	2	NOW THAT'S WHAT I CALL MUSIC 6	Various Artists (EMI/Virgin)
6	3	PROMISE	Sade (Epic)
3	4	HITS 3	Various Artists (CBS/WEA)
8	5	LIKE A VIRGIN	Madonna (Sire)
5	6	THE LOVE SONGS	George Benson (K-Tel)
13	7	WHITNEY HOUSTON	Whitney Houston (Arista)
2	8	NOW - THE CHRISTMAS ALBUM	Various Artists (EMI/Virgin)
9	9	THE LOVE ALBUM	Various Artists (Telstar)
15	10	WORLD MACHINE	Level 42 (Polydor)
12	11	JENNIFER RUSH	Jennifer Rush (CBS)
31	12	ALED JONES WITH THE BBC WELSH CHORUS	Aled Jones (10/BBC)
7	13	THE SINGLES COLLECTION	Spandau Ballet (Chrysalis)
11	14	GOLD	Barbara Dickson (K-Tel)
21	15	JAMBOREE BAG NO.3	Chas & Dave (Rockney)
17	16	LOVE HURTS	Elaine Paige (WEA)
20	17	FINE YOUNG CANNIBALS	Fine Young Cannibals (London)
22	18	ISLAND LIFE	Grace Jones (Island)
23	19	STREET SOUNDS EDITION 15	Various Artists (Street Sounds)
19	20	EASY PIECES	Lloyd Cole & the Commotions (Polydor)
16	21	LEAVE THE BEST TO LAST	James Last (Polydor)
27	22	GREATEST HITS VOL 1 & VOL 2	Billy Joel (CBS)
14	23	GREATEST HITS OF '85	Various Artists (Portrait)
36	24	GO WEST/BANGS AND CRASHES	Go West (Chrysalis)
30	25	FEARGAL SHARKEY	Feargal Sharkey (Virgin)
37	26	SONGS TO LEARN AND SING	Echo & the Bunnymen (Korova)
41	27	STREETSOUNDS ELECTRO 10	Various Artists (Street Sounds)
10	28	ICE ON FIRE	Elton John (Rocket)
42	29	THE CLASSIC TOUCH	Richard Clayderman (Decca/Delphine)
18	30	I LOVE A PARTY	Russ Abbot (K-Tel)
-	31	BLUE SKIES	Kiri Te Kanawa (London)
-	32	MADONNA	Madonna (Epic)
-	33	LITTLE CREATURES	Talking Heads (EMI)
33	34	HOUNDS OF LOVE	Kate Bush (EMI)
34	35	ONCE UPON A TIME	Simple Minds (Virgin)
29	36	NO JACKET REQUIRED	Phil Collins (Virgin)
24	37	THE POWER OF CLASSIC ROCK	LSO (Portrait)
44	38	PSYCHOCANDY	Jesus & Mary Chain (Blanco Y Negro)
28	39	THE VERY BEST OF THE COMMODORES	Commodores (Telstar)
32	40	PARTY PARTY 2	Black Lace (Telstar)
25	41	REMINISCING – THE HOWARD KEEL COLLECTION	Howard Keel (Telstar)
46	42	VELVET WATERS	Various Artists (Stylus)
35	43	SONGS FROM THE BIG CHAIR	Tears for Fears (Mercury)
-	44	THE COMPLETE MIKE OLDFIELD	Mike Oldfield (Virgin)
-	45	THE DREAM OF THE BLUE TURTLES	Sting (A&M)
26	46	CRACKERS – THE SLADE CHRISTMAS PARTY ALBUM	Slade (Telstar)
47	47	THE HEART OF THE MATTER	Kenny Rogers (RCA)
48	48	HEART AND SOUL	Barry White (K-Tel)
-	49	FRANKENCHRIST	Dead Kennedys (Alternative Tentacles)
-	50	ALCHEMY – DIRE STRAITS LIVE	Dire Straits (Vertigo)

18 January 1986

last	this	Title	Artist (Label)
1	1	BROTHERS IN ARMS	Dire Straits (Vertigo)
2	2	NOW THAT'S WHAT I CALL MUSIC 6	Various Artists (EMI/Virgin)
5	3	LIKE A VIRGIN	Madonna (Sire)
3	4	PROMISE	Sade (Epic)
4	5	HITS 3	Various Artists (CBS/WEA)
7	6	WHITNEY HOUSTON	Whitney Houston (Arista)
10	7	WORLD MACHINE	Level 42 (Polydor)
18	8	ISLAND LIFE	Grace Jones (Island)
13	9	THE SINGLES COLLECTION	Spandau Ballet (Chrysalis)
6	10	THE LOVE SONGS	George Benson (K-Tel)
-	11	HUNTING HIGH AND LOW	A-Ha (Warner Bros.)
11	12	JENNIFER RUSH	Jennifer Rush (CBS)
24	13	GO WEST/BANGS AND CRASHES	Go West (Chrysalis)
43	14	SONGS FROM THE BIG CHAIR	Tears for Fears (Mercury)
28	15	ICE ON FIRE	Elton John (Rocket)
20	16	EASY PIECES	Lloyd Cole & the Commotions (Polydor)
23	17	GREATEST HITS OF '85	Various Artists (Telstar)
45	18	THE DREAM OF THE BLUE TURTLES	Sting (A&M)
22	19	GREATEST HITS VOL 1 & VOL 2	Billy Joel (CBS)
35	20	ONCE UPON A TIME	Simple Minds (Virgin)
34	21	HOUNDS OF LOVE	Kate Bush (EMI)
36	22	NO JACKET REQUIRED	Phil Collins (Virgin)
17	23	FINE YOUNG CANNIBALS	Fine Young Cannibals (London)
-	24	THE BROADWAY ALBUM	Barbra Streisand (CBS)
9	25	THE LOVE ALBUM	Various Artists (Telstar)
25	26	FEARGAL SHARKEY	Feargal Sharkey (Virgin)
14	27	GOLD	Barbara Dickson (K-Tel)
29	28	THE CLASSIC TOUCH	Richard Clayderman (Decca/Delphine)
37	29	THE POWER OF CLASSIC ROCK	LSO (Portrait)
19	30	STREET SOUNDS EDITION 15	Various Artists (Street Sounds)
-	31	LUXURY OF LIFE	Five Star (Tent)
-	32	ELIMINATOR	ZZ Top (Warner Bros.)
32	33	MADONNA	Madonna (Epic)
41	34	REMINISCING – THE HOWARD KEEL COLLECTION	Howard Keel (Telstar)
21	35	LEAVE THE BEST TO LAST	James Last (Polydor)
16	36	LOVE HURTS	Elaine Paige (WEA)
15	37	JAMBOREE BAG NO.3	Chas & Dave (Rockney)
48	38	HEART AND SOUL	Barry White (K-Tel)
44	39	THE COMPLETE MIKE OLDFIELD	Mike Oldfield (Virgin)
39	40	THE VERY BEST OF THE COMMODORES	Commodores (Telstar)
-	41	BITTER SWEET	King (CBS)
-	42	PRIVATE DANCER	Tina Turner (Capitol)
-	43	BAGGARADDIM	UB40 (DEP Int)
-	44	WHO'S ZOOMIN' WHO	Aretha Franklin (Arista)
47	45	THE HEART OF THE MATTER	Kenny Rogers (RCA)
26	46	SONGS TO LEARN AND SING	Echo & the Bunnymen (Korova)
27	47	STREETSOUNDS ELECTRO 10	Various Artists (Street Sounds)
38	48	PSYCHOCANDY	Jesus & Mary Chain (Blanco Y Negro)
12	49	ALED JONES WITH THE BBC WELSH CHORUS	Aled Jones (10/BBC)
33	50	LITTLE CREATURES	Talking Heads (EMI)

As the hits compilations lost some of their impetus after Christmas, Dire Straits' *Brothers In Arms* reasserted itself at the top of the charts again, helped once more by the Top 5 success of an extracted single - *Walk Of Life*. By the end of the 1980s, this album would have passed three million sales in the UK alone, putting it second only to the Beatles' *Sergeant Pepper* as the country's all-time best-seller.

January – February 1986

last week	this week	25 January 1986
1	1	BROTHERS IN ARMS Dire Straits (Vertigo)
11	2	HUNTING HIGH AND LOW A-Ha (Warner Bros.)
18	3	THE DREAM OF THE BLUE TURTLE Sting (A&M)
8	4	ISLAND LIFE Grace Jones (Island)
7	5	WORLD MACHINE Level 42 (Polydor)
6	6	WHITNEY HOUSTON Whitney Houston (Arista)
4	7	PROMISE Sade (Epic)
3	8	LIKE A VIRGIN Madonna (Sire)
24	9	THE BROADWAY ALBUM Barbra Streisand (CBS)
2	10	NOW THAT'S WHAT I CALL MUSIC 6 Various Artists (EMI/Virgin)
13	11	GO WEST/BANGS AND CRASHES Go West (Chrysalis)
26	12	FEARGAL SHARKEY Feargal Sharkey (Virgin)
23	13	FINE YOUNG CANNIBALS Fine Young Cannibals (London)
9	14	THE SINGLES COLLECTION Spandau Ballet (Chrysalis)
16	15	EASY PIECES Lloyd Cole & the Commotions (Polydor)
15	16	ICE ON FIRE Elton John (Rocket)
14	17	SONGS FROM THE BIG CHAIR Tears for Fears (Mercury)
22	18	NO JACKET REQUIRED Phil Collins (Virgin)
12	19	JENNIFER RUSH Jennifer Rush (CBS)
5	20	HITS 3 Various Artists (CBS/WEA)
20	21	ONCE UPON A TIME Simple Minds (Virgin)
-	22	BE YOURSELF TONIGHT Eurythmics (RCA)
46	23	SONGS TO LEARN AND SING Echo & the Bunnymen (Korova)
25	24	THE LOVE ALBUM Various Artists (Telstar)
-	25	HIGH PRIORITY Cherrelle (Tabu)
31	26	LUXURY OF LIFE Five Star (Tent)
30	27	STREET SOUNDS EDITION 15 Various Artists (Street Sounds)
21	28	HOUNDS OF LOVE Kate Bush (EMI)
10	29	THE LOVE SONGS George Benson (K-Tel)
42	30	PRIVATE DANCER Tina Turner (Capitol)
19	31	GREATEST HITS VOL 1 & VOL 2 Billy Joel (CBS)
-	32	RECKLESS Bryan Adams (A&M)
17	33	GREATEST HITS OF '85 Various Artists (Telstar)
36	34	LOVE HURTS Elaine Paige (WEA)
38	35	HEART AND SOUL Barry White (K-Tel)
44	36	WHO'S ZOOMIN' WHO Aretha Franklin (Arista)
50	37	LITTLE CREATURES Talking Heads (EMI)
27	38	GOLD Barbara Dickson (K-Tel)
49	39	ALED JONES WITH THE BBC WELSH CHORUS Aled Jones (10/BBC)
39	40	THE COMPLETE MIKE OLDFIELD Mike Oldfield (Virgin)
28	41	THE CLASSIC TOUCH Richard Clayderman (Decca/Delphine))
-	42	BORN IN THE USA Bruce Springsteen (CBS)
-	43	THE JAZZ SINGER Neil Diamond (Capitol)
-	44	THE SECRET OF ASSOCIATION Paul Young (CBS)
-	45	FULL FORCE Full Force (CBS)
-	46	LISTEN LIKE THIEVES INXS (Mercury)
41	47	BITTER SWEET King (CBS)
47	48	STREETSOUNDS ELECTRO 10 Various Artists (Street Sounds)
-	49	THE BEST OF ANDREW LLOYD WEBBER Various Artists (K-Tel)
-	50	DOUBLE TROUBLE Molly Hatchet (Epic)

last week	this week	1 February 1986
1	1	BROTHERS IN ARMS Dire Straits (Vertigo)
2	2	HUNTING HIGH AND LOW A-Ha (Warner Bros.)
5	3	WORLD MACHINE Level 42 (Polydor)
4	4	THE DREAM OF THE BLUE TURTLES Sting (A&M)
6	5	WHITNEY HOUSTON Whitney Houston (Arista)
9	6	THE BROADWAY ALBUM Barbra Streisand (CBS)
12	7	FEARGAL SHARKEY Feargal Sharkey (Virgin)
4	8	ISLAND LIFE Grace Jones (Island)
8	9	LIKE A VIRGIN Madonna (Sire)
11	10	GO WEST/BANGS AND CRASHES Go West (Chrysalis)
7	11	PROMISE Sade (Epic)
13	12	FINE YOUNG CANNIBALS Fine Young Cannibals (London)
22	13	BE YOURSELF TONIGHT Eurythmics (RCA)
25	14	HIGH PRIORITY Cherrelle (Tabu)
10	15	NOW THAT'S WHAT I CALL MUSIC 6 Various Artists (EMI/Virgin)
21	16	ONCE UPON A TIME Simple Minds (Virgin)
15	17	EASY PIECES Lloyd Cole & the Commotions (Polydor)
26	18	LUXURY OF LIFE Five Star (Tent)
19	19	JENNIFER RUSH Jennifer Rush (CBS)
17	20	SONGS FROM THE BIG CHAIR Tears for Fears (Mercury)
29	21	THE LOVE SONGS George Benson (K-Tel)
14	22	THE SINGLES COLLECTION Spandau Ballet (Chrysalis)
18	23	NO JACKET REQUIRED Phil Collins (Virgin)
30	24	PRIVATE DANCER Tina Turner (Capitol)
16	25	ICE ON FIRE Elton John (Rocket)
27	26	STREET SOUNDS EDITION 15 Various Artists (Street Sounds)
36	27	WHO'S ZOOMIN' WHO Aretha Franklin (Arista)
-	28	SUZANNE VEGA Suzanne Vega (A&M)
35	29	HEART AND SOUL Barry White (K-Tel)
41	30	THE CLASSIC TOUCH Richard Clayderman (Decca)
43	31	THE JAZZ SINGER Neil Diamond (Capitol)
-	32	MACALLA Clannad (RCA)
-	33	ROCK A LITTLE Stevie Nicks (Modern)
32	34	RECKLESS Bryan Adams (A&M)
-	35	THE UNFORGETTABLE FIRE U2 (Island)
20	36	HITS 3 Various Artists (CBS/WEA)
23	37	SONGS TO LEARN AND SING Echo & the Bunnymen (Korova)
28	38	HOUNDS OF LOVE Kate Bush (EMI)
24	39	THE LOVE ALBUM Various Artists (Telstar)
-	40	ALEXANDER O'NEAL Alexander O'Neal (Tabu/Epic)
-	41	BLACK AND WHITE Terraplane (Epic)
-	42	ROCK ME TONIGHT Freddie Jackson (Capitol)
47	43	BITTER SWEET King (CBS)
46	44	LISTEN LIKE THIEVES INXS (Mercury)
50	45	DOUBLE TROUBLE Molly Hatchet (Epic)
34	46	LOVE HURTS Elaine Paige (WEA)
42	47	BORN IN THE USA Bruce Springsteen (CBS)
-	48	THE BEST OF INCANTATION Incantation (West Five)
-	49	ALL THROUGH THE NIGHT Aled Jones (BBC)
-	50	LEAVE THE BEST TO LAST James Last (Polydor)

last week	this week	8 February 1986
1	1	BROTHERS IN ARMS Dire Straits (Vertigo)
2	2	HUNTING HIGH AND LOW A-Ha (Warner Bros.)
4	3	THE DREAM OF THE BLUE TURTLES Sting (A&M)
3	4	WORLD MACHINE Level 42 (Polydor)
8	5	ISLAND LIFE Grace Jones (Island)
5	6	WHITNEY HOUSTON Whitney Houston (Arista)
6	7	THE BROADWAY ALBUM Barbra Streisand (CBS)
9	8	LIKE A VIRGIN Madonna (Sire)
13	9	BE YOURSELF TONIGHT Eurythmics (RCA)
10	10	GO WEST/BANGS AND CRASHES Go West (Chrysalis)
7	11	FEARGAL SHARKEY Feargal Sharkey (Virgin)
12	12	FINE YOUNG CANNIBALS Fine Young Cannibals (London)
14	13	HIGH PRIORITY Cherrelle (Tabu)
18	14	LUXURY OF LIFE Five Star (Tent)
11	15	PROMISE Sade (Epic)
16	16	ONCE UPON A TIME Simple Minds (Virgin)
20	17	SONGS FROM THE BIG CHAIR Tears for Fears (Mercury)
15	18	NOW THAT'S WHAT I CALL MUSIC 6 Various Artists (EMI/Virgin)
17	19	EASY PIECES Lloyd Cole & the Commotions (Polydor)
32	20	MACALLA Clannad (RCA)
27	21	WHO'S ZOOMIN' WHO Aretha Franklin (Arista)
-	22	THIS IS BIG AUDIO DYNAMITE Big Audio Dynamite (CBS)
-	23	ROCKY IV Soundtrack (Scotti Brothers)
-	24	LITTLE CREATURES Talking Heads (EMI)
19	25	JENNIFER RUSH Jennifer Rush (CBS)
26	26	STREET SOUNDS EDITION 15 Various Artists (Street Sounds)
-	27	BACK IN THE DHSS Half Man Half Biscuit (Probe Plus)
24	28	PRIVATE DANCER Tina Turner (Capitol)
34	29	RECKLESS Bryan Adams (A&M)
25	30	ICE ON FIRE Elton John (Rocket)
30	31	THE CLASSIC TOUCH Richard Clayderman (Decca)
28	32	SUZANNE VEGA Suzanne Vega (A&M)
42	33	ROCK ME TONIGHT Freddie Jackson (Capitol)
40	34	ALEXANDER O'NEAL Alexander O'Neal (Tabu/Epic)
21	35	THE LOVE SONGS George Benson (K-Tel)
38	36	BORN IN THE USA Bruce Springsteen (CBS)
38	37	HOUNDS OF LOVE Kate Bush (EMI)
39	38	THE LOVE ALBUM Various Artists (Telstar)
44	39	LISTEN LIKE THIEVES INXS (Mercury)
22	40	THE SINGLES COLLECTION Spandau Ballet (Chrysalis)
29	41	HEART AND SOUL Barry White (K-Tel)
-	42	DAMNED BUT NOT FORGOTTEN Damned (Dojo)
31	43	THE JAZZ SINGER Neil Diamond (Capitol)
37	44	SONGS TO LEARN AND SING Echo & the Bunnymen (Korova)
23	45	NO JACKET REQUIRED Phil Collins (Virgin)
-	46	SOUNDTRACK FROM MISTRAL'S DAUGHTER Vladimir Cosma (Carrere)
45	47	DOUBLE TROUBLE Molly Hatchet (Epic)
48	48	THE BEST OF INCANTATION - MUSIC FROM THE ANDES Incantation (West Five)
41	49	BLACK AND WHITE Terraplane (Epic)
36	50	HITS 3 Various Artists (CBS/WEA)

Sting's resurgence into the Top 3 with the seven-month-old *The Dream Of The Blue Turtles* was largely attributable to extensive airplay for its track *Russians*, which made the Top 10 as a single at the same time. Barbra Streisand made the Top 10 for the first time since her *Love Songs* compilation in 1982 with an album of Broadway show tunes which, stylistically, went back to her early 1960s stage roots.

February – March 1986

15 February 1986

		Title	Artist (Label)
1	1	BROTHERS IN ARMS	Dire Straits (Vertigo)
2	2	HUNTING HIGH AND LOW	A-Ha (Warner Bros.)
4	3	WORLD MACHINE	Level 42 (Polydor)
3	4	THE DREAM OF THE BLUE TURTLES	Sting (A&M)
5	5	ISLAND LIFE	Grace Jones (Island)
6	6	WHITNEY HOUSTON	Whitney Houston (Arista)
9	7	BE YOURSELF TONIGHT	Eurythmics (RCA)
7	8	THE BROADWAY ALBUM	Barbra Streisand (CBS)
16	9	ONCE UPON A TIME	Simple Minds (Virgin)
8	10	LIKE A VIRGIN	Madonna (Sire)
12	11	FINE YOUNG CANNIBALS	Fine Young Cannibals (London)
14	12	LUXURY OF LIFE	Five Star (Tent)
11	13	FEARGAL SHARKEY	Feargal Sharkey (Virgin)
10	14	GO WEST/BANGS AND CRASHES	Go West (Chrysalis)
24	15	LITTLE CREATURES	Talking Heads (EMI)
23	16	ROCKY IV	Soundtrack (Scotti Brothers)
13	17	HIGH PRIORITY	Cherrelle (Tabu)
15	18	PROMISE	Sade (Epic)
19	19	EASY PIECES	Lloyd Cole & the Commotions (Polydor)
-	20	ALBUM/CASSETTE	Public Image Limited (Virgin)
20	21	MACALLA	Clannad (RCA)
21	22	WHO'S ZOOMIN' WHO	Aretha Franklin (Arista)
35	23	THE LOVE SONGS	George Benson (K-Tel)
28	24	PRIVATE DANCER	Tina Turner (Capitol)
18	25	NOW THAT'S WHAT I CALL MUSIC 6	Various Artists (EMI/Virgin)
31	26	THE CLASSIC TOUCH	Richard Clayderman (Decca/Delphine)
17	27	SONGS FROM THE BIG CHAIR	Tears for Fears (Mercury)
30	28	ICE ON FIRE	Elton John (Rocket)
25	29	JENNIFER RUSH	Jennifer Rush (CBS)
-	30	U2 LIVE: UNDER A BLOOD RED SKY	U2 (Island)
27	31	BACK IN THE DHSS	Half Man Half Biscuit (Probe Plus)
45	32	NO JACKET REQUIRED	Phil Collins (Virgin)
39	33	LISTEN LIKE THIEVES	INXS (Mercury)
32	34	SUZANNE VEGA	Suzanne Vega (A&M)
48	35	THE BEST OF INCANTATION - MUSIC FROM THE ANDES	Incantation (West Five)
34	36	ALEXANDER O'NEAL	Alexander O'Neal (Tabu)
-	37	PSYCHOCANDY	Jesus & Mary Chain (Blanco Y Negro)
-	38	STEVE McQUEEN	Prefab Sprout (Kitchenware)
38	39	THE LOVE ALBUM	Various Artists (Telstar)
33	40	ROCK ME TONIGHT	Freddie Jackson (Capitol)
-	41	ALCHEMY – DIRE STRAITS LIVE	Dire Straits (Vertigo)
44	42	SONGS TO LEARN AND SING	Echo & the Bunnymen (Korova)
43	43	THE JAZZ SINGER	Neil Diamond (Capitol)
-	44	ROCK A LITTLE	Stevie Nicks (Modern)
40	45	THE SINGLES COLLECTION	Spandau Ballet (Chrysalis)
-	46	THE POWER OF CLASSIC ROCK	London Symphony Orchestra (Portrait)
47	47	THE FIRST ALBUM	Madonna (Sire)
48	48	MISPLACED CHILDHOOD	Marillion (EMI)
-	49	STRENGTH	Alarm (IRS/MCA)
-	50	THE VERY BEST OF THE COMMODORES	Commodores (Telstar)

22 February 1986

		Title	Artist (Label)
1	1	BROTHERS IN ARMS	Dire Straits (Vertigo)
2	2	HUNTING HIGH AND LOW	A-Ha (Warner Bros.)
20	3	ALBUM/CASSETTE	Public Image Limited (Virgin)
6	4	WHITNEY HOUSTON	Whitney Houston (Arista)
3	5	WORLD MACHINE	Level 42 (Polydor)
5	6	ISLAND LIFE	Grace Jones (Island)
16	7	ROCKY IV	Soundtrack (Scotti Brothers)
7	8	BE YOURSELF TONIGHT	Eurythmics (RCA)
8	9	THE BROADWAY ALBUM	Barbra Streisand (CBS)
12	10	LUXURY OF LIFE	Five Star (Tent)
4	11	THE DREAM OF THE BLUE TURTLES	Sting (A&M)
9	12	ONCE UPON A TIME	Simple Minds (Virgin)
14	13	GO WEST/BANGS AND CRASHES	Go West (Chrysalis)
32	14	NO JACKET REQUIRED	Phil Collins (Virgin)
10	15	LIKE A VIRGIN	Madonna (Sire)
13	16	FEARGAL SHARKEY	Feargal Sharkey (Virgin)
-	17	THE ULTIMATE SUN	Ozzy Osbourne (Epic)
11	18	FINE YOUNG CANNIBALS	Fine Young Cannibals (London)
15	19	LITTLE CREATURES	Talking Heads (EMI)
-	20	WELCOME TO THE REAL WORLD	Mr Mister (RCA)
18	21	PROMISE	Sade (Epic)
-	22	THE DANCE HITS ALBUM	Various Artists (Towerbell)
-	23	JONATHAN KING'S ENTERTAINMENT USA	Various Artists (Stylus)
21	24	MACALLA	Clannad (RCA)
-	25	HOUNDS OF LOVE	Kate Bush (EMI)
24	26	PRIVATE DANCER	Tina Turner (Capitol)
17	27	HIGH PRIORITY	Cherrelle (Tabu)
19	28	EASY PIECES	Lloyd Cole & the Commotions (Polydor)
31	29	BACK IN THE DHSS	Half Man Half Biscuit (Probe Plus)
44	30	ROCK A LITTLE	Stevie Nicks (Modern)
22	31	WHO'S ZOOMIN' WHO	Aretha Franklin (Arista)
27	32	SONGS FROM THE BIG CHAIR	Tears for Fears (Mercury)
26	33	THE CLASSIC TOUCH	Richard Clayderman (Decca/Delphine)
-	34	HITS 3	Various Artists (CBS/WEA)
25	35	NOW THAT'S WHAT I CALL MUSIC 6	Various Artists (EMI/Virgin)
36	36	ALEXANDER O'NEAL	Alexander O'Neal (Tabu)
45	37	THE SINGLES COLLECTION	Spandau Ballet (Chrysalis)
28	38	ICE ON FIRE	Elton John (Rocket)
-	39	THE SECRET OF ASSOCIATION	Paul Young (CBS)
-	40	RECKLESS	Bryan Adams (A&M)
33	41	LISTEN LIKE THIEVES	INXS (Mercury)
38	42	STEVE McQUEEN	Prefab Sprout (Kitchenware)
40	43	ROCK ME TONIGHT	Freddie Jackson (Capitol)
23	44	THE LOVE SONGS	George Benson (K-Tel)
-	45	RADIO	L L Cool J (Def Jam)
41	46	ALCHEMY – DIRE STRAITS LIVE	Dire Straits (Vertigo)
48	47	MISPLACED CHILDHOOD	Marillion (EMI)
-	48	LEGEND	Bob Marley & the Wailers (Island)
46	49	THE POWER OF CLASSIC ROCK	London Symphony Orchestra (Portrait)
47	50	THE FIRST ALBUM	Madonna (Sire)

1 March 1986

		Title	Artist (Label)
1	1	BROTHERS IN ARMS	Dire Straits (Vertigo)
4	2	WHITNEY HOUSTON	Whitney Houston (Arista)
2	3	HUNTING HIGH AND LOW	A-Ha (Warner Bros.)
7	4	ROCKY IV	Soundtrack (Scotti Brothers)
6	5	ISLAND LIFE	Grace Jones (Island)
14	6	NO JACKET REQUIRED	Phil Collins (Virgin)
5	7	WORLD MACHINE	Level 42 (Polydor)
8	8	BE YOURSELF TONIGHT	Eurythmics (RCA)
9	9	THE BROADWAY ALBUM	Barbra Streisand (CBS)
17	10	THE ULTIMATE SUN	Ozzy Osbourne (Epic)
11	11	THE DREAM OF THE BLUE TURTLE	Sting (A&M)
3	12	ALBUM/CASSETTE	Public Image Limited (Virgin)
22	13	THE DANCE HITS ALBUM	Various Artists (Towerbell)
10	14	LUXURY OF LIFE	Five Star (Tent)
12	15	ONCE UPON A TIME	Simple Minds (Virgin)
15	16	LIKE A VIRGIN	Madonna (Sire)
16	17	FEARGAL SHARKEY	Feargal Sharkey (Virgin)
-	18	THE COLOUR OF SPRING	Talk Talk (EMI)
13	19	GO WEST/BANGS AND CRASHES	Go West (Chrysalis)
23	20	JONATHAN KING'S ENTERTAINMENT USA	Various Artists (Stylus)
19	21	LITTLE CREATURES	Talking Heads (EMI)
20	22	WELCOME TO THE REAL WORLD	Mr Mister (RCA)
-	23	KING OF AMERICA	Costello Show (F-Beat)
21	24	PROMISE	Sade (Epic)
43	25	ROCK ME TONIGHT	Freddie Jackson (Capitol)
31	26	WHO'S ZOOMIN' WHO	Aretha Franklin (Arista)
-	27	A DATE WITH ELVIS	Cramps (Big Beat)
27	28	HIGH PRIORITY	Cherrelle (Tabu)
18	29	FINE YOUNG CANNIBALS	Fine Young Cannibals (London)
32	30	SONGS FROM THE BIG CHAIR	Tears for Fears (Mercury)
29	31	BACK IN THE DHSS	Half Man Half Biscuit (Probe Plus)
28	32	EASY PIECES	Lloyd Cole & the Commotions (Polydor)
25	33	HOUNDS OF LOVE	Kate Bush (EMI)
-	34	SEVENTH STAR	Black Sabbath (Vertigo)
-	35	ALONE	Nana Mouskouri (Philips)
33	36	THE CLASSIC TOUCH	Richard Clayderman (Decca/Delphine)
-	37	SUDDENLY	Billy Ocean (Jive)
46	38	ALCHEMY – DIRE STRAITS LIVE	Dire Straits (Vertigo)
24	39	MACALLA	Clannad (RCA)
34	40	HITS 3	Various Artists (CBS/WEA)
44	41	THE LOVE SONGS	George Benson (K-Tel)
42	42	STEVE McQUEEN	Prefab Sprout (Kitchenware)
50	43	THE FIRST ALBUM	Madonna (Sire)
-	44	GREATEST HITS VOL 1 & VOL 2	Billy Joel (CBS)
30	45	ROCK A LITTLE	Stevie Nicks (Modern)
35	46	NOW THAT'S WHAT I CALL MUSIC 6	Various Artists (EMI/Virgin)
-	47	THE LOVE ALBUM	Various Artists (Telstar)
-	48	THE BLIND LEADING THE NAKED	Violent Femmes (Slash)
-	49	THE UNFORGETTABLE FIRE	U2 (Island)
-	50	THE WEDGE	Pallas (Harvest)

Whitney Houston's debut album had first charted in December 1985 when her chart-topping single *Saving All My Love For You* took off. It took its time making the Top 10, however, to finally peak at Number 2 in March after a further boost from Whitney's next hit *How Will I Know?* Public Image Ltd's set had a different title depending on which format you bought - i.e. album or cassette (the later CD was called *CD*).

March 1986

8 March 1986

last week	this week	Title	Artist
1	1	BROTHERS IN ARMS	Dire Straits (Vertigo)
6	2	NO JACKET REQUIRED	Phil Collins (Virgin)
2	3	WHITNEY HOUSTON	Whitney Houston (Arista)
4	4	ROCKY IV	Soundtrack (Scotti Brothers)
5	5	ISLAND LIFE	Grace Jones (Island)
3	6	HUNTING HIGH AND LOW	A-Ha (Warner Bros.)
8	7	BE YOURSELF TONIGHT	Eurythmics (RCA)
18	8	THE COLOUR OF SPRING	Talk Talk (EMI)
10	9	THE ULTIMATE SIN	Ozzy Osbourne (Epic)
23	10	KING OF AMERICA	Costello Show (F-Beat)
9	11	THE BROADWAY ALBUM	Barbra Streisand (CBS)
7	12	WORLD MACHINE	Level 42 (Polydor)
15	13	ONCE UPON A TIME	Simple Minds (Virgin)
20	14	JONATHAN KING'S ENTERTAINMENT USA	Various Artists (Stylus)
14	15	LUXURY OF LIFE	Five Star (Tent)
33	16	HOUNDS OF LOVE	Kate Bush (EMI)
11	17	THE DREAM OF THE BLUE TURTLES	Sting (A&M)
21	18	LITTLE CREATURES	Talking Heads (EMI)
12	19	ALBUM/CASSETTE	Public Image Limited (Virgin)
16	20	LIKE A VIRGIN	Madonna (Sire)
19	21	GO WEST/BANGS AND CRASHES	Go West (Chrysalis)
13	22	THE DANCE HITS ALBUM	Various Artists (Towerbell)
22	23	WELCOME TO THE REAL WORLD	Mr Mister (RCA)
30	24	SONGS FROM THE BIG CHAIR	Tears for Fears (Mercury)
35	25	ALONE	Nana Mouskouri (Philips)
-	26	BIG COCK	King Kurt (Stiff)
29	27	FINE YOUNG CANNIBALS	Fine Young Cannibals (London)
37	28	SUDDENLY	Billy Ocean (Jive)
-	29	FINAL VINYL	Rainbow (Polydor)
27	30	A DATE WITH ELVIS	Cramps (Big Beat)
17	31	FEARGAL SHARKEY	Feargal Sharkey (Virgin)
25	32	ROCK ME TONIGHT	Freddie Jackson (Capitol)
28	33	HIGH PRIORITY	Cherrelle (Tabu)
31	34	BACK IN THE DHSS	Half Man Half Biscuit (Probe Plus)
34	35	SEVENTH STAR	Black Sabbath (Vertigo)
48	36	THE BLIND LEADING THE NAKED	Violent Femmes (Slash)
-	37	PIECE BY PIECE	John Martyn (Island)
24	38	PROMISE	Sade (Epic)
26	39	WHO'S ZOOMIN' WHO	Aretha Franklin (Arista)
38	40	ALCHEMY – DIRE STRAITS LIVE	Dire Straits (Vertigo)
-	41	PRECIOUS MEMORIES	Ann Williamson (Emerald)
39	42	MACALLA	Clannad (RCA)
-	43	ALEXANDER O'NEAL	Alexander O'Neal (Tabu)
32	44	EASY PIECES	Lloyd Cole & the Commotions (Polydor)
41	45	THE LOVE SONGS	George Benson (K-Tel)
43	46	THE FIRST ALBUM	Madonna (Sire)
-	47	IT TAKES TWO	Juicy (Epic)
-	48	SEVEN SINGLES DEEP	Icicle Works (Beggars Banquet)
49	49	THE UNFORGETTABLE FIRE	U2 (Island)
46	50	NOW THAT'S WHAT I CALL MUSIC 6	Various Artists (EMI/Virgin)

15 March 1986

last week	this week	Title	Artist
1	1	BROTHERS IN ARMS	Dire Straits (Vertigo)
3	2	WHITNEY HOUSTON	Whitney Houston (Arista)
2	3	NO JACKET REQUIRED	Phil Collins (Virgin)
8	4	THE COLOUR OF SPRING	Talk Talk (EMI)
4	5	ROCKY IV	Soundtrack (Scotti Brothers)
14	6	JONATHAN KING'S ENTERTAINMENT USA	Various Artists (Stylus)
7	7	BE YOURSELF TONIGHT	Eurythmics (RCA)
10	8	KING OF AMERICA	Costello Show (F-Beat)
16	9	HOUNDS OF LOVE	Kate Bush (EMI)
21	10	GO WEST/BANGS AND CRASHES	Go West (Chrysalis)
17	11	THE DREAM OF THE BLUE TURTLES	Sting (A&M)
-	12	HITS FOR LOVERS	Various Artists (Epic)
6	13	HUNTING HIGH AND LOW	A-Ha (Warner Bros.)
5	14	ISLAND LIFE	Grace Jones (Island)
13	15	ONCE UPON A TIME	Simple Minds (Virgin)
18	16	LITTLE CREATURES	Talking Heads (EMI)
37	17	PIECE BY PIECE	John Martyn (Island)
11	18	THE BROADWAY ALBUM	Barbra Streisand (CBS)
12	19	WORLD MACHINE	Level 42 (Polydor)
-	20	LIVES IN THE BALANCE	Jackson Browne (Asylum)
22	21	THE DANCE HITS ALBUM	Various Artists (Towerbell)
23	22	WELCOME TO THE REAL WORLD	Mr Mister (RCA)
9	23	THE ULTIMATE SIN	Ozzy Osbourne (Epic)
25	24	ALONE	Nana Mouskouri (Philips)
-	25	BALANCE OF POWER	Electric Light Orchestra (Epic)
29	26	FINAL VINYL	Rainbow (Polydor)
26	27	BIG COCK	King Kurt (Stiff)
34	28	BACK IN THE DHSS	Half Man Half Biscuit (Probe Plus)
-	29	LIVE IN NEW YORK CITY	John Lennon (Parlophone)
35	30	SEVENTH STAR	Black Sabbath (Vertigo)
-	31	DIFFERENT LIGHT	Bangles (CBS)
-	32	MASTER OF PUPPETS	Metallica (Music For Nations)
15	33	LUXURY OF LIFE	Five Star (Tent)
19	34	ALBUM/CASSETTE	Public Image Limited (Virgin)
20	35	LIKE A VIRGIN	Madonna (Sire)
43	36	ALEXANDER O'NEAL	Alexander O'Neal (Tabu)
24	37	SONGS FROM THE BIG CHAIR	Tears for Fears (Mercury)
28	38	SUDDENLY	Billy Ocean (Jive)
30	39	A DATE WITH ELVIS	Cramps (Big Beat)
-	40	TOTAL CONTRAST	Total Contrast (London)
-	41	PASSION	William Bell (Wilbe import)
32	42	ROCK ME TONIGHT	Freddie Jackson (Capitol)
33	43	HIGH PRIORITY	Cherrelle (Tabu)
40	44	ALCHEMY – DIRE STRAITS LIVE	Dire Straits (Vertigo)
31	45	FEARGAL SHARKEY	Feargal Sharkey (Virgin)
-	46	MEETS THE MOTHERS OF PREVENTION	Frank Zappa (EMI)
-	47	NIGHT BEAT 2	Various Artists (Stylus)
41	48	PRECIOUS MEMORIES	Ann Williamson (Emerald)
38	49	PROMISE	Sade (Epic)
39	50	WHO'S ZOOMIN' WHO	Aretha Franklin (Arista)

22 March 1986

last week	this week	Title	Artist
1	1	BROTHERS IN ARMS	Dire Straits (Vertigo)
3	2	NO JACKET REQUIRED	Phil Collins (Virgin)
12	3	HITS FOR LOVERS	Various Artists (Epic)
9	4	HOUNDS OF LOVE	Kate Bush (EMI)
2	5	WHITNEY HOUSTON	Whitney Houston (Arista)
5	6	ROCKY IV	Soundtrack (Scotti Brothers)
7	7	BE YOURSELF TONIGHT	Eurythmics (RCA)
16	8	LITTLE CREATURES	Talking Heads (EMI)
4	9	THE COLOUR OF SPRING	Talk Talk (EMI)
25	10	BALANCE OF POWER	Electric Light Orchestra (Epic)
8	11	KING OF AMERICA	Costello Show (F-Beat)
6	12	JONATHAN KING'S ENTERTAINMENT USA	Various Artists (Stylus)
15	13	ONCE UPON A TIME	Simple Minds (Virgin)
36	14	ALEXANDER O'NEAL	Alexander O'Neal (Tabu/Epic)
10	15	GO WEST/BANGS AND CRASHES	Go West (Chrysalis)
18	16	THE BROADWAY ALBUM	Barbra Streisand (CBS)
13	17	HUNTING HIGH AND LOW	A-Ha (Warner Bros.)
14	18	ISLAND LIFE	Grace Jones (Island)
22	19	WELCOME TO THE REAL WORLD	Mr Mister (RCA)
31	20	DIFFERENT LIGHT	Bangles (CBS)
11	21	THE DREAM OF THE BLUE TURTLES	Sting (A&M)
17	22	PIECE BY PIECE	John Martyn (Island)
19	23	WORLD MACHINE	Level 42 (Polydor)
32	24	MASTER OF PUPPETS	Metallica (Music For Nations)
20	25	LIVES IN THE BALANCE	Jackson Browne (Asylum)
-	26	NEITHER MOSCOW NOR WASHINGTON	Redskins (Decca)
47	27	NIGHT BEAT 2	Various Artists (Stylus)
24	28	ALONE	Nana Mouskouri (Philips)
-	29	MATT BIANCO	Matt Bianco (WEA)
27	30	BIG COCK	King Kurt (Stiff)
-	31	CUTS LIKE A KNIFE	Bryan Adams (Capitol)
48	32	PRECIOUS MEMORIES	Ann Williamson (Emerald)
35	33	LIKE A VIRGIN	Madonna (Sire)
-	34	NEW YORK, NEW YORK (GREATEST HITS)	Frank Sinatra (Reprise)
26	35	FINAL VINYL	Rainbow (Polydor)
42	36	ROCK ME TONIGHT	Freddie Jackson (Capitol)
-	37	HYMNS	Huddersfield Choral Society (HMV)
38	38	SUDDENLY	Billy Ocean (Jive)
45	39	FEARGAL SHARKEY	Feargal Sharkey (Virgin)
34	40	ALBUM/CASSETTE	Public Image Limited (Virgin)
33	41	LUXURY OF LIFE	Five Star (Tent)
30	42	SEVENTH STAR	Black Sabbath (Vertigo)
-	43	THE CINEMA HITS ALBUM	Various Artists (Towerbell)
29	44	LIVE IN NEW YORK CITY	John Lennon (Parlophone)
39	45	A DATE WITH ELVIS	Cramps (Big Beat)
46	46	DAMNED BUT NOT FORGOTTEN	Damned (Dojo)
21	47	THE DANCE HITS ALBUM	Various (Towerbell)
-	48	IT TAKES TWO	Juicy (Epic)
28	49	BACK IN THE DHSS	Half Man Half Biscuit (Probe Plus)
40	50	TOTAL CONTRAST	Total Contrast (London)

Brothers In Arms' early 1986 stretch at the top of the chart lasted for exactly 3 months with no gaps - one of the longest consecutive stays of modern times. Among the albums which just failed to dislodge it in March was Phil Collins' *No Jacket Required*, now a chart resident for just over a year! ELO returned after a three-year recording absence with what would be their last Top 10 album, *Balance Of Power*.

March – April 1986

29 March 1986

last week	this week	title	artist (label)
1	1	BROTHERS IN ARMS	Dire Straits (Vertigo)
5	2	WHITNEY HOUSTON	Whitney Houston (Arista)
2	3	NO JACKET REQUIRED	Phil Collins (Virgin)
4	4	HOUNDS OF LOVE	Kate Bush (EMI)
10	5	BALANCE OF POWER	Electric Light Orchestra (Epic)
3	6	HITS FOR LOVERS	Various Artists (Epic)
6	7	ROCKY IV	Soundtrack (Scotti Brothers)
19	8	WELCOME TO THE REAL WORLD	Mr Mister (RCA)
9	9	THE COLOUR OF SPRING	Talk Talk (EMI)
-	10	HITS 4	Various Artists (CBS/WEA)
7	11	BE YOURSELF TONIGHT	Eurythmics (RCA)
14	12	ALEXANDER O'NEAL	Alexander O'Neal (Tabu)
-	13	EATEN ALIVE	Diana Ross (Capitol)
29	14	MATT BIANCO	Matt Bianco (WEA)
8	15	LITTLE CREATURES	Talking Heads (EMI)
12	16	JONATHAN KING'S ENTERTAINMENT USA	Various Artists (Stylus)
18	17	ISLAND LIFE	Grace Jones (Island)
31	18	CUTS LIKE A KNIFE	Bryan Adams (Capitol)
20	19	DIFFERENT LIGHT	Bangles (CBS)
26	20	NEITHER MOSCOW NOR WASHINGTON	Redskins (Decca)
27	21	NIGHT BEAT 2	Various Artists (Stylus)
-	22	BLACK CELEBRATION	Depeche Mode (Mute)
13	23	ONCE UPON A TIME	Simple Minds (Virgin)
17	24	HUNTING HIGH AND LOW	A-Ha (Warner Bros.)
11	25	KING OF AMERICA	Costello Show (F-Beat)
34	26	NEW YORK, NEW YORK (GREATEST HITS)	Frank Sinatra (Reprise)
16	27	THE BROADWAY ALBUM	Barbra Streisand (CBS)
25	28	LIVES IN THE BALANCE	Jackson Browne (Asylum)
49	29	BACK IN THE DHSS	Half Man Half Biscuit (Probe Plus)
-	30	STREET SOUNDS HIP HOP ELECTRO 11	Various Artists (Street Sounds)
37	31	HYMNS	Huddersfield Choral Society (HMV)
36	32	ROCK ME TONIGHT	Freddie Jackson (Capitol)
21	33	THE DREAM OF THE BLUE TURTLES	Sting (A&M)
24	34	MASTER OF PUPPETS	Metallica (Music For Nations)
-	35	9012 LIVE: THESOLOS	Yes (Atlantic)
22	36	PIECE BY PIECE	John Martyn (Island)
38	37	SUDDENLY	Billy Ocean (Jive)
47	38	THE DANCE HITS ALBUM	Various Artists (Towerbell)
23	39	WORLD MACHINE	Level 42 (Polydor)
15	40	GO WEST/BANGS AND CRASHES	Go West (Chrysalis)
45	41	A DATE WITH ELVIS	Cramps (Big Beat)
-	42	CANDY APPLE GREY	Husker Du (Warner Bros.)
48	43	IT TAKES TWO	Juicy (Epic)
50	44	TOTAL CONTRAST	Total Contrast (London)
35	45	FINAL VINYL	Rainbow (Polydor)
41	46	LUXURY OF LIFE	Five Star (Tent)
43	47	THE CINEMA HITS ALBUM	Various (Towerbell)
-	48	PAINT YOUR WAGON	Red Lorry Yellow Lorry (Red Rhino)
46	49	DAMNED BUT NOT FORGOTTEN	Damned (Dojo)
28	50	ALONE	Nana Mouskouri (Philips)

5 April 1986

last week	this week	title	artist (label)
1	1	BROTHERS IN ARMS	Dire Straits (Vertigo)
10	2	HITS 4	Various Artists (CBS/WEA)
2	3	WHITNEY HOUSTON	Whitney Houston (Arista)
11	4	BE YOURSELF TONIGHT	Eurythmics (RCA)
3	5	NO JACKET REQUIRED	Phil Collins (Virgin)
9	6	THE COLOUR OF SPRING	Talk Talk (EMI)
5	7	BALANCE OF POWER	Electric Light Orchestra (Epic)
-	8	DIRTY WORK	Rolling Stones (CBS)
22	9	BLACK CELEBRATION	Depeche Mode (Mute)
6	10	HITS FOR LOVERS	Various Artists (Epic)
8	11	WELCOME TO THE REAL WORLD	Mr Mister (RCA)
13	12	EATEN ALIVE	Diana Ross (Capitol)
4	13	HOUNDS OF LOVE	Kate Bush (EMI)
7	14	ROCKY IV	Soundtrack (Scotti Brothers)
24	15	HUNTING HIGH AND LOW	A-Ha (Warner Bros.)
30	16	STREET SOUNDS HIP HOP ELECTRO 11	Various Artists (Street Sounds)
32	17	ROCK ME TONIGHT	Freddie Jackson (Capitol)
14	18	MATT BIANCO	Matt Bianco (WEA)
31	19	HYMNS	Huddersfield Choral Society (HMV)
15	20	LITTLE CREATURES	Talking Heads (EMI)
26	21	NEW YORK, NEW YORK (GREATEST HITS)	Frank Sinatra (Reprise)
12	22	ALEXANDER O'NEAL	Alexander O'Neal (Tabu)
18	23	CUTS LIKE A KNIFE	Bryan Adams (Capitol)
20	24	NEITHER MOSCOW NOR WASHINGTON	Redskins (Decca)
23	25	ONCE UPON A TIME	Simple Minds (Virgin)
33	26	THE DREAM OF THE BLUE TURTLES	Sting (A&M)
17	27	ISLAND LIFE	Grace Jones (Island)
16	28	JONATHAN KING'S ENTERTAINMENT USA	Various Artists (Stylus)
-	29	5150	Van Halen (Warner Bros.)
-	30	MEAN BUSINESS	Firm (Atlantic)
35	31	9012 LIVE: THESOLOS	Yes (Atlantic)
-	32	PLEASE	Pet Shop Boys (Parlophone)
50	33	ALONE	Nana Mouskouri (Philips)
-	34	THE ALBUM	Mantronix (10)
19	35	DIFFERENT LIGHT	Bangles (CBS)
-	36	THIS IS BIG AUDIO DYNAMITE	Big Audio Dynamite (CBS)
34	37	MASTER OF PUPPETS	Metallica (Music For Nations)
48	38	PAINT YOUR WAGON	Red Lorry Yellow Lorry (Red Rhino)
47	39	THE CINEMA HITS ALBUM	Various Artists (Towerbell)
-	40	PHANTASMAGORIA	Damned (MCA)
28	41	LIVES IN THE BALANCE	Jackson Browne (Asylum)
25	42	KING OF AMERICA	Costello Show (F-Beat)
27	43	THE BROADWAY ALBUM	Barbra Streisand (CBS)
29	44	BACK IN THE DHSS	Half Man Half Biscuit (Probe Plus)
42	45	CANDY APPLE GREY	Husker Du (Warner Bros.)
-	46	SPORTS	Huey Lewis and the News (Chrysalis)
-	47	BIG WORLD	Joe Jackson (A&M)
21	48	NIGHT BEAT 2	Various Artists (Stylus)
-	49	MASTERS OF METAL	Various Artists (Powersaw/K-Tel)
40	50	GO WEST/BANGS AND CRASHES	Go West (Chrysalis)

12 April 1986

last week	this week	title	artist (label)
2	1	HITS 4	Various Artists (CBS/WEA)
1	2	BROTHERS IN ARMS	Dire Straits (Vertigo)
3	3	WHITNEY HOUSTON	Whitney Houston (Arista)
9	4	BLACK CELEBRATION	Depeche Mode (Mute)
11	5	WELCOME TO THE REAL WORLD	Mr Mister (RCA)
8	6	DIRTY WORK	Rolling Stones (CBS)
10	7	HITS FOR LOVERS	Various Artists (Epic)
5	8	NO JACKET REQUIRED	Phil Collins (Virgin)
12	9	EATEN ALIVE	Diana Ross (Capitol)
32	10	PLEASE	Pet Shop Boys (Parlophone)
14	11	ROCKY IV	Soundtrack (Scotti Brothers)
29	12	5150	Van Halen (Warner Bros.)
6	13	THE COLOUR OF SPRING	Talk Talk (EMI)
17	14	ROCK ME TONIGHT	Freddie Jackson (Capitol)
21	15	NEW YORK, NEW YORK (GREATEST HITS)	Frank Sinatra (Reprise)
22	16	ALEXANDER O'NEAL	Alexander O'Neal (Tabu/Epic)
25	17	ONCE UPON A TIME	Simple Minds (Virgin)
4	18	BE YOURSELF TONIGHT	Eurythmics (RCA)
13	19	HOUNDS OF LOVE	Kate Bush (EMI)
7	20	BALANCE OF POWER	Electric Light Orchestra (Epic)
19	21	HYMNS	Huddersfield Choral Society (HMV)
15	22	HUNTING HIGH AND LOW	A-Ha (Warner Bros.)
16	23	STREET SOUNDS HIP HOP ELECTRO 11	Various Artists (Street Sounds)
-	24	PARADE	Prince & the Revolution (Warner Bros.)
27	25	ISLAND LIFE	Grace Jones (Island)
26	26	THE DREAM OF THE BLUE TURTLES	Sting (A&M)
30	27	MEAN BUSINESS	Firm (Atlantic)
18	28	MATT BIANCO	Matt Bianco (WEA)
-	29	SONGS FROM THE BIG CHAIR	Tears for Fears (Mercury)
-	30	ABSOLUTE BEGINNERS	Soundtrack (Virgin)
-	31	STREET SOUNDS EDITION 16	Various Artists (Street Sounds)
40	32	PHANTASMAGORIA	Damned (MCA)
-	33	FROM LUXURY TO HEARTACHE	Culture Club (Virgin)
36	34	THIS IS BIG AUDIO DYNAMITE	Big Audio Dynamite (CBS)
35	35	DIFFERENT LIGHT	Bangles (CBS)
20	36	LITTLE CREATURES	Talking Heads (EMI)
48	37	NIGHT BEAT 2	Various Artists (Stylus)
34	38	THE ALBUM	Mantronix (10)
23	39	CUTS LIKE A KNIFE	Bryan Adams (Capitol)
39	40	THE CINEMA HITS ALBUM	Various Artists (Towerbell)
46	41	SPORTS	Huey Lewis and the News (Chrysalis)
41	42	LIVES IN THE BALANCE	Jackson Browne (Asylum)
24	43	NEITHER MOSCOW NOR WASHINGTON	Redskins (Decca)
28	44	JONATHAN KING'S ENTERTAINMENT USA	Various Artists (Stylus)
43	45	THE BROADWAY ALBUM	Barbra Streisand (CBS)
42	46	KING OF AMERICA	Costello Show (F-Beat)
50	47	GO WEST/BANGS AND CRASHES	Go West (Chrysalis)
31	48	9012 LIVE: THESOLOS	Yes (Atlantic)
47	49	BIG WORLD	Joe Jackson (A&M)
-	50	STREET SOUNDS EDITION 15	Various Artists (Street Sounds)

Acts celebrating their first UK Top 10 albums after finding singles success included Talk Talk with *The Colour Of Spring* and Mr Mister with *Welcome To The Real World*, while Depeche Mode had their sixth Top Tenner in a row with *Black Celebration*. James Brown could also claim his first hit UK album with the *Rocky IV* soundtrack, which was dominated by his hit single from the movie, *Living In America*.

19 April 1986

last week	this week		
1	1	HITS 4	Various Artists (CBS/WEA)
2	2	BROTHERS IN ARMS	Dire Straits (Vertigo)
10	3	PLEASE	Pet Shop Boys (Parlophone)
3	4	WHITNEY HOUSTON	Whitney Houston (Arista)
24	5	PARADE	Prince & the Revolution (Warner Bros.)
6	6	DIRTY WORK	Rolling Stones (CBS)
5	7	WELCOME TO THE REAL WORLD	Mr Mister (RCA)
22	8	HUNTING HIGH AND LOW	A-Ha (Warner Bros.)
33	9	FROM LUXURY TO HEARTACHE	Culture Club (Virgin)
12	10	5150	Van Halen (Warner Bros.)
8	11	NO JACKET REQUIRED	Phil Collins (Virgin)
7	12	HITS FOR LOVERS	Various Artists (Epic)
15	13	NEW YORK, NEW YORK (GREATEST HITS)	Frank Sinatra (Reprise)
30	14	ABSOLUTE BEGINNERS	Soundtrack (Virgin)
18	15	BE YOURSELF TONIGHT	Eurythmics (RCA)
-	16	RENDEZ-VOUS	Jean Michel Jarre (Polydor)
31	17	STREET SOUNDS EDITION 16	Various Artists (Street Sounds)
4	18	BLACK CELEBRATION	Depeche Mode (Mute)
17	19	ONCE UPON A TIME	Simple Minds (Virgin)
16	20	ALEXANDER O'NEAL	Alexander O'Neal (Tabu)
11	21	ROCKY IV	Soundtrack (Scotti Brothers)
9	22	EATEN ALIVE	Diana Ross (Capitol)
-	23	ANIMAL MAGIC	Blow Monkeys (RCA)
34	24	THIS IS BIG AUDIO DYNAMITE	Big Audio Dynamite (CBS)
13	25	THE COLOUR OF SPRING	Talk Talk (EMI)
26	26	THE DREAM OF THE BLUE TURTLES	Sting (A&M)
-	27	LITTLE MISS DANGEROUS	Ted Nugent (WEA)
49	28	BIG WORLD	Joe Jackson (A&M)
19	29	HOUNDS OF LOVE	Kate Bush (EMI)
-	30	HEART TO HEART	Various Artists (K-Tel)
-	31	SHALAMAR: THE GREATEST HITS	Shalamar (Stylus)
-	32	WORLD MACHINE	Level 42 (Polydor)
21	33	HYMNS	Huddersfield Choral Society (HMV)
32	34	PHANTASMAGORIA	Damned (MCA)
14	35	ROCK ME TONIGHT	Freddie Jackson (Capitol)
23	36	STREET SOUNDS HIP HOP ELECTRO 11	Various Artists (Street Sounds)
27	37	MEAN BUSINESS	Firm (Atlantic)
-	38	TURBO	Judas Priest (CBS)
-	39	CONTROL	Janet Jackson (A&M)
-	40	LIKE A VIRGIN	Madonna (Sire)
-	41	THE TV ALBUM TWO	Various Artists (Towerbell)
-	42	AS THE BAND TURNS	Atlantic Star (A&M)
38	43	THE ALBUM	Mantronix (10)
20	44	BALANCE OF POWER	Electric Light Orchestra (Epic)
36	45	LITTLE CREATURES	Talking Heads (EMI)
-	46	HOME OF THE BRAVE	Laurie Anderson (Warner Bros.)
37	47	NIGHT BEAT 2	Various Artists (Stylus)
35	48	DIFFERENT LIGHT	Bangles (CBS)
-	49	LUXURY OF LIFE	Five Star (Tent)
-	50	SUZANNE VEGA	Suzanne Vega (A&M)

26 April 1986

1	1	HITS 4	Various Artists (CBS/WEA)
2	2	BROTHERS IN ARMS	Dire Straits (Vertigo)
5	3	PARADE	Prince & the Revolution (Warner Bros.)
4	4	WHITNEY HOUSTON	Whitney Houston (Arista)
3	5	PLEASE	Pet Shop Boys (Parlophone)
7	6	WELCOME TO THE REAL WORLD	Mr Mister (RCA)
11	7	NO JACKET REQUIRED	Phil Collins (Virgin)
8	8	HUNTING HIGH AND LOW	A-Ha (Warner Bros.)
10	9	5150	Van Halen (Warner Bros.)
-	10	STREET LIFE - 20 GREAT HITS	Bryan Ferry & Roxy Music (EG)
6	11	DIRTY WORK	Rolling Stones (CBS)
19	12	ONCE UPON A TIME	Simple Minds (Virgin)
16	13	RENDEZ-VOUS	Jean Michel Jarre (Polydor)
24	14	THIS IS BIG AUDIO DYNAMITE	Big Audio Dynamite (CBS)
38	15	TURBO	Judas Priest (CBS)
-	16	TINDERBOX	Siouxsie & the Banshees (Wonderland)
12	17	HITS FOR LOVERS	Various Artists (Epic)
-	18	VICTORIALAND	Cocteau Twins (4AD)
31	19	SHALAMAR: THE GREATEST HITS	Shalamar (Stylus)
14	20	ABSOLUTE BEGINNERS	Soundtrack (Virgin)
23	21	ANIMAL MAGIC	Blow Monkeys (RCA)
9	22	FROM LUXURY TO HEARTACHE	Culture Club (Virgin)
30	23	HEART TO HEART	Various Artists (K-Tel)
17	24	STREET SOUNDS EDITION 16	Various Artists (Street Sounds)
25	25	ON THE BEACH	Chris Rea (Magnet)
18	26	BLACK CELEBRATION	Depeche Mode (Mute)
21	27	ROCKY IV	Soundtrack (Scotti Brothers)
15	28	BE YOURSELF TONIGHT	Eurythmics (RCA)
29	29	HOUNDS OF LOVE	Kate Bush (EMI)
-	30	HIPSWAY	Hipsway (Mercury)
-	31	THE MAN AND HIS MUSIC	Sam Cooke (RCA)
-	32	LIKE A ROCK	Bob Seger (Capitol)
25	33	THE COLOUR OF SPRING	Talk Talk (EMI)
20	34	ALEXANDER O'NEAL	Alexander O'Neal (Tabu)
35	35	ROCK ME TONIGHT	Freddie Jackson (Capitol)
-	36	IN VISIBLE SILENCE	Art Of Noise (China)
50	37	SUZANNE VEGA	Suzanne Vega (A&M)
13	38	NEW YORK, NEW YORK (GREATEST HITS)	Frank Sinatra (Reprise)
39	39	CONTROL	Janet Jackson (A&M)
28	40	BIG WORLD	Joe Jackson (A&M)
-	41	ROCK ANTHEMS VOLUME TWO	Various (K-Tel)
-	42	GO WEST/BANGS AND CRASHES	Go West (Chrysalis)
22	43	EATEN ALIVE	Diana Ross (Capitol)
26	44	THE DREAM OF THE BLUE TURTLES	Sting (A&M)
27	45	LITTLE MISS DANGEROUS	Ted Nugent (WEA)
40	46	LIKE A VIRGIN	Madonna (Sire)
-	47	IT TAKES TWO	Juicy (Epic)
43	48	THE ALBUM	Mantronix (10)
41	49	THE TV ALBUM TWO	Various Artists (Towerbell)
-	50	CHILDREN OF THE NIGHT	52nd Street (10/)

3 May 1986

10	1	STREET LIFE - 20 GREAT HITS	Bryan Ferry & Roxy Music (EG)
1	2	HITS 4	Various Artists (CBS/WEA)
2	3	BROTHERS IN ARMS	Dire Straits (Vertigo)
4	4	WHITNEY HOUSTON	Whitney Houston (Arista)
5	5	PLEASE	Pet Shop Boys (Parlophone)
16	6	TINDERBOX	Siouxsie & the Banshees (Wonderland)
8	7	HUNTING HIGH AND LOW	A-Ha (Warner Bros.)
19	8	SHALAMAR: THE GREATEST HITS	Shalamar (Stylus)
20	9	ABSOLUTE BEGINNERS	Soundtrack (Virgin)
3	10	PARADE	Prince & the Revolution (Warner Bros.)
25	11	ON THE BEACH	Chris Rea (Magnet)
13	12	RENDEZ-VOUS	Jean Michel Jarre (Polydor)
6	13	WELCOME TO THE REAL WORLD	Mr Mister (RCA)
18	14	VICTORIALAND	Cocteau Twins (4AD)
31	15	THE MAN AND HIS MUSIC	Sam Cooke (RCA)
16	16	ONCE UPON A TIME	Simple Minds (Virgin)
23	17	HEART TO HEART	Various Artists (K-Tel)
7	18	NO JACKET REQUIRED	Phil Collins (Virgin)
9	19	5150	Van Halen (Warner Bros.)
14	20	THIS IS BIG AUDIO DYNAMITE	Big Audio Dynamite (CBS)
36	21	IN VISIBLE SILENCE	Art Of Noise (China)
37	22	SUZANNE VEGA	Suzanne Vega (A&M)
11	23	DIRTY WORK	Rolling Stones (CBS)
17	24	HITS FOR LOVERS	Various Artists (Epic)
32	25	LIKE A ROCK	Bob Seger (Capitol)
21	26	ANIMAL MAGIC	Blow Monkeys (RCA)
49	27	THE TV ALBUM TWO	Various Artists (Towerbell)
15	28	TURBO	Judas Priest (CBS)
24	29	STREET SOUNDS EDITION 16	Various Artists (Street Sounds)
30	30	HIPSWAY	Hipsway (Mercury)
-	31	WORLD MACHINE	Level 42 (Polydor)
27	32	ROCKY IV	Soundtrack (Scotti Brothers)
-	33	BACK TO THE CENTRE	Paul Brady (Mercury)
-	34	FALCO 3	Falco (A&M)
41	35	ROCK ANTHEMS VOLUME TWO	Various (K-Tel)
26	36	BLACK CELEBRATION	Depeche Mode (Mute)
35	37	ROCK ME TONIGHT	Freddie Jackson (Capitol)
-	38	DO ME BABY	Meli'sa Morgan (Capitol)
33	39	THE COLOUR OF SPRING	Talk Talk (EMI)
28	40	BE YOURSELF TONIGHT	Eurythmics (RCA)
-	41	LITTLE CREATURES	Talking Heads (EMI)
22	42	FROM LUXURY TO HEARTACHE	Culture Club (Virgin)
-	43	QUEEN'S GREATEST HITS	Queen (EMI)
34	44	ALEXANDER O'NEAL	Alexander O'Neal (Tabu)
46	45	LIKE A VIRGIN	Madonna (Sire)
29	46	HOUNDS OF LOVE	Kate Bush (EMI)
-	47	SONGS FROM THE BIG CHAIR	Tears for Fears (Mercury)
39	48	CONTROL	Janet Jackson (A&M)
43	49	EATEN ALIVE	Diana Ross (Capitol)
-	50	PORTRAIT	Diana Ross (Telstar)

In the absence of new recordings either by Bryan Ferry or his erstwhile band Roxy Music, the TV-promoted compilation *Street Life* filled the gap effectively by combining for the first time the hit recordings by both band and soloist. Also scoring with hits compilations were Frank Sinatra (his sixth such collection to make the charts) and Shalamar - the latter group's compilation also being TV-advertised.

May 1986

10 May 1986

last week	this week	Title	Artist
1	1	STREET LIFE - 20 GREAT HITS	Bryan Ferry & Roxy Music (EG)
4	2	WHITNEY HOUSTON	Whitney Houston (Arista)
3	3	BROTHERS IN ARMS	Dire Straits (Vertigo)
2	4	HITS 4	Various Artists (CBS/WEA)
6	5	TINDERBOX	Siouxsie & the Banshees (Wonderland)
8	6	SHALAMAR: THE GREATEST HITS	Shalamar (Stylus)
15	7	THE MAN AND HIS MUSIC	Sam Cooke (RCA)
14	8	VICTORIALAND	Cocteau Twins (4AD)
7	9	HUNTING HIGH AND LOW	A-Ha (Warner Bros.)
5	10	PLEASE	Pet Shop Boys (Parlophone)
11	11	ON THE BEACH	Chris Rea (Magnet)
16	12	ONCE UPON A TIME	Simple Minds (Virgin)
19	13	5150	Van Halen (Warner Bros.)
12	14	RENDEZ-VOUS	Jean Michel Jarre (Polydor)
10	15	PARADE	Prince & the Revolution (Warner Bros.)
18	16	NO JACKET REQUIRED	Phil Collins (Virgin)
22	17	SUZANNE VEGA	Suzanne Vega (A&M)
13	18	WELCOME TO THE REAL WORLD	Mr Mister (RCA)
17	19	HEART TO HEART	Various Artists (K-Tel)
20	20	THIS IS BIG AUDIO DYNAMITE	Big Audio Dynamite (CBS)
31	21	WORLD MACHINE	Level 42 (Polydor)
23	22	DIRTY WORK	Rolling Stones (CBS)
35	23	ROCK ANTHEMS VOLUME TWO	Various (K-Tel)
-	24	TRUTHDARE DOUBLEDARE	Bronski Beat (London)
-	25	RAPTURE	Anita Baker (Elektra)
-	26	LUXURY OF LIFE	Five Star (Tent)
24	27	HITS FOR LOVERS	Various Artists (Epic)
21	28	IN VISIBLE SILENCE	Art Of Noise (China)
36	29	BLACK CELEBRATION	Depeche Mode (Mute)
26	30	ANIMAL MAGIC	Blow Monkeys (RCA)
9	31	ABSOLUTE BEGINNERS	Soundtrack (Virgin)
27	32	THE TV ALBUM TWO	Various Artists (Towerbell)
-	33	SANDS OF TIME	SOS Band (Tabu)
46	34	HOUNDS OF LOVE	Kate Bush (EMI)
32	35	ROCKY IV	Soundtrack (Scotti Brothers)
25	36	LIKE A ROCK	Bob Seger (Capitol)
48	37	CONTROL	Janet Jackson (A&M)
28	38	TURBO	Judas Priest (CBS)
-	39	RUSSIAN ROULETTE	Accept (Portrait)
-	40	GETTING THE HOLY GHOST ACROSS	Bill Nelson (Portrait)
49	41	EATEN ALIVE	Diana Ross (Capitol)
44	42	ALEXANDER O'NEAL	Alexander O'Neal (Tabu)
33	43	BACK TO THE CENTRE	Paul Brady (Mercury)
-	44	THE OTHER SIDE OF LIFE	Moody Blues (Threshold)
-	45	THE COLLECTION	Earth Wind & Fire (K-Tel)
30	46	HIPSWAY	Hipsway (Mercury)
-	47	OUT OF AFRICA	Soundtrack (MCA)
-	48	BACK IN THE DHSS	Half Man Half Biscuit (Probe Plus)
34	49	FALCO 3	Falco (A&M)
-	50	MOVIN'	Jennifer Rush (CBS)

17 May 1986

last week	this week	Title	Artist
1	1	STREET LIFE - 20 GREAT HITS	Bryan Ferry & Roxy Music (EG)
3	2	BROTHERS IN ARMS	Dire Straits (Vertigo)
6	3	SHALAMAR: THE GREATEST HITS	Shalamar (Stylus)
2	4	WHITNEY HOUSTON	Whitney Houston (Arista)
12	5	ONCE UPON A TIME	Simple Minds (Virgin)
4	6	HITS 4	Various Artists (CBS/WEA)
21	7	WORLD MACHINE	Level 42 (Polydor)
9	8	HUNTING HIGH AND LOW	A-Ha (Warner Bros.)
7	9	THE MAN AND HIS MUSIC	Sam Cooke (RCA)
16	10	ON THE BEACH	Chris Rea (Magnet)
16	11	NO JACKET REQUIRED	Phil Collins (Virgin)
10	12	PLEASE	Pet Shop Boys (Parlophone)
17	13	SUZANNE VEGA	Suzanne Vega (A&M)
-	14	UTTERLY UTTERLY LIVE!	Comic Relief (Comic Relief/WEA)
19	15	HEART TO HEART	Various Artists (K-Tel)
-	16	HOME AND ABROAD	Style Council (Polydor)
45	17	THE COLLECTION	Earth Wind & Fire (K-Tel)
14	18	RENDEZ-VOUS	Jean Michel Jarre (Polydor)
26	19	LUXURY OF LIFE	Five Star (Tent)
24	20	TRUTHDARE DOUBLEDARE	Bronski Beat (London)
13	21	5150	Van Halen (Warner Bros.)
8	22	VICTORIALAND	Cocteau Twins (4AD)
5	23	TINDERBOX	Siouxsie & the Banshees (Wonderland)
15	24	PARADE	Prince & the Revolution (Warner Bros.)
20	25	THIS IS BIG AUDIO DYNAMITE	Big Audio Dynamite (CBS)
25	26	RAPTURE	Anita Baker (Elektra)
-	27	LOVE ZONE	Billy Ocean (Jive)
18	28	WELCOME TO THE REAL WORLD	Mr Mister (RCA)
33	29	SANDS OF TIME	SOS Band (Tabu)
31	30	ABSOLUTE BEGINNERS	Soundtrack (Virgin)
34	31	HOUNDS OF LOVE	Kate Bush (EMI)
30	32	ANIMAL MAGIC	Blow Monkeys (RCA)
36	33	LIKE A ROCK	Bob Seger (Capitol)
-	34	DO ME BABY	Meli'sa Morgan (Capitol)
37	35	CONTROL	Janet Jackson (A&M)
48	36	BACK IN THE DHSS	Half Man Half Biscuit (Probe Plus)
27	37	HITS FOR LOVERS	Various Artists (Epic)
32	38	THE TV ALBUM TWO	Various Artists (Towerbell)
-	39	DIFFERENT LIGHT	Bangles (CBS)
-	40	HEART	Heart (Capitol)
-	41	DAVE CLARK'S TIME	Various Artists (EMI)
28	42	IN VISIBLE SILENCE	Art Of Noise (China)
43	43	BACK TO THE CENTRE	Paul Brady (Mercury)
46	44	HIPSWAY	Hipsway (Mercury)
-	45	QUEEN'S GREATEST HITS	Queen (EMI)
-	46	ROCK ME TONIGHT	Freddie Jackson (Capitol)
49	47	FALCO 3	Falco (A&M)
-	48	LISTEN LIKE THIEVES	INXS (Mercury)
22	49	DIRTY WORK	Rolling Stones (CBS)
29	50	BLACK CELEBRATION	Depeche Mode (Mute)

24 May 1986

last week	this week	Title	Artist
1	1	STREET LIFE - 20 GREAT HITS	Bryan Ferry & Roxy Music (EG)
2	2	BROTHERS IN ARMS	Dire Straits (Vertigo)
16	3	HOME AND ABROAD	Style Council (Polydor)
27	4	LOVE ZONE	Billy Ocean (Jive)
4	5	WHITNEY HOUSTON	Whitney Houston (Arista)
17	6	THE COLLECTION	Earth Wind & Fire (K-Tel)
3	7	SHALAMAR'S GREATEST HITS	Shalamar (Stylus)
5	8	ONCE UPON A TIME	Simple Minds (Virgin)
29	9	SANDS OF TIME	SOS Band (Tabu)
7	10	WORLD MACHINE	Level 42 (Polydor)
6	11	HITS 4	Various Artists (CBS/WEA)
14	12	UTTERLY UTTERLY LIVE!	Comic Relief (Comic Relief/WEA)
-	13	PRINCESS	Princess (Supreme)
21	14	5150	Van Halen (Warner Bros.)
13	15	SUZANNE VEGA	Suzanne Vega (A&M)
9	16	THE MAN AND HIS MUSIC	Sam Cooke (RCA)
11	17	NO JACKET REQUIRED	Phil Collins (Virgin)
8	18	HUNTING HIGH AND LOW	A-Ha (Warner Bros.)
15	19	HEART TO HEART	Various Artists (K-Tel)
-	20	RAISED ON RADIO	Journey (CBS)
10	21	ON THE BEACH	Chris Rea (Magnet)
12	22	PLEASE	Pet Shop Boys (Parlophone)
-	23	SECRET DREAMS AND FORBIDDEN FIRE	Bonnie Tyler (CBS)
20	24	TRUTHDARE DOUBLEDARE	Bronski Beat (London)
41	25	DAVE CLARK'S TIME	Various Artists (EMI)
28	26	WELCOME TO THE REAL WORLD	Mr Mister (RCA)
22	27	VICTORIALAND	Cocteau Twins (4AD)
18	28	RENDEZ-VOUS	Jean Michel Jarre (Polydor)
19	29	LUXURY OF LIFE	Five Star (Tent)
26	30	RAPTURE	Anita Baker (Elektra)
31	31	HOUNDS OF LOVE	Kate Bush (EMI)
-	32	THE FINAL FRONTIER	Keel (Vertigo)
35	33	CONTROL	Janet Jackson (A&M)
36	34	BACK IN THE DHSS	Half Man Half Biscuit (Probe Plus)
-	35	URBAN BEACHES	Cactus World News (MCA)
-	36	MOONLIGHT SHADOWS	Shadows (Polydor)
32	37	ANIMAL MAGIC	Blow Monkeys (RCA)
-	38	GUN SHY	Screaming Blue Messiahs (WEA)
23	39	TINDERBOX	Siouxsie & the Banshees (Wonderland)
24	40	PARADE	Prince & the Revolution (Warner Bros.)
25	41	THIS IS BIG AUDIO DYNAMITE	Big Audio Dynamite (CBS)
-	42	THE WINNER IN YOU	Patti LaBelle (MCA)
-	43	MANIC POP THRILL	That Petrol Emotion (Demon)
-	44	SPEED KILLS II	Various Artists (Under One Flag)
-	45	BOXED SET	Velvet Underground (Polydor)
30	46	ABSOLUTE BEGINNERS	Soundtrack (Virgin)
34	47	DO ME BABY	Meli'sa Morgan (Capitol)
42	48	IN VISIBLE SILENCE	Art Of Noise (China)
44	49	HIPSWAY	Hipsway (Mercury)
45	50	QUEEN'S GREATEST HITS	Queen (EMI)

Sam Cooke's *The Man And His Music*, its profile boosted by the recent Number 2 single success of the 21-years-dead singer with *Wonderful World* (itself attributable to exposure on a Levi's Jeans TV ad), was a double album anthologising the biggest selection available to date of Cooke's hit recordings from the 1950s and '60s. Ironically, this was his only album ever to make the UK chart, never mind the Top 10!

31 May 1986

last week	this week	Title	Artist (Label)
1	1	STREET LIFE - 20 GREAT HITS	Bryan Ferry & Roxy Music (EG)
2	2	BROTHERS IN ARMS	Dire Straits (Vertigo)
4	3	LOVE ZONE	Billy Ocean (Jive)
-	4	SO	Peter Gabriel (Virgin)
3	5	HOME AND ABROAD	Style Council (Polydor)
6	6	THE COLLECTION	Earth Wind & Fire (K-Tel)
10	7	WORLD MACHINE	Level 42 (Polydor)
5	8	WHITNEY HOUSTON	Whitney Houston (Arista)
18	9	HUNTING HIGH AND LOW	A-Ha (Warner Bros.)
11	10	HITS 4	Various Artists (CBS/WEA)
-	11	PICTURE BOOK	Simply Red (Elektra)
20	12	RAISED ON RADIO	Journey (CBS)
16	13	THE MAN AND HIS MUSIC	Sam Cooke (RCA)
8	14	ONCE UPON A TIME	Simple Minds (Virgin)
36	15	MOONLIGHT SHADOWS	Shadows (Polydor)
9	16	SANDS OF TIME	SOS Band (Tabu)
7	17	SHALAMAR: THE GREATEST HITS	Shalamar (Stylus)
21	18	ON THE BEACH	Chris Rea (Magnet)
13	19	PRINCESS	Princess (Supreme)
-	20	STANDING ON THE BEACH - THE SINGLES	Cure (Fiction)
12	21	UTTERLY UTTERLY LIVE!	Comic Relief (Comic Relief/WEA)
29	22	LUXURY OF LIFE	Five Star (Tent)
-	23	BANGS AND CRASHES	Go West (Chrysalis)
-	24	LET'S HEAR IT FROM THE GIRLS	Various Artists (Stylus)
22	25	PLEASE	Pet Shop Boys (Parlophone)
-	26	SLEIGHT OF HAND	Joan Armatrading (A&M)
42	27	THE WINNER IN YOU	Patti LaBelle (MCA)
14	28	5150	Van Halen (Warner Bros.)
-	29	ANIMAL BOY	Ramones (Beggers Banquet)
15	30	SUZANNE VEGA	Suzanne Vega (A&M)
17	31	NO JACKET REQUIRED	Phil Collins (Virgin)
33	32	CONTROL	Janet Jackson (A&M)
26	33	WELCOME TO THE REAL WORLD	Mr Mister (RCA)
25	34	DAVE CLARK'S TIME	Various Artists (EMI)
41	35	THIS IS BIG AUDIO DYNAMITE	Big Audio Dynamite (CBS)
37	36	ANIMAL MAGIC	Blow Monkeys (RCA)
35	37	URBAN BEACHES	Cactus World News (MCA)
-	38	MISTRIAL	Lou Reed (RCA)
27	39	VICTORIALAND	Cocteau Twins (4AD)
39	40	TINDERBOX	Siouxsie & the Banshees (Wonderland)
19	41	HEART TO HEART	Various Artists (K-Tel)
40	42	PARADE	Prince & the Revolution (Warner Bros.)
24	43	TRUTHDARE DOUBLEDARE	Bronski Beat (London)
23	44	SECRET DREAMS AND FORBIDDEN FIRE	Bonnie Tyler (CBS)
-	45	ALCHEMY – DIRE STRAITS LIVE	Dire Straits (Vertigo)
31	46	HOUNDS OF LOVE	Kate Bush (EMI)
43	47	MANIC POP THRILL	That Petrol Emotion (Demon)
48	48	IN VISIBLE SILENCE	Art Of Noise (China)
-	49	HEADED FOR THE FUTURE	Neil Diamond (CBS)
-	50	SISTERS ARE DOIN' IT	Various Artists (Towerbell)

7 June 1986

Title	Artist (Label)
4 1 SO	Peter Gabriel (Virgin)
1 2 STREET LIFE - 20 GREAT HITS	Bryan Ferry & Roxy Music (EG)
20 3 STANDING ON THE BEACH - THE SINGLES	Cure (Fiction)
2 4 BROTHERS IN ARMS	Dire Straits (Vertigo)
11 5 PICTURE BOOK	Simply Red (Elektra)
3 6 LOVE ZONE	Billy Ocean (Jive)
7 7 WORLD MACHINE	Level 42 (Polydor)
6 8 THE COLLECTION	Earth Wind & Fire (K-Tel)
23 9 BANGS AND CRASHES	Go West (Chrysalis)
8 10 WHITNEY HOUSTON	Whitney Houston (Arista)
13 11 THE MAN AND HIS MUSIC	Sam Cooke (RCA)
28 12 5150	Van Halen (Warner Bros.)
14 13 ONCE UPON A TIME	Simple Minds (Virgin)
18 14 ON THE BEACH	Chris Rea (Magnet)
- 15 WHO MADE WHO	AC/DC (Atlantic)
10 16 HITS 4	Various Artists (CBS/WEA)
9 17 HUNTING HIGH AND LOW	A-Ha (Warner Bros.)
25 18 PLEASE	Pet Shop Boys (Parlophone)
5 19 HOME AND ABROAD	Style Council (Polydor)
27 20 THE WINNER IN YOU	Patti LaBelle (MCA)
12 21 RAISED ON RADIO	Journey (CBS)
21 22 UTTERLY UTTERLY LIVE!	Comic Relief (Comic Relief/WEA)
17 23 SHALAMAR: THE GREATEST HITS	Shalamar (Stylus)
29 24 ANIMAL BOY	Ramones (Beggers Banquet)
15 25 MOONLIGHT SHADOWS	Shadows (Polydor)
24 26 LET'S HEAR IT FROM THE GIRLS	Various Artists (Stylus)
38 27 MISTRIAL	Lou Reed (RCA)
33 28 WELCOME TO THE REAL WORLD	Mr Mister (RCA)
16 29 SANDS OF TIME	SOS Band (Tabu)
19 30 PRINCESS	Princess (Supreme)
31 31 NO JACKET REQUIRED	Phil Collins (Virgin)
22 32 LUXURY OF LIFE	Five Star (Tent)
30 33 SUZANNE VEGA	Suzanne Vega (A&M)
- 34 THE COLOUR OF SPRING	Talk Talk (EMI)
26 35 SLEIGHT OF HAND	Joan Armatrading (A&M)
50 36 SISTERS ARE DOIN' IT	Various Artists (Towerbell)
- 37 QUEEN'S GREATEST HITS	Queen (EMI)
46 38 HOUNDS OF LOVE	Kate Bush (EMI)
- 39 INTO THE LIGHT	Chris DeBurgh (A&M)
- 40 WHERE YOU GONNA BE TONIGHT?	Willie Collins (Capitol)
35 41 THIS IS BIG AUDIO DYNAMITE	Big Audio Dynamite (CBS)
49 42 HEADED FOR THE FUTURE	Neil Diamond (CBS)
37 43 URBAN BEACHES	Cactus World News (MCA)
39 44 VICTORIALAND	Cocteau Twins (4AD)
47 45 MANIC POP THRILL	That Petrol Emotion (Demon)
- 46 RIPTIDE	Robert Palmer (Island)
32 47 CONTROL	Janet Jackson (A&M)
34 48 DAVE CLARK'S TIME	Various Artists (EMI)
36 49 ANIMAL MAGIC	Blow Monkeys (RCA)
43 50 TRUTHDARE DOUBLEDARE	Bronski Beat (London)

14 June 1986

Title	Artist (Label)
1 1 SO	Peter Gabriel (Virgin)
5 2 PICTURE BOOK	Simply Red (Elektra)
2 3 STREET LIFE - 20 GREAT HITS	Bryan Ferry & Roxy Music (EG)
3 4 STANDING ON THE BEACH - THE SINGLES	Cure (Fiction)
4 5 BROTHERS IN ARMS	Dire Straits (Vertigo)
7 6 WORLD MACHINE	Level 42 (Polydor)
9 7 BANGS AND CRASHES	Go West (Chrysalis)
39 8 INTO THE LIGHT	Chris DeBurgh (A&M)
6 9 LOVE ZONE	Billy Ocean (Jive)
- 10 A KIND OF MAGIC	Queen (EMI)
15 11 WHO MADE WHO	AC/DC (Atlantic)
10 12 WHITNEY HOUSTON	Whitney Houston (Arista)
8 13 THE COLLECTION	Earth Wind & Fire (K-Tel)
11 14 THE MAN AND HIS MUSIC	Sam Cooke (RCA)
25 15 MOONLIGHT SHADOWS	Shadows (Polydor)
16 16 PLEASE	Pet Shop Boys (Parlophone)
17 17 HUNTING HIGH AND LOW	A-Ha (Warner Bros.)
13 18 ONCE UPON A TIME	Simple Minds (Virgin)
14 19 ON THE BEACH	Chris Rea (Magnet)
33 20 SUZANNE VEGA	Suzanne Vega (A&M)
21 21 RAISED ON RADIO	Journey (CBS)
- 22 UPFRONT1	Various Artists (Serious)
31 23 NO JACKET REQUIRED	Phil Collins (Virgin)
32 24 LUXURY OF LIFE	Five Star (Tent)
23 25 SHALAMAR: THE GREATEST HITS	Shalamar (Stylus)
12 26 5150	Van Halen (Warner Bros.)
20 27 THE WINNER IN YOU	Patti LaBelle (MCA)
30 28 PRINCESS	Princess (Supreme)
24 29 ANIMAL BOY	Ramones (Beggers Banquet)
34 30 THE COLOUR OF SPRING	Talk Talk (EMI)
47 31 CONTROL	Janet Jackson (A&M)
19 32 HOME AND ABROAD	Style Council (Polydor)
29 33 SANDS OF TIME	SOS Band (Tabu)
16 34 HITS 4	Various Artists (CBS/WEA)
22 35 UTTERLY UTTERLY LIVE!	Comic Relief (Comic Relief/WEA)
26 36 LET'S HEAR IT FROM THE GIRLS	Various Artists (Stylus)
- 37 MARVIN GAYE'S GREATEST HITS	Marvin Gaye (Telstar)
41 38 THIS IS BIG AUDIO DYNAMITE	Big Audio Dynamite (CBS)
- 39 RAPTURE	Anita Baker (Elektra)
43 40 URBAN BEACHES	Cactus World News (MCA)
27 41 MISTRIAL	Lou Reed (RCA)
35 42 SLEIGHT OF HAND	Joan Armatrading (A&M)
38 43 HOUNDS OF LOVE	Kate Bush (EMI)
28 44 WELCOME TO THE REAL WORLD	Mr Mister (RCA)
46 45 RIPTIDE	Robert Palmer (Island)
44 46 VICTORIALAND	Cocteau Twins (4AD)
- 47 BE YOURSELF TONIGHT	Eurythmics (RCA)
- 48 SECRET DREAMS AND FORBIDDEN FIRE	Bonnie Tyler (CBS)
- 49 LITTLE CREATURES	Talking Heads (EMI)
- 50 DIRTY WORK	Rolling Stones (CBS)

Seven albums into his solo career (including his soundtrack set for the film *Birdy*), Peter Gabriel scored his all-time biggest seller with *So* (which was only his third album - again including the soundtrack - not to be titled *Peter Gabriel*!) A vital factor in the initial success of this set, which by 1992 would be Virgin Records' eighth best-seller of all time, was the single *Sledgehammer* and its award-winning video.

June – July 1986

Genesis replaced their former lead singer Peter Gabriel at Number 1 in typically swift chart-topping style with *Invisible Touch* (though the title track had failed to get anywhere near Gabriel's *Sledgehammer* in the singles chart). Both acts, in the process of this exchange, kept Queen to another Number 2 album with *A Kind Of Magic*. Meanwhile, almost unnoticed at the foot of the chart, Erasure made a quiet debut.

July 1986

12 July 1986

last week	this week		
1	1	INVISIBLE TOUCH	Genesis (Charisma)
3	2	SO	Peter Gabriel (Virgin)
2	3	A KIND OF MAGIC	Queen (EMI)
-	4	TRUE BLUE	Madonna (Sire)
10	5	LONDON 0 - HULL 4	Housemartins (Go! Discs)
4	6	THE QUEEN IS DEAD	Smiths (Rough Trade)
5	7	PICTURE BOOK	Simply Red (Elektra)
19	8	EVERY BEAT OF MY HEART	Rod Stewart (Warner Bros.)
-	9	REVENGE	Eurythmics (RCA)
12	10	BRING ON THE NIGHT	Sting (A&M)
16	11	SUZANNE VEGA	Suzanne Vega (A&M)
6	12	BROTHERS IN ARMS	Dire Straits (Vertigo)
-	13	INTERMISSION	Dio (Vertigo)
18	14	INTO THE LIGHT	Chris DeBurgh (A&M)
8	15	HUNTING HIGH AND LOW	A-Ha (Warner Bros.)
-	16	BACK IN THE HIGH LIFE	Stevie Winwood (Island)
11	17	WHITNEY HOUSTON	Whitney Houston (Arista)
13	18	RIPTIDE	Robert Palmer (Island)
7	19	STREET LIFE - 20 GREAT HITS	Bryan Ferry & Roxy Music (EG)
24	20	WORLD MACHINE	Level 42 (Polydor)
22	21	ONCE UPON A TIME	Simple Minds (Virgin)
49	22	STANDING ON THE BEACH - THE SINGLES	Cure (Fiction)
9	23	LOVE ZONE	Billy Ocean (Jive)
17	24	PLEASE	Pet Shop Boys (Parlophone)
14	25	MOONLIGHT SHADOWS	Shadows (Polydor)
15	26	THE MAN AND HIS MUSIC	Sam Cooke (RCA)
-	27	CASHFLOW	Cashflow (Club)
-	28	LABYRINTH - ORIGINAL SOUNDTRACK	David Bowie (EMI America)
23	29	BANGS AND CRASHES	Go West (Chrysalis)
-	30	GIANT	Woodentops (Rough Trade)
35	31	POOLSIDE	Nu Shooz (Atlantic)
28	32	STREET SOUNDS ELECTRO 12	Various Artists (Street Sounds)
41	33	HEADLINES	Midnight Star (MCA)
20	34	UPFRONT1	Various Artists (Serious)
50	35	DANCE HITS 2	Various Artists (Towerbell)
30	36	THE WINNER IN YOU	Patti LaBelle (MCA)
47	37	WHEREYOU GONNA BE TONIGHT?	Willie Collins (Capitol)
-	38	TO THE TOP	Aswad (Simba)
31	39	NO JACKET REQUIRED	Phil Collins (Virgin)
26	40	ON THE BEACH	Chris Rea (Magnet)
-	41	SHALAMAR: THE GREATEST HITS	Shalamar (Stylus)
-	42	PRINCESS	Princess (Supreme)
-	43	BEST OF THE REAL THING	Real Thing (PRT)
32	44	BORN SANDY DEVOTIONAL	Triffids (Hot)
33	45	WHO MADE WHO	AC/DC (Atlantic)
-	46	SHRINE	D C Lee (CBS)
42	47	CONTROL	Janet Jackson (A&M)
44	48	FALCO 3	Falco (A&M)
-	49	MAKE IT BIG	Wham! (Epic)
-	50	OUT OF THE GREY	Dream Syndicate (Chrysalis)

19 July 1986

4	1	TRUE BLUE	Madonna (Sire)
9	2	REVENGE	Eurythmics (RCA)
1	3	INVISIBLE TOUCH	Genesis (Charisma)
5	4	LONDON 0 - HULL 4	Housemartins (Go! Discs)
3	5	A KIND OF MAGIC	Queen (EMI)
8	6	EVERY BEAT OF MY HEART	Rod Stewart (Warner Bros.)
-	7	THE SEER	Big Country (Mercury)
16	8	BACK IN THE HIGH LIFE	Stevie Winwood (Island)
7	9	PICTURE BOOK	Simply Red (Elektra)
-	10	THE FINAL	Wham! (Epic)
2	11	SO	Peter Gabriel (Virgin)
6	12	THE QUEEN IS DEAD	Smiths (Rough Trade)
14	13	INTO THE LIGHT	Chris DeBurgh (A&M)
12	14	BROTHERS IN ARMS	Dire Straits (Vertigo)
15	15	HUNTING HIGH AND LOW	A-Ha (Warner Bros.)
11	16	SUZANNE VEGA	Suzanne Vega (A&M)
-	17	NOW – THE SUMMER ALBUM	Various Artists (EMI/Virgin)
19	18	STREET LIFE - 20 GREAT HITS	Bryan Ferry & Roxy Music (EG)
-	19	DISCOVER	Gene Love Jezebel (Beggars Banquet)
10	20	BRING ON THE NIGHT	Sting (A&M)
18	21	RIPTIDE	Robert Palmer (Island)
17	22	WHITNEY HOUSTON	Whitney Houston (Arista)
20	23	WORLD MACHINE	Level 42 (Polydor)
22	24	STANDING ON THE BEACH - THE SINGLES	Cure (Fiction)
13	25	INTERMISSION	Dio (Vertigo)
24	26	PLEASE	Pet Shop Boys (Parlophone)
40	27	ON THE BEACH	Chris Rea (Magnet)
30	28	GIANT	Woodentops (Rough Trade)
26	29	THE MAN AND HIS MUSIC	Sam Cooke (RCA)
43	30	BEST OF THE REAL THING	Real Thing (PRT)
-	31	EAT 'EM AND SMILE	David Lee Roth (Warner Bros.)
21	32	ONCE UPON A TIME	Simple Minds (Virgin)
25	33	MOONLIGHT SHADOWS	Shadows (Polydor)
23	34	LOVE ZONE	Billy Ocean (Jive)
29	35	BANGS AND CRASHES	Go West (Chrysalis)
47	36	CONTROL	Janet Jackson (A&M)
27	37	CASHFLOW	Cashflow (Club)
35	38	DANCE HITS 2	Various Artists (Towerbell)
38	39	TO THE TOP	Aswad (Simba)
33	40	HEADLINES	Midnight Star (MCA)
32	41	STREET SOUNDS ELECTRO 12	Various Artists (Street Sounds)
39	42	NO JACKET REQUIRED	Phil Collins (Virgin)
45	43	WHO MADE WHO	AC/DC (Atlantic)
31	44	POOLSIDE	Nu Shooz (Atlantic)
49	45	MAKE IT BIG	Wham! (Epic)
37	46	WHERE YOU GONNA BE TONIGHT?	Willie Collins (Capitol)
-	47	DISCO BEACH PARTY	Various Artists (Stylus)
36	48	THE WINNER IN YOU	Patti LaBelle (MCA)
48	49	FALCO 3	Falco (A&M)
44	50	BORN SANDY DEVOTIONAL	Triffids (Hot)

26 July 1986

1	1	TRUE BLUE	Madonna (Sire)
2	2	REVENGE	Eurythmics (RCA)
8	3	BACK IN THE HIGH LIFE	Stevie Winwood (Island)
10	4	THE FINAL	Wham! (Epic)
7	5	THE SEER	Big Country (Mercury)
5	6	A KIND OF MAGIC	Queen (EMI)
6	7	EVERY BEAT OF MY HEART	Rod Stewart (Warner Bros)
3	8	INVISIBLE TOUCH	Genesis (Charisma)
17	9	NOW – THE SUMMER ALBUM	Various Artists (EMI/Virgin)
4	10	LONDON 0 - HULL 4	Housemartins (Go! Discs)
13	11	INTO THE LIGHT	Chris DeBurgh (A&M)
14	12	BROTHERS IN ARMS	Dire Straits (Vertigo)
9	13	PICTURE BOOK	Simply Red (Elektra)
11	14	SO	Peter Gabriel (Virgin)
15	15	HUNTING HIGH AND LOW	A-Ha (Warner Bros.)
16	16	SUZANNE VEGA	Suzanne Vega (A&M)
21	17	RIPTIDE	Robert Palmer (Island)
12	18	THE QUEEN IS DEAD	Smiths (Rough Trade)
31	19	EAT 'EM AND SMILE	David Lee Roth (Warner Bros.)
24	20	STANDING ON THE BEACH - THE SINGLES	Cure (Fiction)
18	21	STREET LIFE - 20 GREAT HITS	Bryan Ferry & Roxy Music (EG)
32	22	ONCE UPON A TIME	Simple Minds (Virgin)
22	23	WHITNEY HOUSTON	Whitney Houston (Arista)
19	24	DISCOVER	Gene Love Jezebel (Beggars Banquet)
34	25	LOVE ZONE	Billy Ocean (Jive)
20	26	BRING ON THE NIGHT	Sting (A&M)
28	27	GIANT	Woodentops (Rough Trade)
30	28	BEST OF THE REAL THING	Real Thing (PRT)
38	29	DANCE HITS 2	Various Artists (Towerbell)
42	30	NO JACKET REQUIRED	
27	31	ON THE BEACH	Phil Collins (Virgin) Chris Rea (Magnet)
-	32	STREET SOUNDS EDITION 17	Various Artists (Street Sounds)
-	33	TOUCH ME	Samantha Fox (Jive)
25	34	INTERMISSION	Dio (Vertigo)
23	35	WORLD MACHINE	Level 42 (Polydor)
40	36	HEADLINES	Midnight Star (MCA)
-	37	QUEEN'S GREATEST HITS	Queen (EMI)
29	38	THE MAN AND HIS MUSIC	Sam Cooke (RCA)
26	39	PLEASE	Pet Shop Boys (Parlophone)
-	40	PIE JESU	Aled Jones (10)
-	41	DRIVE TIME USA	Various Artists (K-Tel)
-	42	GIFT	Sisterhood (Merciful Release)
-	43	TRUE CONFESSIONS	Bananarama (London)
35	44	BANGS AND CRASHES	Go West (Chrysalis)
-	45	GTR	GTR (Arista)
-	46	PRINCESS	Princess (Supreme)
41	47	STREET SOUNDS ELECTRO 12	Various Artists (Street Sounds)
43	48	WHO MADE WHO	AC/DC (Atlantic)
-	49	UPFRONT1	Various Artists (Serious)
36	50	CONTROL	Janet Jackson (A&M)

Madonna's third album *True Blue*, eagerly awaited some 18 months after the release of her second, was predictably her biggest seller yet - indeed, the ninth biggest-selling album of the 1980s by the end of the decade. It was obviously not going to have the long, slow climb to the chart top that *Like A Virgin* had displayed, and almost immediately unseated Genesis to stake a five-week residence at the summit.

August 1986

Into The Light was Chris De Burgh's best-selling album yet, easily eclipsing his previous Top 10 entry in 1984 with a hits compilation. The key to the new set's success was what would probably prove to be De Burgh's most enduring song, *The Lady In Red*. This topped the singles chart in the week that *Into The Light* reached the Top 3 - and would ironically drop in the very week that the album finally hit Number 1.

August – September 1986

23 August 1986

last week	this week	Title	Artist (Label)
2	1	INTO THE LIGHT	Chris DeBurgh (A&M)
1	2	TRUE BLUE	Madonna (Sire)
6	3	A KIND OF MAGIC	Queen (EMI)
-	4	NOW THAT'S WHAT I CALL MUSIC 7	Various Artists (EMI Virgin)
4	5	RIPTIDE	Robert Palmer (Island)
7	6	REVENGE	Eurythmics (RCA)
3	7	THE FINAL	Wham! (Epic)
5	8	RAT IN THE KITCHEN	UB40 (DEP Int)
8	9	BROTHERS IN ARMS	Dire Straits (Vertigo)
11	10	BACK IN THE HIGH LIFE	Stevie Winwood (Island)
-	11	DANCING ON THE CEILING	Lionel Richie (Motown)
10	12	PICTURE BOOK	Simply Red (Elektra)
12	13	EVERY BEAT OF MY HEART	Rod Stewart (Warner Bros.)
-	14	THE ORIGINALS	Various Artists (Towerbell)
24	15	THE BRIDGE	Billy Joel (CBS)
15	16	INVISIBLE TOUCH	Genesis (Charisma)
26	17	COMMUNARDS	Communards (London)
16	18	NOW – THE SUMMER ALBUM	Various Artists (EMI/Virgin)
9	19	FLAUNT IT	Sigue Sigue Sputnik (Parlophone)
14	20	SO	Peter Gabriel (Virgin)
18	21	HUNTING HIGH AND LOW	A-Ha (Warner Bros.)
-	22	THREE HEARTS IN THE HAPPY ENDING MACHINE	Daryl Hall (RCA)
-	23	THE PAVAROTTI COLLECTION	Luciano Pavarotti (Stylus)
13	24	ORGASMATRON	Motorhead (GWR)
29	25	QUEEN'S GREATEST HITS	Queen (EMI)
17	26	KNOCKED OUT LOADED	Bob Dylan (CBS)
20	27	THE SEER	Big Country (Mercury)
31	28	THE QUEEN IS DEAD	Smiths (Rough Trade)
19	29	EAT 'EM AND SMILE	David Lee Roth (Warner Bros.)
21	30	LONDON O - HULL 4	Housemartins (Go! Discs)
-	31	PARADE	Prince & the Revolution (Warner Bros.)
23	32	NO GURU, NO METHOD, NO TEACHER	Van Morrison (Mercury)
28	33	STREET LIFE - 20 GREAT HITS	Bryan Ferry & Roxy Music (EG)
-	34	ONCE UPON A TIME	Simple Minds (Virgin)
25	35	WHITNEY HOUSTON	Whitney Houston (Arista)
-	36	RENDEZ-VOUS	Jean Michel Jarre (Polydor)
22	37	LANDING ON WATER	Neil Young (Geffen)
27	38	RAISING HELL	Run DMC (Profile/London)
44	39	RAPTURE	Anita Baker (Elektra)
43	40	QR3	Quiet Riot (Epic)
-	41	UPFRONT1	Various Artists (Serious)
33	42	STANDING ON THE BEACH - THE SINGLES	Cure (Fiction)
45	43	LISTEN LIKE THIEVES	INXS (Mercury)
46	44	LIKE A VIRGIN	Madonna (Sire)
-	45	THE GREATEST STORY EVER TOLD	Balaam & the Angel (Virgin)
-	46	LOVE ZONE	Billy Ocean (Jive)
32	47	DRIVE TIME USA	Various Artists (K-Tel)
36	48	SUZANNE VEGA	Suzanne Vega (A&M)
-	49	THE HEAT IS ON	Various Artists (Portrait)
42	50	GIANT	Woodentops (Rough Trade)

30 August 1986

last week	this week	Title	Artist (Label)
4	1	NOW THAT'S WHAT I CALL MUSIC 7	Various Artists (EMI Virgin)
2	2	TRUE BLUE	Madonna (Sire)
11	3	DANCING ON THE CEILING	Lionel Richie (Motown)
1	4	INTO THE LIGHT	Chris DeBurgh (A&M)
3	5	A KIND OF MAGIC	Queen (EMI)
7	6	THE FINAL	Wham! (Epic)
6	7	REVENGE	Eurythmics (RCA)
5	8	RIPTIDE	Robert Palmer (Island)
12	9	PICTURE BOOK	Simply Red (Elektra)
8	10	RAT IN THE KITCHEN	UB40 (DEP Int)
9	11	BROTHERS IN ARMS	Dire Straits (Vertigo)
36	12	RENDEZ-VOUS	Jean Michel Jarre (Polydor)
-	13	SILK AND STEEL	Five Star (Tent/RCA)
22	14	THREE HEARTS IN THE HAPPY ENDING MACHINE	Daryl Hall (RCA)
13	15	EVERY BEAT OF MY HEART	Rod Stewart (Warner Bros.)
49	16	THE HEAT IS ON	Various Artists (Portrait)
10	17	BACK IN THE HIGH LIFE	Stevie Winwood (Island)
28	18	THE QUEEN IS DEAD	Smiths (Rough Trade)
19	19	FLAUNT IT	Sigue Sigue Sputnik (Parlophone)
15	20	THE BRIDGE	Billy Joel (CBS)
29	21	EAT 'EM AND SMILE	David Lee Roth (Warner Bros.)
21	22	HUNTING HIGH AND LOW	A-Ha (Warner Bros.)
20	23	SO	Peter Gabriel (Virgin)
-	24	KICKING AGAINST THE PRICKS	Nick Cave & the Bad Seeds (Mute)
16	25	INVISIBLE TOUCH	Genesis (Charisma)
23	26	THE PAVAROTTI COLLECTION	Luciano Pavarotti (Stylus)
30	27	LONDON O - HULL 4	Housemartins (Go! Discs)
-	28	WORLD MACHINE	Level 42 (Polydor)
25	29	QUEEN'S GREATEST HITS	Queen (EMI)
24	30	ORGASMATRON	Motorhead (GWR)
43	31	LISTEN LIKE THIEVES	INXS (Mercury)
39	32	RAPTURE	Anita Baker (Elektra)
-	33	UPFRONT 2	Various Artists (Serious)
27	34	THE SEER	Big Country (Mercury)
-	35	GOOD TO GO LOVER	Gwen Guthrie (Boiling Point)
32	36	NO GURU, NO METHOD, NO TEACHER	Van Morrison (Mercury)
47	37	DRIVE TIME USA	Various Artists (K-Tel)
31	38	PARADE	Prince & the Revolution (Warner Bros.)
-	39	A LOT OF LOVE	Melba Moore (Capitol)
41	40	UPFRONT1	Various Artists (Serious)
18	41	NOW – THE SUMMER ALBUM	Various Artists (EMI/Virgin)
-	42	ALWAYS IN THE MOOD	Shirley Jones (Philly Int)
-	43	TAKE IT FROM ME	Glenn Jones (RCA)
40	44	QR3	Quiet Riot (Epic)
38	45	RAISING HELL	Run DMC (Profile/London)
35	46	WHITNEY HOUSTON	Whitney Houston (Arista)
33	47	STREET LIFE - 20 GREAT HITS	Bryan Ferry & Roxy Music (EG)
48	48	SUZANNE VEGA	Suzanne Vega (A&M)
-	49	DESTINY	Chaka Khan (Warner Bros.)
14	50	THE ORIGINALS	Various Artists (Towerbell)

6 September 1986

last week	this week	Title	Artist (Label)
1	1	NOW THAT'S WHAT I CALL MUSIC 7	Various Artists (EMI Virgin)
2	2	TRUE BLUE	Madonna (Sire)
3	3	DANCING ON THE CEILING	Lionel Richie (Motown)
5	4	A KIND OF MAGIC	Queen (EMI)
4	5	INTO THE LIGHT	Chris DeBurgh (A&M)
13	6	SILK AND STEEL	Five Star (Tent/RCA)
12	7	RENDEZ-VOUS	Jean Michel Jarre (Polydor)
6	8	THE FINAL	Wham! (Epic)
7	9	REVENGE	Eurythmics (RCA)
9	10	PICTURE BOOK	Simply Red (Elektra)
8	11	RIPTIDE	Robert Palmer (Island)
16	12	THE HEAT IS ON	Various Artists (Portrait)
-	13	IN THE ARMY NOW	Status Quo (Vertigo)
10	14	RAT IN THE KITCHEN	UB40 (DEP Int)
-	15	LIFE'S RICH PAGEANT	REM (IRS)
11	16	BROTHERS IN ARMS	Dire Straits (Vertigo)
14	17	THREE HEARTS IN THE HAPPY ENDING MACHINE	Daryl Hall (RCA)
17	18	BACK IN THE HIGH LIFE	Stevie Winwood (Island)
-	19	BABY THE STARS SHINE BRIGHT	Everything But The Girl (Blanco y Negro)
25	20	INVISIBLE TOUCH	Genesis (Charisma)
-	21	COMMUNARDS	Communards (London)
15	22	EVERY BEAT OF MY HEART	Rod Stewart (Warner Bros.)
35	23	GOOD TO GO LOVER	Gwen Guthrie (Boiling Point)
26	24	THE PAVAROTTI COLLECTION	Luciano Pavarotti (Stylus)
20	25	THE BRIDGE	Billy Joel (CBS)
24	26	KICKING AGAINST THE PRICKS	Nick Cave and the Bad Seeds (Mute)
33	27	UPFRONT 2	Various Artists (Serious)
38	28	PARADE	Prince & the Revolution (Warner Bros.)
29	29	QUEEN'S GREATEST HITS	Queen (EMI)
50	30	THE ORIGINALS	Various Artists (Towerbell)
22	31	HUNTING HIGH AND LOW	A-Ha (Warner Bros.)
-	32	WATCH YOUR STEP	Ted Hawkins (Windows of the World)
18	33	THE QUEEN IS DEAD	Smiths (Rough Trade)
23	34	SO	Peter Gabriel (Virgin)
47	35	STREET LIFE - 20 GREAT HITS	Bryan Ferry & Roxy Music (EG)
-	36	CONTROL	Janet Jackson (A&M)
-	37	STREET SOUNDS HIP-HOP ELECTRO 13	Various Artists (Street Sounds)
32	38	RAPTURE	Anita Baker (Elektra)
44	39	QR3	Quiet Riot (Epic)
48	40	SUZANNE VEGA	Suzanne Vega (A&M)
30	41	ORGASMATRON	Motorhead (GWR)
-	42	GUITAR TOWN	Steve Earle (MCA)
46	43	WHITNEY HOUSTON	Whitney Houston (Arista)
19	44	FLAUNT IT	Sigue Sigue Sputnik (Parlophone)
21	45	EAT 'EM AND SMILE	David Lee Roth (Warner Bros.)
-	46	THE BIG LAD IN THE WINDMILL	It Bites (Virgin)
-	47	WHILE THE CITY SLEEPS	George Benson (Warner Bros.)
-	48	NEVER FELT SO GOOD	James Ingram (Qwest)
28	49	WORLD MACHINE	Level 42 (Polydor)
27	50	LONDON O - HULL 4	Housemartins (Go! Discs)

Now That's What I Call Music 7 kept up the remarkable chart success of this series, becoming an easy late summer chart-topper with no sign of opposition from the opposing *Hits* camp (which, in fact, had also had an unopposed chart-topper in April with its fourth volume). With equal ease, Lionel Richie made it three Top 10 albums from as many realeases, with *Dancing On The Ceiling.*

293

September 1986

13 September 1986

last week	this week	Title	Artist
1	1	NOW THAT'S WHAT I CALL MUSIC 7	Various Artists (EMI Virgin)
3	2	DANCING ON THE CEILING	Lionel Richie (Motown)
2	3	TRUE BLUE	Madonna (Sire)
4	4	A KIND OF MAGIC	Queen (EMI)
9	5	REVENGE	Eurythmics (RCA)
5	6	INTO THE LIGHT	Chris DeBurgh (A&M)
47	7	WHILE THE CITY SLEEPS	George Benson (Warner Bros.)
13	8	IN THE ARMY NOW	Status Quo (Vertigo)
6	9	SILK AND STEEL	Five Star (Tent/RCA)
21	10	COMMUNARDS	Communards (London)
7	11	RENDEZ-VOUS	Jean Michel Jarre (Polydor)
10	12	PICTURE BOOK	Simply Red (Elektra)
16	13	BROTHERS IN ARMS	Dire Straits (Vertigo)
12	14	THE HEAT IS ON	Various Artists (Portrait)
8	15	THE FINAL	Wham! (Epic)
19	16	BABY THE STARS SHINE BRIGHT	Everything But The Girl (Blanco y Negro)
11	17	RIPTIDE	Robert Palmer (Island)
36	18	CONTROL	Janet Jackson (A&M)
20	19	INVISIBLE TOUCH	Genesis (Charisma)
37	20	STREET SOUNDS HIP-HOP ELECTRO 13	Various Artists (Street Sounds)
28	21	PARADE	Prince & the Revolution (Warner Bros.)
46	22	THE BIG LAD IN THE WINDMILL	It Bites (Virgin)
-	23	PRESS TO PLAY	Paul McCartney (EMI)
-	24	GRACELAND	Paul Simon (Virgin)
15	25	LIFE'S RICH PAGEANT	REM (IRS)
24	26	THE PAVAROTTI COLLECTION	Luciano Pavarotti (Stylus)
32	27	WATCH YOUR STEP	Ted Hawkins (Windows of the World)
18	28	BACK IN THE HIGH LIFE	Stevie Winwood (Island)
17	29	THREE HEARTS IN THE HAPPY ENDING MACHINE	Daryl Hall (RCA)
31	30	HUNTING HIGH AND LOW	A-Ha (Warner Bros.)
-	31	GONE TO EARTH	David Sylvian (Virgin)
-	32	LOVE ZONE	Billy Ocean (Jive)
29	33	QUEEN'S GREATEST HITS	Queen (EMI)
22	34	EVERY BEAT OF MY HEART	Rod Stewart (Warner Bros.)
14	35	RAT IN THE KITCHEN	UB40 (DEP Int)
27	36	UPFRONT 2	Various Artists (Serious)
23	37	GOOD TO GO LOVER	Gwen Guthrie (Boiling Point)
30	38	THE ORIGINALS	Various Artists (Towerball)
-	39	THE BEST OF 10 YEARS	Boney M (Stylus)
38	40	RAPTURE	Anita Baker (Elektra)
-	41	RAISING HELL	Run DMC (Profile)
25	42	THE BRIDGE	Billy Joel (CBS)
-	43	ONCE UPON A TIME	Simple Minds (Virgin)
43	44	WHITNEY HOUSTON	Whitney Houston (Arista)
50	45	LONDON O - HULL 4	Housemartins (Go! Discs)
-	46	THE WAY IT IS	Bruce Hornsby & the Range (RCA)
26	47	KICKING AGAINST THE PRICKS	Nick Cave and the Bad Seeds (Mute)
34	48	SO	Peter Gabriel (Virgin)
35	49	STREET LIFE - 20 GREAT HITS	Bryan Ferry & Roxy Music (EG)
42	50	GUITAR TOWN	Steve Earle (MCA)

20 September 1986

last week	this week	Title	Artist
1	1	NOW THAT'S WHAT I CALL MUSIC 7	Various Artists (EMI Virgin)
24	2	GRACELAND	Paul Simon (Warner Bros.)
2	3	DANCING ON THE CEILING	Lionel Richie (Motown)
9	4	SILK AND STEEL	Five Star (Tent/RCA)
3	5	TRUE BLUE	Madonna (Sire)
5	6	REVENGE	Eurythmics (RCA)
10	7	COMMUNARDS	Communards (London)
23	8	PRESS TO PLAY	Paul McCartney (EMI)
46	9	THE WAY IT IS	Bruce Hornsby & the Range (RCA)
8	10	IN THE ARMY NOW	Status Quo (Vertigo)
4	11	A KIND OF MAGIC	Queen (EMI)
7	12	WHILE THE CITY SLEEPS	George Benson (Warner Bros.)
6	13	INTO THE LIGHT	Chris DeBurgh (A&M)
-	14	BREAK EVERY RULE	Tina Turner (Capitol)
-	15	CRASH	Human League (Virgin)
-	16	SLIPPERY WHEN WET	Bon Jovi (Vertigo)
18	17	CONTROL	Janet Jackson (A&M)
14	18	THE HEAT IS ON	Various Artists (Portrait)
16	19	BABY THE STARS SHINE BRIGHT	Everything But The Girl (Blanco y Negro)
19	20	INVISIBLE TOUCH	Genesis (Charisma)
21	21	PARADE	Prince & the Revolution (Warner Bros.)
20	22	STREET SOUNDS HIP-HOP ELECTRO 13	Various Artists (Street Sounds)
12	23	PICTURE BOOK	Simply Red (Elektra)
13	24	BROTHERS IN ARMS	Dire Straits (Vertigo)
31	25	GONE TO EARTH	David Sylvian (Virgin)
11	26	RENDEZ-VOUS	Jean Michel Jarre (Polydor)
15	27	THE FINAL	Wham! (Epic)
-	28	FORE!	Huey Lewis & the News (Chrysalis)
17	29	RIPTIDE	Robert Palmer (Island)
35	30	RAT IN THE KITCHEN	UB40 (DEP Int)
22	31	THE BIG LAD IN THE WINDMILL	It Bites (Virgin)
25	32	LIFE'S RICH PAGEANT	REM (IRS)
26	33	THE PAVAROTTI COLLECTION	Luciano Pavarotti (Stylus)
42	34	THE BRIDGE	Billy Joel (CBS)
27	35	WATCH YOUR STEP	Ted Hawkins (Windows of the World)
-	36	STANDING ON THE BEACH - THE SINGLES	Cure (Fiction)
49	37	STREET LIFE - 20 GREAT HITS	Bryan Ferry & Roxy Music (EG)
-	38	INDISCREET	FM (Portrait)
28	39	BACK IN THE HIGH LIFE	Stevie Winwood (Island)
30	40	HUNTING HIGH AND LOW	A-Ha (Warner Bros.)
40	41	RAPTURE	Anita Baker (Elektra)
43	42	ONCE UPON A TIME	Simple Minds (Virgin)
-	43	BREAKING AWAY	Jaki Graham (EMI)
29	44	THREE HEARTS IN THE HAPPY ENDING MACHINE	Daryl Hall (RCA)
-	45	STRANGE TIMES	Chameleons (Geffen)
-	46	OFF THE BEATEN TRACK	Stranglers (Liberty)
-	47	A LOT OF LOVE	Melba Moore (Capitol)
48	48	SO	Peter Gabriel (Virgin)
44	49	WHITNEY HOUSTON	Whitney Houston (Arista)
47	50	KICKING AGAINST THE PRICKS	Nick Cave and the Bad Seeds (Mute)

27 September 1986

last week	this week	Title	Artist
14	1	BREAK EVERY RULE	Tina Turner (Capitol)
2	2	GRACELAND	Paul Simon (Warner Bros.)
1	3	NOW THAT'S WHAT I CALL MUSIC 7	Various Artists (EMI Virgin)
16	4	SLIPPERY WHEN WET	Bon Jovi (Vertigo)
28	5	FORE!	Huey Lewis & the News (Chrysalis)
6	6	REVENGE	Eurythmics (RCA)
5	7	TRUE BLUE	Madonna (Sire)
4	8	SILK AND STEEL	Five Star (Tent/RCA)
3	9	A KIND OF MAGIC	Queen (EMI)
3	10	DANCING ON THE CEILING	Lionel Richie (Motown)
15	11	CRASH	Human League (Virgin)
13	12	INTO THE LIGHT	Chris DeBurgh (A&M)
7	13	COMMUNARDS	Communards (London)
-	14	TRUE STORIES	Talking Heads (EMI)
-	15	BLOOD AND CHOCOLATE	Elvis Costello (Imp)
8	16	PRESS TO PLAY	Paul McCartney (EMI)
9	17	THE WAY IT IS	Bruce Hornsby & the Range (RCA)
12	18	WHILE THE CITY SLEEPS	George Benson (Warner Bros.)
10	19	IN THE ARMY NOW	Status Quo (Vertigo)
18	20	THE HEAT IS ON	Various Artists (Portrait)
23	21	PICTURE BOOK	Simply Red (Elektra)
24	22	BROTHERS IN ARMS	Dire Straits (Vertigo)
45	23	STRANGE TIMES	Chameleons (Geffen)
17	24	CONTROL	Janet Jackson (A&M)
19	25	BABY THE STARS SHINE BRIGHT	Everything But The Girl (Blanco y Negro)
-	26	ROCK THE NATION	Saxon (EMI)
31	27	THE BIG LAD IN THE WINDMILL	It Bites (Virgin)
20	28	INVISIBLE TOUCH	Genesis (Charisma)
32	29	LIFE'S RICH PAGEANT	REM (IRS)
43	30	BREAKING AWAY	Jaki Graham (EMI)
-	31	GOOD TO GO LOVER	Gwen Guthrie (Boiling Point)
-	32	COMPANEROS	Working Week (Virgin)
21	33	PARADE	Prince & the Revolution (Warner Bros.)
22	34	STREET SOUNDS HIP-HOP ELECTRO 13	Various Artists (Street Sounds)
34	35	THE BRIDGE	Billy Joel (CBS)
-	36	L IS FOR LOVER	Al Jarreau (WEA)
26	37	RENDEZ-VOUS	Jean Michel Jarre (Polydor)
27	38	THE FINAL	Wham! (Epic)
25	39	GONE TO EARTH	David Sylvian (Virgin)
-	40	EVERY BEAT OF MY HEART	Rod Stewart (Warner Bros.)
-	41	ON THE BOARDWALK	Ted Hawkins (Brave)
29	42	RIPTIDE	Robert Palmer (Island)
30	43	RAT IN THE KITCHEN	UB40 (DEP Int)
33	44	THE PAVAROTTI COLLECTION	Luciano Pavarotti (Stylus)
39	45	BACK IN THE HIGH LIFE	Stevie Winwood (Island)
46	46	STREET LIFE - 20 GREAT HITS	Bryan Ferry & Roxy Music (EG)
48	47	SO	Peter Gabriel (Virgin)
49	48	WHITNEY HOUSTON	Whitney Houston (Arista)
42	49	ONCE UPON A TIME	Simple Minds (Virgin)
40	50	HUNTING HIGH AND LOW	A-Ha (Warner Bros.)

Graceland was Paul Simon's first album since 1983's *Hearts And Bones*, which had barely sniffed at chart success. The reception for this one was to be quite different, as its mixture of first and third-world rhythms brought Simon a huge new following. *Graceland* would be the decade's 11th best-selling album - but even so, it was (albeit briefly) beaten to the Number 1 slot by Tina Turner's *Break Every Rule*.

October 1986

last week	this week	4 October 1986	
2	1	GRACELAND	Paul Simon (Warner Bros.)
8	2	SILK AND STEEL	Five Star (Tent/RCA)
1	3	BREAK EVERY RULE	Tina Turner (Capitol)
14	4	TRUE STORIES	Talking Heads (EMI)
3	5	NOW THAT'S WHAT I CALL MUSIC 7	
			Various Artists (EMI Virgin)
6	6	REVENGE	Eurythmics (RCA)
7	7	TRUE BLUE	Madonna (Sire)
5	8	FORE!	Huey Lewis & the News (Chrysalis)
4	9	SLIPPERY WHEN WET	Bon Jovi (Vertigo)
11	10	CRASH	Human League (Virgin)
13	11	COMMUNARDS	Communards (London)
-	12	TALKING WITH THE TAXMAN	
			Billy Bragg (Go! Discs)
15	13	BLOOD AND CHOCOLATE	
			Elvis Costello (Imp)
9	14	A KIND OF MAGIC	Queen (EMI)
10	15	DANCING ON THE CEILING	
			Lionel Richie (Motown)
12	16	INTO THE LIGHT	Chris DeBurgh (A&M)
17	17	THE WAY IT IS	
			Bruce Hornsby & the Range (RCA)
19	18	IN THE ARMY NOW	Status Quo (Vertigo)
26	19	ROCK THE NATION	Saxon (EMI)
18	20	WHILE THE CITY SLEEPS	
			George Benson (Warner Bros.)
22	21	BROTHERS IN ARMS	Dire Straits (Vertigo)
-	22	HAPPY HEAD	Might Lemon Drops (Chrysalis)
-	23	VIGILANTE	Magnum (Polydor)
21	24	PICTURE BOOK	Simply Red (Elektra)
20	25	THE HEAT IS ON	Various Artists (Portrait)
-	26	EYE OF THE ZOMBIE	
			John Fogerty (Warner Bros.)
16	27	PRESS TO PLAY	Paul McCartney (EMI)
28	28	INVISIBLE TOUCH	
			Genesis (Charisma)
23	29	STRANGE TIMES	Chameleons (Geffen)
32	30	COMPANEROS	Working Week (Virgin)
24	31	CONTROL	Janet Jackson (A&M)
-	32	RAISING HELL	Run DMC (Profile)
-	33	LIVE IN LOS ANGELES	Maze (Capitol)
30	34	BREAKING AWAY	Jaki Graham (EMI)
47	35	SO	Peter Gabriel (Virgin)
38	36	THE FINAL	Wham! (Epic)
25	37	BABY THE STARS SHINE BRIGHT	
			Everything But The Girl (Blanco y Negro)
41	38	ON THE BOARDWALK	Ted Hawkins (Brave)
-	39	LONDON O - HULL 4	
			Housemartins (Go! Discs)
33	40	PARADE	
			Prince & the Revolution (Warner Bros.)
39	41	GONE TO EARTH	David Sylvian (Virgin)
43	42	RAT IN THE KITCHEN	UB40 (DEP Int)
36	43	L IS FOR LOVER	Al Jarreau (WEA)
48	44	WHITNEY HOUSTON	Whitney Houston (Arista)
49	45	ONCE UPON A TIME	Simple Minds (Virgin)
27	46	THE BIG LAD IN THE WINDMILL	
			It Bites (Virgin)
29	47	LIFE'S RICH PAGEANT	REM (IRS)
35	48	THE BRIDGE	Billy Joel (CBS)
31	49	GOOD TO GO LOVER	
			Gwen Guthrie (Boiling Point)
46	50	STREET LIFE - 20 GREAT HITS	
			Bryan Ferry & Roxy Music (EG)

		11 October 1986	
1	1	GRACELAND	Paul Simon (Warner Bros.)
2	2	SILK AND STEEL	Five Star (Tent/RCA)
7	3	TRUE BLUE	Madonna (Sire)
6	4	REVENGE	Eurythmics (RCA)
12	5	TALKING WITH THE TAXMAN ABOUT POETRY	
			Billy Bragg (Go! Discs)
3	6	BREAK EVERY RULE	Tina Turner (Capitol)
4	7	TRUE STORIES	Talking Heads (EMI)
5	8	NOW THAT'S WHAT I CALL MUSIC 7	
			Various Artists (EMI Virgin)
11	9	COMMUNARDS	Communards (London)
8	10	FORE!	Huey Lewis & the News (Chrysalis)
9	11	SLIPPERY WHEN WET	Bon Jovi (Vertigo)
-	12	SOMEWHERE IN TIME	Iron Maiden (EMI)
16	13	INTO THE LIGHT	Chris DeBurgh (A&M)
14	14	A KIND OF MAGIC	Queen (EMI)
15	15	DANCING ON THE CEILING	
			Lionel Richie (Motown)
18	16	IN THE ARMY NOW	Status Quo (Vertigo)
-	17	BROTHERHOOD	New Order (Factory)
23	18	VIGILANTE	Magnum (Polydor)
28	19	INVISIBLE TOUCH	
			Genesis (Charisma)
20	20	BROTHERS IN ARMS	Dire Straits (Vertigo)
24	21	PICTURE BOOK	Simply Red (Elektra)
13	22	BLOOD AND CHOCOLATE	
			Elvis Costello (Imp)
-	23	THE GHOST OF CAIN	
			New Model Army (EMI)
-	24	TRUE COLORS	Cyndi Lauper (CBS)
-	25	HUNTING HIGH AND LOW	A-Ha (Warner Bros.)
17	26	THE WAY IT IS	
			Bruce Hornsby & the Range (RCA)
31	27	CONTROL	Janet Jackson (A&M)
-	28	THE PACIFIC AGE	
			Orchestral Manoeuvres in the Dark (Virgin)
10	29	CRASH	Human League (Virgin)
-	30	FRANTIC ROMANTIC	
			Jermain Stewart (10/Virgin)
-	31	BLAH BLAH BLAH	Iggy Pop (A&M)
-	32	INDISCREET	FM (Portrait)
25	33	THE HEAT IS ON	Various Artists (Portrait)
27	34	PRESS TO PLAY	Paul McCartney (EMI)
20	35	WHILE THE CITY SLEEPS	
			George Benson (Warner Bros.)
33	36	LIVE IN LOS ANGELES	Maze (Capitol)
34	37	BREAKING AWAY	Jaki Graham (EMI)
38	38	LONDON O - HULL 4	
			Housemartins (Go! Discs)
38	39	ON THE BOARDWALK	Ted Hawkins (Brave)
-	40	WHO'S BEEN TALKING	Robert Cray (Charly)
-	41	BLIND BEFORE I STOP	Meat Loaf (Arista)
19	42	ROCK THE NATION	Saxon (EMI)
-	43	BEND SINISTER	Fall (Beggars Banquet)
-	44	STREET SOUNDS HIP-HOP ELECTRO 14	
			Various Artists (Street Sounds)
-	45	RAPTURE	Anita Baker (Elektra)
-	46	DIFFERENT LIGHT	Bangles (CBS)
22	47	HAPPY HEAD	
			Might Lemon Drops (Chrysalis)
35	48	SO	Peter Gabriel (Virgin)
44	49	WHITNEY HOUSTON	
			Whitney Houston (Arista)
45	50	ONCE UPON A TIME	Simple Minds (Virgin)

		18 October 1986	
1	1	GRACELAND	Paul Simon (Warner Bros.)
2	2	SILK AND STEEL	Five Star (Tent/RCA)
12	3	SOMEWHERE IN TIME	Iron Maiden (EMI)
3	4	TRUE BLUE	Madonna (Sire)
4	5	REVENGE	Eurythmics (RCA)
25	6	HUNTING HIGH AND LOW	A-Ha (Warner Bros.)
-	7	SOUTH PACIFIC	Various Artists (CBS)
17	8	BROTHERHOOD	New Order (Factory)
6	9	BREAK EVERY RULE	Tina Turner (Capitol)
9	10	COMMUNARDS	Communards (London)
5	11	TALKING WITH THE TAXMAN ABOUT POETRY	
			Billy Bragg (Go! Discs)
28	12	THE PACIFIC AGE	
			Orchestral Manoeuvres in the Dark (Virgin)
7	13	TRUE STORIES	Talking Heads (EMI)
10	14	FORE!	Huey Lewis & the News (Chrysalis)
13	15	INTO THE LIGHT	Chris DeBurgh (A&M)
-	16	STREET SOUNDS EDITION 18	
			Various Artists (Street Sounds)
8	17	NOW THAT'S WHAT I CALL MUSIC 7	
			Various Artists (EMI Virgin)
-	18	WORD UP	Cameo (Club)
16	19	IN THE ARMY NOW	Status Quo (Vertigo)
14	20	A KIND OF MAGIC	Queen (EMI)
15	21	DANCING ON THE CEILING	
			Lionel Richie (Motown)
20	22	BROTHERS IN ARMS	Dire Straits (Vertigo)
23	23	THE GHOST OF CAIN	New Model Army (EMI)
24	24	TRUE COLORS	Cyndi Lauper (CBS)
38	25	LONDON O - HULL 4	
			Housemartins (Go! Discs)
-	26	THIRD STAGE	Boston (MCA)
19	27	INVISIBLE TOUCH	Genesis (Charisma)
41	28	BLIND BEFORE I STOP	Meat Loaf (Arista)
11	29	SLIPPERY WHEN WET	Bon Jovi (Vertigo)
-	30	ZAGORA	Loose Ends (Virgin)
43	31	BEND SINISTER	Fall (Beggars Banquet)
-	32	FILIGREE AND SHADOW	
			This Mortal Coil (4AD)
18	33	VIGILANTE	Magnum (Polydor)
47	34	HAPPY HEAD	Might Lemon Drops (Chrysalis)
31	35	BLAH BLAH BLAH	Iggy Pop (A&M)
-	36	NASTY, NASTY	Black 'n' Blue (Atlantic)
27	37	CONTROL	Janet Jackson (A&M)
22	38	BLOOD AND CHOCOLATE	
			Elvis Costello (Imp)
44	39	STREET SOUNDS HIP-HOP ELECTRO 14	
			Various Artists (Street Sounds)
26	40	THE WAY IT IS	
			Bruce Hornsby & the Range (RCA)
21	41	PICTURE BOOK	Simply Red (Elektra)
30	42	FRANTIC ROMANTIC	
			Jermain Stewart (10/Virgin)
-	43	GOOD TO GO LOVER	
			Gwen Guthrie (Boiling Point)
29	44	CRASH	Human League (Virgin)
35	45	WHILE THE CITY SLEEPS	
			George Benson (Warner Bros.)
45	46	RAPTURE	Anita Baker (Elektra)
32	47	INDISCREET	FM (Portrait)
36	48	LIVE IN LOS ANGELES	Maze (Capitol)
-	49	THE AUTOBIOGRAPHY OF SUPERTRAMP	
			Supertramp (A&M)
-	50	THE FINAL	Wham! (Epic)

Graceland settled into a six-week straight run at the chart top, which meant that the UK family vocal group Five Star had to be content with three weeks at Number 2 for their biggest-selling album *Silk And Steel* (the title of which was taken from a phrase in the song *Rain Or Shine*, simultaneously a Number 2 single). Meanwhile, Billy Bragg made the Top 10 for the first time with his intriguingly-titled third album.

October – November 1986

25 October 1986

last	this	Title	Artist (Label)
1	1	GRACELAND	Paul Simon (Warner Bros.)
-	2	SCOUNDREL DAYS	A-Ha (Warner Bros.)
4	3	TRUE BLUE	Madonna (Sire)
2	4	SILK AND STEEL	Five Star (Tent/RCA)
3	5	SOMEWHERE IN TIME	Iron Maiden (EMI)
5	6	REVENGE	Eurythmics (RCA)
7	7	SOUTH PACIFIC	Various Artists (CBS)
18	8	WORD UP	Cameo (Club)
10	9	COMMUNARDS	Communards (London)
30	10	ZAGORA	Loose Ends (Virgin)
8	11	BROTHERHOOD	New Order (Factory)
14	12	FORE!	Huey Lewis & the News (Chrysalis)
-	13	U-VOX	Ultravox (Chrysalis)
25	14	LONDON O - HULL 4	Housemartins (Go! Discs)
26	15	THIRD STAGE	Boston (MCA)
9	16	BREAK EVERY RULE	Tina Turner (Capitol)
20	17	A KIND OF MAGIC	Queen (EMI)
15	18	INTO THE LIGHT	Chris DeBurgh (A&M)
-	19	THE CHART	Various Artists (Telstar)
-	20	ONE TO ONE	Howard Jones (WEA)
17	21	NOW THAT'S WHAT I CALL MUSIC 7	Various Artists (EMI Virgin)
33	22	VIGILANTE	Magnum (Polydor)
19	23	IN THE ARMY NOW	Status Quo (Vertigo)
11	24	TALKING WITH THE TAXMAN ABOUT POETRY	Billy Bragg (Go! Discs)
12	25	THE PACIFIC AGE	Orchestral Manoeuvres in the Dark (Virgin)
27	26	INVISIBLE TOUCH	Genesis (Charisma)
-	27	POWER OF LOVE	Various Artists (West Five)
6	28	HUNTING HIGH AND LOW	A-Ha (Warner Bros.)
-	29	DANCE UNDERCOVER	Ratt (Atlantic)
13	30	TRUE STORIES	Talking Heads (EMI)
21	31	DANCING ON THE CEILING	Lionel Richie (Motown)
22	32	BROTHERS IN ARMS	Dire Straits (Vertigo)
16	33	STREET SOUNDS EDITION 18	Various Artists (Street Sounds)
-	34	JOURNEY TO THE URGE WITHIN	Courtney Pine (Island)
-	35	TOP GUN	Soundtrack (CBS)
49	36	THE AUTOBIOGRAPHY OF SUPERTRAMP	Supertramp (A&M)
-	37	DARING ADVENTURES	Richard Thompson (Polydor)
24	38	TRUE COLORS	Cyndi Lauper (CBS)
-	39	TUTU	Miles Davis (Warner Bros.)
50	40	THE FINAL	Wham! (Epic)
45	41	WHILE THE CITY SLEEPS	George Benson (Warner Bros.)
-	42	WHO'S BEEN TALKING	Robert Cray (Charly)
32	43	FILIGREE AND SHADOW	This Mortal Coil (4AD)
39	44	STREET SOUNDS HIP-HOP ELECTRO 14	Various Artists (Street Sounds)
29	45	SLIPPERY WHEN WET	Bon Jovi (Vertigo)
23	46	THE GHOST OF CAIN	New Model Army (EMI)
28	47	BLIND BEFORE I STOP	Meat Loaf (Arista)
-	48	SPIT IN YOUR EAR	Spitting Image (Virgin)
-	49	WOMEN HOLD UP HALF THE SKY	Ruby Turner (Jive)
31	50	BEND SINISTER	Fall (Beggars Banquet)

1 November 1986

last	this	Title	Artist (Label)
1	1	GRACELAND	Paul Simon (Warner Bros.)
3	2	TRUE BLUE	Madonna (Sire)
2	3	SCOUNDREL DAYS	A-Ha (Warner Bros.)
5	4	SOMEWHERE IN TIME	Iron Maiden (EMI)
4	5	SILK AND STEEL	Five Star (Tent/RCA)
-	6	GET CLOSE	Pretenders (Real)
-	7	LIVERPOOL	Frankie Goes To Hollywood (ZZT)
19	8	THE CHART	Various Artists (Telstar)
6	9	REVENGE	Eurythmics (RCA)
7	10	SOUTH PACIFIC	Various Artists (CBS)
20	11	ONE TO ONE	Howard Jones (WEA)
8	12	WORD UP	Cameo (Club)
-	13	BETWEEN TWO FIRES	Paul Young (CBS)
14	14	U-VOX	Ultravox (Chrysalis)
14	15	LONDON O - HULL 4	Housemartins (Go! Discs)
9	16	COMMUNARDS	Communards (London)
35	17	TOP GUN	Soundtrack (CBS)
-	18	WHIPLASH SMILE	Billy Idol (Chrysalis)
12	19	FORE!	Huey Lewis & the News (Chrysalis)
16	20	BREAK EVERY RULE	Tina Turner (Capitol)
38	21	TRUE COLORS	Cyndi Lauper (CBS)
32	22	BROTHERS IN ARMS	Dire Straits (Vertigo)
17	23	A KIND OF MAGIC	Queen (EMI)
18	24	INTO THE LIGHT	Chris DeBurgh (A&M)
-	25	PLEASE	Pet Shop Boys (EMI)
30	26	TRUE STORIES	Talking Heads (EMI)
24	27	TALKING WITH THE TAXMAN ABOUT POETRY	Billy Bragg (Go! Discs)
15	28	THIRD STAGE	Boston (MCA)
34	29	JOURNEY TO THE URGE WITHIN	Courtney Pine (Island)
11	30	BROTHERHOOD	New Order (Factory)
10	31	ZAGORA	Loose Ends (Virgin)
36	32	THE AUTOBIOGRAPHY OF SUPERTRAMP	Supertramp (A&M)
23	33	IN THE ARMY NOW	Status Quo (Vertigo)
-	34	CONSTRICTOR	Alice Cooper (WEA)
29	35	DANCE UNDERCOVER	Ratt (Atlantic)
-	36	GIVE ME THE REASON	Luther Vandross (Epic)
21	37	NOW THAT'S WHAT I CALL MUSIC 7	Various Artists (EMI Virgin)
31	38	DANCING ON THE CEILING	Lionel Richie (Motown)
40	39	THE FINAL	Wham! (Epic)
26	40	INVISIBLE TOUCH	Genesis (Charisma)
-	41	ENTERTAINMENT USA II	Various Artists (Priority)
33	42	STREET SOUNDS EDITION 18	Various Artists (Street Sounds)
41	43	WHILE THE CITY SLEEPS	George Benson (Warner Bros.)
25	44	THE PACIFIC AGE	Orchestral Manoeuvres in the Dark (Virgin)
39	45	TUTU	Miles Davis (Warner Bros.)
50	46	BEND SINISTER	Fall (Beggars Banquet)
45	47	SLIPPERY WHEN WET	Bon Jovi (Vertigo)
46	48	THE GHOST OF CAIN	New Model Army (EMI)
-	49	DIESEL RIVER	Weather Prophets (Rough Trade)
-	50	SO	Peter Gabriel (Virgin)

8 November 1986

last	this	Title	Artist (Label)
1	1	GRACELAND	Paul Simon (Warner Bros.)
18	2	WHIPLASH SMILE	Billy Idol (Chrysalis)
6	3	GET CLOSE	Pretenders (Real)
7	4	LIVERPOOL	Frankie Goes To Hollywood (ZZT)
2	5	TRUE BLUE	Madonna (Sire)
3	6	SCOUNDREL DAYS	A-Ha (Warner Bros.)
5	7	SILK AND STEEL	Five Star (Tent/RCA)
13	8	BETWEEN TWO FIRES	Paul Young (CBS)
17	9	TOP GUN	Soundtrack (CBS)
15	10	LONDON O - HULL 4	Housemartins (Go! Discs)
8	11	THE CHART	Various Artists (Telstar)
-	12	EVERY BREATH YOU TAKE - THE SINGLES	Police (A&M)
36	13	GIVE ME THE REASON	Luther Vandross (Epic)
12	14	WORD UP	Cameo (Club)
-	15	NO. 10 UPPING STREET	Big Audio Dynamite (CBS)
21	16	TRUE COLORS	Cyndi Lauper (CBS)
-	17	DREAMTIME	Stranglers (Epic)
9	18	REVENGE	Eurythmics (RCA)
10	19	SOUTH PACIFIC	Various Artists (CBS)
19	20	FORE!	Huey Lewis & the News (Chrysalis)
34	21	SOMEWHERE IN TIME	Iron Maiden (EMI)
-	22	CONSTRICTOR	Alice Cooper (WEA)
28	23	THIRD STAGE	Boston (MCA)
-	24	INSIDE THE ELECTRIC CIRCUS	W.A.S.P. (Capitol)
-	25	NOW DANCE '86	Various Artists (EMI/Virgin)
-	26	JUST LIKE THE FIRST TIME	Freddie Jackson (Capitol)
14	27	U-VOX	Ultravox (Chrysalis)
-	28	UPFRONT 3	Various Artists (Serious)
11	29	ONE TO ONE	Howard Jones (WEA)
22	30	BROTHERS IN ARMS	Dire Straits (Vertigo)
33	31	IN THE ARMY NOW	Status Quo (Vertigo)
32	32	THE AUTOBIOGRAPHY OF SUPERTRAMP	Supertramp (A&M)
38	33	DANCING ON THE CEILING	Lionel Richie (Motown)
47	34	SLIPPERY WHEN WET	Bon Jovi (Vertigo)
20	35	BREAK EVERY RULE	Tina Turner (Capitol)
16	36	COMMUNARDS	Communards (London)
25	37	PLEASE	Pet Shop Boys (EMI)
-	38	REMINISCING	Foster & Allen (Stylus)
-	39	SHELTER	Lone Justice (Geffen)
-	40	HOW GREEN IS THE VALLEY	Men They Couldn't Hang (MCA)
23	41	A KIND OF MAGIC	Queen (EMI)
27	42	TALKING WITH THE TAXMAN ABOUT POETRY	Billy Bragg (Go! Discs)
39	43	THE FINAL	Wham! (Epic)
-	44	THE PAVAROTTI COLLECTION	Luciano Pavarotti (Stylus)
45	45	WHITNEY HOUSTON	Whitney Houston (Arista)
31	46	ZAGORA	Loose Ends (Virgin)
-	47	PICTURE BOOK	Simply Red (Elektra)
24	48	INTO THE LIGHT	Chris DeBurgh (A&M)
-	49	SIMON BATES - OUR TUNE	Various Artists (Polydor)
-	50	AN IMITATION OF LOVE	Millie Jackson (Jive)

New albums by a plethora of major names failed to to dislodge Paul Simon from the chart top, with A-Ha and Billy Idol coming closest with Number 2 placings. Frankie Goes To Hollywood's second album *Liverpool* proved not to have the sales stamina of their debut release, peaking at Number 4, while Paul Young's *Between Two Fires*, his follow-up to a duo of chart-toppers, had to be content with Number 7.

15 November 1986

last week	this week	Title	Artist (Label)
12	1	EVERY BREATH YOU TAKE - THE SINGLES	Police (A&M)
1	2	GRACELAND	Paul Simon (Warner Bros.)
9	3	TOP GUN	Soundtrack (CBS)
4	4	LIVERPOOL	Frankie Goes To Hollywood (ZZT)
2	5	WHIPLASH SMILE	Billy Idol (Chrysalis)
15	6	NO. 10 UPPING STREET	Big Audio Dynamite (CBS)
8	7	BETWEEN TWO FIRES	Paul Young (CBS)
7	8	SILK AND STEEL	Five Star (Tent/RCA)
3	9	GET CLOSE	Pretenders (Real)
17	10	DREAMTIME	Stranglers (Epic)
25	11	NOW DANCE '86	Various Artists (EMI/Virgin)
5	12	TRUE BLUE	Madonna (Sire)
6	13	SCOUNDREL DAYS	A-Ha (Warner Bros.)
10	14	LONDON O - HULL 4	Housemartins (Go! Discs)
26	15	JUST LIKE THE FIRST TIME	Freddie Jackson (Capitol)
14	16	WORD UP	Cameo (Club)
11	17	THE CHART	Various Artists (Telstar)
18	18	REVENGE	Eurythmics (RCA)
20	19	FORE!	Huey Lewis & the News (Chrysalis)
34	20	SLIPPERY WHEN WET	Bon Jovi (Vertigo)
19	21	SOUTH PACIFIC	Various Artists (CBS)
13	22	GIVE ME THE REASON	Luther Vandross (Epic)
41	23	A KIND OF MAGIC	Queen (EMI)
33	24	DANCING ON THE CEILING	Lionel Richie (Motown)
32	25	THE AUTOBIOGRAPHY OF SUPERTRAMP	Supertramp (A&M)
-	26	LEATHER JACKET	Elton John (Rocket)
31	27	IN THE ARMY NOW	Status Quo (Vertigo)
46	28	ZAGORA	Loose Ends (Virgin)
24	29	INSIDE THE ELECTRIC CIRCUS	W.A.S.P. (Capitol)
16	30	TRUE COLORS	Cyndi Lauper (CBS)
38	31	REMINISCING	Foster & Allen (Stylus)
30	32	BROTHERS IN ARMS	Dire Straits (Vertigo)
-	33	SO	Peter Gabriel (Virgin)
-	34	THE GREATEST HITS OF 1986	Various Artists (Telstar)
28	35	UPFRONT 3	Various Artists (Serious)
-	36	JOURNEY TO THE URGE WITHIN	Courtney Pine (Island)
21	37	SOMEWHERE IN TIME	Iron Maiden (EMI)
40	38	HOW GREEN IS THE VALLEY	Men They Couldn't Hang (MCA)
-	39	TOGETHER	Various Artists (K-Tel)
35	40	BREAK EVERY RULE	Tina Turner (Capitol)
36	41	COMMUNARDS	Communards (London)
-	42	RADIO MUSICOLA	Nik Kershaw (MCA)
47	43	PICTURE BOOK	Simply Red (Elektra)
27	44	U-VOX	Ultravox (Chrysalis)
42	45	TALKING WITH THE TAXMAN ABOUT POETRY	Billy Bragg (Go! Discs)
23	46	THIRD STAGE	Boston (MCA)
-	47	ULTIMATE TRAX VOL 1	Various Artists (Champion)
-	48	ARETHA	Aretha Franklin (Arista)
39	49	SHELTER	Lone Justice (Geffen)
50	50	AN IMITATION OF LOVE	Millie Jackson (Jive)

22 November 1986

last week	this week	Title	Artist (Label)
1	1	EVERY BREATH YOU TAKE - THE SINGLES	Police (A&M)
2	2	GRACELAND	Paul Simon (Warner Bros.)
3	3	TOP GUN	Soundtrack (CBS)
-	4	LIVE 1975-85	Bruce Springsteen & the E Street Band (CBS)
11	5	NOW DANCE '86	Various Artists (EMI/Virgin)
12	6	TRUE BLUE	Madonna (Sire)
8	7	SILK AND STEEL	Five Star (Tent/RCA)
20	8	SLIPPERY WHEN WET	Bon Jovi (Vertigo)
-	9	THE WHOLE STORY	Kate Bush (EMI)
9	10	GET CLOSE	Pretenders (Real)
34	11	THE GREATEST HITS OF 1986	Various Artists (Telstar)
26	12	LEATHER JACKET	Elton John (Rocket)
-	13	HIT MIX '86	Various Artists (Stylus)
18	14	REVENGE	Eurythmics (RCA)
4	15	LIVERPOOL	Frankie Goes To Hollywood (ZZT)
7	16	BETWEEN TWO FIRES	Paul Young (CBS)
6	17	NO. 10 UPPING STREET	Big Audio Dynamite (CBS)
10	18	HITS 5	Various Artists (CBS/WEA)
5	19	WHIPLASH SMILE	Billy Idol (Chrysalis)
25	20	THE AUTOBIOGRAPHY OF SUPERTRAMP	Supertramp (A&M)
31	21	REMINISCING	Foster & Allen (Stylus)
13	22	SCOUNDREL DAYS	A-Ha (Warner Bros.)
-	23	GOD'S OWN MEDICINE	Mission (Mercury)
10	24	DREAMTIME	Stranglers (Epic)
33	25	SO	Peter Gabriel (Virgin)
14	26	LONDON O - HULL 4	Housemartins (Go! Discs)
-	27	THE FINAL COUNTDOWN	Europe (Epic)
16	28	WORD UP	Cameo (Club)
22	29	GIVE ME THE REASON	Luther Vandross (CBS)
-	30	DIFFERENT LIGHT	Bangles (CBS)
-	31	BRIGHTER THAN A THOUSAND SUNS	Killing Joke (EG)
15	32	JUST LIKE THE FIRST TIME	Freddie Jackson (Capitol)
23	33	A KIND OF MAGIC	Queen (EMI)
36	34	JOURNEY TO THE URGE WITHIN	Courtney Pine (Island)
-	35	STRONG PERSUADER	Robert Cray Band (Mercury)
29	36	INSIDE THE ELECTRIC CIRCUS	W.A.S.P. (Capitol)
-	37	TOGETHER	Various Artists (K-Tel)
32	38	BROTHERS IN ARMS	Dire Straits (Vertigo)
19	39	FORE!	Huey Lewis & the News (Chrysalis)
-	40	ELECTRIC CAFE	Kraftwerk (EMI)
-	41	SAY WHAT	Trouble Funk (Fourth & Broadway)
-	42	YOUR FUNERAL ...... MY TRIAL	Nick Cave and the Bad Seeds (Mute)
17	43	THE CHART	Various Artists (Telstar)
-	44	BLACK MAGIC	Various Artists (Stylus)
27	45	IN THE ARMY NOW	Status Quo (Vertigo)
40	46	BREAK EVERY RULE	Tina Turner (Capitol)
28	47	ZAGORA	Loose Ends (Virgin)
-	48	THE FINAL	Wham! (Epic)
-	49	THEIR VERY BEST BACK-TO-BACK	Various Artists (Priority)
49	50	SHELTER	Lone Justice (Geffen)

29 November 1986

last week	this week	Title	Artist (Label)
1	1	EVERY BREATH YOU TAKE - THE SINGLES	Police (A&M)
18	2	HITS 5	Various Artists (CBS/WEA)
9	3	THE WHOLE STORY	Kate Bush (EMI)
4	4	LIVE 1975-85	Bruce Springsteen & the E Street Band (CBS)
3	5	TOP GUN	Soundtrack (CBS)
2	6	GRACELAND	Paul Simon (Warner Bros.)
8	7	SLIPPERY WHEN WET	Bon Jovi (Vertigo)
6	8	TRUE BLUE	Madonna (Sire)
7	9	SILK AND STEEL	Five Star (Tent/RCA)
13	10	HIT MIX '86	Various Artists (Stylus)
5	11	NOW DANCE '86	Various Artists (EMI/Virgin)
23	12	GOD'S OWN MEDICINE	Mission (Mercury)
11	13	THE GREATEST HITS OF 1986	Various Artists (Telstar)
20	14	THE AUTOBIOGRAPHY OF SUPERTRAMP	Supertramp (A&M)
15	15	LIVERPOOL	Frankie Goes To Hollywood (ZZT)
10	16	GET CLOSE	Pretenders (Real)
25	17	SO	Peter Gabriel (Virgin)
38	18	BROTHERS IN ARMS	Dire Straits (Vertigo)
-	19	SWEET FREEDOM	Michael McDonald (Warner Bros.)
-	20	INFECTED	The The (Some Bizzare)
21	21	REMINISCING	Foster & Allen (Stylus)
-	22	THROUGH THE BARRICADES	Spandau Ballet (Reformation)
17	23	NO. 10 UPPING STREET	Big Audio Dynamite (CBS)
27	24	THE FINAL COUNTDOWN	Europe (Epic)
-	25	WHITNEY HOUSTON	Whitney Houston (Arista)
16	26	BETWEEN TWO FIRES	Paul Young (CBS)
28	27	WORD UP	Cameo (Club)
29	28	GIVE ME THE REASON	Luther Vandross (CBS)
32	29	JUST LIKE THE FIRST TIME	Freddie Jackson (Capitol)
35	30	STRONG PERSUADER	Robert Cray Band (Mercury)
44	31	BLACK MAGIC	Various Artists (Stylus)
26	32	LONDON O - HULL 4	Housemartins (Go! Discs)
14	33	REVENGE	Eurythmics (RCA)
33	34	A KIND OF MAGIC	Queen (EMI)
37	35	TOGETHER	Various Artists (K-Tel)
12	36	LEATHER JACKET	Elton John (Rocket)
22	37	SCOUNDREL DAYS	A-Ha (Warner Bros.)
24	38	DREAMTIME	Stranglers (Epic)
-	39	RAPTURE	Anita Baker (Elektra)
49	40	THEIR VERY BEST BACK-TO-BACK	Various Artists (Priority)
-	41	THE MOON AND THE MELODIES	Harold Budd with the Cocteau Twins (4AD)
47	42	ZAGORA	Loose Ends (Virgin)
-	43	TRILOGY	Yngwie J Malmsteen (Polydor)
30	44	DIFFERENT LIGHT	Bangles (CBS)
40	45	ELECTRIC CAFE	Kraftwerk (EMI)
-	46	INSIDE STORY	Grace Jones (Manhattan)
-	47	ROCKBIRD	Debbie Harry (Chrysalis)
31	48	BRIGHTER THAN A THOUSAND SUNS	Killing Joke (EG)
36	49	INSIDE THE ELECTRIC CIRCUS	W.A.S.P. (Capitol)
34	50	JOURNEY TO THE URGE WITHIN	Courtney Pine (Island)

Although the Police had been disbanded, and the three former members busily embroiled in solo careers, for some years by the end of 1986, their commercial profile was still high, as proved by the success of the belated hits compilation *Every Breath You Take - The Singles*. One unusual highlight of this set was a radically remixed version of the 1980 hit *Don't Stand So Close To Me*, also issued as a single.

December 1986

6 December 1986

last week	this week	Title	Artist (Label)
2	1	HITS 5	Various Artists (CBS/WEA)
3	2	THE WHOLE STORY	Kate Bush (EMI)
1	3	EVERY BREATH YOU TAKE - THE SINGLES	Police (A&M)
7	4	SLIPPERY WHEN WET	Bon Jovi (Vertigo)
4	5	LIVE 1975-85	Bruce Springsteen and the E Street Band (CBS)
22	6	THROUGH THE BARRICADES	Spandau Ballet (Reformation)
5	7	TOP GUN	Soundtrack (CBS)
-	8	NOW THAT'S WHAT I CALL MUSIC 8	Various Artists (EMI/Virgin/PolyGram)
6	9	GRACELAND	Paul Simon (Warner Bros.)
20	10	INFECTED	The The (Some Bizzare)
-	11	DISCO	Pet Shop Boys (Parlophone)
9	12	SILK AND STEEL	Five Star (Tent/RCA)
8	13	TRUE BLUE	Madonna (Sire)
10	14	HIT MIX '86	Various Artists (Stylus)
47	15	ROCKBIRD	Debbie Harry (Chrysalis)
24	16	THE FINAL COUNTDOWN	Europe (Epic)
12	17	GOD'S OWN MEDICINE	Mission (Mercury)
46	18	INSIDE STORY	Grace Jones (Manhattan)
-	19	NOTORIOUS	Duran Duran (EMI)
-	20	AUGUST	Eric Clapton (Duck)
17	21	SO	Peter Gabriel (Virgin)
11	22	NOW DANCE '86	Various Artists (EMI/Virgin)
18	23	BROTHERS IN ARMS	Dire Straits (Vertigo)
33	24	REVENGE	Eurythmics (RCA)
14	25	THE AUTOBIOGRAPHY OF SUPERTRAMP	Supertramp (A&M)
21	26	REMINISCING	Foster & Allen (Stylus)
28	27	GIVE ME THE REASON	Luther Vandross (Epic)
19	28	SWEET FREEDOM	Michael McDonald (Warner Bros.)
13	29	THE GREATEST HITS OF 1986	Various Artists (Telstar)
39	30	RAPTURE	Anita Baker (Elektra)
-	31	UTTER MADNESS	Madness (Zarjazz)
-	32	THE VERY BEST OF THE DRIFTERS	Drifters (Telstar)
25	33	WHITNEY HOUSTON	Whitney Houston (Arista)
34	34	A KIND OF MAGIC	Queen (EMI)
16	35	GET CLOSE	Pretenders (Real)
-	36	WHAT PRICE PARADISE	China Crisis (Virgin)
-	37	SHOP ASSISTANTS	Shop Assistants (Blue Guitar)
-	38	THE CIRCLE AND THE SQUARE	Red Box (WEA)
-	39	IN THE ARMY NOW	Status Quo (Vertigo)
-	40	INTENTIONS	Maxi Priest (10)
27	41	WORD UP	Cameo (Club)
29	42	JUST LIKE THE FIRST TIME	Freddie Jackson (Capitol)
15	43	LIVERPOOL	Frankie Goes To Hollywood (ZZT)
26	44	BETWEEN TWO FIRES	Paul Young (CBS)
42	45	ZAGORA	Loose Ends (Virgin)
40	46	THEIR VERY BEST BACK-TO-BACK	Various Artists (Priority)
37	47	SCOUNDREL DAYS	A-Ha (Warner Bros.)
-	48	BROADCAST	Cutting Crew (Siren)
-	49	LOVERS	Various Artists (Telstar)
-	50	TOGETHER	Various Artists (K-Tel)

13 December 1986

last week	this week	Title	Artist (Label)
8	1	NOW THAT'S WHAT I CALL MUSIC 8	Various Artists (EMI/Virgin/PolyGram)
2	2	THE WHOLE STORY	Kate Bush (EMI)
1	3	HITS 5	Various Artists (CBS/WEA)
3	4	EVERY BREATH YOU TAKE - THE SINGLES	Police (A&M)
4	5	SLIPPERY WHEN WET	Bon Jovi (Vertigo)
7	6	TOP GUN	Soundtrack (CBS)
9	7	GRACELAND	Paul Simon (Warner Bros.)
6	8	THROUGH THE BARRICADES	Spandau Ballet (Reformation)
5	9	LIVE 1975-85	Bruce Springsteen & the E Street Band (CBS)
13	10	TRUE BLUE	Madonna (Sire)
-	11	LIVE MAGIC	Queen (EMI)
12	12	SILK AND STEEL	Five Star (Tent/RCA)
11	13	DISCO	Pet Shop Boys (Parlophone)
20	14	AUGUST	Eric Clapton (Duck)
14	15	HIT MIX '86	Various Artists (Stylus)
15	16	ROCKBIRD	Debbie Harry (Chrysalis)
-	17	ANYTHING	Damned (MCA)
16	18	THE FINAL COUNTDOWN	Europe (Epic)
22	19	NOW DANCE '86	Various Artists (EMI/Virgin)
29	20	THE GREATEST HITS OF 1986	Various Artists (Telstar)
49	21	LOVERS	Various Artists (Telstar)
23	22	BROTHERS IN ARMS	Dire Straits (Vertigo)
31	23	UTTER MADNESS	Madness (Zarjazz)
10	24	INFECTED	The The (Some Bizzare)
26	25	REMINISCING	Foster & Allen (Stylus)
-	26	DIFFERENT LIGHT	Bangles (CBS)
19	27	NOTORIOUS	Duran Duran (EMI)
21	28	SO	Peter Gabriel (Virgin)
30	29	RAPTURE	Anita Baker (Elektra)
24	30	REVENGE	Eurythmics (RCA)
25	31	THE AUTOBIOGRAPHY OF SUPERTRAMP	Supertramp (A&M)
32	32	THE VERY BEST OF THE DRIFTERS	Drifters (Telstar)
28	33	SWEET FREEDOM	Michael McDonald (Warner Bros.)
-	34	NOW - THE CHRISTMAS ALBUM	Various Artists (EMI/Virgin)
36	35	WHAT PRICE PARADISE	China Crisis (Virgin)
17	36	GOD'S OWN MEDICINE	Mission (Mercury)
-	37	SIXTIES MANIA	Various Artists (Telstar)
-	38	FORE!	Huey Lewis & the News (Chrysalis)
39	39	IN THE ARMY NOW	Status Quo (Vertigo)
46	40	THEIR VERY BEST BACK-TO-BACK	Various Artists (Priority)
-	41	DEEP IN THE HEART OF NOWHERE	Bob Geldof (Mercury)
-	42	MUSIC FROM THE SINGING DETECTIVE	Various Artists (BBC)
33	43	WHITNEY HOUSTON	Whitney Houston (Arista)
47	44	SCOUNDREL DAYS	A-Ha (Warner Bros.)
34	45	A KIND OF MAGIC	Queen (EMI)
-	46	THE FINAL	Wham! (Epic)
18	47	INSIDE STORY	Grace Jones (Manhattan)
-	48	SOUTH PACIFIC	Various Artists (CBS)
-	49	JAZZ FROM HELL	Frank Zappa (EMI)
-	50	STREET SOUNDS EDITION 19	Various Artists (Street Sounds)

20 December 1986

last week	this week	Title	Artist (Label)
1	1	NOW THAT'S WHAT I CALL MUSIC 8	Various Artists (EMI/Virgin/PolyGram)
3	2	HITS 5	Various Artists (CBS/WEA)
2	3	THE WHOLE STORY	Kate Bush (EMI)
4	4	EVERY BREATH YOU TAKE - THE SINGLES	Police (A&M)
11	5	LIVE MAGIC	Queen (EMI)
7	6	GRACELAND	Paul Simon (Warner Bros.)
5	7	SLIPPERY WHEN WET	Bon Jovi (Vertigo)
10	8	TRUE BLUE	Madonna (Sire)
6	9	TOP GUN	Soundtrack (CBS)
9	10	LIVE 1975-85	Bruce Springsteen & the E Street Band (CBS)
12	11	SILK AND STEEL	Five Star (Tent/RCA)
26	12	DIFFERENT LIGHT	Bangles (CBS)
30	13	REVENGE	Eurythmics (RCA)
14	14	AUGUST	Eric Clapton (Duck)
21	15	LOVERS	Various Artists (Telstar)
8	16	THROUGH THE BARRICADES	Spandau Ballet (Reformation)
22	17	BROTHERS IN ARMS	Dire Straits (Vertigo)
25	18	REMINISCING	Foster & Allen (Stylus)
48	19	SOUTH PACIFIC	Various Artists (CBS)
17	20	ANYTHING	Damned (MCA)
38	21	FORE!	Huey Lewis & the News (Chrysalis)
34	22	NOW - THE CHRISTMAS ALBUM	Various Artists (EMI/Virgin)
24	23	INFECTED	The The (Some Bizzare)
37	24	SIXTIES MANIA	Various Artists (Telstar)
20	25	THE GREATEST HITS OF 1986	Various Artists (Telstar)
15	26	HIT MIX '86	Various Artists (Stylus)
44	27	SCOUNDREL DAYS	A-Ha (Warner Bros.)
19	28	NOW DANCE '86	Various Artists (EMI/Virgin)
13	29	DISCO	Pet Shop Boys (Parlophone)
18	30	THE FINAL COUNTDOWN	Europe (Epic)
27	31	NOTORIOUS	Duran Duran (EMI)
29	32	RAPTURE	Anita Baker (Elektra)
39	33	IN THE ARMY NOW	Status Quo (Vertigo)
46	34	THE FINAL	Wham! (Epic)
36	35	GOD'S OWN MEDICINE	Mission (Mercury)
-	36	LONDON 0 - HULL 4	Housemartins (Go! Discs)
33	37	SWEET FREEDOM	Michael McDonald (Warner Bros.)
-	38	MUSIC MADNESS	Mantronix (10/Virgin)
-	39	BOSTIN' STEVE AUSTIN	We've Got A Fuzzbox And We're Gonna Use It (Vindaloo WEA)
16	40	ROCKBIRD	Debbie Harry (Chrysalis)
-	41	MOTOWN CHARTBUSTERS	Various Artists (Telstar)
43	42	WHITNEY HOUSTON	Whitney Houston (Arista)
-	43	COMMUNARDS	Communards (London)
-	44	THE CAROLS ALBUM	Huddersfield Choral Society (EMI)
-	45	WOMAGIC	Bobby Womack (MCA)
28	46	SO	Peter Gabriel (Virgin)
-	47	AN ALBUM OF HYMNS	Aled Jones (EMI)
23	48	UTTER MADNESS	Madness (Zarjazz)
-	49	TOGETHER	Various Artists (K-Tel)
-	50	BEDTIME FOR DEMOCRACY	Dead Kennedys (Alternative Tentacles)

Kate Bush's *The Whole Story*, an anthology of her hit singles and key work to date, narrowly failed to give her another chart-topping album. The inevitable December culprits were the year-end volumes in the *Hits* and *Now* compilation series, which squared their third Christmas scorecard with a draw - this time, both *Hits 5* and *Now Music 8* made Number 1 (though EMI/Virgin might claim the final Yule advantage).

3 January 1987

last week	this week		
1	1	NOW THAT'S WHAT I CALL MUSIC 8	Various Artists (EMI/Virgin/PolyGram)
3	2	THE WHOLE STORY	Kate Bush (EMI)
2	3	HITS 5	Various Artists (CBS/WEA)
5	4	LIVE MAGIC	Queen (EMI)
6	5	GRACELAND	Paul Simon (Warner Bros.)
4	6	EVERY BREATH YOU TAKE - THE SINGLES	Police (A&M)
8	7	TRUE BLUE	Madonna (Sire)
7	8	SLIPPERY WHEN WET	Bon Jovi (Vertigo)
21	9	FORE!	Huey Lewis & the News (Chrysalis)
37	10	SWEET FREEDOM	Michael McDonald (Warner Bros.)
11	11	SILK AND STEEL	Five Star (Tent/RCA)
9	12	TOP GUN	Soundtrack (CBS)
13	13	REVENGE	Eurythmics (RCA)
12	14	DIFFERENT LIGHT	Bangles (CBS)
14	15	AUGUST	Eric Clapton (Duck)
22	16	NOW - THE CHRISTMAS ALBUM	Various Artists (EMI/Virgin/PolyGram)
18	17	REMINISCING	Foster & Allen (Stylus)
19	18	SOUTH PACIFIC	Various Artists (CBS)
10	19	LIVE 1975-85	Bruce Springsteen and the E Street Band (CBS)
15	20	LOVERS	Various Artists (Telstar)
16	21	THROUGH THE BARRICADES	Spandau Ballet (Reformation)
30	22	THE FINAL COUNTDOWN	Europe (Epic)
36	23	LONDON O - HULL 4	Housemartins (Go! Discs)
34	24	THE FINAL	Wham! (Epic)
-	25	CHRISTMAS	Elaine Paige (WEA)
-	26	MUSIC FROM THE SINGING DETECTIVE	Various Artists (BBC)
24	27	SIXTIES MANIA	Various Artists (Telstar)
-	28	BONNIE TYLER'S GREATEST HITS	Bonnie Tyler (Telstar)
26	29	HIT MIX '86	Various Artists (Stylus)
-	30	HIGHWAY OF LIFE	Harry Secombe (Telstar)
47	31	AN ALBUM OF HYMNS	Aled Jones (EMI)
44	32	THE CAROLS ALBUM	Huddersfield Choral Society (EMI)
42	33	WHITNEY HOUSTON	Whitney Houston (Arista)
32	34	RAPTURE	Anita Baker (Elektra)
33	35	IN THE ARMY NOW	Status Quo (Vertigo)
17	36	BROTHERS IN ARMS	Dire Straits (Vertigo)
20	37	ANYTHING	Damned (MCA)
27	38	SCOUNDREL DAYS	A-Ha (Warner Bros.)
31	39	NOTORIOUS	Duran Duran (EMI)
35	40	GOD'S OWN MEDICINE	Mission (Mercury)
39	41	BOSTIN' STEVE AUSTIN	We've Got A Fuzzbox And We're Gonna Use It (Vindaloo WEA)
46	42	SO	Peter Gabriel (Virgin)
43	43	COMMUNARDS	Communards (London)
41	44	MOTOWN CHARTBUSTERS	Various Artists (Telstar)
25	45	THE GREATEST HITS OF 1986	Various Artists (Telstar)
-	46	JAZZ FROM HELL	Frank Zappa (EMI)
-	47	CHRISTMAS WITH KIRI	Kiri Te Kanawa (Decca)
-	48	INVISIBLE TOUCH	Genesis (Charisma)
23	49	INFECTED	The The (Some Bizzare)
29	50	DISCO	Pet Shop Boys (Parlophone)

10 January 1987

1	1	NOW THAT'S WHAT I CALL MUSIC 8	Various Artists (EMI/Virgin/PolyGram)
5	2	GRACELAND	Paul Simon (Warner Bros.)
3	3	HITS 5	Various Artists (CBS/WEA)
2	4	THE WHOLE STORY	Kate Bush (EMI)
6	5	EVERY BREATH YOU TAKE - THE SINGLES	Police (A&M)
8	6	SLIPPERY WHEN WET	Bon Jovi (Vertigo)
7	7	TRUE BLUE	Madonna (Sire)
4	8	LIVE MAGIC	Queen (EMI)
11	9	SILK AND STEEL	Five Star (Tent/RCA)
13	10	REVENGE	Eurythmics (RCA)
9	11	FORE!	Huey Lewis & the News (Chrysalis)
23	12	LONDON O - HULL 4	Housemartins (Go! Discs)
10	13	SWEET FREEDOM	Michael McDonald (Warner Bros.)
26	14	MUSIC FROM THE SINGING DETECTIVE	Various Artists (BBC)
14	15	DIFFERENT LIGHT	Bangles (CBS)
38	16	SCOUNDREL DAYS	A-Ha (Warner Bros.)
12	17	TOP GUN	Soundtrack (CBS)
24	18	THE FINAL	Wham! (Epic)
31	19	AN ALBUM OF HYMNS	Aled Jones (EMI)
36	20	BROTHERS IN ARMS	Dire Straits (Vertigo)
20	21	LOVERS	Various Artists (Telstar)
17	22	REMINISCING	Foster & Allen (Stylus)
18	23	SOUTH PACIFIC	Various Artists (CBS)
16	24	NOW - THE CHRISTMAS ALBUM	Various Artists (EMI/Virgin/PolyGram)
-	25	GET CLOSE	Pretenders (WEA)
49	26	INFECTED	The The (Some Bizzare)
43	27	COMMUNARDS	Communards (London)
35	28	IN THE ARMY NOW	Status Quo (Vertigo)
19	29	LIVE 1975-85	Bruce Springsteen & the E Street Band (CBS)
15	30	AUGUST	Eric Clapton (Duck)
27	31	SIXTIES MANIA	Various Artists (Telstar)
44	32	MOTOWN CHARTBUSTERS	Various Artists (Telstar)
-	33	DANCING ON THE CEILING	Lionel Ritchie (Motown)
33	34	WHITNEY HOUSTON	Whitney Houston (Arista)
22	35	THE FINAL COUNTDOWN	Europe (Epic)
-	36	WONDERLAND	Erasure (Mute)
29	37	HIT MIX '86	Various Artists (Stylus)
30	38	HIGHWAY OF LIFE	Harry Secombe (Telstar)
34	39	RAPTURE	Anita Baker (Elektra)
21	40	THROUGH THE BARRICADES	Spandau Ballet (Reformation)
28	41	BONNIE TYLER'S GREATEST HITS	Bonnie Tyler (Telstar)
39	42	NOTORIOUS	Duran Duran (EMI)
25	43	CHRISTMAS	Elaine Paige (WEA)
-	44	JUST GOOD FRIENDS	Paul Nicholas (K-Tel)
42	45	SO	Peter Gabriel (Virgin)
-	46	A KIND OF MAGIC	Queen (EMI)
48	47	INVISIBLE TOUCH	Genesis (Charisma)
50	48	DISCO	Pet Shop Boys (Parlophone)
-	49	NO MORE THE FOOL	Elkie Brooks (Legend)
-	50	HOLLYWOOD AND BROADWAY	Richard Clayderman (Decca/Delphine)

17 January 1987

2	1	GRACELAND	Paul Simon (Warner Bros.)
1	2	NOW THAT'S WHAT I CALL MUSIC 8	Various Artists (EMI/Virgin/PolyGram)
4	3	THE WHOLE STORY	Kate Bush (EMI)
7	4	TRUE BLUE	Madonna (Sire)
6	5	SLIPPERY WHEN WET	Bon Jovi (Vertigo)
8	6	LIVE MAGIC	Queen (EMI)
9	7	SILK AND STEEL	Five Star (Tent/RCA)
3	8	HITS 5	Various Artists (CBS/WEA)
5	9	EVERY BREATH YOU TAKE - THE SINGLES	Police (A&M)
13	10	SWEET FREEDOM	Michael McDonald (Warner Bros.)
10	11	REVENGE	Eurythmics (RCA)
15	12	DIFFERENT LIGHT	Bangles (CBS)
12	13	LONDON O - HULL 4	Housemartins (Go! Discs)
16	14	SCOUNDREL DAYS	A-Ha (Warner Bros.)
27	15	COMMUNARDS	Communards (London)
14	16	MUSIC FROM THE SINGING DETECTIVE	Various Artists (BBC)
11	17	FORE!	Huey Lewis & the News (Chrysalis)
17	18	TOP GUN	Soundtrack (CBS)
48	19	DISCO	Pet Shop Boys (Parlophone)
49	20	NO MORE THE FOOL	Elkie Brooks (Legend)
20	21	BROTHERS IN ARMS	Dire Straits (Vertigo)
35	22	THE FINAL COUNTDOWN	Europe (Epic)
18	23	THE FINAL	Wham! (Epic)
23	24	SOUTH PACIFIC	Various Artists (CBS)
41	25	BONNIE TYLER'S GREATEST HITS	Bonnie Tyler (Telstar)
25	26	GET CLOSE	Pretenders (WEA)
30	27	AUGUST	Eric Clapton (Duck)
45	28	SO	Peter Gabriel (Virgin)
26	29	INFECTED	The The (Some Bizzare)
-	30	SUZANNE VEGA	Suzanne Vega (A&M)
-	31	GIVE ME THE REASON	Luther Vandross (Epic)
33	32	DANCING ON THE CEILING	Lionel Ritchie (Motown)
31	33	SIXTIES MANIA	Various Artists (Telstar)
37	34	HIT MIX '86	Various Artists (Stylus)
28	35	IN THE ARMY NOW	Status Quo (Vertigo)
39	36	RAPTURE	Anita Baker (Elektra)
-	37	CROOKED MILE	Microdisney (Virgin)
-	38	JUST LIKE THE FIRST TIME	Freddie Jackson (Capitol)
21	39	LOVERS	Various Artists (Telstar)
-	40	WORD UP	Cameo (Club)
32	41	MOTOWN CHARTBUSTERS	Various Artists (Telstar)
-	42	BEDTIME FOR DEMOCRACY	Dead Kennedys (Alternative Tentacles)
-	43	LICENCED TO ILL	Beastie Boys (Def Jam)
22	44	REMINISCING	Foster & Allen (Stylus)
36	45	WONDERLAND	Erasure (Mute)
34	46	WHITNEY HOUSTON	Whitney Houston (Arista)
40	47	THROUGH THE BARRICADES	Spandau Ballet (Reformation)
19	48	AN ALBUM OF HYMNS	Aled Jones (EMI)
-	49	BREAK EVERY RULE	Tina Turner (Capitol)
46	50	A KIND OF MAGIC	Queen (EMI)

Top US vocalist Michael McDonald opened 1987 in the Top 10 with his only significant UK album success, the compilation *Sweet Freedom*, which was titled after his biggest solo success (a hit in 1986), and also included his even better-known duets with James Ingram (*Yah Mo Be There*) and Patti LaBelle (*On My Own*). Springsteen's *Live 1975-85* box set, still huge in the US, dropped rapidly out of the Top 10 here.

January – February 1987

Graceland took to the top of the chart again for another extended stay - a further six consecutive weeks. Showing similar longevity was Kate Bush's *The Whole Story* compilation, which saw off the pre-Christmas Various Artists compilations that kept it from Number 1, and held on doggedly for a further month at 2. Elkie Brooks attacked the Top 20 with simultaneous hit albums, one of them a hits package.

February 1987

14 February 1987

last week	this week	Title	Artist (Label)
1	1	GRACELAND	Paul Simon (Warner Bros.)
2	2	THE WHOLE STORY	Kate Bush (EMI)
4	3	DIFFERENT LIGHT	Bangles (CBS)
5	4	LIVE MAGIC	Queen (EMI)
10	5	AUGUST	Eric Clapton (Duck)
3	6	SLIPPERY WHEN WET	Bon Jovi (Vertigo)
15	7	ZAZU	Rosie Vela (A&M)
6	8	TRUE BLUE	Madonna (Sire)
11	9	SWEET FREEDOM	Michael McDonald (Warner Bros.)
12	10	THE VERY BEST OF ELKIE BROOKS	Elkie Brooks (Telstar)
9	11	NO MORE THE FOOL	Elkie Brooks (Legend)
17	12	SILK AND STEEL	Five Star (Tent/RCA)
19	13	THE FINAL COUNTDOWN	Europe (Epic)
27	14	RAPTURE	Anita Baker (Elektra)
-	15	THE COST OF LOVING	Style Council (Polydor)
8	16	GET CLOSE	Pretenders (WEA)
13	17	REVENGE	Eurythmics (RCA)
26	18	BROTHERS IN ARMS	Dire Straits (Vertigo)
23	19	UPFRONT 4	Various Artists (Serious)
-	20	MIDNIGHT TO MIDNIGHT	Psychedelic Furs (CBS)
20	21	NOW THAT'S WHAT I CALL MUSIC 8	Various Artists (EMI/Virgin/PolyGram)
16	22	EVERY BREATH YOU TAKE - THE SINGLES	Police (A&M)
45	23	GIVE ME THE REASON	Luther Vandross (Epic)
7	24	THE HOUSE OF BLUE LIGHT	Deep Purple (Polydor)
25	25	DANCING ON THE CEILING	Lionel Ritchie (Motown)
-	26	GAP BAND VIII	Gap Band (Total Experience)
46	27	GEORGIA SATELLITES	Georgia Satellites (Elektra)
18	28	DISCO	Pet Shop Boys (Parlophone)
28	29	BY THE LIGHT OF THE MOON	Los Lobos (London)
30	30	FORE!	Huey Lewis & the News (Chrysalis)
-	31	ABSTRACT EMOTIONS	Randy Crawford (Warner Bros.)
-	32	MASTER OF PUPPETS	Metallica (Music for Nations)
42	33	BLAH BLAH BLAH	Iggy Pop (A&M)
14	34	GOD'S OWN MEDICINE	Mission (Mercury)
35	35	SO	Peter Gabriel (Virgin)
-	36	WAREHOUSE: SONGS AND STORIES	Husker Du (Warner Bros.)
33	37	SCOUNDREL DAYS	A-Ha (Warner Bros.)
21	38	COMMUNARDS	Communards (London)
24	39	LONDON 0 - HULL 4	Housemartins (Go! Discs)
-	40	PICTURE BOOK	Simply Red (Elektra)
41	41	THE HOUSE SOUND OF CHICAGO	Various Artists (D J Int)
40	42	RAT IN THE KITCHEN	UB40 (DEP International)
44	43	LICENCED TO ILL	Beastie Boys (Def Jam)
47	44	THE WEST END STORY	Various Artists (Stre Sounds)
22	45	INFECTED	The The (Some Bizzare)
38	46	STREET SOUNDS CRUCIAL ELECTRO 3	Various Artists (Street Sounds)
29	47	MUSIC FROM THE SINGING DETECTIVE	Various Artists (BBC)
31	48	INVISIBLE TOUCH	Genesis (Charisma)
36	49	WHITNEY HOUSTON	Whitney Houston (Arista)
-	50	IMPRESSIONS	Various Artists (K-Tel)

21 February 1987

last week	this week	Title	Artist (Label)
1	1	GRACELAND	Paul Simon (Warner Bros.)
5	2	AUGUST	Eric Clapton (Duck)
15	3	THE COST OF LOVING	Style Council (Polydor)
2	4	THE WHOLE STORY	Kate Bush (EMI)
3	5	DIFFERENT LIGHT	Bangles (CBS)
-	6	THE PHANTOM OF THE OPERA	Original Cast (Polydor)
20	7	MIDNIGHT TO MIDNIGHT	Psychedelic Furs (CBS)
7	8	ZAZU	Rosie Vela (A&M)
-	9	SILK AND STEEL	Five Star (Tent/RCA)
8	10	TRUE BLUE	Madonna (Sire)
4	11	LIVE MAGIC	Queen (EMI)
9	12	SWEET FREEDOM	Michael McDonald (Warner Bros.)
16	13	GET CLOSE	Pretenders (WEA)
31	14	ABSTRACT EMOTIONS	Randy Crawford (Warner Bros.)
6	15	SLIPPERY WHEN WET	Bon Jovi (Vertigo)
23	16	GIVE ME THE REASON	Luther Vandross (Epic)
14	17	RAPTURE	Anita Baker (Elektra)
17	18	REVENGE	Eurythmics (RCA)
10	19	THE VERY BEST OF ELKIE BROOKS	Elkie Brooks (Telstar)
-	20	MAD, BAD AND DANGEROUS TO KNOW	Dead or Alive (Epic)
11	21	NO MORE THE FOOL	Elkie Brooks (Legend)
28	22	DISCO	Pet Shop Boys (Parlophone)
13	23	THE FINAL COUNTDOWN	Europe (Epic)
22	24	EVERY BREATH YOU TAKE - THE SINGLES	Police (A&M)
-	25	STREET SOUNDS EDITION 20	Various Artists (Street Sounds)
21	26	NOW THAT'S WHAT I CALL MUSIC 8	Various Artists (EMI/Virgin/PolyGram)
35	27	SO	Peter Gabriel (Virgin)
24	28	THE HOUSE OF BLUE LIGHT	Deep Purple (Polydor)
29	29	BY THE LIGHT OF THE MOON	Los Lobos (London)
18	30	BROTHERS IN ARMS	Dire Straits (Vertigo)
40	31	PICTURE BOOK	Simply Red (Elektra)
19	32	UPFRONT 4	Various Artists (Serious)
27	33	GEORGIA SATELLITES	Georgia Satellites (Elektra)
37	34	SCOUNDREL DAYS	A-Ha (Warner Bros.)
30	35	FORE!	Huey Lewis & the News (Chrysalis)
45	36	INFECTED	The The (Some Bizzare)
39	37	CHASIN' A DREAM	Tashan (Def Jam)
38	38	LONDON O - HULL 4	Housemartins (Go! Discs)
49	39	WHITNEY HOUSTON	Whitney Houston (Arista)
-	40	SURFACE	Surface (CBS)
38	41	COMMUNARDS	Communards (London)
-	42	BACK IN THE HIGH LIFE	Steve Winwood (Island)
34	43	GOD'S OWN MEDICINE	Mission (Mercury)
-	44	BACK AGAIN IN THE DHSS	Half Man Half Biscuit (Probe Plus)
32	45	MASTER OF PUPPETS	Metallica (Music for Nations)
-	46	JUST LIKE THE FIRST TIME	Freddie Jackson (Capitol)
43	47	LICENCED TO ILL	Beastie Boys (Def Jam)
25	48	DANCING ON THE CEILING	Lionel Ritchie (Motown)
26	49	GAP BAND VIII	Gap Band (Total Experience)
36	50	WAREHOUSE: SONGS AND STORIES	Husker Du (Warner Bros.)

28 February 1987

last week	this week	Title	Artist (Label)
6	1	THE PHANTOM OF THE OPERA	Original Cast (Polydor)
1	2	GRACELAND	Paul Simon (Warner Bros.)
2	3	AUGUST	Eric Clapton (Duck)
9	4	SILK AND STEEL	Five Star (Tent/RCA)
27	5	SO	Peter Gabriel (Virgin)
5	6	DIFFERENT LIGHT	Bangles (CBS)
4	7	THE WHOLE STORY	Kate Bush (EMI)
16	8	GIVE ME THE REASON	Luther Vandross (Epic)
3	9	THE COST OF LOVING	Style Council (Polydor)
31	10	PICTURE BOOK	Simply Red (Elektra)
-	11	THE VERY BEST OF HOT CHOCOLATE	Hot Chocolate (RAK)
17	12	RAPTURE	Anita Baker (Elektra)
15	13	SLIPPERY WHEN WET	Bon Jovi (Vertigo)
8	14	ZAZU	Rosie Vela (A&M)
12	15	SWEET FREEDOM	Michael McDonald (Warner Bros.)
30	16	BROTHERS IN ARMS	Dire Straits (Vertigo)
14	17	ABSTRACT EMOTIONS	Randy Crawford (Warner Bros.)
18	18	REVENGE	Eurythmics (RCA)
7	19	MIDNIGHT TO MIDNIGHT	Psychedelic Furs (CBS)
10	20	TRUE BLUE	Madonna (Sire)
11	21	LIVE MAGIC	Queen (EMI)
23	22	THE FINAL COUNTDOWN	Europe (Epic)
20	23	MAD, BAD AND DANGEROUS TO KNOW	Dead or Alive (Epic)
47	24	LICENCED TO ILL	Beastie Boys (Def Jam)
50	25	WAREHOUSE: SONGS AND STORIES	Husker Du (Warner Bros.)
39	26	WHITNEY HOUSTON	Whitney Houston (Arista)
22	27	DISCO	Pet Shop Boys (Parlophone)
19	28	THE VERY BEST OF ELKIE BROOKS	Elkie Brooks (Telstar)
44	29	BACK AGAIN IN THE DHSS	Half Man Half Biscuit (Probe Plus)
13	30	GET CLOSE	Pretenders (WEA)
48	31	DANCING ON THE CEILING	Lionel Ritchie (Motown)
41	32	COMMUNARDS	Communards (London)
34	33	SCOUNDREL DAYS	A-Ha (Warner Bros.)
33	34	GEORGIA SATELLITES	Georgia Satellites (Elektra)
37	35	CHASIN' A DREAM	Tashan (Def Jam)
49	36	GAP BAND VIII	Gap Band (Total Experience)
26	37	NOW THAT'S WHAT I CALL MUSIC 8	Various Artists (EMI/Virgin/PolyGram)
29	38	BY THE LIGHT OF THE MOON	Los Lobos (London)
46	39	JUST LIKE THE FIRST TIME	Freddie Jackson (Capitol)
32	40	UPFRONT 4	Various Artists (Serious)
21	41	NO MORE THE FOOL	Elkie Brooks (Legend)
38	42	LONDON O - HULL 4	Housemartins (Go! Discs)
25	43	STREET SOUNDS EDITION 20	Various Artists (Street Sounds)
-	44	ARETHA	Aretha Franklin (Arista)
-	45	ALIVE AND SCREAMING	Krokus (Arista)
24	46	EVERY BREATH YOU TAKE - THE SINGLES	Police (A&M)
35	47	FORE!	Huey Lewis & the News (Chrysalis)
42	48	BACK IN THE HIGH LIFE	Steve Winwood (Island)
43	49	GOD'S OWN MEDICINE	Mission (Mercury)
-	50	COUNT THREE AND PRAY	Berlin (Mercury)

The most successful stage musical on record for many years proved to be Andrew Lloyd Webber's adaptation of a much-filmed chiller, *The Phantom Of The Opera*, starring Michael Crawford and Sarah Brightman. The original cast album was snapped up so readily that it reached Number 1 in its second chart week, while the show itself would still be playing to capacity West End audiences six years later.

March 1987

The Beatles' first four albums (*Please Please Me, With The Beatles, A Hard Day's Night* and *Beatles For Sale*) were issued for the first time on CD in March, and such was the interest created that all four jumped back into the chart simultaneously, entirely on their digital format sales - many of these undoubtedly to people who had first bought the same releases on vinyl 23 and 24 years previously!

28 March 1987

last week	this week	Title	Artist
1	1	THE JOSHUA TREE	U2 (Island)
31	2	MEN AND WOMEN	Simply Red (WEA)
3	3	THE WORLD WON'T LISTEN	Smiths (Rough Trade)
4	4	GRACELAND	Paul Simon (Warner Bros.)
6	5	THE VERY BEST OF HOT CHOCOLATE	Hot Chocolate (RAK)
36	6	RUNNING IN THE FAMILY	Level 42 (Polydor)
19	7	PICTURE BOOK	Simply Red (Elektra)
2	8	THE PHANTOM OF THE OPERA	Original Cast (Polydor)
8	9	WILD FRONTIER	Gary Moore (10)
24	10	MOVE CLOSER	Various Artists (CBS)
13	11	SILK AND STEEL	Five Star (Tent/RCA)
5	12	AUGUST	Eric Clapton (Duck)
14	13	STAND BY ME	Ben E King (Atlantic)
30	14	IF YOU WANT TO DEFEAT YOUR ENEMY, SING HIS SONG	Icicle Works (Beggars Banquet)
10	15	THE FINAL COUNTDOWN	Europe (Epic)
15	16	LICENCED TO ILL	Beastie Boys (Def Jam)
16	17	LIVE MAGIC	Queen (EMI)
12	18	GIVE ME THE REASON	Luther Vandross (Epic)
25	19	COMMUNARDS	Communards (London)
7	20	SAINT JULIAN	Julian Cope (Island)
9	21	THROUGH THE LOOKING GLASS	Siouxsie and the Banshees (Wonderland)
21	22	DIFFERENT LIGHT	Bangles (CBS)
27	23	IMPRESSIONS	Various Artists (K-Tel)
22	24	SO	Peter Gabriel (Virgin)
11	25	BROTHERS IN ARMS	Dire Straits (Vertigo)
23	26	TRUE BLUE	Madonna (Sire)
26	27	WHEN A MAN LOVES A WOMAN	Percy Sledge (Atlantic)
38	28	SHEILA E	Sheila E (Paisley Park)
-	29	CONTROL	Janet Jackson (A&M)
-	30	UPFRONT 5	Various Artists (Serious)
47	31	JUST LIKE THE FIRST TIME	Freddie Jackson (Capitol)
-	32	LICENSED TO KILL	Malice (Atlantic)
-	33	STRONG PERSUADER	Robert Cray Band (Mercury)
18	34	THE WHOLE STORY	Kate Bush (EMI)
-	35	THE FINER THINGS IN LIFE	Chuck Stanley (Def Jam)
20	36	SLIPPERY WHEN WET	Bon Jovi (Vertigo)
-	37	GET CLOSE	Pretenders (WEA)
-	38	ULTIMATE TRAX VOL 2	Various Artists (Champion)
-	39	LOVE ME RIGHT	Millie Scott (Fourth & Broadway)
-	40	TRIO	Parton/Ronstadt/Harris (Warner Bros.)
-	41	RHYTHM OF THE NIGHT	Various Artists (K-Tel)
-	42	INVISIBLE TOUCH	Genesis (Charisma)
-	43	THE DANCE CHART	Various Artists (Telstar)
40	44	A CHANGE OF HEART	David Sanborn (Warner Bros.)
-	45	CLASSIC SONGS	James Taylor (CBS/WEA)
-	46	PRIVATE REVOLUTION	World Party (Chrysalis)
28	47	SCOUNDREL DAYS	A-Ha (Warner Bros.)
45	48	DANCING ON THE CEILING	Lionel Richie (Motown)
49	49	THE COST OF LOVING	Style Council (Polydor)
33	50	RAPTURE	Anita Baker (Elektra)

4 April 1987

last week	this week	Title	Artist
1	1	THE JOSHUA TREE	U2 (Island)
2	2	MEN AND WOMEN	Simply Red (WEA)
6	3	RUNNING IN THE FAMILY	Level 42 (Polydor)
4	4	GRACELAND	Paul Simon (Warner Bros.)
8	5	THE PHANTOM OF THE OPERA	Original Cast (Polydor)
5	6	THE VERY BEST OF HOT CHOCOLATE	Hot Chocolate (RAK)
-	7	NOW THAT'S WHAT I CALL MUSIC 9	Various Artists (EMI/Virgin/PolyGram)
12	8	AUGUST	Eric Clapton (Duck)
11	9	SILK AND STEEL	Five Star (Tent/RCA)
42	10	INVISIBLE TOUCH	Genesis (Charisma)
9	11	WILD FRONTIER	Gary Moore (10)
10	12	MOVE CLOSER	Various Artists (CBS)
24	13	SO	Peter Gabriel (Virgin)
16	14	LICENCED TO ILL	Beastie Boys (Def Jam)
3	15	THE WORLD WON'T LISTEN	Smiths (Rough Trade)
18	16	GIVE ME THE REASON	Luther Vandross (Epic)
7	17	PICTURE BOOK	Simply Red (Elektra)
17	18	LIVE MAGIC	Queen (EMI)
23	19	IMPRESSIONS	Various Artists (K-Tel)
29	20	CONTROL	Janet Jackson (A&M)
26	21	TRUE BLUE	Madonna (Sire)
19	22	COMMUNARDS	Communards (London)
13	23	STAND BY ME	Ben E King (Atlantic)
14	24	IF YOU WANT TO DEFEAT YOUR ENEMY, SING HIS SONG	Icicle Works (Beggars Banquet)
-	25	REVENGE	Eurythmics (RCA)
15	26	THE FINAL COUNTDOWN	Europe (Epic)
48	27	DANCING ON THE CEILING	Lionel Richie (Motown)
21	28	THROUGH THE LOOKING GLASS	Siouxsie and the Banshees (Wonderland)
20	29	SAINT JULIAN	Julian Cope (Island)
30	30	UPFRONT 5	Various Artists (Serious)
25	31	BROTHERS IN ARMS	Dire Straits (Vertigo)
22	32	DIFFERENT LIGHT	Bangles (CBS)
46	33	PRIVATE REVOLUTION	World Party (Chrysalis)
32	34	LICENSED TO KILL	Malice (Atlantic)
35	35	THE FINER THINGS IN LIFE	Chuck Stanley (Def Jam)
43	36	THE DANCE CHART	Various Artists (Telstar)
50	37	RAPTURE	Anita Baker (Elektra)
36	38	SLIPPERY WHEN WET	Bon Jovi (Vertigo)
47	39	SCOUNDREL DAYS	A-Ha (Warner Bros.)
27	40	WHEN A MAN LOVES A WOMAN	Percy Sledge (Atlantic)
37	42	GET CLOSE	Pretenders (WEA)
39	43	LOVE ME RIGHT	Millie Scott (4th & Broadway)
-	44	THE KILLER INSIDE ME	Green On Red (Mercury)
-	45	GOD'S OWN MEDICINE	Mission (Mercury)
45	46	CLASSIC SONGS	James Taylor (CBS/WEA)
-	47	A HARD DAY'S NIGHT	Beatles (Parlophone)
-	48	OPUS DEI	Laibach (Mute)
-	49	DISCO	Pet Shop Boys (Parlophone)
-	50	SWEET FREEDOM	Michael McDonald (Warner Bros.)

11 April 1987

last week	this week	Title	Artist
1	1	THE JOSHUA TREE	U2 (Island)
3	2	RUNNING IN THE FAMILY	Level 42 (Polydor)
2	3	MEN AND WOMEN	Simply Red (WEA)
7	4	NOW THAT'S WHAT I CALL MUSIC 9	Various Artists (EMI/Virgin/PolyGram)
4	5	GRACELAND	Paul Simon (Warner Bros.)
5	6	THE PHANTOM OF THE OPERA	Original Cast (Polydor)
13	7	SO	Peter Gabriel (Virgin)
12	8	MOVE CLOSER	Various Artists (CBS)
6	9	THE VERY BEST OF HOT CHOCOLATE	Hot Chocolate (RAK)
-	10	SIGN 'O' THE TIMES	Prince (Paisley Park)
8	11	AUGUST	Eric Clapton (Duck)
-	12	WHITESNAKE 1987	Whitesnake (EMI)
20	13	CONTROL	Janet Jackson (A&M)
14	14	LICENCED TO ILL	Beastie Boys (Def Jam)
-	15	THE CIRCUS	Erasure (Mute)
17	16	PICTURE BOOK	Simply Red (Elektra)
15	17	THE WORLD WON'T LISTEN	Smiths (Rough Trade)
-	18	INTO THE FIRE	Bryan Adams (A&M)
18	19	LIVE MAGIC	Queen (EMI)
10	20	INVISIBLE TOUCH	Genesis (Charisma)
21	21	TRUE BLUE	Madonna (Sire)
11	22	WILD FRONTIER	Gary Moore (10)
9	23	SILK AND STEEL	Five Star (Tent/RCA)
19	24	IMPRESSIONS	Various Artists (K-Tel)
16	25	GIVE ME THE REASON	Luther Vandross (Epic)
31	26	BROTHERS IN ARMS	Dire Straits (Vertigo)
36	27	THE DANCE CHART	Various Artists (Telstar)
22	28	COMMUNARDS	Communards (London)
30	29	UPFRONT 5	Various Artists (Serious)
23	30	STAND BY ME	Ben E King (Atlantic)
26	31	THE FINAL COUNTDOWN	Europe (Epic)
27	32	DANCING ON THE CEILING	Lionel Richie (Motown)
25	33	REVENGE	Eurythmics (RCA)
28	34	THROUGH THE LOOKING GLASS	Siouxsie and the Banshees (Wonderland)
-	35	FIGHTIN' THE WORLD	ManOWar (Atlantic)
-	36	THE PAVAROTTI COLLECTION	Luciano Pavarotti (Stylus)
24	37	IF YOU WANT TO DEFEAT YOUR ENEMY, SING HIS SONG	Icicle Works (Beggars Banquet)
29	38	SAINT JULIAN	Julian Cope (Island)
-	39	REUNION WILDERNESS	Railway Children (Factory)
43	40	LOVE ME RIGHT	Millie Scott (4th & Broadway)
32	41	DIFFERENT LIGHT	Bangles (CBS)
-	42	L IS FOR LOVER	Al Jarreau (WEA)
33	43	PRIVATE REVOLUTION	World Party (Chrysalis)
-	44	SIGNS OF LIFE	Penguin Cafe Orchestra (Editons EG)
39	45	THE WHOLE STORY	Kate Bush (EMI)
-	46	U2 LIVE: UNDER A BLOOD RED SKY	U2 (Island)
37	47	RAPTURE	Anita Baker (Elektra)
38	48	SLIPPERY WHEN WET	Bon Jovi (Vertigo)
49	49	DISCO	Pet Shop Boys (Parlophone)
-	50	ALF	Alison Moyet (CBS)

U2 had allowed a gap of almost two-and-a-half years between their previous album *The Unforgettable Fire* and the new set *The Joshua Tree* - a hiatus which made it all the more eagerly awaited, particularly as their status as international performers had climbed to superstar level in the interim. This album was their first to debut at Number 1(where it stayed for six weeks), and became the10th-best seller of the 1980s.

April – May 1987

18 April 1987

last week	this week	Title	Artist
1	1	THE JOSHUA TREE	U2 (Island)
4	2	NOW THAT'S WHAT I CALL MUSIC 9	Various Artists (EMI/Virgin/PolyGram)
2	3	RUNNING IN THE FAMILY	Level 42 (Polydor)
3	4	MEN AND WOMEN	Simply Red (WEA)
10	5	SIGN 'O' THE TIMES	Prince (Paisley Park)
18	6	INTO THE FIRE	Bryan Adams (A&M)
12	7	WHITESNAKE 1987	Whitesnake (EMI)
-	8	RAINDANCING	Alison Moyet (CBS)
15	9	THE CIRCUS	Erasure (Mute)
5	10	GRACELAND	Paul Simon (Warner Bros.)
-	11	ELECTRIC	Cult (Beggars Banquet)
6	12	THE PHANTOM OF THE OPERA	Original Cast (Polydor)
13	13	CONTROL	Janet Jackson (A&M)
7	14	SO	Peter Gabriel (Virgin)
8	15	MOVE CLOSER	Various Artists (CBS)
11	16	AUGUST	Eric Clapton (Duck)
9	17	THE VERY BEST OF HOT CHOCOLATE	Hot Chocolate (RAK)
14	18	LICENCED TO ILL	Beastie Boys (Def Jam)
-	19	AMONG THE LIVING	Anthrax (Island)
-	20	THIS TIME	Culture Club (Virgin)
16	21	PICTURE BOOK	Simply Red (Elektra)
21	22	TRUE BLUE	Madonna (Sire)
23	23	SILK AND STEEL	Five Star (Tent/RCA)
25	24	GIVE ME THE REASON	Luther Vandross (Epic)
17	25	THE WORLD WON'T LISTEN	Smiths (Rough Trade)
27	26	THE DANCE CHART	Various Artists (Telstar)
20	27	INVISIBLE TOUCH	Genesis (Charisma)
48	28	SLIPPERY WHEN WET	Bon Jovi (Vertigo)
22	29	WILD FRONTIER	Gary Moore (10)
19	30	LIVE MAGIC	Queen (EMI)
26	31	BROTHERS IN ARMS	Dire Straits (Vertigo)
24	32	IMPRESSIONS	Various Artists (K-Tel)
38	33	SAINT JULIAN	Julian Cope (Island)
-	34	CLASSIC SONGS	James Taylor (CBS/WEA)
28	35	COMMUNARDS	Communards (London)
45	36	THE WHOLE STORY	Kate Bush (EMI)
-	37	THE ENGELBERT HUMPERDINCK COLLECTION	Engelbert Humperdinck (Telstar)
29	38	UPFRONT 5	Various Artists (Serious)
34	39	THROUGH THE LOOKING GLASS	Siouxsie and the Banshees (Wonderland)
-	40	THE HOUSE SOUND OF CHICAGO 2	Various Artists (DJ International)
-	41	STRONG PERSUADER	Robert Cray Band (Mercury)
41	42	DIFFERENT LIGHT	Bangles (CBS)
42	43	L IS FOR LOVER	Al Jarreau (WEA)
39	44	REUNION WILDERNESS	Railway Children (Factory)
-	45	CRUSH ON YOU	Jets (MCA)
31	46	THE FINAL COUNTDOWN	Europe (Epic)
32	47	DANCING ON THE CEILING	Lionel Richie (Motown)
-	48	SHAKA ZULU	Ladysmith Black Mambazo (Warner Bros.)
33	49	REVENGE	Eurythmics (RCA)
36	50	THE PAVAROTTI COLLECTION	Luciano Pavarotti (Stylus)

25 April 1987

last week	this week	Title	Artist
1	1	THE JOSHUA TREE	U2 (Island)
5	2	SIGN 'O' THE TIMES	Prince (Paisley Park)
2	3	NOW THAT'S WHAT I CALL MUSIC 9	Various Artists (EMI/Virgin/PolyGram)
8	4	RAINDANCING	Alison Moyet (CBS)
3	5	RUNNING IN THE FAMILY	Level 42 (Polydor)
11	6	ELECTRIC	Cult (Beggars Banquet)
6	7	INTO THE FIRE	Bryan Adams (A&M)
7	8	WHITESNAKE 1987	Whitesnake (EMI)
4	9	MEN AND WOMEN	Simply Red (WEA)
9	10	THE CIRCUS	Erasure (Mute)
10	11	GRACELAND	Paul Simon (Warner Bros.)
19	12	AMONG THE LIVING	Anthrax (Island)
22	13	TRUE BLUE	Madonna (Sire)
13	14	CONTROL	Janet Jackson (A&M)
14	15	SO	Peter Gabriel (Virgin)
-	16	TANGO IN THE NIGHT	Fleetwood Mac (Warner Bros.)
15	17	MOVE CLOSER	Various Artists (CBS)
20	18	THIS TIME	Culture Club (Virgin)
17	19	THE VERY BEST OF HOT CHOCOLATE	Hot Chocolate (RAK)
-	20	FLM	Mel & Kim (Supreme)
16	21	AUGUST	Eric Clapton (Duck)
12	22	THE PHANTOM OF THE OPERA	Original Cast (Polydor)
18	23	LICENCED TO ILL	Beastie Boys (Def Jam)
23	24	SILK AND STEEL	Five Star (Tent/RCA)
21	25	PICTURE BOOK	Simply Red (Elektra)
30	26	LIVE MAGIC	Queen (EMI)
48	27	SHAKA ZULU	Ladysmith Black Mambazo (Warner Bros.)
27	28	INVISIBLE TOUCH	Genesis (Charisma)
46	29	THE FINAL COUNTDOWN	Europe (Epic)
-	30	THE RETURN OF BRUNO	Bruce Willis (Motown)
31	31	BROTHERS IN ARMS	Dire Straits (Vertigo)
28	32	SLIPPERY WHEN WET	Bon Jovi (Vertigo)
47	33	DANCING ON THE CEILING	Lionel Richie (Motown)
37	34	THE ENGELBERT HUMPERDINCK COLLECTION	Engelbert Humperdinck (Telstar)
-	35	NICK KAMEN	Nick Kamen (WEA)
49	36	REVENGE	Eurythmics (RCA)
40	37	THE HOUSE SOUND OF CHICAGO 2	Various Artists (DJ International)
-	38	MOTHER FIST AND HER FIVE DAUGHTERS	Marc Almond (Some Bizzare)
-	39	UH! TEARS BABY	Win (London)
-	40	SHE WAS ONLY A GROCER'S DAUGHTER	Blow Monkeys (RCA)
-	41	HYPNO BEAT	Woodentops (Rough Trade)
39	42	THROUGH THE LOOKING GLASS	Siouxsie and the Banshees (Wonderland)
35	43	COMMUNARDS	Communards (London)
42	44	DIFFERENT LIGHT	Bangles (CBS)
24	45	GIVE ME THE REASON	Luther Vandross (Epic)
25	46	THE WORLD WON'T LISTEN	Smiths (Rough Trade)
41	47	STRONG PERSUADER	Robert Cray Band (Mercury)
-	48	HEART OVER MIND	Jennifer Rush (CBS)
26	49	THE DANCE CHART	Various Artists (Telstar)
36	50	THE WHOLE STORY	Kate Bush (EMI)

2 May 1987

last week	this week	Title	Artist
4	1	RAINDANCING	Alison Moyet (CBS)
3	2	NOW THAT'S WHAT I CALL MUSIC 9	Various Artists (EMI/Virgin/PolyGram)
1	3	THE JOSHUA TREE	U2 (Island)
6	4	ELECTRIC	Cult (Beggars Banquet)
16	5	TANGO IN THE NIGHT	Fleetwood Mac (Warner Bros.)
20	6	FLM	Mel & Kim (Supreme)
5	7	RUNNING IN THE FAMILY	Level 42 (Polydor)
2	8	SIGN 'O' THE TIMES	Prince (Paisley Park)
11	9	GRACELAND	Paul Simon (Warner Bros.)
9	10	MEN AND WOMEN	Simply Red (WEA)
18	11	THIS TIME	Culture Club (Virgin)
12	12	AMONG THE LIVING	Anthrax (Island)
-	13	NEVER LET ME DOWN	David Bowie (EMI America)
17	14	MOVE CLOSER	Various Artists (CBS)
28	15	INVISIBLE TOUCH	Genesis (Charisma)
8	16	WHITESNAKE 1987	Whitesnake (EMI)
10	17	THE CIRCUS	Erasure (Mute)
7	18	INTO THE FIRE	Bryan Adams (A&M)
13	19	TRUE BLUE	Madonna (Sire)
24	20	SILK AND STEEL	Five Star (Tent/RCA)
40	21	SHE WAS ONLY A GROCER'S DAUGHTER	Blow Monkeys (RCA)
15	22	SO	Peter Gabriel (Virgin)
14	23	CONTROL	Janet Jackson (A&M)
19	24	THE VERY BEST OF HOT CHOCOLATE	Hot Chocolate (RAK)
-	25	OUTLAND	Spear Of Destiny (10)
-	26	REIGN IN BLOOD	Slayer (Def Jam)
30	27	THE RETURN OF BRUNO	Bruce Willis (Motown)
45	28	GIVE ME THE REASON	Luther Vandross (Epic)
32	29	SLIPPERY WHEN WET	Bon Jovi (Vertigo)
31	30	BROTHERS IN ARMS	Dire Straits (Vertigo)
46	31	THE WORLD WON'T LISTEN	Smiths (Rough Trade)
27	32	SHAKA ZULU	Ladysmith Black Mambazo (Warner Bros.)
23	33	LICENCED TO ILL	Beastie Boys (Def Jam)
34	34	THE HOUSE SOUND OF CHICAGO 2	Various Artists (London)
-	35	BIG LIFE	Nightranger (MCA)
-	36	CLOSE TO THE BONE	Thompson Twins (Arista)
22	37	THE PHANTOM OF THE OPERA	Original Cast (Polydor)
-	38	FORE!	Huey Lewis & the News (Chrysalis)
21	39	AUGUST	Eric Clapton (Duck)
26	40	LIVE MAGIC	Queen (EMI)
25	41	PICTURE BOOK	Simply Red (Elektra)
35	42	NICK KAMEN	Nick Kamen (WEA)
-	43	HAPPY HOUR	Ted Hawkins (Windows on the World)
29	44	THE FINAL COUNTDOWN	Europe (Epic)
50	45	THE WHOLE STORY	Kate Bush (EMI)
49	46	THE DANCE CHART	Various Artists (Telstar)
34	47	THE ENGELBERT HUMPERDINCK COLLECTION	Engelbert Humperdinck (Telstar)
36	48	REVENGE	Eurythmics (RCA)
-	49	BY REQUEST	James Last (Polydor)
-	50	SWEET FREEDOM	Michael McDonald (Warner Bros.)

Continuing massive sales for U2's *The Joshua Tree* kept the ninth volume of *Now Music* at Number 2 on the chart, while U2 were eventually deposed by Alison Moyet's *Raindancing* - a release which hoisted her into the tiny club of female atists to have had Number 1 sellers with consecutive albums. Actor Bruce Willis from TV's *Moonlighting*, meanwhile, charted his *Return Of Bruno* album - on Motown!

May 1987

last this
week

9 May 1987

last	this	Title	Artist
3	1	THE JOSHUA TREE	U2 (Island)
5	2	TANGO IN THE NIGHT	Fleetwood Mac (Warner Bros.)
6	3	FLM	Mel & Kim (Supreme)
1	4	RAINDANCING	Alison Moyet (CBS)
13	5	NEVER LET ME DOWN	David Bowie (EMI America)
7	6	RUNNING IN THE FAMILY	Level 42 (Polydor)
2	7	NOW THAT'S WHAT I CALL MUSIC 9	Various Artists (EMI/Virgin/PolyGram)
15	8	INVISIBLE TOUCH	Genesis (Charisma)
8	9	SIGN 'O' THE TIMES	Prince (Paisley Park)
10	10	MEN AND WOMEN	Simply Red (WEA)
4	11	ELECTRIC	Cult (Beggars Banquet)
-	12	KEEP YOUR DISTANCE	Curiosity Killed The Cat (Mercury)
11	13	THIS TIME	Culture Club (Virgin)
25	14	OUTLAND	Spear Of Destiny (10)
9	15	GRACELAND	Paul Simon (Warner Bros.)
17	16	THE CIRCUS	Erasure (Mute)
-	17	SOLITUDE STANDING	Suzanne Vega (A&M)
19	18	TRUE BLUE	Madonna (Sire)
21	19	SHE WAS ONLY A GROCER'S DAUGHTER	Blow Monkeys (RCA)
16	20	WHITESNAKE 1987	Whitesnake (EMI)
12	21	AMONG THE LIVING	Anthrax (Island)
20	22	SILK AND STEEL	Five Star (Tent/RCA)
23	23	CONTROL	Janet Jackson (A&M)
29	24	SLIPPERY WHEN WET	Bon Jovi (Vertigo)
22	25	SO	Peter Gabriel (Virgin)
26	26	REIGN IN BLOOD	Slayer (Def Jam)
14	27	MOVE CLOSER	Various Artists (CBS)
37	28	THE PHANTOM OF THE OPERA	Original Cast (Polydor)
18	29	INTO THE FIRE	Bryan Adams (A&M)
32	30	SHAKA ZULU	Ladysmith Black Mambazo (Warner Bros.)
-	31	LILLO	Lillo Thomas (Capitol)
28	32	GIVE ME THE REASON	Luther Vandross (Epic)
31	33	THE WORLD WON'T LISTEN	Smiths (Rough Trade)
27	34	THE RETURN OF BRUNO	Bruce Willis ((Motown)
-	35	LET ME UP (I'VE HAD ENOUGH)	Tom Petty & the Heartbreakers (MCA)
36	36	CLOSE TO THE BONE	Thompson Twins (Arista)
24	37	THE VERY BEST OF HOT CHOCOLATE	Hot Chocolate (RAK)
-	38	BOYS' NIGHT OUT	First Circle (EMI America)
50	39	SWEET FREEDOM	Michael McDonald (Warner Bros.)
33	40	LICENCED TO ILL	Beastie Boys (Def Jam)
30	41	BROTHERS IN ARMS	Dire Straits (Vertigo)
44	42	THE FINAL COUNTDOWN	Europe (Epic)
41	43	PICTURE BOOK	Simply Red (Elektra)
38	44	FORE!	Huey Lewis & the News (Chrysalis)
39	45	AUGUST	Eric Clapton (Duck)
40	46	LIVE MAGIC	Queen (EMI)
45	47	THE WHOLE STORY	Kate Bush (EMI)
-	48	BREAK EVERY RULE	Tina Turner (Capitol)
-	49	DANCING ON THE CEILING	Lionel Richie (Motown)
43	50	HAPPY HOUR	Ted Hawkins (Windows on the World)

16 May 1987

last	this	Title	Artist
12	1	KEEP YOUR DISTANCE	Curiosity Killed The Cat (Mercury)
2	2	TANGO IN THE NIGHT	Fleetwood Mac (Warner Bros.)
17	3	SOLITUDE STANDING	Suzanne Vega (A&M)
1	4	THE JOSHUA TREE	U2 (Island)
4	5	RAINDANCING	Alison Moyet (CBS)
5	6	NEVER LET ME DOWN	David Bowie (EMI America)
8	7	INVISIBLE TOUCH	Genesis (Charisma)
3	8	FLM	Mel & Kim (Supreme)
7	9	NOW THAT'S WHAT I CALL MUSIC 9	Various Artists (EMI/Virgin/PolyGram)
6	10	RUNNING IN THE FAMILY	Level 42 (Polydor)
14	11	OUTLAND	Spear Of Destiny (10)
15	12	GRACELAND	Paul Simon (Warner Bros.)
11	13	ELECTRIC	Cult (Beggars Banquet)
10	14	MEN AND WOMEN	Simply Red (WEA)
18	15	TRUE BLUE	Madonna (Sire)
16	16	MEN AND WOMEN	Simply Red (WEA)
-	17	LIVING IN A BOX	Living in a Box (Chrysalis)
22	18	SILK AND STEEL	Five Star (Tent/RCA)
20	19	WHITESNAKE 1987	Whitesnake (EMI)
23	20	CONTROL	Janet Jackson (A&M)
26	21	REIGN IN BLOOD	Slayer (Def Jam)
13	22	THIS TIME	Culture Club (Virgin)
25	23	SO	Peter Gabriel (Virgin)
29	24	INTO THE FIRE	Bryan Adams (A&M)
19	25	SHE WAS ONLY A GROCER'S DAUGHTER	Blow Monkeys (RCA)
16	26	THE CIRCUS	Erasure (Mute)
-	27	HILLBILLY DELUXE	Dwight Yoakam (Reprise)
21	28	AMONG THE LIVING	Anthrax (Island)
-	29	RHYTHM KILLERS	Sly & Robbie (Fourth & Broadway)
31	30	LILLO	Lillo Thomas (Capitol)
27	31	MOVE CLOSER	Various Artists (CBS)
-	32	COMING ROUND AGAIN	Carly Simon (Arista)
35	33	LET ME UP (I'VE HAD ENOUGH)	Tom Petty & the Heartbreakers (MCA)
30	34	SHAKA ZULU	Ladysmith Black Mambazo (Warner Bros.)
-	35	JOIN THE ARMY	Suicidal Tendencies (Virgin)
24	36	SLIPPERY WHEN WET	Bon Jovi (Vertigo)
32	37	GIVE ME THE REASON	Luther Vandross (Epic)
28	38	THE PHANTOM OF THE OPERA	Original Cast (Polydor)
39	39	SWEET FREEDOM	Michael McDonald (Warner Bros.)
37	40	THE VERY BEST OF HOT CHOCOLATE	Hot Chocolate (RAK)
38	41	BOYS' NIGHT OUT	First Circle (EMI America)
40	42	LICENCED TO ILL	Beastie Boys (Def Jam)
-	43	THE FINER THINGS IN LIFE	Chuck Stanley (Def Jam)
-	44	MAYFLOWER	Weather Prophets (Elevation)
-	45	THIS IS THE STORY	Proclaimers (Chrysalis)
-	46	CAN'T BE WITH YOU TONIGHT	Judy Boucher (Orbitone)
-	47	S. O. D. – THE EPIC YEARS	Spear of Destiny (Epic)
33	48	THE WORLD WON'T LISTEN	Smiths (Rough Trade)
41	49	BROTHERS IN ARMS	Dire Straits (Vertigo)
42	50	THE FINAL COUNTDOWN	Europe (Epic)

23 May 1987

last	this	Title	Artist
3	1	SOLITUDE STANDING	Suzanne Vega (A&M)
1	2	KEEP YOUR DISTANCE	Curiosity Killed The Cat (Mercury)
2	3	TANGO IN THE NIGHT	Fleetwood Mac (Warner Bros.)
4	4	THE JOSHUA TREE	U2 (Island)
7	5	INVISIBLE TOUCH	Genesis (Charisma)
5	6	RAINDANCING	Alison Moyet (CBS)
10	7	RUNNING IN THE FAMILY	Level 42 (Polydor)
8	8	FLM	Mel & Kim (Supreme)
13	9	ELECTRIC	Cult (Beggars Banquet)
-	10	IT'S BETTER TO TRAVEL	Swing Out Sister (Mercury)
-	11	TRIBUTE	Ozzy Osbourne (Epic)
23	12	SO	Peter Gabriel (Virgin)
11	13	OUTLAND	Spear Of Destiny (10)
6	14	NEVER LET ME DOWN	David Bowie (EMI America)
9	15	NOW THAT'S WHAT I CALL MUSIC 9	Various Artists (EMI/Virgin/PolyGram)
15	16	TRUE BLUE	Madonna (Sire)
12	17	GRACELAND	Paul Simon (Warner Bros.)
16	18	MEN AND WOMEN	Simply Red (WEA)
18	19	SILK AND STEEL	Five Star (Tent/RCA)
26	20	THE CIRCUS	Erasure (Mute)
17	21	LIVING IN A BOX	Living in a Box (Chrysalis)
20	22	CONTROL	Janet Jackson (A&M)
22	23	THIS TIME	Culture Club (Virgin)
14	24	SIGN 'O' THE TIMES	Prince (Paisley Park)
32	25	COMING ROUND AGAIN	Carly Simon (Arista)
35	26	JOIN THE ARMY	Suicidal Tendencies (Virgin)
-	27	UPFRONT 6	Various Artists (Upfront)
29	28	RHYTHM KILLERS	Sly & Robbie (Fourth & Broadway)
25	29	SHE WAS ONLY A GROCER'S DAUGHTER	Blow Monkeys (RCA)
38	30	THE PHANTOM OF THE OPERA	Original Cast (Polydor)
19	31	WHITESNAKE 1987	Whitesnake (EMI)
-	32	TOM JONES' GREATEST HITS	Tom Jones (Telstar)
42	33	LICENCED TO ILL	Beastie Boys (Def Jam)
28	34	AMONG THE LIVING	Anthrax (Island)
27	35	HILLBILLY DELUXE	Dwight Yoakam (Reprise)
21	36	REIGN IN BLOOD	Slayer (Def Jam)
-	37	BY REQUEST	James Last (Polydor)
31	38	MOVE CLOSER	Various Artists (CBS)
36	39	SLIPPERY WHEN WET	Bon Jovi (Vertigo)
50	40	THE FINAL COUNTDOWN	Europe (Epic)
30	41	GIVE ME THE REASON	Luther Vandross (Epic)
-	42	LILLO	Lillo Thomas (Capitol)
24	43	INTO THE FIRE	Bryan Adams (A&M)
33	44	LET ME UP (I'VE HAD ENOUGH)	Tom Petty & the Heartbreakers (MCA)
-	45	REVOLVER	Beatles (Parlophone)
-	46	PUBLIC ENEMY	Public Enemy (Def Jam)
-	47	WALLS OF JERICHO	Helloween (Noise International)
39	48	SWEET FREEDOM	Michael McDonald (Warner Bros.)
40	49	THE VERY BEST OF HOT CHOCOLATE	Hot Chocolate (RAK)
-	50	DEAD LETTER OFFICE	REM (IRS)

Though it was not, incredibly, to reach Number 1 until November, Fleetwood Mac's *Tango In The Night* was the most consistently high-selling album of May 1987, sitting doggedly at Number 2 in the chart while short-lived Number 1s rose and fell in brief shows of glory around it. Eventually the seventh biggest-selling album of the 1980s, it sales would rival that of Mac's yardstick *Rumours* from 1977.

May – June 1987

30 May 1987

last week	this week	Title	Artist (Label)
10	1	IT'S BETTER TO TRAVEL	Swing Out Sister (Mercury)
1	2	SOLITUDE STANDING	Suzanne Vega (A&M)
2	3	KEEP YOUR DISTANCE	Curiosity Killed The Cat (Mercury)
3	4	TANGO IN THE NIGHT	Fleetwood Mac (Warner Bros.)
7	5	RUNNING IN THE FAMILY	Level 42 (Polydor)
4	6	THE JOSHUA TREE	U2 (Island)
12	7	SO	Peter Gabriel (Virgin)
6	8	RAINDANCING	Alison Moyet (CBS)
8	9	FLM	Mel & Kim (Supreme)
11	10	TRIBUTE	Ozzy Osbourne (Epic)
9	11	ELECTRIC	Cult (Beggars Banquet)
5	12	INVISIBLE TOUCH	Genesis (Charisma)
18	13	MEN AND WOMEN	Simply Red (WEA)
13	14	OUTLAND	Spear Of Destiny (10)
-	15	BABBLE	That Petrol Emotion (Polydor)
22	16	CONTROL	Janet Jackson (A&M)
-	17	GIRLS GIRLS GIRLS	Motley Crue (Elektra)
15	18	NOW THAT'S WHAT I CALL MUSIC 9	Various Artists (EMI/Virgin/PolyGram)
17	19	GRACELAND	Paul Simon (Warner Bros.)
20	20	SILK AND STEEL	Five Star (Tent/RCA)
16	21	TRUE BLUE	Madonna (Sire)
21	22	LIVING IN A BOX	Living in a Box (Chrysalis)
40	23	THE FINAL COUNTDOWN	Europe (Epic)
27	24	UPFRONT 6	Various Artists (Upfront)
25	25	COMING ROUND AGAIN	Carly Simon (Arista)
32	26	TOM JONES' GREATEST HITS	Tom Jones (Telstar)
33	27	LICENCED TO ILL	Beastie Boys (Def Jam)
28	28	RHYTHM KILLERS	Sly & Robbie (Fourth & Broadway)
20	29	THE CIRCUS	Erasure (Mute)
-	30	ONE VOICE	Barbra Streisand (CBS)
41	31	GIVE ME THE REASON	Luther Vandross (Epic)
29	32	SHE WAS ONLY A GROCER'S DAUGHTER	Blow Monkeys (RCA)
-	33	THE WORLD WON'T LISTEN	Smiths (Rough Trade)
-	34	S. O. D. – THE EPIC YEARS	Spear of Destiny (Epic)
-	35	THIS IS THE STORY	Proclaimers (Chrysalis)
38	36	MOVE CLOSER	Various Artists (CBS)
30	37	THE PHANTOM OF THE OPERA	Original Cast (Polydor)
-	38	PLEASED TO MEET YOU	Replacements (Sire)
45	39	REVOLVER	Beatles (Parlophone)
50	40	DEAD LETTER OFFICE	REM (IRS)
35	41	HILLBILLY DELUXE	Dwight Yoakam (Reprise)
39	42	SLIPPERY WHEN WET	Bon Jovi (Vertigo)
23	43	THIS TIME	Culture Club (Virgin)
37	44	BY REQUEST	James Last (Polydor)
31	45	WHITESNAKE 1987	Whitesnake (EMI)
24	46	SIGN 'O' THE TIMES	Prince (Paisley Park)
42	47	LILLO	Lillo Thomas (Capitol)
-	48	ROGER WHITTAKER'S FINEST COLLECTION	Roger Whittaker (Tembo)
43	49	INTO THE FIRE	Bryan Adams (A&M)
49	50	THE VERY BEST OF HOT CHOCOLATE	Hot Chocolate (RAK)

6 June 1987

last week	this week	Title	Artist (Label)
2	1	SOLITUDE STANDING	Suzanne Vega (A&M)
1	2	IT'S BETTER TO TRAVEL	Swing Out Sister (Mercury)
-	3	LIVE IN THE CITY OF LIGHT	Simple Minds (Virgin)
3	4	KEEP YOUR DISTANCE	Curiosity Killed The Cat (Mercury)
6	5	THE JOSHUA TREE	U2 (Island)
7	6	SO	Peter Gabriel (Virgin)
4	7	TANGO IN THE NIGHT	Fleetwood Mac (Warner Bros.)
-	8	KISS ME KISS ME KISS ME	Cure (Fiction)
5	9	RUNNING IN THE FAMILY	Level 42 (Polydor)
10	10	TRIBUTE	Ozzy Osbourne (Epic)
9	11	FLM	Mel & Kim (Supreme)
13	12	MEN AND WOMEN	Simply Red (WEA)
17	13	GIRLS GIRLS GIRLS	Motley Crue (Elektra)
8	14	RAINDANCING	Alison Moyet (CBS)
11	15	ELECTRIC	Cult (Beggars Banquet)
19	16	GRACELAND	Paul Simon (Warner Bros.)
27	17	LICENCED TO ILL	Beastie Boys (Def Jam)
22	18	LIVING IN A BOX	Living in a Box (Chrysalis)
12	19	INVISIBLE TOUCH	Genesis (Charisma)
20	20	TRUE BLUE	Madonna (Sire)
14	21	OUTLAND	Spear Of Destiny (10)
-	22	LOUDER THAN BOMBS	Smiths (Rough Trade)
-	23	FREEDOM NO COMPROMISE	Little Steven (Manhattan)
-	24	DANCING ON THE COUCH	Go West (Chrysalis)
26	25	TOM JONES' GREATEST HITS	Tom Jones (Telstar)
-	26	BAD ANIMALS	Heart (Capitol)
28	27	RHYTHM KILLERS	Sly & Robbie (Fourth & Broadway)
15	28	BABBLE	That Petrol Emotion (Polydor)
20	29	SILK AND STEEL	Five Star (Tent/RCA)
18	30	NOW THAT'S WHAT I CALL MUSIC 9	Various Artists (EMI/Virgin/PolyGram)
29	31	THE CIRCUS	Erasure (Mute)
30	32	ONE VOICE	Barbra Streisand (CBS)
25	33	COMING ROUND AGAIN	Carly Simon (Arista)
24	34	UPFRONT 6	Various Artists (Upfront)
-	35	RED HOT RHYTHM 'N' BLUES	Diana Ross (EMI)
-	36	MICK AND CAROLINE	Latin Quarter (Rockin' Horse)
16	37	CONTROL	Janet Jackson (A&M)
36	38	MOVE CLOSER	Various Artists (CBS)
34	39	S. O. D. – THE EPIC YEARS	Spear of Destiny (Epic)
-	40	WHITNEY	Whitney Houston (Arista)
-	41	THUNDER	Andy Taylor (MCA)
23	42	THE FINAL COUNTDOWN	Europe (Epic)
48	43	ROGER WHITTAKER'S FINEST COLLECTION	Roger Whittaker (Tembo)
-	44	NEVER LET ME DOWN	David Bowie (EMI America)
-	45	DAWNRAZOR	Fields of the Nephilim (Situation 2)
47	46	LILLO	Lillo Thomas (Capitol)
45	47	WHITESNAKE 1987	Whitesnake (EMI)
-	48	BLUE MOODS	Keni Stevens (Jam Today)
41	49	HILLBILLY DELUXE	Dwight Yoakam (Reprise)
-	50	ATLANTIC SOUL	Various Artists (Atlantic)

13 June 1987

last week	this week	Title	Artist (Label)
3	1	LIVE IN THE CITY OF LIGHT	Simple Minds (Virgin)
2	2	IT'S BETTER TO TRAVEL	Swing Out Sister (Mercury)
8	3	KISS ME KISS ME KISS ME	Cure (Fiction)
1	4	SOLITUDE STANDING	Suzanne Vega (A&M)
40	5	WHITNEY	Whitney Houston (Arista)
5	6	THE JOSHUA TREE	U2 (Island)
4	7	KEEP YOUR DISTANCE	Curiosity Killed The Cat (Mercury)
7	8	TANGO IN THE NIGHT	Fleetwood Mac (Warner Bros.)
13	9	GIRLS GIRLS GIRLS	Motley Crue (Elektra)
17	10	LICENCED TO ILL	Beastie Boys (Def Jam)
14	11	RAINDANCING	Alison Moyet (CBS)
26	12	BAD ANIMALS	Heart (Capitol)
9	13	RUNNING IN THE FAMILY	Level 42 (Polydor)
11	14	FLM	Mel & Kim (Supreme)
15	15	ELECTRIC	Cult (Beggars Banquet)
16	16	INVISIBLE TOUCH	Genesis (Charisma)
12	17	MEN AND WOMEN	Simply Red (WEA)
-	18	SGT PEPPER'S LONELY HEARTS CLUB BAND	Beatles (Parlophone)
6	19	SO	Peter Gabriel (Virgin)
31	20	THE CIRCUS	Erasure (Mute)
50	21	ATLANTIC SOUL	Various Artists (Atlantic)
22	22	LOUDER THAN BOMBS	Smiths (Rough Trade)
20	23	TRUE BLUE	Madonna (Sire)
29	24	SILK AND STEEL	Five Star (Tent/RCA)
25	25	TOM JONES' GREATEST HITS	Tom Jones (Telstar)
16	26	GRACELAND	Paul Simon (Warner Bros.)
18	27	LIVING IN A BOX	Living in a Box (Chrysalis)
10	28	TRIBUTE	Ozzy Osbourne (Epic)
24	29	DANCING ON THE COUCH	Go West (Chrysalis)
21	30	OUTLAND	Spear Of Destiny (10)
27	31	RHYTHM KILLERS	Sly & Robbie (Fourth & Broadway)
28	32	BABBLE	That Petrol Emotion (Polydor)
-	33	JUST GETS BETTER WITH TIME	Whispers (Solar)
23	34	FREEDOM NO COMPROMISE	Little Steven (Manhattan)
-	35	TALLULAH	Go-Betweens (Beggars Banquet)
-	36	PRIEST LIVE	Judas Priest (CBS)
32	37	ONE VOICE	Barbra Streisand (CBS)
30	38	NOW THAT'S WHAT I CALL MUSIC 9	Various Artists (EMI/Virgin/PolyGram)
-	39	GIVE ME THE REASON	Luther Vandross (Epic)
43	40	ROGER WHITTAKER'S FINEST COLLECTION	Roger Whittaker (Tembo)
34	41	UPFRONT 6	Various Artists (Upfront)
42	42	ANNIVERSARY	Tammy Wynette (Epic)
46	43	LILLO	Lillo Thomas (Capitol)
45	44	DAWNRAZOR	Fields of the Nephilim (Situation 2)
41	45	THUNDER	Andy Taylor (MCA)
-	46	I CAN'T LET YOU GO	Norwood (MCA)
-	47	TWO-FISTED TALES	Long Ryders (Island)
33	48	COMING ROUND AGAIN	Carly Simon (Arista)
36	49	MICK AND CAROLINE	Latin Quarter (Rockin' Horse)
37	50	CONTROL	Janet Jackson (A&M)

Suzanne Vega, the most prominent of a new wave of mid-1980s female singer-songwriters, topped the chart for a week with her second album, while new British group Swing Out Sister went one better by reaching the summit - again, for one week only - with their debut package. Whitney Houston's second album started modestly on the chart, but her concurrent Number 1 single success quickly boosted it.

June – July 1987

Once into its stride, there was no holding Whitney Houston's *Whitney*. Her first album had been a long stayer near the top of the chart a year earlier. but had actually peaked at Number 2. The follow-up managed six straight weeks at Number 1, and would eventually become the second biggest-selling album of the 1980s by a female artist, outselling Madonna's *True Blue*, and beaten only by Kylie Minogue's debut.

July 1987

11 July 1987

last week	this week	Title	Artist
1	1	WHITNEY	Whitney Houston (Arista)
6	2	CLUTCHING AT STRAWS	Marillion (EMI)
2	3	THE JOSHUA TREE	U2 (Island)
5	4	THE RETURN OF BRUNO	Bruce Willis (Motown)
3	5	LIVE IN THE CITY OF LIGHT	Simple Minds (Virgin)
7	6	KEEP YOUR DISTANCE	Curiosity Killed The Cat (Mercury)
4	7	SOLITUDE STANDING	Suzanne Vega (A&M)
11	8	INVISIBLE TOUCH	Genesis (Charisma)
9	9	ATLANTIC SOUL	Various Artists (Atlantic)
10	10	LICENCED TO ILL	Beastie Boys (Def Jam)
8	11	IT'S BETTER TO TRAVEL	Swing Out Sister (Mercury)
16	12	THE CIRCUS	Erasure (Mute)
21	13	BAD ANIMALS	Heart (Capitol)
25	14	HITS REVIVAL	Various Artists (K-Tel)
14	15	TANGO IN THE NIGHT	Fleetwood Mac (Warner Bros.)
28	16	WHITESNAKE 1987	Whitesnake (EMI)
17	17	NEVER LET ME DOWN	David Bowie (EMI America)
12	18	FRIENDS AND LOVERS	Various Artists (K-Tel)
13	19	SGT PEPPER'S LONELY HEARTS CLUB BAND	Beatles (Parlophone)
27	20	FLM	Mel & Kim (Supreme)
24	21	GRACELAND	Paul Simon (Warner Bros.)
15	22	RADIO K.A.O.S.	Roger Waters (EMI)
20	23	RAINDANCING	Alison Moyet (CBS)
30	24	FIRST CHAPTER	Mission (Mercury)
-	25	FOREVER, FOR ALWAYS, FOR LOVE	Luther Vandross (Epic)
-	26	GIVE ME CONVENIENCE	Dead Kennedys (Alternative Tentacles)
48	27	THE HOLIDAY ALBUM	Various Artists (CBS)
19	28	MEN AND WOMEN	Simply Red (WEA)
35	29	SIGN 'O' THE TIMES	Prince (Paisley Park)
40	30	SO	Peter Gabriel (Virgin)
33	31	TRUE BLUE	Madonna (Sire)
-	32	WHISPERING JACK	John Farnham (RCA)
-	33	LIVE AT THE HOLLYWOOD BOWL	Doors (Elektra)
18	34	ROGER WHITTAKER'S FINEST COLLECTION	Roger Whittaker (Tembo)
-	35	CONTROL	Janet Jackson (A&M)
23	36	TOM JONES' GREATEST HITS	Tom Jones (Telstar)
22	37	KISS ME KISS ME KISS ME	Cure (Fiction)
32	38	RUNNING IN THE FAMILY	Level 42 (Polydor)
-	39	DISCO	Pet Shop Boys (Parlophone)
29	40	LIFE	Neil Young (Geffen)
-	41	ONE SECOND	Yello (Mercury)
31	42	EXIT 0	Steve Earle (MCA)
-	43	SAMMY HAGAR	Sammy Hagar (Geffen)
-	44	TALLULAH	Go-Betweens (Beggars Banquet)
-	45	LONELY IS AN EYESORE	Various Artists (4AD)
37	46	SOLD	Boy George (Virgin)
45	47	THE MARIA CALLAS COLLECTION	Maria Callas (Stylus)
38	48	STRONG PERSUADER	Robert Cray Band (Mercury)
-	49	STREET SOUNDS DANCE MUSIC '87	Various Artists (Street Sounds)
26	50	BIGGER AND DEFFER	LL Cool J (Def Jam)

18 July 1987

last week	this week	Title	Artist
1	1	WHITNEY	Whitney Houston (Arista)
3	2	THE JOSHUA TREE	U2 (Island)
2	3	CLUTCHING AT STRAWS	Marillion (EMI)
8	4	INVISIBLE TOUCH	Genesis (Charisma)
4	5	THE RETURN OF BRUNO	Bruce Willis (Motown)
5	6	LIVE IN THE CITY OF LIGHT	Simple Minds (Virgin)
6	7	KEEP YOUR DISTANCE	Curiosity Killed The Cat (Mercury)
7	8	SOLITUDE STANDING	Suzanne Vega (A&M)
13	9	BAD ANIMALS	Heart (Capitol)
14	10	HITS REVIVAL	Various Artists (K-Tel)
-	11	ECHO AND THE BUNNYMEN	Echo & the Bunnymen (WEA)
9	12	ATLANTIC SOUL	Various Artists (Atlantic)
11	13	IT'S BETTER TO TRAVEL	Swing Out Sister (Mercury)
10	14	LICENCED TO ILL	Beastie Boys (Def Jam)
25	15	FOREVER, FOR ALWAYS, FOR LOVE	Luther Vandross (Epic)
20	16	FLM	Mel & Kim (Supreme)
27	17	THE HOLIDAY ALBUM	Various Artists (CBS)
16	18	WHITESNAKE 1987	Whitesnake (EMI)
32	19	WHISPERING JACK	John Farnham (RCA)
35	20	CONTROL	Janet Jackson (A&M)
15	21	TANGO IN THE NIGHT	Fleetwood Mac (Warner Bros.)
29	22	SIGN 'O' THE TIMES	Prince (Paisley Park)
12	23	THE CIRCUS	Erasure (Mute)
30	24	SO	Peter Gabriel (Virgin)
17	25	NEVER LET ME DOWN	David Bowie (EMI America)
37	26	KISS ME KISS ME KISS ME	Cure (Fiction)
24	27	FIRST CHAPTER	Mission (Mercury)
31	28	TRUE BLUE	Madonna (Sire)
23	29	RAINDANCING	Alison Moyet (CBS)
48	30	STRONG PERSUADER	Robert Cray Band (Mercury)
-	31	THE ISLAND STORY	Various Artists (Island)
-	32	IN CONCERT - LYON AND HOUSTON	Jean Michel Jarre (Polydor)
-	33	NO PROTECTION	Starship (Grunt)
45	34	LONELY IS AN EYESORE	Various Artists (4AD)
33	35	LIVE AT THE HOLLYWOOD BOWL	Doors (Elektra)
26	36	GIVE ME CONVENIENCE	Dead Kennedys (Alternative Tentacles)
38	37	RUNNING IN THE FAMILY	Level 42 (Polydor)
19	38	SGT PEPPER'S LONELY HEARTS CLUB BAND	Beatles (Parlophone)
21	39	GRACELAND	Paul Simon (Warner Bros.)
41	40	ONE SECOND	Yello (Mercury)
40	41	LIFE	Neil Young (Geffen)
28	42	MEN AND WOMEN	Simply Red (WEA)
49	43	STREET SOUNDS DANCE MUSIC '87	Various Artists (Street Sounds)
39	44	DISCO	Pet Shop Boys (Parlophone)
-	45	QUEEN'S GREATEST HITS	Queen (EMI)
46	46	SOLD	Boy George (Virgin)
42	47	EXIT 0	Steve Earle (MCA)
-	48	THE PLAGUE	Nuclear Assault (Under One Flag)
18	49	FRIENDS AND LOVERS	Various Artists (K-Tel)
34	50	ROGER WHITTAKER'S FINEST COLLECTION	Roger Whittaker (Tembo)

25 July 1987

last week	this week	Title	Artist
1	1	WHITNEY	Whitney Houston (Arista)
2	2	THE JOSHUA TREE	U2 (Island)
11	3	ECHO AND THE BUNNYMEN	Echo & the Bunnymen (WEA)
5	4	THE RETURN OF BRUNO	Bruce Willis (Motown)
4	5	INVISIBLE TOUCH	Genesis (Charisma)
3	6	CLUTCHING AT STRAWS	Marillion (EMI)
6	7	LIVE IN THE CITY OF LIGHT	Simple Minds (Virgin)
-	8	INTRODUCING THE HARDLINE ACCORDING TO	Terence Trent D'Arby (CBS)
7	9	KEEP YOUR DISTANCE	Curiosity Killed The Cat (Mercury)
9	10	BAD ANIMALS	Heart (Capitol)
31	11	THE ISLAND STORY	Various Artists (Island)
8	12	SOLITUDE STANDING	Suzanne Vega (A&M)
20	13	CONTROL	Janet Jackson (A&M)
12	14	ATLANTIC SOUL	Various Artists (Atlantic)
-	15	HITS 6	Various Artists (CBS/WEA/BMG)
32	16	IN CONCERT - LYON AND HOUSTON	Jean Michel Jarre (Polydor)
16	17	FLM	Mel & Kim (Supreme)
10	18	HITS REVIVAL	Various Artists (K-Tel)
21	19	TANGO IN THE NIGHT	Fleetwood Mac (Warner Bros.)
14	20	LICENCED TO ILL	Beastie Boys (Def Jam)
15	21	FOREVER, FOR ALWAYS, FOR LOVE	Luther Vandross (Epic)
-	22	SIXTIES MIX	Various Artists (Stylus)
30	23	STRONG PERSUADER	Robert Cray Band (Mercury)
13	24	IT'S BETTER TO TRAVEL	Swing Out Sister (Mercury)
23	25	THE CIRCUS	Erasure (Mute)
18	26	WHITESNAKE 1987	Whitesnake (EMI)
33	27	NO PROTECTION	Starship (Grunt)
19	28	WHISPERING JACK	John Farnham (RCA)
-	29	SHABINI	Bhundu Boys (Discafrique)
26	30	KISS ME KISS ME KISS ME	Cure (Fiction)
28	31	TRUE BLUE	Madonna (Sire)
-	32	COLLABORATION	George Benson & Earl Klugh (Warner Bros.)
41	33	LIFE	Neil Young (Geffen)
22	34	SIGN 'O' THE TIMES	Prince (Paisley Park)
-	35	FAMOUS BLUE RAINCOAT	Jennifer Warnes (RCA)
42	36	MEN AND WOMEN	Simply Red (WEA)
43	37	STREET SOUNDS DANCE MUSIC '87	Various Artists (Street Sounds)
37	38	RUNNING IN THE FAMILY	Level 42 (Polydor)
-	39	ALL IN THE NAME OF LOVE	Atlantic Starr (Warner Bros.)
-	40	RADIO K.A.O.S.	Roger Waters (EMI)
24	41	SO	Peter Gabriel (Virgin)
34	42	THE HOLIDAY ALBUM	Various Artists (CBS)
43	43	LONELY IS AN EYESORE	Various Artists (4AD)
44	44	DISCO	Pet Shop Boys (Parlophone)
-	45	U2 LIVE: UNDER A BLOOD RED SKY	U2 (Island)
36	46	GIVE ME CONVENIENCE	Dead Kennedys (Alternative Tentacles)
47	47	EXIT 0	Steve Earle (MCA)
50	48	ROGER WHITTAKER'S FINEST COLLECTION	Roger Whittaker (Tembo)
25	49	NEVER LET ME DOWN	David Bowie (EMI America)
29	50	RAINDANCING	Alison Moyet (CBS)

Bruce Willis' *The Return Of Bruno* had seemed an unlikely major album seller at first, notwithstanding the actor's TV popularity. However, the singles taken from it were giving Willis huge success in the singles chart - *Under The Boardwalk* was at Number 2 in the week the album peaked at 4 - and the benefits of the resulting airplay fed back to the parent package. This was, however, his only hit album.

1 August 1987

last week	this week	Title	Artist (Label)
8	1	INTRODUCING THE HARDLINE ACCORDING TO	Terence Trent D'Arby (CBS)
15	2	HITS 6	Various Artists (CBS/WEA/BMG)
1	3	WHITNEY	Whitney Houston (Arista)
2	4	THE JOSHUA TREE	U2 (Island)
5	5	INVISIBLE TOUCH	Genesis (Charisma)
10	6	BAD ANIMALS	Heart (Capitol)
4	7	THE RETURN OF BRUNO	Bruce Willis (Motown)
22	8	SIXTIES MIX	Various Artists (Stylus)
3	9	ECHO AND THE BUNNYMEN	Echo & the Bunnymen (WEA)
17	10	FLM	Mel & Kim (Supreme)
11	11	THE ISLAND STORY	Various Artists (Island)
9	12	KEEP YOUR DISTANCE	Curiosity Killed The Cat (Mercury)
-	13	WHO'S THAT GIRL	Soundtrack (Warner Bros.)
7	14	LIVE IN THE CITY OF LIGHT	Simple Minds (Virgin)
12	15	SOLITUDE STANDING	Suzanne Vega (A&M)
20	16	LICENCED TO ILL	Beastie Boys (Def Jam)
13	17	CONTROL	Janet Jackson (A&M)
6	18	CLUTCHING AT STRAWS	Marillion (EMI)
16	19	IN CONCERT - LYON AND HOUSTON	Jean Michel Jarre (Polydor)
24	20	IT'S BETTER TO TRAVEL	Swing Out Sister (Mercury)
31	21	TRUE BLUE	Madonna (Sire)
21	22	FOREVER, FOR ALWAYS, FOR LOVE	Luther Vandross (Epic)
14	23	ATLANTIC SOUL	Various Artists (Atlantic)
35	24	FAMOUS BLUE RAINCOAT	Jennifer Warnes (RCA)
-	25	LOVE IS FOR SUCKERS	Twisted Sister (Atlantic)
25	26	THE CIRCUS	Erasure (Mute)
19	27	TANGO IN THE NIGHT	Fleetwood Mac (Warner Bros.)
18	28	HITS REVIVAL	Various Artists (K-Tel)
26	29	WHITESNAKE 1987	Whitesnake (EMI)
48	30	ROGER WHITTAKER'S FINEST COLLECTION	Roger Whittaker (Tembo)
49	31	NEVER LET ME DOWN	David Bowie (EMI America)
-	32	THE LIVING DAYLIGHTS	Soundtrack (Warner Bros.)
27	33	NO PROTECTION	Starship (Grunt)
32	34	COLLABORATION	George Benson & Earl Klugh (Warner Bros.)
-	35	APPETITE FOR DESTRUCTION	Guns 'N' Roses (Geffen)
42	36	THE HOLIDAY ALBUM	Various Artists (CBS)
-	37	BROTHERS IN ARMS	Dire Straits (Vertigo)
23	38	STRONG PERSUADER	Robert Cray Band (Mercury)
39	39	ALL IN THE NAME OF LOVE	Atlantic Starr (Warner Bros.)
40	40	RADIO K.A.O.S.	Roger Waters (EMI)
37	41	STREET SOUNDS DANCE MUSIC '87	Various Artists (Street Sounds)
-	42	ALL BY MYSELF	Regina Belle (CBS)
-	43	LILLO	Lillo Thomas (Capitol)
28	44	WHISPERING JACK	John Farnham (RCA)
44	45	DISCO	Pet Shop Boys (Parlophone)
38	46	RUNNING IN THE FAMILY	Level 42 (Polydor)
30	47	KISS ME KISS ME KISS ME	Cure (Fiction)
36	48	MEN AND WOMEN	Simply Red (WEA)
50	49	RAINDANCING	Alison Moyet (CBS)
-	50	SGT PEPPER'S LONELY HEARTS CLUB BAND	Beatles (Parlophone)

8 August 1987

last week	this week	Title	Artist (Label)
1	1	INTRODUCING THE HARDLINE ACCORDING TO	Terence Trent D'Arby (CBS)
2	2	HITS 6	Various Artists (CBS/WEA/BMG)
3	3	WHITNEY	Whitney Houston (Arista)
13	4	THE JOSHUA TREE	U2 (Island)
-	5	WHO'S THAT GIRL	Soundtrack (Warner Bros.)
6	6	BAD ANIMALS	Heart (Capitol)
7	7	THE RETURN OF BRUNO	Bruce Willis (Motown)
8	8	SIXTIES MIX	Various Artists (Stylus)
14	9	LIVE IN THE CITY OF LIGHT	Simple Minds (Virgin)
5	10	INVISIBLE TOUCH	Genesis (Charisma)
10	11	FLM	Mel & Kim (Supreme)
15	12	SOLITUDE STANDING	Suzanne Vega (A&M)
16	13	LICENCED TO ILL	Beastie Boys (Def Jam)
11	14	THE ISLAND STORY	Various Artists (Island)
12	15	KEEP YOUR DISTANCE	Curiosity Killed The Cat (Mercury)
16	16	CLUTCHING AT STRAWS	Marillion (EMI)
21	17	TRUE BLUE	Madonna (Sire)
20	18	IT'S BETTER TO TRAVEL	Swing Out Sister (Mercury)
22	19	FOREVER, FOR ALWAYS, FOR LOVE	Luther Vandross (Epic)
-	20	SAMANTHA FOX	Samantha Fox (Jive)
35	21	APPETITE FOR DESTRUCTION	Guns 'N' Roses (Geffen)
9	22	ECHO AND THE BUNNYMEN	Echo & the Bunnymen (WEA)
23	23	ATLANTIC SOUL	Various Artists (Atlantic)
17	24	CONTROL	Janet Jackson (A&M)
27	25	TANGO IN THE NIGHT	Fleetwood Mac (Warner Bros.)
24	26	HEARSAY	Alexander O'Neal (Tabu)
24	27	FAMOUS BLUE RAINCOAT	Jennifer Warnes (RCA)
34	28	COLLABORATION	George Benson & Earl Klugh (Warner Bros.)
32	29	THE LIVING DAYLIGHTS	Soundtrack (Warner Bros.)
45	30	DISCO	Pet Shop Boys (Parlophone)
-	31	FASTER PUSSYCAT	Faster Pussycat (Elektra)
19	32	IN CONCERT - LYON AND HOUSTON	Jean Michel Jarre (Polydor)
26	33	THE CIRCUS	Erasure (Mute)
29	34	WHITESNAKE 1987	Whitesnake (EMI)
28	35	HITS REVIVAL	Various Artists (K-Tel)
39	36	ALL IN THE NAME OF LOVE	Atlantic Starr (Warner Bros.)
25	37	LOVE IS FOR SUCKERS	Twisted Sister (Atlantic)
-	38	FIERCE	Various Artists (Cooltempo)
42	39	ALL BY MYSELF	Regina Belle (CBS)
30	40	ROGER WHITTAKER'S FINEST COLLECTION	Roger Whittaker (Tembo)
37	41	BROTHERS IN ARMS	Dire Straits (Vertigo)
44	42	WHISPERING JACK	John Farnham (RCA)
46	43	RUNNING IN THE FAMILY	Level 42 (Polydor)
47	44	KISS ME KISS ME KISS ME	Cure (Fiction)
49	45	RAINDANCING	Alison Moyet (CBS)
-	46	GRACELAND	Paul Simon (Warner Bros.)
-	47	SO	Peter Gabriel (Virgin)
48	48	MEN AND WOMEN	Simply Red (WEA)
-	49	BOUNCING OFF SATELLITES	B-52s (Island)
50	50	SGT PEPPER'S LONELY HEARTS CLUB BAND	Beatles (Parlophone)

15 August 1987

last week	this week	Title	Artist (Label)
2	1	HITS 6	Various Artists (CBS/WEA/BMG)
1	2	INTRODUCING THE HARDLINE ACCORDING TO	Terence Trent D'Arby (CBS)
4	3	THE JOSHUA TREE	U2 (Island)
8	4	SIXTIES MIX	Various Artists (Stylus)
6	5	BAD ANIMALS	Heart (Capitol)
3	6	WHITNEY	Whitney Houston (Arista)
5	7	WHO'S THAT GIRL	Soundtrack (Warner Bros.)
10	8	INVISIBLE TOUCH	Genesis (Charisma)
17	9	TRUE BLUE	Madonna (Sire)
11	10	FLM	Mel & Kim (Supreme)
7	11	THE RETURN OF BRUNO	Bruce Willis (Motown)
-	12	KICK IT - THE DEF JAM SAMPLER	Various Artists (Def Jam)
26	13	HEARSAY	Alexander O'Neal (Tabu)
13	14	LICENCED TO ILL	Beastie Boys (Def Jam)
9	15	LIVE IN THE CITY OF LIGHT	Simple Minds (Virgin)
-	16	DUOTONES	Kenny G (Arista)
12	17	SOLITUDE STANDING	Suzanne Vega (A&M)
16	18	CLUTCHING AT STRAWS	Marillion (EMI)
-	19	U2 LIVE: UNDER A BLOOD RED SKY	U2 (Island)
15	20	KEEP YOUR DISTANCE	Curiosity Killed The Cat (Mercury)
21	21	APPETITE FOR DESTRUCTION	Guns 'N' Roses (Geffen)
22	22	ECHO AND THE BUNNYMEN	Echo & the Bunnymen (WEA)
18	23	IT'S BETTER TO TRAVEL	Swing Out Sister (Mercury)
-	24	MIRACLE	Kane Gang (Kitchenware)
14	25	THE ISLAND STORY	Various Artists (Island)
19	26	FOREVER, FOR ALWAYS, FOR LOVE	Luther Vandross (Epic)
36	27	ALL IN THE NAME OF LOVE	Atlantic Starr (Warner Bros.)
39	28	ALL BY MYSELF	Regina Belle (CBS)
-	29	GIRLS GIRLS GIRLS	Motley Crue (Elektra)
-	30	PRIDE	White Lion (Atlantic)
32	31	IN CONCERT - LYON AND HOUSTON	Jean Michel Jarre (Polydor)
20	32	SAMANTHA FOX	Samantha Fox (Jive)
23	33	ATLANTIC SOUL	Various Artists (Atlantic)
25	34	TANGO IN THE NIGHT	Fleetwood Mac (Warner Bros.)
-	35	FIERCE	Various Artists (Cooltempo)
24	36	CONTROL	Janet Jackson (A&M)
27	37	FAMOUS BLUE RAINCOAT	Jennifer Warnes (RCA)
-	38	STRANGE WEATHER	Marianne Faithfull (Island)
-	39	THE UNFORGETTABLE FIRE	U2 (Island)
-	40	DEFENDER	Rory Gallagher (Demon)
-	41	MUSICAL MADNESS	Mantronix (10)
-	42	UNDER THE INFLUENCE	Mary Coughlan (WEA)
29	43	THE LIVING DAYLIGHTS	Soundtrack (Warner Bros.)
34	44	WHITESNAKE 1987	Whitesnake (EMI)
35	45	HITS REVIVAL	Various Artists (K-Tel)
44	46	KISS ME KISS ME KISS ME	Cure (Fiction)
30	47	DISCO	Pet Shop Boys (Parlophone)
49	48	BOUNCING OFF SATELLITES	B-52s (Island)
28	49	COLLABORATION	George Benson & Earl Klugh (Warner Bros.)
31	50	FASTER PUSSYCAT	Faster Pussycat (Elektra)

Terence Trent D'Arby, a startling songwriting and performing talent in a credible R&B idiom, broke from obscurity to mega-success almost overnight, with one of the most highly-praised and successful debut albums of recent years, from which also flowed a number of major hit singles. D'Arby's major flaw was an apparent arrogance based on his appreciation of his own talent, and the critics soon turned on him.

August – September 1987

Elvis Presley's *The All Time Greatest Hits*, his first major chart album for many years despite a constant archive-raiding policy by RCA, was a double-album package of his most familiar chartmakers, compiled to mark the 10th anniversary (August 16) of his death. Def Leppard scored their first UK Number 1 with *Hysteria*, after huge US successes, while Heart had their first ever UK Top-Tenner with *Bad Animals*.

September 1987

12 September 1987

last week	this week	Title	Artist (Label)
1	1	HYSTERIA	Def Leppard (Bludgen Riffola)
-	2	BAD	Michael Jackson (Epic)
2	3	HITS 6	Various Artists (CBS/WEA/BMG)
3	4	SUBSTANCE	New Order (Factory)
4	5	WHITNEY	Whitney Houston (Arista)
11	6	ELVIS PRESLEY - THE ALL TIME GREATEST HITS	Elvis Presley (RCA)
6	7	INTRODUCING THE HARDLINE ACCORDING TO	Terence Trent D'Arby (CBS)
17	8	CHANGING FACES – THE VERY BEST OF 10 c.c. AND GODLEY AND CREME	10c.c. & Godley & Creme (Phonogram)
7	9	THE JOSHUA TREE	U2 (Island)
12	10	TRUE BLUE	Madonna (Sire)
10	11	BAD ANIMALS	Heart (Capitol)
5	12	WHO'S THAT GIRL	Soundtrack (Warner Bros.)
8	13	SIXTIES MIX	Various Artists (Stylus)
-	14	DARKLANDS	Jesus & Mary Chain (Blanco y Negro)
18	15	GIVE ME THE REASON	Luther Vandross (Epic)
24	16	FRANK'S WILD YEARS	Tom Waits (Island)
13	17	HEARSAY	Alexander O'Neal (Tabu)
14	18	INVISIBLE TOUCH	Genesis (Charisma)
28	19	THE RETURN OF BRUNO	Bruce Willis (Motown)
21	20	SHERRICK	Sherrick (Warner Bros.)
19	21	PERMANENT VACATION	Aerosmith (Geffen)
9	22	DREAM EVIL	Dio (Vertigo)
25	23	LICENCED TO ILL	Beastie Boys (Def Jam)
15	24	SLIPPERY WHEN WET	Bon Jovi (Vertigo)
16	25	FLM	Mel & Kim (Supreme)
20	26	KEEP YOUR DISTANCE	Curiosity Killed The Cat (Mercury)
37	27	TANGO IN THE NIGHT	Fleetwood Mac (Warner Bros.)
27	28	ROCK 'N' ROLL	Motorhead (GWR)
49	29	LIVE IN THE CITY OF LIGHT	Simple Minds (Virgin)
-	30	THE BEATLES	Beatles (Parlophone)
30	31	SOLITUDE STANDING	Suzanne Vega (A&M)
-	32	SIGN 'O' THE TIMES	Prince (Paisley Park)
-	33	WHERE THE ACTION IS	Westworld (RCA)
29	34	CLUTCHING AT STRAWS	Marillion (EMI)
-	35	TROUBLE OVER HERE	Trouble Funk (Fourth & Broadway)
22	36	LA BAMBA	Soundtrack (London)
38	37	FAMOUS BLUE RAINCOAT	Jennifer Warnes (RCA)
32	38	THE BIG THROWDOWN	Levert (Atlantic)
-	39	JONATHAN BUTLER	Jonathan Butler (Jive)
23	40	FOREVER, FOR ALWAYS, FOR LOVE	Luther Vandross (Epic)
41	41	ATLANTIC SOUL	Various Artists (Atlantic)
35	42	U2 LIVE: UNDER A BLOOD RED SKY	U2 (Island)
-	43	JODY WATLEY	Jody Watley (MCA)
26	44	APPETITE FOR DESTRUCTION	Guns 'N' Roses (Geffen)
-	45	RARE	Various Artists (CBS)
-	46	DOOR TO DOOR	Cars (Elektra)
40	47	IT'S BETTER TO TRAVEL	Swing Out Sister (Mercury)
47	48	SGT PEPPER'S LONELY HEARTS CLUB BAND	Beatles (Parlophone)
33	49	KICK IT - THE DEF JAM SAMPLER	Various Artists (Def Jam)
31	50	IF I WERE YOUR WOMAN	Stephanie Mills (MCA)

19 September 1987

last week	this week	Title	Artist (Label)
2	1	BAD	Michael Jackson (Epic)
1	2	HYSTERIA	Def Leppard (Bludgen Riffola)
4	3	SUBSTANCE	New Order (Factory)
14	4	DARKLANDS	Jesus & Mary Chain (Blanco y Negro)
3	5	HITS 6	Various Artists (CBS/WEA/BMG)
9	6	THE JOSHUA TREE	U2 (Island)
8	7	CHANGING FACES – THE VERY BEST OF 10 c.c. AND GODLEY AND CREME	10c.c. & Godley & Creme (Phonogram)
5	8	WHITNEY	Whitney Houston (Arista)
6	9	ELVIS PRESLEY - THE ALL TIME GREATEST HITS	Elvis Presley (RCA)
10	10	ACTUALLY	Pet Shop Boys (Parlophone)
11	11	A MOMENTARY LAPSE OF REASON	Pink Floyd (EMI)
7	12	INTRODUCING THE HARDLINE ACCORDING TO	Terence Trent D'Arby (CBS)
39	13	JONATHAN BUTLER	Jonathan Butler (Jive)
15	14	GIVE ME THE REASON	Luther Vandross (Epic)
18	15	INVISIBLE TOUCH	Genesis (Charisma)
19	16	THE RETURN OF BRUNO	Bruce Willis (Motown)
12	17	WHO'S THAT GIRL	Soundtrack (Warner Bros.)
11	18	BAD ANIMALS	Heart (Capitol)
10	19	TRUE BLUE	Madonna (Sire)
13	20	HEARSAY	Alexander O'Neal (Tabu)
13	21	SIXTIES MIX	Various Artists (Stylus)
-	22	RUNNING IN THE FAMILY	Level 42 (Polydor)
27	23	TANGO IN THE NIGHT	Fleetwood Mac (Warner Bros.)
16	24	FRANK'S WILD YEARS	Tom Waits (Island)
26	25	KEEP YOUR DISTANCE	Curiosity Killed The Cat (Mercury)
20	26	SHERRICK	Sherrick (Warner Bros.)
-	27	BEST OF HOUSE VOL 2	Various Artists (Serious)
-	28	POETIC CHAMPIONS COMPOSE	Van Morrison (Mercury)
21	29	PERMANENT VACATION	Aerosmith (Geffen)
25	30	FLM	Mel & Kim (Supreme)
29	31	LIVE IN THE CITY OF LIGHT	Simple Minds (Virgin)
-	32	CREST OF A KNAVE	Jethro Tull (Chrysalis)
23	33	LICENCED TO ILL	Beastie Boys (Def Jam)
38	34	THE BIG THROWDOWN	Levert (Atlantic)
22	35	DREAM EVIL	Dio (Vertigo)
-	36	PAID IN FULL	Eric B & Rakim (Fourth & Broadway)
-	37	WHITESNAKE 1987	Whitesnake (EMI)
31	38	SOLITUDE STANDING	Suzanne Vega (A&M)
24	39	SLIPPERY WHEN WET	Bon Jovi (Vertigo)
40	40	FOREVER, FOR ALWAYS, FOR LOVE	Luther Vandross (Epic)
-	42	THRILLER	Michael Jackson (Epic)
41	43	ATLANTIC SOUL	Various Artists (Atlantic)
-	44	AMERICAN ENGLISH	Wax (RCA)
-	45	IN THE DARK	Grateful Dead (Arista)
28	46	ROCK 'N' ROLL	Motorhead (GWR)
-	47	WELCOME TO MY ROOM	Randy Brown (Threeway)
32	48	SIGN 'O' THE TIMES	Prince (Paisley Park)
33	49	WHERE THE ACTION IS	Westworld (RCA)
35	50	TROUBLE OVER HERE	Trouble Funk (Fourth & Broadway)

26 September 1987

last week	this week	Title	Artist (Label)
1	1	BAD	Michael Jackson (Epic)
10	2	ACTUALLY	Pet Shop Boys (Parlophone)
11	3	A MOMENTARY LAPSE OF REASON	Pink Floyd (EMI)
2	4	HYSTERIA	Def Leppard (Bludgen Riffola)
7	5	CHANGING FACES – THE VERY BEST OF 10 c.c. AND GODLEY AND CREME	10c.c. & Godley & Creme (Phonogram)
5	6	HITS 6	Various Artists (CBS/WEA/BMG)
3	7	SUBSTANCE	New Order (Factory)
6	8	THE JOSHUA TREE	U2 (Island)
4	9	DARKLANDS	Jesus & Mary Chain (Blanco y Negro)
-	10	DANCING WITH STRANGERS	Chris Rea (Magnet)
-	11	WONDERFUL LIFE	Black (A&M)
13	12	JONATHAN BUTLER	Jonathan Butler (Jive)
8	13	WHITNEY	Whitney Houston (Arista)
9	14	ELVIS PRESLEY - THE ALL TIME GREATEST HITS	Elvis Presley (RCA)
-	15	ALWAYS GUARANTEED	Cliff Richard (EMI)
-	16	BABYLON AND ON	Squeeze (A&M)
12	17	INTRODUCING THE HARDLINE ACCORDING TO	Terence Trent D'Arby (CBS)
-	18	BETWEEN THE LINES	Five Star (RCA)
28	19	POETIC CHAMPIONS COMPOSE	Van Morrison (Mercury)
-	20	LIFE IN THE RAW	W.A.S.P. (Capitol)
19	21	TRUE BLUE	Madonna (Sire)
32	22	CREST OF A KNAVE	Jethro Tull (Chrysalis)
14	23	GIVE ME THE REASON	Luther Vandross (Epic)
17	24	WHO'S THAT GIRL	Soundtrack (Warner Bros.)
22	25	RUNNING IN THE FAMILY	Level 42 (Polydor)
-	26	DOCUMENT	REM (IRS)
-	27	THE CREAM OF ERIC CLAPTON	Eric Clapton (Polydor)
41	28	FOREVER, FOR ALWAYS, FOR LOVE	Luther Vandross (Epic)
-	29	RAINDANCING	Alison Moyet (CBS)
30	30	INVISIBLE TOUCH	Genesis (Charisma)
31	31	LIVE IN THE CITY OF LIGHT	Simple Minds (Virgin)
21	32	SIXTIES MIX	Various Artists (Stylus)
16	33	THE RETURN OF BRUNO	Bruce Willis (Motown)
45	34	IN THE DARK	Grateful Dead (Arista)
43	35	ATLANTIC SOUL	Various Artists (Atlantic)
42	36	THRILLER	Michael Jackson (Epic)
48	37	SIGN 'O' THE TIMES	Prince (Paisley Park)
30	38	FLM	Mel & Kim (Supreme)
37	39	WHITESNAKE 1987	Whitesnake (EMI)
29	40	PERMANENT VACATION	Aerosmith (Geffen)
23	41	TANGO IN THE NIGHT	Fleetwood Mac (Warner Bros.)
39	42	SOLITUDE STANDING	Suzanne Vega (A&M)
27	43	BEST OF HOUSE VOL 2	Various Artists (Serious)
24	44	FRANK'S WILD YEARS	Tom Waits (Island)
26	45	SHERRICK	Sherrick (Warner Bros.)
20	46	HEARSAY	Alexander O'Neal (Tabu)
44	47	AMERICAN ENGLISH	Wax (RCA)
-	48	HAPPY?	PiL (Virgin)
-	49	WOW!	Bananarama (London)
34	50	THE BIG THROWDOWN	Levert (Atlantic)

Michael Jackson's *Bad* broke all existing UK records for first-week sales by a new album, moving over 340,000 copies in its first seven days, and demolishing the existing record of 230,000 set only a few months previously by U2's *The Joshua Tree*. In its first week at the top, it was estimated to be outselling the Number 1 single (Rick Astley's *Never Gonna Give You Up*) by a factor of four to one.

October 1987

3 October 1987

last week	this week		
1	1	BAD	Michael Jackson (Epic)
10	2	DANCING WITH STRANGERS	Chris Rea (Magnet)
11	3	WONDERFUL LIFE	Black (A&M)
2	4	ACTUALLY	Pet Shop Boys (Parlophone)
3	5	A MOMENTARY LAPSE OF REASON	Pink Floyd (EMI)
15	6	ALWAYS GUARANTEED	Cliff Richard (EMI)
18	7	BETWEEN THE LINES	Five Star (RCA)
5	8	CHANGING FACES – THE VERY BEST OF 10 c.c. AND GODLEY AND CREME	10c.c. & Godley Creme (Phonogram)
4	9	HYSTERIA	Def Leppard (Bludgen Riffola)
-	10	NOW! SMASH HITS	Various Artists (Virgin/EMI)
27	11	THE CREAM OF ERIC CLAPTON	Eric Clapton (Polydor)
-	12	THE PEOPLE WHO GRINNED THEMSELVES TO DEATH	Housemartins (Go! Discs)
26	13	DOCUMENT	REM (IRS)
8	14	THE JOSHUA TREE	U2 (Island)
20	15	LIFE IN THE RAW	W.A.S.P. (Capitol)
-	16	POPPED IN SOULED OUT	Wet Wet Wet (Precious)
13	17	WHITNEY	Whitney Houston (Arista)
-	18	BRIDGE OF SPIES	T'Pau (Siren)
12	19	JONATHAN BUTLER	Jonathan Butler (Jive)
22	20	CREST OF A KNAVE	Jethro Tull (Chrysalis)
14	21	ELVIS PRESLEY - THE ALL TIME GREATEST HITS	Elvis Presley (RCA)
6	22	HITS 6	Various Artists (CBS/WEA/BMG)
19	23	POETIC CHAMPIONS COMPOSE	Van Morrison (Mercury)
21	24	TRUE BLUE	Madonna (Sire)
16	25	BABYLON AND ON	Squeeze (A&M)
7	26	SUBSTANCE	New Order (Factory)
41	27	TANGO IN THE NIGHT	Fleetwood Mac (Warner Bros.)
23	28	GIVE ME THE REASON	Luther Vandross (Epic)
17	29	INTRODUCING THE HARDLINE ACCORDING TO	Terence Trent D'Arby (CBS)
9	30	DARKLANDS	Jesus & Mary Chain (Blanco y Negro)
25	31	RUNNING IN THE FAMILY	Level 42 (Polydor)
44	32	FRANK'S WILD YEARS	Tom Waits (Island)
-	33	A SAMPLE OF BLUE NOTE	Various Artists (Blue Note)
48	34	HAPPY?	PiL (Virgin)
24	35	WHO'S THAT GIRL	Soundtrack (Warner Bros.)
-	36	EXHIBITION	Gary Numan (Beggars Banquet)
-	37	PRIMITIVE COOL	Mick Jagger (CBS)
-	38	LONESOME JUBILEE	John Cougar Mellencamp (Mercury)
-	39	LINDA'S PARTY	Bolshoi (Beggars Banquet)
45	40	SHERRICK	Sherrick (Warner Bros.)
-	41	ANOTHER STEP	Kim Wilde (MCA)
46	42	HEARSAY	Alexander O'Neal (Tabu)
43	43	BEST OF HOUSE VOL 2	Various Artists (Serious)
33	44	THE RETURN OF BRUNO	Bruce Willis (Motown)
34	45	IN THE DARK	Grateful Dead (Arista)
39	46	WHITESNAKE 1987	Whitesnake (EMI)
49	47	WOW!	Bananarama (London)
47	48	AMERICAN ENGLISH	Wax (RCA)
-	49	PORTRAIT	Andres Segovia (Stylus)
-	50	ODYSSEY - THE GREATEST HITS	Odyssey (Stylus)

10 October 1987

last week	this week		
1	1	BAD	Michael Jackson (Epic)
2	2	DANCING WITH STRANGERS	Chris Rea (Magnet)
3	3	WONDERFUL LIFE	Black (A&M)
10	4	NOW! SMASH HITS	Various Artists (Virgin/EMI)
4	5	ACTUALLY	Pet Shop Boys (Parlophone)
16	6	POPPED IN SOULED OUT	Wet Wet Wet (Precious)
11	7	THE CREAM OF ERIC CLAPTON	Eric Clapton (Polydor)
-	8	STRANGEWAYS HERE WE COME	Smiths (Rough Trade)
6	9	ALWAYS GUARANTEED	Cliff Richard (EMI)
12	10	THE PEOPLE WHO GRINNED THEMSELVES TO DEATH	Housemartins (Go! Discs)
9	11	HYSTERIA	Def Leppard (Bludgen Riffola)
7	12	BETWEEN THE LINES	Five Star (RCA)
5	13	A MOMENTARY LAPSE OF REASON	Pink Floyd (EMI)
14	14	THE JOSHUA TREE	U2 (Island)
8	15	CHANGING FACES – THE VERY BEST OF 10 c.c. AND GODLEY AND CREME	10c.c. & Godley & Creme (Phonogram)
-	16	MUSIC FOR THE MASSES	Depeche Mode (Mute)
17	17	WHITNEY	Whitney Houston (Arista)
-	18	BIG GENERATOR	Yes (Atco)
26	19	SUBSTANCE	New Order (Factory)
28	20	DOCUMENT	REM (IRS)
21	21	GIVE ME THE REASON	Luther Vandross (Epic)
37	22	PRIMITIVE COOL	Mick Jagger (CBS)
19	23	JONATHAN BUTLER	Jonathan Butler (Jive)
-	24	HALFWAY TO SANITY	Ramones (Beggars Banquet)
18	25	BRIDGE OF SPIES	T'Pau (Siren)
15	26	LIFE IN THE RAW	W.A.S.P. (Capitol)
24	27	TRUE BLUE	Madonna (Sire)
22	28	HITS 6	Various Artists (CBS/WEA/BMG)
29	29	INTRODUCING THE HARDLINE ACCORDING TO	Terence Trent D'Arby (CBS)
21	30	ELVIS PRESLEY - THE ALL TIME GREATEST HITS	Elvis Presley (RCA)
30	31	DARKLANDS	Jesus & Mary Chain (Blanco y Negro)
27	32	TANGO IN THE NIGHT	Fleetwood Mac (Warner Bros.)
-	33	FIRST (THE SOUND OF MUSIC)	Then Jerico (London)
23	34	POETIC CHAMPIONS COMPOSE	Van Morrison (Mercury)
-	35	ISLANDS	Mike Oldfield (Virgin)
-	36	ATLANTIC SOUL	Various Artists (Atlantic)
-	37	ESP	Bee Gees (Warner Bros.)
20	38	CREST OF A KNAVE	Jethro Tull (Chrysalis)
31	39	RUNNING IN THE FAMILY	Level 42 (Polydor)
34	40	HAPPY?	PiL (Virgin)
25	41	BABYLON AND ON	Squeeze (A&M)
35	42	WHO'S THAT GIRL	Soundtrack (Warner Bros.)
-	43	BAD ANIMALS	Heart (Capitol)
42	44	HEARSAY	Alexander O'Neal (Tabu)
36	45	EXHIBITION	Gary Numan (Beggars Banquet)
38	46	LONESOME JUBILEE	John Cougar Mellencamp (Mercury)
47	47	TRACKS OF MY TEARS	Various Artists (Telstar)
32	48	FRANK'S WILD YEARS	Tom Waits (Island)
-	49	CRUSHIN'	Fat Boys (Urban)
39	50	LINDA'S PARTY	Bolshoi (Beggars Banquet)

17 October 1987

last week	this week		
1	1	BAD	Michael Jackson (Epic)
8	2	STRANGEWAYS HERE WE COME	Smiths (Rough Trade)
2	3	DANCING WITH STRANGERS	Chris Rea (Magnet)
-	4	TUNNEL OF LOVE	Bruce Springsteen (CBS)
5	5	ACTUALLY	Pet Shop Boys (Parlophone)
6	6	POPPED IN SOULED OUT	Wet Wet Wet (Precious)
16	7	MUSIC FOR THE MASSES	Depeche Mode (Mute)
7	8	THE CREAM OF ERIC CLAPTON	Eric Clapton (Polydor)
3	9	WONDERFUL LIFE	Black (A&M)
9	10	ALWAYS GUARANTEED	Cliff Richard (EMI)
11	11	HYSTERIA	Def Leppard (Bludgen Riffola)
4	12	NOW! SMASH HITS	Various Artists (Virgin/EMI)
10	13	THE PEOPLE WHO GRINNED THEMSELVES TO DEATH	Housemartins (Go! Discs)
12	14	BETWEEN THE LINES	Five Star (RCA)
14	15	THE JOSHUA TREE	U2 (Island)
18	16	BIG GENERATOR	Yes (Atco)
13	17	A MOMENTARY LAPSE OF REASON	Pink Floyd (EMI)
-	18	RED	Communards (London)
15	19	CHANGING FACES – THE VERY BEST OF 10 c.c. AND GODLEY AND CREME	10c.c. & Godley Creme (Phonogram)
29	20	INTRODUCING THE HARDLINE ACCORDING TO	Terence Trent D'Arby (CBS)
17	21	WHITNEY	Whitney Houston (Arista)
19	22	SUBSTANCE	New Order (Factory)
21	23	GIVE ME THE REASON	Luther Vandross (Epic)
37	24	ESP	Bee Gees (Warner Bros.)
32	25	TANGO IN THE NIGHT	Fleetwood Mac (Warner Bros.)
23	26	JONATHAN BUTLER	Jonathan Butler (Jive)
46	27	LONESOME JUBILEE	John Cougar Mellencamp (Mercury)
39	28	RUNNING IN THE FAMILY	Level 42 (Polydor)
27	29	TRUE BLUE	Madonna (Sire)
-	30	THE CIRCUS	Erasure (Mute)
38	31	CREST OF A KNAVE	Jethro Tull (Chrysalis)
24	32	HALFWAY TO SANITY	Ramones (Beggars Banquet)
-	33	PERMANENT VACATION	Aerosmith (Geffen)
20	34	DOCUMENT	REM (IRS)
25	35	BRIDGE OF SPIES	T'Pau (Siren)
28	36	HITS 6	Various Artists (CBS/WEA/BMG)
30	37	ELVIS PRESLEY - THE ALL TIME GREATEST HITS	Elvis Presley (RCA)
35	38	ISLANDS	Mike Oldfield (Virgin)
-	39	IN NO SENSE/NONSENSE	Art of Noise (China)
36	41	ATLANTIC SOUL	Various Artists (Atlantic)
-	42	DO IT AGAIN - THE VERY BEST OF STEELY DAN	Steely Dan (Telstar)
31	43	DARKLANDS	Jesus & Mary Chain (Blanco y Negro)
44	44	BEST OF JAMES BROWN	James Brown (K-Tel)
33	45	FIRST (THE SOUND OF MUSIC)	Then Jerico (London)
26	46	LIFE IN THE RAW	W.A.S.P. (Capitol)
-	47	REFLECTIONS	Foster & Allen (Stylus)
41	48	BABYLON AND ON	Squeeze (A&M)
43	49	BAD ANIMALS	Heart (Capitol)
-	50	ODYSSEY - GREATEST HITS	Odyssey (Stylus)

Chris Rea had by far his biggest-selling album to date (and first Top 5 entry) with *Dancing With Strangers*, even though at Number 2 it was hardly denting the sort of sales which were keeping *Bad* in place at the chart top. The Number 13 placing for *Document* was also the highest UK chart position yet reached by the still somewhat cultish US band REM, whose mega-sales were to arrive during the 1990s.

24 October 1987

last week	this week		
4	1	TUNNEL OF LOVE	Bruce Springsteen (CBS)
1	2	BAD	Michael Jackson (Epic)
2	3	STRANGEWAYS HERE WE COME	Smiths (Rough Trade)
9	4	WONDERFUL LIFE	Black (A&M)
18	5	RED	Communards (London)
8	6	THE CREAM OF ERIC CLAPTON	Eric Clapton (Polydor)
5	7	ACTUALLY	Pet Shop Boys (Parlophone)
3	8	DANCING WITH STRANGERS	Chris Rea (Magnet)
6	9	POPPED IN SOULED OUT	Wet Wet Wet (Precious)
-	10	NOTHING LIKE THE SUN	Sting (A&M)
12	11	NOW! SMASH HITS	Various Artists (Virgin/EMI)
19	12	CHANGING FACES – THE VERY BEST OF 10 c.c. AND GODLEY AND CREME	10c.c. & Godley & Creme (Phonogram)
24	13	ESP	Bee Gees (Warner Bros.)
-	14	ALPHABET CITY	ABC (Neutron)
25	15	TANGO IN THE NIGHT	Fleetwood Mac (Warner Bros.)
14	16	BETWEEN THE LINES	Five Star (RCA)
10	17	ALWAYS GUARANTEED	Cliff Richard (EMI)
11	18	HYSTERIA	Def Leppard (Bludgen Riffola)
7	19	MUSIC FOR THE MASSES	Depeche Mode (Mute)
15	20	THE JOSHUA TREE	U2 (Island)
21	21	WHITNEY	Whitney Houston (Arista)
20	22	INTRODUCING THE HARDLINE ACCORDING TO	Terence Trent D'Arby (CBS)
17	23	A MOMENTARY LAPSE OF REASON	Pink Floyd (EMI)
16	24	BIG GENERATOR	Yes (Atco)
-	25	HIT FACTORY	Various Artists (Stylus)
-	26	UPFRONT 8	Various Artists (Serious)
13	27	THE PEOPLE WHO GRINNED THEMSELVES TO DEATH	Housemartins (Go! Discs)
44	28	BEST OF JAMES BROWN	James Brown (K-Tel)
23	29	GIVE ME THE REASON	Luther Vandross (Epic)
27	30	LONESOME JUBILEE	John Cougar Mellencamp (Mercury)
38	31	ISLANDS	Mike Oldfield (Virgin)
-	32	AFTER DARK	Ray Parker Jnr (Warner Bros.)
-	33	RARE GROOVES	Various Artists (RCA/Arista)
-	34	CRUSHIN'	Fat Boys (Urban)
28	35	RUNNING IN THE FAMILY	Level 42 (Polydor)
30	36	THE CIRCUS	Erasure (Mute)
49	37	BAD ANIMALS	Heart (Capitol)
-	38	THE RIGHT NIGHT AND BARRY WHITE	Barry White (A&M)
-	39	TRACKS OF MY TEARS	Various Artists (Telstar)
-	40	TRUE LOVE	Various Artists (K-Tel)
22	41	SUBSTANCE	New Order (Factory)
29	42	TRUE BLUE	Madonna (Sire)
26	43	JONATHAN BUTLER	Jonathan Butler (Jive)
-	44	SONIC FLOWER GROOVE	Primal Scream (Elevation)
-	45	MIAMI VICE 2	Various Artists (MCA)
35	46	BRIDGE OF SPIES	T'Pau (Siren)
-	47	THE HOUSE OF DOLLS	Gene Loves Jezebel (Beggars Banquet)
32	48	HALFWAY TO SANITY	Ramones (Beggars Banquet)
40	49	PRIMITIVE COOL	Mick Jagger (CBS)
48	50	BABYLON AND ON	Squeeze (A&M)

31 October 1987

1	1	TUNNEL OF LOVE	Bruce Springsteen (CBS)
10	2	NOTHING LIKE THE SUN	Sting (A&M)
2	3	BAD	Michael Jackson (Epic)
13	4	ESP	Bee Gees (Warner Bros.)
14	5	ALPHABET CITY	ABC (Neutron)
6	6	THE CREAM OF ERIC CLAPTON	Eric Clapton (Polydor)
5	7	RED	Communards (London)
15	8	TANGO IN THE NIGHT	Fleetwood Mac (Warner Bros.)
4	9	WONDERFUL LIFE	Black (A&M)
8	10	DANCING WITH STRANGERS	Chris Rea (Magnet)
16	11	BETWEEN THE LINES	Five Star (RCA)
9	12	POPPED IN SOULED OUT	Wet Wet Wet (Precious)
3	13	STRANGEWAYS HERE WE COME	Smiths (Rough Trade)
7	14	ACTUALLY	Pet Shop Boys (Parlophone)
22	15	INTRODUCING THE HARDLINE ACCORDING TO	Terence Trent D'Arby (CBS)
12	16	CHANGING FACES – THE VERY BEST OF 10 c.c. AND GODLEY AND CREME	10c.c. & Godley & Creme (Phonogram)
-	17	SIMPLY SHADOWS	Shadows (Polydor)
-	18	THE CHRISTIANS	Christians (Island)
11	19	NOW! SMASH HITS	Various Artists (Virgin/EMI)
20	20	THE JOSHUA TREE	U2 (Island)
28	21	BEST OF JAMES BROWN	James Brown (K-Tel)
-	22	REFLECTIONS	Foster & Allen (Stylus)
30	23	LONESOME JUBILEE	John Cougar Mellencamp (Mercury)
24	24	UPFRONT 8	Various Artists (Serious)
21	25	WHITNEY	Whitney Houston (Arista)
36	26	THE CIRCUS	Erasure (Mute)
23	27	A MOMENTARY LAPSE OF REASON	Pink Floyd (EMI)
37	28	BAD ANIMALS	Heart (Capitol)
27	29	THE PEOPLE WHO GRINNED THEMSELVES TO DEATH	Housemartins (Go! Discs)
-	30	GEORGE BEST	Wedding Present (Reception)
31	31	ALWAYS GUARANTEED	Cliff Richard (EMI)
18	32	HYSTERIA	Def Leppard (Bludgen Riffola)
24	33	BIG GENERATOR	Yes (Atco)
46	34	BRIDGE OF SPIES	T'Pau (Siren)
25	35	HIT FACTORY	Various Artists (Stylus)
19	36	MUSIC FOR THE MASSES	Depeche Mode (Mute)
32	37	AFTER DARK	Ray Parker Jnr (Warner Bros.)
-	38	PERMANENT VACATION	Aerosmith (Geffen)
-	39	GLENN JONES	Glenn Jones (Jive)
-	40	STREET SOUNDS HIP HOP 18	Various Artists (Street Sounds)
29	41	GIVE ME THE REASON	Luther Vandross (Epic)
-	42	HIT FACTORY	Various Artists (Stylus)
-	43	ODYSSEY - THE GREATEST HITS	Odyssey (Stylus)
35	44	RUNNING IN THE FAMILY	Level 42 (Polydor)
-	45	JUST VISITING THIS PLANET	Jellybean (Chrysalis)
43	46	JONATHAN BUTLER	Jonathan Butler (Jive)
50	47	BABYLON AND ON	Squeeze (A&M)
39	48	TRACKS OF MY TEARS	Various Artists (Telstar)
41	49	SUBSTANCE	New Order (Factory)
-	50	PERFECT TIMING	MSG (EMI)

7 November 1987

2	1	NOTHING LIKE THE SUN	Sting (A&M)
4	2	ESP	Bee Gees (Warner Bros.)
8	3	TANGO IN THE NIGHT	Fleetwood Mac (Warner Bros.)
3	4	BAD	Michael Jackson (Epic)
1	5	TUNNEL OF LOVE	Bruce Springsteen (CBS)
18	6	THE CHRISTIANS	Christians (Island)
14	7	ACTUALLY	Pet Shop Boys (Parlophone)
34	8	BRIDGE OF SPIES	T'Pau (Siren)
6	9	THE CREAM OF ERIC CLAPTON	Eric Clapton (Polydor)
-	10	CRAZY NIGHTS	Kiss (Vertigo)
13	11	STRANGEWAYS HERE WE COME	Smiths (Rough Trade)
-	12	BEST OF UB40 VOL 1	UB40 (Virgin)
5	13	ALPHABET CITY	ABC (Neutron)
-	14	MAINSTREAM	Lloyd Cole & the Commotions (Polydor)
20	15	THE JOSHUA TREE	U2 (Island)
15	16	INTRODUCING THE HARDLINE ACCORDING TO	Terence Trent D'Arby (CBS)
17	17	SIMPLY SHADOWS	Shadows (Polydor)
-	18	THE SINGLES	Pretenders (WEA)
-	19	CHRONICLES	Steve Winwood (Island)
21	20	BEST OF JAMES BROWN	James Brown (K-Tel)
9	21	WONDERFUL LIFE	Black (A&M)
10	22	DANCING WITH STRANGERS	Chris Rea (Magnet)
7	23	RED	Communards (London)
11	24	BETWEEN THE LINES	Five Star (RCA)
22	25	REFLECTIONS	Foster & Allen (Stylus)
-	26	BEST SHOTS	Pat Benatar (Chrysalis)
31	27	ALWAYS GUARANTEED	Cliff Richard (EMI)
16	28	CHANGING FACES – THE VERY BEST OF 10 c.c. AND GODLEY AND CREME	10c.c. & Godley & Creme (Phonogram)
27	29	A MOMENTARY LAPSE OF REASON	Pink Floyd (EMI)
12	30	POPPED IN SOULED OUT	Wet Wet Wet (Precious)
-	31	RAISE YOUR FIST AND YELL	Alice Cooper (MCA)
25	32	WHITNEY	Whitney Houston (Arista)
35	33	HIT FACTORY	Various Artists (Stylus)
-	34	SIRIUS	Clannad (RCA)
39	35	GLENN JONES	Glenn Jones (Jive)
26	36	THE CIRCUS	Erasure (Mute)
19	37	NOW! SMASH HITS	Various Artists (Virgin/EMI)
-	38	ABBEY ROAD	Beatles (Parlophone)
24	39	UPFRONT 8	Various Artists (Serious)
23	40	LONESOME JUBILEE	John Cougar Mellencamp (Mercury)
37	41	AFTER DARK	Ray Parker Jnr (Warner Bros.)
-	42	HEARSAY	Alexander O'Neal (Tabu)
45	43	JUST VISITING THIS PLANET	Jellybean (Chrysalis)
30	44	GEORGE BEST	Wedding Present (Reception)
32	45	HYSTERIA	Def Leppard (Bludgen Riffola)
-	46	FROM MOTOWN WITH LOVE	Various Artists (K-Tel)
41	47	GIVE ME THE REASON	Luther Vandross (Epic)
28	48	BAD ANIMALS	Heart (Capitol)
-	49	JACKMASTER VOL 1	Various Artists (DJ International)
43	50	ODYSSEY - THE GREATEST HITS	Odyssey (Stylus)

It took the long-awaited new album by Bruce Springsteen, *Tunnel Of Love*, to muster enough sales to overtake Michael Jackson and snatch Number 1. Also in close contention were the Bee Gees, whose *ESP* was their first UK chart album since their greatest hits set made the Top 10 almost eight years earlier. The trio were simultaneously back at the top of the singles chart, with *You Win Again*.

November 1987

14 November 1987

last	this	Title	Artist (Label)
3	1	TANGO IN THE NIGHT	Fleetwood Mac (Warner Bros.)
8	2	BRIDGE OF SPIES	T'Pau (Siren)
18	3	THE SINGLES	Pretenders (WEA)
12	4	BEST OF UB40 VOL 1	UB40 (Virgin)
10	5	CRAZY NIGHTS	Kiss (Vertigo)
-	6	FAITH	George Michael (Epic)
1	7	NOTHING LIKE THE SUN	Sting (A&M)
14	8	MAINSTREAM	Lloyd Cole & the Commotions (Polydor)
19	9	CHRONICLES	Steve Winwood (Island)
6	10	THE CHRISTIANS	Christians (Island)
4	11	BAD	Michael Jackson (Epic)
2	12	ESP	Bee Gees (Warner Bros.)
26	13	BEST SHOTS	Pat Benatar (Chrysalis)
5	14	TUNNEL OF LOVE	Bruce Springsteen (CBS)
-	15	BETE NOIRE	Bryan Ferry (Virgin)
-	16	ALL THE BEST!	Paul McCartney (Parlophone)
7	17	ACTUALLY	Pet Shop Boys (Parlophone)
9	18	THE CREAM OF ERIC CLAPTON	Eric Clapton (Polydor)
17	19	SIMPLY SHADOWS	Shadows (Polydor)
16	20	INTRODUCING THE HARDLINE ACCORDING TO	Terence Trent D'Arby (CBS)
25	21	REFLECTIONS	Foster & Allen (Stylus)
-	22	SEDUCED AND ABANDONED	Hue And Cry (Circa)
31	23	RAISE YOUR FIST AND YELL	Alice Cooper (MCA)
24	24	BETWEEN THE LINES	Five Star (RCA)
-	25	CLOUD NINE	George Harrison (Dark Horse)
22	26	DANCING WITH STRANGERS	Chris Rea (Magnet)
36	27	THE CIRCUS	Erasure (Mute)
15	28	THE JOSHUA TREE	U2 (Island)
-	29	EYE OF THE HURRICANE	Alarm (IRS)
34	30	SIRIUS	Clannad (RCA)
41	31	AFTER DARK	Ray Parker Jnr (Warner Bros.)
11	32	STRANGEWAYS HERE WE COME	Smiths (Rough Trade)
21	33	WONDERFUL LIFE	Black (A&M)
33	34	HIT FACTORY	Various Artists (Stylus)
20	35	BEST OF JAMES BROWN	James Brown (K-Tel)
23	36	RED	Communards (London)
47	37	GIVE ME THE REASON	Luther Vandross (Epic)
46	38	FROM MOTOWN WITH LOVE	Various Artists (K-Tel)
28	39	CHANGING FACES – THE VERY BEST OF 10 c.c. AND GODLEY AND CREME	10c.c. & Godley & Creme (Phonogram)
-	40	RUNNING IN THE FAMILY	Level 42 (Polydor)
-	41	DIRTY DANCING	Soundtrack (RCA)
-	42	DRILL YOUR OWN HOLE	Gaye Bykers On Acid (Virgin)
27	43	ALWAYS GUARANTEED	Cliff Richard (EMI)
13	44	ALPHABET CITY	ABC (Neutron)
-	45	SECRETS OF THE BEEHIVE	David Sylvian (Virgin)
29	46	A MOMENTARY LAPSE OF REASON	Pink Floyd (EMI)
-	47	LIVE AT WEMBLEY	Meat Loaf (RCA)
-	48	CALENTURE	Triffids (Island)
30	49	POPPED IN SOULED OUT	Wet Wet Wet (Precious)
32	50	WHITNEY	Whitney Houston (Arista)

21 November 1987

last	this	Title	Artist (Label)
6	1	FAITH	George Michael (Epic)
2	2	BRIDGE OF SPIES	T'Pau (Siren)
1	3	TANGO IN THE NIGHT	Fleetwood Mac (Warner Bros.)
16	4	ALL THE BEST!	Paul McCartney (Parlophone)
4	5	BEST OF UB40 VOL 1	UB40 (Virgin)
3	6	THE SINGLES	Pretenders (WEA)
15	7	BETE NOIRE	Bryan Ferry (Virgin)
25	8	CLOUD NINE	George Harrison (Dark Horse)
13	9	BEST SHOTS	Pat Benatar (Chrysalis)
12	10	ESP	Bee Gees (Warner Bros.)
10	11	THE CHRISTIANS	Christians (Island)
11	12	BAD	Michael Jackson (Epic)
-	13	SAVAGE	Eurythmics (RCA)
7	14	NOTHING LIKE THE SUN	Sting (A&M)
40	15	RUNNING IN THE FAMILY	Level 42 (Polydor)
-	16	HOLD YOUR FIRE	Rush (Vertigo)
38	17	FROM MOTOWN WITH LOVE	Various Artists (K-Tel)
9	18	CHRONICLES	Steve Winwood (Island)
14	19	TUNNEL OF LOVE	Bruce Springsteen (CBS)
8	20	MAINSTREAM	Lloyd Cole & the Commotions (Polydor)
29	21	EYE OF THE HURRICANE	Alarm (IRS)
-	22	CONTROL - THE REMIXES	Janet Jackson (Breakout)
36	23	RED	Communards (London)
19	24	SIMPLY SHADOWS	Shadows (Polydor)
5	25	CRAZY NIGHTS	Kiss (Vertigo)
17	26	ACTUALLY	Pet Shop Boys (Parlophone)
41	27	DIRTY DANCING	Soundtrack (RCA)
-	28	GET RHYTHM	Ry Cooder (Warner Bros.)
20	29	INTRODUCING THE HARDLINE ACCORDING TO	Terence Trent D'Arby (CBS)
18	30	THE CREAM OF ERIC CLAPTON	Eric Clapton (Polydor)
-	31	HEARSAY	Alexander O'Neal (Tabu)
26	32	DANCING WITH STRANGERS	Chris Rea (Magnet)
30	33	SIRIUS	Clannad (RCA)
31	34	AFTER DARK	Ray Parker Jnr (Warner Bros.)
34	35	HIT FACTORY	Various Artists (Stylus)
32	36	STRANGEWAYS HERE WE COME	Smiths (Rough Trade)
42	37	DRILL YOUR OWN HOLE	Gaye Bykers On Acid (Virgin)
-	38	URBAN CLASSICS	Various Artists (Urban)
-	39	IT'S CALLED LOVE	Aztec Camera (WEA)
48	40	CALENTURE	Triffids (Island)
35	41	BEST OF JAMES BROWN	James Brown (K-Tel)
-	42	THE LOVE SONGS	Randy Crawford (Telstar)
21	43	REFLECTIONS	Foster & Allen (Stylus)
-	44	ROBBIE ROBERTSON	Robbie Robertson (Geffen)
33	45	WONDERFUL LIFE	Black (A&M)
-	46	ESCAPE FROM TV	Jan Hammer (MCA)
-	47	BEST OF HOUSE VOL 3	Various Artists (Serious)
45	48	SECRETS OF THE BEEHIVE	David Sylvian (Virgin)
22	49	SEDUCED AND ABANDONED	Hue And Cry (Circa)
23	50	RAISE YOUR FIST AND YELL	Alice Cooper (MCA)

28 November 1987

last	this	Title	Artist (Label)
2	1	BRIDGE OF SPIES	T'Pau (Siren)
4	2	ALL THE BEST!	Paul McCartney (Parlophone)
5	3	BEST OF UB40 VOL 1	UB40 (Virgin)
3	4	TANGO IN THE NIGHT	Fleetwood Mac (Warner Bros.)
13	5	SAVAGE	Eurythmics (RCA)
1	6	FAITH	George Michael (Epic)
6	7	THE SINGLES	Pretenders (WEA)
8	8	CLOUD NINE	George Harrison (Dark Horse)
9	9	BEST SHOTS	Pat Benatar (Chrysalis)
16	10	HOLD YOUR FIRE	Rush (Vertigo)
-	11	YOU CAN DANCE	Madonna (Sire)
-	12	FLOODLANDS	Sisters of Mercy (WEA)
-	13	WHENEVER YOU NEED SOMEBODY	Rick Astley (RCA)
17	14	FROM MOTOWN WITH LOVE	Various Artists (K-Tel)
10	15	ESP	Bee Gees (Warner Bros.)
12	16	BAD	Michael Jackson (Epic)
-	17	GREATEST HITS OF '87	Various Artists (Telstar)
15	18	RUNNING IN THE FAMILY	Level 42 (Polydor)
26	19	ACTUALLY	Pet Shop Boys (Parlophone)
7	20	BETE NOIRE	Bryan Ferry (Virgin)
35	21	HIT FACTORY	Various Artists (Stylus)
43	22	REFLECTIONS	Foster & Allen (Stylus)
30	23	THE CREAM OF ERIC CLAPTON	Eric Clapton (Polydor)
22	24	CONTROL - THE REMIXES	Janet Jackson (Breakout)
-	25	WHITNEY	Whitney Houston (Arista)
14	26	NOTHING LIKE THE SUN	Sting (A&M)
25	27	CRAZY NIGHTS	Kiss (Vertigo)
-	28	MY BABY JUST CARES FOR ME	Nina Simone (Charly)
21	29	EYE OF THE HURRICANE	Alarm (IRS)
11	30	THE CHRISTIANS	Christians (Island)
18	31	CHRONICLES	Steve Winwood (Island)
19	32	TUNNEL OF LOVE	Bruce Springsteen (CBS)
24	33	SIMPLY SHADOWS	Shadows (Polydor)
-	34	CHARACTERS	Stevie Wonder (Motown)
42	35	THE LOVE SONGS	Randy Crawford (Telstar)
23	36	RED	Communards (London)
36	37	STRANGEWAYS HERE WE COME	Smiths (Rough Trade)
39	38	IT'S CALLED LOVE	Aztec Camera (WEA)
27	39	DIRTY DANCING	Soundtrack (RCA)
28	40	GET RHYTHM	Ry Cooder (Warner Bros.)
-	41	KICK	INXS (Mercury)
20	42	MAINSTREAM	Lloyd Cole & the Commotions (Polydor)
31	43	HEARSAY	Alexander O'Neal (Tabu)
-	44	SIXTIES MIX	Various Artists (Stylus)
-	45	THE LOVE SONGS	Michael Jackson & Diana Ross (Telstar)
-	46	KOHYEP - LIVE IN LENINGRAD	Billy Joel (CBS)
32	47	DANCING WITH STRANGERS	Chris Rea (Magnet)
29	48	INTRODUCING THE HARDLINE ACCORDING TO	Terence Trent D'Arby (CBS)
44	49	ROBBIE ROBERTSON	Robbie Robertson (Geffen)
-	50	MY FAIR LADY	Kiri Te Kanawa (Decca)

After originally peaking at Number 2 shortly after its release in April, Fleetwood Mac's *Tango In The Night* finally made Number 1 six months later, having in the interim descended as low as 41 before reasserting itself. A factor in the resurrection was certainly the Top 5 success of the extracted single *Little Lies*, but *Tango* would now remain a highly-charted album for some months to come.

5 December 1987

last week	this week	Title	Artist (Label)
13	1	WHENEVER YOU NEED SOMEBODY	Rick Astley (RCA)
1	2	BRIDGE OF SPIES	T'Pau (Siren)
3	3	BEST OF UB40 VOL 1	UB40 (Virgin)
2	4	ALL THE BEST!	Paul McCartney (Parlophone)
11	5	YOU CAN DANCE	Madonna (Sire)
6	6	FAITH	George Michael (Epic)
4	7	TANGO IN THE NIGHT	Fleetwood Mac (Warner Bros.)
7	8	THE SINGLES	Pretenders (WEA)
-	9	HITS 7	Various Artists (CBS/WEA/BMG)
-	10	NOW THAT'S WHAT I CALL MUSIC10	Various Artists (EMI/Virgin/PolyGram)
12	11	FLOODLANDS	Sisters of Mercy (WEA)
9	12	BEST SHOTS	Pat Benatar (Chrysalis)
14	13	FROM MOTOWN WITH LOVE	Various Artists (K-Tel)
5	14	SAVAGE	Eurythmics (RCA)
16	15	BAD	Michael Jackson (Epic)
17	16	GREATEST HITS OF '87	Various Artists (Telstar)
8	17	CLOUD NINE	George Harrison (Dark Horse)
18	18	ACTUALLY	Pet Shop Boys (Parlophone)
43	19	HEARSAY	Alexander O'Neal (Tabu)
32	20	TUNNEL OF LOVE	Bruce Springsteen (CBS)
33	21	SIMPLY SHADOWS	Shadows (Polydor)
25	22	WHITNEY	Whitney Houston (Arista)
41	23	KICK	INXS (Mercury)
30	24	THE CHRISTIANS	Christians (Island)
15	25	ESP	Bee Gees (Warner Bros.)
34	26	CHARACTERS	Stevie Wonder (Motown)
42	27	MAINSTREAM	Lloyd Cole & the Commotions (Polydor)
18	28	RUNNING IN THE FAMILY	Level 42 (Polydor)
22	29	REFLECTIONS	Foster & Allen (Stylus)
-	30	SPECIAL OLYMPICS – A VERY SPECIAL CHRISTMAS	Various Artists (A&M)
45	31	THE LOVE SONGS	Michael Jackson & Diana Ross (Telstar)
20	32	BETE NOIRE	Bryan Ferry (Virgin)
26	33	NOTHING LIKE THE SUN	Sting (A&M)
44	34	SIXTIES MIX	Various Artists (Stylus)
36	35	RED	Communards (London)
-	36	ALWAYS GUARANTEED	Cliff Richard (EMI)
39	37	DIRTY DANCING	Soundtrack (RCA)
10	38	HOLD YOUR FIRE	Rush (Vertigo)
-	39	BACK FOR THE ATTACK	Dokken (Elektra)
28	40	MY BABY JUST CARES FOR ME	Nina Simone (Charly)
37	41	STRANGEWAYS HERE WE COME	Smiths (Rough Trade)
21	42	HIT FACTORY	Various Artists (Stylus)
23	43	THE CREAM OF ERIC CLAPTON	Eric Clapton (Polydor)
31	44	CHRONICLES	Steve Winwood (Island)
24	45	CONTROL - THE REMIXES	Janet Jackson (Breakout)
40	46	GET RHYTHM	Ry Cooder (Warner Bros.)
48	47	INTRODUCING THE HARDLINE ACCORDING TO	Terence Trent D'Arby (CBS)
47	48	DANCING WITH STRANGERS	Chris Rea (Magnet)
-	49	LOVE CHANGES	Kashif (Arista)
46	50	KOHYEPT- LIVE IN LENINGRAD	Billy Joel (CBS)

12 December 1987

last week	this week	Title	Artist (Label)
10	1	NOW THAT'S WHAT I CALL MUSIC10	Various Artists (EMI/Virgin/PolyGram)
1	2	WHENEVER YOU NEED SOMEBODY	Rick Astley (RCA)
9	3	HITS 7	Various Artists (CBS/WEA/BMG)
2	4	BRIDGE OF SPIES	T'Pau (Siren)
3	5	BEST OF UB40 VOL 1	UB40 (Virgin)
4	6	ALL THE BEST!	Paul McCartney (Parlophone)
8	7	THE SINGLES	Pretenders (WEA)
7	8	TANGO IN THE NIGHT	Fleetwood Mac (Warner Bros.)
5	9	YOU CAN DANCE	Madonna (Sire)
15	10	BAD	Michael Jackson (Epic)
31	11	THE LOVE SONGS	Michael Jackson & Diana Ross (Telstar)
6	12	FAITH	George Michael (Epic)
21	13	SIMPLY SHADOWS	Shadows (Polydor)
12	14	BEST SHOTS	Pat Benatar (Chrysalis)
18	15	ACTUALLY	Pet Shop Boys (Parlophone)
13	16	FROM MOTOWN WITH LOVE	Various Artists (K-Tel)
19	17	HEARSAY	Alexander O'Neal (Tabu)
22	18	WHITNEY	Whitney Houston (Arista)
-	19	ALWAYS GUARANTEED	Cliff Richard (EMI)
-	20	SONGS FROM STAGE AND SCREEN	Michael Crawford (Telstar)
17	21	CLOUD NINE	George Harrison (Dark Horse)
11	22	FLOODLANDS	Sisters of Mercy (WEA)
14	23	SAVAGE	Eurythmics (RCA)
-	24	MAXI	Maxi Priest (10)
29	25	REFLECTIONS	Foster & Allen (Stylus)
35	26	RED	Communards (London)
28	27	RUNNING IN THE FAMILY	Level 42 (Polydor)
47	28	INTRODUCING THE HARDLINE ACCORDING TO	Terence Trent D'Arby (CBS)
16	29	GREATEST HITS OF '87	Various Artists (Telstar)
-	30	SENTIMENTALLY YOURS	Rose Marie (Telstar)
-	31	THE JOSHUA TREE	U2 (Island)
27	32	MAINSTREAM	Lloyd Cole & the Commotions (Polydor)
-	33	THE LIGHT AT THE END OF THE TUNNEL	Damned (MCA)
34	34	SIXTIES MIX	Various Artists (Stylus)
25	35	ESP	Bee Gees (Warner Bros.)
33	36	NOTHING LIKE THE SUN	Sting (A&M)
45	37	CONTROL - THE REMIXES	Janet Jackson (Breakout)
41	38	STRANGEWAYS HERE WE COME	Smiths (Rough Trade)
40	39	WHITESNAKE 1987	Whitesnake (EMI)
40	40	MY BABY JUST CARES FOR ME	Nina Simone (Charly)
49	41	LOVE CHANGES	Kashif (Arista)
43	42	THE CREAM OF ERIC CLAPTON	Eric Clapton (Polydor)
20	43	TUNNEL OF LOVE	Bruce Springsteen (CBS)
24	44	THE CHRISTIANS	Christians (Island)
30	45	SPECIAL OLYMPICS – A VERY SPECIAL CHRISTMAS	Various Artists (A&M)
37	46	DIRTY DANCING	Soundtrack (RCA)
23	47	KICK	INXS (Mercury)
-	48	MEMORIES	Elaine Paige (Telstar)
26	49	CHARACTERS	Stevie Wonder (Motown)
-	50	ALWAYS AND FOREVER	Various Artists (Telstar)

19 December 1987

last week	this week	Title	Artist (Label)
1	1	NOW THAT'S WHAT I CALL MUSIC10	Various Artists (EMI/Virgin/PolyGram)
3	2	HITS 7	Various Artists (CBS/WEA/BMG)
2	3	WHENEVER YOU NEED SOMEBODY	Rick Astley (RCA)
6	4	ALL THE BEST!	Paul McCartney (Parlophone)
4	5	BRIDGE OF SPIES	T'Pau (Siren)
10	6	BAD	Michael Jackson (Epic)
7	7	THE SINGLES	Pretenders (WEA)
5	8	BEST OF UB40 VOL 1	UB40 (Virgin)
8	9	TANGO IN THE NIGHT	Fleetwood Mac (Warner Bros.)
12	10	FAITH	George Michael (Epic)
9	11	YOU CAN DANCE	Madonna (Sire)
13	12	SIMPLY SHADOWS	Shadows (Polydor)
15	13	ACTUALLY	Pet Shop Boys (Parlophone)
20	14	SONGS FROM STAGE AND SCREEN	Michael Crawford (Telstar)
17	15	HEARSAY	Alexander O'Neal (Tabu)
18	16	WHITNEY	Whitney Houston (Arista)
19	17	ALWAYS GUARANTEED	Cliff Richard (EMI)
34	18	SIXTIES MIX	Various Artists (Stylus)
11	19	THE LOVE SONGS	Michael Jackson & Diana Ross (Telstar)
14	20	BEST SHOTS	Pat Benatar (Chrysalis)
42	21	THE CREAM OF ERIC CLAPTON	Eric Clapton (Polydor)
39	22	WHITESNAKE 1987	Whitesnake (EMI)
-	23	RAINDANCING	Alison Moyet (CBS)
-	24	THIS IS THE STORY	Proclaimers (Chrysalis)
-	25	SONGS OF LOVE	Richard Clayderman (Decca)
25	26	REFLECTIONS	Foster & Allen (Stylus)
23	27	SAVAGE	Eurythmics (RCA)
16	28	FROM MOTOWN WITH LOVE	Various Artists (K-Tel)
29	29	MEMORIES	Elaine Paige (Telstar)
30	30	SENTIMENTALLY YOURS	Rose Marie (Telstar)
21	31	CLOUD NINE	George Harrison (Dark Horse)
-	32	BETWEEN THE LINES	Five Star (RCA)
26	33	RED	Communards (London)
35	34	ESP	Bee Gees (Warner Bros.)
32	35	MAINSTREAM	Lloyd Cole & the Commotions (Polydor)
-	36	A PORTRAIT OF MARIO LANZA	Mario Lanza (Stylus)
24	37	MAXI	Maxi Priest (10)
44	38	THE CHRISTIANS	Christians (Island)
33	39	THE LIGHT AT THE END OF THE TUNNEL	Damned (MCA)
-	40	NO MORE COCOONS	Jello Biafra (Alternative Tentacles)
40	41	MY BABY JUST CARES FOR ME	Nina Simone (Charly)
28	42	INTRODUCING THE HARDLINE ACCORDING TO	Terence Trent D'Arby (CBS)
31	43	THE JOSHUA TREE	U2 (Island)
27	44	RUNNING IN THE FAMILY	Level 42 (Polydor)
36	45	NOTHING LIKE THE SUN	Sting (A&M)
29	46	GREATEST HITS OF '87	Various Artists (Telstar)
-	47	POPPED IN SOULED OUT	Wet Wet Wet (Precious)
45	48	SPECIAL OLYMPICS – A VERY SPECIAL CHRISTMAS	Various Artists (A&M)
-	49	GOOD LOVE	M'lissa Morgan (Capitol)
-	50	THE CIRCUS	Erasure (Mute)

Although Rick Asley's debut album was hotly tipped as the likely biggest seller for the end of the year (and did reach Number 1), the actual battle, with more than a touch of deja vu about it, was between the inevitable *Now* and *Hits* compilations. In a repeat of the previous year's result, the *Now* volume won the contest, settling into its second week at the top as its rival moved up to Number 2 during Christmas week.

315

Tina Turner's been singing since the 60s, but made it biggest in the late 80s.
Bottom left: Pet Shop Boys
Below: Whitney Houston

January 1988

9 January 1988

last week	this week	Title / Artist (Label)
1	1	NOW THAT'S WHAT I CALL MUSIC10 Various Artists (EMI/Virgin/PolyGram)
2	2	HITS 7 Various Artists (CBS/WEA/BMG)
3	3	WHENEVER YOU NEED SOMEBODY Rick Astley (RCA)
4	4	ALL THE BEST! Paul McCartney (Parlophone)
5	5	BRIDGE OF SPIES T'Pau (Siren)
6	6	BAD Michael Jackson (Epic)
9	7	TANGO IN THE NIGHT Fleetwood Mac (Warner Bros.)
7	8	THE SINGLES Pretenders (WEA)
8	9	BEST OF UB40 VOL 1 UB40 (Virgin)
23	10	RAINDANCING Alison Moyet (CBS)
10	11	FAITH George Michael (Epic)
13	12	ACTUALLY Pet Shop Boys (Parlophone)
14	13	SONGS FROM STAGE AND SCREEN Michael Crawford (Telstar)
11	14	YOU CAN DANCE Madonna (Sire)
17	15	ALWAYS GUARANTEED Cliff Richard (EMI)
-	16	NOW – THE CHRISTMAS ALBUM Various Artists (EMI/Virgin/PolyGram)
12	17	SIMPLY SHADOWS Shadows (Polydor)
15	18	HEARSAY Alexander O'Neal (Tabu)
29	19	MEMORIES Elaine Paige (Telstar)
28	20	FROM MOTOWN WITH LOVE Various Artists (K-Tel)
19	21	THE LOVE SONGS Michael Jackson & Diana Ross (Telstar)
30	22	SENTIMENTALLY YOURS Rose Marie (Telstar)
21	23	THE CREAM OF CLAPTON Eric Clapton (Polydor)
33	24	RED Communards (London)
22	25	WHITESNAKE 1987 Whitesnake (EMI)
20	26	BEST SHOTS Pat Benatar (Chrysalis)
16	27	WHITNEY Whitney Houston (Arista)
18	28	SIXTIES MIX Various Artists (Stylus)
-	29	INSIDE INFORMATION Foreigner (Atlantic)
25	30	SONGS OF LOVE Richard Clayderman (Decca)
47	31	POPPED IN SOULED OUT Wet Wet Wet (Precious)
27	32	SAVAGE Eurythmics (RCA)
-	33	THE PHANTOM OF THE OPERA Original Cast (Polydor)
26	34	REFLECTIONS Foster & Allen (Stylus)
31	35	CLOUD NINE George Harrison (Dark Horse)
46	36	GREATEST HITS OF '87 Various Artists (Telstar)
-	37	UPFRONT 9 Various Artists (Serious)
36	38	A PORTRAIT OF MARIO LANZA Mario Lanza (Stylus)
-	39	CLASSIC ROCK COUNTDOWN London Symphony Orchestra (CBS)
24	40	THIS IS THE STORY Proclaimers (Chrysalis)
34	41	ESP Bee Gees (Warner Bros.)
32	42	BETWEEN THE LINES Five Star (Tent)
48	43	SPECIAL OLYMPICS – A VERY SPECIAL CHRISTMAS Various Artists (A&M)
49	44	GOOD LOVE M'lissa Morgan (Capitol)
38	45	THE CHRISTIANS Christians (Island)
43	46	THE JOSHUA TREE U2 (Island)
42	47	INTRODUCING THE HARDLINE ... Terence Trent D'Arby (CBS)
-	48	ALWAYS AND FOREVER Various Artists (Telstar)
45	49	NOTHING LIKE THE SUN Sting (A&M)
-	50	THE PEOPLE WHO GRINNED THEMSELVES TO DEATH Housemartins (Go! Discs)

16 January 1988

last week	this week	Title / Artist (Label)
1	1	NOW THAT'S WHAT I CALL MUSIC10 Various Artists (EMI/Virgin/PolyGram)
6	2	BAD Michael Jackson (Epic)
12	3	ACTUALLY Pet Shop Boys (Parlophone)
2	4	HITS 7 Various Artists (CBS/WEA/BMG)
3	5	WHENEVER YOU NEED SOMEBODY Rick Astley (RCA)
7	6	TANGO IN THE NIGHT Fleetwood Mac (Warner Bros.)
31	7	BRIDGE OF SPIES T'Pau (Siren)
-	8	POPPED IN SOULED OUT Wet Wet Wet (Precious)
4	9	ALL THE BEST! Paul McCartney (Parlophone)
8	10	THE SINGLES Pretenders (WEA)
27	11	WHITNEY Whitney Houston (Arista)
45	12	THE CHRISTIANS Christians (Island)
11	13	FAITH George Michael (Epic)
23	14	THE CREAM OF CLAPTON Eric Clapton (Polydor)
10	15	RAINDANCING Alison Moyet (CBS)
9	16	BEST OF UB40 VOL 1 UB40 (Virgin)
46	17	THE JOSHUA TREE U2 (Island)
25	18	WHITESNAKE 1987 Whitesnake (EMI)
18	19	HEARSAY Alexander O'Neal (Tabu)
14	20	YOU CAN DANCE Madonna (Sire)
-	21	KICK INXS (Mercury)
-	22	LIFE IN THE FAST LANE Various Artists (Telstar)
-	23	THE MICHAEL JACKSON MIX Michael Jackson (Stylus)
-	24	HYSTERIA Def Leppard (Bludgeon Riffola)
-	25	THE BEST OF MIRAGE JACK MIX 88 Mirage (Stylus)
26	26	THE GREATEST LOVE Various Artists (Telstar)
19	27	MEMORIES Elaine Paige (Telstar)
-	28	THE CIRCUS Erasure (Mute)
21	29	THE LOVE SONGS Michael Jackson & Diana Ross (Telstar)
-	30	RUNNING IN THE FAMILY Level 42 (Polydor)
20	31	FROM MOTOWN WITH LOVE Various Artists (K-Tel)
32	32	SAVAGE Eurythmics (RCA)
-	33	HEAVEN ON EARTH Belinda Carlisle (Virgin)
-	34	JUST VISITING THIS PLANET Jellybean (Chrysalis)
15	35	COME INTO MY LIFE Joyce Sims (London)
22	36	ALWAYS GUARANTEED Cliff Richard (EMI)
22	37	SENTIMENTALLY YOURS Rose Marie (Telstar)
-	38	SUBSTANCE New Order (Factory)
17	39	SIMPLY SHADOWS Shadows (Polydor)
24	40	RED Communards (London)
-	41	RUM, SODOMY AND THE LASH Pogues (Stiff)
26	42	BEST SHOTS Pat Benatar (Chrysalis)
43	43	GOOD LOVE M'lissa Morgan (Capitol)
35	44	CLOUD NINE George Harrison (Dark Horse)
47	45	INTRODUCING THE HARDLINE ACCORDING TO Terence Trent D'Arby (CBS)
42	46	BETWEEN THE LINES Five Star (Tent)
28	47	SIXTIES MIX Various Artists (Stylus)
49	48	NOTHING LIKE THE SUN Sting (A&M)
-	49	BROTHERS IN ARMS Dire Straits (Vertigo)
48	50	ALWAYS AND FOREVER Various Artists (Telstar)

23 January 1988

last week	this week	Title / Artist (Label)
8	1	POPPED IN SOULED OUT Wet Wet Wet (Precious)
45	2	INTRODUCING THE HARDLINE ACCORDING TO Terence Trent D'Arby (CBS)
3	3	ACTUALLY Pet Shop Boys (Parlophone)
2	4	BAD Michael Jackson (Epic)
5	5	WHENEVER YOU NEED SOMEBODY Rick Astley (RCA)
6	6	TANGO IN THE NIGHT Fleetwood Mac (Warner Bros.)
1	7	NOW THAT'S WHAT I CALL MUSIC10 Various Artists (EMI/Virgin/PolyGram)
12	8	THE CHRISTIANS Christians (Island)
7	9	BRIDGE OF SPIES T'Pau (Siren)
13	10	FAITH George Michael (Epic)
33	11	HEAVEN ON EARTH Belinda Carlisle (Virgin)
17	12	THE JOSHUA TREE U2 (Island)
4	13	HITS 7 Various Artists (CBS/WEA/BMG)
11	14	WHITNEY Whitney Houston (Arista)
15	15	RAINDANCING Alison Moyet (CBS)
-	16	TURN BACK THE CLOCK Johnny Hates Jazz (Virgin)
8	17	THE SINGLES Pretenders (WEA)
25	18	THE BEST OF MIRAGE JACK MIX 88 Mirage (Stylus)
35	19	COME INTO MY LIFE Joyce Sims (London)
9	20	ALL THE BEST! Paul McCartney (Parlophone)
22	21	LIFE IN THE FAST LANE Various Artists (Telstar)
18	22	WHITESNAKE 1987 Whitesnake (EMI)
21	23	KICK INXS (Mercury)
19	24	HEARSAY Alexander O'Neal (Tabu)
16	25	BEST OF UB40 VOL 1 UB40 (Virgin)
14	26	THE CREAM OF CLAPTON Eric Clapton (Polydor)
-	27	CHER Cher (Geffen)
28	28	YOU CAN DANCE Madonna (Sire)
23	29	THE MICHAEL JACKSON MIX Michael Jackson (Stylus)
34	30	JUST VISITING THIS PLANET Jellybean (Chrysalis)
44	31	CLOUD NINE George Harrison (Dark Horse)
30	32	RUNNING IN THE FAMILY Level 42 (Polydor)
28	33	THE CIRCUS Erasure (Mute)
-	34	SINITTA Sinitta (Fanfare)
-	35	DIRTY DANCING Soundtrack (RCA)
-	36	GIVE ME THE REASON Luther Vandross (Epic)
-	37	MAKE IT LAST FOREVER Keith Sweat (Elektra)
26	38	GOOD LOVE M'lissa Morgan (Capitol)
26	39	THE GREATEST LOVE Various Artists (Telstar)
27	40	MEMORIES Elaine Paige (Telstar)
24	41	HYSTERIA Def Leppard (Bludgeon Riffola)
29	42	THE LOVE SONGS Michael Jackson & Diana Ross (Telstar)
-	43	GRACELAND Paul Simon (Warner Bros.)
42	44	BEST SHOTS Pat Benatar (Chrysalis)
31	45	FROM MOTOWN WITH LOVE Various Artists (K-Tel)
32	46	SAVAGE Eurythmics (RCA)
-	47	MEN AND WOMEN Simply Red (Elektra)
40	48	RED Communards (London)
49	49	BROTHERS IN ARMS Dire Straits (Vertigo)
-	50	DANCING WITH STRANGERS Chris Rea (Magnet)

The success of current singles seemed to be a factor in many people's New Year album buying as 1988 opened: the Top 10 hit *Angel Eyes* helped Wet Wet Wet's *Popped In Souled Out* to a stronger second chart run than its first in the previous October, this time snatching a week at Number 1. Terence Trent D'Arby also soared upwards again after almost dropping out, boosted by the single *Sign Your Name*.

January – February 1988

30 January 1988

Last week	This week	Title	Artist
16	1	TURN BACK THE CLOCK	Johnny Hates Jazz (Virgin)
1	2	POPPED IN SOULED OUT	Wet Wet Wet (Precious)
2	3	INTRODUCING THE HARDLINE ACCORDING TO	Terence Trent D'Arby (CBS)
11	4	HEAVEN ON EARTH	Belinda Carlisle (Virgin)
8	5	THE CHRISTIANS	Christians (Island)
4	6	BAD	Michael Jackson (Epic)
5	7	WHENEVER YOU NEED SOMEBODY	Rick Astley (RCA)
-	8	IF I SHOULD FALL FROM GRACE WITH GOD	Pogues (Pogue Mahone)
6	9	TANGO IN THE NIGHT	Fleetwood Mac (Warner Bros.)
21	10	LIFE IN THE FAST LANE	Various Artists (Telstar)
10	11	FAITH	George Michael (Epic)
18	12	THE BEST OF MIRAGE JACK MIX 88	Mirage (Stylus)
3	13	ACTUALLY	Pet Shop Boys (Parlophone)
23	14	KICK	INXS (Mercury)
9	15	BRIDGE OF SPIES	T'Pau (Siren)
19	16	COME INTO MY LIFE	Joyce Sims (London)
12	17	THE JOSHUA TREE	U2 (Island)
7	18	NOW THAT'S WHAT I CALL MUSIC10	Various Artists (EMI/Virgin/PolyGram)
14	19	WHITNEY	Whitney Houston (Arista)
17	20	THE SINGLES	Pretenders (WEA)
22	21	WHITESNAKE 1987	Whitesnake (EMI)
27	22	CHER	Cher (Geffen)
39	23	THE GREATEST LOVE	Various Artists (Telstar)
15	24	RAINDANCING	Alison Moyet (CBS)
24	25	HEARSAY	Alexander O'Neal (Tabu)
30	26	JUST VISITING THIS PLANET	Jellybean (Chrysalis)
13	27	HITS 7	Various Artists (CBS/WEA/BMG)
35	28	DIRTY DANCING	Soundtrack (RCA)
25	29	BEST OF UB40 VOL 1	UB40 (Virgin)
26	30	THE CREAM OF CLAPTON	Eric Clapton (Polydor)
20	31	ALL THE BEST!	Paul McCartney (Parlophone)
42	32	THE LOVE SONGS	Michael Jackson & Diana Ross (Telstar)
28	33	YOU CAN DANCE	Madonna (Sire)
36	34	GIVE ME THE REASON	Luther Vandross (Epic)
37	35	MAKE IT LAST FOREVER	Keith Sweat (Elektra)
29	36	THE MICHAEL JACKSON MIX	Michael Jackson (Stylus)
32	37	RUNNING IN THE FAMILY	Level 42 (Polydor)
44	38	BEST SHOTS	Pat Benatar (Chrysalis)
33	39	THE CIRCUS	Erasure (Mute)
43	40	GRACELAND	Paul Simon (Warner Bros.)
-	41	MAINSTREAM	Lloyd Cole & the Commotions (Polydor)
34	42	SINITTA	Sinitta (Fanfare)
45	43	FROM MOTOWN WITH LOVE	Various Artists (K-Tel)
41	44	HYSTERIA	Def Leppard (Bludgeon Riffola)
40	45	MEMORIES	Elaine Paige (Telstar)
46	46	SAVAGE	Eurythmics (RCA)
50	47	DANCING WITH STRANGERS	Chris Rea (Magnet)
-	48	THE LION AND THE COBRA	Sinead O'Connor (Ensign)
47	49	MEN AND WOMEN	Simply Red (Elektra)
49	50	BROTHERS IN ARMS	Dire Straits (Vertigo)

6 February 1988

Last week	This week	Title	Artist
3	1	INTRODUCING THE HARDLINE ACCORDING TO	Terence Trent D'Arby (CBS)
1	2	TURN BACK THE CLOCK	Johnny Hates Jazz (Virgin)
8	3	IF I SHOULD FALL FROM GRACE WITH GOD	Pogues (Pogue Mahone)
2	4	POPPED IN SOULED OUT	Wet Wet Wet (Precious)
5	5	THE CHRISTIANS	Christians (Island)
4	6	HEAVEN ON EARTH	Belinda Carlisle (Virgin)
7	7	KICK	INXS (Mercury)
6	8	BAD	Michael Jackson (Epic)
9	9	TANGO IN THE NIGHT	Fleetwood Mac (Warner Bros.)
16	10	COME INTO MY LIFE	Joyce Sims (London)
12	11	THE BEST OF MIRAGE JACK MIX 88	Mirage (Stylus)
15	12	BRIDGE OF SPIES	T'Pau (Siren)
11	13	FAITH	George Michael (Epic)
7	14	WHENEVER YOU NEED SOMEBODY	Rick Astley (RCA)
-	15	SKYSCRAPER	David Lee Roth (Warner Bros.)
36	16	THE MICHAEL JACKSON MIX	Michael Jackson (Stylus)
13	17	ACTUALLY	Pet Shop Boys (Parlophone)
24	18	RAINDANCING	Alison Moyet (CBS)
19	19	WHITNEY	Whitney Houston (Arista)
26	20	JUST VISITING THIS PLANET	Jellybean (Chrysalis)
22	21	CHER	Cher (Geffen)
-	22	DUSTY - THE SILVER COLLECTION	Dusty Springfield (Philips)
48	23	THE LION AND THE COBRA	Sinead O'Connor (Ensign)
23	24	THE GREATEST LOVE	Various Artists (Telstar)
10	25	LIFE IN THE FAST LANE	Various Artists (Telstar)
20	26	THE SINGLES	Pretenders (WEA)
25	27	HEARSAY	Alexander O'Neal (Tabu)
17	28	THE JOSHUA TREE	U2 (Island)
18	30	NOW THAT'S WHAT I CALL MUSIC10	Various Artists (EMI/Virgin/PolyGram)
34	31	GIVE ME THE REASON	Luther Vandross (Epic)
21	32	WHITESNAKE 1987	Whitesnake (EMI)
30	33	THE CREAM OF CLAPTON	Eric Clapton (Polydor)
-	34	DESTINY'S SONG	Courtney Pine (Island)
35	35	MAKE IT LAST FOREVER	Keith Sweat (Elektra)
-	36	GOOD LOVE	M'lissa Morgan (Capitol)
28	37	DIRTY DANCING	Soundtrack (RCA)
29	38	BEST OF UB40 VOL 1	UB40 (Virgin)
47	39	DANCING WITH STRANGERS	Chris Rea (Magnet)
42	40	SINITTA	Sinitta (Fanfare)
-	41	THE HOUSE SOUND OF CHICAGO 3	Various Artists (DJ International)
-	42	PENETENTIARY	Soundtrack (RCA)
31	43	ALL THE BEST!	Paul McCartney (Parlophone)
-	44	RADIO K.A.O.S.	Roger Waters (EMI)
32	45	THE LOVE SONGS	Michael Jackson & Diana Ross (Telstar)
-	46	YOU CAN DANCE	Madonna (Sire)
40	47	GRACELAND	Paul Simon (Warner Bros.)
37	48	RUNNING IN THE FAMILY	Level 42 (Polydor)
-	49	CLASSIC ROCK COUNTDOWN	London Symphony Orchestra (CBS)
38	50	BEST SHOTS	Pat Benatar (Chrysalis)

13 February 1988

Last week	This week	Title	Artist
1	1	INTRODUCING THE HARDLINE ACCORDING TO	Terence Trent D'Arby (CBS)
3	2	IF I SHOULD FALL FROM GRACE WITH GOD	Pogues (Pogue Mahone)
5	3	THE CHRISTIANS	Christians (Island)
4	4	POPPED IN SOULED OUT	Wet Wet Wet (Precious)
2	5	TURN BACK THE CLOCK	Johnny Hates Jazz (Virgin)
7	6	KICK	INXS (Mercury)
12	7	BRIDGE OF SPIES	T'Pau (Siren)
15	8	SKYSCRAPER	David Lee Roth (Warner Bros.)
-	9	BLOW UP YOUR VIDEO	AC/DC (Atlantic)
10	10	COME INTO MY LIFE	Joyce Sims (London)
11	11	THE BEST OF MIRAGE JACK MIX 88	Mirage (Stylus)
8	12	BAD	Michael Jackson (Epic)
6	13	HEAVEN ON EARTH	Belinda Carlisle (Virgin)
13	14	FAITH	George Michael (Epic)
20	15	JUST VISITING THIS PLANET	Jellybean (Chrysalis)
9	16	TANGO IN THE NIGHT	Fleetwood Mac (Warner Bros.)
17	17	ACTUALLY	Pet Shop Boys (Parlophone)
14	18	WHENEVER YOU NEED SOMEBODY	Rick Astley (RCA)
23	19	THE LION AND THE COBRA	Sinead O'Connor (Ensign)
16	20	THE MICHAEL JACKSON MIX	Michael Jackson (Stylus)
19	21	WHITNEY	Whitney Houston (Arista)
21	22	CHER	Cher (Geffen)
18	23	RAINDANCING	Alison Moyet (CBS)
22	24	DUSTY - THE SILVER COLLECTION	Dusty Springfield (Philips)
35	25	MAKE IT LAST FOREVER	Keith Sweat (Elektra)
24	26	THE GREATEST LOVE	Various Artists (Telstar)
32	27	WHITESNAKE 1987	Whitesnake (EMI)
34	28	DESTINY'S SONG	Courtney Pine (Island)
25	29	LIFE IN THE FAST LANE	Various Artists (Telstar)
-	30	THE PHANTOM OF THE OPERA	Original Cast (Polydor)
30	31	NOW THAT'S WHAT I CALL MUSIC10	Various Artists (EMI/Virgin/PolyGram)
27	32	HEARSAY	Alexander O'Neal (Tabu)
26	33	THE SINGLES	Pretenders (WEA)
28	34	THE JOSHUA TREE	U2 (Island)
31	35	GIVE ME THE REASON	Luther Vandross (Epic)
-	36	EVERYTHING	Climie Fisher (EMI)
33	37	THE CREAM OF CLAPTON	Eric Clapton (Polydor)
-	38	MAINSTREAM	Lloyd Cole & the Commotions (Polydor)
37	39	DIRTY DANCING	Soundtrack (RCA)
-	40	OUT OF THE BLUE	Debbie Gibson (Atlantic)
46	41	YOU CAN DANCE	Madonna (Sire)
41	42	THE HOUSE SOUND OF CHICAGO 3	Various Artists (DJ International)
29	43	HITS 7	Various Artists (CBS/WEA/BMG)
38	44	BEST OF UB40 VOL 1	UB40 (Virgin)
-	45	SHOVE IT	Cross (Virgin)
39	46	DANCING WITH STRANGERS	Chris Rea (Magnet)
-	47	THE CIRCUS	Erasure (Mute)
43	48	ALL THE BEST!	Paul McCartney (Parlophone)
48	49	RUNNING IN THE FAMILY	Level 42 (Polydor)
47	50	GRACELAND	Paul Simon (Warner Bros.)

Johnny Hates Jazz joined the honour roll of acts to have achieved a Number 1 album with their first release, although they had a brief stay before Terence Trent Darby's *Hardline* re-established itself at the top for a second spell which was to last most of the next month and a half. The Pogues also enjoyed their best-selling album yet with their third release, *If I Should Fall From Grace With God*, which peaked at 2.

February – March 1988

20 February 1988

9	1	BLOW UP YOUR VIDEO	AC/DC (Atlantic)
1	2	INTRODUCING THE HARDLINE ACCORDING TO	Terence Trent D'Arby (CBS)
3	3	THE CHRISTIANS	Christians (Island)
4	4	POPPED IN SOULED OUT	Wet Wet Wet (Precious)
5	5	TURN BACK THE CLOCK	Johnny Hates J (Virgin)
2	6	IF I SHOULD FALL FROM GRACE WITH GOD	Pogues (Pogue Mahone)
7	7	BRIDGE OF SPIES	T'Pau (Siren)
10	8	COME INTO MY LIFE	Joyce Sims (London)
6	9	KICK	INXS (Mercury)
8	10	SKYSCRAPER	David Lee Roth (Warner Bros.)
11	11	THE BEST OF MIRAGE JACK MIX 88	Mirage (Stylus)
16	12	TANGO IN THE NIGHT	Fleetwood Mac (Warn Bros.)
13	13	HEAVEN ON EARTH	Belinda Carlisle (Virgin)
-	14	ALL LIVE AND ALL OF THE NIGHT	Stranglers (Epic)
12	15	BAD	Michael Jackson (Epic)
15	16	JUST VISITING THIS PLANET	Jellybean (Chrysalis)
19	17	THE LION AND THE COBRA	Sinead O'Connor (Ensign)
18	18	WHENEVER YOU NEED SOMEBODY	Rick Astley (RCA)
24	19	DUSTY - THE SILVER COLLECTION	Dusty Springfield (Philips)
14	20	FAITH	George Michael (Epic)
35	21	GIVE ME THE REASON	Luther Vandross (Epic)
36	22	EVERYTHING	Climie Fisher (EMI)
26	23	THE GREATEST LOVE	Various Artists (Telstar)
17	24	ACTUALLY	Pet Shop Boys (Parlophone)
23	25	RAINDANCING	Alison Moyet (CBS)
20	26	THE MICHAEL JACKSON MIX	Michael Jackson (Stylus)
22	27	CHER	Cher (Geffen)
25	28	MAKE IT LAST FOREVER	Keith Sweat (Elektra)
28	29	DESTINY'S SONG	Courtney Pine (Island)
37	30	THE CREAM OF CLAPTON	Eric Clapton (Polydor)
32	31	HEARSAY	Alexander O'Neal (Tabu)
34	32	THE JOSHUA TREE	U2 (Island)
40	33	OUT OF THE BLUE	Debbie Gibson (Atlantic)
-	34	WHO KILLED THE JAMS	Justified Ancients of Mu Mu (Jams)
-	35	SCALLYWAG JAZ	Thomas Lang (Epic)
21	36	WHITNEY	Whitney Houston (Arista)
27	37	WHITESNAKE 1987	Whitesnake (EMI)
29	38	LIFE IN THE FAST LANE	Various Artists (Telstar)
39	39	DIRTY DANCING	Soundtrack (RCA)
-	40	TIME AND TIDE	Basia (Portrait)
42	41	THE HOUSE SOUND OF CHICAGO 3	Various Artists DJ International)
45	42	SHOVE IT	Cross (Virgin)
-	43	GEORGE THOROGOOD	George Thorogood (EMI)
30	44	THE PHANTOM OF THE OPERA	Original Cast (Polydor)
-	45	FATAL ATTRACTION	Lion (Polydor)
31	46	NOW THAT'S WHAT I CALL MUSIC10	Various Artists (EMI/Virgin/PolyGram)
-	47	BIRTH SCHOOL WORK DEATH	Godfathers (Epic)
-	48	ELVIS PRESLEY – THE ALL TIME GREATEST HITS	Elvis Presley (RCA)
33	49	THE SINGLES	Pretenders (WEA)
43	50	HITS 7	Various Artists (CBS/WEA/BMG)

27 February 1988

2	1	INTRODUCING THE HARDLINE ACCORDING TO	Terence Trent D'Arby (CBS)
3	2	THE CHRISTIANS	Christians (Island)
7	3	BRIDGE OF SPIES	T'Pau (Siren)
4	4	POPPED IN SOULED OUT	Wet Wet Wet (Precious)
1	5	BLOW UP YOUR VIDEO	AC/DC (Atlantic)
14	6	ALL LIVE AND ALL OF THE NIGHT	Stranglers (Epic)
9	7	KICK	INXS (Mercury)
5	8	TURN BACK THE CLOCK	Johnny Hates Jazz (Virgin)
15	9	BAD	Michael Jackson (Epic)
24	10	ACTUALLY	Pet Shop Boys (Parlophone)
19	11	DUSTY - THE SILVER COLLECTION	Dusty Springfield (Philips)
18	12	WHENEVER YOU NEED SOMEBODY	Rick Astley (RCA)
8	13	COME INTO MY LIFE	Joyce Sims (London)
32	14	THE JOSHUA TREE	U2 (Island)
10	15	SKYSCRAPER	David Lee Roth (Warner Bros.)
6	16	IF I SHOULD FALL FROM GRACE WITH GOD	Pogues (Pogue Mahone)
17	17	THE LION AND THE COBRA	Sinead O'Connor (Ensign)
-	18	ALL ABOUT EVE	All About Eve (Mercury)
12	19	TANGO IN THE NIGHT	Fleetwood Mac (Warner Bros.)
21	20	GIVE ME THE REASON	Luther Vandross (Epic)
-	21	I'M YOUR MAN	Leonard Cohen (CBS)
16	22	JUST VISITING THIS PLANET	Jellybean (Chrysalis)
23	23	THE GREATEST LOVE	Various Artists (Telstar)
20	24	FAITH	George Michael (Epic)
11	25	THE BEST OF MIRAGE JACK MIX 88	
25	26	RAINDANCING	Alison Moyet (CBS)
13	27	HEAVEN ON EARTH	Belinda Carlisle (Virgin)
22	28	EVERYTHING	Climie Fisher (EMI)
31	29	HEARSAY	Alexander O'Neal (Tabu)
26	30	THE MICHAEL JACKSON MIX	Michael Jackson (Stylus)
35	31	SCALLYWAG JAZ	Thomas Lang (Epic)
43	32	GEORGE THOROGOOD	George Thorogood (EMI)
-	33	ALL OUR LOVE	Gladys Knight & the Pips (MCA)
-	34	WALTER BEASLEY	Walter Beasley (Urban)
-	35	ESP	Bee Gees (Warner Bros.)
28	36	MAKE IT LAST FOREVER	Keith Sweat (Elektra)
40	37	TIME AND TIDE	Basia (Portrait)
38	38	LIFE PLUS ONE	Frehley's Comet (Atlantic)
-	39	WE CARE A LOT	Faith No More (Mordam)
33	40	OUT OF THE BLUE	Debbie Gibson (Atlantic)
44	41	THE PHANTOM OF THE OPERA	Original Cast (Polydor)
27	42	CHER	Cher (Geffen)
39	43	DIRTY DANCING	Soundtrack (RCA)
47	44	BIRTH SCHOOL WORK DEATH	Godfathers (Epic)
-	45	GLOBE OF FROGS	Robyn Hitchcock (A&M)
-	46	WOW	Bananarama (London)
30	47	THE CREAM OF CLAPTON	Eric Clapton (Polydor)
36	48	WHITNEY	Whitney Houston (Arista)
-	49	VITAL IDOL	Billy Idol (Chrysalis)
49	50	THE SINGLES	Pretenders (WEA)

5 March 1988

1	1	INTRODUCING THE HARDLINE ACCORDING TO	Terence Trent D'Arby (CBS)
2	2	THE CHRISTIANS	Christians (Island)
4	3	POPPED IN SOULED OUT	Wet Wet Wet (Precious)
-	4	TIFFANY	Tiffany (MCA)
3	5	BRIDGE OF SPIES	T'Pau (Siren)
18	6	ALL ABOUT EVE	All About Eve (Mercury)
8	7	TURN BACK THE CLOCK	Johnny Hates Jazz (Virgin)
5	8	BLOW UP YOUR VIDEO	AC/DC (Atlantic)
12	9	WHENEVER YOU NEED SOMEBODY	Rick Astley (RCA)
9	10	BAD	Michael Jackson (Epic)
13	11	COME INTO MY LIFE	Joyce Sims (London)
10	12	ACTUALLY	Pet Shop Boys (Parlophone)
7	13	KICK	INXS (Mercury)
19	14	TANGO IN THE NIGHT	Fleetwood Mac (Warner Bros.)
11	15	DUSTY - THE SILVER COLLECTION	Dusty Springfield (Philips)
16	16	ALL LIVE AND ALL OF THE NIGHT	Stranglers (Epic)
15	17	SKYSCRAPER	David Lee Roth (Warner Bros.)
16	18	IF I SHOULD FALL FROM GRACE WITH GOD	Pogues (Pogue Mahone)
20	19	GIVE ME THE REASON	Luther Vandross (Epic)
-	20	TATTOOED BEAT MESSIAH	Zodiac Mindwarp (Mercury)
-	21	THE WORLD WITHOUT END	Mighty Lemondrops (Blue Guitar)
22	22	I'M YOUR MAN	Leonard Cohen (CBS)
-	23	NOTHING LIKE THE SUN	Sting (A&M)
27	24	HEAVEN ON EARTH	Belinda Carlisle (Virgin)
14	25	THE JOSHUA TREE	U2 (Island)
17	26	THE LION AND THE COBRA	Sinead O'Connor (Ensign)
36	27	MAKE IT LAST FOREVER	Keith Sweat (Elektra)
-	28	WOODEN FOOT COPS ON THE HIGHWAY	Woodentops (Rough Trade)
24	29	FAITH	George Michael (Epic)
-	30	CRY FREEDOM	Soundtrack (MCA)
44	31	BIRTH SCHOOL WORK DEATH	Godfathers (Epic)
-	32	TELL IT TO MY HEART	Taylor Dayne (Arista)
33	33	ALL OUR LOVE	Gladys Knight & the Pips (MCA)
25	34	THE BEST OF MIRAGE JACK MIX 88	Mirage (Stylus)
-	35	LA GUNS	LA Guns (Vertigo)
38	36	LIFE PLUS ONE	Frehley's Comet (Atlantic)
23	37	THE GREATEST LOVE	Various Artists (Telstar)
-	38	FOREVER YOURS	Tony Terry (Epic)
-	39	RAINTOWN	Deacon Blue (CBS)
46	40	WOW	Bananarama (London)
22	41	JUST VISITING THIS PLANET	Jellybean (Chrysalis)
29	42	HEARSAY	Alexander O'Neal (Tabu)
-	43	WHITESNAKE 1987	Whitesnake (EMI)
-	44	IF YOU CAN'T LICK 'EM, LICK 'EM	Ted Nugent (WEA)
34	45	WALTER BEASLEY	Walter Beasley (Urban)
40	46	OUT OF THE BLUE	Debbie Gibson (Atlantic)
-	47	GET HERE	Brenda Russell (A&M)
-	48	MAXI	Maxi Priest (10/Virgin)
-	49	LIVE IN AUSTRALIA	Elton John (Rocket)
-	50	SAY IT AGAIN	Jermaine Stewart (Siren)

Dusty Springfield's *The Silver Collection* was a compilation of most of her 1960s hits, released to mark the 25th anniversary of the start of her solo recording career. It was her first chart album since the mid-60s. By contrast, another female soloist, Sinead O'Connor, was having her first chart entry of any kind with *The Lion And The Cobra*, and teenager Tiffany's eponymous debut was even more spectacular.

March 1988

last week	this week	12 March 1988
1	1	INTRODUCING THE HARDLINE ACCORDING TO Terence Trent D'Arby (CBS)
5	2	BRIDGE OF SPIES T'Pau (Siren)
7	3	TURN BACK THE CLOCK Johnny Hates Jazz (Virgin)
2	4	THE CHRISTIANS Christians (Island)
4	5	TIFFANY Tiffany (MCA)
3	6	POPPED IN SOULED OUT Wet Wet Wet (Precious)
9	7	WHENEVER YOU NEED SOMEBODY Rick Astley (RCA)
10	8	BAD Michael Jackson (Epic)
19	9	GIVE ME THE REASON Luther Vandross (Epic)
6	10	ALL ABOUT EVE All About Eve (Mercury)
-	11	LITTLE CHILDREN Mission (Mercury)
24	12	HEAVEN ON EARTH Belinda Carlisle (Virgin)
20	13	TATTOOED BEAT MESSIAH Zodiac Mindwarp (Mercury)
23	14	NOTHING LIKE THE SUN Sting (A&M)
13	15	KICK INXS (Mercury)
-	16	NOW AND ZEN Robert Plant (Ez paranza)
12	17	ACTUALLY Pet Shop Boys (Parlophone)
42	18	HEARSAY Alexander O'Neal (Tabu)
26	19	THE LION AND THE COBRA Sinead O'Connor (Ensign)
37	20	THE GREATEST LOVE Various Artists (Telstar)
14	21	TANGO IN THE NIGHT Fleetwood Mac (Warner Bros.)
11	22	COME INTO MY LIFE Joyce Sims (London)
25	23	THE JOSHUA TREE U2 (Island)
8	24	BLOW UP YOUR VIDEO AC/DC (Atlantic)
18	25	IF I SHOULD FALL FROM GRACE WITH GOD Pogues (Pogue Mahone)
-	26	THE FRENZ EXPERIMENT Fall (Beggars Banquet)
29	27	FAITH George Michael (Epic)
15	28	DUSTY - THE SILVER COLLECTION Dusty Springfield (Philips)
32	29	TELL IT TO MY HEART Taylor Dayne (Arista)
16	30	ALL LIVE AND ALL OF THE NIGHT Stranglers (Epic)
-	31	IDLEWILD Everything But The Girl (Blanco Y Negro)
-	32	THE BEST OF OMD Orchestral Manoeuvres in the Dark (Virgin)
43	33	WHITESNAKE 1987 Whitesnake (EMI)
50	34	SAY IT AGAIN Jermaine Stewart (Siren)
39	35	RAINTOWN Deacon Blue (CBS)
17	36	SKYSCRAPER David Lee Roth (Warner Bros.)
28	37	WOODEN FOOT COPS ON THE HIGHWAY Woodentops (Rough Trade)
35	38	LA GUNS LA Guns (Vertigo)
44	39	IF YOU CAN'T LICK 'EM, LICK 'EM Ted Nugent (WEA)
-	40	UNFORGETTABLE Various Artists (EMI)
27	41	MAKE IT LAST FOREVER Keith Sweat (Elektra)
22	42	I'M YOUR MAN Leonard Cohen (CBS)
47	43	GET HERE Brenda Russell (A&M)
21	44	THE WORLD WITHOUT END Mighty Lemondrops (Blue Guitar)
33	45	ALL OUR LOVE Gladys Knight & the Pips (MCA)
49	46	LIVE IN AUSTRALIA Elton John (Rocket)
-	47	THE ISLEY BROTHERS' GREATEST HITS Isley Brothers (Telstar)
40	48	WOW Bananarama (London)
46	49	OUT OF THE BLUE Debbie Gibson (Atlantic)
34	50	THE BEST OF MIRAGE JACK MIX 88 Mirage (Stylus)

last week	this week	19 March 1988
1	1	INTRODUCING THE HARDLINE ACCORDING TO Terence Trent D'Arby (CBS)
11	2	LITTLE CHILDREN Mission (Mercury)
16	3	BRIDGE OF SPIES T'Pau (Siren)
16	4	NOW AND ZEN Robert Plant (Ez paranza)
32	5	THE BEST OF OMD Orchestral Manoeuvres in the Dark (Virgin)
9	6	GIVE ME THE REASON Luther Vandross (Epic)
6	7	POPPED IN SOULED OUT Wet Wet Wet (Precious)
7	8	WHENEVER YOU NEED SOMEBODY Rick Astley (RCA)
31	9	IDLEWILD Everything But The Girl (Blanco Y Negro)
3	10	TURN BACK THE CLOCK Johnny Hates Jazz (Virgin)
26	11	THE FRENZ EXPERIMENT Fall (Beggars Banquet)
4	12	THE CHRISTIANS Christians (Island)
12	13	HEAVEN ON EARTH Belinda Carlisle (Virgin)
40	14	UNFORGETTABLE Various Artists (EMI)
5	15	TIFFANY Tiffany (MCA)
18	16	HEARSAY Alexander O'Neal (Tabu)
-	17	TEAR DOWN THESE WALLS Billy Ocean (Jive)
23	18	THE JOSHUA TREE U2 (Island)
10	19	ALL ABOUT EVE All About Eve (Mercury)
21	20	TANGO IN THE NIGHT Fleetwood Mac (Warner Bros.)
15	21	KICK INXS (Mercury)
-	22	BEST OF HOUSE VOL 4 Various Artists (Serious)
-	23	WHO'S BETTER, WHO'S BEST Who (Polydor)
29	24	TELL IT TO MY HEART Taylor Dayne (Arista)
13	25	TATTOOED BEAT MESSIAH Zodiac Mindwarp (Mercury)
20	26	THE GREATEST LOVE Various Artists (Telstar)
14	27	NOTHING LIKE THE SUN Sting (A&M)
22	28	ACTUALLY Pet Shop Boys (Parlophone)
22	29	COME INTO MY LIFE Joyce Sims (London)
-	30	WHITNEY Whitney Houston (Arista)
-	31	FLOODLAND Sisters of Mercy (Merciful Release)
25	32	IF I SHOULD FALL FROM GRACE WITH GOD Pogues (Pogue Mahone)
36	33	SKYSCRAPER David Lee Roth (Warner Bros.)
-	34	BAD ANIMALS Heart (Capitol)
19	35	THE LION AND THE COBRA Sinead O'Connor (Ensign)
35	36	RAINTOWN Deacon Blue (CBS)
37	37	WOODEN FOOT COPS ON THE HIGHWAY Woodentops (Rough Trade)
24	38	BLOW UP YOUR VIDEO AC/DC (Atlantic)
28	39	DUSTY - THE SILVER COLLECTION Dusty Springfield (Philips)
42	40	I'M YOUR MAN Leonard Cohen (CBS)
-	41	YOU'RE A PART OF ME Jean Carne (RCA)
45	42	ALL OUR LOVE Gladys Knight & the Pips (MCA)
-	43	WALTER BEASLEY Walter Beasley (Polydor)
27	44	FAITH George Michael (Epic)
-	45	THE CIRCUS Erasure (Mute)
-	46	HORIZONS Various Artists (K-Tel)
33	47	WHITESNAKE 1987 Whitesnake (EMI)
46	48	LIVE IN AUSTRALIA Elton John (Rocket)
50	49	THE BEST OF MIRAGE JACK MIX 88 Mirage (Stylus)
44	50	THE WORLD WITHOUT END Mighty Lemondrops (Blue Guitar)

last week	this week	26 March 1988
5	1	THE BEST OF OMD Orchestral Manoeuvres in the Dark (Virgin)
1	2	INTRODUCING THE HARDLINE ACCORDING TO Terence Trent D'Arby (CBS)
2	3	LITTLE CHILDREN Mission (Mercury)
23	4	WHO'S BETTER, WHO'S BEST Who (Polydor)
-	5	VIVA HATE Morrissey (HMV)
17	6	TEAR DOWN THESE WALLS Billy Ocean (Jive)
7	7	POPPED IN SOULED OUT Wet Wet Wet (Precious)
14	8	UNFORGETTABLE Various Artists (EMI)
16	9	HEARSAY Alexander O'Neal (Tabu)
6	10	GIVE ME THE REASON Luther Vandross (Epic)
8	11	WHENEVER YOU NEED SOMEBODY Rick Astley (RCA)
-	12	NAKED Talking Heads (EMI)
10	13	TURN BACK THE CLOCK Johnny Hates Jazz (Virgin)
9	14	IDLEWILD Everything But The Girl (Blanco Y Negro)
13	15	HEAVEN ON EARTH Belinda Carlisle (Virgin)
4	16	NOW AND ZEN Robert Plant (Ez paranza)
3	17	BRIDGE OF SPIES T'Pau (Siren)
-	18	SO FAR SO GOOD...SO WHAT! Megadeth (Capitol)
30	19	WHITNEY Whitney Houston (Arista)
20	20	TANGO IN THE NIGHT Fleetwood Mac (Warner Bros.)
12	21	THE CHRISTIANS Christians (Island)
-	22	BAD Michael Jackson (Epic)
15	23	TIFFANY Tiffany (MCA)
21	24	KICK INXS (Mercury)
11	25	THE FRENZ EXPERIMENT Fall (Beggars Banquet)
-	26	KINGDOM COME Kingdom Come (Polydor)
26	27	THE GREATEST LOVE Various Artists (Telstar)
33	28	SKYSCRAPER David Lee Roth (Warner Bros.)
18	29	THE JOSHUA TREE U2 (Island)
25	30	TATTOOED BEAT MESSIAH Zodiac Mindwarp (Mercury)
27	31	NOTHING LIKE THE SUN Sting (A&M)
-	32	ROCK THE NATION Various Artists (Dover)
19	33	ALL ABOUT EVE All About Eve (Mercury)
22	34	BEST OF HOUSE VOL 4 Various Artists (Serious)
28	35	ACTUALLY Pet Shop Boys (Parlophone)
34	36	BAD ANIMALS Heart (Capitol)
40	37	I'M YOUR MAN Leonard Cohen (CBS)
-	38	DIRTY DANCING Soundtrack (RCA)
-	39	STREET SOUNDS HIP HOP 20 Various Artists (Street Sounds)
-	40	PAST MASTERS VOL 1 Beatles (Parlophone)
41	41	YOU'RE A PART OF ME Jean Carne (RCA)
-	42	PAST MASTERS VOL 2 Beatles (Parlophone)
-	43	LA GUNS LA Guns (Vertigo)
29	44	COME INTO MY LIFE Joyce Sims (London)
45	45	THE CIRCUS Erasure (Mute)
-	46	YOU SEND ME Roy Ayers (Polydor)
-	47	WILL DOWNING Will Downing (Fourth & Broadway)
31	48	FLOODLAND Sisters of Mercy (Merciful Release)
24	49	TELL IT TO MY HEART Taylor Dayne (Arista)
-	50	STREET SOUNDS 88-1 Various Artists (Street Sounds)

Orchestral Manoeuvres In The Dark (now more commonly known by the snappier acronym OMD) punctuated Terence Trent D'Arby's Number 1 run with just a week of their own at the summit with a compilation of their string of hit singles to date. It was the Liverpudlians' first album release for well over a year, and their highest-placed ever. The Mission also had their best seller to date with *Little Children*.

April 1988

2 April 1988

Last	This	Title	Artist (Label)
5	1	VIVA HATE	Morrissey (HMV)
12	2	NAKED	Talking Heads (EMI)
1	3	THE BEST OF OMD	Orchestral Manoeuvres in the Dark (Virgin)
-	4	FROM LANGLEY PARK TO MEMPHIS	Prefab Sprout (Kitchenware)
6	5	TEAR DOWN THESE WALLS	Billy Ocean (Jive)
7	6	POPPED IN SOULED OUT	Wet Wet Wet (Precious Organisation)
9	7	HEARSAY	Alexander O'Neal (Tabu)
2	8	INTRODUCING THE HARDLINE ACCORDING TO	Terence Trent D'Arby (CBS)
4	9	WHO'S BETTER, WHO'S BEST	Who (Polydor)
13	10	TURN BACK THE CLOCK	Johnny Hates Jazz (Virgin)
18	11	SO FAR SO GOOD...SO WHAT!	Megadeth (Capitol)
-	12	NOW THAT'S WHAT I CALL MUSIC 11	Various Artists (EMI/Virgin/PolyGram)
8	13	UNFORGETTABLE	Various Artists (EMI)
17	14	BRIDGE OF SPIES	T'Pau (Siren)
-	15	THE STORY OF THE CLASH	Clash (CBS)
11	16	WHENEVER YOU NEED SOMEBODY	Rick Astley (RCA)
24	17	KICK	INXS (Mercury)
32	18	ROCK THE NATION	Various Artists (Dover)
3	19	LITTLE CHILDREN	Mission (Mercury)
-	20	LIVE IN EUROPE	Tina Turner (Capitol)
15	21	HEAVEN ON EARTH	Belinda Carlisle (Virgin)
10	22	GIVE ME THE REASON	Luther Vandross (Epic)
19	23	WHITNEY	Whitney Houston (Arista)
21	24	THE CHRISTIANS	Christians (Island)
23	25	TIFFANY	Tiffany (MCA)
22	26	BAD	Michael Jackson (Epic)
14	27	IDLEWILD	Everything But The Girl (Blanco Y Negro)
-	28	HORIZONS	Various Artists (K-Tel)
26	29	KINGDOM COME	Kingdom Come (Polydor)
47	30	WILL DOWNING	Will Downing (Fourth & Broadway)
-	31	CHALK MARKS IN A RAIN STORM	Joni Mitchell (Geffen)
20	32	TANGO IN THE NIGHT	Fleetwood Mac (Warner Bros.)
35	33	ACTUALLY	Pet Shop Boys (Parlophone)
31	34	NOTHING LIKE THE SUN	Sting (A&M)
38	35	DIRTY DANCING	Soundtrack (RCA)
45	36	THE CIRCUS	Erasure (Mute)
16	37	NOW AND ZEN	Robert Plant (Ez paranza)
27	38	THE GREATEST LOVE	Various Artists (Telstar)
-	39	LITTLE LOVE AFFAIRS	Nanci Griffith (MCA)
-	40	IN FULL EFFECT	Mantronix (10)
29	41	THE JOSHUA TREE	U2 (Island)
33	42	ALL ABOUT EVE	All About Eve (Mercury)
41	43	YOU'RE A PART OF ME	Jean Carne (CBS)
43	44	LA GUNS	LA Guns (Vertigo)
25	45	THE FRENZ EXPERIMENT	Fall (Beggars Banquet)
-	46	TAJA SEVELLE	Taja Sevelle (Paisley Park)
-	47	ALL OUR LOVE	Gladys Knight & the Pips (MCA)
28	48	SKYSCRAPER	David Lee Roth (Warner Bros.)
36	49	BAD ANIMALS	Heart (Capitol)
-	50	THE WORD VOL 2	Various Artists (Jive)

9 April 1988

Last	This	Title	Artist (Label)
12	1	NOW THAT'S WHAT I CALL MUSIC 11	Various Artists (EMI/Virgin/PolyGram)
1	2	VIVA HATE	Morrissey (HMV)
3	3	THE BEST OF OMD	Orchestral Manoeuvres in the Dark (Virgin)
20	4	LIVE IN EUROPE	Tina Turner (Capitol)
2	5	NAKED	Talking Heads (EMI)
15	6	THE STORY OF THE CLASH	Clash (CBS)
6	7	POPPED IN SOULED OUT	Wet Wet Wet (Precious)
4	8	FROM LANGLEY PARK TO MEMPHIS	Prefab Sprout (Kitchenware)
8	9	INTRODUCING THE HARDLINE ACCORDING TO	Terence Trent D'Arby (CBS)
7	10	HEARSAY	Alexander O'Neal (Tabu)
10	11	TURN BACK THE CLOCK	Johnny Hates Jazz (Virgin)
5	12	TEAR DOWN THESE WALLS	Billy Ocean (Jive)
13	13	HORIZONS	Various Artists (K-Tel)
23	14	WHITNEY	Whitney Houston (Arista)
9	15	WHO'S BETTER, WHO'S BEST	Who (Polydor)
-	16	PUSH	Bros (CBS)
31	17	CHALK MARKS IN A RAIN STORM	Joni Mitchell (Geffen)
11	18	SO FAR SO GOOD...SO WHAT!	Megadeth (Capitol)
35	19	DIRTY DANCING	Soundtrack (RCA)
16	20	WHENEVER YOU NEED SOMEBODY	Rick Astley (RCA)
13	21	UNFORGETTABLE	Various Artists (EMI)
17	22	KICK	INXS (Mercury)
21	23	HEAVEN ON EARTH	Belinda Carlisle (Virgin)
32	24	TANGO IN THE NIGHT	Fleetwood Mac (Warner Bros.)
25	25	TIFFANY	Tiffany (MCA)
19	26	LITTLE CHILDREN	Mission (Mercury)
22	27	GIVE ME THE REASON	Luther Vandross (Epic)
28	28	ROCK THE NATION	Various Artists (Dover)
14	29	BRIDGE OF SPIES	T'Pau (Siren)
26	30	BAD	Michael Jackson (Epic)
33	31	ACTUALLY	Pet Shop Boys (Parlophone)
30	32	WILL DOWNING	Will Downing (Fourth & Broadway)
-	33	DISTANT THUNDER	Aswad (Mango)
38	34	THE GREATEST LOVE	Various Artists (Telstar)
29	35	KINGDOM COME	Kingdom Come (Polydor)
24	36	THE CHRISTIANS	Christians (Island)
-	37	HIP HOP AND RAPPING IN THE HOUSE	Various Artists (Stylus)
-	38	EVERYTHING	Climie Fisher (EMI)
46	39	TAJA SEVELLE	Taja Sevelle (Paisley Park)
37	40	NOW AND ZEN	Robert Plant (Ez paranza)
-	41	PAID IN FULL	Eric & Rakim (4th & Broadway)
40	42	IN FULL EFFECT	Mantronix (10)
43	43	ONCE AROUND THE WORLD	It Bites (Virgin)
27	44	IDLEWILD	Everything But The Girl (Blanco Y Negro)
34	45	NOTHING LIKE THE SUN	Sting (A&M)
-	46	PLIGHT AND PREMONITION	David Sylvian & Holger Czukay (Vertigo)
-	47	A PORTRAIT OF ELLA FITZGERALD	Ella Fitzgerald (Stylus)
49	48	BAD ANIMALS	Heart (Capitol)
-	49	THE ISLEY BROTHERS' GREATEST HITS	Isley Brothers (Telstar)
-	50	TELL IT TO MY HEART	Taylor Dayne (Arista)

16 April 1988

Last	This	Title	Artist (Label)
1	1	NOW THAT'S WHAT I CALL MUSIC 11	Various Artists (EMI/Virgin/PolyGram)
3	2	THE BEST OF OMD	Orchestral Manoeuvres in the Dark (Virgin)
16	3	PUSH	Bros (CBS)
4	4	LIVE IN EUROPE	Tina Turner (Capitol)
7	5	POPPED IN SOULED OUT	Wet Wet Wet (Precious Organisation)
2	6	VIVA HATE	Morrissey (HMV)
-	7	LOVELY	Primitives (RCA)
-	8	WINGS OF HEAVEN	Magnum (Polydor)
5	9	NAKED	Talking Heads (EMI)
33	10	DISTANT THUNDER	Aswad (Mango)
24	11	TANGO IN THE NIGHT	Fleetwood Mac (Warner Bros.)
6	12	THE STORY OF THE CLASH	Clash (CBS)
11	13	TURN BACK THE CLOCK	Johnny Hates Jazz (Virgin)
9	14	INTRODUCING THE HARDLINE ACCORDING TO	Terence Trent D'Arby (CBS)
14	15	WHITNEY	Whitney Houston (Arista)
19	16	DIRTY DANCING	Soundtrack (RCA)
8	17	FROM LANGLEY PARK TO MEMPHIS	Prefab Sprout (Kitchenware)
31	18	ACTUALLY	Pet Shop Boys (Parlophone)
25	19	TIFFANY	Tiffany (MCA)
20	20	WHENEVER YOU NEED SOMEBODY	Rick Astley (RCA)
29	21	BRIDGE OF SPIES	T'Pau (Siren)
10	22	HEARSAY	Alexander O'Neal (Tabu)
17	23	CHALK MARKS IN A RAIN STORM	Joni Mitchell (Geffen)
37	24	HIP HOP AND RAPPING IN THE HOUSE	Various Artists (Stylus)
23	25	HEAVEN ON EARTH	Belinda Carlisle (Virgin)
28	26	ROCK THE NATION	Various Artists (Dover)
15	27	WHO'S BETTER, WHO'S BEST	Who (Polydor)
-	28	WHAT'S UP DOG	Was Not Was (Fontana)
12	29	TEAR DOWN THESE WALLS	Billy Ocean (Jive)
18	30	SO FAR SO GOOD...SO WHAT!	Megadeth (Capitol)
-	31	RICHARD MARX	Richard Marx (Manhattan)
-	32	GLADSOME, HUMOUR AND BLUE	Martin Stephenson & the Daintees (Kitchenwear)
32	33	WILL DOWNING	Will Downing (Fourth & Broadway)
-	34	DESTINY	Saxon (EMI)
21	35	UNFORGETTABLE	Various Artists (EMI)
36	36	THE CHRISTIANS	Christians (Island)
22	37	KICK	INXS (Mercury)
48	38	BAD ANIMALS	Heart (Capitol)
-	39	HEART	Heart (Capitol)
26	40	LITTLE CHILDREN	Mission (Mercury)
-	41	FILE UNDER ROCK	Eddy Grant (Parlophone)
13	42	HORIZONS	Various Artists (K-Tel)
27	43	GIVE ME THE REASON	Luther Vandross (Epic)
35	44	KINGDOM COME	Kingdom Come (Polydor)
-	45	SGT PEPPER KNEW MY FATHER	Various Artists (NME/Island)
-	46	IN HEAT	Black 'n' Blue (Geffen)
-	47	PASSION	Norman Connors (Capitol)
-	48	UPFRONT 10	Various Artists (Serious)
30	49	BAD	Michael Jackson (Epic)
38	50	EVERYTHING	Climie Fisher (EMI)

Previously the lead singer with the Smiths, who had split amid general acrimony between key members himself and Johnny Marr, Morrissey wasted no time launching what would be an equally high-profile solo career, and began it by topping the Smiths' former album chart successes with an immediate Number 1 release, *Viva Hate*. No doubt he was unimpressed to then be deposed almost immediately by *Now 11*!

April – May 1988

23 April 1988

last week	this week	title	artist (label)
3	1	PUSH	Bros (CBS)
1	2	NOW THAT'S WHAT I CALL MUSIC 11	Various Artists (EMI/Virgin/PolyGram)
-	3	SEVENTH SON OF A SEVENTH SON	Iron Maiden (EMI)
2	4	THE BEST OF OMD	Orchestral Manoeuvres in the Dark (Virgin)
5	5	POPPED IN SOULED OUT	Wet Wet Wet (Precious)
11	6	TANGO IN THE NIGHT	Fleetwood Mac (Warner Bros.)
16	7	DIRTY DANCING	Soundtrack (RCA)
7	8	LOVELY	Primitives (RCA)
8	9	WINGS OF HEAVEN	Magnum (Polydor)
18	10	ACTUALLY	Pet Shop Boys (Parlophone)
10	11	DISTANT THUNDER	Aswad (Mango)
24	12	HIP HOP AND RAPPING IN THE HOUSE	Various Artists (Stylus)
4	13	LIVE IN EUROPE	Tina Turner (Capitol)
6	14	VIVA HATE	Morrissey (HMV)
21	15	BRIDGE OF SPIES	T'Pau (Siren)
14	16	INTRODUCING THE HARDLINE ACCORDING TO	Terence Trent D'Arby (CBS)
9	17	NAKED	Talking Heads (EMI)
27	18	WHO'S BETTER, WHO'S BEST	Who (Polydor)
32	19	GLADSOME, HUMOUR AND BLUE	Martin Stephenson & the Daintees (Kitchenwear)
13	20	TURN BACK THE CLOCK	Johnny Hates Jazz (Virgin)
15	21	WHITNEY	Whitney Houston (Arista)
19	22	TIFFANY	Tiffany (MCA)
12	23	THE STORY OF THE CLASH	Clash (CBS)
17	24	FROM LANGLEY PARK TO MEMPHIS	Prefab Sprout (Kitchenware)
39	25	HEART	Heart (Capitol)
50	26	EVERYTHING	Cimie Fisher (EMI)
33	27	WILL DOWNING	Will Downing (Fourth & Broadway)
22	28	HEARSAY	Alexander O'Neal (Tabu)
25	29	HEAVEN ON EARTH	Belinda Carlisle (Virgin)
49	30	BAD	Michael Jackson (Epic)
23	31	CHALK MARKS IN A RAIN STORM	Joni Mitchell (Geffen)
20	32	WHENEVER YOU NEED SOMEBODY	Rick Astley (RCA)
29	33	TEAR DOWN THESE WALLS	Billy Ocean (Jive)
42	34	HORIZONS	Various Artists (K-Tel)
43	35	GIVE ME THE REASON	Luther Vandross (Epic)
26	36	ROCK THE NATION	Various Artists (Dover)
36	37	THE CHRISTIANS	Christians (Island)
38	38	BAD ANIMALS	Heart (Capitol)
-	39	CHER	Cher (Geffen)
37	40	KICK	INXS (Mercury)
-	41	GREATEST HITS	Isley Brothers (Telstar)
44	42	KINGDOM COME	Kingdom Come (Polydor)
-	43	SOUTHERN BY THE GRACE OF GOD	Lynyrd Skynyrd (MCA)
34	44	DESTINY	Saxon (EMI)
47	45	PASSION	Norman Connors (Capitol)
-	46	YOU'RE A PART OF ME	Jean Carne (RCA)
-	47	WAITING FOR BONAPARTE	Men They Couldn't Hang (Magnet)
-	48	RARE GROOVE 2	Various Artists (RCA/Arista)
-	49	THE ESSENTIAL KARAJAN	Herbert Von Karajan (Deutsche Grammophon)
-	50	RAINTOWN	Deacon Blue (CBS)

30 April 1988

last week	this week	title	artist (label)
3	1	SEVENTH SON OF A SEVENTH SON	Iron Maiden (EMI)
6	2	TANGO IN THE NIGHT	Fleetwood Mac (Warner Bros.)
2	3	NOW THAT'S WHAT I CALL MUSIC 11	Various Artists (EMI/Virgin/PolyGram)
4	4	THE BEST OF OMD	Orchestral Manoeuvres in the Dark (Virgin)
1	5	PUSH	Bros (CBS)
7	7	DIRTY DANCING	Soundtrack (RCA)
10	8	ACTUALLY	Pet Shop Boys (Parlophone)
17	9	NAKED	Talking Heads (EMI)
8	10	LOVELY	Primitives (RCA)
12	11	HIP HOP AND RAPPING IN THE HOUSE	Various Artists (Stylus)
26	12	EVERYTHING	Cimie Fisher (EMI)
13	13	LIVE IN EUROPE	Tina Turner (Capitol)
-	14	THE INNOCENTS	Erasure (Mute)
15	15	BRIDGE OF SPIES	T'Pau (Siren)
28	16	HEARSAY	Alexander O'Neal (Tabu)
37	17	THE CHRISTIANS	Christians (Island)
11	18	DISTANT THUNDER	Aswad (Mango)
-	19	BARBED WIRE KISS	Jesus & Mary Chain (Blanco Y Negro)
27	20	WILL DOWNING	Will Downing (Fourth & Broadway)
14	21	VIVA HATE	Morrissey (HMV)
21	22	WHITNEY	Whitney Houston (Arista)
9	23	WINGS OF HEAVEN	Magnum (Polydor)
22	24	TIFFANY	Tiffany (MCA)
20	25	TURN BACK THE CLOCK	Johnny Hates Jazz (Virgin)
18	26	WHO'S BETTER, WHO'S BEST	Who (Polydor)
47	27	WAITING FOR BONAPARTE	Men They Couldn't Hang (Magnet)
16	28	INTRODUCING THE HARDLINE ACCORDING TO	Terence Trent D'Arby (CBS)
25	29	HEART	Heart (Capitol)
29	30	HEAVEN ON EARTH	Belinda Carlisle (Virgin)
19	31	GLADSOME, HUMOUR AND BLUE	Martin Stephenson & the Daintees (Kitchenwear)
-	32	THIS NOTE'S FOR YOU	Neil Young & the Blue Notes (Reprise)
24	33	FROM LANGLEY PARK TO MEMPHIS	Prefab Sprout (Kitchenware)
-	34	FAITH	George Michael (Epic)
30	35	BAD	Michael Jackson (Epic)
32	36	WHENEVER YOU NEED SOMEBODY	Rick Astley (RCA)
33	37	TEAR DOWN THESE WALLS	Billy Ocean (Jive)
48	38	ALL ABOUT EVE	All About Eve (Mercury)
-	39	GREATEST LOVE SONGS	Placido Domingo (CBS)
40	40	LOVE	Aztec Camera (Warner Bros.)
31	41	CHALK MARKS IN A RAIN STORM	Joni Mitchell (Geffen)
23	42	THE STORY OF THE CLASH	Clash (CBS)
48	43	RARE GROOVE 2	Various Artists (RCA-Arista)
34	44	HORIZONS	Various Artists (K-Tel)
50	45	RAINTOWN	Deacon Blue (CBS)
46	46	YOU'RE A PART OF ME	Jean Carne (RCA)
47	47	NITE FLITE	Various Artists (CBS)
35	48	GIVE ME THE REASON	Luther Vandross (Epic)
-	49	TELL IT TO MY HEART	Taylor Dayne (Arista)
40	50	KICK	INXS (Mercury)

7 May 1988

last week	this week	title	artist (label)
14	1	THE INNOCENTS	Erasure (Mute)
2	2	TANGO IN THE NIGHT	Fleetwood Mac (Warner Bros.)
3	3	NOW THAT'S WHAT I CALL MUSIC 11	Various Artists (EMI/Virgin/PolyGram)
1	4	SEVENTH SON OF A SEVENTH SON	Iron Maiden (EMI)
5	5	DIRTY DANCING	Soundtrack (RCA)
4	6	THE BEST OF OMD	Orchestral Manoeuvres in the Dark (Virgin)
5	7	PUSH	Bros (CBS)
11	8	HIP HOP AND RAPPING IN THE HOUSE	Various Artists (Stylus)
19	9	BARBED WIRE KISS	Jesus & Mary Chain (Blanco Y Negro)
12	10	EVERYTHING	Cimie Fisher (EMI)
6	11	POPPED IN SOULED OUT	Wet Wet Wet (Precious)
8	12	ACTUALLY	Pet Shop Boys (Parlophone)
17	13	THE CHRISTIANS	Christians (Island)
15	14	BRIDGE OF SPIES	T'Pau (Siren)
9	15	NAKED	Talking Heads (EMI)
32	16	THIS NOTE'S FOR YOU	Neil Young & the Blue Notes (Reprise)
20	17	WILL DOWNING	Will Downing (Fourth & Broadway)
-	18	LIFE'S TOO GOOD	Sugarcubes (One Little Indian)
13	19	LIVE IN EUROPE	Tina Turner (Capitol)
47	20	NITE FLITE	Various Artists (CBS)
34	21	FAITH	George Michael (Epic)
30	22	HEAVEN ON EARTH	Belinda Carlisle (Virgin)
22	23	WHITNEY	Whitney Houston (Arista)
10	24	LOVELY	Primitives (RCA)
21	25	VIVA HATE	Morrissey (HMV)
33	26	FROM LANGLEY PARK TO MEMPHIS	Prefab Sprout (Kitchenware)
18	27	DISTANT THUNDER	Aswad (Mango)
28	28	INTRODUCING THE HARDLINE ACCORDING TO	Terence Trent D'Arby (CBS)
16	29	HEARSAY	Alexander O'Neal (Tabu)
25	30	TURN BACK THE CLOCK	Johnny Hates Jazz (Virgin)
23	31	WINGS OF HEAVEN	Magnum (Polydor)
40	32	LOVE	Aztec Camera (Warner Bros.)
-	33	THE MADNESS	Madness (Virgin)
-	34	REMEMBER YOU'RE MINE	Foster & Allen (Stylus)
48	35	GIVE ME THE REASON	Luther Vandross (Epic)
38	36	ALL ABOUT EVE	All About Eve (Mercury)
-	37	CHER	Cher (Geffen)
45	38	RAINTOWN	Deacon Blue (CBS)
37	39	TEAR DOWN THESE WALLS	Billy Ocean (Jive)
24	40	TIFFANY	Tiffany (MCA)
26	41	WHO'S BETTER, WHO'S BEST	Who (Polydor)
-	42	JOE JACKSON LIVE 1980-86	Joe Jackson (A&M)
-	43	ALIENS ARE AT MY BUICK	Thomas Dolby (EMI)
-	44	MEET DANNY WILSON	Danny Wilson (Virgin)
-	45	MAKE IT LAST FOREVER	Keith Sweat (Elektra)
-	46	YOU CAN'T DO THAT ON STAGE ANYMORE	Frank Zappa (Music for Nations)
47	47	PASSION	Norman Connors (Capitol)
29	48	HEART	Heart (Capitol)
35	49	BAD	Michael Jackson (Epic)
-	50	THIS IS OUR ART	Soup Dragons (Sire)

Bros had just had two Number 2 singles - *When Will I Be Famous* and *Drop The Boy* - in quick succession, when their *Push* album was released, and were already shaping up as the latest UK teen sensation. The surprise, then, was not that the album should reach Number 1, but that it should come and go from the summit quite so fast. Possibly, most of the trio's young fans were exclusively singles buyers.

14 May 1988

last week	this week	Title	Artist (Label)
2	1	TANGO IN THE NIGHT	Fleetwood Mac (Warner Bros.)
1	2	THE INNOCENTS	Erasure (Mute)
4	3	SEVENTH SON OF A SEVENTH SON	Iron Maiden (EMI)
5	4	DIRTY DANCING	Soundtrack (RCA)
6	5	THE BEST OF OMD	Orchestral Manoeuvres in the Dark (Virgin)
12	6	ACTUALLY	Pet Shop Boys (Parlophone)
3	7	NOW THAT'S WHAT I CALL MUSIC 11	Various Artists (EMI/Virgin/PolyGram)
7	8	PUSH	Bros (CBS)
8	9	HIP HOP AND RAPPING IN THE HOUSE	Various Artists (Stylus)
-	10	STRONGER THAN PRIDE	Sade (Epic)
11	11	POPPED IN SOULED OUT	Wet Wet Wet (Precious)
14	12	BRIDGE OF SPIES	T'Pau (Siren)
18	13	LIFE'S TOO GOOD	Sugarcubes (One Little Indian)
-	14	STAY ON THESE ROADS	A-Ha (WEA)
9	15	BARBED WIRE KISS	Jesus & Mary Chain (Blanco Y Negro)
-	16	MORE DIRTY DANCING	Various Artists (RCA)
23	17	WHITNEY	Whitney Houston (Arista)
20	18	NITE FLITE	Various Artists (CBS)
13	19	THE CHRISTIANS	Christians (Island)
10	20	EVERYTHING	Cimie Fisher (EMI)
17	21	WILL DOWNING	Will Downing (Fourth & Broadway)
-	22	SIXTIES MIX 2	Various Artists (Stylus)
43	23	ALIENS ATE MY BUICK	Thomas Dolby (EMI)
21	24	FAITH	George Michael (Epic)
26	25	FROM LANGLEY PARK TO MEMPHIS	Prefab Sprout (Kitchenware)
15	26	NAKED	Talking Heads (EMI)
16	27	THIS NOTE'S FOR YOU	Neil Young & the Blue Notes (Reprise)
22	28	HEAVEN ON EARTH	Belinda Carlisle (Virgin)
34	29	REMEMBER YOU'RE MINE	Foster & Allen (Stylus)
28	30	INTRODUCING THE HARDLINE ACCORDING TO	Terence Trent D'Arby (CBS)
49	31	BAD	Michael Jackson (Epic)
-	32	BLIND	Icicle Works (Beggars Banquet)
-	33	SCENES FROM THE SOUTHSIDE	Bruce Hornsby and the Range (RCA)
24	34	LOVELY	Primitives (RCA)
29	35	HEARSAY	Alexander O'Neal (Tabu)
19	36	LIVE IN EUROPE	Tina Turner (Capitol)
27	37	DISTANT THUNDER	Aswad (Mango)
50	38	THIS IS OUR ART	Soup Dragons (Sire)
-	39	EVERLASTING	Natalie Cole (Manhattan)
45	40	MAKE IT LAST FOREVER	Keith Sweat (Elektra)
31	41	WINGS OF HEAVEN	Magnum (Polydor)
-	42	PEBBLES	Pebbles (MCA)
-	43	NARADA	Narada Michael Walden (Warner Bros.)
25	44	VIVA-HaTE	Morrissey (HMV)
30	45	TURN BACK THE CLOCK	Johnny Hates Jazz (Virgin)
32	46	LOVE	Aztec Camera (Warner Bros.)
37	47	CHER	Cher (Geffen)
42	48	JOE JACKSON LIVE 1980-86	Joe Jackson (A&M)
35	49	GIVE ME THE REASON	Luther Vandross (Epic)
38	50	RAINTOWN	Deacon Blue (CBS)

21 May 1988

last week	this week	Title	Artist (Label)
1	1	TANGO IN THE NIGHT	Fleetwood Mac (Warner Bros.)
10	2	STRONGER THAN PRIDE	Sade (Epic)
14	3	STAY ON THESE ROADS	A-Ha (WEA)
2	4	THE INNOCENTS	Erasure (Mute)
4	5	DIRTY DANCING	Soundtrack (RCA)
16	6	MORE DIRTY DANCING	Various Artists (RCA)
-	7	LOVESEXY	Prince (Paisley Park)
11	8	POPPED IN SOULED OUT	Wet Wet Wet (Precious)
19	9	THE CHRISTIANS	Christians (Island)
5	10	THE BEST OF OMD	Orchestral Manoeuvres in the Dark (Virgin)
17	11	WHITNEY	Whitney Houston (Arista)
7	12	NOW THAT'S WHAT I CALL MUSIC 11	Various Artists (EMI/Virgin/PolyGram)
9	13	HIP HOP AND RAPPING IN THE HOUSE	Various Artists (Stylus)
-	14	SAVAGE AMUSEMENT	Scorpions (Harvest)
8	15	PUSH	Bros (CBS)
13	16	LIFE'S TOO GOOD	Sugarcubes (One Little Indian)
6	17	ACTUALLY	Pet Shop Boys (Parlophone)
22	18	SIXTIES MIX 2	Various Artists (Stylus)
3	19	SEVENTH SON OF A SEVENTH SON	Iron Maiden (EMI)
-	20	OPEN UP AND SAY AHH	Poison (Capitol)
18	21	NITE FLITE	Various Artists (CBS)
25	22	FROM LANGLEY PARK TO MEMPHIS	Prefab Sprout (Kitchenware)
-	23	SGT PEPPER KNEW MY FATHER	Various Artists (NME/Island)
20	24	EVERYTHING	Cimie Fisher (EMI)
32	25	BLIND	Icicle Works (Beggars Banquet)
-	26	RUMOURS	Fleetwood Mac (Warner Bros.)
12	27	BRIDGE OF SPIES	T'Pau (Siren)
30	28	INTRODUCING THE HARDLINE ACCORDING TO	Terence Trent D'Arby (CBS)
33	29	SCENES FROM THE SOUTHSIDE	Bruce Hornsby and the Range (RCA)
-	30	NOW THATS WHAT I CALL QUITE GOOD	Housemartins (Go! Discs)
-	31	ODYSSEY	Yngwie Malmsteen (Polydor)
28	32	HEAVEN ON EARTH	Belinda Carlisle (Virgin)
43	33	NARADA	Narada Michael Walden (Warner Bros.)
34	34	HOUSE HITS	Various Artists (Needle)
34	35	LOVELY	Primitives (RCA)
24	36	FAITH	George Michael (Epic)
15	37	BARBED WIRE KISS	Jesus & Mary Chain (Blanco Y Negro)
41	38	WINGS OF HEAVEN	Magnum (Polydor)
46	39	LOVE	Aztec Camera (Warner Bros.)
-	40	THE XENON CODE	Hawkwind (GWR)
21	41	WILL DOWNING	Will Downing (Fourth & Broadway)
26	42	NAKED	Talking Heads (EMI)
29	43	REMEMBER YOU'RE MINE	Foster & Allen (Stylus)
31	44	BAD	Michael Jackson (Epic)
-	45	TSOP - THE SOUND OF PHILADELPHIA	Various Artists (K-Tel)
42	46	PEBBLES	Pebbles (MCA)
35	47	HEARSAY	Alexander O'Neal (Tabu)
-	48	WOW	Bananarama (London)
36	49	LIVE IN EUROPE	Tina Turner (Capitol)
50	50	RAINTOWN	Deacon Blue (CBS)

28 May 1988

last week	this week	Title	Artist (Label)
7	1	LOVESEXY	Prince (Paisley Park)
2	2	STRONGER THAN PRIDE	Sade (Epic)
1	3	TANGO IN THE NIGHT	Fleetwood Mac (Warner Bros.)
9	4	THE CHRISTIANS	Christians (Island)
8	5	POPPED IN SOULED OUT	Wet Wet Wet (Precious)
30	6	NOW THATS WHAT I CALL QUITE GOOD	Housemartins (Go! Discs)
3	7	STAY ON THESE ROADS	A-Ha (WEA)
5	8	DIRTY DANCING	Soundtrack (RCA)
11	9	WHITNEY	Whitney Houston (Arista)
4	10	MORE DIRTY DANCING	Various Artists (RCA)
4	11	THE INNOCENTS	Erasure (Mute)
-	12	MOTOWN DANCE PARTY	Various Artists (Motown)
-	13	BULLET FROM A GUN	Derek B (Tuff Audio)
18	14	SIXTIES MIX 2	Various Artists (Stylus)
32	15	HEAVEN ON EARTH	Belinda Carlisle (Virgin)
29	16	SCENES FROM THE SOUTHSIDE	Bruce Hornsby and the Range (RCA)
10	17	THE BEST OF OMD	Orchestral Manoeuvres in the Dark (Virgin)
-	18	THE SEA OF LOVE	Adventures (Elektra)
20	19	OPEN UP AND SAY AHH	Poison (Capitol)
24	20	EVERYTHING	Cimie Fisher (EMI)
31	21	ODYSSEY	Yngwie Malmsteen (Polydor)
22	22	FROM LANGLEY PARK TO MEMPHIS	Prefab Sprout (Kitchenware)
26	23	RUMOURS	Fleetwood Mac (Warner Bros.)
21	24	NITE FLITE	Various Artists (CBS)
19	25	SEVENTH SON OF A SEVENTH SON	Iron Maiden (EMI)
12	26	NOW THAT'S WHAT I CALL MUSIC 11	Various Artists (EMI/Virgin/PolyGram)
-	27	RAM IT DOWN	Judas Priest (CBS)
15	28	PUSH	Bros (CBS)
-	29	THE FIRST OF A MILLION KISSES	Fairground Attraction (RCA)
13	30	HIP HOP AND RAPPING IN THE HOUSE	Various Artists (Stylus)
17	31	ACTUALLY	Pet Shop Boys (Parlophone)
34	32	HOUSE HITS	Various Artists (Needle)
-	33	JOY	Teddy Pendergrass (Elektra)
16	34	LIFE'S TOO GOOD	Sugarcubes (One Little Indian)
-	35	ALL SYSTEMS GO	Vinnie Vincent (Chrysalis)
14	36	SAVAGE AMUSEMENT	Scorpions (Harvest)
23	37	SGT PEPPER KNEW MY FATHER	Various Artists (NME/Island)
27	38	BRIDGE OF SPIES	T'Pau (Siren)
33	39	NARADA	Narada Michael Walden (Warner Bros.)
-	40	THE NEW ORDER	Testament (Atlantic)
36	41	FAITH	George Michael (Epic)
37	42	BARBED WIRE KISS	Jesus & Mary Chain (Blanco Y Negro)
-	43	NORTH AND SOUTH	Gerry Rafferty (London)
47	44	HEARSAY	Alexander O'Neal (Tabu)
28	45	INTRODUCING THE HARDLINE ACCORDING TO	Terence Trent D'Arby (CBS)
25	46	BLIND	Icicle Works (Beggars Banquet)
42	47	NAKED	Talking Heads (EMI)
-	48	HE'S THE DJ, I'M THE RAPPER	DJ Jazzy Jeff & the Fresh Prince (Jive)
13	49	IN EFFECT MODE	Al B Sure (Warner Bros.)
-	50	BROOMFIELD	Broomfield (Vision)

After five previous UK charting albums since his 1984 breakthrough with *Purple Rain*, Prince's *Lovesexy* was the first to take him all the way to Number 1, the previous year's *Sign 'O' The Times* having halted at 2. The album he replaced at Number 1 was none other than Fleetwood Mac's *Tango In The Night*, resurgent once again after more than a year in the chart, and enjoying its second spell at the top.

June 1988

4 June 1988

last	this		
3	1	TANGO IN THE NIGHT	
			Fleetwood Mac (Warner Bros.)
1	2	LOVESEXY	Prince (Paisley Park)
8	3	DIRTY DANCING	Soundtrack (RCA)
10	4	MORE DIRTY DANCING	Various Artists (RCA)
2	5	STRONGER THAN PRIDE	Sade (Epic)
29	6	THE FIRST OF A MILLION KISSES	
			Fairground Attraction (RCA)
13	7	BULLET FROM A GUN	Derek B (Tuff Audio)
9	8	WHITNEY	Whitney Houston (Arista)
5	9	POPPED IN SOULED OUT	Wet Wet Wet (Precious)
24	10	NITE FLITE	Various Artists (CBS)
4	11	THE CHRISTIANS	Christians (Island)
12	12	MOTOWN DANCE PARTY	Various Artists (Motown)
6	13	NOW THATS WHAT I CALL QUITE GOOD	
			Housemartins (Go! Discs)
27	14	RAM IT DOWN	Judas Priest (CBS)
-	15	OU812	Van Halen (Warner Bros.)
15	16	HEAVEN ON EARTH	Belinda Carlisle (Virgin)
7	17	STAY ON THESE ROADS	A-Ha (WEA)
-	18	LOVE	Aztec Camera (Warner Bros.)
36	19	SAVAGE AMUSEMENT	Scorpions (Harvest)
16	20	SCENES FROM THE SOUTHSIDE	
			Bruce Hornsby and the Range (RCA)
11	21	THE INNOCENTS	Erasure (Mute)
23	22	RUMOURS	Fleetwood Mac (Warner Bros.)
19	23	OPEN UP AND SAY AHH	Poison (Capitol)
22	24	FROM LANGLEY PARK TO MEMPHIS	
			Prefab Sprout (Kitchenware)
37	25	SGT PEPPER KNEW MY FATHER	
			Various Artists (NME/Island)
-	26	OUT OF ORDER	Rod Stewart (Warner Bros.)
40	27	THE NEW ORDER	Testament (Atlantic)
14	28	SIXTIES MIX 2	Various Artists (Stylus)
26	29	NOW THAT'S WHAT I CALL MUSIC 11	
			Various Artists (EMI/Virgin/PolyGram)
-	30	REMEMBER YOU'RE MINE	Foster & Allen (Stylus)
18	31	THE SEA OF LOVE	Adventures (Elektra)
-	32	TSOP - THE SOUND OF PHILADELPHIA	
			Various Artists (K-Tel)
35	33	ALL SYSTEMS GO	Vinnie Vincent (Chrysalis)
21	34	ODYSSEY	Yngwie Malmsteen (Polydor)
25	35	TOUGHER THAN LEATHER	Run DMC (London)
30	36	HIP HOP AND RAPPING IN THE HOUSE	
			Various Artists (Stylus)
-	37	OPERATION MINDCRIME	
			Queensryche (Manhattan)
17	38	THE BEST OF OMD	
			Orchestral Manoeuvres in the Dark (Virgin)
20	39	EVERYTHING	Cimie Fisher (EMI)
31	40	ACTUALLY	Pet Shop Boys (Parlophone)
44	41	HEARSAY	Alexander O'Neal (Tabu)
34	42	LIFE'S TOO GOOD	
			Sugarcubes (One Little Indian)
43	43	NORTH AND SOUTH	Gerry Rafferty (London)
33	44	JOY	Teddy Pendergrass (Elektra)
-	45	REGGAE CLASSICS VOL 2	
			Various Artists (Trojan)
28	46	PUSH	Bros (CBS)
32	47	HOUSE HITS	Various Artists (Needle)
38	48	BRIDGE OF SPIES	T'Pau (Siren)
-	49	DISTANT THUNDER	Aswad (Mango)
-	50	SLAUGHTERHOUSE	
			Various Artists (Lambs to the Slaughter)

11 June 1988

last	this		
1	1	TANGO IN THE NIGHT	
			Fleetwood Mac (Warner Bros.)
10	2	NITE FLITE	Various Artists (CBS)
5	3	STRONGER THAN PRIDE	Sade (Epic)
3	4	DIRTY DANCING	Soundtrack (RCA)
2	5	LOVESEXY	Prince (Paisley Park)
9	6	POPPED IN SOULED OUT	Wet Wet Wet (Precious)
4	7	MOTOWN DANCE PARTY	Various Artists (Motown)
4	8	MORE DIRTY DANCING	Various Artists (RCA)
8	9	WHITNEY	Whitney Houston (Arista)
6	10	THE FIRST OF A MILLION KISSES	
			Fairground Attraction (RCA)
16	11	HEAVEN ON EARTH	Belinda Carlisle (Virgin)
26	12	OUT OF ORDER	Rod Stewart (Warner Bros.)
35	13	TOUGHER THAN LEATHER	Run DMC (London)
15	14	OU812	Van Halen (Warner Bros.)
18	15	LOVE	Aztec Camera (Warner Bros.)
7	16	BULLET FROM A GUN	Derek B (Tuff Audio)
11	17	THE CHRISTIANS	Christians (Island)
21	18	THE INNOCENTS	Erasure (Mute)
24	19	FROM LANGLEY PARK TO MEMPHIS	
			Prefab Sprout (Kitchenware)
20	20	SCENES FROM THE SOUTHSIDE	
			Bruce Hornsby and the Range (RCA)
30	21	REMEMBER YOU'RE MINE	
			Foster & Allen (Stylus)
25	22	SGT PEPPER KNEW MY FATHER	
			Various Artists (NME/Island)
39	23	EVERYTHING	Cimie Fisher (EMI)
28	24	SIXTIES MIX 2	Various Artists (Stylus)
22	25	RUMOURS	Fleetwood Mac (Warner Bros.)
38	26	THE BEST OF OMD	
			Orchestral Manoeuvres in the Dark (Virgin)
46	27	PUSH	Bros (CBS)
17	28	STAY ON THESE ROADS	A-Ha (WEA)
32	29	TSOP - THE SOUND OF PHILADELPHIA	
			Various Artists (K-Tel)
14	30	RAM IT DOWN	Judas Priest (CBS)
34	31	ODYSSEY	Yngwie Malmstein (Polydor)
37	32	OPERATION MINDCRIME	
			Queensryche (Manhattan)
45	33	REGGAE CLASSICS VOL 2	
			Various Artists (Trojan)
-	34	TIME ODYSSEY	Vinny Moore (Phonogram)
13	35	NOW THAT'S WHAT I CALL QUITE GOOD	
			Housemartins (Go! Discs)
-	36	OUT OF THE BLUE	Debbie Gibson (Atlantic)
40	37	ACTUALLY	Pet Shop Boys (Parlophone)
-	38	GIVE ME THE REASON	Luther Vandross (Epic)
41	39	HEARSAY	Alexander O'Neal (Tabu)
-	40	SUBSTANCE	New Order (Factory)
27	41	THE NEW ORDER	Testament (Atlantic)
-	42	TRACY CHAPMAN	Tracy Chapman (Elektra)
19	43	SAVAGE AMUSEMENT	Scorpions (Harvest)
29	44	NOW THAT'S WHAT I CALL MUSIC 11	
			Various Artists (EMI/Virgin/PolyGram)
33	45	ALL SYSTEMS GO	Vinnie Vincent (Chrysalis)
31	46	THE SEA OF LOVE	Adventures (Elektra)
36	47	HIP HOP AND RAPPING IN THE HOUSE	
			Various Artists (Stylus)
44	48	JOY	Teddy Pendergrass (Elektra)
-	49	EUREKA	Bible (Chrysalis)
-	50	STREET SOUNDS HIP HOP 21	
			Various Artists (Street Sounds)

18 June 1988

last	this		
2	1	NITE FLITE	Various Artists (CBS)
1	2	TANGO IN THE NIGHT	
			Fleetwood Mac (Warner Bros.)
7	3	MOTOWN DANCE PARTY	Various Artists (Motown)
11	4	HEAVEN ON EARTH	Belinda Carlisle (Virgin)
4	5	DIRTY DANCING	Soundtrack (RCA)
15	6	LOVE	Aztec Camera (Warner Bros.)
-	7	PROVISION	Scritti Politti (Virgin)
27	8	PUSH	Bros (CBS)
-	9	PEOPLE	Hothouse Flowers (London)
3	10	STRONGER THAN PRIDE	Sade (Epic)
6	11	POPPED IN SOULED OUT	
			Wet Wet Wet (Precious)
8	12	MORE DIRTY DANCING	Various Artists (RCA)
9	13	WHITNEY	Whitney Houston (Arista)
10	14	THE FIRST OF A MILLION KISSES	
			Fairground Attraction (RCA)
-	15	AIN'T COMPLAINING	Status Quo (Vertigo)
39	16	HEARSAY	
			Alexander O'Neal (Tabu)
17	17	THE CHRISTIANS	Christians (Island)
-	18	HEART	Heart (Capitol)
12	19	OUT OF ORDER	Rod Stewart (Warner Bros.)
18	20	THE INNOCENTS	Erasure (Mute)
24	21	SIXTIES MIX 2	Various Artists (Stylus)
-	22	BAD	Michael Jackson (Epic)
26	23	THE BEST OF OMD	
			Orchestral Manoeuvres in the Dark (Virgin)
5	24	LOVESEXY	Prince (Paisley Park)
19	25	FROM LANGLEY PARK TO MEMPHIS	
			Prefab Sprout (Kitchenware)
29	26	TSOP - THE SOUND OF PHILADELPHIA	
			Various Artists (K-Tel)
21	27	REMEMBER YOU'RE MINE	
			Foster & Allen (Stylus)
37	28	ACTUALLY	Pet Shop Boys (Parlophone)
13	29	TOUGHER THAN LEATHER	Run DMC (London)
20	30	SCENES FROM THE SOUTHSIDE	
			Bruce Hornsby and the Range (RCA)
28	31	STAY ON THESE ROADS	A-Ha (WEA)
14	32	OU812	Van Halen (Warner Bros.)
-	33	TIFFANY	Tiffany (MCA)
35	34	NOW THATS WHAT I CALL QUITE GOOD	
			Housemartins (Go! Discs)
44	35	NOW THAT'S WHAT I CALL MUSIC 11	
			Various Artists (EMI/Virgin/PolyGram)
-	36	FAITH	George Michael (Epic)
-	37	DISTANT THUNDER	Aswad (Mango)
36	38	OUT OF THE BLUE	Debbie Gibson (Atlantic)
42	39	TRACY CHAPMAN	Tracy Chapman (Elektra)
23	40	EVERYTHING	Cimie Fisher (EMI)
-	41	BACK ON THE ROAD	Various Artists (Stylus)
-	42	VIVA-HaTE	Morrissey (HMV)
-	43	BRIDGE OF SPIES	T'Pau (Siren)
25	44	RUMOURS	Fleetwood Mac (Warner Bros.)
-	45	THE HITS OF HOUSE ARE HERE	
			Various Artists (K-Tel)
-	46	INTRODUCING THE HARDLINE ACCORDING TO	
			Terence Trent D'Arby (CBS)
38	47	GIVE ME THE REASON	Luther Vandross (Epic)
16	48	BULLET FROM A GUN	Derek B (Tuff Audio)
-	49	THE COLLECTION - 20 GREATEST HITS	
			Frankie Valli & the Four Seasons (Telstar)
-	50	WOLF	Hugh Cornwell (Virgin)

The *Sgt. Pepper Knew My Father* compilation owes its origins to he NME, and was first made available by mail order to the paper's readers, prior to going on general sale through Island Records. A charity project (for Childline), the album featured all the songs from the Beatles' *Sgt.Pepper* album as covered by 1980s acts, and it spun off the chart-topping Wet Wet Wet single *With A Little Help From My Friends*.

324

June – July 1988

25 June 1988

last week	this week		
1	1	NITE FLITE	Various Artists (CBS)
2	2	TANGO IN THE NIGHT	
			Fleetwood Mac (Warner Bros.)
9	3	PEOPLE	Hothouse Flowers (London)
3	4	MOTOWN DANCE PARTY	
			Various Artists (Motown)
4	5	HEAVEN ON EARTH	Belinda Carlisle (Virgin)
8	6	PUSH	Bros (CBS)
5	7	DIRTY DANCING	Soundtrack (RCA)
39	8	TRACY CHAPMAN	Tracy Chapman (Elektra)
7	9	PROVISION	Scritti Politti (Virgin)
13	10	WHITNEY	Whitney Houston (Arista)
11	11	POPPED IN SOULED OUT	
			Wet Wet Wet (Precious)
10	12	STRONGER THAN PRIDE	Sade (Epic)
45	13	THE HITS OF HOUSE ARE HERE Various Artists (K-Tel)	
40	14	EVERYTHING	Cimie Fisher (EMI)
20	15	THE INNOCENTS	Erasure (Mute)
6	16	LOVE	Aztec Camera (Warner Bros.)
12	17	MORE DIRTY DANCING	Various Artists (RCA)
26	18	TSOP - THE SOUND OF PHILADELPHIA	
			Various Artists (K-Tel)
19	19	AIN'T COMPLAINING	Status Quo (Vertigo)
14	20	THE FIRST OF A MILLION KISSES	
			Fairground Attraction (RCA)
17	21	THE CHRISTIANS	Christians (Island)
-	22	DOWN IN THE GROOVE	Bob Dylan (CBS)
18	23	HEART	Heart (Capitol)
36	24	FAITH	George Michael (Epic)
16	25	HEARSAY	
			Alexander O'Neal (Tabu)
22	26	BAD	Michael Jackson (Epic)
31	27	STAY ON THESE ROADS	A-Ha (WEA)
19	28	OUT OF ORDER	Rod Stewart (Warner Bros.)
23	29	THE BEST OF OMD	
			Orchestral Manoeuvres in the Dark (Virgin)
27	30	REMEMBER YOU'RE MINE	
			Foster & Allen (Stylus)
21	31	SIXTIES MIX 2	Various Artists (Stylus)
-	32	I'M REAL	
			James Brown with Full Force (Scotti Brothers)
24	33	LOVESEXY	Prince (Paisley Park)
30	34	SCENES FROM THE SOUTHSIDE	
			Bruce Hornsby and the Range (RCA)
-	35	BROTHERS IN ARMS	Dire Straits (Vertigo)
42	36	VIVA-HaTE	Morrissey (HMV)
41	37	BACK ON THE ROAD	Various Artists (Stylus)
28	38	ACTUALLY	Pet Shop Boys (Parlophone)
-	39	SAVAGE	Eurythmics (RCA)
-	40	BY ALL MEANS NECESSARY	
			Boogie Down Productions (Jive)
25	41	FROM LANGLEY PARK TO MEMPHIS	
			Prefab Sprout (Kitchenware)
38	42	OUT OF THE BLUE	Debbie Gibson (Atlantic)
-	43	SUR LA MER	Moody Blues (Polydor)
44	44	RUMOURS	Fleetwood Mac (Warner Bros.)
35	45	NOW THAT'S WHAT I CALL MUSIC 11	
			Various Artists (EMI/Virgin/PolyGram)
29	46	TOUGHER THAN LEATHER	Run DMC (London)
43	47	BRIDGE OF SPIES	T'Pau (Siren)
37	48	DISTANT THUNDER	Aswad (Mango)
32	49	OU812	Van Halen (Warner Bros.)
-	50	FACE VALUE	Phil Collins (Virgin)

2 July 1988

8	1	TRACY CHAPMAN	Tracy Chapman (Elektra)
1	2	NITE FLITE	Various Artists (CBS)
2	3	TANGO IN THE NIGHT	
			Fleetwood Mac (Warner Bros.)
6	4	PUSH	Bros (CBS)
-	5	ROLL WITH IT	Steve Winwood (Virgin)
10	6	WHITNEY	Whitney Houston (Arista)
7	7	DIRTY DANCING	Soundtrack (RCA)
5	8	HEAVEN ON EARTH	Belinda Carlisle (Virgin)
-	9	IDOL SONGS - 11 OF THE BEST	
			Billy Idol (Chrysalis)
12	10	STRONGER THAN PRIDE	Sade (Epic)
11	11	POPPED IN SOULED OUT	
			Wet Wet Wet (Precious)
4	12	MOTOWN DANCE PARTY	
			Various Artists (Motown)
3	13	PEOPLE	Hothouse Flowers (London)
13	14	THE HITS OF HOUSE ARE HERE	
			Various Artists (K-Tel)
9	15	PROVISION	Scritti Politti (Virgin)
17	16	MORE DIRTY DANCING	Various Artists (RCA)
35	17	BROTHERS IN ARMS	Dire Straits (Vertigo)
38	18	ACTUALLY	Pet Shop Boys (Parlophone)
19	19	LET IT BEE	Voice of the Beehive (London)
15	20	THE INNOCENTS	Erasure (Mute)
16	21	LOVE	Aztec Camera (Warner Bros.)
14	22	EVERYTHING	Cimie Fisher (EMI)
43	23	SUR LA MER	Moody Blues (Polydor)
-	24	JACK MIX IN FULL EFFECT	Mirage (Stylus)
24	25	FAITH	George Michael (Epic)
-	26	CONFESSIONS OF A POP GROUP	
			Style Council (Polydor)
39	27	SAVAGE	Eurythmics (RCA)
18	28	TSOP - THE SOUND OF PHILADELPHIA	
			Various Artists (K-Tel)
21	29	THE CHRISTIANS	Christians (Island)
32	30	I'M REAL	
			James Brown with Full Force (Scotti Brothers)
23	31	HEART	Heart (Capitol)
26	32	BAD	Michael Jackson (Epic)
19	33	AIN'T COMPLAINING	Status Quo (Vertigo)
30	34	REMEMBER YOU'RE MINE	
			Foster & Allen (Stylus)
33	35	LOVESEXY	Prince (Paisley Park)
20	36	THE FIRST OF A MILLION KISSES	
			Fairground Attraction (RCA)
31	37	SIXTIES MIX 2	Various Artists (Stylus)
50	38	FACE VALUE	Phil Collins (Virgin)
22	39	DOWN IN THE GROOVE	Bob Dylan (CBS)
-	40	TUNNEL OF LOVE	Bruce Springsteen (CBS)
29	41	THE BEST OF OMD	
			Orchestral Manoeuvres in the Dark (Virgin)
-	42	BEST OF HOUSE VOL 5	
			Various Artists (Serious)
25	43	HEARSAY	Alexander O'Neal (Tabu)
27	44	STAY ON THESE ROADS	A-Ha (WEA)
44	45	RUMOURS	Fleetwood Mac (Warner Bros.)
47	46	BRIDGE OF SPIES	T'Pau (Siren)
41	47	BACK ON THE ROAD	Various Artists (Stylus)
34	48	SCENES FROM THE SOUTHSIDE	
			Bruce Hornsby and the Range (RCA)
-	49	IRISH HEARTBEAT	
			Van Morrison with the Chieftains (Mercury)
-	50	THE OUTRIDER	Jimmy Page (Geffen)

9 July 1988

1	1	TRACY CHAPMAN	Tracy Chapman (Elektra)
9	2	IDOL SONGS - 11 OF THE BEST	
			Billy Idol (Chrysalis)
4	3	PUSH	Bros (CBS)
5	4	ROLL WITH IT	Steve Winwood (Virgin)
3	5	TANGO IN THE NIGHT	
			Fleetwood Mac (Warner Bros.)
2	6	NITE FLITE	Various Artists (CBS)
7	7	DIRTY DANCING	Soundtrack (RCA)
-	8	HEAVY NOVA	Robert Palmer (EMI)
8	9	HEAVEN ON EARTH	Belinda Carlisle (Virgin)
-	10	THE COLLECTION	Barry White (Mercury)
6	11	WHITNEY	Whitney Houston (Arista)
40	12	TUNNEL OF LOVE	Bruce Springsteen (CBS)
10	13	STRONGER THAN PRIDE	Sade (Epic)
14	14	THE HITS OF HOUSE ARE HERE	
			Various Artists (K-Tel)
19	15	LET IT BEE	Voice of the Beehive (London)
11	16	POPPED IN SOULED OUT	
			Wet Wet Wet (Precious Organisation)
13	17	PEOPLE	Hothouse Flowers (London)
-	18	TIGHTEN UP VOL 88	
			Big Audio Dynamite (CBS)
49	19	IRISH HEARTBEAT	
			Van Morrison with the Chieftains (Mercury)
24	20	JACK MIX IN FULL EFFECT	Mirage (Stylus)
12	21	MOTOWN DANCE PARTY	
			Various Artists (Motown)
18	22	ACTUALLY	Pet Shop Boys (Parlophone)
26	23	CONFESSIONS OF A POP GROUP	
			Style Council (Polydor)
16	24	MORE DIRTY DANCING	
			Various Artists (RCA)
27	25	SAVAGE	Eurythmics (RCA)
20	26	THE INNOCENTS	Erasure (Mute)
15	27	PROVISION	Scritti Politti (Virgin)
25	28	FAITH	George Michael (Epic)
17	29	BROTHERS IN ARMS	Dire Straits (Vertigo)
32	30	BAD	Michael Jackson (Epic)
22	31	EVERYTHING	Cimie Fisher (EMI)
46	32	BRIDGE OF SPIES	T'Pau (Siren)
23	33	SUR LA MER	Moody Blues (Polydor)
21	34	LOVE	Aztec Camera (Warner Bros.)
29	35	THE CHRISTIANS	Christians (Island)
50	36	THE OUTRIDER	Jimmy Page (Geffen)
47	37	BACK ON THE ROAD	
			Various Artists (Stylus)
38	38	FACE VALUE	Phil Collins (Virgin)
31	39	HEART	Heart (Capitol)
-	40	INDIGO	Matt Bianco (WEA)
43	41	HEARSAY	
			Alexander O'Neal (Tabu)
36	42	THE FIRST OF A MILLION KISSES	
			Fairground Attraction (RCA)
-	43	OPEN ALL NIGHT	Georgia Satellites (Elektra)
37	44	SIXTIES MIX 2	Various Artists (Stylus)
-	45	KICK	INXS (Mercury)
-	46	OUT OF THE BLUE	Debbie Gibson (Atlantic)
-	47	JULIA FORDHAM	Julia Fordham (Circa)
30	48	I'M REAL	
			James Brown with Full Force (Scotti Brothers)
-	49	OUTSIDE THE GATE	Killing Joke (EG)
41	50	THE BEST OF OMD	
			Orchestral Manoeuvres in the Dark (Virgin)

Singer-songwriter Tracy Chapman suddenly found herself atop the album chart with her eponymous debut set after a memorable performance (as a virtual unknown) at the internationally televised Nelson Mandela Birthday Party concert at London's Wembley Stadium. Whitney Houston, another performer at the same concert, also saw her perennial *Whitney* album rebound into the Top 10.

July 1988

16 July 1988

Kylie Minogue's first album was an eagerly awaited item, since the teenage Australian actress had already registered a Number 1 and a Number 2 single with her first two UK releases. Near the top of the chart for the rest of the year, moving over a million copies, it would become the best-selling debut album ever in the UK, the top all-time seller by a female artist, and the fifth biggest UK seller of the 1980s.

August 1988

6 August 1988

Last	This	Title	Artist (Label)
1	1	NOW THAT'S WHAT I CALL MUSIC 12	Various Artists (EMI/Virgin/Polygram)
3	2	THE HITS ALBUM – HITS 8	Various Artists (CBS/WEA/BMG)
2	3	TRACY CHAPMAN	Tracy Chapman (Elektra)
5	4	KYLIE	Kylie Minogue (PWL)
4	5	BAD	Michael Jackson (Epic)
6	6	IDOL SONGS - 11 OF THE BEST	Billy Idol (Chrysalis)
7	7	IT TAKES A NATION OF MILLIONS TO HOLD US BACK	Public Enemy (Def Jam)
10	8	PUSH	Bros (CBS)
9	9	TANGO IN THE NIGHT	Fleetwood Mac (Warner Bros.)
12	10	DIRTY DANCING	Soundtrack (RCA)
13	11	TUNNEL OF LOVE	Bruce Springsteen (CBS)
-	12	FOLLOW THE LEADER	Eric B & Rakim (MCA)
15	13	POPPED IN SOULED OUT	Wet Wet Wet (Precious)
11	14	THE COLLECTION	Barry White (Mercury)
8	15	SUBSTANCE 1977-1980	Joy Division (Factory)
18	16	THRILLER	Michael Jackson (Epic)
14	17	KICK	INXS (Mercury)
16	18	UB40	UB40 (DEP International)
-	19	A SALT WITH A DEADLY PEPA	Salt 'N' Pepa (London)
27	20	LOVE	Aztec Camera (Warner Bros.)
17	21	FAITH	George Michael (Epic)
22	22	HEAVEN ON EARTH	Belinda Carlisle (Virgin)
43	23	HYSTERIA	Def Leppard (Bludgeon Riffola)
34	24	LOVESEXY	Prince (Paisley Park)
25	25	STRONGER THAN PRIDE	Sade (Epic)
20	26	WIDE AWAKE IN DREAMLAND	Pat Benatar (Chrysalis)
28	27	JACK MIX IN FULL EFFECT	Mirage (Stylus)
46	28	THE FIRST OF A MILLION KISSES	Fairground Attraction (RCA)
-	29	SMALL WORLD	Huey Lewis & the News (Chrysalis)
30	30	DON'T LET LOVE SLIP AWAY	Freddie Jackson (Capitol)
21	31	WHITNEY	Whitney Houston (Arista)
40	32	OUT OF THE BLUE	Debbie Gibson (Atlantic)
29	33	MORE DIRTY DANCING	Various Artists (RCA)
44	34	HEARSAY	Alexander O'Neal (Tabu)
23	35	ROLL WITH IT	Steve Winwood (Virgin)
38	36	THE MICHAEL JACKSON MIX	Michael Jackson (Stylus)
24	37	BRIDGE OF SPIES	T'Pau (Siren)
33	38	BROTHERS IN ARMS	Dire Straits (Vertigo)
19	39	WHAT YOU SEE IS WHAT YOU GET	Glen Goldsmith (Reproduction)
-	40	RAINTOWN	Deacon Blue (CBS)
31	41	PEOPLE	Hothouse Flowers (London)
-	42	THE GREATEST EVER ROCK 'N' ROLL MIX	Various Artists (Stylus)
-	43	OFF THE WALL	Michael Jackson (Epic)
41	44	SAVAGE	Eurythmics (RCA)
35	45	INDIGO	Matt Bianco (WEA)
49	46	LET IT BEE	Voice of the Beehive (London)
-	47	THE CHRISTIANS	Christians (Island)
-	48	IDLEWILD	Everything But The Girl (Blanco Y Negro)
32	49	REG STRIKES BACK	Elton John (Rocket)
-	50	OLD 8 X 10	Randy Travis (Warner Bros.)

13 August 1988

Last	This	Title	Artist (Label)
1	1	NOW THAT'S WHAT I CALL MUSIC 12	Various Artists (EMI/Virgin/Polygram)
2	2	THE HITS ALBUM – HITS 8	Various Artists (CBS/WEA/BMG)
3	3	TRACY CHAPMAN	Tracy Chapman (Elektra)
4	4	KYLIE	Kylie Minogue (PWL)
6	5	IDOL SONGS - 11 OF THE BEST	Billy Idol (Chrysalis)
5	6	BAD	Michael Jackson (Epic)
28	7	THE FIRST OF A MILLION KISSES	Fairground Attraction (RCA)
8	8	PUSH	Bros (CBS)
9	9	TANGO IN THE NIGHT	Fleetwood Mac (Warner Bros.)
14	10	THE COLLECTION	Barry White (Mercury)
10	11	DIRTY DANCING	Soundtrack (RCA)
42	12	THE GREATEST EVER ROCK 'N' ROLL MIX	Various Artists (Stylus)
29	13	SMALL WORLD	Huey Lewis & the News (Chrysalis)
24	14	LOVESEXY	Prince (Paisley Park)
13	15	POPPED IN SOULED OUT	Wet Wet Wet (Precious)
16	16	THRILLER	Michael Jackson (Epic)
17	17	KICK	INXS (Mercury)
48	18	IDLEWILD	Everything But The Girl (Blanco Y Negro)
26	19	WIDE AWAKE IN DREAMLAND	Pat Benatar (Chrysalis)
20	20	LOVE	Aztec Camera (Warner Bros.)
19	21	A SALT WITH A DEADLY PEPA	Salt 'N' Pepa (London)
31	22	WHITNEY	Whitney Houston (Arista)
11	23	TUNNEL OF LOVE	Bruce Springsteen (CBS)
34	24	HEARSAY	Alexander O'Neal (Tabu)
22	25	HEAVEN ON EARTH	Belinda Carlisle (Virgin)
7	26	IT TAKES A NATION OF MILLIONS TO HOLD US BACK	Public Enemy (Def Jam)
15	27	SUBSTANCE 1977-1980	Joy Division (Factory)
21	28	FAITH	George Michael (Epic)
12	29	FOLLOW THE LEADER	Eric B & Rakim (MCA)
40	30	RAINTOWN	Deacon Blue (CBS)
23	31	HYSTERIA	Def Leppard (Bludgeon Riffola)
41	32	PEOPLE	Hothouse Flowers (London)
35	33	ROLL WITH IT	Steve Winwood (Virgin)
-	34	JULIA FORDHAM	Julia Fordham (Virgin)
18	35	UB40	UB40 (DEP International)
33	36	MORE DIRTY DANCING	Various Artists (RCA)
36	37	THE MICHAEL JACKSON MIX	Michael Jackson (Stylus)
38	38	BROTHERS IN ARMS	Dire Straits (Vertigo)
25	39	STRONGER THAN PRIDE	Sade (Epic)
47	40	THE CHRISTIANS	Christians (Island)
-	41	ALL OF THIS AND NOTHING	Psychedelic Furs (CBS)
30	42	DON'T LET LOVE SLIP AWAY	Freddie Jackson (Capitol)
44	43	SAVAGE	Eurythmics (RCA)
46	44	LET IT BEE	Voice of the Beehive (London)
37	45	BRIDGE OF SPIES	T'Pau (Siren)
32	46	OUT OF THE BLUE	Debbie Gibson (Atlantic)
45	47	INDIGO	Matt Bianco (WEA)
-	48	BUENOS NOCHES FROM A LONELY ROOM	Dwight Yoakam (Warner Bros.)
39	49	WHAT YOU SEE IS WHAT YOU GET	Glen Goldsmith (Reproduction)
-	50	LONG COLD WINTER	Cinderella (Vertigo)

20 August 1988

Last	This	Title	Artist (Label)
1	1	NOW THAT'S WHAT I CALL MUSIC 12	Various Artists (EMI/Virgin/Polygram)
4	2	KYLIE	Kylie Minogue (PWL)
3	3	TRACY CHAPMAN	Tracy Chapman (Elektra)
5	4	IDOL SONGS - 11 OF THE BEST	Billy Idol (Chrysalis)
2	5	THE HITS ALBUM – HITS 8	Various Artists (CBS/WEA/BMG)
7	6	THE FIRST OF A MILLION KISSES	Fairground Attraction (RCA)
6	7	BAD	Michael Jackson (Epic)
12	8	THE GREATEST EVER ROCK 'N' ROLL MIX	Various Artists (Stylus)
9	9	TANGO IN THE NIGHT	Fleetwood Mac (Warner Bros.)
-	10	BEST OF THE EAGLES	Eagles (Asylum)
8	11	PUSH	Bros (CBS)
30	12	RAINTOWN	Deacon Blue (CBS)
11	13	DIRTY DANCING	Soundtrack (RCA)
10	14	THE COLLECTION	Barry White (Mercury)
13	15	SMALL WORLD	Huey Lewis & the News (Chrysalis)
18	16	IDLEWILD	Everything But The Girl (Blanco Y Negro)
14	17	LOVESEXY	Prince (Paisley Park)
15	18	POPPED IN SOULED OUT	Wet Wet Wet (Precious)
20	19	LOVE	Aztec Camera (Warner Bros.)
17	20	KICK	INXS (Mercury)
19	21	WIDE AWAKE IN DREAMLAND	Pat Benatar (Chrysalis)
22	22	WHITNEY	Whitney Houston (Arista)
25	23	HEAVEN ON EARTH	Belinda Carlisle (Virgin)
24	24	HEARSAY	Alexander O'Neal (Tabu)
31	25	HYSTERIA	Def Leppard (Bludgeon Riffola)
34	26	JULIA FORDHAM	Julia Fordham (Virgin)
21	27	A SALT WITH A DEADLY PEPA	Salt 'N' Pepa (London)
16	28	THRILLER	Michael Jackson (Epic)
44	29	LET IT BEE	Voice of the Beehive (London)
33	30	ROLL WITH IT	Steve Winwood (Virgin)
23	31	TUNNEL OF LOVE	Bruce Springsteen (CBS)
32	32	PEOPLE	Hothouse Flowers (London)
35	33	UB40	UB40 (DEP International)
26	34	IT TAKES A NATION OF MILLIONS TO HOLD US BACK	Public Enemy (Def Jam)
36	35	MORE DIRTY DANCING	Various Artists (RCA)
46	36	OUT OF THE BLUE	Debbie Gibson (Atlantic)
28	37	FAITH	George Michael (Epic)
38	38	BROTHERS IN ARMS	Dire Straits (Vertigo)
43	39	SAVAGE	Eurythmics (RCA)
-	40	ON THE BEACH	Chris Rea (WEA)
27	41	SUBSTANCE 1977-1980	Joy Division (Factory)
40	42	THE CHRISTIANS	Christians (Island)
-	43	APPETITE FOR DESTRUCTION	Guns 'N' Roses (Geffen)
29	44	FOLLOW THE LEADER	Eric B & Rakim (MCA)
45	45	BRIDGE OF SPIES	T'Pau (Siren)
-	46	ALL ABOUT EVE	All About Eve (Mercury)
-	47	CLOSE	Kim Wilde (MCA)
42	48	DON'T LET LOVE SLIP AWAY	Freddie Jackson (Capitol)
47	49	INDIGO	Matt Bianco (WEA)
-	50	INTRODUCING THE HARDLINE ACCORDING TO	Terence Trent D'Arby (CBS)

August saw another head-to-head between the *Now* and *Hits* compilation series, with volume 12 of the former series having the sales edge, as was becoming the consistent pattern. Many were surprised to see the militant black rap group Public Enemy riding the UK Top 10; in fact, they never quite managed to replicate the success of *It Takes A Nation Of Millions To Hold Us Back*, either on the single or album charts.

August – September 1988

27 August 1988

last week	this week	title / artist
1	1	NOW THAT'S WHAT I CALL MUSIC 12 — Various Artists (EMI/Virgin/Polygram)
2	2	KYLIE — Kylie Minogue (PWL)
6	3	THE FIRST OF A MILLION KISSES — Fairground Attraction (RCA)
3	4	TRACY CHAPMAN — Tracy Chapman (Elektra)
4	5	IDOL SONGS - 11 OF THE BEST — Billy Idol (Chrysalis)
10	6	BEST OF THE EAGLES — Eagles (Asylum)
8	7	THE GREATEST EVER ROCK 'N' ROLL MIX — Various Artists (Stylus)
5	8	THE HITS ALBUM – HITS 8 — Various Artists (CBS/WEA/BMG)
7	9	BAD — Michael Jackson (Epic)
-	10	TURN BACK THE CLOCK — Johnny Hates Jazz (Virgin)
13	11	DIRTY DANCING — Soundtrack (RCA)
9	12	TANGO IN THE NIGHT — Fleetwood Mac (Warner Bros.)
25	13	HYSTERIA — Def Leppard (Bludgeon Riffola)
-	14	ROCK THE WORLD — Five Star (Tent)
11	15	PUSH — Bros (CBS)
20	16	KICK — INXS (Mercury)
19	17	LOVE — Aztec Camera (Warner Bros.)
12	18	RAINTOWN — Deacon Blue (CBS)
14	19	THE COLLECTION — Barry White (Mercury)
-	20	EIGHT LEGGED GROOVE MACHINE — Wonder Stuff (Polydor)
15	21	SMALL WORLD — Huey Lewis & the News (Chrysalis)
22	22	WHITNEY — Whitney Houston (Arista)
23	23	HEAVEN ON EARTH — Belinda Carlisle (Virgin)
18	24	POPPED IN SOULED OUT — Wet Wet Wet (Precious)
30	25	ROLL WITH IT — Steve Winwood (Virgin)
21	26	WIDE AWAKE IN DREAMLAND — Pat Benatar (Chrysalis)
24	27	HEARSAY — Alexander O'Neal (Tabu)
16	28	IDLEWILD — Everything But The Girl (Blanco Y Negro)
27	29	A SALT WITH A DEADLY PEPA — Salt 'N' Pepa (London)
46	30	ALL ABOUT EVE — All About Eve (Mercury)
17	31	LOVESEXY — Prince (Paisley Park)
32	32	UB40 — UB40 (DEP International)
29	33	LET IT BEE — Voice of the Beehive (London)
38	34	BROTHERS IN ARMS — Dire Straits (Vertigo)
43	35	APPETITE FOR DESTRUCTION — Guns 'N' Roses (Geffen)
40	36	ON THE BEACH — Chris Rea (WEA)
-	37	A MOMENTARY LAPSE OF REASON — Pink Floyd (EMI)
-	38	HOT CITY NIGHTS — Various Artists (Vertigo)
35	39	MORE DIRTY DANCING — Various Artists (RCA)
26	40	JULIA FORDHAM — Julia Fordham (Virgin)
-	41	ROBBIE ROBERTSON — Robbie Robertson (Geffen)
28	42	THRILLER — Michael Jackson (Epic)
31	43	TUNNEL OF LOVE — Bruce Springsteen (CBS)
47	44	CLOSE — Kim Wilde (MCA)
50	45	INTRODUCING THE HARDLINE ACCORDING TO — Terence Trent D'Arby (CBS)
37	46	FAITH — George Michael (Epic)
34	47	IT TAKES A NATION OF MILLIONS TO HOLD US BACK — Public Enemy (Def Jam)
-	48	SEVENTH SON OF A SEVENTH SON — Iron Maiden (EMI)
42	49	THE CHRISTIANS — Christians (Island)
-	50	EVERLASTING — Natalie Cole (Capitol)

3 September 1988

last week	this week	title / artist
3	1	THE FIRST OF A MILLION KISSES — Fairground Attraction (RCA)
2	2	KYLIE — Kylie Minogue (PWL)
4	3	TRACY CHAPMAN — Tracy Chapman (Elektra)
1	4	NOW THAT'S WHAT I CALL MUSIC 12 — Various Artists (EMI/Virgin/Polygram)
7	5	THE GREATEST EVER ROCK 'N' ROLL MIX — Various Artists (Stylus)
6	6	BEST OF THE EAGLES — Eagles (Asylum)
5	7	IDOL SONGS - 11 OF THE BEST — Billy Idol (Chrysalis)
10	8	TURN BACK THE CLOCK — Johnny Hates Jazz (Virgin)
9	9	BAD — Michael Jackson (Epic)
11	10	DIRTY DANCING — Soundtrack (RCA)
38	11	HOT CITY NIGHTS — Various Artists (Vertigo)
8	12	THE HITS ALBUM – HITS 8 — Various Artists (CBS/WEA/BMG)
13	13	HYSTERIA — Def Leppard (Bludgeon Riffola)
12	14	TANGO IN THE NIGHT — Fleetwood Mac (Warner Bros.)
41	15	ROBBIE ROBERTSON — Robbie Robertson (Geffen)
16	16	KICK — INXS (Mercury)
-	17	SO GOOD — Mica Paris (Fourth & Broadway)
17	18	LOVE — Aztec Camera (Warner Bros.)
19	19	THE COLLECTION — Barry White (Mercury)
14	20	ROCK THE WORLD — Five Star (Tent)
18	21	PUSH — Bros (CBS)
30	22	RAINTOWN — Deacon Blue (CBS)
-	23	ALL ABOUT EVE — All About Eve (Mercury)
36	24	ON THE BEACH — Chris Rea (WEA)
22	25	WHITNEY — Whitney Houston (Arista)
29	26	A SALT WITH A DEADLY PEPA — Salt 'N' Pepa (London)
20	27	EIGHT LEGGED GROOVE MACHINE — Wonder Stuff (Polydor)
34	28	BROTHERS IN ARMS — Dire Straits (Vertigo)
24	29	POPPED IN SOULED OUT — Wet Wet Wet (Precious)
23	30	HEAVEN ON EARTH — Belinda Carlisle (Virgin)
39	31	MORE DIRTY DANCING — Various Artists (RCA)
-	32	NON STOP — Julio Iglesias (CBS)
31	33	LOVESEXY — Prince (Paisley Park)
35	34	APPETITE FOR DESTRUCTION — Guns 'N' Roses (Geffen)
25	35	HOUSE SOUND OF LONDON – THE JACKIN' ZONE VOL 4 — Various Artists (London)
21	36	ROLL WITH IT — Steve Winwood (Virgin)
-	37	SMALL WORLD — Huey Lewis & the News (Chrysalis)
-	38	CONSCIENCE — Womack & Womack (Fourth & Broadway)
-	39	ROCKS THE HOUSE! — Jellybean (Chrysalis)
26	40	WIDE AWAKE IN DREAMLAND — Pat Benatar (Chrysalis)
46	41	FAITH — George Michael (Epic)
27	42	HEARSAY — Alexander O'Neal (Tabu)
42	43	THRILLER — Michael Jackson (Epic)
44	44	CLOSE — Kim Wilde (MCA)
-	45	DON'T BE AFRAID OF THE DARK — Robert Cray Band (Mercury)
-	46	INDIGO — Matt Bianco (WEA)
-	47	OUT OF THE BLUE — Debbie Gibson (Atlantic)
28	48	IDLEWILD Everything But The Girl (Blanco Y Negro)
40	49	JULIA FORDHAM — Julia Fordham (Virgin)
32	50	UB40 — UB40 (DEP International)

10 September 1988

last week	this week	title / artist
2	1	KYLIE — Kylie Minogue (PWL)
1	2	THE FIRST OF A MILLION KISSES — Fairground Attraction (RCA)
3	3	TRACY CHAPMAN — Tracy Chapman (Elektra)
4	4	NOW THAT'S WHAT I CALL MUSIC 12 — Various Artists (EMI/Virgin/Polygram)
11	5	HOT CITY NIGHTS — Various Artists (Vertigo)
6	6	BEST OF THE EAGLES — Eagles (Asylum)
17	7	SO GOOD — Mica Paris (Fourth & Broadway)
9	8	BAD — Michael Jackson (Epic)
7	9	IDOL SONGS - 11 OF THE BEST — Billy Idol (Chrysalis)
8	10	TURN BACK THE CLOCK — Johnny Hates Jazz (Virgin)
5	11	THE GREATEST EVER ROCK 'N' ROLL MIX — Various Artists (Stylus)
45	12	DON'T BE AFRAID OF THE DARK — Robert Cray Band (Mercury)
38	13	CONSCIENCE — Womack & Womack (Fourth & Broadway)
12	14	THE HITS ALBUM – HITS 8 — Various Artists (CBS/WEA/BMG)
15	15	ROBBIE ROBERTSON — Robbie Robertson (Geffen)
10	16	DIRTY DANCING — Soundtrack (RCA)
18	17	LOVE — Aztec Camera (Warner Bros.)
34	18	APPETITE FOR DESTRUCTION — Guns 'N' Roses (Geffen)
39	19	ROCKS THE HOUSE! — Jellybean (Chrysalis)
13	20	HYSTERIA — Def Leppard (Bludgeon Riffola)
14	21	TANGO IN THE NIGHT — Fleetwood Mac (Warner)
16	22	KICK — INXS (Mercury)
-	23	RAP TRAX — Various Artists (Stylus)
-	24	PURPLE RAIN — Prince & the Revolution (Warner Bros.)
21	25	PUSH — Bros (CBS)
23	26	ALL ABOUT EVE — All About Eve (Mercury)
31	27	MORE DIRTY DANCING — Various Artists (RCA)
33	28	LOVESEXY — Prince (Paisley Park)
22	29	RAINTOWN — Deacon Blue (CBS)
-	30	TWICE THE LOVE — George Benson (Warner Bros.)
24	31	POPPED IN SOULED OUT — Wet Wet Wet (Precious)
32	32	ON THE BEACH — Chris Rea (WEA)
25	33	WHITNEY — Whitney Houston (Arista)
32	34	NON STOP — Julio Iglesias (CBS)
27	35	EIGHT LEGGED GROOVE MACHINE — Wonder Stuff (Polydor)
-	36	SHORT SHARP SHOCKED — Michelle Shocked (Cooking Vinyl)
28	37	BROTHERS IN ARMS — Dire Straits (Vertigo)
42	38	HEARSAY — Alexander O'Neal (Tabu)
40	39	WIDE AWAKE IN DREAMLAND — Pat Benatar (Chrysalis)
19	40	THE COLLECTION — Barry White (Mercury)
30	41	HEAVEN ON EARTH — Belinda Carlisle (Virgin)
20	42	ROCK THE WORLD — Five Star (Tent)
43	43	THRILLER — Michael Jackson (Epic)
26	44	CLOSE — Kim Wilde (MCA)
26	45	A SALT WITH A DEADLY PEPA — Salt 'N' Pepa (London)
36	46	ROLL WITH IT — Steve Winwood (Virgin)
46	47	INDIGO — Matt Bianco (WEA)
41	48	FAITH — George Michael (Epic)
37	49	SMALL WORLD — Huey Lewis & the News (Chrysalis)
-	50	PEOPLE — Hothouse Flowers (London)

Fairground Attraction added their name to the several who had scored a chart-topper with their debut albums in 1988. The group got a head start from their singles *Perfect* (which topped the chart in May) and *Find My Love* (Number 6 in August), but the album had initially peaked at only Number 6 in June, before dropping away for a while and then reasserting itself all the way to the top (for the obligatory single week!)

September – October 1988

17 September 1988

Last	This	Title	Artist (Label)
-	1	RANK	Smiths (Rough Trade)
1	2	KYLIE	Kylie Minogue (PWL)
23	3	RAP TRAX	Various Artists (Stylus)
-	4	...AND JUSTICE FOR ALL	Metallica (Vertigo)
3	5	TRACY CHAPMAN	Tracy Chapman (Elektra)
2	6	THE FIRST OF A MILLION KISSES	Fairground Attraction (RCA)
8	7	BAD	Michael Jackson (Epic)
5	8	HOT CITY NIGHTS	Various Artists (Vertigo)
25	9	PUSH	Bros (CBS)
4	10	NOW THAT'S WHAT I CALL MUSIC 12	Various Artists (EMI/Virgin/Polygram)
6	11	BEST OF THE EAGLES	Eagles (Asylum)
-	12	THE NEPHILIM	Fields of the Nephilim (Situation Two)
11	13	THE GREATEST EVER ROCK 'N' ROLL MIX	Various Artists (Stylus)
7	14	SO GOOD	Mica Paris (Fourth & Broadway)
-	15	PEEPSHOW	Siouxsie & the Banshees (Wonderland)
18	16	APPETITE FOR DESTRUCTION	Guns 'N' Roses (Geffen)
9	17	IDOL SONGS - 11 OF THE BEST	Billy Idol (Chrysalis)
20	18	HYSTERIA	Def Leppard (Bludgeon Riffola)
12	19	DON'T BE AFRAID OF THE DARK	Robert Cray Band (Mercury)
41	20	HEAVEN ON EARTH	Belinda Carlisle (Virgin)
30	21	TWICE THE LOVE	George Benson (Warner Bros.)
16	22	DIRTY DANCING	Soundtrack (RCA)
21	23	TANGO IN THE NIGHT	Fleetwood Mac (Warner Bros.)
-	24	OUT OF THIS WORLD	Europe (Epic)
33	25	WHITNEY	Whitney Houston (Arista)
13	26	CONSCIENCE	Womack & Womack (Broadway)
14	27	THE HITS ALBUM – HITS 8	Various Artists (CBS/WEA/BMG)
22	28	KICK	INXS (Mercury)
15	29	ROBBIE ROBERTSON	Robbie Robertson (Geffen)
19	30	ROCKS THE HOUSE!	Jellybean (Chrysalis)
31	31	POPPED IN SOULED OUT	Wet Wet Wet (Precious)
10	32	TURN BACK THE CLOCK	Johnny Hates Jazz (Virgin)
43	33	THRILLER	Michael Jackson (Epic)
24	34	PURPLE RAIN	Prince & the Revolution (Warner Bros.)
17	35	LOVE	Aztec Camera (Warner Bros.)
34	36	NON STOP	Julio Iglesias (CBS)
-	37	ANSWERS TO NOTHING	Midge Ure (Chrysalis)
27	38	MORE DIRTY DANCING	Various Artists (RCA)
37	39	BROTHERS IN ARMS	Dire Straits (Vertigo)
26	40	ALL ABOUT EVE	All About Eve (Mercury)
36	41	SHORT SHARP SHOCKED	Michelle Shocked (Cooking Vinyl)
29	42	RAINTOWN	Deacon Blue (CBS)
45	43	A SALT WITH A DEADLY PEPA	Salt 'N' Pepa (London)
50	44	PEOPLE	Hothouse Flowers (London)
38	45	HEARSAY	Alexander O'Neal (Tabu)
46	46	ROLL WITH IT	Steve Winwood (Virgin)
32	47	ON THE BEACH	Chris Rea (WEA)
-	48	KEEPER OF THE 7 KEYS PT 2	Helloween (Noise)
28	49	LOVESEXY	Prince (Paisley Park)
48	50	FAITH	George Michael (Epic)

24 September 1988

Last	This	Title	Artist (Label)
2	1	KYLIE	Kylie Minogue (PWL)
8	2	HOT CITY NIGHTS	Various Artists (Vertigo)
3	3	RAP TRAX	Various Artists (Stylus)
1	4	RANK	Smiths (Rough Trade)
5	5	TRACY CHAPMAN	Tracy Chapman (Elektra)
9	6	PUSH	Bros (CBS)
6	7	THE FIRST OF A MILLION KISSES	Fairground Attraction (RCA)
7	8	BAD	Michael Jackson (Epic)
-	9	STATE OF EUPHORIA	Anthrax (Island)
10	10	NOW THAT'S WHAT I CALL MUSIC 12	Various Artists (EMI/Virgin/Polygram)
13	11	THE GREATEST EVER ROCK 'N' ROLL MIX	Various Artists (Stylus)
4	12	...AND JUSTICE FOR ALL	Metallica (Vertigo)
11	13	BEST OF THE EAGLES	Eagles (Asylum)
24	14	OUT OF THIS WORLD	Europe (Epic)
22	15	DIRTY DANCING	Soundtrack (RCA)
17	16	IDOL SONGS - 11 OF THE BEST	Billy Idol (Chrysalis)
-	17	BUSTER	Soundtrack (Virgin)
20	18	HEAVEN ON EARTH	Belinda Carlisle (Virgin)
26	19	CONSCIENCE	Womack & Womack (Broadway)
16	20	APPETITE FOR DESTRUCTION	Guns 'N' Roses (Geffen)
14	21	SO GOOD	Mica Paris (Fourth & Broadway)
-	22	SPIRIT OF EDEN	Talk Talk (Parlophone)
23	23	TANGO IN THE NIGHT	Fleetwood Mac (Warner Bros.)
21	24	TWICE THE LOVE	George Benson (Warner Bros.)
31	25	POPPED IN SOULED OUT	Wet Wet Wet (Precious)
12	26	THE NEPHILIM	Fields of the Nephilim (Situation Two)
25	27	WHITNEY	Whitney Houston (Arista)
18	28	HYSTERIA	Def Leppard (Bludgeon Riffola)
-	29	SUNSHINE ON LEITH	Proclaimers (Chrysalis)
28	30	KICK	INXS (Mercury)
43	31	A SALT WITH A DEADLY PEPA	Salt 'N' Pepa (London)
19	32	DON'T BE AFRAID OF THE DARK	Robert Cray Band (Mercury)
27	33	THE HITS ALBUM – HITS 8	Various Artists (CBS/WEA/BMG)
15	34	PEEPSHOW	Siouxsie & the Banshees (Wonderland)
30	35	ROCKS THE HOUSE!	Jellybean (Chrysalis)
34	36	PURPLE RAIN	Prince & the Revolution (Warne Bros.)
45	37	HEARSAY	Alexander O'Neal (Tabu)
48	38	KEEPER OF THE SEVEN KEYS PART 2	Helloween (Noise)
36	39	NON STOP	Julio Iglesias (CBS)
29	40	ROBBIE ROBERTSON	Robbie Robertson (Geffen)
39	41	BROTHERS IN ARMS	Dire Straits (Vertigo)
-	42	ANCIENT HEART	Tanita Tikaram (WEA)
32	43	TURN BACK THE CLOCK	Johnny Hates Jazz (Virgin)
41	44	SHORT SHARP SHOCKED	Michelle Shocked (Cooking Vinyl)
49	45	LOVESEXY	Prince (Paisley Park)
38	46	MORE DIRTY DANCING	Various Artists (RCA)
47	47	FUR	Jane Wiedlin (EMI Manhattan)
40	48	ALL THE HITS AND MORE	Hollies (EMI)
40	49	ALL ABOUT EVE	All About Eve (Mercury)
-	50	GREATEST HITS	Bill Withers (CBS)

1 October 1988

Last	This	Title	Artist (Label)
-	1	STARING AT THE SUN	Level 42 (Polydor)
-	2	NEW JERSEY	Bon Jovi (Vertigo)
2	3	HOT CITY NIGHTS	Various Artists (Vertigo)
1	4	KYLIE	Kylie Minogue (PWL)
8	5	BAD	Michael Jackson (Epic)
3	6	RAP TRAX	Various Artists (Stylus)
5	7	TRACY CHAPMAN	Tracy Chapman (Elektra)
17	8	BUSTER	Soundtrack (Virgin)
19	9	CONSCIENCE	Womack & Womack (Fourth & Broadway)
7	10	THE FIRST OF A MILLION KISSES	Fairground Attraction (RCA)
6	11	PUSH	Bros (CBS)
29	12	SUNSHINE ON LEITH	Proclaimers (Chrysalis)
10	13	NOW THAT'S WHAT I CALL MUSIC 12	Various Artists (EMI/Virgin/Polygram)
42	14	ANCIENT HEART	Tanita Tikaram (WEA)
15	15	DIRTY DANCING	Soundtrack (RCA)
4	16	RANK	Smiths (Rough Trade)
17	17	BLUE BELL KNOLL	Cocteau Twins (4AD)
22	18	SPIRIT OF EDEN	Talk Talk (Parlophone)
11	19	THE GREATEST EVER ROCK 'N' ROLL MIX	Various Artists (Stylus)
27	20	WHITNEY	Whitney Houston (Arista)
-	21	WORKER'S PLAYTIME	Billy Bragg (Go! Discs)
18	22	HEAVEN ON EARTH	Belinda Carlisle (Virgin)
9	23	STATE OF EUPHORIA	Anthrax (Island)
16	24	IDOL SONGS - 11 OF THE BEST	Billy Idol (Chrysalis)
23	25	TANGO IN THE NIGHT	Fleetwood Mac (Warner Bros.)
20	26	APPETITE FOR DESTRUCTION	Guns 'N' Roses (Geffen)
37	27	HEARSAY	Alexander O'Neal (Tabu)
13	28	BEST OF THE EAGLES	Eagles (Asylum)
28	29	HYSTERIA	Def Leppard (Bludgeon Riffola)
30	30	KICK	INXS (Mercury)
25	31	POPPED IN SOULED OUT	Wet Wet Wet (Precious)
12	32	...AND JUSTICE FOR ALL	Metallica (Vertigo)
21	33	SO GOOD	Mica Paris (Fourth & Broadway)
14	34	OUT OF THIS WORLD	Europe (Epic)
31	35	A SALT WITH A DEADLY PEPA	Salt 'N' Pepa (London)
24	36	TWICE THE LOVE	George Benson (Warner Bros.)
33	37	THE HITS ALBUM – HITS 8	Various Artists (CBS/WEA/BMG)
41	38	BROTHERS IN ARMS	Dire Straits (Vertigo)
47	39	FUR	Jane Wiedlin (EMI Manhattan)
-	40	THE RARE GROOVE MIX	Various Artists (Stylus)
-	41	EIGHT LEGGED GROOVE MACHINE	Wonderstuff (Polydor)
36	42	PURPLE RAIN	Prince & the Revolution (Warner Bros.)
-	44	THRILLER	Michael Jackson (Epic)
48	43	ALL THE HITS AND MORE	Hollies (EMI)
45	45	LOVESEXY	Prince (Paisley Park)
46	46	ROBBIE ROBERTSON	Robbie Robertson (Geffen)
43	47	TURN BACK THE CLOCK	Johnny Hates Jazz (Virgin)
-	48	THE JOSHUA TREE	U2 (Island)
44	49	SHORT SHARP SHOCKED	Michelle Shocked (Cooking Vinyl)
32	50	DON'T BE AFRAID OF THE DARK	Robert Cray Band (Mercury)

The posthumous release *Rank* by the Smiths demonstrated a sales pattern more frequently displayed by singles in the late 1980s, concentrating all its sales very shortly after release (usually a sign that avid fans are buying, and few others are following up). After debuting at Number 1, it immediately dropped to 4, in its third chart week fell out of the Top 15, and after a month - had vanished!

October 1988

8 October 1988

last week	this week	Title	Artist (Label)
2	1	NEW JERSEY	Bon Jovi (Vertigo)
1	2	STARING AT THE SUN	Level 42 (Polydor)
9	3	CONSCIENCE	Womack & Womack (Fourth & Broadway)
-	4	MOONLIGHTING	VariousArtists (WEA)
6	5	RAP TRAX	Various Artists (Stylus)
8	6	BUSTER	Soundtrack (Virgin)
-	7	PEACE IN OUR TIME	Big Country (Mercury)
3	8	HOT CITY NIGHTS	Various Artists (Vertigo)
4	9	KYLIE	Kylie Minogue (PWL)
-	10	REVOLUTIONS	Jean Michel Jarre (Polydor)
7	11	TRACY CHAPMAN	Tracy Chapman (Elektra)
12	12	SUNSHINE ON LEITH	Proclaimers (Chrysalis)
5	13	BAD	Michael Jackson (Epic)
14	14	ANCIENT HEART	Tanita Tikaram (WEA)
-	15	...AND THE BEAT GOES ON	Various Artists (Telstar)
11	16	PUSH	Bros (CBS)
10	17	THE FIRST OF A MILLION KISSES	Fairground Attraction (RCA)
22	18	HEAVEN ON EARTH	Belinda Carlisle (Virgin)
-	19	THE STARS WE ARE	Marc Almond (Parlophone)
20	20	WHITNEY	Whitney Houston (Arista)
15	21	DIRTY DANCING	Soundtrack (RCA)
-	22	BIG TIME	Tom Waits (Island)
13	23	NOW THAT'S WHAT I CALL MUSIC 12	Various Artists (EMI/Virgin/Polygram)
17	24	BLUE BELL KNOLL	Cocteau Twins (4AD)
27	25	HEARSAY	Alexander O'Neal (Tabu)
24	26	IDOL SONGS - 11 OF THE BEST	Billy Idol (Chrysalis)
21	27	WORKER'S PLAYTIME	Billy Bragg (Go! Discs)
-	28	THE WORLDS OF FOSTER AND ALLEN	Foster & Allen (Stylus)
25	29	TANGO IN THE NIGHT	Fleetwood Mac (Warner Bros.)
40	30	THE RARE GROOVE MIX	Various Artists (Stylus)
26	31	APPETITE FOR DESTRUCTION	Guns 'N' Rose (Geffen)
18	32	SPIRIT OF EDEN	Talk Talk (Parlophone)
28	33	BEST OF THE EAGLES	Eagles (Asylum)
-	34	METAL RHYTHM	Gary Numan (Illegal)
16	35	RANK	Smiths (Rough Trade)
19	36	THE GREATEST EVER ROCK 'N' ROLL MIX	Various Artists (Stylus)
33	37	SO GOOD	Mica Paris (Fourth & Broadway)
23	38	STATE OF EUPHORIA	Anthrax (Island)
29	39	HYSTERIA	Def Leppard (Bludgeon Riffola)
43	40	ALL THE HITS AND MORE	Hollies (EMI)
-	41	THE INNOCENTS	Erasure (Mute)
30	42	KICK	INXS (Mercury)
-	43	ALL THAT JAZZ	Breathe (Siren)
35	44	A SALT WITH A DEADLY PEPA	Salt 'N' Pepa (London)
-	45	ONES ON 1	Various Artists (BBC)
49	46	SHORT SHARP SHOCKED	Michelle Shocked (Cooking Vinyl)
-	47	NOT ME	Glenn Medeiros (London)
31	48	POPPED IN SOULED OUT	Wet Wet Wet (Precious)
38	49	BROTHERS IN ARMS	Dire Straits (Vertigo)
-	50	VIXEN	Vixen (EMI Manhattan)

15 October 1988

last week	this week	Title	Artist (Label)
1	1	NEW JERSEY	Bon Jovi (Vertigo)
10	2	REVOLUTIONS	Jean Michel Jarre (Polydor)
4	3	MOONLIGHTING	VariousArtists (WEA)
3	4	CONSCIENCE	Womack & Womack (Fourth & Broadway)
2	5	STARING AT THE SUN	Level 42 (Polydor)
5	6	RAP TRAX	Various Artists (Stylus)
7	7	PEACE IN OUR TIME	Big Country (Mercury)
-	8	FLYING COLOURS	Chris De Burgh (A&M)
8	9	HOT CITY NIGHTS	Various Artists (Vertigo)
-	10	POP ART	Transvision Vamp (MCA)
9	11	KYLIE	Kylie Minogue (PWL)
11	12	TRACY CHAPMAN	Tracy Chapman (Elektra)
45	13	ONES ON 1	Various Artists (BBC)
15	14	...AND THE BEAT GOES ON	Various Artists (Telstar)
6	15	BUSTER	Soundtrack (Virgin)
13	16	BAD	Michael Jackson (Epic)
21	17	DIRTY DANCING	Soundtrack (RCA)
30	18	THE RARE GROOVE MIX	Various Artists (Stylus)
16	19	PUSH	Bros (CBS)
12	20	SUNSHINE ON LEITH	Proclaimers (Chrysalis)
18	21	HEAVEN ON EARTH	Belinda Carlisle (Virgin)
25	22	HEARSAY	Alexander O'Neal (Tabu)
20	23	WHITNEY	Whitney Houston (Arista)
17	24	THE FIRST OF A MILLION KISSES	Fairground Attraction (RCA)
23	25	NOW THAT'S WHAT I CALL MUSIC 12	Various Artists (EMI/Virgin/Polygram)
14	26	ANCIENT HEART	Tanita Tikaram (WEA)
28	27	THE WORLDS OF FOSTER AND ALLEN	Foster & Allen (Stylus)
43	28	ALL THAT JAZZ	Breathe (Siren)
31	29	APPETITE FOR DESTRUCTION	Guns 'N' Roses (Geffen)
42	30	KICK	INXS (Mercury)
29	31	TANGO IN THE NIGHT	Fleetwood Mac (Warner Bros.)
-	32	BROTHERS IN RHYTHM	Various Artists (Ariola)
46	33	SHORT SHARP SHOCKED	Michelle Shocked (Cooking Vinyl)
41	34	THE INNOCENTS	Erasure (Mute)
32	35	SPIRIT OF EDEN	Talk Talk (Parlophone)
26	36	IDOL SONGS - 11 OF THE BEST	Billy Idol (Chrysalis)
-	37	THE MOTOWN SONGBOOK	Ruby Turner (Jive)
19	39	THE STARS WE ARE	Marc Almond (Parlophone)
44	40	A SALT WITH A DEADLY PEPA	Salt 'N' Pepa (London)
33	41	BEST OF THE EAGLES	Eagles (Asylum)
-	42	BEST OF AL GREEN: HI LIFE	Al Green (K-Tel)
-	43	PURPLE RAIN	Prince & the Revolution (Warner Bros.)
39	44	HYSTERIA	Def Leppard (Bludgeon Riffola)
34	45	METAL RHYTHM	Gary Numan (Illegal)
22	46	BIG TIME	Tom Waits (Island)
-	47	ONE MOMENT IN TIME	Various Artists (Arista)
37	48	SO GOOD	Mica Paris (Fourth & Broadway)
-	49	NO SLEEP AT ALL	Motorhead (GWR)
24	50	BLUE BELL KNOLL	Cocteau Twins (4AD)

22 October 1988

last week	this week	Title	Artist (Label)
-	1	RATTLE AND HUM	U2 (Island)
2	2	REVOLUTIONS	Jean Michel Jarre (Polydor)
-	3	INTROSPECTIVE	Pet Shop Boys (Parlophone)
8	4	FLYING COLOURS	Chris De Burgh (A&M)
1	5	NEW JERSEY	Bon Jovi (Vertigo)
11	6	KYLIE	Kylie Minogue (PWL)
-	7	TO WHOM IT MAY CONCERN	Pasadenas (CBS)
3	8	MOONLIGHTING	VariousArtists (WEA)
4	9	CONSCIENCE	Womack & Womack (Fourth & Broadway)
13	10	ONES ON 1	Various Artists (BBC)
10	11	POP ART	Transvision Vamp (MCA)
5	12	STARING AT THE SUN	Level 42 (Polydor)
6	13	RAP TRAX	Various Artists (Stylus)
12	14	TRACY CHAPMAN	Tracy Chapman (Elektra)
-	15	THE GREATEST HITS COLLECTION	Bananarama (London)
17	16	DIRTY DANCING	Soundtrack (RCA)
16	17	BAD	Michael Jackson (Epic)
9	18	HOT CITY NIGHTS	Various Artists (Vertigo)
23	19	WHITNEY	Whitney Houston (Arista)
-	20	WATERMARK	Enya (WEA)
14	21	...AND THE BEAT GOES ON	Various Artists (Telstar)
22	22	HEARSAY	Alexander O'Neal (Tabu)
7	23	PEACE IN OUR TIME	Big Country (Mercury)
34	24	THE INNOCENTS	Erasure (Mute)
20	25	SUNSHINE ON LEITH	Proclaimers (Chrysalis)
-	26	NO REST FOR THE WICKED	Ozzy Osbourne (CBS)
15	27	BUSTER	Soundtrack (Virgin)
19	28	PUSH	Bros (CBS)
-	29	INTO THE DRAGON	Bomb the Brass (Rhythm King)
42	30	BEST OF AL GREEN: HI LIFE	Al Green (K-Tel)
37	31	THE MOTOWN SONGBOOK	Ruby Turner (Jive)
18	32	THE RARE GROOVE MIX	Various Artists (Stylus)
24	33	THE FIRST OF A MILLION KISSES	Fairground Attraction (RCA)
32	34	BROTHERS IN RHYTHM	Various Artists (Ariola)
21	35	HEAVEN ON EARTH	Belinda Carlisle (Virgin)
26	36	ANCIENT HEART	Tanita Tikaram (WEA)
30	37	KICK	INXS (Mercury)
31	38	TANGO IN THE NIGHT	Fleetwood Mac (Warner Bros.)
40	39	A SALT WITH A DEADLY PEPA	Salt 'N' Pepa (London)
48	40	SO GOOD	Mica Paris (Fourth & Broadway)
-	41	URBAN ACID	Various Artists (Urban)
25	42	NOW THAT'S WHAT I CALL MUSIC 12	Various Artists (EMI/Virgin/Polygram)
-	43	THE MAGIC OF NANA MOUSKOURI	Nana Mouskouri (Philips)
47	44	ONE MOMENT IN TIME	Various Artists (Arista)
36	45	IDOL SONGS - 11 OF THE BEST	Billy Idol (Chrysalis)
27	46	THE WORLDS OF FOSTER AND ALLEN	Foster & Allen (Stylus)
-	47	THE PRICE YOU PAY	Spear of Destiny (Virgin)
29	48	APPETITE FOR DESTRUCTION	Guns 'N' Roses (Geffen)
-	49	BARCELONA	Freddie Mercury & Montserrat Caballe (Polydor)
38	50	TALK IS CHEAP	Keith Richards (Virgin)

Exactly two years on from their first Top 5 album *Slippery When Wet*, US heavy rockers Bon Jovi - who were indeed from New Jersey - scored their first chart-topper with *New Jersey*. Also enjoying their biggest-ever album were the husband-and-wife soul vocal team Womack & Womack (the "he" being Cecil Womack, brother of chartmaker Bobby), with *Conscience*, their first Fourth & Broadway recording.

October – November 1988

last week	this week	29 October 1988	
1	1	RATTLE AND HUM	U2 (Island)
-	2	MONEY FOR NOTHING	Dire Straits (Vertigo)
3	3	INTROSPECTIVE	Pet Shop Boys (Parlophone)
15	4	THE GREATEST HITS COLLECTION	Bananarama (London)
-	5	THE BEST OF CHRIS REA - NEW LIGHT THROUGH OLD WINDOWS	Chris Rea (WEA)
6	6	KYLIE	Kylie Minogue (PWL)
-	7	ANY LOVE	Luther Vandross (Epic)
7	8	TO WHOM IT MAY CONCERN	Pasadenas (CBS)
8	9	MOONLIGHTING	Various Artists (WEA)
20	10	WATERMARK	Enya (WEA)
2	11	REVOLUTIONS	Jean Michel Jarre (Polydor)
4	12	FLYING COLOURS	Chris De Burgh (A&M)
-	13	GIVING YOU THE BEST THAT I GOT	Anita Baker (Elektra)
9	14	CONSCIENCE	Womack & Womack (Fourth & Broadway)
13	15	RAP TRAX	Various Artists (Stylus)
10	16	ONES ON 1	Various Artists (BBC)
-	17	BIG THING	Duran Duran (EMI)
5	18	NEW JERSEY	Bon Jovi (Vertigo)
-	19	FISHERMAN'S BLUES	Waterboys (Chrysalis)
12	20	STARING AT THE SUN	Level 42 (Polydor)
14	21	TRACY CHAPMAN	Tracy Chapman (Elektra)
29	22	INTO THE DRAGON	Bomb the Brass (Rhythm King)
16	23	DIRTY DANCING	Soundtrack (RCA)
36	24	ANCIENT HEART	Tanita Tikaram (WEA)
11	25	POP ART	Transvision Vamp (MCA)
-	26	MY NATION UNDERGROUND	Julian Cope (Island)
17	27	BAD	Michael Jackson (Epic)
18	28	HOT CITY NIGHTS	Various Artists (Vertigo)
-	29	COMEDY	Black (A&M)
24	30	THE INNOCENTS	Erasure (Mute)
19	31	WHITNEY	Whitney Houston (Arista)
-	32	THE CLASSICAL EXPERIENCE	Various Artists (EMI)
25	33	SUNSHINE ON LEITH	Proclaimers (Chrysalis)
21	34	...AND THE BEAT GOES ON	Various Artists (Stylus)
30	35	BEST OF AL GREEN: HI LIFE	Al Green (K-Tel)
26	36	NO REST FOR THE WICKED	Ozzy Osbourne (CBS)
27	37	BUSTER	Soundtrack (Virgin)
46	38	THE WORLDS OF FOSTER AND ALLEN	Foster & Allen (Stylus)
49	39	BARCELONA	Freddie Mercury & Montserrat Caballe (Polydor)
22	40	HEARSAY	Alexander O'Neal (Tabu)
-	41	THE GREATEST LOVE	Various Artists (Telstar)
23	42	PEACE IN OUR TIME	Big Country (Mercury)
31	43	THE MOTOWN SONGBOOK	Ruby Turner (Jive)
28	44	PUSH	Bros (CBS)
-	45	LOVE	Aztec Camera (Warner Bros.)
41	46	URBAN ACID	Various Artists (Urban)
-	47	MOTOWN IN MOTION	Various Artists (K-Tel)
-	48	RAINTOWN	Deacon Blue (CBS)
-	49	EPONYMOUS	REM (IRS)
40	50	SO GOOD	Mica Paris (Fourth & Broadway)

last week	this week	5 November 1988	
2	1	MONEY FOR NOTHING	Dire Straits (Vertigo)
1	2	RATTLE AND HUM	U2 (Island)
7	3	ANY LOVE	Luther Vandross (Epic)
6	4	KYLIE	Kylie Minogue (PWL)
10	5	WATERMARK	Enya (WEA)
3	6	INTROSPECTIVE	Pet Shop Boys (Parlophone)
5	7	THE BEST OF CHRIS REA - NEW LIGHT THROUGH OLD WINDOWS	Chris Rea (WEA)
-	8	RAGE	T'Pau (Siren)
13	9	GIVING YOU THE BEST THAT I GOT	Anita Baker (Elektra)
4	10	THE GREATEST HITS COLLECTION	Bananarama (London)
-	11	SMASH HITS PARTY '88	Various Artists (Chrysalis)
8	12	TO WHOM IT MAY CONCERN	Pasadenas (CBS)
12	13	FLYING COLOURS	Chris De Burgh (A&M)
41	14	THE GREATEST LOVE	Various Artists (Telstar)
11	15	REVOLUTIONS	Jean Michel Jarre (Polydor)
30	16	THE INNOCENTS	Erasure (Mute)
19	17	FISHERMAN'S BLUES	Waterboys (Chrysalis)
14	18	CONSCIENCE	Womack & Womack (Fourth & Broadway)
24	19	ANCIENT HEART	Tanita Tikaram (WEA)
21	20	TRACY CHAPMAN	Tracy Chapman (Elektra)
20	21	STARING AT THE SUN	Level 42 (Polydor)
17	22	BIG THING	Duran Duran (EMI)
-	23	NEGOTIATIONS AND LOVE SONGS 1971-1986	Paul Simon (Warner Bros.)
31	24	WHITNEY	Whitney Houston (Arista)
23	25	DIRTY DANCING	Soundtrack (RCA)
9	26	MOONLIGHTING	VariousArtists (WEA)
-	27	SOFT METAL	Various Artists (Stylus)
32	28	THE CLASSICAL EXPERIENCE	Various Artists (EMI)
18	29	NEW JERSEY	Bon Jovi (Vertigo)
38	30	THE WORLDS OF FOSTER AND ALLEN	Foster & Allen (Stylus)
25	31	POP ART	Transvision Vamp (MCA)
-	32	THE RARE GROOVE MIX	Various Artists (Stylus)
27	33	BAD	Michael Jackson (Epic)
16	34	ONES ON 1	Various Artists (BBC)
15	35	RAP TRAX	Various Artists (Stylus)
37	36	BUSTER	Soundtrack (Virgin)
-	37	HEAVY NOVA	Robert Palmer (EMI)
29	38	COMEDY	Black (A&M)
47	39	MOTOWN IN MOTION	Various Artists (K-Tel)
33	40	SUNSHINE ON LEITH	Proclaimers (Chrysalis)
-	41	ELECTRIC FOLKLORE	Alarm (IRS)
-	42	THE LEGENDARY ROY ORBISON	Roy Orbison (Telstar)
43	43	THE BEAT THE RHYME THE NOISE	Wee Papa Girl Rappers (Jive)
48	44	RAINTOWN	Deacon Blue (CBS)
50	45	SO GOOD	Mica Paris (Fourth & Broadway)
-	46	THE TRAVELING WILBURYS VOL 1	Traveling Wilburys (Wilbury)
22	47	INTO THE DRAGON	Bomb the Brass (Rhythm King)
44	48	PUSH	Bros (CBS)
-	49	KICK	INXS (Mercury)
26	50	MY NATION UNDERGROUND	Julian Cope (Island)

last week	this week	12 November 1988	
1	1	MONEY FOR NOTHING	Dire Straits (Vertigo)
2	2	RATTLE AND HUM	U2 (Island)
5	3	WATERMARK	Enya (WEA)
4	4	KYLIE	Kylie Minogue (PWL)
11	5	SMASH HITS PARTY '88	Various Artists (Chrysalis)
8	6	RAGE	T'Pau (Siren)
-	7	GREATEST HITS	Human League (Virgin)
13	8	FLYING COLOURS	Chris De Burgh (A&M)
27	9	SOFT METAL	Various Artists (Stylus)
3	10	ANY LOVE	Luther Vandross (Epic)
-	11	UNFORGETTABLE	Various Artists (EMI)
6	12	INTROSPECTIVE	Pet Shop Boys (Parlophone)
10	13	THE GREATEST HITS COLLECTION	Bananarama (London)
7	14	THE BEST OF CHRIS REA - NEW LIGHT THROUGH OLD WINDOWS	Chris Rea (WEA)
14	15	THE GREATEST LOVE	Various Artists (Telstar)
12	16	TO WHOM IT MAY CONCERN	Pasadenas (CBS)
15	17	REVOLUTIONS	Jean Michel Jarre (Polydor)
19	18	ANCIENT HEART	Tanita Tikaram (WEA)
23	19	NEGOTIATIONS AND LOVE SONGS 1971-1986	Paul Simon (Warner Bros.)
9	20	GIVING YOU THE BEST THAT I GOT	Anita Baker (Elektra)
16	21	THE INNOCENTS	Erasure (Mute)
48	22	PUSH	Bros (CBS)
20	23	TRACY CHAPMAN	Tracy Chapman (Elektra)
40	24	SUNSHINE ON LEITH	Proclaimers (Chrysalis)
17	25	FISHERMAN'S BLUES	Waterboys (Chrysalis)
25	26	DIRTY DANCING	Soundtrack (RCA)
37	27	HEAVY NOVA	Robert Palmer (EMI)
30	28	THE WORLDS OF FOSTER AND ALLEN	Foster & Allen (Stylus)
-	29	THE PREMIERE COLLECTION: THE BEST OF ANDREW LLOYD WEBBER	Various Artists (Really Useful)
18	30	CONSCIENCE	Womack & Womack (Fourth & Broadway)
-	31	THE HIT FACTORY: THE BEST OF STOCK AITKEN WATERMAN VOL 2	Various Artists (PWL)
24	32	WHITNEY	Whitney Houston (Arista)
28	33	THE CLASSICAL EXPERIENCE	Various Artists (EMI)
-	34	THE LOVERS	Various Artists (K-Tel)
33	35	BAD	Michael Jackson (Epic)
21	36	STARING AT THE SUN	Level 42 (Polydor)
36	37	BUSTER	Soundtrack (Virgin)
44	38	RAINTOWN	Deacon Blue (CBS)
29	39	NEW JERSEY	Bon Jovi (Vertigo)
32	40	THE RARE GROOVE MIX	Various Artists (Stylus)
49	41	KICK	INXS (Mercury)
39	42	MOTOWN IN MOTION	Various Artists (K-Tel)
-	43	...AND THE BEAT GOES ON	Various Artists (Telstar)
-	44	THE SINGLES COLLECTION	Kool & the Gang (De-Lite)
-	45	A SALT WITH A DEADLY PEPA	Salt 'N' Pepa (London)
-	46	I AM KURIOUS ORANJ	Fall (Beggars Banquet)
31	47	POP ART	Transvision Vamp (MCA)
-	48	THE HEART AND SOUL OF ROCK 'N' ROLL	Various Artists (Stylus)
35	49	RAP TRAX	Various Artists (Stylus)
43	50	THE BEAT THE RHYME THE NOISE	Wee Papa Girl Rappers (Jive)

Hits compilations began to dominate the late autumn charts of 1988, the most successful, predictably, being Dire Straits' *Money For Nothing*, which anthologised the best of the band's material since 1978. Other hits packages selling particularly well were those by Chris Rea, the Human League and Bananarama, all Top 5 items. Enya's New Age-styled *Watermark* followed her Number 1 single *Orinoco Flow* to the heights.

November – December 1988

19 November 1988

last week	this week	Title	Artist
1	1	MONEY FOR NOTHING	Dire Straits (Vertigo)
4	2	KYLIE	Kylie Minogue (PWL)
7	3	GREATEST HITS	Human League (Virgin)
3	4	WATERMARK	Enya (WEA)
2	5	RATTLE AND HUM	U2 (Island)
14	6	THE BEST OF CHRIS REA - NEW LIGHT THROUGH OLD WINDOWS	Chris Rea (WEA)
8	7	FLYING COLOURS	Chris De Burgh (A&M)
13	8	THE GREATEST HITS COLLECTION	Bananarama (London)
-	9	THE MEMPHIS SESSIONS	Wet Wet Wet (Precious)
5	10	SMASH HITS PARTY '88	Various Artists (Chrysalis)
9	11	SOFT METAL	Various Artists (Stylus)
6	12	RAGE	T'Pau (Siren)
11	13	UNFORGETTABLE	Various Artists (EMI)
-	14	THE ULTIMATE COLLECTION	Bryan Ferry with Roxy Music (EG)
12	15	INTROSPECTIVE	Pet Shop Boys (Parlophone)
-	16	THE TRAVELING WILBURYS VOL 1	Traveling Wilburys (Wilbury)
31	17	THE HIT FACTORY: THE BEST OF STOCK AITKEN WATERMAN VOL 2	Various Artists (PWL)
41	18	KICK	INXS (Mercury)
10	19	ANY LOVE	Luther Vandross (Epic)
-	20	PRIVATE COLLECTION (1979-1988)	Cliff Richard (EMI)
15	21	THE GREATEST LOVE	Various Artists (Telstar)
29	22	THE PREMIERE COLLECTION: THE BEST OF ANDREW LLOYD WEBBER	Various Artists (Really Useful)
18	23	ANCIENT HEART	Tanita Tikaram (WEA)
24	24	SUNSHINE ON LEITH	Proclaimers (Chrysalis)
37	25	BUSTER	Soundtrack (Virgin)
19	26	NEGOTIATIONS AND LOVE SONGS 1971-1986	Paul Simon (Warner Bros.)
27	27	HEAVY NOVA	Robert Palmer (EMI)
16	28	TO WHOM IT MAY CONCERN	Pasadenas (CBS)
21	29	THE INNOCENTS	Erasure (Mute)
38	30	RAINTOWN	Deacon Blue (CBS)
26	31	DIRTY DANCING	Soundtrack (RCA)
28	32	THE WORLDS OF FOSTER AND ALLEN	Foster & Allen (Stylus)
34	33	THE LOVERS	Various Artists (K-Tel)
44	34	THE SINGLES COLLECTION	Kool & the Gang (De-Lite)
-	35	SO GOOD	Mica Paris (Fourth & Broadway)
-	36	THE LEGENDARY ROY ORBISON	Roy Orbison (Telstar)
22	37	PUSH	Bros (CBS)
30	38	CONSCIENCE	Womack & Womac (Fourth & Broadway)
-	39	APPETITE FOR DESTRUCTION	Guns 'N' Roses (Geffen)
-	40	GREEN	REM (Warner Bros.)
20	41	GIVING YOU THE BEST THAT I GOT	Anita Baker (Elektra)
23	42	TRACY CHAPMAN	Tracy Chapman (Elektra)
35	43	BAD	Michael Jackson (Epic)
32	44	WHITNEY	Whitney Houston (Arista)
17	45	REVOLUTIONS	Jean Michel Jarre (Polydor)
42	46	MOTOWN IN MOTION	Various Artists (K-Tel)
-	47	COPPERHEAD ROAD	Steve Earle (MCA)
-	48	GOOD MORNING VIETNAM - ORIGINAL SOUNDTRACK	Various Artists (A&M)
-	49	ANYTHING FOR YOU	Gloria Estefan & Miami Sound Machine (Epic)
39	50	NEW JERSEY	Bon Jovi (Vertigo)

26 November 1988

		Title	Artist
2	1	KYLIE	Kylie Minogue (PWL)
1	2	MONEY FOR NOTHING	Dire Straits (Vertigo)
3	3	GREATEST HITS	Human League (Virgin)
9	4	THE MEMPHIS SESSIONS	Wet Wet Wet (Precious)
-	5	WANTED	Yazz (Big Life)
20	6	PRIVATE COLLECTION (1979-1988)	Cliff Richard (EMI)
14	7	THE ULTIMATE COLLECTION	Bryan Ferry with Roxy Music (EG)
6	8	THE BEST OF CHRIS REA - NEW LIGHT THROUGH OLD WINDOWS	Chris Rea (WEA)
18	9	KICK	INXS (Mercury)
-	10	THE GREATEST HITS OF '88	Various Artists (Telstar)
5	11	RATTLE AND HUM	U2 (Island)
16	12	THE TRAVELING WILBURYS VOL 1	Traveling Wilburys (Wilbury)
7	13	FLYING COLOURS	Chris De Burgh (A&M)
8	14	THE GREATEST HITS COLLECTION	Bananarama (London)
11	15	SOFT METAL	Various Artists (Stylus)
4	16	WATERMARK	Enya (WEA)
-	17	GET EVEN	Brother Beyond (Parlophone)
22	18	THE PREMIERE COLLECTION: THE BEST OF ANDREW LLOYD WEBBER	Various Artists (Really Useful Records)
17	19	THE HIT FACTORY: THE BEST OF STOCK AITKEN WATERMAN VOL 2	Various Artists (PWL)
15	20	INTROSPECTIVE	Pet Shop Boys (Parlophone)
49	21	ANYTHING FOR YOU	Gloria Estefan & Miami Sound Machine (Epic)
21	22	THE GREATEST LOVE	Various Artists (Telstar)
10	23	SMASH HITS PARTY '88	Various Artists (Chrysalis)
12	24	RAGE	T'Pau (Siren)
19	25	ANY LOVE	Luther Vandross (Epic)
28	26	TO WHOM IT MAY CONCERN	Pasadenas (CBS)
23	27	ANCIENT HEART	Tanita Tikaram (WEA)
-	28	HEARSAY	Alexander O'Neal (Tabu)
35	29	SO GOOD	Mica Paris (Fourth & Broadway)
25	30	BUSTER	Soundtrack (Virgin)
27	31	HEAVY NOVA	Robert Palmer (EMI)
40	32	GREEN	REM (Warner Bros.)
13	33	UNFORGETTABLE	Various Artists (EMI)
24	34	SUNSHINE ON LEITH	Proclaimers (Chrysalis)
43	35	BAD	Michael Jackson (Epic)
26	36	NEGOTIATIONS AND LOVE SONGS 1971-1986	Paul Simon (Warner Bros.)
30	37	RAINTOWN	Deacon Blue (CBS)
37	38	PUSH	Bros (CBS)
33	39	THE LOVERS	Various Artists (K-Tel)
-	40	THE LOVE ALBUM '88	Various Artists (Telstar)
34	41	THE SINGLES COLLECTION	Kool & the Gang (De-Lite)
-	42	NITE FLITE	Various Artists (CBS)
31	43	DIRTY DANCING	Soundtrack (RCA)
44	44	MACHISMO	Cameo (Club)
29	45	THE INNOCENTS	Erasure (Mute)
38	46	CONSCIENCE	Womack & Womack (Fourth & Broadway)
48	47	GOOD MORNING VIETNAM - ORIGINAL SOUNDTRACK	Various Artists (A&M)
32	48	THE WORLDS OF FOSTER AND ALLEN	Foster & Allen (Stylus)
-	49	HIT MIX '88	Various Artists (Stylus)
-	50	A SALT WITH A DEADLY PEPA	Salt 'N' Pepa (London)

3 December 1988

		Title	Artist
-	1	NOW THAT'S WHAT I CALL MUSIC 13	Various Artists (EMI/Virgin/Polygram)
1	2	KYLIE	Kylie Minogue (PWL)
6	3	PRIVATE COLLECTION (1979-1988)	Cliff Richard (EMI)
-	4	FLEETWOOD MAC'S GREATEST HITS	Fleetwood Mac (Warner Bros.)
2	5	MONEY FOR NOTHING	Dire Straits (Vertigo)
5	6	WANTED	Yazz (Big Life)
9	7	KICK	INXS (Mercury)
7	8	THE ULTIMATE COLLECTION	Bryan Ferry with Roxy Music (EG)
3	9	GREATEST HITS	Human League (Virgin)
-	10	DELICATE SOUND OF THUNDER	Pink Floyd (EMI)
18	11	THE PREMIERE COLLECTION: THE BEST OF ANDREW LLOYD WEBBER	Various Artists (Really Useful)
4	12	THE MEMPHIS SESSIONS	Wet Wet Wet (Precious)
13	13	FLYING COLOURS	Chris De Burgh (A&M)
8	14	THE BEST OF CHRIS REA - NEW LIGHT THROUGH OLD WINDOWS	Chris Rea (WEA)
23	15	SMASH HITS PARTY '88	Various Artists (Chrysalis)
15	16	SOFT METAL	Various Artists (Stylus)
10	17	THE GREATEST HITS OF '88	Various Artists (Telstar)
28	18	HEARSAY	Alexander O'Neal (Tabu)
19	19	THE HIT FACTORY: THE BEST OF STOCK AITKEN WATERMAN VOL 2	Various Artists (PWL)
14	20	THE GREATEST HITS COLLECTION	Bananarama (London)
11	21	RATTLE AND HUM	U2 (Island)
-	22	TILL I LOVED YOU	Barbra Streisand (CBS)
22	23	THE GREATEST LOVE	Various Artists (Telstar)
24	24	RAGE	T'Pau (Siren)
25	25	BEST OF THE ART OF NOISE	Art of Noise (China)
20	26	INTROSPECTIVE	Pet Shop Boys (Parlophone)
16	27	WATERMARK	Enya (WEA)
12	28	THE TRAVELING WILBURYS VOL 1	Traveling Wilburys (Wilbury)
36	29	NEGOTIATIONS AND LOVE SONGS 1971-1986	Paul Simon (Warner Bros.)
35	30	BAD	Michael Jackson (Epic)
17	31	GET EVEN	Brother Beyond (Parlophone)
43	32	DIRTY DANCING	Soundtrack (RCA)
33	33	PUSH	Bros (CBS)
30	34	BUSTER	Soundtrack (Virgin)
26	35	TO WHOM IT MAY CONCERN	Pasadenas (CBS)
21	36	ANYTHING FOR YOU	Gloria Estefan & Miami Sound Machine (Epic)
49	37	HIT MIX '88	Various Artists (Stylus)
37	38	RAINTOWN	Deacon Blue (CBS)
27	39	ANCIENT HEART	Tanita Tikaram (WEA)
25	40	ANY LOVE	Luther Vandross (Epic)
-	41	HOUSE HITS '88	Various Artists (Telstar)
41	42	THE SINGLES COLLECTION	Kool & the Gang (De-Lite)
29	43	SO GOOD	Mica Paris (Fourth & Broadway)
-	44	RAPPIN' IN THE HOUSE	Various Artists (K-Tel)
31	45	HEAVY NOVA	Robert Palmer (EMI)
-	46	GIVING YOU THE BEST THAT I GOT	Anita Baker (Elektra)
47	47	CONSCIENCE	Womack & Womack (Fourth & Broadway)
34	48	SUNSHINE ON LEITH	Proclaimers (Chrysalis)
48	49	THE WORLDS OF FOSTER AND ALLEN	Foster & Allen (Stylus)
50	50	A SALT WITH A DEADLY PEPA	Salt 'N' Pepa (London)

Kylie made the top of the chart for the second time in November, as the Minogue hit singles continued to roll, and the album began to build to its really major sales in the run-up to Christmas. It was joined by still more hits compilations - Cliff Richard's *Private Collection*, Bryan Ferry & Roxy Music's *Ultimate Collection*, and *Fleetwood Mac's Greatest Hits* - plus the inevitable *Now Music*, currently up to volume 13.

December 1988

last	this	10 December 1988
1	1	NOW THAT'S WHAT I CALL MUSIC 13 Various Artists (EMI/Virgin/Polygram)
3	2	PRIVATE COLLECTION (1979-1988) Cliff Richard (EMI)
2	3	KYLIE Kylie Minogue (PWL)
4	4	FLEETWOOD MAC'S GREATEST HITS Fleetwood Mac (Warner Bros.)
5	5	MONEY FOR NOTHING Dire Straits (Vertigo)
11	6	THE PREMIERE COLLECTION: THE BEST OF ANDREW LLOYD WEBBER Various Artists (Really Useful Records)
-	7	THE THIEVING MAGPIE Marillion (EMI)
8	8	THE ULTIMATE COLLECTION Bryan Ferry with Roxy Music (EG)
16	9	SOFT METAL Various Artists (Stylus)
-	10	HOLD ME IN YOUR ARMS Rick Astley (RCA)
9	11	GREATEST HITS Human League (Virgin)
7	12	KICK INXS (Mercury)
17	13	THE GREATEST HITS OF '88 Various Artists (Telstar)
6	14	WANTED Yazz (Big Life)
33	15	PUSH Bros (CBS)
10	16	DELICATE SOUND OF THUNDER Pink Floyd (EMI)
14	17	THE BEST OF CHRIS REA - NEW LIGHT THROUGH OLD WINDOWS Chris Rea (WEA)
20	18	THE GREATEST HITS COLLECTION Bananarama (London)
31	19	GET EVEN Brother Beyond (Parlophone)
13	20	FLYING COLOURS Chris De Burgh (A&M)
21	21	RATTLE AND HUM U2 (Island)
19	22	THE HIT FACTORY: THE BEST OF STOCK AITKEN WATERMAN VOL 2 Various Artists (PWL)
12	23	THE MEMPHIS SESSIONS Wet Wet Wet (Precious)
18	24	HEARSAY Alexander O'Neal (Tabu)
23	25	THE GREATEST LOVE Various Artists (Telstar)
42	26	THE SINGLES COLLECTION Kool & the Gang (De-Lite)
-	27	SMASHES, THRASHES AND HITS Kiss (Vertigo)
15	28	SMASH HITS PARTY '88 Various Artists (Chrysalis)
34	29	BUSTER Soundtrack (Virgin)
41	30	HOUSE HITS '88 Various Artists (London)
29	31	NEGOTIATIONS AND LOVE SONGS 1971-1986 Paul Simon (Warner Bros.)
30	32	BAD Michael Jackson (Epic)
27	33	WATERMARK Enya (WEA)
44	34	RAPPIN' IN THE HOUSE Various Artists (K-Tel)
24	35	RAGE T'Pau (Siren)
26	36	INTROSPECTIVE Pet Shop Boys (Parlophone)
22	37	TILL I LOVED YOU Barbra Streisand (CBS)
37	38	HIT MIX '88 Various Artists (Stylus)
-	39	THE INNOCENTS Erasure (Mute)
-	40	DANCE DANCE DANCE James Last (Polydor)
25	41	BEST OF THE ART OF NOISE Art of Noise (China)
-	42	THE FLAG Yello (Mercury)
35	43	TO WHOM IT MAY CONCERN Pasadenas (CBS)
50	44	A SALT WITH A DEADLY PEPA Salt 'N' Pepa (London)
39	45	ANCIENT HEART Tanita Tikaram (WEA)
-	46	THE CLASSICAL EXPERIENCE Various Artists (EMI)
-	47	THE QUEEN ALBUM Elaine Paige (Siren)
-	48	REMOTE Hue & Cry (Circa)
-	49	EVERYTHING Bangles (CBS)
32	50	DIRTY DANCING Soundtrack (RCA)

last	this	17 December 1988
1	1	NOW THAT'S WHAT I CALL MUSIC 13 Various Artists (EMI/Virgin/Polygram)
2	2	PRIVATE COLLECTION (1979-1988) Cliff Richard (EMI)
3	3	KYLIE Kylie Minogue (PWL)
-	4	THE HITS ALBUM Various Artists (CBS/WEA/BMG)
5	5	MONEY FOR NOTHING Dire Straits (Vertigo)
6	6	THE PREMIERE COLLECTION: THE BEST OF ANDREW LLOYD WEBBER Various Artists (Really Useful)
4	7	FLEETWOOD MAC'S GREATEST HITS Fleetwood Mac (Warner Bros.)
18	8	THE GREATEST HITS COLLECTION Bananarama (London)
8	9	THE ULTIMATE COLLECTION Bryan Ferry with Roxy Music (EG)
10	10	HOLD ME IN YOUR ARMS Rick Astley (RCA)
9	11	SOFT METAL Various Artists (Stylus)
12	12	PUSH Bros (CBS)
36	13	INTROSPECTIVE Pet Shop Boys (Parlophone)
11	14	GREATEST HITS Human League (Virgin)
13	15	THE GREATEST HITS OF '88 Various Artists (Telstar)
12	16	KICK INXS (Mercury)
21	17	RATTLE AND HUM U2 (Island)
17	18	THE BEST OF CHRIS REA - NEW LIGHT THROUGH OLD WINDOWS Chris Rea (WEA)
32	19	BAD Michael Jackson (Epic)
14	20	WANTED Yazz (Big Life)
20	21	FLYING COLOURS Chris De Burgh (A&M)
29	22	BUSTER Soundtrack (Virgin)
23	23	GET EVEN Brother Beyond (Parlophone)
23	24	THE MEMPHIS SESSIONS Wet Wet Wet (Precious)
39	25	THE INNOCENTS Erasure (Mute)
-	26	G N' R LIES Guns N' Roses (Geffen)
7	27	THE THIEVING MAGPIE Marillion (EMI)
22	28	THE HIT FACTORY: THE BEST OF STOCK AITKEN WATERMAN VOL 2 Various Artists (PWL)
26	29	THE SINGLES COLLECTION Kool & the Gang (De-Lite)
-	30	MY GIFT TO YOU Alexander O'Neal (Tabu)
16	31	DELICATE SOUND OF THUNDER Pink Floyd (EMI)
28	32	SMASH HITS PARTY '88 Various Artists (Chrysalis)
43	33	TO WHOM IT MAY CONCERN Pasadenas (CBS)
30	34	HOUSE HITS '88 Various Artists (London)
25	35	THE GREATEST LOVE Various Artists (Telstar)
44	36	A SALT WITH A DEADLY PEPA Salt 'N' Pepa (London)
31	37	NEGOTIATIONS AND LOVE SONGS 1971-1986 Paul Simon (Warner Bros.)
37	38	TILL I LOVED YOU Barbra Streisand (CBS)
-	39	TRACY CHAPMAN Tracy Chapman (Elektra)
-	40	CHRISTMAS WITH NAT 'KING' COLE Nat 'King' Cole (Stylus)
-	41	THE LEGENDARY ROY ORBISON Roy Orbison (Telstar)
24	42	HEARSAY Alexander O'Neal (Tabu)
-	43	THE TRAVELING WILBURYS VOL 1 Traveling Wilburys (Wilbury)
-	44	NOW - THE CHRISTMAS ALBUM Various Artists (EMI/Virgin/PolyGram)
-	45	SO GOOD Mica Paris (Fourth & Broadway)
45	46	ANCIENT HEART Tanita Tikaram (WEA)
33	47	WATERMARK Enya (WEA)
-	48	SUNSHINE ON LEITH Proclaimers (Chrysalis)
50	49	DIRTY DANCING Soundtrack (RCA)
27	50	SMASHES, THRASHES AND HITS Kiss (Vertigo)

last	this	24 December 1988
2	1	PRIVATE COLLECTION (1979-1988) Cliff Richard (EMI)
1	2	NOW THAT'S WHAT I CALL MUSIC 13 Various Artists (EMI/Virgin/Polygram)
3	3	KYLIE Kylie Minogue (PWL)
4	4	THE HITS ALBUM Various Artists (CBS/WEA/BMG)
5	5	MONEY FOR NOTHING Dire Straits (Vertigo)
7	6	GREATEST HITS Fleetwood Mac (Warner Bros.)
41	7	THE LEGENDARY ROY ORBISON Roy Orbison (Telstar)
6	8	THE PREMIERE COLLECTION: THE BEST OF ANDREW LLOYD WEBBER Various Artists (Really Useful)
8	9	THE GREATEST HITS COLLECTION Bananarama (London)
12	10	PUSH Bros (CBS)
9	11	THE ULTIMATE COLLECTION Bryan Ferry with Roxy Music (EG)
10	12	HOLD ME IN YOUR ARMS Rick Astley (RCA)
43	13	THE TRAVELING WILBURYS VOL 1 Traveling Wilburys (Wilbury)
17	14	RATTLE AND HUM U2 (Island)
15	15	GREATEST HITS Human League (Virgin)
15	16	THE GREATEST HITS OF '88 Various Artists (Telstar)
11	17	SOFT METAL Various Artists (Stylus)
13	18	INTROSPECTIVE Pet Shop Boys (Parlophone)
18	19	THE BEST OF CHRIS REA - NEW LIGHT THROUGH OLD WINDOWS Chris Rea (WEA)
44	20	NOW - THE CHRISTMAS ALBUM Various Artists (EMI/Virgin/PolyGram)
19	21	BAD Michael Jackson (Epic)
16	22	KICK INXS (Mercury)
-	23	THE JOE LONGTHORNE SONGBOOK Joe Longthorne (Telstar)
22	24	BUSTER Soundtrack (Virgin)
25	25	THE INNOCENTS Erasure (Mute)
20	26	WANTED Yazz (Big Life)
21	27	FLYING COLOURS Chris De Burgh (A&M)
23	28	GET EVEN Brother Beyond (Parlophone)
28	29	THE HIT FACTORY: THE BEST OF STOCK AITKEN WATERMAN VOL 2 Various Artists (PWL)
-	30	THE GREATEST HITS OF HOUSE Various (Stylus)
34	31	THE MEMPHIS SESSIONS Wet Wet Wet (Precious)
32	32	SMASH HITS PARTY '88 Various Artists (Chrysalis)
29	33	THE SINGLES COLLECTION Kool & the Gang (De-Lite)
40	34	CHRISTMAS WITH NAT 'KING' COLE Nat 'King' Cole (Stylus)
35	35	THE GREATEST LOVE Various Artists (Telstar)
33	36	TO WHOM IT MAY CONCERN Pasadenas (CBS)
30	37	MY GIFT TO YOU Alexander O'Neal (Tabu)
39	38	TRACY CHAPMAN Tracy Chapman (Elektra)
37	39	NEGOTIATIONS AND LOVE SONGS 1971-1986 Paul Simon (Warner Bros.)
31	40	DELICATE SOUND OF THUNDER Pink Floyd (EMI)
36	41	A SALT WITH A DEADLY PEPA Salt 'N' Pepa (London)
26	42	G N' R LIES Guns N' Roses (Geffen)
47	43	WATERMARK Enya (WEA)
38	44	TILL I LOVED YOU Barbra Streisand (CBS)
46	45	HOUSE HITS '88 Various Artists (London)
46	46	ANCIENT HEART Tanita Tikaram (WEA)
49	47	DIRTY DANCING Soundtrack (RCA)
-	48	DANCE DANCE DANCE James Last (Polydor)
-	49	BACK TO THE 60'S Various Artists (Telstar)
-	50	NEW JERSEY Bon Jovi (Vertigo)

The *Premiere Collection* of Andrew Lloyd Webber favourites anthologised the original or hit versions of most of the best-known tracks from virtually every Lloyd Webber musical, thereby saving a lot of people the need to buy individual cast albums! *Kylie* emerged as 1988's top-selling album by year's end, but the actual year-end No. 1 went to Cliff Richard, also topping the singles chart with *Mistletoe & Wine*.

January 1989

14 January 1989

last week	this week	Title	Artist (Label)
3	1	KYLIE	Kylie Minogue (PWL)
2	2	NOW THAT'S WHAT I CALL MUSIC 13	Various Artists (EMI/Virgin/PolyGram)
9	3	THE GREATEST HITS	Bananarama (London)
6	4	GREATEST HITS	Fleetwood Mac (Warner Bros.)
1	5	PRIVATE COLLECTION (1979-1988)	Cliff Richard (EMI)
5	6	MONEY FOR NOTHING	Dire Straits (Vertigo)
10	7	PUSH	Bros (CBS)
25	8	THE INNOCENTS	Erasure (Mute)
4	9	THE HITS ALBUM	Various Artists (CBS/WEA/BMG)
21	10	BAD	Michael Jackson (Epic)
18	11	INTROSPECTIVE	Pet Shop Boys (Parlophone)
22	12	KICK	INXS (Mercury)
8	13	THE PREMIERE COLLECTION: THE BEST OF ANDREW LLOYD WEBBER	Various Artists (Really Useful)
7	14	THE LEGENDARY ...	Roy Orbison (Telstar)
12	15	HOLD ME IN YOUR ARMS	Rick Astley (RCA)
11	16	THE ULTIMATE COLLECTION	Bryan Ferry & Roxy Music (EG)
14	17	RATTLE AND HUM	U2 (Island)
26	18	WANTED	Yazz (Big Life)
15	19	GREATEST HITS	Human League (Virgin)
19	20	THE BEST OF CHRIS REA - NEW LIGHT THROUGH OLD WINDOWS	Chris Rea (WEA)
-	21	ANYTHING FOR YOU	Gloria Estefan & the Miami Sound Machine (Epic)
22	22	GET EVEN	Brother Beyond (Parlophone)
13	23	TRAVELING WILBURYS VOL.1	Traveling Wilburys (Wilbury)
30	24	THE GREATEST HITS OF HOUSE	Various Artists (Stylus)
24	25	BUSTER - SOUNDTRACK	Various Artists (Virgin)
16	26	GREATEST HITS OF '88	Various Artists (Telstar)
-	27	THE GREATEST LOVE 2	Various Artists (Telstar)
17	28	SOFT METAL	Various Artists (Stylus)
31	29	THE MEMPHIS SESSIONS	Wet Wet Wet (Precious Organisation)
-	30	HEARSAY	Alexander O'Neal (Tabu)
46	31	ANCIENT HEART	Tanita Tikaram (WEA)
36	32	TO WHOM IT MAY CONCERN	Pasadenas (CBS)
38	33	TRACY CHAPMAN	Tracy Chapman (Elektra)
-	34	DIRTY DANCING - SOUNDTRACK	Various Artists (RCA)
43	35	WATERMARK	Enya (WEA)
27	36	FLYING COLOURS	Chris De Burgh (A&M)
29	37	THE HIT FACTORY - THE BEST OF STOCK AITKEN WATERMAN VOL.2	Various Artists (PWL)
33	38	THE SINGLES COLLECTION	Kool & the Gang (De-Lite)
23	39	THE JOE LONGTHORNE SONGBOOK	Joe Longthorne (Telstar)
-	40	ROYAL MIX '89	Mirage (Stylus)
50	41	NEW JERSEY	Bon Jovi (Vertigo)
41	42	A SALT WITH A DEADLY PEPA	Salt'n'Pepa (ffrr)
40	43	DELICATE SOUND OF THUNDER	Pink Floyd (EMI)
-	44	RAINTOWN	Deacon Blue (CBS)
45	45	HOUSE HITS '88	Various Artists (Dover)
32	46	SMASH HITS PARTY '88	Various Artists (Dover)
-	47	REVOLUTIONS	Jean-Michel Jarre (Polydor)
39	48	NEGOTIATIONS AND LOVE SONGS 1971-1986	Paul Simon (Warner Bros.)
-	49	CLOSE	Kim Wilde (MCA)
-	50	SO GOOD	Mica Paris (Fourth & Broadway)

21 January 1989

last week	this week	Title	Artist (Label)
8	1	THE INNOCENTS	Erasure (Mute)
14	2	THE LEGENDARY ROY ORBISON	Roy Orbison (Telstar)
1	3	KYLIE	Kylie Minogue (PWL)
4	4	GREATEST HITS	Fleetwood Mac (Warner Bros.)
13	5	THE PREMIERE COLLECTION: THE BEST OF ANDREW LLOYD WEBBER	Various Artists (Really Useful)
2	6	NOW THAT'S WHAT I CALL MUSIC 13	Various Artists (EMI/Virgin/PolyGram)
3	7	THE GREATEST HITS	Bananarama (London)
10	8	BAD	Michael Jackson (Epic)
6	9	MONEY FOR NOTHING	Dire Straits (Vertigo)
5	10	PRIVATE COLLECTION (1979-1988)	Cliff Richard (EMI)
11	11	INTROSPECTIVE	Pet Shop Boys (Parlophone)
12	12	KICK	INXS (Mercury)
21	13	ANYTHING FOR YOU	Gloria Estefan & the Miami Sound Machine (Epic)
7	14	PUSH	Bros (CBS)
35	15	WATERMARK	Enya (WEA)
-	16	THE LIVING YEARS	Mike & the Mechanics (WEA)
23	17	TRAVELING WILBURYS VOL.1	Traveling Wilburys (Wilbury)
25	18	BUSTER - SOUNDTRACK	Various Artists (Virgin)
16	19	THE ULTIMATE COLLECTION	Bryan Ferry & Roxy Music (EG)
28	20	SOFT METAL	Various Artists (Stylus)
27	21	THE GREATEST LOVE 2	Various Artists (Telstar)
9	22	THE HITS ALBUM	Various Artists (CBS/WEA/BMG)
22	23	GET EVEN	Brother Beyond (Parlophone)
17	24	RATTLE AND HUM	U2 (Island)
20	25	THE BEST OF CHRIS REA - NEW LIGHT THROUGH OLD WINDOWS	Chris Rea (WEA)
-	26	LOVE SUPREME	Supremes featuring Diana Ross (Motown)
18	27	WANTED	Yazz (Big Life)
15	28	HOLD ME IN YOUR ARMS	Rick Astley (RCA)
24	29	THE GREATEST HITS OF HOUSE	Various Artists (Stylus)
19	30	GREATEST HITS	Human League (Virgin)
29	31	THE MEMPHIS SESSIONS	Wet Wet Wet (Precious Organisation)
36	32	FLYING COLOURS	Chris De Burgh (A&M)
31	33	ANCIENT HEART	Tanita Tikaram (WEA)
33	34	TRACY CHAPMAN	Tracy Chapman (Elektra)
49	35	CLOSE	Kim Wilde (MCA)
32	36	TO WHOM IT MAY CONCERN	Pasadenas (CBS)
30	37	HEARSAY	Alexander O'Neal (Tabu)
40	38	ROYAL MIX '89	Mirage (Stylus)
34	39	DIRTY DANCING - SOUNDTRACK	Various Artists (RCA)
43	40	DELICATE SOUND OF THUNDER	Pink Floyd (EMI)
41	41	NEW JERSEY	Bon Jovi (Vertigo)
26	42	THE GREATEST HITS OF '88	Various Artists (Telstar)
-	43	WHITNEY	Whitney Houston (Arista)
50	44	SO GOOD	Mica Paris (Fourth & Broadway)
44	45	RAINTOWN	Deacon Blue (CBS)
38	46	THE SINGLES COLLECTION	Kool & the Gang (De-Lite)
-	47	THE GREATEST LOVE	Various Artists (Telstar)
47	48	REVOLUTIONS	Jean-Michel Jarre (Polydor)
42	49	A SALT WITH A DEADLY PEPA	Salt'n'Pepa (ffrr)
-	50	FISHERMAN'S BLUES	Waterboys (Ensign)

28 January 1989

last week	this week	Title	Artist (Label)
2	1	THE LEGENDARY ROY ORBISON	Roy Orbison (Telstar)
1	2	THE INNOCENTS	Erasure (Mute)
13	3	ANYTHING FOR YOU	Gloria Estefan & the Miami Sound Machine (Epic)
4	4	GREATEST HITS	Fleetwood Mac (Warner Bros.)
5	5	THE PREMIERE COLLECTION: THE BEST OF ANDREW LLOYD WEBBER	Various Artists (Really Useful)
3	6	KYLIE	Kylie Minogue (PWL)
16	7	THE LIVING YEARS	Mike & the Mechanics (WEA)
8	8	BAD	Michael Jackson (Epic)
7	9	THE GREATEST HITS COLLECTION	Bananarama (London)
19	10	THE ULTIMATE COLLECTION	Bryan Ferry & Roxy Music (EG)
12	11	KICK	INXS (Mercury)
9	12	MONEY FOR NOTHING	Dire Straits (Vertigo)
21	13	THE GREATEST LOVE 2	Various Artists (Telstar)
15	14	WATERMARK	Enya (WEA)
18	15	BUSTER - SOUNDTRACK	Various Artists (Virgin)
6	16	NOW THAT'S WHAT I CALL MUSIC 13	Various Artists (EMI/Virgin/PolyGram)
35	17	CLOSE	Kim Wilde (MCA)
11	18	INTROSPECTIVE	Pet Shop Boys (Parlophone)
17	19	TRAVELING WILBURYS VOL.1	Traveling Wilburys (Wilbury)
-	20	A SHOW OF HANDS	Rush (Vertigo)
10	21	PRIVATE COLLECTION (1979-1988)	Cliff Richard (EMI)
22	22	WANTED	Yazz (Big Life)
26	23	LOVE SUPREME	Supremes featuring Diana Ross (Motown)
29	24	THE GREATEST HITS OF HOUSE	Various Artists (Stylus)
14	25	PUSH	Bros (CBS)
23	26	GET EVEN	Brother Beyond (Parlophone)
25	27	THE BEST OF CHRIS REA - NEW LIGHT THROUGH OLD WINDOWS	Chris Rea (WEA)
44	28	SO GOOD	Mica Paris (Fourth & Broadway)
30	29	GREATEST HITS	Human League (Virgin)
24	30	RATTLE AND HUM	U2 (Island)
33	31	FISHERMAN'S BLUES	Waterboys (Ensign)
33	32	ANCIENT HEART	Tanita Tikaram (WEA)
41	33	NEW JERSEY	Bon Jovi (Vertigo)
28	34	HOLD ME IN YOUR ARMS	Rick Astley (RCA)
22	35	THE HITS ALBUM	Various Artists (CBS/WEA/BMG)
20	36	SOFT METAL	Various Artists (Stylus)
37	37	HEARSAY	Alexander O'Neal (Tabu)
32	38	FLYING COLOURS	Chris De Burgh (A&M)
45	39	RAINTOWN	Deacon Blue (CBS)
34	40	TRACY CHAPMAN	Tracy Chapman (Elektra)
39	41	DIRTY DANCING - SOUNDTRACK	Various Artists (RCA)
31	42	THE MEMPHIS SESSIONS	Wet Wet Wet (Precious Organisation)
-	43	ALL OR NOTHING	Milli Vanilli (Cooltempo)
36	44	TO WHOM IT MAY CONCERN	Pasadenas (CBS)
-	45	NEW YORK	Lou Reed (Sire)
47	46	THE GREATEST LOVE	Various Artists (Telstar)
40	47	DELICATE SOUND OF THUNDER	Pink Floyd (EMI)
-	48	REMOTE	Hue & Cry (Circa)
49	49	WHITNEY	Whitney Houston (Arista)
-	50	SEE THE LIGHT	Jeff Healey Band (Arista)

With her duet with Jason Donovan, *Especially For You*, topping the singles chart, Kylie Minogue picked up the record-token-for-Christmas market to return to the Number 1 slot at the beginning of the New Year, before being dethroned by Erasure's *The Innocents* - which had been in the chart for more than eight months before getting its biggest sales boost from the success of the duo's *Crackers International* EP.

February 1989

Roy Orbison's sudden death in December 1988, just as he was returning to prominence as a member of the all-star Traveling Wilburys, brought him a posthumous flurry of chart success reminiscent of that which had followed John Lennon's assassination exactly eight years earlier. While the hits compilation went to Number 1, the all-new *Mystery Girl*, the Big O's last recordings, crashed in at 2.

February – March 1989

25 February 1989

-	1	A NEW FLAME	Simply Red (Elektra)
10	2	ANYTHING FOR YOU	Gloria Estefan & the Miami Sound Machine (Epic)
1	3	THE RAW AND THE COOKED	Fine Young Cannibals (London)
2	4	MYSTERY GIRL	Roy Orbison (Virgin)
9	5	SPIKE	Elvis Costello (Warner Bros.)
16	6	WANTED	Yazz (Big Life)
7	7	ANCIENT HEART	Tanita Tikaram (WEA)
4	8	THE LEGENDARY ...	Roy Orbison (Telstar)
5	9	THE LIVING YEARS	Mike & the Mechanics (WEA)
6	10	THE MARQUEE 30 LEGENDARY YEARS	Various Artists (Polydor)
31	11	BUSTER - SOUNDTRACK	Various Artists (Virgin)
8	12	THE INNOCENTS	Erasure (Mute)
3	13	TECHNIQUE	New Order (Factory)
30	14	HOLD ME IN YOUR ARMS	Rick Astley (RCA)
11	15	COCKTAIL - SOUNDTRACK	Various Artists (Elektra)
13	16	WATERMARK	Enya (WEA)
28	17	BAD	Michael Jackson (Epic)
-	18	TRUE LOVE WAYS	Buddy Holly & the Crickets (Telstar)
12	19	ROACHFORD	Roachford (CBS)
42	20	HYSTERIA	Def Leppard (Bludgeon Riffola)
14	21	REMOTE	Hue & Cry (Circa)
19	22	KICK	INXS (Mercury)
29	23	FOUNDATION	Ten City (Atlantic)
18	24	KYLIE	Kylie Minogue (PWL)
22	25	MONEY FOR NOTHING	Dire Straits (Vertigo)
24	26	THE ULTIMATE COLLECTION	Bryan Ferry & Roxy Music (EG)
39	27	SHOOTING RUBBERBANDS AT THE STARS	Edie Brickell & New Bohemians (Geffen)
27	28	CLOSE	Kim Wilde (MCA)
20	29	GREATEST HITS	Fleetwood Mac (Warner Bros.)
38	30	THE BEST OF CHRIS REA - NEW LIGHT THROUGH OLD WINDOWS	Chris Rea (WEA)
-	31	THE FIRST OF A MILLION KISSES	Fairground Attraction (RCA)
23	32	THE PREMIERE COLLECTION: THE BEST OF ANDREW LLOYD WEBBER	Various Artists (Really Useful)
15	33	ELECTRIC YOUTH	Debbie Gibson (Atlantic)
26	34	THE GREATEST HITS	Bananarama (London)
-	35	TRACY CHAPMAN	Tracy Chapman (Elektra)
17	36	LOVE SUPREME	Supremes featuring Diana Ross (Motown)
37	37	HEARSAY	Alexander O'Neal (Tabu)
25	38	POP SAID	Darling Buds (CBS)
36	39	NEW YORK	Lou Reed (Sire)
50	40	PUSH	Bros (CBS)
44	41	GET EVEN	Brother Beyond (Parlophone)
21	42	THUNDER AND CONSOLATION	New Model Army (EMI)
33	43	DYLAN AND THE DEAD	Bob Dylan & the Grateful Dead (CBS)
43	44	PRIVATE COLLECTION (1979-1988)	Cliff Richard (EMI)
45	45	RAINTOWN	Deacon Blue (CBS)
-	46	STOP	Sam Brown (A&M)
40	47	FLYING COLOURS	Chris De Burgh (A&M)
-	48	THE BEST YEARS OF OUR LIVES	Neil Diamond (CBS)
41	49	THE GREATEST LOVE 2	Various Artists (Telstar)
-	50	GIVING YOU THE BEST THAT I GOT	Anita Baker (Elektra)

4 March 1989

1	1	A NEW FLAME	Simply Red (Elektra)
2	2	ANYTHING FOR YOU	Gloria Estefan & the Miami Sound Machine (Epic)
7	3	ANCIENT HEART	Tanita Tikaram (WEA)
3	4	THE RAW AND THE COOKED	Fine Young Cannibals (London)
-	5	THE BIG AREA	Then Jerico (London)
20	6	HYSTERIA	Def Leppard (Bludgeon Riffola)
4	7	MYSTERY GIRL	Roy Orbison (Virgin)
8	8	THE LEGENDARY ROY ORBISON	Roy Orbiso (Telstar)
17	9	BAD	Michael Jackson (Epic)
5	10	SPIKE	Elvis Costello (Warner Bros.)
9	11	THE LIVING YEARS	Mike & the Mechanics (WEA)
6	12	WANTED	Yazz (Big Life)
31	13	THE FIRST OF A MILLION KISSES	Fairground Attraction (RCA)
15	14	COCKTAIL - SOUNDTRACK	Various Artists (Elektra)
29	15	GREATEST HITS	Fleetwood Mac (Warner Bros.)
10	16	THE MARQUEE 30 LEGENDARY YEARS	Various Artists (Polydor)
16	17	THE INNOCENTS	Erasure (Mute)
16	18	WATERMARK	Enya (WEA)
11	19	BUSTER - SOUNDTRACK	Various Artists (Virgin)
24	20	KYLIE	Kylie Minogue (PWL)
30	21	THE BEST OF CHRIS REA - NEW LIGHT THROUGH OLD WINDOWS	Chris Rea (WEA)
18	22	TRUE LOVE WAYS	Buddy Holly & the Crickets (Telstar)
14	23	HOLD ME IN YOUR ARMS	Rick Astley (RCA)
22	24	KICK	INXS (Mercury)
35	25	TRACY CHAPMAN	Tracy Chapman (Elektra)
21	26	REMOTE	Hue & Cry (Circa)
13	27	TECHNIQUE	New Order (Factory)
25	28	MONEY FOR NOTHING	Dire Straits (Vertigo)
19	29	ROACHFORD	Roachford (CBS)
28	30	CLOSE	Kim Wilde (MCA)
26	31	THE ULTIMATE COLLECTION	Bryan Ferry & Roxy Music (EG)
46	32	STOP	Sam Brown (A&M)
23	33	FOUNDATION	Ten City (Atlantic)
32	34	THE PREMIERE COLLECTION: THE BEST OF ANDREW LLOYD WEBBER	Various Artists (Really Useful)
27	35	SHOOTING RUBBERBANDS AT THE STARS	Edie Brickell & New Bohemians (Geffen)
37	36	HEARSAY	Alexander O'Neal (Tabu)
41	37	GET EVEN	Brother Beyond (Parlophone)
38	38	SO GOOD	Mica Paris (Fourth & Broadway)
40	39	PUSH	Bros (CBS)
34	40	THE GREATEST HITS	Bananarama (London)
44	41	PRIVATE COLLECTION (1979-1988)	Cliff Richard (EMI)
-	42	DON'T BE CRUEL	Bobby Brown (MCA)
33	43	ELECTRIC YOUTH	Debbie Gibson (Atlantic)
-	44	THE LOVER IN ME	Sheena Easton (MCA)
-	45	THE AWARDS 1989	Various Artists (Telstar)
36	46	LOVE SUPREME	Supremes featuring Diana Ross (Motown)
-	47	CONSCIENCE	Womack & Womack (Fourth & Broadway)
-	48	TRAVELING WILBURYS VOL.1	Traveling Wilburys (Wilbury)
49	49	THE GREATEST LOVE 2	Various Artists (Telstar)
-	50	AND ALL BECAUSE THE LADY LOVES ...	Various Artists (Dover)

11 March 1989

1	1	A NEW FLAME	Simply Red (Elektra)
2	2	ANYTHING FOR YOU	Gloria Estefan & the Miami Sound Machine (Epic)
3	3	ANCIENT HEART	Tanita Tikaram (WEA)
10	4	SPIKE	Elvis Costello (Warner Bros.)
9	5	BAD	Michael Jackson (Epic)
4	6	THE RAW AND THE COOKED	Fine Young Cannibals (London)
6	7	HYSTERIA	Def Leppard (Bludgeon Riffola)
7	8	MYSTERY GIRL	Roy Orbison (Virgin)
5	9	THE BIG AREA	Then Jerico (London)
-	10	CHEEK TO CHEEK	Various Artists (CBS)
22	11	TRUE LOVE WAYS	Buddy Holly & the Crickets (Telstar)
12	12	WANTED	Yazz (Big Life)
-	13	DEEP HEAT	Various Artists (Telstar)
8	14	THE LEGENDARY ROY ORBISON	Roy Orbison (Telstar)
25	15	TRACY CHAPMAN	Tracy Chapman (Elektra)
11	16	THE LIVING YEARS	Mike & the Mechanics (WEA)
17	17	THE INNOCENTS	Erasure (Mute)
16	18	THE MARQUEE 30 LEGENDARY YEARS	Various Artists (Polydor)
26	19	REMOTE	Hue & Cry (Circa)
32	20	STOP	Sam Brown (A&M)
45	21	THE AWARDS 1989	Various Artists (Telstar)
50	22	AND ALL BECAUSE THE LADY LOVES ...	Various Artists (Dover)
15	23	GREATEST HITS	Fleetwood Mac (Warner Bros.)
18	24	WATERMARK	Enya (WEA)
47	25	CONSCIENCE	Womack & Womack (Fourth & Broadway)
19	26	BUSTER - SOUNDTRACK	Various Artists (Virgin)
13	27	THE FIRST OF A MILLION KISSES	Fairground Attraction (RCA)
35	28	SHOOTING RUBBERBANDS AT THE STARS	Edie Brickell & New Bohemians (Geffen)
44	29	THE LOVER IN ME	Sheena Easton (MCA)
-	30	ORANGES AND LEMONS	XTC (Virgin)
31	31	KYLIE	Kylie Minogue (PWL)
41	32	PRIVATE COLLECTION (1979-1988)	Cliff Richard (EMI)
14	33	COCKTAIL - SOUNDTRACK	Various Artists (Elektra)
21	34	THE BEST OF CHRIS REA - NEW LIGHT THROUGH OLD WINDOWS	Chris Rea (WEA)
24	35	KICK	INXS (Mercury)
-	36	FLYING COLOURS	Chris De Burgh (A&M)
-	37	NEW YORK	Lou Reed (Sire)
23	38	HOLD ME IN YOUR ARMS	Rick Astley (RCA)
42	39	DON'T BE CRUEL	Bobby Brown (MCA)
-	40	RAINTOWN	Deacon Blue (CBS)
30	41	CLOSE	Kim Wilde (MCA)
27	42	TECHNIQUE	New Order (Factory)
39	43	PUSH	Bros (CBS)
28	44	MONEY FOR NOTHING	Dire Straits (Vertigo)
36	45	HEARSAY	Alexander O'Neal (Tabu)
-	46	BEAT THIS - 20 HITS OF RHYTHM KING	Various Artists (Stylus)
38	47	SO GOOD	Mica Paris (Fourth & Broadway)
29	48	ROACHFORD	Roachford (CBS)
48	49	TRAVELING WILBURYS VOL.1	Traveling Wilburys (Wilbury)
-	50	INTROSPECTIVE	Pet Shop Boys (Parlophone)

Simly Red had made the Top 3 with both their previous albums, but *A New Flame* was the release which established the Mick Hucknall-led group as mega-record sellers. After an initial five weeks at Number 1, the album would never be far from the top of the chart for much of the year - and indeed would be 1989's top seller until it was overtaken in the closing days of December (about which more later).

last week	this week	18 March 1989	
1	1	A NEW FLAME	Simply Red (Elektra)
10	2	CHEEK TO CHEEK	Various Artists (CBS)
2	3	ANYTHING FOR YOU	Gloria Estefan & the Miami Sound Machine (Epic)
3	4	ANCIENT HEART	Tanita Tikaram (WEA)
20	5	STOP	Sam Brown (A&M)
-	6	THE SINGULAR ADVENTURES OF THE STYLE COUNCIL - GREATEST HITS VOLUME 1	Style Council (Polydor)
39	7	DON'T BE CRUEL	Bobby Brown (MCA)
4	8	SPIKE	Elvis Costello (Warner Bros.)
6	9	THE RAW AND THE COOKED	Fine Young Cannibals (London)
11	10	TRUE LOVE WAYS	Buddy Holly & the Crickets (Telstar)
13	11	DEEP HEAT	Various Artists (Telstar)
8	12	MYSTERY GIRL	Roy Orbison (Virgin)
22	13	AND ALL BECAUSE THE LADY LOVES ..	Various Artists (Dover)
12	14	WANTED	Yazz (Big Life)
7	15	HYSTERIA	Def Leppard (Bludgeon Riffola)
36	16	FLYING COLOURS	Chris De Burgh (A&M)
5	17	BAD	Michael Jackson (Epic)
32	18	PRIVATE COLLECTION (1979-1988)	Cliff Richard (EMI)
17	19	THE INNOCENTS	Erasure (Mute)
38	20	HOLD ME IN YOUR ARMS	Rick Astley (RCA)
14	21	THE LEGENDARY...	Roy Orbison (Telstar)
9	22	THE BIG AREA	Then Jerico (London)
-	23	OPEN UP AND SAY ... AAH!	Poison (Capitol)
16	24	THE LIVING YEARS	Mike & the Mechanics (WEA)
15	25	TRACY CHAPMAN	Tracy Chapman (Elektra)
23	26	GREATEST HITS	Fleetwood Mac (Warner Bros.)
-	27	JULIA FORDHAM	Julia Fordham (Circa)
19	28	REMOTE	Hue & Cry (Circa)
41	29	CLOSE	Kim Wilde (MCA)
-	30	UNFORGETTABLE 2	Various Artists (EMI)
25	31	CONSCIENCE	Womack & Womack (Fourth & Broadway)
-	32	THE PREMIERE COLLECTION: THE BEST OF ANDREW LLOYD WEBBER	Various Artists (Really Useful)
24	33	WATERMARK	Enya (WEA)
50	34	INTROSPECTIVE	Pet Shop Boys (Parlophone)
18	35	THE MARQUEE 30 LEGENDARY YEARS	Various Artists (Polydor)
-	36	RADIO ONE	Jimi Hendrix Experience (Castle Collectors Series)
34	37	THE BEST OF CHRIS REA - NEW LIGHT THROUGH OLD WINDOWS	Chris Rea (WEA)
49	38	TRAVELING WILBURYS VOL.1	Traveling Wilburys (Wilbury)
31	39	KYLIE	Kylie Minogue (PWL)
21	40	THE AWARDS 1989	Various Artists (Telstar)
-	41	FOUNDATION	Ten City (Atlantic)
26	42	BUSTER - SOUNDTRACK	Various Artists (Virgin)
40	43	RAINTOWN	Deacon Blue (CBS)
-	44	SCANDAL - SOUNDTRACK	Various Artists (Parlophone)
30	45	ORANGES AND LEMONS	XTC (Virgin)
42	46	TECHNIQUE	New Order (Factory)
48	47	ROACHFORD	Roachford (CBS)
44	48	MONEY FOR NOTHING	Dire Straits (Vertigo)
27	49	THE FIRST OF A MILLION KISSES	Fairground Attraction (RCA)
35	50	KICK	INXS (Mercury)

		25 March 1989	
1	1	A NEW FLAME	Simply Red (Elektra)
3	2	ANYTHING FOR YOU	Gloria Estefan & the Miami Sound Machine (Epic)
-	3	101	Depeche Mode (Mute)
11	4	DEEP HEAT	Various Artists (Telstar)
4	5	ANCIENT HEART	Tanita Tikaram (WEA)
2	6	CHEEK TO CHEEK	Various Artists (CBS)
5	7	STOP	Sam Brown (A&M)
30	8	UNFORGETTABLE 2	Various Artists (EMI)
-	9	SOUTHSIDE	Texas (Mercury)
6	10	THE SINGULAR ADVENTURES OF THE STYLE COUNCIL	Style Council (Polydor)
7	11	DON'T BE CRUEL	Bobby Brown (MCA)
8	12	SPIKE	Elvis Costello (Warner Bros.)
-	13	THE GREATEST HITS	Bananarama (London)
10	14	TRUE LOVE WAYS	Buddy Holly & the Crickets (Telstar)
17	15	BAD	Michael Jackson (Epic)
9	16	THE RAW AND THE COOKED	Fine Young Cannibals (London)
14	17	WANTED	Yazz (Big Life)
12	18	MYSTERY GIRL	Roy Orbison (Virgin)
27	19	JULIA FORDHAM	Julia Fordham (Circa)
46	20	TECHNIQUE	New Order (Factory)
39	21	KYLIE	Kylie Minogue (PWL)
15	22	HYSTERIA	Def Leppard (Bludgeon Riffola)
19	23	THE INNOCENTS	Erasure (Mute)
23	24	OPEN UP AND SAY ... AAH!	Poison (Capitol)
21	25	THE LEGENDARY...	Roy Orbison (Telstar)
-	26	A GRAVEYARD OF EMPTY BOTTLES	Dogs D'Amour (China)
26	27	GREATEST HITS	Fleetwood Mac (Warner Bros.)
22	28	THE BIG AREA	Then Jerico (London)
13	29	AND ALL BECAUSE THE LADY LOVES ...	Various Artists (Dover)
28	30	REMOTE	Hue & Cry (Circa)
43	31	RAINTOWN	Deacon Blue (CBS)
38	32	TRAVELING WILBURYS VOL.1	Traveling Wilburys (Wilbury)
25	33	TRACY CHAPMAN	Tracy Chapman (Elektra)
33	34	WATERMARK	Enya (WEA)
49	35	THE FIRST OF A MILLION KISSES	Fairground Attraction (RCA)
16	36	FLYING COLOURS	Chris De Burgh (A&M)
24	37	THE LIVING YEARS	Mike & the Mechanics (WEA)
-	38	ANOTHER PLACE AND TIME	Donna Summer (Warner Bros.)
31	39	CONSCIENCE	Womack & Womack (Fourth & Broadway)
18	40	PRIVATE COLLECTION (1979-1988)	Cliff Richard (EMI)
-	41	HIP HOUSE - 20 HIP HOUSE HITS	Various Artists (Stylus)
29	42	CLOSE	Kim Wilde (MCA)
20	43	HOLD ME IN YOUR ARMS	Rick Astley (RCA)
47	44	ROACHFORD	Roachford (CBS)
34	45	INTROSPECTIVE	Pet Shop Boys (Parlophone)
-	46	THE LOVER IN ME	Sheena Easton (MCA)
48	47	MONEY FOR NOTHING	Dire Straits (Vertigo)
37	48	THE BEST OF CHRIS REA - NEW LIGHT THROUGH OLD WINDOWS	Chris Rea (WEA)
35	49	THE MARQUEE 30 LEGENDARY YEARS	Various Artists (Polydor)
-	50	BEAT THIS - 20 HITS OF RHYTHM KING	Various Artists (Stylus)

		1 April 1989	
-	1	LIKE A PRAYER	Madonna (Sire)
2	2	ANYTHING FOR YOU	Gloria Estefan & the Miami Sound Machine (Epic)
-	3	NOW THAT'S WHAT I CALL MUSIC 14	Various Artists (EMI/Virgin/PolyGram)
1	4	A NEW FLAME	Simply Red (Elektra)
9	5	SOUTHSIDE	Texas (Mercury)
8	6	UNFORGETTABLE 2	Various Artists (EMI)
4	7	DEEP HEAT	Various Artists (Telstar)
3	8	101	Depeche Mode (Mute)
7	9	STOP	Sam Brown (A&M)
-	10	ORIGINAL SOUNDTRACK	S'Express (Rhythm King)
5	11	ANCIENT HEART	Tanita Tikaram (WEA)
18	12	MYSTERY GIRL	Roy Orbison (Virgin)
11	13	DON'T BE CRUEL	Bobby Brown (MCA)
6	14	CHEEK TO CHEEK	Various Artists (CBS)
10	15	THE SINGULAR ADVENTURES OF THE STYLE COUNCIL - GREATEST HITS VOLUME 1	Style Council (Polydor)
38	16	ANOTHER PLACE AND TIME	Donna Summer (Warner Bros.)
13	17	THE GREATEST HITS	Bananarama (London)
14	18	TRUE LOVE WAYS	Buddy Holly & the Crickets (Telstar)
41	19	HIP HOUSE - 20 HIP HOUSE HITS	Various Artists (Stylus)
-	20	APPETITE FOR DESTRUCTION	Guns N' Roses (Geffen)
15	21	BAD	Michael Jackson (Epic)
12	22	SPIKE	Elvis Costello (Warner Bros.)
22	23	HYSTERIA	Def Leppard (Bludgeon Riffola)
24	24	KYLIE	Kylie Minogue (PWL)
16	25	THE RAW AND THE COOKED	Fine Young Cannibals (London)
31	26	RAINTOWN	Deacon Blue (CBS)
44	27	ROACHFORD	Roachford (CBS)
23	28	THE INNOCENTS	Erasure (Mute)
25	29	THE LEGENDARY ROY ORBISON	Roy Orbison (Telstar)
17	30	WANTED	Yazz (Big Life)
20	31	TECHNIQUE	New Order (Factory)
-	32	HIP HOUSE	Various Artists (K-Tel)
28	33	THE BIG AREA	Then Jerico (London)
19	34	JULIA FORDHAM	Julia Fordham (Circa)
32	35	TRAVELING WILBURYS VOL.1	Traveling Wilburys (Wilbury)
42	36	CLOSE	Kim Wilde (MCA)
33	37	TRACY CHAPMAN	Tracy Chapman (Elektra)
-	38	3 FEET HIGH AND RISING	De La Soul (Big Life)
27	39	GREATEST HITS	Fleetwood Mac (Warner Bros.)
34	40	WATERMARK	Enya (WEA)
-	41	RAW	Alyson Williams (Def Jam)
-	42	KICK	INXS (Mercury)
-	43	RATTLE AND HUM	U2 (Island)
35	44	THE FIRST OF A MILLION KISSES	Fairground Attraction (RCA)
39	45	CONSCIENCE	Womack & Womack (Fourth & Broadway)
29	46	AND ALL BECAUSE THE LADY LOVES ...	Various Artists (Dover)
24	47	OPEN UP AND SAY ... AAH!	Poison (Capitol)
46	48	THE LOVER IN ME	Sheena Easton (MCA)
30	49	REMOTE	Hue & Cry (Circa)
26	50	A GRAVEYARD OF EMPTY BOTTLES	Dogs D'Amour (China)

The times were proving fruitful for female recording artists, with Gloria Estefan, Sam Brown and Tanita Tikaram (the latter two with their debut albums) all riding the Top 5 (simultaneously, on March 18), and the likes of Yazz, Julia Fordham and a revitalised (by Stock/Aitken/Waterman) Donna Summer selling extremely well. Madonna's immediate Number 1 with *Like A Prayer* was just the icing on the distaff cake.

April 1989

Guns N' Roses, still not the worldwide superstars they would become during the 1990s, made the Top 10 for the first time with their *Appetite For Destruction*, while another Top 10 debutant was Bobby Bown, whose *Don't Be Cruel* was his first solo album sucess, but who had originally been a member of the best selling black vocal group First Edition in the early 1980s, reaching No. 1 with the single *Candy Girl*.

338

April – May 1989

29 April 1989

last	this		
2	1	A NEW FLAME	Simply Red (Elektra)
1	2	WHEN THE WORLD KNOWS YOUR NAME	
			Deacon Blue (CBS)
6	3	CLUB CLASSICS VOL.1	Soul II Soul (10)
3	4	LIKE A PRAYER	Madonna (Sire)
7	5	ANYTHING FOR YOU	Gloria Estefan
			& the Miami Sound Machine (Epic)
4	6	NOW THAT'S WHAT I CALL MUSIC 14	
			Various Artists (EMI/Virgin/PolyGram)
5	7	SONIC TEMPLE	Cult (Beggars Banquet)
8	8	THE RAW AND THE COOKED	
			Fine Young Cannibals (London)
9	9	APPETITE FOR DESTRUCTION	
			Guns N' Roses (Geffen)
14	10	EVERYTHING	Bangles (CBS)
10	11	FOREVER YOUR GIRL	Paula Abdul (Siren)
48	12	HEY HEY IT'S THE MONKEES - GREATEST HITS	
		Monkees (K-Tel)	
11	13	DON'T BE CRUEL	Bobby Brown (MCA)
24	14	KICK	INXS (Mercury)
15	15	SOUTHSIDE	Texas (Mercury)
22	16	GIPSY KINGS	Gipsy Kings (Telstar)
13	17	MYSTERY GIRL	Roy Orbison (Virgin)
31	18	POP ART	Transvision Vamp (MCA)
-	19	HEADLESS CROSS	Black Sabbath (IRS)
50	20	GOOD DEEDS AND DIRTY RAGS	
			Goodbye Mr. Mackenzie (Capitol)
21	21	3 FEET HIGH AND RISING	De La Soul (Big Life)
12	22	THE SINGULAR ADVENTURES OF THE STYLE	
		COUNCIL	Style Council (Polydor)
17	23	CHEEK TO CHEEK	Various Artists (CBS)
16	24	ORIGINAL SOUNDTRACK S'Express (Rhythm King)	
-	25	WHAT'S THAT NOISE? Coldcut (Ahead Of Our Time)	
26	26	KYLIE	Kylie Minogue (PWL)
27	27	1984-1989 Lloyd Cole and the Commotions (Polydor)	
-	28	UKRAINSKI VISTUPI V JOHNA PEELA	
			Wedding Present (RCA)
18	29	ANCIENT HEART	Tanita Tikaram (WEA)
-	30	DEEP HEAT - THE SECOND BURN	
			Various Artists (Telstar)
23	31	BAD	Michael Jackson (Epic)
40	32	RATTLE AND HUM	U2 (Island)
29	33	ANOTHER PLACE AND TIME	
			Donna Summer (Warner Bros.)
25	34	HYSTERIA	Def Leppard (Bludgeon Riffola)
26	35	STOP	Sam Brown (A&M)
20	36	UNFORGETTABLE 2	Various Artists (EMI)
-	37	ONE	Bee Gees (Warner Bros.)
-	38	BLAZE OF GLORY	Joe Jackson (A&M)
32	39	ROACHFORD	Roachford (CBS)
-	40	DOOLITTLE	Pixies (4AD)
19	41	THE HEADLESS CHILDREN	W.A.S.P. (Capitol)
42	42	DIRTY DANCING - SOUNDTRACK	
			Various Artists (RCA)
39	43	SPIKE	Elvis Costello (Warner Bros.)
47	44	THE BIG AREA	Then Jerico (London)
35	45	THE INNOCENTS	Erasure (Mute)
34	46	TRAVELING WILBURYS VOL.1	
			Traveling Wilburys (Wilbury)
33	47	THE GREATEST HITS COLLECTION	
			Bananarama (London)
38	48	DEEP HEAT	Various Artists (Telstar)
30	49	TECHNIQUE	New Order (Factory)
46	50	THE LEGENDARY...	Roy Orbison (Telstar)

6 May 1989

last	this		
-	1	BLAST	Holly Johnson (MCA)
1	2	A NEW FLAME	Simply Red (Elektra)
5	3	ANYTHING FOR YOU	Gloria Estefan
			& the Miami Sound Machine (Epic)
2	4	WHEN THE WORLD KNOWS YOUR NAME	
			Deacon Blue (CBS)
8	5	THE RAW AND THE COOKED	
			Fine Young Cannibals (London)
4	6	LIKE A PRAYER	Madonna (Sire)
3	7	CLUB CLASSICS VOL.1	Soul II Soul (10)
14	8	KICK	INXS (Mercury)
10	9	EVERYTHING	Bangles (CBS)
40	10	DOOLITTLE	Pixies (4AD)
6	11	NOW THAT'S WHAT I CALL MUSIC 14	
			Various Artists (EMI/Virgin/PolyGram)
9	12	APPETITE FOR DESTRUCTION	
			Guns N' Roses (Geffen)
18	13	POP ART	Transvision Vamp (MCA)
12	14	HEY HEY IT'S THE MONKEES - GREATEST HITS	
		Monkees (K-Tel)	
30	15	DEEP HEAT - THE SECOND BURN	
			Various Artists (Telstar)
13	16	DON'T BE CRUEL	Bobby Brown (MCA)
15	17	SOUTHSIDE	Texas (Mercury)
11	18	FOREVER YOUR GIRL	Paula Abdul (Siren)
17	19	MYSTERY GIRL	Roy Orbison (Virgin)
7	20	SONIC TEMPLE	Cult (Beggars Banquet)
16	21	GIPSY KINGS	Gipsy Kings (Telstar)
25	22	WHAT'S THAT NOISE? Coldcut (Ahead Of Our Time)	
22	23	THE SINGULAR ADVENTURES OF THE STYLE	
		COUNCIL	Style Council (Polydor)
-	24	BORN THIS WAY!	Cookie Crew (London)
26	25	KYLIE	Kylie Minogue (PWL)
23	26	CHEEK TO CHEEK	Various Artists (CBS)
37	27	ONE	Bee Gees (Warner Bros.)
28	28	ANCIENT HEART	Tanita Tikaram (WEA)
27	29	1984-1989 Lloyd Cole and the Commotions (Polydor)	
-	30	PASTPRESENT	Clannad (RCA)
45	31	THE INNOCENTS	Erasure (Mute)
32	32	RATTLE AND HUM	U2 (Island)
21	33	3 FEET HIGH AND RISING	De La Soul (Big Life)
31	34	BAD	Michael Jackson (Epic)
28	35	UKRAINSKI VISTUPI V JOHNA PEELA	
			Wedding Present (RCA)
19	36	HEADLESS CROSS	Black Sabbath (IRS)
42	37	DIRTY DANCING - SOUNDTRACK	
			Various Artists (RCA)
24	38	ORIGINAL SOUNDTRACK S'Express (Rhythm King)	
34	39	HYSTERIA	Def Leppard (Bludgeon Riffola)
-	40	OPEN UP AND SAY ... AAH!	Poison (Capitol)
35	41	STOP	Sam Brown (A&M)
38	42	BLAZE OF GLORY	Joe Jackson (A&M)
46	43	TRAVELING WILBURYS VOL.1	
			Traveling Wilburys (Wilbury)
39	44	ROACHFORD	Roachford (CBS)
20	45	GOOD DEEDS AND DIRTY RAGS	
			Goodbye Mr. Mackenzie (Capitol)
47	46	THE GREATEST HITS	Bananarama (London)
33	47	ANOTHER PLACE AND TIME	
			Donna Summer (Warner Bros.)
-	48	GET EVEN	Brother Beyond (Parlophone)
-	49	DIESEL AND DUST	Midnight Oil (CBS)
-	50	THE SINGER AND THE SONG	•
			Various Artists (Stylus)

13 May 1989

last	this		
-	1	STREET FIGHTING YEARS Simple Minds (Virgin)	
-	2	TEN GOOD REASONS	Jason Donovan (PWL)
-	3	DISINTEGRATION	Cure (Fiction)
4	4	A NEW FLAME	Simply Red (Elektra)
1	5	BLAST	Holly Johnson (MCA)
3	6	ANYTHING FOR YOU	Gloria Estefan
			& the Miami Sound Machine (Epic)
5	7	THE RAW AND THE COOKED	
			Fine Young Cannibals (London)
9	8	EVERYTHING	Bangles (CBS)
6	9	LIKE A PRAYER	Madonna (Sire)
4	10	WHEN THE WORLD KNOWS YOUR NAME	
			Deacon Blue (CBS)
7	11	CLUB CLASSICS VOL.1	Soul II Soul (10)
15	12	DEEP HEAT - THE SECOND BURN	
			Various Artists (Telstar)
30	13	PASTPRESENT	Clannad (RCA)
8	14	KICK	INXS (Mercury)
13	15	POP ART	Transvision Vamp (MCA)
16	16	DON'T BE CRUEL	Bobby Brown (MCA)
12	17	APPETITE FOR DESTRUCTION	
			Guns N' Roses (Geffen)
11	18	NOW THAT'S WHAT I CALL MUSIC 14	
			Various Artists (EMI/Virgin/PolyGram)
25	19	KYLIE	Kylie Minogue (PWL)
18	20	FOREVER YOUR GIRL	Paula Abdul (Siren)
14	21	HEY HEY IT'S THE MONKEES - GREATEST HITS	
		Monkees (K-Tel)	
19	22	MYSTERY GIRL	Roy Orbison (Virgin)
-	23	WANTED	Yazz (Big Life)
17	24	SOUTHSIDE	Texas (Mercury)
21	25	GIPSY KINGS	Gipsy Kings (Telstar)
-	26	THIS IS THE DAY, THIS IS THE HOUR	
			Pop Will Eat Itself (RCA)
23	27	THE SINGULAR ADVENTURES OF THE STYLE	
		COUNCIL	Style Council (Polydor)
34	28	BAD	Michael Jackson (Epic)
10	29	DOOLITTLE	Pixies (4AD)
-	30	IN YOUR FACE	Kingdom Come (Polydor)
20	31	SONIC TEMPLE	Cult (Beggars Banquet)
28	32	ANCIENT HEART	Tanita Tikaram (WEA)
24	33	BORN THIS WAY!	Cookie Crew (London)
40	34	OPEN UP AND SAY ... AAH!	Poison (Capitol)
49	35	DIESEL AND DUST	Midnight Oil (CBS)
22	36	WHAT'S THAT NOISE?	
			Coldcut (Ahead Of Our Time)
43	37	TRAVELING WILBURYS (Wilbury)	
-	38	MONEY FOR NOTHING	Dire Straits (Vertigo)
-	39	SILVERTOWN	
			Men They Couldn't Hang (Silvertone)
37	40	DIRTY DANCING - SOUNDTRACK	
			Various Artists (RCA)
31	41	THE INNOCENTS	Erasure (Mute)
50	42	THE SINGER AND THE SONG	
			Various Artists (Stylus)
-	43	BLUE MURDER	Blue Murder (Geffen)
26	44	CHEEK TO CHEEK	Various Artists (CBS)
32	45	RATTLE AND HUM	U2 (Island)
27	46	ONE	Bee Gees (Warner Bros.)
41	47	STOP	Sam Brown (A&M)
33	48	3 FEET HIGH AND RISING De La Soul (Big Life)	
-	49	GREATEST HITS Fleetwood Mac (Warner Bros.)	
-	50	REMOTE	Hue & Cry (Circa)

Holly Johnson, former lead singer with Frankie Goes To Hollywood, got off to the best possible start with his debut solo album *Blast*, entering the chart at Number 1. He was, however, quickly eclipsed after one week by the rare instance of three new titles debuting simultaneously in the chart's top three places - by Simple Minds, newcomer (and growing teen idol) Jason Donovan, and the Cure.

May – June 1989

last week	this week	20 May 1989	
2	1	TEN GOOD REASONS	Jason Donovan (PWL)
1	2	STREET FIGHTING YEARS	Simple Minds (Virgin)
3	3	DISINTEGRATION	Cure (Fiction)
7	4	THE RAW AND THE COOKED	
			Fine Young Cannibals (London)
-	5	PARADISE	Inner City (10)
-	6	NITE FLITE 2	Various Artists (CBS)
5	7	BLAST	Holly Johnson (MCA)
4	8	A NEW FLAME	Simply Red (Elektra)
6	9	ANYTHING FOR YOU	Gloria Estefan
			& the Miami Sound Machine (Epic)
8	10	EVERYTHING	Bangles (CBS)
11	11	CLUB CLASSICS VOL.1	Soul II Soul (10)
10	12	WHEN THE WORLD KNOWS YOUR NAME	
			Deacon Blue (CBS)
9	13	LIKE A PRAYER	Madonna (Sire)
13	14	PASTPRESENT	Clannad (RCA)
16	15	DON'T BE CRUEL	Bobby Brown (MCA)
-	16	GOOD TO BE BACK	Natalie Cole (EMI Manhattan)
14	17	KICK	INXS (Mercury)
35	18	DIESEL AND DUST	Midnight Oil (CBS)
-	19	KALEIDOSCOPE WORLD	
			Swing Out Sister (Fontana)
19	20	KYLIE	Kylie Minogue (PWL)
15	21	POP ART	Transvision Vamp (MCA)
17	22	APPETITE FOR DESTRUCTION	
			Guns N' Roses (Geffen)
20	23	FOREVER YOUR GIRL	Paula Abdul (Siren)
23	24	WANTED	Yazz (Big Life)
12	25	DEEP HEAT - THE SECOND BURN	
			Various Artists (Telstar)
18	26	NOW THAT'S WHAT I CALL MUSIC 14	
			Various Artists (EMI/Virgin/PolyGram)
21	27	HEY HEY IT'S THE MONKEES - GREATEST HITS	
50	28	REMOTE	Hue & Cry (Circa)
-	29	THE STONE ROSES	Stone Roses (Silvertone)
24	30	SOUTHSIDE	Texas (Mercury)
31	31	SONIC TEMPLE	Cult (Beggars Banquet)
-	32	SONGS TO MAKE THE WHOLE WORLD SING	
			Barry Manilow (Arista)
25	33	GIPSY KINGS	Gipsy Kings (Telstar)
26	34	THIS IS THE DAY, THIS IS THE HOUR	
			Pop Will Eat Itself (RCA)
28	35	BAD	Michael Jackson (Epic)
-	36	IN SEARCH OF SANITY	Onslaught (London)
27	37	THE SINGULAR ADVENTURES OF THE STYLE	
		COUNCIL - GREATEST HITS VOLUME 1	
			Style Council (Polydor)
-	38	STEPPIN' TO THE SHADOWS	Shadows (Polydor)
22	39	MYSTERY GIRL	Roy Orbison (Virgin)
-	40	ROACHFORD	Roachford (CBS)
30	41	IN YOUR FACE	Kingdom Come (Polydor)
34	42	OPEN UP AND SAY ... AAH!	Poison (Capitol)
49	43	GREATEST HITS Fleetwood Mac (Warner Bros.)	
-	44	AT THIS MOMENT	Various Artists (Jive)
47	45	STOP	Sam Brown (A&M)
40	46	DIRTY DANCING - SOUNDTRACK	
			Various Artists (RCA)
41	47	THE INNOCENTS	Erasure (Mute)
42	48	THE SINGER AND THE SONG	
			Various Artists (Stylus)
45	49	RATTLE AND HUM	U2 (Island)
32	50	ANCIENT HEART	Tanita Tikaram (WEA)

last week	this week	27 May 1989	
1	1	TEN GOOD REASONS	Jason Donovan (PWL)
2	2	STREET FIGHTING YEARS	
			Simple Minds (Virgin)
6	3	NITE FLITE 2	Various Artists (CBS)
-	4	MIND BOMB	The The (Epic)
5	5	PARADISE	Inner City (10)
4	6	THE RAW AND THE COOKED	
			Fine Young Cannibals (London)
12	7	WHEN THE WORLD KNOWS YOUR NAME	
			Deacon Blue (CBS)
8	8	A NEW FLAME	Simply Red (Elektra)
14	9	PASTPRESENT	Clannad (RCA)
16	10	GOOD TO BE BACK	
			Natalie Cole (EMI Manhattan)
19	11	KALEIDOSCOPE WORLD	
			Swing Out Sister (Fontana)
7	12	BLAST	Holly Johnson (MCA)
38	13	STEPPIN' TO THE SHADOWS	Shadows (Polydor)
9	14	ANYTHING FOR YOU	Gloria Estefan
			& the Miami Sound Machine (Epic)
11	15	CLUB CLASSICS VOL.1	Soul II Soul (10)
-	16	BLIND MAN'S ZOO	10,000 Maniacs (Elektra)
3	17	DISINTEGRATION	Cure (Fiction)
15	18	DON'T BE CRUEL	Bobby Brown (MCA)
13	19	LIKE A PRAYER	Madonna (Sire)
32	20	SONGS TO MAKE THE WHOLE WORLD SING	
			Barry Manilow (Arista)
10	21	EVERYTHING	Bangles (CBS)
28	22	REMOTE	Hue & Cry (Circa)
17	23	KICK	INXS (Mercury)
21	24	POP ART	Transvision Vamp (MCA)
18	25	DIESEL AND DUST	Midnight Oil (CBS)
-	26	BIG DADDY John Cougar Mellencamp (Mercury)	
20	27	KYLIE	Kylie Minogue (PWL)
23	28	FOREVER YOUR GIRL	Paula Abdul (Siren)
22	29	APPETITE FOR DESTRUCTION	
			Guns N' Roses (Geffen)
-	30	LARGER THAN LIFE	Jody Watley (MCA)
24	31	WANTED	Yazz (Big Life)
26	32	NOW THAT'S WHAT I CALL MUSIC 14	
			Various Artists (EMI/Virgin/PolyGram)
33	33	GIPSY KINGS	Gipsy Kings (Telstar)
42	34	OPEN UP AND SAY ... AAH!	Poison (Capitol)
-	35	WORKIN' OVERTIME	Diana Ross (EMI)
35	36	BAD	Michael Jackson (Epic)
30	37	SOUTHSIDE	Texas (Mercury)
27	38	HEY HEY IT'S THE MONKEES - GREATEST HITS	
			Monkees (K-Tel)
-	39	COMING ALIVE AGAIN Barbara Dickson (Telstar)	
25	40	DEEP HEAT - THE SECOND BURN	
			Various Artists (Telstar)
45	41	STOP	Sam Brown (A&M)
-	42	PRECIOUS METAL	Various Artists (Stylus)
44	43	AT THIS MOMENT	Various Artists (Jive)
37	44	THE SINGULAR ADVENTURES OF THE STYLE	
		COUNCIL - GREATEST HITS VOLUME 1	
			Style Council (Polydor)
-	45	WATERMARK	Enya (WEA)
-	46	HYSTERIA	Def Leppard (Bludgeon Riffola)
39	47	MYSTERY GIRL	Roy Orbison (Virgin)
31	48	SONIC TEMPLE	Cult (Beggars Banquet)
-	49	CHART SHOW ROCK THE NATION VOL.II	
			Various Artists (Dover)
47	50	THE INNOCENTS	Erasure (Mute)

last week	this week	3 June 1989	
-	1	THE MIRACLE	Queen (Parlophone)
-	2	TEN GOOD REASONS	Jason Donovan (PWL)
-	3	TIN MACHINE	Tin Machine (EMI USA)
2	4	STREET FIGHTING YEARS	Simple Minds (Virgin)
3	5	NITE FLITE 2	Various Artists (CBS)
9	6	PASTPRESENT	Clannad (RCA)
-	7	THE HITS ALBUM 10	
			Various Artists (CBS/WEA/BMG)
18	8	DON'T BE CRUEL	Bobby Brown (MCA)
5	9	PARADISE	Inner City (10)
7	10	WHEN THE WORLD KNOWS YOUR NAME	
			Deacon Blue (CBS)
4	11	MIND BOMB	The The (Epic)
15	12	CLUB CLASSICS VOL.1	Soul II Soul (10)
6	13	THE RAW AND THE COOKED	
			Fine Young Cannibals (London)
8	14	A NEW FLAME	Simply Red (Elektra)
29	15	APPETITE FOR DESTRUCTION	
			Guns N' Roses (Geffen)
22	16	REMOTE	Hue & Cry (Circa)
12	17	BLAST	Holly Johnson (MCA)
14	18	ANYTHING FOR YOU	Gloria Estefan
			& the Miami Sound Machine (Epic)
10	19	GOOD TO BE BACK	Natalie Cole (EMI Manhattan)
16	20	BLIND MAN'S ZOO	10,000 Maniacs (Elektra)
13	21	STEPPIN' TO THE SHADOWS	Shadows (Polydor)
42	22	PRECIOUS METAL	Various Artists (Stylus)
19	23	LIKE A PRAYER	Madonna (Sire)
11	24	KALEIDOSCOPE WORLD	
			Swing Out Sister (Fontana)
21	25	EVERYTHING	Bangles (CBS)
-	26	LIFE IS A DANCE (THE REMIX PROJECT)	
			Chaka Khan (Warner Bros.)
35	27	WORKIN' OVERTIME	Diana Ross (EMI)
17	28	DISINTEGRATION	Cure (Fiction)
23	29	KICK	INXS (Mercury)
27	30	KYLIE	Kylie Minogue (PWL)
28	31	FOREVER YOUR GIRL	Paula Abdul (Siren)
41	32	STOP	Sam Brown (A&M)
24	33	POP ART	Transvision Vamp (MCA)
26	34	BIG DADDY John Cougar Mellencamp (Mercury)	
33	35	GIPSY KINGS	Gipsy Kings (Telstar)
36	36	BAD	Michael Jackson (Epic)
20	37	SONGS TO MAKE THE WHOLE WORLD SING	
			Barry Manilow (Arista)
32	38	NOW THAT'S WHAT I CALL MUSIC 14	
			Various Artists (EMI/Virgin/PolyGram)
25	39	DIESEL AND DUST	Midnight Oil (CBS)
-	40	ELECTRIC YOUTH	Debbie Gibson (Atlantic)
37	41	SOUTHSIDE	Texas (Mercury)
31	42	WANTED	Yazz (Big Life)
45	43	WATERMARK	Enya (WEA)
44	44	LOC'ED AFTER DARK	Tone Loc (Delicious)
30	45	LARGER THAN LIFE	Jody Watley (MCA)
-	46	ANOTHER PLACE AND TIME	
			Donna Summer (Warner Bros.)
34	47	OPEN UP AND SAY ... AAH!	Poison (Capitol)
44	48	THE SINGULAR ADVENTURES OF THE STYLE	
		COUNCIL - GREATEST HITS VOLUME 1	
			Style Council (Polydor)
40	49	DEEP HEAT - THE SECOND BURN	
			Various Artists (Telstar)
38	50	HEY HEY IT'S THE MONKEES - GREATEST HITS	
			Monkees (K-Tel)

Jason Donovan's *Ten Good Reasons* (which actually had eleven tracks - a source of puzzlement to many until it was ascertained that the title was actually a phrase from one of the songs, *Too Many Broken Hearts*) turned the chart tables on Simple Minds' *Street Fighting Years* in their second week of sales, and after two weeks at Number 1 would settle in near the chart top for most of the rest of 1989.

June 1989

10 June 1989

last week	this week	Title	Artist (Label)
1	1	THE MIRACLE	Queen (Parlophone)
7	2	THE HITS ALBUM 10	Various Artists (CBS/WEA/BMG)
2	3	TEN GOOD REASONS	Jason Donovan (PWL)
3	4	TIN MACHINE	Tin Machine (EMI USA)
-	5	THE OTHER SIDE OF THE MIRROR	Stevie Nicks (EMI)
8	6	DON'T BE CRUEL	Bobby Brown (MCA)
4	7	STREET FIGHTING YEARS	Simple Minds (Virgin)
5	8	NITE FLITE 2	Various Artists (CBS)
12	9	CLUB CLASSICS VOL.1	Soul II Soul (10)
6	10	PASTPRESENT	Clannad (RCA)
19	11	GOOD TO BE BACK	Natalie Cole (EMI Manhattan)
10	12	WHEN THE WORLD KNOWS YOUR NAME	Deacon Blue (CBS)
9	13	PARADISE	Inner City (10)
26	14	LIFE IS A DANCE (THE REMIX PROJECT)	Chaka Khan (Warner Bros.)
15	15	APPETITE FOR DESTRUCTION	Guns N' Roses (Geffen)
13	16	THE RAW AND THE COOKED	Fine Young Cannibals (London)
11	17	MIND BOMB	The The (Epic)
14	18	A NEW FLAME	Simply Red (Elektra)
21	19	STEPPIN' TO THE SHADOWS	Shadows (Polydor)
18	20	ANYTHING FOR YOU	Gloria Estefan & the Miami Sound Machine (Epic)
-	21	AVALON SUNSET	Van Morrison (Polydor)
23	22	LIKE A PRAYER	Madonna (Sire)
30	23	KYLIE	Kylie Minogue (PWL)
22	24	PRECIOUS METAL	Various Artists (Stylus)
17	25	BLAST	Holly Johnson (MCA)
16	26	REMOTE	Hue & Cry (Circa)
-	27	THE CHART SHOW DANCE MASTERS	Various Artists (Dover)
31	28	FOREVER YOUR GIRL	Paula Abdul (Siren)
27	29	WORKIN' OVERTIME	Diana Ross (EMI)
20	30	BLIND MAN'S ZOO	10,000 Maniacs (Elektra)
44	31	LOC'ED AFTER DARK	Tone Loc (Delicious)
24	32	KALEIDOSCOPE WORLD	Swing Out Sister (Fontana)
32	33	STOP	Sam Brown (A&M)
25	34	EVERYTHING	Bangles (CBS)
28	35	DISINTEGRATION	Cure (Fiction)
49	36	DEEP HEAT - THE SECOND BURN	Various Artists (Telstar)
29	37	KICK	INXS (Mercury)
47	38	OPEN UP AND SAY ... AAH!	Poison (Capitol)
46	39	ANOTHER PLACE AND TIME	Donna Summer (Warner Bros.)
-	40	9	Public Image Ltd. (Virgin)
36	41	BAD	Michael Jackson (Epic)
33	42	POP ART	Transvision Vamp (MCA)
34	43	BIG DADDY	John Cougar Mellencamp (Mercury)
35	44	GIPSY KINGS	Gipsy Kings (Telstar)
-	45	THROUGH THE STORM	Aretha Franklin (Arista)
38	46	NOW THAT'S WHAT I CALL MUSIC 14	Various Artists (EMI/Virgin/PolyGram)
-	47	DIRTY DANCING - SOUNDTRACK	Various Artists (RCA)
39	48	DIESEL AND DUST	Midnight Oil (CBS)
-	49	ANCIENT HEART	Tanita Tikaram (WEA)
48	50	THE SINGULAR ADVENTURES OF THE STYLE COUNCIL	Style Council (Polydor)

17 June 1989

last week	this week	Title	Artist (Label)
2	1	THE HITS ALBUM 10	Various Artists (CBS/WEA/BMG)
3	2	TEN GOOD REASONS	Jason Donovan (PWL)
1	3	THE MIRACLE	Queen (Parlophone)
5	4	THE OTHER SIDE OF THE MIRROR	Stevie Nicks (EMI)
6	5	DON'T BE CRUEL	Bobby Brown (MCA)
4	6	TIN MACHINE	Tin Machine (EMI USA)
15	7	APPETITE FOR DESTRUCTION	Guns N' Roses (Geffen)
9	8	CLUB CLASSICS VOL.1	Soul II Soul (10)
21	9	AVALON SUNSET	Van Morrison (Polydor)
12	10	WHEN THE WORLD KNOWS YOUR NAME	Deacon Blue (CBS)
8	11	NITE FLITE 2	Various Artists (CBS)
-	12	FLOWERS IN THE DIRT	Paul McCartney (Parlophone)
7	13	STREET FIGHTING YEARS	Simple Minds (Virgin)
10	14	PASTPRESENT	Clannad (RCA)
11	15	GOOD TO BE BACK	Natalie Cole (EMI Manhattan)
13	16	PARADISE	Inner City (10)
-	17	RAW LIKE SUSHI	Neneh Cherry (Circa)
16	18	THE RAW AND THE COOKED	Fine Young Cannibals (London)
-	19	WATERMARK	Enya (WEA)
-	20	ffrr - SILVER ON BLACK	Various Artists (ffrr)
22	21	LIKE A PRAYER	Madonna (Sire)
18	22	A NEW FLAME	Simply Red (Elektra)
23	23	KYLIE	Kylie Minogue (PWL)
24	24	PRECIOUS METAL	Various Artists (Stylus)
14	25	LIFE IS A DANCE (THE REMIX PROJECT)	Chaka Khan (Warner Bros.)
20	26	ANYTHING FOR YOU	Gloria Estefan & the Miami Sound Machine (Epic)
17	27	MIND BOMB	The The (Epic)
31	28	LOC'ED AFTER DARK	Tone Loc (Delicious)
27	29	THE CHART SHOW DANCE MASTERS	Various Artists (Dover)
30	30	BLIND MAN'S ZOO	10,000 Maniacs (Elektra)
34	31	EVERYTHING	Bangles (CBS)
32	32	STOP	Sam Brown (A&M)
33	33	KICK	INXS (Mercury)
19	34	STEPPIN' TO THE SHADOWS	Shadows (Polydor)
-	35	STAGE HEROES	Colm Wilkinson (RCA)
-	36	PASSION	Peter Gabriel (Virgin)
28	37	FOREVER YOUR GIRL	Paula Abdul (Siren)
39	38	ANOTHER PLACE AND TIME	Donna Summer (Warner Bros.)
36	39	DEEP HEAT - THE SECOND BURN	Various Artists (Telstar)
46	40	NOW THAT'S WHAT I CALL MUSIC 14	Various Artists (EMI/Virgin/PolyGram)
47	41	DIRTY DANCING - SOUNDTRACK	Various Artists (RCA)
43	42	BIG DADDY	John Cougar Mellencamp (Mercury)
25	43	BLAST	Holly Johnson (MCA)
26	44	REMOTE	Hue & Cry (Circa)
42	45	POP ART	Transvision Vamp (MCA)
-	46	GREEN	R.E.M. (Warner Bros.)
-	47	NEW YORK	Lou Reed (Sire)
48	48	ANCIENT HEART	Tanita Tikaram (WEA)
44	49	GIPSY KINGS	Gipsy Kings (Telstar)
38	50	OPEN UP AND SAY ... AAH!	Poison (Capitol)

24 June 1989

last week	this week	Title	Artist (Label)
1	1	THE HITS ALBUM 10	Various Artists (CBS/WEA/BMG)
2	2	TEN GOOD REASONS	Jason Donovan (PWL)
17	3	RAW LIKE SUSHI	Neneh Cherry (Circa)
8	4	CLUB CLASSICS VOL.1	Soul II Soul (10)
3	5	THE MIRACLE	Queen (Parlophone)
4	6	THE OTHER SIDE OF THE MIRROR	Stevie Nicks (EMI)
12	7	FLOWERS IN THE DIRT	Paul McCartney (Parlophone)
11	8	NITE FLITE 2	Various Artists (CBS)
-	9	RAINBOW WARRIORS	Various Artists (RCA)
19	10	WATERMARK	Enya (WEA)
5	11	DON'T BE CRUEL	Bobby Brown (MCA)
7	12	APPETITE FOR DESTRUCTION	Guns N' Roses (Geffen)
14	13	PASTPRESENT	Clannad (RCA)
6	14	TIN MACHINE	Tin Machine (EMI USA)
9	15	AVALON SUNSET	Van Morrison (Polydor)
10	16	WHEN THE WORLD KNOWS YOUR NAME	Deacon Blue (CBS)
13	17	STREET FIGHTING YEARS	Simple Minds (Virgin)
15	18	GOOD TO BE BACK	Natalie Cole (EMI Manhattan)
16	19	PARADISE	Inner City (10)
24	20	PRECIOUS METAL	Various Artists (Stylus)
23	21	KYLIE	Kylie Minogue (PWL)
35	22	STAGE HEROES	Colm Wilkinson (RCA)
18	23	THE RAW AND THE COOKED	Fine Young Cannibals (London)
22	24	A NEW FLAME	Simply Red (Elektra)
21	25	LIKE A PRAYER	Madonna (Sire)
31	26	EVERYTHING	Bangles (CBS)
37	27	FOREVER YOUR GIRL	Paula Abdul (Siren)
28	28	LOC'ED AFTER DARK	Tone Loc (Delicious)
26	29	ANYTHING FOR YOU	Gloria Estefan & the Miami Sound Machine (Epic)
25	30	LIFE IS A DANCE (THE REMIX PROJECT)	Chaka Khan (Warner Bros.)
29	31	THE CHART SHOW DANCE MASTERS	Various Artists (Dover)
30	32	BLIND MAN'S ZOO	10,000 Maniacs (Elektra)
27	33	MIND BOMB	The The (Epic)
32	34	STOP	Sam Brown (A&M)
20	35	ffrr - SILVER ON BLACK	Various Artists (ffrr)
46	36	GREEN	R.E.M. (Warner Bros.)
45	37	POP ART	Transvision Vamp (MCA)
33	38	KICK	INXS (Mercury)
40	39	NOW THAT'S WHAT I CALL MUSIC 14	Various Artists (EMI/Virgin/PolyGram)
34	40	STEPPIN' TO THE SHADOWS	Shadows (Polydor)
36	41	PASSION	Peter Gabriel (Virgin)
39	42	DEEP HEAT - THE SECOND BURN	Various Artists (Telstar)
43	43	BLAST	Holly Johnson (MCA)
38	44	ANOTHER PLACE AND TIME	Donna Summer (Warner Bros.)
44	45	REMOTE	Hue & Cry (Circa)
-	46	BAD	Michael Jackson (Epic)
41	47	DIRTY DANCING	Various Artists (RCA)
-	48	THE SONGS THAT GOT AWAY	Sarah Brightman (Really Useful)
-	49	DISINTEGRATION	Cure (Fiction)
-	50	THE ESSENTIAL DOMINGO	Placido Domingo (Deutsche Grammophon)

Queen had released a fair number of albums which had sold strongly but peaked at Number 2 during the 1980s, and so must have been gratified by the instant Number 1 success of *The Miracle*, their first release for over two years, and first studio recording since mid-1986. It was dethroned by the *Hits 10* compilation, notable for restoring the identifying number (abandoned on volume 9) to the title.

July 1989

1 July 1989

last week	this week	Title	Artist (Label)
-	1	BATMAN	Prince (Warner Bros.)
4	2	CLUB CLASSICS VOL.1	Soul II Soul (10)
1	3	THE HITS ALBUM 10	Various Artists (CBS/WEA/BMG)
7	4	FLOWERS IN THE DIRT	Paul McCartney (Parlophone)
9	5	RAINBOW WARRIORS	Various Artists (RCA)
2	6	TEN GOOD REASONS	Jason Donovan (PWL)
3	7	RAW LIKE SUSHI	Neneh Cherry (Circa)
12	8	APPETITE FOR DESTRUCTION	Guns N' Roses (Geffen)
5	9	THE MIRACLE	Queen (Parlophone)
13	10	PASTPRESENT	Clannad (RCA)
11	11	DON'T BE CRUEL	Bobby Brown (MCA)
10	12	WATERMARK	Enya (WEA)
8	13	NITE FLITE 2	Various Artists (CBS)
6	14	THE OTHER SIDE OF THE MIRROR	Stevie Nicks (EMI)
17	15	STREET FIGHTING YEARS	Simple Minds (Virgin)
24	16	A NEW FLAME	Simply Red (Elektra)
-	17	ANYWAYAWANNA	Beatmasters (Rhythm King)
16	18	WHEN THE WORLD KNOWS YOUR NAME	Deacon Blue (CBS)
25	19	LIKE A PRAYER	Madonna (Sire)
40	20	STEPPIN' TO THE SHADOWS	Shadows (Polydor)
23	21	THE RAW AND THE COOKED	Fine Young Cannibals (London)
50	22	THE ESSENTIAL DOMINGO	Placido Domingo (Deutsche Grammophon)
-	23	A NIGHT TO REMEMBER	Cyndi Lauper (Epic)
20	24	PRECIOUS METAL	Various Artists (Stylus)
36	25	GREEN	R.E.M. (Warner Bros.)
19	26	PARADISE	Inner City (10)
14	27	TIN MACHINE	Tin Machine (EMI USA)
21	28	KYLIE	Kylie Minogue (PWL)
29	29	ANYTHING FOR YOU	Gloria Estefan & the Miami Sound Machine (Epic)
15	30	AVALON SUNSET	Van Morrison (Polydor)
18	31	GOOD TO BE BACK	Natalie Cole (EMI Manhattan)
32	32	LOC'ED AFTER DARK	Tone Loc (Delicious)
22	33	STAGE HEROES	Colm Wilkinson (RCA)
30	34	LIFE IS A DANCE (THE REMIX PROJECT)	Chaka Khan (Warner Bros.)
-	35	EAT ME IN ST. LOUIS	It Bites (Virgin)
-	36	KARYN WHITE	Karyn White (Warner Bros.)
43	37	BLAST	Holly Johnson (MCA)
31	38	THE CHART SHOW DANCE MASTERS	Various Artists (Dover)
26	39	EVERYTHING	Bangles (CBS)
27	40	FOREVER YOUR GIRL	Paula Abdul (Siren)
-	41	PROTEST SONGS	Prefab Sprout (Kitchenware)
-	42	BADLANDS	Badlands (Atlantic)
-	43	RATTLE AND HUM	U2 (Island)
-	44	GIPSY KINGS	Gipsy Kings (Telstar)
-	45	PRIVATE COLLECTION (1979-1988)	Cliff Richard (EMI)
46	46	BAD	Michael Jackson (Epic)
-	47	ANCIENT HEART	Tanita Tikaram (WEA)
-	48	HEAVY NOVA	Robert Palmer (EMI)
32	49	BLIND MAN'S ZOO	10,000 Maniacs (Elektra)
44	50	ANOTHER PLACE AND TIME	Donna Summer (Warner Bros.)

8 July 1989

this week	Title	Artist (Label)
1	BATMAN	Prince (Warner Bros.)
2	VELVETEEN	Transvision Vamp (MCA)
3	CLUB CLASSICS VOL.1	Soul II Soul (10)
4	DON'T BE CRUEL	Bobby Brown (MCA)
5	TEN GOOD REASONS	Jason Donovan (PWL)
6	PASTPRESENT	Clannad (RCA)
7	FULL MOON FEVER	Tom Petty (MCA)
8	THE HITS ALBUM 10	Various Artists (CBS/WEA/BMG)
9	RAW LIKE SUSHI	Neneh Cherry (Circa)
10	RAINBOW WARRIORS	Various Artists (RCA)
11	A NIGHT TO REMEMBER	Cyndi Lauper (Epic)
12	FLOWERS IN THE DIRT	Paul McCartney (Parlophone)
13	APPETITE FOR DESTRUCTION	Guns N' Roses (Geffen)
14	WHEN THE WORLD KNOWS YOUR NAME	Deacon Blue (CBS)
15	PROTEST SONGS	Prefab Sprout (Kitchenware)
16	THE MIRACLE	Queen (Parlophone)
17	NITE FLITE 2	Various Artists (CBS)
18	WALKING ON SUNSHINE - VERY BEST OF EDDY GRANT	Eddy Grant (Parlophone)
19	EVERYTHING	Bangles (CBS)
20	LIKE A PRAYER	Madonna (Sire)
21	WATERMARK	Enya (WEA)
22	A NEW FLAME	Simply Red (Elektra)
23	THE RAW AND THE COOKED	Fine Young Cannibals (London)
24	STREET FIGHTING YEARS	Simple Minds (Virgin)
25	PRECIOUS METAL	Various Artists (Stylus)
26	THE OTHER SIDE OF THE MIRROR	Stevie Nicks (EMI)
27	ANYTHING FOR YOU	Gloria Estefan & the Miami Sound Machine (Epic)
28	BLAST	Holly Johnson (MCA)
29	PARADISE	Inner City (10)
30	ANYWAYAWANNA	Beatmasters (Rhythm King)
31	AVALON SUNSET	Van Morrison (Polydor)
32	KYLIE	Kylie Minogue (PWL)
33	ANDERSON BRUFORD WAKEMAN AND HOWE	Anderson Bruford Wakeman & Howe (Arista)
34	STEPPIN' TO THE SHADOWS	Shadows (Polydor)
35	LOC'ED AFTER DARK	Tone Loc (Delicious)
36	G N' R LIES	Guns N' Roses (Geffen)
37	KARYN WHITE	Karyn White (Warner Bros)
38	LIFE IS A DANCE (THE REMIX PROJECT)	Chaka Khan (Warner Bros.)
39	GOOD TO BE BACK	Natalie Cole (EMI Manhattan)
40	GREEN	R.E.M. (Warner Bros.)
41	THE ESSENTIAL DOMINGO	Placido Domingo (Deutsche Grammophon)
42	DON'T STOP THE MUSIC	Various Artists (Stylus)
43	GATECRASHING	Living In A Box (Chrysalis)
44	TIN MACHINE	Tin Machine (EMI USA)
45	RATTLE AND HUM	U2 (Island)
46	STAGE HEROES	Colm Wilkinson (RCA)
47	BIG GAME	White Lion (Atlantic)
48	2300 JACKSON STREET	Jacksons (Epic)
49	DOOLITTLE	Pixies (4AD)
50	ANOTHER PLACE AND TIME	Donna Summer (Warner Bros.)

15 July 1989

last week	this week	Title	Artist (Label)
3	1	CLUB CLASSICS VOL.1	Soul II Soul (10)
2	2	VELVETEEN	Transvision Vamp (MCA)
4	3	DON'T BE CRUEL	Bobby Brown (MCA)
1	4	BATMAN	Prince (Warner Bros.)
22	5	A NEW FLAME	Simply Red (Elektra)
6	6	PASTPRESENT	Clannad (RCA)
13	7	APPETITE FOR DESTRUCTION	Guns N' Roses (Geffen)
5	8	TEN GOOD REASONS	Jason Donovan (PWL)
-	9	NOW DANCE '89	Various Artists (EMI/Virgin)
7	10	FULL MOON FEVER	Tom Petty (MCA)
16	11	THE MIRACLE	Queen (Parlophone)
9	12	RAW LIKE SUSHI	Neneh Cherry (Circa)
19	13	EVERYTHING	Bangles (CBS)
11	14	A NIGHT TO REMEMBER	Cyndi Lauper (Epic)
10	15	RAINBOW WARRIORS	Various Artists (RCA)
8	16	THE HITS ALBUM 10	Various Artists (CBS/WEA/BMG)
33	17	ANDERSON BRUFORD WAKEMAN AND HOWE	Anderson Bruford Wakeman & Howe (Arista)
12	18	FLOWERS IN THE DIRT	Paul McCartney (Parlophone)
20	19	LIKE A PRAYER	Madonna (Sire)
36	20	G N' R LIES	Guns N' Roses (Geffen)
14	21	WHEN THE WORLD KNOWS YOUR NAME	Deacon Blue (CBS)
38	22	LIFE IS A DANCE (THE REMIX PROJECT)	Chaka Khan (Warner Bros.)
43	23	GATECRASHING	Living In A Box (Chrysalis)
-	24	HIT FACTORY 3	Various Artists (PWL)
21	25	WATERMARK	Enya (WEA)
26	26	THE OTHER SIDE OF THE MIRROR	Stevie Nicks (EMI)
23	27	THE RAW AND THE COOKED	Fine Young Cannibals (London)
29	28	PARADISE	Inner City (10)
24	29	STREET FIGHTING YEARS	Simple Minds (Virgin)
-	30	WALTZ DARLING	Malcolm McLaren & the Bootzilla Orchestra (Epic)
37	31	KARYN WHITE	Karyn White (Warner Bros)
44	32	TIN MACHINE	Tin Machine (EMI USA)
39	33	GOOD TO BE BACK	Natalie Cole (EMI Manhattan)
27	34	ANYTHING FOR YOU	Gloria Estefan & the Miami Sound Machine (Epic)
17	35	NITE FLITE 2	Various Artists (CBS)
-	36	REMOTE	Hue & Cry (Circa)
37	37	BAD	Michael Jackson (Epic)
18	38	WALKING ON SUNSHINE - VERY BEST OF EDDY GRANT	Eddy Grant (Parlophone)
28	39	BLAST	Holly Johnson (MCA)
15	40	PROTEST SONGS	Prefab Sprout (Kitchenware)
25	41	PRECIOUS METAL	Various Artists (Stylus)
32	42	KYLIE	Kylie Minogue (PWL)
35	43	LOC'ED AFTER DARK	Tone Loc (Delicious)
40	44	GREEN	R.E.M. (Warner Bros.)
31	45	AVALON SUNSET	Van Morrison (Polydor)
-	46	WALKING WITH A PANTHER	L.L. Cool J. (Def Jam)
-	47	SEMINAL LIVE	Fall (Beggars Banquet)
-	48	STEPPIN' TO THE SHADOWS	Shadows (Polydor)
41	49	THE ESSENTIAL DOMINGO	Placido Domingo (Deutsche Grammophon)
-	50	ROACHFORD	Roachford (CBS)

It might have been his raised profile as a Traveling Wilbury which made the difference, but Tom Petty had by far his highest-charted album yet with the Heartbreakers on *Full Moon Fever* - which actually debuted inside the Top 10 which previous Petty offerings had been unable to climb to. Also riding a new high was Prince, whose LP had some of the best movie promotion ever via the blockbusting *Batman*.

July – August 1989

22 July 1989

last week	this week	Title	Artist
1	1	CLUB CLASSICS VOL.1	Soul II Soul (10)
5	2	A NEW FLAME	Simply Red (Elektra)
9	3	NOW DANCE '89	Various Artists (EMI/Virgin)
3	4	DON'T BE CRUEL	Bobby Brown (MCA)
2	5	VELVETEEN	Transvision Vamp (MCA)
7	6	APPETITE FOR DESTRUCTION	Guns N' Roses (Geffen)
4	7	BATMAN	Prince (Warner Bros.)
6	8	PASTPRESENT	Clannad (RCA)
8	9	TEN GOOD REASONS	Jason Donovan (PWL)
11	10	THE MIRACLE	Queen (Parlophone)
19	11	LIKE A PRAYER	Madonna (Sire)
12	12	RAW LIKE SUSHI	Neneh Cherry (Circa)
21	13	WHEN THE WORLD KNOWS YOUR NAME	Deacon Blue (CBS)
13	14	EVERYTHING	Bangles (CBS)
27	15	THE RAW AND THE COOKED	Fine Young Cannibals (London)
10	16	FULL MOON FEVER	Tom Petty (MCA)
22	17	LIFE IS A DANCE (THE REMIX PROJECT)	Chaka Khan (Warner Bros.)
18	18	FLOWERS IN THE DIRT	Paul McCartney (Parlophone)
24	19	HIT FACTORY 3	Various Artists (PWL)
15	20	RAINBOW WARRIORS	Various Artists (RCA)
37	21	BAD	Michael Jackson (Epic)
14	22	A NIGHT TO REMEMBER	Cyndi Lauper (Epic)
25	23	WATERMARK	Enya (WEA)
31	24	KARYN WHITE	Karyn White (Warner Bros)
-	25	BEACHES	Soundtrack (Atlantic)
20	26	G N' R LIES	Guns N' Roses (Geffen)
16	27	THE HITS ALBUM 10	Various Artists (CBS/WEA/BMG)
29	28	STREET FIGHTING YEARS	Simple Minds (Virgin)
38	29	WALKING ON SUNSHINE - VERY BEST OF EDDY GRANT	Eddy Grant (Parlophone)
-	30	THEMES	Vangelis (Polydor)
17	31	ANDERSON BRUFORD WAKEMAN AND HOWE	Anderson Bruford Wakeman & Howe (Arista)
28	32	PARADISE	Inner City (10)
34	33	ANYTHING FOR YOU	Gloria Estefan & the Miami Sound Machine (Epic)
26	34	THE OTHER SIDE OF THE MIRROR	Stevie Nicks (EMI)
41	35	PRECIOUS METAL	Various Artists (Stylus)
30	36	WALTZ DARLING	Malcolm McLaren & the Bootzilla Orchestra (Epic)
-	37	RATTLE AND HUM	U2 (Island)
32	38	TIN MACHINE	Tin Machine (EMI USA)
-	39	DEEP HEAT 3 - THE THIRD DEGREE	Various Artists (Telstar)
49	40	THE ESSENTIAL DOMINGO	Placido Domingo (Deutsche Grammophon)
-	41	GIPSY KINGS	Gipsy Kings (Telstar)
23	42	GATECRASHING	Living In A Box (Chrysalis)
33	43	GOOD TO BE BACK	Natalie Cole (EMI Manhattan)
-	44	EARTH MOVING	Mike Oldfield (Virgin)
-	45	PROTECT THE INNOCENT	Various Artists (Telstar)
-	46	FOREVER YOUR GIRL	Paula Abdul (Siren)
-	47	AFTER DARK	Tom Jones (Stylus)
45	48	AVALON SUNSET	Van Morrison (Polydor)
39	49	BLAST	Holly Johnson (MCA)
-	50	KICK	INXS (Mercury)

29 July 1989

last week	this week	Title	Artist
2	1	A NEW FLAME	Simply Red (Elektra)
1	2	CLUB CLASSICS VOL.1	Soul II Soul (10)
3	3	NOW DANCE '89	Various Artists (EMI/Virgin)
4	4	DON'T BE CRUEL	Bobby Brown (MCA)
-	5	PEACE AND LOVE	Pogues (Pogue Mahone)
9	6	TEN GOOD REASONS	Jason Donovan (PWL)
6	7	APPETITE FOR DESTRUCTION	Guns N' Roses (Geffen)
7	8	BATMAN	Prince (Warner Bros.)
33	9	ANYTHING FOR YOU	Gloria Estefan & the Miami Sound Machine (Epic)
5	10	VELVETEEN	Transvision Vamp (MCA)
30	11	THEMES	Vangelis (Polydor)
28	12	STREET FIGHTING YEARS	Simple Minds (Virgin)
8	13	PASTPRESENT	Clannad (RCA)
14	14	THE MIRACLE	Queen (Parlophone)
13	15	WHEN THE WORLD KNOWS YOUR NAME	Deacon Blue (CBS)
12	16	RAW LIKE SUSHI	Neneh Cherry (Circa)
19	17	HIT FACTORY 3	Various Artists (PWL)
39	18	DEEP HEAT 3 - THE THIRD DEGREE	Various Artists (Telstar)
11	19	LIKE A PRAYER	Madonna (Sire)
15	20	THE RAW AND THE COOKED	Fine Young Cannibals (London)
25	21	BEACHES	Soundtrack (Atlantic)
14	22	EVERYTHING	Bangles (CBS)
24	23	KARYN WHITE	Karyn White (Warner Bros)
22	24	A NIGHT TO REMEMBER	Cyndi Lauper (Epic)
18	25	FLOWERS IN THE DIRT	Paul McCartney (Parlophone)
23	26	WATERMARK	Enya (WEA)
16	27	FULL MOON FEVER	Tom Petty (MCA)
21	28	BAD	Michael Jackson (Epic)
17	29	LIFE IS A DANCE (THE REMIX PROJECT)	Chaka Khan (Warner Bros.)
-	30	THE 12 COMMANDMENTS OF DANCE	London Boys (WEA)
32	31	PARADISE	Inner City (10)
44	32	EARTH MOVING	Mike Oldfield (Virgin)
43	33	GOOD TO BE BACK	Natalie Cole (EMI Manhattan)
40	34	THE ESSENTIAL DOMINGO	Placido Domingo (Deutsche Grammophon)
-	35	GHETTO MUSIC	Boogie Down Productions (Jive)
26	36	G N' R LIES	Guns N' Roses (Geffen)
35	37	PRECIOUS METAL	Various Artists (Stylus)
20	38	RAINBOW WARRIORS	Various Artists (RCA)
39	39	3 FEET HIGH AND RISING	De La Soul (Big Life)
-	40	BEEBOP MOPTOP	Danny Wilson (Virgin)
31	41	ANDERSON BRUFORD WAKEMAN AND HOWE	Anderson Bruford Wakeman & Howe (Arista)
29	42	WALKING ON SUNSHINE - VERY BEST OF EDDY GRANT	Eddy Grant (Parlophone)
48	43	AVALON SUNSET	Van Morrison (Polydor)
34	44	THE OTHER SIDE OF THE MIRROR	Stevie Nicks (EMI)
27	45	THE HITS ALBUM 10	Various Artists (CBS/WEA/BMG)
36	46	WALTZ DARLING	Malcolm McLaren & the Bootzilla Orchestra (Epic)
-	47	THE COMPLETE	Glen Campbell (Stylus)
-	48	THE END OF THE INNOCENCE	Don Henley (Geffen)
41	49	GIPSY KINGS	Gipsy Kings (Telstar)
-	50	JUMP - THE BEST OF THE POINTER SISTERS	Pointer Sisters (RCA)

5 August 1989

last week	this week	Title	Artist
-	1	CUTS BOTH WAYS	Gloria Estefan (Epic)
1	2	A NEW FLAME	Simply Red (Elektra)
2	3	CLUB CLASSICS VOL.1	Soul II Soul (10)
3	4	NOW DANCE '89	Various Artists (EMI/Virgin)
30	5	THE 12 COMMANDMENTS OF DANCE	London Boys (WEA)
4	6	DON'T BE CRUEL	Bobby Brown (MCA)
18	7	DEEP HEAT 3 - THE THIRD DEGREE	Various Artists (Telstar)
5	8	PEACE AND LOVE	Pogues (Pogue Mahone)
6	9	TEN GOOD REASONS	Jason Donovan (PWL)
7	10	APPETITE FOR DESTRUCTION	Guns N' Roses (Geffen)
10	11	VELVETEEN	Transvision Vamp (MCA)
8	12	BATMAN	Prince (Warner Bros.)
12	13	STREET FIGHTING YEARS	Simple Minds (Virgin)
11	14	THEMES	Vangelis (Polydor)
14	15	THE MIRACLE	Queen (Parlophone)
16	16	RAW LIKE SUSHI	Neneh Cherry (Circa)
15	17	WHEN THE WORLD KNOWS YOUR NAME	Deacon Blue (CBS)
9	18	ANYTHING FOR YOU	Gloria Estefan & the Miami Sound Machine (Epic)
13	19	PASTPRESENT	Clannad (RCA)
20	20	THE RAW AND THE COOKED	Fine Young Cannibals (London)
19	21	LIKE A PRAYER	Madonna (Sire)
40	22	BEEBOP MOPTOP	Danny Wilson (Virgin)
21	23	BEACHES	Soundtrack (Atlantic)
17	24	HIT FACTORY 3	Various Artists (PWL)
25	25	FLOWERS IN THE DIRT	Paul McCartney (Parlophone)
39	26	3 FEET HIGH AND RISING	De La Soul (Big Life)
24	27	A NIGHT TO REMEMBER	Cyndi Lauper (Epic)
31	28	PARADISE	Inner City (10)
27	29	FULL MOON FEVER	Tom Petty (MCA)
22	30	EVERYTHING	Bangles (CBS)
23	31	KARYN WHITE	Karyn White (Warner Bros)
-	32	ESPECIALLY FOR YOU	Joe Longthorne (Telstar)
26	33	WATERMARK	Enya (WEA)
28	34	BAD	Michael Jackson (Epic)
36	35	G N' R LIES	Guns N' Roses (Geffen)
29	36	LIFE IS A DANCE (THE REMIX PROJECT)	Chaka Khan (Warner Bros.)
48	37	THE END OF THE INNOCENCE	Don Henley (Geffen)
50	38	JUMP - THE BEST OF THE POINTER SISTERS	Pointer Sisters (RCA)
-	39	KYLIE	Kylie Minogue (PWL)
-	40	HOT SUMMER NIGHTS	Various Artists (Stylus)
49	41	GIPSY KINGS	Gipsy Kings (Telstar)
-	42	PAUL'S BOUTIQUE	Beastie Boys (Capitol)
44	43	THE OTHER SIDE OF THE MIRROR	Stevie Nicks (EMI)
-	44	BLAST	Holly Johnson (MCA)
33	45	GOOD TO BE BACK	Natalie Cole (EMI Manhattan)
42	46	WALKING ON SUNSHINE - VERY BEST OF EDDY GRANT	Eddy Grant (Parlophone)
-	47	KICK	INXS (Mercury)
-	48	NITE FLITE 2	Various Artists (CBS)
37	49	PRECIOUS METAL	Various Artists (Stylus)
-	50	THE STONE ROSES	Stone Roses (Silvertone)

With *Cuts Both Ways*, Gloria Estefan, who had begun her recorded career without an identifying credit as part of Miami Sound Machine, then graduated (on *Anything For You*) to promotion up front, finally made it to ostensible solo billing - though in fact there had been no material change, and she still sang fronting the band (which was led by her husband and producer Emilio Estefan).

343

August 1989

Following Soul II Soul's July Number 1 album with *Club Classics Vol.1*, several dance-oriented acts, whom received record industry wisdom suggested were incapable of "sustaining" hit albums, were making the upper echelons of the chart. WEA's gimmicky dance duo the London Boys actually made the Top 3, while Inner City and club-style girl singers Karyn White and Nena Cherry also sold strongly.

September 1989

2 September 1989

last week	this week	Title	Artist (Label)
2	1	NOW THAT'S WHAT I CALL MUSIC 15	Various Artists (EMI/Virgin/PolyGram)
1	2	CUTS BOTH WAYS	Gloria Estefan (Epic)
3	3	TEN GOOD REASONS	Jason Donovan (PWL)
10	4	TRASH	Alice Cooper (Epic)
5	5	HEART AND SOUL - 18 CLASSIC SOUL CUTS	Various Artists (Polydor)
4	6	A NEW FLAME	Simply Red (Elektra)
9	7	BATMAN	Prince (Warner Bros.)
26	8	BIG BANG	Fuzzbox (WEA)
7	9	VELVETEEN	Transvision Vamp (MCA)
30	10	CHOICES - THE SINGLES CONNECTION	Blow Monkeys (RCA)
12	11	RAW LIKE SUSHI	Neneh Cherry (Circa)
8	12	DON'T BE CRUEL	Bobby Brown (MCA)
11	13	CLUB CLASSICS VOL.1	Soul II Soul (10)
6	14	THE 12 COMMANDMENTS OF DANCE	London Boys (WEA)
13	15	JUMP - THE BEST OF THE POINTER SISTERS	Pointer Sisters (RCA)
20	16	THE MIRACLE	Queen (Parlophone)
23	17	ALL THE HITS	Imagination (Stylus)
17	18	ANYTHING FOR YOU	Gloria Estefan & the Miami Sound Machine (Epic)
-	19	SACRED HEART	Shakespear's Sister (London)
15	20	THEMES	Vangelis (Polydor)
16	21	APPETITE FOR DESTRUCTION	Guns N' Roses (Geffen)
14	22	NOW DANCE '89	Various Artists (EMI/Virgin)
21	23	THE RAW AND THE COOKED	Fine Young Cannibals (London)
18	24	STREET FIGHTING YEARS	Simple Minds (Virgin)
24	25	A NIGHT TO REMEMBER	Cyndi Lauper (Epic)
-	26	ROCK ISLAND	Jethro Tull (Chrysalis)
33	27	WHEN THE WORLD KNOWS YOUR NAME	Deacon Blue (CBS)
19	28	PARADISE	Inner City (10)
22	29	DEEP HEAT 3 - THE THIRD DEGREE	Various Artists (Telstar)
28	30	THE END OF THE INNOCENCE	Don Henley (Geffen)
35	31	LIKE A PRAYER	Madonna (Sire)
40	32	WATERMARK	Enya (WEA)
43	33	THE BIG AREA	Then Jerico (London)
-	34	FRENCH KISS: THE COMPLETE MIX COLLECTION (EP)	L'il Louis (ffrr)
36	35	FULL MOON FEVER	Tom Petty (MCA)
25	36	FLOWERS IN THE DIRT	Paul McCartney (Parlophone)
27	37	KYLIE	Kylie Minogue (PWL)
48	38	ELECTRIC YOUTH	Debbie Gibson (Atlantic)
32	39	PASTPRESENT	Clannad (RCA)
29	40	HOT SUMMER NIGHTS	Various Artists (Stylus)
34	41	SOUTHSIDE	Texas (Mercury)
43	42	G N' R LIES	Guns N' Roses (Geffen)
-	43	KICK	INXS (Mercury)
39	44	KARYN WHITE	Karyn White (Warner Bros)
-	45	NEW JERSEY	Bon Jovi (Vertigo)
31	46	ESPECIALLY FOR YOU	Joe Longthorne (Telstar)
44	47	BAD	Michael Jackson (Epic)
-	48	SINGALONGWARYEARS	Max Bygraves (Parkfield Music)
50	49	DISINTEGRATION	Cure (Fiction)
45	50	WALTZ DARLING	Malcolm McLaren & the Bootzilla Orchestra (Epic)

9 September 1989

last week	this week	Title	Artist (Label)
1	1	NOW THAT'S WHAT I CALL MUSIC 15	Various Artists (EMI/Virgin/PolyGram)
2	2	CUTS BOTH WAYS	Gloria Estefan (Epic)
3	3	TEN GOOD REASONS	Jason Donovan (PWL)
4	4	TRASH	Alice Cooper (Epic)
5	5	HEART AND SOUL - 18 CLASSIC SOUL CUTS	Various Artists (Polydor)
11	6	RAW LIKE SUSHI	Neneh Cherry (Circa)
6	7	A NEW FLAME	Simply Red (Elektra)
7	8	BATMAN	Prince (Warner Bros.)
10	9	CHOICES - THE SINGLES CONNECTION	Blow Monkeys (RCA)
19	10	SACRED HEART	Shakespear's Sister (London)
12	11	DON'T BE CRUEL	Bobby Brown (MCA)
17	12	ALL THE HITS	Imagination (Stylus)
9	13	VELVETEEN	Transvision Vamp (MCA)
13	14	CLUB CLASSICS VOL.1	Soul II Soul (10)
16	15	THE MIRACLE	Queen (Parlophone)
20	16	THEMES	Vangelis (Polydor)
14	17	THE 12 COMMANDMENTS OF DANCE	London Boys (WEA)
8	18	BIG BANG	Fuzzbox (WEA)
26	19	ROCK ISLAND	Jethro Tull (Chrysalis)
18	20	ANYTHING FOR YOU	Gloria Estefan & the Miami Sound Machine (Epic)
23	21	THE RAW AND THE COOKED	Fine Young Cannibals (London)
48	22	SINGALONGWARYEARS	Max Bygraves (Parkfield Music)
21	23	APPETITE FOR DESTRUCTION	Guns N' Roses (Geffen)
31	24	LIKE A PRAYER	Madonna (Sire)
27	25	WHEN THE WORLD KNOWS YOUR NAME	Deacon Blue (CBS)
-	26	ADEVA	Adeva (Cooltempo)
15	27	JUMP - THE BEST OF	Pointer Sisters (RCA)
24	28	STREET FIGHTING YEARS	Simple Minds (Virgin)
29	29	PARADISE	Inner City (10)
44	30	KARYN WHITE	Karyn White (Warner Bros)
35	31	FULL MOON FEVER	Tom Petty (MCA)
32	32	NOW DANCE '89	Various Artists (EMI/Virgin)
33	33	WATERMARK	Enya (WEA)
37	34	KYLIE	Kylie Minogue (PWL)
30	35	THE END OF THE INNOCENCE	Don Henley (Geffen)
25	36	A NIGHT TO REMEMBER	Cyndi Lauper (Epic)
46	37	ESPECIALLY FOR YOU	Joe Longthorne (Telstar)
38	38	ELECTRIC YOUTH	Debbie Gibson (Atlantic)
33	39	THE BIG AREA	Then Jerico (London)
-	40	REPEAT OFFENDER	Richard Marx (EMI USA)
-	41	DIRTY DANCING - SOUNDTRACK	Various Artists (RCA)
39	42	PASTPRESENT	Clannad (RCA)
29	43	DEEP HEAT 3 - THE THIRD DEGREE	Various Artists (Telstar)
34	44	FRENCH KISS: THE COMPLETE MIX COLLECTION (EP)	L'il Louis (ffrr)
-	45	HYSTERIA	Def Leppard (Bludgeon Riffola)
36	46	FLOWERS IN THE DIRT	Paul McCartney (Parlophone)
41	47	SOUTHSIDE	Texas (Mercury)
43	48	KICK	INXS (Mercury)
-	49	GREATEST EVER ROCK'N'ROLL MIX	Various Artists (Stylus)
-	50	ANYWAYAWANNA	Beatmasters (Rhythm King)

16 September 1989

last week	this week	Title	Artist (Label)
1	1	NOW THAT'S WHAT I CALL MUSIC 15	Various Artists (EMI/Virgin/PolyGram)
2	2	CUTS BOTH WAYS	Gloria Estefan (Epic)
3	3	TEN GOOD REASONS	Jason Donovan (PWL)
21	4	THE RAW AND THE COOKED	Fine Young Cannibals (London)
7	5	A NEW FLAME	Simply Red (Elektra)
4	6	TRASH	Alice Cooper (Epic)
8	7	BATMAN	Prince (Warner Bros.)
-	8	ASPECTS OF LOVE	Various Artists (Really Useful)
26	9	ADEVA	Adeva (Cooltempo)
12	10	ALL THE HITS	Imagination (Stylus)
22	11	SINGALONGWARYEARS	Max Bygraves (Parkfield Music)
6	12	RAW LIKE SUSHI	Neneh Cherry (Circa)
-	13	DR. FEELGOOD	Motley Crue (Elektra)
9	14	CHOICES - THE SINGLES CONNECTION	Blow Monkeys (RCA)
24	15	LIKE A PRAYER	Madonna (Sire)
11	16	DON'T BE CRUEL	Bobby Brown (MCA)
5	17	HEART AND SOUL - 18 CLASSIC SOUL CUTS	Various Artists (Polydor)
25	18	WHEN THE WORLD KNOWS YOUR NAME	Deacon Blue (CBS)
14	19	CLUB CLASSICS VOL.1	Soul II Soul (10)
40	20	REPEAT OFFENDER	Richard Marx (EMI USA)
15	21	THE MIRACLE	Queen (Parlophone)
17	22	THE 12 COMMANDMENTS OF DANCE	London Boys (WEA)
23	23	APPETITE FOR DESTRUCTION	Guns N' Roses (Geffen)
13	24	VELVETEEN	Transvision Vamp (MCA)
20	25	ANYTHING FOR YOU	Gloria Estefan & the Miami Sound Machine (Epic)
16	26	THEMES	Vangelis (Polydor)
29	27	PARADISE	Inner City (10)
31	28	FULL MOON FEVER	Tom Petty (MCA)
47	29	SOUTHSIDE	Texas (Mercury)
10	30	SACRED HEART	Shakespear's Sister (London)
28	31	STREET FIGHTING YEARS	Simple Minds (Virgin)
18	32	BIG BANG	Fuzzbox (WEA)
41	33	DIRTY DANCING - SOUNDTRACK	Various Artists (RCA)
30	34	KARYN WHITE	Karyn White (Warner Bros)
19	35	ROCK ISLAND	Jethro Tull (Chrysalis)
35	36	THE END OF THE INNOCENCE	Don Henley (Geffen)
-	37	A SHADE OF RED	Redhead Kingpin & the FBI (10)
33	38	WATERMARK	Enya (WEA)
-	39	MEGATOP PHOENIX	Big Audio Dynamite (CBS)
34	40	KYLIE	Kylie Minogue (PWL)
-	41	RAW	Alyson Williams (Def Jam)
38	42	ELECTRIC YOUTH	Debbie Gibson (Atlantic)
-	43	WE'LL MEET AGAIN	Vera Lynn (Telstar)
27	44	JUMP - THE BEST OF THE POINTER SISTERS	Pointer Sisters (RCA)
-	45	MARTIKA	Martika (CBS)
37	46	ESPECIALLY FOR YOU	Joe Longthorne (Telstar)
45	47	HYSTERIA	Def Leppard (Bludgeon Riffola)
50	48	ANYWAYAWANNA	Beatmasters (Rhythm King)
32	49	NOW DANCE '89	Various Artists (EMI/Virgin)
36	50	A NIGHT TO REMEMBER	Cyndi Lauper (Epic)

Trash was Alice Coper's first UK Top 10 album since *Billion Dollar Babies*, over 16 years previously; its success was spurred by Cooper's Top 5 single *Poison* - also his first big hit single since 1973. Meanwhile, hits compilations abounded in the chart much as they had prior to the previous Christmas, with Imagination, the Blow Monkeys, the Pointer Sisters and even Vangelis all finding major hit anthology success.

September – October 1989

23 September 1989

last	this	Title	Artist (Label)
8	1	ASPECTS OF LOVE	Various Artists (Really Useful)
1	2	NOW THAT'S WHAT I CALL MUSIC 15	Various Artists (EMI/Virgin/PolyGram)
-	3	WE TOO ARE ONE	Eurythmics (RCA)
2	4	CUTS BOTH WAYS	Gloria Estefan (Epic)
3	5	TEN GOOD REASONS	Jason Donovan (PWL)
-	6	PUMP	Aerosmith (Geffen)
13	7	DR. FEELGOOD	Motley Crue (Elektra)
5	8	A NEW FLAME	Simply Red (Elektra)
4	9	THE RAW AND THE COOKED	Fine Young Cannibals (London)
20	10	REPEAT OFFENDER	Richard Marx (EMI USA)
7	11	BATMAN	Prince (Warner Bros.)
-	12	STEEL WHEELS	Rolling Stones (CBS)
15	13	LIKE A PRAYER	Madonna (Sire)
6	14	TRASH	Alice Cooper (Epic)
10	15	ALL THE HITS	Imagination (Stylus)
12	16	RAW LIKE SUSHI	Neneh Cherry (Circa)
12	17	SINGALONGAWARYEARS	Max Bygraves (Parkfield Music)
16	18	DON'T BE CRUEL	Bobby Brown (MCA)
-	19	SLEEPING WITH THE PAST	Elton John (Rocket)
26	20	THEMES	Vangelis (Polydor)
41	21	RAW	Alyson Williams (Def Jam)
23	22	APPETITE FOR DESTRUCTION	Guns N' Roses (Geffen)
18	23	WHEN THE WORLD KNOWS YOUR NAME	Deacon Blue (CBS)
9	24	ADEVA	Adeva (Cooltempo)
17	25	HEART AND SOUL - 18 CLASSIC SOUL CUTS	Various Artists (Polydor)
14	26	CHOICES - THE SINGLES CONNECTION	Blow Monkeys (RCA)
45	27	MARTIKA	Martika (CBS)
34	28	KARYN WHITE	Karyn White (Warner Bros.)
25	29	ANYTHING FOR YOU	Gloria Estefan & the Miami Sound Machine (Epic)
19	30	CLUB CLASSICS VOL.1	Soul II Soul (10)
24	31	VELVETEEN	Transvision Vamp (MCA)
21	32	THE MIRACLE	Queen (Parlophone)
27	33	PARADISE	Inner City (10)
39	34	MEGATOP PHOENIX	Big Audio Dynamite (CBS)
22	35	THE 12 COMMANDMENTS OF DANCE	London Boys (WEA)
31	36	STREET FIGHTING YEARS	Simple Minds (Virgin)
29	37	SOUTHSIDE	Texas (Mercury)
36	38	THE END OF THE INNOCENCE	Don Henley (Geffen)
40	39	KYLIE	Kylie Minogue (PWL)
28	40	FULL MOON FEVER	Tom Petty (MCA)
-	41	THE ULTIMATE COLLECTION	Kinks (Castle Communications)
30	42	SACRED HEART	Shakespear's Sister (London)
-	43	WAKE ME UP WHEN IT'S OVER	Faster Pussycat (Elektra)
33	44	DIRTY DANCING - SOUNDTRACK	Various Artists (RCA)
32	45	BIG BANG	Fuzzbox (WEA)
35	46	ROCK ISLAND	Jethro Tull (Chrysalis)
42	47	ELECTRIC YOUTH	Debbie Gibson (Atlantic)
-	48	DISINTEGRATION	Cure (Fiction)
37	49	A SHADE OF RED	Redhead Kingpin & the FBI (10)
-	50	STORMS	Nanci Griffith (MCA)

30 September 1989

last	this	Title	Artist (Label)
3	1	WE TOO ARE ONE	Eurythmics (RCA)
-	2	FOREIGN AFFAIR	Tina Turner (Capitol)
12	3	STEEL WHEELS	Rolling Stones (CBS)
6	4	PUMP	Aerosmith (Geffen)
2	5	NOW THAT'S WHAT I CALL MUSIC 15	Various Artists (EMI/Virgin/PolyGram)
4	6	CUTS BOTH WAYS	Gloria Estefan (Epic)
19	7	SLEEPING WITH THE PAST	Elton John (Rocket)
-	8	JANET JACKSON'S RHYTHM NATION 1814	Janet Jackson (A&M)
1	9	ASPECTS OF LOVE	Various Artists (Really Useful)
10	10	REPEAT OFFENDER	Richard Marx (EMI USA)
-	11	JUST SEVENTEEN - HEARTBEATS	Various Artists (Fanfare)
13	12	LIKE A PRAYER	Madonna (Sire)
5	13	TEN GOOD REASONS	Jason Donovan (PWL)
-	14	DEEP HEAT 4 - PLAY WITH FIRE	Various Artists (Telstar)
8	15	A NEW FLAME	Simply Red (Elektra)
9	16	THE RAW AND THE COOKED	Fine Young Cannibals (London)
11	17	BATMAN	Prince (Warner Bros.)
24	18	ADEVA	Adeva (Cooltempo)
23	19	WHEN THE WORLD KNOWS YOUR NAME	Deacon Blue (CBS)
16	20	RAW LIKE SUSHI	Neneh Cherry (Circa)
7	21	DR. FEELGOOD	Motley Crue (Elektra)
14	22	TRASH	Alice Cooper (Epic)
22	23	APPETITE FOR DESTRUCTION	Guns N' Roses (Geffen)
-	24	ERROL FLYNN	Dogs D'Amour (China)
15	25	ALL THE HITS	Imagination (Stylus)
18	26	DON'T BE CRUEL	Bobby Brown (MCA)
30	27	CLUB CLASSICS VOL.1	Soul II Soul (10)
25	28	HEART AND SOUL	Various Artists (Polydor)
-	29	LOVEHOUSE	Various Artists (K-Tel)
-	30	CHANGE	Alarm (IRS)
29	31	ANYTHING FOR YOU	Gloria Estefan & the Miami Sound Machine (Epic)
-	32	ANOTHER PLACE AND TIME	Donna Summer (Warner Bros.)
21	33	RAW	Alyson Williams (Def Jam)
50	34	STORMS	Nanci Griffith (MCA)
17	35	SINGALONGAWARYEARS	Max Bygraves (Parkfield Music)
26	36	CHOICES	Blow Monkeys (RCA)
35	37	THE 12 COMMANDMENTS OF DANCE	London Boys (WEA)
41	38	THE ULTIMATE COLLECTION	Kinks (Castle Communications)
31	39	VELVETEEN	Transvision Vamp (MCA)
32	40	THE MIRACLE	Queen (Parlophone)
-	41	HEART LIKE A SKY	Spandau Ballet (CBS)
33	42	PARADISE	Inner City (10)
-	43	STRAIGHT OUTTA COMPTON	NWA (Fourth & Broadway)
20	44	THEMES	Vangelis (Polydor)
-	45	LEGENDS AND HEROES	Various Artists (Stylus)
36	46	STREET FIGHTING YEARS	Simple Minds (Virgin)
-	47	IS THIS LOVE	Various Artists (EMI)
-	48	SATURDAY NIGHT SUNDAY MORNING	River Detectives (WEA)
-	49	COCKED AND LOADED	L.A. Guns (Vertigo)
-	50	HOME LOVIN' MAN	Roger Whittaker (Tembo)

7 October 1989

last	this	Title	Artist (Label)
-	1	THE SEEDS OF LOVE	Tears For Fears (Fontana)
2	2	FOREIGN AFFAIR	Tina Turner (Capitol)
14	3	DEEP HEAT 4 - PLAY WITH FIRE	Various Artists (Telstar)
1	4	WE TOO ARE ONE	Eurythmics (RCA)
6	5	CUTS BOTH WAYS	Gloria Estefan (Epic)
4	6	PUMP	Aerosmith (Geffen)
10	7	REPEAT OFFENDER	Richard Marx (EMI USA)
8	8	JANET JACKSON'S RHYTHM NATION 1814	Janet Jackson (A&M)
12	9	LIKE A PRAYER	Madonna (Sire)
13	10	TEN GOOD REASONS	Jason Donovan (PWL)
11	11	JUST SEVENTEEN - HEARTBEATS	Various Artists (Fanfare)
5	12	NOW THAT'S WHAT I CALL MUSIC 15	Various Artists (EMI/Virgin/PolyGram)
3	13	STEEL WHEELS	Rolling Stones (CBS)
32	14	ANOTHER PLACE AND TIME	Donna Summer (Warner Bros.)
-	15	SEASONS END	Marillion (EMI)
15	16	A NEW FLAME	Simply Red (Elektra)
29	17	LOVEHOUSE	Various Artists (K-Tel)
7	18	SLEEPING WITH THE PAST	Elton John (Rocket)
37	19	THE 12 COMMANDMENTS OF DANCE	London Boys (WEA)
18	20	ADEVA	Adeva (Cooltempo)
47	21	IS THIS LOVE	Various Artists (EMI)
9	22	ASPECTS OF LOVE	Various Artists (Really Useful)
20	23	RAW LIKE SUSHI	Neneh Cherry (Circa)
16	24	THE RAW AND THE COOKED	Fine Young Cannibals (London)
19	25	WHEN THE WORLD KNOWS YOUR NAME	Deacon Blue (CBS)
22	26	TRASH	Alice Cooper (Epic)
17	27	BATMAN	Prince (Warner Bros.)
27	28	CLUB CLASSICS VOL.1	Soul II Soul (10)
26	29	DON'T BE CRUEL	Bobby Brown (MCA)
28	30	HEART AND SOUL - 18 CLASSIC SOUL CUTS	Various Artists (Polydor)
30	31	CHANGE	Alarm (IRS)
-	32	KARYN WHITE	Karyn White (Warner Bros.)
31	33	ANYTHING FOR YOU	Gloria Estefan & the Miami Sound Machine (Epic)
50	34	HOME LOVIN' MAN	Roger Whittaker (Tembo)
23	35	APPETITE FOR DESTRUCTION	Guns N' Roses (Geffen)
33	36	RAW	Alyson Williams (Def Jam)
25	37	ALL THE HITS	Imagination (Stylus)
-	38	CANDLELAND	Ian McCulloch (WEA)
41	39	HEART LIKE A SKY	Spandau Ballet (CBS)
21	40	DR. FEELGOOD	Motley Crue (Elektra)
36	41	CHOICES	Blow Monkeys (RCA)
24	42	ERROL FLYNN	Dogs D'Amour (China)
43	43	STRAIGHT OUTTA COMPTON	NWA (Fourth & Broadway)
39	44	VELVETEEN	Transvision Vamp (MCA)
40	45	THE MIRACLE	Queen (Parlophone)
-	46	IT'S A BIG DADDY THING	Big Daddy Kane (Cold Chillin')
42	47	PARADISE	Inner City (10)
-	48	HEART OF STONE	Cher (Geffen)
38	49	THE ULTIMATE COLLECTION	Kinks (Castle Communications)
-	50	FLYING COWBOYS	Rickie Lee Jones (Geffen)

Like *The Phantom Of The Opera* before it, another new hit Andrew Lloyd Webber West End musical, *Aspects Of Love*, managed to place its original cast album at the top of the chart. The show's most popular song was *Love Changes Everything*, which, sung by Michael Ball, had been a major hit single at the beginning of the year. *Aspects'* most unusual aspect was its odd chart moves from 8 to 1, and back to 9.

October 1989

14 October 1989

last week	this week	Title	Artist (Label)
1	1	THE SEEDS OF LOVE	Tears For Fears (Fontana)
-	2	CROSSROADS	Tracy Chapman (Elektra)
3	3	DEEP HEAT 4 - PLAY WITH FIRE	Various Artists (Telstar)
2	4	FOREIGN AFFAIR	Tina Turner (Capitol)
5	5	CUTS BOTH WAYS	Gloria Estefan (Epic)
9	6	LIKE A PRAYER	Madonna (Sire)
21	7	IS THIS LOVE	Various Artists (EMI)
4	8	WE TOO ARE ONE	Eurythmics (RCA)
8	9	JANET JACKSON'S RHYTHM NATION 1814	Janet Jackson (A&M)
10	10	TEN GOOD REASONS	Jason Donovan (PWL)
6	11	PUMP	Aerosmith (Geffen)
-	12	OH MERCY	Bob Dylan (CBS)
7	13	REPEAT OFFENDER	Richard Marx (EMI USA)
13	14	STEEL WHEELS	Rolling Stones (CBS)
25	15	WHEN THE WORLD KNOWS YOUR NAME	Deacon Blue (CBS)
-	16	HUP	Wonder Stuff (Polydor)
33	17	ANYTHING FOR YOU	Gloria Estefan & the Miami Sound Machine (Epic)
16	18	A NEW FLAME	Simply Red (Elektra)
19	19	THE 12 COMMANDMENTS OF DANCE	London Boys (WEA)
20	20	ADEVA	Adeva (Cooltempo)
12	21	NOW THAT'S WHAT I CALL MUSIC 15	Various Artists (EMI/Virgin/PolyGram)
38	22	CANDLELAND	Ian McCulloch (WEA)
23	23	RAW LIKE SUSHI	Neneh Cherry (Circa)
-	24	SEARCHLIGHT	Runrig (Chrysalis)
15	25	SEASONS END	Marillion (EMI)
22	26	ASPECTS OF LOVE	Various Artists (Really Useful)
14	27	ANOTHER PLACE AND TIME	Donna Summer (Warner Bros.)
17	28	LOVEHOUSE	Various Artists (K-Tel)
24	29	THE RAW AND THE COOKED	Fine Young Cannibals (London)
48	30	HEART OF STONE	Cher (Geffen)
11	31	JUST SEVENTEEN - HEARTBEATS	Various Artists (Fanfare)
18	32	SLEEPING WITH THE PAST	Elton John (Rocket)
28	33	CLUB CLASSICS VOL.1	Soul II Soul (10)
32	34	KARYN WHITE	Karyn White (Warner Bros.)
44	35	VELVETEEN	Transvision Vamp (MCA)
30	36	HEART AND SOUL - 18 CLASSIC SOUL CUTS	Various Artists (Polydor)
29	37	DON'T BE CRUEL	Bobby Brown (MCA)
26	38	TRASH	Alice Cooper (Epic)
27	39	BATMAN	Prince (Warner Bros.)
-	40	JARRE LIVE	Jean-Michel Jarre (Polydor)
-	41	SACRED HEART	Shakespear's Sister (London)
-	42	TOUGH IT OUT	FM (Epic)
35	43	APPETITE FOR DESTRUCTION	Guns N' Roses (Geffen)
-	44	ETERNAL LOVE	Various Artists (K-tel)
36	45	RAW	Alyson Williams (Def Jam)
-	46	STREET FIGHTING YEARS	Simple Minds (Virgin)
-	47	VIVALDI: THE FOUR SEASONS	Nigel Kennedy with the English Chamber Orchestra (EMI)
34	48	HOME LOVIN' MAN	Roger Whittaker (Tembo)
-	49	HERE TODAY, TOMORROW, NEXT WEEK	Sugarcubes (One Little Indian)
-	50	LIQUIDIZER	Jesus Jones (Food)

21 October 1989

last week	this week	Title	Artist (Label)
-	1	ENJOY YOURSELF	Kylie Minogue (PWL)
2	2	CROSSROADS	Tracy Chapman (Elektra)
3	3	DEEP HEAT 4 - PLAY WITH FIRE	Various Artists (Telstar)
4	4	FOREIGN AFFAIR	Tina Turner (Capitol)
1	5	THE SEEDS OF LOVE	Tears For Fears (Fontana)
12	6	OH MERCY	Bob Dylan (CBS)
5	7	CUTS BOTH WAYS	Gloria Estefan (Epic)
6	8	LIKE A PRAYER	Madonna (Sire)
7	9	IS THIS LOVE	Various Artists (EMI)
-	10	AUTOMATIC	Jesus & Mary Chain (blanco y negro)
10	11	TEN GOOD REASONS	Jason Donovan (PWL)
8	12	WE TOO ARE ONE	Eurythmics (RCA)
-	13	RESULTS	Liza Minnelli (Epic)
19	14	THE 12 COMMANDMENTS OF DANCE	London Boys (WEA)
16	15	HUP	Wonder Stuff (Polydor)
9	16	JANET JACKSON'S RHYTHM NATION 1814	Janet Jackson (A&M)
49	17	HERE TODAY, TOMORROW, NEXT WEEK	Sugarcubes (One Little Indian)
40	18	JARRE LIVE	Jean-Michel Jarre (Polydor)
18	19	A NEW FLAME	Simply Red (Elektra)
15	20	WHEN THE WORLD KNOWS YOUR NAME	Deacon Blue (CBS)
11	21	PUMP	Aerosmith (Geffen)
29	22	THE RAW AND THE COOKED	Fine Young Cannibals (London)
17	23	ANYTHING FOR YOU	Gloria Estefan & the Miami Sound Machine (Epic)
13	24	REPEAT OFFENDER	Richard Marx (EMI USA)
-	25	ITALIA - DANCE MUSIC FROM ITALY	Various Artists (deConstruction)
14	26	STEEL WHEELS	Rolling Stones (CBS)
20	27	ADEVA	Adeva (Cooltempo)
30	28	HEART OF STONE	Cher (Geffen)
23	29	RAW LIKE SUSHI	Neneh Cherry (Circa)
34	30	KARYN WHITE	Karyn White (Warner Bros.)
-	31	RETRO	Lou Reed (RCA)
35	32	VELVETEEN	Transvision Vamp (MCA)
27	33	ANOTHER PLACE AND TIME	Donna Summer (Warner Bros.)
33	34	CLUB CLASSICS VOL.1	Soul II Soul (10)
21	35	NOW THAT'S WHAT I CALL MUSIC 15	Various Artists (EMI/Virgin/PolyGram)
-	36	HATS	Blue Nile (Linn)
50	37	LIQUIDIZER	Jesus Jones (Food)
26	38	ASPECTS OF LOVE	Various Artists (Really Useful)
32	39	SLEEPING WITH THE PAST	Elton John (Rocket)
37	40	DON'T BE CRUEL	Bobby Brown (MCA)
-	41	COMING IN FOR THE KILL	Climie Fisher (EMI)
44	42	ETERNAL LOVE	Various Artists (K-tel)
38	43	TRASH	Alice Cooper (Epic)
25	44	SEASONS END	Marillion (EMI)
39	45	BATMAN	Prince (Warner Bros.)
24	46	SEARCHLIGHT	Runrig (Chrysalis)
-	47	FREEDOM	Neil Young (Reprise)
-	48	PORCELAIN	Julia Fordham (Circa)
43	49	APPETITE FOR DESTRUCTION	Guns N' Roses (Geffen)
42	50	TOUGH IT OUT	FM (Epic)

28 October 1989

last week	this week	Title	Artist (Label)
-	1	WILD!	Erasure (Mute)
-	2	THE SENSUAL WORLD	Kate Bush (EMI)
1	3	ENJOY YOURSELF	Kylie Minogue (PWL)
2	4	CROSSROADS	Tracy Chapman (Elektra)
-	5	THE TIME	Bros (CBS)
3	6	DEEP HEAT 4 - PLAY WITH FIRE	Various Artists (Telstar)
5	7	THE SEEDS OF LOVE	Tears For Fears (Fontana)
4	8	FOREIGN AFFAIR	Tina Turner (Capitol)
7	9	CUTS BOTH WAYS	Gloria Estefan (Epic)
-	10	SCARLET AND OTHER STORIES	All About Eve (Mercury)
14	11	THE 12 COMMANDMENTS OF DANCE	London Boys (WEA)
36	12	HATS	Blue Nile (Linn)
8	13	LIKE A PRAYER	Madonna (Sire)
11	14	TEN GOOD REASONS	Jason Donovan (PWL)
6	15	OH MERCY	Bob Dylan (CBS)
47	16	FREEDOM	Neil Young (Reprise)
9	17	IS THIS LOVE	Various Artists (EMI)
12	18	WE TOO ARE ONE	Eurythmics (RCA)
-	19	PURE	Primitives (RCA)
10	20	AUTOMATIC	Jesus & Mary Chain (blanco y negro)
13	21	RESULTS	Liza Minnelli (Epic)
48	22	PORCELAIN	Julia Fordham (Circa)
-	23	DEF, DUMB AND BLONDE	Deborah Harry (Chrysalis)
28	24	HEART OF STONE	Cher (Geffen)
-	25	THE RIGHT STUFF REMIX '89	Various Artists (Stylus)
19	26	A NEW FLAME	Simply Red (Elektra)
31	27	RETRO	Lou Reed (RCA)
20	28	WHEN THE WORLD KNOWS YOUR NAME	Deacon Blue (CBS)
-	29	2X2	Milli Vanilli (Cooltempo)
-	30	MOTOWN HEARTBREAKERS	Various Artists (Telstar)
49	31	APPETITE FOR DESTRUCTION	Guns N' Roses (Geffen)
23	32	ANYTHING FOR YOU	Gloria Estefan & the Miami Sound Machine (Epic)
16	33	JANET JACKSON'S RHYTHM NATION 1814	Janet Jackson (A&M)
27	34	ADEVA	Adeva (Cooltempo)
21	35	PUMP	Aerosmith (Geffen)
15	36	HUP	Wonder Stuff (Polydor)
22	37	THE RAW AND THE COOKED	Fine Young Cannibals (London)
18	38	JARRE LIVE	Jean-Michel Jarre (Polydor)
26	39	STEEL WHEELS	Rolling Stones (CBS)
34	40	CLUB CLASSICS VOL.1	Soul II Soul (10)
-	41	FREE	Sydney Youngblood (Circa)
-	42	SMASH HITS PARTY '89	Various Artists (Dover)
33	43	ANOTHER PLACE AND TIME	Donna Summer (Warner Bros.)
17	44	HERE TODAY, TOMORROW, NEXT WEEK	Sugarcubes (One Little Indian)
-	45	3 FEET HIGH AND RISING	De La Soul (Big Life)
40	46	DON'T BE CRUEL	Bobby Brown (MCA)
38	47	ASPECTS OF LOVE	Various Artists (Really Useful)
-	48	GREATEST HITS	Five Star (Tent)
24	49	REPEAT OFFENDER	Richard Marx (EMI USA)
29	50	RAW LIKE SUSHI	Neneh Cherry (Circa)

Another strong chart period for female singers, who occupied all three top places and two more slots in the Top 10 at the end of October. Tracy Chapman's second album just failed to emulate its chart-topping predecessor, but Kylie Minogue's *Enjoy Yourself* equalled her debut's Number 1 status, without having the same chart longevity, while *The Sensual World* just failed to extend Kate Bush's Number 1 tally.

November 1989

4 November 1989

last	this	title	artist
1	1	WILD!	Erasure (Mute)
3	2	ENJOY YOURSELF	Kylie Minogue (PWL)
2	3	THE SENSUAL WORLD	Kate Bush (EMI)
-	4	WELCOME TO THE BEAUTIFUL SOUTH	Beautiful South (Go! Discs)
-	5	RUNAWAY HORSES	Belinda Carlisle (Virgin)
-	6	NEITHER FISH NOR FLESH	Terence Trent D'Arby (CBS)
29	7	2X2	Milli Vanilli (Cooltempo)
9	8	CUTS BOTH WAYS	Gloria Estefan (Epic)
4	9	CROSSROADS	Tracy Chapman (Elektra)
8	10	FOREIGN AFFAIR	Tina Turner (Capitol)
25	11	THE RIGHT STUFF REMIX '89	Various Artists (Stylus)
34	12	ADEVA	Adeva (Cooltempo)
5	13	THE TIME	Bros (CBS)
-	14	BIZARRO	Wedding Present (RCA)
7	15	THE SEEDS OF LOVE	Tears For Fears (Fontana)
-	16	SPARK TO A FLAME - THE VERY BEST OF CHRIS DE BURGH	Chris De Burgh (A&M)
11	17	THE 12 COMMANDMENTS OF DANCE	London Boys (WEA)
-	18	GREATEST HITS	Billy Ocean (Jive)
-	19	STORM FRONT	Billy Joel (CBS)
26	20	A NEW FLAME	Simply Red (Elektra)
6	21	DEEP HEAT 4 - PLAY WITH FIRE	Various Artists (Telstar)
10	22	SCARLET AND OTHER STORIES	All About Eve (Mercury)
-	23	THE SINGLES ALBUM	Gladys Knight & the Pips (PolyGram TV)
24	24	HEART OF STONE	Cher (Geffen)
42	25	SMASH HITS PARTY '89	Various Artists (Dover)
-	26	HOT IN THE SHADE	Kiss (Fontana)
45	27	3 FEET HIGH AND RISING	De La Soul (Big Life)
14	28	TEN GOOD REASONS	Jason Donovan (PWL)
13	29	LIKE A PRAYER	Madonna (Sire)
18	30	WE TOO ARE ONE	Eurythmics (RCA)
23	31	DEF, DUMB AND BLONDE	Deborah Harry (Chrysalis)
-	32	RAP ATTACK	Various Artists (K-tel)
17	33	IS THIS LOVE	Various Artists (Jive)
41	34	FEELING FREE	Sydney Youngblood (Circa)
21	35	RESULTS	Liza Minnelli (Epic)
32	36	ANYTHING FOR YOU	Gloria Estefan & the Miami Sound Machine (Epic)
12	37	HATS	Blue Nile (Linn)
31	38	APPETITE FOR DESTRUCTION	Guns N' Roses (Geffen)
15	39	OH MERCY	Bob Dylan (CBS)
-	40	GETAHEAD	Curiosity Killed The Cat (Mercury)
16	41	FREEDOM	Neil Young (Reprise)
-	42	VELVETEEN	Transvision Vamp (MCA)
20	43	AUTOMATIC	Jesus & Mary Chain (blanco y negro)
22	44	PORCELAIN	Julia Fordham (Circa)
37	45	THE RAW AND THE COOKED	Fine Young Cannibals (London)
-	46	THE GREATEST LOVE 3	Various Artists (Telstar)
19	47	PURE	Primitives (RCA)
33	48	JANET JACKSON'S RHYTHM NATION 1814	Janet Jackson (A&M)
-	49	THEIR GREATEST HITS	Foster & Allen (Stylus)
35	50	PUMP	Aerosmith (Geffen)

11 November 1989

last	this	title	artist
1	1	WILD!	Erasure (Mute)
-	2	THE ROAD TO HELL	Chris Rea (WEA)
-	3	HOLDING BACK THE RIVER	Wet Wet Wet (Precious Organisation)
4	4	WELCOME TO THE BEAUTIFUL SOUTH	Beautiful South (Go! Discs)
2	5	ENJOY YOURSELF	Kylie Minogue (PWL)
5	6	RUNAWAY HORSES	Belinda Carlisle (Virgin)
16	7	SPARK TO A FLAME - THE VERY BEST OF CHRIS DE BURGH	Chris De Burgh (A&M)
19	8	STORM FRONT	Billy Joel (CBS)
7	9	2X2	Milli Vanilli (Cooltempo)
-	10	STRONGER	Cliff Richard (EMI)
18	11	GREATEST HITS	Billy Ocean (Jive)
3	12	THE SENSUAL WORLD	Kate Bush (EMI)
25	13	SMASH HITS PARTY '89	Various Artists (Dover)
-	14	THE BEST OF LUTHER VANDROSS - THE BEST OF LOVE	Luther Vandross (Epic)
23	15	THE SINGLES ALBUM	Gladys Knight & the Pips (PolyGram TV)
8	16	CUTS BOTH WAYS	Gloria Estefan (Epic)
9	17	CROSSROADS	Tracy Chapman (Elektra)
11	18	THE RIGHT STUFF REMIX '89	Various (Stylus)
10	19	FOREIGN AFFAIR	Tina Turner (Capitol)
6	20	NEITHER FISH NOR FLESH	Terence Trent D'Arby (CBS)
20	21	A NEW FLAME	Simply Red (Elektra)
24	22	HEART OF STONE	Cher (Geffen)
30	23	WE TOO ARE ONE	Eurythmics (RCA)
12	24	ADEVA	Adeva (Cooltempo)
-	25	ROCK CITY NIGHTS	Various Artists (Vertigo)
26	26	TEN GOOD REASONS	Jason Donovan (PWL)
27	27	3 FEET HIGH AND RISING	De La Soul (Big Life)
13	28	THE TIME	Bros (CBS)
17	29	THE 12 COMMANDMENTS OF DANCE	London Boys (WEA)
40	30	GETAHEAD	Curiosity Killed The Cat (Mercury)
15	31	THE SEEDS OF LOVE	Tears For Fears (Fontana)
29	32	LIKE A PRAYER	Madonna (Sire)
21	33	DEEP HEAT 4 - PLAY WITH FIRE	Various Artists (Telstar)
14	34	BIZARRO	Wedding Present (RCA)
-	35	GATECRASHING	Living In A Box (Chrysalis)
31	36	DEF, DUMB AND BLONDE	Deborah Harry (Chrysalis)
-	37	MONSTER HITS	Various Artists (CBS/WEA/BMG)
42	38	VELVETEEN	Transvision Vamp (MCA)
-	39	WHEN THE WORLD KNOWS YOUR NAME	Deacon Blue (CBS)
34	40	FEELING FREE	Sydney Youngblood (Circa)
46	41	THE GREATEST LOVE 3	Various Artists (Telstar)
-	42	HUP	Wonder Stuff (Polydor)
45	43	THE RAW AND THE COOKED	Fine Young Cannibals (London)
26	44	HOT IN THE SHADE	Kiss (Fontana)
-	45	"ADDICTIONS" VOLUME ONE	Robert Palmer (Island)
22	46	SCARLET AND OTHER STORIES	All About Eve (Mercury)
36	47	ANYTHING FOR YOU	Gloria Estefan & the Miami Sound Machine (Epic)
-	48	A LITTLE BIT OF THIS A LITTLE BIT OF THAT	D Mob (ffrr)
-	49	THOUGHTS OF HOME	Daniel O'Donnell (Telstar)
38	50	APPETITE FOR DESTRUCTION	Guns N' Roses (Geffen)

18 November 1989

last	this	title	artist
2	1	THE ROAD TO HELL	Chris Rea (WEA)
3	2	HOLDING BACK THE RIVER	Wet Wet Wet (Precious Organisation)
-	3	JOURNEYMAN	Eric Clapton (Duck)
5	4	ENJOY YOURSELF	Kylie Minogue (PWL)
-	5	LEVEL BEST	Level 42 (Polydor)
11	6	GREATEST HITS	Billy Ocean (Jive)
1	7	WILD!	Erasure (Mute)
14	8	THE BEST OF LUTHER VANDROSS - THE BEST OF LOVE	Luther Vandross (Epic)
6	9	RUNAWAY HORSES	Belinda Carlisle (Virgin)
18	10	THE RIGHT STUFF REMIX '89	Various (Stylus)
10	11	STRONGER	Cliff Richard (EMI)
9	12	2X2	Milli Vanilli (Cooltempo)
13	13	SMASH HITS PARTY '89	Various Artists (Dover)
7	14	SPARK TO A FLAME - THE VERY BEST OF CHRIS DE BURGH	Chris De Burgh (A&M)
15	15	THE SINGLES ALBUM	Gladys Knight & the Pips (PolyGram TV)
4	16	WELCOME TO THE BEAUTIFUL SOUTH	Beautiful South (Go! Discs)
8	17	STORM FRONT	Billy Joel (CBS)
23	18	WE TOO ARE ONE	Eurythmics (RCA)
45	19	"ADDICTIONS" VOLUME ONE	Robert Palmer (Island)
16	20	CUTS BOTH WAYS	Gloria Estefan (Epic)
41	21	THE GREATEST LOVE 3	Various Artists (Telstar)
12	22	THE SENSUAL WORLD	Kate Bush (EMI)
25	23	ROCK CITY NIGHTS	Various Artists (Vertigo)
17	24	CROSSROADS	Tracy Chapman (Elektra)
-	25	MARTIKA	Martika (CBS)
21	26	A NEW FLAME	Simply Red (Elektra)
26	27	TEN GOOD REASONS	Jason Donovan (PWL)
-	28	JANET JACKSON'S RHYTHM NATION 1814	Janet Jackson (A&M)
22	29	HEART OF STONE	Cher (Geffen)
-	30	CRY LIKE A RAINSTORM - HOWL LIKE THE WIND	Linda Ronstadt (Elektra)
29	31	THE 12 COMMANDMENTS OF DANCE	London Boys (WEA)
19	32	FOREIGN AFFAIR	Tina Turner (Capitol)
31	33	THE SEEDS OF LOVE	Tears For Fears (Fontana)
20	34	NEITHER FISH NOR FLESH	Terence Trent D'Arby (CBS)
38	35	VELVETEEN	Transvision Vamp (MCA)
27	36	3 FEET HIGH AND RISING	De La Soul (Big Life)
35	37	GATECRASHING	Living In A Box (Chrysalis)
24	38	ADEVA	Adeva (Cooltempo)
-	39	THE CLASSIC EXPERIENCE	Various Artists (EMI)
28	40	THE TIME	Bros (CBS)
-	41	CAPTAIN SWING	Michelle Shocked (Cooking Vinyl)
36	42	DEF, DUMB AND BLONDE	Deborah Harry (Chrysalis)
37	43	MONSTER HITS	Various Artists (CBS/WEA/BMG)
44	44	DANCE DECADE - DANCE HITS OF THE 80'S	Various Artists (London)
32	45	LIKE A PRAYER	Madonna (Sire)
43	46	THE RAW AND THE COOKED	Fine Young Cannibals (London)
40	47	FEELING FREE	Sydney Youngblood (Circa)
-	48	THE 80'S - ALBUM OF THE DECADE	Various (EMI)
-	49	MOTOWN HEARTBREAKERS	Various Artists (Telstar)
-	50	QUADRASTATE	808 State (Creed)

Unlike their previous album *The Innocents*, Erasure's *Wild!* was an instant chart-topper, marking the duo's status, after several years of steadily growing popularity, as one of the major pop/rock attractions of the late 80s. The same sort of status, after something of a wilderness period, had now accrued to Chris Rea, whose *The Road To Hell* album and its namesake hit single were his all-time biggest sellers.

November – December 1989

25 November 1989

last	this	Title	Artist (Label)
1	1	THE ROAD TO HELL	Chris Rea (WEA)
5	2	LEVEL BEST	Level 42 (Polydor)
3	3	JOURNEYMAN	Eric Clapton (Duck)
6	4	GREATEST HITS	Billy Ocean (Jive)
4	5	ENJOY YOURSELF	Kylie Minogue (PWL)
14	6	SPARK TO A FLAME - THE VERY BEST OF CHRIS DE BURGH	Chris De Burgh (A&M)
-	7	SLIP OF THE TONGUE	Whitesnake (EMI)
9	8	RUNAWAY HORSES	Belinda Carlisle (Virgin)
11	9	STRONGER	Cliff Richard (EMI)
12	10	2X2	Milli Vanilli (Cooltempo)
-	11	DECADE	Duran Duran (EMI)
48	12	THE 80'S - ALBUM OF THE DECADE	Various (EMI)
2	13	HOLDING BACK THE RIVER	Wet Wet Wet (Precious Organisation)
7	14	WILD!	Erasure (Mute)
8	15	THE BEST OF LUTHER VANDROSS - THE BEST OF LOVE	Luther Vandross (Epic)
-	16	THE GREATEST HITS OF THE '80S	Various (Telstar)
19	17	"ADDICTIONS" VOLUME ONE	Robert Palm (Island)
13	18	SMASH HITS PARTY '89	Various Artists (Dover)
16	19	WELCOME TO THE BEAUTIFUL SOUTH	Beautiful South (Go! Discs)
15	20	THE SINGLES ALBUM	Gladys Knight & the Pips (PolyGram TV)
18	21	WE TOO ARE ONE	Eurythmics (RCA)
17	22	STORM FRONT	Billy Joel (CBS)
27	23	TEN GOOD REASONS	Jason Donovan (PWL)
33	24	THE SEEDS OF LOVE	Tears For Fears (Fontana)
-	25	THE BEST OF ROD STEWART	Rod Stewart (Warner Bros.)
30	26	CRY LIKE A RAINSTORM - HOWL LIKE THE WIND	Linda Ronstadt (Elektra)
-	27	THE GREATEST HITS OF '89	Various (Telstar)
26	28	A NEW FLAME	Simply Red (Elektra)
20	29	CUTS BOTH WAYS	Gloria Estefan (Epic)
22	30	THE SENSUAL WORLD	Kate Bush (EMI)
10	31	THE RIGHT STUFF REMIX '89	Various (Stylus)
46	32	THE RAW AND THE COOKED	Fine Young Cannibals (London)
21	33	THE GREATEST LOVE 3	Various Artists (Telstar)
24	34	CROSSROADS	Tracy Chapman (Elektra)
29	35	HEART OF STONE	Cher (Geffen)
32	36	FOREIGN AFFAIR	Tina Turner (Capitol)
31	37	THE 12 COMMANDMENTS OF DANCE	London Boys (WEA)
41	38	CAPTAIN SWING	Michelle Shocked (Cooking Vinyl)
-	39	A PORTRAIT OF DORIS DAY	Doris Day (Stylus)
-	40	COME TOGETHER AS ONE	Will Downing (Fourth & Broadway)
-	41	DEEP HEAT '89 - FIGHT THE FLAME	Various Artists (Telstar)
25	42	MARTIKA	Martika (CBS)
36	43	3 FEET HIGH AND RISING	De La Soul (Big Life)
50	44	QUADRASTATE	808 State (Creed)
28	45	JANET JACKSON'S RHYTHM NATION 1814	Janet Jackson (A&M)
-	46	THE WANTED REMIXES	Yazz (Big Life)
-	47	TRUST	Brother Beyond (Parlophone)
38	48	ADEVA	Adeva (Cooltempo)
-	49	THE BEST YEARS OF OUR LIVES	Neil Diamond (CBS)
42	50	DEF, DUMB AND BLONDE	Deborah Harry (Chrysalis)

2 December 1989

last	this	Title	Artist (Label)
-	1	... BUT SERIOUSLY	Phil Collins (Virgin)
1	2	THE ROAD TO HELL	Chris Rea (WEA)
-	3	AFFECTION	Lisa Stansfield (Arista)
-	4	NOW THAT'S WHAT I CALL MUSIC 16	Various Artists (EMI/Virgin/PolyGram)
5	5	ENJOY YOURSELF	Kylie Minogue (PWL)
25	6	THE BEST OF ROD STEWART	Rod Stewart (Warner Bros.)
11	7	DECADE	Duran Duran (EMI)
6	8	SPARK TO A FLAME - THE VERY BEST OF CHRIS DE BURGH	Chris De Burgh (A&M)
9	9	STRONGER	Cliff Richard (EMI)
2	10	LEVEL BEST	Level 42 (Polydor)
16	11	THE GREATEST HITS OF THE '80S	Various (Telstar)
12	12	THE 80'S - ALBUM OF THE DECADE	Various (EMI)
7	13	SLIP OF THE TONGUE	Whitesnake (EMI)
14	14	GREATEST HITS	Billy Ocean (Jive)
20	15	THE SINGLES ALBUM	Gladys Knight & the Pips (PolyGram TV)
23	16	TEN GOOD REASONS	Jason Donovan (PWL)
3	17	JOURNEYMAN	Eric Clapton (Duck)
10	18	2X2	Milli Vanilli (Cooltempo)
-	19	DANCE ... YA KNOW IT	Bobby Brown (MCA)
17	20	"ADDICTIONS" VOLUME ONE	Robert Palm (Island)
8	21	RUNAWAY HORSES	Belinda Carlisle (Virgin)
29	22	CUTS BOTH WAYS	Gloria Estefan (Epic)
-	23	THE HEART OF CHICAGO	Chicago (WEA)
-	24	MONSTER HITS	Various Artists (CBS/WEA/BMG)
24	25	THE SEEDS OF LOVE	Tears For Fears (Fontana)
14	26	WILD!	Erasure (Mute)
19	27	WELCOME TO THE BEAUTIFUL SOUTH	Beautiful South (Go! Discs)
21	28	WE TOO ARE ONE	Eurythmics (RCA)
13	29	HOLDING BACK THE RIVER	Wet Wet Wet (Precious Organisation)
22	30	STORM FRONT	Billy Joel (CBS)
15	31	THE BEST OF LUTHER VANDROSS - THE BEST OF LOVE	Luther Vandross (Epic)
32	32	THE RAW AND THE COOKED	Fine Young Cannibals (London)
41	33	DEEP HEAT '89 - FIGHT THE FLAME	Various Artists (Telstar)
-	34	THEIR GREATEST HITS	Foster & Allen (Stylus)
-	35	AFTER THE LAUGHTER	Freddie Starr (Dover)
26	36	CRY LIKE A RAINSTORM - HOWL LIKE THE WIND	Linda Ronstadt (Elektra)
28	37	A NEW FLAME	Simply Red (Elektra)
-	38	GREATEST HITS LIVE	Diana Ross (EMI)
27	39	THE GREATEST HITS OF '89	Various Artists (Telstar)
30	40	THE SENSUAL WORLD	Kate Bush (EMI)
-	41	A COLLECTION - GREATEST HITS ... AND MORE	Barbra Streisand (CBS)
-	42	THE STONE ROSES	Stone Roses (Silvertone)
18	43	SMASH HITS PARTY '89	Various Artists (Dover)
31	44	THE RIGHT STUFF REMIX '89	Various Artists (Stylus)
34	45	CROSSROADS	Tracy Chapman (Elektra)
36	46	FOREIGN AFFAIR	Tina Turner (Capitol)
-	47	THE LOVE SONGS OF ANDREW LLOYD WEBBER	Richard Clayderman (Decca Delphine)
42	48	MARTIKA	Martika (CBS)
45	49	JANET JACKSON'S RHYTHM NATION 1814	Janet Jackson (A&M)
-	50	JUKE BOX JIVE MIX	Various Artists (Stylus)

9 December 1989

last	this	Title	Artist (Label)
1	1	... BUT SERIOUSLY	Phil Collins (Virgin)
4	2	NOW THAT'S WHAT I CALL MUSIC 16	Various Artists (EMI/Virgin/PolyGram)
24	3	MONSTER HITS	Various Artists (CBS/WEA/BMG)
3	4	AFFECTION	Lisa Stansfield (Arista)
5	5	ENJOY YOURSELF	Kylie Minogue (PWL)
6	6	THE BEST OF ROD STEWART	Rod Stewart (Warner Bros.)
-	7	LABOUR OF LOVE II	UB40 (DEP International)
16	8	TEN GOOD REASONS	Jason Donovan (PWL)
2	9	THE ROAD TO HELL	Chris Rea (WEA)
8	10	SPARK TO A FLAME - THE VERY BEST OF CHRIS DE BURGH	Chris De Burgh (A&M)
20	11	"ADDICTIONS" VOLUME ONE	Robert Palm (Island)
-	12	HANGIN' TOUGH	New Kids On The Block (CBS)
9	13	STRONGER	Cliff Richard (EMI)
11	14	THE GREATEST HITS OF THE '80S	Various Artists (Telstar)
12	15	THE 80'S - ALBUM OF THE DECADE	Various Artists (EMI)
10	16	LEVEL BEST	Level 42 (Polydor)
47	17	THE LOVE SONGS OF ANDREW LLOYD WEBBER	Richard Clayderman (Decca Delphine)
25	18	THE SEEDS OF LOVE	Tears For Fears (Fontana)
-	19	READ MY LIPS	Jimmy Somerville (London)
14	20	GREATEST HITS	Billy Ocean (Jive)
7	21	DECADE	Duran Duran (EMI)
22	22	CUTS BOTH WAYS	Gloria Estefan (Epic)
-	23	JIVE BUNNY - THE ALBUM	Jive Bunny & the Mastermixers (Telstar)
18	24	2X2	Milli Vanilli (Cooltempo)
45	25	FOREIGN AFFAIR	Tina Turner (Capitol)
17	26	JOURNEYMAN	Eric Clapton (Duck)
35	27	AFTER THE LAUGHTER	Freddie Starr (Dover)
26	28	WILD!	Erasure (Mute)
23	29	THE HEART OF CHICAGO	Chicago (WEA)
19	30	DANCE ... YA KNOW IT	Bobby Brown (MCA)
15	31	THE SINGLES ALBUM	Gladys Knight & the Pips (PolyGram TV)
27	32	WELCOME TO THE BEAUTIFUL SOUTH	Beautiful South (Go! Discs)
33	33	DEEP HEAT '89 - FIGHT THE FLAME	Various Artists (Telstar)
21	34	RUNAWAY HORSES	Belinda Carlisle (Virgin)
28	35	WE TOO ARE ONE	Eurythmics (RCA)
13	36	SLIP OF THE TONGUE	Whitesnake (EMI)
30	37	STORM FRONT	Billy Joel (CBS)
42	38	THE STONE ROSES	Stone Roses (Silvertone)
40	39	THE SENSUAL WORLD	Kate Bush (EMI)
29	40	HOLDING BACK THE RIVER	Wet Wet Wet (Precious Organisation)
34	41	THEIR GREATEST HITS	Foster & Allen (Stylus)
-	42	PRESTO	Rush (Atlantic)
32	43	THE RAW AND THE COOKED	Fine Young Cannibals (London)
36	44	CRY LIKE A RAINSTORM - HOWL LIKE THE WIND	Linda Ronstadt (Elektra)
48	45	MARTIKA	Martika (CBS)
39	46	THE GREATEST HITS OF '89	Various (Telstar)
31	47	THE BEST OF LUTHER VANDROSS - THE BEST OF LOVE	Luther Vandross (Epic)
-	48	JUKE BOX JIVE MIX	Various Artists (Stylus)
37	49	A NEW FLAME	Simply Red (Elektra)
-	50	MOSAIQUE	Gipsy Kings (Telstar)

Phil Collins' ...*But Seriously* was to become his all-time best-seller and also the biggest-ever for Virgin Records, overtaking Mike Oldfield's *Tubular Bells*. Its initial sales were prodigious enough: it went double Platinum (600,000 copies sold) during just its first four weeks in the chart. For once, the customary year-end *Now That's What I Call Music* compilation was to be held from the top by a stronger album.

December 1989

16 December 1989

last	this	Title	Artist
1	1	... BUT SERIOUSLY	Phil Collins (Virgin)
2	2	NOW THAT'S WHAT I CALL MUSIC 16	Various Artists (EMI/Virgin/PolyGram)
23	3	JIVE BUNNY - THE ALBUM	Jive Bunny & the Mastermixers (Telstar)
5	4	ENJOY YOURSELF	Kylie Minogue (PWL)
3	5	MONSTER HITS	Various Artists (CBS/WEA/BMG)
4	6	AFFECTION	Lisa Stansfield (Arista)
12	7	HANGIN' TOUGH	New Kids On The Block (CBS)
9	8	THE ROAD TO HELL	Chris Rea (WEA)
25	9	FOREIGN AFFAIR	Tina Turner (Capitol)
10	10	SPARK TO A FLAME - THE VERY BEST OF CHRIS DE BURGH	Chris De Burgh (A&M)
6	11	THE BEST OF ROD STEWART	Rod Stewart (Warner Bros.)
8	12	TEN GOOD REASONS	Jason Donovan (PWL)
7	13	LABOUR OF LOVE II	UB40 (DEP International)
11	14	"ADDICTIONS" VOLUME ONE	Robert Palmer (Island)
14	15	THE GREATEST HITS OF THE '80S	Various (Telstar)
13	16	STRONGER	Cliff Richard (EMI)
29	17	THE HEART OF CHICAGO	Chicago (WEA)
16	18	LEVEL BEST	Level 42 (Polydor)
33	19	DEEP HEAT '89 - FIGHT THE FLAME	Various Artists (Telstar)
-	20	IT'S CHRISTMAS	Various Artists (EMI)
18	21	THE SEEDS OF LOVE	Tears For Fears (Fontana)
22	22	CUTS BOTH WAYS	Gloria Estefan (Epic)
15	23	THE 80'S - ALBUM OF THE DECADE	Various Artists (EMI)
21	24	DECADE	Duran Duran (EMI)
17	25	THE LOVE SONGS OF ANDREW LLOYD WEBBER	Richard Clayderman (Decca Delphine)
50	26	MOSAIQUE	Gipsy Kings (Telstar)
26	27	JOURNEYMAN	Eric Clapton (Duck)
27	28	AFTER THE LAUGHTER	Freddie Starr (Dover)
43	29	THE RAW AND THE COOKED	Fine Young Cannibals (London)
20	30	GREATEST HITS	Billy Ocean (Jive)
-	31	ASPECTS OF LOVE	Various Artists (Polydor)
28	32	WILD!	Erasure (Mute)
24	33	2X2	Milli Vanilli (Cooltempo)
34	34	RUNAWAY HORSES	Belinda Carlisle (Virgin)
19	35	READ MY LIPS	Jimmy Somerville (London)
39	36	THE SENSUAL WORLD	Kate Bush (EMI)
49	37	A NEW FLAME	Simply Red (Elektra)
32	38	WELCOME TO THE BEAUTIFUL SOUTH	Beautiful South (Go! Discs)
-	39	A PORTRAIT OF DORIS DAY	Doris Day (Stylus)
-	40	NINETY	808 State (ZTT)
35	41	WE TOO ARE ONE	Eurythmics (RCA)
40	42	HOLDING BACK THE RIVER	Wet Wet Wet (Precious Organisation)
-	43	WAR OF THE WORLDS	Jeff Wayne (CBS)
-	44	THE JOE LONGTHORNE CHRISTMAS ALBUM	Joe Longthorne (Telstar)
30	45	DANCE ... YA KNOW IT	Bobby Brown (MCA)
45	46	MARTIKA	Martika (CBS)
-	47	FOSTER AND ALLEN CHRISTMAS COLLECTION	Foster & Allen (Stylus)
31	48	THE SINGLES ALBUM	Gladys Knight & the Pips (PolyGram TV)
-	49	QUEEN AT THE BEEB	Queen (Band Of Joy)
37	50	STORM FRONT	Billy Joel (CBS)

23 December 1989

last	this	Title	Artist
1	1	... BUT SERIOUSLY	Phil Collins (Virgin)
3	2	JIVE BUNNY - THE ALBUM	Jive Bunny & the Mastermixers (Telstar)
9	3	FOREIGN AFFAIR	Tina Turner (Capitol)
4	4	ENJOY YOURSELF	Kylie Minogue (PWL)
2	5	NOW THAT'S WHAT I CALL MUSIC 16	Various Artists (EMI/Virgin/PolyGram)
12	6	TEN GOOD REASONS	Jason Donovan (PWL)
20	7	IT'S CHRISTMAS	Various Artists (EMI)
8	8	THE ROAD TO HELL	Chris Rea (WEA)
6	9	AFFECTION	Lisa Stansfield (Arista)
5	10	MONSTER HITS	Various Artists (CBS/WEA/BMG)
10	11	SPARK TO A FLAME - THE VERY BEST OF CHRIS DE BURGH	Chris De Burgh (A&M)
29	12	THE RAW AND THE COOKED	Fine Young Cannibals (London)
11	13	THE BEST OF ROD STEWART	Rod Stewart (Warner Bros.)
13	14	LABOUR OF LOVE II	UB40 (DEP International)
7	15	HANGIN' TOUGH	New Kids On The Block (CBS)
18	16	LEVEL BEST	Level 42 (Polydor)
16	17	STRONGER	Cliff Richard (EMI)
15	18	THE GREATEST HITS OF THE '80S	Various(Telstar)
14	19	"ADDICTIONS" VOLUME ONE	Robert Palmer (Island)
32	20	WILD!	Erasure (Mute)
21	21	CUTS BOTH WAYS	Gloria Estefan (Epic)
42	22	HOLDING BACK THE RIVER	Wet Wet Wet (Precious Organisation)
21	23	THE SEEDS OF LOVE	Tears For Fears (Fontana)
24	24	DECADE	Duran Duran (EMI)
27	25	JOURNEYMAN	Eric Clapton (Duck)
25	26	THE LOVE SONGS OF ANDREW LLOYD WEBBER	Richard Clayderman (Decca Delphine)
30	27	GREATEST HITS	Billy Ocean (Jive)
17	28	THE HEART OF CHICAGO	Chicago (WEA)
-	29	AT THEIR VERY BEST	Shadows (Polydor)
26	30	MOSAIQUE	Gipsy Kings (Telstar)
19	31	DEEP HEAT '89 - FIGHT THE FLAME	Various (EMI)
37	32	A NEW FLAME	Simply Red (Elektra)
28	33	AFTER THE LAUGHTER	Freddie Starr (Dover)
-	34	THE 12 COMMANDMENTS OF DANCE	London Boys (WEA)
31	35	ASPECTS OF LOVE	Various Artists (Polydor)
33	36	2X2	Milli Vanilli (Cooltempo)
-	37	THE VERY BEST OF ELECTRIC LIGHT ORCHESTRA	Electric Light Orchestra (CBS)
23	38	THE 80'S - ALBUM OF THE DECADE	Various (EMI)
34	39	RUNAWAY HORSES	Belinda Carlisle (Virgin)
36	40	THE SENSUAL WORLD	Kate Bush (EMI)
47	41	FOSTER AND ALLEN CHRISTMAS COLLECTION	Foster & Allen (Stylus)
41	42	WE TOO ARE ONE	Eurythmics (RCA)
-	43	CRY LIKE A RAINSTORM - HOWL LIKE THE WIND	Linda Ronstadt (Elektra)
-	44	WITH LOVE	Michael Crawford (Telstar)
-	45	THE BEST OF LUTHER VANDROSS - THE BEST OF LOVE	Luther Vandross (Epic)
-	46	PUMP UP THE JAM	Technotronic (Swanyard)
38	47	WELCOME TO THE BEAUTIFUL SOUTH	Beautiful South (Go! Discs)
50	48	STORM FRONT	Billy Joel (CBS)
-	49	CROSSROADS	Tracy Chapman (Elektra)
-	50	LIKE A PRAYER	Madonna (Sire)

Though Phil Collins ruled the Christmas roost, selling upwards of 20,000 copies a day, the year-end also belonged to Jason Donovan's *Ten Good Reasons*, which, as it went into a Yule sales spurt, topped sales of one-and-a-half million, and just pipped (on Christmas Eve, before the shops closed for the holiday) Simply Red's *A New Flame* as the biggest-selling album of 1989.

Making it at the end of the 80s, and into the 90s: Clockwise from top; Guns N' Roses Elton John Nigel Kennedy REM

January 1990

13 January 1990

last week / this week

last	this	Title	Artist
1	1	... BUT SERIOUSLY	Phil Collins (Vertigo)
4	2	ENJOY YOURSELF	Kylie Minogue (PWL)
3	3	FOREIGN AFFAIR	Tina Turner (Capitol)
5	4	TEN GOOD REASONS	Jason Donovan (PWL)
2	5	JIVE BUNNY - THE ALBUM	Jive Bunny & the Mastermixers (Telstar)
27	6	HANGIN' TOUGH	New Kids On The Block (CBS)
14	7	THE BEST OF ROD STEWART	Rod Stewart (Warner Bros.)
9	8	THE ROAD TO HELL	Chris Rea (WEA)
6	9	NOW THAT'S WHAT I CALL MUSIC 16	Various Artists (EMI/Virgin/PolyGram)
11	10	AFFECTION	Lisa Stansfield (Arista)
41	11	CLUB CLASSICS VOL 1	Soul II Soul (10)
10	12	MONSTER HITS	Various Artists (CBS/WEA/BMG)
7	13	HOLDING BACK THE RIVER	Wet Wet Wet (Precious Organisation)
44	14	LIKE A PRAYER	Madonna (Sire)
12	15	CUTS BOTH WAYS	Gloria Estefan (Epic)
17	16	THE GREATEST HITS OF THE 80S	Various (Telstar)
16	17	LEVEL BEST	Level 42 (Polydor)
18	18	WILD!	Erasure (Mute)
-	19	3 FEET HIGH AND RISING	De La Soul (Big Life)
13	20	SPARK TO A FLAME - THE VERY BESTOF CHRIS DE BURGH	Chris De Burgh (A&M)
24	21	DECADE	Duran Duran (EMI)
20	22	THE RAW AND THE COOKED	Fine Young Cannibals (London)
29	23	A NEW FLAME	Simply Red (Elektra)
21	24	LABOUR OF LOVE II	UB40 (DEP International)
38	25	2X2	Milli Vanilli (Cooltempo)
15	26	STRONGER	Cliff Richard (EMI)
25	27	DEEP HEAT '89 - FIGHT THE FLAME	Various Artists (Telstar)
22	28	"ADDICTIONS" VOLUME 1	Robert Palmer (Island)
28	29	THE SENSUAL WORLD	Kate Bush (EMI)
40	30	STORM FRONT	Billy Joel (CBS)
26	31	THE SEEDS OF LOVE	Tears For Fears (Fontana)
30	32	JOURNEYMAN	Eric Clapton (Duck)
-	33	THE STONE ROSES	Stone Roses (Silvertone)
33	34	THE 12 COMMANDMENTS OF DANCE	London Boys (WEA)
50	35	RUNAWAY HORSES	Belinda Carlisle (Virgin)
-	36	WARE'S THE HOUSE	Various Artists (Stylus)
-	37	MARTIKA	Martika (CBS)
38	38	GREATEST HITS	Billy Ocean (Jive)
45	39	THE TIME	Bros (CBS)
-	40	THE LOVE SONGS	Dionne Warwick (Arista)
43	41	THE BEST OF LUTHER VANDROSS - THE BEST OF LOVE	Luther Vandross (Epic)
19	42	AT THEIR VERY BEST	Shadows (Polydor)
-	43	RAW LIKE SUSHI	Neneh Cherry (Circa)
-	44	WHEN THE WORLD KNOWS YOUR NAME	Deacon Blue (CBS)
31	45	THE LOVE SONGS OF ANDREW LLOYD-WEBBER	Richard Clayderman (Decca Delphine)
39	46	THE '80S: ALBUM OF THE DECADE	Various Artists (EMI)
47	47	WELCOME TO THE BEAUTIFUL SOUTH	Beautiful South (Go! Discs)
-	48	FEELING FREE	Sydney Youngblood (Circa)
32	49	MOSAIQUE	Gipsy Kings (Telstar)
23	50	VERY BEST OF ELO	Electric Light Orchestra (Telstar)

20 January 1990

last	this	Title	Artist
1	1	... BUT SERIOUSLY	Phil Collins (Vertigo)
2	2	ENJOY YOURSELF	Kylie Minogue (PWL)
6	3	HANGIN' TOUGH	New Kids On The Block (CBS)
3	4	FOREIGN AFFAIR	Tina Turner (Capitol)
4	5	TEN GOOD REASONS	Jason Donovan (PWL)
8	6	THE ROAD TO HELL	Chris Rea (WEA)
5	7	JIVE BUNNY - THE ALBUM	Jive Bunny & the Mastermixers (Telstar)
10	8	AFFECTION	Lisa Stansfield (Arista)
40	9	THE LOVE SONGS	Dionne Warwick (Arista)
7	10	THE BEST OF ROD STEWART	Rod Stewart (Warner Bros.)
13	11	HOLDING BACK THE RIVER	Wet Wet Wet (Precious Organisation)
14	12	LIKE A PRAYER	Madonna (Sire)
11	13	CLUB CLASSICS VOL 1	Soul II Soul (10)
9	14	NOW THAT'S WHAT I CALL MUSIC 16	Various Artists (EMI/Virgin/PolyGram)
22	15	THE RAW AND THE COOKED	Fine Young Cannibals (London)
36	16	WARE'S THE HOUSE	Various Artists (Stylus)
12	17	MONSTER HITS	Various Artists (CBS/WEA/BMG)
19	18	3 FEET HIGH AND RISING	De La Soul (Big Life)
23	19	A NEW FLAME	Simply Red (Elektra)
20	20	WILD!	Erasure (Mute)
21	21	DECADE	Duran Duran (EMI)
33	22	THE STONE ROSES	Stone Roses (Silvertone)
15	23	CUTS BOTH WAYS	Gloria Estefan (Epic)
20	24	SPARK TO A FLAME - THE VERY BESTOF CHRIS DE BURGH	Chris De Burgh (A&M)
37	25	MARTIKA	Martika (CBS)
17	26	LEVEL BEST	Level 42 (Polydor)
27	27	PURE SOFT METAL	Various Artists (Stylus)
-	28	DEEP HEAT '89 - FIGHT THE FLAME	Various Artists (Telstar)
29	29	THE SINGLES 1969-1973	Carpenters (A&M)
24	30	LABOUR OF LOVE II	UB40 (DEP International)
30	31	STORM FRONT	Billy Joel (CBS)
16	32	THE GREATEST HITS OF THE 80S	Various (Telstar)
47	33	WELCOME TO THE BEAUTIFUL SOUTH	Beautiful South (Go! Discs)
26	34	STRONGER	Cliff Richard (EMI)
28	35	"ADDICTIONS" VOLUME 1	Robert Palmer (Island)
31	36	THE SEEDS OF LOVE	Tears For Fears (Fontana)
25	37	2X2	Milli Vanilli (Cooltempo)
-	38	VIVALDI: THE FOUR SEASONS	Nigel Kennedy with the English Chamber Orchestra
34	39	THE 12 COMMANDMENTS OF DANCE	London Boys (WEA)
50	40	VERY BEST OF ELO	Electric Light Orchestra (Telstar)
29	41	THE SENSUAL WORLD	Kate Bush (EMI)
41	42	THE BEST OF LUTHER VANDROSS - THE BEST OF LOVE	Luther Vandross (Epic)
32	43	JOURNEYMAN	Eric Clapton (Duck)
-	44	THE SINGLES 1974-1978	Carpenters (A&M)
35	45	RUNAWAY HORSES	Belinda Carlisle (Virgin)
44	46	WHEN THE WORLD KNOWS YOUR NAME	Deacon Blue (CBS)
42	47	AT THEIR VERY BEST	Shadows (Polydor)
-	48	READ MY LIPS	Jimmy Somerville (London)
-	49	A COLLECTION - GREATEST HITS ... AND MORE	Barbra Streisand (CBS)
38	50	GREATEST HITS	Billy Ocean (Jive)

27 January 1990

last	this	Title	Artist
-	1	COLOUR	Christians (Island)
1	2	... BUT SERIOUSLY	Phil Collins (Vertigo)
3	3	HANGIN' TOUGH	New Kids On The Block (CBS)
2	4	ENJOY YOURSELF	Kylie Minogue (PWL)
4	5	FOREIGN AFFAIR	Tina Turner (Capitol)
6	6	THE ROAD TO HELL	Chris Rea (WEA)
8	7	AFFECTION	Lisa Stansfield (Arista)
27	8	PURE SOFT METAL	Various Artists (Stylus)
10	9	THE BEST OF ROD STEWART	Rod Stewart (Warner Bros.)
5	10	TEN GOOD REASONS	Jason Donovan (PWL)
9	11	THE LOVE SONGS	Dionne Warwick (Arista)
13	12	CLUB CLASSICS VOL 1	Soul II Soul (10)
7	13	JIVE BUNNY - THE ALBUM	Jive Bunny & the Mastermixers (Telstar)
14	14	THE STONE ROSES	Stone Roses (Silvertone)
11	15	HOLDING BACK THE RIVER	Wet Wet Wet (Precious Organisation)
43	16	JOURNEYMAN	Eric Clapton (Duck)
16	17	WARE'S THE HOUSE	Various Artists (Stylus)
12	18	LIKE A PRAYER	Madonna (Sire)
-	19	READING, WRITING AND ARITHMETIC	Sundays (Rough Trade)
25	20	MARTIKA	Martika (CBS)
23	21	CUTS BOTH WAYS	Gloria Estefan (Epic)
15	22	THE RAW AND THE COOKED	Fine Young Cannibals (London)
49	23	A COLLECTION - GREATEST HITS ... AND MORE	Barbra Streisand (CBS)
18	24	3 FEET HIGH AND RISING	De La Soul (Big Life)
19	25	A NEW FLAME	Simply Red (Elektra)
33	26	WELCOME TO THE BEAUTIFUL SOUTH	Beautiful South (Go! Discs)
30	27	LABOUR OF LOVE II	UB40 (DEP International)
17	28	MONSTER HITS	Various Artists (CBS/WEA/BMG)
24	29	SPARK TO A FLAME - THE VERY BESTOF CHRIS DE BURGH	Chris De Burgh (A&M)
20	30	WILD!	Erasure (Mute)
-	31	WE TOO ARE ONE	Eurythmics (RCA)
38	32	VIVALDI: THE FOUR SEASONS	Nigel Kennedy with the English Chamber Orchestra
14	33	NOW THAT'S WHAT I CALL MUSIC 16	Various Artists (EMI/Virgin/PolyGram)
21	34	DECADE	Duran Duran (EMI)
48	35	READ MY LIPS	Jimmy Somerville (London)
29	36	THE SINGLES 1969-1973	Carpenters (A&M)
46	37	WHEN THE WORLD KNOWS YOUR NAME	Deacon Blue (CBS)
-	38	RAW LIKE SUSHI	Neneh Cherry (Circa)
-	39	FLOWERS IN THE DIRT	Paul McCartney (Parlophone)
26	40	LEVEL BEST	Level 42 (Polydor)
28	41	DEEP HEAT '89 - FIGHT THE FLAME	Various Artists (Telstar)
-	42	PUMP UP THE JAM	Technotronic (Swanyard)
47	43	AT THEIR VERY BEST	Shadows (Polydor)
35	44	"ADDICTIONS" VOLUME 1	Robert Palmer (Island)
31	45	STORM FRONT	Billy Joel (CBS)
-	46	BACK ON THE BLOCK	Quincy Jones (Qwest)
-	47	HEART OF STONE	Cher (Geffen)
44	48	THE SINGLES 1974-1978	Carpenters (A&M)
36	49	THE SEEDS OF LOVE	Tears For Fears (Fontana)
34	50	STRONGER	Cliff Richard (EMI)

Apart from the two weeks when the Christians' *Colour* overtook it, Phil Collins' *...But Seriously* was to totally dominate album sales during the early months of 1990, clocking up another two months at Number 1 to add to its tally from the previous year. Its eventual UK sales total would reach about two-and-a-half million, making it one of the half-dozen best-selling albums of all time.

3 February 1990

last week	this week	Title	Artist (label)
1	1	COLOUR	Christians (Island)
2	2	... BUT SERIOUSLY	Phil Collins (Vertigo)
8	3	PURE SOFT METAL	Various Artists (Stylus)
19	4	READING, WRITING AND ARITHMETIC	Sundays (Rough Trade)
3	5	HANGIN' TOUGH	New Kids On The Block (CBS)
16	6	JOURNEYMAN	Eric Clapton (Duck)
11	7	THE LOVE SONGS	Dionne Warwick (Arista)
4	8	ENJOY YOURSELF	Kylie Minogue (PWL)
5	9	FOREIGN AFFAIR	Tina Turner (Capitol)
7	10	AFFECTION	Lisa Stansfield (Arista)
-	11	DEEP HEAT 5 - FEED THE FEVER	Various(Telstar)
6	12	THE ROAD TO HELL	Chris Rea (WEA)
9	13	THE BEST OF ROD STEWART	Rod Stewart (Warner Bros.)
14	14	THE STONE ROSES	Stone Roses (Silvertone)
24	15	3 FEET HIGH AND RISING	De La Soul (Big Life)
12	16	CLUB CLASSICS VOL 1	Soul II Soul (10)
20	17	MARTIKA	Martika (CBS)
15	18	HOLDING BACK THE RIVER	Wet Wet Wet (Precious Organisation)
10	19	TEN GOOD REASONS	Jason Donovan (PWL)
17	20	WARE'S THE HOUSE	Various Artists (Stylus)
42	21	PUMP UP THE JAM	Technotronic (Swanyard)
22	22	THE RAW AND THE COOKED	Fine Young Cannibals (London)
13	23	JIVE BUNNY - THE ALBUM	Jive Bunny & the Mastermixers (Telstar)
47	24	HEART OF STONE	Cher (Geffen)
18	25	LIKE A PRAYER	Madonna (Sire)
32	26	VIVALDI: THE FOUR SEASONS	Nigel Kennedy with the English Chamber Orchestra
21	27	CUTS BOTH WAYS	Gloria Estefan (Epic)
-	28	DONE BY THE FORCES OF NATURE	Jungle Brothers (Eternal)
23	29	A COLLECTION - GREATEST HITS ... AND MORE	Barbra Streisand (CBS)
-	30	THE VERY BEST OF CAT STEVENS	Cat Stevens (Island)
31	31	WE TOO ARE ONE	Eurythmics (RCA)
26	32	WELCOME TO THE BEAUTIFUL SOUTH	Beautiful South (Go! Discs)
25	33	A NEW FLAME	Simply Red (Elektra)
27	34	LABOUR OF LOVE II	UB40 (DEP International)
35	35	READ MY LIPS	Jimmy Somerville (London)
36	36	THE SINGLES 1969-1973	Carpenters (A&M)
30	37	WILD!	Erasure (Mute)
46	38	BACK ON THE BLOCK	Quincy Jones (Qwest)
28	39	MONSTER HITS	Various Artists (CBS/WEA/BMG)
38	40	RAW LIKE SUSHI	Neneh Cherry (Circa)
29	41	SPARK TO A FLAME - THE VERY BESTOF CHRIS DE BURGH	Chris De Burgh (A&M)
-	42	A GILDED ETERNITY	Loop (Situation Two)
37	43	WHEN THE WORLD KNOWS YOUR NAME	Deacon Blue (CBS)
33	44	NOW THAT'S WHAT I CALL MUSIC 16	Various Artists (EMI/Virgin/PolyGram)
34	45	DECADE	Duran Duran (EMI)
-	46	GREATEST HITS	Billy Ocean (Jive)
49	47	THE SEEDS OF LOVE	Tears For Fears (Fontana)
40	48	LEVEL BEST	Level 42 (Polydor)
44	49	"ADDICTIONS" VOLUME 1	Robert Palmer (Island)
39	50	FLOWERS IN THE DIRT	Paul McCartney (Parlophone)

10 February 1990

last week	this week	Title	Artist (label)
2	1	... BUT SERIOUSLY	Phil Collins (Vertigo)
-	2	THE SWEET KEEPER	Tanita Tikaram (East West)
11	3	DEEP HEAT 5 - FEED THE FEVER	Various (Telstar)
-	4	A BIT OF WHAT YOU FANCY	Quireboys (Parlophone)
1	5	COLOUR	Christians (Island)
30	6	THE VERY BEST OF CAT STEVENS	Cat Stevens (Island)
6	7	JOURNEYMAN	Eric Clapton (Duck)
10	8	AFFECTION	Lisa Stansfield (Arista)
12	9	THE ROAD TO HELL	Chris Rea (WEA)
9	16	FOREIGN AFFAIR	Tina Turner (Capitol)
-	11	VIGIL IN A WILDERNESS OF MIRRORS	Fish (EMI)
21	12	PUMP UP THE JAM	Technotronic (Swanyard)
3	13	PURE SOFT METAL	Various Artists (Stylus)
24	14	HEART OF STONE	Cher (Geffen)
8	15	ENJOY YOURSELF	Kylie Minogue (PWL)
12	16	FOREIGN AFFAIR	Tina Turner (Capitol)
7	17	THE LOVE SONGS	Dionne Warwick (Arista)
14	18	THE STONE ROSES	Stone Roses (Silvertone)
4	19	READING, WRITING AND ARITHMETIC	Sundays (Rough Trade)
13	20	THE BEST OF ...	Rod Stewart (Warner Bros.)
16	21	CLUB CLASSICS VOL 1	Soul II Soul (10)
19	22	TEN GOOD REASONS	Jason Donovan (PWL)
22	23	THE RAW AND THE COOKED	Fine Young Cannibals (London)
33	24	A NEW FLAME	Simply Red (Elektra)
20	25	WARE'S THE HOUSE	Various Artists (Stylus)
15	26	3 FEET HIGH AND RISING	De La Soul (Big Life)
35	27	READ MY LIPS	Jimmy Somerville (London)
17	28	MARTIKA	Martika (CBS)
31	29	WE TOO ARE ONE	Eurythmics (RCA)
26	30	VIVALDI: THE FOUR SEASONS	Nigel Kennedy with the English Chamber Orchestra
43	31	WHEN THE WORLD KNOWS YOUR NAME	Deacon Blue (CBS)
18	32	HOLDING BACK THE RIVER	Wet Wet Wet (Precious Organisation)
27	33	CUTS BOTH WAYS	Gloria Estefan (Epic)
-	34	PARADISE REMIXED	Inner City (10)
25	35	LIKE A PRAYER	Madonna (Sire)
28	36	DONE BY THE FORCES OF NATURE	Jungle Brothers (Eternal)
-	37	THE CREAM OF ERIC CLAPTON	Eric Clapton & Cream (Polydor)
23	38	JIVE BUNNY - THE ALBUM	Jive Bunny & the Mastermixers (Telstar)
38	39	BACK ON THE BLOCK	Quincy Jones (Qwest)
29	40	A COLLECTION - GREATEST HITS ... AND MORE	Barbra Streisand (CBS)
32	41	WELCOME TO THE BEAUTIFUL SOUTH	Beautiful South (Go! Discs)
-	42	SKID ROW	Skid Row (Atlntic)
-	43	THE LION AND THE COBRA	Sinead O'Connor (Ensign)
37	44	WILD!	Erasure (Mute)
34	45	LABOUR OF LOVE II	UB40 (DEP International)
-	46	BUMMED	Happy Mondays (Factory)
49	47	"ADDICTIONS" VOLUME 1	Robert Palmer (Island)
40	48	RAW LIKE SUSHI	Neneh Cherry (Circa)
42	49	A GILDED ETERNITY	Loop (Situation Two)
-	50	APPETITE FOR DESTRUCTION	Guns N' Roses (Geffen)

17 February 1990

last week	this week	Title	Artist (label)
1	1	... BUT SERIOUSLY	Phil Collins (Vertigo)
-	2	CARVED IN SAND	Mission (Mercury)
3	3	DEEP HEAT 5 - FEED THE FEVER	Various(Telstar)
7	4	JOURNEYMAN	Eric Clapton (Duck)
4	5	A BIT OF WHAT YOU FANCY	Quireboys (Parlophone)
2	6	THE SWEET KEEPER	Tanita Tikaram (East West)
6	7	THE VERY BEST OF CAT STEVENS	Cat Stevens (Island)
5	8	COLOUR	Christians (Island)
12	9	PUMP UP THE JAM	Technotronic (Swanyard)
11	10	VIGIL IN A WILDERNESS OF MIRRORS	Fish (EMI)
8	11	AFFECTION	Lisa Stansfield (Arista)
-	12	THE LANGUAGE OF LIFE	Everything But The Girl (blanco y negro)
20	13	THE BEST OF ROD STEWART	Rod Stewart (Warner Bros.)
9	14	THE ROAD TO HELL	Chris Rea (WEA)
13	15	PURE SOFT METAL	Various Artists (Stylus)
15	16	HANGIN' TOUGH	New Kids On The Block (CBS)
14	17	HEART OF STONE	Cher (Geffen)
18	18	THE STONE ROSES	Stone Roses (Silvertone)
16	19	FOREIGN AFFAIR	Tina Turner (Capitol)
34	20	PARADISE REMIXED	Inner City (10)
15	21	ENJOY YOURSELF	Kylie Minogue (PWL)
19	22	READING, WRITING AND ARITHMETIC	Sundays (Rough Trade)
28	23	MARTIKA	Martika (CBS)
-	24	THIS SHOULD MOVE YA	Mantronix (Capitol)
29	25	WE TOO ARE ONE	Eurythmics (RCA)
17	26	THE LOVE SONGS	Dionne Warwick (Arista)
39	27	BACK ON THE BLOCK	Quincy Jones (Qwest)
24	28	A NEW FLAME	Simply Red (Elektra)
21	29	CLUB CLASSICS VOL 1	Soul II Soul (10)
-	30	BODY AND SOUL - HEART AND SOUL II	Various Artists (Heart & Soul)
26	31	3 FEET HIGH AND RISING	De La Soul (Big Life)
22	32	TEN GOOD REASONS	Jason Donovan (PWL)
37	33	THE CREAM OF ERIC CLAPTON	Eric Clapton & Cream (Polydor)
40	34	A COLLECTION - GREATEST HITS ... AND MORE	Barbra Streisand (CBS)
30	35	VIVALDI: THE FOUR SEASONS	Nigel Kennedy with the English Chamber Orchestra
23	36	THE RAW AND THE COOKED	Fine Young Cannibals (London)
-	37	DECADE	Duran Duran (EMI)
42	38	SKID ROW	Skid Row (Atlntic)
-	39	ALL BY MYSELF	Various Artists (Dover)
25	40	WARE'S THE HOUSE	Various Artists (Stylus)
31	41	WHEN THE WORLD KNOWS YOUR NAME	Deacon Blue (CBS)
45	42	LABOUR OF LOVE II	UB40 (DEP International)
27	43	READ MY LIPS	Jimmy Somerville (London)
32	44	HOLDING BACK THE RIVER	Wet Wet Wet (Precious Organisation)
35	45	LIKE A PRAYER	Madonna (Sire)
44	46	WILD!	Erasure (Mute)
43	47	THE LION AND THE COBRA	Sinead O'Connor (Ensign)
33	48	CUTS BOTH WAYS	Gloria Estefan (Epic)
41	49	WELCOME TO THE BEAUTIFUL SOUTH	Beautiful South (Go! Discs)
48	50	RAW LIKE SUSHI	Neneh Cherry (Circa)

Despite a curious lack of hit singles after 1988, Tanita Tikaram proved her consistency as an album seller when her second set *The Sweet Keeper* actually bettered its predecessor *Ancient Heart* by one place on the chart, reaching Number 2. The former lead singer with Marillion, Fish, made his solo debut with *Vigil In A Wilderness Of Mirrors*, and achieved something approaching Marillion-like sales with it.

February – March 1990

Journeyman was a slightly self-deprecating album title for one whom many still considered a god of the electric guitar. But the album in question was to prove one of Eric Clapton's best sellers. Joining it in the Top 10 (albeit briefly) was the original UK cast recording of another hit West End stage musical, *Miss Saigon*. Possibly the most unusual thing about this successful show was its *lack* of Lloyd Webber involvement!

17 March 1990

last week	this week	title	artist
1	1	... BUT SERIOUSLY	Phil Collins (Vertigo)
10	2	NOW DANCE 901	Various Artists (EMI/Virgin/PolyGram)
4	3	PUMP UP THE JAM	Technotronic (Swanyard)
2	4	AFFECTION	Lisa Stansfield (Arista)
7	5	THE BEST OF ROD STEWART	Rod Stewart (Warner Bros.)
6	6	THE ROAD TO HELL	Chris Rea (WEA)
8	7	FOREIGN AFFAIR	Tina Turner (Capitol)
5	8	THE HOUSE OF LOVE	House Of Love (Fontana)
-	9	RUN TO THE HILLS/THE NUMBER OF THE BEAST	Iron Maiden (EMI)
3	10	JOURNEYMAN	Eric Clapton (Duck)
9	11	HEART OF STONE	Cher (Geffen)
-	12	MISSING ... PRESUMED HAVING A GOOD TIME	Notting Hillbillies (Vertigo)
12	13	THE RAW AND THE COOKED	Fine Young Cannibals (London)
38	14	THE RIGHT STUFF 2 - NOTHIN' BUT A HOUSE PARTY	Various Artists (Stylus)
24	15	CUTS BOTH WAYS	Gloria Estefan (Epic)
16	16	THE VERY BEST OF CAT STEVENS	Cat Stevens (Island)
33	17	THE SYNTHESIZER ALBUM	Project D (Telstar)
18	18	WAKING HOURS	Del Amitri (A&M)
21	19	THE STONE ROSES	Stone Roses (Silvertone)
17	20	MISS SAIGON	London Cast (Warner Bros.)
11	21	CLUB CLASSICS VOL 1	Soul II Soul (10)
39	22	WILD!	Erasure (Mute)
-	23	10	Stranglers (Epic)
28	24	VIVALDI: THE FOUR SEASONS	Nigel Kennedy with the English Chamber Orchestra
13	25	LLOYD COLE	Lloyd Cole (Polydor)
19	26	RAW LIKE SUSHI	Neneh Cherry (Circa)
-	27	SOUL PROVIDER	Michael Bolton (CBS)
48	28	MOVE YOUR SKIN	And Why Not! (Island)
-	29	BACK STREET SYMPHONY	Thunder (EMI)
49	30	HOLDING BACK THE RIVER	Wet Wet Wet (Precious Organisation)
15	31	HAPPINESS	Beloved (East West)
22	32	THE SWEET KEEPER	Tanita Tikaram (East West)
30	33	THE LOVE SONGS	Dionne Warwick (Arista)
27	34	MARTIKA	Martika (CBS)
40	35	HANGIN' TOUGH	New Kids On The Block (CBS)
32	36	A NEW FLAME	Simply Red (Elektra)
20	37	BODY AND SOUL - HEART AND SOUL II	Various Artists (Heart & Soul)
34	38	BLUE SKY MINING	Midnight Oil (CBS)
29	39	3 FEET HIGH AND RISING	De La Soul (Big Life)
26	40	THE SEEDS OF LOVE	Tears For Fears (Fontana)
46	41	CARVED IN SAND	Mission (Mercury)
23	42	PURE SOFT METAL	Various Artists (Stylus)
14	43	PURGATORY/MAIDEN JAPAN	Iron Maiden (EMI)
-	44	LIVE ON BROADWAY	Barry Manilow (Arista)
31	45	THE 49ERS	49ers (Fourth & Broadway)
25	46	THE AWARDS 1990	Various Artists (Telstar)
37	47	COLOUR	Christians (Island)
36	48	ALL BY MYSELF	Various Artists (Dover)
-	49	THE ESSENTIAL PAVAROTTI	Luciano Pavarotti (Decca)
-	50	THE GREATEST HITS	Thompson Twins (Stylus)

24 March 1990

last week	this week	title	artist
-	1	I DO NOT WANT WHAT I HAVEN'T GOT	Sinead O'Connor (Ensign)
2	2	NOW DANCE 901	Various Artists (EMI/Virgin/PolyGram)
1	3	... BUT SERIOUSLY	Phil Collins (Vertigo)
12	4	MISSING ... PRESUMED HAVING A GOOD TIME	Notting Hillbillies (Vertigo)
5	5	CHANGESBOWIE	David Bowie (EMI)
24	6	VIVALDI: THE FOUR SEASONS	Nigel Kennedy with the English Chamber Orchestra
-	7	FLIGHT OF ICARUS/THE TROOPER	Iron Maiden (EMI)
27	8	SOUL PROVIDER	Michael Bolton (CBS)
14	9	THE RIGHT STUFF 2 - NOTHIN' BUT A HOUSE PARTY	Various Artists (Stylus)
49	10	THE ESSENTIAL PAVAROTTI	Luciano Pavarotti (Decca)
35	11	HANGIN' TOUGH	New Kids On The Block (CBS)
6	12	THE ROAD TO HELL	Chris Rea (WEA)
7	13	FOREIGN AFFAIR	Tina Turner (Capitol)
3	14	PUMP UP THE JAM	Technotronic (Swanyard)
5	15	THE BEST OF ROD STEWART	Rod Stewart (Warner Bros.)
44	16	LIVE ON BROADWAY	Barry Manilow (Arista)
4	17	AFFECTION	Lisa Stansfield (Arista)
23	18	10	Stranglers (Epic)
11	19	HEART OF STONE	Cher (Geffen)
10	20	JOURNEYMAN	Eric Clapton (Duck)
22	21	WILD!	Erasure (Mute)
50	22	THE GREATEST HITS	Thompson Twins (Stylus)
15	23	CUTS BOTH WAYS	Gloria Estefan (Epic)
8	24	THE HOUSE OF LOVE	House Of Love (Fontana)
19	25	THE STONE ROSES	Stone Roses (Silvertone)
16	26	THE VERY BEST OF CAT STEVENS	Cat Stevens (Island)
13	27	THE RAW AND THE COOKED	Fine Young Cannibals (London)
18	28	WAKING HOURS	Del Amitri (A&M)
40	29	THE SEEDS OF LOVE	Tears For Fears (Fontana)
-	30	MANNERS AND PHYSIQUE	Adam Ant (MCA)
17	31	THE SYNTHESIZER ALBUM	Project D (Telstar)
25	32	LLOYD COLE	Lloyd Cole (Polydor)
21	33	CLUB CLASSICS VOL 1	Soul II Soul (10)
-	34	LABOUR OF LOVE II	UB40 (DEP International)
26	35	RAW LIKE SUSHI	Neneh Cherry (Circa)
36	36	A NEW FLAME	Simply Red (Elektra)
20	37	MISS SAIGON	London Cast (Warner Bros.)
29	38	BACK STREET SYMPHONY	Thunder (EMI)
34	39	MARTIKA	Martika (CBS)
39	40	3 FEET HIGH AND RISING	De La Soul (Big Life)
-	41	JIVE BUNNY - THE ALBUM	Jive Bunny & the Mastermixers (Telstar)
-	42	PENNIES FROM HEAVEN	Various Artists (BBC)
30	43	HOLDING BACK THE RIVER	Wet Wet Wet (Precious Organisation)
-	44	JOIN TOGETHER	Who (Virgin)
28	45	MOVE YOUR SKIN	And Why Not! (Island)
-	46	WE TOO ARE ONE	Eurythmics (RCA)
41	47	CARVED IN SAND	Mission (Mercury)
31	48	HAPPINESS	Beloved (East West)
38	49	BLUE SKY MINING	Midnight Oil (CBS)
33	50	THE LOVE SONGS	Dionne Warwick (Arista)

31 March 1990

last week	this week	title	artist
1	1	I DO NOT WANT WHAT I HAVEN'T GOT	Sinead O'Connor (Ensign)
-	2	VIOLATOR	Depeche Mode (Mute)
5	3	CHANGESBOWIE	David Bowie (EMI)
2	4	NOW DANCE 901	Various Artists (EMI/Virgin/PolyGram)
6	5	VIVALDI: THE FOUR SEASONS	Nigel Kennedy with the English Chamber Orchestra
-	6	DEEP HEAT 6 - THE SIXTH SENSE	Various Artists (Telstar)
3	7	... BUT SERIOUSLY	Phil Collins (Vertigo)
-	8	2 MINUTES TO MIDNIGHT/ACES HIGH	Iron Maiden (EMI)
4	9	MISSING ... PRESUMED HAVING A GOOD TIME	Notting Hillbillies (Vertigo)
10	10	THE ESSENTIAL PAVAROTTI	Luciano Pavarotti (Decca)
-	11	COSMIC THING	B-52's (Reprise)
9	12	THE RIGHT STUFF 2 - NOTHIN' BUT A HOUSE PARTY	Various Artists (Stylus)
12	13	THE ROAD TO HELL	Chris Rea (WEA)
28	14	WAKING HOURS	Del Amitri (A&M)
11	15	HANGIN' TOUGH	New Kids On The Block (CBS)
13	16	FOREIGN AFFAIR	Tina Turner (Capitol)
8	17	SOUL PROVIDER	Michael Bolton (CBS)
-	18	MANIC NIRVANA	Robert Plant (Es Paranza)
23	19	CUTS BOTH WAYS	Gloria Estefan (Epic)
17	20	AFFECTION	Lisa Stansfield (Arista)
14	21	PUMP UP THE JAM	Technotronic (Swanyard)
15	22	THE BEST OF ROD STEWART	Rod Stewart (Warner Bros.)
21	23	WILD!	Erasure (Mute)
19	24	HEART OF STONE	Cher (Geffen)
25	25	THE STONE ROSES	Stone Roses (Silvertone)
24	26	THE HOUSE OF LOVE	House Of Love (Fontana)
30	27	MANNERS AND PHYSIQUE	Adam Ant (MCA)
-	28	JUST THE TWO OF US	Various (Columbia)
20	29	JOURNEYMAN	Eric Clapton (Duck)
-	30	ONLY YESTERDAY	Carpenters (A&M)
-	31	THE CAUTION HORSES	Cowboy Junkies (RCA)
34	32	LABOUR OF LOVE II	UB40 (DEP International)
22	33	THE GREATEST HITS	Thompson Twins (Stylus)
26	34	THE VERY BEST OF CAT STEVENS	Cat Stevens (Island)
48	35	HAPPINESS	Beloved (East West)
29	36	THE SEEDS OF LOVE	Tears For Fears (Fontana)
33	37	CLUB CLASSICS VOL 1	Soul II Soul (10)
31	38	THE SYNTHESIZER ALBUM	Project D (Telstar)
7	39	FLIGHT OF ICARUS/THE TROOPER	Iron Maiden (EMI)
-	40	10	Stranglers (Epic)
27	41	THE RAW AND THE COOKED	Fine Young Cannibals (London)
43	42	HOLDING BACK THE RIVER	Wet Wet Wet (Precious Organisation)
-	43	COLLECTION: RAY CHARLES	Ray Charles (Arcade)
35	44	RAW LIKE SUSHI	Neneh Cherry (Circa)
32	45	LLOYD COLE	Lloyd Cole (Polydor)
16	46	LIVE ON BROADWAY	Barry Manilow (Arista)
44	47	JOIN TOGETHER	Who (Virgin)
36	48	A NEW FLAME	Simply Red (Elektra)
-	49	WILD AND LONELY	Associates (Circa)
-	50	SKID ROW	Skid Row (Atlntic)

The somewhat odd Top 10 entries by Iron Maiden in three consecutive charts, each surviving for barely more than a week, were listed, in a sense, by default. Each was a double package of two original Maiden 12-inch singles, released as a limited collectors edition, but their length and number of tracks precluded their inclusion in the singles chart, so with the albums, briefly, they were lumped.

April 1990

7 April 1990

last	this	Title	Artist (Label)
3	1	CHANGESBOWIE	David Bowie (EMI)
1	2	I DO NOT WANT WHAT I HAVEN'T GOT	Sinead O'Connor (Ensign)
30	3	ONLY YESTERDAY	Carpenters (A&M)
2	4	VIOLATOR	Depeche Mode (Mute)
6	5	DEEP HEAT 6 - THE SIXTH SENSE	Various (Telstar)
7	6	... BUT SERIOUSLY	Phil Collins (Vertigo)
10	7	THE ESSENTIAL PAVAROTTI	Luciano Pavarotti (Decca)
11	8	COSMIC THING	B-52's (Reprise)
5	9	VIVALDI: THE FOUR SEASONS	Nigel Kennedy with the English Chamber Orchestra
4	10	NOW DANCE 901	Various Artists (EMI/Virgin/PolyGram)
16	11	FOREIGN AFFAIR	Tina Turner (Capitol)
13	12	THE ROAD TO HELL	Chris Rea (WEA)
9	13	MISSING ... PRESUMED HAVING A GOOD TIME	Notting Hillbillies (Vertigo)
-	14	THE BEST OF VAN MORRISON	Van Morrison (Polydor)
-	15	RUNNING FREE (LIVE)/RUN TO THE HILLS (LIVE)	Iron Maiden (EMI)
22	16	THE BEST OF ROD STEWART	Rod Stewart (Warner Bros.)
12	17	THE RIGHT STUFF 2 - NOTHIN' BUT A HOUSE PARTY	Various Artists (Stylus)
17	18	SOUL PROVIDER	Michael Bolton (CBS)
18	19	MANIC NIRVANA	Robert Plant (Es Paranza)
23	20	WILD!	Erasure (Mute)
14	21	WAKING HOURS	Del Amitri (A&M)
19	22	CUTS BOTH WAYS	Gloria Estefan (Epic)
-	23	FLOOD	They Might Be Giants (Elektra)
20	24	AFFECTION	Lisa Stansfield (Arista)
24	25	HEART OF STONE	Cher (Geffen)
15	26	HANGIN' TOUGH	New Kids On The Block (CBS)
32	27	LABOUR OF LOVE II	UB40 (DEP International)
21	28	PUMP UP THE JAM	Technotronic (Swanyard)
25	29	THE STONE ROSES	Stone Roses (Silvertone)
28	30	JUST THE TWO OF US	Various Artists (Columbia)
-	31	MISS SAIGON	London Cast (Warner Bros.)
26	32	THE HOUSE OF LOVE	House Of Love (Fontana)
42	33	HOLDING BACK THE RIVER	Wet Wet Wet (Precious Organisation)
29	34	JOURNEYMAN	Eric Clapton (Duck)
-	35	STILL GOT THE BLUES	Gary Moore (Virgin)
35	36	HAPPINESS	Beloved (East West)
37	37	THE CAUTION HORSES	Cowboy Junkies (RCA)
34	38	THE VERY BEST OF CAT STEVENS	Cat Stevens (Island)
37	39	CLUB CLASSICS VOL 1	Soul II Soul (10)
50	40	SKID ROW	Skid Row (Atlntic)
33	41	THE GREATEST HITS	Thompson Twins (Stylus)
27	42	MANNERS AND PHYSIQUE	Adam Ant (MCA)
38	43	THE SYNTHESIZER ALBUM	Project D (Telstar)
43	44	COLLECTION	Ray Charles (Arcade)
-	45	SKINBEAT - THE FIRST TOUCH	Various (Polydor)
-	46	A COLLECTION - GREATEST HITS ... AND MORE	Barbra Streisand (CBS)
8	47	2 MINUTES TO MIDNIGHT/ACES HIGH	Iron Maiden (EMI)
41	48	THE RAW AND THE COOKED	Fine Young Cannibals (London)
-	49	JANET JACKSON'S RHYTHM NATION 1814	Janet Jackson (A&M)
36	50	THE SEEDS OF LOVE	Tears For Fears (Fontana)

14 April 1990

last	this	Title	Artist (Label)
3	1	ONLY YESTERDAY	Carpenters (A&M)
1	2	CHANGESBOWIE	David Bowie (EMI)
14	3	THE BEST OF VAN MORRISON	Van Morrison (Polydor)
2	4	I DO NOT WANT WHAT I HAVEN'T GOT	Sinead O'Connor (Ensign)
6	5	... BUT SERIOUSLY	Phil Collins (Vertigo)
5	6	DEEP HEAT 6 - THE SIXTH SENSE	Various (Telstar)
4	7	VIOLATOR	Depeche Mode (Mute)
-	8	BRIGADE	Heart (Capitol)
-	9	WASTED YEARS/STRANGER IN A STRANGE LAND	Iron Maiden (EMI)
8	10	COSMIC THING	B-52's (Reprise)
9	11	VIVALDI: THE FOUR SEASONS	Nigel Kennedy with the English Chamber Orchestra
7	12	THE ESSENTIAL PAVAROTTI	Luciano Pavarotti (Decca)
23	13	FLOOD	They Might Be Giants (Elektra)
12	14	THE ROAD TO HELL	Chris Rea (WEA)
17	15	THE RIGHT STUFF 2 - NOTHIN' BUT A HOUSE PARTY	Various Artists (Stylus)
13	16	MISSING ... PRESUMED HAVING A GOOD TIME	Notting Hillbillies (Vertigo)
35	17	STILL GOT THE BLUES	Gary Moore (Virgin)
27	18	LABOUR OF LOVE II	UB40 (DEP International)
20	19	WILD!	Erasure (Mute)
-	20	LET THEM EAT BINGO	Beats International (Go Beat)
11	21	FOREIGN AFFAIR	Tina Turner (Capitol)
22	22	CUTS BOTH WAYS	Gloria Estefan (Epic)
16	23	THE BEST OF ROD STEWART	Rod Stewart (Warner Bros.)
28	24	PUMP UP THE JAM	Technotronic (Swanyard)
25	25	HEART OF STONE	Cher (Geffen)
10	26	NOW DANCE 901	Various Artists (EMI/Virgin/PolyGram)
21	27	WAKING HOURS	Del Amitri (A&M)
26	28	HANGIN' TOUGH	New Kids On The Block (CBS)
34	29	JOURNEYMAN	Eric Clapton (Duck)
24	30	AFFECTION	Lisa Stansfield (Arista)
45	31	SKINBEAT - THE FIRST TOUCH	Various Artists (Polydor)
18	32	SOUL PROVIDER	Michael Bolton (CBS)
30	33	JUST THE TWO OF US	Various Artists (Columbia)
32	34	THE HOUSE OF LOVE	House Of Love (Fontana)
29	35	THE STONE ROSES	Stone Roses (Silvertone)
41	36	THE GREATEST HITS	Thompson Twins (Stylus)
-	37	LILY WAS HERE - ORIGINAL SOUNDTRACK	David A. Stewart featuring Candy Dulfer (AnXious)
33	38	HOLDING BACK THE RIVER	Wet Wet Wet (Precious Organisation)
19	39	MANIC NIRVANA	Robert Plant (Es Paranza)
-	40	RAW LIKE SUSHI	Neneh Cherry (Circa)
-	41	BEZERK	Tigertailz (Music For Nations)
36	42	HAPPINESS	Beloved (East West)
-	43	HUNKY DORY	David Bowie (EMI)
-	44	3 FEET HIGH AND RISING	De La Soul (Big Life)
-	45	APRIL MOON	Sam Brown (A&M)
-	46	THE MAN WHO SOLD THE WORLD	David Bowie (EMI)
39	47	CLUB CLASSICS VOL 1	Soul II Soul (10)
-	48	WITNESS	Halo James (Epic)
49	49	JANET JACKSON'S RHYTHM NATION 1814	Janet Jackson (A&M)
-	50	SPACE ODDITY	David Bowie (EMI)

21 April 1990

last	this	Title	Artist (Label)
-	1	BEHIND THE MASK	Fleetwood Mac (Warner Bros.)
1	2	ONLY YESTERDAY	Carpenters (A&M)
2	3	CHANGESBOWIE	David Bowie (EMI)
8	4	BRIGADE	Heart (Capitol)
3	5	THE BEST OF VAN MORRISON	Van Morrison (Polydor)
5	6	... BUT SERIOUSLY	Phil Collins (Vertigo)
18	7	LABOUR OF LOVE II	UB40 (DEP International)
4	8	I DO NOT WANT WHAT I HAVEN'T GOT	Sinead O'Connor (Ensign)
-	9	CAN I PLAY WITH MADNESS/THE EVIL THAT MEN DO	Iron Maiden (EMI)
6	10	DEEP HEAT 6 - THE SIXTH SENSE	Various (Telstar)
11	11	VIVALDI: THE FOUR SEASONS	Nigel Kennedy with the English Chamber Orchestra
7	12	VIOLATOR	Depeche Mode (Mute)
10	13	COSMIC THING	B-52's (Reprise)
25	14	HEART OF STONE	Cher (Geffen)
14	15	THE ROAD TO HELL	Chris Rea (WEA)
16	16	MISSING ... PRESUMED HAVING A GOOD TIME	Notting Hillbillies (Vertigo)
-	17	ABSOLUTELY	ABC (Neutron)
24	18	PUMP UP THE JAM	Technotronic (Swanyard)
20	19	LET THEM EAT BINGO	Beats International (Go Beat)
48	20	WITNESS	Halo James (Epic)
12	21	THE ESSENTIAL PAVAROTTI	Luciano Pavarotti (Decca)
15	22	THE RIGHT STUFF 2 - NOTHIN' BUT A HOUSE PARTY	Various Artists (Stylus)
13	23	FLOOD	They Might Be Giants (Elektra)
19	24	WILD!	Erasure (Mute)
33	25	JUST THE TWO OF US	Various Artists (Columbia)
23	26	THE BEST OF ROD STEWART	Rod Stewart (Warner Bros.)
27	27	WAKING HOURS	Del Amitri (A&M)
-	28	CLASSICS BY MOONLIGHT	James Last (Polydor)
21	29	FOREIGN AFFAIR	Tina Turner (Capitol)
-	30	MONTAGE	Kenny G (Arista)
17	31	STILL GOT THE BLUES	Gary Moore (Virgin)
29	32	JOURNEYMAN	Eric Clapton (Duck)
22	33	CUTS BOTH WAYS	Gloria Estefan (Epic)
45	34	APRIL MOON	Sam Brown (A&M)
9	35	WASTED YEARS/STRANGER IN A STRANGE LAND	Iron Maiden (EMI)
28	36	HANGIN' TOUGH	New Kids On The Block (CBS)
-	37	THE VOICE	Brenda Cochrane (Polydor)
26	38	NOW DANCE 901	Various Artists (EMI/Virgin/PolyGram)
30	39	AFFECTION	Lisa Stansfield (Arista)
-	40	MARTIKA	Martika (CBS)
35	41	THE STONE ROSES	Stone Roses (Silvertone)
32	42	SOUL PROVIDER	Michael Bolton (CBS)
34	43	THE HOUSE OF LOVE	House Of Love (Fontana)
38	44	HOLDING BACK THE RIVER	Wet Wet Wet (Precious Organisation)
-	45	THE BLUES BROTHERS - SOUNDTRACK	Various Artists (Atlantic)
31	46	SKINBEAT - THE FIRST TOUCH	Various Artists (Polydor)
-	47	HUNKY DORY	David Bowie (EMI)
36	48	THE GREATEST HITS	Thompson Twins (Stylus)
49	49	JANET JACKSON'S RHYTHM NATION 1814	Janet Jackson (A&M)
-	50	COLOUR	Christians (Island)

Seven years after the death of Karen Carpenter, the timeless appeal of the Carpenters' music proved itself once again as their *Only Yesterday* retrospective package gave the duo their first Number 1 album since the 1970s. It displaced another hits package, David Bowie's *Changesbowie*. Meanwhile, for the first time ever, there were two classical albums, by Pavarotti and Nigel Kennedy, in the Top 10.

April – May 1990

last week	this week	28 April 1990		5 May 1990		12 May 1990

28 April 1990

last week	this week	Title	Artist (Label)
1	1	BEHIND THE MASK	Fleetwood Mac (Warner Bros.)
2	2	ONLY YESTERDAY	Carpenters (A&M)
3	3	CHANGESBOWIE	David Bowie (EMI)
6	4	... BUT SERIOUSLY	Phil Collins (Vertigo)
17	5	ABSOLUTELY	ABC (Neutron)
4	6	BRIGADE	Heart (Capitol)
7	7	LABOUR OF LOVE II	UB40 (DEP International)
-	8	DAYS OF OPEN HAND	Suzanne Vega (A&M)
5	9	THE BEST OF VAN MORRISON	Van Morrison (Polydor)
8	10	I DO NOT WANT WHAT I HAVEN'T GOT	Sinead O'Connor (Ensign)
-	11	FEAR OF A BLACK PLANET	Public Enemy (Def Jam)
11	12	VIVALDI: THE FOUR SEASONS	Nigel Kennedy with the English Chamber Orchestra
-	13	THE CLAIRVOYANT/INFINITE DREAMS (LIVE)	Iron Maiden (EMI)
14	14	HEART OF STONE	Cher (Geffen)
25	15	JUST THE TWO OF US	Various Artists (Columbia)
10	16	DEEP HEAT 6 - THE SIXTH SENSE	Various (Telstar)
18	17	PUMP UP THE JAM	Technotronic (Swanyard)
12	18	VIOLATOR	Depeche Mode (Mute)
-	19	ALANNAH MYLES	Alannah Myles (Atlantic)
15	20	THE ROAD TO HELL	Chris Rea (WEA)
21	21	THE ESSENTIAL PAVAROTTI	Luciano Pavarotti (Decca)
16	22	MISSING ... PRESUMED HAVING A GOOD TIME	Notting Hillbillies (Vertigo)
13	23	COSMIC THING	B-52's (Reprise)
36	24	HANGIN' TOUGH	New Kids On The Block (CBS)
29	25	FOREIGN AFFAIR	Tina Turner (Capitol)
28	26	CLASSICS BY MOONLIGHT	James Last (Polydor)
31	27	STILL GOT THE BLUES	Gary Moore (Virgin)
33	28	CUTS BOTH WAYS	Gloria Estefan (Epic)
-	29	REBEL MUSIC	Rebel MC (Desire)
45	30	THE BLUES BROTHERS - SOUNDTRACK	Various Artists (Atlantic)
24	31	WILD!	Erasure (Mute)
40	32	MARTIKA	Martika (CBS)
30	33	MONTAGE	Kenny G (Arista)
26	34	THE BEST OF ROD STEWART	Rod Stewart (Warner Bros.)
9	35	CAN I PLAY WITH MADNESS/THE EVIL THAT MEN DO	Iron Maiden (EMI)
20	36	WITNESS	Halo James (Epic)
39	37	AFFECTION	Lisa Stansfield (Arista)
19	38	LET THEM EAT BINGO	Beats International (Go Beat)
27	39	WAKING HOURS	Del Amitri (A&M)
41	40	THE STONE ROSES	Stone Roses (Silvertone)
42	41	SOUL PROVIDER	Michael Bolton (CBS)
32	42	JOURNEYMAN	Eric Clapton (Duck)
22	43	THE RIGHT STUFF 2 - NOTHIN' BUT A HOUSE PARTY	Various Artists (Stylus)
-	44	LIKE A PRAYER	Madonna (Sire)
23	45	FLOOD	They Might Be Giants (Elektra)
-	46	A BIT OF WHAT YOU FANCY	Quireboys (Parlophone)
-	47	THE GOOD SON	Nick Cave & the Bad Seeds (Mute)
43	48	THE HOUSE OF LOVE	House Of Love (Fontana)
37	49	THE VOICE	Brenda Cochrane (Polydor)
-	50	A LITTLE BIT OF THIS A LITTLE BIT OF THAT	D Mob (ffrr)

5 May 1990

last week	this week	Title	Artist (Label)
1	1	BEHIND THE MASK	Fleetwood Mac (Warner Bros.)
2	2	ONLY YESTERDAY	Carpenters (A&M)
4	3	... BUT SERIOUSLY	Phil Collins (Vertigo)
19	4	ALANNAH MYLES	Alannah Myles (Atlantic)
12	5	VIVALDI: THE FOUR SEASONS	Nigel Kennedy with the English Chamber Orchestra
-	6	LIFE	Inspiral Carpets (Cow)
11	7	FEAR OF A BLACK PLANET	Public Enemy (Def Jam)
3	8	CHANGESBOWIE	David Bowie (EMI)
6	9	BRIGADE	Heart (Capitol)
-	10	NOW THAT'S WHAT I CALL MUSIC 17	Various Artists (EMI/Virgin/PolyGram)
8	11	DAYS OF OPEN HAND	Suzanne Vega (A&M)
7	12	LABOUR OF LOVE II	UB40 (DEP International)
5	13	ABSOLUTELY	ABC (Neutron)
10	14	I DO NOT WANT WHAT I HAVEN'T GOT	Sinead O'Connor (Ensign)
9	15	THE BEST OF VAN MORRISON	Van Morrison (Polydor)
15	16	JUST THE TWO OF US	Various Artists (Columbia)
14	17	HEART OF STONE	Cher (Geffen)
16	18	DEEP HEAT 6 - THE SIXTH SENSE	Various Artists (Telstar)
17	19	PUMP UP THE JAM	Technotronic (Swanyard)
-	20	DREAMLAND	Black Box (deConstruction)
20	21	THE ROAD TO HELL	Chris Rea (WEA)
29	22	REBEL MUSIC	Rebel MC (Desire)
24	23	HANGIN' TOUGH	New Kids On The Block (CBS)
25	24	FOREIGN AFFAIR	Tina Turner (Capitol)
22	25	MISSING ... PRESUMED HAVING A GOOD TIME	Notting Hillbillies (Vertigo)
32	26	MARTIKA	Martika (CBS)
30	27	THE BLUES BROTHERS - SOUNDTRACK	Various Artists (Atlantic)
18	28	VIOLATOR	Depeche Mode (Mute)
-	29	SONGS FOR DRELLA	Lou Reed & John Cale (Sire)
23	30	COSMIC THING	B-52's (Reprise)
21	31	THE ESSENTIAL PAVAROTTI	Luciano Pavarotti (Decca)
26	32	CLASSICS BY MOONLIGHT	James Last (Polydor)
49	33	THE VOICE	Brenda Cochrane (Polydor)
31	34	WILD!	Erasure (Mute)
28	35	CUTS BOTH WAYS	Gloria Estefan (Epic)
34	36	THE BEST OF ROD STEWART	Rod Stewart (Warner Bros.)
-	37	THE REAL THING	Faith No More (Slash)
27	38	STILL GOT THE BLUES	Gary Moore (Virgin)
37	39	AFFECTION	Lisa Stansfield (Arista)
-	40	EVERYBODY KNOWS	Sonia (Chrysalis)
13	41	THE CLAIRVOYANT/INFINITE DREAMS (LIVE)	Iron Maiden (EMI)
-	42	MANIC NIRVANA	Robert Plant (Es Paranza)
40	43	THE STONE ROSES	Stone Roses (Silvertone)
33	44	MONTAGE	Kenny G (Arista)
-	45	CLUB CLASSICS VOL 1	Soul II Soul (10)
-	46	NICK OF TIME	Bonnie Raitt (Capitol)
-	47	ECLIPSE	Yngwie J. Malmsteen (Polydor)
39	48	WAKING HOURS	Del Amitri (A&M)
38	49	LET THEM EAT BINGO	Beats International (Go Beat)
42	50	JOURNEYMAN	Eric Clapton (Duck)

12 May 1990

last week	this week	Title	Artist (Label)
10	1	NOW THAT'S WHAT I CALL MUSIC 17	Various Artists (EMI/Virgin/PolyGram)
3	2	... BUT SERIOUSLY	Phil Collins (Vertigo)
2	3	ONLY YESTERDAY	Carpenters (A&M)
6	4	LIFE	Inspiral Carpets (Cow)
5	5	VIVALDI: THE FOUR SEASONS	Nigel Kennedy with the English Chamber Orchestra
1	6	BEHIND THE MASK	Fleetwood Mac (Warner Bros.)
4	7	ALANNAH MYLES	Alannah Myles (Atlantic)
-	8	CHARMED LIFE	Billy Idol (Chrysalis)
9	9	BRIGADE	Heart (Capitol)
12	10	LABOUR OF LOVE II	UB40 (DEP International)
13	11	ABSOLUTELY	ABC (Neutron)
8	12	CHANGESBOWIE	David Bowie (EMI)
40	13	EVERYBODY KNOWS	Sonia (Chrysalis)
16	14	JUST THE TWO OF US	Various Artists (Columbia)
11	15	DAYS OF OPEN HAND	Suzanne Vega (A&M)
14	16	I DO NOT WANT WHAT I HAVEN'T GOT	Sinead O'Connor (Ensign)
20	17	DREAMLAND	Black Box (deConstruction)
23	18	HANGIN' TOUGH	New Kids On The Block (CBS)
29	19	SONGS FOR DRELLA	Lou Reed & John Cale (Sire)
7	20	FEAR OF A BLACK PLANET	Public Enemy (Def Jam)
-	21	GET ON THIS!!! 30 DANCE HITS VOLUME 1	Various Artists (Telstar)
15	22	THE BEST OF VAN MORRISON	Van Morrison (Polydor)
-	23	SOUL PROVIDER	Michael Bolton (CBS)
-	24	A POCKETFUL OF DREAMS	Big Fun (Jive)
38	25	STILL GOT THE BLUES	Gary Moore (Virgin)
17	26	HEART OF STONE	Cher (Geffen)
22	27	REBEL MUSIC	Rebel MC (Desire)
-	28	FOREVER YOUR GIRL	Paula Abdul (Siren)
21	29	THE ROAD TO HELL	Chris Rea (WEA)
18	30	DEEP HEAT 6 - THE SIXTH SENSE	Various Artists (Telstar)
37	31	THE REAL THING	Faith No More (Slash)
19	32	PUMP UP THE JAM	Technotronic (Swanyard)
27	33	THE BLUES BROTHERS - SOUNDTRACK	Various Artists (Atlantic)
24	34	FOREIGN AFFAIR	Tina Turner (Capitol)
35	35	CUTS BOTH WAYS	Gloria Estefan (Epic)
-	36	DISINTEGRATION	Cure (Fiction)
46	37	NICK OF TIME	Bonnie Raitt (Capitol)
33	38	THE VOICE	Brenda Cochrane (Polydor)
25	39	MISSING ... PRESUMED HAVING A GOOD TIME	Notting Hillbillies (Vertigo)
32	40	CLASSICS BY MOONLIGHT	James Last (Polydor)
-	41	HELLO, I MUST BE GOING!	Phil Collins (Vertigo)
26	42	MARTIKA	Martika (CBS)
30	43	COSMIC THING	B-52's (Reprise)
42	44	MANIC NIRVANA	Robert Plant (Es Paranza)
34	45	WILD!	Erasure (Mute)
-	46	APRIL MOON	Sam Brown (A&M)
-	47	NO JACKET REQUIRED	Phil Collins (Vertigo)
43	48	THE STONE ROSES	Stone Roses (Silvertone)
28	49	VIOLATOR	Depeche Mode (Mute)
36	50	THE BEST OF ROD STEWART	Rod Stewart (Warner Bros.)

The last of the Iron Maiden 12-inch packages hit the Top 20 briefly at the end of April, after which the album charts belonged to the albums again - and notably, at that point in time, to Fleetwood Mac, whose *Behind The Mask* album has never been one of their most highly-regarded releases, but nevertheless at its time of release managed three straight weeks at Number 1 without a hit single.

May – June 1990

19 May 1990

last week	this week	
1	1	NOW THAT'S WHAT I CALL MUSIC 17 — Various Artists (EMI/Virgin/PolyGram)
2	2	... BUT SERIOUSLY — Phil Collins (Vertigo)
3	3	ONLY YESTERDAY — Carpenters (A&M)
28	4	FOREVER YOUR GIRL — Paula Abdul (Siren)
6	5	BEHIND THE MASK — Fleetwood Mac (Warner Bros.)
7	6	ALANNAH MYLES — Alannah Myles (Atlantic)
5	7	VIVALDI: THE FOUR SEASONS — Nigel Kennedy with the English Chamber Orchestra
18	8	HANGIN' TOUGH — New Kids On The Block (CBS)
21	9	GET ON THIS!!! 30 DANCE HITS VOLUME 1 — Various Artists (Telstar)
10	10	LABOUR OF LOVE II — UB40 (DEP International)
-	11	TATTOOED MILLIONAIRE — Bruce Dickinson (EMI)
24	12	A POCKETFUL OF DREAMS — Big Fun (Jive)
9	13	BRIGADE — Heart (Capitol)
4	14	LIFE — Inspiral Carpets (Cow)
14	15	JUST THE TWO OF US — Various Artists (Columbia)
23	16	SOUL PROVIDER — Michael Bolton (CBS)
8	17	CHARMED LIFE — Billy Idol (Chrysalis)
11	18	ABSOLUTELY — ABC (Neutron)
12	19	CHANGESBOWIE — David Bowie (EMI)
13	20	EVERYBODY KNOWS — Sonia (Chrysalis)
43	21	COSMIC THING — B-52's (Reprise)
15	22	DAYS OF OPEN HAND — Suzanne Vega (A&M)
-	23	THE EARTHQUAKE ALBUM - ROCK AID ARMENIA — Various Artists (Live Aid Armenia)
26	24	HEART OF STONE — Cher (Geffen)
-	25	JANET JACKSON'S RHYTHM NATION 1814 — Janet Jackson (A&M)
16	26	I DO NOT WANT WHAT I HAVEN'T GOT — Sinead O'Connor (Ensign)
-	27	THE ESSENTIAL PAVAROTTI — Luciano Pavarotti (Decca)
17	28	DREAMLAND — Black Box (deConstruction)
25	29	STILL GOT THE BLUES — Gary Moore (Virgin)
-	30	LIVE AND DIRECT — Adamski (MCA)
46	31	APRIL MOON — Sam Brown (A&M)
37	32	NICK OF TIME — Bonnie Raitt (Capitol)
29	33	THE ROAD TO HELL — Chris Rea (WEA)
32	34	PUMP UP THE JAM — Technotronic (Swanyard)
34	35	FOREIGN AFFAIR — Tina Turner (Capitol)
49	36	VIOLATOR — Depeche Mode (Mute)
35	37	CUTS BOTH WAYS — Gloria Estefan (Epic)
22	38	THE BEST OF VAN MORRISON — Van Morrison (Polydor)
33	39	THE BLUES BROTHERS - SOUNDTRACK — Various Artists (Atlantic)
-	40	GOODBYE JUMBO — World Party (Ensign)
-	41	THE INTERNATIONALE — Billy Bragg (Utility)
20	42	FEAR OF A BLACK PLANET — Public Enemy (Def Jam)
-	43	THE GOOD THE BAD AND THE LIVE (THE 6 1/2 YEAR ANNIVERSARY 12" COLLECTION) — Metallica (Vertigo)
27	44	REBEL MUSIC — Rebel MC (Desire)
19	45	SONGS FOR DRELLA — Lou Reed & John Cale (Sire)
40	46	CLASSICS BY MOONLIGHT — James Last (Polydor)
38	47	THE VOICE — Brenda Cochrane (Polydor)
31	48	THE REAL THING — Faith No More (Slash)
-	49	ENERGY ORCHARD — Energy Orchard (MCA)
-	50	SALUTATION ROAD — Martin Stephenson & the Daintees (Kitchenware)

26 May 1990

last week	this week	
1	1	NOW THAT'S WHAT I CALL MUSIC 17 — Various Artists (EMI/Virgin/PolyGram)
3	2	ONLY YESTERDAY — Carpenters (A&M)
2	3	... BUT SERIOUSLY — Phil Collins (Vertigo)
4	4	FOREVER YOUR GIRL — Paula Abdul (Siren)
-	5	THROUGH A BIG COUNTRY - GREATEST HITS — Big Country (Mercury)
10	6	LABOUR OF LOVE II — UB40 (DEP International)
7	7	VIVALDI: THE FOUR SEASONS — Nigel Kennedy with the English Chamber Orchestra
-	8	PACKED! — Pretenders (WEA)
9	9	GET ON THIS!!! 30 DANCE HITS VOLUME 1 — Various Artists (Telstar)
8	10	HANGIN' TOUGH — New Kids On The Block (CBS)
6	11	ALANNAH MYLES — Alannah Myles (Atlantic)
12	12	A POCKETFUL OF DREAMS — Big Fun (Jive)
5	13	BEHIND THE MASK — Fleetwood Mac (Warner Bros.)
14	14	LIFE — Inspiral Carpets (Cow)
16	15	SOUL PROVIDER — Michael Bolton (CBS)
21	16	COSMIC THING — B-52's (Reprise)
26	17	I DO NOT WANT WHAT I HAVEN'T GOT — Sinead O'Connor (Ensign)
13	18	BRIGADE — Heart (Capitol)
24	19	HEART OF STONE — Cher (Geffen)
27	20	THE ESSENTIAL PAVAROTTI — Luciano Pavarotti (Decca)
11	21	TATTOOED MILLIONAIRE — Bruce Dickinson (EMI)
18	22	ABSOLUTELY — ABC (Neutron)
29	23	STILL GOT THE BLUES — Gary Moore (Virgin)
15	24	JUST THE TWO OF US — Various Artists (Columbia)
33	25	THE ROAD TO HELL — Chris Rea (WEA)
22	26	DAYS OF OPEN HAND — Suzanne Vega (A&M)
25	27	JANET JACKSON'S RHYTHM NATION 1814 — Janet Jackson (A&M)
-	28	LOCK UP THE WOLVES — Dio (Vertigo)
19	29	CHANGESBOWIE — David Bowie (EMI)
17	30	CHARMED LIFE — Billy Idol (Chrysalis)
30	31	LIVE AND DIRECT — Adamski (MCA)
31	32	APRIL MOON — Sam Brown (A&M)
-	33	MENDELSOHN VIOLIN CONCERTO IN E MINOR — Nigel Kennedy with Jeffrey Tate & the English Chamber Orchestra
20	34	EVERYBODY KNOWS — Sonia (Chrysalis)
-	35	LET THEM EAT BINGO — Beats International (Go Beat)
-	36	FREEDOM TO PARTY - FIRST LEGAL RAVE — Various Artists (Trax)
28	37	DREAMLAND — Black Box (deConstruction)
-	38	WORLD POWER — Snap (Arista)
40	39	GOODBYE JUMBO — World Party (Ensign)
36	40	VIOLATOR — Depeche Mode (Mute)
42	41	FEAR OF A BLACK PLANET — Public Enemy (Def Jam)
50	42	SALUTATION ROAD — Martin Stephenson & the Daintees (Kitchenware)
-	43	MISSING ... PRESUMED HAVING A GOOD TIME — Notting Hillbillies (Vertigo)
-	44	TAKE IT TO HEART — Michael McDonald (Reprise)
46	45	CLASSICS BY MOONLIGHT — James Last (Polydor)
-	46	A NIGHT AT THE OPERA — Various Artists (Telstar)
-	47	CIRCLE OF ONE — Oleta Adams (Fontana)
48	48	THE BEST OF VAN MORRISON — Van Morrison (Polydor)
-	49	CLASSIC EXPERIENCE II — Various Artists (EMI)
-	50	AFFECTION — Lisa Stansfield (Arista)

2 June 1990

last week	this week	
-	1	I'M BREATHLESS — Madonna (Sire)
-	2	VOLUME II - 1990 A NEW DECADE — Soul II Soul (10)
1	3	NOW THAT'S WHAT I CALL MUSIC 17 — Various Artists (EMI/Virgin/PolyGram)
2	4	ONLY YESTERDAY — Carpenters (A&M)
5	5	THROUGH A BIG COUNTRY - GREATEST HITS — Big Country (Mercury)
3	6	... BUT SERIOUSLY — Phil Collins (Vertigo)
6	7	LABOUR OF LOVE II — UB40 (DEP International)
10	8	HANGIN' TOUGH — New Kids On The Block (CBS)
49	9	CLASSIC EXPERIENCE II — Various Artists (EMI)
4	10	FOREVER YOUR GIRL — Paula Abdul (Siren)
16	11	COSMIC THING — B-52's (Reprise)
7	12	VIVALDI: THE FOUR SEASONS — Nigel Kennedy with the English Chamber Orchestra
15	13	SOUL PROVIDER — Michael Bolton (CBS)
20	14	THE ESSENTIAL PAVAROTTI — Luciano Pavarotti (Decca)
9	15	GET ON THIS!!! 30 DANCE HITS VOLUME 1 — Various Artists (Telstar)
8	16	PACKED! — Pretenders (WEA)
11	17	ALANNAH MYLES — Alannah Myles (Atlantic)
23	18	STILL GOT THE BLUES — Gary Moore (Virgin)
13	19	BEHIND THE MASK — Fleetwood Mac (Warner Bros.)
17	20	I DO NOT WANT WHAT I HAVEN'T GOT — Sinead O'Connor (Ensign)
19	21	HEART OF STONE — Cher (Geffen)
40	22	VIOLATOR — Depeche Mode (Mute)
18	23	BRIGADE — Heart (Capitol)
12	24	A POCKETFUL OF DREAMS — Big Fun (Jive)
25	25	THE ROAD TO HELL — Chris Rea (WEA)
22	26	ABSOLUTELY — ABC (Neutron)
14	27	LIFE — Inspiral Carpets (Cow)
24	28	JUST THE TWO OF US — Various Artists (Columbia)
37	29	DREAMLAND — Black Box (deConstruction)
-	30	FOREIGN AFFAIR — Tina Turner (Capitol)
44	31	TAKE IT TO HEART — Michael McDonald (Reprise)
29	32	CHANGESBOWIE — David Bowie (EMI)
-	33	SIXTIES MIX 3 — Various Artists (Stylus)
32	34	APRIL MOON — Sam Brown (A&M)
39	35	GOODBYE JUMBO — World Party (Ensign)
30	36	CHARMED LIFE — Billy Idol (Chrysalis)
33	37	MENDELSOHN VIOLIN CONCERTO IN E MINOR — Nigel Kennedy with Jeffrey Tate & the English Chamber Orchestra
-	38	LOVE MOVES — Kim Wilde (MCA)
-	39	PASSION AND WARFARE — Steve Vai (Food For Thought)
26	40	DAYS OF OPEN HAND — Suzanne Vega (A&M)
21	41	TATTOOED MILLIONAIRE — Bruce Dickinson (EMI)
47	42	CIRCLE OF ONE — Oleta Adams (Fontana)
27	43	JANET JACKSON'S RHYTHM NATION 1814 — Janet Jackson (A&M)
36	44	FREEDOM TO PARTY - FIRST LEGAL RAVE — Various Artists (Trax)
-	45	LET LOVE RULE — Lenny Kravitz (Virgin America)
48	46	THE BEST OF VAN MORRISON — Van Morrison (Polydor)
31	47	LIVE AND DIRECT — Adamski (MCA)
35	48	LET THEM EAT BINGO — Beats International (Go Beat)
28	49	LOCK UP THE WOLVES — Dio (Vertigo)
43	50	MISSING ... PRESUMED HAVING A GOOD TIME — Notting Hillbillies (Vertigo)

Paula Abdul's *Forever Your Girl*, which had originally charted in 1989, swept back in favour alongside the singer's smash hit single *Opposites Attract*. In the US, this had been one of the biggest-selling debut albums ever released, but Abdul's UK singles success was patchier, with the LP reflecting this. Madonna's *I'm Breathless*, meanwhile, drew its inspiration from her role in the film *Dick Tracy*.

June 1990

9 June 1990

Last	This	Title / Artist
2	1	VOLUME II - 1990 A NEW DECADE Soul II Soul (10)
-	2	BETWEEN THE LINES Jason Donovan (PWL)
1	3	I'M BREATHLESS Madonna (Sire)
4	4	ONLY YESTERDAY Carpenters (A&M)
3	5	NOW THAT'S WHAT I CALL MUSIC 17 Various Artists (EMI/Virgin/PolyGram)
5	6	THROUGH A BIG COUNTRY - GREATEST HITS Big Country (Mercury)
6	7	... BUT SERIOUSLY Phil Collins (Vertigo)
9	8	CLASSIC EXPERIENCE II Various Artists (EMI)
11	9	COSMIC THING B-52's (Reprise)
13	10	SOUL PROVIDER Michael Bolton (CBS)
7	11	LABOUR OF LOVE II UB40 (DEP International)
14	12	THE ESSENTIAL PAVAROTTI Luciano Pavarotti (Decca)
12	13	VIVALDI: THE FOUR SEASONS Nigel Kennedy with the English Chamber Orchestra
39	14	PASSION AND WARFARE Steve Vai (Food For Thought)
10	15	FOREVER YOUR GIRL Paula Abdul (Siren)
8	16	HANGIN' TOUGH New Kids On The Block (CBS)
18	17	STILL GOT THE BLUES Gary Moore (Virgin)
-	18	THE VERY BEST OF TALK TALK - NATURAL HISTORY Talk Talk (Parlophone)
26	19	ABSOLUTELY ABC (Neutron)
20	20	I DO NOT WANT WHAT I HAVEN'T GOT Sinead O'Connor (Ensign)
17	21	ALANNAH MYLES Alannah Myles (Atlantic)
19	22	BEHIND THE MASK Fleetwood Mac (Warner Bros.)
22	23	VIOLATOR Depeche Mode (Mute)
-	24	GREATEST HITS Bangles (CBS)
15	25	GET ON THIS!!! 30 DANCE HITS VOLUME 1 Various Artists (Telstar)
48	26	LET THEM EAT BINGO Beats International (Go Beat)
35	27	GOODBYE JUMBO World Party (Ensign)
33	28	SIXTIES MIX 3 Various Artists (Stylus)
-	29	NITEFLITE 3 - BEING WITH YOU Various Artists (Columbia)
-	30	BORN TO SING En Vogue (Atlantic)
23	31	BRIGADE Heart (Capitol)
21	32	HEART OF STONE Cher (Geffen)
29	33	DREAMLAND Black Box (deConstruction)
37	34	MENDELSOHN VIOLIN CONCERTO IN E MINOR Nigel Kennedy with Jeffrey Tate & the English Chamber Orchestra
46	35	THE BEST OF VAN MORRISON Van Morrison (Polydor)
30	36	FOREIGN AFFAIR Tina Turner (Capitol)
25	37	THE ROAD TO HELL Chris Rea (WEA)
32	38	CHANGESBOWIE David Bowie (EMI)
24	39	A POCKETFUL OF DREAMS Big Fun (Jive)
27	40	LIFE Inspiral Carpets (Cow)
-	41	CUTS BOTH WAYS Gloria Estefan (Epic)
-	42	AFFECTION Lisa Stansfield (Arista)
28	43	JUST THE TWO OF US Various Artists (Columbia)
16	44	PACKED! Pretenders (WEA)
-	45	POD Breeders (4AD)
34	46	APRIL MOON Sam Brown (A&M)
31	47	TAKE IT TO HEART Michael McDonald (WEA)
-	48	WILD! Erasure (Mute)
-	49	PUMP UP THE JAM Technotronic (Swanyard)
-	50	HELL TO PAY Jeff Healey Band (Arista)

16 June 1990

Last	This	Title / Artist
1	1	VOLUME II - 1990 A NEW DECADE Soul II Soul (10)
18	2	THE VERY BEST OF TALK TALK - NATURAL HISTORY Talk Talk (Parlophone)
3	3	I'M BREATHLESS Madonna (Sire)
2	4	BETWEEN THE LINES Jason Donovan (PWL)
24	5	GREATEST HITS Bangles (CBS)
4	6	ONLY YESTERDAY Carpenters (A&M)
8	7	CLASSIC EXPERIENCE II Various Artists (EMI)
-	8	HOME Hothouse Flowers (London)
7	9	... BUT SERIOUSLY Phil Collins (Vertigo)
6	10	THROUGH A BIG COUNTRY - GREATEST HITS Big Country (Mercury)
9	11	COSMIC THING B-52's (Reprise)
12	12	THE ESSENTIAL PAVAROTTI Luciano Pavarotti (Decca)
11	13	LABOUR OF LOVE II UB40 (DEP International)
-	14	OTHER VOICES Paul Young (CBS)
29	15	NITEFLITE 3 - BEING WITH YOU Various Artists (Columbia)
10	16	SOUL PROVIDER Michael Bolton (CBS)
-	17	GOLD MOTHER James (Fontana)
13	18	VIVALDI: THE FOUR SEASONS Nigel Kennedy with the English Chamber Orchestra
19	19	HANGIN' TOUGH New Kids On The Block (CBS)
50	20	HELL TO PAY Jeff Healey Band (Arista)
5	21	NOW THAT'S WHAT I CALL MUSIC 17 Various Artists (EMI/Virgin/PolyGram)
20	22	I DO NOT WANT WHAT I HAVEN'T GOT Sinead O'Connor (Ensign)
-	23	ONE WORLD ONE VOICE Various Artists (Virgin)
45	24	POD Breeders (4AD)
17	25	STILL GOT THE BLUES Gary Moore (Virgin)
22	26	BEHIND THE MASK Fleetwood Mac (Warner Bros.)
15	27	FOREVER YOUR GIRL Paula Abdul (Siren)
34	28	MENDELSOHN VIOLIN CONCERTO IN E MINOR Nigel Kennedy with Jeffrey Tate & the English Chamber Orchestra
21	29	ALANNAH MYLES Alannah Myles (Atlantic)
14	30	PASSION AND WARFARE Steve Vai (Food For Thought)
-	31	ENCHANTED Marc Almond (Some Bizzare)
32	32	HEART OF STONE Cher (Geffen)
19	33	ABSOLUTELY ABC (Neutron)
27	34	GOODBYE JUMBO World Party (Ensign)
23	35	VIOLATOR Depeche Mode (Mute)
36	36	FOREIGN AFFAIR Tina Turner (Capitol)
-	37	STRAY Aztec Camera (WEA)
26	38	LET THEM EAT BINGO Beats International (Go Beat)
31	39	BRIGADE Heart (Capitol)
33	40	DREAMLAND Black Box (deConstruction)
35	41	THE BEST OF VAN MORRISON Van Morrison (Polydor)
40	42	LIFE Inspiral Carpets (Cow)
25	43	GET ON THIS!!! 30 DANCE HITS VOLUME 1 Various Artists (Telstar)
43	44	JUST THE TWO OF US Various Artists (Columbia)
28	45	SIXTIES MIX 3 Various Artists (Stylus)
-	46	1234 Propaganda (Virgin)
38	47	CHANGESBOWIE David Bowie (EMI)
37	48	THE ROAD TO HELL Chris Rea (WEA)
-	49	PRETTY WOMAN - SOUNDTRACK Various Artists (EMI USA)
-	50	HEARTS AND FLOWERS Joan Armatrading (A&M)

23 June 1990

Last	This	Title / Artist
1	1	VOLUME II - 1990 A NEW DECADE Soul II Soul (10)
2	2	THE VERY BEST OF TALK TALK - NATURAL HISTORY Talk Talk (Parlophone)
12	3	THE ESSENTIAL PAVAROTTI Luciano Pavarotti (Decca)
4	4	BETWEEN THE LINES Jason Donovan (PWL)
14	5	OTHER VOICES Paul Young (CBS)
8	6	HOME Hothouse Flowers (London)
7	7	CLASSIC EXPERIENCE II Various Artists (EMI)
3	8	I'M BREATHLESS Madonna (Sire)
-	9	THE CHIMES Chimes (CBS)
5	10	GREATEST HITS Bangles (CBS)
6	11	ONLY YESTERDAY Carpenters (A&M)
9	12	... BUT SERIOUSLY Phil Collins (Vertigo)
10	13	THROUGH A BIG COUNTRY - GREATEST HITS
19	14	HANGIN' TOUGH New Kids On The Block (CBS)
15	15	NITEFLITE 3 - BEING WITH YOU Various Artists (Columbia)
13	16	LABOUR OF LOVE II UB40 (DEP International)
17	17	GOLD MOTHER James (Fontana)
11	18	COSMIC THING B-52's (Reprise)
16	19	SOUL PROVIDER Michael Bolton (CBS)
-	20	WAITING FOR COUSTEAU Jean-Michel Jarre (Dreyfus)
37	21	STRAY Aztec Camera (WEA)
18	22	VIVALDI: THE FOUR SEASONS Nigel Kennedy with the English Chamber Orchestra
-	23	THE RISE AND FALL OF ZIGGY STARDUST AND THE SPIDERS FROM MARS David Bowie (EMI)
50	24	HEARTS AND FLOWERS Joan Armatrading (A&M)
25	25	STILL GOT THE BLUES Gary Moore (Virgin)
22	26	I DO NOT WANT WHAT I HAVEN'T GOT Sinead O'Connor (Ensign)
27	27	FOREVER YOUR GIRL Paula Abdul (Siren)
45	28	SIXTIES MIX 3 Various Artists (Stylus)
34	29	GOODBYE JUMBO World Party (Ensign)
-	30	SUMMER DREAMS Beach Boys (Capitol)
-	31	CUTS BOTH WAYS Gloria Estefan (Epic)
26	32	BEHIND THE MASK Fleetwood Mac (Warner Bros.)
32	33	HEART OF STONE Cher (Geffen)
33	34	ABSOLUTELY ABC (Neutron)
36	35	FOREIGN AFFAIR Tina Turner (Capitol)
28	36	MENDELSOHN VIOLIN CONCERTO IN E MINOR Nigel Kennedy with Jeffrey Tate & the English Chamber Orchestra
29	37	ALANNAH MYLES Alannah Myles (Atlantic)
35	38	VIOLATOR Depeche Mode (Mute)
21	39	NOW THAT'S WHAT I CALL MUSIC 17 Various Artists (EMI/Virgin/PolyGram)
20	40	HELL TO PAY Jeff Healey Band (Arista)
-	41	WILD! Erasure (Mute)
-	42	SLEEPING WITH THE PAST Elton John (Rocket)
41	43	THE BEST OF VAN MORRISON Van Morrison (Polydor)
39	44	BRIGADE Heart (Capitol)
24	45	POD Breeders (4AD)
30	46	PASSION AND WARFARE Steve Vai (Food For Thought)
47	47	WAKING HOURS Del Amitri (A&M)
-	48	THE NORTHERN BEAT Various Artists (London)
23	49	ONE WORLD ONE VOICE Various Artists (Virgin)
-	50	THE STONE ROSES Stone Roses (Silvertone)

As their *Volume II - 1990 A New Decade* hit the chart top, Soul II Soul became the first UK dance/R&B act ever to have two consecutive Number 1 albums. It significantly outsold Jason Donovan's second album *Between The Lines*, which could only eventually muster a fraction of the huge sales of its predecessor, failing to reach Number 1 and only spending just over a month in the Top 10.

June – July 1990

30 June 1990

Last	This	Title / Artist (Label)
3	1	THE ESSENTIAL PAVAROTTI — Luciano Pavarotti (Decca)
30	2	SUMMER DREAMS — Beach Boys (Capitol)
-	3	STEP BY STEP — New Kids On The Block (CBS)
1	4	VOLUME II - 1990 A NEW DECADE — Soul II Soul (10)
10	5	GREATEST HITS — Bangles (CBS)
2	6	THE VERY BEST OF TALK TALK - NATURAL HISTORY — Talk Talk (Parlophone)
4	7	BETWEEN THE LINES — Jason Donovan (PWL)
7	8	CLASSIC EXPERIENCE II — Various Artists (EMI)
-	9	THE SONGS 1975-1990 — Barry Manilow (Arista)
11	10	ONLY YESTERDAY — Carpenters (A&M)
12	11	... BUT SERIOUSLY — Phil Collins (Vertigo)
8	12	I'M BREATHLESS — Madonna (Sire)
13	13	THROUGH A BIG COUNTRY - GREATEST HITS — Big Country (Mercury)
16	14	LABOUR OF LOVE II — UB40 (DEP International)
20	15	WAITING FOR COUSTEAU — Jean-Michel Jarre (Dreyfus)
9	16	THE CHIMES — Chimes (CBS)
-	17	A NIGHT AT THE OPERA — Various Artists (Telstar)
5	18	OTHER VOICES — Paul Young (CBS)
6	19	HOME — Hothouse Flowers (London)
22	20	VIVALDI: THE FOUR SEASONS — Nigel Kennedy with the English Chamber Orchestra
-	21	PRETTY WOMAN - SOUNDTRACK — Various Artists (EMI USA)
19	22	SOUL PROVIDER — Michael Bolton (CBS)
25	23	STILL GOT THE BLUES — Gary Moore (Virgin)
18	24	COSMIC THING — B-52's (Reprise)
35	25	FOREIGN AFFAIR — Tina Turner (Capitol)
36	26	MENDELSOHN VIOLIN CONCERTO IN E MINOR — Nigel Kennedy with Jeffrey Tate & the English Chamber Orchestra
26	27	I DO NOT WANT WHAT I HAVEN'T GOT — Sinead O'Connor (Ensign)
-	28	A NIGHT ON THE TOWN — Bruce Hornsby & the Range (RCA)
15	29	NITEFLITE 3 - BEING WITH YOU — Various Artists (Columbia)
23	30	THE RISE AND FALL OF ZIGGY STARDUST AND THE SPIDERS FROM MARS — David Bowie (EMI)
31	31	CUTS BOTH WAYS — Gloria Estefan (Epic)
42	32	SLEEPING WITH THE PAST — Elton John (Rocket)
17	33	GOLD MOTHER — James (Fontana)
37	34	ALANNAH MYLES — Alannah Myles (Atlantic)
14	35	HANGIN' TOUGH — New Kids On The Block (CBS)
21	36	STRAY — Aztec Camera (WEA)
27	37	FOREVER YOUR GIRL — Paula Abdul (Siren)
-	38	WILSON PHILLIPS — Wilson Phillips (SBK)
-	39	LEATHER AND LACE — Various Artists (Dino)
-	40	THE ROAD TO HELL — Chris Rea (WEA)
32	41	BEHIND THE MASK — Fleetwood Mac (Warner Bros.)
28	42	SIXTIES MIX 3 — Various Artists (Stylus)
38	43	VIOLATOR — Depeche Mode (Mute)
-	44	CHANGESBOWIE — David Bowie (EMI)
-	45	THE SAME SKY — Horse (Echo Chamber)
33	46	HEART OF STONE — Cher (Geffen)
29	47	GOODBYE JUMBO — World Party (Ensign)
24	48	HEARTS AND FLOWERS — Joan Armatrading (A&M)
-	49	ONE TRUE PASSION — Revenge (Factory)
44	50	BRIGADE — Heart (Capitol)

7 July 1990

Last	This	Title / Artist (Label)
3	1	STEP BY STEP — New Kids On The Block (CBS)
1	2	THE ESSENTIAL PAVAROTTI — Luciano Pavarotti (Decca)
2	3	SUMMER DREAMS — Beach Boys (Capitol)
4	4	VOLUME II - 1990 A NEW DECADE — Soul II Soul (10)
6	5	THE VERY BEST OF TALK TALK - NATURAL HISTORY — Talk Talk (Parlophone)
5	6	GREATEST HITS — Bangles (CBS)
9	7	THE SONGS 1975-1990 — Barry Manilow (Arista)
38	8	WILSON PHILLIPS — Wilson Phillips (SBK)
7	9	BETWEEN THE LINES — Jason Donovan (PWL)
8	10	CLASSIC EXPERIENCE II — Various Artists (EMI)
21	11	PRETTY WOMAN - SOUNDTRACK — Various Artists (EMI USA)
11	12	... BUT SERIOUSLY — Phil Collins (Vertigo)
10	13	ONLY YESTERDAY — Carpenters (A&M)
14	14	THROUGH A BIG COUNTRY - GREATEST HITS — Big Country (Mercury)
14	15	LABOUR OF LOVE II — UB40 (DEP International)
-	16	REPUTATION — Dusty Springfield (Parlophone)
16	17	THE CHIMES — Chimes (CBS)
20	18	VIVALDI: THE FOUR SEASONS — Nigel Kennedy with the English Chamber Orchestra
19	19	HOT ROCKS 1964-1971 — Rolling Stones (London)
12	20	I'M BREATHLESS — Madonna (Sire)
28	21	A NIGHT ON THE TOWN — Bruce Hornsby & the Range (RCA)
-	22	DEEP HEAT 7 - SEVENTH HEAVEN — Various Artists (Telstar)
18	23	OTHER VOICES — Paul Young (CBS)
32	24	SLEEPING WITH THE PAST — Elton John (Rocket)
15	25	WAITING FOR COUSTEAU — Jean-Michel Jarre (Dreyfus)
-	26	GOO — Sonic Youth (DGC)
31	27	CUTS BOTH WAYS — Gloria Estefan (Epic)
17	28	A NIGHT AT THE OPERA — Various Artists (Telstar)
25	29	FOREIGN AFFAIR — Tina Turner (Capitol)
19	30	HOME — Hothouse Flowers (London)
22	31	SOUL PROVIDER — Michael Bolton (CBS)
-	32	WILD! — Erasure (Mute)
23	33	STILL GOT THE BLUES — Gary Moore (Virgin)
39	34	LEATHER AND LACE — Various Artists (Dino)
34	35	ALANNAH MYLES — Alannah Myles (Atlantic)
24	36	COSMIC THING — B-52's (Reprise)
27	37	I DO NOT WANT WHAT I HAVEN'T GOT — Sinead O'Connor (Ensign)
40	38	THE ROAD TO HELL — Chris Rea (WEA)
-	39	WORLD POWER — Snap (Arista)
26	40	MENDELSOHN VIOLIN CONCERTO IN E MINOR — Nigel Kennedy with Jeffrey Tate & the English Chamber Orchestra
-	41	THE HARD WAY — Steve Earle & the Dukes (MCA)
30	42	THE RISE AND FALL OF ZIGGY STARDUST AND THE SPIDERS FROM MARS — David Bowie (EMI)
35	43	HANGIN' TOUGH — New Kids On The Block (CBS)
41	44	BEHIND THE MASK — Fleetwood Mac (Warner Bros.)
47	45	GOODBYE JUMBO — World Party (Ensign)
-	46	THE STONE ROSES — Stone Roses (Silvertone)
36	47	STRAY — Aztec Camera (WEA)
29	48	NITEFLITE 3 - BEING WITH YOU — Various Artists (Columbia)
43	49	VIOLATOR — Depeche Mode (Mute)
37	50	FOREVER YOUR GIRL — Paula Abdul (Siren)

14 July 1990

Last	This	Title / Artist (Label)
2	1	THE ESSENTIAL PAVAROTTI — Luciano Pavarotti (Decca)
19	2	HOT ROCKS 1964-1971 — Rolling Stones (London)
24	3	SLEEPING WITH THE PAST — Elton John (Rocket)
3	4	SUMMER DREAMS — Beach Boys (Capitol)
1	5	STEP BY STEP — New Kids On The Block (CBS)
22	6	DEEP HEAT 7 - SEVENTH HEAVEN — Various Artists (Telstar)
4	7	VOLUME II - 1990 A NEW DECADE — Soul II Soul (10)
6	8	GREATEST HITS — Bangles (CBS)
11	9	PRETTY WOMAN - SOUNDTRACK — Various Artists (EMI USA)
10	10	COMPOSITIONS — Anita Baker (Elektra)
8	11	WILSON PHILLIPS — Wilson Phillips (SBK)
5	12	THE VERY BEST OF TALK TALK - NATURAL HISTORY — Talk Talk (Parlophone)
12	13	... BUT SERIOUSLY — Phil Collins (Vertigo)
20	14	I'M BREATHLESS — Madonna (Sire)
9	15	BETWEEN THE LINES — Jason Donovan (PWL)
16	16	REPUTATION — Dusty Springfield (Parlophone)
7	17	THE SONGS 1975-1990 — Barry Manilow (Arista)
13	18	ONLY YESTERDAY — Carpenters (A&M)
41	19	THE HARD WAY — Steve Earle & the Dukes (MCA)
14	20	THROUGH A BIG COUNTRY - GREATEST HITS — Big Country (Mercury)
15	21	LABOUR OF LOVE II — UB40 (DEP International)
18	22	VIVALDI: THE FOUR SEASONS — Nigel Kennedy with the English Chamber Orchestra
10	23	CLASSIC EXPERIENCE II — Various Artists (EMI)
17	24	THE CHIMES — Chimes (CBS)
33	25	STILL GOT THE BLUES — Gary Moore (Virgin)
36	26	COSMIC THING — B-52's (Reprise)
23	27	OTHER VOICES — Paul Young (CBS)
26	28	GOO — Sonic Youth (DGC)
27	29	CUTS BOTH WAYS — Gloria Estefan (Epic)
30	30	HOME — Hothouse Flowers (London)
45	31	GOODBYE JUMBO — World Party (Ensign)
21	32	A NIGHT ON THE TOWN — Bruce Hornsby & the Range (RCA)
-	33	WAKING HOURS — Del Amitri (A&M)
31	34	SOUL PROVIDER — Michael Bolton (CBS)
-	35	BONAFIDE — Maxi Priest (10)
37	36	I DO NOT WANT WHAT I HAVEN'T GOT — Sinead O'Connor (Ensign)
-	37	STEEL WHEELS — Rolling Stones (CBS)
25	38	WAITING FOR COUSTEAU — Jean-Michel Jarre (Dreyfus)
32	39	WILD! — Erasure (Mute)
40	40	LIFE — Inspiral Carpets (Cow)
49	41	VIOLATOR — Depeche Mode (Mute)
-	42	THE NORTHERN BEAT — Various Artists (London)
38	43	THE ROAD TO HELL — Chris Rea (WEA)
44	44	BEHIND THE MASK — Fleetwood Mac (Warner Bros.)
29	45	FOREIGN AFFAIR — Tina Turner (Capitol)
35	46	ALANNAH MYLES — Alannah Myles (Atlantic)
-	47	SMASH HITS - RAVE! — Various Artists (Dover)
46	48	THE STONE ROSES — Stone Roses (Silvertone)
-	49	PUMP UP THE JAM — Technotronic (Swanyard)
39	50	WORLD POWER — Snap (Arista)

As World Cup fever hit much of the world, the greatest non-footballing beneficiary was Luciano Pavarotti, one of the world's greatest tenors, whose recording of Puccini's *Nessun Dorma* was chosen as the theme to the BBC's coverage of the tournament from Italy. His compilation album *The Essential Pavarotti*, including the aria, became, historically, the first ever classical album to top the UK chart.

21 July 1990

last week	this week	Album	Artist
1	1	THE ESSENTIAL PAVAROTTI	Luciano Pavarotti (Decca)
3	2	SLEEPING WITH THE PAST	Elton John (Rocket)
2	3	HOT ROCKS 1964-1971	Rolling Stones (London)
-	4	FLESH AND BLOOD	Poison (Enigma)
10	5	COMPOSITIONS	Anita Baker (Elektra)
9	6	PRETTY WOMAN - SOUNDTRACK	Various Artists (EMI USA)
47	7	SMASH HITS - RAVE!	Various Artists (Dover)
4	8	SUMMER DREAMS	Beach Boys (Capitol)
5	9	STEP BY STEP	New Kids On The Block (CBS)
12	10	THE VERY BEST OF TALK TALK - NATURAL HISTORY	Talk Talk (Parlophone)
8	11	GREATEST HITS	Bangles (CBS)
13	12	... BUT SERIOUSLY	Phil Collins (Vertigo)
35	13	BONAFIDE	Maxi Priest (10)
15	14	BETWEEN THE LINES	Jason Donovan (PWL)
7	15	VOLUME II - 1990 A NEW DECADE	Soul II Soul (10)
14	16	I'M BREATHLESS	Madonna (Sire)
22	17	VIVALDI: THE FOUR SEASONS Nigel Kennedy with the English Chamber Orchestra	
6	18	DEEP HEAT 7 - SEVENTH HEAVEN	Various Artists (Telstar)
17	19	THE SONGS 1975-1990	Barry Manilow (Arista)
37	20	STEEL WHEELS	Rolling Stones (CBS)
11	21	WILSON PHILLIPS	Wilson Phillips (SBK)
-	22	GOODNIGHT L.A.	Magnum (Polydor)
18	23	ONLY YESTERDAY	Carpenters (A&M)
34	24	SOUL PROVIDER	Michael Bolton (CBS)
21	25	LABOUR OF LOVE II	UB40 (DEP International)
36	26	I DO NOT WANT WHAT I HAVEN'T GOT	Sinead O'Connor (Ensign)
-	27	THE ULTIMATE '60S COLLECTION	Various Artists (Castle Communications)
20	28	THROUGH A BIG COUNTRY - GREATEST HITS	Big Country (Mercury)
-	29	DANCE THIS MESS AROUND (BEST OF THE B52'S)	B-52's (Island)
50	30	WORLD POWER	Snap (Arista)
29	31	CUTS BOTH WAYS	Gloria Estefan (Epic)
-	32	ARE YOU OKAY?	Was (Not Was) (Fontana)
16	33	REPUTATION	Dusty Springfield (Parlophone)
45	34	FOREIGN AFFAIR	Tina Turner (Capitol)
26	35	COSMIC THING	B-52's (Reprise)
25	36	STILL GOT THE BLUES	Gary Moore (Virgin)
48	37	THE STONE ROSES	Stone Roses (Silvertone)
19	38	THE HARD WAY	Steve Earle & the Dukes (MCA)
49	39	PUMP UP THE JAM	Technotronic (Swanyard)
39	40	WILD!	Erasure (Mute)
27	41	OTHER VOICES	Paul Young (CBS)
-	42	CRAIG MCLACHLAN AND CHECK 1-2	Craig McLachlan & Check 1-2 (Epic)
33	43	WAKING HOURS	Del Amitri (A&M)
41	44	VIOLATOR	Depeche Mode (Mute)
-	45	CHANGESBOWIE	David Bowie (EMI)
30	46	HOME	Hothouse Flowers (London)
24	47	THE CHIMES	Chimes (CBS)
32	48	A NIGHT ON THE TOWN	Bruce Hornsby & the Range (RCA)
23	49	CLASSIC EXPERIENCE II	Various Artists (EMI)
-	50	BRICK BY BRICK	Iggy Pop (Virgin America)

28 July 1990

last week	this week	Album	Artist
2	1	SLEEPING WITH THE PAST	Elton John (Rocket)
1	2	THE ESSENTIAL PAVAROTTI	Luciano Pavarotti (Decca)
3	3	HOT ROCKS 1964-1971	Rolling Stones (London)
4	4	FLESH AND BLOOD	Poison (Enigma)
6	5	PRETTY WOMAN - SOUNDTRACK	Various Artists (EMI USA)
16	6	I'M BREATHLESS	Madonna (Sire)
8	7	SUMMER DREAMS	Beach Boys (Capitol)
7	8	SMASH HITS - RAVE!	Various Artists (Dover)
12	9	... BUT SERIOUSLY	Phil Collins (Vertigo)
-	10	NOW DANCE 902	Various Artists (EMI/Virgin/PolyGram)
5	11	COMPOSITIONS	Anita Baker (Elektra)
9	12	STEP BY STEP	New Kids On The Block (CBS)
22	13	GOODNIGHT L.A.	Magnum (Polydor)
14	14	BETWEEN THE LINES	Jason Donovan (PWL)
11	15	GREATEST HITS	Bangles (CBS)
10	16	THE VERY BEST OF TALK TALK - NATURAL HISTORY	Talk Talk (Parlophone)
18	17	DEEP HEAT 7 - SEVENTH HEAVEN	Various Artists (Telstar)
26	18	I DO NOT WANT WHAT I HAVEN'T GOT	Sinead O'Connor (Ensign)
15	19	VOLUME II - 1990 A NEW DECADE	Soul II Soul (10)
28	20	THROUGH A BIG COUNTRY - GREATEST HITS	Big Country (Mercury)
42	21	CRAIG MCLACHLAN AND CHECK 1-2	Craig McLachlan & Check 1-2 (Epic)
23	22	ONLY YESTERDAY	Carpenters (A&M)
24	23	SOUL PROVIDER	Michael Bolton (CBS)
20	24	STEEL WHEELS	Rolling Stones (CBS)
-	25	PLEASE HAMMER DON'T HURT 'EM	MC Hammer (Capitol)
21	26	WILSON PHILLIPS	Wilson Phillips (SBK)
37	27	THE STONE ROSES	Stone Roses (Silvertone)
33	28	REPUTATION	Dusty Springfield (Parlophone)
13	29	BONAFIDE	Maxi Priest (10)
-	30	TEENAGE NINJA MUTANT TURTLES - SOUNDTRACK	Various Artists (SBK)
17	31	VIVALDI: THE FOUR SEASONS Nigel Kennedy with the English Chamber Orchestra	
-	32	ALADDIN SANE	David Bowie (EMI)
41	33	OTHER VOICES	Paul Young (CBS)
25	34	LABOUR OF LOVE II	UB40 (DEP International)
32	35	ARE YOU OKAY?	Was (Not Was) (Fontana)
19	36	THE SONGS 1975-1990	Barry Manilow (Arista)
30	37	WORLD POWER	Snap (Arista)
34	38	FOREIGN AFFAIR	Tina Turner (Capitol)
46	39	HOME	Hothouse Flowers (London)
27	40	THE ULTIMATE '60S COLLECTION	Various Artists (Castle Communications)
-	41	PIN UPS	David Bowie (EMI)
39	42	PUMP UP THE JAM	Technotronic (Swanyard)
31	43	CUTS BOTH WAYS	Gloria Estefan (Epic)
48	44	A NIGHT ON THE TOWN	Bruce Hornsby & the Range (RCA)
40	45	WILD!	Erasure (Mute)
35	46	COSMIC THING	B-52's (Reprise)
-	47	LIKE A PRAYER	Madonna (Sire)
36	48	STILL GOT THE BLUES	Gary Moore (Virgin)
47	49	THE CHIMES	Chimes (CBS)
38	50	THE HARD WAY	Steve Earle & the Dukes (MCA)

4 August 1990

last week	this week	Album	Artist
10	1	NOW DANCE 902	Various Artists (EMI/Virgin/PolyGram)
1	2	SLEEPING WITH THE PAST	Elton John (Rocket)
6	3	I'M BREATHLESS	Madonna (Sire)
2	4	THE ESSENTIAL PAVAROTTI	Luciano Pavarotti (Decca)
7	5	SUMMER DREAMS	Beach Boys (Capitol)
5	6	PRETTY WOMAN - SOUNDTRACK	Various Artists (EMI USA)
3	7	HOT ROCKS 1964-1971	Rolling Stones (London)
9	8	... BUT SERIOUSLY	Phil Collins (Vertigo)
15	9	GREATEST HITS	Bangles (CBS)
4	10	FLESH AND BLOOD	Poison (Enigma)
19	11	VOLUME II - 1990 A NEW DECADE	Soul II Soul (10)
12	12	STEP BY STEP	New Kids On The Block (CBS)
14	13	BETWEEN THE LINES	Jason Donovan (PWL)
21	14	CRAIG MCLACHLAN AND CHECK 1-2	Craig McLachlan & Check 1-2 (Epic)
18	15	I DO NOT WANT WHAT I HAVEN'T GOT	Sinead O'Connor (Ensign)
8	16	SMASH HITS - RAVE!	Various Artists (Dover)
20	17	THROUGH A BIG COUNTRY - GREATEST HITS	Big Country (Mercury)
25	18	PLEASE HAMMER DON'T HURT 'EM	MC Hammer (Capitol)
22	19	ONLY YESTERDAY	Carpenters (A&M)
16	20	THE VERY BEST OF TALK TALK - NATURAL HISTORY	Talk Talk (Parlophone)
30	21	TEENAGE NINJA MUTANT TURTLES - SOUNDTRACK	Various Artists (SBK)
11	22	COMPOSITIONS	Anita Baker (Elektra)
34	23	LABOUR OF LOVE II	UB40 (DEP International)
23	24	SOUL PROVIDER	Michael Bolton (CBS)
-	25	EROICA	Wendy & Lisa (Virgin)
29	26	BONAFIDE	Maxi Priest (10)
-	27	WAKING HOURS	Del Amitri (A&M)
37	28	WORLD POWER	Snap (Arista)
-	29	HEART & SOUL III - HEART FULL OF SOUL	Various Artists (Heart & Soul)
39	30	HOME	Hothouse Flowers (London)
26	31	WILSON PHILLIPS	Wilson Phillips (SBK)
13	32	GOODNIGHT L.A.	Magnum (Polydor)
31	33	VIVALDI: THE FOUR SEASONS Nigel Kennedy with the English Chamber Orchestra	
33	34	OTHER VOICES	Paul Young (CBS)
27	35	THE STONE ROSES	Stone Roses (Silvertone)
36	36	THE SONGS 1975-1990	Barry Manilow (Arista)
-	37	THE VEGETARIANS OF LOVE	Bob Geldof (Mercury)
24	38	STEEL WHEELS	Rolling Stones (CBS)
28	39	REPUTATION	Dusty Springfield (Parlophone)
-	40	ARMCHAIR THEATRE	Jeff Lynne (Reprise)
43	41	FOREIGN AFFAIR	Tina Turner (Capitol)
42	42	PUMP UP THE JAM	Technotronic (Swanyard)
17	43	DEEP HEAT 7 - SEVENTH HEAVEN	Various Artists (Telstar)
40	44	THE ULTIMATE '60S COLLECTION	Various Artists (Castle Communications)
48	45	STILL GOT THE BLUES	Gary Moore (Virgin)
49	46	THE CHIMES	Chimes (CBS)
-	47	THE WILD ONE	Various Artists (EMI)
43	48	CUTS BOTH WAYS	Gloria Estefan (Epic)
-	49	JUST THE TWO OF US	Various Artists (Columbia)
50	50	WILD!	Erasure (Mute)

Elton John, whose single *Sacrifice* prevented Pavarotti's *Nessun Dorma* from giving him an historic double Number 1 in both album and singles charts, coincidentally also removed the Italian from the Number 1 album slot with *Sleeping In The Past* - although this too quickly surrendered the summit, being replaced by the second volume of EMI/Virgin's newly-inaugurated *Now Dance 90* compilation series.

August 1990

11 August 1990

last week	this week	
1	1	NOW DANCE 902 — Various Artists (EMI/Virgin/PolyGram)
2	2	SLEEPING WITH THE PAST — Elton John (Rocket)
3	3	I'M BREATHLESS — Madonna (Sire)
8	4	... BUT SERIOUSLY — Phil Collins (Vertigo)
4	5	THE ESSENTIAL PAVAROTTI — Luciano Pavarotti (Decca)
5	6	SUMMER DREAMS — Beach Boys (Capitol)
6	7	PRETTY WOMAN - SOUNDTRACK — Various Artists (EMI USA)
7	8	HOT ROCKS 1964-1971 — Rolling Stones (London)
29	9	HEART & SOUL III - HEART FULL OF SOUL — Various Artists (Heart & Soul)
18	10	PLEASE HAMMER DON'T HURT 'EM — MC Hammer (Capitol)
15	11	I DO NOT WANT WHAT I HAVEN'T GOT — Sinead O'Connor (Ensign)
10	12	FLESH AND BLOOD — Poison (Enigma)
9	13	GREATEST HITS — Bangles (CBS)
14	14	CRAIG MCLACHLAN AND CHECK 1-2 — Craig McLachlan & Check 1-2 (Epic)
13	15	BETWEEN THE LINES — Jason Donovan (PWL)
12	16	STEP BY STEP — New Kids On The Block (CBS)
23	17	LABOUR OF LOVE II — UB40 (DEP International)
24	18	SOUL PROVIDER — Michael Bolton (CBS)
19	19	ONLY YESTERDAY — Carpenters (A&M)
31	20	WILSON PHILLIPS — Wilson Phillips (SBK)
21	21	TEENAGE NINJA MUTANT TURTLES - SOUNDTRACK — Various Artists (SBK)
11	22	VOLUME II - 1990 A NEW DECADE — Soul II Soul (10)
37	23	THE VEGETARIANS OF LOVE — Bob Geldof (Mercury)
40	24	ARMCHAIR THEATRE — Jeff Lynne (Reprise)
20	25	THE VERY BEST OF TALK TALK - NATURAL HISTORY — Talk Talk (Parlophone)
41	26	FOREIGN AFFAIR — Tina Turner (Capitol)
17	27	THROUGH A BIG COUNTRY - GREATEST HITS — Big Country (Mercury)
-	28	SNAP IT UP - MONSTER HITS 2 — Various Artists (CBS/WEA/BMG)
33	29	VIVALDI: THE FOUR SEASONS — Nigel Kennedy with the English Chamber Orchestra
22	30	COMPOSITIONS — Anita Baker (Elektra)
47	31	THE WILD ONE — Various Artists (EMI)
26	32	BONAFIDE — Maxi Priest (10)
28	33	WORLD POWER — Snap (Arista)
49	34	JUST THE TWO OF US — Various Artists (Columbia)
25	35	EROICA — Wendy & Lisa (Virgin)
-	36	FOREVER YOUR GIRL — Paula Abdul (Siren)
27	37	WAKING HOURS — Del Amitri (A&M)
16	38	SMASH HITS - RAVE! — Various Artists (Dover)
42	39	PUMP UP THE JAM — Technotronic (Swanyard)
-	40	LIFE — Inspiral Carpets (Cow)
30	41	HOME — Hothouse Flowers (London)
48	42	CUTS BOTH WAYS — Gloria Estefan (Epic)
-	43	NEVER NEVER LAND — Annihilator (Road Runner)
-	44	THE WALL — Pink Floyd (Harvest)
-	45	COSMIC THING — B-52's (Reprise)
34	46	OTHER VOICES — Paul Young (CBS)
35	47	THE STONE ROSES — Stone Roses (Silvertone)
-	48	VIOLATOR — Depeche Mode (Mute)
46	49	THE CHIMES — Chimes (CBS)
-	50	BORN TO SING — En Vogue (Atlantic)

18 August 1990

last week	this week	
1	1	NOW DANCE 902 — Various Artists (EMI/Virgin/PolyGram)
28	2	SNAP IT UP - MONSTER HITS 2 — Various Artists (CBS/WEA/BMG)
2	3	SLEEPING WITH THE PAST — Elton John (Rocket)
3	4	I'M BREATHLESS — Madonna (Sire)
-	5	KNEBWORTH - THE ALBUM — Various Artists (Polydor)
4	6	... BUT SERIOUSLY — Phil Collins (Vertigo)
6	7	SUMMER DREAMS — Beach Boys (Capitol)
16	8	STEP BY STEP — New Kids On The Block (CBS)
10	9	PLEASE HAMMER DON'T HURT 'EM — MC Hammer (Capitol)
5	10	THE ESSENTIAL PAVAROTTI — Luciano Pavarotti (Decca)
8	11	HOT ROCKS 1964-1971 — Rolling Stones (London)
7	12	PRETTY WOMAN - SOUNDTRACK — Various Artists (EMI USA)
26	13	FOREIGN AFFAIR — Tina Turner (Capitol)
9	14	HEART & SOUL III - HEART FULL OF SOUL — Various Artists (Heart & Soul)
15	15	GREATEST HITS — Bangles (CBS)
11	16	I DO NOT WANT WHAT I HAVEN'T GOT — Sinead O'Connor (Ensign)
14	17	CRAIG MCLACHLAN AND CHECK 1-2 — Craig McLachlan & Check 1-2 (Epic)
20	18	WILSON PHILLIPS — Wilson Phillips (SBK)
41	19	HOME — Hothouse Flowers (London)
12	20	FLESH AND BLOOD — Poison (Enigma)
31	21	THE WILD ONE — Various Artists (EMI)
21	22	TEENAGE NINJA MUTANT TURTLES - SOUNDTRACK — Various Artists (SBK)
17	23	LABOUR OF LOVE II — UB40 (DEP International)
-	24	LOVEGOD — Soup Dragons (Raw TV)
39	25	PUMP UP THE JAM — Technotronic (Swanyard)
18	26	SOUL PROVIDER — Michael Bolton (CBS)
-	27	LOOK SHARP! — Roxette (EMI)
19	28	ONLY YESTERDAY — Carpenters (A&M)
22	29	VOLUME II - 1990 A NEW DECADE — Soul II Soul (10)
-	30	BROTHER'S KEEPER — Neville Brothers (A&M)
15	31	BETWEEN THE LINES — Jason Donovan (PWL)
30	32	COMPOSITIONS — Anita Baker (Elektra)
25	33	THE VERY BEST OF TALK TALK - NATURAL HISTORY — Talk Talk (Parlophone)
-	34	WILD! — Erasure (Mute)
33	35	WORLD POWER — Snap (Arista)
-	36	THE SUMMER OF LOVE — Various Artists (Dino)
29	37	VIVALDI: THE FOUR SEASONS — Nigel Kennedy with the English Chamber Orchestra
27	38	THROUGH A BIG COUNTRY - GREATEST HITS — Big Country (Mercury)
-	39	CHANGESONEBOWIE — David Bowie (EMI)
34	40	JUST THE TWO OF US — Various Artists (Columbia)
-	41	THE HUNGER — Michael Bolton (CBS)
42	42	REV IT UP — Vixen (EMI USA)
23	43	THE VEGETARIANS OF LOVE — Bob Geldof (Mercury)
36	44	FOREVER YOUR GIRL — Paula Abdul (Siren)
42	45	CUTS BOTH WAYS — Gloria Estefan (Epic)
48	46	VIOLATOR — Depeche Mode (Mute)
32	47	BONAFIDE — Maxi Priest (10)
24	48	ARMCHAIR THEATRE — Jeff Lynne (Reprise)
37	49	WAKING HOURS — Del Amitri (A&M)
47	50	THE STONE ROSES — Stone Roses (Silvertone)

25 August 1990

last week	this week	
5	1	KNEBWORTH - THE ALBUM — Various Artists (Polydor)
3	2	SLEEPING WITH THE PAST — Elton John (Rocket)
2	3	SNAP IT UP - MONSTER HITS 2 — Various Artists (CBS/WEA/BMG)
-	4	MEGABASS — Various Artists (Telstar)
10	5	THE ESSENTIAL PAVAROTTI — Luciano Pavarotti (Decca)
-	6	BOSSANOVA — Pixies (4AD)
1	7	NOW DANCE 902 — Various Artists (EMI/Virgin/PolyGram)
6	8	... BUT SERIOUSLY — Phil Collins (Vertigo)
8	9	STEP BY STEP — New Kids On The Block (CBS)
-	10	BLAZE OF GLORY/YOUNG GUNS II — Jon Bon Jovi (Vertigo)
24	11	LOVEGOD — Soup Dragons (Raw TV)
7	12	SUMMER DREAMS — Beach Boys (Capitol)
12	13	PRETTY WOMAN - SOUNDTRACK — Various Artists (EMI USA)
14	14	I'M BREATHLESS — Madonna (Sire)
11	15	HOT ROCKS 1964-1971 — Rolling Stones (London)
16	16	FOREIGN AFFAIR — Tina Turner (Capitol)
19	17	HOME — Hothouse Flowers (London)
9	18	PLEASE HAMMER DON'T HURT 'EM — MC Hammer (Capitol)
23	19	LABOUR OF LOVE II — UB40 (DEP International)
18	20	WILSON PHILLIPS — Wilson Phillips (SBK)
15	21	GREATEST HITS — Bangles (CBS)
14	22	HEART & SOUL III - HEART FULL OF SOUL — Various Artists (Heart & Soul)
17	23	CRAIG MCLACHLAN AND CHECK 1-2 — Craig McLachlan & Check 1-2 (Epic)
27	24	LOOK SHARP! — Roxette (EMI)
25	25	BROTHER'S KEEPER — Neville Brothers (A&M)
42	26	REV IT UP — Vixen (EMI USA)
25	27	PUMP UP THE JAM — Technotronic (Swanyard)
20	28	FLESH AND BLOOD — Poison (Enigma)
22	29	TEENAGE NINJA MUTANT TURTLES - SOUNDTRACK — Various Artists (SBK)
30	30	SAXUALITY — Candy Dulfer (RCA)
37	31	VIVALDI: THE FOUR SEASONS — Nigel Kennedy with the English Chamber Orchestra
16	32	I DO NOT WANT WHAT I HAVEN'T GOT — Sinead O'Connor (Ensign)
29	33	VOLUME II - 1990 A NEW DECADE — Soul II Soul (10)
33	34	THE VERY BEST OF TALK TALK - NATURAL HISTORY — Talk Talk (Parlophone)
-	35	GET ON THIS!!! 2 — Various Artists (Telstar)
26	36	SOUL PROVIDER — Michael Bolton (CBS)
31	37	BETWEEN THE LINES — Jason Donovan (PWL)
28	38	ONLY YESTERDAY — Carpenters (A&M)
39	39	CHANGESONEBOWIE — David Bowie (EMI)
40	40	COMPOSITIONS — Anita Baker (Elektra)
38	41	THROUGH A BIG COUNTRY - GREATEST HITS — Big Country (Mercury)
41	42	THE HUNGER — Michael Bolton (CBS)
-	43	HEART OF STONE — Cher (Geffen)
-	44	STILL GOT THE BLUES — Gary Moore (Virgin)
21	45	THE WILD ONE — Various Artists (EMI)
-	46	SAY SOMETHING GOOD — River City People (EMI)
50	47	THE STONE ROSES — Stone Roses (Silvertone)
-	48	AN EMOTIONAL FISH — An Emotional Fish (East West)
36	49	THE SUMMER OF LOVE — Various Artists (Dino)
44	50	FOREVER YOUR GIRL — Paula Abdul (Siren)

The chart-topping Knebworth compilation album consisted of live recordings of some of the biggest names from over 30 years of UK recording history, all captured at the Silver Clef Award Winners Show, in aid of the Music Therapy charity, at Knebworth Park. Participants in the show and album included Phil Collins, Dire Straits, Elton John, Eric Clapton, Paul McCartney, Pink Floyd and Cliff & the Shadows.

September 1990

1 September 1990

last week	this week	title	artist (label)
-	1	MUSIC FROM GRAFFITI BRIDGE	Prince (Paisley Park)
2	2	SLEEPING WITH THE PAST	Elton John (Rocket)
10	3	BLAZE OF GLORY/YOUNG GUNS II	Jon Bon Jovi (Vertigo)
6	4	BOSSANOVA	Pixies (4AD)
1	5	KNEBWORTH - THE ALBUM	Various (Polydor)
3	6	SNAP IT UP - MONSTER HITS 2	Various Artists (CBS/WEA/BMG)
4	7	MEGABASS	Various Artists (Telstar)
9	8	STEP BY STEP	New Kids On The Block (CBS)
-	9	IN CONCERT	Luciano Pavarotti, Placido Domingo & José Carreras (Decca)
8	10	... BUT SERIOUSLY	Phil Collins (Vertigo)
-	11	LIBERTY	Duran Duran (Parlophone)
5	12	THE ESSENTIAL PAVAROTTI	Luciano Pavarotti (Decca)
20	13	WILSON PHILLIPS	Wilson Phillips (SBK)
12	14	SUMMER DREAMS	Beach Boys (Capitol)
16	15	FOREIGN AFFAIR	Tina Turner (Capitol)
36	16	SOUL PROVIDER	Michael Bolton (CBS)
24	17	LOOK SHARP!	Roxette (EMI)
11	18	LOVEGOD	Soup Dragons (Raw TV)
7	19	NOW DANCE 902	Various Artists (EMI/Virgin/PolyGram)
14	20	I'M BREATHLESS	Madonna (Sire)
13	21	PRETTY WOMAN - SOUNDTRACK	Various Artists (EMI USA)
18	22	PLEASE HAMMER DON'T HURT 'EM	MC Hammer (Capitol)
15	23	HOT ROCKS 1964-1971	Rolling Stones (London)
19	24	LABOUR OF LOVE II	UB40 (DEP International)
21	25	GREATEST HITS	Bangles (CBS)
38	26	ONLY YESTERDAY	Carpenters (A&M)
-	27	TYR	Black Sabbath (IRS)
17	28	HOME	Hothouse Flowers (London)
30	29	SAXUALITY	Candy Dulfer (RCA)
27	30	PUMP UP THE JAM	Technotronic (Swanyard)
35	31	GET ON THIS!!! 2	Various Artists (Telstar)
46	32	SAY SOMETHING GOOD	River City People (EMI)
23	33	CRAIG MCLACHLAN AND CHECK 1-2	Craig McLachlan & Check 1-2 (Epic)
28	34	FLESH AND BLOOD	Poison (Enigma)
31	35	VIVALDI: THE FOUR SEASONS	Nigel Kennedy with the English Chamber Orchestra
33	36	VOLUME II - 1990 A NEW DECADE	Soul II Soul (10)
34	37	THE VERY BEST OF TALK TALK - NATURAL HISTORY	Talk Talk (Parlophone)
39	38	CHANGESONEBOWIE	David Bowie (EMI)
43	39	HEART OF STONE	Cher (Geffen)
29	40	TEENAGE NINJA MUTANT TURTLES - SOUNDTRACK	Various Artists (SBK)
47	41	THE STONE ROSES	Stone Roses (Silvertone)
32	42	I DO NOT WANT WHAT I HAVEN'T GOT	Sinead O'Connor (Ensign)
26	43	REV IT UP	Vixen (EMI)
40	44	COMPOSITIONS	Anita Baker (Elektra)
37	45	BETWEEN THE LINES	Jason Donovan (PWL)
22	46	HEART & SOUL III - HEART FULL OF SOUL	Various Artists (Heart & Soul)
-	47	THE VEGETARIANS OF LOVE	Bob Geldof (Mercury)
42	48	THE HUNGER	Michael Bolton (CBS)
25	49	BROTHER'S KEEPER	Neville Brothers (A&M)
41	50	THROUGH A BIG COUNTRY - GREATEST HITS	Big Country (Mercury)

8 September 1990

last week	this week	title	artist (label)
1	1	MUSIC FROM GRAFFITI BRIDGE	Prince (Paisley Park)
9	2	IN CONCERT	Placido Domingo & José Carreras (Decca)
2	3	SLEEPING WITH THE PAST	Elton John (Rocket)
7	4	MEGABASS	Various Artists (Telstar)
16	5	SOUL PROVIDER	Michael Bolton (CBS)
3	6	BLAZE OF GLORY/YOUNG GUNS II	Jon Bon Jovi (Vertigo)
17	7	LOOK SHARP!	Roxette (EMI)
-	8	PERSISTENCE OF TIME	Anthrax (Island)
8	9	STEP BY STEP	New Kids On The Block (CBS)
-	10	JORDAN: THE COMEBACK	Prefab Sprout (Kitchenware)
10	11	... BUT SERIOUSLY	Phil Collins (Vertigo)
4	12	BOSSANOVA	Pixies (4AD)
31	13	GET ON THIS!!! 2	Various Artists (Telstar)
11	14	LIBERTY	Duran Duran (Parlophone)
14	15	SUMMER DREAMS	Beach Boys (Capitol)
20	16	I'M BREATHLESS	Madonna (Sire)
13	17	WILSON PHILLIPS	Wilson Phillips (SBK)
12	18	THE ESSENTIAL PAVAROTTI	Luciano Pavarotti (Decca)
6	19	SNAP IT UP - MONSTER HITS 2	Various Artists (CBS/WEA/BMG)
22	20	PLEASE HAMMER DON'T HURT 'EM	MC Hammer (Capitol)
15	21	FOREIGN AFFAIR	Tina Turner (Capitol)
-	22	JUST THE TWO OF US	Various Artists (Columbia)
18	23	LOVEGOD	Soup Dragons (Raw TV)
34	24	FLESH AND BLOOD	Poison (Enigma)
5	25	KNEBWORTH - THE ALBUM	Various Artists (Polydor)
21	26	PRETTY WOMAN - SOUNDTRACK	Various Artists (EMI USA)
25	27	GREATEST HITS	Bangles (CBS)
28	28	HOME	Hothouse Flowers (London)
37	29	THE VERY BEST OF TALK TALK - NATURAL HISTORY	Talk Talk (Parlophone)
19	31	NOW DANCE 902	Various (EMI/Virgin/PolyGram)
23	33	HOT ROCKS 1964-1971	Rolling Stones (London)
26	34	ONLY YESTERDAY	Carpenters (A&M)
29	35	SAXUALITY	Candy Dulfer (RCA)
35	37	VIVALDI: THE FOUR SEASONS	Nigel Kennedy with the English Chamber Orchestra
30	38	PUMP UP THE JAM	Technotronic (Swanyard)
33	39	CRAIG MCLACHLAN AND CHECK 1-2	Craig McLachlan & Check 1-2 (Epic)
41	40	THE STONE ROSES	Stone Roses (Silvertone)
-	41	POISON	Bell Biv Devoe (MCA)
45	42	BETWEEN THE LINES	Jason Donovan (PWL)
42	43	I DO NOT WANT WHAT I HAVEN'T GOT	Sinead O'Connor (Ensign)
36	44	VOLUME II - 1990 A NEW DECADE	Soul II Soul (10)
32	45	SAY SOMETHING GOOD	River City People (EMI)
-	46	WHEN THE WORLD KNOWS YOUR NAME	Deacon Blue (CBS)
-	47	BACK STREET SYMPHONY	Thunder (EMI)
39	48	HEART OF STONE	Cher (Geffen)
38	49	CHANGESONEBOWIE	David Bowie (EMI)
-	50	RITUAL DE LO HABITUAL	Jane's Addiction (Warner Bros.)

15 September 1990

last week	this week	title	artist (label)
-	1	LISTEN WITHOUT PREJUDICE VOLUME 1	George Michael (Epic)
2	2	IN CONCERT	Placido Domingo & José Carreras (Decca)
1	3	MUSIC FROM GRAFFITI BRIDGE	Prince (Paisley Park)
5	4	SOUL PROVIDER	Michael Bolton (CBS)
3	5	SLEEPING WITH THE PAST	Elton John (Rocket)
6	6	BLAZE OF GLORY/YOUNG GUNS II	Jon Bon Jovi (Vertigo)
10	7	JORDAN: THE COMEBACK	Prefab Sprout (Kitchenware)
4	8	MEGABASS	Various Artists (Telstar)
7	9	LOOK SHARP!	Roxette (EMI)
9	10	STEP BY STEP	New Kids On The Block (CBS)
11	11	... BUT SERIOUSLY	Phil Collins (Vertigo)
17	12	WILSON PHILLIPS	Wilson Phillips (SBK)
8	13	PERSISTENCE OF TIME	Anthrax (Island)
14	14	WORLD CLIQUE	Deee-Lite (Elektra)
21	15	FOREIGN AFFAIR	Tina Turner (Capitol)
12	16	BOSSANOVA	Pixies (4AD)
15	17	SUMMER DREAMS	Beach Boys (Capitol)
26	18	PRETTY WOMAN - SOUNDTRACK	Various Artists (EMI USA)
-	19	MARIAH CAREY	Mariah Carey (CBS)
13	20	GET ON THIS!!! 2	Various Artists (Telstar)
22	21	JUST THE TWO OF US	Various Artists (Columbia)
16	22	I'M BREATHLESS	Madonna (Sire)
18	23	THE ESSENTIAL PAVAROTTI	Luciano Pavarotti (Decca)
23	24	LOVEGOD	Soup Dragons (Raw TV)
20	25	PLEASE HAMMER DON'T HURT 'EM	MC Hammer (Capitol)
27	26	GREATEST HITS	Bangles (CBS)
29	27	THE VERY BEST OF TALK TALK - NATURAL HISTORY	Talk Talk (Parlophone)
-	28	TIME'S UP	Living Colour (Epic)
34	29	ONLY YESTERDAY	Carpenters (A&M)
28	30	HOME	Hothouse Flowers (London)
31	31	LABOUR OF LOVE II	UB40 (DEP International)
24	32	FLESH AND BLOOD	Poison (Enigma)
14	33	LIBERTY	Duran Duran (Parlophone)
33	34	HOT ROCKS 1964-1971	Rolling Stones (London)
25	35	KNEBWORTH - THE ALBUM	Various (Polydor)
44	36	VOLUME II - 1990 A NEW DECADE	Soul II Soul (10)
35	37	SAXUALITY	Candy Dulfer (RCA)
-	38	THE REAL THING	Faith No More (Slash)
32	39	BONAFIDE	Maxi Priest (10)
19	40	SNAP IT UP - MONSTER HITS 2	Various Artists (CBS/WEA/BMG)
-	41	45 84 89 (A-SIDES)	Fall (Beggars Banquet)
37	42	VIVALDI: THE FOUR SEASONS	Nigel Kennedy with the English Chamber Orchestra
50	43	RITUAL DE LO HABITUAL	Jane's Addiction (Warner Bros.)
31	44	NOW DANCE 902	Various (EMI/Virgin/PolyGram)
45	45	WORLD POWER	Snap (Arista)
-	46	JANET JACKSON'S RHYTHM NATION 1814	Janet Jackson (A&M)
38	47	PUMP UP THE JAM	Technotronic (Swanyard)
43	48	I DO NOT WANT WHAT I HAVEN'T GOT	Sinead O'Connor (Ensign)
-	49	CUTS BOTH WAYS	Gloria Estefan (Epic)
-	50	HARMONY OF CORRUPTION	Napalm Death (Earache)

Prince's fourth soundtrack album from his own movie *Graffiti Bridge*, became his second such release to top the chart, following *Batman* the previous year. Another act whose success was fuelled by a film was Jon Bon Jovi, who worked as a soloist on *Blaze Of Glory*, which contained the soundtrack songs from the western *Young Guns II*. George Michael returned with his first album for three years.

September – October 1990

22 September 1990

last	this	title	artist (label)
1	1	LISTEN WITHOUT PREJUDICE VOLUME 1	George Michael (Epic)
2	2	IN CONCERT	Luciano Pavarotti, Placido Domingo & José Carreras (Decca)
-	3	OOH LAS VEGAS	Deacon Blue (CBS)
5	4	SLEEPING WITH THE PAST	Elton John (Rocket)
19	5	MARIAH CAREY	Mariah Carey (CBS)
9	6	LOOK SHARP!	Roxette (EMI)
-	7	STEPPING OUT - THE VERY BEST OF JOE JACKSON	Joe Jackson (A&M)
4	8	SOUL PROVIDER	Michael Bolton (CBS)
3	9	MUSIC FROM GRAFFITI BRIDGE	Prince (Paisley Park)
7	10	JORDAN: THE COMEBACK	Prefab Sprout (Kitchenware)
10	11	WORLD CLIQUE	Deee-Lite (Elektra)
11	12	... BUT SERIOUSLY	Phil Collins (Vertigo)
6	13	BLAZE OF GLORY/YOUNG GUNS II	Jon Bon Jovi (Vertigo)
10	14	STEP BY STEP	New Kids On The Block (CBS)
27	15	THE VERY BEST OF TALK TALK - NATURAL HISTORY	Talk Talk (Parlophone)
-	16	BOOMANIA	Betty Boo (Rhythm King)
12	17	WILSON PHILLIPS	Wilson Phillips (SBK)
-	18	EMPIRE	Queensryche (EMI-USA)
15	19	FOREIGN AFFAIR	Tina Turner (Capitol)
8	20	MEGABASS	Various Artists (Telstar)
-	21	RAGGED GLORY	Neil Young & Crazy Horse (Reprise)
28	22	TIME'S UP	Living Colour (Epic)
17	23	SUMMER DREAMS	Beach Boys (Capitol)
22	24	I'M BREATHLESS	Madonna (Sire)
18	25	PRETTY WOMAN - SOUNDTRACK	Various Artists (EMI USA)
16	26	BOSSANOVA	Pixies (4AD)
-	27	CHINA CRISIS COLLECTION	China Crisis (Virgin)
23	28	THE ESSENTIAL PAVAROTTI	Luciano Pavarotti (Decca)
21	29	JUST THE TWO OF US	Various Artists (Columbia)
24	30	LOVEGOD	Soup Dragons (Raw TV)
38	31	THE REAL THING	Faith No More (Slash)
46	32	JANET JACKSON'S RHYTHM NATION 1814	Janet Jackson (A&M)
25	33	PLEASE HAMMER DON'T HURT 'EM	MC Hammer (Capitol)
-	34	HIGH ON EMOTION - LIVE FROM DUBLIN	Chris De Burgh (A&M)
20	35	GET ON THIS!!! 2	Various Artists (Telstar)
29	36	ONLY YESTERDAY	Carpenters (A&M)
34	37	HOT ROCKS 1964-1971	Rolling Stones (London)
-	38	DAYS OF THUNDER - SOUNDTRACK	Various Artists (Epic)
-	39	SAY SOMETHING GOOD	River City People (EMI)
-	40	DAVE STEWART AND THE SPIRITUAL COWBOYS	Dave Stewart & the Spiritual Cowboys (RCA)
48	41	I DO NOT WANT WHAT I HAVEN'T GOT	Sinead O'Connor (Ensign)
13	42	PERSISTENCE OF TIME	Anthrax (Island)
26	43	GREATEST HITS	Bangles (CBS)
31	44	LABOUR OF LOVE II	UB40 (DEP International)
-	45	FAITH	George Michael (Epic)
35	46	KNEBWORTH - THE ALBUM	Various (Polydor)
-	47	STILL GOT THE BLUES	Gary Moore (Virgin)
32	48	FLESH AND BLOOD	Poison (Enigma)
47	49	PUMP UP THE JAM	Technotronic (Swanyard)
36	50	VOLUME II - 1990 A NEW DECADE	Soul II Soul (10)

29 September 1990

last	this	title	artist (label)
1	1	LISTEN WITHOUT PREJUDICE VOLUME 1	George Michael (Epic)
2	2	IN CONCERT	Luciano Pavarotti, Placido Domingo & José Carreras (Decca)
3	3	OOH LAS VEGAS	Deacon Blue (CBS)
4	4	SLEEPING WITH THE PAST	Elton John (Rocket)
16	5	BOOMANIA	Betty Boo (Rhythm King)
6	6	LOOK SHARP!	Roxette (EMI)
5	7	MARIAH CAREY	Mariah Carey (CBS)
8	8	HEAVEN OR LAS VEGAS	Cocteau Twins (4AD)
8	9	SOUL PROVIDER	Michael Bolton (CBS)
7	10	STEPPING OUT - THE VERY BEST OF JOE JACKSON	Joe Jackson (A&M)
19	11	FOREIGN AFFAIR	Tina Turner (Capitol)
12	12	... BUT SERIOUSLY	Phil Collins (Vertigo)
17	13	WILSON PHILLIPS	Wilson Phillips (SBK)
21	14	RAGGED GLORY	Neil Young & Crazy Horse (Reprise)
-	15	ROOM TO ROAM	Waterboys (Ensign)
16	16	WORLD CLIQUE	Deee-Lite (Elektra)
14	17	STEP BY STEP	New Kids On The Block (CBS)
-	18	JUST SEVENTEEN - GET KICKIN'	Various Artists (Dover)
9	19	UNDER THE RED SKY	Bob Dylan (CBS)
-	20	MUSIC FROM GRAFFITI BRIDGE	Prince (Paisley Park)
34	21	HIGH ON EMOTION - LIVE FROM DUBLIN	Chris De Burgh (A&M)
20	22	MEGABASS	Various Artists (Telstar)
15	23	THE VERY BEST OF TALK TALK - NATURAL HISTORY	Talk Talk (Parlophone)
29	24	JUST THE TWO OF US	Various Artists (Columbia)
13	25	BLAZE OF GLORY/YOUNG GUNS II	Jon Bon Jovi (Vertigo)
31	26	THE REAL THING	Faith No More (Slash)
-	27	THE WALL - LIVE IN BERLIN	Roger Waters (Mercury)
18	28	EMPIRE	Queensryche (EMI-USA)
39	29	SAY SOMETHING GOOD	River City People (EMI)
50	30	VOLUME II - 1990 A NEW DECADE	Soul II Soul (10)
24	31	I'M BREATHLESS	Madonna (Sire)
28	32	THE ESSENTIAL PAVAROTTI	Luciano Pavarotti (Decca)
41	33	I DO NOT WANT WHAT I HAVEN'T GOT	Sinead O'Connor (Ensign)
38	34	DAYS OF THUNDER - SOUNDTRACK	Various (Epic)
10	35	JORDAN: THE COMEBACK	Prefab Sprout (Kitchenware)
32	36	JANET JACKSON'S RHYTHM NATION 1814	Janet Jackson (A&M)
23	37	SUMMER DREAMS	Beach Boys (Capitol)
33	38	PLEASE HAMMER DON'T HURT 'EM	MC Hammer (Capitol)
-	39	MIDNIGHT STROLL	Robert Cray Band (Mercury)
43	40	GREATEST HITS	Bangles (CBS)
25	41	PRETTY WOMAN - SOUNDTRACK	Various Artists (EMI USA)
-	42	ROMANTIC?	Human League (Virgin)
30	43	LOVEGOD	Soup Dragons (Raw TV)
27	44	CHINA CRISIS COLLECTION	China Crisis (Virgin)
-	45	TOO WICKED	Aswad (Mango)
49	46	PUMP UP THE JAM	Technotronic (Swanyard)
-	47	PAINKILLER	Judas Priest (CBS)
-	48	LOOK HOW LONG	Loose Ends (10)
26	49	BOSSANOVA	Pixies (4AD)
36	50	ONLY YESTERDAY	Carpenters (A&M)

6 October 1990

last	this	title	artist (label)
-	1	X	INXS (Mercury)
2	2	IN CONCERT	Luciano Pavarotti, Placido Domingo & José Carreras (Decca)
1	3	LISTEN WITHOUT PREJUDICE VOLUME 1	George Michael (Epic)
-	4	THE RAZOR'S EDGE	AC/DC (Atco)
3	5	OOH LAS VEGAS	Deacon Blue (CBS)
15	6	ROOM TO ROAM	Waterboys (Ensign)
8	7	HEAVEN OR LAS VEGAS	Cocteau Twins (4AD)
-	8	SLAMMIN'	Various Artists (A&M)
4	9	SLEEPING WITH THE PAST	Elton John (Rocket)
5	10	BOOMANIA	Betty Boo (Rhythm King)
-	11	RUST IN PEACE	Megadeth (Capitol)
7	12	MARIAH CAREY	Mariah Carey (CBS)
11	13	FOREIGN AFFAIR	Tina Turner (Capitol)
9	14	SOUL PROVIDER	Michael Bolton (CBS)
6	15	LOOK SHARP!	Roxette (EMI)
19	16	UNDER THE RED SKY	Bob Dylan (CBS)
12	17	... BUT SERIOUSLY	Phil Collins (Vertigo)
18	18	JUST SEVENTEEN - GET KICKIN'	Various Artists (Dover)
13	19	WILSON PHILLIPS	Wilson Phillips (SBK)
10	20	STEPPING OUT - THE VERY BEST OF JOE JACKSON	Joe Jackson (A&M)
39	21	MIDNIGHT STROLL	Robert Cray Band (Mercury)
-	22	SEASONS IN THE ABYSS	Slayer (Def American)
48	23	LOOK HOW LONG	Loose Ends (10)
-	24	IMPURITY	New Model Army (EMI)
35	25	JORDAN: THE COMEBACK	Prefab Sprout (Kitchenware)
16	26	WORLD CLIQUE	Deee-Lite (Elektra)
17	27	STEP BY STEP	New Kids On The Block (CBS)
42	28	ROMANTIC?	Human League (Virgin)
-	29	ELIZIUM	Fields Of The Nephilim (Beggars Banquet)
23	30	THE VERY BEST OF TALK TALK - NATURAL HISTORY	Talk Talk (Parlophone)
21	31	HIGH ON EMOTION - LIVE FROM DUBLIN	Chris De Burgh (A&M)
14	32	RAGGED GLORY	Neil Young & Crazy Horse (Reprise)
34	33	DAYS OF THUNDER - SOUNDTRACK	Various Artists (Epic)
47	34	PAINKILLER	Judas Priest (CBS)
-	35	BETWEEN THE LINES	Jason Donovan (PWL)
27	36	THE WALL - LIVE IN BERLIN	Roger Waters (Mercury)
25	37	BLAZE OF GLORY/YOUNG GUNS II	Jon Bon Jovi (Vertigo)
38	38	PLEASE HAMMER DON'T HURT 'EM	MC Hammer (Capitol)
50	39	ONLY YESTERDAY	Carpenters (A&M)
20	40	MUSIC FROM GRAFFITI BRIDGE	Prince (Paisley Park)
32	41	THE ESSENTIAL PAVAROTTI	Luciano Pavarotti (Decca)
-	42	STRAIGHT	Dogs D'Amour (China)
43	43	LABOUR OF LOVE II	UB40 (DEP International)
41	44	PRETTY WOMAN - SOUNDTRACK	Various Artists (EMI USA)
24	45	JUST THE TWO OF US	Various Artists (Columbia)
30	46	VOLUME II - 1990 A NEW DECADE	Soul II Soul (10)
31	47	I'M BREATHLESS	Madonna (Sire)
-	48	SOULS OF BLACK	Testament (Megaforce)
22	49	MEGABASS	Various Artists (Telstar)
29	50	SAY SOMETHING GOOD	River City People (EMI)

Listen Without Prejudice Volume 1 was, as its title suggested, designed as the first part of a longer project, and George Michael originally intimated that *Volume 2* would be following hot on its heels. These plans were clearly drastically changed somewhere along the line, since the follow-up is still awaited in 1993, and Michael has turned his attention to suing his record company instead.

October 1990

13 October 1990

last	this	title / artist
-	1	NO PRAYER FOR THE DYING Iron Maiden (EMI)
1	2	X INXS (Mercury)
2	3	IN CONCERT Luciano Pavarotti, Placido Domingo & José Carreras (Decca)
3	4	LISTEN WITHOUT PREJUDICE VOLUME 1 George Michael (Epic)
4	5	THE RAZOR'S EDGE AC/DC (Atco)
14	6	SOUL PROVIDER Michael Bolton (CBS)
9	7	SLEEPING WITH THE PAST Elton John (Rocket)
5	8	OOH LAS VEGAS Deacon Blue (CBS)
-	9	HELL'S DITCH Pogues (Pogue Mahone)
-	10	THAT LOVING FEELING VOL. 3 Various Artists (Dino)
11	11	RUST IN PEACE Megadeth (Capitol)
6	12	ROOM TO ROAM Waterboys (Ensign)
8	13	SLAMMIN' Various Artists (A&M)
12	14	MARIAH CAREY Mariah Carey (CBS)
10	15	BOOMANIA Betty Boo (Rhythm King)
17	16	... BUT SERIOUSLY Phil Collins (Vertigo)
-	17	DOCTOR ADAMSKI'S MUSICAL PHARMACY Adamski (MCA)
13	18	FOREIGN AFFAIR Tina Turner (Capitol)
15	19	LOOK SHARP! Roxette (EMI)
22	20	SEASONS IN THE ABYSS Slayer (Def American)
7	21	HEAVEN OR LAS VEGAS Cocteau Twins (4AD)
-	22	WE ARE IN LOVE Harry Connick Jr. (CBS)
19	23	WILSON PHILLIPS Wilson Phillips (SBK)
23	24	LOOK HOW LONG Loose Ends (10)
20	25	STEPPING OUT - THE VERY BEST OF JOE JACKSON Joe Jackson (A&M)
25	26	JORDAN: THE COMEBACK Prefab Sprout (Kitchenware)
29	27	ELIZIUM Fields Of The Nephilim (Beggars Banquet)
18	28	JUST SEVENTEEN - GET KICKIN' Various Artists (Dover)
16	29	UNDER THE RED SKY Bob Dylan (CBS)
26	30	WORLD CLIQUE Deee-Lite (Elektra)
-	31	THE BEST OF 1968-1973 Steve Miller Band (Capitol)
27	32	STEP BY STEP New Kids On The Block (CBS)
-	33	THE LA'S La's (Go! Discs)
38	34	PLEASE HAMMER DON'T HURT 'EM MC Hammer (Capitol)
30	35	THE VERY BEST OF TALK TALK - NATURAL HISTORY Talk Talk (Parlophone)
24	36	IMPURITY New Model Army (EMI)
-	37	UK BLAK Caron Wheeler (RCA)
21	38	MIDNIGHT STROLL Robert Cray Band (Mercury)
37	39	BLAZE OF GLORY/YOUNG GUNS II Jon Bon Jovi (Vertigo)
31	40	HIGH ON EMOTION - LIVE FROM DUBLIN Chris De Burgh (A&M)
33	41	DAYS OF THUNDER - SOUNDTRACK Various Artists (Epic)
45	42	JUST THE TWO OF US Various Artists (Columbia)
35	43	BETWEEN THE LINES Jason Donovan (PWL)
39	44	ONLY YESTERDAY Carpenters (A&M)
-	45	JANET JACKSON'S RHYTHM NATION 1814 Janet Jackson (A&M)
32	46	RAGGED GLORY Neil Young & Crazy Horse (Reprise)
43	47	LABOUR OF LOVE II UB40 (DEP International)
-	48	PUMP UP THE JAM Technotronic (Swanyard)
40	49	MUSIC FROM GRAFFITI BRIDGE Prince (Paisley Park)
-	50	THE NORTH AT ITS HEIGHTS MC Tunes (ZTT)

20 October 1990

last	this	title / artist
3	1	IN CONCERT Luciano Pavarotti, Placido Domingo & José Carreras (Decca)
1	2	NO PRAYER FOR THE DYING Iron Maiden (EMI)
2	3	SOME FRIENDLY Charlatans (Situation Two)
4	4	X INXS (Mercury)
-	5	LISTEN WITHOUT PREJUDICE VOLUME 1 George Michael (Epic)
6	6	SOUL PROVIDER Michael Bolton (CBS)
7	7	SLEEPING WITH THE PAST Elton John (Rocket)
17	8	DOCTOR ADAMSKI'S MUSICAL PHARMACY Adamski (MCA)
10	9	THAT LOVING FEELING VOL. 3 Various Artists (Dino)
-	10	ENLIGHTENMENT Van Morrison (Polydor)
8	11	OOH LAS VEGAS Deacon Blue (CBS)
9	12	HELL'S DITCH Pogues (Pogue Mahone)
5	13	THE RAZOR'S EDGE AC/DC (Atco)
34	14	PLEASE HAMMER DON'T HURT 'EM MC Hammer (Capitol)
18	15	FOREIGN AFFAIR Tina Turner (Capitol)
16	16	... BUT SERIOUSLY Phil Collins (Vertigo)
14	17	MARIAH CAREY Mariah Carey (CBS)
-	18	ROCKING ALL OVER THE YEARS Status Quo (Vertigo)
37	19	UK BLAK Caron Wheeler (RCA)
-	20	REFLECTION Shadows (Roll Over)
-	21	SOUL DECADE: THE SIXTIES Various Artists (Motown)
15	22	BOOMANIA Betty Boo (Rhythm King)
22	23	WE ARE IN LOVE Harry Connick Jr. (CBS)
12	24	ROOM TO ROAM Waterboys (Ensign)
45	25	JANET JACKSON'S RHYTHM NATION 1814 Janet Jackson (A&M)
42	26	JUST THE TWO OF US Various Artists (Columbia)
19	27	LOOK SHARP! Roxette (EMI)
23	28	WILSON PHILLIPS Wilson Phillips (SBK)
26	29	JORDAN: THE COMEBACK Prefab Sprout (Kitchenware)
-	30	DOWN TO EARTH Monie Love (Cooltempo)
32	31	STEP BY STEP New Kids On The Block (CBS)
11	32	RUST IN PEACE Megadeth (Capitol)
25	33	STEPPING OUT - THE VERY BEST OF JOE JACKSON Joe Jackson (A&M)
50	34	THE NORTH AT ITS HEIGHTS MC Tunes (ZTT)
41	35	DAYS OF THUNDER - SOUNDTRACK Various Artists (Epic)
-	36	IN THE BLOOD Londonbeat (AnXious)
33	37	THE LA'S La's (Go! Discs)
30	38	WORLD CLIQUE Deee-Lite (Elektra)
-	39	ANAM Clannad (RCA)
39	40	BLAZE OF GLORY/YOUNG GUNS II Jon Bon Jovi (Vertigo)
-	41	MISSING YOU - AN ALBUM OF LOVE Various Artists (EMI)
21	42	HEAVEN OR LAS VEGAS Cocteau Twins (4AD)
-	43	ELECTRIBAL MEMORIES Electribe 101 (Mercury)
35	44	THE VERY BEST OF TALK TALK - NATURAL HISTORY Talk Talk (Parlophone)
24	45	LOOK HOW LONG Loose Ends (10)
31	46	THE BEST OF 1968-1973 Steve Miller Band (Capitol)
13	47	SLAMMIN' Various Artists (A&M)
-	48	ESSENTIAL CLASSICS Various Artists (Deutsche Grammophon)
-	49	SAY SOMETHING GOOD River City People (EMI)
48	50	PUMP UP THE JAM Technotronic (Swanyard)

27 October 1990

last	this	title / artist
-	1	RHYTHM OF THE SAINTS Paul Simon (Warner Bros.)
3	2	SOME FRIENDLY Charlatans (Situation Two)
18	3	ROCKING ALL OVER THE YEARS Status Quo (Vertigo)
5	4	LISTEN WITHOUT PREJUDICE VOLUME 1 George Michael (Epic)
1	5	IN CONCERT Placido Domingo & José Carreras (Decca)
41	6	MISSING YOU - AN ALBUM OF LOVE Various Artists (EMI)
10	7	ENLIGHTENMENT Van Morrison (Polydor)
4	8	X INXS (Mercury)
-	9	BONA DRAG Morrissey (HMV)
-	10	RECYCLER ZZ Top (Warner Bros.)
6	11	SOUL PROVIDER Michael Bolton (CBS)
7	12	SLEEPING WITH THE PAST Elton John (Rocket)
-	13	NOWHERE Ride (Creation)
2	14	NO PRAYER FOR THE DYING Iron Maiden (EMI)
39	15	ANAM Clannad (RCA)
15	16	FOREIGN AFFAIR Tina Turner (Capitol)
9	17	THAT LOVING FEELING VOL. 3 Various Artists (Dino)
-	18	REMASTERS Led Zeppelin (Atlantic)
8	19	DOCTOR ADAMSKI'S MUSICAL PHARMACY Adamski (MCA)
16	20	... BUT SERIOUSLY Phil Collins (Vertigo)
22	21	BOOMANIA Betty Boo (Rhythm King)
11	22	OOH LAS VEGAS Deacon Blue (CBS)
14	23	PLEASE HAMMER DON'T HURT 'EM MC Hammer (Capitol)
24	24	JUST THE TWO OF US Various Artists (Columbia)
12	25	HELL'S DITCH Pogues (Pogue Mahone)
20	26	REFLECTION Shadows (Roll Over)
17	27	MARIAH CAREY Mariah Carey (CBS)
27	28	LOOK SHARP! Roxette (EMI)
31	29	STEP BY STEP New Kids On The Block (CBS)
-	30	TOP GUN - SOUNDTRACK Various Artists (CBS)
23	31	WE ARE IN LOVE Harry Connick Jr. (CBS)
-	32	CONTRIBUTION Mica Paris (Fourth & Broadway)
43	33	ELECTRIBAL MEMORIES Electribe 101 (Mercury)
19	34	UK BLAK Caron Wheeler (RCA)
13	35	THE RAZOR'S EDGE AC/DC (Atco)
28	36	WILSON PHILLIPS Wilson Phillips (SBK)
25	37	JANET JACKSON'S RHYTHM NATION 1814 Janet Jackson (A&M)
-	38	DEEP HEAT 8 - THE HAND OF FATE Various (Telstar)
29	39	JORDAN: THE COMEBACK Prefab Sprout (Kitchenware)
-	40	THE BEST OF BEN E. KING AND THE DRIFTERS Ben E. King & the Drifters (Telstar)
21	41	SOUL DECADE: THE SIXTIES Various Artists (Motown)
-	42	THE SYNTHESIZER ALBUM Project D (Telstar)
-	43	VERY BEST OF ELO Electric Light Orchestra (Telstar)
30	44	DOWN TO EARTH Monie Love (Cooltempo)
24	45	ROOM TO ROAM Waterboys (Ensign)
36	46	IN THE BLOOD Londonbeat (AnXious)
33	47	STEPPING OUT - THE VERY BEST OF JOE JACKSON Joe Jackson (A&M)
38	48	WORLD CLIQUE Deee-Lite (Elektra)
35	49	DAYS OF THUNDER - SOUNDTRACK Various Artists (Epic)
50	50	PUMP UP THE JAM Technotronic (Swanyard)

For the second time this year, a classical album achieved the previously-thought-impossible by topping the UK chart, and once again Luciano Pavarotti was involved. *In Concert* was a recording of the historic coming together of three of the world's most celebrated tenors - Pavarotti, Placido Domingo and Jose Carreras - at a gala concert staged in Italy as part of the general World Cup extravaganza.

November 1990

3 November 1990

last week	this week	title	artist (label)
1	1	RHYTHM OF THE SAINTS	Paul Simon (Warner Bros.)
-	2	BEHAVIOUR	Pet Shop Boys (Parlophone)
3	3	ROCKING ALL OVER THE YEARS	Status Quo (Vertigo)
5	4	IN CONCERT	Luciano Pavarotti, Placido Domingo & José Carreras (Decca)
4	5	LISTEN WITHOUT PREJUDICE VOLUME 1	George Michael (Epic)
6	6	MISSING YOU - AN ALBUM OF LOVE	Various (EMI)
-	7	VISION THING	Sisters Of Mercy (Merciful Release)
2	8	SOME FRIENDLY	Charlatans (Situation Two)
10	9	RECYCLER	ZZ Top (Warner Bros.)
11	10	SOUL PROVIDER	Michael Bolton (CBS)
38	11	DEEP HEAT 8 - THE HAND OF FATE	Various (Telstar)
12	12	SLEEPING WITH THE PAST	Elton John (Rocket)
13	13	NOWHERE	Ride (Creation)
18	14	REMASTERS	Led Zeppelin (Atlantic)
7	15	ENLIGHTENMENT	Van Morrison (Polydor)
23	16	PLEASE HAMMER DON'T HURT 'EM	MC Hammer (Capitol)
16	17	FOREIGN AFFAIR	Tina Turner (Capitol)
8	18	X	INXS (Mercury)
-	19	GRAINS OF SAND	Mission (Mercury)
20	20	... BUT SERIOUSLY	Phil Collins (Vertigo)
9	21	BONA DRAG	Morrissey (HMV)
40	22	THE BEST OF BEN E. KING AND THE DRIFTERS	Ben E. King & the Drifters (Telstar)
28	23	LOOK SHARP!	Roxette (EMI)
-	24	EAST OF THE SUN, WEST OF THE MOON	A-ha (Warner Bros.)
14	25	NO PRAYER FOR THE DYING	Iron Maiden (EMI)
-	26	CORNERSTONES 1967-1970	Jimi Hendrix (Polydor)
26	27	REFLECTION	Shadows (Roll Over)
15	28	ANAM	Clannad (RCA)
-	29	LLOYD WEBBER PLAYS LLOYD WEBBER	Julian Lloyd Webber (Philips)
43	30	VERY BEST OF ELO	Electric Light Orchestra (Telstar)
-	31	RED HOT + BLUE	Various Artists (Chrysalis)
19	32	DOCTOR ADAMSKI'S MUSICAL PHARMACY	Adamski (MCA)
32	33	CONTRIBUTION	Mica Paris (Fourth & Broadway)
17	34	THAT LOVING FEELING VOL. 3	Various Artists (Dino)
-	35	BACKSTAGE - THE GREATEST HITS AND MORE	Gene Pitney (Polydor)
29	36	STEP BY STEP	New Kids On The Block (CBS)
27	37	MARIAH CAREY	Mariah Carey (CBS)
-	38	THE FINAL COUNTDOWN - THE VERY BEST OF SOFT METAL	Various Artists (Telstar)
22	39	OOH LAS VEGAS	Deacon Blue (CBS)
-	40	SMASH HITS 1990	Various Artists (Dover)
21	41	BOOMANIA	Betty Boo (Rhythm King)
-	42	EN TACT	Shamen (One Little Indian)
31	43	WE ARE IN LOVE	Harry Connick Jr. (CBS)
-	44	CURE FOR SANITY	Pop Will Eat Itself (RCA)
-	45	SYNTHESIZER GREATEST	Ed Starink (Arcade)
-	46	NEW KIDS ON THE BLOCK	New Kids On The Block (CBS)
36	47	WILSON PHILLIPS	Wilson Phillips (SBK)
37	48	JANET JACKSON'S RHYTHM NATION 1814	Janet Jackson (A&M)
-	49	SLAVES AND MASTERS	Deep Purple (RCA)
25	50	HELL'S DITCH	Pogues (Pogue Mahone)

10 November 1990

last week	this week	title	artist (label)
1	1	RHYTHM OF THE SAINTS	Paul Simon (Warner Bros.)
-	2	CHOKE	Beautiful South (Go! Discs)
2	3	BEHAVIOUR	Pet Shop Boys (Parlophone)
-	4	THE VERY BEST OF ELTON JOHN	Elton John (Rocket)
3	5	ROCKING ALL OVER THE YEARS	Status Quo (Vertigo)
4	6	IN CONCERT	Placido Domingo & José Carreras (Decca)
26	7	CORNERSTONES 1967-1970	Jimi Hendrix (Polydor)
5	8	LISTEN WITHOUT PREJUDICE VOLUME 1	George Michael (Epic)
6	9	MISSING YOU - AN ALBUM OF LOVE	Various (EMI)
46	10	NEW KIDS ON THE BLOCK	New Kids On The Block (CBS)
7	11	VISION THING	Sisters Of Mercy (Merciful Release)
24	12	EAST OF THE SUN, WEST OF THE MOON	A-ha (Warner Bros.)
10	13	SOUL PROVIDER	Michael Bolton (CBS)
14	14	REMASTERS	Led Zeppelin (Atlantic)
8	15	SOME FRIENDLY	Charlatans (Situation Two)
-	16	TRIP ON THIS - THE REMIXES	Technotronic (Swanyard)
31	17	RED HOT + BLUE	Various Artists (Chrysalis)
34	18	THAT LOVING FEELING VOL. 3	Various (Dino)
9	19	RECYCLER	ZZ Top (Warner Bros.)
-	20	TRAVELING WILBURYS VOLUME 3	Traveling Wilburys (Wilbury)
23	21	LOOK SHARP!	Roxette (EMI)
40	22	SMASH HITS 1990	Various Artists (Dover)
27	23	REFLECTION	Shadows (Roll Over)
12	24	SLEEPING WITH THE PAST	Elton John (Rocket)
-	25	THE VERY BEST OF THE GREATEST LOVE	Various Artists (Telstar)
16	26	PLEASE HAMMER DON'T HURT 'EM	MC Hammer (Capitol)
29	27	LLOYD WEBBER PLAYS LLOYD WEBBER	Julian Lloyd Webber (Philips)
18	28	X	INXS (Mercury)
-	29	BELIEF	Innocence (Cooltempo)
30	30	NOW DANCE 903	Various (EMI/Virgin/PolyGram)
11	31	DEEP HEAT 8 - THE HAND OF FATE	Various (Telstar)
41	32	BOOMANIA	Betty Boo (Rhythm King)
15	33	ENLIGHTENMENT	Van Morrison (Polydor)
-	34	THE GREATEST HITS SO FAR	Public Image Ltd. (Virgin)
42	35	EN TACT	Shamen (One Little Indian)
13	36	NOWHERE	Ride (Creation)
17	37	FOREIGN AFFAIR	Tina Turner (Capitol)
20	38	... BUT SERIOUSLY	Phil Collins (Vertigo)
30	39	VERY BEST OF ELO	Electric Light Orchestra (Telstar)
21	40	BONA DRAG	Morrissey (HMV)
-	41	I DO NOT WANT WHAT I HAVEN'T GOT	Sinead O'Connor (Ensign)
-	42	GHOST	Soundtrack (Milan)
-	43	THE HOUSE OF LOVE	House Of Love (Fontana)
44	44	OOH LAS VEGAS	Deacon Blue (CBS)
19	45	GRAINS OF SAND	Mission (Mercury)
28	46	ANAM	Clannad (RCA)
-	47	THE BEST OF MATT BIANCO	Matt Bianco (East West)
36	48	STEP BY STEP	New Kids On The Block (CBS)
-	49	WORLD CLIQUE	Deee-Lite (Elektra)
-	50	GHOST OF A DOG	Edie Brickell & New Bohemians (Geffen)

17 November 1990

last week	this week	title	artist (label)
4	1	THE VERY BEST OF ELTON JOHN	Elton John (Rocket)
-	2	PILLS 'N' THRILLS AND BELLYACHES	Happy Mondays (Factory)
2	3	CHOKE	Beautiful South (Go! Discs)
-	4	SERIOUS HITS ... LIVE!	Phil Collins (Vertigo)
1	5	RHYTHM OF THE SAINTS	Paul Simon (Warner Bros.)
-	6	MIXED UP	Cure (Fiction)
3	7	BEHAVIOUR	Pet Shop Boys (Parlophone)
-	8	I'M YOUR BABY TONIGHT	Whitney Houston (Arista)
5	9	ROCKING ALL OVER THE YEARS	Status Quo (Vertigo)
-	10	TRIPPING THE LIVE FANTASTIC	Paul McCartney (Parlophone)
8	11	LISTEN WITHOUT PREJUDICE VOLUME 1	George Michael (Epic)
6	12	IN CONCERT	Placido Domingo & José Carreras (Decca)
20	13	VOLUME 3	Traveling Wilburys (Wilbury)
-	14	FROM A DISTANCE ... THE EVENT	Cliff Richard (EMI)
30	15	NOW DANCE 903	Various (EMI/Virgin/PolyGram)
14	16	REMASTERS	Led Zeppelin (Atlantic)
7	17	CORNERSTONES 1967-1970	Jimi Hendrix (Polydor)
9	18	MISSING YOU - AN ALBUM OF LOVE	Various (EMI)
13	19	SOUL PROVIDER	Michael Bolton (CBS)
16	20	TRIP ON THIS - THE REMIXES	Technotronic (Swanyard)
12	21	EAST OF THE SUN, WEST OF THE MOON	A-ha (Warner Bros.)
22	22	SMASH HITS 1990	Various Artists (Dover)
11	23	VISION THING	Sisters Of Mercy (Merciful Release)
-	24	THE VERY BEST OF ...	Bee Gees (Polydor)
15	25	SOME FRIENDLY	Charlatans (Situation Two)
34	26	THE GREATEST HITS SO FAR	Public Image Ltd. (Virgin)
21	27	LOOK SHARP!	Roxette (EMI)
10	28	NEW KIDS ON THE BLOCK	New Kids On The Block (CBS)
19	29	RECYCLER	ZZ Top (Warner Bros.)
-	30	REFUGEES OF THE HEART	Steve Winwood (Virgin)
23	31	REFLECTION	Shadows (Roll Over)
42	32	GHOST	Soundtrack (Milan)
25	33	THE VERY BEST OF THE GREATEST LOVE	Various Artists (Telstar)
27	34	LLOYD WEBBER PLAYS LLOYD WEBBER	Julian Lloyd Webber (Philips)
28	35	X	INXS (Mercury)
-	36	DON'T EXPLAIN	Robert Palmer (EMI)
33	37	ENLIGHTENMENT	Van Morrison (Polydor)
-	38	BEST OF...	Ben E. King & the Drifters (Telstar)
29	39	BELIEF	Innocence (Cooltempo)
-	40	SHUT UP AND DANCE (THE DANCE REMIXES)	Paula Abdul (Virgin America)
24	41	SLEEPING WITH THE PAST	Elton John (Rocket)
26	42	PLEASE HAMMER DON'T HURT 'EM	MC Hammer (Capitol)
31	43	DEEP HEAT 8 - THE HAND OF FATE	Various (Telstar)
41	44	I DO NOT WANT WHAT I HAVEN'T GOT	Sinead O'Connor (Ensign)
37	45	FOREIGN AFFAIR	Tina Turner (Capitol)
-	46	PIGEONHOLE	New Fast Automatic Daffodils (Play It Again Sam)
18	47	THAT LOVING FEELING VOL. 3	Various Artists (Dino)
-	48	BALLADS	Roy Orbison (Telstar)
39	49	VERY BEST OF...	Electric Light Orchestra (Telstar)
43	50	THE HOUSE OF LOVE	House Of Love (Fontana)

Though it was not to have quite the mega-success worldwide of his 1986 project *Graceland*, Paul Simon's *Rhythm Of The Saints* shared some of its predecessor's characteristics - notably in influx of World Music influences, particularly this time from South America. *Cornerstones 1967-1970* was a high-profile repackage of Jimi Hendrix tracks - the first of several such compilations dominating late-year sales.

24 November 1990

last week	this week	album	artist (label)
1	1	THE VERY BEST OF ELTON JOHN	Elton John (Rocket)
-	2	THE IMMACULATE COLLECTION	Madonna (Sire)
4	3	SERIOUS HITS ... LIVE!	Phil Collins (Vertigo)
-	4	RHYTHM OF LOVE	Kylie Minogue (PWL)
5	5	RHYTHM OF THE SAINTS	Paul Simon (Warner Bros.)
8	6	I'M YOUR BABY TONIGHT	Whitney Houston (Arista)
2	7	PILLS 'N' THRILLS AND BELLYACHES	Happy Mondays (Factory)
3	8	CHOKE	Beautiful South (Go! Discs)
9	9	ROCKING ALL OVER THE YEARS	Status Quo (Vertigo)
15	10	NOW DANCE 903	Various (EMI/Virgin/PolyGram)
24	11	THE VERY BEST OF ...	Bee Gees (Polydor)
6	12	MIXED UP	Cure (Fiction)
12	13	IN CONCERT	Luciano Pavarotti, Placido Domingo & José Carreras (Decca)
-	14	THE SINGLES COLLECTION 1984-1990	Jimmy Somerville (London)
22	15	SMASH HITS 1990	Various Artists (Dover)
18	16	MISSING YOU - AN ALBUM OF LOVE	Various (EMI)
14	17	FROM A DISTANCE ... THE EVENT	Cliff Richard (EMI)
7	18	BEHAVIOUR	Pet Shop Boys (Parlophone)
20	19	TRIP ON THIS - THE REMIXES	Technotronic (Swanyard)
16	20	REMASTERS	Led Zeppelin (Atlantic)
11	21	LISTEN WITHOUT PREJUDICE VOLUME 1	George Michael (Epic)
17	22	CORNERSTONES 1967-1970	Jimi Hendrix (Polydor)
13	23	VOLUME 3	Traveling Wilburys (Wilbury)
19	24	SOUL PROVIDER	Michael Bolton (CBS)
30	25	REFUGEES OF THE HEART	Steve Winwood (Virgin)
10	26	TRIPPING THE LIVE FANTASTIC	Paul McCartney (Parlophone)
27	27	LOOK SHARP!	Roxette (EMI)
28	28	NEW KIDS ON THE BLOCK	New Kids On The Block (CBS)
-	29	TRULY UNFORGETTABLE	Various Artists (EMI)
26	30	DON'T EXPLAIN	Robert Palmer (EMI)
25	31	SOME FRIENDLY	Charlatans (Situation Two)
-	32	THE GREATEST HITS OF 1990	Various (Telstar)
33	33	LLOYD WEBBER PLAYS LLOYD WEBBER	Julian Lloyd Webber (Philips)
31	34	REFLECTION	Shadows (Roll Over)
45	35	FOREIGN AFFAIR	Tina Turner (Capitol)
29	36	RECYCLER	ZZ Top (Warner Bros.)
35	37	X	INXS (Mercury)
44	38	I DO NOT WANT WHAT I HAVEN'T GOT	Sinead O'Connor (Ensign)
32	39	GHOST	Soundtrack (Milan)
33	40	THE VERY BEST OF THE GREATEST LOVE	Various Artists (Telstar)
21	41	EAST OF THE SUN, WEST OF THE MOON	A-ha (Warner Bros.)
26	42	THE GREATEST HITS SO FAR	Public Image Ltd. (Virgin)
42	43	PLEASE HAMMER DON'T HURT 'EM	MC Hammer (Capitol)
-	44	BOOMANIA	Betty Boo (Rhythm King)
38	45	BEST OF ...	Ben E. King & the Drifters (Telstar)
-	46	THE WANDERER	Freddie Starr (Dover)
48	47	BALLADS	Roy Orbison (Telstar)
-	48	DO ME AGAIN	Freddie Jackson (Capitol)
-	49	NECK AND NECK	Chet Atkins & Mark Knopfler (CBS)
-	50	BLAZE OF GLORY/YOUNG GUNS II	Jon Bon Jovi (Vertigo)

1 December 1990

last week	this week	album	artist (label)
2	1	THE IMMACULATE COLLECTION	Madonna (Sire)
1	2	THE VERY BEST OF ELTON JOHN	Elton John (Rocket)
3	3	SERIOUS HITS ... LIVE!	Phil Collins (Vertigo)
5	4	RHYTHM OF THE SAINTS	Paul Simon (Warner Bros.)
14	5	THE SINGLES COLLECTION 1984-1990	Jimmy Somerville (London)
-	6	NOW THAT'S WHAT I CALL MUSIC 18	Various Artists (EMI/Virgin/PolyGram)
8	7	CHOKE	Beautiful South (Go! Discs)
13	8	IN CONCERT	Luciano Pavarotti, Placido Domingo & José Carreras (Decca)
9	9	ROCKING ALL OVER THE YEARS	Status Quo (Vertigo)
7	10	PILLS 'N' THRILLS AND BELLYACHES	Happy Mondays (Factory)
6	11	I'M YOUR BABY TONIGHT	Whitney Houston (Arista)
11	12	THE VERY BEST OF ...	Bee Gees (Polydor)
4	13	RHYTHM OF LOVE	Kylie Minogue (PWL)
16	14	MISSING YOU - AN ALBUM OF LOVE	Various (EMI)
-	15	SHAKING THE TREE - GOLDEN GREATS	Peter Gabriel (Virgin)
17	16	FROM A DISTANCE ... THE EVENT	Cliff Richard (EMI)
10	17	NOW DANCE 903	Various (EMI/Virgin/PolyGram)
18	18	BEHAVIOUR	Pet Shop Boys (Parlophone)
21	19	LISTEN WITHOUT PREJUDICE VOLUME 1	George Michael (Epic)
12	20	MIXED UP	Cure (Fiction)
24	21	SOUL PROVIDER	Michael Bolton (CBS)
-	22	DEEP HEAT 90	Various Artists (Telstar)
23	23	SMASH HITS 1990	Various Artists (Dover)
32	24	THE GREATEST HITS OF 1990	Various (Telstar)
-	25	HEARTBREAK STATION	Cinderella (Vertigo)
19	26	TRIP ON THIS - THE REMIXES	Technotronic (Swanyard)
-	27	MUSIC FROM TWIN PEAKS	Angelo Badalamenti (Warner Bros.)
-	28	BE MY LOVE ...	Placido Domingo (EMI)
27	29	LOOK SHARP!	Roxette (EMI)
20	30	REMASTERS	Led Zeppelin (Atlantic)
-	31	THE BEST OF ... Donna Summer (Warner Bros.)	
22	32	CORNERSTONES 1967-1970 Jimi Hendrix (Polydor)	
-	33	ROCK'N'ROLL LOVE SONGS	Various Artists (Dino)
37	34	X	INXS (Mercury)
49	35	NECK AND NECK	Chet Atkins & Mark Knopfler (CBS)
-	36	REASON TO BELIEVE	Rita MacNeil (Polydor)
29	37	TRULY UNFORGETTABLE	Various Artists (EMI)
-	38	UNCHAINED MELODY - THE VERY BEST OF ...	Righteous Brothers (Verve)
28	39	NEW KIDS ON THE BLOCK	New Kids On The Block (CBS)
23	40	VOLUME 3	Traveling Wilburys (Wilbury)
33	41	LLOYD WEBBER PLAYS LLOYD WEBBER	Julian Lloyd Webber (Philips)
30	42	DON'T EXPLAIN	Robert Palmer (EMI)
25	43	REFUGEES OF THE HEART	Steve Winwood (Virgin)
44	44	BOOMANIA	Betty Boo (Rhythm King)
38	45	I DO NOT WANT WHAT I HAVEN'T GOT	Sinead O'Connor (Ensign)
31	46	SOME FRIENDLY	Charlatans (Situation Two)
26	47	TRIPPING THE LIVE FANTASTIC	Paul McCartney (Parlophone)
-	48	BLISSED OUT	Beloved (East West)
-	49	SOUVENIRS	Foster & Allen (Telstar)
35	50	FOREIGN AFFAIR	Tina Turner (Capitol)

8 December 1990

last week	this week	album	artist (label)
6	1	NOW THAT'S WHAT I CALL MUSIC 18	Various Artists (EMI/Virgin/PolyGram)
1	2	THE IMMACULATE COLLECTION	Madonna (Sire)
3	3	THE VERY BEST OF ELTON JOHN	Elton John (Rocket)
3	4	SERIOUS HITS ... LIVE!	Phil Collins (Vertigo)
5	5	THE SINGLES COLLECTION 1984-1990	Jimmy Somerville (London)
16	6	FROM A DISTANCE ... THE EVENT	Cliff Richard (EMI)
8	7	IN CONCERT	Luciano Pavarotti, Placido Domingo & José Carreras (Decca)
4	8	RHYTHM OF THE SAINTS	Paul Simon (Warner Bros.)
38	9	UNCHAINED MELODY - THE VERY BEST OF ...	Righteous Brothers (Verve)
7	10	CHOKE	Beautiful South (Go! Discs)
9	11	ROCKING ALL OVER THE YEARS	Status Quo (Vertigo)
12	12	THE VERY BEST OF ...	Bee Gees (Polydor)
15	13	SHAKING THE TREE - GOLDEN GREATS	Peter Gabriel (Virgin)
11	14	I'M YOUR BABY TONIGHT	Whitney Houston (Arista)
21	15	SOUL PROVIDER	Michael Bolton (CBS)
10	16	PILLS 'N' THRILLS AND BELLYACHES	Happy Mondays (Factory)
22	17	DEEP HEAT 90	Various Artists (Telstar)
18	18	BEHAVIOUR	Pet Shop Boys (Parlophone)
19	19	LISTEN WITHOUT PREJUDICE VOLUME 1	George Michael (Epic)
28	20	BE MY LOVE ...	Placido Domingo (EMI)
14	21	MISSING YOU - AN ALBUM OF LOVE	Various (EMI)
30	22	REMASTERS	Led Zeppelin (Atlantic)
23	23	SMASH HITS 1990	Various Artists (Dover)
31	24	THE BEST OF ...	Donna Summer (Warner Bros.)
-	25	STARRY NIGHT	Julio Iglesias (CBS)
13	26	RHYTHM OF LOVE	Kylie Minogue (PWL)
27	27	MUSIC FROM TWIN PEAKS	Angelo Badalamenti (Warner Bros.)
-	28	KIM APPLEBY	Kim Appleby (Parlophone)
-	29	MY CLASSIC COLLECTION	Richard Clayderman (Decca Delphine)
44	30	BOOMANIA	Betty Boo (Rhythm King)
-	31	PLEASE HAMMER DON'T HURT 'EM	MC Hammer (Capitol)
17	32	NOW DANCE 903	Various (EMI/Virgin/PolyGram)
20	33	MIXED UP	Cure (Fiction)
26	34	TRIP ON THIS - THE REMIXES	Technotronic (Swanyard)
49	35	SOUVENIRS	Foster & Allen (Telstar)
29	36	LOOK SHARP!	Roxette (EMI)
-	37	THE LA'S	La's (Go! Discs)
24	38	THE GREATEST HITS OF 1990	Various (Telstar)
48	39	BLISSED OUT	Beloved (East West)
34	40	X	INXS (Mercury)
41	41	LLOYD WEBBER PLAYS LLOYD WEBBER	Julian Lloyd Webber (Philips)
-	42	REFLECTION	Shadows (Roll Over)
25	43	HEARTBREAK STATION	Cinderella (Vertigo)
45	44	I DO NOT WANT WHAT I HAVEN'T GOT	Sinead O'Connor (Ensign)
35	45	NECK AND NECK	Chet Atkins & Mark Knopfle (CBS)
32	46	CORNERSTONES 1967-1970	Jimi Hendrix (Polydor)
-	47	GREATEST HITS 1977-1990	Stranglers (Epic)
47	48	TRIPPING THE LIVE FANTASTIC	Paul McCartney (Parlophone)
33	49	ROCK'N'ROLL LOVE SONGS	Various Artists (Dino)
-	50	BEST OF ...	Ben E. King & the Drifters (Telstar)

The flavour of the end of the year was to be greatest hits compilations - no rare thing in the pre-Christmas market, but in 1990 they involved some of the most bankable album sellers around. Elton John was the first to see his anthology top the charts, but it was then quickly eclipsed by Madonna's *Immaculate Collection*, which comprehensively rounded up the material girl's many hit singles to date.

December 1990

15 December 1990

last week	this week		
2	1	THE IMMACULATE COLLECTION	Madonna (Sire)
3	2	THE VERY BEST OF ELTON JOHN	Elton John (Rocket)
4	3	SERIOUS HITS ... LIVE!	Phil Collins (Vertigo)
7	4	IN CONCERT	Luciano Pavarotti, Placido Domingo & José Carreras (Decca)
5	5	THE SINGLES COLLECTION 1984-1990	Jimmy Somerville (London)
6	6	FROM A DISTANCE ... THE EVENT	Cliff Richard (EMI)
12	7	THE VERY BEST OF ...	Bee Gees (Polydor)
11	8	ROCKING ALL OVER THE YEARS	Status Quo (Vertigo)
13	9	SHAKING THE TREE	Peter Gabriel (Virgin)
14	10	I'M YOUR BABY TONIGHT	Whitney Houston (Arista)
8	11	RHYTHM OF THE SAINTS	Paul Simon (Warner Bros.)
10	12	CHOKE	Beautiful South (Go! Discs)
9	13	UNCHAINED MELODY - THE VERY BEST OF...	Righteous Brothers (Verve)
15	14	SOUL PROVIDER	Michael Bolton (CBS)
19	15	LISTEN WITHOUT PREJUDICE VOLUME 1	George Michael (Epic)
-	16	TO THE EXTREME	Vanilla Ice (SBK)
20	17	BE MY LOVE ...	Placido Domingo (EMI)
40	18	X	INXS (Mercury)
16	19	PILLS 'N' THRILLS AND BELLYACHES	Happy Mondays (Factory)
-	20	MERRY MERRY CHRISTMAS	New Kids On The Block (CBS)
-	21	ONLY YESTERDAY	Carpenters (A&M)
28	22	KIM APPLEBY	Kim Appleby (Parlophone)
18	23	BEHAVIOUR	Pet Shop Boys (Parlophone)
35	24	SOUVENIRS	Foster & Allen (Telstar)
22	25	REMASTERS	Led Zeppelin (Atlantic)
25	26	STARRY NIGHT	Julio Iglesias (CBS)
29	27	MY CLASSIC COLLECTION	Richard Clayderman (Decca Delphine)
42	28	REFLECTION	Shadows (Roll Over)
26	29	RHYTHM OF LOVE	Kylie Minogue (PWL)
30	30	BOOMANIA	Betty Boo (Rhythm King)
27	31	MUSIC FROM TWIN PEAKS	Angelo Badalamenti (Warner Bros.)
31	32	PLEASE HAMMER DON'T HURT 'EM	MC Hammer (Capitol)
-	33	STEP BY STEP	New Kids On The Block (CBS)
34	34	TRIP ON THIS - THE REMIXES	Technotronic (Swanyard)
41	35	LLOYD WEBBER PLAYS LLOYD WEBBER	Julian Lloyd Webber (Philips)
36	36	LOOK SHARP!	Roxette (EMI)
-	37	TEENAGE NINJA MUTANT TURTLES	Various (SBK)
24	38	THE BEST OF ...	Donna Summer (Warner Bros.)
37	39	THE LA'S	La's (Go! Discs)
44	40	I DO NOT WANT WHAT I HAVEN'T GOT	Sinead O'Connor (Ensign)
33	41	MIXED UP	Cure (Fiction)
50	42	BEST OF ...	Ben E. King & the Drifters (Telstar)
46	43	CORNERSTONES 1967-1970	Jimi Hendrix (Polydor)
-	44	FOREIGN AFFAIR	Tina Turner (Capitol)
48	45	TRIPPING THE LIVE FANTASTIC	Paul McCartney (Parlophone)
-	46	... BUT SERIOUSLY	Phil Collins (Vertigo)
-	47	RED HOT + BLUE	Various Artists (Chrysalis)
-	48	BELIEF	Innocence (Cooltempo)
-	49	THE RAW AND THE REMIX	Fine Young Cannibals (London)
-	50	VOLUME 3	Traveling Wilburys (Wilbury)

22 December 1990

last week	this week		
1	1	THE IMMACULATE COLLECTION	Madonna (Sire)
2	2	THE VERY BEST OF ELTON JOHN	Elton John (Rocket)
3	3	SERIOUS HITS ... LIVE!	Phil Collins (Vertigo)
4	4	IN CONCERT	Luciano Pavarotti, Placido Domingo & José Carreras (Decca)
5	5	THE SINGLES COLLECTION 1984-1990	Jimmy Somerville (London)
7	6	THE VERY BEST OF ...	Bee Gees (Polydor)
6	7	FROM A DISTANCE ... THE EVENT	Cliff Richard (EMI)
14	8	SOUL PROVIDER	Michael Bolton (CBS)
10	9	I'M YOUR BABY TONIGHT	Whitney Houston (Arista)
11	10	RHYTHM OF THE SAINTS	Paul Simon (Warner Bros.)
15	11	LISTEN WITHOUT PREJUDICE VOLUME 1	George Michael (Epic)
8	12	ROCKING ALL OVER THE YEARS	Status Quo (Vertigo)
13	13	UNCHAINED MELODY - THE VERY BEST OF ...	Righteous Brothers (Verve)
12	14	CHOKE	Beautiful South (Go! Discs)
16	15	TO THE EXTREME	Vanilla Ice (SBK)
18	16	X	INXS (Mercury)
21	17	ONLY YESTERDAY	Carpenters (A&M)
20	18	MERRY MERRY CHRISTMAS	New Kids On The Block (CBS)
9	19	SHAKING THE TREE	Peter Gabriel (Virgin)
29	20	RHYTHM OF LOVE	Kylie Minogue (PWL)
23	21	BEHAVIOUR	Pet Shop Boys (Parlophone)
25	22	REMASTERS	Led Zeppelin (Atlantic)
19	23	PILLS 'N' THRILLS AND BELLYACHES	Happy Mondays (Factory)
17	24	BE MY LOVE ...	Placido Domingo (EMI)
31	25	MUSIC FROM TWIN PEAKS	Angelo Badalamenti (Warner Bros.)
24	26	SOUVENIRS	Foster & Allen (Telstar)
22	27	KIM APPLEBY	Kim Appleby (Parlophone)
26	28	STARRY NIGHT	Julio Iglesias (CBS)
28	29	REFLECTION	Shadows (Roll Over)
30	30	BOOMANIA	Betty Boo (Rhythm King)
27	31	MY CLASSIC COLLECTION	Richard Clayderman (Decca Delphine)
32	32	PLEASE HAMMER DON'T HURT 'EM	MC Hammer (Capitol)
33	33	STEP BY STEP	New Kids On The Block (CBS)
36	34	LOOK SHARP!	Roxette (EMI)
35	35	LLOYD WEBBER PLAYS LLOYD WEBBER	Julian Lloyd Webber (Philips)
-	36	THE ESSENTIAL PAVAROTTI	Luciano Pavarotti (Decca)
49	37	THE RAW AND THE REMIX	Fine Young Cannibals (London)
44	38	FOREIGN AFFAIR	Tina Turner (Capitol)
40	39	I DO NOT WANT WHAT I HAVEN'T GOT	Sinead O'Connor (Ensign)
45	40	TRIPPING THE LIVE FANTASTIC	Paul McCartney (Parlophone)
34	41	TRIP ON THIS - THE REMIXES	Technotronic (Swanyard)
37	42	TEENAGE NINJA MUTANT TURTLES	Various (SBK)
38	43	THE BEST OF...	Donna Summer (Warner Bros.)
39	44	THE LA'S	La's (Go! Discs)
46	45	... BUT SERIOUSLY	Phil Collins (Vertigo)
42	46	BEST OF...	Ben E. King & the Drifters (Telstar)
-	47	PRETTY WOMAN - SOUNDTRACK	Various (EMI USA)
-	48	NECK AND NECK	Chet Atkins & Mark Knopfler (CBS)
41	49	MIXED UP	Cure (Fiction)
43	50	CORNERSTONES 1967-1970	Jimi Hendrix (Polydor)

The compilations came in thick and fast to see the year out, with Madonna and Elton joined by Jimmy Somerville, The Bee Gees, Status Quo and (spurred by their chart-topping single with the reissued *Unchained Melody*) the Righteous Brothers.

January 1991

5 January 1991

last week	this week	Title	Artist
1	1	THE IMMACULATE COLLECTION	Madonna (Sire)
2	2	THE VERY BEST OF ELTON JOHN	Elton John (Rocket)
3	3	SERIOUS HITS ... LIVE!	Phil Collins (Virgin)
4	4	IN CONCERT	Luciano Pavarotti, Placido Domingo and José Carreras (Decca)
7	5	FROM A DISTANCE ...THE EVENT	Cliff Richard (EMI)
5	6	THE SINGLES COLLECTION 1984-1990	Jimmy Somerville (London)
9	7	I'M YOUR BABY TONIGHT	Whitney Houston (Arista)
8	8	SOUL PROVIDER	Michael Bolton (CBS)
10	9	THE RHYTHM OF THE SAINTS	Paul Simon (Warner Bros.)
6	10	THE VERY BEST OF...	Bee Gees (Polydor)
11	11	LISTEN WITHOUT PREJUDICE VOLUME 1	George Michael (Epic)
12	12	ROCKING ALL OVER THE YEARS	Status Quo (Vertigo)
19	13	SHAKING THE TREE	Peter Gabriel (Virgin)
15	14	TO THE EXTREME	Vanilla Ice (SBK)
13	15	UNCHAINED MELODY - THE VERY BEST OF	Righteous Brothers (Verve)
16	16	X	INXS (Mercury)
17	17	ONLY YESTERDAY	Carpenters (A&M)
22	18	REMASTERS	Led Zeppelin (Atlantic)
26	19	SOUVENIRS	Foster & Allen (Telstar)
18	20	MERRY MERRY CHRISTMAS	New Kids On The Block (CBS)
14	21	CHOKE	Beautiful South (Go! Discs)
36	22	THE ESSENTIAL ...	Luciano Pavarotti (Decca)
20	23	RHYTHM OF LOVE	Kylie Minogue (PWL)
23	24	PILLS 'N' THRILLS	Happy Mondays (Factory)
30	25	BOOMANIA	Betty Boo (Rhythm King)
24	26	BE MY LOVE ...	Placido Domingo (EMI)
21	27	BEHAVIOUR	Pet Shop Boys (Parlophone)
27	28	KIM APPLEBY	Kim Appleby (Parlophone)
29	29	REFLECTION	Shadows (Roll Over)
32	30	PLEASE HAMMER DON'T HURT 'EM	MC Hammer (Capitol)
31	31	MY CLASSIC COLLECTION	Richard Clayderman (Decca Delphine)
28	32	STARRY NIGHT	Julio Iglesias (CBS)
33	33	STEP BY STEP	New Kids On The Block (CBS)
-	34	TRIPPING THE LIVE FANTASTIC - HIGHLIGHTS	Paul McCartney (Parlophone)
35	35	LLOYD WEBBER PLAYS LLOYD WEBBER	Julian Lloyd Webber (Philips)
25	36	MUSIC FROM TWIN PEAKS	Angelo Badalamenti (Warner Bros.)
38	37	FOREIGN AFFAIR	Tina Turner (Capitol)
-	38	VIVALDI: THE FOUR SEASONS	Nigel Kennedy with the English Chamber Orchestra (EMI)
34	39	LOOK SHARP!	Roxette (EMI)
47	40	PRETTY WOMAN	Various (EMI USA)
45	41	... BUT SERIOUSLY	Phil Collins (Virgin)
41	42	TRIP ON THIS - THE REMIXES	Technotronic (Telstar)
39	43	I DO NOT WANT WHAT I HAVEN'T GOT	Sinead O'Connor (Ensign)
37	44	THE RAW AND THE REMIX	Fine Young Cannibals (London)
42	45	TEENAGE NINJA MUTANT TURTLES	Various (SBK)
-	46	CHRISTMAS COLLECTION	Foster & Allen (Telstar)
49	47	MIXED UP	Cure (Fiction)
40	48	TRIPPING THE LIVE FANTASTIC	Paul McCartney (Parlophone)
-	49	MCMXC AD	Enigma (Virgin International)
48	50	NECK AND NECK	Chet Atkins & Mark Knopfler (CBS)

12 January 1991

last week	this week	Title	Artist
1	1	THE IMMACULATE COLLECTION	Madonna (Sire)
2	2	THE VERY BEST OF ELTON JOHN	Elton John (Rocket)
3	3	SERIOUS HITS ... LIVE!	Phil Collins (Virgin)
7	4	I'M YOUR BABY TONIGHT	Whitney Houston (Arista)
13	5	SHAKING THE TREE	Peter Gabriel (Virgin)
11	6	LISTEN WITHOUT PREJUDICE VOLUME 1	George Michael (Epic)
4	7	IN CONCERT	Luciano Pavarotti, Placido Domingo and José Carreras (Decca)
6	8	THE SINGLES COLLECTION 1984-1990	Jimmy Somerville (London)
8	9	SOUL PROVIDER	Michael Bolton (CBS)
5	10	FROM A DISTANCE ... THE EVENT	Cliff Richard (EMI)
9	11	THE RHYTHM OF THE SAINTS	Paul Simon (Warner Bros.)
14	12	TO THE EXTREME	Vanilla Ice (SBK)
10	13	THE VERY BEST OF...	Bee Gees (Polydor)
12	14	ROCKING ALL OVER THE YEARS	Status Quo (Vertigo)
15	15	UNCHAINED MELODY - THE VERY BEST OF ...	Righteous Brothers (Verve)
21	16	CHOKE	Beautiful South (Go! Discs)
16	17	X	INXS (Mercury)
30	18	PLEASE HAMMER DON'T HURT 'EM	MC Hammer (Capitol)
23	19	RHYTHM OF LOVE	Kylie Minogue (PWL)
17	20	ONLY YESTERDAY	Carpenters (A&M)
27	21	BEHAVIOUR	Pet Shop Boys (Parlophone)
18	22	REMASTERS	Led Zeppelin (Atlantic)
24	23	PILLS 'N' THRILLS AND BELLYACHES	Happy Mondays (Factory)
49	24	MCMXC AD	Enigma (Virgin International)
22	25	THE ESSENTIAL PAVAROTTI	Luciano Pavarotti (Decca)
25	26	BOOMANIA	Betty Boo (Rhythm King)
38	27	VIVALDI: THE FOUR SEASONS	Nigel Kennedy with the English Chamber Orchestra (EMI)
-	28	DIRTY DANCING - SOUNDTRACK	Various(RCA)
19	29	SOUVENIRS	Foster & Allen (Telstar)
28	30	KIM APPLEBY	Kim Appleby (Parlophone)
34	31	TRIPPING THE LIVE FANTASTIC - HIGHLIGHTS	Paul McCartney (Parlophone)
-	32	CORNERSTONES 1967-1970	Jimi Hendrix (Polydor)
40	33	PRETTY WOMAN	Various (EMI USA)
26	34	BE MY LOVE ...	Placido Domingo (EMI)
33	35	STEP BY STEP	New Kids On The Block (CBS)
43	36	I DO NOT WANT WHAT I HAVEN'T GOT	Sinead O'Connor (Ensign)
39	37	LOOK SHARP!	Roxette (EMI)
42	38	TRIP ON THIS - THE REMIXES	Technotronic (Telstar)
-	39	DREAMLAND	Black Box (deConstruction)
-	40	NO PRAYER FOR THE DYING	Iron Maiden (EMI)
-	41	WORLD POWER	Snap (Arista)
29	42	REFLECTION	Shadows (Roll Over)
41	43	... BUT SERIOUSLY	Phil Collins (Virgin)
37	44	FOREIGN AFFAIR	Tina Turner (Capitol)
45	45	MIXED UP	Cure (Fiction)
-	46	THE LA'S	La's (Go! Discs)
47	47	BELIEF	Innocence (Cooltempo)
31	48	MY CLASSIC COLLECTION	Richard Clayderman (Decca Delphine)
20	49	MERRY MERRY CHRISTMAS	New Kids On The Block (CBS)
32	50	STARRY NIGHT	Julio Iglesias (CBS)

19 January 1991

last week	this week	Title	Artist
1	1	THE IMMACULATE COLLECTION	Madonna (Sire)
2	2	THE VERY BEST OF ELTON JOHN	Elton John (Rocket)
3	3	SERIOUS HITS ... LIVE!	Phil Collins (Virgin)
6	4	LISTEN WITHOUT PREJUDICE VOLUME 1	George Michael (Epic)
4	5	I'M YOUR BABY TONIGHT	Whitney Houston (Arista)
24	6	MCMXC AD	Enigma (Virgin International)
12	7	TO THE EXTREME	Vanilla Ice (SBK)
5	8	SHAKING THE TREE	Peter Gabriel (Virgin)
7	9	IN CONCERT	Luciano Pavarotti Placido Domingo and José Carreras (Decca)
9	10	SOUL PROVIDER	Michael Bolton (CBS)
8	11	THE SINGLES COLLECTION 1984-1990	Jimmy Somerville (London)
17	12	X	INXS (Mercury)
16	13	CHOKE	Beautiful South (Go! Discs)
11	14	THE RHYTHM OF THE SAINTS	Paul Simon (Warner Bros.)
28	15	DIRTY DANCING - SOUNDTRACK	Various (RCA)
14	16	ROCKING ALL OVER THE YEARS	Status Quo (Vertigo)
18	17	PLEASE HAMMER DON'T HURT 'EM	MC Hammer (Capitol)
15	18	UNCHAINED MELODY - THE VERY BEST OF ...	Righteous Brothers (Verve)
13	19	THE VERY BEST OF...	Bee Gees (Polydor)
22	20	REMASTERS	Led Zeppelin (Atlantic)
21	21	FROM A DISTANCE ... THE EVENT	Cliff Richard (EMI)
23	22	PILLS 'N' THRILLS AND BELLYACHES	Happy Mondays (Factory)
20	23	ONLY YESTERDAY	Carpenters (A&M)
24	24	BEHAVIOUR	Pet Shop Boys (Parlophone)
25	25	THE ESSENTIAL PAVAROTTI	Luciano Pavarotti (Decca)
26	26	BOOMANIA	Betty Boo (Rhythm King)
36	27	I DO NOT WANT WHAT I HAVEN'T GOT	Sinead O'Connor (Ensign)
27	28	VIVALDI: THE FOUR SEASONS	Nigel Kennedy with the English Chamber Orchestra (EMI)
40	29	NO PRAYER FOR THE DYING	Iron Maiden (EMI)
33	30	PRETTY WOMAN	Various (EMI USA)
19	31	RHYTHM OF LOVE	Kylie Minogue (PWL)
32	32	CORNERSTONES 1967-1970	Jimi Hendrix (Polydor)
34	33	BE MY LOVE ... AN ALBUM OF LOVE	Placido Domingo (EMI)
30	34	KIM APPLEBY	Kim Appleby (Parlophone)
39	35	DREAMLAND	Black Box (deConstruction)
-	36	THE LOST BOYS - SOUNDTRACK	Various (Atlantic)
46	37	THE LA'S	La's (Go! Discs)
47	38	BELIEF	Innocence (Cooltempo)
41	39	WORLD POWER	Snap (Arista)
31	40	TRIPPING THE LIVE FANTASTIC - HIGHLIGHTS	Paul McCartney (Parlophone)
37	41	LOOK SHARP!	Roxette (EMI)
38	42	TRIP ON THIS - THE REMIXES	Technotronic (Telstar)
45	43	MIXED UP	Cure (Fiction)
35	44	STEP BY STEP	New Kids On The Block (CBS)
-	45	NECK AND NECK	Chet Atkins & Mark Knopfler (CBS)
43	46	... BUT SERIOUSLY	Phil Collins (Virgin)
-	47	SOME FRIENDLY	Charlatans (Situation Two)
-	48	MUSIC FROM TWIN PEAKS	Angelo Badalamenti (Warner Bros.)
-	49	VERY BEST OF	Ben E. King & the Drifters (Telstar)
-	50	THE RAZOR'S EDGE	AC/DC (Atco)

Just prior to the end of 1990, a decision had been taken by MRIB, compiler and supplier of the NME album chart, to henceforth exclude Various Artists compilations from the chart, making it totally artist-orientated (the British record industry's own chart had taken a similar decision a year earlier). Thus, there were no such compilations to be seen in the Top 50 when 1991 began, nor would there be in future charts.

January – February 1991

26 January 1991

last week	this week	title
1	1	THE IMMACULATE COLLECTION Madonna (Sire)
2	2	THE VERY BEST OF ELTON JOHN Elton John (Rocket)
6	3	MCMXC AD Enigma (Virgin International)
4	4	LISTEN WITHOUT PREJUDICE VOLUME 1 George Michael (Epic)
5	5	I'M YOUR BABY TONIGHT Whitney Houston (Arista)
3	6	SERIOUS HITS ... LIVE! Phil Collins (Virgin)
8	7	SHAKING THE TREE Peter Gabriel (Virgin)
11	8	THE SINGLES COLLECTION 1984-1990 Jimmy Somerville (London)
-	9	A LITTLE AIN'T ENOUGH David Lee Roth (Warner Bros.)
7	10	TO THE EXTREME Vanilla Ice (SBK)
12	11	X INXS (Mercury)
9	12	IN CONCERT Luciano Pavarotti, Placido Domingo and José Carreras (Decca)
10	13	SOUL PROVIDER Michael Bolton (CBS)
15	14	DIRTY DANCING - SOUNDTRACK Various(RCA)
13	15	CHOKE Beautiful South (Go! Discs)
22	16	PILLS 'N' THRILLS AND BELLYACHES Happy Mondays (Factory)
18	17	UNCHAINED MELODY - THE VERY BEST OF ... Righteous Brothers (Verve)
-	18	WICKED GAME Chris Isaak (Reprise)
17	19	PLEASE HAMMER DON'T HURT 'EM MC Hammer (Capitol)
20	20	REMASTERS Led Zeppelin (Atlantic)
14	21	THE RHYTHM OF THE SAINTS Paul Simon (Warner Bros.)
16	22	ROCKING ALL OVER THE YEARS Status Quo (Vertigo)
21	23	FROM A DISTANCE ... THE EVENT Cliff Richard (EMI)
19	24	THE VERY BEST OF THE BEE GEES Bee Gees (Polydor)
27	25	I DO NOT WANT WHAT I HAVEN'T GOT Sinead O'Connor (Ensign)
36	26	THE LOST BOYS - SOUNDTRACK Various (Atlantic)
29	27	NO PRAYER FOR THE DYING Iron Maiden (EMI)
23	28	ONLY YESTERDAY Carpenters (A&M)
-	29	DON'T EXPLAIN Robert Palmer (EMI)
24	30	BEHAVIOUR Pet Shop Boys (Parlophone)
25	31	THE ESSENTIAL PAVAROTTI Luciano Pavarotti (Decca)
39	32	WORLD POWER Snap (Arista)
30	33	PRETTY WOMAN Various (EMI USA)
26	34	BOOMANIA Betty Boo (Rhythm King)
28	35	VIVALDI: THE FOUR SEASONS Nigel Kennedy with the English Chamber Orchestra (EMI)
38	36	BELIEF Innocence (Cooltempo)
35	37	DREAMLAND Black Box (deConstruction)
32	38	CORNERSTONES 1967-1970 Jimi Hendrix (Polydor)
31	39	RHYTHM OF LOVE Kylie Minogue (PWL)
43	40	MIXED UP Cure (Fiction)
-	41	GREATEST HITS 1977-1990 Stranglers (Epic)
41	42	LOOK SHARP! Roxette (EMI)
-	43	SWEET DREAMS Patsy Cline (MCA)
33	44	BE MY LOVE ... Placido Domingo (EMI)
45	45	NECK AND NECK Chet Atkins & Mark Knopfler (CBS)
50	46	THE RAZOR'S EDGE AC/DC (Atco)
37	47	THE LA'S La's (Go! Discs)
-	48	RUNAWAY HORSES Belinda Carlisle (Virgin)
48	49	MUSIC FROM TWIN PEAKS Angelo Badalamenti (Warner Bros.)
-	50	JORDAN: THE COMEBACK Prefab Sprout (Kitchenware)

2 February 1991

last week	this week	title
3	1	MCMXC AD Enigma (Virgin International)
9	2	A LITTLE AIN'T ENOUGH David Lee Roth (Warner Bros.)
1	3	THE IMMACULATE COLLECTION Madonna (Sire)
2	4	THE VERY BEST OF ELTON JOHN Elton John (Rocket)
-	5	THE SOUL CAGES Sting (A&M)
18	6	WICKED GAME Chris Isaak (Reprise)
6	7	SERIOUS HITS ... LIVE! Phil Collins (Virgin)
-	8	ALL TRUE MAN Alexander O'Neal (Tabu)
5	9	I'M YOUR BABY TONIGHT Whitney Houston (Arista)
10	10	TO THE EXTREME Vanilla Ice (SBK)
4	11	LISTEN WITHOUT PREJUDICE VOLUME 1 George Michael (Epic)
14	12	DIRTY DANCING - SOUNDTRACK Various (RCA)
13	13	SOUL PROVIDER Michael Bolton (CBS)
7	14	SHAKING THE TREE Peter Gabriel (Virgin)
12	15	IN CONCERT Luciano Pavarotti, Placido Domingo and José Carreras (Decca)
29	16	DON'T EXPLAIN Robert Palmer (EMI)
8	17	THE SINGLES COLLECTION 1984-1990 Jimmy Somerville (London)
16	18	PILLS 'N' THRILLS AND BELLYACHES Happy Mondays (Factory)
11	19	X INXS (Mercury)
26	20	THE LOST BOYS - SOUNDTRACK Various (Atlantic)
19	21	PLEASE HAMMER DON'T HURT 'EM MC Hammer (Capitol)
21	22	THE RHYTHM OF THE SAINTS Paul Simon (Warner Bros.)
15	23	CHOKE Beautiful South (Go! Discs)
-	24	1916 Motorhead (Epic)
17	25	UNCHAINED MELODY - THE VERY BEST OF ... Righteous Brothers (Verve)
20	26	REMASTERS Led Zeppelin (Atlantic)
32	27	WORLD POWER Snap (Arista)
22	28	ROCKING ALL OVER THE YEARS Status Quo (Vertigo)
25	29	I DO NOT WANT WHAT I HAVEN'T GOT Sinead O'Connor (Ensign)
24	30	THE VERY BEST OF... Bee Gees (Polydor)
28	31	ONLY YESTERDAY Carpenters (A&M)
43	32	SWEET DREAMS Patsy Cline (MCA)
41	33	GREATEST HITS 1977-1990 Stranglers (Epic)
39	34	RHYTHM OF LOVE Kylie Minogue (PWL)
23	35	FROM A DISTANCE ... THE EVENT Cliff Richard (EMI)
48	36	RUNAWAY HORSES Belinda Carlisle (Virgin)
31	37	THE ESSENTIAL PAVAROTTI Luciano Pavarotti (Decca)
37	38	DREAMLAND Black Box (deConstruction)
36	39	BELIEF Innocence (Cooltempo)
30	40	BEHAVIOUR Pet Shop Boys (Parlophone)
27	41	NO PRAYER FOR THE DYING Iron Maiden (EMI)
38	42	CORNERSTONES 1967-1970 Jimi Hendrix (Polydor)
-	43	STEP IN THE ARENA Gang Starr (Cooltempo)
34	44	BOOMANIA Betty Boo (Rhythm King)
49	45	MUSIC FROM TWIN PEAKS Angelo Badalamenti (Warner Bros.)
35	46	VIVALDI: THE FOUR SEASONS Nigel Kennedy with the English Chamber Orchestra (EMI)
33	47	PRETTY WOMAN - SOUNDTRACK Various (EMI USA)
40	48	MIXED UP Cure (Fiction)
42	49	LOOK SHARP! Roxette (EMI)
-	50	SHAKE YOUR MONEY MAKER Black Crowes (Def American)

9 February 1991

last week	this week	title
5	1	THE SOUL CAGES Sting (A&M)
8	2	ALL TRUE MAN Alexander O'Neal (Tabu)
1	3	MCMXC AD Enigma (Virgin International)
3	4	THE IMMACULATE COLLECTION Madonna (Sire)
-	5	DOUBT Jesus Jones (Food)
6	6	WICKED GAME Chris Isaak (Reprise)
4	7	THE VERY BEST OF ELTON JOHN Elton John (Rocket)
9	8	I'M YOUR BABY TONIGHT Whitney Houston (Arista)
7	9	SERIOUS HITS ... LIVE! Phil Collins (Virgin)
2	10	A LITTLE AIN'T ENOUGH David Lee Roth (Warner Bros.)
11	11	LISTEN WITHOUT PREJUDICE VOLUME 1 George Michael (Epic)
16	12	DON'T EXPLAIN Robert Palmer (EMI)
17	13	THE SINGLES COLLECTION 1984-1990 Jimmy Somerville (London)
12	14	DIRTY DANCING - SOUNDTRACK Various (RCA)
10	15	TO THE EXTREME Vanilla Ice (SBK)
13	16	SOUL PROVIDER Michael Bolton (CBS)
27	17	WORLD POWER Snap (Arista)
15	18	IN CONCERT Luciano Pavarotti, Placido Domingo and José Carreras (Decca)
20	19	THE LOST BOYS - SOUNDTRACK Various (Atlantic)
14	20	SHAKING THE TREE Peter Gabriel (Virgin)
24	21	1916 Motorhead (Epic)
19	22	X INXS (Mercury)
32	23	SWEET DREAMS Patsy Cline (MCA)
18	24	PILLS 'N' THRILLS AND BELLYACHES Happy Mondays (Factory)
21	25	PLEASE HAMMER DON'T HURT 'EM MC Hammer (Capitol)
23	26	CHOKE Beautiful South (Go! Discs)
25	27	UNCHAINED MELODY - THE VERY BEST OF ... Righteous Brothers (Verve)
33	28	GREATEST HITS 1977-1990 Stranglers (Epic)
22	29	THE RHYTHM OF THE SAINTS Paul Simon (Warner Bros.)
36	30	RUNAWAY HORSES Belinda Carlisle (Virgin)
34	31	RHYTHM OF LOVE Kylie Minogue (PWL)
28	32	ROCKING ALL OVER THE YEARS Status Quo (Vertigo)
30	33	THE VERY BEST OF ... Bee Gees (Polydor)
26	34	REMASTERS Led Zeppelin (Atlantic)
-	35	ROCKY V - SOUNDTRACK Various (Capitol)
-	36	STARRY NIGHT Julio Iglesias (CBS)
31	37	ONLY YESTERDAY Carpenters (A&M)
-	38	THE SIMPSONS SING THE BLUES Simpsons (Geffen)
29	39	I DO NOT WANT WHAT I HAVEN'T GOT Sinead O'Connor (Ensign)
-	40	GONNA MAKE YOU SWEAT C&C Music Factory (Columbia)
38	41	DREAMLAND Black Box (deConstruction)
43	42	STEP IN THE ARENA Gang Starr (Cooltempo)
-	43	BACK FROM RIO Roger McGuinn (Arista)
45	44	MUSIC FROM TWIN PEAKS Angelo Badalamenti (Warner Bros.)
39	45	BELIEF Innocence (Cooltempo)
47	46	PRETTY WOMAN - SOUNDTRACK Various (EMI USA)
-	47	MARIAH CAREY Mariah Carey (CBS)
46	48	VIVALDI: THE FOUR SEASONS Nigel Kennedy with the English Chamber Orchestra (EMI)
-	49	ENLIGHTENMENT Van Morrison (Polydor)
-	50	SOMEWHERE SOON High (London)

Enigma's album, with its mysterious Roman numeral title, rose to Number 1 on the back of their haunting hit single *Sadness*, which topped the chart at the same time. Groups were in a comparative minority among the top album sellers at this point, however, as an influx of male solo vocalists virtually took over the Top 10 - Alexander O'Neal, Peter Gabriel, David Lee Roth, Chris Isaak, and Sting, who also hit Number 1.

February – March 1991

16 February 1991

-	1	INNUENDO	Queen (Parlophone)
5	2	DOUBT	Jesus Jones (Food)
1	3	THE SOUL CAGES	Sting (A&M)
3	4	MCMXC AD	Enigma (Virgin International)
6	5	WICKED GAME	Chris Isaak (Reprise)
2	6	ALL TRUE MAN	Alexander O'Neal (Tabu)
4	7	THE IMMACULATE COLLECTION	Madonna (Sire)
7	8	THE VERY BEST OF ELTON JOHN	Elton John (Rocket)
-	9	INTO THE LIGHT	Gloria Estefan (Epic)
8	10	I'M YOUR BABY TONIGHT	Whitney Houston (Arista)
9	11	SERIOUS HITS ... LIVE!	Phil Collins (Virgin)
12	12	DON'T EXPLAIN	Robert Palmer (EMI)
11	13	LISTEN WITHOUT PREJUDICE VOLUME 1	George Michael (Epic)
30	14	RUNAWAY HORSES	Belinda Carlisle (Virgin)
23	15	SWEET DREAMS	Patsy Cline (MCA)
13	16	THE SINGLES COLLECTION 1984-1990	Jimmy Somerville (London)
15	17	TO THE EXTREME	Vanilla Ice (SBK)
19	18	THE LOST BOYS - SOUNDTRACK	Various (Atlantic)
22	19	X	INXS (Mercury)
14	20	DIRTY DANCING - SOUNDTRACK	Various (RCA)
-	21	DEDICATION - THE VERY BEST OF THIN LIZZY	Thin Lizzy (Vertigo)
18	22	IN CONCERT	Luciano Pavarotti, Placido Domingo and José Carreras (Decca)
17	23	WORLD POWER	Snap (Arista)
16	24	SOUL PROVIDER	Michael Bolton (CBS)
10	25	A LITTLE AIN'T ENOUGH	David Lee Roth (Warner Bros.)
20	26	SHAKING THE TREE	Peter Gabriel (Virgin)
25	27	PLEASE HAMMER DON'T HURT 'EM	MC Hammer (Capitol)
38	28	THE SIMPSONS SING THE BLUES	Simpsons (Geffen)
31	29	RHYTHM OF LOVE	Kylie Minogue (PWL)
27	30	THE RHYTHM OF THE SAINTS	Paul Simon (Warner Bros.)
-	31	AND NOW THE LEGACY BEGINS	Dream Warriors (Fourth & Broadway)
28	32	GREATEST HITS 1977-1990	Stranglers (Epic)
-	33	EVERYBODY'S ANGEL	Tanita Tikaram (East West)
24	34	PILLS 'N' THRILLS AND BELLYACHES	Happy Mondays (Factory)
-	35	THE TRACKS OF MY TEARS	Smokey Robinson and Various Artists (Motown)
-	36	LIVE AT THE BRIXTON ACADEMY	Faith No More (Slash)
40	37	GONNA MAKE YOU SWEAT	C&C Music Factory (Columbia)
26	38	CHOKE	Beautiful South (Go! Discs)
36	39	STARRY NIGHT	Julio Iglesias (CBS)
35	40	ROCKY V - SOUNDTRACK	Various (Capitol)
21	41	1916	Motorhead (Epic)
27	42	UNCHAINED MELODY - THE VERY BEST OF ...	Righteous Brothers (Verve)
43	43	BACK FROM RIO	Roger McGuinn (Arista)
33	44	THE VERY BEST OF ...	Bee Gees (Polydor)
44	45	MUSIC FROM TWIN PEAKS	Angelo Badalamenti (Warner Bros.)
41	46	DREAMLAND	Black Box (deConstruction)
45	47	BELIEF	Innocence (Cooltempo)
46	48	PRETTY WOMAN	Various (EMI USA)
-	49	WAKING HOURS	Del Amitri (A&M)
-	50	JORDAN: THE COMEBACK	Prefab Sprout (Kitchenware)

23 February 1991

1	1	INNUENDO	Queen (Parlophone)
9	2	INTO THE LIGHT	Gloria Estefan (Epic)
5	3	WICKED GAME	Chris Isaak (Reprise)
8	4	THE VERY BEST OF ELTON JOHN	Elton John (Rocket)
2	5	DOUBT	Jesus Jones (Food)
21	6	DEDICATION - THE VERY BEST OF THIN LIZZY	Thin Lizzy (Vertigo)
13	7	LISTEN WITHOUT PREJUDICE VOLUME 1	George Michael (Epic)
3	8	THE SOUL CAGES	Sting (A&M)
7	9	THE IMMACULATE COLLECTION	Madonna (Sire)
4	10	MCMXC AD	Enigma (Virgin International)
6	11	ALL TRUE MAN	Alexander O'Neal (Tabu)
14	12	RUNAWAY HORSES	Belinda Carlisle (Virgin)
31	13	AND NOW THE LEGACY BEGINS	Dream Warriors (Fourth & Broadway)
11	14	SERIOUS HITS ... LIVE!	Phil Collins (Virgin)
22	15	IN CONCERT	Luciano Pavarotti, Placido Domingo and José Carreras (Decca)
10	16	I'M YOUR BABY TONIGHT	Whitney Houston (Arista)
19	17	X	INXS (Mercury)
33	18	EVERYBODY'S ANGEL	Tanita Tikaram (East West)
16	19	THE SINGLES COLLECTION 1984-1990	Jimmy Somerville (London)
28	20	THE SIMPSONS SING THE BLUES	Simpsons (Geffen)
18	21	THE LOST BOYS - SOUNDTRACK	Various (Atlantic)
36	22	LIVE AT THE BRIXTON ACADEMY	Faith No More (Slash)
12	23	DON'T EXPLAIN	Robert Palmer (EMI)
15	24	SWEET DREAMS	Patsy Cline (MCA)
17	25	TO THE EXTREME	Vanilla Ice (SBK)
20	26	DIRTY DANCING - SOUNDTRACK	Various (RCA)
30	27	THE RHYTHM OF THE SAINTS	Paul Simon (Warner Bros.)
24	28	SOUL PROVIDER	Michael Bolton (CBS)
38	29	CHOKE	Beautiful South (Go! Discs)
34	30	PILLS 'N' THRILLS AND BELLYACHES	Happy Mondays (Factory)
25	31	A LITTLE AIN'T ENOUGH	David Lee Roth (Warner Bros.)
32	32	GREATEST HITS 1977-1990	Stranglers (Epic)
23	33	WORLD POWER	Snap (Arista)
27	34	PLEASE HAMMER DON'T HURT 'EM	MC Hammer (Capitol)
29	35	RHYTHM OF LOVE	Kylie Minogue (PWL)
35	36	THE TRACKS OF MY TEARS	Smokey Robinson and Various Artists (Motown)
-	37	THE COLLECTION	Barry White (Mercury)
45	38	MUSIC FROM TWIN PEAKS	Angelo Badalamenti (Warner Bros.)
42	39	UNCHAINED MELODY - THE VERY BEST OF ...	Righteous Brothers (Verve)
26	40	SHAKING THE TREE	Peter Gabriel (Virgin)
40	41	ROCKY V - SOUNDTRACK	Various (Capitol)
44	42	THE VERY BEST OF...	Bee Gees (Polydor)
37	43	GONNA MAKE YOU SWEAT	C&C Music Factory (Columbia)
-	44	THE BEST OF THE DOORS	Doors (Elektra)
43	45	BACK FROM RIO	Roger McGuinn (Arista)
39	46	STARRY NIGHT	Julio Iglesias (CBS)
-	47	ROCKING ALL OVER THE YEARS	Status Quo (Vertigo)
-	48	BITE	Ned's Atomic Dustbin (Rough Trade)
-	49	KIM APPLEBY	Kim Appleby (Parlophone)
50	50	SATELLITES	Big Dish (East West)

2 March 1991

1	1	INNUENDO	Queen (Parlophone)
3	2	WICKED GAME	Chris Isaak (Reprise)
2	3	INTO THE LIGHT	Gloria Estefan (Epic)
7	4	LISTEN WITHOUT PREJUDICE VOLUME 1	George Michael (Epic)
-	5	CIRCLE OF ONE	Oleta Adams (Fontana)
4	6	THE VERY BEST OF ELTON JOHN	Elton John (Rocket)
6	7	DEDICATION - THE VERY BEST OF THIN LIZZY	Thin Lizzy (Vertigo)
9	8	THE IMMACULATE COLLECTION	Madonna (Sire)
5	9	DOUBT	Jesus Jones (Food)
12	10	RUNAWAY HORSES	Belinda Carlisle (Virgin)
20	11	THE SIMPSONS SING THE BLUES	Simpsons (Geffen)
16	12	I'M YOUR BABY TONIGHT	Whitney Houston (Arista)
-	13	FREE	Rick Astley (RCA)
-	14	THE BEST OF FREE - ALL RIGHT NOW	Free (Island)
11	15	ALL TRUE MAN	Alexander O'Neal (Tabu)
10	16	MCMXC AD	Enigma (Virgin International)
14	17	SERIOUS HITS ... LIVE!	Phil Collins (Virgin)
8	18	THE SOUL CAGES	Sting (A&M)
17	19	X	INXS (Mercury)
21	20	THE LOST BOYS - SOUNDTRACK	Various (Atlantic)
15	21	IN CONCERT	Luciano Pavarotti, Placido Domingo and José Carreras (Decca)
30	22	PILLS 'N' THRILLS AND BELLYACHES	Happy Mondays (Factory)
-	23	30 SOMETHING	Carter - The Unstoppable Sex Machine (Rough Trade)
19	24	THE SINGLES COLLECTION 1984-1990	Jimmy Somerville (London)
-	25	THE ESSENTIAL JOSE CARRERAS	José Carreras (Philips)
13	26	AND NOW THE LEGACY BEGINS	Dream Warriors (Fourth & Broadway)
29	27	CHOKE	Beautiful South (Go! Discs)
23	28	DON'T EXPLAIN	Robert Palmer (EMI)
24	29	SWEET DREAMS	Patsy Cline (MCA)
-	30	NO MORE GAMES - THE REMIX ALBUM	New Kids On The Block (CBS)
25	31	TO THE EXTREME	Vanilla Ice (SBK)
28	32	SOUL PROVIDER	Michael Bolton (CBS)
34	33	PLEASE HAMMER DON'T HURT 'EM	MC Hammer (Capitol)
26	34	DIRTY DANCING - SOUNDTRACK	Various (RCA)
-	35	YOUNG GODS	Little Angels (Polydor)
37	36	THE COLLECTION	Barry White (Mercury)
22	37	LIVE AT THE BRIXTON ACADEMY	Faith No More (Slash)
18	38	EVERYBODY'S ANGEL	Tanita Tikaram (East West)
32	39	GREATEST HITS 1977-1990	Stranglers (Epic)
-	40	GREEN MIND	DinosaurJr. (blanco y negro)
41	41	ROCKY V - SOUNDTRACK	Various (Capitol)
27	42	THE RHYTHM OF THE SAINTS	Paul Simon (Warner Bros.)
50	43	SATELLITES	Big Dish (East West)
-	44	THE REAL RAMONA	Throwing Muses (4AD)
-	45	THE ROAD TO HELL	Chris Rea (WEA)
35	46	RHYTHM OF LOVE	Kylie Minogue (PWL)
33	47	WORLD POWER	Snap (Arista)
36	48	THE TRACKS OF MY TEARS	Smokey Robinson and Various Artists (Motown)
-	49	RALPH TRESVANT	Ralph Tresvant (MCA)
31	50	A LITTLE AIN'T ENOUGH	David Lee Roth (Warner Bros.)

Queen's *Innuendo* album topped the chart alongside its title track, which made Number 1 as a single; these were the last chart-toppers singer Freedie Mercury would have during his lifetime. Meanwhile, Patsy Cline's *Sweet Dreams* compilation was spurred to big sales by the Top 10 reissue of her 1961 single *Crazy*. These were the biggest chart successes ever for the country vocalist who had died way back in 1963.

March 1991

9 March 1991

last week	this week	Title	Artist (Label)
-	1	AUBERGE	Chris Rea (East West)
5	2	CIRCLE OF ONE	Oleta Adams (Fontana)
1	3	INNUENDO	Queen (Parlophone)
2	4	WICKED GAME	Chris Isaak (Reprise)
14	5	THE BEST OF FREE - ALL RIGHT NOW	Free (Island)
3	6	INTO THE LIGHT	Gloria Estefan (Epic)
4	7	LISTEN WITHOUT PREJUDICE VOLUME 1	George Michael (Epic)
8	8	THE IMMACULATE COLLECTION	Madonna (Sire)
6	9	THE VERY BEST OF ELTON JOHN	Elton John (Rocket)
11	10	THE SIMPSONS SING THE BLUES	Simpsons (Geffen)
13	11	FREE	Rick Astley (RCA)
7	12	DEDICATION - THE VERY BEST OF THIN LIZZY	Thin Lizzy (Vertigo)
23	13	30 SOMETHING	Carter - The Unstoppable Sex Machine (Rough Trade)
17	14	SERIOUS HITS ... LIVE!	Phil Collins (Virgin)
20	15	THE LOST BOYS - SOUNDTRACK	Various (Atlantic)
9	16	DOUBT	Jesus Jones (Food)
16	17	MCMXC AD	Enigma (Virgin International)
12	18	I'M YOUR BABY TONIGHT	Whitney Houston (Arista)
10	19	RUNAWAY HORSES	Belinda Carlisle (Virgin)
22	20	PILLS 'N' THRILLS AND BELLYACHES	Happy Mondays (Factory)
26	21	AND NOW THE LEGACY BEGINS	Dream Warriors (Fourth & Broadway)
19	22	X	INXS (Mercury)
18	23	THE SOUL CAGES	Sting (A&M)
15	24	ALL TRUE MAN	Alexander O'Neal (Tabu)
35	25	YOUNG GODS	Little Angels (Polydor)
33	26	PLEASE HAMMER DON'T HURT 'EM	MC Hammer (Capitol)
21	27	IN CONCERT	Luciano Pavarotti, Placido Domingo and José Carreras (Decca)
28	28	DON'T EXPLAIN	Robert Palmer (EMI)
30	29	NO MORE GAMES - THE REMIX ALBUM	New Kids On The Block (CBS)
-	30	NIGHT RIDE HOME	Joni Mitchell (Geffen)
-	31	THE VERY BEST OF...	Bee Gees (Polydor)
24	32	THE SINGLES COLLECTION 1984-1990	Jimmy Somerville (London)
34	33	DIRTY DANCING - SOUNDTRACK	Various (RCA)
31	34	TO THE EXTREME	Vanilla Ice (SBK)
40	35	GREEN MIND	Dinosaur Jr. (blanco y negro)
39	36	GREATEST HITS 1977-1990	Stranglers (Epic)
25	37	THE ESSENTIAL	José Carreras (Philips)
32	38	SOUL PROVIDER	Michael Bolton (CBS)
44	39	THE REAL RAMONA	Throwing Muses (4AD)
-	40	MUSIC FROM TWIN PEAKS	Angelo Badalamenti (Warner Bros.)
29	41	SWEET DREAMS	Patsy Cline (MCA)
41	42	ROCKY V - SOUNDTRACK	Various (Capitol)
-	43	BIRDLAND	Birdland (Lazy)
42	44	THE RHYTHM OF THE SAINTS	Paul Simon (Warner Bros.)
45	45	THE ROAD TO HELL	Chris Rea (WEA)
27	46	CHOKE	Beautiful South (Go! Discs)
-	47	GODDESS	Soho (S&M)
36	48	THE COLLECTION	Barry White (Mercury)
-	49	GREASE	Soundtrack (Polydor)
37	50	LIVE AT THE BRIXTON ACADEMY	Faith No More (Slash)

16 March 1991

last week	this week	Title	Artist (Label)
-	1	SPARTACUS	Farm (Produce)
1	2	AUBERGE	Chris Rea (East West)
2	3	CIRCLE OF ONE	Oleta Adams (Fontana)
-	4	EX : EL	808 State (ZTT)
-	5	KILL UNCLE	Morrissey (HMV)
3	6	INNUENDO	Queen (Parlophone)
-	7	THE WHITE ROOM	KLF (KLF Communications)
8	8	THE IMMACULATE COLLECTION	Madonna (Sire)
7	9	LISTEN WITHOUT PREJUDICE VOLUME 1	George Michael (Epic)
4	10	WICKED GAME	Chris Isaak (Reprise)
5	11	THE BEST OF FREE - ALL RIGHT NOW	Free (Island)
6	12	INTO THE LIGHT	Gloria Estefan (Epic)
9	13	THE VERY BEST OF ELTON JOHN	Elton John (Rocket)
10	14	THE SIMPSONS SING THE BLUES	Simpsons (Geffen)
12	15	DEDICATION	Thin Lizzy (Vertigo)
36	16	GREATEST HITS 1977-1990	Stranglers (Epic)
-	17	INSPECTOR MORSE	Barrington Pheloung (Virgin Television)
11	18	FREE	Rick Astley (RCA)
14	19	SERIOUS HITS ... LIVE!	Phil Collins (Virgin)
13	20	30 SOMETHING	Carter - The Unstoppable Sex Machine (Rough Trade)
16	21	DOUBT	Jesus Jones (Food)
17	22	MCMXC AD	Enigma (Virgin International)
-	23	THE COMPLETE PICTURE	Deborah Harry and Blondie (Chrysalis)
18	24	I'M YOUR BABY TONIGHT	Whitney Houston (Arista)
-	25	PEGGY SUICIDE	Julian Cope (Island)
27	26	IN CONCERT	Luciano Pavarotti, Placido Domingo and José Carreras (Decca)
20	27	PILLS 'N' THRILLS AND BELLYACHES	Happy Mondays (Factory)
15	28	THE LOST BOYS - SOUNDTRACK	Various (Atlantic)
37	29	THE ESSENTIAL	José Carreras (Philips)
22	30	X	INXS (Mercury)
31	31	THE VERY BEST OF ...	Bee Gees (Polydor)
26	32	PLEASE HAMMER DON'T HURT 'EM	MC Hammer (Capitol)
19	33	RUNAWAY HORSES	Belinda Carlisle (Virgin)
23	34	THE SOUL CAGES	Sting (A&M)
30	35	NIGHT RIDE HOME	Joni Mitchell (Geffen)
24	36	ALL TRUE MAN	Alexander O'Neal (Tabu)
25	37	YOUNG GODS	Little Angels (Polydor)
40	38	MUSIC FROM TWIN PEAKS	Angelo Badalamenti (Warner Bros.)
21	39	AND NOW THE LEGACY BEGINS	Dream Warriors (Fourth & Broadway)
-	40	THE VERY BEST OF ...	Joan Armatrading (A&M)
32	41	THE SINGLES COLLECTION 1984-1990	Jimmy Somerville (London)
-	42	WORLD POWER	Snap (Arista)
45	43	THE ROAD TO HELL	Chris Rea (WEA)
28	44	DON'T EXPLAIN	Robert Palmer (EMI)
33	45	DIRTY DANCING - SOUNDTRACK	Various Artists (RCA)
-	46	TIME'S UP	Living Colour (Epic)
-	47	EVERYBODY'S ANGEL	Tanita Tikaram (East West)
49	48	GREASE	Soundtrack (Polydor)
42	49	ROCKY V - SOUNDTRACK	Various (Capitol)
34	50	TO THE EXTREME	Vanilla Ice (SBK)

23 March 1991

last week	this week	Title	Artist (Label)
1	1	SPARTACUS	Farm (Produce)
2	2	AUBERGE	Chris Rea (East West)
-	3	OUT OF TIME	R.E.M. (Warner Bros.)
7	4	THE WHITE ROOM	KLF (KLF Communications)
4	5	EX : EL	808 State (ZTT)
23	6	THE COMPLETE PICTURE	Deborah Harry and Blondie (Chrysalis)
3	7	CIRCLE OF ONE	Oleta Adams (Fontana)
10	8	WICKED GAME	Chris Isaak (Reprise)
8	9	THE IMMACULATE COLLECTION	Madonna (Sire)
5	10	KILL UNCLE	Morrissey (HMV)
9	11	LISTEN WITHOUT PREJUDICE VOLUME 1	George Michael (Epic)
6	12	INNUENDO	Queen (Parlophone)
17	13	INSPECTOR MORSE	Barrington Pheloung (Virgin Television)
13	14	THE VERY BEST OF ELTON JOHN	Elton John (Rocket)
40	15	THE VERY BEST OF JOAN ARMATRADING	Joan Armatrading (A&M)
12	16	INTO THE LIGHT	Gloria Estefan (Epic)
46	17	TIME'S UP	Living Colour (Epic)
16	18	GREATEST HITS 1977-1990	Stranglers (Epic)
11	19	THE BEST OF FREE - ALL RIGHT NOW	Free (Island)
15	20	DEDICATION	Thin Lizzy (Vertigo)
26	21	IN CONCERT	Luciano Pavarotti, Placido Domingo and José Carreras (Decca)
14	22	THE SIMPSONS SING THE BLUES	Simpsons (Geffen)
25	23	PEGGY SUICIDE	Julian Cope (Island)
35	24	NIGHT RIDE HOME	Joni Mitchell (Geffen)
21	25	DOUBT	Jesus Jones (Food)
29	26	THE ESSENTIAL	José Carreras (Philips)
18	27	FREE	Rick Astley (RCA)
24	28	I'M YOUR BABY TONIGHT	Whitney Houston (Arista)
19	29	SERIOUS HITS ... LIVE!	Phil Collins (Virgin)
-	30	PINK BUBBLES GO APE	Helloween (EMI)
22	31	MCMXC AD	Enigma (Virgin International)
20	32	30 SOMETHING	Carter - The Unstoppable Sex Machine (Rough Trade)
31	33	THE VERY BEST OF ...	Bee Gees (Polydor)
27	34	PILLS 'N' THRILLS AND BELLYACHES	Happy Mondays (Factory)
41	35	THE SINGLES COLLECTION 1984-1990	Jimmy Somerville (London)
28	36	THE LOST BOYS - SOUNDTRACK	Various (Atlantic)
32	37	PLEASE HAMMER DON'T HURT 'EM	MC Hammer (Capitol)
38	38	MUSIC FROM TWIN PEAKS	Angelo Badalamenti (Warner Bros.)
30	39	X	INXS (Mercury)
33	40	RUNAWAY HORSES	Belinda Carlisle (Virgin)
43	41	THE ROAD TO HELL	Chris Rea (WEA)
37	42	YOUNG GODS	Little Angels (Polydor)
-	43	LLOYD WEBBER PLAYS LLOYD WEBBER	Julian Lloyd Webber & the Royal Philharmonic Orchestra (Philips)
36	44	ALL TRUE MAN	Alexander O'Neal (Tabu)
34	45	THE SOUL CAGES	Sting (A&M)
46	46	CHOKE	Beautiful South (Go! Discs)
45	47	DIRTY DANCING - SOUNDTRACK	Various Artists (RCA)
-	48	LOOK SHARP!	Roxette (EMI)
-	49	THE COLLECTION	Barry White (Mercury)
-	50	SWEET DREAMS	Patsy Cline (MCA)

Auberge gave Chris Rea his second consecutive chart-topper, following *The Road To Hell*, while Morrissey's second solo album, *Kill Uncle*, did not quite scale the same heights as its short-lived predecessor - it did vanish from contention just as rapidly, however, with all its notable sales being packed into two Top 10 weeks and three more much further down the Top 50.

March – April 1991

30 March 1991

last week	this week	Title	Artist
3	1	OUT OF TIME	R.E.M. (Warner Bros.)
-	2	GREATEST HITS	Eurythmics (RCA)
2	3	AUBERGE	Chris Rea (East West)
6	4	THE COMPLETE PICTURE	Deborah Harry and Blondie (Chrysalis)
1	5	SPARTACUS	Farm (Produce)
13	6	INSPECTOR MORSE	Barrington Pheloung (Virgin Television)
5	7	EX : EL	808 State (ZTT)
4	8	THE WHITE ROOM	KLF (KLF Communications)
8	9	WICKED GAME	Chris Isaak (Reprise)
15	10	THE VERY BEST OF ...	Joan Armatrading (A&M)
9	11	THE IMMACULATE COLLECTION	Madonna (Sire)
11	12	LISTEN WITHOUT PREJUDICE VOLUME 1	George Michael (Epic)
14	13	THE VERY BEST OF ELTON JOHN	Elton John (Rocket)
7	14	CIRCLE OF ONE	Oleta Adams (Fontana)
12	15	INNUENDO	Queen (Parlophone)
16	16	INTO THE LIGHT	Gloria Estefan (Epic)
19	17	THE BEST OF FREE - ALL RIGHT NOW	Free (Island)
18	18	GREATEST HITS 1977-1990	Stranglers (Epic)
17	19	TIME'S UP	Living Colour (Epic)
-	20	THE STORY OF THE CLASH VOLUME 1	Clash (CBS)
20	21	DEDICATION	Thin Lizzy (Vertigo)
34	22	PILLS 'N' THRILLS AND BELLYACHES	Happy Mondays (Factory)
10	23	KILL UNCLE	Morrissey (HMV)
25	24	DOUBT	Jesus Jones (Food)
28	25	I'M YOUR BABY TONIGHT	Whitney Houston (Arista)
33	26	THE VERY BEST OF ...	Bee Gees (Polydor)
31	27	MCMXC AD	Enigma (Virgin International)
21	28	IN CONCERT	Placido Domingo and José Carreras (Decca)
22	29	THE SIMPSONS SING THE BLUES	Simpsons (Geffen)
23	30	PEGGY SUICIDE	Julian Cope (Island)
27	31	FREE	Rick Astley (RCA)
-	32	SLINKY	Milltown Brothers (A&M)
26	33	THE ESSENTIAL	José Carreras (Philips)
39	34	X	INXS (Mercury)
-	35	SOUL DESTRUCTION	Almighty (Polydor)
45	36	THE SOUL CAGES	Sting (A&M)
29	37	SERIOUS HITS ... LIVE!	Phil Collins (Virgin)
44	38	ALL TRUE MAN	Alexander O'Neal (Tabu)
32	39	30 SOMETHING	Carter - The Unstoppable Sex Machine (Rough Trade)
-	40	THE INCREDIBLE SOUND MACHINE	Mantronix (Capitol)
24	41	NIGHT RIDE HOME	Joni Mitchell (Geffen)
36	42	THE LOST BOYS - SOUNDTRACK	Various (Atlantic)
37	43	PLEASE HAMMER DON'T HURT 'EM	MC Hammer (Capitol)
35	44	THE SINGLES COLLECTION 1984-1990	Jimmy Somerville (London)
-	45	SOUL PROVIDER	Michael Bolton (CBS)
48	46	LOOK SHARP!	Roxette (EMI)
40	47	RUNAWAY HORSES	Belinda Carlisle (Virgin)
38	48	MUSIC FROM TWIN PEAKS	Angelo Badalamenti (Warner Bros.)
30	49	PINK BUBBLES GO APE	Helloween (EMI)
46	50	CHOKE	Beautiful South (Go! Discs)

5 April 1991

last week	this week	Title	Artist
2	1	GREATEST HITS	Eurythmics (RCA)
1	2	OUT OF TIME	R.E.M. (Warner Bros.)
3	3	AUBERGE	Chris Rea (East West)
4	4	THE COMPLETE PICTURE	Deborah Harry and Blondie (Chrysalis)
6	5	INSPECTOR MORSE	Barrington Pheloung (Virgin Television)
5	6	SPARTACUS	Farm (Produce)
12	7	LISTEN WITHOUT PREJUDICE VOLUME 1	George Michael (Epic)
10	8	THE VERY BEST OF ...	Joan Armatrading (A&M)
-	9	VAGABOND HEART	Rod Stewart (Warner Bros.)
11	10	THE IMMACULATE COLLECTION	Madonna (Sire)
-	11	ENTREAT	Cure (Fiction)
20	12	THE STORY OF THE CLASH VOLUME 1	Clash (CBS)
7	13	EX : EL	808 State (ZTT)
9	14	WICKED GAME	Chris Isaak (Reprise)
13	15	THE VERY BEST OF ELTON JOHN	Elton John (Rocket)
14	16	CIRCLE OF ONE	Oleta Adams (Fontana)
8	17	THE WHITE ROOM	KLF (KLF Communications)
15	18	INNUENDO	Queen (Parlophone)
16	19	INTO THE LIGHT	Gloria Estefan (Epic)
19	20	TIME'S UP	Living Colour (Epic)
24	21	DOUBT	Jesus Jones (Food)
18	22	GREATEST HITS 1977-1990	Stranglers (Epic)
22	23	PILLS 'N' THRILLS AND BELLYACHES	Happy Mondays (Factory)
-	24	THE DOORS - SOUNDTRACK	Doors (Elektra)
17	25	THE BEST OF FREE - ALL RIGHT NOW	Free (Island)
28	26	IN CONCERT	Placido Domingo and José Carreras (Decca)
34	27	X	INXS (Mercury)
-	28	BRAHMS VIOLIN CONCERTO	Nigel Kennedy (EMI)
29	29	THE SIMPSONS SING THE BLUES	Simpsons (Geffen)
35	30	SOUL DESTRUCTION	Almighty (Polydor)
31	31	FREE	Rick Astley (RCA)
21	32	DEDICATION - THE VERY BEST OF THIN LIZZY	Thin Lizzy (Vertigo)
26	33	THE VERY BEST OF ...	Bee Gees (Polydor)
27	34	MCMXC AD	Enigma (Virgin International)
-	35	HIGH CIVILIZATION	Bee Gees (Warner Bros.)
33	36	THE ESSENTIAL JOSE CARRERAS	José Carreras (Philips)
38	37	ALL TRUE MAN	Alexander O'Neal (Tabu)
25	38	I'M YOUR BABY TONIGHT	Whitney Houston (Arista)
36	39	THE SOUL CAGES	Sting (A&M)
-	40	EARTH INFERNO	Fields Of The Nephilim (Beggars Banquet)
43	41	PLEASE HAMMER DON'T HURT 'EM	MC Hammer (Capitol)
-	42	WHEN YOU'RE A BOY	Susanna Hoffs (Columbia)
23	43	KILL UNCLE	Morrissey (HMV)
45	44	SOUL PROVIDER	Michael Bolton (CBS)
42	45	THE LOST BOYS - SOUNDTRACK	Various (Atlantic)
32	46	SLINKY	Milltown Brothers (A&M)
30	47	PEGGY SUICIDE	Julian Cope (Island)
37	48	SERIOUS HITS ... LIVE!	Phil Collins (Virgin)
50	49	CHOKE	Beautiful South (Go! Discs)
41	50	NIGHT RIDE HOME	Joni Mitchell (Geffen)

12 April 1991

last week	this week	Title	Artist
1	1	GREATEST HITS	Eurythmics (RCA)
9	2	VAGABOND HEART	Rod Stewart (Warner Bros.)
2	3	OUT OF TIME	R.E.M. (Warner Bros.)
-	4	JOYRIDE	Roxette (EMI)
4	5	THE COMPLETE PICTURE	Deborah Harry and Blondie (Chrysalis)
3	6	AUBERGE	Chris Rea (East West)
5	7	INSPECTOR MORSE	Barrington Pheloung (Virgin Television)
11	8	ENTREAT	Cure (Fiction)
24	9	THE DOORS - SOUNDTRACK	Doors (Elektra)
-	10	GOD FODDER	Ned's Atomic Dustbin (Furtive)
7	11	LISTEN WITHOUT PREJUDICE VOLUME 1	George Michael (Epic)
10	12	THE IMMACULATE COLLECTION	Madonna (Sire)
6	13	SPARTACUS	Farm (Produce)
12	14	THE STORY OF THE CLASH VOLUME 1	Clash (CBS)
14	15	WICKED GAME	Chris Isaak (Reprise)
28	16	BRAHMS VIOLIN CONCERTO	Nigel Kennedy (EMI)
35	17	HIGH CIVILIZATION	Bee Gees (Warner Bros.)
8	18	THE VERY BEST OF JOAN ARMATRADING	Joan Armatrading (A&M)
15	19	THE VERY BEST OF ELTON JOHN	Elton John (Rocket)
-	20	MAMA SAID	Lenny Kravitz (Virgin America)
21	21	DOUBT	Jesus Jones (Food)
18	22	INNUENDO	Queen (Parlophone)
29	23	THE SIMPSONS SING THE BLUES	Simpsons (Geffen)
19	24	INTO THE LIGHT	Gloria Estefan (Epic)
20	25	TIME'S UP	Living Colour (Epic)
16	26	CIRCLE OF ONE	Oleta Adams (Fontana)
13	27	EX : EL	808 State (ZTT)
22	28	GREATEST HITS 1977-1990	Stranglers (Epic)
-	29	HISTORY REVISITED - THE REMIXES	Talk Talk (Parlophone)
17	30	THE WHITE ROOM	KLF (KLF Communications)
26	31	IN CONCERT	Placido Domingo and José Carreras (Decca)
27	32	X	INXS (Mercury)
23	33	PILLS 'N' THRILLS AND BELLYACHES	Happy Mondays (Factory)
32	34	DEDICATION	Thin Lizzy (Vertigo)
-	35	THE BEST OF THE DOORS	Doors (Elektra)
40	36	EARTH INFERNO	Fields Of The Nephilim (Beggars Banquet)
42	37	WHEN YOU'RE A BOY	Susanna Hoffs (Columbia)
-	38	THE BOOTLEG SERIES VOLUMES 1-3 (RARE & UNRELEASED) 196-1991	Bob Dylan (CBS)
46	39	SLINKY	Milltown Brothers (A&M)
30	40	SOUL DESTRUCTION	Almighty (Polydor)
33	41	THE VERY BEST OF ...	Bee Gees (Polydor)
34	42	MCMXC AD	Enigma (Virgin International)
25	43	THE BEST OF FREE - ALL RIGHT NOW	Free (Island)
36	44	THE ESSENTIAL JOSE CARRERAS	José Carreras (Philips)
31	45	FREE	Rick Astley (RCA)
48	46	SERIOUS HITS ... LIVE!	Phil Collins (Virgin)
47	47	PEGGY SUICIDE	Julian Cope (Island)
43	48	KILL UNCLE	Morrissey (HMV)
-	49	RIPE	Banderas (London)
-	50	A DREAM FULFILLED	Will Downing (Fourth & Broadway)

The chart-topping success of *Out Of Time*, coupled with the strong showings of the several singles which would be taken from it, confirmed the rise of REM - cult favourites for much of the 1980s - to the position of one of the world's top rock bands. *Out Of Time* remained in the Top 10 for much of the remainder of the year. The unusual spectacle of a TV soundtrack in the Top 10 was provided by *Inspector Morse*.

April – May 1991

last week	this week	20 April 1991	
-	1	REAL LIFE	Simple Minds (Virgin)
1	2	GREATEST HITS	Eurythmics (RCA)
4	3	JOYRIDE	Roxette (EMI)
2	4	VAGABOND HEART	Rod Stewart (Warner Bros.)
3	5	OUT OF TIME	R.E.M. (Warner Bros.)
10	6	GOD FODDER	Ned's Atomic Dustbin (Furtive)
-	7	FLASHPOINT	Rolling Stones (Rolling Stones)
20	8	MAMA SAID	Lenny Kravitz (Virgin America)
5	9	THE COMPLETE PICTURE	
			Deborah Harry and Blondie (Chrysalis)
9	10	THE DOORS - SOUNDTRACK	Doors (Elektra)
6	11	AUBERGE	Chris Rea (East West)
12	12	THE IMMACULATE COLLECTION	Madonna (Sire)
7	13	INSPECTOR MORSE (ORIGINAL MUSIC FROM	
		THE ITV SERIES)	
			Barrington Pheloung (Virgin Television)
23	14	THE SIMPSONS SING THE BLUES	
			Simpsons (Geffen)
-	15	BLUE LINES	Massive Attack (Wild Bunch)
14	16	THE STORY OF THE CLASH VOLUME 1	
			Clash (CBS)
24	17	INTO THE LIGHT	Gloria Estefan (Epic)
13	18	SPARTACUS	Farm (Produce)
11	19	LISTEN WITHOUT PREJUDICE VOLUME 1	
			George Michael (Epic)
26	20	CIRCLE OF ONE	Oleta Adams (Fontana)
8	21	ENTREAT	Cure (Fiction)
15	22	WICKED GAME	Chris Isaak (Reprise)
21	23	DOUBT	Jesus Jones (Food)
16	24	BRAHMS VIOLIN CONCERTO	
			Nigel Kennedy (EMI)
19	25	THE VERY BEST OF ELTON JOHN	
			Elton John (Rocket)
35	26	THE BEST OF THE DOORS	Doors (Elektra)
38	27	THE BOOTLEG SERIES VOLUMES 1-3 (RARE &	
		UNRELEASED) 196-1991	Bob Dylan (CBS)
28	28	THE WHITE ROOM	KLF (KLF Communications)
-	29	RAIN TREE CROW	Rain Tree Crow (Virgin)
25	30	TIME'S UP	Living Colour (Epic)
18	31	THE VERY BEST OF...	Joan Armatrading (A&M)
22	32	INNUENDO	Queen (Parlophone)
28	33	GREATEST HITS 1977-1990	Stranglers (Epic)
-	34	BUDDY'S SONG	Chesney Hawkes (Chrysalis)
17	35	HIGH CIVILIZATION	Bee Gees (Warner Bros.)
33	36	PILLS 'N' THRILLS AND BELLYACHES	
			Happy Mondays (Factory)
27	37	EX : EL	808 State (ZTT)
34	38	DEDICATION	Thin Lizzy (Vertigo)
-	39	MANE ATTRACTION	White Lion (Atlantic)
-	40	PLEASE HAMMER DON'T HURT 'EM	
			MC Hammer (Capitol)
32	41	X	INXS (Mercury)
42	42	MCMXC AD	Enigma (Virgin International)
31	43	IN CONCERT	Luciano Pavarotti
		, Placido Domingo and José Carreras (Decca)	
47	44	PEGGY SUICIDE	Julian Cope (Island)
43	45	THE BEST OF FREE - ALL RIGHT NOW	
			Free (Island)
49	46	RIPE	Banderas (London)
40	47	SOUL DESTRUCTION	Almighty (Polydor)
29	48	HISTORY REVISITED - THE REMIXES	
			Talk Talk (Parlophone)
39	49	SLINKY	Milltown Brothers (A&M)
-	50	LOOK SHARP!	Roxette (EMI)

last week	this week	27 April 1991	
2	1	GREATEST HITS	Eurythmics (RCA)
1	2	REAL LIFE	Simple Minds (Virgin)
7	3	FLASHPOINT	Rolling Stones (Rolling Stones)
3	4	JOYRIDE	Roxette (EMI)
4	5	VAGABOND HEART	Rod Stewart (Warner Bros.)
5	6	OUT OF TIME	R.E.M. (Warner Bros.)
12	7	THE IMMACULATE COLLECTION	Madonna (Sire)
15	8	BLUE LINES	Massive Attack (Wild Bunch)
9	9	THE COMPLETE PICTURE	
			Deborah Harry and Blondie (Chrysalis)
8	10	MAMA SAID	Lenny Kravitz (Virgin America)
10	11	THE DOORS - SOUNDTRACK	Doors (Elektra)
11	12	AUBERGE	Chris Rea (East West)
17	13	INTO THE LIGHT	Gloria Estefan (Epic)
14	14	THE SIMPSONS SING THE BLUES	
			Simpsons (Geffen)
19	15	LISTEN WITHOUT PREJUDICE VOLUME 1	
			George Michael (Epic)
26	16	THE BEST OF THE DOORS	Doors (Elektra)
16	17	THE STORY OF THE CLASH VOLUME 1	
			Clash (CBS)
13	18	INSPECTOR MORSE	
			Barrington Pheloung (Virgin Television)
25	19	THE VERY BEST OF ELTON JOHN	
			Elton John (Rocket)
22	20	WICKED GAME	Chris Isaak (Reprise)
20	21	CIRCLE OF ONE	Oleta Adams (Fontana)
24	22	BRAHMS VIOLIN CONCERTO	Nigel Kennedy (EMI)
29	23	RAIN TREE CROW	Rain Tree Crow (Virgin)
6	24	GOD FODDER	Ned's Atomic Dustbin (Furtive)
18	25	SPARTACUS	Farm (Produce)
33	26	GREATEST HITS 1977-1990	Stranglers (Epic)
-	27	SONGS FROM THE MARDI GRAS	
			Feargal Sharkey (Virgin)
31	28	THE VERY BEST OF ...	Joan Armatrading (A&M)
23	29	DOUBT	Jesus Jones (Food)
34	30	BUDDY'S SONG	Chesney Hawkes (Chrysalis)
40	31	PLEASE HAMMER DON'T HURT 'EM	
			MC Hammer (Capitol)
-	32	WORD OF MOUTH	Mike & the Mechanics (Virgin)
32	33	INNUENDO	Queen (Parlophone)
41	34	X	INXS (Mercury)
43	35	IN CONCERT	Luciano Pavarotti,
			Placido Domingo and José Carreras (Decca)
28	36	THE WHITE ROOM	KLF (KLF Communications)
27	37	THE BOOTLEG SERIES VOLUMES 1-3 (RARE &	
		UNRELEASED) 196-1991	Bob Dylan (CBS)
21	38	ENTREAT	Cure (Fiction)
36	39	PILLS 'N' THRILLS AND BELLYACHES	
			Happy Mondays (Factory)
37	40	EX : EL	808 State (ZTT)
42	41	MCMXC AD	Enigma (Virgin International)
35	42	HIGH CIVILIZATION	Bee Gees (Warner Bros.)
38	43	DEDICATION - THE VERY BEST OF THIN LIZZY	
			Thin Lizzy (Vertigo)
30	44	TIME'S UP	Living Colour (Epic)
-	45	DANCES WITH WOLVES - SOUNDTRACK	
			John Barry (Epic)
39	46	MANE ATTRACTION	White Lion (Atlantic)
44	47	PEGGY SUICIDE	Julian Cope (Island)
46	48	RIPE	Banderas (London)
50	49	LOOK SHARP!	Roxette (EMI)
-	50	ADVENTURES BEYOND THE ULTRAWORLD	
			Orb (Big Life)

last week	this week	4 May 1991	
1	1	GREATEST HITS	Eurythmics (RCA)
2	2	REAL LIFE	Simple Minds (Virgin)
4	3	JOYRIDE	Roxette (EMI)
6	4	OUT OF TIME	R.E.M. (Warner Bros.)
-	5	THE BEAST INSIDE	Inspiral Carpets (Cow)
5	6	VAGABOND HEART	Rod Stewart (Warner Bros.)
11	7	THE DOORS - SOUNDTRACK	Doors (Elektra)
13	8	INTO THE LIGHT	Gloria Estefan (Epic)
-	9	GOLD MOTHER	James (Fontana)
7	10	THE IMMACULATE COLLECTION	Madonna (Sire)
9	11	THE COMPLETE PICTURE	
			Deborah Harry and Blondie (Chrysalis)
32	12	WORD OF MOUTH	Mike & the Mechanics (Virgin)
3	13	FLASHPOINT	Rolling Stones (Rolling Stones)
12	14	AUBERGE	Chris Rea (East West)
26	15	GREATEST HITS 1977-1990	Stranglers (Epic)
16	16	THE BEST OF THE DOORS	Doors (Elektra)
19	17	THE VERY BEST OF ELTON JOHN	
			Elton John (Rocket)
-	18	HOODOO	Alison Moyet (Columbia)
14	19	THE SIMPSONS SING THE BLUES	
			Simpsons (Geffen)
10	20	MAMA SAID	Lenny Kravitz (Virgin America)
15	21	LISTEN WITHOUT PREJUDICE VOLUME 1	
			George Michael (Epic)
20	22	WICKED GAME	Chris Isaak (Reprise)
8	23	BLUE LINES	Massive Attack (Wild Bunch)
21	24	CIRCLE OF ONE	Oleta Adams (Fontana)
25	25	SPARTACUS	Farm (Produce)
17	26	THE STORY OF THE CLASH VOLUME 1	
			Clash (CBS)
18	27	INSPECTOR MORSE (ORIGINAL MUSIC FROM	
		THE ITV SERIES)	
			Barrington Pheloung (Virgin Television)
27	28	SONGS FROM THE MARDI GRAS	
			Feargal Sharkey (Virgin)
31	29	PLEASE HAMMER DON'T HURT 'EM	
			MC Hammer (Capitol)
22	30	BRAHMS VIOLIN CONCERTO	Nigel Kennedy (EMI)
-	31	SHIFT-WORK	Fall (Beggars Banquet)
30	32	BUDDY'S SONG	Chesney Hawkes (Chrysalis)
36	33	THE WHITE ROOM	KLF (KLF Communications)
29	34	DOUBT	Jesus Jones (Food)
34	35	X	INXS (Mercury)
35	36	IN CONCERT	Luciano Pavarotti
			Placido Domingo and José Carreras (Decca)
-	37	THE EMOTIONAL HOOLIGAN	
			Gary Clail On-U Sound System (Perfecto)
33	38	INNUENDO	Queen (Parlophone)
50	39	ADVENTURES BEYOND THE ULTRAWORLD	
			Orb (Big Life)
-	40	RAW	Alarm (IRS)
40	41	EX : EL	808 State (ZTT)
39	42	PILLS 'N' THRILLS AND BELLYACHES	
			Happy Mondays (Factory)
24	43	GOD FODDER	Ned's Atomic Dustbin (Furtive)
28	44	THE VERY BEST OF JOAN ARMATRADING	
			Joan Armatrading (A&M)
42	45	HIGH CIVILIZATION	Bee Gees (Warner Bros.)
41	46	MCMXC AD	Enigma (Virgin International)
-	47	LOVE CAN DO THAT	Elaine Paige (RCA)
-	48	THE DOORS	Doors (Elektra)
-	49	THE VERY BEST OF ...	Bee Gees (Polydor)
38	50	ENTREAT	Cure (Fiction)

The Eurythmics had eschewed the Christmas 1990 compilation scramble, but cannily released their *Greatest Hits* set at Easter instead, when it got the top of the chart to itself after dethroning Simple Minds. Four weeks at the top and a stay of several months in the Top 10 helped make it the duo's bigest-selling album ever. The *Doors* soundtrack music, by the way, was provided by the band's original records.

May 1991

11 May 1991

last week	this week	Title	Artist (Label)
1	1	GREATEST HITS	Eurythmics (RCA)
-	2	THE BEST OF THE WATERBOYS '81-'91	Waterboys (Ensign)
9	3	GOLD MOTHER	James (Fontana)
3	4	JOYRIDE	Roxette (EMI)
2	5	REAL LIFE	Simple Minds (Virgin)
5	6	THE BEAST INSIDE	Inspiral Carpets (Cow)
4	7	OUT OF TIME	R.E.M. (Warner Bros.)
8	8	INTO THE LIGHT	Gloria Estefan (Epic)
15	9	GREATEST HITS 1977-1990	Stranglers (Epic)
18	10	HOODOO	Alison Moyet (Columbia)
6	11	VAGABOND HEART	Rod Stewart (Warner Bros.)
10	12	THE IMMACULATE COLLECTION	Madonna (Sire)
7	13	THE DOORS - SOUNDTRACK	Doors (Elektra)
33	14	THE WHITE ROOM	KLF (KLF Communications)
14	15	AUBERGE	Chris Rea (East West)
11	16	THE COMPLETE PICTURE	Deborah Harry and Blondie (Chrysalis)
-	17	UNION	Yes (Arista)
16	18	THE BEST OF THE DOORS	Doors (Elektra)
29	19	PLEASE HAMMER DON'T HURT 'EM	MC Hammer (Capitol)
31	20	SHIFT-WORK	Fall (Beggars Banquet)
12	21	WORD OF MOUTH	Mike & the Mechanics (Virgin)
25	22	SPARTACUS	Farm (Produce)
19	23	THE SIMPSONS SING THE BLUES	Simpsons (Geffen)
17	24	THE VERY BEST OF ELTON JOHN	Elton John (Rocket)
24	25	CIRCLE OF ONE	Oleta Adams (Fontana)
22	26	WICKED GAME	Chris Isaak (Reprise)
21	27	LISTEN WITHOUT PREJUDICE VOLUME 1	George Michael (Epic)
37	28	THE EMOTIONAL HOOLIGAN	Gary Clail On-U Sound System (Perfecto)
20	29	MAMA SAID	Lenny Kravitz (Virgin America)
-	30	TRUE LOVE	Pat Benatar (Chrysalis)
26	31	THE STORY OF THE CLASH VOLUME 1	Clash (CBS)
40	32	RAW	Alarm (IRS)
36	33	IN CONCERT	Placido Domingo and José Carreras (Decca)
27	34	INSPECTOR MORSE (ORIGINAL MUSIC FROM THE ITV SERIES)	Barrington Pheloung (Virgin Television)
30	35	BRAHMS VIOLIN CONCERTO	Nigel Kennedy (EMI)
32	36	BUDDY'S SONG	Chesney Hawkes (Chrysalis)
13	37	FLASHPOINT	Rolling Stones (Rolling Stones)
-	38	WHIRLPOOL	Chapterhouse (Dedicated)
28	39	SONGS FROM THE MARDI GRAS	Feargal Sharkey (Virgin)
-	40	BLOOD	This Mortal Coil (4AD)
23	41	BLUE LINES	Massive Attack (Wild Bunch)
34	42	DOUBT	Jesus Jones (Food)
-	43	SOUL PROVIDER	Michael Bolton (CBS)
42	44	PILLS 'N' THRILLS AND BELLYACHES	Happy Mondays (Factory)
38	45	INNUENDO	Queen (Parlophone)
46	46	MCMXC AD	Enigma (Virgin International)
41	47	EX : EL	808 State (ZTT)
49	48	THE VERY BEST OF...	Bee Gees (Polydor)
35	49	X	INXS (Mercury)
-	50	SMOKE & STRONG WHISKEY	Christy Moore (Newberry)

18 May 1991

last week	this week	Title	Artist (Label)
1	1	GREATEST HITS	Eurythmics (RCA)
-	2	SCHUBERT DIP	EMF (Parlophone)
2	3	THE BEST OF THE WATERBOYS '81-'91	Waterboys (Ensign)
-	4	TIME, LOVE & TENDERNESS	Michael Bolton (Columbia)
3	5	GOLD MOTHER	James (Fontana)
4	6	JOYRIDE	Roxette (EMI)
14	7	THE WHITE ROOM	KLF (KLF Communications)
7	8	OUT OF TIME	R.E.M. (Warner Bros.)
5	9	REAL LIFE	Simple Minds (Virgin)
-	10	SUGAR TAX	Orchestral Manoeuvres In The Dark (Virgin)
17	11	UNION	Yes (Arista)
8	12	INTO THE LIGHT	Gloria Estefan (Epic)
9	13	GREATEST HITS 1977-1990	Stranglers (Epic)
19	14	PLEASE HAMMER DON'T HURT 'EM	MC Hammer (Capitol)
12	15	THE IMMACULATE COLLECTION	Madonna (Sire)
11	16	VAGABOND HEART	Rod Stewart (Warner Bros.)
15	17	AUBERGE	Chris Rea (East West)
13	18	THE DOORS - SOUNDTRACK	Doors (Elektra)
6	19	THE BEAST INSIDE	Inspiral Carpets (Cow)
23	20	THE SIMPSONS SING THE BLUES	Simpsons (Geffen)
22	21	SPARTACUS	Farm (Produce)
10	22	HOODOO	Alison Moyet (Columbia)
16	23	THE COMPLETE PICTURE	Deborah Harry and Blondie (Chrysalis)
-	24	GET READY!	Roachford (Columbia)
18	25	THE BEST OF THE DOORS	Doors (Elektra)
25	26	CIRCLE OF ONE	Oleta Adams (Fontana)
24	27	THE VERY BEST OF ELTON JOHN	Elton John (Rocket)
26	28	WICKED GAME	Chris Isaak (Reprise)
27	29	LISTEN WITHOUT PREJUDICE VOLUME 1	George Michael (Epic)
-	30	ZUCCHERO	Zucchero (A&M)
29	31	MAMA SAID	Lenny Kravitz (Virgin America)
21	32	WORD OF MOUTH	Mike & the Mechanics (Virgin)
38	33	WHIRLPOOL	Chapterhouse (Dedicated)
43	34	SOUL PROVIDER	Michael Bolton (CBS)
31	35	THE STORY OF THE CLASH VOLUME 1	Clash (CBS)
35	36	BRAHMS VIOLIN CONCERTO	Nigel Kennedy (EMI)
33	37	IN CONCERT	Placido Domingo and José Carreras (Decca)
30	38	TRUE LOVE	Pat Benatar (Chrysalis)
37	39	FLASHPOINT	Rolling Stones (Rolling Stones)
36	40	BUDDY'S SONG	Chesney Hawkes (Chrysalis)
34	41	INSPECTOR MORSE (ORIGINAL MUSIC FROM THE ITV SERIES)	Barrington Pheloung (Virg Television)
48	42	THE VERY BEST OF...	Bee Gees (Polydor)
-	43	LAUGHTER & LUST	Joe Jackson (Virgin America)
44	44	INNUENDO	Queen (Parlophone)
41	45	BLUE LINES	Massive Attack (Wild Bunch)
20	46	SHIFT-WORK	Fall (Beggars Banquet)
44	47	PILLS 'N' THRILLS AND BELLYACHES	Happy Mondays (Factory)
46	48	MCMXC AD	Enigma (Virgin International)
-	49	HARD AT PLAY	Huey Lewis & the News (Chrysalis)
-	50	HEART OF STONE	Cher (Geffen)

25 May 1991

last week	this week	Title	Artist (Label)
4	1	TIME, LOVE & TENDERNESS	Michael Bolton (Columbia)
1	2	GREATEST HITS	Eurythmics (RCA)
2	3	SCHUBERT DIP	EMF (Parlophone)
8	4	OUT OF TIME	R.E.M. (Warner Bros.)
-	5	MIGHTY LIKE A ROSE	Elvis Costello (Warner Bros.)
6	6	JOYRIDE	Roxette (EMI)
10	7	SUGAR TAX	Orchestral Manoeuvres In The Dark (Virgin)
-	8	DE LA SOUL IS DEAD	De La Soul (Big Life)
3	9	THE BEST OF THE WATERBOYS '81-'91	Waterboys (Ensign)
7	10	THE WHITE ROOM	KLF (KLF Communications)
9	11	REAL LIFE	Simple Minds (Virgin)
14	12	PLEASE HAMMER DON'T HURT 'EM	MC Hammer (Capitol)
15	13	THE IMMACULATE COLLECTION	Madonna (Sire)
-	14	POWER OF LOVE	Luther Vandross (Epic)
5	15	GOLD MOTHER	James (Fontana)
12	16	INTO THE LIGHT	Gloria Estefan (Epic)
18	17	THE DOORS - SOUNDTRACK	Doors (Elektra)
16	18	VAGABOND HEART	Rod Stewart (Warner Bros.)
13	19	GREATEST HITS 1977-1990	Stranglers (Epic)
11	20	UNION	Yes (Arista)
31	21	MAMA SAID	Lenny Kravitz (Virgin America)
24	22	GET READY!	Roachford (Columbia)
17	23	AUBERGE	Chris Rea (East West)
20	24	THE SIMPSONS SING THE BLUES	Simpsons (Geffen)
25	25	THE BEST OF THE DOORS	Doors (Elektra)
23	26	THE COMPLETE PICTURE	Deborah Harry and Blondie (Chrysalis)
-	27	LEGEND	Bob Marley & the Wailers (Island)
27	28	THE VERY BEST OF ELTON JOHN	Elton John (Rocket)
30	29	ZUCCHERO	Zucchero (A&M)
-	30	KEEP THE MUSIC PLAYING	Shirley Bassey (Dino)
26	31	CIRCLE OF ONE	Oleta Adams (Fontana)
21	32	SPARTACUS	Farm (Produce)
29	33	LISTEN WITHOUT PREJUDICE VOLUME 1	George Michael (Epic)
28	34	WICKED GAME	Chris Isaak (Reprise)
36	35	BRAHMS VIOLIN CONCERTO	Nigel Kennedy (EMI)
34	36	SOUL PROVIDER	Michael Bolton (CBS)
35	37	THE STORY OF THE CLASH VOLUME 1	Clash (CBS)
-	38	POP LIFE	Bananarama (London)
19	39	THE BEAST INSIDE	Inspiral Carpets (Cow)
37	40	IN CONCERT	Placido Domingo and José Carreras (Decca)
22	41	HOODOO	Alison Moyet (Columbia)
41	42	INSPECTOR MORSE (ORIGINAL MUSIC FROM THE ITV SERIES)	Barrington Pheloung (Virgin Television)
-	43	THE RHYTHM OF THE SAINTS	Paul Simon (Warner Bros.)
32	44	WORD OF MOUTH	Mike & the Mechanics (Virgin)
-	45	THE SOUL CAGES	Sting (A&M)
-	46	X	INXS (Mercury)
-	47	5,000,000	Dread Zeppelin (IRS)
-	48	MARIAH CAREY	Mariah Carey (CBS)
49	49	HARD AT PLAY	Huey Lewis & the News (Chrysalis)
-	50	TURTLE SOUP	Mock Turtles (Imaginary)

The Waterboys were another group to benefit from a strong-selling springtime compilation of the pick of their oldies, but *The Best Of '81-'91* just failed to unseat the Euythmics from the top. That honour went to US singer Michael Bolton, whose previous *Soul Provider* set had been a solid Top-Tenner in 1990, but whose new *Time, Love And Tenderness* outpaced the more hotly tipped EMF and James albums to the top.

June 1991

last week	this week	1 June 1991	
2	1	GREATEST HITS	Eurythmics (RCA)
1	2	TIME, LOVE & TENDERNESS	Michael Bolton (Columbia)
-	3	UNPLUGGED (THE OFFICIAL BOOTLEG)	Paul McCartney (Parlophone)
-	4	SEAL	Seal (ZTT)
5	5	MIGHTY LIKE A ROSE Elvis Costello (Warner Bros.)	
4	6	OUT OF TIME	R.E.M. (Warner Bros.)
3	7	SCHUBERT DIP	EMF (Parlophone)
6	8	JOYRIDE	Roxette (EMI)
8	9	DE LA SOUL IS DEAD	De La Soul (Big Life)
-	10	BEVERLY CRAVEN Beverly Craven (Columbia)	
10	11	THE WHITE ROOM KLF (KLF Communications)	
14	12	POWER OF LOVE	Luther Vandross (Epic)
17	13	THE DOORS - SOUNDTRACK	Doors (Elektra)
7	14	SUGAR TAX	Orchestral Manoeuvres in The Dark (Virgin)
-	15	MEMORABILIA - THE SINGLES	Soft Cell/Marc Almond (Some Bizzare)
9	16	THE BEST OF THE WATERBOYS '81-'91	Waterboys (Ensign)
11	17	REAL LIFE	Simple Minds (Virgin)
12	18	PLEASE HAMMER DON'T HURT 'EM	MC Hammer (Capitol)
27	19	LEGEND	Bob Marley & the Wailers (Island)
13	20	THE IMMACULATE COLLECTION Madonna (Sire)	
19	21	GREATEST HITS 1977-1990	Stranglers (Epic)
25	22	THE BEST OF THE DOORS	Doors (Elektra)
16	23	INTO THE LIGHT	Gloria Estefan (Epic)
15	24	GOLD MOTHER	James (Fontana)
18	25	VAGABOND HEART Rod Stewart (Warner Bros.)	
28	26	THE VERY BEST OF ELTON JOHN	Elton John (Rocket)
30	27	KEEP THE MUSIC PLAYING Shirley Bassey (Dino)	
20	28	UNION	Yes (Arista)
-	29	IN CONCERT	Doors (Elektra)
21	30	MAMA SAID	Lenny Kravitz (Virgin America)
26	31	THE COMPLETE PICTURE	Deborah Harry and Blondie (Chrysalis)
32	32	SPARTACUS	Farm (Produce)
22	33	GET READY!	Roachford (Columbia)
38	34	POP LIFE	Bananarama (London)
24	35	THE SIMPSONS SING THE BLUES	Simpsons (Geffen)
23	36	AUBERGE	Chris Rea (East West)
37	37	CIRCLE OF ONE	Oleta Adams (Fontana)
29	38	ZUCCHERO	Zucchero (A&M)
33	39	LISTEN WITHOUT PREJUDICE VOLUME 1	George Michael (Epic)
40	40	IN CONCERT	Luciano Pavarotti, Placido Domingo and José Carreras (Decca)
-	41	WILSON PHILLIPS	Wilson Phillips (SBK)
43	42	THE RHYTHM OF THE SAINTS	Paul Simon (Warner Bros.)
36	43	SOUL PROVIDER	Michael Bolton (CBS)
-	44	INNUENDO	Queen (Parlophone)
42	45	INSPECTOR MORSE (ORIGINAL MUSIC FROM THE ITV SERIES)	Barrington Pheloung (Virgin Television)
48	46	MARIAH CAREY	Mariah Carey (CBS)
34	47	WICKED GAME	Chris Isaak (Reprise)
35	48	BRAHMS VIOLIN CONCERTO	Nigel Kennedy (EMI)
-	49	O.G.: ORIGINAL GANGSTER	Ice-T (Sire)
46	50	X	INXS (Mercury)

last week	this week	8 June 1991	
4	1	SEAL	Seal (ZTT)
-	2	NEVER LOVED ELVIS	Wonder Stuff (Polydor)
1	3	GREATEST HITS	Eurythmics (RCA)
-	4	ELECTRONIC	Electronic (Factory)
6	5	OUT OF TIME	R.E.M. (Warner Bros.)
2	6	TIME, LOVE & TENDERNESS	Michael Bolton (Columbia)
3	7	UNPLUGGED (THE OFFICIAL BOOTLEG)	Paul McCartney (Parlophone)
10	8	BEVERLY CRAVEN Beverly Craven (Columbia)	
8	9	JOYRIDE	Roxette (EMI)
15	10	MEMORABILIA - THE SINGLES	Soft Cell/Marc Almond (Some Bizzare)
7	11	SCHUBERT DIP	EMF (Parlophone)
19	12	LEGEND	Bob Marley & the Wailers (Island)
-	13	SEAMONSTERS	Wedding Present (RCA)
22	14	THE BEST OF THE DOORS	Doors (Elektra)
17	15	REAL LIFE	Simple Minds (Virgin)
5	16	MIGHTY LIKE A ROSE Elvis Costello (Warner Bros.)	
11	17	THE WHITE ROOM KLF (KLF Communications)	
13	18	THE DOORS - SOUNDTRACK	Doors (Elektra)
9	19	DE LA SOUL IS DEAD	De La Soul (Big Life)
20	20	THE IMMACULATE COLLECTION Madonna (Sire)	
16	21	THE BEST OF THE WATERBOYS '81-'91	Waterboys (Ensign)
14	22	SUGAR TAX	Orchestral Manoeuvres in The Dark (Virgin)
-	23	WE ARE IN LOVE	Harry Connick Jr. (CBS)
21	24	GREATEST HITS 1977-1990	Stranglers (Epic)
29	25	IN CONCERT	Doors (Elektra)
18	26	PLEASE HAMMER DON'T HURT 'EM	MC Hammer (Capitol)
12	27	POWER OF LOVE	Luther Vandross (Epic)
-	28	THE VERY BEST OF DEXY'S MIDNIGHT RUNNERS Dexy's Midnight Runners (Mercury)	
26	29	THE VERY BEST OF ELTON JOHN	Elton John (Rocket)
25	30	VAGABOND HEART Rod Stewart (Warner Bros.)	
23	31	INTO THE LIGHT	Gloria Estefan (Epic)
24	32	GOLD MOTHER	James (Fontana)
27	33	KEEP THE MUSIC PLAYING Shirley Bassey (Dino)	
-	34	JUNGLE FEVER SOUNDTRACK	Stevie Wonder (Motown)
35	35	THE SIMPSONS SING THE BLUES	Simpsons (Geffen)
28	36	UNION	Yes (Arista)
30	37	MAMA SAID	Lenny Kravitz (Virgin America)
36	38	AUBERGE	Chris Rea (East West)
31	39	THE COMPLETE PICTURE - THE VERY BEST OF DEBORAH HARRY AND BLONDIE	Deborah Harry and Blondie (Chrysalis)
39	40	LISTEN WITHOUT PREJUDICE VOLUME 1	George Michael (Epic)
37	41	CIRCLE OF ONE	Oleta Adams (Fontana)
-	42	ELECTRIC LIGHT ORCHESTRA PART 2	Electric Light Orchestra Part 2 (Telstar)
40	43	IN CONCERT	Luciano Pavarotti, Placido Domingo and José Carreras (Decca)
41	44	WILSON PHILLIPS	Wilson Phillips (SBK)
32	45	SPARTACUS	Farm (Produce)
-	46	BLACK	Black (A&M)
44	47	INNUENDO	Queen (Parlophone)
-	48	MERMAIDS - SOUNDTRACK	Various (Epic)
33	49	GET READY!	Roachford (Columbia)
38	50	ZUCCHERO	Zucchero (A&M)

last week	this week	15 June 1991	
1	1	SEAL	Seal (ZTT)
4	2	ELECTRONIC	Electronic (Factory)
2	3	NEVER LOVED ELVIS	Wonder Stuff (Polydor)
-	4	FELLOW HOODLUMS	Deacon Blue (Columbia)
3	5	GREATEST HITS	Eurythmics (RCA)
5	6	OUT OF TIME	R.E.M. (Warner Bros.)
8	7	BEVERLY CRAVEN Beverly Craven (Columbia)	
6	8	TIME, LOVE & TENDERNESS	Michael Bolton (Columbia)
12	9	LEGEND	Bob Marley & the Wailers (Island)
28	10	THE VERY BEST OF DEXY'S MIDNIGHT RUNNERS Dexy's Midnight Runners (Mercury)	
18	11	THE DOORS - SOUNDTRACK	Doors (Elektra)
11	12	SCHUBERT DIP	EMF (Parlophone)
-	13	LOVE AND KISSES	Dannii Minogue (MCA)
9	14	JOYRIDE	Roxette (EMI)
10	15	MEMORABILIA - THE SINGLES	Soft Cell/Marc Almond (Some Bizzare)
17	16	THE WHITE ROOM KLF (KLF Communications)	
14	17	THE BEST OF THE DOORS	Doors (Elektra)
20	18	THE IMMACULATE COLLECTION Madonna (Sire)	
26	19	PLEASE HAMMER DON'T HURT 'EM	MC Hammer (Capitol)
24	20	GREATEST HITS 1977-1990	Stranglers (Epic)
15	21	REAL LIFE	Simple Minds (Virgin)
23	22	WE ARE IN LOVE	Harry Connick Jr. (CBS)
22	23	SUGAR TAX	Orchestral Manoeuvres in The Dark (Virgin)
13	24	SEAMONSTERS	Wedding Present (RCA)
21	25	THE BEST OF THE WATERBOYS '81-'91	Waterboys (Ensign)
30	26	VAGABOND HEART Rod Stewart (Warner Bros.)	
16	27	MIGHTY LIKE A ROSE Elvis Costello (Warner Bros.)	
37	28	MAMA SAID	Lenny Kravitz (Virgin America)
29	29	THE VERY BEST OF ELTON JOHN	Elton John (Rocket)
25	30	IN CONCERT	Doors (Elektra)
7	31	UNPLUGGED (THE OFFICIAL BOOTLEG)	Paul McCartney (Parlophone)
19	32	DE LA SOUL IS DEAD	De La Soul (Big Life)
27	33	POWER OF LOVE	Luther Vandross (Epic)
38	34	AUBERGE	Chris Rea (East West)
31	35	INTO THE LIGHT	Gloria Estefan (Epic)
35	36	THE SIMPSONS SING THE BLUES	Simpsons (Geffen)
41	37	CIRCLE OF ONE	Oleta Adams (Fontana)
32	38	GOLD MOTHER	James (Fontana)
-	39	EXTREME II PORNOGRAFFITTI	Extreme (A&M)
39	40	THE COMPLETE PICTURE	Deborah Harry and Blondie (Chrysalis)
33	41	KEEP THE MUSIC PLAYING	Shirley Bassey (Dino)
43	42	IN CONCERT	Luciano Pavarotti, Placido Domingo and José Carreras (Decca)
40	43	LISTEN WITHOUT PREJUDICE VOLUME 1	George Michael (Epic)
44	44	WILSON PHILLIPS	Wilson Phillips (SBK)
-	45	EFIL4ZREGGIN	NWA (Fourth & Broadway)
34	46	JUNGLE FEVER SOUNDTRACK	Stevie Wonder (Motown)
45	47	SPARTACUS	Farm (Produce)
48	48	MERMAIDS - SOUNDTRACK	Various (Epic)
49	49	BLUE LINES	Massive Attack (Wild Bunch)
42	50	ELECTRIC LIGHT ORCHESTRA PART 2	Electric Light Orchestra (Telstar)

Paul McCartney's *Unplugged (The Official Bootleg)* was a recording of the unique accoustic live set which McCartney and current band performed on cable TV channel MTV's new showcase programme, also titled *Unplugged*. Over the next couple of years, many acts, from Eric Clapton to Rod Stewart, would also have major chart success by releasing their acoustic sets like this after appearing on the MTV show.

376

22 June 1991

last week	this week	Title	Artist (label)
1	1	SEAL	Seal (ZTT)
4	2	FELLOW HOODLUMS	Deacon Blue (Columbia)
6	3	OUT OF TIME	R.E.M. (Warner Bros.)
-	4	SLAVE TO THE GRIND	Skid Row (Atlantic)
5	5	GREATEST HITS	Eurythmics (RCA)
2	6	ELECTRONIC	Electronic (Factory)
3	7	NEVER LOVED ELVIS	Wonder Stuff (Polydor)
7	8	BEVERLY CRAVEN	Beverly Craven (Columbia)
8	9	TIME, LOVE & TENDERNESS	Michael Bolton (Columbia)
-	10	THE MIX	Kraftwerk (EMI)
-	11	SUPERSTITION	Siouxsie & the Banshees (Wonderland)
14	12	JOYRIDE	Roxette (EMI)
13	13	LOVE AND KISSES	Dannii Minogue (MCA)
9	14	LEGEND	Bob Marley & the Wailers (Island)
11	15	THE DOORS - SOUNDTRACK	Doors (Elektra)
10	16	THE VERY BEST OF DEXY'S MIDNIGHT RUNNERS	Dexy's Midnight Runners (Mercury)
12	17	SCHUBERT DIP	EMF (Parlophone)
15	18	MEMORABILIA - THE SINGLES	Soft Cell/Marc Almond (Some Bizzare)
21	19	REAL LIFE	Simple Minds (Virgin)
20	20	GREATEST HITS 1977-1990	Stranglers (Epic)
16	21	THE WHITE ROOM	KLF (KLF Communications)
-	22	THE PROMISE	T'Pau (China)
18	23	THE IMMACULATE COLLECTION	Madonna (Sire)
17	24	THE BEST OF THE DOORS	Doors (Elektra)
26	25	VAGABOND HEART	Rod Stewart (Warner Bros.)
-	26	POP SYMPHONIES	James Last (Polydor)
28	27	MAMA SAID	Lenny Kravitz (Virgin America)
19	28	PLEASE HAMMER DON'T HURT 'EM	MC Hammer (Capitol)
22	29	WE ARE IN LOVE	Harry Connick Jr. (CBS)
-	30	RAW MELODY MEN	New Model Army (EMI)
23	31	SUGAR TAX	Orchestral Manoeuvres In The Dark (Virgin)
35	32	INTO THE LIGHT	Gloria Estefan (Epic)
39	33	EXTREME II PORNOGRAFFITI	Extreme (A&M)
45	34	EFIL4ZREGGIN	NWA (Fourth & Broadway)
25	35	THE BEST OF THE WATERBOYS '81-'91	Waterboys (Ensign)
34	36	AUBERGE	Chris Rea (East West)
-	37	BODY TO BODY	Technotronic (ARS)
37	38	CIRCLE OF ONE	Oleta Adams (Fontana)
29	39	THE VERY BEST OF ELTON JOHN	Elton John (Rocket)
-	40	CHANGING CABINS	Nomad (Rumour)
32	41	DE LA SOUL IS DEAD	De La Soul (Big Life)
24	42	SEAMONSTERS	Wedding Present (RCA)
41	43	KEEP THE MUSIC PLAYING	Shirley Bassey (Dino)
-	44	THE BIG WHEEL	Runrig (Chrysalis)
49	45	BLUE LINES	Massive Attack (Wild Bunch)
-	46	HEART IN MOTION	Amy Grant (A&M)
27	47	MIGHTY LIKE A ROSE	Elvis Costello (Warner Bros.)
30	48	IN CONCERT	Doors (Elektra)
33	49	POWER OF LOVE	Luther Vandross (Epic)
31	50	UNPLUGGED (THE OFFICIAL BOOTLEG)	Paul McCartney (Parlophone)

29 June 1991

last week	this week	Title	Artist (label)
-	1	LOVE HURTS	Cher (Geffen)
3	2	OUT OF TIME	R.E.M. (Warner Bros.)
1	3	SEAL	Seal (ZTT)
5	4	GREATEST HITS	Eurythmics (RCA)
4	5	SLAVE TO THE GRIND	Skid Row (Atlantic)
20	6	GREATEST HITS 1977-1990	Stranglers (Epic)
2	7	FELLOW HOODLUMS	Deacon Blue (Columbia)
9	8	TIME, LOVE & TENDERNESS	Michael Bolton (Columbia)
6	9	ELECTRONIC	Electronic (Factory)
8	10	BEVERLY CRAVEN	Beverly Craven (Columbia)
26	11	POP SYMPHONIES	James Last (Polydor)
10	12	THE MIX	Kraftwerk (EMI)
29	13	WE ARE IN LOVE	Harry Connick Jr. (CBS)
-	14	FOR UNLAWFUL CARNAL KNOWLEDGE	Van Halen (Warner Bros.)
22	15	THE PROMISE	T'Pau (China)
25	16	VAGABOND HEART	Rod Stewart (Warner Bros.)
27	17	MAMA SAID	Lenny Kravitz (Virgin America)
7	18	NEVER LOVED ELVIS	Wonder Stuff (Polydor)
16	19	THE VERY BEST OF DEXY'S MIDNIGHT RUNNERS	Dexy's Midnight Runners (Mercury)
-	20	CHICKEN RHYTHMS	Northside (Factory)
12	21	JOYRIDE	Roxette (EMI)
19	22	REAL LIFE	Simple Minds (Virgin)
11	23	SUPERSTITION	Siouxsie & the Banshees (Wonderland)
14	24	LEGEND	Bob Marley & the Wailers (Island)
44	25	THE BIG WHEEL	Runrig (Chrysalis)
23	26	THE IMMACULATE COLLECTION	Madonna (Sire)
18	27	MEMORABILIA - THE SINGLES	Soft Cell/Marc Almond (Some Bizzare)
33	28	EXTREME II PORNOGRAFFITI	Extreme (A&M)
15	29	THE DOORS - SOUNDTRACK	Doors (Elektra)
-	30	STARS CRASH DOWN	Hue & Cry (Circa)
13	31	LOVE AND KISSES	Dannii Minogue (MCA)
32	32	INTO THE LIGHT	Gloria Estefan (Epic)
21	33	THE WHITE ROOM	KLF (KLF Communications)
24	34	THE BEST OF THE DOORS	Doors (Elektra)
36	35	AUBERGE	Chris Rea (East West)
46	36	HEART IN MOTION	Amy Grant (A&M)
17	37	SCHUBERT DIP	EMF (Parlophone)
28	38	PLEASE HAMMER DON'T HURT 'EM	MC Hammer (Capitol)
38	39	CIRCLE OF ONE	Oleta Adams (Fontana)
-	40	BABY	Yello (Mercury)
31	41	SUGAR TAX	Orchestral Manoeuvres In The Dark (Virgin)
39	42	THE VERY BEST OF ELTON JOHN	Elton John (Rocket)
-	43	IN CONCERT	Placido Domingo and José Carreras (Decca)
-	44	LOVE AND LIFE - A JOURNEY WITH THE CHAMELEONS	Definition Of Sound (Circa)
35	45	THE BEST OF THE WATERBOYS '81-'91	Waterboys (Ensign)
30	46	RAW MELODY MEN	New Model Army (EMI)
43	47	KEEP THE MUSIC PLAYING	Shirley Bassey (Dino)
37	48	BODY TO BODY	Technotronic (ARS)
40	49	CHANGING CABINS	Nomad (Rumour)
45	50	BLUE LINES	Massive Attack (Wild Bunch)

6 July 1991

last week	this week	Title	Artist (label)
1	1	LOVE HURTS	Cher (Geffen)
2	2	OUT OF TIME	R.E.M. (Warner Bros.)
4	3	GREATEST HITS	Eurythmics (RCA)
3	4	SEAL	Seal (ZTT)
6	5	GREATEST HITS 1977-1990	Stranglers (Epic)
10	6	BEVERLY CRAVEN	Beverly Craven (Columbia)
-	7	HOLIDAYS IN EDEN	Marillion (EMI)
14	8	FOR UNLAWFUL CARNAL KNOWLEDGE	Van Halen (Warner Bros.)
13	9	WE ARE IN LOVE	Harry Connick Jr. (CBS)
7	10	FELLOW HOODLUMS	Deacon Blue (Columbia)
8	11	TIME, LOVE & TENDERNESS	Michael Bolton (Columbia)
17	12	MAMA SAID	Lenny Kravitz (Virgin America)
16	13	VAGABOND HEART	Rod Stewart (Warner Bros.)
5	14	SLAVE TO THE GRIND	Skid Row (Atlantic)
11	15	POP SYMPHONIES	James Last (Polydor)
9	16	ELECTRONIC	Electronic (Factory)
15	17	THE PROMISE	T'Pau (China)
18	18	THE VERY BEST OF DEXY'S MIDNIGHT RUNNERS	Dexy's Midnight Runners (Mercury)
19	19	CHICKEN RHYTHMS	Northside (Factory)
21	20	JOYRIDE	Roxette (EMI)
30	21	STARS CRASH DOWN	Hue & Cry (Circa)
-	22	ELECTRIC LANDLADY	Kirsty MacColl (Virgin)
12	23	THE MIX	Kraftwerk (EMI)
25	24	THE BIG WHEEL	Runrig (Chrysalis)
26	25	THE IMMACULATE COLLECTION	Madonna (Sire)
27	26	MEMORABILIA - THE SINGLES	Soft Cell/Marc Almond (Some Bizzare)
22	27	REAL LIFE	Simple Minds (Virgin)
24	28	LEGEND	Bob Marley & the Wailers (Island)
28	29	EXTREME II PORNOGRAFFITI	Extreme (A&M)
33	30	THE WHITE ROOM	KLF (KLF Communications)
32	31	INTO THE LIGHT	Gloria Estefan (Epic)
-	32	LUCK OF THE DRAW	Bonnie Raitt (Capitol)
18	33	NEVER LOVED ELVIS	Wonder Stuff (Polydor)
34	34	THE BEST OF THE DOORS	Doors (Elektra)
35	35	AUBERGE	Chris Rea (East West)
-	36	EXTREMELY LIVE	Vanilla Ice (SBK)
23	37	SUPERSTITION	Siouxsie & the Banshees (Wonderland)
29	38	THE DOORS - SOUNDTRACK	Doors (Elektra)
38	39	PLEASE HAMMER DON'T HURT 'EM	MC Hammer (Capitol)
39	40	CIRCLE OF ONE	Oleta Adams (Fontana)
31	41	LOVE AND KISSES	Dannii Minogue (MCA)
36	42	HEART IN MOTION	Amy Grant (A&M)
42	43	THE VERY BEST OF ELTON JOHN	Elton John (Rocket)
41	44	SUGAR TAX	Orchestral Manoeuvres In The Dark (Virgin)
37	45	SCHUBERT DIP	EMF (Parlophone)
-	46	UNUSUAL HEAT	Foreigner (Atlantic)
40	47	BABY	Yello (Mercury)
44	48	LOVE AND LIFE - A JOURNEY WITH THE CHAMELEONS	Definition Of Sound (Circa)
50	49	BLUE LINES	Massive Attack (Wild Bunch)
45	50	THE BEST OF THE WATERBOYS '81-'91	Waterboys (Ensign)

When it debuted at the top, Cher's *Love Hurts* gave the singer her first-ever UK Number 1 album - either as a soloist or as half of Sonny & Cher - after 26 years of hitmaking. Its sales were boosted by the inclusion of her revival of the oldie *The Shoop Shoop Song (It's In His Kiss)*, which she also performed in the movie Mermaids; this had already been a Number 1 hit during May as a single.

July 1991

13 July 1991

last week	this week	Title	Artist
1	1	LOVE HURTS	Cher (Geffen)
2	2	OUT OF TIME	R.E.M. (Warner Bros.)
3	3	GREATEST HITS	Eurythmics (RCA)
-	4	HEY STOOPID	Alice Cooper (Epic)
-	5	GREATEST HITS	Jam (Polydor)
5	6	GREATEST HITS 1977-1990	Stranglers (Epic)
4	7	SEAL	Seal (ZTT)
7	8	HOLIDAYS IN EDEN	Marillion (EMI)
11	9	TIME, LOVE & TENDERNESS	Michael Bolton (Columbia)
6	10	BEVERLY CRAVEN	Beverly Craven (Columbia)
12	11	MAMA SAID	Lenny Kravitz (Virgin America)
9	12	WE ARE IN LOVE	Harry Connick Jr. (CBS)
13	13	VAGABOND HEART	Rod Stewart (Warner Bros.)
15	14	POP SYMPHONIES	James Last (Polydor)
-	15	SOME PEOPLE'S LIVES	Bette Midler (Atlantic)
18	16	THE VERY BEST OF DEXY'S MIDNIGHT RUNNERS	Dexy's Midnight Runners (Mercury)
20	17	JOYRIDE	Roxette (EMI)
22	18	ELECTRIC LANDLADY	Kirsty MacColl (Virgin)
25	19	THE IMMACULATE COLLECTION	Madonna (Sire)
16	20	ELECTRONIC	Electronic (Factory)
10	21	FELLOW HOODLUMS	Deacon Blue (Columbia)
26	22	MEMORABILIA - THE SINGLES	Soft Cell/Marc Almond (Some Bizzare)
35	23	AUBERGE	Chris Rea (East West)
8	24	FOR UNLAWFUL CARNAL KNOWLEDGE	Van Halen (Warner Bros.)
28	25	LEGEND	Bob Marley & the Wailers (Island)
27	26	REAL LIFE	Simple Minds (Virgin)
24	27	THE BIG WHEEL	Runrig (Chrysalis)
29	28	EXTREME II PORNOGRAFFITI	Extreme (A&M)
36	29	EXTREMELY LIVE	Vanilla Ice (SBK)
14	30	SLAVE TO THE GRIND	Skid Row (Atlantic)
34	31	THE BEST OF THE DOORS	Doors (Elektra)
31	32	INTO THE LIGHT	Gloria Estefan (Epic)
32	33	LUCK OF THE DRAW	Bonnie Raitt (Capitol)
30	34	THE WHITE ROOM	KLF (KLF Communications)
17	35	THE PROMISE	T'Pau (China)
40	36	CIRCLE OF ONE	Oleta Adams (Fontana)
21	37	STARS CRASH DOWN	Hue & Cry (Circa)
-	38	WOODFACE	Crowded House (Capitol)
-	39	HOLLYWOOD VAMPIRES	L.A. Guns (Mercury)
39	40	PLEASE HAMMER DON'T HURT 'EM	MC Hammer (Capitol)
19	41	CHICKEN RHYTHMS	Northside (Factory)
44	42	SUGAR TAX	Orchestral Manoeuvres In The Dark (Virgin)
43	43	NEVER LOVED ELVIS	Wonder Stuff (Polydor)
38	44	THE DOORS - SOUNDTRACK	Doors (Elektra)
45	45	THE VERY BEST OF ELTON JOHN	Elton John (Rocket)
42	46	HEART IN MOTION	Amy Grant (A&M)
37	47	SUPERSTITION	Siouxsie & the Banshees (Wonderland)
23	48	THE MIX	Kraftwerk (EMI)
45	49	SCHUBERT DIP	EMF (Parlophone)
46	50	UNUSUAL HEAT	Foreigner (Atlantic)

20 July 1991

last week	this week	Title	Artist
5	1	GREATEST HITS	Jam (Polydor)
1	2	LOVE HURTS	Cher (Geffen)
4	3	HEY STOOPID	Alice Cooper (Epic)
-	4	INTO THE GREAT WIDE OPEN	Tom Petty & the Heartbreakers (MCA)
2	5	OUT OF TIME	R.E.M. (Warner Bros.)
3	6	GREATEST HITS	Eurythmics (RCA)
7	7	SEAL	Seal (ZTT)
6	8	GREATEST HITS 1977-1990	Stranglers (Epic)
10	9	BEVERLY CRAVEN	Beverly Craven (Columbia)
-	10	ATTACK OF THE KILLER B'S	Anthrax (Island)
11	11	MAMA SAID	Lenny Kravitz (Virgin America)
13	12	VAGABOND HEART	Rod Stewart (Warner Bros.)
17	13	JOYRIDE	Roxette (EMI)
-	14	ESSENTIAL PAVAROTTI II	Luciano Pavarotti (Decca)
15	15	SOME PEOPLE'S LIVES	Bette Midler (Atlantic)
9	16	TIME, LOVE & TENDERNESS	Michael Bolton (Columbia)
22	17	MEMORABILIA - THE SINGLES	Soft Cell/Marc Almond (Some Bizzare)
16	18	THE VERY BEST OF DEXY'S MIDNIGHT RUNNERS	Dexy's Midnight Runners (Mercury)
21	19	FELLOW HOODLUMS	Deacon Blue (Columbia)
-	20	ESTE MUNDO	Gipsy Kings (Columbia)
19	21	THE IMMACULATE COLLECTION	Madonna (Sire)
12	22	WE ARE IN LOVE	Harry Connick Jr. (CBS)
14	23	POP SYMPHONIES	James Last (Polydor)
23	24	AUBERGE	Chris Rea (East West)
38	25	WOODFACE	Crowded House (Capitol)
20	26	ELECTRONIC	Electronic (Factory)
25	27	LEGEND	Bob Marley & the Wailers (Island)
42	28	SUGAR TAX	Orchestral Manoeuvres In The Dark (Virgin)
8	29	HOLIDAYS IN EDEN	Marillion (EMI)
27	30	THE BIG WHEEL	Runrig (Chrysalis)
28	31	EXTREME II PORNOGRAFFITI	Extreme (A&M)
34	32	THE WHITE ROOM	KLF (KLF Communications)
30	33	SLAVE TO THE GRIND	Skid Row (Atlantic)
18	34	ELECTRIC LANDLADY	Kirsty MacColl (Virgin)
-	35	BLACK MEANING GOOD	Rebel MC (Desire)
33	36	LUCK OF THE DRAW	Bonnie Raitt (Capitol)
24	37	FOR UNLAWFUL CARNAL KNOWLEDGE	Van Halen (Warner Bros.)
26	38	REAL LIFE	Simple Minds (Virgin)
32	39	INTO THE LIGHT	Gloria Estefan (Epic)
40	40	PLEASE HAMMER DON'T HURT 'EM	MC Hammer (Capitol)
37	41	STARS CRASH DOWN	Hue & Cry (Circa)
39	42	HOLLYWOOD VAMPIRES	L.A. Guns (Mercury)
-	43	X	INXS (Mercury)
31	44	THE BEST OF THE DOORS	Doors (Elektra)
43	45	NEVER LOVED ELVIS	Wonder Stuff (Polydor)
45	46	THE VERY BEST OF ELTON JOHN	Elton John (Rocket)
49	47	SCHUBERT DIP	EMF (Parlophone)
46	48	HEART IN MOTION	Amy Grant (A&M)
-	49	DERELICTS OF DIALECT	3rd Bass (Def Jam)
35	50	THE PROMISE	T'Pau (China)

27 July 1991

last week	this week	Title	Artist
1	1	GREATEST HITS	Jam (Polydor)
2	2	LOVE HURTS	Cher (Geffen)
4	3	INTO THE GREAT WIDE OPEN	Tom Petty & the Heartbreakers (MCA)
5	4	OUT OF TIME	R.E.M. (Warner Bros.)
14	5	ESSENTIAL PAVAROTTI II	Luciano Pavarotti (Decca)
6	6	GREATEST HITS	Eurythmics (RCA)
7	7	SEAL	Seal (ZTT)
15	8	SOME PEOPLE'S LIVES	Bette Midler (Atlantic)
-	9	SPELLBOUND	Paula Abdul (Virgin America)
9	10	BEVERLY CRAVEN	Beverly Craven (Columbia)
11	11	MAMA SAID	Lenny Kravitz (Virgin America)
21	12	THE IMMACULATE COLLECTION	Madonna (Sire)
8	13	GREATEST HITS 1977-1990	Stranglers (Epic)
-	14	THE HEAT	Dan Reed Network (Mercury)
3	15	HEY STOOPID	Alice Cooper (Epic)
12	16	VAGABOND HEART	Rod Stewart (Warner Bros.)
13	17	JOYRIDE	Roxette (EMI)
-	18	UNFORGETTABLE - WITH LOVE	Natalie Cole (Elektra)
10	19	ATTACK OF THE KILLER B'S	Anthrax (Island)
16	20	TIME, LOVE & TENDERNESS	Michael Bolton (Columbia)
17	21	MEMORABILIA - THE SINGLES	Soft Cell/Marc Almond (Some Bizzare)
19	22	FELLOW HOODLUMS	Deacon Blue (Columbia)
24	23	AUBERGE	Chris Rea (East West)
18	24	THE VERY BEST OF DEXY'S MIDNIGHT RUNNERS	Dexy's Midnight Runners (Mercury)
28	25	SUGAR TAX	Orchestral Manoeuvres In The Dark (Virgin)
20	26	ESTE MUNDO	Gipsy Kings (Columbia)
22	27	WE ARE IN LOVE	Harry Connick Jr. (CBS)
26	28	ELECTRONIC	Electronic (Factory)
31	29	EXTREME II PORNOGRAFFITI	Extreme (A&M)
-	30	THERE'S NOTHING LIKE THIS	Omar (Kongo Dance)
27	31	LEGEND	Bob Marley & the Wailers (Island)
43	32	X	INXS (Mercury)
30	33	THE BIG WHEEL	Runrig (Chrysalis)
23	34	POP SYMPHONIES	James Last (Polydor)
32	35	THE WHITE ROOM	KLF (KLF Communications)
40	36	PLEASE HAMMER DON'T HURT 'EM	MC Hammer (Capitol)
39	37	INTO THE LIGHT	Gloria Estefan (Epic)
38	38	REAL LIFE	Simple Minds (Virgin)
41	39	STARS CRASH DOWN	Hue & Cry (Circa)
35	40	BLACK MEANING GOOD	Rebel MC (Desire)
25	41	WOODFACE	Crowded House (Capitol)
-	42	TWO SIDES	Mock Turtles (Imaginary)
46	43	THE VERY BEST OF ELTON JOHN	Elton John (Rocket)
-	44	RECKLESS	Bryan Adams (A&M)
29	45	HOLIDAYS IN EDEN	Marillion (EMI)
44	46	THE BEST OF THE DOORS	Doors (Elektra)
-	47	DIVINYLS	Divinyls (Virgin America)
47	48	SCHUBERT DIP	EMF (Parlophone)
-	49	ROBIN HOOD - PRINCE OF THIEVES	Soundtrack (Polydor)
-	50	LOVE AND KISSES	Dannii Minogue (MCA)

Pavarotti once again proved the pop-sized fervour for his brand of grand opera when a new compilation of his best songs and arias, *Essential Pavarotti II*, gave him another Top 5 hit. Meanwhile, into the Top 5 for the first time came Tom Petty & The Heartbreakers, whose *Into The Great Wide Open* seemed to be benefitting from Petty's hit profile as a Traveling Wilbury, since it had no major hit single to lean on.

3 August 1991

last week	this week	Title	Artist (Label)
1	1	GREATEST HITS	Jam (Polydor)
2	2	LOVE HURTS	Cher (Geffen)
9	3	SPELLBOUND	Paula Abdul (Virgin America)
5	4	ESSENTIAL PAVAROTTI II	Luciano Pavarotti (Decca)
7	5	SEAL	Seal (ZTT)
4	6	OUT OF TIME	R.E.M. (Warner Bros.)
18	7	UNFORGETTABLE - WITH LOVE	Natalie Cole (Elektra)
6	8	GREATEST HITS	Eurythmics (RCA)
3	9	INTO THE GREAT WIDE OPEN	Tom Petty & the Heartbreakers (MCA)
25	10	SUGAR TAX	Orchestral Manoeuvres In The Dark (Virgin)
8	11	SOME PEOPLE'S LIVES	Bette Midler (Atlantic)
29	12	EXTREME II PORNOGRAFFITI	Extreme (A&M)
12	13	THE IMMACULATE COLLECTION	Madonna (Sire)
16	14	VAGABOND HEART	Rod Stewart (Warner Bros.)
22	15	FELLOW HOODLUMS	Deacon Blue (Columbia)
10	16	BEVERLY CRAVEN	Beverly Craven (Columbia)
14	17	THE HEAT	Dan Reed Network (Mercury)
20	18	TIME, LOVE & TENDERNESS	Michael Bolton (Columbia)
13	19	GREATEST HITS 1977-1990	Stranglers (Epic)
17	20	JOYRIDE	Roxette (EMI)
11	21	MAMA SAID	Lenny Kravitz (Virgin America)
-	22	BAT OUT OF HELL	Meatloaf (Epic)
31	23	LEGEND	Bob Marley & the Wailers (Island)
21	24	MEMORABILIA - THE SINGLES	Soft Cell/Marc Almond (Some Bizzare)
30	25	THERE'S NOTHING LIKE THIS	Omar (Kongo Dance)
32	26	X	INXS (Mercury)
24	27	THE VERY BEST OF DEXY'S MIDNIGHT RUNNERS	Dexy's Midnight Runners (Mercury)
27	28	WE ARE IN LOVE	Harry Connick Jr. (CBS)
49	29	ROBIN HOOD - PRINCE OF THIEVES	Soundtrack (Polydor)
42	30	TWO SIDES	Mock Turtles (Imaginary)
15	31	HEY STOOPID	Alice Cooper (Epic)
38	32	REAL LIFE	Simple Minds (Virgin)
37	33	INTO THE LIGHT	Gloria Estefan (Epic)
35	34	THE WHITE ROOM	KLF (KLF Communications)
26	35	ESTE MUNDO	Gipsy Kings (Columbia)
23	36	AUBERGE	Chris Rea (East West)
36	37	PLEASE HAMMER DON'T HURT 'EM	MC Hammer (Capitol)
50	38	LOVE AND KISSES	Dannii Minogue (MCA)
19	39	ATTACK OF THE KILLER B'S	Anthrax (Island)
28	40	ELECTRONIC	Electronic (Factory)
-	41	DOUBT	Jesus Jones (Food)
43	42	THE VERY BEST OF ELTON JOHN	Elton John (Rocket)
-	43	CHIC AND ROSE ROYCE - THEIR GREATEST HITS SIDE BY SIDE	Chic/Rose Royce (Dino)
48	44	SCHUBERT DIP	EMF (Parlophone)
46	45	THE BEST OF THE DOORS	Doors (Elektra)
44	46	RECKLESS	Bryan Adams (A&M)
34	47	POP SYMPHONIES	James Last (Polydor)
-	48	FREQUENCIES	LFO (Warp)
-	49	THE BEST OF ROD STEWART	Rod Stewart (Warner Bros.)
33	50	THE BIG WHEEL	Runrig (Chrysalis)

10 August 1991

last week	this week	Title	Artist (Label)
4	1	ESSENTIAL PAVAROTTI II	Luciano Pavarotti (Decca)
2	2	LOVE HURTS	Cher (Geffen)
5	3	SEAL	Seal (ZTT)
8	4	GREATEST HITS	Eurythmics (RCA)
6	5	OUT OF TIME	R.E.M. (Warner Bros.)
12	6	EXTREME II PORNOGRAFFITI	Extreme (A&M)
13	7	THE IMMACULATE COLLECTION	Madonna (Sire)
1	8	GREATEST HITS	Jam (Polydor)
3	9	SPELLBOUND	Paula Abdul (Virgin America)
-	10	GONNA MAKE YOU SWEAT	C&C Music Factory (Columbia)
15	11	FELLOW HOODLUMS	Deacon Blue (Columbia)
10	12	SUGAR TAX	Orchestral Manoeuvres In The Dark (Virgin)
9	13	INTO THE GREAT WIDE OPEN	Tom Petty & the Heartbreakers (MCA)
14	14	BEVERLY CRAVEN	Beverly Craven (Columbia)
18	15	TIME, LOVE & TENDERNESS	Michael Bolton (Columbia)
19	16	GREATEST HITS 1977-1990	Stranglers (Epic)
14	17	VAGABOND HEART	Rod Stewart (Warner Bros.)
7	18	UNFORGETTABLE - WITH LOVE	Natalie Cole (Elektra)
-	19	MOVE TO THIS	Cathy Dennis (Polydor)
22	20	BAT OUT OF HELL	Meatloaf (Epic)
11	21	SOME PEOPLE'S LIVES	Bette Midler (Atlantic)
23	22	LEGEND	Bob Marley & the Wailers (Island)
20	23	JOYRIDE	Roxette (EMI)
21	24	MAMA SAID	Lenny Kravitz (Virgin America)
29	25	ROBIN HOOD - PRINCE OF THIEVES	Soundtrack (Polydor)
33	26	INTO THE LIGHT	Gloria Estefan (Epic)
28	27	WE ARE IN LOVE	Harry Connick Jr. (CBS)
26	28	X	INXS (Mercury)
34	29	THE WHITE ROOM	KLF (KLF Communications)
38	30	LOVE AND KISSES	Dannii Minogue (MCA)
25	31	THERE'S NOTHING LIKE THIS	Omar (Kongo Dance)
17	32	THE HEAT	Dan Reed Network (Mercury)
-	33	PEACEFUL JOURNEY	Heavy D & the Boyz (MCA)
27	34	THE VERY BEST OF DEXY'S MIDNIGHT RUNNERS	Dexy's Midnight Runners (Mercury)
-	35	IN CONCERT	Luciano Pavarotti, Placido Domingo and José Carreras (Decca)
41	36	DOUBT	Jesus Jones (Food)
48	37	FREQUENCIES	LFO (Warp)
37	38	PLEASE HAMMER DON'T HURT 'EM	MC Hammer (Capitol)
46	39	RECKLESS	Bryan Adams (A&M)
24	40	MEMORABILIA - THE SINGLES	Soft Cell/Marc Almond (Some Bizzare)
32	41	REAL LIFE	Simple Minds (Virgin)
-	42	THE ESSENTIAL PAVAROTTI	Luciano Pavarotti (Decca)
36	43	AUBERGE	Chris Rea (East West)
35	44	ESTE MUNDO	Gipsy Kings (Columbia)
30	45	TWO SIDES	Mock Turtles (Imaginary)
31	46	HEY STOOPID	Alice Cooper (Epic)
42	47	THE VERY BEST OF...	Elton John (Rocket)
43	48	CHIC AND ROSE ROYCE - THEIR GREATEST HITS SIDE BY SIDE	Chic/Rose Royce (Dino)
49	49	THE BEST OF ROD STEWART	Rod Stewart (Warner Bros.)
40	50	ELECTRONIC	Electronic (Factory)

17 August 1991

last week	this week	Title	Artist (Label)
1	1	ESSENTIAL PAVAROTTI II	Luciano Pavarotti (Decca)
2	2	LOVE HURTS	Cher (Geffen)
3	3	SEAL	Seal (ZTT)
19	4	MOVE TO THIS	Cathy Dennis (Polydor)
12	5	SUGAR TAX	Orchestral Manoeuvres In The Dark (Virgin)
4	6	GREATEST HITS	Eurythmics (RCA)
5	7	OUT OF TIME	R.E.M. (Warner Bros.)
11	8	FELLOW HOODLUMS	Deacon Blue (Columbia)
10	9	GONNA MAKE YOU SWEAT	C&C Music Factory (Columbia)
6	10	EXTREME II PORNOGRAFFITI	Extreme (A&M)
7	11	THE IMMACULATE COLLECTION	Madonna (Sire)
14	12	BEVERLY CRAVEN	Beverly Craven (Columbia)
8	13	GREATEST HITS	Jam (Polydor)
16	14	GREATEST HITS 1977-1990	Stranglers (Epic)
15	15	TIME, LOVE & TENDERNESS	Michael Bolton (Columbia)
13	16	INTO THE GREAT WIDE OPEN	Tom Petty & the Heartbreakers (MCA)
9	17	SPELLBOUND	Paula Abdul (Virgin America)
18	18	UNFORGETTABLE - WITH LOVE	Natalie Cole (Elektra)
17	19	VAGABOND HEART	Rod Stewart (Warner Bros.)
42	20	THE ESSENTIAL PAVAROTTI	Luciano Pavarotti (Decca)
23	21	JOYRIDE	Roxette (EMI)
20	22	BAT OUT OF HELL	Meatloaf (Epic)
22	23	LEGEND	Bob Marley & the Wailers (Island)
35	24	IN CONCERT	Luciano Pavarotti, Placido Domingo and José Carreras (Decca)
21	25	SOME PEOPLE'S LIVES	Bette Midler (Atlantic)
39	26	RECKLESS	Bryan Adams (A&M)
26	27	INTO THE LIGHT	Gloria Estefan (Epic)
25	28	ROBIN HOOD - PRINCE OF THIEVES	Soundtrack (Polydor)
29	29	MAMA SAID	Lenny Kravitz (Virgin America)
29	30	THE WHITE ROOM	KLF (KLF Communications)
27	31	WE ARE IN LOVE	Harry Connick Jr. (CBS)
28	33	X	INXS (Mercury)
36	34	DOUBT	Jesus Jones (Food)
-	35	DE LA SOUL IS DEAD	De La Soul (Big Life)
30	36	LOVE AND KISSES	Dannii Minogue (MCA)
32	37	THE HEAT	Dan Reed Network (Mercury)
-	38	HEART IN MOTION	Amy Grant (A&M)
49	39	THE BEST OF ROD STEWART	Rod Stewart (Warner Bros.)
-	40	SCHUBERT DIP	EMF (Parlophone)
33	41	PEACEFUL JOURNEY	Heavy D & the Boyz (MCA)
43	42	AUBERGE	Chris Rea (East West)
47	43	THE VERY BEST OF ELTON JOHN	Elton John (Rocket)
44	44	ESTE MUNDO	Gipsy Kings (Columbia)
38	45	PLEASE HAMMER DON'T HURT 'EM	MC Hammer (Capitol)
-	46	HEART OF STONE	Cher (Geffen)
-	47	HOLIDAYS IN EDEN	Marillion (EMI)
-	48	THE BEST OF THE DOORS	Doors (Elektra)
31	49	THERE'S NOTHING LIKE THIS	Omar (Kongo Dance)
34	50	THE VERY BEST OF DEXY'S MIDNIGHT RUNNERS	Dexy's Midnight Runners (Mercury)

There could hardly have been two more contrasting compilation albums than the Jam's *Greatest Hits* and the second *Essential Pavarotti* - which did not prevent the latter from succeeding the former at the chart top - amazingly, Pavarotti's third Number 1 album (including the three tenors' *In Concert*). Natalie Cole's *Unforgettable* included a studio-created "duet" with her late father Nat 'King' Cole on the title track.

August – September 1991

24 August 1991

last week	this week	Title	Artist (Label)
-	1	METALLICA	Metallica (Vertigo)
1	2	ESSENTIAL PAVAROTTI II	Luciano Pavarotti (Decca)
2	3	LOVE HURTS	Cher (Geffen)
7	4	OUT OF TIME	R.E.M. (Warner Bros.)
3	5	SEAL	Seal (ZTT)
5	6	SUGAR TAX	Orchestral Manoeuvres In The Dark (Virgin)
8	7	FELLOW HOODLUMS	Deacon Blue (Columbia)
6	8	GREATEST HITS	Eurythmics (RCA)
4	9	MOVE TO THIS	Cathy Dennis (Polydor)
10	10	EXTREME II PORNOGRAFFITI	Extreme (A&M)
12	11	BEVERLY CRAVEN	Beverly Craven (Columbia)
9	12	GONNA MAKE YOU SWEAT	C&C Music Factory (Columbia)
15	13	TIME, LOVE & TENDERNESS	Michael Bolton (Columbia)
11	14	THE IMMACULATE COLLECTION	Madonna (Sire)
13	15	GREATEST HITS	Jam (Polydor)
-	16	CMB	Color Me Badd (Giant)
14	17	GREATEST HITS 1977-1990	Stranglers (Epic)
17	18	SPELLBOUND	Paula Abdul (Virgin America)
20	19	THE ESSENTIAL PAVAROTTI	Luciano Pavarotti (Decca)
16	20	INTO THE GREAT WIDE OPEN	Tom Petty & the Heartbreakers (MCA)
-	21	HONEY LINGERS	Voice Of The Beehive (London)
18	22	UNFORGETTABLE - WITH LOVE	Natalie Cole (Elektra)
-	23	MARC COHN	Marc Cohn (Atlantic)
22	24	BAT OUT OF HELL	Meatloaf (Epic)
19	25	VAGABOND HEART	Rod Stewart (Warner Bros.)
21	26	JOYRIDE	Roxette (EMI)
23	27	LEGEND	Bob Marley & the Wailers (Island)
24	28	IN CONCERT	Luciano Pavarotti, Placido Domingo and José Carreras (Decca)
26	29	RECKLESS	Bryan Adams (A&M)
27	30	INTO THE LIGHT	Gloria Estefan (Epic)
30	31	THE WHITE ROOM KLF	(KLF Communications)
25	32	SOME PEOPLE'S LIVES	Bette Midler (Atlantic)
-	33	ABRACADABRA	ABC (Parlophone)
28	34	ROBIN HOOD - PRINCE OF THIEVES	Soundtrack (Polydor)
32	35	REAL LIFE	Simple Minds (Virgin)
38	36	HEART IN MOTION	Amy Grant (A&M)
35	37	DE LA SOUL IS DEAD	De La Soul (Big Life)
29	38	MAMA SAID	Lenny Kravitz (Virgin America)
31	39	WE ARE IN LOVE	Harry Connick Jr. (CBS)
36	40	LOVE AND KISSES	Dannii Minogue (MCA)
42	41	AUBERGE	Chris Rea (East West)
47	42	HOLIDAYS IN EDEN	Marillion (EMI)
-	43	MCMXC AD	Enigma (Virgin International)
33	44	X	INXS (Mercury)
-	45	EN-TACT	Shamen (One Little Indian)
39	46	THE BEST OF ROD STEWART	Rod Stewart (Warner Bros.)
34	47	DOUBT	Jesus Jones (Food)
43	48	THE VERY BEST OF ELTON JOHN	Elton John (Rocket)
45	49	PLEASE HAMMER DON'T HURT 'EM	MC Hammer (Capitol)
-	50	BEATSONGS	Blue Aeroplanes (Ensign)

31 August 1991

last week	this week	Title	Artist (Label)
1	1	METALLICA	Metallica (Vertigo)
2	2	ESSENTIAL PAVAROTTI II	Luciano Pavarotti (Decca)
3	3	LOVE HURTS	Cher (Geffen)
-	4	JOSEPH AND THE AMAZING TECHNICOLOUR DREAMCOAT	Original Cast (Really Useful)
4	5	OUT OF TIME	R.E.M. (Warner Bros.)
6	6	SUGAR TAX	Orchestral Manoeuvres In The Dark (Virgin)
11	7	BEVERLY CRAVEN	Beverly Craven (Columbia)
7	8	FELLOW HOODLUMS	Deacon Blue (Columbia)
16	9	CMB	Color Me Badd (Giant)
5	10	SEAL	Seal (ZTT)
8	11	GREATEST HITS	Eurythmics (RCA)
13	12	TIME, LOVE & TENDERNESS	Michael Bolton (Columbia)
10	13	EXTREME II PORNOGRAFFITI	Extreme (A&M)
21	14	HONEY LINGERS	Voice Of The Beehive (London)
14	15	THE IMMACULATE COLLECTION	Madonna (Sire)
12	16	GONNA MAKE YOU SWEAT	C&C Music Factory (Columbia)
-	17	UNKNOWN TERRITORY	Bomb The Bass (Rhythm King)
18	18	GREATEST HITS 1977-1990	Stranglers (Epic)
15	19	GREATEST HITS	Jam (Polydor)
9	20	MOVE TO THIS	Cathy Dennis (Polydor)
20	21	INTO THE GREAT WIDE OPEN	Tom Petty & the Heartbreakers (MCA)
24	22	BAT OUT OF HELL	Meatloaf (Epic)
23	23	MARC COHN	Marc Cohn (Atlantic)
27	24	LEGEND	Bob Marley & the Wailers (Island)
22	25	UNFORGETTABLE - WITH LOVE	Natalie Cole (Elektra)
35	26	REAL LIFE	Simple Minds (Virgin)
18	27	SPELLBOUND	Paula Abdul (Virgin America)
26	28	RECKLESS	Bryan Adams (A&M)
25	29	VAGABOND HEART	Rod Stewart (Warner Bros.)
-	30	ROAD TO FREEDOM	Young Disciples (Talkin' Loud)
31	31	THE WHITE ROOM	KLF (KLF Communications)
26	32	JOYRIDE	Roxette (EMI)
19	33	THE ESSENTIAL PAVAROTTI	Luciano Pavarotti (Decca)
34	34	MAMA SAID	Lenny Kravitz (Virgin America)
28	35	IN CONCERT	Luciano Pavarotti, Placido Domingo and José Carreras (Decca)
-	36	EVERY GOOD BOY DESERVES FUDGE	Mudhoney (Subpop)
34	37	ROBIN HOOD - PRINCE OF THIEVES	Soundtrack (Polydor)
36	38	HEART IN MOTION	Amy Grant (A&M)
39	39	X	INXS (Mercury)
30	40	INTO THE LIGHT	Gloria Estefan (Epic)
-	41	SHAKE YOUR MONEY MAKER	Black Crowes (Def American)
32	42	SOME PEOPLE'S LIVES	Bette Midler (Atlantic)
41	43	AUBERGE	Chris Rea (East West)
39	44	WE ARE IN LOVE	Harry Connick Jr. (CBS)
43	45	MCMXC AD	Enigma (Virgin International)
48	46	THE VERY BEST OF...	Elton John (Rocket)
-	47	HEART OF STONE	Cher (Geffen)
45	48	EN-TACT	Shamen (One Little Indian)
40	49	LOVE AND KISSES	Dannii Minogue (MCA)
49	50	PLEASE HAMMER DON'T HURT 'EM	MC Hammer (Capitol)

7 September 1991

last week	this week	Title	Artist (Label)
4	1	JOSEPH AND THE AMAZING TECHNICOLOUR DREAMCOAT	Original Cast (Really Useful)
-	2	LEISURE	Blur (Food)
2	3	ESSENTIAL PAVAROTTI II	Luciano Pavarotti (Decca)
3	4	LOVE HURTS	Cher (Geffen)
5	5	OUT OF TIME	R.E.M. (Warner Bros.)
10	6	SEAL	Seal (ZTT)
1	7	METALLICA	Metallica (Vertigo)
9	8	CMB	Color Me Badd (Giant)
7	9	BEVERLY CRAVEN	Beverly Craven (Columbia)
8	10	FELLOW HOODLUMS	Deacon Blue (Columbia)
12	11	TIME, LOVE & TENDERNESS	Michael Bolton (Columbia)
11	12	GREATEST HITS	Eurythmics (RCA)
15	13	THE IMMACULATE COLLECTION	Madonna (Sire)
6	14	SUGAR TAX	Orchestral Manoeuvres In The Dark (Virgin)
13	15	EXTREME II PORNOGRAFFITI	Extreme (A&M)
17	16	UNKNOWN TERRITORY	Bomb The Bass (Rhythm King)
-	17	TOUCHED BY JESUS	All About Eve (Vertigo)
16	18	GONNA MAKE YOU SWEAT	C&C Music Factory (Columbia)
19	19	GREATEST HITS	Jam (Polydor)
18	20	GREATEST HITS 1977-1990	Stranglers (Epic)
20	21	MOVE TO THIS	Cathy Dennis (Polydor)
22	22	BAT OUT OF HELL	Meatloaf (Epic)
30	23	ROAD TO FREEDOM	Young Disciples (Talkin' Loud)
14	24	HONEY LINGERS	Voice Of The Beehive (London)
-	25	A LIFE WITH BRIAN	Flowered Up (London)
24	26	LEGEND	Bob Marley & the Wailers (Island)
26	27	REAL LIFE	Simple Minds (Virgin)
21	28	INTO THE GREAT WIDE OPEN	Tom Petty & the Heartbreakers (MCA)
28	29	RECKLESS	Bryan Adams (A&M)
29	30	VAGABOND HEART	Rod Stewart (Warner Bros.)
23	31	MARC COHN	Marc Cohn (Atlantic)
27	32	SPELLBOUND	Paula Abdul (Virgin America)
32	33	JOYRIDE	Roxette (EMI)
-	34	TERMINATOR 2: JUDGEMENT DAY - ORIGINAL SOUNDTRACK	Brad Fiedel (Varese Sarabande)
41	35	SHAKE YOUR MONEY MAKER	Black Crowes (Def American)
25	36	UNFORGETTABLE - WITH LOVE	Natalie Cole (Elektra)
34	37	MAMA SAID	Lenny Kravitz (Virgin America)
35	38	IN CONCERT	Luciano Pavarotti, Placido Domingo and José Carreras (Decca)
-	39	MARTIKA'S KITCHEN	Martika (Columbia)
37	40	ROBIN HOOD - PRINCE OF THIEVES	Soundtrack (Polydor)
31	41	THE WHITE ROOM	KLF (KLF Communications)
33	42	THE ESSENTIAL PAVAROTTI	Luciano Pavarotti (Decca)
-	43	SINGLES	Specials (2 Tone)
44	44	WE ARE IN LOVE	Harry Connick Jr. (CBS)
-	45	SCHUBERT DIP	EMF (Parlophone)
49	46	LOVE AND KISSES	Dannii Minogue (MCA)
39	47	X	INXS (Mercury)
46	48	THE VERY BEST OF ELTON JOHN	Elton John (Rocket)
38	49	HEART IN MOTION	Amy Grant (A&M)
-	50	PLAY	Squeeze (Reprise)

More dramatic contrasts among the top sellers, as heavy metallurgists Metallica took over the Number 1 slot from Pavarotti, only to then surrender it to a musical cast album, in the shape of another Andrew Lloyd Webber success. *Joseph And The Amazing Technicolour Dreamcoat*, featuring Jason Donovan both on West End stage and record, was a revival of Lloyd Webber and Tim Rice's first-ever collaboration.

September 1991

14 September 1991

last week	this week	Title	Artist (Label)
1	1	JOSEPH AND THE AMAZING TECHNICOLOUR DREAMCOAT	Original Cast (Really Useful)
8	2	CMB	Color Me Badd (Giant)
4	3	LOVE HURTS	Cher (Geffen)
5	4	OUT OF TIME	R.E.M. (Warner Bros.)
6	5	SEAL	Seal (ZTT)
-	6	GUARANTEED	Level 42 (Polydor)
2	7	LEISURE	Blur (Food)
3	8	ESSENTIAL PAVAROTTI II	Luciano Pavarotti (Decca)
12	9	GREATEST HITS	Eurythmics (RCA)
-	10	FROM TIME TO TIME	Paul Young (Columbia)
10	11	FELLOW HOODLUMS	Deacon Blue (Columbia)
13	12	THE IMMACULATE COLLECTION	Madonna (Sire)
-	13	ROLL THE BONES	Rush (Atlantic)
-	14	OF THE HEART, OF THE SOUL AND OF THE CROSS: THE UTOPIAN EXPERIENCE	PM Dawn (Gee Street)
-	15	TIN MACHINE II	Tin Machine (London)
14	16	SUGAR TAX	Orchestral Manoeuvres In The Dark (Virgin)
11	17	TIME, LOVE & TENDERNESS	Michael Bolton (Columbia)
22	18	BAT OUT OF HELL	Meatloaf (Epic)
-	19	TIMESPACE - THE BEST OF...	Stevie Nicks (EMI)
9	20	BEVERLY CRAVEN	Beverly Craven (Columbia)
7	21	METALLICA	Metallica (Vertigo)
15	22	EXTREME II PORNOGRAFFITI	Extreme (A&M)
39	23	MARTIKA'S KITCHEN	Martika (Columbia)
17	24	TOUCHED BY JESUS	All About Eve (Vertigo)
43	25	SINGLES	Specials (2 Tone)
-	26	STRANGER IN THIS TOWN	Richie Sambora (Mercury)
18	27	GONNA MAKE YOU SWEAT	C&C Music Factory (Columbia)
20	28	GREATEST HITS 1977-1990	
16	29	UNKNOWN TERRITORY	Bomb The Bass (Rhythm King)
27	30	REAL LIFE	Simple Minds (Virgin)
29	31	RECKLESS	Bryan Adams (A&M)
32	32	SPELLBOUND	Paula Abdul (Virgin America)
19	33	GREATEST HITS	Jam (Polydor)
33	34	JOYRIDE	Roxette (EMI)
-	35	CATFISH RISING	Jethro Tull (Chrysalis)
21	36	MOVE TO THIS	Cathy Dennis (Polydor)
24	37	HONEY LINGERS	Voice Of The Beehive (London)
28	38	INTO THE GREAT WIDE OPEN	Tom Petty & the Heartbreakers (MCA)
30	39	VAGABOND HEART	Rod Stewart (Warner Bros.)
26	40	LEGEND	Bob Marley & the Wailers (Island)
23	41	ROAD TO FREEDOM	Young Disciples (Talkin' Loud)
25	42	A LIFE WITH BRIAN	Flowered Up (London)
-	43	APPETITE FOR DESTRUCTION	Guns N' Roses (Geffen)
35	44	SHAKE YOUR MONEY MAKER	Black Crowes (Def American)
36	45	UNFORGETTABLE - WITH LOVE	Natalie Cole (Elektra)
42	46	THE ESSENTIAL PAVAROTTI	Luciano Pavarotti (Decca)
34	47	TERMINATOR 2: JUDGEMENT DAY - ORIGINAL SOUNDTRACK	Brad Fiedel (Varese Sarabande)
49	48	HEART IN MOTION	Amy Grant (A&M)
48	49	THE VERY BEST OF...	Elton John (Rocket)
-	50	THE SPIRIT	Magnum (Polydor)

21 September 1991

last week	this week	Title	Artist (Label)
-	1	ON EVERY STREET	Dire Straits (Vertigo)
10	2	FROM TIME TO TIME - THE SINGLES COLLECTION	Paul Young (Columbia)
1	3	JOSEPH AND THE AMAZING TECHNICOLOUR DREAMCOAT	Original Cast (Really Useful)
4	4	OUT OF TIME	R.E.M. (Warner Bros.)
6	5	GUARANTEED	Level 42 (Polydor)
2	6	CMB	Color Me Badd (Giant)
3	7	LOVE HURTS	Cher (Geffen)
14	8	OF THE HEART, OF THE SOUL AND OF THE CROSS: THE UTOPIAN EXPERIENCE	PM Dawn (Gee Street)
5	9	SEAL	Seal (ZTT)
-	10	MR. LUCKY	John Lee Hooker (Silvertone)
13	11	ROLL THE BONES	Rush (Atlantic)
-	12	HYMNS TO THE SILENCE	Van Morrison (Polydor)
17	13	TIME, LOVE & TENDERNESS	Michael Bolton (Columbia)
19	14	TIMESPACE - THE BEST OF...	Stevie Nicks (EMI)
25	15	SINGLES	Specials (2 Tone)
12	16	THE IMMACULATE COLLECTION	Madonna (Sire)
11	17	FELLOW HOODLUMS	Deacon Blue (Columbia)
9	18	GREATEST HITS	Eurythmics (RCA)
18	19	BAT OUT OF HELL	Meatloaf (Epic)
16	20	SUGAR TAX	Orchestral Manoeuvres In The Dark (Virgin)
8	21	ESSENTIAL PAVAROTTI II	Luciano Pavarotti (Decca)
7	22	LEISURE	Blur (Food)
26	23	STRANGER IN THIS TOWN	Richie Sambora (Mercury)
24	24	EXTREME II PORNOGRAFFITI	Extreme (A&M)
23	25	MARTIKA'S KITCHEN	Martika (Columbia)
15	26	TIN MACHINE II	Tin Machine (London)
34	27	JOYRIDE	Roxette (EMI)
28	28	GREATEST HITS 1977-1990	Stranglers (Epic)
20	29	BEVERLY CRAVEN	Beverly Craven (Columbia)
31	30	RECKLESS	Bryan Adams (A&M)
-	31	VAGABOND HEART	Rod Stewart (Warner Bros.)
44	32	SHAKE YOUR MONEY MAKER	Black Crowes (Def American)
27	33	GONNA MAKE YOU SWEAT	C&C Music Factory (Columbia)
-	34	METALLICA	Metallica (Vertigo)
35	35	CATFISH RISING	Jethro Tull (Chrysalis)
33	36	GREATEST HITS	Jam (Polydor)
37	37	REAL LIFE	Simple Minds (Virgin)
36	38	MOVE TO THIS	Cathy Dennis (Polydor)
38	39	INTO THE GREAT WIDE OPEN	Tom Petty & the Heartbreakers (MCA)
43	40	APPETITE FOR DESTRUCTION	Guns N' Roses (Geffen)
24	41	TOUCHED BY JESUS	All About Eve (Vertigo)
40	42	LEGEND	Bob Marley & the Wailers (Island)
48	43	HEART IN MOTION	Amy Grant (A&M)
-	44	PSYCHOTIC SUPPER	Tesla (Geffen)
37	45	HONEY LINGERS	Voice Of The Beehive (London)
45	46	UNFORGETTABLE - WITH LOVE	Natalie Cole (Elektra)
46	47	THE ESSENTIAL PAVAROTTI	Luciano Pavarotti (Decca)
-	48	SCHUBERT DIP	EMF (Parlophone)
-	49	THE BIG WHEEL	Runrig (Chrysalis)
-	50	RITUAL OF LOVE	Karyn White (Warner Bros.)

28 September 1991

last week	this week	Title	Artist (Label)
-	1	USE YOUR ILLUSION I	Guns N' Roses (Geffen)
-	2	USE YOUR ILLUSION II	Guns N' Roses (Geffen)
1	3	ON EVERY STREET	Dire Straits (Vertigo)
10	4	MR. LUCKY	John Lee Hooker (Silvertone)
2	5	FROM TIME TO TIME - THE SINGLES COLLECTION	Paul Young (Columbia)
12	6	HYMNS TO THE SILENCE	Van Morrison (Polydor)
-	7	GREATEST HITS	Jason Donovan (PWL)
4	8	OUT OF TIME	R.E.M. (Warner Bros.)
15	9	SINGLES	Specials (2 Tone)
3	10	JOSEPH AND THE AMAZING TECHNICOLOUR DREAMCOAT	Original Cast (Really Useful)
9	11	SEAL	Seal (ZTT)
46	12	UNFORGETTABLE - WITH LOVE	Natalie Cole (Elektra)
13	13	DON'T TRY THIS AT HOME	Billy Bragg (Go! Discs)
14	14	TIMESPACE - THE BEST OF...	Stevie Nicks (EMI)
8	15	OF THE HEART, OF THE SOUL AND OF THE CROSS ...	PM Dawn (Gee Street)
7	16	LOVE HURTS	Cher (Geffen)
6	17	CMB	Color Me Badd (Giant)
-	18	THE ULTIMATE COLLECTION	Marc Bolan & T. Rex (Telstar)
18	19	GREATEST HITS	Eurythmics (RCA)
5	20	GUARANTEED	Level 42 (Polydor)
13	21	TIME, LOVE & TENDERNESS	Michael Bolton (Columbia)
19	22	BAT OUT OF HELL	Meatloaf (Epic)
20	23	SUGAR TAX	Orchestral Manoeuvres In The Dark (Virgin)
25	24	MARTIKA'S KITCHEN	Martika (Columbia)
-	25	PROGENY	Shamen (One Little Indian)
16	26	THE IMMACULATE COLLECTION	Madonna (Sire)
-	27	DON'T GET WEIRD ON ME BABE	Lloyd Cole (Polydor)
-	28	LAUGHING STOCK	Talk Talk (Verve)
24	29	EXTREME II PORNOGRAFFITI	Extreme (A&M)
-	30	NO PLACE LIKE HOME	Big Country (Vertigo)
17	31	FELLOW HOODLUMS	Deacon Blue (Columbia)
27	32	JOYRIDE	Roxette (EMI)
21	33	ESSENTIAL PAVAROTTI II	Luciano Pavarotti (Decca)
28	34	GREATEST HITS 1977-1990	Stranglers (Epic)
29	35	BEVERLY CRAVEN	Beverly Craven (Columbia)
33	36	GONNA MAKE YOU SWEAT	C&C Music Factory (Columbia)
-	37	PURE	Midge Ure (Arista)
30	38	RECKLESS	Bryan Adams (A&M)
-	39	WINGS OF JOY	Cranes (Dedicated)
11	40	ROLL THE BONES	Rush (Atlantic)
22	41	LEISURE	Blur (Food)
-	42	THE BEST OF SPANDAU BALLET	Spandau Ballet (Chrysalis)
34	43	METALLICA	Metallica (Vertigo)
23	44	STRANGER IN THIS TOWN	Richie Sambora (Mercury)
36	45	GREATEST HITS	Jam (Polydor)
26	46	TIN MACHINE II	Tin Machine (London)
50	47	RITUAL OF LOVE	Karyn White (Warner Bros.)
-	48	101 DAMNATIONS	Carter - The Unstoppable Sex Machine (Big Cat)
31	49	VAGABOND HEART	Rod Stewart (Warner Bros.)
32	50	SHAKE YOUR MONEY MAKER	Black Crowes (Def American)

Much was expected of Dire Straits' *On Every Street*, since it was an album many people had never expcted to be made - an official follow-up to 1985's *Brothers In Arms*, now the second-biggest-selling album ever in the UK. In the interim, the group had disbanded, ostensibly for good, then eventually reunited in revised form. The new album sold well, but without the legs to stride the summit for more than a week.

October 1991

Many had scoffed at Guns N' Roses' announcement of two simultaneously-released albums, with the suggestion that the idea was little more than a gimmick, and that the heavy rock group could not muster sufficient strong material to satisfy such a pair of releases. Fans and buyers thought differently, and Axl Rose & Co made history by debuting at Numbers 1 and 2 with the two parts of *Use Your Illusion*.

October – November 1991

last week	this week	26 October 1991	
1	1	STARS	Simply Red (East West)
4	2	SIMPLY THE BEST	Tina Turner (Capitol)
-	3	CHORUS	Erasure (Mute)
3	4	WAKING UP THE NEIGHBOURS	Bryan Adams (A&M)
-	5	VOICES	Kenny Thomas (Cooltempo)
5	6	ON EVERY STREET	Dire Straits (Vertigo)
6	7	FROM TIME TO TIME	Paul Young (Columbia)
2	8	DIAMONDS AND PEARLS	Prince & the New Power Generation (Paisley Park)
18	9	LOOKING BACK	Daryl Hall & John Oates (RCA)
8	10	THE BEST OF R.E.M.	R.E.M. (IRS)
14	11	THE BEST OF ...	Pogues (Pogue Mahone)
-	12	THE GREATEST HITS	Salt 'n' Pepa (ffrr)
7	13	USE YOUR ILLUSION II	Guns N' Roses (Geffen)
15	14	OUT OF TIME	R.E.M. (Warner Bros.)
-	15	LIVE YOUR LIFE BE FREE	Belinda Carlisle (Virgin)
9	16	USE YOUR ILLUSION I	Guns N' Roses (Geffen)
-	17	HIS GREATEST HITS	David Essex (Mercury)
-	18	TWO ROOMS - CELEBRATING THE SONGS OF ELTON JOHN AND BERNIE TAUPIN	Various (Mercury)
10	19	APOCALYPSE '91 ... THE ENEMY STRIKES BLACK	Public Enemy (Def Jam)
-	20	LET'S GET TO IT	Kylie Minogue (PWL)
11	21	THE ULTIMATE COLLECTION	Marc Bolan & T. Rex (Telstar)
-	22	EMOTIONS	Mariah Carey (Columbia)
49	23	LEVELLING THE LAND	Levellers (China)
-	24	TENEMENT SYMPHONY - GRIT AND GLITTER	Marc Almond (Some Bizzare)
-	25	BLUE LIGHT, RED LIGHT	Harry Connick Jr. (Columbia)
16	26	NO MORE TEARS	Ozzy Osbourne (Epic)
26	27	GREATEST HITS	Eurythmics (RCA)
-	28	24 NIGHTS	Eric Clapton (Duck)
12	29	MR. LUCKY	John Lee Hooker (Silvertone)
-	30	IMAGES	Jean-Michel Jarre (Dreyfus)
19	31	LOVE HURTS	Cher (Geffen)
21	32	DECADE OF DECADENCE '81-'91	Motley Crue (Elektra)
34	33	THE IMMACULATE COLLECTION	Madonna (Sire)
42	34	MOVE TO THIS	Cathy Dennis (Polydor)
-	35	PAUL MCCARTNEY'S LIVERPOOL ORATORIO	Carl Davis & the Royal Liverpool Philharmonic Orchestra (EMI Classics)
13	36	TROMPE LE MONDE	Pixies (4AD)
20	37	ROCK 'TIL YOU DROP	Status Quo (Vertigo)
-	38	SONIA	Sonia (IQ)
25	39	GREATEST HITS	Jason Donovan (PWL)
27	40	TIME, LOVE & TENDERNESS	Michael Bolton (Columbia)
29	41	BAT OUT OF HELL	Meatloaf (Epic)
17	42	SCREAMADELICA	Primal Scream (Creation)
35	43	JOSEPH AND THE AMAZING TECHNICOLOUR DREAMCOAT	Original Cast (Really Useful)
41	44	FELLOW HOODLUMS	Deacon Blue (Columbia)
31	45	SEAL	Seal (ZTT)
45	46	SINGLES	Specials (2 Tone)
36	47	CMB	Color Me Badd (Giant)
-	48	JOYRIDE	Roxette (EMI)
32	49	BEVERLY CRAVEN	Beverly Craven (Columbia)
-	50	MIDNIGHT MOODS - THE LOVE COLLECTION	George Benson (Telstar)

last week	this week	2 November 1991	
3	1	CHORUS	Erasure (Mute)
1	2	STARS	Simply Red (East West)
5	3	VOICES	Kenny Thomas (Cooltempo)
4	4	WAKING UP THE NEIGHBOURS	Bryan Adams (A&M)
2	5	SIMPLY THE BEST	Tina Turner (Capitol)
15	6	LIVE YOUR LIFE BE FREE	Belinda Carlisle (Virgin)
22	7	EMOTIONS	Mariah Carey (Columbia)
18	8	TWO ROOMS - CELEBRATING THE SONGS OF ELTON JOHN AND BERNIE TAUPIN	Various (Mercury)
7	9	FROM TIME TO TIME - THE SINGLES COLLECTION	Paul Young (Columbia)
8	10	DIAMONDS AND PEARLS	Prince & the New Power Generation (Paisley Park)
-	11	THE COMMITMENTS	Commitments (MCA)
9	12	THE BEST OF DARYL HALL & JOHN OATES - LOOKING BACK	Daryl Hall & John Oates (RCA)
-	13	WELD	Neil Young & Crazy Horse (Reprise)
6	14	ON EVERY STREET	Dire Straits (Vertigo)
30	15	IMAGES	Jean-Michel Jarre (Dreyfus)
25	16	BLUE LIGHT, RED LIGHT	Harry Connick Jr. (Columbia)
28	17	24 NIGHTS	Eric Clapton (Duck)
12	18	THE GREATEST HITS	Salt 'n' Pepa (ffrr)
13	19	USE YOUR ILLUSION II	Guns N' Roses (Geffen)
20	20	LET'S GET TO IT	Kylie Minogue (PWL)
21	21	THE ULTIMATE COLLECTION	Marc Bolan & T. Rex (Telstar)
10	22	THE BEST OF R.E.M.	R.E.M. (IRS)
11	23	THE BEST OF	Pogues (Pogue Mahone)
17	24	HIS GREATEST HITS	David Essex (Mercury)
14	25	OUT OF TIME	R.E.M. (Warner Bros.)
31	26	LOVE HURTS	Cher (Geffen)
34	27	MOVE TO THIS	Cathy Dennis (Polydor)
27	28	GREATEST HITS	Eurythmics (RCA)
29	29	MR. LUCKY	John Lee Hooker (Silvertone)
16	30	USE YOUR ILLUSION I	Guns N' Roses (Geffen)
40	31	TIME, LOVE & TENDERNESS	Michael Bolton (Columbia)
33	32	THE IMMACULATE COLLECTION	Madonna (Sire)
49	33	BEVERLY CRAVEN	Beverly Craven (Columbia)
-	34	DECADE OF AGGRESSION LIVE	Slayer (Def American)
19	35	APOCALYPSE '91 ... THE ENEMY STRIKES BLACK	Public Enemy (Def Jam)
-	36	FOXBASE ALPHA	Saint Etienne (Heavenly)
-	37	WORLD IN UNION	Union (Columbia)
-	38	TOO LEGIT TO QUIT	Hammer (Capitol)
-	39	CRAZY WORLD	Scorpions (Vertigo)
24	40	TENEMENT SYMPHONY - GRIT AND GLITTER	Marc Almond (Some Bizzare)
-	41	SWEPT	Julia Fordham (Circa)
23	42	LEVELLING THE LAND	Levellers (China)
41	43	BAT OUT OF HELL	Meatloaf (Epic)
37	44	ROCK 'TIL YOU DROP	Status Quo (Vertigo)
-	45	SUGAR TAX	Orchestral Manoeuvres In The Dark (Virgin)
46	46	SEAL	Seal (ZTT)
26	47	NO MORE TEARS	Ozzy Osbourne (Epic)
-	48	THIS IS THE WORLD	River City People (EMI)
-	49	WATERMARK	Enya (WEA)
44	50	FELLOW HOODLUMS	Deacon Blue (Columbia)

last week	this week	9 November 1991	
-	1	GREATEST HITS II	Queen (Parlophone)
2	2	STARS	Simply Red (East West)
3	3	VOICES	Kenny Thomas (Cooltempo)
5	4	SIMPLY THE BEST	Tina Turner (Capitol)
1	5	CHORUS	Erasure (Mute)
4	6	WAKING UP THE NEIGHBOURS	Bryan Adams (A&M)
7	7	THE COMMITMENTS	Commitments (MCA)
9	8	FROM TIME TO TIME	Paul Young (Columbia)
7	9	EMOTIONS	Mariah Carey (Columbia)
10	10	DIAMONDS AND PEARLS	Prince & the New Power Generation (Paisley Park)
8	11	TWO ROOMS - CELEBRATING THE SONGS OF ELTON JOHN AND BERNIE TAUPIN	Various (Mercury)
-	12	INTERNAL EXILE	Fish (Polydor)
15	13	IMAGES	Jean-Michel Jarre (Dreyfus)
14	14	ON EVERY STREET	Dire Straits (Vertigo)
13	15	WELD	Neil Young & Crazy Horse (Reprise)
6	16	LIVE YOUR LIFE BE FREE	Belinda Carlisle (Virgin)
24	17	HIS GREATEST HITS	David Essex (Mercury)
12	18	THE BEST OF DARYL HALL & JOHN OATES - LOOKING BACK	Daryl Hall & John Oates (RCA)
26	19	LOVE HURTS	Cher (Geffen)
-	20	TIMELESS - THE VERY BEST OF NEIL SEDAKA	Neil Sedaka (Flying Music/Polydor)
31	21	TIME, LOVE & TENDERNESS	Michael Bolton (Columbia)
18	22	THE GREATEST HITS	Salt 'n' Pepa (ffrr)
20	23	LET'S GET TO IT	Kylie Minogue (PWL)
21	24	THE ULTIMATE COLLECTION	Marc Bolan & T. Rex (Telstar)
27	25	MOVE TO THIS	Cathy Dennis (Polydor)
16	26	BLUE LIGHT, RED LIGHT	Harry Connick Jr. (Columbia)
37	27	WORLD IN UNION	Union (Columbia)
19	28	USE YOUR ILLUSION II	Guns N' Roses (Geffen)
22	29	THE BEST OF R.E.M.	R.E.M. (IRS)
39	30	CRAZY WORLD	Scorpions (Vertigo)
33	31	BEVERLY CRAVEN	Beverly Craven (Columbia)
34	32	DECADE OF AGGRESSION LIVE	Slayer (Def American)
28	33	GREATEST HITS	Eurythmics (RCA)
25	34	OUT OF TIME	R.E.M. (Warner Bros.)
23	35	24 NIGHTS	Eric Clapton (Duck)
23	36	THE BEST OF THE POGUES	Pogues (Pogue Mahone)
30	37	USE YOUR ILLUSION I	Guns N' Roses (Geffen)
32	38	THE IMMACULATE COLLECTION	Madonna (Sire)
-	39	BEST OF ME	Maxi Priest (10)
46	40	SEAL	Seal (ZTT)
29	41	MR. LUCKY	John Lee Hooker (Silvertone)
43	42	BAT OUT OF HELL	Meatloaf (Epic)
38	43	TOO LEGIT TO QUIT	Hammer (Capitol)
35	44	APOCALYPSE '91 ... THE ENEMY STRIKES BLACK	Public Enemy (Def Jam)
42	45	LEVELLING THE LAND	Levellers (China)
36	46	FOXBASE ALPHA	Saint Etienne (Heavenly)
45	47	SUGAR TAX	Orchestral Manoeuvres In The Dark (Virgin)
43	48	FELLOW HOODLUMS	Deacon Blue (Columbia)
49	49	WATERMARK	Enya (WEA)
-	50	MIDNIGHT MOODS - THE LOVE COLLECTION	George Benson (Telstar)

Simply Red's *Stars* was destined to outstrip even the group's one-and-a-half million-selling *A New Flame*, to become their most successful recording to date and take up what seemed like almost permanent residence close to the top end of the chart. Meanwhile, the *Two Rooms* compilation, which escaped the "Various Artists" exclusion rule because of its thematic approach, featured Elton John/Bernie Taupin classics.

November 1991

16 November 1991

last	this	Album	Artist (Label)
-	1	SHEPHERD MOONS	Enya (WEA)
-	2	DISCOGRAPHY - THE COMPLETE SINGLES COLLECTION	Pet Shop Boys (Parlophone)
1	3	GREATEST HITS II	Queen (Parlophone)
2	4	STARS	Simply Red (East West)
4	5	SIMPLY THE BEST	Tina Turner (Capitol)
7	6	THE COMMITMENTS	Commitments (MCA)
-	7	LIVE BABY LIVE	INXS (Mercury)
8	8	FROM TIME TO TIME	Paul Young (Columbia)
3	9	VOICES	Kenny Thomas (Cooltempo)
6	10	WAKING UP THE NEIGHBOURS	Bryan Adams (A&M)
5	11	CHORUS	Erasure (Mute)
9	12	EMOTIONS	Mariah Carey (Columbia)
10	13	DIAMONDS AND PEARLS	Prince & the New Power Generation (Paisley Park)
19	14	LOVE HURTS	Cher (Geffen)
20	15	TIMELESS	Neil Sedaka (Flying Music/Polydor)
13	16	IMAGES	Jean-Michel Jarre (Dreyfus)
14	17	ON EVERY STREET	Dire Straits (Vertigo)
11	18	TWO ROOMS - CELEBRATING THE SONGS OF ELTON JOHN AND BERNIE TAUPIN	Various (Mercury)
-	19	HEADLINES AND DEADLINES - THE HITS OF A-HA	A-ha (Warner Bros.)
18	20	THE BEST OF DARYL HALL & JOHN OATES - LOOKING BACK	Daryl Hall & John Oates (RCA)
27	21	WORLD IN UNION	Union (Columbia)
50	22	MIDNIGHT MOODS - THE LOVE COLLECTION	George Benson (Telstar)
16	23	LIVE YOUR LIFE BE FREE	Belinda Carlisle (Virgin)
22	24	THE GREATEST HITS	Salt 'n' Pepa (ffrr)
17	25	HIS GREATEST HITS	David Essex (Mercury)
21	26	TIME, LOVE & TENDERNESS	Michael Bolton (Columbia)
-	27	I WILL CURE YOU	Vic Reeves (Sense)
12	28	INTERNAL EXILE	Fish (Polydor)
-	29	BANDWAGONESQUE	Teenage Fanclub (Creation)
-	30	CMB	Color Me Badd (Giant)
33	31	GREATEST HITS	Eurythmics (RCA)
34	32	OUT OF TIME	R.E.M. (Warner Bros.)
-	33	MEMORIES	Foster & Allen (Telstar)
40	34	SEAL	Seal (ZTT)
-	35	TOGETHER AT LAST	Richard Clayderman & James Last (Delphine)
23	36	LET'S GET TO IT	Kylie Minogue (PWL)
-	37	THE VERY BEST OF DANIEL O'DONNELL	Daniel O'Donnell (Ritz)
24	38	THE ULTIMATE COLLECTION	Marc Bolan & T. Rex (Telstar)
28	39	USE YOUR ILLUSION II	Guns N' Roses (Geffen)
39	40	BEST OF ME	Maxi Priest (10)
29	41	THE BEST OF R.E.M.	R.E.M. (IRS)
15	42	WELD	Neil Young & Crazy Horse (Reprise)
31	43	BEVERLY CRAVEN	Beverly Craven (Columbia)
25	44	MOVE TO THIS	Cathy Dennis (Polydor)
26	45	BLUE LIGHT, RED LIGHT	Harry Connick Jr. (Columbia)
-	46	THE SINGLES	Clash (Columbia)
36	47	THE BEST OF THE POGUES	Pogues (Pogue Mahone)
30	48	CRAZY WORLD	Scorpions (Vertigo)
37	49	USE YOUR ILLUSION I	Guns N' Roses (Geffen)
35	50	24 NIGHTS	Eric Clapton (Duck)

23 November 1991

last	this	Album	Artist (Label)
-	1	WE CAN'T DANCE	Genesis (Virgin)
1	2	SHEPHERD MOONS	Enya (WEA)
3	3	GREATEST HITS II	Queen (Parlophone)
2	4	DISCOGRAPHY - THE COMPLETE SINGLES COLLECTION	Pet Shop Boys (Parlophone)
-	5	REAL LOVE	Lisa Stansfield (Arista)
4	6	STARS	Simply Red (East West)
6	7	THE COMMITMENTS	Commitments (MCA)
8	8	FROM TIME TO TIME	Paul Young (Columbia)
7	10	LIVE BABY LIVE	INXS (Mercury)
10	11	WAKING UP THE NEIGHBOURS	Bryan Adams (A&M)
9	12	VOICES	Kenny Thomas (Cooltempo)
15	13	TIMELESS	Neil Sedaka (Flying Music/Polydor)
19	14	HEADLINES AND DEADLINES - THE HITS OF A-HA	A-ha (Warner Bros.)
-	15	LOVELESS	My Bloody Valentine (Creation)
16	16	CHORUS	Erasure (Mute)
17	17	IMAGES	Jean-Michel Jarre (Dreyfus)
27	18	I WILL CURE YOU	Vic Reeves (Sense)
13	19	DIAMONDS AND PEARLS	Prince & the New Power Generation (Paisley Park)
26	20	TIME, LOVE & TENDERNESS	Michael Bolton (Columbia)
14	21	LOVE HURTS	Cher (Geffen)
12	22	EMOTIONS	Mariah Carey (Columbia)
33	23	MEMORIES	Foster & Allen (Telstar)
29	24	BANDWAGONESQUE	Teenage Fanclub (Creation)
-	25	SEX MACHINE - THE VERY BEST OF JAMES BROWN	James Brown (Polydor)
22	26	MIDNIGHT MOODS - THE LOVE COLLECTION	George Benson (Telstar)
18	27	TWO ROOMS - CELEBRATING THE SONGS OF ELTON JOHN AND BERNIE TAUPIN	Various (Mercury)
34	28	SEAL	Seal (ZTT)
17	29	ON EVERY STREET	Dire Straits (Vertigo)
-	30	THE CONCERT IN THE PARK - AUGUST 15TH 1991	Paul Simon (Warner Bros.)
23	31	LIVE YOUR LIFE BE FREE	Belinda Carlisle (Virgin)
20	32	THE BEST OF DARYL HALL & JOHN OATES - LOOKING BACK	Daryl Hall & John Oates (RCA)
-	33	WALL OF HITS	Slade (Polydor)
35	34	TOGETHER AT LAST	Richard Clayderman & James Last (Delphine)
43	35	BEVERLY CRAVEN	Beverly Craven (Columbia)
-	36	THEMES AND DREAMS	Shadows (Polydor)
32	37	THE GREATEST HITS	Salt 'n' Pepa (ffrr)
30	38	OUT OF TIME	R.E.M. (Warner Bros.)
25	39	CMB	Color Me Badd (Giant)
25	40	HIS GREATEST HITS	David Essex (Mercury)
31	41	GREATEST HITS	Eurythmics (RCA)
41	42	THE BEST OF R.E.M.	R.E.M. (IRS)
37	43	THE VERY BEST OF DANIEL O'DONNELL	Daniel O'Donnell (Ritz)
40	44	BEST OF ME	Maxi Priest (10)
-	45	LOVESCAPE	Neil Diamond (Columbia)
46	46	WORLD IN UNION	Union (Columbia)
39	47	USE YOUR ILLUSION II	Guns N' Roses (Geffen)
-	48	THE UNFORGETTABLE NAT 'KING' COLE	Nat King Cole (EMI)
-	49	EXTREME II PORNOGRAFFITI	Extreme (A&M)
-	50	THE IMMACULATE COLLECTION	Madonna (Sire)

30 November 1991

last	this	Album	Artist (Label)
-	1	ACHTUNG BABY	U2 (Island)
1	2	WE CAN'T DANCE	Genesis (Virgin)
2	3	SHEPHERD MOONS	Enya (WEA)
3	4	GREATEST HITS II	Queen (Parlophone)
6	5	STARS	Simply Red (East West)
5	6	REAL LOVE	Lisa Stansfield (Arista)
8	7	FROM TIME TO TIME	Paul Young (Columbia)
4	8	DISCOGRAPHY - THE COMPLETE SINGLES COLLECTION	Pet Shop Boys (Parlophone)
9	9	SIMPLY THE BEST	Tina Turner (Capitol)
7	10	THE COMMITMENTS	Commitments (MCA)
20	11	TIME, LOVE & TENDERNESS	Michael Bolton (Columbia)
11	12	WAKING UP THE NEIGHBOURS	Bryan Adams (A&M)
12	13	VOICES	Kenny Thomas (Cooltempo)
-	14	DANGEROUS	Michael Jackson (Epic)
28	15	SEAL	Seal (ZTT)
-	16	TOGETHER WITH CLIFF RICHARD	Cliff Richard (EMI)
16	17	CHORUS	Erasure (Mute)
13	18	TIMELESS	Neil Sedaka (Flying Music/Polydor)
23	19	MEMORIES	Foster & Allen (Telstar)
10	20	LIVE BABY LIVE	INXS (Mercury)
19	21	DIAMONDS AND PEARLS	Prince & the New Power Generation (Paisley Park)
27	22	TWO ROOMS - CELEBRATING THE SONGS OF ELTON JOHN AND BERNIE TAUPIN	Various (Mercury)
-	23	THE DEFINITIVE SIMON AND GARFUNKEL	Simon & Garfunkel (Columbia)
34	24	TOGETHER AT LAST	Richard Clayderman & James Last (Delphine)
29	25	ON EVERY STREET	Dire Straits (Vertigo)
33	26	WALL OF HITS	Slade (Polydor)
25	27	SEX MACHINE - THE VERY BEST OF JAMES BROWN	James Brown (Polydor)
35	28	BEVERLY CRAVEN	Beverly Craven (Columbia)
14	29	HEADLINES AND DEADLINES - THE HITS OF A-HA	A-ha (Warner Bros.)
37	30	THE GREATEST HITS	Salt 'n' Pepa (ffrr)
21	31	LOVE HURTS	Cher (Geffen)
15	32	LOVELESS	My Bloody Valentine (Creation)
38	33	OUT OF TIME	R.E.M. (Warner Bros.)
32	34	THE BEST OF DARYL HALL & JOHN OATES - LOOKING BACK	Daryl Hall & John Oates (RCA)
41	35	GREATEST HITS	Eurythmics (RCA)
36	36	THEMES AND DREAMS	Shadows (Polydor)
31	37	LIVE YOUR LIFE BE FREE	Belinda Carlisle (Virgin)
40	38	HIS GREATEST HITS	David Essex (Mercury)
49	39	EXTREME II PORNOGRAFFITI	Extreme (A&M)
48	40	THE UNFORGETTABLE..	Nat King Cole (EMI)
17	41	IMAGES	Jean-Michel Jarre (Dreyfus)
22	42	EMOTIONS	Mariah Carey (Columbia)
39	43	CMB	Color Me Badd (Giant)
26	44	MIDNIGHT MOODS - THE LOVE COLLECTION	George Benson (Telstar)
30	45	THE CONCERT IN THE PARK - AUGUST 15TH 1991	Paul Simon (Warner Bros.)
18	46	I WILL CURE YOU	Vic Reeves (Sense)
44	47	BEST OF ME	Maxi Priest (10)
50	48	THE IMMACULATE COLLECTION	Madonna (Sire)
-	49	NEVERMIND	Nirvana (DGC)
47	50	USE YOUR ILLUSION II	Guns N' Roses (Geffen)

Major names weighed in with a vengeance for a share of the lucrative 1991 pre-Christmas market, arriving on the chart at a rate of one or two a week with a new album or compilation, and generally denying each other more than a week's peace at Number 1 before abrupt removal. Hence, Queen, Enya, Genesis, U2 and Michael Jackson all topped the chart in possibly the most rapid star-studded succession ever.

December 1991

7 December 1991

last week	this week	title	artist
14	1	DANGEROUS	Michael Jackson (Epic)
4	2	GREATEST HITS II	Queen (Parlophone)
1	3	ACHTUNG BABY	U2 (Island)
5	4	STARS	Simply Red (East West)
2	5	WE CAN'T DANCE	Genesis (Virgin)
9	6	SIMPLY THE BEST	Tina Turner (Capitol)
11	7	TIME, LOVE & TENDERNESS	Michael Bolton (Columbia)
3	8	SHEPHERD MOONS	Enya (WEA)
7	9	FROM TIME TO TIME	Paul Young (Columbia)
16	10	TOGETHER WITH CLIFF RICHARD	Cliff Richard (EMI)
10	11	THE COMMITMENTS	Commitments (MCA)
6	12	REAL LOVE	Lisa Stansfield (Arista)
8	13	DISCOGRAPHY - THE COMPLETE SINGLES COLLECTION	Pet Shop Boys (Parlophone)
15	14	SEAL	Seal (ZTT)
12	15	WAKING UP THE NEIGHBOURS	Bryan Adams (A&M)
23	16	THE DEFINITIVE SIMON AND GARFUNKEL	Simon & Garfunkel (Columbia)
-	17	GREATEST HITS	Queen (EMI)
17	18	CHORUS	Erasure (Mute)
13	19	VOICES	Kenny Thomas (Cooltempo)
18	20	TIMELESS	Neil Sedaka (Flying Music/Polydor)
22	21	TWO ROOMS - CELEBRATING THE SONGS OF ELTON JOHN AND BERNIE TAUPIN	Various (Mercury)
28	22	BEVERLY CRAVEN	Beverly Craven (Columbia)
19	23	MEMORIES	Foster & Allen (Telstar)
21	24	DIAMONDS AND PEARLS	Prince & the New Power Generation (Paisley Park)
24	25	TOGETHER AT LAST	Richard Clayderman & James Last (Delphine)
25	26	ON EVERY STREET	Dire Straits (Vertigo)
35	27	GREATEST HITS	Eurythmics (RCA)
30	28	THE GREATEST HITS	Salt 'n' Pepa (ffrr)
40	29	THE UNFORGETTABLE ...	Nat King Cole (EMI)
33	30	OUT OF TIME	R.E.M. (Warner Bros.)
31	31	LOVE HURTS	Cher (Geffen)
36	32	THEMES AND DREAMS	Shadows (Polydor)
49	33	NEVERMIND	Nirvana (DGC)
38	34	HIS GREATEST HITS	David Essex (Mercury)
37	35	LIVE YOUR LIFE BE FREE	Belinda Carlisle (Virgin)
20	36	LIVE BABY LIVE	INXS (Mercury)
27	37	SEX MACHINE - THE VERY BEST OF JAMES BROWN	James Brown (Polydor)
39	38	EXTREME II PORNOGRAFFITI	Extreme (A&M)
29	39	HEADLINES AND DEADLINES - THE HITS OF A-HA	A-ha (Warner Bros.)
34	40	THE BEST OF DARYL HALL & JOHN OATES - LOOKING BACK	Daryl Hall & John Oates (RCA)
-	41	MICHAEL CRAWFORD PERFORMS ANDREW LLOYD WEBBER	Michael Crawford (Telstar)
48	42	THE IMMACULATE COLLECTION	Madonna (Sire)
41	43	IMAGES	Jean-Michel Jarre (Dreyfus)
43	44	CMB	Color Me Badd (Giant)
42	45	EMOTIONS	Mariah Carey (Columbia)
44	46	MIDNIGHT MOODS - THE LOVE COLLECTION	George Benson (Telstar)
-	47	INNUENDO	Queen (Parlophone)
46	48	I WILL CURE YOU	Vic Reeves (Sense)
-	49	ESSENTIAL PAVAROTTI II	Luciano Pavarotti (Decca)
50	50	USE YOUR ILLUSION II	Guns N' Roses (Geffen)

14 December 1991

last week	this week	title	artist
2	1	GREATEST HITS II	Queen (Parlophone)
1	2	DANGEROUS	Michael Jackson (Epic)
4	3	STARS	Simply Red (East West)
17	4	GREATEST HITS	Queen (EMI)
3	5	ACHTUNG BABY	U2 (Island)
5	6	WE CAN'T DANCE	Genesis (Virgin)
7	7	TIME, LOVE & TENDERNESS	Michael Bolton (Columbia)
6	8	SIMPLY THE BEST	Tina Turner (Capitol)
9	9	FROM TIME TO TIME	Paul Young (Columbia)
8	10	SHEPHERD MOONS	Enya (WEA)
12	11	REAL LOVE	Lisa Stansfield (Arista)
16	12	THE DEFINITIVE SIMON AND GARFUNKEL	Simon & Garfunkel (Columbia)
10	13	TOGETHER WITH CLIFF RICHARD	Cliff Richard (EMI)
14	14	DISCOGRAPHY - THE COMPLETE SINGLES COLLECTION	Pet Shop Boys (Parlophone)
47	15	INNUENDO	Queen (Parlophone)
21	16	TWO ROOMS - CELEBRATING THE SONGS OF ELTON JOHN AND BERNIE TAUPIN	Various (Mercury)
19	17	VOICES	Kenny Thomas (Cooltempo)
11	18	THE COMMITMENTS	Commitments (MCA)
15	19	WAKING UP THE NEIGHBOURS	Bryan Adams (A&M)
18	20	CHORUS	Erasure (Mute)
33	21	NEVERMIND	Nirvana (DGC)
14	22	SEAL	Seal (ZTT)
30	23	OUT OF TIME	R.E.M. (Warner Bros.)
25	24	TOGETHER AT LAST	Richard Clayderman & James Last (Delphine)
20	25	TIMELESS	Neil Sedaka (Flying Music/Polydor)
24	26	DIAMONDS AND PEARLS	Prince & the New Power Generation (Paisley Park)
26	27	ON EVERY STREET	Dire Straits (Vertigo)
22	28	BEVERLY CRAVEN	Beverly Craven (Columbia)
41	29	MICHAEL CRAWFORD PERFORMS ANDREW LLOYD WEBBER	Michael Crawford (Telstar)
-	30	SWALLOW THIS LIVE	Poison (Capitol)
-	31	THE FORCE BEHIND THE POWER	Diana Ross (EMI)
29	32	THE UNFORGETTABLE...	Nat King Cole (EMI)
27	33	GREATEST HITS	Eurythmics (RCA)
31	34	LOVE HURTS	Cher (Geffen)
23	35	MEMORIES	Foster & Allen (Telstar)
28	36	THE GREATEST HITS	Salt 'n' Pepa (ffrr)
32	37	THEMES AND DREAMS	Shadows (Polydor)
37	38	SEX MACHINE - THE VERY BEST OF JAMES BROWN	James Brown (Polydor)
38	39	EXTREME II PORNOGRAFFITI	Extreme (A&M)
34	40	HIS GREATEST HITS	David Essex (Mercury)
42	41	THE IMMACULATE COLLECTION	Madonna (Sire)
46	42	MIDNIGHT MOODS - THE LOVE COLLECTION	George Benson (Telstar)
-	43	JOSEPH AND THE AMAZING TECHNICOLOUR DREAMCOAT	Original Cast (Really Useful)
-	44	AUBERGE	Chris Rea (East West)
45	45	MOVE TO THIS	Cathy Dennis (Polydor)
44	46	LIVE YOUR LIFE BE FREE	Belinda Carlisle (Virgin)
44	47	CMB	Color Me Badd (Giant)
-	48	THE VERY BEST OF DANIEL O'DONNELL	Daniel O'Donnell (Ritz)
49	49	ESSENTIAL PAVAROTTI II	Luciano Pavarotti (Decca)
36	50	LIVE BABY LIVE	INXS (Mercury)

21 December 1991

last week	this week	title	artist
1	1	GREATEST HITS II	Queen (Parlophone)
3	2	STARS	Simply Red (East West)
4	3	GREATEST HITS	Queen (EMI)
2	4	DANGEROUS	Michael Jackson (Epic)
29	5	MICHAEL CRAWFORD PERFORMS ANDREW LLOYD WEBBER	Michael Crawford (Telstar)
8	6	SIMPLY THE BEST	Tina Turner (Capitol)
7	7	TIME, LOVE & TENDERNESS	Michael Bolton (Columbia)
31	8	THE FORCE BEHIND THE POWER	Diana Ross (EMI)
6	9	WE CAN'T DANCE	Genesis (Virgin)
5	10	ACHTUNG BABY	U2 (Island)
11	11	SHEPHERD MOONS	Enya (WEA)
13	12	TOGETHER WITH CLIFF RICHARD	Cliff Richard (EMI)
12	13	THE DEFINITIVE SIMON AND GARFUNKEL	Simon & Garfunkel (Columbia)
9	14	FROM TIME TO TIME	Paul Young (Columbia)
16	15	TWO ROOMS - CELEBRATING THE SONGS OF ELTON JOHN AND BERNIE TAUPIN	Various (Mercury)
17	16	VOICES	Kenny Thomas (Cooltempo)
11	17	REAL LOVE	Lisa Stansfield (Arista)
18	18	THE COMMITMENTS	Commitments (MCA)
14	19	DISCOGRAPHY - THE COMPLETE SINGLES COLLECTION	Pet Shop Boys (Parlophone)
24	20	TOGETHER AT LAST	Richard Clayderman & James Last (Delphine)
19	21	WAKING UP THE NEIGHBOURS	Bryan Adams (A&M)
23	22	OUT OF TIME	R.E.M. (Warner Bros.)
25	23	TIMELESS	Neil Sedaka (Flying Music/Polydor)
28	24	BEVERLY CRAVEN	Beverly Craven (Columbia)
21	25	NEVERMIND	Nirvana (DGC)
20	26	CHORUS	Erasure (Mute)
27	27	LOVE HURTS	Cher (Geffen)
15	28	INNUENDO	Queen (Parlophone)
27	29	ON EVERY STREET	Dire Straits (Vertigo)
35	30	MEMORIES	Foster & Allen (Telstar)
-	31	H.I.T.S.	New Kids On The Block (CBS)
36	32	THE GREATEST HITS	Salt 'n' Pepa (ffrr)
43	33	SEAL	Seal (ZTT)
43	34	JOSEPH AND THE AMAZING TECHNICOLOUR DREAMCOAT	Original Cast (Really Useful)
33	35	GREATEST HITS	Eurythmics (RCA)
32	36	THE UNFORGETTABLE...	Nat King Cole (EMI)
37	37	THEMES AND DREAMS	Shadows (Polydor)
26	38	DIAMONDS AND PEARLS	Prince & the New Power Generation (Paisley Park)
41	39	THE IMMACULATE COLLECTION	Madonna (Sire)
48	40	THE VERY BEST OF DANIEL O'DONNELL	Daniel O'Donnell (Ritz)
39	41	EXTREME II PORNOGRAFFITI	Extreme (A&M)
46	42	LIVE YOUR LIFE BE FREE	Belinda Carlisle (Virgin)
40	43	HIS GREATEST HITS	David Essex (Mercury)
49	44	ESSENTIAL PAVAROTTI II	Luciano Pavarotti (Decca)
-	45	THE VERY BEST OF...	Elton John (Rocket)
45	46	MOVE TO THIS	Cathy Dennis (Polydor)
-	47	USE YOUR ILLUSION I	Guns N' Roses (Geffen)
-	48	JOYRIDE	Roxette (EMI)
44	49	AUBERGE	Chris Rea (East West)
-	50	THE BEST OF DARYL HALL & JOHN OATES - LOOKING BACK	Daryl Hall & John Oates (RCA)

A significant and tragic event towards the end of the year was the death of Queen's Freddie Mercury. Inevitably, the magnitude of this loss to the music world sent the sales of Queen material into orbit, putting their recently-issued *Greatest Hits II* set back at Number 1, the original *Greatest Hits* (now approaching 3 million sales) close behind it, and the reissued *Bohemian Rhapsody* atop the singles chart.

January 1992

11 January 1992

last week	this week		
2	1	STARS	Simply Red (East West)
1	2	GREATEST HITS II	Queen (Parlophone)
6	3	SIMPLY THE BEST	Tina Turner (Capitol)
4	4	DANGEROUS	Michael Jackson (Epic)
17	5	REAL LOVE	Lisa Stansfield (Arista)
10	6	ACHTUNG BABY	U2 (Island)
7	7	TIME, LOVE & TENDERNESS	Michael Bolton (Columbia)
5	8	MICHAEL CRAWFORD PERFORMS ANDREW LLOYD WEBBER	Michael Crawford (Telstar)
13	9	THE DEFINITIVE SIMON AND GARFUNKEL	Simon & Garfunkel (Columbia)
9	10	WE CAN'T DANCE	Genesis (Virgin)
3	11	GREATEST HITS	Queen (EMI)
11	12	SHEPHERD MOONS	Enya (WEA)
14	13	FROM TIME TO TIME	Paul Young (Columbia)
8	14	THE FORCE BEHIND THE POWER	Diana Ross (EMI)
16	15	VOICES	Kenny Thomas (Cooltempo)
21	16	WAKING UP THE NEIGHBOURS	Bryan Adams (A&M)
38	17	DIAMONDS AND PEARLS	Prince & the New Power Generation (Paisley Park)
15	18	TWO ROOMS - CELEBRATING THE SONGS OF ELTON JOHN AND BERNIE TAUPIN	Various Artists (Mercury)
22	19	OUT OF TIME	R.E.M. (Warner Bros.)
12	20	TOGETHER WITH CLIFF RICHARD	Cliff Richard (EMI)
19	21	DISCOGRAPHY - THE COMPLETE SINGLES COLLECTION	Pet Shop Boys (Parlophone)
26	22	CHORUS	Erasure (Mute)
34	23	JOSEPH AND THE AMAZING TECHNICOLOUR DREAMCOAT	Original Cast (Really Useful)
27	24	LOVE HURTS	Cher (Geffen)
29	25	ON EVERY STREET	Dire Straits (Vertigo)
33	26	SEAL	Seal (ZTT)
32	27	THE GREATEST HITS	Salt 'n' Pepa (ffrr)
25	28	NEVERMIND	Nirvana (DGC)
45	29	THE VERY BEST OF...	Elton John (Rocket)
18	30	THE COMMITMENTS	Commitments (MCA)
24	31	BEVERLEY CRAVEN	Beverley Craven (Epic)
35	32	GREATEST HITS	Eurythmics (RCA)
20	33	TOGETHER AT LAST	Richard Clayderman & James Last (Decca Delphine)
37	34	THEMES AND DREAMS	Shadows (Polydor)
47	35	USE YOUR ILLUSION I	Guns N' Roses (Geffen)
28	36	INNUENDO	Queen (Parlophone)
41	37	EXTREME II PORNOGRAFFITTI	Extreme (A&M)
30	38	MEMORIES	Foster & Allen (Telstar)
44	39	ESSENTIAL PAVAROTTI II	Luciano Pavarotti (Decca)
36	40	THE UNFORGETTABLE...	Nat King Cole (EMI)
-	41	USE YOUR ILLUSION II	Guns N' Roses (Geffen)
39	42	THE IMMACULATE COLLECTION	Madonna (Sire)
46	43	MOVE TO THIS	Cathy Dennis (Polydor)
-	44	IN CONCERT	Luciano Pavarotti, Placido Domingo & José Carreras (Decca)
-	45	GREATEST HITS	Jason Donovan (PWL)
48	46	JOYRIDE	Roxette (EMI)
23	47	TIMELESS	Neil Sedaka (Flying Music/Polydor)
42	48	LIVE YOUR LIFE BE FREE	Belinda Carlisle (Virgin)
40	49	THE VERY BEST OF DANIEL O'DONNELL	Daniel O'Donnell (Ritz)
50	50	THE BEST OF DARYL HALL & JOHN OATES - LOOKING BACK	Daryl Hall & John Oates (RCA)

18 January 1992

last week	this week		
1	1	STARS	Simply Red (East West)
2	2	GREATEST HITS II	Queen (Parlophone)
3	3	SIMPLY THE BEST	Tina Turner (Capitol)
4	4	DANGEROUS	Michael Jackson (Epic)
5	5	REAL LOVE	Lisa Stansfield (Arista)
6	6	ACHTUNG BABY	U2 (Island)
10	7	WE CAN'T DANCE	Genesis (Virgin)
11	8	GREATEST HITS	Queen (EMI)
13	9	FROM TIME TO TIME - THE SINGLES COLLECTION	Paul Young (Columbia)
15	10	VOICES	Kenny Thomas (Cooltempo)
17	11	DIAMONDS AND PEARLS	the New Power Generation (Paisley Park)
28	12	NEVERMIND	Nirvana (DGC)
9	13	THE DEFINITIVE SIMON AND GARFUNKEL	Simon & Garfunkel (Columbia)
19	14	OUT OF TIME	R.E.M. (Warner Bros.)
12	15	SHEPHERD MOONS	Enya (WEA)
21	16	DISCOGRAPHY - THE COMPLETE SINGLES COLLECTION	Pet Shop Boys (Parlophone)
16	17	WAKING UP THE NEIGHBOURS	Bryan Adams (A&M)
7	18	TIME, LOVE & TENDERNESS	Michael Bolton (Columbia)
24	19	LOVE HURTS	Cher (Geffen)
30	20	THE COMMITMENTS	Commitments (MCA)
8	21	MICHAEL CRAWFORD PERFORMS ANDREW LLOYD WEBBER	Michael Crawford (Telstar)
14	22	THE FORCE BEHIND THE POWER	Diana Ross (EMI)
22	23	CHORUS	Erasure (Mute)
23	24	JOSEPH AND THE AMAZING TECHNICOLOUR DREAMCOAT	Original Cast (Really Useful)
37	25	EXTREME II PORNOGRAFFITTI	Extreme (A&M)
35	26	USE YOUR ILLUSION I	Guns N' Roses (Geffen)
18	27	TWO ROOMS - CELEBRATING THE SONGS OF ELTON JOHN AND BERNIE TAUPIN	Various Artists (Mercury)
26	28	SEAL	Seal (ZTT)
41	29	USE YOUR ILLUSION II	Guns N' Roses (Geffen)
43	30	MOVE TO THIS	Cathy Dennis (Polydor)
27	31	THE GREATEST HITS	Salt 'n' Pepa (ffrr)
36	32	INNUENDO	Queen (Parlophone)
46	33	JOYRIDE	Roxette (EMI)
32	34	GREATEST HITS	Eurythmics (RCA)
42	35	THE IMMACULATE COLLECTION	Madonna (Sire)
-	36	LITTLE EARTHQUAKES	Tori Amos (East West)
25	37	ON EVERY STREET	Dire Straits (Vertigo)
29	38	THE VERY BEST OF ELTON JOHN	Elton John (Rocket)
31	39	BEVERLEY CRAVEN	Beverley Craven (Epic)
-	40	EMOTIONS	Mariah Carey (Columbia)
48	41	LIVE YOUR LIFE BE FREE	Belinda Carlisle (Virgin)
39	42	ESSENTIAL PAVAROTTI II	Luciano Pavarotti (Decca)
-	43	MARTIKA'S KITCHEN	Martika (Columbia)
44	44	THE BEST OF R.E.M.	R.E.M. (IRS)
33	45	TOGETHER AT LAST	Richard Clayderman & James Last (Decca Delphine)
44	46	IN CONCERT	Luciano Pavarotti, Iacido Domingo & José Carreras (Decca)
-	47	THE WHITE ROOM	KLF (KLF Communications)
45	48	GREATEST HITS	Jason Donovan (PWL)
50	49	THE BEST OF DARYL HALL & JOHN OATES - LOOKING BACK	Daryl Hall & John Oates (RCA)
-	50	LIVE BABY LIVE	INXS (Mercury)

25 January 1992

last week	this week		
1	1	STARS	Simply Red (East West)
7	2	WE CAN'T DANCE	Genesis (Virgin)
2	3	GREATEST HITS II	Queen (Parlophone)
3	4	SIMPLY THE BEST	Tina Turner (Capitol)
6	5	ACHTUNG BABY	U2 (Island)
5	6	REAL LOVE	Lisa Stansfield (Arista)
4	7	DANGEROUS	Michael Jackson (Epic)
-	8	MAGIC AND LOSS	Lou Reed (Sire)
12	9	NEVERMIND	Nirvana (DGC)
8	10	GREATEST HITS	Queen (EMI)
36	11	LITTLE EARTHQUAKES	Tori Amos (East West)
11	12	DIAMONDS AND PEARLS	the New Power Generation (Paisley Park)
14	13	OUT OF TIME	R.E.M. (Warner Bros.)
9	14	FROM TIME TO TIME	Paul Young (Columbia)
15	15	SHEPHERD MOONS	Enya (WEA)
10	16	VOICES	Kenny Thomas (Cooltempo)
20	17	THE COMMITMENTS	Commitments (MCA)
21	18	MICHAEL CRAWFORD PERFORMS ANDREW LLOYD WEBBER	Michael Crawford (Telstar)
13	19	THE DEFINITIVE SIMON AND GARFUNKEL	Simon & Garfunkel (Columbia)
16	20	DISCOGRAPHY - THE COMPLETE SINGLES COLLECTION	Pet Shop Boys (Parlophone)
18	21	TIME, LOVE & TENDERNESS	Michael Bolton (Columbia)
17	22	WAKING UP THE NEIGHBOURS	Bryan Adams (A&M)
19	23	LOVE HURTS	Cher (Geffen)
22	24	THE FORCE BEHIND THE POWER	Diana Ross (EMI)
23	25	CHORUS	Erasure (Mute)
24	26	JOSEPH AND THE AMAZING TECHNICOLOUR DREAMCOAT	Original Cast (Really Useful)
28	27	SEAL	Seal (ZTT)
26	28	USE YOUR ILLUSION I	Guns N' Roses (Geffen)
25	29	EXTREME II PORNOGRAFFITTI	Extreme (A&M)
29	30	USE YOUR ILLUSION II	Guns N' Roses (Geffen)
35	31	THE IMMACULATE COLLECTION	Madonna (Sire)
31	32	THE GREATEST HITS	Salt 'n' Pepa (ffrr)
34	33	GREATEST HITS	Eurythmics (RCA)
30	34	MOVE TO THIS	Cathy Dennis (Polydor)
27	35	TWO ROOMS - CELEBRATING THE SONGS OF ELTON JOHN AND BERNIE TAUPIN	Various Artists (Mercury)
43	36	MARTIKA'S KITCHEN	Martika (Columbia)
38	37	THE VERY BEST OF ELTON JOHN	Elton John (Rocket)
32	38	INNUENDO	Queen (Parlophone)
-	39	BILL AND TED'S BOGUS JOURNEY - SOUNDTRACK	Various Artists (Interscope)
44	40	THE BEST OF R.E.M.	R.E.M. (IRS)
47	41	THE WHITE ROOM	KLF (KLF Communications)
37	42	ON EVERY STREET	Dire Straits (Vertigo)
33	43	JOYRIDE	Roxette (EMI)
39	44	BEVERLEY CRAVEN	Beverley Craven (Epic)
41	45	LIVE YOUR LIFE BE FREE	Belinda Carlisle (Virgin)
-	46	NO REGRETS - 1965-1976	Scott Walker & the Walker Brothers (Fontana)
40	47	EMOTIONS	Mariah Carey (Columbia)
49	48	THE BEST OF DARYL HALL & JOHN OATES - LOOKING BACK	Daryl Hall & John Oates (RCA)
46	49	IN CONCERT	Luciano Pavarotti, Placido Domingo & José Carreras (Decca)
-	50	SEX MACHINE - THE VERY BEST OF JAMES BROWN	James Brown (Polydor)

Simply Red's *Stars* took its second turn at the top for the first month of 1992 - it would not be the album's only visit to the summit during the year. Genesis' *We Can't Dance* also rebounded as far as Number 2, with a prod coming from the success of its title track as a Top 10 single. In the Top 10 for the first time were Nirvana, whose *Nevermind* album was the commercial spearhead of the rootsy US grunge style.

1 February 1992

Last	This	Album	Artist (Label)
1	1	STARS	Simply Red (East West)
2	2	WE CAN'T DANCE	Genesis (Virgin)
3	3	GREATEST HITS II	Queen (Parlophone)
6	4	REAL LOVE	Lisa Stansfield (Arista)
4	5	SIMPLY THE BEST	Tina Turner (Capitol)
8	6	MAGIC AND LOSS	Lou Reed (Sire)
9	7	NEVERMIND	Nirvana (DGC)
5	8	ACHTUNG BABY	U2 (Island)
11	9	LITTLE EARTHQUAKES	Tori Amos (East West)
10	10	GREATEST HITS	Queen (EMI)
12	11	DIAMONDS AND PEARLS	Prince & the New Power Generation (Paisley Park)
7	12	DANGEROUS	Michael Jackson (Epic)
-	13	30 SOMETHING	Carter The Unstoppable Sex Machine (Chrysalis)
46	14	NO REGRETS 1965-1976	Scott Walker & the Walker Brothers (Fontana)
15	15	SHEPHERD MOONS	Enya (WEA)
13	16	OUT OF TIME	R.E.M. (Warner Bros.)
18	17	MICHAEL CRAWFORD PERFORMS ANDREW LLOYD WEBBER	Michael Crawford (Telstar)
17	18	THE COMMITMENTS	Commitments (MCA)
16	19	VOICES	Kenny Thomas (Cooltempo)
14	20	FROM TIME TO TIME - THE SINGLES COLLECTION	Paul Young (Columbia)
19	21	THE DEFINITIVE SIMON AND GARFUNKEL	Simon & Garfunkel (Columbia)
21	22	TIME, LOVE & TENDERNESS	Michael Bolton (Columbia)
24	23	THE FORCE BEHIND THE POWER	Diana Ross (EMI)
23	24	LOVE HURTS	Cher (Geffen)
-	25	BOING	Airhead (Korova)
39	26	BILL AND TED'S BOGUS JOURNEY - SOUNDTRACK	Various Artists (Interscope)
26	27	JOSEPH AND THE AMAZING TECHNICOLOUR DREAMCOAT	Original Cast (Really Useful)
27	28	SEAL	Seal (ZTT)
-	29	WIND OF CHANGE - CLASSIC ROCK	London Symphony Orchestra (Columbia)
22	30	WAKING UP THE NEIGHBOURS	Bryan Adams (A&M)
28	31	USE YOUR ILLUSION I	Guns N' Roses (Geffen)
36	32	MARTIKA'S KITCHEN	Martika (Columbia)
37	33	THE VERY BEST OF ELTON JOHN	Elton John (Rocket)
47	34	EMOTIONS	Mariah Carey (Columbia)
30	35	USE YOUR ILLUSION II	Guns N' Roses (Geffen)
20	36	DISCOGRAPHY - THE COMPLETE SINGLES COLLECTION	Pet Shop Boys (Parlophone)
41	37	THE WHITE ROOM	KLF (KLF Communications)
29	38	EXTREME II PORNOGRAFFITTI	Extreme (A&M)
34	39	MOVE TO THIS	Cathy Dennis (Polydor)
25	40	CHORUS	Erasure (Mute)
33	41	GREATEST HITS	Eurythmics (RCA)
-	42	SCREAMADELICA	Primal Scream (Creation)
32	43	THE GREATEST HITS	Salt 'n' Pepa (ffrr)
38	44	INNUENDO	Queen (Parlophone)
-	45	MCMXC AD	Enigma (Virgin International)
35	46	TWO ROOMS - CELEBRATING THE SONGS OF ELTON JOHN AND BERNIE TAUPIN	Various Artists (Mercury)
31	47	THE IMMACULATE COLLECTION	Madonna (Sire)
44	48	BEVERLEY CRAVEN	Beverley Craven (Epic)
43	49	JOYRIDE	Roxette (EMI)
42	50	ON EVERY STREET	Dire Straits (Vertigo)

8 February 1992

Last	This	Album	Artist (Label)
-	1	HIGH ON THE HAPPY SIDE	Wet Wet Wet (Precious Organisation)
1	2	STARS	Simply Red (East West)
2	3	WE CAN'T DANCE	Genesis (Virgin)
3	4	GREATEST HITS II	Queen (Parlophone)
4	5	REAL LOVE	Lisa Stansfield (Arista)
7	6	NEVERMIND	Nirvana (DGC)
14	7	NO REGRETS 1965-1976	Scott Walker & the Walker Brothers (Fontana)
5	8	SIMPLY THE BEST	Tina Turner (Capitol)
-	9	SPOOKY	Lush (4AD)
-	10	FINALLY	Ce Ce Peniston (A&M)
11	11	DIAMONDS AND PEARLS	Prince & the New Power Generation (Paisley Park)
34	12	EMOTIONS	Mariah Carey (Columbia)
12	13	DANGEROUS	Michael Jackson (Epic)
8	14	ACHTUNG BABY	U2 (Island)
22	15	TIME, LOVE & TENDERNESS	Michael Bolton (Columbia)
16	16	GREATEST HITS	Queen (EMI)
9	17	LITTLE EARTHQUAKES	Tori Amos (East West)
21	18	THE DEFINITIVE SIMON AND GARFUNKEL	Simon & Garfunkel (Columbia)
15	19	SHEPHERD MOONS	Enya (WEA)
42	20	SCREAMADELICA	Primal Scream (Creation)
16	21	OUT OF TIME	R.E.M. (Warner Bros.)
6	22	MAGIC AND LOSS	Lou Reed (Sire)
18	23	THE COMMITMENTS	Commitments (MCA)
20	24	FROM TIME TO TIME - THE SINGLES COLLECTION	Paul Young (Columbia)
24	25	LOVE HURTS	Cher (Geffen)
17	26	MICHAEL CRAWFORD PERFORMS ANDREW LLOYD WEBBER	Michael Crawford (Telstar)
19	27	VOICES	Kenny Thomas (Cooltempo)
30	28	WAKING UP THE NEIGHBOURS	Bryan Adams (A&M)
13	29	30 SOMETHING	Carter The Unstoppable Sex Machine (Chrysalis)
23	30	THE FORCE BEHIND THE POWER	Diana Ross (EMI)
25	31	BOING	Airhead (Korova)
41	32	GREATEST HITS	Eurythmics (RCA)
27	33	JOSEPH AND THE AMAZING TECHNICOLOUR DREAMCOAT	Original Cast (Really Useful)
29	34	WIND OF CHANGE - CLASSIC ROCK	London Symphony Orchestra (Columbia)
37	35	THE WHITE ROOM	KLF (KLF Communications)
26	36	BILL AND TED'S BOGUS JOURNEY - SOUNDTRACK	Various Artists (Interscope)
28	37	SEAL	Seal (ZTT)
31	38	USE YOUR ILLUSION I	Guns N' Roses (Geffen)
-	39	INTO THE GREAT WIDE OPEN	Tom Petty & the Heartbreakers (MCA)
38	40	EXTREME II PORNOGRAFFITTI	Extreme (A&M)
48	41	BEVERLEY CRAVEN	Beverley Craven (Epic)
47	42	THE IMMACULATE COLLECTION	Madonna (Sire)
44	43	INNUENDO	Queen (Parlophone)
39	44	MOVE TO THIS	Cathy Dennis (Polydor)
36	45	DISCOGRAPHY - THE COMPLETE SINGLES COLLECTION	Pet Shop Boys (Parlophone)
-	46	SWEPT	Julia Fordham (Circa)
33	47	THE VERY BEST OF ELTON JOHN	Elton John (Rocket)
35	48	USE YOUR ILLUSION II	Guns N' Roses (Geffen)
-	49	EAT YOURSELF WHOLE	Kingmaker (Scorch)
40	50	CHORUS	Erasure (Mute)

15 February 1992

Last	This	Album	Artist (Label)
1	1	HIGH ON THE HAPPY SIDE	Wet Wet Wet (Precious Organisation)
2	2	STARS	Simply Red (East West)
3	3	WE CAN'T DANCE	Genesis (Virgin)
7	4	NO REGRETS 1965-1976	Scott Walker & the Walker Brothers (Fontana)
5	5	REAL LOVE	Lisa Stansfield (Arista)
13	6	DANGEROUS	Michael Jackson (Epic)
4	7	GREATEST HITS II	Queen (Parlophone)
10	8	FINALLY	Ce Ce Peniston (A&M)
6	9	NEVERMIND	Nirvana (DGC)
8	10	SIMPLY THE BEST	Tina Turner (Capitol)
12	11	EMOTIONS	Mariah Carey (Columbia)
9	12	SPOOKY	Lush (4AD)
15	13	TIME, LOVE & TENDERNESS	Michael Bolton (Columbia)
11	14	DIAMONDS AND PEARLS	Prince & the New Power Generation (Paisley Park)
14	15	ACHTUNG BABY	U2 (Island)
20	16	SCREAMADELICA	Primal Scream (Creation)
16	17	GREATEST HITS	Queen (EMI)
23	18	THE COMMITMENTS	Commitments (MCA)
19	19	SHEPHERD MOONS	Enya (WEA)
17	20	LITTLE EARTHQUAKES	Tori Amos (East West)
21	21	OUT OF TIME	R.E.M. (Warner Bros.)
22	22	MAGIC AND LOSS	Lou Reed (Sire)
28	23	WAKING UP THE NEIGHBOURS	Bryan Adams (A&M)
26	24	MICHAEL CRAWFORD PERFORMS ANDREW LLOYD WEBBER	Michael Crawford (Telstar)
25	25	LOVE HURTS	Cher (Geffen)
-	26	BLACK EYED MAN	Cowboy Junkies (RCA)
24	27	FROM TIME TO TIME - THE SINGLES COLLECTION	Paul Young (Columbia)
30	28	THE FORCE BEHIND THE POWER	Diana Ross (EMI)
27	29	VOICES	Kenny Thomas (Cooltempo)
-	30	DECENCY	Diesel Park West (Food)
18	31	THE DEFINITIVE SIMON AND GARFUNKEL	Simon & Garfunkel (Columbia)
33	32	JOSEPH AND THE AMAZING TECHNICOLOUR DREAMCOAT	Original Cast (Really Useful)
-	33	ROPIN' THE WIND	Garth Brooks (Capitol)
35	34	THE WHITE ROOM	KLF (KLF Communications)
-	35	PAVAROTTI IN HYDE PARK	Luciano Pavarotti (Decca)
36	36	BILL AND TED'S BOGUS JOURNEY - SOUNDTRACK	Various Artists (Interscope)
45	37	DISCOGRAPHY - THE COMPLETE SINGLES COLLECTION	Pet Shop Boys (Parlophone)
41	38	BEVERLEY CRAVEN	Beverley Craven (Epic)
37	39	SEAL	Seal (ZTT)
32	40	GREATEST HITS	Eurythmics (RCA)
34	41	WIND OF CHANGE - CLASSIC ROCK	London Symphony Orchestra (Columbia)
43	42	INNUENDO	Queen (Parlophone)
38	43	USE YOUR ILLUSION I	Guns N' Roses (Geffen)
29	44	30 SOMETHING	Carter The Unstoppable Sex Machine (Chrysalis)
49	45	EAT YOURSELF WHOLE	Kingmaker (Scorch)
-	46	THE GREATEST HITS	Salt 'n' Pepa (ffrr)
-	47	BANDWAGONESQUE	Teenage Fanclub (Creation)
40	48	EXTREME II PORNOGRAFFITTI	Extreme (A&M)
42	49	THE IMMACULATE COLLECTION	Madonna (Sire)
50	50	T.V. SKY	Young Gods (Play It Again Sam)

Wet Wet Wet's resurrection to major album sales, which brought their *High On The Happy Side* straight in at Number 1, was initiated by the success of their single *Goodnight Girl*, which was already topping the chart when the album was released. Initial copies of the CD of *High On The Happy side* carried an entire bonus disc, also performed by Wet Wet Wet, but in the spurious guise of "Maggie Pie & The Imposters".

February – March 1992

22 February 1992

2	1	STARS	Simply Red (East West)
1	2	HIGH ON THE HAPPY SIDE	Wet Wet Wet (Precious Organisation)
3	3	WE CAN'T DANCE	Genesis (Virgin)
5	4	REAL LOVE	Lisa Stansfield (Arista)
11	5	EMOTIONS	Mariah Carey (Columbia)
6	6	DANGEROUS	Michael Jackson (Epic)
7	7	GREATEST HITS II	Queen (Parlophone)
4	8	NO REGRETS 1965-1976	Scott Walker & the Walker Brothers (Fontana)
13	9	TIME, LOVE & TENDERNESS	Michael Bolton (Columbia)
14	10	DIAMONDS AND PEARLS	the New Power Generation (Paisley Park)
39	11	SEAL	Seal (ZTT)
-	12	STICK AROUND FOR JOY	Sugarcubes (One Little Indian)
10	13	SIMPLY THE BEST	Tina Turner (Capitol)
21	14	OUT OF TIME	R.E.M. (Warner Bros.)
9	15	NEVERMIND	Nirvana (DGC)
-	16	GENERATION TERRORISTS	Manic Street Preachers (Columbia)
18	17	THE COMMITMENTS	Commitments (MCA)
-	18	FROM THE HEART - HIS GREATEST LOVE SONGS	Elvis Presley (RCA)
38	19	BEVERLEY CRAVEN	Beverley Craven (Epic)
34	20	THE WHITE ROOM	KLF (KLF Communications)
19	21	SHEPHERD MOONS	Enya (WEA)
28	22	THE FORCE BEHIND THE POWER	Diana Ross (EMI)
35	23	PAVAROTTI IN HYDE PARK	Luciano Pavarotti (Decca)
17	24	GREATEST HITS	Queen (EMI)
23	25	WAKING UP THE NEIGHBOURS	Bryan Adams (A&M)
8	26	FINALLY	Ce Ce Peniston (A&M)
15	27	ACHTUNG BABY	U2 (Island)
24	28	MICHAEL CRAWFORD PERFORMS ANDREW LLOYD WEBBER	Michael Crawford (Telstar)
16	29	SCREAMADELICA	Primal Scream (Creation)
20	30	LITTLE EARTHQUAKES	Tori Amos (East West)
29	31	VOICES	Kenny Thomas (Cooltempo)
27	32	FROM TIME TO TIME	Paul Young (Columbia)
48	33	EXTREME II PORNOGRAFFITTI	Extreme (A&M)
26	34	BLACK EYED MAN	Cowboy Junkies (RCA)
25	35	LOVE HURTS	Cher (Geffen)
40	36	GREATEST HITS	Eurythmics (RCA)
32	37	JOSEPH AND THE AMAZING TECHNICOLOUR DREAMCOAT	Original Cast (Really Useful)
12	38	SPOOKY	Lush (4AD)
-	39	LOVESCAPE	Neil Diamond (Columbia)
37	40	DISCOGRAPHY - THE COMPLETE SINGLES COLLECTION	Pet Shop Boys (Parlophone)
31	41	THE DEFINITIVE SIMON AND GARFUNKEL	Simon & Garfunkel (Columbia)
22	42	MAGIC AND LOSS	Lou Reed (Sire)
-	43	THE VERY BEST OF ELTON JOHN	Elton John (Rocket)
49	44	THE IMMACULATE COLLECTION	Madonna (Sire)
42	45	INNUENDO	Queen (Parlophone)
43	46	USE YOUR ILLUSION I	Guns N' Roses (Geffen)
-	47	NEVER LOVED ELVIS	Wonder Stuff (Polydor)
36	48	BILL AND TED'S BOGUS JOURNEY - SOUNDTRACK	Various Artists (Interscope)
33	49	ROPIN' THE WIND	Garth Brooks (Capitol)
-	50	MOVE TO THIS	Cathy Dennis (Polydor)

29 February 1992

-	1	SEVEN	Jam (Polydor)
1	2	STARS	Simply Red (East West)
2	3	HIGH ON THE HAPPY SIDE	Wet Wet Wet (Precious Organisation)
-	4	HORMONALLY YOURS	Shakespear's Sister (London)
3	5	WE CAN'T DANCE	Genesis (Virgin)
11	6	SEAL	Seal (ZTT)
19	7	BEVERLEY CRAVEN	Beverley Craven (Epic)
4	8	REAL LOVE	Lisa Stansfield (Arista)
6	9	DANGEROUS	Michael Jackson (Epic)
18	10	FROM THE HEART - HIS GREATEST LOVE SONGS	Elvis Presley (RCA)
-	11	CURTIS STIGERS	Curtis Stigers (Arista)
5	12	EMOTIONS	Mariah Carey (Columbia)
7	13	GREATEST HITS II	Queen (Parlophone)
10	14	DIAMONDS AND PEARLS	Prince & the New Power Generation (Paisley Park)
25	15	WAKING UP THE NEIGHBOURS	Bryan Adams (A&M)
9	16	TIME, LOVE & TENDERNESS	Michael Bolton (Columbia)
13	17	SIMPLY THE BEST	Tina Turner (Capitol)
16	18	GENERATION TERRORISTS	Manic Street Preachers (Columbia)
17	19	THE COMMITMENTS	Commitments (MCA)
12	20	STICK AROUND FOR JOY	Sugarcubes (One Little Indian)
8	21	NO REGRETS 1965-1976	Scott Walker & the Walker Brothers (Fontana)
14	22	OUT OF TIME	R.E.M. (Warner Bros.)
15	23	NEVERMIND	Nirvana (DGC)
21	24	SHEPHERD MOONS	Enya (WEA)
20	25	THE WHITE ROOM	KLF (KLF Communications)
24	26	GREATEST HITS	Queen (EMI)
27	27	ACHTUNG BABY	U2 (Island)
33	28	EXTREME II PORNOGRAFFITTI	Extreme (A&M)
28	29	MICHAEL CRAWFORD PERFORMS ANDREW LLOYD WEBBER	Michael Crawford (Telstar)
22	30	THE FORCE BEHIND THE POWER	Diana Ross (EMI)
29	31	SCREAMADELICA	Primal Scream (Creation)
31	32	VOICES	Kenny Thomas (Cooltempo)
35	33	LOVE HURTS	Cher (Geffen)
-	34	MIND ADVENTURES	Des'ree (Dusted Sound)
36	35	GREATEST HITS	Eurythmics (RCA)
32	36	FROM TIME TO TIME	Paul Young (Columbia)
23	37	PAVAROTTI IN HYDE PARK	Luciano Pavarotti (Decca)
-	38	THE ESSENTIAL KIRI	Kiri Te Kanawa (Decca)
26	39	FINALLY	Ce Ce Peniston (A&M)
45	40	INNUENDO	Queen (Parlophone)
37	41	JOSEPH AND THE AMAZING TECHNICOLOUR DREAMCOAT	Original Cast (Really Useful)
41	42	THE DEFINITIVE SIMON AND GARFUNKEL	Simon & Garfunkel (Columbia)
46	43	USE YOUR ILLUSION I	Guns N' Roses (Geffen)
39	44	LOVESCAPE	Neil Diamond (Columbia)
34	45	BLACK EYED MAN	Cowboy Junkies (RCA)
30	46	LITTLE EARTHQUAKES	Tori Amos (East West)
-	47	ON EVERY STREET	Dire Straits (Vertigo)
40	48	DISCOGRAPHY - THE COMPLETE SINGLES COLLECTION	Pet Shop Boys (Parlophone)
43	49	THE VERY BEST OF ELTON JOHN	Elton John (Rocket)
44	50	THE IMMACULATE COLLECTION	Madonna (Sire)

7 March 1992

2	1	STARS	Simply Red (East West)
1	2	SEVEN	Jam (Polydor)
4	3	HORMONALLY YOURS	Shakespear's Sister (London)
-	4	DIVINE MADNESS	Madness (Virgin)
5	5	WE CAN'T DANCE	Genesis (Virgin)
6	6	DANGEROUS	Michael Jackson (Epic)
-	7	TEN	Pearl Jam (Epic)
3	8	HIGH ON THE HAPPY SIDE	Wet Wet Wet (Precious Organisation)
6	9	SEAL	Seal (ZTT)
10	10	FROM THE HEART - HIS GREATEST LOVE SONGS	Elvis Presley (RCA)
11	11	CURTIS STIGERS	Curtis Stigers (Arista)
7	12	BEVERLEY CRAVEN	Beverley Craven (Epic)
-	13	YOURS SINCERELY	Pasadenas (Columbia)
8	14	REAL LOVE	Lisa Stansfield (Arista)
17	15	SIMPLY THE BEST	Tina Turner (Capitol)
12	16	EMOTIONS	Mariah Carey (Columbia)
13	17	GREATEST HITS II	Queen (Parlophone)
-	18	WASTED IN AMERICA	Love/Hate (Columbia)
15	19	WAKING UP THE NEIGHBOURS	Bryan Adams (A&M)
27	20	ACHTUNG BABY	U2 (Island)
-	21	SEBASTOPOL RD	Mega City Four (Big Life)
14	22	DIAMONDS AND PEARLS	Prince & the New Power Generation (Paisley Park)
22	23	OUT OF TIME	R.E.M. (Warner Bros.)
23	24	NEVERMIND	Nirvana (DGC)
16	25	TIME, LOVE & TENDERNESS	Michael Bolton (Columbia)
-	26	BLEACH	Nirvana (Tupelo)
21	27	NO REGRETS - THE BEST OF SCOTT WALKER AND THE WALKER BROTHERS 1965-1976	Scott Walker & the Walker Brothers (Fontana)
-	28	LITTLE VILLAGE	Little Village (Reprise)
25	29	THE WHITE ROOM	KLF (KLF Communications)
34	30	SHEPHERD MOONS	Enya (WEA)
34	31	MIND ADVENTURES	Des'ree (Dusted Sound)
-	32	MIRMAMA	Eddie Reader with the Patron Saints Of Imperfection (RCA)
3	33	THAT WHAT IS NOT	Public Image Ltd. (Virgin)
19	34	THE COMMITMENTS	Commitments (MCA)
43	35	USE YOUR ILLUSION I	Guns N' Roses (Geffen)
26	36	GREATEST HITS	Queen (EMI)
28	37	EXTREME II PORNOGRAFFITTI	Extreme (A&M)
38	38	THE ESSENTIAL KIRI	Kiri Te Kanawa (Decca)
18	39	GENERATION TERRORISTS	Manic Street Preachers (Columbia)
29	40	MICHAEL CRAWFORD PERFORMS ANDREW LLOYD WEBBER	Michael Crawford (Telstar)
-	41	WOODFACE	Crowded House (Capitol)
20	42	STICK AROUND FOR JOY	Sugarcubes (One Little Indian)
-	43	HANDS ON	Thousand Yard Stare (Polydor)
35	44	GREATEST HITS	Eurythmics (RCA)
-	45	FERMENT	Catherine Wheel (Fontana)
-	46	MOTOWN'S GREATEST HITS	Diana Ross (Motown)
48	47	DISCOGRAPHY - THE COMPLETE SINGLES COLLECTION	Pet Shop Boys (Parlophone)
33	48	LOVE HURTS	Cher (Geffen)
30	49	THE FORCE BEHIND THE POWER	Diana Ross (EMI)
32	50	VOICES	Kenny Thomas (Cooltempo)

All at once the album chart was strong with Top 10-registering solo female artists once again: joining Lisa Stansfield's *Real Love* and Tina Turner's hits compilation *Simply The Best*, were albums by Ce Ce Peniston, Mariah Carey, Beverley Craven and girl duo Shakespear's Sister, who were just into a six-week stay at Number 1 on the singles chart with *Stay*. Their LP *Hormonally Yours*, however, peaked at 3.

March 1992

14 March 1992

Last	This	Title / Artist (Label)
-	1	TEARS ROLL DOWN (GREATEST HITS '82-'92) / Tears For Fears (Fontana)
4	2	DIVINE MADNESS / Madness (Virgin)
1	3	STARS / Simply Red (East West)
3	4	HORMONALLY YOURS / Shakespear's Sister (London)
2	5	SEVEN / Jam (Polydor)
13	6	YOURS SINCERELY / Pasadenas (Columbia)
6	7	DANGEROUS / Michael Jackson (Epic)
8	8	HIGH ON THE HAPPY SIDE / Wet Wet Wet (Precious Organisation)
5	9	WE CAN'T DANCE / Genesis (Virgin)
15	10	SIMPLY THE BEST / Tina Turner (Capitol)
10	11	FROM THE HEART - HIS GREATEST LOVE SONGS / Elvis Presley (RCA)
14	12	REAL LOVE / Lisa Stansfield (Arista)
11	13	CURTIS STIGERS / Curtis Stigers (Arista)
7	14	TEN / Pearl Jam (Epic)
9	15	SEAL / Seal (ZTT)
-	16	THE VERY BEST OF... / Frankie Valli & the Four Seasons (Flying Music/PolyGram TV)
20	17	ACHTUNG BABY / U2 (Island)
24	18	NEVERMIND / Nirvana (DGC)
19	19	WAKING UP THE NEIGHBOURS / Bryan Adams (A&M)
12	20	BEVERLEY CRAVEN / Beverley Craven (Epic)
17	21	GREATEST HITS II / Queen (Parlophone)
22	22	DIAMONDS AND PEARLS / Prince & the New Power Generation (Paisley Park)
25	23	TIME, LOVE & TENDERNESS / Michael Bolton (Columbia)
23	24	OUT OF TIME / R.E.M. (Warner Bros.)
16	25	EMOTIONS / Mariah Carey (Columbia)
-	26	BRAND NEW HEAVIES / Brand New Heavies (Acid Jazz)
29	27	THE WHITE ROOM KLF / KLF Communications
26	28	BLEACH / Nirvana (Tupelo)
41	29	WOODFACE / Crowded House (Capitol)
18	30	WASTED IN AMERICA / Love/Hate (Columbia)
35	31	USE YOUR ILLUSION I / Guns N' Roses (Geffen)
27	32	NO REGRETS - THE BEST OF SCOTT WALKER AND THE WALKER BROTHERS 1965-1976 / Scott Walker & the Walker Brothers (Fontana)
28	33	LITTLE VILLAGE / Little Village (Reprise)
30	34	SHEPHERD MOONS / Enya (WEA)
-	35	MUSIC FROM THE ITV SERIES INSPECTOR MORSE VOLUME 2 / Barrington Pheloung (Virgin Television)
36	36	GREATEST HITS / Queen (EMI)
38	37	THE ESSENTIAL KIRI / Kiri Te Kanawa (Decca)
37	38	EXTREME II PORNOGRAFFITTI / Extreme (A&M)
34	39	THE COMMITMENTS / Commitments (MCA)
-	40	GET READY / 2 Unlimited (PWL International)
46	41	MOTOWN'S GREATEST HITS / Diana Ross (Motown)
-	42	USE YOUR ILLUSION II / Guns N' Roses (Geffen)
21	43	SEBASTOPOL RD / Mega City Four (Big Life)
44	44	GREATEST HITS / Eurythmics (RCA)
33	45	THAT WHAT IS NOT / Public Image Ltd. (Virgin)
40	46	MICHAEL CRAWFORD PERFORMS ANDREW LLOYD WEBBER / Michael Crawford (Telstar)
48	47	LOVE HURTS / Cher (Geffen)
32	48	MIRMAMA / Eddie Reader with the Patron Saints Of Imperfection (RCA)
31	49	MIND ADVENTURES / Des'ree (Dusted Sound)
-	50	UH-OH / David Byrne (Luaka Bop)

21 March 1992

Last	This	Title / Artist (Label)
2	1	DIVINE MADNESS / Madness (Virgin)
1	2	TEARS ROLL DOWN (GREATEST HITS '82-'92) / Tears For Fears (Fontana)
3	3	STARS / Simply Red (East West)
-	4	AFTER HOURS / Gary Moore (Virgin)
-	5	GOING BLANK AGAIN / Ride (Creation)
4	6	HORMONALLY YOURS / Shakespear's Sister (London)
5	7	SEVEN / Jam (Polydor)
-	8	DOPPELGANGER / Curve (AnXious)
8	9	HIGH ON THE HAPPY SIDE / Wet Wet Wet (Precious Organisation)
29	10	WOODFACE / Crowded House (Capitol)
17	11	ACHTUNG BABY / U2 (Island)
12	12	REAL LOVE / Lisa Stansfield (Arista)
11	13	FROM THE HEART - HIS GREATEST LOVE SONGS / Elvis Presley (RCA)
10	14	SIMPLY THE BEST / Tina Turner (Capitol)
18	15	NEVERMIND / Nirvana (DGC)
19	16	WAKING UP THE NEIGHBOURS / Bryan Adams (A&M)
9	17	WE CAN'T DANCE / Genesis (Virgin)
7	18	DANGEROUS / Michael Jackson (Epic)
6	19	YOURS SINCERELY / Pasadenas (Columbia)
13	20	CURTIS STIGERS / Curtis Stigers (Arista)
16	21	THE VERY BEST OF FRANKIE VALLI AND THE FOUR SEASONS / Frankie Valli & the Four Seasons (Flying Music/PolyGram TV)
15	22	SEAL / Seal (ZTT)
21	23	GREATEST HITS II / Queen (Parlophone)
23	24	TIME, LOVE & TENDERNESS / Michael Bolton (Columbia)
27	25	THE WHITE ROOM KLF / KLF Communications
24	26	OUT OF TIME / R.E.M. (Warner Bros.)
22	27	DIAMONDS AND PEARLS / Prince & the New Power Generation (Paisley Park)
20	28	BEVERLEY CRAVEN / Beverley Craven (Epic)
14	29	TEN / Pearl Jam (Epic)
50	30	UH-OH / David Byrne (Luaka Bop)
31	31	USE YOUR ILLUSION I / Guns N' Roses (Geffen)
-	32	INNER CHILD / Shanice (Motown)
28	33	BLEACH / Nirvana (Tupelo)
26	34	BRAND NEW HEAVIES / Brand New Heavies (Acid Jazz)
37	35	THE ESSENTIAL KIRI / Kiri Te Kanawa (Decca)
36	36	THE COMMITMENTS / Commitments (MCA)
33	37	LITTLE VILLAGE / Little Village (Reprise)
42	38	USE YOUR ILLUSION II / Guns N' Roses (Geffen)
38	39	EXTREME II PORNOGRAFFITTI / Extreme (A&M)
-	40	COINCIDENCE AND LIKELY STORIES / Buffy Sainte-Marie (Ensign)
25	41	EMOTIONS / Mariah Carey (Columbia)
32	42	NO REGRETS - THE BEST OF SCOTT WALKER AND THE WALKER BROTHERS 1965-1976 / Scott Walker & the Walker Brothers (Fontana)
34	43	SHEPHERD MOONS / Enya (WEA)
36	44	GREATEST HITS / Queen (EMI)
35	45	MUSIC FROM THE ITV SERIES INSPECTOR MORSE VOLUME 2 / Barrington Pheloung (Virgin Television)
44	46	GREATEST HITS / Eurythmics (RCA)
30	47	WASTED IN AMERICA / Love/Hate (Columbia)
46	48	MICHAEL CRAWFORD PERFORMS ANDREW LLOYD WEBBER / Michael Crawford (Telstar)
-	49	MYSTERIO / Ian McCulloch (East West)
-	50	THE IMMACULATE COLLECTION / Madonna (Sire)

28 March 1992

Last	This	Title / Artist (Label)
1	1	DIVINE MADNESS / Madness (Virgin)
2	2	TEARS ROLL DOWN (GREATEST HITS '82-'92) / Tears For Fears (Fontana)
3	3	STARS / Simply Red (East West)
4	4	AFTER HOURS / Gary Moore (Virgin)
6	5	HORMONALLY YOURS / Shakespear's Sister (London)
10	6	WOODFACE / Crowded House (Capitol)
12	7	REAL LOVE / Lisa Stansfield (Arista)
9	8	HIGH ON THE HAPPY SIDE / Wet Wet Wet (Precious Organisation)
15	9	NEVERMIND / Nirvana (DGC)
-	10	UP / Right Said Fred (Tug)
5	11	GOING BLANK AGAIN / Ride (Creation)
16	12	WAKING UP THE NEIGHBOURS / Bryan Adams (A&M)
21	13	THE VERY BEST OF FRANKIE VALLI AND THE FOUR SEASONS / Frankie Valli & the Four Seasons (Flying Music/PolyGram TV)
11	14	ACHTUNG BABY / U2 (Island)
14	15	SIMPLY THE BEST / Tina Turner (Capitol)
13	16	FROM THE HEART - HIS GREATEST LOVE SONGS / Elvis Presley (RCA)
7	17	SEVEN / Jam (Polydor)
8	18	DOPPELGANGER / Curve (AnXious)
18	19	DANGEROUS / Michael Jackson (Epic)
17	20	WE CAN'T DANCE / Genesis (Virgin)
24	21	TIME, LOVE & TENDERNESS / Michael Bolton (Columbia)
20	22	CURTIS STIGERS / Curtis Stigers (Arista)
23	23	GREATEST HITS II / Queen (Parlophone)
27	24	DIAMONDS AND PEARLS / Prince & the New Power Generation (Paisley Park)
22	25	SEAL / Seal (ZTT)
26	26	OUT OF TIME / R.E.M. (Warner Bros.)
32	27	INNER CHILD / Shanice (Motown)
41	28	EMOTIONS / Mariah Carey (Columbia)
-	29	CODE: SELFISH / Fall (Cog Sinister)
19	30	YOURS SINCERELY / Pasadenas (Columbia)
-	31	GREATEST REMIXES VOL.1 / Clivilles & Cole (Columbia)
25	32	THE WHITE ROOM / KLF (KLF Communications)
36	33	THE COMMITMENTS / Commitments (MCA)
31	34	USE YOUR ILLUSION I / Guns N' Roses (Geffen)
28	35	BEVERLEY CRAVEN / Beverley Craven (Epic)
35	36	THE ESSENTIAL KIRI / Kiri Te Kanawa (Decca)
29	37	TEN / Pearl Jam (Epic)
33	38	BLEACH / Nirvana (Tupelo)
43	39	SHEPHERD MOONS / Enya (WEA)
-	40	FINALLY / Ce Ce Peniston (A&M)
40	41	COINCIDENCE AND LIKELY STORIES / Buffy Sainte-Marie (Ensign)
38	42	USE YOUR ILLUSION II / Guns N' Roses (Geffen)
34	43	BRAND NEW HEAVIES / Brand New Heavies (Acid Jazz)
44	44	EXTREME II PORNOGRAFFITTI / Extreme (A&M)
46	45	GREATEST HITS / Eurythmics (RCA)
30	46	UH-OH / David Byrne (Luaka Bop)
-	47	KING'S X / King's X (Atlantic)
50	48	THE IMMACULATE COLLECTION / Madonna (Sire)
45	49	MUSIC FROM THE ITV SERIES INSPECTOR MORSE VOLUME 2 / Barrington Pheloung (Virgin Television)
-	50	INGENUE / k.d. lang (Sire)

Two established groups from the 1980s looked back on their past successes with Number 1 compilation albums: Tears For Fears with *Tears Roll Down*, and Madness with *Divine Madness*. The latter was the third in a series of compilations which began with *Complete Madness* as far back as 1982, and continued with *Utter Madness* in 1986; the new album effectively anthologised its two predecessors.

April 1992

4 April 1992

last week	this week	Title	Artist (Label)
1	1	DIVINE MADNESS	Madness (Virgin)
10	2	UP	Right Said Fred (Tug)
3	3	STARS	Simply Red (East West)
2	4	TEARS ROLL DOWN (GREATEST HITS '82-'92)	Tears For Fears (Fontana)
4	5	AFTER HOURS	Gary Moore (Virgin)
6	6	WOODFACE	Crowded House (Capitol)
5	7	HORMONALLY YOURS	Shakespear's Sister (London)
9	8	NEVERMIND	Nirvana (DGC)
-	9	HONEY'S DEAD	Jesus & Mary Chain (blanco y negro)
-	10	BETWEEN 10TH AND 11TH	Charlatans (Situation Two)
7	11	REAL LOVE	Lisa Stansfield (Arista)
12	12	WAKING UP THE NEIGHBOURS	Bryan Adams (A&M)
8	13	HIGH ON THE HAPPY SIDE	Wet Wet Wet (Precious Organisation)
14	14	ACHTUNG BABY	U2 (Island)
-	15	"ADDICTIONS" VOLUME 2	Robert Palmer (Island)
15	16	SIMPLY THE BEST	Tina Turner (Capitol)
11	17	GOING BLANK AGAIN	Ride (Creation)
17	18	SEVEN	Jam (Polydor)
13	19	THE VERY BEST OF ...	Frankie Valli & the Four Seasons (Flying Music/PolyGram TV)
18	20	DOPPELGANGER	Curve (AnXious)
19	21	DANGEROUS	Michael Jackson (Epic)
21	22	TIME, LOVE & TENDERNESS	Michael Bolton (Columbia)
16	23	FROM THE HEART - HIS GREATEST LOVE SONGS	Elvis Presley (RCA)
20	24	WE CAN'T DANCE	Genesis (Virgin)
24	25	DIAMONDS AND PEARLS	Prince & the New Power Generation (Paisley Park)
40	26	FINALLY	Ce Ce Peniston (A&M)
22	27	CURTIS STIGERS	Curtis Stigers (Arista)
28	28	EMOTIONS	Mariah Carey (Columbia)
29	29	CODE: SELFISH	Fall (Cog Sinister)
-	30	HISTORY - THE SINGLES '85-'91	New Model Army (EMI)
26	31	OUT OF TIME	R.E.M. (Warner Bros.)
23	32	GREATEST HITS II	Queen (Parlophone)
33	33	THE COMMITMENTS	Commitments (MCA)
25	34	SEAL	Seal (ZTT)
37	35	TEN	Pearl Jam (Epic)
-	36	EVERYTHING'S ALRIGHT FOREVER	Boo Radleys (Creation)
-	37	BLOOD SUGAR SEX MAGIK	Red Hot Chili Peppers (Warner Bros.)
34	38	USE YOUR ILLUSION I	Guns N' Roses (Geffen)
27	39	INNER CHILD	Shanice (Motown)
49	40	MUSIC FROM INSPECTOR MORSE VOLUME 2	Barrington Pheloung (Virgin Television)
50	41	INGENUE	k.d. lang (Sire)
32	42	THE WHITE ROOM	KLF (KLF Communications)
-	43	IN RIBBONS	Pale Saints (4AD)
30	44	YOURS SINCERELY	Pasadenas (Columbia)
-	45	EVERYBODY'S FREE	Rozalla (Pulse 8)
35	46	BEVERLEY CRAVEN	Beverley Craven (Epic)
31	47	GREATEST REMIXES VOL.1	Clivilles & Cole (Columbia)
36	48	THE ESSENTIAL KIRI	Kiri Te Kanawa (Decca)
38	49	BLEACH	Nirvana (Tupelo)
-	50	MICHAEL CRAWFORD PERFORMS ANDREW LLOYD WEBBER	Michael Crawford (Telstar)

11 April 1992

last week	this week	Title	Artist (Label)
-	1	ADRENALIZE	Def Leppard (Bludgeon Riffola)
-	2	HUMAN TOUCH	Bruce Springsteen (Columbia)
-	3	LUCKY TOWN	Bruce Springsteen (Columbia)
2	4	UP	Right Said Fred (Tug)
3	5	STARS	Simply Red (East West)
1	6	DIVINE MADNESS	Madness (Virgin)
-	7	0898	Beautiful South (Go! Discs)
4	8	TEARS ROLL DOWN (GREATEST HITS '82-'92)	Tears For Fears (Fontana)
11	9	REAL LOVE	Lisa Stansfield (Arista)
13	10	HIGH ON THE HAPPY SIDE	Wet Wet Wet (Precious Organisation)
6	11	WOODFACE	Crowded House (Capitol)
7	12	HORMONALLY YOURS	Shakespear's Sister (London)
16	13	SIMPLY THE BEST	Tina Turner (Capitol)
19	14	THE VERY BEST OF FRANKIE VALLI AND THE FOUR SEASONS	Frankie Valli & the Four Seasons (Flying Music/PolyGram TV)
15	15	"ADDICTIONS" VOLUME 2	Robert Palmer (Island)
12	16	WAKING UP THE NEIGHBOURS	Bryan Adams (A&M)
5	17	AFTER HOURS	Gary Moore (Virgin)
-	18	HEAR MY SONG (THE BEST OF JOSEF LOCKE)	Josef Locke (EMI)
8	19	NEVERMIND	Nirvana (DGC)
9	20	HONEY'S DEAD	Jesus & Mary Chain (blanco y negro)
14	21	ACHTUNG BABY	U2 (Island)
22	22	CURTIS STIGERS	Curtis Stigers (Arista)
22	23	TIME, LOVE & TENDERNESS	Michael Bolton (Columbia)
10	24	BETWEEN 10TH AND 11TH	Charlatans (Situation Two)
23	25	FROM THE HEART - HIS GREATEST LOVE SONGS	Elvis Presley (RCA)
25	26	DIAMONDS AND PEARLS	Prince & the New Power Generation (Paisley Park)
18	27	SEVEN	Jam (Polydor)
21	28	DANGEROUS	Michael Jackson (Epic)
-	29	LEAN INTO IT	Mr. Big (Atlantic)
24	30	WE CAN'T DANCE	Genesis (Virgin)
32	31	GREATEST HITS II	Queen (Parlophone)
-	32	DRY	PJ Harvey (Too Pure)
-	33	THE DEFINITIVE SIMON AND GARFUNKEL	Simon & Garfunkel (Columbia)
33	34	THE COMMITMENTS	Commitments (MCA)
-	35	CHORUS	Erasure (Mute)
-	36	LAZER GUIDED MELODIES	Spiritualized (Dedicated)
31	37	OUT OF TIME	R.E.M. (Warner Bros.)
-	38	NIGHT CALLS	Joe Cocker (Capitol)
-	39	ARKANSAS TRAVELER	Michelle Shocked (London)
28	40	EMOTIONS	Mariah Carey (Columbia)
40	41	MUSIC FROM THE ITV SERIES INSPECTOR MORSE VOLUME 2	Barrington Pheloung (Virgin Television)
45	42	EVERYBODY'S FREE	Rozalla (Pulse 8)
17	43	GOING BLANK AGAIN	Ride (Creation)
44	44	YOURS SINCERELY	Pasadenas (Columbia)
20	45	DOPPELGANGER	Curve (AnXious)
34	46	SEAL	Seal (ZTT)
46	47	BEVERLEY CRAVEN	Beverley Craven (Epic)
48	48	THE ESSENTIAL KIRI	Kiri Te Kanawa (Decca)
26	49	FINALLY	Ce Ce Peniston (A&M)

18 April 1992

last week	this week	Title	Artist (Label)
-	1	DIVA	Annie Lennox (RCA)
1	2	ADRENALIZE	Def Leppard (Bludgeon Riffola)
4	3	UP	Right Said Fred (Tug)
6	4	DIVINE MADNESS	Madness (Virgin)
2	5	HUMAN TOUCH	Bruce Springsteen (Columbia)
7	6	0898	Beautiful South (Go! Discs)
3	7	LUCKY TOWN	Bruce Springsteen (Columbia)
5	8	STARS	Simply Red (East West)
8	9	TEARS ROLL DOWN (GREATEST HITS '82-'92)	Tears For Fears (Fontana)
18	10	HEAR MY SONG (THE BEST OF JOSEF LOCKE)	Josef Locke (EMI)
12	11	HORMONALLY YOURS	Shakespear's Sister (London)
9	12	REAL LOVE	Lisa Stansfield (Arista)
32	13	DRY	PJ Harvey (Too Pure)
11	14	WOODFACE	Crowded House (Capitol)
-	15	GALLUS	Gun (A&M)
22	16	CURTIS STIGERS	Curtis Stigers (Arista)
16	17	WAKING UP THE NEIGHBOURS	Bryan Adams (A&M)
10	18	HIGH ON THE HAPPY SIDE	Wet Wet Wet (Precious Organisation)
15	19	"ADDICTIONS" VOLUME 2	Robert Palmer (Island)
29	20	LEAN INTO IT	Mr. Big (Atlantic)
19	21	NEVERMIND	Nirvana (DGC)
21	22	ACHTUNG BABY	U2 (Island)
17	23	AFTER HOURS	Gary Moore (Virgin)
30	24	WE CAN'T DANCE	Genesis (Virgin)
14	25	THE VERY BEST OF...	Frankie Valli & the Four Seasons (Flying Music/PolyGram TV)
13	26	SIMPLY THE BEST	Tina Turner (Capitol)
38	27	NIGHT CALLS	Joe Cocker (Capitol)
23	28	TIME, LOVE & TENDERNESS	Michael Bolton (Columbia)
26	29	DIAMONDS AND PEARLS	Prince & the New Power Generation (Paisley Park)
35	30	CHORUS	Erasure (Mute)
28	31	DANGEROUS	Michael Jackson (Epic)
27	32	SEVEN	Jam (Polydor)
-	33	EXTRAS	Jam (Polydor)
-	34	MOTOWN'S GREATEST HITS	Temptations (Motown)
33	35	THE DEFINITIVE SIMON AND GARFUNKEL	Simon & Garfunkel (Columbia)
34	36	THE COMMITMENTS	Commitments (MCA)
37	37	SENSE	Lightning Seeds (Virgin)
36	38	LAZER GUIDED MELODIES	Spiritualized (Dedicated)
37	39	OUT OF TIME	R.E.M. (Warner Bros.)
-	40	JOYRIDE	Roxette (EMI)
-	41	GREATEST HITS	Eurythmics (RCA)
31	42	GREATEST HITS II	Queen (Parlophone)
25	43	FROM THE HEART - HIS GREATEST LOVE SONGS	Elvis Presley (RCA)
44	44	YOURS SINCERELY	Pasadenas (Columbia)
48	45	BEVERLEY CRAVEN	Beverley Craven (Epic)
47	46	SEAL	Seal (ZTT)
40	47	EMOTIONS	Mariah Carey (Columbia)
24	48	BETWEEN 10TH AND 11TH	Charlatans (Situation Two)
41	49	MUSIC FROM THE ITV SERIES INSPECTOR MORSE VOLUME 2	Barrington Pheloung (Virgin Television)
39	50	ARKANSAS TRAVELER	Michelle Shocked (London)

Following (though for certain not intentionally) in the footsteps of Guns N' Roses a few months earlier, Bruce Springsteen released two new albums simultaneously. Unlike the GN'R set, though, *Human Touch* and *Lucky Town* were not presented as two halves of a single project, but rather two differently-styled projects - one more deliberately commercial, the other more laid back - completed simultaneously.

25 April 1992

last week	this week	Title	Artist (Label)
1	1	DIVA	Annie Lennox (RCA)
3	2	UP	Right Said Fred (Tug)
2	3	ADRENALIZE	Def Leppard (Bludgeon Riffola)
-	4	VOLUME III JUST RIGHT	Soul II Soul (10)
4	5	DIVINE MADNESS	Madness (Virgin)
8	6	STARS	Simply Red (East West)
-	7	GREATEST HITS	ZZ Top (Warner Bros.)
9	8	TEARS ROLL DOWN (GREATEST HITS '82-'92)	Tears For Fears (Fontana)
6	9	0898	Beautiful South (Go! Discs)
16	10	CURTIS STIGERS	Curtis Stigers (Arista)
10	11	HEAR MY SONG (THE BEST OF JOSEF LOCKE)	Josef Locke (EMI)
12	12	REAL LOVE	Lisa Stansfield (Arista)
5	13	HUMAN TOUCH	Bruce Springsteen (Columbia)
11	14	HORMONALLY YOURS	Shakespear's Sister (London)
33	15	EXTRAS	Jam (Polydor)
24	16	WE CAN'T DANCE	Genesis (Virgin)
14	17	WOODFACE	Crowded House (Capitol)
7	18	LUCKY TOWN	Bruce Springsteen (Columbia)
15	19	GALLUS	Gun (A&M)
34	20	MOTOWN'S GREATEST HITS	Temptations (Motown)
17	21	WAKING UP THE NEIGHBOURS	Bryan Adams (A&M)
21	22	NEVERMIND	Nirvana (DGC)
19	23	"ADDICTIONS" VOLUME 2	Robert Palmer (Island)
-	24	THE COMMITMENTS VOL.2	Commitments (MCA)
29	25	DIAMONDS AND PEARLS	Prince & the New Power Generation (Paisley Park)
18	26	HIGH ON THE HAPPY SIDE	Wet Wet Wet (Precious Organisation)
23	27	AFTER HOURS	Gary Moore (Virgin)
26	28	SIMPLY THE BEST	Tina Turner (Capitol)
27	29	NIGHT CALLS	Joe Cocker (Capitol)
30	30	CHORUS	Erasure (Mute)
25	31	THE VERY BEST OF	Frankie Valli & the Four Seasons (Flying Music/PolyGram TV)
22	32	ACHTUNG BABY	U2 (Island)
31	33	DANGEROUS	Michael Jackson (Epic)
20	34	LEAN INTO IT	Mr. Big (Atlantic)
32	35	SEVEN	Jam (Polydor)
28	36	TIME, LOVE & TENDERNESS	Michael Bolton (Columbia)
47	37	EMOTIONS	Mariah Carey (Columbia)
13	38	DRY	PJ Harvey (Too Pure)
42	39	GREATEST HITS II	Queen (Parlophone)
49	40	MUSIC FROM THE ITV SERIES INSPECTOR MORSE VOLUME 2	Barrington Pheloung (Virgin Television)
44	41	YOURS SINCERELY	Pasadenas (Columbia)
35	42	THE DEFINITIVE SIMON AND GARFUNKEL	Simon & Garfunkel (Columbia)
37	43	SENSE	Lightning Seeds (Virgin)
-	44	FINALLY	Ce Ce Peniston (A&M)
-	45	THE COMFORT ZONE	Vanessa Williams (Polydor)
-	46	TEN	Pearl Jam (Epic)
39	47	OUT OF TIME	R.E.M. (Warner Bros.)
-	48	TOO BLIND TO SEE IT	Kym Sims (Atco)
36	49	THE COMMITMENTS	Commitments (MCA)
43	50	FROM THE HEART - HIS GREATEST LOVE SONGS	Elvis Presley (RCA)

2 May 1992

last week	this week	Title	Artist (Label)
-	1	WISH	Cure (Fiction)
1	2	DIVA	Annie Lennox (RCA)
2	3	UP	Right Said Fred (Tug)
7	4	GREATEST HITS	ZZ Top (Warner Bros.)
5	5	DIVINE MADNESS	Madness (Virgin)
6	6	STARS	Simply Red (East West)
4	7	VOLUME III JUST RIGHT	Soul II Soul (10)
8	8	TEARS ROLL DOWN (GREATEST HITS '82-'92)	Tears For Fears (Fontana)
12	9	REAL LOVE	Lisa Stansfield (Arista)
39	10	GREATEST HITS II	Queen (Parlophone)
3	11	ADRENALIZE	Def Leppard (Bludgeon Riffola)
10	12	CURTIS STIGERS	Curtis Stigers (Arista)
24	13	THE COMMITMENTS VOL.2	Commitments (MCA)
11	14	HEAR MY SONG (THE BEST OF JOSEF LOCKE)	Josef Locke (EMI)
9	15	0898	Beautiful South (Go! Discs)
16	16	WE CAN'T DANCE	Genesis (Virgin)
14	17	HORMONALLY YOURS	Shakespear's Sister (London)
18	18	WOODFACE	Crowded House (Capitol)
13	19	HUMAN TOUCH	Bruce Springsteen (Columbia)
20	20	MOTOWN'S GREATEST HITS	Temptations (Motown)
28	21	SIMPLY THE BEST	Tina Turner (Capitol)
22	22	NEVERMIND	Nirvana (DGC)
26	23	HIGH ON THE HAPPY SIDE	Wet Wet Wet (Precious Organisation)
21	24	WAKING UP THE NEIGHBOURS	Bryan Adams (A&M)
33	25	DANGEROUS	Michael Jackson (Epic)
25	26	DIAMONDS AND PEARLS	Prince & the New Power Generation (Paisley Park)
-	27	GREATEST HITS	Queen (EMI)
27	28	AFTER HOURS	Gary Moore (Virgin)
18	29	LUCKY TOWN	Bruce Springsteen (Columbia)
-	30	GREATEST HITS	Foreigner (Atlantic)
-	31	USE YOUR ILLUSION I	Guns N' Roses (Geffen)
23	32	"ADDICTIONS" VOLUME 2	Robert Palmer (Island)
-	33	BRICKS ARE HEAVY	L7 (Slash)
49	34	THE COMMITMENTS	Commitments (MCA)
45	35	THE COMFORT ZONE	Vanessa Williams (Polydor)
32	36	ACHTUNG BABY	U2 (Island)
-	37	LOVE HURTS	Cher (Geffen)
19	38	GALLUS	Gun (A&M)
44	39	FINALLY	Ce Ce Peniston (A&M)
30	40	CHORUS	Erasure (Mute)
-	41	SEAL	Seal (ZTT)
15	42	EXTRAS	Jam (Polydor)
35	43	SEVEN	Jam (Polydor)
-	44	USE YOUR ILLUSION II	Guns N' Roses (Geffen)
34	45	LEAN INTO IT	Mr. Big (Atlantic)
36	46	TIME, LOVE & TENDERNESS	Michael Bolton (Columbia)
31	47	THE VERY BEST OF FRANKIE VALLI AND THE FOUR SEASONS	Frankie Valli & the Four Seasons (Flying Music/PolyGram TV)
29	48	NIGHT CALLS	Joe Cocker (Capitol)
40	49	MUSIC FROM THE ITV SERIES INSPECTOR MORSE VOLUME 2	Barrington Pheloung (Virgin Television)
-	50	EXTREME II PORNOGRAFFITTI	Extreme (A&M)

9 May 1992

last week	this week	Title	Artist (Label)
1	1	WISH	Cure (Fiction)
2	2	DIVA	Annie Lennox (RCA)
3	3	UP	Right Said Fred (Tug)
4	4	GREATEST HITS	ZZ Top (Warner Bros.)
6	5	STARS	Simply Red (East West)
5	6	DIVINE MADNESS	Madness (Virgin)
10	7	GREATEST HITS II	Queen (Parlophone)
-	8	POWER OF TEN	Chris De Burgh (A&M)
8	9	TEARS ROLL DOWN (GREATEST HITS '82-'92)	Tears For Fears (Fontana)
7	10	VOLUME III JUST RIGHT	Soul II Soul (10)
-	11	SOME GIRLS WANDER BY MISTAKE	Sisters Of Mercy (Merciful Release)
11	12	ADRENALIZE	Def Leppard (Bludgeon Riffola)
12	13	CURTIS STIGERS	Curtis Stigers (Arista)
9	14	REAL LOVE	Lisa Stansfield (Arista)
30	15	GREATEST HITS	Foreigner (Atlantic)
13	16	THE COMMITMENTS VOL.2	Commitments (MCA)
22	17	NEVERMIND	Nirvana (DGC)
16	18	WE CAN'T DANCE	Genesis (Virgin)
17	19	HORMONALLY YOURS	Shakespear's Sister (London)
14	20	HEAR MY SONG (THE BEST OF JOSEF LOCKE)	Josef Locke (EMI)
50	21	EXTREME II PORNOGRAFFITTI	Extreme (A&M)
31	22	USE YOUR ILLUSION I	Guns N' Roses (Geffen)
15	23	0898	Beautiful South (Go! Discs)
27	24	GREATEST HITS	Queen (EMI)
-	25	MATTERS OF THE HEART	Tracy Chapman (Elektra)
25	26	DANGEROUS	Michael Jackson (Epic)
34	27	THE COMMITMENTS	Commitments (MCA)
18	28	WOODFACE	Crowded House (Capitol)
19	29	HUMAN TOUCH	Bruce Springsteen (Columbia)
21	30	SIMPLY THE BEST	Tina Turner (Capitol)
20	31	MOTOWN'S GREATEST HITS	Temptations (Motown)
44	32	USE YOUR ILLUSION II	Guns N' Roses (Geffen)
-	33	NONSUCH	XTC (Virgin)
24	34	WAKING UP THE NEIGHBOURS	Bryan Adams (A&M)
33	35	BRICKS ARE HEAVY	L7 (Slash)
37	36	LOVE HURTS	Cher (Geffen)
-	37	HENRY'S DREAM	Nick Cave & the Bad Seeds (Mute)
23	38	HIGH ON THE HAPPY SIDE	Wet Wet Wet (Precious Organisation)
26	39	DIAMONDS AND PEARLS	Prince & the New Power Generation (Paisley Park)
36	40	ACHTUNG BABY	U2 (Island)
29	41	LUCKY TOWN	Bruce Springsteen (Columbia)
-	42	OUT OF TIME	R.E.M. (Warner Bros.)
35	43	THE COMFORT ZONE	Vanessa Williams (Polydor)
-	44	APPETITE FOR DESTRUCTION	Guns N' Roses (Geffen)
32	45	"ADDICTIONS" VOLUME 2	Robert Palmer (Island)
46	46	GALLUS	Gun (A&M)
46	47	TIME, LOVE & TENDERNESS	Michael Bolton (Columbia)
28	48	AFTER HOURS	Gary Moore (Virgin)
-	49	UNDER THE WATER-LINE	Ten Sharp (Columbia)
40	50	CHORUS	Erasure (Mute)

The success of Right Said Fred's debut album *Up* coincided with that of their third consecutive hit single, and first Number 1, *Deeply Dippy*, which was engaged on a 4-week chart-topping run. Perhaps surprisingly, the album itself failed to make Number 1, held at bay by the success of Def Leppard's *Adrenalise*, Annie Lennox' first solo set *Diva* and the Cure's equally succinctly-titled *Wish*.

May 1992

16 May 1992

last	this		
-	1	1992 THE LOVE ALBUM	Carter The Unstoppable Sex Machine (Chrysalis)
5	2	STARS	Simply Red (East West)
3	3	UP	Right Said Fred (Tug)
2	4	DIVA	Annie Lennox (RCA)
4	5	GREATEST HITS	ZZ Top (Warner Bros.)
8	6	POWER OF TEN	Chris De Burgh (A&M)
1	7	WISH	Cure (Fiction)
11	8	SOME GIRLS WANDER BY MISTAKE	Sisters Of Mercy (Merciful Release)
6	9	DIVINE MADNESS	Madness (Virgin)
13	10	CURTIS STIGERS	Curtis Stigers (Arista)
12	11	ADRENALIZE	Def Leppard (Bludgeon Riffola)
7	12	GREATEST HITS II	Queen (Parlophone)
10	13	VOLUME III JUST RIGHT	Soul II Soul (10)
9	14	TEARS ROLL DOWN (GREATEST HITS '82-'92)	Tears For Fears (Fontana)
19	15	HORMONALLY YOURS	Shakespear's Sister (London)
14	16	REAL LOVE	Lisa Stansfield (Arista)
27	17	THE COMMITMENTS	Commitments (MCA)
17	18	NEVERMIND	Nirvana (DGC)
15	19	GREATEST HITS	Foreigner (Atlantic)
18	20	WE CAN'T DANCE	Genesis (Virgin)
20	21	HEAR MY SONG (THE BEST OF JOSEF LOCKE)	Josef Locke (EMI)
16	22	THE COMMITMENTS VOL.2	Commitments (MCA)
21	23	EXTREME II PORNOGRAFFITTI	Extreme (A&M)
26	24	DANGEROUS	Michael Jackson (Epic)
-	25	EMOTIONS	Mariah Carey (Columbia)
32	26	USE YOUR ILLUSION II	Guns N' Roses (Geffen)
23	27	0898	Beautiful South (Go! Discs)
24	28	GREATEST HITS	Queen (EMI)
30	29	SIMPLY THE BEST	Tina Turner (Capitol)
22	30	USE YOUR ILLUSION I	Guns N' Roses (Geffen)
-	31	GET IN TOUCH WITH YOURSELF	Swing Out Sister (Fontana)
25	32	MATTERS OF THE HEART	Tracy Chapman (Elektra)
36	33	LOVE HURTS	Cher (Geffen)
40	34	ACHTUNG BABY	U2 (Island)
31	35	MOTOWN'S GREATEST HITS	Temptations (Motown)
33	36	NONSUCH	XTC (Virgin)
-	37	METALLICA	Metallica (Vertigo)
47	38	TIME, LOVE & TENDERNESS	Michael Bolton (Columbia)
28	39	WOODFACE	Crowded House (Capitol)
37	40	HENRY'S DREAM	Nick Cave and the Bad Seeds (Mute)
39	41	DIAMONDS AND PEARLS	Prince & the New Power Generation (Paisley Park)
29	42	HUMAN TOUCH	Bruce Springsteen (Columbia)
42	43	OUT OF TIME	R.E.M. (Warner Bros.)
-	44	BRAND NEW HEAVIES	Brand New Heavies (Acid Jazz)
-	45	TENEMENT SYMPHONY	Marc Almond (Some Bizzare)
34	46	WAKING UP THE NEIGHBOURS	Bryan Adams (A&M)
35	47	BRICKS ARE HEAVY	L7 (Slash)
38	48	HIGH ON THE HAPPY SIDE	Wet Wet Wet (Precious Organisation)
49	49	UNDER THE WATER-LINE	Ten Sharp (Columbia)
-	50	NEED FOR NOT	Levitation (Rough Trade)

23 May 1992

last	this		
-	1	FEAR OF THE DARK	Iron Maiden (EMI)
1	2	1992 THE LOVE ALBUM	Carter The Unstoppable Sex Machine (Chrysalis)
-	3	THE SOUTHERN HARMONY AND MUSICAL COMPANION	Black Crowes (Def American)
2	4	STARS	Simply Red (East West)
3	5	UP	Right Said Fred (Tug)
5	6	GREATEST HITS	ZZ Top (Warner Bros.)
4	7	DIVA	Annie Lennox (RCA)
6	8	POWER OF TEN	Chris De Burgh (A&M)
20	9	WE CAN'T DANCE	Genesis (Virgin)
-	10	GREATEST HITS	Squeeze (A&M)
9	11	DIVINE MADNESS	Madness (Virgin)
-	12	REVENGE	Kiss (Mercury)
15	13	HORMONALLY YOURS	Shakespear's Sister (London)
7	14	WISH	Cure (Fiction)
11	15	ADRENALIZE	Def Leppard (Bludgeon Riffola)
12	16	GREATEST HITS II	Queen (Parlophone)
17	17	THE COMMITMENTS	Commitments (MCA)
23	18	EXTREME II PORNOGRAFFITTI	Extreme (A&M)
10	19	CURTIS STIGERS	Curtis Stigers (Arista)
19	20	GREATEST HITS	Foreigner (Atlantic)
16	21	REAL LOVE	Lisa Stansfield (Arista)
26	22	USE YOUR ILLUSION II	Guns N' Roses (Geffen)
14	23	TEARS ROLL DOWN (GREATEST HITS '82-'92)	Tears For Fears (Fontana)
13	24	VOLUME III JUST RIGHT	Soul II Soul (10)
24	25	DANGEROUS	Michael Jackson (Epic)
18	26	NEVERMIND	Nirvana (DGC)
33	27	LOVE HURTS	Cher (Geffen)
28	28	GREATEST HITS	Queen (EMI)
22	29	THE COMMITMENTS VOL.2	Commitments (MCA)
34	30	ACHTUNG BABY	U2 (Island)
8	31	SOME GIRLS WANDER BY MISTAKE	Sisters Of Mercy (Merciful Release)
30	32	USE YOUR ILLUSION I	Guns N' Roses (Geffen)
37	33	METALLICA	Metallica (Vertigo)
21	34	HEAR MY SONG (THE BEST OF JOSEF LOCKE)	Josef Locke (EMI)
25	35	EMOTIONS	Mariah Carey (Columbia)
29	36	SIMPLY THE BEST	Tina Turner (Capitol)
42	37	HUMAN TOUCH	Bruce Springsteen (Columbia)
27	38	0898	Beautiful South (Go! Discs)
31	39	GET IN TOUCH WITH YOURSELF	Swing Out Sister (Fontana)
35	40	MOTOWN'S GREATEST HITS	Temptations (Motown)
41	41	DIAMONDS AND PEARLS	Prince & the New Power Generation (Paisley Park)
45	42	TENEMENT SYMPHONY	Marc Almond (Some Bizzare)
39	43	WOODFACE	Crowded House (Capitol)
32	44	MATTERS OF THE HEART	Tracy Chapman (Elektra)
43	45	OUT OF TIME	R.E.M. (Warner Bros.)
46	46	WAKING UP THE NEIGHBOURS	Bryan Adams (A&M)
47	47	LUCKY TOWN	Bruce Springsteen (Columbia)
38	48	TIME, LOVE & TENDERNESS	Michael Bolton (Columbia)
40	49	HENRY'S DREAM	Nick Cave & the Bad Seeds (Mute)
-	50	NIGHT CALLS	Joe Cocker (Capitol)

30 May 1992

last	this		
1	1	FEAR OF THE DARK	Iron Maiden (EMI)
3	2	THE SOUTHERN HARMONY AND MUSICAL COMPANION	Black Crowes (Def American)
4	3	STARS	Simply Red (East West)
5	4	UP	Right Said Fred (Tug)
10	5	GREATEST HITS	Squeeze (A&M)
13	6	HORMONALLY YOURS	Shakespear's Sister (London)
2	7	1992 THE LOVE ALBUM	Carter The Unstoppable Sex Machine (Chrysalis)
7	8	DIVA	Annie Lennox (RCA)
6	9	GREATEST HITS	ZZ Top (Warner Bros.)
-	10	THIS THING CALLED LOVE - THE GREATEST HITS OF ALEXANDER O'NEAL	Alexander O'Neal (Tabu)
14	11	WISH	Cure (Fiction)
8	12	POWER OF TEN	Chris De Burgh (A&M)
9	13	WE CAN'T DANCE	Genesis (Virgin)
12	14	REVENGE	Kiss (Mercury)
-	15	ADRENALIZE	Def Leppard (Bludgeon Riffola)
11	16	DIVINE MADNESS	Madness (Virgin)
-	17	MICHAEL BALL	Michael Ball (Polydor)
18	18	EXTREME II PORNOGRAFFITTI	Extreme (A&M)
19	19	CURTIS STIGERS	Curtis Stigers (Arista)
16	20	GREATEST HITS II	Queen (Parlophone)
17	21	THE COMMITMENTS	Commitments (MCA)
22	22	USE YOUR ILLUSION II	Guns N' Roses (Geffen)
21	23	REAL LOVE	Lisa Stansfield (Arista)
26	24	NEVERMIND	Nirvana (DGC)
20	25	GREATEST HITS	Foreigner (Atlantic)
24	26	VOLUME III JUST RIGHT	Soul II Soul (10)
23	27	TEARS ROLL DOWN (GREATEST HITS '82-'92)	Tears For Fears (Fontana)
-	28	UNFORGETTABLE - WITH LOVE	Natalie Cole (Elektra)
29	29	THE COMMITMENTS VOL.2	Commitments (MCA)
27	30	LOVE HURTS	Cher (Geffen)
25	31	DANGEROUS	Michael Jackson (Epic)
28	32	GREATEST HITS	Queen (EMI)
30	33	ACHTUNG BABY	U2 (Island)
32	34	USE YOUR ILLUSION I	Guns N' Roses (Geffen)
-	35	INGENUE	k.d. lang (Sire)
33	36	METALLICA	Metallica (Vertigo)
34	37	HEAR MY SONG (THE BEST OF JOSEF LOCKE)	Josef Locke (EMI)
35	38	EMOTIONS	Mariah Carey (Columbia)
37	39	HUMAN TOUCH	Bruce Springsteen (Columbia)
-	40	LOVE IS	Kim Wilde (MCA)
36	41	SIMPLY THE BEST	Tina Turner (Capitol)
31	42	SOME GIRLS WANDER BY MISTAKE	Sisters Of Mercy (Merciful Release)
45	43	OUT OF TIME	R.E.M. (Warner Bros.)
46	44	WAKING UP THE NEIGHBOURS	Bryan Adams (A&M)
41	45	DIAMONDS AND PEARLS	Prince & the New Power Generation (Paisley Park)
50	46	NIGHT CALLS	Joe Cocker (Capitol)
-	47	APPETITE FOR DESTRUCTION	Guns N' Roses (Geffen)
38	48	0898	Beautiful South (Go! Discs)
47	49	LUCKY TOWN	Bruce Springsteen (Columbia)
43	50	WOODFACE	Crowded House (Capitol)

Carter The Unstoppable Sex Machine (or just Carter to their more celibate friends and fans) became the seventh act already in 1992 to enter the album chart at Number 1. *1992 The Love Album* had but a week there, though, before being ousted by a further chart-topper from heavy mob Iron Maiden, *Fear Of The Dark*. American hard rockers the Black Crowes, meanwhile, made an impressive debut at 3.

June 1992

6 June 1992

last	this	Title	Artist (Label)
-	1	LIVE AT WEMBLEY '86	Queen (Parlophone)
-	2	BACK TO FRONT	Lionel Richie (Motown)
3	3	STARS	Simply Red (East West)
8	4	DIVA	Annie Lennox (RCA)
17	5	MICHAEL BALL	Michael Ball (Polydor)
6	6	HORMONALLY YOURS	Shakespear's Sister (London)
4	7	UP	Right Said Fred (Tug)
10	8	THIS THING CALLED LOVE - THE GREATEST HITS OF ALEXANDER O'NEAL	Alexander O'Neal (Tabu)
5	9	GREATEST HITS	Squeeze (A&M)
2	10	THE SOUTHERN HARMONY AND MUSICAL COMPANION	Black Crowes (Def American)
22	11	USE YOUR ILLUSION II	Guns N' Roses (Geffen)
9	12	GREATEST HITS	ZZ Top (Warner Bros.)
1	13	FEAR OF THE DARK	Iron Maiden (EMI)
11	14	WISH	Cure (Fiction)
21	15	THE COMMITMENTS	Commitments (MCA)
16	16	DIVINE MADNESS	Madness (Virgin)
7	17	1992 THE LOVE ALBUM	Carter The Unstoppable Sex Machine (Chrysalis)
23	18	REAL LOVE	Lisa Stansfield (Arista)
19	19	EXTREME II PORNOGRAFFITTI	Extreme (A&M)
12	20	POWER OF TEN	Chris De Burgh (A&M)
19	21	CURTIS STIGERS	Curtis Stigers (Arista)
34	22	USE YOUR ILLUSION I	Guns N' Roses (Geffen)
15	23	ADRENALIZE	Def Leppard (Bludgeon Riffola)
35	24	INGENUE	k.d. lang (Sire)
24	25	NEVERMIND	Nirvana (DGC)
13	26	WE CAN'T DANCE	Genesis (Virgin)
28	27	UNFORGETTABLE - WITH LOVE	Natalie Cole (Elektra)
20	28	GREATEST HITS II	Queen (Parlophone)
27	29	TEARS ROLL DOWN (GREATEST HITS '82-'92)	Tears For Fears (Fontana)
33	30	ACHTUNG BABY	U2 (Island)
29	31	THE COMMITMENTS VOL.2	Commitments (MCA)
-	32	FINALLY	Ce Ce Peniston (A&M)
26	33	VOLUME III JUST RIGHT	Soul II Soul (10)
38	34	EMOTIONS	Mariah Carey (Columbia)
14	35	REVENGE	Kiss (Mercury)
25	36	GREATEST HITS	Foreigner (Atlantic)
41	37	SIMPLY THE BEST	Tina Turner (Capitol)
40	38	LOVE IS	Kim Wilde (MCA)
31	39	DANGEROUS	Michael Jackson (Epic)
30	40	LOVE HURTS	Cher (Geffen)
39	41	HUMAN TOUCH	Bruce Springsteen (Columbia)
32	42	GREATEST HITS	Queen (EMI)
46	43	NIGHT CALLS	Joe Cocker (Capitol)
47	44	APPETITE FOR DESTRUCTION	Guns N' Roses (Geffen)
-	45	WAYNE'S WORLD - SOUNDTRACK	Various Artists (Warner Bros.)
-	46	GROOVUS MAXIMUS	Electric Boys (Vertigo)
36	47	METALLICA	Metallica (Vertigo)
37	48	HEAR MY SONG (THE BEST OF JOSEF LOCKE)	Josef Locke (EMI)
-	49	VALHALLA AVENUE	Fatima Mansions (Radioactive)
44	50	WAKING UP THE NEIGHBOURS	Bryan Adams (A&M)

13 June 1992

last	this	Title	Artist (Label)
2	1	BACK TO FRONT	Lionel Richie (Motown)
-	2	CHANGE EVERYTHING	Del Amitri (A&M)
1	3	LIVE AT WEMBLEY '86	Queen (Parlophone)
3	4	STARS	Simply Red (East West)
5	5	MICHAEL BALL	Michael Ball (Polydor)
4	6	DIVA	Annie Lennox (RCA)
6	7	HORMONALLY YOURS	Shakespear's Sister (London)
-	8	AS UGLY AS THEY WANNA BE	Ugly Kid Joe (Mercury)
7	9	UP	Right Said Fred (Tug)
8	10	SHADOWS AND LIGHT	Wilson Phillips (SBK)
8	11	THIS THING CALLED LOVE - THE GREATEST HITS OF ALEXANDER O'NEAL	Alexander O'Neal (Tabu)
9	12	GREATEST HITS	Squeeze (A&M)
12	13	GREATEST HITS	ZZ Top (Warner Bros.)
11	14	USE YOUR ILLUSION II	Guns N' Roses (Geffen)
14	15	WISH	Cure (Fiction)
18	16	REAL LOVE	Lisa Stansfield (Arista)
15	17	THE COMMITMENTS	Commitments (MCA)
-	18	COMPLETELY HOOKED - THE BEST OF DR. HOOK	Dr. Hook (Capitol)
10	19	THE SOUTHERN HARMONY AND MUSICAL COMPANION	Black Crowes (Def American)
30	20	ACHTUNG BABY	U2 (Island)
16	21	DIVINE MADNESS	Madness (Virgin)
19	22	EXTREME II PORNOGRAFFITTI	Extreme (A&M)
22	23	USE YOUR ILLUSION I	Guns N' Roses (Geffen)
24	24	NEVERMIND	Nirvana (DGC)
45	25	WAYNE'S WORLD - SOUNDTRACK	Various Artists (Warner Bros.)
21	26	CURTIS STIGERS	Curtis Stigers (Arista)
20	27	POWER OF TEN	Chris De Burgh (A&M)
24	28	INGENUE	k.d. lang (Sire)
23	29	ADRENALIZE	Def Leppard (Bludgeon Riffola)
37	30	SIMPLY THE BEST	Tina Turner (Capitol)
28	31	GREATEST HITS II	Queen (Parlophone)
13	32	FEAR OF THE DARK	Iron Maiden (EMI)
26	33	WE CAN'T DANCE	Genesis (Virgin)
-	34	FUNKY DIVAS	En Vogue (East West America)
31	35	THE COMMITMENTS VOL.2	Commitments (MCA)
29	36	TEARS ROLL DOWN (GREATEST HITS '82-'92)	Tears For Fears (Fontana)
27	37	UNFORGETTABLE - WITH LOVE	Natalie Cole (Elektra)
33	38	VOLUME III JUST RIGHT	Soul II Soul (10)
17	39	1992 THE LOVE ALBUM	Carter The Unstoppable Sex Machine (Chrysalis)
39	40	DANGEROUS	Michael Jackson (Epic)
32	41	FINALLY	Ce Ce Peniston (A&M)
-	42	0898	Beautiful South (Go! Discs)
44	43	APPETITE FOR DESTRUCTION	Guns N' Roses (Geffen)
34	44	EMOTIONS	Mariah Carey (Columbia)
43	45	NIGHT CALLS	Joe Cocker (Capitol)
42	46	GREATEST HITS	Queen (EMI)
40	47	LOVE HURTS	Cher (Geffen)
36	48	GREATEST HITS	Foreigner (Atlantic)
47	49	METALLICA	Metallica (Vertigo)
-	50	DIAMONDS AND PEARLS	Prince & the New Power Generation (Paisley Park)

20 June 1992

last	this	Title	Artist (Label)
1	1	BACK TO FRONT	Lionel Richie (Motown)
2	2	CHANGE EVERYTHING	Del Amitri (A&M)
-	3	ANGEL DUST	Faith No More (Slash)
3	4	LIVE AT WEMBLEY '86	Queen (Parlophone)
4	5	STARS	Simply Red (East West)
18	6	COMPLETELY HOOKED - THE BEST OF DR. HOOK	Dr. Hook (Capitol)
11	7	THIS THING CALLED LOVE - THE GREATEST HITS OF ALEXANDER O'NEAL	Alexander O'Neal (Tabu)
6	8	DIVA	Annie Lennox (RCA)
9	9	AS UGLY AS THEY WANNA BE	Ugly Kid Joe (Mercury)
10	10	SHADOWS AND LIGHT	Wilson Phillips (SBK)
-	11	RUSH STREET	Richard Marx (Capitol)
7	12	HORMONALLY YOURS	Shakespear's Sister (London)
14	13	USE YOUR ILLUSION II	Guns N' Roses (Geffen)
-	14	THE CRIMSON IDOL	W.A.S.P. (Parlophone)
5	15	MICHAEL BALL	Michael Ball (Polydor)
16	16	WISH	Cure (Fiction)
-	17	HIT PARADE 1	Wedding Present (RCA)
20	18	ACHTUNG BABY	U2 (Island)
9	19	UP	Right Said Fred (Tug)
16	20	REAL LOVE	Lisa Stansfield (Arista)
-	21	A SINGLES COLLECTION 1982-1992	Marillion (EMI)
25	22	WAYNE'S WORLD - SOUNDTRACK	Various Artists (Warner Bros.)
12	23	GREATEST HITS	Squeeze (A&M)
13	24	GREATEST HITS	ZZ Top (Warner Bros.)
23	25	USE YOUR ILLUSION I	Guns N' Roses (Geffen)
17	26	THE COMMITMENTS	Commitments (MCA)
41	27	FINALLY	Ce Ce Peniston (A&M)
21	28	DIVINE MADNESS	Madness (Virgin)
24	29	NEVERMIND	Nirvana (DGC)
22	30	EXTREME II PORNOGRAFFITTI	Extreme (A&M)
31	31	GREATEST HITS II	Queen (Parlophone)
19	32	THE SOUTHERN HARMONY AND MUSICAL COMPANION	Black Crowes (Def American)
44	33	EMOTIONS	Mariah Carey (Columbia)
33	34	WE CAN'T DANCE	Genesis (Virgin)
26	35	CURTIS STIGERS	Curtis Stigers (Arista)
30	36	SIMPLY THE BEST	Tina Turner (Capitol)
34	37	FUNKY DIVAS	En Vogue (East West America)
43	38	APPETITE FOR DESTRUCTION	Guns N' Roses (Geffen)
42	39	0898	Beautiful South (Go! Discs)
-	40	LEVELLING THE LAND	Levellers (China)
-	41	SQUARE THE CIRCLE	Joan Armatrading (A&M)
27	42	POWER OF TEN	Chris De Burgh (A&M)
-	43	WOODFACE	Crowded House (Capitol)
29	44	ADRENALIZE	Def Leppard (Bludgeon Riffola)
40	45	DANGEROUS	Michael Jackson (Epic)
28	46	INGENUE	k.d. lang (Sire)
37	47	UNFORGETTABLE - WITH LOVE	Natalie Cole (Elektra)
32	48	FEAR OF THE DARK	Iron Maiden (EMI)
39	49	1992 THE LOVE ALBUM	Carter The Unstoppable Sex Machine (Chrysalis)
36	50	TEARS ROLL DOWN (GREATEST HITS '82-'92)	Tears For Fears (Fontana)

The release of a vintage live performance by Queen on record reiterated the public's hunger for the now officially disbanded supergroup's material by debuting at the top. An album with more eventual staying power, however, was Lionel Richie's *Back To Front*, with his first solo recordings for nearly 5 years.

June – July 1992

27 June 1992

last week	this week	Title	Artist (Label)
-	1	THE ONE	Elton John (Rocket)
1	2	BACK TO FRONT	Lionel Richie (Motown)
5	3	STARS	Simply Red (East West)
7	4	THIS THING CALLED LOVE - THE GREATEST HITS OF ALEXANDER O'NEAL	Alexander O'Neal (Tabu)
6	5	COMPLETELY HOOKED - THE BEST OF DR. HOOK	Dr. Hook (Capitol)
2	6	CHANGE EVERYTHING	Del Amitri (A&M)
3	7	ANGEL DUST	Faith No More (Slash)
13	8	USE YOUR ILLUSION II	Guns N' Roses (Geffen)
4	9	LIVE AT WEMBLEY '86	Queen (Parlophone)
11	10	RUSH STREET	Richard Marx (Capitol)
8	11	DIVA	Annie Lennox (RCA)
18	12	ACHTUNG BABY	U2 (Island)
19	13	UP	Right Said Fred (Tug)
10	14	SHADOWS AND LIGHT	Wilson Phillips (SBK)
12	15	HORMONALLY YOURS	Shakespear's Sister (London)
9	16	AS UGLY AS THEY WANNA BE	Ugly Kid Joe (Mercury)
16	17	WISH	Cure (Fiction)
25	18	USE YOUR ILLUSION I	Guns N' Roses (Geffen)
15	19	MICHAEL BALL	Michael Ball (Polydor)
26	20	THE COMMITMENTS	Commitments (MCA)
39	21	0898	Beautiful South (Go! Discs)
-	22	THE COMPLETE TOM JONES	Tom Jones (London/The Hit Label)
-	23	DIAMONDS AND PEARLS	Prince & the New Power Generation (Paisley Park)
21	24	A SINGLES COLLECTION 1982-1992	Marillion (EMI)
22	25	WAYNE'S WORLD - SOUNDTRACK	Various Artists (Warner Bros.)
43	26	WOODFACE	Crowded House (Capitol)
20	27	REAL LOVE	Lisa Stansfield (Arista)
23	28	GREATEST HITS	Squeeze (A&M)
29	29	DIVINE MADNESS	Madness (Virgin)
28	30	APPETITE FOR DESTRUCTION	Guns N' Roses (Geffen)
-	31	THE LEGEND - THE ESSENTIAL COLLECTION	Joe Cocker (PolyGram TV)
29	32	NEVERMIND	Nirvana (DGC)
33	33	EMOTIONS	Mariah Carey (Columbia)
31	34	GREATEST HITS II	Queen (Parlophone)
14	35	THE CRIMSON IDOL	W.A.S.P. (Parlophone)
27	36	FINALLY	Ce Ce Peniston (A&M)
17	37	HIT PARADE 1	Wedding Present (RCA)
44	38	ADRENALIZE	Def Leppard (Bludgeon Riffola)
24	39	GREATEST HITS	ZZ Top (Warner Bros.)
-	40	VOLUME III JUST RIGHT	Soul II Soul (10)
-	41	HEARTBEAT - MUSIC FROM THE YORKSHIRE TV SERIES	Various Artists (Columbia)
40	42	LEVELLING THE LAND	Levellers (China)
-	43	TOTALLY KROSSED OUT	Kris Kross (Columbia)
45	44	DANGEROUS	Michael Jackson (Epic)
32	45	THE SOUTHERN HARMONY AND MUSICAL COMPANION	Black Crowes (Def American)
30	46	EXTREME II PORNOGRAFFITTI	Extreme (A&M)
42	47	POWER OF TEN	Chris De Burgh (A&M)
34	48	WE CAN'T DANCE	Genesis (Virgin)
-	49	DEATH IS NOT THE END	Shut Up And Dance (Shut Up And Dance)
35	50	CURTIS STIGERS	Curtis Stigers (Arista)

4 July 1992

last week	this week	Title	Artist (Label)
1	1	THE ONE	Elton John (Rocket)
2	2	BACK TO FRONT	Lionel Richie (Motown)
41	3	HEARTBEAT - MUSIC FROM THE YORKSHIRE TV SERIES	Various Artists (Columbia)
5	4	COMPLETELY HOOKED	Dr. Hook (Capitol)
3	5	STARS	Simply Red (East West)
4	6	THIS THING CALLED LOVE - THE GREATEST HITS OF ALEXANDER O'NEAL	Alexander O'Neal (Tabu)
31	7	THE LEGEND - THE ESSENTIAL COLLECTION	Joe Cocker (PolyGram TV)
-	8	SGT PEPPER'S LONELY HEARTS CLUB BAND	Beatles (Parlophone)
9	9	LIVE AT WEMBLEY '86	Queen (Parlophone)
12	10	ACHTUNG BABY	U2 (Island)
10	11	RUSH STREET	Richard Marx (Capitol)
8	12	USE YOUR ILLUSION II	Guns N' Roses (Geffen)
15	13	HORMONALLY YOURS	Shakespear's Sister (London)
22	14	THE COMPLETE TOM JONES	Tom Jones (London/The Hit Label)
-	15	THE GREATEST HITS 1966-1992	Neil Diamond (Columbia)
23	16	DIAMONDS AND PEARLS	Prince & the New Power Generation (Paisley Park)
6	17	CHANGE EVERYTHING	Del Amitri (A&M)
27	18	REAL LOVE	Lisa Stansfield (Arista)
-	19	MASQUE	Mission (Vertigo)
7	20	ANGEL DUST	Faith No More (Slash)
18	21	USE YOUR ILLUSION I	Guns N' Roses (Geffen)
11	22	DIVA	Annie Lennox (RCA)
13	23	UP	Right Said Fred (Tug)
16	24	AS UGLY AS THEY WANNA BE	Ugly Kid Joe (Mercury)
20	25	THE COMMITMENTS	Commitments (MCA)
17	26	WISH	Cure (Fiction)
-	27	DEHUMANIZE	Black Sabbath (IRS)
26	28	WOODFACE	Crowded House (Capitol)
38	29	ADRENALIZE	Def Leppard (Bludgeon Riffola)
33	30	EMOTIONS	Mariah Carey (Columbia)
14	31	SHADOWS AND LIGHT	Wilson Phillips (SBK)
29	32	DIVINE MADNESS	Madness (Virgin)
21	33	0898	Beautiful South (Go! Discs)
39	34	GREATEST HITS	ZZ Top (Warner Bros.)
19	35	MICHAEL BALL	Michael Ball (Polydor)
32	36	NEVERMIND	Nirvana (DGC)
28	37	GREATEST HITS	Squeeze (A&M)
-	38	INFINITY WITHIN	Deee-Lite (Elektra)
-	39	TRIBES, VIBES AND SCRIBES	Incognito (Talkin' Loud)
30	40	APPETITE FOR DESTRUCTION	Guns N' Roses (Geffen)
34	41	GREATEST HITS II	Queen (Parlophone)
43	42	TOTALLY KROSSED OUT	Kris Kross (Columbia)
44	43	DANGEROUS	Michael Jackson (Epic)
-	44	SIMPLY THE BEST	Tina Turner (Capitol)
49	45	DEATH IS NOT THE END	Shut Up And Dance (Shut Up And Dance)
48	46	WE CAN'T DANCE	Genesis (Virgin)
36	47	FINALLY	Ce Ce Peniston (A&M)
47	48	POWER OF TEN	Chris De Burgh (A&M)
24	49	A SINGLES COLLECTION 1982-1992	Marillion (EMI)

11 July 1992

last week	this week	Title	Artist (Label)
1	1	THE ONE	Elton John (Rocket)
2	2	BACK TO FRONT	Lionel Richie (Motown)
3	3	HEARTBEAT - MUSIC FROM THE YORKSHIRE TV SERIES	Various Artists (Columbia)
15	4	THE GREATEST HITS 1966-1992	Neil Diamond (Columbia)
5	5	STARS	Simply Red (East West)
7	6	THE LEGEND - THE ESSENTIAL COLLECTION	Joe Cocker (PolyGram TV)
6	7	THIS THING CALLED LOVE - THE GREATEST HITS	Alexander O'Neal (Tabu)
4	8	COMPLETELY HOOKED	Dr. Hook (Capitol)
-	9	GOOD STUFF	B52's (Epic)
10	10	ACHTUNG BABY	U2 (Island)
-	11	THE BEST OF PREFAB SPROUT: A LIFE OF SURPRISES	Prefab Sprout (Kitchenware)
16	12	DIAMONDS AND PEARLS	Prince & the New Power Generation (Paisley Park)
17	13	CHANGE EVERYTHING	Del Amitri (A&M)
11	14	RUSH STREET	Richard Marx (Capitol)
14	15	THE COMPLETE TOM JONES	Tom Jones (London/The Hit Label)
12	16	USE YOUR ILLUSION II	Guns N' Roses (Geffen)
8	17	SGT PEPPER'S LONELY HEARTS CLUB BAND	Beatles (Parlophone)
25	18	THE COMMITMENTS	Commitments (MCA)
29	19	ADRENALIZE	Def Leppard (Bludgeon Riffola)
9	20	LIVE AT WEMBLEY '86	Queen (Parlophone)
18	21	REAL LOVE	Lisa Stansfield (Arista)
22	22	DIVA	Annie Lennox (RCA)
28	23	WOODFACE	Crowded House (Capitol)
20	24	ANGEL DUST	Faith No More (Slash)
19	25	MASQUE	Mission (Vertigo)
23	26	UP	Right Said Fred (Tug)
13	27	HORMONALLY YOURS	Shakespear's Sister (London)
30	28	EMOTIONS	Mariah Carey (Columbia)
36	29	NEVERMIND	Nirvana (DGC)
21	30	USE YOUR ILLUSION I	Guns N' Roses (Geffen)
24	31	AS UGLY AS THEY WANNA BE	Ugly Kid Joe (Mercury)
31	32	SHADOWS AND LIGHT	Wilson Phillips (SBK)
32	33	DIVINE MADNESS	Madness (Virgin)
-	34	ASQUARIUS	Cud (A&M)
37	35	WAYNE'S WORLD - SOUNDTRACK	Various Artists (Warner Bros.)
-	36	LEVELLING THE LAND	Levellers (China)
26	37	WISH	Cure (Fiction)
33	38	0898	Beautiful South (Go! Discs)
-	39	CURTIS STIGERS	Curtis Stigers (Arista)
40	40	GREATEST HITS II	Queen (Parlophone)
39	41	INFINITY WITHIN	Deee-Lite (Elektra)
41	42	APPETITE FOR DESTRUCTION	Guns N' Roses (Geffen)
27	43	DEHUMANIZE	Black Sabbath (IRS)
40	44	TRIBES, VIBES AND SCRIBES	Incognito (Talkin' Loud)
44	45	DANGEROUS	Michael Jackson (Epic)
-	46	1992 THE LOVE ALBUM	Carter The Unstoppable Sex Machine (Chrysalis)
42	47	GREATEST HITS	ZZ Top (Warner Bros.)
38	48	GREATEST HITS	Squeeze (A&M)
-	49	PRAISE	Inner City (10)
47	50	WE CAN'T DANCE	Genesis (Virgin)

Emulating his previous two albums, *Sleeping With The Past* and *The Very Best Of* in 1990, Elton John's *The One* soared easily to a three-week spell at the top.

Meanwhile, the sudden reappearance in the Top 10 of the Beatles' *Sgt Pepper* album was mostly due to wide media coverage of its own 25th anniversary!

July – August 1992

last week	this week	18 July 1992	
-	1	U.F. ORB	Orb (Big Life)
2	2	BACK TO FRONT	Lionel Richie (Motown)
3	3	HEARTBEAT - MUSIC FROM THE YORKSHIRE TV SERIES	Various Artists (Columbia)
1	4	THE ONE	Elton John (Rocket)
-	5	COUNTDOWN TO EXTINCTION	Megadeth (Capitol)
4	6	THE GREATEST HITS 1966-1992	Neil Diamond (Columbia)
6	7	THE LEGEND - THE ESSENTIAL COLLECTION	Joe Cocker (PolyGram TV)
-	8	MTV UNPLUGGED (EP)	Mariah Carey (Columbia)
11	9	THE BEST OF PREFAB SPROUT: A LIFE OF SURPRISES	Prefab Sprout (Kitchenware)
9	10	GOOD STUFF	B52's (Epic)
14	11	RUSH STREET	Richard Marx (Capitol)
5	12	STARS	Simply Red (East West)
10	13	ACHTUNG BABY	U2 (Island)
13	14	CHANGE EVERYTHING	Del Amitri (A&M)
8	15	COMPLETELY HOOKED - THE BEST OF DR. HOOK	Dr. Hook (Capitol)
12	16	DIAMONDS AND PEARLS	Prince & the New Power Generation (Paisley Park)
7	17	THIS THING CALLED LOVE - THE GREATEST HITS	Alexander O'Neal (Tabu)
19	18	ADRENALIZE	Def Leppard (Bludgeon Riffola)
27	19	HORMONALLY YOURS	Shakespear's Sister (London)
18	20	THE COMMITMENTS	Commitments (MCA)
-	21	MICHAEL CRAWFORD PERFORMS ANDREW LLOYD WEBBER	Michael Crawford (Telstar)
23	22	WOODFACE	Crowded House (Capitol)
39	23	CURTIS STIGERS	Curtis Stigers (Arista)
16	24	USE YOUR ILLUSION II	Guns N' Roses (Geffen)
22	25	DIVA	Annie Lennox (RCA)
17	26	SGT PEPPER'S LONELY HEARTS CLUB BAND	Beatles (Parlophone)
15	27	THE COMPLETE TOM JONES	Tom Jones (London/The Hit Label)
21	28	REAL LOVE	Lisa Stansfield (Arista)
29	29	NEVERMIND	Nirvana (DGC)
24	30	ANGEL DUST	Faith No More (Slash)
30	31	USE YOUR ILLUSION I	Guns N' Roses (Geffen)
28	32	EMOTIONS	Mariah Carey (Columbia)
20	33	LIVE AT WEMBLEY '86	Queen (Parlophone)
26	34	UP	Right Said Fred (Tug)
-	35	BABE RAINBOW	House Of Love (Fontana)
-	37	THE FORCE BEHIND THE POWER Diana Ross (EMI)	
31	38	AS UGLY AS THEY WANNA BE	Ugly Kid Joe (Mercury)
45	39	DANGEROUS	Michael Jackson (Epic)
-	40	LITTLE EARTHQUAKES	Tori Amos (East West)
34	41	AQUARIUS	Cud (A&M)
40	42	GREATEST HITS II	Queen (Parlophone)
42	43	APPETITE FOR DESTRUCTION	Guns N' Roses (Geffen)
33	44	DIVINE MADNESS	Madness (Virgin)
38	45	0898 - Beautiful South (Go! Discs)	
46	46	1992 THE LOVE ALBUM	Carter The Unstoppable Sex Machine (Chrysalis)
36	47	LEVELLING THE LAND	Levellers (China)
35	48	WAYNE'S WORLD	Various Artists (Warner Bros.)
32	49	SHADOWS AND LIGHT	Wilson Phillips (SBK)
47	50	GREATEST HITS	ZZ Top (Warner Bros.)

last week	this week	25 July 1992	
2	1	BACK TO FRONT	Lionel Richie (Motown)
8	2	MTV UNPLUGGED (EP)	Mariah Carey (Columbia)
1	3	U.F. ORB	Orb (Big Life)
6	4	THE GREATEST HITS 1966-1992	Neil Diamond (Columbia)
7	5	THE LEGEND - THE ESSENTIAL COLLECTION	Joe Cocker (PolyGram TV)
3	6	HEARTBEAT - MUSIC FROM THE YORKSHIRE TV SERIES	Various Artists (Columbia)
12	7	STARS	Simply Red (East West)
4	8	THE ONE	Elton John (Rocket)
9	9	THE BEST OF PREFAB SPROUT: A LIFE OF SURPRISES	Prefab Sprout (Kitchenware)
11	10	RUSH STREET	Richard Marx (Capitol)
5	11	COUNTDOWN TO EXTINCTION Megadeth (Capitol)	
14	12	CHANGE EVERYTHING	Del Amitri (A&M)
10	13	GOOD STUFF	B52's (Epic)
17	14	THIS THING CALLED LOVE - THE GREATEST HITS	Alexander O'Neal (Tabu)
15	15	COMPLETELY HOOKED - THE BEST OF DR. HOOK	Dr. Hook (Capitol)
13	16	ACHTUNG BABY	U2 (Island)
16	17	DIAMONDS AND PEARLS	Prince & the New Power Generation (Paisley Park)
-	18	FULL ON ... MASK HYSTERIA Altern 8 (Network)	
19	19	HORMONALLY YOURS	Shakespear's Sister (London)
23	20	CURTIS STIGERS	Curtis Stigers (Arista)
22	21	WOODFACE	Crowded House (Capitol)
20	22	THE COMMITMENTS	Commitments (MCA)
37	23	THE FORCE BEHIND THE POWER Diana Ross (EMI)	
21	24	MICHAEL CRAWFORD PERFORMS ANDREW LLOYD WEBBER	Michael Crawford (Telstar)
24	25	USE YOUR ILLUSION II	Guns N' Roses (Geffen)
18	26	ADRENALIZE	Def Leppard (Bludgeon Riffola)
29	27	NEVERMIND	Nirvana (DGC)
25	28	DIVA	Annie Lennox (RCA)
28	29	REAL LOVE	Lisa Stansfield (Arista)
34	30	UP	Right Said Fred (Tug)
36	31	WE CAN'T DANCE	Genesis (Virgin)
39	32	DANGEROUS	Michael Jackson (Epic)
31	33	USE YOUR ILLUSION I	Guns N' Roses (Geffen)
33	34	LIVE AT WEMBLEY '86	Queen (Parlophone)
27	35	THE COMPLETE TOM JONES	Tom Jones (London/The Hit Label)
26	36	SGT PEPPER'S LONELY HEARTS CLUB BAND	Beatles (Parlophone)
30	37	ANGEL DUST	Faith No More (Slash)
43	38	APPETITE FOR DESTRUCTION	Guns N' Roses (Geffen)
50	39	GREATEST HITS	ZZ Top (Warner Bros.)
-	40	BACK TO BASICS: THE ESSENTIAL COLLECTION 1971-1992	Olivia Newton-John (Mercury)
-	41	PSALM 69: THE WAY TO SUCCEED AND THE WAY TO SUCK EGGS	Ministry (Sire)
-	42	HIGH ON THE HAPPY SIDE	Wet Wet Wet (Precious Organisation)
-	43	OUT OF TIME	R.E.M. (Warner Bros.)
44	44	DIVINE MADNESS	Madness (Virgin)
-	45	LIVE IN JAPAN	George Harrison (Dark Horse)
42	46	GREATEST HITS II	Queen (Parlophone)
-	47	SIMPLY THE BEST	Tina Turner (Capitol)
32	48	EMOTIONS	Mariah Carey (Columbia)
35	49	BABE RAINBOW	House Of Love (Fontana)
40	50	LITTLE EARTHQUAKES	Tori Amos (East West)

last week	this week	1 August 1992	
4	1	THE GREATEST HITS 1966-1992	Neil Diamond (Columbia)
7	2	STARS	Simply Red (East West)
1	3	BACK TO FRONT	Lionel Richie (Motown)
2	4	MTV UNPLUGGED (EP)	Mariah Carey (Columbia)
5	5	THE LEGEND - THE ESSENTIAL COLLECTION	Joe Cocker (PolyGram TV)
9	6	THE BEST OF PREFAB SPROUT: A LIFE OF SURPRISES	Prefab Sprout (Kitchenware)
14	7	THIS THING CALLED LOVE - THE GREATEST HITS	Alexander O'Neal (Tabu)
8	8	THE ONE	Elton John (Rocket)
-	9	DIRTY	Sonic Youth (DGC)
3	10	U.F. ORB	Orb (Big Life)
6	11	HEARTBEAT - MUSIC FROM THE YORKSHIRE TV SERIES	Various Artists (Columbia)
12	12	CHANGE EVERYTHING	Del Amitri (A&M)
27	13	NEVERMIND	Nirvana (DGC)
10	14	RUSH STREET	Richard Marx (Capitol)
32	15	DANGEROUS	Michael Jackson (Epic)
16	16	ACHTUNG BABY	U2 (Island)
19	17	HORMONALLY YOURS	Shakespear's Sister (London)
17	18	DIAMONDS AND PEARLS	Prince & the New Power Generation (Paisley Park)
31	19	WE CAN'T DANCE	Genesis (Virgin)
13	20	GOOD STUFF	B52's (Epic)
18	21	FULL ON ... MASK HYSTERIA Altern 8 (Network)	
40	22	BACK TO BASICS: THE ESSENTIAL COLLECTION 1971-1992	Olivia Newton-John (Mercury)
25	23	USE YOUR ILLUSION II	Guns N' Roses (Geffen)
22	24	THE COMMITMENTS	Commitments (MCA)
-	25	WAKING UP THE NEIGHBOURS	Bryan Adams (A&M)
30	26	UP	Right Said Fred (Tug)
24	27	MICHAEL CRAWFORD PERFORMS ANDREW LLOYD WEBBER	Michael Crawford (Telstar)
21	28	WOODFACE	Crowded House (Capitol)
15	29	COMPLETELY HOOKED	Dr. Hook (Capitol)
28	30	DIVA	Annie Lennox (RCA)
11	31	COUNTDOWN TO EXTINCTION Megadeth (Capitol)	
20	32	CURTIS STIGERS	Curtis Stigers (Arista)
29	33	REAL LOVE	Lisa Stansfield (Arista)
23	34	THE FORCE BEHIND THE POWER Diana Ross (EMI)	
26	35	ADRENALIZE	Def Leppard (Bludgeon Riffola)
33	36	USE YOUR ILLUSION I	Guns N' Roses (Geffen)
34	37	LIVE AT WEMBLEY '86	Queen (Parlophone)
38	38	APPETITE FOR DESTRUCTION	Guns N' Roses (Geffen)
42	39	HIGH ON THE HAPPY SIDE	Wet Wet Wet (Precious Organisation)
-	40	TONGUES AND TAILS	Sophie B. Hawkins (Columbia)
44	41	DIVINE MADNESS	Madness (Virgin)
37	42	ANGEL DUST	Faith No More (Slash)
41	43	PSALM 69: THE WAY TO SUCCEED AND THE WAY TO SUCK EGGS	Ministry (Sire)
-	44	TURNS INTO STONE	Stone Roses (Silvertone)
39	45	GREATEST HITS	ZZ Top (Warner Bros.)
-	46	SHEPHERD MOONS	Enya (WEA)
46	47	GREATEST HITS II	Queen (Parlophone)
47	48	SIMPLY THE BEST	Tina Turner (Capitol)
36	49	SGT PEPPER'S LONELY HEARTS CLUB BAND	Beatles (Parlophone)
43	50	OUT OF TIME	R.E.M. (Warner Bros.)

The soundtrack to the TV series *Heartbeat* was another of the occasional "Various Artists" sets still allowed in the chart, the reason being that it was regarded as a soundtrack *rather* than a compilation. Nevertheless, there was only one new track on board - *Heartbeat*, as sung by the show's star Nick Berry.

August 1992

8 August 1992

last week	this week	Title	Artist (Label)
1	1	THE GREATEST HITS 1966-1992	Neil Diamond (Columbia)
2	2	STARS	Simply Red (East West)
3	3	BACK TO FRONT	Lionel Richie (Motown)
-	4	YOUR ARSENAL	Morrissey (HMV)
5	5	THE LEGEND - THE ESSENTIAL COLLECTION	Joe Cocker (PolyGram TV)
6	6	THE BEST OF PREFAB SPROUT: A LIFE OF SURPRISES	Prefab Sprout (Kitchenware)
13	7	NEVERMIND	Nirvana (DGC)
4	8	MTV UNPLUGGED (EP)	Mariah Carey (Columbia)
7	9	THIS THING CALLED LOVE - THE GREATEST HITS	Alexander O'Neal (Tabu)
15	10	DANGEROUS	Michael Jackson (Epic)
8	11	THE ONE	Elton John (Rocket)
9	12	DIRTY	Sonic Youth (DGC)
-	13	GROWING UP IN PUBLIC	Jimmy Nail (East West)
26	14	UP	Right Said Fred (Tug)
17	15	HORMONALLY YOURS	Shakespear's Sister (London)
14	16	RUSH STREET	Richard Marx (Capitol)
19	17	WE CAN'T DANCE	Genesis (Virgin)
18	18	DIAMONDS AND PEARLS	Prince & the New Power Generation (Paisley Park)
16	19	ACHTUNG BABY	U2 (Island)
24	20	THE COMMITMENTS	Commitments (MCA)
-	21	ASTRONAUTS & HERETICS	Thomas Dolby (Virgin)
23	22	USE YOUR ILLUSION II	Guns N' Roses (Geffen)
-	23	THE MADMAN'S RETURN	Snap (Arista)
30	24	DIVA	Annie Lennox (RCA)
46	25	SHEPHERD MOONS	Enya (WEA)
25	26	WAKING UP THE NEIGHBOURS	Bryan Adams (A&M)
22	27	BACK TO BASICS: THE ESSENTIAL COLLECTION 1971-1992	Olivia Newton-John (Mercury)
12	28	CHANGE EVERYTHING	Del Amitri (A&M)
-	29	OUT OF THE CRADLE	Lindsey Buckingham (Mercury)
36	30	USE YOUR ILLUSION I	Guns N' Roses (Geffen)
28	31	WOODFACE	Crowded House (Capitol)
29	32	COMPLETELY HOOKED - THE BEST OF DR. HOOK	Dr. Hook (Capitol)
11	33	HEARTBEAT - MUSIC FROM THE YORKSHIRE TV SERIES	Various Artists (Columbia)
20	34	GOOD STUFF	B52's (Epic)
27	35	MICHAEL CRAWFORD PERFORMS ANDREW LLOYD WEBBER	Michael Crawford (Telstar)
10	36	U.F. ORB	Orb (Big Life)
33	37	REAL LOVE	Lisa Stansfield (Arista)
41	38	DIVINE MADNESS	Madness (Virgin)
-	39	MARCH OR DIE	Motorhead (Epic)
21	40	FULL ON ... MASK HYSTERIA	Altern 8 (Network)
-	41	THE DEFINITIVE...	Jim Reeves (Arcade)
35	42	ADRENALIZE	Def Leppard (Bludgeon Riffola)
37	43	LIVE AT WEMBLEY '86	Queen (Parlophone)
44	44	TURNS INTO STONE	Stone Roses (Silvertone)
40	45	TONGUES AND TAILS	Sophie B. Hawkins (Columbia)
39	46	HIGH ON THE HAPPY SIDE	Wet Wet Wet (Precious Organisation)
38	47	APPETITE FOR DESTRUCTION	Guns N' Roses (Geffen)
47	48	GREATEST HITS II	Queen (Parlophone)
32	49	CURTIS STIGERS	Curtis Stigers (Arista)
48	50	SIMPLY THE BEST	Tina Turner (Capitol)

15 August 1992

last week	this week	Title	Artist (Label)
-	1	WELCOME TO WHEREVER YOU ARE	INXS (Mercury)
1	2	THE GREATEST HITS 1966-1992	Neil Diamond (Columbia)
13	3	GROWING UP IN PUBLIC	Jimmy Nail (East West)
2	4	STARS	Simply Red (East West)
5	5	THE LEGEND - THE ESSENTIAL COLLECTION	Joe Cocker (PolyGram TV)
10	6	DANGEROUS	Michael Jackson (Epic)
25	7	SHEPHERD MOONS	Enya (WEA)
17	8	WE CAN'T DANCE	Genesis (Virgin)
3	9	BACK TO FRONT	Lionel Richie (Motown)
7	10	NEVERMIND	Nirvana (DGC)
4	11	YOUR ARSENAL	Morrissey (HMV)
8	12	MTV UNPLUGGED (EP)	Mariah Carey (Columbia)
-	13	FLOORED GENIUS - THE BEST OF...	Julian Cope/Teardrop Explodes (Island)
14	14	UP	Right Said Fred (Tug)
41	15	THE DEFINITIVE...	Jim Reeves (Arcade)
9	16	THIS THING CALLED LOVE - THE GREATEST HITS	Alexander O'Neal (Tabu)
38	17	DIVINE MADNESS	Madness (Virgin)
16	18	RUSH STREET	Richard Marx (Capitol)
11	19	THE ONE	Elton John (Rocket)
24	20	DIVA	Annie Lennox (RCA)
20	21	THE COMMITMENTS	Commitments (MCA)
6	22	THE BEST OF PREFAB SPROUT: A LIFE OF SURPRISES	Prefab Sprout (Kitchenware)
15	23	HORMONALLY YOURS	Shakespear's Sister (London)
22	24	USE YOUR ILLUSION II	Guns N' Roses (Geffen)
18	25	DIAMONDS AND PEARLS	Prince & the New Power Generation (Paisley Park)
19	26	ACHTUNG BABY	U2 (Island)
48	27	GREATEST HITS II	Queen (Parlophone)
-	28	BAD	Michael Jackson (Epic)
26	29	WAKING UP THE NEIGHBOURS	Bryan Adams (A&M)
27	30	BACK TO BASICS: THE ESSENTIAL COLLECTION 1971-1992	Olivia Newton-John (Mercury)
-	31	TOUR SOUVENIR PACK	Michael Jackson (Epic)
32	32	USE YOUR ILLUSION I	Guns N' Roses (Geffen)
21	33	ASTRONAUTS & HERETICS	Thomas Dolby (Virgin)
-	34	ANGEL DUST	Faith No More (Slash)
-	35	THRILLER	Michael Jackson (Epic)
23	36	THE MADMAN'S RETURN	Snap (Arista)
37	37	REAL LOVE	Lisa Stansfield (Arista)
12	38	DIRTY	Sonic Youth (DGC)
34	39	GOOD STUFF	B52's (Epic)
31	40	WOODFACE	Crowded House (Capitol)
36	41	U.F. ORB	Orb (Big Life)
-	42	THE EXTREMIST	Joe Satriani (Epic)
29	43	OUT OF THE CRADLE	Lindsey Buckingham (Mercury)
43	44	LIVE AT WEMBLEY '86	Queen (Parlophone)
28	45	CHANGE EVERYTHING	Del Amitri (A&M)
-	46	BARCELONA GAMES	Placido Domingo, Jose Carreras, Montserrat Caballé (RCA Red Seal)
44	47	TURNS INTO STONE	Stone Roses (Silvertone)
32	48	COMPLETELY HOOKED - THE BEST OF DR. HOOK	Dr. Hook (Capitol)
46	49	HIGH ON THE HAPPY SIDE	Wet Wet Wet (Precious Organisation)
47	50	APPETITE FOR DESTRUCTION	Guns N' Roses (Geffen)

22 August 1992

last week	this week	Title	Artist (Label)
1	1	WELCOME TO WHEREVER YOU ARE	INXS (Mercury)
2	2	THE GREATEST HITS 1966-1992	Neil Diamond (Columbia)
8	3	WE CAN'T DANCE	Genesis (Virgin)
-	4	RED HEAVEN	Throwing Muses (4AD)
4	5	STARS	Simply Red (East West)
6	6	SHEPHERD MOONS	Enya (WEA)
6	7	DANGEROUS	Michael Jackson (Epic)
10	8	NEVERMIND	Nirvana (DGC)
3	9	GROWING UP IN PUBLIC	Jimmy Nail (East West)
17	10	DIVINE MADNESS	Madness (Virgin)
5	11	THE LEGEND - THE ESSENTIAL COLLECTION	Joe Cocker (PolyGram TV)
9	12	BACK TO FRONT	Lionel Richie (Motown)
15	13	THE DEFINITIVE...	Jim Reeves (Arcade)
12	14	MTV UNPLUGGED (EP)	Mariah Carey (Columbia)
-	15	BARCELONA	Freddie Mercury & Montserrat Caballé (Polydor)
20	16	DIVA	Annie Lennox (RCA)
14	17	UP	Right Said Fred (Tug)
26	18	ACHTUNG BABY	U2 (Island)
16	19	THIS THING CALLED LOVE - THE GREATEST HITS	Alexander O'Neal (Tabu)
34	20	ANGEL DUST	Faith No More (Slash)
18	21	RUSH STREET	Richard Marx (Capitol)
42	22	THE EXTREMIST	Joe Satriani (Epic)
24	23	USE YOUR ILLUSION II	Guns N' Roses (Geffen)
-	24	THE VERY BEST OF...	Supertramp (A&M)
22	25	THE BEST OF PREFAB SPROUT: A LIFE OF SURPRISES	Prefab Sprout (Kitchenware)
36	26	THE MADMAN'S RETURN	Snap (Arista)
19	27	THE ONE	Elton John (Rocket)
11	28	YOUR ARSENAL	Morrissey (HMV)
13	29	FLOORED GENIUS - THE BEST OF ...	Julian Cope/Teardrop Explodes (Island)
-	30	BRAND NEW HEAVIES	Brand New Heavies (Acid Jazz)
21	31	THE COMMITMENTS	Commitments (MCA)
25	32	DIAMONDS AND PEARLS	Prince & the New Power Generation (Paisley Park)
32	33	USE YOUR ILLUSION I	Guns N' Roses (Geffen)
-	34	CURTIS STIGERS	Curtis Stigers (Arista)
23	35	HORMONALLY YOURS	Shakespear's Sister (London)
-	36	BLOOD SUGAR SEX MAGIK	Red Hot Chili Peppers (Warner Bros.)
27	37	GREATEST HITS II	Queen (Parlophone)
28	38	BAD	Michael Jackson (Epic)
40	39	WOODFACE	Crowded House (Capitol)
-	40	MACHINE + SOUL	Gary Numan (Numan)
-	41	WHIPPED!	Faster Pussycat (Elektra)
31	42	TOUR SOUVENIR PACK	Michael Jackson (Epic)
29	43	WAKING UP THE NEIGHBOURS	Bryan Adams (A&M)
-	44	UNBREAKABLE	Don-E (Fourth & Broadway)
50	45	APPETITE FOR DESTRUCTION	Guns N' Roses (Geffen)
30	46	BACK TO BASICS: THE ESSENTIAL COLLECTION 1971-1992	Olivia Newton-John (Mercury)
37	47	REAL LOVE	Lisa Stansfield (Arista)
-	48	ROUGH AND READY - VOLUME 1	Shabba Ranks (Epic)
38	49	DIRTY	Sonic Youth (DGC)
44	50	LIVE AT WEMBLEY '86	Queen (Parlophone)

Neil Diamond's chart-topping double compilation, featuring the mid-60s hits from the beginning of his career, plus an overview of his 15-odd years with Columbia, was his first major UK album seller since *Primitive* in 1984, but its success demonstrated the amount of silent majority support he clearly still had.

August – September 1992

last week	this week	29 August 1992	
-	1	BEST … 1	Smiths (WEA)
3	2	WE CAN'T DANCE	Genesis (Virgin)
2	3	THE GREATEST HITS 1966-1992	Neil Diamond (Columbia)
1	4	WELCOME TO WHEREVER YOU ARE	INXS (Mercury)
7	5	DANGEROUS	Michael Jackson (Epic)
5	6	STARS	Simply Red (East West)
6	7	SHEPHERD MOONS	Enya (WEA)
8	8	NEVERMIND	Nirvana (DGC)
10	9	DIVINE MADNESS	Madness (Virgin)
9	10	GROWING UP IN PUBLIC	Jimmy Nail (East West)
17	11	UP	Right Said Fred (Tug)
-	12	SOME GAVE ALL	Billy Ray Cyrus (Mercury)
16	13	DIVA	Annie Lennox (RCA)
12	14	BACK TO FRONT	Lionel Richie (Motown)
11	15	THE LEGEND - THE ESSENTIAL COLLECTION	Joe Cocker (PolyGram TV)
13	16	THE DEFINITIVE...	Jim Reeves (Arcade)
15	17	BARCELONA	Freddie Mercury & Montserrat Caballé (Polydor)
20	18	ANGEL DUST	Faith No More (Slash)
23	19	USE YOUR ILLUSION II	Guns N' Roses (Geffen)
21	20	RUSH STREET	Richard Marx (Capitol)
26	21	THE MADMAN'S RETURN	Snap (Arista)
31	22	THE COMMITMENTS	Commitments (MCA)
18	23	ACHTUNG BABY	U2 (Island)
19	24	THIS THING CALLED LOVE - THE GREATEST HITS	Alexander O'Neal (Tabu)
22	25	THE EXTREMIST	Joe Satriani (Epic)
24	26	THE VERY BEST OF SUPERTRAMP	Supertramp (A&M)
25	27	THE BEST OF PREFAB SPROUT: A LIFE OF SURPRISES	Prefab Sprout (Kitchenware)
28	28	YOUR ARSENAL	Morrissey (HMV)
4	29	RED HEAVEN	Throwing Muses (4AD)
35	30	HORMONALLY YOURS	Shakespear's Sister (London)
14	31	MTV UNPLUGGED (EP)	Mariah Carey (Columbia)
32	32	DIAMONDS AND PEARLS	Prince & the New Power Generation (Paisley Park)
37	33	GREATEST HITS II	Queen (Parlophone)
27	34	THE ONE	Elton John (Rocket)
33	35	USE YOUR ILLUSION I	Guns N' Roses (Geffen)
34	36	CURTIS STIGERS	Curtis Stigers (Arista)
29	37	FLOORED GENIUS - THE BEST OF...	Julian Cope/Teardrop Explodes (Island)
36	38	BLOOD SUGAR SEX MAGIK	Red Hot Chili Peppers (Warner Bros.)
38	39	BAD	Michael Jackson (Epic)
30	40	BRAND NEW HEAVIES	Brand New Heavies (Acid Jazz)
39	41	WOODFACE	Crowded House (Capitol)
45	42	APPETITE FOR DESTRUCTION	Guns N' Roses (Geffen)
43	43	WAKING UP THE NEIGHBOURS	Bryan Adams (A&M)
50	44	LIVE AT WEMBLEY '86	Queen (Parlophone)
-	45	WATERMARK	Enya (WEA)
47	46	REAL LOVE	Lisa Stansfield (Arista)
42	47	TOUR SOUVENIR PACK	Michael Jackson (Epic)
-	48	SIMPLY THE BEST	Tina Turner (Capitol)
46	49	BACK TO BASICS: THE ESSENTIAL COLLECTION 1971-1992	Olivia Newton-John (Mercury)
-	50	TRUTH AND LOVE	Hue & Cry (Fidelity)

last week	this week	5 September 1992	
-	1	GREATEST HITS	Kylie Minogue (PWL)
-	2	LAUGHING ON JUDGEMENT DAY	Thunder (EMI)
1	3	BEST … 1	Smiths (WEA)
12	4	SOME GAVE ALL	Billy Ray Cyrus (Mercury)
5	5	DANGEROUS	Michael Jackson (Epic)
4	6	WELCOME TO WHEREVER YOU ARE	INXS (Mercury)
2	7	WE CAN'T DANCE	Genesis (Virgin)
13	8	DIVA	Annie Lennox (RCA)
8	9	NEVERMIND	Nirvana (DGC)
3	10	THE GREATEST HITS 1966-1992	Neil Diamond (Columbia)
14	11	BACK TO FRONT	Lionel Richie (Motown)
-	12	BOBBY	Bobby Brown (MCA)
6	13	STARS	Simply Red (East West)
7	14	SHEPHERD MOONS	Enya (WEA)
9	15	DIVINE MADNESS	Madness (Virgin)
10	16	GROWING UP IN PUBLIC	Jimmy Nail (East West)
-	17	TAKE THAT AND PARTY	Take That (RCA)
11	18	UP	Right Said Fred (Tug)
15	19	THE LEGEND - THE ESSENTIAL COLLECTION	Joe Cocker (PolyGram TV)
22	20	THE COMMITMENTS	Commitments (MCA)
21	21	THE MADMAN'S RETURN	Snap (Arista)
18	22	ANGEL DUST	Faith No More (Slash)
19	23	USE YOUR ILLUSION II	Guns N' Roses (Geffen)
16	24	THE DEFINITIVE JIM REEVES	Jim Reeves (Arcade)
20	25	RUSH STREET	Richard Marx (Capitol)
27	26	THE BEST OF PREFAB SPROUT: A LIFE OF SURPRISES	Prefab Sprout (Kitchenware)
24	27	THIS THING CALLED LOVE - THE GREATEST HITS	Alexander O'Neal (Tabu)
23	28	ACHTUNG BABY	U2 (Island)
-	29	FONTANELLE	Babes In Toyland (Southern)
-	30	HEAVY RHYME EXPERIENCE: VOL. 1	Brand New Heavies (Acid Jazz)
25	31	THE EXTREMIST	Joe Satriani (Epic)
31	32	MTV UNPLUGGED (EP)	Mariah Carey (Columbia)
-	33	THE DEFINITIVE PATSY CLINE	Patsy Cline (Arcade)
28	34	YOUR ARSENAL	Morrissey (HMV)
33	35	GREATEST HITS II	Queen (Parlophone)
30	36	HORMONALLY YOURS	Shakespear's Sister (London)
37	37	USE YOUR ILLUSION I	Guns N' Roses (Geffen)
32	38	DIAMONDS AND PEARLS	Prince & the New Power Generation (Paisley Park)
17	39	BARCELONA	Freddie Mercury & Montserrat Caballé (Polydor)
-	40	JON SECADA	Jon Secada (SBK)
34	41	THE ONE	Elton John (Rocket)
26	42	THE VERY BEST OF SUPERTRAMP	Supertramp (A&M)
42	43	APPETITE FOR DESTRUCTION	Guns N' Roses (Geffen)
38	44	BLOOD SUGAR SEX MAGIK	Red Hot Chili Peppers (Warner Bros.)
36	45	CURTIS STIGERS	Curtis Stigers (Arista)
-	46	TEN	Pearl Jam (Epic)
39	47	BAD	Michael Jackson (Epic)
45	48	WATERMARK	Enya (WEA)
-	49	DON'T TREAD	Damn Yankees (Warner Bros.)
-	50	CHANGE EVERYTHING	Del Amitri (A&M)

last week	this week	12 September 1992	
-	1	TUBULAR BELLS II	Mike Oldfield (WEA)
1	2	GREATEST HITS	Kylie Minogue (PWL)
2	3	LAUGHING ON JUDGEMENT DAY	Thunder (EMI)
-	4	UNPLUGGED	Eric Clapton (Duck)
-	5	TOURISM	Roxette (EMI)
3	6	BEST … 1	Smiths (WEA)
5	7	DANGEROUS	Michael Jackson (Epic)
4	8	SOME GAVE ALL	Billy Ray Cyrus (Mercury)
17	9	TAKE THAT AND PARTY	Take That (RCA)
8	10	DIVA	Annie Lennox (RCA)
11	11	BACK TO FRONT	Lionel Richie (Motown)
10	12	THE GREATEST HITS 1966-1992	Neil Diamond (Columbia)
6	13	WELCOME TO WHEREVER YOU ARE	INXS (Mercury)
7	14	WE CAN'T DANCE	Genesis (Virgin)
12	15	BOBBY	Bobby Brown (MCA)
-	16	PAUL WELLER	Paul Weller (Go! Discs)
-	17	AMERICA'S LEAST WANTED	Ugly Kid Joe (Vertigo)
9	18	NEVERMIND	Nirvana (DGC)
13	19	STARS	Simply Red (East West)
33	20	THE DEFINITIVE PATSY CLINE	Patsy Cline (Arcade)
14	21	SHEPHERD MOONS	Enya (WEA)
15	22	DIVINE MADNESS	Madness (Virgin)
16	23	GROWING UP IN PUBLIC	Jimmy Nail (East West)
22	24	ANGEL DUST	Faith No More (Slash)
25	25	RUSH STREET	Richard Marx (Capitol)
-	26	I WAS WARNED	Robert Cray Band (Mercury)
18	27	UP	Right Said Fred (Tug)
19	28	THE LEGEND - THE ESSENTIAL COLLECTION	Joe Cocker (PolyGram TV)
20	29	THE COMMITMENTS	Commitments (MCA)
40	30	JON SECADA	Jon Secada (SBK)
23	31	USE YOUR ILLUSION II	Guns N' Roses (Geffen)
21	32	THE MADMAN'S RETURN	Snap (Arista)
28	33	ACHTUNG BABY	U2 (Island)
35	34	GREATEST HITS II	Queen (Parlophone)
26	35	THE BEST OF PREFAB SPROUT: A LIFE OF SURPRISES	Prefab Sprout (Kitchenware)
24	36	THE DEFINITIVE JIM REEVES	Jim Reeves (Arcade)
27	37	THIS THING CALLED LOVE - THE GREATEST HITS OF ALEXANDER O'NEAL	Alexander O'Neal (Tabu)
32	38	MTV UNPLUGGED (EP)	Mariah Carey (Columbia)
31	39	THE EXTREMIST	Joe Satriani (Epic)
37	40	USE YOUR ILLUSION I	Guns N' Roses (Geffen)
34	41	YOUR ARSENAL	Morrissey (HMV)
30	42	HEAVY RHYME EXPERIENCE: VOL. 1	Brand New Heavies (Acid Jazz)
-	43	ADRENALIZE	Def Leppard (Bludgeon Riffola)
-	44	LITTLE EARTHQUAKES	Tori Amos (East West)
43	45	APPETITE FOR DESTRUCTION	Guns N' Roses (Geffen)
38	46	DIAMONDS AND PEARLS	Prince & the New Power Generation (Paisley Park)
41	47	THE ONE	Elton John (Rocket)
-	48	VIVA ESPANA	James Last (PolyGram TV)
50	49	CHANGE EVERYTHING	Del Amitri (A&M)
44	50	BLOOD SUGAR SEX MAGIK	Red Hot Chili Peppers (Warner Bros.)

Genesis' *We Can't Dance*, like Simply Red's *Stars* an album which simply would not go away from the Top 10, had its strongest resurgence yet, moving back to Number 2. Billy Ray Cyrus' success with *Some Gave All* was almost unique - he was a new US country artist, a breed woefully short of UK chart recognition.

September – October 1992

19 September 1992

last week	this week	Title	Artist (Label)
1	1	TUBULAR BELLS II	Mike Oldfield (WEA)
5	2	TOURISM	Roxette (EMI)
2	3	GREATEST HITS	Kylie Minogue (PWL)
4	4	UNPLUGGED	Eric Clapton (Duck)
-	5	THE BEST OF BELINDA CARLISLE VOLUME 1	Belinda Carlisle (Virgin)
10	6	DIVA	Annie Lennox (RCA)
11	7	BACK TO FRONT	Lionel Richie (Motown)
-	8	AMUSED TO DEATH	Roger Waters (Columbia)
6	9	BEST ... 1	Smiths (WEA)
12	10	THE GREATEST HITS 1966-1992	Neil Diamond (Columbia)
8	11	SOME GAVE ALL	Billy Ray Cyrus (Mercury)
16	12	PAUL WELLER	Paul Weller (Go! Discs)
17	13	AMERICA'S LEAST WANTED	Ugly Kid Joe (Vertigo)
7	14	DANGEROUS	Michael Jackson (Epic)
13	15	WELCOME TO WHEREVER YOU ARE	INXS (Mercury)
3	16	LAUGHING ON JUDGEMENT DAY	Thunder (EMI)
18	17	NEVERMIND	Nirvana (DGC)
19	18	STARS	Simply Red (East West)
14	19	WE CAN'T DANCE	Genesis (Virgin)
20	20	THE DEFINITIVE PATSY CLINE	Patsy Cline (Arcade)
21	21	SHEPHERD MOONS	Enya (WEA)
22	22	RUSH STREET	Richard Marx (Capitol)
9	23	TAKE THAT AND PARTY	Take That (RCA)
15	24	ANGEL DUST	Bobby Brown (MCA)
22	25	DIVINE MADNESS	Madness (Virgin)
27	26	UP	Right Said Fred (Tug)
23	27	GROWING UP IN PUBLIC	Jimmy Nail (East West)
26	28	I WAS WARNED	Robert Cray Band (Mercury)
-	29	THE LOOKS OR THE LIFESTYLE	Pop Will Eat Itself (RCA)
30	30	ANGEL DUST	Faith No More (Slash)
29	31	THE COMMITMENTS	Commitments (MCA)
-	32	COPPER BLUE	Sugar (Creation)
48	33	VIVA ESPANA	James Last (PolyGram TV)
32	34	THE MADMAN'S RETURN	Snap (Arista)
-	35	LEGEND	Bob Marley & the Wailers (Island)
34	36	GREATEST HITS II	Queen (Parlophone)
30	37	JON SECADA	Jon Secada (SBK)
35	38	THE BEST OF PREFAB SPROUT: A LIFE OF SURPRISES	Prefab Sprout (Kitchenware)
28	39	THE LEGEND - THE ESSENTIAL COLLECTION	Joe Cocker (PolyGram TV)
31	40	USE YOUR ILLUSION II	Guns N' Roses (Geffen)
-	41	BONE MACHINE	Tom Waits (Island)
49	42	CHANGE EVERYTHING	Del Amitri (A&M)
-	43	99.9F	Suzanne Vega (A&M)
33	44	ACHTUNG BABY	U2 (Island)
-	45	TUBULAR BELLS	Mike Oldfield (Virgin)
43	46	ADRENALIZE	Def Leppard (Bludgeon Riffola)
46	47	DIAMONDS AND PEARLS	Prince & the New Power Generation (Paisley Park)
-	48	THE SINGLES COLLECTION	Four Tops (PolyGram TV)
-	49	IN THE NIGHT	Stranglers (Psycho)
40	50	USE YOUR ILLUSION I	Guns N' Roses (Geffen)

26 September 1992

last week	this week	Title	Artist (Label)
-	1	III SIDES TO EVERY STORY	Extreme (A&M)
-	2	BOSS DRUM	Shamen (One Little Indian)
1	3	TUBULAR BELLS II	Mike Oldfield (WEA)
5	4	THE BEST OF BELINDA CARLISLE VOLUME 1	Belinda Carlisle (Virgin)
-	5	AM I NOT YOUR GIRL?	Sinead O'Connor (Ensign)
2	6	TOURISM	Roxette (EMI)
7	7	BACK TO FRONT	Lionel Richie (Motown)
4	8	UNPLUGGED	Eric Clapton (Duck)
6	9	DIVA	Annie Lennox (RCA)
3	10	GREATEST HITS	Kylie Minogue (PWL)
9	11	BEST ... 1	Smiths (WEA)
8	12	AMUSED TO DEATH	Roger Waters (Columbia)
18	13	STARS	Simply Red (East West)
17	14	NEVERMIND	Nirvana (DGC)
15	15	WELCOME TO WHEREVER YOU ARE	INXS (Mercury)
19	16	WE CAN'T DANCE	Genesis (Virgin)
20	17	THE DEFINITIVE PATSY CLINE	Patsy Cline (Arcade)
10	18	THE GREATEST HITS 1966-1992	Neil Diamond (Columbia)
11	19	SOME GAVE ALL	Billy Ray Cyrus (Mercury)
14	20	DANGEROUS	Michael Jackson (Epic)
22	21	RUSH STREET	Richard Marx (Capitol)
21	22	SHEPHERD MOONS	Enya (WEA)
32	23	COPPER BLUE	Sugar (Creation)
16	24	LAUGHING ON JUDGEMENT DAY	Thunder (EMI)
43	25	99.9F	Suzanne Vega (A&M)
29	26	THE LOOKS OR THE LIFESTYLE	Pop Will Eat Itself (RCA)
13	27	AMERICA'S LEAST WANTED	Ugly Kid Joe (Vertigo)
12	28	PAUL WELLER	Paul Weller (Go! Discs)
25	29	DIVINE MADNESS	Madness (Virgin)
35	30	LEGEND	Bob Marley & the Wailers (Island)
42	31	CHANGE EVERYTHING	Del Amitri (A&M)
31	32	THE COMMITMENTS	Commitments (MCA)
33	33	VIVA ESPANA	James Last (PolyGram TV)
48	34	THE SINGLES COLLECTION	Four Tops (PolyGram TV)
28	35	I WAS WARNED	Robert Cray Band (Mercury)
41	36	BONE MACHINE	Tom Waits (Island)
24	37	BOBBY	Bobby Brown (MCA)
-	38	A LITTLE LIGHT MUSIC	Jethro Tull (Chrysalis)
44	39	ACHTUNG BABY	U2 (Island)
37	40	JON SECADA	Jon Secada (SBK)
40	41	USE YOUR ILLUSION II	Guns N' Roses (Geffen)
26	42	UP	Right Said Fred (Tug)
27	43	GROWING UP IN PUBLIC	Jimmy Nail (East West)
30	44	ANGEL DUST	Faith No More (Slash)
-	45	NUMBER 10	J.J. Cale (Silvertone)
45	46	TUBULAR BELLS	Mike Oldfield (Virgin)
34	47	THE MADMAN'S RETURN	Snap (Arista)
49	48	IN THE NIGHT	Stranglers (Psycho)
-	49	TEN	Pearl Jam (Epic)
-	50	... XYZ	Moose (Hut)

3 October 1992

last week	this week	Title	Artist (Label)
-	1	GOLD - GREATEST HITS	Abba (Polydor)
4	2	THE BEST OF BELINDA CARLISLE VOLUME 1	Belinda Carlisle (Virgin)
1	3	III SIDES TO EVERY STORY	Extreme (A&M)
3	4	TUBULAR BELLS II	Mike Oldfield (WEA)
2	5	BOSS DRUM	Shamen (One Little Indian)
7	6	BACK TO FRONT	Lionel Richie (Motown)
5	7	AM I NOT YOUR GIRL?	Sinead O'Connor (Ensign)
8	8	UNPLUGGED	Eric Clapton (Duck)
9	9	DIVA	Annie Lennox (RCA)
6	10	TOURISM	Roxette (EMI)
-	11	SONGS OF FREEDOM	Bob Marley & the Wailers (Tuff Gong)
10	12	GREATEST HITS	Kylie Minogue (PWL)
14	13	NEVERMIND	Nirvana (DGC)
11	14	BEST ... 1	Smiths (WEA)
15	15	WELCOME TO WHEREVER YOU ARE	INXS (Mercury)
13	16	STARS	Simply Red (East West)
20	17	DANGEROUS	Michael Jackson (Epic)
18	18	THE GREATEST HITS 1966-1992	Neil Diamond (Columbia)
16	19	WE CAN'T DANCE	Genesis (Virgin)
-	20	GREATEST MISSES	Public Enemy (Def Jam)
19	21	SOME GAVE ALL	Billy Ray Cyrus (Mercury)
22	22	RUSH STREET	Richard Marx (Capitol)
22	23	SHEPHERD MOONS	Enya (WEA)
17	24	THE DEFINITIVE PATSY CLINE	Patsy Cline (Arcade)
34	25	THE SINGLES COLLECTION	Four Tops (PolyGram TV)
30	26	LEGEND	Bob Marley & the Wailers (Island)
24	27	LAUGHING ON JUDGEMENT DAY	Thunder (EMI)
-	28	JEFF WAYNE'S MUSICAL VERSION OF SPARTACUS	Jeff Wayne (Columbia)
31	29	CHANGE EVERYTHING	Del Amitri (A&M)
12	30	AMUSED TO DEATH	Roger Waters (Columbia)
-	31	WOODFACE	Crowded House (Capitol)
25	32	99.9F	Suzanne Vega (A&M)
33	33	THE COMMITMENTS	Commitments (MCA)
28	34	PAUL WELLER	Paul Weller (Go! Discs)
29	35	DIVINE MADNESS	Madness (Virgin)
23	36	COPPER BLUE	Sugar (Creation)
27	37	AMERICA'S LEAST WANTED	Ugly Kid Joe (Vertigo)
39	38	ACHTUNG BABY	U2 (Island)
-	39	ADRENALIZE	Def Leppard (Bludgeon Riffola)
33	40	VIVA ESPANA	James Last (PolyGram TV)
49	41	TEN	Pearl Jam (Epic)
-	42	BLOOD SUGAR SEX MAGIK	Red Hot Chili Peppers (Warner Bros.)
43	43	GROWING UP IN PUBLIC	Jimmy Nail (East West)
-	44	WAKING UP THE NEIGHBOURS	Bryan Adams (A&M)
37	45	BOBBY	Bobby Brown (MCA)
41	46	USE YOUR ILLUSION II	Guns N' Roses (Geffen)
46	47	TUBULAR BELLS	Mike Oldfield (Virgin)
44	48	ANGEL DUST	Faith No More (Slash)
42	49	UP	Right Said Fred (Tug)
40	50	JON SECADA	Jon Secada (SBK)

Mike Oldfield's *Tubular Bells II* was a virtual re-run of the original piece using the new studio techniques and possibilities not available 20 years before when *Tubular Bells* was cut for release as Virgin's first-ever album. Inevitably, *II* was not to have anything like its predecessor's incredible chart longevity.

October 1992

10 October 1992

last week	this week	Title	Artist
-	1	AUTOMATIC FOR THE PEOPLE	R.E.M. (Warner Bros.)
-	2	US	Peter Gabriel (Realworld)
1	3	GOLD - GREATEST HITS	Abba (Polydor)
-	4	BACK TO THE LIGHT	Brian May (Parlophone)
-	5	TIMELESS - THE CLASSICS	Michael Bolton (Columbia)
4	6	TUBULAR BELLS II	Mike Oldfield (WEA)
2	7	THE BEST OF BELINDA CARLISLE VOLUME 1	Belinda Carlisle (Virgin)
-	8	... YES PLEASE!	Happy Mondays (Factory)
-	9	GREATEST HITS	Police (A&M)
5	10	BOSS DRUM	Shamen (One Little Indian)
3	11	III SIDES TO EVERY STORY	Extreme (A&M)
6	12	BACK TO FRONT	Lionel Richie (Motown)
11	13	SONGS OF FREEDOM	Bob Marley & the Wailers (Tuff Gong)
-	14	STIGMA	EMF (Parlophone)
8	15	UNPLUGGED	Eric Clapton (Duck)
7	16	AM I NOT YOUR GIRL?	Sinead O'Connor (Ensign)
9	17	DIVA	Annie Lennox (RCA)
10	18	TOURISM	Roxette (EMI)
-	19	HAPPY IN HELL	Christians (Island)
12	20	GREATEST HITS	Kylie Minogue (PWL)
19	21	WE CAN'T DANCE	Genesis (Virgin)
-	22	THE PRODIGY EXPERIENCE	Prodigy (XL Recordings)
17	23	DANGEROUS	Michael Jackson (Epic)
16	24	STARS	Simply Red (East West)
15	25	WELCOME TO WHEREVER YOU ARE	INXS (Mercury)
13	26	NEVERMIND	Nirvana (DGC)
41	27	TEN	Pearl Jam (Epic)
31	28	WOODFACE	Crowded House (Capitol)
26	29	LEGEND	Bob Marley & the Wailers (Island)
14	30	BEST ... 1	Smiths (WEA)
31	31	SOME GAVE ALL	Billy Ray Cyrus (Mercury)
-	32	OUR TIME IN EDEN	10,000 Maniacs (Elektra)
18	33	THE GREATEST HITS 1966-1992	Neil Diamond (Columbia)
20	34	GREATEST MISSES	Public Enemy (Def Jam)
25	35	THE SINGLES COLLECTION	Four Tops (PolyGram TV)
27	36	LAUGHING ON JUDGEMENT DAY	Thunder (EMI)
23	37	SHEPHERD MOONS	Enya (WEA)
22	38	RUSH STREET	Richard Marx (Capitol)
34	39	PAUL WELLER	Paul Weller (Go! Discs)
24	40	THE DEFINITIVE PATSY CLINE	Patsy Cline (Arcade)
28	41	JEFF WAYNE'S MUSICAL VERSION OF SPARTACUS	Jeff Wayne (Columbia)
43	42	GROWING UP IN PUBLIC	Jimmy Nail (East West)
30	43	AMUSED TO DEATH	Roger Waters (Columbia)
29	44	CHANGE EVERYTHING	Del Amitri (A&M)
33	45	THE COMMITMENTS	Commitments (MCA)
32	46	99.9F	Suzanne Vega (A&M)
-	47	GENERATION TERRORISTS	Manic Street Preachers (Columbia)
38	48	ACHTUNG BABY	U2 (Island)
36	49	COPPER BLUE	Sugar (Creation)
35	50	DIVINE MADNESS	Madness (Virgin)

17 October 1992

last week	this week	Title	Artist
1	1	AUTOMATIC FOR THE PEOPLE	R.E.M. (Warner Bros.)
-	2	SYMBOL	Prince & the New Power Generation (Paisley Park)
2	3	US	Peter Gabriel (Realworld)
3	4	GOLD - GREATEST HITS	Abba (Polydor)
5	5	TIMELESS - THE CLASSICS	Michael Bolton (Columbia)
6	6	TUBULAR BELLS II	Mike Oldfield (WEA)
4	7	BACK TO THE LIGHT	Brian May (Parlophone)
-	8	KISS THIS	Sex Pistols (Virgin)
7	9	THE BEST OF BELINDA CARLISLE VOLUME 1	Belinda Carlisle (Virgin)
10	10	GREATEST HITS	Police (A&M)
10	11	BOSS DRUM	Shamen (One Little Indian)
12	12	BACK TO FRONT	Lionel Richie (Motown)
-	13	REVENGE OF THE GOLDFISH	Inspiral Carpets (Cow)
8	14	... YES PLEASE!	Happy Mondays (Factory)
-	15	WHAT HITS!?	Red Hot Chili Peppers (EMI USA)
11	16	III SIDES TO EVERY STORY	Extreme (A&M)
15	17	UNPLUGGED	Eric Clapton (Duck)
17	18	DIVA	Annie Lennox (RCA)
14	19	STIGMA	EMF (Parlophone)
13	20	SONGS OF FREEDOM	Bob Marley & the Wailers (Tuff Gong)
-	21	PIECE OF CAKE	Mudhoney (Reprise)
19	22	HAPPY IN HELL	Christians (Island)
-	23	TWICE UPON A TIME - THE SINGLES	Siouxsie & the Banshees (Wonderland)
28	24	WOODFACE	Crowded House (Capitol)
-	25	BROKEN	Nine Inch Nails (Interscope)
16	26	AM I NOT YOUR GIRL?	Sinead O'Connor (Ensign)
23	27	DANGEROUS	Michael Jackson (Epic)
22	28	THE PRODIGY EXPERIENCE	Prodigy (XL Recordings)
24	29	STARS	Simply Red (East West)
18	30	TOURISM	Roxette (EMI)
21	31	WE CAN'T DANCE	Genesis (Virgin)
20	32	GREATEST HITS	Kylie Minogue (PWL)
26	33	NEVERMIND	Nirvana (DGC)
27	34	TEN	Pearl Jam (Epic)
31	35	SOME GAVE ALL	Billy Ray Cyrus (Mercury)
25	36	WELCOME TO WHEREVER YOU ARE	INXS (Mercury)
-	37	IT'S - IT	Sugarcubes (One Little Indian)
29	38	LEGEND	Bob Marley & the Wailers (Island)
-	39	OUR TIME IN EDEN	10,000 Maniacs (Elektra)
36	40	LAUGHING ON JUDGEMENT DAY	Thunder (EMI)
33	41	THE GREATEST HITS 1966-1992	Neil Diamond (Columbia)
37	42	SHEPHERD MOONS	Enya (WEA)
35	43	THE SINGLES COLLECTION	Four Tops (PolyGram TV)
45	44	THE COMMITMENTS	Commitments (MCA)
47	45	GENERATION TERRORISTS	Manic Street Preachers (Columbia)
30	46	BEST ... 1	Smiths (WEA)
34	47	GREATEST MISSES	Public Enemy (Def Jam)
39	48	PAUL WELLER	Paul Weller (Go! Discs)
38	49	RUSH STREET	Richard Marx (Capitol)
40	50	THE DEFINITIVE PATSY CLINE	Patsy Cline (Arcade)

24 October 1992

last week	this week	Title	Artist
-	1	GLITTERING PRIZE 81/92	Simple Minds (Virgin)
1	2	AUTOMATIC FOR THE PEOPLE	R.E.M. (Warner Bros.)
2	3	SYMBOL	Prince & the New Power Generation (Paisley Park)
-	4	EROTICA	Madonna (Maverick)
4	5	GOLD - GREATEST HITS	Abba (Polydor)
5	6	TIMELESS - THE CLASSICS	Michael Bolton (Columbia)
6	7	TUBULAR BELLS II	Mike Oldfield (WEA)
3	8	US	Peter Gabriel (Realworld)
8	9	KISS THIS	Sex Pistols (Virgin)
9	10	THE BEST OF BELINDA CARLISLE VOLUME 1	Belinda Carlisle (Virgin)
12	11	BACK TO FRONT	Lionel Richie (Motown)
7	12	BACK TO THE LIGHT	Brian May (Parlophone)
10	13	GREATEST HITS	Police (A&M)
-	14	THE BEST OF - ONCE IN A LIFETIME	Talking Heads (EMI)
11	15	BOSS DRUM	Shamen (One Little Indian)
24	16	WOODFACE	Crowded House (Capitol)
17	17	UNPLUGGED	Eric Clapton (Duck)
18	18	DIVA	Annie Lennox (RCA)
27	19	DANGEROUS	Michael Jackson (Epic)
16	20	III SIDES TO EVERY STORY	Extreme (A&M)
15	21	WHAT HITS!?	Red Hot Chili Peppers (EMI USA)
13	22	REVENGE OF THE GOLDFISH	Inspiral Carpets (Cow)
29	23	STARS	Simply Red (East West)
25	24	BROKEN	Nine Inch Nails (Interscope)
23	25	TWICE UPON A TIME - THE SINGLES	Siouxsie & the Banshees (Wonderland)
33	26	NEVERMIND	Nirvana (DGC)
38	27	LEGEND	Bob Marley & the Wailers (Island)
14	28	... YES PLEASE!	Happy Mondays (Factory)
26	29	AM I NOT YOUR GIRL?	Sinead O'Connor (Ensign)
20	30	SONGS OF FREEDOM	Bob Marley & the Wailers (Tuff Gong)
21	31	PIECE OF CAKE	Mudhoney (Reprise)
22	32	HAPPY IN HELL	Christians (Island)
31	33	WE CAN'T DANCE	Genesis (Virgin)
35	34	SOME GAVE ALL	Billy Ray Cyrus (Mercury)
28	35	THE PRODIGY EXPERIENCE	Prodigy (XL Recordings)
40	36	LAUGHING ON JUDGEMENT DAY	Thunder (EMI)
-	37	IZZY STRADLIN AND THE JU JU HOUNDS	Izzy Stradlin & the Ju Ju Hounds (Geffen)
34	38	TEN	Pearl Jam (Epic)
30	39	TOURISM	Roxette (EMI)
41	40	THE GREATEST HITS 1966-1992	Neil Diamond (Columbia)
-	41	TAKE THAT AND PARTY	Take That (RCA)
42	42	SHEPHERD MOONS	Enya (WEA)
32	43	GREATEST HITS	Kylie Minogue (PWL)
36	44	WELCOME TO WHEREVER YOU ARE	INXS (Mercury)
-	45	GREATEST HITS II	Queen (Parlophone)
46	46	BEST ... 1	Smiths (WEA)
-	47	SAND IN THE VASELINE - POPULAR FAVOURITES 1976-1992	Talking Heads (EMI)
19	48	STIGMA	EMF (Parlophone)
44	49	THE COMMITMENTS	Commitments (MCA)
-	50	CURTIS STIGERS	Curtis Stigers (Arista)

Their previous album had already established them in rock's top echelon, but REM's *Automatic For The People* was their first superstar release, while still gathering critical acclaim from those who might normally be ready by now to shoot the band down. It would still be in the Top 5 by the end of this book....

October – November 1992

31 October 1992

last week	this week	Title / Artist
4	1	EROTICA Madonna (Maverick)
1	2	GLITTERING PRIZE 81/92 Simple Minds (Virgin)
2	3	AUTOMATIC FOR THE PEOPLE R.E.M. (Warner Bros.)
3	4	SYMBOL Prince & the New Power Generation (Paisley Park)
-	5	GREAT EXPECTATIONS Tasmin Archer (EMI)
5	6	GOLD - GREATEST HITS Abba (Polydor)
6	7	TIMELESS - THE CLASSICS Michael Bolton (Columbia)
14	8	THE BEST OF - ONCE IN A LIFETIME Talking Heads (EMI)
-	9	ARE YOU NORMAL? Ned's Atomic Dustbin (Furtive)
7	10	TUBULAR BELLS II Mike Oldfield (WEA)
10	11	THE BEST OF BELINDA CARLISLE VOLUME 1 Belinda Carlisle (Virgin)
-	12	BLIND Sundays (Parlophone)
11	13	BACK TO FRONT Lionel Richie (Motown)
13	14	GREATEST HITS Police (A&M)
18	15	DIVA Annie Lennox (RCA)
-	16	COOLEYHIGHHARMONY Boyz II Men (Motown)
8	17	US Peter Gabriel (Realworld)
15	18	BOSS DRUM Shamen (One Little Indian)
17	19	UNPLUGGED Eric Clapton (Duck)
9	20	KISS THIS Sex Pistols (Virgin)
12	21	BACK TO THE LIGHT Brian May (Parlophone)
19	22	DANGEROUS Michael Jackson (Epic)
-	23	JEHOVAH KILL Julian Cope (Island)
16	24	WOODFACE Crowded House (Capitol)
50	25	CURTIS STIGERS Curtis Stigers (Arista)
20	26	III SIDES TO EVERY STORY Extreme (A&M)
-	27	ALL THE WAY FROM TUAM Saw Doctors (Solid)
21	28	WHAT HITS!? Red Hot Chili Peppers (EMI USA)
23	29	STARS Simply Red (East West)
26	30	NEVERMIND Nirvana (DGC)
29	31	AM I NOT YOUR GIRL? Sinead O'Connor (Ensign)
47	32	SAND IN THE VASELINE - POPULAR FAVOURITES 1976-1992 Talking Heads (EMI)
27	33	LEGEND Bob Marley & the Wailers (Island)
36	34	LAUGHING ON JUDGEMENT DAY Thunder (EMI)
24	35	BROKEN Nine Inch Nails (Interscope)
39	36	TOURISM Roxette (EMI)
38	37	TEN Pearl Jam (Epic)
-	38	RIDIN' HIGH Robert Palmer (EMI)
33	39	WE CAN'T DANCE Genesis (Virgin)
35	40	THE PRODIGY EXPERIENCE Prodigy (XL Recordings)
25	41	TWICE UPON A TIME - THE SINGLES Siouxsie & the Banshees (Wonderland)
-	42	THE COLLECTION Mary Black (Telstar)
22	43	REVENGE OF THE GOLDFISH Inspiral Carpets (Cow)
-	44	INTO THE LIGHT Hank Marvin (Polydor)
-	45	ORIGINAL SOUNDTRACK - 1492 CONQUEST OF PARADISE Vangelis (East West)
34	46	SOME GAVE ALL Billy Ray Cyrus (Mercury)
31	47	PIECE OF CAKE Mudhoney (Reprise)
42	48	SHEPHERD MOONS Enya (WEA)
46	49	BEST ... 1 Smiths (WEA)
-	50	MAIN OFFENDER Keith Richards (Virgin America)

7 November 1992

last week	this week	Title / Artist
2	1	GLITTERING PRIZE 81/92 Simple Minds (Virgin)
1	2	EROTICA Madonna (Maverick)
7	3	TIMELESS - THE CLASSICS Michael Bolton (Columbia)
-	4	LIVE AC/DC (Atco)
3	5	AUTOMATIC FOR THE PEOPLE R.E.M. (Warner Bros.)
6	6	GOLD - GREATEST HITS Abba (Polydor)
4	7	SYMBOL Prince & the New Power Generation (Paisley Park)
5	8	GREAT EXPECTATIONS Tasmin Archer (EMI)
8	9	THE BEST OF - ONCE IN A LIFETIME Talking Heads (EMI)
-	10	BOOM BOOM John Lee Hooker (Pointblank)
11	11	THE BEST OF BELINDA CARLISLE VOLUME 1 Belinda Carlisle (Virgin)
16	12	COOLEYHIGHHARMONY Boyz II Men (Motown)
10	13	TUBULAR BELLS II Mike Oldfield (WEA)
13	14	BACK TO FRONT Lionel Richie (Motown)
15	15	DIVA Annie Lennox (RCA)
18	16	BOSS DRUM Shamen (One Little Indian)
14	17	GREATEST HITS Police (A&M)
25	18	CURTIS STIGERS Curtis Stigers (Arista)
-	19	LOVE DELUXE Sade (Epic)
9	20	ARE YOU NORMAL? Ned's Atomic Dustbin (Furtive)
17	21	US Peter Gabriel (Realworld)
19	22	UNPLUGGED Eric Clapton (Duck)
23	23	BLIND Sundays (Parlophone)
22	24	DANGEROUS Michael Jackson (Epic)
-	25	HOMEBREW Neneh Cherry (Circa)
29	26	STARS Simply Red (East West)
23	27	JEHOVAH KILL Julian Cope (Island)
21	28	BACK TO THE LIGHT Brian May (Parlophone)
30	29	NEVERMIND Nirvana (DGC)
-	30	3 YEARS, 5 MONTHS AND 2 DAYS IN THE LIFE Arrested Development (Cooltempo)
-	31	ULTRAVIOLET All About Eve (MCA)
27	32	ALL THE WAY FROM TUAM Saw Doctors (Solid)
44	33	INTO THE LIGHT Hank Marvin (Polydor)
26	34	III SIDES TO EVERY STORY Extreme (A&M)
24	35	WOODFACE Crowded House (Capitol)
28	36	WHAT HITS!? Red Hot Chili Peppers (EMI USA)
37	37	TOURISM Roxette (EMI)
20	38	KISS THIS Sex Pistols (Virgin)
33	39	LEGEND Bob Marley & the Wailers (Island)
-	40	TAKE THAT AND PARTY Take That (RCA)
39	41	WE CAN'T DANCE Genesis (Virgin)
32	42	SAND IN THE VASELINE - POPULAR FAVOURITES 1976-1992 Talking Heads (EMI)
38	43	RIDIN' HIGH Robert Palmer (EMI)
-	44	ENERGIQUE Bizarre Inc. (Vinyl Solution)
34	45	LAUGHING ON JUDGEMENT DAY Thunder (EMI)
-	46	TRAINS, BOATS AND PLANES Frank & Walters (Setanta)
40	47	THE PRODIGY EXPERIENCE Prodigy (XL Recordings)
45	48	ORIGINAL SOUNDTRACK - 1492 CONQUEST OF PARADISE Vangelis (East West)
-	49	THE EPIC YEARS Shaky (Epic)
50	50	MAIN OFFENDER Keith Richards (Virgin America)

14 November 1992

last week	this week	Title / Artist
1	1	GLITTERING PRIZE 81/92 Simple Minds (Virgin)
-	2	KEEP THE FAITH Bon Jovi (Jambco)
3	3	TIMELESS - THE CLASSICS Michael Bolton (Columbia)
2	4	EROTICA Madonna (Maverick)
-	5	GOD'S GREAT BANANA SKIN Chris Rea (East West)
4	6	LIVE AC/DC (Atco)
5	7	AUTOMATIC FOR THE PEOPLE R.E.M. (Warner Bros.)
6	8	GOLD - GREATEST HITS Abba (Polydor)
-	9	GREATEST HITS Gloria Estefan (Epic)
-	10	HARVEST MOON Neil Young (Reprise)
12	11	COOLEYHIGHHARMONY Boyz II Men (Motown)
8	12	GREAT EXPECTATIONS Tasmin Archer (EMI)
16	13	BOSS DRUM Shamen (One Little Indian)
7	14	SYMBOL Prince & the New Power Generation (Paisley Park)
11	15	THE BEST OF BELINDA CARLISLE VOLUME 1 Belinda Carlisle (Virgin)
13	16	TUBULAR BELLS II Mike Oldfield (WEA)
-	17	BEST ... II Smiths (WEA)
10	18	BOOM BOOM John Lee Hooker (Pointblank)
9	19	THE BEST OF - ONCE IN A LIFETIME Talking Heads (EMI)
-	20	GOOD AS I BEEN TO YOU Bob Dylan (CBS)
14	21	BACK TO FRONT Lionel Richie (Motown)
19	22	LOVE DELUXE Sade (Epic)
15	23	DIVA Annie Lennox (RCA)
21	24	US Peter Gabriel (Realworld)
30	25	3 YEARS, 5 MONTHS AND 2 DAYS IN THE LIFE Arrested Development (Cooltempo)
17	26	GREATEST HITS Police (A&M)
18	27	CURTIS STIGERS Curtis Stigers (Arista)
26	28	STARS Simply Red (East West)
25	29	HOMEBREW Neneh Cherry (Circa)
29	30	NEVERMIND Nirvana (DGC)
-	31	MADSTOCK Madness (Go! Discs)
22	32	UNPLUGGED Eric Clapton (Duck)
40	33	TAKE THAT AND PARTY Take That (RCA)
34	34	DANGEROUS Michael Jackson (Epic)
33	35	INTO THE LIGHT Hank Marvin (Polydor)
35	36	WOODFACE Crowded House (Capitol)
36	37	WHAT HITS!? Red Hot Chili Peppers (EMI USA)
38	38	KISS THIS Sex Pistols (Virgin)
-	39	NURSE Therapy? (A&M)
41	40	WE CAN'T DANCE Genesis (Virgin)
39	41	LEGEND Bob Marley & the Wailers (Island)
-	42	LIVE ALIVE QUO Status Quo (Polydor)
-	43	LOVE SEE NO COLOUR Farm (End Product)
28	44	BACK TO THE LIGHT Brian May (Parlophone)
23	45	BLIND Sundays (Parlophone)
20	46	ARE YOU NORMAL? Ned's Atomic Dustbin (Furtive)
34	47	III SIDES TO EVERY STORY Extreme (A&M)
-	48	HORMONALLY YOURS Shakespear's Sister (London)
-	49	THE ULTIMATE EXPERIENCE Jimi Hendrix (PolyGram TV)
-	50	UP Right Said Fred (Tug)

Madonna's *Erotica* album (available, at least initially, in the equivalent of PG and 18-rated versions) was part of her general multi-media attempt to apparently present herself as the world's most sex-obsessed woman - the other half of the equation being her fantasy-photo book *Sex* (strictly 18-rated only).

November – December 1992

21 November 1992

last week	this week		
-	1	CHER'S GREATEST HITS: 1965-1992	Cher (Geffen)
2	2	KEEP THE FAITH	Bon Jovi (Jambco)
1	3	GLITTERING PRIZE 81/92	Simple Minds (Virgin)
3	4	TIMELESS - THE CLASSICS	Michael Bolton (Columbia)
5	5	GOD'S GREAT BANANA SKIN	Chris Rea (East West)
10	6	HARVEST MOON	Neil Young (Reprise)
9	7	GREATEST HITS	Gloria Estefan (Epic)
8	8	GOLD - GREATEST HITS	Abba (Polydor)
7	9	AUTOMATIC FOR THE PEOPLE	R.E.M. (Warner Bros.)
4	10	EROTICA	Madonna (Maverick)
11	11	COOLEYHIGHHARMONY	Boyz II Men (Motown)
13	12	BOSS DRUM	Shamen (One Little Indian)
20	13	GOOD AS I BEEN TO YOU	Bob Dylan (CBS)
14	14	SYMBOL	the New Power Generation (Paisley Park)
6	15	LIVE	AC/DC (Atco)
17	16	BEST ... II	Smiths (WEA)
15	17	THE BEST OF BELINDA CARLISLE VOLUME 1	Belinda Carlisle (Virgin)
25	18	3 YEARS, 5 MONTHS AND 2 DAYS IN THE LIFE	Arrested Development (Cooltempo)
16	19	TUBULAR BELLS II	Mike Oldfield (WEA)
21	20	BACK TO FRONT	Lionel Richie (Motown)
19	21	THE BEST OF - ONCE IN A LIFETIME	Talking Heads (EMI)
49	22	THE ULTIMATE EXPERIENCE	Jimi Hendrix (PolyGram TV)
12	23	GREAT EXPECTATIONS	Tasmin Archer (EMI)
33	24	TAKE THAT AND PARTY	Take That (RCA)
23	25	DIVA	Annie Lennox (RCA)
27	26	CURTIS STIGERS	Curtis Stigers (Arista)
31	27	MADSTOCK	Madness (Go! Discs)
28	28	STARS	Simply Red (East West)
-	29	INDIAN SUMMER	Go West (Chrysalis)
26	30	GREATEST HITS	Police (A&M)
-	31	FOLLOW YOUR DREAM	Daniel O'Donnell (Ritz)
18	32	BOOM BOOM	John Lee Hooker (Pointblank)
34	33	DANGEROUS	Michael Jackson (Epic)
30	34	NEVERMIND	Nirvana (DGC)
39	35	NURSE	Therapy? (A&M)
32	36	UNPLUGGED	Eric Clapton (Duck)
40	37	WE CAN'T DANCE	Genesis (Virgin)
35	38	INTO THE LIGHT	Hank Marvin (Polydor)
-	39	THE ONE	Elton John (Rocket)
-	40	MANY HAPPY RETURNS - THE HITS	Gary Glitter (EMI)
22	41	LOVE DELUXE	Sade (Epic)
41	42	LEGEND	Bob Marley & the Wailers (Island)
42	43	LIVE ALIVE QUO	Status Quo (Polydor)
24	44	US	Peter Gabriel (Realworld)
36	45	WOODFACE	Crowded House (Capitol)
37	46	WHAT HITS!?	Red Hot Chili Peppers (EMI USA)
-	47	HEART STRINGS	Foster & Allen (Telstar)
-	48	THE VERY BEST OF RICHARD CLAYDERMAN	Richard Clayderman (Decca Delphine)
48	49	HORMONALLY YOURS	Shakespear's Sister (London)
44	50	BACK TO THE LIGHT	Brian May (Parlophone)

28 November 1992

-	1	POP! - THE FIRST 20 HITS	Erasure (Mute)
1	2	GREATEST HITS: 1965-1992	Cher (Geffen)
-	3	LIVE - THE WAY WE WALK VOL. 1: THE SHORTS	Genesis (Virgin)
3	4	GLITTERING PRIZE 81/92	Simple Minds (Virgin)
4	5	TIMELESS - THE CLASSICS	Michael Bolton (Columbia)
-	6	THE FREDDIE MERCURY ALBUM	Freddie Mercury (Parlophone)
7	7	GREATEST HITS	Gloria Estefan (Epic)
9	8	AUTOMATIC FOR THE PEOPLE	R.E.M. (Warner Bros.)
8	9	GOLD - GREATEST HITS	Abba (Polydor)
2	10	KEEP THE FAITH	Bon Jovi (Jambco)
5	11	GOD'S GREAT BANANA SKIN	Chris Rea (East West)
10	12	EROTICA	Madonna (Maverick)
12	13	BOSS DRUM	Shamen (One Little Indian)
11	14	COOLEYHIGHHARMONY	Boyz II Men (Motown)
20	15	BACK TO FRONT	Lionel Richie (Motown)
17	16	THE BEST OF BELINDA CARLISLE VOLUME 1	Belinda Carlisle (Virgin)
49	17	HORMONALLY YOURS	Shakespear's Sister (London)
24	18	TAKE THAT AND PARTY	Take That (RCA)
31	19	FOLLOW YOUR DREAM	Daniel O'Donnell (Ritz)
19	20	TUBULAR BELLS II	Mike Oldfield (WEA)
18	21	3 YEARS, 5 MONTHS AND 2 DAYS IN THE LIFE	Arrested Development (Cooltempo)
6	22	HARVEST MOON	Neil Young (Reprise)
28	23	STARS	Simply Red (East West)
14	24	SYMBOL	the New Power Generation (Paisley Park)
25	25	DIVA	Annie Lennox (RCA)
26	26	CURTIS STIGERS	Curtis Stigers (Arista)
-	27	KING OF HEARTS	Roy Orbison (Virgin America)
15	28	LIVE	AC/DC (Atco)
29	29	INDIAN SUMMER	Go West (Chrysalis)
-	30	THE CELTS	Enya (WEA)
27	31	MADSTOCK	Madness (Go! Discs)
22	32	THE ULTIMATE EXPERIENCE	Jimi Hendrix (PolyGram TV)
30	33	GREATEST HITS	Police (A&M)
13	34	GOOD AS I BEEN TO YOU	Bob Dylan (CBS)
16	35	BEST ... II	Smiths (WEA)
23	36	GREAT EXPECTATIONS	Tasmin Archer (EMI)
32	37	BOOM BOOM	John Lee Hooker (Pointblank)
-	38	THE HEART OF ROCK & ROLL: THE BEST OF	Huey Lewis & the News (Chrysalis)
-	39	FEEL THIS	Jeff Healey Band (Arista)
21	40	THE BEST OF - ONCE IN A LIFETIME	Talking Heads (EMI)
41	41	LOVE DELUXE	Sade (Epic)
-	42	PORTRAIT	Des O'Connor (Columbia)
37	43	WE CAN'T DANCE	Genesis (Virgin)
42	44	LEGEND	Bob Marley & the Wailers (Island)
40	45	MANY HAPPY RETURNS - THE HITS	Gary Glitter (EMI)
33	46	DANGEROUS	Michael Jackson (Epic)
34	47	NEVERMIND	Nirvana (DGC)
-	48	SHEPHERD MOONS	Enya (WEA)
49	49	THE BODYGUARD - SOUNDTRACK	Various (Arista)
-	50	BEETHOVEN VIOLIN CONCERTO	Nigel Kennedy/Klaus Tennstedt (EMI Classics)

5 December 1992

1	1	POP! - THE FIRST 20 HITS	Erasure (Mute)
3	2	LIVE - THE WAY WE WALK VOL. 1: THE SHORTS	Genesis (Virgin)
2	3	GREATEST HITS: 1965-1992	Cher (Geffen)
6	4	THE FREDDIE MERCURY ALBUM	Freddie Mercury (Parlophone)
5	5	TIMELESS - THE CLASSICS	Michael Bolton (Columbia)
4	6	GLITTERING PRIZE 81/92	Simple Minds (Virgin)
7	7	GREATEST HITS	Gloria Estefan (Epic)
8	8	AUTOMATIC FOR THE PEOPLE	R.E.M. (Warner Bros.)
9	9	GOLD - GREATEST HITS	Abba (Polydor)
30	10	THE CELTS	Enya (WEA)
15	11	BACK TO FRONT	Lionel Richie (Motown)
12	12	EROTICA	Madonna (Maverick)
11	13	GOD'S GREAT BANANA SKIN	Chris Rea (East West)
13	14	BOSS DRUM	Shamen (One Little Indian)
10	15	KEEP THE FAITH	Bon Jovi (Jambco)
16	16	THE BEST OF BELINDA CARLISLE VOLUME 1	Belinda Carlisle (Virgin)
18	17	TAKE THAT AND PARTY	Take That (RCA)
17	18	HORMONALLY YOURS	Shakespear's Sister (London)
20	19	TUBULAR BELLS II	Mike Oldfield (WEA)
19	20	FOLLOW YOUR DREAM	Daniel O'Donnell (Ritz)
14	21	COOLEYHIGHHARMONY	Boyz II Men (Motown)
27	22	KING OF HEARTS	Roy Orbison (Virgin America)
23	23	STARS	Simply Red (East West)
25	24	DIVA	Annie Lennox (RCA)
49	25	THE BODYGUARD - SOUNDTRACK	Various (Arista)
24	26	SYMBOL	the New Power Generation (Paisley Park)
26	27	CURTIS STIGERS	Curtis Stigers (Arista)
21	28	3 YEARS, 5 MONTHS AND 2 DAYS IN THE LIFE	Arrested Development (Cooltempo)
46	29	DANGEROUS	Michael Jackson (Epic)
-	30	INTO THE LIGHT	Hank Marvin (Polydor)
22	31	HARVEST MOON	Neil Young (Reprise)
29	32	INDIAN SUMMER	Go West (Chrysalis)
33	33	GREATEST HITS	Police (A&M)
34	34	THE HEART OF ROCK & ROLL: THE BEST OF	Huey Lewis & the News (Chrysalis)
28	35	LIVE	AC/DC (Atco)
-	36	NICK BERRY	Nick Berry (Columbia)
31	37	MADSTOCK	Madness (Go! Discs)
32	38	THE ULTIMATE EXPERIENCE	Jimi Hendrix (PolyGram TV)
36	39	GREAT EXPECTATIONS	Tasmin Archer (EMI)
44	40	LEGEND	Bob Marley & the Wailers (Island)
-	41	THE FUTURE	Leonard Cohen (Columbia)
-	42	UP	Right Said Fred (Tug)
-	43	CHECK OUT THE GROOVE	Undercover (PWL Continental)
41	44	LOVE DELUXE	Sade (Epic)
45	45	MANY HAPPY RETURNS	Gary Glitter (EMI)
43	46	WE CAN'T DANCE	Genesis (Virgin)
-	47	THE CHRISTMAS ALBUM	Neil Diamond (Columbia)
40	48	THE BEST OF - ONCE IN A LIFETIME	Talking Heads (EMI)
47	49	NEVERMIND	Nirvana (DGC)
-	50	THE PRODIGY EXPERIENCE	Prodigy (XL Recordings)

As at the end of 1991, the major-name compilations vied with each other for year-end chart-topping sales, and it was Cher (with a 27-year career overview stretching back to Sonny & Cher days) and Erasure (rather fewer years to anthologise), who were to toss the Number 1 position back and forth between them.

December 1992

12 December 1992

last	this	Title	Artist
1	1	POP! - THE FIRST 20 HITS	Erasure (Mute)
3	2	GREATEST HITS: 1965-1992	Cher (Geffen)
5	3	TIMELESS - THE CLASSICS	Michael Bolton (Columbia)
4	4	THE FREDDIE MERCURY ALBUM	Freddie Mercury (Parlophone)
2	5	LIVE - THE WAY WE WALK VOL. 1: THE SHORTS	Genesis (Virgin)
7	6	GREATEST HITS	Gloria Estefan (Epic)
8	7	AUTOMATIC FOR THE PEOPLE	R.E.M. (Warner Bros.)
6	8	GLITTERING PRIZE 81/92	Simple Minds (Virgin)
9	9	GOLD - GREATEST HITS	Abba (Polydor)
10	10	THE CELTS	Enya (WEA)
12	11	EROTICA	Madonna (Maverick)
-	12	DUOPHONIC	Charles & Eddie (Capitol)
17	13	TAKE THAT AND PARTY	Take That (RCA)
11	14	BACK TO FRONT	Lionel Richie (Motown)
14	15	BOSS DRUM	Shamen (One Little Indian)
13	16	GOD'S GREAT BANANA SKIN	Chris Rea (East West)
16	17	THE BEST OF BELINDA CARLISLE VOLUME 1	Belinda Carlisle (Virgin)
15	18	KEEP THE FAITH	Bon Jovi (Jambco)
23	19	STARS	Simply Red (East West)
19	20	TUBULAR BELLS II	Mike Oldfield (WEA)
24	21	DIVA	Annie Lennox (RCA)
27	22	CURTIS STIGERS	Curtis Stigers (Arista)
25	23	THE BODYGUARD - SOUNDTRACK	Various (Arista)
20	24	FOLLOW YOUR DREAM	Daniel O'Donnell (Ritz)
29	25	DANGEROUS	Michael Jackson (Epic)
18	26	HORMONALLY YOURS	Shakespear's Sister (London)
43	27	CHECK OUT THE GROOVE	Undercover (PWL Continental)
26	28	SYMBOL	Prince & the New Power Generation (Paisley Park)
30	29	INTO THE LIGHT	Hank Marvin (Polydor)
21	30	COOLEYHIGHHARMONY	Boyz II Men (Motown)
28	31	3 YEARS, 5 MONTHS AND 2 DAYS IN THE LIFE	Arrested Development (Cooltempo)
22	32	KING OF HEARTS	Roy Orbison (Virgin America)
42	33	UP	Right Said Fred (Tug)
-	34	THE BEST OF...	Shirley Bassey (Dino)
36	35	NICK BERRY	Nick Berry (Columbia)
-	36	WELCOME TO WHEREVER YOU ARE	INXS (Mercury)
41	37	THE FUTURE	Leonard Cohen (Columbia)
-	38	THE VERY BEST OF ELAINE PAIGE AND BARBARA DICKSON - TOGETHER	Elaine Paige & Barbara Dickson (Telstar)
38	39	THE ULTIMATE EXPERIENCE	Jimi Hendrix (PolyGram TV)
49	40	NEVERMIND	Nirvana (DGC)
34	41	THE HEART OF ROCK & ROLL: THE BEST OF ...	Huey Lewis & the News (Chrysalis)
40	42	LEGEND	Bob Marley & the Wailers (Island)
33	43	GREATEST HITS	Police (A&M)
31	44	HARVEST MOON	Neil Young (Reprise)
-	45	GREATEST HITS II	Queen (Parlophone)
-	46	ACHTUNG BABY	U2 (Island)
-	47	THE VERY BEST OF	Earth Wind & Fire (Telstar)
46	48	WE CAN'T DANCE	Genesis (Virgin)
50	49	THE PRODIGY EXPERIENCE	Prodigy (XL Recordings)
39	50	GREAT EXPECTATIONS	Tasmin Archer (EMI)

19 December 1992

last	this	Title	Artist
2	1	GREATEST HITS: 1965-1992	Cher (Geffen)
1	2	POP! - THE FIRST 20 HITS	Erasure (Mute)
3	3	TIMELESS - THE CLASSICS	Michael Bolton (Columbia)
6	4	GREATEST HITS	Gloria Estefan (Epic)
5	5	LIVE - THE WAY WE WALK VOL. 1: THE SHORTS	Genesis (Virgin)
8	6	GLITTERING PRIZE 81/92	Simple Minds (Virgin)
4	7	THE FREDDIE MERCURY ALBUM	Freddie Mercury (Parlophone)
9	8	GOLD - GREATEST HITS	Abba (Polydor)
7	9	AUTOMATIC FOR THE PEOPLE	R.E.M. (Warner Bros.)
23	10	THE BODYGUARD - SOUNDTRACK	Various (Arista)
19	11	STARS	Simply Red (East West)
14	12	BACK TO FRONT	Lionel Richie (Motown)
25	13	DANGEROUS	Michael Jackson (Epic)
11	14	EROTICA	Madonna (Maverick)
13	15	TAKE THAT AND PARTY	Take That (RCA)
16	16	GOD'S GREAT BANANA SKIN	Chris Rea (East West)
10	17	THE CELTS	Enya (WEA)
15	18	BOSS DRUM	Shamen (One Little Indian)
-	19	FIXED	Nine Inch Nail (TVT)
12	20	DUOPHONIC	Charles & Eddie (Capitol)
17	21	THE BEST OF BELINDA CARLISLE VOLUME 1	Belinda Carlisle (Virgin)
21	22	DIVA	Annie Lennox (RCA)
24	23	FOLLOW YOUR DREAM	Daniel O'Donnell (Ritz)
18	24	KEEP THE FAITH	Bon Jovi (Jambco)
22	25	CURTIS STIGERS	Curtis Stigers (Arista)
20	26	TUBULAR BELLS II	Mike Oldfield (WEA)
26	27	HORMONALLY YOURS	Shakespear's Sister (London)
38	28	THE VERY BEST - TOGETHER	Elaine Paige & Barbara Dickson (Telstar)
-	29	THE GREATEST HITS 1966-1992	Neil Diamond (Columbia)
45	30	GREATEST HITS II	Queen (Parlophone)
27	31	CHECK OUT THE GROOVE	Undercover (PWL Continental)
34	32	THE BEST OF...	Shirley Bassey (Dino)
33	33	UP	Right Said Fred (Tug)
-	34	ONCE IN A LIFETIME	Talking Heads (EMI)
28	35	SYMBOL	Prince & the New Power Generation (Paisley Park)
29	36	INTO THE LIGHT	Hank Marvin (Polydor)
31	37	3 YEARS, 5 MONTHS AND 2 DAYS IN THE LIFE	Arrested Development (Cooltempo)
-	38	HEART STRINGS	Foster & Allen (Telstar)
46	39	ACHTUNG BABY	U2 (Island)
35	40	NICK BERRY	Nick Berry (Columbia)
36	41	WELCOME TO WHEREVER YOU ARE	INXS (Mercury)
30	42	COOLEYHIGHHARMONY	Boyz II Men (Motown)
40	43	NEVERMIND	Nirvana (DGC)
42	44	LEGEND	Bob Marley & the Wailers (Island)
41	45	THE HEART OF ROCK & ROLL: THE BEST OF	Huey Lewis & the News (Chrysalis)
47	46	THE VERY BEST OF...Earth Wind & Fire (Telstar)	
39	47	THE ULTIMATE EXPERIENCE	Jimi Hendrix (PolyGram TV)
49	48	THE PRODIGY EXPERIENCE	Prodigy (XL Recordings)
-	49	THE CHRISTMAS ALBUM	Neil Diamond (Columbia)
-	50	THE FORCE BEHIND THE POWER	Diana Ross (EMI)

Michael Bolton's Number 3 album was not a set of his own hits (he hadn't yet had enough), but covers of classic pop songs - mainly ballads. Most of the rest of the Top 10 was hits anthologies (or hit album tracks recorded live by Genesis) with only REM raising the contemporary flag.

9 January 1993

last week	this week	Title	Artist (Label)
1	1	GREATEST HITS: 1965-1992	Cher (Geffen)
4	2	GREATEST HITS	Gloria Estefan (Epic)
10	3	THE BODYGUARD - SOUNDTRACK	Various (Arista)
2	4	POP! - THE FIRST 20 HITS	Erasure (Mute)
3	5	TIMELESS - THE CLASSICS	Michael Bolton (Columbia)
5	6	LIVE - THE WAY WE WALK VOLUME ONE: THE SHORTS	Genesis (Virgin)
6	7	GLITTERING PRIZE 81/92	Simple Minds (Virgin)
7	8	THE FREDDIE MERCURY ALBUM	Freddie Mercury (Parlophone)
11	9	STARS	Simply Red (East West)
15	10	TAKE THAT AND PARTY	Take That (RCA)
8	11	GOLD - GREATEST HITS	Abba (Polydor)
12	12	BACK TO FRONT	Lionel Richie (Motown)
13	13	DANGEROUS	Michael Jackson (Epic)
18	14	BOSS DRUM	Shamen (One Little Indian)
9	15	AUTOMATIC FOR THE PEOPLE	R.E.M. (Warner Bros.)
29	16	THE GREATEST HITS 1966-1992	Neil Diamond (Columbia)
14	17	EROTICA	Madonna (Maverick)
50	18	THE FORCE BEHIND THE POWER	Diana Ross (EMI)
-	19	INCESTICIDE	Nirvana (Geffen)
22	20	DIVA	Annie Lennox (RCA)
21	21	THE BEST OF BELINDA CARLISLE VOLUME 1	Belinda Carlisle (Virgin)
28	22	THE BEST OF - TOGETHER	Elaine Paige & Barbara Dickson (Telstar)
20	23	DUOPHONIC	Charles & Eddie (Capitol)
24	24	TUBULAR BELLS II	Mike Oldfield (WEA)
16	25	GOD'S GREAT BANANA SKIN	Chris Rea (East West)
17	26	THE CELTS	Enya (WEA)
23	27	FOLLOW YOUR DREAM	Daniel O'Donnell (Ritz)
24	28	KEEP THE FAITH	Bon Jovi (Jambco)
30	29	GREATEST HITS II	Queen (Parlophone)
34	30	THE BEST OF - ONCE IN A LIFETIME	Talking Heads (EMI)
-	31	SIMPLY THE BEST	Tina Turner (Capitol)
27	32	HORMONALLY YOURS	Shakespear's Sister (London)
25	33	CURTIS STIGERS	Curtis Stigers (Arista)
33	34	UP	Right Said Fred (Tug)
43	35	NEVERMIND	Nirvana (DGC)
37	36	3 YEARS, 5 MONTHS AND 2 DAYS IN THE LIFE	Arrested Development (Cooltempo)
-	37	MICHAEL CRAWFORD PERFORMS ANDREW LLOYD WEBBER	Michael Crawford (Ritz)
38	38	HEART STRINGS	Foster & Allen (Telstar)
32	39	THE BEST OF ...	Shirley Bassey (Dino)
44	40	LEGEND	Bob Marley & the Wailers (Island)
39	41	ACHTUNG BABY	U2 (Island)
36	42	INTO THE LIGHT	Hank Marvin (Polydor)
41	43	WELCOME TO WHEREVER YOU ARE	INXS (Mercury)
-	44	FROM BOTH SIDES NOW	Ian McShane (PolyGram TV)
-	45	GREATEST HITS	Queen (EMI)
35	46	SYMBOL	Prince & the New Power Generation (Paisley Park)
46	47	THE VERY BEST OF	Earth Wind & Fire (Telstar)
-	48	UNPLUGGED	Eric Clapton (Duck)
40	49	NICK BERRY	Nick Berry (Columbia)
42	50	COOLEYHIGHHARMONY	Boyz II Men (Motown)

16 January 1993

last week	this week	Title	Artist (Label)
3	1	THE BODYGUARD - SOUNDTRACK	Various (Arista)
1	2	GREATEST HITS: 1965-1992	Cher (Geffen)
4	3	POP! - THE FIRST 20 HITS	Erasure (Mute)
2	4	GREATEST HITS	Gloria Estefan (Epic)
10	5	TAKE THAT AND PARTY	Take That (RCA)
7	6	GLITTERING PRIZE 81/92	Simple Minds (Virgin)
14	7	BOSS DRUM	Shamen (One Little Indian)
6	8	LIVE - THE WAY WE WALK VOLUME ONE: THE SHORTS	Genesis (Virgin)
15	9	AUTOMATIC FOR THE PEOPLE	R.E.M. (Warner Bros.)
5	10	TIMELESS - THE CLASSICS	Michael Bolton (Columbia)
11	11	GOLD - GREATEST HITS	Abba (Polydor)
9	12	STARS	Simply Red (East West)
12	13	BACK TO FRONT	Lionel Richie (Motown)
13	14	DANGEROUS	Michael Jackson (Epic)
8	15	THE FREDDIE MERCURY ALBUM	Freddie Mercury (Parlophone)
17	16	EROTICA	Madonna (Maverick)
36	17	3 YEARS, 5 MONTHS AND 2 DAYS IN THE LIFE	Arrested Development (Cooltempo)
19	18	INCESTICIDE	Nirvana (Geffen)
35	19	NEVERMIND	Nirvana (DGC)
-	20	HIT PARADE 2	Wedding Present (RCA)
21	21	THE BEST OF - VOL 1	Belinda Carlisle (Virgin)
20	22	DIVA	Annie Lennox (RCA)
28	23	KEEP THE FAITH	Bon Jovi (Jambco)
23	24	DUOPHONIC	Charles & Eddie (Capitol)
32	25	HORMONALLY YOURS	Shakespear's Sister (London)
26	26	THE CELTS	Enya (WEA)
27	27	TUBULAR BELLS II	Mike Oldfield (WEA)
29	28	GREATEST HITS II	Queen (Parlophone)
48	29	UNPLUGGED	Eric Clapton (Duck)
25	30	GOD'S GREAT BANANA SKIN	Chris Rea (East West)
41	31	ACHTUNG BABY	U2 (Island)
33	32	CURTIS STIGERS	Curtis Stigers (Arista)
30	33	THE BEST OF - ONCE IN A LIFETIME	Talking Heads (EMI)
34	34	UP	Right Said Fred (Tug)
-	35	THE PRODIGY EXPERIENCE	Prodigy (XL Recordings)
46	36	SYMBOL	Prince & the New Power Generation (Paisley Park)
18	37	THE FORCE BEHIND THE POWER	Diana Ross (EMI)
16	38	THE GREATEST HITS 1966-1992	Neil Diamond (Columbia)
31	39	SIMPLY THE BEST	Tina Turner (Capitol)
-	40	IT'S A SHAME ABOUT RAY	Lemonheads (Atlantic)
43	41	WELCOME TO WHEREVER YOU ARE	INXS (Mercury)
50	42	COOLEYHIGHHARMONY	Boyz II Men (Motown)
-	43	USE YOUR ILLUSION II	Guns N' Roses (Geffen)
45	44	GREATEST HITS	Queen (EMI)
-	45	TEN	Pearl Jam (Sony)
-	46	USE YOUR ILLUSION I	Guns N' Roses (Geffen)
-	47	THE ULTIMATE EXPERIENCE	Jimi Hendrix (PolyGram TV)
40	48	LEGEND	Bob Marley & the Wailers (Island)
22	49	THE BEST OF - TOGETHER	Elaine Paige & Barbara Dickson (Telstar)
-	50	DIVINE MADNESS	Madness (Virgin)

23 January 1993

last week	this week	Title	Artist (Label)
1	1	THE BODYGUARD - SOUNDTRACK	Various (Arista)
-	2	LIVE - THE WAY WE WALK VOLUME TWO: THE LONGS	Genesis (Virgin)
2	3	GREATEST HITS: 1965-1992	Cher (Geffen)
7	4	BOSS DRUM	Shamen (One Little Indian)
5	5	TAKE THAT AND PARTY	Take That (RCA)
9	6	AUTOMATIC FOR THE PEOPLE	R.E.M. (Warner Bros.)
-	7	CONNECTED	Stereo MCs (Fourth & Broadway)
3	8	POP! - THE FIRST 20 HITS	Erasure (Mute)
6	9	GLITTERING PRIZE 81/92	Simple Minds (Virgin)
4	10	GREATEST HITS	Gloria Estefan (Epic)
11	11	GOLD - GREATEST HITS	Abba (Polydor)
8	12	LIVE - THE WAY WE WALK VOLUME ONE: THE SHORTS	Genesis (Virgin)
18	13	INCESTICIDE	Nirvana (Geffen)
17	14	3 YEARS, 5 MONTHS AND 2 DAYS IN THE LIFE	Arrested Development (Cooltempo)
10	15	TIMELESS - THE CLASSICS	Michael Bolton (Columbia)
13	16	BACK TO FRONT	Lionel Richie (Motown)
12	17	STARS	Simply Red (East West)
14	18	DANGEROUS	Michael Jackson (Epic)
16	19	EROTICA	Madonna (Maverick)
15	20	THE FREDDIE MERCURY ALBUM	Freddie Mercury (Parlophone)
-	21	INTO THE SKYLINE	Cathy Dennis (Polydor)
23	22	KEEP THE FAITH	Bon Jovi (Jambco)
19	23	NEVERMIND	Nirvana (DGC)
20	24	HIT PARADE 2	Wedding Present (RCA)
34	25	UP	Right Said Fred (Tug)
-	26	ONLY YESTERDAY - THE CARPENTER'S GREATEST HITS	Carpenters (A&M)
29	27	UNPLUGGED	Eric Clapton (Duck)
24	28	DUOPHONIC	Charles & Eddie (Capitol)
-	29	LUCKY THIRTEEN	Neil Young (Geffen)
30	30	GOD'S GREAT BANANA SKIN	Chris Rea (East West)
22	31	DIVA	Annie Lennox (RCA)
35	32	THE PRODIGY EXPERIENCE	Prodigy (XL Recordings)
26	33	THE CELTS	Enya (WEA)
-	34	US	Peter Gabriel (Realworld)
21	35	THE BEST OF BELINDA CARLISLE VOLUME 1	Belinda Carlisle (Virgin)
-	36	AGES OF MANN - 22 CLASSIC HITS OF THE '60S	Manfred Mann (PolyGram TV)
25	37	HORMONALLY YOURS	Shakespear's Sister (London)
27	38	TUBULAR BELLS II	Mike Oldfield (WEA)
40	39	IT'S A SHAME ABOUT RAY	Lemonheads (Atlantic)
36	40	SYMBOL	Prince & the New Power Generation (Paisley Park)
28	41	GREATEST HITS II	Queen (Parlophone)
32	42	CURTIS STIGERS	Curtis Stigers (Arista)
31	43	ACHTUNG BABY	U2 (Island)
42	44	COOLEYHIGHHARMONY	Boyz II Men (Motown)
-	45	INSPECTOR MORSE, VOL. 3	Barrington Pheloung (Virgin)
38	46	THE GREATEST HITS 1966-1992	Neil Diamond (Columbia)
39	47	SIMPLY THE BEST	Tina Turner (Capitol)
-	48	ANGEL DUST	Faith No More (Slash)
-	49	SYNTHESIZER GOLD	Ed Starink (Arcade)
33	50	ONCE IN A LIFETIME	Talking Heads (EMI)

The Bodyguard soundtrack album, mostly consisting of songs by the film's leading lady Whitney Houston, was something of a phenomenon. In the US it was estimated to be selling almost a million copies a week at its peak, and the UK release was also to hit the 7-figure sales mark, with two months of consistent Number 1 sales to its credit. It also spawned the million-selling single *I Will Always Love You.*

January – February 1993

30 January 1993

last week	this week	
1	1	THE BODYGUARD - SOUNDTRACK Various (Arista)
2	2	LIVE - THE WAY WE WALK VOLUME TWO: THE LONGS Genesis (Virgin)
7	3	CONNECTED Stereo MCs (Fourth & Broadway)
6	4	AUTOMATIC FOR THE PEOPLE R.E.M. (Warner Bros.)
14	5	3 YEARS, 5 MONTHS AND 2 DAYS IN THE LIFE Arrested Development (Cooltempo)
3	6	GREATEST HITS: 1965-1992 Cher (Geffen)
4	7	BOSS DRUM Shamen (One Little Indian)
5	8	TAKE THAT AND PARTY Take That (RCA)
-	9	SO CLOSE Dina Carroll (A&M PM)
8	10	POP! - THE FIRST 20 HITS Erasure (Mute)
21	11	INTO THE SKYLINE Cathy Dennis (Polydor)
9	12	GLITTERING PRIZE 81/92 Simple Minds (Virgin)
12	13	LIVE - THE WAY WE WALK VOLUME ONE: THE SHORTS Genesis (Virgin)
13	14	INCESTICIDE Nirvana (Geffen)
10	15	GREATEST HITS Gloria Estefan (Epic)
11	16	GOLD - GREATEST HITS Abba (Polydor)
16	17	BACK TO FRONT Lionel Richie (Motown)
22	18	KEEP THE FAITH Bon Jovi (Jambco)
17	19	STARS Simply Red (East West)
34	20	US Peter Gabriel (Realworld)
15	21	TIMELESS - THE CLASSICS Michael Bolton (Columbia)
-	22	SONGS FROM THE MIRROR Fish (Polydor)
36	23	AGES OF MANN - 22 CLASSIC HITS OF THE '60S Manfred Mann (PolyGram TV)
23	24	NEVERMIND Nirvana (DGC)
-	25	THE JULIET LETTERS Elvis Costello & the Brodsky Quartet (Warner Bros.)
18	26	DANGEROUS Michael Jackson (Epic)
27	27	UNPLUGGED Eric Clapton (Duck)
32	28	THE PRODIGY EXPERIENCE Prodigy (XL Recordings)
19	29	EROTICA Madonna (Maverick)
31	30	DIVA Annie Lennox (RCA)
-	31	25 Harry Connick Jr. (Columbia)
20	32	THE FREDDIE MERCURY ALBUM Freddie Mercury (Parlophone)
28	33	DUOPHONIC Charles & Eddie (Capitol)
30	34	GOD'S GREAT BANANA SKIN Chris Rea (East West)
39	35	IT'S A SHAME ABOUT RAY Lemonheads (Atlantic)
33	36	THE CELTS Enya (WEA)
26	37	ONLY YESTERDAY - THE CARPENTER'S GREATEST HITS Carpenters (A&M)
45	38	MUSIC FROM THE ITV SERIES INSPECTOR MORSE, VOL. 3 Barrington Pheloung (Virgin)
35	39	THE BEST OF BELINDA CARLISLE VOLUME 1 Belinda Carlisle (Virgin)
37	40	HORMONALLY YOURS Shakespear's Sister (London)
-	41	FROM THE HEART - HIS GREATEST HITS Elvis Presley (RCA)
48	42	ANGEL DUST Faith No More (Slash)
-	43	COPPER BLUE Sugar (Creation)
-	44	FUNKY DIVAS En Vogue (East West)
43	45	ACHTUNG BABY U2 (Island)
38	46	TUBULAR BELLS II Mike Oldfield (WEA)
-	47	INDIAN SUMMER Go West (Chrysalis)
41	48	GREATEST HITS II Queen (Parlophone)
44	49	COOLEYHIGHHARMONY Boyz II Men (Motown)
49	50	SYNTHESIZER GOLD Ed Starink (Arcade)

6 February 1993

last week	this week	
1	1	THE BODYGUARD - SOUNDTRACK Various (Arista)
-	2	JAM Little Angels (Jam)
2	3	LIVE - THE WAY WE WALK VOLUME TWO: THE LONGS Genesis (Virgin)
9	4	SO CLOSE Dina Carroll (A&M PM)
-	5	DUSK The The (Epic)
4	6	AUTOMATIC FOR THE PEOPLE R.E.M. (Warner Bros.)
5	7	3 YEARS, 5 MONTHS AND 2 DAYS IN THE LIFE Arrested Development (Cooltempo)
8	8	PERVERSE Jesus Jones (Food)
3	9	CONNECTED Stereo MCs (Fourth & Broadway)
7	10	BOSS DRUM Shamen (One Little Indian)
8	11	TAKE THAT AND PARTY Take That (RCA)
6	12	GREATEST HITS: 1965-1992 Cher (Geffen)
18	13	KEEP THE FAITH Bon Jovi (Jambco)
10	14	POP! - THE FIRST 20 HITS Erasure (Mute)
20	15	US Peter Gabriel (Realworld)
13	16	LIVE - THE WAY WE WALK VOLUME ONE: THE SHORTS Genesis (Virgin)
42	17	ANGEL DUST Faith No More (Slash)
12	18	GLITTERING PRIZE 81/92 Simple Minds (Virgin)
16	19	GOLD - GREATEST HITS Abba (Polydor)
11	20	INTO THE SKYLINE Cathy Dennis (Polydor)
15	21	GREATEST HITS Gloria Estefan (Epic)
25	22	THE JULIET LETTERS Elvis Costello & the Brodsky Quartet (Warner Bros.)
19	23	STARS Simply Red (East West)
17	24	BACK TO FRONT Lionel Richie (Motown)
14	25	INCESTICIDE Nirvana (Geffen)
-	26	NO RESERVATIONS Apache Indian (Island)
21	27	TIMELESS - THE CLASSICS Michael Bolton (Columbia)
24	28	NEVERMIND Nirvana (DGC)
27	29	UNPLUGGED Eric Clapton (Duck)
38	30	MUSIC FROM THE ITV SERIES INSPECTOR MORSE, VOL. 3 Barrington Pheloung (Virgin)
28	31	THE PRODIGY EXPERIENCE Prodigy (XL Recordings)
30	32	DIVA Annie Lennox (RCA)
26	33	DANGEROUS Michael Jackson (Epic)
31	34	25 Harry Connick Jr. (Columbia)
35	35	IT'S A SHAME ABOUT RAY Lemonheads (Atlantic)
43	36	COPPER BLUE Sugar (Creation)
33	37	DUOPHONIC Charles & Eddie (Capitol)
-	38	APPOLONIA BM-EX (UCR)
22	39	SONGS FROM THE MIRROR Fish (Polydor)
47	40	INDIAN SUMMER Go West (Chrysalis)
41	41	DIRT Alice In Chains (Columbia)
36	42	THE CELTS Enya (WEA)
34	43	GOD'S GREAT BANANA SKIN Chris Rea (East West)
37	44	ONLY YESTERDAY - RICHARD AND KAREN CARPENTER'S GREATEST HITS Carpenters (A&M)
45	45	ACHTUNG BABY U2 (Island)
32	46	THE FREDDIE MERCURY ALBUM Freddie Mercury (Parlophone)
29	47	EROTICA Madonna (Maverick)
23	48	AGES OF MANN - 22 CLASSIC HITS OF THE '60S Manfred Mann (PolyGram TV)
44	49	FUNKY DIVAS En Vogue (East West)
48	50	GREATEST HITS II Queen (Parlophone)

13 February 1993

last week	this week	
1	1	THE BODYGUARD - SOUNDTRACK Various (Arista)
2	2	JAM Little Angels (Jam)
-	3	OFF THE GROUND Paul McCartney (Parlophone)
-	4	PURE CULT - FOR ROCKERS, RAVERS, LOVERS AND SINNERS Cult (Beggars Banquet)
5	5	DUSK The The (Epic)
-	6	STAR Belly (4AD)
7	7	3 YEARS, 5 MONTHS AND 2 DAYS IN THE LIFE Arrested Development (Cooltempo)
4	8	SO CLOSE Dina Carroll (A&M PM)
3	9	LIVE - THE WAY WE WALK VOLUME TWO: THE LONGS Genesis (Virgin)
6	10	AUTOMATIC FOR THE PEOPLE R.E.M. (Warner Bros.)
8	11	PERVERSE Jesus Jones (Food)
9	12	CONNECTED Stereo MCs (Fourth & Broadway)
10	13	BOSS DRUM Shamen (One Little Indian)
11	14	TAKE THAT AND PARTY Take That (RCA)
40	15	INDIAN SUMMER Go West (Chrysalis)
12	16	GREATEST HITS: 1965-1992 Cher (Geffen)
-	17	GORECKI: SYMPHONY NO. 3 DaUpshaw/London Sinfonietta/David Zinman (Elektra Nonesuch)
49	18	FUNKY DIVAS En Vogue (East West)
13	19	KEEP THE FAITH Bon Jovi (Jambco)
32	20	DIVA Annie Lennox (RCA)
15	21	US Peter Gabriel (Realworld)
16	22	LIVE - THE WAY WE WALK VOLUME ONE: THE SHORTS Genesis (Virgin)
17	23	ANGEL DUST Faith No More (Slash)
19	24	GOLD - GREATEST HITS Abba (Polydor)
14	25	POP! - THE FIRST 20 HITS Erasure (Mute)
-	26	CASUAL SEX IN THE CINEPLEX Sultans Of Ping FC (Rhythm King)
18	27	GLITTERING PRIZE 81/92 Simple Minds (Virgin)
24	28	BACK TO FRONT Lionel Richie (Motown)
23	29	STARS Simply Red (East West)
-	30	THE MADMAN'S RETURN Snap (Logic)
28	31	NEVERMIND Nirvana (DGC)
30	32	MUSIC FROM THE ITV SERIES INSPECTOR MORSE, VOL. 3 Barrington Pheloung (Virgin)
21	33	GREATEST HITS Gloria Estefan (Epic)
35	34	IT'S A SHAME ABOUT RAY Lemonheads (Atlantic)
-	35	GORGEOUS 808 State (ZTT)
-	36	O3 Sunscreem (Sony Soho Square)
29	37	UNPLUGGED Eric Clapton (Duck)
31	38	THE PRODIGY EXPERIENCE Prodigy (XL Recordings)
27	39	TIMELESS - THE CLASSICS Michael Bolton (Columbia)
25	40	INCESTICIDE Nirvana (Geffen)
41	41	DIRT Alice In Chains (Columbia)
33	42	DANGEROUS Michael Jackson (Epic)
22	43	THE JULIET LETTERS Elvis Costello & the Brodsky Quartet (Warner Bros.)
26	44	NO RESERVATIONS Apache Indian (Island)
-	45	ON A WING AND A PRAYER Gerry Rafferty (A&M)
46	46	THE FREDDIE MERCURY ALBUM Freddie Mercury (Parlophone)
36	47	COPPER BLUE Sugar (Creation)
44	48	ONLY YESTERDAY - THE CARPENTER'S GREATEST HITS Carpenters (A&M)
42	49	THE CELTS Enya (WEA)
20	50	INTO THE SKYLINE Cathy Dennis (Polydor)

Genesis' two oddled-titled live albums actually gave straight descriptions of what they contained - *The Shorts* featured the trio's short in-concert numbers, and *The Longs* the extended songs. Elvis Costello's collaboration with the avant-garde classical Brodsky Quartet on *The Juliet Letters* did not bring him universal critical approval, but certainly showed how far Costello had moved on from *My Aim Is True*.

February – March 1993

20 February 1993

1	1	THE BODYGUARD - SOUNDTRACK	Various (Arista)
4	2	PURE CULT - FOR ROCKERS, RAVERS, LOVERS AND SINNERS	Cult (Beggars Banquet)
-	3	CONSCIENCE	Beloved (East West)
-	4	WHERE YOU BEEN	Dinosaur Jr. (blanco y negro)
-	5	WANDERING SPIRIT	Mick Jagger (Atlantic)
6	6	STAR	Belly (4AD)
7	7	3 YEARS, 5 MONTHS AND 2 DAYS IN THE LIFE	Arrested Development (Cooltempo)
18	8	FUNKY DIVAS	En Vogue (East West)
3	9	OFF THE GROUND	Paul McCartney (Parlophone)
10	10	AUTOMATIC FOR THE PEOPLE	R.E.M. (Warner Bros.)
12	11	CONNECTED	Stereo MCs (Fourth & Broadway)
20	12	DIVA	Annie Lennox (RCA)
14	13	TAKE THAT AND PARTY	Take That (RCA)
17	14	GORECKI: SYMPHONY NO. 3	Dawn Upshaw/London Sinfonietta/David Zinman (Elektra Nonesuch)
8	15	SO CLOSE	Dina Carroll (A&M PM)
2	16	JAM	Little Angels (Jam)
30	17	THE MADMAN'S RETURN	Snap (Logic)
9	18	LIVE - THE WAY WE WALK VOLUME TWO: THE LONGS	Genesis (Virgin)
13	19	BOSS DRUM	Shamen (One Little Indian)
-	20	LOVE MAKES NO SENSE	Alexander O'Neal (Tabu)
5	21	DUSK	The The (Epic)
15	22	INDIAN SUMMER	Go West (Chrysalis)
-	23	HEAD OVER HEELS	Various Artists (Telstar)
-	24	THE VERY BEST OF SISTER SLEDGE 1973-1993	Sister Sledge (Atlantic)
16	25	GREATEST HITS: 1965-1992	Cher (Geffen)
19	26	KEEP THE FAITH	Bon Jovi (Jambco)
35	27	GORGEOUS	808 State (ZTT)
24	28	GOLD - GREATEST HITS	Abba (Polydor)
25	29	POP! - THE FIRST 20 HITS	Erasure (Mute)
21	30	US	Peter Gabriel (Realworld)
-	31	WORDS OF LOVE - 22 CLASSIC HITS	Buddy Holly & the Crickets (MCA)
22	32	LIVE - THE WAY WE WALK VOLUME ONE: THE SHORTS	Genesis (Virgin)
11	33	PERVERSE	Jesus Jones (Food)
23	34	ANGEL DUST	Faith No More (Slash)
-	35	SCENES FROM THE SECOND STOREY	God Machine (Fiction)
26	36	CASUAL SEX IN THE CINEPLEX	Sultans Of Ping FC (Rhythm King)
29	37	STARS	Simply Red (East West)
28	38	BACK TO FRONT	Lionel Richie (Motown)
27	39	GLITTERING PRIZE 81/92	Simple Minds (Virgin)
36	40	O3	Sunscreem (Sony Soho Square)
31	41	NEVERMIND	Nirvana (DGC)
34	42	IT'S A SHAME ABOUT RAY	Lemonheads (Atlantic)
37	43	UNPLUGGED	Eric Clapton (Duck)
32	44	MUSIC FROM THE ITV SERIES INSPECTOR MORSE, VOL. 3	Barrington Pheloung (Virgin)
38	45	THE PRODIGY EXPERIENCE	Prodigy (XL Recordings)
42	46	DANGEROUS	Michael Jackson (Epic)
-	47	DUOPHONIC	Charles & Eddie (Capitol)
-	48	ACHTUNG BABY	U2 (Island)
33	49	GREATEST HITS	Gloria Estefan (Epic)
39	50	TIMELESS - THE CLASSICS	Michael Bolton (Columbia)

27 February 1993

1	1	THE BODYGUARD - SOUNDTRACK	Various (Arista)
10	2	AUTOMATIC FOR THE PEOPLE	R.E.M. (Warner Bros.)
31	3	WORDS OF LOVE - 22 CLASSIC HITS	Buddy Holly & the Crickets (MCA)
-	4	DURAN DURAN	Duran Duran (Parlophone)
-	5	WALTHAMSTOW	East 17 (London)
12	6	DIVA	Annie Lennox (RCA)
13	7	TAKE THAT AND PARTY	Take That (RCA)
2	8	PURE CULT - FOR ROCKERS, RAVERS, LOVERS AND SINNERS	Cult (Beggars Banquet)
7	10	3 YEARS, 5 MONTHS AND 2 DAYS IN THE LIFE	Arrested Development (Cooltempo)
8	11	FUNKY DIVAS	En Vogue (East West)
15	12	SO CLOSE	Dina Carroll (A&M PM)
11	13	CONNECTED	Stereo MCs (Fourth & Broadway)
14	14	GORECKI: SYMPHONY NO. 3	Dawn Upshaw/London Sinfonietta/David Zinman (Elektra Nonesuch)
37	15	STARS	Simply Red (East West)
5	16	WANDERING SPIRIT	Mick Jagger (Atlantic)
-	17	THE BEST OF VAN MORRISON VOLUME TWO	Van Morrison (Virgin)
20	18	LOVE MAKES NO SENSE	Alexander O'Neal (Tabu)
46	19	DANGEROUS	Michael Jackson (Epic)
47	20	DUOPHONIC	Charles & Eddie (Capitol)
4	21	WHERE YOU BEEN	Dinosaur Jr. (blanco y negro)
-	22	GREAT EXPECTATIONS	Tasmin Archer (EMI)
6	23	STAR	Belly (4AD)
30	24	US	Peter Gabriel (Realworld)
48	25	ACHTUNG BABY	U2 (Island)
9	26	OFF THE GROUND	Paul McCartney (Parlophone)
43	27	UNPLUGGED	Eric Clapton (Duck)
41	28	NEVERMIND	Nirvana (DGC)
19	29	BOSS DRUM	Shamen (One Little Indian)
18	30	LIVE - THE WAY WE WALK VOLUME TWO: THE LONGS	Genesis (Virgin)
-	31	HORMONALLY YOURS	Shakespear's Sister (London)
29	32	POP! - THE FIRST 20 HITS	Erasure (Mute)
25	33	GREATEST HITS: 1965-1992	Cher (Geffen)
22	34	INDIAN SUMMER	Go West (Chrysalis)
26	35	KEEP THE FAITH	Bon Jovi (Jambco)
17	36	THE MADMAN'S RETURN	Snap (Logic)
-	37	WELCOME TO WHEREVER YOU ARE	INXS (Mercury)
28	38	GOLD - GREATEST HITS	Abba (Polydor)
-	39	HEART AND SOUL	T'Pau (Virgin)
32	40	LIVE - THE WAY WE WALK VOLUME ONE: THE SHORTS	Genesis (Virgin)
38	41	BACK TO FRONT	Lionel Richie (Motown)
39	42	GLITTERING PRIZE 81/92	Simple Minds (Virgin)
-	43	INCESTICIDE	Nirvana (Geffen)
-	44	ONLY YESTERDAY - THE CARPENTER'S GREATEST HITS	Carpenters (A&M)
23	45	HEAD OVER HEELS	Various Artists (Telstar)
16	46	JAM	Little Angels (Jam)
21	47	DUSK	The The (Epic)
-	48	METALLICA	Metallica (Vertigo)
24	49	THE VERY BEST OF SISTER SLEDGE 1973-1993	Sister Sledge (Atlantic)
50	50	TIMELESS - THE CLASSICS	Michael Bolton (Columbia)

6 March 1993

1	1	THE BODYGUARD - SOUNDTRACK	Various (Arista)
2	2	AUTOMATIC FOR THE PEOPLE	R.E.M. (Warner Bros.)
5	3	WALTHAMSTOW	East 17 (London)
-	4	LEAD VOCALIST	Rod Stewart (Warner Bros.)
-	5	SO TOUGH	Saint Etienne (Heavenly)
6	6	DIVA	Annie Lennox (RCA)
7	7	TAKE THAT AND PARTY	Take That (RCA)
-	8	NATIVE TONGUE	Poison (EMI)
4	9	DURAN DURAN	Duran Duran (Parlophone)
15	10	STARS	Simply Red (East West)
-	11	STAIN	Living Colour (Stain)
19	12	DANGEROUS	Michael Jackson (Epic)
3	13	WORDS OF LOVE - 22 CLASSIC HITS	Buddy Holly & the Crickets (MCA)
8	14	PURE CULT - FOR ROCKERS, RAVERS, LOVERS AND SINNERS	Cult (Beggars Banquet)
22	15	GREAT EXPECTATIONS	Tasmin Archer (EMI)
11	16	FUNKY DIVAS	En Vogue (East West)
-	17	LIVE: RIGHT HERE, RIGHT NOW	Van Halen (Warner Bros.)
10	18	3 YEARS, 5 MONTHS AND 2 DAYS IN THE LIFE	Arrested Development (Cooltempo)
13	19	CONNECTED	Stereo MCs (Fourth & Broadway)
14	20	GORECKI: SYMPHONY NO. 3	Dawn Upshaw/London Sinfonietta/David Zinman (Elektra Nonesuch)
24	21	US	Peter Gabriel (Realworld)
12	22	SO CLOSE	Dina Carroll (A&M PM)
-	23	IF I WAS: THE VERY BEST OF MIDGE URE AND ULTRAVOX	Midge Ure & Ultravox (Chrysalis)
24	24	WEIRD'S BAR & GRILL	Pop Will Eat Itself (RCA)
29	25	BOSS DRUM	Shamen (One Little Indian)
-	26	INGENUE	k.d. lang (Sire)
9	27	CONSCIENCE	Beloved (East West)
49	28	THE VERY BEST OF SISTER SLEDGE 1973-1993	Sister Sledge (Atlantic)
28	29	NEVERMIND	Nirvana (DGC)
-	30	PABLO HONEY	Radiohead (Parlophone)
27	31	UNPLUGGED	Eric Clapton (Duck)
31	32	HORMONALLY YOURS	Shakespear's Sister (London)
32	33	POP! - THE FIRST 20 HITS	Erasure (Mute)
16	34	WANDERING SPIRIT	Mick Jagger (Atlantic)
33	35	GREATEST HITS: 1965-1992	Cher (Geffen)
25	36	ACHTUNG BABY	U2 (Island)
17	37	THE BEST OF VAN MORRISON VOLUME TWO	Van Morrison (Virgin)
23	38	STAR	Belly (4AD)
30	39	LIVE - THE WAY WE WALK VOLUME TWO: THE LONGS	Genesis (Virgin)
-	40	HARVEST MOON	Neil Young (Reprise)
48	41	METALLICA	Metallica (Vertigo)
38	42	GOLD - GREATEST HITS	Abba (Polydor)
34	43	THE MADMAN'S RETURN	Snap (Logic)
35	44	KEEP THE FAITH	Bon Jovi (Jambco)
34	45	INDIAN SUMMER	Go West (Chrysalis)
37	46	WELCOME TO WHEREVER YOU ARE	INXS (Mercury)
42	47	GLITTERING PRIZE 81/92	Simple Minds (Virgin)
18	48	LOVE MAKES NO SENSE	Alexander O'Neal (Tabu)
20	49	DUOPHONIC	Charles & Eddie (Capitol)
26	50	OFF THE GROUND	Paul McCartney (Parlophone)

Though, thanks to the three tenors and Nigel Kennedy, classical albums in the chart were no longer a cause of utter wonder, the success of Polish composer Gorecki's relatively obscure *3rd Symphony* was still extraordinary, and a notable tribute to the widening influence of the new nationwide commercial classic radio station, Classic FM, which playlisted the work recurrently.

March 1993

Lenny Kravitz, a writer/singer/guitarist whose attitude and mode of dress seemed straight out of 1967, with a firm nod at Jimi Hendrix, nonetheless shaped up in early 1993 as one of the likely bright musical stars of the 90s, his material mixing traditional rock and R&B influences and eschewing modern computer-generations in favour of "real" instruments in a way which gave him an ironically fresh flavour.

April 1993

3 April 1993

last	this	title	artist (label)
-	1	SONGS OF FAITH AND DEVOTION	Depeche Mode (Mute)
-	2	A REAL LIVE ONE	Iron Maiden (EMI)
16	3	THEIR GREATEST HITS	Hot Chocolate (EMI)
1	4	COVERDALE/PAGE	Coverdale/Page (EMI)
2	5	ARE YOU GONNA GO MY WAY	Lenny Kravitz (Virgin America)
8	6	AMAZING THINGS	Runrig (Chrysalis)
3	7	UNPLUGGED	Eric Clapton (Duck)
6	8	THE BODYGUARD - SOUNDTRACK	Various (Arista)
5	9	INGENUE	k.d. lang (Sire)
-	10	TAXI	Bryan Ferry (Virgin)
-	11	THE BLISS ALBUM...	PM Dawn (Gee Street)
10	12	AUTOMATIC FOR THE PEOPLE	R.E.M. (Warner Bros.)
12	13	LIPSTICK ON YOUR COLLAR	Various Artists (PolyGram TV)
7	14	TEN SUMMONER'S TALES	Sting (A&M)
4	15	THE DARK SIDE OF THE MOON - 20TH ANNIVERSARY	Pink Floyd (EMI)
11	16	DIVA	Annie Lennox (RCA)
-	17	HOME INVASION	Ice-T (Rhyme Syndicate)
28	18	THE VERY BEST OF...	Randy Crawford (Dino)
27	19	THE ULTIMATE...	Glenn Miller (Telstar)
-	20	THE BUFFALO SKINNERS	Big Country (Compulsion)
14	21	SO CLOSE	Dina Carroll (A&M PM)
13	22	DANGEROUS	Michael Jackson (Epic)
15	23	LEAD VOCALIST	Rod Stewart (Warner Bros.)
9	24	SONGS FROM THE RAIN	Hothouse Flowers (London)
18	25	STARS	Simply Red (East West)
23	26	TAKE THAT AND PARTY	Take That (RCA)
36	27	THE GREATEST HITS	Boney M (Telstar)
22	28	RAGE AGAINST THE MACHINE	Rage Against The Machine (Epic)
17	29	WHATEVER YOU SAY, SAY NOTHING	Deacon Blue (Columbia)
26	30	3 YEARS, 5 MONTHS AND 2 DAYS IN THE LIFE	Arrested Development (Cooltempo)
30	31	WALTHAMSTOW	East 17 (London)
24	32	FUNKY DIVAS	En Vogue (East West)
25	33	CONNECTED	Stereo MCs (Fourth & Broadway)
19	34	BITTER SWEET & TWISTED	Quireboys (Parlophone)
45	35	ROUND MIDNIGHT	Elkie Brooks (Castle)
39	36	BOSS DRUM	Shamen (One Little Indian)
20	37	FRANK BLACK	Frank Black (4AD)
-	38	THE AIR THAT I BREATHE - GREATEST HITS	Hollies (EMI)
29	39	GREAT EXPECTATIONS	Tasmin Archer (EMI)
31	40	WORDS OF LOVE - 22 CLASSIC HITS	Buddy Holly & the Crickets (MCA)
32	41	DURAN DURAN	Duran Duran (Parlophone)
33	42	IF I WAS: THE VERY BEST OF MIDGE URE AND ULTRAVOX	Midge Ure & Ultravox (Chrysalis)
21	43	OTHER VOICES, OTHER ROOMS	Nanci Griffith (MCA)
44	44	MERCURY	American Music Club (Virgin)
38	45	GORECKI: SYMPHONY NO. 3	Dawn Upshaw/London Sinfonietta/David Zinman (Elektra Nonesuch)
-	46	GOLD - GREATEST HITS	Abba (Polydor)
-	47	HIDDEN TREASURES	Barry Manilow (Arista)
-	48	AMERICA'S LEAST WANTED	Ugly Kid Joe (Vertigo)
35	49	HIGHER AND HIGHER	Heaven 17 (Virgin)
41	50	DIRT	Alice In Chains (Columbia)

10 April 1993

last	this	title	artist (label)
-	1	SUEDE	Suede (Nude)
1	2	SONGS OF FAITH AND DEVOTION	Depeche Mode (Mute)
10	3	TAXI	Bryan Ferry (Virgin)
3	4	THEIR GREATEST HITS	Hot Chocolate (EMI)
5	5	ARE YOU GONNA GO MY WAY	Lenny Kravitz (Virgin America)
8	6	THE BODYGUARD - SOUNDTRACK	Various (Arista)
7	7	UNPLUGGED	Eric Clapton (Duck)
18	8	THE VERY BEST OF...	Randy Crawford (Dino)
12	9	AUTOMATIC FOR THE PEOPLE	R.E.M. (Warner Bros.)
16	10	DIVA	Annie Lennox (RCA)
9	11	INGENUE	k.d. lang (Sire)
13	12	LIPSTICK ON YOUR COLLAR	Various Artists (PolyGram TV)
2	13	A REAL LIVE ONE	Iron Maiden (EMI)
11	14	THE BLISS ALBUM...	PM Dawn (Gee Street)
4	15	COVERDALE/PAGE	Coverdale/Page (EMI)
14	16	TEN SUMMONER'S TALES	Sting (A&M)
21	17	SO CLOSE	Dina Carroll (A&M PM)
-	18	COVER SHOT	David Essex (PolyGram TV)
30	19	3 YEARS, 5 MONTHS AND 2 DAYS IN THE LIFE	Arrested Development (Cooltempo)
-	20	THE LOVE OF HOPELESS CAUSES	New Model Army (Epic)
15	21	THE DARK SIDE OF THE MOON - 20TH ANNIVERSARY	Pink Floyd (EMI)
17	22	HOME INVASION	Ice-T (Rhyme Syndicate)
22	23	DANGEROUS	Michael Jackson (Epic)
6	24	AMAZING THINGS	Runrig (Chrysalis)
25	25	STARS	Simply Red (East West)
-	26	NUMBER ONE	Felix (deConstruction)
27	27	THE GREATEST HITS	Boney M (Telstar)
-	28	LABOURS OF LOVE - THE BEST OF HUE AND CRY	Hue & Cry (Circa)
38	29	THE AIR THAT I BREATHE - GREATEST HITS	Hollies (EMI)
39	30	GREAT EXPECTATIONS	Tasmin Archer (EMI)
28	31	RAGE AGAINST THE MACHINE	Rage Against The Machine (Epic)
41	32	DURAN DURAN	Duran Duran (Parlophone)
31	33	WALTHAMSTOW	East 17 (London)
23	34	LEAD VOCALIST	Rod Stewart (Warner Bros.)
19	35	THE ULTIMATE...	Glenn Miller (Telstar)
20	36	THE BUFFALO SKINNERS	Big Country (Compulsion)
29	37	WHATEVER YOU SAY, SAY NOTHING	Deacon Blue (Columbia)
32	38	FUNKY DIVAS	En Vogue (East West)
-	39	GREATEST HITS	Sheep On Drugs (Transglobal)
-	40	UNPLUGGED	Arrested Development (EMI)
26	41	TAKE THAT AND PARTY	Take That (RCA)
48	42	AMERICA'S LEAST WANTED	Ugly Kid Joe (Vertigo)
33	43	CONNECTED	Stereo MCs (Fourth & Broadway)
24	44	SONGS FROM THE RAIN	Hothouse Flowers (London)
-	45	PLEASE YOURSELF	Bananarama (London)
43	46	OTHER VOICES, OTHER ROOMS	Nanci Griffith (MCA)
47	47	HIDDEN TREASURES	Barry Manilow (Arista)
45	48	GORECKI: SYMPHONY NO. 3	Dawn Upshaw/London Sinfonietta/David Zinman (Elektra Nonesuch)
-	49	NURSE	Therapy? (A&M)
-	50	THE NEW STARLIGHT EXPRESS	Andrew Lloyd Webber (Really Useful)

17 April 1993

last	this	title	artist (label)
1	1	SUEDE	Suede (Nude)
-	2	BLACK TIE WHITE NOISE	David Bowie (Savage)
2	3	SONGS OF FAITH AND DEVOTION	Depeche Mode (Mute)
-	4	POWERTRIPPIN'	Almighty (Powertrippin')
-	5	BEASTER	Sugar (Creation)
5	6	ARE YOU GONNA GO MY WAY	Lenny Kravitz (Virgin America)
4	7	THEIR GREATEST HITS	Hot Chocolate (EMI)
7	8	UNPLUGGED	Eric Clapton (Duck)
9	9	AUTOMATIC FOR THE PEOPLE	R.E.M. (Warner Bros.)
10	10	DIVA	Annie Lennox (RCA)
17	11	SO CLOSE	Dina Carroll (A&M PM)
18	12	COVER SHOT	David Essex (PolyGram TV)
12	13	LIPSTICK ON YOUR COLLAR	Various (PolyGram TV)
6	14	THE BODYGUARD - SOUNDTRACK	Various(Arista)
8	15	THE VERY BEST OF...	Randy Crawford (Dino)
3	16	TAXI	Bryan Ferry (Virgin)
11	17	INGENUE	k.d. lang (Sire)
16	18	TEN SUMMONER'S TALES	Sting (A&M)
27	19	THE GREATEST HITS	Boney M (Telstar)
19	20	3 YEARS, 5 MONTHS AND 2 DAYS IN THE LIFE	Arrested Development (Cooltempo)
29	21	THE AIR THAT I BREATHE - GREATEST HITS	Hollies (EMI)
23	22	DANGEROUS	Michael Jackson (Epic)
15	23	COVERDALE/PAGE	Coverdale/Page (EMI)
13	24	A REAL LIVE ONE	Iron Maiden (EMI)
14	25	THE BLISS ALBUM...?	PM Dawn (Gee Street)
21	26	THE DARK SIDE OF THE MOON - 20TH ANNIVERSARY	Pink Floyd (EMI)
-	27	GLAD ALL OVER AGAIN	Dave Clark Five (EMI)
41	28	TAKE THAT AND PARTY	Take That (RCA)
-	29	WRESTLEMANIA	WWF Superstars (Arista)
22	30	HOME INVASION	Ice-T (Rhyme Syndicate)
-	31	THE SINGLES COLLECTION	Bluebells (London)
26	32	NUMBER ONE	Felix (deConstruction)
30	33	GREAT EXPECTATIONS	Tasmin Archer (EMI)
31	34	RAGE AGAINST THE MACHINE	Rage Against The Machine (Epic)
25	35	STARS	Simply Red (East West)
-	36	LEONARD BERNSTEIN'S WEST SIDE STORY	Various Artists (IMG)
20	37	THE LOVE OF HOPELESS CAUSES	New Model Army (Epic)
28	38	LABOURS OF LOVE - THE BEST OF HUE AND CRY	Hue & Cry (Circa)
33	39	WALTHAMSTOW	East 17 (London)
32	40	DURAN DURAN	Duran Duran (Parlophone)
38	41	FUNKY DIVAS	En Vogue (East West)
42	42	UNPLUGGED	Arrested Development (EMI)
42	43	AMERICA'S LEAST WANTED	Ugly Kid Joe (Vertigo)
55	44	THE ULTIMATE GLENN MILLER	Glenn Miller (Telstar)
-	45	GREATEST HITS	Gloria Estefan (Epic)
48	46	GORECKI: SYMPHONY NO. 3	Dawn Upshaw/London Sinfonietta/David Zinman (Elektra Nonesuch)
34	47	LEAD VOCALIST	Rod Stewart (Warner Bros.)
37	48	WHATEVER YOU SAY, SAY NOTHING	Deacon Blue (Columbia)
43	49	CONNECTED	Stereo MCs (Fourth & Broadway)
24	50	AMAZING THINGS	Runrig (Chrysalis)

Coverdale/Page were, as their name suggests, a collaboration between David Coverdale, the former lead vocalist of Deep Purple and Whitesnake, and Jimmy Page, once the guitarist with Led Zeppelin and role model to a whole world of heavy-style axe-wielders. Many expected a tired recreation of Zeppelin, with Coverdale in the Robert Plant role, but their album won both critical approval and big sales.

April – May 1993

24 April 1993

last week	this week		
2	1	BLACK TIE WHITE NOISE	David Bowie (Savage)
-	2	IN CONCERT - MTV UNPLUGGED	Bruce Springsteen (Columbia)
1	3	SUEDE	Suede (Nude)
9	4	AUTOMATIC FOR THE PEOPLE	R.E.M. (Warner Bros.)
12	5	COVER SHOT	David Essex (PolyGram TV)
14	6	THE BODYGUARD - SOUNDTRACK	Various (Arista)
20	7	3 YEARS, 5 MONTHS AND 2 DAYS IN THE LIFE	Arrested Development (Cooltempo)
10	8	DIVA	Annie Lennox (RCA)
4	9	POWERTRIPPIN'	Almighty (Powertrippin')
5	10	BEASTER	Sugar (Creation)
8	11	UNPLUGGED	Eric Clapton (Duck)
-	12	SAN FRANCISCO DAYS	Chris Isaak (Reprise)
18	13	TEN SUMMONER'S TALES	Sting (A&M)
6	14	ARE YOU GONNA GO MY WAY	Lenny Kravitz (Virgin America)
3	15	SONGS OF FAITH AND DEVOTION	Depeche Mode (Mute)
11	16	SO CLOSE	Dina Carroll (A&M PM)
7	17	THEIR GREATEST HITS	Hot Chocolate (EMI)
28	18	TAKE THAT AND PARTY	Take That (RCA)
17	19	INGENUE	k.d. lang (Sire)
13	20	LIPSTICK ON YOUR COLLAR	Various (PolyGram TV)
15	21	THE VERY BEST OF...	Randy Crawford (Dino)
19	22	THE GREATEST HITS	Boney M (Telstar)
39	23	WALTHAMSTOW	East 17 (London)
32	24	DURAN DURAN	Duran Duran (Parlophone)
21	25	THE AIR THAT I BREATHE - GREATEST HITS	Hollies (EMI)
46	26	GORECKI: SYMPHONY NO. 3	Dawn Upshaw/London Sinfonietta/David Zinman (Elektra Nonesuch)
22	27	DANGEROUS	Michael Jackson (Epic)
45	28	GREATEST HITS	Gloria Estefan (Epic)
16	29	TAXI	Bryan Ferry (Virgin)
31	30	THE SINGLES COLLECTION	Bluebells (London)
29	31	WRESTLEMANIA	WWF Superstars (Arista)
23	32	COVERDALE/PAGE	Coverdale/Page (EMI)
48	33	WHATEVER YOU SAY, SAY NOTHING	Deacon Blue (Columbia)
26	34	THE DARK SIDE OF THE MOON - 20TH ANNIVERSARY	Pink Floyd (EMI)
27	35	GLAD ALL OVER AGAIN	Dave Clark Five (EMI)
35	36	STARS	Simply Red (East West)
33	37	GREAT EXPECTATIONS	Tasmin Archer (EMI)
34	38	RAGE AGAINST THE MACHINE	Rage Against The Machine (Epic)
-	39	XTRA NAKED	Shabba Ranks (Epic)
-	40	DIANA ROSS LIVE...	Diana Ross (EMI)
24	41	A REAL LIVE ONE	Iron Maiden (EMI)
-	42	THE SINGLES COLLECTION	Connie Francis (PolyGram TV)
43	43	AMERICA'S LEAST WANTED	Ugly Kid Joe (Vertigo)
36	44	LEONARD BERNSTEIN'S WEST SIDE STORY	Various Artists (IMG)
25	45	THE BLISS ALBUM...? (VIBRATIONS AND LOVE AND ANGER AND THE PONDERANCE OF LIFE AND EXISTENCE)	PM Dawn (Gee Street)
30	46	HOME INVASION	Ice-T (Rhyme Syndicate)
41	47	FUNKY DIVAS	En Vogue (East West)
38	48	LABOURS OF LOVE	Hue & Cry (Circa)
-	49	CONSCIENCE	Beloved (East West)
49	50	CONNECTED	Stereo MCs (Fourth & Broadway)

1 May 1993

-	1	GET A GRIP	Aerosmith (Geffen)
-	2	CLIFF RICHARD - THE ALBUM	Cliff Richard (EMI)
4	3	AUTOMATIC FOR THE PEOPLE	R.E.M. (Warner Bros.)
1	4	BLACK TIE WHITE NOISE	David Bowie (Savage)
5	5	COVER SHOT	David Essex (PolyGram TV)
2	6	IN CONCERT - MTV UNPLUGGED	Bruce Springsteen (Columbia)
6	7	THE BODYGUARD - SOUNDTRACK	Various (Arista)
3	8	SUEDE	Suede (Nude)
7	9	3 YEARS, 5 MONTHS AND 2 DAYS IN THE LIFE	Arrested Development (Cooltempo)
8	10	DIVA	Annie Lennox (RCA)
16	11	SO CLOSE	Dina Carroll (A&M PM)
23	12	WALTHAMSTOW	East 17 (London)
24	13	DURAN DURAN	Duran Duran (Parlophone)
13	14	TEN SUMMONER'S TALES	Sting (A&M)
11	15	UNPLUGGED	Eric Clapton (Duck)
18	16	TAKE THAT AND PARTY	Take That (RCA)
12	17	SAN FRANCISCO DAYS	Chris Isaak (Reprise)
14	18	ARE YOU GONNA GO MY WAY	Lenny Kravitz (Virgin America)
42	19	THE SINGLES COLLECTION	Connie Francis (PolyGram TV)
28	20	GREATEST HITS	Gloria Estefan (Epic)
31	21	WRESTLEMANIA	WWF Superstars (Arista)
19	22	INGENUE	k.d. lang (Sire)
27	23	DANGEROUS	Michael Jackson (Epic)
17	24	THEIR GREATEST HITS	Hot Chocolate (EMI)
-	25	EARTH AND SUN AND MOON	Midnight Oil (Columbia)
22	26	THE GREATEST HITS	Boney M (Telstar)
-	27	JURASSIC SHIFT	Ozric Tentacles (Dovetail)
15	28	SONGS OF FAITH AND DEVOTION	Depeche Mode (Mute)
21	29	THE VERY BEST OF...	Randy Crawford (Dino)
20	30	LIPSTICK ON YOUR COLLAR	Various Artists (PolyGram TV)
25	31	THE AIR THAT I BREATHE - GREATEST HITS	Hollies (EMI)
30	32	THE SINGLES COLLECTION	Bluebells (London)
9	33	POWERTRIPPIN'	Almighty (Powertrippin')
10	34	BEASTER	Sugar (Creation)
35	35	GLAD ALL OVER AGAIN	Dave Clark Five (EMI)
36	36	STARS	Simply Red (East West)
32	37	COVERDALE/PAGE	Coverdale/Page (EMI)
38	38	RAGE AGAINST THE MACHINE	Rage Against The Machine (Epic)
39	39	XTRA NAKED	Shabba Ranks (Epic)
43	40	AMERICA'S LEAST WANTED	Ugly Kid Joe (Vertigo)
-	41	MASTERPIECES - THE ESSENTIAL FLUTE OF JAMES GALWAY	James Galway (RCA Red Seal)
29	42	TAXI	Bryan Ferry (Virgin)
26	43	GORECKI: SYMPHONY NO. 3	Dawn Upshaw/London Sinfonietta/David Zinman (Elektra Nonesuch)
47	44	FUNKY DIVAS	En Vogue (East West)
50	45	CONNECTED	Stereo MCs (Fourth & Broadway)
40	46	DIANA ROSS LIVE...	Diana Ross (EMI)
33	47	WHATEVER YOU SAY, SAY NOTHING	Deacon Blue (Columbia)
37	48	GREAT EXPECTATIONS	Tasmin Archer (EMI)
34	49	THE DARK SIDE OF THE MOON - 20TH ANNIVERSARY	Pink Floyd (EMI)
-	50	OUT OF TIME	R.E.M. (Warner Bros.)

8 May 1993

-	1	BANG!	World Party (Ensign)
-	2	RID OF ME	PJ Harvey (Island)
2	3	CLIFF RICHARD - THE ALBUM	Cliff Richard (EMI)
1	4	GET A GRIP	Aerosmith (Geffen)
3	5	AUTOMATIC FOR THE PEOPLE	R.E.M. (Warner Bros.)
7	6	THE BODYGUARD - SOUNDTRACK	Various (Arista)
14	7	TEN SUMMONER'S TALES	Sting (A&M)
13	8	DURAN DURAN	Duran Duran (Parlophone)
11	9	SO CLOSE	Dina Carroll (A&M PM)
-	10	THE INFOTAINMENT SCAN	Fall (Cog Sinister)
5	11	COVER SHOT	David Essex (PolyGram TV)
15	12	UNPLUGGED	Eric Clapton (Duck)
4	13	BLACK TIE WHITE NOISE	David Bowie (Savage)
6	14	IN CONCERT - MTV UNPLUGGED	Bruce Springsteen (Columbia)
9	15	3 YEARS, 5 MONTHS AND 2 DAYS IN THE LIFE	Arrested Development (Cooltempo)
-	16	PORNO FOR PYROS	Porno For Pyros (Warner Bros.)
10	17	DIVA	Annie Lennox (RCA)
8	18	SUEDE	Suede (Nude)
19	19	THE SINGLES COLLECTION	Connie Francis (PolyGram TV)
18	20	ARE YOU GONNA GO MY WAY	Lenny Kravitz (Virgin America)
28	21	SONGS OF FAITH AND DEVOTION	Depeche Mode (Mute)
12	22	WALTHAMSTOW	East 17 (London)
20	23	GREATEST HITS	Gloria Estefan (Epic)
-	24	TEN SHORT SONGS ABOUT LOVE	Gary Clark (Circa)
22	25	INGENUE	k.d. lang (Sire)
16	26	TAKE THAT AND PARTY	Take That (RCA)
17	27	SAN FRANCISCO DAYS	Chris Isaak (Reprise)
21	28	WRESTLEMANIA	WWF Superstars (Arista)
29	29	THE VERY BEST OF ...	Randy Crawford (Dino)
35	30	GLAD ALL OVER AGAIN	Dave Clark Five (EMI)
-	31	METAL WORKS 73-93	Judas Priest (Columbia)
47	32	WHATEVER YOU SAY, SAY NOTHING	Deacon Blue (Columbia)
26	33	THE GREATEST HITS	Boney M (Telstar)
-	34	FOREVER	Cranes (Dedicated)
27	35	JURASSIC SHIFT	Ozric Tentacles (Dovetail)
-	36	HARBOR LIGHTS	Bruce Hornsby (RCA)
38	37	RAGE AGAINST THE MACHINE	Rage Against The Machine (Epic)
25	38	EARTH AND SUN AND MOON	Midnight Oil (Columbia)
24	39	THEIR GREATEST HITS	Hot Chocolate (EMI)
36	40	STARS	Simply Red (East West)
-	41	EXPOSED	Vince Neil (Warner Bros.)
23	42	DANGEROUS	Michael Jackson (Epic)
41	43	MASTERPIECES - THE ESSENTIAL FLUTE OF JAMES GALWAY	James Galway (RCA Red Seal)
30	44	LIPSTICK ON YOUR COLLAR	Various Artists (PolyGram TV)
32	45	THE SINGLES COLLECTION	Bluebells (London)
39	46	XTRA NAKED	Shabba Ranks (Epic)
31	47	THE AIR THAT I BREATHE - GREATEST HITS	Hollies (EMI)
40	48	AMERICA'S LEAST WANTED	Ugly Kid Joe (Vertigo)
37	49	COVERDALE/PAGE	Coverdale/Page (EMI)
34	50	BEASTER	Sugar (Creation)

After some years hiding away in the band format of Tin Machine (to most people's continued bemusement), David Bowie emerged once again as a soloist with a new recording deal - although after the release and initial chart success of *Black Tie, White Noise*, this new career move would suffer a setback when the label to which he had signed (in the US), collapsed and went out of business.

408

May 1993

last week	this week	15 May 1993	
-	1	REPUBLIC	New Order (London)
5	2	AUTOMATIC FOR THE PEOPLE	R.E.M. (Warner Bros.)
-	3	SYMPHONY OR DAMN	Terence Trent D'Arby (Columbia)
1	4	BANG!	World Party (Ensign)
7	5	TEN SUMMONER'S TALES	Sting (A&M)
6	6	THE BODYGUARD - SOUNDTRACK	Various (Arista)
3	7	CLIFF RICHARD - THE ALBUM	Cliff Richard (EMI)
2	8	RID OF ME	PJ Harvey (Island)
9	9	SO CLOSE	Dina Carroll (A&M PM)
8	10	DURAN DURAN	Duran Duran (Parlophone)
4	11	GET A GRIP	Aerosmith (Geffen)
12	12	UNPLUGGED	Eric Clapton (Duck)
-	13	BANBA	Clannad (RCA)
21	14	SONGS OF FAITH AND DEVOTION	Depeche Mode (Mute)
15	15	3 YEARS, 5 MONTHS AND 2 DAYS IN THE LIFE	Arrested Development (Cooltempo)
17	16	DIVA	Annie Lennox (RCA)
20	17	ARE YOU GONNA GO MY WAY	Lenny Kravitz (Virgin America)
14	18	IN CONCERT - MTV UNPLUGGED	Bruce Springsteen (Columbia)
26	19	TAKE THAT AND PARTY	Take That (RCA)
25	20	INGENUE	k.d. lang (Sire)
11	21	COVER SHOT	David Essex (PolyGram TV)
37	22	RAGE AGAINST THE MACHINE	Rage Against The Machine (Epic)
18	23	SUEDE	Suede (Nude)
-	24	BREATHLESS	Kenny G (Arista)
13	25	BLACK TIE WHITE NOISE	David Bowie (Savage)
10	26	THE INFOTAINMENT SCAN	Fall (Cog Sinister)
22	27	WALTHAMSTOW	East 17 (London)
23	28	GREATEST HITS	Gloria Estefan (Epic)
16	29	PORNO FOR PYROS	Porno For Pyros (Warner Bros.)
19	30	THE SINGLES COLLECTION	Connie Francis (PolyGram TV)
40	31	STARS	Simply Red (East West)
-	32	TESTAMENT '93	Inner City (Virgin)
30	33	GLAD ALL OVER AGAIN	Dave Clark Five (EMI)
48	34	AMERICA'S LEAST WANTED	Ugly Kid Joe (Vertigo)
24	35	TEN SHORT SONGS ABOUT LOVE	Gary Clark (Circa)
-	36	SHADOWS IN THE NIGHT	Shadows (PolyGram TV)
36	37	HARBOR LIGHTS	Bruce Hornsby (RCA)
29	38	THE VERY BEST OF...	Randy Crawford (Dino)
27	39	SAN FRANCISCO DAYS	Chris Isaak (Reprise)
-	40	I'VE SEEN EVERYTHING	Trash Can Sinatras (Go! Discs)
28	41	WRESTLEMANIA	WWF Superstars (Arista)
33	42	THE GREATEST HITS	Boney M (Telstar)
42	43	DANGEROUS	Michael Jackson (Epic)
46	44	XTRA NAKED	Shabba Ranks (Epic)
-	45	MORE UNCHARTERED HEIGHTS OF DISGRACE	Dogs D'Amour (China)
32	46	WHATEVER YOU SAY, SAY NOTHING	Deacon Blue (Columbia)
31	47	METAL WORKS 73-93	Judas Priest (Columbia)
35	48	JURASSIC SHIFT	Ozric Tentacles (Dovetail)
47	49	THE AIR THAT I BREATHE - GREATEST HITS	Hollies (EMI)
39	50	THEIR GREATEST HITS	Hot Chocolate (EMI)

last week	this week	22 May 1993	
-	1	ON THE NIGHT	Dire Straits (Vertigo)
2	2	AUTOMATIC FOR THE PEOPLE	R.E.M. (Warner Bros.)
1	3	REPUBLIC	New Order (London)
-	4	NO LIMITS	2 Unlimited (PWL Continental)
-	5	BEETHOVEN WAS DEAF	Morrissey (HMV)
13	6	BANBA	Clannad (RCA)
3	7	SYMPHONY OR DAMN	Terence Trent D'Arby (Columbia)
5	8	TEN SUMMONER'S TALES	Sting (A&M)
-	9	BLUES ALIVE	Gary Moore (Virgin)
6	10	THE BODYGUARD - SOUNDTRACK	Various Artists (Arista)
9	11	SO CLOSE	Dina Carroll (A&M PM)
4	12	BANG!	World Party (Ensign)
10	13	DURAN DURAN	Duran Duran (Parlophone)
-	14	HOME MOVIES - THE BEST OF...	Everything But The Girl (blanco y negro)
-	15	MODERN LIFE IS RUBBISH	Blur (Food)
17	16	ARE YOU GONNA GO MY WAY	Lenny Kravitz (Virgin America)
7	18	CLIFF RICHARD - THE ALBUM	Cliff Richard (EMI)
12	19	UNPLUGGED	Eric Clapton (Duck)
22	21	RAGE AGAINST THE MACHINE	Rage Against The Machine (Epic)
11	22	GET A GRIP	Aerosmith (Geffen)
14	23	SONGS OF FAITH AND DEVOTION	Depeche Mode (Mute)
16	24	DIVA	Annie Lennox (RCA)
36	25	SHADOWS IN THE NIGHT	Shadows (PolyGram TV)
8	26	RID OF ME	PJ Harvey (Island)
19	27	TAKE THAT AND PARTY	Take That (RCA)
-	28	KEEP THE FAITH	Bon Jovi (Jambco)
15	29	3 YEARS, 5 MONTHS AND 2 DAYS IN THE LIFE	Arrested Development (Cooltempo)
23	30	SUEDE	Suede (Nude)
18	31	IN CONCERT - MTV UNPLUGGED	Bruce Springsteen (Columbia)
20	32	INGENUE	k.d. lang (Sire)
31	33	STARS	Simply Red (East West)
21	34	COVER SHOT	David Essex (PolyGram TV)
27	36	WALTHAMSTOW	East 17 (London)
42	38	THE GREATEST HITS	Boney M (Telstar)
34	39	AMERICA'S LEAST WANTED	Ugly Kid Joe (Vertigo)
37	40	HARBOR LIGHTS	Bruce Hornsby (RCA)
32	41	TESTAMENT '93	Inner City (Virgin)
45	42	MORE UNCHARTERED HEIGHTS OF DISGRACE	Dogs D'Amour (China)
44	43	XTRA NAKED	Shabba Ranks (Epic)
-	44	CONNECTED	Stereo MCs (Fourth & Broadway)
-	45	SONGS FROM THE RAIN	Hothouse Flowers (London)
38	46	THE VERY BEST OF...	Randy Crawford (Dino)
-	47	OUT OF TIME	R.E.M. (Warner Bros.)
29	48	PORNO FOR PYROS	Porno For Pyros (Warner Bros.)
30	49	THE SINGLES COLLECTION	Connie Francis (PolyGram TV)
43	50	DANGEROUS	Michael Jackson (Epic)

last week	this week	29 May 1993	
-	1	JANET	Janet Jackson (Virgin)
2	2	AUTOMATIC FOR THE PEOPLE	R.E.M. (Warner Bros.)
4	3	NO LIMITS	2 Unlimited (PWL Continental)
3	4	REPUBLIC	New Order (London)
1	5	ON THE NIGHT	Dire Straits (Vertigo)
14	6	HOME MOVIES - THE BEST OF EVERYTHING BUT THE GIRL	Everything But The Girl (blanco y negro)
11	7	SO CLOSE	Dina Carroll (A&M PM)
-	8	LIVE AT THE ROYAL ALBERT HALL	Wet Wet Wet with the Wren Orchestra (Precious Organisation)
16	9	BREATHLESS	Kenny G (Arista)
10	10	THE BODYGUARD - SOUNDTRACK	Various Artists (Arista)
6	11	BANBA	Clannad (RCA)
9	12	BLUES ALIVE	Gary Moore (Virgin)
28	13	KEEP THE FAITH	Bon Jovi (Jambco)
8	14	TEN SUMMONER'S TALES	Sting (A&M)
-	15	SLEEPWALKING	Kingmaker (Scorch)
-	16	SOUND OF WHITE NOISE	Anthrax (Elektra)
5	17	BEETHOVEN WAS DEAF	Morrissey (HMV)
13	18	DURAN DURAN	Duran Duran (Parlophone)
17	19	ARE YOU GONNA GO MY WAY	Lenny Kravitz (Virgin America)
12	20	BANG!	World Party (Ensign)
-	21	DREAMLAND	Aztec Camera (WEA)
-	22	ALIVE III	Kiss (Mercury)
7	23	SYMPHONY OR DAMN	Terence Trent D'Arby (Columbia)
21	24	RAGE AGAINST THE MACHINE	Rage Against The Machine (Epic)
20	25	UNPLUGGED	Eric Clapton (Duck)
-	26	POCKET FULL OF KRYPTONITE	Spin Doctors (Epic)
-	27	JIM DIAMOND	Jim Diamond (PolyGram TV)
30	28	SUEDE	Suede (Nude)
15	29	MODERN LIFE IS RUBBISH	Blur (Food)
18	30	CLIFF RICHARD - THE ALBUM	Cliff Richard (EMI)
19	31	SPILT MILK	Jellyfish (Charisma)
24	32	DIVA	Annie Lennox (RCA)
23	33	SONGS OF FAITH AND DEVOTION	Depeche Mode (Mute)
25	34	SHADOWS IN THE NIGHT	Shadows (PolyGram TV)
-	35	BETTER THE DEVIL YOU KNOW	Sonia (Arista)
27	36	TAKE THAT AND PARTY	Take That (RCA)
33	37	STARS	Simply Red (East West)
-	38	THE GOLDEN YEARS OF THE EVERLY BROTHERS	Everly Brothers (Warner Bros.)
44	39	CONNECTED	Stereo MCs (Fourth & Broadway)
31	40	IN CONCERT - MTV UNPLUGGED	Bruce Springsteen (Columbia)
22	41	GET A GRIP	Aerosmith (Geffen)
26	42	RID OF ME	PJ Harvey (Island)
32	43	INGENUE	k.d. lang (Sire)
29	44	3 YEARS, 5 MONTHS AND 2 DAYS IN THE LIFE	Arrested Development (Cooltempo)
34	45	COVER SHOT	David Essex (PolyGram TV)
47	46	OUT OF TIME	R.E.M. (Warner Bros.)
35	47	BLACK TIE WHITE NOISE	David Bowie (Savage)
36	48	WALTHAMSTOW	East 17 (London)
50	49	DANGEROUS	Michael Jackson (Epic)
-	50	JADE TO THE MAX	Jade (Giant)

Label-less for some time since the demise of Factory Records, their home since their days as Joy Division, New Order were signed by London and immediately showed their old commercial muscle (if not universal ability to please the critics) with a convincing Number 1 entry for *Republic*. This was the second of four albums in consecutive weeks which debuted at the top and were then immediately shunted aside!

June 1993

5 June 1993

last	this		
1	1	JANET	Janet Jackson (Virgin)
-	2	KAMAKIRIAD	Donald Fagen (Reprise)
2	3	AUTOMATIC FOR THE PEOPLE	R.E.M. (Warner Bros.)
-	4	DREAM HARDER	Waterboys (Geffen)
-	5	FATE OF NATIONS	Robert Plant (Es Paranza)
3	6	NO LIMITS	2 Unlimited (PWL Continental)
9	7	BREATHLESS	Kenny G (Arista)
7	8	SO CLOSE	Dina Carroll (A&M PM)
-	9	UNPLUGGED ... AND SEATED	Rod Stewart (Warner Bros.)
4	10	REPUBLIC	New Order (London)
13	11	KEEP THE FAITH	Bon Jovi (Jambco)
26	12	POCKET FULL OF KRYPTONITE	Spin Doctors (Epic)
6	13	HOME MOVIES - THE BEST OF EVERYTHING BUT THE GIRL	Everything But The Girl (blanco y negro)
-	14	MORE ABBA GOLD - MORE ABBA HITS	Abba (Polydor)
-	15	CHRONOLOGIE	Jean-Michel Jarre (Dreyfus)
5	16	ON THE NIGHT	Dire Straits (Vertigo)
10	17	THE BODYGUARD - SOUNDTRACK	Various Artists (Arista)
12	18	BLUES ALIVE	Gary Moore (Virgin)
14	19	TEN SUMMONER'S TALES	Sting (A&M)
8	20	LIVE AT THE ROYAL ALBERT HALL	Wet Wet Wet with the Wren Orchestra (Precious Organisation)
-	21	UTAH SAINTS	Utah Saints (ffrr)
11	22	BANBA	Clannad (RCA)
19	23	ARE YOU GONNA GO MY WAY	Lenny Kravitz (Virgin America)
18	24	DURAN DURAN	Duran Duran (Parlophone)
25	25	UNPLUGGED	Eric Clapton (Duck)
38	26	THE GOLDEN YEARS OF THE EVERLY BROTHERS	Everly Brothers (Warner Bros.)
23	27	SYMPHONY OR DAMN	Terence Trent D'Arby (Columbia)
28	28	SUEDE	Suede (Nude)
24	29	RAGE AGAINST THE MACHINE	Rage Against The Machine (Epic)
20	30	BANG!	World Party (Ensign)
39	31	CONNECTED	Stereo MCs (Fourth & Broadway)
27	32	JIM DIAMOND	Jim Diamond (PolyGram TV)
32	33	DIVA	Annie Lennox (RCA)
16	34	SOUND OF WHITE NOISE	Anthrax (Elektra)
21	35	DREAMLAND	Aztec Camera (WEA)
-	36	TAXI	Bryan Ferry (Virgin)
30	37	CLIFF RICHARD - THE ALBUM	Cliff Richard (EMI)
37	38	STARS	Simply Red (East West)
15	39	SLEEPWALKING	Kingmaker (Scorch)
34	40	SHADOWS IN THE NIGHT	Shadows (PolyGram TV)
33	41	SONGS OF FAITH AND DEVOTION	Depeche Mode (Mute)
35	42	BETTER THE DEVIL YOU KNOW	Sonia (Arista)
36	43	TAKE THAT AND PARTY	Take That (RCA)
-	44	GREAT EXPECTATIONS	Tasmin Archer (EMI)
50	45	JADE TO THE MAX	Jade (Giant)
-	46	BAD TO THE BONE	Inner Circle (Magnet)
-	47	LOVE DELUXE	Sade (Epic)
29	48	MODERN LIFE IS RUBBISH	Blur (Food)
31	49	SPILT MILK	Jellyfish (Charisma)
46	50	OUT OF TIME	R.E.M. (Warner Bros.)

12 June 1993

last	this		
1	1	JANET	Janet Jackson (Virgin)
3	2	AUTOMATIC FOR THE PEOPLE	R.E.M. (Warner Bros.)
6	3	NO LIMITS	2 Unlimited (PWL Continental)
2	4	KAMAKIRIAD	Donald Fagen (Reprise)
-	5	TOO LONG IN EXILE	Van Morrison (Polydor)
9	6	UNPLUGGED ... AND SEATED	Rod Stewart (Warner Bros.)
12	7	POCKET FULL OF KRYPTONITE	Spin Doctors (Epic)
4	8	DREAM HARDER	Waterboys (Geffen)
5	9	FATE OF NATIONS	Robert Plant (Es Paranza)
8	10	SO CLOSE	Dina Carroll (A&M PM)
7	11	BREATHLESS	Kenny G (Arista)
21	12	UTAH SAINTS	Utah Saints (ffrr)
-	13	NEVER LET ME GO	Luther Vandross (Epic)
11	14	KEEP THE FAITH	Bon Jovi (Jambco)
14	15	MORE ABBA GOLD - MORE ABBA HITS	Abba (Polydor)
-	16	GOOD AND READY	Sybil (PWL International)
15	17	CHRONOLOGIE	Jean-Michel Jarre (Dreyfus)
23	18	ARE YOU GONNA GO MY WAY	Lenny Kravitz (Virgin America)
10	19	REPUBLIC	New Order (London)
31	20	CONNECTED	Stereo MCs (Fourth & Broadway)
17	21	THE BODYGUARD - SOUNDTRACK	Various Artists (Arista)
13	22	HOME MOVIES	Everything But The Girl (blanco y negro)
19	23	TEN SUMMONER'S TALES	Sting (A&M)
43	24	TAKE THAT AND PARTY	Take That (RCA)
25	25	UNPLUGGED	Eric Clapton (Duck)
-	26	THE RAINY SEASON	Marc Cohn (Atlantic)
16	27	ON THE NIGHT	Dire Straits (Vertigo)
37	28	CLIFF RICHARD - THE ALBUM	Cliff Richard (EMI)
18	29	BLUES ALIVE	Gary Moore (Virgin)
28	30	SUEDE	Suede (Nude)
29	31	RAGE AGAINST THE MACHINE	Rage Against The Machine (Epic)
-	32	YOU GOTTA SIN TO BE SAVED	Maria McKee (Geffen)
22	33	BANBA	Clannad (RCA)
36	34	TAXI	Bryan Ferry (Virgin)
33	35	DIVA	Annie Lennox (RCA)
-	36	ORBITAL	Orbital (Internal)
24	37	DURAN DURAN	Duran Duran (Parlophone)
30	38	BANG!	World Party (Ensign)
20	39	LIVE AT THE ROYAL ALBERT HALL	Wet Wet Wet with the Wren Orchestra (Precious Organisation)
26	40	THE GOLDEN YEARS OF THE EVERLY BROTHERS	Everly Brothers (Warner Bros.)
46	41	BAD TO THE BONE	Inner Circle (Magnet)
32	42	JIM DIAMOND	Jim Diamond (PolyGram TV)
44	43	GREAT EXPECTATIONS	Tasmin Archer (EMI)
-	44	THE BEST OF...	Howard Jones (East West)
47	45	LOVE DELUXE	Sade (Epic)
38	46	STARS	Simply Red (East West)
27	47	SYMPHONY OR DAMN	Terence Trent D'Arby (Columbia)
-	48	FOREVER FOR NOW - THE VERY BEST OF ...	Harry Connick Jr. (Columbia)
45	49	JADE TO THE MAX	Jade (Giant)
-	50	SOUVLAKI	Slowdive (Creation)

19 June 1993

last	this		
-	1	WHAT'S LOVE GOT TO DO WITH IT	Tina Turner (Parlophone)
-	2	ELEMENTAL	Tears For Fears (Mercury)
3	3	NO LIMITS	2 Unlimited (PWL Continental)
1	4	JANET	Janet Jackson (Virgin)
2	5	AUTOMATIC FOR THE PEOPLE	R.E.M. (Warner Bros.)
7	6	POCKET FULL OF KRYPTONITE	Spin Doctors (Epic)
5	7	TOO LONG IN EXILE	Van Morrison (Polydor)
6	8	UNPLUGGED ... AND SEATED	Rod Stewart (Warner Bros.)
10	9	SO CLOSE	Dina Carroll (A&M PM)
20	10	CONNECTED	Stereo MCs (Fourth & Broadway)
4	11	KAMAKIRIAD	Donald Fagen (Reprise)
13	12	NEVER LET ME GO	Luther Vandross (Epic)
8	13	DREAM HARDER	Waterboys (Geffen)
15	14	MORE ABBA GOLD - MORE ABBA HITS	Abba (Polydor)
11	15	BREATHLESS	Kenny G (Arista)
-	16	HAPPY NATION	Ace Of Base (Mega)
16	17	GOOD AND READY	Sybil (PWL International)
14	18	KEEP THE FAITH	Bon Jovi (Jambco)
9	19	FATE OF NATIONS	Robert Plant (Es Paranza)
23	20	TEN SUMMONER'S TALES	Sting (A&M)
18	21	ARE YOU GONNA GO MY WAY	Lenny Kravitz (Virgin America)
12	22	UTAH SAINTS	Utah Saints (ffrr)
25	23	UNPLUGGED	Eric Clapton (Duck)
21	24	THE BODYGUARD - SOUNDTRACK	Various Artists (Arista)
17	25	CHRONOLOGIE	Jean-Michel Jarre (Dreyfus)
28	26	CLIFF RICHARD - THE ALBUM	Cliff Richard (EMI)
26	27	THE RAINY SEASON	Marc Cohn (Atlantic)
-	28	USE YOUR ILLUSION II	Guns N' Roses (Geffen)
24	29	TAKE THAT AND PARTY	Take That (RCA)
19	30	REPUBLIC	New Order (London)
30	31	SUEDE	Suede (Nude)
33	32	BANBA	Clannad (RCA)
43	33	GREAT EXPECTATIONS	Tasmin Archer (EMI)
22	34	HOME MOVIES - THE BEST OF EVERYTHING BUT THE GIRL	Everything But The Girl (blanco y negro)
34	35	TAXI	Bryan Ferry (Virgin)
35	36	DIVA	Annie Lennox (RCA)
32	37	YOU GOTTA SIN TO BE SAVED	Maria McKee (Geffen)
48	38	FOREVER FOR NOW - THE VERY BEST OF HARRY CONNICK JR.	Harry Connick Jr. (Columbia)
-	39	THOUSAND ROADS	David Crosby (Atlantic)
-	40	USE YOUR ILLUSION I	Guns N' Roses (Geffen)
-	41	IN ON THE KILL TAKER	Fugazi (Dischord)
31	42	RAGE AGAINST THE MACHINE	Rage Against The Machine (Epic)
27	43	ON THE NIGHT	Dire Straits (Vertigo)
1	44	GOLD - GREATEST HITS	Abba (Polydor)
37	45	DURAN DURAN	Duran Duran (Parlophone)
46	46	STARS	Simply Red (East West)
-	47	PROVOCATIVE	Johnny Gill (Motown)
29	48	BLUES ALIVE	Gary Moore (Virgin)
45	49	LOVE DELUXE	Sade (Epic)
-	50	AMERICA'S LEAST WANTED	Ugly Kid Joe (Vertigo)

Janet Jackson had failed to make the chart-top in the UK with either of her US mega-selling albums of the 80s, *Control* and *Rhythm Nation 1814*, but it was *Janet*, the first product of her new deal with Virgin, that did the required trick. It was replaced at the top by the doyenne of hard-working female performers, Tina Turner, whose *What's Love Got To Do With It* was the soundtrack to the movie of her life and career.

26 June 1993

last week	this week	Title / Artist (Label)
-	1	EMERGENCY ON PLANET EARTH — Jamiroquai (Orenda)
-	2	UNPLUGGED — Neil Young (Reprise)
1	3	WHAT'S LOVE GOT TO DO WITH IT — Tina Turner (Parlophone)
8	4	UNPLUGGED ... AND SEATED — Rod Stewart (Warner Bros.)
6	5	POCKET FULL OF KRYPTONITE — Spin Doctors (Epic)
5	6	AUTOMATIC FOR THE PEOPLE — R.E.M. (Warner Bros.)
3	7	NO LIMITS — 2 Unlimited (PWL Continental)
2	8	ELEMENTAL — Tears For Fears (Mercury)
4	9	JANET — Janet Jackson (Virgin)
-	10	LIBERATOR — Orchestral Manoeuvres In The Dark (Virgin)
10	11	CONNECTED — Stereo MCs (Fourth & Broadway)
9	12	SO CLOSE — Dina Carroll (A&M PM)
20	13	TEN SUMMONER'S TALES — Sting (A&M)
7	14	TOO LONG IN EXILE — Van Morrison (Polydor)
-	15	MEMORIAL BEACH — A-ha (Warner Bros.)
15	16	BREATHLESS — Kenny G (Arista)
-	17	WHISPER A PRAYER — Mica Paris (4th & Broadway)
17	18	GOOD AND READY — Sybil (PWL International)
11	19	KAMAKIRIAD — Donald Fagen (Reprise)
14	20	MORE ABBA GOLD - MORE ABBA HITS — Abba (Polydor)
16	21	HAPPY NATION — Ace Of Base (Mega)
18	22	KEEP THE FAITH — Bon Jovi (Jambco)
23	23	UNPLUGGED — Eric Clapton (Duck)
12	24	NEVER LET ME GO — Luther Vandross (Epic)
13	25	DREAM HARDER — Waterboys (Geffen)
21	26	ARE YOU GONNA GO MY WAY — Lenny Kravitz (Virgin America)
24	27	THE BODYGUARD - SOUNDTRACK — Various Artists (Arista)
19	28	FATE OF NATIONS — Robert Plant (Es Paranza)
22	29	UTAH SAINTS — Utah Saints (ffrr)
26	30	CLIFF RICHARD - THE ALBUM — Cliff Richard (EMI)
25	31	CHRONOLOGIE — Jean-Michel Jarre (Dreyfus)
-	32	TAKE A LOOK — Natalie Cole (Elektra)
38	33	FOREVER FOR NOW - THE VERY BEST OF ... — Harry Connick Jr. (Columbia)
49	34	LOVE DELUXE — Sade (Epic)
32	35	BANBA — Clannad (RCA)
35	36	TAXI — Bryan Ferry (Virgin)
-	37	SYMPHONY OR DAMN — Terence Trent D'Arby (Columbia)
27	38	THE RAINY SEASON — Marc Cohn (Atlantic)
36	39	DIVA — Annie Lennox (RCA)
29	40	TAKE THAT AND PARTY — Take That (RCA)
28	41	USE YOUR ILLUSION II — Guns N' Roses (Geffen)
44	42	GOLD - GREATEST HITS — Abba (Polydor)
30	43	REPUBLIC — New Order (London)
33	44	GREAT EXPECTATIONS — Tasmin Archer (EMI)
34	45	HOME MOVIES — Everything But The Girl (blanco y negro)
31	46	SUEDE — Suede (Nude)
-	47	SIMPLY THE BEST — Tina Turner (Capitol)
-	48	METALLICA — Metallica (Vertigo)
37	49	YOU GOTTA SIN TO BE SAVED — Maria McKee (Geffen)
41	50	IN ON THE KILL TAKER — Fugazi (Dischord)

3 July 1993

last week	this week	Title / Artist (Label)
1	1	EMERGENCY ON PLANET EARTH — Jamiroquai (Orenda)
4	2	UNPLUGGED ... AND SEATED — Rod Stewart (Warner Bros.)
3	3	WHAT'S LOVE GOT TO DO WITH IT — Tina Turner (Parlophone)
2	4	UNPLUGGED — Neil Young (Reprise)
-	5	GOLD AGAINST THE SOUL — Manic Street Preachers (Columbia)
6	6	POCKET FULL OF KRYPTONITE — Spin Doctors (Epic)
7	7	AUTOMATIC FOR THE PEOPLE — R.E.M. (Warner Bros.)
13	8	TEN SUMMONER'S TALES — Sting (A&M)
7	9	NO LIMITS — 2 Unlimited (PWL Continental)
10	10	JANET — Janet Jackson (Virgin)
11	11	CONNECTED — Stereo MCs (Fourth & Broadway)
12	12	SO CLOSE — Dina Carroll (A&M PM)
19	13	KAMAKIRIAD — Donald Fagen (Reprise)
14	14	TOO LONG IN EXILE — Van Morrison (Polydor)
10	15	LIBERATOR — Orchestral Manoeuvres In The Dark (Virgin)
-	16	MUDDY WATERS BLUES - A TRIBUTE TO MUDDY WATERS — Paul Rodgers (Victory)
8	17	ELEMENTAL — Tears For Fears (Mercury)
16	18	BREATHLESS — Kenny G (Arista)
23	19	UNPLUGGED — Eric Clapton (Duck)
32	20	TAKE A LOOK — Natalie Cole (Elektra)
22	21	KEEP THE FAITH — Bon Jovi (Jambco)
27	22	THE BODYGUARD - SOUNDTRACK — Various Artists (Arista)
15	23	MEMORIAL BEACH — A-ha (Warner Bros.)
18	24	GOOD AND READY — Sybil (PWL International)
17	25	WHISPER A PRAYER — Mica Paris (4th & Broadway)
20	26	MORE ABBA GOLD - MORE ABBA HITS — Abba (Polydor)
21	27	HAPPY NATION — Ace Of Base (Mega)
28	28	LOVE DELUXE — Sade (Epic)
28	29	FATE OF NATIONS — Robert Plant (Es Paranza)
30	30	DREAM HARDER — Waterboys (Geffen)
35	31	BANBA — Clannad (RCA)
40	32	TAKE THAT AND PARTY — Take That (RCA)
37	33	SYMPHONY OR DAMN — Terence Trent D'Arby (Columbia)
26	34	ARE YOU GONNA GO MY WAY — Lenny Kravitz (Virgin America)
42	35	GOLD - GREATEST HITS — Abba (Polydor)
31	36	CHRONOLOGIE — Jean-Michel Jarre (Dreyfus)
-	37	A STORM IN HEAVEN — Verve (Hut)
-	38	AUDIENCE WITH THE MIND — House Of Love (Fontana)
29	39	UTAH SAINTS — Utah Saints (ffrr)
36	40	TAXI — Bryan Ferry (Virgin)
24	41	NEVER LET ME GO — Luther Vandross (Epic)
33	42	CLIFF RICHARD - THE ALBUM — Cliff Richard (EMI)
33	43	FOREVER FOR NOW - THE VERY BEST OF ... — Harry Connick Jr. (Columbia)
47	44	SIMPLY THE BEST — Tina Turner (Capitol)
39	45	DIVA — Annie Lennox (RCA)
43	46	REPUBLIC — New Order (London)
-	47	CEREAL KILLER — Green Jelly (Zoo)
41	48	USE YOUR ILLUSION II — Guns N' Roses (Geffen)
38	49	THE RAINY SEASON — Marc Cohn (Atlantic)
-	50	STARS — Simply Red (East West)

10 July 1993

last week	this week	Title / Artist (Label)
1	1	EMERGENCY ON PLANET EARTH — Jamiroquai (Orenda)
2	2	UNPLUGGED ... AND SEATED — Rod Stewart (Warner Bros.)
6	3	POCKET FULL OF KRYPTONITE — Spin Doctors (Epic)
7	4	AUTOMATIC FOR THE PEOPLE — R.E.M. (Warner Bros.)
3	5	WHAT'S LOVE GOT TO DO WITH IT — Tina Turner (Parlophone)
4	6	UNPLUGGED — Neil Young (Reprise)
8	7	TEN SUMMONER'S TALES — Sting (A&M)
5	8	GOLD AGAINST THE SOUL — Manic Street Preachers (Columbia)
16	9	MUDDY WATERS BLUES - A TRIBUTE TO MUDDY WATERS — Paul Rodgers (Victory)
9	10	NO LIMITS — 2 Unlimited (PWL Continental)
-	11	BACK TO BROADWAY — Barbra Streisand (Columbia)
12	12	SO CLOSE — Dina Carroll (A&M PM)
11	13	CONNECTED — Stereo MCs (Fourth & Broadway)
10	14	JANET — Janet Jackson (Virgin)
13	15	KAMAKIRIAD — Donald Fagen (Reprise)
22	16	THE BODYGUARD - SOUNDTRACK — Various Artists (Arista)
-	17	MI TIERRA — Gloria Estefan (Epic)
18	18	BREATHLESS — Kenny G (Arista)
14	19	TOO LONG IN EXILE — Van Morrison (Polydor)
21	20	KEEP THE FAITH — Bon Jovi (Jambco)
19	21	UNPLUGGED — Eric Clapton (Duck)
-	22	CYBERPUNK — Billy Idol (Chrysalis)
23	23	THE BEST OF... — Eric Clapton (Polydor)
15	24	LIBERATOR — Orchestral Manoeuvres In The Dark (Virgin)
47	25	CEREAL KILLER — Green Jelly (Zoo)
20	26	TAKE A LOOK — Natalie Cole (Elektra)
33	27	SYMPHONY OR DAMN — Terence Trent D'Arby (Columbia)
-	28	BEFORE & AFTER — Tim Finn (Capitol)
39	29	UTAH SAINTS — Utah Saints (ffrr)
17	30	ELEMENTAL — Tears For Fears (Mercury)
25	31	WHISPER A PRAYER — Mica Paris (4th & Broadway)
28	32	LOVE DELUXE — Sade (Epic)
27	33	HAPPY NATION — Ace Of Base (Mega)
-	34	LIVE & LOUD — Ozzy Osbourne (Epic)
26	35	MORE ABBA GOLD - MORE ABBA HITS — Abba (Polydor)
35	36	GOLD - GREATEST HITS — Abba (Polydor)
-	37	TEASE ME — Chaka Demus & Pliers (Mango)
30	38	DREAM HARDER — Waterboys (Geffen)
24	39	GOOD AND READY — Sybil (PWL International)
29	40	FATE OF NATIONS — Robert Plant (Es Paranza)
34	41	ARE YOU GONNA GO MY WAY — Lenny Kravitz (Virgin America)
37	42	A STORM IN HEAVEN — Verve (Hut)
-	43	DANGEROUS — Michael Jackson (Epic)
46	44	REPUBLIC — New Order (London)
32	45	TAKE THAT AND PARTY — Take That (RCA)
23	46	MEMORIAL BEACH — A-ha (Warner Bros.)
31	47	BANBA — Clannad (RCA)
-	48	THE MADMAN'S RETURN — Snap (Logic)
-	49	INGENUE — k.d. lang (Sire)
42	50	CLIFF RICHARD - THE ALBUM — Cliff Richard (EMI)

Take note of the Number 50 in the final chart - the ever youthful Cliff who was, of course, at Number 5 in the NME's very first album chart, along with the Shadows, with *The Young Ones*. Cliff has outlasted the George Mitchell Minstrels, and even Elvis and Frank Sinatra from that first chart. Thirty one years on he shows no more sign of retiring than "pop" does of being the passing fad that was so widely predicted.

411

July 1993

17 July 1993

LW	TW	Title	Artist (Label)
-	1	ZOOROPA	U2 (Island)
1	2	EMERGENCY ON PLANET EARTH	Jamiroquai (Orenda)
2	3	UNPLUGGED ... AND SEATED	Rod Stewart (Warner Bros.)
3	4	POCKET FULL OF KRYPTONITE	Spin Doctors (Epic)
4	5	AUTOMATIC FOR THE PEOPLE	R.E.M. (Warner Bros.)
11	6	BACK TO BROADWAY	Barbra Streisand (Columbia)
7	7	TEN SUMMONER'S TALES	Sting (A&M)
6	8	UNPLUGGED	Neil Young (Reprise)
5	9	WHAT'S LOVE GOT TO DO WITH IT	Tina Turner (Parlophone)
-	10	ALWAYS	Michael Ball (PolyGram TV)
17	11	MI TIERRA	Gloria Estefan (Epic)
16	12	THE BODYGUARD - SOUNDTRACK	Various Artists (Arista)
-	13	BIGGER, BETTER, FASTER, MORE!	4 Non Blondes (Interscope)
-	14	DEBUT	Bjork (One Little Indian)
10	15	NO LIMITS	2 Unlimited (PWL Continental)
9	16	MUDDY WATERS BLUES - A TRIBUTE TO MUDDY WATERS	Paul Rodgers (Victory)
14	17	JANET	Janet Jackson (Virgin)
12	18	SO CLOSE	Dina Carroll (A&M PM)
13	19	CONNECTED	Stereo MCs (Fourth & Broadway)
20	20	KEEP THE FAITH	Bon Jovi (Jambco)
8	21	GOLD AGAINST THE SOUL	Manic Street Preachers (Columbia)
-	22	THE FIRST DAY	David Sylvian & Robert Fripp (Virgin)
23	23	THE BEST OF ERIC CLAPTON	Eric Clapton (Polydor)
45	24	TAKE THAT AND PARTY	Take That (RCA)
18	25	BREATHLESS	Kenny G (Arista)
41	26	ARE YOU GONNA GO MY WAY	Lenny Kravitz (Virgin America)
21	27	UNPLUGGED	Eric Clapton (Duck)
22	28	CYBERPUNK	Billy Idol (Chrysalis)
15	29	KAMAKIRIAD	Donald Fagen (Reprise)
-	30	WALTHAMSTOW	East 17 (London)
19	31	TOO LONG IN EXILE	Van Morrison (Polydor)
37	32	TEASE ME	Chaka Demus & Pliers (Mango)
24	33	LIBERATOR	Orchestral Manoeuvres In The Dark (Virgin)
43	34	DANGEROUS	Michael Jackson (Epic)
28	35	BEFORE & AFTER	Tim Finn (Capitol)
25	36	CEREAL KILLER	Green Jelly (Zoo)
32	37	LOVE DELUXE	Sade (Epic)
27	38	SYMPHONY OR DAMN	Terence Trent D'Arby (Columbia)
29	39	UTAH SAINTS	Utah Saints (ffrr)
31	40	WHISPER A PRAYER	Mica Paris (4th & Broadway)
-	41	IT'S ABOUT TIME	SWV (RCA)
44	42	REPUBLIC	New Order (London)
26	43	TAKE A LOOK	Natalie Cole (Elektra)
33	44	HAPPY NATION	Ace Of Base (Mega)
-	45	RAGE AGAINST THE MACHINE	Rage Against The Machine (Epic)
47	46	BANBA	Clannad (RCA)
30	47	ELEMENTAL	Tears For Fears (Mercury)
38	48	DREAM HARDER	Waterboys (Geffen)
40	49	FATE OF NATIONS	Robert Plant (Es Paranza)
48	50	THE MADMAN'S RETURN	Snap (Logic)

24 July 1993

LW	TW	Title	Artist (Label)
1	1	ZOOROPA	U2 (Island)
-	2	PROMISES AND LIES	UB40 (DEP International)
2	3	EMERGENCY ON PLANET EARTH	Jamiroquai (Orenda)
4	4	POCKET FULL OF KRYPTONITE	Spin Doctors (Epic)
3	5	UNPLUGGED ... AND SEATED	Rod Stewart (Warner Bros.)
14	6	DEBUT	Bjork (One Little Indian)
5	7	AUTOMATIC FOR THE PEOPLE	R.E.M. (Warner Bros.)
10	8	ALWAYS	Michael Ball (PolyGram TV)
6	9	BACK TO BROADWAY	Barbra Streisand (Columbia)
7	10	TEN SUMMONER'S TALES	Sting (A&M)
13	11	BIGGER, BETTER, FASTER, MORE!	4 Non Blondes (Interscope)
12	12	THE BODYGUARD - SOUNDTRACK	Various Artists (Arista)
-	13	LAST ACTION HERO - SOUNDTRACK	Various Artists (Arista)
-	14	THE SOUND OF SPEED	Jesus & Mary Chain (blanco y negro)
8	15	UNPLUGGED	Neil Young (Reprise)
9	16	WHAT'S LOVE GOT TO DO WITH IT	Tina Turner (Parlophone)
11	17	MI TIERRA	Gloria Estefan (Epic)
16	18	MUDDY WATERS BLUES - A TRIBUTE TO MUDDY WATERS	Paul Rodgers (Victory)
20	19	KEEP THE FAITH	Bon Jovi (Jambco)
19	20	CONNECTED	Stereo MCs (Fourth & Broadway)
-	21	LET'S RUMBLE	Love/Hate (RCA)
27	22	UNPLUGGED	Eric Clapton (Duck)
24	23	TAKE THAT AND PARTY	Take That (RCA)
18	24	SO CLOSE	Dina Carroll (A&M PM)
17	25	JANET	Janet Jackson (Virgin)
15	26	NO LIMITS	2 Unlimited (PWL Continental)
30	27	WALTHAMSTOW	East 17 (London)
34	28	DANGEROUS	Michael Jackson (Epic)
22	29	THE FIRST DAY	David Sylvian & Robert Fripp (Virgin)
21	30	GOLD AGAINST THE SOUL	Manic Street Preachers (Columbia)
23	31	THE BEST OF ERIC CLAPTON	Eric Clapton (Polydor)
25	32	BREATHLESS	Kenny G (Arista)
26	33	ARE YOU GONNA GO MY WAY	Lenny Kravitz (Virgin America)
29	34	KAMAKIRIAD	Donald Fagen (Reprise)
32	35	TEASE ME	Chaka Demus & Pliers (Mango)
41	36	IT'S ABOUT TIME	SWV (RCA)
39	37	UTAH SAINTS	Utah Saints (ffrr)
28	38	CYBERPUNK	Billy Idol (Chrysalis)
31	39	TOO LONG IN EXILE	Van Morrison (Polydor)
35	40	BEFORE & AFTER	Tim Finn (Capitol)
36	41	CEREAL KILLER	Green Jelly (Zoo)
-	42	SUBSTANCE	New Order (Factory)
37	43	LOVE DELUXE	Sade (Epic)
48	44	DREAM HARDER	Waterboys (Geffen)
45	45	ELEMENTAL	Tears For Fears (Mercury)
-	46	SUEDE	Suede (Nude)
-	47	THE COMMITMENTS - SOUNDTRACK	Commitments (MCA)
49	48	FATE OF NATIONS	Robert Plant (Es Paranza)
45	49	RAGE AGAINST THE MACHINE	Rage Against The Machine (Epic)
42	50	REPUBLIC	New Order (London)

31 July 1993

LW	TW	Title	Artist (Label)
2	1	PROMISES AND LIES	UB40 (DEP International)
1	2	ZOOROPA	U2 (Island)
8	3	ALWAYS	Michael Ball (PolyGram TV)
11	4	BIGGER, BETTER, FASTER, MORE!	4 Non Blondes (Interscope)
4	5	POCKET FULL OF KRYPTONITE	Spin Doctors (Epic)
5	6	UNPLUGGED ... AND SEATED	Rod Stewart (Warner Bros.)
7	7	AUTOMATIC FOR THE PEOPLE	R.E.M. (Warner Bros.)
3	8	EMERGENCY ON PLANET EARTH	Jamiroquai (Orenda)
12	9	THE BODYGUARD - SOUNDTRACK	Various Artists (Arista)
23	10	TAKE THAT AND PARTY	Take That (RCA)
-	11	SIAMESE DREAM	Smashing Pumpkins (Hut)
9	12	BACK TO BROADWAY	Barbra Streisand (Columbia)
10	13	TEN SUMMONER'S TALES	Sting (A&M)
15	14	UNPLUGGED	Neil Young (Reprise)
19	15	KEEP THE FAITH	Bon Jovi (Jambco)
16	16	JANET	Janet Jackson (Virgin)
16	17	WHAT'S LOVE GOT TO DO WITH IT	Tina Turner (Parlophone)
13	18	LAST ACTION HERO - S'TRACK	Various (Arista)
6	19	DEBUT	Bjork (One Little Indian)
22	20	UNPLUGGED	Eric Clapton (Duck)
28	21	DANGEROUS	Michael Jackson (Epic)
20	22	CONNECTED	Stereo MCs (Fourth & Broadway)
-	23	DEBRAVATION	Deborah Harry (Chrysalis)
14	24	THE SOUND OF SPEED	Jesus & Mary Chain (blanco y negro)
17	25	MI TIERRA	Gloria Estefan (Epic)
18	26	MUDDY WATERS BLUES - A TRIBUTE TO MUDDY WATERS	Paul Rodgers (Victory)
-	27	GOLD - GREATEST HITS	Abba (Polydor)
24	28	SO CLOSE	Dina Carroll (A&M PM)
26	29	NO LIMITS	2 Unlimited (PWL Continental)
32	30	BREATHLESS	Kenny G (Arista)
21	31	LET'S RUMBLE	Love/Hate (RCA)
27	32	WALTHAMSTOW	East 17 (London)
33	33	ARE YOU GONNA GO MY WAY	Lenny Kravitz (Virgin America)
31	34	THE BEST OF ERIC CLAPTON	Eric Clapton (Polydor)
37	35	UTAH SAINTS	Utah Saints (ffrr)
43	36	LOVE DELUXE	Sade (Epic)
-	37	LIBERATOR	Orchestral Manoeuvres In The Dark (Virgin)
36	38	IT'S ABOUT TIME	SWV (RCA)
34	39	KAMAKIRIAD	Donald Fagen (Reprise)
-	40	OUT OF TIME	R.E.M. (Warner Bros.)
44	41	DREAM HARDER	Waterboys (Geffen)
41	42	CEREAL KILLER	Green Jelly (Zoo)
30	43	GOLD AGAINST THE SOUL	Manic Street Preachers (Columbia)
49	44	RAGE AGAINST THE MACHINE	Rage Against The Machine (Epic)
39	45	TOO LONG IN EXILE	Van Morrison (Polydor)
-	46	SYMPHONY OR DAMN	Terence Trent D'Arby (Columbia)
47	47	THE COMMITMENTS - SOUNDTRACK	Commitments (MCA)
45	48	ELEMENTAL	Tears For Fears (Mercury)
29	49	THE FIRST DAY	David Sylvian /Robert Fripp (Virgin)
-	50	STARS	Simply Red (East West)

Zooropa continued the trend of entering the chart at Number One and then gradually drifting downwards. Though more musically inventive it didn't sell the zillions that earlier LPs managed. Polydor had craftily acquired the rights to Abba's back catalogue, and were about to rake in the profits of a 1970s revival.

August 1993

last week	this week	7 August 1993	
1	1	PROMISES AND LIES	UB40 (DEP International)
2	2	ZOOROPA	U2 (Island)
3	3	ALWAYS	Michael Ball (PolyGram TV)
4	4	BIGGER, BETTER, FASTER, MORE!	4 Non Blondes (Interscope)
5	5	POCKET FULL OF KRYPTONITE	Spin Doctors (Epic)
7	6	AUTOMATIC FOR THE PEOPLE	R.E.M. (Warner Bros.)
11	7	SIAMESE DREAM	Smashing Pumpkins (Hut)
27	8	GOLD - GREATEST HITS	Abba (Polydor)
9	9	THE BODYGUARD - SOUNDTRACK	Various Artists (Arista)
6	10	UNPLUGGED ... AND SEATED	Rod Stewart (Warner Bros.)
10	11	TAKE THAT AND PARTY	Take That (RCA)
-	12	EVOLUTION	Oleta Adams (Fontana)
8	13	EMERGENCY ON PLANET EARTH	Jamiroquai (Orenda)
15	14	KEEP THE FAITH	Bon Jovi (Jambco)
-	15	SEX AND RELIGION	Vai (Relativity)
-	16	BLACK SUNDAY	Cypress Hill (Ruff House)
13	17	TEN SUMMONER'S TALES	Sting (A&M)
12	18	BACK TO BROADWAY	Barbra Streisand (Columbia)
16	19	JANET	Janet Jackson (Virgin)
21	20	DANGEROUS	Michael Jackson (Epic)
20	21	UNPLUGGED	Eric Clapton (Duck)
19	22	DEBUT	Bjork (One Little Indian)
14	23	UNPLUGGED	Neil Young (Reprise)
18	24	LAST ACTION HERO - SOUNDTRACK	Various Artists (Arista)
-	25	THE BATTLE RAGES ON	Deep Purple (RCA)
17	26	WHAT'S LOVE GOT TO DO WITH IT	Tina Turner (Parlophone)
-	27	MORE ABBA GOLD - MORE ABBA HITS	Abba (Polydor)
22	28	CONNECTED	Stereo MCs (Fourth & Broadway)
36	29	LOVE DELUXE	Sade (Epic)
-	30	WELCOME TO WHEREVER YOU ARE	INXS (Mercury)
28	31	SO CLOSE	Dina Carroll (A&M PM)
23	32	DEBRAVATION	Deborah Harry (Chrysalis)
30	33	BREATHLESS	Kenny G (Arista)
25	34	MI TIERRA	Gloria Estefan (Epic)
-	35	JOEY LAWRENCE	Joey Lawrence (Impact)
26	36	MUDDY WATERS BLUES - A TRIBUTE TO MUDDY WATERS	Paul Rodgers (Victory)
29	37	NO LIMITS	2 Unlimited (PWL Continental)
32	38	WALTHAMSTOW	East 17 (London)
33	39	ARE YOU GONNA GO MY WAY	Lenny Kravitz (Virgin America)
-	40	OUI LOVE YOU	Oui 3 (MCA)
41	41	DREAM HARDER	Waterboys (Geffen)
40	42	OUT OF TIME	R.E.M. (Warner Bros.)
35	43	UTAH SAINTS	Utah Saints (ffrr)
38	44	IT'S ABOUT TIME	SWV (RCA)
37	45	LIBERATOR	Orchestral Manoeuvres In The Dark (Virgin)
50	46	STARS	Simply Red (East West)
-	47	TEN	Pearl Jam (Epic)
44	48	RAGE AGAINST THE MACHINE	Rage Against The Machine (Epic)
47	49	THE COMMITMENTS - SOUNDTRACK	Commitments (MCA)
-	50	KICK	INXS (Mercury)

last week	this week	14 August 1993	
1	1	PROMISES AND LIES	UB40 (DEP International)
2	2	ZOOROPA	U2 (Island)
4	3	BIGGER, BETTER, FASTER, MORE!	4 Non Blondes (Interscope)
6	4	AUTOMATIC FOR THE PEOPLE	R.E.M. (Warner Bros.)
-	5	RIVER OF DREAMS	Billy Joel (Columbia)
5	6	POCKET FULL OF KRYPTONITE	Spin Doctors (Epic)
3	7	ALWAYS	Michael Ball (PolyGram TV)
11	8	TAKE THAT AND PARTY	Take That (RCA)
9	9	THE BODYGUARD - SOUNDTRACK	Various Artists (Arista)
13	10	EMERGENCY ON PLANET EARTH	Jamiroquai (Orenda)
10	11	UNPLUGGED ... AND SEATED	Rod Stewart (Warner Bros.)
12	12	EVOLUTION	Oleta Adams (Fontana)
14	13	KEEP THE FAITH	Bon Jovi (Jambco)
17	14	TEN SUMMONER'S TALES	Sting (A&M)
7	15	SIAMESE DREAM	Smashing Pumpkins (Hut)
18	16	BACK TO BROADWAY	Barbra Streisand (Columbia)
20	17	DANGEROUS	Michael Jackson (Epic)
16	18	BLACK SUNDAY	Cypress Hill (Ruff House)
19	19	JANET	Janet Jackson (Virgin)
8	20	GOLD - GREATEST HITS	Abba (Polydor)
21	21	UNPLUGGED	Eric Clapton (Duck)
22	22	DEBUT	Bjork (One Little Indian)
15	23	SEX AND RELIGION	Vai (Relativity)
26	24	WHAT'S LOVE GOT TO DO WITH IT	Tina Turner (Parlophone)
28	25	CONNECTED	Stereo MCs (Fourth & Broadway)
23	26	UNPLUGGED	Neil Young (Reprise)
37	27	NO LIMITS	2 Unlimited (PWL Continental)
24	28	LAST ACTION HERO - SOUNDTRACK	Various Artists (Arista)
29	29	MI TIERRA	Gloria Estefan (Epic)
25	30	THE BATTLE RAGES ON	Deep Purple (RCA)
-	31	EROTICA	Madonna (Maverick)
27	32	MORE ABBA GOLD - MORE ABBA HITS	Abba (Polydor)
29	33	LOVE DELUXE	Sade (Epic)
33	34	BREATHLESS	Kenny G (Arista)
31	35	SO CLOSE	Dina Carroll (A&M PM)
48	36	RAGE AGAINST THE MACHINE	Rage Against The Machine (Epic)
42	37	OUT OF TIME	R.E.M. (Warner Bros.)
39	38	ARE YOU GONNA GO MY WAY	Lenny Kravitz (Virgin America)
38	39	WALTHAMSTOW	East 17 (London)
-	40	THE FREDDIE MERCURY ALBUM	Freddie Mercury (Parlophone)
47	41	TEN	Pearl Jam (Epic)
-	42	JURASSIC PARK - S'TRACK	John Williams (MCA)
35	43	JOEY LAWRENCE	Joey Lawrence (Impact)
43	44	UTAH SAINTS	Utah Saints (ffrr)
-	45	GOLD AGAINST THE SOUL	Manic Street Preachers (Columbia)
30	46	WELCOME TO WHEREVER YOU ARE	INXS (Mercury)
44	47	IT'S ABOUT TIME	SWV (RCA)
46	48	STARS	Simply Red (East West)
40	49	OUI LOVE YOU	Oui 3 (MCA)
49	50	THE COMMITMENTS - SOUNDTRACK	Commitments (MCA)

last week	this week	21 August 1993	
1	1	PROMISES AND LIES	UB40 (DEP International)
2	2	ZOOROPA	U2 (Island)
4	3	AUTOMATIC FOR THE PEOPLE	R.E.M. (Warner Bros.)
5	4	RIVER OF DREAMS	Billy Joel (Columbia)
6	5	POCKET FULL OF KRYPTONITE	Spin Doctors (Epic)
3	6	BIGGER, BETTER, FASTER, MORE!	4 Non Blondes (Interscope)
10	7	EMERGENCY ON PLANET EARTH	Jamiroquai (Orenda)
7	8	ALWAYS	Michael Ball (PolyGram TV)
8	9	TAKE THAT AND PARTY	Take That (RCA)
9	10	THE BODYGUARD - SOUNDTRACK	Various Artists (Arista)
11	11	UNPLUGGED ... AND SEATED	Rod Stewart (Warner Bros.)
13	12	KEEP THE FAITH	Bon Jovi (Jambco)
14	13	TEN SUMMONER'S TALES	Sting (A&M)
24	14	WHAT'S LOVE GOT TO DO WITH IT	Tina Turner (Parlophone)
20	15	GOLD - GREATEST HITS	Abba (Polydor)
17	16	DANGEROUS	Michael Jackson (Epic)
19	17	JANET	Janet Jackson (Virgin)
40	18	THE FREDDIE MERCURY ALBUM	Freddie Mercury (Parlophone)
16	19	BACK TO BROADWAY	Barbra Streisand (Columbia)
18	20	BLACK SUNDAY	Cypress Hill (Ruff House)
15	21	SIAMESE DREAM	Smashing Pumpkins (Hut)
21	22	UNPLUGGED	Eric Clapton (Duck)
22	23	DEBUT	Bjork (One Little Indian)
29	24	MI TIERRA	Gloria Estefan (Epic)
25	25	CONNECTED	Stereo MCs (Fourth & Broadway)
12	26	EVOLUTION	Oleta Adams (Fontana)
31	27	EROTICA	Madonna (Maverick)
27	28	NO LIMITS	2 Unlimited (PWL Continental)
36	29	RAGE AGAINST THE MACHINE	Rage Against The Machine (Epic)
23	30	SEX AND RELIGION	Vai (Relativity)
38	31	ARE YOU GONNA GO MY WAY	Lenny Kravitz (Virgin America)
26	32	UNPLUGGED	Neil Young (Reprise)
28	33	LAST ACTION HERO - SOUNDTRACK	Various Artists (Arista)
32	34	MORE ABBA GOLD - MORE ABBA HITS	Abba (polydor)
34	35	BREATHLESS	Kenny G (Arista)
47	36	IT'S ABOUT TIME	SWV (RCA)
-	37	CEREAL KILLER	Green Jelly (Zoo)
33	38	LOVE DELUXE	Sade (Epic)
45	39	GOLD AGAINST THE SOUL	Manic Street Preachers (Columbia)
37	40	OUT OF TIME	R.E.M. (Warner Bros.)
41	41	TEN	Pearl Jam (Epic)
30	42	THE BATTLE RAGES ON	Deep Purple (RCA)
35	43	SO CLOSE	Dina Carroll (A&M PM)
42	44	JURASSIC PARK - SOUNDTRACK	John Williams (MCA)
45	45	UTAH SAINTS	Utah Saints (ffrr)
-	46	USE YOUR ILLUSION II	Guns N' Roses (Geffen)
-	47	ACHTUNG BABY	U2 (Island)
39	48	WALTHAMSTOW	East 17 (London)
50	49	THE COMMITMENTS - SOUNDTRACK	Commitments (MCA)
-	50	USE YOUR ILLUSION I	Guns N' Roses (Geffen)

UB40 were turning into one of Britain's most enduring bands. Washed in on the ska and reggae revival of 1980, they've managed to stick around for the last 14 years. *Promises And Lies* was their first Number One album since *Labour Of Love* hit the top for 3 weeks in October 1983.

413

August – September 1993

28 August 1993

LW	TW	Title	Artist (Label)
1	1	PROMISES AND LIES	UB40 (DEP International)
2	2	ZOOROPA	U2 (Island)
4	3	RIVER OF DREAMS	Billy Joel (Columbia)
5	4	POCKET FULL OF KRYPTONITE	Spin Doctors (Epic)
3	5	AUTOMATIC FOR THE PEOPLE	R.E.M. (Warner Bros.)
12	6	KEEP THE FAITH	Bon Jovi (Jambco)
7	7	EMERGENCY ON PLANET EARTH	Jamiroquai (Orenda)
6	8	BIGGER, BETTER, FASTER, MORE!	4 Non Blondes (Interscope)
10	9	THE BODYGUARD - SOUNDTRACK	Various Artists (Arista)
14	10	WHAT'S LOVE GOT TO DO WITH IT	Tina Turner (Parlophone)
8	11	ALWAYS	Michael Ball (PolyGram TV)
9	12	TAKE THAT AND PARTY	Take That (RCA)
13	13	UNPLUGGED ... AND SEATED	Rod Stewart (Warner Bros.)
13	14	TEN SUMMONER'S TALES	Sting (A&M)
18	15	THE FREDDIE MERCURY ALBUM	Freddie Mercury (Parlophone)
23	16	DEBUT	Bjork (One Little Indian)
15	17	GOLD - GREATEST HITS	Abba (Polydor)
17	18	JANET	Janet Jackson (Virgin)
-	19	GIANT STEPS	Boo Radleys (Creation)
-	20	ANTMUSIC - THE VERY BEST OF ADAM ANT	Adam Ant
16	21	DANGEROUS	Michael Jackson (Epic)
25	22	CONNECTED	Stereo MCs (Fourth & Broadway)
47	23	ACHTUNG BABY	U2 (Island)
20	24	BLACK SUNDAY	Cypress Hill (Ruff House)
22	25	UNPLUGGED	Eric Clapton (Duck)
31	26	ARE YOU GONNA GO MY WAY	Lenny Kravitz (Virgin America)
36	27	IT'S ABOUT TIME	SWV (RCA)
19	28	BACK TO BROADWAY	Barbra Streisand (Columbia)
29	29	RAGE AGAINST THE MACHINE	Rage Against The Machine (Epic)
24	30	MI TIERRA	Gloria Estefan (Epic)
26	31	EVOLUTION	Oleta Adams (Fontana)
21	32	SIAMESE DREAM	Smashing Pumpkins (Hut)
27	33	EROTICA	Madonna (Maverick)
28	34	NO LIMITS	2 Unlimited (PWL Continental)
37	35	CEREAL KILLER	Green Jelly (Zoo)
39	36	GOLD AGAINST THE SOUL	Manic Street Preachers (Columbia)
43	37	SO CLOSE	Dina Carroll (A&M PM)
33	38	LAST ACTION HERO - SOUNDTRACK	Various Artists (Arista)
34	39	MORE ABBA GOLD - MORE ABBA HITS	Abba (polydor)
38	40	LOVE DELUXE	Sade (Epic)
-	41	THE JOSHUA TREE	U2 (Island)
30	42	SEX AND RELIGION	Vai (Relativity)
32	43	UNPLUGGED	Neil Young (Reprise)
35	44	BREATHLESS	Kenny G (Arista)
-	45	GREAT EXPECTATIONS	Tasmin Archer (EMI)
40	46	OUT OF TIME	R.E.M. (Warner Bros.)
-	47	RATTLE AND HUM	U2 (Island)
45	48	UTAH SAINTS	Utah Saints (ffrr)
41	49	TEN	Pearl Jam (Epic)
-	50	THE VERY BEST OF CAT STEVENS	Cat Stevens (PolyGram TV)

4 September 1993

LW	TW	Title	Artist (Label)
-	1	THE LEVELLERS	Levellers (China)
1	2	PROMISES AND LIES	UB40 (DEP International)
3	3	RIVER OF DREAMS	Billy Joel (Columbia)
4	4	POCKET FULL OF KRYPTONITE	Spin Doctors (Epic)
2	5	ZOOROPA	U2 (Island)
6	6	KEEP THE FAITH	Bon Jovi (Jambco)
20	7	ANTMUSIC - THE VERY BEST OF ADAM ANT	Adam Ant
5	8	AUTOMATIC FOR THE PEOPLE	R.E.M. (Warner Bros.)
7	9	EMERGENCY ON PLANET EARTH	Jamiroquai (Orenda)
8	10	BIGGER, BETTER, FASTER, MORE!	4 Non Blondes (Interscope)
10	11	WHAT'S LOVE GOT TO DO WITH IT	Tina Turner (Parlophone)
9	12	THE BODYGUARD - SOUNDTRACK	Various Artists (Arista)
14	13	TEN SUMMONER'S TALES	Sting (A&M)
-	14	A SLIGHT CASE OF OVERBOMBING - GREATEST HITS	Sisters Of Mercy (Merciful Release)
13	15	UNPLUGGED ... AND SEATED	Rod Stewart (Warner Bros.)
16	16	DEBUT	Bjork (One Little Indian)
12	17	TAKE THAT AND PARTY	Take That (RCA)
11	18	ALWAYS	Michael Ball (PolyGram TV)
15	19	THE FREDDIE MERCURY ALBUM	Freddie Mercury (Parlophone)
27	20	IT'S ABOUT TIME	SWV (RCA)
17	21	GOLD - GREATEST HITS	Abba (Polydor)
18	22	JANET	Janet Jackson (Virgin)
22	23	CONNECTED	Stereo MCs (Fourth & Broadway)
21	24	DANGEROUS	Michael Jackson (Epic)
23	25	ACHTUNG BABY	U2 (Island)
29	26	RAGE AGAINST THE MACHINE	Rage Against The Machine (Epic)
19	27	GIANT STEPS	Boo Radleys (Creation)
25	28	UNPLUGGED	Eric Clapton (Duck)
24	29	BLACK SUNDAY	Cypress Hill (Ruff House)
-	30	SYMPHONY OR DAMN	Terence Trent D'Arby (Columbia)
34	31	NO LIMITS	2 Unlimited (PWL Continental)
26	32	ARE YOU GONNA GO MY WAY	Lenny Kravitz (Virgin America)
32	33	SIAMESE DREAM	Smashing Pumpkins (Hut)
34	34	BACK TO BROADWAY	Barbra Streisand (Columbia)
30	35	MI TIERRA	Gloria Estefan (Epic)
31	36	EVOLUTION	Oleta Adams (Fontana)
45	37	GREAT EXPECTATIONS	Tasmin Archer (EMI)
40	38	LOVE DELUXE	Sade (Epic)
33	39	EROTICA	Madonna (Maverick)
-	40	05:22:09:12 OFF	Front 242 (RRE)
-	41	SHOW ME LOVE	Robin S (Champion)
41	42	THE JOSHUA TREE	U2 (Island)
36	43	GOLD AGAINST THE SOUL	Manic Street Preachers (Columbia)
35	44	CEREAL KILLER	Green Jelly (Zoo)
44	45	BREATHLESS	Kenny G (Arista)
37	46	SO CLOSE	Dina Carroll (A&M PM)
48	47	UTAH SAINTS	Utah Saints (ffrr)
49	48	TEN	Pearl Jam (Epic)
-	49	UNITED KINGDOMS	Ultramarino (blanco y negro)
-	50	THE COMMITMENTS - SOUNDTRACK	Commitments (MCA)

11 September 1993

LW	TW	Title	Artist (Label)
-	1	MUSIC BOX	Mariah Carey (Columbia)
2	2	PROMISES AND LIES	UB40 (DEP International)
1	3	THE LEVELLERS	Levellers (China)
3	4	RIVER OF DREAMS	Billy Joel (Columbia)
4	5	POCKET FULL OF KRYPTONITE	Spin Doctors (Epic)
7	6	ANTMUSIC - THE VERY BEST OF ADAM ANT	Adam Ant
5	7	ZOOROPA	U2 (Island)
6	8	KEEP THE FAITH	Bon Jovi (Jambco)
8	9	AUTOMATIC FOR THE PEOPLE	R.E.M. (Warner Bros.)
-	10	SUNSET BOULEVARD	Various (Really Useful)
13	11	TEN SUMMONER'S TALES	Sting (A&M)
-	12	LAST SPLASH	Breeders (4AD)
10	13	BIGGER, BETTER, FASTER, MORE!	4 Non Blondes (Interscope)
9	14	EMERGENCY ON PLANET EARTH	Jamiroquai (Orenda)
11	15	WHAT'S LOVE GOT TO DO WITH IT	Tina Turner (Parlophone)
16	16	DEBUT	Bjork (One Little Indian)
12	17	THE BODYGUARD - SOUNDTRACK	Various Artists (Arista)
19	18	THE FREDDIE MERCURY ALBUM	Freddie Mercury (Parlophone)
14	19	A SLIGHT CASE OF OVERBOMBING - GREATEST HITS	Sisters Of Mercy (Merciful Release)
20	20	IT'S ABOUT TIME	SWV (RCA)
15	21	UNPLUGGED ... AND SEATED	Rod Stewart (Warner Bros.)
-	22	WAITING FOR HERB	Pogues (Pogue Mahone)
-	23	TI AMO - PUCCINI'S GREATEST LOVE SONGS	Luciano Pavarotti (Decca)
17	24	TAKE THAT AND PARTY	Take That (RCA)
18	25	ALWAYS	Michael Ball (PolyGram TV)
23	26	CONNECTED	Stereo MCs (Fourth & Broadway)
26	27	RAGE AGAINST THE MACHINE	Rage Against The Machine (Epic)
-	28	ALL AROUND THE WORLD	Jason Donovan (Polydor)
32	29	ARE YOU GONNA GO MY WAY	Lenny Kravitz (Virgin America)
22	30	JANET	Janet Jackson (Virgin)
21	31	GOLD - GREATEST HITS	Abba (Polydor)
24	32	UNPLUGGED	Eric Clapton (Duck)
24	33	DANGEROUS	Michael Jackson (Epic)
25	34	ACHTUNG BABY	U2 (Island)
29	35	BLACK SUNDAY	Cypress Hill (Ruff House)
30	36	SYMPHONY OR DAMN	Terence Trent D'Arby (Columbia)
33	37	SIAMESE DREAM	Smashing Pumpkins (Hut)
31	38	NO LIMITS	2 Unlimited (PWL Continental)
39	39	GREAT EXPECTATIONS	Tasmin Archer (EMI)
27	40	GIANT STEPS	Boo Radleys (Creation)
41	41	SHOW ME LOVE	Robin S (Champion)
38	42	LOVE DELUXE	Sade (Epic)
35	43	MI TIERRA	Gloria Estefan (Epic)
34	44	BACK TO BROADWAY	Barbra Streisand (Columbia)
36	45	EVOLUTION	Oleta Adams (Fontana)
40	46	05:22:09:12 OFF	Front 242 (RRE)
39	47	EROTICA	Madonna (Maverick)
46	48	SO CLOSE	Dina Carroll (A&M PM)
50	49	THE COMMITMENTS - SOUNDTRACK	Commitments (MCA)
-	50	CHRONOLOGIE	Jean-Michel Jarre (Dreyfus)

The Levellers (name based on a seventeenth century bunch of land squatters and social reformers) had previously charted with *Levelling The Land* in 1991 and 1992, though failed to get higher than Number 23 that time. Now protecting the land was big – and so, temporarily, were the Levellers.

September – October 1993

last week	this week	18 September 1993	Artist (Label)
-	1	BAT OUT OF HELL II – BACK INTO HELL...	Meatloaf (Virgin)
-	2	WILD WOOD	Paul Weller (Go! Discs)
1	3	MUSIC BOX	Mariah Carey (Columbia)
2	4	PROMISES AND LIES	UB40 (DEP International)
-	5	POST HISTORIC MONSTERS	Carter USM (Chrysalis)
5	6	POCKET FULL OF KRYPTONITE	Spin Doctors (Epic)
4	7	RIVER OF DREAMS	Billy Joel (Columbia)
3	8	THE LEVELLERS	Levellers (China)
7	9	ZOOROPA	U2 (Island)
12	10	LAST SPLASH	Breeders (4AD)
9	11	AUTOMATIC FOR THE PEOPLE	R.E.M. (Warner Bros.)
6	12	ANTMUSIC - THE VERY BEST OF ADAM ANT	Adam Ant (Arcade)
11	13	TEN SUMMONER'S TALES	Sting (A&M)
8	14	KEEP THE FAITH	Bon Jovi (Jambco)
16	15	DEBUT	Bjork (One Little Indian)
10	16	SUNSET BOULEVARD	Various (Really Useful)
14	17	EMERGENCY ON PLANET EARTH	Jamiroquai (Orenda)
13	18	BIGGER, BETTER, FASTER, MORE!	4 Non Blondes (Interscope)
15	19	WHAT'S LOVE GOT TO DO WITH IT	Tina Turner (Parlophone)
18	20	THE FREDDIE MERCURY ALBUM	Freddie Mercury (Parlophone)
29	21	ARE YOU GONNA GO MY WAY	Lenny Kravitz (Virgin America)
17	22	THE BODYGUARD - S'TRACK	Various s (Arista)
20	23	IT'S ABOUT TIME	SWV (RCA)
19	24	A SLIGHT CASE OF OVERBOMBING – GREATEST HITS	Sisters Of Mercy (Merciful Release)
21	25	UNPLUGGED ... AND SEATED	Rod Stewart (Warner Bros.)
23	26	TI AMO – PUCCINI'S GREATEST LOVE SONGS	Luciano Pavarotti (Decca)
22	27	WAITING FOR HERB	Pogues (Pogue Mahone)
24	28	TAKE THAT AND PARTY	Take That (RCA)
27	29	RAGE AGAINST THE MACHINE	Rage Against The Machine (Epic)
26	30	CONNECTED	Stereo MCs (Fourth & Broadway)
-	31	MIND AND SOUL COLLABORATORS	Back To The Planet (Parallel)
-	32	CORE	Stone Temple Pilots (Atlantic)
38	33	NO LIMITS	2 Unlimited (PWL Continental)
25	34	ALWAYS	Michael Ball (PolyGram TV)
-	35	PRETTY WOMAN – S'TRACK	Various (EMI USA)
-	36	WHATEVER	Aimee Mann (Imago)
-	37	REPUBLIC	New Order (London)
30	38	JANET	Janet Jackson (Virgin)
-	39	HUMAN WHEELS	John Mellencamp (Mercury)
28	40	ALL AROUND THE WORLD	Jason Donovan (Polydor)
33	41	DANGEROUS	Michael Jackson (Epic)
32	42	UNPLUGGED	Eric Clapton (Duck)
31	43	GOLD - GREATEST HITS	Abba (Polydor)
35	44	BLACK SUNDAY	Cypress Hill (Ruff House)
36	45	SYMPHONY OR DAMN	Terence Trent D'Arby (Columbia)
-	46	BAT OUT OF HELL	Meatloaf (Epic)
39	47	GREAT EXPECTATIONS	Tasmin Archer (EMI)
37	48	SIAMESE DREAM	Smashing Pumpkins (Hut)
50	49	CHRONOLOGIE	Jean-Michel Jarre (Dreyfus)
34	50	ACHTUNG BABY	U2 (Island)

last week	this week	25 September 1993	Artist (Label)
-	1	IN UTERO	Nirvana (Geffen)
1	2	BAT OUT OF HELL II – BACK INTO HELL...	Meatloaf (Virgin)
-	3	THE HITS/THE B-SIDES	Prince (Paisley Park)
-	4	THE HITS 1	Prince (Paisley Park)
-	5	THE HITS 2	Prince (Paisley Park)
2	6	WILD WOOD	Paul Weller (Go! Discs)
3	7	MUSIC BOX	Mariah Carey (Columbia)
4	8	PROMISES AND LIES	UB40 (DEP International)
-	9	ELEMENTS – THE BEST OF MIKE OLDFIELD	Mike Oldfield (Virgin)
6	10	POCKET FULL OF KRYPTONITE	Spin Doctors (Epic)
-	11	WAIT FOR ME	Kenny Thomas (Cooltempo)
5	12	POST HISTORIC MONSTERS	Carter USM (Chrysalis)
7	13	RIVER OF DREAMS	Billy Joel (Columbia)
11	14	AUTOMATIC FOR THE PEOPLE	R.E.M. (Warner Bros.)
-	15	THE SINGLES COLLECTION 1981-1993	Kim Wilde (MCA)
8	16	THE LEVELLERS	Levellers (China)
-	17	CUCKOO	Curve (Anxious)
9	18	ZOOROPA	U2 (Island)
12	19	ANTMUSIC - THE VERY BEST OF ADAM ANT	Adam Ant (Arcade)
21	20	ARE YOU GONNA GO MY WAY	Lenny Kravitz (Virgin America)
15	21	DEBUT	Bjork (One Little Indian)
13	22	TEN SUMMONER'S TALES	Sting (A&M)
-	23	SOME FANTASTIC PLACE	Squeeze (A&M)
-	24	SHOW	Cure (Fiction)
-	25	THE DEFINITIVE COLLECTION	Kinks (PolyGram TV)
14	26	KEEP THE FAITH	Bon Jovi (Jambco)
19	27	WHAT'S LOVE GOT TO DO WITH IT	Tina Turner (Parlophone)
17	28	EMERGENCY ON PLANET EARTH	Jamiroquai (Orenda)
18	29	BIGGER, BETTER, FASTER, MORE!	4 Non Blondes (Interscope)
22	30	THE BODYGUARD - S'TRACK	Various (Arista)
46	31	BAT OUT OF HELL	Meatloaf (Epic)
32	32	CORE	Stone Temple Pilots (Atlantic)
10	33	LAST SPLASH	Breeders (4AD)
-	34	SIZE ISN'T EVERYTHING	Bee Gees (Polydor)
20	35	THE FREDDIE MERCURY ALBUM	Freddie Mercury (Parlophone)
24	36	A SLIGHT CASE OF OVERBOMBING – GREATEST HITS	Sisters Of Mercy (Merciful Release)
30	37	CONNECTED	Stereo MCs (Fourth & Broadway)
37	38	REPUBLIC	New Order (London)
16	39	SUNSET BOULEVARD	Various (Really Useful)
23	40	IT'S ABOUT TIME	SWV (RCA)
38	41	JANET	Janet Jackson (Virgin)
25	42	UNPLUGGED ... AND SEATED	Rod Stewart (Warner Bros.)
26	43	TI AMO – PUCCINI'S GREATEST LOVE SONGS	Luciano Pavarotti (Decca)
-	44	MORNING DOVE WHITE	One Dove (Boy's Own)
-	45	AMERICAN CAESAR	Iggy Pop (Virgin)
35	46	PRETTY WOMAN – S'TRACK	Various (EMI USA)
28	47	TAKE THAT AND PARTY	Take That (RCA)
29	48	RAGE AGAINST THE MACHINE	Rage Again The Machine (Epic)
33	49	NO LIMITS	2 Unlimited (PWL Continental)
41	50	DANGEROUS	Michael Jackson (Epic)

last week	this week	2 October 1993	Artist (Label)
2	1	BAT OUT OF HELL II – BACK INTO HELL...	Meatloaf (Virgin)
1	2	IN UTERO	Nirvana (Geffen)
-	3	THE BEATLES 1962-1966	Beatles (Apple)
-	4	THE BEATLES 1967-1970	Beatles (Apple)
9	5	ELEMENTS – THE BEST OF MIKE OLDFIELD	Mike Oldfield (Virgin)
6	6	WILD WOOD	Paul Weller (Go! Discs)
5	7	THE HITS 2	Prince (Paisley Park)
4	8	THE HITS 1	Prince (Paisley Park)
3	9	THE HITS/THE B-SIDES	Prince (Paisley Park)
8	10	PROMISES AND LIES	UB40 (DEP International)
7	11	MUSIC BOX	Mariah Carey (Columbia)
15	12	THE SINGLES COLLECTION 1981-1993	Kim Wilde (MCA)
11	13	WAIT FOR ME	Kenny Thomas (Cooltempo)
10	14	POCKET FULL OF KRYPTONITE	Spin Doctors (Epic)
13	15	RIVER OF DREAMS	Billy Joel (Columbia)
14	16	AUTOMATIC FOR THE PEOPLE	R.E.M. (Warner Bros.)
17	17	KEEP THE FAITH	Bon Jovi (Jambco)
20	18	ARE YOU GONNA GO MY WAY	Lenny Kravitz (Virgin America)
22	19	TEN SUMMONER'S TALES	Sting (A&M)
18	20	ZOOROPA	U2 (Island)
21	21	DEBUT	Bjork (One Little Indian)
-	22	DAYTIME FRIENDS – THE VERY BEST OF KENNY ROGERS	Kenny Rogers (EMI)
-	23	GREASE	Original London Cast (Epic)
28	24	EMERGENCY ON PLANET EARTH	Jamiroquai (Orenda)
16	25	THE LEVELLERS	Levellers (China)
-	26	WHAT SILENCE KNOWS	Shara Nelson (Cooltempo)
-	27	AT WORST...THE BEST OF BOY GEORGE AND CULTURE CLUB	Boy George and Culture Club (Virgin)
27	28	WHAT'S LOVE GOT TO DO WITH IT	Tina Turner (Parlophone)
25	29	THE DEFINITIVE COLLECTION	Kinks (PolyGram TV)
19	30	ANTMUSIC - THE VERY BEST OF ADAM ANT	Adam Ant
12	31	POST HISTORIC MONSTERS	Carter USM (Chrysalis)
30	32	THE BODYGUARD - S'TRACK	Various(Arista)
17	33	CUCKOO	Curve (Anxious)
38	34	REPUBLIC	New Order (London)
23	35	SOME FANTASTIC PLACE	Squeeze (A&M)
47	36	TAKE THAT AND PARTY	Take That (RCA)
29	37	BIGGER, BETTER, FASTER, MORE!	4 Non Blondes (Interscope)
24	38	SHOW	Cure (Fiction)
31	39	BAT OUT OF HELL	Meatloaf (Epic)
34	40	SIZE ISN'T EVERYTHING	Bee Gees (Polydor)
37	41	CONNECTED	Stereo MCs (Fourth & Broadway)
35	42	THE FREDDIE MERCURY ALBUM	Freddie Mercury (Parlophone)
32	43	CORE	Stone Temple Pilots (Atlantic)
44	44	MORNING DOVE WHITE	One Dove (Boy's Own)
40	45	TUBULAR BELLS II	Mike Oldfield (WEA)
36	46	A SLIGHT CASE OF OVERBOMBING – GREATEST HITS	Sisters Of Mercy (Merciful Release)
40	47	IT'S ABOUT TIME	SWV (RCA)
-	48	THROUGH THE YEARS	Cilla Black (Columbia)
-	49	PABLO HONEY	Radiohead (Parlophone)
33	50	LAST SPLASH	Breeders (4AD)

Notable entries in September – *Music Box*, Mariah Carey's fourth album, is still in the Top 50 as this book goes to press – 64 weeks after entering at Number One. *Bat Out Of Hell II* was to become the most successful chart album of 1993. Nirvana confirmed their status as the seminal band of the time.

October 1993

9 October 1993

last	this		
-	1	VERY	Pet Shop Boys (Parlophone)
1	2	BAT OUT OF HELL II – BACK INTO HELL...	Meatloaf (Virgin)
2	3	IN UTERO	Nirvana (Geffen)
3	4	THE BEATLES 1962-1966	Beatles (Apple)
4	5	THE BEATLES 1967-1970	Beatles (Apple)
-	6	VERY RELENTLESS	Pet Shop Boys (Parlophone)
5	7	ELEMENTS – THE BEST OF MIKE OLDFIELD	Mike Oldfield (Virgin)
-	8	LAID	James (Fontana)
6	9	WILD WOOD	Paul Weller (Go! Discs)
7	10	THE HITS 2	Prince (Paisley Park)
8	11	THE HITS 1	Prince (Paisley Park)
-	12	LOVE SCENES	Beverley Craven (Epic)
11	13	MUSIC BOX	Mariah Carey (Columbia)
10	14	PROMISES AND LIES	UB40 (DEP International)
14	15	POCKET FULL OF KRYPTONITE	Spin Doctors (Epic)
16	16	AUTOMATIC FOR THE PEOPLE	R.E.M. (Warner Bros.)
12	17	THE SINGLES COLLECTION 1981-1993	Kim Wilde (MCA)
22	18	DAYTIME FRIENDS – THE VERY BEST OF KENNY ROGERS	Kenny Rogers (EMI)
9	19	THE HITS/THE B-SIDES	Prince (Paisley Park)
15	20	RIVER OF DREAMS	Billy Joel (Columbia)
13	21	WAIT FOR ME	Kenny Thomas (Cooltempo)
17	22	KEEP THE FAITH	Bon Jovi (Jambco)
19	23	TEN SUMMONER'S TALES	Sting (A&M)
21	24	DEBUT	Bjork (One Little Indian)
18	25	ARE YOU GONNA GO MY WAY	Lenny Kravitz (Virgin America)
23	26	GREASE	Original London Cast (Epic)
27	27	AT WORST...THE BEST OF BOY GEORGE AND CULTURE CLUB	Boy George and Culture Club (Virgin)
20	28	ZOOROPA	U2 (Island)
24	29	EMERGENCY ON PLANET EARTH	Jamiroquai (Orenda)
26	30	WHAT SILENCE KNOWS	Shara Nelson (Cooltempo)
28	31	WHAT'S LOVE GOT TO DO WITH IT	Tina Turner (Parlophone)
-	32	TEASE ME	Chaka Demus & Pliers (Mango)
25	33	THE LEVELLERS	Levellers (China)
32	34	THE BODYGUARD - SOUNDTRACK	Various Artists (Arista)
-	35	UP ON THE ROOF	Neil Diamond (Columbia)
49	36	PABLO HONEY	Radiohead (Parlophone)
-	37	BLACK SUNDAY	Cypress Hill (Ruff House)
29	38	THE DEFINITIVE COLLECTION	Kinks (PolyGram TV)
30	39	ANTMUSIC - THE VERY BEST OF ADAM ANT	Adam Ant
-	40	BIG RED LETTER DAY	Buffalo Tom (Beggars Banquet)
34	41	REPUBLIC	New Order (London)
-	42	BULLHOONE MIND STATE	De La Soul (Big Life)
47	43	IT'S ABOUT TIME	SWV (RCA)
44	44	TUBULAR BELLS II	Mike Oldfield (WEA)
36	45	TAKE THAT AND PARTY	Take That (RCA)
35	46	SOME FANTASTIC PLACE	Squeeze (A&M)
37	47	BIGGER, BETTER, FASTER, MORE!	4 Non Blondes (Interscope)
39	48	BAT OUT OF HELL	Meatloaf (Epic)
41	49	CONNECTED	Stereo MCs (Fourth & Broadway)
31	50	POST HISTORIC MONSTERS	Carter USM (Chrysalis)

16 October 1993

last	this		
2	1	BAT OUT OF HELL II – BACK INTO HELL...	Meatloaf (Virgin)
1	2	VERY	Pet Shop Boys (Parlophone)
-	3	CONSTRUCTION FOR THE MODERN IDIOT	Wonder Stuff (Polydor)
8	4	LAID	James (Fontana)
7	5	ELEMENTS – THE BEST OF MIKE OLDFIELD	Mike Oldfield (Virgin)
12	6	LOVE SCENES	Beverley Craven (Epic)
3	7	IN UTERO	Nirvana (Geffen)
6	8	VERY RELENTLESS	Pet Shop Boys (Parlophone)
11	9	THE HITS 1	Prince (Paisley Park)
10	10	THE HITS 2	Prince (Paisley Park)
-	11	RETRO ACTIVE	Def Leppard (Bludgeon Riffola)
4	12	THE BEATLES 1962-1966	Beatles (Apple)
5	13	THE BEATLES 1967-1970	Beatles (Apple)
9	14	WILD WOOD	Paul Weller (Go! Discs)
13	15	MUSIC BOX	Mariah Carey (Columbia)
-	16	ELEGANT SLUMMING	M People (deConstruction)
14	17	PROMISES AND LIES	UB40 (DEP International)
15	18	POCKET FULL OF KRYPTONITE	Spin Doctors (Epic)
17	19	THE SINGLES COLLECTION 1981-1993	Kim Wilde (MCA)
16	20	AUTOMATIC FOR THE PEOPLE	R.E.M. (Warner Bros.)
-	21	THIRTEEN	Teenage Fan Club (Creation)
19	22	THE HITS/THE B-SIDES	Prince (Paisley Park)
24	23	DEBUT	Bjork (One Little Indian)
-	24	ACES AND KINGS – THE BEST OF GO WEST	Go West (Chrysalis)
40	25	BIG RED LETTER DAY	Buffalo Tom (Beggars Banquet)
25	26	ARE YOU GONNA GO MY WAY	Lenny Kravitz (Virgin America)
18	27	DAYTIME FRIENDS – THE VERY BEST OF KENNY ROGERS	Kenny Rogers (EMI)
20	28	RIVER OF DREAMS	Billy Joel (Columbia)
23	29	TEN SUMMONER'S TALES	Sting (A&M)
21	30	WAIT FOR ME	Kenny Thomas (Cooltempo)
22	31	KEEP THE FAITH	Bon Jovi (Jambco)
35	32	UP ON THE ROOF	Neil Diamond (Columbia)
-	33	BELIEVE ME	Duff McKagan (Geffen)
32	34	TEASE ME	Chaka Demus & Pliers (Mango)
28	35	ZOOROPA	U2 (Island)
27	36	AT WORST...THE BEST OF BOY GEORGE AND CULTURE CLUB	Boy George and Culture Club (Virgin)
31	37	WHAT'S LOVE GOT TO DO WITH IT	Tina Turner (Parlophone)
-	38	SHAME AND SIN	Robert Cray (Mercury)
26	39	GREASE	Original London Cast (Epic)
34	40	THE BODYGUARD - SOUNDTRACK	Various Artists (Arista)
30	41	WHAT SILENCE KNOWS	Shara Nelson (Cooltempo)
29	42	EMERGENCY ON PLANET EARTH	Jamiroquai (Orenda)
37	43	BLACK SUNDAY	Cypress Hill (Ruff House)
-	44	GET INTO YOU	Dannii Minogue (MCA)
33	45	THE LEVELLERS	Levellers (China)
47	46	BIGGER, BETTER, FASTER, MORE!	4 Non Blondes (Interscope)
-	47	GENTLEMEN	Afghan Whigs (Blast First)
36	48	PABLO HONEY	Radiohead (Parlophone)
49	49	CONNECTED	Stereo MCs (Fourth & Broadway)
-	50	UNPLUGGED	Eric Clapton (Duck)

23 October 1993

last	this		
-	1	EVERYTHING CHANGES	Take That (RCA)
-	2	VS	Pearl Jam (Epic)
-	3	TOGETHER ALONE	Crowded House (Capitol)
1	4	BAT OUT OF HELL II – BACK INTO HELL...	Meatloaf (Virgin)
16	5	ELEGANT SLUMMING	M People (deConstruction)
-	6	COME ON FEEL THE LEMONHEADS	Lemonheads (Atlantic)
7	7	IN UTERO	Nirvana (Geffen)
2	8	VERY	Pet Shop Boys (Parlophone)
11	9	RETRO ACTIVE	Def Leppard (Bludgeon Riffola)
-	10	REAL	Belinda Carlisle (Offside)
24	11	ACES AND KINGS – THE BEST OF GO WEST	Go West (Chrysalis)
18	12	POCKET FULL OF KRYPTONITE	Spin Doctors (Epic)
6	13	LOVE SCENES	Beverley Craven (Epic)
3	14	CONSTRUCTION FOR THE MODERN IDIOT	Wonder Stuff (Polydor)
14	15	WILD WOOD	Paul Weller (Go! Discs)
10	16	THE HITS 2	Prince (Paisley Park)
5	17	ELEMENTS – THE BEST OF MIKE OLDFIELD	Mike Oldfield (Virgin)
23	18	DEBUT	Bjork (One Little Indian)
9	19	THE HITS 1	Prince (Paisley Park)
12	20	THE BEATLES 1962-1966	Beatles (Apple)
17	21	PROMISES AND LIES	UB40 (DEP International)
13	22	THE BEATLES 1967-1970	Beatles (Apple)
34	23	TEASE ME	Chaka Demus & Pliers (Mango)
15	24	MUSIC BOX	Mariah Carey (Columbia)
-	25	THE CROSSING	Paul Young (Columbia)
31	26	KEEP THE FAITH	Bon Jovi (Jambco)
4	27	LAID	James (Fontana)
35	28	ZOOROPA	U2 (Island)
-	29	BAD VIBES	Lloyd Cole (Fontana)
-	30	THE ALBUM	Haddaway (Logic)
19	31	THE SINGLES COLLECTION 1981-1993	Kim Wilde (MCA)
20	32	AUTOMATIC FOR THE PEOPLE	R.E.M. (Warner Bros.)
36	33	AT WORST...THE BEST OF BOY GEORGE AND CULTURE CLUB	Boy George and Culture Club (Virgin)
22	34	THE HITS/THE B-SIDES	Prince (Paisley Park)
21	35	THIRTEEN	Teenage Fan Club (Creation)
-	36	SIX WHEELS ON MY WAGON	Fluke (Circa)
37	37	WHAT'S LOVE GOT TO DO WITH IT	Tina Turner (Parlophone)
26	38	ARE YOU GONNA GO MY WAY	Lenny Kravitz (Virgin America)
25	39	BIG RED LETTER DAY	Buffalo Tom (Beggars Banquet)
-	40	SO CLOSE	Dina Carroll (A&M)
28	41	RIVER OF DREAMS	Billy Joel (Columbia)
45	42	THE LEVELLERS	Levellers (China)
27	43	DAYTIME FRIENDS – THE VERY BEST OF KENNY ROGERS	Kenny Rogers (EMI)
46	44	BIGGER, BETTER, FASTER, MORE!	4 Non Blondes (Interscope)
-	45	IT'S ABOUT TIME	SWV (RCA)
-	46	SLIPPERY WHEN WET	Bon Jovi (Vertigo)
32	47	UP ON THE ROOF	Neil Diamond (Columbia)
29	48	TEN SUMMONER'S TALES	Sting (A&M)
38	49	SHAME AND SIN	(Mercury)
-	50	SOUL ALONE	Daryl Hall (Epic)

Contrasting hit compilations in the chart. The Beatles collections, a curious mixture of singles and album tracks that someone decided were their best, were first issued in 1973. This was the CD version. Prince found enough Hits to fill three albums, and the B-sides went higher than the others – funny old world.

last week	this week	30 October 1993	
1	1	EVERYTHING CHANGES	Take That (RCA)
4	2	BAT OUT OF HELL II – BACK INTO HELL...	
			Meatloaf (Virgin)
-	3	ONE WOMAN – THE ULTIMATE COLLECTION	
			Diana Ross (EMI)
2	4	VS	Pearl Jam (Epic)
-	5	BANG!...THE GREATEST HITS	
			Frankie Goes To Hollywood (ZTT)
5	6	ELEGANT SLUMMING	M People (deConstruction)
3	7	TOGETHER ALONE	Crowded House (Capitol)
11	8	ACES AND KINGS – THE BEST OF GO WEST	
			Go West (Chrysalis)
6	9	COME ON FEEL THE LEMONHEADS	
			Lemonheads (Atlantic)
-	10	FOUR CALENDAR CAFE	
			Cocteau Twins (Fontana)
-	11	COUNTERPARTS	Rush (Anthem)
-	12	FIND YOUR WAY	Gabrielle (Go Beat)
-	13	A REAL DEAD ONE	Iron Maiden (EMI)
10	14	REAL	Belinda Carlisle (Offside)
8	15	VERY	Pet Shop Boys (Parlophone)
16	16	THE HITS 2	Prince (Paisley Park)
40	17	SO CLOSE	Dina Carroll (A&M)
-	18	EXPERIENCE THE DIVINE BETTE MIDLER	
			Bette Midler (Atlantic)
-	19	CHAOS AD	Sepultura (Roadrunner)
19	20	THE HITS 1	Prince (Paisley Park)
18	21	DEBUT	Bjork (One Little Indian)
24	22	MUSIC BOX	Mariah Carey (Columbia)
12	23	POCKET FULL OF KRYPTONITE	
			Spin Doctors (Epic)
7	24	IN UTERO	Nirvana (Geffen)
9	25	RETRO ACTIVE	Def Leppard (Bludgeon Riffola)
30	26	THE ALBUM	Haddaway (Logic)
21	27	PROMISES AND LIES	UB40 (DEP International)
-	28	4-TRACK DEMOS	P J Harvey (Island)
13	29	LOVE SCENES	Beverley Craven (Epic)
32	30	AUTOMATIC FOR THE PEOPLE	
			R.E.M. (Warner Bros.)
15	31	WILD WOOD	Paul Weller (Go! Discs)
20	32	THE BEATLES 1962-1966	Beatles (Apple)
22	33	THE BEATLES 1967-1970	Beatles (Apple)
14	34	CONSTRUCTION FOR THE MODERN IDIOT	
			Wonder Stuff (Polydor)
17	35	ELEMENTS – THE BEST OF MIKE OLDFIELD	
			Mike Oldfield (Virgin)
25	36	THE CROSSING	Paul Young (Columbia)
37	37	WHAT'S LOVE GOT TO DO WITH IT	
			Tina Turner (Parlophone)
23	38	TEASE ME	Chaka Demus & Pliers (Mango)
-	39	SABRESONIC	Sabres Of Paradise (Warp)
31	40	THE SINGLES COLLECTION 1981-1993	
			Kim Wilde (MCA)
-	41	D:REAM ON VOLUME 1	D:Ream (Magnet)
27	42	LAID	James (Fontana)
33	43	AT WORST...THE BEST OF BOY GEORGE AND CULTURE CLUB	
			Boy George and Culture Club (Virgin)
41	44	RIVER OF DREAMS	Billy Joel (Columbia)
26	45	KEEP THE FAITH	Bon Jovi (Jambco)
28	46	ZOOROPA	U2 (Island)
38	47	ARE YOU GONNA GO MY WAY	
			Lenny Kravitz (Virgin America)
-	48	BAT OUT OF HELL	Meatloaf (Epic)
-	49	RED HOUSE PAINTERS	
			Red House Painters (4AD)
-	50	HITS OUT OF HELL	Meatloaf (Epic)

last week	this week	6 November 1993	
2	1	BAT OUT OF HELL II – BACK INTO HELL...	
			Meatloaf (Virgin)
3	2	ONE WOMAN – THE ULTIMATE COLLECTION	
			Diana Ross (EMI)
1	3	EVERYTHING CHANGES	Take That (RCA)
-	4	DUETS	Frank Sinatra (Capitol)
5	5	BANG!...THE GREATEST HITS	
			Frankie Goes To Hollywood (ZTT)
18	6	EXPERIENCE THE DIVINE BETTE MIDLER	
			Bette Midler (Atlantic)
17	7	SO CLOSE	Dina Carroll (A&M)
6	8	ELEGANT SLUMMING	
			M People (deConstruction)
4	9	VS	Pearl Jam (Epic)
7	10	TOGETHER ALONE	Crowded House (Capitol)
12	11	FIND YOUR WAY	Gabrielle (Go Beat)
8	12	ACES AND KINGS – THE BEST OF GO WEST	
			Go West (Chrysalis)
9	13	COME ON FEEL THE LEMONHEADS	
			Lemonheads (Atlantic)
21	14	DEBUT	Bjork (One Little Indian)
22	15	MUSIC BOX	Mariah Carey (Columbia)
15	16	VERY	Pet Shop Boys (Parlophone)
11	17	COUNTERPARTS	Rush (Anthem)
10	18	FOUR CALENDAR CAFE	
			Cocteau Twins (Fontana)
13	19	A REAL DEAD ONE	Iron Maiden (EMI)
16	20	THE HITS 2	Prince (Paisley Park)
-	21	BY REQUEST	Foster & Allen (Telstar)
30	22	AUTOMATIC FOR THE PEOPLE	
			R.E.M. (Warner Bros.)
23	23	POCKET FULL OF KRYPTONITE	
			Spin Doctors (Epic)
24	24	IN UTERO	Nirvana (Geffen)
20	25	THE HITS 1	Prince (Paisley Park)
27	26	PROMISES AND LIES	UB40 (DEP International)
14	27	REAL	Belinda Carlisle (Offside)
26	28	THE ALBUM	Haddaway (Logic)
-	29	A DATE WITH DANIEL – LIVE	
			Daniel O'Donnell (Ritz)
28	30	4-TRACK DEMOS	P J Harvey (Island)
37	31	WHAT'S LOVE GOT TO DO WITH IT	
			Tina Turner (Parlophone)
-	32	TIME MACHINE	Joe Satriani (Relativity)
48	33	BAT OUT OF HELL	Meatloaf (Epic)
32	34	THE BEATLES 1962-1966	Beatles (Apple)
33	35	THE BEATLES 1967-1970	Beatles (Apple)
31	36	WILD WOOD	Paul Weller (Go! Discs)
-	37	THE BODYGUARD – SOUNDTRACK	
			Various Artists (Arista)
-	38	LIVE JAM	Jam (Polydor)
-	39	UNPLUGGED	10,000 Maniacs (Elektra)
29	40	LOVE SCENES	Beverley Craven (Epic)
34	41	CONSTRUCTION FOR THE MODERN IDIOT	
			Wonder Stuff (Polydor)
19	42	CHAOS AD	Sepultura (Roadrunner)
25	43	RETRO ACTIVE	
			Def Leppard (Bludgeon Riffola)
44	44	RIVER OF DREAMS	Billy Joel (Columbia)
-	45	I'M ALIVE	Jackson Browne (Elektra)
-	46	DREAM OF 100 NATIONS	
			Trans Global Underground (Nation)
42	47	LAID	James (Fontana)
-	48	FUNKY DIVAS	En Vogue (East West America)
-	49	THE LEVELLERS	Levellers (China)
35	50	ELEMENTS – THE BEST OF MIKE OLDFIELD	
			Mike Oldfield (Virgin)

last week	this week	13 November 1993	
-	1	THE RED SHOES	Kate Bush (EMI)
1	2	BAT OUT OF HELL II – BACK INTO HELL...	
			Meatloaf (Virgin)
-	3	FULL MOON, DIRTY HEARTS	INXS (Mercury)
6	4	EXPERIENCE THE DIVINE BETTE MIDLER	
			Bette Midler (Atlantic)
2	5	ONE WOMAN – THE ULTIMATE COLLECTION	
			Diana Ross (EMI)
-	6	ESPRESSO LOGIC	Chris Rea (East West)
4	7	DUETS	Frank Sinatra (Capitol)
3	8	EVERYTHING CHANGES	Take That (RCA)
7	9	SO CLOSE	Dina Carroll (A&M)
5	10	BANG!...THE GREATEST HITS	
			Frankie Goes To Hollywood (ZTT)
8	11	ELEGANT SLUMMING	
			M People (deConstruction)
10	12	TOGETHER ALONE	Crowded House (Capitol)
9	13	VS	Pearl Jam (Epic)
15	14	MUSIC BOX	Mariah Carey (Columbia)
-	15	GREATEST HITS	
			Tom Petty & the Heartbreakers (MCA)
21	16	BY REQUEST	Foster & Allen (Telstar)
-	17	RICK'S ROAD	Texas (Vertigo)
11	18	FIND YOUR WAY	Gabrielle (Go Beat)
14	19	DEBUT	Bjork (One Little Indian)
12	20	ACES AND KINGS – THE BEST OF GO WEST	
			Go West (Chrysalis)
-	21	A TOUCH OF MUSIC IN THE NIGHT	
			Michael Crawford (Telstar)
16	22	VERY	Pet Shop Boys (Parlophone)
13	23	COME ON FEEL THE LEMONHEADS	
			Lemonheads (Atlantic)
22	24	AUTOMATIC FOR THE PEOPLE	
			R.E.M. (Warner Bros.)
23	25	POCKET FULL OF KRYPTONITE	
			Spin Doctors (Epic)
33	26	BAT OUT OF HELL	Meatloaf (Epic)
-	27	THE BEST OF NANCI GRIFFITH	
			Nanci Griffith (MCA)
29	28	A DATE WITH DANIEL – LIVE	
			Daniel O'Donnell (Ritz)
20	29	THE HITS 2	Prince (Paisley Park)
37	30	THE BODYGUARD – SOUNDTRACK	
			Various Artists (Arista)
49	31	THE LEVELLERS	Levellers (China)
24	32	IN UTERO	Nirvana (Geffen)
17	33	COUNTERPARTS	Rush (Anthem)
31	34	WHAT'S LOVE GOT TO DO WITH IT	
			Tina Turner (Parlophone)
25	35	THE HITS 1	Prince (Paisley Park)
26	36	PROMISES AND LIES	UB40 (DEP International)
35	37	THE BEATLES 1967-1970	Beatles (Apple)
36	38	WILD WOOD	Paul Weller (Go! Discs)
34	39	THE BEATLES 1962-1966	Beatles (Apple)
19	40	A REAL DEAD ONE	Iron Maiden (EMI)
-	41	EVEN COWGIRLS GET THE BLUES	
			kd lang (Sire)
-	42	SEX AND TRAVEL	Right Said Fred (Tug)
39	43	UNPLUGGED	10,000 Maniacs (Elektra)
38	44	LIVE JAM	Jam (Polydor)
18	45	FOUR CALENDAR CAFE	
			Cocteau Twins (Fontana)
32	46	TIME MACHINE	Joe Satriani (Relativity)
45	47	I'M ALIVE	Jackson Browne (Elektra)
27	48	REAL	Belinda Carlisle (Offside)
28	49	THE ALBUM	Haddaway (Logic)
44	50	RIVER OF DREAMS	Billy Joel (Columbia)

Teen idol pop sensation Take That made it to the top of the album chart for the first time, while Kate Bush had been there before – but not for eight years. Frank Sinatra duetted with people who didn't even bother to come to the same studio – what a way to go. Down in the depths the original *Bat Out Of Hell* was a re-entry.

November – December 1993

20 November 1993

last	this		
-	1	BOTH SIDES	Phil Collins (Virgin)
-	2	SO FAR SO GOOD	Bryan Adams (A&M)
2	3	BAT OUT OF HELL II – BACK INTO HELL...	Meatloaf (Virgin)
-	4	END OF PART ONE – THEIR GREATEST HITS	Wet Wet Wet (Precious)
1	5	THE RED SHOES	Kate Bush (EMI)
-	6	SO NATURAL	Lisa Stansfield (Arista)
5	7	ONE WOMAN – THE ULTIMATE COLLECTION	Diana Ross (EMI)
8	8	EVERYTHING CHANGES	Take That (RCA)
9	9	SO CLOSE	Dina Carroll (A&M)
4	10	EXPERIENCE THE DIVINE BETTE MIDLER	Bette Midler (Atlantic)
-	11	THE SINGLES COLLECTION	David Bowie (EMI)
6	12	ESPRESSO LOGIC	Chris Rea (East West)
7	13	DUETS	Frank Sinatra (Capitol)
3	14	FULL MOON, DIRTY HEARTS	INXS (Mercury)
16	15	BY REQUEST	Foster & Allen (Telstar)
11	16	ELEGANT SLUMMING	M People (deConstruction)
15	17	GREATEST HITS	Tom Petty & the Heartbreakers (MCA)
12	18	TOGETHER ALONE	Crowded House (Capitol)
10	19	BANG!...THE GREATEST HITS	Frankie Goes To Hollywood (ZTT)
14	20	MUSIC BOX	Mariah Carey (Columbia)
13	21	VS	Pearl Jam (Epic)
-	22	THE HIT SINGLES COLLECTION	Doris Day (Telstar)
29	23	THE HITS 2	Prince (Paisley Park)
26	24	BAT OUT OF HELL	Meatloaf (Epic)
20	25	ACES AND KINGS – THE BEST OF GO WEST	Go West (Chrysalis)
24	26	AUTOMATIC FOR THE PEOPLE	R.E.M. (Warner Bros.)
23	27	COME ON FEEL THE LEMONHEADS	Lemonheads (Atlantic)
-	28	PAUL IS LIVE	Paul McCartney (Parlophone)
18	29	FIND YOUR WAY	Gabrielle (Go Beat)
22	30	VERY	Pet Shop Boys (Parlophone)
27	31	THE BEST OF NANCI GRIFFITH	Nanci Griffith (MCA)
25	32	POCKET FULL OF KRYPTONITE	Spin Doctors (Epic)
21	33	A TOUCH OF MUSIC IN THE NIGHT	Michael Crawford (Telstar)
17	34	RICK'S ROAD	Texas (Vertigo)
34	35	WHAT'S LOVE GOT TO DO WITH IT	Tina Turner (Parlophone)
28	36	A DATE WITH DANIEL – LIVE	Daniel O'Donnell (Ritz)
30	37	THE BODYGUARD - S'TRACK	Various (Arista)
19	38	DEBUT	Bjork (One Little Indian)
35	39	THE HITS 1	Prince (Paisley Park)
36	40	PROMISES AND LIES	UB40 (DEP International)
-	41	LIVE AT DONNINGTON AUGUST 22, 1993	Iron Maiden (EMI)
37	42	THE BEATLES 1967-1970	Beatles (Apple)
-	43	WORLD GONE WRONG	Bob Dylan (Columbia)
-	44	BLACK RIDER	Tom Waits (Island)
42	45	SEX AND TRAVEL	Right Said Fred (Tug)
-	46	REMASTERED – THE BEST OF STEELY DAN	Steely Dan (MCA)
-	47	THE BEST OF THE CHRISTIANS	Christians (Island)
39	48	THE BEATLES 1962-1966	Beatles (Apple)
38	49	WILD WOOD	Paul Weller (Go! Discs)
32	50	IN UTERO	Nirvana (Geffen)

27 November 1993

last	this		
1	1	BOTH SIDES	Phil Collins (Virgin)
2	2	SO FAR SO GOOD	Bryan Adams (A&M)
3	3	BAT OUT OF HELL II – BACK INTO HELL...	Meatloaf (Virgin)
-	4	THE ONE THING	Michael Bolton (Columbia)
7	5	ONE WOMAN – THE ULTIMATE COLLECTION	Diana Ross (EMI)
4	6	END OF PART ONE – THEIR GREATEST HITS	Wet Wet Wet (Precious)
9	7	SO CLOSE	Dina Carroll (A&M)
8	8	EVERYTHING CHANGES	Take That (RCA)
11	9	THE SINGLES COLLECTION	David Bowie (EMI)
5	10	THE RED SHOES	Kate Bush (EMI)
6	11	SO NATURAL	Lisa Stansfield (Arista)
10	12	EXPERIENCE THE DIVINE BETTE MIDLER	Bette Midler (Atlantic)
13	13	DUETS	Frank Sinatra (Capitol)
12	14	ESPRESSO LOGIC	Chris Rea (East West)
15	15	BY REQUEST	Foster & Allen (Telstar)
-	16	VOLUME 4 – THE CLASSIC SINGLES	Soul II Soul (Virgin)
38	17	DEBUT	Bjork (One Little Indian)
-	18	LIVE 1983-1989	Eurythmics (RCA)
20	19	MUSIC BOX	Mariah Carey (Columbia)
16	20	ELEGANT SLUMMING	M People (deConstruction)
22	21	THE HIT SINGLES COLLECTION	Doris Day (Telstar)
18	22	TOGETHER ALONE	Crowded House (Capitol)
17	23	GREATEST HITS	Tom Petty & the Heartbreakers (MCA)
19	24	BANG!...THE GREATEST HITS	Frankie Goes To Hollywood (ZTT)
47	25	THE BEST OF THE CHRISTIANS	Christians (Island)
23	26	THE HITS 2	Prince (Paisley Park)
28	27	PAUL IS LIVE	Paul McCartney (Parlophone)
-	28	HEARTBEAT	Hank Marvin (PolyGram TV)
14	29	FULL MOON, DIRTY HEARTS	INXS (Mercury)
25	30	ACES AND KINGS – THE BEST OF GO WEST	Go West (Chrysalis)
-	31	THE PLATINUM COLLECTION	Barry Manilow (Arista)
21	32	VS	Pearl Jam (Epic)
24	33	BAT OUT OF HELL	Meatloaf (Epic)
26	34	AUTOMATIC FOR THE PEOPLE	R.E.M. (Warner Bros.)
37	35	THE BODYGUARD - S'TRACK	Various (Arista)
39	36	THE HITS 1	Prince (Paisley Park)
31	37	THE BEST OF NANCI GRIFFITH	Nanci Griffith (MCA)
27	38	COME ON FEEL THE LEMONHEADS	Lemonheads (Atlantic)
30	39	VERY	Pet Shop Boys (Parlophone)
32	40	POCKET FULL OF KRYPTONITE	Spin Doctors (Epic)
35	41	WHAT'S LOVE GOT TO DO WITH IT	Tina Turner (Parlophone)
-	42	HATFUL OF STARS	Cyndi Lauper (Epic)
46	43	REMASTERED – THE BEST OF..	Steely Dan (MCA)
-	44	JAMES LAST PLAYS ANDREW LLOYD WEBBER	James Last (Polydor)
36	45	A DATE WITH DANIEL – LIVE	Daniel O'Donnell (Ritz)
48	46	THE BEATLES 1962-1966	Beatles (Apple)
33	47	A TOUCH OF MUSIC IN THE NIGHT	Michael Crawford (Telstar)
-	48	RIVER OF DREAMS	Billy Joel (Columbia)
42	49	THE BEATLES 1967-1970	Beatles (Apple)
40	50	PROMISES AND LIES	UB40 (DEP International)

4 December 1993

last	this		
-	1	THE SPAGHETTI INCIDENT?	Guns N' Roses (Geffen)
3	2	BAT OUT OF HELL II – BACK INTO HELL...	Meatloaf (Virgin)
2	3	SO FAR SO GOOD	Bryan Adams (A&M)
1	4	BOTH SIDES	Phil Collins (Virgin)
-	5	DUETS	Elton John (Rocket)
4	6	THE ONE THING	Michael Bolton (Columbia)
5	7	ONE WOMAN – THE ULTIMATE COLLECTION	Diana Ross (EMI)
8	8	EVERYTHING CHANGES	Take That (RCA)
7	9	SO CLOSE	Dina Carroll (A&M)
10	10	THE RED SHOES	Kate Bush (EMI)
6	11	END OF PART ONE – THEIR GREATEST HITS	Wet Wet Wet (Precious)
19	12	MUSIC BOX	Mariah Carey (Columbia)
9	13	THE SINGLES COLLECTION	David Bowie (EMI)
12	14	EXPERIENCE THE DIVINE BETTE MIDLER	Bette Midler (Atlantic)
13	15	DUETS	Frank Sinatra (Capitol)
17	16	DEBUT	Bjork (One Little Indian)
11	17	SO NATURAL	Lisa Stansfield (Arista)
16	18	VOLUME 4 – THE CLASSIC SINGLES	Soul II Soul (Virgin)
15	19	BY REQUEST	Foster & Allen (Telstar)
14	20	ESPRESSO LOGIC	Chris Rea (East West)
21	21	THE HIT SINGLES	Doris Day (Telstar)
44	22	JAMES LAST PLAYS ANDREW LLOYD WEBBER	James Last (Polydor)
-	23	LIVE 93	Orb (Island)
24	24	BANG!...THE GREATEST HITS	Frankie Goes To Hollywood (ZTT)
18	25	LIVE 1983-1989	Eurythmics (RCA)
20	26	ELEGANT SLUMMING	M People (deConstruction)
28	27	HEARTBEAT	Hank Marvin (PolyGram TV)
23	28	GREATEST HITS	Tom Petty & the Heartbreakers (MCA)
-	29	JUMP BACK – THE BEST OF THE ROLLING STONES 1971-1993	Rolling Stones (Virgin)
22	30	TOGETHER ALONE	Crowded House (Capitol)
25	31	THE BEST OF THE CHRISTIANS	Christians (Island)
26	32	THE HITS 2	Prince (Paisley Park)
32	33	VS	Pearl Jam (Epic)
30	34	ACES AND KINGS – THE BEST OF GO WEST	Go West (Chrysalis)
47	35	A TOUCH OF MUSIC IN THE NIGHT	Michael Crawford (Telstar)
29	36	FULL MOON, DIRTY HEARTS	INXS (Mercury)
35	37	THE BODYGUARD - S'TRACK	Various (Arista)
45	38	A DATE WITH DANIEL – LIVE	Daniel O'Donnell (Ritz)
48	39	RIVER OF DREAMS	Billy Joel (Columbia)
-	40	YOU NEED A MESS OF HELP TO STAND ALONE	Saint Etienne (Heavenly)
36	41	THE HITS 1	Prince (Paisley Park)
31	42	THE PLATINUM COLLECTION	Barry Manilow (Arista)
33	43	BAT OUT OF HELL	Meatloaf (Epic)
34	44	AUTOMATIC FOR THE PEOPLE	R.E.M. (Warner Bros.)
-	45	LOVE SCENES	Beverley Craven (Epic)
43	46	REMASTERED – THE BEST OF STEELY DAN	Steely Dan (MCA)
-	47	MIDNIGHT POSTCARDS	Adam Faith (PolyGram TV)
46	48	THE BEATLES 1962-1966	Beatles (Apple)
38	49	COME ON FEEL THE LEMONHEADS	Lemonheads (Atlantic)
-	50	GRAVE DANCERS UNION	Soul Asylum (Columbia)

Just when you thought it was safe here comes Phil Collins again. His first album for three years, but they have a habit of staying in the chart. Now Elton John is singing duets too – money for old rope really. Nice to see Doris Day back – at least she really did have some hit singles. Is it Christmas shopping time?

418

December 1993

11 December 1993

last week	this week	Title	Artist
2	1	BAT OUT OF HELL II – BACK INTO HELL...	Meatloaf (Virgin)
3	2	SO FAR SO GOOD	Bryan Adams (A&M)
4	3	BOTH SIDES	Phil Collins (Virgin)
5	4	DUETS	Elton John (Rocket)
6	5	THE ONE THING	Michael Bolton (Columbia)
8	6	EVERYTHING CHANGES	Take That (RCA)
7	7	ONE WOMAN – THE ULTIMATE COLLECTION	Diana Ross (EMI)
1	8	THE SPAGHETTI INCIDENT?	Guns N' Roses (Geffen)
12	9	MUSIC BOX	Mariah Carey (Columbia)
9	10	SO CLOSE	Dina Carroll (A&M)
11	11	END OF PART ONE – THEIR GREATEST HITS	Wet Wet Wet (Precious)
35	12	A TOUCH OF MUSIC IN THE NIGHT	Michael Crawford (Telstar)
10	13	THE RED SHOES	Kate Bush (EMI)
14	14	EXPERIENCE THE DIVINE BETTE MIDLER	Bette Midler (Atlantic)
29	15	JUMP BACK – THE BEST OF THE ROLLING STONES 1971-1993	Rolling Stones (Virgin)
18	16	VOLUME 4 – THE CLASSIC SINGLES	Soul II Soul (Virgin)
13	17	THE SINGLES COLLECTION	David Bowie (EMI)
15	18	DUETS	Frank Sinatra (Capitol)
21	19	THE HIT SINGLES	Doris Day (Telstar)
17	20	SO NATURAL	Lisa Stansfield (Arista)
19	21	BY REQUEST	Foster & Allen (Telstar)
16	22	DEBUT	Bjork (One Little Indian)
22	23	JAMES LAST PLAYS ANDREW LLOYD WEBBER	James Last (Polydor)
24	24	BANG!...THE GREATEST HITS	Frankie Goes To Hollywood (ZTT)
20	25	ESPRESSO LOGIC	Chris Rea (East West)
26	26	ELEGANT SLUMMING	M People (deConstruction)
27	27	HEARTBEAT	Hank Marvin (PolyGram TV)
37	28	THE BODYGUARD - SOUNDTRACK	Various Artists (Arista)
28	29	GREATEST HITS	Tom Petty & the Heartbreakers (MCA)
30	30	RIVER OF DREAMS	Billy Joel (Columbia)
25	31	LIVE 1983-1989	Eurythmics (RCA)
32	32	TOGETHER ALONE	Crowded House (Capitol)
-	33	DESIRE WALKS ON	Heart (Capitol)
38	34	A DATE WITH DANIEL – LIVE	Daniel O'Donnell (Ritz)
31	35	THE BEST OF THE CHRISTIANS	Christians (Island)
-	36	PROMISES AND LIES	UB40 (DEP International)
32	37	THE HITS 2	Prince (Paisley Park)
42	38	THE PLATINUM COLLECTION	Barry Manilow (Arista)
41	39	THE HITS 1	Prince (Paisley Park)
33	40	VS	Pearl Jam (Epic)
-	41	DOGGY STYLE	Snoop Doggy Dogg (Death Row)
-	42	CODE RED	Jazzy Jeff & the Fresh Prince (Jive)
-	43	ALWAYS AND FOREVER	Eternal (EMI)
34	44	ACES AND KINGS – THE BEST OF GO WEST	Go West (Chrysalis)
-	45	THE BEST OF THE VILLAGE PEOPLE	Village People
36	46	FULL MOON, DIRTY HEARTS	INXS (Mercury)
23	47	LIVE 93	Orb (Island)
43	48	BAT OUT OF HELL	Meatloaf (Epic)
-	49	JANET	Janet Jackson (Virgin)
-	50	THE OTHER TWO AND YOU	The Other Two (Centredate)

18 December 1993

last	this	Title	Artist
1	1	BAT OUT OF HELL II – BACK INTO HELL...	Meatloaf (Virgin)
2	2	SO FAR SO GOOD	Bryan Adams (A&M)
6	3	EVERYTHING CHANGES	Take That (RCA)
3	4	BOTH SIDES	Phil Collins (Virgin)
7	5	ONE WOMAN – THE ULTIMATE COLLECTION	Diana Ross (EMI)
4	6	DUETS	Elton John (Rocket)
5	7	THE ONE THING	Michael Bolton (Columbia)
10	8	SO CLOSE	Dina Carroll (A&M)
9	9	MUSIC BOX	Mariah Carey (Columbia)
14	10	EXPERIENCE THE DIVINE BETTE MIDLER	Bette Midler (Atlantic)
11	11	END OF PART ONE – THEIR GREATEST HITS	Wet Wet Wet (Precious)
12	12	A TOUCH OF MUSIC IN THE NIGHT	Michael Crawford (Telstar)
18	13	DUETS	Frank Sinatra (Capitol)
16	14	VOLUME 4 – THE CLASSIC SINGLES	Soul II Soul (Virgin)
23	15	JAMES LAST PLAYS ANDREW LLOYD WEBBER	James Last (Polydor)
13	16	THE RED SHOES	Kate Bush (EMI)
8	17	THE SPAGHETTI INCIDENT?	Guns N' Roses (Geffen)
21	18	BY REQUEST	Foster & Allen (Telstar)
20	19	SO NATURAL	Lisa Stansfield (Arista)
26	20	ELEGANT SLUMMING	M People (deConstruction)
15	21	JUMP BACK – THE BEST OF THE ROLLING STONES 1971-1993	Rolling Stones (Virgin)
17	22	THE SINGLES COLLECTION	David Bowie (EMI)
19	23	THE HIT SINGLES	Doris Day (Telstar)
22	24	DEBUT	Bjork (One Little Indian)
24	25	BANG!...THE GREATEST HITS	Frankie Goes To Hollywood (ZTT)
28	26	THE BODYGUARD - SOUNDTRACK	Various Artists (Arista)
27	27	HEARTBEAT	Hank Marvin (PolyGram TV)
49	28	JANET	Janet Jackson (Virgin)
36	29	PROMISES AND LIES	UB40 (DEP International)
30	30	RIVER OF DREAMS	Billy Joel (Columbia)
35	31	THE BEST OF THE CHRISTIANS	Christians (Island)
29	32	GREATEST HITS	Tom Petty & the Heartbreakers (MCA)
25	33	ESPRESSO LOGIC	Chris Rea (East West)
32	34	TOGETHER ALONE	Crowded House (Capitol)
44	35	ACES AND KINGS – THE BEST OF GO WEST	Go West (Chrysalis)
34	36	A DATE WITH DANIEL – LIVE	Daniel O'Donnell (Ritz)
43	37	ALWAYS AND FOREVER	Eternal (EMI)
37	38	THE HITS 2	Prince (Paisley Park)
39	39	THE HITS 1	Prince (Paisley Park)
-	40	SONGS OF FAITH AND DEVOTION	Depeche Mode (Mute)
33	41	DESIRE WALKS ON	Heart (Capitol)
41	42	DOGGY STYLE	Snoop Doggy Dogg (Death Row)
31	43	LIVE 1983-1989	Eurythmics (RCA)
-	44	A GIFT OF LOVE	Bill Tarney (EMI)
38	45	THE PLATINUM COLLECTION	Barry Manilow (Arista)
-	46	VERY	Pet Shop Boys (Parlophone)
48	47	BAT OUT OF HELL	Meatloaf (Epic)
40	48	VS	Pearl Jam (Epic)
-	49	AUTOMATIC FOR THE PEOPLE	R.E.M. (Warner Bros.)
-	50	THE BEATLES 1962-1966	Beatles (Apple)

25 December 1993

last	this	Title	Artist
1	1	BAT OUT OF HELL II – BACK INTO HELL...	Meatloaf (Virgin)
2	2	SO FAR SO GOOD	Bryan Adams (A&M)
5	3	ONE WOMAN – THE ULTIMATE COLLECTION	Diana Ross (EMI)
3	4	EVERYTHING CHANGES	Take That (RCA)
6	5	DUETS	Elton John (Rocket)
8	6	SO CLOSE	Dina Carroll (A&M)
4	7	BOTH SIDES	Phil Collins (Virgin)
7	8	THE ONE THING	Michael Bolton (Columbia)
9	9	MUSIC BOX	Mariah Carey (Columbia)
10	10	EXPERIENCE THE DIVINE BETTE MIDLER	Bette Midler (Atlantic)
11	11	END OF PART ONE – THEIR GREATEST HITS	Wet Wet Wet (Precious)
12	12	A TOUCH OF MUSIC IN THE NIGHT	Michael Crawford (Telstar)
15	13	JAMES LAST PLAYS ANDREW LLOYD WEBBER	James Last (Polydor)
13	14	DUETS	Frank Sinatra (Capitol)
20	15	ELEGANT SLUMMING	M People (deConstruction)
19	16	SO NATURAL	Lisa Stansfield (Arista)
14	17	VOLUME 4 – THE CLASSIC SINGLES	Soul II Soul (Virgin)
16	18	THE RED SHOES	Kate Bush (EMI)
21	19	JUMP BACK – THE BEST OF THE ROLLING STONES 1971-1993	Rolling Stones (Virgin)
17	20	THE SPAGHETTI INCIDENT?	Guns N' Roses (Geffen)
18	21	BY REQUEST	Foster & Allen (Telstar)
27	22	HEARTBEAT	Hank Marvin (PolyGram TV)
23	23	THE HIT SINGLES	Doris Day (Telstar)
24	24	DEBUT	Bjork (One Little Indian)
22	25	THE SINGLES COLLECTION	David Bowie (EMI)
26	26	THE BODYGUARD - SOUNDTRACK	Various Artists (Arista)
-	27	SIZE ISN'T EVERYTHING	Bee Gees (Polydor)
29	28	PROMISES AND LIES	UB40 (DEP International)
28	29	JANET	Janet Jackson (Virgin)
30	30	RIVER OF DREAMS	Billy Joel (Columbia)
44	31	A GIFT OF LOVE	Bill Tarney (EMI)
25	32	BANG!...THE GREATEST HITS	Frankie Goes To Hollywood (ZTT)
35	33	ACES AND KINGS – THE BEST OF GO WEST	Go West (Chrysalis)
46	34	VERY	Pet Shop Boys (Parlophone)
33	35	ESPRESSO LOGIC	Chris Rea (East West)
38	36	THE HITS 2	Prince (Paisley Park)
37	37	THE BEST OF THE CHRISTIANS	Christians (Island)
39	38	THE HITS 1	Prince (Paisley Park)
-	39	FIND YOUR WAY	Gabrielle (Go Beat)
34	40	TOGETHER ALONE	Crowded House (Capitol)
47	41	BAT OUT OF HELL	Meatloaf (Epic)
-	42	WALTHAMSTOW	East 17 (London)
50	43	THE BEATLES 1962-1966	Beatles (Apple)
37	44	ALWAYS AND FOREVER	Eternal (EMI)
36	45	A DATE WITH DANIEL – LIVE	Daniel O'Donnell (Ritz)
-	46	THE BEATLES 1967-1970	Beatles (Apple)
32	47	GREATEST HITS	Tom Petty & the Heartbreakers (MCA)
-	48	WHAT'S LOVE GOT TO DO WITH IT	Tina Turner (Parlophone)
45	49	THE PLATINUM COLLECTION	Barry Manilow (Arista)
40	50	SONGS OF FAITH AND DEVOTION	Depeche Mode (Mute)

Slightly slimmer, but still big enough, Meatloaf had the best-selling single too in 1993 with *I'll Do Anything For Love (But I Won't Do That)*. The Beatles, REM and UB40 all came back in for the festive market. Elsewhere *James Last Plays Andrew Lloyd Webber* – the nightmare continues.

419

January 1994

The soundtrack of the movie *The Bodyguard* featuring Whitney Houston as a singer just like, well, Whitney Houston was second only to Meatloaf in the previous year's overall album stakes. There were to be some long stayers in 1994, chief among them Mariah Carey's *Music Box* – in the Top 50 for the whole year.

February 1994

5 February 1994

last week	this week		
1	1	TEASE ME	Chaka Demus & Pliers (Mango)
-	2	JAR OF FLIES	Alice In Chains (Columbia)
3	3	ONE WOMAN – THE ULTIMATE COLLECTION	Diana Ross (EMI)
-	4	ANTENNA	ZZ Top (RCA)
-	5	D:REAM ON VOL 1	D:Ream (Magnet)
5	6	DEBUT	Bjork (One Little Indian)
2	7	SO CLOSE	Dina Carroll (A&M)
4	8	SO FAR SO GOOD	Bryan Adams (A&M)
6	9	ELEGANT SLUMMING	M People (deConstruction)
9	10	MUSIC BOX	Mariah Carey (Columbia)
-	11	HIPS AND MAKERS	Kristin Hersh (4AD)
-	12	DUB NO BASS WITH MY HEAD MAN	Underworld (Junior Boy's Own)
8	13	BOTH SIDES	Phil Collins (Virgin)
7	14	EVERYTHING CHANGES	Take That (RCA)
10	15	BAT OUT OF HELL II – BACK INTO HELL...	Meatloaf (Virgin)
13	16	ALWAYS AND FOREVER	Eternal (EMI)
17	17	INGENUE	kd lang (Sire)
15	18	PROMISES AND LIES	UB40 (DEP International)
50	19	SERENITY	Culture Beat (Epic)
12	20	THE BODYGUARD - SOUNDTRACK	Various Artists (Arista)
18	21	DUETS	Elton John (Rocket)
16	22	THE ONE THING	Michael Bolton (Columbia)
11	23	END OF PART ONE – THEIR GREATEST HITS	Wet Wet Wet (Precious)
14	24	BAT OUT OF HELL	Meatloaf (Epic)
21	25	THE RED SHOES	Kate Bush (EMI)
22	26	WALTHAMSTOW	East 17 (London)
19	27	AUTOMATIC FOR THE PEOPLE	REM (Warner Bros.)
36	28	GRAVE DANCERS UNION	Soul Asylum (Columbia)
-	29	TONI BRAXTON	Toni Braxton (Arista)
20	30	BLACK SUNDAY	Cypress Hill (Ruff House)
-	31	THOUGHT YA KNEW	Ce Ce Peniston (A&M)
25	32	VS	Pearl Jam (Epic)
-	33	SWING BATTA SWING	K7 (Big Life)
37	34	FIND YOUR WAY	Gabrielle (Go Beat)
28	35	MIRROR BLUE	Richard Thompson (Capitol)
23	36	JUMP BACK – THE BEST OF THE ROLLING STONES 1971-1993	Rolling Stones (Virgin)
-	37	THE ALBUM	Haddaway (Logic)
24	38	VOLUME 4 – THE CLASSIC SINGLES	Soul II Soul (Virgin)
31	39	STARS	Simply Red (East West)
32	40	JANET	Janet Jackson (Virgin)
29	41	THE SPAGHETTI INCIDENT?	Guns N' Roses
26	42	SO NATURAL	Lisa Stansfield (Arista)
27	43	ZOOROPA	U2 (Island)
43	44	THE BEATLES 1962-1966	Beatles (Apple)
30	45	THE HITS 2	Prince (Paisley Park)
35	46	SIZE ISN'T EVERYTHING	Bee Gees (Polydor)
47	47	THE BEATLES 1967-1970	Beatles (Apple)
40	48	DIRTY DANCING – SOUNDTRACK	Various Artists (RCA)
38	49	TEN SUMMONER'S TALES	Sting (A&M)
34	50	THE HITS 1	Prince (Paisley Park)

12 February 1994

last week	this week		
-	1	UNDER THE PINK	Tori Amos (East West)
1	2	TEASE ME	Chaka Demus & Pliers (Mango)
3	3	ONE WOMAN – THE ULTIMATE COLLECTION	Diana Ross (EMI)
4	4	IN PIECES	Garth Brooks (Liberty)
5	5	D:REAM ON VOL 1	D:Ream (Magnet)
13	6	BOTH SIDES	Phil Collins (Virgin)
8	7	SO FAR SO GOOD	Bryan Adams (A&M)
9	8	ELEGANT SLUMMING	M People (deConstruction)
4	9	ANTENNA	ZZ Top (RCA)
7	10	SO CLOSE	Dina Carroll (A&M)
2	11	JAR OF FLIES	Alice In Chains (Columbia)
6	12	DEBUT	Bjork (One Little Indian)
10	13	MUSIC BOX	Mariah Carey (Columbia)
15	14	BAT OUT OF HELL II – BACK INTO HELL...	Meatloaf (Virgin)
18	15	PROMISES AND LIES	UB40 (DEP International)
14	16	EVERYTHING CHANGES	Take That (RCA)
19	17	SERENITY	Culture Beat (Epic)
17	18	INGENUE	kd lang (Sire)
16	19	ALWAYS AND FOREVER	Eternal (EMI)
20	20	THE BODYGUARD - SOUNDTRACK	Various Artists (Arista)
29	21	TONI BRAXTON	Toni Braxton (Arista)
21	22	DUETS	Elton John (Rocket)
23	23	END OF PART ONE – THEIR GREATEST HITS	Wet Wet Wet (Precious)
24	24	BAT OUT OF HELL	Meatloaf (Epic)
22	25	THE ONE THING	Michael Bolton (Columbia)
11	26	HIPS AND MAKERS	Kristin Hersh (4AD)
12	27	DUB NO BASS WITH MY HEAD MAN	Underworld (Junior Boy's Own)
25	28	THE RED SHOES	Kate Bush (EMI)
46	29	SIZE ISN'T EVERYTHING	Bee Gees (Polydor)
26	30	WALTHAMSTOW	East 17 (London)
33	31	SWING BATTA SWING	K7 (Big Life)
27	32	AUTOMATIC FOR THE PEOPLE	REM (Warner Bros.)
32	33	VS	Pearl Jam (Epic)
28	34	GRAVE DANCERS UNION	Soul Asylum (Columbia)
30	35	BLACK SUNDAY	Cypress Hill (Ruff House)
37	36	HADDAWAY – THE ALBUM	Haddaway (Logic)
31	37	THOUGHT YA KNEW	Ce Ce Peniston (A&M)
-	38	TOGETHER ALONE	Crowded House (Capitol)
-	39	SHIRLEY BASSEY SINGS ANDREW LLOYD WEBBER	Shirley Bassey (Premier)
36	40	JUMP BACK – THE BEST OF THE ROLLING STONES 1971-1993	Rolling Stones (Virgin)
34	41	FIND YOUR WAY	Gabrielle (Go Beat)
40	42	JANET	Janet Jackson (Virgin)
38	43	VOLUME 4 – THE CLASSIC SINGLES	Soul II Soul (Virgin)
-	44	BREATHLESS	Kenny G (Arista)
-	45	ALADDIN – SOUNDTRACK	Various Artists (Pickwick)
-	46	THE LESLEY GARRETT ALBUM	Lesley Garrett (Telstar)
41	47	THE SPAGHETTI INCIDENT?	Guns N' Roses
35	48	MIRROR BLUE	Richard Thompson (Capitol)
39	49	STARS	Simply Red (East West)
-	50	WAYNE'S WORLD 2 – SOUNDTRACK	Various Artists (Reprise)

19 February 1994

last week	this week		
-	1	THE CROSS OF CHANGES	Enigma (Virgin)
1	2	UNDER THE PINK	Tori Amos (East West)
4	3	IN PIECES	Garth Brooks (Liberty)
2	4	TEASE ME	Chaka Demus & Pliers (Mango)
13	5	MUSIC BOX	Mariah Carey (Columbia)
-	6	TROUBLEGUM	Therapy? (A&M)
3	7	ONE WOMAN – THE ULTIMATE COLLECTION	Diana Ross (EMI)
7	8	SO FAR SO GOOD	Bryan Adams (A&M)
8	9	ELEGANT SLUMMING	M People (deConstruction)
-	10	BRAVE	Marillion (EMI)
5	11	D:REAM ON VOL 1	D:Ream (Magnet)
10	12	SO CLOSE	Dina Carroll (A&M)
-	13	PAID VACATION	Richard Marx (Capitol)
-	14	LIVE AT THE BRIXTON ACADEMY	Brian May Band (Parlophone)
14	15	BAT OUT OF HELL II – BACK INTO HELL...	Meatloaf (Virgin)
6	16	BOTH SIDES	Phil Collins (Virgin)
21	17	TONI BRAXTON	Toni Braxton (Arista)
12	18	DEBUT	Bjork (One Little Indian)
17	19	SERENITY	Culture Beat (Epic)
-	20	JUST TO LET YOU KNOW	Bitty McLean (Brillian)
9	21	ANTENNA	ZZ Top (RCA)
16	22	EVERYTHING CHANGES	Take That (RCA)
15	23	PROMISES AND LIES	UB40 (DEP International)
19	24	ALWAYS AND FOREVER	Eternal (EMI)
18	25	INGENUE	kd lang (Sire)
24	26	BAT OUT OF HELL	Meatloaf (Epic)
20	27	THE BODYGUARD - SOUNDTRACK	Various Artists (Arista)
23	28	END OF PART ONE – THEIR GREATEST HITS	Wet Wet Wet (Precious)
-	29	SOFTLY WITH THESE SONGS – THE BEST OF ROBERTA FLACK	Roberta Flack (Atlantic)
38	30	TOGETHER ALONE	Crowded House (Capitol)
22	31	DUETS	Elton John (Rocket)
32	32	AUTOMATIC FOR THE PEOPLE	REM (Warner Bros.)
-	33	PAULINE	Pauline Henry (Sony Soho Square)
11	34	JAR OF FLIES	Alice In Chains (Columbia)
44	35	BREATHLESS	Kenny G (Arista)
25	36	THE ONE THING	Michael Bolton (Columbia)
29	37	SIZE ISN'T EVERYTHING	Bee Gees (Polydor)
26	38	HIPS AND MAKERS	Kristin Hersh (4AD)
31	39	SWING BATTA SWING	K7 (Big Life)
34	40	GRAVE DANCERS UNION	Soul Asylum (Columbia)
33	41	VS	Pearl Jam (Epic)
28	42	THE RED SHOES	Kate Bush (EMI)
30	43	WALTHAMSTOW	East 17 (London)
35	44	BLACK SUNDAY	Cypress Hill (Ruff House)
40	45	JUMP BACK – THE BEST OF THE ROLLING STONES 1971-1993	Rolling Stones (Virgin)
46	46	THE LESLEY GARRETT ALBUM	Lesley Garrett (Telstar)
-	47	THE HEART OF CHICAGO	Chicago (Reprise)
-	48	SUM AND SUBSTANCE	Mission (Vertigo)
50	49	WAYNE'S WORLD 2 – SOUNDTRACK	Various Artists (Reprise)
-	50	TUESDAY NIGHT MUSIC CLUB	Sheryl Crow (A&M)

More albums entering the chart at Number One – evidence of massive advance publicity or a fragmented market? But these weren't necessarily the biggest sellers. A relief from the Greatest Hits Collections post-Christmas, but Roberta Flack entered in February and the Rolling Stones lingered on.

February – March 1994

26 February 1994

last week	this week	title	artist (label)
1	1	THE CROSS OF CHANGES	Enigma (Virgin)
5	2	MUSIC BOX	Mariah Carey (Columbia)
12	3	SO CLOSE	Dina Carroll (A&M)
2	4	UNDER THE PINK	Tori Amos (East West)
18	5	DEBUT	Bjork (One Little Indian)
15	6	BAT OUT OF HELL II – BACK INTO HELL...	Meatloaf (Virgin)
4	7	TEASE ME	Chaka Demus & Pliers (Mango)
9	8	ELEGANT SLUMMING	M People (deConstruction)
3	9	IN PIECES	Garth Brooks (Liberty)
7	10	ONE WOMAN – THE ULTIMATE COLLECTION	Diana Ross (EMI)
29	11	SOFTLY WITH THESE SONGS – THE BEST OF ROBERTA FLACK	Roberta Flack (Atlantic)
47	12	THE HEART OF CHICAGO	Chicago (Reprise)
22	13	EVERYTHING CHANGES	Take That (RCA)
8	14	SO FAR SO GOOD	Bryan Adams (A&M)
6	15	TROUBLEGUM	Therapy? (A&M)
-	16	DEEP FOREST	Deep Forest (Columbia)
13	17	PAID VACATION	Richard Marx (Capitol)
-	18	CROOKED RAIN CROOKED RAIN	Pavement (Big Cat)
16	19	BOTH SIDES	Phil Collins (Virgin)
19	20	SERENITY	Culture Beat (Epic)
26	21	BAT OUT OF HELL	Meatloaf (Epic)
-	22	TEN SUMMONER'S TALES	Sting (A&M)
17	23	TONI BRAXTON	Toni Braxton (Arista)
10	24	BRAVE	Marillion (EMI)
-	25	CONNECTED	Stereo MCs (4th & Broadway)
30	26	TOGETHER ALONE	Crowded House (Capitol)
31	27	DUETS	Elton John (Rocket)
11	28	D:REAM ON VOL 1	D:Ream (Magnet)
20	29	JUST TO LET YOU KNOW	Bitty McLean (Brilliant)
24	30	ALWAYS AND FOREVER	Eternal (EMI)
-	31	WHAT SILENCE KNOWS	Shara Nelson (Cooltempo)
14	32	LIVE AT THE BRIXTON ACADEMY	Brian May Band (Parlophone)
27	33	THE BODYGUARD - SOUNDTRACK	Various Artists (Arista)
-	34	THE BEST OF VAN MORRISON	Van Morrison (Polydor)
36	35	THE ONE THING	Michael Bolton (Columbia)
32	36	AUTOMATIC FOR THE PEOPLE	REM (Warner Bros.)
23	37	PROMISES AND LIES	UB40 (DEP International)
-	38	EMERGENCY ON PLANET EARTH	Jamiroquai (Sony Soho Square)
28	39	END OF PART ONE – THEIR GREATEST HITS	Wet Wet Wet (Precious)
-	40	WOODFACE	Crowded House (Capitol)
25	41	INGENUE	kd lang (Sire)
-	42	FIND YOUR WAY	Gabrielle (Go Beat)
21	43	ANTENNA	ZZ Top (RCA)
35	44	BREATHLESS	Kenny G (Arista)
46	45	THE LESLEY GARRETT ALBUM	Lesley Garrett (Telstar)
-	46	VERY	Pet Shop Boys (Parlophone)
49	47	WAYNE'S WORLD 2 - SOUNDTRACK	Various Artists (Reprise)
44	48	BLACK SUNDAY	Cypress Hill (Ruff House)
-	49	A GIFT OF LOVE	Bill Tarney (EMI)
-	50	THE COLLECTION	Barry White (PolyGram TV)

5 March 1994

last week	this week	title	artist (label)
2	1	MUSIC BOX	Mariah Carey (Columbia)
1	2	THE CROSS OF CHANGES	Enigma (Virgin)
3	3	SO CLOSE	Dina Carroll (A&M)
5	4	DEBUT	Bjork (One Little Indian)
6	5	BAT OUT OF HELL II – BACK INTO HELL...	Meatloaf (Virgin)
4	6	UNDER THE PINK	Tori Amos (East West)
8	7	ELEGANT SLUMMING	M People (deConstruction)
7	8	TEASE ME	Chaka Demus & Pliers (Mango)
22	9	TEN SUMMONER'S TALES	Sting (A&M)
25	10	CONNECTED	Stereo MCs (4th & Broadway)
13	11	EVERYTHING CHANGES	Take That (RCA)
12	12	THE HEART OF CHICAGO	Chicago (Reprise)
26	13	TOGETHER ALONE	Crowded House (Capitol)
11	14	SOFTLY WITH THESE SONGS – THE BEST OF ROBERTA FLACK	Roberta Flack (Atlantic)
10	15	ONE WOMAN – THE ULTIMATE COLLECTION	Diana Ross (EMI)
16	16	DEEP FOREST	Deep Forest (Columbia)
-	17	THE COLOUR OF MY LOVE	Celine Dion (Epic)
9	18	IN PIECES	Garth Brooks (Liberty)
14	19	SO FAR SO GOOD	Bryan Adams (A&M)
34	20	THE BEST OF VAN MORRISON	Van Morrison (Polydor)
17	21	PAID VACATION	Richard Marx (Capitol)
15	22	TROUBLEGUM	Therapy? (A&M)
23	23	TONI BRAXTON	Toni Braxton (Arista)
19	24	BOTH SIDES	Phil Collins (Virgin)
20	25	SERENITY	Culture Beat (Epic)
18	26	CROOKED RAIN CROOKED RAIN	Pavement (Big Cat)
21	27	BAT OUT OF HELL	Meatloaf (Epic)
28	28	D:REAM ON VOL 1	D:Ream (Magnet)
27	29	DUETS	Elton John (Rocket)
42	30	FIND YOUR WAY	Gabrielle (Go Beat)
48	31	BLACK SUNDAY	Cypress Hill (Ruff House)
31	32	WHAT SILENCE KNOWS	Shara Nelson (Cooltempo)
38	33	EMERGENCY ON PLANET EARTH	Jamiroquai (Sony Soho Square)
33	34	THE BODYGUARD - SOUNDTRACK	Various Artists (Arista)
24	35	BRAVE	Marillion (EMI)
41	36	INGENUE	kd lang (Sire)
30	37	ALWAYS AND FOREVER	Eternal (EMI)
35	38	THE ONE THING	Michael Bolton (Columbia)
37	39	PROMISES AND LIES	UB40 (DEP International)
36	40	AUTOMATIC FOR THE PEOPLE	REM (Warner Bros.)
-	41	SUEDE	Suede (Nude)
29	42	JUST TO LET YOU KNOW	Bitty McLean (Brillian)
46	43	VERY	Pet Shop Boys (Parlophone)
-	44	DOGGYSTYLE	Snoop Doggy Dogg (Death Row)
45	45	THE LESLEY GARRETT ALBUM	Lesley Garrett (Telstar)
40	46	WOODFACE	Crowded House (Capitol)
-	47	KEEP THE FAITH	Bon Jovi (Jambco)
39	48	END OF PART ONE – THEIR GREATEST HITS	Wet Wet Wet (Precious)
-	49	HITS OUT OF HELL	Meatloaf (Epic)
32	50	LIVE AT THE BRIXTON ACADEMY	Brian May Band (Parlophone)

12 March 1994

last week	this week	title	artist (label)
1	1	MUSIC BOX	Mariah Carey (Columbia)
2	2	THE CROSS OF CHANGES	Enigma (Virgin)
4	3	DEBUT	Bjork (One Little Indian)
-	4	EVERYBODY ELSE IS DOING IT, SO WHY CAN'T WE	Cranberries (Island)
3	5	SO CLOSE	Dina Carroll (A&M)
5	6	BAT OUT OF HELL II – BACK INTO HELL...	Meatloaf (Virgin)
7	7	ELEGANT SLUMMING	M People (deConstruction)
-	8	TIGER BAY	Saint Etienne (Heavenly)
9	9	TEN SUMMONER'S TALES	Sting (A&M)
6	10	UNDER THE PINK	Tori Amos (East West)
12	11	THE HEART OF CHICAGO	Chicago (Reprise)
10	12	CONNECTED	Stereo MCs (4th & Broadway)
17	13	THE COLOUR OF MY LOVE	Celine Dion (Epic)
8	14	TEASE ME	Chaka Demus & Pliers (Mango)
23	15	TONI BRAXTON	Toni Braxton (Arista)
11	16	EVERYTHING CHANGES	Take That (RCA)
16	17	DEEP FOREST	Deep Forest (Nude)
-	18	AUGUST AND EVERYTHING AFTER	Counting Crows (Geffen)
13	19	TOGETHER ALONE	Crowded House (Capitol)
14	20	SOFTLY WITH THESE SONGS – THE BEST OF ROBERTA FLACK	Roberta Flack (Atlantic)
20	21	THE BEST OF VAN MORRISON	Van Morrison (Polydor)
-	22	THE DEVIL IN SISTER GEORGE EP	Boy George (Virgin)
15	23	ONE WOMAN – THE ULTIMATE COLLECTION	Diana Ross (EMI)
30	24	FIND YOUR WAY	Gabrielle (Go Beat)
-	25	HARD TO EARN	Gang Starr (Cooltempo)
19	26	SO FAR SO GOOD	Bryan Adams (A&M)
18	27	IN PIECES	Garth Brooks (Liberty)
-	28	FACE THE MUSIC	NKOTB (Columbia)
-	29	MAYA	Banco De Gaia (Planet Dog)
22	30	TROUBLEGUM	Therapy? (A&M)
21	31	PAID VACATION	Richard Marx (Capitol)
26	32	CROOKED RAIN CROOKED RAIN	Pavement (Big Cat)
31	33	BLACK SUNDAY	Cypress Hill (Ruff House)
25	34	SERENITY	Culture Beat (Epic)
28	35	D:REAM ON VOL 1	D:Ream (Magnet)
24	36	BOTH SIDES	Phil Collins (Virgin)
27	37	BAT OUT OF HELL	Meatloaf (Epic)
37	38	ALWAYS AND FOREVER	Eternal (EMI)
45	39	THE LESLEY GARRETT ALBUM	Lesley Garrett (Telstar)
44	40	DOGGYSTYLE	Snoop Doggy Dogg (Death Row)
41	41	SUEDE	Suede (Nude)
34	42	THE BODYGUARD - SOUNDTRACK	Various Artists (Arista)
32	43	WHAT SILENCE KNOWS	Shara Nelson (Cooltempo)
-	44	PARCEL OF ROGUES	Barbara Dickson (Castle Communications)
40	45	AUTOMATIC FOR THE PEOPLE	REM (Warner Bros.)
38	46	THE ONE THING	Michael Bolton (Columbia)
46	47	WOODFACE	Crowded House (Capitol)
42	48	JUST TO LET YOU KNOW	Bitty McLean (Brillian)
33	49	EMERGENCY ON PLANET EARTH	Jamiroquai (Sony Soho Square)
-	50	THE ULTIMATE COLLECTION	Mario Lanza (RCA)

The Best Of Van Morrison was a curious collection of album tracks from an artist whose popularity and influence has grown over the years. Paradoxically his first and most important album, *Astral Weeks*, never made it into the charts at all. Long chart stays for new acts – M People and Jamiroquai still selling well.

19 March 1994

last week	this week	
1	1	MUSIC BOX — Mariah Carey (Columbia)
2	2	THE CROSS OF CHANGES — Enigma (Virgin)
-	3	BRUTAL YOUTH — Elvis Costello (Warner Bros.)
3	4	DEBUT — Bjork (One Little Indian)
4	5	EVERYBODY ELSE IS DOING IT, SO WHY CAN'T WE — Cranberries (Island)
7	6	ELEGANT SLUMMING — M People (deConstruction)
9	7	TEN SUMMONER'S TALES — Sting (A&M)
-	8	SUPERUNKNOWN — Soundgarden (A&M)
-	9	THE DOWNWARD SPIRAL — Nine Inch Nails (Island)
5	10	SO CLOSE — Dina Carroll (A&M)
-	11	DEVIL HOPPING — Inspiral Carpets (Cow)
-	12	HIT THE HIGHWAY — Proclaimers (Chrysalis)
-	13	SELECTED AMBIENT WORKS VOLUME 2 — Aphex Twin (Warp)
6	14	BAT OUT OF HELL II – BACK INTO HELL... — Meatloaf (Virgin)
10	15	UNDER THE PINK — Tori Amos (East West)
8	16	TIGER BAY — Saint Etienne (Heavenly)
-	17	GREATEST HITS (1980-1994) — Aretha Franklin (Arista)
15	18	TONI BRAXTON — Toni Braxton (Arista)
20	19	SOFTLY WITH THESE SONGS – THE BEST OF ROBERTA FLACK — Roberta Flack (Atlantic)
-	20	MAJOR WORKS OF CANTO GREGORIANO — Monks' Chorus Silos (EMI Classics)
11	21	THE HEART OF CHICAGO — Chicago (Reprise)
14	22	TEASE ME — Chaka Demus & Pliers (Mango)
12	23	CONNECTED — Stereo MCs (4th & Broadway)
23	24	ONE WOMAN – THE ULTIMATE COLLECTION — Diana Ross (EMI)
-	25	YOUR FILTHY LITTLE MOUTH — David Lee Roth (A&M)
13	26	THE COLOUR OF MY LOVE — Celine Dion (Epic)
18	27	AUGUST AND EVERYTHING AFTER — Counting Crows (Geffen)
16	28	EVERYTHING CHANGES — Take That (RCA)
17	29	DEEP FOREST — Deep Forest (Columbia)
26	30	SO FAR SO GOOD — Bryan Adams (A&M)
19	31	TOGETHER ALONE — Crowded House (Capitol)
-	32	PEEL SESSION — Orbital (Internal)
21	33	THE BEST OF VAN MORRISON — Van Morrison (Polydor)
24	34	FIND YOUR WAY — Gabrielle (Go Beat)
33	35	BLACK SUNDAY — Cypress Hill (Ruff House)
-	36	PHILADELPHIA - SOUNDTRACK — Various Artists (Epic)
42	37	THE BODYGUARD - SOUNDTRACK — Various Artists (Arista)
46	38	THE ONE THING — Michael Bolton (Columbia)
30	39	TROUBLEGUM — Therapy? (A&M)
-	40	WENDY MOTEN — Wendy Moten (EMI)
22	41	THE DEVIL IN SISTER GEORGE EP — Boy George (Virgin)
28	42	FACE THE MUSIC — NKOTB (Columbia)
27	43	IN PIECES — Garth Brooks (Liberty)
32	44	CROOKED RAIN CROOKED RAIN — Pavement (Big Cat)
29	45	MAYA — Banco De Gaia (Planet Dog)
31	46	PAID VACATION — Richard Marx (Capitol)
36	47	BOTH SIDES — Phil Collins (Virgin)
35	48	D:REAM ON VOL 1 — D:Ream (Magnet)
25	49	HARD TO EARN — Gang Starr (Cooltempo)
44	50	PARCEL OF ROGUES — Barbara Dickson (Castle Communications)

26 March 1994

last week	this week	
-	1	VAUXHALL AND I — Morrissey (Parlophone)
1	2	MUSIC BOX — Mariah Carey (Columbia)
2	3	THE CROSS OF CHANGES — Enigma (Virgin)
3	4	BRUTAL YOUTH — Elvis Costello (Warner Bros.)
6	5	ELEGANT SLUMMING — M People (deConstruction)
-	6	HAPPY NATION (US VERSION) — Ace Of Base (Metronome)
5	7	EVERYBODY ELSE IS DOING IT, SO WHY CAN'T WE — Cranberries (Island)
8	8	SUPERUNKNOWN — Soundgarden (A&M)
4	9	DEBUT — Bjork (One Little Indian)
-	10	FOREVER NOW — Level 42 (RCA)
-	11	U GOT 2 KNOW — Cappella (Internal)
12	12	HIT THE HIGHWAY — Proclaimers (Chrysalis)
15	13	UNDER THE PINK — Tori Amos (East West)
7	14	TEN SUMMONER'S TALES — Sting (A&M)
-	15	MOTLEY CRUE — Motley Crue (Elektra)
20	16	MAJOR WORKS OF CANTO GREGORIANO — Monks' Chorus Silos (EMI Classics)
9	17	THE DOWNWARD SPIRAL — Nine Inch Nails (Island)
21	18	THE HEART OF CHICAGO — Chicago (Reprise)
10	19	SO CLOSE — Dina Carroll (A&M)
11	20	DEVIL HOPPING — Inspiral Carpets (Cow)
18	21	TONI BRAXTON — Toni Braxton (Arista)
19	22	SOFTLY WITH THESE SONGS – THE BEST OF ROBERTA FLACK — Roberta Flack (Atlantic)
13	23	SELECTED AMBIENT WORKS VOLUME 2 — Aphex Twin (Warp)
14	24	BAT OUT OF HELL II – BACK INTO HELL... — Meatloaf (Virgin)
22	25	TEASE ME — Chaka Demus & Pliers (Mango)
24	26	ONE WOMAN – THE ULTIMATE COLLECTION — Diana Ross (EMI)
38	27	THE ONE THING — Michael Bolton (Columbia)
-	28	STARRY EYED AND BOLLOCK NAKED — Carter USM (Chrysalis)
30	29	SO FAR SO GOOD — Bryan Adams (A&M)
28	30	EVERYTHING CHANGES — Take That (RCA)
17	31	GREATEST HITS (1980-1994) — Aretha Franklin (Arista)
32	32	CONNECTED — Stereo MCs (4th & Broadway)
36	33	PHILADELPHIA – SOUNDTRACK — Various Artists (Epic)
-	34	HIGH ON A HAPPY VIBE — Urban Cookie Collective (Pulse 8)
16	35	TIGER BAY — Saint Etienne (Heavenly)
26	36	THE COLOUR OF MY LOVE — Celine Dion (Epic)
48	37	D:REAM ON VOL 1 — D:Ream (Magnet)
31	38	TOGETHER ALONE — Crowded House (Capitol)
29	39	DEEP FOREST — Deep Forest (Columbia)
-	40	THE ULTIMATE COLLECTION — Mario Lanza (RCA)
35	41	BLACK SUNDAY — Cypress Hill (Ruff House)
25	42	YOUR FILTHY LITTLE MOUTH — David Lee Roth (A&M)
32	43	PEEL SESSION — Orbital (Internal)
37	44	THE BODYGUARD - SOUNDTRACK — Various Artists (Arista)
34	45	FIND YOUR WAY — Gabrielle (Go Beat)
-	46	ANTMUSIC – THE VERY BEST OF ADAM ANT — Adam Ant (Arcade)
27	47	AUGUST AND EVERYTHING AFTER — Counting Crows (Geffen)
40	48	WENDY MOTEN — Wendy Moten (EMI)
-	49	BAT OUT OF HELL — Meatloaf (Epic)
39	50	TROUBLEGUM — Therapy? (A&M)

2 April 1994

last week	this week	
2	1	MUSIC BOX — Mariah Carey (Columbia)
6	2	HAPPY NATION (US VERSION) — Ace Of Base (Metronome)
-	3	FAR BEYOND DRIVEN — Pantera (East West)
1	4	VAUXHALL AND I — Morrissey (Parlophone)
3	5	THE CROSS OF CHANGES — Enigma (Virgin)
5	6	ELEGANT SLUMMING — M People (deConstruction)
16	7	MAJOR WORKS OF CANTO GREGORIANO — Monks' Chorus Silos (EMI Classics)
9	8	DEBUT — Bjork (One Little Indian)
-	9	UP TO OUR HIPS — Charlatans (Beggars Banquet)
7	10	EVERYBODY ELSE IS DOING IT, SO WHY CAN'T WE — Cranberries (Island)
4	11	BRUTAL YOUTH — Elvis Costello (Warner Bros.)
11	12	U GOT 2 KNOW — Cappella (Internal)
14	13	TEN SUMMONER'S TALES — Sting (A&M)
13	14	UNDER THE PINK — Tori Amos (East West)
21	15	TONI BRAXTON — Toni Braxton (Arista)
10	16	FOREVER NOW — Level 42 (RCA)
8	17	SUPERUNKNOWN — Soundgarden (A&M)
22	18	SOFTLY WITH THESE SONGS – THE BEST OF ROBERTA FLACK — Roberta Flack (Atlantic)
33	19	PHILADELPHIA – SOUNDTRACK — Various Artists (Epic)
18	20	THE HEART OF CHICAGO — Chicago (Reprise)
30	21	EVERYTHING CHANGES — Take That (RCA)
37	22	D:REAM ON VOL 1 — D:Ream (Magnet)
19	23	SO CLOSE — Dina Carroll (A&M)
-	24	TALK — Yes (Victory)
15	25	MOTLEY CRUE — Motley Crue (Elektra)
26	26	ONE WOMAN – THE ULTIMATE COLLECTION — Diana Ross (EMI)
12	27	HIT THE HIGHWAY — Proclaimers (Chrysalis)
24	28	BAT OUT OF HELL II – BACK INTO HELL... — Meatloaf (Virgin)
25	29	TEASE ME — Chaka Demus & Pliers (Mango)
28	30	STARRY EYED AND BOLLOCK NAKED — Carter USM (Chrysalis)
17	31	THE DOWNWARD SPIRAL — Nine Inch Nails (Island)
40	32	THE ULTIMATE COLLECTION — Mario Lanza (RCA)
-	33	S*M*A*S*H* — S*M*A*S*H* (Hi Rise)
41	34	BLACK SUNDAY — Cypress Hill (Ruff House)
-	35	ESSEX — Alison Moyet (Columbia)
23	36	SELECTED AMBIENT WORKS VOLUME 2 — Aphex Twin (Warp)
20	37	DEVIL HOPPING — Inspiral Carpets (Cow)
38	38	THE ONE THING — Michael Bolton (Columbia)
34	39	HIGH ON A HAPPY VIBE — Urban Cookie Collective (Pulse 8)
38	40	TOGETHER ALONE — Crowded House (Capitol)
29	41	SO FAR SO GOOD — Bryan Adams (A&M)
32	42	CONNECTED — Stereo MCs (4th & Broadway)
39	43	DEEP FOREST — Deep Forest (Columbia)
46	44	ANTMUSIC – THE VERY BEST OF ADAM ANT — Adam Ant (Arcade)
44	45	THE BODYGUARD - SOUNDTRACK — Various Artists (Arista)
49	46	BAT OUT OF HELL — Meatloaf (Epic)
-	47	THE BEST OF THE AVERAGE WHITE BAND – LET'S GO ROUND AGAIN — Average White Band (The Hit Label)
-	48	MELLOW GOLD — Beck (Geffen)
35	49	TIGER BAY — Saint Etienne (Heavenly)
45	50	FIND YOUR WAY — Gabrielle (Go Beat)

If you add in the Smiths' albums, this was Morrissey's sixteenth appearance in the album chart, though his first entry at Number One. The latest teen fad was for Gregorian chants, combined with ambient music – you know, that stuff they play in airports. Elvis Costello still tried to convince us youth was brutal.

April 1994

Back in the summer of love in 1967, Pink Floyd charted with their first album *Piper At The Gates Of Dawn*. In between they'd said goodbye to Syd Barrett and, amid much acrimony, to Roger Waters. *The Division Bell* was thought by many to be a pale imitation of previous LPs, but sold to hardcore fans.

last week	this week	30 April 1994	
1	1	THE DIVISION BELL	Pink Floyd (EMI)
2	2	OUR TOWN – THE GREATEST HITS	Deacon Blue (Columbia)
3	3	CRASH! BOOM! BANG!	Roxette (EMI)
4	4	THE VERY BEST OF MARVIN GAYE	Marvin Gaye (Motown)
5	5	HAPPY NATION (US VERSION)	Ace Of Base (Metronome)
7	6	MUSIC BOX	Mariah Carey (Columbia)
6	7	BROTHER SISTER	Brand New Heavies (ffrr)
17	8	D:REAM ON VOL 1	D:Ream (Magnet)
9	9	GIVE OUT BUT DON'T GIVE UP	Primal Scream (Creation)
8	10	EVERYTHING CHANGES	Take That (RCA)
-	11	LET LOVE IN	Nick Cave & the Bad Seeds (Mute)
-	12	BLUES	Jimi Hendrix (Polydor)
-	13	A NIGHT IN SAN FRANCISCO	Van Morrison (Polydor)
-	14	HIS 'N' HERS	Pulp (Island)
33	15	HADDAWAY – THE ALBUM	Haddaway (Logic)
12	16	PHILADELPHIA – SOUNDTRACK	Various Artists (Epic)
21	17	EVERYBODY ELSE IS DOING IT, SO WHY CAN'T WE	Cranberries (Island)
13	18	MAJOR WORKS OF CANTO GREGORIANO	Monks' Chorus Silos (EMI Classics)
-	19	HOW TO MAKE FRIENDS AND INFLUENCE PEOPLE	Terrorvision (Total Vegas)
11	20	THE CROSS OF CHANGES	Enigma (Virgin)
16	21	NEVERMIND	Nirvana (Geffen)
18	22	DEBUT	Bjork (One Little Indian)
23	23	TONI BRAXTON	Toni Braxton (Arista)
10	24	MIAOW	Beautiful South (Go! Discs)
36	25	IN UTERO	Nirvana (Geffen)
14	26	ELEGANT SLUMMING	M People (deConstruction)
45	27	A CARNIVAL OF HITS	Judith Durham & the Seekers (EMI)
-	28	TOGETHER	Worlds Apart (Arista)
27	29	BAT OUT OF HELL II – BACK INTO HELL...	Meatloaf (Virgin)
22	30	UNDER THE PINK	Tori Amos (East West)
15	31	LITTLE OF THE PAST	Little Angels (Polydor)
47	32	BACKBEAT – SOUNDTRACK	Backbeat Band (Virgin)
-	33	AFRICA TO AMERICA: THE JOURNEY OF THE DRUM	Sounds Of Blackness (A&M)
-	34	BACK TO BROADWAY	Barbra Streisand (Columbia)
37	35	JUST TO LET YOU KNOW	Bitty McLean (Brilliant)
20	36	LIVE THROUGH THIS	Hole (City Slang)
29	37	JEWEL	Marcella Detroit (London)
24	38	ONE WOMAN – THE ULTIMATE COLLECTION	Diana Ross (EMI)
30	39	LONGING IN THEIR HEARTS	Bonnie Raitt (Capitol)
31	40	PERMANENT SHADE OF BLUE	Roachford (Columbia)
41	41	VERY NECESSARY	Salt 'N' Pepa (ffrr)
19	42	WEIGHT	Rollins Band (Imago)
26	43	KIRI!	Kiri Te Kanawa (Decca)
28	44	THE HEART OF CHICAGO	Chicago (Reprise)
32	45	VAUXHALL AND I	Morrissey (Parlophone)
35	46	IN PIECES	Garth Brooks (Liberty)
39	47	FAR BEYOND DRIVEN	Pantera (East West)
34	48	TEASE ME	Chaka Demus & Pliers (Mango)
44	49	TEN SUMMONER'S TALES	Sting (A&M)
48	50	RHYTHM COUNTRY AND BLUES	Various (MCA)

last week	this week	7 May 1994	
-	1	PARKLIFE	Blur (Food)
1	2	THE DIVISION BELL	Pink Floyd (EMI)
2	3	OUR TOWN – THE GREATEST HITS	Deacon Blue (Columbia)
4	4	THE VERY BEST OF MARVIN GAYE	Marvin Gaye (Motown)
-	5	STACKED UP	Senser (Ultimate)
5	6	HAPPY NATION (US VERSION)	Ace Of Base (Metronome)
17	7	EVERYBODY ELSE IS DOING IT, SO WHY CAN'T WE	Cranberries (Island)
6	8	MUSIC BOX	Mariah Carey (Columbia)
3	9	CRASH! BOOM! BANG!	Roxette (EMI)
8	10	D:REAM ON VOL 1	D:Ream (Magnet)
7	11	BROTHER SISTER	Brand New Heavies (ffrr)
16	12	PHILADELPHIA – SOUNDTRACK	Various (Epic)
23	13	TONI BRAXTON	Toni Braxton (Arista)
14	14	A NIGHT IN SAN FRANCISCO	Van Morrison (Polydor)
-	15	ANARCHY	Chumbawumba (One Little Indian)
10	16	EVERYTHING CHANGES	Take That (RCA)
12	17	BLUES	Jimi Hendrix (Polydor)
15	18	HADDAWAY – THE ALBUM	Haddaway (Logic)
27	19	A CARNIVAL OF HITS	Judith Durham & the Seekers (EMI)
9	20	GIVE OUT BUT DON'T GIVE UP	Primal Scream (Creation)
19	21	HOW TO MAKE FRIENDS AND INFLUENCE PEOPLE	Terrorvision (Total Vegas)
14	22	HIS 'N' HERS	Pulp (Island)
18	23	MAJOR WORKS OF CANTO GREGORIANO	Monks' Chorus Silos (EMI Classics)
20	24	THE CROSS OF CHANGES	Enigma (Virgin)
11	25	LET LOVE IN	Nick Cave & the Bad Seeds (Mute)
34	26	BACK TO BROADWAY	Barbra Streisand (Columbia)
33	27	AFRICA TO AMERICA: THE JOURNEY OF THE DRUM	Sounds Of Blackness (A&M)
26	28	ELEGANT SLUMMING	M People (deConstruction)
21	29	NEVERMIND	Nirvana (Geffen)
22	30	DEBUT	Bjork (One Little Indian)
24	31	MIAOW	Beautiful South (Go! Discs)
-	32	LISTEN	Urban Species (Talkin Loud)
25	33	IN UTERO	Nirvana (Geffen)
32	34	BACKBEAT – S'TRACK	Backbeat Band (Virgin)
30	35	UNDER THE PINK	Tori Amos (East West)
29	36	BAT OUT OF HELL II – BACK INTO HELL...	Meatloaf (Virgin)
-	37	WILD WOOD	Paul Weller (Go! Discs)
-	38	SANTA MONICA '72	David Bowie (Mainman)
-	39	GREATEST HITS...AND MORE	Barbra Streisand (Columbia)
35	40	JUST TO LET YOU KNOW	Bitty McLean (Brilliant)
38	41	ONE WOMAN – THE ULTIMATE COLLECTION	Diana Ross (EMI)
-	42	AUGUST AND EVERYTHING AFTER	Counting Crows (Geffen)
-	43	ALWAYS AND FOREVER	Eternal (EMI)
37	44	JEWEL	Marcella Detroit (London)
46	45	IN PIECES	Garth Brooks (Liberty)
40	46	PERMANENT SHADE OF BLUE	Roachford (Columbia)
31	47	LITTLE OF THE PAST	Little Angels (Polydor)
47	48	VERY	Pet Shop Boys (Parlophone)
36	49	LIVE THROUGH THIS	Hole (City Slang)
39	50	LONGING IN THEIR HEARTS	Bonnie Raitt (Capitol)

last week	this week	14 May 1994	
3	1	OUR TOWN – THE GREATEST HITS	Deacon Blue (Columbia)
1	2	PARKLIFE	Blur (Food)
2	3	THE DIVISION BELL	Pink Floyd (EMI)
4	4	THE VERY BEST OF MARVIN GAYE	Marvin Gaye (Motown)
-	5	GOD SHUFFLED HIS FEET	Crash Test Dummies (RCA)
7	6	EVERYBODY ELSE IS DOING IT, SO WHY CAN'T WE	Cranberries (Island)
6	7	HAPPY NATION (US VERSION)	Ace Of Base (Metronome)
-	8	GOIN' BACK – THE VERY BEST OF DUSTY SPRINGFIELD 1962-1994	Dusty Springfield (Philips)
19	9	A CARNIVAL OF HITS	Judith Durham & the Seekers (EMI)
8	10	MUSIC BOX	Mariah Carey (Columbia)
5	11	STACKED UP	Senser (Ultimate)
10	12	D:REAM ON VOL 1	D:Ream (Magnet)
13	13	TONI BRAXTON	Toni Braxton (Arista)
9	14	CRASH! BOOM! BANG!	Roxette (EMI)
-	15	SKIN	Skin (Parlophone)
16	16	EVERYTHING CHANGES	Take That (RCA)
11	17	BROTHER SISTER	Brand New Heavies (ffrr)
14	18	A NIGHT IN SAN FRANCISCO	Van Morrison (Polydor)
43	19	ALWAYS AND FOREVER	Eternal (EMI)
12	20	PHILADELPHIA – SOUNDTRACK	Various (Epic)
40	21	JUST TO LET YOU KNOW	Bitty McLean (Brilliant)
18	22	HADDAWAY – THE ALBUM	Haddaway (Logic)
-	23	MIDDLE CLASS REVOLT	Fall (Permanent)
24	24	THE CROSS OF CHANGES	Enigma (Virgin)
17	25	BLUES	Jimi Hendrix (Polydor)
36	26	BAT OUT OF HELL II – BACK INTO HELL...	Meatloaf (Virgin)
20	27	GIVE OUT BUT DON'T GIVE UP	Primal Scream (Creation)
15	28	ANARCHY	Chumbawumba (One Little Indian)
28	29	ELEGANT SLUMMING	M People (deConstruction)
30	30	DEBUT	Bjork (One Little Indian)
29	31	NEVERMIND	Nirvana (Geffen)
26	32	BACK TO BROADWAY	Barbra Streisand (Columbia)
31	33	MIAOW	Beautiful South (Go! Discs)
27	34	AFRICA TO AMERICA: THE JOURNEY OF THE DRUM	Sounds Of Blackness (A&M)
33	35	IN UTERO	Nirvana (Geffen)
21	36	HOW TO MAKE FRIENDS AND INFLUENCE PEOPLE	Terrorvision (Total Vegas)
37	37	WILD WOOD	Paul Weller (Go! Discs)
23	38	MAJOR WORKS OF CANTO GREGORIANO	Monks' Chorus Silos (EMI Classics)
-	39	HOME INVASION/THE LAST TEMPTATION	Ice-T (Virgin)
22	40	HIS 'N' HERS	Pulp (Island)
34	41	BACKBEAT – S'TRACK	Backbeat Band (Virgin)
-	42	ABOVE THE RIM – S'TRACK	Various (Interscope)
35	43	UNDER THE PINK	Tori Amos (East West)
39	44	GREATEST HITS...AND MORE	Barbra Streisand (Columbia)
-	45	HEAVEN AND HULL	Mick Ronson (Epic)
25	46	LET LOVE IN	Nick Cave & the Bad Seeds (Mute)
-	47	AUTOMATIC FOR THE PEOPLE	REM (Warner Bros.)
48	48	VERY	Pet Shop Boys (Parlophone)
-	49	BOTH SIDES	Phil Collins (Virgin)
42	50	AUGUST AND EVERYTHING AFTER	Counting Crows (Geffen)

Parklife hailed the revival of British pop/rock music, as Blur became rivals to Suede for the affections of the nation's thinking youth. In the same month Dusty Springfield and Judith Durham and the Seekers were an echo of the time of the first great British Beat Boom – though they were all from the antipodes.

425

May – June 1994

21 May 1994

Last	This	Title – Artist	Label
1	1	OUR TOWN – THE GREATEST HITS	Deacon Blue (Columbia)
5	2	GOD SHUFFLED HIS FEET	Crash Test Dummies (RCA)
3	3	THE DIVISION BELL	Pink Floyd (EMI)
2	4	PARKLIFE	Blur (Food)
6	5	EVERYBODY ELSE IS DOING IT, SO WHY CAN'T WE	Cranberries (Island)
8	6	GOIN' BACK – THE VERY BEST OF DUSTY SPRINGFIELD 1962-1994	Dusty Springfield (Philips)
19	7	ALWAYS AND FOREVER	Eternal (EMI)
-	8	LAST OF THE INDEPENDENTS	Pretenders (WEA)
9	9	A CARNIVAL OF HITS	Judith Durham & the Seekers (EMI)
10	10	MUSIC BOX	Mariah Carey (Columbia)
7	11	HAPPY NATION (US VERSION)	Ace Of Base (Metronome)
-	12	EXPERIMENTAL JET SET, TRASH AND NO STAR	Sonic Youth (Geffen)
4	13	THE VERY BEST OF...	Marvin Gaye (Motown)
24	14	THE CROSS OF CHANGES	Enigma (Virgin)
-	15	I AIN'T MOVIN'	Des'ree (Dusted Sound)
13	16	TONI BRAXTON	Toni Braxton (Arista)
-	17	NOW I'M A COWBOY	Auteurs (Hut)
16	18	EVERYTHING CHANGES	Take That (RCA)
11	19	STACKED UP	Senser (Ultimate)
-	20	FALLING FORWARD	Julia Fordham (Circa)
12	21	D:REAM ON VOL 1	D:Ream (Magnet)
20	22	PHILADELPHIA – SOUNDTRACK	Various (Epic)
14	23	CRASH! BOOM! BANG!	Roxette (EMI)
15	24	SKIN	Skin (Parlophone)
5	25	FAR FROM HOME	Traffic (Virgin)
17	26	BROTHER SISTER	Brand New Heavies (ffrr)
21	27	JUST TO LET YOU KNOW	Bitty McLean (Brilliant)
18	28	A NIGHT IN SAN FRANCISCO	Van Morrison (Polydor)
27	29	GIVE OUT BUT DON'T GIVE UP	Primal Scream (Creation)
30	30	DEBUT	Bjork (One Little Indian)
29	31	ELEGANT SLUMMING	M People (deConstruction)
31	32	NEVERMIND	Nirvana (Geffen)
26	33	BAT OUT OF HELL II – BACK INTO HELL...	Meatloaf (Virgin)
22	34	HADDAWAY – THE ALBUM	Haddaway (Logic)
25	35	BLUES	Jimi Hendrix (Polydor)
35	36	IN UTERO	Nirvana (Geffen)
33	37	MIAOW	Beautiful South (Go! Discs)
32	38	BACK TO BROADWAY	Barbra Streisand (Columbia)
23	39	MIDDLE CLASS REVOLT	Fall (Permanent)
37	40	WILD WOOD	Paul Weller (Go! Discs)
39	41	HOME INVASION/THE LAST TEMPTATION	Ice-T (Virgin)
34	42	AFRICA TO AMERICA: THE JOURNEY OF THE DRUM	Sounds Of Blackness (A&M)
-	43	THE ULTIMATE COLLECTION	Louis Armstrong (RCA)
38	44	MAJOR WORKS OF CANTO GREGORIANO	Monks' Chorus Silos (EMI Classics)
45	45	HEAVEN AND HULL	Mick Ronson (Epic)
41	46	BACKBEAT – S'TRACK	Backbeat Band (Ruff House)
-	47	BLACK SUNDAY	Cypress Hill (Ruff House)
-	48	FOUR WEDDINGS AND A FUNERAL – SOUNDTRACK	Various Artists (Vertigo)
-	49	JEWEL	Marcella Detroit (London)
-	50	FEAR, EMPTINESS, DESPAIR	Napalm Death (Earache)

28 May 1994

Last	This	Title – Artist	Label
-	1	I SAY, I SAY, I SAY	Erasure (Mute)
1	2	OUR TOWN – THE GREATEST HITS	Deacon Blue (Columbia)
5	3	EVERYBODY ELSE IS DOING IT, SO WHY CAN'T WE	Cranberries (Island)
3	4	THE DIVISION BELL	Pink Floyd (EMI)
2	5	GOD SHUFFLED HIS FEET	Crash Test Dummies (RCA)
4	6	PARKLIFE	Blur (Food)
7	7	THIS WAY UP	Chris De Burgh (A&M)
9	8	A CARNIVAL OF HITS	Judith Durham & the Seekers (EMI)
8	9	LAST OF THE INDEPENDENTS	Pretenders (WEA)
7	10	ALWAYS AND FOREVER	Eternal (EMI)
6	11	GOIN' BACK – THE VERY BEST OF DUSTY SPRINGFIELD 1962-1994	Dusty Springfield (Philips)
10	12	MUSIC BOX	Mariah Carey (Columbia)
14	13	THE CROSS OF CHANGES	Enigma (Virgin)
11	14	HAPPY NATION (US VERSION)	Ace Of Base (Metronome)
15	15	I AIN'T MOVIN'	Des'ree (Dusted Sound)
-	16	TAKE ME TO GOD	Jah Wobble's Invaders Of The Heart (Island)
16	17	TONI BRAXTON	Toni Braxton (Arista)
13	18	THE VERY BEST OF MARVIN GAYE	Marvin Gaye (Motown)
18	19	EVERYTHING CHANGES	Take That (RCA)
32	20	NEVERMIND	Nirvana (Geffen)
12	21	EXPERIMENTAL JET SET, TRASH AND NO STAR	Sonic Youth (Geffen)
22	22	PHILADELPHIA – SOUNDTRACK	Various (Epic)
21	23	D:REAM ON VOL 1	D:Ream (Magnet)
48	24	FOUR WEDDINGS AND A FUNERAL – SOUNDTRACK	Various Artists (Vertigo)
25	25	FAR FROM HOME	Traffic (Virgin)
23	26	CRASH! BOOM! BANG!	Roxette (EMI)
20	27	FALLING FORWARD	Julia Fordham (Circa)
31	28	ELEGANT SLUMMING	M People (deConstruction)
36	29	IN UTERO	Nirvana (Geffen)
-	30	CHRONOLOGIE 6	Jean Michel Jarre (Polydor)
17	31	NOW I'M A COWBOY	Auteurs (Hut)
26	32	BROTHER SISTER	Brand New Heavies (ffrr)
19	33	STACKED UP	Senser (Ultimate)
30	34	DEBUT	Bjork (One Little Indian)
-	35	CRAZY	Julio Iglesias (Columbia)
24	36	SKIN	Skin (Parlophone)
33	37	BAT OUT OF HELL II – BACK INTO HELL...	Meatloaf (Virgin)
34	38	HADDAWAY – THE ALBUM	Haddaway (Logic)
29	39	GIVE OUT BUT DON'T GIVE UP	Primal Scream (Creation)
35	40	BLUES	Jimi Hendrix (Polydor)
28	41	A NIGHT IN SAN FRANCISCO	Van Morrison (Polydor)
27	42	JUST TO LET YOU KNOW	Bitty McLean (Brilliant)
37	43	MIAOW	Beautiful South (Go! Discs)
43	44	THE ULTIMATE COLLECTION	Louis Armstrong (RCA)
-	45	UNDER THE PINK	Tori Amos (East West)
44	46	MAJOR WORKS OF CANTO GREGORIANO	Monks' Chorus Silos (EMI Classics)
47	47	BLACK SUNDAY	Cypress Hill (Ruff House)
46	48	BACKBEAT – S'TRACK	Backbeat Band (Ruff House)
-	49	RE-LOAD – FRANKIE: THE WHOLE 12 INCHES	Frankie Goes To Hollywood (ZTT)
49	50	JEWEL	Marcella Detroit (London)

4 June 1994

Last	This	Title – Artist	Label
-	1	SEAL	Seal (ZTT)
1	2	I SAY, I SAY, I SAY	Erasure (Mute)
4	3	THE DIVISION BELL	Pink Floyd (EMI)
3	4	EVERYBODY ELSE IS DOING IT, SO WHY CAN'T WE	Cranberries (Island)
-	5	THE BEAUTIFUL EXPERIENCE	Prince (Symbol)
2	6	OUR TOWN – THE GREATEST HITS	Deacon Blue (Columbia)
7	7	THIS WAY UP	Chris De Burgh (A&M)
6	8	PARKLIFE	Blur (Food)
10	9	ALWAYS AND FOREVER	Eternal (EMI)
8	10	A CARNIVAL OF HITS	Judith Durham & the Seekers (EMI)
5	11	GOD SHUFFLED HIS FEET	Crash Test Dummies (RCA)
12	12	MUSIC BOX	Mariah Carey (Columbia)
9	13	LAST OF THE INDEPENDENTS	Pretenders (WEA)
13	14	THE CROSS OF CHANGES	Enigma (Virgin)
-	15	LIFEFORMS	Future Sound Of London (Virgin)
11	16	GOIN' BACK – THE VERY BEST OF DUSTY SPRINGFIELD 1962-1994	Dusty Springfield (Philips)
16	17	TAKE ME TO GOD	Jah Wobble's Invaders Of The Heart (Island)
-	18	ILL COMMUNICATIONS	Beastie Boys (Capitol)
35	19	CRAZY	Julio Iglesias (Columbia)
24	20	FOUR WEDDINGS AND A FUNERAL – SOUNDTRACK	Various Artists (Vertigo)
18	21	THE VERY BEST OF MARVIN GAYE	Marvin Gaye (Motown)
-	22	STREET ANGEL	Stevie Nicks (EMI)
-	23	TEENAGER OF THE YEAR	Frank Black (4AD)
14	24	HAPPY NATION (US VERSION)	Ace Of Base (Metronome)
20	25	NEVERMIND	Nirvana (Geffen)
19	26	EVERYTHING CHANGES	Take That (RCA)
17	27	TONI BRAXTON	Toni Braxton (Arista)
-	28	DAVID BYRNE	David Byrne (Luaka Bop)
26	29	CRASH! BOOM! BANG!	Roxette (EMI)
15	30	I AIN'T MOVIN'	Des'ree (Dusted Sound)
28	31	ELEGANT SLUMMING	M People (deConstruction)
23	32	D:REAM ON VOL 1	D:Ream (Magnet)
22	33	PHILADELPHIA – SOUNDTRACK	Various Artists (Epic)
25	34	FAR FROM HOME	Traffic (Virgin)
-	35	HEART, SOUL AND VOICE	Jon Secada (SBK)
29	36	IN UTERO	Nirvana (Geffen)
21	37	EXPERIMENTAL JET SET, TRASH AND NO STAR	Sonic Youth (Geffen)
32	38	BROTHER SISTER	Brand New Heavies (ffrr)
34	39	DEBUT	Bjork (One Little Indian)
40	40	UNDER THE PINK	Tori Amos (East West)
37	41	BAT OUT OF HELL II – BACK INTO HELL...	Meatloaf (Virgin)
-	42	FOUR CHORDS AND SEVERAL YEARS AGO	Huey Lewis & the News (Elektra)
27	43	FALLING FORWARD	Julia Fordham (Circa)
30	44	MAGIC HAPPENS	Family Cat (Dedicated)
30	45	CHRONOLOGIE 6	Jean Michel Jarre (Polydor)
43	46	MIAOW	Beautiful South (Go! Discs)
40	47	BLUES	Jimi Hendrix (Polydor)
48	48	NOW I'M A COWBOY	Auteurs (Hut)
38	49	HADDAWAY – THE ALBUM	Haddaway (Logic)
-	50	COWGIRL'S PRAYER	Emmylou Harris (Grapevine)

More in-at-Number-Ones. And more reminders that some acts were still around. Most notably the Pretenders and David Byrne, former leading light of Talking Heads. Latest person to benefit from the power of TV advertising was Louis Armstrong, who happened to have re-invented jazz back in the 1920s.

11 June 1994

last week	this week		
1	1	SEAL	Seal (ZTT)
4	2	EVERBODY ELSE IS DOING IT, SO WHY CAN'T WE	Cranberries (Island)
6	3	OUR TOWN – THE GREATEST HITS	Deacon Blue (Columbia)
3	4	THE DIVISION BELL	Pink Floyd (EMI)
8	5	PARKLIFE	Blur (Food)
2	6	I SAY, I SAY, I SAY	Erasure (Mute)
15	7	LIFEFORMS	Future Sound Of London (Virgin)
9	8	ALWAYS AND FOREVER	Eternal (EMI)
5	9	THE BEAUTIFUL EXPERIENCE	Prince (Symbol)
-	10	THE PLOT THICKENS	Galliano (Talkin' Loud)
12	11	MUSIC BOX	Mariah Carey (Columbia)
14	12	THE CROSS OF CHANGES	Enigma (Virgin)
19	13	CRAZY	Julio Iglesias (Columbia)
11	14	GOD SHUFFLED HIS FEET	Crash Test Dummies (RCA)
18	15	ILL COMMUNICATIONS	Beastie Boys (Capitol)
24	16	HAPPY NATION (US VERSION)	Ace Of Base (Metronome)
10	17	A CARNIVAL OF HITS	Judith Durham & the Seekers (EMI)
7	18	THIS WAY UP	Chris De Burgh (A&M)
16	19	GOIN' BACK – THE VERY BEST OF DUSTY SPRINGFIELD 1962-1994	Dusty Springfield (Philips)
20	20	FOUR WEDDINGS AND A FUNERAL – SOUNDTRACK	Various Artists (Vertigo)
17	21	TAKE ME TO GOD	Jah Wobble's Invaders Of The Heart (Island)
26	22	EVERYTHING CHANGES	Take That (RCA)
35	23	HEART, SOUL AND VOICE	Jon Secada (SBK)
21	24	THE VERY BEST OF MARVIN GAYE	Marvin Gaye (Motown)
13	25	LAST OF THE INDEPENDENTS	Pretenders (WEA)
25	26	NEVERMIND	Nirvana (Geffen)
22	27	STREET ANGEL	Stevie Nicks (EMI)
29	28	CRASH! BOOM! BANG!	Roxette (EMI)
31	29	ELEGANT SLUMMING	M People (deConstruction)
46	30	MIAOW	Beautiful South (Go! Discs)
28	31	DAVID BYRNE	David Byrne (Luaka Bop)
23	32	TEENAGER OF THE YEAR	Frank Black (4AD)
38	33	BROTHER SISTER	Brand New Heavies (ffrr)
27	34	TONI BRAXTON	Toni Braxton (Arista)
33	35	PHILADELPHIA – SOUNDTRACK	Various Artists (Epic)
32	36	D:REAM ON VOL 1	D:Ream (Magnet)
-	37	TOGETHER ALONE	Crowded House (Capitol)
36	38	IN UTERO	Nirvana (Geffen)
34	39	FAR FROM HOME	Traffic (Virgin)
40	40	UNDER THE PINK	Tori Amos (East West)
41	41	BAT OUT OF HELL II – BACK INTO HELL...	Meatloaf (Virgin)
-	42	SUITS	Fish (Dick Brothers)
39	43	DEBUT	Bjork (One Little Indian)
-	44	HAND ON THE TORCH/JAZZ MIXES	Us3 (Blue Note)
37	45	EXPERIMENTAL JET SET, TRASH AND NO STAR	Sonic Youth (Geffen)
30	46	I AIN'T MOVIN'	Des'ree (Dusted Sound)
-	47	GIVE OUT BUT DON'T GIVE UP	Primal Scream (Creation)
42	48	FOUR CHORDS AND SEVERAL YEARS AGO	Huey Lewis & the News (Elektra)
-	49	HIS 'N' HERS	Pulp (Island)
47	50	BLUES	Jimi Hendrix (Polydor)

18 June 1994

2	1	EVERBODY ELSE IS DOING IT, SO WHY CAN'T WE	Cranberries (Island)
1	2	SEAL	Seal (ZTT)
3	3	REAL THINGS	2 Unlimited (PWL Continental)
3	4	OUR TOWN – THE GREATEST HITS	Deacon Blue (Columbia)
-	5	THE LAST TEMPTATION	Alice Cooper (Epic)
4	6	THE DIVISION BELL	Pink Floyd (EMI)
-	7	AROUND THE NEXT DREAM	BBM (Virgin)
11	8	MUSIC BOX	Mariah Carey (Columbia)
5	9	PARKLIFE	Blur (Food)
8	10	ALWAYS AND FOREVER	Eternal (EMI)
-	11	PURPLE	Stone Temple Pilots (Atlantic)
10	12	THE PLOT THICKENS.	Galliano (Talkin' Loud)
-	13	TRUE SPIRIT	Carleen Anderson (Circa)
6	14	I SAY, I SAY, I SAY	Erasure (Mute)
-	15	ZINGALAMADUNI	Arrested Development (Cooltempo)
16	16	HAPPY NATION (US VERSION)	Ace Of Base (Metronome)
14	17	GOD SHUFFLED HIS FEET	Crash Test Dummies (RCA)
13	18	CRAZY	Julio Iglesias (Columbia)
9	19	BAD BOYS INC	Bad Boys Inc (A&M)
7	20	LIFEFORMS	Future Sound Of London (Virgin)
12	21	THE CROSS OF CHANGES	Enigma (Virgin)
-	22	BALLS TO PICASSO	Bruce Dickinson (EMI)
-	23	BLADERUNNER – SOUNDTRACK	Vangelis (East West)
9	24	THE BEAUTIFUL EXPERIENCE	Prince (Symbol)
42	25	SUITS	Fish (Dick Brothers)
20	26	FOUR WEDDINGS AND A FUNERAL – SOUNDTRACK	Various Artists (Vertigo)
33	27	BROTHER SISTER	Brand New Heavies (ffrr)
22	28	EVERYTHING CHANGES	Take That (RCA)
-	29	DOMINATOR	Time Frequency (Internal Affairs)
30	30	MIAOW	Beautiful South (Go! Discs)
26	31	NEVERMIND	Nirvana (Geffen)
15	32	ILL COMMUNICATIONS	Beastie Boys (Capitol)
23	33	HEART, SOUL AND VOICE	Jon Secada (SBK)
17	34	A CARNIVAL OF HITS	Judith Durham & the Seekers (EMI)
-	35	WOODFACE	Crowded House (Capitol)
28	36	CRASH! BOOM! BANG!	Roxette (EMI)
37	37	TOGETHER ALONE	Crowded House (Capitol)
19	38	GOIN' BACK – THE VERY BEST OF DUSTY SPRINGFIELD 1962-1994	Dusty Springfield (Philips)
18	39	THIS WAY UP	Chris De Burgh (A&M)
25	40	LAST OF THE INDEPENDENTS	Pretenders (WEA)
35	41	PHILADELPHIA – SOUNDTRACK	Various Artists (Epic)
36	42	D:REAM ON VOL 1	D:Ream (Magnet)
24	43	THE VERY BEST OF MARVIN GAYE	Marvin Gaye (Motown)
31	44	DAVID BYRNE	David Byrne (Luaka Bop)
29	45	ELEGANT SLUMMING	M People (deConstruction)
27	46	STREET ANGEL	Stevie Nicks (EMI)
47	47	GIVE OUT BUT DON'T GIVE UP	Primal Scream (Creation)
38	48	IN UTERO	Nirvana (Geffen)
-	49	LIVE: WITHOUT THE AID OF A SAFETY NET	Big Country (Compulsion)
-	50	ULTRAVIOLET	Ed Alleyne-Johnson (China)

25 June 1994

-	1	POMME FRITZ	Orb (Island)
1	2	EVERBODY ELSE IS DOING IT, SO WHY CAN'T WE	Cranberries (Island)
3	3	REAL THINGS	2 Unlimited (PWL Continental)
8	4	MUSIC BOX	Mariah Carey (Columbia)
4	5	OUR TOWN – THE GREATEST HITS	Deacon Blue (Columbia)
2	6	SEAL	Seal (ZTT)
6	7	THE DIVISION BELL	Pink Floyd (EMI)
5	8	THE LAST TEMPTATION	Alice Cooper (Epic)
9	9	PARKLIFE	Blur (Food)
10	10	ALWAYS AND FOREVER	Eternal (EMI)
7	11	AROUND THE NEXT DREAM	BBM (Virgin)
11	12	PURPLE	Stone Temple Pilots (Atlantic)
16	13	HAPPY NATION (US VERSION)	Ace Of Base (Metronome)
21	14	THE CROSS OF CHANGES	Enigma (Virgin)
13	15	TRUE SPIRIT	Carleen Anderson (Circa)
12	16	THE PLOT THICKENS	Galliano (Talkin' Loud)
18	17	CRAZY	Julio Iglesias (Columbia)
15	18	ZINGALAMADUNI	Arrested Development (Cooltempo)
-	19	AMPLIFIED HEART	Everything But The Girl (blanco y negro)
26	20	FOUR WEDDINGS AND A FUNERAL – SOUNDTRACK	Various Artists (Vertigo)
19	21	BAD BOYS INC	Bad Boys Inc (A&M)
-	22	SPLIT	Lush (4AD)
30	23	MIAOW	Beautiful South (Go! Discs)
17	24	GOD SHUFFLED HIS FEET	Crash Test Dummies (RCA)
27	25	BROTHER SISTER	Brand New Heavies (ffrr)
23	26	BLADERUNNER – SOUNDTRACK	Vangelis (East West)
14	27	I SAY, I SAY, I SAY	Erasure (Mute)
35	28	WOODFACE	Crowded House (Capitol)
37	29	TOGETHER ALONE	Crowded House (Capitol)
28	30	EVERYTHING CHANGES	Take That (RCA)
32	31	BALLS TO PICASSO	Bruce Dickinson (EMI)
36	32	CRASH! BOOM! BANG!	Roxette (EMI)
20	33	LIFEFORMS	Future Sound Of London (Virgin)
31	34	NEVERMIND	Nirvana (Geffen)
32	35	ILL COMMUNICATIONS	Beastie Boys (Capitol)
34	36	A CARNIVAL OF HITS	Judith Durham & the Seekers (EMI)
40	37	LAST OF THE INDEPENDENTS	Pretenders (WEA)
39	38	THIS WAY UP	Chris De Burgh (A&M)
24	39	THE BEAUTIFUL EXPERIENCE	Prince (Symbol)
-	40	KEROSENE HAT	Cracker (Virgin)
49	41	LIVE: WITHOUT THE AID OF A SAFETY NET	Big Country (Compulsion)
42	42	D:REAM ON VOL 1	D:Ream (Magnet)
47	43	GIVE OUT BUT DON'T GIVE UP	Primal Scream (Creation)
29	44	DOMINATOR	Time Frequency (Internal Affairs)
41	45	PHILADELPHIA – SOUNDTRACK	Various Artists (Epic)
-	46	TAKE ME TO GOD	Jah Wobble's Invaders Of The Heart (Island)
43	47	THE VERY BEST OF MARVIN GAYE	Marvin Gaye (Motown)
-	48	WALK ON	Boston (MCA)
-	49	CLOSER TO YOU	JJ Cale (Delabel)
-	50	IMPLANT	Eat Static (Ultimate)

The soundtrack to *Four Weddings And A Funeral* – the most successful British movie of all time – included *Love Is All Around* by Wet Wet Wet, which was topping the singles chart for the whole summer. The soundtrack from *Bladerunner* was revived as Ridley Scott's 'Director's Cut' was offered up.

July 1994

Lots of women singers entering the chart in February, including Eddie Reader – a bluesy Nana Mouskouri lokalike – Toni Braxton and the ever-youthful Diana Ross. Prodigy were big among all the twelve-year-old boys I asked, and now here comes Bob and the Rats – always suspected of being a bit too self-knowing.

428

July – August 1994

23 July 1994

last week	this week	Title	Artist (Label)
-	1	VOODOO LOUNGE	Rolling Stones (Virgin)
1	2	MUSIC FOR THE JILTED GENERATION	Prodigy (XL)
13	3	END OF PART ONE – THEIR GREATEST HITS	Wet Wet Wet (Precious)
7	4	GREATEST HITS	Whitesnake (EMI)
2	5	HAPPY NATION (US VERSION)	Ace Of Base (Metronome)
5	6	EVERYBODY ELSE IS DOING IT, SO WHY CAN'T WE	Cranberries (Island)
4	7	MUSIC BOX	Mariah Carey (Columbia)
6	8	THE VERY BEST OF THE ELECTRIC LIGHT ORCHESTRA	Electric Light Orchestra (Dino)
3	9	TURN IT UPSIDE DOWN	Spin Doctors (Epic)
-	10	THE VERY BEST OF THE EAGLES	Eagles (Elektra)
30	11	FEELING GOOD – THE BEST OF NINA SIMONE	Nina Simone (Verve)
10	12	THE DIVISION BELL	Pink Floyd (EMI)
8	13	PARKLIFE	Blur (Food)
9	14	EDDI READER	Eddi Reader (blanco y negro)
-	15	HUNGRY FOR STINK	L7 (London)
17	16	GOD SHUFFLED HIS FEET	Crash Test Dummies (RCA)
18	17	EVERYTHING CHANGES	Take That (RCA)
11	18	OUR TOWN – THE GREATEST HITS	Deacon Blue (Columbia)
24	19	AUTOGEDDON	Julian Cope (Echo)
15	20	FOUR WEDDINGS AND A FUNERAL – SOUNDTRACK	Various Artists (Vertigo)
16	21	ILL COMMUNICATIONS	Beastie Boys (Capitol)
20	22	SEAL	Seal (ZTT)
19	23	ONE WOMAN – THE ULTIMATE COLLECTION	Diana Ross (EMI)
14	24	CRAZY	Julio Iglesias (Columbia)
27	25	THE CROSS OF CHANGES	Enigma (Virgin)
-	26	ALL-4-ONE	All-4-One (Atlantic)
22	27	ALWAYS AND FOREVER	Eternal (EMI)
21	28	REAL THINGS	2 Unlimited (PWL Continental)
12	29	LOUDMOUTH: THE BEST OF THE BOOMTOWN RATS AND BOB GELDOF	Boomtown Rats and Bob Geldof (Vertigo)
23	30	MIAOW	Beautiful South (Go! Discs)
50	31	GREATEST HITS	Troggs (PolyGram TV)
39	32	NEVERMIND	Nirvana (Geffen)
28	33	TONI BRAXTON	Toni Braxton (Arista)
29	34	HEAD LIKE A ROCK	Ian McNabb (This Way Up)
33	35	BROTHER SISTER	Brand New Heavies (ffrr)
34	36	BLACKSTREET	Blackstreet (Interscope)
35	37	THE PLOT THICKENS	Galliano (Talkin' Loud)
38	38	ELEGANT SLUMMING	M People (deConstruction)
-	39	AGE AIN'T NOTHING BUT A NUMBER	Aaliyah (Jive)
31	40	CARNIVAL OF LIGHT	Ride (Creation)
40	41	GET A GRIP	Aerosmith (Geffen)
49	42	HIS 'N' HERS	Pulp (Island)
32	43	POMME FRITZ	Orb (Island)
37	44	WOODFACE	Crowded House (Capitol)
41	45	D:REAM ON VOL 1	D:Ream (Magnet)
45	46	LAST OF THE INDEPENDENTS	Pretenders (WEA)
-	47	MAJOR WORKS OF CANTO GRGORIANO	Monks'Chorus Silos (EMI Classics)
46	48	RISE AND SHINE	Aswad (Bubblin')
43	49	BLADERUNNER – SOUNDTRACK	Vangelis (East West)
-	50	TO THE MAXIMUM	Maxx (Pulse 8)

30 July 1994

last week	this week	Title	Artist (Label)
1	1	VOODOO LOUNGE	Rolling Stones (Virgin)
2	2	MUSIC FOR THE JILTED GENERATION	Prodigy (XL)
3	3	END OF PART ONE – THEIR GREATEST HITS	Wet Wet Wet (Precious)
10	4	THE VERY BEST OF THE EAGLES	E (Elektra)
4	5	GREATEST HITS	Whitesnake (EMI)
5	6	HAPPY NATION (US VERSION)	Ace Of Base (Metronome)
7	7	MUSIC BOX	Mariah Carey (Columbia)
6	8	EVERYBODY ELSE IS DOING IT, SO WHY CAN'T WE	Cranberries (Island)
16	9	GOD SHUFFLED HIS FEET	Crash Test Dummies (RCA)
-	10	SAME AS IT EVER WAS	House Of Pain (Ruffness)
8	11	THE VERY BEST OF THE ELECTRIC LIGHT ORCHESTRA	Electric Light Orchestra (Dino)
11	12	FEELING GOOD – THE BEST OF NINA SIMONE	Nina Simone (Verve)
9	13	TURN IT UPSIDE DOWN	Spin Doctors (Epic)
13	14	PARKLIFE	Blur (Food)
12	15	THE DIVISION BELL	Pink Floyd (EMI)
17	16	EVERYTHING CHANGES	Take That (RCA)
22	17	SEAL	Seal (ZTT)
14	18	EDDI READER	Eddi Reader (blanco y negro)
18	19	OUR TOWN – THE GREATEST HITS	Deacon Blue (Columbia)
20	20	FOUR WEDDINGS AND A FUNERAL – SOUNDTRACK	Various Artists (Vertigo)
21	21	ILL COMMUNICATIONS	Beastie Boys (Capitol)
26	22	ALL-4-ONE	All-4-One (Atlantic)
24	23	CRAZY	Julio Iglesias (Columbia)
25	24	THE CROSS OF CHANGES	Enigma (Virgin)
25	25	IN CONCERT	Carreras, Domingo, Pavarotti, Mehta (Decca)
23	26	ONE WOMAN – THE ULTIMATE COLLECTION	Diana Ross (EMI)
39	27	AGE AIN'T NOTHING BUT A NUMBER	Aaliyah (Jive)
15	28	HUNGRY FOR STINK	L7 (London)
27	29	ALWAYS AND FOREVER	Eternal (EMI)
32	30	NEVERMIND	Nirvana (Geffen)
33	31	TONI BRAXTON	Toni Braxton (Arista)
19	32	BROTHER SISTER	Brand New Heavies (ffrr)
19	33	AUTOGEDDON	Julian Cope (Echo)
28	34	REAL THINGS	2 Unlimited (PWL Continental)
37	35	THE PLOT THICKENS	Galliano (Talkin' Loud)
36	36	ELEGANT SLUMMING	M People (deConstruction)
31	37	GREATEST HITS	Troggs (PolyGram TV)
30	38	MIAOW	Beautiful South (Go! Discs)
41	39	GET A GRIP	Aerosmith (Geffen)
45	40	D:REAM ON VOL 1	D:Ream (Magnet)
-	41	I SAY I SAY I SAY	Erasure (Mute)
46	42	LAST OF THE INDEPENDENTS	Pretenders (WEA)
42	43	HIS 'N' HERS	Pulp (Island)
47	44	MAJOR WORKS OF CANTO GRGORIANO	Monks'Chorus Silos (EMI Classics)
44	45	BLACKSTREET	Blackstreet (Interscope)
29	46	LOUDMOUTH: THE BEST OF...	Boomtown Rats and Bob Geldof (Vertigo)
44	47	WOODFACE	Crowded House (Capitol)
48	48	RISE AND SHINE	Aswad (Bubblin')
-	49	BUSINESS OF PUNISHMENT	Consolidated (London)
-	50	LIVE IN AMERICA	Neil Diamond (Columbia)

6 August 1994

last week	this week	Title	Artist (Label)
3	1	END OF PART ONE – THEIR GREATEST HITS	Wet Wet Wet (Precious)
2	2	MUSIC FOR THE JILTED GENERATION	Prodigy (XL)
1	3	VOODOO LOUNGE	Rolling Stones (Virgin)
4	4	THE VERY BEST OF THE EAGLES	Eagles (Elektra)
5	5	GREATEST HITS	Whitesnake (EMI)
6	6	HAPPY NATION (US VERSION)	Ace Of Base (Metronome)
7	7	MUSIC BOX	Mariah Carey (Columbia)
9	8	GOD SHUFFLED HIS FEET	Crash Test Dummies (RCA)
-	9	THE GLORY OF GERSHWIN	Various Artists (Mercury)
10	10	SAME AS IT EVER WAS	House Of Pain (Ruffness)
11	11	THE VERY BEST OF THE ELECTRIC LIGHT ORCHESTRA	Electric Light Orchestra (Dino)
8	12	EVERYBODY ELSE IS DOING IT, SO WHY CAN'T WE	Cranberries (Island)
14	13	PARKLIFE	Blur (Food)
-	14	SEAL	Seal (ZTT)
-	15	PANDEMONIUM	Killing Joke (Big Life)
16	16	EVERYTHING CHANGES	Take That (RCA)
12	17	FEELING GOOD – THE BEST OF NINA SIMONE	Nina Simone (Verve)
19	18	OUR TOWN – THE GREATEST HITS	Deacon Blue (Columbia)
25	19	IN CONCERT	Carreras, Domingo, Pavarotti, Mehta (Decca)
-	20	LIVE! LIVE! LIVE!	Bryan Adams (A&M)
13	21	TURN IT UPSIDE DOWN	Spin Doctors (Epic)
15	22	THE DIVISION BELL	Pink Floyd (EMI)
-	23	GREATEST HITS	Gipsy Kings (Columbia)
23	24	CRAZY	Julio Iglesias (Columbia)
20	25	FOUR WEDDINGS AND A FUNERAL – SOUNDTRACK	Various Artists (Vertigo)
30	26	NEVERMIND	Nirvana (Geffen)
32	27	BROTHER SISTER	Brand New Heavies (ffrr)
31	28	TONI BRAXTON	Toni Braxton (Arista)
18	29	EDDI READER	Eddi Reader (blanco y negro)
41	30	I SAY I SAY I SAY	Erasure (Mute)
22	31	ALL-4-ONE	All-4-One (Atlantic)
21	32	ILL COMMUNICATIONS	Beastie Boys (Capitol)
29	33	ALWAYS AND FOREVER	Eternal (EMI)
-	34	REGULATE...G FUNK ERA	Warren G (Island)
24	35	THE CROSS OF CHANGES	Enigma (Virgin)
26	36	ELEGANT SLUMMING	M People (deConstruction)
26	37	ONE WOMAN – THE ULTIMATE COLLECTION	Diana Ross (EMI)
34	38	REAL THINGS	2 Unlimited (PWL Continental)
-	39	PAWNSHOP GUITARS	Gilby Clarke (Virgin America)
-	40	COHEN LIVE	Leonard Cohen (Columbia)
39	41	GET A GRIP	Aerosmith (Geffen)
27	42	AGE AIN'T NOTHING BUT A NUMBER	Aaliyah (Jive)
35	43	THE PLOT THICKENS	Galliano (Talkin' Loud)
40	44	D:REAM ON VOL 1	D:Ream (Magnet)
38	45	MIAOW	Beautiful South (Go! Discs)
42	46	LAST OF THE INDEPENDENTS	Pretenders (WEA)
47	47	RISE AND SHINE	Aswad (Bubblin')
28	48	HUNGRY FOR STINK	L7 (London)
47	49	WOODFACE	Crowded House (Capitol)
-	50	TREAT U RIGHT	Blackgirl (RCA)

Another entry at Number One for a band with over 30 years of recording behind them. The Stones' eponymous first album also went straight in at the top, in April 1964 – but *it* manged to stay there for twelve weeks. Other veterans entering this month: the Eagles, George Gerschwin and those three old tenors.

August 1994

last week	this week	13 August 1994	
1	1	END OF PART ONE – THEIR GREATEST HITS	Wet Wet Wet (Precious)
9	2	THE GLORY OF GERSHWIN	Various Artists (Mercury)
2	3	MUSIC FOR THE JILTED GENERATION	Prodigy (XL)
3	4	VOODOO LOUNGE	Rolling Stones (Virgin)
4	5	THE VERY BEST OF THE EAGLES	Eagles (Elektra)
-	6	SWAGGER	Gun (A&M)
6	7	HAPPY NATION (US VERSION)	Ace Of Base (Metronome)
8	8	GOD SHUFFLED HIS FEET	Crash Test Dummies (RCA)
-	9	ONE CAREFUL OWNER Michael Ball (Columbia)	
7	10	MUSIC BOX	Mariah Carey (Columbia)
5	11	GREATEST HITS	Whitesnake (EMI)
23	12	GREATEST HITS	Gipsy Kings (Columbia)
13	13	PARKLIFE	Blur (Food)
14	14	SEAL	Seal (ZTT)
12	15	EVERYBODY ELSE IS DOING IT, SO WHY CAN'T WE	Cranberries (Island)
10	16	SAME AS IT EVER WAS	House Of Pain (Ruffness)
11	17	THE VERY BEST OF THE ELECTRIC LIGHT ORCHESTRA	Electric Light Orchestra (Dino)
27	18	BROTHER SISTER	Brand New Heavies (ffrr)
22	19	THE DIVISION BELL	Pink Floyd (EMI)
19	20	IN CONCERT	Carreras, Domingo, Pavarotti, Mehta (Decca)
20	21	LIVE! LIVE! LIVE!	Bryan Adams (A&M)
15	22	PANDEMONIUM	Killing Joke (Big Life)
16	23	EVERYTHING CHANGES	Take That (RCA)
34	24	REGULATE...G FUNK ERA	Warren G (Island)
24	25	CRAZY	Julio Iglesias (Columbia)
18	26	OUR TOWN – THE GREATEST HITS	Deacon Blue (Columbia)
17	27	FEELING GOOD – THE BEST OF NINA SIMONE	Nina Simone (Verve)
29	28	EDDI READER	Eddi Reader (blanco y negro)
21	29	TURN IT UPSIDE DOWN	Spin Doctors (Epic)
32	30	ILL COMMUNICATIONS	Beastie Boys (Capitol)
33	31	ALWAYS AND FOREVER	Eternal (EMI)
-	32	WOODSTOCK	Jimi Hendrix (Polydor)
25	33	FOUR WEDDINGS AND A FUNERAL – SOUNDTRACK	Various Artists (Vertigo)
26	34	NEVERMIND	Nirvana (Geffen)
28	35	TONI BRAXTON	Toni Braxton (Arista)
30	36	I SAY I SAY I SAY	Erasure (Mute)
36	37	ELEGANT SLUMMING M People (deConstruction)	
31	38	ALL-4-ONE	All-4-One (Atlantic)
35	39	THE CROSS OF CHANGES	Enigma (Virgin)
40	40	COHEN LIVE	Leonard Cohen (Columbia)
41	41	GET A GRIP	Aerosmith (Geffen)
-	42	FFWD	FFWD (Inter-Modo)
43	43	THE PLOT THICKENS	Galliano (Talkin' Loud)
37	44	ONE WOMAN – THE ULTIMATE COLLECTION	Diana Ross (EMI)
-	45	THE FLINTSTONES – S'TRACK	Various (MCA)
38	46	REAL THINGS	2 Unlimited (PWL Continental)
39	47	PAWNSHOP GUITARS	Gilby Clarke (Virgin America)
42	48	AGE AIN'T NOTHING BUT A NUMBER	Aaliyah (Jive)
-	49	NO PRIMA DONNA – THE SONGS OF VAN MORRISON	Various Artists (Exile)
-	50	SUPERUNKNOWN	Soundgarden (A&M)

last week	this week	20 August 1994	
1	1	END OF PART ONE – THEIR GREATEST HITS	Wet Wet Wet (Precious)
2	2	THE GLORY OF GERSHWIN	Various Artists (Mercury)
3	3	MUSIC FOR THE JILTED GENERATION	Prodigy (XL)
4	4	VOODOO LOUNGE	Rolling Stones (Virgin)
5	5	THE VERY BEST OF THE EAGLES	Eagles (Elektra)
-	6	SNIVILISATION	Orbital (Internal)
6	7	SWAGGER	Gun (A&M)
9	8	ONE CAREFUL OWNER Michael Ball (Columbia)	
8	9	GOD SHUFFLED HIS FEET	Crash Test Dummies (RCA)
10	10	MUSIC BOX	Mariah Carey (Columbia)
7	11	HAPPY NATION (US VERSION)	Ace Of Base (Metronome)
14	12	SEAL	Seal (ZTT)
11	13	GREATEST HITS	Whitesnake (EMI)
13	14	PARKLIFE	Blur (Food)
15	15	EVERYBODY ELSE IS DOING IT, SO WHY CAN'T WE	Cranberries (Island)
19	16	THE DIVISION BELL	Pink Floyd (EMI)
12	17	GREATEST HITS	Gipsy Kings (Columbia)
18	18	BROTHER SISTER	Brand New Heavies (ffrr)
25	19	CRAZY	Julio Iglesias (Columbia)
16	20	SAME AS IT EVER WAS	House Of Pain (Ruffness)
17	21	THE VERY BEST OF THE ELECTRIC LIGHT ORCHESTRA	Electric Light Orchestra (Dino)
20	22	IN CONCERT	Carreras, Domingo, Pavarotti, Mehta (Decca)
31	23	ALWAYS AND FOREVER	Eternal (EMI)
24	24	REGULATE...G FUNK ERA	Warren G (Island)
23	25	EVERYTHING CHANGES	Take That (RCA)
26	26	OUR TOWN – THE GREATEST HITS	Deacon Blue (Columbia)
-	27	MARS AUDIAC QUINTET	Stereolab (Duophonic UHF)
28	28	EDDI READER	Eddi Reader (blanco y negro)
30	29	ILL COMMUNICATIONS	Beastie Boys (Capitol)
27	30	FEELING GOOD – THE BEST OF NINA SIMONE	Nina Simone (Verve)
29	31	TURN IT UPSIDE DOWN	Spin Doctors (Epic)
32	32	WOODSTOCK	Jimi Hendrix (Polydor)
21	33	LIVE! LIVE! LIVE!	Bryan Adams (A&M)
-	34	BURN MY EYES	Machine Head (Roadrunner)
50	35	SUPERUNKNOWN	Soundgarden (A&M)
34	36	NEVERMIND	Nirvana (Geffen)
33	37	FOUR WEDDINGS AND A FUNERAL – SOUNDTRACK	Various Artists (Vertigo)
35	38	TONI BRAXTON	Toni Braxton (Arista)
37	39	ELEGANT SLUMMINGM People (deConstruction)	
39	40	THE CROSS OF CHANGES	Enigma (Virgin)
36	41	I SAY I SAY I SAY	Erasure (Mute)
43	42	THE PLOT THICKENS	Galliano (Talkin' Loud)
-	43	PARIS	Malcolm McLaren (No!)
44	44	ONE WOMAN – THE ULTIMATE COLLECTION	Diana Ross (EMI)
41	45	GET A GRIP	Aerosmith (Geffen)
40	46	COHEN LIVE	Leonard Cohen (Columbia)
-	47	DEBUT	Bjork (One Little Indian)
-	48	1-800-NEW-FUNK	Various Artists (NPG)
45	49	THE FLINTSTONES – SOUNDTRACK	Various Artists (MCA)
22	50	PANDEMONIUM	Killing Joke (Big Life)

last week	this week	27 August 1994	
-	1	COME	Prince (Warner Bros.)
-	2	SLEEPS WITH ANGELS	Neil Young & Crazy Horse (Reprise)
1	3	END OF PART ONE – THEIR GREATEST HITS	Wet Wet Wet (Precious)
2	4	THE GLORY OF GERSHWIN	Various Artists (Mercury)
5	5	THE VERY BEST OF THE EAGLES Eagles (Elektra)	
3	6	MUSIC FOR THE JILTED GENERATION	Prodigy (XL)
4	7	VOODOO LOUNGE	Rolling Stones (Virgin)
14	8	PARKLIFE	Blur (Food)
12	9	SEAL	Seal (ZTT)
18	10	BROTHER SISTER	Brand New Heavies (ffrr)
-	11	STONED AND DETHRONED	Jesus & Mary Chain (blanco y negro)
6	12	SNIVILISATION	Orbital (Internal)
10	13	MUSIC BOX	Mariah Carey (Columbia)
23	14	ALWAYS AND FOREVER	Eternal (EMI)
8	15	ONE CAREFUL OWNER Michael Ball (Columbia)	
13	16	GREATEST HITS	Whitesnake (EMI)
16	17	THE DIVISION BELL	Pink Floyd (EMI)
9	18	GOD SHUFFLED HIS FEET	Crash Test Dummies (RCA)
11	19	HAPPY NATION (US VERSION)	Ace Of Base (Metronome)
7	20	SWAGGER	Gun (A&M)
15	21	EVERYBODY ELSE IS DOING IT, SO WHY CAN'T WE	Cranberries (Island)
17	22	GREATEST HITS	Gipsy Kings (Columbia)
19	23	CRAZY	Julio Iglesias (Columbia)
26	24	OUR TOWN – THE GREATEST HITS	Deacon Blue (Columbia)
25	25	EVERYTHING CHANGES	Take That (RCA)
35	26	SUPERUNKNOWN	Soundgarden (A&M)
24	27	REGULATE...G FUNK ERA	Warren G (Island)
27	28	MARS AUDIAC QUINTET	Stereolab (Duophonic UHF)
22	29	IN CONCERT	Carreras, Domingo, Pavarotti, Mehta (Decca)
34	30	BURN MY EYES	Machine Head (Roadrunner)
21	31	THE VERY BEST OF THE ELECTRIC LIGHT ORCHESTRA	Electric Light Orchestra (Dino)
-	32	SHE	Harry Connick Jr (Columbia)
-	33	THE MAN IN BLACK – THE DEFINITIVE COLLECTION	Johnny Cash (Columbia)
20	34	SAME AS IT EVER WAS	House Of Pain (Ruffness)
28	35	EDDI READER	Eddi Reader (blanco y negro)
48	36	1-800-NEW-FUNK	Various Artists (NPG)
36	37	NEVERMIND	Nirvana (Geffen)
29	38	ILL COMMUNICATIONS	Beastie Boys (Capitol)
37	39	FOUR WEDDINGS AND A FUNERAL – SOUNDTRACK	Various Artists (Vertigo)
40	40	THE CROSS OF CHANGES	Enigma (Virgin)
39	41	ELEGANT SLUMMING M People (deConstruction)	
-	42	PERMANENT SHADE OF BLUE	Roachford (Columbia)
38	43	TONI BRAXTON	Toni Braxton (Arista)
31	44	TURN IT UPSIDE DOWN	Spin Doctors (Epic)
32	45	WOODSTOCK	Jimi Hendrix (Polydor)
42	46	THE PLOT THICKENS	Galliano (Talkin' Loud)
46	47	COHEN LIVE	Leonard Cohen (Columbia)
-	48	MIAOW	Beautiful South (Go! Discs)
30	49	FEELING GOOD – THE BEST OF NINA SIMONE	Nina Simone (Verve)
45	50	GET A GRIP	Aerosmith (Geffen)

Prince was producing so much material it was difficult to keep up. There were still enough fans to bring *Come* in at Number One, followed closely by Neil Young, who had found a new audience as the godfather of grunge. Jimi Hendrix also enjoyed cult status among young record-buyers, hence *Woodstock*.

last week	this week	3 September 1994	
1	1	COME	Prince (Warner Bros.)
3	2	END OF PART ONE – THEIR GREATEST HITS	Wet Wet Wet (Precious)
2	3	SLEEPS WITH ANGELS	Neil Young & Crazy Horse (Reprise)
14	4	ALWAYS AND FOREVER	Eternal (EMI)
8	5	PARKLIFE	Blur (Food)
4	6	THE GLORY OF GERSHWIN	Various Artists (Mercury)
-	7	TWELVE DEADLY CYNS...AND THEN SOME	Cyndi Lauper (Epic)
-	8	MUSE SICK-N-HOUR MESS AGE	Public Enemy (Def Jam)
9	9	THIRSTY WORK	Status Quo (Polydor)
-	10	EVERYBODY'S GOT ONE	Echobelly (Fauve)
6	11	MUSIC FOR THE JILTED GENERATION	Prodigy (XL)
23	12	CRAZY	Julio Iglesias (Columbia)
5	13	THE VERY BEST OF THE EAGLES	Eagles (Elektra)
9	14	SEAL	Seal (ZTT)
10	15	BROTHER SISTER	Brand New Heavies (ffrr)
33	16	THE MAN IN BLACK – THE DEFINITIVE COLLECTION	Johnny Cash (Columbia)
7	17	VOODOO LOUNGE	Rolling Stones (Virgin)
13	18	MUSIC BOX	Mariah Carey (Columbia)
17	19	THE DIVISION BELL	Pink Floyd (EMI)
16	20	GREATEST HITS	Whitesnake (EMI)
19	21	HAPPY NATION (US VERSION)	Ace Of Base (Metronome)
11	22	STONED AND DETHRONED	Jesus & Mary Chain (blanco y negro)
21	23	EVERYBODY ELSE IS DOING IT, SO WHY CAN'T WE	Cranberries (Island)
26	24	SUPERUNKNOWN	Soundgarden (A&M)
15	25	ONE CAREFUL OWNER	Michael Ball (Columbia)
18	26	GOD SHUFFLED HIS FEET	Crash Test Dummies (RCA)
12	27	SNIVILISATION	Orbital (Internal)
28	28	SHE	Harry Connick Jr (Columbia)
20	29	SWAGGER	Gun (A&M)
25	30	EVERYTHING CHANGES	Take That (RCA)
22	31	GREATEST HITS	Gipsy Kings (Island)
24	32	OUR TOWN – THE GREATEST HITS	Deacon Blue (Columbia)
27	33	REGULATE...G FUNK ERA	Warren G (Island)
37	34	NEVERMIND	Nirvana (Geffen)
35	35	EDDI READER	Eddi Reader (blanco y negro)
-	36	DUMMY	Portishead (Go Beat)
40	37	THE CROSS OF CHANGES	Enigma (Virgin)
29	38	IN CONCERT	Carreras, Domingo, Pavarotti, Mehta (Decca)
31	39	THE VERY BEST OF THE ELECTRIC LIGHT ORCHESTRA	Electric Light Orchestra (Dino)
41	40	ELEGANT SLUMMING	M People (deConstruction)
39	41	FOUR WEDDINGS AND A FUNERAL – SOUNDTRACK	Various Artists (Vertigo)
30	42	BURN MY EYES	Machine Head (Roadrunner)
42	43	PERMANENT SHADE OF BLUE	Roachford (Columbia)
34	44	SAME AS IT EVER WAS	House Of Pain (Ruffness)
50	45	GET A GRIP	Aerosmith (Geffen)
48	46	MIAOW	Beautiful South (Go! Discs)
-	47	WHALER	Sophie B Hawkins (Columbia)
-	48	DEBUT	Bjork (One Little Indian)
-	49	BAKESALE	Sebadoh (Domino)
-	50	DOLLARS	CJ Lewis (MCA)

		10 September 1994	
-	1	DEFINITELY MAYBE	Oasis (Creation)
-	2	THE THREE TENORS – IN CONCERT 1994	Carreras/Domingo/Pavarotti/Mehta (Teldec)
2	3	END OF PART ONE – THEIR GREATEST HITS	Wet Wet Wet (Precious)
7	4	TWELVE DEADLY CYNS...AND THEN SOME	Cyndi Lauper (Epic)
5	5	PARKLIFE	Blur (Food)
1	6	COME	Prince (Warner Bros.)
-	7	THE HOLY BIBLE	Manic Street Preachers (Epic)
4	8	ALWAYS AND FOREVER	Eternal (EMI)
3	9	SLEEPS WITH ANGELS	Neil Young & Crazy Horse (Reprise)
15	10	BROTHER SISTER	Brand New Heavies (ffrr)
12	11	CRAZY	Julio Iglesias (Columbia)
10	12	EVERYBODY'S GOT ONE	Echobelly (Fauve)
6	13	THE GLORY OF GERSHWIN	Various (Mercury)
11	14	MUSIC FOR THE JILTED GENERATION	Prodigy (XL)
-	15	THE ESSENTIAL COLLECTION	Elvis Presley (RCA)
-	16	SECRET WORLD LIVE	Peter Gabriel (Real World)
8	17	MUSE SICK-N-HOUR MESS AGE	Public Enemy (Def Jam)
14	18	SEAL	Seal (ZTT)
13	19	THE VERY BEST OF THE EAGLES	Eagles (Elektra)
16	20	THE MAN IN BLACK – THE DEFINITIVE COLLECTION	Johnny Cash (Columbia)
9	21	THIRSTY WORK	Status Quo (Polydor)
20	22	GREATEST HITS	Whitesnake (EMI)
18	23	MUSIC BOX	Mariah Carey (Columbia)
-	24	WITHOUT A SOUND	Dinosaur Jr (blanco y negro)
19	25	THE DIVISION BELL	Pink Floyd (EMI)
17	26	VOODOO LOUNGE	Rolling Stones (Virgin)
24	27	SUPERUNKNOWN	Soundgarden (A&M)
23	28	EVERBODY ELSE IS DOING IT, SO WHY CAN'T WE	Cranberries (Island)
26	29	GOD SHUFFLED HIS FEET	Crash Test Dummies (RCA)
21	30	HAPPY NATION (US VERSION)	Ace Of Base (Metronome)
30	31	EVERYTHING CHANGES	Take That (RCA)
25	32	ONE CAREFUL OWNER	Michael Ball (Columbia)
-	33	THE VERY BEST OF RANDY CRAWFORD	Randy Crawford (Dino)
31	34	GREATEST HITS	Gipsy Kings (Island)
29	35	SWAGGER	Gun (A&M)
32	36	OUR TOWN – THE GREATEST HITS	Deacon Blue (Columbia)
28	37	SHE	Harry Connick Jr (Columbia)
27	38	SNIVILISATION	Orbital (Internal)
36	39	DUMMY	Portishead (Go Beat)
40	40	ELEGANT SLUMMING	M People (deConstruction)
34	41	NEVERMIND	Nirvana (Geffen)
-	42	HOW TO MAKE FRIENDS AND INFLUENCE PEOPLE	Terrorvision (Total Vegas)
46	43	MIAOW	Beautiful South (Go! Discs)
43	44	PERMANENT SHADE OF BLUE	Roachford (Columbia)
22	45	STONED AND DETHRONED	Jesus & Mary Chain (blanco y negro)
33	46	REGULATE...G FUNK ERA	Warren G (Island)
35	47	EDDI READER	Eddi Reader (blanco Y negro)
41	48	FOUR WEDDINGS AND A FUNERAL – SOUNDTRACK	Various Artists (Vertigo)
-	49	DOWN	Jesus Lizard (Touch & Go)
-	50	LOST IN THE FORMER WEST	Fatima Mansions (Radioactive)

		17 September 1994	
1	1	DEFINITELY MAYBE	Oasis (Creation)
2	2	THE THREE TENORS – IN CONCERT 1994	Carreras/Domingo/Pavarotti/Mehta (Teldec)
3	3	END OF PART ONE – THEIR GREATEST HITS	Wet Wet Wet (Precious)
4	4	TWELVE DEADLY CYNS...AND THEN SOME	Cyndi Lauper (Epic)
5	5	PARKLIFE	Blur (Food)
15	6	THE ESSENTIAL COLLECTION	Elvis Presley (RCA)
-	7	FILE UNDER: EASY LISTENING	Sugar (Creation)
8	8	ALWAYS AND FOREVER	Eternal (EMI)
-	9	MAMOUNA	Bryan Ferry (Virgin)
6	10	COME	Prince (Warner Bros.)
9	11	SLEEPS WITH ANGELS	Neil Young & Crazy Horse (Reprise)
10	12	BROTHER SISTER	Brand New Heavies (ffrr)
7	13	THE HOLY BIBLE	Manic Street Preachers (Epic)
14	14	MUSIC FOR THE JILTED GENERATION	Prodigy (XL)
16	15	SECRET WORLD LIVE	Peter Gabriel (Real World)
11	16	CRAZY	Julio Iglesias (Columbia)
-	17	HAVE A LITTLE FAITH	Joe Cocker (Capitol)
-	18	CHANGE OVER	Shed Seven (Polydor)
-	19	HAPPINESS?	Roger Taylor (Parlophone)
13	20	THE GLORY OF GERSHWIN	Various Artists (Mercury)
18	21	SEAL	Seal (ZTT)
23	22	MUSIC BOX	Mariah Carey (Columbia)
20	23	THE MAN IN BLACK – THE DEFINITIVE COLLECTION	Johnny Cash (Columbia)
17	24	MUSE SICK-N-HOUR MESS AGE	Public Enemy (Def Jam)
12	25	EVERYBODY'S GOT ONE	Echobelly (Fauve)
22	26	GREATEST HITS	Whitesnake (EMI)
25	27	THE DIVISION BELL	Pink Floyd (EMI)
19	28	THE VERY BEST OF THE EAGLES	Eagles (Elektra)
28	29	EVERBODY ELSE IS DOING IT, SO WHY CAN'T WE	Cranberries (Island)
33	30	THE VERY BEST OF RANDY CRAWFORD	Randy Crawford (Dino)
27	31	SUPERUNKNOWN	Soundgarden (A&M)
24	32	WITHOUT A SOUND	Dinosaur Jr (blanco y negro)
-	33	SELF ABUSED	S*M*A*S*H* (Hi-Rise)
26	34	VOODOO LOUNGE	Rolling Stones (Virgin)
29	35	GOD SHUFFLED HIS FEET	Crash Test Dummies (RCA)
30	36	HAPPY NATION (US VERSION)	Ace Of Base (Metronome)
31	37	EVERYTHING CHANGES	Take That (RCA)
32	38	ONE CAREFUL OWNER	Michael Ball (Columbia)
40	39	ELEGANT SLUMMING	M People (deConstruction)
48	40	FOUR WEDDINGS AND A FUNERAL – SOUNDTRACK	Various Artists (Vertigo)
42	41	HOW TO MAKE FRIENDS AND INFLUENCE PEOPLE	Terrorvision (Total Vegas)
36	42	OUR TOWN – THE GREATEST HITS	Deacon Blue (Columbia)
35	43	SWAGGER	Gun (A&M)
39	44	DUMMY	Portishead (Go Beat)
-	45	BORN DEAD	Body Count (Rhyme Syndicate)
41	46	NEVERMIND	Nirvana (Geffen)
38	47	SNIVILISATION	Orbital (Internal)
-	48	WORLD DEMISE	Obituary (Roadrunner)
21	49	THIRSTY WORK	Status Quo (Polydor)
-	50	JOLLIFICATION	Lightning Seeds (Epic)

Oasis crashed in at the top with the album destined to be voted LP of the year by the NME writers. They thus joined Blur and Suede at the vanguard of a new kind of British music, though many people said it sounded awfully like something they'd heard before. Still there was always the sublime Elvis, in at No. 15.

431

September – October 1994

24 September 1994

last week	this week	Title	Artist
-	1	FROM THE CRADLE	Eric Clapton (Duck)
2	2	THE THREE TENORS – IN CONCERT 1994	Carreras/Domingo/Pavarotti/Mehta (Teldec)
1	3	DEFINITELY MAYBE	Oasis (Creation)
3	4	END OF PART ONE – THEIR GREATEST HITS	Wet Wet Wet (Precious)
5	5	PARKLIFE	Blur (Food)
4	6	TWELVE DEADLY CYNS...AND THEN SOME	Cyndi Lauper (Epic)
6	7	THE ESSENTIAL COLLECTION	Elvis Presley (RCA)
-	8	DISCO 2	Pet Shop Boys (Parlophone)
-	9	LIVE WOOD	Paul Weller (Go! Discs)
14	10	MUSIC FOR THE JILTED GENERATION	Prodigy (XL)
17	11	HAVE A LITTLE FAITH	Joe Cocker (Capitol)
-	12	WAH WAH	James (Fontana)
8	13	ALWAYS AND FOREVER	Eternal (EMI)
16	14	CRAZY	Julio Iglesias (Columbia)
12	15	BROTHER SISTER	Brand New Heavies (ffrr)
9	16	MAMOUNA	Bryan Ferry (Virgin)
7	17	FILE UNDER: EASY LISTENING	Sugar (Creation)
11	18	SLEEPS WITH ANGELS	Neil Young & Crazy Horse (Reprise)
-	19	THE RHYTHM OF LOVE	Anita Baker (Elektra)
10	20	COME	Prince (Warner Bros.)
-	21	II	Boyz II Men (Motown)
13	22	THE HOLY BIBLE	Manic Street Preachers (Epic)
20	23	THE GLORY OF GERSHWIN	Various Artists (Mercury)
27	24	THE DIVISION BELL	Pink Floyd (EMI)
21	25	SEAL	Seal (ZTT)
15	26	SECRET WORLD LIVE	Peter Gabriel (Real World)
18	27	CHANGE OVER	Shed Seven (Polydor)
45	28	BORN DEAD	Body Count (Rhyme Syndicate)
19	29	HAPPINESS?	Roger Taylor (Parlophone)
39	30	ELEGANT SLUMMING	M People (deConstruction)
22	31	MUSIC BOX	Mariah Carey (Columbia)
24	32	MUSE SICK-N-HOUR MESS AGE	Public Enemy (Def Jam)
-	33	WATUSI	Wedding Present (Island)
23	34	THE MAN IN BLACK – THE DEFINITIVE COLLECTION	Johnny Cash (Columbia)
31	35	SUPERUNKNOWN	Soundgarden (A&M)
26	36	GREATEST HITS	Whitesnake (EMI)
34	37	VOODOO LOUNGE	Rolling Stones (Virgin)
28	38	THE VERY BEST OF THE EAGLES	Eagles (Elektra)
-	39	HONEY	Robert Palmer (EMI)
40	40	FOUR WEDDINGS AND A FUNERAL – SOUNDTRACK	Various Artists (Vertigo)
-	41	SAN FRANCISCO	American Music Club (Virgin)
25	42	EVERYBODY'S GOT ONE	Echobelly (Fauve)
37	43	EVERYTHING CHANGES	Take That (RCA)
30	44	THE VERY BEST OF RANDY CRAWFORD	Randy Crawford (Dino)
29	45	EVERBODY ELSE IS DOING IT, SO WHY CAN'T WE	Cranberries (Island)
36	46	HAPPY NATION (US VERSION)	Ace Of Base (Metronome)
43	47	SWAGGER	Gun (A&M)
48	48	NEVERMIND	Nirvana (Geffen)
33	49	SELF ABUSED	S*M*A*S*H (Hi-Rise)
38	50	ONE CAREFUL OWNER	Michael Ball (Columbia)

1 October 1994

last week	this week	Title	Artist
1	1	FROM THE CRADLE	Eric Clapton (Duck)
-	2	KYLIE MINOGUE	Kylie Minogue (deConstruction)
3	3	SONGS	Luther Vandross (Epic)
2	4	THE THREE TENORS – IN CONCERT 1994	Carreras/Domingo/Pavarotti/Mehta (Teldec)
3	5	DEFINITELY MAYBE	Oasis (Creation)
6	6	TWELVE DEADLY CYNS...AND THEN SOME	Cyndi Lauper (Epic)
5	7	PARKLIFE	Blur (Food)
4	8	END OF PART ONE – THEIR GREATEST HITS	Wet Wet Wet (Precious)
7	9	THE ESSENTIAL COLLECTION	Elvis Presley (RCA)
8	10	DISCO 2	Pet Shop Boys (Parlophone)
10	11	MUSIC FOR THE JILTED GENERATION	Prodigy (XL)
-	12	UNIVERSAL MOTHER	Sinead O'Connor (Ensign)
-	13	DOS DEDOS MES AMIGOS	Pop Will Eat Itself (Infectious)
19	14	THE RHYTHM OF LOVE	Anita Baker (Elektra)
14	15	CRAZY	Julio Iglesias (Columbia)
9	16	EVOLVER	Grid (deConstruction)
9	17	LIVE WOOD	Paul Weller (Go! Discs)
13	18	ALWAYS AND FOREVER	Eternal (EMI)
11	19	HAVE A LITTLE FAITH	Joe Cocker (Capitol)
12	20	WAH WAH	James (Fontana)
15	21	BROTHER SISTER	Brand New Heavies (ffrr)
21	22	II	Boyz II Men (Motown)
30	23	ELEGANT SLUMMING	M People (deConstruction)
-	24	MIGHTY JOE MOON	Grant Lee Buffalo (London)
39	25	HONEY	Robert Palmer (EMI)
23	26	THE GLORY OF GERSHWIN	Various Artists (Mercury)
-	27	FLYER	Nanci Griffith (MCA)
17	28	FILE UNDER: EASY LISTENING	Sugar (Creation)
16	29	MAMOUNA	Bryan Ferry (Virgin)
18	30	SLEEPS WITH ANGELS	Neil Young & Crazy Horse (Reprise)
31	31	MUSIC BOX	Mariah Carey (Columbia)
25	32	SEAL	Seal (ZTT)
24	33	THE DIVISION BELL	Pink Floyd (EMI)
20	34	COME	Prince (Warner Bros.)
22	35	THE HOLY BIBLE	Manic Street Preachers (Epic)
33	36	WATUSI	Wedding Present (Island)
32	37	MUSE SICK-N-HOUR MESS AGE	Public Enemy (Def Jam)
26	38	SECRET WORLD LIVE	Peter Gabriel (Real World)
27	39	CHANGE OVER	Shed Seven (Polydor)
34	40	THE MAN IN BLACK – THE DEFINITIVE COLLECTION	Johnny Cash (Columbia)
37	41	VOODOO LOUNGE	Rolling Stones (Virgin)
38	42	THE VERY BEST OF THE EAGLES	Eagles (Elektra)
35	43	SUPERUNKNOWN	Soundgarden (A&M)
46	44	HAPPY NATION (US VERSION)	Ace Of Base (Metronome)
36	45	GREATEST HITS	Whitesnake (EMI)
29	46	HAPPINESS?	Roger Taylor (Parlophone)
40	47	FOUR WEDDINGS AND A FUNERAL – SOUNDTRACK	Various Artists (Vertigo)
43	48	EVERYTHING CHANGES	Take That (RCA)
-	49	PERMANENT SHADE OF BLUE	Roachford (Columbia)
28	50	BORN DEAD	Body Count (Rhyme Syndicate)

8 October 1994

last week	this week	Title	Artist
-	1	MONSTER	REM (Warner Bros.)
3	2	SONGS	Luther Vandross (Epic)
-	3	PROTECTION	Massive Attack (Circa)
6	4	TWELVE DEADLY CYNS...AND THEN SOME	Cyndi Lauper (Epic)
1	5	FROM THE CRADLE	Eric Clapton (Duck)
-	6	IF THE BEATLES HAD READ HUNTER...THE SINGLES	Wonder Stuff (Polydor)
5	7	DEFINITELY MAYBE	Oasis (Creation)
2	8	KYLIE MINOGUE	Kylie Minogue (deConstruction)
4	9	THE THREE TENORS – IN CONCERT 1994	Carreras/Domingo/Pavarotti/Mehta (Teldec)
7	10	PARKLIFE	Blur (Food)
8	11	END OF PART ONE – THEIR GREATEST HITS	Wet Wet Wet (Precious)
11	12	MUSIC FOR THE JILTED GENERATION	Prodigy (XL)
9	13	THE ESSENTIAL COLLECTION	Elvis Presley (RCA)
-	14	THE BEST MIXES FROM THE ALBUM, DEBUT	Bjork (One Little Indian)
-	15	CRANK	Almighty (Chrysalis)
16	16	EVOLVER	Grid (deConstruction)
10	17	DISCO 2	Pet Shop Boys (Parlophone)
12	18	UNIVERSAL MOTHER	Sinead O'Connor (Ensign)
13	19	DOS DEDOS MES AMIGOS	Pop Will Eat Itself (Infectious)
14	20	THE RHYTHM OF LOVE	Anita Baker (Elektra)
22	21	II	Boyz II Men (Motown)
15	22	CRAZY	Julio Iglesias (Columbia)
18	23	ALWAYS AND FOREVER	Eternal (EMI)
27	24	FLYER	Nanci Griffith (MCA)
21	25	BROTHER SISTER	Brand New Heavies (ffrr)
24	26	MIGHTY JOE MOON	Grant Lee Buffalo (London)
23	27	ELEGANT SLUMMING	M People (deConstruction)
33	28	THE DIVISION BELL	Pink Floyd (EMI)
31	29	MUSIC BOX	Mariah Carey (Columbia)
-	30	EVERYBODY ELSE IS DOING IT, SO WHY CAN'T WE	Cranberries (Island)
19	31	HAVE A LITTLE FAITH	Joe Cocker (Capitol)
17	32	LIVE WOOD	Paul Weller (Go! Discs)
41	33	VOODOO LOUNGE	Rolling Stones (Virgin)
32	34	SEAL	Seal (ZTT)
29	35	MAMOUNA	Bryan Ferry (Virgin)
26	36	THE GLORY OF GERSHWIN	Various Artists (Mercury)
25	37	HONEY	Robert Palmer (EMI)
30	38	SLEEPS WITH ANGELS	Neil Young & Crazy Horse (Reprise)
-	39	(COME ON, JOIN) THE HIGH SOCIETY	These Animal Men (Hi-Rise)
44	40	HAPPY NATION (US VERSION)	Ace Of Base (Metronome)
-	41	DON'T ASK, DON'T TELL	Come (Beggars Banquet)
38	42	SECRET WORLD LIVE	Peter Gabriel (Real World)
49	43	PERMANENT SHADE OF BLUE	Roachford (Columbia)
43	44	SUPERUNKNOWN	Soundgarden (A&M)
34	45	COME	Prince (Warner Bros.)
28	46	FILE UNDER: EASY LISTENING	Sugar (Creation)
-	47	I LOVE EVERYBODY	Lyle Lovett (MCA)
46	48	HAPPINESS?	Roger Taylor (Parlophone)
20	49	WAH WAH	James (Fontana)
48	50	EVERYTHING CHANGES	Take That (RCA)

These old buggers kept on doing it in 1994. Clapton was back at Number One, 28 years after *Blues Breakers*, recorded with John Mayall, first made it into the album chart. In the intervening decades there has hardly been a year when an Eric Clapton album wasn't around on the chart somewhere.

October 1994

15 October 1994

last week	this week	Title	Artist (Label)
1	1	MONSTER	REM (Warner Bros.)
-	2	NO NEED TO ARGUE	Cranberries (Island)
-	3	THE HIT LIST	Cliff Richard (EMI)
4	4	TWELVE DEADLY CYNS...AND THEN SOME	Cyndi Lauper (Epic)
3	5	PROTECTION	Massive Attack (Circa)
2	6	SONGS	Luther Vandross (Epic)
9	7	THE THREE TENORS – IN CONCERT 1994	Carreras/Domingo/Pavarotti/Mehta (Teldec)
6	8	IF THE BEATLES HAD READ HUNTER...THE SINGLES	Wonder Stuff (Polydor)
5	9	FROM THE CRADLE	Eric Clapton (Duck)
10	10	PARKLIFE	Blur (Food)
7	11	DEFINITELY MAYBE	Oasis (Creation)
12	12	MUSIC FOR THE JILTED GENERATION	Prodigy (XL)
11	13	END OF PART ONE – THEIR GREATEST HITS	Wet Wet Wet (Precious)
8	14	KYLIE MINOGUE	Kylie Minogue (deConstruction)
13	15	THE ESSENTIAL COLLECTION	Elvis Presley (RCA)
22	16	CRAZY	Julio Iglesias (Columbia)
-	17	DIVINE INTERVENTION	Slayer (American)
14	18	THE BEST MIXES FROM THE ALBUM, DEBUT	Bjork (One Little Indian)
15	19	CRANK	Almighty (Chrysalis)
30	20	EVERYBODY ELSE IS DOING IT, SO WHY CAN'T WE	Cranberries (Island)
16	21	VOODOO LOUNGE	Grid (deConstruction)
21	22	II	Boyz II Men (Motown)
20	23	THE RHYTHM OF LOVE	Anita Baker (Elektra)
28	24	THE DIVISION BELL	Pink Floyd (EMI)
23	25	ALWAYS AND FOREVER	Eternal (EMI)
25	26	BROTHER SISTER	Brand New Heavies (ffrr)
18	27	UNIVERSAL MOTHER	Sinead O'Connor (Ensign)
24	28	FLYER	Nanci Griffith (MCA)
33	29	VOODOO LOUNGE	Rolling Stones (Virgin)
29	30	MUSIC BOX	Mariah Carey (Columbia)
17	31	DISCO 2	Pet Shop Boys (Parlophone)
27	32	ELEGANT SLUMMING	M People (deConstruction)
31	33	HAVE A LITTLE FAITH	Joe Cocker (Capitol)
-	34	INTERPRETATIONS	Carpenters (A&M)
19	35	DOS DEDOS MES AMIGOS	Pop Will Eat Itself (Infectious)
34	36	SEAL	Seal (ZTT)
26	37	MIGHTY JOE MOON	Grant Lee Buffalo (London)
40	38	HAPPY NATION (US VERSION)	Ace Of Base (Metronome)
36	39	THE GLORY OF GERSHWIN	Various Artists (Mercury)
-	40	WELCOME TO TOMORROW	Snap (Arista)
-	41	AMERICAN THIGHS	Veronica Salt (Hi-Rise)
32	42	LIVE WOOD	Paul Weller (Go! Discs)
-	43	WITH LOVE – THE BEST OF BRENDA LEE	Brenda Lee (Telstar)
35	44	MAMOUNA	Bryan Ferry (Virgin)
43	45	PERMANENT SHADE OF BLUE	Roachford (Columbia)
50	46	EVERYTHING CHANGES	Take That (RCA)
44	47	SUPERUNKNOWN	Soundgarden (A&M)
37	48	HONEY	Robert Palmer (EMI)
38	49	SLEEPS WITH ANGELS	Neil Young & Crazy Horse (Reprise)
-	50	THE HOLY BIBLE	Manic Street Preachers (Epic)

22 October 1994

last week	this week	Title	Artist (Label)
-	1	CROSS ROAD – THE BEST OF BON JOVI	Bon Jovi (Jambco)
1	2	MONSTER	REM (Warner Bros.)
2	3	DOG MAN STAR	Suede (Nude)
3	4	NO NEED TO ARGUE	Cranberries (Island)
5	5	THE HIT LIST	Cliff Richard (EMI)
4	6	TWELVE DEADLY CYNS...AND THEN SOME	Cyndi Lauper (Epic)
7	7	THE THREE TENORS – IN CONCERT 1994	Carreras/Domingo/Pavarotti/Mehta (Teldec)
6	8	SONGS	Luther Vandross (Epic)
11	9	DEFINITELY MAYBE	Oasis (Creation)
10	10	PARKLIFE	Blur (Food)
30	11	MUSIC BOX	Mariah Carey (Columbia)
9	12	FROM THE CRADLE	Eric Clapton (Duck)
5	13	PROTECTION	Massive Attack (Circa)
12	14	MUSIC FOR THE JILTED GENERATION	Prodigy (XL)
13	15	END OF PART ONE – THEIR GREATEST HITS	Wet Wet Wet (Precious)
-	16	PROMISED LAND	Queensryche (EMI)
15	17	THE ESSENTIAL COLLECTION	Elvis Presley (RCA)
17	18	DIVINE INTERVENTION	Slayer (American)
20	19	EVERYBODY ELSE IS DOING IT, SO WHY CAN'T WE	Cranberries (Island)
-	20	MOVE IT!	Reel 2 Real featuring the Mad Stuntman (Positiva)
-	21	THE CULT	Cult (Beggars Banquet)
8	22	IF THE BEATLES HAD READ HUNTER...THE SINGLES	Wonder Stuff (Polydor)
24	23	THE DIVISION BELL	Pink Floyd (EMI)
18	24	THE BEST MIXES FROM THE ALBUM, DEBUT	Bjork (One Little Indian)
14	25	KYLIE MINOGUE	Kylie Minogue (deConstruction)
16	26	CRAZY	Julio Iglesias (Columbia)
-	27	FORREST GUMP – SOUNDTRACK	Various (Epic)
26	28	BROTHER SISTER	Brand New Heavies (ffrr)
-	29	THE LION KING – SOUNDTRACK	Various Artists (Mercury)
-	30	MICHELLE GAYLE	Michelle Gayle (RCA)
25	31	ALWAYS AND FOREVER	Eternal (EMI)
43	32	WITH LOVE – THE BEST OF BRENDA LEE	Brenda Lee (Telstar)
34	33	INTERPRETATIONS	Carpenters (A&M)
28	34	FLYER	Nanci Griffith (MCA)
-	35	BACK TO BACK	David Essex (PolyGram TV)
27	36	UNIVERSAL MOTHER	Sinead O'Connor (Ensign)
29	37	VOODOO LOUNGE	Rolling Stones (Virgin)
22	38	II	Boyz II Men (Motown)
32	39	ELEGANT SLUMMING	M People (deConstruction)
39	40	THE GLORY OF GERSHWIN	Various Artists (Mercury)
23	41	THE RHYTHM OF LOVE	Anita Baker (Elektra)
-	42	AUTOMATIC FOR THE PEOPLE	REM (Warner Bros.)
36	43	SEAL	Seal (ZTT)
38	44	HAPPY NATION (US VERSION)	Ace Of Base (Metronome)
19	45	CRANK	Almighty (Chrysalis)
44	46	MAMOUNA	Bryan Ferry (Virgin)
-	47	ALIVE IN HELL	Meatloaf (Pure Music)
-	48	THE BEST OF HANK MARVIN & THE SHADOWS	Hank Marvin & the Shadows (PolyGram TV)
40	49	WELCOME TO TOMORROW	Snap (Arista)
-	50	WORST CASE SCENARIO	dEUS (Island)

29 October 1994

last week	this week	Title	Artist (Label)
1	1	CROSS ROAD – THE BEST OF BON JOVI	Bon Jovi (Jambco)
2	2	MONSTER	REM (Warner Bros.)
-	3	THE RETURN OF THE SPACE COWBOY	Jamiroquai (Sony Soho Square)
4	4	NO NEED TO ARGUE	Cranberries (Island)
3	5	DOG MAN STAR	Suede (Nude)
-	6	STEAM	East17 (London)
6	7	TWELVE DEADLY CYNS...AND THEN SOME	Cyndi Lauper (Epic)
5	8	THE HIT LIST	Cliff Richard (EMI)
-	9	HOLD ME, THRILL ME, KISS ME	Gloria Estefan (Epic)
10	10	DEFINITELY MAYBE	Oasis (Creation)
7	11	THE THREE TENORS – IN CONCERT 1994	Carreras/Domingo/Pavarotti/Mehta (Teldec)
11	12	MUSIC BOX	Mariah Carey (Columbia)
8	13	SONGS	Luther Vandross (Epic)
20	14	MOVE IT!	Reel 2 Real featuring the Mad Stuntman (Positiva)
10	15	PARKLIFE	Blur (Food)
23	16	THE DIVISION BELL	Pink Floyd (EMI)
16	17	PROMISED LAND	Queensryche (EMI)
12	18	FROM THE CRADLE	Eric Clapton (Duck)
14	19	MUSIC FOR THE JILTED GENERATION	Prodigy (XL)
27	20	FORREST GUMP – SOUNDTRACK	Various (Epic)
13	21	PROTECTION	Massive Attack (Circa)
29	22	THE LION KING – S'TRACK	Various (Mercury)
17	23	THE ESSENTIAL COLLECTION	Elvis Presley (RCA)
15	24	END OF PART ONE – THEIR GREATEST HITS	Wet Wet Wet (Precious)
21	25	THE CULT	Cult (Beggars Banquet)
19	26	EVERYBODY ELSE IS DOING IT, SO WHY CAN'T WE	Cranberries (Island)
-	27	ESPECIALLY FOR YOU	Daniel O'Donnell (Ritz)
48	28	THE BEST OF HANK MARVIN & THE SHADOWS	Hank Marvin & the Shadows (PolyGram TV)
-	29	THE MIND'S EYE	Stiltskin (White Water)
-	30	STONES IN THE ROAD	Mary Chapin Carpenter (Columbia)
31	31	ALWAYS AND FOREVER	Eternal (EMI)
30	32	MICHELLE GAYLE	Michelle Gayle (RCA)
26	33	CRAZY	Julio Iglesias (Columbia)
32	34	WITH LOVE – THE BEST OF BRENDA LEE	Brenda Lee (Telstar)
28	35	BROTHER SISTER	Brand New Heavies (ffrr)
47	36	ALIVE IN HELL	Meatloaf (Pure Music)
22	37	IF THE BEATLES HAD READ HUNTER...THE SINGLES	Wonder Stuff (Polydor)
18	38	DIVINE INTERVENTION	Slayer (American)
42	39	AUTOMATIC FOR THE PEOPLE	REM (Warner Bros.)
-	40	THE SNAKE	Shane MacGowan & the Popes (ZTT)
33	41	INTERPRETATIONS	Carpenters (A&M)
35	42	BACK TO BACK	David Essex (PolyGram TV)
-	43	INTERNATIONAL TIMES	Trans Global Underground (Nation)
25	44	KYLIE MINOGUE	Kylie Minogue (deConstruction)
37	45	VOODOO LOUNGE	Rolling Stones (Virgin)
38	46	II	Boyz II Men (Motown)
43	47	SEAL	Seal (ZTT)
41	48	THE RHYTHM OF LOVE	Anita Baker (Elektra)
39	49	ELEGANT SLUMMING	M People (deConstruction)
34	50	FLYER	Nanci Griffith (MCA)

Monster was the follow up to the awesomely successful *Automatic For The People*, still on the chart two years after its release in October 1992. Jamiroquai was also in there with a follow up to a big first album. And then there was Cliff and Hank Marvin and the Shads – but in separate packages.

November 1994

5 November 1994

LW	TW	Title	Artist (Label)
1	1	CROSS ROAD – THE BEST OF BON JOVI	Bon Jovi (Jambco)
-	2	BEDTIME STORIES	Madonna (Maverick)
2	3	MONSTER	REM (Warner Bros.)
3	4	THE RETURN OF THE SPACE COWBOY	Jamiroquai (Sony Soho Square)
4	5	NO NEED TO ARGUE	Cranberries (Island)
-	6	YOUTHANASIA	Megadeth (Capitol)
6	7	STEAM	East17 (London)
-	8	THE BEST OF CHRIS REA	Chris Rea (East West)
9	9	HOLD ME, THRILL ME, KISS ME	Gloria Estefan (Epic)
7	10	TWELVE DEADLY CYNS...AND THEN SOME	Cyndi Lauper (Epic)
8	11	THE HIT LIST	Cliff Richard (EMI)
10	12	DEFINITELY MAYBE	Oasis (Creation)
5	13	DOG MAN STAR	Suede (Nude)
16	14	THE DIVISION BELL	Pink Floyd (EMI)
11	15	THE THREE TENORS – IN CONCERT 1994	Carreras/Domingo/Pavarotti/Mehta (Teldec)
15	16	PARKLIFE	Blur (Food)
12	17	MUSIC BOX	Mariah Carey (Columbia)
22	18	THE LION KING – S'TRACK	Various (Mercury)
13	19	SONGS	Luther Vandross (Epic)
20	20	FORREST GUMP – SOUNDTRACK	Various (Epic)
-	21	QUEEN OF SOUL – THE VERY BEST OF ARETHA FRANKLIN	Aretha Franklin (Atlantic)
29	22	THE MIND'S EYE	Stiltskin (White Water)
18	23	FROM THE CRADLE	Eric Clapton (Duck)
14	24	MOVE IT!	Reel 2 Real featuring the Mad Stuntman (Positiva)
27	25	ESPECIALLY FOR YOU	Daniel O'Donnell (Ritz)
-	26	HOMEGROWN	Dodgy (A&M)
24	27	END OF PART ONE – THEIR GREATEST HITS	Wet Wet Wet (Precious)
28	28	THE BEST OF HANK MARVIN & THE SHADOWS	Hank Marvin & the Shadows (PolyGram TV)
19	29	MUSIC FOR THE JILTED GENERATION	Prodigy (XL)
32	30	MICHELLE GAYLE	Michelle Gayle (RCA)
31	31	ALWAYS AND FOREVER	Eternal (EMI)
40	32	THE SNAKE	Shane MacGowan & the Popes (ZTT)
23	33	THE ESSENTIAL COLLECTION	Elvis Presley (RCA)
26	34	EVERYBODY ELSE IS DOING IT, SO WHY CAN'T WE	Cranberries (Island)
34	35	WITH LOVE – THE BEST OF BRENDA LEE	Brenda Lee (Telstar)
21	36	PROTECTION	Massive Attack (Circa)
30	37	STONES IN THE ROAD	Mary Chapin Carpenter (Columbia)
-	38	SONGS WE LOVE TO SING	Foster & Allen (Telstar)
33	39	CRAZY	Julio Iglesias (Columbia)
36	40	ALIVE IN HELL	Meatloaf (Pure Music)
35	41	BROTHER SISTER	Brand New Heavies (ffrr)
41	42	INTERPRETATIONS	Carpenters (A&M)
17	43	PROMISED LAND	Queensryche (EMI)
-	44	WE ARE SHAMPOO	Shampoo (Food)
45	45	VOODOO LOUNGE	Rolling Stones (Virgin)
43	46	INTERNATIONAL TIMES	Trans Global Underground (Nation)
-	47	SINGIN! WITH THE BIG BANDS	Barry Manilow (Arista)
25	48	THE CULT	Cult (Beggars Banquet)
-	49	EVERYTHING CHANGES	Take That (RCA)
-	50	TURBULENT INDIGO	Joni Mitchell (Warner Bros.)

12 November 1994

LW	TW	Title	Artist (Label)
-	1	UNPLUGGED IN NEW YORK	Nirvana (Geffen)
1	2	CROSS ROAD – THE BEST OF BON JOVI	Bon Jovi (Jambco)
2	3	BEDTIME STORIES	Madonna (Maverick)
-	4	GREATEST HITS	INXS (Mercury)
3	5	MONSTER	REM (Warner Bros.)
8	6	THE BEST OF CHRIS REA	Chris Rea (East West)
-	7	AMORICA	Black Crowes (American)
-	8	BIG ONES	Aerosmith (Geffen)
-	9	THE DIVISION BELL	Pink Floyd (EMI)
10	10	TWELVE DEADLY CYNS...AND THEN SOME	Cyndi Lauper (Epic)
4	11	THE RETURN OF THE SPACE COWBOY	Jamiroquai (Sony Soho Square)
-	12	THE BEST OF SADE	Sade (Epic)
5	13	NO NEED TO ARGUE	Cranberries (Island)
9	14	HOLD ME, THRILL ME, KISS ME	Gloria Estefan (Epic)
7	15	STEAM	East17 (London)
15	16	THE THREE TENORS – IN CONCERT 1994	Carreras/Domingo/Pavarotti/Mehta (Teldec)
6	17	YOUTHANASIA	Megadeth (Capitol)
20	18	FORREST GUMP – SOUNDTRACK	Various Artists (Epic)
12	19	DEFINITELY MAYBE	Oasis (Creation)
18	20	THE LION KING – SOUNDTRACK	Various Artists (Mercury)
11	21	THE HIT LIST	Cliff Richard (EMI)
16	22	PARKLIFE	Blur (Food)
31	23	ALWAYS AND FOREVER	Eternal (EMI)
17	24	MUSIC BOX	Mariah Carey (Columbia)
19	25	SONGS	Luther Vandross (Epic)
13	26	DOG MAN STAR	Suede (Nude)
21	27	QUEEN OF SOUL – THE VERY BEST OF ARETHA FRANKLIN	Aretha Franklin (Atlantic)
-	28	WILDFLOWERS	Tom Petty (Warner Bros.)
23	29	FROM THE CRADLE	Eric Clapton (Duck)
27	30	END OF PART ONE – THEIR GREATEST HITS	Wet Wet Wet (Precious)
28	31	THE BEST OF HANK MARVIN & THE SHADOWS	Hank Marvin & the Shadows (PolyGram TV)
41	32	BROTHER SISTER	Brand New Heavies (ffrr)
33	33	THE ESSENTIAL COLLECTION	Elvis Presley (RCA)
26	34	HOMEGROWN	Dodgy (A&M)
-	35	LABOUR OF LOVE 1 & 2	UB40 (DEP International)
24	36	DOOKIE	Green Day (Reprise)
-	37	MOVE IT!	Reel 2 Real featuring the Mad Stuntman (Positiva)
25	38	ESPECIALLY FOR YOU	Daniel O'Donnell (Ritz)
-	39	TIME FOR LOVE	Bill Tarney (EMI)
36	40	PROTECTION	Massive Attack (Circa)
22	41	THE MIND'S EYE	Stiltskin (White Water)
35	42	WITH LOVE – THE BEST OF BRENDA LEE	Brenda Lee (Telstar)
43	43	MICHELLE GAYLE	Michelle Gayle (RCA)
39	44	CRAZY	Julio Iglesias (Columbia)
40	45	ALIVE IN HELL	Meatloaf (Pure Music)
32	46	THE SNAKE	Shane MacGowan & the Popes (ZTT)
29	47	MUSIC FOR THE JILTED GENERATION	Prodigy (XL)
34	48	EVERYBODY ELSE IS DOING IT, SO WHY CAN'T WE	Cranberries (Island)
38	49	SONGS WE LOVE TO SING	Foster & Allen (Telstar)
-	50	PULP FICTION – SOUNDTRACK	Various (MCA)

19 November 1994

LW	TW	Title	Artist (Label)
2	1	CROSS ROAD – THE BEST OF BON JOVI	Bon Jovi (Jambco)
1	2	UNPLUGGED IN NEW YORK	Nirvana (Geffen)
-	3	FIELDS OF GOLD – THE BEST OF STING 1984–1994	Sting (A&M)
4	4	GREATEST HITS	INXS (Mercury)
-	5	NO QUARTER	Jimmy Page & Robert Plant (Fontana)
3	6	BEDTIME STORIES	Madonna (Maverick)
5	7	MONSTER	REM (Warner Bros.)
-	8	CARRY ON UP THE CHARTS – THE BEST OF THE BEAUTIFUL SOUTH	Beautiful South (Go! Discs)
6	9	THE BEST OF CHRIS REA	Chris Rea (East West)
8	10	BIG ONES	Aerosmith (Geffen)
12	11	THE BEST OF SADE	Sade (Epic)
10	12	TWELVE DEADLY CYNS...AND THEN SOME	Cyndi Lauper (Epic)
23	13	ALWAYS AND FOREVER	Eternal (EMI)
21	14	THE HIT LIST	Cliff Richard (EMI)
7	15	AMORICA	Black Crowes (American)
11	16	THE RETURN OF THE SPACE COWBOY	Jamiroquai (Sony Soho Square)
13	17	NO NEED TO ARGUE	Cranberries (Island)
35	18	LABOUR OF LOVE 1 & 2	UB40 (DEP International)
9	19	THE DIVISION BELL	Pink Floyd (EMI)
14	20	HOLD ME, THRILL ME, KISS ME	Gloria Estefan (Epic)
16	21	THE THREE TENORS – IN CONCERT 1994	Carreras/Domingo/Pavarotti/Mehta (Teldec)
18	22	FORREST GUMP – SOUNDTRACK	Various Artists (Epic)
19	23	DEFINITELY MAYBE	Oasis (Creation)
22	24	PARKLIFE	Blur (Food)
20	25	THE LION KING – SOUNDTRACK	Various Artists (Mercury)
24	26	MUSIC BOX	Mariah Carey (Columbia)
15	27	STEAM	East17 (London)
33	28	THE ESSENTIAL COLLECTION	Elvis Presley (RCA)
25	29	SONGS	Luther Vandross (Epic)
-	30	HELL FREEZES OVER	Eagles (Geffen)
29	31	FROM THE CRADLE	Eric Clapton (Duck)
26	32	YOUTHANASIA	Megadeth (Capitol)
13	33	DOG MAN STAR	Suede (Nude)
32	34	BROTHER SISTER	Brand New Heavies (ffrr)
-	35	LET LOOSE	Let Loose (Mercury)
-	36	PSYCHE	PJ & Duncan (XS Rhythm)
39	37	TIME FOR LOVE	Bill Tarney (EMI)
30	38	END OF PART ONE – THEIR GREATEST HITS	Wet Wet Wet (Precious)
28	39	WILDFLOWERS	Tom Petty (Warner Bros.)
50	40	PULP FICTION – SOUNDTRACK	Various Artists (MCA)
31	41	THE BEST OF HANK MARVIN & THE SHADOWS	Hank Marvin & the Shadows (PolyGram TV)
38	42	ESPECIALLY FOR YOU	Daniel O'Donnell (Ritz)
43	43	CRAZY	Julio Iglesias (Columbia)
27	44	QUEEN OF SOUL – THE VERY BEST OF ARETHA FRANKLIN	Aretha Franklin (Atlantic)
36	45	DOOKIE	Green Day (Reprise)
-	46	HOW TO MAKE FRIENDS AND INFLUENCE PEOPLE	Terrorvision (Total Vegas)
40	47	PROTECTION	Massive Attack (Circa)
37	48	MOVE IT!	Reel 2 Real featuring the Mad Stuntman (Positiva)
-	49	EVERYTHING CHANGES	Take That (RCA)
-	50	OUT IN L.A.	Red Hot Chili Peppers (EMI)

Here come the 'Best Of' albums as Christmas shopping time approaches: Chris Rea, Sting, Sade, etc. Most interesting was Aretha Franklin's Atlantic recordings, Arista having already given us the best of her 'second' career. Joni Mitchell made a return to the chart, 24 years on from *Ladies Of The Canyon*.

November – December 1994

26 November 1994

last	this	Title / Artist (Label)
1	1	CROSS ROAD – THE BEST OF BON JOVI Bon Jovi (Jambco)
3	2	FIELDS OF GOLD – THE BEST OF STING 1984–1994 Sting (A&M)
8	3	CARRY ON UP THE CHARTS – THE BEST OF THE BEAUTIFUL SOUTH Beautiful South (Go! Discs)
2	4	UNPLUGGED IN NEW YORK Nirvana (Geffen)
-	5	BIZARRE FRUIT M People (deConstruction)
5	6	NO QUARTER Jimmy Page & Robert Plant (Fontana)
4	7	GREATEST HITS INXS (Mercury)
18	8	LABOUR OF LOVE 1 & 2 UB40 (DEP International)
9	9	THE BEST OF CHRIS REA Chris Rea (East West)
14	10	THE HIT LIST Cliff Richard (EMI)
11	11	THE BEST OF SADE Sade (Epic)
7	12	MONSTER REM (Warner Bros.)
6	13	BEDTIME STORIES Madonna (Maverick)
10	14	BIG ONES Aerosmith (Geffen)
19	15	THE DIVISION BELL Pink Floyd (EMI)
13	16	ALWAYS AND FOREVER Eternal (EMI)
12	17	TWELVE DEADLY CYNS...AND THEN SOME Cyndi Lauper (Epic)
21	18	THE THREE TENORS – IN CONCERT 1994 Carreras/Domingo/Pavarotti/Mehta (Teldec)
26	19	MUSIC BOX Mariah Carey (Columbia)
17	20	NO NEED TO ARGUE Cranberries (Island)
20	21	HOLD ME, THRILL ME, KISS ME Gloria Estefan (Epic)
16	22	THE RETURN OF THE SPACE COWBOY Jamiroquai (Sony Soho Square)
23	23	DEFINITELY MAYBE Oasis (Creation)
36	24	PSYCHE PJ & Duncan (XS Rhythm)
24	25	PARKLIFE Blur (Food)
41	26	THE BEST OF HANK MARVIN & THE SHADOWS Hank Marvin & the Shadows (PolyGram TV)
-	27	TUESDAY NIGHT MUSIC CLUB Sheryl Crow (A&M)
25	28	THE LION KING – SOUNDTRACK Various Artists (Mercury)
22	29	FORREST GUMP – SOUNDTRACK Various Artists (Epic)
28	30	THE ESSENTIAL COLLECTION Elvis Presley (RCA)
27	31	STEAM East17 (London)
29	32	SONGS Luther Vandross (Epic)
40	33	PULP FICTION – SOUNDTRACK Various Artists (MCA)
15	34	AMORICA Black Crowes (American)
30	35	HELL FREEZES OVER Eagles (Geffen)
35	36	LET LOOSE Let Loose (Mercury)
43	37	CRAZY Julio Iglesias (Columbia)
-	38	DUETS II Frank Sinatra (Capitol)
-	39	THE BEST OF MICHAEL BALL Michael Ball (PolyGram TV)
31	40	FROM THE CRADLE Eric Clapton (Duck)
37	41	TIME FOR LOVE Bill Tarney (EMI)
-	42	GREATEST HITS I & II Queen (EMI)
33	43	DOG MAN STAR Suede (Nude)
-	44	BALLADS AND BLUES 1982–1984 Gary Moore (Virgin)
-	45	12 PLAY R Kelly (Jive)
34	46	BROTHER SISTER Brand New Heavies (ffrr)
38	47	END OF PART ONE – THEIR GREATEST HITS Wet Wet Wet (Precious)
42	48	ESPECIALLY FOR YOU Daniel O'Donnell (Ritz)
-	49	MERRY CHRISTMAS Mariah Carey (Columbia)
-	50	TRANSMITTING LOVE Runrig (Chrysalis)

3 December 1994

last	this	Title / Artist (Label)
1	1	CROSS ROAD – THE BEST OF BON JOVI Bon Jovi (Jambco)
3	2	CARRY ON UP THE CHARTS – THE BEST OF THE BEAUTIFUL SOUTH Beautiful South (Go! Discs)
2	3	FIELDS OF GOLD – THE BEST OF STING 1984–1994 Sting (A&M)
-	4	(THE BEST OF) NEW ORDER New Order (London)
5	5	BIZARRE FRUIT M People (deConstruction)
8	6	LABOUR OF LOVE 1 & 2 UB40 (DEP International)
14	7	BIG ONES Aerosmith (Geffen)
4	8	UNPLUGGED IN NEW YORK Nirvana (Geffen)
7	9	GREATEST HITS INXS (Mercury)
16	10	ALWAYS AND FOREVER Eternal (EMI)
11	11	THE BEST OF SADE Sade (Epic)
9	12	THE BEST OF CHRIS REA Chris Rea (East West)
10	13	THE HIT LIST Cliff Richard (EMI)
13	14	BEDTIME STORIES Madonna (Maverick)
12	15	MONSTER REM (Warner Bros.)
17	16	TWELVE DEADLY CYNS...AND THEN SOME Cyndi Lauper (Epic)
6	17	NO QUARTER Jimmy Page & Robert Plant (Fontana)
18	18	THE THREE TENORS – IN CONCERT 1994 Carreras/Domingo/Pavarotti/Mehta (Teldec)
15	19	THE DIVISION BELL Pink Floyd (EMI)
21	20	HOLD ME, THRILL ME, KISS ME Gloria Estefan (Epic)
33	21	PULP FICTION – SOUNDTRACK Various Artists (MCA)
32	22	SONGS Luther Vandross (Epic)
23	23	PARKLIFE Blur (Food)
19	24	MUSIC BOX Mariah Carey (Columbia)
24	25	PSYCHE PJ & Duncan (XS Rhythm)
22	26	THE RETURN OF THE SPACE COWBOY Jamiroquai (Sony Soho Square)
27	27	TUESDAY NIGHT MUSIC CLUB Sheryl Crow (A&M)
39	28	THE BEST OF MICHAEL BALL Michael Ball (PolyGram TV)
20	29	NO NEED TO ARGUE Cranberries (Island)
23	30	DEFINITELY MAYBE Oasis (Creation)
31	31	STEAM East17 (London)
-	32	SONGS OF DISTANT EARTH Mike Oldfield (WEA)
37	33	CRAZY Julio Iglesias (Columbia)
28	34	THE LION KING – SOUNDTRACK Various Artists (Mercury)
30	35	THE ESSENTIAL COLLECTION Elvis Presley (RCA)
29	36	FORREST GUMP – SOUNDTRACK Various Artists (Epic)
26	37	THE BEST OF HANK MARVIN & THE SHADOWS Hank Marvin & the Shadows (PolyGram TV)
38	38	DUETS II Frank Sinatra (Capitol)
-	39	THE BLACK ALBUM Prince (Warner Bros.)
44	40	BALLADS AND BLUES 1982–1984 Gary Moore (Virgin)
35	41	HELL FREEZES OVER Eagles (Geffen)
45	42	12 PLAY R Kelly (Jive)
40	43	FROM THE CRADLE Eric Clapton (Duck)
42	44	GREATEST HITS I & II Queen (EMI)
48	45	ESPECIALLY FOR YOU Daniel O'Donnell (Ritz)
46	46	BROTHER SISTER Brand New Heavies (ffrr)
-	47	ENDLESS SUMMER Donna Summer (Mercury)
43	48	DOG MAN STAR Suede (Nude)
49	49	MERRY CHRISTMAS Mariah Carey (Columbia)
-	50	CROCODILE SHOES Jimmy Nail (East West)

10 December 1994

last	this	Title / Artist (Label)
2	1	CARRY ON UP THE CHARTS – THE BEST OF THE BEAUTIFUL SOUTH Beautiful South (Go! Discs)
1	2	CROSS ROAD – THE BEST OF BON JOVI Bon Jovi (Jambco)
-	3	VITALOGY Pearl Jam (Epic)
-	4	LIVE AT THE BBC Beatles (Apple)
3	5	FIELDS OF GOLD – THE BEST OF STING 1984–1994 Sting (A&M)
4	6	(THE BEST OF) NEW ORDER New Order (London)
10	7	ALWAYS AND FOREVER Eternal (EMI)
5	8	BIZARRE FRUIT M People (deConstruction)
6	9	LABOUR OF LOVE 1 & 2 UB40 (DEP International)
13	10	THE HIT LIST Cliff Richard (EMI)
7	11	BIG ONES Aerosmith (Geffen)
15	12	MONSTER REM (Warner Bros.)
9	13	GREATEST HITS INXS (Mercury)
8	14	UNPLUGGED IN NEW YORK Nirvana (Geffen)
11	15	THE BEST OF SADE Sade (Epic)
18	16	THE THREE TENORS – IN CONCERT 1994 Carreras/Domingo/Pavarotti/Mehta (Teldec)
22	17	SONGS Luther Vandross (Epic)
16	18	TWELVE DEADLY CYNS...AND THEN SOME Cyndi Lauper (Epic)
50	19	CROCODILE SHOES Jimmy Nail (East West)
14	20	BEDTIME STORIES Madonna (Maverick)
12	21	THE BEST OF CHRIS REA Chris Rea (East West)
23	22	PARKLIFE Blur (Food)
20	23	HOLD ME, THRILL ME, KISS ME Gloria Estefan (Epic)
31	24	STEAM East17 (London)
21	25	PULP FICTION – SOUNDTRACK Various Artists (MCA)
19	26	THE DIVISION BELL Pink Floyd (EMI)
29	27	NO NEED TO ARGUE Cranberries (Island)
17	28	NO QUARTER Jimmy Page & Robert Plant (Fontana)
24	29	MUSIC BOX Mariah Carey (Columbia)
30	30	DEFINITELY MAYBE Oasis (Creation)
26	31	THE RETURN OF THE SPACE COWBOY Jamiroquai (Sony Soho Square)
37	32	THE BEST OF HANK MARVIN & THE SHADOWS Hank Marvin & the Shadows (PolyGram TV)
27	33	TUESDAY NIGHT MUSIC CLUB Sheryl Crow (A&M)
28	34	THE BEST OF MICHAEL BALL Michael Ball (PolyGram TV)
33	35	CRAZY Julio Iglesias (Columbia)
25	36	PSYCHE PJ & Duncan (XS Rhythm)
34	37	THE LION KING – SOUNDTRACK Various Artists (Mercury)
32	38	SONGS OF DISTANT EARTH Mike Oldfield (WEA)
36	39	FORREST GUMP – SOUNDTRACK Various Artists (Epic)
-	40	TIME FOR LOVE Bill Tarney (EMI)
-	41	ESSENTIAL ELLA Ella Fitzgerald (PolyGram TV)
39	42	THE BLACK ALBUM Prince (Warner Bros.)
-	43	HAUNTED DANCEHALL Sabres of Paradise (Sabres Of Paradise)
-	44	CHRISTMAS WITH DANIEL Daniel O'Donnell (Ritz)
-	45	KYLIE MINOGUE Kylie Minogue (deConstruction)
35	46	THE ESSENTIAL COLLECTION Elvis Presley (RCA)
38	47	DUETS II Frank Sinatra (Capitol)
49	48	MERRY CHRISTMAS Mariah Carey (Columbia)
-	49	BALLADS AND BLUES 1982–1984 Gary Moore (Virgin)
-	50	BOOTLEGS AND B-SIDES Ice Cube (4th & Broadway)

M People entered high with the follow-up to the long-running *Elegant Slumming*, while *Pulp Fiction* added to the list of soundtrack albums. Most intriguing was *Live At The BBC*, a set of live recordings and out-takes from TV shows by the Beatles. An odd choice of tracks, would the Beatles name make it a winner?

December 1994

last this
week

		17 December 1994				24 December 1994	
-	1	SECOND COMING	Stone Roses (Geffen)	3	1	CARRY ON UP THE CHARTS – THE BEST OF THE	
4	2	LIVE AT THE BBC	Beatles (Apple)			BEAUTIFUL SOUTH	Beautiful South (Go! Discs)
1	3	CARRY ON UP THE CHARTS – THE BEST OF THE		2	2	LIVE AT THE BBC	Beatles (Apple)
		BEAUTIFUL SOUTH	Beautiful South (Go! Discs)	7	3	STEAM	East17 (London)
2	4	CROSS ROAD – THE BEST OF BON JOVI		4	4	CROSS ROAD – THE BEST OF BON JOVI	
			Bon Jovi (Jambco)				Bon Jovi (Jambco)
7	5	ALWAYS AND FOREVER	Eternal (EMI)	12	5	CROCODILE SHOES	Jimmy Nail (East West)
5	6	FIELDS OF GOLD – THE BEST OF STING		1	6	SECOND COMING	Stone Roses (Geffen)
		1984–1994	Sting (A&M)	5	7	ALWAYS AND FOREVER	Eternal (EMI)
24	7	STEAM	East17 (London)	6	8	FIELDS OF GOLD – THE BEST OF STING	
8	8	BIZARRE FRUIT	M People (deConstruction)			1984–1994	Sting (A&M)
6	9	(THE BEST OF) NEW ORDER	New Order (London)	9	9	(THE BEST OF) NEW ORDER	New Order (London)
10	10	THE HIT LIST	Cliff Richard (EMI)	10	10	THE HIT LIST	Cliff Richard (EMI)
3	11	VITALOGY	Pearl Jam (Epic)	8	11	BIZARRE FRUIT	M People (deConstruction)
19	12	CROCODILE SHOES	Jimmy Nail (East West)	13	12	THE THREE TENORS – IN CONCERT 1994	
16	13	THE THREE TENORS – IN CONCERT 1994					Carreras/Domingo/Pavarotti/Mehta (Teldec)
			Carreras/Domingo/Pavarotti/Mehta (Teldec)	37	13	THE PURE GENIUS OF LOUIS ARMSTRONG	
9	14	LABOUR OF LOVE 1 & 2	UB40 (DEP International)				Louis Armstrong (EMI)
11	15	BIG ONES	Aerosmith (Geffen)	14	14	LABOUR OF LOVE 1 & 2	UB40 (DEP International)
20	16	BEDTIME STORIES	Madonna (Maverick)	16	15	BEDTIME STORIES	Madonna (Maverick)
12	17	MONSTER	REM (Warner Bros.)	17	16	MONSTER	REM (Warner Bros.)
13	18	GREATEST HITS	INXS (Mercury)	15	17	BIG ONES	Aerosmith (Geffen)
15	19	THE BEST OF SADE	Sade (Epic)	23	18	PSYCHE	PJ & Duncan (XS Rhythm)
18	20	TWELVE DEADLY CYNS...AND THEN SOME		18	19	GREATEST HITS	INXS (Mercury)
			Cyndi Lauper (Epic)	11	20	VITALOGY	Pearl Jam (Epic)
14	21	UNPLUGGED IN NEW YORK	Nirvana (Geffen)	22	21	PARKLIFE	Blur (Food)
22	22	PARKLIFE	Blur (Food)	26	22	THE BEST OF CHRIS REA	Chris Rea (East West)
36	23	PSYCHE	PJ & Duncan (XS Rhythm)	19	23	THE BEST OF SADE	Sade (Epic)
17	24	SONGS	Luther Vandross (Epic)	25	24	HOLD ME, THRILL ME, KISS ME	
23	25	HOLD ME, THRILL ME, KISS ME					Gloria Estefan (Epic)
			Gloria Estefan (Epic)	20	25	TWELVE DEADLY CYNS...AND THEN SOME	
21	26	THE BEST OF CHRIS REA	Chris Rea (East West)				Cyndi Lauper (Epic)
26	27	THE DIVISION BELL	Pink Floyd (EMI)	33	26	THE ESSENTIAL COLLECTION	
29	28	MUSIC BOX	Mariah Carey (Columbia)				Elvis Presley (RCA)
27	29	NO NEED TO ARGUE	Cranberries (Island)	27	27	THE DIVISION BELL	Pink Floyd (EMI)
32	30	THE BEST OF HANK MARVIN & THE SHADOWS		21	28	UNPLUGGED IN NEW YORK	Nirvana (Geffen)
		Hank Marvin & the Shadows (PolyGram TV)		24	29	SONGS	Luther Vandross (Epic)
28	31	NO QUARTER		28	30	MUSIC BOX	Mariah Carey (Columbia)
			Jimmy Page & Robert Plant (Fontana)	29	31	NO NEED TO ARGUE	Cranberries (Island)
35	32	CRAZY	Julio Iglesias (Columbia)	40	32	END OF PART ONE – THEIR GREATEST HITS	
46	33	THE ESSENTIAL COLLECTION					Wet Wet Wet (Precious)
			Elvis Presley (RCA)	30	33	THE BEST OF HANK MARVIN & THE SHADOWS	
34	34	THE BEST OF MICHAEL BALL				Hank Marvin & the Shadows (PolyGram TV)	
			Michael Ball (PolyGram TV)	32	34	CRAZY	Julio Iglesias (Columbia)
30	35	DEFINITELY MAYBE	Oasis (Creation)	34	35	THE BEST OF MICHAEL BALL	
31	36	THE RETURN OF THE SPACE COWBOY					Michael Ball (PolyGram TV)
			Jamiroquai (Sony Soho Square)	35	36	DEFINITELY MAYBE	Oasis (Creation)
-	37	THE PURE GENIUS OF LOUIS ARMSTRONG		39	37	THE LION KING – SOUNDTRACK	
			Louis Armstrong (EMI)				Various Artists (Mercury)
39	38	FORREST GUMP – SOUNDTRACK	Various (Epic)	42	38	IN HARMONY	
37	39	THE LION KING – SOUNDTRACK					Richard Clayderman & James Last (Polydor)
			Various Artists (Mercury)	48	39	MERRY CHRISTMAS	Mariah Carey (Columbia)
-	40	END OF PART ONE – THEIR GREATEST HITS		38	40	FORREST GUMP – SOUNDTRACK	
			Wet Wet Wet (Precious)				Various Artists (Epic)
33	41	TUESDAY NIGHT MUSIC CLUB		31	41	NO QUARTER	
			Sheryl Crow (A&M)				Jimmy Page & Robert Plant (Fontana)
-	42	IN HARMONY		-	42	A VERY SPECIAL SEASON	Diana Ross (EMI)
		Richard Clayderman & James Last (Polydor)		36	43	THE RETURN OF THE SPACE COWBOY	
25	43	PULP FICTION – SOUNDTRACK					Jamiroquai (Sony Soho Square)
			Various Artists (MCA)	45	44	ESSENTIAL ELLA	Ella Fitzgerald (PolyGram TV)
45	44	KYLIE MINOGUE	Kylie Minogue (deConstruction)	-	45	HELL FREEZES OVER	Eagles (Geffen)
41	45	ESSENTIAL ELLA	Ella Fitzgerald (PolyGram TV)	-	46	GREATEST HITS I & II	Queen (EMI)
40	46	TIME FOR LOVE	Bill Tarney (EMI)	41	47	TUESDAY NIGHT MUSIC CLUB	
38	47	SONGS OF DISTANT EARTH	Mike Oldfield (WEA)				Sheryl Crow (A&M)
48	48	MERRY CHRISTMAS	Mariah Carey (Columbia)	46	48	TIME FOR LOVE	Bill Tarney (EMI)
47	49	DUETS II	Frank Sinatra (Capitol)	44	49	KYLIE MINOGUE	Kylie Minogue (deConstruction)
-	50	ISDN	Future Sound Of London (Virgin)	49	50	DUETS II	Frank Sinatra (Capitol)

Biggest news of the month, if not the year, was *Second Coming*. The band's first album since the hugely influential *Stone Roses* was released in 1989. Alas, the wait was too long, the album good, but not good enough.

Title Index

443

445

447

Artist Index

In the Artist Index records are listed once, at their first date of chart entry. Please note that the Artist Index is arranged in order of the first name of the artist, whether a person or a group. To find Elvis Presley, for example, look under 'E'. Records by 'Various Artists', and Cast and Soundtrack albums are not included in the Artist Index. Artist's names that begin with numerals are placed at the end of the index.

471

Iron Maiden THE NUMBER OF THE BEAST	17/04/82	
Iron Maiden PIECE OF MIND	28/05/83	
Iron Maiden POWERSLAVE	15/09/84	
Iron Maiden LIVE AFTER DEATH	26/10/85	
Iron Maiden SOMEWHERE IN TIME	11/10/86	
Iron Maiden SEVENTH SON OF A SEVENTH SON		
	23/04/88	
Iron Maiden RUNNING FREE/SANCTUARY	24/02/90	
Iron Maiden WOMEN IN UNIFORM/TWILIGHT ZONE		
	03/03/90	
Iron Maiden PURGATORY/MAIDEN JAPAN	10/03/90	
Iron Maiden RUN TO THE HILLS/THE NUMBER OF		
THE BEAST	17/03/90	
Iron Maiden FLIGHT OF ICARUS/THE TROOPER		
	24/03/90	
Iron Maiden 2 MINUTES TO MIDNIGHT/ACES HIGH		
	31/03/90	
Iron Maiden RUNNING FREE (LIVE)/RUN TO THE		
HILLS (LIVE)	07/04/90	
Iron Maiden WASTED YEARS/STRANGER IN A		
STRANGE LAND	14/04/90	
Iron Maiden CAN I PLAY WITH MADNESS/THE EVIL		
THAT MEN DO	21/04/90	
Iron Maiden THE CLAIRVOYANT/INFINITE DREAMS		
(LIVE)	28/04/90	
Iron Maiden NO PRAYER FOR THE DYING	13/10/90	
Iron Maiden FEAR OF THE DARK	23/05/92	
Iron Maiden A REAL LIVE ONE	03/04/93	
Iron Maiden A REAL DEAD ONE	30/10/93	
Iron Maiden LIVE AT DONNINGTON AUGUST 22, 1993		
	20/11/93	
Isaac Hayes SHAFT	04/12/71	
Isley Brothers THE ISLEY BROTHERS'		
GREATEST HITS	12/03/88	
It Bites THE BIG LAD IN THE WINDMILL	06/09/86	
It Bites ONCE AROUND THE WORLD	09/04/88	
It Bites EAT ME IN ST. LOUIS	01/07/89	
Izzy Stradlin & the Ju Ju Hounds IZZY STRADLIN AND		
THE JU JU HOUNDS	24/10/92	
J Geils Band FREEZE FRAME	06/03/82	
J J Cale NO. 8	24/09/83	
J J Cale NUMBER 10	26/09/92	
J J Cale CLOSER TO YOU	25/06/94	
Jack Bruce SONGS FOR A TAILOR	27/09/69	
Jack Bruce HARMONY ROW	07/08/71	
Jack Jones A SONG FOR YOU	20/05/72	
Jack Jones BREADWINNERS	27/05/72	
Jack Jones SIMPLY	19/08/72	
Jack Jones TOGETHER	14/04/73	
Jack Jones HARBOUR	16/02/74	
Jack Jones ALL TO YOURSELF	14/05/77	
Jackson Browne RUNNING ON EMPTY	28/01/78	
Jackson Browne LAWYERS IN LOVE	13/08/83	
Jackson Browne LIVES IN THE BALANCE	15/03/86	
Jackson Browne I'M ALIVE	06/11/93	
Jackson Five DIANA ROSS PRESENTS THE JACKSON		
FIVE	14/03/70	
Jackson Five JACKSON FIVE'S GREATEST HITS		
	02/09/72	
Jackson Five LOOKIN' THROUGH THE WINDOWS		
	02/12/72	
Jacksons TRIUMPH	18/10/80	
Jacksons VICTORY	21/07/84	
Jacksons 2300 JACKSON STREET	08/07/89	
Jade JADE TO THE MAX	29/05/93	
Jah Wobble SNAKE CHARMER	19/11/83	
Jah Wobble's Invaders Of The Heart TAKE ME TO GOD		
	28/05/94	
Jaki Graham HEAVEN KNOWS	21/09/85	
Jaki Graham BREAKING AWAY	20/09/86	
Jam IN THE CITY	28/05/77	
Jam ALL MOD CONS	11/11/78	
Jam SETTING SONS	24/11/79	
Jam SOUND AFFECTS	13/12/80	
Jam THE GIFT	20/03/82	
Jam DIG THE NEW BREED	25/12/82	
Jam SNAP!	22/10/83	
Jam GREATEST HITS	13/07/91	
Jam SEVEN	29/02/92	
Jam EXTRAS	18/04/92	
Jam LIVE JAM	06/11/93	
James STUTTER	09/08/86	
James GOLD MOTHER	16/06/90	
James LAID	09/10/93	

James WAH WAH	24/09/94	
James Brown BEST OF JAMES BROWN	17/10/87	
James Brown SEX MACHINE - THE VERY BEST OF		
JAMES BROWN	23/11/91	
James Brown with Full Force I'M REAL	25/06/88	
James Galway JAMES GALWAY PLAYS SONGS FOR		
ANNIE	02/09/78	
James Galway MASTERPIECES - THE ESSENTIAL		
FLUTE OF JAMES GALWAY	01/05/93	
James Ingram IT'S YOUR NIGHT	07/04/84	
James Ingram IT'S YOUR NIGHT	09/02/85	
James Ingram NEVER FELT SO GOOD	06/09/86	
James Last THIS IS JAMES LAST	22/04/67	
James Last JAMES LAST IN RUSSIA	03/03/73	
James Last TEN YEARS NON STOP JUBILEE	02/08/75	
James Last MAKE THE PARTY LAST	22/11/75	
James Last LAST THE WHOLE NIGHT THROUGH		
	28/04/79	
James Last CLASSICS FOR DREAMING	13/12/80	
James Last HANSIMANIA	05/12/81	
James Last THE ROSE OF TRALEE	07/04/84	
James Last LEAVE THE BEST TO LAST	28/09/85	
James Last BY REQUEST	02/05/87	
James Last DANCE DANCE DANCE	10/12/88	
James Last CLASSICS BY MOONLIGHT	21/04/90	
James Last POP SYMPHONIES	22/06/91	
James Last VIVA ESPANA	12/09/92	
James Last JAMES LAST PLAYS ANDREW LLOYD		
WEBBER	27/11/93	
James Taylor SWEET BABY JAMES	28/11/70	
James Taylor MUD SLIDE SLIM	22/05/71	
James Taylor CLASSIC SONGS	28/03/87	
Jamiroquai EMERGENCY ON PLANET EARTH	26/06/93	
Jamiroquai THE RETURN OF THE SPACE COWBOY		
	29/10/94	
Jan Hammer ESCAPE FROM TV	21/11/87	
Jane Fonda JANE FONDA'S WORKOUT ALBUM		
	05/03/83	
Jane Wiedlin FUR	24/09/88	
Jane's Addiction RITUAL DE LO HABITUAL	08/09/90	
Janet Jackson CONTROL	19/04/86	
Janet Jackson CONTROL - THE REMIXES	21/11/87	
Janet Jackson JANET JACKSON'S		
RHYTHM NATION 1814	30/09/89	
Janet Jackson JANET	29/05/93	
Janis Joplin JANIS JOPLIN IN CONCERT	12/08/72	
Japan ASSEMBLAGE	10/10/81	
Japan TIN DRUM	28/11/81	
Japan ASSEMBLAGE	14/08/82	
Japan OIL ON CANVAS	18/06/83	
Japan EXORCISING GHOSTS	08/12/84	
Jason Donovan TEN GOOD REASONS	13/05/89	
Jason Donovan BETWEEN THE LINES	09/06/90	
Jason Donovan GREATEST HITS	28/09/91	
Jason Donovan ALL AROUND THE WORLD	11/09/93	
Jason & the Scorchers LOST AND FOUND	02/03/85	
Jasper Carrott RABBITS ON AND ON	01/11/75	
Jasper Carrott THE UNRECORDED JASPER CARROTT		
	27/10/79	
Jasper Carrott BEAT THE CARROTT	10/10/81	
Jazzy Jeff & the Fresh Prince CODE RED	11/12/93	
Jean Carne YOU'RE A PART OF ME	19/03/88	
Jean Michel Jarre OXYGENE	20/08/77	
Jean Michel Jarre EQUINOXE	23/12/78	
Jean Michel Jarre MAGNETIC FIELDS	13/06/81	
Jean Michel Jarre THE CONCERTS IN CHINA	22/05/82	
Jean Michel Jarre THE ESSENTIAL JEAN MICHEL		
JARRE	19/11/83	
Jean Michel Jarre ZOOLOOK	01/12/84	
Jean Michel Jarre RENDEZ-VOUS	24/01/87	
Jean Michel Jarre RENDEZ-VOUS	19/04/86	
Jean Michel Jarre IN CONCERT - LYON AND HOUSTON		
	18/07/87	
Jean Michel Jarre REVOLUTIONS	15/10/88	
Jean Michel Jarre JARRE LIVE	14/10/89	
Jean Michel Jarre WAITING FOR COUSTEAU	23/06/90	
Jean Michel Jarre IMAGES - THE BEST OF JEAN-		
MICHEL JARRE	26/10/91	
Jean Michel Jarre CHRONOLOGIE	05/06/93	
Jean Michel Jarre CHRONOLOGIE 6	28/05/94	
Jeff Beck WIRED	31/07/76	
Jeff Beck FLASH	17/08/85	
Jeff Beck, Tim Bogert & Carmine Appice		
BECK, BOGERT & APPICE	21/04/73	

Jeff Healey Band SEE THE LIGHT	28/01/89	
Jeff Healey Band HELL TO PAY	09/06/90	
Jeff Healey Band FEEL THIS	28/11/92	
Jeff Lorber STEP BY STEP	01/06/85	
Jeff Lynne ARMCHAIR THEATRE	04/08/90	
Jeff Wayne WAR OF THE WORLDS	08/07/78	
Jeff Wayne JEFF WAYNE'S MUSICAL VERSION OF		
SPARTACUS	03/10/92	
Jefferson Starship SPITFIRE	04/09/76	
Jefferson Starship FREEDOM AT POINT ZERO	22/03/80	
Jefferson Starship RED OCTOPUS	21/07/84	
Jeffrey Lee Pierce WILDWEED	04/05/85	
Jeffrey Osborne DON'T STOP	20/10/84	
Jello Biafra NO MORE COCOONS	19/12/87	
Jellybean JUST VISITING THIS PLANET	31/10/87	
Jellybean ROCKS THE HOUSE!	03/09/88	
Jellyfish SPILT MILK	22/05/93	
Jennifer Rush JENNIFER RUSH	16/11/85	
Jennifer Rush MOVIN'	10/05/86	
Jennifer Rush HEART OVER MIND	25/04/87	
Jennifer Warnes FAMOUS BLUE RAINCOAT	25/07/87	
Jermain Stewart FRANTIC ROMANTIC	11/10/86	
Jermaine Jackson LET'S GET SERIOUS	07/06/80	
Jermaine Jackson DYNAMITE	26/05/84	
Jermaine Stewart SAY IT AGAIN	05/03/88	
Jesus Jones LIQUIDIZER	14/10/89	
Jesus Jones DOUBT	09/02/91	
Jesus Jones PERVERSE	06/02/93	
Jesus Lizard DOWN	10/09/94	
Jesus & Mary Chain PSYCHOCANDY	30/11/85	
Jesus & Mary Chain DARKLANDS	12/09/87	
Jesus & Mary Chain BARBED WIRE KISS	30/04/88	
Jesus & Mary Chain AUTOMATIC	21/10/89	
Jesus & Mary Chain HONEY'S DEAD	04/04/92	
Jesus & Mary Chain THE SOUND OF SPEED	24/07/93	
Jesus & Mary Chain STONED AND DETHRONED		
	27/08/94	
Jethro Tull THIS WAS	26/10/68	
Jethro Tull STAND UP	02/08/69	
Jethro Tull BENEFIT	09/05/70	
Jethro Tull AQUALUNG	27/03/71	
Jethro Tull THICK AS A BRICK	11/03/72	
Jethro Tull LIVING IN THE PAST	01/07/72	
Jethro Tull PASSION PLAY	21/07/73	
Jethro Tull WAR CHILD	09/11/74	
Jethro Tull MINSTREL IN THE GALLERY	04/10/75	
Jethro Tull TOO OLD TO ROCK 'N' ROLL	29/05/76	
Jethro Tull SONGS FROM THE WOOD	26/02/77	
Jethro Tull HEAVY HORSES	06/05/78	
Jethro Tull BURSTING OUT	21/10/78	
Jethro Tull THE BROADSWORD AND THE BEAST		
	08/05/82	
Jethro Tull UNDER WRAPS	15/09/84	
Jethro Tull CREST OF A KNAVE	19/09/87	
Jethro Tull ROCK ISLAND	02/09/89	
Jethro Tull CATFISH RISING	14/09/91	
Jethro Tull A LITTLE LIGHT MUSIC	26/09/92	
Jets 100 PER CENT COTTON	17/04/82	
Jets CRUSH ON YOU	18/04/87	
Jim Diamond JIM DIAMOND	29/05/93	
Jim Reeves GOOD 'N' COUNTRY	04/04/64	
Jim Reeves A TOUCH OF VELVET	15/08/64	
Jim Reeves GENTLEMAN JIM	15/08/64	
Jim Reeves HE'LL HAVE TO GO	29/08/64	
Jim Reeves MOONLIGHT AND ROSES	05/09/64	
Jim Reeves GOD BE WITH YOU	19/09/64	
Jim Reeves TWELVE SONGS OF CHRISTMAS	05/12/64	
Jim Reeves BEST OF JIM REEVES	30/01/65	
Jim Reeves HAVE I TOLD YOU LATELY THAT I LOVE		
YOU	10/04/65	
Jim Reeves THE JIM REEVES WAY	08/05/65	
Jim Reeves DISTANT DRUMS	05/11/66	
Jim Reeves A TOUCH OF SADNESS	04/01/69	
Jim Reeves ACCORDING TO MY HEART	28/06/69	
Jim Reeves JIM REEVES AND SOME FRIENDS	30/08/69	
Jim Reeves THE COUNTRY SIDE OF JIM REEVES		
	18/10/69	
Jim Reeves JIM REEVES' GOLDEN RECORDS	28/03/70	
Jim Reeves INTIMATE JIM REEVES	28/08/71	
Jim Reeves JIM REEVES' 40 GOLDEN GREATS	04/10/75	
Jim Reeves THE DEFINITIVE JIM REEVES	08/08/92	
Jim Steinman BAD FOR GOOD	23/05/81	
Jimi Hendrix BAND OF GYPSIES	04/07/70	
Jimi Hendrix CRY OF LOVE	27/03/71	